P9-DVM-891

FIREFLY ATLAS OF
North America

UNITED STATES, CANADA & MEXICO

FIREFLY ATLAS OF
North America

UNITED STATES, CANADA & MEXICO

FIREFLY BOOKS

DEC 1 3 2006

DOUGLAS COLLEGE LIBRARY

A FIREFLY BOOK

Published by Firefly Books Ltd. 2006
Copyright © 2006 Philip's

All rights reserved. No part of this publication may be reproduced, stored in a retrieval system, or transmitted in any form or by any means, electronic, mechanical, photocopying, recording or otherwise, without the prior written permission of the Publisher.

First printing

Publisher Cataloging-in-Publication Data (U.S.)
   Firefly atlas of North America : United States, Canada & Mexico.
[270] p : col. photos. ; cm.
Included index.
ISBN-13: 978-1-55407-207-1
ISBN-10: 1-55407-207-7
1. North America - Maps. I. Title.
912.7 c22   G1105.F3 2006

Library and Archives Canada Cataloguing in Publication
   Firefly atlas of North America [cartographic material] : United States, Canada & Mexico.
Includes index.
ISBN-13: 978-1-55407-207-1
ISBN-10: 1-55407-207-7
1. North America--Maps.
G1105.F4 2006   912.7   C2006-903367-6

Published in the United States by
Firefly Books (U.S.) Inc.
P.O. Box 1338, Ellicott Station
Buffalo, New York 14205

Published in Canada by
Firefly Books Ltd.
66 Leek Crescent
Richmond Hill, Ontario L4B 1H1

Picture Acknowledgements
Gazetteer
All images copyright © Corbis and Alberta **Tibor Bognár**, British Columbia **Gunter Marx**, Manitoba **John Conrad**, New Brunswick **Paul A. Souders**, Newfoundland **Wolfgang Kaehler**, Nova Scotia **Ron Watts**, Nunavut **Rob Howard**, NW Territories **Lowell Georgia**, Ontario **Jose Fuste Raga**, Prince Edward Island **Paul A. Souders**, Quebec **Richard T. Nowitz**, Saskatchewan **Craig Aurness**, Yukon **Charlie Munsey**, Alabama **David Muench**, Alaska **Frans Lanting**, Arizona **Paul C. Pet**, Arkansas **John Wigmore**, California **Richard Glover; Ecoscene** Colorado **David Muench**, Connecticut **Robert Holmes**, Delaware **Bob Krist**, Florida **Roger Ressmeyer**, Georgia **David Muench**, Hawaii **Jim Sugar**, Idaho **David Stoecklein**, Illinois **Jose Fuste Raga**, Indiana **Neil Rabinowitz**, Iowa **Louie Psihoyos**, Kansas **Eric Nguyen/Jim Reed Photography**, Kentucky **David Muench**, Louisiana **Philip Gould**, Maine **Tom Stewart**, Maryland **Mark E. Gibson**, Massachusetts **Royalty free**, Michigan **W. Cody**, Minnesota **Ed Bock**, Mississippi **Richard Cummins**, Missouri **Royalty free**, Montana **George Huey**, Nebraska **David Muench**, Nevada **Bob Krist**, New Hampshire **Erik Freeland**, New Jersey **Kelly-Mooney Photography**, New Mexico **Macduff Everton**, New York **Jason Hawkes**, North Carolina **Owaki - Kulla**, North Dakota **Tom Bean**, Ohio **William Manning**, Oklahoma **Richard Hamilton Smith**, Oregon **Steve Terrill**, Pensylvania **Royalty free**, Rhode Island **Bob Krist**, South Carolina **Kevin Fleming**, South Dakota **Lester Lefkowitz**, Tennessee **W. Cody**, Texas **David Muench**, Utah **Bill Stormont**, Vermont **Franz Marc Frei**, Virginia **Richard A. Cooke**, Washington **Tim McGuire**, West Virginia **Ron Watts**, Wisconsin **Royalty free**, Wyoming **Robert Y. Ono**, Northern Mexico (top) **George H. H. Huey**, Northern Mexico (bottom) **Danny Lehman**, Central Mexico (first) **Peter M. Wilson**, Central Mexico (second) **Angelo Hornak**, Southern Mexico **Bob Krist**.
End papers
Satellite images are courtesy of NPA Group, Edenbridge, Kent (www.satmaps.com).

City Maps
The following city maps utilize base data supplied courtesy of MapQuest.com, inc. (© MapQuest).
United States Baltimore, Cleveland, Dallas–Fort Worth, Denver, Detroit, Houston, Las Vegas, Memphis, Milwaukee, Minneapolis–St. Paul, New Orleans, Orlando, Philadelphia, Phoenix, Pittsburgh, Portland, St. Louis, Salt Lake City, San Antonio, San Diego, Seattle, Tampa & St. Petersburg.
Canada Ottawa, Vancouver.
Mexico Guadalajara, Monterrey.

Cartography by Philip's

Cover design by Sideways Design

Printed in Spain

Contents

Statistics   6

Gazetteer   7

United States Maps   🇺🇸

Map symbols   71
United States   72
   1:10 100 000
United States Midwest and
  North-East   74
   1:5 625 000
North Dakota and South Dakota   76
   1:2 500 000
Minnesota   77
   1:2 100 000
Wisconsin   78
   1:2 100 000
Michigan   79
   1:2 100 000
Nebraska   80
   1:2 100 000
Iowa   81
   1:2 100 000
Kansas   82
   1:2 100 000
Missouri   83
   1:2 100 000
Illinois   84
   1:2 100 000
Indiana   85
   1:2 100 000
Ohio   86
   1:2 100 000
Pennsylvania   87
   1:2 100 000
New York   88
   1:2 100 000
New Hampshire and Vermont   89
   1:1 050 000
Maine   90
   1:2 100 000
Massachusetts, Connecticut and
  Rhode Island   91
   1:1 050 000
New Jersey   92
   1:1 050 000
Maryland, Delaware and
  District of Columbia   93
   1:1 050 000
Minneapolis–St. Paul, Milwaukee,
  St. Louis   94
Chicago   95
Boston   96
New York City   97
Detroit, Cleveland, Pittsburgh,
  Philadelphia   98
Baltimore, Washington D.C.   99
United States – South   100
   1:5 625 000
West Virginia and Virginia   102
   1:2 100 000
North Carolina and South Carolina   103
   1:2 500 000
Tennessee and
  Kentucky   104
   1:2 100 000
Arkansas   106
   1:2 100 000

Oklahoma   107
   1:2 100 000
Texas   108
   1:2 500 000
Louisiana   110
   1:2 100 000
Mississippi   111
   1:2 100 000
Alabama   112
   1:2 100 000
Georgia   113
   1:2 100 000
Florida   114
   1:2 100 000
Tampa–St. Petersburg,
  Miami–Fort Lauderdale,
  Orlando,   115
Dallas–Fort Worth
  Houston, San Antonio   116
New Orleans, Memphis,
  Atlanta   117
United States – West   118
   1:5 625 000
Washington   120
   1:2 100 000
Oregon   121
   1:2 100 000
Idaho   122
   1:2 100 000
Montana   123
   1:3 150 000
Wyoming   124
   1:2 100 000
Colorado   125
   1:2 100 000
California   126
   1:2 100 000
Nevada   128
   1:2 100 000
Utah   129
   1:2 100 000
Arizona   130
   1:2 100 000
New Mexico   131
   1:2 200 000
Seattle, Portland,
  San Francisco   132
Los Angeles,
  San Diego   133
Salt Lake City, Denver,
  Las Vegas, Phoenix   134
Alaska   135
   1:8 400 000
Hawaii   136
   1:2 100 000
  Oahu
   1:4 200 000
  Hawaiian Islands
   1:16 800 000

Canada Maps   🇨🇦

Map Symbols   137
Canada   138
   1:12 600 000
Atlantic Provinces   140
   1:2 100 000
Newfoundland   142
   1:2 100 000

Northern Quebec and Labrador   143
   1:5 900 000
Southern Quebec   144
   1:2 100 000
Southern Ontario   146
   1:2 100 000
Central Ontario – Lake Superior   148
   1:2 100 000
Southern Manitoba and
  Saskatchewan   150
   1:2 100 000
Southern Alberta   152
   1:2 100 000
Southern British Columbia   154
   1:2 100 000
Canada Northwest   156
   1:6 700 000
Nunavut   158
   1:6 700 000
Montreal, Ottawa   160
Toronto, Vancouver   161

Greenland   162
   1:10 500 000

Mexico Maps   🇲🇽

Map symbols   163
Mexico   164
   1:6 700 000
Baja California   166
   1:2 100 000
Sonora and Chihuahua   168
   1:2 100 000
Coahuila, Nuevo León,
  Tamaulipas and San Luis Potosí   170
   1:2 100 000
Nayarit, Sinaloa, Durango,
  Zacatecas and Aguascalientes   172
   1:2 100 000
Central Mexico   174
   1:2 100 000
Veracruz, Puebla and Oaxaca   176
   1:2 100 000
Tabasco and Chiapas   178
   1:2 100 000
Yucatán, Quintana Roo and
  Campeche   179
   1:2 100 000
Guadalajara, Monterrey   180
Mexico City   181

Central America and the
  Caribbean   182
   1:6 700 000

Puerto Rico and
the U.S. Pacific Territories   184
  Puerto Rico 1:1 450 000
  U.S. Outlying Territories 1:80 000 000
  Northern Marianas 1:16 800 000
  Samoan Islands 1:21 000 000
  Guam, Saipan, Tutuila, Manua Islands
  1:800 000

Index to Maps   185–272

Statistics

LARGEST METROPOLITAN AREAS

These figures represent urban agglomerations (continuous metropolitan areas). For the United States and Mexico, these are considerably larger than the cities themselves.

UNITED STATES

Metropolitan area	Population
New York-Northern New Jersey-Long Island (NY-NJ-PA)	18,323,002
Los Angeles-Long Beach-Santa Ana (CA)	12,365,627
Chicago-Naperville-Joliet (IL-IN-WI)	9,098,316
Philadelphia-Camden-Wilmington (PA-NJ-DE)	5,687,147
Dallas-Fort Worth-Arlington (TX)	5,161,544
Miami-Fort Lauderdale-Miami Beach (FL)	5,007,564
Washington-Arlington-Alexandria (DC-VA-MD)	4,796,183
Houston-Baytown-Sugar Land (TX)	4,715,407
Detroit-Warren-Livonia (MI)	4,452,557
Boston-Cambridge-Quincy (MA-NH)	4,391,344
Atlanta-Sandy Springs-Marietta (GA)	4,247,981
San Francisco-Oakland-Fremont (CA)	4,123,740
Riverside-San Bernardino-Ontario (CA)	3,254,821
Phoenix-Mesa-Scottsdale (AZ)	3,251,876
Seattle-Tacoma-Bellevue (WA)	3,043,878
Minneapolis-St. Paul-Bloomington (MN-WI)	2,968,806
San Diego-Carlsbad-San Marcos (CA)	2,813,833
St. Louis (MO-IL)	2,698,687
Baltimore-Towson (MD)	2,552,994
Pittsburgh (PA)	2,431,087
Tampa-St. Petersburg-Clearwater (FL)	2,395,997
Denver-Aurora (CO)	2,179,240
Cleveland-Elyria-Mentor (OH)	2,148,143
Cincinnati-Middletown (OH-KY-IN)	2,009,632
Portland-Vancouver-Beaverton (OR-WA)	1,927,881

CANADA

Metropolitan area	Population
Toronto (Ontario)	4,683,000
Montreal (Quebec)	3,426,350
Vancouver (British Columbia)	2,173,100
Calgary (Alberta)	933,495
Ottawa (Ontario)	845,875
Edmonton (Alberta)	712,391
Winnipeg (Manitoba)	706,854
Quebec (Quebec)	682,757
Hamilton (Ontario)	662,401
London (Ontario)	457,200
Kitchener (Ontario)	444,100
St. Catharines-Niagara (Ontario)	393,600
Halifax (Nova Scotia)	379,800
Windsor (Ontario)	329,000
Victoria (British Columbia)	330,200

MEXICO

Metropolitan area	Population
Ciudad de México (Distrito Federal)	17,806,527
Guadalajara (Jalisco)	3,677,531
Monterrey (Nuevo León)	3,243,466
Puebla (Puebla)	2,220,236
Tijuana (Baja California)	1,274,240
León (Guanajuato)	1,235,081
Ciudad Juárez (Chihuahua)	1,187,275
Toluca (México)	1,151,651
Torreón (Coahuila)	1,007,291
San Luis Potosí (San Luis Potosí)	850,828
Mérida (Yucatán)	842,188
Querétaro (Querétaro)	787,341
Aguascalientes (Aguascalientes)	707,516
Cuernavaca (Morelos)	705,405
Chihuahua (Chihuahua)	677,117

WEATHER

Highest Temperature	°F	°C	Date
Death Valley, California	134	56.7	July 10, 1913

Lowest Temperature	°F	°C	Date
Snag, Yukon Territory	−81.4	−63	February 3, 1947

Highest Wind Speed	mph	km/h	Date
Mt. Washington, New Hampshire	231	372	April 12, 1934

Highest Annual Rainfall	inches	cm	Date
Henderson Lake, British Columbia	256	650.2	1990

Lowest Annual Rainfall	inches	cm	Date
Batagues, Mexico	1.2	3	1990

Highest Daily Rainfall	inches	cm	Date
Alvin, Texas	42.9	109.0	July 28, 1979

Most Snowfall (single season)	inches	cm	Date
Mt. Baker Ski Area, Washington	1,140	2,895.6	July 1998 – June 1999

Largest Hailstone	Diameter	Circumference	Date
Aurora, Nebraska	7 in (17.8 cm)	18.75 in (47.6 cm)	June 22, 2003

HIGHEST MOUNTAINS

Name	feet	meters	Country
Mt. McKinley (Denali)	20,320	6,194	U.S.
Mt. Logan	19,551	5,959	Canada
Pico de Orizaba (Citlaltepetl)	18,707	5,702	Mexico
Mt. St. Elias	18,015	5,491	U.S./Canada
Popocatépetl	17,887	5,452	Mexico
Mt. Foraker	17,402	5,304	U.S.
Iztaccihuatl	17,159	5,230	Mexico
Mt. Lucania	17,142	5,225	Canada
Mt. King	16,972	5,173	Canada
Mt. Steele	16,644	5,073	Canada
Mt. Bona	16,421	5,005	U.S.
Mt. Blackburn	16,391	4,996	U.S.
Mt. Sanford	16,237	4,949	U.S.
Mt. Wood	15,886	4,842	Canada
Mt. Vancouver	15,699	4,785	Canada

LONGEST RIVERS

Name	miles	km	Feeds into
Mississippi-Missouri	3,740	6,020	Gulf of Mexico
Mackenzie	2,630	4,240	Arctic Ocean
Mississippi	2,350	3,780	Gulf of Mexico
Missouri	2,350	3,780	Mississippi
Yukon	1,980	3,185	Pacific Ocean
Rio Grande	1,880	3,030	Gulf of Mexico
Arkansas	1,450	2,340	Mississippi
Colorado	1,445	2,330	Pacific Ocean
Red	1,270	2,040	Mississippi
Columbia	1,210	1,950	Pacific Ocean
Saskatchewan	1,205	1,940	Lake Winnipeg
Snake	1,040	1,674	Columbia
Platte	990	1,594	Missouri
Ohio	981	1,579	Mississippi
Pecos	926	1,491	Rio Grande

LARGEST ISLANDS

Name	sq. miles	sq. km	Country
Baffin	196,100	508,000	Canada
Victoria	81,900	212,200	Canada
Ellesmere	81,800	212,000	Canada
Newfoundland	42,031	108,860	Canada
Banks	27,038	70,028	Canada
Devon	21,331	55,247	Canada
Axel Heiberg	16,671	43,178	Canada
Melville	16,274	42,149	Canada
Southampton	15,913	41,214	Canada
Prince of Wales	12,872	33,339	Canada
Vancouver	12,079	31,285	Canada
Somerset	9,570	24,786	Canada
Bathurst	6,194	16,042	Canada
Prince Patrick	6,119	15,848	Canada
King William	5,062	13,111	Canada

LARGEST LAKES

Name	sq. miles	sq. km	Country
Lake Superior	31,800	82,350	Canada/U.S.
Lake Huron	23,010	59,600	Canada/U.S.
Lake Michigan	22,400	58,000	U.S.
Great Bear Lake	12,280	31,800	Canada
Great Slave Lake	11,000	28,500	Canada
Lake Erie	9,900	25,700	Canada/U.S.
Lake Winnipeg	9,400	24,400	Canada
Lake Ontario	7,500	19,500	Canada/U.S.
Lake Athabasca	3,058	7,920	Canada
Lake Reindeer	2,444	6,330	Canada
Lake Winnipegosis	2,086	5,403	Canada
Lake Nettilling	1,950	5,051	Canada
Lake Nipigon	1,870	4,843	Canada
Lake Manitoba	1,817	4,706	Canada
Great Salt Lake	1,800	4,662	U.S.

Gazetteer

CANADA 🍁

Alberta	8
British Columbia	9
Manitoba	10
New Brunswick	10
Newfoundland and Labrador	11
Northwest Territories	12
Nova Scotia	13
Nunavut	14
Ontario	15
Prince Edward Island	16
Quebec	16
Saskatchewan	17
Yukon Territory	18

UNITED STATES 🇺🇸

Alabama	19
Alaska	20
Arizona	21
Arkansas	22
California	23
Colorado	24
Connecticut	25
Delaware	26
Florida	27
Georgia	28
Hawaii	29
Idaho	30
Illinois	31
Indiana	32
Iowa	33
Kansas	34
Kentucky	35
Louisiana	36
Maine	37
Maryland, District of Columbia	37
Massachusetts	38
Michigan	40
Minnesota	41
Mississippi	42
Missouri	43
Montana	44
Nebraska	44
Nevada	45
New Hampshire	46
New Jersey	47
New Mexico	48
New York	49
North Carolina	50
North Dakota	51
Ohio	52
Oklahoma	53
Oregon	54
Pennsylvania	55
Rhode Island	56
South Carolina	57
South Dakota	58
Tennessee	59
Texas	60
Utah	61
Vermont	62
Virginia	63
Washington	64
West Virginia	65
Wisconsin	66
Wyoming	67

MEXICO 🇲🇽

Northern Mexico	68
Central Mexico	69
Southern Mexico	70

ALBERTA

Alberta is a province of western Canada, bordered on the west by British Columbia, east by Saskatchewan, north by the Northwest Territories, and south by the state of Montana. It has two large cities, Edmonton and Calgary.

LAND AND ECONOMY

Except for the **Rocky Mountain** ranges, Alberta is part of the high plains of central North America, with a few hills and deep river valleys. The principal rivers are the Athabasca, Peace, Saskatchewan, and Milk. **Lesser Slave Lake** is the largest of the many lakes; **Lake Louise**, in the Rockies, is noted for its beauty. The fertile plains support vast wheat and livestock farming, and the oil and natural gas fields of central Alberta make a major contribution to the economy. Manufacturing is mostly concentrated in the areas of Edmonton and Calgary. The economy is boosted by tourism, which includes numerous mountain and water activities. The province has five national parks, with three of these located in the Rocky Mountains. **Banff National Park** was the nation's first national park and is the most popular; also well known is **Jasper National Park**.

Settlement did not begin on a large scale until the late 19th century, when immigrants came from other Canadian provinces, the United States, and Europe. Besides the British and French, main groups include Germans, Ukrainians, and Scandinavians.

Centers of higher education include the University of Alberta, in Edmonton, the University of Calgary and the University of Lethbridge.

HISTORY

The area was first home to the **Plains Indians**, including the Blackfoot, Peigan, Cree, and Sarcee. It was part of a huge territory granted in 1670 by King Charles II to the **Hudson's Bay Company**, a fur-trading enterprise. In 1870 the government of Canada bought the region from the company. Also in the late 1800s, the Sioux tribe moved here from the south. The North West Mounted Police were established here in the 1870s, later becoming the **Royal Canadian Mounted Police**. Farming pioneers arrived and, in 1885, the **transcontinental railroad** was completed. The area was part of the **Northwest Territories** and was governed from Ottawa, but in 1882 this was divided into four districts, with Alberta being one.

The province was named after Princess Louise Caroline Alberta, the fourth daughter of Queen Victoria. In 1905 it was admitted to the Confederation along with Saskatchewan. **Natural gas** was discovered as early as 1914, but rich **oil fields** found after World War II were a major stimulus to the economy. With the current demands on the global oil and gas market, Alberta's rich natural resources have led to a boom in the province's economy and job market.

MAIN CITIES

EDMONTON The capital of Alberta, it is in the province's south-central region on the North Saskatchewan River. It was first populated by the Cree and Blackfoot peoples. Founded in 1795 as Fort Edmonton, it became a major fur-trading post by the 19th century, developed rapidly with the arrival of the railway in 1891 and became the capital in 1906. The **University of Alberta** opened two years later.

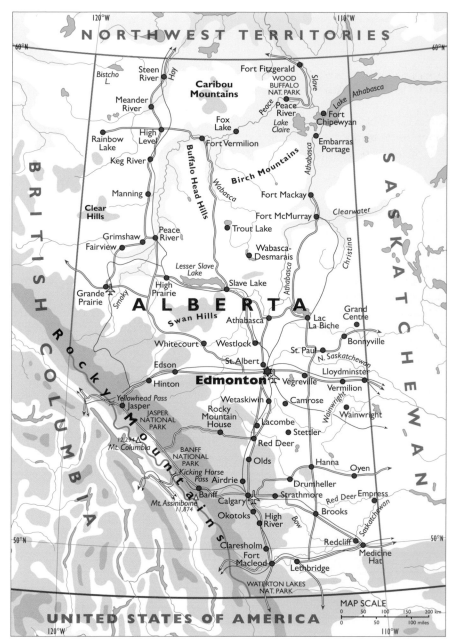

North America's first mosque was built here in 1938. Edmonton enjoyed a boom with the discovery of oil after World War II. The **West Edmonton Mall**, built from 1981–1998, is one of the world's largest, covering 48 city blocks. The main industries are coal mining, natural gas, petrochemicals, and oil refining. Population (2005) 712,391.

CALGARY City at the confluence of the Bow and Elbow rivers, in southern Alberta. The city was founded in 1875 as a post of the North West Mounted Police. It is an industrial and commercial center and has a university (est. 1966). The **Calgary Stampede** is a famous annual rodeo, which began in 1912. Vast deposits of oil were discovered in Alberta in the 1960s, leading to some 450 oil companies opening headquarters in Calgary. The city hosted the **Winter Olympic Games** in 1988. Industries include flour milling, lumber, brick, cement, natural gas, and oil refining. Population (2004) 933,495.

Two Jack Lake is one of the many beautiful lakes in Banff National Park, Alberta. The park is Canada's oldest, created as a small reserve in 1885 and expanded from 1887 onwards, with 2,564 sq mi (6,641 sq km) now under its protection.

PROVINCIAL FACTS

Admitted to Confederation September 1, 1905
National Parliament Representatives Senate 6, House of Commons 28
Population 3,256,800; ranked 4th
Capital Edmonton
Provincial legislature 83 members
Area 255,285 sq mi (661,188 sq km); ranked 6th
Elevation Highest 12,294 ft (3,750 m), Mount Columbia; lowest 600 ft (183 m), Salt River
Motto Strong and free
Provincial flower Wild rose
Provincial tree Lodgepole pine
Provincial bird Great horned owl

BRITISH COLUMBIA

British Columbia is a province of western Canada, on the Pacific Ocean, bordered on the south by the states of Washington, Idaho, and Montana, and in the northwest by the state of Alaska. Its major city is Vancouver and the capital is Victoria.

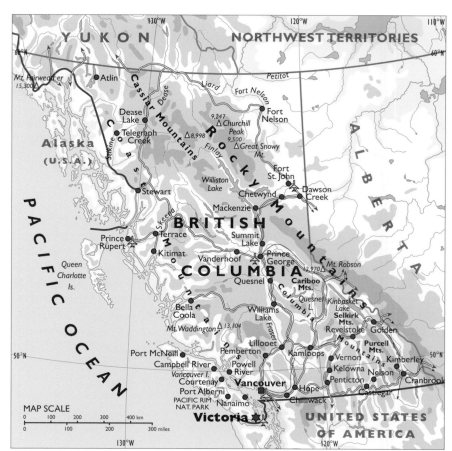

LAND AND ECONOMY

British Columbia is mountainous, with many ranges of the **Rocky Mountains** running from south to north with deep river valleys among them. The Pacific coastline is broken by many inlets with hundreds of islands, of which **Vancouver Island** in the southwest is the most important. Vast forests cover three-quarters of the province and yield the **lumber** that is a mainstay of the economy. The many rivers provide abundant hydroelectric power. Fishing is a major industry along the Pacific coast.

Manufacturing in the province is centered in the cities of the southwest, and agriculture is largely confined to the valleys. Dairying and fruit growing are the most important farming activities. The beautiful mountain and coast scenery, as well as the extensive parks system, attracts a profitable tourist trade.

The cities of the south and on the south end of Vancouver Island contain more than 70% of the population. The majority of the population originated from other Canadian provinces, and most trace their origins to the British Isles; more recently, the pattern of immigration has shifted from European to Asian countries.

There are several universities supported by the province, including the University of British Columbia, at Vancouver; Simon Fraser University, in Burnaby, a Vancouver suburb; and the University of Victoria.

HISTORY

The area was originally settled by groups from Asia some 10,000 years ago. These included the Salish, Haida, Nootka, and Kwakiutl. The region was sighted by the English navigator **Sir Francis Drake** in 1578, and **Captain James Cook** of Britain landed on the coast in 1778 while searching for the Northwest Passage, a water route across Canada. Russians and Spaniards sought to exploit the fur trade, and the British government sent **Captain George Vancouver** to map the area from 1792–1794 and to take possession of the land. In 1793, the Scottish explorer Alexander MacKenzie arrived as the first European to complete an overland journey across North America above Mexico. Other British explorers pushed west, and the region came to be called **New Caledonia**. In 1800, trading posts were established in the region by the North West Company, later part of the **Hudson's Bay Company**. In 1846, the southern boundary with the United States was fixed, and in 1849 Vancouver Island became a British colony. A boom resulted when **gold** was discovered in New Caledonia along the Fraser River in 1858 and then in the Cariboo region.

The island and New Caledonia were united as British Columbia in 1866 and became a Canadian province in 1871. The population increased when the first **transcontinental railroad** was completed in 1885, but the province encountered economic difficulties during the early 20th century. The economy improved with the completion of the Panama Canal in 1914, which allowed ships to reach the Atlantic more easily and so increased the province's trade with Europe and the eastern United States. British Columbia now has the most balanced export market of all territories and provinces with the U.S., Japan, European Union, and Pacific Rim countries.

MAIN CITIES

VANCOUVER City on the south shore of Burrard Inlet in southern British Columbia. It is Canada's third-largest city and principal Pacific port. The area was first explored by Europeans in 1792 by British Captain George Vancouver. The building of the Canadian Pacific Railway led to the city's incorporation in 1886 and allowed Vancouver to grow into the largest city on Canada's west coast. Some 30% of its population today is of Chinese ancestry. The excellent sea and air links make it one of North America's leading centers for transportation and communication. The beautiful harbor setting, pleasant climate, and railroad terminus make it a magnet for tourists. In 1986 the city had a world's fair, Expo 86, and it will host the Winter Olympic Games in 2010. It has two universities: the University of British Columbia (1908) and Simon Fraser University (1965). Industries include tourism, lumber, oil refining, shipbuilding, and fish processing. Population (2004) 2,173,100.
VICTORIA The capital of British Columbia and the province's second largest city. It is located on the southeastern end of Vancouver Island and has Canada's mildest

PROVINCIAL FACTS

Admitted to Confederation July 20, 1871
National Parliament Representatives Senate 6; House of Commons 36
Population 4,254,500; ranked 3rd
Capital Victoria
Provincial legislature 79 members
Area 366,255 sq mi (948,600 sq km); ranked 5th
Elevation Highest 15,300 ft (4,663 m), Mount Fairweather; lowest, sea level
Motto Splendor without diminishment
Provincial flower Flowering dogwood
Provincial tree Western red cedar
Provincial bird Steller's jay

False Creek – in fact, an ocean inlet from the Strait of Georgia – lies at the heart of downtown Vancouver. The south shore, with its towering office buildings, was once a traditional wintering area of the Squamish nation, who used it because of the rich fishing in the shallow waters of the inlet.

climate. Founded in 1843, Victoria developed during the 1858 gold rush as a supply base for prospectors. The University of Victoria (1963) traces its origins to the city's Victoria College (1903). Victoria's leading industries are lumber, paper, shipbuilding, fishing, and tourism. A large naval base is on its western edge in the township of Esquimalt. Population (2004) 330,200.

MANITOBA

Manitoba is a province in the plains region of south-central Canada. It is bordered on the east by Ontario, south by the states of Minnesota and North Dakota, west by Saskatchewan, and north by Nunavut and Hudson Bay.

LAND AND ECONOMY

In the south the land is chiefly prairie, while the north has rolling country and low hills. Three great lakes – Winnipeg, Winnipegosis, and Manitoba – lie in the central portion. The major rivers are the Red, Saskatchewan, Nelson, Winnipeg, and Assiniboine. More than one-third of the land is **forest**, but the rich farmlands of the south and center support agriculture, such as the extensive **wheat fields**, which were once a mainstay of the economy, but has now diversified to include cattle, hogs, poultry, oil seeds, barley, and oats. Large **oil fields** are in the southwest. Major industries include manufacturing, agriculture, hydroelectricity production, and mining of copper, gold, zinc, silver, nickel, and petroleum.

The south is the most heavily populated area. Most people are of British origin, but there are many French, Ukrainians, Germans, and Scandinavians. Manitoba is home to the University of Manitoba, the University of Winnipeg, and Brandon University.

HISTORY

The region's main First Nation groups were the Assiniboine and Cree. French and English fur traders entered the region in the 1600s, and in 1670 **King Charles II** granted the area, first called Rupert's Land, to the **Hudson's Bay Company**, a fur enterprise. The first settlers were Scots led by **Lord Selkirk** in 1812. The Canadian government bought the rights of the Hudson's Bay Company in 1870, and Manitoba joined the Confederation. Railroad building in the 1880s accelerated the development of the economy. After new ore discoveries in the Flin Flon area (1915) a mining boom began, to be followed by another in the 1960s.

MAIN CITY

WINNIPEG The capital of Manitoba is at the confluence of the Assiniboine and Red rivers. It was founded in 1812 by the Hudson's Bay Company and came under the control of the Canadian government in 1870. It grew after the completion of the **Canadian Pacific Railway** in 1885. In 2003 it opened the $76 million twin **Provencher Bridges** over the Red River. Today, with an extensive service sector and manufacturing industries, Winnipeg claims the most diverse economy of any Canadian city. Population (2005) 706,854.

Polar bears crossing a snowfield near Churchill, Manitoba. Churchill, standing at the edge of the arctic tundra, is on the bears' autumn route to the Hudson Bay.

PROVINCIAL FACTS

Admitted to Confederation July 15, 1870
National Parliament Representatives Senate 6; House of Commons 14
Population 1,119,600; ranked 5th
Capital Winnipeg
Provincial legislature 57 members
Area 250,947 sq mi (649,953 sq km); ranked 8th
Elevation Highest 2,729 ft (832 m), Baldy Mountain; lowest 400 ft (122 m)
Motto Glorious and free
Provincial flower Prairie crocus (pasqueflower)
Provincial tree White spruce
Provincial bird Great gray owl

NEW BRUNSWICK

New Brunswick, a province in eastern Canada, is one of the country's three **Maritime Provinces.** It is bordered in the north by Quebec, east by Nova Scotia, and west by the state of Maine.

LAND AND ECONOMY

The Gulf of St. Lawrence is on the east, and the Bay of Fundy, with the highest tides in the world at 52 ft (16 m), is on the south. The Saint John is the principal river. More than 75% of the province is **forest**, a valuable resource. **Fisheries** and **mineral deposits**, such as copper, zinc, and silver, are major sources of income. Agriculture products include potatoes and fruit.

New Brunswick is Canada's only official **bilingual province** (English and French). The original settlers were French, and 37% of the population speak that language. Institutions of higher education include the University of New Brunswick, St. Thomas University, Mount Allison University and Université de Moncton.

HISTORY

The first natives included the Mi'kmaq (Micmac), Maliseet, and Passamaquoddy peoples. The region was discovered by the French explorer **Jacques Cartier** in 1534, and the first French settlement was in 1604 at the mouth of the St. Croix River. With Nova Scotia, it formed the French colony of **Acadia**, ceded to Great

Britain in 1713. By 1755 the British had expelled more than 5,000 Acadians, many settling in Louisiana and northeastern New Brunswick, now the **Acadian Peninsula**. During the American Revolution, over 12,000 Loyalists from the American colonies arrived, helping to create the province in 1784. In 1867 it joined Nova Scotia, Quebec, and Ontario to establish the Dominion of Canada. In the 20th century, New Brunswick's economy moved into mining, manufacturing, and forestry.

MAIN CITIES

SAINT JOHN Canada's first incorporated city, located at the mouth of the Saint John River on the Bay of Fundy, was settled in 1785 by some 4,000 Loyalists fleeing the American colonies. The Saint John Waterfront Development Partnership is working toward revitalizing the historic harbor for residents and tourists. Population (2001) 122,680.

FREDERICTON New Brunswick's capital is on the Saint John River. The French established the village of **Ste. Anne's Point** there as the capital of **Acadia** from 1692 to 1698, but the British burned it. They named their new town Fredericton for the second son of King George III. About 2,000 American Loyalists fled here in 1783. Population (2004) 81,346.

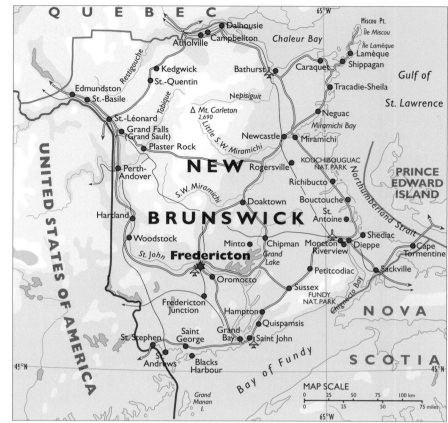

Cape Enrage Lighthouse stands on the southern tip of Barn Marsh Island in Albert County, New Brunswick. It is near the mouth of the Bay of Fundy, where local conditions magnify the tides to extreme ranges of up to 52 ft (16 m).

PROVINCIAL FACTS

Admitted to Confederation July 1, 1867; one of the original provinces of the Dominion of Canada
National Parliament Representatives Senate 10, House of Commons 10
Population 752,000; ranked 8th
Capital Fredericton
Provincial legislature 66 members
Area 28,354 sq mi (73,437 sq km); ranked 11th
Elevation Highest 2,690 ft (820 m), Mount Carleton; lowest, sea level
Motto Hope was restored
Provincial flower Purple violet
Provincial tree Balsam fir
Provincial bird Black-capped chickadee

NEWFOUNDLAND AND LABRADOR

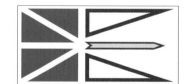

Newfoundland is the large island part of this Canadian province on the Atlantic Ocean, while Labrador is on the mainland. They are separated by the **Strait of Belle Isle**, and though similar in many ways, each has its own culture and history.

LAND AND ECONOMY

The surface of the island and mainland, which are separated by the Strait of Belle Isle, is generally rolling. Newfoundland's **Cape Spear** is the most easterly point in North America. The coastline is broken by deep bays and inlets with many islands, and is the site of the main national parks, including **Gros Morne National Park.** Whales and icebergs can be viewed around the coast. Forests cover much of the land and are a major sector of the economy. Newfoundland's **cod fisheries**, famous for nearly 500 years, have been affected by international over-fishing. Another popular ocean product is lobster. Offshore oil sales account for a large percentage of the export sector. Great mineral deposits as yet have not been accessed. The discovery of nickel reserves at Voisey's Bay leads forecasters to predict extensive economic growth for the province in years to come. Wilderness tourism is a developing economic sector.

Nearly all of the population live along the coasts, mainly in Newfoundland. **Memorial University of Newfoundland** at St. John's is the province's only institution of higher education.

Part of the vast tundra landscape of Labrador, seen in fall. Although the ground never completely thaws, it warms enough in summer to support grasses, moss, and lichens, and the animals, such as caribou and deer, that feed on them.

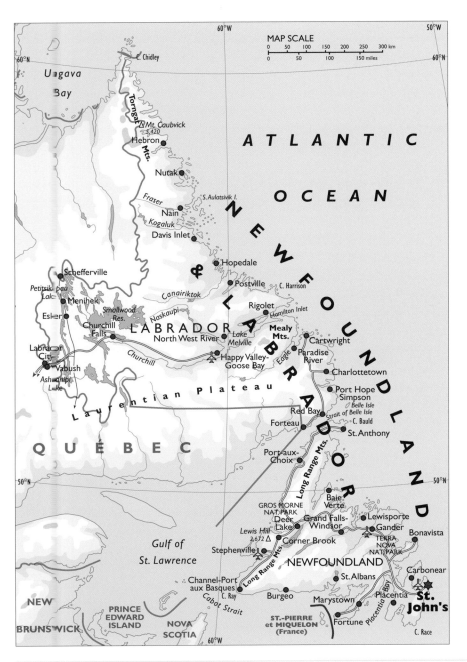

HISTORY

Norsemen probably reached Labrador about AD 1000 and established a short-lived settlement on the northern tip of Newfoundland. English navigator **John Cabot** found the island in 1497 and the Labrador coast in 1498. Sir **Humphrey Gilbert** formally claimed the island for England in 1583, and the population grew slowly until it became a British colony in 1832. Labrador was under the jurisdiction of the governor of Newfoundland, and both remained separate from the Dominion of Canada until joining the Confederation in 1949 as the province of Newfoundland, with Labrador added to the name in 2001. **Queen Elizabeth** visited in 1997 for the 500th anniversary of Cabot's discovery.

MAIN CITY

ST. JOHN'S The province's capital and largest city is North America's oldest city and the closest to Europe. Discovered by John Cabot in 1497, it became Britain's first overseas colony. It has North America's oldest continuing sporting event, the **Royal St. John's Regatta**, begun in 1826. **Guglielmo Marconi** sent the first transatlantic wireless transmission in 1901 from Cornwall, England, to Signal Hill overlooking the city. In 1919, **John Alcock** and **Arthur Brown** made the first nonstop transatlantic flight, flying from St. John's to Ireland. Population (2001) 172,918.

PROVINCIAL FACTS

Admitted to Confederation March 31, 1949
National Parliament Representatives Senate 5,
House of Commons 7
Population 514,409; ranked 9th
Capital St. John's
Provincial legislature 48 members
Area 156,185 sq mi (404,420 sq km); ranked 10th
Elevation Highest 5,420 ft (1,652 m), Mount
Caubrick; lowest, sea level
Motto Seek ye first the kingdom of God
Provincial flower Pitcher plant
Provincial tree Black spruce
Provincial bird Atlantic puffin

NORTHWEST TERRITORIES

A territory in northern Canada between two other territories, Yukon to the west and Nunavut to the east; its southern border is shared with the provinces of Saskatchewan, Alberta, and part of British Columbia.

LAND AND ECONOMY

This vast wilderness contains forests, tundra, clean rivers, and thousands of lakes. Two major lakes are **Great Bear** and **Great Slave** in the Mackenzie district. The principal river is the **Mackenzie**, flowing into the Arctic Ocean. Among the islands in the **Arctic Archipelago** are Banks and parts of Victoria and Melville. About 15% of the land is forested, and beyond the treeline there is virtually no vegetation of importance. Permafrost – perennially frozen ground – underlies much of the territory. Diamonds and gold are mined, as well as uranium, petroleum, nickel, and copper. Few roads accessible by car exist outside the district of Mackenzie.

Many Native peoples live on the land and hunt; however, today as part of mining development agreements, First Nations and Inuit people are finding employment at the mines. The main cluster of the population is around **Yellowknife** on Great Slave Lake in south Mackenzie. The territory recognizes eight official languages: English, French, and six native ones. Schools are few and dispersed. There are no universities, but **Aurora College** offers continuing education at Inuvik, Fort Smith, and Yellowknife.

HISTORY

The first inhabitants in the region, moving from Asia, were the **Dene**, or Athapaskans, and later the **Inuit**. The **Vikings** were the first Europeans to arrive,

The western edge of the Mackenzie Delta, seen from the air in winter. The river and its floodplain are frozen, but thaw in summer and are prone to flooding. The Richardson mountains of the Yukon are in the distance.

around AD 1000. In 1670, the **Hudson's Bay Company**, a fur-trading enterprise, received a charter to much of the huge lands west of Hudson Bay from King Charles II. In 1870, the Canadian government bought the lands from the company. The boundaries of the territory and of the interior districts were changed several times. During the 1960s an extensive road-building program made many mineral deposits – especially lead and zinc – more accessible; exploration boomed during the 1970s and early 1980s. The largest land claim in Canadian history by the native Inuit resulted in the creation in 1999 of **Nunavut territory** in the east, which took 808,185 sq mi (2,093,190 sq km) from the Northwest Territories.

MAIN CITY

YELLOWKNIFE The capital and largest city of the territory is on the northern shores of **Great Slave Lake**. It is an administrative and commercial center that also serves as a base for outdoor activities. Gold was discovered here in the early 1930s, and in the 1990s diamond mining began 200 miles (300 km) north of the city. Today it is known as the "Diamond Capital of North America." The city's name comes from the copper knives once used by the native **Slavey** people. Population (2005) 19,429.

TERRITORIAL FACTS

Admitted as Territory July 15, 1870
National Parliament Representatives Senate 1, House of Commons 1
Population 42,982, ranked 11th
Capital Yellowknife
Territorial legislature 19 members
Area 519,734 sq mi (1,346,106 sq km); ranked 3rd
Elevation: Highest 9,098 ft (2,775 m), Mount Nirvana; lowest, sea level
Motto No official motto
Territorial flower Mountain avens
Territorial tree Tamarack
Territorial bird Gyrfalcon

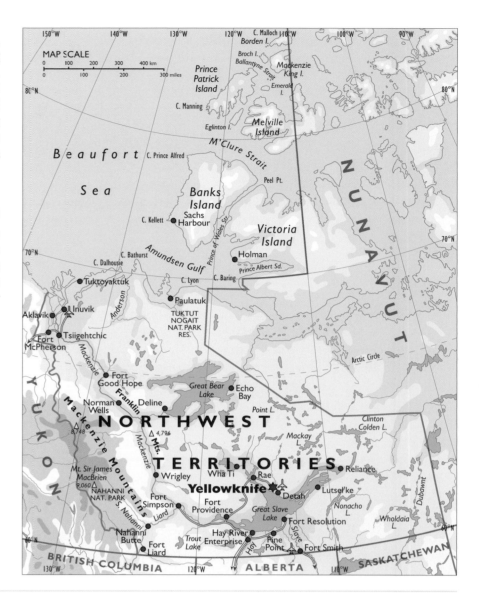

NOVA SCOTIA

Nova Scotia is one of the **Maritime Provinces** of Canada, on the Atlantic Ocean. It is connected to its **Cape Breton Island** in the north by a narrow strait and to the province of New Brunswick on its west by the **Isthmus of Chignecto**.

LAND AND ECONOMY

Nova Scotia is virtually surrounded by the Atlantic Ocean and its bays. The land, nearly level or gently rolling, has been compared with Scotland; its name is derived from the Latin for "New Scotland." There are some 3,000 lakes, but no rivers of importance.

PROVINCIAL FACTS

Admitted to Confederation July 1, 1867; one of the original provinces of the Dominion of Canada
National Parliament Representatives Senate 10, House of Commons 11
Population 937,900; ranked 7th
Capital Halifax
Provincial legislature 52 members
Area 21,425 sq mi (55,491 sq km); ranked 12th
Elevation Highest 1,747 ft (533 m), White Hill; lowest, sea level
Motto One defends and the other conquers
Provincial flower Trailing arbutus (pink mayflower)
Provincial tree Red spruce
Provincial bird Osprey

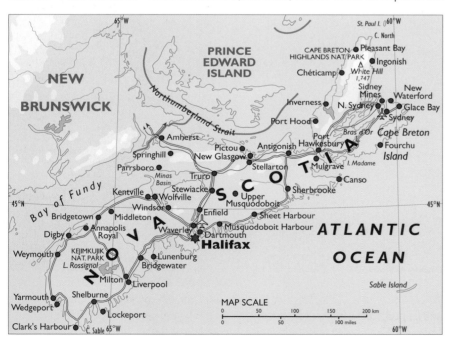

Extensive forests and rich fishing grounds have been the traditional base of the economy. The port city of **Halifax** is an important manufacturing center. The province has been a leader in Canadian coal production, though many mines have closed. The fishing industry supplies products like lobster, scallops and other shellfish. The farming sector is highly varied, and major minerals are coal, gypsum, salt, clay, sand, gravel, and stone. Industries include shipbuilding, pulp and paper, steelmaking, and food processing.

The bulk of the population are descendants of British immigrants, especially from Scotland, although there remains a sizable proportion of French ancestry.

Dalhousie University, in Halifax, is the largest of 11 universities. Others include Acadia University, St. Mary's University, St. Francis Xavier University, Mount St. Vincent University, and the University of King's College.

HISTORY

The original settlers were the native **Mi'kmaq** (Micmac) peoples but Nova Scotia's strategic position made it a prize in a struggle of empires. The first settlement was by the French at **Port Royal** in 1605 – the first permanent European community in North America north of Florida. Other settlers came to the area, and the French

named the land **Acadia**. Nova Scotia was taken and retaken eight times by the British and French. The mainland was awarded to the British in 1713, and Cape Breton Island was seized from the French in 1758. The British deported more than 4,000 Acadians. After the mid-18th century came steady immigration from the British Isles. The **American Revolution** resulted in the province receiving thousands of British Loyalists from New England. Today, many historic sites, like Louisbourg, have been reconstructed to tell the stories of the past.

MAIN CITY

HALIFAX Nova Scotia's capital is the largest Canadian city east of Montréal. Its harbor on the Atlantic is one of the world's largest. **Mi'kmaqs** (Micmacs) first settled there, and the British founded Halifax in 1749. It had Canada's first representative government, first post office, first Protestant church, and first newspaper. It was home to a British naval base during the American Revolution and both world wars; a large Canadian naval base remains. Population (2004) 379,800.

The lighthouse on Peggys Point, south of Peggys Cove, on Nova Scotia's south coast. One of the many small fishing communities that lie on St. Margarets Bay, Peggys Cove is today a focus for tourism.

NUNAVUT

Nunavut is a territory in northern Canada that was until 1999 part of the **Northwest Territories,** now on its western border. Manitoba is in the south, and Nunavut's many islands stretch north to Greenland and south to Quebec.

LAND AND ECONOMY

Nunavut extends above the treeline to the **North Pole**, and this vast area of land and water is one-fifth the size of Canada. None of the territory's 26 communities is accessible by road or rail, which contributes to the highest cost of living in Canada. Fishing is a growth industry, with the main products being turbot, shrimp, and char. Mineral exploration continues for diamonds, gold, and base metal deposits, with a diamond mine proposed for the **Kitikmeot** region in the north. Oil and gas reserves are also set for future development. The largest employer in the territory is the government, but growth is occurring in the mining and fishing industries, native arts, and tourism.

The territory has Canada's youngest population, with an average age of just over 22 years. The **Inuit** people represent about 85% of the population, which has the extremely low density of one person per 27 sq mi (70 sq km). There are four official languages: Inuktitut, Inuinaqtun, English, and French.

Nunavut Arctic College offers post-secondary education and training programs at campuses in Iqaluit, Cambridge Bay, and Rankin Inlet.

HISTORY

Until 1999, Nunavut was part of the Northwest Territories. Its creation was proposed in 1976 as a settlement of **Inuit land claims**. In 1992, the majority of voters in the Northwest Territories approved the new boundary for division and the allocation of 808,185 sq mi (2,093,190 sq km) to the new territory. On April 1, 1999, Nunavut (the name means "our land" in Inuktitut) became Canada's third territory. The **Government of Nunavut** embraces traditional knowledge with modern innovation – a blending of parliamentary democracy with Aboriginal customs and values.

MAIN CITY

IQALUIT The territory's capital and only city is on **Baffin Island** in hills above Koojesse Inlet of **Frobisher Bay,** one of the most easterly points from Nunavut's mainland. It came into existence in 1942 as a U.S. air base and was named Frobisher Bay. The Americans left in 1963, and the name was changed in 1987 to Iqaluit, which means "place of many fish" in the Inuktitut language. It was selected as the future territory's capital in 1995. It is accessible from mainland Canada only by air and sea. In the years to come, economic growth sectors are expected to be in tourism, retail, and the service sector. Population (2006) 6,000.

TERRITORIAL FACTS

Admitted as territory 1999
National Parliament Representatives Senate 1, House of Commons 1
Population 29,300; ranked 13th
Capital Iqaluit
Territorial legislature 19 members
Area: 808,185 sq mi (2,093,190 sq km); ranked 1st
Elevation: Highest 8,583 ft (2,618 m), Barbeau Peak, Ellesmere Island; lowest, sea level
Motto Nunavut, our strength
Territorial flower Purple saxifrage
Territorial bird Rock ptarmigan

An Inuit hunter with sled dogs on Nunavut's ice fields. Many Inuit preserve traditional practices.

ONTARIO

Province in southeast Canada, bordered to the south by four of the **Great Lakes.** As the most populous province and the site of the federal capital at Ottawa, it exerts considerable influence in national affairs.

LAND AND ECONOMY

The country is rolling or level, of generally even elevation. Forests cover the land in the north toward **Hudson Bay**, while the center and south offer good farming land. Many rivers supply hydroelectric power for industry. The famous **Niagara Falls** are on the Niagara River on the southeastern border. The Great Lakes and the St. Lawrence River provide excellent water transportation; since the opening of the **St. Lawrence Seaway,** ocean-going vessels have been able to use Ontario's ports. Ontario is Canada's most industrialized province, with transportation equipment, iron and steel, paper, and processed foods the leading products.

About 90% of the population live in the southern part of the province on about 15% of the total area. About 80% dwell in urban areas.

There are more than 20 institutions of higher education, including the University of Toronto, the University of Western Ontario, the University of Ottawa, Queen's University, McMaster University, and York University.

HISTORY

French explorers roamed through the region early in the 17th century and established fur-trading posts. The area became part of **New France,** the French colonies in North America, but was ceded to Great Britain in 1763. Its population was expanded by thousands of **British Loyalists** fleeing the American colonies during and after the American Revolution. Most of the population has British ancestry, but about 10% is French-speaking. For 50 years after 1791, Ontario was known as **Upper Canada,** separate from Quebec. The two were reunited in 1841 and known as Canada until 1867, when the separate provinces of Ontario and Quebec were created and the Dominion of Canada was formed.

Ontario's mining industries began to develop during the late 19th century. The development of cheap hydroelectric power fueled further industrial growth from the beginning of the 20th century, and the region became Canada's economic center. After World War II Ontario received about 1.5 million immigrants from war-torn countries in Europe. The province now contains the highest proportion of people born outside of Canada.

MAIN CITIES

OTTAWA Capital of Canada, situated in southeastern Ontario on the Ottawa River and the Rideau Canal. Founded in 1826 as Bytown, it acquired its present name in 1854. **Queen Victoria** chose it as capital of the United Provinces in 1858, and in 1867 it became the national capital of the Dominion of Canada. Its economy now revolves around the administration of the Canadian government and high-technology industry, though other industries include printing, publishing, and lumber products. Population (2004) 845,875.

TORONTO Capital of Ontario and Canada's largest city, situated on the northern shore of **Lake Ontario**. An inland port at the mouth of the Don River, it is Canada's main financial and manufacturing center. The site was first visited in 1615 by the French explorer **Étienne Brulé**. In 1787, the British purchased the area from Native Americans, and the settlement of York was founded in 1793. U.S. troops captured the city twice during the War of 1812. In 1834 it was renamed Toronto, from a Huron word for "meeting place," and it became the capital of Ontario province in 1867. Its development was spurred by the opening in 1959 of the **St. Lawrence Seaway**. Toronto produces more than half of all Canada's manufacturing products. Industries include electrical equipment, iron and steel, meat packing, and the manufacture of aircraft and motor vehicles. The city is part of the "**Golden Horseshoe,**" a densely populated region of Ontario containing approximately one-quarter of the Canadian population. The city is home to people from over 100 cultures, resulting in a rich and vibrant multicultural city. Population (2001) 4,683,000.

HAMILTON City in southeastern Ontario, 40 miles (65 km) southwest of Toronto. Founded in 1815, it grew into a major industrial center in the second half of the 19th century. By the early 1900s it was dominated by the iron and steel industries. Though it is still an important communication and manufacturing center, Hamilton's heavy industries are being replaced by diversification into services and technology. Industries include vehicles, electrical equipment, and textiles. Population (2001) 662,401.

PROVINCIAL FACTS

Admitted to Confederation July 1, 1867; one of the original provinces of the Dominion of Canada
National Parliament Representatives Senate 24; House of Commons 106
Population 11,410,046; ranked 1st
Capital Toronto
Provincial legislature 103 members
Area 412,582 sq mi (1,068,587 sq km); ranked 4th
Elevation Highest 2,275 ft (693 m), Ishpatina Ridge; lowest, sea level at Hudson and James bays
Motto Loyal she began, loyal she remains
Provincial flower White trillium
Provincial tree Eastern white pine
Provincial bird Common loon

Downtown Toronto seen from the CN Tower. The provincial capital of Ontario, Toronto stands on the northern shore of Lake Ontario. The CN Tower, opened in 1976, is the world's tallest free-standing structure at 1,815 ft (553 m). It attracts some 2 million tourists a year.

PRINCE EDWARD ISLAND

Prince Edward Island is a province of eastern Canada, in the southern part of the **Gulf of St. Lawrence**. It is Canada's smallest province both in population and land, but is the most densely populated.

LAND AND ECONOMY

High cliffs rise along the coast, but the land is low and rolling. Fertile soils and a temperate climate are favorable to agriculture, which has long been the province's chief source of income. Fishing and tourism are also important. Manufacturing is limited to a few small plants. The University of Prince Edward Island is at **Charlottetown**.

Because of its small size, Prince Edward Island is the most densely populated province in Canada. Most of the population have English, Irish, or French ancestry.

HISTORY

The first European to discover the island was **Jacques Cartier** in 1534. Under the name of **Ile St. Jean** (St. John's Island), the island was a French fishing station until it was captured by the British in 1745. Retaken by the French, it finally passed to the British by treaty in 1763. The name was changed to Prince Edward Island in 1798. As the forest was cleared, agriculture broadened the economic base, which had been founded on fishing. Prince Edward Island joined the Dominion of Canada in 1873, hoping to alleviate its economic difficulties. The province was granted extensive economic aid during the 1940s, and in 1969 a comprehensive economic development plan was launched.

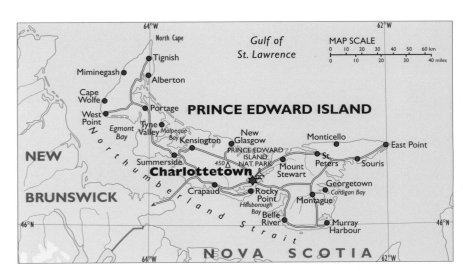

MAIN CITY

CHARLOTTETOWN Capital and major port of Prince Edward Island. It is linked to mainland Canada by the 8-mile (13-km) long **Confederation Bridge**, and is the smallest of Canada's provincial capitals. The city was founded by the French circa 1720 as Port La Joie; Charlottetown was was laid out in its present location by the British in 1768. It is named for the wife of **George III** of England. In 1864, Charlottetown hosted the **Conference of the Maritime Provinces**, which led to the Confederation of Canada. In 1992, it was the site of the signing of the **Charlottetown Accord**, which amended the Canadian constitution. Charlottetown's economy, as with most provincial capitals in Canada, is dominated by the public sector. Other important economic activities include the technology sector, tourism, and light manufacturing such as chemicals, biotechnology, and machining. Population (2001) 58,358.

An aerial view of the western coastline of Prince Edward Island. The island's coastline has many small bays, low cliffs and beaches, some with a distinctive red-tinted sand that results from iron oxide in the rock. The island lies in the Gulf of St. Lawrence, which opens into the North Atlantic.

PROVINCIAL FACTS
Admitted to Confederation July 1, 1873
National Parliament Representatives Senate 4; House of Commons 4
Population 135,294; ranked 10th
Capital Charlottetown
Provincial Legislature 27 members
Area 2,184 sq mi (5,657 sq km); ranked 13th
Elevation Highest, 466 ft (142 m); lowest, sea level
Motto The small under the protection of the great
Provincial flower Lady's slipper
Provincial tree Red oak
Provincial bird Blue jay

QUEBEC

Quebec is a province in eastern Canada, the largest in area and second in population among the provinces and territories. It is bordered in the northeast by Labrador, south by New Brunswick and New England states, and west by Ontario.

LAND AND ECONOMY

A rugged wilderness covers most of the north, reaching along the east shore of **Hudson Bay** to Hudson Strait. This land is rich in minerals. The **St. Lawrence River** in the extreme south, flowing from the Great Lakes to the Atlantic Ocean, has been vital in Quebec's history and economy. In its valley and to the south lie the agricultural lands. The **Appalachian Mountains** of eastern North America extend into the far southeast. Quebec's wealth in natural resources, especially lumber and minerals, has sustained its economy at a high level. Hydroelectric power is extensive, and Quebec is a major paper producer in North America. Manufacturing is centered in the cities along the St. Lawrence and in the south. **Montreal** is a major port and financial center. Tourism makes an important year-round contri-bution to the province's income. Major industrial products are pulp and paper, aluminum, petroleum products, electrical equipment, railroad equipment, textiles, clothing, and food

products. Agricultural products include hay, oats, potatoes, cattle, dairy products, and maple sugar. Among the chief minerals are iron, copper, and asbestos.

More than 80% of the population is of French descent and French-speaking – the remainder of the population is chiefly of English ancestry.

There are six major institutions of higher education: Laval University, the University of Montreal, the University of Sherbrooke, McGill University, Bishop's University, and Concordia University.

HISTORY

The Frenchman **Jacques Cartier** found the east coast in 1534 and later sailed up the St. Lawrence. The first permanent settlement in the area was **Quebec City**, founded on the St. Lawrence by **Samuel de Champlain** in 1608. **Montreal** was settled in 1642. From the expanding colony, the French pushed trading and military posts to the west. Quebec City fell to the British in 1759 during the **Seven Years' War**, Montreal surrendered in 1760, and in 1763 the entire area was ceded by treaty to Great Britain and became a British colony. Thousands of American Loyalists fleeing the American Revolution resulted in the country being divided in 1791 into Lower Canada (Quebec) and Upper Canada (Ontario); in 1841 the parts were united as the province of Canada.

With the establishment of the Dominion of Canada in 1867, Quebec became a province under that name. In the mid-20th century, francophone (French-speaking) elements intensified their demands for recognition of their cultural heritage. In 1976 the separatist **Parti Québécois**, under the leadership of René

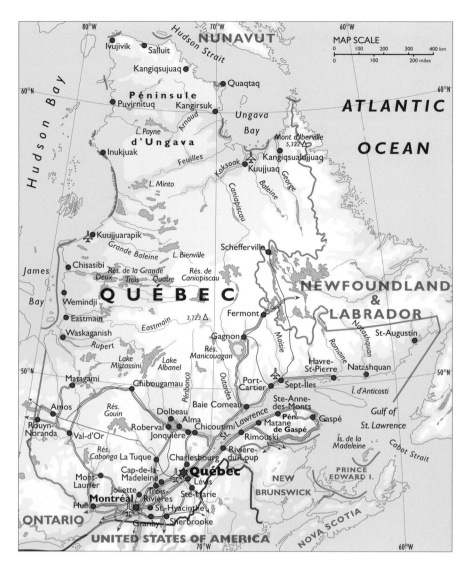

PROVINCIAL FACTS

Admitted to Confederation July 1, 1867; one of the original provinces of the Dominion of Canada
National Parliament Representatives Senate 24, House of Commons 75
Population 7,237,479; ranked 2nd
Capital Quebec City
Provincial legislature 125 members
Area 594,860 sq mi (1,540,687 sq km); ranked 2nd
Elevation Highest 5,420 ft (1,652 m), Mount D'Iberville; lowest, sea level
Motto Je me souviens
Provincial flower Blue flag iris
Provincial tree Yellow birch
Provincial bird Snowy owl

Old Quebec City, here at dusk in winter, is an important tourist attraction and has original city walls. The Château Frontenac (1893), one of the first of many château-style hotels built for the Canadian Pacific Railway, dominates the skyline.

Lévesque was elected, and the following year French was made the official language of the province. The Canadian Supreme Court struck down the law in 1979. In a 1980 referendum, Quebec voters rejected a separate status for the province, but unity remains an issue in the province.

MAIN CITIES

MONTREAL The province's largest city and Canada's second largest is on **Montreal Island** and the north bank of the St. Lawrence River. An extinct volcano rises 764 ft (233 m) in the middle of the island. Montreal is the country's chief port. The French settled the site in 1642 and remained until the British seized control in 1760. Its growth accelerated with the opening of the **Lachine Canal** in 1825, connecting it to the Great Lakes. Montreal has a huge **underground city** at its center, constructed to ease the harsh winter weather and traffic congestion. Its industries include aircraft, electrical equipment, textiles, and oil refining. The city hosted the Summer Olympic Games in 1976. Population (2001) 3,426,350.

QUEBEC CITY The capital of Quebec is a port at the confluence of the St. Lawrence and St. Charles rivers. **Samuel de Champlain** established a French trading post there in 1608. It was the capital of **New France** before Britain took control in 1763. American revolutionaries tried unsuccessfully to capture the city in 1775. The British completed the French **Citadel** in 1820 that dominates Quebec from the **Old Upper Town**. The city is a focal point for Canada's French-speaking separatists. Industries include shipbuilding, paper, leather, and textiles. Tourism profits from its annual 17-day **Winter Carnival**. Population (2001) 682,757.

SASKATCHEWAN

Saskatchewan is a province in west-central Canada, in the plains region. It is bordered on the east by Manitoba, west by Alberta, north by the Northwest Territories, and south by the states of Montana and North Dakota.

LAND AND ECONOMY

Saskatchewan's southern half is on the fertile **Interior Plains**, and the northern half is in the lake-strewn **Canadian Shield.** The country is gently rolling with the highest elevations in the southwest. The south is chiefly agricultural land; the north is forested wilderness. Rivers cut deep valleys, and there are more than 100,000 lakes, rivers, and streams. **Prince Albert National Park** in the province's center is a large wilderness area. Saskatchewan has over one-third of Canada's farmland. Mining is also important, with the **Athabasca Basin** region being the world's largest exporter of uranium and having nearly two-thirds of the world's recoverable potash reserves. Other minerals include copper, zinc, gold, natural gas, and coal.

People of English descent form the largest sector of the population. The three universities are the University of Saskatchewan, in Saskatoon; the University of Regina; and the First Nations University of Canada in Regina.

Fields and a farmhouse on the plains of Saskatchewan. The province has about one-third of Canada's farmland and grows many crops, particularly great amounts of wheat.

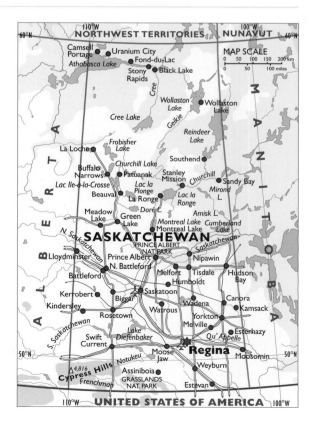

HISTORY

The region's First Nation peoples were mainly the Cree. The Hudson's Bay Company ceded rights to the Canadian government in 1870, and the region became part of the Northwest Territories. Major settlement did not begin until the 19th century when immigrants came from eastern Canada, the United States, and Europe.

The Metis people, led by **Louis Riel**, staged the North-West Rebellion in 1885. They formed a provisional government, but were defeated later that year. Slow immigration created farming communities through the 19th century, but the main influx of population did not begin until the completion of the **Canadian Pacific Railway** in 1885. The Canadian government provided free land to encourage settlers. Saskatchewan joined the Confederation on the same day as Alberta in 1905. Almost a million Europeans settlers had moved to the province by 1930. Under Saskatchewan's Socialist government (1944–1964), many

PROVINCIAL FACTS

Admitted to Confederation September 1, 1905
National Parliament Representatives Senate 6, House of Commons 14
Population 994,100; ranked 6th
Capital Regina
Provincial Legislature 58 members
Area 251,100 sq mi (651,903 sq km); ranked 7th
Elevation Highest 4,816 ft (1,468 m), Cypress Hills; lowest 699 ft (213 m), Lake Athabasca
Motto From many peoples, strength
Provincial flower Western red lily
Provincial tree White birch
Provincial bird Sharp-tailed grouse

social welfare programs were introduced that were later adopted by the national government.

MAIN CITIES

REGINA The province's capital is located in the center of the Canadian plains. The Canadian Pacific Railway arrived in 1882, and the town was named Regina that year in honor of Queen Victoria. **The North West Mounted Police** were headquartered here for several years. Regina became the capital of the province in 1906. Buildings in its downtown area are connected by enclosed walkways. Population (2001) 192,000.
SASKATOON The largest city in the province is located on the the Saskatchewan River. The first Europeans arrived in 1883 – members of the **Temperance Colonization Society** from Ontario, and the city was incorporated in 1906. The city is the agriculture biotechnology capital of Canada. Population (2001) 225,927.

YUKON TERRITORY

Yukon Territory is in the extreme northwest of Canada, bounded on the north by the Beaufort Sea, on the east by Northwest Territories, on the south by British Columbia, and on the west by the state of Alaska.

LAND AND ECONOMY

The territory's north consists of Arctic wilderness and is virtually uninhabited. Further south there is spectacular mountain scenery with lakes and coniferous forests. **Mount Logan** in **Kluane National Park** in the southwest is the highest point in Canada. The region is drained by the **Yukon** and **Mackenzie** rivers. The climate is harsh, with freezing winters and short summers. The principal activity is mining, with deposits including lead, zinc, silver, and gold. Forestry and tourism are important.

Nearly half of today's population is of British ancestry, more than one-third have other European connections, and about one-quarter are First Nations peoples.

HISTORY

The **Athapaskan** people were the first occupiers of the region. In 1789, Scotland's **Alexander Mackenzie** explored down the river now bearing his name, and England's **John Franklin,** searching for the Northwest Passage, mapped the Arctic coastline of the province. The **Hudson's Bay Company** set up trading posts in the 1840s, and the Canadian government acquired the land in 1870, dividing it from the **Northwest Territories** in 1898. The **Klondike Gold Rush** brought over 30,000 prospectors in the late 1890s, and more than $95 million was mined from 1896 to 1903 before the gold was depleted. In 1900, the **White Pass and Yukon Railway** was completed and the building of the **Alaska Highway** in 1942 and 1943 brought over 30,000 U.S. Army personnel into the territory and made it accessible to cars.

MAIN CITY

WHITEHORSE The capital and Yukon's largest city is in the south-central area of the territory. It is Canada's most westerly capital city. The capital was moved here in 1953 from Dawson City. Whitehorse is now an important communication and transportation center. Its name was given by gold miners who thought the rapids at Miles Canyon looked like the manes of charging white horses. Population (2005) 23,511.

A kayaker paddles near icebergs on Lowell Lake in the Yukon Territory. The icebergs have "calved" from the Lowell Glacier, one of many glaciers that feed water into the territory's lakes and rivers.

TERRITORIAL FACTS

Admitted as territory June 13, 1898
National Parliament Representatives Senate 1, House of Commons 1
Population 31,587; ranked 12th
Capital Whitehorse
Provincial legislature 18 members
Area 186,675 sq mi (483,450 sq km); ranked 9th
Elevation Highest 19,551 ft (5,959 m), Mount Logan, St. Elias Mountains; lowest, sea level
Motto No official motto
Provincial flower Fireweed
Provincial tree Subalpine fir
Provincial bird Common raven

ALABAMA

Alabama is a southeastern U.S. state that borders the Gulf of Mexico in the south, and three states: Georgia is east, Mississippi west, and Tennessee north. It was one of the six original states of the Confederacy.

LAND AND ECONOMY

Roughly the north half of the state lies in the Appalachian Highlands, which have deposits of coal and other minerals; the remainder is in the Gulf Coastal Plain, which is crossed by the **Black Belt**, a wide strip of rich, black soil valuable for farming. The chief river system is the Tennessee-Tombigbee Waterway, a project completed in 1985 to connect those two rivers. The Mobile River, with its tributaries, the Alabama and Tombigbee, flows to the Gulf of Mexico. On the Tennessee River in the north are hydroelectric power dams and a **Tennessee Valley Authority** nuclear power plant.

Traditionally agrarian, the economy has been altered by industrial growth. Birmingham is a leading steel center, Mobile is a major international port, and Huntsville has NASA's **George C. Marshall Space Flight Center** for rocket and missile research. Major industrial products include iron and steel products, automobiles, chemicals, processed foods, paper and paper products, and textiles. Among agriculture's main products are cotton, poultry, and cattle. The chief minerals are coal, petroleum, and stone, especially marble and limestone. In the 21st century the state has become a center of **automobile production**, with foreign companies like Mercedes, Toyota, and Honda opening facilities.

The five largest reported ancestry groups in Alabama are African American, American, English, Irish, and German. The state is part of the "**Bible Belt**," an area in which Christian Evangelical Protestantism is an integral part of the culture.

There are about 60 institutions of higher education. The major state-supported schools are the University of Alabama, which has a renowned medical school, Auburn University, and the University of South Alabama. Tuskegee University is ranked as one of America's best colleges; **George Washington Carver** was one of its most noteworthy professors.

HISTORY

Alabama was first inhabited by Native American peoples, mostly the Cherokee, Creek, Chickasaw, Choctaw, and Alabama. The Spanish explorer **Hernando de Soto** visited in 1540, but the first European settlers were the French in 1701 on **Mobile Bay**. Great Britain acquired the region from France in 1763 and ceded most of it to the United States after the American Revolution (1783). Some of the south, part of Florida then, was in Spanish hands until 1812. **Andrew Jackson** defeated the powerful Creek Confederacy in 1814, and three years later the Territory of Alabama was created. Alabama seceded on January 11, 1861, and Montgomery was briefly the first Confederate capital. The state was readmitted to the Union in June 1868.

During the 1950s and 1960s it was a center of civil rights activities when **Martin Luther King, Jr.** began his civil rights campaign with a Montgomery bus boycott after **Rosa Parks** refused to yield her bus seat to a white person. **Governor George C. Wallace** achieved national prominence as a proponent of segregation. An independent presidential candidate in 1968, Wallace withdrew from national politics in 1972 after an assassination attempt left him partially paralyzed. He then gained African American support and was reelected governor in 1982.

MAIN CITIES

BIRMINGHAM Alabama's largest city is in the state's north central region, founded after the Civil War in 1871 as a steel town, known as "the Pittsburgh of the South" and, because of its rapid growth, "the Magic City." The Vulcan statue on Red Mountain is the world's largest cast-iron statue. The city was a focus for civil rights in the 1960s. Today, the Birmingham Civil Rights Institute provides educational programs about the roots and history of the civil rights movement. Population (2004) 233,149.

Camellias, the state flower of Alabama, grace the DeSoto Falls in DeSoto State Park, Alabama. The park lies on the slopes of Lookout Mountain. In 1570, an expedition sent by Hernando de Soto camped at the falls as they searched for gold and precious stones.

STATE FACTS

Admitted to Union December 14, 1819; ranked 22nd
U.S. Congress Senate 2, House of Representatives 7
Population 4,557,808; ranked 23rd
Capital Montgomery
State legislature Senate 35, House of Representatives 105
Area 52,419 sq mi (135,765 sq km); ranked 30th
Elevation Highest 2,405 ft (733 m), Mount Cheaha; lowest, sea level
State nicknames Heart of Dixie, Camellia State
State motto We dare defend our rights
State bird Yellowhammer
State flower Camellia
State tree Longleaf pine

MOBILE A port city founded in 1710, it was the capital of French Louisiana from 1710 to 1719. The nation's first Mardi Gras celebrations were held here and remain a major attraction. During the Civil War, the Battle of Mobile Bay occurred on August 5, 1864, with the victorious U.S. Admiral David Farragut ordering, "Damn the torpedoes, full speed ahead." The port of Mobile today has the world's largest terminal for forest products. Population (2004) 192,759.

MONTGOMERY Located in the state's east-central region, Montgomery was the city in which the Confederate government was established in 1861 and its president, Jefferson Davis, inaugurated; it served that year as capital of the Confederacy. Martin Luther King, a Baptist pastor here from 1954 to 1960, led a year-long boycott in the city against segregated buses in 1955 and 1956. Population (2004) 201,568.

ALASKA

Alaska is a state in the far northwest, separated from the continental United States by the Canadian province of British Columbia. It is the largest state in area, being about one-fifth the size of the rest of the United States.

LAND AND ECONOMY

About 25% of Alaska lies north of the Arctic Circle. The **Alaska Range** in the south-central area includes the highest peaks in North America. The chief river is the **Yukon**, flowing to the Bering Sea. The **Aleutian Island** chain extends southwest and west, while the **Alexander Archipelago**, containing hundreds of islands, is in the southeast. Alaska has larger earthquakes than any other state – and more of them. Its natural resources include fish, lumber, and petroleum. Vast northern oil deposits are tapped via a pipeline running 800 mi (1,288 km) from **Prudhoe Bay** on the Arctic Ocean to Valdez on the south coast. Tourism is also a major revenue source.

Alaska has a younger population and higher proportion of males to females than any other state (103.2 males to 100 females). Its population density of 1.2 persons per square mile is the lowest U.S. figure. About 16% of the population is of Inuit or Native American extraction, including the Athabascan, Yupik, Aleut, and Eyak.

Alaska has several colleges and universities including the University of Alaska and Alaska Pacific University.

HISTORY

Alaska was first inhabited by humans who crossed th Bering Land Bridge. It was later populated by the Inupiaq, Inuit and Aleut peoples. **Vitus Bering**, a Danish navigator serving Russia, made the first recorded landing in July 1741, and Russian hunters followed. The United States purchased Alaska from Russia on October 18,1867. After gold was discovered in the 1890s, the population doubled in 10 years and in 1913 Alaska became a territory. In World War II, after Japanese forces occupied Attu and Kiska in the Aleutians, Alaska became a major military area. In 1942, U.S. troops constructed the 1,523 mi (2,451 km) **Alaska Highway**. The development of oil deposits and completion of a pipeline in 1977 transformed the economy. The controversial Alaska Lands bill of 1980 protected over 1,000,000 acres (400,000 ha) of wilderness. In 2006, however, the federal government was debating a proposal to drill for oil in Alaska's **Arctic National Wildlife Refuge**.

MAIN CITY

ANCHORAGE Located in the south central area, Anchorage is by far Alaska's largest city, with over one-third of the state's population. It was established as a railroad town in 1914 and became the supply center for the region's gold and coal mines. It suffered a severe earthquake in 1964, and there are frequent small earthquakes; active volcanoes lie nearby. Its industries include tourism, oil, and natural gas. Population (2004) 265,176.

STATE FACTS

Admitted to Union January 3, 1959; ranked 49th

U.S. Congress Senate 2, House of Representatives 1

Population 663,661; ranked 47th

Capital Juneau

State legislature Senate 20, House of Representatives 40

Area 616,240 sq mi (1,596,061 sq km); ranked 1st

Elevation Highest 20,320 ft (6,194 m), Mount McKinley (Denali, the highest point in North America); lowest, sea level

State nickname The Last Frontier

State motto North to the Future

State bird Willow ptarmigan

State fish King salmon

State flower Forget-me-not

State tree Sitka spruce

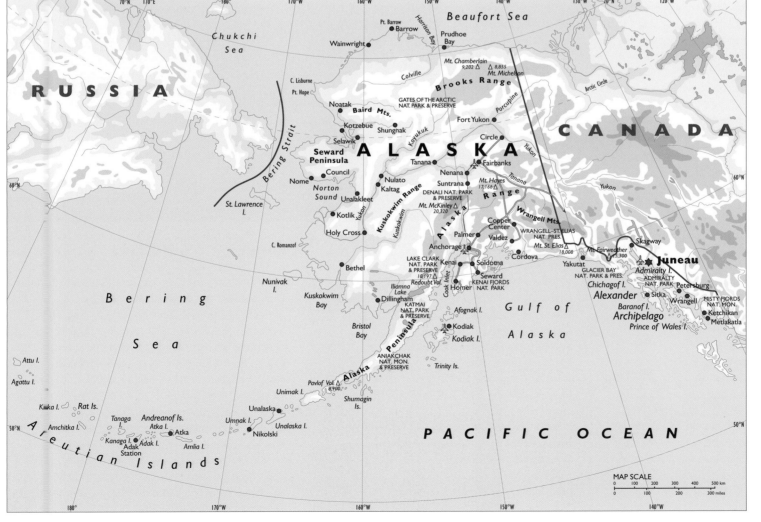

A brown bear and her cub wading in Katmai National Park and Preserve. More than 60% of Alaska is comprised of national parks, forests and wildlife refuges. Wildlife and wilderness tourism forms a significant part of the Alaskan economy.

ARIZONA

Arizona is a state in the southwestern United States, bordered on the south by Mexico, east by New Mexico, north by Utah, and west (across the Colorado River) by Nevada and California.

LAND AND ECONOMY

The Colorado Plateau, at elevations of 4,500 to 10,000 ft (1,373 to 3,050 m), occupies the northern part of the state. It is cut by many steep canyons, notably the **Grand Canyon** of the Colorado River, which became a national park in 1919. The Colorado is the principal river, flowing about 700 mi (1,127 km) through the state and along its western boundary. The construction of **Hoover Dam**, at the Arizona-Nevada border, created **Lake Mead** for irrigation and water supply to distant points. Other scenic landmarks are **Monument Valley**, **the Painted Desert**, and the **Petrified Forest**. The Mexican Highlands, a mountain mass running northwest to southeast, separates the plateau from the **Sonoran Desert** region in the southwest and south.

Arizona's mineral resources and its grazing and farming land have long been mainstays of the economy. Mining and agriculture are still important. Among the chief agricultural products are cotton, citrus fruits, corn, barley, wheat, cattle, sheep, and hogs. Minerals include copper, gold, silver, and molybdenum. Since the 1950s construction and manufacturing have been profitable sectors, with industrial products including electronic components, aircraft and missiles, metals, and printing and publishing. Tourism is also a major source of income.

Between 1990 and 2000, Arizona was the second fastest growing state (after Nevada), increasing its population by 40%. New residents have come from all parts of the United States, with Arizona being a popular retirement region because of its climate. Nearly 80% of the population is urban. The largest reported ancestry groups in Arizona are Mexican, German, English, Irish and Native Americans. The state has the second highest number of Native Americans (after California).

Major institutions of higher education include the University of Arizona, in Tucson, and Arizona State University, in Tempe. The Lowell Observatory in Flagstaff, and the Kitt Peak National Observatory, in Tucson, are leading centers of astronomical research.

HISTORY

Before European explorers arrived, peoples such as the Cochise, Hohokam, and Anasazi lived on the land. Spanish explorers visited the region from 1539 to 1540, with **Francisco Vázquez de Coronado** claiming the region for Spain. Jesuit missionaries taught the Native Americans after 1690. The area became part of Mexico, which kept it after winning independence from Spain in 1821. At the end of the Mexican War in 1848, Mexico ceded most of the present state to the United States, and in 1853 land was acquired from Mexico by the **Gadsden Purchase**. During the Civil War, Confederate forces invaded but were defeated.

In 1863, Arizona became a U.S. territory, and in 1864 **Kit Carson** led troops to defeat the **Navajo**. The Indian wars ended in 1886 with the surrender of **Geronimo**. Silver mining boomed from the 1870s, but copper became more important by 1888. These were lawless years that in 1881 saw the gunfight at the **OK Corral** in Tombstone won by Deputy Marshal Wyatt Earp's side over the Clanton gang.

Arizona became a state in 1912, the last of the 48 contiguous states to join, and major growth began after World War II. Its Native Americans gained the vote in 1948. Rapid population increases and development of high technology industries have continued, placing a strain on resources, especially scarce water supplies. In 1975, Arizona elected its first Hispanic governor, **Raul Castro**, and in 1999, the state's top five executive posts went to women, including **Janet Napolitano**, now Governor.

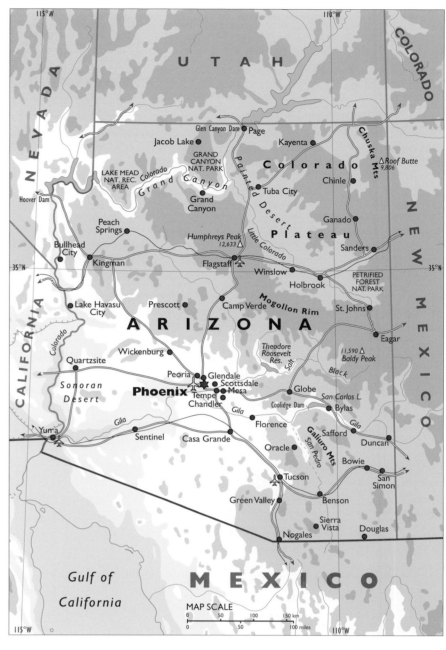

STATE FACTS

Admitted to Union February 14, 1912; ranked 48th

U.S. Congress Senate 2, House of Representatives 8

Population 5,939,292; ranked 17th

Capital Phoenix

State legislature Senate 30, House of Representatives 60

Area 113,998 sq mi (295,254 sq km); ranked 6th

Elevation Highest 12,633 ft (3,851 m), Humphreys Peak; lowest 100 ft (31 m), Colorado River

State nickname Grand Canyon State

State motto *Ditat Deus* (God Enriches)

State bird Cactus wren

State flower Saguaro cactus blossom

State tree Palo verde

MAIN CITIES

PHOENIX Arizona's capital and largest city is on the **Salt River** in the south-central region. Founded in 1868, the city expanded after agriculture in the area was made possible by irrigation. It became the territorial capital in 1889. It now covers 500 sq mi (1,295 sq km), an area larger than Los Angeles. Phoenix is a popular resort for its warm winter weather. Industries include computer parts, aircraft, textiles, clothing, and food products. Population (2004) 1,418,041.

TUCSON City on the **Santa Cruz River** in southeastern Arizona. The Spanish built a fort here in 1776, and the city was territorial capital from 1867 to 1877. It is now a foothills resort with a sunny climate. It is a port for cotton and cattle. Industries include textiles, meat packing, and aircraft parts. Population (2004) 512,023.

The Grand Canyon in northern Arizona plummets to depths of over 1 mi (1.6 km) in places. It is one of the world's great natural wonders.

21

ARKANSAS

Arkansas is a state in the south-central United States, bordered on the west by Oklahoma, north by Missouri, east over the Mississippi River by Tennessee and Mississippi, south by Louisiana, and on its southwest tip by Texas.

LAND AND ECONOMY

In the east and south the land is low, providing excellent soil for farming, while rugged hills of moderate height mark the west and north. All of the drainage flows into the **Mississippi River**. The state's principal river is the **Arkansas**, flowing southeast across the central area. Nearly half the state is forested, and lumber contributes greatly to the economy.

Agriculture is an important economic sector for Arkansas, but manufacturing is expanding. **Hot Springs National Park** is a major attraction for tourists. Industrial products include wood products and chemicals. The state leads the nation in rice and poultry production. Among other major agricultural products are sorghum, grain, cotton, soybeans, and grapes. Arkansas is a diamond-producing state and has the only public diamond mine in the world at the **Crater of Diamonds State Park** in Murfreesboro. It is the world's largest producer of bromine and leads the nation in producing bauxite (aluminum ore), quartz crystal, and silica stone. Also important to the state's economy are petroleum, natural gas, and coal.

An Arkansas cotton grower inspects a mature boll in his harvest-ready cotton field.

STATE FACTS

Admitted to Union June 15, 1836; ranked 25th
U.S. Congress Senate 2, House of Representatives 4
Population 2,779,154; ranked 32nd
Capital Little Rock
State legislature Senate 35, House of Representatives 100
Area 53,179 sq mi (137,732 sq km); ranked 29th
Elevation Highest 2,753 ft (839 m), Mount Magazine; lowest 55 ft (11 m), Ouachita River
State nickname Land of Opportunity
State motto *Regnat populus* (The people rule)
State bird Mockingbird
State flower Apple blossom
State tree Pine

Most residents are descended from immigrants who moved westward from the South Atlantic states after 1815. A rural way of life in isolated communities prevailed generally until after World War II, but by 1970 around half the population was classified as urban.

There are over 20 institutions of higher education; these include the University of Arkansas, in Fayetteville; Arkansas State University, in Jonesboro; the University of Central Arkansas, in Conway; the University of the Ozarks, in Clarksville; and Arkansas Tech University, in Russellville.

HISTORY

Native American groups included the Osage, Quapaw, and Caddo. **Hernando de Soto** and other Spaniard explorers visited the region in 1541 and 1542, and by 1673 the French descended the Mississippi as far as the Arkansas River. In 1682 **Robert Cavelier, Sieur de La Salle**, established the first permanent European settlement, **Arkansas Post**, on the lower Arkansas River and claimed all of the Mississippi valley for France. French missionaries and traders were active until 1762, when France ceded the area to Spain. Returned to France in 1800, it passed to the United States through the **Louisiana Purchase** in 1803. It was made part of the **Missouri Territory** in 1812 and became a separate territory in 1819 with the capital first at Arkansas Post and then two years later at Little Rock.

Large **cotton plantations** were established in the lowlands along the Mississippi River. With nearly one-fourth of its inhabitants being African-American slaves, Arkansas was the ninth state to secede and join the Confederacy in 1861, and several battles were fought in the state. It rejoined the Union in 1868. Railroads brought in European immigrants from such nations as Germany, Austria, and Italy. In 1906, diamonds were discovered, and in 1921 the discovery of oil created a boom. Development of the state's resources proceeded slowly until the 1950s. **Bill Clinton** was governor from 1978 to 1980 and 1983 to 1992 before becoming the first Arkansas citizen to be elected U.S. President, a post he held from 1993–2001.

MAIN CITIES

LITTLE ROCK Arkansas' capital and largest city lies on the Arkansas River. In 1682, the French explorer La Salle landed at "**La Petite Roche**," a little rock on the bank of the river. Founded in 1814, it became the territorial capital in 1821 and state capital in 1836. It is the only state capital with three capitol buildings (new, old, and territorial) still standing. In 1957, about 1,000 federal troops enforced the integration of **Central High School** after rioting and the national guard prevented the "Little Rock Nine" from enrolling. Little Rock effectively became a river port in 1969 when new locks and dams were opened on the river. The **William J. Clinton Presidential Center** is in the city, opened in 2004. Industries include electronics and textiles. Population (2004) 183,133.

FORT SMITH Located in northwest Arkansas where the Arkansas and Poteau rivers meet, the town grew up next to a military post established in 1817. One of its commanders was the future president **Zachary Taylor**. In 1848 the city became a supply center for gold prospectors. The **United States National Cemetery** is located there. Important manufacturing products include appliances, air conditioning systems, and wood and paper products. Population (2004) 81,849.

CALIFORNIA

California, the largest U.S. state in population and third largest in area, is situated in the west on the Pacific Ocean. It is bordered in the north by Oregon, east by Nevada and Arizona, and south by the Mexican state of Baja California.

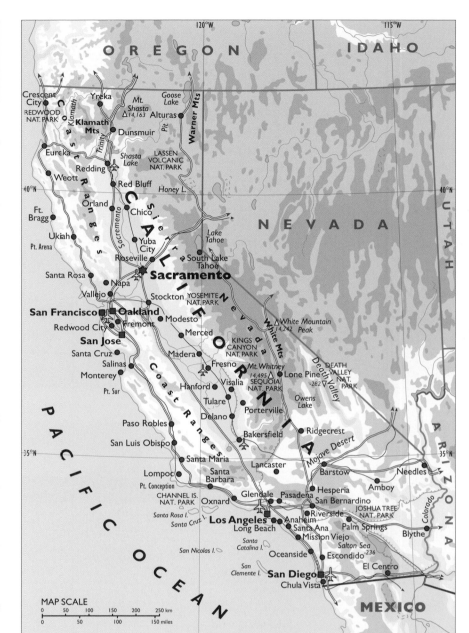

LAND AND ECONOMY

In the west, the low **Coast Ranges** run north and south, paralleling the high **Sierra Nevada** in the east. Between these ranges lies the fertile **Central Valley**, drained by the Sacramento and San Joaquin rivers. In the southeast are broad desert areas; the north is mountainous. The state lies on the **San Andreas Fault**, an active earthquake zone that has caused disasters in San Francisco and Los Angeles. National parks include **Yosemite**, established in 1890, and **Redwood**, having the world's tallest trees. Forests covering about 40% of the land support an important lumber industry. Mineral deposits include petroleum, borax, stone, sand and gravel, and soda ash.

California had the world's fifth largest economy in 2002. Services comprise one-fourth of its businesses. Chief industries include computer and software design, electronic equipment, entertainment, chemicals, engineering, automobiles, aircraft, banking, processed food, and health care. With an all-year growing season and vast irrigation projects, the state is the nation's leading agricultural producer and earns one-eighth of all U.S. farming receipts. The main crops include grapes, oranges, strawberries, cotton, rice, asparagus, and almonds. Farming contributes poultry, cattle, and dairy products. The state also ranks high in commercial fisheries. A year-round tourist industry is especially important to the economy. Among the major attractions are **Disneyland**, in Anaheim; **Universal Studios**, in Hollywood; and the **Queen Mary**, in Long Beach.

Between the 1950 and 1970 censuses, the population nearly doubled; it is now the 13th fastest-growing state. About 90% of the people live in urban areas. One-third of Californians are Hispanic, and one-fourth of the state's population are now foreign-born, with about one-third of these being Asian.

There are more than 200 institutions of higher education. The University of California, which has more than 190,000 students, opened its 10th campus in 2005. Its best known campuses are in Los Angeles (UCLA) and Berkeley. California State University has 23 campuses with over 400,000 students. Among privately endowed institutions are Stanford University, California Institute of Technology (Caltech), in Pasadena, and the University of Southern California, in Los Angeles. The Lick, Mount Wilson, and Palomar observatories are leaders in astronomical research. Other important facilities are the Jet Propulsion Lab, Scripps Institution of Oceanography, and the Lawrence Radiation Laboratory.

HISTORY

More than 100 Native American groups were the first residents of California. Spanish sailors explored the coast in 1542, and **Sir Francis Drake** reached north of today's San Francisco and named it "Nova Albion" (New England). The first European settlement, however, was not until 1769, when Spaniards from Mexico founded a mission at **San Diego**. Other missions and military posts were established, and California was joined to Mexico, then a Spanish colony. The lands of 21 Franciscan missions were broken up by law, and land grants created huge cattle ranches. In 1812, Russian fur traders settled in northern California. New settlers came from the east, and in 1846, early in the Mexican War, U.S. forces occupied California, which was ceded to the United States at the war's end. That same year, 1848, gold was discovered at Sutter's Mill, and the **gold rush** swelled the population from 15,000 to 250,000 in four years.

In November 1849 the people voted California into the Union without the approval of Congress, which did not come until September 9,1850. The opening of the **Union Pacific Railroad in** 1868 brought an era of great expansion. Waves of refugees from the **Dust Bowl** of Oklahoma and Arkansas arrived in the 1930s. During and immediately after Word War II the spread of manufacturing plants speeded the shift from agricul-

ture to industry, especially aerospace and electronics. Since the 1960s, worldwide computer corporations have developed in **Silicon Valley** centered around **San Jose**. The wine industry in **Napa Valley** is now world famous. Two Californians have became president of the United States, **Richard Nixon** (1969–1974) and **Ronald Reagan** (1981–1989). California's governors have included two actors, Reagan (1967–1975) and Austrian-born **Arnold Schwarzenegger** (2003–).

MAIN CITIES

LOS ANGELES California's largest city, located on its southwest coast, is the second most populated U.S. city. Greater Los Angeles covers 465 sq mi (1,200 sq km). **Hollywood** is located downtown, and Los Angeles surrounds the opulent independent city of **Beverly Hills**. Mexican settlers founded the city in 1781, and its Spanish name has generated the nickname "City of Angels." In 1965, riots in **Watts** left 34 dead, and a 1994 earthquake killed 57. The city is noted for its poor air **quality**. Its industries include tourism, aerospace, motion pictures and television, oil refining, and electronic equipment. Population (2004) 3,745,742.

SAN FRANCISCO This city on California's north central coast is situated on a hilly peninsula between the Pacific Ocean and San Francisco Bay, connected by the **Golden Gate Strait**. Founded by the Spanish in 1776, it was captured in 1846 by the U.S. in the **Mexican War**. A gold rush in 1848 swelled the population. Devastated by an earthquake and fire in 1906 that killed some 3,000 people, it was rebuilt in nine years and prospered. (A centennial memorial service in 2006 included some survivors.) Another devastating earthquake struck in 1989 with 63 deaths. Tourists are attracted to its cable cars, Victorian houses, **Golden Gate Bridge**, **Chinatown**, the now-defunct

STATE FACTS

Admitted to Union September 9, 1850; ranked 31st
U.S. Congress Senate 2, House of Representatives, 53
Population 36,132,147; ranked, 1st
Capital Sacramento
State legislature Senate 40, Assembly 80
Area 163,696 sq mi (423,970 sq km); ranked, 3rd
Elevation Highest 14,495 ft (4,418 m), Mount Whitney; Lowest 282 ft (86 m) below sea level, Badwater Death Valley
State nickname Golden State
State motto Eureka
State bird California quail
State flower California poppy
State tree Redwood

Alcatraz prison in the bay, and the **Haight-Ashbury** area renowned in the 1960s for its hippies. Industries include finance, shipbuilding, food processing, aircraft, and printing and publishing. Population (2004) 744,230.

SAN DIEGO This city on a natural harbor on California's southern coast almost adjoins **Tijuana** on the Mexican border. It was founded in 1769 as a mission. It has a huge naval base and is an important center for scientific research, especially oceanography. Among the main industries are aerospace, electronics, fishing, shipbuilding, food processing, and tourism. Population (2004) 1,241,338.

The Golden Gate Bridge spans the opening of San Francisco Bay into the Pacific Ocean. The bridge is some 1.7 mi (2.7 km) long, and the main span is 4,200 ft (1,280 m). Since it opened in 1937, is has become recognized as a symbol of San Francisco.

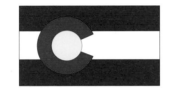

COLORADO

Colorado is a state in the west-central United States, and is bordered by six states: Wyoming in the north, Nebraska northeast, Kansas east, Oklahoma southeast, New Mexico south, and Utah west.

LAND AND ECONOMY

The north to south ranges of the **Rocky Mountains** traverse the western half with more than 50 peaks over 14,000 ft (4,270 m). Their crests form the **Continental Divide**. The rest of the state is covered by the western portion of the **Great Plains**, grazing and farming land. Major rivers rise in the state: the Colorado, Rio Grande, Arkansas, North Platte, and South Platte.

Colorado's economy has been dominated successively by mining, agriculture, and manufacturing. Huge reserves of petroleum, natural gas, and coal remain. Irrigation has made possible the varied agriculture of the plains. The chief agricultural products are sugar beets, cattle, sheep, wheat, corn, barley, and fruit. Manufacture of military material in government plants is an important sector. Among the main industrial products are processed food, electronics, aerospace parts, and metals. The major minerals are molybdenum, tin, vanadium, tungsten, uranium, lead, zinc, coal, and oil shale.

The facilities for year-round recreation make tourism a major aspect of the economy, with world-renowned skiing at **Aspen**, **Vail**, **Breckenridge**, **Steamboat**, and many other centers. The small town of Aspen, once a mining community, has

developed beyond its skiing fame into a cultural center; it is home to the Aspen Music Festival and School.

More than 75% of the population resides in urban areas in a strip north and south of Denver in the center of the state.

There are about 30 institutions of higher education. The public ones include the University of Colorado, in Boulder; Colorado State University, in Fort Collins; and the Colorado School of Mines, in Golden. The U.S. Air Force Academy is near Colorado Springs.

HISTORY

The **Anasazi** cliff dwellers lived in southwestern Colorado until about 1299, and other groups have included the **Utes**, **Cheyenne**, **Arapahoe**, **Comanches**, and **Pawnee**. The state's name came from Spanish explorers calling the river "*Colorado*" because of its red stone gorges. The United States acquired the eastern part of Colorado from France by **the Louisiana Purchase** of 1803. The remainder was ceded by Mexico in 1848 after the **Mexican War**. Two years later, the present borders were established when the federal government purchased from Mexico lands east of the Rio Grande that were claimed by Texas in what is known as the Compromise of 1850.

Gold was discovered in 1858, and explorers flocked to the area, with some 100,000 arriving during 1859, who came to be known as "Fifty-Niners." A provisional government called this the territory of Jefferson. The slogan of fortune seekers was "**Pikes Peak or bust**" since this mountain was at **Ute Pass** leading to the gold fields. Colorado became a territory in 1861. Building of railroads after 1870 led to the rapid expansion of the population, and statehood came in 1876. A year later silver was discovered, and then a second gold rush occurred in 1891.

STATE FACTS

Admitted to Union August 1,1876; ranked 38th

U.S. Congress Senate 2, House of Representatives 7

Population 4,665,177; ranked 22nd

Capital Denver

State legislature Senate 36, House of Representatives 68

Area 104,094 sq mi (269,601 sq km); ranked 8th

Elevation Highest 14,432 ft (4,399 m), Mount Elbert; lowest 3,350ft (1,022 m), Arkansas River

State nickname Centennial State

State motto *Nil sine numine* (Nothing without Providence)

State bird Lark bunting

State flower Rocky Mountain columbine

State tree Colorado blue spruce

Great Sand Dunes National Park and Preserve in southern Colorado contains North America's tallest dunes, which rise to some 750 ft (230 m) high. The dunes, sculpted by the wind, cover more than 30 sq mi (80 sq km). Behind them lie the rugged Sangre de Cristo Mountains.

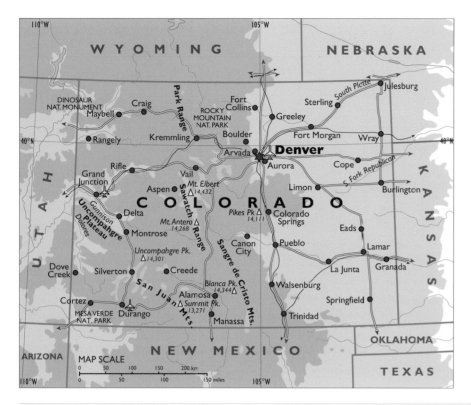

World War I stimulated agriculture, while World War II shifted the economic emphasis to manufacturing. Another economic boom began during the 1970s with development of energy-related industries. Today its diversified economy includes scientific research and high-tech industry.

MAIN CITIES

DENVER The state's capital and largest city is in the north-central area at the foot of the **Rocky Mountains**. It borders the city of **Aurora**, which has a population of 291,843. At an altitude of 5,280 ft (1,608 m), Denver is called the "**Mile High City**." Founded in 1860 by gold prospectors and miners, it became the territorial capital in 1867 and the state capital in 1876. It is the site of a **U.S. Mint** and has the world's largest airport in area. Fifteen colleges and universities are there. Denver is a major tourist center and has many high-technology industries, especially aerospace and electronics. Population (2004) 544,116.

COLORADO SPRINGS Established in 1871, the city is in the state's central region at the foot of **Pikes Peak** on the Monument and Fountain creeks. It is next to the popular **Garden of the Gods**, large rosy-tinted rocks rising from the earth. Silver and gold brought miners, and at the beginning of the 20th century, it was the wealthiest U.S. city per capita. The area has the **United States Air Force Academy** and the **North American Air Defense Command (NORAD)**. Colorado Springs is a year-round vacation center, and produces electronic, aerospace, and mining equipment. Population (2004) 369,363.

CONNECTICUT

Connecticut, the third smallest U.S. state, is in the northeast U.S. in the New England region. It is bordered by the states of Massachusetts in the north, Rhode Island in the east, and New York in the west, with the Atlantic coastline along the south.

LAND AND ECONOMY

A narrow plain lies along the shore of **Long Island Sound** in the south of the state. In the west and east, hill ridges run north and south, with the highest in the northwest corner. More than half of the state is forested, and the northern region has a number of ski centers. The **Connecticut River Valley** between the ridges is fertile farmland. Other major rivers are the Housatonic (west) and the Thames (east). The Connecticut shoreline contains expensive real estate; it is an area that is popular for sailing and home to yacht clubs.

Agricultural products include milk, cattle, poultry, and hogs. Among the main crops are mushrooms, corn, tobacco, apples, and Christmas trees. Major minerals are stone, sand, gravel, and clay. The major industrial products include aircraft engines and parts, helicopters, submarines, machinery, computer equipment, household appliances, pharmaceuticals, hardware, and silverware. Defense contracts, including building nuclear submarines, are important, as well as services, finances, and real estate.

In the 19th century, Connecticut received thousands of immigrants from Europe, creating a mixture of nationalities and races, but by the late 20th century about 90% of its population was U.S.-born. More than 75% of the population lives in urban areas. Thousands of residents in the southwest section of the state commute to jobs in **New York City.**

Yale University, the nation's fourth oldest institution of higher learning, was founded in 1701 at New Haven. The University of Connecticut's principal campus is in Storrs. Trinity College, Wesleyan University, and Connecticut College are leading privately endowed schools. There are 54 institutions of higher education. The **U.S. Coast Guard Academy** is in New London.

HISTORY

Native Americans in the region were **Algonquian** peoples, such as the Mohegan and Pequot. In 1614, the Dutch navigator **Adriaen Block** explored the area, seeking to establish a fur trade with the native peoples. The first permanent European settlements were made by 1634 in the Connecticut River Valley around present-day **Hartford** by English arrivals from the Massachusetts Bay Colony. Three years later they defeated the local Pequots. Other settlements were established along Long Island Sound, and in 1662 the colony received a charter from King Charles II, and added the colony of **New Haven** in 1665.

When the **American Revolution** began, the colony of nearly 200,000 inhabitants had 30,000 men join the Continental Army. After the war, many migrated to neighboring states, but later Connecticut's growing light industry drew new residents. In 1839, slaves who had seized their ship, *Amistad*, and killed the captain and cook, were imprisoned in New Haven before the U.S. Supreme Court eventually freed them. The state abolished slavery in 1848 and contributed nearly 60,000 soldiers to the **Civil War**. In each of the country's major wars, Connecticut was a prime supplier of arms, munitions, and tools. In 1974, **Ella T. Grasso** was elected governor, the first woman in the nation to be elected to this office.

STATE FACTS

Admitted to Union January 9, 1788; 5th of the 13 original states to ratify the U.S. Constitution
U.S. Congress Senate 2, House of Representatives 5
Population 3,510,297; ranked 29th
Capital Hartford
State legislature Senate 36, House of Representatives 151
Area 5,543 sq mi (14,357 sq km); ranked 48th
Elevation Highest 2,380 ft (725 m), Mount Frissell; lowest, sea level
State nicknames Constitution State, Nutmeg State
State motto *Qui transtulit sustinet* (He who transplanted, still sustains)
State bird American robin
State flower Mountain laurel
State tree White oak

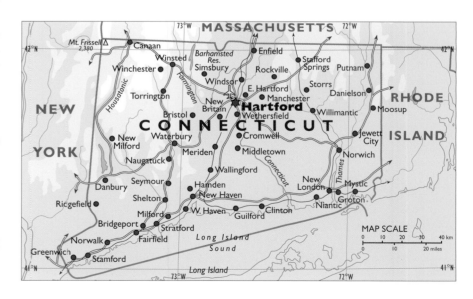

Connecticut has been the home to many inventors during its history. In the 19th century **Charles Goodyear** discovered the process to vulcanize rubber, **Linus Yale** invented the cylinder lock, **Seth Thomas** developed modern mass-produced clocks, and **Ezra J. Warner** invented the first can opener, which was widely used by soldiers during the Civil War.

MAIN CITIES

HARTFORD The state capital is on the Connecticut River. English settlers formed a colony there in 1636 named for Hertford, England. Many large insurance companies have their headquarters in the city. The *Hartford Courant*, begun in 1764, is the nation's oldest continuously published newspaper. Manufactured products include precision instruments and electrical equipment. Population (2004) 124,848.

BRIDGEPORT Located on Long Island Sound, Bridgeport is the state's chief industrial and largest city. Settled in 1639 as a fishing community, it is now a port of entry. Industries include electrical appliances, transportation equipment, helicopters, and machine tools. Population (2004) 139,910.

NEW HAVEN A port on Long Island Sound, New Haven was founded by **Puritans** in 1638 and shared the role of capital of Connecticut with Hartford from 1701 to 1875. It had the world's first telephone exchange in 1877. The presence of **Yale University** has made the city a cultural center. Industries include firearms and ammunition, rubber products, locks, and tools. Population (2004) 124,829.

Many of the the buildings of Yale University in downtown New Haven are Gothic in style, but were mostly built in the early 20th century.

DELAWARE

Delaware, the second smallest state, is in the eastern United States on the Atlantic Ocean and **Delaware Bay**. It is bordered by Pennsylvania in the north, New Jersey in the northeast, and Maryland in the east and south.

LAND AND ECONOMY

Delaware occupies the northern portion of the **Delmarva Peninsula** between the Atlantic Ocean and Chesapeake Bay. Most of the state is a coastal plain, and the higher elevations are in the extreme north. The **Delaware River** forms part of the eastern boundary. The economy's mainstay is manufacturing, principally in the Wilmington area, which is the center of the huge **E. I. du Pont de Nemours** chemical industry. Products of the state include food, paper, rubber, plastics, and printed materials. The chief agricultural products are poultry, soybeans, corn, and milk. Crabs and clams are an important product of Delaware Bay. Major minerals include sand, gravel, and magnesium compounds.

The five largest reported ancestries in Delaware are Irish, German, English, Italian, and African American. The state had the largest population of free Blacks prior to the Civil War.

The **University of Delaware**, founded in 1743, is in Newark, and there are six other institutions of higher education in the state.

An aerial view of the Delaware River looking northeast from Point Pleasant, Pennsylvania.

HISTORY

The first permanent European settlement was made by Swedes at Fort Christina (Wilmington) in 1638. Called **New Sweden**, it spread north and south along the Delaware River. in 1655 the Dutch conquered New Sweden and added it to **New Netherlands**. The English seized New Netherlands in 1664, naming it New York; the Delaware area remained part of that colony until 1682, when the Duke of York ceded it to William Penn and **Pennsylvania**. In 1704, Penn allowed the three "Lower Counties" to elect an assembly of their own. The state was loyal to the Union in the **Civil War** but retained slaves until they were freed in 1865 by the 13th Amendment. Delaware's first woman governor, **Ruth Ann Minner**, was elected in 2000.

MAIN CITIES

WILMINGTON The state's largest city is located at the junction of the Delaware and Christina rivers and Brandywine Creek. The first settlement in 1638 was founded by Swedes then enlarged by Dutch and British settlers. The first iron steamer built in the nation was launched there in 1836. Wilmington was a main stop on the slaves' "**Underground Railway**" before the Civil War. It is an important industrial center with shipyards, rail yards, and chemical plants. Population (2004) 72,784.

DOVER The state capital of Delaware was founded in 1683 by William Penn, and was officially laid out by a commission of the Delaware General Assembly in 1717. The largest employer is the state government. Population (2000) 32,135.

STATE FACTS

Admitted to Union December 7, 1787; 1st of the original states to ratify the U.S. Constitution
U.S. Congress Senate 2, House of Representatives 1
Population 843,524; ranked 45th
Capital Dover
State legislature Senate 21, House of Representatives 41
Area 2,489 sq mi (6,447 sq km); ranked 49th
Elevation Highest 442 ft (135 m), Ebright Azimuth; lowest, sea level
State nicknames First State, Diamond State
State motto Liberty and Independence
State bird Blue hen chicken
State flower Peach blossom
State tree American holly

FLORIDA

Florida is a southeastern U.S. peninsula state that extends farther south than any continental state. It lies between the Atlantic Ocean and the Gulf of Mexico, and is bordered on the north by Alabama and Georgia.

LAND AND ECONOMY

Florida is about 500 mi (805 km) long with an average width of 120 mi (193 km). At its southern end are the **Florida Keys**, a chain of 43 small islands connected by the world's longest road over water stretching about 150 mi (241 km) west to **Key West**. Florida's land is mostly level, with thousands of lakes and vast swamplands, the most notable being the **Everglades** in the south comprising 1.4 million acres (567,000 ha). The **St. John's** in the northeast and the **Apalachicola** in the west are the largest of many rivers. Florida is especially vulnerable to hurricanes, with **Hurricane Andrew** destroying 60,000 homes in 1992 and five other major hurricanes causing devastation in the two-year period of 2004 and 2005.

The subtropical climate favors two major elements in the economy – tourism and agriculture. World-renowned attractions are gathered around **Orlando**, including Walt Disney World, Epcot, Universal Studios, Cypress Gardens, and SeaWorld Orlando. In agriculture, Florida is a leader in the production of citrus fruits, sugarcane, and vegetables. Other important farm products are cotton, poultry, and cattle. The chief minerals include phosphate rock and titanium.

The **John F. Kennedy Space Center** at Cape Canaveral is the nucleus of an aeronautics, electronics, and research industry. Major industrial products include processed foods, chemicals, electrical equipment, transportation equipment, and paper.

One of the fastest-growing states, Florida increased its population by 250% between 1950 and 1970, and by nearly 9% from 2000 to 2004. The influx has come mainly from states of the north and the Midwest and includes many retirees. More than 80% of the people reside in urban areas.

There are more than 60 institutions of higher education, including the **University of Florida**, in Gainesville, and **Florida State University**, in Tallahassee.

HISTORY

The first Native Americans in the area included the Apalachee, Timucua, and Calusa. The Spanish explorer **Ponce de León** landed on the east coast in 1513 and claimed the land for Spain. He also brought the first horses, oranges, and sugarcane to the area. France began the **Fort Caroline** colony in 1564 on the St. Johns River, but most of the colonists were killed by Spaniards who in 1565 established the permanent settlement of **St. Augustine**, the oldest European community in the present-day U.S. It became the center of East Florida but was burned in an 1586 attack by England's **Sir Francis Drake**. The center of West Florida was **Pensacola**, founded in 1698. In the early 1700s, the **Seminole** migrated from Georgia to become the largest group of Native Americans. Both Floridas were ceded to Great Britain in 1763 after the Seven Years' War and remained the only loyal British region during the American Revolution. The two Floridas were returned to Spain in 1783 after that war.

Andrew Jackson led U.S. troops into the area in 1818, and all of Florida was purchased from Spain the following year by the United States for $5 million and became a territory in 1821. Between 1835 and 1842 many of the Seminoles were killed in war and many others were removed to the Oklahoma territory. Some took refuge in the Everglades to become known as the "Unconquered People," the last Native Americans to sign a treaty (1957) with the U.S. government. Florida became a state in 1845 but seceded in 1861 to join the Confederacy; it was little affected by the Civil War.

After 1880, the building of railroads, clearing of forests, and draining of swamps signaled an era of growth. A real estate boom occurred after World War I with 2.5 million new residents in 1925 alone. A huge Cuban community has now been established in southern Florida, beginning in 1959 after Fidel Castro assumed

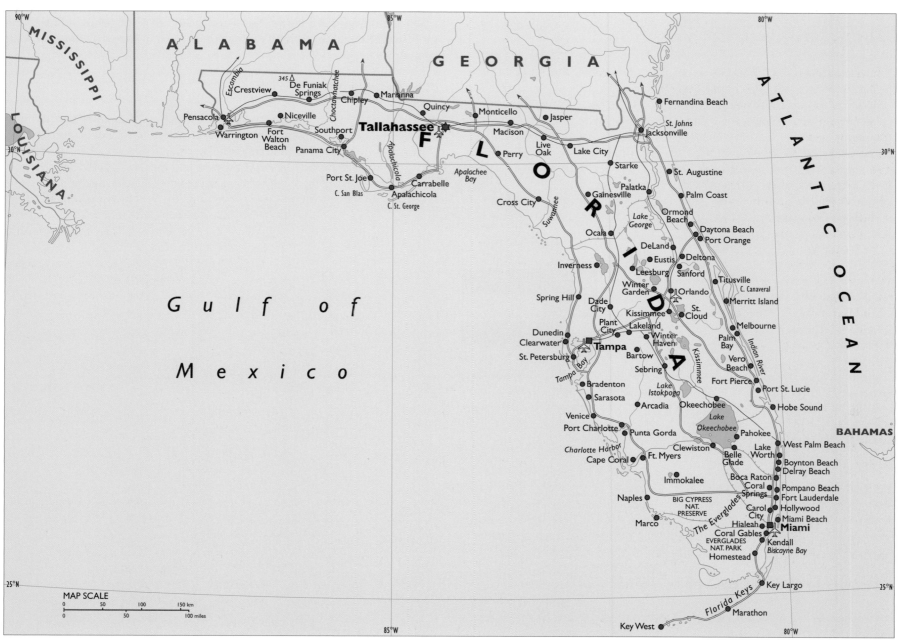

The space shuttle Discovery lifts off its launching pad at the Kennedy Space Center, causing a large flock of birds to erupt into flight. NASA's presence in the area is important to the local economy.

power, and it has transformed **Miami** into a center of Latin American culture and trade. In 1961, some 1,500 Cuban exiles returned to overthow Castro, but their attempt failed at the Bay of Pigs.

Space exploration from **Cape Canaveral** began in the 1950s, and it was the site of most of NASA's space launches, including **Neil Armstrong's** epic 1969 voyage to become the first person to stand on the Moon, and space shuttle missions since the first obital flight in 1981.

MAIN CITIES

MIAMI Florida's famous resort city is on **Biscayne Bay** in the state's southeast. A fort was there in 1836. Originally a small agricultural community, it developed quickly after 1895 when the railroad was extended and the harbor dredged. Modern Miami is a popular tourist resort with luxury hotels along **Miami Beach** across the bay. The city has a large Cuban population and many immigrants from Central and South America and Haiti. Its industries include clothing, concrete, metal products, and fishing. It has six universities and colleges. Population (2004) 324,508.

JACKSONVILLE A seaport on both sides of the **St. Johns River** in northeastern Florida, it is the largest city in the state. Settled as Cowford in 1816, it was renamed for Andrew Jackson in 1822. The city served as a Confederate base during the Civil War, and developed as a port in the 19th century. Fire devastated it in 1901, burning down 2,400 buildings. Its boundaries cover most of **Duval County** making it one of the largest U.S. cities in land area, covering 841 sq mi (2,178 sq km). Industries include fruit, canning, and wood products. It has 10 universities and 5 colleges. Population (2004) 765,994.

TALLAHASSEE The state capital of Florida is in the west end of the **Panhandle** in the northern area. First discovered by Europeans in 1539, it was the site of a Spanish mission. Tallahassee became the territorial capital of Florida in 1824. During the Civil War, it repulsed a Union force and kept the capital uncaptured during the conflict. **Florida State University** and **Florida A & M University** are located here. Among the important industries are chemicals, lumber, and paper. Population (2004) 156,612.

STATE FACTS

Admitted to Union March 3, 1845; ranked 27th

U.S. Congress Senate 2, House of Representatives 25

Population 17,789,864; ranked 4th

Capital Tallahassee

State legislature Senate 40, House of Representatives 120

Area 65,755 sq mi (170,304 sq km); ranked 22nd

Elevation Highest 345 ft (105 m), Britton Hill; lowest, sea level

State nickname Sunshine State

State motto In God we trust

State bird Mockingbird

State flower Orange blossom

State tree Sabal palm

GEORGIA

Georgia is in the southeastern U.S. on the Atlantic Ocean. It is bordered by five states: Tennessee and North Carolina are north, South Carolina is east, Florida is south, and Alabama is west. Georgia was one of the six original states of the Confederacy.

LAND AND ECONOMY

A coastal plain in the east and south occupies about half the state. To the north is the **Piedmont**, a region of rolling hills and farmland. In the extreme north, the **Blue Ridge Mountains** run from east to west. Of the many rivers that flow southeast, the Savannah, the Ogeechee, and the Altamaha are the largest. The products of Georgia's forests and farms, which formed its economic base from earliest times, are still important. They include lumber, groundnuts and other nuts, soybeans, cotton, tobacco, hay, peaches, cattle, poultry, and hogs.

Manufacturing development during World War II moved the main emphasis to industry. Making aircraft, automobile and truck bodies, and boats has become a major enterprise. Other major industries produce textiles, paper, processed foods, and chemicals. The chief minerals are clays, marble, gravel, and bauxite.

The great majority of Georgia's current population was born in the United States. Business expansion has attracted thousands of residents from northern states. Urban growth came late and slowly. The state's five largest reported ancestries are African American, American, English, German, and Irish.

There are more than 60 institutions of higher education, including the University of Georgia, in Athens; Georgia Institute of Technology (Georgia Tech), in Atlanta; and Emory University, in Atlanta.

HISTORY

In 1732, King George II gave **General James E. Oglethorpe** a large land grant in the area. Oglethorpe founded a settlement on the Savannah River the next year. At the **Battle of Bloody Marsh** in 1742, he defeated the Spaniards, who threatened the colony from Florida. Georgia became a royal province in 1754. Its delegates to the Continental Congress in 1776 supported national independence, and Georgia was among the earliest to ratify the U.S. Constitution. In 1792, **Eli Whitney**, a Massachusetts native living in Savannah, invented the cotton gin that simplified the processing of cotton, bringing prosperity to Southern planters but, as a result, strengthening slavery. The state seceded in 1861 and near the end of the Civil War it was ravaged in 1864 by Union General William T. Sherman's "**March through Georgia**" from Atlanta to Savannah. The state was readmitted to the Union in 1870, but its economy and society were slow in recovering from the effects of the war. The economy was finally driven to recovery by Atlanta's boom in the 1960s. In 1976 Georgia's **Jimmy Carter** was elected the 39th president of the United States. In 2001 the state flag was changed to remove the Confederate battle flag, which formed a large part of it, and changed again in 2003.

The Okefenokee Swamp provides an important refuge for many endangered species, including alligators. This once seriously endangered species is recovering in numbers because of strict regulations against habitat destruction and hunting.

MAIN CITIES

ATLANTA The state's capital is in the northwest center. It was founded in 1837 at the east end of the Western and Atlantic Railroad, and originally called Terminus, then renamed Marthasville in 1843 and Atlanta in 1845. It served as a Confederate supply depot and communications center during the Civil War, falling on September 2, 1864, to **General William T. Sherman**'s troops. Atlanta rapidly rebuilt and developed into a transportation and cotton manufacturing center. It became the capital in 1887 and a major U.S. city by the late 20th century, being the financial center of a multistate region. Its metropolitan population has grown 40% in a decade to 4.7 million. **Hartsfield Atlanta International Airport** is one of the busiest in the nation. **Martin Luther King, Jr.**, the civil rights leader, had his home church here. Atlanta contains Coca-Cola's headquarters, the U.S. Centers of Disease Control and Prevention, and two major universities: Georgia Tech and Emory. The city hosted the 1996 Summer Olympics. Industries include textiles, chemicals, iron and steel, and electronics. Population (2004) 419,122.

SAVANNAH Georgia's oldest city is an eastern port on the **Savannah River**. It was founded in 1733 and became the seat of the colonial government in 1754. During the American Revolution, it was initially captured by the British in 1778 and resisted all attempts at invasion until 1782. The city prospered on the tobacco and cotton trade, despite a devastating fire in 1796. During the Civil War, it remained a Confederate stronghold until December 1864. Today, many tourists are attracted by its historic district, with much fine 18th- and 19th-century architecture, and its reputation for representing the traditional South. It is a major port whose exports include tobacco, cotton, and sugar. Industries include chemicals, petroleum, paper products, rubber, and tourism. Population (2004) 129,808.

STATE FACTS

Admitted to Union January 2, 1788; 4th of the 13 original states to ratify the U.S. Constitution
U.S. Congress Senate 2, House of Representatives 13
Population 9,072,576; ranked 9th
Capital Atlanta
State legislature Senate 56, House of Representatives 180
Area 59,425 sq mi (153,909 sq km); ranked 24th
Elevation Highest 4,784 ft (1,458 m), Brasstown Bald; lowest, sea level
State nicknames Peach State
State motto Wisdom, Justice, and Moderation
State bird Brown thrasher
State flower Cherokee rose
State tree Live oak

HAWAII

Hawaii is a state of the United States, situated in the Pacific Ocean about 2,400 mi (3,864 km) southwest of California. It was the last to join the Union.

LAND AND ECONOMY

Hawaii is an archipelago of 8 large and 124 small islands, many of them uninhabited, stretching over 2,000 mi (3,220 km) southeast to northwest. The four main islands are **Oahu**, **Hawaii**, **Kaui**, and **Maui**, which are all of volcanic origin. Maui and Hawaii have volcanic activity at intervals. Valleys support rich agriculture, with products including sugar, pineapples, and vegetables. Among the minerals are sand and gravel. Federal defense establishments and tourism invigorate the economy. Industrial products include processed foods, concrete, and electronic components.

Hawaii's population displays a mixture of origins, reflecting the 19th- and 20th-century immigrations from Asia, the continental U.S., and Europe. In the 2000 census, 41.6% identified themselves as Asian, 24.3% Caucasian, and 6.6% as Native Hawaiian. Hawaii is the only state with an official native language, **Hawaiian**, along with English.

Universities in the state include the University of Hawaii, Hawaii Pacific University, and Chaminade University.

HISTORY

Voyagers from Polynesian islands to the south reached the Hawaiian Islands as early as AD 800. The first European was Britain's **Captain James Cook** in 1778 who named the chain the Sandwich Islands for the Earl of Sandwich. The next year, Cook was killed by the natives. In 1782 **Kamehameha I** united the islands, and in 1820 U.S. missionaries arrived, followed by businessmen who started the sugar industry. In 1893 a group of U.S. citizens deposed **Queen Liliuokalani** and set up a republic. In August 1898, the United States annexed the islands. They became a territory in 1900, but not a state until 1959. The naval base

at **Pearl Harbor** on Oahu was attacked by the Japanese in December 1941, taking the United States into World War II. In 1993, President Bill Clinton signed a resolution apologizing to native Hawaiians for the U.S. ending their kingdom.

MAIN CITY

HONOLULU The capital and chief port of Hawaii is on the southeastern coast of Oahu Island. It became the capital of the **Kingdom of Hawaii** in 1845, and remained the capital after the U.S. annexation in 1898. Landmarks include the Iolani Palace (the only former royal palace in the U.S.), Waikiki Beach (the center of the main tourist district), the Diamond Head Crater, and the memorial to the USS *Arizona* sunk by the Japanese. The **U.S. Naval Base** remains a major facility at Pearl Harbor. There are two universities and several colleges. Tourism is of major importance and industries include sugar refining and pineapple canning. Population (2004) 362,262.

STATE FACTS

Admitted to Union August 21, 1959; ranked 50th
US Congress Senate 2, House of Representatives 2
Population 1,275,194; ranked 42nd
Capital Honolulu
State legislature Senate 25, House of Representatives 52
Area 10,931 sq mi (28,311 sq km); ranked 43rd
Elevation Highest 13,796 ft (4,205 m), Mauna Kea (on island of Hawaii); lowest, sea level
State nickname Aloha State
State motto *Ua mau ke ea o ka ajna i ka pono* (The Life of the Land is Perpetuated in Righteousness)
State bird Nene (Hawaiian goose)
State flower Hawaiian hibiscus
State tree Kukui (candlenut)

Pu'u 'O'o, the easternmost of Kilauea's volcanic vents, spews molten lava.

IDAHO

Idaho is a state in the northwestern United States, bordered on the north by the Canadian province of British Columbia, and by six states: Washington and Oregon in the west, Nevada and Utah south, and Montana and Wyoming east.

LAND AND ECONOMY

Much of the state is mountainous and forested, with many lakes. The **Snake River**, along the west boundary, flows for 40 mi (64 km) through **Hells Canyon**, the deepest river gorge in North America. In the south, irrigation projects have created agricultural areas. Crops include the famous Idaho potatoes and peas, sugar beets, wheat, hops, and barley. Among the main minerals are silver, lead, zinc, and phosphate rock. Major industrial products include computer equipment, processed foods, lumber, paper, and chemicals. Year-round resorts and wilderness hunting and fishing have made tourism a major source of income.

Idaho is the sixth fastest-growing state; its population has increased by 38% since 1990. The institutions of higher education include the University of Idaho, Idaho State University, and Boise State University. The **Idaho National Laboratory** in the southeast Idaho desert is the U.S. Department of Energy center for advanced civilian nuclear technology research and development.

HISTORY

In 1805, the U.S. explorers **Meriwether Lewis** and **William Clark** traversed the region. In a few years fur trappers were active and trading posts were established, with missionaries moving among the Indians. Discovery of gold in 1860 brought a rush of immigrants, and Idaho Territory was created in 1863. War with the Indians ended in 1877 with the surrender of **Chief Joseph** of the Nez Perce. After Idaho joined the Union in 1890, violent labor disputes racked the state. The world's first usable electricity from nuclear power was generated in 1951 at the **National Reactor Testing Station** (now the Idaho National Laboratory), but the nation's first fatal nuclear accident occurred there in 1961 killing three employees. The signing of the **Central Idaho**

Wilderness Act (1980) protected more than 2,300,000 acres (930,000 ha) of undeveloped land.

MAIN CITIES

BOISE The capital and largest city of Idaho is in the **Boise River** valley in the foothills of the Rocky Mountains. Founded in 1863 as a supply post for gold miners, it is now a trade center for the agricultural region. It is home to Idaho's largest university, **Boise State University**. The chief industries produce steel, sheet metal, computer equipment, furniture, and lumber products. Population (2004) 185,787.

IDAHO FALLS In the southeast of the state, Idaho Falls grew up on the Oregon trail. Originally named Eagle Rock, it expanded when gold was discovered. It is an important distribution and processing center for local agricultural produce. It is home to the Idaho National Laboratory. Population (2003) 51,507.

STATE FACTS

Admitted to Union July 3, 1890; ranked 43rd
U.S. Congress Senate 2, House of Representatives 2
Population 1,429,096; ranked 39th
Capital Boise
State legislature Senate 35, House of Representatives 70
Area 83,570 sq mi (216,446 sq km); ranked 14th
Elevation Highest 12,662 ft (3,859 m), Borah Peak; lowest 710 ft (217 m), Snake River
State nickname Gem State
State motto *Esto perpetua* (Let it be perpetual)
State bird Mountain bluebird
State flowe Syringa
State tree Western white pine

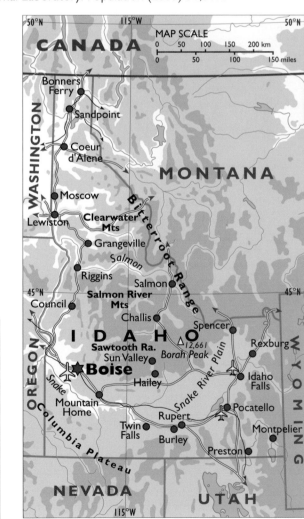

Idaho's mountain scenery and fast-flowing rivers make it a popular destination for adventure sports enthusiasts.

ILLINOIS

ILLINOIS

Illinois is a state in the north-central United States on the east bank of the Mississippi River. It is bordered by Wisconsin in the north, Iowa and Missouri west, Kentucky south, and Indiana east. Lake Michigan's shoreline runs along the northeast of the state.

LAND AND ECONOMY

Except for rolling hills in the northwest, the land is virtually level. The **Illinois River** is the largest of many flowing southwest into the Mississippi. The black fertile soil is enormously productive, and the state is among the top producers of such products as corn, soybeans, hogs, and cattle.

Illinois has a well-developed industrial sector dominated by heavy industry, including steel, farm and construction machinery, communications equipment, electronic components, appliances, transportation equipment, and processed foods. Reserves of bituminous coal are extensive, and there is some oil. Illinois' products are widely distributed throughout the country and overseas. **Chicago** is the focus of many railroads and highways. Since the **St. Lawrence Seaway** was opened in 1959, the city's port on **Lake Michigan** has received large ocean-going vessels.

Farmlands and factories have attracted immigrants from other states and foreign nations since the early 19th century. Many residents are of German, Scandinavian, Russian, Irish, and Italian descent. There are about 140 institutions of higher education. The University of Illinois, in Urbana, has many branches. Private institutions include the University of Chicago and Northwestern University, in Evanston. The **Argonne National Laboratory**, operated by the University of Chicago, carries on basic science and national security research. The **Fermi National Accelerator Laboratory** for high-energy physics research is at Batavia.

HISTORY

Illinois was occupied by the **Algonquin** people when **Father Jacques Marquette** and **Louis Jolliet**, French explorers, sailed up the Illinois River in 1673; a few French settlements were made in the next century. In 1763 the land was ceded to Great Britain; it was occupied by American troops in the Revolution.

STATE FACTS

Admitted to Union December 3, 1818; ranked 21st

U.S. Congress Senate 2, House of Representatives 19

Population 12,763,371; ranked 5th

Capital Springfield

State legislature Senate 59, House of Representatives 118

Area 57,914 sq mi (149,998 sq km); ranked 25th

Elevation Highest 1,235 ft (376 m), Charles Mound; lowest 279 ft (85 m), Mississippi River

State nickname Prairie State

State motto State Sovereignty, National Union

State bird Cardinal

State flower Purple violet

State tree White oak

Traditionally a manufacturing city and transportation hub, with extensive railroad links and access to the North Atlantic via the St. Lawrence Seaway, Chicago has in recent years begun to reinvent itself as a vibrant commercial center, attracting large multinationals and financial services companies.

The Illinois Territory was organized in 1809, becoming a state nine years later. The opening of the **Erie Canal** in 1825 and railway access led to a boom in settlers; between 1840 and 1890, the state's population rose from 476,000 to almost 4 million. Around 1839 the **Mormons** moved to Illinois from Missouri, and their leader, **Joseph Smith**, was murdered in 1844; they then moved west to Salt Lake City, Utah. Illinois became a power in national politics with the emergence of **Abraham Lincoln** as a voice of the pro-Union, antislavery policies that led to his election as president. The Illinois legislature was the first to ratify the 13th Amendment that abolished slavery. In 1942 the atomic age was inaugurated at the **University of Chicago** when researchers set off the first self-sustaining atomic chain reaction.

MAIN CITIES

CHICAGO America's third most populous city (after New York and Los Angeles) is on the southwest shore of **Lake Michigan** in the state's northeast. **Fort Dearborn** was established here in 1803. One-third of the city was destroyed by fire in 1871. During the Prohibition era in the 1920s, **Al Capone** and other gangsters held sway. As mayor of Chicago from 1955 until his death in 1976,

Richard J. Daley dominated Illinois politics, but riots in Chicago at the Democratic National Convention in 1968 hurt his image. **Harold Washington** became Chicago's first African American mayor in 1983, and Daley's son **Richard M. Daley**, became mayor in 1989, becoming the first to serve five consecutive terms. The city has the largest rail terminal in the world and one of the world's busiest airports, **O'Hare**. "**The Loop**," an elevated railway, circles the downtown area. The **University of Chicago** is among many colleges and universities. The world's first skyscraper was built here in 1885, and the **Sears Tower** (1,729 ft/527 m) was the world's tallest building from 1974 to 1996. Chicago is the major industrial, commercial, and cultural center of the Midwest. Population (2004) 2,719,290.

SPRINGFIELD Illinois' capital is near the center of the state on the **Sangamon River**. Founded in 1818, it became the capital in 1837. That same year Abraham Lincoln moved there until being elected president in 1860; he is buried nearby. The **Abraham Lincoln Presidential Museum** opened in 2005. Springfield is in the center of a fertile farming area and coal region. It is a governmental, medical, and insurance center. The main industries include machinery, electronics, and fertilizers. Population (2004) 111,454.

INDIANA

Indiana is a state in the north-central United States, in one of the country's richest farming regions. It is bordered by Michigan in the north, Illinois west, Kentucky south, and Ohio east. Lake Michigan's shoreline is along the northwest corner.

LAND AND ECONOMY

The land slopes gradually to the west and south, and many rivers, of which the **Wabash** is the largest, flow in this direction. There are numerous lakes, especially in the north. The original forests were cleared by the first settlers for farming, which remains a major sector of the economy; the state ranks high in agricultural production. Major farm products include corn, wheat, soybeans, fruit, tobacco, cattle, sheep, hogs, and chickens. Among the chief minerals are coal, petroleum, and limestone.

Development of varied manufacturing, particularly in heavy industry complexes in the northwest along **Lake Michigan**, has placed Indiana among the nation's leaders in this category. Access to the lake and to the **Ohio River** in the south, with an extensive highway and railroad system, ensures efficient distribution of Indiana's farm and manufactured products, which include steel, electrical machinery, aircraft, musical instruments, motor vehicles, automobile parts, farm machinery, and processed foods.

Early settlement was made largely by people from states to the east and southeast, and their descendents form the bulk of the population. About 95% were born in the United States and about 75% in Indiana. The five largest reported ancestries in the state are German, American, Irish, English, and African American. There are nearly 40 institutions of higher education. Indiana University and Purdue University both have several campuses. The University of Notre Dame is a Roman Catholic institution in South Bend.

STATE FACTS

Admitted to Union December 11, 1816; ranked 19th

U.S. Congress Senate 2, House of Representatives 9

Population 6,271,973; ranked 15th

Capital Indianapolis

State legislature Senate 50, House of Representatives 100

Area 36,418 sq mi (94,321 sq km); ranked 38th

Elevation Highest 1,257 ft (383 m), Hoosier Hill; lowest 320 ft (98 m), Ohio River

State nickname Hoosier State

State motto Crossroads of America

State bird Cardinal

State flower Peony

State tree Tulip poplar

HISTORY

The first three main Native American groups in Indiana were the Delaware, Potawatomi, and Miami. The first European to visit the region was the French explorer **Robert Cavelier**, **Sieur de La Salle**, in 1673. More French explorers and fur trappers arrived, and several forts were established to protect their trade. France ceded the area to Great Britain in 1763. During the American Revolution, U.S. troops successfully attacked the British garrison at **Fort Vincennes** in 1779. The region passed to the United States at the war's end, and Indiana Territory was created in 1800. Severe fighting was used to subdue the Native Americans. They were forced to sign a treaty in 1795 by **General Anthony Wayne** but were soon threatening the settlements. The Shawnee's **Chief Tecumseh** was finally defeated in 1811 at the **Battle of Tippecanoe** by the territorial governor, **William Henry Harrison**, who later became the 9th U.S. president. A year later, a land rush occurred with many newcomers settling near **Vincennes**, the first capital and oldest town (c. 1730). After achieving statehood in 1816, Indiana remained a rural area until late in the 19th century. Before and during the Civil War, many escaping slaves found refuge in Indiana cities along the "**Underground Railroad**." In 1880, **Wabash** became the first U.S. city to be electrically lighted. The famous **Indianapolis 500** auto race began in 1911 and is still held each Memorial Day.

MAIN CITIES

INDIANAPOLIS The capital and by far largest city of Indiana is in the center of the state on the **White River**. It was laid out like Washington, D.C., with wide streets and avenues on a specially se-lected site, becoming the state capital in 1825. It is home to the **Indianapolis Motor Speedway**, where the Indianapolis 500 auto race – the largest single-day sporting event in the world – takes place. The city is the major cereal and livestock market in a fertile agricultural area. It is a center for the trucking industry. It has eight universities and colleges. Many insurance companies are located here, and industries include electronic equipment, vehicle parts, pharmaceuticals, and meat packing. Population (2004) 766,094.

FORT WAYNE City in northeast Indiana where the St. Joseph and St. Mary rivers meet to form the Maumee River. A French fort was established in 1680 and captured by the British during the French and Indian War (1755–1763) and held by Native Americans in 1763 during **Pontiac's Rebellion**. It became a U.S. fort in 1794 built by **General Anthony Wayne**. The city was settled by 1832 and its development spurred in the 1850s by the **Wabash** and **Erie** canals and the railroads. Industries include heavy vehicles, copper wire, stainless steel, mining machinery, and pumps. Five universities and four colleges are here. Population (2004) 219,351.

The Indianapolis Motor Speedway was first proposed in 1906 and built in 1909 as a 2.5-mile (4k m) test track. The first auto races took place that year and the inaugural Indianapolis 500 race was held in 1911.

IOWA

Iowa is a state in the north-central United States, on the west bank of the Mississippi River. It borders Minnesota in the north, South Dakota and Nebraska west, Missouri south, and Wisconsin and Illinois east.

LAND AND ECONOMY

Level or slightly rolling, the land rises gradually to the west and north. The elevation of two-thirds of the land is from 800 to 1,400 ft (244 to 427 m). Iowa was originally prairie, covered with high grass that was plowed to create farmland. Lumber is found primarily along the rivers. The state is bounded on the east by the **Mississippi River** and on most of the west by the **Missouri River**; the principal river in the state is the **Des Moines**. As an income source, agriculture maintains a fair balance with industry, which has grown steadily. Farm-related products are important, such as hogs, cattle, corn, soybeans, alfalfa, and fruit (such as the popular "Delicious" apple that originated in the state). Among the chief minerals are cement components: limestone, sand, and gravel. The state's industrial production is broadly diversified, including processed foods, farm and construction machinery, and electrical machinery.

The first settlers came in the 1830s from the eastern and southern states. Later, farmers from Europe, notably Germans, Scandinavians, Scottish, Irish, and Dutch, came to work the soil. About 80% of Iowa's people were born in the state. There are nearly 60 institutions of higher education. The **University of Iowa**, **Iowa State University** and the **University of Northern Iowa** are all state-supported. Agricultural research at these and other institutions has contributed largely to the state's development and use of the land.

HISTORY

The first inhabitants in the region were Mound Builders and later the Iowa and Yankton Sioux. The first European visitors were **Father Jacques Marquette** and **Louis Jolliet**. As part of the Mississippi valley, Iowa was included in the claim by **Robert Cavelier**, **Sieur de La Salle** to the region for France in 1682. French hunters and trappers explored the region. It was ceded briefly to Spain but was regained in 1800. The land was sold to the United States in the Louisiana Purchase of 1803. Native Americans still occupied the land, and it was not legally opened for settlement until after the **Black Hawk War** in 1832. It was successively atttached to other territories – Indiana, Louisiana, Missouri, Michigan, and Wisconsin – before 1838, when Congress created the Territory of Iowa. After admission to the Union in 1846, Iowa grew rapidly as a farming area. The first capital at **Burlington** was moved to **Iowa City** in 1839 and then **Des Moines** in 1857. Two groups moving into its southeastern area were the Swiss **Amish** in 1846 to Amana, and German **Inspirationists** in 1855 to Kalona; both communities still exist. In 1856, Iowa had the first bridge spanning the Mississippi River, linking Davenport and Rock Island. U.S. President **Herbert Hoover** was born in 1874 at West Branch in southeast Iowa. Industrial development was intensive after World War II. In 1959, the Soviet Premier **Nikita Khrushchev** visited Iowa to learn about its farming methods. The state experienced widespread flooding in 1993. Diversification of agriculture is a current trend.

MAIN CITIES

DES MOINES The state's capital and largest city is in south-central Iowa near the confluence of the Des Moines and Raccoon rivers. Founded in 1843 as a fort, it is now an industrial and transportation center for the **Corn Belt**. In 1857 its name was shortened from Fort Des Moines and the city became the capital. Its commission form of government, the **Des Moines Plan**, has been adopted by many other U.S. cities. It has a downtown system of climate-controlled skywalks connecting major buildings. Industries include mechanical and aerospace engineering, publishing, and chemicals. Population (2004) 198,682.

CEDAR RAPIDS Located in east central Iowa on the Cedar River, Iowa's second most populous city began as one cabin in 1838. The town was named Rapids City in 1841 for the rapids on the river and seven years later renamed Cedar Rapids. Many Czechs arrived in 1852, and it was incorporated in 1856. The **National Czech and Slovak Museum and Library** opened here in 1974. Cedar Rapids is a distribution center for the agricultural region and manufactures such products as communications equipment, farm machinery, paper products, and cereals. Population (2004) 122,206.

Almost 90% of Iowa's land is farmed, with major crops including corn and soybeans. In order to avoid further erosion and put agricultre at risk, farmers are encouraged to plant field buffers and plant round waterways. Iowa is one of the United States's leading producers of crops for ethanol, an alternative fuel source.

STATE FACTS

Admitted to Union December 28, 1846; ranked 29th
U.S. Congress Senate 2, House of Representatives 5
Population 2,966,334; ranked 30th
Capital Des Moines
State legislature Senate 50, House of Representatives 100
Area 56,272 sq mi (145,743 sq km); ranked 26th
Elevation Highest 1,670 ft (509 m), Hawkeye Point; lowest 480 ft (146 m), Mississippi River
State nickname Hawkeye State
State motto Our liberties we prize and our rights we will maintain
State bird Eastern goldfinch
State flower Wild rose
State tree Oak

KANSAS

KANSAS

Kansas is a state in the central United States. It is bordered by Nebraska in the north, Colorado west, Oklahoma south and Missouri east. The geographical center of the 48 contiguous states is in Smith County near the northern boundary.

LAND AND ECONOMY

The land rises gradually from east to west, marked by some level areas and hill ranges. The highest portions are on a high plateau in the west, while the **Osage Plains** are in the east. Important rivers are the **Kansas** and the **Arkansas**. The only lakes are human-made. In much of the state the soil is especially suitable for wheat-growing, and the state ranks first in wheat production. Other crops include sorghum, hay, corn, soybeans, and sunflowers. In all sections pasturage is plentiful for raising beef and dairy cattle. Manufacturing is centered in the cities of the east and south. Finance, insurance, and real estate are also important. The major industrial products include aircraft, transportation equipment, processed foods, machinery, and chemicals. Oil is drilled and refined in the southeast, and large natural gas deposits occur in the southeast and southwest.

Pioneers from the eastern and southern states flocked to Kansas when settlement began in 1854, followed by German, Swedish, Czech, and Russian farmers. Many African Americans in the state are descended from the "**Exodusters**," newly freed Blacks who fled the south after the Civil War for land in Kansas. There are over 50 institutions of higher education, including the **University of Kansas**, in Lawrence and **Kansas State University**, in Manhattan.

HISTORY

The Spanish explorer **Francisco Vázquez de Coronado** crossed the region in 1541 and French hunters and traders followed. The land passed from France to the United States in the Louisiana Purchase of 1803. Native Americans were moved to other lands, and in 1854 the Territory of Kansas was created and opened for settlement under the Kansas-Nebraska Act that allowed residents to decide if slavery was permitted. The **Pony Express** was founded in 1860 in **Leavenworth**. Immigrants came from the slave states of the South and the free states of the East causing violence between the factions. Kansas was admitted to the Union as a free state in 1861, just before the Civil War began. The Confederate raider William Quantrill attacked **Lawrence** in 1863, killing 150 civilians and burning 200 buildings. After the war, cattle were driven up the **Chisholm Trail** to **Abilene** in 1867 and five years later came the establishment of **Dodge City**, home to Wyatt Earp,

Wild Bill Hickock, and Bat Masterson. Kansas became an assembly and supply area for thousands of immigrants bound for the Far West. The state's own population grew from 364,000 in 1870 to over 1,400,000 in 1890 as its agricultural potential was realized. In 1954, the Supreme Court ruled against the segregated **Topeka** school system, beginning integration in public schools throughout the nation.

MAIN CITIES

WICHITA Kansas's largest city by far is in the south-central area of the state at the confluence of the Arkansas and Little Arkansas rivers. Established in 1864 as a trading post, it developed with the arrivals of the **Chisholm Trail** and the railroad (1872). A cattle town and later a wheat center, its commercial growth was spurred by the discovery of oil in 1915 and by the development of its aircraft industry in 1920. It is home to the **Mid-American All-Indian Center** which preserves the heritage of many Native American groups. Industries include aviation, railroad workshops, oil refining, grain processing, and meat-packing. Population (2004) 345,810.

KANSAS CITY Located in the state's northeast, the city is adjacent to the larger Kansas City, Missouri. Part of an Indian reservation, it was acquired by the Wyandotte people in 1843 and sold to the U.S. government in 1855. The modern city was established in 1886. The **Kansas Speedway** was opened here in 2001 for major auto races. The industries include livestock, vehicles, metal products, and chemicals. Population (2004) 145,004.

TOPEKA The capital is in the state's northeast on the Kansas River. Founded by settlers from New England in 1854, it became the state capital in 1861. It is a major transportation center for cattle and wheat. The city is home to the **Brown v. Board of Education National Park**, opened in 2003 to commemorate the Supreme Court decision ending segregation in public schools. Industries include printing, rubber goods, steel products, and footwear. Population (2004) 122,377.

STATE FACTS

Admitted to Union January 29, 1861; ranked 34th

U.S. Congress Senate 2, House of Representatives 4

Population 2,744,687; ranked 33rd

Capital Topeka

State legislature Senate 40, House of Representatives 125

Area 82,277 sq mi (213,096 sq km); ranked 15th

Elevation Highest 4,039 ft (1,231 m), Mount Sunflower; lowest, 700 ft (214 m), Verdigris River

State nickname Sunflower State

State motto *Ad astra per aspera* (To the stars through difficulties)

State bird Western meadowlark

State flower Sunflower

State tree Cottonwood

Kansas is at the heart of "Tornado Alley," the area of the U.S. Midwest most commonly at risk of their occurrence, which also includes Nebraska, Oklahoma, and Texas, as well as Colorado and Arkansas. The tornado season runs from March to August, but they can occur at any time of year in the right weather conditions.

KENTUCKY

The Commonwealth of Kentucky is a state in the east central United States. It is surrounded by seven states: Indiana and Ohio in the north, West Virginia and Virginia east, Tennessee south, and Illinois and Missouri west.

LAND AND ECONOMY

The land is generally rolling except in the southeast, where the Cumberland and Pine mountains dominate a rugged plateau. **Mammoth Cave** in the central region is the world's longest cave. The **Ohio River** forms the north boundary and the **Mississippi River** the west. The Kentucky and Tennessee rivers are the largest in the state. About 40% of the land is forested, and Kentucky is a major hardwood producing state. It has about 91,000 farms, and the main agricultural crops are tobacco, corn, hay, soybeans, winter wheat, and fruit, while livestock includes dairy cattle, poultry, and hogs. Grasslands (including **bluegrass** which has bluish green stems) provide pasturage for horses, for which Kentucky is famous, and cattle. Manufacturing expanded after World War II, and major products include processed foods, machinery, and chemicals. Kentucky is the nation's third largest coal producer, and other major minerals are petroleum, natural gas, fluorite, stone, sand, and gravel.

Kentucky was first settled by European immigrants from the eastern states. The five largest reported ancestries in the state are American, German, Irish, British, and African American. Rural dwellers outnumbered urban ones until 1970. There are eight state-supported institutions of higher education, including the University of Kentucky, in Lexington; Kentucky State University, in Frankfort; and the University of Louisville. Some 20 independent colleges and universities exist.

HISTORY

Before European settlers arrived, Native American groups such as the **Shawnees**, **Cherokees**, and **Chickasaws**, lived in the region. The area was the first to be colonized west of the Allegheny Mountains. **Dr. Thomas Walker** led the first surveying party in 1750, and **James Harrod** established the first settlement in 1774 at **Fort Harrod**. In the 1770s, the frontiersman **Daniel Boone** blazed the **Wilderness Road** from Virginia and North Carolina through the **Cumberland Gap** in the southeast corner of Kentucky. Thousands of settlers followed this route, while others came down the Ohio River. Kentucky was originally a part of Virginia. After a period of war with Native Americans and a series of land disputes, it was admitted to the Union in 1792. The final western area of the state was purchased from the Chickasaws in 1818. At the outbreak of the Civil War, the state remained in the Union but Kentuckians fought in both armies. The opposing presidents, **Abraham Lincoln** and **Jefferson Davis**, were both born in Kentucky. The state's largest battle was in 1862 at **Perryville**, in which 1,600 soldiers were killed. After the war, Kentucky prospered, with burley tobacco being developed. **Fort Knox** was established in 1936 as a U.S. Treasury Gold Vault and now contains roughly $6 billion. The increased price of imported oil to the United States during the 1970s Energy Crisis, as well as today, has created more activity in coal mining.

MAIN CITIES

LOUISVILLE The state's largest city is located in northwest Kentucky and is a port on the **Ohio River**. It was established as a military base in 1778 by **George Rogers Clark** and named after King Louis XVI. It is host to the famous **Kentucky Derby**, which has been run on Churchill Downs since 1875; the city has many stud stables. The world's first electric light was demonstrated here by **Thomas Edison** in 1883 at the Southern Exposition. The most important industries include tobacco, bourbon whiskey, domestic appliances, and synthetic rubber. Population (2004) 556,332.

LEXINGTON In the bluegrass region of northeast-central Kentucky, Lexington is a famous breeding ground for thoroughbred horses. It has the world's largest tobacco market. Other key industries are electrical machinery and distilling. The **University of Kentucky** is here. Population (2004) 266,358.

FRANKFORT The state's capital is in north-central Kentucky at a double curve of the **Kentucky River**. First settled in 1779, it was made the state capital in 1792 after winning a contest to make the most generous contribution for the capitol building ($3,000 and construction materials). During the Civil War, it was the only Union capital occupied by Confederate troops. The city has "**Liberty Hall**" (1796), reportedly designed by Thomas Jefferson, and the **Old Capitol** (1827–1830). Its industries include tobacco, whiskey distilling, textiles, electronic parts, and furniture. Population (2004) 27,742.

STATE FACTS

Admitted to Union June 1, 1792; ranked 15th
U.S. Congress Senate 2, House of Representatives 6
Population 4,173,405; ranked 26th
Capital Frankfort
State legislature Senate 38, House of Representatives 100
Area 40,409 sq mi (104,659 sq km); ranked 37th
Elevation Highest 4,139 ft (1,262 m), Black Mountain; lowest 257 ft (78 m), Mississippi River
State nickname Bluegrass State
State motto United we stand, divided we fall
State bird Cardinal
State flower Goldenrod
State tree Tulip poplar

The Cumberland Falls State Park forms part of the Daniel Boone National Forest. The falls are 125 ft (37 m) wide, with a 60 ft (18 m) drop.

LOUISIANA

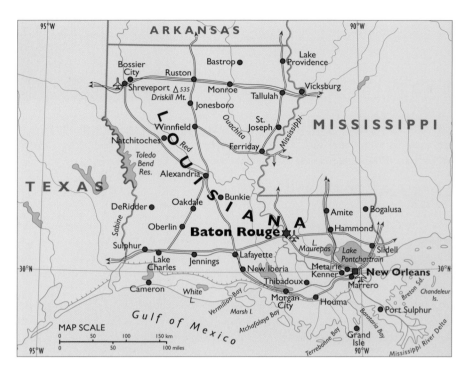

Louisiana is a state in the south-central United States, on the Gulf of Mexico at the mouth of the Mississippi River. It has boundaries with Texas in the west, Arkansas north, and Mississippi east, with the Gulf of Mexico on the south.

LAND AND ECONOMY

The state is a level coastal plain. The **Mississippi River** bisects its southern half; and the Red and Ouachita are other major rivers. Vast marshes lie along the southern coast. Agricultural production is widespread, with major products including rice, sugarcane, sweet potatoes, soybeans, cotton, and cattle. Commercial fishing in the **Gulf of Mexico** is important. Key manufacturing includes chemicals, petroleum products, and processed foods. The main mineral resources are petroleum, natural gas, sulfur, and salt. Much oil is obtained from offshore wells. The Mississippi has long been a commercial route with northern states, and **New Orleans** is one of the nation's leading ports.

The French began settling Louisiana about 1700 and were followed by Germans. Many Acadian French deported by the British from Nova Scotia arrived in the 1750s and Spaniards joined the colony a few years later. Americans from other states settled in the north. Slaves were brought in to work on cotton and sugar plantations. French and Spanish influences are strongest in the south, and New Orleans is notably cosmopolitan. There are nearly 30 institutions of higher education. **Louisiana State University** and the **University of Louisiana** have eight campuses each. Among private universities are two in New Orleans: Tulane University and Loyola University.

HISTORY

Robert Cavelier, **Sieur de La Salle**, claimed the area for France in 1682. By secret treaty, in 1762, France ceded it to Spain, which ceded it back in 1800. France sold it to the United States as part of the **Louisiana Purchase** in 1803. In 1804 the Territory of Orleans, comprising the present state, was organized. On its admission to the Union in 1812, it was renamed Louisiana. The **Battle of New Orleans**, won by the Americans on January 8, 1815, was the last engagement of the War of 1812 (the troops did not know it was over). The state joined the Confederacy in January 1861, and Union troops took New Orleans in 1862 and controlled the Mississippi a year later. Louisiana's economy was wrecked by the Civil War, and industrial growth did not come until the 20th century. For most of that century, the Long family dominated Louisiana politics, especially the populist governor **Huey Long**, who was assassinated on the capitol steps in 1936. Drilling of Louisiana's offshore oil resources, begun on a large scale after World War II, transformed the state's economy. **Hurricane Katrina** was a disaster in 2005, killing some 1,300 people in the state and virtually turning New Orleans into a deserted city.

MAIN CITIES

NEW ORLEANS City and river port at the tip of southeast Louisiana, between **Lake Pontchartrain** and the **Mississippi River**. Founded by the French in 1718, it was ceded to Spain in 1763 and acquired by the United States under the Louisiana Purchase. Its industries expanded rapidly in the 20th century after the discovery of oil and natural gas. New Orleans is known for its jazz, the largest annual **Mardi Gras** festival, and its old **French Quarter**. The city was devastated on August 29, 2005, by floods caused by **Hurricane Katrina**, which engulfed 80% of the city. (About 550 persons are known to be dead, but some estimates are much higher.) Residents were made homeless, with some 30,000 crowded in unsanitary and dangerous conditions for days in the **Superdome**. About 240,000 people, almost half of the city's population, were evacuated to Houston and others were housed throughout the nation. Repairs on the broken levees that let in the water from Lake Ponchartrain, were being finished in 2006, and the city celebrated a reduced Mardi Gras six months after the tragedy. Population (2006) 181,400.

BATON ROUGE The capital of Louisiana is on the Mississippi River in the state's southeast. Baton Rouge means "red stick" and was named by the French explorer **Pierre LeMoyne**, **Sieur d'Iberville**, in 1699 when he saw a red stick used there as a Native American boundary. Founded in 1719 by French colonists, it was ceded to Britain by France in 1763 and to the United States with the Louisiana Purchase, becoming the capital in 1849. It is home to Louisiana State University and Southern University. Baton Rouge is also the site of a large petrochemical complex, and industries include natural gas, chemicals, plastics, and wood products. Population (2004) 227,818.

The Statue of Andrew Jackson on his horse in Jackson Square in front of St. Louis Cathedral in New Orleans. The motto on the base reads "The Union Must and Shall Be Preserved."

STATE FACTS

Admitted to Union April 30, 1812; ranked 18th
U.S. Congress Senate 2, House of Representatives 7
Population 4,523,628; ranked 24th
Capital Baton Rouge
State legislature Senate 39, House of Representatives 105
Area 51,840 sq mi (134,264 sq km); ranked 31st
Elevation Highest 535 ft (163 m), Driskill Mountain; lowest, 5 ft (2 m) below sea level, at New Orleans
State nickname Pelican State
State motto Union, Justice, and Confidence
State bird Eastern brown pelican
State flower Magnolia
State tree Bald cypress

MAINE

Maine is a state in the extreme northeast United States bordered by the Canadian provinces of Quebec on the west and New Brunswick north and by the U.S. state of New Hampshire southwest. The Atlantic coastline is on the east.

LAND AND ECONOMY

The coastline is broken by bays and inlets; hundreds of islands lie offshore. The land is generally rolling, the highest mountains being in the central part. Principal rivers are the **Penobscot**, **Kennebec**, and **Androscoggin**. About 89% of the state is forested, and there are thousands of lakes. Among the main minerals are granite, cement, and feldspar. Coastal fisheries catch 90% of the nation's lobsters, and also clams and herring. Maine is a large producer of potatoes, and produces 90% of low-bush blueberries in the U.S. Other major crops are apples, maple syrup, and vegetables. Key industrial products include wood products, lumber, paper, textiles, and processed foods. Tourism is an important source of revenue.

Most of the residents are descended from English, Scottish, Irish, and French settlers. Among the institutions of higher education are the **University of Maine**, in Orono, near Bangor, while private schools include **Bowdoin College** (founded 1794) in Brunswick.

HISTORY

A colony was established in 1604 at the mouth of the **St. Croix River** by the French explorer **Pierre du Guast**, **Sieur de Monts**. Scattered English settlements were made soon after 1600, when the name "Maine" was applied by **Sir Ferdinando Gorges** to the mainland as distinct from the islands. The province received a charter from King Charles I in 1639. **York** became America's first chartered city in 1641, being first named Agamenticus and then Gorgeana. In 1691, the region became part of the colony of Massachusetts Bay. It remained part of the state of Massachusetts until achieving statehood in 1820. World War II spurred shipbuilding and brought military establishments to the state. In 1948, Skowhegan native **Margaret Chase Smith** became the nation's first woman elected as a U.S. senator.

The University of Maine is the most important institution of post-secondary education in the state. Originally the Maine College of Agriculture and the Mechanic Arts, it has a wide range of academic programs in the natural and social sciences, business, engineering, and liberal arts.

MAIN CITIES

PORTLAND Maine's largest city and port is on a deep natural harbor on **Casco Bay**. A settlement called Falmouth was established here in 1632. The town grew rapidly under the **Massachusetts Bay Company**. In 1775 it was devastated by the British during the American Revolution. From 1820–1827, it was the state capital. The modern city is an oil and shipping center with important commercial links with Montreal, Quebec. Population (2004) 63,905.

AUGUSTA At the highest tidal eddy point of the **Kennebec River**, the site of Maine's capital city was first explored by English settlers in 1604 and settled as a trading post in 1625. The town was renamed Augusta in 1797 and became the state capital in 1827. Population (2000) 18,650.

STATE FACTS

Admitted to Union March 15, 1820; ranked 23rd
U.S. Congress Senate 2, House of Representatives 2
Population 1,321,505; ranked 40th
Capital Augusta
State legislature Senate 35, House of Representatives 151
Area 35,385 sq mi (91,646 sq km); ranked 39th
Elevation Highest 5,268 ft (1,606 m), Mount Katahdin; lowest, sea level
State nickname Pine Tree State
State motto *Dirigo* (I direct)
State bird Chickadee
State flower White pinecone and tassel
State tree Eastern white pine

MARYLAND & D.C.

Maryland is a state in the eastern United States on the Atlantic Ocean. It is bordered by Pennsylvania in the north, Delaware east, Virginia south and West Virginia southwest.

LAND AND ECONOMY

Maryland is divided nearly in half by **Chesapeake Bay**. East of the bay lies a coastal plain, a center of agriculture, with major products including tobacco, corn, soybeans, apples, and poultry. To the west the land is rolling; the **Blue Ridge Mountains** cross the western tip of the state. The **Potomac River** forms the irregular west boundary of most of Maryland. **Baltimore**, on the west shore of Chesapeake Bay, is one of the nation's leading ports. Among the state's major industrial products are steel, copper, aircraft, ships, processed foods, and chemicals.

Maryland's first settlers were largely English, while the industrialized Baltimore area drew immigrants of varied stock. The state has about 50 institutions of higher education, including the **University of Maryland**. Best-known of the private institutions is **Johns Hopkins University**. The **U.S. Naval Academy** is in Annapolis.

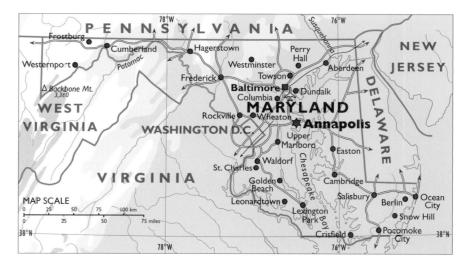

HISTORY

A charter that included the present Maryland was granted in 1632 by King Charles I to **Cecilius Calvert**, **2nd Lord Baltimore**. The first settlements came two years later. In 1791, Maryland ceded a section of land on the Potomac River to create the **District of Columbia** for the nation's capital. In 1814, **Francis Scott Key** wrote a poem that became "The Star-Spangled Banner" while watching the

37

MAIN CITIES

BALTIMORE The city is in north Maryland at the mouth of the **Patapsco River** on Chesapeake Bay. It was founded in 1729 by the Irish family of Baltimore as a tobacco port. During the 19th century, it became an important shipbuilding center. The world's first telegraph line was established in 1844 from Baltimore to Washington. In 1904 the city was destroyed by fire. The metropolitan areas of Baltimore and Washington, D.C., virtually merge. A major port, its industries include steelworks, oil refineries, shipbuilding, and aerospace equipment. Population (2005) 609,779.

ANNAPOLIS Maryland's state capital is on the south bank of the **Severn River** on Chesapeake Bay. Founded in 1649 by Puritans from Virginia, it was laid out as a state capital in 1694. Its **State House** (1796) is the oldest in the nation still in use. The peace treaty that ended the American Revolution was signed there. Annapolis is the seat of the **U.S. Naval Academy** (1845) and **St. John's College** (1784), the third oldest U.S. institute of higher education. Industries include boatyards and seafood packing. Population (2004) 35,838.

Johns Hopkins University was founded in 1876 as the first research university in the United States, aimed not only at teaching students, but furthering human knowledge. One of three major universities in Baltimore, it is home to a world-renowned medical school.

DISTRICT FACTS

U.S. Congress Senate 2 (nonvoting), House of Representatives 2 (1 with some voting rights)
Population 550,521
Area 68 sq mi (177 sq km)
Elevation 410 ft (125 m), Tenleytown; lowest 1 ft (0.3 m), Potomac River
District motto *Justitia omnibus* (Justice for All)
District bird Wood thrush
District flower American beauty rose
District tree Scarlet oak

STATE FACTS

Admitted to Union April 28, 1788; 7th of the 13 original states to ratify the U.S. Constitution
U.S. Congress Senate 2, House of Representatives 8
Population 5,600,388; ranked 19th
Capital Annapolis
State legislature Senate 47, House of Representatives, 141
Area 12,407 sq mi (32,133 sq km); ranked 42nd
Elevation Highest 3,360 ft (1,024 m), Hoye-Crest, Backbone Mountain; lowest sea level
State nicknames Old Line State, Free State
State motto *Fatti maschii, parole femine* (Manly deeds, womanly words)
State bird Baltimore oriole
State flower Black-eyed Susan
State tree White oak

DISTRICT OF COLUMBIA

The District of Columbia and **Washington**, the U.S. capital, are coextensive on the east bank of the **Potomac River**. It is independent of any state; it wasn't until 1961 that residents were given the right by the 23rd Amendment to vote for the U.S. president and vice president, and in 1974 to elect their mayor and to levy taxes. They still have no representation in Congress, only a non-voting delegate. Congress retains the right to veto the city council's actions.

The area was chosen in 1790 by **President George Washington** as the seat of government. **Maryland** and **Virginia** donated the land, although Virginia's land was returned in 1846. During the **War of 1812**, it was occupied by the British and almost totally burned. The president's home was first painted white to disguise the scars of the fire. Washington has seen many peaceful protest marches, including the one led in 1963 by **Martin Luther King, Jr.** who made his "I have a dream" speech then. In 2001, terrorists flew a plane into the **Pentagon**, killing 189 people and destroying part of the building.

Landmarks include the White House, Capitol, Washington Monument, Lincoln Memorial, Jefferson Memorial, Franklin Delano Roosevelt Memorial, Smithsonian Institution, Library of Congress, Pentagon, Supreme Court, Federal Bureau of Investigation, Holocaust Memorial Museum, National Gallery of Art, and John F. Kennedy Center for the Performing Arts. Military memorials are the Vietnam Veterans Memorial, National World War II Memorial, and Korean War Veterans Memorial. Universities there include Georgetown University, George Washington University, Catholic University, Howard University, and American University.

British shell **Fort McHenry** in Baltimore harbor. In the Civil War, Maryland was one of the border states that did not secede, but its citizens served in both armies. The battle of **Antietam** was fought in west Maryland on September 17, 1862, resulting in more than 23,000 killed, wounded, or missing. In both world wars, the city was a major center of war material production.

The **Chesapeake Bay Bridge** was opened in 1952, and the parallel span in 1973. In 1967 **Thurgood Marshall** from Baltimore became the first African American to serve on the Supreme Court. **Spiro Agnew**, a former governor of Maryland, resigned in 1973 as U.S. vice president after being charged with previous corruption in Maryland.

MASSACHUSETTS

The Commonwealth of Massachusetts is a state in the northeastern United States on the Atlantic Ocean in the New England region. It is bordered by five states: Vermont and New Hampshire in the north, New York west, and Connecticut and Rhode Island south.

LAND AND ECONOMY

The coastline is indented by bays and inlets, creating many small harbors. Fishhook-shaped **Cape Cod** in the southeast is a distinctive feature. To the west the land is rolling. The broad valley of the **Connecticut River** crosses the state from north to south. The **Berkshire Hills** are in the west. Besides the Connecticut, the principal rivers are the Housatonic (west) and the Merrimack (northeast). Many smaller streams supply abundant water power to generate electricity. The **Connecticut Valley** is a notable farming area. The major agricultural products are cranberries, dairy products, vegetables, cattle, hogs, sheep, and poultry. Among key minerals are clay, lime, marble, silica, quartz, sand, and gravel. No metal mining is done. Industrial products include electrical machinery, computer equipment,

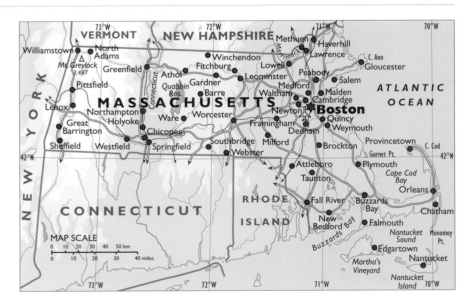

instruments, chemicals, metal products, communications equipment, printing and publishing, apparel, and processed foods. Since the 1950s, the Boston area has emerged as a leader in computer and high-tech industries. Also important to the state are financial services, health care, and tourism, which includes the popular summer resorts on the islands of **Martha's Vineyard** and **Nantucket**.

Massachusetts is one of the most densely populated states in the country, with about 818 people per square mile. More than half of the population lives in the greater **Boston** area. Some are descended from the first English settlers, but in the 19th century many overseas immigrants, largely Irish, Polish, and Italians, were drawn to employment in the factories. The reported ancestry today is 21% Irish, 14.5% English, 13.6% Italian, and 9.9% French.

A pioneer in public education, Massachusetts has many universities and colleges. **Harvard University** in Cambridge (1636) is the oldest U.S. university. The **Massachusetts Institute of Technology** (MIT), also in Cambridge, is a major center of scientific training and research. The **University of Massachusetts**, with its central campus in Amherst, is the state university.

HISTORY

Native American groups in the area included the Massachuset, Wampanoag, and Nauset. The first settlement, the **Plymouth Colony**, was made in 1620 on Massachusetts Bay by the **Pilgrim Fathers**, a group of English settlers seeking religious freedom. They landed at **Plymouth Rock**, a large rock now preserved under a protective roof. Boston was founded by English Puritans in 1630 and became the center of the colony of **Massachusetts Bay**. Through the years several wars were waged against Native Americans who ravaged frontier towns. The **Salem** witch trials occurred in 1692 with 20 people executed and 17 dying in prison. The first regularly issued American newspaper, *The Boston News-Letter*, began publishing in 1704.

Massachusetts strongly resisted the policies of the British crown that led to the Revolution. The **Boston Massacre** occurred on March 5, 1770, when British soldiers killed five colonists, and the **Boston Tea Party** was on December 16, 1773, when colonists dumped 342 large boxes of tea from three British ships into the harbor to protest a tea tax. The silversmith **Paul Revere** made his "midnight ride" on April 18, 1775, to warn **Samuel Adams** and **John Hancock** about British troop movements, and the following day the first battles of the war were at **Lexington** and **Concord**. **Bunker Hill** (June 17, 1775) was the first major battle of the Revolution, but the last battle in the colony.

After achieving statehood in 1788, Massachusetts prospered. Its fishing and whaling fleets were famous, and large vessels carried on a lucrative worldwide trade. Manufacturing flourished, especially in textiles and shoes. The state's John Chapman (1774–1845), popularly known as "**Johnny Appleseed**," planted apple trees from New England to the Ohio River valley. He is now the official Folk Hero of Massachusetts. The 19th century was a time of intellectual ferment, marked by the work of Massachusetts-born writers such as Ralph Waldo Emerson, Henry David Thoreau, Nathaniel Hawthorne, Emily Dickinson, and Edgar Allan Poe. In the Civil War, Massachusetts was a foremost supporter of the Union with men, money, and supplies. During the 1920s traditional industries such as textiles

STATE FACTS

Admitted to Union February 6,1788; 6th of 13 original states to ratify the U.S. Constitution
U.S. Congress Senate 2, House of Representatives 10
Population 6,398,743; ranked 13th
Capital Boston
State legislature Senate 40, House of Representatives 159
Area 10,555 sq mi (27,336 sq km); ranked 44th
Elevation Highest 3,487 ft (1,063 m), Mount Greylock; lowest, sea level
State nickname Bay State
State motto *Ense petit placidam sub libertate quietem* (By the sword we seek peace, but peace only under liberty)
State bird Chickadee
State flower Mayflower
State tree American elm

declined, but later in the century the economy was revitalized through the aerospace and electronics industries. The Kennedys, a nationally prominent political family, are from Massachusetts. In addition to John F. Kennedy, presidents from Massachusetts were John Adams, John Quincy Adams, Calvin Coolidge, and George H.W. Bush.

MAIN CITIES

BOSTON The state capital is a seaport at the mouth of the **Charles River** on Massachusetts Bay. Founded in 1630, it became a Puritan stronghold and the scene of several incidents leading to the outbreak of the American Revolution. At **Independence Hall**, the Declaration of Independence was written and signed, and the U.S. Constitution was written and approved; the Liberty Bell is also there. A religious and cultural center, Boston is the home of many important educational establishments such as Harvard and the Massachusetts Institute of Technology (MIT), both across the river in Cambridge, which has a population of 100,771 (2004). The **Boston Marathon**, first run in 1897, is an annual event. In 2006 the city completed the largest ever U.S. urban transportation project, the $14.6 billion **Central Artery/Tunnel Project**, popularly called the "Big Dig," in which a central elevated highway was replaced by an underground one. Industries include publishing, banking and insurance, shipbuilding, electronics, fishing, and clothing manufacture. Population (2004) 523,683.

WORCESTER The city is on the Blackstone River in central Massachusetts. It was settled in the 1670s, but Native American attacks occurred two years later and again in 1683. **Shays's Rebellion** in 1786 and 1787 brought fighting to the area. In 1850 the first national women's rights conventions was held there. In the 1920s, **Robert Goddard**, known as the father of modern rocketry, made his first experiments in Worcester when a professor at **Clark University**. The **College of the Holy Cross** is also there. Industries include machinery, chemicals, pharmaceuticals, and plastics. Population (2004) 175,966.

SPRINGFIELD Located in southwest Massachusetts, the city is a port on the Connecticut River. It was settled by Puritans in 1636. **Daniel Shays** led Shays's Rebellion there in 1787 when poor farmers unsuccessfully attacked the Springfield arsenal to protest taxes. The new armory saw the development in 1795 of Springfield army rifles and the use, before the Civil War, of interchangeable rifle parts for mass production, which created the concept of the assembly line. Basketball was invented at Springfield College by **Dr. James Naismith**. Springfield is now the regional center for banking and other types of finance. Population (2004) 152,091.

Boston is an economic and cultural center, and is home to three major orchestras and several museums and galleries with internationally important collections.

MICHIGAN

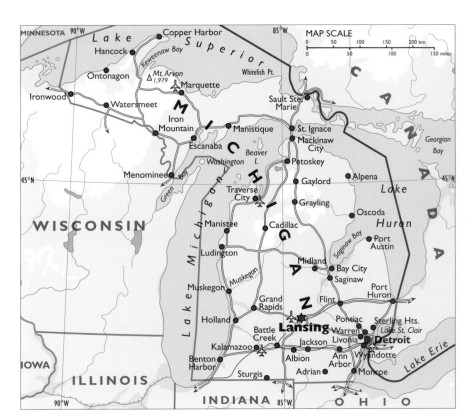

Michigan is a state in the north-central United States that borders on four of the five Great Lakes – Superior, Michigan, Huron, and Erie – and three states, Wisconsin west, and Indiana and Ohio south.

LAND AND ECONOMY

Michigan comprises two peninsulas separated by the narrow **Straits of Mackinac**, which connect lakes Michigan and Huron. The **Upper Peninsula** in the north lies between lakes Superior and Michigan; to the south, the **Lower Peninsula** is between Lake Michigan and lakes Huron, St. Clair, and Erie. The Lower Peninsula, level or rolling, contains most of the population. About 50% of the state is forested, and there are more than 11,000 inland lakes. The motor vehicle industry is centered in **Detroit**, and other state products are machinery, chemicals, pharmaceuticals, baby food, lumber, and furniture. Mineral deposits include iron ore, salt, gypsum, and limestone. Oil and gas fields exist. The state, with about 53,000 farms, produces the most blueberries in the nation. Among other main crops are soybeans, spearmint, dairy products, cherries, apples, pears, and sugar beets, while livestock includes sheep, hogs, and turkeys.

Michigan was settled by pioneers from the eastern states. The Dutch, Germans, Swedes, Norwegians, Finns, and some Canadians came in the 19th century and early 20th century as lumberjacks and miners. Before World War I, the motor industry drew immigrants from Italy and eastern Europe. During World War II, an influx of African Americans joined the labor force. Asian and Spanish immigrants have arrived more recently. There are nearly 90 institutions of higher education, including the **University of Michigan**, in Ann Arbor, and **Michigan State University**, in East Lansing, which pioneered agricultural education and was the nation's first land-grant college.

HISTORY

The original inhabitants were the Native American groups of the Ojibwa, Ottawa and Potawatomi. Beginning with a settlement at **Sault Ste. Marie** between lakes Superior and Huron in 1641, the French built forts and settlements through the area, but lost control to Great Britain by the 1763 treaty that ended the Seven Years War. After the American Revolution, the British did not evacuate the region until 1796. Michigan became a U.S. territory on July 1, 1805. In the War of 1812, the British captured **Detroit**, and their Native American allies terrorized the settlements. In 1819 the treaty of Saginaw ceded nearly 6 million acres (2.4 million ha) of Native American lands to Michigan settlers. The opening of the **Erie Canal** in New York in 1825 aided Michigan's growth by linking it with the Atlantic through the lakes. After joining the Union, the state rapidly developed its lumber and mining resources, which were superseded by the industrial boom, led by the automobile sector, beginning about 1914. The auto industry switched to wartime production during World War II but fell into decline during the late 1970s and early 1980s. Michigan's **Gerald Ford** served as U.S. president from 1974 to 1977, and **Jennifer Granholm** became the state's first woman governor in 2002.

MAIN CITIES

DETROIT Michigan's largest city is on the Detroit River. It is the oldest city in the Midwest, founded in 1701 as **Fort Pontchartrain** by Antoine de la Mothe Cadillac. It was captured by the British in 1760 and used as a base during the American Revolution. They evacuated it in 1796. Detroit was devastated by fire in 1805, the year it became the territorial capital. It was lost to Britain in the war of 1812, but retaken by U.S. forces the next year. The city suffered a five-day race riot in 1967 resulting in 43 deaths. Detroit is headquarters for General Motors, DaimlerChrysler, and Ford, giving the city its "Motown" (motor town) nickname. Universities include the **University of Detroit Mercy** and **Wayne State University**. Besides automobiles, industries include steel, pharmaceuticals, food processing, machine tools, tires, and paint. There are also salt mines in the area. Population (2004) 840,006.

LANSING The state capital is at the confluence of the Grand and Red Cedar rivers in south Michigan. First settled in the 1840s, it became the capital in 1847. Its growth was rapidly increased by the arrival of the railroad in the 1870s and then the automobile industry in 1897. It has a historic **City Market** still operating. **Michigan State University** is in the suburb of **East Lansing**. The main industries are automobiles, metal goods, and machinery. Population (2004) 119,128.

STATE FACTS

Admitted to Union January 26, 1837; ranked 26th
U.S. Congress Senate 2, House of Representatives 15
Population 10,120,860; ranked 8th
Capital Lansing
State legislature Senate 38; House of Representatives 110
Area 96,716 sq mi (250,494 sq km); ranked 11th
Elevation Highest 1,979 ft (603 m), Mount Arvon; lowest 572 ft (174 m), Lake Erie
State nicknames Great Lakes State, Wolverine State
State motto *Si quaeris peninsulam amoenam, circumspice* (If you seek a pleasant peninsula, look about you)
State bird Robin
State flower Apple blossom
State tree White pine

Fort Michilimackinac was originally built by French settlers on the south side of the Straits of Mackinac in about 1715. The reconstructed trading post is now a National Historic Landmark.

MINNESOTA

Minnesota is in the north-central United States, bordered on the north by the Canadian provinces of Manitoba and Ontario, and by four states: North Dakota and South Dakota west, Iowa south, and Wisconsin east. Lake Superior is northeast.

LAND AND ECONOMY

The land is level or rolling except in the rugged hills of the northeast. Much of it is richly fertile. Among the key agricultural products are dairy products, oats, corn, soybeans, and poultry. The north is forested. There are more than 10,000 lakes, some of which are sources of the **Mississippi River**. Shipments of iron ore found in the **Mesabi Range** north of Lake Superior pass through the port of **Duluth**. Taconite, a rock containing low-grade iron, is also mined. The major industrial products include processed foods, machinery, electrical equipment, chemicals, and paper.

In the late 19th century, thousands of immigrants from Europe, chiefly Germans, Swedes, Norwegians, and Finns, came to work the state's forests, farms, and mines. Their descendants comprise a sizable element of the population. The metropolitan area of **Minneapolis-St. Paul** has recently gained large refugee groups of Hmong and Somali peoples from, respectively, Asia and Africa. There are nearly 60 institutions of higher education, and the state-supported University of Minnesota has several campuses. The **Mayo Clinic** at Rochester, founded in 1883, is one of the world's greatest medical centers.

HISTORY

Minnesota's original settlers were mainly two Native American groups, the **Sioux** and **Chippewa**. French fur traders entered the region in the 17th century and controlled it until 1763, when the part east of the Mississippi River passed to Great Britain by the Treaty ending the Seven Years' War. After the American Revolution, this area was ceded to the United States, which acquired the lands west of the river from France by the Louisiana Purchase in 1803. Fort Anthony, now **Fort Snelling**, was built in 1820 at the junction of the Minnesota and Mississippi rivers; other tracts of land were bought from the Native Americans, and settlement began. Minnesota Territory was organized in 1849 and the eastern half of the current state gained statehood 1858.

Minnesota was the first state to respond to President Lincoln's call for troops in the Civil War. A Sioux uprising occurred during the war in 1862, resulting in 38 being hanged in Mankato. The state grew rapidly after the war; its population, which numbered 172,000 in 1860, increased to 1,310,000 in 1890. During the 20th

STATE FACTS

Admitted to Union May 11, 1858; ranked 32nd
U.S. Congress Senate 2, House of Representatives 8
Population 5,132,799; ranked 21st
Capital St. Paul
State legislature Senate 67, House of Representatives 134
Area 86,939 sq mi (225,171 sq km); ranked 12th
Elevation Highest 2,301 ft (701 m), Eagle Mountain; lowest 602 ft (184 m), Lake Superior
State nicknames Gopher State, North Star State
State motto L'Étoile du Nord (The Star of the North)
State bird Common loon
State flower Pink and white lady's-slipper
State tree Red pine

After soybeans, corn is Minnesota's most important agricultural product and the state is in the top four U.S. corn producers. Drought conditions in recent years have led to fears of another "Dust Bowl" across the agricultural heartland of the United States.

century, mining and manufacturing began to dominate Minnesota's economy. Two U.S. senators from the state served as U.S. vice presidents: **Hubert Humphrey** (1965–1969) and **Walter Mondale** (1977–1981), both of whom later lost bids for the U.S. presidency.

MAIN CITIES

MINNEAPOLIS Located in the state's east at the head of navigation on the Mississippi River, Minneapolis is the state's largest city. It and **St. Paul** across the river are known as the "**Twin Cities**." First settled in the 1840s, Minneapolis was the nation's leading lumber center in the 19th century and developed flour milling. Now it is an important processing and distribution center for grain and cattle. Industries include farm machinery, food processing, electronic equipment, computers, and printing and publishing. The **University of Minnesota** is here, and the **Mall of America**, the nation's most visited mall, with 40 million visitors annually, was opened in 1992. Population (2004) 346,104.

ST. PAUL The state's capital and port of entry is on the east bank of the Mississippi River next to Minneapolis. The site was first called **Pig's Eye Landing**, until a chapel was built there in 1841. In 1848, St. Paul became the capital of the territory and continued as capital when Minnesota was admitted to the Union. The capitol building has the world's largest unsupported marble dome. The railroad arrived in 1862 and the city became a transportation center. Today it is a major manufacturing and distribution center. The city is known for its parks and **Winter Carnival**. Population (2004) 258,422.

DULUTH The second largest port on the Great Lakes, Duluth is in northeastern Minnesota on **Lake Superior**. It was settled about 1852 and named for the 17th-century French explorer **Daniel Greysolon, Sieur de Lhut**. It became a center for shipping lumber and then iron ore that was discovered in 1865 in the Mesabi Range. Ocean traffic arrived with the opening of the **St. Lawrence Seaway** in 1959. Duluth also now ships grain and bulk cargo. Population (2004) 85,556.

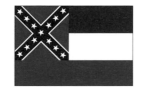

MISSISSIPPI

Mississippi is a state in the south-central United States that borders the Gulf of Mexico in the south, and four states: Arkansas and Louisiana west across the Mississippi River, Tennessee north, and Alabama east.

LAND AND ECONOMY

The land slopes from the hills in the northeast. An east-west strip across the center, known as the **Black Prairie**, has exceptionally rich soil. Pine forests are widespread. The principal rivers in the state are the **Yazoo** and its tributaries and the **Pearl**. Mississippi's soils and its warm climate have made agriculture and forestry the mainstays of the economy. The chief farming products are soybeans, cotton, dairy products, cattle, and poultry. Commercial fisheries operate on the **Gulf Coast**. Since the mid-20th century, efforts to attract industry have been successful. Among the major products are lumber, paper, furniture, apparel, and chemicals. Petroleum and natural gas are extracted chiefly in the south and offshore.

The early settlers were English, Scottish, and Irish from states along the Atlantic coast. Thousands of slaves were brought in to work the cotton plantations. Mississippi's 11 universities include the University of Mississippi, Mississippi State University, the University of Southern Mississippi, and Mississippi University for Women, which in 1884 became the nation's first state-supported college for women; there are also 16 community colleges and 9 private colleges.

STATE FACTS

Admitted to Union December 10, 1817; ranked 20th
U.S. Congress Senate 2, House of Representatives 4
Population 2,921,088; ranked 31st
Capital Jackson
State legislature Senate 52, House of Representatives 122
Area 48,430 sq mi (125,434 sq km); ranked 32nd
Elevation Highest 806 ft (246 m), Woodall Mountain; lowest, sea level
State nickname Magnolia State
State motto *Virtute et armis* (By valor and arms)
State bird Mockingbird
State flower Magnolia
State tree Magnolia

HISTORY

Native American groups in the area included the Natchez, Choctaw, and Chickasaw. The region was explored in 1540 by **Hernando de Soto**. **Robert Cavelier**, **Sieur de La Salle** claimed the region for France in 1682, and a French settlement was made on the Gulf Coast in 1699. Great Britain received the area in 1763 by the treaty ending the Seven Years' War, but during the American Revolution the Spanish gained control and refused to transfer the land to the United States after the war. Spain finally yielded in 1798, and the Territory of Mississippi was organized that year.

One of the six original states of the Confederacy, Mississippi seceded from the Union on January 9, 1861, and **Jefferson Davis**, a U.S. senator from the state and former U.S. secretary of war, became president of the **Confederate States of America**. The state was a battleground in the Civil War: **Jackson** and **Meridian** were burned by Union forces, and **Vicksburg**, on the Mississippi, fell on July 4, 1863, after a long siege by Union General **Ulysses S. Grant**. The state was re-admitted to the Union in 1870, but it took years to repair the ravages of war and the political turmoil of the Reconstruction era.

William Faulkner, Nobel Prize–winning novelist, won his fame writing about life in his native state, as did the Pulitzer Prize–winning writer **Eudora Welty**. The Mississippi River flooded in 1927 causing disaster but leading to a federal flood-control program. The state was a focus of the civil rights movement of the 1960s. In 1962, Mississippi's governor **Ross Barnett** failed to block the admission of an African-American student to the University of Mississippi. The following year saw the murder of the African-American civil rights leader **Medgar Evers**, whose murderer was finally convicted in 1994 after three trials.

On August 29, 2005, the state's Gulf Coast was hit by **Hurricane Katrina**, which caused 224 confirmed deaths and severely damaged or destroyed two-thirds of homes across the region, including **Beauvoir**, the home of Confederate President Jefferson Davis at **Biloxi**. Katrina virtually blew away much of Biloxi and **Gulfport**. Oil and gas production from the Gulf was significantly reduced and oil spills occurred. Although rebuilding continues, many Mississippians feel that their area has received much less attention and volunteer efforts than New Orleans.

MAIN CITY

JACKSON The capital and largest city, Jackson is on the **Pearl River** in southwest Mississippi. It was established as a trading post in the 1790s and first known as LeFleur's Bluff. It was chosen as the capital in 1821 and named for General **Andrew Jackson** (who later became the seventh U.S. president). During the Civil War it was burned three times by Union troops led by General **William T. Sherman**. The old capitol building (1839) has become a museum. In 1997, Jackson elected its first African American mayor, **Harvey Johnson**. The city hosts the **U.S.A. International Ballet Competition** every four years. Industries include natural gas, glass, processed food, and textiles. Population (2004) 184,256.

The classic era of Mississippi paddlewheel steamboats is long gone, but they remain popular tourist attractions in Mississippi and Louisiana.

MISSOURI

Missouri is a state in the central United States on the west bank of the Mississippi River. It is bordered by eight states: Iowa is north and then clockwise are Illinois, Kentucky, Tennessee, Arkansas, Oklahoma, Kansas, and Nebraska.

LAND AND ECONOMY

In the north and west the land is prairie and rolling hills. In the south, the low ridges of the **Ozark Mountains** run northeast to southwest. The **Missouri River** flows west to east across the state to its junction with the **Mississippi**. The two great rivers have been major influences on the state's history. Much of the farmland lies north of the Missouri and includes soybeans, corn, wheat, hay, hogs, cattle, and poultry. The major portion of industry is in **St. Louis** and **Kansas City**, the chief products being chemicals, processed foods, and transportation equipment, including automobiles, aircraft, rocket engines, and space capsules. The Ozark region is the center of most mining, with key minerals including lead, barite, and limestone.

Missouri's early settlers came mostly from Kentucky, Tennessee, Virginia, and North Carolina. Germans, Irish, and English moved into the St. Louis area in the mid-19th century. More than 90% of the present population was born in the United States. The state's universities include the **University of Missouri-Columbia**, where the nation's first school of journalism was established in 1908; the private **Washington University in St. Louis**; and **Saint Louis University**, a Catholic school.

HISTORY

The Native American settlers included the Missouri and Osage. **Robert Cavelier, Sieur de La Salle** claimed the region for France in 1682, and the French made the first settlements in the mid-18th century. The United States acquired the region from France in the Louisiana Purchase of 1803, and it became a territory in 1812. The **Lewis and Clark Expedition** began in St. Louis in 1804 to explore to the Pacific Ocean. In the following decades, Missouri was the main corridor of the westward migrations, and **St. Louis** became a supply center. Wagon trails to Oregon, California, and the Southwest began at **St. Joseph** and **Independence**. Vivid pictures of these years in Missouri appear in the writings of **Mark Twain** (Samuel Clemens), a native of Hannibal. Missouri was admitted to the Union under the **Missouri Compromise** of 1821 as a slave state, and **Jefferson City** became its capital in 1826. When the Civil War began, sympathies were divided. Guerrilla fighting and pitched battles ensued before the state was kept in the Union. One Confederate guerrilla, **Jesse James**, became a renowned bank and train robber between 1866 and 1879. After the war and into the 20th century, the state's development was steady. The two world wars, especially, stimulated the growth of St. Louis and **Kansas City** as industrial and distribution centers, and following World War II, Missouri was a large producer of automobiles. **Harry S. Truman** from Independence became the 33rd U.S. president (1945–1953).

The Gateway Arch in St. Louis sits beside the Mississippi River. Its unique transport system conveys passengers to the observation room at the top of the 630 ft (192 m) arch in capsules.

STATE FACTS

Admitted to Union August 10 1821; ranked 24th
U.S. Congress Senate 2, House of Representatives 9
Population 5,800,310; ranked 18th
Capital Jefferson City
State legislature Senate 34, House of Representatives 163
Area 69,704 sq mi (180,533 sq km); ranked 21st
Elevation Highest 1,772 ft (540 m), Taum Sauk Mountain; lowest 230 ft (70 m), St. Francis River
State nickname Show Me State
State motto *Salus populi suprema lex esto* (Let the welfare of the people be the supreme law)
State bird Bluebird
State flower Hawthorn
State tree Flowering dogwood

MAIN CITIES

KANSAS CITY Located in northwest Missouri on the Missouri River, the state's largest city is next to Kansas City, Kansas. Established in 1821 as a trading post, it developed in the 1860s with the introduction of the railroad and growth in the cattle trade. It was a center for jazz in the 1920s when **Count Basie** and **Duke Ellington** began their careers. The city has the **Liberty Memorial Museum**, a 21-story tower that is the national World War I museum opened in 1926. Kansas City supposedly has more fountains than any city except Rome. Industries include aerospace equipment, vehicles, chemicals, petroleum products, livestock, and grain. Population (2004) 419,664.

ST. LOUIS A city and port in east Missouri, St. Louis is on the Mississippi River near its confluence with the Missouri. The second largest city in the state, St. Louis was founded as a fur-trading post in 1763 by the French who named it for **King Louis IX**. It was held by Spain from 1770 to 1800, returning briefly to France, and then ceded to the U.S. in the Louisiana Purchase of 1803. St. Louis grew rapidly and is now the second largest U.S. inland port. In 1904 it held a large world's fair, the **Louisiana Purchase Exposition**. The city is nicknamed "the Gateway to the West" and has a symbolic **Gateway Arch** rising 630 ft (192 m), the nation's tallest monument. St. Louis is one of the country's largest railroad centers, and industries include brewing, chemicals, tourism, and transportation equipment. Population (2004) 343,279.

MONTANA

MONTANA

Montana is a state in the northwestern United States bordered on the north by Canada, and by four states: North Dakota and South Dakota in the east, Wyoming south and Idaho west and south.

LAND AND ECONOMY

The west is 40% mountainous. The **Rocky Mountains** run south to north, with many subsidiary ranges. The rest of the state is largely high plains, where grazing and farming produce a major part of the state's income. Farm products include wheat, barley, potatoes, sheep, and cattle. The **Missouri River** flows west to east across the state and other large rivers are the **Muk** and the **Yellowstone**. Key minerals include copper, zinc, phosphate rock, petroleum, natural gas, and coal. Among industrial products are lumber and wood processed primary metals, and processed foods. Tourism is a major source of revenue.

Montana is among the least populated states. Native Americans make up 6.4% of the population with seven reservations housing 11 tribes. The main institutions of higher education are the University of Montana and Montana State University.

STATE FACTS

Admitted to Union November 8, 1889; ranked 41st
U.S. Congress Senate 2, House of Representatives 1
Population 935,670; ranked 44th
Capital Helena
State legislature Senate 50; House of Representatives 100
Area 147,042 sq mi (380,838 sq km); ranked 4th
Elevation Highest 12,799 ft (3,901 m), Granite Peak; lowest 1,800 ft (549 m), Kootenai River
State nickname Treasure State
State motto Oro y plata (Gold and silver)
State bird Western meadowlark
State flower Bitterroot
State tree Ponderosa pine

HISTORY

French and Spanish fur traders and prospectors were active before 1800, and the United States acquired the region from France by the **Louisiana Purchase** in 1803. Reports by the **Lewis and Clark Expedition** of 1804–1806 led to the development of the fur trade and the establishment of settlements, army posts, and missions. Discovery of gold brought a rush of immigrants after 1852, and Montana Territory was organized in 1864. Military action over many years subdued the Native Americans. In 1876, Colonel George Custer and his 259 troops of the 7th Cavalry were killed by Sioux and Cheyennes led by Crazy Horse and Sitting Bull, an event known as "Custer's Last Stand." The opening of the **Northern Pacific Railroad** in 1883 was an enormous stimulus, and statehood came in 1889. During the 1980s copper mining slumped, but the strip mining of coal expanded. The state has become important to the military; the **U.S. Air Force** maintains 200 missile silos here.

MAIN CITY

BILLINGS Situated on the **Yellowstone River** in southern Montana, the city is surrounded by four mountain ranges. The site was officially established in 1882 by the **Northern Pacific Railroad**, and named for the company's former president; it was incorporated three years later. It developed as a fur-trading and shipping center and now has such products as oil, natural gas, coal, wheat, barley, corn, and beef and dairy cattle. One of **Montana State University**'s campuses is here. Population (2004) 96,977.

The Little Bighorn Battlefield National Monument marks the defeat of the U.S. 7th Cavalry by Crazy Horse's Cheyenne and Sioux warriors.

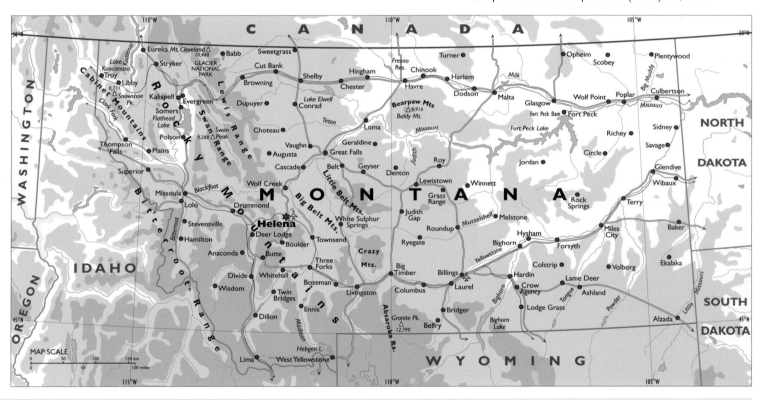

NEBRASKA

Nebraska is a state in the west-central United States, in the Great Plains region. It is bordered by six states: South Dakota in the north, Wyoming west, Colorado southwest, Kansas south, Missouri southeast, and Iowa east.

LAND AND ECONOMY

Nebraska is a rolling prairie that rises steadily from east to west. Grasses are the principal native vegetation. The **Missouri River** forms the east and part of

Many thousands of pioneers crossed Nebraska in covered wagons like these modern replicas.

STATE FACTS

Admitted to Union: March 1, 1867; ranked 37th
U.S. Congress Senate 2, House of Representatives 3
Population 1,758,787; ranked 38th
Capital Lincoln
State legislature (unicameral): 49 senators
Area 77,354 sq mi (200,345 sq km); ranked 16th
Elevation Highest 5,424 ft (1,653 m), Panorama Point; lowest, 840 ft (256 m), Missouri River
State nickname Cornhusker State
State motto Equality before the law
State bird Western meadowlark
State flower Goldenrod
State tree Cottonwood

HISTORY

Native Americans have included the Omaha, Pawnee, Sioux, Arapahoe, and Cheyenne. The region, part of the **Louisiana Purchase** from France in 1803, was little known until the **Lewis and Clark Expedition** (1804–1806). After 1830, the migration of pioneers bound for Oregon and California followed the **Platte Valley** westward. Nebraska Territory was created in 1854 by the **Kansas-Nebraska Act**. After the **Homestead Act** was passed in 1862, thousands of settlers occupied the free lands that it offered. Building of the transcontinental railroads brought prosperity to the farms, and the state developed industry in the 20th century to diversify its economy.

MAIN CITIES

OMAHA A port on the Missouri River in eastern Nebraska, Omaha was ceded to the U.S. government in 1854. It was the capital of Nebraska Territory from 1854 to 1867. The state's largest city, it is across the river from **Council Bluffs, Iowa**. Omaha has just undergone a $2-billion development of its downtown and riverfront areas. It is a center for telecommunications, food-processing, and insurance. Former president **Gerald Ford** was born here. Population (2004) 371,592.

LINCOLN The state's capital and second largest city is in southeastern Nebraska. Founded in 1856 as **Lancaster**, its name was changed in honor of **Abraham Lincoln**. The city was made the state capital when Nebraska joined the Union in 1867. The capitol building is a skyscraper with a golden dome. Lincoln is a center for livestock and grain, and more recently for insurance. **The University of Nebraska** is here. Population (2004) 225,581.

the north boundary. The main rivers within the state are the **Platte** in the central area, which drains into the Missouri, and the **Niobrara** in the north. Farm production includes cattle, hogs, wheat, corn, rye, soybeans, and sorghum. Manufacturing industries, largely related to agriculture, produce processed meat, grain, dairy products, farm equipment, electrical machinery, and railroad equipment. Petroleum drilling takes place in the southwestern area.

Early immigration came from eastern states. In the late 19th century, Germans, Swedes, and Danes arrived to work the farmlands. Most of the present population were born in the United States. There are nearly 30 institutions of higher education, including the University of Nebraska.

NEVADA

Nevada is a state that lies in the western United States, in the Great Basin region. It is bordered by California in the west, Oregon and Idaho north, and Utah and Arizona east.

LAND AND ECONOMY

Nevada is a semidesert region of nearly 100 basins separated by short mountain ranges running north to south with an average altitude of 5,500 ft (1,676 m). Its climate is dry, and there are few rivers. The **Humboldt**, which is the longest, runs 290 miles (467 km). **Pyramid Lake** is the only natural lake. Grazing and mining are important to the economy. Farming's main products include cattle and other livestock, hay, alfalfa seed, potatoes, wheat, and barley. The chief minerals are copper, gold, mercury, and lithium. The main industrial output includes aerospace products, plastics, food, and irrigation equipment. Tourism is the state's major source of income. Visitors are drawn by the legalized gambling and the lenient divorce laws, which require only a brief residence. The city of **Las Vegas** offers a wide range of entertainment. Resort areas such as Lake Tahoe, which is partly in California, and Lake Mead, formed by dams on the Colorado River on the southern border, are year-round recreation centers.

Nevada is not a densely populated state but one of the fastest growing. Most of the new residents move to Nevada's cities, and the population is more than 80% urban. Las Vegas more than doubled its population from 1990 to 2004. The state-supported **University of Nevada** has campuses in Las Vegas and Reno.

HISTORY

Native American groups in the region included the Paiute, Shoshone, and Washoe. Spaniards visited the area in 1776, but the first explorations were not begun until 1825 by British fur trappers. In 1833 a party bound for California crossed the region along the Humboldt River. Their route became the **Overland Trail**, which took thousands west after gold was discovered in California in 1848. In that year, the United States acquired Nevada by the treaty that ended the Mexican War. When the **Comstock Lode**, a rich deposit of silver and gold, was found in western Nevada in 1859, settlers flocked to the land. Nevada Territory was organized in 1861, only three years before it became a state. The mining rush created several boom towns, but changes in the prices of precious metals and depletion of the ores led to them becoming ghost towns. The World War II quest for useful metals

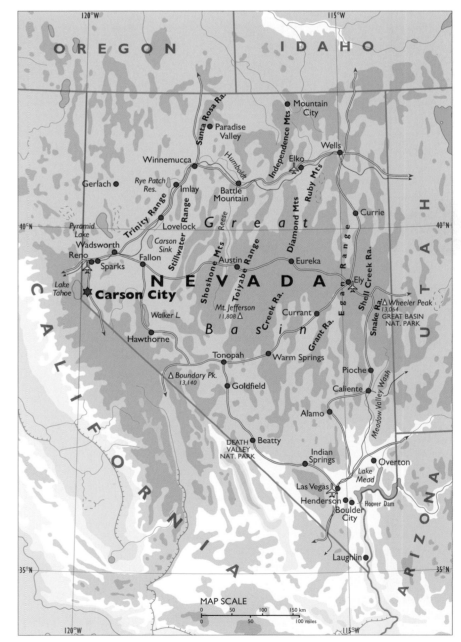

revived the mining industry, especially in copper. **Boulder Dam**, one of the world's largest, was completed in 1935 on the Nevada-Arizona border and renamed Hoover Dam in 1947 to honor U.S. President **Herbert Hoover**.

MAIN CITIES

LAS VEGAS Nevada's largest city is in the southern part of the state. It is a world-famous gambling and entertainment center. With more than 37 million visitors a year, it is the nation's second most popular vacation destination after Disney World. The **Mormons** established a colony on the site in 1855–1857. The modern city of Las Vegas was founded in 1905, and is now the largest U.S. city begun in the 20th century. Nevada legalized gambling in 1931, and the city grew rapidly. Its first big gambling casino opened in 1946, and by the 1970s gambling was earning the city more than $1 million a day. Once associated with organized crime and adult-only entertainment, the city restyled itself for families at the end of the 20th century, including theme parks with mixed results. It has more large hotels than any city in the world, and the **Stratosphere Hotel and Tower**, at over 1,100 ft (336 m), is the tallest U.S. building west of the Mississippi. Population (2004) 536,119.

RENO The city is located on the **Truckee River** in western Nevada. Like Las Vegas, Reno is a gambling and entertainment center with 5 million visitors a year. It is also famous worldwide for its provision of quick divorces. Reno was established in 1868 and named for the Civil War's Union **General Jesse Reno**. Mining and agriculture are also significant. Population (2004) 197,963.

CARSON CITY Named after the frontiersman **Kit Carson**, the state capital is in west Nevada 30 miles (48 km) south of Reno. It boomed after silver was discovered in the Comstock Lode in 1859. It became the territorial capital in 1861 and continued as state capital three years later. Its famous **U.S. Mint** was established in 1866, closed in 1893, and is now the **Nevada State Museum**. Gambling is important to the economy. Population (2004) 52,457.

"The Strip" runs for approximately 4 mi (6.7 km) through Las Vegas and Paradise, Clark County.

STATE FACTS

Admitted to Union October 31, 1864; ranked 36th
U.S. Congress Senate 2, House of Representatives 3
Population 2,414,807; ranked 35th
Capital Carson City
State legislature Senate 21, House of Representatives 42
Area 110,561 sq mi (286,351 sq km); ranked 7th
Elevation Highest 13,140 ft (4,005 m), Boundary Peak; lowest 470 ft (143 m), Colorado River
State nicknames Sagebrush State, Silver State
State motto All for our country
State bird Mountain bluebird
State flower Sagebrush
State trees Single-leaf piñon and bristlecone pine

NEW HAMPSHIRE

New Hampshire is a state in the northeastern United States in the **New England** region. It is bordered by the Canadian province of Quebec in the north and by three states: Maine in the northeast, Vermont west and Massachusetts south.

LAND AND ECONOMY

The state touches the Atlantic Ocean in the southeast for 13 mi (21 km). To the west and north, the land is hilly. In the north are the rugged **White Mountains**, where **Mount Washington** is the highest peak in the northeastern United States. The **Connecticut River** forms the west boundary, while the **Merrimack** is the largest river. There are more than 1,300 lakes. About 85% of the state is forested. Tourists are important, and large numbers of them are attracted by the fall foliage. Industrial products include textiles, electrical equipment, and wood products. Among the main farm output are dairy products, maple syrup, and apples.

Most inhabitants are descended from the original settlers but there is a strong French-Canadian element. Many workers today commute to jobs in Boston, Massachusetts. The **University of New Hampshire**, in Durham, also has a major campus in Manchester. Private **Dartmouth College**, in Hanover, was founded in 1769 and is one of the nation's oldest colleges.

HISTORY

English explorers visited the coast as early as 1603, and the first settlement was made at the mouth of the **Piscataqua River** in 1623. New Hampshire became an English royal province in 1679. Native American raids harassed the frontier towns until 1759. In one of the first armed moves against Britain, New Hampshire men captured **Fort William and Mary** at Portsmouth in 1774. The first free public library in the United States was established in **Dublin** in 1822. During presidential election years, New Hampshire holds the first primary election.

MAIN CITIES

MANCHESTER The state's largest city is located in south New Hampshire. Settled in 1722, it had the world's largest cotton textile mill in the 19th century, the Amoskeag Manufacturing Company. It has widened its industries, producing such products as electronic and electrical equipment and shoes. Its nickname is the "**Queen City**." Population (2004) 109,310.

CONCORD The state's capital is on the **Merrimack River**. Founded as a trading post in 1660, it was settled in 1727. It was the scene of New Hampshire's ratification of the U.S. Constitution in 1788 and became the capital in 1808. Quarries north of the city produce the famous white granite used for the Library of Congress in Washington, D.C. Concord was home to the 14th U.S. president, **Franklin Pierce**, and to **Christa McAuliffe**, the first civilian astronaut, who died in the *Challenger* space shuttle explosion in 1986. Population (2004) 40,687.

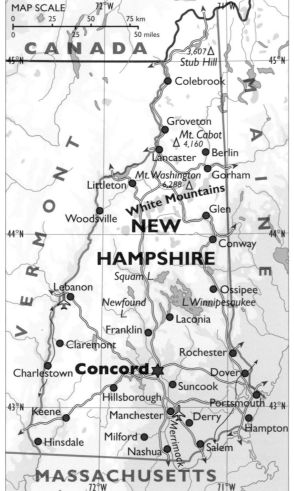

MAP SCALE
0 25 50 75 km
0 25 50 miles

CANADA

3,607 △
Stub Hill

Colebrook

Groveton
Mt. Cabot
△ 4,160
Lancaster
Berlin
Mt. Washington
Gorham
6,288 △
Littleton
White Mountains
Glen
Woodsville
NEW
Conway
HAMPSHIRE
Squam L.
Lebanon
Ossipee
Newfound L.
L. Winnipesaukee
Franklin
Laconia
Claremont
Rochester
Charlestown
Concord★
Dover
Suncook
Hillsborough
Portsmouth
Keene
Manchester
Derry
Hampton
Milford
Hinsdale
Salem
Nashua

VERMONT

MAINE

MASSACHUSETTS

Keene, New Hampshire: Pumpkin Festival.

STATE FACTS

Admitted to Union June 21, 1788; 9th of the 13 original states to ratify the U.S. Constitution
U.S. Congress Senate 2, House of Representatives 2
Population 1,309,940; ranked 41st
Capital Concord
State legislature Senate 24, House of Representatives 400
Area 9,350 sq mi (24,216 sq km); ranked 46th
Elevation Highest 6,288 ft (1,917 m), Mount Washington; lowest, sea level
State nickname Granite State
State motto Live free or die
State bird Purple finch
State flower Purple lilac
State tree White birch

NEW JERSEY

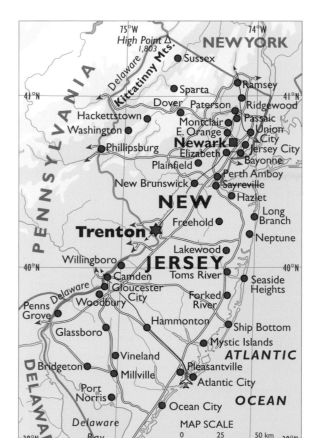

New Jersey is situated in the eastern United States, on the Atlantic coast. It is bordered by New York in the north, Pennsylvania west and Delaware southwest. It is the most densely populated state, and one of the most highly industrialized.

LAND AND ECONOMY

The southern 60% of the state is nearly level, or gently sloping up to the west. In the north, ranges of hills run southwest to northeast; the highest elevations are in the **Kittatinny Mountains** in the extreme northwest. The Delaware River forms the boundary with Delaware and Pennsylvania; the **Hudson** forms part of the boundary with New York. The **Hackensack**, **Passaic**, and **Raritan** are the principal rivers in the state.

The economy is greatly influenced by two cities outside the state: **New York**, which lies just across the Hudson River, and **Philadelphia**, across the Delaware. Much of the state's industry is concentrated in the 90 mi (145 km) between these two cities, which constitutes virtually a continuous metropolitan area. Each of the cities is one of the nation's leading ports, with huge docking facilities on the New Jersey side of the rivers. A network of highways and railroads, feeding from the cities, crosses the state. Thousands of New Jersey residents commute to jobs in New York and Philadelphia. Agriculture, which is based on large-scale truck farms supplying the cities, operates principally in the center and the south. The Atlantic coast of the state is a notable tourist area.

New Jersey is the most densely populated state. Nearly 90% of the people reside in urban areas. It is one of the most diverse states in the country with a large portion of the country's Jewish, Muslim, and Italian American populations.

There are more than 60 institutions of higher education in the state. **Rutgers University**, with its main campus in New Brunswick, is the state university; until 1956 it was run as a private institution. **Princeton University** – one of the oldest colleges in the United States, founded in 1746 – is the leading privately endowed institution in the country.

HISTORY

The first peoples were the Delaware and Algonquin. In 1524, the Italian explorer **Giovanni da Verrazano**, in the service of France, explored the New Jersey. European settlement did not begin until the 1620s, when the Dutch founded the colony of **New Netherland** (later New York). Some of these pioneers settled in northeastern New Jersey. In 1664, the English seized New Netherland. The land between the Hudson and the Delaware was separated and renamed New Jersey. The colony supported the Revolution, and its strategic position led to almost 100 engagements between American and British troops being fought on its soil.

After achieving statehood, New Jersey began the development of its industry and transportation system. In the 19th century many overseas immigrants settled in the industrial cities, and their descendants form a large segment of the population. In the Civil War and both world wars, the state was a major supplier of war material. The administration of **Woodrow Wilson**, governor from 1910, initiated many progressive measures of government. He resigned in 1913 to become president of the United States.

During the era following World War II, this heavily urbanized state has faced the problems of decaying city centers and flight to the suburbs. In 1978 the state legalized casino gambling in **Atlantic City** in a successful effort to revitalize its tourist industry.

Autumn foliated trees cling to the sides of the New Jersey Palisades overlooking the Hudson River in Bergen County. The cliffs run for some 20 mi (30 km) north of Jersey City, and reach heights of 550 ft (170 m). They are a popular recreational area.

STATE FACTS

Admitted to Union December 18, 1787; 3rd of 13 original states to ratify the U.S. Constitution
U.S. Congress Senate 2, House of Representatives 15
Population 8,717,925; ranked 10th
Capital Trenton
State legislature Senate 40; House of Representatives 80
Area 8,721 sq mi (22,588 sq km); ranked 47th
Elevation Highest 1,803 ft (550 m), High Point Mountain; lowest, sea level
State nickname Garden State
State motto Liberty and Prosperity
State bird Eastern goldfinch
State flower Purple violet
State tree Red oak

MAIN CITIES

TRENTON The state capital, on the Delaware River, was first settled by British **Quakers** in the 1670s. It became a manufacturing center in the late 1800s and early 1900s; its major industries included steel, rubber, wire, rope, and ceramics. Industry went into decline in the late 20th century, but the city is now moving into commerce. Government administration is the largest economic sector. Population (2004) 85,379.

NEWARK City in northeastern New Jersey, situated on the Passaic River and Newark Bay. It is connected to New York City by tunnel. Founded in 1666 by the **Puritans**, it is the third oldest major city in the U.S. after Boston and New York. Newark began rapid industrial growth after the American Revolution. Today it is an important commercial and financial center, particularly in insurance. Industries include chemicals and electrical equipment. Population (2004) 280,451.

NEW MEXICO

New Mexico is a state in the southwest United States. It borders Mexico and Texas in the south, Arizona west, Colorado north, Oklahoma northeast, and touches on Utah in the far northwest.

LAND AND ECONOMY

The state occupies a plateau with a mean elevation of 5,700 ft (1,739 m). It has a diverse landscape ranging from deserts to forested mountains. The **Sangre de Cristo Mountains**, a southern extension of the **Rocky Mountains**, are in the north-central part. Shorter ranges rise in other sections. The **Rio Grande**, flowing south through the center, is the principal river. Dams on the Rio Grande and other rivers have created artificial lakes for water storage and irrigation.

Mineral production is the major sector of the economy. Military installations and nuclear and space research, directed by the U.S. government, are important. Tourism is a valuable source of income.

New Mexico has a high proportion of residents of Spanish ancestry, as well as a large Native American population. The **Navaho Nation** is the largest Native American nation, with over 70,000 people living in the state. About 70% of the population lives in urban areas. There are more than 20 institutions of higher education.

HISTORY

From 1539, Spanish adventurers seeking gold traversed the region. In 1609 it became a province of the Spanish colony of Mexico; **Santa Fe** was founded and became capital the next year. Mexico won independence in 1821, and that year the **Santa Fe Trail**, a major trade route from Missouri, was opened. U.S. troops occupied the province on the outbreak of the Mexican War in 1846, and the Territory of New Mexico was organized in 1850. In the Civil War, a Confederate invasion was repulsed; fighting with Native Americans continued until the 1880s. Today there are 22 sovereign Indian nations in the state.

The New Mexican desert was the site of early research on nuclear weapons. The first atomic bomb was produced at Los Alamos and exploded at **Alamogordo** on July 16, 1945. Uranium mining began during the 1950s, and both the mining and research industries expanded during the 1970s and early 1980s.

MAIN CITIES

ALBUQUERQUE City in west-central New Mexico, on the Upper Rio Grande. The state's largest city, it was traditionally a center for railroad workshops and the livestock trade. Albuquerque is now a center for high-technology industries and home to the **U.S. Atomic Energy Commission**. The city is a popular health resort, and its population increased by nearly 20% between 1980 and 1992. Population (2004) 471,856.

SANTA FE Capital of New Mexico at the foot of the

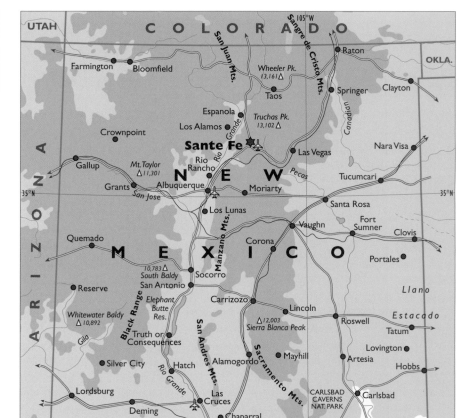

Sangre de Cristo Mountains. The oldest U.S. capital city, it was founded in c.1609 by the Spanish, and acted as a center of trade between the Spanish and Native Americans for more than 200 years. Mexico's independence in 1821 opened trade with the U.S., and Santa Fe functioned as the western terminus of the Santa Fe Trail. In 1846 U.S. troops captured the city as part of their conquest of New Mexico. In the later 19th century it went into economic decline when the surrounding mountains led the town to be bypassed by major railroads, but it was chosen as capital when New Mexico became a state in 1912. Today it is primarily an administrative, tourist, and resort center. Population (2004) 68,041.

Desert hills colored with a variety of different minerals near Abiquiu, New Mexico. Desert scenery and desert vegetation are particularly associated with New Mexico, but the state also has large areas of mountain forest in the Rockies, and rough pastureland in the northern parts of the state.

STATE FACTS

Admitted to Union January 6, 1912; ranked 47th
U.S. Congress Senate 2; House of Representatives 3
Population 1,928,384; ranked 36th
Capital Santa Fe
State legislature Senate, 42, House of Representatives 70
Area 121,589 sq mi (314,915 sq km); ranked 5th
Elevation Highest 13,161 ft (4,011 m), Wheeler Peak; lowest 2,817 ft (859 m), Red Bluff Reservoir
State nickname Land of Enchantment
State motto *Crescit eundo* (It Grows as It Goes)
State bird Roadrunner
State flower Yucca
State tree Piñon pine

NEW YORK

New York is a state in the northeastern United States. It is bordered by the Canadian provinces of Ontario and Quebec, the Atlantic Ocean in the east, and the states of Massachusetts, Connecticut, Vermont, Pennsylvania, and New Jersey.

LAND AND ECONOMY

The seacoast is short, but New York Harbor is one of the world's finest. The state's interior is mountainous in the east; the **Catskills** in the southeast and the **Adirondacks** in the northeast are the main systems. To the west stretches a gently rolling plateau. The **Hudson River** in the east empties into New York Bay; its main tributary is the Mohawk River. Other important rivers are the Delaware and the Genesee. It is the only state that touches the ocean and the **Great Lakes**. In the northeast, **Lake Champlain** forms a border with Vermont, and there are more than 2,000 other lakes.

New York's economy is one of the nation's richest. The chief farm output includes dairy products, apples, grapes, maple syrup, and wine. Among the major minerals are stone, zinc, and salt. The port of New York is among the world's leaders, and the city is a transportation and distribution center. It is also the nation's financial capital and many corporations have their headquarters in the city and its suburbs. Heavy industry is concentrated in the "upstate" cities. The major industrial products include apparel, publications, instruments, pharmaceuticals, processed foods, paper and paper products, jewelry, and sporting goods.

From 1820 to 1964, when California surpassed it, New York was the most populous state. About 85% of its inhabitants live in urban areas. Traditionally, the population has been ethnically diverse. In the 19th century, New York was the port of entry through **Ellis Island** for hundreds of thousands of immigrants from overseas. Many remained in the state to work, and their descendants constitute a large segment of the population.

There are more than 250 institutions of higher education. The **State University of New York** comprises 64 campuses. The leading private institutions are **Columbia University** and **New York University** (the largest U.S. private university), in New York City; **Cornell University**, in Ithaca; and **Syracuse University**. The **U.S. Military Academy** is at West Point.

HISTORY

Henry Hudson, an English navigator who was in the service of the Netherlands, discovered New York Bay and sailed up the river that bears his name in 1609 laying claim to the surrounding territory. Settlement began up the Hudson Valley, and the colony was named New Netherland. The English seized it in 1664 and renamed it New York. As a royal province, New York became a leader among the American colonies, playing a major role in the American Revolution. Almost 100 engagements (nearly one-third of the war's total) were fought in the colony,

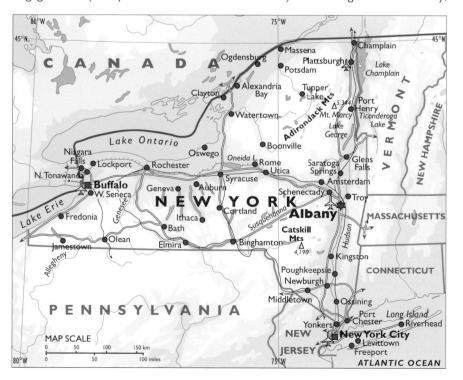

The Statue of Liberty stands on an island about 1.6 mi (2.6 km) southwest of Manhattan. It was a gift from France, and was dedicated on October 28, 1886. The statue is made of copper on a steel skeleton and is 151 ft (46 m) tall. With the base, the top of the statue is 305 ft (93 m) from the ground.

including the battle of Saratoga in 1777, which was a turning point of the war. The city became the first capital of the United States, and George Washington was inaugurated president there in 1789.

The **New York Stock Exchange** was founded in 1792. The opening of the **Erie Canal** in 1825, creating a water route to the west through the Great Lakes, was an enormous economic stimulus. New York sent about 500,000 men into the Union army in the Civil War, one-sixth of the entire army. The **Winter Olympics** were held in **Lake Placid** twice: in 1932 and in 1980. Five presidents have come from the state: Martin Van Buren, Chester A. Arthur, Grover Cleveland, Theodore Roosevelt, and Franklin D. Roosevelt.

MAIN CITIES

NEW YORK CITY The largest U.S. city is a port in southeastern New York State at the mouth of the **Hudson River**. It is made up of five boroughs: Manhattan, the Bronx, Brooklyn, Queens, and Staten Island. **Manhattan Island** was settled in 1624 and bought two years later from Native Americans by the Dutch West India Company. **New Amsterdam** was founded at the south end of the island. In 1664, the British took the colony and renamed it New York. The founding of the **Bank of New York** by Alexander Hamilton and the opening of the **Erie Canal** in 1825 made New York the principal commercial and financial center of the nation. After the Civil War and in the early 20th century, the city received a great influx of immigrants. The **Statue of Liberty** was dedicated in 1886. The

United Nations moved its headquarters to New York City in 1953.

The city suffered America's worst civilian attack on September 11, 2001, when terrorists flew two jet liners into the **World Trade Center**, killing some 2,800 people and destroying the **Twin Towers** (this was the second major terrorist attack on the World Trade Center; it had been damaged when bombed in 1993, killing six people and injuring more than 1,000). The removal of the debris from "**Ground Zero**" took until May 2002.

The **World Trade Center Memorial and Museum** was opened in March 2006, and the first new building on the site, the 750 ft (229 m) **7 World Trade Center**, was opened a month later. Construction was also begun in 2006 on **Freedom Tower**, the skyscraper replacing the twin towers.

Nicknamed the "**Big Apple**," New York's most popular tourist sights in Manhattan include Central Park, Broadway, the Statue of Liberty, the Empire State Building, Rockefeller Center, the Metropolitan Museum of Art, the Museum of Modern Art, the

STATE FACTS

Admitted to Union July 26, 1788; 11th of the 13 original states to ratify the U.S. Constitution

U.S. Congress Senate 2, House of Representatives 29

Population 19,254,630; ranked 3rd

Capital Albany

State legislature Senate 60, House of Representatives 150

Area 54,556 sq mi (141,299 sq km); ranked 27th

Elevation Highest 5,344 ft (1,629 m), Mount Marcy; lowest, sea level

State nickname Empire State

State motto Excelsior! (Ever upward)

State bird Eastern bluebird

State flower Rose

State tree Sugar maple

Guggenheim Museum, Lincoln Center, and Carnegie Hall. The city is known for hosting lavish ticker-tape parades to celebrate the achievements of heroes, and special events include **Macy's Thanksgiving Parade**, which has been held each year since 1924. Population (2004) 7,918,562.

BUFFALO The industrial city and port of Buffalo lies on the east shore of **Lake Erie**, at the beginning of the Niagara River, in the northwest of New York state. It was first settled in 1803 by the Holland Land Company. Its rapid industrial growth was encouraged by its position at the western terminus of the Erie Canal. **President William McKinley** was assassinated at the **Pan-American Exposition** here in 1901. The city has two universities. Important industries include flour milling, automobiles, chemicals, and railway engineering. Population (2004) 282,864.

ALBANY New York State's capital lies to the south of the juncture between the Hudson and Mohawk rivers. It is the oldest chartered city in the nation. "The Egg" at Empire State Plaza is an impressive-looking performance arts center. Population (2004) 93,919.

NORTH CAROLINA

North Carolina is a state in the eastern United States on the Atlantic Ocean about midway along the eastern coastline. It shares borders with Virginia in the north South Carolina and Georgia south, and Tennessee west.

LAND AND ECONOMY

Along the coast stretches a chain of islands enclosing several large sounds. Beyond the broad coastal plain is the **Piedmont Plateau**, a rolling, fertile region. In the extreme west are the **Blue Ridge Mountains** and **Great Smoky Mountains**, some of which rise to over 6,000 ft (1,830 m). **Mount Mitchell** is the highest peak in the United States east of the Mississippi River. There are many small rivers.

A mild climate and productive soil made agriculture the base of the economy through the 19th century, and major crops include tobacco, yams, soybeans, groundnuts, wheat, cotton, and corn. Among the livestock are cattle, sheep, hogs, and chickens. Abundant water power and natural resources encouraged manufacturing. Key

U.S.A. Mansion at Orton Plantation originated in the 18th century as the house of a rice-growing plantation owner. The mansion took its present form around 1840, with wings added in 1910. The gardens are now open to the public.

industrial products include textiles, tobacco products, food products, industrial machinery, furniture, and apparel. Major minerals include mica, lithium, and feldspar.

The population is largely of English origin, with elements of Scottish-Irish and Germans. Most of the early settlers came from other colonies. North Carolina's Hispanic population, estimated at 600,000 in 2006, grew 400% from 1990 to 2000, the largest U.S. increase during that period.

There are over 100 institutions of higher education. The **University of North Carolina**, in Chapel Hill, established in 1789, is one of the oldest state universities and now has five other campuses. **Duke University**, in Durham, and **Wake Forest University**, in Winston-Salem, are outstanding among the private institutions.

HISTORY

Native Americans in the region included the Cherokee, Algonquin, and Catawba. In 1524, the first explorer was the Italian **Giovanni da Verrazano** in the service of France. The first two English colonies in North America were on **Roanoke Island**. The first in 1585 under Ralph Lane ended in failure. The second, established by John White in 1587 with 110 settlers, had disappeared when White returned in 1590, with only the word "Croatoan" carved on a tree. It became known as the "Lost Colony." Settlers began moving into the region from Virginia about 1660. The coast became popular with pirates, and the feared **Blackbeard** was killed by the British navy in 1718.

A royal charter was granted to eight proprietors in 1663, and North Carolina became a royal province in 1729. It was the first colony to assert its will for independence from Great Britain, and in the American Revolution contributed strongly to the Continental cause. The important battles of **Kings Mountain** and **Guilford Courthouse** were fought in North Carolina. In 1790 western land was ceded to the federal government and became the **Tennessee Territory**. North Carolina was the last state to join the Confederacy, which it did on May 20, 1861. It supplied more men and material to the South than any other state. On December 17, 1903, Wilbur and Orville Wright made the first successful flight in a propelled "heavier-than-air" plane at **Kitty Hawk** on the coast. The industrial development of the state was spurred by both world wars. In 1999, **Hurricane Floyd** killed 35 people and caused $5.1 billion in damages (mostly in North Carolina).

MAIN CITIES

CHARLOTTE North Carolina's largest city is in the south-central region near the South Carolina border. It was settled by Scottish-Irish immigrants, who named it for Queen Charlotte, the wife of George III. It was incorporated in 1768 and occupied by British **General Lord Cornwallis** in 1780 during the American Revolution – he famously described the city as a "hornet's nest of rebellion." In 1799, the first major U.S. gold discovery was made here. Charlotte has now become the nation's second largest banking center. The 11th U.S. president, **James K. Polk**, was born here. The **University of North Carolina** has a campus here, and the city is home to the **Billy Graham Evangelistic Association**. Population (2004) 582,502.

RALEIGH The state capital is in the east central part of the state. Founded in 1792 as the capital, it was named after **Sir Walter Raleigh**. During the Civil War, it was occupied by **General William T. Sherman**'s Union troops. In 1996, **Hurricane Fran** caused $275 million damage. Raleigh was the birthplace of the 17th U.S. president, **Andrew Johnson**. The city is a market center for the cotton and tobacco trade. It has six colleges and universities, including **North Carolina State University**. Industries include food processing, textiles, and electronic equipment. Population (2004) 317,651.

STATE FACTS

Admitted to Union November 21, 1789; 12th of the 13 original states to ratify the U.S. Constitution
U.S. Congress Senate 2, House of Representatives 13
Population 8,683,242; ranked 11th
Capital Raleigh
State legislature Senate 50, House of Representatives 120
Area 53,819 sq mi (139,389 sq km); ranked 28th
Elevation Highest 6,684 ft (2,037 m), Mount Mitchell; lowest, sea level
State nicknames Tar Heel State, Old North State
State motto *Esse quam videri* (To be rather than to seem)
State bird Cardinal
State flower Dogwood
State tree Longleaf pine

NORTH DAKOTA

North Dakota is a state in the north-central United States bordered by the Canadian provinces of Saskatchewan and Manitoba in the north, and by three U.S. states: Minnesota in the east, South Dakota south, and Montana west.

LAND AND ECONOMY

The land rises from the fertile valley of the **Red River** on the eastern boundary. The **Missouri River** flows east and south. **Garrison Reservoir**, formed by a dam on the Missouri, is the largest artificial lake, while **Devil's Lake** is the largest natural one. Agriculture remains the heart of the economy, especially producing wheat, barley, flaxseed, rye, oats, and cattle. Petroleum was discovered in the 1950s, and other minerals include natural gas, coal, and clay.

North Dakota's settlers chiefly came from other states and Europe, chiefly Norwegians, Germans, Russians, Scottish, Irish, and English. More than 50% now live in cities and towns.

The North Dakota university system has 11 colleges and universities, including the **University of North Dakota** and **North Dakota State University**; there are five private institutions of higher education and five tribal colleges.

HISTORY

The Native Americans included the Sioux groups of Dakota and Lakota, as well as Cheyenne and Assiniboine. French explorers visited as early as 1738, and in 1797 a British trading post was established. The United States acquired roughly the region's western half from France in the Louisiana Purchase of 1803, and the

remainder from Great Britain in 1818. **Dakota Territory** was created in 1861 and divided into North and South Dakota in 1889, the year both achieved statehood on November 2. Fire destroyed the old state capitol in 1930 and the new skyscraper capitol was completed in 1935. Oil was discovered at **Tioga** in 1951, and the nation's first coal-to-synthetic gas conversion facility opened in 1983 at **Beulah**.

MAIN CITIES

FARGO North Dakota's largest city lies on the **Red River** across from Moorhead, Minnesota. Fargo was established when the railroad arrived in 1871 and became known as the "Gateway to the West." It was called Centralia before being renamed for **William Fargo** who founded the Fargo Express Company. The city is a financial center and a hub for the wheat and livestock region. It is home to the main campus of **North Dakota State University**. Population (2004) 91,048.

BISMARCK The state capital overlooks the **Missouri River** in south-central North Dakota. It originated in the 1830s, becoming the territorial capital in 1883 and the state capital six years later. It became a distribution center for grain and cattle and was later an important stop on the **Northern Pacific Railroad**. Industries include livestock raising, dairying, and woodworking. The **Bismarck State College** campus of the **North Dakota State University** is here. Population (2004) 55,532.

STATE FACTS

Admitted to Union November 2, 1889; ranked 39th
U.S. Congress Senate 2, House of Representatives 1
Population 636,677; ranked 48th
Capital Bismarck
State legislature Senate 47, House of Representatives 94
Area 70,700 sq mi (183,112 sq km); ranked 19th
Elevation Highest 3,506 ft (1,067 m), White Butte; lowest 750 ft (229 m), Red River
State nickname Peace Garden State
State motto Liberty and union, now and forever, one and inseparable
State bird Western meadowlark
State flower Wild prairie rose
State tree American elm

A bull bison stands in the prairie of Theodore Roosevelt National Park. The American bison (also called the American buffalo) once roamed the the Plains in vast herds, but commercial hunting almost exterminated them by the late 19th century.

OHIO

Ohio is a state in the east-central United States. Lake Erie marks most of its northern boundary, along with the state of Michigan. Other borders are with Indiana in the west, Kentucky south, West Virginia southeast, and Pennsylvania east.

LAND AND ECONOMY

The land is a rolling plain with many rivers, including the Muskingum, Scioto, Miami, and Maumee. Water transportation on **Lake Erie** and the **Ohio River**, which forms the southern boundary, is of great importance to the economy. Agriculture is profitable in most sections, with the major products including corn, hay, wheat, oats, grapes, soybeans, cattle, hogs, sheep, and dairy products.

Because of its proximity to iron and coal as well as excellent transportation links, Ohio developed as a major center of heavy manufacturing. **Akron** became the center of rubber manufacturing after **Benjamin F. Goodrich** and **Harvey Firestone** established factories there. By the late 1970s, however, many industries experienced a serious downturn. Industry is widely distributed in cities and towns, with key products being automobiles, parts and accessories, tires, aircraft, boats, industrial machinery, household appliances, and processed foods. The main minerals are coal, lime, clay, salt, and sand and gravel. **Wright-Patterson Air Force Base** at Dayton is one of the nation's largest Air Force facilities.

Ohio was settled originally by pioneers from New England, Pennsylvania, and Virginia. Immigrants from overseas, principally Germans and Irish, flocked to the state in the early 19th century. For most of that century, the state ranked third in the nation in the size of its population; its decline in rank reflects the later growth of other states.

There are more than 100 institutions of higher education in the state, including 12 state-supported universities. **Ohio State University**, in Columbus, has four more campuses, while **Ohio University**, in Athens, has five other locations.

HISTORY

The region had prehistoric people dwelling there some 5,000 to 7,000 years ago, and a group of 24 prehistoric Indian burial mounds is now maintained in **Hopewell Culture National Historical Park**. When Europeans arrived, the main Native American groups were the Shawnee, Delaware, Wyandot, and Miami. French and English traders operated in the region in the early 18th century. Great Britain acquired it in 1763 at the end of the French and Indian War. It became U.S. soil after the Revolution, and in 1787 Congress created the **Northwest Territory** which included the present states of Ohio, Indiana, and Ilinois, and lands to the north.

The first settlement in Ohio was at **Marietta** in 1788, founded by General Rufus Putnam and named for Marie Antoinette, Queen of France. In 1795, the **Treaty of Green Ville** saw the Native Americans give up much of their land. Ohio was separated from the Northwest Territory in 1800 and was accepted as a state three years later. (In 1953, the U.S. Congress discovered it had failed to recognize Ohio's statehood officially and passed a resolution declaring it had been a state since 1803.) **Oberlin College**, founded in 1833, was the first U.S. institution of higher education for both men and women.

The development of railroads and canals enhanced Ohio's geographical position midway between the Atlantic seaboard and the Mississippi Valley, and the state exerted great influence in national affairs. The inventor **Thomas Edison** was born in Milan in 1847. Before 1860, Ohio was a leader in helping slaves to

The Scioto River flows through downtown Columbus. The Art Deco skyscraper, the LeVeque Tower (center) was the fifth tallest building in the world when completed in 1927 – at 555.5 ft (169.5 m), it is half a foot taller than the Washington Monument. The Rhodes State Office Tower (629 ft/192 m) is now the tallest in Columbus.

STATE FACTS

Admitted to Union March 1, 1803; ranked 17th
U.S. Congress Senate 2, House of Representatives 18
Population 11,464,042; ranked 7th
Capital Columbus
State legislature Senate 33, House of Representatives 99
Area 44,825 sq mi (116,096 sq km); ranked 34th
Elevation Highest 1,549 ft (472 m), Campbell Hill; lowest 433 ft (132 m), Ohio River
State nickname Buckeye State
State motto With God, all things are possible
State bird Cardinal
State flower Scarlet carnation
State tree Buckeye

escape via the "**Underground Railroad**." During the Civil War, several Confederate raids were made on the state. Seven Ohio citizens have become U.S. presidents, (second only to Virginia's eight presidents). They were Ulysses S. Grant, Rutherford B. Hayes, James Garfield, Benjamin Harrison, William McKinley, William Howard Taft, and Warren G. Harding.

Wilbur and Orville Wright, credited with the first successful flight in a propelled "heavier-than-air"plane in 1903, were bicycle shop owners in Dayton. The first man on the moon, **Neil Armstrong**, was born in Wapakoneta in 1930. The **Ohio Turnpike** was opened in 1955. Four students at **Kent State University** were shot and killed by National Guardsmen in 1970 while protesting the Vietnam War. In 1986, Astronaut **Judith Resnick** of Akron died in the *Challenger* space shuttle explosion. The **Dayton Accord**, ending the war in Bosnia-Hercegovina, was signed in 1995 at Wright-Patterson Air Force Base.

MAIN CITIES

COLUMBUS The state's capital and largest city is on the **Scioto River** in central Ohio. Founded in 1812, it grew rapidly with the arrival of the railroad in 1850. It is a major transportation, industrial, and trading center for a rich agricultural region. It has a historic **German Village** and **Italian Village**. Columbus had the nation's first major league soccer stadium. It is home to **Ohio State University** and to the **Battelle Memorial Institute**, which does research for 800 federal, state, and local governments. Columbus industries include machinery, transportation equipment, textiles, aircraft, and printing and publishing. Population (2004) 700,874.

CLEVELAND The city is a port at the mouth of the **Cuyahoga River** on **Lake Erie** in northeastern Ohio. Founded in 1796 by Moses Cleaveland, it grew rapidly with the opening of the **Ohio and Erie Canal** and the arrival of the railroad in 1851. It annexed Ohio City in 1854. **John D. Rockefeller** founded **Standard Oil Company** there in 1870. Cleveland was the world's first city to be electrically lighted in 1879. **Carl Stokes** became mayor in 1967, the first African-American mayor of a large U.S. city. Cleveland is a major Great Lakes shipping port and an important iron and steel center. **Case Western Reserve University** and NASA's **Glenn Research Center** are major research centers. Industries include chemicals, oil refining, engineering, and electronics. Population (2004) 458,864.

CINCINNATI Located on the **Ohio River** in southwest Ohio, the city was originally named Losantiville. It grew around Fort Washington (established 1789). The **University of Cincinnati** was established in 1819. The completion of the **Miami and Erie Canal** in 1832 made the city a shipping center for farm produce. In order to compete with Chicago and St. Louis, Cincinnati built its own railroad in 1880. It had the first all-professional baseball team, the **Cincinnati Red Stockings**, in 1869, and held major league baseball's first night game at **Crosley Field**. The **Procter & Gamble** corporation has its headquarters here. Industries include machine tools, soap products, brewing, meat packing, and aircraft engines. Population (2004) 314,154.

OKLAHOMA

Oklahoma is a state in the south-central United States in the Great Plains region. It is bordered by Kansas and Colorado in the north, New Mexico west, Texas south and west, and Arkansas and Missouri east.

LAND AND ECONOMY

From high plains in the northwest, the land slopes to the southeast, broken by hills and low mountains. Much of the state is grassland, with 24% covered by forests. The **Arkansas River** flows east through the center of the state; the **Red River** marks most of the southern boundary. There are no large natural lakes, but Oklahoma has 200 human-made lakes, more than any other state; many reservoirs have been created by dams. Oklahoma's grazing land and resources of petroleum and natural gas are widely distributed in the state; in 2004 it was the state with the second largest production of natural gas in the U.S. Major minerals also include helium, gypsum, coal, and zinc. The world's largest single deposit of pure alabaster is in caverns near **Freedom**. Manufacturing is largely involved with processing the products of natural resources. The main industrial products include petroleum products, machinery (construction and oil equipment), and processed foods. Among the main agricultural products are wheat, corn, sorghum, groundnuts, and cattle.

European settlement of the region, which did not come until the 19th century, was principally by immigrants from other states. Oklahoma has the largest Native-American population in the United States, with 35 tribes headquartered here. There are no reservations, unlike in other states.

There are 43 institutions of higher education. The **University of Oklahoma**'s main campus is in Norman, with another in Tulsa. **Oklahoma State University**, in Stillwater, has three other large campuses.

A walking beam pump (often called a "pump-jack" or "nodding donkey") in a field raises oil from one of the many underground pools in Oklahoma. There are thousands of oil and natural gas wells in the state. Oil brought wealth to Oklahoma in the early 20th century, and many historic buildings date from this period.

STATE FACTS

Admitted to Union November 16, 1907; ranked 46th
U.S. Congress Senate 2, House of Representatives 5
Population 3,547,884; ranked 28th
Capital Oklahoma City
State legislature Senate 48, House of Representatives 101
Area 69,898 sq mi (181,035 sq km); ranked 20th
Elevation Highest 4,973 ft (1,516 m), Black Mesa; lowest 287 ft (88 m), Little River
State nickname Sooner State
State motto *Labor vincit omnia* (Labor conquers all things)
State bird Scissor-tailed flycatcher
State flower Mistletoe
State tree Redbud

HISTORY

Most of the area was acquired by the United States from France in the Louisiana Purchase of 1803. If was successively part of several new larger territories. In 1834, **Indian Territory** was created as a home for the "Five Civilized Tribes" – Cherokees, Chickasaws, Creeks, Choctaws, and Seminoles – who had been moved by the federal government from states in the east. The federal government opened 2 million acres (800,000 ha) of "Unassigned Lands" on April 22, 1889, at noon, when thousands rushed to claim it. Those who staked a claim ahead of time were called "**Sooners**." The region was organized in 1890 as the Territory of Oklahoma. This was merged with Indian Territory to become one state. By the early 20th century, oil production had begun, and industry, based on processing oil and natural gas, gradually developed. During the depression of the 1930s, poverty-stricken "Okie" families left their farms to migrate to California, as portrayed in John Steinbeck's novel *The Grapes of Wrath* (1939).

MAIN CITIES

OKLAHOMA CITY The capital and largest city is on the **North Canadian River** in the center of the state. The area was settled in 1889 during the land rush: 10,000 people camped on the empty site the first night. The city was made the state capital in 1910 and prospered with the discovery of rich oil deposits in 1928; oil wells arose throughout the city, with one even on the lawn of the capitol building. In April 1995, a bomb destroyed the federal office building, killing 168 people and injuring more than 400 others in what was the nation's largest domestic terrorist attack. It is commemorated by the **Oklahoma City National Memorial**, which was dedicated in 1997 and has 168 memorial chairs. The city has 20 universities and colleges, including campuses of the **University of Oklahoma** and **Oklahoma State University,** as well as **Oklahoma City University**. Industries include oil refining, grain milling, cotton processing, steel products, electronic equipment, and aircraft. Population (2004) 520,421.

TULSA A port on the **Arkansas River** in northeastern Oklahoma, Tulsa is the state's second-largest city. Creek Indians settled there in 1836. It developed with the 1882 arrival of the **Atlantic and Pacific Railroad**; the 1901 discovery of oil further accelerated development. The **1921 Tulsa Race Riot** left 39 people dead. In 1971, the Tulsa port of **Catoosa** opened a year after the **Arkansas River Navigation** project connected the area to the Mississippi River. Tulsa has become a major center for the telecommunications industry. There are eight universities and colleges, including the **University of Tulsa** and **Oral Roberts University** founded by the Christian evangelist of the same name. Tulsa has more than 300 aerospace and aviation companies. The city has a system of 80 sirens to warn of tornadoes, floods, and other disasters. Industries include oil refining and research, petroleum products, oilfield equipment, mining, metal goods, and aerospace. Population (2004) 383,764.

OREGON

Oregon is a state in the northwest United States on the Pacific Ocean. It has borders with Washington state in the north, Idaho east, and California and Nevada south. The Coast and Cascade ranges rise eastward to the Columbia plateau.

LAND AND ECONOMY

The fertile **Willamette Valley** reaches north and south between the Coast Range on the west and the Cascade Range east. About 65% of the state is a plateau east of the Cascades. **Crater Lake** is the nation's deepest at 1,932 ft (589 m). The **Columbia River** on the northern boundary is of great economic importance, supplying hydroelectric power to a wide region. Its lower section is navigable by ocean vessels. **Portland**, on the Willamette River near its junction with the Columbia, is a major seaport. Dense forests of Douglas fir and ponderosa pine, especially in the mountains, help make Oregon the nation's leading lumber producer, providing some 20% of the national output. Agriculture is largely centered in the Willamette Valley. The state's main agricultural products include wheat, hops, fruit, nuts, potatoes, oats, cattle, and dairy products. Fishing includes salmon in the rivers and tuna in the sea. Among the key minerals are nickel, stone, and sand and

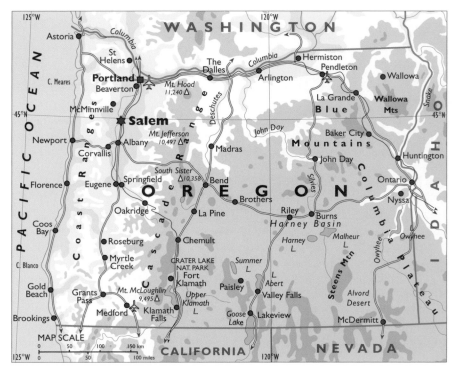

gravel. The chief industrial products include lumber and other forest products, furniture, paper, processed foods, and transportation equipment.

Most of the population is descended from the 19th-century settlers who came from other states. There are about 40 institutions of higher education. The Oregon University System has eight universities, including the **University of Oregon**, in Eugene, and **Oregon State University**, in Corvallis, with another campus in Bend. There are 16 private institutions of higher education.

HISTORY

More than 100 Native American groups were living in the region when Europeans arrived. They included the Yakima, Cayuse, Chinook, and Nez Perce. "Oregon" was a Native American name for the Columbia River. The British explorer, **Sir Francis Drake**, may have reached Oregon's southern coast in 1579. **Robert Gray**, a U.S. sea captain, discovered the mouth of the Columbia River in 1792. He sailed up it, traded with Native Americans, and named the river for his ship, the *Columbia*. The **Lewis and Clark Expedition** reached the river in 1805 and a U.S. trading post, Astoria, was established there in 1811 by John Jacob Astor's fur company. This was sold to British interests, and the British regarded the region as their territory. The United States claimed it by right of prior discovery and settlement,

Hells Canyon was carved by the Snake River from the Owyhee Mountains. The gorge is on average more than 5,000 ft (1,500 m) deep, and at one point nearly 8,000 ft (2,400 m), making it the deepest river gorge in the U.S.

and settlers began arriving by the **Oregon Trail** in 1843. In 1846, the boundary with Canada was fixed at its current latitude.

U.S. pioneers had been entering the area since the 1830s, and the **Oregon Territory** was organized in 1848. It included the present state of **Washington**, which was separated in 1853. After Oregon became a state, settlement and development proceeded steadily. Industrial development took place during the 20th century, particularly following the construction of the **Bonneville Dam** in 1943 on the Columbus River, but the state is still heavily dependent upon its lumber industry.

MAIN CITIES

PORTLAND Located on the **Willamette River** in the northwest of Oregon in the foothills of the Coast and Cascade ranges, Portland is the state's largest city. Its name was chosen over "Boston" by a flip of a coin. First settled in 1845, it developed rapidly as a major port for exporting lumber and grain after 1850. It was a supply station for the California gold fields, which also drew away half its male population, and for the

STATE FACTS

Admitted to Union February 14, 1859; ranked 33rd
U.S. Congress Senate 2, House of Representatives 5
Population 3,641,056; ranked 27th
Capital Salem
State legislature Senate 30, House of Representatives 60
Area 98,381 sq mi (254,805 sq km); ranked 9th
Elevation Highest 11,240 ft (3,426 m), Mount Hood; lowest, sea level
State nickname Beaver State
State motto She flies with her own wings
State bird Western meadowlark
State flower Oregon grape
State tree Douglas fir

Alaska gold rush. In 1883, the transcontinental railroad reached the city, opening it up to the east. Educational institutions include **Portland State University**, **Oregon Health & Science University**, and the **University of Portland**. Industries include shipbuilding, lumber, wood products, textiles, metals, and machinery. Population (2004) 524,944.

SALEM The state capital is on the Willamette River in northwest Oregon. Founded in 1840 by Methodist missionaries, Salem was made the capital of the Oregon Territory in 1851 and state capital in 1859. In 1998, it dedicated the **Riverfront Park**. The city is home to **Willamette University** and **Chemeketa Community College**. Major industries here include lumber, paper, textiles, food canning, meat packing, and the manufacture of high-technology equipment. Population (2004) 146,120.

EUGENE Located in a farm area, Eugene is on the Willamette River in western Oregon. It is home to the **University of Oregon** and **Lane Community College**. The city's annual **Oregon Bach Festival** has been held since 1970. Eugene has more than 70 public parks. Its industries include lumber and food-processing, with tourism important. Population (2004) 142,681.

PENNSYLVANIA

Pennsylvania is a state in the Middle Atlantic region of the eastern United States. It shares boundaries with New York to the north, Ohio west, Delaware and New Jersey east, and Maryland and West Virginia south.

LAND AND ECONOMY

Mountain ranges of medium height run roughly northeast to southwest across much of the state, interspersed with fertile valleys. In the southeast lies a rich agricultural area. The **Delaware River** forms the eastern boundary and ends at Delaware Bay, an arm of the Atlantic Ocean. Other important rivers are the **Susquehanna**, flowing north to south in the state's center, and the **Allegheny** in the west. In the extreme northwest, the state borders **Lake Erie**.

Pennsylvania's productive soil and abundant mineral deposits, especially of coal and iron, contributed to the growth of the manufacturing industries that have kept the economy in a prosperous balance. Manufacturing is centered in 12 metropolitan areas, notably Philadelphia, Pittsburgh, and Allentown-Bethlehem-Easton.

Philadelphia, with access to the sea by the Delaware River, is one of the nation's major ports. More than 70% of the state's population lives in urban areas.

There are about 150 institutions of higher education in the state. **Pennsylvania State University** is state-supported. The **University of Pennsylvania** is the leading privately funded institution.

STATE FACTS

Admitted to Union December 12, 1787; 2nd of the 13 original states to ratify the U.S. Constitution
U.S. Congress Senate 2, House of Representatives 19
Population 12,281,054; ranked 6th
Capital Harrisburg
State legislature Senate 50, House of Representatives 203
Area 46,055 sq mi (119,283 sq km); ranked 33rd
Elevation Highest 3,213 ft (979 m), Mount Davis; lowest, sea level, Delaware River
State nickname Keystone State
State motto Virtue, Liberty, and Independence
State bird Ruffed grouse
State flower Mountain laurel
State tree Eastern hemlock

An Amish farmer uses a horse team to plow a field in Pennsylvania Dutch Country – a popular destination for tourists. Many members of some 15 Christian sects, mostly of German and Swiss origin, avoid the use of modern machinery.

HISTORY

Swedish and Dutch settlements were made along the Delaware River in the mid-17th century, but by 1674 the area was under the control of the British. The original settlers were mostly from the British Isles. **William Penn** received a charter from Charles II in 1681 to create what is now Pennsylvania, with Philadelphia as the provincial capital. The English settlers were followed in the 18th century by Germans, erroneously called the "**Pennsylvania Dutch**," who occupied farmlands in the east and southeast. **Philadelphia** was the capital of the colonies during the American Revolution, and the national capital from 1790 to 1800.

The **Continental Congresses** were held in the Philadelphia, where the **Declaration of Independence** was signed in 1776. **The Constitutional Convention** met here, and adopted the **U.S. Constitution** in 1787. In the 19th century Pennsylvania industrialized; mines and mills drew immigrants from Italy, Poland, Russia, Czechoslovakia, and Hungary. The Union victory at the **Battle of Gettysburg** (July 1863) was a turning point of the Civil War.

During both world wars, Pennsylvania was a major source of military supplies, shipbuilding being especially important. In 1979, in the country's most serious nuclear accident, a nuclear power plant at **Three Mile Island** malfunctioned badly, leaked radioactive material, and had to be shut down.

MAIN CITIES

HARRISBURG The state capital of Pennsylvania, situated in the southeast of the state on the Susquehanna River. Established as a trading post in about 1718, Harrisburg had become a town by 1785. It was the scene of the **Harrisburg Convention** of 1788, and became the state capital in 1812. Industries include textiles, machinery, and electronic equipment. Population (2004) 47,635.

PHILADELPHIA City and port at the confluence of the Delaware and Schuylkill rivers in southeast Pennsylvania. The site was first settled by Swedes in the early 17th century, but the city was founded by **William Penn**. By 1774 it was a major commercial, cultural, and industrial center and played an important part in the fight for independence. Industries include shipbuilding, textiles, chemicals, clothing, electrical equipment, metal products, publishing and printing, oil refining, and food processing. It is known as the "**City of Brotherly Love**." Population (2004) 1,470,151.

PITTSBURGH City and port at the confluence of the Allegheny and Monongahela rivers in southwest Pennsylvania. The British captured a French fort on the site in 1758, renaming it **Fort Pitt**. Pittsburgh grew as a major industrial center, particularly for steel, from the early 19th century. The steel industry in the city is now in decline. Other industries include glass, machinery, petroleum products, electrical equipment, publishing, coal mining, and oil and natural gas extraction. Population (2004) 322,450.

RHODE ISLAND

Rhode Island is a state in the northeastern United States, on the Atlantic Ocean in the New England region. It shares a border with Connecticut to the west and Massachusetts north and east.

LAND AND ECONOMY

The land is level or gently rolling. **Narragansett Bay**, which contains many islands, cuts deeply into the eastern section. There are no rivers of importance, but nearly 300 lakes and ponds. Manufacturing, centered in the larger cities, is the economy's mainstay. Fish and shellfish are harvested in coastal waters. Tourism is a valuable source of income.

About 87% of the population lives in urban areas, most in the **Providence** metropolitan area. There are 13 institutions of higher education. The privately financed **Brown University**, founded in 1764, is the seventh oldest in the United States. The University of Rhode Island is state supported.

HISTORY

The first European settlers came in 1636, led by **Roger Williams**, who had been banished from Massachusetts for his liberal religious and political views. The town he founded at Providence joined later settlements in 1644 to form the colony of **Providence Plantations**, but in 1663 the charter was revoked by Charles II. The area, including some islands that had been governed separately, became the State of Rhode Island and Providence Plantations. This remains the official name of the state.

Wars with Native Americans shook the colony in the late 17th century. Rhode Island was one of the first colonies to show a spirit of revolt against the British crown. A British revenue cutter was burned by colonists in 1772, and on May 4, 1776, two months before the national **Declaration of Independence**, the General Assembly declared Rhode Island free of Great Britain. A French fleet aiding the Americans was based at Newport during the Revolution.

The first settlers in the state were mostly English, but immigrants from many European countries arrived in the 19th century to work in the factories. In the 19th century, the state became an important center of the textile industry, but by the 1940s most of this industry had moved to southern states. Health services and tourism are the largest economic sectors.

A fishing boat lies moored in a cove near Castle Hill Inn in Newport, Rhode Island, along Rhode Island Sound. Newport, a major naval training center, is famous for its magnificent mansions dating from the Gilded Age (c.1876–1914) and has many hotels and resorts.

MAIN CITIES

PROVIDENCE Capital of Rhode Island, a port on Providence Bay in the northeast of the state. The city was founded in 1636 as a refuge for religious dissenters from Massachusetts. It later enjoyed prosperity through trade with the West Indies, and played an active role in the American Revolution. It was one of the first industrial cities in the U.S. Industry has declined, though it is still notable for jewelry and silverware. A financial sector revived the city's economy. Population (2004) 176,365.

WARWICK City in central Rhode Island, 10 mi (16 km) south of Providence on the Pawtuxet River at Narragansett Bay. Originally called Shawomet after the Native American tribe from which the land was purchased, it was renamed after the Earl of Warwick in 1648. It is the site of Rocky Point, one of the oldest seaside resorts in New England. Its industries include tourism and the production of aluminum, clothing, and electronic equipment. Population (2004) 87,365.

PAWTUCKET City in northern Rhode Island, 4 mi (6 km) northeast of Providence, on Blackstone River. It is the site of **Slater Mill**, the first water-powered textile mill in the U.S., and thus of the beginning of America's Industrial Revolution. Today its major industries include textiles, clothing, and brass and iron foundries. Population (2004) 74,330.

STATE FACTS

Admitted to Union May 29, 1790; 13th of the 13 original states to ratify the U.S. Constitution
U.S. Congress Senate 2, House of Representatives 2
Population 1,048,319; ranked 43rd
Capital Providence
State legislature Senate 50, House of Representatives 100
Area 1,545 sq mi (4,002 sq km); ranked 50th
Elevation Highest 812 ft (247 m), Jerimoth Hill; lowest, sea level
State nicknames Little Rhody, Ocean State
State motto Hope
State bird Rhode Island red chicken
State flower Violet
State tree Red maple

SOUTH CAROLINA

South Carolina is a state in the southeast United States on the Atlantic Ocean. It is bordered by North Carolina in the north and Georgia southwest. It was the first state to secede from the Union before the Civil War.

LAND AND ECONOMY

From the seacoast the land rolls gradually up to the **Blue Ridge Mountains** in the extreme northwest. Many rivers flow southeast to the Atlantic, including the Pee Dee, the Santee, and the Edisto. The **Savannah River** forms the southwest boundary. The principal lakes are human-made, providing hydroelectric power and flood control. Fertile soils and a mild climate have made South Carolina a productive agricultural region. The major products are tobacco, soybeans, cotton, peaches, groundnuts, and poultry. Forests yield an abundant supply of lumber. Key minerals are clay, cement, limestone, and vermiculite. Manufacturing did not become important until the 20th century; it was widely diversified after World War II. The main industrial products are textiles, lumber, pulp and paper, chemicals, apparel, and machinery. Tourists are important, drawn to the beaches, fine public gardens, and the old-world charm of Charleston.

The original British settlers in the region were followed by the French Huguenots, Germans, and Swiss. Slaves were brought into work the plantations, and for many years they were a majority of the population. When South Carolina celebrated its **Tricentennial** in 1970, more than 80% of its residents had been born in the state.

There are nearly 50 institutions of higher education, including the **University of South Carolina** and **Clemson University**.

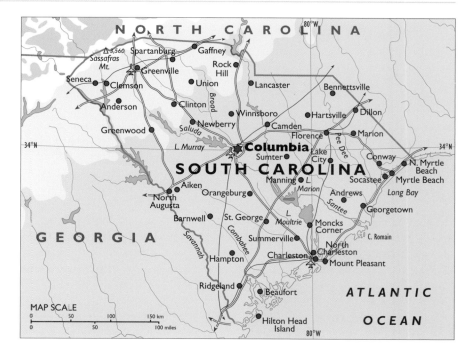

HISTORY

The Spanish and French had short-lived settlements on the coast in the 16th century, but permanent occupation did not begin until the English came a century later. **Charles II** granted the land to eight proprietors in 1663, and the first settlers arrived in 1670. **Charleston** (then known as Charles Town) was founded in 1680. In 1729 South Carolina became a royal colony. A plantation society arose, with rice, indigo, and cotton the major crops. In the **American Revolution**, the battles of Camden, Cowpens, and Eutaw Springs were fought. The nation's first steam locomotive for regular passenger service, "Best Friend of Charleston," began service in 1830.

After joining the Union, South Carolina was a strong defender of states' rights and a leader in forming the Confederacy. The first shots of the Civil War were fired on **Fort Sumter** in Charleston harbor on April 12, 1861. The first ever submarine used in warfare was the Confederate's *Hunley* in 1863 in **Charleston harbor**, but it sank the following year. It was raised in 2000 and is now being conserved. In 1865, a Union army devastated the state and burned **Columbia**, the capital. South Carolina was readmitted to the Union in 1868, but recovery from the

The Battery Street neighborhood in Charleston has many historic homes in a traditional southern style and attracts large numbers of tourists.

catastrophe was long and difficult. Development of the textile industry, beginning in the 1880s, helped to stabilize the economy. During the 20th century, industry became more diversified and now dominates the economy. The state was devastated in 1989 by **Hurricane Hugo**, which claimed 13 lives and caused $3.7 billion in damages.

MAIN CITIES

COLUMBIA The capital and largest city of South Carolina is located in the center of the state on a bluff overlooking the **Congaree River**. Founded as the state capital in 1786, it was nearly destroyed in the Civil War when burned by **General William T. Sherman**'s Union troops. It is home to the **University of South Carolina** and **Columbia College**. Its **Riverbanks Zoo** has been rated one of the top 10 in the nation. **Fort Jackson** in Columbia is the largest U.S. military

STATE FACTS

Admitted to Union May 23, 1788; 8th of the 13 original states to ratify the U.S. Constitution
U.S. Congress Senate 2, House of Representatives 6
Population 4,255,083; ranked 25th
Capital Columbia
State legislature Senate 46, House of Representatives 124
Area 32,020 sq mi (82,932 sq km); ranked 40th
Elevation Highest 3,560 ft (1,085 m), Sassafras Mountain; lowest, sea level
State nickname Palmetto State
State motto *Dum spiro, spero* (While I breathe, I hope)
State bird Carolina wren
State flower Yellow jessamine
State tree Palmetto

training base. Industries in the city include textiles, printing, and electronic equipment. Population (2004) 116,278.

CHARLESTON The city of Charleston is a port in southeastern South Carolina, lying between the Ashley and Cooper rivers. It was founded in the 1670s by **William Sayle**, and soon became the major southeast seaport. Charleston had the first opera performed in the U.S. in 1735. The South Carolina Ordinance of Secession was signed here in 1860, and the firing on **Fort Sumter** began the Civil War. The city lures many tourists with its picturesque colonial buildings and the Fort Sumter National Monument. **Charleston Museum**, established in 1773 and still open, is the nation's oldest museum. The area has many gardens, including **Cypress Gardens**. It is the site of an important naval base. Industries include paper, textiles, chemicals, and steel. Population (2004) 104,883.

SOUTH DAKOTA

South Dakota is a state in the north-central United States in the Plains region. It is bordered by North Dakota in the north, Montana and Wyoming west, Nebraska south, and Minnesota and Iowa east.

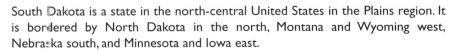

LAND AND ECONOMY

The land rises gradually from east to west. In the southwest are the **Badlands** of strangely formed, broken terrain and the rugged forest region of the **Black Hills**, where **Mount Rushmore** has carved into it a gigantic sculpture of presidents Washington, Jefferson, Lincoln, and Theodore Roosevelt. The **Missouri River** flows from north to south, with fertile farmlands east of the river and grasslands west. Major agricultural products include rye, wheat, sheep, and cattle. Rich mineral deposits are in the Black Hills. Among the state's main minerals are gold, beryllium, silver, petroleum, and uranium. Key industrial products include processed foods, lumber, and farm equipment.

Settlement began in the 19th century with pioneers from Minnesota, Wisconsin, Illinois and Iowa. Some came from Canada and a number from Sweden, Norway, Germany, the Netherlands, and Russia. A small number of Native Americans live on reservations. Universities include the University of South Dakota, South Dakota State University, and South Dakota School of Mines and Technology.

STATE FACTS

Admitted to Union November 2, 1889; ranked 40th
U.S. Congress Senate 2, House of Representatives 1
Population 775,933; ranked 46th
Capital Pierre
State legislature Senate 35, House of Representatives 70
Area 77,116 sq mi (199,731 sq km); ranked 17th
Elevation Highest 7,242 ft (2,207 m), Harney Peak; lowest 962 ft (293 m), Big Stone Lake
State nickname Mount Rushmore State
State motto Under God the people rule
State bird Ring-necked pheasant
State flower Pasqueflower
State tree Black Hills spruce

The colossal carvings on Mount Rushmore are some 60 ft (18 m) high and were completed in 1941. From left to right they are U.S. presidents Washington, Jefferson, Theodore Roosevelt, and Lincoln. The original aim was to attract tourists to the Black Hills; more than two million a year now visit the monument.

HISTORY

The first peoples in this area were the Plains Indians and Sioux Nation. French trappers in the 1740s claimed the land for France, and it was then acquired by the United States in the Louisiana Purchase of 1803. The **Lewis and Clark Expedition** explored it in 1804 and 1805. Settlers arrived in the 1850s, the **Dakota Territory** was formed in 1861, and the two Dakotas separated as states in 1889. Gold was discovered in the **Black Hills** in 1874. The last major armed conflict between the U.S. Army and Indians in the Plains was **The Wounded Knee Massacre** on December 29, 1890, when more than 200 Sioux were killed. In 1973, Wounded Knee was the site of a 71-day standoff between the authorities and Indian Movement militants.

MAIN CITIES

SIOUX FALLS The state's largest city is on the **Big Sioux River** in the southeastern part of the state. It was settled in 1856 but burned by Indians six years later. Settlers returned when **Fort Dakota** was built there in 1865. It has stockyards as well as financial institutions. Among the institutions of higher education are the **University of Sioux Falls** and **Augustina College**. The city celebrated its sesquicentennial in 2006. Population (2004) 136,695.

PIERRE The state capital is on the **Missouri River** in central South Dakota opposite **Fort Pierre**. It was a trading settlement in the early 19th century before becoming a railroad terminus in 1880 and the state capital in 1904. Government services and agriculture are especially important. Nearby is **Lake Oahe**, South Dakota's largest lake. Population (2004) 13,876.

TENNESSEE

Tennessee is a state in the southeast-central United States. It is bordered by eight states: Kentucky and Virginia in the north, North Carolina east, Mississippi, Alabama, and Georgia south, and Missouri and Arkansas west across the Mississippi River.

LAND AND ECONOMY

The **Great Smoky Mountains** of the Appalachian chain, with elevations of more than 6,000 ft (1,830 m) rise along the eastern boundary. West of them is the **Great Valley** of east Tennessee and the **Cumberland Plateau**. Beyond, the land slopes to the **Mississippi River** on the western border. The principal river is the **Tennessee**, which rises in the east, flows south into Alabama, and turns north to flow across the western part of the state. Mountain valleys in the east and the lower lands in the center and west are the primary agricultural regions. The state's main farm products include corn, soybeans, tobacco, cotton, dairy products, cattle, sheep, and hogs.

A diversified manufacturing industry was created by plentiful electric power from the network of the **Tennessee Valley Authority** (TVA), as well as an efficient transportation system and the state's proximity to major markets. Among the main industrial products are chemicals, textiles, apparel, electrical machinery, processed foods, transportation equipment, forest products, and printing and publishing. Industrial research facilities include the federal government's nuclear installation at Oak Ridge, which produced material for the first atom bomb and now carries out nuclear studies. The state's major minerals include zinc, limestone, marble, sandstone, and coal. Tourism is important, with the **Great Smoky Mountains National Park** being the most popular national park in the nation, attracting more than 9 million visitors a year, including walkers on the Appalachian Trail, which runs through the center of the protected area.

The first settlers were pioneers who crossed the mountains from states on the Atlantic seaboard, and their descendants form a major part of the population. There are more than 60 institutions of higher education, including the **University of Tennessee** and the private **Vanderbilt University**.

HISTORY

Native American groups in the region included the Creek and Yuchi and later the Cherokee. The region was visited by Spaniards in the 16th century and by the English and French a century later. The first permanent settlement was made in the **Watauga River Valley** in the northeast of the region in 1769. Sparsely settled and far removed from military action in the American Revolution, the area was little affected by the war. North Carolina relinquished its claim to the land in 1784, and dwellers in east Tennessee organized what they called the **State of Franklin**, although this was never recognized by the United States. In 1790, Congress created the **Southwest Territory**, out of which the state of Tennessee was established six years later.

As the Civil War approached, Union sentiment was strong in Tennessee, but the state seceded in 1861. Tennesseans served on both sides. More than 400 engagements, including several major battles, were fought in the state. The battle of **Nashville** in 1864 was the final forward action of the Confederate army and resulted in a crushing defeat. Tennessee rejoined the Union in 1866 and was the only former Confederate state to avoid a Reconstruction military government. Industrial development began in the 19th century and was greatly stimulated by World War II. In 1968 civil rights leader **Martin Luther King, Jr.** was assassinated in Memphis. In 1982, the **Knoxville World's Fair** was hosted in that city, drawing 11 million visitors.

MAIN CITIES

MEMPHIS Tennessee's largest city is a river port on the Mississippi River in southwest Tennessee. Strategically located on Chickasaw Bluff, Memphis was a French (1682), Spanish (1794), and U.S. (1797) fort before the first permanent settlement in 1819. The city is home to the **University of Memphis**. Tourists are drawn to **Beale Street**, center of the "Birthplace of the Blues," and to **Graceland**, which was Elvis Presley's home. Memphis is a major transportation center and livestock market. Industries include lumber, farm machinery, cotton, and pharmaceuticals. Population (2004) 627,802.

NASHVILLE The state's capital is a port on the Cumberland River. Settled in 1779, it became the capital in 1843. During the Civil War, it was the scene of a decisive Union victory. The city merged with Davidson County in 1963. **Vanderbilt University** is there. Centennial Park has **The Parthenon**, the world's only full-scale reproduction of the Greek temple. Nashville is a country music center and the home of the **Grand Ole Opry** and the **Country Music Hall of Fame and Museum.** The city has many neoclassical buildings. Industries include music and publishing. Population (2004) 525,849.

The Great Smoky Mountains National Park, Tennessee. With an area of 315 sq mi (2,110 sq km), it is one of the largest protected areas in the U.S. It is very rich in wildlife, including more than 60 species of mammals, among them a large population of black bears, and more than 200 species of birds. The park was designated a UNESCO World Heritage Site in 1983.

STATE FACTS

Admitted to Union June 1, 1796, ranked 16th

U.S. Congress Senate 2, House of Representatives 9

Population 5,962,959; ranked 16th

Capital Nashville

State legislature Senate 33, House of Representatives 99

Area 42,143 sq mi (109,151 sq km); ranked 36th

Elevation Highest 6,642 ft (2,024 m), Clingmans Dome; lowest 182 ft (56 m), Mississippi River

State nickname Volunteer State

State motto Agriculture and commerce

State bird Mockingbird

State flower Iris

State tree Tulip poplar

TEXAS

Texas is in the southwest-central United States on the Gulf of Mexico and separated from Mexico by the Rio Grande. The Gulf is in the southeast, and Texas is bordered by Oklahoma in the north, New Mexico west, and Louisiana and Arkansas east.

LAND AND ECONOMY

The largest of the contiguous 48 states, Texas covers about 12% of that U.S. land mass. A broad coastal plain lies along the **Gulf of Mexico**. West and north, the land rises to plains and plateaus. Highest elevations are in the far western mountains. Besides the **Rio Grande**, the principal rivers are the Brazos, Colorado, Guadalupe, and Nueces. There are few natural lakes, but throughout the state dams create reservoirs for irrigation and flood control. Irrigation aided the growth of ranching and farming on the plains in the west and north.

Among the state's agricultural products are rice, sorghum, fruits, vegetables, nuts, cattle, sheep, and poultry. Manufacturing is largely centered in the populous east and south. The key industrial products include chemicals, refined petroleum, aircraft, aerospace equipment, automobiles, ships and boats, machinery, and processed foods. Major petroleum deposits and refineries are on or near the Gulf Coast, although wells are also in the northwest. Other minerals include natural gas, sulfur, helium, cement, and clay.

Seaborne transportation is a major asset. **Houston**, linked to the Gulf by a ship canal, is a leading port; others are **Beaumont**, **Port Arthur**, **Galveston**, and **Corpus Christi**. Networks of railroads and highways cover the state's vast interior. NASA's **Lyndon B. Johnson Space Center**, located outside Houston, directs U.S. manned space flights.

Texas is the second most populous state (after California) and one of the fastest growing. Most Texans were born in the state, descendants of settlers from other states. More than 34% of the population is Hispanic. The German towns of **Fredericksburg** and **New Braufels** in the hill country have retained much of their culture. Institutions of higher education include the systems of the University of Texas, Texas A & M University, and the University of Houston, as well as Texas Tech University. Private universities include Southern Methodist University, Baylor University, Rice University, and Texas Christian University.

HISTORY

Before Europeans arrived, nine Native American tribes lived in what is now Texas. Spaniards explored the region after 1519 and claimed it. **Robert Cavelier, Sieur de La Salle**, descending the Mississippi River in 1682, asserted a French claim by building a fort on **Matagorda Bay**. The French went no farther, but the Spaniards made a few settlements, and the area became part of Mexico, then a Spanish colony. Mexico won independence in 1821, and in that year Americans began settling Texas in large numbers. They revolted against Mexican rule, and after defeating a Mexican army, established the **Republic of Texas** in 1837. It lasted eight years before being admitted to the Union.

Texas seceded in 1861 and was an active member of the Confederacy. The first major oil discovery was at **Spindletop** near Beaumont in 1901, ushering in the modern economy. **Miriam "Ma" Ferguson** became Texas's first woman governor in 1925, a figurehead for her husband, former Gov. James E. Ferguson. In 1962,

STATE FACTS

Admitted to Union December 29, 1845; ranked 28th
U.S. Congress Senate 2, House of Representatives 32
Population 22,859,968; ranked 2nd
Capital Austin
State legislature Senate 31, House of Representatives 150
Area 268,581 sq mi (695,621 sq km); ranked 2nd
Elevation Highest 8,749 ft (2,667m), Guadalupe Peak; lowest, sea level
State nickname Lone Star State
State motto Friendship
State bird Mockingbird
State flower Bluebonnet
State tree Pecan

In the southwest of Texas, Big Bend National park spans more than 1,000 mi (1,600 km) of the border between Texas and Mexico along the Rio Grande. In the higher parts of the park, such as the Chisos Mountains, the climate is very dry. There are traces of human habitation from 10,500 years ago.

NASA opened its **Manned Spacecraft Center** in Houston (renamed in 1973 as the Lyndon B. Johnson Space Center). **Ann Richards** became the first woman governor in her own right in 1990. Federal agents stormed the compound of cult leader David Koresh near **Waco** in 1993, leading to the deaths of four agents and 86 Branch Davidian members.

MAIN CITIES

HOUSTON The state's largest city is a deep-water port connected to the Gulf of Mexico by the **Houston Ship Canal**. Founded in 1836, it became the capital of the Republic of Texas (1837–1839, 1842–1845). Its greatest growth came after the opening of the canal in 1914. It is a major cultural center with five universities, including the **University of Houston** and **Rice University**, a symphony orchestra, and many art galleries and museums. It is also a leading industrial, commercial, and financial center, with vast oil refineries and a massive petrochemical complex. Other industries include space research, with the **Lyndon B. Johnson Space Center** nearby, shipbuilding, meat-packing, electronics, chemicals, brewing, sugar and rice processing, and printing and publishing. Population (2004) 1,946,484.
DALLAS Located in northeast Texas, the city was first settled in the 1840s. It expanded with the 20th-century development of its oil fields. **President John F. Kennedy** was assassinated here on November 22, 1963. **Annette Strauss** became the first woman mayor in 1987. The city celebrated its 150th anniversary

in 1991. It is home to the **State Fair of Texas**, an annual event since 1886, and to college football's **Cotton Bowl**. Dallas is a leading commercial and transportation center for the U.S. Southwest. It has many educational and cultural institutions. Industries include oil refining, electronic equipment, clothing, and aircraft. Population (2004) 1,193,433.
SAN ANTONIO The city is in the state's south-central area and the **San Antonio River** meanders through its center. The **River Walk** (Paseo Del Rio) is a tourist attraction. The city was founded on the site of the mission-fort **San Antonio de Valero** (the Alamo) where, in 1836, about 180 defenders were killed by thousands of Mexicans led by **General Santa Anna**. "Remember the Alamo" became a Texas rallying cry. The city hosted a world's fair, the **HemisFair**, in 1968. San Antonio's industries include aircraft, meat-packing, electronics, oil-refining, chemicals, wood products, financial services, and tourism. Population (2004) 1,144,646.
AUSTIN The state capital is in the south central hill country on the **Colorado River**. Originally called Waterloo, it was first settled in 1835 and four years later renamed for **Stephen Austin**, the "father of Texas." It became the capital of the **Republic of Texas** in 1839. The capitol building is the largest state one, second only to the nation's capitol in Washington, D.C. The **Lyndon B. Johnson Library and Museum**, dedicated in 1971, is on the **University of Texas** campus. Austin is called the "Live Music Capital of the World" for having some 150 music venues each evening. Industries include high-tech electronics, furniture, machinery, building materials, and food processing. Population (2004) 681,804.

UTAH

Utah is a state in the western United States in the Rocky Mountain region. It is bordered by Idaho and Wyoming in the north, Colorado east, Arizona south, and Nevada west. The southeast corner touches on New Mexico.

LAND AND ECONOMY

About 90% of the land is desert or mountains, with 65% owned by the U.S. government. The **Wasatch Range** of the **Rocky Mountains** crosses the state from north to south. To the west of this range is a basin of desert land. **Great Salt Lake**, a saline body of water 72 mi (116 km) long and 30 mi (48 km) wide, is in the northeastern part of the basin. East of the Wasatch Range, the **Unita Mountains**, with 11 peaks over 13,000 ft (3,965 m), run east and west. Much of the southern and eastern portions of the state consist of desert plateaus cut by canyons, making spectacular, but very harsh landscapes.

Agriculture is largely confined to the valleys on the west front of the Wasatch. The main farm products include sheep, turkeys, apricots, corn, apples, cherries, barley, sugar beets, hay, and wheat. Irrigation projects have aided production. Manufacturing is concentrated in the area of Ogden-Salt Lake City-Provo. Among the major industrial products are electronic components, medical instruments, transportation equipment, fabricated steel, and food products. Mining is carried out in many parts of the state, with the key minerals including copper, gold, silver, petroleum, and uranium. Utah's scenery, especially in the national parks in the south, attracts an important tourist trade.

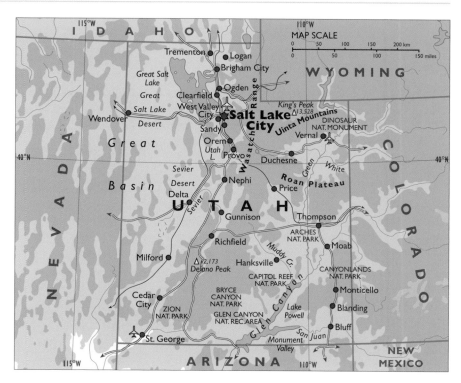

The first non-Native settlement was by pioneers from other states, whose descendants form the bulk of the population. About 76% of the population lives along the Wasatch front. More than 70% of the residents belong to the **Church of Jesus Christ of Latter-day Saints** (Mormonism), and the church exerts a strong influence in Utah. The University of Utah and Utah State University are state-supported, while Brigham Young University is a Mormon institution.

HISTORY

In 1776 two Franciscan friars seeking a way to California crossed the region, which was Mexican territory until ceded to the United States in 1848. The first non-Native settlement came in 1847, when **Brigham Young** led a party of Mormons to the valley between the Wasatch and Great Salt Lake. Through irrigation they created good farmland. Immigrants from Eastern states and Europe established new communities. In 1849 the Mormons organized the **State of Deseret** and sought admission to the Union, but Congress instead created the Territory of Utah. The transcontinental railroad was completed in 1869 at **Promontory Point**. A long conflict with federal authorities ended in 1890, when the Mormons agreed to abandon their practice of polygamy. Mining long dominated Utah's economy. Following World War II, defense-related manufacturing became important, but the leasing of lands with oil-shale deposits during the 1970s continued to make minerals important.

Goblin Valley State Park, Utah, is named for the strange shapes of its rock formations, caused by differential weathering of its sandstone. The region is very dry, with average annual rainfall of less than 8 in (20 cm).

MAIN CITIES

SALT LAKE CITY The state capital is in north-central Utah 13 mi (21 km) east of the Great Salt Lake. Founded in 1847 by the Mormons led by Brigham Young, it grew rapidly to become capital of the Territory of Utah in 1856 and of the state in 1896. It is the world headquarters of the Mormon Church. The historic **Temple Square** has the six-spired **Salt Lake Temple** and the domed **Tabernacle**, home of the world-famous **Mormon Tabernacle Choir**. In 1999, a tornado hit the downtown area, causing $100 million in damages. The city hosted the **2002 Winter Olympics**. Industries include missiles, rocket engines, oil-refining, tourism and printing and publishing. Population (2004) 181,743.

PROVO The city is on the **Provo River** in north-central Utah near **Utah Lake**. It was settled by Mormons in 1849 and named for a fur trapper, Etienne Provost. The city had wool mills and steel plants, and is also a shipping center for mines in the area. It s home to **Brigham Young University**. Industries include iron and steel, and textiles. Population (2004) 99,624.

OGDEN Located at the confluence of the **Ogden** and **Weber** rivers in northern Utah, Ogden was founded (as Fort Buenaventura) in 1846, settled in 1847 by Mormons, who named it Brownsville then gave it its current name in 1851. During World War II, German and Italian prisoners were interned in the area. **Weber**

STATE FACTS

Admitted to Union January 4, 1896; ranked 45th
U.S. Congress Senate 2, House of Representatives 3
Population 2,469,585; ranked 34th
Capital Salt Lake City
State legislature Senate 29, House of Representatives 75
Area 84,899 sq mi (219,887 sq km); ranked 13th
Elevation Highest 13,528 ft (4,123 m) Kings Peak; lowest 2,000 ft (607 m), Beaver Dam Wash
State nickname Beehive State
State motto Industry
State bird Seagull
State flower Sego lily
State tree Blue spruce

State University is located here. The city is a mountain resort, and industries include aerospace and defense companies. Population (2004) 78,519.

VERMONT

Vermont is a state in the northeastern United States in the New England region. It is bordered by the Canadian province of Quebec in the north and three states: New Hampshire in the east, Massachusetts in the south, and New York in the west.

LAND AND ECONOMY

The north-south ranges of the **Green Mountains** occupy most of the state. A plain lies along **Lake Champlain**, which forms almost half the western boundary. The **Connecticut River** runs along the eastern border. The state is the largest producer of maple syrup, and other agricultural products include apples potatoes, honey, and dairy products. Among the industrial products are machine tools, lumber, furniture, and stone products. Key minerals include marble, granite, limestone, and asbestos. Tourism is a major source of income.

Vermont settlers came from other New England states. In the 19th century, the Irish came to build railroads, and Italians, Scottish, and Welsh to work the quarries. There is also a French-Canadian element. The **University of Vermont** was founded in 1791, and **Norwich University**, begun in 1819, is the nation's oldest private military college.

HISTORY

Originally inhabited by the Iroquois, Algonquin, and Abenaki peoples, it was claimed by France in 1609. **Samuel de Champlain** discovered the lake that bears his name, but the first permanent settlement was in 1724 at Britain's **Fort Drummer**. In the American Revolution, the **Green Mountain Boys**, an independent force, took **Fort Ticonderoga** and **Crown Point**. In 1777, Vermont declared independence as the republic of **New Connecticut** and preserved this unrecognized status until becoming a state in 1791. Agriculture began to decline during the 19th century and into the 20th century. In 1964, Victory, Granby, and Jamaica became the last Vermont towns to receive electricity. Many towns and villages hold a **Town Meeting Day** to debate and decide on local issues once a year, usually in March, continuing a 200-year tradition.

STATE FACTS

Admitted to Union March 4, 1791; ranked 14th
U.S. Congress Senate 2, House of Representatives 1
Population 623,050; ranked 49th
Capital Montpelier
State legislature Senate 30, House of Representatives 150
Area 9,614 sq mi (24,901 sq km); ranked 45th
Elevation Highest 4,393 ft (1,339 m), Mount Mansfield; lowest 95 ft (29 m), Lake Champlain
State nickname Green Mountain State
State motto Freedom and unity
State bird Hermit thrush
State flower Red clover
State tree Sugar maple

MAIN CITY

BURLINGTON The largest city in Vermont is located on **Lake Champlain** in the northwest. It was settled in 1773 and during the War of 1812 its naval base was the scene of an attack by the British navy launched up the river Richelieu from their base on the Isle de Noix. It is the site of the **University of Vermont** and **Champlain College**. Burlington is surrounded by ski resorts in the Green Mountains. Industries include tourism, missile parts, textiles, ice-cream manufacturing, and wood products. Population (2004) 38,934.

MONTPELIER The state capital is located at the confluence of the **Winooski** and **North Branch**, in north-central Vermont. It has the smallest population of any state capital. First settled in the 1780s, it became the state capital in 1805. It is in the heart of ski country. Industries include tourism, machinery, granite, quarrying, plastics, and maple syrup. Population (2004) 8,035.

A white-painted wooden church near Burlington. Such churches are a familiar sight throughout New England. They developed from the prototype, Trinity Church in Newport, Rhode Island, completed in 1726. The arched and round windows and tall, thin spire are typical of the style.

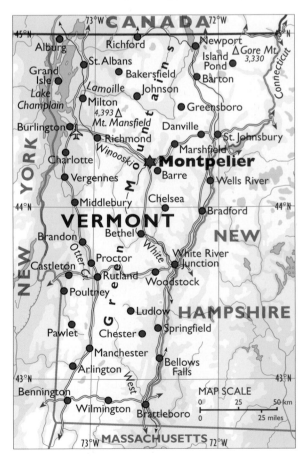

VIRGINIA

The Commonwealth of Virginia is a state in the eastern United States on the Atlantic. It is bordered by Maryland and the District of Columbia in the north, West Virginia and Kentucky west, and Tennessee and North Carolina south.

LAND AND ECONOMY

From the coast, the land rises gently to the **Blue Ridge Mountains**. Beyond the Blue Ridge, the **Shenandoah Valley** is a rich farming region. In the far west, the rugged **Allegheny Mountains** lie along the state boundary. **Chesapeake Bay**, a large arm of the Atlantic, cuts into the east section; flowing into it are the **James**, the **York**, and the **Rappahannock** rivers. The **Potomac River** forms much of the state's northern boundary. The rich farmland that long sustained the economy is east of the mountains. The main agricultural products include tobacco, corn, soybeans, groundnuts, apples, poultry, and hogs. Among the key minerals are coal, zinc, and limestone. The major industrial products include chemicals, tobacco products, food products, textiles, transportation equipment, apparel, lumber, and furniture. The state's historical sites are prime attractions for the important tourist industry.

Early settlers were English; in the early 18th century, numbers of Scottish-Irish and Germans arrived, but immigration decreased after 1800. The **College of William and Mary**, founded in 1693, is the second oldest in the U.S. **Washington and Lee University**, founded in 1749, had the former General Robert E. Lee as its president when it was Washington College. The state-supported **University of Virginia** was founded by Thomas Jefferson in 1819. The **Virginia Military Institute**, established in 1839, sent many cadets to fight in the Civil War. **Arlington National Cemetery** was founded in 1864 in the grounds of General Lee's wife's family home.

HISTORY

Native American groups in the region included the Algonquin, Iroquois, and Sioux. The first permanent settlement by Europeans in the New World was made at **Jamestown** in 1607. The General Assembly of 1619 was the first representative local government in the U.S. Virginia became a royal colony in 1624 and developed an aristocratic plantation society in the east, with vast holdings in tobacco acreage. The west was settled by immigrants from overseas and from other colonies in the early 18th century.

Virginia's leaders, including **Thomas Jefferson**, **Patrick Henry**, and **Richard Henry Lee**, were foremost in the drive for independence from Great Britain. Jefferson was the principal author of the **Declaration of Independence**, and **George Washington**, a Virginian, was commander-in-chief of the Continental Army during the American Revolution. Lord Cornwallis surrendered his British troops at **Yorktown** on October 19, 1781.

Four of the first five presidents of the United States were Virginians, and the state, called the "Mother of Presidents," leads the nation in having produced eight: George Washington, Thomas Jefferson, James Madison, James Monroe, William Henry Harrison, John Tyler, Zachary Taylor, and Woodrow Wilson.

Virginia was one of the last states to join the Confederacy in the Civil War, but Richmond became the Confederate capital, and the state's **General Robert E. Lee** commanded its army. Virginia was the principal battleground of the war. Lee surrendered his army to U.S. **General Ulysses S. Grant** at **Appomattox Court House**, on April 9, 1865. Social and economic recovery was slow after the war, but was followed by industrial growth during the 20th century. After World War II, rapid growth was experienced by the **Norfolk** metropolitan area and Virginia's suburbs outside Washington, D.C., where the **Pentagon** and **CIA** have headquarters. In 1990, **L. Douglas Wilder** became the nation's first African American governor.

MAIN CITIES

RICHMOND The state's capital is a port on the **James River** in east central Virginia. Settled in 1637, the city became state capital in 1779. During the Civil War, it was the Confederate capital from 1861–1865 and was badly burned when it fell in 1865 to Union forces. Industries include metal products, tobacco processing, textiles, clothing, chemicals, and publishing. Population (2004) 197,790.

VIRGINIA BEACH The largest city in the state, it is a major resort and is listed in the *Guinness Book of Records* as having the longest pleasure beach in the world. Real estate and tourism are the major economic sectors. Population (2005) 438,416.

NORFOLK CITY is on the **Elizabeth River** in southeastern Virginia. Founded in 1682, it forms the port of **Hampton Roads** with **Newport News** and **Portsmouth**. The oldest structure is **St. Paul's Episcopal Church** (1739). The **Norfolk Navy Base** (Naval Station Norfolk) is the largest in the world, with 75 ships and 134 aircraft. Industries include shipbuilding, automobiles, and chemicals. Population (2004) 234,403.

The strategically important Shenendoah Valley was the scene of repeated battles during the American Civil War. Its national park was founded 1935 to protect the landscape from development.

STATE FACTS

Admitted to the Union June 25, 1788; 10th of the 13 original states to ratify the U.S. Constitution
U.S. Congress Senate 2, House of Representatives 11
Population 7,567,465; ranked 12th
Capital Richmond
State legislature Senate 40, House of Representatives 100
Area 42,774 sq mi (110,785 sq km); ranked 35th
Elevation Highest 5,729 ft (1,746 m), Mount Rogers; lowest, sea level
State nickname Old Dominion
State motto *Sic semper tyrannis* (Thus always to tyrants)
State bird Cardinal
State flower Dogwood
State tree Dogwood

WASHINGTON

Washington is a state in the northwestern United States on the Pacific Ocean. It is bordered by the Canadian province of British Columbia in the north and the states of Oregon south and Idaho east.

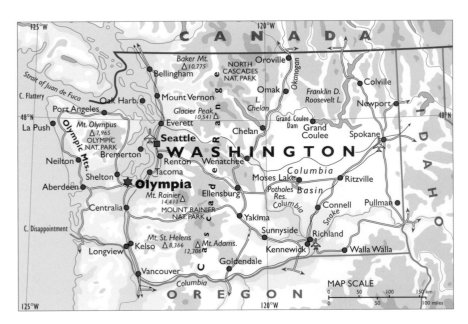

LAND AND ECONOMY

Puget Sound, an arm of the Pacific, extends about 125 mi (201 km) into the northwestern part of the state. If contains hundreds of islands and its broken shoreline provides many harbors. West of the Sound, the **Olympic Mountains** dominate the **Olympic Peninsula**. The densely forested, volcanic **Cascade Range** splits the state north to south, with an average elevation of 8,000 ft (2,440 m). East of the Cascades, the land is largely farming and grazing country. Washington is the leading producer of apples; other farm products are hay, hops, dairy products, pears, blueberries, apricots, potatoes, cattle, and sheep. Among major minerals are zinc, sand, and gravel. The **Columbia River** enters from Canada in the northeast and flows south, turning west to form much of the state's southern boundary.

Manufacturing is centered principally in the cities along Puget Sound. Industrial products include computer technology, biotechnology, aerospace, food processing, pulp and paper, aluminum, lumber, and chemicals. **Seattle** is a major port for connections with Alaska and the Pacific area. Washington was settled by pioneers from other states as well as Canadians, Norwegians, and Swedes. There are more than 40 institutions of higher education, including the **University of Washington** based in Seattle and **Washington State University** based in Pullman.

HISTORY

Native Americans in the area included the Nez Perce, Yakima, Spokan, and Chinock. **Bruno Heceta**, a Spanish navigator, discovered the mouth of the **Columbia River** in 1775 and laid claim to the area. British explorer **George Vancouver** mapped the **Puget Sound** area in 1792. U.S. fur traders established a post at Spokane in 1810. Missionaries came to the site of **Walla Walla** in 1843. The region's boundary with Canada was fixed by treaty with Great Britain in 1846, and in 1848 the **Oregon Territory** was organized, including the present states of Oregon and Washington. **Washington Territory** was created separately in 1853. The railroad reached the area in 1883, and a few years later **Seattle** became the supply center for gold-seekers flocking to Alaska. World War I brought a boom to the state, especially in shipbuilding. In World War II, the Hanford nuclear plant produced the plutonium used in the Nagasaki atomic bomb. The nuclear plant was closed in 1990, and the federal government is constructing a treatment plant for radioactive waste. On May 18, 1980, Mount St. Helens erupted, toppling the north face of the mountain. The state held its first presidential primary in 1992. Washington had the nation's closest gubernatorial race in history in 2004 when **Christine Gregoire** was elected by a 133-vote margin after two recounts.

MAIN CITIES

SEATTLE The state's largest city is a seaport in western Washington on **Elliott Bay** between Lake Washington and Puget Sound. Settled in 1851, it was called Duwamps until 1852. Fire destroyed the downtown area in 1889, but it developed rapidly after the arrival of the railway in 1893. Seattle served as the gateway for the Alaska Gold Rush in 1897. It is home to the **University of Washington**. The city has been the center of the U.S. aerospace industry since **William Boeing** opened his first factory there in 1916, but the Boeing corporation moved its headquarters to Chicago in 2001. The computer company, **Microsoft**, has had its headquarters there since 1979. Other industries include shipbuilding, precision instruments, chemicals, lumber, fishing, and tourism. Population (2004) 557,046.

SPOKANE Located at the falls of the **Spokane River** in east Washington, it was incorporated in 1881 as Spokan Falls. Eight years later 32 downtown blocks were destroyed by fire. In 1974, it held a world's fair, "Expo '74" that left the city its **Riverfront Park**. A campus of **Washington State University** is here. Spokane is an industrial, commercial, and transportation center for the region. Population (2004) 196,721.

TACOMA North America's sixth largest container port, Tacoma is at the mouth of the **Puyallup River** on Puget Sound and Commencement Bay. The city is home to the **Washington State History Museum**. It is a popular tourist destination. Industries include chemicals, boats, and wood products. Population (2004) 196,094.

The most distinctive feature of Seattle's skyline is the Space Needle. At 605 ft (184 m) high, it was built for the World's Fair in 1962. It is designed to withstand magnitude 9 earthquakes and winds of up to 200 mph (330 km/h), and has 25 lightning rods on the roof. The observation platform is at 520 ft (159 m).

STATE FACTS

Admitted to Union November 11, 1889; ranked 42nd
U.S. Congress Senate 2, House of Representatives 9
Population 6,287,759; ranked 14th
Capital Olympia
State legislature Senate 49, House of Representatives 98
Area 71,300 sq mi (184,665 sq km); ranked 18th
Elevation Highest 14,411 ft (4,392 m), Mount Rainier; lowest, sea level
State nickname Evergreen State
State motto Alki (Bye and bye)
State bird American goldfinch
State flower Coast rhododendron
State tree Western hemlock

WEST VIRGINIA

West Virginia is a state in the eastern United States in the Appalachian Mountain region. It is bordered by Pennsylvania and Maryland (the latter partly along the Potomac River) in the north, Virginia south and east, and Ohio and Kentucky west.

LAND AND ECONOMY

The **Allegheny Mountain** ranges run northeast-southwest in much of the eastern half of the state. The west portion is a plateau dropping gradually to the **Ohio River**, which marks the western boundary with Ohio. The state's mineral resources supply the manufacturing industries and are the mainstay of the economy. Among the key minerals are coal, natural gas, petroleum, salt, and stone. Industries are located principally in the cities along the Ohio River, which is a valuable transportation artery. The major industrial products include chemicals, plastics, steel, machinery, fabricated metals, automobile parts, glass, and pottery. Agriculture is a smaller element in the state, with the main products being poultry, apples, dairy products, cattle, and sheep.

The early settlers came from states to the east. Most were of English, Scottish-Irish, and German descent. Later, immigrants from Poland, Hungary, and other central European countries came to work in the mining industry. There are 25 institutions of higher education, including the state-supported **West Virginia University**, in Morgantown; **West Virginia State University**, in Institute; and the private schools of the **University of Charleston**, **Salem International University**, and **Wheeling Jesuit University**.

HISTORY

Archeological evidence in the form of human-made earthen mounds indicate the presence of early Native American civilizations. In 1671 the British explorers Thomas Batts and Robert Fallam reached the **New River**, and **George Washington** explored the region in 1753. **Daniel Boone** was another explorer and eventually a resident. Pioneers from Virginia pushed across the mountains into the region in the late 18th century. During the American Revolution, the battle of **Fort Henry** (now Wheeling) was fought in 1782 nearly a year after the war had ended elsewhere. Settlement expanded in the early 19th century, especially along the Ohio River. The area was part of the state of **Virginia**, but political and economic tensions arose between the new settlements and the older society to the east. When Virginia seceded in 1861, a convention of westerners who supported the Union repudiated the act. Later that year they formed a new state named **Kanawha**, which was admitted to the Union two years later as West Virginia. During the Civil War, the state saw many battles and Confederate raids, with the town or **Romney** near the Virginia border changing hands between the two armies 56 times. In later years, the state's fortune depended on the varying prosperity of the coal-mining industry. During the 1960s, the federal government began an Appalachian aid program, and the increased demand led to expansion of coal mining beginning in the mid-1970s.

STATE FACTS

Admitted to Union June 20, 1863; ranked 35th
U.S. Congress Senate 2, House of Representatives 3
Population 1,816,856; ranked 37th
Capital Charleston
State legislature Senate 34, House of
Representatives 100
Area 24,230 sq mi (62,755 sq km); ranked 41st
Elevation Highest 4,861 ft (1,481 m), Spruce Knob;
lowest 240 ft (73 m), Potomac River
State nickname Mountain State
State motto *Montani semper liberi* (Mountaineers
are always free)
State bird Cardinal
State flower Rhododendron
State tree Sugar maple

Glade Creek Grist Mill, Babcock State Park, is a working reconstruction of a type of water mill once common in West Virginia, when grain was more commonly grown. It is reconstructed from parts of several other mills in the region.

The coal industry set a production record in 1996 of 174 million tons. There have also been disasters, including 125 killed in 1972 when the **Buffalo Creek** coal waste dam collapsed, and in 2006 the explosion in the **Sago** mine that killed 12 coal miners. Peace talks between Israel and Syria were held at **Shepherdstown** in 2000.

MAIN CITIES

CHARLESTON West Virginia's capital and largest city is in the west of the state on the **River Kanawha** where it joins the **Elk River**. The city grew around **Fort Lee** in the 1780s. **Daniel Boone** lived there from 1789 to 1795. The state capital from 1870 to 1875, it has been so since 1885. The private **University of Charleston** is there. The **Charleston Town Center Mall** was the largest urban shopping center east of the Mississippi when it opened in 1983. The **Clay Center for the Arts and Sciences** was dedicated in 2003. Charleston is an important trade and transportation center for the industrialized **Kanawha Valley**. Industries include chemicals, glass, metallurgy, lumber, oil, gas, and coal. Population (2004) 53,421.

HUNTINGTON A port on the **Ohio River** in the state's west, the city is the center of the bituminous coal trade. It was established in 1871 as the western terminus of the **Chesapeake & Ohio Railroad**. A great flood in 1937 led to flood walls being constructed. Industries include glass and chemicals. Huntington is the home of the state-supported **Marshall University** and the **Heritage Farm Museum and Village**. Population (2004) 49,891.

WISCONSIN
1848

WISCONSIN

Wisconsin is a state in the north-central United States in the Great Lakes region. It shares borders with Michigan in the northeast, Minnesota west, Iowa southwest, and Illinois south. The Mississippi forms part of the western boundary.

LAND AND ECONOMY

The land is a rolling plain that slopes down from the high ground in the north. **The state is bordered on the east by Lake Michigan and on the north partly by Lake Superior.** Many small rivers lie within the state, and there are more than 8,000 lakes in total. Fertile pasturelands through most of the state support the dairy herds that make Wisconsin the nation's leader in the production of milk and other dairy products. The state also leads the nation in producing cranberries, snap beans, and ginseng. Other agricultural products include hay, corn, Christmas trees, hogs, and poultry.

Manufacturing is chiefly in the cities along **Lake Michigan**, which gives a water outlet to markets. **Milwaukee, Racine, Sheboygan,** and **Green Bay** have developed harbors. In the far northwest, **Superior** is part of the Lake Superior port of **Duluth**, Minnesota, a center for iron-ore shipping. Other main minerals include zinc, lime, cement, stone, and sand. Wisconsin's major industrial products include machinery, food products, beer, automobile parts and equipment, steel, metal products, and paper.

Early settlers came from eastern states, especially New England. They were followed by New England immigrants, chiefly Germans, Norwegians, and Swedes. **Milwaukee** became a center of German culture in the nation. There are about 60 institutions of higher education. The state-supported **University of Wisconsin** is in **Madison** and has 12 other campuses.

HISTORY

Six Native American nations, including the Oneida, Ojibway, and Winnebago, were the first peoples in this area. **Jean Nicolet** landed at **Green Bay** in 1634 and claimed the region for France. French fur trappers were active there through the 18th century. The area was ceded in 1763 to Great Britain, which yielded it to the United States in 1783 following the Treaty of Paris. Settlement began slowly with exploitation of the sand deposits in the southwest. Land was obtained by treaties with Native Americans, and the **Territory of Wisconsin** was created on July 3, 1836.

After admission to the Union, the new state was a leader in growing wheat. This declined after 1870, and dairy farming dominated the economy. In the 20th century, Wisconsin was known for its progressive state governments, which pioneered many liberal political measures. In 1919, it was the first state to ratify the **19th Amendment** giving women the right to vote, and in 1970 it celebrated the nation's first **Earth Day**.

STATE FACTS

Admitted to Union May 29, 1848; ranked 30th
U.S. Congress Senate 2, House of Representatives 8
Population 5,503,533; ranked 20th
Capital Madison
State legislature Senate 33, House of Representatives 98
Area 65,498 sq mi (169,639 sq km); ranked 23rd
Elevation Highest 1,951 ft (595 m), Timms Hill; lowest 581 ft (177 m), Lake Michigan
State nickname Badger State
State motto Forward
State bird Robin
State flower Wood violet
State tree Sugar maple

As well as the traditional crops of corn, cranberries and snap peas, Wisconsin is a leading producer of alfalfa (lucerne), which is grown primarily as premium-quality hay for feeding cattle and horses. As a leguminous plant, it fixes nitrogen in the soil and so produces a high-protein feed.

MAIN CITIES

MILWAUKEE The state's largest city is on the western shore of **Lake Michigan** in southeastern Wisconsin. It was founded in 1846 by the merger of three small towns. The first settlers were French trappers and traders, and then many Germans arrived during the 19th century. It is home to **Marquette University**, and the **University of Wisconsin at Milwaukee**. In 2001, the **Milwaukee Art Museum** opened its architecturally dramatic Quadracci Pavilion, the first design by **Santiago Calatrava** in the United States. Industries include healthcare, brewing, diesel and gas engines, construction, and electrical equipment. Population (2004) 554,965.

MADISON The state's capital and second largest city is partially sited on an isthmus that lies between lakes **Mendota** and **Monona**. Founded as the territorial capital in 1836, it continued as the state capital in 1848. The capitol building has the nation's only granite dome. Madison is an educational and manufacturing center in a dairy farming region. It is home to the main campus of the **University of Wisconsin** and the **Olbrich Botanical Gardens**. The **Dane Country Farmer's Market**, begun in 1972, is held twice a week with only Wisconsin produce sold. Madison celebrated its sesquicentennial in 2006. Industries include agricultural machinery, meat and dairy products, and medical equipment. Population (2004) 208,054.

GREEN BAY Wisconsin's oldest city is on Green Bay at the mouth of the **Fox River** in northeastern Wisconsin. A French fur-trading post was established there in 1634 and a permanent settlement in 1765. The U.S. established **Fort Howard** in 1816. The borough of Green Bay, founded in 1838, merged with the borough of Fort Howard in 1895 to form the city. Two years later, the first paper mill opened. The city's meat-packing industry gave its name to the **Green Bay Packers** professional football team, which has won the most National Football League championships. A campus of the **University of Wisconsin** is here. Products include paper, automobile parts, and food products. Population (2004) 101,100.

WYOMING

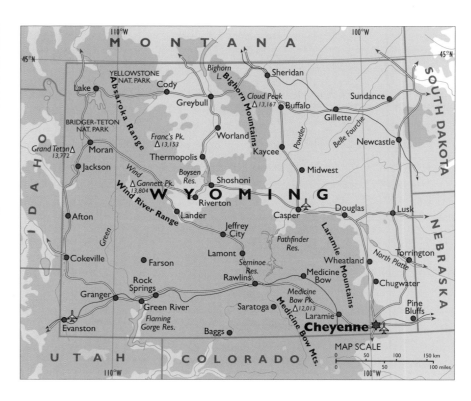

Wyoming is a state in the northwestern United States in the Rocky Mountain region. It is bordered by Montana in the north, Idaho west, Utah southwest, Colorado south, and South Dakota and Nebraska east.

LAND AND ECONOMY

The eastern half of the state is part of the **Great Plains**, rising to the ranges of the **Rocky Mountains** in the west. High plateaus lie among the ranges. Rivers include the Belle Fourche, Cheyenne, and North Platte flowing east; the Big Horn and Powder flowing north, the Snake flowing northwest, and the Green flowing south. Much of the open country is grazing land. Hay, wheat, barley, oats, beans, and sugar beets are among the chief crops grown. Among other farm products are cattle, sheep, and dairy products. Mineral resources supply the greater part of income. Wyoming has the largest coal resources in the nation. Also mined are petroleum, natural gas, uranium, and iron ore. The state is one of the least industrialized states. The major products include refined petroleum, processed foods, aircraft, electronics, wood, and clay products. Tourism and recreation are important to the economy.

Wyoming has the smallest population of any state, with a density of about 5 persons per sq mi. There are eight institutions of higher education, including the **University of Wyoming**, in Laramie.

HISTORY

Early settlers in Wyoming were the **Plains Indians**, including the Arapaho, Cheyenne, Blackfeet, Crow, Sioux, Shoshone, Ute, and Nez Perce. In the early 19th century, U.S. trappers roamed the region, which had been visited by the French a century before. In 1807 **John Colter** discovered the geysers in the area that later became **Yellowstone National Park**. His reports on the region were considered at the time to be fictional. Wagon trains bringing supplies were often accompanied by scientists and missionaries. **Fort Laramie** was established in 1834.

Beginning in the 1840s, thousands of immigrants to California and Oregon followed the **Oregon Trail** through south Wyoming, obtaining supplies at Fort Laramie in the southeast and **Fort Bridger** in the southwest, the only posts in the area. The **Union Pacific Railroad** was built through south Wyoming in 1867, and the cities of **Cheyenne**, **Laramie**, **Rawlins**, and **Rock Springs** arose along its route.

Yellowstone National Park became the world's first national park in 1872, and in 1891 **Shoshone National Forest** was the nation's first national forest. In 1906, **Devils Tower** became the first U.S. national monument. **Grand Teton National Park** is another important site for wildlife and recreation. **Wyoming Territory** was created by Congress in 1868, and a year later the territory's women were the first in the nation given the right to vote. In 1925, **Nellie Tayloe Ross** became the first woman governor in the U.S. (16 days before Texas's Miriam "Ma" Ferguson). From 1933 to 1953, Ross was also the first woman to head the U.S. Mint.

In the development of nuclear weapons after World War II, the state gained from its uranium deposits, and a missile launching site was located near Cheyenne. During the 1970s, increased demand for domestic coal and petroleum resulted in growth for Wyoming's energy-related industries. In 1978 the world's largest radio telescope was built on **Jelm Mountain** near Laramie. Wyoming celebrated its centennial in 1990. In 1995, wolves were reintroduced into Yellowstone National Park, where they are now thriving.

MAIN CITIES

CHEYENNE The state capital is in southeastern Wyoming near the border with Colorado. It began as a center for transporting goods and livestock by railroad. It grew rapidly after the arrival in 1867 of the **Union Pacific Railroad** and two years later became the territorial capital. The city was famous for its lawlessness and connections with such figures as **Buffalo Bill**, **Calamity Jane**, and **Wild Bill Hickok**. During its **Frontier Days**, Cheyenne has the oldest and largest outdoor rodeo in the world, celebrated annually since 1897. Industries include packing plants and oil refineries, and among the products are petroleum and plastics. Population (2004) 53,001.

CASPER Located on the **North Platte River** in east central Wyoming, Casper was established when the railroad arrived in 1888. Two years later, an oil discovery began a boom. When the **Pathfinder Reservoir** was built in 1909, it was the largest human-made reservoir in the U.S. In an agricultural region, Casper also produces oil, gas, coal, and uranium. The **College National Finals Rodeo** and the **Central Wyoming Fair and Rodeo** are annual events. In 2001, **Richard (Dick) Cheney**, who grew up in Casper, was inaugurated as the U.S. vice president. Population (2004) 51,240.

STATE FACTS

Admitted to Union July 10, 1890; ranked 44th
U.S. Congress Senate 2, House of Representatives 1
Population 509,294; ranked 50th
Capital Cheyenne
State legislature Senate 30, House of Representatives 62
Area 97,814 sq mi (253,336 sq km); ranked 10th
Elevation Highest 13,804 ft (4,207 m), Gannett Peak; lowest 3,100 ft (945 m), Belle Fourche River
State nicknames Equality State, Cowboy State
State motto Equal rights
State bird Western meadowlark
State flower Indian paintbrush
State tree Cottonwood

Rodeos, such as the one pictured here at Jackson Hole, Wyoming, developed as a way for ranch hands in the U.S. and gauchos in Mexico to show off their skills.

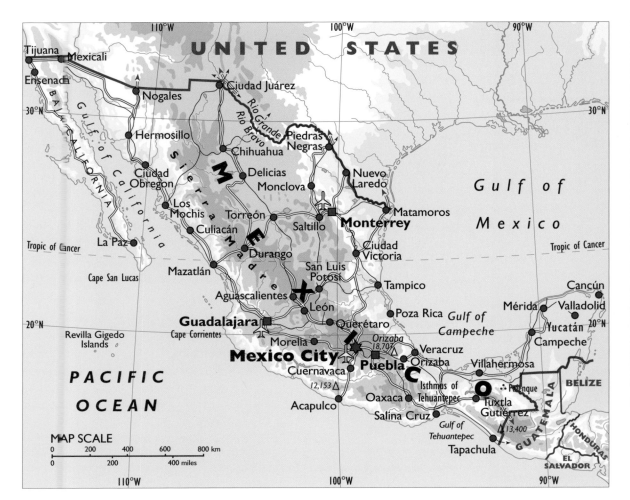

Senita Cacti Growing on Isla Datil, Sonora, in the Gulf of California (Sea of Cortes). The gulf is an important area for large marine mammals, and whale-watching operations provide valuable tourist income.

NORTHERN MEXICO

Northern Mexico extends from the Gulf of Mexico to the Pacific Ocean and from the United States to the central region of the Southern Plateau. It has 12 states: in the north (west to east) Baja California, Sonora, Chihuahua, Coahuila, and Tamaulipas; in the center Baja California Sur, Sinaloa, Durango, and Nuevo León; and in the south Nayarit, Zacatecas, and San Luis Potosí.

LAND AND ECONOMY

Northern Mexico generally has an arid to semiarid climate in the **Mesa del Norte** (Northern Plateau). The mountainous **Baja California** (Lower California) peninsula lies between the Pacific Ocean and Gulf of California. The main rivers are the **Rio Bravo del Norte** (Rio Grande) that forms a border with the United States, the Conchos in the north-central region, and six northwestern rivers: the Colorado, Culiacán, Fuerte, Tamazula, Tijuana, and Yaqui. The north's interior has a varied landscape of mountains, steppes, plains, and deserts. The two mountain ranges of the **Sierra Madre Occidental** and **Sierra Madre Oriental** run parallel north to south, separated by the large **Chihuahua Desert**. The **Barrancas del Cobre** (Copper Canyons) of Chihuahua are deeper than the Grand Canyon, reaching a depth of 6,161 ft (1,879 m).

The north is home to farming and mining villages. **Zacatecas** has numerous silver, gold, copper, and iron mines. **Tamaulipas** is a rich petroleum-producing state.

Among northern farm products are corn, cattle, sheep, and goats. Industrial products include electrical items, automobile parts, textiles, leather goods, and lumber. This region has received Mexico's greatest economic boost from the **North American Free Trade Agreement** (NAFTA) with the United States and Canada, in effect since 1994.

The region is a melting pot of people classified as European, Indian, and Mestizo (mixed). A national university with campuses throughout Mexico is Monterrey's private **Instituto Tecnológico y de Estudios Superiores de Monterrey** (Monterrey Institute of Technology and Higher Studies). Other key universities are those of Chihuahua, Sonora, Nayarit, and Baja California.

HISTORY

Native American groups in the region have included the Tarahumara, Yaqui, Pima, Cocopah, and Huichol. The region has seen explorers and missionaries since the 16th century. Silver mines were operating in the latter part of that century in the state of **Chihuahua**. The present border with the United States was

STATE FACTS

State	Population	Area sq mi (sq km)	Capital
Baja California	424,041	185,197 (479,660)	Mexicali
Baja California Sur	2,487,367	191,524 (496,047)	La Paz
Chihuahua	3,052,907	634,387 (1,643,062)	Chihuahua
Coahuila	2,298,070	388,452 (1,006,091)	Saltillo
Durango	1,448,661	319,037 (826,306)	Durango
Nayarit	920,185	69,875 (180,976)	Tepic
Nuevo León	3,834,141	168,152 (435,514)	Monterrey
San Luis Potosí	2,299,360	163,345 (423,064)	San Luis Potosí
Sinaloa	2,536,844	151,069 (391,269)	Culiacán
Sonora	2,216,969	471,513 (1,221,219)	Hermosillo
Tamaulipas	2,753,222	205,604 (532,514)	Ciudad Victoria
Zacatecas	1,353,610	189,722 (491,380)	Zacatecas

Paquimé was the center of the thriving Casas Grandes culture in the 13th–15th centuries. Its ruins include a ball court, temple structures, ritual area, pyramids, and a parrot hatchery. Its buildings were made of rammed earth and painted white or in bright colors. It became a UNESCO World Heritage site in 1998.

established by the **Mexican War** (1846–1848) when California and New Mexico became part of the United States. The revolutionary, **Pancho Villa**, was born in the state of **Durango** and lived in the city of Chihuahua. In 1916, he ordered the shooting of U.S. citizens in Mexico and an attack on Columbus, New Mexico, leading to a retaliatory attack by the U.S. military. Mexico's north is the gateway for illegal immigration into the United States. However, the country itself receives illegal immmigrants from Central America, many of whom are trying to ultimately enter the U.S.

MAIN CITIES

MONTERREY The country's third largest city, nicknamed the "Sultan of the North," is in a mountain valley in northeastern Mexico. It is the capital of the state of **Nuevo León**. Established in 1579, it was captured by U.S. forces in 1846 during the Mexican War. It has the nation's largest steel and iron foundries and also produces cement, chemicals, glass, and beer. Tourists are attracted to the scenery,

historic sites, bullfights, and rodeos. The city's **Faro del Comercio** is a 229 ft (70 m) monument to the local Chamber of Commerce. Population (2004) 1,110,909.

CIUDAD JUÁREZ The city, often shortened to Juárez, is in the state of **Chihuahua** on the **Rio Bravo del Norte** (Rio Grande) connected by bridges to **El Paso**, Texas. It was established by Spanish explorers in 1659. It is a transportation center, has processing industries for the surrounding cotton-growing region, and has increasing numbers of assembly plants, often owned by U.S. companies. The city was captured by Pancho Villa's forces in 1910 during the **Mexican Revolution**. It has now become an industrial center. Population (2000) 1,210,820.

TIJUANA The largest city in the state of **Baja California** is on the border to the U.S. state of **California**. This is the most used international border in the world, with some 64 million crossings a year. A mission was founded in 1769, and the city was officially established in 1889. Revolutionaries occupied the city in 1911 during the Mexican Revolution. Tijuana relies heavily upon tourism. Universities include the **Colegio de la Frontera Norte** (College of the Northern Border) and the private **Universidad Iberoamericana**. Population (2000) 1,210,820.

CENTRAL MEXICO

Central Mexico lies on the Southern Plateau, from the Pacific Ocean to the state of Veracruz. It has Mexico City in the Distrito Federal (Federal District), which is surrounded by the five states of Hidalgo, Tlaxcala, Puebla, Morelos, and México. The six other states to the north and west are Aguascalientes, Jalisco, Guanajuato, Querétaro, Colima, and Michoacán.

LAND AND ECONOMY

A variety of landscapes lie between the **South Sierra Madre** range in its north to the towering volcanoes in the state of **Puebla**, where the active, snow-capped **Popocatépetl** soars to 17,802 ft (5,430 m) – it can be seen from Mexico City in good weather. There are also forests, fertile valleys, lakes, desert-like tablelands, and semiarid zones. River systems include the **Moctezuma-Pánuco** flowing to the Gulf of Mexico, and the **Mexcala-Balsas** and **Lerma-Grande de Santiago** systems running into the Pacific Ocean. Other rivers include the Verde, Laja, Turbio, Zahuapan, San Martin, and Salado. Central Mexico is famed for its numerous silver and gold mines. Agricultural products include corn, grain, cattle, sheep, and goats. Among industrial products are textiles, processed food, and ceramics. Tourism is important, with **Mexico City** being the magnet for the area.

Most of the population has Spanish and Indian ancestry, with Mestizos being a mixture of the two. There are a large number of indigenous minorities. Institutions of higher education in Mexico City include the famous **Universidad Nacional Autónoma de México**, Universidad Anáhuac del Sur, Universidad Autónoma Metropolitana, and the Alliant International University. Major state universities include those in Aguascalientes, Colima, Guanajuato, Jalisco, Puebla, and Querétaro.

HISTORY

In 1325, the Aztec people established **Tenochtitlán** as their capital, later replaced by **Mexico City**. Another ancient capital was the Toltecs' city of **Tula** (Hidalgo). Spain's **Nuño de Guzmán** conquered **Jalisco** on the Pacific coast in the 1530s and conquistadors occupied the north-central area after silver was discovered. In 1810 **Miguel Hidalgo y Costilla**, a priest of Dolores, **Guanajuato**, began the War of Independence. His demand on September 16 for racial equality and land reform is now celebrated as Mexico's Independence Day. Despite his capture and death, the uprising led to the Mexican Republic in 1823. In the Mexican War, U.S. forces of **General Winfield Scott** captured Mexico City in 1846. It was again taken in 1860 during the civil war by the army of **González Ortega**, and in 1863 by French forces who installed **Maximilian of Hapsburg** as emperor. He was besieged in 1867 in **Querétaro**

State	Population	Area sq mi (sq km)	Capital
Aguascalientes	944,285	14,170 (36,700)	Aguascalientes
Colima	542,627	13,445 (34,823)	Colima
Distrito Federal	8,605239	4,007 (10,378)	Mexico City
Guanajuato	4,663,032	78,971 (204,535)	Guanajuato
Hidalgo	2,235,591	53,905 (139,614)	Pachuca
Jalisco	6,322,002	209,364 (542,253)	Guadalajara
México	13,096,686	55,309 (143,250)	Toluca
Michoacán	3,985,667	155,213 (402,002)	Morelia
Morelos	1,555,296	12,820 (33,204)	Cuernavaca
Puebla	5,076,686	87,806 (227,418)	Puebla
Querétaro	1,404,306	29,653 (76,801)	Querétaro
Tlaxcala	962,646	10,401 (26,939)	Tlaxcala

and executed. In 1934, the **Michoacán** native, **Lázaro Cárdenas**, became president and carried out extensive land reforms. The region suffers earthquakes, with 9,500 killed in the Michoacán quake in 1985 that devastated Mexico City. In 2003, another 29 deaths occurred in **Colima**.

MAIN CITIES

MEXICO CITY The capital and largest city of Mexico sits in a volcanic basin at an altitude of 7,800 ft (2,380 m) in the center of the country. It is the nation's political, economic, and cultural center, with several universities, and is classified as a megalopolis. **Hernán Cortés** destroyed the Aztec capital there in 1521, and the new city was capital of Spain's New World colonies for 300 years. It fell to U.S. troops in the Mexican War and French ones in 1863, but **Benito Juárez's** forces recaptured it in 1867. Between 1914 and 1915, the revoutionary forces of **Pancho Villa** and **Emiliano Zapata** captured and lost the city three times. Mexico City is a major tourist center. Traffic congestion and air pollution are two serious issues facing the local government. The city is also vulnerable to earthquakes. Population (2004) 8,605,239.

GUADALAJARA Located in west-central Mexico, the nation's second largest city is the capital of **Jalisco** state. Founded in 1531, it has fine Spanish colonial architecture, such as the cathedral and governor's palace. It was the birthplace of Mariachi bands. The **Universidad de Guadalajara** is Mexico's second largest university. The city's **Mercado Libertad** is

The 1985 earthquake destroyed much of Mexico City's infrastructure. Strict building regulations now apply to private and public buildings, such as the Stock Exchange.

Teotihuacán's Avenue of the Dead stretches south for 2.5 mi (4 km) from the Pyramid of the Moon past the Pyramid of the Sun and the Temple of Quetzalcoatl.

claimed to be Latin America's largest covered market. Population (2004) 1,646,183.

PUEBLA The capital of **Puebla** state is located in east-central Mexico. It is a tourist resort renowned for its buildings' colored tiles and colonial architecture Established in 1531 by the Spanish, Puebla became a key link for **Mexico City** to the port city of **Veracruz** on the Gulf of Mexico. Tourists are drawn to its a 100-block **El Centro Histórico** (Central Historic District). Many buildings were damaged by an earthquake in 1999. Population (2004) 1,271,673.

SOUTHERN MEXICO

Southern Mexico extends from the nation's central Southern Plateau to the borders with Guatemala and Belize. The Gulf of Mexico is in the north, the Pacific Ocean south, and Caribbean southeast. The eight states include three on the Yucatán Peninsula – Campeche, Quintana Roo, and Yucatán – and Chiapas, Guerrero, Oaxaca, Tabasco, and Veracruz.

LAND AND ECONOMY

The region includes diverse landscapes, from the **Yucatán Peninsula** tableland to the dormant volcano **Pico de Orizaba** (or Citlaltépetl) on the border of **Veracruz** and **Puebla**, rising to 18,619 ft (5,679 m) as Mexico's highest elevation. Among the South's highlights are canyons, waterfalls, cloud forests, seacoasts, plains, volcanoes, and mountain ranges. **Chiapas** is known for its green jungles, **Tabasco** for mangrove swamps and palm trees, and **Veracruz** for beaches, lagoons, and waterfalls. Rivers include the **Usumacinta** in the states of Chiapas and Tabasco, the **Hondo** in Quintana Roo, and the **Papaloapan** and **Pánuco** in Veracruz.

The region's main agricultural product is coffee, and fishing is important on both coasts. Mexico's major oil production comes from under **Campeche Bay** and the **Gulf of Mexico**. Industrial products include oil, lumber, textiles, ceramics, light industry, and assembly plants. Tourism is vital, with destinations including Mayan ruins, such as Chichen Itzá, Palenque, Uxmal, the Olmec/Toltec site of Monte Albán and such world famous resorts as **Acapulco** (Acapulco de Juárez) on the Pacific coast in the state of **Guerrero**, and **Cancún** on the Gulf of Mexico in **Quintana Roo**.

The people of the south have come from the indigenous Indians and colonial settlers, with the modern Mayans still predominating in today's Yucatán population. Public universities include the Universidad Autónoma de Campeche, the Universidad del Mar at Oaxaca, the Universidad de Quintana Roo, the Universidad Juárez Autónoma de Tabasco, the Universidad Veracruzana, and the Universidad Autónoma de Yucatan.

HISTORY

Impressive ancient civilizations arose in the region, with the **Olmecs** (800–400 BC) on the south coast of the Gulf of Mexico and the **Mayans** (AD 300–900) in the Yucatán Peninsula. Other groups included the **Huastecs** and **Totonacs** in Veracruz on the Gulf. The Mayans declined in the 10th century and much was destroyed after the Spanish conquest in the 16th century. The region continued to see occupying forces from Spain and France until 1867 when republican rule was restored.

The poor indigenous peoples of the south were seldom affected by the political reforms of the 20th century. In 1994, southern Mexico saw a two-week armed revolt in the state of **Chiapas** of guerrillas of the **Zapatista National Liberation Army** (Ejército Zapatista de Liberación Nacional, or EZLN). They called for land reforms and recognition of Indigenous

STATE FACTS

State	Population	Area sq mi (sq km)	Capital
Campeche	690,689	131,602 (340,849)	Campeche
Chiapas	3,920,892	192,206 (497,814)	Tuxtia Gutiérrez
Guerrero	3,079,649	166,487 (431,201)	Chilpancingo
Oaxaca	3,438,765	243,335 (630,238)	Oaxaca
Quintana Roo	874,963	130,048 (336,824)	Chetumal
Tabasco	1,891,829	65,441 (169,492)	Villahermosa
Veracruz	6,908,975	185,700 (480,963)	Xalapa
Yucatán	1,658,210	99,461 (257,604)	Mérida

peoples' rights. The government signed accords in 1996 promising autonomy for indigenous groups, but the next year armed attackers massacred 45 peasants in the state of Chiapas. In 2001, the Zapatistas held a nationwide march that resulted in the Mexican parliament passing a new rights' bill for indigenous peoples.

Recent natural disasters have included **Hurricane Wilma** in 2005 that caused great destruction along the Yucatán Peninsula, including the resort of Cancún.

MAIN CITIES

MÉRIDA The capital of the state of **Yucatán** was founded by the Spaniard **Francisco de Montejo** on the site of the Mayan city of **T'ho**. After conquering it, the Spaniards used stones from the Mayan pyramids to build the **Cathedral of San Idelfonso** from 1556 to 1599, the oldest cathedral in North America. Mérida is called the "White City" because of the white limestone used for its buildings. It is a center for tourists touring the area's Mayan ruins and home to four universities. Population (2004) 549,996.

OAXACA The city, officially Oaxaca de Juárez, is the capital of the state of **Oaxaca**. It was founded by the Aztecs as a fortress in 1486, and the Spanish established the city there in 1529. It played a major role in Mexico's struggle for independence. The city is renowned for its beautiful gold and silver jewelry and hand-woven textiles. Tourists use it as a base for exploring archeological sites, such as **Monte Albán**. Population (2004) 437,634.

TUXTIA GUTIÉRREZ The capital of the state of **Chiapas** is located on the site of a former native village established by the **Zoques** in 1240. It became the permanent capital in 1892. The town prospered with the coming in the 1940s of the **Pan-American Highway** and many moved there from the northeastern countryside in 1994 to avoid the armed clashes between Zapatista rebels and government forces. A few miles to the east of the city is the spectacular **Sumidero Canyon**. Population (2004) 424,579.

Cancún's hotel zone is vital for the local economy: rapid reconstruction work in the aftermath of 2005's Hurricane Wilma sought to minimize the loss of tourist revenue.

UNITED STATES

STATE MAPS

Settlements
(number of inhabitants)

■ **NEW YORK** — Over 5,000,000
■ **SEATTLE** — 2,000,000 – 5,000,000
■ **SACRAMENTO** — 1,000,000 – 2,000,000
◉ **Albuquerque** — 500,000 – 1,000,000
⊙ **Omaha** — 250,000 – 500,000
◉ Abilene — 100,000 – 250,000
◎ Charleston — 50,000 – 100,000
⊙ Sandusky — 20,000 – 50,000
○ *Twentynine Palms* — 10,000 – 20,000
○ *Pecos* — 5,000 – 10,000
○ *Deadwood* — Less than 5,000
▢ — Extent of urban areas (over 1,000,000 inhabitants)

Population figures for settlements are from the U.S. Census 2000 Summary file. Population figures for settlements with over 500,000 inhabitants are for urban areas.

Administration

International boundaries
State boundaries
County boundaries (parishes in Louisiana and census areas in Alaska)
CALHOUN — County names
MESA VERDE NAT. PARK — National parks *
NANTAHALA NAT. FOREST — National forests and grasslands
FORT A.P. HILL ⊞ — Military and federal reserves
WASHINGTON D.C. ■ — National capital
PHOENIX ✪ — State capitals with over 1,000,000 inhabitants
Dover ⊛ — State capitals with less than 1,000,000 inhabitants
■ JOHN F KENNEDY SPACE CENTER — Selected points of interest

* Includes national monuments, national preserves, national recreation areas, national scenic areas, national memorials, national historic sites, national seashores, national wildlife refuges, and selected state parks.

Communications

Limited-access highways
Limited-access highways under construction
Other highways
70 — Interstate route numbers
40 — U.S. route numbers
13 — State route numbers
Principal railroads (Amtrak)
Other railroads
Railroad tunnels
JFK ✈ — Principal airports (with location identifiers)
✈ — Other airports
Transportation canals and aqueducts

CITY MAPS

⊖ — Free limited-access highways (with interchange)
Toll limited-access highways
Tunnels
Primary divided highways
Primary undivided highways
Secondary divided highways
Secondary undivided highways
Other roads
70 — Interstate route numbers
40 — U.S. route numbers
13 — State route numbers
Railroads
Union Terminal — Principal railroad stations
✈ — Principal airports
✈ — Other airports
□ — City centers
City center map coverage
Urban areas
Lynn / **Clifton** / Swampscott — Suburbs (size of type indicates relative populations)
Woodlands and parks
■ Zoo — Points of interest

CITY CENTER MAPS

Free limited-access highways
Toll limited-access highways
Through routes
Secondary routes
Divided highways
Other roads
Tunnels
Railroads
Central Sta. — Railroad stations
Ⓢ Ⓜ — Subway stations
Urban areas
BEACON HILL — Suburbs
Woodlands and parks
□ — Public buildings
† — Churches
✝ — Cathedrals
Museum — Points of interest

STATE MAPS
Physical features

Perennial streams and rivers
Intermittent streams and rivers
Perennial lakes and reservoirs
Intermittent lakes
Dry lakes
Swamps and marshes
Reservoirs (with dams)
Permanent ice and glaciers
▲ 4301 — Elevations in meters
▼ 2731 — Sea and lake depths in meters
1134 — Height of lake surface above sea level in meters
C. Fear — Capes, points and mountain passes
Blue Ridge — Islands, peninsulas, mountain ranges and peaks
Tennessee — Rivers, lakes, bays, straits, glaciers, marshes and deserts
Columbia Plateau — Plateaus, basins and valleys

1:10 100 000

State capitals

COPYRIGHT PHILIP'S

COPYRIGHT PHILIP'S

1:2 500 000

10 0 10 20 30 40 50 km
10 0 10 20 30 miles

SASKATCHEWAN

CANADA

MANITOBA

MONTANA

NORTH DAKOTA

SOUTH DAKOTA

MINNESOTA

NEBRASKA

Williston
Minot
Lake Sakakawea
New Town
THEODORE ROOSEVELT NAT. PARK
Dickinson
Bismarck
Mandan
Devils Lake
Grand Forks
Fargo
Moorhead
Jamestown
Valley City
Aberdeen
Rapid City
BLACK HILLS
Pierre
Fort Pierre
Lake Oahe
Huron
Brookings
Watertown
Mitchell
Sioux Falls
Yankton

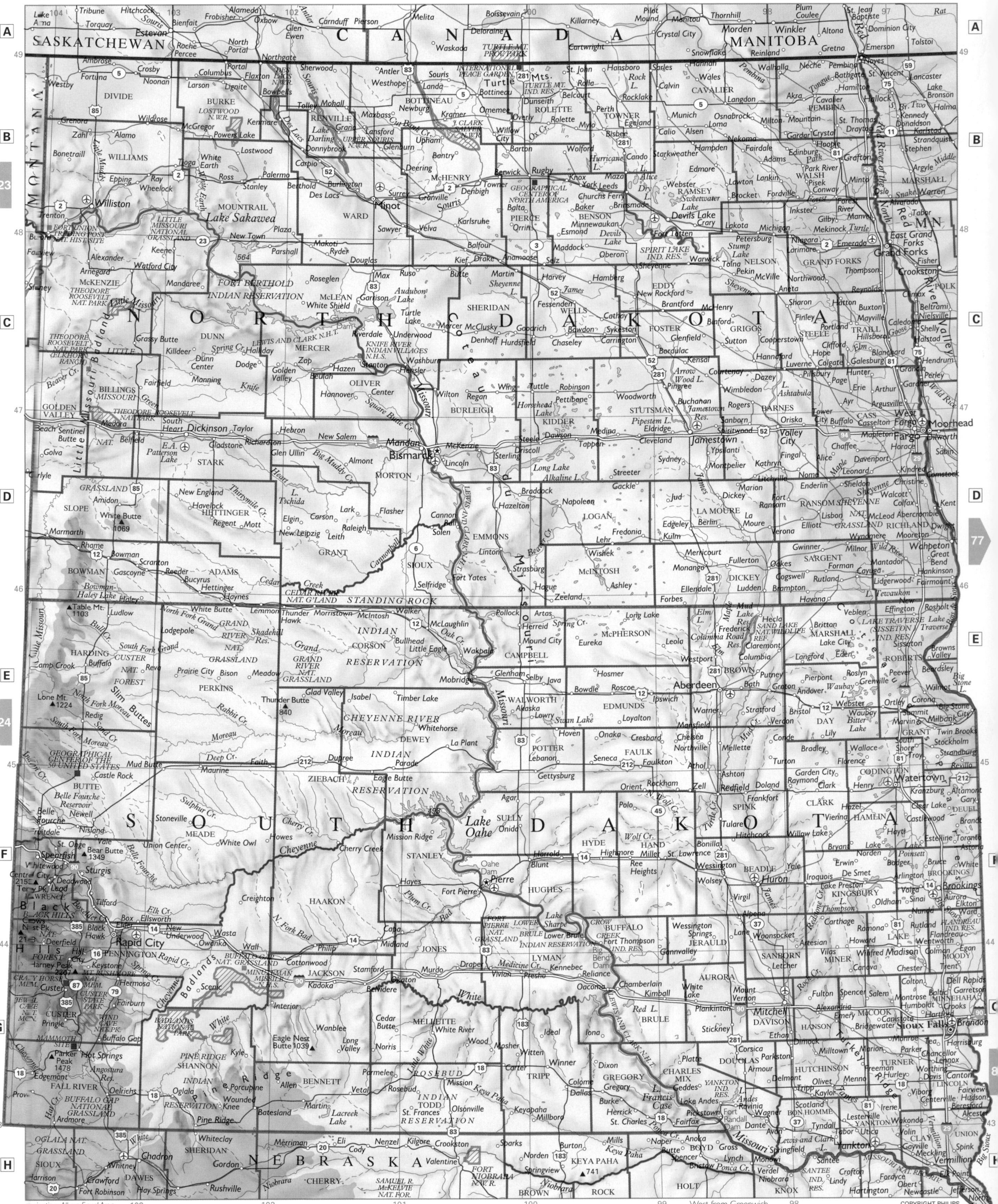

Projection: Albers Equal Area

West from Greenwich

COPYRIGHT PHILIPS '97

400 1500 2000 m
1200 3000 4500 6000 ft

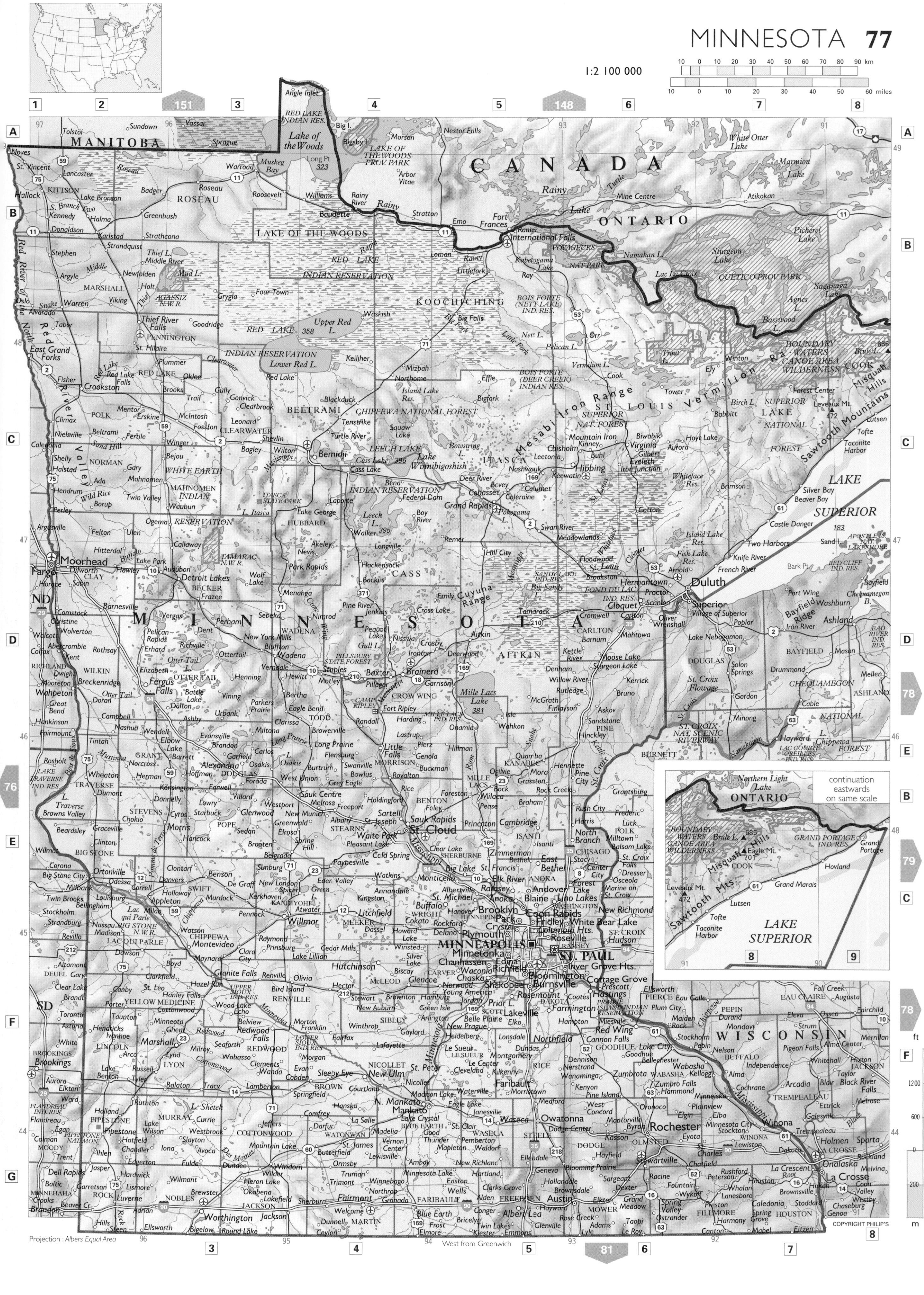

1:2 100 000
km
miles
CANADA
MANITOBA
ONTARIO
MINNESOTA
WISCONSIN
LAKE SUPERIOR
Lake of the Woods
Upper Red L.
Lower Red L.
Mille Lacs Lake
Rainy Lake
Fargo
Moorhead
Grand Forks
East Grand Forks
Duluth
Superior
International Falls
Bemidji
Brainerd
St. Cloud
MINNEAPOLIS
ST. PAUL
Rochester
Mankato
La Crosse
Winona
Austin
Albert Lea
Willmar
Brookings
Worthington
Hibbing
Grand Rapids
Fergus Falls
Detroit Lakes
Alexandria
Thief River Falls
Crookston
Marshall
New Ulm
Owatonna
Faribault
Red Wing
continuation eastwards on same scale
Projection : Albers Equal Area
West from Greenwich
COPYRIGHT PHILIP'S

1:2 100 000

0 10 20 30 40 50 60 70 80 100 km
10 0 10 20 30 40 50 60 miles

MINNESOTA

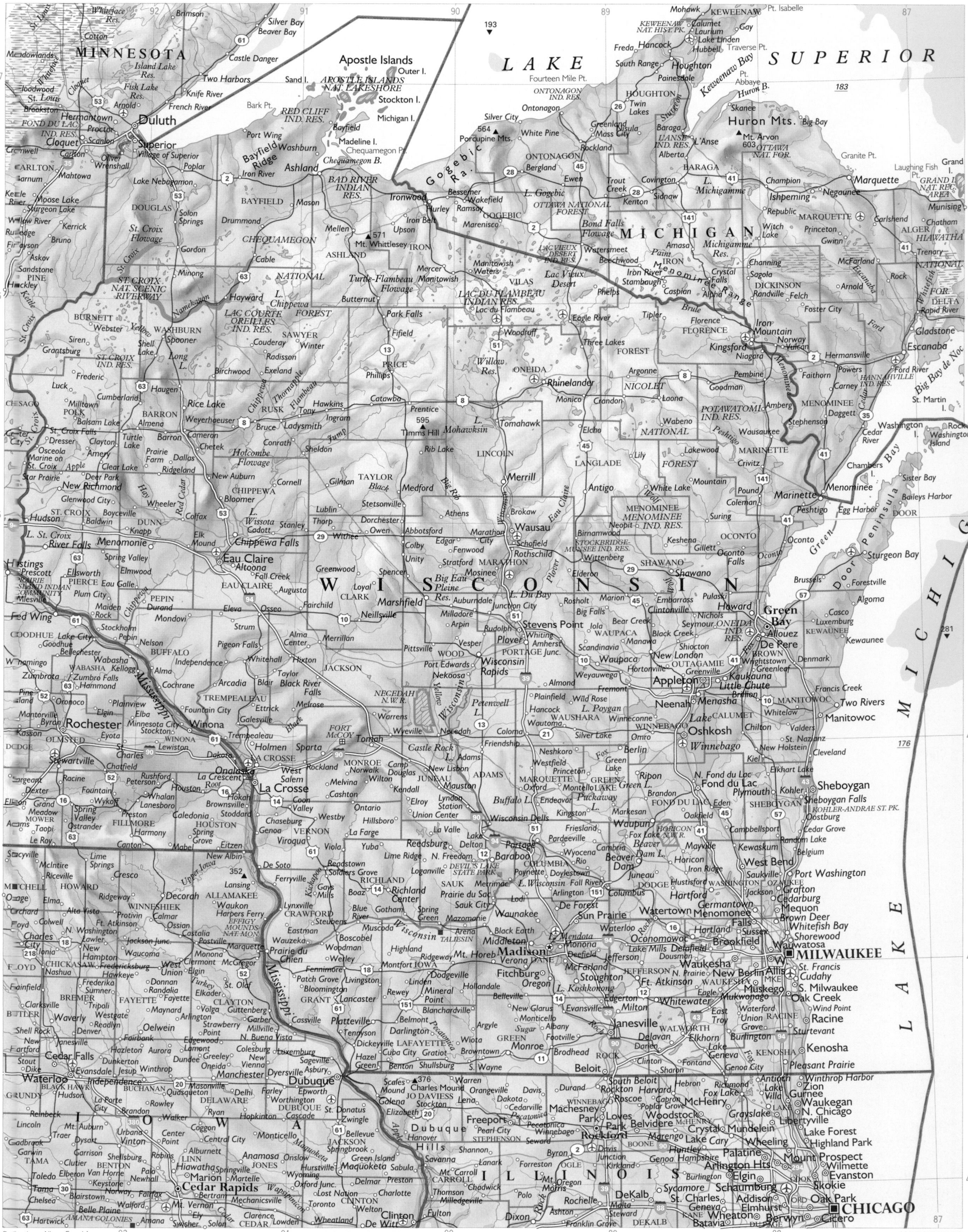

LAKE SUPERIOR

Apostle Islands

APOSTLE ISLANDS NAT. LAKESHORE

Duluth
Superior

MICHIGAN

Gogebic Range

OTTAWA NATIONAL FOREST

Marquette
Escanaba

CHEQUAMEGON NATIONAL FOREST

NICOLET NATIONAL FOREST

Rhinelander

WISCONSIN

Eau Claire
Wausau
Stevens Point

Green Bay
De Pere
Appleton
Neenah
Menasha
Oshkosh
Manitowoc
Two Rivers

La Crosse
Wisconsin Dells
Wisconsin Rapids

Madison
Janesville
Beloit

Milwaukee
Waukesha
Racine
Kenosha
Sheboygan
Fond du Lac

IOWA

Dubuque
Cedar Rapids
Waterloo
Rochester

ILLINOIS

Rockford
Freeport

CHICAGO
Oak Park
Evanston
Elgin
Schaumburg

LAKE MICHIGAN

Door Peninsula
Sturgeon Bay

Mississippi R.

Projection: Albers Equal Area

West from Greenwich

COPYRIGHT PHILIP'S

1:2 100 000

extension north-westwards on same scale

extension westwards on same scale

LAKE SUPERIOR

CANADA
ONTARIO

Isle Royale
ISLE ROYALE NAT PARK
MICHIGAN
LAKE SUPERIOR

Apostle Islands
APOSTLE ISLANDS NAT LAKESHORE
Stockton I.
Michigan I.
ASHLAND
WISCONSIN
PORCUPINE MOUNTAINS WILDERNESS STATE PARK
Porcupine Mts.
Gogebic Range
OTTAWA NATIONAL FOREST
MICHIGAN
ONTONAGON

LAKE SUPERIOR

Keweenaw Pen.
Copper Harbor
Keweenaw Pt.
Houghton
Hancock
Huron Mts.
Marquette
Ishpeming
Negaunee
Munising
PICTURED ROCKS NAT. LAKESHORE
Grand Marais
Whitefish Point
Paradise
Sault Ste. Marie
Newberry
HIAWATHA NATIONAL FOREST
Mackinac Island
CANADA
ONTARIO
Manitoulin Island

MICHIGAN

Escanaba
Gladstone
Garden Pen.
Beaver I.
CHARLEVOIX
Petoskey
Cheboygan
Alpena
Gaylord

WISCONSIN
Marinette
Menominee
Green Bay
DOOR
Sturgeon Bay

LAKE MICHIGAN

Sleeping Bear
SLEEPING BEAR DUNES NAT. LAKESHORE
Traverse City
Grayling
HURON NATIONAL FOREST
Tawas City

Manistee
Cadillac
Houghton Lake
West Branch

Ludington
MANISTEE NATIONAL FOREST
Big Rapids
Mt. Pleasant
Midland
Bay City
Saginaw

Muskegon
Muskegon Heights
Norton Shores
Grand Haven
Grand Rapids
Wyoming
Holland
Lansing
East Lansing
Flint
Port Huron

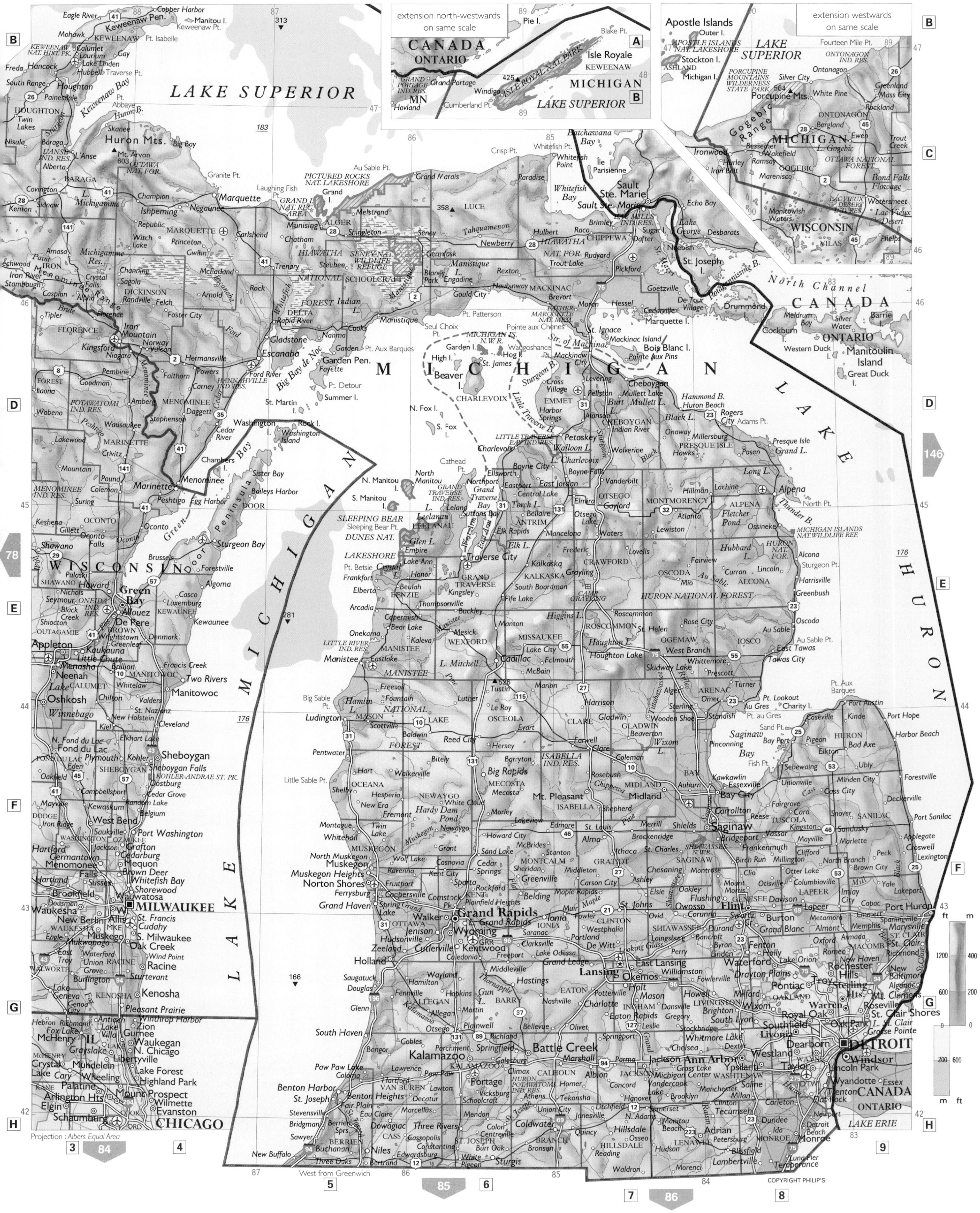

Kalamazoo
Battle Creek
Jackson
Ann Arbor
Ypsilanti
DETROIT
Dearborn
Windsor
CANADA
ONTARIO

Benton Harbor
St. Joseph
Niles
Sturgis
Coldwater
Adrian
Monroe

CHICAGO
Milwaukee
Racine
Kenosha
Waukesha
WISCONSIN
IL

LAKE HURON

LAKE ERIE

Projection : Albers Equal Area

COPYRIGHT PHILIP'S

West from Greenwich

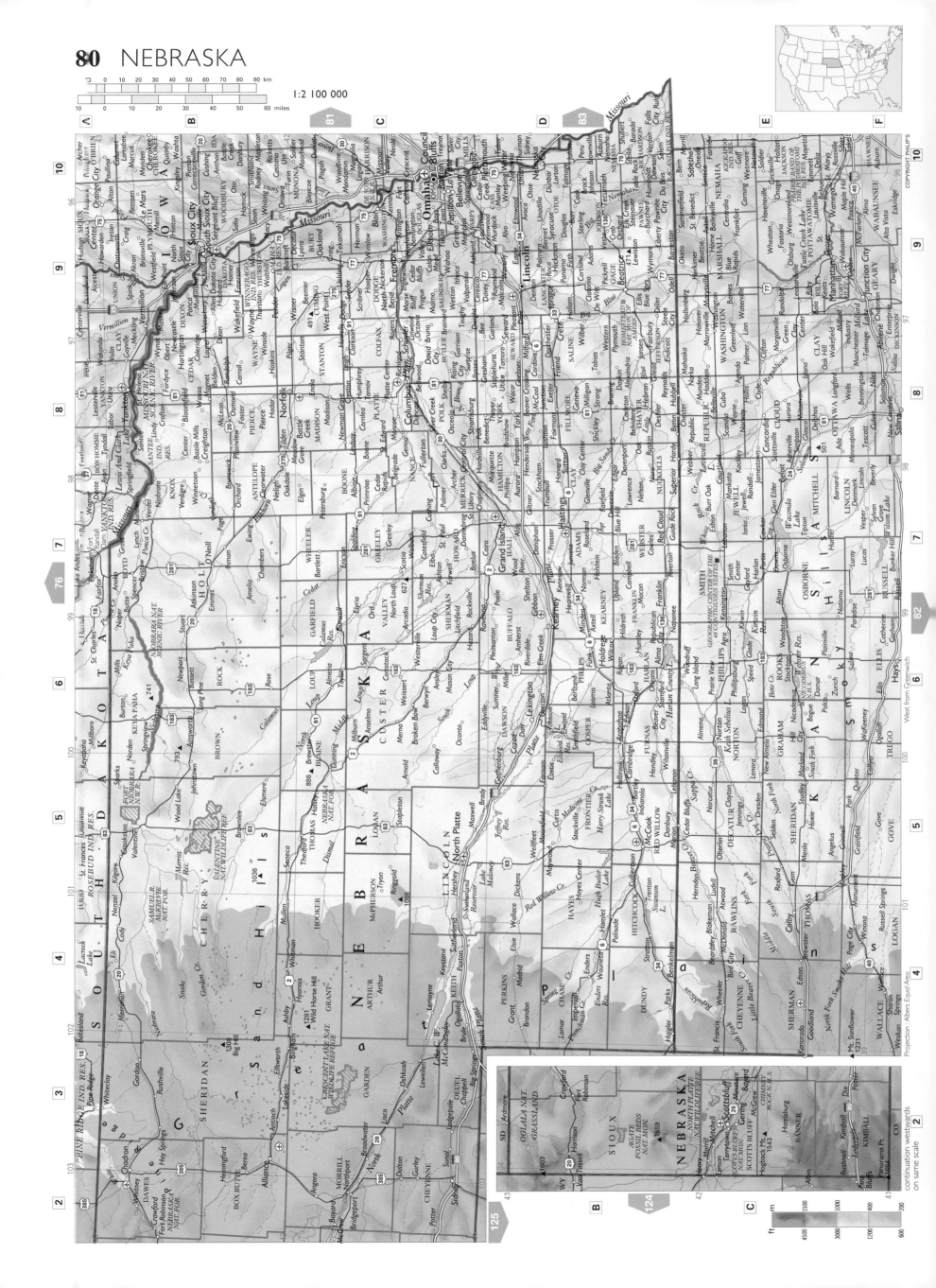

1:2 100 000

Projection: Albers Equal Area

COPYRIGHT PHILIP'S

continuation westwards on same scale

1:2 100 000

10 0 10 20 30 40 50 60 70 80 100 km
10 0 10 20 30 40 50 60 miles

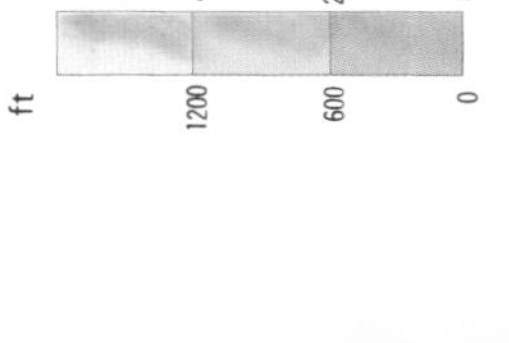

COPYRIGHT PHILIP'S

Projection: Albers Equal Area

West from Greenwich

0 10 20 30 40 50 60 70 80 90 km

1:2 100 000

10 0 10 20 30 40 50 60 miles

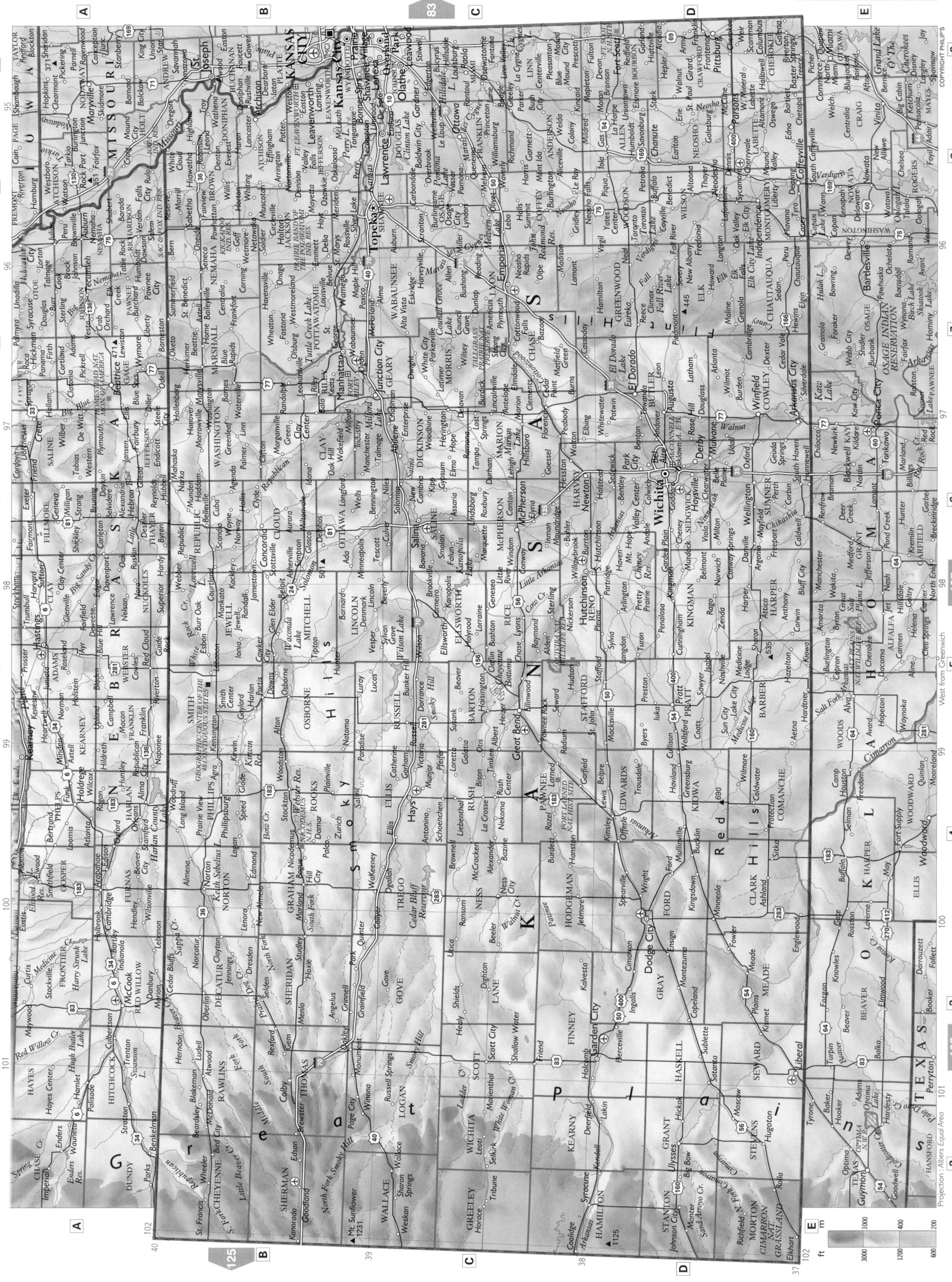

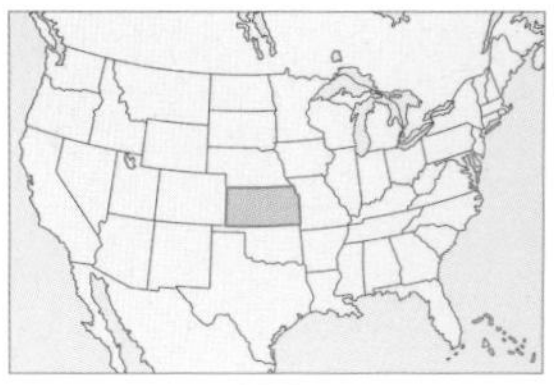

1:2 100 000

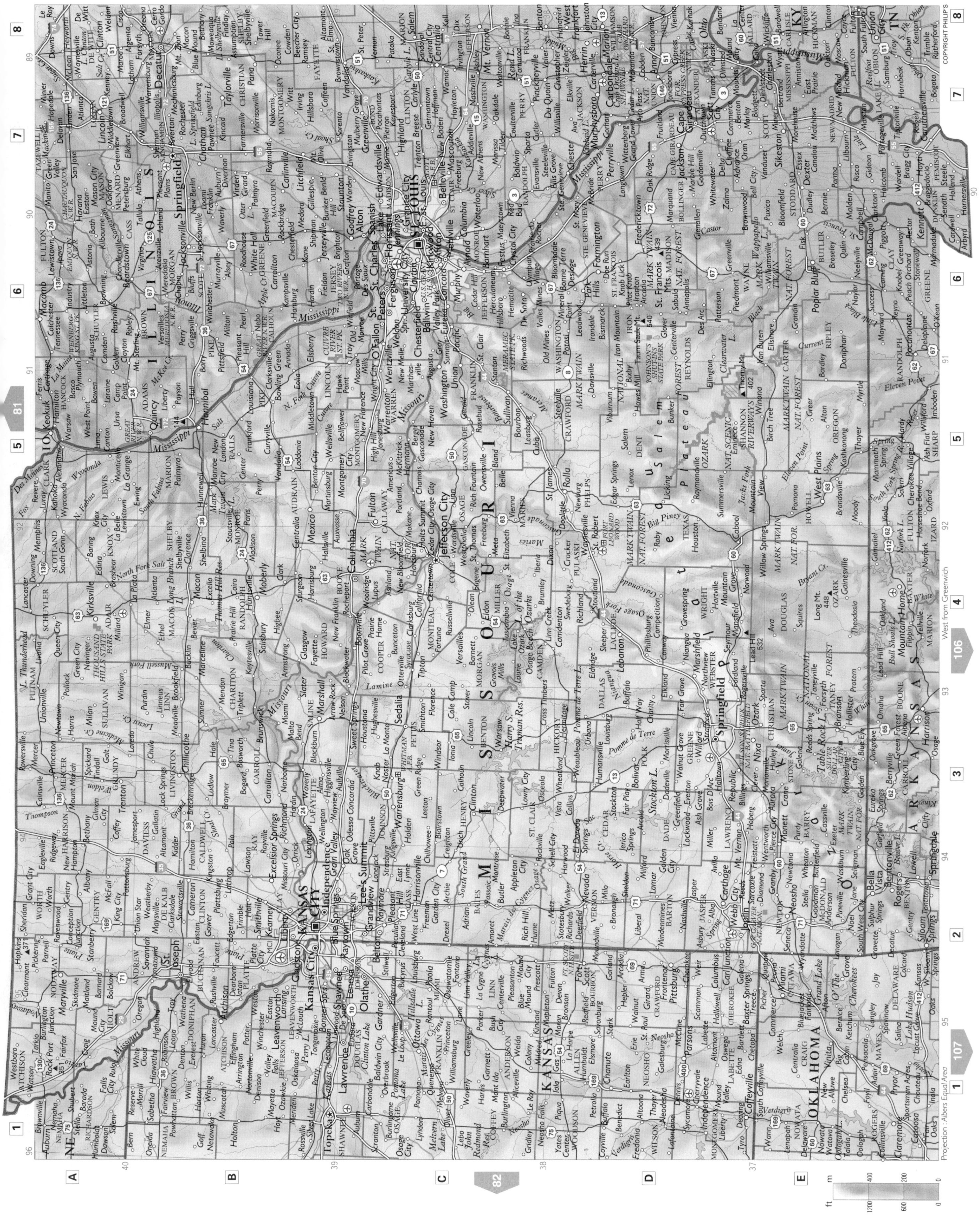

10 0 10 20 30 40 50 60 70 80 90 km

10 0 10 20 30 40 50 60 miles

COPYRIGHT PHILIP'S

West from Greenwich

Projection : Albers Equal Area

1:2 100 000

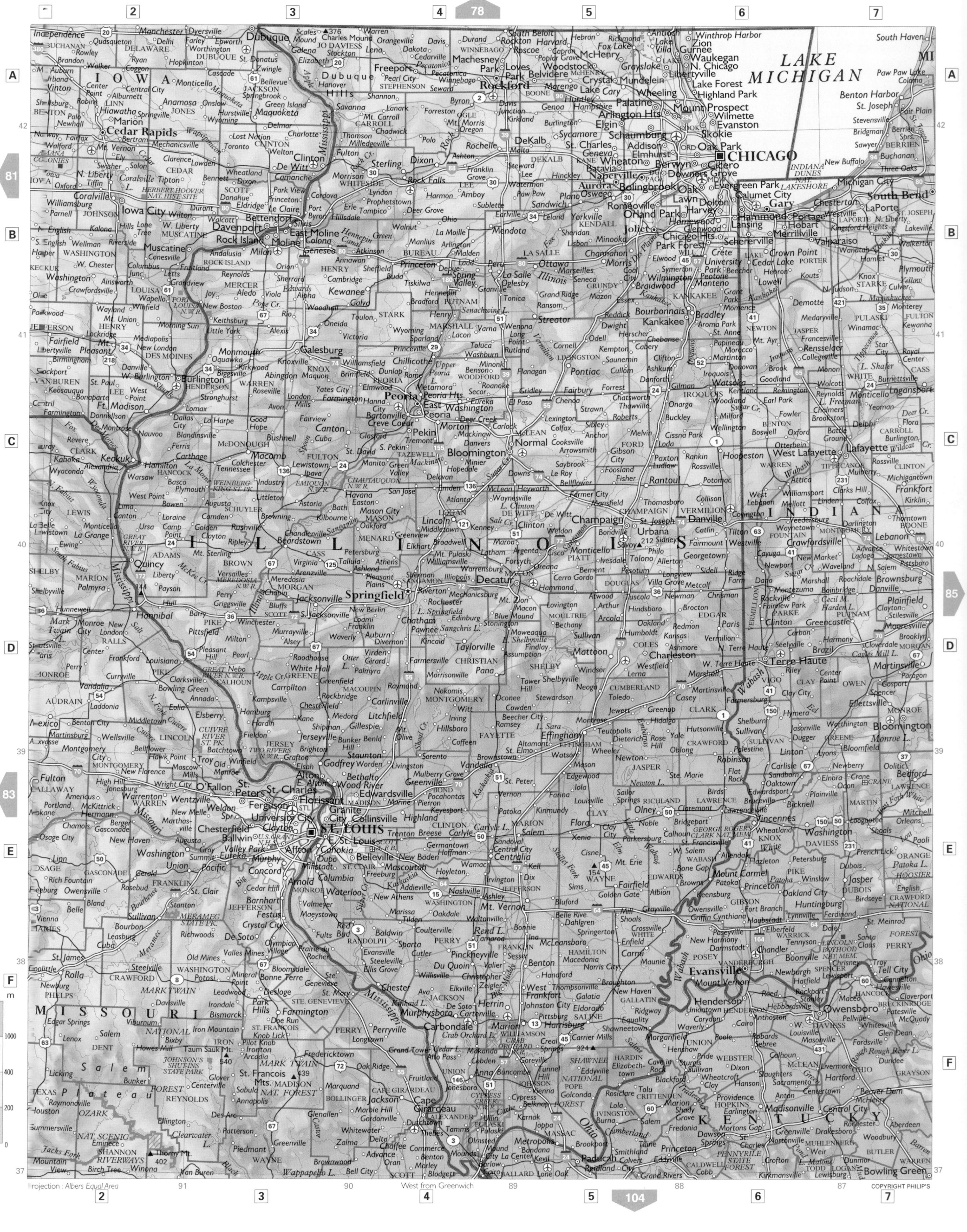

Projection: Albers Equal Area

West from Greenwich

COPYRIGHT PHILIP'S

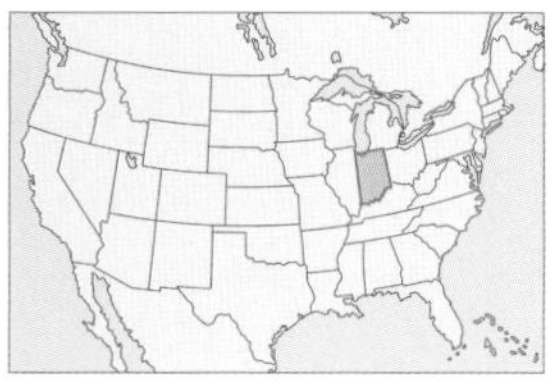

1:2 100 000

10 0 10 20 30 40 50 60 70 80 90 km

10 0 10 20 30 40 50 60 miles

79

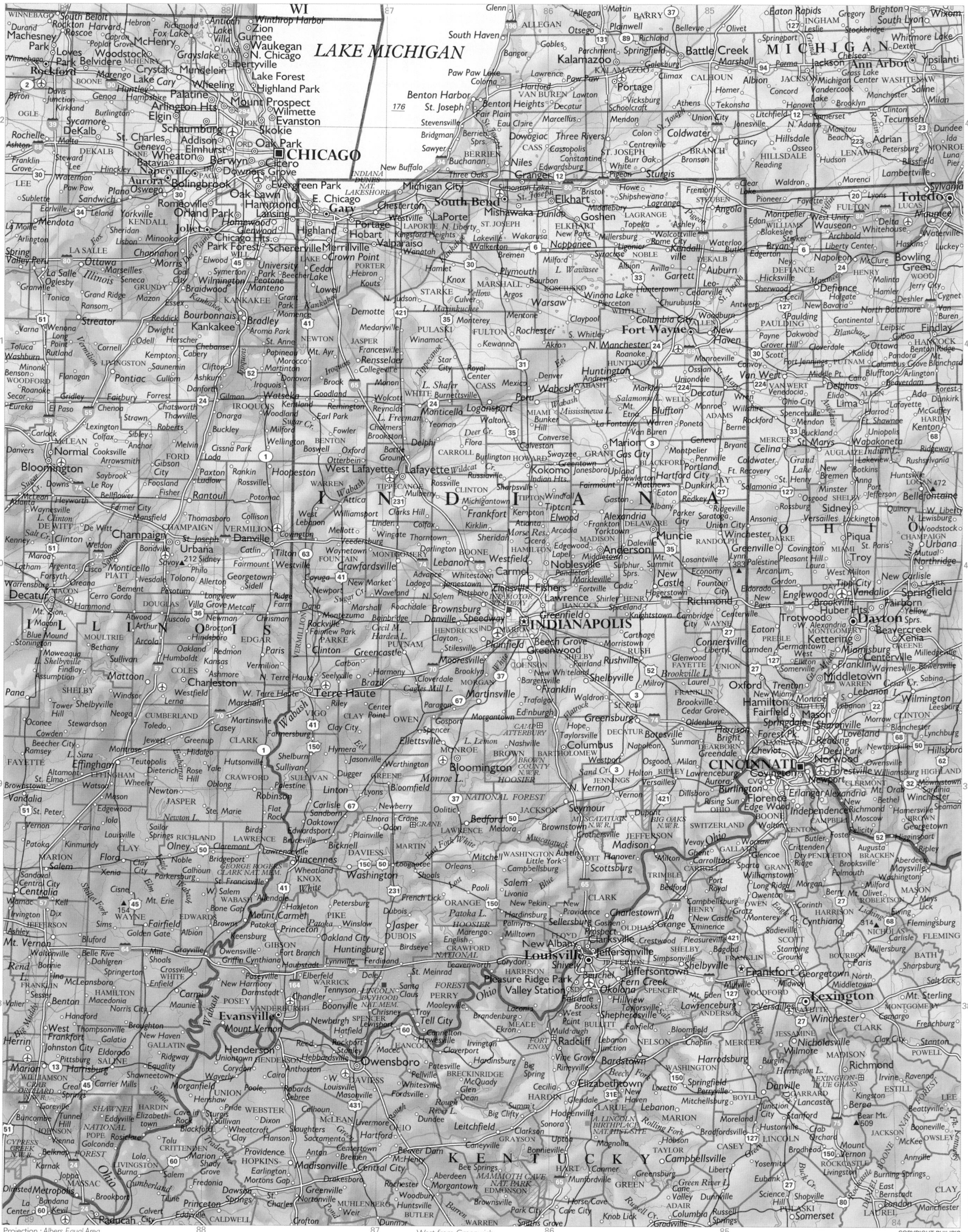

Projection : Albers Equal Area

West from Greenwich

COPYRIGHT PHILIP'S

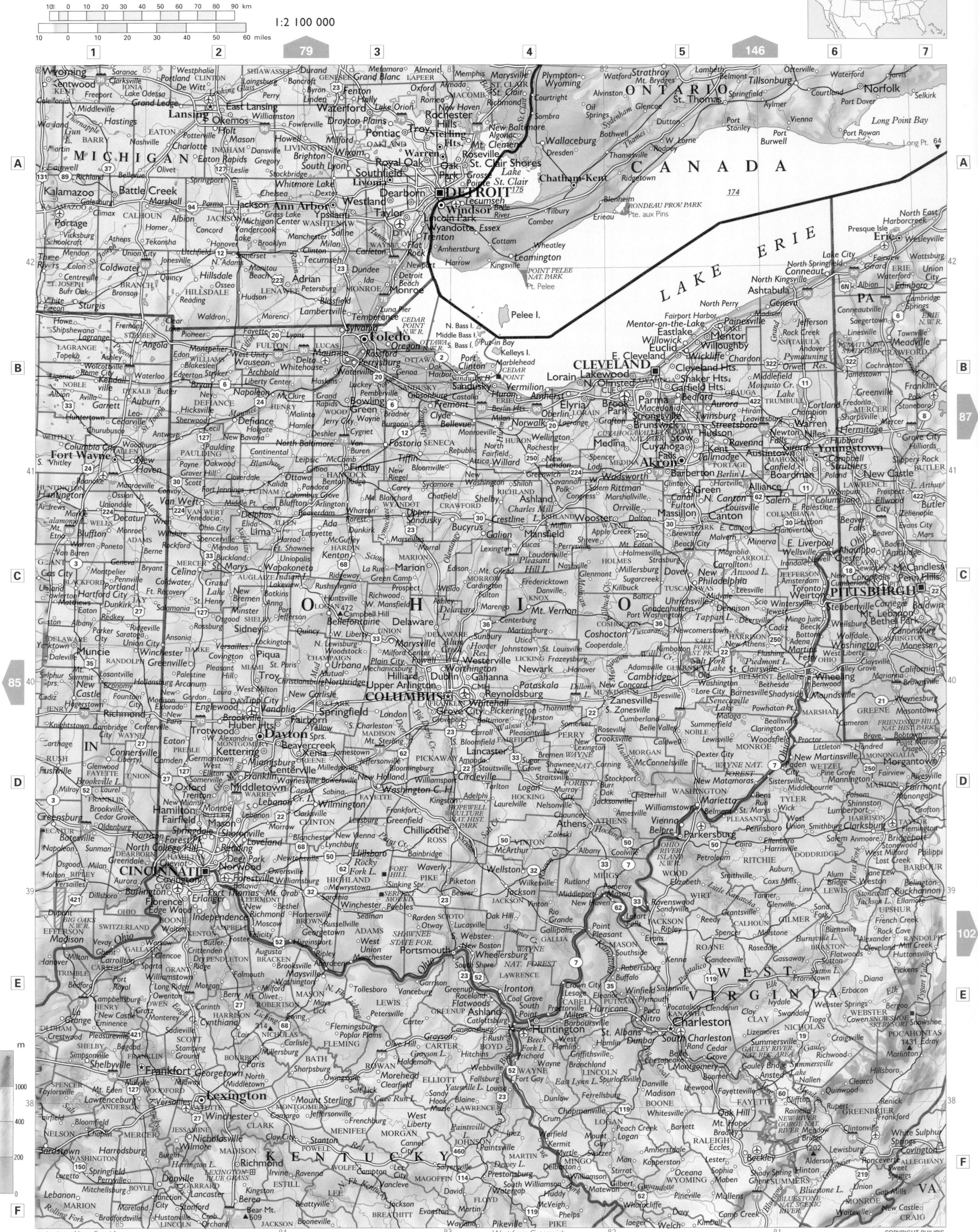
1:2 100 000
km
miles
79
146
87
85
102
105
MICHIGAN
ONTARIO
CANADA
LAKE ERIE
OHIO
PA
IN
KENTUCKY
WEST VIRGINIA
VA
Lake St. Clair
DETROIT
Windsor
Toledo
CLEVELAND
Akron
Canton
Youngstown
Erie
PITTSBURGH
Wheeling
COLUMBUS
Dayton
Springfield
CINCINNATI
Lexington
Frankfort
Huntington
Charleston
Parkersburg
Marietta
Lansing
Ann Arbor
Fort Wayne
Muncie
Findlay
Lima
Mansfield
Zanesville
Portsmouth
Sandusky
Lorain
Chatham-Kent
Pelee I.
Long Point Bay
Projection : Albers Equal Area
West from Greenwich
COPYRIGHT PHILIP'S

1:2 100 000

10 0 10 20 30 40 50 60 70 80 90 100 km
10 0 10 20 30 40 50 60 miles

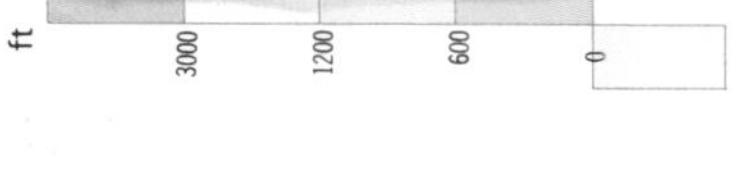

COPYRIGHT PHILIP'S

1. HOPEWELL FURNACE NAT. HIST. PARK
2. VALLEY FORGE NAT. HIST. PARK
3. ALLEGHENY PORTAGE RAILROAD NAT. HIST. SITE

Underlined settlements give their name
to the county in which they stand.

West from Greenwich

Projection : Albers Equal Area

ATLANTIC OCEAN

LAKE ERIE

CANADA

ONTARIO

NEW YORK

NEW JERSEY

PENNSYLVANIA

OHIO

WEST VIRGINIA

VIRGINIA

MARYLAND

DELAWARE

WASHINGTON D.C.

PHILADELPHIA

PITTSBURGH

BALTIMORE

BUFFALO

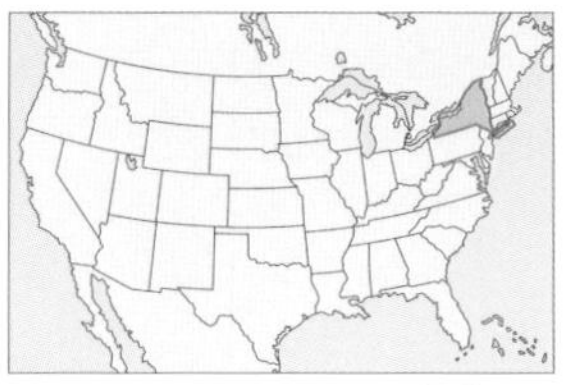

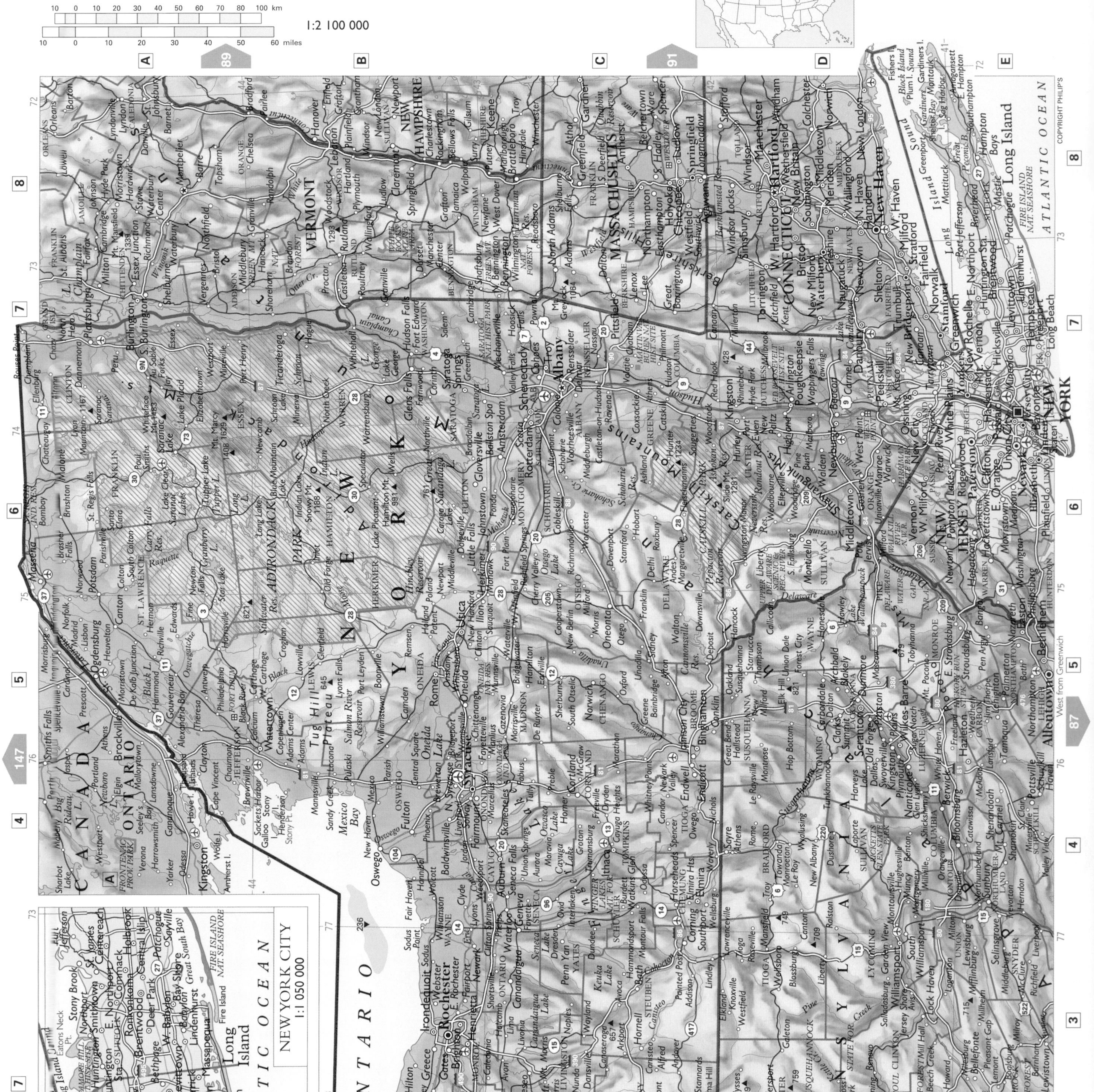

1:2 100 000

10 0 10 20 30 40 50 60 70 80 100 km
10 0 10 20 30 40 50 60 miles

NEW YORK CITY
1:1 050 000

ATLANTIC OCEAN

LAKE ONTARIO

LAKE ERIE

CANADA

ONTARIO

VERMONT

NEW HAMPSHIRE

MASSACHUSETTS

CONNECTICUT

NEW JERSEY

PENNSYLVANIA

N E W   Y O R K

ADIRONDACK PARK

CATSKILL MOUNTAINS

Long Island

Projection: Albers' Equal Area

COPYRIGHT PHILIP'S

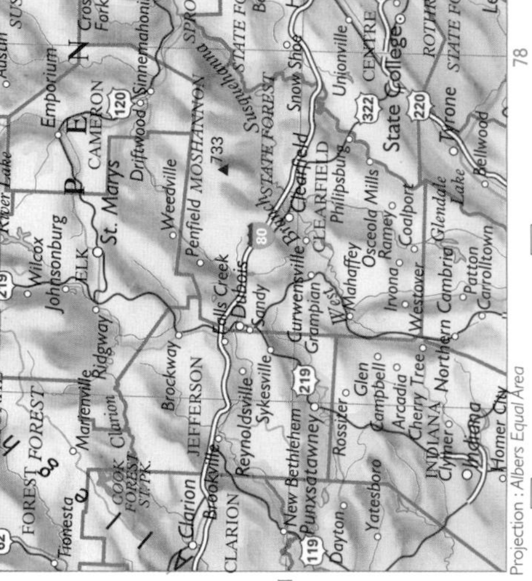

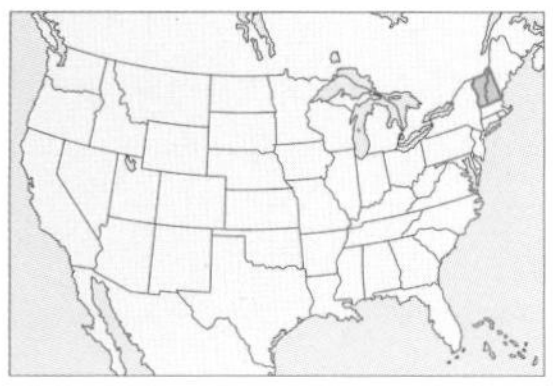

1:1 050 000

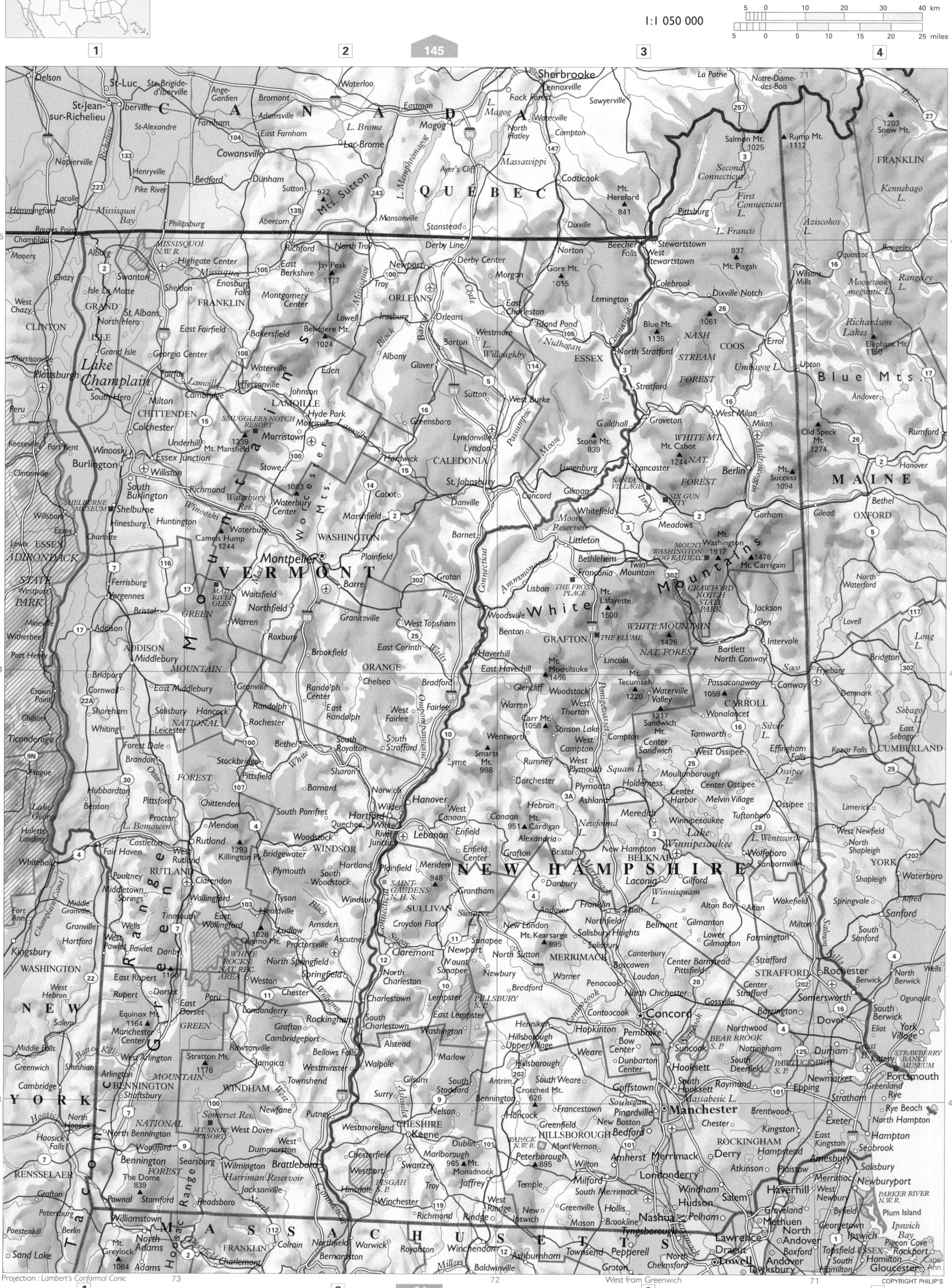

5 0 10 20 30 40 km
5 0 5 10 15 20 25 miles
1 2 3 4
A B C D
145
90
88
91
QUEBEC
CANADA
VERMONT
NEW HAMPSHIRE
MAINE
NEW YORK
MASSACHUSETTS
Lake Champlain
Green Mountains
White Mountains
Blue Mts.
Taconic Range
Hoosac Range
Worcester Mts.
Montpelier
Burlington
Concord
Manchester
Nashua
Portsmouth
Sherbrooke
Plattsburgh
Rutland
Keene
Berlin
Lake Winnipesaukee
Mt. Washington 1917
Mt. Mansfield 1339
WHITE MOUNTAIN NAT. FOREST
GREEN MOUNTAIN NATIONAL FOREST
ADIRONDACK STATE PARK
45
44
43
73
72
71
Projection : Lambert's Conformal Conic
West from Greenwich

ft
m
4500
1500
3000
1000
1200
400
600
200
0
0

COPYRIGHT PHILIP'S

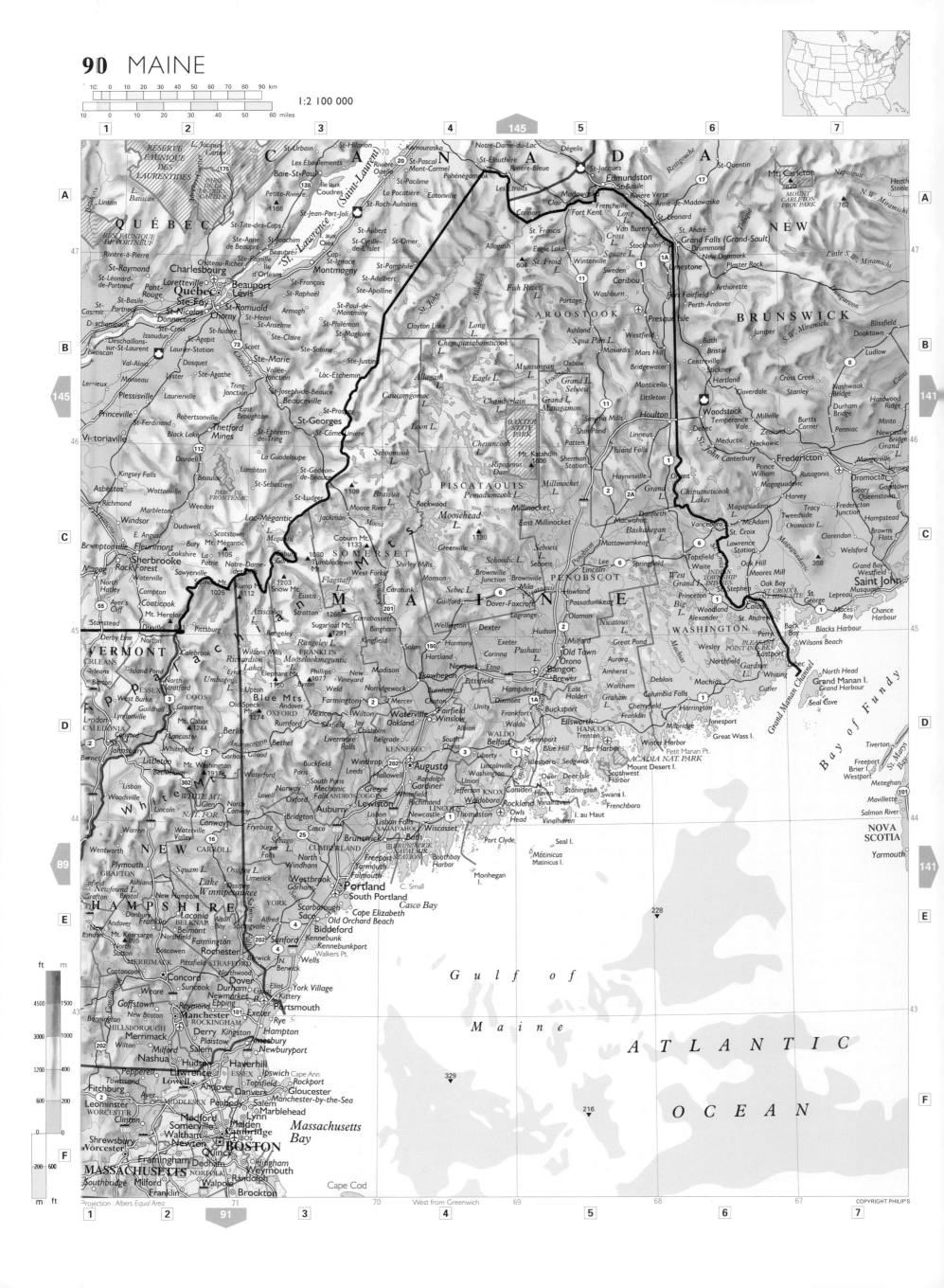

1:1 050 000

40 km
25 miles

COPYRIGHT PHILIP'S

Gulf of Maine

MAINE

Massachusetts Bay

Cape Cod Bay

CAPE COD NATIONAL SEASHORE

Cape Cod

Provincetown
Race Point

North Truro
Wellfleet
South Wellfleet
Eastham
North Eastham
Orleans
Brewster
Dennis
Harwich
Chatham
MONOMOY N.W.R.
Monomoy I.
Monomoy Point

Barnstable
Yarmouth
Hyannis
Centerville
Osterville
Mashpee
Falmouth
Woods Hole
Oak Bluffs
Edgartown

Nantucket Sound

Great Point
Nantucket Harbor
Nantucket
NANTUCKET
Nantucket Island
Siasconset
Chappaquiddick Island

Martha's Vineyard
Vineyard Haven
West Tisbury
Chilmark
DUKES
NOMANS LAND NAT WILDLIFE REFUGE
Nomans Land

ATLANTIC OCEAN

NEW HAMPSHIRE

VERMONT
GREEN MOUNTAIN NATIONAL FOREST
Bennington
BENNINGTON
WINDHAM

NEW YORK
RENSSELAER
COLUMBIA
DUTCHESS
Hudson

MASSACHUSETTS
BERKSHIRE
WORCESTER
HAMPSHIRE
HAMPDEN
FRANKLIN
NORFOLK
BRISTOL
PLYMOUTH
MIDDLESEX
ESSEX
SUFFOLK

BOSTON
Cambridge
Quincy
Newton
Brockton
Plymouth
Springfield
Worcester
New Bedford
Fall River

Gloucester
Rockport
Newburyport
Salem
Marblehead
Lynn

QUABBIN RESERVOIR

CONNECTICUT
HARTFORD
NEW HAVEN
TOLLAND
WINDHAM
NEW LONDON
MIDDLESEX
LITCHFIELD
FAIRFIELD

New Haven
Bridgeport
Norwalk
Stamford
Greenwich
Waterbury
New Britain
Meriden
Norwich
New London

RHODE ISLAND
PROVIDENCE
Warwick
Cranston
Pawtucket
Newport
NEWPORT
Narragansett Bay
Block Island Sound
Block Island (R.I.)

Rhode Island Sound

Long Island Sound

Long Island

NEW YORK
SUFFOLK
WESTCHESTER

Fishers I. (N.Y.)
Gardiners I.
Montauk Point

Projection: Lambert's Conformal Conic

West from Greenwich

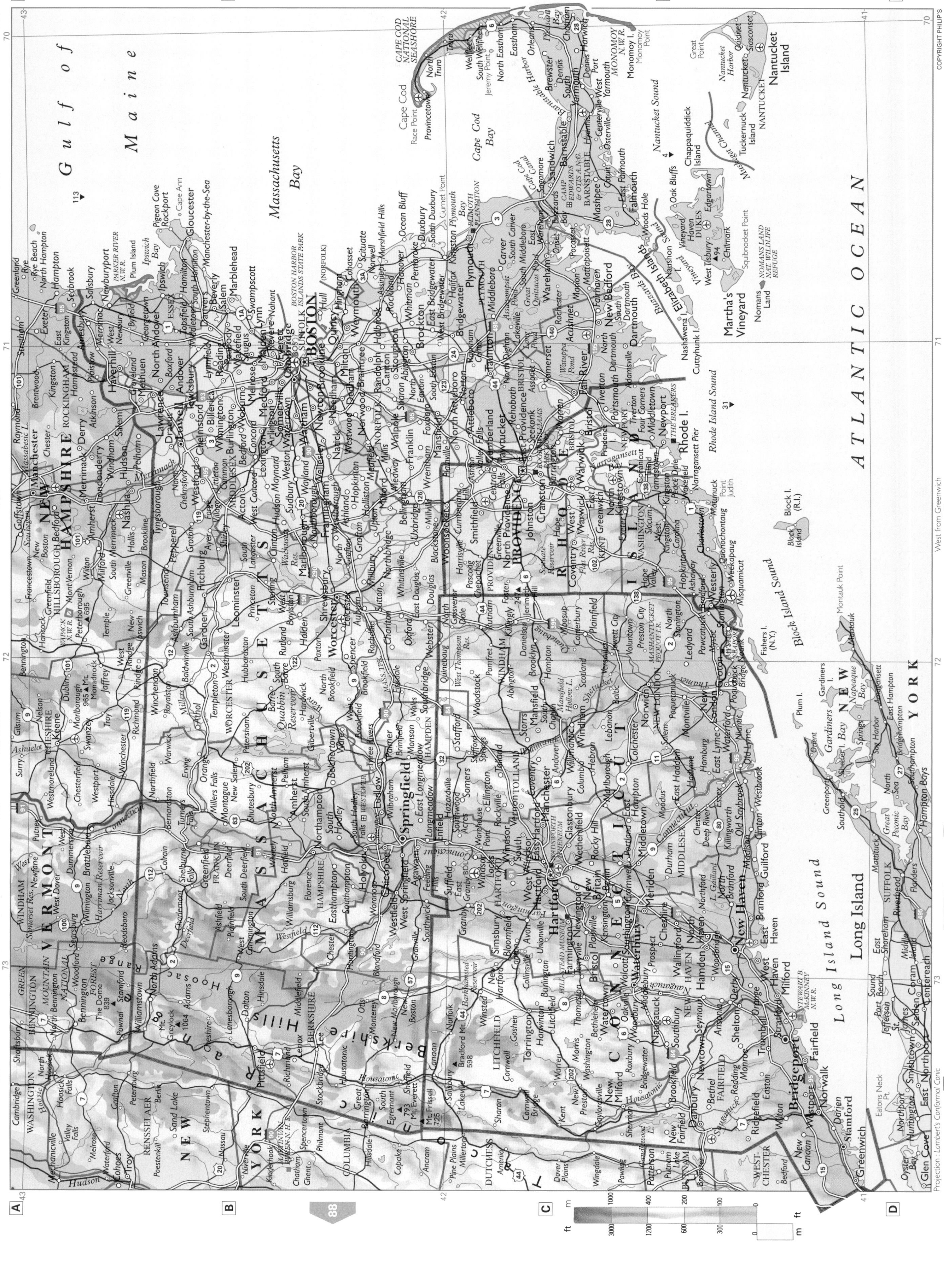

1:1 050 000

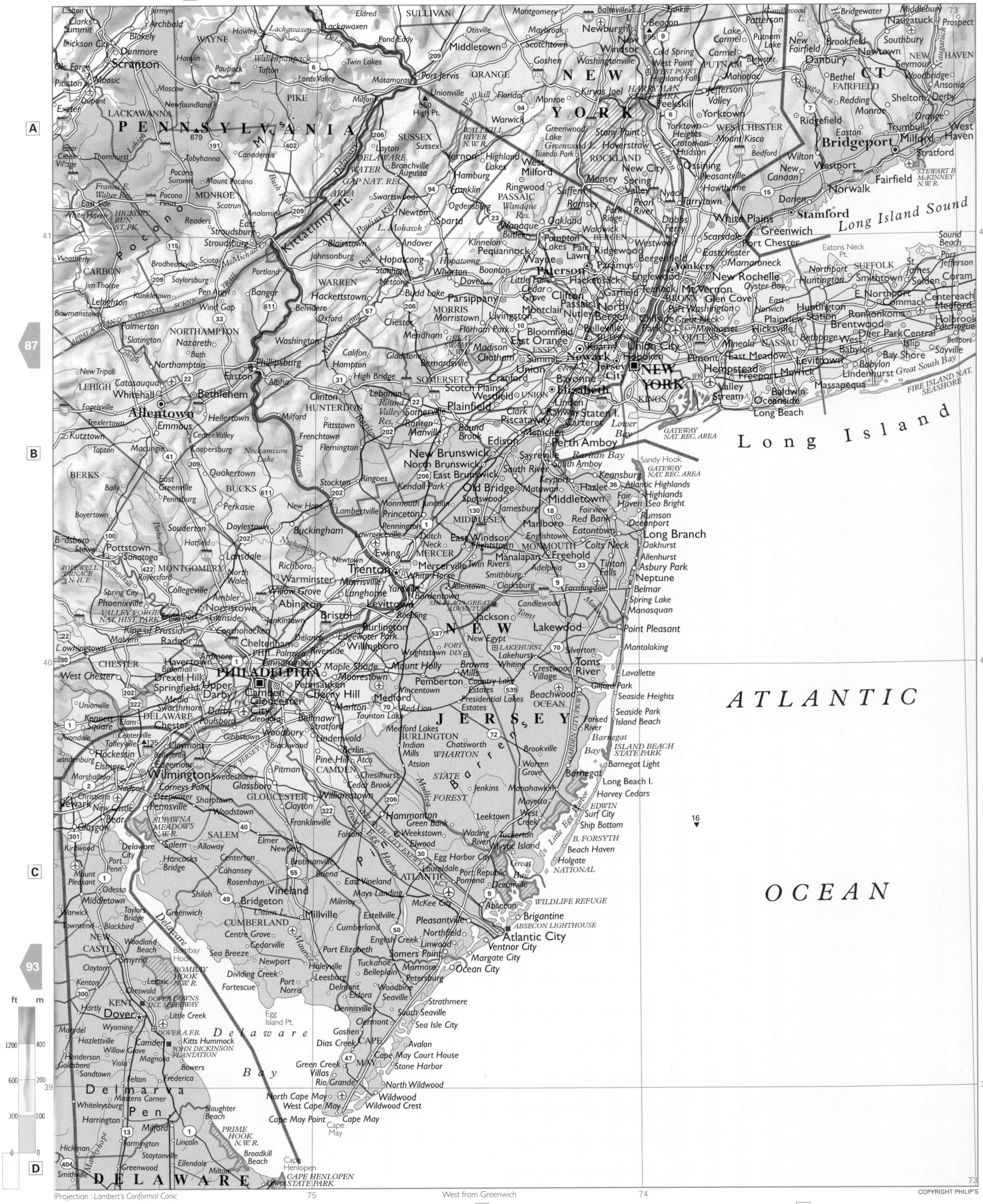

Projection: Lambert's Conformal Conic

West from Greenwich

COPYRIGHT PHILIP'S

PENNSYLVANIA

NEW YORK

NEW JERSEY

DELAWARE

CT

Delaware Bay

ATLANTIC OCEAN

Long Island

Long Island Sound

Delmarva Pen

PHILADELPHIA

NEW YORK

Trenton

Atlantic City

Scranton

Allentown

Wilmington

Dover

1:1 050 000

5   10   20   30   40 km
5   10   15   20   25 miles

ATLANTIC OCEAN

Delaware Bay

Chesapeake Bay

NEW JERSEY

PENNSYLVANIA

DELAWARE

MARYLAND

VIRGINIA

WEST VIRGINIA

PHILADELPHIA

Wilmington

Dover

Baltimore

Annapolis

WASHINGTON

D.C.

continuation westwards on same scale

Projection: Lambert's Conformal Conic

West from Greenwich

COPYRIGHT PHILIP'S

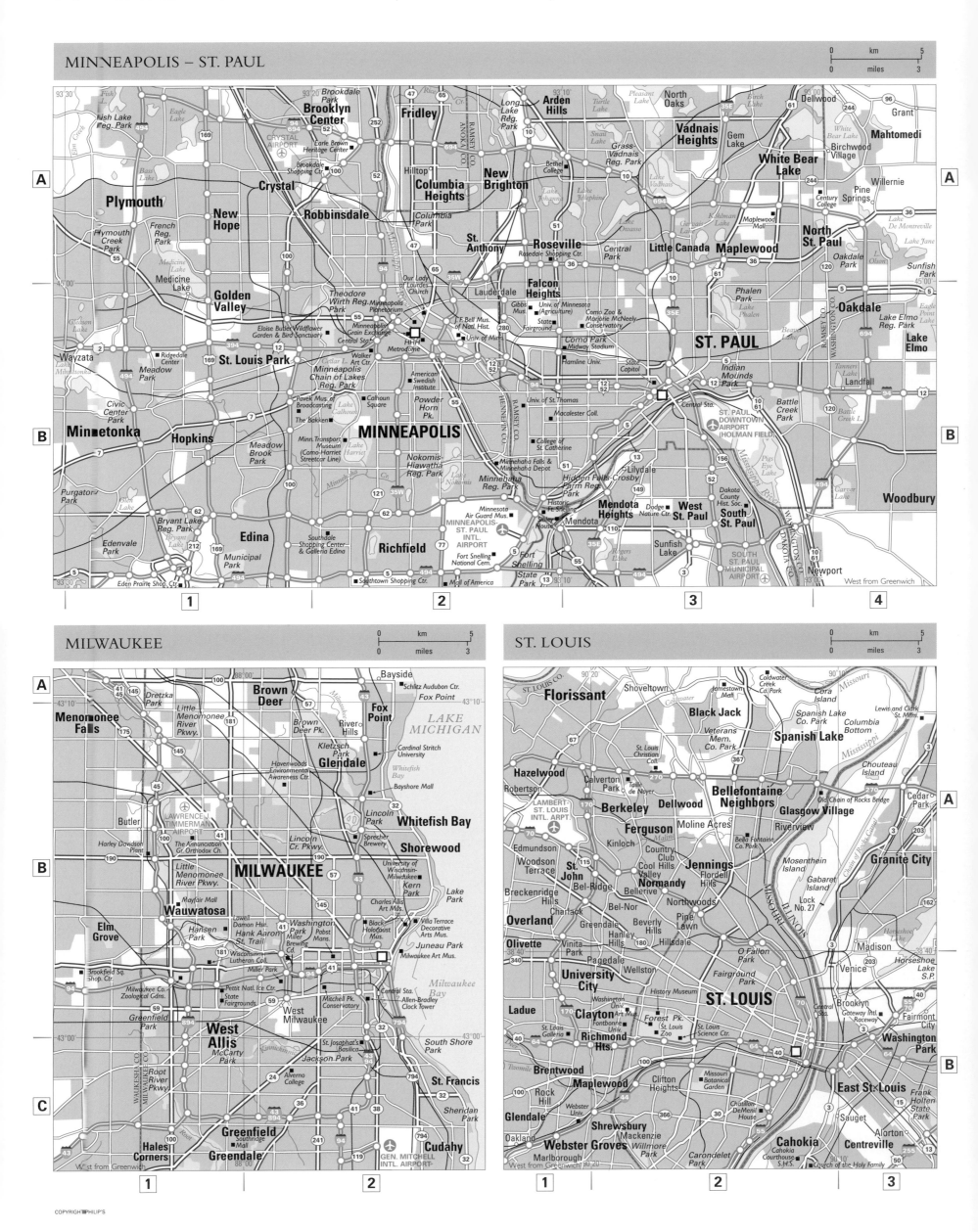

MINNEAPOLIS – ST. PAUL

MILWAUKEE

ST. LOUIS

COPYRIGHT PHILIP'S

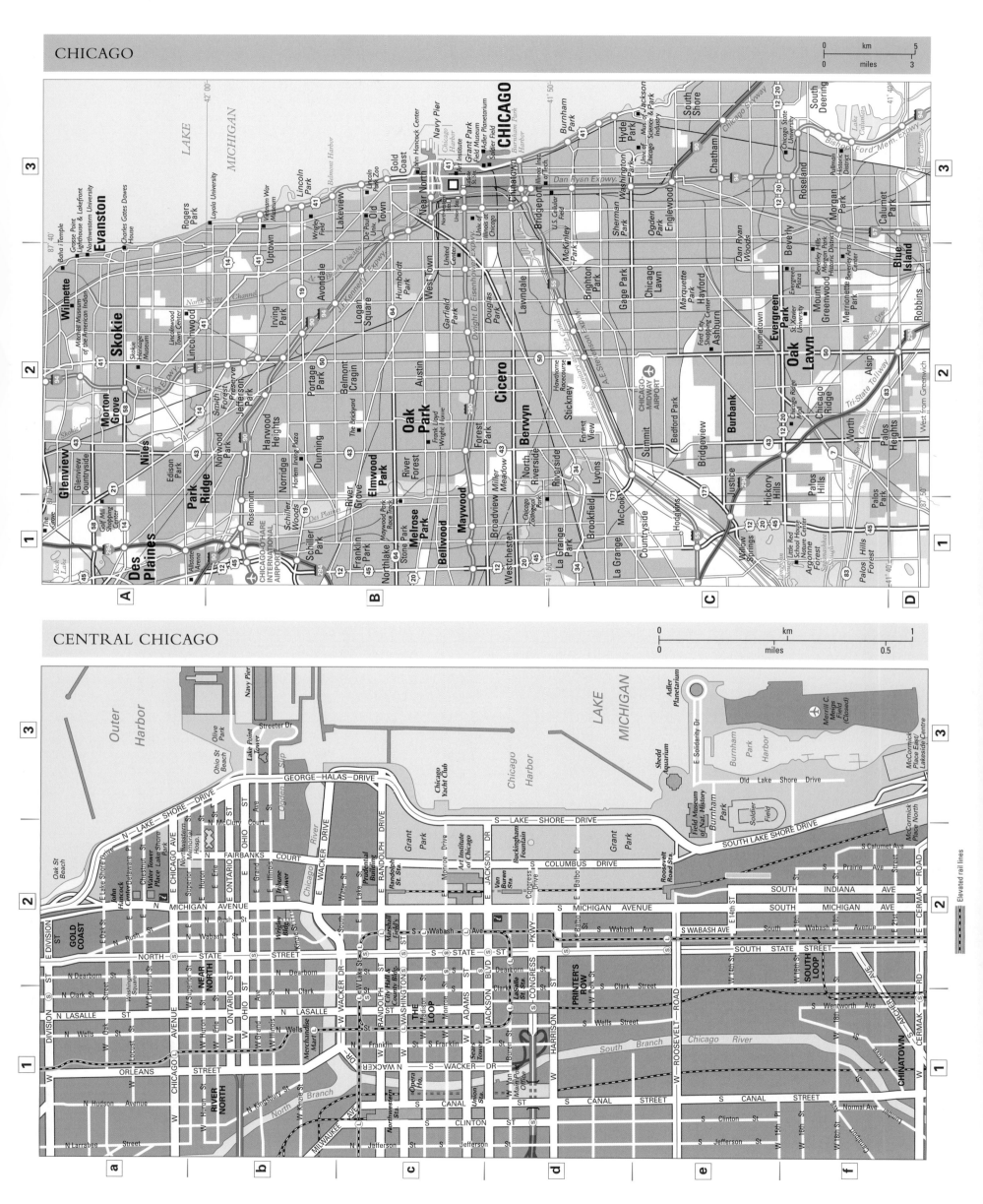

BOSTON

km 5
miles 3

Bedford · Burlington 3A · 71 10 · Wakefield · 129
62 · 225 · Woburn · 38 · North Saugus Breakheart Reservation · Lynn Woods Reservation · 71 00
North Lexington · 3 · Stoneham · 28 · Walter D. Stone Mem. Zoo · Greenwood · 1 Broadway
95 · Middlesex Fells Reservation · 93 · Saugus · Cliftondale
Lexington · 128 · 225 · 114 · Winchester · 38 · West Medford · South Res. · Melrose · Mt. Hood Mem. Park · 107
2A · East Lexington · Arlington Heights · Medford · 28 · Malden · 60
A · Concord Turnpike · 2 · Arlington · 60 · East Arlington · 3 · Tufts Univ. · Wellington · 16 · Everett · Revere · 60 · 16 · 1A · Orient Heights
Belmont · Radcliffe Coll. · Somerville · 93 · Chelsea · Logan Int. Airport
Waltham · 60 · Waverley · Fresh Pond · Harvard University · 28 · Charlestown · East Boston · 145
Prospect Hill Park · Brandeis Univ. · Charles R. · Watertown · 20 · Allston · Mass. Inst. of Tech. · 3 · Bunker Hill Mem. · BOSTON · Ted Williams Tunnel
95 · Auburndale · 90 · Brighton · John F. Kennedy Nat. Hist. Site · Boston Common · Northeastern University · South Boston · Spectacle Island
42 20 · Newton · Newtonville · 9 · Chestnut Hill · Museum of Fine Arts · 3 · Dorchester Hts. Nat. Hist. Site · Old Harbor
16 · Brookline · Roxbury · Blake House · 1 · Thompson Island · 42 20
Wellesley Hills · Newton Heights · Oak Hill · Jamaica Plain · Franklin Park · Grove Hall · Fields Corner · Dorchester Bay · Squantum
B · Needham · 128 · Cutler Park · 203 · Arnold Arboretum · 28 · Dorchester · 203 · North Quincy · Quincy Bay
135 · 95 · W. Roxbury · Roslindale · 203 · Wollaston
109 · Mattapan · Hyde Park · Stony Brook Res. · 93 · 138 · Milton · 3A · Wollaston
Dedham · 10 · 28 · Quincy · 71 00

1 · **2**

CENTRAL BOSTON

km 1
miles 0.5

CHARLESTOWN · Old Ironside (U.S.S. Constitution) · Boston Harbor
MSGR. O'BRIEN HIGHWAY · RUTHERFORD AVE · Hoosac Pier · **a**
Museum of Science · North Point Park · Paul Revere Park · ZAKIM BRIDGE · CHARLESTOWN BRIDGE · North End Playground · Battery Wharf · Sumner Tunnel
Charles River · Nashua Street Park · North Station · WASHINGTON ST · NORTH END · Commercial · Battery St. · Lincoln Wharf · Callahan Tunnel
WEST END · Fleet Center · Copper · Union Wharf · **A**
LONGFELLOW BRIDGE · Mass General Hospital · Merrimac St · Revere House · Sargents Wharf · Lewis Wharf
CAMBRIDGE STREET · City Hall · Holocaust Memorial · Clinton St · Commercial Wharf
BEACON HILL · Myrtle St · Pinckney St · Vernon · State House · Faneuil Hall Marketplace · Long Wharf · **b**
STORROW DRIVE · Mount · Charles · Chestnut · Frog Pond · Post Office Square Park · New England Aquarium
BEACON · STREET · Boston Common · Franklin · Channel
Common Wealth Ave · Newbury · Boylston · Public Garden · Avery St · Chauncy · Federal Courthouse
ARLINGTON ST · BOYLSTON ST · Park Plaza · Bedford St · Boston Tea Party Ship & Mus. · MOAKLEY BRIDGE
St James Ave · Essex St · Beach · South Station · Children's Museum · **c**
COLUMBUS AVE · STUART ST · TREMONT · CHINATOWN · Purchase · SOUTH BOSTON
Stuart · Piedmont St · Kneeland · The Wang Center · Bus Terminal · Fort

1 · **2** · **3**

CENTRAL NEW YORK

km 2
miles 1

HARLEM · QUEENS · To JFK International Airport · WILLIAMSBURG · **3**
Central Park · Jacqueline Kennedy Onassis Res. · Metropolitan Museum of Art · UPPER EAST SIDE · JACKSON AVE · McGuinness BOULEVARD · GREENPOINT · BROOKLYN
Transverse Rd No. 4 · Guggenheim · Roosevelt Island · United Nations Headquarters · Queens-Midtown Tunnel · East River · US Naval Reserve Center
UPPER WEST SIDE · Transverse Rd No. 3 · The Lake · Transverse Rd No. 2 · Frick Collection · Central Park Zoo · QUEENSBORO BRIDGE · Wallabout Bay · WILLIAMSBURG BRIDGE
American Mus. of Natural History · EAST 57TH ST · St. Patrick's Cathedral · Chrysler Building · LOWER EAST SIDE · Kent · Navy
Lincoln Center for Performing Arts · WEST 57TH ST · Rockefeller Center · Grand Central Sta. · Bellevue Medical Center · EAST VILLAGE · FLATBUSH AVE · **2**
Columbus Circle · Times Square · Bryant Park · Main Library · Empire State Building · MANHATTAN · Madison Square · ADAMS ST
Broadway · Port Authority Bus Terminal · Penn Sta. · Madison Square · Flatiron Building · Union Square · GREENWICH VILLAGE · LITTLE ITALY · Criminal Ct. Bldg. · N.Y. State Office · MANHATTAN BRIDGE · BROOKLYN HEIGHTS
Passenger Ship Terminal · CHELSEA · SOHO · CHINA TOWN · Municipal Bldg. · BROOKLYN BRIDGE
Intrepid Air & Space Museum · Jacob Javits Convention Center · TWELFTH AVENUE · ELEVENTH AVE · WEST STREET · Woolworth City Hall Building · South St Seaport
Hudson River · WEST NEW YORK · GUTTENBERG · **1**
WEEHAWKEN · Lincoln Tunnel · Holland Tunnel to Newark · World Financial Center · Ground Zero (Site of former World Trade Center) · Battery Park · Ellis I. & Statue of Liberty · Governors Island · Staten Island Ferry · Brooklyn-Battery Tunnel
UNION CITY · HOBOKEN · Hudson River · J.F. KENNEDY BOULEVARD · 10 AVE

a · **b** · **c** · **d** · **e** · **f**

COPYRIGHT PHILIP'S

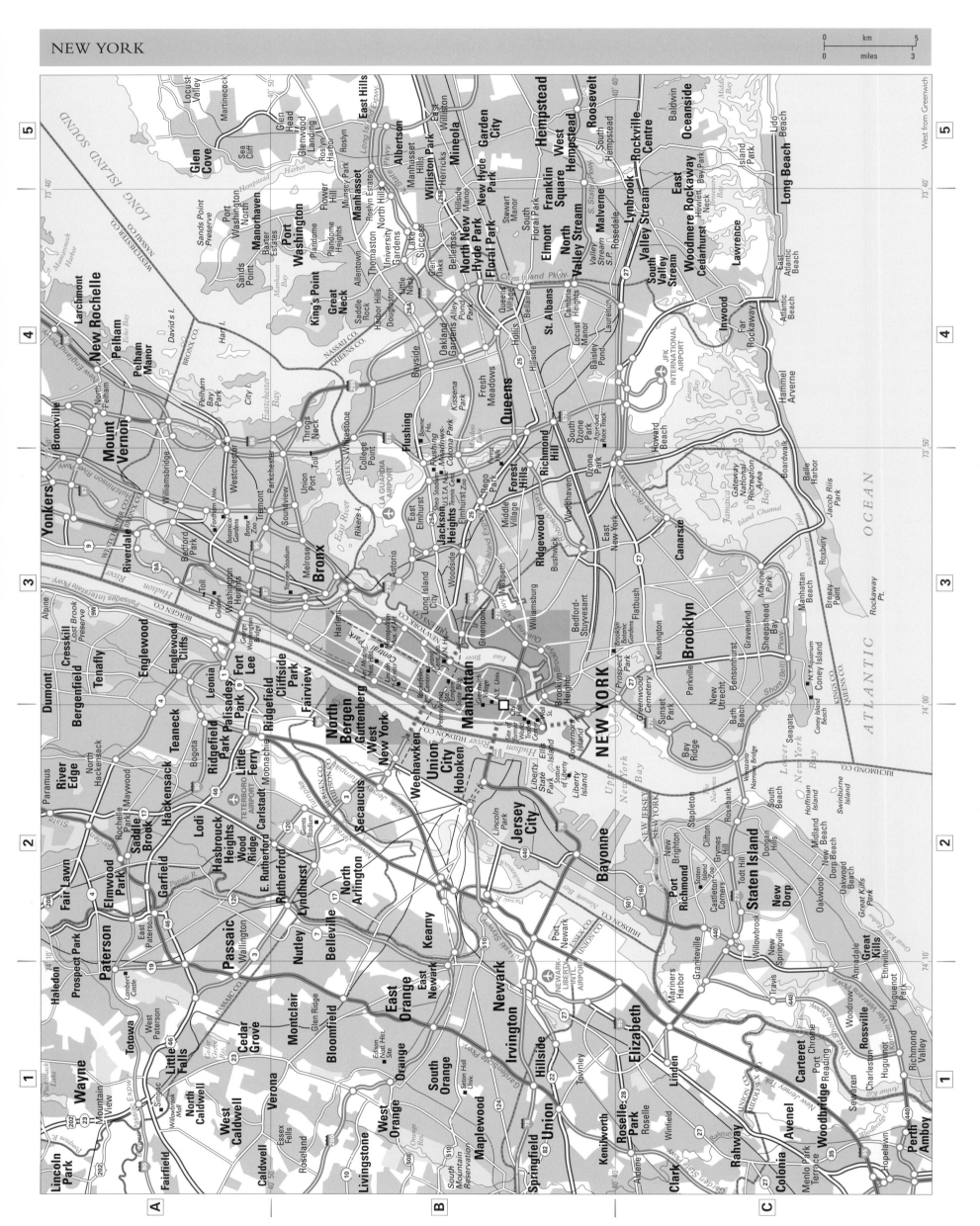

COPYRIGHT PHILIP'S

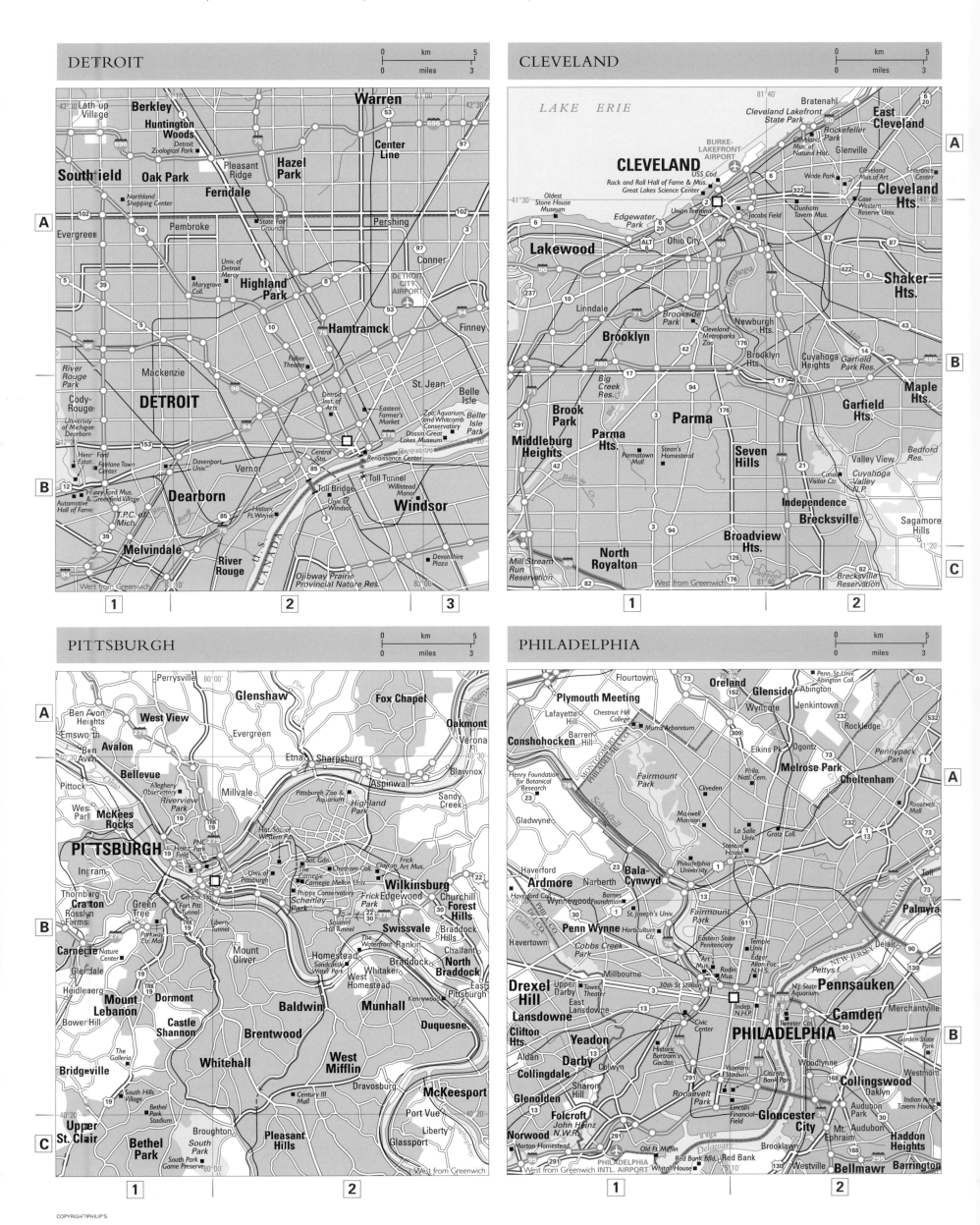

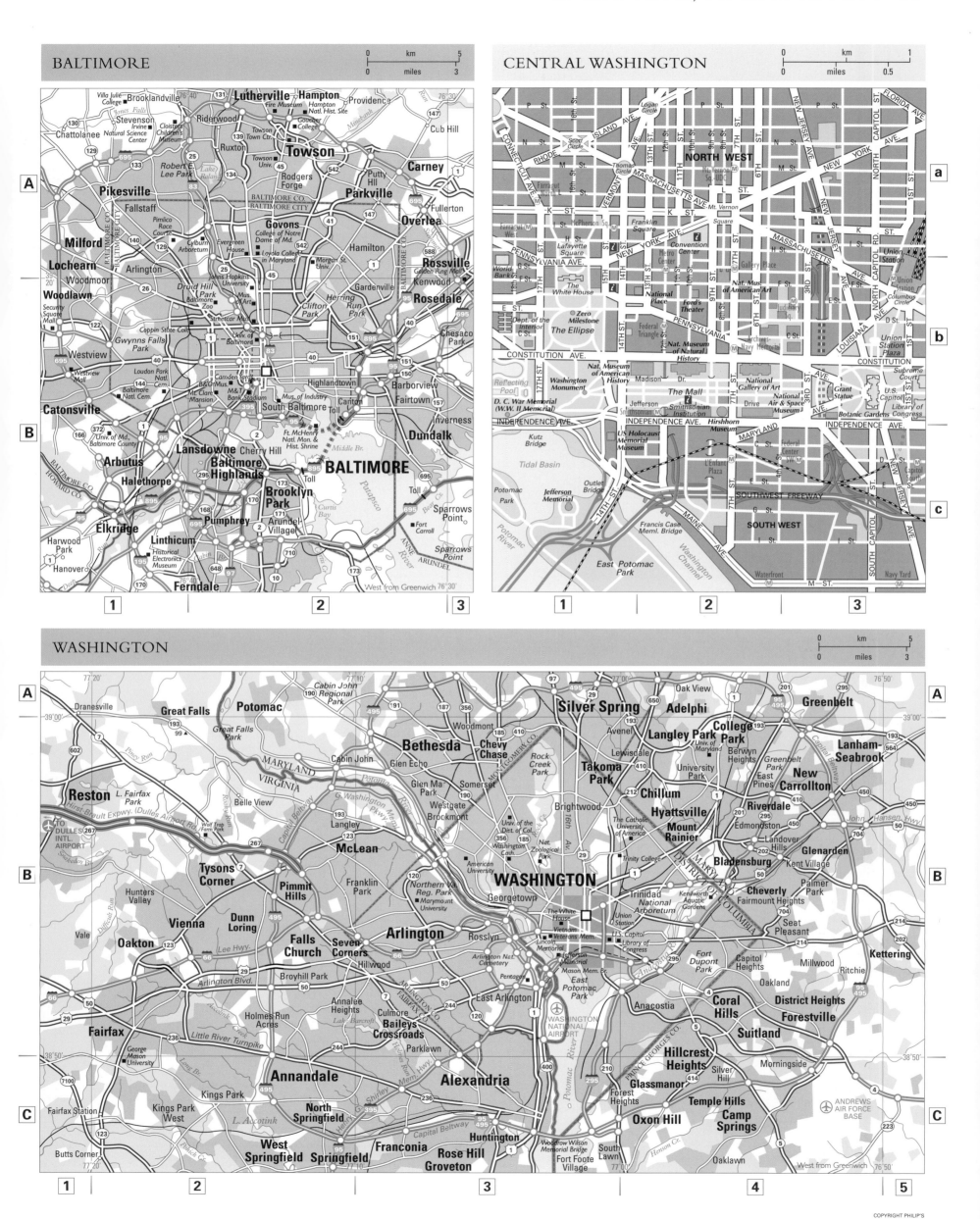

BALTIMORE

km 5
miles 3

Villa Julie College
Brooklandville
Jones Falls
Stevenson
Cloisters Children's Museum
Irvine Natural Science Center
Chattolanee
Lutherville
Hampton
Fire Museum
Hampton Natl. Hist. Site
Providence
Riderwood
Ruxton
Towson Town Ctr.
Towson Univ.
Rodgers Forge
Towson
Carney
Cub Hill
Putty Hill
Parkville
Pikesville
Fallstaff
Baltimore Co.
Baltimore City
Robert E. Lee Park
Lake Roland
Pimlico Race Course
Govons
College of Notre Dame of Md.
Fullerton
Overlea
Milford
Cylburn Arboretum
Evergreen House
Loyola College in Maryland
Morgan St. Univ.
Hamilton
Rossville
Golden Ring Mall
Lochearn
Woodmoor
Arlington
Druid Hill Park
Baltimore Zoo
Johns Hopkins University
Mus. of Art
Gardenville
Kenwood
Woodlawn
Security Square Mall
Coppin State Coll.
Gwynns Falls Park
Streetcar Mus.
Univ. of Baltimore
Clifton Park
Herring Run Park
Rosedale
Westview
Westview Mall
Loudon Park Natl. Cem.
Baltimore Natl. Cem.
Highlandtown
Chesaco Park
Catonsville
Univ. of Md. Baltimore County
Mt. Clare Mansion
B&O Mus.
Camden Yards
M&T Bank Stadium
Mus. of Industry
Canton
South Baltimore
Barborview
Fairtown
Inverness
Arbutus
Halethorpe
Cherry Hill
Baltimore Highlands
BALTIMORE
Middle Br.
Dundalk
Lansdowne
Brooklyn Park
Fort Carroll
Sparrows Point
Elkridge
Pumphrey
Arundel Village
Curtis Bay
Sparrows Point
Harwood Park
Hanover
Linthicum
Historical Electronics Museum
Ferndale
West from Greenwich

CENTRAL WASHINGTON

km 1
miles 0.5

Logan Circle
NORTH WEST
Scott Circle
Mt. Vernon Sq.-UDC
Thomas Circle
Farragut North
Terraplein West
McPherson Sq.
Franklin Square
Lafayette Square
Convention Center
Metro Center
Gallery Place
Union Station
World Bank Co.
The White House
National Place
Ford's Theater
Nat. Mus. of American Art
Judiciary
Union Station Plaza
Columbus Circle
Dept. of the Interior
Zero Milestone
The Ellipse
Federal Triangle
Pennsylvania
Archives-Navy Memorial
Supreme Court
CONSTITUTION AVE.
Nat. Museum of Natural History
Nat. Museum of American History
Madison
National Gallery of Art
Grant Statue
U.S. Capitol
Library of Congress
Reflecting Pool
Washington Monument
The Mall
Jefferson
Smithsonian Institution
National Air & Space Museum
Botanic Gardens
D. C. War Memorial (W.W. II Memorial)
INDEPENDENCE AVE.
Hirshhorn Museum
INDEPENDENCE AVE.
Kutz Bridge
US Holocaust Memorial Museum
L'Enfant Plaza
Federal Center
Tidal Basin
Potomac Park
Outlet Bridge
SOUTHWEST FREEWAY
Jefferson Memorial
SOUTH WEST
Francis Case Meml. Bridge
Potomac River
East Potomac Park
Washington Channel
Waterfront
Navy Yard

WASHINGTON

km 5
miles 3

Dranesville
Cabin John Regional Park
Oak View
Greenbelt
Great Falls
Potomac
Silver Spring
Adelphi
Great Falls Park
Woodmont
Langley Park
College Park
Lanham-Seabrook
Reston
L. Fairfax Park
Bethesda
Chevy Chase
Avenel
Univ. of Maryland
Berwyn Heights
Hirst-Brault Expwy. (Dulles Airport Rd.)
Wolf Trap Farm Park
Cabin John
Glen Echo
Lewisdale
University Park
Greenbelt Park
East Pines
New Carrollton
TO DULLES INTL. AIRPORT
Glen Mar Park
Somerset
Takoma Park
Chillum
Riverdale
MARYLAND
VIRGINIA
Westgate
Brockmont
Rock Creek Park
Hyattsville
Mount Rainier
Edmonston
Landover Hills
Langley
Brightwood
Glenarden
McLean
Univ. of the Dist. of Col.
Washington Cath.
Nat. Zoological Park
The Catholic University of America
Kent Village
Tysons Corner
Franklin Park
American University
Trinity College
District of Columbia
Bladensburg
Palmer Park
Pimmit Hills
Northern Va. Reg. Park
Marymount University
WASHINGTON
Cheverly
Fairmount Heights
Vienna
Dunn Loring
Georgetown
Trinidad National Arboretum
Kenilworth Aquatic Gardens
Seat Pleasant
Oakton
Falls Church
Seven Corners
Arlington
Rosslyn
The White House
Union Station
U.S. Capitol
Library of Congress
Kettering
Hillwood
Vietnam
Veterans Mem.
Lincoln Memorial
Jefferson Memorial
Fort Dupont Park
Oakland
Ritchie
Broyhill Park
Arlington Blvd.
Arlington Nat. Cemetery
Pentagon
Mason Mem. Br.
East Potomac Park
Capitol Heights
Millwood
Annalee Heights
Culmore
East Arlington
Fort Dupont Park
Coral Hills
District Heights
Fairfax
Holmes Run Acres
Little River Turnpike
Baileys Crossroads
Parklawn
Anacostia
Forestville
WASHINGTON NATIONAL AIRPORT
Suitland
George Mason University
Hillcrest Heights
Morningside
Annandale
Alexandria
Silver Hill
Glassmanor
Forest Heights
Temple Hills
Camp Springs
ANDREWS AIR FORCE BASE
Kings Park
North Springfield
Oxon Hill
Fairfax Station
Kings Park West
L. Accotink
West Springfield
Springfield
Franconia
Rose Hill
Groveton
Huntington
Woodrow Wilson Memorial Bridge
Fort Foote Village
South Lawn
Fort Foote
Oaklawn
Butts Corner
West from Greenwich

COPYRIGHT PHILIP'S

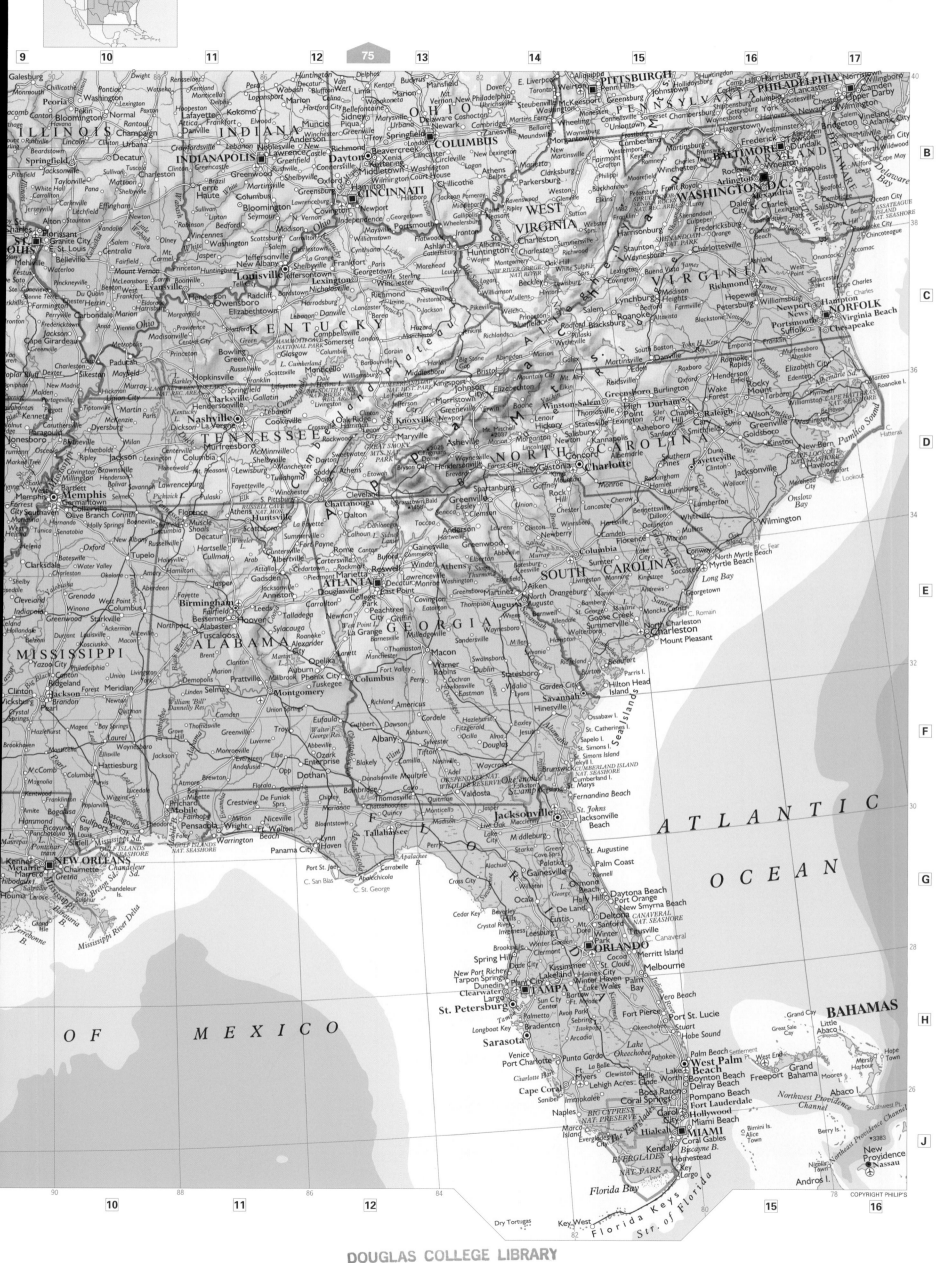

DOUGLAS COLLEGE LIBRARY

Underlined settlements give their name
to the county in which they stand

1:2 100 000

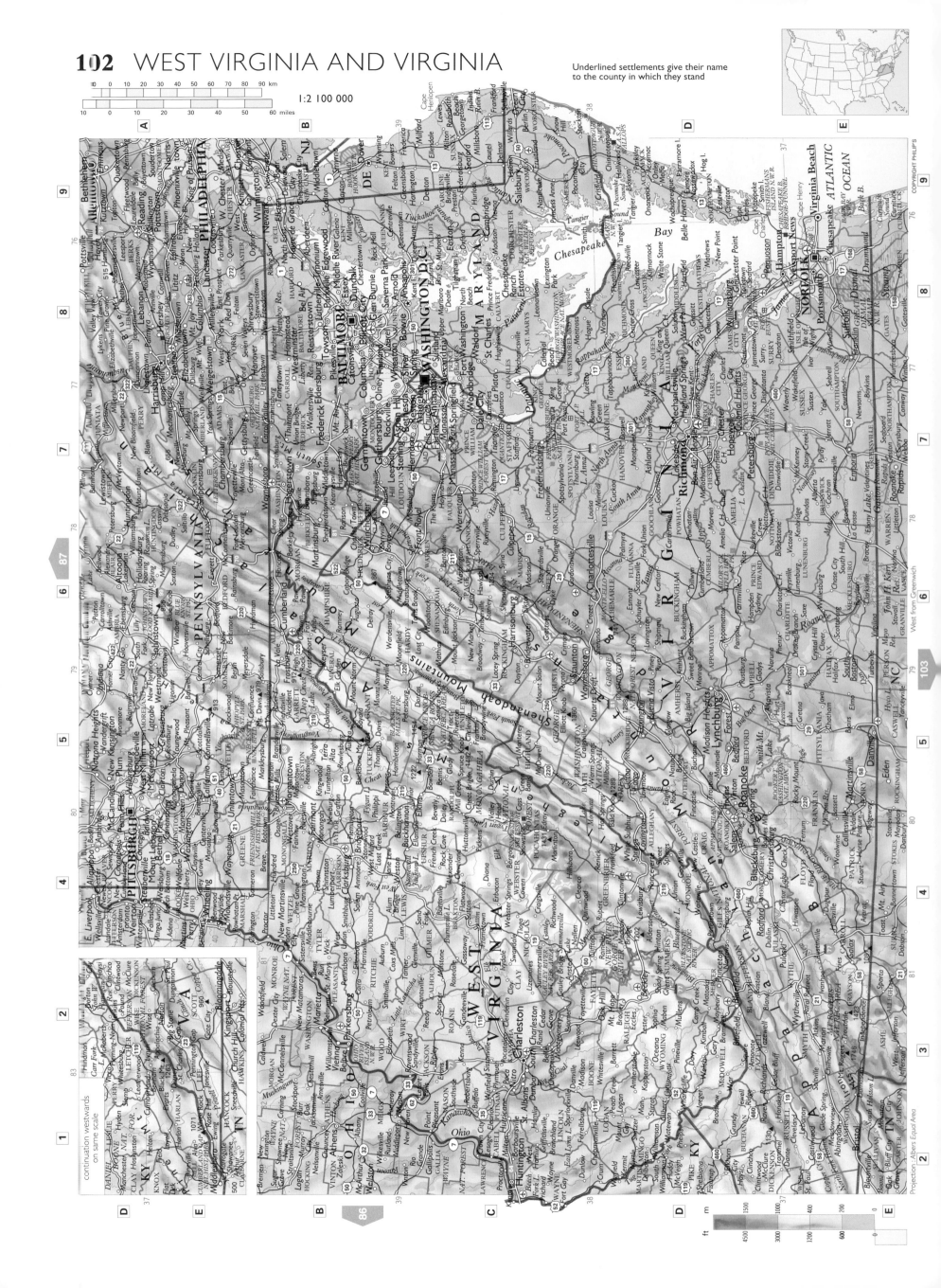

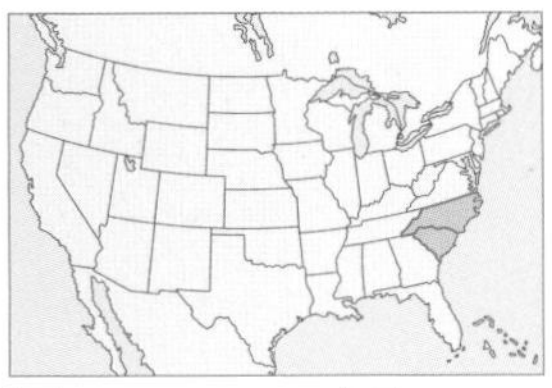

1:2 500 000

ATLANTIC OCEAN

VIRGINIA

NORTH CAROLINA

SOUTH CAROLINA

GEORGIA

TN

Norfolk
Virginia Beach
Hampton
Newport News
Chesapeake
Portsmouth
Suffolk

Raleigh
Durham
Chapel Hill
Greensboro
Winston-Salem
High Point
Charlotte
Gastonia
Asheville
Rocky Mount
Greenville
Wilson
Goldsboro
New Bern
Jacksonville
Wilmington
Myrtle Beach
North Myrtle Beach
Georgetown
Charleston
Mount Pleasant
Columbia
Sumter
Florence
Spartanburg
Greenville
Augusta
Savannah
Hilton Head
Beaufort

continuation westwards on same scale

West from Greenwich

Projection: Albers Equal Area

COPYRIGHT PHILIP'S

m ft
4500 / 15000
3000 / 9000
1200 / 3000
600 / 1200
400 / 600
200 / 0
0 / -200
-600

km
100 0 10 20 30 40 50 60 70 80 90 100 km
miles
10 0 10 20 30 40 50 60 70 miles

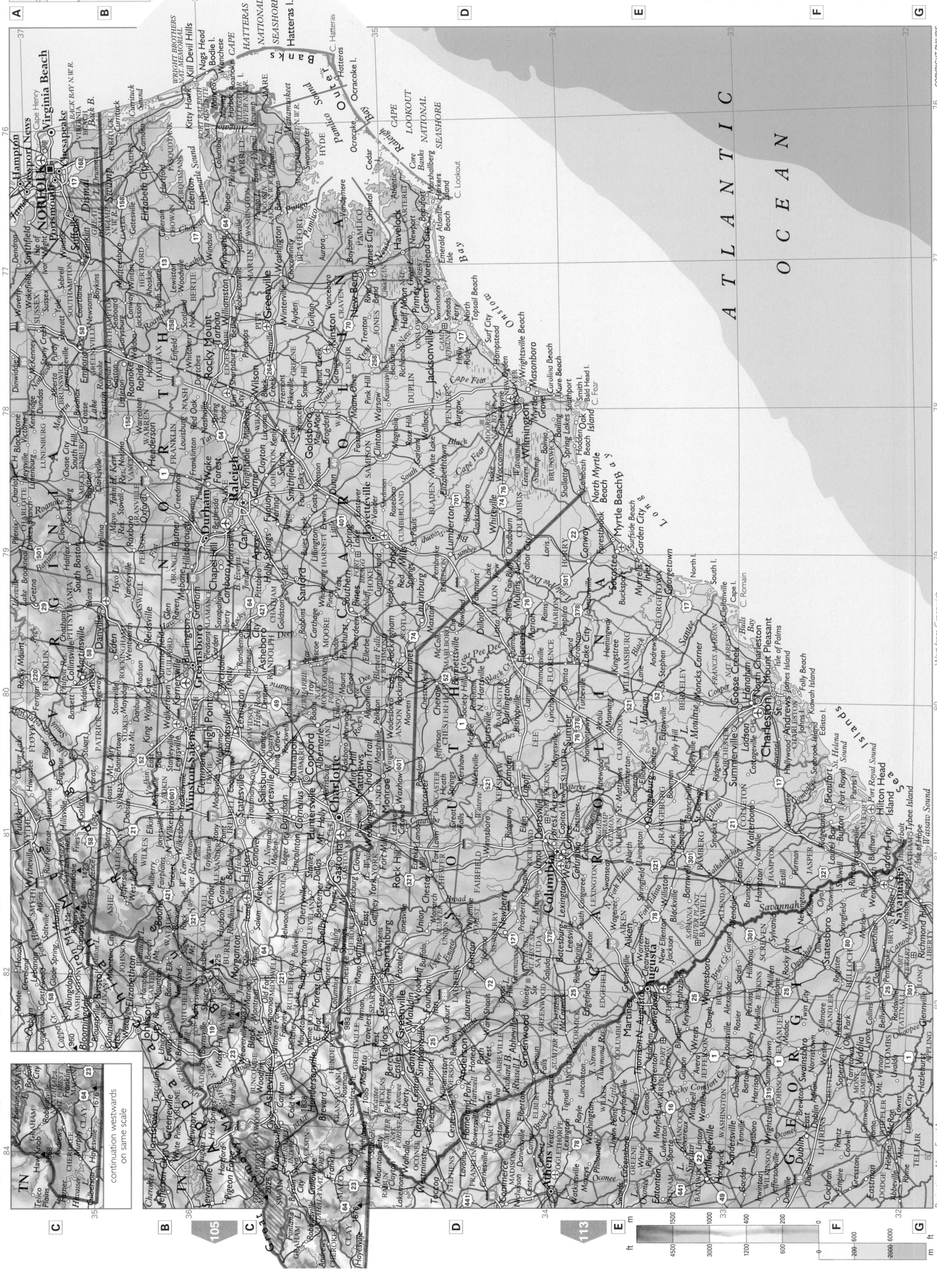

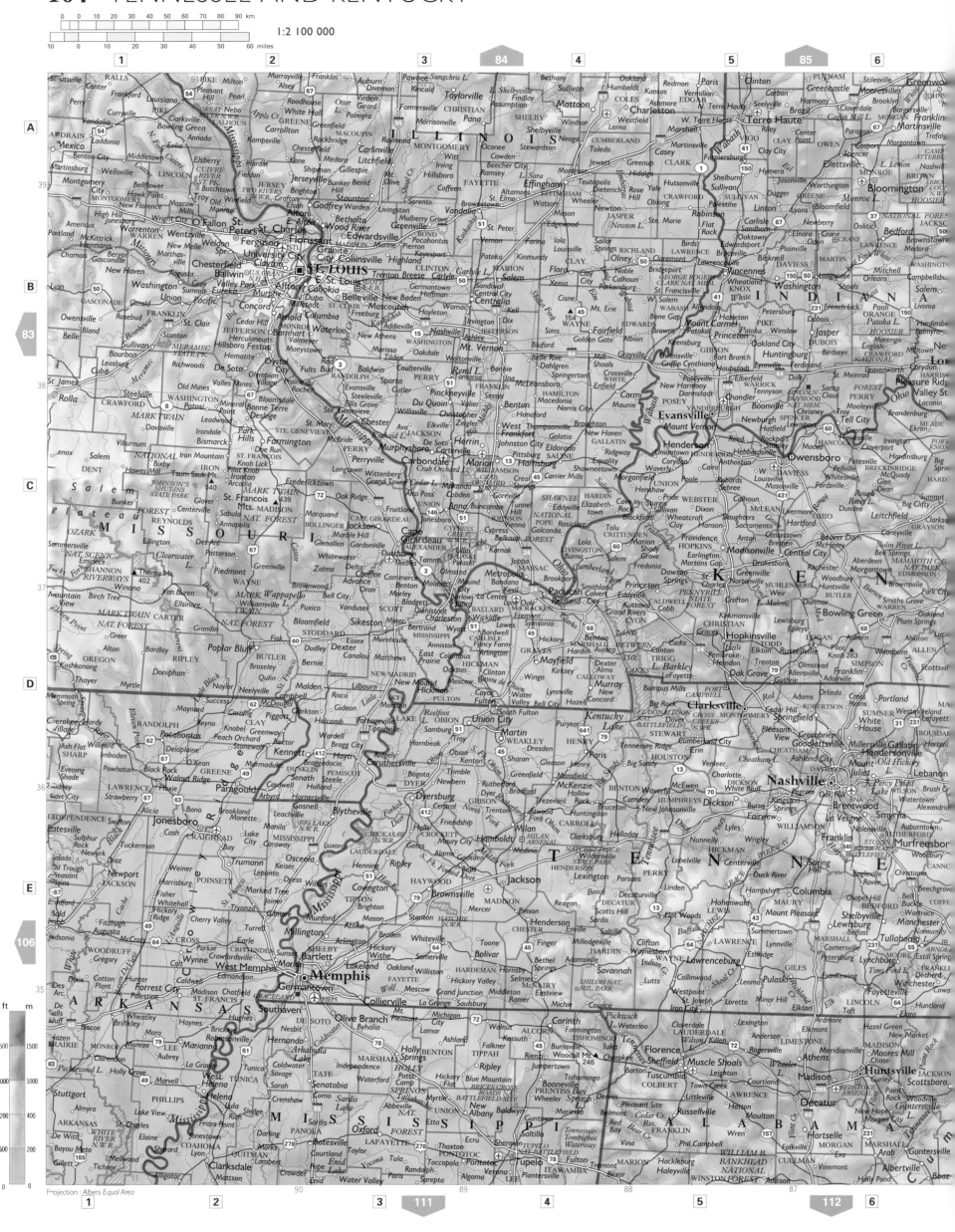

1:2 100 000

Projection: Albers Equal Area

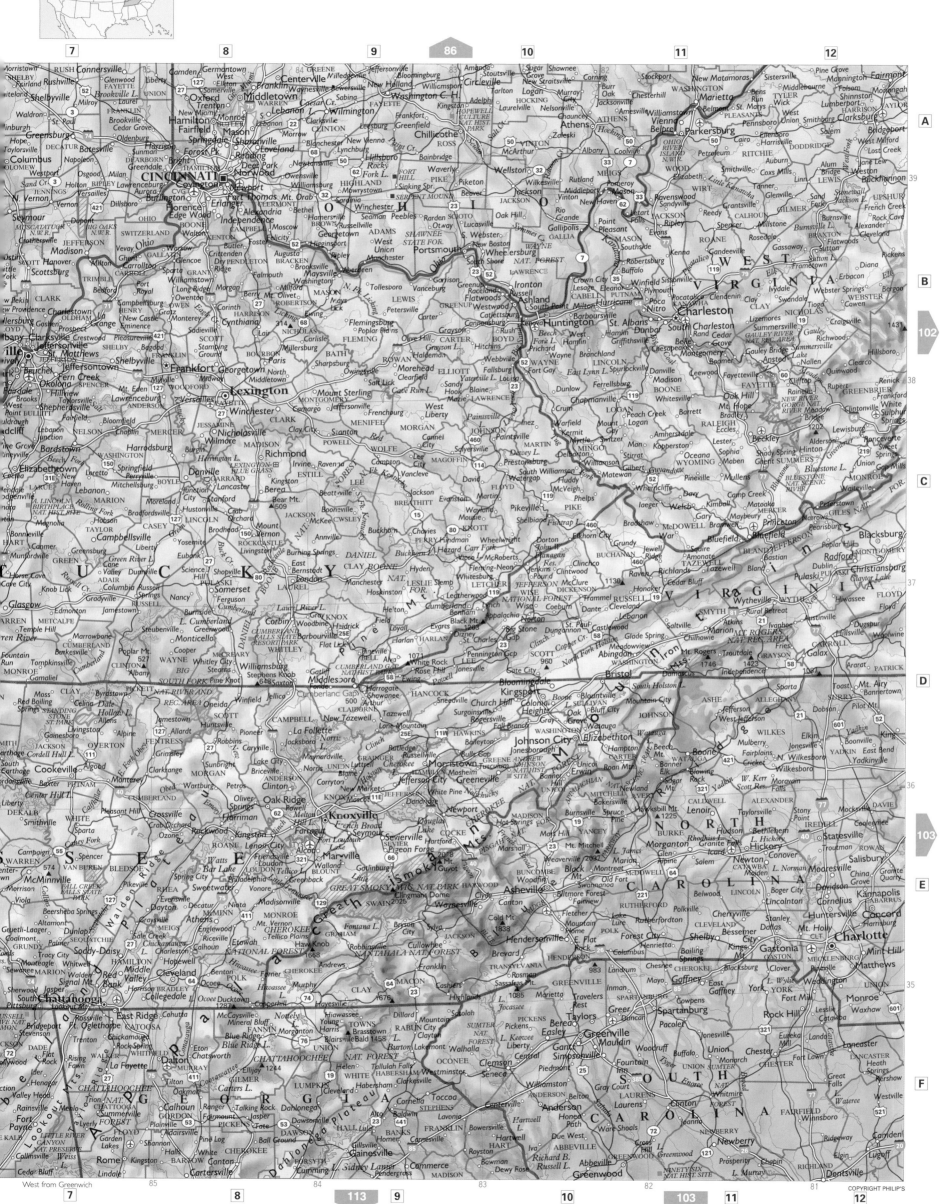

10 0 10 20 30 40 50 60 70 80 100 km

1:2 100 000

10 0 10 20 30 40 50 60 miles

1 2 3 83 4 5 6

States / Regions

KS · OK · MISSOURI · TENNESSEE (TN) · MISSISSIPPI · LOUISIANA · TEXAS

ARKANSAS

OZARK · MARK TWAIN NATIONAL FOREST · OZARK NATIONAL FOREST · OUACHITA NATIONAL FOREST · Boston Mts. · Ouachita Mts. · Buffalo National River

Selected cities and towns

Springfield · Little Rock · North Little Rock · Fort Smith · Fayetteville · Springdale · Rogers · Bentonville · Jonesboro · Paragould · Memphis · Pine Bluff · Hot Springs · Texarkana · El Dorado · Camden · Magnolia · Monroe · Shreveport · Bossier City · Jackson · Vicksburg · Greenville · Conway · Russellville · Searcy · Harrison · Mountain Home · Batesville · Newport · Blytheville · West Memphis · Forrest City · Helena

107 · 104 · 108 · 111 · 110

ft m

3000 / 1000 · 1200 / 400 · 600 / 200 · 0 / 0

Projection : Albers Equal Area

West from Greenwich

94 · 93 · 92 · 91 · 90

COPYRIGHT PHILIP'S

37 · 36 · 35 · 34 · 33 · 32

A B C D E F

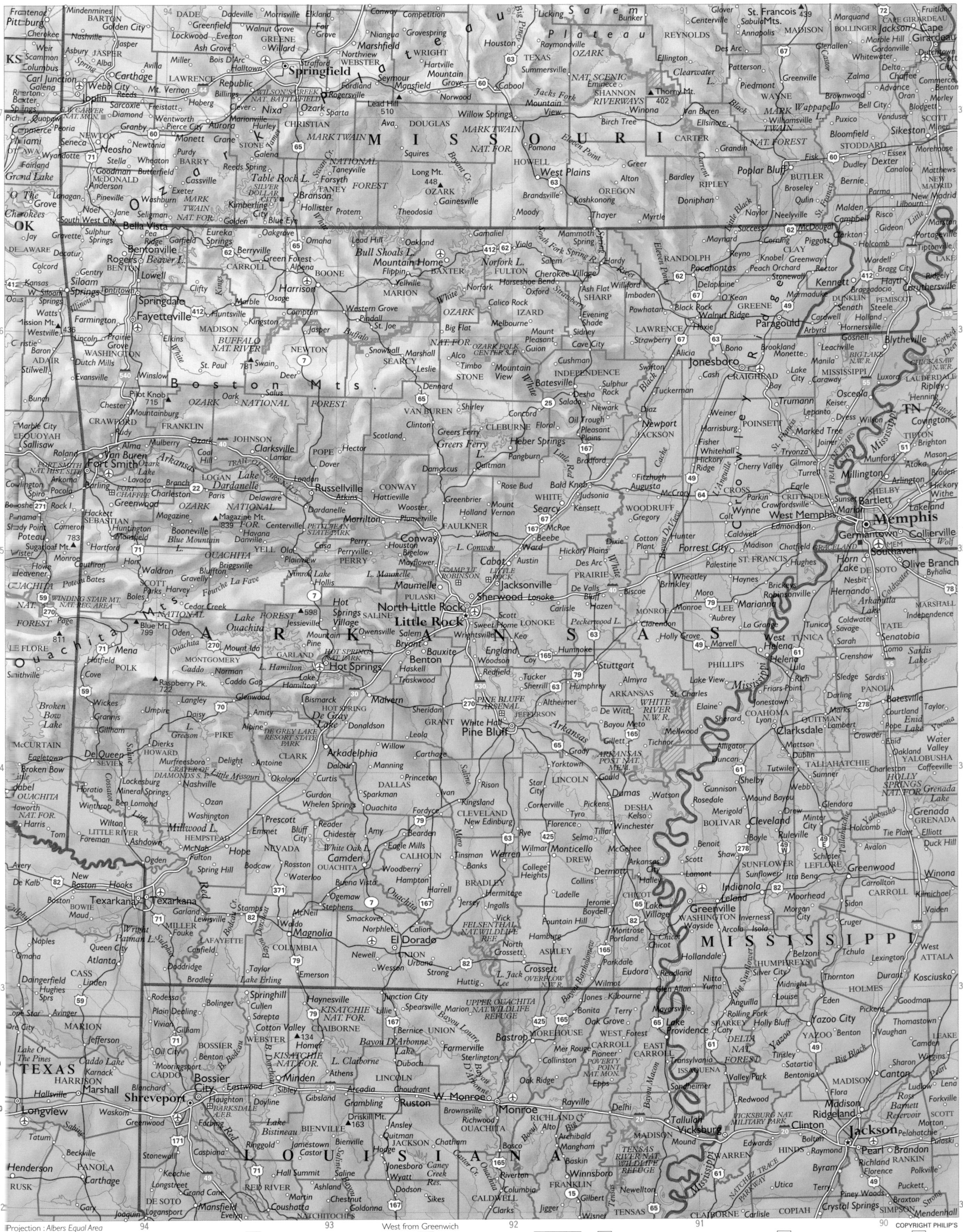

1:2 100 000

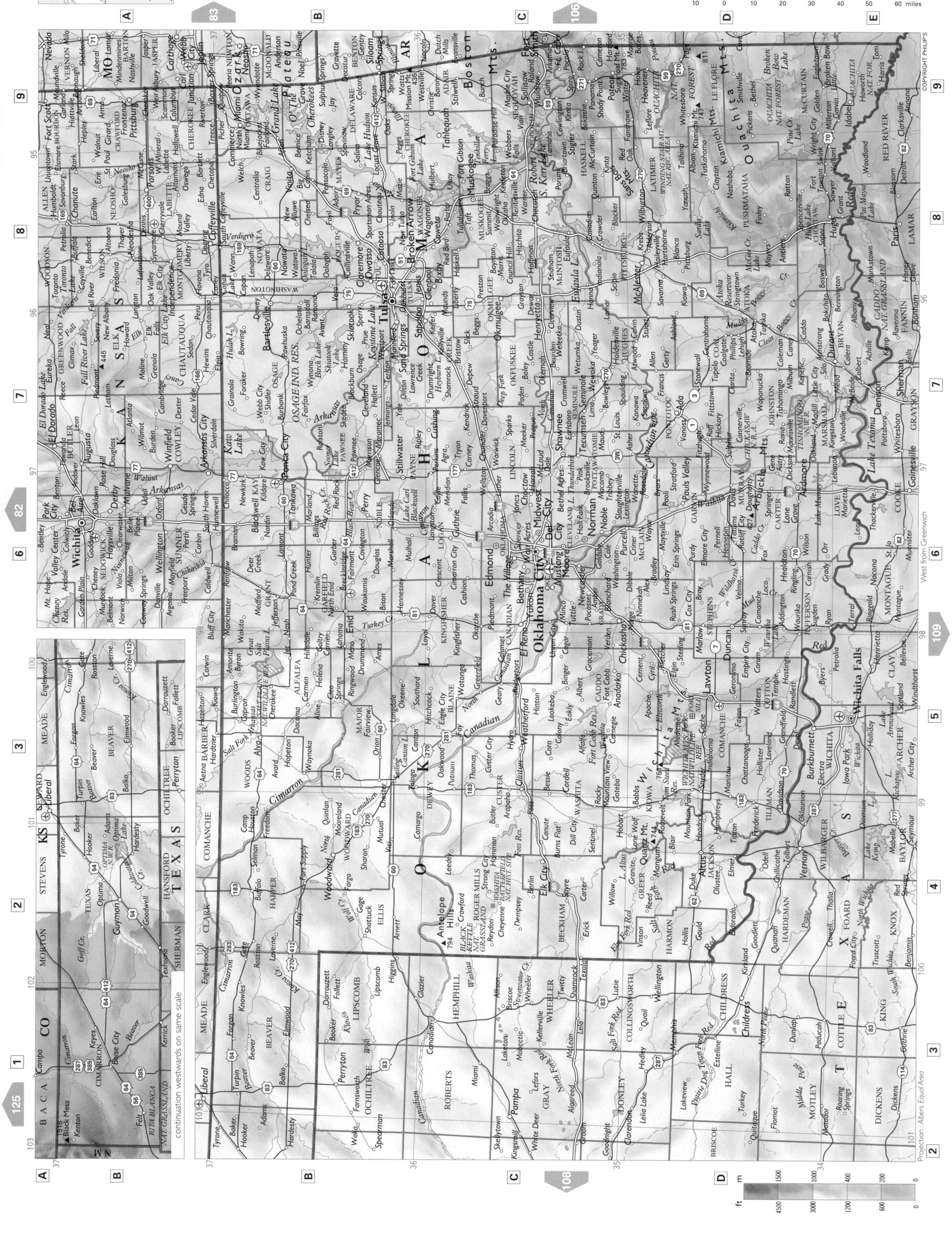

West from Greenwich

Projection : Albers Equal Area

COPYRIGHT PHILIP'S

continuation westwards on same scale

MO
KS
AR
KANSAS
TEXAS
OKLAHOMA

Wichita
Tulsa
Oklahoma City
Norman
Lawton
Enid
Ponca City
Stillwater
Muskogee
McAlester
Ardmore
Duncan
Shawnee
Bartlesville
Wichita Falls

Ozark Plateau
Boston Mts.
Ouachita Mts.
Kiamichi Mts.
Wichita Mts.
Arbuckle Mts.

Osage Ind. Res.
Black Kettle Nat. Grassland
Rita Blanca Nat. Grassland
Wichita Mts. Nat. Wildlife Ref.

Red River
Arkansas
Canadian
Cimarron
North Canadian

Lake Texoma
Grand Lake
Eufaula L.
Kaw Lake
Keystone Lake

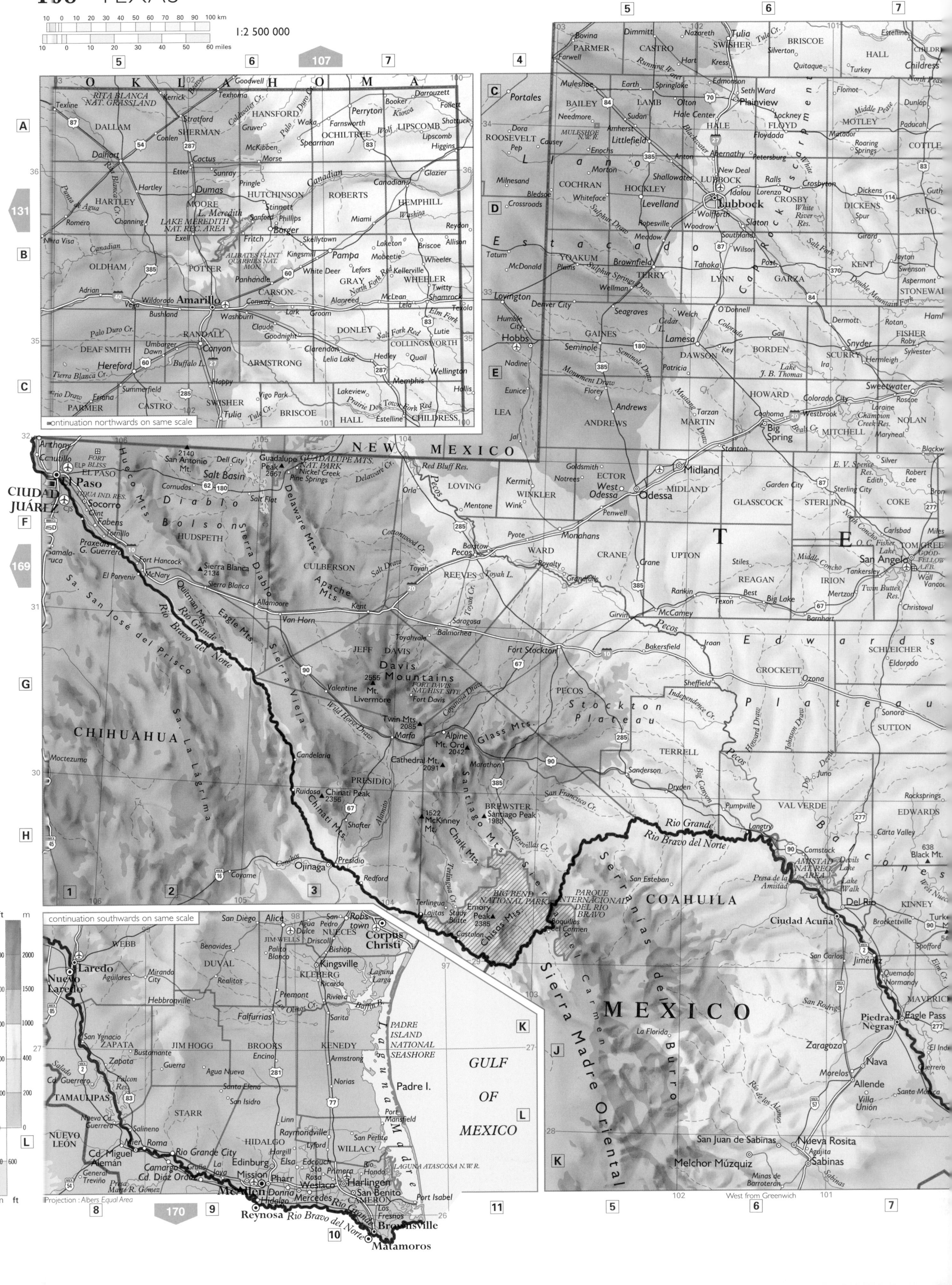

1:2 500 000

10 0 10 20 30 40 50 60 70 80 90 100 km
10 0 10 20 30 40 50 60 miles

OKLAHOMA

NEW MEXICO

TEXAS

MEXICO

CHIHUAHUA

COAHUILA

NUEVO LEÓN

TAMAULIPAS

GULF OF MEXICO

El Paso
CIUDAD JUÁREZ
Amarillo
Lubbock
Odessa
Midland
Big Spring
San Angelo
Del Rio
Ciudad Acuña
Piedras Negras
Eagle Pass
Laredo
Nuevo Laredo
Corpus Christi
Kingsville
McAllen
Reynosa
Brownsville
Matamoros
Harlingen

DALLAM SHERMAN HANSFORD OCHILTREE LIPSCOMB
HARTLEY MOORE HUTCHINSON ROBERTS HEMPHILL
OLDHAM POTTER CARSON GRAY WHEELER
DEAF SMITH RANDALL ARMSTRONG DONLEY COLLINGSWORTH
PARMER CASTRO SWISHER BRISCOE HALL CHILDRESS

BAILEY LAMB HALE FLOYD MOTLEY COTTLE
COCHRAN HOCKLEY LUBBOCK CROSBY DICKENS KING
YOAKUM TERRY LYNN GARZA KENT STONEWALL
GAINES DAWSON BORDEN SCURRY FISHER
ANDREWS MARTIN HOWARD MITCHELL NOLAN

Guadalupe Mts. Nat. Park
Guadalupe Peak 2667
GUADALUPE MTS. NAT PARK

HUDSPETH CULBERSON REEVES WARD CRANE UPTON
LOVING WINKLER ECTOR MIDLAND GLASSCOCK STERLING COKE
PECOS CRANE IRION

JEFF DAVIS
Davis Mountains
Mt. Livermore 2555
Fort Davis
Marfa
Alpine Mt. Ord 2042
Glass Mts.
BREWSTER
Santiago Peak 1983
STOCKTON PLATEAU
BIG BEND NATIONAL PARK
Chisos Mts.
Emory Peak 2385
PRESIDIO
Chinati Peak 2356
Ojinaga
Presidio

TERRELL VAL VERDE EDWARDS KINNEY
AMISTAD NAT REC AREA
Rio Grande / Rio Bravo del Norte

Sierra Madre Oriental

WEBB DUVAL JIM WELLS NUECES
ZAPATA JIM HOGG BROOKS KENEDY
STARR HIDALGO WILLACY CAMERON

PADRE ISLAND NATIONAL SEASHORE
Padre I.

Projection: Albers Equal Area

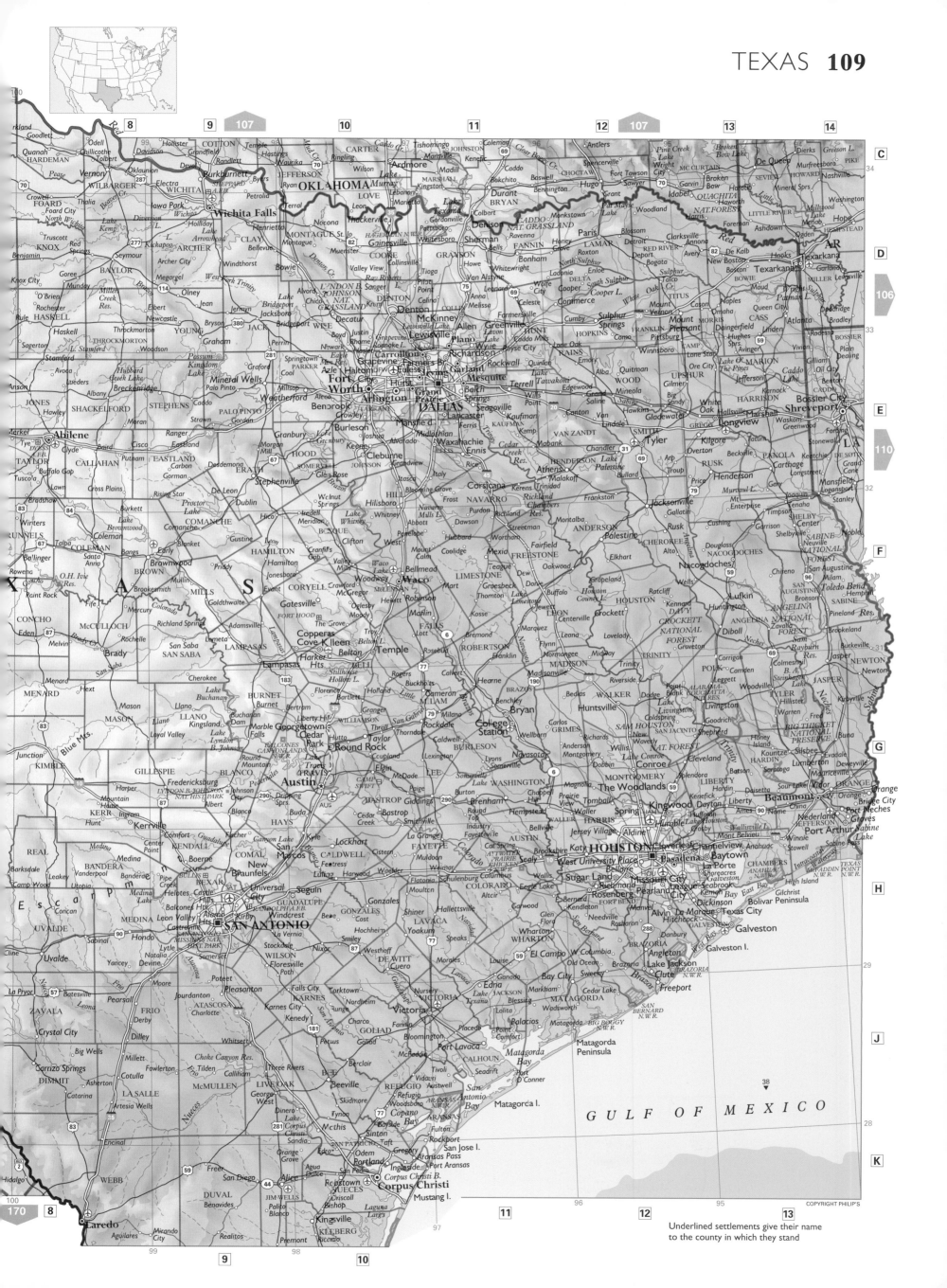

GULF OF MEXICO

COPYRIGHT PHILIP'S

Underlined settlements give their name
to the county in which they stand

1:2 100 000

Projection: Albers Equal Area

West from Greenwich

COPYRIGHT PHILIP'S

State names: ALABAMA · MISSISSIPPI · LOUISIANA · ARKANSAS · TEXAS

Major features: GULF OF MEXICO · Mississippi River Delta · Lake Pontchartrain · Lake Borgne · Atchafalaya Bay · Vermilion Bay · Chandeleur Sound · Chandeleur Islands · Breton Sound · Mississippi Sound

Major cities: New Orleans · Baton Rouge · Shreveport · Bossier City · Monroe · Alexandria · Lafayette · Lake Charles · Jackson · Meridian · Mobile · Biloxi · Gulfport · Hattiesburg · Natchez · Vicksburg

National areas: KISATCHIE NATIONAL FOREST · DE SOTO NATIONAL FOREST · BIENVILLE NATIONAL FOREST · HOMOCHITTO NATIONAL FOREST · DELTA NATIONAL WILDLIFE REFUGE · BRETON NATIONAL WILDLIFE RESERVE · GULF ISLANDS NAT. SEASHORE · SABINE NATIONAL WILDLIFE REFUGE · ANGELINA NATIONAL FOREST · SABINE NATIONAL FOREST

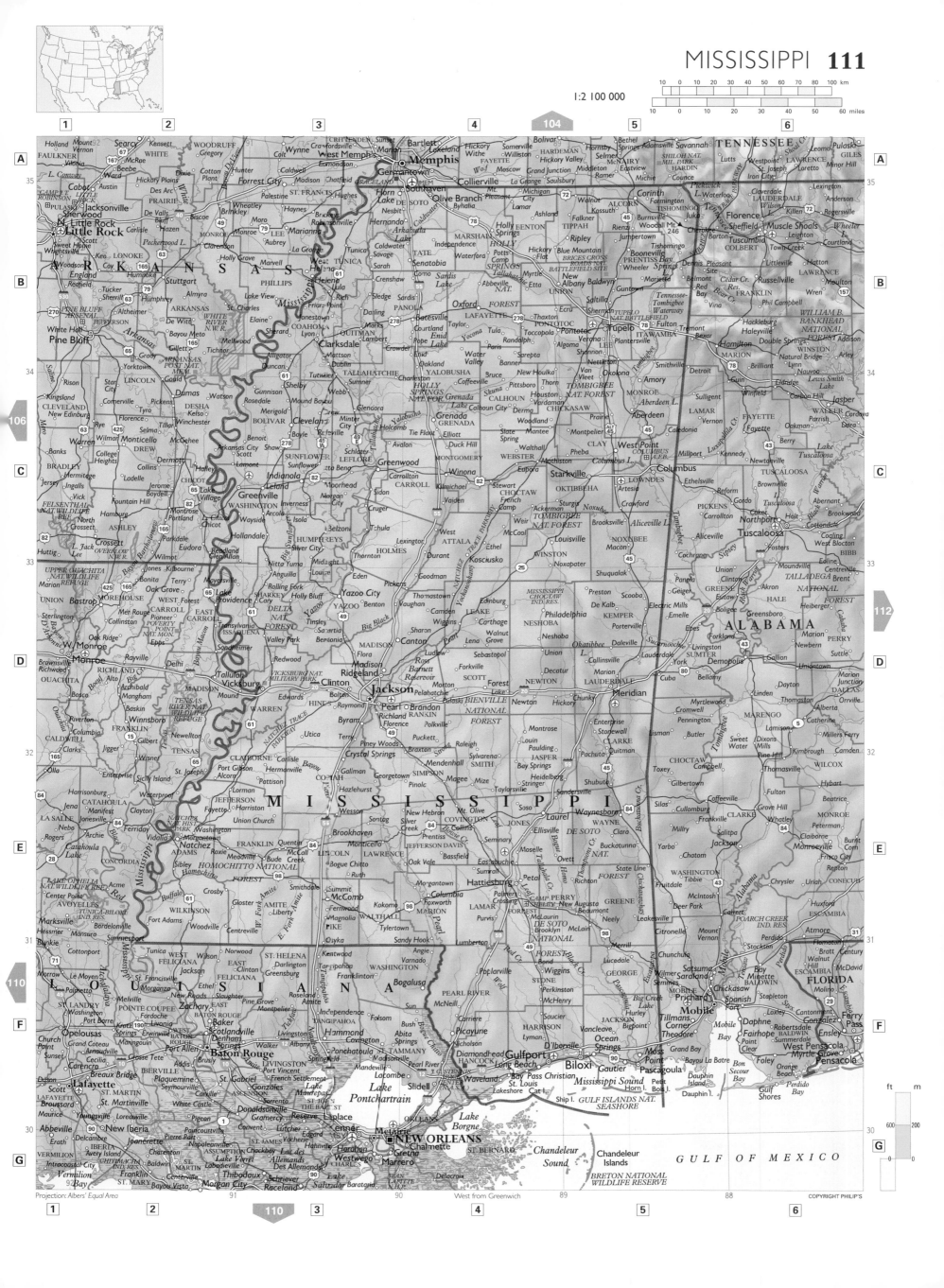

0 10 20 30 40 50 60 70 80 90 km

10 0 10 20 30 40 50 60 miles

1:2 100 000

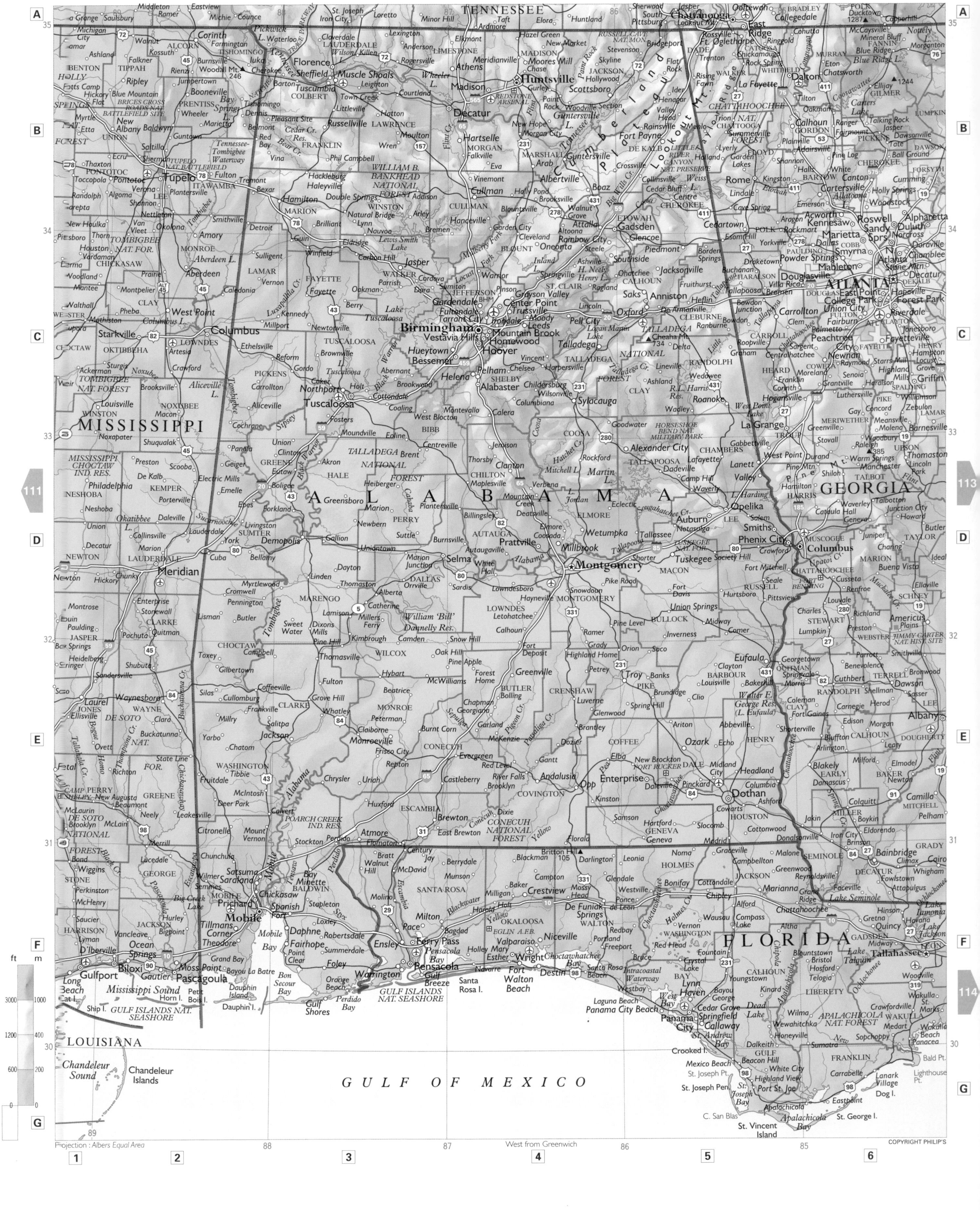

1 **104** **2** **3** **4** **5** **105** **6**

TENNESSEE

MISSISSIPPI

A L A B A M A

GEORGIA

FLORIDA

LOUISIANA

GULF OF MEXICO

Huntsville

Decatur

Tupelo

Birmingham

Tuscaloosa

Columbus

Meridian

Gadsden

Anniston

ATLANTA

Montgomery

Columbus

Opelika · Auburn

Phenix City

Tuskegee

Selma

Demopolis

Laurel

Dothan

Enterprise

Andalusia

Brewton

Mobile

Pascagoula

Biloxi · Gulfport

Pensacola

Fort Walton Beach

Panama City

Tallahassee

Apalachicola

Chandeleur Sound

Chandeleur Islands

Mississippi Sound

Gulf Islands Nat. Seashore

Gulf Shores

Dauphin I.

Projection : Albers Equal Area

West from Greenwich

COPYRIGHT PHILIP'S

1 **2** **3** **4** **5** **6**

1:2 100 000

Projection : Albers Equal Area

West from Greenwich

COPYRIGHT PHILIP'S

TENNESSEE

NORTH CAROLINA

SOUTH CAROLINA

ALABAMA

GEORGIA

FLORIDA

ATLANTIC OCEAN

Gulf of Mexico

Sea Islands

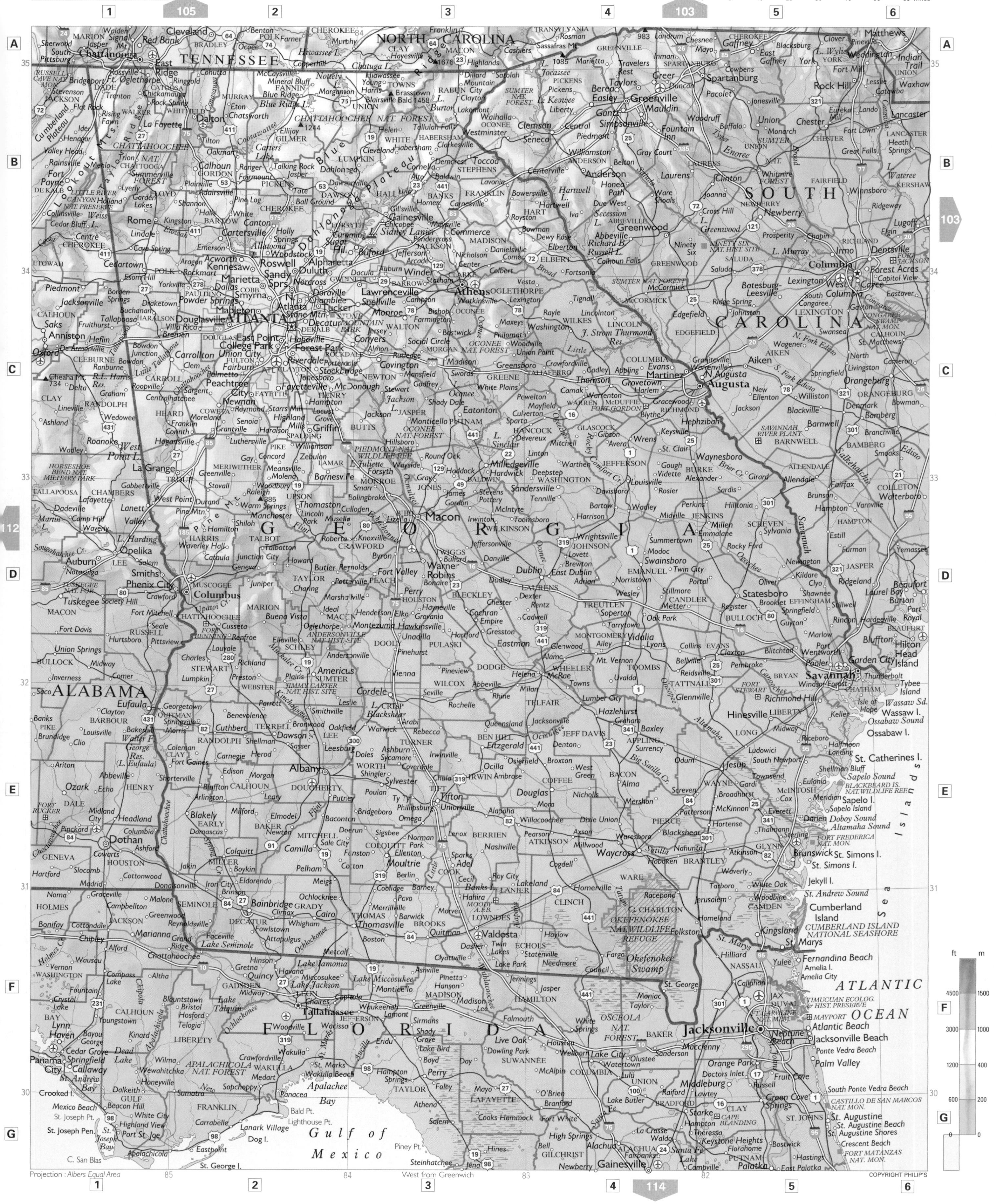

1:2 100 000

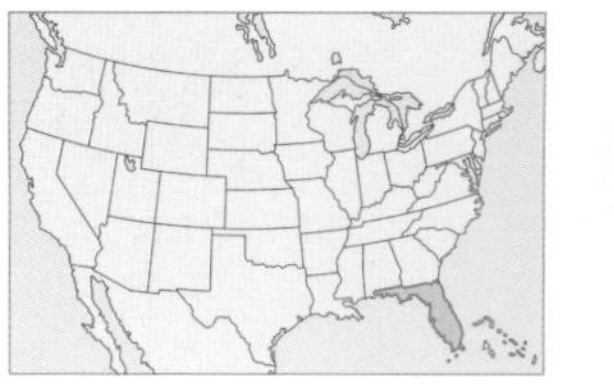

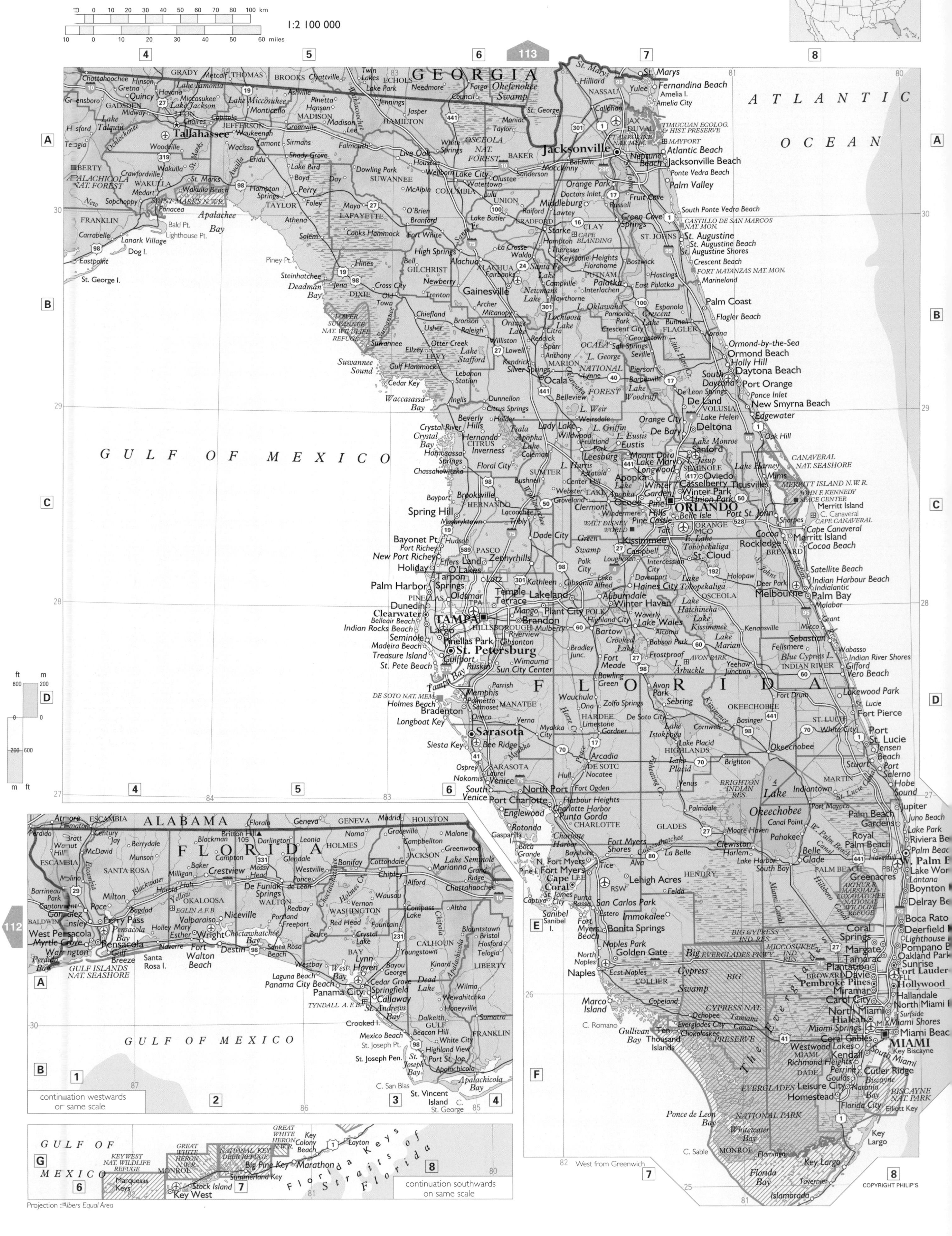

0 10 20 30 40 50 60 70 80 100 km
10 0 10 20 30 40 50 60 miles

113 | 4 | 5 | 6 | 7 | 8

GEORGIA

ATLANTIC OCEAN

GULF OF MEXICO

F L O R I D A

Tallahassee

Jacksonville

ORLANDO

TAMPA

St. Petersburg

Sarasota

MIAMI

Miami Beach

W. Palm Beach

Fort Lauderdale

Hollywood

Key West

Key Largo

ALABAMA

FLORIDA

Pensacola

Panama City

continuation westwards
or same scale

continuation southwards
on same scale

Projection : Albers Equal Area

COPYRIGHT PHILIP'S

West from Greenwich

112

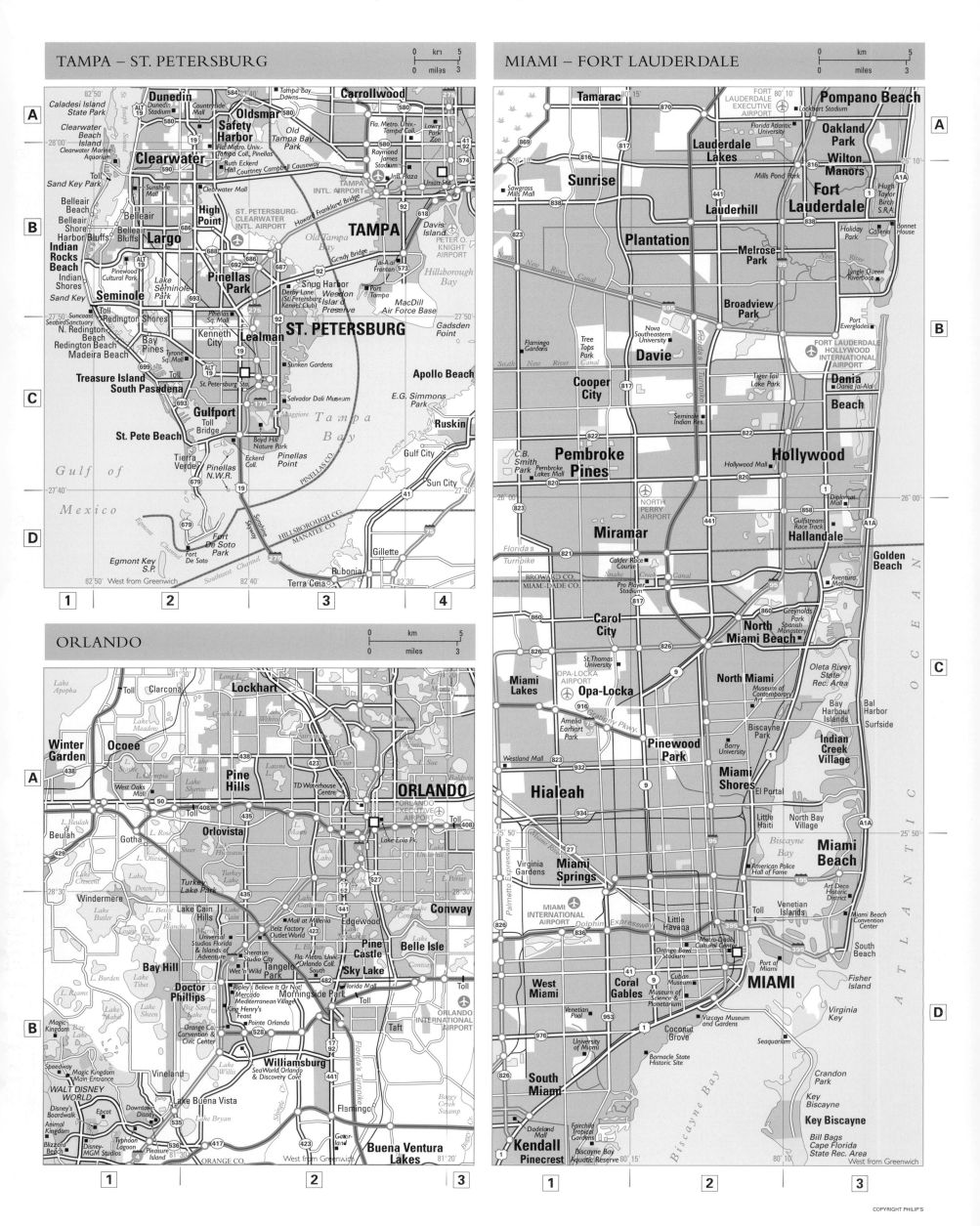

DALLAS – FORT WORTH

0 km 5
0 miles 3

A

Keller
Southlake
Grapevine Rec. Area
Grapevine Mills
Grapevine
Grapevine Steam Railroad
97°10'
97°00'
Coppell
96°50' Toll
Richardson
96°40'
78 190
A

N. Richland Hills
Watauga
Colleyville
Dragon Stadium
114
26
DALLAS-FT. WORTH INTL. AIRPORT
121
635
North Lake Park
Farmers Branch
Galleria
289
Richardson Sq. Mall
Saginaw
Blue Mound
Bedford
Euless
360
97
NRH2O Water Park
348
354
Mustangs of Las Colinas
Biblical Arts Center
NorthPark Center
Harry S. Moss Park
635
78
Garland

B
32°50'
FT. WORTH-MEACHAM INTL. APT.
Haltom City
Hurst
Richland Hills
North East Mall
American Airlines C.R. Smith Mus.
Irving
114
Univ. of Dallas
482
183
University Park
DALLAS LOVE FIELD
Southern Methodist Univ.
Highland Park
White Rock Lake
Arboretum & Botanical Gdn.
Town East Mall
B

Sansom Park
Sansom
820
Gateway Park
Pantego
Univ. of TX-Arlington
The Palace of Wax & Ripley's Believe it or Not!
Lone Star Park
NextStage
Irving Heritage Dist.
Trinity River Greenbelt Park
DALLAS
Dallas Theater Center
Central Sta.
Cotton Bowl Fair Park
Big Town Mall
80

Stockyards Natl. Hist. District
Ct. Hse.
F.W. Cult. Dt. & Will Rogers Ctr.
C.H. Central Sta.
Ft. Worth Zoo
Forest Park
Texas Christian University
FORT WORTH
Dalworthington Gardens
Six Flags Hurricane Harbor
Arlington Conv. Ctr.
The Ballpark in Arlington
Six Flags Over Texas
Six Flags Mall
MILLENNIUM DALLAS AIRPORT
Arcadia Park
Cockrell Hill
Dallas Zoo
Rochester Park
Balch Springs

Forest Hill
Lake Arlington
Univ. of TX-Arlington
Forum 303 Mall
Mountain Creek Lake Park
Dallas Baptist Univ.
DALLAS EXECUTIVE AIRPORT
Paul Quinn Coll.
Lake Lemmon
Kelberg

C
32°40'
Edgecliff
35W
Kennedale
Everman
277
Arlington
ARLINGTON MUNICIPAL AIRPORT
Grand Prairie
Southwest Center Mall
Duncanville
De Soto
342
Cedar Valley College
Hutchins
C

Crowley
97°10'
Mansfield
BUS 287
360
Joe Pool Lake
Cedar Hill State Park
Cedar Hill
67
Lancaster
Wilmer
96°40'
West from Greenwich

1 | 2 | 3 | 4 | 5 | 6

HOUSTON

0 km 5
0 miles 3

Jersey Village
95°30'
North Houston
249
Hardy Toll Road
95°20'
59
A

8
Toll
290
Highland Heights
45
261
Scenic Woods
Northline Mall
East Houston

Lois
Spring Valley
Hilshire Village
Memorial City Mall
Antique Car Mus.
BUS 90
Anheuser-Busch Brewery
Jacinto City
Port of Houston Turning Basin

Hedwig Village
Hunters Creek Village
Piney Point Village
Briargrove
Nature Center
Mem. Park
Bayou Bend
Compaq Center
HOUSTON
Union Sta.
Minute Maid Park
Buffalo Soldiers Natl. Mus.
Texas Southern Univ.
610

B
Bunker Hill Village
Jeanetta
Post Oak Galleria
Mus. of St. Thomas
W. Univ. Place
Rice Univ.
Mus. of Fine Arts
Mus. of Natural Science
Univ. of Houston
5
45
B

Sharpstown Center
Southside Place
Zoo
Texas Medical Center
Houston Baptist Univ.
Bellaire
Reliant Park
Mayfair

Westwood Mall
Meyerland
59
Sunny Side
610
Six Flags AstroWorld

C
29°40'
Stafford
ALT 90
Myrtle
288
Minnetex The Reef
WILLIAM P. HOBBY AIRPORT
35
C

Missouri City
HARRIS CO. FORT BEND CO.
8
Toll
Tom Bass Reg. Park
95°30'
Brookside Village
95°20'
El Franco Lee Park
8
Pearland
35

1 | 2 | 3

SAN ANTONIO

0 km 5
0 miles 3

98°40'
Camp Bullis
281
98°30'
Garden Ridge
Bracken
29°40'
35
A

10
Grey Forest
Six Flags Fiesta Texas
Hollywood Park
1604
Rolling Oaks Mall
Retama Park
Schertz
Selma
A

Helotes
Univ. of Texas-San Antonio
53
Shavano Park
Hill Country Village
McAllister Park
Texas Transportation Mus.
SAN ANTONIO INTL. ARPT.
Universal City
Live Oak
Windcrest
Randolph A.F.B.
1604
B

16
1604
Leon Valley
87
Malibu Grand Prix
Castle Hills
North Star Mall
Alamo Hts.
McNay Art Mus.
368
Windsor Park Mall
Converse
29°30'
90
B

151
SeaWorld San Antonio
Ingram Park Mall
345
Pear Apple Co. Fair
Balcones Hts.
Olmos Park
Olmos Basin Park
Terrell Hills
Botanic Gdns.
Kirby
Splashtown San Antonio
C

St. Mary's Univ. of San Antonio
421
Trinity Univ.
Central Sta.
Gardendale

Westlakes Mercado
151
Our Lady of the Lake Univ.
Westwood Village
90
SAN ANTONIO
13
China Grove
Savers

C
29°30'
Lackland City
16
Wolff Mun. Stadium
371
35
South Park Mall
410
13
87
Boldtville
D

410
353
San Antonio Missions N.H.P.
422
536
Brooks A.F.B.
122
Calaveras Lake

Macdona
29°20'
Von Ormy
Mitchell Lake
San Antonio Missions N.H.P.
Southton
181
1604

35
16
Leon Cr.
281
Buena Vista
35
Elmendorf
TEXAS CO. WILSON CO.

1604
98°40'
West from Greenwich
98°30'
98°20'
Saspanico
29°20'

1 | 2 | 3 | 4

COPYRIGHT PHILIP'S

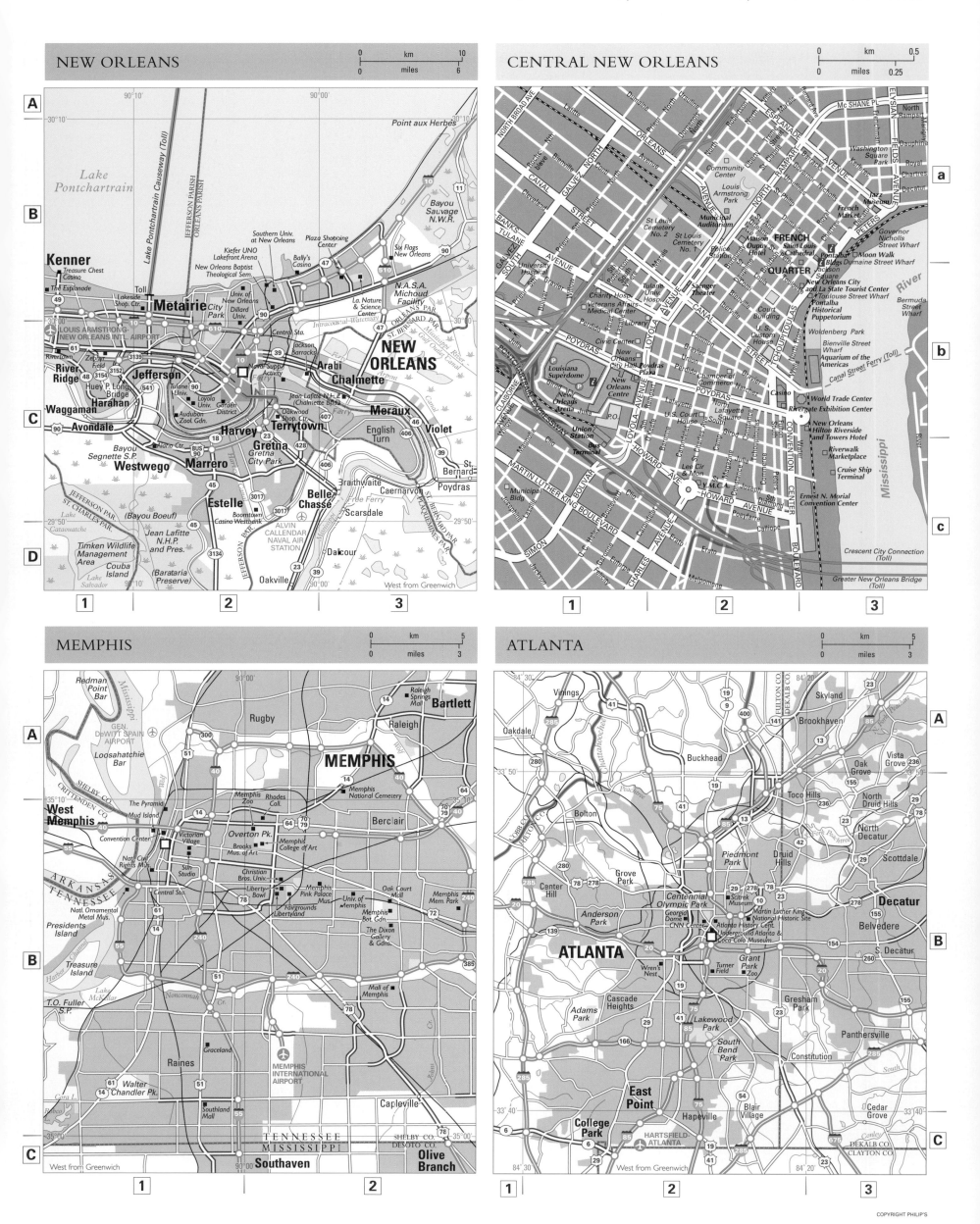

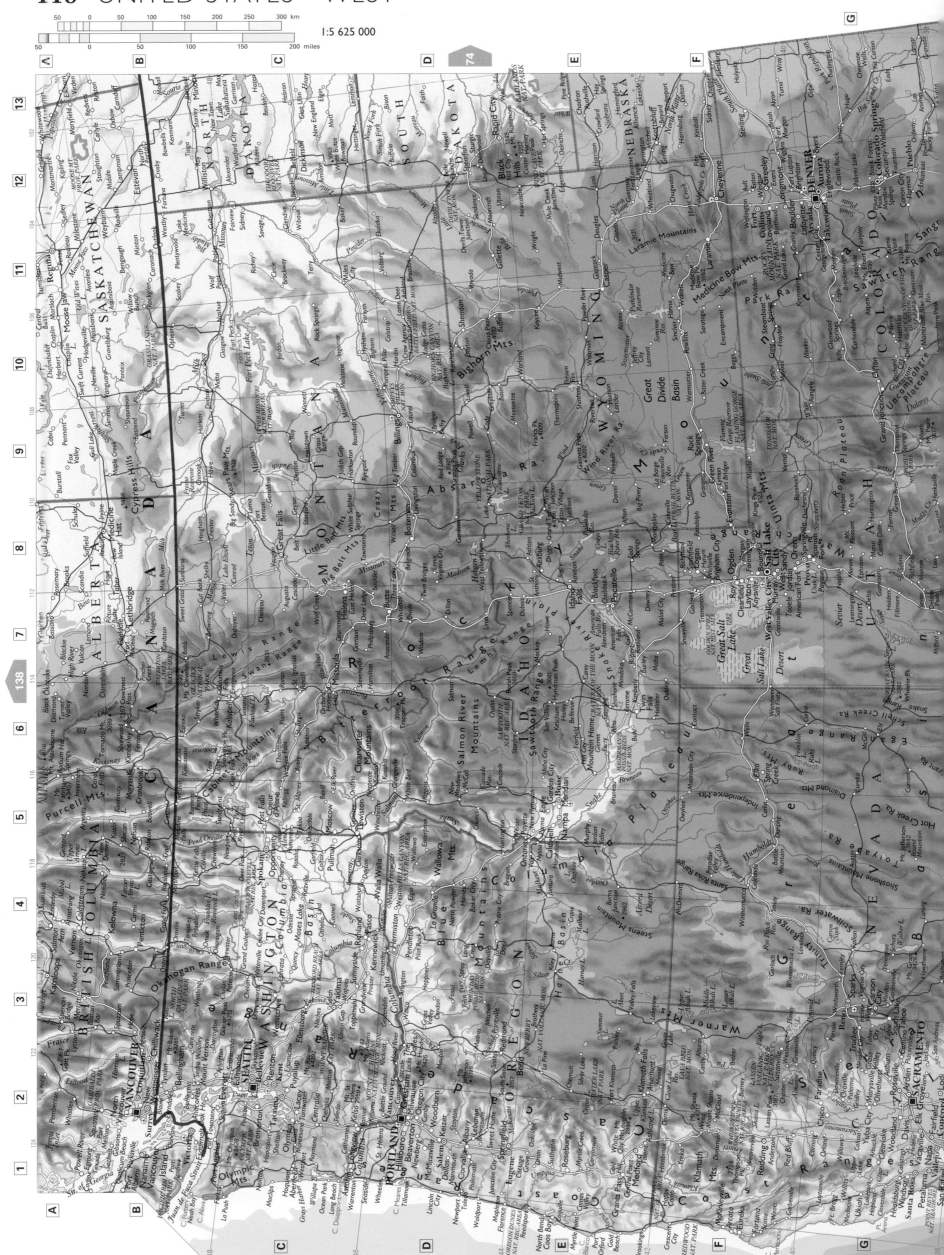

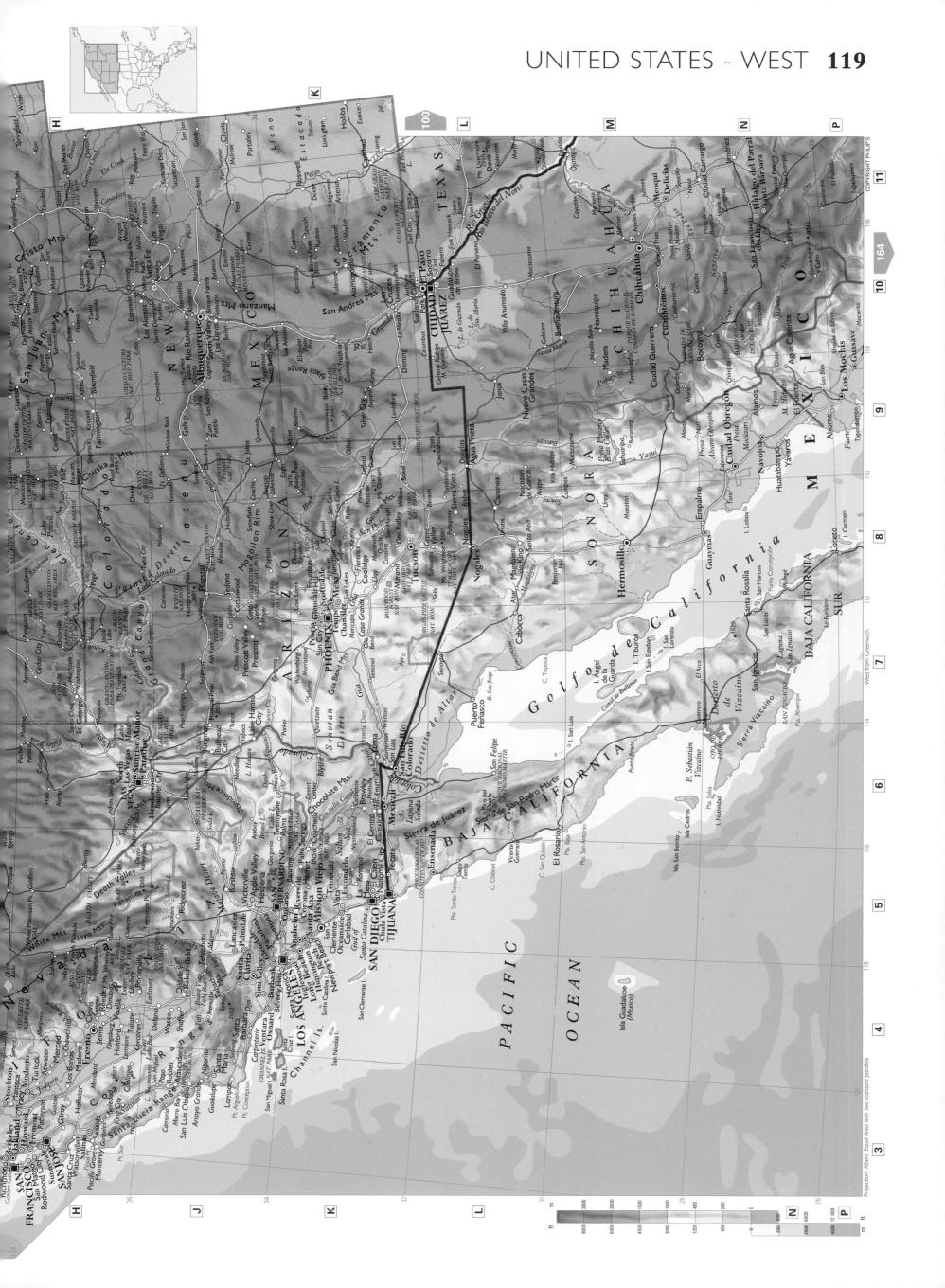

COPYRIGHT PHILIP'S

1:2 100 000

COPYRIGHT PHILIP'S

Projection: Albers Equal Area

West from Greenwich

PACIFIC OCEAN

CANADA

BRITISH COLUMBIA

WASHINGTON

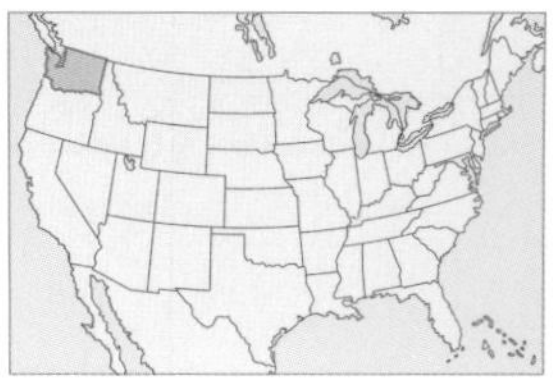

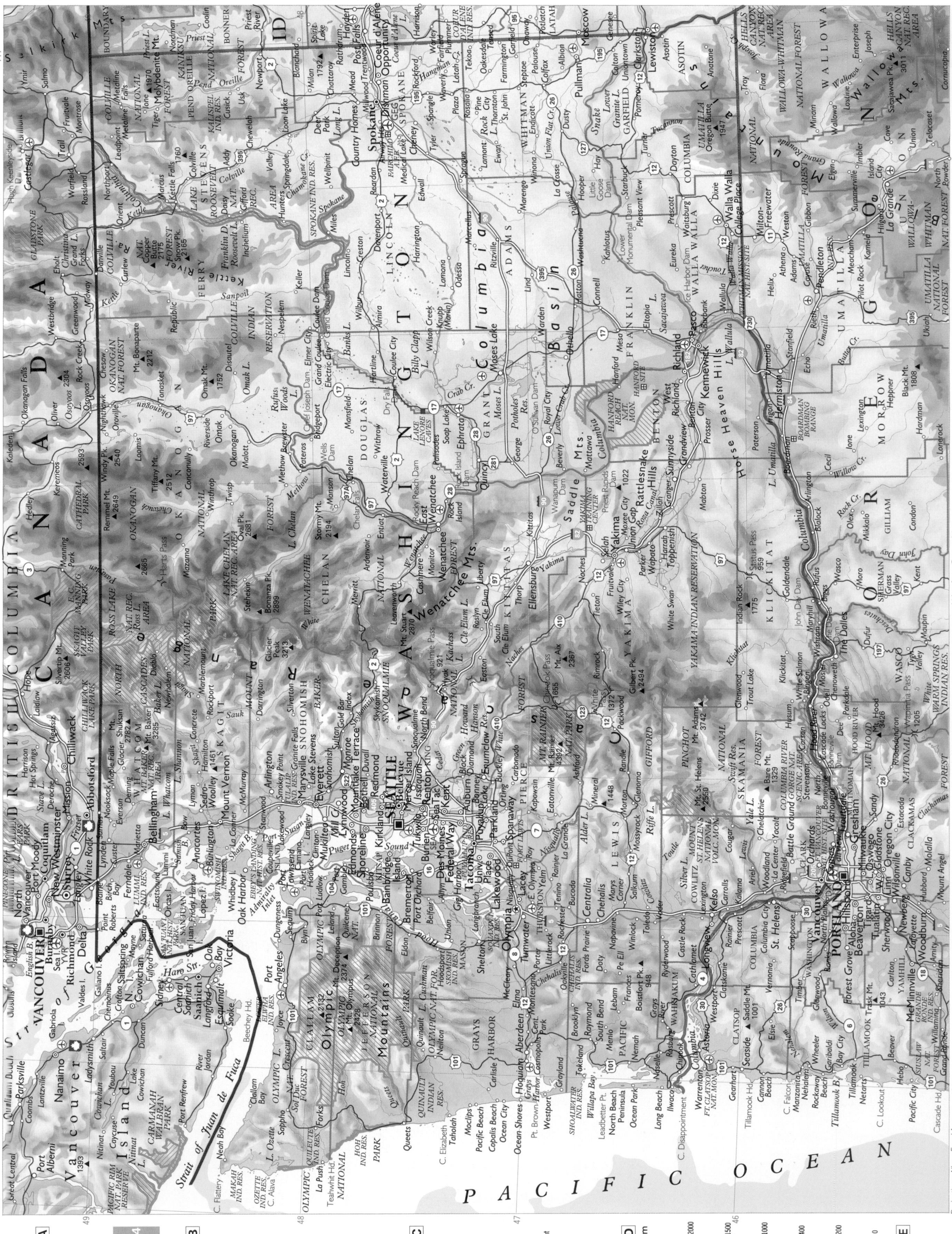

OREGON

IDAHO

Vancouver Island

Strait of Juan de Fuca

Puget Sound

Olympic Mountains

OLYMPIC NATIONAL PARK

NORTH CASCADES NATIONAL PARK

MOUNT RAINIER NATIONAL PARK

Columbia Basin

Cascade Range

Permanent ice

1:2 100 000

COPYRIGHT PHILIP'S

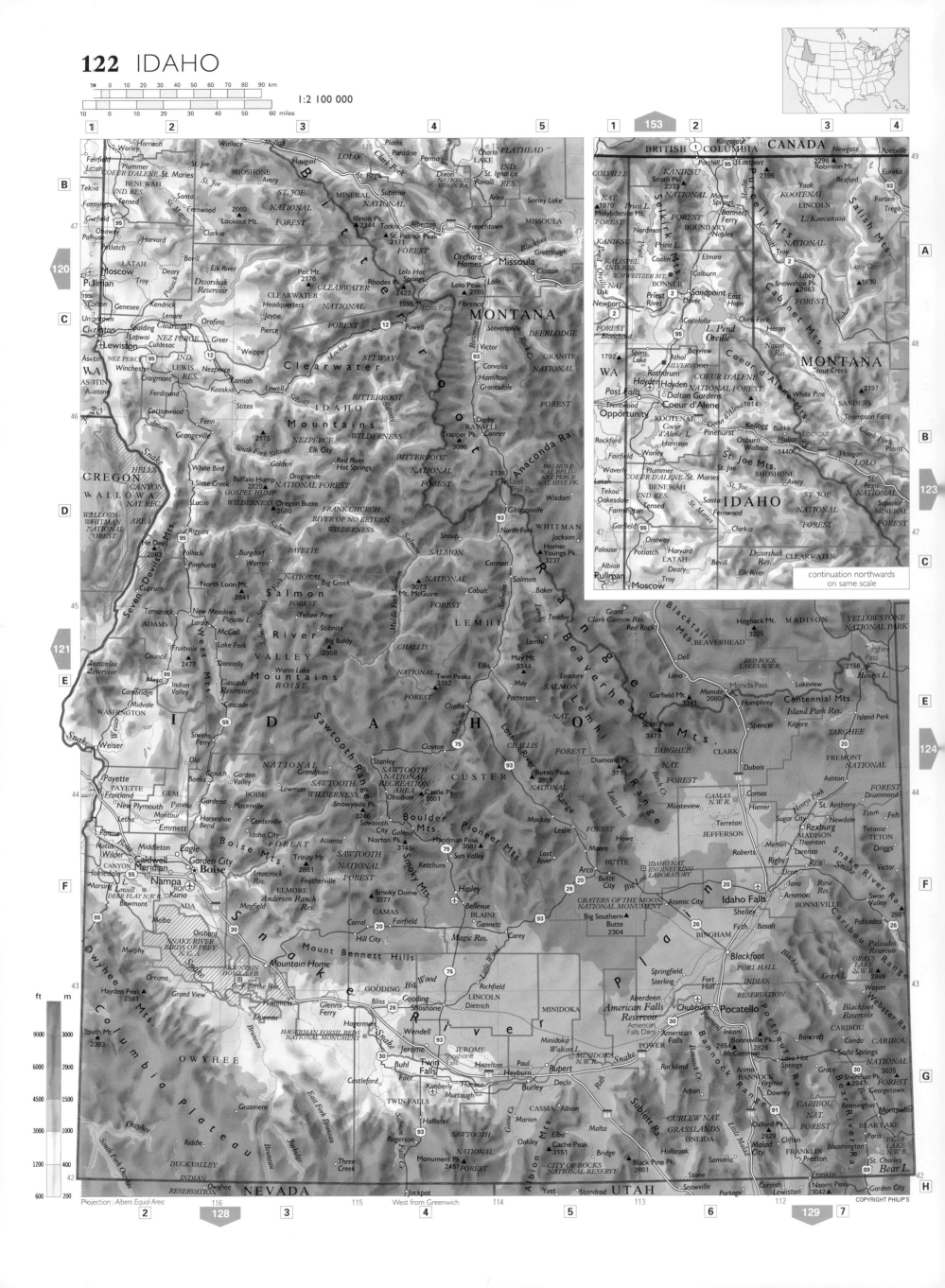

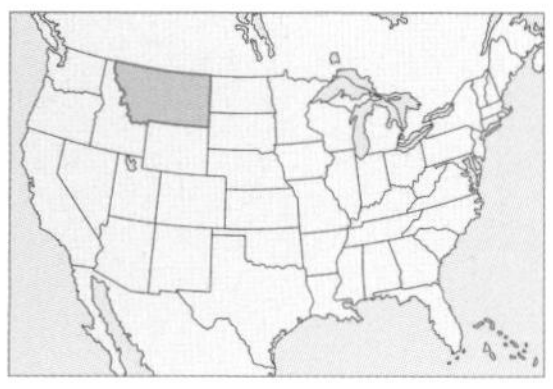

1:3 150 000

COPYRIGHT PHILIP'S

Projection: Albers' Equal Area

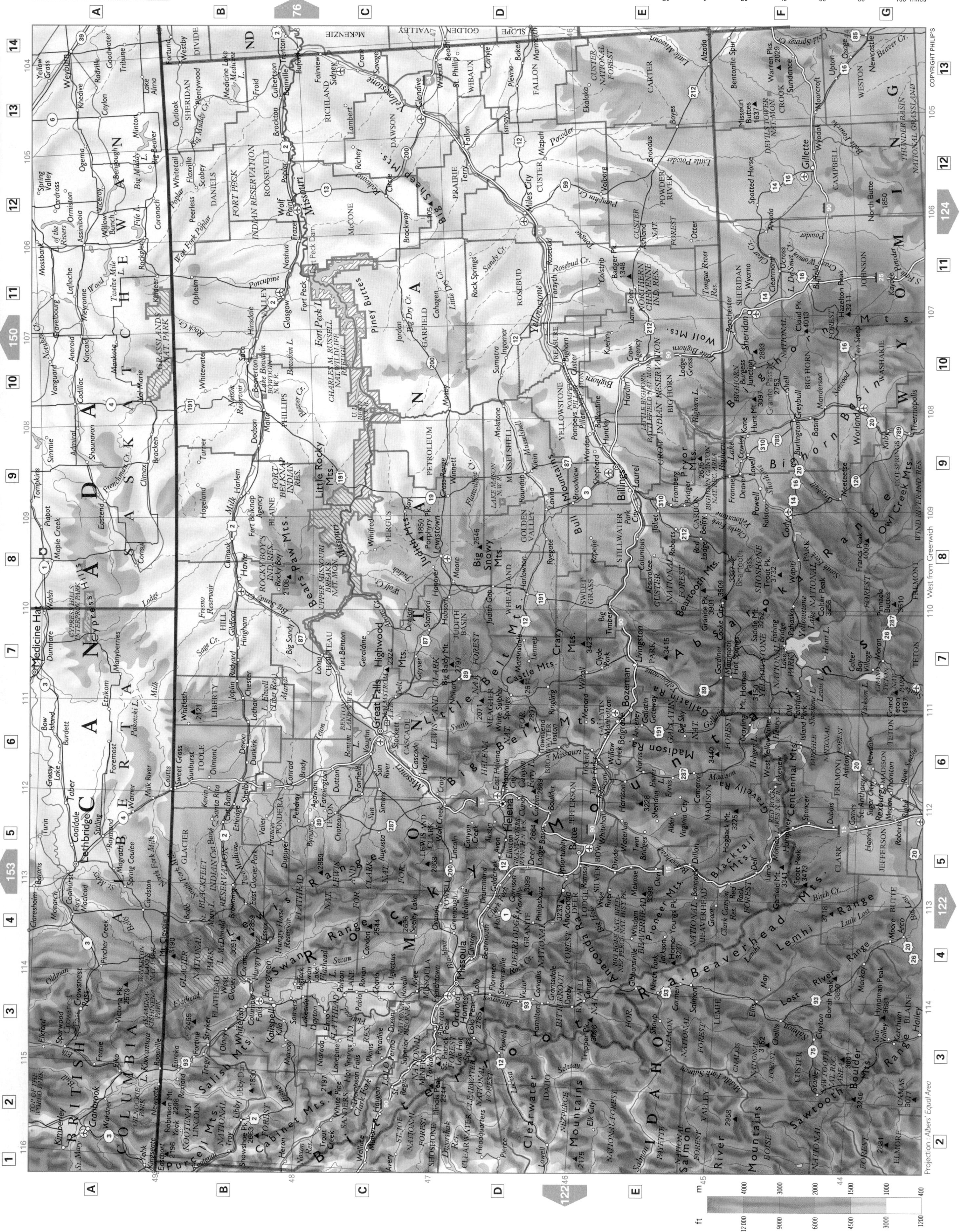

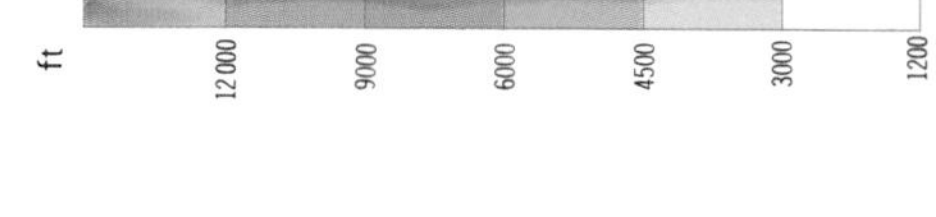

0 10 20 30 40 50 60 70 80 90 km
10   0   10   20   30   40   50   60 miles

1:2 100 000

COPYRIGHT PHILIPS

West from Greenwich 107

Projection: Albers Equal Area

1:2 100 000

10 0 10 20 30 40 50 60 70 80 100 km
10 0 10 20 30 40 50 60 miles

Projection: Albers Equal Area

COPYRIGHT PHILIP'S

West from Greenwich

KANSAS

NEBRASKA

WYOMING

UTAH

NEW MEXICO

OKLAHOMA

COLORADO

Counties and regions: DEUEL, SEDGWICK, PHILLIPS, YUMA, WASHINGTON, LOGAN, MORGAN, WELD, LARIMER, KIMBALL, LARAMIE, ALBANY, MOFFAT, ROUTT, JACKSON, GRAND, BOULDER, ADAMS, ARAPAHOE, DENVER, JEFFERSON, CLEAR CREEK, GILPIN, SUMMIT, EAGLE, PITKIN, GARFIELD, RIO BLANCO, MESA, DELTA, GUNNISON, MONTROSE, OURAY, SAN MIGUEL, DOLORES, MONTEZUMA, LA PLATA, HINSDALE, MINERAL, SAN JUAN, ARCHULETA, CONEJOS, RIO GRANDE, SAGUACHE, COSTILLA, ALAMOSA, CHAFFEE, LAKE, PARK, TELLER, FREMONT, CUSTER, HUERFANO, LAS ANIMAS, PUEBLO, EL PASO, DOUGLAS, ELBERT, LINCOLN, KIT CARSON, CHEYENNE, KIOWA, CROWLEY, OTERO, BENT, PROWERS, BACA, DENVER

Rocky Mountains, Front Range, Sangre de Cristo Mountains, San Juan Mountains, Sawatch Range, Park Range, Medicine Bow Mountains, Gore Range, Elk Mountains, West Elk Mountains, Wet Mountains, San Luis Valley, Colorado Plateau, Uncompahgre Plateau, Grand Mesa, Roan Plateau, Book Cliffs, Danforth Hills, Flat Tops, Rio Grande

National forests and parks: ROCKY MT. NAT. PARK, PAWNEE NATIONAL GRASSLAND, ROOSEVELT NATIONAL FOREST, ARAPAHO NATIONAL FOREST, PIKE NATIONAL FOREST, WHITE RIVER NATIONAL FOREST, GUNNISON NATIONAL FOREST, ROUTT NATIONAL FOREST, MEDICINE BOW NATIONAL FOREST, GRAND MESA NATIONAL FOREST, UNCOMPAHGRE NATIONAL FOREST, SAN JUAN NATIONAL FOREST, RIO GRANDE NATIONAL FOREST, SAN ISABEL NATIONAL FOREST, COMANCHE NATIONAL GRASSLAND, DINOSAUR NAT. MON., COLORADO NAT. MON., BLACK CANYON OF THE GUNNISON NAT. PARK, GREAT SAND DUNES NAT. MON., MESA VERDE NATIONAL PARK, HOVENWEEP NAT. MON., CANYONS OF THE ANCIENTS NAT. MON., YUCCA HOUSE NAT. MON., AZTEC RUINS NAT. MON., FLORISSANT FOSSIL BEDS NAT. MON., BENT'S OLD FORT NAT. HISTORIC SITE, GREAT PLAINS RESERVOIRS, CURECANTI NAT. REC. AREA, SOUTHERN UTE INDIAN RESERVATION, UTE MOUNTAIN RESERVATION, NAVAJO INDIAN RES., UINTAH AND OURAY INDIAN RESERVATION, BROWNS PARK NAT. W.R.

Cities and towns: Denver, Colorado Springs, Pueblo, Fort Collins, Greeley, Boulder, Longmont, Loveland, Aurora, Lakewood, Arvada, Westminster, Thornton, Englewood, Littleton, Golden, Centennial, Castle Rock, Parker, Brighton, Commerce City, Northglenn, Federal Heights, Lafayette, Louisville, Broomfield, Estes Park, Sterling, Fort Morgan, Brush, Wray, Burlington, Limon, Lamar, La Junta, Rocky Ford, Las Animas, Trinidad, Walsenburg, Alamosa, Monte Vista, Del Norte, Creede, Durango, Cortez, Telluride, Ouray, Silverton, Montrose, Delta, Grand Junction, Fruita, Rifle, Glenwood Springs, Aspen, Carbondale, Leadville, Breckenridge, Vail, Steamboat Springs, Craig, Meeker, Gunnison, Salida, Cañon City, Florence, Woodland Park, Manitou Springs, Cheyenne Wells, Eads, Springfield, Campo, Holly, Granada

Elevations (m): Mt. Elbert 4398, Mt. Massive, Mt. Harvard 4395, La Plata Pk., Uncompahgre Pk. 4361, Crestone Pk., Mt. Lincoln, Grays Pk., Mt. Antero 4349, Pikes Pk. 4301, Mt. Evans 4348, Longs Pk., Mt. Wilson 4342, Blanca Pk. 4372, San Luis Pk. 4271, Summit Pk. 4285, Wheeler Peak 4011, Mt. Sneffels, Windom Pk.

1:2 100 000

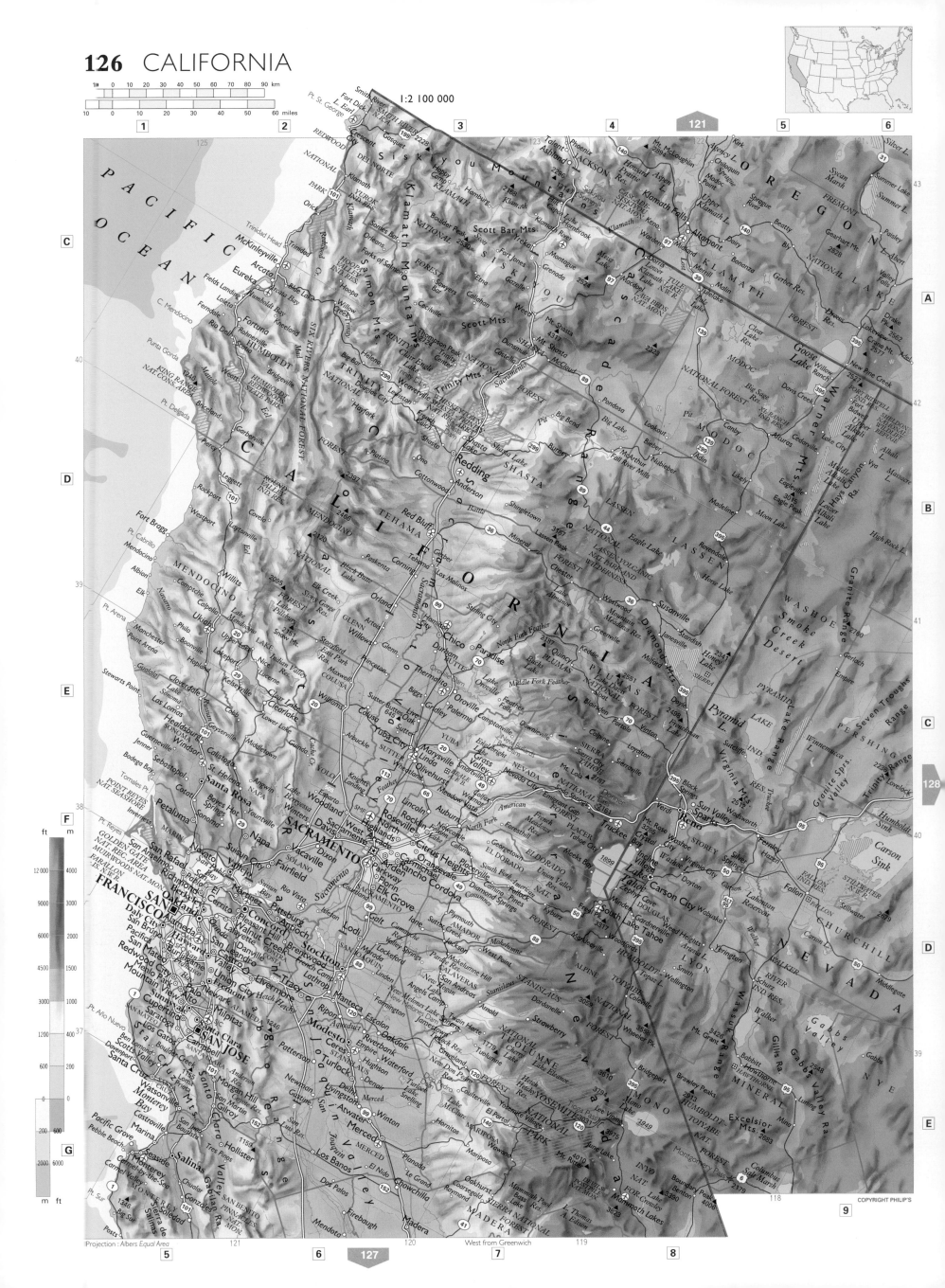

COPYRIGHT PHILIP'S

Projection : Albers Equal Area

West from Greenwich

NEVADA

ESMERALDA

NYE

CLARK

ARIZONA

YUMA

MEXICO

BAJA CALIFORNIA

PACIFIC OCEAN

Channel Islands

Gulf of Santa Catalina

Santa Barbara Channel

LOS ANGELES

SAN DIEGO

SAN BERNARDINO

Bakersfield

Fresno

Clovis

Tijuana

Mexicali

Calexico

Barstow

Lancaster

Palmdale

Victorville

Death Valley National Park

SEQUOIA NATIONAL PARK

KINGS CANYON NATIONAL PARK

JOSHUA TREE NAT. PARK

CHANNEL ISLANDS NAT. PARK

Salton Sea

Imperial Valley

Mojave Desert

Santa Barbara

Ventura

Oxnard

Oceanside

Carlsbad

Escondido

Chula Vista

National City

Long Beach

Santa Monica

Pasadena

Burbank

Glendale

Anaheim

Santa Ana

Riverside

Redlands

Palm Springs

San Luis Obispo

Paso Robles

Morro Bay

Santa Maria

Lompoc

Goleta

Needles

Blythe

Mt. Whitney 4418

Projection : Albers Equal Area

West from Greenwich

COPYRIGHT PHILIP'S

126

128

130

166

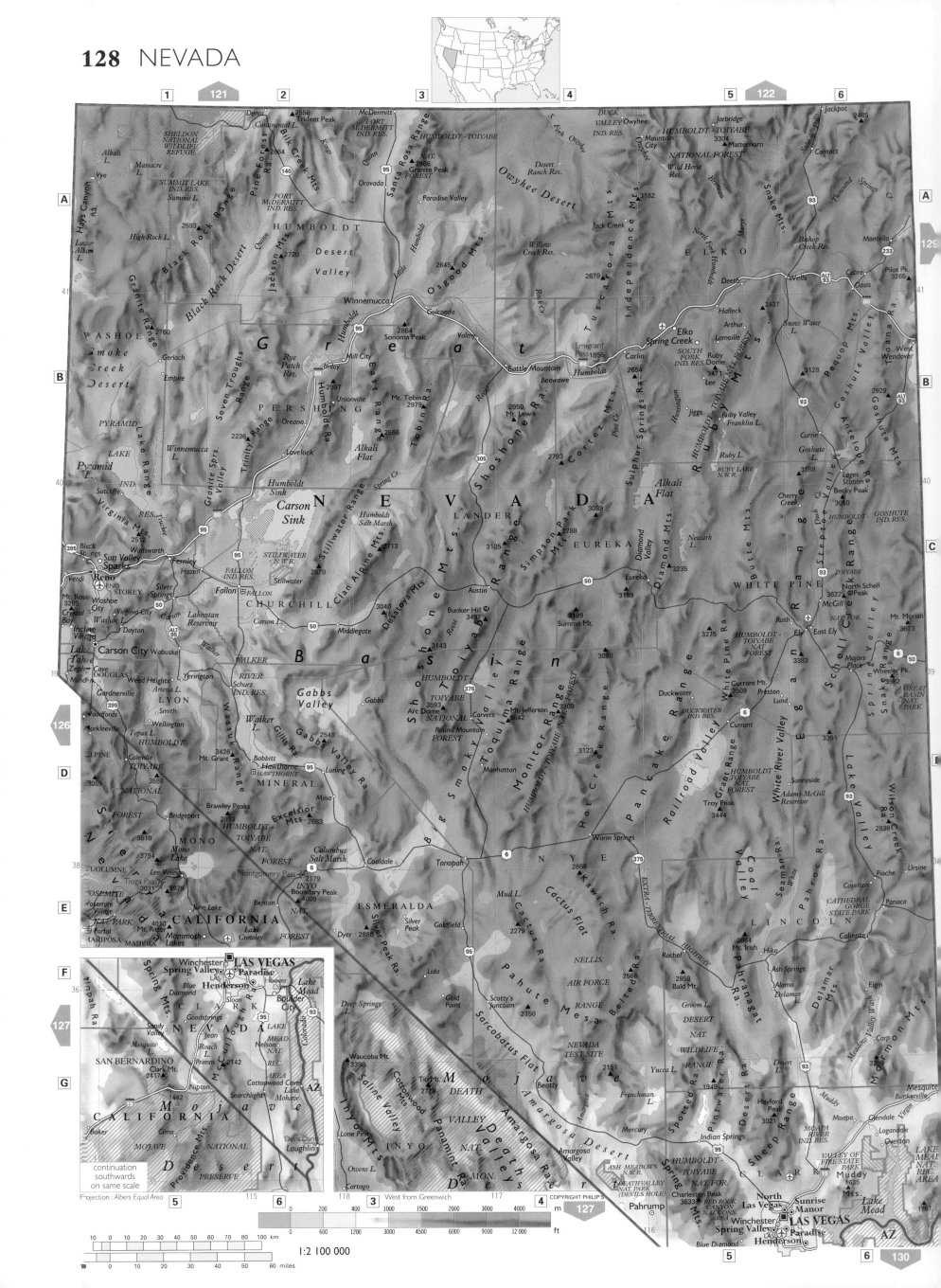

1:2 100 000

10 0 10 20 30 40 50 60 70 80 90 km
10 0 10 20 30 40 50 60 miles

1 **2** **3** **4** **5** **6** **7**

122 124

A
SAWTOOTH
2457 ▲ Monument Pk.
NAT. FOR.
Cache Peak ▲ 3151
CASSIA
Holbrook
ONEIDA
Malad City
Cliifton
Samaria
15
FRANKLIN
Preston
Paris
Bloomington
NEAR
LAKE
N.W.R.
Border
Cokeville
LINCOLN
Eden
Reservoir
Farson
Fontenelle
Reservoir
A

Albion Mts.
Bridge 2861
Black
Pine Pk.
CITY OF ROCKS
NATIONAL RESERVE
Cornish
Lewiston
Richmond
91
Smithfield
N. Logan
WASATCH-
St. Charles
Bear L.
Garden City
Laketown
189
Fontenelle
Opal
Kemmerer
Sage
Elkol
Diamondville
SEEDSKADEE
NATIONAL WILDLIFE
REFUGE
Spring Butte
2314 Superior
Point of
Rocks

2485 ▲
Yost
Standrod
Howell
Stone
Snowville
Portage
Clarkston
Plymouth, Trenton
Logan
CACHE
Providence
Hyrum
Paradise
NAT. FOR.
RICH
Randolph
Woodruff
WYOMING
FOSSIL BUTTE
NAT. MON.
Frontier
30
Naomi Peak
3042
Elkol
Almy
Granger
Little
America
191
80
Rock Springs
Bitter Cr.

B
ELKO
Montello
Cobre
233
Grouse Creek
Etna
Lynn
Raft River Mts.
Rosette
Park Valley
GOLDEN SPIKE
NAT. HIST. SITE
HOGUP
Mts.
BOX
ELDER
2247 ▲
Great
Tremonton
Garland
Fielding
Honeyville
Bear River City
Corinne
Brigham City
Perry
Willard
Wellsville
Mantua
Woodruff
WEBER
2976 ▲
189
Evanston
Mountain View
Fort Bridger
Lyman
Carter
Muddy Cr.
UINTA
Robertson
Bear
Blacks Fork
FLAMING
GORGE
NATIONAL
REC. AREA
Manila
Flaming
Gorge
Reservoir
Pine Mountain
2911 ▲
B

SWEETWATER
Green River

C
Thousand Springs Cr.
Toana Ra.
30
West
Wendover
ALT
93
Wendover
UTAH TEST
RANGE NORTH
Desert Peak
2135 ▲
Lakeside
Newfoundland
Mts.
2135
Salt
Newfoundland
Evaporation
Basin
Lake
1282
Rowley
Stansbury I.
Antelope I.
Farmington
DAVIS
Woods Cross
North Salt Lake
Bountiful
Centerville
Kaysville
Layton
Clearfield
Clinton
Roy
Washington Terrace
South Ogden
Ogden
North Ogden
Pleasant View
Plain City
Huntsville
MORGAN
Morgan
Henefer
Coalville
80
SUMMIT
Oakley
Park City
Kamas
3157 ▲
3804 ▲
WASATCH-CACHE
NATIONAL FOREST
Uinta Mountains
Kings Peak
4123
3731
Marsh Peak
2977
Flaming
Gorge Dam
Dutch John
Mt. Lena
DAGGETT
Burntfork
DINOSAUR
NAT. MON.
Greystone
Yampa
C

Pilot Pk.
3265 ▲
G
O
Bonneville
Salt Flats
SLC
Salt Lake City
Magna
West Valley City
Murray
Midvale
Holladay
Millcreek
Cottonwood
Sandy Heights
Draper
Francis
Heber City
Midway
WASATCH
Daniels
Pass 2437
Hanna
Tabiona
Altamont
Neola
ASHLEY
NAT. FOREST
Whiterocks
UINTA AND
OURAY
INDIAN
Maeser
Vernal
Naples
Jensen
Blue
Mountain
Dinosaur
UINTAH
Randlett
MOFFAT

2929 ▲
GREAT
SALT
Grantsville
Erda
Tooele
WASATCH-
CACHE
NAT. FOR.
3362 ▲
Stockton
Deseret Peak
Eagle Mountain
South Jordan
Riverton
Alpine
Lehi
American Fork
Lindon
Pleasant Grove
Orem
Provo
Wallsburg
Charleston
Lake Fork
Starvation
Res.
Duchesne
191
DUCHESNE
Fruitland
Strawberry Res.
40
Myton
Roosevelt
Fort Duchesne
Ouray
RESERVATION
Bonanza
UINTAH
RIO
BLANCO
CO
Rangely

D
WHITE
PINE
GOSHUTE
IND. RES.
Goshute
Ibapah Pk.
3684 ▲
Callao
FISH SPRINGS
NAT. WILDLIFE
REFUGE
SKULL VALLEY
IND. RES.
Rush
Valley
36
Vernon
Faust
Dugway
DUGWAY
PROVING
GROUND
Eureka
Elberta
Goshen
6
Santaquin
Rocky Ridge
3636 ▲
Mt. Nebo
NAT.
Mona
Nephi
SALT
UTAH
Utah
Lake
Springville
Mapleton
Spanish Fork
Salem
Payson
Fountain Green
Fairview
Moroni
Mount
Pleasant
JUAB
Levan
Elk Ridge
UINTA
Spring City
WASATCH
UTAH
NAT.
FOREST
ASHLEY NAT. FOR.
Soldier
Summit
Scofield Res.
Scofield
Colton
6
Helper
Spring Glen
Price
Wellington
East Carbon
West Tavaputs
Plateau
3104 ▲
Bruin Point
Sunnyside
CARBON
Nine Mile Cr.
191
UINTAH AND
OURAY
IND. RES.
East Tavaputs
Plateau
GARFIELD
Roan
Plateau
D
125

Mt. Moriah
3673 ▲
Deep Creek Ra.
Snake Valley
Trout Creek
SEVIER
DESERT
Lynndyl
Leamington
Oak City
Scipio
Sevier
Bridge
Res.
Fayette
Mayfield
Centerfield
SANPETE
Ephraim
Manti
3197 ▲
Sterling
Swedish Knoll
MANTI-LA
SAL.
NATIONAL
FOREST
Hiawatha
Cleveland
Elmo
Huntington
Castle Dale
Emery
Crangeville
Ferron
3392 ▲
Heliotrope
Mt
EMERY
Moore
Green
River
Price River
Roan
Book
Cliffs
Green
Crescent
Junction
Thompson
Springs
Cisco
GRAND
Cliffs
Mack
Fruita
Lama
COLORADO
NAT. MON.
MESA
E

Salt Marsh
L.
Swasey
Peak
2947 ▲
House Ra.
2943 ▲
Notch Peak
6
50
2545 ▲
Tule Valley
Confusion Ra.
Cricket Mts.
MILLARD
Clear L.
Holden
Delta
Deseret
Hinckley
Sugarville
Sevier
Fillmore
Meadow
Kanosh
3133 ▲
Oasis
Redmond
Salina
Richfield
Glenwood
Annabella
Sigurd
SEVIER
NATIONAL
FOREST
FISHLAKE
Emery
3539 ▲
Mt. Marvine
Last Chance Cr.
Fremont Junction
San Rafael Swell
2414 ▲
24
San Rafael
Desert
San
Rafael
70
191
ARCHES
NAT.
PARK
Moab
Castle Valley
La Sal Mts.
Mt. Peale
3877 ▲
MANTI-LA SAL
NAT. FOR.
MONTROSE
Uravan
E
128

NV
Wheeler Pk.
3982 ▲
GREAT
BASIN
NAT.
PARK
Garrison
6
50
50
Wilson Creek Ra.
Indian Peak Range
2982 ▲
Indian Peak
Milford
Minersville
Beaver
Frisco Peak
2944 ▲
Wah Wah Mts.
Mineral Mts.
BEAVER
Tushar Mts.
3710 ▲
Delano Peak
Marysvale
Sevier
Joseph
Monroe
Cove
Fort
Elsinore
FISHLAKE
NATIONAL
FOREST
Koosharem
Fish L.
Fremont
Loa
Lyman
Bicknell
Torrey
Teasdale
Grover
Fremont
Caineville
Hanksville
WAYNE
Dirty Devil
Dry
GLEN
CANYON
NAT. REC.
AREA
CANYONLANDS
NATIONAL
PARK
Summit
Point
La Sal
Bedrock
SAN
MIGUEL
Slick Rock
Egnar
F

WHITE
PINE
Ursine
Beryl
Modena
Uvada
Newcastle
LINCOLN
Enterprise
Lund
Little Salt
L.
Escalante Desert
IRON
Paragonah
Parowan
Enoch
Cedar City
Summit
89
DIXIE
NAT.
Brian Head
3446 ▲
Panguitch
Hatch
PIUTE
3454 ▲
Circleville Mt.
Circleville
Junction
Kingston
Antimony
Otter Creek
Res.
Otter Creek
3365 ▲
Mt. Dutton
Circle
Cliffs
Aquarius
Plateau
DIXIE
NAT.
FOR.
Boulder
Escalante
3216 ▲
GARFIELD
3453 ▲
CAPITOL
REEF
NATIONAL
PARK
Henry
Mountains
3466 ▲
Mt. Pennell
3463 ▲
Mt. Peale
COLORADO
Colorado
Lockhart
Glen Canyon
Ticaboo
Fry Canyon
95
2761 ▲
Bears Ears
NATURAL
BRIDGES
NAT. MON.
Blanding
SAN JUAN
Abajo Peak
3463 ▲
MANTI-LA SAL
NATIONAL
FOREST
491
Monticello
Dove
Creek
F
ft   m
F

Mt. Bangs
2442 ▲
Littlefield
Mesquite
Bunkerville
Virgin Mts.
St. George
Santa Clara
Washington
Hurricane
Ivins
La Verkin
Leeds
Toquerville
New Harmony
Central
Pine Valley
Kanarraville
PAIUTE
IND. RES.
DIXIE NAT.
FOR.
Signal Peak 3159 ▲
Lost Peak
2290 ▲
PAIUTE
IND. RES.
14
CEDAR BREAKS
NAT. MON.
Alton
BRYCE
CANYON
NAT. PARK
Tropic
Cannonville
Henrieville
Pink
Cliffs
ZION
NAT.
PARK
Springdale
Rockville
Virgin
9
Glendale
Orderville
Mt. Carmel
KANE
GRAND STAIRCASE-
ESCALANTE
NATIONAL MONUMENT
Kaiparowits Plateau
Escalante
Plateau
San
Powell
HOVENWEEP
NAT. MON.
Montezuma
Creek
Bluff
Aneth
UTE MT.
IND. RES.
NM
CANYONS OF
THE ANCIENTS
NAT. MON.
DOLORES
Cahone
Pleasant
View
12000
9000
6000
4500
3000
1200
4000
3000
2000
1500
1000
400
F

G
Colorado City
Moccasin
Fredonia
KAIBAB
IND. RES.
Kanab
Paria
Plateau
Big Water
89
VERMILION
CLIFFS NAT. MON.
Rainbow Plateau
Page
RAINBOW
BRIDGE
NAT. MON.
Navajo Mt.
3166 ▲
Navajo Cr.
Monument
1609 Pass
163
Mexican
Water
Dennehotso
160
Mexican Hat
Monument Valley
NAVAJO
NAVAJO NATION INDIAN RESERVATION
Pastora Pk.
2869 ▲
Teec Nos Pos
FOUR
CORNERS
64
Beklabito
San Juan
NM
G

Jacob Lake
VERMILION CLIFFS
Colorado
Vermilion Cliffs
Hurricane
Cliffs
Kaibab
PIPE SPRING
NAT. MON.
GRAND CANYON-
PARASHANT NAT. MON.
MOHAVE
ARIZONA
COCONINO
Kayenta
APACHE

1:2 100 000

10 0 10 20 30 40 50 60 70 80 90 km
10 0 10 20 30 40 50 60 miles

UTAH

NEVADA

Littlefield
Colorado City
Moccasin
Fredonia
Mt. Bangs 2442
Bunkerville
Mesquite
Virgin Mts.
Hurricane Cliffs
Kenab Plateau
Kaibab Plateau
L. Powell
Page
VERMILION CLIFFS
Paria Plateau
NAT. MON.
Glen Canyon Dam
Marble Canyon
Rainbow Plateau
Monument Pass 1609
Monument Valley
Mexican Water
Teec Nos Pos
Dennehotso
Pastora Pk. 2869

Logandale
Overton
Mesquite
CLARK
Lake Mead
GRAND CANYON-PARASHANT NAT. MON.
Mt. Trumbull 2447
Shivwits Plateau
Kaibab IND. RES.
KAIBAB IND. RES.
Jacob Lake
PIPE SPRING NAT. MON.
Kaibab
Kanab Cr.
Supai
HAVASUPAI IND. RES.
North Rim
Point Imperial 2683
Colorado
Echo Cliffs
Kaibito Plateau
Kaibito
Shonto
Marsh Pass 2041
Kayenta
Black Mesa
Round Rock
Rock Point
Red Rock
Roof Butte 2989
Lukachukai
Matthews Pk. 2899
Tsaile

Jumbo Pk. 1757
LAKE MEAD NAT. REC. AREA
GRAND CANYON NATIONAL PARK
GRAND CANYON NATIONAL PARK
Grand Canyon
Tusayan
COCONINO
Tonalea
Navajo Cr.
NAVAJO NAT. MON.
Many Farms
CANYON DE CHELLY NAT. MON.
Chinle
Fort Defiance
Window Rock

Hoover Dam
LAKE MEAD NAT. REC. AREA
Lake Mead
Supai
Havasu Cr.
KAIBAB
NATIONAL FOREST
Tuba City
Moenkopi
Moenkopi Wash
Dinnebito Wash
Pinon
Salina
Steamboat Canyon
Ganado
HUBBELL TRADING POST NAT. HIST. SITE

Davis Dam
Black Mts.
Dolan Springs
Red L.
Cerbat Mts.
MOHAVE
HUALAPAI INDIAN RESERVATION
Peach Springs
Aubrey Cliffs
Coconino Plateau
Little Colorado
NAVAJO
Hotevilla
Kykotsmovi Village
HOPI
Polacca
Second Mesa
Keams Canyon
INDIAN
RESERVATION
Dilkon
NAVAJO INDIAN RESERVATION
Chambers
Houck
Sanders
Lupton

Lake Mohave
Mt. Tipton 2179
Truxton
Nelson
WUPATKI NAT. MON.
Polacca Wash
Black Cr.

Kingman
Hualapai Pk. 2566
Valentine
Hackberry
Seligman
Williams
2821
Ash Fork
Bill Williams Mt.
San Francisco Mts.
Humphreys Pk. 3851
SUNSET CRATER VOLCANO NAT. MON.
Flagstaff
WALNUT CANYON NAT. MON.
Winslow
Joseph City
Holbrook
APACHE
Leupp Corner
Little Colorado
PETRIFIED FOREST NAT. PARK
Navajo
ZUNI INDIAN RESERVATION
Zion Res.
St. Johns

Bullhead City
Riviera
FORT MOHAVE IND. RES.
Oatman
Mohave Mts.
Juniper Mts.
Big Chino Wash
Mountainaire
COCONINO
NATIONAL
FOREST
Mormon Lake
Mormon L.
Hutch Mt. 2601
Happy Jack
Concho
Snowflake
Clay Springs
Taylor
Lyman L.
Springerville

Yucca
Mohon Pk. 2285
Paulden
Drake
Chino Valley
Clarkdale
Jerome
TUZIGOOT NAT. MON.
Sedona
OAK
Cottonwood
Cornville
MONTEZUMA CASTLE NAT. MON.
Lake Montezuma
Baker Butte 2461
APACHE
Mogollon Plateau
SITGREAVES
Heber
Show Low
NATIONAL
FOREST
Pinetop-Lakeside
McNary
Eagar
Nutrioso

L. Havasu
Aquarius Mts.
PRESCOTT
Skull Valley
Prescott
Cornville
Dewey
Humboldt
YAVAPAI 2345
Camp Verde
Pine
Payson 1459
Mogollon Rim
Cibecue
FORT APACHE INDIAN RESERVATION
Whiteriver
White Mts.
Baldy Pk. 3476
Alpine

Lake Havasu City
Parker Dam
CHEMEHUEVI IND. RES.
Bill Williams
Alamo L.
Big Sandy
Santa Maria
Kirkland
Spruce Mt. 2297
Kirkland Junction
Mayer
AGUA FRIA NAT. MON.
Verde
TONTO
2409
Payson
Aztec Pk. 2345
FOREST
White R.
Black R.

CALIFORNIA
Parker
Buckskin Mts. 1197
LA PAZ
Bouse
Harcuvar Mts. 1598
Hillside
Yarnell
Congress
Black Canyon City
Horseshoe Res.
Mazatzal Mts.
Theodore 2345
Roosevelt L.
Roosevelt
GILA
Aztec Pk.
SAN CARLOS INDIAN RESERVATION
Rose Pk. 2678
GREENLEE

Colorado
Poston
COLORADO RIVER IND. RES.
Bill Williams River
N.W.R.
ARIZONA
Wickenburg
Morristown
Wittmann
Cave Creek
Carefree
L. Pleasant
Bartlett Res.
2334
FORT McDOWELL IND. RES.
Apache L.
TONTO NAT. FOREST
Claypool
Miami
Globe
San Carlos
Peridot
San Carlos L.
2224
Morenci
Clifton

Ehrenberg
Harquahala Mts.
Aguila
Wenden
Salome
Hope
Vicksburg
Vulture Mts. 1115
Salome
Hassayampa
Surprise
Sun City West
Sun City
Peoria
El Mirage
Glendale
Paradise Valley
Fountain Hills
SALT RIVER IND. RES.
Scottsdale
Tempe
Mesa
Apache Junction
Tortilla Flat
Queen Creek
Superior
60
Kearny
Winkelman
Hayden
Dudleyville
Mammoth
Pinaleno Mts.
Mt. Graham 3267
CORONADO
Safford
Solomon
GRAHAM
Thatcher
Pima
Duncan

Quartzsite
KOFA
Kofa Mts.
Signal Peak 1487
KOFA NAT. WILDLIFE REFUGE
Castle Dome Pk. 1155
Eagletail Mts.
1006
Centennial Wash
1732
Tonopah
Litchfield Park
Goodyear
Avondale
Tolleson
PHOENIX
PHX
Guadalupe
Gilbert
Chandler
HOHOKAM PIMA NAT. MON.
GILA RIVER INDIAN RES.
Sacaton
Coolidge
CASA GRANDE RUINS NAT. MON.
Florence
PINAL
Gila
La Palma
Coolidge Dam
Bylas
Galiuro Mts. 2336
San Simon
Franklin
San Simon

Cibola
Trigo Mts.
Chocolate Mts.
Martinez Lake
Imperial Dam
IMPERIAL NAT. WILDLIFE REFUGE
Yuma
SONORAN
Arlington
Palo Verde
Buckeye
966
Gila Bend Mts.
MARICOPA
Komatke
Maricopa
Santa Cruz Wash
Mobile
GILA BEND IND. RES.
MARICOPA (AK-CHIN) IND. RES.
Olberg
Casa Grande
Eloy
Picacho
Picacho Pass
549
Red Rock
Marana
Oracle
San Manuel
SAN CARLOS INDIAN RESERVATION

Somerton
Gadsden
San Luis
Yuma
YUMA PROVING GROUND
Roll
Wellton
Tacna
Dateland
Sentinel
BARRY M. GOLDWATER AIR FORCE RANGE
Gila Bend
Stanfield
Casa Grande
Arizona City
Eloy
IRONWOOD FOREST NAT. MON.
Rillito
Silver Bell
Catalina
CORONADO NAT. FOR.
2791
Oro Valley
SAGUARO NAT. PARK
Tucson
TUS
South Tucson
Vail
Willcox
FORT BOWIE NAT. HIST. SITE
Bowie
San Simon

Yuma Desert
Gila Mts. 960
Mohawk Mts. 846
Coyote Wash
Growler Wash
Cabeza Prieta Wash
DESERT
Sand Tank Mts.
NAT. MON.
Table Top 1333
Santa Rosa Wash
Sand
Tank Mts.
SAUCEDA MTS.
1252
Santa Rosa
Anegam
Sil Nakya 1459
TOHONO O'ODHAM INDIAN RESERVATION
Sells
Comobabi Mts.
Bradley Wash
TOHONO O'ODHAM (SAN XAVIER) IND. RES.
Sahuarita
Green Valley
Benson
St. David
COCHISE
Willcox Playa
Dragoon
CHIRICAHUA NAT. MON.
Pearce
Tombstone
191

MEXICO
SONORA
Gran Desierto de Altar
Río Sonoyta
Sonoyta
1206
CABEZA PRIETA N.W.R.
SIERRA PINTA
899
GRANITE MTS.
Growler
ORGAN PIPE CACTUS NAT. MON.
Mt. Ajo 1465
Lukeville
Pisinimo
Topawa
Cowlic
Babaquivari Pk. 2356
BUENOS AIRES N.W.R.
Keystone Pk. 1892
TUMACACORI NAT. HIST. PARK
Sasabe
Tubac
Mt. Wrightson 2881
Patagonia
SANTA CRUZ
Nogales
Sierra Vista
Hereford
Huachuca City
FORT HUACHUCA
CORONADO NAT. FOREST
Elfrida
Chiricahua Pk. 2986
Portal
NAT. FOREST
Bisbee
Naco
Douglas
McNeal

Projection: Albers Equal Area
West from Greenwich
COPYRIGHT PHILIP'S

0 200 400 1000 1500 2000 3000 m
600 1200 3000 4500 6000 9000 ft

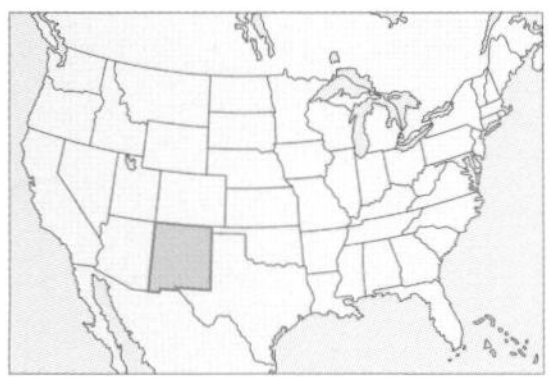

1:2 200 000

10 0 10 20 30 40 50 60 70 80 100 km

10 0 10 20 30 40 50 60 miles

Projection : Albers Equal Area

108 107 106 West from Greenwich 105 104

400 1000 1500 2000 3000 4000 m

1200 3000 4500 6000 9000 12 000 ft

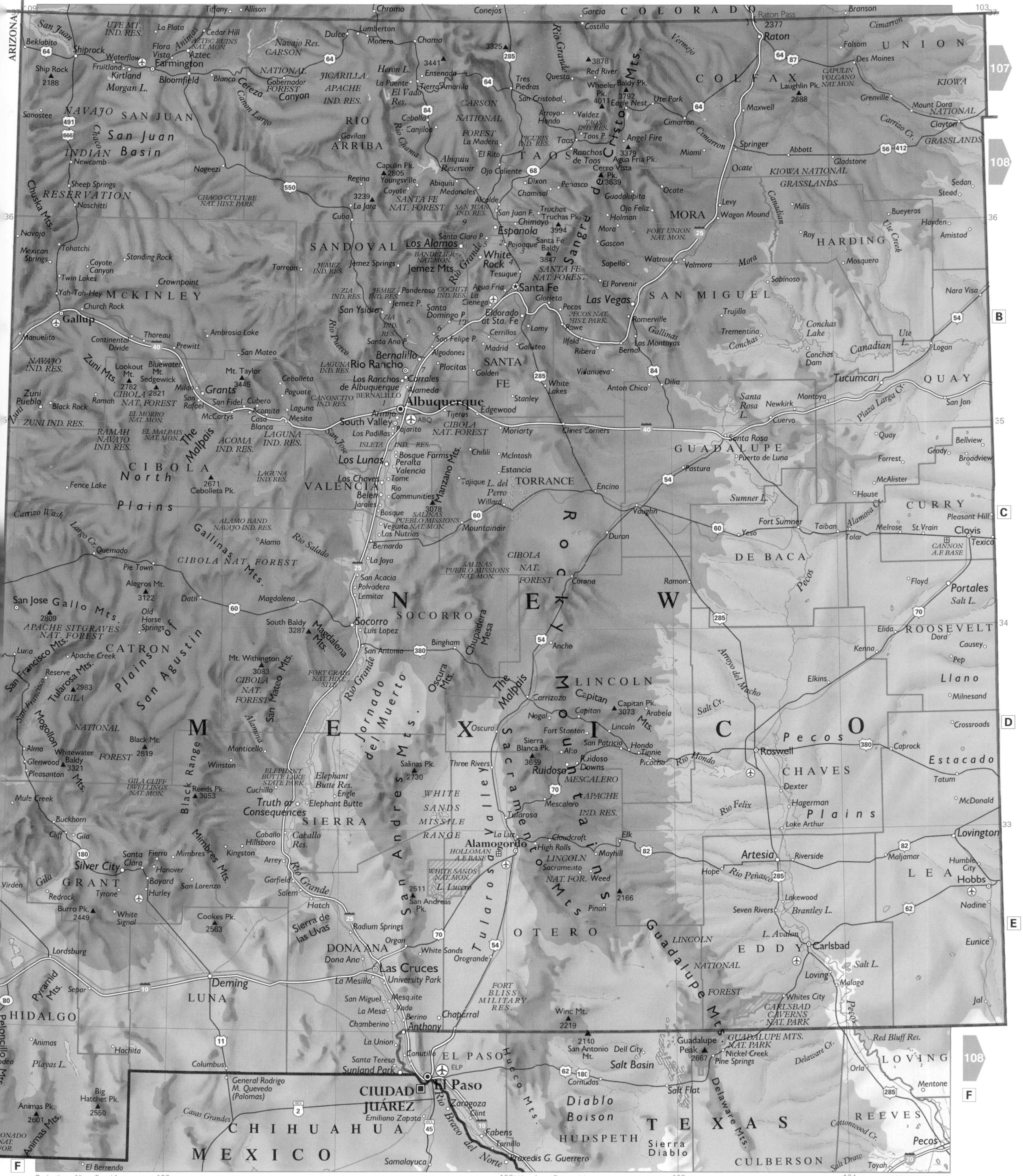

Underlined settlements give their name to the county in which they stand.

1 PETROGLYPH NAT. MON.
2 POJOAQUE IND. RES.
3 NAMBE IND. RES.
4 TESUQUE IND. RES.
5 SAN ILDEFONSO IND. RES.
6 SAN FELIPE IND. RES.
7 SANDIA IND. RES.
8 SANTA ANA IND. RES.
9 SANTA CLARA IND. RES.
10 SANTO DOMINGO IND. RES.

COPYRIGHT PHILIP'S

125 107 108 68

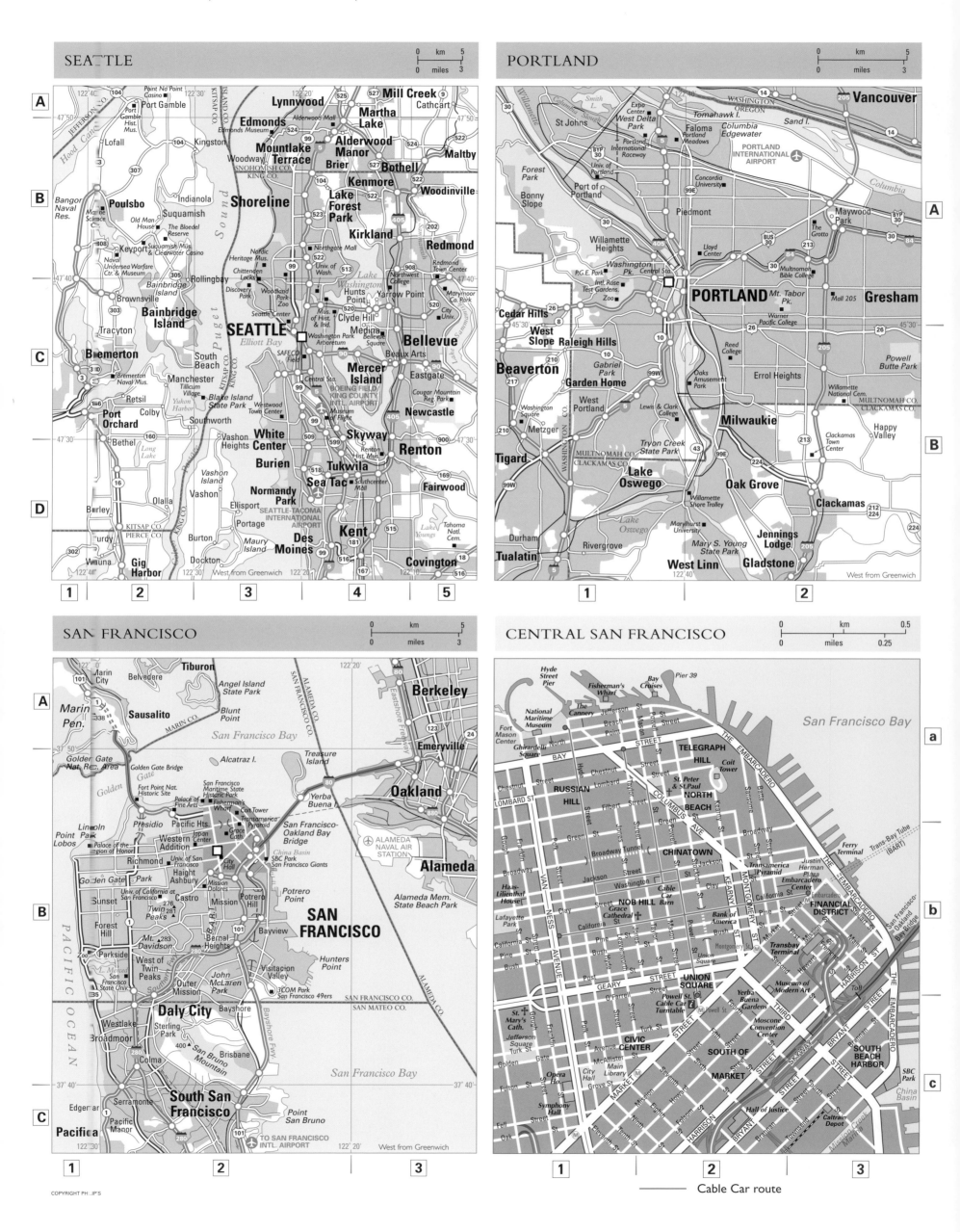

SEATTLE

km 5 / miles 3

A
104 Point Nd Point Casino
Port Gamble
Port Gamble Mus.
Lofall
Kingston
Hood Canal
Edmonds
Edmonds Museum
Alderwood Mall
Lynnwood 525
Martha Lake
Mill Creek 9 Cathcart
527

B
Bangor Naval Res.
Poulsbo
Indianola
Suquamish
Old Man House
The Bloedel Reserve
Suquamish Mus. & Clearwater Casino
Keyport
Marine Science
Naval Undersea Warfare Ctr. & Museum
308
305
Rollingbay
Bainbridge Island
Shoreline
Mountlake Terrace 524
Woodway
Brier 527
Alderwood Manor 524
Bothell
Kenmore 522
Maltby 522
Woodinville
Lake Forest Park 522
523
Kirkland
Redmond
Northgate Mall
Nordic Heritage Mus.
Chittenden Locks
Discovery Park
Woodland Park Zoo
Univ. of Wash. 513
Northwest College 908
Redmond Town Center
202
405

C
Bremerton 3
Bremerton Naval Mus.
Manchester
Tillicum Village
Blake Island State Park
Yukon Harbor
South Beach
Westwood Town Center
SAFECO Field
Central Sta. 90
Hunts Point
Yarrow Point
Clyde Hill
Medina
Bellevue Square
Beaux Arts
Mercer Island
Eastgate
Cougar Mountain Reg. Park
Bellevue
47°40'

D
Port Orchard 160
Colby
Retsil
Bethel
Southworth
Vashon Heights
White Center
Burien
Sea Tac 518
Normandy Park
Des Moines
Kent 181
520
521
Seattle Center
SEATTLE
Washington Park Arboretum
Elliott Bay
Mus. of Hist. & Ind.
509
599
Skyway
Renton Hist. Mus.
Tukwila
Southcenter Mall
Renton 900
Fairwood 169
SEATTLE-TACOMA INTERNATIONAL AIRPORT
Covington 18

PORTLAND

km 5 / miles 3

A
St Johns
Smith L.
Columbia Slough
Expo Center
West Delta Park
Vancouver 205
Tomahawk I.
Sand I.
Faloma
Portland Meadows
Portland International Raceway
Columbia
Edgewater
WASHINGTON OREGON
14
PORTLAND INTERNATIONAL AIRPORT
Maywood Park
The Grotto
Multnomah Bible College
213
Forest Park
Port of Portland
Bonny Slope
Piedmont
Concordia University
Univ. of Portland
99E
Willamette Heights
Lloyd Center
P.G.E. Park
Washington Pk.
Central Sta.
Intl. Rose Test Gardens
Zoo
PORTLAND
Mt. Tabor Pk.
Warner Pacific College
Mall 205
Gresham
26
10

B
Cedar Hills 8
West Slope
Raleigh Hills
Beaverton 217 210
Garden Home
West Portland
Washington Square
Metzger
Tigard 99W
Tualatin
Durham
Rivergrove
West Linn
Reed College
Oaks Amusement Park
Lewis & Clark College
Tryon Creek State Park
Lake Oswego
Willamette Shore Trolley
Marylhurst University
Mary S. Young State Park
Errol Heights
Powell Butte Park
Willamette National Cem.
MULTNOMAH CO. CLACKAMAS CO.
Milwaukie
Oak Grove
Jennings Lodge
Gladstone
Clackamas Town Center
Clackamas 212 224
Happy Valley

SAN FRANCISCO

km 5 / miles 3

A
Marin City 101
Tiburon
Belvedere
Angel Island State Park
Sausalito
Blunt Point
Marin Pen.
Golden Gate Nat. Rec. Area
Alcatraz I.
Treasure Island
Yerba Buena I.
San Francisco Bay
Berkeley 80
Emeryville 123
Oakland 24
880

B
Golden Gate Bridge
Fort Point Nat. Historic Site
Palace of Fine Arts
Presidio
Lincoln Point Park Lobos
Palace of the Legion of Honor
Pacific Hts.
Fisherman's Wharf
Coit Tower
Transamerica Pyramid
Japan Center
Western Addition
Richmond
Univ. of San Francisco
Haight Ashbury
Castro
Mission Dolores
Golden Gate Park
Sunset
Forest Hill
Twin Peaks
Mission
Potrero Hill
Potrero Point
San Francisco-Oakland Bay Bridge
Grace Cath.
City Hall
SBC Park
San Francisco Giants
China Basin
Bayview
Hunters Point
SAN FRANCISCO
Alameda Mem. State Beach Park
Alameda
ALAMEDA NAVAL AIR STATION

C
West of Twin Peaks
John McLaren Park
Visitacion Valley
Outer Mission
3COM Park
San Francisco 49ers
SAN FRANCISCO CO.
SAN MATEO CO.
Daly City
Bayshore
Colma
Sterling Park
San Bruno Mountain
Brisbane
South San Francisco
Pacifica
Pacific Manor
Point San Bruno
TO SAN FRANCISCO INTL. AIRPORT

CENTRAL SAN FRANCISCO

km 0.5 / miles 0.25

Hyde Street Pier
Fisherman's Wharf
Bay Cruises
Pier 39
National Maritime Museum
The Cannery
Fort Mason Center
Ghirardelli Square
TELEGRAPH HILL
Coit Tower
San Francisco Bay
RUSSIAN HILL
NORTH BEACH
St. Peter & St.Paul
THE EMBARCADERO
Broadway Tunnel
CHINATOWN
Transamerica Pyramid
Justin Herman Plaza
Embarcadero Center
Ferry Terminal
Trans Bay Tube (BART)
Haas-Lilienthal House
NOB HILL
Cable Car Barn
Lafayette Park
Grace Cathedral
Bank of America
FINANCIAL DISTRICT
San Francisco-Oakland Bay Bridge
Union Square
Transbay Terminal
St. Mary's Cath.
UNION SQUARE
Powell St. Cable Car Turntable
Yerba Buena Gardens
Museum of Modern Art
SOUTH OF MARKET
Moscone Convention Center
SOUTH BEACH HARBOR
SBC Park
CIVIC CENTER
Opera Ho.
City Hall
McAllister Main Library
Jefferson Square
Symphony Hall
Hall of Justice
Caltrain Depot
China Basin
Mission Creek

Cable Car route

COPYRIGHT PHILIP'S

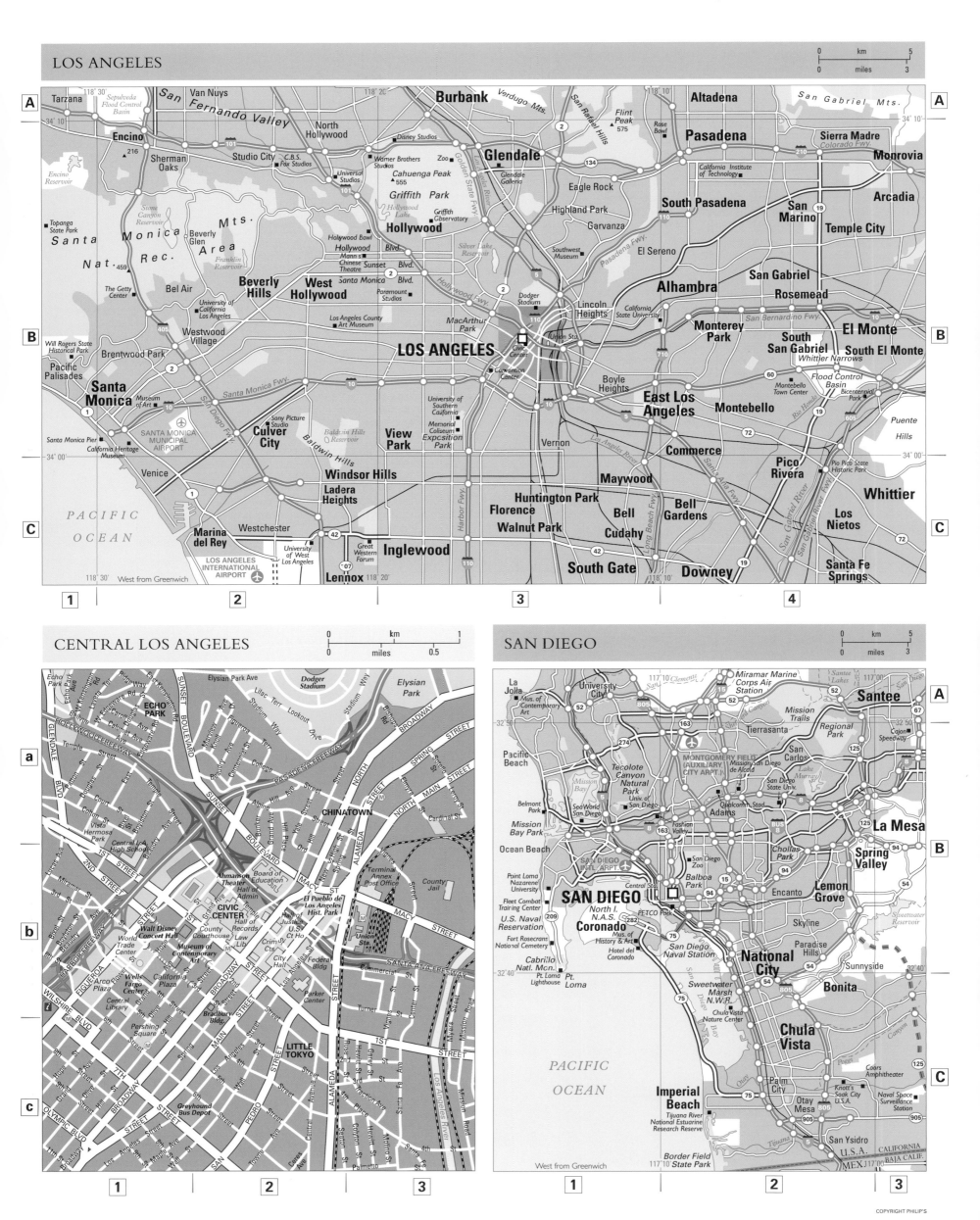

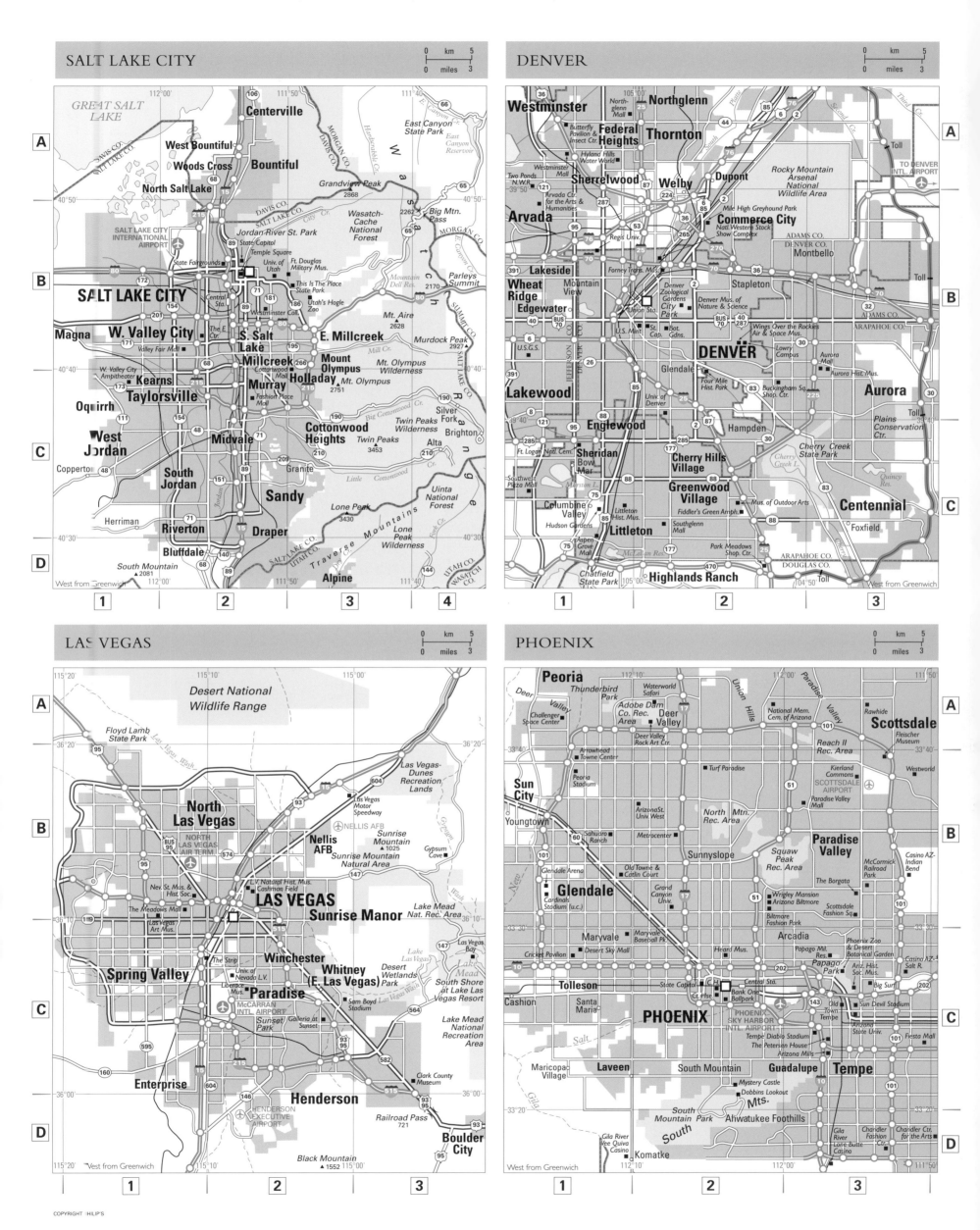

SALT LAKE CITY

km 5 / miles 3

GREAT SALT LAKE

Davis Co.
Centerville
West Bountiful
Woods Cross
Bountiful
North Salt Lake
Grandview Peak 2868

Morgan Co.
East Canyon State Park
East Canyon Reservoir

SALT LAKE CITY INTERNATIONAL AIRPORT
Jordan River St. Park
State Capitol
Temple Square
Univ. of Utah
Ft. Douglas Military Mus.
State Fairgrounds

SALT LAKE CITY
Central Sta.
Westminster Coll.
This Is The Place State Park
Utah's Hogle Zoo

Magna
W. Valley City
The E Ctr.
S. Salt Lake
E. Millcreek
Mount Olympus
Mt. Olympus Wilderness
Mt. Aire 2628
Murdock Peak 2927

Kearns
Taylorsville
Millcreek
Holladay
Mt. Olympus 2751

Oquirrh
Valley Fair Mall
Cottonwood Mall
Fashion Place Mall
Silver Fork
Brighton

West Jordan
Midvale
Cottonwood Heights
Twin Peaks Wilderness
Twin Peaks 3453
Alta

Copperton
Granite
Little Cottonwood

South Jordan
Sandy
Lone Peak 3430
Uinta National Forest

Herriman
Riverton
Draper
Lone Peak Wilderness

Bluffdale
South Mountain ▲ 2081
Alpine
Traverse Mountains
Wasatch Co.

West from Greenwich

DENVER

km 5 / miles 3

Westminster
Northglenn
Federal Heights
Thornton
Sherrelwood
Welby
Dupont
Arvada
Rocky Mountain Arsenal National Wildlife Area
Commerce City
Natl. Western Stock Show Complex
Montbello
Lakeside
Wheat Ridge
Edgewater
Mountain View
Denver Zoological Gardens
City Park
Denver Mus. of Nature & Science
Stapleton
Wings Over the Rockies Air & Space Mus.
U.S. Mint
St. Cap.
Bot. Gdns.
DENVER
Lowry Campus
Aurora Mall
Aurora Hist. Mus.
U.S.G.S.
Lakewood
Univ. of Denver
Glendale
Four Mile Hist. Park
Buckingham Shop. Ctr.
Aurora
Plains Conservation Ctr.
Englewood
Hampden
Sheridan
Ft. Logan Natl. Cem.
Bow Mar
Cherry Hills Village
Cherry Creek State Park
Southwest Plaza Mall
Columbine Valley
Littleton Hist. Mus.
Greenwood Village
Mus. of Outdoor Arts
Fiddler's Green Amph.
Centennial
Hudson Gardens
Southglenn Mall
Foxfield
Aspen Grove Mall
Littleton
Park Meadows Shop. Ctr.
McLellan Res.
Chatfield State Park
Highlands Ranch
Douglas Co.
Arapahoe Co.

West from Greenwich

LAS VEGAS

km 5 / miles 3

Desert National Wildlife Range
Floyd Lamb State Park
Las Vegas Wash
Las Vegas-Dunes Recreation Lands
North Las Vegas
Las Vegas Motor Speedway
Nellis AFB
Sunrise Mountain 1025
Sunrise Mountain Natural Area
Gypsum Cave
North Las Vegas Air Term.
L.V. Natural Hist. Mus.
Cashman Field
Nev. St. Mus. & Hist. Soc.
The Meadows Mall
LAS VEGAS
Sunrise Manor
Lake Mead Nat. Rec. Area
Las Vegas Art Mus.
Winchester
Whitney (E. Las Vegas)
Desert Wetlands Park
Lake Las Vegas
Spring Valley
The Strip
Univ. of Nevada L.V.
Liberace Mus.
Paradise
Sam Boyd Stadium
South Shore at Lake Las Vegas Resort
McCARRAN INTL. AIRPORT
Sunset Park
Galleria at Sunset
Lake Mead National Recreation Area
Clark County Museum
Enterprise
Henderson
HENDERSON EXECUTIVE AIRPORT
Railroad Pass 721
Boulder City
Black Mountain ▲ 1552

West from Greenwich

PHOENIX

km 5 / miles 3

Peoria
Thunderbird Park
Waterworld Safari
Adobe Dam Co. Rec. Area
Deer Valley
National Mem. Cem. of Arizona
Rawhide
Scottsdale
Fleischer Museum
Challenger Space Center
Deer Valley Rock Art Ctr.
Reach II Rec. Area
Westworld
Arrowhead Towne Center
Sun City
Turf Paradise
Kierland Commons
Youngtown
Peoria Stadium
SCOTTSDALE AIRPORT
Paradise Valley Mall
Sahuaro Ranch
Arizona St. Univ. West
North Mtn. Rec. Area
Metrocenter
Paradise Valley
Glendale Arena
Old Towne & Catlin Court
Sunnyslope
Squaw Peak Rec. Area
McCormick Railroad Park
Casino AZ-Indian Bend
Glendale
Cardinals Stadium (u.c.)
Grand Canyon Univ.
Wrigley Mansion
Arizona Biltmore
Biltmore Fashion Park
Scottsdale Fashion Sq.
The Borgata
Maryvale
Maryvale Baseball Pk.
Arcadia
Phoenix Zoo & Desert Botanical Garden
Cricket Pavilion
Desert Sky Mall
Heard Mus.
Papago Pk.
Papago Park
Ariz. Hist. Soc. Mus.
Casino AZ-Salt R.
Tolleson
State Capitol
Bank One Ballpark
Central Sta.
PHOENIX
Cashion
Santa Maria
PHOENIX SKY HARBOR INTL. AIRPORT
Tempe Diablo Stadium
The Petersen House
Old Town Tempe
Arizona Mills
Sun Devil Stadium
Arizona State Univ.
Fiesta Mall
Laveen
South Mountain
Guadalupe
Tempe
Maricopa Village
Mystery Castle
Dobbins Lookout
South Mountain Park
South Mtns.
Ahwatukee Foothills
Gila River Vee Quiva Casino
Komatke
Gila River
Lone Butte Casino
Chandler Fashion Ctr.
Chandler Ctr. for the Arts

West from Greenwich

COPYRIGHT PHILIP'S

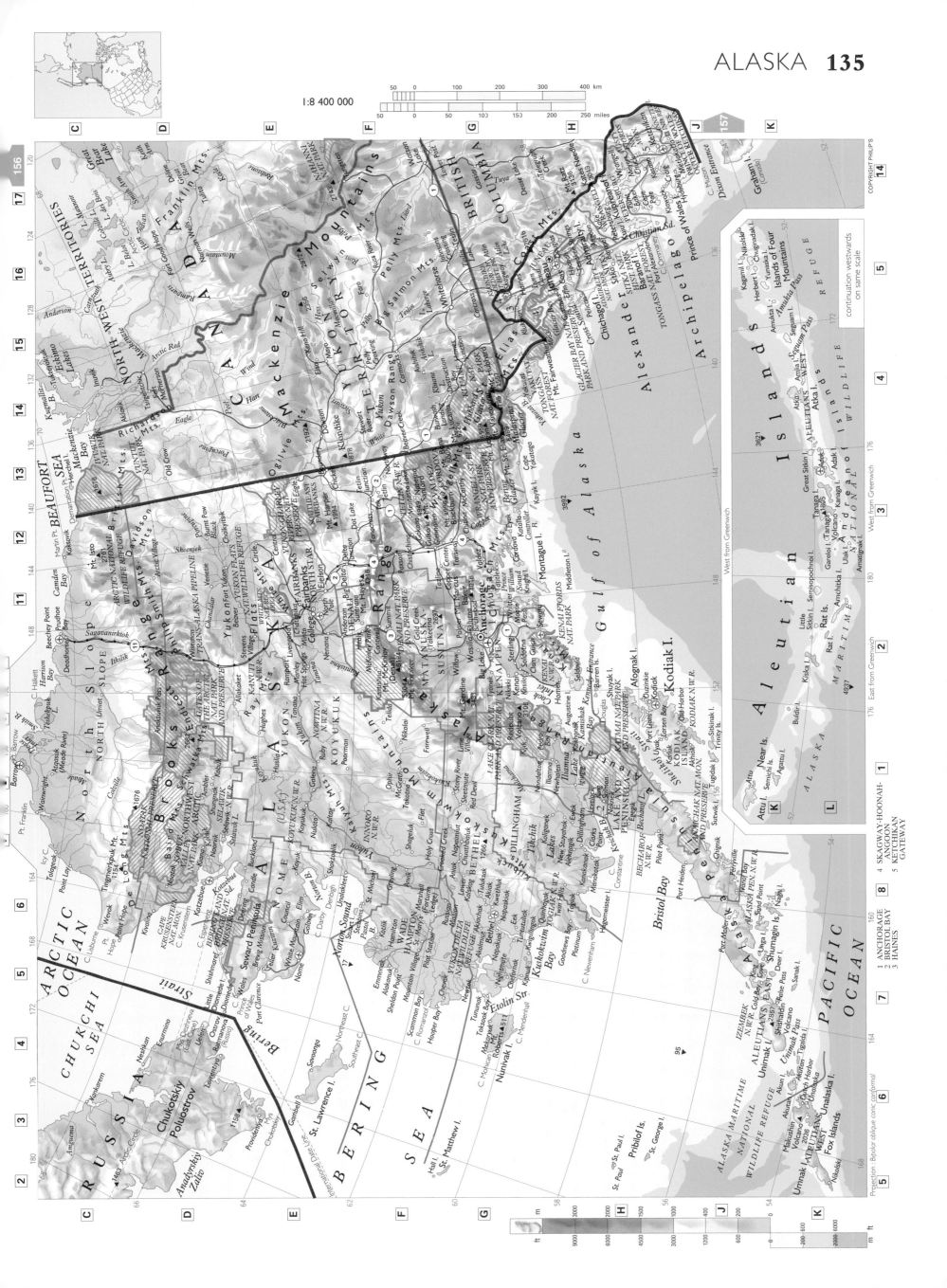

0 10 20 30 40 50 60 70 80 90 km

10 0 10 20 30 40 50 60 miles

1:2 100 000

COPYRIGHT PHILIP'S

HAWAIIAN ISLANDS

1:16 800 000

HAWAI'I

KAUA'I COUNTY

O'ahu
HONOLULU
COUNTY

Moloka'i
KALAWAO COUNTY

MAUI COUNTY

Lāna'i

Maui

Kaho'olawe

HAWAI'I COUNTY

HAWAIIAN ISLANDS (inset)

Kauai
Ni'ihau
Kaua'i

O'ahu
Moloka'i
Lāna'i
Maui
Kaho'olawe
Hawai'i

Tropic of Cancer

Kure I.
Midway Is.
HONOLULU COUNTY

Pearl and Hermes Reef

Lisianski I.
Laysan I.

Gardiner Pinnacles
French Frigate Shoals

Necker I.
Nihoa

Maro Reef

PACIFIC OCEAN

P A C I F I C   O C E A N

H a w a i i a n   I s l a n d s

West from Greenwich

Projection: Albers Equal Area

Kaua'i / Ni'ihau

KAUA'I COUNTY

Nāpali Coast
Hā'ena
Princeville
Hanalei
Kīlauea
Wai'ale'ale
1598
Kapa'a
Anahola
Waimea
KOKE'E STATE PARK
Kekaha
Kalāheo
Līhu'e
50
Kōloa
Kōloa
Po'ipū
Wai'ta Res.
Nāwiliwili Pt.
Makahuena Pt.

Waimea
1231
Mt.
Mauna Kea
4205

Nohili Pt.
Māna
Pānā'ū
1390
Pu'uwai
Lehua I.
Kawaihoa Pt.

Ni'ihau
Ka'ena Pt.

Kaulakahi Channel

▲3026

P A C I F I C   O C E A N

O'ahu

O'ahu
Kahuku Pt.
Lā'ie
Hau'ula
Kahalu'u
Waialua
Hale'iwa
Ka'ena Pt.
83
Wahiawā
99
Kāne'ohe
Kailua
72
Waimānalo
HONOLULU COUNTY
Wai'anae
Nānākuli
'Ewa Beach
Barbers Pt.
Makapu'u Pt.
Honolulu
HNL
★

Kauaʻi Channel

Ka'iwi Channel

▲446

Moloka'i / Lāna'i

KALAWAO NAT. HIST. PARK
Kalaupapa
Kalawao
'Īlio Pt.
Ho'olehua
Kaunakakai
Maunaloa
1515
Pūkō'o
Kamalō
Moloka'i
Lā'au Pt.

Kaloni Channel
Pā'ilolo Channel

Lāna'i City
1027
Lāna'i
Lāna'ihale
Kaumālapau
Kaunolū Pt.
Palaoa Pt.

Maui

Honokōhau
Wailuku
Napili
Lahaina
Olowalu
Mā'alaea
Kīhei
Wailea-Mākena
Waihe'e
Waiehu
Kahului
Pā'ia
Makawao
Pu'unēnē
Kula
Pu'u'ula'ula
450
Wailua
Wailua
Kapalua
Haiku-Pauwela
Hana
Kaupō
HALEAKALĀ NAT. PARK
MAUI COUNTY
ROAD TO HANA

37
30

Kamalō
Molokini I.

Kaho'olawe

Lua Makiki
Lae o Kealaikahiki
Kākā
450

Kealaikahiki Channel
'Alalākeiki Channel

Pailolo Channel

'Au'au Channel

'Alenuihāhā Channel

Hawai'i

Hawai'i

HAWAI'I COUNTY

Honomū
Pepe'ekeo
Papa'ikou
Hilo
Hilo Bay
Leleiwi Pt.
Honoka'a
Kukuihaele
Pa'auilo
Honomu
'Ō'ōkala
Laupāhoehoe
Pāpa'aloa
'Akaka Falls
Honoka'a
19
Waimea (Kamuela)
Kamuela
MAUNA KEA FOREST RES.
Mauna Kea
▲4205
Waikōloa Village
200
190
Mauna Loa
▲4169
Pu'u'ō'ō
2521
HAWAI'I VOLCANOES NATIONAL PARK
Kīlauea Caldera
1243
Kīlauea
Volcano
KA'Ū DESERT
Hilina
PUNA FOR. RES.
130
Kapoho
Cape Kumukahi
Keā'au
Pāhoa
Kalapana
'Ōpihikao

KOHALA FOR. RES.
Kohala Mts.
1678
'Upolu Pt.
Hāwī
Kapa'au
Kaupulehu
Kalāhuipua'a
Kawaihae
Kawaihae Bay
PU'UKOHOLĀ HEIAU NAT. HISTORIC SITE
Kailua
KONA
Keahole Pt.
Kiholo Bay
Hualālai
KALOKO-HONOKŌHAU NAT. HISTORICAL PARK
Keāhole
Keōkea
Keauhou
Kealakekua
Captain Cook
Hōnaunau
PU'UHONUA O HŌNAUNAU NAT. HISTORICAL PARK
Keālia
Hōlualoa
Miloli'i
2096
Ka Lae (South Pt.)
Kaunā Pt.
Pōhue Bay
Nā'ālehu
Wai'ōhinu
Pāhala
Ka Lae

11
19
270
200
190

▼1340

P A C I F I C   O C E A N

P A C I F I C   O C E A N

Projection: Lambert's Conformal Conic

O'AHU (inset map)

O'AHU

1:420 000

KOOLAULOA DISTRICT
KO'OLAUPOKO DISTRICT
WAI'ANAE DISTRICT
WAIALUA DISTRICT
'EWA DISTRICT
HONOLULU DISTRICT
HONOLULU COUNTY

KO'OLAU RANGE
WAI'ANAE RANGE

Kahuku Pt.
Kahuku
Kawela
Waialua Bay
Pūpūkea
Sunset Beach
Waimea
Hale'iwa
Waialua
Mokulē'ia
Ka'ena Pt.
930
99

Lā'ie
Hau'ula
Punalu'u
Kahana Bay
Ka'a'awa
Kualoa
KAHANA VALLEY STATE PARK
Waiāhole
Ka'alaea
Kāne'ohe Bay
He'eia
Kāne'ohe
Kailua
Maunawili
Waimānalo
Waimānalo Bay
72
83
63

Mōkapu Peninsula
Mōkōlea Rock
Mokolea Pt.
Mōkapu Pt.
Kapapa I.
Mōkōlea I.
Kualoa I.
Kāne'ohe MC Air Station
Mokumanu
Mānana I.
Makapu'u Pt.
Hanauma Bay
Koko Head
232
Diamond Head
Waikīkī

POLYNESIAN CULTURAL CENTER
Ku Tree Res.
818
817
946
Pu'u 'ō'ūmaka'oko

ANAHULU
KAWAILOA FOREST RESERVE
WAIALUA FOREST RESERVE
EWA FOREST RESERVE
Wahiawā
Schofield Barracks
Whitmore Village
Mililani Town
Mililani
Waipi'o Acres
Waipi'o
Pearl City
Waipahu
Wai'anae
LUALUALEI
MĀKUA KAHANAHANA
MT. KA'ALA NAT. AREA RESERVE
Mt. Ka'ala
1231
944
750
HONOULIULI FOREST RESERVE
Mā'ili
Nānākuli
Mā'ili Pt.
93
Kūpono
Mākaha
Mikilua
Waimānalo
Kea'au
Makua
MĀKUA MIL. RES.
Mākua Valley
Ka'ena Pt.

Pearl Harbor
Pearl City
NAVAL RESERVATION
'Aiea
Hickam AFB
Honolulu
HNL
★
HICKAM
FORD I.
'Ewa Villages
Ewa
'Ewa Beach
Iroquois Pt.
Keahi Pt.
Barbers Pt.
Kalaeloa
Sand I.

Honolulu
Halawa Heights
Pacific Palisades
Pālolo
Waialae
Mānoa
Niu Valley
Kuli'ou'ou
Kuapā Pd.
Hawai'i Kai
Koko Head

Puʻu Loa

Makahoa Pt.
Mokuau'ia I.
Kahuku Pt.
Hukilau Beach

78
76
61

Mā'ama Bay
M ā m a l a   B a y

N o r t h   S h o r e

W a i ' a n a e   C o a s t

K a i w i   C h a n n e l

Ka'ie'ie Waho Channel

Kaua'i Channel

P A C I F I C   O C E A N

P A C I F I C   O C E A N

Elevation scale

m   ft
4000 12 000
3000 9000
2000 6000
1500 4500
1000 3000
400   1200
200   600
0   0
200   600
2000 6000
6000 12 000
m   ft

20 km
15
10
5
0
10 miles
5
0

CANADA

PROVINCIAL MAPS

Settlements
(number of inhabitants)

- ■ **TORONTO** Over 2,000,000
- ■ **MONTRÉAL** 1,000,000 – 2,000,000
- ◉ **Winnipeg** 500,000 – 1,000,000
- ◉ **Windsor** 250,000 – 500,000
- ◉ **Kitchener** 100,000 – 250,000
- ◎ **Brantford** 50,000 – 100,000
- ◎ St. Thomas 20,000 – 50,000
- ○ Elliot Lake 10,000 – 20,000
- ○ Elmira 5,000 – 10,000
- ° Palmerston Less than 5,000
- ☐ Urban areas

Communications

- Limited-access highways
- Principal highways
- Secondary highways
- Trans-Canada highway
- (27) Provincial route numbers
- Principal railroads
- Other railroads
- Railroad tunnels
- YYZ ✈ Principal airports (with location identifiers)
- ✈ Other airports

Physical features

- Perennial streams and rivers
- Perennial lakes and reservoirs
- Intermittent lakes
- Reservoirs (with dams)
- Permanent ice and glaciers
- ▲ 4301 Elevations in meters
- ▼ 2731 Sea and lake depths in meters
- 1134 Height of lake surface above sea level in meters
- C.Rich Capes, waterfalls, points and mountain passes
- Great Duck I. Islands, peninsulas, mountain ranges and peaks
- Cape Breton Island Regions, coasts and large islands
- Ottawa Rivers, lakes, bays, straits, channels and glaciers

Administration

- International boundaries
- Provincial boundaries
- National parks
- Provincial parks and national wildlife areas
- PRINCE EDWARD ISLAND Names of provinces and territories
- **OTTAWA** ■ National capital

CITY MAPS

- Free limited-access highways (with interchange)
- Toll limited-access highways
- Tunnels
- Primary divided highways
- Primary undivided highways
- Secondary divided highways
- Secondary undivided highways
- Other roads
- Trans-Canada route numbers
- (19) Canadian autoroute numbers
- (27) Provincial route numbers
- Railroads
- Gare Windsor Principal railroad stations
- ✈ Principal airports
- ✈ Other airports
- ☐ City centers
- City center map coverage
- Urban areas
- **Verdun** **Hampstead** Chicot Suburbs (size of type indicates relative populations)
- Woodlands and parks
- ■ Zoo Points of interest

CITY CENTER MAPS

- Free limited-access highways
- Toll limited-access highways
- Through routes
- Secondary routes
- Divided highways
- Other roads
- Tunnels
- Railroads
- Union Station Railroad stations
- Ⓢ Ⓜ Subway stations
- Urban areas
- **ST.-LOUIS** Suburbs
- Woodlands and parks
- ☐ Public buildings
- † Churches
- ✝ Cathedrals
- Museum Points of interest

1:12 600 000

Projection : Bonne

Provincial Capitals

NORTHERN CANADA
Continuation northwards
on same scale

Devon I.
Lancaster Sound

Baffin Bay

2136

Arctic Bay   1951
Nanisivik   Bylot I.
Brodeur   Borden   Eclipse   Pond Inlet
Peninsula   Pen.   Sd.

C. Adair

Clyde River

C. Raper

ARCTIC
OCEAN

North
Magnetic
Pole

C. Columbia
2616
Alert

GREENLAND

Meighen   Sverdrup
Islands

Borden I.

Brock I.   Mackenzie
King I.   Amund
Ringnes I.   Ringnes I.
Eglinton   Lougheed
Prince Patrick I.

Cornwall

Axel
Heiberg
I.

Eureka

Grise
Fiord

Ellesmere Island

Nares Str.

Smith Sound

Jones Sound

Norwegian
Bay

Queen
Elizabeth
Is.

Bathurst   Cornwallis

Devon Island

Banks
Island

McClure Strait

Viscount Melville
Sound

Resolute

Lancaster
Sound

Arctic
Bay

Nanisivik   1951
Bylot I.

747

Prince Albert
Pen.

Holman

M'Clintock
Channel

Prince
of
Wales Island

Somerset
Island

Brodeur
Peninsula

Pond
Inlet

NORTHWEST
TERRITORIES

Victoria Island

NUNAVUT

Baffin Island

Baffin   Island

Gulf
of
Boothia

Fury and Hecla Str.
Igloolik

Simpson
Pen.
Kugaaruk

Melville
Peninsula

Committee B.

Hall Beach

Prince
Charles
I.

Air
Force
I.

Qikiqtarjuaq

Cumberland
Peninsula

C. Dyer

Rae Isthmus
Repulse
Bay

Foxe
Basin

Nettilling L.

Pangnirtung

Hoare B.

C. Mercy

Ware R.

C. Dorchester

Foxe
Pen.

Amadjuak
L.

Meta

Hall
Peninsula

Cumberland
Sd.

Chesterfield Inlet

Southampton
I.
Coral Harbour

Coats
I.

Mansel
I.

Foxe Channel

Cape Dorset

Iqaluit

Incognita
Kimmirut
Peninsula

Frobisher Bay

NUNAVUT

Salisbury
I.

Hudson   Strait

Resolution I.

Bell
Pen.

Nottingham
I.

Ivujivik
Salluit

Quaqtaq

Akpatok I.

C. Chidley

Hudson

Ottawa Is.

Kangiqsujuaq

Péninsule

Kangirsuk

Ungava Bay

Hebron

1652

Kangiqsualujjuaq

Labrador

Bay

257

Sleeper Is.

King George Is.

Bakers
Dozen
Is.

Belcher Is.

Puvirnituq

d'Ungava

Inukjuak

Arnaud

L. Payne

Feuilles

Kuujjuaq

Baleine

Caniapiscau

George

Nain

Sea

3809

Peawanuck

C. Henrietta
Maria

Kuujjuarapik

A

Kanaaupscow

L. Minto

L. Bienville

Kawawachikamach
(Schefferville)

Petitsikapau L.

Esker

Smallwood
Res.

North West River

Labrador

Hopedale

Rigolet

C. Harrison

Cartwright

Port Hope Simpson

Winisk

Tatnam

Big
Trout L.

Seven

Chisasibi

La Grande

Grande r. de la Baleine

L. à l'Eau
Claire

L.
Caniapiscau

1135

Labrador
City

Ashuanipi L.

Fermont

Churchill
Falls

Happy Valley-
Goose Bay

St-Augustin

Str. of Belle Isle

Belle Isle

St. Anthony

L'Anse aux Meadows

Churchill

Gagnon

Manicouagan

Moisie

Natashquan

R.

Havre-
St-Pierre

Natashquan

Baie
Verte

Grand
Falls-
Windsor

Lewisporte

Gander

Notre Dame B.

Bonavista

Bonavista B.

Carbonear

St. John's

ATLANTIC

James Bay

Akimiski I.

Charlton

Wemindji

Eastmain

Waskaganish

Eastmain

Rupert

L.
Albanel

L.
Mistassini

NEWFOUNDLAND

QUÉBEC

Rés.
Manicouagan

Sept-Îles

I. d'Anticosti

Port-Cartier

Deer
Lake

Corner Brook

Stephenville

814

Newfoundland

Marystown

Placentia

Placentia B.

C. Race

Fort Albany

Attawapiskat

Attawapiskat

Moosonee

Harricana

Nottaway

Chibougamau

Mistassini R.

Baie-Comeau

Gulf of
St. Lawrence

Ray
Cabot Str.

North

Channel-Port
aux Basques

ST-PIERRE
ST-PIERRE et MIQUELON (Fr.)

Albany

L. St. Joseph

Albany

Misinaibi

Matagami

L. Matagami

Dolbeau-
Mistassini

St-Jean

Lac-
St-Jean

Chicoutimi

Rimouski

Matane

Pén. de
la Gaspésie

Gaspé

Campbellton

Bathurst

Miramichi

Îs. de la Madeleine

Cape Breton I.

Sydney

Glace Bay

Nakina

Kenogami

L.
Nipigon

Greenstone

Nipigon

Marathon

Oba

Hearst

Kapuskasing

Cochrane

L. Abitibi

Timmins

Amos

Val-d'Or

Rouyn-
Noranda

Rés. Gouin

Roberval

Jonquière

La Tuque

1190

Grand-Falls

Rivière-du-Loup

Edmundston

Woodstock

NEW
BRUNSWICK

Moncton

Fredericton

Northumberland Str.

PR. EDWARD I.
Summerside

Charlottetown

New
Glasgow

Antigonish

Port Hawkesbury

NOVA SCOTIA

Thunder Bay

Lake Superior

Houghton   183

Wawa

Chapleau

Kirkland
Lake

New
Liskeard

Mont-
Laurier

Rés.
Cabonga

Shawinigan

Trois-Rivières

Québec

Lévis

Thetford
Mines

Sherbrooke

St-Hyacinthe

St-Jean

Drummondville

Granby

Joliette

Sorel

Grand
Falls

MAINE

Augusta

Bangor

Fredericton

Saint
John

Amherst

Kentville

Truro

Dartmouth

Halifax

Bridgewater

Liverpool

Yarmouth

B. of Fundy

Digby

C. Sable

Sable I.
(Nova Scotia)

6309

Ironwood

Marquette

Elliot
Lake

Sudbury

North
Bay

L. Nipissing

Pembroke

Hull

MONTRÉAL

Cornwall

Champlain

Montpelier

VERMONT

Concord

NEW
HAMPSHIRE

Manchester

Portland

Manistique

Escanaba

Menominee

Sault Ste.
Marie

Sault Ste.
Marie

Manitoulin I.

Georgian
Bay

Parry
Sound

Huntsville

OTTAWA

Outaouais

Burlington

Lewiston

Rhinelander

Wausau

Green
Bay

Traverse City

Lake
Huron

Owen Sound

Barrie

Peterborough

Kingston

Belleville

Oshawa

L. Ontario

Syracuse

Utica

Albany

MASS.

BOSTON

C. Cod

PROVIDENCE

Appleton

Sheboygan

Cadillac

Petoskey

Lake
Michigan

Saginaw

Flint

London

Kitchener

Hamilton

TORONTO

Niagara
Falls

Rochester

NEW YORK

Binghamton

Scranton

Springfield

Hartford

CONN.

New Haven

Bridgeport

R.I.

NEW YORK

MILWAUKEE

Madison

Racine

Kenosha

WISCONSIN

Rockford

CHICAGO

Gary

South Bend

Grand
Rapids

Lansing

DETROIT

Windsor

Toledo

CLEVELAND

L. Erie

Erie

Buffalo

Jamestown

Elmira

Allentown

Trenton

Newark

N.J.

PENNSYLVANIA

OHIO

INDIANA

ILLINOIS

I 74

I 74

ONTARIO

1:2 100 000

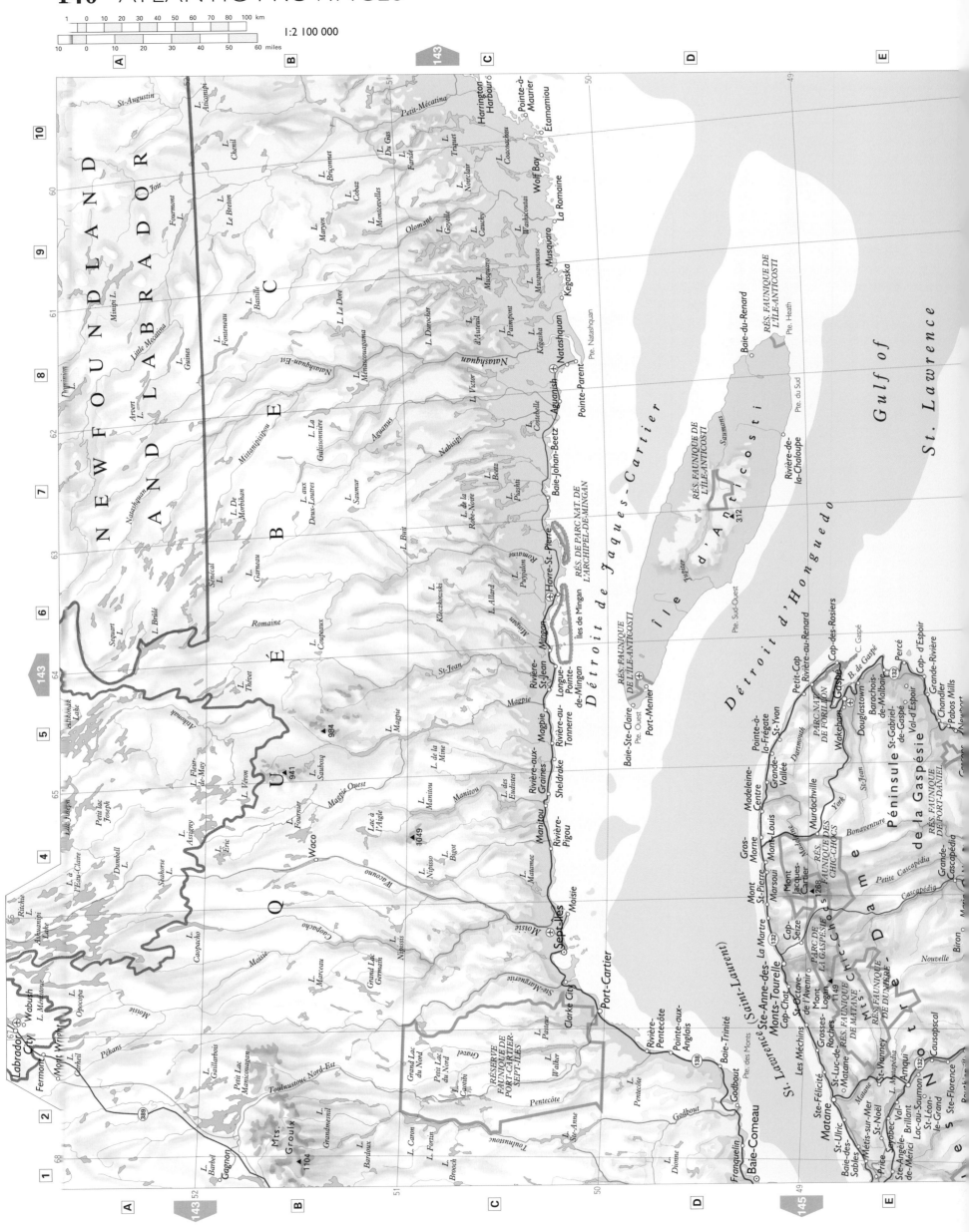

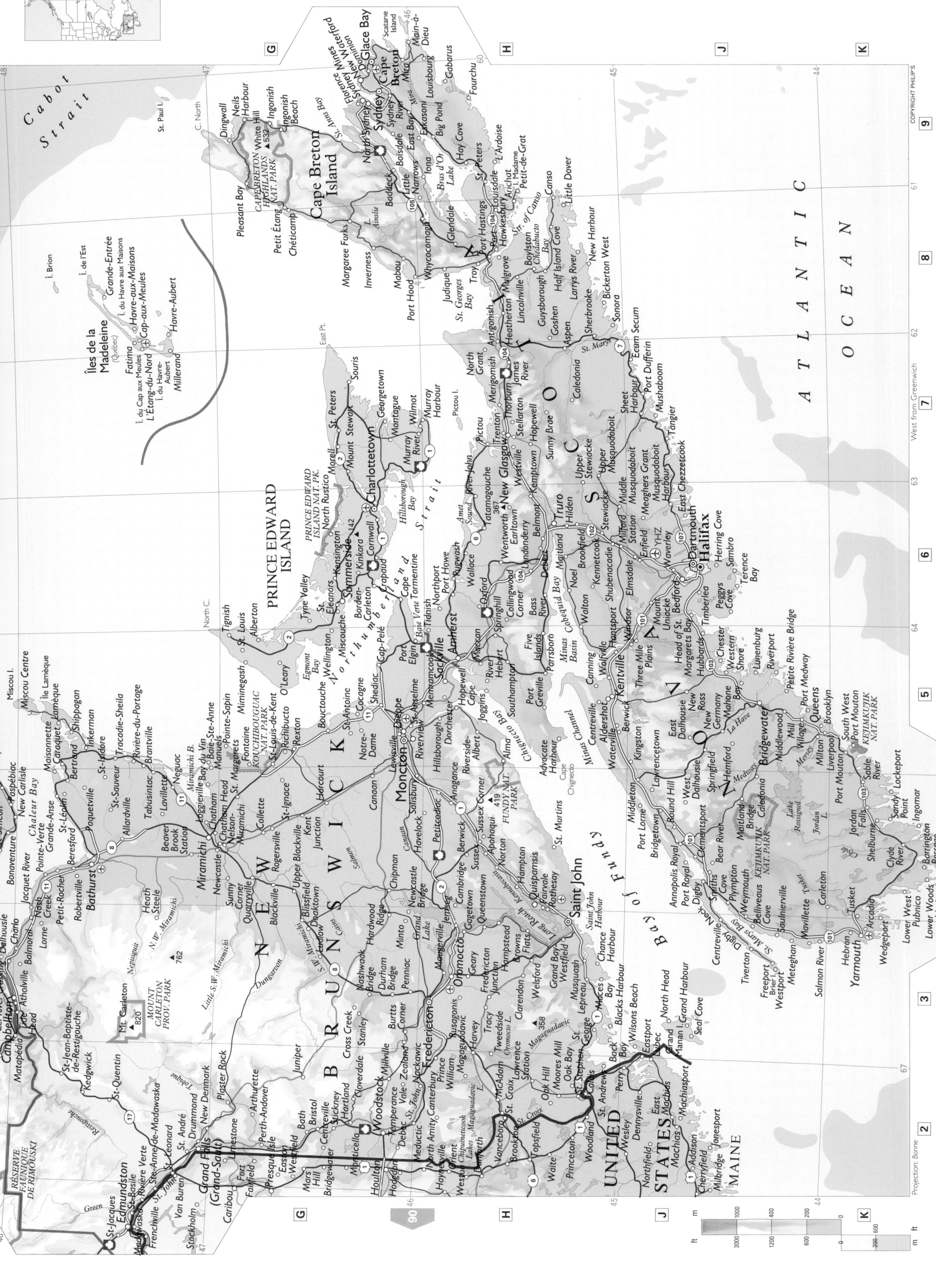

COPYRIGHT PHILIP'S

Cabot Strait

Îles de la Madeleine (Québec)

Cape Breton Island

CAPE BRETON HIGHLANDS NAT. PARK

PRINCE EDWARD ISLAND

PRINCE EDWARD ISLAND NAT. PK.

Northumberland Strait

NEW BRUNSWICK

NOVA SCOTIA

MOUNT CARLETON PROV. PARK

KOUCHIBOUGUAC NAT. PARK

FUNDY NAT. PARK

KEJIMKUJIK NAT. PARK

Bay of Fundy

Minas Basin

Chignecto Bay

ATLANTIC OCEAN

UNITED STATES

MAINE

RÉSERVE FAUNIQUE DE RIMOUSKI

West from Greenwich

Projection: Bonne

ft m
3000 1200
1000 400
600 200
0 0
-200 -600 m ft

1:2 100 000

100 km
60 miles

143

1 2 3 143 4 5 6 7 8

Labrador

QUÉBEC

Henley Harbour
Belle Isle
Pinware
Red Bay
Strait of Belle Isle
Cook's Harbour
Pistolet Bay
C. Bauld
L'Anse aux Meadows
Raleigh
St. Lunaire-Griquet
St. Anthony

St. Paul
St. Augustin
Rivière-St-Paul
Middle Bay
Bradore Bay
L'Anse au Loup
Forteau
L'Anse-au-Clair
Lourdes-de-Blanc-Sablon
Flower's Cove
Sandy Cove
Hare Bay
Goose Cove East
L. Robertson
Île de la Grande Passe
Île Monger
Main Brook

Northern Peninsula

Bird Cove
Ten Mile L.
La Tabatière
Bartletts Harbour
St. John Bay
St. John I.
Roddickton
Conche
Groais I.
Grey Islands
Tête-à-la-Baleine
Île du Petit-Mécatina
Port au Choix
Pte. Riche
Port Saunders
Igornachoix Bay
Englee
Canada Bay
Bell I.
Hawke's Bay
River of Ponds
Granite Pt.

NEWFOUNDLAND AND LABRADOR

Bellburns
River of Ponds L.
Great Harbour Deep
Horse Islands

ATLANTIC OCEAN

Gulf of St. Lawrence

Daniel's Harbour
Portland Creek Pond
Partridge Pt.
Fleur de Lys

Parson's Pond
Parsons Pond
Baie Verte
Pacquet
C. St. John

Cow Head
Jackson's Arm
Seal Cove
White Bay
La Scie
St. Pauls
Sop's Arm
Baie Verte Peninsula
Nippers Harbour
Notre Dame Bay
Funk I.
Sally's Cove
GROS MORNE NAT. PARK
Westport
Burlington
Green Bay
Joe Batt's Arm-Barr'd Islands-Shoal Bay
Fogo
Rocky Harbour
806
King's Point
Little Bay
Beaumont
Twillingate
Fogo I.
C. Fogo
Woody Point
Norris Point
Hampden
Springdale
Triton
New World I.
Hamilton Sound
Trout River
Change Islands
Summerford
686
Robert's Arm
Bay of Exploits
Horwood
Musgrave Harbour
Cormack
South Brook
North Twin L.
Leamington
Little Burnt Bay
Birchy Bay
Carmanville

Range
Mountains
Long
Long Range Mountains

Upper Humber

Deer Lake
Sandy L.
Sheffield L.
South Twin L.
Lewisporte
Campbellton
Lumsden
C. Freels
New-Wes-Valley
South Hd.
Bay of Islands
Deer L.
Howley
663
Hodges Hill
570
Botwood
Peterview
Norris Arm
Gander
Ten Mile Pond
Lark Harbour
Cox's Cove
Summerside
Pasadena
Centreville-Wareham-Trinity
Humber Arm South
Mount Moriah
Corner Brook
Grand Lake
Hinds L.
Badger
Buchans Junction
Exploits
Bishop's Falls
Glenwood
Gander L.
Hare Bay
Dover
Bonavista Bay
St. Brendan's Bay
814
Glover I.
Buchans
Millertown
Grand Falls-Windsor
Gambo
Glovertown
C. Bonavista
Lewis Hills
Red Indian L.
400
Bonavista
Elliston

Newfoundland

Port au Port Bay
Lourdes
Port au Port Peninsula
Kippens
Piccadilly
Stephenville
Stephenville Crossing
De Grau
St. George's
Flat Bay
St. George's Bay
C. St. George
667
Island Pond
Crooked L.
Deer Pond
Terra Nova
TERRA NOVA NAT. PARK
Summerville
Catalina
Trinity
St. David's
Heatherton
Lloyds L.
Victoria
L.
341
MIDDLE RIDGE WILDLIFE RESERVE
St. John
Port Blandford
Lethbridge
Trinity Bay
Anguille Mts.
Codroy Pond
Victoria L.
Meelpaeg Lake
Great Burnt L.
376
Kaegudeck L.
BAY DU NORD WILDERNESS RESERVE
Clarenville-Shoal Harbour
Random I.
Baccalieu
Old Perlican
Cape Anguille
Co-roy
South Branch
Granite L.
Round Pond
Teddore Lake
Jubilee L.
Hickman's Harbour
Hant's Harbour
Bay de Verde
Doyles
St. Andrew's
La Poile
Grand Bruit
Grey
St. Alban's
Milltown-Head of Bay D'Espoir
Gisborne L.
Swift Current
Come By Chance
Heart's Content
Winterton
Conception Bay
Pouch Cove
Cape Ray
Burnt Islands
Bois I.
Grand Le Pierre
Sunnyside
Victoria
C. Ray
Isle aux Morts
Rose Blanche-Harbour Le Cou
Burgeo
Grey River
François
McCallum
Long I.
Gaultois
Hermitage
Rencontre East
English Harbour East
Terrenceville
Arnold's Cove
Norman's Cove-St. Philip's
Harbour Grace
Spaniard's Bay
Bell I.
Wabana
Carbonear
Torbay
St. John
Mount
Channel-Port aux Basques
Ramea
Ramea Is.
Pass Island
Seal Cove
Harbour Bretón
Belleoram
St. Bernard's-Jacques Fontaine
Bay L'Argent
Boat Harbour
Merasheen I.
Monkstown
Red I.
Whitbourne
Bay Roberts
Conception Bay South
Paradise
Brunette I.
Garnish
Fortune Bay
Burin Peninsula
Rushoon
Placentia Bay
Dunville
Carmel-Mitchells Brook-St. Catherines
Colinet
Holyrood
Bay Bulls
Grand Bank
Marystown
Jude I.
Placentia
Avondale
Avalon Peninsula
Witless Bay
Miquelon
Fortune
Burin
Argentia
Admiral's Beach
Riverhead
AVALON WILDERNESS RESERVE
Cape Broyle
ST-PIERRE et MIQUELON
(France)
Lamaline
Lawn
Lord's Cove
St. Lawrence
St. Bride's
Patrick's Cove
Branch
St. Mary's Bay
Ferryland
Langlade
Î. St-Pierre
St-Pierre
C. St. Mary's
C. Pine
Trepassey
C. Race
Trepassey Bay

Cabot Strait

West from Greenwich

Projection: Lambert's Conformal Conic

COPYRIGHT PHILIP'S

ft m
1200 400
600 200
200 600
m ft

52 51 50 49 48 47
59 58 57 56 55 54 53

1 2 3 4 5 6 7 8

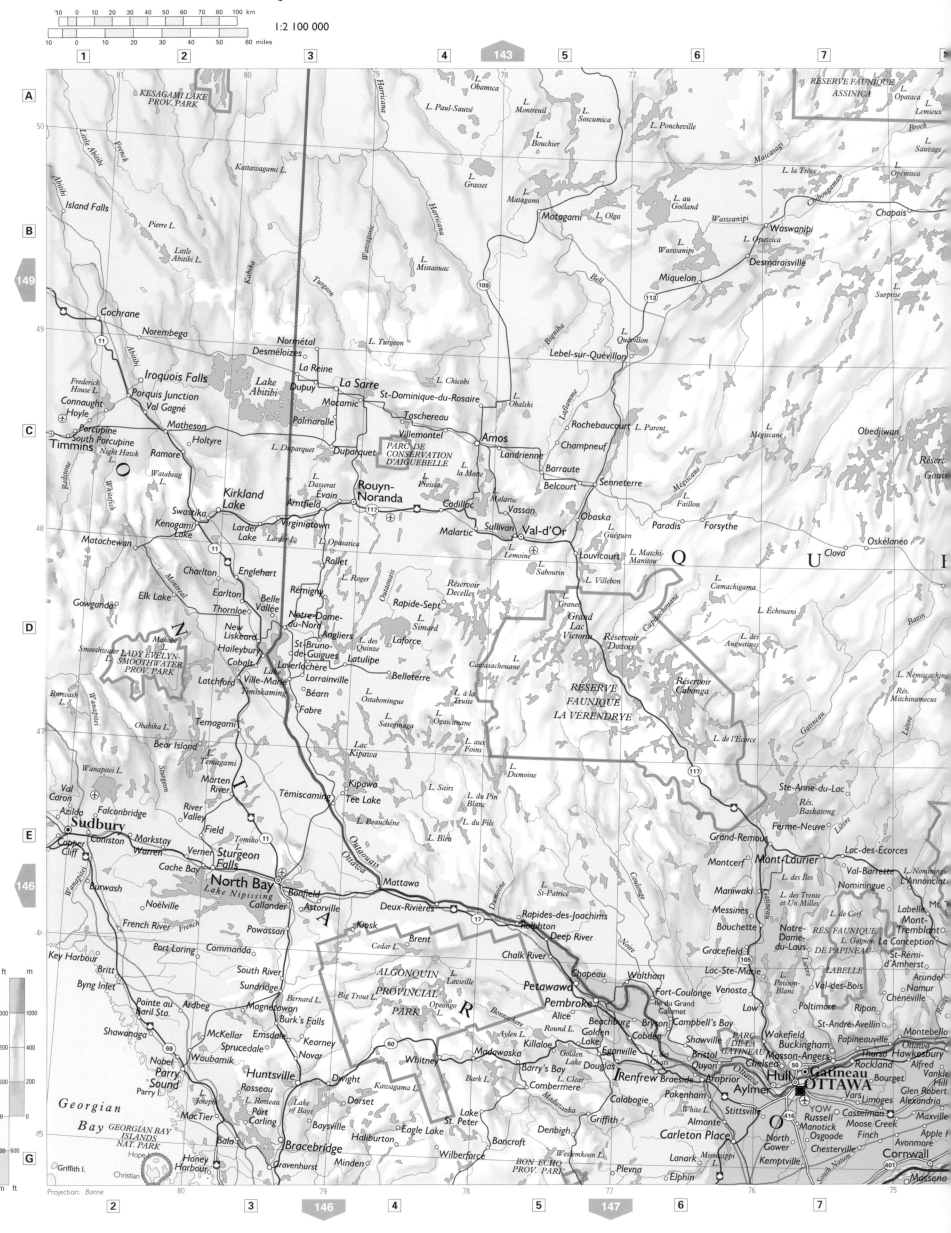

1:2 100 000

Projection: Bonne

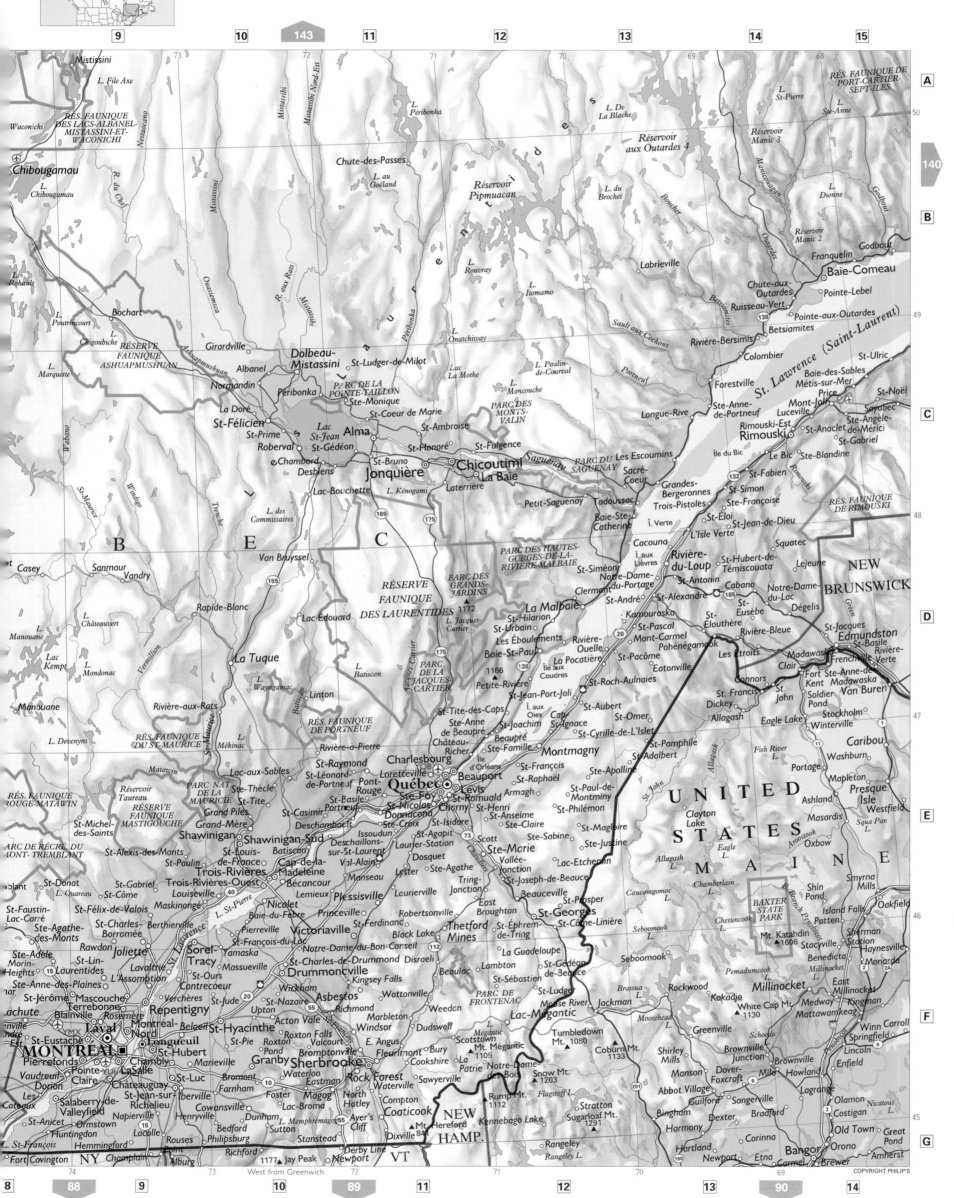

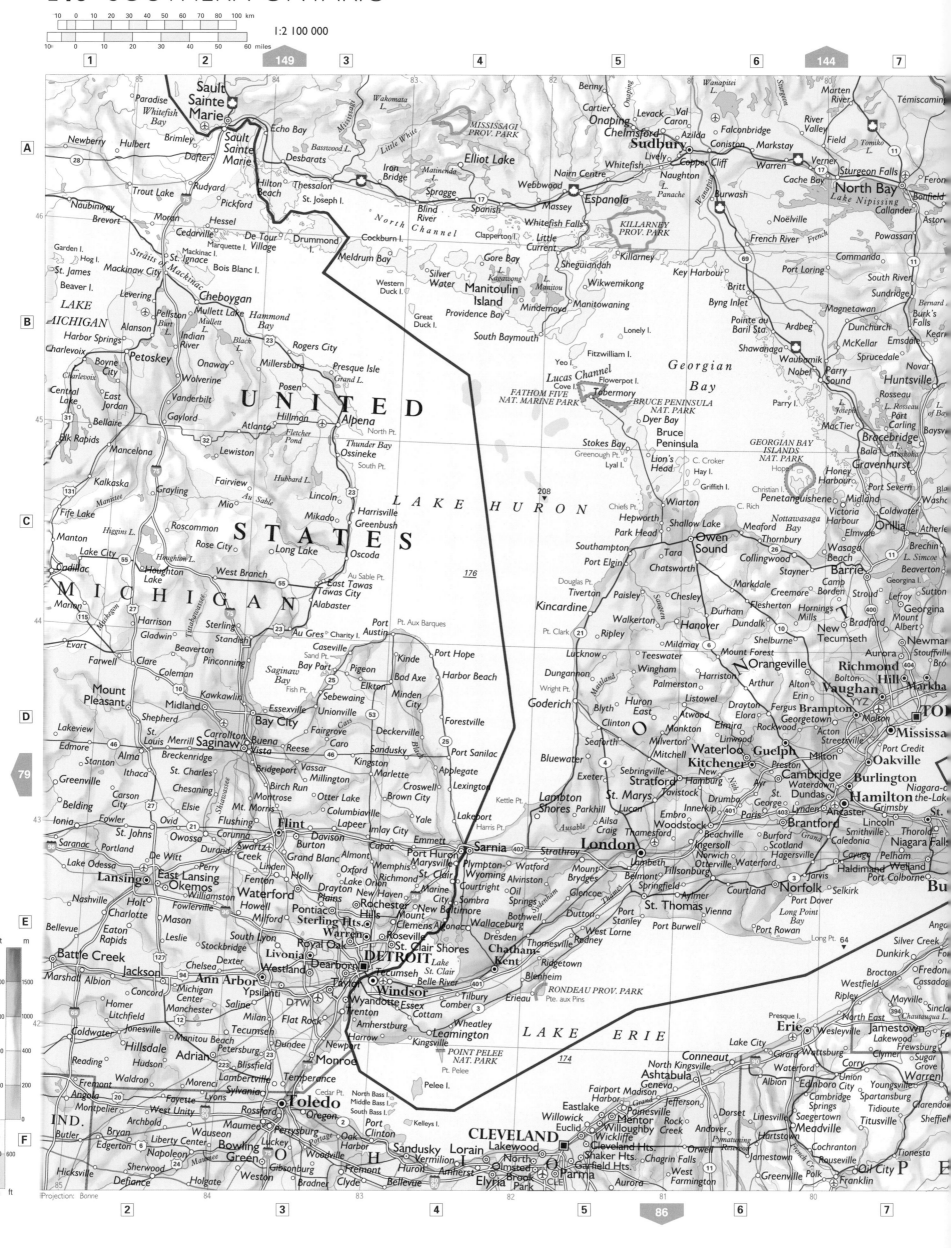

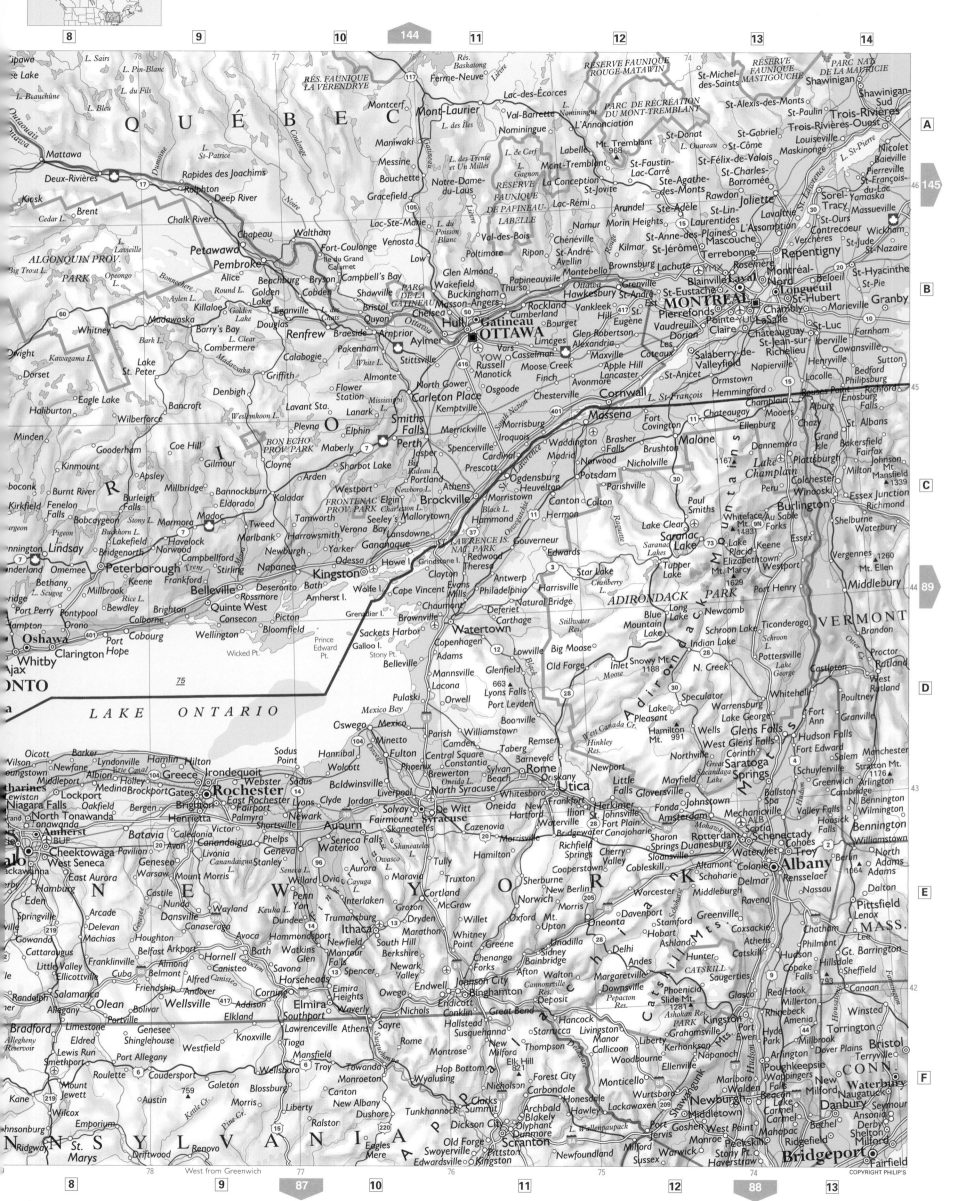

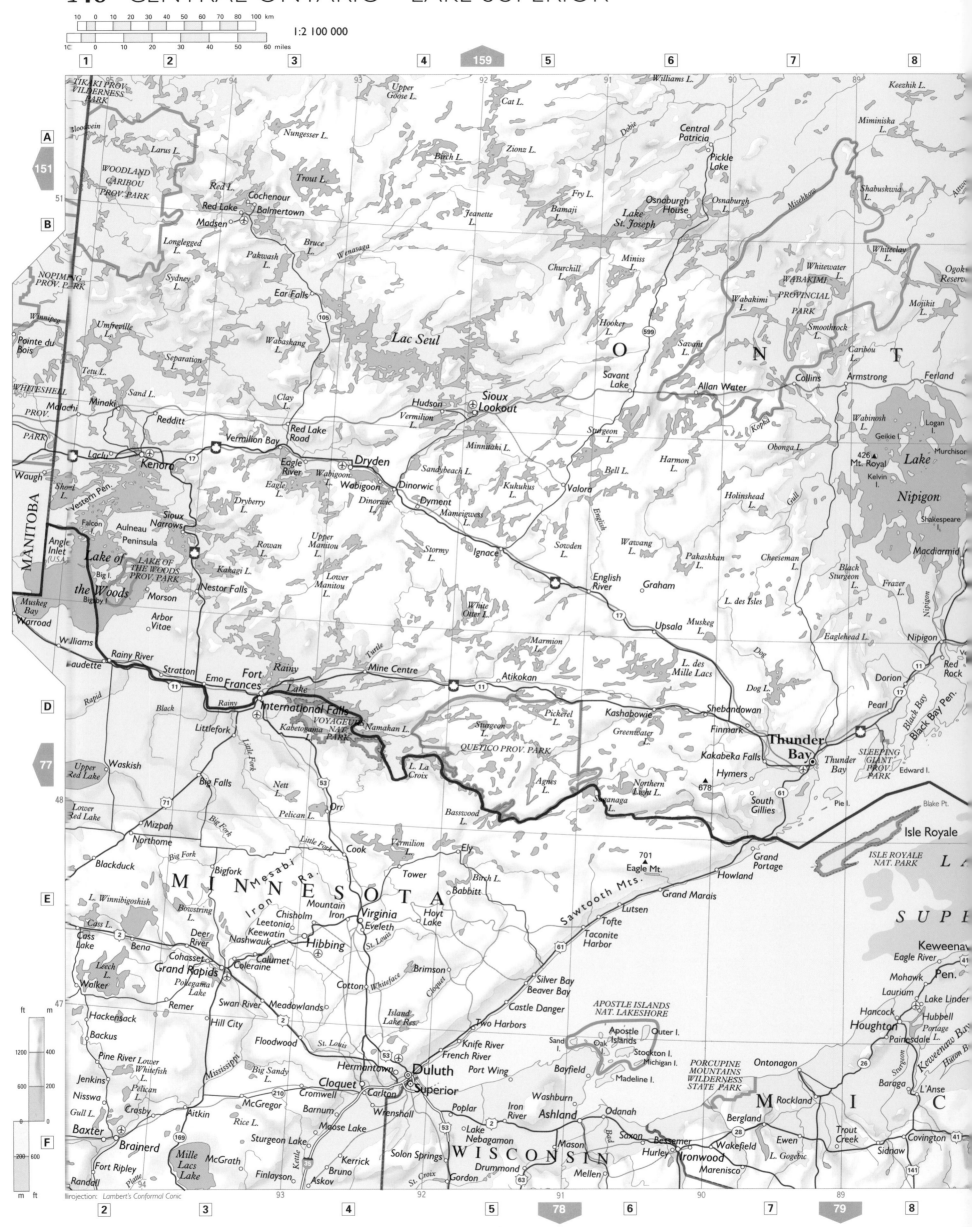

1:2 100 000

Projection: Lambert's Conformal Conic

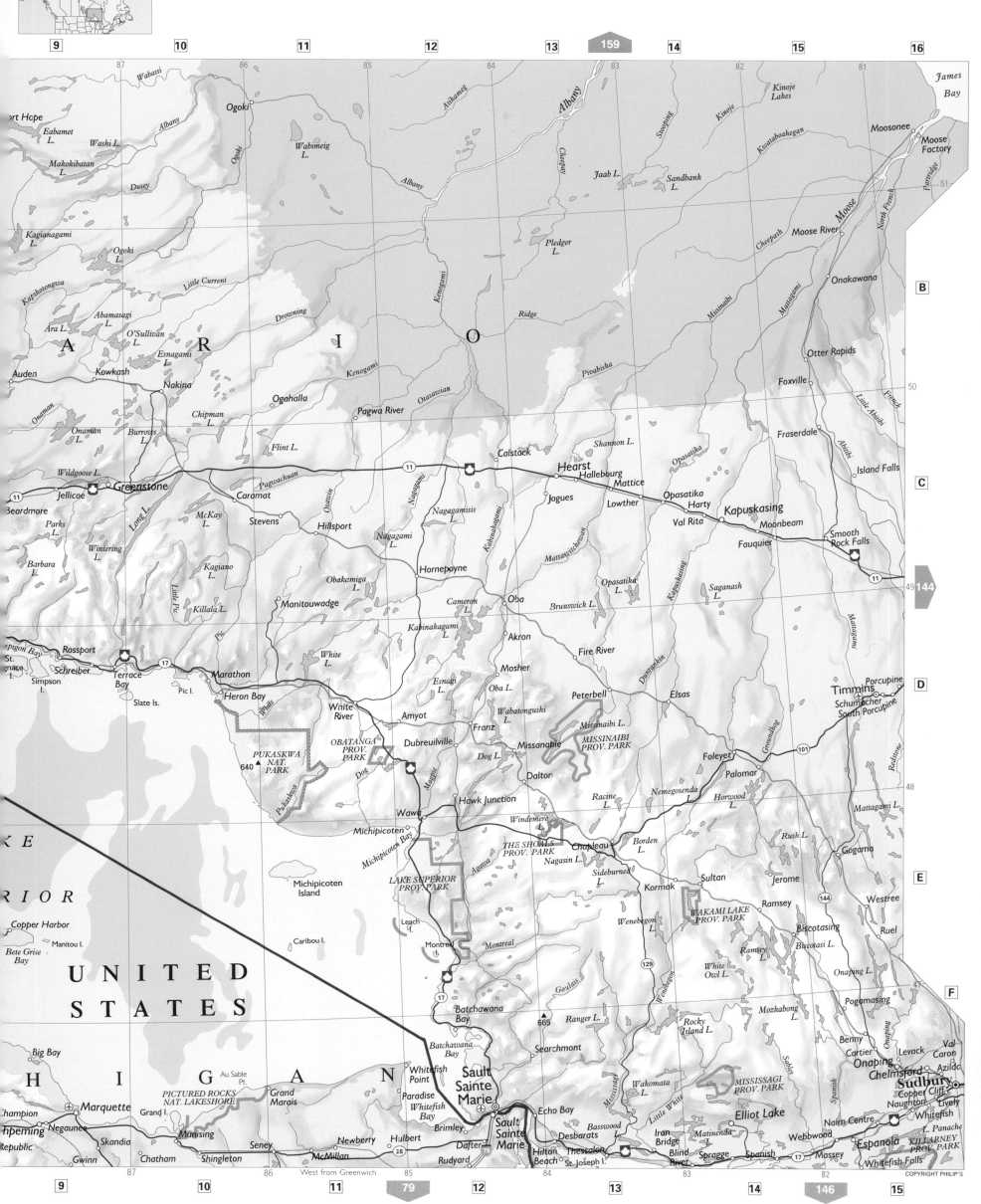

COPYRIGHT PHILIP'S

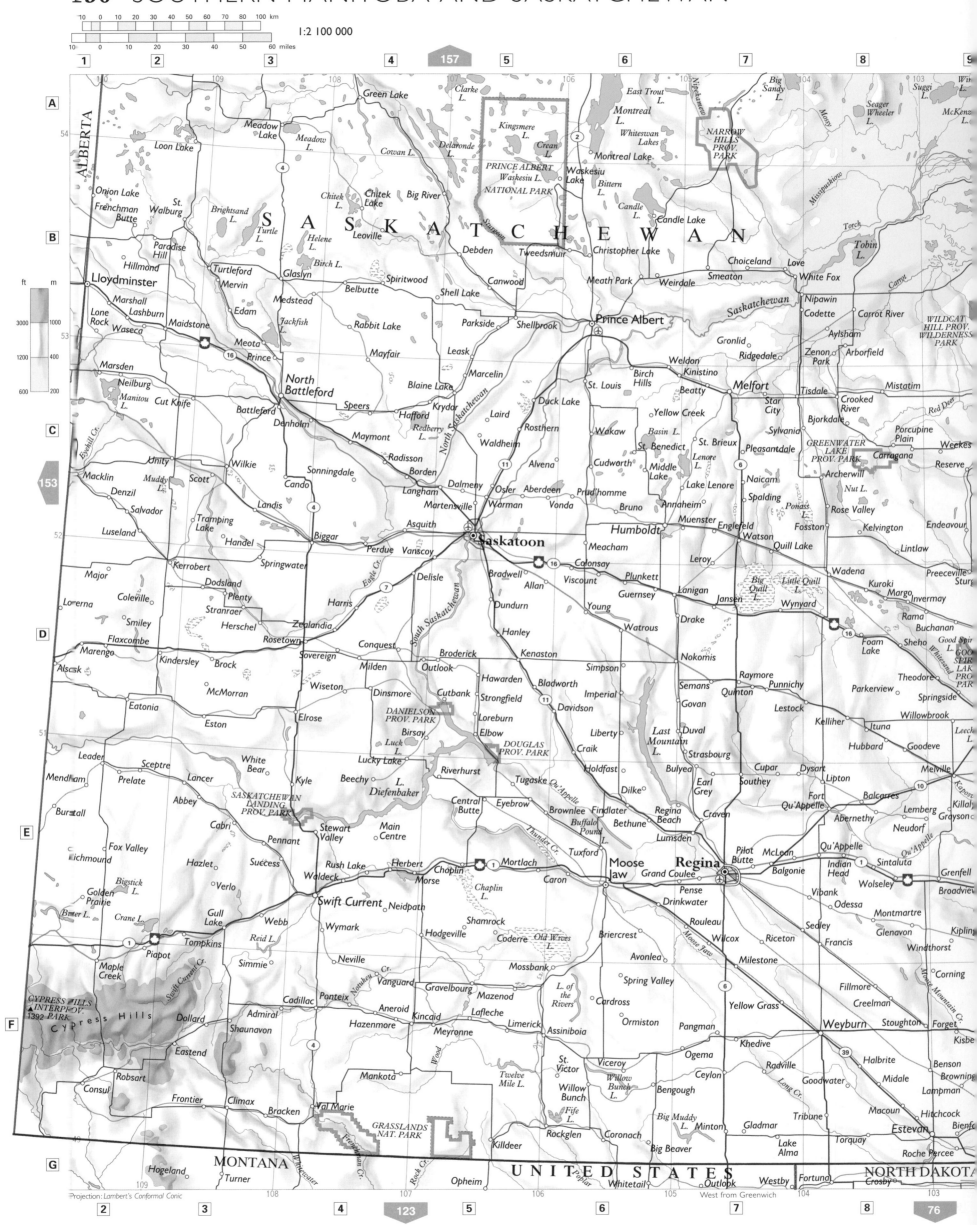

10 0 10 20 30 40 50 60 70 80 100 km

1:2 100 000

10 0 10 20 30 40 50 60 miles

157

153

123

76

Projection: Lambert's Conformal Conic

West from Greenwich

1:2 100 000

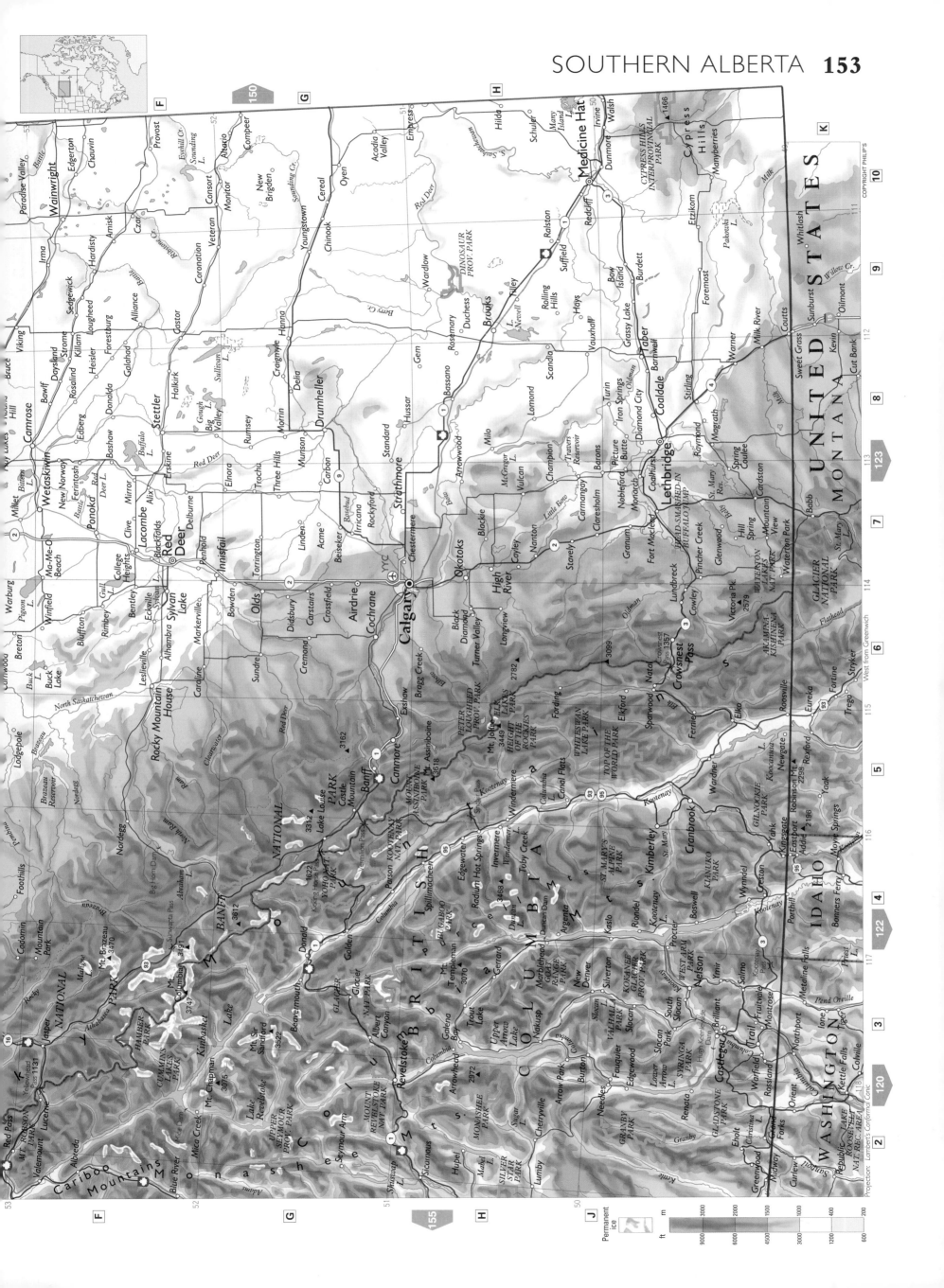

1:2 100 000

Projection: Lambert's Conformal Conic

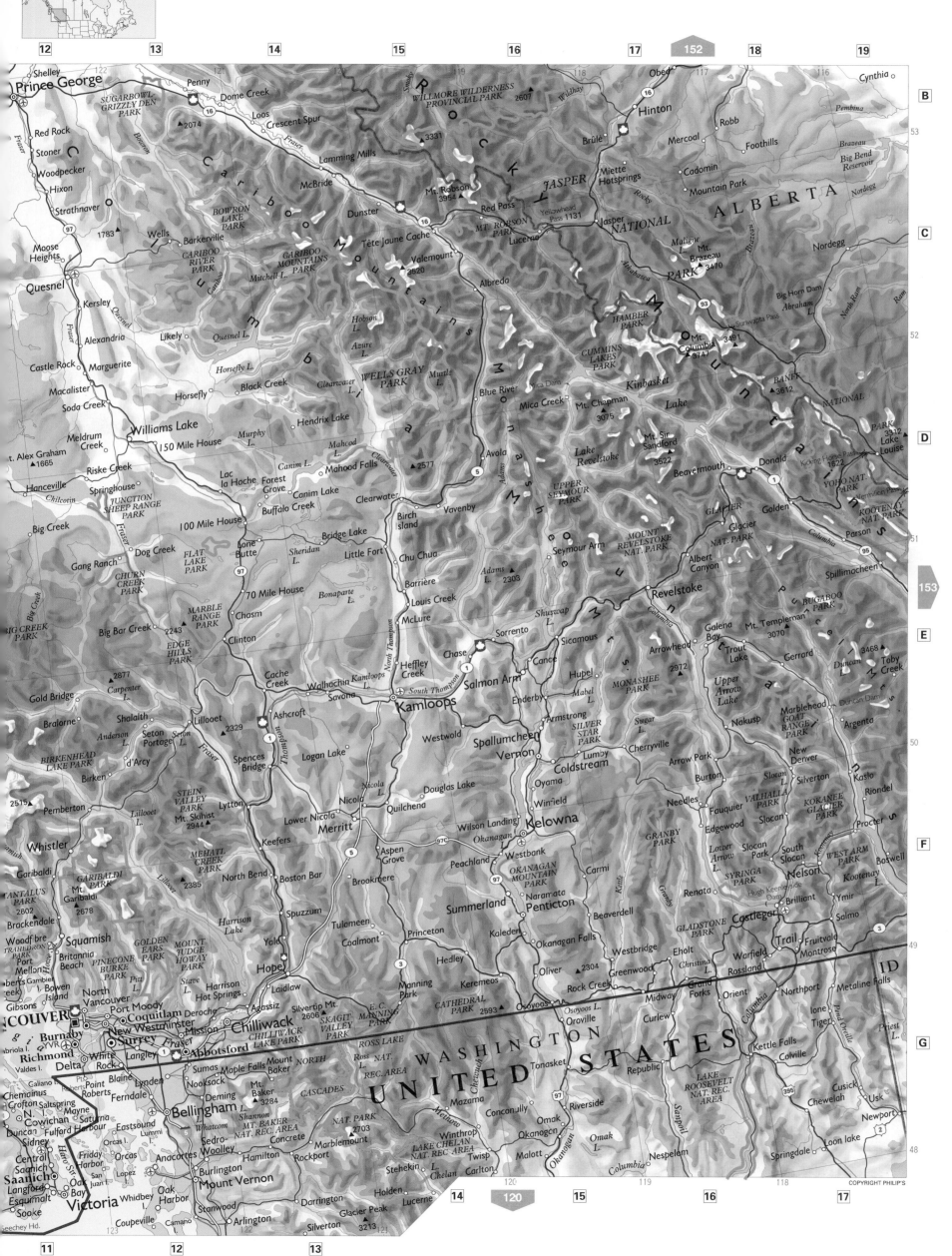

Shelley
Prince George
Red Rock
Stoner
Woodpecker
Hixon
Strathnaver
Moose
Heights
Quesnel
Kersley
Alexandria
Castle Rock
Marguerite
Macalister
Soda Creek
Meldrum
Creek
t. Alex Graham
Hanceville
Springhouse
Big Creek
Williams Lake
150 Mile House
Riske Creek
Dog Creek
Gang Ranch
Big Bar Creek
Gold Bridge
Bralorne
Shalalth
Lillooet
Pemberton
Whistler
Garibaldi
Brackendale
Squamish
Britannia
Beach
Port
Mellon
North
Vancouver
Gibsons
VANCOUVER
Burnaby
Richmond
Delta
Surrey
Langley
White
Rock
Victoria

SUGARBOWL-
GRIZZLY DEN
PARK

Penny
Dome Creek
Loos
Crescent Spur
Lamming Mills
McBride
Dunster
Tête Jaune Cache
Valemount

Barkerville
Wells
Cariboo
River
Park

BOWRON
LAKE
PARK

GARIBOO
MOUNTAINS
PARK

Mitchell L.
Likely
Quesnel L.

Horsefly L.
Horsefly
Black Creek
Hendrix Lake

Lac
la Hache
Forest
Grove
Canim Lake
Buffalo Creek
100 Mile House
Lone
Butte
Bridge Lake
Sheridan
Little Fort
70 Mile House
Chasm
Clinton
Cache
Creek
Ashcroft
Spences
Bridge
Lytton
Lower Nicola
Merritt
Boston Bar
North Bend
Yale
Hope
Laidlaw
Agassiz
Chilliwack
Abbotsford
Mission

WELLS GRAY
PARK

Mahood Falls
Clearwater
Birch
island
Vavenby
Chu Chua
Barrière
Louis Creek
McLure
Heffley
Creek
Kamloops
Walhachin
Savona
Westwold
Logan Lake
Douglas Lake
Nicola
Quilchena
Aspen
Grove
Brookmere
Tulameen
Princeton
Coalmont
Hedley
Manning
Park
Keremeos

Blue River
Avola
Seymour Arm
Sorrento
Chase
Salmon Arm
Sicamous
Canoe
Enderby
Armstrong
Spallumcheen
Vernon
Coldstream
Oyama
Winfield
Kelowna
Westbank
Peachland
Summerland
Penticton
Naramata
Kaleden
Okanagan Falls
Oliver
Osoyoos
Keremeos
Rock Creek

WASHINGTON

UNITED STATES

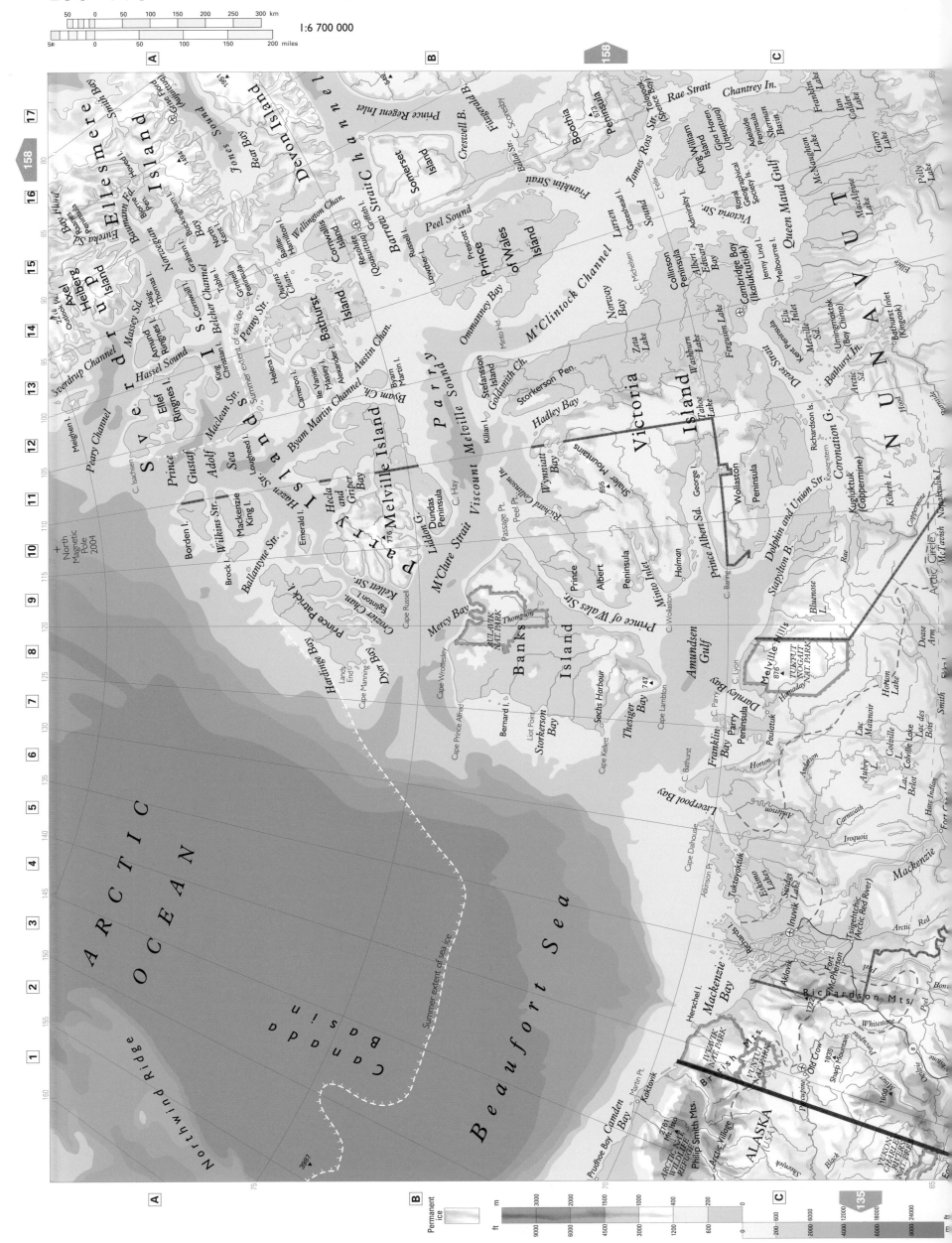

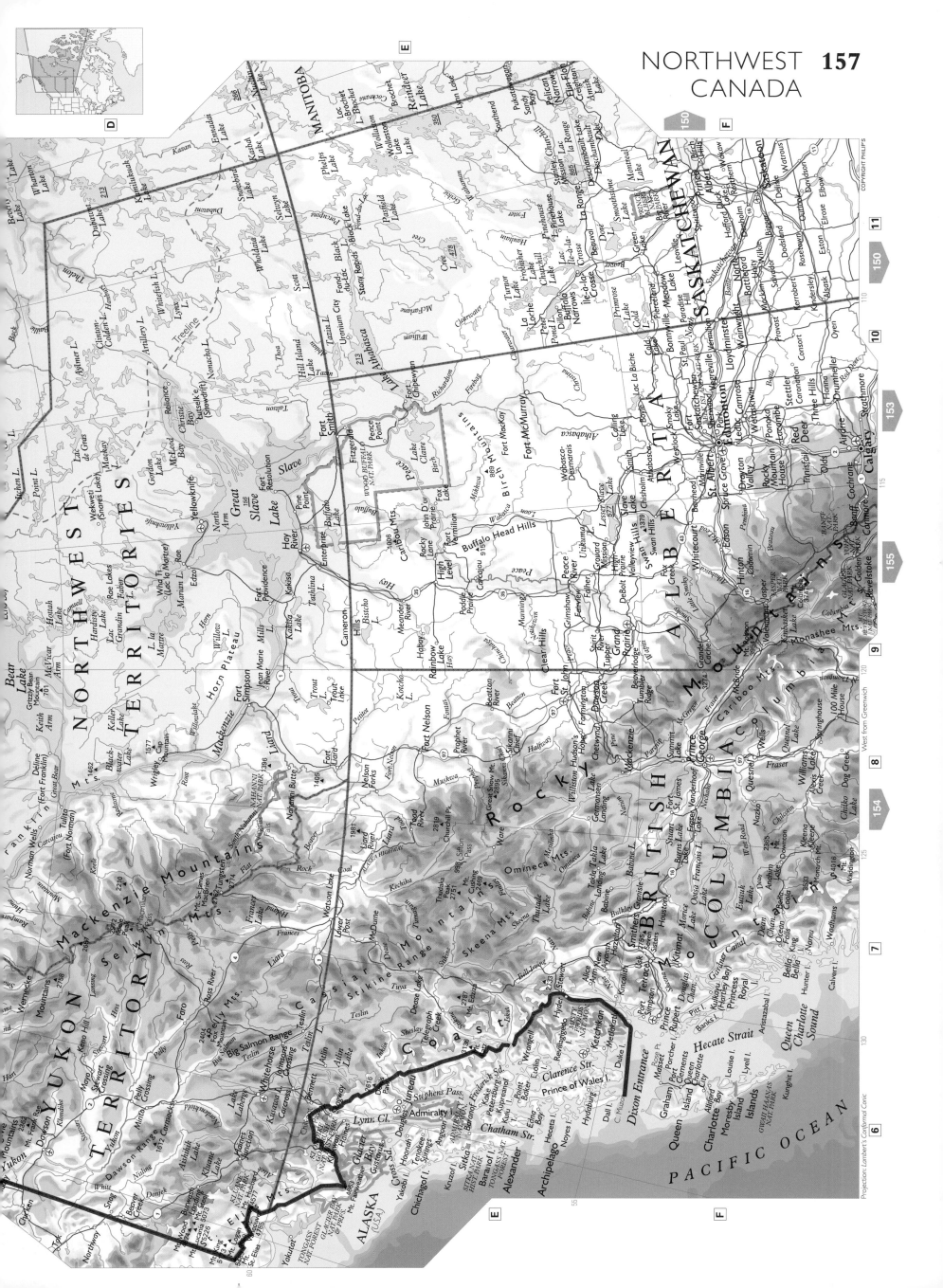

COPYRIGHT PHILIP'S

Projection: Lambert's Conformal Conic

West from Greenwich

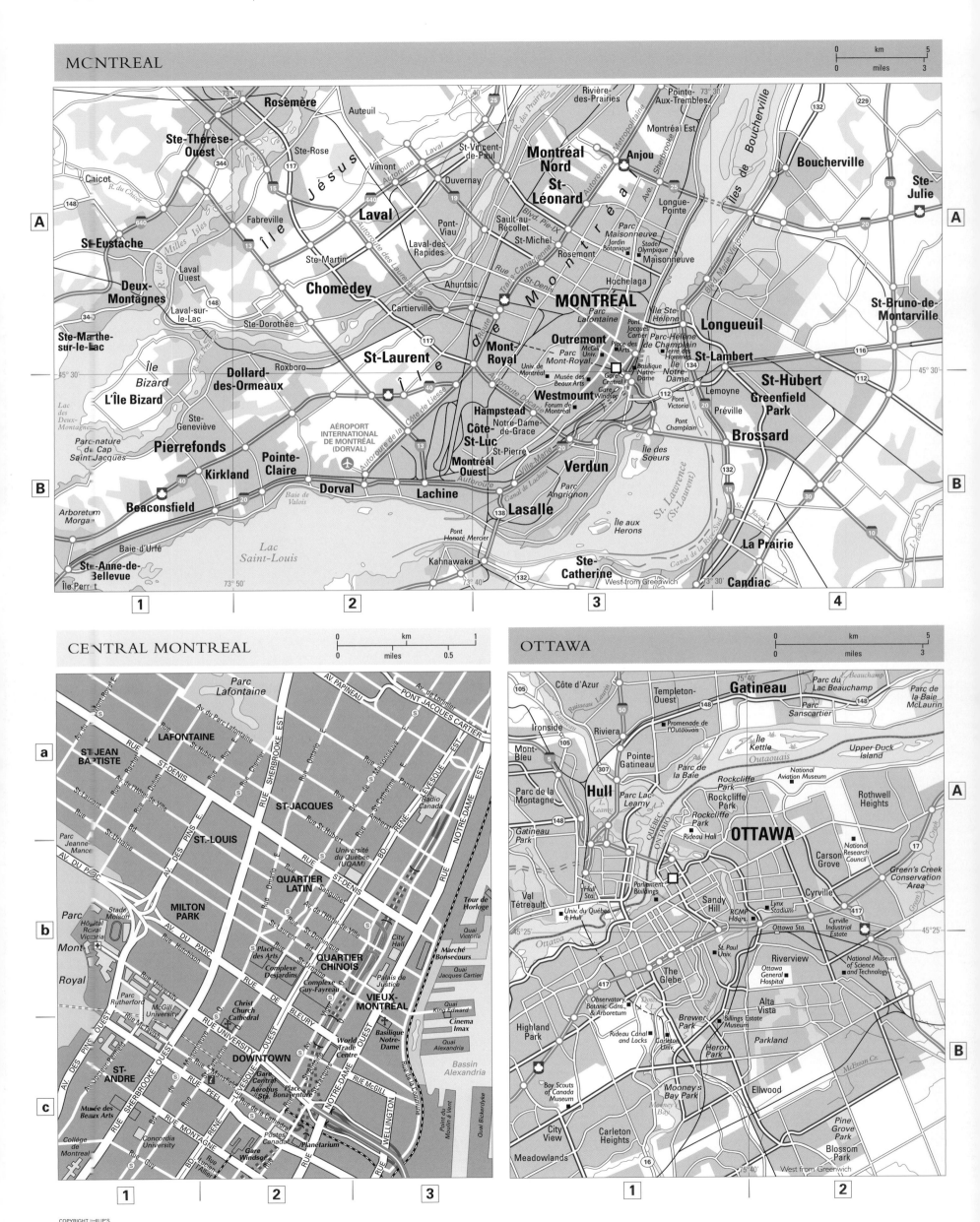

MONTREAL

Rosèmere
Auteuil
Rivière-des-Prairies
Pointe-Aux-Trembles
Boucherville
Ste-Thérèse-Ouest
Ste-Rose
Vimont
Ste-Vincent-de-Paul
Montréal Est
Montréal Nord
St-Léonard
Anjou
Longue-Pointe
Boucherville
Ste-Julie
St-Eustache
Fabreville
Duvernay
Sault-au-Récollet
St-Michel
Parc Maisonneuve
Jardin Botanique
Stade Olympique
Maisonneuve
Chicot
Laval
Pont-Viau
Laval-des-Rapides
Ahuntsic
Rosemont
Hochelaga
Deux-Montagnes
Ste-Martin
Cartierville
Rue Canadienne
MONTREAL
Île Ste-Hélène
Parc Maisonneuve
Chomedey
Laval-sur-le-Lac
Ste-Dorothée
Mont Royal
Outremont
Parc Mont-Royal
Parc Lafontaine
Place des Arts
Parc-Hélène de Champlain
Terre des Hommes
Longueuil
St-Bruno-de-Montarville
Ste-Marthe-sur-le-Lac
Île Bizard
L'Île Bizard
Roxboro
St-Laurent
Univ. de Montréal
Musée des Beaux Arts
Gare Central
Basilique Notre-Dame
St-Lambert
St-Hubert
Pierrefonds
Ste-Geneviève
Dollard-des-Ormeaux
AÉROPORT INTERNATIONAL DE MONTRÉAL (DORVAL)
Hampstead
Côte-St-Luc
Westmount
Forum de Montréal
Notre-Dame-de-Grace
St-Pierre
Lemoyne
Préville
Greenfield Park
Kirkland
Pointe-Claire
Verdun
Île des Soeurs
Brossard
Beaconsfield
Dorval
Lachine
Montréal Ouest
Parc Angrignon
St. Laurence (St-Laurent)
Baie-d'Urfé
Baie de Valois
Lasalle
Île aux Herons
La Prairie
St-Anne-de-Bellevue
Lac Saint-Louis
Pont Honoré Mercier
Kahnawake
Ste-Catherine
Candiac
Île Perrot

CENTRAL MONTREAL

Parc Lafontaine
LAFONTAINE
ST JEAN BAPTISTE
ST-JACQUES
Radio Canada
ST.-LOUIS
Université du Québec (UQAM)
QUARTIER LATIN
Tour de l'Horloge
Parc Jeanne-Mance
MILTON PARK
Quai Victoria
City Hall
Marché Bonsecours
Quai Jacques Cartier
Mont Royal
Place des Arts
Complexe Desjardins
QUARTIER CHINOIS
Palais de Justice
Quai King Edward
Cinema Imax
Parc Rutherford
McGill University
Christ Church Cathedral
Complexe Guy-Favreau
VIEUX-MONTREAL
Quai Alexandria
World Trade Centre
Basilique Notre-Dame
Bassin Alexandria
ST-ANDRE
Musée des Beaux Arts
DOWNTOWN
Gare Centrale Autobus Sta.
Place Bonaventure
Collège de Montréal
Concordia University
Gare Windsor
Cathédrale Postes Canada
Planétarium
Pointe du Moulin à Vent
Quai Bickerdyke

OTTAWA

Côte d'Azur
Templeton-Ouest
Gatineau
Parc du Lac Beauchamp
Parc de la Baie McLaurin
Ironside
Riviera
Promenade de l'Outaouais
Parc Sanscartier
Mont-Bleu
Pointe-Gatineau
Île Kettle
Upper Duck Island
Parc de la Montagne
Hull
Parc Lac Leamy
Parc de la Baie
National Aviation Museum
Rothwell Heights
Gatineau Park
Rockcliffe Park
Rockcliffe Park
Rideau Hall
OTTAWA
Carson Grove
National Research Council
Green's Creek Conservation Area
Val Tétreault
Hull Sta.
Parliament Buildings
Sandy Hill
Lynx Stadium
Cyrville
Univ. du Québec à Hull
RCMP Hqdrs.
Ottawa Sta.
Cyrville Industrial Estate
The Glebe
St. Paul Univ.
Riverview
National Museum of Science and Technology
Observatory, Botanic Gdns. & Arboretum
Ottawa General Hospital
Alta Vista
Highland Park
Rideau Canal and Locks
Carleton Univ.
Brewer Park
Billings Estate Museum
Parkland
Heron Park
Boy Scouts of Canada Museum
Mooney's Bay Park
Ellwood
City View
Carleton Heights
Meadowlands
Pine Grove Park
Blossom Park

COPYRIGHT PHILIP'S

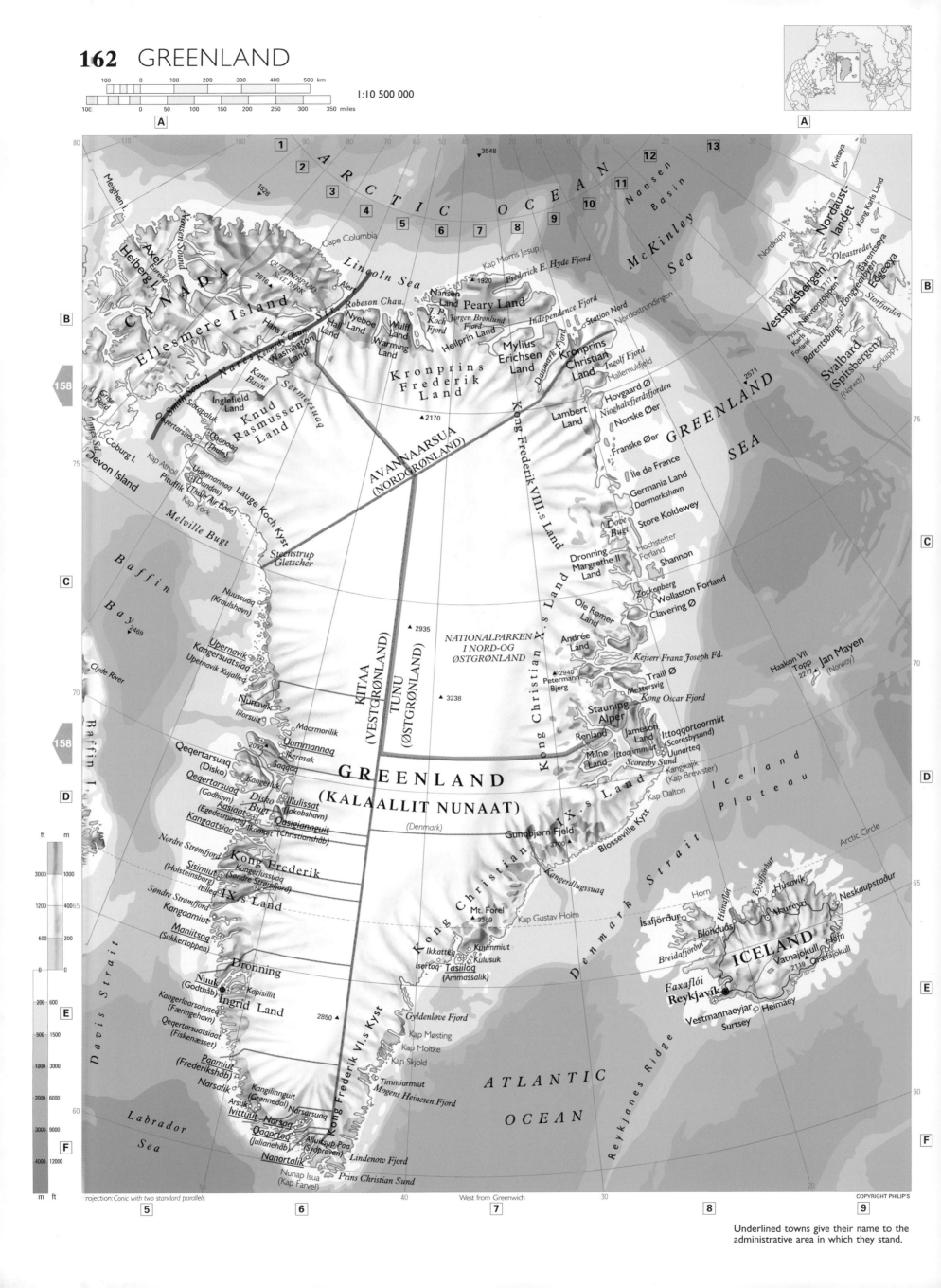

100   0   100   200   300   400   500 km

1:10 500 000

100   0   50   100   150   200   250   300   350 miles

A

A

ARCTIC OCEAN

▾ 3548

QUTTINIRPAAQ NAT. PARK
▲ 2616

Cape Columbia

Lincoln Sea

Kap Morris Jesup

▲ 1626

Meighen I.

Axel Heiberg I.

Nansen Sound

Eureka

Ellesmere Island

CANADA

Alert

Robeson Chan.

Hans I. (Chall.)

Nyeboe Land

Wulff Land

Warming Land

Hall Land

Washington Land

Koch Fjord

Nansen Land J.P. Peary Land

Jørgen Brønlund Fjord

Hellprin Land

Independence Fjord

▲ 1920 Frederick E. Hyde Fjord

Kronprins Christian Land

Mylius Erichsen Land

Daumark Fjord

Station Nord

Nordostrundingen

Ingolf Fjord

Mallemukfjeld

Kap Atholl

Nares Str.

Kennedy Chan.

Smith Sound

Kane Basin

Inglefield Land

Qeqertarsuaq

Siorapaluk

Qaanaaq (Thule)

Savissivik

Knud Rasmussen Land

Sermersuaq

Kronprins Frederik Land

▲ 2170

Kong Frederik VIII.s Land

AVANNAARSUA
(NORDGRØNLAND)

Hovgaard Ø

Nioghalvfjerdsfjorden

Norske Øer

Lambert Land

Franske Øer

Île de France

Germania Land

Danmarkshavn

Store Koldewey

Dove Bugt

Hochstetter Forland

Dronning Margrethe II Land

Shannon

GREENLAND SEA

▲ 2571

Devon Island

Coburg I.

Jones Sd.

Baffin Bay

Kap Atholl

Uummannaq (Dundas)

Pituffik (Thule Air Base)

Kap York

Melville Bugt

Steenstrup Gletscher

Nuussuaq (Kraulshavn)

Upernavik

Kangersuatsiaq

Upernavik Kujalleq

Nunavik

Illorsuit

Maarmorilik

Uummannaq

Ikerasak

Saqqaq

▲ 2092

▲ 2469

Clyde River

Baffin I.

NATIONALPARKEN I NORD-OG ØSTGRØNLAND

▲ 2935

KITAA (VESTGRØNLAND)

TUNU (ØSTGRØNLAND)

▲ 3238

Zackenberg

Wollaston Forland

Clavering Ø

Ole Rømer Land

Andrée Land

▲ 2940

Kejser Franz Joseph Fd.

Petermann Bjerg

Traill Ø

Mestersvig

Kong Oscar Fjord

Stauning Alper

Renland

Jameson Land

Milne Land

Ittoqqortoormiit (Scoresbysund)

Uunarteq

Scoresby Sund

Kangikajik (Kap Brewster)

Haakon VII Topp ▲ 2277

Jan Mayen (Norway)

Iceland Plateau

Kong Christian X.s Land

Kong Christian IX.s Land

Qeqertarsuaq (Disko)

Qeqertarsuaq (Godhavn)

Aasiaat (Egedesminde)

Kangerlussuaq

Kangerluk

Disko Bugt

Ilulissat (Jakobshavn)

Qasigiannguit (Christianshåb)

Ikamiut

GREENLAND
(KALAALLIT NUNAAT)

(Denmark)

Gunnbjørn Field ▲ 3700

Kap Dalton

Blosseville Kyst

Nordre Strømfjord

Sisimiut (Holsteinsborg)

Kangerlussuaq (Søndre Strømfjord)

Søndre Strømfjord

Kangaamiut

Itilleq

Kong Frederik IX.s Land

Maniitsoq (Sukkertoppen)

Mt. Forel ▲ 3360

Kap Gustav Holm

Ikkatteq

Kuummiut

Kulusuk

Dronning Ingrid Land

Nuuk (Godthåb)

Kapisillit

Kangerluarsoruseq (Færingehavn)

Qeqertarsuatsiaat (Fiskenæsset)

Isortoq

Tasiilaq (Ammassalik)

▲ 2850

Paamiut (Frederikshåb)

Gyldenløve Fjord

Kap Møsting

Kap Moltke

Kap Skjold

Narsalik

Kong Frederik VI.s Kyst

Arsuk

Kangilinnguit (Grønnedal)

Ivittuut

Narsaq

Narsarsuaq

Timmiarmiut

Mogens Heinesen Fjord

Qaqortoq (Julianehåb)

Alluitsup Paa (Sydprøven)

Lindenow Fjord

Nanortalik

Prins Christian Sund

Nunap Isua (Kap Farvel)

Davis Strait

Labrador Sea

ATLANTIC OCEAN

Denmark Strait

Reykjanes Ridge

Arctic Circle

Horn

Ísafjörður

Breidafjörður

Húsavík

Akureyri

Neskaupstaður

Húnaflói

Blönduós

Eyjafjörður

ICELAND

Vatnajökull ▲ 2119

Höfn

Faxaflói

Reykjavík

Vestmannaeyjar

Heimaey

Surtsey

Kvitøya

Nordaust-landet

Kong Karls Land

Nordkapp

Olgastredet

Barentsøya

Edgeøya

Vestspitsbergen

Prins Karls Forland

Ny-Ålesund

Longyearbyen

Storfjorden

Svalbard (Spitsbergen) (Norway)

McKinley Sea

Nansen Basin

West from Greenwich

projection: Conic with two standard parallels

COPYRIGHT PHILIP'S

ft   m

3000   1000

1200

600   400

200

0   0

200   600

500   1500

1000   3000

2000   6000

3000   9000

4000   12000

m   ft

158

158

Underlined towns give their name to the administrative area in which they stand.

MEXICO

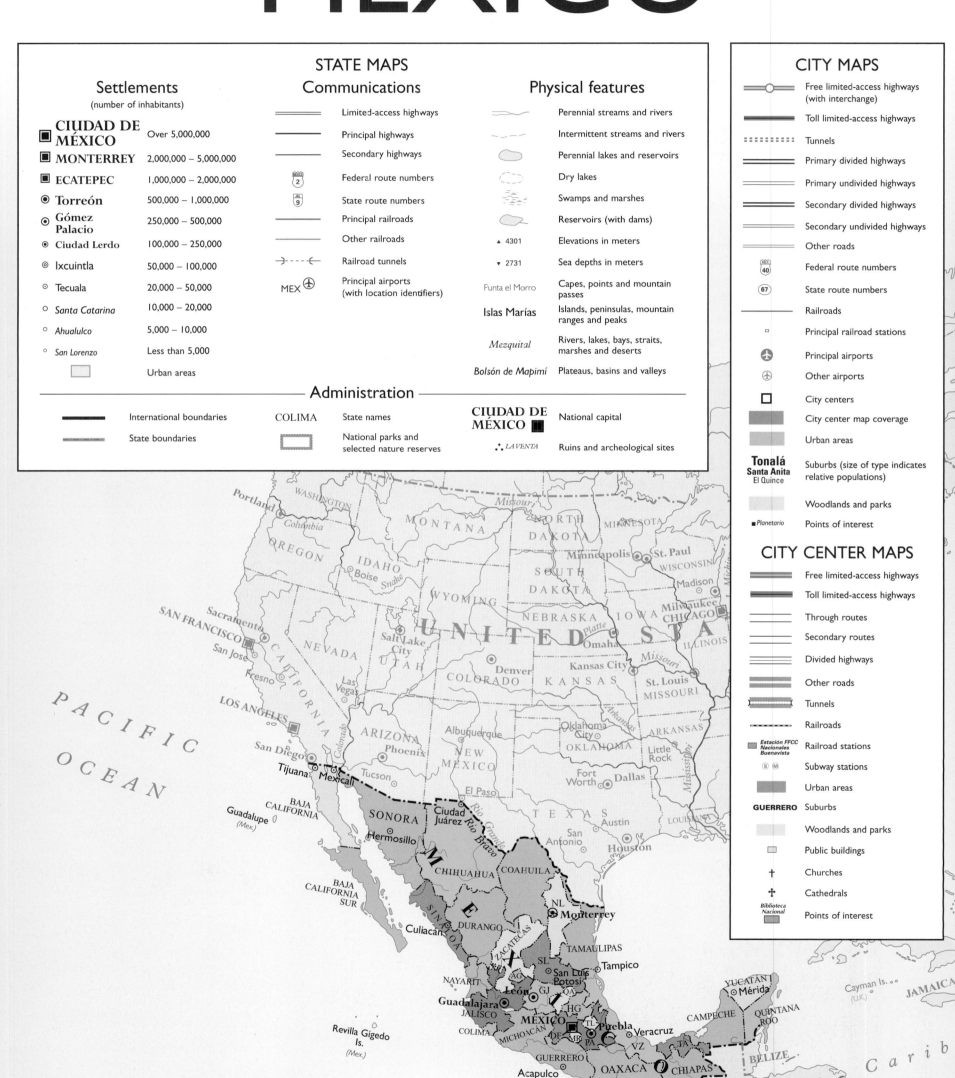

STATE MAPS

Settlements
(number of inhabitants)

■ **CIUDAD DE MÉXICO**	Over 5,000,000
■ **MONTERREY**	2,000,000 – 5,000,000
■ **ECATEPEC**	1,000,000 – 2,000,000
◉ **Torreón**	500,000 – 1,000,000
◉ **Gómez Palacio**	250,000 – 500,000
◉ Ciudad Lerdo	100,000 – 250,000
◉ Ixcuintla	50,000 – 100,000
○ Tecuala	20,000 – 50,000
○ Santa Catarina	10,000 – 20,000
○ Ahualulco	5,000 – 10,000
○ San Lorenzo	Less than 5,000
▢	Urban areas

Communications

	Limited-access highways
	Principal highways
	Secondary highways
2	Federal route numbers
9	State route numbers
	Principal railroads
	Other railroads
→--←	Railroad tunnels
MEX ✈	Principal airports (with location identifiers)

Physical features

	Perennial streams and rivers
	Intermittent streams and rivers
	Perennial lakes and reservoirs
	Dry lakes
	Swamps and marshes
	Reservoirs (with dams)
▲ 4301	Elevations in meters
▼ 2731	Sea depths in meters
Punta el Morro	Capes, points and mountain passes
Islas Marías	Islands, peninsulas, mountain ranges and peaks
Mezquital	Rivers, lakes, bays, straits, marshes and deserts
Bolsón de Mapimí	Plateaus, basins and valleys

Administration

	International boundaries
	State boundaries
COLIMA	State names
▢	National parks and selected nature reserves
CIUDAD DE MÉXICO ■	National capital
∴ LA VENTA	Ruins and archeological sites

CITY MAPS

	Free limited-access highways (with interchange)
	Toll limited-access highways
··········	Tunnels
	Primary divided highways
	Primary undivided highways
	Secondary divided highways
	Secondary undivided highways
	Other roads
40	Federal route numbers
67	State route numbers
	Railroads
□	Principal railroad stations
✈	Principal airports
✈	Other airports
□	City centers
	City center map coverage
	Urban areas
Tonalá Santa Anita El Quince	Suburbs (size of type indicates relative populations)
	Woodlands and parks
■ Planetario	Points of interest

CITY CENTER MAPS

	Free limited-access highways
	Toll limited-access highways
	Through routes
	Secondary routes
	Divided highways
	Other roads
	Tunnels
·-·-·-·	Railroads
Estación FFCC Nacionales Buenavista	Railroad stations
Ⓢ Ⓜ	Subway stations
	Urban areas
GUERRERO	Suburbs
	Woodlands and parks
□	Public buildings
†	Churches
✝	Cathedrals
Biblioteca Nacional	Points of interest

50 0   50   100 150 200 250 300 km

1:6 700 000

50   0   50   100   150   200 miles

119

100

1   2   3   4

A

B

C

D

Projection: Bi-polar oblique Conical Orthomorphic

West from Greenwich

State names in Central Mexico

1 DISTRITO FEDERAL   5 MÉXICO
2 AGUASCALIENTES   6 MORELOS
3 GUANAJUATO   7 QUERÉTARO
4 HIDALGO   8 TLAXCALA

GULF OF MEXICO

Golfo de Campeche

Banco Campeche

Yucatan Basin

Canal de Yucatán

CUBA

UNITED STATES

ARKANSAS

MISSISSIPPI

ALABAMA

GEORGIA

FLORIDA

LOUISIANA

TEXAS

Wichita Falls
Denison
Sherman
Paris
Denton
Greenville
Fort Worth
DALLAS
Ranger
Cleburne
Longview
Marshall
Texarkana
El Dorado
Camden
Greenville
Tuscaloosa
Opelika
Columbus
McRae
Abilene
Hillsboro
Corsicana
Tyler
Monroe
Vicksburg
Jackson
Meridian
Selma
Montgomery
Phenix City
Americus
Cordele
Albany
Tifton
Waycross
Brownwood
Waco
Palestine
Lufkin
Nacogdoches
Alexandria
Natchez
Laurel
Hattiesburg
Brewton
Dothan
Valdosta
Lake City
Temple
Bryan
Huntsville
College Station
Lake Charles
Lafayette
Baton Rouge
McComb
Bogalusa
Biloxi
Mobile
Pensacola
Panama City
Tallahassee
Austin
Houston
Rosenberg
Beaumont
Port Arthur
NEW ORLEANS
Gulfport
Apalachee Bay
Clearwater
San Antonio
Victoria
Galveston
Corpus Christi
Padre Island
Laredo
Kingsville
Nuevo Laredo
Zapata
McAllen
Harlingen
Brownsville
Reynosa
Río Bravo
Matamoros
Valle Hermoso
Santa Teresa
Laguna Madre
San Fernando
Linares
Villa Hidalgo
Zaragoza
Ciudad Victoria
La Pesca
Soto la Marina
Aldama
Ciudad Madero
Altamira
Tampico
Pánuco
Ciudad Mante
Ciudad Valles
Ebano
Ozuluama
Naranjos
Tuxpan
Poza Rica
Papantla
Nautla
Misantla
Huauchinango
Tulancingo
Teziutlán
Xalapa
Veracruz
Boca del Río
Pachuca
Zumpango
MEXICO
ECATEPEC
Tlaxcala
Apizaco
PUEBLA
Orizaba
Córdoba
Coatepec
Alvarado
Cuernavaca
Cuautla
Izúcar de Matamoros
Tehuacán
Cosamaloapan
Tierra Blanca
San Andrés Tuxtla
Acayucan
Minatitlán
Coatzacoalcos
Villahermosa
Frontera
Ciudad del Carmen
Campeche
Champotón
Escárcega
Chetumal
Belize City
Belmopan
BELIZE
Mérida
Progreso
Motul
Izamal
Tizimín
Cancún
Valladolid
Cozumel
Playa del Carmen
Acapulco
Chilpancingo
Oaxaca
Tehuantepec
Juchitán de Zaragoza
Salina Cruz
Tuxtla Gutiérrez
San Cristóbal de las Casas
Comitán de Domínguez
Tapachula
GUATEMALA
HONDURAS
Tegucigalpa
San Pedro Sula

Tropic of Cancer

Istmo de Tehuantepec

Golfo de Tehuantepec

CHIAPAS

TABASCO

CAMPECHE

QUINTANA ROO

YUCATAN

OAXACA

GUERRERO

VERACRUZ

COPYRIGHT PHILIP'S

1:2 100 000

km scale: 10 0 10 20 30 40 50 60 70 80 90 km
miles scale: 10 0 10 20 30 40 50 60 miles

PINAL

ARIZONA

PIMA

MARICOPA

U.S.A.

YUMA

IMPERIAL

CALIFORNIA

SAN DIEGO

San Diego
La Mesa
El Cajon
Santee
National City
Chula Vista
Spring Valley
Imperial Beach
Tijuana
Rosarito

Mexicali
Tecate

Ensenada

Sierra de Juárez

Sierra Cucapá

PARQUE NACIONAL CONSTITUCIÓN DE 1857

PARQUE NACIONAL SIERRA DE SAN PEDRO MÁRTIR

Sierra de San Pedro Mártir
Pico de Diablo 3078

BAJA CALIFORNIA

El Rosario

Gran Desierto de Altar

PARQUE NACIONAL DEL GRAN DESIERTO DEL PINACATE

Sierra El Pinacate

Puerto Peñasco

Bahía Adair

Golfo de California (Mar de Cortés)

Bahía San Jorge

Bahía San Felipe

San Felipe

Bahía Santa María

Puertecitos

SONORA

Caborca

Sierra El Viejo

Sierra El Alamo

Llanura

Costa

Isla Tiburón

PARQUE NATURAL ISLA TIBURÓN

Isla San Esteban
Isla San Lorenzo

Isla Ángel de la Guarda

PARQUE NATURAL ISLA ÁNGEL DE LA GUARDA

Canal de Ballenas

Bahía de los Ángeles

BAJA CALIFORNIA

PARQUE NATURAL DEL DESIERTO CENTRAL DE BAJA CALIFORNIA

Casas Grandes

PACIFIC OCEAN

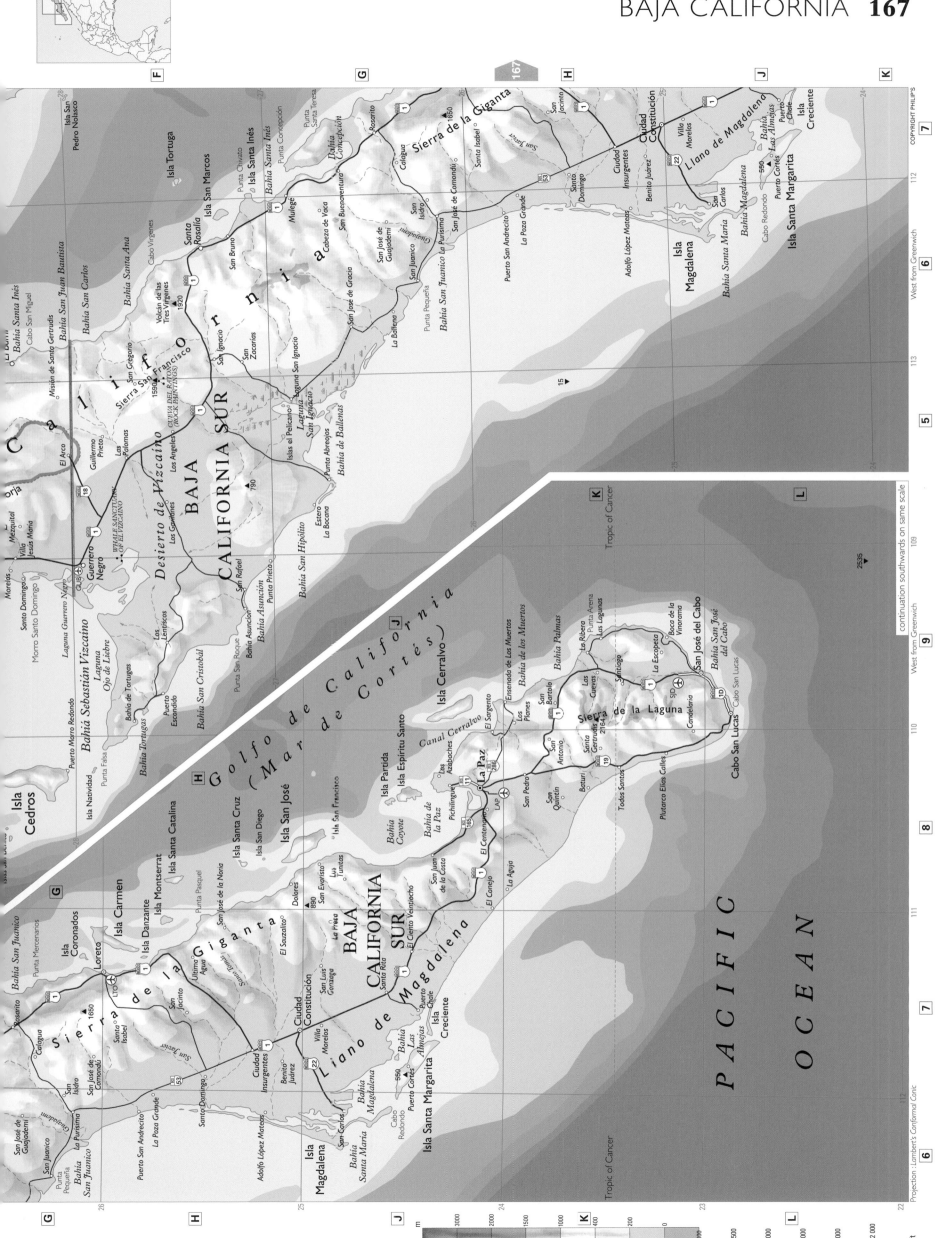

Projection : Lambert's Conformal Conic

1:2 100 000

10 0 10 20 30 40 50 60 70 80 90 km
10 0 10 20 30 40 50 60 miles

ARIZONA

COCHISE

HIDALGO

Animas Mts.

Bisbee
Nogales
Nogales
NOG
Douglas
Agua Prieta
Naco
Morelos
Santa Cruz
José Maria
2510

B

Bahia Lair
L. Choya
Puerto Peñasco
Bahia San Jorge
Punta Salina
Isla San Jorge

Cerro San Carlos
1213
San Luisito
El Plomo
Sierra El Humo
1667
El Sásabe
SANTA CRUZ

Cuba
Los Molinos
Sáric

Sahuaro
Las Enchilayas
Villa Guadalupe
Vicente Guerrero
Punta Jagüey
San Pedro

La Discordia
El Carrizal
Altar
Sierra San Juan
Tubutama
Valle
Imuris
Cananea
Sa. de los Ajos
Fronteras
Morelos
Pancho Villa

31

Isla San Jorge
San Isidro
El Coyote
Jesús García
Caborca
Pitiquito
948

Tajitos
Sierra La Gloria
Oquitoa
Altar
Atil
Santa Ana
San Ignacio
Magdalena de Kino
Cerro Azul
2450
Bacanuchi
Bacoachi
Esqueda
2450
Sierra San Diego
San Miguelito
2700
Bacerac

C

El Desemboque
Las Calenturas
San Juan
Bamuri
Sierra El Rajón
Trincheras
El Claro
Cucurpé
Arizpe
Nacozari de García
La Angostura
Presa la Angostura
Huachinera

Cabo Tepoca
El Plomito
Sierra El Viejo
Benjamín Hill
Banámichi
Opodepe
Huépac
San Felipe de Jesús
2180
Aconchi
Moctezuma
Cumpas
Huásabas
Granados
Bacadéhuachi
Villa Hidalgo
Mesa Tres Rios

30

Puerto Lobos
La Golondrina
Punta Tepoca
Puerto Libertad
San Ignacio
Sierra Tordilla
Sierra Santa Rosa
La Inmaculadita
El Cuatro
San Benito
1080
Carbó
Rayón
Baviácora
Divisaderos
Tepache
Nácori Chico

Isla Mejia
Isla Ángel de la Guarda
1315
Parque Natural Isla Ángel de la Guarda
El Desemboque
Pozo Coyote
San Miguel de Horcasitas
Pesqueira
Ures
San Pedro de la Cueva
1700
Presa Plutarco Elias Calles

D

Isla Coronado
Isla Partida
Punta Las Ánimas
Isla Patos
Parque Natural Isla Tiburón
Isla Tiburón
1218
Casas Grandes
Santa Martha
La Manga
HMO
Hermosillo
Mesa del Seri
Nacori Grande
Villa Pesqueira
1460
El Novillo
Sahuaripa
Natora

29

Isla Rasa
Isla Las Ánimas
Isla San Esteban
Punta Chueca
La Mocha
Los Pinitos
Santa María
El Triunfo
Miguel Alemán
Ignacio Ramírez
Mazatán
La Colorada
Rebeico
Bacanora
Arivechi
Soyopa
1520
Mulatos

BAJA CALIFORNIA
Bahia San Rafael
Isla San Lorenzo
Kino Nuevo
Bahia Kino
Valle Verde
Campo Cuatro
Rosario
La Palma
La Misa
San José de Moradillos
Tecoripa
San Javier
Tonichi
Santa Rosa
Cerro Mochomos
1100
San Nicolás
Yécora

E

Sierra La Libertad
Cerro La Sandía
1810
San Pedro
Punta San Francisquito
San Francisquito
Miguel Alemán
Los Arrieros
Ortiz
Onavas
Nuri
1860

Parque Natural del Desierto Central de Baja California
El Barril
Bahia Santa Inés
Cabo San Miguel
Misión de Santa Gertrudis
El Arco
Bahia San Juan Bautista
Isla San Pedro Nolasco
Playa Algodones
San Carlos
Empalme
Guaymas
El Pochote
Vicam
Suaqui Grande
Agua Caliente
2320

28

CALIFORNIA
U.S.A.
Gila
Aztec
Sentinel
MARICOPA
Esperanza
Ciudad Obregón
San Bernardo
Chinapa

Yuma
Wellton
Tacna
Roll
Dateland
Sonoran Desert
Bácum
San Ignacio
Quiriego
Gasoriachic

Mérida
Vicente Guerrero
Somerton
Gadsden
San Luis
YUMA
Yuma Desert
Mohawk Mts.
846
Growler Wash
85
Granite Mts.
Sauceda Mts.
San Simon Wash
Isla Lobos
Liliba
Pueblo Yaqui
Villa Guadalupe
Presa Adolfo Ruiz Cortines
Milpillas

San Luis Río Colorado
Lagunitas
Ignacio Zaragoza
Ajo
1252
ARIZONA
PIMA
Los Médanos
Villa Juárez
Jecopaca
148
Navojoa
13
Alamos

Riito
Sierra Pinta
Coyote Wash
Mt. Ajo
1465
Lukeville
Pisinimo
Isla Huivulai
Buaysiacobe
Bacobampo
El Cuchujaqui
1250

Gran Desierto de Altar
40
Los Vidrios
Sierra El Pinacate
PARQUE NACIONAL DEL GRAN DESIERTO DEL PINACATE
Cerro del Pinacate
1190
Sonoyta
Cerro Cubabi
1366
San Emeterio
Sells
Topawa
Cowlic
Baboquivari Pk.
2356
Huatabampo
Las Milpas
Etchoropo
56
Huatabampito
Yávaros
Cerro Colorado

BAJA CALIFORNIA
Isla Pelicano
Golfo de Santa Clara
Villagrán
8
Guadalupe
SONORA
2
El Gato
El Patricio
1036
El Sásabe
Masiaca
Agiabampo

Isla Montague
La Trinidad (El Chinero)
La Choya
Puerto Peñasco
Cerro San Carlos
1213
San Luisito
El Plomo
Sierra El Humo
1667
Los Molinos
Sasabe
Bahia Jitzamuri
Niños Héroes de Chapultepec
Chihuahuita
Presa Josefa Ortiz de Dominguez
El Fuerte
Hoyonila
La Lajitas
San Blas

Golfo de California
Bahia Adair
Bahia San Jorge
West from Greenwich
Presa Miguel Hidalgo

Continuation westwards on same scale
Projection : Lambert's Conformal Conic

8   131   9

7

108 LUNA **NEW MEXICO** 107 DONA ANA
General Rodrigo
M. Quevedo (Palomas)
▲2100
Cerro El Grande 24
▲2300   Casas Grandes

CIUDAD JUÁREZ

El Paso
Socorro
CJS
2

Nuevo Cuauhtémoc

Emiliano Zapata
San Isidro 35D
Fabens

10

Guadalupe de Bravo
Samalayuca Práxedis G. Guerrero
2

Fort Hancock

HUDSPETH

U.S.A.
CULBERSON

10   108   11   12

Pecos

El Berrendo
El Barreal
Laguna de Guzmán
Guzmán
El Porvenir
2134
Toyah

REEVES

B

La Palotada
Ascensión
2
Sierra El Fresnal
▲2320
El Mirador
Laguna
El Barreal
2140▲
Quitman Mts.
Río Grande
Apache Mts.
Kent
Van Horn

Saragosa
31

Janos
Campo Cinco
Santa María
El Consuelo
2200
Sierra San José del Prisco
Sierra Diablo
Eagle Mts.
Sierra Vieja

T E X A S

JEFF DAVIS
Davis
Mt. Livermore
2555
Valentine
Mountains

40
67

C

Casas Grandes
Hidalgo
Dublán
Nuevo Casas Grandes
PAQUIME
Juárez
Progreso
Villa Ahumada
Villa Ahumada
y Anexas
El Veinticuatro
Moctezuma
El Cuervo
Las Cuatas
San Eduardo
El Cuervo
El Llano
Sierra La Esperanza
Marfa
Twin Mts.
2085
Alpine
Mt. Ord
2042▲
Cathedral Mt.
2091
Marathon

PRESIDIO
Chinati Peak
▲2356
Chinati Mts.
McKinney Mt.
1522
Santiago Peak
1988▲
Santiago Mts.
Chalk Mts.

90
Glass Mts.

30

Ignacio
Zaragoza
Juan Mata Ortiz
Galeana
Laguna
La Vieja
Benito Juárez
Ricardo Flores Magón
La Constitución
Ojo del Carrizo
Sierra La Lágrima

D

El Colorado
▲2640
La Mesa
del Huracán
CUERENTA
CASAS
Las Varas
Buenaventura
San Lorenzo
La Trasquila
2820
10
45D
Laguna
Encinillas
Loma Blanca
2200
Coyame
Cuchillo
Parado
Sierra Matasaguas
Ojinaga
Presidio
Alamo Chapo

BREWSTER

BIG BEND
NATIONAL
PARK
Emory Peak
2388

La Esmeralda
Madera
ANASAZI
Gómez Farías
San José de Bavicora
Cerro Tres Picos
3040
Namiquipa
Ojos Azules
Benito Juárez
Laguna
El Cuervo
El Peñol
El Scuz
Estación Colonias
Plomosa
Maclovio Herrera
Chilicote
2400
Manuel Benavides
PARQUE NATURAL
CAÑÓN DE
SANTA ELENA
Paso de
San Antonio
San Antonio

29

Chico
Siripa
Oscar Soto Maynes
Temosachic
2978
San José
y Anexas
Campo
Sesenta y Uno
2720
PARQUE NACIONAL
CUMBRES DE MAJALCA
C H I H U A H U A
Lázaro
Cárdenas
Luis L. León
Presa
Luis L. León
Chorreras
Polvorillas
Cruces y Anexas
1980
Los Alamos
de Márquez

E

Tres Ojitos
Matachic
Cocomorachic
Bachíniva
Álvaro
Obregón
Cumbres
de Majaka
45
CUU
Chihuahua
Aldama
Dolores
San Diego
de Alcalá
2140
El Becerro
Santa Fe

Tosanachic
**Ciudad
Guerrero**
Adolfo
López Mateos
Anáhuac
10
Laguna
Bustillos
Chihuahua
Riva Palacio
Aquiles
Serdán
45D
Julimes

Salto
16
Tomochic
Cuauhtémoc
16D
General
Trías
Meoqui
Rosales
La Perla
San Miguel
Santa Anita

28

campo
PARQUE NACIONAL
CASCADAS DE
BASASEACHIC
Terrero
3060
San Miguel
Cerro
Prieto
Cusihuiriachic
Gran Morelos
Delicias
El Orranteño
Santa Isabel
Hércules

Ana Casas
Cascadas
de Basaseachic
2820
Cajurichic
San Juanito
Carichic
Dr. Belisario
Domínguez
La Joya
La Capilla
de los Remedios
Tajirachic
Santa Cruz
Presa
Francisco
I. Madero
Kilometro
Noventa y Uno
Satevó
Saucillo
Ancón de Carros
Texcoco
El Alicante

Uruachic
2520
Bocoyna
San Francisco
de Borja
Santa
María
de Cuevas
San Pedro
Estación Conchos
45
Naica
La Cruz
45D
COAHUILA
Hormigas
San José
de Carranza
Cenzontle

170

F

Guasizaco
Creel
Sisoguichi
Panalachic
Cusárare
San José
Baqueachi
San Francisco
del Orc
Valerio
Monte
Redondo
Ciudad Camargo
San Francisco
de Conchos
30
Laguna
Colorada
Las Norias

Maguarichic
San José
Guacayvo
Conchos
La Libertad
Nonoava
Boquilla
de Abajo
Valle
del Rosario
2792
Valle
de Zaragoza
Presa
la Boquilla
La Boquilla
del Conchos
Florido
Las Pampas
2058▲
Sierra Las Pampas
Maravillas
Sierra Mojada
2463

Guazapares
San Rafael
Guaguachique
Rochéachic
Huejotitán
San Antonio
del Potrero
Búfalo
Jiménez
49
La Providencia
Laguna del Rey
27

Urique
Batopilas
Buenavista
23
20
Balleza
La Magdalena
Hidalgo del Parral
Villa López
División
del Norte
Guimbalete
Laguna
del Rey
Zona del Silencio
El Cinco

La Reforma
Fuerte
Guachochi
Cabórachi
San Francisco del Oro
Santa
Bárbara
Torreón
de Mata
Villa
Coronada
Guadalupe
de Bafues
45
Carrillo
Laguna
Palomas
El Cinco
Santa María
de Mohovano

G

Tasajeras
Choix
23
Morelos
2671▲
La Providencia
Orestes
Pereyra
3315
Villa
Matamoros
Escalón
PARQUE
NATURAL
MAPIMÍ
Ceballos
Las Tortugas
49

Yecorato
Chinobampa
Las
Palomas
2692
Baborigame
El Caldillo
Verde
3310
Villa Ocampo
Canutillo
San Fermín
44
El Diamante
Conejos

SINALOA
Válgame
Dios
3010
3050
La Logunita
Cerro Prieto
Sexto
D U R A N G O
Revolución
Villa
Hidalgo
El Jaralito
Tlahualilo
de Zaragoza

Presa Guillermo
Blake Agular
Guadalupe
y Calvo
Yerbitas
Sardinas
Potrero
del Llano
26

108   West from Greenwich   107   106   105   104   COPYRIGHT PHILIP'S

7   8   9   172   10   11   12

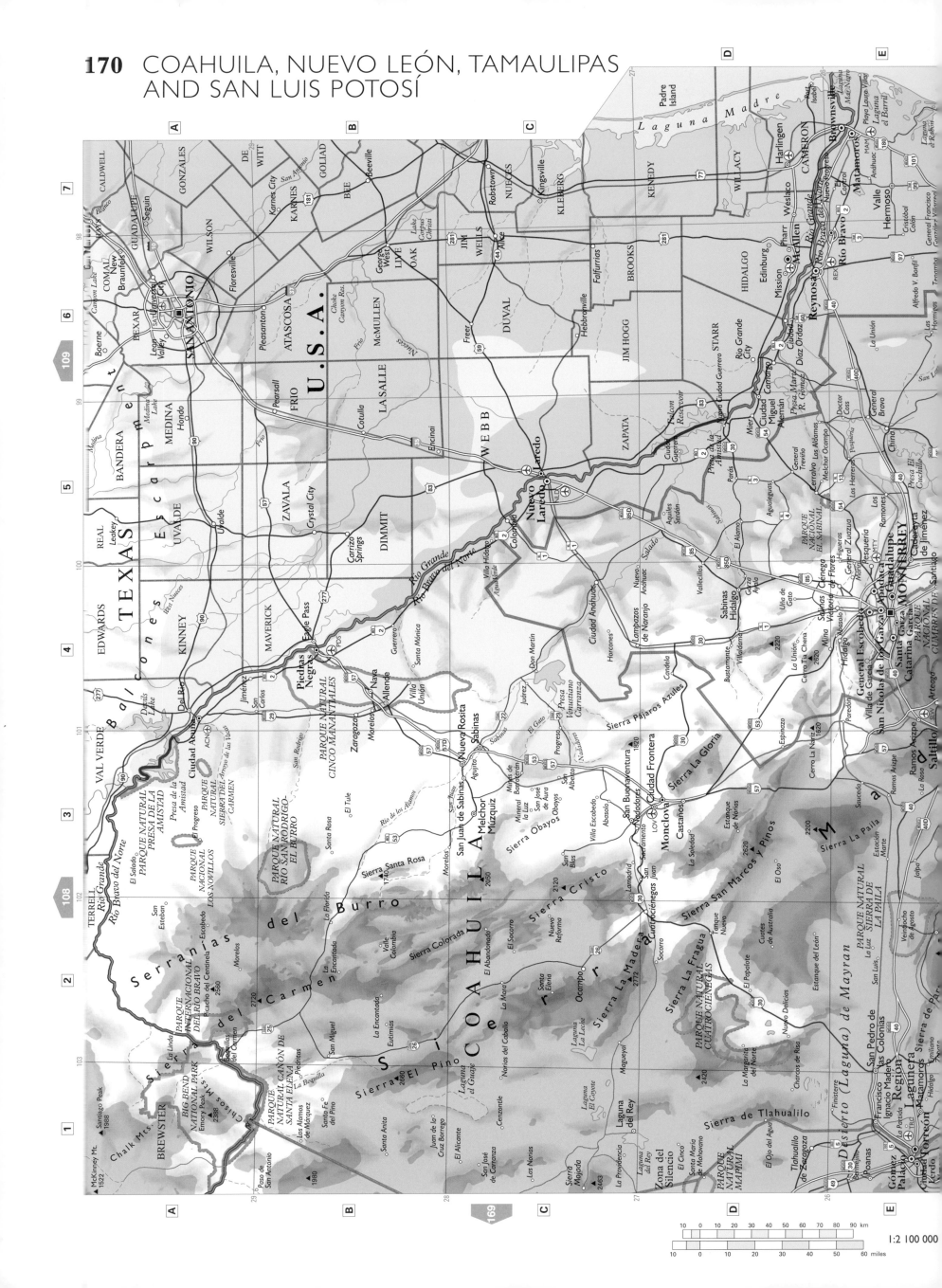

A   B   C

7

6

109

5

4

3

108

2

1

A   B   **169**   C   D   E

Padre Island

L a g u n a   M a d r e

CALDWELL
GONZALES
DE WITT
GUADALUPE
COMAL
New Braunfels
Seguin
San Antonio
Boerne
BEXAR
SAN ANTONIO
WILSON
KARNES
Karnes City
Floresville
GOLIAD
BEE
Beeville
Leon Valley
Pleasanton
ATASCOSA
McMULLEN
Lake Corpus Christi
Choke Canyon Res.
LIVE OAK
George West
JIM WELLS
Alice
Robstown
NUECES
Kingsville
KLEBERG
KENEDY
WILLACY
Harlingen
Weslaco
Brownsville
Matamoros
CAMERON
Playa Lauro Villar
Laguna Madre
Valle Hermoso
Río Bravo

REAL
Leakey
Bandera
BANDERA
Medina
MEDINA
Hondo
Pearsall
FRIO
LA SALLE
U.S.A.
Cotulla
Encinal
WEBB
DUVAL
Freer
Falfurrias
BROOKS
Hebbronville
JIM HOGG
Rio Grande City
STARR
HIDALGO
Edinburg
Mission
McAllen
Pharr
Reynosa
Río Bravo
Ciudad Díaz Ordaz
Camargo
Ciudad Miguel Alemán
ZAPATA
Falcon Reservoir
Ciudad Guerrero
Mier
Nuevo Ciudad Guerrero

EDWARDS
TEXAS
Vance Nueces
KINNEY
Del Rio
Ciudad Acuña
Presa de la Amistad
PARQUE NATURAL PRESA DE LA AMISTAD
UVALDE
Uvalde
ZAVALA
Crystal City
Carrizo Springs
DIMMIT
Guerrero
Santa Mónica
Nuevo Laredo
Laredo
Colombia
Villa Hidalgo
Aguaverde
Anáhuac
Nuevo Anáhuac
Ciudad Anáhuac
Aguileños
Aguilas Serdán
El Alamo
Sabinas Hidalgo
Vallecillos
General Treviño
Cerralvo
Los Aldamas
China
Melchor Ocampo
General Bravo

VAL VERDE
Río Bravo del Norte
Río Grande
Jiménez
San Carlos
Piedras Negras
Nava
Allende
Villa Unión
Morelos
Zaragoza
Sierra Pájaros Azules
Lampazos de Naranjo
Horcones
Doctor Coss
MONTERREY
General Zuazua
Salinas Victoria
Ciénega de Flores
Pesquería
Higueras
PARQUE NACIONAL EL SABINAL
Marín
Mina
Cadereyta de Jiménez
Guadalupe

TERRELL
BREWSTER
Chalk Mts.
McKinney Mt. 1522
Santiago Peak 1988
Emory Peak 2386
Chisos Mts.
BIG BEND NATIONAL PARK
PARQUE INTERNACIONAL DEL RIO BRAVO
Picacho del Centinela 2560
PARQUE NATURAL CAÑON DE SANTA ELENA
Escobedo
Morelos
La Encantada
Vale Colombia
Sierra Colorada
El Socorro
El Abandonado
Nuevo Reforma
Socorro
PARQUE NATURAL RIO SAN RODRIGO-EL BURRO
San Rodrigo
El Tule
Santa Rosa
Rio de los Alamos
Sierra Santa Rosa 1740
Sierra del Carmen 2720
Serranías del Burro
S i e r r a   L a   M a d e r a
2772
COAHUILA
Sierra La Madera
Sierra El Pino 2660
Sierra La Fragua
Laguna el Guaje
Norias del Caballo
Santa Elena
Ocampo
2426
Sierra La Gloria
Ciudad Frontera
Monclova
Castaños
San Buenaventura
Nadadores
Progreso
San José de Aura
Mineral la Luz
Villa Escobedo
Abasolo
Lamadrid
Nuevo Reforma
Cuatrociénegas
PARQUE NATURAL CUATROCIÉNEGAS
El Oso
Tanque Nuevo
El Papalote
Estanque de Norias
Sierra San Marcos y Pinos 2620
M
2200
Sierra La Paila
Estación Marte
PARQUE NATURAL SIERRA DE LA PAILA
Veinticho de Agosto

Nueva Rosita
Sabinas
Agujita
San Juan de Sabinas
Melchor Múzquiz
2050
Minas de Barroterán
El Gato
Presa Venustiano Carranza
Juárez
Don Martin
Presa Don Martin
Candela
Bustamante
Villaldama
La Unión
Cerro Tía Chena
Ramos Arizpe
Saltillo
Santa Catarina
San Nicolás de los Garza
General Escobedo
Villa de García
Sierra Mojada 2463
Zona del Silencio
Laguna del Rey
Laguna El Coyote
Laguna La Leche
San Pedro de las Colonias
PARQUE NATURAL MAPIMÍ
Desierto (Laguna) de Mayran
Sierra de Tlahualilo
Francisco Ignacio Madero
Laguna Region
Gómez Palacio
Torreón

10   90   99   100   101   102   103

28   27   26

Golfo de California

C a l i f o r n i a

Isla Cerralvo

DURANGO

SINALOA

SONORA

CHIHUAHUA

DURA

SINALOA

Tropic of Cancer

PACIFIC OCEAN

NAYARIT

JALISCO

PACIFIC OCEAN

Culiacán

Mazatlán

Tepic

Puerto Vallarta

JALISCO

Islas Marías

Isla María Madre

Isla María Magdalena

Isla María Cleofas

PARQUE NACIONAL ISLA ISABEL

PARQUE NACIONAL PUERTO DE LOS ANGELES

Nayarit on same scale

Projection : Lambert's Conformal Conic

1:2 100 000

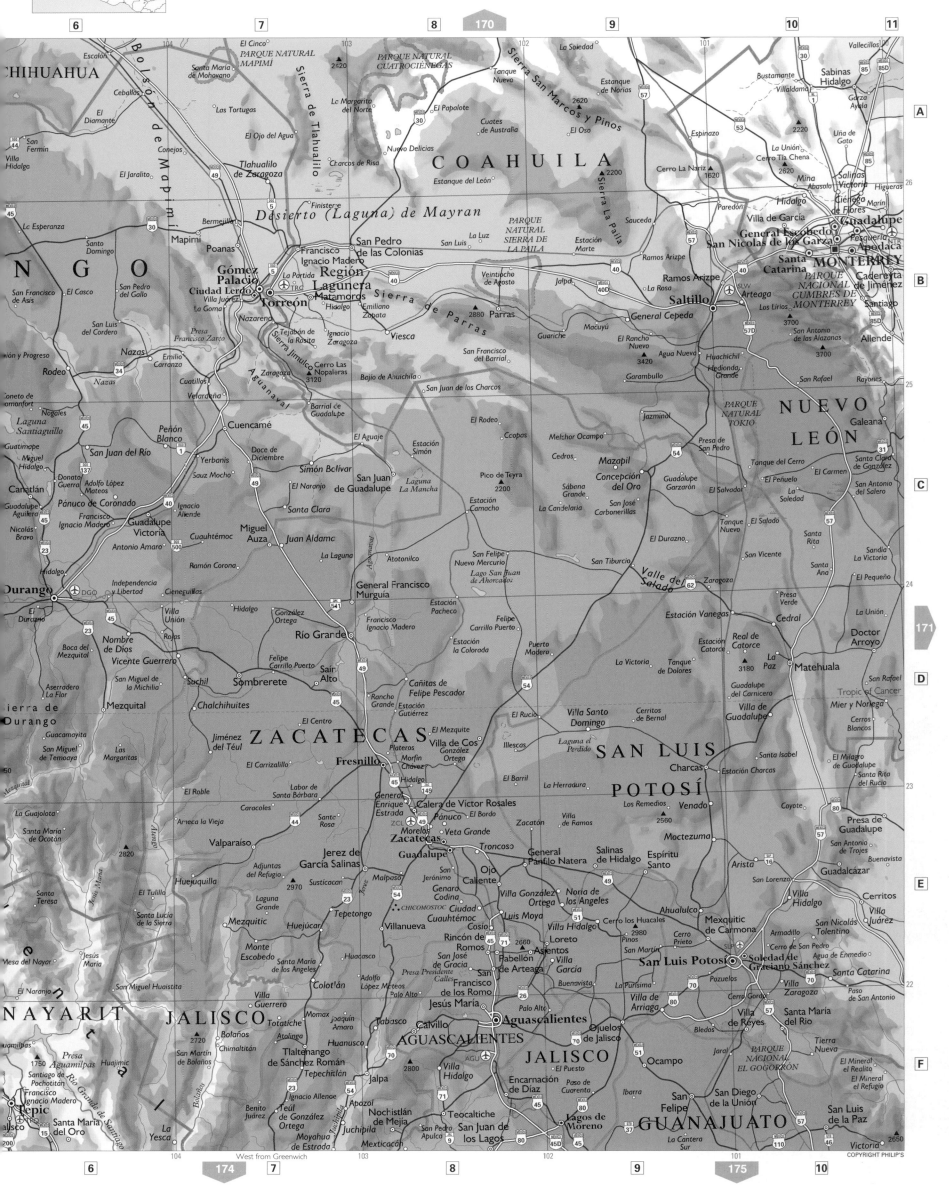

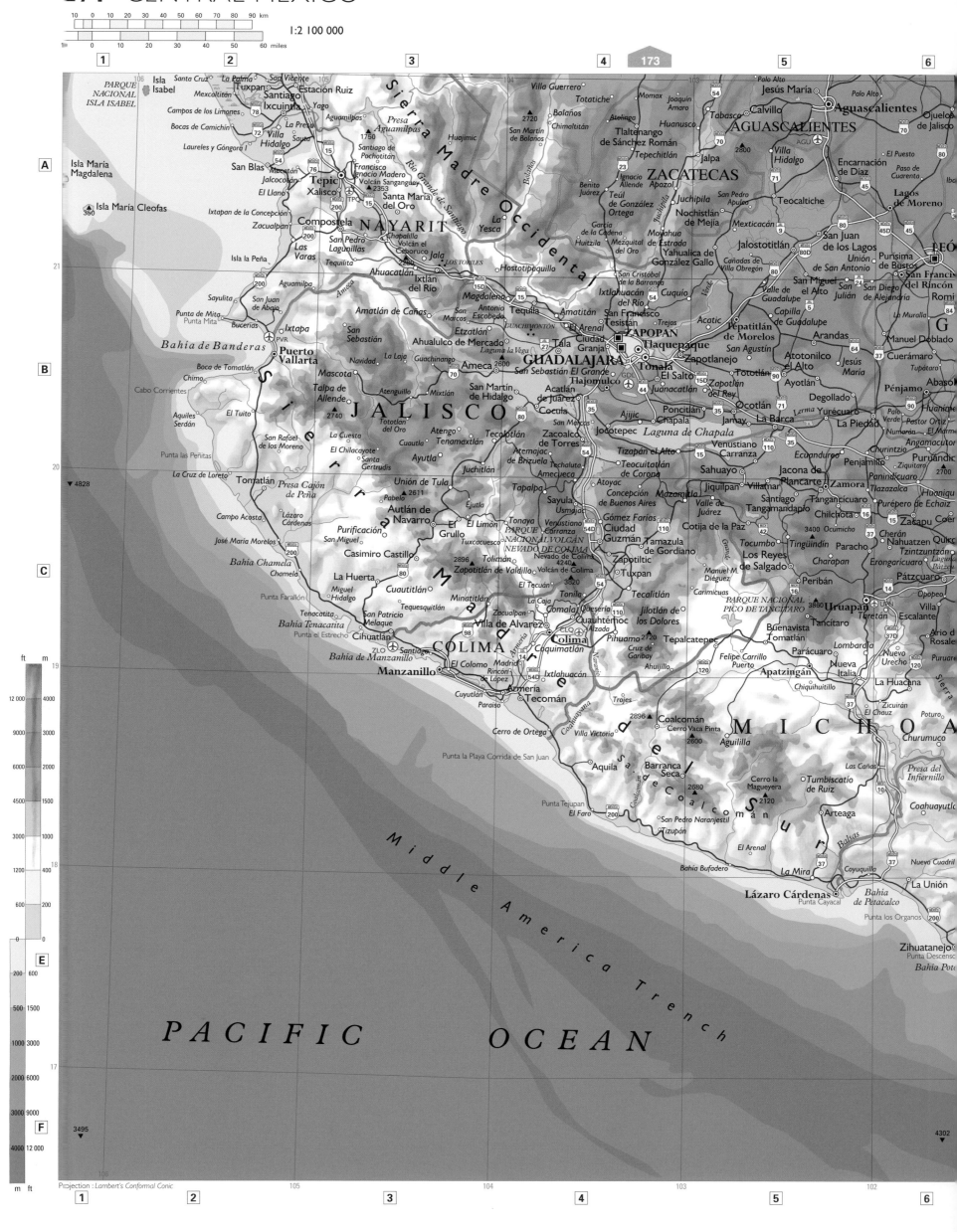

10 0 10 20 30 40 50 60 70 80 90 km
1:2 100 000
0 10 20 30 40 50 60 miles

173

Projection : Lambert's Conformal Conic

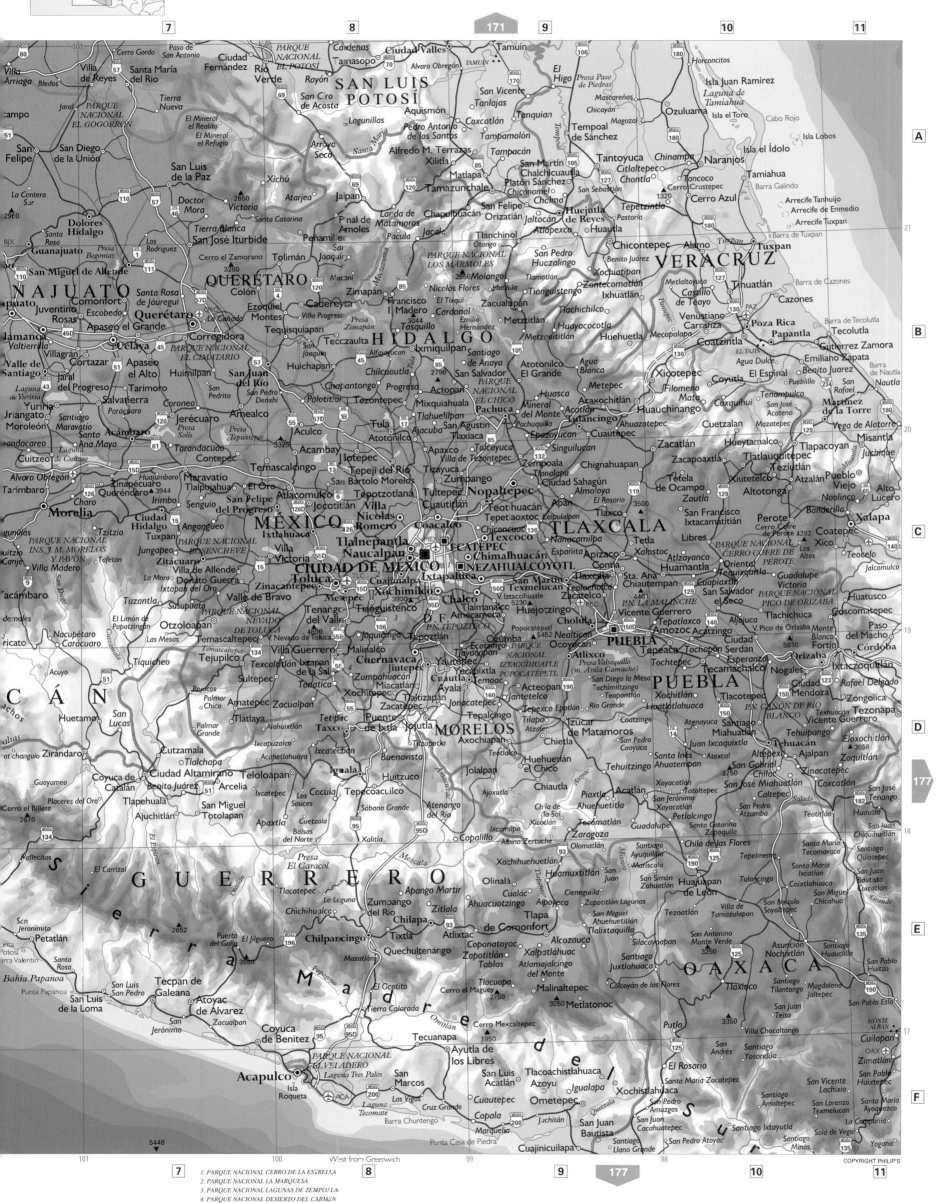

1:2 100 000

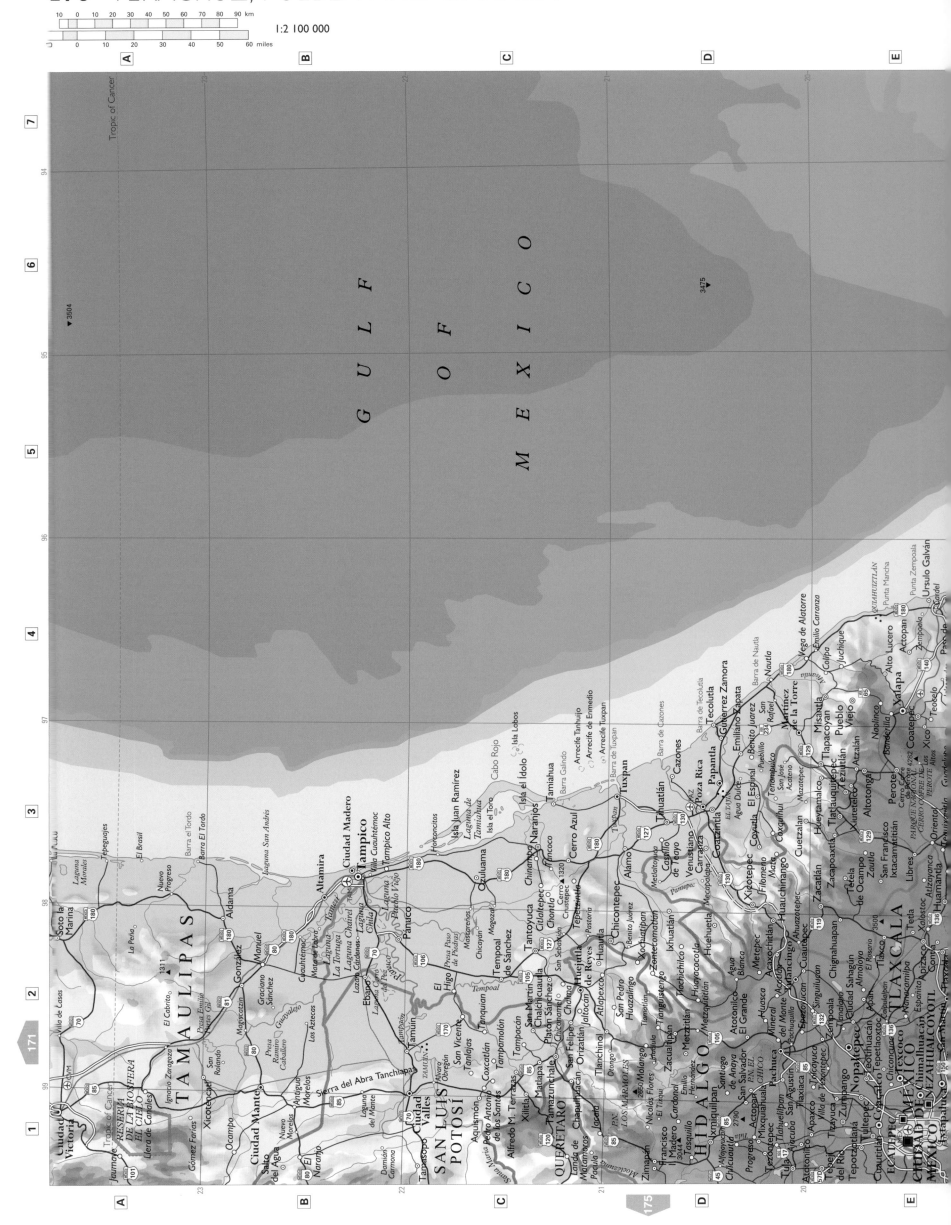

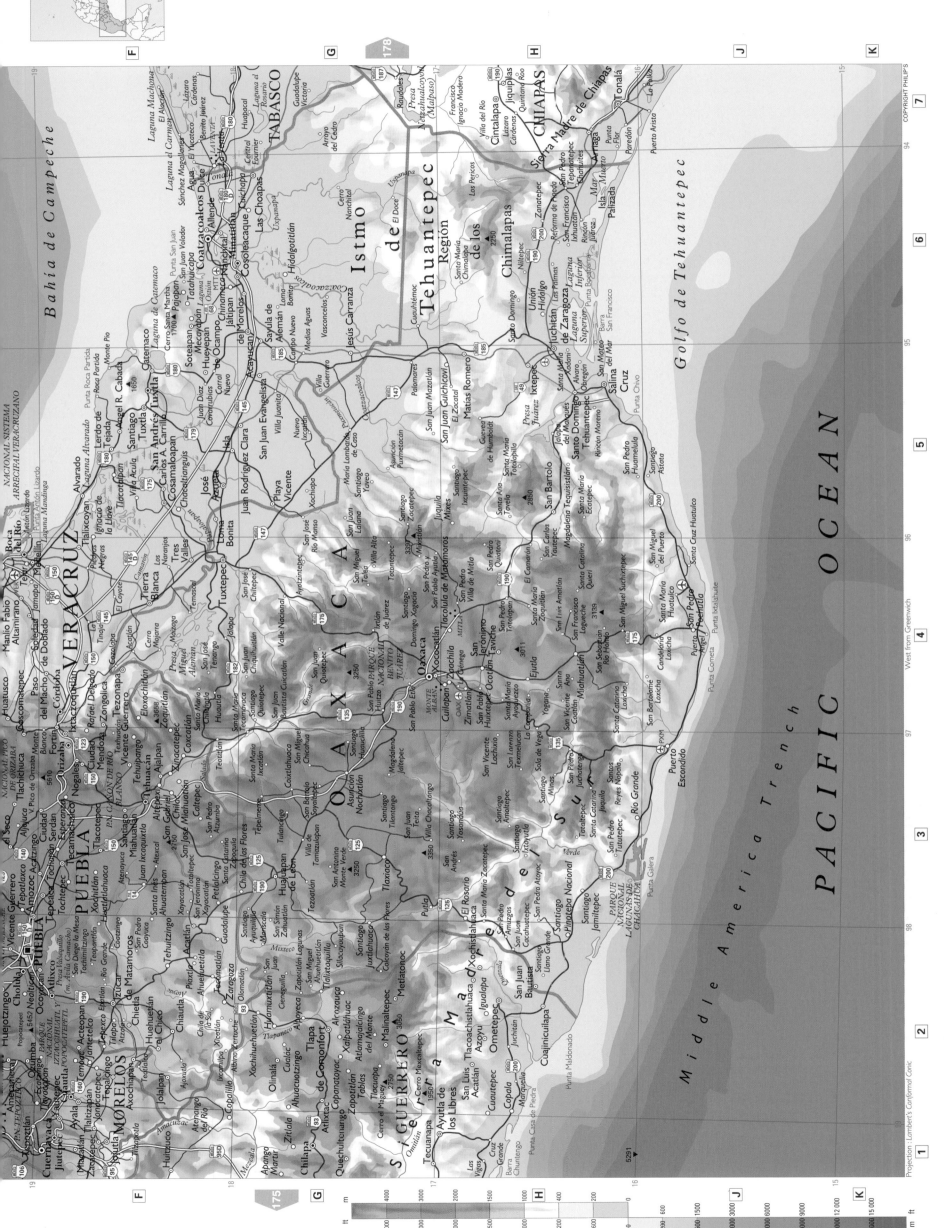

COPYRIGHT PHILIP'S

Projection : Lambert's Conformal Conic

1:1 925 000

Projection: Lambert's Conformal Conic

West from Greenwich

COPYRIGHT PHILIP'S

CAMPECHE

PETÉN

GUATEMALA

ALTA VERAPAZ

BAJA VERAPAZ

QUICHÉ

HUEHUETENANGO

SAN MARCOS

TABASCO

VERACRUZ

OAXACA

CHIAPAS

Sierra Madre de Chiapas

Sierra del Norte de Chiapas

Istmo de Tehuantepec

Región de los Chimalapas

Bahía de Campeche

Golfo de Tehuantepec

PACIFIC OCEAN

RESERVA DE LA BIOSFERA CALAKMUL

PARQUE NACIONAL LAGUNA DEL TIGRE

PARQUE NACIONAL SIERRA DE LACANDÓN

PARQUE NATURAL MONTES AZULES

RESERVA DE LA BIOSFERA MONTES AZULES

RESERVA DE LA BIOSFERA LACANTÚN

PARQUE NACIONAL LAGUNAS DE MONTEBELLO

PARQUE NATURAL LAGUNA LACHUÁ

PARQUE NACIONAL PALENQUE

Laguna de Términos

Villahermosa

Tuxtla Gutiérrez

San Cristóbal de las Casas

Palenque

Comitán de Domínguez

Tapachula

Escárcega

Ciudad del Carmen

Coatzacoalcos

Minatitlán

Tonalá

Tehuantepec

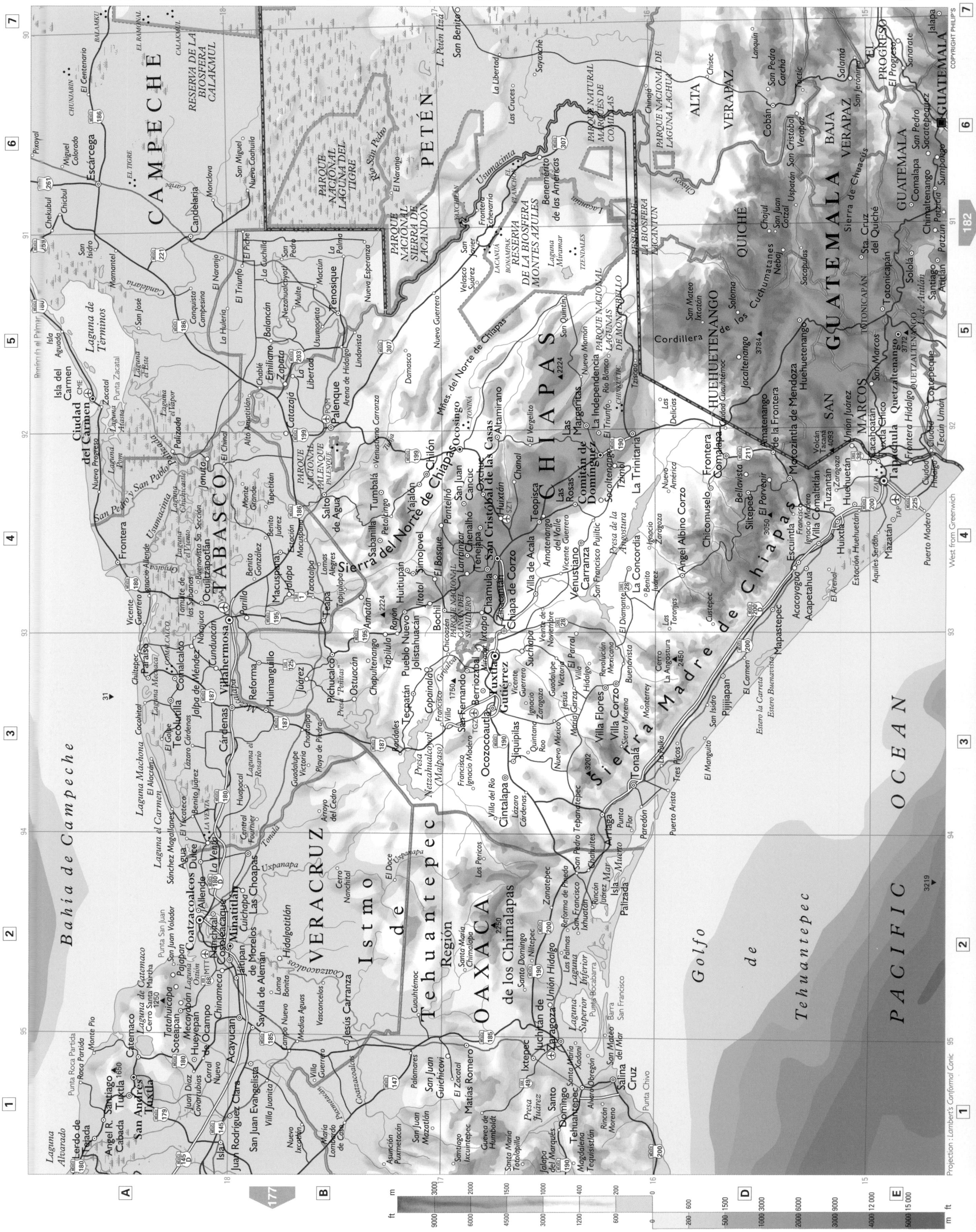

1:2 100 000

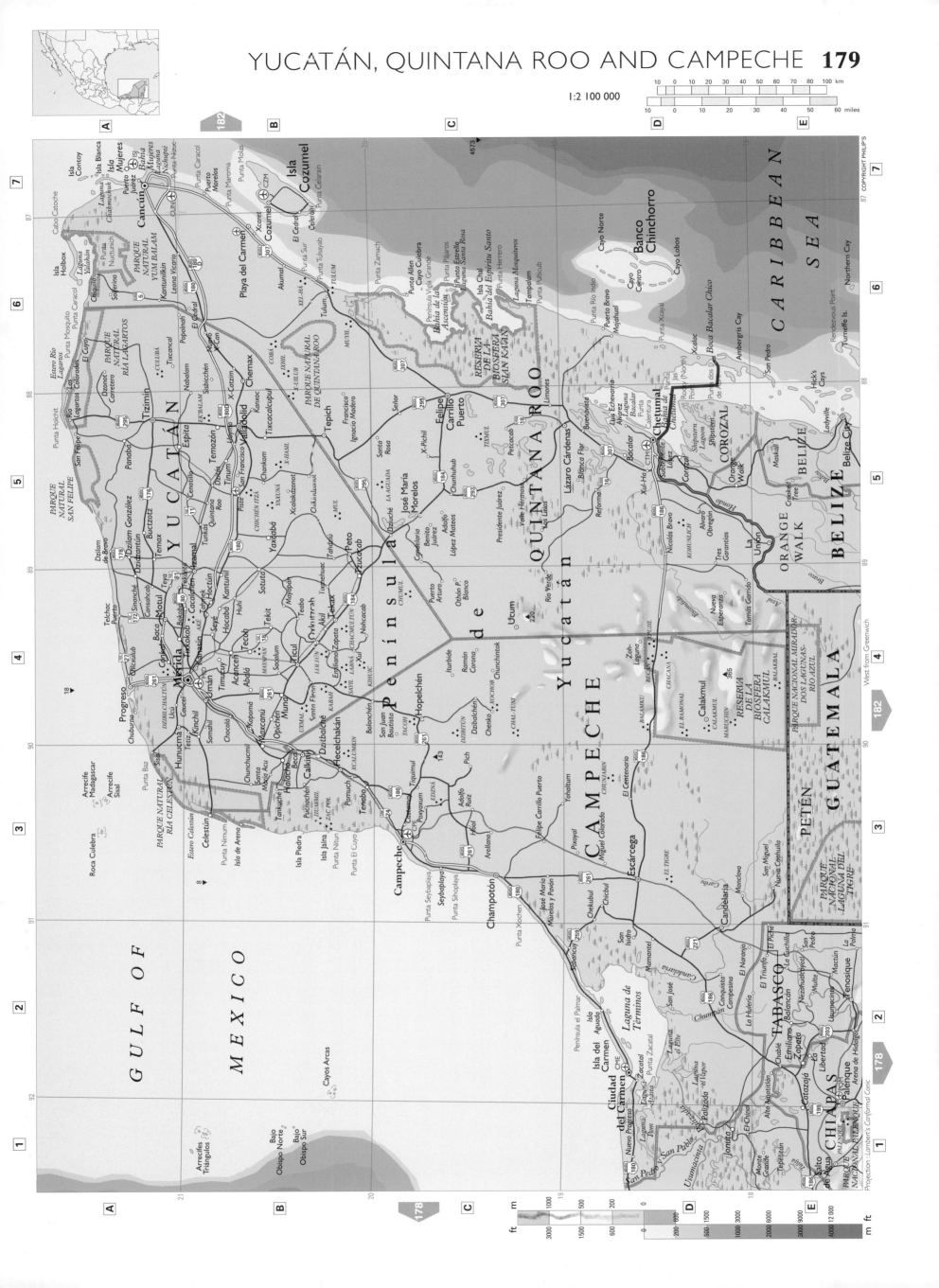

CARIBBEAN SEA

Banco Chinchorro

GULF OF MEXICO

YUCATÁN

QUINTANA ROO

CAMPECHE

BELIZE

GUATEMALA

PETÉN

Península de Yucatán

Cancún
Isla Mujeres
Isla Contoy
Isla Holbox
Cabo Catoche

Isla Cozumel

Playa del Carmen

Tulum

Mérida
Progreso
Valladolid
Chichén Itzá
Tizimín

RESERVA DE LA BIOSFERA SIAN KA'AN

Felipe Carrillo Puerto

Chetumal
COROZAL
Corozal

Campeche
Champotón
Escárcega

Ciudad del Carmen
Laguna de Términos

Calakmul
RESERVA DE LA BIOSFERA CALAKMUL

PARQUE NACIONAL LAGUNA DEL TIGRE

TABASCO

CHIAPAS
Palenque

COPYRIGHT PHILIPS

Projection: Lambert's Conformal Conic

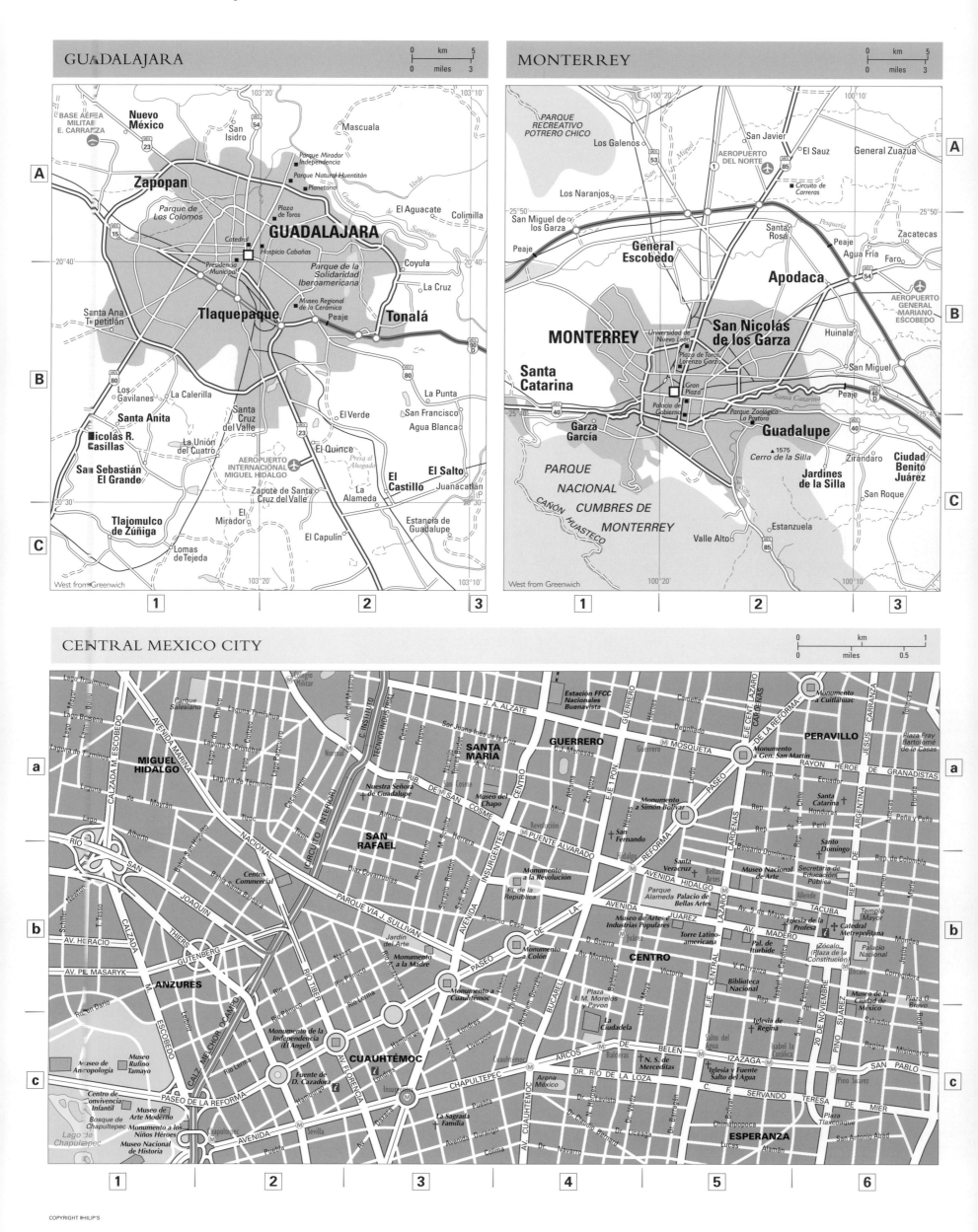

GUADALAJARA

km 5 / miles 3

Base Aérea Militar E. Carranza
Nuevo México
San Isidro
Mascuala
54
23
Zapopan
Parque Mirador Independencia
Parque Natural Huentitán
Planetario
Parque de Los Colomos
Plaza de Toros
Verde Grande de El Aguacate
Colimilla
Santiago
GUADALAJARA
Catedral
Hospicio Cabañas
Coyula
Presidencia Municipal
Parque de la Solidaridad Iberoamericana
La Cruz
15
Santa Ana Tepetitlán
Tlaquepaque
Museo Regional de la Cerámica
Peaje
Tonalá
80
La Punta
80
Los Gavilanes
La Calerilla
Santa Cruz del Valle
El Verde
La Punta
San Francisco
90
Santa Anita
La Unión del Cuatro
Agua Blanca
Nicolás R. Casillas
Aeropuerto Internacional Miguel Hidalgo
El Quince
23
San Sebastián El Grande
Presa el Ahogado
La Alameda
El Castillo
El Salto
Zapote de Santa Cruz del Valle
Juanacatlán
Tlajomulco de Zúñiga
El Mirador
El Capulín
Estancia de Guadalupe
Lomas de Tejeda
West from Greenwich
103°20' 103°10'

MONTERREY

km 5 / miles 3

PARQUE RECREATIVO POTRERO CHICO
Los Galenos
San Javier
El Sauz
General Zuazúa
AEROPUERTO DEL NORTE
85
Circuito de Carreras
Los Naranjos
San Miguel de los Garza
Santa Rosa
Zacatecas
Peaje
General Escobedo
Agua Fría
Faro
54
Apodaca
AEROPUERTO GENERAL MARIANO ESCOBEDO
Universidad de Nuevo León
MONTERREY
Plaza de Toros Lorenzo Garza
San Nicolás de los Garza
Huinala
San Miguel
Santa Catarina
Gran Plaza
Palacio de Gobierno
Parque Zoológico La Pastora
Santa Catarina
Peaje
40
Garza García
40
Guadalupe
1575 Cerro de la Silla
Zirándaro
Ciudad Benito Juárez
PARQUE NACIONAL CUMBRES DE MONTERREY
Jardines de la Silla
San Roque
CAÑÓN HUASTECO
Valle Alto
Estanzuela
85
West from Greenwich
100°20' 100°10'

CENTRAL MEXICO CITY

km 1 / miles 0.5

Colegio Militar
Parque Salesiano
Lago Tresmeno
Lago Becena
Laguna Tenlagua
Estación FFCC Nacionales Buenavista
J.A. ALZATE
Monumento a Cuitláhuac
MIGUEL HIDALGO
Laguna S. Cristóbal
Laguna de Términos
GUERRERO
Camelia
PERAVILLO
Plaza Fray Bartolomé de la Casas
AVENIDA MARINA
Nuestra Señora de Guadalupe
SANTA MARÍA
Monumento a Gen. San Martín
Monumento a Simón Bolívar
Santa Catarina
Museo del Chapo
SAN RAFAEL
San Fernando
CIRCUITO INTERIOR
PUENTE ALVARADO
Monumento a la Revolución
Museo Nacional de Arte
Secretaría de Educación Pública
Santo Domingo
Pl. de la República
Bellas Artes
Parque Alameda
Palacio de Bellas Artes
Templo Mayor
PARQUE VÍA J. SULLIVAN
Jardín del Arte
Museo de Artes e Industrias Populares
JUÁREZ
Iglesia de la Profesa
Catedral Metropolitana
ANZURES
Monumento a la Madre
Monumento a Colón
Torre Latinoamericana
Pal. de Iturbide
TACUBA
MADERO
Palacio Nacional
Museo de Antropología
Museo Rufino Tamayo
Monumento a Cuauhtémoc
CENTRO
Zócalo (Plaza de la Constitución)
Biblioteca Nacional
Museo de la Ciudad de México
Plaza del Bravo
Monumento de la Independencia (El Ángel)
CUAUHTÉMOC
Plaza J. M. Morelos y Pavón
La Ciudadela
Iglesia de Regina
Centro de Convivencia Infantil
Fuente de D. Cazadora
N. S. de Mercedítas
Iglesia y Fuente Salto del Agua
Museo de Arte Moderno
Bosque de Chapultepec
Monumento a los Niños Héroes
Museo Nacional de Historia
Lago de Chapultepec
La Sagrada Familia
Arena México
ESPERANZA
Plaza Tlaxcoaque
COPYRIGHT PHILIP'S

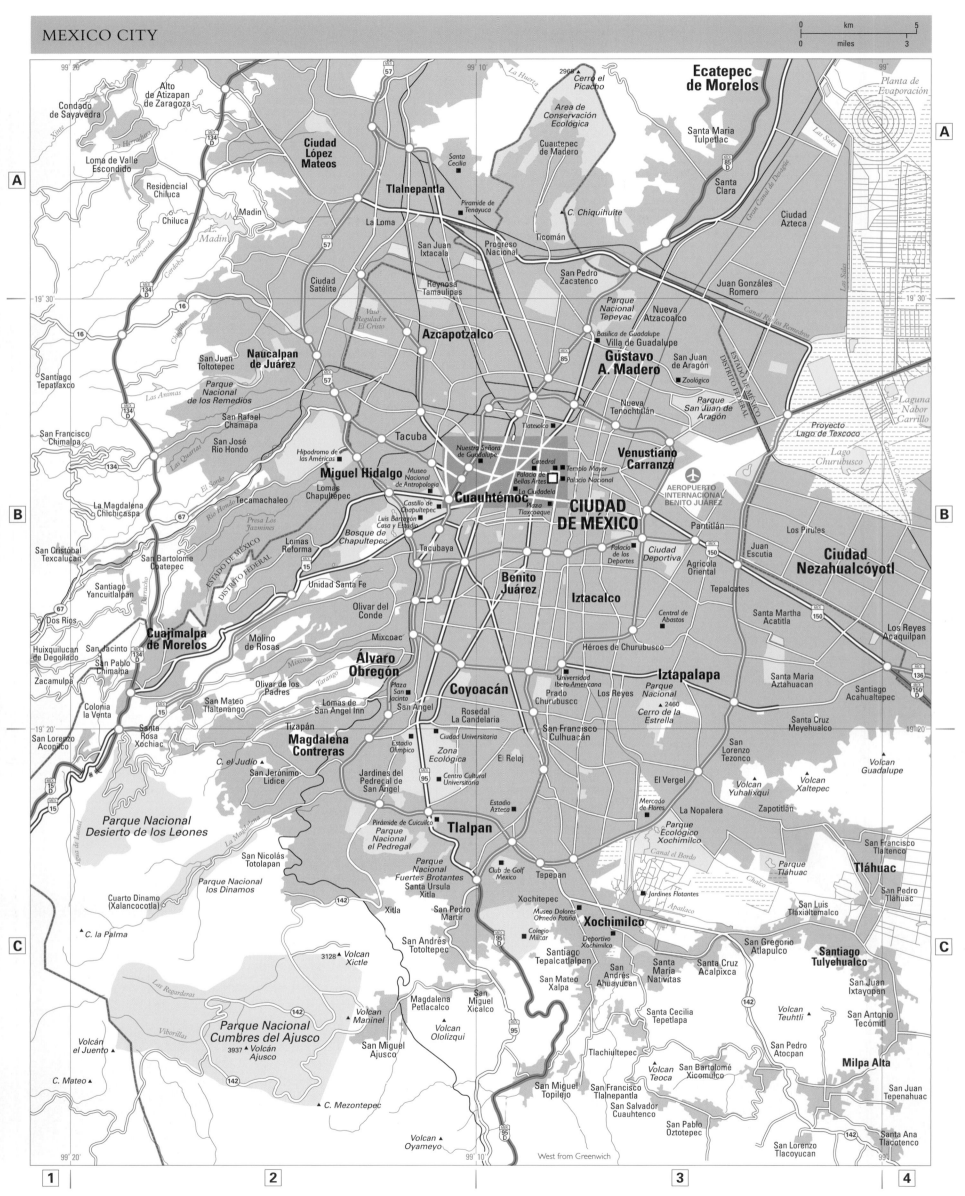

MEXICO CITY

| 0 | km | 5 |
| 0 | miles | 3 |

Condado de Sayavedra
Alto de Atizapan de Zaragoza
Loma de Valle Escondido
Residencial Chiluca
Madin
Chiluca
Ciudad López Mateos
La Loma
Pirámide de Tenayuca
Santa Cecilia
Tlalnepantla
Cerro el Picacho
2968
Area de Conservación Ecológica
Cuautepec de Madero
C. Chiquihuite
Ticomán
Santa María Tulpetlac
Santa Clara
Ciudad Azteca
Ecatepec de Morelos

Planta de Evaporación

La Herradura
Santiago Tepatlaxco
San Juan Toltotepec
Naucalpan de Juárez
Parque Nacional de los Remedios
San Rafael Chamapa
Le Madin
Vaso Regulador El Cristo
San Juan Ixtacala
Reynosa Tamaulipas
Ciudad Satélite
Azcapotzalco
Progreso Nacional
San Pedro Zacatenco
Parque Nacional Tepeyac
Nueva Atzacoalco
Juan Gonzáles Romero

San Francisco Chimalpa
San José Río Hondo
Las Animas
Tacuba
Nuestra Señora de Guadalupe
Basílica de Guadalupe
Villa de Guadalupe
Gustavo A. Madero
San Juan de Aragón
Nueva Tenochtitlán
Parque San Juan de Aragón
Zoológico
Laguna Nabor Carrillo

La Magdalena Chichicaspa
San Cristóbal Texcalucan
San Bartolome Coatepec
Santiago Yancuitlalpan
Dos Rios
Tecamachaleo
Lomas Chapultepec
Miguel Hidalgo
Hipodromo de las Américas
Museo Nacional de Antropología
Castillo de Chapultepec
Luis Barragán Casa y Estudio
Bosque de Chapultepec
Presa Los Jazmines
Lomas Reforma
Tlatelolco
Catedral
Templo Mayor
Palacio de Bellas Artes
Palacio Nacional
La Ciudadela
Plaza Tlaxcoaque
Cuauhtémoc
CIUDAD DE MÉXICO
Venustiano Carranza
AEROPUERTO INTERNACIONAL BENITO JUÁREZ
Pantitlán
Los Pirules
Juan Escutia
Ciudad Nezahualcóyotl
Lago Churubusco
Proyecto Lago de Texcoco

Huixquilucan de Degollado
San Jacinto
San Pablo Chimalpa
Zacamulpa
Cuajimalpa de Morelos
Molino de Rosas
Olivar del Conde
Tacubaya
Unidad Santa Fe
Mixcoac
Palacio de los Deportes
Ciudad Deportiva
Agrícola Oriental
Tepalcates
Benito Juárez
Iztacalco
Central de Abastos
Santa Martha Acatitla
Los Reyes Acaquilpan

Colonia la Venta
Santa Rosa Xochiac
San Mateo Tlaltenango
Olivar de los Padres
Lomas de San Angel Inn
Plaza San Jacinto
San Angel
Álvaro Obregón
Rosedal La Candelaria
Coyoacán
Prado Churubusco
Los Reyes
Universidad Ibero-Americana
San Francisco Culhuacán
Héroes de Churubusco
Iztapalapa
Cerro de la Estrella
2460
Santa María Aztahuacan
Santa Cruz Meyehualco
Santiago Acahualtepec

San Lorenzo Acopilco
C. el Judío
San Jerónimo Lidice
Magdalena Contreras
Estadio Olímpico
Zona Ecológica
Ciudad Universitaria
Centro Cultural Universitário
El Reloj
Estadio Azteca
Jardines del Pedregal de San Angel
San Lorenzo Tezonco
El Vergel
Mercado de Flores
La Nopalera
Volcán Yuhalixqui
Volcán Xaltepec
Volcán Guadalupe
Zapotitlán

Parque Nacional Desierto de los Leones
Pirámide de Cuicuilco
Parque Nacional el Pedregal
Tlalpan
Parque Nacional Fuertes Brotantes
Club de Golf Mexico
Tepepan
Jardines Flotantes
Parque Ecológico Xochimilco
Parque Tláhuac
Tláhuac
San Francisco Tlaltenco

San Nicolás Totolapan
Santa Ursula Xitla
Xochitepec
Canal el Bordo
San Pedro Tláhuac

Cuarto Dinamo (Xalancocotla)
Parque Nacional los Dinamos
Xitla
San Pedro Mártir
Museo Dolores Olmedo Patiño
Xochimilco
Deportivo Xochimilco
San Luis Tlaxialtemalco

C. la Palma
3128
Volcán Xictle
San Andrés Totoltepec
Colegio Militar
Santiago Tepalcatlalpan
San Andrés Ahuayucan
Santa María Nativitas
Santa Cruz Acalpixca
San Gregorio Atlapulco
Santiago Tulyehualco
San Juan Ixtayopan

Volcán Maninel
Magdalena Petlacalco
San Miguel Xicalco
San Mateo Xalpa
Santa Cecilia Tepetlapa
Volcán Teuhtli
San Antonio Tecómitl

Parque Nacional Cumbres del Ajusco
3937
Volcán Ajusco
San Miguel Ajusco
Volcán Ololizqui
Tlachiultepec
Volcán Teoca
San Bartolomé Xicomulco
San Pedro Atocpan
Milpa Alta

Volcán el Juento
C. Mateo
C. Mezontepec
Volcán Oyameyo
San Miguel Topilejo
San Francisco Tlalnepantla
San Salvador Cuauhtenco
San Pablo Oztotepec
San Lorenzo Tlacoyucan
San Juan Tepenahuac
Santa Ana Tlacotenco

West from Greenwich

DISTRITO FEDERAL
ESTADO DE MÉXICO

COPYRIGHT PHILIP'S

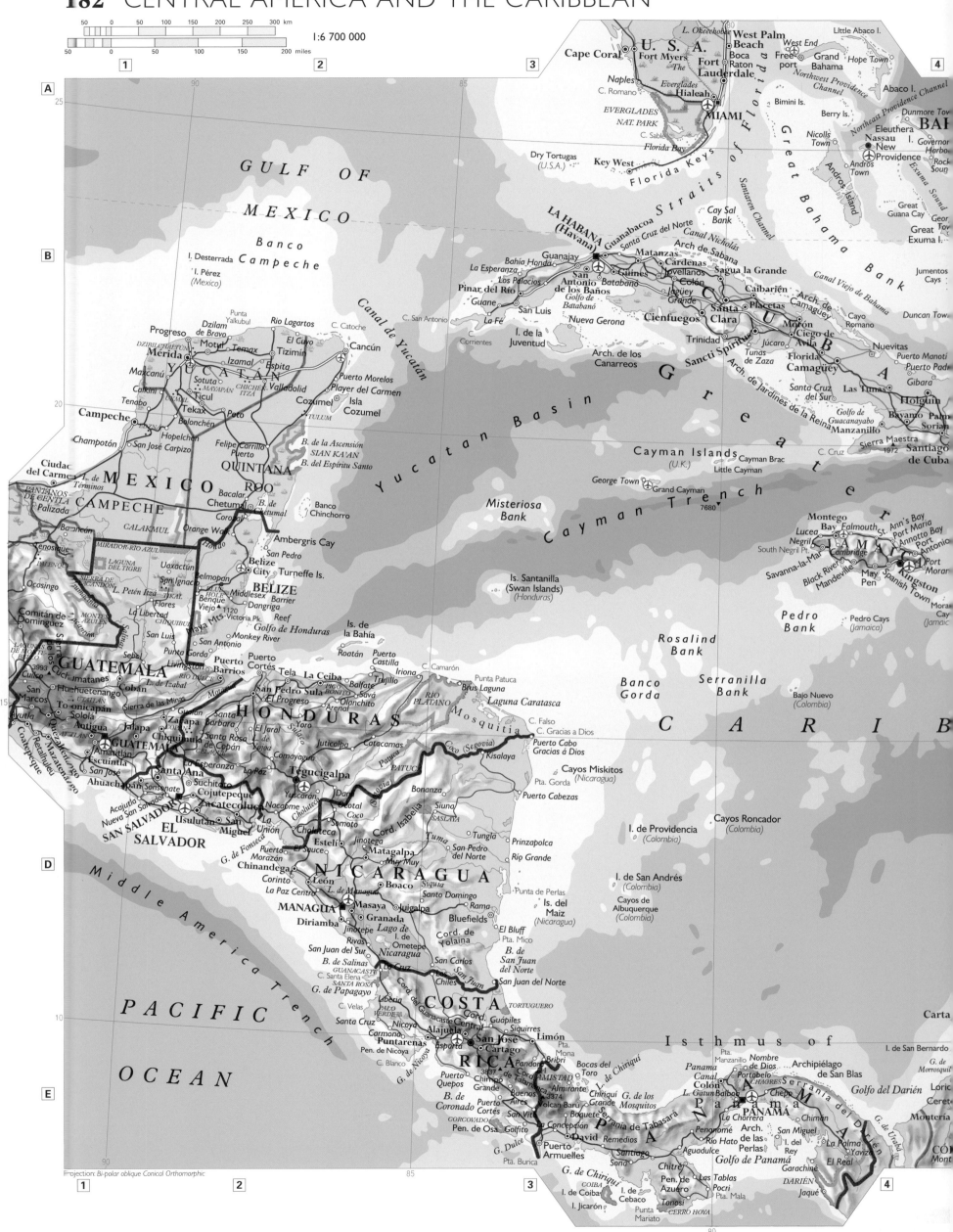

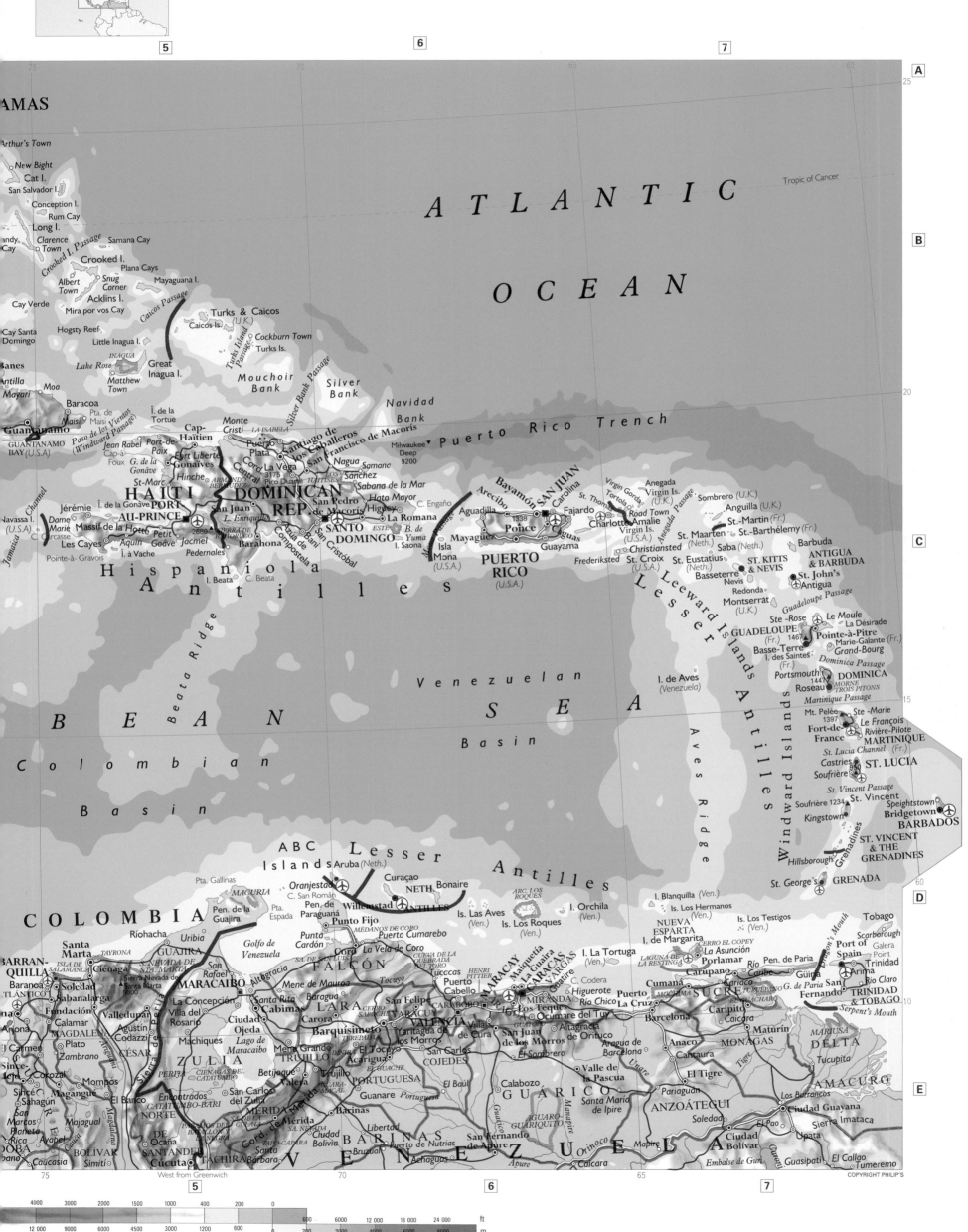

AMAS

Arthur's Town
New Bight
Cat I.
San Salvador I.
Conception I.
Rum Cay
Long I.
andy
Clarence
Cay
Town
Samana Cay
Crooked I.
Albert
Town
Plana Cays
Snug
Corner
Acklins I.
Mayaguana I.
Cay Verde
Mira por vos Cay
Caicos Passage
Turks & Caicos
(U.K.)
Hogsty Reef
Caicos Is.
Cockburn Town
Cay Santa
Domingo
Little Inagua I.
Turks Island
Passage
Turks Is.
Banes
Lake Rose
INAGUA
Antilla
Matthew
Town
Mouchoir
Bank
Mayari
Moa
Great
Inagua I.
Silver Bank Passage
Silver
Bank
Navidad
Bank
Baracoa
Pta. de
Maisí Maisí
Î. de la
Tortue
Monte
Cristi
LA ISABELA
Puerto
Rico
Trench
Milwaukee▾
Deep
9200
Guantanamo
Cap-
Haïtien
Puerto
Plata
Santiago de
los Caballeros
San Francisco de Macorís
GUANTANAMO
BAY (U.S.A.)
Jean Rabel Port-de-
Paix
Cap-à-
Foux
Central
Corail
3175
La Vega
Pico Duarte
Nagua
Samaná
Bayamón
SAN JUAN
Virgin Gorda
Anegada
Virgin Is.
Sombrero (U.K.)
Paso de los Vientos
(Windward Passage)
Fort Liberté
Gonaïves
Hinche
ARMANDO
BERMÚDEZ
HAITISES
Sánchez
Sabana de la Mar
Arecibo
Carolina
St. Thomas
(U.S.A.)
Tortola
Road Town
Anguilla (U.K.)
Jérémie
Î. de la Gonâve
G. de la
Gonâve
St-Marc
HAITI
PORT
AU-PRINCE
San Juan
DOMINICAN
REP.
San Pedro
de Macorís
Higüey
Aguadilla
1338
Ponce
Mayagüez
Aguas
Charlotte Amalie
Virgin Is.
(U.K.)
St-Martin (Fr.)
St.-Barthélemy (Fr.)
Navassa I.
(U.S.A.)
Dame
Marie
Massif de la Hotte
Carcasse
2680
SANTO
DOMINGO
SIERRA DE
BAORUCO
Agua
de Enriquillo
San Cristóbal
ESTE
B. de
Yuma
I. Saona
C. Engaño
Guayama
Christiansted
Frederiksted
St. Croix
(U.S.A.)
St. Eustatius
(Neth.)
Saba (Neth.)
Basseterre
ST. KITTS
& NEVIS
Barbuda
Les Cayes
Aquin
Jacmel
Godve
Barahona
Compostela
Pedernales
Isla
Mona
(U.S.A.)
PUERTO
RICO
(U.S.A.)
St. Maarten
(Neth.)
Nevis
Redonda
Montserrat
(U.K.)
ANTIGUA
& BARBUDA
St. John's
Antigua
Jamaica Channel
Hispaniola
I. Beata
C. Beata
Antilles
Guadeloupe Passage
Ste-Rose
Le Moule
La Désirade
Pointe-à-Pitre
Marie-Galante (Fr.)
Basse-Terre
Grand-Bourg
I. des Saintes (Fr.)
B
E
A
N
SEA
Beata Ridge
Venezuelan
Basin
I. de Aves
(Venezuela)
Leeward Islands
Lesser
Antilles
Portsmouth
Roseau
Dominica Passage
1447
DOMINICA
MORNE
TROIS PITONS
Martinique Passage
Mt. Pelée
1397
Ste-Marie
Le François
Fort-de-
France
Rivière-Pilote
MARTINIQUE (Fr.)
C O
l o m b i a n
Basin
Colombian
Basin
Aves Ridge
St. Lucia Channel
Castries
Soufrière
ST. LUCIA
St. Vincent Passage
Soufrière 1234
St. Vincent
Speightstown
Kingstown
Bridgetown
BARBADOS
ABC
Lesser
Antilles
Windward Islands
Grenadines
ST. VINCENT
& THE
GRENADINES
Islands
Aruba (Neth.)
Curaçao
NETH.
Bonaire
ARC. LOS
ROQUES
I. Blanquilla (Ven.)
Hillsborough
St. George's
GRENADA
Pta. Gallinas
MACUIRA
Oranjestad
C. San Román
Willemstad
ANTILLES
Is. Las Aves
(Ven.)
Is. Los Roques
(Ven.)
I. Orchila
(Ven.)
Is. Los Hermanos
(Ven.)
Is. Los Testigos
(Ven.)
Tobago
Scarborough
COLOMBIA
Pen. de la
Guajira
Pta.
Espada
Punta
Cardón
MÉDANOS DE CORO
Puerto Cumarebo
NUEVA
ESPARTA
I. La Tortuga
(Ven.)
CERRO EL COPEY
I. de Margarita
Port of
Spain
Galera
Point
Trinidad
Santa
Marta
Ríohacha
Uribia
GUAJIRA
Golfo de
Venezuela
La Vela de Coro
Coro
FALCÓN
La Guaira
MARACAY
CARACAS
VARGAS
Maiquetía
Pen. de Paria
Porlamar
Río
Carúpano
Cariaco
Güiria
Arima
Rio Claro
BARRAN-
QUILLA
ISLA DE
SALAMANCA
Ciénaga
SA. NEVADA DE
STA. MARTA
Sierra Nevada de
Santa Marta
5800
San
Rafael
Altagracia
Mene de Mauroa
Tocuyo
Puerto
Cabello
C. Codera
HENRI
PITTIER
MIRANDA
Higuerote
Ocumare del Tuy
Puerto
La Cruz
MOCHIMA
SUCRE
Cumaná
G. de Paria
TRINIDAD
& TOBAGO
Serpent's Mouth
Baranoa
Soledad
Sabanalarga
TLÁNTICO
Fundación
Valledupar
Villa del
Rosario
La Concepción
MARACAIBO
Santa Rita
Cabimas
Baragua
San Felipe
YARACUY
Tinaquillo de
Cura
Villa
de Cura
San Juan
de los Morros
Aragua de
Barcelona
Barcelona
Anaco
Caicara
Maturín
MONAGAS
MARIUSA
DELTA
Calamar
MAGDALENA
Plato
Agustín
Codazzi
CÉSAR
Machiques
Ciudad
Ojeda
Lago de
Maracaibo
Mene Grande
Carora
LARA
Barquisimeto
Tinaco
El Tocuyo
TEREPAIMA
EL GUACHE
Tinaquillo
Villa
COJEDES
San Carlos
Los Morros
El Sombrero
Valle de
la Pascua
Cantaura
El Tigre
Soledad
Ciudad Guayana
Sierra Imataca
Arjona
MAGDALE
Zambrano
Mompós
La Concepción
PERIJÁ
CIÉNAGAS DEL
CATATUMBO
Betijoque
TRUJILLO
Trujillo
PORTUGUESA
El Guache
Guanare
El Baúl
GUÁRICO
Santa María
de Ipire
Pariaguán
ANZOÁTEGUI
El Pao
Ciudad Bolívar
Upata
El Callao
Tumeremo
Sincé
Corozal
Magangué
El Banco
Encontrados
San Carlos
del Zulia
ZULIA
CATATUMBO-BARI
NORTE
MÉRIDA
SA. NEVADA
Ciudad
Bolivia
Barinas
Libertad
Portuguesa
Calabozo
AGUARO-
GUARIQUITO
MAMO
Soledad
MANAPIRE
AMACURO
Majagual
COBA
Caucasia
El Carmen
Since
San
Marcos
San
Planeto
Ayapel
Ábrego
BOLÍVAR
Simití
SANTANDER
Cúcuta
TÁCHIRA
Santa
Bárbara
V E N E Z U E L A
MÉRIDA
SA. NEVADA
CORD. DE MÉRIDA
TAPO-CAPARRO
BARINAS
Puerto de Nutrias
San Fernando
de Apure
Achaguas
Apure
Arauca
San Carlos
Calcara
Orinoco
Mapire
Guasipati

4000 3000 2000 1500 1000 400 200 0
12 000 9000 6000 4500 3000 1200 600 0
600 6000 12 000 18 000 24 000 ft
200 2000 4000 6000 8000 m

U.S. OUTLYING AREAS
1:80 000 000
Projection: Mercator

West from Greenwich
Arctic Circle
ALASKA (U.S.A.)
Anchorage

Sea of Okhotsk
Kamchatka
Bering Sea
Sakhalin
Kuril Is.
Aleutian Islands (U.S.A.)
Gulf of Alaska

CANADA
Hudson Bay
Edmonton
NORTH AMERICA
Vancouver
Winnipeg
Seattle
Montreal
Toronto
Boston
Detroit
Chicago
New York
UNITED STATES
Washington D.C.
Philadelphia
San Francisco
Atlanta
Los Angeles
Phoenix
Houston
ATLANTIC OCEAN
Monterrey
Miami
BAHAMAS
Gulf of Mexico
Guadalajara
Havana
Guantanamo Bay (U.S.A.)
CUBA
DOM. REP.
MEXICO
Mexico
Navassa (U.S.A.)
HAITI
Virgin Is. (U.S.A.)
BELIZE
PUERTO RICO (U.S.A.)
GUATEMALA
HONDURAS
Caribbean Sea
EL SALVADOR
NICARAGUA
VENEZUELA
COSTA RICA
PANAMA
Bogotá
GUYANA
COLOMBIA
ECUADOR
Guayaquil
PERU
SOUTH AMERICA
BRAZIL

CHINA
ASIA
Vladivostok
N. KOREA
Beijing
S. KOREA
Seoul
JAPAN
Tokyo
Osaka
Shanghai
Taipei
TAIWAN
Manila
PHILIPPINES
Mindanao
PALAU
INDONESIA
Celebes
PAPUA NEW GUINEA
SOLOMON IS.
AUSTRALIA
VANUATU
FIJI

PACIFIC OCEAN
Midway Is. (U.S.A.)
Tropic of Cancer
Honolulu HAWAI'I
Wake I. (U.S.A.)
Johnston I. (U.S.A.)
NORTHERN MARIANAS (U.S.A.)
GUAM (U.S.A.)
MARSHALL IS.
FEDERATED STATES OF MICRONESIA
NAURU
Howland I. (U.S.A.)
Baker I. (U.S.A.)
Jarvis I. (U.S.A.)
Palmyra Is. (U.S.A.)
Equator
International Date Line
TUVALU
KIRIBATI
Tokelau Is. (N.Z.)
SAMOA
AMERICAN SAMOA (U.S.A.)
FRENCH POLYNESIA
TONGA

PUERTO RICO AND THE VIRGIN IS.
1:1 450 000

ATLANTIC OCEAN

Ruffling Pt.
The Settlement
Anegada
East Pt.
VIRGIN ISLANDS (U.K.)
Jost Van Dyke I.
Great Camanoe
Guana I.
Virgin Gorda
Hans Lollik I.
Beef I.
Spanish Town
Tortola
Road Town
Cruz Bay
VIRGIN IS. NAT. PARK
Peter I.
Charlotte Amalie
St. Thomas I.
St. John I.
VIRGIN ISLANDS (U.S.A.)

Pta. Agujereada
F.a. Agujereada
Isabela
Quebradillas
Camuy
Hatillo
Arecibo
Aguadilla
Barceloneta
Vega Baja
Moca
Manati
Vega Alta
Levittown
San Juan
Aguada
Florida
Ciales
Carolina
Rincón
PARQUE DE LAS CAVERNAS DEL RIO CAMUY
OBSERVATORIO DE ARECIBO
Corozal
Bayamón
Catano
Guaynabo
Río Grande
Trujillo Alto
Luquillo
Fajardo
Añasco
San Sebastián
Lares
Utuado
PUERTO RICO
Comerio
Gurabo
Sierra de Luquillo
EL YUNQUE
Ceiba
Mayagüez
Maricao
Cordillera Central
Caguas
Naguabo
1338
Cerro de Punta
Villalba
Barranquitas
Juncos
Las Piedras
Humacao
Mts. de Uroyan
Adjuntas
Juana Díaz
Cidra
Cayey
Pta. Puerca
Cabo Rojo
Yauco
Coamo
Yabucoa
Hormigueros
Sabana Grande
Ponce
Salinas
Guayama
Maunabo
San German
Parguera
Guayanilla
Guánica
Santa Isabel
Patillas
Isabel Segunda
Dewey
Culebra
Esperanza
Vieques
Pta. Arenas
Pta. Aguila
I. Caja de Muertos

CARIBBEAN SEA

353
Christiansted
Mt. Eagle
East Pt.
Frederiksted
Southwest Pt.
St. Croix I. (U.S.A.)
West from Greenwich

NORTHERN MARIANAS
1:16 800 000

Farallon de Pajaros
Maug Is.
Asuncion
Agrihan
NORTHERN
Mariana Islands
Pagan
Alamagan
Guguan
Sarigan
MARIANAS
Anatahan
Farallon de Medinilla
PACIFIC
Saipan
Tinian
(U.S.A.)
Rota
OCEAN
GUAM (U.S.A.)
Agana
9650
Mariana Trench

GUAM
1:800 000

Ritidian Pt.
Pati Pt.
ANDERSEN A.F.B.
Mt. Santa Rosa 252
Yigo
Dededo
Tumon Bay
Tamuning
GUM
Agana
Barrigada
Piti
Yona
Pago Bay
Orote Peninsula
WAR IN THE PACIFIC N.H.P.
Santa Rita
Agat
Talofofo
406
Mt. Lamlam
Umatac
Merizo
Jalaihai Pt.
Cocos I.
Inarajan
PACIFIC OCEAN

SAIPAN & TINIAN (NORTHERN MARIANAS)
1:800 000

Sabaneta Pt.
Tanapag
Garapan
Capitol Hill
Mt. Tagpochau 465
Chalan Kanoa
Bahia Laulau
Saipan
PACIFIC OCEAN
Tahgong Pt.
Saipan Channel
Naftan Pt.
Tinian
Masalog Pt.
Diablo Pt.
San Jose 178
Tinian Channel
Carolinas Pt.

SAMOAN ISLANDS
1:21 000 000

PACIFIC OCEAN
KIRIBATI
International Date Line
Tokelau Is. (N.Z.)
SAMOA
Savai'i
Apia
'Upolu
AMERICAN SAMOA
Tutuila
Manua Is.
Vava'u Group
Niue (N.Z.)
Ha'apai Group
TONGA

TUTUILA (AMER. SAMOA)
1:800 000

PACIFIC OCEAN
Vatia
Cape Matatula
Pago Pago
Aua
Tula
Fagasa
652
Aunuu
Amanave
Nu'uuli
Leone
Pago Pago Harbor
Futiga
C. Taputapu
Steps Pt.

MANUA IS. (AMER. SAMOA)
1:800 000

PACIFIC OCEAN
Olosega
639
Ofu 484
Piumafua Mt.
Luma 931
Leusoalii
Lata Mt.
Siufaalele Pt.
Tau

3000
1200
600
200
0
200
1000
2000
4000
ft m
1000
400
200
0
600
3000
6000
12000
m ft

10 0 10 20 30 km
1:1 450 000
10 0 10 20 miles

100 0 100 200 300 400 500 600 700 800 km
1:16 800 000
100 0 100 200 300 400 500 miles

5 0 5 10 km
1:800 000
5 0 5 10 miles

COPYRIGHT PHILIP'S

INDEX

How to use the index

The index contains the names of the principal places and features shown on the maps. Each name is followed by an additional entry in italics giving the state, province, city, region or country within which it is located.

The alphabetical order of names composed of two or more words is governed primarily by the first word and then by the second. This is an example of the rule:

Middle River *Md., U.S.A.*	39°20N 76°27W	**93** A4
Middle River *Minn., U.S.A.*	48°26N 96°10W	**77** B2
Middle Valley *Tenn., U.S.A.*	35°12N 85°11W	**105** E7
Middle Village *N.Y., U.S.A.*	40°43N 73°52W	**97** B3
Middleboro *Mass., U.S.A.*	41°54N 70°55W	**91** C4

Physical features composed of a proper name (Erie) and a description (Lake) are positioned alphabetically by the proper name. The description is positioned after the proper name and is usually abbreviated:

Erie, L. *N. Amer.*	42°15N 81°0W	**146** E5

Where a description forms part of a settlement or administrative name, however, it is always written in full and put in its true alphabetical position:

Mount Olive *Ill., U.S.A.*	9°4N 89°44W	**84** D4

Names beginning with M' and Mc are indexed as if they were spelled Mac. Names beginning St. are alphabetized under Saint, but Sant', Santa and San are all spelled in full and are alphabetized accordingly.

The geographical coordinates that follow each name give the latitude and longitude of that place. The first coordinate indicates latitude – the distance north or south of the Equator. The second coordinate indicates longitude – the distance east or west of the Greenwich Meridian. Both latitude and longitude are measured in degrees and minutes (there are 60 minutes in a degree).

The latitude is followed by N(orth) or S(outh) and the longitude by E(ast) or W(est).

The number in bold type that follows the geographical coordinates refers to the number of the map page where that feature or place will be found. This is usually the largest scale at which the place or feature appears

The letter and figure that are in bold type immediately after the page number give the grid square on the map page, within which the feature is situated. The letter represents the latitude and the figure the longitude. A lower-case letter immediately after the page number refers to an inset map on that page.

In some cases the feature itself may fall within the specified square, while the name is outside. This is usually the case only with features that are larger than a grid square.

Rivers are indexed to their mouths or confluences, and carry the symbol ➤ after their names. The following symbols are also used in the index: ■ country, ☑ overseas territory or dependency, □ state or province, ☆ county, △ national park, ▵ other park (national monuments and recreation areas, state and provincial parks, and wildlife reserves), and ✈ (DCA) principal airport (and location identifier).

Abbreviations

Ala. – Alabama	*Minn.* – Minnesota	*Pt.* – Point
Alta. – Alberta	*Miss.* – Mississippi	*Pta.* – Punta
Amer. – America(n)	*Mo.* – Missouri	*Qué.* – Québec
Ariz. – Arizona	*Mont.* – Montana	*R.* – Rio, River
Ark. – Arkansas	*Mt.(s).* – Mont, Montaña, Mount,	*R.I.* – Rhode Island
B. – Baie, Bahía, Bay	Mountain	*Range* – Range
B.C. – British Columbia	*N.* – Nord, Norte, North, Northern	*Recr.* – Recreational
Br. – British	*N.B.* – New Brunswick	*Res.* – Reserve, Reservoir
C. – Cabo, Cap, Cape	*N.C.* – North Carolina	*S.* – South, Southern
Calif. – California	*N.Dak.* – North Dakota	*S.C.* – South Carolina
Colo. – Colorado	*N.H.* – New Hampshire	*S.D.* – South Dakota
Conn. – Connecticut	*N.J.* – New Jersey	*Sa.* – Serra, Sierra
D.C. – District of Columbia	*N.Mex.* – New Mexico	*Sask.* – Saskatchewan
Del. – Delaware	*N.S.* – Nova Scotia	*Sd.* – Sound
E. – East	*N.W.T.* – North West Territory	*Sprs.* – Springs
Fla. – Florida	*N.Y.* – New York	*St.* – Saint
G. – Golfe, Golfo, Gulf	*Nac.* – Nacional	*Sta.* – Santa
Ga. – Georgia	*Nat.* – National	*Ste.* – Sainte
Harb. – Harbor, Harbour	*Nebr.* – Nebraska	*Sto.* – Santo
Hd. – Head	*Nev.* – Nevada	*St-P. & M.* – Saint Pierre
Hts. – Heights	*Nfld. & L.* – Newfoundland	et Miquelon
I.(s). – Île, Isla, Island, Isle	and Labrador	*Str.* – Strait, Stretto
Ill. – Illinois	*Okla.* – Oklahoma	*Tenn.* – Tennessee
Ind. – Indiana	*Ont.* – Ontario	*Terr.* – Territory, Territoire
Kans. – Kansas	*Oreg.* – Oregon	*Tex.* – Texas
Ky. – Kentucky	*P.* – Pass	*Va.* – Virginia
L. – Lac, Lago, Lake	*P.E.I.* – Prince Edward Island	*Vt.* – Vermont
La. – Louisiana	*Pa.* – Pennsylvania	*W.* – West
Man. – Manitoba	*Pac. Oc.* – Pacific Ocean	*W.Va.* – West Virginia
Mass. – Massachusetts	*Pass.* – Passage	*Wash.* – Washington
Md. – Maryland	*Pen.* – Peninsula, Péninsule	*Wis.* – Wisconsin
Me. – Maine	*Pk.* – Peak	*Wyo.* – Wyoming
Mich. – Michigan	*Plat.* – Plateau	

A

Aasiaat *Greenland* 68°43N 52°56W **162** D5
Abaco I. *Bahamas* 26°25N 77°10W **182** A4
Abajo Peak *Utah, U.S.A.* 37°51N 109°27W **129** F6
Abalá *Yucatán, Mexico* 20°38N 89°41W **179** B4
Abamasagi L. *Ont., Canada* 50°28N 87°15W **149** B9
Abasolo *Coahuila, Mexico* 27°12N 101°24W **170** C3
Abasolo *Guanajuato, Mexico* 20°28N 101°32W **174** B6
Abasolo *Nuevo León, Mexico* 25°58N 100°26W **170** E4
Abasolo *Tamaulipas, Mexico* 24°4N 98°22W **171** F6
Abbaye, Pt. *Mich., U.S.A.* 46°58N 88°8W **79** C3
Abbeville *Ala., U.S.A.* 31°34N 85°15W **112** E5
Abbeville *Ga., U.S.A.* 31°59N 83°18W **113** E3
Abbeville *La., U.S.A.* 29°58N 92°8W **110** E3
Abbeville *Miss., U.S.A.* 34°30N 89°30W **111** B4
Abbeville *S.C., U.S.A.* 34°11N 82°23W **103** D3
Abbeville County ☆ *S.C., U.S.A.* 34°11N 82°23W **103** D3
Abbey *Sask., Canada* 50°44N 108°45W **150** E3
Abbotsford *B.C., Canada* 49°5N 122°20W **155** F12
Abbotsford *Wis., U.S.A.* 44°57N 90°19W **78** D3
Abbott *N. Mex., U.S.A.* 36°18N 104°16W **131** A6
Abbott *Tex., U.S.A.* 31°53N 97°4W **109** F10
Abbottstown *Pa., U.S.A.* 39°53N 76°59W **93** A4
Abercorn *Qué., Canada* 45°2N 72°40W **89** A2
Abercrombie *N. Dak., U.S.A.* 46°27N 96°44W **76** D9
Aberdeen *Sask., Canada* 52°20N 106°8W **150** C5
Aberdeen *Ala., U.S.A.* 33°49N 88°33W **111** C5
Aberdeen *Idaho, U.S.A.* 42°57N 112°50W **122** G6
Aberdeen *Ky., U.S.A.* 37°15N 86°41W **104** C6
Aberdeen *Md., U.S.A.* 39°31N 76°10W **93** A4
Aberdeen *N.C., U.S.A.* 35°8N 79°26W **103** C6
Aberdeen *Ohio, U.S.A.* 38°39N 83°46W **86** E3
Aberdeen *S. Dak., U.S.A.* 45°28N 98°29W **76** E7
Aberdeen *Wash., U.S.A.* 46°59N 123°50W **120** D2
Aberdeen L. *Nunavut, Canada* 64°30N 99°0W **159** E6
Aberdeen L. *Miss., U.S.A.* 33°50N 88°31W **111** C5
Aberdeen Proving Ground *Md., U.S.A.* 39°29N 76°10W **93** A4
Abernant *Ala., U.S.A.* 33°17N 87°12W **112** C3
Abernathy *Tex., U.S.A.* 33°50N 101°51W **108** D6
Abernethy *Sask., Canada* 50°45N 103°25W **150** E8
Abert, L. *Oreg., U.S.A.* 42°38N 120°14W **121** E5
Abilene *Kans., U.S.A.* 38°55N 97°13W **82** C6
Abilene *Tex., U.S.A.* 32°28N 99°43W **109** E8
Abingdon *Ill., U.S.A.* 40°48N 90°24W **84** C3
Abingdon *Va., U.S.A.* 36°43N 81°59W **102** E3
Abington *Conn., U.S.A.* 41°52N 72°1W **91** C2
Abington *Mass., U.S.A.* 42°6N 70°57W **91** B4
Abington *Pa., U.S.A.* 40°7N 75°7W **98** A2
Abiquiu *N. Mex., U.S.A.* 36°13N 106°19W **131** A4
Abiquiu Res. *N. Mex., U.S.A.* 36°16N 106°27W **131** A4
Abita Springs *La., U.S.A.* 30°29N 90°2W **110** D5
Abitau → *Canada* 59°53N 109°3W **157** E11
Abitibi → *Ont., Canada* 51°3N 80°55W **149** A16
Abitibi, L. *Ont., Canada* 48°40N 79°40W **144** C3
Abra Tanchipas, Sa. del *San Luis Potosí, Mexico* 22°15N 98°57W **171** H6
Abraham González, Presa *Chihuahua, Mexico* 28°28N 107°28W **169** E8
Abraham L. *Alta., Canada* 52°15N 116°35W **153** F4
Abraham Lincoln Birthplace Nat. Historic Site △ *Ky., U.S.A.* 37°32N 85°44W **105** C7
Absaroka Range *Wyo., U.S.A.* 44°45N 109°50W **124** B3
Absarokee *Mont., U.S.A.* 45°31N 109°27W **123** E8
Absecon *N.J., U.S.A.* 39°26N 74°30W **92** C2
Absecon Lighthouse *N.J., U.S.A.* 39°22N 74°27W **92** C2
Acacoyagua *Chiapas, Mexico* 15°21N 92°39W **178** D4
Acadia Nat. Park △ *Maine, U.S.A.* 44°20N 68°13W **90** D5
Acadia Parish ☆ *La., U.S.A.* 30°13N 92°22W **110** D4
Acadia Valley *Alta., Canada* 51°8N 110°13W **153** G10
Acajutla *El Salv.* 13°36N 89°50W **182** D2
Acámbaro *Guanajuato, Mexico* 20°2N 100°44W **175** B7
Acambay *Mexico, Mexico* 19°58N 99°52W **175** C8
Acancéh *Yucatán, Mexico* 20°49N 89°27W **179** B4
Acapetahua *Chiapas, Mexico* 15°17N 92°42W **178** D4
Acapetlahuaya *Guerrero, Mexico* 18°26N 100°4W **175** D7
Acaponeta *Nayarit, Mexico* 22°30N 105°22W **172** E5
Acapulco *Guerrero, Mexico* 16°51N 99°55W **175** E8
Acapulco Trench *Pac. Oc.* 12°0N 88°0W **182** D2
Acatic *Jalisco, Mexico* 20°47N 102°53W **174** B5
Acatlán *Hidalgo, Mexico* 20°9N 98°27W **175** B9
Acatlán *Oaxaca, Mexico* 18°32N 96°47W **177** F4
Acatlán *Puebla, Mexico* 18°12N 98°3W **177** F2
Acatlán de Juárez *Jalisco, Mexico* 20°26N 103°38W **174** B4
Acatzingo *Puebla, Mexico* 18°59N 97°47W **177** F3
Acayucan *Veracruz, Mexico* 17°57N 94°55W **177** F6
Accident *Md., U.S.A.* 39°38N 79°19W **93** A1
Accokeek *Md., U.S.A.* 38°40N 77°2W **93** B3
Accomac *Va., U.S.A.* 37°43N 75°40W **102** D9
Accomack County ☆ *Va., U.S.A.* 37°45N 75°40W **102** D9
Accotink *Va., U.S.A.* 38°47N 77°13W **99** C2
Accotink Cr. → *Va., U.S.A.* 38°51N 77°15W **99** B2
Achille *Okla., U.S.A.* 33°50N 96°23W **107** E7
Ackerman *Miss., U.S.A.* 33°19N 89°11W **111** C4
Ackley *Iowa, U.S.A.* 42°33N 93°3W **81** C5
Acklins I. *Bahamas* 22°30N 74°0W **183** B5
Acme *Alta., Canada* 51°33N 113°30W **153** G7
Acme *La., U.S.A.* 31°17N 91°49W **110** C4
Acoma Indian Reservation *N. Mex., U.S.A.* 34°45N 107°30W **131** C3
Acomita *N. Mex., U.S.A.* 35°3N 107°34W **131** B3
Aconchi *Sonora, Mexico* 29°50N 110°12W **168** D5
Acteopan *Puebla, Mexico* 18°47N 98°41W **177** F2
Acton *Ont., Canada* 43°38N 80°3W **146** C4
Acton *Mass., U.S.A.* 42°29N 71°26W **91** B3
Acton Vale *Qué., Canada* 45°39N 72°34W **145** F10
Actopan *Hidalgo, Mexico* 20°16N 98°56W **175** B9
Actopan *Veracruz, Mexico* 19°30N 96°37W **176** E4
Acuitzio del Canje *Michoacan, Mexico* 19°29N 101°20W **175** C6
Aculco *Mexico, Mexico* 20°7N 99°49W **175** B8
Acushnet *Mass., U.S.A.* 41°41N 70°55W **91** C4
Acuyo *Michoacan, Mexico* 18°53N 101°11W **175** D6
Acworth *Ga., U.S.A.* 34°4N 84°41W **113** B2
Ada *Kans., U.S.A.* 39°9N 97°53W **82** B6
Ada *Minn., U.S.A.* 47°18N 96°31W **77** C2
Ada *Ohio, U.S.A.* 40°46N 83°49W **86** C3
Ada *Okla., U.S.A.* 34°46N 96°41W **107** D7
Ada County ☆ *Idaho, U.S.A.* 43°30N 116°15W **122** F2
Adair *Iowa, U.S.A.* 41°30N 94°39W **81** C4
Adair *Okla., U.S.A.* 36°26N 95°16W **107** B8
Adair, C. *Nunavut, Canada* 71°30N 71°34W **158** C11
Adair County ☆ *Iowa, U.S.A.* 41°20N 94°30W **81** C4
Adair County ☆ *Ky., U.S.A.* 37°5N 85°20W **105** C7

Adair County ☆ *Mo., U.S.A.* 40°10N 92°35W **83** A4
Adair County ☆ *Okla., U.S.A.* 35°55N 94°45W **107** C9
Adairsville *Ga., U.S.A.* 34°22N 84°56W **113** B2
Adairville *Ky., U.S.A.* 36°40N 86°51W **104** D6
Adak *Alaska, U.S.A.* 51°45N 176°45W **135** L3
Adak I. *Alaska, U.S.A.* 51°45N 176°45W **135** L3
Adams *Calif., U.S.A.* 32°45N 117°7W **133** B2
Adams *Mass., U.S.A.* 42°38N 73°7W **91** B1
Adams *Minn., U.S.A.* 43°34N 92°43W **77** G6
Adams *N. Dak., U.S.A.* 48°25N 98°5W **76** B7
Adams *N.Y., U.S.A.* 43°49N 76°1W **88** B6
Adams *Nebr., U.S.A.* 40°28N 96°31W **80** D9
Adams *Okla., U.S.A.* 36°45N 101°5W **107** B2
Adams *Oreg., U.S.A.* 45°46N 118°34W **121** B7
Adams *Tenn., U.S.A.* 36°35N 87°4W **104** D5
Adams *Wis., U.S.A.* 43°57N 89°49W **78** E41
Adams → *B.C., Canada* 51°25N 119°27W **155** D15
Adams, Mt. *Wash., U.S.A.* 46°12N 121°30W **120** D4
Adams Center *N.Y., U.S.A.* 43°52N 76°0W **88** B5
Adams County ☆ *Colo., U.S.A.* 39°50N 104°10W **125** C6
Adams County ☆ *Idaho, U.S.A.* 45°0N 116°30W **122** E2
Adams County ☆ *Ill., U.S.A.* 40°0N 91°10W **84** D2
Adams County ☆ *Ind., U.S.A.* 40°45N 85°0W **85** D6
Adams County ☆ *Iowa, U.S.A.* 41°0N 94°40W **81** D4
Adams County ☆ *Miss., U.S.A.* 31°23N 91°24W **111** E2
Adams County ☆ *N. Dak., U.S.A.* 46°0N 102°30W **76** D3
Adams County ☆ *Nebr., U.S.A.* 40°30N 98°30W **80** D7
Adams County ☆ *Ohio, U.S.A.* 38°48N 83°33W **86** E3
Adams County ☆ *Pa., U.S.A.* 39°50N 77°14W **87** E5
Adams County ☆ *Wash., U.S.A.* 47°0N 118°30W **120** C7
Adams County ☆ *Wis., U.S.A.* 44°0N 89°50W **78** E41
Adams L. *B.C., Canada* 51°10N 119°40W **155** D15
Adams-McGill Res. *Nev., U.S.A.* 38°22N 115°3W **128** D5
Adams Park *Georgia, U.S.A.* 33°43N 84°27W **117** B2
Adamstown *Pa., U.S.A.* 40°15N 76°3W **87** D6
Adamsville *Qué., Canada* 45°17N 72°47W **89** A2
Adamsville *Ohio, U.S.A.* 40°4N 81°53W **86** C5
Adamsville *R.I., U.S.A.* 41°30N 71°10W **91** C3
Adamsville *Tenn., U.S.A.* 35°14N 88°23W **104** B2
Addieville *Ill., U.S.A.* 38°23N 89°29W **84** E4
Addis *La., U.S.A.* 30°21N 91°16W **110** D4
Addison *Ala., U.S.A.* 34°12N 87°11W **112** B3
Addison *Ill., U.S.A.* 41°55N 88°0W **84** B5
Addison *N.Y., U.S.A.* 42°1N 77°14W **88** C3
Addison *Ohio, U.S.A.* 38°53N 82°9W **86** E4
Addison *Vt., U.S.A.* 44°8N 73°20W **89** B1
Addison County ☆ *Vt., U.S.A.* 44°0N 73°15W **89** B1
Addy *Wash., U.S.A.* 48°21N 117°50W **120** B8
Adel *Ga., U.S.A.* 31°8N 83°25W **113** E3
Adel *Iowa, U.S.A.* 41°37N 94°1W **81** D4
Adel *Oreg., U.S.A.* 42°11N 119°54W **121** E6
Adelaide Pen. *Nunavut, Canada* 68°15N 97°30W **158** D6
Adelaide Village *Bahamas* 25°0N 77°31W **182** A4
Adelanto *Calif., U.S.A.* 34°35N 117°22W **127** J9
Adelphi *Md., U.S.A.* 39°0N 76°58W **99** A4
Adelphi *Ohio, U.S.A.* 39°28N 82°45W **86** D4
Adelphia *N.J., U.S.A.* 40°13N 74°15W **92** B2
Adena *Ohio, U.S.A.* 40°13N 80°53W **86** C6
Adin *Calif., U.S.A.* 41°12N 120°57W **126** B6
Adirondack Mts. *N.Y., U.S.A.* 44°0N 74°0W **88** B7
Adirondack Park △ *N.Y., U.S.A.* 44°0N 74°20W **88** B6
Adjuntas *Puerto Rico* 18°10N 66°43W **184** G16
Adjuntas del Refugio *Zacatecas, Mexico* 22°39N 103°24W **173** E7
Adlavik Is. *Nfld. & L., Canada* 55°0N 58°40W **143** C6
Adler Planetarium *Ill., U.S.A.* 41°51N 87°36W **95** B3
Admiral *Sask., Canada* 49°43N 108°1W **150** F3
Admiral's Beach *Nfld. & L., Canada* 47°1N 53°39W **142** E7
Admiralty I. *N.W.T., Canada* 69°25N 101°10W **158** D5
Admiralty I. *Alaska, U.S.A.* 57°30N 134°30W **135** H14
Admiralty Inlet *N.W.T., Canada* 72°30N 86°0W **158** C8
Admiralty Inlet *Wash., U.S.A.* 48°8N 122°58W **120** B3
Admiralty Island Nat. Monument △ *U.S.A.* 57°40N 134°10W **135** H14
Adobe Creek Res. *Colo., U.S.A.* 38°14N 103°17W **125** D7
Adobe Dam County Recreation Area *Ariz., U.S.A.* 33°41N 112°9W **134** A1
Adolfo López Mateos *Baja Calif. S., Mexico* 25°11N 112°8W **167** H6
Adolfo López Mateos *Chihuahua, Mexico* 28°28N 107°20W **169** E8
Adolfo López Mateos *Durango, Mexico* 24°32N 104°17W **173** C6
Adolfo López Mateos *Quintana Roo, Mexico* 19°37N 88°42W **179** C5
Adolfo López Mateos *Zacatecas, Mexico* 22°7N 103°1W **173** E7
Adolfo López Mateos, Presa *Sinaloa, Mexico* 25°10N 107°24W **172** E3
Adolfo Ruiz *Campeche, Mexico* 19°30N 90°21W **179** C3
Adolfo Ruiz Cortines, Presa *Sonora, Mexico* 27°15N 109°6W **168** F6
Adrian *Ga., U.S.A.* 32°33N 82°35W **113** D4
Adrian *Mich., U.S.A.* 41°54N 84°2W **79** H7
Adrian *Minn., U.S.A.* 43°38N 95°56W **77** G3
Adrian *Mo., U.S.A.* 38°24N 94°21W **83** C2
Adrian *Oreg., U.S.A.* 43°45N 117°4W **121** D9
Adrian *Tex., U.S.A.* 35°16N 102°40W **108** B5
Advance *Ind., U.S.A.* 40°0N 86°40W **85** D4
Advance *Mo., U.S.A.* 37°6N 89°55W **83** D7
Advocate Harbour *N.S., Canada* 45°20N 64°47W **141** H5
Aetna *Kans., U.S.A.* 37°5N 98°58W **82** D5
Afton *Mo., U.S.A.* 38°33N 90°20W **83** C6
Afognak I. *Alaska, U.S.A.* 58°15N 152°30W **135** G9
Afton *Iowa, U.S.A.* 41°2N 94°12W **81** D4
Afton *N.Y., U.S.A.* 42°14N 75°32W **88** C5
Afton *Okla., U.S.A.* 36°42N 94°58W **107** B9
Afton *Wyo., U.S.A.* 42°44N 110°56W **124** D2
Agana *Guam* 13°28N 144°45E **184** b
Agar *S. Dak., U.S.A.* 44°50N 100°5W **76** F5
Agassiz *B.C., Canada* 49°14N 121°46W **155** F13
Agassiz Icecap *Nunavut, Canada* 80°15N 76°0W **158** A10
Agassiz Nat. Wildlife Refuge △ *Minn., U.S.A.* 48°21N 95°57W **77** B3
Agassiz Pool *Minn., U.S.A.* 48°20N 95°59W **77** B3
Agat *Guam* 13°25N 144°40E **184** b
Agate *Colo., U.S.A.* 39°28N 103°57W **125** C7
Agate Fossil Beds Nat. Monument △ *Nebr., U.S.A.* 42°25N 103°44W **80** C1
Agawa → *Ont., Canada* 47°23N 84°40W **149** E12
Agawam *S. Dak., U.S.A.* 43°56N 102°13W **76** G3
Agawam *Mass., U.S.A.* 42°5N 72°37W **91** B2
Agawam *Mont., U.S.A.* 48°0N 112°10W **123** C5
Agency *Iowa, U.S.A.* 41°0N 92°18W **81** E6

Agency L. *Oreg., U.S.A.* 42°33N 121°58W **121** E4
Agenda *Kans., U.S.A.* 39°43N 97°26W **82** B6
Agiabampo *Sonora, Mexico* 26°24N 109°8W **168** G6
Agincourt *Ont., Canada* 43°47N 79°16W **161** A3
Agnes L. *Ont., Canada* 48°15N 91°20W **148** D5
Agra *Kans., U.S.A.* 39°46N 99°7W **82** B4
Agra *Okla., U.S.A.* 35°54N 96°53W **107** C7
Agricola Oriental *Distrito Federal, Mexico* 19°23N 99°4W **181** B3
Agrihan *N. Marianas* 18°46N 145°40E **184** a
Agua Blanca *Guadalajara, Mexico* 20°33N 103°10W **180** B2
Agua Blanca *Hidalgo, Mexico* 20°22N 98°20W **175** B9
Agua Brava, L. de *Nayarit, Mexico* 22°10N 105°32W **172** E5
Agua Caliente *Chihuahua, Mexico* 27°55N 108°50W **168** F7
Agua Caliente *Sinaloa, Mexico* 23°36N 106°6W **172** D4
Agua Caliente *Sonora, Mexico* 28°5N 110°10W **168** E5
Agua Caliente → *Chihuahua, Mexico* 27°57N 108°30W **168** F7
Agua de Enmedio *San Luis Potosí, Mexico* 22°9N 100°15W **171** H4
Agua Dulce *Veracruz, Mexico* 20°21N 97°17W **176** D3
Agua Dulce *Zacatecas, Mexico* 18°8N 94°8W **177** F6
Agua Dulce *Tex., U.S.A.* 27°47N 97°55W **109** K10
Agua Escondida → *Baja Calif., Mexico* 30°31N 115°43W **166** C3
Agua Fría *Monterrey, Mexico* 25°38N 100°10W **180** B3
Agua Fria *N. Mex., U.S.A.* 35°39N 106°1W **131** B4
Agua Fria → *Ariz., U.S.A.* 33°23N 112°22W **130** D3
Agua Fria Nat. Monument △ *Ariz., U.S.A.* 34°14N 112°0W **130** C3
Agua Fria Pk. *N. Mex., U.S.A.* 36°22N 105°13W **131** A5
Agua Grande, L. *Sinaloa, Mexico* 22°37N 105°40W **172** E5
Agua Nueva *Coahuila, Mexico* 25°12N 101°6W **171** E3
Agua Nueva *Tex., U.S.A.* 26°54N 98°36W **108** L9
Agua Nueva del Norte *San Luis Potosí, Mexico* 22°37N 99°48W **171** H5
Agua Prieta *Sonora, Mexico* 31°18N 109°34W **168** B6
Agua Verde *Sinaloa, Mexico* 22°54N 105°59W **172** E5
Agua Verde → *Mexico* 27°0N 99°52W **170** C5
Aguada *Puerto Rico* 18°23N 67°11W **184** G15
Aguadilla *Puerto Rico* 18°26N 67°10W **184** G15
Aguadulce *Panama* 8°15N 80°32W **182** E3
Agualeguas *Nuevo León, Mexico* 26°18N 99°34W **170** D5
Aguamilpa *Nayarit, Mexico* 20°56N 105°2W **172** E5
Aguamilpas, Presa *Nayarit, Mexico* 21°47N 104°46W **172** F6
Aguamilpas, Presa *Nayarit, Mexico* 21°38N 104°37W **172** F6
Aguanaval → *Mexico* 25°28N 102°53W **173** C8
Aguanaval, Sa. *Durango, Mexico* 25°3N 103°28W **173** B7
Aguanish *Qué., Canada* 50°14N 62°2W **143** C5
Aguanus → *Qué., Canada* 50°13N 62°5W **143** C5
Aguapepito *Sinaloa, Mexico* 24°35N 107°42W **172** C3
Aguaruto *Sinaloa, Mexico* 24°47N 107°29W **172** C3
Aguascalientes *Aguascalientes, Mexico* 21°53N 102°18W **173** F8
Aguascalientes □ *Mexico* 22°0N 102°20W **173** F8
Aguila *Ariz., U.S.A.* 33°57N 113°11W **130** D2
Aguila, Punta *Puerto Rico* 17°57N 67°13W **184** H15
Aguilar *Colo., U.S.A.* 37°24N 104°39W **125** E6
Aguilares *Tex., U.S.A.* 27°27N 99°5W **108** K3
Aguililla *Michoacan, Mexico* 18°44N 102°44W **174** D5
Ahome *Sinaloa, Mexico* 25°55N 109°11W **172** B1
Ahoskie *N.C., U.S.A.* 36°17N 76°59W **103** B9
Ahuacatlán *El Salv.* 13°54N 89°52W **182** D2
Ahuacuotzingo *Guerrero, Mexico* 17°43N 98°59W **175** E9
Ahualulco *San Luis Potosí, Mexico* 22°24N 101°10W **171** H3
Ahualulco de Mercado *Jalisco, Mexico* 20°42N 103°59W **174** B4
Ahuazotepec *Puebla, Mexico* 20°3N 98°9W **176** D2
Ahuehuetitla *Puebla, Mexico* 18°12N 97°12W **177** F2
Ahuijillo *Jalisco, Mexico* 19°3N 103°5W **174** C4
'Āhuimanu *Hawai'i, U.S.A.* 21°26N 157°50W **136** K14
Ahuntsic *Qué., Canada* 45°32N 73°41W **160** A2
Ahwatukee Foothills *Ariz., U.S.A.* 33°20N 111°59W **134** D2
'Aiea *Hawai'i, U.S.A.* 21°23N 157°56W **136** K14
Aiguebelle, Parc de Conservation d' △ *Qué., Canada* 48°30N 78°45W **144** C4
Aiken *S.C., U.S.A.* 33°34N 81°43W **103** D4
Aiken County ☆ *S.C., U.S.A.* 33°30N 81°40W **103** D4
Ailey *Ga., U.S.A.* 32°11N 82°34W **113** D4
Aillik *Nfld. & L., Canada* 55°11N 59°18W **143** B6
Ailsa Craig *Ont., Canada* 43°8N 81°33W **146** D3
Ainsworth *Iowa, U.S.A.* 41°17N 91°33W **81** D7
Ainsworth *Nebr., U.S.A.* 42°33N 99°52W **80** B6
Air Force I. *Nunavut, Canada* 67°58N 74°5W **158** D11
Airdrie *Alta., Canada* 51°18N 114°2W **153** G6
Aire, Mt. *Utah, U.S.A.* 40°43N 111°41W **134** B3
Airway Heights *Wash., U.S.A.* 47°39N 117°36W **120** C8
Aishihik L. *Yukon, Canada* 61°26N 137°15W **157** D5
Aitkin *Minn., U.S.A.* 46°32N 93°42W **77** D5
Aitkin County ☆ *Minn., U.S.A.* 46°30N 93°25W **77** D5
Aix, Mt. *Wash., U.S.A.* 46°47N 121°15W **120** D4
Ajacuba *Hidalgo, Mexico* 20°5N 99°8W **175** B8
Ajalpan *Puebla, Mexico* 18°22N 97°15W **177** F3
Ajax *Ont., Canada* 43°50N 79°1W **147** D7
Ajijic *Jalisco, Mexico* 20°18N 103°17W **174** B4
Ajo *Ariz., U.S.A.* 32°22N 112°52W **130** E3
Ajo Mt. *Ariz., U.S.A.* 32°25N 112°45W **130** E3
Ajos, Sa. de los *Sonora, Mexico* 30°57N 109°54W **168** C6
Ajoxutla *Puebla, Mexico* 18°15N 98°45W **177** F2
Ajoya *Sinaloa, Mexico* 24°7N 106°21W **172** C4
Ajuchitlán *Guerrero, Mexico* 18°10N 100°30W **175** D7
Ajusco, Volcán *Distrito Federal, Mexico* 19°12N 99°15W **181** C2
Ak-Chin = Maricopa Indian Reservation *Ariz., U.S.A.* 33°0N 112°1W **130** E3
Akamina-Kishinena Park △ *B.C., Canada* 49°1N 114°12W **153** J6
Akaska *S. Dak., U.S.A.* 45°20N 100°7W **76** E5
Aké *Yucatán, Mexico* 20°55N 89°21W **179** B4
Akil *Yucatán, Mexico* 20°15N 89°21W **179** B4
Akimiski I. *Nunavut, Canada* 52°50N 81°30W **159** G9
Aklavik *N.W.T., Canada* 68°12N 135°0W **156** C5
Akolmiut *Alaska, U.S.A.* 60°55N 162°20W **135** F7
Akpatok I. *Nunavut, Canada* 60°25N 68°8W **143** A4
Akra *N.D., U.S.A.* 48°47N 97°44W **76** B8
Akron *Ont., Canada* 48°55N 84°7W **149** D12
Akron *Ala., U.S.A.* 32°53N 87°45W **112** D3
Akron *Colo., U.S.A.* 40°10N 103°13W **125** B7
Akron *Iowa, U.S.A.* 42°50N 96°34W **81** C2
Akron *Ohio, U.S.A.* 41°5N 81°31W **86** B5
Akron *Pa., U.S.A.* 40°9N 76°12W **87** D6

Akulivik *Qué., Canada* 60°48N 78°12W **143** A12
Akumal *Quintana Roo, Mexico* 20°25N 87°18W **179** B6
Akun I. *Alaska, U.S.A.* 54°11N 165°32W **135** J6
Akutan *Alaska, U.S.A.* 54°8N 165°46W **135** J6
Akutan I. *Alaska, U.S.A.* 54°7N 165°55W **135** J6
Alabama □ *U.S.A.* 33°0N 87°0W **112** C4
Alabama → *Ala., U.S.A.* 31°8N 87°57W **112** E3
Alabama-Coushatta Indian Reservation *Tex., U.S.A.* 30°33N 94°42W **109** G13
Alabaster *Ala., U.S.A.* 33°15N 86°49W **112** C4
Alachua *Fla., U.S.A.* 29°47N 82°30W **114** B6
Alachua County ☆ *Fla., U.S.A.* 29°45N 82°20W **114** B6
Aladdin *Wyo., U.S.A.* 44°38N 104°11W **124** B8
Alahuixtlán *Guerrero, Mexico* 18°36N 100°3W **175** D7
Alajuela *Costa Rica* 10°2N 84°8W **182** D3
Alakanuk *Alaska, U.S.A.* 62°41N 164°37W **135** E6
'Alalākeiki Channel *Hawai'i, U.S.A.* 20°30N 156°30W **136** C5
Alamagan *N. Marianas* 17°36N 145°50E **184** a
Alamance County ☆ *N.C., U.S.A.* 36°0N 79°25W **103** B6
Alameda *Sask., Canada* 49°16N 102°17W **151** F9
Alameda *Calif., U.S.A.* 37°46N 122°15W **132** B3
Alameda *N. Mex., U.S.A.* 35°11N 106°37W **131** B4
Alameda County ☆ *Calif., U.S.A.* 37°40N 121°50W **126** F5
Alameda Memorial State Beach Park *Calif., U.S.A.* 37°45N 122°16W **132** B3
Alamito → *Tex., U.S.A.* 29°45N 104°18W **108** H3
Alamo *Veracruz, Mexico* 20°55N 97°41W **176** D3
Alamo *Ga., U.S.A.* 32°9N 82°47W **113** D4
Alamo *N. Dak., U.S.A.* 48°35N 103°28W **76** B2
Alamo *N. Mex., U.S.A.* 34°25N 107°31W **131** C3
Alamo *Nev., U.S.A.* 37°22N 115°10W **128** E5
Alamo *Tenn., U.S.A.* 35°47N 89°7W **104** C3
Alamo *Calif., U.S.A.* 33°13N 115°37W **127** K11
Alamo Chapo *Chihuahua, Mexico* 29°20N 104°23W **169** D11
Alamo Heights *Tex., U.S.A.* 29°29N 98°27W **116** B3
Alamo Indian Reservation *N. Mex., U.S.A.* 34°20N 107°30W **131** C3
Alamo L. *Ariz., U.S.A.* 34°10N 113°35W **130** C2
Alamogordo *N. Mex., U.S.A.* 32°54N 105°57W **131** E5
Álamos *Sonora, Mexico* 27°1N 108°56W **168** F7
Álamos, Río de los → *Coahuila, Mexico* 27°53N 101°12W **170** C3
Alamosa *Colo., U.S.A.* 37°22N 105°46W **125** E5
Alamosa → *Colo., U.S.A.* 37°22N 105°46W **125** E5
Alamosa → *N. Mex., U.S.A.* 33°25N 107°15W **131** D3
Alamosa County ☆ *Colo., U.S.A.* 37°40N 105°40W **125** E5
Alamosa Cr. → *N. Mex., U.S.A.* 34°20N 104°10W **131** C6
Alanreed *Tex., U.S.A.* 35°13N 100°44W **108** B7
Alanson *Mich., U.S.A.* 45°27N 84°47W **79** D7
Alapaha *Ga., U.S.A.* 31°23N 83°13W **113** E3
Alapaha → *Ga., U.S.A.* 30°27N 83°6W **113** F3
Alaquines *San Luis Potosí, Mexico* 22°8N 99°36W **171** H5
Alaska □ *U.S.A.* 64°0N 154°0W **135** D9
Alaska, G. of *Pac. Oc.* 58°0N 145°0W **135** G11
Alaska Maritime Nat. Wildlife Refuge △ *Alaska, U.S.A.* 52°0N 174°0W **135** L4
Alaska Peninsula *Alaska, U.S.A.* 56°0N 159°0W **135** H8
Alaska Peninsula Nat. Wildlife Refuge △ *Alaska, U.S.A.* 56°0N 159°0W **135** J8
Alaska Range *Alaska, U.S.A.* 62°50N 151°0W **135** E10
Alava, C. *Wash., U.S.A.* 48°10N 124°44W **120** B1
Alba *Mo., U.S.A.* 37°14N 94°25W **83** D2
Alba *Tex., U.S.A.* 32°48N 95°38W **109** E12
Albanel *Qué., Canada* 48°53N 72°27W **145** C10
Albanel, L. *Qué., Canada* 50°55N 73°12W **143** C3
Albany *B.C., Canada* 31°35N 84°10W **113** E2
Albany *Ind., U.S.A.* 40°18N 85°14W **85** C5
Albany *Ky., U.S.A.* 36°42N 85°8W **105** D7
Albany *La., U.S.A.* 30°30N 90°35W **110** D5
Albany *Minn., U.S.A.* 45°38N 94°34W **77** E4
Albany *Mo., U.S.A.* 40°15N 94°20W **83** A2
Albany *N.Y., U.S.A.* 42°39N 73°45W **88** C7
Albany *Ohio, U.S.A.* 39°14N 82°12W **86** D4
Albany *Okla., U.S.A.* 33°53N 96°10W **107** E7
Albany *Oreg., U.S.A.* 44°38N 123°6W **121** C2
Albany *Tex., U.S.A.* 32°44N 99°18W **109** E8
Albany *Vt., U.S.A.* 44°43N 72°23W **89** B2
Albany *Wis., U.S.A.* 42°42N 89°26W **78** F4
Albany → *Ont., Canada* 52°17N 81°31W **159** G9
Albany County ☆ *N.Y., U.S.A.* 42°30N 74°0W **88** C7
Albany County ☆ *Wyo., U.S.A.* 41°50N 105°42W **124** E6
Albany Int. ✈ (ALB) *N.Y., U.S.A.* 42°45N 73°48W **88** C7
Albemarle *N.C., U.S.A.* 35°21N 80°12W **103** C5
Albemarle County ☆ *Va., U.S.A.* 38°2N 78°30W **102** C6
Albemarle Sd. *N.C., U.S.A.* 36°5N 76°0W **103** B9
Albert *Kans., U.S.A.* 38°27N 99°1W **82** C4
Albert *Okla., U.S.A.* 35°14N 98°25W **107** C5
Albert City *Iowa, U.S.A.* 42°47N 94°57W **81** C4
Albert Canyon *B.C., Canada* 51°8N 117°41W **155** D17
Albert Edward B. *Nunavut, Canada* 69°32N 102°25W **158** D5
Albert Lea *Minn., U.S.A.* 43°39N 93°22W **77** G5
Albert Town *Bahamas* 22°37N 74°33W **183** B5
Alberta □ *Canada* 32°14N 87°25W **112** D3
Alberta *Mich., U.S.A.* 46°39N 88°29W **79** C3
Alberta *Va., U.S.A.* 36°52N 77°53W **102** E7
Alberta □ *Canada* 54°40N 115°0W **152** E6
Alberta Beach *Alta., Canada* 53°40N 114°21W **152** E6
Alberton *P.E.I., Canada* 46°50N 64°0W **141** G5
Alberton *Mont., U.S.A.* 47°0N 114°29W **123** D3
Albertson *N.Y., U.S.A.* 40°46N 73°38W **97** B5
Albertville *Ala., U.S.A.* 34°16N 86°13W **112** B4
Albertville *Minn., U.S.A.* 45°14N 93°39W **77** E5
Albia *Iowa, U.S.A.* 41°2N 92°48W **81** D61
Albin *Wyo., U.S.A.* 41°25N 104°6W **124** E8
Albino Zertuche *Puebla, Mexico* 18°1N 98°33W **177** F2
Albion *Calif., U.S.A.* 39°14N 123°46W **126** E3
Albion *Idaho, U.S.A.* 42°25N 113°35W **122** G5
Albion *Ill., U.S.A.* 38°23N 88°4W **84** E5
Albion *Ind., U.S.A.* 41°24N 85°25W **85** B6
Albion *Iowa, U.S.A.* 42°7N 92°59W **81** C6
Albion *Maine, U.S.A.* 44°32N 69°27W **90** D4
Albion *Mich., U.S.A.* 42°15N 84°45W **79** G7
Albion *N.Y., U.S.A.* 43°15N 78°12W **88** B2
Albion *Nebr., U.S.A.* 41°42N 98°0W **80** C7
Albion *Okla., U.S.A.* 34°40N 95°6W **107** D8
Albion *Pa., U.S.A.* 41°53N 80°22W **87** C2
Albion *Wash., U.S.A.* 46°48N 117°15W **120** D8
Albion Mts. *Idaho, U.S.A.* 42°13N 113°43W **122** G5
Albreda *B.C., Canada* 52°35N 119°10W **155** C15
Albright *W. Va., U.S.A.* 39°30N 79°39W **102** B4
Albuquerque *N. Mex., U.S.A.* 35°5N 106°39W **131** B4
Albuquerque, Cayos de *Caribbean* 12°10N 81°50W **182** D3
Albuquerque Int. ✈ (ABQ) *N. Mex., U.S.A.* 35°3N 106°36W **131** B4

Alburg *Vt., U.S.A.* 44°59N 73°18W **89** B1
Alburnett *Iowa, U.S.A.* 42°9N 91°37W **81** C7
Alcalde *N. Mex., U.S.A.* 36°5N 106°3W **131** A4
Alcester *S. Dak., U.S.A.* 43°1N 96°38W **76** G9
Alco *Ark., U.S.A.* 35°53N 92°22W **106** C3
Alcoa *Tenn., U.S.A.* 35°48N 83°59W **105** E9
Alcolu *S.C., U.S.A.* 33°45N 80°13W **103** E5
Alcoma *Fla., U.S.A.* 27°54N 81°29W **114** D7
Alcona *Mich., U.S.A.* 44°45N 83°17W **79** E8
Alcona County ☆ *Mich., U.S.A.* 44°40N 83°40W **79** E8
Alcorn *Miss., U.S.A.* 31°53N 91°8W **111** E2
Alcorn County ☆ *Miss., U.S.A.* 34°56N 88°31W **111** B5
Alcova *Wyo., U.S.A.* 42°34N 106°43W **124** D6
Alcova Res. *Wyo., U.S.A.* 42°33N 106°42W **124** D6
Alcozauca *Guerrero, Mexico* 17°28N 98°23W **175** E9
Alda *Nebr., U.S.A.* 40°52N 98°28W **80** D7
Aldama *Chihuahua, Mexico* 28°51N 105°54W **169** D10
Aldama *Tamaulipas, Mexico* 22°55N 98°4W **171** H6
Aldan *Pa., U.S.A.* 39°55N 75°17W **98** B1
Alden *Iowa, U.S.A.* 42°31N 93°22W **81** C5
Alden *Kans., U.S.A.* 38°15N 98°19W **82** C5
Alden *Minn., U.S.A.* 43°40N 93°34W **77** G5
Alden *N.Y., U.S.A.* 42°54N 78°30W **88** C2
Aldene *N.J., U.S.A.* 40°39N 74°16W **97** C1
Alder *Mont., U.S.A.* 45°19N 112°6W **123** E5
Alder L. *Wash., U.S.A.* 46°48N 122°18W **120** D3
Aldershot *N.S., Canada* 45°6N 64°31W **141** H5
Alderson *Okla., U.S.A.* 34°54N 95°41W **107** D8
Alderson *W. Va., U.S.A.* 37°44N 80°38W **102** D4
Alderwood Manor *Wash., U.S.A.* 47°49N 122°16W **120** C4
Aldie *Va., U.S.A.* 38°59N 77°39W **93** B3
Aldine *Tex., U.S.A.* 29°56N 95°23W **109** H12
Aledo *Ill., U.S.A.* 41°12N 90°45W **84** B3
Aledo *Tex., U.S.A.* 32°42N 97°36W **109** E10
Alegros Mt. *N. Mex., U.S.A.* 34°9N 108°11W **131** C2
Aleknagik *Alaska, U.S.A.* 59°17N 158°36W **135** G8
ʻAlenuihāhā Channel *Hawaiʻi, U.S.A.* 20°30N 156°0W **136** C5
Alert *Nunavut, Canada* 83°2N 60°0W **158** A13
Alert Bay *B.C., Canada* 50°30N 126°55W **154** E8
Alesia *Md., U.S.A.* 39°43N 76°51W **93** A4
Aleutian Is. *Pac. Oc.* 52°0N 175°0W **135** K3
Aleutian Range *Alaska, U.S.A.* 60°0N 154°0W **135** G9
Aleutians East ☆ *Alaska, U.S.A.* 54°51N 163°25W **135** J7
Aleutians West ☆ *Alaska, U.S.A.* 52°15N 175°7W **135** K4
Alex *Okla., U.S.A.* 34°55N 97°47W **107** D6
Alex Graham, Mt. *B.C., Canada* 52°4N 122°52W **155** C12
Alexander *Man., Canada* 49°49N 100°17W **151** F11
Alexander *Ga., U.S.A.* 33°1N 81°53W **113** C6
Alexander *Iowa, U.S.A.* 42°48N 93°29W **81** C5
Alexander *Kans., U.S.A.* 38°28N 99°33W **82** C4
Alexander *Maine, U.S.A.* 45°5N 67°28W **90** C6
Alexander *N. Dak., U.S.A.* 47°51N 103°39W **76** C2
Alexander *W. Va., U.S.A.* 38°47N 80°13W **102** C4
Alexander Arch. *Alaska, U.S.A.* 56°0N 136°0W **135** J14
Alexander City *Ala., U.S.A.* 32°56N 85°58W **112** D5
Alexander County ☆ *Ill., U.S.A.* 37°10N 89°20W **84** F4
Alexander County ☆ *N.C., U.S.A.* 35°50N 81°10W **103** B4
Alexander I. *Nunavut, Canada* 75°52N 102°37W **158** B5
Alexandria *B.C., Canada* 52°35N 122°27W **155** C12
Alexandria *Ont., Canada* 45°19N 74°38W **147** B12
Alexandria *Ind., U.S.A.* 40°16N 85°41W **85** C5
Alexandria *Ky., U.S.A.* 38°58N 84°23W **105** B8
Alexandria *La., U.S.A.* 31°18N 92°27W **110** C3
Alexandria *Minn., U.S.A.* 45°53N 95°22W **77** E3
Alexandria *Mo., U.S.A.* 40°27N 91°28W **83** A5
Alexandria *N.H., U.S.A.* 43°37N 71°47W **89** C3
Alexandria *Nebr., U.S.A.* 40°15N 97°23W **80** D8
Alexandria *Pa., U.S.A.* 40°34N 78°6W **87** D4
Alexandria *S. Dak., U.S.A.* 43°39N 97°47W **76** G8
Alexandria *Tenn., U.S.A.* 36°5N 86°2W **104** D6
Alexandria *Va., U.S.A.* 38°49N 77°5W **99** C3
Alexandria Bay *N.Y., U.S.A.* 44°20N 75°55W **88** A5
Alexis *Ill., U.S.A.* 41°4N 90°33W **84** B3
Alexis → *Nfld. & L., Canada* 52°33N 56°8W **143** C6
Alexis Creek *B.C., Canada* 52°10N 123°20W **154** C11
Alfajayucan *Hidalgo, Mexico* 20°25N 99°20W **175** B8
Alfalfa *Okla., U.S.A.* 35°13N 98°36W **107** C5
Alfalfa County ☆ *Okla., U.S.A.* 36°45N 98°15W **107** B5
Alford *Fla., U.S.A.* 30°42N 85°24W **114** A3
Alfred *Qué., Canada* 45°33N 74°52W **144** F8
Alfred *Maine, U.S.A.* 43°29N 70°43W **90** E3
Alfred *N.Y., U.S.A.* 42°16N 77°48W **88** C3
Alfred M. Terrazas *San Luis Potosí, Mexico* 21°28N 98°51W **171** J6
Alfred V. Bonfil *Tamaulipas, Mexico* 25°33N 98°14W **170** E6
Alger County ☆ *Mich., U.S.A.* 46°20N 86°50W **79** C5
Algodones *N. Mex., U.S.A.* 35°23N 106°29W **131** B4
Algodones, Pta. de *Tamaulipas, Mexico* 24°26N 97°45W **171** F7
Algoma *Miss., U.S.A.* 34°11N 89°2W **111** B4
Algoma *Wis., U.S.A.* 44°36N 87°26W **78** D6
Algona *Iowa, U.S.A.* 43°4N 94°14W **81** B4
Algonac *Mich., U.S.A.* 42°37N 82°32W **79** G9
Algonquin *Ill., U.S.A.* 42°10N 88°18W **84** A5
Algonquin Prov. Park △ *Ont., Canada* 45°50N 78°30W **147** B8
Algood *Tenn., U.S.A.* 36°12N 85°27W **105** D7
Alhambra *Alta., Canada* 52°20N 114°40W **153** F6
Alhambra *Calif., U.S.A.* 34°5N 118°7W **133** B4
Alibates Flint Quarries Nat. Monument △ *U.S.A.* 35°34N 101°41W **108** B6
Alice *Ont., Canada* 45°47N 77°14W **147** B9
Alice *N. Dak., U.S.A.* 46°46N 97°33W **76** D8
Alice *Tex., U.S.A.* 27°45N 98°5W **109** K9
Alice, L. *N. Dak., U.S.A.* 48°20N 99°7W **76** B6
Alice Arm *B.C., Canada* 55°29N 129°31W **157** E7
Aliceville *Ala., U.S.A.* 33°8N 88°9W **112** C2
Aliceville *Kans., U.S.A.* 38°9N 95°33W **82** C8
Aliceville L. *U.S.A.* 33°15N 88°17W **112** C2
Alicia *Ark., U.S.A.* 35°54N 91°5W **106** C4
Alida *Sask., Canada* 49°25N 101°55W **151** F10
Aline *Okla., U.S.A.* 36°31N 98°27W **107** B5
Aliquippa *Pa., U.S.A.* 40°38N 80°15W **87** D2
Aljojuca *Puebla, Mexico* 19°6N 97°31W **177** E3
Alix *Alta., Canada* 52°24N 113°11W **153** F7
Alkali Flat *Nev., U.S.A.* 40°24N 117°21W **128** B3
Alkali Flat *Nev., U.S.A.* 40°0N 115°58W **128** C5
Alkali L. *Nev., U.S.A.* 41°42N 119°51W **128** A1
Alkali L. *Oreg., U.S.A.* 42°58N 120°2W **121** E5
Alkaline L. *N. Dak., U.S.A.* 46°40N 99°34W **76** D6
All American Canal *Calif., U.S.A.* 32°45N 115°15W **127** L11
Allagash *Maine, U.S.A.* 47°5N 69°3W **90** A4
Allagash → *Maine, U.S.A.* 47°5N 69°3W **90** A4
Allagash L. *Maine, U.S.A.* 46°18N 69°35W **90** B4
Allakaket *Alaska, U.S.A.* 66°34N 152°39W **135** C9
Allamakee County ☆ *Iowa, U.S.A.* 43°15N 91°20W **81** B7

Allamoore *Tex., U.S.A.* 31°5N 105°0W **108** F3
Allan *Sask., Canada* 51°53N 106°4W **150** D5
Allan Water *Ont., Canada* 50°14N 90°10W **148** B6
Allard, L. *Qué., Canada* 50°32N 63°31W **140** C4
Allardt *Tenn., U.S.A.* 36°23N 84°53W **105** D8
Allardville *N.B., Canada* 47°28N 65°29W **141** F4
Allatoona L. *Ga., U.S.A.* 34°10N 84°44W **113** B2
Allegan *Mich., U.S.A.* 42°32N 85°51W **79** G6
Allegan County ☆ *Mich., U.S.A.* 42°35N 85°50W **79** G6
Allegany *N.Y., U.S.A.* 42°6N 78°30W **88** C2
Allegany *Oreg., U.S.A.* 43°26N 124°2W **121** D1
Allegany County ☆ *Md., U.S.A.* 39°40N 78°40W **93** A2
Allegany County ☆ *N.Y., U.S.A.* 42°15N 78°0W **88** C2
Allegany Indian Reservation *N.Y., U.S.A.* 42°6N 78°55W **88** C2
Allegany State Park △ *N.Y., U.S.A.* 42°3N 78°48W **88** C2
Alleghany County ☆ *N.C., U.S.A.* 36°25N 81°10W **103** B4
Alleghany County ☆ *Va., U.S.A.* 37°50N 80°0W **102** D4
Allegheny → *Pa., U.S.A.* 40°27N 80°1W **87** D2
Allegheny County ☆ *Pa., U.S.A.* 40°25N 80°0W **87** D2
Allegheny Mts. *W. Va., U.S.A.* 38°15N 80°10W **102** C4
Allegheny Nat. Forest *Pa., U.S.A.* 41°45N 79°5W **87** C3
Allegheny Plateau *Pa., U.S.A.* 41°30N 78°30W **87** C4
Allegheny Portage Railroad Nat. Historic Site △ *Pa., U.S.A.* 40°22N 78°51W **87** D4
Allegheny Res. *Pa., U.S.A.* 41°50N 79°0W **87** C4
Allemands, L. des *La., U.S.A.* 29°55N 90°35W **110** E5
Allen *Kans., U.S.A.* 38°39N 96°10W **82** C7
Allen *Md., U.S.A.* 38°17N 75°42W **93** B5
Allen *Nebr., U.S.A.* 42°25N 96°51W **80** B9
Allen *Okla., U.S.A.* 34°53N 96°25W **107** D7
Allen *S. Dak., U.S.A.* 43°17N 101°56W **76** G4
Allen *Tex., U.S.A.* 33°6N 96°40W **109** D11
Allen County ☆ *Ind., U.S.A.* 41°5N 85°5W **85** B5
Allen County ☆ *Kans., U.S.A.* 37°50N 95°15W **82** D8
Allen County ☆ *Ky., U.S.A.* 36°45N 86°10W **104** D6
Allen County ☆ *Ohio, U.S.A.* 40°44N 84°6W **86** C2
Allen Parish ☆ *La., U.S.A.* 30°37N 92°46W **110** D3
Allendale *Ill., U.S.A.* 38°32N 87°43W **84** E6
Allendale *S.C., U.S.A.* 33°1N 81°18W **103** E4
Allendale County ☆ *S.C., U.S.A.* 33°0N 81°20W **103** E4
Allende *Coahuila, Mexico* 28°20N 100°51W **170** B4
Allende *Nuevo León, Mexico* 25°17N 100°1W **171** E4
Allende *Veracruz, Mexico* 18°4N 94°22W **177** F6
Allenhurst *N.J., U.S.A.* 40°15N 73°59W **92** B3
Allensville *Ky., U.S.A.* 36°43N 87°4W **104** D5
Allentown *N.J., U.S.A.* 40°11N 74°35W **92** B2
Allentown *N.Y., U.S.A.* 40°47N 73°43W **97** B4
Allentown *Pa., U.S.A.* 40°37N 75°29W **92** B1
Allerton *Ill., U.S.A.* 39°55N 87°56W **84** D6
Allerton *Iowa, U.S.A.* 40°42N 93°22W **81** E5
Alley Pond Park *N.Y., U.S.A.* 40°44N 73°43W **97** B4
Alliance *Alta., Canada* 52°26N 111°47W **153** F9
Alliance *Nebr., U.S.A.* 42°6N 102°52W **80** B2
Alliance *Ohio, U.S.A.* 40°55N 81°6W **86** C5
Alliford Bay *B.C., Canada* 53°12N 131°58W **154** B3
Alligator *Miss., U.S.A.* 34°6N 90°43W **111** B3
Alligator → *N.C., U.S.A.* 35°55N 76°7W **103** C9
Alligator Alley = Everglades Parkway *Fla., U.S.A.* 26°10N 81°0W **114** E7
Alligator L. = New L. *N.C., U.S.A.* 35°39N 76°21W **103** C9
Allison *Colo., U.S.A.* 37°2N 107°29W **125** E3
Allison *Iowa, U.S.A.* 42°45N 92°48W **81** C6
Allison *Tex., U.S.A.* 35°36N 100°6W **108** B7
Alliston = New Tecumseth *Ont., Canada* 44°9N 79°52W **146** C7
Allons *Tenn., U.S.A.* 36°27N 85°21W **105** D7
Allouez *Wis., U.S.A.* 44°27N 88°4W **78** D5
Alloway *N.J., U.S.A.* 39°34N 75°22W **92** C1
Allstate Arena *Ill., U.S.A.* 42°2N 87°54W **95** A1
Allston *Mass., U.S.A.* 42°21N 71°7W **96** A2
Alluitsup Paa *Greenland* 60°30N 45°35W **162** E6
Alluviaq Fjord *Qué., Canada* 59°27N 65°10W **143** B4
Allyn *Wash., U.S.A.* 47°23N 122°50W **120** C3
Alma *N.B., Canada* 45°36N 64°57W **141** H5
Alma *Qué., Canada* 48°35N 71°40W **145** C11
Alma *Ark., U.S.A.* 35°29N 94°13W **106** C1
Alma *Colo., U.S.A.* 39°17N 106°4W **125** C4
Alma *Ga., U.S.A.* 31°33N 82°28W **113** E4
Alma *Kans., U.S.A.* 39°1N 96°17W **82** B7
Alma *Mich., U.S.A.* 43°23N 84°39W **79** F7
Alma *Mo., U.S.A.* 39°6N 93°33W **83** B3
Alma *N. Mex., U.S.A.* 33°23N 108°54W **131** D2
Alma *Nebr., U.S.A.* 40°6N 99°22W **80** D6
Alma *Wis., U.S.A.* 44°20N 91°55W **78** D21
Alma Center *Wis., U.S.A.* 44°26N 90°55W **78** D3
Alma Hill *N.Y., U.S.A.* 42°3N 78°0W **88** C3
Almagre, L. *Tamaulipas, Mexico* 23°48N 97°48W **171** G7
Almanor, L. *Calif., U.S.A.* 40°14N 121°9W **126** C5
Almena *Kans., U.S.A.* 39°54N 99°43W **82** B4
Almena *Wis., U.S.A.* 45°25N 92°2W **78** C1
Almeria *Nebr., U.S.A.* 41°50N 99°31W **80** C6
Almira *Wash., U.S.A.* 47°43N 118°56W **120** C7
Almirante *Panama* 9°10N 82°30W **182** E3
Almo *Ky., U.S.A.* 36°42N 88°16W **104** D4
Almoloya *Hidalgo, Mexico* 19°44N 98°24W **175** C9
Almond *Wis., U.S.A.* 44°16N 89°25W **78** D4
Almont *Colo., U.S.A.* 38°40N 106°51W **125** D4
Almont *Mich., U.S.A.* 42°55N 83°3W **79** G8
Almont *N. Dak., U.S.A.* 46°44N 101°30W **76** D4
Almonte *Ont., Canada* 45°14N 76°12W **144** F6
Almy *Wyo., U.S.A.* 41°19N 111°0W **124** D2
Almyra *Ark., U.S.A.* 34°24N 91°25W **106** D4
Aloha *Oreg., U.S.A.* 45°29N 122°52W **121** B3
Alorton *Ill., U.S.A.* 38°35N 90°7W **94** B3
Alpaugh *Calif., U.S.A.* 35°53N 119°29W **127** H7
Alpena *Ark., U.S.A.* 36°18N 93°18W **106** B2
Alpena *Mich., U.S.A.* 45°4N 83°27W **79** D8
Alpena *S. Dak., U.S.A.* 44°11N 98°22W **76** F7
Alpena County ☆ *Mich., U.S.A.* 45°0N 83°40W **79** D8
Alpha *Ill., U.S.A.* 41°12N 90°23W **84** B3
Alpha *Mich., U.S.A.* 46°3N 88°23W **79** C3
Alpha *N.J., U.S.A.* 40°40N 75°9W **92** B1
Alpharetta *Ga., U.S.A.* 34°5N 84°18W **113** B2
Alpine *Ariz., U.S.A.* 33°51N 109°9W **130** D6
Alpine *Ark., U.S.A.* 34°14N 93°23W **106** D2
Alpine *Calif., U.S.A.* 32°50N 116°46W **127** L10
Alpine *N.J., U.S.A.* 40°57N 73°57W **97** B4
Alpine *Tenn., U.S.A.* 36°24N 85°13W **105** D7
Alpine *Tex., U.S.A.* 30°22N 103°40W **108** G4
Alpine *Utah, U.S.A.* 40°27N 111°46W **134** D3
Alpine *Wyo., U.S.A.* 43°11N 111°3W **124** C1
Alpine County ☆ *Calif., U.S.A.* 38°40N 119°50W **126** E7
Alpoyeca *Guerrero, Mexico* 17°40N 98°31W **175** E9
Alsask *Sask., Canada* 51°21N 109°59W **150** D2
Alsea → *Oreg., U.S.A.* 44°26N 124°5W **121** C1

Alsek → *Alaska, U.S.A.* 59°10N 138°12W **157** E5
Alsen *N. Dak., U.S.A.* 48°38N 98°42W **76** B7
Alsey *Ill., U.S.A.* 39°34N 90°26W **84** D3
Alsip *Ill., U.S.A.* 41°40N 87°44W **95** C2
Alston *N.H., U.S.A.* 43°9N 72°22W **89** C2
Alta *Iowa, U.S.A.* 42°40N 95°18W **81** C3
Alta *Utah, U.S.A.* 40°35N 111°38W **134** C4
Alta Vista *Ont., Canada* 45°23N 75°39W **160** B2
Alta Vista *Iowa, U.S.A.* 43°12N 92°25W **81** B6
Alta Vista *Kans., U.S.A.* 38°52N 96°29W **82** C7
Altadena *Calif., U.S.A.* 34°11N 118°8W **133** A4
Altair *Tex., U.S.A.* 29°34N 96°27W **109** H11
Altamaha → *Ga., U.S.A.* 31°20N 81°20W **113** E5
Altamaha Sound *Ga., U.S.A.* 31°19N 81°17W **113** E5
Altamira *Tamaulipas, Mexico* 22°24N 97°55W **171** H7
Altamirano *Chiapas, Mexico* 16°53N 92°9W **178** C4
Altamont *Ill., U.S.A.* 39°4N 88°45W **84** D5
Altamont *Kans., U.S.A.* 37°12N 95°18W **82** D8
Altamont *Mo., U.S.A.* 39°53N 94°5W **83** B2
Altamont *Oreg., U.S.A.* 42°12N 121°44W **121** E4
Altamont *S. Dak., U.S.A.* 44°50N 96°42W **76** F9
Altamont *Tenn., U.S.A.* 35°26N 85°44W **105** E7
Altamont *Utah, U.S.A.* 40°22N 110°17W **129** C5
Altamura *Ill., U.S.A.* 25°0N 108°10W **172** B2
Altar *Sonora, Mexico* 30°43N 111°44W **168** C4
Altar → *Sonora, Mexico* 30°39N 111°53W **168** C4
Altar, Gran Desierto de *Sonora, Mexico* 31°50N 114°10W **168** B1
Altario *Alta., Canada* 51°55N 110°9W **153** G10
Altata *Sinaloa, Mexico* 24°40N 107°55W **172** C3
Altavista *Va., U.S.A.* 37°6N 79°17W **102** D5
Altepexi *Puebla, Mexico* 18°24N 97°17W **177** F3
Altha *Fla., U.S.A.* 30°34N 85°8W **114** A4
Altheimer *Ark., U.S.A.* 34°19N 91°51W **106** D4
Alto *Ga., U.S.A.* 34°28N 83°35W **113** B3
Alto *La., U.S.A.* 32°22N 91°52W **110** B4
Alto *N. Mex., U.S.A.* 33°23N 105°41W **131** D5
Alto *Tex., U.S.A.* 31°39N 95°4W **109** F12
Alto Amatitlán *Tabasco, Mexico* 17°54N 91°47W **178** B5
Alto Cuchumatanes = Cuchumatanes, Sierra de los *Guatemala* 15°35N 91°25W **182** C1
Alto de Atizapan de Zaragoza *México, Mexico* 19°36N 99°18W **181** A2
Alto Lucero *Veracruz, Mexico* 19°37N 96°43W **176** E4
Alto Pass *Ill., U.S.A.* 37°34N 89°19W **84** F4
Alton *Ont., Canada* 43°54N 80°5W **146** D6
Alton *Ill., U.S.A.* 38°53N 90°11W **84** E3
Alton *Iowa, U.S.A.* 42°59N 96°1W **81** C2
Alton *Kans., U.S.A.* 39°28N 98°57W **82** B5
Alton *Mo., U.S.A.* 36°42N 91°24W **83** E5
Alton *N.H., U.S.A.* 43°27N 71°13W **89** C3
Alton *Utah, U.S.A.* 37°26N 112°29W **129** F3
Alton Bay *N.H., U.S.A.* 43°27N 71°13W **89** C3
Altona *Man., Canada* 49°6N 97°33W **151** F14
Altona *N.Y., U.S.A.* 44°53N 73°39W **88** A7
Altoona *Ala., U.S.A.* 34°2N 86°20W **112** C4
Altoona *Iowa, U.S.A.* 41°39N 93°28W **81** D5
Altoona *Kans., U.S.A.* 37°32N 95°40W **82** D8
Altoona *Pa., U.S.A.* 40°31N 78°24W **87** D4
Altoona *Wis., U.S.A.* 44°48N 91°26W **78** D2
Alto Amatitlán ... *Tex., U.S.A.* 19°46N 97°14W **176** E3
Altus *Okla., U.S.A.* 34°38N 99°20W **107** D4
Altus, L. *Okla., U.S.A.* 34°53N 99°18W **107** D4
Altus *Ark., U.S.A.* 35°26N 93°46W **106** C2
Alum Bridge *W. Va., U.S.A.* 39°2N 80°40W **102** B4
Alum Creek L. *Ohio, U.S.A.* 40°11N 82°57W **86** C4
Alva *Fla., U.S.A.* 26°43N 81°37W **114** E7
Alva *Ky., U.S.A.* 36°44N 83°25W **105** D9
Alva *Okla., U.S.A.* 36°48N 98°40W **107** B5
Alvarado *Veracruz, Mexico* 18°46N 95°46W **177** F5
Alvarado *Minn., U.S.A.* 48°10N 96°59W **77** B2
Alvarado *Tex., U.S.A.* 32°24N 97°13W **109** E10
Alvaro → *La., U.S.A.* 18°45N 95°50W **177** F5
Alvaro Obregón *Chihuahua, Mexico* 28°45N 106°55W **169** D9
Alvaro Obregón *Distrito Federal, Mexico* 19°22N 99°13W **181** B2
Alvaro Obregón *Michoacán, Mexico* 19°50N 101°5W **175** C6
Alvaro Obregón *Oaxaca, Mexico* 16°18N 95°44W **177** H6
Alvaro Obregón *Quintana Roo, Mexico* 18°16N 88°41W **179** D5
Alvaro Obregón *San Luis Potosí, Mexico* 21°51N 98°56W **171** J6
Alvaro Obregón, Presa *Sonora, Mexico* 27°52N 109°52W **168** F6
Alvaton *Ky., U.S.A.* 36°53N 86°21W **104** D6
Alvena *Sask., Canada* 52°31N 106°1W **150** D5
Alvin *Tex., U.S.A.* 29°26N 95°15W **109** H12
Alvinston *Ont., Canada* 42°49N 81°52W **146** E5
Alvo *Nebr., U.S.A.* 40°52N 96°23W **80** D9
Alvord *Tex., U.S.A.* 33°22N 97°42W **109** D10
Alvord Desert *Oreg., U.S.A.* 42°23N 118°25W **121** E7
Alvord L. *Oreg., U.S.A.* 42°23N 118°35W **121** E7
Alzada *Colima, Mexico* 19°14N 103°32W **174** C4
Alzada *Mont., U.S.A.* 45°2N 104°25W **123** E13
Amacueca *Jalisco, Mexico* 20°1N 103°37W **174** B4
Amaculi *Durango, Mexico* 24°38N 106°37W **172** C4
Amacuzac → *Guerrero, Mexico* 17°53N 99°12W **175** E8
Amadjuak L. *Nunavut, Canada* 65°0N 71°8W **159** E11
Amador County ☆ *Calif., U.S.A.* 38°25N 120°45W **126** E6
Amagansett *N.Y., U.S.A.* 40°59N 72°9W **91** D2
Amana *Iowa, U.S.A.* 41°48N 91°52W **81** D7
Amana Colonies *Iowa, U.S.A.* 41°48N 91°56W **81** D7
Amanda *Ohio, U.S.A.* 39°39N 82°45W **86** D4
Amarante *Man., Canada* 50°36N 98°43W **151** E13
Amargosa → *Calif., U.S.A.* 36°14N 116°51W **127** G10
Amargosa Desert *U.S.A.* 36°40N 116°30W **128** F4
Amargosa Range *Calif., U.S.A.* 36°20N 116°45W **127** G10
Amargosa Valley *Nev., U.S.A.* 36°39N 116°24W **128** F4
Amarillo *Tex., U.S.A.* 35°13N 101°50W **108** B6
Amasa *Mich., U.S.A.* 46°14N 88°27W **79** C3
Amatán *Chiapas, Mexico* 17°21N 92°45W **178** B4
Amatenango de la Frontera *Chiapas, Mexico* 15°26N 92°7W **178** D2
Amatenango del Valle *Chiapas, Mexico* 16°31N 92°27W **178** C4
Amatepec *México, Mexico* 18°39N 100°9W **175** D7
Amatignak I. *Alaska, U.S.A.* 51°16N 179°6W **135** L3
Amatitán *Jalisco, Mexico* 20°50N 103°43W **174** B4
Amatitlán *Guatemala* 14°29N 90°38W **182** C1
Amatlán de Cañas *Nayarit, Mexico* 20°52N 104°22W **172** D6
Amazonia *Mo., U.S.A.* 39°53N 94°54W **83** B2
Amazonia *Mo., U.S.A.* 35°10N 90°53W **106** C5
Amberg *Wis., U.S.A.* 45°30N 88°0W **78** C5
Ambergris Cay *Belize* 18°0N 87°55W **182** C2
Ambler *Alaska, U.S.A.* 67°5N 157°52W **135** C8

Ambler *Pa., U.S.A.* 40°9N 75°13W **92** B1
Ambleside *B.C., Canada* 49°19N 123°9W **161** B2
Ambleside Park *B.C., Canada* 49°19N 123°9W **161** B2
Amboy *Calif., U.S.A.* 34°33N 115°45W **127** J11
Amboy *Ill., U.S.A.* 41°44N 89°20W **84** B4
Amboy *Minn., U.S.A.* 43°53N 94°10W **77** G4
Ambridge *Pa., U.S.A.* 40°36N 80°14W **87** D2
Ambrose *Ga., U.S.A.* 31°36N 83°1W **113** E3
Ambrose *N. Dak., U.S.A.* 48°57N 103°29W **76** B2
Ambrosia Lake *N. Mex., U.S.A.* 35°26N 107°54W **131** B3
Amchitka I. *Alaska, U.S.A.* 51°32N 179°0E **135** L2
Amealco *Querétaro, Mexico* 20°11N 100°9W **175** B7
Ameca *Jalisco, Mexico* 20°33N 104°2W **174** B3
Ameca → *Mexico* 20°41N 105°18W **174** B2
Ameca la Vieja *Zacatecas, Mexico* 22°56N 104°0W **173** F7
Amecameca de Juárez *México, Mexico* 19°8N 98°46W **175** C9
Amelia *La., U.S.A.* 29°40N 91°6W **110** E4
Amelia *Nebr., U.S.A.* 42°14N 98°55W **80** B7
Amelia City *Fla., U.S.A.* 30°35N 81°28W **114** A7
Amelia County ☆ *Va., U.S.A.* 37°21N 77°59W **102** D7
Amelia Court House *Va., U.S.A.* 37°21N 77°59W **102** D7
Amelia Earhart Park *Fla., U.S.A.* 25°53N 80°16W **115** C1
Amelia I. *Fla., U.S.A.* 30°40N 81°25W **114** A7
Amenia *N.Y., U.S.A.* 41°51N 73°33W **91** C1
American Corners *Md., U.S.A.* 38°47N 75°51W **93** B5
American Falls *Idaho, U.S.A.* 42°47N 112°51W **122** G6
American Falls Dam *Idaho, U.S.A.* 42°47N 112°52W **122** G6
American Falls Res. *Idaho, U.S.A.* 42°47N 112°52W **122** G6
American Fork *Utah, U.S.A.* 40°23N 111°48W **129** C4
American Samoa ☐ *Pac. Oc.* 14°20S 170°40W **184** d
American University *D.C., U.S.A.* 38°56N 77°5W **99** B3
Americans, Barra los *Tamaulipas, Mexico* 24°48N 97°37W **171** F7
Americus *Ga., U.S.A.* 32°4N 84°14W **113** D2
Americus *Kans., U.S.A.* 38°30N 96°16W **82** C7
Americus *Mo., U.S.A.* 38°47N 91°34W **83** C5
Amery *Wis., U.S.A.* 45°19N 92°22W **78** C1
Ames *Iowa, U.S.A.* 42°2N 93°37W **81** C5
Ames *Okla., U.S.A.* 36°15N 98°11W **107** B5
Ames *Tex., U.S.A.* 30°3N 94°45W **109** G13
Amesbury *Mass., U.S.A.* 42°51N 70°56W **96** A4
Amesville *Ohio, U.S.A.* 39°24N 81°57W **86** D5
Amet Sound *N.S., Canada* 45°47N 63°10W **141** H6
Amherst *N.S., Canada* 45°48N 64°8W **141** H5
Amherst *Colo., U.S.A.* 40°41N 102°10W **125** B8
Amherst *Maine, U.S.A.* 44°50N 68°22W **90** D5
Amherst *Mass., U.S.A.* 42°23N 72°31W **91** B2
Amherst *N.H., U.S.A.* 42°52N 71°38W **89** D3
Amherst *N.Y., U.S.A.* 42°58N 78°48W **88** C2
Amherst *Nebr., U.S.A.* 40°46N 99°16W **80** D6
Amherst *Ohio, U.S.A.* 41°24N 82°14W **86** B4
Amherst *Tex., U.S.A.* 34°1N 102°25W **108** C5
Amherst *Va., U.S.A.* 37°35N 79°3W **102** D5
Amherst County ☆ *Va., U.S.A.* 37°35N 79°3W **102** D5
Amherst I. *Ont., Canada* 44°8N 76°43W **147** C10
Amherst Junction *Wis., U.S.A.* 44°28N 89°19W **78** D4
Amherstburg *Ont., Canada* 42°6N 83°6W **146** E3
Amherstdale *W. Va., U.S.A.* 37°47N 81°49W **102** D3
Amidon *N. Dak., U.S.A.* 46°29N 103°19W **76** D2
Amisk *Alta., Canada* 52°33N 111°4W **153** F9
Amisk L. *Sask., Canada* 54°35N 102°15W **157** F12
Amistad *N. Mex., U.S.A.* 35°55N 103°9W **131** B7
Amistad, Presa de la *Coahuila, Mexico* 29°26N 101°3W **108** H6
Amistad Nat. Recr. Area △ *Tex., U.S.A.* 29°32N 101°12W **108** H6
Amite *La., U.S.A.* 30°44N 90°30W **110** D5
Amite → *La., U.S.A.* 30°18N 90°34W **110** D5
Amite County ☆ *Miss., U.S.A.* 31°10N 90°49W **111** E4
Amity *Ark., U.S.A.* 34°16N 93°28W **106** D2
Amity *Oreg., U.S.A.* 45°7N 123°12W **121** B2
Amlia I. *Alaska, U.S.A.* 52°4N 173°30W **135** K4
Ammassalik = Tasiilaq *Greenland* 65°40N 37°20W **162** D7
Ammon *Idaho, U.S.A.* 43°28N 111°58W **122** F7
Ammonoonoosuc → *N.H., U.S.A.* 44°10N 72°2W **89** B2
Amonate *Va., U.S.A.* 37°12N 81°38W **102** D3
Amoret *Mo., U.S.A.* 38°15N 94°35W **83** C2
Amorita *Okla., U.S.A.* 36°56N 98°18W **107** B5
Amory *Miss., U.S.A.* 33°59N 88°29W **111** C5
Amos *Qué., Canada* 48°35N 78°5W **144** C4
Amozoc *Puebla, Mexico* 19°1N 98°1W **177** E2
Ampliación San Germán *Tamaulipas, Mexico* 25°6N 98°3W **171** E6
Amqui *Qué., Canada* 48°28N 67°27W **140** C2
Amsden *Vt., U.S.A.* 43°25N 72°30W **89** C2
Amsterdam *N.Y., U.S.A.* 42°56N 74°11W **88** C6
Amsterdam *Ohio, U.S.A.* 40°29N 80°56W **86** C6
Amukta I. *Alaska, U.S.A.* 52°30N 171°16W **135** K5
Amukta Pass *Alaska, U.S.A.* 52°0N 171°0W **135** K5
Amund Ringnes I. *Nunavut, Canada* 78°20N 96°25W **158** B6
Amundsen Gulf *Canada* 71°0N 124°0W **156** B8
Amy *Ark., U.S.A.* 34°20N 92°20W **106** E3
Amyot *Ont., Canada* 48°29N 84°57W **149** D12
Anacapa I. *Calif., U.S.A.* 34°1N 119°26W **127** J7
Anacoco *La., U.S.A.* 31°15N 93°21W **110** C2
Anaconda *Mont., U.S.A.* 46°8N 112°57W **123** D5
Anaconda Ra. *Mont., U.S.A.* 45°30N 113°30W **123** E4
Anacortes *Wash., U.S.A.* 48°30N 122°37W **120** B3
Anacosta → *D.C., U.S.A.* 38°52N 77°1W **99** B4
Anacostia *D.C., U.S.A.* 38°51N 76°59W **99** B4
Anadarko *Okla., U.S.A.* 35°4N 98°15W **107** C5
Anaheim *Calif., U.S.A.* 33°50N 117°55W **127** K9
Anahim Lake *B.C., Canada* 52°28N 125°18W **154** C10
Anahola *Hawaiʻi, U.S.A.* 22°9N 159°19W **136** A2
Anáhuac *Chihuahua, Mexico* 28°28N 106°45W **169** E9
Anáhuac *Tamaulipas, Mexico* 25°50N 97°48W **170** E7
Anahuac *Tex., U.S.A.* 29°46N 94°41W **109** H13
Anahuac Nat. Wildlife Refuge △ *Tex., U.S.A.* 29°34N 94°32W **109** H13
ʻAnahulu → *Hawaiʻi, U.S.A.* 21°37N 158°6W **136** J13
Aniakchak Nat. Monument and Preserve △ *Alaska, U.S.A.* 56°50N 158°15W **135** H8
Anaktuvuk Pass *Alaska, U.S.A.* 68°8N 151°45W **135** B10
Analalik *Alaska, U.S.A.* 41°3N 75°13W **92** B1
Anamoose *N. Dak., U.S.A.* 47°53N 100°15W **76** C5
Anamosa *Iowa, U.S.A.* 42°7N 91°17W **81** C71
Anandale *La., U.S.A.* 31°16N 92°27W **110** C3
Anasazi *Chihuahua, Mexico* 28°3N 108°15W **169** E7
Añasco *Puerto Rico* 18°17N 67°8W **184** G15
Anatahan *N. Marianas* 16°21N 145°40E **184** a
Anatone *Wash., U.S.A.* 46°8N 117°8W **120** D8
Anceney *Mont., U.S.A.* 45°39N 111°21W **123** E6
Ancho *N. Mex., U.S.A.* 33°56N 105°45W **131** D5
Anchor *Ill., U.S.A.* 40°34N 88°32W **84** C5
Anchorage *Alaska, U.S.A.* 61°13N 149°54W **135** F10
Anchorage ☆ *Alaska, U.S.A.* 61°10N 149°15W **135** F10

Anchorage ✈ (ANC) Alaska, U.S.A. 61°10N 150°0W **135** F10
Ancón de Carros Chihuahua, Mexico 27°58N 105°15W **169** F10
Ancram N.Y., U.S.A. 42°3N 73°38W **91** B1
Andale Kans., U.S.A. 37°48N 97°38W **82** D6
Andalusia Ala., U.S.A. 31°18N 86°29W **112** E4
Andalusia Ill., U.S.A. 41°26N 90°43W **84** B3
Ande de Piedra, L. Tamaulipas, Mexico 25°0N 97°49W **171** F7
Andersen Air Force Base Guam 13°35N 144°55E **184** b
Anderson Ala., U.S.A. 34°55N 87°16W **112** B3
Anderson Alaska, U.S.A. 64°25N 149°15W **135** D10
Anderson Cal., U.S.A. 40°27N 122°18W **126** C4
Anderson Ind., U.S.A. 40°10N 85°41W **85** C5
Anderson Mo., U.S.A. 36°39N 94°27W **83** E2
Anderson S.C., U.S.A. 34°31N 82°39W **103** D3
Anderson Tex., U.S.A. 30°29N 95°59W **109** G12
Anderson → N.W.T., Canada 69°42N 129°0W **156** C7
Anderson County ☆ Kans., U.S.A. 38°15N 95°15W **82** C8
Anderson County ☆ Ky., U.S.A. 38°0N 85°0W **105** C8
Anderson County ☆ S.C., U.S.A. 34°30N 82°40W **103** D3
Anderson County ☆ Tenn., U.S.A. 36°6N 84°8W **105** D8
Anderson County ☆ Tex., U.S.A. 31°46N 95°38W **109** F12
Anderson L. B.C., Canada 50°37N 122°25W **155** E12
Anderson Park Georgia, U.S.A. 33°45N 84°27W **117** B2
Anderson Ranch Res. Idaho, U.S.A. 43°22N 115°27W **122** F3
Anderson Res. Calif., U.S.A. 37°10N 121°38W **126** F5
Andersonville Ga., U.S.A. 32°12N 84°9W **113** D2
Andersonville Nat. Historic Site △ Ga., U.S.A. 32°12N 84°11W **113** D2
Andes N.Y., U.S.A. 42°11N 74°47W **88** C6
Andes, L. S. Dak., U.S.A. 43°11N 98°27W **76** G7
Andover Conn., U.S.A. 41°44N 72°23W **91** C2
Andover Kans., U.S.A. 37°43N 97°7W **82** D6
Andover Maine, U.S.A. 44°38N 70°45W **90** D3
Andover Mass., U.S.A. 42°40N 71°8W **91** B3
Andover Minn., U.S.A. 45°17N 93°21W **77** E5
Andover N.H., U.S.A. 43°26N 71°49W **89** C3
Andover N.J., U.S.A. 40°59N 74°45W **92** B2
Andover N.Y., U.S.A. 42°10N 77°48W **88** C3
Andover Ohio, U.S.A. 41°36N 80°34W **86** B6
Andover S. Dak., U.S.A. 45°25N 97°54W **76** E8
Andreanof Is. Alaska, U.S.A. 51°30N 176°0W **135** L4
Andrée Land Greenland 73°40N 26°0W **162** C8
Andrew Alta., Canada 53°53N 112°21W **152** E8
Andrew County ☆ Mo., U.S.A. 40°0N 94°45W **83** B2
Andrew Johnson Nat. Historic Site △ Tenn., U.S.A. 36°10N 82°50W **105** D10
Andrews Ind., U.S.A. 40°52N 85°36W **85** C5
Andrews Md., U.S.A. 38°20N 76°10W **93** B4
Andrews N.C., U.S.A. 35°12N 83°49W **103** C2
Andrews S.C., U.S.A. 33°27N 79°34W **103** E6
Andrews Tex., U.S.A. 32°19N 102°33W **108** E5
Andrews County ☆ Tex., U.S.A. 32°19N 102°33W **108** E5
Andros I. Bahamas 24°30N 78°0W **182** B4
Andros Town Bahamas 24°43N 77°47W **182** B4
Androscoggin → Maine, U.S.A. 43°58N 69°52W **90** E4
Androscoggin County ☆ Maine, U.S.A. 44°5N 70°10W **90** D3
Anegada Br. Virgin Is. 18°45N 64°20W **184** G18
Anegada Passage W. Indies 18°15N 63°45W **183** C7
Anegam Ariz., U.S.A. 32°22N 112°2W **130** E3
Aneroid Sask., Canada 49°43N 107°18W **150** F4
Aneta N. Dak., U.S.A. 47°41N 97°59W **76** C8
Aneth Utah, U.S.A. 37°13N 109°11W **129** F6
Angamacutiro Michoacan, Mexico 20°8N 101°42W **174** B6
Angangueo Michoacan, Mexico 19°37N 100°18W **175** C7
Ange-Gardien Qué., Canada 45°21N 72°56W **89** A2
Angel Albino Corzo Chiapas, Mexico 15°55N 92°43W **178** D3
Ángel de la Guarda, I. Baja Calif., Mexico 29°20N 113°25W **166** D5
Angel Fire N. Mex., U.S.A. 36°24N 105°17W **131** A5
Angel I. Calif., U.S.A. 37°52N 122°25W **132** A2
Angel Island State Park △ Calif., U.S.A. 37°52N 122°25W **132** A2
Ángel R. Cabada Veracruz, Mexico 18°36N 95°26W **177** F5
Angeles Nat. Forest Calif., U.S.A. 34°15N 118°0W **127** J9
Angelina → Tex., U.S.A. 30°54N 94°12W **109** G13
Angelina County ☆ Tex., U.S.A. 31°21N 94°44W **109** F13
Angelina Nat. Forest Tex., U.S.A. 31°7N 94°15W **109** F13
Angels Camp Calif., U.S.A. 38°4N 120°32W **126** E6
Angelus Kans., U.S.A. 39°11N 100°41W **82** B3
Angie La., U.S.A. 30°58N 89°49W **110** D6
Angier N.C., U.S.A. 35°31N 78°44W **103** C7
Angikuni L. Nunavut, Canada 62°12N 99°59W **159** E6
Angle Inlet Minn., U.S.A. 49°21N 95°4W **77** A3
Angleton Tex., U.S.A. 29°10N 95°26W **109** H12
Angliers Qué., Canada 47°33N 79°14W **144** D3
Angmagssalik = Tasiilaq Greenland 65°40N 37°20W **162** D7
Angola Del., U.S.A. 38°40N 75°10W **93** B5
Angola Ind., U.S.A. 41°38N 85°0W **85** B6
Angola N.Y., U.S.A. 42°38N 79°2W **88** C1
Angoon Alaska, U.S.A. 57°30N 134°35W **135** H14
Angora Nebr., U.S.A. 41°51N 103°8W **80** C2
Angostura Sinaloa, Mexico 25°22N 108°11W **172** B2
Angostura, Presa de la Chiapas, Mexico 16°10N 92°35W **178** C4
Angostura, Presa de la Sonora, Mexico 30°30N 109°22W **168** C6
Angostura Res. S. Dak., U.S.A. 43°21N 103°26W **76** G2
Angrignon, Parc Qué., Canada 45°25N 73°36W **160** B3
Anguilla Del., U.S.A. 38°40N 75°10W **111** D3
Anguilla ☑ W. Indies 18°14N 63°5W **183** C7
Anguille, C. Nfld. & L., Canada 47°55N 59°24W **142** E1
Anguille Mts. Nfld. & L., Canada 48°0N 59°11W **142** E1
Angus Ont., Canada 44°19N 79°53W **146** C7
Angusville Man., Canada 50°44N 101°1W **151** E10
Angwin Calif., U.S.A. 38°34N 122°26W **126** E4
Aniak Alaska, U.S.A. 61°35N 159°32W **135** F8
Animas N. Mex., U.S.A. 31°57N 108°48W **131** F2
Animas → N. Mex., U.S.A. 36°43N 108°13W **131** A2
Animas Mts. N. Mex., U.S.A. 31°33N 108°47W **131** F2
Animas Peak N. Mex., U.S.A. 31°35N 108°47W **131** F2
Anita Iowa, U.S.A. 41°27N 94°46W **81** D4
Anjou Qué., Canada 45°36N 73°33W **160** A3
Ankeny Iowa, U.S.A. 41°44N 93°36W **81** D5
Anmoore W. Va., U.S.A. 39°16N 80°18W **102** B4
Ann, C. Mass., U.S.A. 42°38N 70°35W **91** B4
Ann Arbor Mich., U.S.A. 42°17N 83°45W **79** G8
Anna Ill., U.S.A. 37°28N 89°15W **84** F12
Anna Ohio, U.S.A. 40°24N 84°11W **86** C2
Anna Tex., U.S.A. 33°21N 96°33W **109** D11
Anna, L. Va., U.S.A. 38°4N 77°45W **102** C7
Annabella Utah, U.S.A. 38°43N 112°4W **129** E3
Annada Mo., U.S.A. 39°16N 90°50W **83** B6
Annaheim Sask., Canada 52°19N 104°43W **150** C7
Annalee Heights Va., U.S.A. 38°51N 77°10W **98** B2
Annandale Minn., U.S.A. 45°16N 94°8W **77** E4
Annandale Va., U.S.A. 38°50N 77°11W **99** C2

Annapolis Md., U.S.A. 38°59N 76°30W **93** B4
Annapolis Mo., U.S.A. 37°22N 90°42W **83** D6
Annapolis Royal N.S., Canada 44°44N 65°32W **141** J4
Annawan Ill., U.S.A. 41°24N 89°55W **84** B4
Anne Arundel County ☆ Md., U.S.A. 39°0N 76°40W **93** A4
Annette Island Indian Reservation Alaska, U.S.A. 55°9N 131°28W **135** J15
Annieopsquotch Mts. Nfld. & L., Canada 48°20N 57°30W **142** D3
Anniston Ala., U.S.A. 33°39N 85°50W **112** C5
Anniston Mo., U.S.A. 36°50N 89°20W **83** E8
Annona Tex., U.S.A. 33°35N 94°55W **109** D13
Annotto B. Jamaica 18°17N 76°45W **182** C4
Annville Ky., U.S.A. 37°19N 83°58W **105** C9
Annville Pa., U.S.A. 40°20N 76°31W **87** D6
Año Nuevo, Pt. Calif., U.S.A. 37°7N 122°19W **126** F4
Anoka Minn., U.S.A. 45°12N 93°23W **77** E5
Anoka Nebr., U.S.A. 42°57N 98°50W **80** B7
Anoka County ☆ Minn., U.S.A. 45°15N 93°15W **77** E5
Anola Man., Canada 49°53N 96°38W **151** F15
Anselmo Nebr., U.S.A. 41°37N 99°52W **80** C6
Ansley La., U.S.A. 32°24N 92°42W **110** B3
Ansley Nebr., U.S.A. 41°18N 99°23W **80** C6
Anson Tex., U.S.A. 32°45N 99°54W **108** E6
Anson County ☆ N.C., U.S.A. 35°0N 80°0W **103** D5
Ansonia Conn., U.S.A. 41°21N 73°5W **91** C1
Ansonia Ohio, U.S.A. 40°13N 84°38W **86** C2
Ansonville N.C., U.S.A. 35°6N 80°7W **103** C5
Ansted W. Va., U.S.A. 38°8N 81°6W **102** C3
Antelope Kans., U.S.A. 38°26N 96°59W **82** C7
Antelope Oreg., U.S.A. 44°55N 120°43W **121** C5
Antelope County ☆ Nebr., U.S.A. 42°15N 98°0W **80** B7
Antelope Hills Okla., U.S.A. 35°55N 99°50W **107** C4
Antelope Hills Wyo., U.S.A. 42°20N 108°25W **124** D4
Antelope I. Utah, U.S.A. 40°51N 112°10W **129** C3
Antelope Range Nev., U.S.A. 40°10N 114°30W **128** B6
Antelope Res. Oreg., U.S.A. 42°54N 117°14W **121** E8
Antero, Mt. Colo., U.S.A. 38°41N 106°15W **125** D4
Antero Res. Colo., U.S.A. 38°56N 105°55W **125** D5
Anthon Iowa, U.S.A. 42°23N 95°52W **81** C3
Anthony Fla., U.S.A. 29°18N 82°7W **114** B6
Anthony Kans., U.S.A. 37°9N 98°2W **82** D5
Anthony N. Mex., U.S.A. 32°0N 106°36W **131** E4
Anthoston Ky., U.S.A. 37°46N 87°32W **104** C5
Anticosti, Î. d' Qué., Canada 49°30N 63°0W **140** D6
Antigo Wis., U.S.A. 45°9N 89°9W **78** C4
Antigonish N.S., Canada 45°38N 61°58W **141** H8
Antigua Guatemala 14°34N 90°41W **182** D1
Antigua W. Indies 17°0N 61°50W **183** C7
Antigua & Barbuda ■ W. Indies 17°20N 61°48W **183** C7
Antiguo Morelos Tamaulipas, Mexico 22°33N 99°5W **171** H5
Antilla Cuba 20°40N 75°50W **182** B4
Antilles = West Indies Cent. Amer. 15°0N 65°0W **183** D7
Antimony Utah, U.S.A. 38°7N 112°0W **129** E4
Antioch Calif., U.S.A. 38°1N 121°48W **126** E5
Antioch Ill., U.S.A. 42°29N 88°6W **84** A5
Antioch Nebr., U.S.A. 42°4N 102°35W **80** B3
Antler Sask., Canada 49°34N 101°27W **151** F10
Antler N. Dak., U.S.A. 48°59N 101°17W **76** B4
Antler → Man., Canada 49°8N 101°0W **151** F10
Antlers Okla., U.S.A. 34°14N 95°37W **107** D8
Antoine Ark., U.S.A. 34°1N 93°25W **106** C2
Anton Colo., U.S.A. 39°45N 103°13W **125** C7
Anton Ky., U.S.A. 37°21N 87°24W **104** C5
Anton Tex., U.S.A. 33°49N 102°10W **108** D5
Anton Chico N. Mex., U.S.A. 35°12N 105°9W **131** B5
Antón Lizardo Veracruz, Mexico 19°3N 95°59W **177** F5
Antón Lizardo, Pta. Veracruz, Mexico 19°1N 95°58W **177** E5
Antonino Kans., U.S.A. 38°47N 99°24W **82** C4
Antonio Amaro Durango, Mexico 24°17N 104°2W **173** C6
Antonio B. Won Pat Int. ✈ (GUM) Guam 13°29N 144°48E **184** D3
Antonio Escobedo Jalisco, Mexico 20°46N 103°57W **174** B4
Antonito Colo., U.S.A. 37°5N 106°0W **125** E4
Antrim N.H., U.S.A. 43°2N 71°56W **89** C3
Antrim County ☆ Mich., U.S.A. 45°0N 85°10W **79** E6
Antwerp N.Y., U.S.A. 44°12N 75°37W **88** A5
Antwerp Ohio, U.S.A. 41°11N 84°45W **86** B2
Anvik Alaska, U.S.A. 62°39N 160°13W **135** E7
Anza Borrego Desert State Park △ Calif., U.S.A. 33°0N 116°26W **127** L10
Apache Okla., U.S.A. 34°54N 98°22W **107** D5
Apache County ☆ Ariz., U.S.A. 35°0N 109°30W **130** B6
Apache Creek N. Mex., U.S.A. 33°50N 108°37W **131** D2
Apache Junction Ariz., U.S.A. 33°25N 111°33W **130** D4
Apache L. Ariz., U.S.A. 33°36N 111°21W **130** D4
Apache Mts. Tex., U.S.A. 31°12N 104°35W **108** F3
Apache Sitgreaves Nat. Forest Ariz., U.S.A. 34°30N 110°30W **130** C5
Apalachee B. Fla., U.S.A. 30°0N 84°0W **114** B5
Apalachicola Fla., U.S.A. 29°43N 84°59W **114** B4
Apalachicola → Fla., U.S.A. 29°43N 84°58W **114** B4
Apalachicola B. Fla., U.S.A. 29°40N 85°0W **114** B4
Apalachicola Nat. Forest Fla., U.S.A. 30°10N 85°0W **114** A4
Apan Hidalgo, Mexico 19°43N 98°25W **175** C9
Apango Mártir Guerrero, Mexico 17°44N 99°20W **175** E8
Apaseo el Alto Guanajuato, Mexico 20°27N 100°37W **175** B7
Apaseo el Grande Guanajuato, Mexico 20°33N 100°41W **175** B7
Apatzingán Michoacan, Mexico 19°5N 102°21W **174** C5
Apaxco México, Mexico 19°59N 99°10W **175** C8
Apaxtla de Castrejón Guerrero, Mexico 18°8N 99°56W **175** D8
Apex N.C., U.S.A. 35°44N 78°51W **103** C7
Apishapa → Colo., U.S.A. 38°8N 103°57W **125** D7
Apizaco Tlaxcala, Mexico 19°25N 98°8W **175** C9
Apodaca Nuevo León, Mexico 25°46N 100°12W **180** B2
Apohaqui N.B., Canada 45°42N 65°36W **141** H4
Apollo Beach Tampa, U.S.A. 27°46N 82°24W **115** C4
Apopka Fla., U.S.A. 28°40N 81°31W **114** C7
Apopka, L. Fla., U.S.A. 28°37N 81°37W **115** A1
Apostle Is. Wis., U.S.A. 47°0N 90°40W **78** A3
Apostle Islands Nat. Lakeshore △ Wis., U.S.A. 46°55N 91°0W **78** B31
Apozol Zacatecas, Mexico 21°29N 103°6W **173** E7
Appalachia Va., U.S.A. 36°54N 82°47W **102** E2
Appalachian Nat. Scenic Trail △ U.S.A. 34°44N 83°59W **113** B3
Appanoose County ☆ Iowa, U.S.A. 40°45N 92°50W **81** E6
Apple → Ill., U.S.A. 42°11N 90°14W **84** A3
Apple → Wis., U.S.A. 45°9N 92°45W **78** C1
Apple Creek Ohio, U.S.A. 40°45N 81°51W **86** C5
Apple Creek → Ill., U.S.A. 39°22N 90°37W **84** D3
Apple Hill Ont., Canada 45°13N 74°46W **147** B12
Apple Valley Calif., U.S.A. 34°32N 117°14W **127** J9
Applegate Mich., U.S.A. 43°21N 82°38W **79** F9
Applegate Oreg., U.S.A. 42°16N 123°10W **121** E2

Appleton Minn., U.S.A. 45°12N 96°1W **77** E2
Appleton Wis., U.S.A. 44°16N 88°25W **78** D5
Appleton City Mo., U.S.A. 38°11N 94°2W **83** C2
Appling Ga., U.S.A. 33°33N 82°19W **113** C4
Appling County ☆ Ga., U.S.A. 31°45N 82°15W **113** E4
Appomattox Va., U.S.A. 37°21N 78°50W **102** D6
Appomattox → Va., U.S.A. 37°19N 77°17W **102** D7
Appomattox County ☆ Va., U.S.A. 37°21N 78°50W **102** D6
Apsley Ont., Canada 44°45N 78°6W **147** C8
Aquarius Mts. Ariz., U.S.A. 34°45N 113°20W **130** C2
Aquarius Plateau Utah, U.S.A. 38°0N 111°40W **129** F4
Aquasco Md., U.S.A. 38°35N 76°43W **93** B4
Aquila Michoacan, Mexico 18°36N 103°30W **174** D4
Aquiles Serdán Chiapas, Mexico 14°55N 92°30W **178** E4
Aquiles Serdán Chihuahua, Mexico 28°36N 105°53W **169** G10
Aquiles Serdán Jalisco, Mexico 20°17N 105°37W **174** B2
Aquiles Serdán Nuevo León, Mexico 26°53N 99°43W **170** D5
Aquin Haiti 18°16N 73°24W **183** C5
Ara L. Ont., Canada 50°33N 87°28W **149** B9
Arab Ala., U.S.A. 34°19N 86°30W **112** B4
Arabela N. Mex., U.S.A. 33°35N 105°10W **131** D5
Arabi Ga., U.S.A. 31°50N 83°44W **113** E3
Arabi La., U.S.A. 29°57N 90°0W **117** C3
Arago, C. Oreg., U.S.A. 43°20N 124°30W **121** D1
Aragon Ala., U.S.A. 34°2N 85°3W **113** B1
Aramberri Nuevo León, Mexico 24°6N 99°49W **171** F5
Arandas Jalisco, Mexico 20°42N 102°21W **174** B5
Aransas County ☆ Tex., U.S.A. 28°5N 96°28W **109** J11
Aransas Nat. Wildlife Refuge △ Tex., U.S.A. 28°14N 96°54W **109** J11
Aransas Pass Tex., U.S.A. 27°55N 97°9W **109** K10
Arapaho Okla., U.S.A. 35°34N 98°58W **107** C5
Arapaho Nat. Forest Colo., U.S.A. 39°30N 106°15W **125** C4
Arapahoe Nebr., U.S.A. 40°18N 99°54W **80** D6
Arapahoe Wyo., U.S.A. 42°58N 108°29W **124** D4
Arapahoe County ☆ Colo., U.S.A. 39°40N 104°15W **125** C6
Ararat Va., U.S.A. 36°36N 80°31W **102** E4
Aratichanguio Guerrero, Mexico 18°30N 101°21W **175** D6
Arbon Idaho, U.S.A. 42°27N 112°34W **122** G6
Arbor Vitae Ont., Canada 48°54N 94°18W **148** D2
Arborfield Sask., Canada 53°6N 103°39W **150** C8
Arborg Man., Canada 50°54N 97°13W **151** E14
Arbuckle Calif., U.S.A. 39°1N 122°3W **126** D4
Arbuckle L. Fla., U.S.A. 27°42N 81°24W **114** D7
Arbuckle Mts. Okla., U.S.A. 34°20N 97°10W **107** D6
Arbutus Md., U.S.A. 39°15N 76°42W **99** B1
Arc Dome Nev., U.S.A. 38°51N 117°22W **128** D3
Arcade Calif., U.S.A. 38°38N 121°24W **126** D5
Arcade N.Y., U.S.A. 42°32N 78°25W **88** C2
Arcadia N.S., Canada 43°50N 66°4W **141** K3
Arcadia Ariz., U.S.A. 33°29N 111°58W **134** C3
Arcadia Calif., U.S.A. 34°7N 118°1W **133** B4
Arcadia Fla., U.S.A. 27°13N 81°52W **114** D7
Arcadia Ind., U.S.A. 40°11N 86°1W **85** C4
Arcadia Iowa, U.S.A. 42°5N 95°3W **81** C3
Arcadia Kans., U.S.A. 37°38N 94°37W **82** D9
Arcadia La., U.S.A. 32°33N 92°55W **110** B3
Arcadia Mich., U.S.A. 44°30N 86°14W **79** E5
Arcadia Mo., U.S.A. 37°35N 90°37W **83** D6
Arcadia Nebr., U.S.A. 41°25N 99°8W **80** C6
Arcadia Okla., U.S.A. 35°40N 97°20W **107** C6
Arcadia Pa., U.S.A. 40°47N 78°51W **87** D4
Arcadia Wis., U.S.A. 44°15N 91°30W **78** D2
Arcadia Park Tex., U.S.A. 32°44N 96°54W **116** C3
Arcanum Ohio, U.S.A. 39°59N 84°33W **86** D2
Arcas, Cayos Campeche, Mexico 20°12N 91°58W **179** B2
Arcata Calif., U.S.A. 40°52N 124°5W **126** C2
Arcata B. Calif., U.S.A. 40°52N 124°5W **126** C2
Arcelia Guerrero, Mexico 18°17N 100°16W **175** D7
Archbald Pa., U.S.A. 41°30N 75°32W **92** A1
Archbold Ohio, U.S.A. 41°31N 84°18W **86** B2
Archdale N.C., U.S.A. 35°56N 79°56W **103** C6
Archer Fla., U.S.A. 29°32N 82°32W **114** B6
Archer Iowa, U.S.A. 43°7N 95°45W **81** B3
Archer Nebr., U.S.A. 41°10N 98°8W **80** C7
Archer City Tex., U.S.A. 33°36N 98°38W **109** D9
Archer County ☆ Tex., U.S.A. 33°35N 98°40W **109** D9
Archer Fd. Nunavut, Canada 81°25N 67°0W **158** A12
Archerwill Sask., Canada 52°26N 103°53W **150** C8
Arches Nat. Park △ Utah, U.S.A. 38°45N 109°25W **129** E6
Archibald La., U.S.A. 32°21N 91°47W **110** B4
Archie Mo., U.S.A. 38°29N 94°21W **83** C2
Archipel-de-Mingan, Réserve de Parc Nat. de l' △ Qué., Canada 50°14N 63°37W **140** C6
Archipiélago Los Roques, Parque Nac. △ Venezuela 11°50N 66°44W **183** D6
Archuleta County ☆ Colo., U.S.A. 37°10N 107°0W **125** E4
Arco Idaho, U.S.A. 43°38N 113°18W **122** F5
Arco Minn., U.S.A. 44°23N 96°11W **77** F2
Arcola Sask., Canada 49°40N 102°30W **151** F9
Arcola Ill., U.S.A. 39°41N 88°19W **84** D5
Arcola Miss., U.S.A. 33°16N 90°53W **111** C3
Arcola Mo., U.S.A. 37°33N 93°53W **83** D3
Arcola Va., U.S.A. 38°57N 77°32W **93** B2
Arctic Bay Nunavut, Canada 73°1N 85°7W **158** C8
Arctic Red = N.W.T., Canada 67°26N 133°44W **156** C6
Arctic Red River = Tsiigehtchic N.W.T., Canada 67°15N 134°0W **156** C6
Arctic Sd. Nunavut, Canada 67°32N 108°5W **158** C6
Arctic Village Alaska, U.S.A. 68°8N 145°32W **135** B11
Ardbeg Ont., Canada 45°38N 80°5W **146** B5
Arden Man., Canada 50°17N 99°16W **151** E12
Arden Ont., Canada 44°43N 76°56W **147** C10
Arden Calif., U.S.A. 38°36N 121°23W **126** D5
Arden Hills Minn., U.S.A. 45°3N 93°9W **94** A2
Ardenvoir Wash., U.S.A. 47°44N 120°22W **120** C5
Ardmore Ala., U.S.A. 34°59N 86°52W **112** B4
Ardmore Okla., U.S.A. 34°10N 97°8W **107** D6
Ardmore Pa., U.S.A. 40°2N 75°17W **98** A1
Ardmore S. Dak., U.S.A. 43°1N 103°40W **76** G2
Ardmore Tenn., U.S.A. 35°0N 86°51W **104** F6
Arecibo Puerto Rico 18°29N 66°43W **184** G16
Aredale Iowa, U.S.A. 42°50N 93°0W **81** C5
Arellano Campeche, Mexico 19°24N 90°29W **179** B5
Arena Wis., U.S.A. 43°10N 89°55W **78** E4
Arena, Pt. Calif., U.S.A. 38°57N 123°44W **126** D3
Arena, Pta. Baja Calif. S., Mexico 23°34N 109°27W **167** K6
Arena de Hidalgo Chiapas, Mexico 17°2N 91°35W **178** B5
Arenac County ☆ Mich., U.S.A. 44°0N 83°55W **79** E8
Arenal Honduras 15°21N 86°50W **182** C2

Arenas, Pta. Puerto Rico 18°7N 65°35W **184** G17
Arenzville Ill., U.S.A. 39°53N 90°22W **84** D3
Argenta = North Little Rock Ark., U.S.A. 34°45N 92°16W **106** D3
Argenta B.C., Canada 50°11N 116°56W **155** E13
Argenta Ill., U.S.A. 39°59N 88°49W **84** D5
Argentia Nfld. & L., Canada 47°18N 53°58W **142** E7
Argonia Kans., U.S.A. 37°16N 97°46W **82** D6
Argonne Wis., U.S.A. 45°40N 88°53W **78** C5
Argonne Forest Ill., U.S.A. 41°42N 87°53W **95** C1
Argos Ind., U.S.A. 41°14N 86°15W **85** B4
Arguello, Pt. Calif., U.S.A. 34°35N 120°39W **127** J6
Argus Range Calif., U.S.A. 36°10N 117°40W **127** G9
Argusville N. Dak., U.S.A. 47°3N 96°56W **76** C9
Argyle Man., Canada 50°11N 97°27W **151** E14
Argyle Minn., U.S.A. 48°20N 96°49W **77** B2
Argyle Wis., U.S.A. 42°42N 89°52W **78** F4
Arichat N.S., Canada 45°31N 61°1W **141** H8
Ariel Wash., U.S.A. 45°57N 122°34W **120** E3
Arikaree → U.S.A. 40°1N 101°56W **125** A8
Arima Trin. & Tob. 10°38N 61°17W **183** D7
Arimo Idaho, U.S.A. 42°34N 112°10W **122** G6
Ario de Rosales Michoacan, Mexico 19°12N 101°43W **174** C6
Arion Iowa, U.S.A. 41°57N 95°27W **81** D3
Arispe Iowa, U.S.A. 40°57N 94°13W **81** E4
Arista San Luis Potosí, Mexico 22°39N 100°50W **171** H4
Ariton Ala., U.S.A. 31°36N 85°43W **112** D5
Arivechi Sonora, Mexico 28°56N 109°11W **168** E6
Arizona □ U.S.A. 34°0N 112°0W **130** C4
Arizona City Ariz., U.S.A. 32°45N 111°40W **130** E4
Arizpe Sonora, Mexico 30°20N 110°10W **168** C5
Arkabutla L. Miss., U.S.A. 34°46N 90°8W **111** B3
Arkadelphia Ark., U.S.A. 34°7N 93°4W **106** D2
Arkansas □ U.S.A. 35°0N 92°30W **106** D3
Arkansas → Ark., U.S.A. 33°47N 91°4W **106** E4
Arkansas City Ark., U.S.A. 33°37N 91°12W **106** E4
Arkansas City Kans., U.S.A. 37°4N 97°2W **82** D6
Arkansas County ☆ Ark., U.S.A. 34°18N 91°20W **106** D4
Arkansas Junction N. Mex., U.S.A. 32°42N 103°21W **131** E7
Arkansas Post Nat. Memorial △ Ark., U.S.A. 34°1N 91°21W **106** D4
Arkoma Okla., U.S.A. 35°21N 94°26W **107** D9
Arkona Ont., Canada 43°4N 81°50W **146** D5
Arkport N.Y., U.S.A. 42°24N 77°42W **88** C3
Arlee Mont., U.S.A. 47°10N 114°5W **123** C3
Arley Ala., U.S.A. 34°4N 87°13W **112** B3
Arlington Ariz., U.S.A. 33°20N 112°46W **130** D3
Arlington Baltimore, U.S.A. 39°20N 76°41W **99** A1
Arlington Colo., U.S.A. 38°20N 103°21W **125** D7
Arlington Ga., U.S.A. 31°26N 84°44W **113** E2
Arlington Ill., U.S.A. 41°29N 89°15W **84** B4
Arlington Iowa, U.S.A. 42°45N 91°40W **81** C7
Arlington Kans., U.S.A. 37°54N 98°11W **82** D5
Arlington Ky., U.S.A. 36°47N 89°0W **104** E3
Arlington Mass., U.S.A. 42°24N 71°10W **96** A1
Arlington Minn., U.S.A. 44°36N 94°5W **77** F4
Arlington N.Y., U.S.A. 41°42N 73°54W **88** D7
Arlington Nebr., U.S.A. 41°27N 96°21W **80** C9
Arlington Ohio, U.S.A. 40°54N 83°39W **86** C3
Arlington Oreg., U.S.A. 45°43N 120°12W **121** B5
Arlington S. Dak., U.S.A. 44°22N 97°8W **76** F8
Arlington Tenn., U.S.A. 35°18N 89°40W **104** E3
Arlington Tex., U.S.A. 32°44N 97°6W **116** C3
Arlington Va., U.S.A. 38°53N 77°7W **99** B3
Arlington Vt., U.S.A. 43°5N 73°9W **89** C1
Arlington Wash., U.S.A. 48°12N 122°8W **120** B3
Arlington Wis., U.S.A. 43°20N 89°23W **78** E4
Arlington Wyo., U.S.A. 41°36N 106°12W **124** E6
Arlington, L. Tex., U.S.A. 32°43N 97°11W **116** B2
Arlington Heights Ill., U.S.A. 42°5N 87°59W **84** A6
Arlington Heights Mass., U.S.A. 42°25N 71°10W **96** A1
Arlington Municipal ✈ Tex., U.S.A. 32°39N 97°5W **116** B3
Arlington Nat. Cemetery △ U.S.A. 38°52N 77°4W **99** B3
Arma Kans., U.S.A. 37°33N 94°42W **82** D9
Armada Mich., U.S.A. 42°51N 82°53W **79** G9
Armadillo San Luis Potosí, Mexico 22°15N 100°39W **171** H4
Armagh Qué., Canada 46°41N 70°32W **145** C12
Armando Bermudez, Parque Nac. △ Dom. Rep. 19°3N 71°0W **183** C5
Armería Colima, Mexico 18°56N 103°58W **174** D4
Armería → Colima, Mexico 18°52N 103°59W **174** D4
Armijo N. Mex., U.S.A. 35°4N 106°39W **131** B4
Arminto Wyo., U.S.A. 43°10N 106°49W **124** C6
Armit L. Nunavut, Canada 64°10N 91°32W **159** E7
Armona Calif., U.S.A. 36°19N 119°42W **127** G7
Armour S. Dak., U.S.A. 43°19N 98°21W **76** G7
Armour Heights Ont., Canada 43°45N 79°25W **161** A2
Armstrong B.C., Canada 50°25N 119°10W **155** E15
Armstrong Ont., Canada 50°18N 89°4W **148** B7
Armstrong Iowa, U.S.A. 43°24N 94°29W **81** B4
Armstrong Mo., U.S.A. 39°16N 92°42W **83** B4
Armstrong Okla., U.S.A. 34°3N 96°21W **107** D7
Armstrong Tex., U.S.A. 26°56N 97°47W **108** L10
Armstrong County ☆ Pa., U.S.A. 40°45N 79°25W **87** D3
Armstrong County ☆ Tex., U.S.A. 35°0N 101°20W **108** C6
Arnaud → Qué., Canada 59°59N 69°46W **143** B4
Arnaudville La., U.S.A. 30°24N 91°56W **110** D4
Arnegard N. Dak., U.S.A. 47°49N 103°27W **76** C2
Arnett Okla., U.S.A. 36°8N 99°46W **107** B4
Arnold Calif., U.S.A. 38°15N 120°21W **126** E6
Arnold Md., U.S.A. 39°2N 76°30W **93** A4
Arnold Mich., U.S.A. 46°3N 87°30W **79** C4
Arnold Mo., U.S.A. 38°26N 90°23W **83** C6
Arnold Nebr., U.S.A. 41°26N 100°12W **80** C5
Arnold Arboretum Mass., U.S.A. 42°18N 71°8W **96** B2
Arnold Engineering Development Center Tenn., U.S.A. 35°21N 86°2W **104** E6
Arnolds Park Iowa, U.S.A. 43°22N 95°8W **81** B3
Arnprior Ont., Canada 45°26N 76°21W **147** B10
Arntfield Qué., Canada 48°12N 79°15W **144** C3
Arock Oreg., U.S.A. 42°55N 117°32W **121** E8
Aroma Park Ill., U.S.A. 41°5N 87°48W **84** B6
Aroostook → Maine, U.S.A. 46°48N 67°45W **90** C6
Aroostook County ☆ Maine, U.S.A. 46°39N 68°0W **90** B5
Aros → Sonora, Mexico 29°30N 109°18W **168** D6
Arp Tex., U.S.A. 32°14N 95°4W **109** E12
Arpin Wis., U.S.A. 44°32N 90°1W **78** D3
Arran Sask., Canada 51°53N 101°43W **151** D10
Arrey N. Mex., U.S.A. 32°38N 107°19W **131** E3
Arriaga Chiapas, Mexico 16°14N 93°54W **178** C3
Arriba Colo., U.S.A. 39°17N 103°17W **125** C7
Arrington Kans., U.S.A. 39°28N 95°32W **82** B8
Arrow Cr. → Mont., U.S.A. 47°43N 109°50W **123** C6

Arrow Park B.C., Canada 50°6N 117°57W 155 E17
Arrow Rock Mo., U.S.A. 39°4N 92°57W 83 B4
Arrow Wood L. N. Dak., U.S.A. 47°14N 98°50W 76 C7
Arrowhead B.C., Canada 50°40N 117°55W 155 E17
Arrowhead L. Tex., U.S.A. 33°45N 98°25W 109 D9
Arrowrock Res. Idaho, U.S.A. 43°36N 115°56W 122 F3
Arrowsmith Ill., U.S.A. 40°27N 88°38W 84 C5
Arrowwood Alta., Canada 50°44N 113°9W 153 H7
Arroyo del Cedro Veracruz, Mexico 17°35N 93°54W 177 G7
Arroyo del Macho → N. Mex., U.S.A. 33°49N 104°7W 131 D6
Arroyo el Sáuz Baja Calif., Mexico 32°11N 115°58W 166 A3
Arroyo Grande Calif., U.S.A. 35°7N 120°35W 127 H6
Arroyo Hondo N. Mex., U.S.A. 36°32N 105°40W 131 A5
Arroyo Seco Querétaro, Mexico 21°33N 99°42W 175 A8
Art Institute Ill., U.S.A. 41°52N 87°37W 95 B3
Artas S. Dak., U.S.A. 45°53N 99°49W 76 E8
Arteaga Coahuila, Mexico 25°28N 100°51W 170 E4
Arteaga Michoacan, Mexico 18°28N 102°25W 174 D5
Artesia Miss., U.S.A. 33°25N 88°39W 111 C5
Artesia N. Mex., U.S.A. 32°51N 104°24W 131 E6
Artesia L. Nev., U.S.A. 38°56N 119°22W 128 D1
Artesia Wells Tex., U.S.A. 28°17N 99°17W 109 J8
Artesian S. Dak., U.S.A. 44°1N 97°56W 76 F8
Arthur Ont., Canada 43°50N 80°32W 146 D6
Arthur Ill., U.S.A. 39°43N 88°28W 84 D5
Arthur N. Dak., U.S.A. 47°6N 97°13W 76 C8
Arthur Nebr., U.S.A. 41°35N 101°41W 80 C4
Arthur Nev., U.S.A. 40°48N 115°11W 128 B5
Arthur Tenn., U.S.A. 36°33N 83°40W 105 D9
Arthur, L. Pa., U.S.A. 40°58N 80°7W 87 D2
Arthur County ☆ Nebr., U.S.A. 41°30N 101°40W 80 C4
Arthur R. Marshall-Loxahatchee Nat. Wildlife Refuge ☆ Fla., U.S.A. 26°27N 80°14W 114 E8
Arthurette N.B., Canada 46°47N 67°29W 141 G2
Arthur's Town Bahamas 24°38N 75°42W 183 B4
Artillery L. N.W.T., Canada 63°9N 107°52W 157 D11
Artois Calif., U.S.A. 39°37N 122°12W 126 D4
Arts, Place des Montréal, Canada 160 b2
Aruba ☑ W. Indies 12°30N 70°0W 183 D6
Arundel Qué., Canada 45°58N 74°37W 144 F8
Arundel Village Baltimore, U.S.A. 39°13N 76°36W 99 B2
Arvada Colo., U.S.A. 39°48N 105°5W 134 B1
Arvada Wyo., U.S.A. 44°39N 106°8W 124 B6
Arvert L. Nfld. & L., Canada 52°18N 61°45W 140 A8
Arviat Nunavut, Canada 61°6N 93°59W 159 E7
Arvin Calif., U.S.A. 35°12N 118°50W 127 K8
Arvon, Mt. Mich., U.S.A. 46°45N 88°9W 79 C3
Asbury Iowa, U.S.A. 42°31N 90°45W 81 C8
Asbury Mo., U.S.A. 37°16N 94°36W 83 D2
Asbury Park N.J., U.S.A. 40°13N 74°1W 92 B2
Ascensión Chihuahua, Mexico 31°6N 107°59W 169 B8
Ascensión, B. de la Quintana Roo, Mexico 19°40N 87°30W 179 C6
Ascension Parish ☆ La., U.S.A. 30°14N 90°55W 110 D5
Ascutney Vt., U.S.A. 43°24N 72°25W 89 C2
Aserradero La Flor Durango, Mexico 23°32N 104°43W 173 D4
Ash Flat Ark., U.S.A. 36°13N 91°37W 106 B4
Ash Fork Ariz., U.S.A. 35°13N 112°29W 130 B3
Ash Grove Mo., U.S.A. 37°19N 93°35W 83 D3
Ash Meadows Nat. Wildlife Refuge ☆ Nev., U.S.A. 36°25N 116°19W 128 F4
Ash Springs Nev., U.S.A. 37°28N 115°12W 128 E5
Ashbridge's Bay Park Ont., Canada 43°40N 79°18W 161 B3
Ashburn Ga., U.S.A. 31°43N 83°39W 113 E3
Ashburn Ill., U.S.A. 41°45N 87°43W 95 C2
Ashburn Va., U.S.A. 39°3N 77°29W 93 A3
Ashburnham Mass., U.S.A. 42°38N 71°55W 91 B3
Ashby Minn., U.S.A. 46°6N 95°49W 77 D3
Ashby Nebr., U.S.A. 42°1N 101°56W 80 B4
Ashcroft B.C., Canada 50°40N 121°20W 155 E13
Ashdown Ark., U.S.A. 33°40N 94°8W 106 E1
Ashe County ☆ N.C., U.S.A. 36°25N 81°30W 103 B4
Asheboro N.C., U.S.A. 35°43N 79°49W 103 C6
Asher Okla., U.S.A. 34°59N 96°56W 107 D7
Ashern Man., Canada 51°11N 98°21W 151 D13
Asherton Tex., U.S.A. 28°27N 99°46W 109 J8
Asherville Kans., U.S.A. 39°24N 97°59W 82 B6
Asheville N.C., U.S.A. 35°36N 82°33W 103 C3
Ashfield Mass., U.S.A. 42°32N 72°48W 91 B2
Ashford Ala., U.S.A. 31°11N 85°14W 112 E5
Ashford Wash., U.S.A. 46°46N 122°2W 120 D3
Ashkum Ill., U.S.A. 40°53N 87°57W 84 C6
Ashland Ala., U.S.A. 33°16N 85°50W 112 C5
Ashland Ill., U.S.A. 39°53N 90°1W 84 D3
Ashland Kans., U.S.A. 37°11N 99°46W 82 D4
Ashland Ky., U.S.A. 38°28N 82°38W 105 B10
Ashland La., U.S.A. 32°9N 93°6W 110 B2
Ashland Maine, U.S.A. 46°38N 68°24W 90 B5
Ashland Mass., U.S.A. 42°16N 71°28W 91 B3
Ashland Miss., U.S.A. 34°50N 89°11W 111 B4
Ashland Mo., U.S.A. 38°47N 92°15W 83 C4
Ashland Mont., U.S.A. 45°36N 106°16W 123 E11
Ashland N.H., U.S.A. 43°42N 71°38W 89 C3
Ashland N.Y., U.S.A. 42°18N 74°20W 88 C6
Ashland Nebr., U.S.A. 41°3N 96°23W 80 C9
Ashland Ohio, U.S.A. 40°52N 82°19W 86 C4
Ashland Okla., U.S.A. 34°46N 96°4W 107 D7
Ashland Oreg., U.S.A. 42°12N 122°43W 121 E3
Ashland Va., U.S.A. 37°46N 77°29W 102 D7
Ashland Wis., U.S.A. 46°35N 90°53W 78 B3
Ashland County ☆ Ohio, U.S.A. 40°52N 82°19W 86 C4
Ashland County ☆ Wis., U.S.A. 46°35N 90°45W 78 B3
Ashley Ill., U.S.A. 38°20N 89°11W 84 E4
Ashley Ind., U.S.A. 41°32N 85°4W 85 B5
Ashley Mich., U.S.A. 43°11N 84°29W 79 F7
Ashley N. Dak., U.S.A. 46°2N 99°22W 76 D6
Ashley Ohio, U.S.A. 40°25N 82°57W 86 C4
Ashley County ☆ Ark., U.S.A. 33°14N 91°48W 106 E4
Ashley Cr. → Utah, U.S.A. 40°20N 109°17W 129 C6
Ashley Nat. Forest Utah, U.S.A. 40°55N 110°0W 129 C5
Ashmont Alta., Canada 54°7N 111°35W 152 D9
Ashmore Ill., U.S.A. 39°32N 88°1W 84 D5
Ashokan Res. N.Y., U.S.A. 41°56N 74°13W 88 D6
Ashtabula Ohio, U.S.A. 41°52N 80°47W 86 B6
Ashtabula, L. N. Dak., U.S.A. 47°2N 98°5W 76 C7
Ashtabula County ☆ Ohio, U.S.A. 41°40N 80°50W 86 B6
Ashton Idaho, U.S.A. 44°4N 111°27W 122 E7
Ashton Ill., U.S.A. 41°52N 89°13W 84 B4
Ashton Iowa, U.S.A. 43°19N 95°47W 81 B3
Ashton Nebr., U.S.A. 41°15N 98°48W 80 C7
Ashton R.I., U.S.A. 41°56N 71°26W 91 C3
Ashton S. Dak., U.S.A. 44°59N 98°31W 76 F7
Ashuanipi, L. Nfld. & L., Canada 52°45N 66°15W 143 C4

Ashuapmushuan, Réserve Faunique ☆ Qué., Canada 49°5N 73°32W 145 B9
Ashuelot → N.H., U.S.A. 43°0N 72°29W 89 D2
Ashville Ala., U.S.A. 33°50N 86°15W 112 C4
Ashville Fla., U.S.A. 30°37N 83°39W 114 A5
Ashville Pa., U.S.A. 40°34N 78°33W 87 D4
Ashwood Oreg., U.S.A. 44°44N 120°45W 121 C5
Asientos Aguascalientes, Mexico 22°14N 102°5W 173 E8
Askov Minn., U.S.A. 46°12N 92°47W 77 D6
Asotin Wash., U.S.A. 46°20N 117°3W 120 D8
Asotin County ☆ Wash., U.S.A. 46°20N 117°3W 120 D8
Aspen Colo., U.S.A. 39°11N 106°49W 125 C4
Aspen Grove B.C., Canada 49°57N 120°37W 155 F14
Aspen Hill Md., U.S.A. 39°5N 77°5W 93 A3
Aspen L. Oreg., U.S.A. 42°17N 122°0W 121 E3
Aspermont Tex., U.S.A. 33°8N 100°14W 108 D7
Aspinwall Pa., U.S.A. 40°29N 79°54W 98 B2
Asquith Sask., Canada 52°8N 107°13W 150 C4
Assaria Kans., U.S.A. 38°41N 97°36W 82 C6
Assateague I. Md., U.S.A. 38°15N 75°10W 93 B5
Assateague Island Nat. Seashore ☆ Md., U.S.A. 38°15N 75°10W 93 B5
Assawompset Pond Mass., U.S.A. 41°50N 70°55W 91 C4
Assigny, L. Nfld. & L., Canada 52°0N 65°20W 140 A4
Assiniboia Sask., Canada 49°40N 105°59W 150 F6
Assiniboine → Man., Canada 49°53N 97°8W 151 F14
Assinica, Réserve Faunique ☆ Qué., Canada 50°37N 75°14W 144 A7
Assinippi Mass., U.S.A. 42°10N 70°51W 91 B4
Assonet Mass., U.S.A. 41°48N 71°4W 91 C3
Assumption Ill., U.S.A. 39°31N 89°3W 84 D4
Assumption Parish ☆ La., U.S.A. 30°0N 91°0W 110 E4
Astatula Fla., U.S.A. 28°43N 81°44W 114 C7
Astoria Ill., U.S.A. 40°14N 90°21W 84 C3
Astoria N.Y., U.S.A. 40°46N 73°55W 97 B3
Astoria Oreg., U.S.A. 46°11N 123°50W 121 A2
Astoria S. Dak., U.S.A. 44°34N 96°33W 76 F9
Astorville Ont., Canada 46°11N 79°17W 146 A7
Asuncion N. Marianas 19°40N 145°24E 184 a
Asunción → Sonora, Mexico 30°31N 113°3W 168 C3
Asunción, B. Baja Calif. S., Mexico 27°6N 114°11W 167 F4
Asunción Nochixtlán Oaxaca, Mexico 17°28N 97°14W 177 D3
Asunción Puxmetacán Oaxaca, Mexico 17°15N 95°38W 177 G5
Atacosa → Tex., U.S.A. 29°16N 98°44W 109 H9
Atarjea Guanajuato, Mexico 21°23N 99°52W 175 A8
Atascadero Calif., U.S.A. 35°29N 120°40W 127 H6
Atascosa County ☆ Tex., U.S.A. 28°55N 98°33W 109 J9
Atasta, L. Campeche, Mexico 18°35N 92°7W 178 D1
Atchafalaya → La., U.S.A. 29°53N 91°23W 110 E4
Atchafalaya B. La., U.S.A. 29°25N 91°25W 110 E4
Atchison Kans., U.S.A. 39°34N 95°7W 82 B8
Atchison County ☆ Kans., U.S.A. 39°30N 95°15W 82 B8
Atchison County ☆ Mo., U.S.A. 40°25N 95°25W 83 A1
Atco N.J., U.S.A. 39°46N 74°53W 92 C2
Atemajac de Brizuela Jalisco, Mexico 20°11N 103°42W 174 B4
Atenango del Río Guerrero, Mexico 18°5N 99°6W 175 D8
Atenayuca Puebla, Mexico 18°34N 97°44W 177 F3
Atengo Jalisco, Mexico 20°14N 104°14W 174 B3
Atenguillo Jalisco, Mexico 20°25N 104°3W 174 B3
Atexcal Puebla, Mexico 18°25N 97°44W 177 F3
Athabasca Alta., Canada 54°45N 113°20W 152 D7
Athabasca → Alta., Canada 58°40N 110°50W 157 E10
Athabasca, L. Sask., Canada 59°15N 109°15W 157 E11
Athena Fla., U.S.A. 29°59N 83°30W 114 B5
Athena Oreg., U.S.A. 45°49N 118°30W 121 B7
Athens Ont., Canada 44°38N 75°57W 147 C11
Athens Ala., U.S.A. 34°48N 86°56W 112 B4
Athens Ga., U.S.A. 33°57N 83°23W 113 C3
Athens Ill., U.S.A. 39°58N 89°44W 84 D4
Athens La., U.S.A. 32°39N 93°1W 110 B2
Athens Mich., U.S.A. 42°5N 85°14W 79 G6
Athens N.Y., U.S.A. 42°16N 73°49W 88 C7
Athens Ohio, U.S.A. 39°20N 82°6W 86 D4
Athens Tenn., U.S.A. 35°27N 84°36W 105 E8
Athens Tex., U.S.A. 32°12N 95°51W 109 E12
Athens Wis., U.S.A. 45°2N 90°5W 78 D3
Athens County ☆ Ohio, U.S.A. 39°20N 82°6W 86 D4
Atherley Ont., Canada 44°37N 79°20W 146 C7
Athlone I. B.C., Canada 52°11N 128°24W 154 C6
Athol Idaho, U.S.A. 47°57N 116°42W 122 B2
Athol Mass., U.S.A. 42°36N 72°14W 91 B2
Athol S. Dak., U.S.A. 45°1N 98°36W 76 E7
Atholville N.B., Canada 47°59N 66°43W 141 F3
Aticonipi, L. Qué., Canada 51°52N 59°22W 140 B10
Atikaki Prov. Wilderness Park ☆ Man., Canada 51°30N 95°31W 151 D16
Atikokan Ont., Canada 48°45N 91°37W 148 D5
Atikonak → Nfld. & L., Canada 52°51N 65°16W 140 A4
Atikonak L. Nfld. & L., Canada 52°40N 64°32W 143 C5
Atil Sonora, Mexico 30°52N 111°34W 168 C4
Atitlán, Parque Nac. ☆ Cent. Amer. 14°38N 91°10W 182 D1
Atka Alaska, U.S.A. 52°12N 174°12W 135 K4
Atka I. Alaska, U.S.A. 52°7N 174°30W 135 K4
Atkins Ark., U.S.A. 35°14N 92°56W 106 C3
Atkins Va., U.S.A. 36°20N 81°25W 102 E3
Atkinson Ga., U.S.A. 31°13N 81°41W 113 E5
Atkinson Ill., U.S.A. 41°25N 90°1W 84 B3
Atkinson N.H., U.S.A. 42°50N 71°9W 89 D3
Atkinson Nebr., U.S.A. 42°32N 98°59W 80 B7
Atkinson Pt. N.W.T., Canada 69°57N 131°27W 156 C6
Atlacomulco México, Mexico 19°48N 99°53W 175 C8
Atlamajalcingo del Monte Guerrero, Mexico 17°19N 98°36W 175 E9
Atlanta Ga., U.S.A. 33°45N 84°23W 117 B2
Atlanta Idaho, U.S.A. 43°48N 115°8W 122 F3
Atlanta Ill., U.S.A. 40°16N 89°14W 84 C4
Atlanta Ind., U.S.A. 40°13N 86°2W 85 C6
Atlanta Kans., U.S.A. 37°26N 96°46W 82 D7
Atlanta La., U.S.A. 31°48N 92°45W 110 C3
Atlanta Mich., U.S.A. 45°0N 84°9W 79 E7
Atlanta Mo., U.S.A. 39°54N 92°29W 83 B4
Atlanta Nebr., U.S.A. 40°22N 99°28W 80 D6
Atlanta Tex., U.S.A. 33°7N 94°10W 109 D13
Atlanta Hartsfield Int. ✈ (ATL) Ga., U.S.A. 33°38N 84°26W 117 C2
Atlanta Zoo Georgia, U.S.A. 33°44N 84°22W 117 B2
Atlantic Iowa, U.S.A. 41°24N 95°1W 81 C3
Atlantic Va., U.S.A. 37°54N 75°30W 93 C5
Atlantic Beach Fla., U.S.A. 30°20N 81°24W 114 A7

Atlantic Beach N.C., U.S.A. 34°42N 76°44W 103 D9
Atlantic Beach N.Y., U.S.A. 40°35N 73°45W 97 C4
Atlantic City Wyo., U.S.A. 42°30N 108°45W 124 D4
Atlantic City N.J., U.S.A. 39°30N 74°40W 92 C2
Atlantic Highlands N.J., U.S.A. 40°25N 74°3W 92 B2
Atlantic Pk. Wyo., U.S.A. 42°37N 109°0W 124 D3
Atlapexco Hidalgo, Mexico 21°1N 98°20W 175 A9
Atlatlauca Tlaxcala, Mexico 19°25N 97°49W 177 C10
Atlixco Puebla, Mexico 18°54N 98°26W 177 F2
Atlixtac Guerrero, Mexico 17°34N 98°56W 175 E9
Atlzayanca Tlaxcala, Mexico 19°23N 97°23W 177 C10
Atmore Ala., U.S.A. 31°2N 87°29W 112 E3
Atoka Okla., U.S.A. 34°23N 96°8W 107 D7
Atoka Tenn., U.S.A. 35°26N 89°47W 104 E3
Atoka County ☆ Okla., U.S.A. 34°21N 96°15W 107 D7
Atoka Res. Okla., U.S.A. 34°27N 96°5W 107 D7
Atolinga Zacatecas, Mexico 21°44N 103°28W 173 F7
Atomic City Idaho, U.S.A. 43°27N 112°49W 122 F6
Atotonilco Hidalgo, Mexico 20°1N 99°14W 175 B8
Atotonilco Zacatecas, Mexico 24°15N 102°45W 173 C8
Atotonilco el Alto Jalisco, Mexico 20°33N 102°31W 174 B5
Atotonilco El Grande Hidalgo, Mexico 20°17N 98°40W 175 B9
Atoyac Jalisco, Mexico 19°58N 103°32W 174 C4
Atoyac → Puebla, Mexico 18°10N 98°31W 177 F2
Atoyac de Álvarez Guerrero, Mexico 17°12N 100°26W 175 E7
Atqasuk Alaska, U.S.A. 70°28N 157°24W 135 A8
Atqasuk → Alaska, U.S.A. 70°52N 155°55W 135 A9
Atsion N.J., U.S.A. 39°44N 74°44W 92 C2
Attala County ☆ Miss., U.S.A. 33°4N 89°35W 111 C4
Attalla Ala., U.S.A. 34°1N 86°6W 112 B4
Attapulgus Ga., U.S.A. 30°45N 84°29W 113 F2
Attawapiskat Ont., Canada 52°56N 82°24W 159 G9
Attawapiskat → Ont., Canada 52°57N 82°18W 159 G9
Attica Ind., U.S.A. 40°18N 87°15W 85 C3
Attica Kans., U.S.A. 37°15N 98°13W 82 D5
Attica N.Y., U.S.A. 42°52N 78°17W 88 C2
Attica Ohio, U.S.A. 41°4N 82°53W 86 B4
Attikamagen L. Nfld. & L., Canada 55°0N 66°30W 143 B4
Attleboro Mass., U.S.A. 41°57N 71°17W 91 C3
Attu Alaska, U.S.A. 52°56N 173°15E 135 K1
Attu I. Alaska, U.S.A. 52°55N 172°55E 135 K1
Attwater Prairie Chicken Nat. Wildlife Refuge ☆ Tex., U.S.A. 29°43N 96°20W 109 H11
Attwood → Ont., Canada 51°15N 88°30W 148 C6
Atwater Calif., U.S.A. 37°21N 120°37W 126 F6
Atwater Minn., U.S.A. 45°8N 94°47W 77 E4
Atwood Ont., Canada 43°40N 81°1W 146 D5
Atwood Ill., U.S.A. 39°48N 88°28W 84 D5
Atwood Kans., U.S.A. 39°48N 101°3W 82 B2
Atwood Okla., U.S.A. 34°57N 96°20W 107 D7
Atwood Tenn., U.S.A. 35°59N 88°41W 104 E4
Atwood L. Ohio, U.S.A. 40°33N 81°13W 86 C5
Atzala Puebla, Mexico 18°34N 98°33W 177 F2
Atzalán Veracruz, Mexico 19°46N 97°13W 176 E3
Au Gres Mich., U.S.A. 44°3N 83°42W 79 E8
Au Sable Mich., U.S.A. 44°25N 83°20W 79 E8
Au Sable → Mich., U.S.A. 44°25N 83°20W 79 E8
Au Sable Forks N.Y., U.S.A. 44°27N 73°41W 88 A7
Au Sable Pt. Mich., U.S.A. 46°40N 86°8W 79 C5
Au Sable Pt. Mich., U.S.A. 44°20N 83°20W 79 E8
Aua Amer. Samoa 14°17S 170°40W 184 e
Aubrey Cliffs Ariz., U.S.A. 35°45N 113°0W 130 B3
Aubry L. N.W.T., Canada 67°23N 126°30W 156 C7
Auburn Ala., U.S.A. 32°36N 85°29W 112 D5
Auburn Calif., U.S.A. 38°54N 121°4W 126 E5
Auburn Ga., U.S.A. 34°1N 83°50W 113 B3
Auburn Ill., U.S.A. 39°36N 89°45W 84 D4
Auburn Ind., U.S.A. 41°22N 85°4W 85 B5
Auburn Iowa, U.S.A. 42°15N 94°53W 81 C4
Auburn Kans., U.S.A. 38°54N 95°49W 82 C8
Auburn Ky., U.S.A. 36°52N 86°43W 104 D6
Auburn Maine, U.S.A. 44°6N 70°14W 90 D3
Auburn Mass., U.S.A. 42°12N 71°50W 91 B3
Auburn Mich., U.S.A. 43°36N 84°4W 79 F7
Auburn N.Y., U.S.A. 42°56N 76°34W 88 C4
Auburn Nebr., U.S.A. 40°23N 95°51W 80 D10
Auburn W. Va., U.S.A. 39°6N 80°51W 102 B4
Auburn Wash., U.S.A. 47°18N 122°14W 120 C3
Auburndale Fla., U.S.A. 28°4N 81°48W 114 C7
Auburndale Mass., U.S.A. 42°20N 71°14W 96 A1
Auburntown Tenn., U.S.A. 35°57N 86°5W 104 E6
Aucilla → Fla., U.S.A. 30°5N 83°59W 114 A5
Auden Ont., Canada 50°14N 87°53W 148 B9
Audrain County ☆ Mo., U.S.A. 39°10N 91°50W 83 B5
Audubon Iowa, U.S.A. 41°43N 94°56W 81 C4
Audubon Minn., U.S.A. 46°52N 95°59W 77 D3
Audubon Pa., U.S.A. 39°53N 79°9W 98 B2
Audubon County ☆ Iowa, U.S.A. 41°40N 94°50W 81 C4
Audubon L. N. Dak., U.S.A. 47°36N 101°10W 76 C4
Audubon Park Pa., U.S.A. 39°53N 79°59W 98 B2
Auglaize → Ohio, U.S.A. 41°17N 84°21W 86 B2
Auglaize County ☆ Ohio, U.S.A. 40°34N 84°12W 86 C2
Augusta Ark., U.S.A. 35°17N 91°22W 106 C4
Augusta Ga., U.S.A. 33°28N 81°58W 113 C5
Augusta Ill., U.S.A. 40°14N 90°57W 84 C3
Augusta Kans., U.S.A. 37°41N 96°59W 82 D7
Augusta Ky., U.S.A. 38°47N 84°0W 105 B8
Augusta Maine, U.S.A. 44°19N 69°47W 90 D4
Augusta Mo., U.S.A. 38°34N 90°53W 83 C6
Augusta Mont., U.S.A. 47°30N 112°24W 123 C5
Augusta W. Va., U.S.A. 39°18N 78°38W 93 A2
Augusta County ☆ Va., U.S.A. 38°9N 79°4W 102 C5
Augustine I. Alaska, U.S.A. 59°22N 153°26W 135 G10
Augustines, L. des Qué., Canada 47°37N 75°56W 144 D7
Auyuittuq = Grise Fiord Nunavut, Canada 76°25N 82°57W 158 B9
Aulavik Nat. Park ☆ N.W.T., Canada 73°42N 119°55W 156 B9
Aullville Mo., U.S.A. 39°1N 93°41W 83 C3
Aulneau Pen. Ont., Canada 49°23N 94°29W 148 C2
Ault Colo., U.S.A. 40°35N 104°44W 125 B6
Aumsville Oreg., U.S.A. 44°50N 122°52W 121 C3
Aunuu Amer. Samoa 14°20S 170°33W 184 e
Aupaluk Qué., Canada 59°18N 69°36W 143 B4
Aurelia Iowa, U.S.A. 42°43N 95°26W 81 C3
Aurelio Benassini, Presa Sinaloa, Mexico 24°9N 106°41W 172 C4
Aurora Colo., U.S.A. 39°43N 104°49W 134 B3
Aurora Ill., U.S.A. 41°45N 88°19W 84 B5
Aurora Ind., U.S.A. 39°4N 84°54W 85 D6

Aurora Iowa, U.S.A. 42°37N 91°44W 81 C7
Aurora Kans., U.S.A. 39°27N 97°32W 82 B6
Aurora Maine, U.S.A. 44°51N 68°20W 90 D5
Aurora Minn., U.S.A. 47°32N 92°14W 77 C6
Aurora Mo., U.S.A. 36°58N 93°43W 83 E3
Aurora N.C., U.S.A. 35°18N 76°47W 103 C9
Aurora Nebr., U.S.A. 40°52N 98°0W 80 D7
Aurora Ohio, U.S.A. 41°21N 81°20W 86 B5
Aurora W. Va., U.S.A. 39°19N 79°33W 93 A1
Aurora County ☆ S. Dak., U.S.A. 43°43N 98°29W 76 G7
Ausable → Ont., Canada 43°19N 81°46W 146 D5
Austin Ark., U.S.A. 35°0N 92°0W 106 D4
Austin Ind., U.S.A. 38°45N 85°49W 85 E5
Austin Minn., U.S.A. 43°40N 92°58W 77 G6
Austin Mont., U.S.A. 46°39N 112°15W 123 D5
Austin Nev., U.S.A. 39°30N 117°4W 128 C3
Austin Pa., U.S.A. 41°38N 78°6W 87 C4
Austin Tex., U.S.A. 30°17N 97°45W 109 G10
Austin Bergstrom Int. ✈ (AUS) Tex., U.S.A. 30°12N 97°41W 109 G10
Austin Chan. N.W.T., Canada 75°35N 103°25W 158 B5
Austin County ☆ Tex., U.S.A. 29°57N 96°15W 109 H11
Austintown Ohio, U.S.A. 41°6N 80°48W 86 B6
Austinville Va., U.S.A. 36°51N 80°55W 102 E4
Austwell Tex., U.S.A. 28°23N 96°51W 109 J11
Autauga County ☆ Ala., U.S.A. 32°26N 86°39W 112 D4
Autaugaville Ala., U.S.A. 32°26N 86°39W 112 D4
Auteuil Qué., Canada 45°38N 73°46W 160 A2
Auteuil, L. d' Qué., Canada 50°28N 66°47W 140 B6
Autlán de Navarro Jalisco, Mexico 19°46N 104°22W 174 C3
Auxvasse Mo., U.S.A. 39°1N 91°54W 83 B5
Auyuittuq Nat. Park ☆ Nunavut, Canada 67°30N 66°0W 158 D12
Ava Ill., U.S.A. 37°53N 89°30W 84 F4
Ava Mo., U.S.A. 36°57N 92°40W 83 E4
Avalon Calif., U.S.A. 33°21N 118°20W 127 K8
Avalon Miss., U.S.A. 33°39N 90°5W 111 C3
Avalon N.J., U.S.A. 39°6N 74°43W 92 C2
Avalon Pa., U.S.A. 40°30N 80°4W 98 A1
Avalon, L. N. Mex., U.S.A. 32°27N 104°15W 131 E6
Avalon Pen. Nfld. & L., Canada 47°30N 53°20W 142 E7
Avalon Wilderness Reserve ☆ Nfld. & L., Canada 47°3N 53°15W 142 E7
Avannaarsua ☐ Greenland 80°0N 55°0W 162 B5
Avant Okla., U.S.A. 36°29N 96°4W 107 B7
Avard Okla., U.S.A. 36°42N 98°47W 107 B6
Avawatz Mts. Calif., U.S.A. 35°40N 116°30W 127 H10
Avenal Calif., U.S.A. 36°0N 120°8W 127 H6
Avenel Md., U.S.A. 38°59N 76°59W 99 B4
Avenel N.J., U.S.A. 40°34N 74°17W 97 C1
Avenue Md., U.S.A. 38°16N 76°44W 93 B4
Avera Ga., U.S.A. 33°12N 82°32W 113 C4
Avery Idaho, U.S.A. 47°15N 115°49W 122 B3
Avery Tex., U.S.A. 33°33N 94°47W 109 D13
Avery County ☆ N.C., U.S.A. 36°5N 82°0W 103 B4
Avery Island La., U.S.A. 29°55N 91°54W 110 E4
Aves, I. de W. Indies 15°45N 63°55W 183 C7
Aves, Is. las Venezuela 12°0N 67°30W 183 D6
Aves Ridge W. Indies 14°0N 63°30W 183 D7
Avila y Urbina Tamaulipas, Mexico 23°41N 99°36W 171 G5
Avilla Ind., U.S.A. 41°22N 85°14W 85 B5
Avilla Mo., U.S.A. 37°12N 94°9W 83 D2
Avinger Tex., U.S.A. 32°54N 94°33W 109 E13
Avis Pa., U.S.A. 41°11N 77°19W 87 C5
Avoca Iowa, U.S.A. 41°29N 95°20W 81 D3
Avoca Minn., U.S.A. 43°57N 95°39W 77 G3
Avoca N.Y., U.S.A. 42°25N 77°25W 88 C3
Avoca Tex., U.S.A. 32°52N 99°43W 109 E8
Avola B.C., Canada 51°45N 119°19W 155 D15
Avon Colo., U.S.A. 39°38N 106°31W 125 C4
Avon Conn., U.S.A. 41°49N 72°50W 91 C2
Avon Ill., U.S.A. 40°40N 90°26W 84 C3
Avon Mont., U.S.A. 46°36N 112°36W 123 D5
Avon N.Y., U.S.A. 42°55N 77°45W 88 C3
Avon S. Dak., U.S.A. 43°0N 98°4W 76 H7
Avon Park Fla., U.S.A. 27°36N 81°31W 114 D7
Avon Park Air Force Range Fla., U.S.A. 27°38N 81°33W 114 D7
Avondale Nfld. & L., Canada 47°25N 53°12W 142 E7
Avondale Ariz., U.S.A. 33°26N 112°21W 130 D3
Avondale Colo., U.S.A. 38°14N 104°21W 125 D6
Avondale Ill., U.S.A. 41°56N 87°41W 95 B2
Avondale La., U.S.A. 29°54N 90°12W 117 C1
Avonlea Sask., Canada 50°0N 105°0W 150 E7
Avonmore Ont., Canada 45°10N 74°58W 144 F8
Avonmore Pa., U.S.A. 40°32N 79°28W 87 D3
Avoyelles Parish ☆ La., U.S.A. 31°0N 92°0W 110 C3
Axel Heiberg I. Nunavut, Canada 80°0N 90°0W 158 B7
Axial Colo., U.S.A. 40°17N 107°47W 125 B3
Axochiapan Morelos, Mexico 18°30N 98°44W 175 D9
Axson Ga., U.S.A. 31°17N 82°44W 113 E4
Axtell Kans., U.S.A. 39°52N 96°15W 82 B7
Axtell Nebr., U.S.A. 40°29N 99°8W 80 D6
Ayala Morelos, Mexico 18°46N 98°59W 175 D9
Ayden N.C., U.S.A. 35°28N 77°25W 103 C8
Ayer Mass., U.S.A. 42°34N 71°35W 91 B3
Ayer's Cliff Qué., Canada 45°10N 72°3W 145 F10
Aylen L. Ont., Canada 45°37N 77°51W 147 B9
Aylmer Ont., Canada 42°46N 80°59W 146 E6
Aylmer Qué., Canada 45°24N 75°51W 144 F7
Aylmer, L. N.W.T., Canada 64°5N 108°30W 157 D10
Aylsham Sask., Canada 53°12N 103°49W 150 B8
Ayotlán Jalisco, Mexico 20°32N 102°19W 174 B5
Ayotzintepec Oaxaca, Mexico 17°41N 96°7W 177 G4
Ayr Ont., Canada 43°17N 80°27W 146 D6
Ayr N. Dak., U.S.A. 47°2N 97°29W 76 C8
Ayr Nebr., U.S.A. 40°26N 98°26W 80 D7
Ayshire Iowa, U.S.A. 43°2N 94°50W 81 B4
Ayutla Guatemala 14°40N 92°10W 182 D1
Ayutla Jalisco, Mexico 20°7N 104°22W 174 B3
Ayutla de los Libres Guerrero, Mexico 16°54N 99°13W 175 E8
Azcapotzalco Distrito Federal, Mexico 19°28N 99°10W 181 B2
Azilda Ont., Canada 46°33N 81°6W 146 A5
Aziscohos L. Maine, U.S.A. 45°0N 71°0W 90 C3
Azle Tex., U.S.A. 32°54N 97°32W 109 E10
Azoyu Guerrero, Mexico 16°46N 98°37W 175 F9
Aztec Ariz., U.S.A. 32°49N 113°27W 130 E2
Aztec N. Mex., U.S.A. 36°49N 107°59W 131 A3
Aztec Peak Ariz., U.S.A. 33°49N 110°54W 130 D5

Aztec Ruins Nat. Monument △ N. Mex., U.S.A. 36°50N 108°0W 131 A3
Azteca, Estad. México, Mexico 19°19N 99°9W 181 C3
Azúa de Compostela Dom. Rep. 18°25N 70°44W 183 C5
Azuero, Pen. de Panama 7°30N 80°30W 182 E3
Azul Quintana Roo, Mexico 17°54N 88°52W 179 E4
Azul, Cerro Sonora, Mexico 30°35N 110°35W 168 C5
Azure L. B.C., Canada 52°23N 120°3W 155 C14
Azure L. Calif., U.S.A. 34°8N 117°52W 127 J9

B

B.A. Steinhagen L. Tex., U.S.A. 30°50N 94°15W 109 G13
B. Everett Jordan L. N.C., U.S.A. 35°30N 79°0W 103 C6
Babb Mont., U.S.A. 48°51N 113°27W 123 B4
Babbitt Minn., U.S.A. 47°41N 91°54W 77 C7
Babbitt Nev., U.S.A. 38°32N 118°39W 128 D2
Babbs Okla., U.S.A. 34°57N 99°3W 107 D4
Babine B.C., Canada 55°22N 126°37W 157 E7
Babine → B.C., Canada 55°45N 127°44W 157 E7
Babine L. B.C. Canada 54°48N 126°0W 157 F7
Baboquivari Peak Ariz., U.S.A. 31°46N 111°36W 130 F4
Baborigame Chihuahua, Mexico 26°27N 107°16W 169 G8
Babson Park Fla., U.S.A. 27°49N 81°32W 114 D7
Babylon N.Y., U.S.A. 40°42N 73°19W 92 B3
Baca Sinaloa, Mexico 26°47N 108°28W 169 G7
Baca Yucatán, Mexico 21°6N 89°25W 179 A4
Baca County ☆ Colo., U.S.A. 37°15N 102°30W 125 E8
Bacadéhuachi Sonora, Mexico 29°44N 109°10W 168 D6
Bacalar Quintana Roo, Mexico 18°43N 88°27W 179 D5
Bacalar, L. Quintana Roo, Mexico 18°43N 88°22W 179 D5
Bacalar Chico, Boca Quintana Roo, Mexico 18°12N 87°53W 179 D6
Bacanora Sonora, Mexico 28°59N 109°24W 168 E6
Bacanuchi Sonora, Mexico 30°38N 110°15W 168 C5
Baccalieu I. Nfld. & L., Canada 48°8N 52°48W 142 D8
Baccaro Pt. N.S., Canada 43°27N 65°28W 141 K4
Bacerac Sonora, Mexico 30°18N 108°50W 168 C6
Bache Pen. Nunavut, Canada 79°8N 76°0W 159 B4
Bachelor, Mt. Oreg., U.S.A. 43°59N 121°41W 121 D4
Bachíniva Chihuahua, Mexico 28°45N 107°15W 169 E8
Back → Canada 65°10N 104°0W 159 D5
Back B. Va., U.S.A. 36°35N 75°57W 102 C9
Back Bay N.E., Canada 45°3N 66°52W 141 H3
Back Bay Nat. Wildlife Refuge △ Va., U.S.A. 36°39N 75°56W 102 E9
Backbone Mt. Md., U.S.A. 39°12N 79°28W 93 A1
Backus Minn., U.S.A. 46°49N 94°31W 77 D4
Bacoachi Sonora, Mexico 30°38N 109°56W 168 D6
Bacobampo Sonora, Mexico 26°59N 109°40W 168 G6
Bacon County ☆ Ga., U.S.A. 31°30N 82°30W 113 E4
Baconton Ga., U.S.A. 31°23N 84°10W 113 E2
Bacqueville, L. Qué., Canada 58°7N 73°50W 143 B3
Bácum Sonora, Mexico 27°33N 110°5W 168 F5
Bacurato = Gustavo Díaz Ordaz, Presa Sinaloa, Mexico 25°55N 107°54W 172 B3
Bad → S. Dak., U.S.A. 44°21N 100°22W 76 F5
Bad Axe Mich., U.S.A. 43°48N 83°0W 79 F9
Bad River Indian Reservation Wis., U.S.A. 46°30N 90°45W 78 B3
Baddeck N.S., Canada 46°6N 60°45W 141 G9
Baden Pa., U.S.A. 40°38N 80°14W 87 D2
Badger Nfld. & L., Canada 49°0N 56°4W 142 D4
Badger Iowa, U.S.A. 42°37N 94°9W 81 C4
Badger Minn., U.S.A. 48°47N 96°1W 77 B2
Badger S. Dak., U.S.A. 44°29N 97°12W 76 F8
Badger Cr. → Colo., U.S.A. 40°17N 103°42W 125 B7
Badger Pk. Mont., U.S.A. 45°40N 106°33W 123 E11
Badger's Quay Nfld. & L., Canada 49°7N 53°35W 142 C7
Badin N.C., U.S.A. 35°24N 80°6W 103 C5
Badin L. N.C., U.S.A. 35°25N 80°6W 103 C5
Badiraguato Sinaloa, Mexico 25°22N 107°31W 172 B3
Badlands S. Dak., U.S.A. 43°55N 102°30W 76 G3
Badlands Nat. Park △ S. Dak., U.S.A. 43°38N 102°56W 76 G3
Badwater Cr. → Wyo., U.S.A. 43°17N 108°8W 124 C4
Baffin B. N. Amer. 72°0N 64°0W 158 C13
Baffin B. Tex., U.S.A. 27°18N 97°30W 108 K10
Baffin I. Nunavut, Canada 68°0N 75°0W 158 C10
Bagdad Ariz., U.S.A. 34°34N 113°11W 130 C2
Bagdad Fla., U.S.A. 30°36N 87°2W 114 A1
Bagdad Ky., U.S.A. 38°16N 85°3W 105 D3
Baggs Wyo., U.S.A. 41°2N 107°39W 124 E5
Bagley Minn., U.S.A. 47°32N 95°24W 77 C3
Baha'i Temple Ill., U.S.A. 42°4N 87°41W 95 A2
Bahama, Canal Viejo de W. Indies 22°10N 77°30W 182 B4
Bahamas ■ N. Amer. 24°0N 75°0W 183 B5
Bahía, Is. de la Honduras 16°45N 86°15W 182 C2
Bahía Asunción Baja Calif. S., Mexico 27°9N 114°19W 167 F4
Bahía Bufadero Michoacan, Mexico 18°3N 102°45W 174 F4
Bahía de Tortugas Baja Calif. S., Mexico 27°43N 114°55W 167 F4
Bahía Kino Sonora, Mexico 28°47N 111°58W 168 E4
Baie, Parc de la Qué., Canada 45°27N 75°41W 160 A1
Baie-Comeau Qué., Canada 49°12N 68°10W 140 D1
Baie-des-Sables Qué., Canada 48°43N 67°54W 140 E2
Baie-du-Febvre Qué., Canada 46°8N 72°43W 145 E10
Baie-du-Poste = Mistissini Qué., Canada 50°24N 73°56W 143 C3
Baie-du-Renard Qué., Canada 49°17N 61°50W 140 D8
Baie-d'Urfé Qué., Canada 45°24N 73°53W 160 B1
Baie-Johan-Beetz Qué., Canada 50°17N 62°48W 140 C7
Baie McLaurin, Parc de la Qué., Canada 42°29N 75°35W 160 A2
Baie-St-Paul Qué., Canada 47°28N 70°32W 145 D12
Baie-Ste-Anne N.B., Canada 47°3N 64°58W 141 F5
Baie-Ste-Catherine Qué., Canada 48°6N 69°44W 145 C13
Baie-Ste-Claire Qué., Canada 49°54N 64°30W 140 D2
Baie-Trinité Qué., Canada 49°25N 67°20W 140 D2
Baie Verte N.B., Canada 46°1N 64°6W 141 G5
Baie Verte Nfld. & L., Canada 49°55N 56°12W 142 C4
Baie Verte Pen. Nfld. & L., Canada 49°55N 56°30W 142 C4
Bailey County ☆ Tex., U.S.A. 34°0N 102°50W 108 D3
Baileys Crossroads Va., U.S.A. 38°50N 77°6W 99 B3
Baileys Harbor Wis., U.S.A. 45°4N 87°8W 78 C6
Baileyton Tenn., U.S.A. 36°20N 82°50W 105 D10
Baileyville Kans., U.S.A. 39°51N 96°11W 82 B7
Baillie → Canada 65°7N 104°36W 157 C12
Baillie-Hamilton I. Nunavut, Canada 75°52N 94°35W 158 B7
Bainbridge Ga., U.S.A. 30°55N 84°35W 113 F2
Bainbridge Ind., U.S.A. 39°46N 86°49W 85 D4
Bainbridge N.Y., U.S.A. 42°18N 75°29W 88 A5
Bainbridge Ohio, U.S.A. 39°14N 83°16W 86 D3
Bainbridge Island Wash., U.S.A. 47°38N 122°32W 120 C2
Bainville Mont., U.S.A. 48°8N 104°13W 123 B13
Baird Tex., U.S.A. 32°24N 99°24W 109 E8
Baird Mts. Alaska, U.S.A. 67°0N 160°0W 135 C7
Baird Pen. N.W.T., Canada 68°55N 76°4W 159 D10
Bairoil Wyo., U.S.A. 42°15N 107°33W 124 D5

Baisley Pond N.Y., U.S.A. 40°40N 73°47W 97 B4
Baja, Pta. Baja Calif., Mexico 29°58N 115°49W 166 D3
Baja California Mexico 31°10N 115°12W 166 E5
Baja California □ Mexico 30°0N 115°0W 166 E5
Baja California Sur □ Mexico 25°50N 111°50W 167 H7
Bajío de Ahuichila Coahuila, Mexico 25°6N 102°37W 171 E2
Bajo Nuevo Caribbean 15°40N 78°50W 182 C4
Bajo Obispo Norte Campeche, Mexico 20°29N 92°9W 179 B1
Bajo Obispo Sur Campeche, Mexico 20°25N 92°9W 179 B1
Baker Calif., U.S.A. 35°16N 116°4W 127 H10
Baker Fla., U.S.A. 30°48N 86°41W 114 A2
Baker Idaho, U.S.A. 45°6N 113°44W 122 D5
Baker La., U.S.A. 30°35N 91°10W 110 D4
Baker Mont., U.S.A. 46°22N 104°17W 123 D13
Baker N. Dak., U.S.A. 48°10N 99°33W 76 B6
Baker Okla., U.S.A. 36°52N 101°1W 107 B2
Baker, L. Nunavut, Canada 64°0N 96°0W 159 E6
Baker, Mt. Wash., U.S.A. 48°50N 121°49W 120 B4
Baker Butte Ariz., U.S.A. 34°27N 111°22W 130 C4
Baker City Oreg., U.S.A. 44°47N 117°50W 121 C8
Baker County ☆ Fla., U.S.A. 30°20N 82°15W 114 A6
Baker County ☆ Ga., U.S.A. 31°20N 84°30W 113 E2
Baker County ☆ Oreg., U.S.A. 44°40N 117°50W 121 C8
Baker I. Pac. Oc. 0°10N 176°35W 184 D6
Baker Lake Nunavut, Canada 64°20N 96°3W 159 E6
Bakerhill Ala., U.S.A. 31°47N 85°18W 112 E5
Bakers Dozen Is. Nunavut, Canada 56°45N 78°45W 143 B2
Bakersfield Calif., U.S.A. 35°23N 119°1W 127 H7
Bakersfield Tex., U.S.A. 30°54N 102°18W 108 G5
Bakersfield Vt., U.S.A. 44°45N 72°48W 89 B2
Bakersville N.C., U.S.A. 36°1N 82°10W 103 B3
Bal Harbor Fla., U.S.A. 25°53N 80°7W 115 C3
Bala Ont., Canada 45°1N 79°37W 146 B7
Bala Kans., U.S.A. 39°19N 96°57W 82 B7
Bala-Cynwyd Pa., U.S.A. 40°0N 75°13W 98 A1
Balakbal Campeche, Mexico 17°53N 89°18W 179 E4
Balamku Campeche, Mexico 18°34N 89°54W 179 D4
Balancán Tabasco, Mexico 17°48N 91°32W 179 D4
Balaton Minn., U.S.A. 44°14N 95°52W 77 F3
Balboa Panama 8°57N 79°34W 182 E4
Balboa Park Calif., U.S.A. 32°43N 117°8W 133 B2
Balcarres Sask., Canada 50°50N 103°35W 150 E8
Balch Springs Tex., U.S.A. 32°43N 96°37W 116 B6
Balcones Canyonlands Nat. Wildlife Refuge △ Tex., U.S.A. 30°33N 98°0W 109 G10
Balcones Escarpment Tex., U.S.A. 29°30N 99°15W 108 H7
Balcones Heights Tex., U.S.A. 29°29N 98°33W 116 B2
Bald Head I. N.C., U.S.A. 33°52N 77°59W 103 E8
Bald Knob Ark., U.S.A. 35°19N 91°34W 106 C4
Bald Knob Va., U.S.A. 37°56N 79°51W 102 D5
Bald Knoll Wyo., U.S.A. 42°22N 110°28W 124 D2
Bald Mt. Nev., U.S.A. 37°27N 115°44W 128 E5
Bald Mt. Oreg., U.S.A. 43°16N 121°21W 121 D4
Bald Pt. Fla., U.S.A. 29°57N 84°20W 114 B4
Baldur Man., Canada 49°23N 99°15W 151 F12
Baldwin Fla., U.S.A. 30°18N 81°59W 114 A7
Baldwin Ga., U.S.A. 34°30N 83°32W 113 B3
Baldwin Ill., U.S.A. 38°11N 89°51W 84 E4
Baldwin La., U.S.A. 29°50N 91°33W 110 E4
Baldwin Mich., U.S.A. 43°54N 85°51W 79 F6
Baldwin N.Y., U.S.A. 40°39N 73°36W 97 C5
Baldwin Pa., U.S.A. 40°21N 79°58W 98 B2
Baldwin Wis., U.S.A. 44°58N 92°22W 78 D1
Baldwin, L. Fla., U.S.A. 28°34N 81°19W 118 A3
Baldwin City Kans., U.S.A. 38°47N 95°11W 82 C8
Baldwin County ☆ Ala., U.S.A. 30°53N 87°46W 112 F3
Baldwin County ☆ Ga., U.S.A. 33°5N 83°10W 113 C3
Baldwin Hills Calif., U.S.A. 34°0N 118°21W 133 B2
Baldwin Hills Res. Calif., U.S.A. 34°0N 118°21W 133 B2
Baldwinsville N.Y., U.S.A. 43°10N 76°20W 88 B4
Baldwinville Mass., U.S.A. 42°37N 72°5W 91 B3
Baldwyn Miss., U.S.A. 34°31N 88°38W 111 B5
Baldy Mt. Man., Canada 51°28N 100°43W 151 D11
Baldy Peak Ariz., U.S.A. 33°54N 109°34W 130 D6
Baldy Pk. N. Mex., U.S.A. 36°38N 105°13W 131 A5
Baleine = Whale → Qué., Canada 58°15N 67°40W 143 B4
Baleine, Petite R. de la → Qué., Canada 56°0N 76°45W 143 B2
Baler, L. Wash., U.S.A. 48°44N 121°38W 120 B4
Balfate Honduras 15°48N 86°25W 182 C2
Balfour N. Dak., U.S.A. 47°57N 100°32W 76 C5
Balgonie Sask., Canada 50°29N 104°16W 150 E7
Balko Okla., U.S.A. 36°38N 100°41W 107 B3
Ball La., U.S.A. 31°25N 92°25W 110 C3
Ball Ground Ga., U.S.A. 34°20N 84°23W 113 B2
Ballantine Mont., U.S.A. 45°57N 108°9W 123 E9
Ballantyne Str. N.W.T., Canada 77°35N 115°6W 156 A9
Ballard Utah, U.S.A. 40°17N 109°57W 129 C6
Ballard County ☆ Ky., U.S.A. 37°0N 89°0W 104 C2
Ballenas, B. de Baja Calif. S., Mexico 26°45N 113°26W 167 F4
Ballenas, Canal de Baja Calif., Mexico 29°10N 113°29W 166 D5
Ballenger Creek Md., U.S.A. 39°22N 77°26W 93 A3
Balleza Chihuahua, Mexico 26°56N 106°21W 169 G9
Balleza → Chihuahua, Mexico 26°58N 106°20W 169 G9
Ballinger Tex., U.S.A. 31°45N 99°57W 109 F8
Ballston Spa N.Y., U.S.A. 43°0N 73°51W 88 C7
Balltown Iowa, U.S.A. 42°38N 90°51W 81 C8
Ballwin Mo., U.S.A. 38°36N 90°33W 83 C6
Bally Pa., U.S.A. 40°24N 75°35W 92 B1
Balmertown Ont., Canada 51°4N 93°41W 148 A3
Balmoral Man., Canada 50°15N 97°19W 151 E14
Balmorhea Tex., U.S.A. 30°59N 103°45W 108 G4
Balmville N.Y., U.S.A. 41°32N 74°1W 92 A2
Balsas → Michoacan, Mexico 17°55N 102°10W 174 E5
Balsas del Norte Guerrero, Mexico 18°0N 99°46W 175 E8
Balta N. Dak., U.S.A. 48°10N 100°2W 76 B5
Baltic Ohio, U.S.A. 40°26N 81°42W 86 C5
Baltic S. Dak., U.S.A. 43°46N 96°44W 76 F9
Baltimore Md., U.S.A. 39°17N 76°36W 99 B2
Baltimore Ohio, U.S.A. 39°51N 82°36W 86 D4
Baltimore County ☆ Md., U.S.A. 39°20N 76°40W 93 A4
Baltimore Highlands Baltimore, U.S.A. 39°13N 76°38W 99 B2
Baltimore Washington Int. ✈ (BWI) Md., U.S.A. 39°11N 76°40W 93 A4
Bamaji L. Ont., Canada 51°9N 91°25W 148 A5
Bamberg S.C., U.S.A. 33°18N 81°2W 103 D5
Bamberg County ☆ S.C., U.S.A. 33°10N 81°0W 103 E5
Bamfield B.C., Canada 48°45N 125°10W 154 G9
Bamuri Sonora, Mexico 30°20N 112°5W 168 C3
Banámichi Sonora, Mexico 30°1N 110°10W 168 D5
Bancroft Ont., Canada 45°3N 77°51W 147 B9
Bancroft Idaho, U.S.A. 42°43N 111°53W 122 G7
Bancroft Iowa, U.S.A. 43°18N 94°13W 81 B4
Bancroft La., U.S.A. 30°34N 93°41W 110 D2

Bancroft Mich., U.S.A. 42°53N 84°4W 79 G7
Bancroft Nebr., U.S.A. 42°1N 96°34W 80 B9
Banda, C. Baja Calif., Mexico 31°45N 116°45W 166 B2
Bandana Ky., U.S.A. 37°9N 88°56W 104 C4
Bandelier Nat. Monument △ N. Mex., U.S.A. 35°50N 106°25W 131 B4
Bandera Tex., U.S.A. 29°44N 99°5W 109 H8
Bandera County ☆ Tex., U.S.A. 29°48N 99°15W 109 H8
Bandera del Aguila Durango, Mexico 23°55N 105°21W 172 D5
Banderas Veracruz, Mexico 20°40N 105°25W 174 B2
Banderilla Veracruz, Mexico 19°35N 96°56W 176 E4
Bandon Oreg., U.S.A. 43°7N 124°25W 121 D1
Banes Cuba 21°0N 75°42W 183 B4
Banff Alta., Canada 51°10N 115°34W 153 G5
Banff Nat. Park △ Alta., Canada 51°30N 116°15W 153 G4
Bangor Maine, U.S.A. 44°48N 68°46W 90 D5
Bangor Mich., U.S.A. 42°18N 86°7W 79 G5
Bangor Pa., U.S.A. 40°52N 75°13W 92 B1
Bangor Naval Reserve Wash., U.S.A. 47°43N 122°44W 132 B1
Bangs Tex., U.S.A. 31°43N 99°8W 109 F8
Bangs, Mt. Ariz., U.S.A. 36°48N 113°51W 130 A2
Bani Dom. Rep. 18°16N 70°22W 183 C5
Banister → Va., U.S.A. 36°42N 78°48W 102 E6
Banks Ala., U.S.A. 31°49N 85°51W 112 E5
Banks Ark., U.S.A. 33°35N 92°16W 106 E3
Banks Idaho, U.S.A. 44°5N 116°8W 122 F2
Banks Oreg., U.S.A. 45°37N 123°7W 121 B2
Banks County ☆ Ga., U.S.A. 34°30N 83°30W 113 B3
Banks I. B.C., Canada 53°20N 130°0W 154 B4
Banks I. N.W.T., Canada 73°15N 121°30W 156 B8
Banks L. Ga., U.S.A. 31°2N 83°6W 113 E3
Banks L. Wash., U.S.A. 47°47N 119°19W 120 C6
Bannack Mont., U.S.A. 45°10N 112°59W 123 E5
Banner Miss., U.S.A. 34°5N 89°23W 111 B4
Banner Wyo., U.S.A. 44°36N 106°52W 124 B6
Banner County ☆ Nebr., U.S.A. 41°30N 103°40W 80 C2
Banner Elk N.C., U.S.A. 36°10N 81°52W 103 B4
Banner Hill Tenn., U.S.A. 36°8N 82°25W 105 D10
Bannertown N.C., U.S.A. 36°29N 80°35W 103 B5
Banning Calif., U.S.A. 33°56N 116°53W 127 K10
Bannock County ☆ Idaho, U.S.A. 42°30N 112°10W 122 G6
Bannock Cr. → Idaho, U.S.A. 42°53N 112°40W 122 G6
Bannock Range Idaho, U.S.A. 42°40N 112°30W 122 G6
Bannockburn Ont., Canada 44°39N 77°33W 147 C9
Bantry N. Dak., U.S.A. 48°30N 100°37W 76 B5
Bapchule Ariz., U.S.A. 33°12N 111°50W 130 D4
Bar Nunn Wyo., U.S.A. 42°55N 106°21W 124 D6
Bar Harbor Maine, U.S.A. 44°23N 68°13W 90 D5
Baraboo Wis., U.S.A. 43°28N 89°45W 78 E4
Barachois-de-Malbaie Qué., Canada 48°37N 64°17W 140 E5
Barachois Pond Prov. Park △ Nfld. & L., Canada 48°28N 58°15W 142 D2
Baracoa Cuba 20°20N 74°30W 183 B5
Barada Nebr., U.S.A. 40°13N 95°35W 80 D10
Baraga Mich., U.S.A. 46°47N 88°30W 79 C3
Baraga County ☆ Mich., U.S.A. 46°40N 88°20W 79 C3
Barahona Dom. Rep. 18°13N 71°7W 183 C5
Baranof Alaska, U.S.A. 57°5N 134°50W 135 H14
Baranof I. Alaska, U.S.A. 57°0N 135°0W 135 H14
Barataria La., U.S.A. 29°44N 90°8W 110 E5
Barataria B. La., U.S.A. 29°20N 89°55W 110 F5
Barataria Preserve La., U.S.A. 29°47N 90°7W 117 D2
Barbados ■ W. Indies 13°10N 59°30W 183 D8
Barbara L. Ont., Canada 49°20N 87°47W 149 C9
Barbeau Pk. N.W.T., Canada 81°54N 75°1W 158 A10
Barbel, L. Qué., Canada 51°55N 68°13W 140 B1
Barber, L. Fla., U.S.A. 28°30N 81°19W 115 A3
Barber County ☆ Kans., U.S.A. 37°15N 98°40W 82 D4
Barbers Pt. Hawai'i, U.S.A. 21°18N 158°7W 136 K13
Barberton Ohio, U.S.A. 41°1N 81°39W 86 B5
Barberville Fla., U.S.A. 29°11N 81°26W 114 B7
Barborview Baltimore, U.S.A. 39°16N 76°31W 99 B2
Barbour County ☆ Ala., U.S.A. 31°53N 85°25W 112 E5
Barbour County ☆ W. Va., U.S.A. 39°9N 80°3W 102 B4
Barboursville W. Va., U.S.A. 38°24N 82°18W 102 C2
Barbuda W. Indies 17°30N 61°40W 183 C7
Barceloneta Puerto Rico 18°27N 66°32W 184 G16
Barclay Md., U.S.A. 39°9N 75°52W 93 A5
Barcroft, L. Va., U.S.A. 38°52N 77°9W 99 B3
Bardley Mo., U.S.A. 36°42N 91°7W 83 E5
Bardoux, L. Qué., Canada 51°9N 67°50W 140 B2
Bardstown Ky., U.S.A. 37°49N 85°28W 105 C7
Bardwell Ky., U.S.A. 36°52N 89°1W 104 D3
Bare Mt. Wash., U.S.A. 45°55N 122°4W 120 E3
Barentsøya Svalbard 78°25N 21°20E 162 B13
Bargersville Ind., U.S.A. 39°31N 86°10W 85 D4
Baring Mo., U.S.A. 40°15N 92°12W 83 A4
Baring, C. N.W.T., Canada 70°0N 117°30W 156 D9
Bark L. Ont., Canada 45°27N 77°51W 144 F5
Bark Pt. Wis., U.S.A. 46°53N 91°11W 78 B2
Barker N.Y., U.S.A. 43°20N 78°33W 88 B2
Barkhamsted Res. Conn., U.S.A. 41°53N 72°58W 91 C2
Barkley, L. Tenn., U.S.A. 37°1N 88°14W 104 C4
Barkley Sound B.C., Canada 48°50N 125°10W 154 G9
Barksdale Tex., U.S.A. 29°44N 100°2W 109 H7
Barksdale Air Force Base La., U.S.A. 32°29N 93°42W 110 B2
Barling Ark., U.S.A. 35°20N 94°18W 106 C1
Barlow Ky., U.S.A. 37°3N 89°3W 104 C3
Barlow Pa., U.S.A. 39°45N 77°14W 93 A3
Barnard Kans., U.S.A. 39°11N 98°3W 82 B5
Barnard Mo., U.S.A. 40°10N 94°50W 83 A2
Barnard Vt., U.S.A. 43°43N 72°38W 89 C2
Barnegat N.J., U.S.A. 39°45N 74°14W 92 C2
Barnegat Bay N.J., U.S.A. 39°45N 74°10W 92 C2
Barnegat Light N.J., U.S.A. 39°46N 74°6W 92 C2
Barnes Kans., U.S.A. 39°43N 96°52W 82 B7
Barnes County ☆ N. Dak., U.S.A. 47°0N 98°0W 76 C7
Barnes Icecap N.W.T., Canada 70°0N 73°15W 158 D11
Barneston Nebr., U.S.A. 40°3N 96°34W 80 D9
Barnesville Ga., U.S.A. 33°3N 84°9W 113 C2
Barnesville Minn., U.S.A. 46°43N 96°28W 77 D2
Barnesville Ohio, U.S.A. 39°59N 81°11W 86 D5
Barnet Vt., U.S.A. 44°19N 72°3W 89 B2
Barneveld Wis., U.S.A. 43°1N 89°55W 78 E4
Barnett Mo., U.S.A. 38°18N 92°39W 83 C4
Barney Ga., U.S.A. 31°0N 83°30W 113 E3
Barnhart Mo., U.S.A. 38°21N 90°24W 83 C6
Barnhart Tex., U.S.A. 31°8N 101°10W 108 F6
Barnsdall Okla., U.S.A. 36°34N 96°10W 107 B7
Barnstable Mass., U.S.A. 41°42N 70°18W 91 C4
Barnstable County ☆ Mass., U.S.A. 41°40N 70°15W 91 C4
Barnstable Harbor Mass., U.S.A. 41°42N 70°18W 91 C4

Barnum Minn., U.S.A. 46°30N 92°42W 77 D6
Barnum Wyo., U.S.A. 43°40N 106°55W 124 C6
Barnwell Alta., Canada 49°46N 112°15W 153 H6
Barnwell S.C., U.S.A. 33°15N 81°23W 103 E4
Barnwell County ☆ S.C., U.S.A. 33°15N 81°30W 103 E4
Baron Okla., U.S.A. 35°55N 94°36W 107 C9
Barons Alta., Canada 50°0N 113°5W 153 H7
Barques, Pt. Aux Mich., U.S.A. 44°4N 82°58W 79 E9
Barques, Pt. Aux Mich., U.S.A. 45°48N 86°21W 79 C5
Barra El Tordo Tamaulipas, Mexico 23°3N 97°46W 171 G7
Barranca del Cobre, Parque Natural △ Chihuahua, Mexico 27°18N 107°40W 169 F8
Barranca Seca Michoacan, Mexico 18°11N 103°1W 174 D4
Barranquitas Puerto Rico 18°11N 66°19W 184 G16
Barraute Qué., Canada 48°26N 77°38W 144 C5
Barre Mass., U.S.A. 42°25N 72°6W 91 B2
Barre Vt., U.S.A. 44°12N 72°30W 89 B2
Barren → Ky., U.S.A. 37°1N 86°37W 104 C6
Barren County ☆ Ky., U.S.A. 36°57N 85°57W 105 D7
Barren Hill Pa., U.S.A. 40°5N 75°15W 98 A1
Barren Is. Alaska, U.S.A. 58°55N 152°15W 135 E8
Barren River L. Ky., U.S.A. 36°54N 86°8W 104 D6
Barrett Minn., U.S.A. 45°55N 95°53W 77 E3
Barrett W. Va., U.S.A. 37°53N 81°40W 102 D3
Barrhead Alta., Canada 54°10N 114°24W 152 D6
Barrial de Guadalupe Coahuila, Mexico 24°58N 103°12W 171 F1
Barrie Ont., Canada 44°24N 79°40W 146 C7
Barriefield Ont., Canada 44°14N 76°28W 147 C10
Barrière B.C., Canada 51°12N 120°7W 155 D14
Barrigada Guam 13°28N 144°48E 184 b
Barril, L. el Tamaulipas, Mexico 25°45N 97°18W 171 F7
Barrineau Park Fla., U.S.A. 30°42N 87°26W 114 A1
Barrington N.H., U.S.A. 43°12N 70°59W 89 C4
Barrington N.J., U.S.A. 39°51N 75°3W 98 B2
Barrington R.I., U.S.A. 41°44N 71°18W 91 C3
Barrington Passage N.S., Canada 43°30N 65°38W 141 K4
Barron Wis., U.S.A. 45°24N 91°51W 78 C21
Barron County ☆ Wis., U.S.A. 45°25N 91°50W 78 C2
Barrow Alaska, U.S.A. 71°18N 156°47W 135 A8
Barrow, Pt. Alaska, U.S.A. 71°23N 156°29W 135 A8
Barrow County ☆ Ga., U.S.A. 34°0N 83°40W 113 C3
Barrow Str. Nunavut, Canada 74°20N 95°0W 158 C7
Barrows Man., Canada 52°50N 101°27W 151 C10
Barry Ill., U.S.A. 39°42N 91°2W 84 D2
Barry County ☆ Mich., U.S.A. 42°35N 85°25W 79 G6
Barry County ☆ Mo., U.S.A. 36°45N 93°45W 83 E3
Barry M. Goldwater Air Force Range Ariz., U.S.A. 32°38N 113°3W 130 E2
Barry's Bay Ont., Canada 45°29N 77°41W 147 B8
Barryton Mich., U.S.A. 43°45N 85°9W 79 F6
Barstow Calif., U.S.A. 34°54N 117°1W 127 J9
Barstow Tex., U.S.A. 31°28N 103°24W 108 F4
Bartholomew, Bayou → La., U.S.A. 32°43N 92°4W 110 B3
Bartholomew County ☆ Ind., U.S.A. 39°10N 85°55W 85 D5
Bartlesville Okla., U.S.A. 36°45N 95°59W 107 B8
Bartlett Kans., U.S.A. 37°3N 95°13W 82 D8
Bartlett N.H., U.S.A. 44°5N 71°17W 89 B3
Bartlett Tenn., U.S.A. 35°12N 89°52W 117 A2
Bartlett Tex., U.S.A. 30°48N 97°26W 109 G10
Bartlett Res. Ariz., U.S.A. 33°49N 111°38W 130 D4
Bartletts Harbour Nfld. & L., Canada 50°57N 57°0W 142 B4
Bartley Nebr., U.S.A. 40°15N 100°18W 80 D5
Barton Md., U.S.A. 39°34N 79°2W 93 A1
Barton N. Dak., U.S.A. 48°30N 100°11W 76 B5
Barton Vt., U.S.A. 44°45N 72°11W 89 B2
Barton → Vt., U.S.A. 44°53N 72°13W 89 B2
Barton, L. Fla., U.S.A. 28°33N 81°18W 115 A3
Barton County ☆ Kans., U.S.A. 38°30N 98°40W 82 C5
Barton County ☆ Mo., U.S.A. 37°30N 94°20W 83 D2
Bartow Fla., U.S.A. 27°54N 81°50W 114 D7
Bartow Ga., U.S.A. 32°53N 82°29W 113 D4
Bartow County ☆ Ga., U.S.A. 34°20N 84°50W 113 B2
Barú, Volcan Panama 8°55N 82°35W 182 E3
Barwick Ont., Canada 30°54N 83°44W 113 F3
Basalt Colo., U.S.A. 39°22N 107°2W 125 C3
Basalt Idaho, U.S.A. 43°19N 112°10W 122 F6
Basaseachic, Cascadas de Chihuahua, Mexico 28°10N 108°12W 169 E7
Basco Ill., U.S.A. 40°20N 91°12W 84 C2
Bashaw Alta., Canada 52°35N 112°58W 153 F8
Basile La., U.S.A. 30°29N 92°36W 110 D3
Basin Mont., U.S.A. 46°16N 112°16W 123 D5
Basin Wyo., U.S.A. 44°23N 108°2W 124 B4
Basin L. Sask., Canada 52°38N 105°17W 150 C6
Basinger Fla., U.S.A. 27°23N 81°2W 114 D7
Baskahegan L. Maine, U.S.A. 45°28N 67°50W 90 C6
Baskatong, Rés. Qué., Canada 46°46N 75°50W 144 E7
Baskin La., U.S.A. 32°16N 91°45W 110 B4
Basonopita → Chihuahua, Mexico 26°1N 107°15W 169 G8
Bass Lake Calif., U.S.A. 37°19N 119°33W 126 F7
Bass Lake Minn., U.S.A. 45°3N 93°29W 95 A7
Bass River N.S., Canada 45°25N 63°47W 141 H6
Bassano Alta., Canada 50°48N 112°20W 153 H8
Basse-Terre Guadeloupe 16°0N 61°44W 183 D7
Basseterre St. Kitts & Nevis 17°17N 62°43W 183 C7
Bassett Nebr., U.S.A. 42°35N 99°32W 80 B6
Bassett Va., U.S.A. 36°46N 79°59W 102 E5
Bassfield Miss., U.S.A. 31°30N 89°45W 111 E4
Basswood I. Minn., U.S.A. 48°7N 91°34W 77 B7
Bastian Va., U.S.A. 37°9N 81°9W 102 D3
Bastille, L. Qué., Canada 51°46N 61°11W 140 B8
Bastrop La., U.S.A. 32°47N 91°55W 110 B4
Bastrop Tex., U.S.A. 30°7N 97°19W 109 G10
Bastrop County ☆ Tex., U.S.A. 30°10N 97°20W 109 G10
Batabanó Cuba 22°41N 82°18W 182 B3
Batabanó, G. de Cuba 22°30N 82°30W 182 B3
Batavia Ill., U.S.A. 41°51N 88°19W 84 B5
Batavia Iowa, U.S.A. 41°0N 92°10W 81 E6
Batavia N.Y., U.S.A. 43°0N 78°11W 88 B2
Batavia Ohio, U.S.A. 39°5N 84°11W 86 D2
Batchawana B. Ont., Canada 46°53N 84°35W 149 F12
Batchawana Bay Ont., Canada 46°55N 84°37W 149 F12
Batchtown Ill., U.S.A. 39°2N 90°43W 84 D3
Bates Ark., U.S.A. 34°55N 94°22W 106 C1
Batesville Ind., U.S.A. 39°18N 85°13W 85 D6
Bates County ☆ Mo., U.S.A. 38°15N 94°20W 83 C2
Batesburg-Leesville S.C., U.S.A. 33°54N 81°33W 103 D4
Batesland S. Dak., U.S.A. 43°8N 102°6W 76 G3
Batesville Ark., U.S.A. 35°46N 91°39W 106 C4
Batesville Miss., U.S.A. 34°19N 89°57W 111 B4
Batesville Tex., U.S.A. 28°58N 99°37W 109 J8
Bath N.B., Canada 46°31N 67°36W 141 G2

Bath Ont., Canada 44°11N 76°47W 147 C10
Bath Ill., U.S.A. 40°11N 90°8W 84 C3
Bath Maine, U.S.A. 43°55N 69°49W 90 E4
Bath N.Y., U.S.A. 42°20N 77°19W 88 C3
Bath Pa., U.S.A. 40°44N 75°24W 92 B1
Bath S. Dak., U.S.A. 45°28N 98°20W 76 E7
Bath N.Y., U.S.A. 40°36N 74°0W 97 C2
Bath County ☆ Ky., U.S.A. 38°10N 83°45W 105 B9
Bath County ☆ Va., U.S.A. 38°0N 79°50W 102 C5
Bathgate N. Dak., U.S.A. 48°53N 97°29W 76 B8
Bathurst N.B., Canada 47°37N 65°43W 141 F4
Bathurst, C. N.W.T., Canada 70°34N 128°0W 156 B7
Bathurst I. Nunavut, Canada 76°0N 100°30W 158 B5
Bathurst Inlet Nunavut, Canada 66°50N 108°1W 156 C11
Batiscan Qué., Canada 46°30N 72°15W 145 E10
Batiscan → Qué., Canada 46°16N 72°15W 145 E10
Batiscan, L. Qué., Canada 47°22N 71°55W 145 D11
Baton Rouge La., U.S.A. 30°27N 91°11W 110 D4
Batopilas Chihuahua, Mexico 27°1N 107°44W 169 F8
Batopilas → Chihuahua, Mexico 26°51N 107°50W 169 G8
Batson Tex., U.S.A. 30°15N 94°40W 109 G13
Batten Kill → Vt., U.S.A. 43°6N 73°35W 89 C1
Battle → Sask., Canada 52°43N 108°15W 150 C3
Battle → Calif., U.S.A. 40°21N 122°11W 126 C4
Battle Creek Iowa, U.S.A. 42°19N 95°36W 81 C3
Battle Creek Mich., U.S.A. 42°19N 85°11W 79 G6
Battle Creek Nebr., U.S.A. 42°0N 97°36W 80 C8
Battle Creek Minn., U.S.A. 44°56N 92°58W 94 B3
Battle Creek Park Minn., U.S.A. 44°56N 92°59W 94 B3
Battle Ground Ind., U.S.A. 40°31N 86°50W 85 C4
Battle Ground Wash., U.S.A. 45°47N 122°32W 120 E3
Battle Harbour Nfld. & L., Canada 52°16N 55°35W 143 C6
Battle Lake Minn., U.S.A. 46°17N 95°43W 77 D3
Battle Mountain Nev., U.S.A. 40°38N 116°56W 128 B4
Battle Mt. Wyo., U.S.A. 41°2N 107°16W 124 E5
Battleford Sask., Canada 52°45N 108°15W 150 C3
Baturi Baja Calif. S., Mexico 23°35N 110°20W 167 K8
Baudette Minn., U.S.A. 48°43N 94°36W 77 B4
Bauld, C. Nfld. & L., Canada 51°38N 55°26W 142 A5
Baumann Fiord Nunavut, Canada 77°40N 85°35W 158 B8
Bauxite Ark., U.S.A. 34°33N 92°30W 106 D3
Bavaria Kans., U.S.A. 38°48N 97°45W 82 C6
Baviácora Sonora, Mexico 29°43N 110°9W 168 D5
Bavispe Sonora, Mexico 30°30N 108°54W 168 C7
Bavispe → Sonora, Mexico 29°15N 109°11W 168 D6
Bawlf Alta., Canada 52°55N 112°28W 153 F8
Baxley Ga., U.S.A. 31°47N 82°21W 113 E4
Baxter Iowa, U.S.A. 41°49N 93°9W 81 D5
Baxter Minn., U.S.A. 46°21N 94°17W 77 D4
Baxter Tenn., U.S.A. 36°9N 85°38W 105 D7
Baxter County ☆ Ark., U.S.A. 36°20N 92°23W 106 B3
Baxter Estates N.Y., U.S.A. 40°50N 73°41W 97 A4
Baxter Springs Kans., U.S.A. 37°2N 94°44W 82 D9
Baxter State Park △ U.S.A. 46°5N 68°57W 90 B5
Bay, Ark., U.S.A. 35°45N 90°34W 106 C5
Bay, L. Fla., U.S.A. 28°25N 81°34W 115 A2
Bay Bulls Nfld. & L., Canada 47°19N 52°50W 142 E8
Bay Chimo = Umingmaktok Nunavut, Canada 67°41N 107°56W 158 D4
Bay City Mich., U.S.A. 43°36N 83°54W 79 F8
Bay City Oreg., U.S.A. 45°31N 123°53W 121 B2
Bay City Tex., U.S.A. 28°59N 95°58W 109 J12
Bay City Fla., U.S.A. 30°20N 85°45W 114 A3
Bay County ☆ Mich., U.S.A. 43°45N 84°5W 79 F7
Bay de Verde Nfld. & L., Canada 48°5N 52°54W 142 D8
Bay du Nord Wilderness Reserve △ Nfld. & L., Canada 48°5N 54°48W 142 D6
Bay du Vin N.B., Canada 47°2N 65°8W 141 F4
Bay Fiord Nunavut, Canada 78°55N 83°30W 158 B9
Bay Harbour Islands Fla., U.S.A. 25°53N 80°7W 115 C3
Bay Hill Fla., U.S.A. 28°28N 81°30W 115 B1
Bay L'Argent Nfld. & L., Canada 47°33N 54°54W 142 E6
Bay Mills Indian Reservation Mich., U.S.A. 46°25N 84°15W 79 C7
Bay Minette Ala., U.S.A. 30°53N 87°46W 112 F3
Bay Park N.Y., U.S.A. 40°37N 73°40W 97 C5
Bay Pines Tampa, U.S.A. 27°48N 82°46W 115 C2
Bay Port Mich., U.S.A. 43°51N 83°23W 79 F8
Bay Ridge N.Y., U.S.A. 40°37N 74°1W 97 C2
Bay Roberts Nfld. & L., Canada 47°36N 53°16W 142 E7
Bay St. Louis Miss., U.S.A. 30°19N 89°20W 111 F4
Bay Shore N.Y., U.S.A. 40°43N 73°15W 92 B3
Bay Springs Miss., U.S.A. 31°59N 89°17W 111 E4
Bay Springs L. Miss., U.S.A. 34°31N 88°20W 111 B5
Bay View Md., U.S.A. 39°39N 75°58W 93 A5
Bayamo Cuba 20°20N 76°40W 182 B4
Bayamón Puerto Rico 18°24N 66°9W 184 G16
Bayard Iowa, U.S.A. 41°51N 94°33W 81 D4
Bayard N. Mex., U.S.A. 32°46N 108°8W 131 E2
Bayard Nebr., U.S.A. 41°45N 103°20W 80 C2
Bayard W. Va., U.S.A. 39°16N 79°22W 93 A1
Bayboro N.C., U.S.A. 35°9N 76°46W 103 C9
Bayfield Colo., U.S.A. 37°14N 107°36W 125 E3
Bayfield Wis., U.S.A. 46°49N 90°49W 78 B3
Bayfield County ☆ Wis., U.S.A. 46°25N 91°15W 78 B2
Bayfield Ridge Wis., U.S.A. 46°45N 91°25W 78 B2
Baylor County ☆ Tex., U.S.A. 33°35N 99°16W 109 D8
Bayonet Point Fla., U.S.A. 28°20N 82°41W 114 C6
Bayonne N.J., U.S.A. 40°40N 74°6W 97 B2
Bayou Boeuf La., U.S.A. 29°50N 90°35W 117 C2
Bayou Cane La., U.S.A. 29°37N 90°45W 110 E5
Bayou D'Arbonne L. La., U.S.A. 32°43N 92°21W 110 B3
Bayou de Chien → Ky., U.S.A. 36°35N 89°12W 104 D3
Bayou DeView → Ark., U.S.A. 34°48N 91°18W 106 C4
Bayou George Fla., U.S.A. 30°19N 85°33W 114 A3
Bayou La Batre Ala., U.S.A. 30°24N 88°15W 112 F2
Bayou Meto → Ark., U.S.A. 34°13N 91°31W 106 D4
Bayou Pierre → Miss., U.S.A. 31°55N 91°11W 111 E2
Bayou Sauvage Nat. Wildlife Refuge △ La., U.S.A. 30°1N 89°53W 117 B3
Bayou Segnette State Park △ La., U.S.A. 29°53N 90°10W 117 C1
Bayou Vista La., U.S.A. 29°41N 91°16W 110 E4
Bayport Fla., U.S.A. 28°32N 82°39W 114 C6
Bays, L. of Ont., Canada 45°15N 79°4W 146 B7
Bayshore Calif., U.S.A. 37°42N 122°24W 132 B2
Bayshore Fla., U.S.A. 26°43N 81°50W 114 E7
Bayside Ont., Canada 44°7N 77°30W 147 C9
Bayside N.Y., U.S.A. 40°46N 73°46W 97 B4
Bayside Wis., U.S.A. 43°10N 87°54W 94 A2
Bayside Beach Md., U.S.A. 39°8N 76°27W 93 A4
Baysville Ont., Canada 45°9N 79°7W 146 B7
Baytown Tex., U.S.A. 29°43N 94°59W 109 H13
Bayview Calif., U.S.A. 37°44N 122°23W 132 B2
Bayview Idaho, U.S.A. 47°59N 116°34W 122 B2

Baz, Pta. Yucatán, Mexico 21°10N 90°5W 179 A3
Bazaar Kans., U.S.A. 38°16N 96°32W 82 C7
Bazile Mills Nebr., U.S.A. 42°31N 97°53W 80 B8
Bazine Kans., U.S.A. 38°27N 99°42W 82 C4
Beach N. Dak., U.S.A. 46°58N 104°0W 76 D2
Beach City Ohio, U.S.A. 40°39N 81°35W 86 C5
Beach Haven N.J., U.S.A. 39°34N 74°14W 92 C2
Beachburg Ont., Canada 45°44N 76°51W 147 B10
Beachville Ont., Canada 43°5N 80°49W 146 D6
Beachville Md., U.S.A. 38°8N 76°24W 93 B4
Beachwood N.J., U.S.A. 39°56N 74°12W 92 C2
Beacon Iowa, U.S.A. 41°17N 92°41W 81 D6
Beacon N.Y., U.S.A. 41°30N 73°58W 92 A3
Beacon Hill Fla., U.S.A. 29°55N 85°23W 114 B3
Beaconia Man., Canada 50°25N 96°31W 151 E15
Beaconsfield Qué., Canada 45°26N 73°52W 160 B1
Beadle County ☆ S. Dak., U.S.A. 44°22N 98°13W 76 F7
Beagle Kans., U.S.A. 38°25N 94°57W 82 C9
Beale Air Force Base Calif., U.S.A. 39°7N 121°19W 126 D5
Beallsville Ohio, U.S.A. 39°51N 81°2W 86 D5
Beals Cr. → Tex., U.S.A. 32°10N 100°51W 108 E7
Beamsville Ont., Canada 43°12N 79°28W 146 D7
Bear Del., U.S.A. 39°38N 75°39W 93 A5
Bear → Utah, U.S.A. 41°30N 112°8W 129 B7
Bear Bay Nunavut, Canada 75°47N 87°0W 158 B8
Bear Brook State Park △ N.H., U.S.A. 43°6N 71°21W 89 C3
Bear Cr. → Ala., U.S.A. 33°11N 88°5W 112 C2
Bear Cr. → Wyo., U.S.A. 41°41N 104° 3W 124 E8
Bear Creek Village Pa., U.S.A. 41°11N 75°45W 92 A1
Bear L. Alta., Canada 55°9N 119°4W 152 C1
Bear L. Utah, U.S.A. 41°59N 111°22W 122 G7
Bear Lake Mich., U.S.A. 44°25N 86°9W 79 E5
Bear Lake County ☆ Idaho, U.S.A. 42°10N 111°15W 122 G7
Bear Lake Nat. Wildlife Refuge △ Idaho, U.S.A. 42°10N 111°18W 122 G7
Bear Mt. Ky., U.S.A. 37°32N 84°6W 105 C8
Bear Peak Wyo., U.S.A. 43°4N 109°3W 124 C3
Bear River N.S., Canada 44°34N 65°39W 141 J4
Bear River City Utah, U.S.A. 41°37N 112°8W 129 B7
Bear River Range U.S.A. 42°9N 111°36W 122 G7
Bear Tooth Pass Wyo., U.S.A. 44°58N 109°28W 124 B3
Bearden Ark., U.S.A. 33°43N 92°37W 106 E3
Bearden Okla., U.S.A. 35°21N 96°23W 107 C7
Beardmore Ont., Canada 49°36N 87°57W 149 C9
Beardsley Kans., U.S.A. 39°36N 101°14W 82 B2
Beardsley Minn., U.S.A. 45°33N 96°43W 77 E2
Beardstown Ill., U.S.A. 40°1N 90°26W 84 C3
Béarn Qué., Canada 47°17N 79°20W 144 D7
Bearmouth Mont., U.S.A. 46°48N 113°20W 123 D4
Bearpaw Mts. Mont., U.S.A. 48°12N 109°30W 123 B8
Bears Ears Utah, U.S.A. 37°38N 109°51W 129 F6
Bearskin Lake Ont., Canada 53°58N 91°2W 159 G7
Beartooth Mts. Mont., U.S.A. 45°10N 109°48W 123 E8
Beartooth Pass Wyo., U.S.A. 44°58N 109°28W 124 B3
Beata, C. Dom. Rep. 17°40N 71°30W 183 C5
Beata, I. Dom. Rep. 17°34N 71°31W 183 C5
Beata Ridge W. Indies 16°0N 72°30W 183 C5
Beatrice Ala., U.S.A. 31°44N 87°13W 112 E3
Beatrice Nebr., U.S.A. 40°16N 96°45W 80 D9
Beattie Kans., U.S.A. 39°52N 96°25W 82 B7
Beatton → B.C., Canada 56°15N 120°45W 157 E8
Beatton River B.C., Canada 57°26N 121°20W 157 E8
Beatty Sask., Canada 52°54N 104°48W 150 C7
Beatty Nev., U.S.A. 36°54N 116°46W 128 F4
Beatty Oreg., U.S.A. 42°27N 121°16W 121 E4
Beattyville Ky., U.S.A. 37°35N 83°42W 105 C9
Beauceville Qué., Canada 46°13N 70°46W 145 E12
Beaucham, L. Qué., Canada 45°29N 75°37W 160 A2
Beauchêne, L. Qué., Canada 46°35N 78°55W 144 E4
Beaufort N.C., U.S.A. 34°43N 76°40W 103 D9
Beaufort S.C., U.S.A. 32°26N 80°40W 103 F5
Beaufort County ☆ N.C., U.S.A. 35°30N 76°50W 103 C9
Beaufort County ☆ S.C., U.S.A. 32°20N 80°50W 103 F5
Beaufort Sea Arctic 72°0N 140°0W 156 B4
Beaulac Qué., Canada 45°50N 71°23W 145 F11
Beaumont Alta., Canada 53°21N 113°25W 152 E7
Beaumont Nfld. & L., Canada 49°37N 55°41W 142 C5
Beaumont Calif., U.S.A. 33°57N 116°59W 127 K10
Beaumont Miss., U.S.A. 31°10N 88°55W 111 E5
Beaumont Tex., U.S.A. 30°5N 94°6W 109 G13
Beaumonte Heights Ont., Canada 43°45N 79°34W 161 A3
Beauport Qué., Canada 46°52N 71°11W 145 E11
Beaupré Qué., Canada 47°3N 70°54W 145 D12
Beauregard Parish ☆ La., U.S.A. 30°39N 93°25W 110 D2
Beausejour Man., Canada 50°5N 96°35W 151 E15
Beauval Sask., Canada 55°9N 107°37W 157 F11
Beaux Arts Wash., U.S.A. 47°35N 122°11W 132 C4
Beaver Alaska, U.S.A. 66°22N 147°24W 135 C11
Beaver Kans., U.S.A. 38°38N 98°40W 82 C5
Beaver Ohio, U.S.A. 39°2N 82°50W 86 D4
Beaver Okla., U.S.A. 36°49N 100°31W 107 B3
Beaver Oreg., U.S.A. 45°17N 123°49W 121 B2
Beaver Pa., U.S.A. 40°42N 80°19W 87 D2
Beaver Utah, U.S.A. 38°17N 112°38W 129 E3
Beaver → B.C., Canada 59°52N 124°20W 157 E8
Beaver → Sask., Canada 55°26N 107°45W 157 F11
Beaver → Okla., U.S.A. 36°35N 99°30W 107 B4
Beaver → Utah, U.S.A. 39°10N 112°57W 129 D3
Beaver Bay Minn., U.S.A. 47°16N 91°18W 77 C7
Beaver Brook Station N.B., Canada 46°33N 65°36W 141 F4
Beaver City Nebr., U.S.A. 40°8N 99°50W 80 D6
Beaver County ☆ Okla., U.S.A. 36°45N 100°25W 107 B3
Beaver County ☆ Pa., U.S.A. 40°45N 80°20W 87 D2
Beaver County ☆ Utah, U.S.A. 38°20N 113°10W 129 E2
Beaver Cr. → Colo., U.S.A. 40°20N 103°33W 125 B7
Beaver Cr. → Mont., U.S.A. 48°27N 107°13W 123 B10
Beaver Cr. → N. Dak., U.S.A. 47°20N 103°39W 76 C2
Beaver Cr. → N. Dak., U.S.A. 46°15N 100°32W 76 D5
Beaver Cr. → Nebr., U.S.A. 40°7N 99°29W 80 D6
Beaver Cr. → Tex., U.S.A. 33°53N 98°49W 109 D9
Beaver Cr. → Wyo., U.S.A. 42°58N 108°26W 124 D4
Beaver Creek N.W.T., Canada 63°0N 141°0W 157 D4
Beaver Creek Colo., U.S.A. 43°33N 96°22W 77 G2
Beaver Crossing Nebr., U.S.A. 40°47N 97°17W 80 D8
Beaver Dam Ky., U.S.A. 37°24N 86°52W 104 C6
Beaver Dam Wis., U.S.A. 43°28N 88°50W 78 E5
Beaver Dam L. Wis., U.S.A. 43°31N 88°53W 78 E5
Beaver Falls Pa., U.S.A. 40°46N 80°20W 87 D2
Beaver I. Mich., U.S.A. 45°40N 85°33W 79 D6
Beaver L. Ark., U.S.A. 36°25N 93°51W 106 B2
Beaver Lake Minn., U.S.A. 44°59N 93°0W 94 B3
Beavercreek Ohio, U.S.A. 39°43N 84°11W 86 D2

Beaverdam Ohio, U.S.A. 40°50N 83°59W 86 C3
Beaverdell B.C., Canada 49°27N 119°6W 155 F15
Beaverhead → Mont., U.S.A. 45°31N 112°21W 123 E5
Beaverhead County ☆ Mont., U.S.A. 45°5N 113°10W 123 E4
Beaverhead Mts. Mont., U.S.A. 45°0N 113°20W 122 E5
Beaverhill L. Alta., Canada 53°27N 112°32W 152 E8
Beaverlodge Alta., Canada 55°11N 119°29W 152 C1
Beavermouth B.C., Canada 51°32N 117°23W 155 D17
Beaverton Ont., Canada 44°26N 79°9W 146 C7
Beaverton Mich., U.S.A. 43°53N 84°29W 79 F7
Beaverton Mont., U.S.A. 48°26N 107°15W 123 B10
Beaverton Oreg., U.S.A. 45°29N 122°48W 132 B1
Bebe Tex., U.S.A. 29°25N 97°38W 109 H10
Becal Campeche, Mexico 20°27N 90°2W 179 B2
Bécancour Qué., Canada 46°20N 72°26W 145 E10
Becerra Nfld. & L., Canada 50°20N 57°32W 142 B3
Becharof L. Alaska, U.S.A. 57°56N 156°23W 135 H8
Becharof Nat. Wildlife Refuge △ Alaska, U.S.A. 58°0N 156°15W 135 H8
Beck L. Ill., U.S.A. 42°4N 87°52W 95 A1
Becker County ☆ Minn., U.S.A. 46°50N 95°50W 77 D3
Beckham County ☆ Okla., U.S.A. 35°15N 99°40W 107 C4
Beckley W. Va., U.S.A. 37°47N 81°11W 102 D3
Beckville Tex., U.S.A. 32°15N 94°27W 109 E13
Beckwith Cr. → La., U.S.A. 30°13N 93°13W 110 D2
Becky Pk. Nev., U.S.A. 39°58N 114°36W 128 C6
Bedford N.S., Canada 44°44N 63°40W 141 J6
Bedford Qué., Canada 45°7N 72°59W 145 F10
Bedford Ind., U.S.A. 38°52N 86°29W 85 F4
Bedford Iowa, U.S.A. 40°40N 94°44W 81 E4
Bedford Ky., U.S.A. 38°36N 85°19W 105 B7
Bedford Mass., U.S.A. 42°27N 71°15W 96 A1
Bedford N.H., U.S.A. 42°55N 71°32W 89 D3
Bedford N.Y., U.S.A. 41°12N 73°39W 91 C1
Bedford Ohio, U.S.A. 41°23N 81°32W 86 B5
Bedford Pa., U.S.A. 40°1N 78°30W 87 E4
Bedford Tex., U.S.A. 32°50N 97°8W 116 A3
Bedford County ☆ Pa., U.S.A. 40°0N 78°30W 87 E4
Bedford County ☆ Tenn., U.S.A. 35°29N 86°28W 104 E6
Bedford County ☆ Va., U.S.A. 37°20N 79°31W 102 D5
Bedford Park Ill., U.S.A. 41°46N 87°46W 95 C2
Bedford Reservation Ohio, U.S.A. 41°22N 81°33W 98 B2
Bedford Stuyvesant N.Y., U.S.A. 40°41N 73°56W 97 B3
Bedias Tex., U.S.A. 30°47N 95°57W 109 G12
Bedrock Colo., U.S.A. 38°19N 108°54W 125 D2
Bee Nebr., U.S.A. 41°0N 97°4W 80 C8
Bee County ☆ Tex., U.S.A. 28°24N 97°45W 109 J10
Bee Ridge Fla., U.S.A. 27°17N 82°29W 114 D6
Bee Springs Ky., U.S.A. 37°17N 86°17W 104 C6
Beebe Ark., U.S.A. 35°4N 91°53W 106 C4
Beech → Tenn., U.S.A. 35°37N 88°2W 104 E4
Beech Bottom W. Va., U.S.A. 40°14N 80°39W 102 A4
Beech Creek Pa., U.S.A. 41°5N 77°36W 87 C5
Beech Fork → Ky., U.S.A. 37°46N 85°41W 105 C7
Beech Fork L. W. Va., U.S.A. 38°18N 82°25W 102 C2
Beech Grove Ind., U.S.A. 39°43N 86°5W 85 E4
Beech Mountain N.C., U.S.A. 36°12N 81°53W 103 B4
Beecher Ill., U.S.A. 41°21N 87°38W 84 B6
Beecher City Ill., U.S.A. 39°11N 88°47W 84 D5
Beecher Falls Vt., U.S.A. 45°1N 71°31W 89 A3
Beechey Hd. B.C., Canada 48°10N 123°30W 155 G11
Beechey Point Alaska, U.S.A. 70°29N 149°9W 135 A10
Beechgrove Tenn., U.S.A. 35°38N 86°14W 104 E6
Beechwood Miss., U.S.A. 35°10N 88°46W 104 E5
Beechy Sask., Canada 50°53N 107°24W 150 E4
Beef I. Br. Virg'n Is. 18°26N 64°30W 184 G18
Beeler Kans., U.S.A. 38°26N 100°12W 82 C3
Beemer Nebr., U.S.A. 41°56N 96°48W 80 C9
Beersheba Springs Tenn., U.S.A. 35°28N 85°39W 105 E7
Beeton Ont., Canada 44°5N 79°47W 146 C7
Beetz, L. Qué., Canada 50°34N 62°42W 140 C7
Beeville Tex., U.S.A. 28°24N 97°45W 109 J10
Beggs Okla., U.S.A. 35°45N 96°4W 107 C7
Begonias, Presa Guanajuato, Mexico 20°53N 100°51W 175 B7
Begonias México, Mexico 19°18N 100°25W 175 D7
Beiseker Alta., Canada 51°23N 113°32W 153 G7
Bejacos México, Mexico 18°46N 100°25W 175 D7
Bejou Minn., U.S.A. 47°26N 95°59W 77 C3
Beklabito N. Mex., U.S.A. 36°50N 109°1W 131 A1
Bel Air Calif., U.S.A. 34°4N 118°27W 133 B2
Bel Air Md., U.S.A. 39°32N 76°21W 93 A4
Bel Aire Kans., U.S.A. 37°46N 97°16W 82 D6
Bel Alton Md., U.S.A. 38°28N 76°59W 93 B4
Bel-Nor Mo., U.S.A. 38°42N 90°19W 94 A2
Bel-Ridge Mo., U.S.A. 38°42N 90°19W 94 A2
Bélanger Qué., Canada 45°35N 73°42W 160 A1
Belanger → Man., Canada 53°27N 97°41W 151 B14
Belbutte Sask., Canada 53°22N 107°49W 150 B4
Belcamp Md., U.S.A. 39°28N 76°14W 93 A4
Belcher Chan. Nunavut, Canada 77°15N 95°0W 158 B6
Belcher Is. N.W.T., Canada 56°15N 78°45W 143 B2
Belchertown Mass., U.S.A. 42°17N 72°24W 91 B2
Belcourt Qué., Canada 48°24N 77°21W 144 C5
Belcourt N. Dak., U.S.A. 48°50N 99°45W 76 B6
Belden Nebr., U.S.A. 42°25N 97°13W 80 B8
Belding Mich., U.S.A. 43°6N 85°14W 79 F6
Belen N. Mex., U.S.A. 34°40N 106°46W 131 C4
Belews L. N.C., U.S.A. 36°15N 80°5W 103 B5
Belfair Wash., U.S.A. 47°27N 122°50W 120 C3
Belfast Maine, U.S.A. 44°26N 69°1W 90 D4
Belfast N.Y., U.S.A. 42°21N 78°7W 88 C2
Belfield N. Dak., U.S.A. 46°53N 103°12W 76 D2
Belfry Mont., U.S.A. 45°9N 109°1W 123 E8
Belgium Wis., U.S.A. 43°30N 87°51W 78 E6
Belgrade Maine, U.S.A. 44°27N 69°50W 90 D4
Belgrade Minn., U.S.A. 45°27N 95°0W 77 E3
Belgrade Mont., U.S.A. 45°47N 111°11W 123 E6
Belgrade Nebr., U.S.A. 41°28N 98°4W 80 C7
Belhaven N.C., U.S.A. 35°33N 76°37W 103 C9
Belington W. Va., U.S.A. 39°2N 79°56W 102 B5
Belize ■ Cent. Amer. 17°0N 88°30W 182 C2
Belize City Belize 17°25N 88°10W 182 C2
Belize Inlet B.C., Canada 51°8N 127°20W 154 D7
Belknap Ill., U.S.A. 37°19N 88°56W 84 F5
Belknap County ☆ N.H., U.S.A. 43°30N 71°30W 89 C3
Bell Calif., U.S.A. 33°58N 118°11W 133 C3
Bell Fla., U.S.A. 29°45N 82°52W 114 B6
Bell → Qué., Canada 49°48N 77°38W 144 B5
Bell Buckle Tenn., U.S.A. 35°35N 86°21W 104 E6
Bell City Mo., U.S.A. 37°1N 89°49W 83 D7
Bell County ☆ Ky., U.S.A. 36°45N 83°40W 105 D9

Bell County ☆ Tex., U.S.A. 31°3N 97°28W 109 F10
Bell Gardens Calif., U.S.A. 33°58N 118°9W 133 C4
Bell I. Nfld. & L., Canada 47°38N 52°58W 142 E8
Bell I. Nfld. & L., Canada 50°46N 55°35W 142 B5
Bell-Irving → B.C., Canada 56°12N 129°5W 157 E7
Bell L. Ont., Canada 49°48N 90°58W 148 C6
Bell Peninsula Nunavut, Canada 63°50N 82°0W 159 E12
Bell Ranch N. Mex., U.S.A. 35°32N 104°6W 131 B6
Bella Bella B.C., Canada 52°10N 128°10W 154 C6
Bella Coola B.C., Canada 52°25N 126°40W 154 C8
Bella Vista Ark., U.S.A. 36°28N 94°16W 106 B1
Bellaire Mich., U.S.A. 44°59N 85°13W 79 E6
Bellaire N.Y., U.S.A. 40°42N 73°45W 97 B4
Bellaire Ohio, U.S.A. 40°1N 80°45W 86 C6
Bellaire Tex., U.S.A. 29°42N 95°27W 116 B2
Bellamy Ala., U.S.A. 32°27N 88°8W 112 D2
Bellavista Chiapas, Mexico 15°35N 92°13W 178 D3
Belle Mo., U.S.A. 38°17N 91°43W 83 C5
Belle W. Va., U.S.A. 38°14N 81°33W 102 C3
Belle → Mich., U.S.A. 42°43N 82°30W 98 G9
Belle-Chasse La., U.S.A. 29°51N 90°0W 117 C3
Belle Fourche → S. Dak., U.S.A. 44°40N 103°51W 76 F3
Belle Fourche S. Dak., U.S.A. 44°26N 102°18W 76 F3
Belle Fourche Res. S. Dak., U.S.A. 44°44N 103°41W 76 F2
Belle Glade Fla., U.S.A. 26°41N 80°40W 114 E8
Belle Harbor N.Y., U.S.A. 40°34N 73°51W 97 C3
Belle Haven Va., U.S.A. 37°33N 75°49W 102 D7
Belle Isle Nfld. & L., Canada 51°57N 55°25W 142 A5
Belle Isle Fla., U.S.A. 28°27N 81°21W 115 B2
Belle Isle Mich., U.S.A. 42°20N 82°58W 98 A3
Belle Isle, Str. of Nfld. & L., Canada 51°30N 56°30W 142 A4
Belle Isle Park Mich., U.S.A. 42°20N 82°58W 98 A3
Belle Plaine Iowa, U.S.A. 41°54N 92°17W 81 D6
Belle Plaine Kans., U.S.A. 37°24N 97°17W 82 D6
Belle Plaine Minn., U.S.A. 44°37N 93°46W 77 F5
Belle Rive Ill., U.S.A. 38°14N 88°45W 84 E5
Belle River Ont., Canada 42°18N 82°43W 146 E4
Belle Valley Ohio, U.S.A. 39°47N 81°33W 86 D5
Belle View Va., U.S.A. 38°57N 77°14W 99 B2
Belleair Tampa, U.S.A. 27°56N 82°48W 115 B2
Belleair Beach Tampa, U.S.A. 27°55N 82°50W 115 B1
Belleair Bluffs Tampa, U.S.A. 27°55N 82°49W 115 B2
Belleair Shore Tampa, U.S.A. 27°54N 82°50W 115 B1
Bellechester Minn., U.S.A. 44°22N 92°31W 77 F6
Bellefontaine Ohio, U.S.A. 40°22N 83°46W 86 C3
Bellefontaine Neighbors Mo., U.S.A. 38°44N 90°13W 94 A2
Bellefonte Del., U.S.A. 39°47N 75°30W 93 A5
Bellefonte Pa., U.S.A. 40°55N 77°47W 87 D5
Bellemont Ariz., U.S.A. 35°14N 111°50W 130 B4
Belleoram Nfld. & L., Canada 47°31N 55°25W 142 E5
Belleplain N.J., U.S.A. 39°11N 74°46W 92 C2
Bellerive Mo., U.S.A. 38°42N 90°18W 94 A2
Bellerose N.Y., U.S.A. 40°43N 73°42W 97 B4
Belleterre Qué., Canada 47°25N 78°41W 144 D4
Belleview Fla., U.S.A. 29°4N 82°3W 114 B6
Belleville Ont., Canada 44°10N 77°23W 147 C9
Belleville Ill., U.S.A. 38°31N 89°59W 84 E4
Belleville Kans., U.S.A. 39°50N 97°38W 82 B6
Belleville N.J., U.S.A. 40°47N 74°9W 97 B2
Belleville Wis., U.S.A. 42°52N 89°32W 78 F4
Bellevue Idaho, U.S.A. 43°28N 114°16W 122 F4
Bellevue Iowa, U.S.A. 42°16N 90°26W 81 C8
Bellevue Nebr., U.S.A. 41°9N 95°54W 80 C10
Bellevue Ohio, U.S.A. 41°17N 82°51W 86 B4
Bellevue Pa., U.S.A. 40°29N 80°3W 98 H1
Bellevue Wash., U.S.A. 47°37N 122°12W 132 C5
Bellflower Ill., U.S.A. 40°20N 88°32W 84 C5
Bellflower Mo., U.S.A. 39°0N 91°21W 83 B5
Bellin = Kangirsuk Qué., Canada 60°0N 70°0W 143 A4
Bellingham Mass., U.S.A. 42°5N 71°28W 91 B3
Bellingham Minn., U.S.A. 45°8N 96°17W 77 E2
Bellingham Wash., U.S.A. 48°46N 122°29W 120 B3
Belliveaus Cove N.S., Canada 44°23N 66°4W 141 J3
Bellmawr N.J., U.S.A. 39°52N 75°5W 98 B2
Bellmead Tex., U.S.A. 31°35N 97°6W 109 F10
Bellot Str. Nunavut, Canada 71°59N 94°48W 158 C7
Bellows Falls Vt., U.S.A. 43°8N 72°27W 89 C2
Bellport N.Y., U.S.A. 40°46N 72°56W 92 B4
Bells Tenn., U.S.A. 35°43N 89°5W 104 E3
Bells Tex., U.S.A. 33°37N 96°25W 109 D11
Bells Corners Ont., Canada 45°19N 75°50W 147 B11
Bellsite Man., Canada 52°35N 101°4W 151 C10
Belltown Del., U.S.A. 38°45N 75°11W 93 B5
Belltown N. Mex., U.S.A. 34°49N 103°7W 131 C7
Bellville Ga., U.S.A. 32°9N 81°59W 113 D5
Bellville Tex., U.S.A. 29°57N 96°15W 109 H11
Bellvue Colo., U.S.A. 40°38N 105°10W 125 B5
Bellwood Ill., U.S.A. 41°52N 87°53W 95 B1
Bellwood La., U.S.A. 31°32N 93°12W 110 C2
Bellwood Nebr., U.S.A. 41°21N 97°14W 80 C8
Bellwood Pa., U.S.A. 40°36N 78°20W 87 D4
Belly → Alta., Canada 49°46N 113°2W 153 J7
Belmar N.J., U.S.A. 40°11N 74°2W 92 B2
Belmond Iowa, U.S.A. 42°51N 93°37W 81 C5
Belmont Man., Canada 49°25N 99°27W 151 F12
Belmont N.S., Canada 45°25N 63°23W 141 H6
Belmont Ont., Canada 42°53N 81°5W 146 E5
Belmont Calif., U.S.A. 37°32N 122°16W 132 B2
Belmont Mass., U.S.A. 42°23N 71°10W 96 A1
Belmont Miss., U.S.A. 34°31N 88°13W 111 B5
Belmont N.H., U.S.A. 43°27N 71°29W 89 C3
Belmont N.Y., U.S.A. 42°14N 78°2W 88 C2
Belmont W. Va., U.S.A. 39°23N 81°16W 102 B4
Belmont Wis., U.S.A. 42°44N 90°20W 78 F3
Belmont County ☆ Ohio, U.S.A. 40°1N 81°4W 86 C5
Belmont Cragin Ill., U.S.A. 41°55N 87°45W 95 B2
Belmont Harbor Ill., U.S.A. 41°56N 87°38W 95 B3
Belmopan Belize 17°18N 88°30W 182 C2
Beloeil Qué., Canada 45°34N 73°12W 145 F9
Beloit Kans., U.S.A. 39°28N 98°6W 82 B5
Beloit Wis., U.S.A. 42°31N 89°2W 78 F4
Belot, L. N.W.T., Canada 66°53N 126°16W 156 C7
Belpre Kans., U.S.A. 37°57N 99°6W 82 D4
Belpre Ohio, U.S.A. 39°17N 81°34W 86 D5
Belt Mont., U.S.A. 47°23N 110°55W 123 C7
Belted Ra. Nev., U.S.A. 37°22N 116°8W 128 E4
Belton Mo., U.S.A. 38°49N 94°32W 83 C2
Belton S.C., U.S.A. 34°31N 82°30W 103 D3
Belton Tex., U.S.A. 31°3N 97°28W 109 F10
Belton L. Tex., U.S.A. 31°6N 97°28W 109 F10
Beltrami Minn., U.S.A. 47°33N 96°32W 77 C2
Beltrami County ☆ Minn., U.S.A. 47°45N 94°50W 77 C4

Beltsville *Md., U.S.A.* 39°2N 76°54W **93** A4
Belvedere *Calif., U.S.A.* 37°52N 122°27W **132** A2
Belvedere *Georgia, U.S.A.* 33°45N 84°16W **117** B3
Belvidere *Ill., U.S.A.* 42°15N 88°50W **84** A5
Belvidere *N.J., U.S.A.* 40°50N 75°5W **92** B1
Belvidere *Nebr., U.S.A.* 40°15N 97°33W **80** D8
Belvidere *S. Dak., U.S.A.* 43°50N 101°16W **76** G4
Belvidere Mt. *Vt., U.S.A.* 44°46N 72°33W **89** B2
Belview *Minn., U.S.A.* 44°36N 95°20W **77** F3
Belvue *Kans., U.S.A.* 39°13N 96°11W **82** B7
Belwood *N.C., U.S.A.* 35°29N 81°31W **103** C4
Bement *Ill., U.S.A.* 39°55N 88°34W **84** D5
Bemidji *Minn., U.S.A.* 47°28N 94°53W **77** C4
Bemis *W. Va., U.S.A.* 38°49N 79°45W **102** C5
Ben Avon *Pa., U.S.A.* 40°30N 80°5W **98** A1
Ben Avon Heights *Pa., U.S.A.* 40°30N 80°4W **98** A1
Ben Hill County ☆ *Ga., U.S.A.* 31°45N 83°10W **113** E3
Ben Lomond *Ark., U.S.A.* 33°50N 94°7W **106** E1
Ben Lomond *Calif., U.S.A.* 37°5N 122°5W **126** F4
Bena *Minn., U.S.A.* 47°21N 94°12W **77** C4
Benavides *Tex., U.S.A.* 27°36N 98°25W **108** K9
Benbrook *Tex., U.S.A.* 32°41N 97°28W **109** E10
Benchley *Tex., U.S.A.* 30°45N 96°27W **109** G11
Bend *Oreg., U.S.A.* 44°4N 121°19W **121** C4
Bendale *Ont., Canada* 43°45N 79°13W **161** A3
Benedict *Kans., U.S.A.* 37°38N 95°45W **82** D8
Benedict *Md., U.S.A.* 38°31N 76°41W **93** B4
Benedict *Nebr., U.S.A.* 41°0N 97°36W **80** D8
Benemérito de las Américas *Chiapas, Mexico* 16°31N 90°38W **178** C6
Benevolence *Ga., U.S.A.* 31°53N 84°44W **113** E2
Benewah County ☆ *Idaho, U.S.A.* 47°5N 116°35W **122** B2
Benham *Ky., U.S.A.* 36°58N 82°57W **105** D10
Benito *Man., Canada* 51°55N 101°33W **151** D10
Benito González *Tabasco, Mexico* 17°52N 92°42W **178** B4
Benito Juárez *Baja Calif. S., Mexico* 25°7N 111°50W **167** H7
Benito Juárez *Chiapas, Mexico* 16°2N 92°49W **178** C4
Benito Juárez *Chihuahua, Mexico* 29°10N 106°58W **169** D9
Benito Juárez *Chihuahua, Mexico* 30°10N 106°53W **169** C9
Benito Juárez *Distrito Federal, Mexico* 19°23N 99°9W **181** B3
Benito Juárez *Guerrero, Mexico* 18°17N 100°28W **175** D5
Benito Juárez *Quintana Roo, Mexico* 19°42N 88°47W **179** C5
Benito Juárez *Tabasco, Mexico* 17°50N 92°33W **178** B4
Benito Juárez *Tabasco, Mexico* 18°10N 93°54W **178** A3
Benito Juárez *Veracruz, Mexico* 20°18N 97°9W **176** D3
Benito Juárez *Veracruz, Mexico* 20°54N 98°11W **176** D2
Benito Juárez *Zacatecas, Mexico* 21°30N 103°34W **173** F7
Benito Juárez, Int. ✈ (MEX) *Distrito Federal, Mexico* 19°25N 99°5W **181** B3
Benito Juárez, Parque Nacional △ *Oaxaca, Mexico* 17°8N 96°43W **177** G4
Benjamin *Tex., U.S.A.* 33°35N 99°48W **109** D8
Benjamín Hill *Sonora, Mexico* 30°9N 111°7W **168** C4
Benkelman *Nebr., U.S.A.* 40°3N 101°32W **80** D4
Benld *Ill., U.S.A.* 39°6N 89°48W **84** D4
Bennet *Nebr., U.S.A.* 40°41N 96°30W **80** D9
Bennett *B.C., Canada* 59°51N 135°0W **157** E6
Bennett *Colo., U.S.A.* 39°46N 104°26W **125** C6
Bennett *Iowa, U.S.A.* 41°43N 90°59W **81** D8
Bennett County ☆ *S. Dak., U.S.A.* 43°5N 101°45W **76** G4
Bennettsville *S.C., U.S.A.* 34°37N 79°41W **103** D6
Bennington *Idaho, U.S.A.* 42°24N 111°19W **122** G7
Bennington *Kans., U.S.A.* 39°2N 97°36W **82** B6
Bennington *N.H., U.S.A.* 43°0N 71°55W **89** C3
Bennington *Okla., U.S.A.* 41°22N 96°9W **80** D9
Bennington *Okla., U.S.A.* 34°0N 96°2W **107** E7
Bennington *Vt., U.S.A.* 42°53N 73°12W **89** D1
Bennington County ☆ *Vt., U.S.A.* 43°0N 73°10W **89** D1
Benny *Ont., Canada* 46°47N 81°38W **146** A5
Benoit *Miss., U.S.A.* 33°39N 91°11W **111** C2
Benque Viejo *Belize* 17°5N 89°8W **182** C2
Bens Run *W. Va., U.S.A.* 39°28N 81°6W **102** B3
Bensley *Va., U.S.A.* 37°27N 77°27W **102** D7
Benson *Sask., Canada* 49°27N 103°1W **150** F8
Benson *Ariz., U.S.A.* 31°58N 110°18W **130** F5
Benson *Ill., U.S.A.* 40°51N 89°7W **84** C4
Benson *La., U.S.A.* 31°52N 93°42W **110** C2
Benson *Minn., U.S.A.* 45°19N 95°36W **77** E3
Benson *N.C., U.S.A.* 35°23N 78°33W **103** C7
Benson *Vt., U.S.A.* 43°42N 73°18W **89** C1
Benson County ☆ *N. Dak., U.S.A.* 48°5N 99°25W **76** B6
Bensonhurst *N.Y., U.S.A.* 40°35N 73°59W **97** C3
Bent County ☆ *Colo., U.S.A.* 38°0N 103°0W **125** E7
Bentley *Alta., Canada* 52°28N 114°4W **153** F6
Bentley *Kans., U.S.A.* 37°54N 97°31W **82** D6
Bentleyville *Pa., U.S.A.* 40°7N 80°1W **87** D2
Benton *Ark., U.S.A.* 34°34N 92°35W **106** D3
Benton *Calif., U.S.A.* 37°48N 118°32W **126** F8
Benton *Ill., U.S.A.* 38°0N 88°55W **84** E5
Benton *Kans., U.S.A.* 40°42N 94°42W **81** E4
Benton *Kans., U.S.A.* 37°47N 97°6W **82** D6
Benton *Ky., U.S.A.* 36°52N 88°21W **104** D4
Benton *La., U.S.A.* 32°42N 93°44W **110** B2
Benton *Miss., U.S.A.* 32°50N 90°16W **111** D3
Benton *Mo., U.S.A.* 37°6N 89°34W **83** D7
Benton *N.H., U.S.A.* 44°8N 71°55W **89** B3
Benton *Pa., U.S.A.* 41°12N 76°23W **87** C6
Benton *Tenn., U.S.A.* 35°10N 84°39W **105** E8
Benton *Wis., U.S.A.* 42°34N 90°23W **78** F3
Benton City *Mo., U.S.A.* 39°8N 91°46W **83** B5
Benton City *Wash., U.S.A.* 46°16N 119°29W **120** D6
Benton County ☆ *Ark., U.S.A.* 36°22N 94°13W **106** B1
Benton County ☆ *Ind., U.S.A.* 40°35N 87°20W **85** C3
Benton County ☆ *Iowa, U.S.A.* 42°0N 92°0W **81** C6
Benton County ☆ *Minn., U.S.A.* 45°45N 94°0W **77** E5
Benton County ☆ *Miss., U.S.A.* 34°50N 89°11W **111** B4
Benton County ☆ *Mo., U.S.A.* 38°20N 93°15W **83** C3
Benton County ☆ *Oreg., U.S.A.* 44°30N 123°20W **121** C2
Benton County ☆ *Tenn., U.S.A.* 36°4N 88°6W **104** D4
Benton County ☆ *Wash., U.S.A.* 46°25N 119°25W **120** D6
Benton Harbor *Mich., U.S.A.* 42°6N 86°27W **79** G4
Benton Heights *Mich., U.S.A.* 42°7N 86°24W **79** G5
Benton L. *Mont., U.S.A.* 47°40N 111°20W **123** C6
Benton Lake Nat. Wildlife Refuge △ *Mont., U.S.A.* 47°40N 111°20W **123** C6
Benton Ridge *Ohio, U.S.A.* 41°0N 83°48W **86** C3
Bentonia *Miss., U.S.A.* 32°38N 90°22W **111** D3
Bentonite Spur *Wyo., U.S.A.* 44°52N 104°54W **124** B8
Bentonville *Ark., U.S.A.* 36°22N 94°13W **106** B1
Bentonville *Va., U.S.A.* 38°50N 78°19W **93** B2
Bent's Old Fort Nat. Historic Site △ *Colo., U.S.A.* 38°6N 103°5W **125** D7
Benwood *W. Va., U.S.A.* 40°1N 80°44W **102** A4
Benzie County ☆ *Mich., U.S.A.* 44°40N 86°0W **79** E5

Beowawe *Nev., U.S.A.* 40°35N 116°29W **128** B4
Berclair *Tenn., U.S.A.* 35°8N 89°54W **117** B2
Berclair *Tex., U.S.A.* 28°32N 97°36W **109** J10
Berea *Ky., U.S.A.* 37°34N 84°17W **105** C8
Berea *Nebr., U.S.A.* 42°13N 102°59W **80** B3
Berea *S.C., U.S.A.* 34°50N 82°25W **103** D3
Berea *Ohio, U.S.A.* 41°22N 81°51W **86** B5
Berens → *Man., Canada* 52°25N 97°2W **151** C14
Berens I. *Man., Canada* 52°18N 97°18W **151** C14
Berens River *Man., Canada* 52°25N 97°0W **151** C14
Beresford *N.B., Canada* 47°42N 65°42W **141** F4
Beresford *S. Dak., U.S.A.* 43°5N 96°47W **76** G9
Bergen *N.Y., U.S.A.* 43°5N 77°57W **88** B3
Bergen County ☆ *N.J., U.S.A.* 41°0N 74°10W **92** B2
Bergenfield *N.J., U.S.A.* 40°55N 73°59W **97** A3
Berger *Mo., U.S.A.* 38°41N 91°20W **83** C5
Bergland *Mich., U.S.A.* 46°36N 89°34W **79** C2
Bergoo *W. Va., U.S.A.* 38°29N 80°18W **102** C4
Bergstrom-Austin Int. ✈ (AUS) *Tex., U.S.A.* 30°12N 97°41W **109** G10
Bering Glacier *Alaska, U.S.A.* 60°20N 143°30W **135** F12
Bering Land Bridge Nat. Preserve △ *Alaska, U.S.A.* 66°20N 165°0W **135** C6
Bering Strait *Pac. Oc.* 65°30N 169°0W **135** D5
Berino *N. Mex., U.S.A.* 32°4N 106°37W **131** E4
Berkeley *Calif., U.S.A.* 37°51N 122°16W **132** A3
Berkeley *Mo., U.S.A.* 38°45N 90°19W **94** A2
Berkeley County ☆ *S.C., U.S.A.* 33°15N 80°0W **103** E6
Berkeley County ☆ *W. Va., U.S.A.* 39°27N 77°58W **102** B7
Berkeley Springs *W. Va., U.S.A.* 39°38N 78°14W **93** A2
Berkley *Mich., U.S.A.* 42°30N 83°11W **98** A1
Berks County ☆ *Pa., U.S.A.* 40°25N 76°0W **87** D6
Berkshire County ☆ *Mass., U.S.A.* 42°25N 73°15W **91** B1
Berkshire Hills *Mass., U.S.A.* 42°20N 73°10W **91** B1
Berland → *Alta., Canada* 54°0N 116°50W **152** D4
Berlin = Kitchener *Ont., Canada* 43°27N 80°29W **146** D6
Berlin *Conn., U.S.A.* 41°37N 72°45W **91** C2
Berlin *Ga., U.S.A.* 31°4N 83°37W **113** E3
Berlin *Md., U.S.A.* 38°20N 75°13W **93** B5
Berlin *N. Dak., U.S.A.* 46°23N 98°29W **76** D7
Berlin *N.H., U.S.A.* 44°28N 71°11W **89** B3
Berlin *N.J., U.S.A.* 39°48N 74°56W **92** C2
Berlin *N.Y., U.S.A.* 42°42N 73°23W **91** B1
Berlin *Okla., U.S.A.* 35°27N 99°36W **107** C4
Berlin *Pa., U.S.A.* 39°55N 78°57W **87** E4
Berlin *Wis., U.S.A.* 43°58N 88°57W **78** E5
Berlin Heights *Ohio, U.S.A.* 41°20N 82°30W **86** B4
Berlin L. *Ohio, U.S.A.* 41°3N 81°0W **86** B5
Bermejillo *Durango, Mexico* 25°53N 103°37W **173** B7
Bermen, L. *Qué., Canada* 53°35N 68°55W **143** C4
Bern *Kans., U.S.A.* 39°58N 95°58W **82** B8
Bernal *N. Mex., U.S.A.* 35°24N 105°19W **131** B5
Bernal Heights *Calif., U.S.A.* 37°44N 122°24W **132** B2
Bernalillo *N. Mex., U.S.A.* 35°18N 106°33W **131** B4
Bernalillo County ☆ *N. Mex., U.S.A.* 35°0N 106°45W **131** B4
Bernard *N.W.T., Canada* 73°36N 124°14W **156** B8
Bernard I. *Ont., Canada* 45°45N 79°23W **146** B7
Bernardo *N. Mex., U.S.A.* 34°25N 106°50W **131** C4
Bernardston *Mass., U.S.A.* 42°40N 72°33W **91** B2
Bernardsville *N.J., U.S.A.* 40°43N 74°34W **92** B2
Berne *La., U.S.A.* 40°39N 84°57W **85** C6
Bernice *La., U.S.A.* 32°49N 92°39W **110** B3
Bernice *Okla., U.S.A.* 36°34N 94°57W **107** B9
Bernie *Mo., U.S.A.* 36°40N 89°58W **83** E7
Bernier B. *N.W.T., Canada* 71°5N 88°15W **158** C8
Berrien County ☆ *Ga., U.S.A.* 31°15N 83°10W **113** E3
Berrien County ☆ *Mich., U.S.A.* 42°0N 86°25W **79** H5
Berrien Springs *Mich., U.S.A.* 41°57N 86°20W **79** H5
Berriozábal *Chiapas, Mexico* 16°48N 93°16W **178** C3
Berry *Ala., U.S.A.* 33°40N 87°36W **112** C3
Berry *Ky., U.S.A.* 38°31N 84°22W **105** B8
Berry Cr. → *Alta., Canada* 50°50N 111°33W **153** H9
Berry Is. *Bahamas* 25°40N 77°50W **182** A4
Berrydale *Fla., U.S.A.* 30°53N 87°3W **114** A1
Berryessa, L. *Calif., U.S.A.* 38°31N 122°6W **126** E4
Berryville *Ark., U.S.A.* 36°22N 93°34W **106** B2
Berryville *Va., U.S.A.* 39°9N 77°59W **93** A3
Bertha *Minn., U.S.A.* 46°16N 95°4W **77** D3
Berthierville *Qué., Canada* 46°5N 73°10W **145** E9
Berthold *N. Dak., U.S.A.* 48°19N 101°44W **76** B4
Berthoud *Colo., U.S.A.* 40°19N 105°5W **125** C5
Berthoud Pass *Colo., U.S.A.* 39°48N 105°47W **125** C5
Bertie County ☆ *N.C., U.S.A.* 36°0N 77°0W **103** B8
Bertram *Iowa, U.S.A.* 41°57N 91°32W **81** D7
Bertram *Tex., U.S.A.* 30°45N 98°3W **109** G9
Bertrand *N.B., Canada* 47°45N 65°4W **141** F4
Bertrand *Mich., U.S.A.* 41°47N 86°16W **79** H5
Bertrand *Mo., U.S.A.* 36°55N 89°27W **83** E7
Bertrand *Nebr., U.S.A.* 40°32N 99°38W **80** D6
Berwick *N.B., Canada* 45°47N 65°36W **141** H4
Berwick *N.S., Canada* 45°3N 64°44W **141** H5
Berwick *La., U.S.A.* 29°42N 91°13W **110** E4
Berwick *Maine, U.S.A.* 43°16N 70°52W **90** E3
Berwick *N. Dak., U.S.A.* 48°22N 100°18W **76** B5
Berwick *Pa., U.S.A.* 41°3N 76°14W **87** C6
Berwyn *Alta., Canada* 56°9N 117°44W **152** B3
Berwyn *Ill., U.S.A.* 41°50N 87°47W **95** B2
Berwyn *Nebr., U.S.A.* 41°21N 99°30W **80** D6
Berwyn Heights *Md., U.S.A.* 38°59N 76°55W **99** B4
Beryl *Utah, U.S.A.* 37°54N 113°40W **129** F2
Bessemer *Ala., U.S.A.* 33°24N 86°58W **112** C4
Bessemer *Mich., U.S.A.* 46°29N 90°3W **79** C1
Bessemer *Pa., U.S.A.* 40°59N 80°30W **87** D2
Bessemer City *N.C., U.S.A.* 35°17N 81°17W **103** C4
Bessie *Okla., U.S.A.* 35°23N 98°59W **107** C5
Bessie, L. *Fla., U.S.A.* 28°29N 81°31N **115** B1
Best *Tex., U.S.A.* 31°13N 101°37W **108** F6
Bethalto *Ill., U.S.A.* 38°54N 90°3W **94** A4
Bethany *Ont., Canada* 44°11N 78°34W **147** C8
Bethany *Ill., U.S.A.* 39°39N 88°45W **84** D5
Bethany *Mo., U.S.A.* 40°16N 94°2W **83** A2
Bethany *Okla., U.S.A.* 35°31N 97°39W **107** C6
Bethany Beach *Del., U.S.A.* 38°32N 75°5W **93** B5
Bethel *Alaska, U.S.A.* 60°48N 161°45W **135** F7
Bethel *Conn., U.S.A.* 41°22N 73°25W **91** C1
Bethel *Maine, U.S.A.* 44°25N 70°47W **90** D3
Bethel *Minn., U.S.A.* 45°24N 93°16W **77** E5
Bethel *N.C., U.S.A.* 35°48N 77°22W **103** C8
Bethel *Ohio, U.S.A.* 38°58N 84°5W **86** E2
Bethel *Okla., U.S.A.* 34°22N 94°51W **107** D9
Bethel *Pa., U.S.A.* 40°28N 76°18W **87** D6
Bethel *Vt., U.S.A.* 43°50N 72°38W **89** C2
Bethel ☆ *Alaska, U.S.A.* 60°45N 160°30W **135** F7
Bethel Acres *Okla., U.S.A.* 35°20N 97°3W **107** C6
Bethel Park *Pa., U.S.A.* 40°19N 80°2W **98** C1
Bethel Springs *Tenn., U.S.A.* 35°14N 88°36W **104** E4

Bethesda *Md., U.S.A.* 38°59N 77°6W **99** B3
Bethesda *N.C., U.S.A.* 35°57N 78°50W **103** C7
Bethesda *Ohio, U.S.A.* 40°1N 81°4W **86** C5
Bethlehem *Conn., U.S.A.* 41°38N 73°13W **91** C1
Bethlehem *Ill., U.S.A.* 38°45N 75°57W **93** B5
Bethlehem *N.C., U.S.A.* 35°50N 81°18W **103** C4
Bethlehem *N.H., U.S.A.* 44°17N 71°41W **89** B3
Bethlehem *Pa., U.S.A.* 40°37N 75°23W **92** B1
Bethpage *N.Y., U.S.A.* 40°44N 73°30W **92** B3
Bethune *Sask., Canada* 50°43N 105°13W **150** E6
Bethune *Colo., U.S.A.* 39°18N 102°26W **125** C8
Betsiamites *Qué., Canada* 48°56N 68°40W **145** C14
Betsiamites → *Qué., Canada* 48°56N 68°38W **145** C14
Betsie, Pt. *Mich., U.S.A.* 44°41N 86°15W **79** E5
Bettendorf *Iowa, U.S.A.* 41°32N 90°30W **81** D81
Betterton *Md., U.S.A.* 39°22N 76°4W **93** A4
Beulah *Colo., U.S.A.* 38°5N 104°59W **125** D6
Beulah *Fla., U.S.A.* 28°32N 81°34W **115** A1
Beulah *Mich., U.S.A.* 44°38N 86°6W **79** E5
Beulah *N. Dak., U.S.A.* 47°16N 101°47W **76** C3
Beulah *Wyo., U.S.A.* 44°33N 104°5W **124** B8
Beulah, L. *Wis., U.S.A.* 42°48N 88°31W **78** F5
Beulah Res. *Oreg., U.S.A.* 43°55N 118°9W **121** D7
Beulahville *N.C., U.S.A.* 34°55N 77°46W **103** D8
Beulahville *Va., U.S.A.* 37°51N 77°11W **93** C3
Bevier *Mo., U.S.A.* 39°45N 92°34W **83** B4
Bewdley *Ont., Canada* 44°5N 78°19W **147** C8
Bexar *Ala., U.S.A.* 34°11N 88°9W **112** B2
Bexar County ☆ *Tex., U.S.A.* 29°25N 98°30W **109** H9
Bibb County ☆ *Ala., U.S.A.* 32°57N 87°8W **112** D3
Bibb County ☆ *Ga., U.S.A.* 32°50N 83°45W **113** D3
Bibby I. *Nunavut, Canada* 61°55N 93°0W **159** E7
Bic, Île du *Qué., Canada* 48°24N 68°52W **145** C14
Bicentennial Park *Calif., U.S.A.* 34°1N 118°1W **133** B4
Bickerton West *N.S., Canada* 45°6N 61°44W **141** H8
Bicknell *Ind., U.S.A.* 38°47N 87°19W **85** E3
Bicknell *Utah, U.S.A.* 38°20N 111°33W **129** E4
Biddeford *Maine, U.S.A.* 43°30N 70°28W **90** E3
Bieber *Calif., U.S.A.* 41°7N 121°8W **126** B5
Bieler L. *Nunavut, Canada* 70°23N 73°5W **158** C11
Bienfait *Sask., Canada* 49°10N 102°50W **150** F9
Bienville *La., U.S.A.* 32°22N 92°59W **110** B3
Bienville, L. *Qué., Canada* 55°5N 72°40W **143** B3
Bienville Nat. Forest *Miss., U.S.A.* 32°10N 89°25W **111** D4
Bienville Parish ☆ *La., U.S.A.* 32°20N 93°0W **110** B2
Big → *Nfld. & L., Canada* 54°50N 58°55W **143** C6
Big → *Mo., U.S.A.* 38°28N 90°37W **83** C6
Big Antelope Cr. → *Oreg., U.S.A.* 42°28N 117°13W **121** E8
Big B. *Nfld. & L., Canada* 55°43N 60°35W **143** B5
Big Baldy *Idaho, U.S.A.* 44°47N 115°13W **122** E3
Big Baldy Mountain *Mont., U.S.A.* 46°59N 110°39W **123** D7
Big Bar *Calif., U.S.A.* 40°45N 123°15W **126** C2
Big Bar Creek *B.C., Canada* 51°12N 122°7W **155** D12
Big Bass *Tamaulipas, Mexico* 24°2N 98°41W **171** F6
Big Basswood L. *Ont., Canada* 46°25N 83°23W **146** A3
Big Bay *Mich., U.S.A.* 46°49N 87°44W **79** C4
Big Bay de Noc *Mich., U.S.A.* 45°45N 86°40W **79** D5
Big Bear City *Calif., U.S.A.* 34°16N 116°51W **127** J10
Big Bear Lake *Calif., U.S.A.* 34°15N 116°56W **127** J10
Big Beaver *Sask., Canada* 49°10N 105°10W **150** F6
Big Belt Mts. *Mont., U.S.A.* 46°30N 111°25W **123** D6
Big Bend *Calif., U.S.A.* 41°1N 121°55W **126** B5
Big Bend Dam *S. Dak., U.S.A.* 44°1N 99°23W **76** F6
Big Bend Nat. Park △ *Tex., U.S.A.* 29°20N 103°5W **108** H4
Big Black → *Miss., U.S.A.* 32°3N 91°4W **111** D2
Big Blue → *Kans., U.S.A.* 39°35N 96°34W **82** B7
Big Boggy Nat. Wildlife Refuge △ *Tex., U.S.A.* 28°17N 95°52W **109** J12
Big Bow *Kans., U.S.A.* 37°34N 101°34W **82** D2
Big Cabin *Okla., U.S.A.* 36°32N 95°14W **107** B8
Big Canyon → *Tex., U.S.A.* 29°45N 101°48W **108** F5
Big Chino Wash → *Ariz., U.S.A.* 34°52N 112°28W **130** C3
Big Clifty *Ky., U.S.A.* 37°33N 86°9W **104** C6
Big Coal → *W. Va., U.S.A.* 38°16N 81°48W **102** C3
Big Cr. → *B.C., Canada* 51°42N 122°41W **155** D12
Big Creek *B.C., Canada* 51°43N 123°2W **155** D11
Big Creek *Idaho, U.S.A.* 45°8N 115°20W **122** E3
Big Creek L. *Ala., U.S.A.* 30°43N 88°20W **112** F2
Big Creek Park △ *B.C., Canada* 51°18N 123°10W **155** D11
Big Creek Reservation *Ohio, U.S.A.* 41°26N 81°45W **98** B1
Big Cypress Indian Reservation *Fla., U.S.A.* 26°18N 81°0W **114** E7
Big Cypress Nat. Preserve △ *Fla., U.S.A.* 26°0N 81°10W **114** E7
Big Cypress Swamp *Fla., U.S.A.* 26°15N 81°30W **114** E7
Big Darby Cr. → *Ohio, U.S.A.* 39°37N 82°58W **86** D4
Big Delta *Alaska, U.S.A.* 64°10N 145°51W **135** D11
Big Dry Creek *Mont., U.S.A.* 47°31N 106°17W **123** C10
Big Eau Pleine Res. *Wis., U.S.A.* 44°44N 89°46W **78** D4
Big Falls *Minn., U.S.A.* 48°12N 93°48W **77** B5
Big Falls *Wis., U.S.A.* 44°37N 89°1W **78** D4
Big Flat *Ark., U.S.A.* 36°1N 92°24W **106** B3
Big Fork → *Minn., U.S.A.* 48°31N 93°44W **77** B5
Big Hatchet Peak *N. Mex., U.S.A.* 31°38N 108°24W **131** F2
Big Hill *Nebr., U.S.A.* 42°23N 102°33W **80** B3
Big Hole → *Mont., U.S.A.* 45°43N 112°24W **123** D5
Big Hole Nat. Battlefield-Nez Perce Nat. Historic Park △ *Mont., U.S.A.* 45°39N 113°39W **123** D4
Big Horn *Wyo., U.S.A.* 44°41N 106°59W **124** B6
Big Horn → *Wyo., U.S.A.* 44°41N 106°59W **124** B6
Big Horn County ☆ *Mont., U.S.A.* 45°25N 107°45W **123** E10
Big Horn County ☆ *Wyo., U.S.A.* 44°45N 108°0W **124** B4
Big Horn Dam *Alta., Canada* 52°20N 116°20W **153** F4
Big Horn Mts. = Bighorn Mts. *Wyo., U.S.A.* 44°25N 107°0W **124** B6
Big I. *Nunavut, Canada* 62°43N 70°43W **159** E11
Big I. *Nunavut, Canada* 49°9N 94°40W **148** C2
Big Island *Va., U.S.A.* 37°32N 79°22W **102** D5
Big L. *Ala., U.S.A.* 41°7N 121°25W **126** B5
Big L. *Maine, U.S.A.* 45°11N 67°41W **90** C6
Big Lake *Alaska, U.S.A.* 61°20N 150°0W **135** F10
Big Lake *Minn., U.S.A.* 45°20N 93°45W **77** E5
Big Lake *Tex., U.S.A.* 31°12N 101°28W **108** F6

Big Lake Nat. Wildlife Refuge △ *Ark., U.S.A.* 35°54N 90°7W **106** C6
Big Lookout Mt. *Oreg., U.S.A.* 44°36N 117°17W **121** C8
Big Lost → *Idaho, U.S.A.* 43°50N 112°44W **122** F6
Big Muddy → *Ill., U.S.A.* 37°33N 89°32W **84** F4
Big Muddy Cr. → *Mont., U.S.A.* 48°8N 104°36W **123** B13
Big Muddy Cr. → *N. Dak., U.S.A.* 46°37N 101°24W **76** D4
Big Muddy L. *Sask., Canada* 49°9N 104°51W **150** F7
Big Nemaha → *Nebr., U.S.A.* 40°1N 95°32W **80** D10
Big Oak Nat. Wildlife Refuge △ *Ind., U.S.A.* 38°56N 85°26W **85** E5
Big Otter → *Va., U.S.A.* 37°7N 79°23W **102** D5
Big Pine *Calif., U.S.A.* 37°10N 118°17W **127** F8
Big Pine Key *Fla., U.S.A.* 24°40N 81°21W **114** G7
Big Piney *Wyo., U.S.A.* 42°32N 110°7W **124** D7
Big Pond *N.S., Canada* 45°57N 60°32W **141** H9
Big Quill L. *Sask., Canada* 51°55N 104°50W **150** D7
Big Rapids *Mich., U.S.A.* 43°42N 85°29W **79** F6
Big Rib → *Wis., U.S.A.* 44°56N 89°41W **78** D4
Big Rideau L. *Ont., Canada* 44°40N 76°15W **147** C10
Big River *Sask., Canada* 53°50N 107°0W **150** D4
Big Rock → *N.C., U.S.A.* 36°35N 87°46W **104** D5
Big Sable Pt. *Mich., U.S.A.* 44°3N 86°1W **79** E5
Big Sage Res. *Calif., U.S.A.* 41°35N 120°38W **126** B6
Big Salmon → *Yukon, Canada* 61°52N 134°55W **157** D6
Big Salmon Range *Yukon, Canada* 61°20N 133°45W **157** D6
Big Sand L. *Man., Canada* 57°45N 99°45W **159** F6
Big Sand Lake *Fla., U.S.A.* 28°25N 81°29W **115** B2
Big Sandy *Mont., U.S.A.* 48°11N 110°7W **123** B7
Big Sandy *Tenn., U.S.A.* 36°14N 88°5W **104** D4
Big Sandy *Tex., U.S.A.* 32°35N 95°7W **109** E12
Big Sandy *Wyo., U.S.A.* 42°38N 109°28W **124** D3
Big Sandy → *Ariz., U.S.A.* 34°19N 113°31W **130** C2
Big Sandy → *Ky., U.S.A.* 38°25N 82°36W **105** B10
Big Sandy → *Mont., U.S.A.* 36°14N 88°5W **104** D4
Big Sandy Cr. = Sandy Cr. → *Wyo., U.S.A.* 41°51N 109°47W **124** D3
Big Sandy Cr. → *Colo., U.S.A.* 38°7N 102°29W **125** D8
Big Sandy Cr. → *Mont., U.S.A.* 48°34N 109°48W **123** B8
Big Sandy L. *Sask., Canada* 54°27N 104°56W **150** A7
Big Sandy L. *Minn., U.S.A.* 46°46N 93°17W **77** D5
Big Sandy Res. *Wyo., U.S.A.* 42°15N 109°26W **124** D3
Big Satilla Cr. → *Ga., U.S.A.* 31°27N 82°3W **113** E4
Big Sheep Mt. *Mont., U.S.A.* 47°10N 105°40W **123** C12
Big Sioux → *S. Dak., U.S.A.* 42°29N 96°27W **76** H9
Big Sky *Mont., U.S.A.* 45°17N 111°22W **123** E6
Big Smoky Valley *Nev., U.S.A.* 38°40N 117°10W **128** D3
Big Snowy Mts. *Mont., U.S.A.* 46°45N 109°30W **123** D8
Big South Fork Nat. River and Recr. Area △ *Tenn., U.S.A.* 36°27N 84°47W **105** E8
Big Southern Butte *Idaho, U.S.A.* 43°23N 113°1W **122** F5
Big Spring *Ky., U.S.A.* 37°48N 86°9W **104** C6
Big Spring *Tex., U.S.A.* 32°15N 101°28W **108** E6
Big Springs *Nebr., U.S.A.* 41°4N 102°5W **80** C3
Big Stone City *S. Dak., U.S.A.* 45°18N 96°28W **76** E1
Big Stone County ☆ *Minn., U.S.A.* 45°25N 96°15W **77** E2
Big Stone Gap *Va., U.S.A.* 36°52N 82°47W **102** E2
Big Stone L. *Minn., U.S.A.* 45°18N 96°27W **77** E2
Big Stone Nat. Wildlife Refuge △ *Minn., U.S.A.* 45°12N 96°4W **77** E2
Big Sunflower → *Miss., U.S.A.* 32°40N 90°40W **111** D3
Big Sur *Calif., U.S.A.* 36°15N 121°48W **126** G5
Big Swamp → *N.C., U.S.A.* 34°28N 78°57W **103** D7
Big Thicket Nat. Preserve △ *Tex., U.S.A.* 30°12N 94°7W **109** G13
Big Timber *Mont., U.S.A.* 45°50N 109°57W **123** E8
Big Trails *Wyo., U.S.A.* 43°46N 107°19W **124** C5
Big Trout L. *Ont., Canada* 45°46N 78°37W **147** B8
Big Trout L. *Ont., Canada* 53°40N 90°0W **159** G7
Big Trout Lake *Ont., Canada* 53°45N 90°0W **159** G8
Big Valley *Alta., Canada* 52°2N 112°46W **153** F7
Big Water *Utah, U.S.A.* 37°5N 111°40W **129** F4
Big Wells *Tex., U.S.A.* 28°34N 99°34W **109** J8
Big Wills Cr. → *Ala., U.S.A.* 33°59N 86°0W **112** C5
Big Wood → *Idaho, U.S.A.* 42°52N 114°54W **122** G4
Bigelow *Ark., U.S.A.* 35°0N 92°38W **106** C3
Bigelow *Minn., U.S.A.* 43°30N 95°42W **77** G3
Bigfork *Minn., U.S.A.* 47°45N 93°39W **77** C5
Bigfork *Mont., U.S.A.* 48°4N 114°4W **123** B3
Biggar *Sask., Canada* 52°4N 108°0W **150** C4
Biggs *Calif., U.S.A.* 39°25N 121°43W **126** D5
Biggs *Oreg., U.S.A.* 45°40N 120°50W **121** B5
Biggsville *Ill., U.S.A.* 40°51N 90°52W **84** C3
Bighorn *Mont., U.S.A.* 46°10N 107°27W **123** D10
Bighorn → *Mont., U.S.A.* 46°10N 107°28W **123** D10
Bighorn Basin *Wyo., U.S.A.* 44°15N 108°0W **124** B6
Bighorn Canyon Nat. Recr. Area △ *Mont., U.S.A.* 45°10N 108°0W **123** E9
Bighorn L. *Mont., U.S.A.* 44°55N 108°15W **123** E9
Bighorn Mts. *Wyo., U.S.A.* 44°25N 107°0W **124** B6
Bighorn Nat. Forest *Wyo., U.S.A.* 44°50N 107°25W **124** B5
Bight, The *Bahamas* 24°19N 75°24W **183** B4
Biglerville *Pa., U.S.A.* 39°56N 77°15W **87** E5
Bigniba → *Qué., Canada* 49°18N 77°20W **144** B3
Bigot, L. *Qué., Canada* 50°50N 65°39W **140** C4
Bigpoint *Miss., U.S.A.* 30°35N 88°29W **111** F5
Bigsby I *Ont., Canada* 49°4N 94°34W **148** C2
Bigstick L. *Sask., Canada* 50°16N 109°20W **150** E2
Bigstone L. *Man., Canada* 53°42N 95°44W **151** B16
Bijou Cr. → *Colo., U.S.A.* 40°17N 104°0W **125** B6
Bilk Creek Mts. *Nev., U.S.A.* 41°50N 118°27W **128** A2
Bill *Wyo., U.S.A.* 43°14N 105°16W **124** C7
Bill Baggs Cape Florida State Recr. Area △ *Fla., U.S.A.* 25°40N 80°9W **115** D3
Bill Williams → *Ariz., U.S.A.* 34°18N 114°4W **130** C1
Bill Williams Mt. *Ariz., U.S.A.* 35°12N 112°12W **130** B3
Bill Williams River Nat. Wildlife Refuge △ *Ariz., U.S.A.* 34°20N 114°5W **130** C1
Billerica *Mass., U.S.A.* 42°34N 71°16W **91** B3
Billete, Cerro el *Guerrero, Mexico* 18°11N 101°18W **175** D6
Billings *Mo., U.S.A.* 37°4N 93°33W **83** D3
Billings *Mont., U.S.A.* 45°47N 108°30W **123** E9
Billings *Okla., U.S.A.* 36°32N 97°27W **107** B6
Billings County ☆ *N. Dak., U.S.A.* 47°0N 103°15W **76** C2
Billingsley *Ala., U.S.A.* 32°40N 86°43W **112** D4
Billy Chinook, L. *Oreg., U.S.A.* 44°36N 121°17W **121** C4
Billy Clapp L. *Wash., U.S.A.* 47°29N 119°20W **120** C6
Biloxi *Miss., U.S.A.* 30°24N 88°53W **111** F5
Biltmore Forest *N.C., U.S.A.* 35°34N 82°33W **103** C3
Bimini Is. *Bahamas* 25°42N 79°25W **182** A4
Binford *N. Dak., U.S.A.* 47°34N 98°21W **76** C7
Bingen *Wash., U.S.A.* 45°43N 121°28W **120** E4
Binger *Okla., U.S.A.* 35°18N 98°21W **107** C5
Bingham *Maine, U.S.A.* 45°3N 69°53W **90** C4
Bingham *N. Mex., U.S.A.* 33°55N 106°21W **131** D4

Name	Coordinates	Ref
Bingham *Nebr., U.S.A.*	42°1N 102°5W	80 B3
Bingham Canyon *Utah, U.S.A.*	40°32N 112°9W	129 C3
Bingham County ☆ *Idaho, U.S.A.*	43°15N 112°30W	122 F6
Binghamton *N.Y., U.S.A.*	42°6N 75°55W	88 C5
Binscarth *Man., Canada*	50°37N 101°17W	151 E10
Biola *Calif., U.S.A.*	36°48N 120°1W	127 G6
Birch → *Alta., Canada*	58°28N 112°17W	157 E10
Birch Bay *Wash., U.S.A.*	48°55N 122°45W	120 B3
Birch Cliff *Ont., Canada*	43°41N 79°16W	161 A3
Birch Cr. → *Idaho, U.S.A.*	43°51N 112°43W	122 F6
Birch Hills *Sask., Canada*	52°59N 105°25W	150 C6
Birch I., *Man., Canada*	52°26N 99°54W	151 C12
Birch Island *B.C., Canada*	51°37N 119°54W	155 D15
Birch L. *Alta., Canada*	53°19N 111°35W	152 E9
Birch L. *Ont., Canada*	51°23N 92°18W	148 A4
Birch L. *Sask., Canada*	53°27N 108°10W	150 B3
Birch L. *Minn., U.S.A.*	47°45N 91°51W	77 C7
Birch L. *Okla., U.S.A.*	36°30N 96°27W	107 B7
Birch Lake *Minn., U.S.A.*	45°4N 93°2W	94 A3
Birch Mts. *Alta., Canada*	57°30N 113°10W	157 E10
Birch River *Man., Canada*	52°24N 101°6W	151 C10
Birch Run *Mich., U.S.A.*	43°15N 83°48W	79 F8
Birch Tree *Mo., U.S.A.*	36°59N 91°30W	83 E5
Birchwood *Alaska, U.S.A.*	61°24N 149°28W	135 F10
Birchwood *Wis., U.S.A.*	45°40N 91°33W	78 C2
Birchwood Village *Minn., U.S.A.*	45°3N 92°58W	94 A4
Birchy Bay *Nfld. & L., Canada*	49°21N 54°44W	142 C6
Bird City *Kans., U.S.A.*	39°45N 101°32W	82 B2
Bird Cove *Nfld. & L., Canada*	51°3N 56°56W	142 A4
Bird I. = Aves, I. de *W. Indies*	15°45N 63°55W	183 C7
Bird Island *Minn., U.S.A.*	44°46N 94°54W	77 F4
Birds *Ill., U.S.A.*	38°50N 87°40W	84 E6
Birdsboro *Pa., U.S.A.*	40°16N 75°48W	92 B1
Birdseye *Ind., U.S.A.*	38°19N 86°42W	85 E4
Birdsville *Md., U.S.A.*	38°54N 76°36W	93 B4
Birken *B.C., Canada*	50°28N 122°37W	155 E12
Birkenhead Lake Park △ *B.C., Canada*	50°35N 122°45W	155 E12
Birmingham *Ala., U.S.A.*	33°31N 86°48W	112 C4
Birmingham *Iowa, U.S.A.*	40°53N 91°57W	81 E7
Birmingham ✈ (BHM) *Ala., U.S.A.*	33°34N 86°45W	112 C4
Birnamwood *Wis., U.S.A.*	44°56N 89°13W	78 D4
Biron *Qué., Canada*	48°12N 66°16W	140 E3
Birsay *Sask., Canada*	51°6N 106°59W	150 D5
Birtle *Man., Canada*	50°30N 101°5W	151 D10
Bisbee *Ariz., U.S.A.*	31°27N 109°55W	130 F6
Bisbee *N. Dak., U.S.A.*	48°37N 99°23W	76 B6
Biscay *Minn., U.S.A.*	44°50N 94°16W	77 F4
Biscayne, Key *Fla., U.S.A.*	25°42N 80°10W	114 F8
Biscayne B. *Fla., U.S.A.*	25°40N 80°12W	114 F8
Biscayne Bay Aquatic Reserve *Fla., U.S.A.*	25°33N 80°13W	115 D1
Biscayne Nat. Park △ *Fla., U.S.A.*	25°25N 80°12W	114 F8
Biscayne Park *Fla., U.S.A.*	25°52N 80°10W	115 C2
Biscoe *Ark., U.S.A.*	34°49N 91°25W	106 D4
Biscoe *N.C., U.S.A.*	35°22N 79°47W	103 C6
Biscotasi L. *Ont., Canada*	47°22N 82°1W	149 E14
Biscotasing *Ont., Canada*	47°18N 82°9W	149 E14
Bishop *Calif., U.S.A.*	37°22N 118°24W	127 F8
Bishop *La., U.S.A.*	33°49N 83°26W	113 C3
Bishop *Tex., U.S.A.*	27°35N 97°48W	108 K10
Bishop Creek Res. *Nev., U.S.A.*	41°15N 114°50W	128 A6
Bishop Museum *Hawai'i, U.S.A.*	21°20N 157°52W	136 K14
Bishop River Park △ *B.C., Canada*	50°55N 124°2W	154 E10
Bishop's Falls *Nfld. & L., Canada*	49°2N 55°30W	142 C5
Bishops Head *Md., U.S.A.*	38°16N 76°5W	93 B4
Bishopville *Md., U.S.A.*	38°22N 75°19W	93 B5
Bishopville *S.C., U.S.A.*	34°13N 80°15W	103 D5
Bismarck *Ark., U.S.A.*	34°19N 93°10W	106 D2
Bismarck *Ill., U.S.A.*	40°16N 87°37W	84 C6
Bismarck *Mo., U.S.A.*	37°46N 90°38W	83 D6
Bismarck *N. Dak., U.S.A.*	46°48N 100°47W	76 D5
Bison *Kans., U.S.A.*	38°31N 99°12W	82 C4
Bison *Okla., U.S.A.*	36°12N 97°53W	107 B6
Bison *S. Dak., U.S.A.*	45°31N 102°28W	76 E3
Bison L. *Alta., Canada*	57°12N 116°8W	152 A4
Bissett *Man., Canada*	51°2N 95°41W	151 D16
Bistcho L. *Alta., Canada*	59°45N 118°50W	157 E9
Bistineau, L. *La., U.S.A.*	32°20N 93°25W	110 B2
Bitely *Mich., U.S.A.*	43°45N 85°52W	79 F6
Bithlo *Fla., U.S.A.*	28°33N 81°6W	114 C7
Bitter Cr. → *Utah, U.S.A.*	39°59N 109°19W	129 D6
Bitter Cr. → *Wyo., U.S.A.*	41°31N 109°27W	124 E4
Bitter Creek *Wyo., U.S.A.*	41°33N 108°33W	124 E4
Bitter L. *Sask., Canada*	50°7N 109°48W	150 E2
Bitter L. *S. Dak., U.S.A.*	45°17N 97°19W	76 E8
Bittern L. *Alta., Canada*	53°3N 113°5W	153 E7
Bittern L. *Sask., Canada*	53°56N 105°45W	150 B6
Bitterroot → *Mont., U.S.A.*	46°52N 114°7W	123 D3
Bitterroot Nat. Forest *Idaho, U.S.A.*	45°52N 114°10W	122 D4
Bitterroot Range *Idaho, U.S.A.*	46°0N 114°20W	122 D4
Bittinger *Md., U.S.A.*	39°37N 79°14W	93 A1
Biwabik *Minn., U.S.A.*	47°32N 92°21W	77 C61
Bixby *Mo., U.S.A.*	37°40N 91°7W	83 D5
Bixby *Okla., U.S.A.*	35°57N 95°53W	107 C8
Bizard, Île *Qué., Canada*	45°29N 73°54W	160 B1
Bjorkdale *Sask., Canada*	52°43N 103°39W	150 C8
Bjorne Pen. *Nunavut, Canada*	77°37N 87°0W	158 B8
Blache, L. de la *Qué., Canada*	50°5N 69°29W	145 A13
Black → *Ont., Canada*	44°42N 79°19W	146 C7
Black → *Alaska, U.S.A.*	66°42N 144°42W	135 C11
Black → *Ariz., U.S.A.*	33°44N 110°13W	130 D5
Black → *Ark., U.S.A.*	35°38N 91°20W	106 C4
Black → *La., U.S.A.*	31°16N 91°50W	110 C4
Black → *Mich., U.S.A.*	45°39N 84°31W	79 D7
Black → *Mich., U.S.A.*	42°59N 82°27W	79 G9
Black → *N.Y., U.S.A.*	34°35N 78°19W	88 C4
Black → *N.Y., U.S.A.*	43°59N 76°4W	88 B4
Black → *S.C., U.S.A.*	33°24N 79°15W	103 E6
Black → *Vt., U.S.A.*	44°55N 72°13W	89 B2
Black → *Wis., U.S.A.*	43°57N 91°22W	78 E21
Black B. *Ont., Canada*	48°40N 88°25W	148 D8
Black Bay Pen. *Ont., Canada*	48°38N 88°21W	148 D8
Black Bear Cr. → *Okla., U.S.A.*	36°25N 96°38W	107 B7
Black Butte L. *Calif., U.S.A.*	39°49N 122°20W	126 D4
Black Canyon City *Ariz., U.S.A.*	34°4N 112°5W	130 C3
Black Canyon of the Gunnison Nat. Park △ *Colo., U.S.A.*	38°40N 107°39W	125 D3
Black Cr. → *Ont., Canada*	43°40N 79°30W	161 A2
Black Cr. → *Ariz., U.S.A.*	35°16N 109°14W	130 B6
Black Cr. → *Miss., U.S.A.*	30°39N 88°39W	111 F5
Black Cr. → *Tex., U.S.A.*	34°18N 79°37W	103 D6
Black Creek *B.C., Canada*	49°49N 125°7W	154 F9
Black Creek *Man., Canada*	52°18N 121°6W	155 C13
Black Creek *N.C., U.S.A.*	35°38N 77°56W	103 C8
Black Creek *Wis., U.S.A.*	44°29N 88°27W	78 D5
Black Creek Pioneer Village *Ont., Canada*	43°46N 79°30W	161 A1
Black Diamond = Pittsburg *Calif., U.S.A.*	38°2N 121°53W	126 E5
Black Diamond *Alta., Canada*	50°45N 114°14W	153 H6
Black Diamond *Wash., U.S.A.*	47°19N 122°0W	132 C4
Black Duck → *Ont., Canada*	56°51N 89°2W	159 F8
Black Earth *Wis., U.S.A.*	43°8N 89°45W	78 E4
Black Forest *Colo., U.S.A.*	39°0N 104°43W	125 C6
Black Hawk *Colo., U.S.A.*	39°48N 105°30W	125 C5
Black Hawk *S. Daz., U.S.A.*	44°9N 103°19W	76 F2
Black Hawk County ☆ *Iowa, U.S.A.*	42°25N 92°20W	81 C6
Black Hills *S. Dak., U.S.A.*	44°0N 103°45W	76 F2
Black Hills Nat. Forest *S. Dak., U.S.A.*	44°10N 103°50W	76 F2
Black Hills Nat. Forest *Wyo., U.S.A.*	44°35N 104°25W	124 C9
Black I. *Man., Canada*	51°12N 96°30W	151 D15
Black Jack *Mo., U.S.A.*	38°47N 90°16W	94 A2
Black Kettle Nat. Grassland *Okla., U.S.A.*	35°45N 99°45W	107 C4
Black L. *Sask., Canada*	59°12N 105°15W	157 E11
Black L. *La., U.S.A.*	31°57N 92°53W	110 C2
Black L. *Mich., U.S.A.*	45°28N 84°16W	79 D7
Black L. *N.Y., U.S.A.*	44°31N 75°36W	88 A5
Black Lake *Qué., Canada*	46°1N 71°22W	145 E11
Black Lake *Sask., Canada*	59°11N 105°20W	157 E11
Black Mesa *Ariz., U.S.A.*	36°30N 110°15W	130 A5
Black Mesa *Okla., U.S.A.*	36°58N 102°58W	107 B1
Black Mountain *N.C., U.S.A.*	35°37N 82°19W	103 C3
Black Mt. *Ky., U.S.A.*	36°54N 82°54W	105 D10
Black Mt. *N. Mex., U.S.A.*	33°23N 108°14W	131 D2
Black Mt. *Nev., U.S.A.*	35°55N 115°2W	134 D2
Black Mt. *Oreg., U.S.A.*	45°13N 119°17W	121 B6
Black Mt. *Tex., U.S.A.*	29°38N 100°20W	108 H7
Black Mts. *Ariz., U.S.A.*	35°30N 114°30W	130 B1
Black Pine Pk. *Idaho, U.S.A.*	42°8N 113°8W	122 G5
Black Range *N. Mex., U.S.A.*	33°15N 107°50W	131 D2
Black River *Jamaica*	18°0N 77°50W	182 C4
Black River *N.Y., U.S.A.*	44°1N 75°48W	88 A5
Black River Falls *Wis., U.S.A.*	44°18N 90°51W	78 D3
Black Rock *Ark., U.S.A.*	36°7N 91°6W	106 B4
Black Rock *N. Mex., U.S.A.*	35°5N 108°47W	131 B2
Black Rock Desert *Nev., U.S.A.*	41°10N 118°50W	128 A2
Black Rock Pt. *Nfld. & L., Canada*	60°2N 64°10W	143 A5
Black Rock Range *Nev., U.S.A.*	41°20N 119°8W	128 A1
Black Springs *Nev., U.S.A.*	39°37N 119°51W	128 C1
Black Squirrel Cr. → *Colo., U.S.A.*	38°14N 104°21W	125 D6
Black Sturgeon L. *Ont., Canada*	49°20N 88°53W	148 C8
Black Warrior → *Ala., U.S.A.*	32°32N 87°51W	112 D3
Blackbeard Island Nat. Wildlife Refuge △ *U.S.A.*	31°30N 81°12W	113 E5
Blackbird *Del., U.S.A.*	39°21N 75°40W	93 A5
Blackburn *Mo., U.S.A.*	39°6N 93°29W	83 B3
Blackburn *Okla., U.S.A.*	36°23N 96°38W	107 B7
Blackburn Mt. *Alaska, U.S.A.*	61°44N 143°26W	135 F12
Blackduck *Minn., U.S.A.*	47°44N 94°33W	77 C4
Blackfalds *Alta., Canada*	52°23N 113°47W	153 F7
Blackfeet Indian Reservation *Mont., U.S.A.*	48°45N 113°0W	123 B5
Blackfoot *Alta., Canada*	53°17N 110°10W	152 E10
Blackfoot *Idaho, U.S.A.*	43°11N 112°21W	122 F6
Blackfoot → *Idaho, U.S.A.*	43°8N 112°30W	122 F6
Blackfoot → *Mont., U.S.A.*	46°52N 113°53W	123 D4
Blackfoot Res. *Idaho, U.S.A.*	42°55N 111°59W	122 G7
Blackford *Ky., U.S.A.*	37°27N 87°56W	104 C5
Blackford County ☆ *Ind., U.S.A.*	40°30N 85°20W	85 C5
Blackhall Mt. *Wyo., U.S.A.*	41°2N 106°41W	124 E6
Blackhead *Nfld. & L., Canada*	47°32N 52°59W	142 E8
Blackhead Road *Nfld. & L., Canada*	47°33N 52°43W	142 E8
Blackman *Fla., U.S.A.*	30°56N 86°38W	114 A2
Blacks Fork → *Wyo., U.S.A.*	41°25N 109°27W	124 E3
Blacks Harbour *N.B., Canada*	45°3N 66°49W	141 H3
Blacksburg *S.C., U.S.A.*	35°7N 81°31W	103 C4
Blacksburg *Va., U.S.A.*	37°14N 80°25W	102 D4
Blackshear *Ga., U.S.A.*	31°18N 82°14W	113 E4
Blackshear, L. *Ga., U.S.A.*	31°51N 83°56W	113 E3
Blackstone *Mass., U.S.A.*	42°1N 71°30W	91 B3
Blackstone *Va., U.S.A.*	37°5N 78°0W	102 D6
Blackstone → *Yukon, Canada*	65°51N 137°15W	156 C5
Blacktail Mts. *Mont., U.S.A.*	44°59N 112°35W	123 F5
Blackville *N.B., Canada*	46°44N 65°53W	141 G4
Blackville *S.C., U.S.A.*	33°22N 81°16W	103 E4
Blackwater = West Road → *B.C., Canada*	53°18N 122°53W	154 B11
Blackwater *Mo., U.S.A.*	38°59N 92°59W	83 B4
Blackwater → *Fla., U.S.A.*	30°36N 87°2W	114 A1
Blackwater → *Md., U.S.A.*	38°21N 76°1W	93 B4
Blackwater → *Mo., U.S.A.*	38°56N 92°57W	83 C4
Blackwater → *Tex., U.S.A.*	33°40N 100°47W	108 D7
Blackwater → *Va., U.S.A.*	36°34N 76°55W	102 E8
Blackwater Falls State Park △ *W. Va., U.S.A.*	39°7N 79°30W	102 B5
Blackwater L. *N.W.T., Canada*	64°0N 123°5W	157 D8
Blackwater Nat. Wildlife Refuge △ *Md., U.S.A.*	38°26N 76°5W	93 B4
Blackwell *Okla., U.S.A.*	36°48N 97°17W	107 B6
Blackwell *Tex., U.S.A.*	32°5N 100°19W	108 E7
Blackwells Corner *Calif., U.S.A.*	35°37N 119°47W	127 H7
Blackwood *N.J., U.S.A.*	39°48N 75°4W	92 B1
Bladen *Nebr., U.S.A.*	40°19N 98°36W	80 D7
Bladen County ☆ *N.C., U.S.A.*	34°30N 78°30W	103 D7
Bladenboro *N.C., U.S.A.*	34°33N 78°48W	103 D7
Bladensburg *Md., U.S.A.*	38°55N 76°55W	99 B4
Bladworth *Sask., Canada*	51°22N 106°8W	150 D5
Blain *Pa., U.S.A.*	40°20N 77°31W	87 D5
Blaine *Ky., U.S.A.*	38°2N 82°51W	105 B10
Blaine *Minn., U.S.A.*	45°10N 93°3W	77 E5
Blaine *Tenn., U.S.A.*	36°9N 83°42W	105 D9
Blaine *Wash., U.S.A.*	48°59N 122°45W	120 B3
Blaine County ☆ *Idaho, U.S.A.*	43°30N 114°0W	122 F4
Blaine County ☆ *Mont., U.S.A.*	48°20N 109°0W	123 B9
Blaine County ☆ *Nebr., U.S.A.*	42°0N 100°0W	80 C5
Blaine County ☆ *Okla., U.S.A.*	35°50N 98°25W	107 C5
Blainville *Qué., Canada*	45°40N 73°52W	145 F9
Blair *Nebr., U.S.A.*	41°33N 96°8W	80 C9
Blair *Okla., U.S.A.*	34°47N 99°20W	107 D5
Blair *Wis., U.S.A.*	44°18N 91°14W	78 D2
Blair County ☆ *Pa., U.S.A.*	40°30N 78°20W	87 D4
Blair Village *Georgia, U.S.A.*	33°40N 84°23W	117 C2
Blairs *Va., U.S.A.*	36°41N 79°22W	102 E5
Blairsburg *Iowa, U.S.A.*	42°29N 93°38W	81 C4
Blairsden *Calif., U.S.A.*	39°47N 120°37W	126 D6
Blairstown *Iowa, U.S.A.*	41°55N 92°5W	81 D5
Blairstown *Mo., U.S.A.*	38°34N 93°58W	83 C3
Blairstown *N.J., U.S.A.*	40°59N 74°57W	92 B2
Blairsville *Ga., U.S.A.*	34°53N 83°58W	113 B3
Blairsville *Pa., U.S.A.*	40°26N 79°16W	87 D3
Blake House *Mass., U.S.A.*	42°19N 71°3W	96 B2
Blake Island State Park △ *Wash., U.S.A.*	47°32N 122°39W	132 C3
Blake Pt. *Mich., U.S.A.*	48°11N 88°25W	79 A31
Blakely *Ga., U.S.A.*	31°23N 84°56W	113 E2
Blakely *Pa., U.S.A.*	41°28N 75°37W	92 A1
Blakeman *Kans., U.S.A.*	39°49N 101°7W	82 B2
Blakesburg *Iowa, U.S.A.*	40°58N 92°38W	81 E6
Blakeslee *Ohio, U.S.A.*	41°32N 84°44W	86 B2
Blanc-Sablon *Qué., Canada*	51°24N 57°12W	142 A3
Blanca *Colo., U.S.A.*	37°27N 105°31W	125 E5
Blanca Flor *Quintana Roo, Mexico*	21°24N 86°51W	179 A7
Blanca, I. *Quintana Roo, Mexico*	21°24N 86°51W	179 A7
Blanca, Sierra *Tex., U.S.A.*	31°15N 105°26W	108 F2
Blanca Peak *Colo., U.S.A.*	37°35N 105°29W	125 E5
Blanchard *Iowa, U.S.A.*	40°35N 95°13W	81 E3
Blanchard *La., U.S.A.*	32°35N 93°54W	110 B2
Blanchard *N. Dak., U.S.A.*	47°21N 97°13W	76 C8
Blanchard *Okla., U.S.A.*	35°8N 97°39W	107 C6
Blanchard → *Ohio, U.S.A.*	41°2N 84°18W	86 B2
Blanchardville *Wis., U.S.A.*	42°49N 89°52W	78 F4
Blanche, L. *Fla., U.S.A.*	28°28N 81°30W	115 B1
Blanchester *Ohio, U.S.A.*	39°17N 83°59W	86 D3
Blanco *N. Mex., U.S.A.*	36°43N 107°50W	131 A3
Blanco *Okla., U.S.A.*	34°45N 95°46W	107 D8
Blanco *Tex., U.S.A.*	30°6N 98°25W	109 G9
Blanco → *Tex., U.S.A.*	29°51N 97°55W	109 H10
Blanco, B. *Baja Calif., Mexico*	29°3N 114°43W	166 D4
Blanco, C. *Costa Rica*	9°34N 85°8W	182 E2
Blanco, C. *Oreg., U.S.A.*	42°51N 124°34W	121 E1
Blanco County ☆ *Tex., U.S.A.*	30°17N 98°25W	109 G9
Bland *Mo., U.S.A.*	38°18N 91°38W	83 C5
Bland *Va., U.S.A.*	37°6N 81°7W	102 D3
Bland County ☆ *Va., U.S.A.*	37°6N 81°7W	102 D3
Blandford *Mass., U.S.A.*	42°11N 72°56W	91 B2
Blanding *Utah, U.S.A.*	37°37N 109°29W	129 F6
Blandinsville *Ill., U.S.A.*	40°33N 90°52W	84 C3
Blaney Park *Mich., U.S.A.*	46°9N 85°55W	79 C6
Blanket *Tex., U.S.A.*	31°49N 98°47W	109 F9
Blanquilla *Venezuela*	11°51N 64°37W	183 D7
Blasdell *N.Y., U.S.A.*	42°48N 78°50W	88 C2
Blawnox *Pa., U.S.A.*	40°29N 79°51W	98 B2
Bleckley County ☆ *Ga., U.S.A.*	32°25N 83°15W	113 D3
Bledos *San Luis Potosí, Mexico*	21°50N 101°7W	171 J3
Bledsoe *Tex., U.S.A.*	33°38N 103°1W	108 D4
Bledsoe County ☆ *Tenn., U.S.A.*	35°36N 85°11W	105 E7
Blencoe *Iowa, U.S.A.*	41°56N 96°5W	81 D2
Blenheim *Ont., Canada*	42°20N 82°0W	146 E5
Blessing *Tex., U.S.A.*	28°52N 96°13W	109 J11
Bleu, L. *Qué., Canada*	46°35N 78°24W	144 E4
Blewett Falls L. *N.C., U.S.A.*	35°3N 79°54W	103 C6
Blind River *Ont., Canada*	46°10N 82°58W	146 A4
Bliss *Idaho, U.S.A.*	42°56N 114°57W	122 F4
Blissfield *N.B., Canada*	46°36N 66°5W	141 G3
Blissfield *Mich., U.S.A.*	41°50N 83°52W	79 H8
Blissville *Ohio, U.S.A.*	40°24N 81°58W	86 C5
Blitchton *Ga., U.S.A.*	32°12N 81°26W	113 D5
Block I. *N.Y., U.S.A.*	41°11N 71°35W	91 C3
Block Island Sd. *R.I., U.S.A.*	41°15N 71°40W	91 C3
Blocker *Okla., U.S.A.*	35°4N 95°34W	107 C8
Blockton *Iowa, U.S.A.*	40°37N 94°29W	81 E4
Blodgett *Mo., U.S.A.*	37°0N 89°32W	83 D6
Bloodsworth I. *Md., U.S.A.*	38°10N 76°3W	93 B4
Bloody Mt. *Calif., U.S.A.*	37°34N 118°54W	127 F8
Bloodvein → *Man., Canada*	51°47N 96°43W	151 D15
Bloom = Chicago Heights *Ill., U.S.A.*	41°30N 87°38W	84 B6
Bloomer *Wis., U.S.A.*	45°6N 91°29W	78 C21
Bloomfield *Ont., Canada*	43°59N 77°14W	147 D9
Bloomfield *Ind., U.S.A.*	39°1N 86°57W	85 D4
Bloomfield *Iowa, U.S.A.*	40°45N 92°25W	81 E61
Bloomfield *Ky., U.S.A.*	37°55N 85°19W	105 C7
Bloomfield *N. Mex., U.S.A.*	36°43N 107°59W	131 A3
Bloomfield *N.J., U.S.A.*	40°48N 74°11W	97 B1
Bloomfield *Nebr., U.S.A.*	42°36N 97°39W	80 B8
Blooming Grove *Tex., U.S.A.*	32°6N 96°43W	109 E11
Blooming Prairie *Minn., U.S.A.*	43°52N 93°3W	77 G5
Bloomingburg *Ohio, U.S.A.*	39°36N 83°24W	86 D3
Bloomingdale *Tenn., U.S.A.*	36°34N 82°32W	105 D10
Bloomington *Idaho, U.S.A.*	42°11N 111°24W	122 G7
Bloomington *Ill., U.S.A.*	40°28N 89°0W	84 C4
Bloomington *Ind., U.S.A.*	39°10N 86°32W	85 D4
Bloomington *Iowa, U.S.A.*	40°45N 92°25W	81 E61
Bloomington *Minn., U.S.A.*	44°50N 93°17W	77 F5
Bloomington *Tex., U.S.A.*	28°39N 96°54W	109 J11
Bloomington *Wis., U.S.A.*	42°53N 90°55W	78 F3
Bloomsburg *Pa., U.S.A.*	41°0N 76°27W	87 D6
Bloomsdale *Mo., U.S.A.*	38°1N 90°13W	83 C6
Bloomville *Ohio, U.S.A.*	41°3N 83°1W	86 B3
Blossburg *Pa., U.S.A.*	41°41N 77°4W	87 C5
Blosseville Kyst *Greenland*	68°50N 26°30W	162 D8
Blossom *Tex., U.S.A.*	33°40N 95°23W	109 D12
Blossom Park *Ont., Canada*	45°21N 75°37W	160 B2
Blossom Point Proving Grounds *Md., U.S.A.*	38°26N 76°5W	93 B4
Blount County ☆ *Ala., U.S.A.*	33°57N 86°28W	112 C4
Blount County ☆ *Tenn., U.S.A.*	35°46N 83°58W	105 E9
Blountstown *Fla., U.S.A.*	30°27N 85°3W	114 A3
Blountsville *Ala., U.S.A.*	34°5N 86°35W	112 B4
Blountville *Tenn., U.S.A.*	36°32N 82°19W	105 D10
Blowing Rock *N.C., U.S.A.*	36°8N 81°41W	103 B4
Bloxom *Va., U.S.A.*	37°50N 75°38W	93 C5
Bloxham *Fla., U.S.A.*	30°26N 84°34W	114 A3
Blubber Bay *B.C., Canada*	49°47N 124°37W	154 F10
Blue → *Ind., U.S.A.*	38°11N 86°19W	85 E4
Blue Cypress L. *Fla., U.S.A.*	27°44N 80°45W	114 D8
Blue Diamond *Nev., U.S.A.*	36°3N 115°24W	128 F5
Blue Earth *Minn., U.S.A.*	43°38N 94°6W	77 G4
Blue Earth County ☆ *Minn., U.S.A.*	44°5N 94°0W	77 G4
Blue Eye *Mo., U.S.A.*	36°30N 93°24W	83 E3
Blue Hill *Maine, U.S.A.*	44°25N 68°35W	90 D7
Blue Hill *Nebr., U.S.A.*	40°20N 98°27W	80 D7
Blue Hole Nat. Park △ *Belize*	17°24N 88°30W	182 C2
Blue Island *Ill., U.S.A.*	41°40N 87°40W	98 D2
Blue Knob *Pa., U.S.A.*	40°17N 78°34W	87 D4
Blue Knob State Park △ *Pa., U.S.A.*	40°16N 78°34W	87 D4
Blue Lake *Calif., U.S.A.*	40°53N 123°59W	126 C3
Blue Mesa Res. *Colo., U.S.A.*	38°28N 107°20W	125 D3
Blue Mound *Ill., U.S.A.*	39°42N 89°7W	84 D4
Blue Mound *Kans., U.S.A.*	38°5N 95°0W	82 C9
Blue Mound *Tex., U.S.A.*	32°51N 97°20W	116 A2
Blue Mountain *Colo., U.S.A.*	40°15N 108°52W	125 B2
Blue Mountain *Miss., U.S.A.*	34°40N 89°2W	111 B4
Blue Mountain L. *Ark., U.S.A.*	35°2N 93°53W	106 C2
Blue Mountain Lake *N.Y., U.S.A.*	43°51N 74°27W	88 B6
Blue Mountain Pass *Oreg., U.S.A.*	42°18N 117°49W	121 E8
Blue Mt. *N.H., U.S.A.*	44°47N 71°28W	89 B3
Blue Mt. *Pa., U.S.A.*	40°30N 76°30W	87 D6
Blue Mts. *Maine, U.S.A.*	44°50N 70°35W	90 D3
Blue Mts. *Oreg., U.S.A.*	45°0N 118°20W	121 C7
Blue Mts. *Pa., U.S.A.*	30°34N 99°27W	109 G8
Blue Rapids *Kans., U.S.A.*	39°41N 96°39W	82 B7
Blue Ridge *Alta., Canada*	54°8N 115°22W	152 D5
Blue Ridge *Ga., U.S.A.*	34°52N 84°20W	113 B2
Blue Ridge *Va., U.S.A.*	36°40N 80°50W	103 B5
Blue Ridge L. *Ga., U.S.A.*	34°53N 84°17W	113 B2
Blue Ridge Parkway *Va., U.S.A.*	36°40N 80°39W	103 B5
Blue River *B.C., Canada*	52°6N 119°18W	155 C15
Blue River *Colo., U.S.A.*	44°9N 122°20W	121 C3
Blue River *Wis., U.S.A.*	43°11N 90°34W	78 E3
Blue Springs *Mo., U.S.A.*	39°1N 94°17W	98 B2
Blue Springs *Nebr., U.S.A.*	40°9N 96°40W	80 D9
Blueberry Mountain *Alta., Canada*	55°56N 119°9W	152 C1
Bluefield *Va., U.S.A.*	37°15N 81°17W	102 D3
Bluefield *W. Va., U.S.A.*	37°16N 81°13W	102 D3
Bluefields *Nic.*	12°20N 83°50W	182 E3
Bluejacket *Okla., U.S.A.*	36°48N 95°4W	107 B8
Bluejoint L. *Oreg., U.S.A.*	42°42N 119°38W	121 E6
Bluenose L. *N.W.T., Canada*	68°30N 119°35W	156 C7
Blueridge *B.C., Canada*	49°19N 122°59W	161 B2
Bluestone → *W. Va., U.S.A.*	37°38N 80°53W	102 D4
Bluestone L. *W. Va., U.S.A.*	37°38N 80°53W	102 D4
Bluestone Nat. Scenic River △ *W. Va., U.S.A.*	37°33N 81°0W	102 D4
Bluewater *Ont., Canada*	43°28N 81°36W	146 D5
Bluewater *N. Mex., U.S.A.*	35°15N 107°59W	131 B2
Bluff *Utah, U.S.A.*	37°17N 109°33W	129 F6
Bluff City *Ark., U.S.A.*	33°43N 93°8W	106 E2
Bluff City *Kans., U.S.A.*	37°5N 97°52W	82 D6
Bluff City *Tenn., U.S.A.*	36°28N 82°16W	105 D10
Bluffdale *Utah, U.S.A.*	40°29N 111°56W	134 D2
Bluffers Park *Ont., Canada*	43°43N 79°14W	161 A3
Bluffs *Ill., U.S.A.*	39°45N 90°32W	84 D3
Bluffton *Alta., Canada*	52°45N 114°17W	153 F6
Bluffton *Ark., U.S.A.*	34°54N 93°36W	106 D2
Bluffton *Ga., U.S.A.*	31°31N 84°52W	113 E2
Bluffton *Ind., U.S.A.*	40°44N 85°11W	85 C5
Bluffton *Minn., U.S.A.*	46°28N 95°14W	77 D3
Bluffton *Ohio, U.S.A.*	40°54N 83°54W	86 C3
Bluffton *S.C., U.S.A.*	32°14N 80°52W	103 F5
Bluford *Ill., U.S.A.*	38°20N 88°45W	84 E5
Blumenau = Stettler *Alta., Canada*	52°19N 112°40W	153 F8
Blunt *S. Dak., U.S.A.*	44°31N 99°59W	76 F6
Bluff Pt. *Calif., U.S.A.*	37°51N 122°25W	132 A2
Bly *Oreg., U.S.A.*	42°24N 121°3W	121 E4
Blyn *Wash., U.S.A.*	48°1N 123°0W	120 B2
Blyth *Ont., Canada*	43°44N 81°26W	146 D5
Blythe *Calif., U.S.A.*	33°37N 114°36W	127 K12
Blythe *Ga., U.S.A.*	33°17N 82°12W	113 D4
Blytheville *Ark., U.S.A.*	35°56N 89°55W	106 C6
Boaco *Nic.*	12°29N 85°35W	182 D2
Boalsburg *Pa., U.S.A.*	40°47N 77°49W	87 D5
Boardman *Ohio, U.S.A.*	41°2N 80°40W	86 B6
Boardman *Oreg., U.S.A.*	45°51N 119°43W	121 B6
Boardman Bombing Range *Oreg., U.S.A.*	45°48N 119°45W	121 B6
Boardwalk *N.Y., U.S.A.*	40°34N 73°49W	97 C4
Boat Harbour *Nfld. & L., Canada*	47°24N 54°50W	142 E6
Boaz *Ala., U.S.A.*	34°12N 86°10W	112 B4
Boaz *Wis., U.S.A.*	43°20N 90°32W	78 E3
Bobcaygeon *Ont., Canada*	44°33N 78°33W	147 C8
Bobtown *Pa., U.S.A.*	39°46N 79°59W	87 E2
Boca de la Vinorama *Baja Calif. S., Mexico*	23°11N 109°29W	167 K9
Boca de Tomatlán *Jalisco, Mexico*	20°31N 105°19W	174 B2
Boca del Mezquital *Durango, Mexico*	23°46N 104°27W	173 D6
Boca del Río *Veracruz, Mexico*	19°5N 96°4W	177 E4
Boca Grande *Fla., U.S.A.*	26°45N 82°16W	114 E6
Boca Raton *Fla., U.S.A.*	26°21N 80°5W	114 E8
Bocabarra, Pta. *Oaxaca, Mexico*	16°1N 94°48W	177 H6
Bocas de Camichín *Nayarit, Mexico*	21°44N 105°29W	174 A2
Bocas del Toro *Panama*	9°15N 82°20W	182 E3
Bochart *Qué., Canada*	49°10N 73°30W	145 B9
Bochil *Chiapas, Mexico*	16°59N 92°55W	178 C4
Bock *Minn., U.S.A.*	45°47N 93°33W	77 E5
Bocoyna *Chihuahua, Mexico*	27°52N 107°35W	169 F8
Bodcau, Bayou → *La., U.S.A.*	32°13N 93°30W	110 B2
Bodcaw *Ark., U.S.A.*	33°33N 93°25W	106 E2
Bode *Iowa, U.S.A.*	42°52N 94°17W	81 C4
Bodega Bay *Calif., U.S.A.*	38°20N 123°3W	126 E3
Bodie I. *N.C., U.S.A.*	35°54N 75°35W	103 C10
Boeing Field = King County Int. ✈ (BFI) *Wash., U.S.A.*	47°31N 122°18W	132 C4
Boelus *Nebr., U.S.A.*	41°5N 98°43W	80 C7
Boerne *Tex., U.S.A.*	29°47N 98°44W	109 H9
Bogalusa *La., U.S.A.*	30°47N 89°52W	110 D6
Bogard *Mo., U.S.A.*	39°27N 93°32W	83 B3
Bogata *Tex., U.S.A.*	33°28N 95°13W	109 D12
Boger City *N.C., U.S.A.*	35°28N 81°13W	103 C4
Boggy Creek Swamp *Fla., U.S.A.*	28°22N 81°19W	115 B2
Bogota *N.J., U.S.A.*	40°52N 74°2W	97 A2
Bogota *Tenn., U.S.A.*	36°10N 89°26W	104 D3
Bogue *Kans., U.S.A.*	39°22N 99°41W	82 B4
Bogue Chitto *Miss., U.S.A.*	31°26N 90°27W	111 E3
Bogue Chitto → *La., U.S.A.*	30°34N 89°50W	110 D6
Bogue Homo → *Miss., U.S.A.*	31°10N 88°55W	111 E5
Boiling Spring Lakes *N.C., U.S.A.*	34°2N 78°4W	103 D7
Boiling Springs *N.C., U.S.A.*	35°15N 81°40W	103 C4
Bois, L. des *Alta., Canada*	56°50N 125°9W	156 D7
Bois Blanc I. *Mich., U.S.A.*	45°46N 84°27W	79 D7
Bois D'Arc *Mo., U.S.A.*	37°16N 93°30W	83 D3
Bois de Sioux → *N. Dak., U.S.A.*	46°16N 96°36W	76 D9
Bois Forte (Deer Creek) Indian Reservation *U.S.A.*	47°48N 93°23W	77 C5
Bois Forte (Nett Lake) Indian Reservation *U.S.A.*	48°5N 93°5W	77 B5
Bois I. *Nfld. & L., Canada*	47°44N 56°0W	142 E5
Boisdale *N.S., Canada*	46°6N 60°30W	141 G9
Boise *Idaho, U.S.A.*	43°37N 116°13W	122 F2
Boise ✈ (BOI) *Idaho, U.S.A.*	43°34N 116°14W	122 F2
Boise City *Okla., U.S.A.*	36°44N 102°31W	107 B1
Boise County ☆ *Idaho, U.S.A.*	44°0N 115°45W	122 E3
Boise Mts. *Idaho, U.S.A.*	43°45N 115°30W	122 E3
Boise Nat. Forest *Idaho, U.S.A.*	44°5N 115°30W	122 E3
Boissevain *Man., Canada*	49°15N 100°5W	151 F11
Boistfort Pk. *Wash., U.S.A.*	46°29N 123°12W	120 D2
Bokchito *Okla., U.S.A.*	34°1N 96°9W	107 D7

Bokobá *Yucatán, Mexico* 20°59N 89°13W **179** B4
Bokoshe *Okla., U.S.A.* 35°11N 94°47W **107** C9
Bolaños *Jalisco, Mexico* 21°41N 103°47W **173** F7
Bolaños → *Mexico* 21°12N 104°55W **174** A3
Bolckow *Mo., U.S.A.* 40°7N 94°50W **83** A2
Boldtville *Tex., U.S.A.* 29°21N 98°21W **116** C3
Boles *Ark., U.S.A.* 34°47N 94°3W **106** D1
Boley *Okla., U.S.A.* 35°29N 96°29W **107** C7
Boligee *La., U.S.A.* 32°45N 88°2W **112** D2
Bolingbroke *Ga., U.S.A.* 32°57N 83°48W **113** D3
Bolingbrook *Ill., U.S.A.* 41°42N 88°4W **84** B5
Bolinger *La., U.S.A.* 32°57N 93°41W **110** D2
Bolivar *Mo., U.S.A.* 37°37N 93°25W **83** D3
Bolivar *N.Y., U.S.A.* 42°4N 78°10W **88** C2
Bolivar *Tenn., U.S.A.* 35°12N 89°0W **104** E4
Bolivar *W. Va., U.S.A.* 39°19N 77°45W **93** A3
Bolivar, Mt. *Oreg., U.S.A.* 42°51N 123°26W **121** E2
Bolivar County ☆ *Miss., U.S.A.* 33°50N 90°43W **111** C3
Bolivar Peninsula *Tex., U.S.A.* 29°27N 94°39W **109** H13
Bolivia *N.C., U.S.A.* 34°4N 78°9W **103** D7
Bolling *Ala., U.S.A.* 31°43N 86°42W **112** E4
Bollinger County ☆ *Mo., U.S.A.* 37°20N 90°0W **83** D6
Bolonchén *Campeche, Mexico* 20°1N 89°45W **179** B4
Bolton *Ont., Canada* 43°54N 79°45W **146** D7
Bolton *Georgia, U.S.A.* 33°48N 84°28W **117** B2
Bolton *Miss., U.S.A.* 32°21N 90°28W **111** D3
Bombay *N.Y., U.S.A.* 44°56N 74°34W **88** A4
Bombay Hook *Del., U.S.A.* 39°21N 75°30W **93** A5
Bombay Hook Nat. Wildlife Refuge △ *Del.,*
  U.S.A. 39°16N 75°27W **93** A5
Bomoseen, L. *Vt., U.S.A.* 43°39N 73°13W **89** C1
Bon Accord *Alta., Canada* 53°50N 113°25W **152** C7
Bon Air *Va., U.S.A.* 37°31N 77°34W **102** D7
Bon Echo Prov. Park △ *Ont., Canada* 44°55N 77°16W **147** C9
Bon Homme County ☆ *S. Dak., U.S.A.* 43°0N 97°50W **76** G8
Bon Secour B. *Ala., U.S.A.* 30°15N 87°58W **112** F3
Bona, Mt. *Alaska, U.S.A.* 61°23N 141°45W **135** C12
Bonaire *Neth. Ant.* 12°10N 68°15W **183** D6
Bonaire *Ga., U.S.A.* 32°33N 83°36W **113** D3
Bonampak *Chiapas, Mexico* 16°44N 91°5W **178** C5
Bonanza *Alta., Canada* 55°55N 119°49W **152** C1
Bonanza *Nic.* 13°54N 84°35W **182** D3
Bonanza *Colo., U.S.A.* 38°18N 106°8W **125** D4
Bonanza *Oreg., U.S.A.* 42°12N 121°24W **121** E4
Bonanza *Utah, U.S.A.* 40°1N 109°11W **129** C6
Bonanza Pk. *Wash., U.S.A.* 48°14N 120°52W **120** B5
Bonaparte *Iowa, U.S.A.* 40°42N 91°48W **81** E7
Bonaparte *Wash., U.S.A.* 48°45N 119°8W **120** B6
Bonaparte L. *B.C., Canada* 51°15N 120°34W **155** D14
Bonaventure *Qué., Canada* 48°5N 65°32W **141** C6
Bonavista *Nfld. & L., Canada* 48°40N 53°5W **142** D7
Bonavista, C. *Nfld. & L., Canada* 48°42N 53°5W **142** D7
Bonavista B. *Nfld. & L., Canada* 48°45N 53°25W **142** D7
Bond *Colo., U.S.A.* 39°53N 106°42W **125** C4
Bond *Miss., U.S.A.* 30°54N 89°10W **111** F4
Bond County ☆ *Ill., U.S.A.* 38°50N 89°25W **84** E4
Bond Falls Flowage *Mich., U.S.A.* 46°30N 89°15W **79** C2
Bondurant *Iowa, U.S.A.* 41°42N 93°28W **81** D5
Bondurant *Wyo., U.S.A.* 43°12N 110°24W **124** C2
Bondville *Ill., U.S.A.* 40°7N 88°22W **84** C5
Bone Gap *Ill., U.S.A.* 38°27N 88°0W **84** E6
Bonetraill *N. Dak., U.S.A.* 48°26N 103°51W **76** B2
Bonfield *Ont., Canada* 46°14N 79°9W **146** A7
Bonham *Tex., U.S.A.* 33°35N 96°11W **109** D11
Bonifay *Fla., U.S.A.* 30°47N 85°41W **114** A3
Bonilla *S. Dak., U.S.A.* 44°35N 98°30W **76** F7
Bonilla I. *B.C., Canada* 53°28N 130°37W **154** B4
Bonita *Calif., U.S.A.* 32°39N 117°1W **133** C2
Bonita *La., U.S.A.* 32°55N 91°40W **110** B4
Bonita Springs *Fla., U.S.A.* 26°21N 81°47W **114** E7
Bonne Terre *Mo., U.S.A.* 37°55N 90°33W **83** D61
Bonneauville *Pa., U.S.A.* 39°49N 77°9W **93** A3
Bonnechere → *Ont., Canada* 45°35N 77°50W **147** B9
Bonner County ☆ *Idaho, U.S.A.* 48°20N 116°30W **122** A2
Bonner Springs *Kans., U.S.A.* 39°4N 94°53W **82** B9
Bonners Ferry *Idaho, U.S.A.* 48°42N 116°19W **122** A2
Bonnet, Lac du *Man., Canada* 50°22N 95°55W **151** E16
Bonnet Plume → *Yukon, Canada* 65°56N 134°56W **156** C6
Bonneville County ☆ *Idaho, U.S.A.* 43°20N 111°20W **122** F7
Bonneville Dam *U.S.A.* 45°38N 121°56W **121** B4
Bonneville Pk. *Idaho, U.S.A.* 42°46N 112°8W **122** G6
Bonneville Salt Flats *Utah, U.S.A.* 40°45N 113°50W **129** C2
Bonney Lake *Wash., U.S.A.* 47°11N 122°11W **120** C3
Bonnie *Ill., U.S.A.* 38°12N 88°54W **84** E5
Bonnieville *Ky., U.S.A.* 37°23N 85°54W **105** C7
Bonny Res. *Colo., U.S.A.* 39°37N 102°11W **125** C8
Bonny Slope *Oreg., U.S.A.* 45°32N 122°46W **132** A1
Bonnyville *Alta., Canada* 54°20N 110°45W **152** D10
Bono *Ark., U.S.A.* 35°55N 90°48W **106** C5
Book Cliffs *Colo., U.S.A.* 39°20N 108°45W **125** C2
Book Cliffs *Utah, U.S.A.* 39°20N 109°0W **129** D6
Booker *Tex., U.S.A.* 36°27N 100°32W **108** A7
Booker T. Washington Nat. Monument △ *Va.,*
  U.S.A. 37°7N 79°44W **102** D5
Boomer *W. Va., U.S.A.* 38°9N 81°17W **102** C3
Boone *Colo., U.S.A.* 38°15N 104°15W **125** D6
Boone *Iowa, U.S.A.* 42°4N 93°53W **81** C5
Boone *N.C., U.S.A.* 36°13N 81°41W **103** B4
Boone *Nebr., U.S.A.* 41°38N 97°55W **80** C8
Boone → *Iowa, U.S.A.* 42°19N 93°56W **81** C5
Boone County ☆ *Ark., U.S.A.* 36°14N 93°7W **106** B2
Boone County ☆ *Ill., U.S.A.* 42°20N 89°50W **84** A4
Boone County ☆ *Ind., U.S.A.* 40°5N 86°30W **85** C4
Boone County ☆ *Iowa, U.S.A.* 42°0N 94°0W **81** D5
Boone County ☆ *Ky., U.S.A.* 38°55N 84°45W **105** B8
Boone County ☆ *Nebr., U.S.A.* 41°40N 98°0W **80** C8
Boone County ☆ *W. Va., U.S.A.* 38°4N 81°49W **102** C3
Boone L. *Tenn., U.S.A.* 36°26N 82°26W **105** D10
Boones Mill *Va., U.S.A.* 37°7N 79°57W **102** D5
Booneville *Ark., U.S.A.* 35°8N 93°55W **106** C2
Booneville *Ky., U.S.A.* 37°29N 83°41W **105** C9
Booneville *Miss., U.S.A.* 34°39N 88°34W **111** B5
Boonsboro *Md., U.S.A.* 39°30N 77°39W **93** A3
Boonton *N.J., U.S.A.* 40°54N 74°25W **92** B2
Boonville *Calif., U.S.A.* 39°1N 123°22W **126** D3
Boonville *Ind., U.S.A.* 38°3N 87°16W **85** E3
Boonville *Mo., U.S.A.* 38°58N 92°44W **83** C41
Boonville *N.C., U.S.A.* 36°14N 80°43W **103** B5
Boonville *N.Y., U.S.A.* 43°29N 75°20W **88** B5
Boothbay Harbor *Maine, U.S.A.* 43°51N 69°38W **91** D7
Boothia, Gulf of *Nunavut, Canada* 71°0N 90°0W **158** C7
Boothia Pen. *Nunavut, Canada* 71°0N 94°0W **158** C7
Boothville *La., U.S.A.* 29°20N 89°25W **110** E6
Boquete *Panama* 8°46N 82°27W **182** E3

Boquilla, Presa de la *Chihuahua,*
  Mexico 27°31N 105°30W **169** F10
Boquilla de Abajo *Chihuahua, Mexico* 27°22N 106°31W **169** F9
Boquillas del Carmen *Coahuila, Mexico* 29°11N 102°58W **108** H5
Borah Peak *Idaho, U.S.A.* 44°8N 113°47W **122** E5
Bordeaux *Tenn., U.S.A.* 36°12N 86°50W **104** D6
Bordelonville *La., U.S.A.* 31°6N 91°55W **110** C4
Borden *Sask., Canada* 52°27N 107°14W **150** C4
Borden-Carleton *P.E.I., Canada* 46°18N 63°47W **141** G6
Borden County ☆ *Tex., U.S.A.* 32°46N 101°27W **108** E6
Borden I. *Canada* 78°30N 111°30W **156** A10
Borden L. *Ont., Canada* 47°50N 83°17W **149** C13
Borden Pen. *Nunavut, Canada* 73°0N 83°0W **158** C9
Borden Springs *Ala., U.S.A.* 33°56N 85°28W **112** C5
Bordentown *N.J., U.S.A.* 40°9N 74°43W **92** B2
Border *Wyo., U.S.A.* 42°11N 111°3W **124** D1
Border Field State Park △ *Calif., U.S.A.* 32°32N 117°7W **133** C2
Bordulac *N. Dak., U.S.A.* 47°23N 98°58W **76** C7
Borger *Tex., U.S.A.* 35°39N 101°24W **108** B6
Borgne, L. *La., U.S.A.* 30°1N 89°42W **110** D6
Borinquen *Minn., U.S.A.* 47°11N 96°30W **77** C2
Boron *Calif., U.S.A.* 35°0N 117°39W **127** H9
Borrego Springs *Calif., U.S.A.* 33°15N 116°23W **127** K10
Borup *Minn., U.S.A.* 47°11N 96°30W **77** C2
Boscawen *N.H., U.S.A.* 43°19N 71°37W **89** C3
Bosco *La., U.S.A.* 32°17N 92°5W **110** B3
Boscobel *Wis., U.S.A.* 43°8N 90°42W **78** E3
Bosencheve, Parque Nacional △
  Mexico 19°26N 100°14W **175** C7
Bosler *Wyo., U.S.A.* 41°35N 105°42W **124** E7
Bosque *N. Mex., U.S.A.* 34°34N 106°47W **131** C4
Bosque County ☆ *Tex., U.S.A.* 31°56N 97°39W **109** F10
Bosque Farms *N. Mex., U.S.A.* 35°51N 106°42W **131** B4
Bossier City *La., U.S.A.* 32°31N 93°44W **110** B2
Bossier Parish ☆ *La., U.S.A.* 32°42N 93°44W **110** B2
Boston *Ga., U.S.A.* 30°47N 83°47W **113** F3
Boston *Mass., U.S.A.* 42°22N 71°3W **96** A2
Boston *N.Y., U.S.A.* 33°27N 94°25W **109** D13
Boston Bar *B.C., Canada* 49°52N 121°30W **155** F13
Boston Logan Int. ✈ (BOS) *Mass., U.S.A.* 42°22N 71°1W **96** A2
Boston Mts. *Ark., U.S.A.* 35°42N 93°15W **106** C2
Bostwick *Fla., U.S.A.* 29°46N 81°38W **114** B7
Bostwick *Ga., U.S.A.* 33°44N 83°31W **113** C3
Boswell *B.C., Canada* 49°28N 116°45W **155** F18
Boswell *Ind., U.S.A.* 40°31N 87°23W **85** C3
Boswell *Okla., U.S.A.* 34°2N 95°52W **107** D8
Boswell *Pa., U.S.A.* 40°10N 79°2W **87** D3
Bosworth *Mo., U.S.A.* 39°28N 93°20W **83** B3
Botetourt County ☆ *Va., U.S.A.* 37°32N 79°41W **102** D5
Bothell *Wash., U.S.A.* 47°45N 122°12W **132** B4
Bothwell *Ont., Canada* 42°38N 81°52W **146** E5
Botkins *Ohio, U.S.A.* 40°28N 84°11W **86** C2
Bottineau *N. Dak., U.S.A.* 48°50N 100°27W **76** B5
Bottineau County ☆ *N. Dak., U.S.A.* 48°50N 101°0W **76** B5
Botwood *Nfld. & L., Canada* 49°6N 55°23W **142** C5
Boucher → *Qué., Canada* 49°10N 69°6W **145** B13
Boucherville *Qué., Canada* 45°36N 73°28W **160** A4
Boucherville, Îs. de *Qué., Canada* 45°36N 73°28W **160** A4
Bouchette *Qué., Canada* 46°12N 75°57W **144** E7
Bouchier, L. *Qué., Canada* 50°6N 77°48W **144** A5
Bouctouche *N.B., Canada* 46°30N 64°45W **141** G5
Boulder *Colo., U.S.A.* 40°1N 105°17W **125** B5
Boulder *Mont., U.S.A.* 46°14N 112°7W **123** D5
Boulder *Utah, U.S.A.* 37°55N 111°25W **129** F4
Boulder *Wyo., U.S.A.* 42°45N 109°43W **124** D3
Boulder City *Nev., U.S.A.* 35°58N 114°49W **134** D3
Boulder County ☆ *Colo., U.S.A.* 40°10N 105°15W **125** B5
Boulder Creek *Calif., U.S.A.* 37°7N 122°7W **126** H4
Boulder Dam = Hoover Dam *U.S.A.* 36°1N 114°44W **130** A1
Boulder L. *Wyo., U.S.A.* 42°51N 109°40W **124** D3
Boulder Mts. *Idaho, U.S.A.* 43°53N 114°30W **122** F4
Boulder Peak *Calif., U.S.A.* 41°35N 123°5W **126** B3
Bound Brook *N.J., U.S.A.* 40°34N 74°32W **92** B2
Boundary *Alaska, U.S.A.* 64°5N 141°1W **135** D12
Boundary County ☆ *Idaho, U.S.A.* 48°45N 116°30W **122** A2
Boundary Peak *Nev., U.S.A.* 37°51N 118°21W **128** E2
Boundary Waters Canoe Area Wilderness △
  U.S.A. 47°57N 91°13W **77** C7
Bountiful *Utah, U.S.A.* 40°53N 111°52W **134** A2
Bourbeuse → *Mo., U.S.A.* 38°24N 90°53W **83** C6
Bourbon *Ind., U.S.A.* 41°18N 86°7W **85** B4
Bourbon *Mo., U.S.A.* 38°9N 91°15W **83** C5
Bourbon County ☆ *Kans., U.S.A.* 37°45N 94°45W **82** D9
Bourbon County ☆ *Ky., U.S.A.* 38°10N 84°15W **105** B8
Bourbonnais *Ill., U.S.A.* 41°9N 87°52W **84** B6
Bourget *Ont., Canada* 45°26N 75°9W **144** F7
Bouse *Ariz., U.S.A.* 33°56N 114°0W **130** D1
Bouse Wash → *Ariz., U.S.A.* 34°3N 114°20W **130** C1
Bovey *Minn., U.S.A.* 47°17N 93°25W **77** C5
Bovill *Idaho, U.S.A.* 46°51N 116°24W **122** C2
Bovina *Tex., U.S.A.* 34°31N 102°53W **108** C5
Bow *Wash., U.S.A.* 48°34N 122°24W **120** B3
Bow → *Alta., Canada* 49°57N 111°41W **153** J9
Bow Center *N.H., U.S.A.* 43°10N 71°34W **89** C3
Bow Island *Alta., Canada* 49°50N 111°23W **153** J9
Bow Mar *Colo., U.S.A.* 39°37N 105°2W **134** C1
Bow Pass *Alta., Canada* 51°43N 116°30W **153** G6
Bowbells *N. Dak., U.S.A.* 48°48N 102°15W **76** B3
Bowden *Alta., Canada* 51°55N 114°2W **153** G6
Bowden *W. Va., U.S.A.* 38°55N 79°43W **102** C5
Bowdle *S. Dak., U.S.A.* 45°27N 99°39W **76** E6
Bowdoin Nat. Wildlife Refuge △ *Mont.,*
  U.S.A. 48°24N 107°39W **123** B10
Bowdon *Ga., U.S.A.* 33°32N 85°15W **113** C1
Bowdon *N. Dak., U.S.A.* 47°28N 99°43W **76** C6
Bowdon Junction *Ga., U.S.A.* 33°40N 85°9W **113** C1
Bowen *Ill., U.S.A.* 40°14N 91°4W **84** C2
Bowen Island *B.C., Canada* 49°23N 123°20W **155** F11
Bowens *Md., U.S.A.* 38°30N 76°38W **93** B4
Bower Hill *Pa., U.S.A.* 40°22N 80°5W **98** B1
Bowers *Del., U.S.A.* 39°4N 75°24W **93** A5
Bowersville *Ga., U.S.A.* 34°22N 83°5W **113** B3
Bowersville *Ohio, U.S.A.* 39°35N 83°44W **86** D3
Bowie *Ariz., U.S.A.* 32°19N 109°29W **130** E6
Bowie *Colo., U.S.A.* 38°55N 107°33W **125** D3
Bowie *Md., U.S.A.* 38°57N 76°47W **93** A4
Bowie *Tex., U.S.A.* 33°34N 97°51W **109** D10
Bowie County ☆ *Tex., U.S.A.* 33°27N 94°25W **109** D13
Bowie Cr. → *Miss., U.S.A.* 31°24N 89°27W **111** E4
Bowlegs *Okla., U.S.A.* 35°9N 96°40W **107** C7
Bowling Green *Fla., U.S.A.* 27°38N 81°50W **114** D7
Bowling Green *Ky., U.S.A.* 36°59N 86°27W **104** D6
Bowling Green *Mo., U.S.A.* 39°21N 91°12W **83** B5
Bowling Green *Ohio, U.S.A.* 41°23N 83°39W **86** B3
Bowling Green *Va., U.S.A.* 38°3N 77°21W **93** B3

Bowlus *Minn., U.S.A.* 45°49N 94°24W **77** E4
Bowman *Ga., U.S.A.* 34°12N 83°2W **113** B3
Bowman *N. Dak., U.S.A.* 46°11N 103°24W **76** D2
Bowman *S.C., U.S.A.* 33°21N 80°41W **103** E5
Bowman B. *Nunavut, Canada* 65°30N 73°40W **159** D11
Bowman County ☆ *N. Dak., U.S.A.* 46°2N 103°30W **76** D2
Bowman-Haley Lake *N. Dak., U.S.A.* 45°59N 103°14W **76** E2
Bowmanstown *Pa., U.S.A.* 40°48N 75°40W **92** B1
Bowmanville = Clarington *Ont.,*
  Canada 43°55N 78°41W **147** D8
Bowmont *Idaho, U.S.A.* 43°27N 116°32W **122** F2
Bowron → *B.C., Canada* 54°3N 121°50W **155** A13
Bowron Lake Park △ *B.C., Canada* 53°10N 121°5W **155** B13
Bowser *B.C., Canada* 49°27N 124°40W **154** F10
Bowsman *Man., Canada* 52°14N 101°12W **151** C10
Bowstring L. *Minn., U.S.A.* 47°33N 93°5W **77** C5
Box Butte County ☆ *Nebr., U.S.A.* 42°15N 103°0W **80** B2
Box Elder *S. Dak., U.S.A.* 44°7N 103°4W **76** F2
Box Elder County ☆ *Utah, U.S.A.* 41°30N 113°0W **129** B3
Boxelder → *S. Dak., U.S.A.* 44°1N 102°27W **76** F3
Boxelder Cr. → *S. Dak., U.S.A.* 45°59N 103°57W **76** E2
Boxford *Mass., U.S.A.* 42°40N 71°0W **91** B4
Boxholm *Iowa, U.S.A.* 42°10N 94°6W **81** C4
Boy River *Minn., U.S.A.* 47°10N 94°7W **77** C4
Boyce *La., U.S.A.* 31°23N 92°40W **110** C3
Boyce *Va., U.S.A.* 39°6N 78°4W **93** A2
Boyd *Minn., U.S.A.* 44°51N 95°54W **77** F3
Boyd *Tex., U.S.A.* 33°5N 97°34W **109** D10
Boyd Conservation Area *Ont., Canada* 43°49N 79°35W **161** A1
Boyd County ☆ *Ky., U.S.A.* 38°20N 82°40W **105** B10
Boyd County ☆ *Nebr., U.S.A.* 42°50N 98°40W **80** B7
Boyd L. *Qué., Canada* 52°46N 76°42W **143** C2
Boydell *Ark., U.S.A.* 33°22N 91°29W **106** E4
Boyden *Iowa, U.S.A.* 43°12N 96°0W **81** B3
Boydton *Va., U.S.A.* 36°40N 78°24W **102** E6
Boyer → *Iowa, U.S.A.* 41°27N 95°55W **81** D3
Boyertown *Pa., U.S.A.* 40°20N 75°38W **92** B1
Boyes *Mont., U.S.A.* 45°16N 105°2W **123** E12
Boyes Hot Springs *Calif., U.S.A.* 38°19N 122°29W **126** E4
Boykin *Ala., U.S.A.* 31°6N 84°41W **113** E2
Boykins *Va., U.S.A.* 36°35N 77°12W **102** E7
Boyle *Alta., Canada* 54°35N 112°49W **152** D8
Boyle *Miss., U.S.A.* 33°42N 90°44W **111** C3
Boyle County ☆ *Ky., U.S.A.* 37°35N 84°55W **105** C8
Boyle Heights *Calif., U.S.A.* 34°1N 118°12W **133** B3
Boylston *N.S., Canada* 45°26N 61°30W **141** H8
Boyne City *Mich., U.S.A.* 45°13N 85°1W **79** D6
Boyne Falls *Mich., U.S.A.* 45°10N 84°55W **79** D7
Boynton *Okla., U.S.A.* 35°39N 95°39W **107** C8
Boynton Beach *Fla., U.S.A.* 26°32N 80°4W **114** E8
Boys Town *Nebr., U.S.A.* 41°16N 96°8W **80** C9
Boysen Res. *Wyo., U.S.A.* 43°25N 108°11W **124** C4
Bozeman *Mont., U.S.A.* 45°41N 111°2W **123** E6
Bozman *Md., U.S.A.* 38°46N 76°16W **93** B4
Bracebridge *Ont., Canada* 45°2N 79°19W **146** B7
Bracey *Va., U.S.A.* 36°36N 78°9W **102** E6
Bracken *Sask., Canada* 49°11N 108°6W **150** F3
Bracken *Tex., U.S.A.* 29°36N 98°19W **116** B3
Bracken County ☆ *Ky., U.S.A.* 38°40N 84°5W **105** B8
Brackendale *B.C., Canada* 49°48N 123°8W **155** F11
Brackettville *Tex., U.S.A.* 29°19N 100°25W **108** H7
Braddock *N. Dak., U.S.A.* 46°34N 100°6W **76** D5
Braddock *Pa., U.S.A.* 40°24N 79°52W **98** B2
Braddock Heights *Md., U.S.A.* 39°25N 77°30W **93** A3
Braddock Hills *Pa., U.S.A.* 40°25N 79°51W **98** B2
Braddyville *Iowa, U.S.A.* 40°35N 95°2W **81** E4
Braden *Tenn., U.S.A.* 35°23N 89°34W **104** E3
Bradenton *Fla., U.S.A.* 27°30N 82°34W **114** D6
Bradford *Ont., Canada* 44°7N 79°34W **146** C7
Bradford *Ark., U.S.A.* 35°25N 91°27W **106** C4
Bradford *Ill., U.S.A.* 41°11N 89°39W **84** B4
Bradford *N.H., U.S.A.* 43°17N 71°56W **89** C3
Bradford *Pa., U.S.A.* 41°58N 78°38W **87** C4
Bradford *R.I., U.S.A.* 41°24N 71°45W **91** C3
Bradford *Tenn., U.S.A.* 36°5N 88°49W **104** D4
Bradford *Vt., U.S.A.* 43°59N 72°9W **89** C2
Bradford County ☆ *Fla., U.S.A.* 30°0N 82°15W **114** B6
Bradford County ☆ *Pa., U.S.A.* 41°50N 76°30W **87** C6
Bradfordsville *Ky., U.S.A.* 37°30N 85°9W **105** C7
Bradgate *Iowa, U.S.A.* 42°48N 94°25W **81** C4
Bradley *Ark., U.S.A.* 33°6N 93°39W **106** E2
Bradley *Calif., U.S.A.* 35°52N 120°48W **127** H6
Bradley *Ill., U.S.A.* 41°8N 87°52W **84** B6
Bradley *Okla., U.S.A.* 34°53N 97°42W **107** D6
Bradley *S. Dak., U.S.A.* 45°5N 97°39W **76** E8
Bradley *W. Va., U.S.A.* 37°51N 81°12W **102** D3
Bradley County ☆ *Ark., U.S.A.* 33°27N 92°10W **106** E3
Bradley County ☆ *Tenn., U.S.A.* 35°10N 84°55W **105** E8
Bradley Int., Hartford ✈ (BDL) *Conn.,*
  U.S.A. 41°56N 72°41W **91** B2
Bradley Junction *Fla., U.S.A.* 27°48N 81°59W **114** D7
Bradner *Ohio, U.S.A.* 41°20N 83°26W **86** B3
Bradore Bay *Qué., Canada* 51°27N 57°18W **142** A3
Bradshaw *Nebr., U.S.A.* 40°53N 97°45W **80** D8
Bradshaw *W. Va., U.S.A.* 37°21N 81°48W **102** D3
Bradwell *Sask., Canada* 51°54N 106°14W **150** D5
Brady *Mont., U.S.A.* 48°2N 111°51W **123** B6
Brady *Nebr., U.S.A.* 41°1N 100°22W **80** C5
Brady *Tex., U.S.A.* 31°9N 99°20W **108** F8
Brady Cr. → *Tex., U.S.A.* 31°8N 98°59W **109** F9
Braeside *Ont., Canada* 45°28N 76°24W **144** F6
Bragg City *Mo., U.S.A.* 36°16N 89°55W **83** E7
Bragg Creek *Alta., Canada* 50°57N 114°35W **153** H6
Braggadocio *Mo., U.S.A.* 36°11N 89°50W **83** E7
Braggs *Okla., U.S.A.* 35°40N 95°12W **107** C8
Bragg's Spur = West Memphis *Ark.,*
  U.S.A. 35°8N 90°11W **117** B3
Braham *Minn., U.S.A.* 45°44N 93°10W **77** E5
Braidwood *Ill., U.S.A.* 41°16N 88°13W **84** B5
Brainard *Nebr., U.S.A.* 41°11N 97°0W **80** C9
Brainerd *Minn., U.S.A.* 46°22N 94°12W **77** D4
Braintree *Mass., U.S.A.* 42°13N 71°0W **91** B4
Braithwaite *La., U.S.A.* 29°51N 89°56W **117** C3
Bralorne *B.C., Canada* 50°50N 122°50W **155** E12
Braman *Okla., U.S.A.* 36°56N 97°20W **107** B6
Bramham I. *B.C., Canada* 51°4N 127°34W **154** D7
Brampton *Ont., Canada* 43°45N 79°45W **146** D7
Brampton *N. Dak., U.S.A.* 46°0N 97°52W **76** D8
Bramwell *W. Va., U.S.A.* 37°20N 81°19W **102** D3
Branch *Nfld. & L., Canada* 46°53N 53°57W **142** F7
Branch *Ark., U.S.A.* 35°18N 93°57W **106** C2

Branch County ☆ *Mich., U.S.A.* 41°50N 85°5W **79** H6
Branchland *W. Va., U.S.A.* 38°13N 82°12W **102** C2
Branchville *N.J., U.S.A.* 41°9N 74°45W **92** A2
Branchville *S.C., U.S.A.* 33°15N 80°49W **103** E5
Brandeis University *Mass., U.S.A.* 42°21N 71°17W **96** A1
Brandenburg *Ky., U.S.A.* 38°0N 86°10W **104** C6
Brandon *Man., Canada* 49°50N 99°57W **151** F12
Brandon *Colo., U.S.A.* 38°27N 102°26W **125** D8
Brandon *Fla., U.S.A.* 27°56N 82°17W **114** D6
Brandon *Iowa, U.S.A.* 42°19N 92°0W **81** C7
Brandon *Minn., U.S.A.* 45°58N 95°36W **77** E3
Brandon *S. Dak., U.S.A.* 32°16N 99°59W **111** D4
Brandon *Nebr., U.S.A.* 40°48N 101°55W **80** D4
Brandon *Vt., U.S.A.* 43°48N 73°6W **89** C1
Brandon *Wis., U.S.A.* 43°44N 88°47W **78** E5
Brandonville *W. Va., U.S.A.* 39°40N 79°37W **102** B5
Brandsville *Mo., U.S.A.* 36°39N 91°42W **83** E5
Brandt *S. Dak., U.S.A.* 44°40N 96°38W **76** F9
Brandy Pk. *Oreg., U.S.A.* 42°36N 123°53W **121** E2
Brandywine *Md., U.S.A.* 38°42N 76°51W **93** B4
Brandywine *W. Va., U.S.A.* 38°38N 79°15W **102** C5
Branford *Conn., U.S.A.* 41°17N 72°49W **91** C2
Branford *Fla., U.S.A.* 29°58N 82°56W **114** B6
Branson *Colo., U.S.A.* 37°1N 103°53W **125** E7
Branson *Mo., U.S.A.* 36°39N 93°13W **83** E3
Brantford *Ont., Canada* 43°10N 80°15W **146** D6
Brantford *N. Dak., U.S.A.* 47°36N 98°55W **76** C7
Brantley *Ala., U.S.A.* 31°35N 86°16W **112** E4
Brantley County ☆ *Ga., U.S.A.* 31°10N 82°0W **113** E5
Brantley L. *N. Mex., U.S.A.* 32°32N 104°22W **131** E6
Bras d'Or L. *N.S., Canada* 45°50N 60°50W **141** H9
Brashear *Mo., U.S.A.* 40°9N 92°23W **83** A4
Brasher Falls *N.Y., U.S.A.* 44°49N 74°47W **88** A6
Brasstown Bald *Ga., U.S.A.* 34°53N 83°49W **113** B3
Brassua L. *Maine, U.S.A.* 45°40N 69°55W **90** C4
Bratenahl *Ohio, U.S.A.* 41°32N 81°37W **98** A2
Bratt *Fla., U.S.A.* 30°58N 87°26W **114** A1
Brattleboro *Vt., U.S.A.* 42°51N 72°34W **89** D2
Braunig Lake *Tex., U.S.A.* 29°14N 98°22W **116** D3
Bravo del Norte, Río = Grande, Río →
  N. Amer. 25°58N 97°9W **108** M10
Brawley *Calif., U.S.A.* 32°59N 115°31W **127** L11
Brawley Peaks *Nev., U.S.A.* 38°15N 118°55W **128** D2
Brawley Wash → *Ariz., U.S.A.* 32°34N 111°26W **130** E4
Braxton *Miss., U.S.A.* 32°1N 89°58W **111** D4
Braxton County ☆ *W. Va., U.S.A.* 38°43N 80°39W **102** C4
Bray *Okla., U.S.A.* 34°38N 97°49W **107** D6
Bray I. *Nunavut, Canada* 69°16N 77°0W **158** D10
Braymer *Mo., U.S.A.* 39°35N 93°48W **83** B3
Brayton *Iowa, U.S.A.* 41°33N 94°56W **81** D4
Brazeau → *Alta., Canada* 52°55N 115°14W **153** F5
Brazeau, Mt. *Alta., Canada* 52°33N 117°21W **153** F3
Brazeau Res. *Alta., Canada* 52°59N 115°30W **153** F5
Brazil *Ind., U.S.A.* 39°32N 87°8W **85** D3
Brazoria *Tex., U.S.A.* 29°3N 95°34W **109** H12
Brazoria County ☆ *Tex., U.S.A.* 29°10N 95°26W **109** H12
Brazoria Nat. Wildlife Refuge △ *Tex.,*
  U.S.A. 29°3N 95°15W **109** H12
Brazos → *Tex., U.S.A.* 28°53N 95°23W **109** J12
Brazos County ☆ *Tex., U.S.A.* 30°40N 96°22W **109** G11
Breakers, The *R.I., U.S.A.* 41°28N 71°18W **91** C3
Breakheart Reservation *Mass., U.S.A.* 42°28N 71°1W **96** A2
Breaks Interstate Park △ *U.S.A.* 37°17N 82°18W **105** C10
Breathitt County ☆ *Ky., U.S.A.* 37°30N 83°20W **105** C9
Breaux Bridge *La., U.S.A.* 30°16N 91°54W **110** D4
Brechin *Ont., Canada* 44°32N 79°10W **146** C7
Breckenridge *Colo., U.S.A.* 39°29N 106°3W **125** C4
Breckenridge *Mich., U.S.A.* 43°24N 84°29W **79** F7
Breckenridge *Minn., U.S.A.* 46°16N 96°35W **77** D2
Breckenridge *Mo., U.S.A.* 39°46N 93°48W **83** B3
Breckenridge *Tex., U.S.A.* 32°45N 98°54W **109** E9
Breckenridge Hills *Mo., U.S.A.* 38°42N 90°22W **94** A1
Breckinridge *Okla., U.S.A.* 36°26N 97°44W **107** B6
Breckinridge County ☆ *Ky., U.S.A.* 37°45N 86°25W **104** C6
Brecksville *Ohio, U.S.A.* 41°19N 81°37W **98** B2
Brecksville Reservation *Ohio, U.S.A.* 41°18N 81°36W **98** B2
Breda *Iowa, U.S.A.* 42°11N 94°59W **81** C4
Bredenbury *Sask., Canada* 50°57N 102°3W **151** D11
Breese *Ill., U.S.A.* 38°37N 89°32W **84** E4
Breezy Point *N.Y., U.S.A.* 40°33N 73°56W **97** C3
Bremen *Ala., U.S.A.* 33°59N 86°58W **112** C4
Bremen *Ga., U.S.A.* 33°43N 85°9W **113** C1
Bremen *Ind., U.S.A.* 41°27N 86°9W **85** B4
Bremen *Ohio, U.S.A.* 39°42N 82°26W **86** D4
Bremer County ☆ *Iowa, U.S.A.* 42°45N 92°15W **81** C6
Bremerton *Wash., U.S.A.* 47°34N 122°37W **132** C2
Bremond *Tex., U.S.A.* 31°10N 96°41W **109** F11
Brenham *Tex., U.S.A.* 30°10N 96°24W **109** G11
Brent *Ont., Canada* 46°2N 78°29W **147** A8
Brent *Ala., U.S.A.* 32°56N 87°10W **112** D3
Brentwood *B.C., Canada* 49°16N 122°59W **161** B2
Brentwood *Calif., U.S.A.* 37°56N 121°42W **126** F5
Brentwood *Mo., U.S.A.* 38°37N 90°20W **94** B1
Brentwood *N.H., U.S.A.* 42°58N 71°6W **89** D3
Brentwood *N.Y., U.S.A.* 40°47N 73°15W **92** B3
Brentwood *Pa., U.S.A.* 40°21N 79°58W **98** B2
Brentwood *Tenn., U.S.A.* 36°2N 86°47W **104** D6
Brentwood Park *Calif., U.S.A.* 34°3N 118°29W **133** B2
Breton *Alta., Canada* 53°7N 114°28W **153** E6
Breton Is. *La., U.S.A.* 29°13N 89°12W **110** E6
Breton Nat. Wildlife Refuge △ *La.,*
  U.S.A. 29°50N 88°50W **110** E7
Breton Sd. *La., U.S.A.* 29°35N 89°15W **110** E7
Brevard *N.C., U.S.A.* 35°14N 82°44W **103** C3
Brevard County ☆ *Fla., U.S.A.* 28°20N 80°42W **114** C8
Brevig Mission *Alaska, U.S.A.* 65°20N 166°29W **135** B6
Brevort *Mich., U.S.A.* 46°1N 85°2W **79** C6
Brewer *Maine, U.S.A.* 44°48N 68°46W **90** D5
Brewerton *N.Y., U.S.A.* 43°14N 76°9W **88** B4
Brewster *Kans., U.S.A.* 39°22N 101°23W **82** B2
Brewster *Mass., U.S.A.* 41°46N 70°5W **91** C4
Brewster *Minn., U.S.A.* 43°42N 95°28W **77** G3
Brewster *N.Y., U.S.A.* 41°24N 73°36W **91** C1
Brewster *Nebr., U.S.A.* 41°56N 99°52W **80** C6
Brewster *Ohio, U.S.A.* 40°43N 81°36W **86** C5
Brewster *Wash., U.S.A.* 48°6N 119°47W **120** B6
Brewster, Kap = Kangikajik *Greenland* 70°7N 22°0W **162** B8
Brewster County ☆ *Tex., U.S.A.* 30°0N 103°0W **108** H4
Brewton *Ala., U.S.A.* 31°7N 87°4W **112** E3
Brewton *Ga., U.S.A.* 32°36N 82°48W **113** D4
Brian Head *Utah, U.S.A.* 37°41N 112°50W **129** F3

Briargrove Tex., U.S.A. 29°44N 95°29W 116 B2
Briartown Okla., U.S.A. 35°18N 95°14W 107 C8
Bribri Costa Rica 9°38N 82°50W 182 E3
Briceland Calif., U.S.A. 40°7N 123°54W 126 C3
Bricelyn Minn., U.S.A. 43°34N 93°49W 77 G5
Brices Cross Roads Nat. Battlefield Site △ Miss., U.S.A. 34°30N 88°44W 111 B5
Briceville Tenn., U.S.A. 36°11N 84°11W 105 D8
Brickeys Ark., U.S.A. 34°52N 90°36W 106 D5
Brickyard, The Ill., U.S.A. 41°55N 87°47W 95 B2
Briçonnet, L. Qué., Canada 51°27N 60°10W 140 B9
Bridge Idaho, U.S.A. 42°8N 113°20W 122 G5
Bridge Oreg., U.S.A. 43°1N 124°0W 121 D2
Bridge City Tex., U.S.A. 30°1N 93°51W 109 G14
Bridge Lake B.C., Canada 51°29N 120°43W 155 D14
Bridgeboro Ont., Canada 31°24N 83°59W 113 E3
Bridgehampton N.Y., U.S.A. 40°56N 72°19W 91 D2
Bridgenorth Ont., Canada 44°23N 78°23W 147 C8
Bridgeport Ont., Canada 43°29N 80°29W 146 D6
Bridgeport Ala., U.S.A. 34°57N 85°43W 112 B5
Bridgeport Calif., U.S.A. 38°15N 119°14W 126 E7
Bridgeport Conn., U.S.A. 41°11N 73°12W 91 C1
Bridgeport Ill., U.S.A. 38°43N 87°46W 84 E6
Bridgeport Ill., U.S.A. 41°50N 87°38W 95 B3
Bridgeport Mich., U.S.A. 43°22N 83°53W 79 F8
Bridgeport N.Y., U.S.A. 43°9N 75°58W 88 B5
Bridgeport Nebr., U.S.A. 41°40N 103°6W 80 C2
Bridgeport Okla., U.S.A. 35°33N 98°23W 107 C5
Bridgeport Tex., U.S.A. 33°13N 97°45W 109 D10
Bridgeport W. Va., U.S.A. 39°17N 80°15W 102 B4
Bridgeport Wash., U.S.A. 48°0N 119°40W 120 C6
Bridgeport, L. Tex., U.S.A. 33°13N 97°50W 109 D10
Bridger Mont., U.S.A. 45°18N 108°55W 123 E9
Bridger Peak Wyo., U.S.A. 41°11N 107°2W 124 E5
Bridger-Teton Nat. Forest Wyo., U.S.A. 43°5N 110°5W 124 C2
Bridgeton N.J., U.S.A. 39°26N 75°14W 92 C1
Bridgetown N.S., Canada 44°55N 65°18W 141 J4
Bridgetown Barbados 13°6N 59°37W 183 D8
Bridgetown Md., U.S.A. 39°2N 75°53W 93 A5
Bridgeview Ill., U.S.A. 41°45N 87°48W 95 C2
Bridgeville Calif., U.S.A. 40°25N 123°50W 126 C3
Bridgeville Del., U.S.A. 38°45N 75°36W 93 B5
Bridgeville Pa., U.S.A. 40°21N 80°6W 98 B1
Bridgewater N.S., Canada 44°25N 64°31W 141 J5
Bridgewater Conn., U.S.A. 41°32N 73°22W 91 C1
Bridgewater Iowa, U.S.A. 41°15N 94°40W 81 D4
Bridgewater Maine, U.S.A. 46°25N 67°51W 90 B6
Bridgewater Mass., U.S.A. 41°59N 70°58W 91 C4
Bridgewater N.Y., U.S.A. 42°53N 75°15W 88 C5
Bridgewater S. Dak., U.S.A. 43°33N 97°30W 76 G8
Bridgewater Va., U.S.A. 38°23N 78°59W 102 C6
Bridgewater Vt., U.S.A. 43°35N 72°38W 89 C2
Bridgman Mich., U.S.A. 41°57N 86°33W 79 H5
Bridgton Maine, U.S.A. 44°3N 70°42W 90 D3
Bridport Vt., U.S.A. 43°58N 73°20W 89 C1
Brier Wash., U.S.A. 47°47N 122°16W 132 B4
Brier Cr. → Ga., U.S.A. 32°44N 81°26W 113 D5
Brier I. N.S., Canada 44°16N 66°22W 141 J3
Briercrest Sask., Canada 50°10N 105°16W 150 E6
Brigantine N.J., U.S.A. 39°24N 74°22W 92 C2
Briggsdale Colo., U.S.A. 40°38N 104°20W 125 B6
Briggsville Ark., U.S.A. 34°56N 93°30W 106 D2
Brigham City Utah, U.S.A. 41°31N 112°1W 129 B3
Bright Ind., U.S.A. 39°13N 84°51W 85 D6
Brighton Ont., Canada 44°2N 77°44W 147 C9
Brighton Colo., U.S.A. 39°59N 104°49W 125 C6
Brighton Fla., U.S.A. 27°14N 81°6W 114 D7
Brighton Ill., U.S.A. 39°2N 90°8W 84 D3
Brighton Iowa, U.S.A. 41°10N 91°49W 81 D7
Brighton Mass., U.S.A. 42°21N 71°9W 96 A2
Brighton Mich., U.S.A. 42°32N 83°47W 79 G8
Brighton N.Y., U.S.A. 43°8N 77°34W 88 B3
Brighton Tenn., U.S.A. 35°29N 89°43W 104 E3
Brighton Utah, U.S.A. 40°36N 111°34W 134 C4
Brighton Indian Reservation Fla., U.S.A. 27°0N 81°15W 114 D7
Brighton Park Ill., U.S.A. 41°48N 87°41W 95 C2
Brightsand L. Sask., Canada 53°36N 108°53W 150 B3
Brightwood Oreg., U.S.A. 38°57N 77°1W 99 B3
Brilliant B.C., Canada 49°19N 117°38W 155 F17
Brilliant Ala., U.S.A. 34°1N 87°46W 112 B3
Brillion Wis., U.S.A. 44°11N 88°4W 78 D5
Brimfield Mich., U.S.A. 46°24N 84°34W 79 C7
Brimfield Mass., U.S.A. 42°7N 72°12W 91 B2
Brimson Minn., U.S.A. 47°17N 91°52W 77 C7
Brinkley Ark., U.S.A. 34°53N 91°12W 106 D4
Brinnon Wash., U.S.A. 47°41N 122°54W 120 C3
Brinsmade N. Dak., U.S.A. 48°11N 99°19W 76 B6
Brinson Ga., U.S.A. 30°59N 84°44W 113 F2
Brion, Î. Qué., Canada 47°46N 61°26W 141 F8
Brisbane Calif., U.S.A. 37°40N 122°23W 132 B2
Briscoe Tex., U.S.A. 35°35N 100°17W 108 B7
Briscoe County ☆ Tex., U.S.A. 34°28N 101°19W 108 C6
Bristol N.B., Canada 46°28N 67°35W 141 G2
Bristol Qué., Canada 45°32N 76°28W 144 F6
Bristol Colo., U.S.A. 38°7N 102°19W 125 D8
Bristol Conn., U.S.A. 41°40N 72°57W 91 C2
Bristol Fla., U.S.A. 30°26N 84°59W 114 A4
Bristol Ind., U.S.A. 41°43N 85°49W 85 B5
Bristol Md., U.S.A. 38°47N 76°40W 93 B4
Bristol N.H., U.S.A. 43°36N 71°44W 89 C3
Bristol Pa., U.S.A. 40°6N 74°51W 92 B3
Bristol R.I., U.S.A. 41°40N 71°16W 91 C3
Bristol S. Dak., U.S.A. 45°21N 97°45W 76 E8
Bristol Tenn., U.S.A. 36°36N 82°11W 105 D10
Bristol Vt., U.S.A. 44°8N 73°5W 89 B1
Bristol B. Alaska, U.S.A. 58°0N 160°0W 135 H8
Bristol Bay ☆ Alaska, U.S.A. 58°45N 156°50W 135 G8
Bristol County ☆ Mass., U.S.A. 41°45N 71°10W 91 C3
Bristol County ☆ R.I., U.S.A. 41°40N 71°20W 91 C3
Bristol L. Calif., U.S.A. 34°28N 115°41W 127 J11
Bristol Mts. Calif., U.S.A. 34°30N 115°50W 127 J11
Bristow Nebr., U.S.A. 42°51N 98°35W 80 B7
Bristow Okla., U.S.A. 35°50N 96°23W 107 C7
Bristow Va., U.S.A. 38°43N 77°33W 93 B3
Britannia Beach B.C., Canada 49°38N 123°12W 155 F11
British Columbia □ Canada 55°0N 125°15W 154 B10
British Empire Range Nunavut, Canada 82°21N 77°30W 158 A10
British Honduras = Belize ■ Cent. Amer. 17°0N 88°30W 182 C2
British Mts. N. Amer. 68°50N 140°0W 156 C4
British Virgin Is. ☑ W. Indies 18°30N 64°30W 184 G18
Britt Ont., Canada 45°46N 80°34W 146 B6
Britt Iowa, U.S.A. 43°6N 93°48W 81 B5
Britton S. Dak., U.S.A. 45°48N 97°45W 76 E8

Britton Hill Fla., U.S.A. 30°59N 86°17W 114 A2
Broad → Ga., U.S.A. 33°59N 82°39W 113 C4
Broad → S.C., U.S.A. 34°1N 81°4W 103 D4
Broadalbin N.Y., U.S.A. 43°4N 74°12W 88 B6
Broadback → Qué., Canada 51°21N 78°52W 143 C2
Broadbent Oreg., U.S.A. 43°1N 124°9W 121 D1
Broadhurst Ga., U.S.A. 31°28N 81°55W 113 E5
Broadkill Beach Del., U.S.A. 38°47N 75°10W 93 B5
Broadmoor Calif., U.S.A. 37°41N 122°29W 132 B2
Broadus Mont., U.S.A. 45°27N 105°25W 123 E12
Broadview Sask., Canada 50°22N 102°35W 150 E9
Broadview Ill., U.S.A. 41°51N 87°52W 95 B1
Broadview Mont., U.S.A. 46°6N 108°53W 123 D9
Broadview N. Mex., U.S.A. 34°49N 103°13W 131 C7
Broadview Heights Ohio, U.S.A. 41°18N 81°41W 98 B1
Broadview Park Fla., U.S.A. 26°5N 80°12W 115 B2
Broadwater Nebr., U.S.A. 41°36N 102°51W 80 C3
Broadwater County ☆ Mont., U.S.A. 46°25N 111°30W 123 D8
Broadway Va., U.S.A. 38°37N 78°48W 102 C6
Broadwell Ill., U.S.A. 40°4N 89°27W 84 C4
Brochet Man., Canada 57°53N 101°40W 159 F5
Brochet, L. Man., Canada 58°36N 101°35W 159 F5
Brochet, L. du Qué., Canada 49°40N 69°37W 145 B13
Brock Sask., Canada 51°26N 108°43W 150 D3
Brock Nebr., U.S.A. 40°29N 95°58W 80 D10
Brock → Qué., Canada 50°0N 75°5W 144 A7
Brock I. N.W.T., Canada 77°52N 114°19W 156 A10
Brocket N. Dak., U.S.A. 48°13N 98°21W 76 B7
Brockport N.Y., U.S.A. 43°13N 77°56W 88 B3
Brockton Mass., U.S.A. 42°5N 71°1W 91 B3
Brockton Mont., U.S.A. 48°9N 104°55W 123 B13
Brockville Ont., Canada 44°35N 75°41W 147 C11
Brockway Mont., U.S.A. 47°18N 105°45W 123 C12
Brockway Pa., U.S.A. 41°15N 78°47W 87 C4
Brocton Ill., U.S.A. 39°43N 87°56W 84 D6
Brocton N.Y., U.S.A. 42°23N 79°26W 88 C1
Broderick Sask., Canada 51°30N 106°55W 150 D5
Brodeur Pen. Nunavut, Canada 72°30N 88°0W 158 C8
Brodhead Ky., U.S.A. 37°24N 84°25W 105 C8
Brodhead Wis., U.S.A. 42°37N 89°22W 78 F4
Brodheadsville Pa., U.S.A. 40°55N 75°24W 92 B1
Brodnax Va., U.S.A. 36°43N 78°2W 102 E6
Brogan Oreg., U.S.A. 44°15N 117°31W 121 C8
Brogden N.C., U.S.A. 35°18N 78°2W 103 C7
Brokaw Wis., U.S.A. 45°2N 89°39W 78 C4
Broken Arrow Okla., U.S.A. 36°3N 95°48W 107 B8
Broken Bow Nebr., U.S.A. 41°24N 99°38W 80 C6
Broken Bow Okla., U.S.A. 34°2N 94°44W 107 D9
Broken Bow Lake Okla., U.S.A. 34°9N 94°40W 107 D9
Bromide Okla., U.S.A. 34°24N 96°51W 107 D7
Bromont Qué., Canada 45°17N 72°39W 145 F10
Bromptonville Qué., Canada 45°28N 71°57W 145 F11
Bronaugh Mo., U.S.A. 37°41N 94°28W 83 D2
Bronson Kans., U.S.A. 37°54N 95°4W 82 D8
Bronson Mich., U.S.A. 41°52N 85°12W 79 H6
Bronson Tex., U.S.A. 31°21N 94°1W 109 F13
Bronte Tex., U.S.A. 31°53N 100°18W 108 F7
Bronwood Ga., U.S.A. 31°50N 84°22W 113 E2
Bronx N.Y., U.S.A. 40°51N 73°52W 97 B3
Bronx County ☆ N.Y., U.S.A. 40°50N 73°52W 88 D3
Bronxville N.Y., U.S.A. 40°56N 73°49W 97 A4
Brooch L. Qué., Canada 50°45N 67°52W 140 C2
Brook Ind., U.S.A. 40°52N 87°22W 85 C3
Brook Park Ohio, U.S.A. 41°23N 81°48W 98 B1
Brookdale Man., Canada 50°3N 99°34W 151 E12
Brookdale Park Minn., U.S.A. 45°3N 93°20W 94 A2
Brooke County ☆ W. Va., U.S.A. 40°16N 80°37W 102 A4
Brookeland Tex., U.S.A. 31°10N 94°0W 109 F14
Brookesmith Tex., U.S.A. 31°33N 99°7W 109 F8
Brookfield N.S., Canada 45°15N 63°17W 141 H6
Brookfield Ill., U.S.A. 41°48N 87°50W 95 C1
Brookfield Mass., U.S.A. 42°13N 72°6W 91 B2
Brookfield Mo., U.S.A. 39°47N 93°4W 83 B3
Brookfield Vt., U.S.A. 44°4N 72°38W 89 B2
Brookfield Wis., U.S.A. 43°4N 88°9W 78 E5
Brookhaven Georgia, U.S.A. 33°52N 84°19W 117 A2
Brookhaven Miss., U.S.A. 31°35N 90°26W 111 E3
Brookings Oreg., U.S.A. 42°3N 124°17W 121 E1
Brookings S. Dak., U.S.A. 44°19N 96°48W 76 F9
Brookings County ☆ S. Dak., U.S.A. 44°19N 96°48W 76 F9
Brookland = West Columbia S.C., U.S.A. 33°59N 81°4W 103 E4
Brookland Ark., U.S.A. 35°54N 90°35W 106 C5
Brooklandville Baltimore, U.S.A. 39°25N 76°40W 99 A1
Brooklawn N.J., U.S.A. 39°52N 75°7W 98 B2
Brooklet Ga., U.S.A. 32°23N 81°40W 113 D5
Brookline Mass., U.S.A. 42°19N 71°8W 96 B2
Brookline N.H., U.S.A. 42°44N 71°40W 89 D3
Brooklyn N.S., Canada 44°3N 64°42W 141 J5
Brooklyn Ala., U.S.A. 31°16N 86°46W 112 E4
Brooklyn Conn., U.S.A. 41°47N 71°57W 91 C3
Brooklyn Ill., U.S.A. 38°39N 90°10W 94 B3
Brooklyn Ind., U.S.A. 39°32N 86°22W 85 D4
Brooklyn Iowa, U.S.A. 41°44N 92°27W 81 D6
Brooklyn Mich., U.S.A. 42°7N 84°15W 79 G7
Brooklyn Miss., U.S.A. 31°3N 89°11W 111 E4
Brooklyn New York, U.S.A. 96 f3
Brooklyn Ohio, U.S.A. 41°26N 81°44W 98 B1
Brooklyn Wash., U.S.A. 46°47N 123°31W 120 D2
Brooklyn Center Minn., U.S.A. 45°4N 93°19W 94 A2
Brooklyn Heights New York, U.S.A. 96 f2
Brooklyn Heights Ohio, U.S.A. 41°23N 81°41W 98 B1
Brooklyn Park Md., U.S.A. 39°13N 76°37W 99 B2
Brooklyn Park Minn., U.S.A. 45°6N 93°23W 77 E5
Brookmere B.C., Canada 49°52N 120°53W 155 F14
Brookmont Md., U.S.A. 38°57N 77°7W 99 B3
Brookneal Va., U.S.A. 37°3N 78°57W 102 D6
Brookport Ill., U.S.A. 37°8N 88°38W 84 F5
Brooks Alta., Canada 50°35N 111°55W 153 H9
Brooks Ky., U.S.A. 38°4N 85°43W 105 B7
Brooks Minn., U.S.A. 47°49N 96°0W 77 C3
Brooks Air Force Base Tex., U.S.A. 29°20N 98°25W 116 C3
Brooks B. B.C., Canada 50°15N 127°55W 154 E7
Brooks County ☆ Ga., U.S.A. 30°50N 83°45W 113 F3
Brooks County ☆ Tex., U.S.A. 27°0N 98°5W 108 K9
Brooks Range Alaska, U.S.A. 68°0N 152°0W 135 C9
Brookshire Tex., U.S.A. 29°47N 95°57W 109 H12
Brookside Beach Ohio, U.S.A. 41°27N 81°43W 98 B1
Brookside Village Tex., U.S.A. 29°35N 95°19W 116 C2
Brookston Ind., U.S.A. 40°36N 86°52W 85 C4
Brookston Minn., U.S.A. 46°52N 92°36W 77 D6
Brooksville Ala., U.S.A. 34°10N 86°29W 112 B4
Brooksville Fla., U.S.A. 28°33N 82°23W 114 C6
Brooksville Ky., U.S.A. 38°41N 84°4W 105 B8
Brooksville Miss., U.S.A. 33°14N 88°35W 111 C5
Brooksville Okla., U.S.A. 35°12N 96°58W 107 C7

Brookview Md., U.S.A. 38°35N 75°48W 93 B5
Brookville Ind., U.S.A. 39°25N 85°1W 85 D5
Brookville Kans., U.S.A. 38°46N 97°52W 82 C6
Brookville N.J., U.S.A. 39°44N 74°18W 92 C2
Brookville Ohio, U.S.A. 39°50N 84°24W 86 D2
Brookville Pa., U.S.A. 41°10N 79°5W 87 C3
Brookville L. Ind., U.S.A. 39°28N 85°0W 85 D5
Brookwood Ala., U.S.A. 33°17N 87°18W 112 C3
Broome County ☆ N.Y., U.S.A. 42°5N 75°45W 88 C5
Broomes Island Md., U.S.A. 38°25N 76°33W 93 B4
Broomfield Colo., U.S.A. 39°55N 105°5W 125 C5
Brooten Minn., U.S.A. 45°30N 95°8W 77 E3
Broseley Mo., U.S.A. 36°40N 90°15W 83 E6
Brosewere Bay N.Y., U.S.A. 40°36N 73°42W 97 C4
Brossard Qué., Canada 45°27N 73°28W 160 B4
Brothers Oreg., U.S.A. 43°49N 120°36W 121 D5
Brotmanville N.J., U.S.A. 39°33N 75°3W 92 C1
Broughton Ill., U.S.A. 37°56N 88°27W 84 F5
Broughton Pa., U.S.A. 40°19N 79°59W 98 C2
Broughton I. B.C., Canada 50°48N 126°42W 154 E8
Broughton Island = Qikiqtarjuaq Nunavut, Canada 67°33N 63°0W 158 D13
Broussard La., U.S.A. 30°9N 91°58W 110 D4
Broward County ☆ Fla., U.S.A. 26°15N 80°30W 114 E8
Browerville Minn., U.S.A. 46°5N 94°52W 77 D4
Brown, Pt. Wash., U.S.A. 46°56N 124°10W 120 D1
Brown City Mich., U.S.A. 43°13N 82°59W 79 F9
Brown County ☆ Ill., U.S.A. 39°55N 90°45W 84 D3
Brown County ☆ Ind., U.S.A. 39°10N 86°15W 85 D4
Brown County ☆ Kans., U.S.A. 39°45N 95°30W 82 B8
Brown County ☆ Minn., U.S.A. 44°10N 94°50W 77 F4
Brown County ☆ Nebr., U.S.A. 42°30N 100°0W 80 B6
Brown County ☆ Ohio, U.S.A. 38°55N 83°59W 86 E3
Brown County ☆ S. Dak., U.S.A. 45°37N 98°19W 76 E7
Brown County ☆ Tex., U.S.A. 31°43N 98°59W 109 F9
Brown County ☆ Wis., U.S.A. 44°30N 88°0W 78 D6
Brown County State Park △ Ind., U.S.A. 39°7N 86°16W 85 D4
Brown Deer Wis., U.S.A. 43°9N 87°57W 94 A2
Brown Deer Park Wis., U.S.A. 43°9N 87°57W 94 B2
Brown L. Nunavut, Canada 65°54N 91°15W 159 D7
Brownell Kans., U.S.A. 38°38N 99°45W 82 C4
Brownfield Tex., U.S.A. 33°11N 102°17W 108 D5
Browning Sask., Canada 49°27N 102°38W 150 F9
Browning Ill., U.S.A. 40°8N 90°22W 84 C3
Browning Mont., U.S.A. 48°34N 113°1W 123 B7
Brownlee Sask., Canada 50°43N 106°1W 150 E5
Brownlee Nebr., U.S.A. 42°17N 100°37W 80 B5
Brownlee Res. Idaho, U.S.A. 44°50N 116°54W 122 E2
Browns Ill., U.S.A. 38°23N 87°59W 84 E6
Browns Flats N.B., Canada 45°28N 66°8W 141 H3
Browns Mills N.J., U.S.A. 39°58N 74°34W 92 C2
Browns Park Nat. Wildlife Refuge ○ Colo., U.S.A. 40°50N 108°55W 125 B2
Browns Valley Minn., U.S.A. 45°36N 96°50W 77 E2
Brownsburg Ind., U.S.A. 39°51N 86°24W 85 D4
Brownsdale Minn., U.S.A. 43°45N 92°52W 77 G6
Brownstown Ill., U.S.A. 39°0N 88°57W 84 E5
Brownstown Ind., U.S.A. 38°53N 86°3W 85 E4
Brownsville Ky., U.S.A. 37°12N 86°16W 104 C6
Brownsville La., U.S.A. 32°29N 92°9W 110 B3
Brownsville Minn., U.S.A. 43°42N 91°17W 77 G7
Brownsville Oreg., U.S.A. 44°24N 122°59W 121 C3
Brownsville Pa., U.S.A. 40°1N 79°53W 87 D3
Brownsville Tenn., U.S.A. 35°36N 89°16W 104 E3
Brownsville Tex., U.S.A. 25°54N 97°30W 108 M10
Brownsville Wash., U.S.A. 47°39N 122°36W 132 C2
Brownton Minn., U.S.A. 44°44N 94°21W 77 F4
Browntown Wis., U.S.A. 42°35N 89°48W 78 F4
Brownville Ala., U.S.A. 33°24N 87°52W 112 C3
Brownville Maine, U.S.A. 45°18N 69°2W 90 C4
Brownville N.Y., U.S.A. 44°0N 75°59W 88 A4
Brownville Junction Maine, U.S.A. 45°21N 69°3W 90 C4
Brownwood Mo., U.S.A. 37°5N 89°57W 83 D7
Brownwood Tex., U.S.A. 31°43N 98°59W 109 F9
Brownwood, L. Tex., U.S.A. 31°50N 99°0W 109 F8
Broxton Ga., U.S.A. 31°38N 82°53W 113 E4
Broyhill Park Va., U.S.A. 38°52N 77°12W 99 B2
Bruce Alta., Canada 53°10N 112°2W 153 E8
Bruce Miss., U.S.A. 33°59N 89°21W 111 C4
Bruce S. Dak., U.S.A. 44°26N 96°54W 76 F9
Bruce Wis., U.S.A. 45°28N 91°16W 78 C2
Bruce L. Ont., Canada 50°49N 93°20W 148 B3
Bruce Pen. Ont., Canada 45°0N 81°30W 146 B5
Bruce Peninsula Nat. Park △ Ont., Canada 45°14N 81°36W 146 B5
Bruceton Tenn., U.S.A. 36°3N 88°15W 104 D4
Bruceton Mills W. Va., U.S.A. 39°40N 79°38W 102 B5
Bruceville Ind., U.S.A. 38°46N 87°25W 85 E3
Bruceville Md., U.S.A. 38°40N 75°59W 93 B5
Bruderheim Alta., Canada 53°47N 112°56W 152 E8
Bruin Pa., U.S.A. 41°3N 79°43W 87 C3
Bruin Pt. Utah, U.S.A. 39°30N 110°21W 129 D5
Brûlé Alta., Canada 53°15N 117°58W 152 E3
Brule Nebr., U.S.A. 41°6N 101°53W 80 C4
Brule → Wis., U.S.A. 45°57N 88°10W 78 B5
Brûlé, L. Nfld. & L., Canada 52°30N 63°40W 140 A6
Brule County ☆ S. Dak., U.S.A. 43°45N 99°0W 76 G6
Brule L. Minn., U.S.A. 47°59N 90°37W 77 D8
Brumley Mo., U.S.A. 38°5N 92°29W 83 C4
Brundidge Ala., U.S.A. 31°43N 85°49W 112 E5
Bruneau Idaho, U.S.A. 42°53N 115°48W 122 G3
Bruneau → Idaho, U.S.A. 42°56N 115°57W 122 G3
Brunette I. Nfld. & L., Canada 47°16N 55°55W 142 E5
Bruning Nebr., U.S.A. 40°20N 97°34W 80 D8
Brunkild Man., Canada 49°36N 97°35W 151 F14
Bruno Sask., Canada 52°20N 105°30W 150 C6
Bruno Minn., U.S.A. 46°17N 92°40W 77 D6
Bruno Nebr., U.S.A. 41°17N 96°58W 80 C9
Brunson S.C., U.S.A. 32°56N 81°11W 103 F4
Brunsville Iowa, U.S.A. 42°49N 96°16W 81 C2
Brunswick Ga., U.S.A. 31°10N 81°30W 113 E5
Brunswick Maine, U.S.A. 43°55N 69°58W 90 E4
Brunswick Md., U.S.A. 39°19N 77°38W 93 A2
Brunswick Mo., U.S.A. 39°26N 93°8W 83 B3
Brunswick Ohio, U.S.A. 41°14N 81°51W 86 B5
Brunswick County ☆ N.C., U.S.A. 34°0N 78°20W 103 E7
Brunswick County ☆ Va., U.S.A. 36°46N 77°51W 102 E7
Brunswick L. Ont., Canada 48°58N 83°23W 149 D13
Brunswick Naval Air Station Maine, U.S.A. 43°53N 69°57W 90 E4
Brus Laguna Honduras 15°47N 84°35W 182 C3
Brush Colo., U.S.A. 40°15N 103°37W 125 B7

Brush Creek Tenn., U.S.A. 36°7N 86°2W 104 D6
Brushton N.Y., U.S.A. 44°50N 74°31W 88 A6
Brusly La., U.S.A. 30°23N 91°14W 110 D4
Brussels Wis., U.S.A. 44°44N 87°37W 78 D6
Bryan Ohio, U.S.A. 41°28N 84°33W 86 B2
Bryan Tex., U.S.A. 30°40N 96°22W 109 G11
Bryan, L. Fla., U.S.A. 28°22N 81°29W 115 B2
Bryan County ☆ Ga., U.S.A. 32°0N 81°30W 113 D5
Bryan County ☆ Okla., U.S.A. 34°0N 96°15W 107 E7
Bryans Road Md., U.S.A. 38°38N 77°4W 93 B3
Bryant Ark., U.S.A. 34°36N 92°29W 106 D3
Bryant Ind., U.S.A. 40°32N 84°58W 85 C6
Bryant S. Dak., U.S.A. 44°35N 97°28W 76 F8
Bryant L. Minn., U.S.A. 44°52N 93°25W 94 B1
Bryant Cr. → Mo., U.S.A. 36°56N 92°17W 83 E4
Bryant Lake Regional Park △ Minn., U.S.A. 44°52N 93°25W 94 B1
Bryantown Md., U.S.A. 38°36N 76°52W 93 B4
Bryce Canyon Nat. Park △ Utah, U.S.A. 37°30N 112°10W 129 F3
Bryson Qué., Canada 45°41N 76°37W 144 F6
Bryson Tex., U.S.A. 33°10N 98°23W 109 D9
Bryson City N.C., U.S.A. 35°26N 83°27W 103 C2
Buaysiacobe Sonora, Mexico 27°5N 109°43W 168 F6
Bucerías Nayarit, Mexico 20°46N 105°20W 172 G5
Buchan G. Nunavut, Canada 71°45N 74°20W 158 C11
Buchanan Sask., Canada 51°40N 102°45W 150 D9
Buchanan Ga., U.S.A. 33°48N 85°11W 113 C1
Buchanan Mich., U.S.A. 41°50N 86°22W 79 H5
Buchanan N. Dak., U.S.A. 47°4N 98°50W 76 C7
Buchanan Va., U.S.A. 37°32N 79°41W 102 D5
Buchanan, L. Tex., U.S.A. 30°45N 98°25W 109 G9
Buchanan County ☆ Iowa, U.S.A. 42°30N 91°50W 81 C7
Buchanan County ☆ Mo., U.S.A. 39°40N 94°50W 83 B2
Buchanan County ☆ Va., U.S.A. 37°17N 82°6W 102 D2
Buchanan Dam Tex., U.S.A. 30°45N 98°25W 109 G9
Buchans Nfld. & L., Canada 48°50N 56°52W 142 D4
Buchans Junction Nfld. & L., Canada 48°51N 56°28W 142 D4
Buchon, Pt. Calif., U.S.A. 35°15N 120°54W 127 H6
Buck Cr. → Ky., U.S.A. 36°59N 84°29W 105 D8
Buck Grove Iowa, U.S.A. 41°55N 95°23W 81 D3
Buck L. Alta., Canada 52°59N 114°46W 153 F6
Buck Lake Alta., Canada 52°57N 114°47W 153 F6
Buckatunna Miss., U.S.A. 31°32N 88°32W 111 E5
Buckatunna Cr. → Miss., U.S.A. 31°30N 88°32W 111 E5
Buckeye Ariz., U.S.A. 33°22N 112°35W 130 D3
Buckeye Iowa, U.S.A. 42°25N 93°23W 81 C5
Buckeystown Md., U.S.A. 39°20N 77°26W 93 A3
Buckfield Maine, U.S.A. 44°17N 70°22W 90 D3
Buckhannon W. Va., U.S.A. 39°0N 80°8W 102 C4
Buckhead Georgia, U.S.A. 33°51N 84°24W 117 A2
Buckholts Tex., U.S.A. 30°52N 97°7W 109 G10
Buckhorn Ky., U.S.A. 37°21N 83°28W 105 C9
Buckhorn N. Mex., U.S.A. 33°2N 108°42W 131 D2
Buckhorn L. Ont., Canada 44°29N 78°23W 147 C8
Buckhorn L. Ky., U.S.A. 37°21N 83°28W 105 C9
Buckingham Qué., Canada 45°37N 75°24W 144 F7
Buckingham Colo., U.S.A. 40°37N 103°58W 125 B7
Buckingham Pa., U.S.A. 40°19N 75°4W 92 B1
Buckingham Va., U.S.A. 37°33N 78°33W 102 D6
Buckingham County ☆ Va., U.S.A. 37°40N 78°40W 102 D6
Buckingham I. Nunavut, Canada 77°12N 91°0W 158 B7
Buckland Alaska, U.S.A. 65°59N 161°8W 135 D7
Buckland Ohio, U.S.A. 40°37N 84°16W 86 C2
Buckley Ill., U.S.A. 40°36N 88°2W 84 C5
Buckley Mich., U.S.A. 44°30N 85°41W 79 E6
Buckley Wash., U.S.A. 47°10N 122°2W 120 C3
Bucklin Kans., U.S.A. 37°33N 99°38W 82 D4
Bucklin Mo., U.S.A. 39°47N 92°53W 83 B4
Buckman Minn., U.S.A. 45°54N 94°6W 77 E4
Bucks County ☆ Pa., U.S.A. 40°20N 75°7W 92 B1
Buckskin L. Calif., U.S.A. 39°54N 121°12W 126 D5
Buckskin Mts. Ariz., U.S.A. 34°10N 113°50W 130 C2
Bucksport Maine, U.S.A. 44°34N 68°47W 90 D5
Bucksport S.C., U.S.A. 33°40N 79°6W 103 E6
Bucoda Wash., U.S.A. 46°48N 122°52W 120 D3
Buctzotz Yucatán, Mexico 21°12N 88°47W 179 A5
Bucyrus N. Dak., U.S.A. 46°4N 102°47W 76 D3
Bucyrus Ohio, U.S.A. 40°48N 82°59W 86 C4
Buda Ill., U.S.A. 41°20N 89°41W 84 B4
Buda Tex., U.S.A. 30°5N 97°51W 109 G10
Budd Lake N.J., U.S.A. 40°52N 74°44W 92 B2
Budds Creek Md., U.S.A. 38°23N 76°51W 93 B4
Buechel Ky., U.S.A. 38°12N 85°39W 105 B7
Buena N.J., U.S.A. 39°31N 74°56W 92 C2
Buena Ventura Lakes Fla., U.S.A. 28°21N 81°21W 115 B2
Buena Vista Ark., U.S.A. 33°29N 92°57W 106 E3
Buena Vista Calif., U.S.A. 37°45N 122°26W 132 B2
Buena Vista Colo., U.S.A. 38°51N 106°8W 125 D4
Buena Vista Ga., U.S.A. 32°19N 84°31W 113 D2
Buena Vista Tex., U.S.A. 29°16N 98°27W 116 D3
Buena Vista Va., U.S.A. 37°44N 79°21W 102 D5
Buena Vista County ☆ Iowa, U.S.A. 42°45N 95°10W 81 C3
Buena Vista Lake Bed Calif., U.S.A. 35°12N 119°18W 127 H7
Buenaventura Chihuahua, Mexico 29°51N 107°29W 169 D8
Buenavista Chiapas, Mexico 16°18N 93°10W 178 C3
Buenavista Chihuahua, Mexico 26°59N 107°36W 169 G8
Buenavista Guerrero, Mexico 18°54N 99°25W 175 D8
Buenavista Quintana Roo, Mexico 18°54N 88°15W 179 D5
Buenavista San Luis Potosí, Mexico 22°37N 100°6W 173 F8
Buenavista Zacatecas, Mexico 22°4N 101°44W 173 E9
Buenavista, Estero Chiapas, Mexico 15°9N 93°0W 178 D2
Buenavista Sa. Sección Tabasco, Mexico 18°12N 92°44W 178 A4
Buenavista Tomatlán Michoacán, Mexico 19°12N 102°36W 174 C5
Buenos Aires Costa Rica 9°10N 83°20W 182 E3
Buenos Aires Nat. Wildlife Refuge ○ Ariz., U.S.A. 31°30N 111°30W 130 F4
Bueyeros N. Mex., U.S.A. 35°59N 103°41W 131 B7
Búfalo Chihuahua, Mexico 27°18N 105°10W 169 F10
Buffalo Kans., U.S.A. 37°42N 95°42W 82 D8
Buffalo Minn., U.S.A. 45°10N 93°53W 77 E5
Buffalo Mo., U.S.A. 37°39N 93°6W 83 D3
Buffalo N. Dak., U.S.A. 46°55N 97°33W 76 D8
Buffalo N.Y., U.S.A. 42°53N 78°53W 88 C2
Buffalo Okla., U.S.A. 36°50N 99°38W 107 B4
Buffalo S.C., U.S.A. 34°43N 81°41W 103 D4
Buffalo S. Dak., U.S.A. 45°35N 103°33W 76 E2
Buffalo Tex., U.S.A. 31°28N 96°4W 109 F11
Buffalo Wyo., U.S.A. 44°21N 106°42W 124 B6
Buffalo → Alta., Canada 60°5N 115°5W 157 D9
Buffalo → Ark., U.S.A. 36°10N 92°26W 106 B3

Buffalo → Minn., U.S.A. 47°6N 96°49W **77** C2
Buffalo → Miss., U.S.A. 31°4N 91°34W **111** E2
Buffalo → Tenn., U.S.A. 36°0N 87°50W **104** E5
Buffalo Bill Res. Wyo., U.S.A. 44°30N 109°11W **124** B3
Buffalo Center Iowa, U.S.A. 43°23N 93°57W **81** B5
Buffalo Count ☆ Nebr., U.S.A. 40°50N 99°0W **80** D6
Buffalo Count ☆ S. Dak., U.S.A. 44°0N 99°5W **76** G6
Buffalo Count ☆ Wis., U.S.A. 44°20N 91°50W **78** D2
Buffalo Cr. → Wyo., U.S.A. 43°36N 106°52W **124** C6
Buffalo Creek B.C., Canada 51°44N 121°9W **155** D13
Buffalo Creek Colo., U.S.A. 39°23N 105°17W **125** C5
Buffalo Gap S. Dak., U.S.A. 43°30N 103°19W **76** G2
Buffalo Gap Tex., U.S.A. 32°17N 99°50W **109** E8
Buffalo Gap Nat. Grassland S. Dak.,
  U.S.A. 43°7N 103°30W **76** G2
Buffalo Head Hills Alta., Canada 57°25N 115°55W **157** E9
Buffalo Hump Idaho, U.S.A. 45°37N 115°42W **122** D3
Buffalo L. Alta., Canada 52°27N 112°54W **153** F8
Buffalo L. N.W.T., Canada 60°12N 115°25W **157** D9
Buffalo L. Tex., U.S.A. 34°52N 102°12W **108** C5
Buffalo L. Wis., U.S.A. 43°47N 89°25W **78** E4
Buffalo Narrows Sask., Canada 55°51N 108°29W **157** E11
Buffalo Nat. River △ Ark., U.S.A. 36°14N 92°36W **106** B31
Buffalo Niagara Int. ✈ (BUF) N.Y.,
  U.S.A. 42°56N 78°44W **88** C2
Buffalo Pound L. Sask., Canada 50°39N 105°30W **150** E6
Buford Ga., U.S.A. 34°10N 84°0W **113** B3
Buford N. Dak., U.S.A. 48°0N 103°59W **76** B1
Buford Wyo., U.S.A. 41°7N 105°18W **124** E7
Bugaboo Park △ B.C., Canada 50°48N 116°49W **155** E18
Buhl Idaho, U.S.A. 42°36N 114°46W **122** G4
Buhl Minn., U.S.A. 47°30N 92°45W **77** C6
Buhler Kans., U.S.A. 38°8N 97°46W **82** C6
Buies Creek N.C., U.S.A. 35°25N 78°44W **103** C7
Buit, L. Qué., Canada 50°59N 63°13W **140** C6
Buldir I. Alask., U.S.A. 52°21N 175°56E **135** K1
Bulkley → B.C., Canada 55°15N 127°40W **157** E7
Bull Cr. → S. Dak., U.S.A. 45°40N 103°18W **76** E2
Bull L. Wyo., U.S.A. 43°13N 109°3W **124** C3
Bull Mts. Mont., U.S.A. 46°8N 109°0W **123** D9
Bull Shoals L. Ark., U.S.A. 36°22N 92°35W **106** B31
Bullard Ga., U.S.A. 32°38N 83°30W **113** D3
Bullard Tex., U.S.A. 32°8N 95°19W **109** E12
Bullhead S. Dak., U.S.A. 45°46N 101°5W **76** E4
Bullhead City Ariz., U.S.A. 35°8N 114°32W **130** B1
Bullion Mts. Calif., U.S.A. 34°40N 116°10W **127** J10
Bullitt County ☆ Ky., U.S.A. 38°0N 85°40W **105** C7
Bulloch County ☆ Ga., U.S.A. 32°20N 81°45W **113** D5
Bullock County ☆ Ala., U.S.A. 32°9N 85°43W **112** D5
Bulls B. S.C., U.S.A. 32°59N 79°35W **103** F6
Bulls Gap Tenn., U.S.A. 36°15N 83°5W **105** D9
Bully Cr. → Oreg., U.S.A. 43°58N 117°14W **121** D8
Bulyea Sask., Canada 50°59N 104°52W **150** E7
Bumpus Mills Tenn., U.S.A. 36°36N 87°52W **104** D5
Buna Tex., U.S.A. 30°26N 93°58W **109** G14
Bunceton Mo., U.S.A. 38°47N 92°48W **83** C4
Bunch Okla., U.S.A. 35°41N 94°46W **107** C9
Buncombe Ill., U.S.A. 37°27N 88°58W **84** F5
Buncombe County ☆ N.C., U.S.A. 35°30N 82°30W **103** C3
Bundick L. → La., U.S.A. 30°36N 92°57W **110** D3
Bunker Mo., U.S.A. 37°27N 91°13W **83** D5
Bunker Hill Ill., U.S.A. 39°3N 89°57W **84** D4
Bunker Hill Ind., U.S.A. 40°40N 86°6W **85** C4
Bunker Hill Kans., U.S.A. 38°53N 98°42W **82** C5
Bunker Hill Oreg., U.S.A. 39°15N 117°8W **128** C3
Bunker Hill W. Va., U.S.A. 43°22N 124°12W **121** D1
Bunker Hill W. Va., U.S.A. 39°20N 78°3W **93** A2
Bunker Hill Memorial Mass., U.S.A. 42°22N 71°4W **96** A2
Bunkerville Nev., U.S.A. 36°46N 114°8W **128** F6
Bunkie La., U.S.A. 30°57N 92°11W **110** D3
Bunnell Fla., U.S.A. 29°28N 81°16W **114** B7
Buras La., U.S.A. 29°22N 89°32W **110** E6
Burbank Calif., U.S.A. 34°12N 118°18W **133** A3
Burbank Ill., U.S.A. 41°44N 87°46W **95** C2
Burbank Okla., U.S.A. 36°42N 96°44W **107** B7
Burbank Wash., U.S.A. 46°12N 119°1W **120** D6
Burbank ✈ (BUR) Calif., U.S.A. 34°12N 118°21W **127** J8
Burchard Nebr., U.S.A. 40°9N 96°21W **80** D9
Burden Kans., U.S.A. 37°19N 96°45W **82** D7
Burden, L. Fla., U.S.A. 28°27N 81°33W **115** B1
Burdett Alta., Canada 49°50N 111°32W **153** J9
Burdett Kans., U.S.A. 38°12N 99°32W **82** C4
Burdett N.Y., U.S.A. 42°25N 76°51W **88** C4
Burdick Kans., U.S.A. 38°34N 96°51W **82** C7
Bureau County ☆ Ill., U.S.A. 41°25N 89°30W **84** B4
Burford Ont., Canada 43°7N 80°27W **146** D6
Burgaw N.C., U.S.A. 34°33N 77°56W **103** D8
Burgdorf Idaho, U.S.A. 45°17N 115°55W **122** D3
Burgeo Nfld. & L., Canada 47°37N 57°38W **142** E3
Burgess Va., U.S.A. 37°53N 76°21W **93** C4
Burgess Junction Wyo., U.S.A. 44°46N 107°32W **124** B5
Burgin Ky., U.S.A. 37°45N 84°46W **105** C8
Burgoon Ohio, U.S.A. 41°16N 83°15W **86** B3
Burgos Tamaulipas, Mexico 24°57N 98°47W **171** F6
Burica, Pta. Costa Rica 8°3N 82°51W **182** E3
Burien Wash., U.S.A. 47°28N 122°20W **132** D3
Burin Nfld. & L., Canada 47°1N 55°14W **142** E5
Burin Peninsula Nfld. & L., Canada 47°0N 55°40W **142** E5
Burkburnett Tex., U.S.A. 34°6N 98°34W **109** D9
Burke Idaho, U.S.A. 47°31N 115°49W **122** B3
Burke S. Dak., U.S.A. 43°11N 99°18W **76** G6
Burke Chan. B.C., Canada 52°10N 127°30W **154** E10
Burke County ☆ Ga., U.S.A. 33°0N 82°0W **113** C4
Burke County ☆ N.C., U.S.A. 35°45N 81°40W **103** C4
Burke County ☆ N. Dak., U.S.A. 48°55N 102°30W **76** B3
Burke-Lakefront ✈ (BKL) Ohio, U.S.A. 41°31N 81°41W **98** A1
Burkesville Ky., U.S.A. 36°48N 85°22W **105** D7
Burkett Tex., U.S.A. 32°0N 99°8W **109** E8
Burkettsville Ohio, U.S.A. 40°21N 84°39W **86** C2
Burkeville Tex., U.S.A. 31°0N 93°40W **109** F14
Burkeville Va., U.S.A. 37°11N 78°12W **102** D6
Burkittsville Md., U.S.A. 39°23N 77°38W **93** A3
Burk's Falls Ont., Canada 45°37N 79°24W **146** B7
Burleigh Falls Ont., Canada 44°33N 78°12W **147** C8
Burleson Tex., U.S.A. 32°33N 97°19W **109** E10
Burleson County ☆ Tex., U.S.A. 30°32N 96°36W **109** G11
Burley Idaho, U.S.A. 42°32N 113°48W **122** G5
Burley Wash., U.S.A. 47°25N 122°37W **132** D2
Burlingame Calif., U.S.A. 37°35N 122°21W **126** F4
Burlingame Kans., U.S.A. 38°45N 95°50W **82** C8
Burlington Nfld. & L., Canada 49°45N 56°1W **142** C4
Burlington Ont., Canada 43°18N 79°45W **146** D7
Burlington Colo., U.S.A. 39°18N 102°16W **125** C8
Burlington Conn., U.S.A. 41°46N 72°58W **91** C2

Burlington Ill., U.S.A. 42°3N 88°33W **84** A5
Burlington Ind., U.S.A. 40°29N 86°24W **85** C4
Burlington Iowa, U.S.A. 40°49N 91°14W **81** E7
Burlington Kans., U.S.A. 38°12N 95°45W **82** C8
Burlington Ky., U.S.A. 39°2N 84°43W **105** A8
Burlington Mass., U.S.A. 42°30N 71°13W **96** A1
Burlington N.C., U.S.A. 36°6N 79°26W **103** B6
Burlington N. Dak., U.S.A. 48°17N 101°26W **76** B4
Burlington N.J., U.S.A. 40°4N 74°51W **92** B2
Burlington Okla., U.S.A. 36°54N 98°25W **107** B5
Burlington Vt., U.S.A. 44°29N 73°12W **89** B1
Burlington W. Va., U.S.A. 39°20N 78°55W **93** A2
Burlington Wash., U.S.A. 48°28N 122°20W **120** B3
Burlington Wis., U.S.A. 42°41N 88°17W **78** F5
Burlington Wyo., U.S.A. 44°27N 108°26W **124** B4
Burlington County ☆ N.J., U.S.A. 39°50N 74°45W **92** C2
Burlington Junction Mo., U.S.A. 40°27N 95°4W **83** A1
Burna Ky., U.S.A. 37°15N 88°22W **104** E4
Burnaby B.C., Canada 49°16N 122°57W **155** F12
Burnaby Heights B.C., Canada 49°17N 123°0W **161** B2
Burnaby I. B.C., Canada 52°25N 131°19W **154** C3
Burnet Tex., U.S.A. 30°45N 98°14W **109** G9
Burnet County ☆ Tex., U.S.A. 30°45N 98°15W **109** G9
Burnett County ☆ Wis., U.S.A. 45°50N 92°20W **78** C1
Burnettsville Ind., U.S.A. 40°46N 86°36W **85** C4
Burney Calif., U.S.A. 40°53N 121°40W **126** C5
Burnham Maine, U.S.A. 44°42N 69°26W **90** D4
Burnham Pa., U.S.A. 40°38N 77°34W **87** D5
Burnham Park Ill., U.S.A. 41°49N 87°35W **95** C3
Burnham Park Harbor Ill., U.S.A. 41°51N 87°36W **95** B3
Burnhamthorpe Ont., Canada 43°37N 79°35W **161** B1
Burning Springs Ky., U.S.A. 37°15N 83°49W **105** C9
Burns Colo., U.S.A. 39°52N 106°53W **125** C4
Burns Kans., U.S.A. 38°5N 96°53W **82** C7
Burns Oreg., U.S.A. 43°35N 119°3W **121** D6
Burns Tenn., U.S.A. 36°3N 87°19W **104** D5
Burns Wyo., U.S.A. 41°12N 104°21W **124** E8
Burns Flat Okla., U.S.A. 35°21N 99°10W **107** C4
Burns Junction Oreg., U.S.A. 42°47N 117°51W **121** E8
Burns Lake B.C., Canada 54°14N 125°45W **154** A9
Burns Paiute Indian Reservation Oreg.,
  U.S.A. 43°35N 119°6W **121** D6
Burnside Ky., U.S.A. 36°59N 84°36W **105** D8
Burnside → Nunavut, Canada 66°51N 108°4W **156** C11
Burnsville Ala., U.S.A. 32°28N 86°53W **112** D4
Burnsville Minn., U.S.A. 44°47N 93°17W **77** F5
Burnsville Miss., U.S.A. 34°51N 88°19W **111** B5
Burnsville N.C., U.S.A. 35°55N 82°18W **103** C3
Burnsville W. Va., U.S.A. 38°52N 80°40W **102** C4
Burnsville W. Va., U.S.A. 38°50N 80°37W **102** C4
Burnt → Oreg., U.S.A. 44°22N 117°14W **121** C8
Burnt, L. Nfld. & L., Canada 53°35N 64°4W **143** C5
Burnt Islands Nfld. & L., Canada 47°36N 58°53W **142** E2
Burnt Paw Alaska, U.S.A. 66°54N 143°44W **135** C12
Burnt River Ont., Canada 44°41N 78°42W **147** C8
Burntfork Wyo., U.S.A. 41°2N 109°59W **124** E3
Burntwood → Man., Canada 56°8N 96°34W **159** F6
Burr Oak Kans., U.S.A. 39°52N 98°18W **82** B5
Burr Oak Mich., U.S.A. 41°51N 85°19W **79** H6
Burr Oak Ohio, U.S.A. 39°33N 82°4W **86** D4
Burrard Inlet B.C., Canada 49°18N 123°13W **161** B1
Burrel Calif., U.S.A. 36°29N 119°59W **127** G7
Burris Wyo., U.S.A. 43°22N 109°16W **124** C3
Burro, Serranías del Coahuila, Mexico 28°56N 102°5W **170** B4
Burro Pk. N. Mex., U.S.A. 32°35N 108°26W **131** E2
Burrows L. Ont., Canada 49°57N 86°44W **149** C10
Burrton Kans., U.S.A. 38°2N 97°41W **82** C6
Burstall Sask., Canada 50°39N 109°54W **150** E2
Burt Iowa, U.S.A. 43°12N 94°13W **81** B4
Burt County ☆ Nebr., U.S.A. 41°50N 96°15W **80** C9
Burt L. Mich., U.S.A. 45°28N 84°40W **79** D7
Burton B.C., Canada 50°0N 117°53W **155** F17
Burton Mich., U.S.A. 43°0N 83°40W **79** G8
Burton Nebr., U.S.A. 42°55N 99°35W **80** B6
Burton Ohio, U.S.A. 41°28N 81°8W **98** A4
Burton S.C., U.S.A. 32°26N 80°43W **103** F5
Burton Tex., U.S.A. 30°11N 96°42W **109** G11
Burton Wash., U.S.A. 47°23N 122°27W **132** D3
Burton, L. Qué., Canada 54°45N 78°20W **143** C2
Burton, L. Ga., U.S.A. 34°50N 83°33W **113** B3
Burtrum Minn., U.S.A. 45°52N 94°41W **77** E4
Burtts Corner N.B., Canada 46°3N 66°52W **141** G3
Burwash Ont., Canada 46°14N 80°51W **146** A6
Burwash Landing Yukon, Canada 61°21N 139°0W **157** D3
Burwell Nebr., U.S.A. 41°47N 99°8W **80** C6
Bury Qué., Canada 45°28N 71°30W **145** F11
Bush La., U.S.A. 30°36N 89°54W **110** D6
Bush City Kans., U.S.A. 38°13N 95°9W **82** C8
Bush Kill → Pa., U.S.A. 41°5N 75°0W **92** A1
Bushland Tex., U.S.A. 35°11N 102°4W **108** B5
Bushnell Fla., U.S.A. 28°40N 82°7W **114** C6
Bushnell Ill., U.S.A. 40°33N 90°31W **84** C3
Bushnell Nebr., U.S.A. 41°14N 103°54W **80** C2
Bushong Kans., U.S.A. 38°39N 96°15W **82** C7
Bushton Kans., U.S.A. 38°31N 98°24W **82** C5
Bushwick N.Y., U.S.A. 40°41N 73°54W **97** B3
Bushwood Md., U.S.A. 38°18N 76°47W **93** B4
Bussey Iowa, U.S.A. 41°12N 92°53W **81** D6
Bustamante Nuevo León, Mexico 26°33N 100°30W **170** D4
Bustamante Tamaulipas, Mexico 27°0N 99°7W **108** L8
Bustillos, L. Chihuahua, Mexico 28°33N 106°45W **169** E9
Bute Inlet B.C., Canada 50°40N 124°53W **154** E10
Butedale B.C., Canada 53°8N 128°42W **154** B6
Butler Ala., U.S.A. 32°5N 88°13W **112** D2
Butler Ga., U.S.A. 32°33N 84°14W **113** D2
Butler Ind., U.S.A. 41°26N 84°52W **85** B6
Butler Ky., U.S.A. 38°47N 84°22W **105** B8
Butler N.J., U.S.A. 41°0N 74°20W **92** B2
Butler Okla., U.S.A. 35°38N 99°11W **107** C4
Butler Pa., U.S.A. 40°52N 79°54W **87** D3
Butler Wis., U.S.A. 43°6N 88°4W **94** B1
Butler, L. Fla., U.S.A. 28°29N 81°33W **115** B1
Butler County ☆ Ala., U.S.A. 31°45N 86°38W **112** E4
Butler County ☆ Iowa, U.S.A. 42°45N 92°45W **81** C5
Butler County ☆ Kans., U.S.A. 37°45N 96°45W **82** D7
Butler County ☆ Ky., U.S.A. 37°10N 86°45W **104** C6
Butler County ☆ Mo., U.S.A. 36°45N 90°25W **83** E6
Butler County ☆ Nebr., U.S.A. 41°15N 97°0W **80** C8
Butler County ☆ Ohio, U.S.A. 39°24N 84°34W **86** D2
Butler County ☆ Pa., U.S.A. 41°0N 80°0W **87** D3
Butner N.C., U.S.A. 36°8N 78°45W **103** B7
Butte Mont., U.S.A. 46°0N 112°32W **123** D5
Butte N. Dak., U.S.A. 47°50N 100°40W **76** C5

Butte Nebr., U.S.A. 42°58N 98°51W **80** B7
Butte City Idaho, U.S.A. 43°37N 113°15W **122** F5
Butte County ☆ Calif., U.S.A. 39°40N 121°35W **126** D5
Butte County ☆ Idaho, U.S.A. 43°50N 113°0W **122** F5
Butte County ☆ S. Dak., U.S.A. 45°0N 103°0W **76** F2
Butte Falls Oreg., U.S.A. 42°33N 122°34W **121** E3
Butte Mts. Nev., U.S.A. 39°50N 115°5W **128** C5
Butter Cr. → Oreg., U.S.A. 45°45N 119°20W **121** B6
Butterfield Minn., U.S.A. 43°58N 94°48W **77** G4
Butterfield Mo., U.S.A. 36°45N 93°54W **83** E3
Butternut Wis., U.S.A. 46°1N 90°30W **78** B3
Buttle L. B.C., Canada 49°42N 125°33W **154** F9
Button Is. Nfld. & L., Canada 60°38N 64°40W **143** A5
Buttonwillow Calif., U.S.A. 35°24N 119°28W **127** H7
Butts Corner Va., U.S.A. 38°46N 77°19W **99** C2
Butts County ☆ Ga., U.S.A. 33°20N 84°0W **113** C3
Buxton N. Dak., U.S.A. 47°36N 97°6W **76** C8
Buzzards B. Mass., U.S.A. 41°30N 70°45W **91** C4
Buzzards Bay Mass., U.S.A. 41°45N 70°37W **91** C4
Byam Channel Nunavut, Canada 75°15N 105°15W **158** B4
Byam Martin Chan. Nunavut, Canada 76°15N 105°45W **158** B4
Byam Martin I. Nunavut, Canada 75°15N 104°15W **158** B5
Byars Okla., U.S.A. 34°53N 97°3W **107** D6
Byers Colo., U.S.A. 39°43N 104°14W **125** C6
Byers Kans., U.S.A. 37°48N 98°52W **82** D5
Byers Tex., U.S.A. 34°4N 98°11W **109** C9
Byesville Ohio, U.S.A. 39°58N 81°32W **86** D5
Byfield Mass., U.S.A. 42°46N 70°57W **91** B4
Byhalia Miss., U.S.A. 34°52N 89°41W **111** B4
Bylas Ariz., U.S.A. 33°8N 110°7W **130** D5
Bylot Man., Canada 58°25N 94°8W **159** F7
Bylot I. Nunavut, Canada 73°13N 78°34W **158** C10
Byng Okla., U.S.A. 34°50N 96°42W **107** D7
Byng Inlet Ont., Canada 45°46N 80°33W **146** B6
Bynum Mont., U.S.A. 47°59N 112°19W **123** C5
Byram Miss., U.S.A. 32°11N 90°15W **111** D3
Byram → Conn., U.S.A. 41°0N 73°38W **97** B5
Byrdstown Tenn., U.S.A. 36°34N 85°8W **105** D7
Byron Ill., U.S.A. 42°8N 89°15W **84** A4
Byron Maine, U.S.A. 44°43N 70°38W **90** D3
Byron Mich., U.S.A. 42°49N 83°57W **79** G8
Byron Minn., U.S.A. 44°2N 92°41W **77** F6
Byron Okla., U.S.A. 40°0N 97°46W **80** D8
Byron Okla., U.S.A. 36°54N 98°19W **107** B5
Byron Wyo., U.S.A. 44°48N 108°30W **124** B4

C

C.B.S. Fox Studios Calif., U.S.A. 34°9N 118°24W **133** B2
C.J. Strike Res. Idaho, U.S.A. 42°59N 115°58W **122** G3
C.N.N. Center Georgia, U.S.A. 33°45N 84°23W **117** B2
C.N. Tower Ont., Canada 43°38N 79°23W **161** B2
C.W. McConaughy, L. Nebr., U.S.A. 41°14N 101°40W **80** C4
Caamaño Sd. B.C., Canada 52°55N 129°25W **154** C5
Caballo N. Mex., U.S.A. 32°59N 107°18W **131** E3
Caballo Res. N. Mex., U.S.A. 32°54N 107°18W **131** E3
Cabano Qué., Canada 47°40N 68°56W **145** D14
Cabarrus County ☆ N.C., U.S.A. 35°20N 80°30W **103** C5
Cabazon Calif., U.S.A. 33°55N 116°47W **127** K10
Cabell County ☆ W. Va., U.S.A. 38°26N 82°8W **102** C2
Cabeza de Vaca Baja Calif. S., Mexico 26°44N 112°5W **167** G6
Cabeza Prieta Nat. Wildlife Refuge △ Ariz.,
  U.S.A. 32°15N 113°20W **130** E2
Cabin Branch → Baltimore, U.S.A. 39°12N 76°34W **99** B2
Cabin John Md., U.S.A. 38°58N 77°10W **99** B2
Cabin John Regional Park △ Md., U.S.A. 39°0N 77°10W **99** A2
Cabinet Mts. Mont., U.S.A. 48°10N 115°50W **123** B2
Cable Wis., U.S.A. 46°13N 91°17W **78** B2
Cabo Rojo Puerto Rico 18°5N 67°9W **184** G15
Cabo San Lucas Baja Calif. S., Mexico 22°53N 109°54W **167** L9
Cabonga, Réservoir Qué., Canada 47°20N 76°40W **144** D6
Cabool Mo., U.S.A. 37°7N 92°6W **83** D41
Cabórachi Chihuahua, Mexico 26°49N 106°58W **169** G9
Caborca Sonora, Mexico 30°37N 112°6W **168** C3
Cabot Ark., U.S.A. 34°59N 92°1W **106** D3
Cabot Vt., U.S.A. 44°23N 72°18W **89** B2
Cabot, Mt. N.H., U.S.A. 44°30N 71°25W **89** B3
Cabras, Pta. Baja Calif., Mexico 31°23N 116°32W **166** B2
Cabri Sask., Canada 50°35N 108°25W **150** E3
Cabrillo, Pt. Calif., U.S.A. 39°21N 123°50W **126** D3
Cabrillo Nat. Monument △ Calif.,
  U.S.A. 32°40N 117°14W **133** B1
Cacahoatán Chiapas, Mexico 14°59N 92°10W **178** E4
Cacalchén Yucatán, Mexico 20°59N 89°14W **179** B4
Cacapon → W. Va., U.S.A. 39°37N 78°16W **93** A2
Cache Okla., U.S.A. 34°38N 98°38W **107** D5
Cache → Ark., U.S.A. 34°43N 91°20W **106** D4
Cache → Ill., U.S.A. 37°4N 89°10W **84** F4
Cache Bay Ont., Canada 46°22N 80°0W **146** A6
Cache County ☆ Utah, U.S.A. 41°40N 111°45W **129** B4
Cache Cr. → Calif., U.S.A. 38°42N 121°42W **126** E5
Cache Creek B.C., Canada 50°48N 121°19W **155** E13
Cache la Poudre → Colo., U.S.A. 40°25N 104°36W **125** B6
Cache Peak Idaho, U.S.A. 42°11N 113°40W **122** G5
Cachuma, L. Calif., U.S.A. 34°35N 119°59W **127** J7
Cacouna Qué., Canada 47°55N 69°30W **145** D13
Cactus Tex., U.S.A. 36°4N 101°59W **108** A6
Cactus Flat Nev., U.S.A. 37°45N 116°40W **128** E4
Cactus Ra. Nev., U.S.A. 37°40N 116°50W **128** E4
Cactboro Bay B.C., Canada 48°28N 123°17W **155** G11
Caddo Okla., U.S.A. 34°7N 96°16W **107** D7
Caddo Tex., U.S.A. 32°43N 98°40W **109** E8
Caddo → Ark., U.S.A. 34°10N 93°3W **106** D2
Caddo Cr. → Okla., U.S.A. 34°14N 96°50W **107** D6
Caddo County ☆ Okla., U.S.A. 35°10N 98°20W **107** C5
Caddo Gap Ark., U.S.A. 34°24N 93°37W **106** D2
Caddo Mills Tex., U.S.A. 33°4N 96°14W **109** D11
Caddo Nat. Grassland Tex., U.S.A. 33°33N 95°57W **109** D12
Caddo Parish ☆ La., U.S.A. 32°30N 93°50W **110** B2
Caddoa Colo., U.S.A. 38°4N 102°56W **125** D8
Cadereyta Querétaro, Mexico 20°42N 99°49W **175** D8
Cadereyta de Jiménez Nuevo León,
  Mexico 25°36N 100°0W **170** D2
Cadillac Qué., Canada 48°14N 78°23W **144** C4
Cadillac Sask., Canada 49°44N 107°44W **150** F4
Cadillac Mich., U.S.A. 44°15N 85°24W **79** E6
Cadiz Ind., U.S.A. 39°57N 85°29W **85** D5
Cadiz Ky., U.S.A. 36°52N 87°50W **104** D5
Cadiz Ohio, U.S.A. 40°16N 81°0W **86** C6
Cadiz L. Calif., U.S.A. 34°18N 115°24W **127** J11
Cadley Ga., U.S.A. 33°32N 82°40W **113** C4
Cadogan Alta., Canada 52°4N 110°20W **153** F10
Cadomin Alta., Canada 53°2N 117°20W **153** E3
Cadotte → Alta., Canada 56°43N 117°10W **152** B3

Cadwell Ga., U.S.A. 32°20N 83°3W **113** D3
Caernarvon La., U.S.A. 29°51N 89°54W **117** C4
Cagles Mill L. Ind., U.S.A. 39°29N 86°55W **85** D4
Caguas Puerto Rico 18°14N 66°2W **184** G16
Cahaba → Ala., U.S.A. 32°20N 87°5W **112** D3
Cahokia Ill., U.S.A. 38°34N 90°11W **94** B2
Cahone Colo., U.S.A. 37°39N 108°49W **125** D2
Cahuenga Park Calif., U.S.A. 34°8N 118°19W **133** B3
Cahuilla Indian Reservation Calif.,
  U.S.A. 33°31N 116°43W **127** K10
Caibarién Cuba 22°30N 79°30W **182** B4
Caicos Is. Turks & Caicos 21°40N 71°40W **183** B5
Caicos Passage W. Indies 22°45N 72°45W **183** B5
Caillou B. La., U.S.A. 29°3N 91°0W **110** E5
Cain, L. Fla., U.S.A. 28°28N 81°28W **115** B2
Caineville Utah, U.S.A. 38°20N 111°1W **129** E4
Cains → N.B., Canada 46°40N 65°47W **141** G4
Cainsville Mo., U.S.A. 40°26N 93°47W **83** A3
Cairo Ga., U.S.A. 30°52N 84°13W **113** F2
Cairo Ill., U.S.A. 37°0N 89°11W **84** F4
Cairo Mo., U.S.A. 39°31N 92°27W **83** B4
Cairo Nebr., U.S.A. 41°0N 98°36W **80** C7
Cairo Ohio, U.S.A. 40°50N 84°5W **86** C2
Cairo W. Va., U.S.A. 39°13N 81°9W **102** B3
Caja de Muertos, I. Puerto Rico 17°54N 66°32W **184** H16
Cajón de Peña, Presa Jalisco, Mexico 19°58N 105°6W **174** C2
Cajon Summit Calif., U.S.A. 34°21N 117°27W **127** J9
Cajurichic Chihuahua, Mexico 28°7N 108°11W **169** E7
Calabash N.C., U.S.A. 33°53N 78°34W **103** E7
Calabazas Durango, Mexico 23°13N 105°3W **172** D5
Calabogie Ont., Canada 45°18N 76°43W **147** B10
Caladesi Island State Park △ Tampa,
  U.S.A. 28°1N 82°49W **115** A2
Calagua Baja Calif. S., Mexico 26°20N 111°50W **167** G7
Calais Maine, U.S.A. 45°11N 67°17W **90** C6
Calakmul Campeche, Mexico 18°14N 89°48W **179** D4
Calakmul, Reserva de la Biosfera △ Campeche,
  Mexico 18°30N 89°55W **179** D4
Calamus → Nebr., U.S.A. 41°48N 99°9W **80** C6
Calamus Res. Nebr., U.S.A. 41°50N 99°13W **80** C6
Calapooia → Oreg., U.S.A. 44°38N 123°9W **121** C2
Calaveras County ☆ Calif., U.S.A. 38°15N 120°40W **126** E6
Calaveras Lake Tex., U.S.A. 29°16N 98°18W **116** C4
Calcasieu → La., U.S.A. 30°5N 93°20W **110** D2
Calcasieu L. La., U.S.A. 29°55N 93°18W **110** D2
Calcasieu Parish ☆ La., U.S.A. 30°14N 93°23W **110** D2
Calcium N.Y., U.S.A. 44°1N 75°51W **88** A5
Caldwell Ark., U.S.A. 35°5N 90°49W **106** C5
Caldwell Idaho, U.S.A. 43°40N 116°41W **122** F2
Caldwell Kans., U.S.A. 37°2N 97°37W **82** D6
Caldwell N.J., U.S.A. 40°50N 74°16W **97** A1
Caldwell Ohio, U.S.A. 39°45N 81°31W **86** D5
Caldwell Tex., U.S.A. 30°32N 96°42W **109** G11
Caldwell County ☆ Ky., U.S.A. 37°10N 87°50W **104** C5
Caldwell County ☆ Mo., U.S.A. 39°40N 94°0W **83** B2
Caldwell County ☆ N.C., U.S.A. 36°0N 81°30W **103** C4
Caldwell County ☆ Tex., U.S.A. 29°53N 97°40W **109** H10
Caldwell Parish ☆ La., U.S.A. 32°0N 92°0W **110** B3
Caledonia N.S., Canada 45°17N 62°33W **141** H7
Caledonia N.S., Canada 44°22N 65°2W **141** J4
Caledonia Ont., Canada 43°7N 79°58W **146** D7
Caledonia Mich., U.S.A. 42°47N 85°31W **79** G6
Caledonia Minn., U.S.A. 43°38N 91°30W **77** G7
Caledonia Miss., U.S.A. 33°41N 88°20W **111** C5
Caledonia N. Dak., U.S.A. 47°28N 96°53W **76** C9
Caledonia N.Y., U.S.A. 42°58N 77°51W **88** C3
Caledonia County ☆ Vt., U.S.A. 44°30N 72°10W **89** B2
Calentura, Pta. Quintana Roo, Mexico 18°30N 88°7W **179** D5
Calera Ala., U.S.A. 33°6N 86°45W **112** C4
Calera Okla., U.S.A. 33°52N 96°26W **107** E7
Calera de Víctor Rosales Zacatecas,
  Mexico 22°57N 102°42W **173** E8
Calexico Calif., U.S.A. 32°40N 115°30W **127** L11
Calfkiller → Tenn., U.S.A. 35°49N 85°29W **105** C7
Calgary Alta., Canada 51°0N 114°10W **153** G6
Calgary ✈ (YYC) Alta., Canada 51°4N 114°1W **153** G6
Calhan Colo., U.S.A. 39°2N 104°18W **125** C6
Calhoun Ga., U.S.A. 32°3N 86°33W **112** C4
Calhoun Ga., U.S.A. 34°30N 84°57W **113** B2
Calhoun Ill., U.S.A. 38°39N 88°3W **84** E5
Calhoun Ky., U.S.A. 37°32N 87°16W **104** C5
Calhoun Mo., U.S.A. 38°28N 93°38W **83** C3
Calhoun Tenn., U.S.A. 35°18N 84°45W **105** D8
Calhoun, L. Minn., U.S.A. 44°56N 93°18W **94** B2
Calhoun City Miss., U.S.A. 33°51N 89°19W **111** C4
Calhoun County ☆ Ala., U.S.A. 33°47N 86°0W **112** C4
Calhoun County ☆ Ark., U.S.A. 33°35N 92°31W **106** E3
Calhoun County ☆ Fla., U.S.A. 30°30N 85°10W **114** A3
Calhoun County ☆ Ga., U.S.A. 31°30N 84°35W **113** E2
Calhoun County ☆ Ill., U.S.A. 39°10N 90°40W **84** D3
Calhoun County ☆ Iowa, U.S.A. 42°25N 94°40W **81** C4
Calhoun County ☆ Mich., U.S.A. 42°15N 85°0W **79** G7
Calhoun County ☆ Miss., U.S.A. 33°56N 89°20W **111** C4
Calhoun County ☆ S.C., U.S.A. 33°45N 80°50W **103** E5
Calhoun County ☆ W. Va., U.S.A. 38°55N 81°6W **102** C3
Calhoun Falls S.C., U.S.A. 34°6N 82°36W **103** D3
Calico Rock Ark., U.S.A. 36°7N 92°9W **106** B3
Caliente Calif., U.S.A. 35°17N 118°38W **127** H8
Caliente Nev., U.S.A. 37°37N 114°31W **128** E6
Califon N.J., U.S.A. 40°42N 74°50W **92** B2
California Md., U.S.A. 38°18N 76°32W **93** B4
California Mo., U.S.A. 38°38N 92°34W **83** C4
California Pa., U.S.A. 40°4N 79°54W **87** D3
California ☆ U.S.A. 37°30N 119°30W **126** F7
California, Baja, T.N. = Baja California □
  Mexico 30°0N 115°0W **166** C2
California, Baja, T.S. = Baja California Sur □
  Mexico 25°50N 111°50W **167** H7
California, G. de Mexico 27°0N 111°0W **167** G7
California Aqueduct Calif., U.S.A. 33°52N 117°12W **127** J9
California City Calif., U.S.A. 35°10N 117°55W **127** H9
California Coastal Nat. Monument △ Calif.,
  U.S.A. 36°19N 121°46W **127** G5
California Inst. of Tech. Calif., U.S.A. 34°8N 118°8W **133** B4
California Los Angeles, University of Calif.,
  U.S.A. 34°4N 118°27W **133** B2
California State University Calif., U.S.A. 34°4N 118°10W **133** B3
Calio N. Dak., U.S.A. 48°38N 98°56W **76** B7
Calion Ark., U.S.A. 33°20N 92°32W **106** E3
Calipatria Calif., U.S.A. 33°8N 115°31W **127** K11
Calistoga Calif., U.S.A. 38°35N 122°35W **126** E4
Calkiní Campeche, Mexico 20°22N 90°3W **179** B3
Callahan Fla., U.S.A. 30°34N 81°50W **114** A7

Callahan County ☆ Tex., U.S.A. 32°24N 99°24W 109 E8
Callander Ont., Canada 46°13N 79°22W 146 A7
Callao Utah, U.S.A. 39°54N 113°43W 129 D2
Callaway Fla., U.S.A. 30°8N 85°36W 114 A3
Callaway Minn., U.S.A. 46°59N 95°54W 77 D3
Callaway Nebr., U.S.A. 41°18N 99°56W 80 C6
Callaway County ☆ Mo., U.S.A. 38°50N 91°50W 83 C5
Callender Iowa, U.S.A. 42°22N 94°17W 81 C4
Callicoon N.Y., U.S.A. 41°46N 75°3W 88 D5
Calliham Tex., U.S.A. 28°29N 98°21W 109 J9
Callimont Pa., U.S.A. 39°48N 78°55W 93 A2
Calling L. Alta., Canada 55°15N 113°20W 152 C7
Calling Lake Alta., Canada 55°15N 113°12W 152 C7
Calloway County ☆ Ky., U.S.A. 36°40N 88°15W 104 D4
Calmar Alta., Canada 53°16N 113°49W 152 E7
Calmar Iowa, U.S.A. 43°11N 91°52W 81 B7
Caloosahatchee → Fla., U.S.A. 26°31N 82°1W 114 E6
Calpella Calif., U.S.A. 39°14N 123°12W 126 D3
Calpine Calif., U.S.A. 39°40N 120°27W 126 D6
Calpulalpan Tlaxcala, Mexico 19°35N 98°35W 177 D3
Caltepec Puebla, Mexico 18°11N 97°28W 177 F3
Calumet Iowa, U.S.A. 42°57N 95°33W 81 C3
Calumet Mich., U.S.A. 47°14N 88°27W 79 B3
Calumet Minn., U.S.A. 47°19N 93°17W 77 D5
Calumet Okla., U.S.A. 35°36N 98°7W 107 C5
Calumet City Ill., U.S.A. 41°37N 87°32W 84 B6
Calumet County ☆ Wis., U.S.A. 44°5N 88°10W 78 D5
Calumet L. Ill., U.S.A. 41°41N 87°35W 95 C3
Calumet Park Ill., U.S.A. 41°40N 87°39W 95 C3
Calumet Sag Channel → Ill., U.S.A. 41°40N 87°47W 95 C2
Calvert Ala., U.S.A. 31°9N 88°1W 112 E2
Calvert Md., U.S.A. 39°42N 75°58W 93 A5
Calvert Tex., U.S.A. 30°59N 96°40W 109 G11
Calvert C. B.C., Canada 51°25N 127°53W 154 D7
Calvert City Ky., U.S.A. 37°2N 88°21W 104 C4
Calvert County ☆ Md., U.S.A. 38°30N 76°35W 93 B4
Calvert I. B.C., Canada 51°30N 128°0W 154 D7
Calverton Md., U.S.A. 39°3N 76°56W 93 A4
Calverton Park Mo., U.S.A. 38°45N 90°18W 94 A2
Calvillo Aguascalientes, Mexico 21°51N 102°43W 173 F8
Calvin La., U.S.A. 31°58N 92°47W 110 C3
Calvin N. Dak., U.S.A. 48°51N 98°56W 76 B7
Calvin Okla., U.S.A. 34°58N 96°15W 107 D7
Calwa Calif., U.S.A. 36°42N 119°46W 127 G7
Camachigama, L. Qué., Canada 47°50N 76°19W 144 D6
Camagüey Cuba 21°20N 77°55W 182 B4
Camagüey, Arch. de Cuba 22°18N 78°0W 182 B4
Camak Ga., U.S.A. 33°27N 82°39W 113 C4
Camalú, B. Baja Calif., Mexico 30°47N 116°5W 166 C2
Camanche Iowa, U.S.A. 41°47N 90°15W 81 D8
Camanche Res. Calif., U.S.A. 38°14N 121°1W 126 E5
Camano I. Wash., U.S.A. 48°0N 122°30W 120 B3
Camargo Tamaulipas, Mexico 26°19N 98°50W 170 D6
Camargo Ky., U.S.A. 38°0N 83°53W 105 C9
Camargo Okla., U.S.A. 36°1N 99°17W 107 B4
Camarillo Calif., U.S.A. 34°13N 119°2W 127 J7
Camarón → Veracruz, Mexico 18°50N 95°55W 177 F5
Camarón, C. Honduras 16°0N 85°5W 182 C2
Camas Idaho, U.S.A. 44°0N 112°13W 122 E6
Camas Wash., U.S.A. 45°35N 122°24W 120 E3
Camas County ☆ Idaho, U.S.A. 43°30N 114°50W 122 F4
Camas Nat. Wildlife Refuge ○ Idaho, U.S.A. 43°57N 112°15W 122 F6
Camas Valley Oreg., U.S.A. 43°2N 123°40W 121 D2
Cambria Calif., U.S.A. 35°34N 121°5W 127 H5
Cambria Wis., U.S.A. 43°33N 89°7W 78 E4
Cambria County ☆ Pa., U.S.A. 40°30N 78°52W 87 C4
Cambria Heights N.Y., U.S.A. 40°41N 73°44W 97 B4
Cambridge N.B., Canada 45°50N 65°58W 141 H4
Cambridge Ont., Canada 43°23N 80°15W 146 D6
Cambridge Jamaica 18°18N 77°54W 182 C4
Cambridge Idaho, U.S.A. 44°34N 116°41W 122 E2
Cambridge Ill., U.S.A. 41°18N 90°12W 84 B3
Cambridge Iowa, U.S.A. 41°54N 93°32W 81 D5
Cambridge Kans., U.S.A. 37°19N 96°40W 82 D7
Cambridge Mass., U.S.A. 42°23N 71°7W 96 A2
Cambridge Md., U.S.A. 38°34N 76°5W 93 B4
Cambridge Minn., U.S.A. 45°34N 93°13W 77 E5
Cambridge N.Y., U.S.A. 43°2N 73°22W 91 A1
Cambridge Nebr., U.S.A. 40°17N 100°10W 80 D5
Cambridge Ohio, U.S.A. 40°2N 81°35W 86 C5
Cambridge Vt., U.S.A. 44°39N 72°53W 89 B2
Cambridge Bay = Ikaluktutiak Nunavut, Canada 69°10N 105°0W 158 D4
Cambridge City Ind., U.S.A. 39°49N 85°10W 85 D5
Cambridge Springs Pa., U.S.A. 41°48N 80°4W 87 C2
Cambridgeport Vt., U.S.A. 43°10N 72°35W 89 C2
Camden Ala., U.S.A. 31°59N 87°17W 112 E3
Camden Ark., U.S.A. 33°35N 92°50W 106 E3
Camden Del., U.S.A. 39°7N 75°33W 93 A5
Camden Ill., U.S.A. 40°9N 90°46W 84 C3
Camden Maine, U.S.A. 44°13N 69°4W 90 D4
Camden Miss., U.S.A. 32°47N 89°50W 111 D4
Camden N.C., U.S.A. 36°20N 76°10W 103 B9
Camden N.J., U.S.A. 39°55N 75°7W 98 B2
Camden N.Y., U.S.A. 43°20N 75°45W 88 C5
Camden Ohio, U.S.A. 39°38N 84°39W 86 D2
Camden S.C., U.S.A. 34°16N 80°36W 103 D5
Camden Tenn., U.S.A. 36°4N 88°6W 104 D4
Camden Tex., U.S.A. 30°55N 94°44W 109 G13
Camden Bay Alaska, U.S.A. 70°10N 145°15W 135 A11
Camden County ☆ Ga., U.S.A. 31°0N 81°45W 113 F5
Camden County ☆ Mo., U.S.A. 38°0N 92°45W 83 C4
Camden County ☆ N.J., U.S.A. 39°45N 75°0W 92 C2
Camdenton Mo., U.S.A. 38°1N 92°45W 83 C4
Camels Hump Vt., U.S.A. 44°19N 72°53W 89 B2
Cameron Ariz., U.S.A. 35°53N 111°25W 130 B4
Cameron La., U.S.A. 29°48N 93°20W 110 E2
Cameron Mo., U.S.A. 39°44N 94°14W 83 B2
Cameron Mont., U.S.A. 45°13N 111°41W 123 E6
Cameron Okla., U.S.A. 35°8N 94°32W 107 C9
Cameron Tex., U.S.A. 30°51N 96°59W 109 G11
Cameron W. Va., U.S.A. 39°50N 80°34W 102 B4
Cameron Wis., U.S.A. 45°25N 91°44W 78 C2
Cameron County ☆ Pa., U.S.A. 41°30N 78°8W 87 C4
Cameron County ☆ Tex., U.S.A. 26°12N 97°42W 108 L10
Cameron Hills Alta., Canada 59°48N 118°0W 157 E9
Cameron I. Nunavut, Canada 76°30N 103°50W 158 B5
Cameron L. Ont., Canada 49°1N 84°17W 149 C12
Cameron Parish ☆ La., U.S.A. 29°55N 93°10W 110 E2
Cameron Prairie Nat. Wildlife Refuge ○ La., U.S.A. 29°50N 93°12W 110 E2
Camilla Ga., U.S.A. 31°14N 84°12W 113 E2

Camino Calif., U.S.A. 38°44N 120°41W 126 E6
Camp Atterbury Ind., U.S.A. 39°20N 86°4W 85 D4
Camp Blanding Training Site Fla., U.S.A. 29°56N 81°57W 114 B7
Camp Borden Ont., Canada 44°18N 79°56W 146 C7
Camp Bullis Tex., U.S.A. 29°38N 98°34W 116 B2
Camp Coulter = Powell Wyo., U.S.A. 44°45N 108°46W 124 B4
Camp County ☆ Tex., U.S.A. 33°0N 94°59W 109 E13
Camp Creek W. Va., U.S.A. 37°30N 81°6W 102 D3
Camp Crook S. Dak., U.S.A. 45°33N 103°59W 76 E2
Camp Douglas Wis., U.S.A. 43°55N 90°16W 78 E3
Camp Edwards and Otis A.N.G. Base Mass., U.S.A. 41°39N 70°32W 91 C4
Camp Grayling Mich., U.S.A. 44°37N 84°47W 79 E7
Camp Hill Ala., U.S.A. 32°48N 85°39W 112 D3
Camp Hill Pa., U.S.A. 40°14N 76°55W 87 D6
Camp Houston Okla., U.S.A. 36°49N 99°7W 107 B4
Camp J.T. Robinson Ark., U.S.A. 34°52N 92°12W 106 D3
Camp Lejeune Marine Corps Base N.C., U.S.A. 34°43N 77°22W 103 D8
Camp Pendleton Calif., U.S.A. 33°13N 117°24W 127 K9
Camp Point Ill., U.S.A. 40°3N 91°4W 84 C2
Camp Ripley Minn., U.S.A. 46°9N 94°22W 77 D4
Camp Roberts Calif., U.S.A. 35°47N 120°48W 127 H6
Camp Shelby Training Site Miss., U.S.A. 31°11N 89°15W 111 E4
Camp Springs Md., U.S.A. 38°48N 76°55W 99 C4
Camp Swift Tex., U.S.A. 30°18N 97°20W 109 G10
Camp Verde Ariz., U.S.A. 34°34N 111°51W 130 C4
Camp Wood Tex., U.S.A. 29°40N 100°1W 109 H7
Campaign Tenn., U.S.A. 35°46N 85°38W 105 E7
Campania I. B.C., Canada 53°5N 129°25W 154 B5
Campbell Calif., U.S.A. 37°17N 121°57W 126 F5
Campbell Fla., U.S.A. 28°16N 81°27W 114 C7
Campbell Minn., U.S.A. 46°6N 96°24W 77 D2
Campbell Mo., U.S.A. 36°30N 90°4W 83 E6
Campbell Nebr., U.S.A. 40°18N 98°44W 80 D7
Campbell Ohio, U.S.A. 41°5N 80°37W 86 B6
Campbell County ☆ Ky., U.S.A. 38°55N 84°20W 105 B8
Campbell County ☆ S. Dak., U.S.A. 45°55N 100°0W 76 E4
Campbell County ☆ Tenn., U.S.A. 36°23N 84°7W 105 D8
Campbell County ☆ Va., U.S.A. 37°15N 79°5W 102 D5
Campbell County ☆ Wyo., U.S.A. 44°15N 105°30W 124 B7
Campbell Hill Ohio, U.S.A. 40°22N 83°43W 86 C3
Campbell I. B.C., Canada 52°7N 128°12W 154 C6
Campbell Island B.C., Canada 52°8N 128°12W 154 C6
Campbell River B.C., Canada 50°5N 125°20W 154 E9
Campbellford Ont., Canada 44°18N 77°48W 147 C9
Campbell's Bay Qué., Canada 45°44N 76°36W 144 F6
Campbellsburg Ind., U.S.A. 38°39N 86°16W 85 E4
Campbellsburg Ky., U.S.A. 38°31N 85°12W 105 B7
Campbellsport Wis., U.S.A. 43°36N 88°17W 78 E5
Campbellton N.B., Canada 47°57N 66°43W 141 F3
Campbellton Nfld. & L., Canada 49°11N 54°56W 142 C6
Campbellton Fla., U.S.A. 30°57N 85°24W 114 A3
Campeche Campeche, Mexico 19°51N 90°32W 179 C3
Campeche □ Mexico 19°0N 90°30W 179 D3
Campeche, Banco Mexico 22°30N 88°0W 182 B2
Camperville Man., Canada 51°59N 100°9W 151 D11
Campion Colo., U.S.A. 40°21N 105°5W 125 B5
Campo Colo., U.S.A. 37°6N 102°35W 125 E8
Campo Acosta Jalisco, Mexico 19°45N 105°15W 174 C2
Campo Cinco Chihuahua, Mexico 30°47N 107°55W 169 C8
Campo Cuatro Sonora, Mexico 28°32N 111°35W 168 E4
Campo del Oso → Baja Calif., Mexico 30°49N 115°39W 166 C3
Campo Indian Reservation Calif., U.S.A. 32°37N 116°23W 127 L10
Campo Nuevo Veracruz, Mexico 17°43N 95°5W 177 G5
Campo Sesenta y Uno Chihuahua, Mexico 28°54N 106°40W 169 E9
Campos de los Limones Nayarit, Mexico 21°47N 105°26W 172 F5
Campti La., U.S.A. 31°54N 93°7W 110 C2
Campton Fla., U.S.A. 30°53N 86°31W 114 A2
Campton Ga., U.S.A. 33°52N 83°43W 113 C3
Campton Ky., U.S.A. 37°44N 83°33W 105 C9
Campton N.H., U.S.A. 43°50N 71°39W 89 C3
Camptonville Calif., U.S.A. 39°27N 121°3W 126 D5
Campville Fla., U.S.A. 29°40N 82°7W 114 B6
Camrose Alta., Canada 53°0N 112°50W 153 E8
Camsell → N.W.T., Canada 65°40N 118°17W 157 C9
Camuy Puerto Rico 18°29N 66°51W 184 G16
Canaan N.B., Canada 46°15N 65°4W 141 G4
Canaan Conn., U.S.A. 42°2N 73°20W 91 B1
Canaan N.H., U.S.A. 43°40N 72°1W 89 C2
Canaan N.B., Canada 45°55N 65°47W 141 H4
Canada ■ N. Amer. 60°0N 100°0W 138 D10
Canada B. Nfld. & L., Canada 50°43N 56°8W 142 B4
Canada Basin Arctic 80°0N 145°0W 156 A3
Cañadas de Villa Orbregón Jalisco Mexico 21°7N 102°40W 174 A5
Canadensis Pa., U.S.A. 41°12N 75°15W 92 A1
Canadian Okla., U.S.A. 35°11N 95°39W 107 C8
Canadian Tex., U.S.A. 35°55N 100°23W 108 B7
Canadian → Okla., U.S.A. 35°28N 95°3W 107 C8
Canadian County ☆ Okla., U.S.A. 35°35N 98°0W 107 C6
Canajoharie N.Y., U.S.A. 42°54N 74°35W 88 C6
Canal Flats B.C., Canada 50°10N 115°48W 153 H5
Canal Fulton Ohio, U.S.A. 40°53N 81°36W 86 C5
Canal Point Fla., U.S.A. 26°52N 80°38W 114 D8
Canalou Mo., U.S.A. 36°46N 89°41W 83 E7
Canandaigua N.Y., U.S.A. 42°54N 77°17W 88 C3
Canandaigua L. N.Y., U.S.A. 42°47N 77°19W 88 C3
Cananea Sonora, Mexico 31°0N 110°18W 168 C5
Canarreos, Arch. de los Cuba 21°35N 81°40W 182 B3
Canarsie N.Y., U.S.A. 40°38N 73°53W 97 C3
Canaseraga N.Y., U.S.A. 42°27N 77°45W 88 C3
Canatlán Durango, Mexico 24°31N 104°47W 173 C6
Canaveral, C. Fla., U.S.A. 28°27N 80°32W 114 C8
Canaveral Nat. Seashore ○ Fla., U.S.A. 28°28N 80°34W 114 C8
Canby Calif., U.S.A. 41°27N 120°52W 126 B6
Canby Minn., U.S.A. 44°43N 96°16W 77 F2
Canby Oreg., U.S.A. 45°16N 122°42W 121 B3
Cancún Quintana Roo, Mexico 21°8N 86°44W 179 A7
Cancún ✈ (CUN) Quintana Roo, Mexico 19°1N 86°54W 179 C7
Candela Coahuila, Mexico 26°50N 100°40W 170 D4
Candelaria Baja Calif. S., Mexico 23°4N 110°0W 167 K8
Candelaria Campeche, Mexico 18°18N 91°23W 179 D2
Candelaria Quintana Roo, Mexico 19°45N 88°59W 179 C5
Candelaria Tex., U.S.A. 30°8N 104°41W 108 G3
Candelaria → Campeche, Mexico 18°38N 91°15W 179 D2
Candelaria Loxicha Oaxaca, Mexico 15°56N 96°32W 177 J4
Candiac Qué., Canada 45°23N 73°29W 160 B4
Cándido Aguilar Tamaulipas, Mexico 25°3N 98°47W 171 E6

Candle Alaska, U.S.A. 65°55N 161°56W 135 D7
Candle L., Sask., Canada 53°50N 105°18W 150 B6
Candle Lake Sask., Canada 53°45N 105°15W 150 B6
Candler County ☆ Ga., U.S.A. 32°30N 82°0W 113 D4
Candlewood N.J., U.S.A. 40°9N 74°10W 92 B2
Candlewood, L. Conn., U.S.A. 41°35N 73°27W 91 C1
Cando Sask., Canada 52°23N 108°14W 150 C3
Cando N. Dak., U.S.A. 48°32N 99°12W 76 B6
Candor N.C., U.S.A. 35°18N 79°45W 103 C6
Candor N.Y., U.S.A. 42°14N 76°21W 88 C4
Cane River Creole Nat. Historical Park ○ La., U.S.A. 31°40N 93°11W 110 C2
Cane Valley Ky., U.S.A. 37°11N 85°19W 105 C7
Canelas Durango, Mexico 25°7N 106°34W 172 B4
Caney Kans., U.S.A. 37°1N 95°56W 82 D8
Caney → Tenn., U.S.A. 34°14N 96°13W 107 D7
Caney Fork → Tenn., U.S.A. 36°15N 85°57W 105 D7
Caneyville Ky., U.S.A. 37°26N 86°29W 104 C6
Canfield Ark., U.S.A. 33°11N 93°38W 106 E2
Canfield Ohio, U.S.A. 41°2N 80°46W 86 B6
Caniapiscau → Qué., Canada 56°40N 69°30W 143 B4
Caniapiscau, L. de Qué., Canada 54°10N 69°55W 143 C4
Canim → B.C., Canada 51°45N 120°50W 155 D14
Canim Lake B.C., Canada 51°47N 120°54W 155 D14
Canisteo N.Y., U.S.A. 42°16N 77°36W 88 C3
Canisteo → N.Y., U.S.A. 42°7N 77°8W 88 C3
Canistota S. Dak., U.S.A. 43°36N 97°18W 76 G8
Cañitas de Felipe Pescador Zacatecas, Mexico 23°36N 102°43W 173 D8
Canjilon N. Mex., U.S.A. 36°29N 106°26W 131 A4
Canmer Ky., U.S.A. 37°17N 85°46W 105 C7
Canmore Alta., Canada 51°7N 115°18W 153 G5
Cannel City Ky., U.S.A. 37°47N 83°17W 105 C9
Cannelton Ind., U.S.A. 37°55N 86°45W 85 F4
Canning N.S., Canada 45°9N 64°25W 141 H5
Cannington Ont., Canada 44°20N 79°2W 147 C7
Cannon Air Force Base N. Mex., U.S.A. 34°23N 104°12W 131 D7
Cannon Ball N. Dak., U.S.A. 46°25N 100°38W 76 D5
Cannon Beach Oreg., U.S.A. 45°54N 123°58W 121 B2
Cannon County ☆ Tenn., U.S.A. 35°50N 86°4W 104 E6
Cannon Falls Minn., U.S.A. 44°31N 92°54W 77 F6
Cannonball → N. Dak., U.S.A. 46°26N 100°35W 76 D5
Cannonsburg Ky., U.S.A. 38°23N 82°42W 105 B10
Cannonsville Res. N.Y., U.S.A. 42°4N 75°22W 88 C5
Cannonville Utah, U.S.A. 37°34N 112°3W 129 F3
Canoas, Pta. Baja Calif., Mexico 29°26N 115°12W 166 D3
Canobie Lake N.H., U.S.A. 42°49N 71°12W 89 D3
Canoe B.C., Canada 50°45N 119°13W 155 E15
Canoe → B.C., Canada 52°10N 119°13W 155 C13
Cañon de Río Blanco, Parque Nacional ○ Puebla, Mexico 18°43N 97°15W 177 F3
Cañón de Santa Elena, Parque Natural ○ Mexico 28°57N 103°15W 169 D12
Cañón del Sumidero, Parque Nacional ○ Chiapas, Mexico 16°51N 93°8W 178 C3
Cañon Fiord Nunavut, Canada 80°0N 82°35W 158 B9
Canon Largo → N. Mex., U.S.A. 36°33N 107°49W 131 A3
Canoncito Indian Reservation N. Mex., U.S.A. 35°10N 107°0W 131 B3
Canonsburg Pa., U.S.A. 40°16N 80°11W 87 D2
Canoochee → Ga., U.S.A. 31°59N 81°19W 113 E5
Canora Sask., Canada 51°40N 102°30W 151 D8
Canova S. Dak., U.S.A. 43°53N 97°30W 76 G8
Cansahcab Yucatán, Mexico 21°10N 89°6W 179 A4
Canso N.S., Canada 45°20N 61°0W 141 H9
Canso, Str. of N.S., Canada 45°37N 61°22W 141 H8
Canterbury = Invermere B.C., Canada 50°30N 116°2W 153 H4
Canterbury N.B., Canada 45°54N 67°29W 141 H2
Canterbury Conn., U.S.A. 41°41N 71°57W 91 C3
Canterbury N.H., U.S.A. 43°20N 71°34W 89 C3
Cantil Calif., U.S.A. 35°18N 117°58W 127 H9
Cantin L. Man., Canada 53°25N 95°10W 151 B16
Canton Baltimore, U.S.A. 39°16N 76°34W 99 B2
Canton Conn., U.S.A. 41°49N 72°54W 91 C2
Canton Ga., U.S.A. 34°14N 84°29W 113 B2
Canton Ill., U.S.A. 40°33N 90°2W 84 C3
Canton Kans., U.S.A. 38°23N 97°26W 82 C6
Canton Ky., U.S.A. 36°48N 87°58W 104 D5
Canton Mass., U.S.A. 42°9N 71°9W 91 B3
Canton Minn., U.S.A. 43°32N 91°56W 77 G7
Canton Miss., U.S.A. 32°37N 90°2W 111 D3
Canton Mo., U.S.A. 40°8N 91°32W 83 A5
Canton N.C., U.S.A. 35°32N 82°50W 103 C3
Canton N.Y., U.S.A. 44°36N 75°10W 88 A5
Canton Ohio, U.S.A. 40°48N 81°23W 86 C5
Canton Okla., U.S.A. 36°3N 98°35W 107 B5
Canton Pa., U.S.A. 41°39N 76°51W 87 C6
Canton S. Dak., U.S.A. 43°18N 96°35W 76 G9
Canton Tex., U.S.A. 32°33N 95°52W 109 E12
Canton L. Okla., U.S.A. 36°6N 98°35W 107 B5
Cantonment Fla., U.S.A. 30°37N 87°20W 114 A1
Cantril Iowa, U.S.A. 40°39N 92°4W 81 E6
Cantwell Alaska, U.S.A. 63°24N 148°57W 135 E10
Canute Okla., U.S.A. 35°25N 99°17W 107 C4
Canutillo Durango, Mexico 26°22N 105°25W 172 A5
Canutillo Tex., U.S.A. 31°55N 106°36W 108 F1
Canwood Sask., Canada 53°22N 106°36W 150 B5
Canyon Tex., U.S.A. 34°59N 101°55W 108 C6
Canyon City Oreg., U.S.A. 44°23N 118°57W 121 C7
Canyon County ☆ Idaho, U.S.A. 43°35N 116°50W 122 F2
Canyon Creek Alta., Canada 55°22N 115°55W 152 C5
Canyon Creek → Alta., Canada 46°49N 112°16W 123 D5
Canyon De Chelly Nat. Monument ○ Ariz., U.S.A. 36°10N 109°20W 130 B6
Canyon Ferry L. Mont., U.S.A. 46°39N 111°44W 123 D6
Canyon L. Tex., U.S.A. 29°52N 98°12W 109 H9
Canyon Village Wyo., U.S.A. 44°46N 110°32W 124 B2
Canyonlands Nat. Park ○ Utah, U.S.A. 38°15N 110°0W 129 E6
Canyons of the Ancients Nat. Monument ○ Colo., U.S.A. 37°30N 108°55W 125 E2
Canyonville Oreg., U.S.A. 42°56N 123°17W 121 D2
Caopacho → Qué., Canada 52°56N 66°9W 140 A3
Caopacho, L. Qué., Canada 52°0N 66°9W 140 A3
Caopas Zacatecas, Mexico 24°48N 101°24W 173 C8
Caotibi, L. Qué., Canada 50°46N 67°33W 140 C2
Cap-aux-Meules Qué., Canada 47°23N 61°52W 141 F8
Cap-Chat Qué., Canada 49°6N 66°40W 140 D3
Cap-de-la-Madeleine Qué., Canada 46°22N 72°31W 145 E10
Cap-des-Rosiers Qué., Canada 48°52N 64°13W 140 E5
Cap-d'Espoir Qué., Canada 48°26N 64°20W 140 E5
Cap-Haïtien Haiti 19°40N 72°20W 183 C5
Cap Mt. N.W.T., Canada 63°24N 123°12W 157 D8

Cap-Pelé N.B., Canada 46°13N 64°18W 141 G5
Cap Rock Escarpment Tex., U.S.A. 33°25N 101°11W 108 D6
Cap-St-Ignace Qué., Canada 47°2N 70°28W 145 D12
Cap-St-Jacques, Parc-nature du ○ Qué., Canada 45°28N 73°55W 160 B1
Cap-Seize Qué., Canada 49°1N 66°24W 140 D3
Capa S. Dak., U.S.A. 44°7N 100°59W 76 F5
Capac Mich., U.S.A. 43°1N 82°56W 79 F9
Cape Breton N.S., Canada 46°0N 60°19W 141 G9
Cape Breton Highlands Nat. Park △ N.S., Canada 46°50N 60°40W 141 G9
Cape Breton I. N.S., Canada 46°0N 60°30W 141 G9
Cape Broyle Nfld. & L., Canada 47°6N 52°57W 142 E8
Cape Canaveral Fla., U.S.A. 28°24N 80°36W 114 C8
Cape Canaveral Air Station Fla., U.S.A. 28°28N 80°34W 114 C8
Cape Charles Va., U.S.A. 37°16N 76°1W 102 D8
Cape Cod B. Mass., U.S.A. 41°50N 70°20W 91 C4
Cape Cod Nat. Seashore △ Mass., U.S.A. 41°56N 70°6W 91 C4
Cape Coral Fla., U.S.A. 26°33N 81°57W 114 E7
Cape Dorset Nunavut, Canada 64°14N 76°32W 159 E10
Cape Elizabeth Maine, U.S.A. 43°34N 70°12W 90 E3
Cape Fear → N.C., U.S.A. 33°53N 78°1W 103 E7
Cape Girardeau Mo., U.S.A. 37°19N 89°32W 83 D7
Cape Girardeau County ☆ Mo., U.S.A. 37°25N 89°40W 83 D7
Cape Hatteras Nat. Seashore △ N.C., U.S.A. 35°30N 75°28W 103 C10
Cape Henlopen State Park △ Del., U.S.A. 38°46N 75°5W 93 B5
Cape I. S.C., U.S.A. 33°2N 79°21W 103 E6
Cape Krusenstern Nat. Monument ○ U.S.A. 67°30N 163°30W 135 C7
Cape Lisburne = Wevok Alaska, U.S.A. 68°51N 166°13W 135 B6
Cape Lookout Nat. Seashore △ N.C., U.S.A. 35°45N 76°25W 103 C9
Cape May N.J., U.S.A. 38°56N 74°56W 92 D2
Cape May County ☆ N.J., U.S.A. 39°10N 74°45W 92 C2
Cape May Court House U.S.A. 39°5N 74°50W 92 C2
Cape May Point N.J., U.S.A. 38°56N 74°58W 92 D2
Cape Pole Alaska, U.S.A. 55°58N 133°48W 135 J14
Cape Ray Nfld. & L., Canada 47°38N 59°17W 142 E1
Cape St. Claire Md., U.S.A. 39°3N 76°25W 93 A4
Cape Scott Park ○ B.C., Canada 50°45N 128°20W 154 E6
Cape Tormentine N.B., Canada 46°8N 63°47W 141 G6
Cape Vincent N.Y., U.S.A. 44°8N 76°20W 88 A4
Cape Yakataga Alaska, U.S.A. 60°4N 142°26W 135 F12
Capilano River Regional Park B.C., Canada 49°21N 122°7W 161 A2
Capilla de Guadalupe Jalisco, Mexico 20°50N 102°35W 174 B5
Capitachouane → Qué., Canada 47°40N 76°47W 144 D6
Capitan N. Mex., U.S.A. 33°35N 105°35W 131 D5
Capitan Grande Indian Reservation Calif., U.S.A. 32°54N 116°43W 127 L10
Capitan Mts. N. Mex., U.S.A. 33°36N 105°22W 131 D5
Capitan Pk. N. Mex., U.S.A. 33°36N 105°16W 131 D5
Capitol Heights Md., U.S.A. 38°52N 76°55W 99 B4
Capitol Hill N. Marianas 15°13N 145°45E 184 c
Capitol Reef Nat. Park ○ Utah, U.S.A. 38°15N 111°10W 129 E4
Capitol View S.C., U.S.A. 33°58N 80°55W 103 E5
Capitola Fla., U.S.A. 30°27N 84°5W 114 A4
Caplan N.B., Canada 48°6N 65°40W 141 E4
Capleville Tenn., U.S.A. 35°1N 89°53W 117 B2
Capon Bridge W. Va., U.S.A. 39°18N 78°26W 93 A2
Caprock N. Mex., U.S.A. 33°24N 103°43W 131 D7
Capron Ill., U.S.A. 42°24N 88°44W 84 A5
Capron Okla., U.S.A. 36°54N 98°35W 107 B5
Captain Cook Hawai'i, U.S.A. 19°30N 155°55W 136 D6
Captiva Fla., U.S.A. 26°31N 82°11W 114 E6
Capulin Pk. N. Mex., U.S.A. 36°15N 106°46W 131 A4
Capulin Volcano Nat. Monument ○ U.S.A. 36°47N 103°58W 131 A7
Caracol, Pta. Yucatán, Mexico 21°32N 87°37W 179 A6
Caracoles Zacatecas, Mexico 22°59N 103°28W 173 E7
Carácuaro Michoacan, Mexico 19°1N 101°8W 175 C6
Caramat Ont., Canada 49°37N 86°9W 149 C16
Caratasca, L. Honduras 15°20N 83°40W 182 C3
Caratunk Maine, U.S.A. 45°8N 69°59W 90 C4
Caraway Ark., U.S.A. 35°46N 90°19W 106 C6
Carberry Man., Canada 49°50N 99°25W 151 F12
Carbó Sonora, Mexico 29°42N 110°58W 168 D5
Carbon Alta., Canada 51°30N 113°9W 153 G7
Carbon Ind., U.S.A. 39°36N 87°6W 85 D3
Carbon Iowa, U.S.A. 41°3N 94°50W 81 D4
Carbon Tex., U.S.A. 32°16N 98°50W 109 E8
Carbon County ☆ Mont., U.S.A. 45°10N 109°0W 123 E8
Carbon County ☆ Pa., U.S.A. 40°55N 75°50W 87 D7
Carbon County ☆ Utah, U.S.A. 39°40N 110°30W 129 D5
Carbon County ☆ Wyo., U.S.A. 42°0N 107°0W 124 E6
Carbon Hill Ala., U.S.A. 33°53N 87°32W 112 C3
Carbonado Wash., U.S.A. 47°5N 122°3W 120 C3
Carbondale Colo., U.S.A. 39°24N 107°13W 125 D4
Carbondale Ill., U.S.A. 37°44N 89°13W 84 F4
Carbondale Kans., U.S.A. 38°49N 95°41W 82 C8
Carbondale Pa., U.S.A. 41°35N 75°30W 87 C7
Carbonear Nfld. & L., Canada 47°42N 53°13W 142 E7
Carboneras Tamaulipas, Mexico 24°38N 97°43W 171 F7
Carcajou Alta., Canada 57°47N 117°6W 157 E9
Carcajou → N.W.T., Canada 65°37N 128°43W 157 C7
Carcasse, C. Haiti 18°30N 74°28W 183 C5
Carcross Yukon, Canada 60°13N 134°45W 157 D6
Cardel Veracruz, Mexico 19°22N 96°21W 176 E4
Cárdenas Cuba 23°0N 81°30W 182 B3
Cárdenas San Luis Potosi, Mexico 22°0N 99°38W 171 H5
Cárdenas Tabasco, Mexico 17°59N 93°22W 178 B3
Cardiff Colo., U.S.A. 39°31N 107°19W 125 C3
Cardigan, Mt. N.H., U.S.A. 43°39N 71°54W 89 C3
Cardinal Ont., Canada 44°47N 75°23W 147 C11
Cardinal L. Alta., Canada 56°14N 117°34W 152 B3
Cardington Ohio, U.S.A. 40°30N 82°54W 86 C4
Cardross Sask., Canada 49°50N 105°40W 150 F6
Cardston Alta., Canada 49°15N 113°20W 153 J7
Cardwell Mo., U.S.A. 36°3N 90°17W 83 E6
Carefree Ariz., U.S.A. 33°50N 111°55W 130 D4
Carencro La., U.S.A. 30°19N 92°3W 110 D3
Carey Idaho, U.S.A. 43°19N 113°57W 122 F5
Carey Ohio, U.S.A. 40°57N 83°23W 86 C3
Carheil, L. Qué., Canada 52°40N 67°54W 140 A2
Caribbean Sea W. Indies 15°0N 75°0W 183 D5
Caribe → Campeche, Mexico 18°7N 90°47W 179 D3
Cariboo → B.C., Canada 53°3N 121°20W 155 B13
Cariboo Mountain Park ○ B.C., Canada 52°53N 120°31W 155 C14
Cariboo Mts. B.C., Canada 53°0N 121°0W 155 C14
Cariboo River Park ○ B.C., Canada 52°52N 121°12W 155 C13
Caribou Maine, U.S.A. 46°52N 68°1W 90 B5
Caribou → Man., Canada 59°20N 94°44W 159 F6
Caribou County ☆ Idaho, U.S.A. 42°50N 111°30W 122 G7

Caribou I. Ont., Canada 47°22N 85°49W **149** E11
Caribou L. Ont., Canada 50°25N 89°5W **148** B7
Caribou Mts. Alta., Canada 59°12N 115°40W **157** E9
Caribou Nat. Forest Idaho, U.S.A. 42°50N 111°5W **122** G7
Caribou Range Idaho, U.S.A. 43°10N 111°15W **122** F7
Carichic Chihuahua, Mexico 27°56N 107°3W **169** F8
Carimicuas Jalisco, Mexico 19°27N 102°58W **174** C5
Carl Blackwell, L. Okla., U.S.A. 36°8N 97°11W **107** B6
Carl Junction Mo., U.S.A. 37°11N 94°34W **83** D2
Carleton = Borden Sask., Canada 52°27N 107°14W **150** C4
Carleton N.B., Canada 48°5N 66°4W **141** E3
Carleton N.S., Canada 44°0N 65°56W **141** K4
Carleton Mich., U.S.A. 42°4N 83°24W **79** G8
Carleton Nebr., U.S.A. 40°18N 97°41W **80** D8
Carleton, Mt. N.B., Canada 47°23N 66°53W **141** F3
Carleton Heights Ont., Canada 45°21N 75°43W **160** B1
Carleton Place Ont., Canada 45°8N 76°9W **147** B10
Carlile Wyo., U.S.A. 44°29N 104°48W **124** B8
Carlin Nev., U.S.A. 40°43N 116°7W **128** B4
Carlinville Ill., U.S.A. 39°17N 89°53W **84** D4
Carlisle Ark., U.S.A. 34°47N 91°45W **106** D4
Carlisle Ind., U.S.A. 38°58N 87°24W **85** E3
Carlisle Iowa, U.S.A. 41°30N 93°29W **81** D5
Carlisle Ky., U.S.A. 38°19N 84°1W **105** B8
Carlisle Miss., U.S.A. 32°0N 90°47W **111** E3
Carlisle Pa., U.S.A. 40°12N 77°12W **87** D5
Carlisle Wash., U.S.A. 47°10N 124°6W **120** C1
Carlisle County ☆ Ky., U.S.A. 36°50N 89°0W **104** D4
Carlock Ill., U.S.A. 40°35N 89°8W **84** C4
Carlos Minn., U.S.A. 45°58N 95°18W **77** E3
Carlos Tex., U.S.A. 30°36N 96°5W **109** G11
Carlos A. Carrillo Veracruz, Mexico 18°17N 95°49W **177** F5
Carlsbad Calif., U.S.A. 33°10N 117°21W **127** K9
Carlsbad N. Mex., U.S.A. 32°25N 104°14W **131** E6
Carlsbad Tex., U.S.A. 31°36N 100°38W **108** F7
Carlsbad Caverns Nat. Park △ N. Mex.,
  U.S.A. 32°10N 104°35W **131** E6
Carlshend Mich., U.S.A. 46°19N 87°13W **79** C4
Carlstadt N.J., U.S.A. 40°50N 74°6W **97** A2
Carlton Minn., U.S.A. 46°40N 92°25W **77** D6
Carlton Oreg., U.S.A. 45°18N 123°11W **121** B2
Carlton County ☆ Minn., U.S.A. 46°35N 92°50W **77** D6
Carlyle Sask., Canada 49°40N 102°20W **151** F9
Carlyle Ill., U.S.A. 38°37N 89°22W **84** E4
Carlyle Mont., U.S.A. 46°40N 104°4W **123** D13
Carlyle L. Ill., U.S.A. 38°30N 89°21W **84** E4
Carmacks Yukon, Canada 62°5N 136°16W **157** D5
Carman Man., Canada 49°30N 98°0W **151** F13
Carmanah Walbran Park △ B.C.,
  Canada 48°39N 124°39W **154** G10
Carmangay Alta., Canada 50°10N 113°10W **153** H7
Carmanville Nfld. & L., Canada 49°23N 54°19W **142** C6
Carmel Ind., U.S.A. 39°58N 86°7W **85** D4
Carmel N.Y., U.S.A. 41°26N 73°41W **92** A3
Carmel-by-the-Sea Calif., U.S.A. 36°33N 121°55W **126** G5
Carmel-Michelis Brook-St. Catherines
  Nfld. & L., Canada 47°9N 53°32W **142** E7
Carmel Valley Calif., U.S.A. 36°29N 121°43W **126** G5
Carmen Idaho, U.S.A. 45°15N 113°54W **122** D5
Carmen Okla., U.S.A. 36°35N 98°28W **107** B5
Carmen, I. Baja Calif. S., Mexico 25°57N 111°12W **167** H7
Carmen, I. del Campeche, Mexico 18°16N 91°48W **179** D2
Carmen, L. el Tabasco, Mexico 18°17N 93°48W **178** A3
Carmen, Sa. de Coahuila, Mexico 29°0N 102°28W **170** B2
Carmi B.C., Canada 49°36N 119°8W **155** F15
Carmi Ill., U.S.A. 38°5N 88°10W **84** E5
Carmichael Calif., U.S.A. 38°38N 121°19W **126** F5
Carmona Costa Rica 10°0N 85°15W **182** E2
Carnduff Sask., Canada 49°10N 101°50W **151** F10
Carnegie Ga., U.S.A. 31°39N 84°47W **113** E2
Carnegie Okla., U.S.A. 35°6N 98°36W **107** C5
Carnegie Pa., U.S.A. 40°24N 80°5W **98** B1
Carneiro Kans., U.S.A. 38°44N 98°2W **82** C1
Carnesville Ga., U.S.A. 34°22N 83°14W **113** B3
Carney Md., U.S.A. 39°23N 76°31W **99** A2
Carney Mich., U.S.A. 45°35N 87°34W **79** D4
Carney Okla., U.S.A. 35°48N 97°1W **107** C6
Carneys Point N.J., U.S.A. 39°43N 75°28W **92** C1
Carnwath → N.W.T., Canada 68°26N 128°52W **156** C7
Carnwood Alta., Canada 53°11N 114°38W **153** E6
Caro Mich., U.S.A. 43°29N 83°24W **79** F8
Caroga Lake N.Y., U.S.A. 43°8N 74°29W **88** B6
Carol City Fla., U.S.A. 25°56N 80°14W **115** C1
Carolina Puerto Rico 18°23N 65°58W **184** G17
Carolina R.I., U.S.A. 41°28N 71°40W **91** C3
Carolina Beach N.C., U.S.A. 34°2N 77°54W **103** D8
Carolinas Pt. N. Marianas 14°55N 145°38E **184** c
Caroline Alta., Canada 52°5N 114°45W **153** F6
Caroline County ☆ Md., U.S.A. 38°50N 75°50W **93** B5
Caroline County ☆ Va., U.S.A. 38°3N 77°21W **102** C7
Caron Sask., Canada 50°30N 105°50W **150** E6
Caron, L. Qué., Canada 50°57N 67°44W **140** C2
Carondelet Park Mo., U.S.A. 38°33N 90°15W **94** B2
Carp Nev., U.S.A. 37°7N 114°29W **128** E6
Carpenter Iowa, U.S.A. 43°25N 93°1W **81** B5
Carpenter Wyo., U.S.A. 41°3N 104°22W **124** E8
Carpenter L. B.C., Canada 50°53N 122°37W **155** E12
Carpentersville Oreg., U.S.A. 42°13N 124°17W **121** E1
Carpinteria Calif., U.S.A. 34°24N 119°31W **127** J7
Carpio N. Dak., U.S.A. 48°27N 101°43W **76** B4
Carr Colo., U.S.A. 40°54N 104°53W **125** B6
Carr Fork L. Ky., U.S.A. 37°14N 83°2W **105** C9
Carr Mt. N.H., U.S.A. 43°52N 71°50W **89** C3
Carrabassett Maine, U.S.A. 45°5N 70°13W **90** C3
Carrabelle Fla., U.S.A. 29°51N 84°40W **114** B4
Carragana Sask., Canada 52°35N 103°6W **150** C8
Carrboro N.C., U.S.A. 35°55N 79°5W **103** C6
Carreta, Estero ≈ Chiapas, Mexico 15°33N 93°12W **178** D3
Carrier Okla., U.S.A. 36°29N 98°2W **107** B5
Carrier Mills Ill., U.S.A. 37°41N 88°38W **84** F5
Carriere Miss., U.S.A. 30°37N 89°39W **111** F4
Carrigain, Mt. N.H., U.S.A. 44°6N 71°26W **89** B3
Carrillo Chihuahua, Mexico 26°54N 103°55W **169** G12
Carrington N. Dak., U.S.A. 47°27N 99°8W **76** C6
Carrizo Cr. → N. Mex., U.S.A. 36°55N 103°55W **131** A7
Carrizo Plain Nat. Monument △
  U.S.A. 35°11N 119°47W **127** H7
Carrizo Springs Tex., U.S.A. 28°31N 99°52W **109** J8
Carrizo Wash → U.S.A. 34°36N 109°26W **131** C1
Carrizos Tamaulipas, Mexico 24°23N 99°16W **171** G5
Carrizozo N. Mex. U.S.A. 33°38N 105°53W **131** D5
Carroll Iowa, U.S.A. 42°4N 94°52W **81** C4
Carroll Nebr., U.S.A. 42°17N 97°12W **80** B8
Carroll Ohio, U.S.A. 39°48N 82°43W **86** D4
Carroll County ☆ Ark., U.S.A. 36°22N 93°35W **106** B2
Carroll County ☆ Ga., U.S.A. 33°30N 85°10W **113** C1

Carroll County ☆ Ill., U.S.A. 42°0N 90°0W **84** A4
Carroll County ☆ Ind., U.S.A. 40°35N 86°35W **85** C4
Carroll County ☆ Iowa, U.S.A. 42°0N 94°50W **81** C4
Carroll County ☆ Ky., U.S.A. 38°40N 85°5W **105** B7
Carroll County ☆ Md., U.S.A. 39°30N 77°0W **93** A4
Carroll County ☆ Miss., U.S.A. 33°30N 89°55W **111** C4
Carroll County ☆ Mo., U.S.A. 39°25N 93°30W **83** D3
Carroll County ☆ N.H., U.S.A. 43°50N 71°15W **89** C3
Carroll County ☆ Ohio, U.S.A. 40°34N 81°5W **86** C5
Carroll County ☆ Tenn., U.S.A. 36°0N 88°26W **104** E4
Carroll County ☆ Va., U.S.A. 36°55N 80°50W **102** E4
Carroll Valley Pa., U.S.A. 39°44N 77°23W **93** A3
Carrolls Wash., U.S.A. 46°4N 122°52W **120** D3
Carrollton Ala., U.S.A. 33°16N 88°6W **112** C2
Carrollton Ga., U.S.A. 33°35N 85°5W **113** C1
Carrollton Ill., U.S.A. 39°18N 90°24W **84** D3
Carrollton Ky., U.S.A. 38°41N 85°11W **105** B7
Carrollton Mich., U.S.A. 43°28N 83°55W **79** F8
Carrollton Miss., U.S.A. 33°30N 89°55W **111** C4
Carrollton Mo., U.S.A. 39°22N 93°30W **83** D3
Carrollton Ohio, U.S.A. 40°34N 81°5W **86** C5
Carrollton Tex., U.S.A. 32°57N 96°55W **109** E11
Carrolltown Pa., U.S.A. 40°36N 78°43W **87** D4
Carrollwood Tampa, U.S.A. 28°2N 82°29W **115** A3
Carrot → Sask., Canada 53°50N 101°17W **151** B10
Carrot River Sask., Canada 53°17N 103°35W **150** B8
Carry Falls Res. N.Y., U.S.A. 44°31N 74°45W **88** A6
Carson Calif., U.S.A. 33°49N 118°16W **127** K8
Carson Iowa, U.S.A. 41°14N 95°25W **81** D3
Carson N. Dak., U.S.A. 46°25N 101°34W **76** D4
Carson Wash., U.S.A. 45°44N 121°49W **120** E4
Carson → Nev., U.S.A. 39°45N 118°40W **128** C2
Carson City Mich., U.S.A. 43°11N 84°51W **79** F7
Carson City Nev., U.S.A. 39°10N 119°46W **128** C1
Carson County ☆ Tex., U.S.A. 35°20N 101°20W **108** B6
Carson Grove Ont., Canada 45°26N 75°37W **160** A2
Carson L. Nev., U.S.A. 39°18N 118°43W **128** C2
Carson Nat. Forest N. Mex., U.S.A. 36°30N 106°15W **131** A4
Carson Sink Nev., U.S.A. 39°50N 118°25W **128** C2
Carstairs Alta., Canada 51°34N 114°6W **153** G6
Carta Valley Tex., U.S.A. 29°48N 100°41W **108** H7
Cartago Costa Rica 9°50N 83°55W **182** E3
Cartago Calif., U.S.A. 36°19N 118°2W **127** G8
Carter Ky., U.S.A. 38°26N 83°8W **105** B9
Carter Okla., U.S.A. 35°13N 99°30W **107** C4
Carter S. Dak., U.S.A. 43°23N 100°12W **76** G5
Carter Wyo., U.S.A. 41°26N 110°26W **124** E2
Carter County ☆ Ky., U.S.A. 38°20N 83°0W **105** B9
Carter County ☆ Mo., U.S.A. 37°0N 91°0W **83** E6
Carter County ☆ Mont., U.S.A. 45°30N 104°30W **123** E13
Carter County ☆ Okla., U.S.A. 34°15N 97°15W **107** D6
Carter County ☆ Tenn., U.S.A. 36°17N 82°10W **105** D10
Carter Mt. Wyo., U.S.A. 44°12N 109°25W **124** B3
Carteret N.J., U.S.A. 40°34N 74°13W **97** C1
Carteret County ☆ N.C., U.S.A. 34°50N 76°30W **103** D9
Carters L. Ga., U.S.A. 34°37N 84°40W **113** B2
Cartersville Ga., U.S.A. 34°10N 84°48W **113** B2
Cartersville Va., U.S.A. 37°40N 78°6W **102** D6
Carterville Ill., U.S.A. 37°46N 89°5W **84** F4
Carthage Ark., U.S.A. 34°4N 92°33W **106** D3
Carthage Ill., U.S.A. 40°25N 91°8W **84** C21
Carthage Ind., U.S.A. 39°44N 85°34W **85** D5
Carthage Miss., U.S.A. 32°44N 89°32W **111** D4
Carthage Mo., U.S.A. 37°11N 94°19W **83** D2
Carthage N.C., U.S.A. 35°21N 79°25W **103** C6
Carthage N.Y., U.S.A. 43°59N 75°37W **88** B5
Carthage S. Dak., U.S.A. 44°10N 97°43W **76** F8
Carthage Tenn., U.S.A. 36°15N 85°57W **105** D7
Carthage Tex., U.S.A. 32°9N 94°20W **109** E13
Cartier Ont., Canada 46°42N 81°33W **146** A5
Cartierville Qué., Canada 45°31N 73°42W **160** A2
Cartwright Man., Canada 49°6N 99°20W **151** F12
Cartwright Nfld. & L., Canada 53°41N 56°58W **143** C6
Cartwright Sd. B.C., Canada 53°13N 132°38W **154** B2
Caruthersville Mo., U.S.A. 36°11N 89°39W **83** E71
Carvajal Tamaulipas, Mexico 24°30N 97°45W **171** F7
Carver Minn., U.S.A. 44°54N 92°58W **94** B4
Carver County ☆ Minn., U.S.A. 44°50N 93°45W **77** F5
Carvers Nev., U.S.A. 38°47N 117°11W **128** D3
Carville La., U.S.A. 30°13N 91°6W **110** D4
Cary Ill., U.S.A. 42°13N 88°14W **84** A5
Cary Miss., U.S.A. 32°49N 90°56W **111** D3
Cary N.C., U.S.A. 35°47N 78°46W **103** C7
Caryville Tenn., U.S.A. 36°18N 84°13W **105** D8
Casa Ark., U.S.A. 35°2N 93°3W **106** C2
Casa Blanca N. Mex., U.S.A. 35°3N 107°28W **131** B3
Casa de Piedra, Pta. Guerrero, Mexico 16°32N 98°52W **175** F9
Casa Grande Ariz., U.S.A. 32°53N 111°45W **130** E4
Casa Grande Ruins Nat. Monument △ Ariz.,
  U.S.A. 33°0N 111°30W **130** E4
Casa Loma Ont., Canada 43°41N 79°24W **161** A2
Casas Grandes Chihuahua, Mexico 30°22N 107°57W **169** C8
Casas Grandes Sonora, Mexico 29°12N 111°43W **168** D4
Casas Grandes → Chihuahua, Mexico 31°22N 107°31W **169** B8
Cascada de Basaseachic, Parque Nacional △
  Chihuahua, Mexico 28°9N 108°15W **169** E7
Cascade Colo., U.S.A. 38°54N 104°58W **125** D6
Cascade Idaho, U.S.A. 44°31N 116°2W **122** E2
Cascade Iowa, U.S.A. 42°18N 91°0W **81** C8
Cascade Mont., U.S.A. 47°16N 111°42W **123** C6
Cascade County ☆ Mont., U.S.A. 47°20N 111°30W **123** C6
Cascade Head Oreg., U.S.A. 45°3N 124°1W **121** B1
Cascade Heights B.C., Canada 49°15N 123°1W **161** A2
Cascade Heights Georgia, U.S.A. 33°43N 84°26W **117** B2
Cascade Locks Oreg., U.S.A. 45°40N 121°54W **121** B4
Cascade Ra. Wash., U.S.A. 47°0N 121°30W **121** B4
Cascade Res. Idaho, U.S.A. 44°32N 116°3W **122** E2
Cascadia Oreg., U.S.A. 44°24N 122°29W **121** C3
Casco Maine, U.S.A. 43°56N 70°31W **90** E3
Casco Wis., U.S.A. 44°34N 87°37W **78** D6
Casco B. Maine, U.S.A. 43°45N 70°0W **90** E4
Caselton Nev., U.S.A. 37°55N 114°29W **128** E6
Caseville Mich., U.S.A. 43°56N 83°16W **79** F8
Casey Qué., Canada 47°53N 74°11W **145** D8
Casey Ill., U.S.A. 39°18N 87°59W **84** D6
Casey Iowa, U.S.A. 41°31N 94°32W **81** D4
Casey County ☆ Ky., U.S.A. 37°20N 85°0W **105** C8
Cash Ark., U.S.A. 35°48N 90°56W **106** C5
Cashie → N.C., U.S.A. 35°53N 76°49W **103** C9
Cashiers N.C., U.S.A. 35°6N 83°6W **103** C4
Cashion Ariz., U.S.A. 33°26N 112°17W **134** C1
Cashion Okla., U.S.A. 35°48N 97°41W **107** C6
Cashmere Wash., U.S.A. 47°31N 120°28W **120** C5

Cashton Wis., U.S.A. 43°43N 90°47W **78** E3
Casimiro Castillo Jalisco, Mexico 19°38N 104°28W **174** C3
Caslan Alta., Canada 54°38N 112°31W **152** D8
Casmalia Calif., U.S.A. 34°50N 120°32W **127** J6
Casnovia Mich., U.S.A. 43°14N 85°48W **79** F6
Cason Tex., U.S.A. 33°2N 94°49W **109** D13
Casper Wyo., U.S.A. 42°51N 106°19W **124** D6
Caspian Mich., U.S.A. 46°4N 88°38W **79** C3
Caspiana La., U.S.A. 32°17N 93°33W **110** B2
Cass W. Va., U.S.A. 38°24N 79°55W **102** C5
Cass City Mich., U.S.A. 43°36N 83°11W **79** F8
Cass County ☆ Ill., U.S.A. 40°0N 90°15W **84** D3
Cass County ☆ Ind., U.S.A. 40°45N 86°20W **85** C4
Cass County ☆ Iowa, U.S.A. 41°20N 94°55W **81** D4
Cass County ☆ Mich., U.S.A. 41°50N 86°0W **79** H5
Cass County ☆ Minn., U.S.A. 47°0N 94°10W **77** D4
Cass County ☆ Mo., U.S.A. 38°40N 94°20W **83** D2
Cass County ☆ N. Dak., U.S.A. 47°0N 97°0W **76** D8
Cass County ☆ Nebr., U.S.A. 40°50N 96°10W **80** D9
Cass County ☆ Tex., U.S.A. 33°1N 94°22W **109** D13
Cass L. Minn., U.S.A. 47°27N 94°29W **77** C4
Cass Lake Minn., U.S.A. 47°23N 94°37W **77** C4
Cassadaga N.Y., U.S.A. 42°20N 79°19W **88** C1
Casselberry Fla., U.S.A. 28°41N 81°20W **114** C7
Casselman Ont., Canada 45°19N 75°5W **144** F7
Casselman Pa., U.S.A. 39°53N 79°13W **93** A1
Casselton N. Dak., U.S.A. 46°54N 97°13W **76** D8
Cassia County ☆ Idaho, U.S.A. 42°20N 113°30W **122** G5
Cassiar Mts. Canada 59°30N 130°30W **157** F4
Cassoday Kans., U.S.A. 38°3N 96°38W **82** C7
Cassopolis Mich., U.S.A. 41°55N 86°1W **79** H5
Cassville Mo., U.S.A. 36°41N 93°52W **83** E3
Cassville Pa., U.S.A. 40°18N 78°2W **87** D4
Cassville Wis., U.S.A. 42°43N 90°59W **78** F3
Castaic L. Calif., U.S.A. 34°32N 118°37W **127** J8
Castalia Iowa, U.S.A. 43°7N 91°41W **81** B7
Castalia Ohio, U.S.A. 41°24N 82°49W **86** B4
Castamay Campeche, Mexico 19°51N 90°27W **179** C3
Castana Iowa, U.S.A. 42°4N 95°55W **81** C3
Castaños Coahuila, Mexico 26°47N 101°25W **170** D3
Castella Calif., U.S.A. 41°9N 122°19W **126** B4
Castile N.Y., U.S.A. 42°38N 78°3W **88** C2
Castillo de San Marcos Nat. Monument △
  U.S.A. 29°54N 81°19W **114** B7
Castillo de Teayo Veracruz, Mexico 20°44N 97°37W **176** D3
Castle Okla., U.S.A. 35°28N 96°23W **107** C7
Castle Dale Utah, U.S.A. 39°13N 111°1W **129** D4
Castle Danger Minn., U.S.A. 47°7N 91°30W **77** C7
Castle Dome Peak Ariz., U.S.A. 33°5N 114°9W **130** D1
Castle Hayne N.C., U.S.A. 34°21N 77°54W **103** D8
Castle Hills Tex., U.S.A. 29°31N 98°30W **116** B2
Castle Mountain Alta., Canada 51°16N 115°55W **153** G5
Castle Mts. Mont., U.S.A. 46°28N 110°46W **123** D7
Castle Peak Colo., U.S.A. 39°1N 106°52W **125** D4
Castle Pk. Idaho, U.S.A. 44°1N 114°42W **122** E4
Castle Rock B.C., Canada 52°32N 122°29W **155** C12
Castle Rock Colo., U.S.A. 39°22N 104°51W **125** C6
Castle Rock S. Dak., U.S.A. 45°7N 103°25W **76** F2
Castle Rock Wash., U.S.A. 46°17N 122°54W **120** D3
Castle Rock L. Wis., U.S.A. 43°52N 89°57W **78** E4
Castle Shannon Pa., U.S.A. 40°21N 80°1W **98** B1
Castle Valley Utah, U.S.A. 38°38N 109°25W **129** E6
Castleberry Ala., U.S.A. 31°18N 87°1W **112** E3
Castleford Idaho, U.S.A. 42°31N 114°52W **122** G4
Castlegar B.C., Canada 49°20N 117°40W **155** F17
Castleton Vt., U.S.A. 43°37N 73°11W **89** C1
Castleton Corners N.Y., U.S.A. 40°36N 74°8W **97** C2
Castleton-on-Hudson N.Y., U.S.A. 42°32N 73°45W **88** C7
Castlewood S. Dak., U.S.A. 44°44N 97°2W **76** F8
Castlewood Va., U.S.A. 36°53N 82°17W **102** E2
Castolon Tex., U.S.A. 29°8N 103°31W **108** H4
Castor Alta., Canada 52°15N 111°50W **153** F9
Castor La., U.S.A. 32°15N 93°10W **110** B2
Castor → Que., Canada 53°24N 78°58W **143** C2
Castor → Mo., U.S.A. 36°51N 89°44W **83** E7
Castor Cr. → La., U.S.A. 31°47N 92°22W **110** C3
Castries St. Lucia 14°2N 60°58W **183** D7
Castro Texas, U.S.A. 41°53N 70°46W **91** C4
Castro County ☆ Tex., U.S.A. 34°33N 102°19W **108** C5
Castro Valley Calif., U.S.A. 37°41N 122°5W **126** F4
Castroville Calif., U.S.A. 36°46N 121°45W **126** G5
Castroville Tex., U.S.A. 29°21N 98°53W **109** H9
Caswell County ☆ N.C., U.S.A. 36°20N 79°15W **103** B6
Cat I. Bahamas 24°30N 75°30W **183** B4
Cat L. Miss., U.S.A. 30°14N 89°6W **111** F4
Cat L. Ont., Canada 51°40N 91°50W **148** A5
Cat Spring Tex., U.S.A. 29°51N 96°20W **109** H11
Catacamas Honduras 14°54N 85°56W **182** D2
Catahoula L. La., U.S.A. 31°31N 92°7W **110** C3
Catahoula Parish ☆ La., U.S.A. 31°35N 91°58W **110** C4
Catalina Nfld. & L., Canada 48°31N 53°4W **142** D7
Catalina Ariz., U.S.A. 32°30N 110°50W **130** E5
Cataño Puerto Rico 18°27N 66°7W **184** G16
Cataouatche, L. La., U.S.A. 29°50N 90°14W **117** C1
Cataract Ont., Canada 39°30N 86°53W **85** D4
Cataract L. Ind., U.S.A. 39°29N 86°55W **85** D4
Catarina Tex., U.S.A. 28°21N 99°37W **109** J8
Catasauqua Pa., U.S.A. 40°39N 75°29W **92** B1
Cataula Ga., U.S.A. 32°39N 84°52W **113** D2
Cataviña Baja Calif., Mexico 29°45N 114°45W **166** D4
Catawba Wis., U.S.A. 45°31N 90°55W **103** D5
Catawba → Wis., U.S.A. 45°32N 90°32W **78** C3
Catawba County ☆ N.C., U.S.A. 35°40N 81°10W **103** C4
Catawissa Pa., U.S.A. 40°57N 76°28W **87** D6
Catazajá Chiapas, Mexico 17°45N 92°1W **178** B4
Catemaco Veracruz, Mexico 18°25N 95°7W **177** F5
Catemaco, L. Veracruz, Mexico 18°23N 95°7W **177** F5
Cathay N. Dak., U.S.A. 47°33N 99°25W **76** C6
Cathcart Pt. Mich., U.S.A. 45°11N 85°37W **79** D6
Cathedral City Calif., U.S.A. 33°47N 116°28W **127** K10
Cathedral Gorge State Park △ Nev.,
  U.S.A. 37°49N 114°25W **128** E6
Cathedral Mt. Tex., U.S.A. 30°11N 103°40W **108** H4
Cathedral Park B.C., Canada 49°5N 120°0W **155** F14
Catherine Ala., U.S.A. 32°11N 87°28W **112** D3
Catherine Kans., U.S.A. 38°56N 99°13W **82** C4
Catherine, L. Fla., U.S.A. 28°31N 81°24W **115** B2
Cathlamet Wash., U.S.A. 46°12N 123°23W **120** D2
Catlettsburg Ky., U.S.A. 38°25N 82°36W **105** B10
Catlin Ill., U.S.A. 40°4N 87°42W **84** C6
Catoche, C. Quintana Roo, Mexico 21°35N 87°5W **179** A6
Catoctin Mountain Park △ Md., U.S.A. 39°39N 77°28W **93** A3
Catoctin Mt. Md., U.S.A. 39°35N 77°30W **93** A3

Catonsville Md., U.S.A. 39°16N 76°43W **99** B1
Catoosa Okla., U.S.A. 36°11N 95°45W **107** B8
Catoosa County ☆ Ga., U.S.A. 34°50N 85°10W **113** B1
Catron County ☆ N. Mex., U.S.A. 34°0N 108°15W **131** D2
Catskill N.Y., U.S.A. 42°14N 73°52W **88** C7
Catskill Mts. N.Y., U.S.A. 42°10N 74°25W **88** C6
Catskill Park △ N.Y., U.S.A. 42°8N 74°39W **88** C6
Cattaraugus N.Y., U.S.A. 42°20N 78°52W **88** C2
Cattaraugus County ☆ N.Y., U.S.A. 42°30N 78°45W **88** C2
Cattaraugus Indian Reservation N.Y.,
  U.S.A. 42°30N 79°0W **88** C2
Caubvick, Mt. = Iberville, Mt. d' Nfld. & L.,
  Canada 58°50N 63°50W **143** G12
Caucel Yucatán, Mexico 21°1N 89°43W **179** A4
Cauchy, L. Qué., Canada 50°36N 60°46W **140** C9
Caucomgomoc L. Maine, U.S.A. 46°15N 69°36W **90** B4
Caulfield B.C., Canada 49°21N 123°14W **161** A1
Causapscal Qué., Canada 48°19N 67°12W **140** E2
Causey N. Mex., U.S.A. 33°53N 103°8W **131** D7
Cauthron Ark., U.S.A. 34°55N 94°18W **106** D1
Caution C. B.C., Canada 51°10N 127°47W **154** D7
Cavalier N. Dak., U.S.A. 48°48N 97°37W **76** B8
Cavalier County ☆ N. Dak., U.S.A. 48°55N 97°30W **76** B8
Cave City Ark., U.S.A. 35°57N 91°33W **106** C4
Cave City Ky., U.S.A. 37°8N 85°58W **105** C7
Cave Creek Ariz., U.S.A. 33°50N 111°57W **130** D4
Cave in Rock Ill., U.S.A. 37°28N 88°10W **84** F5
Cave Junction Oreg., U.S.A. 42°10N 123°39W **121** E2
Cave Run L. Ky., U.S.A. 38°5N 83°25W **105** B9
Cave Spring Ga., U.S.A. 34°6N 85°20W **113** B1
Cave Spring Va., U.S.A. 37°47N 79°53W **102** D5
Cavernas del Río Camuy, Parque de las △
  Puerto Rico 18°20N 66°50W **184** G16
Cawasachouane, L. Qué., Canada 47°27N 77°45W **144** D5
Cawker City Kans., U.S.A. 39°31N 98°26W **82** B5
Cay Sal Bank Bahamas 23°45N 80°0W **182** B4
Cayacal, Pta. Michoacan, Mexico 17°53N 102°10W **174** E5
Cayce Ky., U.S.A. 36°33N 89°2W **104** D3
Cayce S.C., U.S.A. 33°58N 81°4W **103** E4
Caycuse B.C., Canada 48°53N 124°22W **154** G10
Cayey Puerto Rico 18°7N 66°10W **184** G16
Cayley Alta., Canada 50°27N 113°51W **153** H7
Cayman Brac Cayman Is. 19°43N 79°49W **182** C4
Cayman Is. ☒ W. Indies 19°40N 80°30W **182** C3
Cayman Trench Caribbean 17°0N 83°0W **182** C3
Cayucos Calif., U.S.A. 35°27N 120°54W **127** H6
Cayuga Ont., Canada 42°59N 79°50W **146** E7
Cayuga Ind., U.S.A. 39°57N 87°28W **85** D6
Cayuga N. Dak., U.S.A. 46°4N 97°23W **76** D8
Cayuga County ☆ N.Y., U.S.A. 43°0N 76°35W **88** C4
Cayuga Heights N.Y., U.S.A. 42°28N 76°30W **88** C4
Cayuga L. N.Y., U.S.A. 42°41N 76°41W **88** C4
Cayuse Oreg., U.S.A. 45°41N 118°32W **121** B7
Cazenovia N.Y., U.S.A. 42°56N 75°51W **88** C5
Cazones Veracruz, Mexico 20°43N 97°19W **176** D3
Cazones, Barra de Veracruz, Mexico 20°45N 97°10W **176** D3
Cearfoss Md., U.S.A. 39°42N 77°46W **93** A3
Cebaco, I. de Panama 7°33N 81°9W **182** E3
Ceballos Durango, Mexico 26°32N 104°9W **173** A6
Cebolla N. Mex., U.S.A. 36°32N 106°29W **131** A4
Cebolleta N. Mex., U.S.A. 35°12N 107°23W **131** B3
Cecil Ga., U.S.A. 31°3N 83°24W **113** E3
Cecil Ohio, U.S.A. 41°13N 84°36W **86** B2
Cecil Oreg., U.S.A. 45°37N 119°58W **121** B6
Cecil County ☆ Md., U.S.A. 39°30N 76°9W **93** A5
Cecil M. Harden L. Ind., U.S.A. 39°43N 87°4W **85** D3
Cecilia Ky., U.S.A. 37°40N 85°57W **105** C7
Cecilia La., U.S.A. 30°20N 91°51W **110** D4
Cecilton Md., U.S.A. 39°24N 75°52W **93** A5
Cecilville Calif., U.S.A. 41°9N 123°8W **126** B3
Cedar → Iowa, U.S.A. 41°17N 91°21W **81** D7
Cedar → Mich., U.S.A. 45°25N 87°26W **79** D4
Cedar → Nebr., U.S.A. 41°22N 97°56W **80** C8
Cedar → Wash., U.S.A. 47°30N 122°13W **120** C3
Cedar Bluff Ala., U.S.A. 34°13N 85°37W **112** B5
Cedar Bluff Res. Kans., U.S.A. 38°47N 99°43W **82** C4
Cedar Bluffs Kans., U.S.A. 39°59N 100°34W **82** B3
Cedar Bluffs Nebr., U.S.A. 41°24N 96°37W **80** C9
Cedar Breaks Nat. Monument △ Utah,
  U.S.A. 37°40N 112°50W **129** F3
Cedar Brook N.J., U.S.A. 39°43N 74°54W **92** C2
Cedar Butte S. Dak., U.S.A. 43°35N 101°1W **76** G4
Cedar City Mo., U.S.A. 38°36N 92°11W **83** D4
Cedar City Utah, U.S.A. 37°41N 113°4W **129** F2
Cedar County ☆ Iowa, U.S.A. 41°45N 91°10W **81** D7
Cedar County ☆ Mo., U.S.A. 37°45N 93°50W **83** D3
Cedar County ☆ Nebr., U.S.A. 42°40N 97°15W **80** B8
Cedar Cr. → N. Dak., U.S.A. 46°8N 101°19W **76** D4
Cedar Creek Ark., U.S.A. 34°47N 93°51W **106** D2
Cedar Creek Nebr., U.S.A. 41°2N 96°6W **80** C9
Cedar Creek Tex., U.S.A. 30°5N 97°30W **109** G10
Cedar Creek Res. Ala., U.S.A. 34°33N 87°59W **112** B3
Cedar Creek Res. Tex., U.S.A. 32°11N 96°4W **109** E11
Cedar Falls Iowa, U.S.A. 42°32N 92°27W **81** C6
Cedar Grove Fla., U.S.A. 30°10N 85°38W **114** A3
Cedar Grove Georgia, U.S.A. 33°40N 84°16W **117** C3
Cedar Grove Ind., U.S.A. 39°22N 84°56W **86** D5
Cedar Grove N.J., U.S.A. 40°51N 74°13W **97** A1
Cedar Grove W. Va., U.S.A. 38°13N 81°26W **102** C3
Cedar Grove Wis., U.S.A. 43°34N 87°49W **78** E6
Cedar Grove Res. N.J., U.S.A. 40°51N 74°12W **97** A1
Cedar Hill N. Mex., U.S.A. 36°56N 107°53W **131** A3
Cedar Hill Tenn., U.S.A. 36°33N 87°0W **104** D5
Cedar Hill Tex., U.S.A. 32°35N 96°59W **116** C4
Cedar Hill State Park △ Tex., U.S.A. 32°36N 96°59W **116** C4
Cedar Hills Oreg., U.S.A. 45°30N 122°47W **121** B3
Cedar I. N.C., U.S.A. 34°57N 76°20W **103** D9
Cedar Key Fla., U.S.A. 29°8N 83°2W **114** B5
Cedar L. Man., Canada 53°10N 100°0W **151** B11
Cedar L. Ont., Canada 46°2N 78°30W **147** B8
Cedar L. Tex., U.S.A. 32°49N 102°17W **108** E5
Cedar Lake Ind., U.S.A. 41°22N 87°26W **85** B3
Cedar Lake Minn., U.S.A. 44°57N 93°19W **94** B2
Cedar Lake Tex., U.S.A. 28°54N 95°38W **109** J12
Cedar Mills Ark., U.S.A. 44°57N 94°31W **77** F4
Cedar Mts. Utah, U.S.A. 40°10N 112°30W **129** C3
Cedar Park Ill., U.S.A. 41°38N 87°47W **95** A2
Cedar Park Tex., U.S.A. 30°30N 97°49W **109** G10
Cedar Point Kans., U.S.A. 38°16N 96°49W **82** C7
Cedar Point Nat. Wildlife Refuge △ Ohio,
  U.S.A. 41°41N 83°19W **86** B3
Cedar Point Ohio, U.S.A. 41°29N 82°41W **86** B4
Cedar Rapids Iowa, U.S.A. 41°59N 91°40W **81** D7

Cedar Rapids *Nebr., U.S.A.* 41°34N 98°9W **80 C7**
Cedar River *Mich., U.S.A.* 45°25N 87°21W **79 D4**
Cedar River Nat. Grassland *N. Dak., U.S.A.* 46°0N 101°45W **76 E4**
Cedar Springs *Mich., U.S.A.* 43°13N 85°33W **79 F6**
Cedar Vale *Kans., U.S.A.* 37°6N 96°30W **82 D7**
Cedarburg *Wis., U.S.A.* 43°18N 87°59W **78 E6**
Cedaredge *Colo., U.S.A.* 38°54N 107°56W **125 D3**
Cedarhurst *N.Y., U.S.A.* 40°37N 73°42W **97 C4**
Cedartown *Ga., U.S.A.* 34°1N 85°15W **113 B1**
Cedarvale Park *Ont., Canada* 43°42N 79°36W **161 A2**
Cedarville *Calif., U.S.A.* 41°32N 120°10W **126 B6**
Cedarville *Ill., U.S.A.* 42°23N 89°38W **84 A4**
Cedarville *Md., U.S.A.* 38°40N 76°47W **93 B4**
Cedarville *Mich., U.S.A.* 46°0N 84°22W **79 D7**
Cedarville *N.J., U.S.A.* 39°18N 75°12W **92 C1**
Cedarwood *Colo., U.S.A.* 37°57N 104°37W **125 E6**
Cedral *San Luis Potosí, Mexico* 23°50N 100°45W **171 G4**
Cedro, Cerro *Baja Calif., Mexico* 32°12N 115°59W **166 A3**
Cedros *Zacatecas, Mexico* 24°41N 101°46W **173 C9**
Cedros, I. *Baja Calif., Mexico* 28°12N 115°15W **167 E3**
Ceiba *Puerto Rico* 18°16N 65°39W **184 G17**
Celaque, Parque Nac. △ *Honduras* 14°30N 88°43W **182 D2**
Celarain, Pta. *Quintana Roo, Mexico* 20°16N 86°59W **179 D7**
Celaya *Guanajuato, Mexico* 20°31N 100°37W **175 B7**
Celerain *Quintana Roo, Mexico* 20°18N 86°58W **179 B7**
Celeste *Tex., U.S.A.* 33°18N 96°12W **109 D11**
Celestún *Yucatán, Mexico* 20°52N 90°24W **179 B3**
Celestún, Estero *Yucatán, Mexico* 20°58N 90°22W **179 B3**
Celina *Ohio, U.S.A.* 40°33N 84°35W **86 C2**
Celina *Tenn., U.S.A.* 36°33N 85°30W **105 D7**
Celina *Tex., U.S.A.* 33°19N 96°47W **109 D11**
Cement *Okla., U.S.A.* 34°56N 98°8W **107 D5**
Cenotillo *Yucatán, Mexico* 20°58N 88°37W **179 B5**
Centennial *Colo., U.S.A.* 39°34N 104°52W **134 C3**
Centennial *Wyo., U.S.A.* 41°18N 106°8W **124 E6**
Centennial Mts. *Idaho, U.S.A.* 44°35N 111°55W **122 E7**
Centennial Olympic Park *Georgia, U.S.A.* 33°46N 84°23W **117 B2**
Centennial Wash → *Ariz., U.S.A.* 33°17N 112°48W **130 D3**
Center *Colo., U.S.A.* 37°45N 106°6W **125 E4**
Center *Ga., U.S.A.* 34°3N 83°25W **113 B3**
Center *Mo., U.S.A.* 39°30N 91°32W **83 B5**
Center *N. Dak., U.S.A.* 47°7N 101°18W **76 C4**
Center *Nebr., U.S.A.* 42°37N 97°53W **80 B8**
Center *Tex., U.S.A.* 31°48N 94°11W **109 F13**
Center Barnstead *N.H., U.S.A.* 43°19N 71°15W **89 C3**
Center City *Minn., U.S.A.* 45°24N 92°49W **77 E6**
Center Cross *Va., U.S.A.* 37°48N 76°47W **93 C4**
Center Harbor *N.H., U.S.A.* 43°42N 71°27W **89 C3**
Center Hill *Fla., U.S.A.* 28°38N 82°3W **114 C6**
Center Hill *Georgia, U.S.A.* 33°46N 84°29W **117 B2**
Center Hill L. *Tenn., U.S.A.* 36°6N 85°50W **105 D7**
Center Line *Mich., U.S.A.* 42°29N 83°1W **98 A2**
Center Ossipee *N.H., U.S.A.* 43°45N 71°9W **89 C3**
Center Point *Ala., U.S.A.* 33°38N 86°41W **112 C4**
Center Point *Ind., U.S.A.* 39°25N 87°4W **85 D3**
Center Point *Iowa, U.S.A.* 42°12N 91°46W **81 C7**
Center Point *La., U.S.A.* 31°15N 92°13W **110 C3**
Center Point *Tex., U.S.A.* 29°57N 99°2W **109 H8**
Center Sandwich *N.H., U.S.A.* 43°39N 71°25W **89 C3**
Center Strafford *N.H., U.S.A.* 43°17N 71°10W **89 C3**
Center Valley *Pa., U.S.A.* 40°32N 75°24W **92 B1**
Centerburg *Ohio, U.S.A.* 40°18N 82°42W **86 C4**
Centereach *N.Y., U.S.A.* 40°52N 73°6W **91 D1**
Centerfield *Utah, U.S.A.* 39°8N 111°49W **129 D4**
Centertown *Ky., U.S.A.* 37°25N 86°59W **104 C6**
Centertown *Mo., U.S.A.* 38°38N 92°25W **83 C4**
Centertown *Tenn., U.S.A.* 35°44N 85°55W **105 E7**
Centerville *Ark., U.S.A.* 35°7N 93°10W **106 C2**
Centerville *Calif., U.S.A.* 36°44N 119°30W **127 G7**
Centerville *Del., U.S.A.* 39°49N 75°37W **93 A5**
Centerville *Idaho, U.S.A.* 43°55N 115°53W **122 F3**
Centerville *Ind., U.S.A.* 39°49N 85°0W **85 D6**
Centerville *Iowa, U.S.A.* 40°44N 92°52W **81 E61**
Centerville *Kans., U.S.A.* 38°13N 95°1W **82 C8**
Centerville *La., U.S.A.* 29°46N 91°26W **110 E4**
Centerville *Mo., U.S.A.* 37°26N 90°58W **83 D6**
Centerville *N.Y., U.S.A.* 42°29N 78°15W **88 C2**
Centerville *Ohio, U.S.A.* 39°38N 84°8W **86 D2**
Centerville *Pa., U.S.A.* 41°44N 79°46W **87 C3**
Centerville *Pa., U.S.A.* 40°3N 79°59W **87 D3**
Centerville *Pa., U.S.A.* 39°50N 78°39W **93 A2**
Centerville *S.C., U.S.A.* 34°32N 82°42W **103 D3**
Centerville *S. Dak., U.S.A.* 43°7N 96°58W **76 G9**
Centerville *Tenn., U.S.A.* 35°47N 87°28W **104 E5**
Centerville *Tex., U.S.A.* 31°16N 95°59W **109 F12**
Centerville *Utah, U.S.A.* 40°55N 111°52W **134 A2**
Centinela, Picacho del *Coahuila, Mexico* 29°14N 102°32W **170 A2**
Centrahoma *Okla., U.S.A.* 34°37N 96°21W **107 D7**
Central *Alaska, U.S.A.* 65°35N 144°48W **135 D11**
Central *S.C., U.S.A.* 34°44N 82°47W **103 D3**
Central *Utah, U.S.A.* 37°25N 113°38W **129 F2**
Central, Cordillera *Costa Rica* 10°10N 84°5W **182 D3**
Central, Cordillera *Dom. Rep.* 19°15N 71°0W **183 C5**
Central, Cordillera *Puerto Rico* 18°8N 66°35W **184 G16**
Central, Gare *Montréal, Canada* **160 c2**
Central Butte *Sask., Canada* 50°48N 106°31W **150 E5**
Central City *Colo., U.S.A.* 39°48N 105°31W **125 C5**
Central City *Ill., U.S.A.* 38°33N 89°8W **84 E4**
Central City *Iowa, U.S.A.* 42°12N 91°32W **81 C7**
Central City *Ky., U.S.A.* 37°18N 87°7W **104 C5**
Central City *Nebr., U.S.A.* 41°7N 98°0W **80 C8**
Central City *Pa., U.S.A.* 40°7N 78°49W **87 D4**
Central City *S. Dak., U.S.A.* 44°22N 103°46W **76 F2**
Central Falls *R.I., U.S.A.* 41°54N 71°23W **91 C3**
Central Fournier *Tabasco, Mexico* 17°52N 93°53W **178 B3**
Central Islip *N.Y., U.S.A.* 40°47N 73°12W **92 B3**
Central Lake *Mich., U.S.A.* 45°4N 85°16W **79 D6**
Central Park *B.C., Canada* 49°13N 123°1W **161 B2**
Central Park *Minn., U.S.A.* 45°1N 93°7W **94 A3**
96 a3
Central Park *New York, U.S.A.*
Central Park *Wash., U.S.A.* 46°58N 123°41W **120 D2**
Central Patricia *Ont., Canada* 51°30N 90°9W **148 A6**
Central Point *Oreg., U.S.A.* 42°23N 122°55W **121 E3**
Central Saanich *B.C., Canada* 48°34N 123°24W **155 G11**
Central Square *N.Y., U.S.A.* 43°17N 76°9W **88 B4**
Centralhatchee *Ga., U.S.A.* 33°22N 85°6W **113 C1**
Centralia *Ill., U.S.A.* 38°32N 89°8W **84 E4**
Centralia *Kans., U.S.A.* 39°44N 96°8W **82 B7**
Centralia *Mo., U.S.A.* 39°13N 92°8W **83 B4**
Centralia *Okla., U.S.A.* 36°48N 95°21W **107 B8**
Centralia *Wash., U.S.A.* 46°43N 122°58W **120 D3**
Centre *Ala., U.S.A.* 34°9N 85°41W **112 B5**
Centre County ☆ *Pa., U.S.A.* 41°0N 78°0W **87 D5**
Centre Grove *N.J., U.S.A.* 39°20N 75°8W **92 C1**
Centreville *N.B., Canada* 46°26N 67°43W **141 G2**
Centreville *N.S., Canada* 45°8N 64°32W **141 H5**
Centreville *Ala., U.S.A.* 32°57N 87°8W **112 D3**
Centreville *Ill., U.S.A.* 38°34N 90°7W **94 B3**
Centreville *Ind., U.S.A.* 39°3N 76°4W **93 A4**
Centreville *Md., U.S.A.* 41°55N 85°32W **79 H6**
Centreville *Mich., U.S.A.* 31°5N 91°4W **111 E2**
Centreville *Miss., U.S.A.* 38°50N 77°26W **93 B3**
Centreville *Va., U.S.A.*
Centreville-Wareham-Trinity *Nfld. & L., Canada* 48°59N 53°59W **142 D7**
Centro *Fla., U.S.A.* 30°58N 87°6W **114 A1**
Century *Fla., U.S.A.* 27°43N 103°21W **170 C1**
Cenzontle *Coahuila, Mexico* 35°30N 114°0W **130 D3**
Cerab Mts. *Ariz., U.S.A.* 37°35N 120°57W **126 F6**
Cereal *Alta., Canada* 51°25N 110°48W **153 G10**
Ceres *Calif., U.S.A.* 36°39N 87°8W **112 B3**
Ceresco *Nebr., U.S.A.* 41°3N 96°39W **80 C9**
Cereze Canyon *N. Mex., U.S.A.* 36°39N 107°42W **131 A4**
Cerf, L. de *Qué., Canada* 46°16N 75°30W **144 E7**
Cero del Pez, L. *San Luis Potosí, Mexico* 22°6N 98°28W **171 H6**
Cerralvo *Nuevo León, Mexico* 26°6N 99°37W **170 D5**
Cerralvo, Canal *Baja Calif. S., Mexico* 24°12N 111°0W **167 J9**
Cerralvo, I. *Baja Calif. S., Mexico* 24°15N 109°55W **167 J9**
Cerrillos *N. Mex., U.S.A.* 35°26N 106°8W **131 B4**
Cerritos *San Luis Potosí, Mexico* 22°25N 100°16W **171 H4**
Cerritos de Bernal *San Luis Potosí, Mexico* 23°23N 101°30W **171 G3**
Cerro Azul *Veracruz, Mexico* 21°12N 97°44W **176 C3**
Cerro Cofre de Perote, Parque Nacional △ *Mexico* 19°29N 97°8W **176 E3**
Cerro Colorado *Sonora, Mexico* 26°45N 108°50W **168 G7**
Cerro de la Estrella, Parque Nacional △ *Distrito Federal, Mexico* 19°23N 99°5W **181 B3**
Cerro de Ortega *Colima, Mexico* 18°44N 103°43W **174 D4**
Cerro de San Pedro *San Luis Potosí, Mexico* 22°3N 100°44W **171 H4**
Cerro del Pez, L. *Veracruz, Mexico* 22°6N 98°18W **176 B2**
Cerro Gordo *San Luis Potosí, Mexico* 21°59N 100°48W **171 J4**
Cerro Gordo *Ill., U.S.A.* 39°53N 88°44W **84 D5**
Cerro Gordo County ☆ *Iowa, U.S.A.* 43°5N 93°15W **81 B5**
Cerro Hoya, Parque Nac. △ *Panamá* 7°17N 80°45W **182 E3**
Cerro Mojarra *Oaxaca, Mexico* 18°24N 96°35W **177 F4**
Cerro Nanchital *Veracruz, Mexico* 17°30N 94°9W **177 G6**
Cerro Prieto *Chihuahua, Mexico* 28°14N 107°9W **169 E8**
Cerro Prieto *Durango, Mexico* 26°20N 106°13W **172 A4**
Cerro Prieto *San Luis Potosí, Mexico* 22°13N 101°17W **171 H3**
Cerro Vista Peak *N. Mex., U.S.A.* 36°14N 105°25W **131 A5**
Cerros Blancos *Nuevo León, Mexico* 23°21N 100°11W **171 G2**
Cesar Creek L. *Ohio, U.S.A.* 39°29N 84°3W **86 D2**
Ceylon *Sask., Canada* 49°27N 104°36W **150 F7**
Ceylon *Minn., U.S.A.* 43°32N 94°38W **77 G4**
Chaati I. *B.C., Canada* 53°7N 132°30W **154 B2**
Chablé *Tabasco, Mexico* 17°51N 91°46W **178 B5**
Chacaltianguis *Veracruz, Mexico* 18°18N 95°51W **177 F5**
Chacana *Campeche, Mexico* 18°29N 89°30W **179 D4**
Chackbay *La., U.S.A.* 29°53N 90°48W **110 E5**
Chacmultún *Yucatán, Mexico* 20°8N 89°20W **179 B4**
Chaco *Nuevo León, Mexico* 26°34N 108°39W **131 A2**
Chaco Canyon Nat. Monument △ *N. Mex., U.S.A.* 36°6N 108°0W **131 A3**
Chaco Culture Nat. Historical Park △ *U.S.A.* 36°3N 107°58W **131 A3**
Chacuaco → *Colo., U.S.A.* 37°34N 103°38W **125 E7**
Chadbourn *N.C., U.S.A.* 34°19N 78°50W **103 D7**
Chadron *Nebr., U.S.A.* 42°50N 103°0W **80 B3**
Chadwick *Ill., U.S.A.* 42°1N 89°53W **84 A4**
Chaffee *Mo., U.S.A.* 37°11N 89°40W **83 D7**
Chaffee *N. Dak., U.S.A.* 46°46N 97°21W **76 D8**
Chaffee County ☆ *Colo., U.S.A.* 38°45N 106°10W **125 D4**
Chahuites *Oaxaca, Mexico* 16°17N 94°11W **177 H6**
Chain of Lakes Regional Park △ *Minn., U.S.A.* 44°56N 93°19W **94 B2**
Chairel, L. *Veracruz, Mexico* 22°19N 98°11W **176 B2**
Chaires *Fla., U.S.A.* 30°26N 84°7W **114 A4**
Chakmochuk, L. *Quintana Roo, Mexico* 21°20N 86°50W **179 A7**
Chakonipau, L. *Qué., Canada* 56°18N 68°30W **143 B4**
Chal, I. *Quintana Roo, Mexico* 19°20N 87°30W **179 C6**
Chal-Tuni *Campeche, Mexico* 19°15N 89°57W **179 C4**
Chalan Kanoa *N. Marianas* 15°N ·45°42E **184 c**
Chalchihuites *Zacatecas, Mexico* 23°29N 103°53W **173 D7**
Chalco *México, Mexico* 19°15N 98°54W **175 B8**
Chaleur B. *N.B., Canada* 47°55N 65°30W **141 F4**
Chalfant *Pa., U.S.A.* 40°24N 79°50W **98 A5**
Chalk Mts. *Tex., U.S.A.* 29°30N 103°18W **108 H4**
Chalk River *Ont., Canada* 46°1N 77°27W **147 A9**
Chalkyitsik *Alaska, U.S.A.* 66°39N 143°43W **135 C12**
Challis *Idaho, U.S.A.* 44°30N 114°14W **122 E4**
Challis Nat. Forest *Idaho, U.S.A.* 44°0N 113°40W **122 E5**
Chalmers *Ind., U.S.A.* 40°40N 86°52W **85 C4**
Chalmette *La., U.S.A.* 29°56N 89°57W **117 C3**
Chama *Colo., U.S.A.* 37°10N 105°23W **125 E5**
Chama *N. Mex., U.S.A.* 36°54N 106°35W **131 A4**
Chama → *N. Mex., U.S.A.* 36°10N 106°10W **131 A4**
Chamberino *N. Mex., U.S.A.* 32°3N 106°41W **131 E4**
Chamberlain *S. Dak., U.S.A.* 43°49N 99°20W **76 G6**
Chamberlain L. *Maine, U.S.A.* 46°14N 69°19W **90 B4**
Chambers *Ariz., U.S.A.* 35°11N 109°26W **130 B6**
Chambers *Nebr., U.S.A.* 42°12N 98°45W **80 B7**
Chambers County ☆ *Ala., U.S.A.* 32°54N 85°24W **112 D5**
Chambers County ☆ *Tex., U.S.A.* 29°47N 94°35W **109 H13**
Chambers I. *Wis., U.S.A.* 45°11N 87°22W **78 C6**
Chambersburg *Pa., U.S.A.* 39°56N 77°40W **87 E5**
Chamblee *Ga., U.S.A.* 33°53N 84°18W **113 C2**
Chambly *Qué., Canada* 45°27N 73°17W **145 F9**
Chambord *Qué., Canada* 48°25N 72°6W **145 C10**
Chamela *Jalisco, Mexico* 19°32N '05°6W **174 C2**
Chamela, B. *Jalisco, Mexico* 19°33N '05°6W **174 C2**
Chamisal *N. Mex., U.S.A.* 36°10N 105°44W **131 A5**
Chamois *Mo., U.S.A.* 38°41N 91°46W **83 C5**
Chamokane Cr. → *Wash., U.S.A.* 47°51N 117°51W **120 C5**
Champaign *Ill., U.S.A.* 40°7N 88°15W **84 C5**
Champaign County ☆ *Ill., U.S.A.* 40°10N 88°10W **84 C5**
Champaign County ☆ *Ohio, U.S.A.* 40°7N 83°45W **86 C3**
Champdoré, L. *Qué., Canada* 55°55N 65°49W **143 B4**
Champion *Alta., Canada* 50°14N 113°9W **153 H7**
Champion *Mich., U.S.A.* 46°31N 87°58W **79 C4**
Champion *Ohio, U.S.A.* 41°19N 80°51W **86 B6**
Champion Creek Res. *Tex., U.S.A.* 32°17N 100°52W **108 E7**
Champlain *N.Y., U.S.A.* 44°59N 73°27W **89 B1**
Champlain, L. *N.Y., U.S.A.* 44°40N 73°20W **89 B1**
Champlain, Pont *Qué., Canada* 45°28N 73°31W **160 B3**
Champlain Canal *N.Y., U.S.A.* 43°30N 73°27W **89 C1**
Champneuf *Qué., Canada* 48°35N 77°30W **144 C5**
Champotón *Campeche, Mexico* 19°21N 90°43W **179 C3**
Chamula *Chiapas, Mexico* 16°47N 92°41W **178 B4**
Chanal *Chiapas, Mexico* 16°43N 92°15W **178 C4**
Chance Harbour *N.B., Canada* 45°7N 66°21W **141 H3**
Chancellor *S. Dak., U.S.A.* 43°22N 96°59W **76 G9**
Chandalar → *Alaska, U.S.A.* 66°37N 146°0W **135 C11**
Chandeleur Is. *La., U.S.A.* 29°55N 88°57W **110 E7**
Chandeleur Sd. *La., U.S.A.* 29°55N 89°0W **110 E6**
Chandler *Qué., Canada* 48°18N 64°46W **140 E5**
Chandler *Ariz., U.S.A.* 33°18N 111°50W **130 D4**
Chandler *Ind., U.S.A.* 38°3N 87°22W **85 E3**
Chandler *Minn., U.S.A.* 43°56N 95°57W **77 G3**
Chandler *Okla., U.S.A.* 35°42N 96°53W **107 C7**
Chandler *Tex., U.S.A.* 32°18N 95°29W **109 E12**
Chandlerville *Ill., U.S.A.* 40°3N 90°9W **84 C3**
Chaneysville *Pa., U.S.A.* 39°49N 78°29W **93 A2**
Change Islands *Nfld. & L., Canada* 49°40N 54°25W **142 C6**
Chanhassen *Minn., U.S.A.* 44°55N 93°32W **77 F5**
Chankom *Yucatán, Mexico* 20°33N 88°31W **179 B5**
Channahon *Ill., U.S.A.* 41°26N 88°14W **84 B5**
Channel Is. *Calif., U.S.A.* 33°40N 119°15W **127 K7**
Channel Islands Nat. Park △ *Calif., U.S.A.* 34°0N 119°24W **127 K7**
Channel-Port aux Basques *Nfld. & L., Canada* 47°30N 59°9W **142 E1**
Channelview *Tex., U.S.A.* 29°47N 95°8W **109 H12**
Channing *Mich., U.S.A.* 46°9N 88°5W **79 C3**
Channing *Tex., U.S.A.* 35°41N 102°20W **108 B5**
Chantilly *Va., U.S.A.* 38°54N 77°26W **93 B3**
Chantrey Inlet *Nunavut, Canada* 67°48N 96°20W **158 D6**
Chanute *Kans., U.S.A.* 37°41N 95°27W **82 D8**
Chapais *Qué., Canada* 49°47N 74°51W **144 B8**
Chapala *Baja Calif., Mexico* 29°24N 114°22W **166 D4**
Chapala *Jalisco, Mexico* 20°18N 103°12W **174 B4**
Chapala, L. de *Jalisco, Mexico* 20°15N 103°0W **174 B4**
Chapalilla *Nayarit, Mexico* 21°10N 104°38W **172 F6**
Chapantongo *Hidalgo, Mexico* 20°17N 99°25W **175 B8**
Chaparral *N. Mex., U.S.A.* 32°4N 106°25W **131 E4**
Chapeau *Qué., Canada* 45°54N 77°4W **144 F5**
Chapel Hill *N.C., U.S.A.* 35°55N 79°4W **103 C6**
Chapel Hill *Tenn., U.S.A.* 35°38N 86°41W **104 E6**
Chapin = Edinburg *Tex., U.S.A.* 26°18N 98°10W **108 L9**
Chapin *Ill., U.S.A.* 39°46N 90°24W **84 D3**
Chapin *S.C., U.S.A.* 34°10N 81°21W **103 D4**
Chapleau *Ont., Canada* 47°50N 83°24W **149 E13**
Chaplin *Sask., Canada* 50°28N 106°40W **150 E5**
Chaplin *Ky., U.S.A.* 37°54N 85°13W **105 C7**
Chaplin L. *Sask., Canada* 50°22N 106°36W **150 E5**
Chapman *Alc., U.S.A.* 31°40N 86°43W **112 E4**
Chapman *Kans., U.S.A.* 38°58N 97°1W **82 C6**
Chapman *Nebr., U.S.A.* 41°2N 98°10W **80 C7**
Chapman, Mt. *B.C., Canada* 51°56N 118°20W **155 D16**
Chapman C. *Nunavut, Canada* 69°17N 89°5W **158 D8**
Chapmanville *W. Va., U.S.A.* 37°59N 82°1W **102 D2**
Chappaquiddick Island *Mass., U.S.A.* 41°22N 70°30W **91 C4**
Chappell *Nebr., U.S.A.* 41°6N 102°28W **80 C3**
Chappell Hill *Tex., U.S.A.* 30°9N 96°15W **109 G11**
Chaptico *Md., U.S.A.* 38°21N 76°49W **93 B4**
Chapulhuacán *Hidalgo, Mexico* 21°10N 98°54W **175 A9**
Chapultenango *Chiapas, Mexico* 17°19N 93°7W **178 B3**
Chapultepec, Bosque de *Distrito Federal, Mexico* 19°25N 99°11W **181 B2**
Chapultepec, Castillo de *Distrito Federal, Mexico* 19°25N 99°10W **181 B2**
Charapan *Michoacan, Mexico* 19°37N 102°14W **174 C5**
Charay *Sinaloa, Mexico* 26°1N 108°50W **172 A2**
Charcas *San Luis Potosí, Mexico* 23°8N 101°7W **171 G3**
Charco *Tex., U.S.A.* 28°44N 97°37W **109 J10**
Charcos de Risa *Coahuila, Mexico* 26°11N 103°7W **170 D1**
Chardon *Ohio, U.S.A.* 41°35N 81°12W **86 B5**
Charenton *La., U.S.A.* 29°53N 91°32W **110 E4**
Charing *Ga., U.S.A.* 32°28N 84°22W **113 D2**
Chariton *Mo., U.S.A.* 41°1N 93°19W **81 D5**
Chariton → *Mo., U.S.A.* 39°19N 92°58W **83 B41**
Chariton County ☆ *Mo., U.S.A.* 39°30N 93°0W **83 B4**
Charity *Ga., U.S.A.* 37°31N 93°1W **83 D3**
Charity I. *Mich., U.S.A.* 44°2N 83°26W **79 E8**
Charlack *Mo., U.S.A.* 38°42N 90°20W **94 A1**
Charleroi *Pa., U.S.A.* 40°9N 79°57W **87 D3**
Charles → *Mass., U.S.A.* 42°22N 71°3W **91 B3**
Charles, C. *Va., U.S.A.* 37°7N 75°58W **102 D9**
Charles City *Iowa, U.S.A.* 43°4N 92°41W **81 B6**
Charles City *Va., U.S.A.* 37°21N 77°4W **102 D7**
Charles City County ☆ *Va., U.S.A.* 37°21N 77°4W **102 D7**
Charles Gates Dawes House *Ill., U.S.A.* 42°2N 87°40W **95 A2**
Charles I. *Nunavut, Canada* 62°39N 74°15W **159 E11**
Charles Mill L. *Ohio, U.S.A.* 40°45N 82°22W **86 C4**
Charles Mix County ☆ *S. Dak., U.S.A.* 43°15N 98°42W **76 G7**
Charles Mound *Ill., U.S.A.* 42°30N 90°14W **84 A3**
Charles Town *W. Va., U.S.A.* 39°17N 77°52W **93 A3**
Charlesbourg *Qué., Canada* 46°51N 71°16W **145 E11**
Charleston *Ark., U.S.A.* 35°18N 94°5W **106 C1**
Charleston *Ill., U.S.A.* 39°30N 88°10W **84 D5**
Charleston *Miss., U.S.A.* 34°1N 90°4W **111 B3**
Charleston *Mo., U.S.A.* 36°55N 89°21W **83 E7**
Charleston *N.Y., U.S.A.* 40°32N 74°14W **97 C1**
Charleston *Oreg., U.S.A.* 43°20N 124°20W **121 D1**
Charleston *S.C., U.S.A.* 32°46N 79°56W **103 F6**
Charleston *Tenn., U.S.A.* 35°17N 84°45W **105 E8**
Charleston *Utah, U.S.A.* 40°28N 111°28W **134 B4**
Charleston *W. Va., U.S.A.* 38°21N 81°38W **102 C3**
Charleston County ☆ *S.C., U.S.A.* 32°50N 80°0W **103 F5**
Charleston Int. ✕ (CHS) *S.C., U.S.A.* 32°54N 80°2W **103 F5**
Charleston L. *Ont., Canada* 44°32N 76°0W **147 C10**
Charleston Peak *Nev., U.S.A.* 36°16N 115°42W **128 F5**
Charlestown *Ind., U.S.A.* 38°27N 85°40W **85 E5**
Charlestown *Mass., U.S.A.* 42°22N 71°4W **96 A2**
Charlestown *Md., U.S.A.* 39°35N 75°59W **93 A5**
Charlestown *N.H., U.S.A.* 43°14N 72°25W **89 C2**
Charlestown *R.I., U.S.A.* 41°23N 71°45W **91 C3**
Charlevoix *Mich., U.S.A.* 45°19N 85°16W **79 D6**
Charlevoix, L. *Mich., U.S.A.* 45°16N 85°9W **79 D6**
Charlevoix County ☆ *Mich., U.S.A.* 45°19N 85°7W **79 D6**
Charlo *N.B., Canada* 47°59N 66°17W **141 F3**
Charlo *Mont., U.S.A.* 47°26N 114°10W **123 C3**
Charlotte *Iowa, U.S.A.* 41°58N 90°28W **81 D8**
Charlotte *Mich., U.S.A.* 42°34N 84°50W **79 G7**
Charlotte *N.C., U.S.A.* 35°13N 80°50W **103 C5**
Charlotte *Tenn., U.S.A.* 36°11N 87°21W **104 D5**
Charlotte *Tex., U.S.A.* 28°52N 98°43W **109 J9**
Charlotte *Vt., U.S.A.* 44°19N 73°16W **89 B1**
Charlotte Amalie *U.S. Virgin Is.* 18°21N 64°56W **184 G18**
Charlotte County ☆ *Fla., U.S.A.* 26°50N 82°0W **114 E7**
Charlotte County ☆ *Va., U.S.A.* 37°0N 78°55W **102 D6**
Charlotte Court House *Va., U.S.A.* 37°3N 78°39W **102 D6**
Charlotte-Douglas Int. ✕ (CLT) *N.C., U.S.A.* 35°12N 80°56W **103 C5**
Charlotte Hall *Md., U.S.A.* 38°28N 76°45W **93 B4**
Charlotte Harbor *Fla., U.S.A.* 26°57N 82°4W **114 E6**
Charlotte, L. *N.S., Canada* 52°12N 125°19W **154 C9**
Charlottesville *Va., U.S.A.* 38°2N 78°30W **102 C6**
Charlottetown *P.E.I., Canada* 46°14N 63°8W **141 G6**
Charlton *Mass., U.S.A.* 42°8N 71°58W **91 B3**
Charlton County ☆ *Ga., U.S.A.* 30°50N 82°10W **113 F4**
Charlton I. *N.W.T., Canada* 52°0N 79°20W **143 C2**
Charny *Qué., Canada* 46°43N 71°15W **145 E11**
Charo *Michoacan, Mexico* 19°45N 101°3W **175 C6**
Charron L. *Man., Canada* 52°44N 95°15W **151 C4**
Charter Oak *Iowa, U.S.A.* 42°4N 95°36W **81 C3**
Chase *B.C., Canada* 50°50N 119°41W **155 E15**
Chase *Ala., U.S.A.* 34°47N 86°33W **112 B4**
Chase *Kans., U.S.A.* 38°21N 98°21W **82 C5**
Chase *Md., U.S.A.* 39°22N 76°22W **93 A4**
Chase, L. *Fla., U.S.A.* 28°28N 81°31W **115 B1**
Chase City *Va., U.S.A.* 36°48N 78°28W **102 E6**
Chase County ☆ *Kans., U.S.A.* 38°15N 96°45W **82 C7**
Chase County ☆ *Nebr., U.S.A.* 40°30N 101°40W **80 D4**
Chaseburg *Wis., U.S.A.* 43°40N 91°6W **78 E2**
Chaseley *N. Dak., U.S.A.* 47°27N 99°49W **76 C6**
Chaska *Minn., U.S.A.* 44°47N 93°36W **77 F5**
Chasm *B.C., Canada* 51°13N 121°30W **155 D13**
Chassahowitzka *Fla., U.S.A.* 28°43N 82°34W **114 C6**
Chataignier *La., U.S.A.* 30°34N 92°19W **110 D3**
Chatanika *Alaska, U.S.A.* 65°7N 147°28W **135 D11**
Château-Richer *Qué., Canada* 46°58N 71°1W **145 E11**
Chateaugay *N.Y., U.S.A.* 44°56N 74°5W **88 A6**
Châteauguay *Qué., Canada* 45°23N 73°45W **145 F9**
Châteauguay, L. *Qué., Canada* 56°26N 70°3W **143 B3**
Châteauvert, L. *Qué., Canada* 47°39N 73°56W **145 D9**
Chatfield *Ark., U.S.A.* 35°0N 90°24W **106 C3**
Chatfield *Minn., U.S.A.* 43°51N 92°11W **77 G6**
Chatfield *Ohio, U.S.A.* 40°57N 82°57W **86 C4**
Chatfield State Park △ *Colo., U.S.A.* 39°32N 105°4W **134 C1**
Chatham = Chatham-Kent *Ont., Canada* 42°24N 82°11W **146 E4**
Chatham = Miramichi *N.B., Canada* 47°2N 65°28W **141 F4**
Chatham *Ill., U.S.A.* 39°40N 89°42W **84 D4**
Chatham *La., U.S.A.* 41°45N 87°36W **95 C3**
Chatham *La., U.S.A.* 32°18N 92°27W **110 B3**
Chatham *Mass., U.S.A.* 41°41N 69°58W **91 C5**
Chatham *N.J., U.S.A.* 46°21N 86°56W **79 C5**
Chatham *N.J., U.S.A.* 40°44N 74°23W **92 B2**
Chatham *N.Y., U.S.A.* 42°21N 73°36W **91 B1**
Chatham *Va., U.S.A.* 39°51N 75°49W **93 A5**
Chatham County ☆ *Ga., U.S.A.* 36°50N 79°24W **102 E5**
Chatham County ☆ *N.C., U.S.A.* 32°0N 81°10W **113 E5**
Chatham Head *N.B., Canada* 35°45N 79°10W **103 C6**
Chatham-Kent *Ont., Canada* 47°0N 65°33W **141 G4**
Chatham L. *Tenn., U.S.A.* 42°24N 82°11W **146 E4**
Chatom *Ala., U.S.A.* 36°19N 87°13W **104 D5**
Chats, L. des *Ont., Canada* 31°28N 88°16W **112 E2**
Chatsworth *Ont., Canada* 45°30N 76°20W **144 F6**
Chatsworth *Ga., U.S.A.* 44°27N 80°54W **146 C6**
Chatsworth *Ill., U.S.A.* 34°46N 84°46W **113 B2**
Chatsworth *Iowa, U.S.A.* 40°45N 88°18W **84 C5**
Chatsworth *N.J., U.S.A.* 42°55N 96°31W **81 C2**
Chattahoochee *Fla., U.S.A.* 39°49N 74°32W **92 C2**
Chattahoochee → *Ga., U.S.A.* 30°42N 84°51W **114 A4**
Chattahoochee County ☆ *Ga., U.S.A.* 30°54N 84°57W **113 F2**
Chattahoochee Nat. Forest *Ga., U.S.A.* 32°20N 84°50W **113 D2**
Chattanooga *Okla., U.S.A.* 34°50N 84°0W **113 B3**
Chattanooga *Tenn., U.S.A.* 34°25N 98°39W **107 D5**
Chattaroy *Wash., U.S.A.* 35°3N 85°19W **105 E8**
Chattolanee *Baltimore, U.S.A.* 47°53N 117°21W **120 C8**
Chattooga County ☆ *Ga., U.S.A.* 39°24N 76°44W **99 A1**
Chattuga L. *U.S.A.* 34°30N 85°24W **113 B1**
Chaudière → *Qué., Canada* 34°30N 83°40W **113 A3**
Chaumont *N.Y., U.S.A.* 46°45N 71°17W **145 E11**
Chauncey *Ohio, U.S.A.* 44°4N 76°8W **88 A4**
Chautauqua *Kans., U.S.A.* 39°24N 82°8W **86 D4**
Chautauqua County ☆ *Kans., U.S.A.* 37°1N 96°11W **82 D7**
Chautauqua County ☆ *N.Y., U.S.A.* 37°15N 96°15W **82 D7**
Chautauquan Nat. Wildlife Refuge △ *Ill., U.S.A.* 42°10N 79°24W **88 C1**
Chauvin *Alta., Canada* 40°23N 89°59W **84 C4**
Chauvin *La., U.S.A.* 52°45N 110°10W **153 F10**
Chaves County ☆ *N. Mex., U.S.A.* 29°26N 90°36W **110 E5**
Chavies *Ky., U.S.A.* 33°15N 104°30W **131 D6**
Chavigny, L. *Qué., Canada* 37°21N 83°21W **105 C9**
Chazy *N.Y., U.S.A.* 58°12N 75°8W **143 B2**
Cheaha Mt. *Ala., U.S.A.* 44°53N 73°26W **89 B1**
Cheat Bridge *W. Va., U.S.A.* 33°29N 85°49W **112 C5**
Cheatham County ☆ *Tenn., U.S.A.* 38°37N 79°52W **102 C5**
Chebanse *Ill., U.S.A.* 36°17N 87°4W **104 D5**
Cheboygan *Mich., U.S.A.* 41°0N 87°54W **84 C6**
Cheboygan County ☆ *Mich., U.S.A.* 45°39N 84°29W **79 D7**
Check *Va., U.S.A.* 45°20N 84°30W **79 D7**
Checleset B. *B.C., Canada* 37°2N 80°10W **102 D4**
Checotah *Okla., U.S.A.* 50°5N 127°35W **154 E7**
Chedabucto B. *N.S., Canada* 35°28N 95°31W **107 C8**
Cheektowaga *N.Y., U.S.A.* 45°25N 61°8W **141 H8**
Cheepash → *Ont., Canada* 42°54N 78°45W **88 C2**
Cheepay → *Ont., Canada* 51°38N 80°59W **149 A16**
Cheeseman L. *Ont., Canada* 51°25N 83°26W **149 A13**
Chef, R. du → *Qué., Canada* 49°2N 73°25W **145 B9**
Chefornak *Alaska, U.S.A.* 49°21N 76°30W **144 B6**
Chehalis *Wash., U.S.A.* 60°13N 164°12W **135 F6**
Chehalis → *Wash., U.S.A.* 46°40N 122°58W **120 D3**
Chehalis Indian Reservation *Wash., U.S.A.* 46°57N 123°50W **120 D2**
Chekubul *Campeche, Mexico* 46°49N 123°12W **120 D2**
Chelan *Wash., U.S.A.* 18°51N 90°58W **179 D3**
Chelan, L. *Wash., U.S.A.* 47°51N 120°1W **120 C5**
Chelan County ☆ *Wash., U.S.A.* 48°11N 120°30W **120 C5**
Chelan Falls *Wash., U.S.A.* 48°0N 120°30W **120 C5**
Chelatchie *Wash., U.S.A.* 47°48N 119°59W **120 C6**
Chelmsford *Mass., U.S.A.* 45°55N 122°25W **120 E3**
Chelsea *Ont., Canada* 42°36N 71°21W **91 A3**
Chelsea *Ala., U.S.A.* 45°30N 75°47W **144 F7**
Chelsea *Iowa, U.S.A.* 33°20N 86°38W **112 C4**
Chelsea *Mass., U.S.A.* 41°55N 92°24W **81 C6**
Chelsea *Mich., U.S.A.* 42°23N 71°1W **96 A2**
Chelsea *Okla., U.S.A.* 42°19N 84°1W **79 G7**
Chelsea *Vt., U.S.A.* 36°32N 95°26W **107 B8**
Cheltenham *Md., U.S.A.* 43°59N 72°27W **89 C2**
Cheltenham *Md., U.S.A.* 38°42N 76°50W **93 B4**

Cheltenham Va., U.S.A. 40°33N 75°5W **98** A2
Chemainus B.C., Canada 48°55N 123°42W **155** G11
Chemax Yucatán, Mexico 20°39N 87°56W **179** B6
Chemehuevi Indian Reservation Calif.,
   U.S.A. 34°30N 114°25W **127** J12
Chemquasabamticook L. Maine, U.S.A. 46°30N 69°37W **90** B4
Chemult Oreg., U.S.A. 43°14N 121°47W **121** D4
Chemung County ☆ N.Y., U.S.A. 42°10N 76°45W **88** C4
Chemung County ☆ N.Y., U.S.A. 42°30N 75°40W **88** C5
Chenal, Pointe aux Mich., U.S.A. 45°55N 84°54W **79** D7
Chénéville Qué., Canada 45°53N 75°3W **144** F7
Cheney Kans., U.S.A. 37°38N 97°47W **82** D6
Cheney Wash., U.S.A. 47°30N 117°35W **120** C8
Cheney Res. Kans., U.S.A. 37°43N 97°48W **82** D6
Cheneyville La., U.S.A. 31°1N 92°17W **110** C3
Chenil, L. Qué Canada 51°51N 59°41W **140** B10
Chenko Campeche, Mexico 19°23N 89°48W **179** C4
Chenoa Ill., U.S.A. 40°45N 88°43W **84** C5
Chenoweth Oreg., U.S.A. 45°37N 121°13W **121** B4
Chepo Panama 9°10N 79°6W **182** E4
Chepachet R.I. U.S.A. 41°55N 71°40W **91** C3
Chepo Panama 9°10N 79°6W **182** E4
Chequamegon B. U.S.A. 46°39N 90°51W **78** B31
Chequamegon Nat. Forest Wis., U.S.A. 46°10N 91°0W **78** B3
Chequamegon Pt. U.S.A. 46°42N 90°45W **78** B3
Cherán Michoacan, Mexico 19°41N 101°57W **174** C6
Cheraw Colo., U.S.A. 38°6N 103°31W **125** D7
Cheraw S.C., U.S.A. 34°42N 79°53W **103** D6
Cherhill Alta., Canada 53°49N 114°41W **152** E6
Cheriton Va., U.S.A. 37°17N 75°58W **102** D7
Cherkee Ala., U.S.A. 34°45N 87°58W **112** B3
Cherokee Iowa, U.S.A. 42°45N 95°33W **81** C3
Cherokee Kans., U.S.A. 37°21N 94°49W **82** D9
Cherokee Okla., U.S.A. 36°45N 98°21W **107** B5
Cherokee Tex., U.S.A. 30°59N 98°43W **109** F9
Cherokee County ☆ Ala., U.S.A. 34°9N 85°41W **112** B5
Cherokee County ☆ Ga., U.S.A. 34°20N 84°20W **113** B2
Cherokee County ☆ Iowa, U.S.A. 42°45N 95°35W **81** C3
Cherokee County ☆ Kans., U.S.A. 37°15N 94°45W **82** D9
Cherokee County ☆ N.C., U.S.A. 35°10N 84°10W **103** C1
Cherokee County ☆ Okla., U.S.A. 36°0N 95°0W **107** B9
Cherokee County ☆ S.C., U.S.A. 35°3N 81°40W **103** C4
Cherokee County ☆ Tex., U.S.A. 31°58N 95°17W **109** F12
Cherokee Indian Reservation N.C.,
   U.S.A. 35°30N 83°20W **103** C2
Cherokee L. Tenn., U.S.A. 36°10N 83°30W **105** C9
Cherokee Nat. Forest Tenn., U.S.A. 36°0N 82°40W **105** E10
Cherokee Village Ark., U.S.A. 36°18N 91°31W **106** B41
Cherokees, Grand Lake O' The Okla.,
   U.S.A. 36°28N 94°55W **107** B9
Cherry County ☆ Nebr., U.S.A. 42°30N 101°0W **80** B4
Cherry Cr. → Colo., U.S.A. 39°45N 105°0W **134** D2
Cherry Cr. → S. Dak., U.S.A. 44°36N 101°30W **76** F4
Cherry Creek Nev., U.S.A. 39°54N 114°53W **128** C6
Cherry Creek Ark., U.S.A. 44°36N 101°30W **76** F4
Cherry Creek L. Colo., U.S.A. 39°39N 104°51W **134** C2
Cherry Creek State Park △ Colo.,
   U.S.A. 39°38N 104°51W **134** C2
Cherry Hill Baltimore, U.S.A. 39°15N 76°38W **99** B2
Cherry Hill N.J. U.S.A. 39°56N 75°2W **92** C1
Cherry Hills Village Colo., U.S.A. 39°38N 104°57W **134** C2
Cherry L., Calif., U.S.A. 37°59N 119°55W **126** F7
Cherry Tree Pa., U.S.A. 40°44N 78°48W **87** D4
Cherry Valley Ark., U.S.A. 35°24N 90°45W **106** C5
Cherry Valley N.Y., U.S.A. 42°48N 74°45W **88** C6
Cherryfield Maine, U.S.A. 44°36N 67°56W **90** D6
Cherryvale Kans., U.S.A. 37°16N 95°33W **82** D8
Cherryville B.C. Canada 50°15N 118°37W **155** E16
Cherryville N.C. U.S.A. 35°23N 81°23W **103** C4
Chesaco Park Baltimore, U.S.A. 39°18N 76°29W **99** B3
Chesaning Mich., U.S.A. 43°11N 84°7W **79** F7
Chesapeake Va., U.S.A. 36°49N 76°16W **102** E8
Chesapeake W. Va., U.S.A. 38°13N 81°32W **102** C3
Chesapeake B. Va., U.S.A. 38°0N 76°10W **102** C8
Chesapeake Bay Bridge-Tunnel Va.,
   U.S.A. 37°2N 76°5W **102** D8
Chesapeake Beach Md., U.S.A. 38°41N 76°32W **93** B4
Chesapeake City Md., U.S.A. 39°32N 75°49W **93** A5
Chesapeake Ranche Estates Md., U.S.A. 38°21N 76°25W **93** B4
Chesaw Wash., U.S.A. 48°57N 119°3W **120** B6
Chesdin, L. Va., U.S.A. 37°20N 77°40W **102** D7
Cheshire Conn., U.S.A. 41°30N 72°54W **91** C2
Cheshire Mass., U.S.A. 42°34N 73°10W **91** B1
Cheshire County ☆ N.H., U.S.A. 43°0N 72°15W **89** D2
Chesilhurst N.J., U.S.A. 39°44N 74°52W **92** C2
Cheslatta B.C., Canada 53°48N 125°48W **154** B9
Cheslatta L. B.C., Canada 53°49N 125°20W **154** B9
Chesley Ont., Canada 44°17N 81°5W **146** C3
Chesnee S.C., U.S.A. 35°9N 81°52W **103** C4
Chester N.S., Canada 44°33N 64°15W **141** J5
Chester Ark., U.S.A. 35°41N 94°11W **106** C1
Chester Calif., U.S.A. 40°19N 121°14W **126** C5
Chester Ga., U.S.A. 32°24N 83°9W **113** D3
Chester Ill., U.S.A. 37°55N 89°49W **84** F41
Chester Mass., U.S.A. 42°17N 72°59W **91** B1
Chester Mont., U.S.A. 48°31N 110°58W **123** B7
Chester N.J., U.S.A. 40°47N 74°42W **92** B2
Chester Nebr., U.S.A. 40°1N 97°37W **80** D8
Chester Okla., U.S.A. 36°13N 98°56W **107** B5
Chester Pa., U.S.A. 39°51N 75°22W **93** A5
Chester S.C., U.S.A. 34°43N 81°12W **103** D4
Chester S. Dak., U.S.A. 43°54N 96°56W **76** G9
Chester Va., U.S.A. 37°21N 77°27W **102** D7
Chester Vt., U.S.A. 43°16N 72°36W **89** C2
Chester W. Va., U.S.A. 40°37N 80°34W **102** A4
Chester → Md., U.S.A. 39°3N 76°16W **93** A4
Chester County ☆ Pa., U.S.A. 39°59N 75°50W **87** E7
Chester County ☆ S.C., U.S.A. 34°30N 81°10W **103** D4
Chester County ☆ Tenn., U.S.A. 35°20N 88°45W **104** E4
Chesterfield Ill., U.S.A. 39°15N 90°4W **84** D3
Chesterfield Mo., U.S.A. 38°40N 90°35W **83** C6
Chesterfield N.H. U.S.A. 42°52N 72°28W **89** D2
Chesterfield S.C., U.S.A. 34°44N 80°5W **103** D5
Chesterfield County ☆ S.C., U.S.A. 34°40N 80°10W **103** D5
Chesterfield County ☆ Va., U.S.A. 37°23N 77°31W **102** D7
Chesterfield Court House Va., U.S.A. 37°23N 77°31W **102** D7
Chesterfield Inlet Nunavut, Canada 63°30N 90°45W **159** E7
Chesterhill Ohio, U.S.A. 39°29N 81°52W **86** D5
Chestermere Alta., Canada 51°2N 113°49W **153** G7
Chesterton Ind., U.S.A. 41°37N 87°4W **85** B3
Chestertown Md., U.S.A. 39°13N 76°4W **93** A4
Chesterville Ont., Canada 45°6N 75°14W **144** F7
Chesterville Md., U.S.A. 39°17N 75°55W **93** A5
Chestnut La., U.S.A. 32°3N 93°1W **110** B2

Chestnut Hill Mass., U.S.A. 42°19N 71°10W **96** B1
Chesuncook L. Maine, U.S.A. 46°0N 69°21W **90** C4
Cheswold Del., U.S.A. 39°13N 75°35W **93** A5
Chetco → Oreg., U.S.A. 42°3N 124°16W **121** E1
Chetek Wis., U.S.A. 45°19N 91°39W **78** C2
Chéticamp N.S., Canada 46°37N 60°59W **141** G9
Chetopa Kans., U.S.A. 37°2N 95°5W **82** D8
Chetumal Quintana Roo, Mexico 18°30N 88°20W **179** D5
Chetumal, B. de Cent. Amer. 18°40N 88°10W **179** D5
Chetwynd B.C., Canada 55°45N 121°36W **157** E8
Chevak Alaska, U.S.A. 61°32N 165°35W **135** F6
Chevelon Cr. → Ariz., U.S.A. 34°55N 110°35W **130** C5
Cheverly Md., U.S.A. 38°55N 76°54W **99** B4
Cheviot Ohio, U.S.A. 39°9N 84°36W **86** D2
Chevreuil, Pt. La., U.S.A. 29°31N 91°33W **110** E4
Chevy Chase Md., U.S.A. 38°59N 77°4W **99** B3
Chewaucan → Oreg., U.S.A. 42°31N 120°15W **121** E5
Chewelah Wash., U.S.A. 48°17N 117°43W **120** B8
Chewuch → Wash., U.S.A. 48°29N 120°11W **120** B5
Cheyenne Okla., U.S.A. 35°37N 99°40W **107** C4
Cheyenne Wyo., U.S.A. 41°8N 104°49W **124** E8
Cheyenne → S. Dak., U.S.A. 44°41N 101°18W **76** F4
Cheyenne Bottoms Kans., U.S.A. 38°27N 98°40W **82** C5
Cheyenne County ☆ Colo., U.S.A. 38°50N 102°35W **125** D8
Cheyenne County ☆ Kans., U.S.A. 39°45N 101°45W **82** B2
Cheyenne County ☆ Nebr., U.S.A. 41°15N 103°0W **80** C3
Cheyenne River Indian Reservation S. Dak.,
   U.S.A. 45°0N 101°0W **76** E4
Cheyenne Wells Colo., U.S.A. 38°49N 102°21W **125** D8
Chezacut B.C., Canada 52°24N 124°1W **154** C10
Chiapa de Corzo Chiapas, Mexico 16°42N 93°0W **178** C4
Chiapas □ Mexico 16°30N 92°0W **178** C4
Chiapas, Sa. Madre de Chiapas, Mexico 15°40N 93°0W **178** C3
Chiautla de Tapia Puebla, Mexico 18°18N 98°36W **177** F2
Chibougamau Qué., Canada 49°56N 74°24W **145** B8
Chibougamau → Qué., Canada 49°50N 75°57W **144** B7
Chibougamau, L. Qué., Canada 49°50N 74°20W **145** B8
Chic-Chocs, Mts. Qué., Canada 48°55N 66°0W **140** E3
Chic-Chocs, Réserve Faunique des △ Qué.,
   Canada 48°55N 66°20W **140** E3
Chicago Ill., U.S.A. 41°52N 87°38W **95** B3
Chicago, University of Ill., U.S.A. 41°47N 87°35W **95** C3
Chicago Harbor Ill., U.S.A. 41°52N 87°36W **95** B3
Chicago Heights Ill., U.S.A. 41°30N 87°38W **84** B6
Chicago Lawn Ill., U.S.A. 41°47N 87°40W **95** C2
Chicago-Midway ✈ (MDW) Ill., U.S.A. 41°47N 87°45W **95** C2
Chicago O'Hare Int. ✈ (ORD) Ill., U.S.A. 41°59N 87°54W **95** B1
Chicago Ridge Ill., U.S.A. 41°41N 87°46W **95** C2
Chicago Sanitary and Ship Canal Ill.,
   U.S.A. 41°49N 87°45W **95** C2
Chicago State University Ill., U.S.A. 41°43N 87°36W **95** C3
Chicago Zoo Ill., U.S.A. 41°50N 87°50W **95** B1
Chicamuxen Md., U.S.A. 38°33N 77°15W **93** B3
Chicayán Veracruz, Mexico 21°37N 98°6W **176** C2
Chicbul Campeche, Mexico 18°48N 90°44W **179** D3
Chichagof I. Alaska, U.S.A. 57°30N 135°30W **135** H14
Chichén-Itzá Yucatán, Mexico 20°37N 88°35W **179** B5
Chichicastle, L. Tabasco, Mexico 18°18N 92°28W **178** A4
Chichihualco Guerrero, Mexico 17°41N 99°39W **175** E8
Chickamauga → Va., U.S.A. 37°14N 76°53W **102** D8
Chickamauga Ga., U.S.A. 34°52N 85°18W **113** B1
Chickamauga L. Tenn., U.S.A. 35°6N 85°14W **105** E7
Chickasaw Ala., U.S.A. 30°46N 88°5W **112** D2
Chickasaw County ☆ Iowa, U.S.A. 43°5N 92°20W **81** B6
Chickasaw County ☆ Miss., U.S.A. 33°54N 89°0W **111** C5
Chickasaw Nat. Recr. Area △ Okla.,
   U.S.A. 34°26N 97°0W **107** D7
Chickasaw Nat. Wildlife Refuge △ Tenn.,
   U.S.A. 35°49N 89°38W **104** E3
Chickasawhay → Miss., U.S.A. 30°59N 88°44W **111** F5
Chickasha Okla., U.S.A. 35°3N 97°58W **107** C6
Chicken Alaska, U.S.A. 64°5N 141°56W **135** D12
Chico Calif., U.S.A. 39°44N 121°50W **126** D5
Chico Tex., U.S.A. 33°18N 97°48W **109** D10
Chico → Chihuahua, Mexico 29°32N 108°29W **169** D7
Chicoasén Chiapas, Mexico 16°58N 93°6W **178** C2
Chicobi, L. Qué., Canada 48°53N 78°30W **144** C4
Chicomostoc Zacatecas, Mexico 22°28N 102°46W **173** E8
Chicomuselo Chiapas, Mexico 15°46N 92°16W **178** C1
Chiconcuac México, Mexico 19°34N 98°54W **175** C9
Chicontepec Veracruz, Mexico 20°58N 98°10W **176** D2
Chicopee Ga., U.S.A. 34°15N 83°51W **113** B3
Chicopee Mass., U.S.A. 42°9N 72°37W **91** B2
Chicopee → Mass., U.S.A. 42°9N 72°37W **91** B2
Chicot Qué., Canada 45°35N 73°56W **144** A1
Chicot Ark., U.S.A. 33°12N 91°17W **106** E4
Chicot County ☆ Ark., U.S.A. 33°12N 91°17W **106** E4
Chicoutimi Qué., Canada 48°28N 71°5W **145** C11
Chicxulub Yucatán, Mexico 21°17N 89°37W **179** A4
Chidester Ark., U.S.A. 33°42N 93°1W **106** E2
Chidley, C. Nfld. & L., Canada 60°23N 64°26W **143** A5
Chief Joseph Dam Wash., U.S.A. 48°0N 119°38W **120** B6
Chiefland Fla., U.S.A. 29°29N 82°52W **114** B6
Chiefs Pt. Ont., Canada 44°41N 81°18W **146** C3
Chietla Puebla, Mexico 18°32N 98°35W **177** F2
Chignahuapan Puebla, Mexico 19°48N 98°2W **176** E2
Chignecto, Cape N.S., Canada 45°20N 64°57W **141** H5
Chignecto B. N.B., Canada 45°30N 64°40W **141** H5
Chignik Alaska, U.S.A. 56°18N 158°24W **135** H8
Chigoubiche, L. Qué., Canada 49°7N 73°30W **145** B9
Chihuahua Chihuahua, Mexico 28°38N 106°5W **169** E9
Chihuahua □ Mexico 28°30N 106°0W **169** D9
Chihuhuita Sinaloa, Mexico 26°8N 109°4W **172** A1
Chikaskia → Okla., U.S.A. 36°37N 97°15W **107** B6
Chikindzonot Yucatán, Mexico 20°20N 88°30W **179** B5
Chila de la Sal Puebla, Mexico 18°7N 97°58W **177** F3
Chila de las Flores Puebla, Mexico 17°58N 97°52W **177** G3
Chilako → B.C., Canada 53°53N 122°57W **154** B11
Chilanko → B.C., Canada 52°7N 123°41W **154** C11
Chilanko Forks B.C., Canada 52°7N 124°5W **154** C11
Chilapa Guerrero, Mexico 17°36N 99°10W **175** E8
Chilchota Michoacan, Mexico 19°49N 102°6W **174** C5
Chilcotin → B.C., Canada 51°44N 122°23W **155** D12
Chilcuautla Hidalgo, Mexico 20°20N 99°14W **175** B8
Childersburg Ala., U.S.A. 33°16N 86°21W **112** C4
Childress Tex., U.S.A. 34°25N 100°13W **108** C7
Childress County ☆ Tex., U.S.A. 34°25N 100°13W **108** C7
Chilhowee Mo., U.S.A. 38°36N 93°51W **83** C3
Chilhowie Va., U.S.A. 36°48N 81°41W **102** E3
Chilicote Chihuahua, Mexico 28°58N 104°52W **169** E11
Chilili N. Mex., U.S.A. 34°53N 106°14W **131** C4
Chilko → B.C., Canada 52°0N 123°40W **154** D11
Chilko L. B.C., Canada 51°20N 124°10W **154** D10
Chillicothe Ill., U.S.A. 40°55N 89°29W **84** C4

Chillicothe Iowa, U.S.A. 41°5N 92°32W **81** D6
Chillicothe Mo., U.S.A. 39°48N 93°33W **83** B3
Chillicothe Ohio, U.S.A. 39°20N 82°59W **86** D4
Chillicothe Tex., U.S.A. 34°15N 99°31W **109** C8
Chilliwack B.C., Canada 49°10N 121°54W **155** F13
Chilliwack Lake Park △ B.C., Canada 49°4N 121°26W **155** F13
Chillum Md., U.S.A. 38°56N 76°58W **99** B4
Chilmark Mass., U.S.A. 41°21N 70°45W **91** D4
Chilocco Okla., U.S.A. 36°59N 97°4W **107** B6
Chiloquin Oreg., U.S.A. 42°35N 121°52W **121** E4
Chilón Chiapas, Mexico 17°14N 92°15W **178** B4
Chiloquin Oreg., U.S.A. 42°35N 121°52W **121** E4
Chilpancingo Guerrero, Mexico 17°33N 99°30W **175** E8
Chilson N.Y., U.S.A. 43°53N 73°32W **89** C1
Chiltepec Tabasco, Mexico 18°25N 93°5W **178** A3
Chilton Wis., U.S.A. 44°2N 88°10W **78** D5
Chiluca México, Mexico 19°31N 99°17W **181** A2
Chimalapas, Región de los Oaxaca,
   Mexico 16°14N 94°30W **177** H6
Chimalhuacán México, Mexico 19°25N 98°57W **175** C9
Chimaltitán Jalisco, Mexico 21°35N 103°50W **173** F7
Chimán Panama 8°45N 78°40W **182** E4
Chimayo N. Mex., U.S.A. 36°0N 105°56W **131** B5
Chimney Rock Colo., U.S.A. 37°13N 107°18W **125** F3
Chimney Rock Nat. Historic Site △ Nebr.,
   U.S.A. 41°42N 103°21W **80** C2
Chimo Jalisco, Mexico 20°28N 105°35W **174** B2
China Nuevo León, Mexico 25°42N 99°14W **170** D5
China Tex., U.S.A. 30°3N 94°20W **109** G13
China Basin San Francisco, U.S.A. **132** c3
China Grove N.C., U.S.A. 35°34N 80°35W **103** C5
China Grove Tex., U.S.A. 29°23N 98°20W **116** C3
China L. Calif., U.S.A. 35°43N 117°20W **127** H9
Chinameca Veracruz, Mexico 17°56N 94°40W **177** F6
Chinampa Veracruz, Mexico 21°22N 97°43W **176** C3
Chinandega Nic. 12°35N 87°12W **182** D2
Chinati Mts. Tex., U.S.A. 29°55N 104°30W **108** H3
Chinati Peak Tex., U.S.A. 29°57N 104°29W **108** H3
Chinchaga → Alta., Canada 58°53N 118°20W **152** A1
Chinchaga Wildland Prov. Park △ Alta.,
   Canada 57°10N 119°30W **152** A1
Chinchorro, Banco Quintana Roo,
   Mexico 18°35N 87°22W **179** D6
Chincoteague Va., U.S.A. 37°56N 75°23W **93** B5
Chincoteague Bay Md., U.S.A. 38°15N 75°15W **93** B5
Chincoteague Nat. Wildlife Refuge △ Va.,
   U.S.A. 37°56N 75°19W **102** D9
Chínipas Chihuahua, Mexico 27°23N 108°32W **168** F7
Chinkultic Chiapas, Mexico 16°13N 91°52W **178** C5
Chinle Ariz., U.S.A. 36°9N 109°33W **130** A6
Chinle Cr. → Utah, U.S.A. 37°12N 109°43W **129** F6
Chino Ariz., U.S.A. 34°1N 117°41W **127** J9
Chino Valley Ariz., U.S.A. 34°45N 112°27W **130** C3
Chinobampo Sinaloa, Mexico 26°26N 108°16W **172** A2
Chinook Alta., Canada 51°28N 110°59W **153** G10
Chinook Mont., U.S.A. 48°35N 109°14W **123** B8
Chinook Wash., U.S.A. 46°16N 123°57W **120** D2
Chinook, L. Oreg., U.S.A. 44°33N 121°10W **121** C4
Chinook Valley Alta., Canada 56°29N 117°39W **152** B3
Chinook Pass Wash., U.S.A. 46°52N 121°32W **120** D4
Chip L. Alta., Canada 53°40N 115°23W **152** E5
Chipley Fla., U.S.A. 30°47N 85°32W **114** A3
Chipman Alta., Canada 53°42N 112°38W **152** E8
Chipman N.B., Canada 46°6N 65°53W **141** G4
Chipman L. Ont., Canada 49°58N 86°15W **149** C10
Chipola → Fla., U.S.A. 30°1N 85°5W **114** A3
Chippewa → Mich., U.S.A. 43°35N 84°17W **79** F7
Chippewa → Minn., U.S.A. 44°56N 95°44W **77** F3
Chippewa → Wis., U.S.A. 44°25N 92°5W **78** D11
Chippewa, L. Wis., U.S.A. 45°57N 91°12W **78** C2
Chippewa County ☆ Mich., U.S.A. 46°20N 84°40W **79** C7
Chippewa County ☆ Minn., U.S.A. 45°0N 95°35W **77** F3
Chippewa County ☆ Wis., U.S.A. 45°5N 91°20W **78** C2
Chippewa Falls Wis., U.S.A. 44°56N 91°24W **78** D2
Chippewa Nat. Forest Minn., U.S.A. 47°45N 94°0W **77** C6
Chiputneticook Lakes N. Amer. 45°35N 67°35W **141** H2
Chiquibul Nat. Park △ Belize 16°49N 88°52W **182** C2
Chiquihuite, Cerro Distrito Federal,
   Mexico 19°32N 99°8W **181** A3
Chiquihuitillo Michoacan, Mexico 18°58N 102°20W **174** D5
Chiquilá Quintana Roo, Mexico 21°26N 87°20W **179** A6
Chiquimula Guatemala 14°51N 89°37W **182** D2
Chireno Tex., U.S.A. 31°30N 94°21W **109** F13
Chiricahua Mts. Ariz., U.S.A. 32°0N 109°15W **130** F6
Chiricahua Nat. Monument △ Ariz.,
   U.S.A. 32°0N 109°20W **130** E6
Chiricahua Peak Ariz., U.S.A. 31°51N 109°18W **130** F6
Chiriquí, G. de Panama 8°0N 82°10W **182** E3
Chiriquí, L. de Panama 9°10N 82°0W **182** E3
Chirripó Grande, Cerro Costa Rica 9°29N 83°29W **182** E3
Chisago County ☆ Minn., U.S.A. 45°30N 92°55W **77** E6
Chisasibi Qué., Canada 53°50N 79°0W **143** D2
Chisholm Alta., Canada 54°55N 114°10W **152** D6
Chisholm Maine, U.S.A. 44°29N 70°12W **90** D3
Chisholm Minn., U.S.A. 47°29N 92°53W **77** C61
Chisos Mts. Tex., U.S.A. 29°5N 103°15W **108** H4
Chistochina Alaska, U.S.A. 62°34N 144°40W **135** E11
Chitek L. Man., Canada 52°25N 99°25W **151** C12
Chitek L. Sask., Canada 53°45N 107°47W **150** B4
Chitek Lake Sask., Canada 53°45N 107°43W **150** B4
Chitimacha Indian Reservation La.,
   U.S.A. 30°33N 92°42W **110** D3
Chitina Alaska, U.S.A. 61°31N 144°26W **135** F11
Chitré Panama 7°59N 80°27W **182** E3
Chittenden Vt., U.S.A. 43°42N 72°55W **89** C2
Chittenden County ☆ Vt., U.S.A. 44°30N 73°0W **89** C1
Chivato, Pta. Baja Calif. S., Mexico 27°5N 111°59W **167** F7
Chivington Colo., U.S.A. 38°26N 102°32W **125** D8
Chivo, Pta. Oaxaca, Mexico 16°1N 95°11W **177** H6
Chloride Ariz., U.S.A. 35°25N 114°12W **130** B1
Chocholá Yucatán, Mexico 20°45N 89°50W **179** B4
Chocolate Mountain Naval Aerial Gunnery
   Calif., U.S.A. 33°14N 115°10W **127** K11
Chocolate Mts. Ariz., U.S.A. 33°15N 114°30W **130** D1
Chocolate Mts. Calif., U.S.A. 33°15N 115°15W **127** K11
Chocowinity N.C., U.S.A. 35°31N 77°6W **103** C8
Choctaw Okla., U.S.A. 35°31N 97°17W **107** C6
Choctaw Bluff Ala., U.S.A. 31°22N 87°46W **112** D3
Choctaw County ☆ Ala., U.S.A. 32°0N 88°10W **112** C2
Choctaw County ☆ Miss., U.S.A. 33°19N 89°11W **111** C4
Choctaw County ☆ Okla., U.S.A. 34°0N 95°30W **107** D7
Choctawhatchee → Fla., U.S.A. 30°25N 86°8W **114** A2
Choctawhatchee B. Fla., U.S.A. 30°20N 86°20W **114** A2
Choelquoit L. B.C., Canada 51°42N 124°12W **154** D10

Choiceland Sask., Canada 53°29N 104°29W **150** B7
Choix Sinaloa, Mexico 26°43N 108°17W **172** A2
Choke Canyon Res. Tex., U.S.A. 28°30N 98°20W **109** J9
Chokio Minn., U.S.A. 45°34N 96°10W **77** E2
Chokoloskee Fla., U.S.A. 25°49N 81°22W **114** F7
Cholame Calif., U.S.A. 35°44N 120°18W **127** H6
Chollas Park Calif., U.S.A. 32°44N 117°3W **133** B2
Cholula Puebla, Mexico 19°4N 98°18W **177** E2
Choluteca Honduras 13°20N 87°14W **182** D2
Choluteca → Honduras 13°0N 87°20W **182** D2
Chomedey Qué., Canada 45°32N 73°45W **144** A2
Chontalpa Tabasco, Mexico 17°42N 93°31W **178** B3
Chontla Veracruz, Mexico 21°18N 97°55W **176** C3
Choptank Md., U.S.A. 38°41N 75°57W **93** B5
Choptank → Md., U.S.A. 38°38N 76°13W **93** B4
Chorkbak Inlet Nunavut, Canada 64°30N 74°25W **159** E11
Chorreras Chihuahua, Mexico 28°51N 105°17W **169** E10
Choteau Mont., U.S.A. 47°49N 112°11W **123** C6
Choudrant La., U.S.A. 32°32N 92°31W **110** B3
Chouteau Okla., U.S.A. 36°11N 95°21W **107** B8
Chouteau County ☆ Mont., U.S.A. 47°55N 110°30W **123** C7
Chouteau I. Ill., U.S.A. 38°46N 90°8W **94** A3
Chowan → N.C., U.S.A. 36°1N 76°40W **103** B9
Chowan County ☆ N.C., U.S.A. 36°10N 76°40W **103** B9
Chowchilla Calif., U.S.A. 37°7N 120°16W **126** F6
Chrisman Ill., U.S.A. 39°48N 87°41W **84** D6
Chrisney Ind., U.S.A. 38°1N 87°2W **85** E3
Christian County ☆ Ill., U.S.A. 39°30N 89°15W **84** D4
Christian County ☆ Ky., U.S.A. 36°50N 87°30W **104** D5
Christian County ☆ Mo., U.S.A. 37°0N 93°10W **83** D3
Christian I. Ont., Canada 44°50N 80°12W **146** C4
Christian Sd. Alaska, U.S.A. 55°56N 134°40W **135** J14
Christiana Del., U.S.A. 39°40N 75°40W **93** A5
Christiana Tenn., U.S.A. 35°43N 86°24W **104** E6
Christiansburg Ohio, U.S.A. 40°3N 84°2W **86** C2
Christiansburg Va., U.S.A. 37°8N 80°25W **102** D4
Christianshåb = Qasigiannguit
   Greenland 68°50N 51°18W **162** D5
Christiansted U.S. Virgin Is. 17°45N 64°42W **184** H18
Christie Okla., U.S.A. 35°57N 94°42W **107** C9
Christie L. N.W.T., Canada 62°32N 111°10W **157** D10
Christina → Alta., Canada 56°40N 111°3W **152** B9
Christina, L. B.C., Canada 49°3N 118°12W **155** F16
Christine N. Dak., U.S.A. 46°35N 96°48W **76** D9
Christopher Ill., U.S.A. 37°59N 89°3W **84** F4
Christopher Lake Sask., Canada 53°32N 105°48W **150** B6
Christoval Tex., U.S.A. 31°12N 100°30W **108** F7
Chrome N.J., U.S.A. 40°34N 74°13W **97** C1
Chromo Colo., U.S.A. 37°2N 106°50W **125** E4
Chrysler Ala., U.S.A. 31°18N 87°42W **112** E3
Chu Chua B.C., Canada 51°22N 120°10W **155** D14
Chualar Calif., U.S.A. 36°34N 121°31W **126** G5
Chuathbaluk Alaska, U.S.A. 61°40N 159°15W **135** F8
Chubbuck Idaho, U.S.A. 42°55N 112°28W **122** G6
Chuburna Yucatán, Mexico 21°16N 89°49W **179** A4
Chuckawalla Mts. Calif., U.S.A. 33°30N 115°20W **127** K11
Chugach Mts. Alaska, U.S.A. 60°45N 147°0W **135** F11
Chuginadak I. Alaska, U.S.A. 52°50N 169°45W **135** K5
Chugwater Wyo., U.S.A. 41°46N 104°50W **124** E8
Chuichu Ariz., U.S.A. 32°45N 111°47W **130** E4
Chula Ga., U.S.A. 31°33N 83°32W **113** E3
Chula Mo., U.S.A. 39°55N 93°29W **83** B3
Chula Va., U.S.A. 37°23N 77°54W **102** D7
Chula Vista Calif., U.S.A. 32°38N 117°5W **133** C2
Chumul Yucatán, Mexico 19°48N 89°9W **179** C4
Chunchintok Campeche, Mexico 19°21N 89°40W **179** C4
Chuncucmil Yucatán, Mexico 20°39N 90°12W **179** B3
Chunchula Ala., U.S.A. 30°55N 88°12W **112** F2
Chunhuhub Quintana Roo, Mexico 19°33N 88°41W **179** C5
Chunky Miss., U.S.A. 32°20N 88°56W **111** D5
Chuntengo, Barra Guerrero, Mexico 16°38N 99°9W **175** F8
Chupadera Mesa N. Mex., U.S.A. 33°52N 106°14W **131** D4
Church Creek Md., U.S.A. 38°30N 76°10W **93** B4
Church Hill Md., U.S.A. 39°9N 75°59W **93** A5
Church Hill Tenn., U.S.A. 36°31N 82°43W **105** D10
Church Point La., U.S.A. 30°24N 92°13W **110** D3
Church Rock N. Mex., U.S.A. 35°32N 108°36W **131** B2
Churchbridge Sask., Canada 50°54N 101°54W **151** D11
Churchill Man., Canada 58°47N 94°11W **159** F7
Churchill Pa., U.S.A. 40°26N 79°50W **98** B2
Churchill → Man., Canada 58°47N 94°12W **159** F7
Churchill → Nfld. & L., Canada 53°19N 60°10W **143** C5
Churchill, C. Man., Canada 58°46N 93°12W **159** F7
Churchill County ☆ Nev., U.S.A. 39°30N 118°20W **128** C2
Churchill Falls Nfld. & L., Canada 53°36N 64°19W **143** C5
Churchill L. Ont., Canada 50°50N 91°0W **148** B3
Churchill L. Sask., Canada 55°55N 108°20W **157** E11
Churchs Ferry N. Dak., U.S.A. 48°16N 99°12W **76** B6
Churchville Md., U.S.A. 39°34N 76°15W **93** A4
Churdan Iowa, U.S.A. 42°9N 94°29W **81** C4
Churintzio Michoacan, Mexico 20°5N 101°39W **174** C6
Churn Creek Park △ B.C., Canada 51°27N 122°20W **155** D12
Churubusco Ind., U.S.A. 41°14N 85°19W **85** B5
Churubusco México, Mexico 19°27N 99°11W **181** B3
Churumuco Michoacan, Mexico 18°40N 101°39W **174** D6
Chuska Mts. Ariz., U.S.A. 36°15N 108°50W **131** B2
Chute-aux-Outardes Qué., Canada 49°7N 68°24W **145** B11
Chute-des-Passes Qué., Canada 49°52N 71°16W **145** B11
Ciales Puerto Rico 18°20N 66°28W **184** G16
Cibecue Ariz., U.S.A. 34°2N 110°29W **130** C5
Cibola Ariz., U.S.A. 33°17N 114°42W **130** D1
Cibola County ☆ N. Mex., U.S.A. 35°0N 108°0W **131** C2
Cibola Nat. Forest N. Mex., U.S.A. 35°0N 108°15W **131** B2
Cicero Ill., U.S.A. 41°51N 87°44W **95** B2
Cicero Ind., U.S.A. 40°8N 86°1W **85** C3
Ciego de Ávila Cuba 21°50N 78°50W **182** B4
Ciénega de Caballos Durango, Mexico 25°41N 106°25W **172** A3
Ciénega de Escobar Durango, Mexico 25°55N 105°45W **172** B5
Ciénega de Flores Nuevo León, Mexico 25°57N 100°11W **170** C4
Cieneguilla Oaxaca, Mexico 17°45N 98°16W **177** G2
Cieneguillas Durango, Mexico 24°3N 104°30W **173** C6
Cienfuegos Cuba 22°10N 80°30W **182** B3
Ciudtlán Jalisco, Mexico 19°14N 104°35W **174** D4
Cima Calif., U.S.A. 35°14N 115°30W **127** H11
Cimarron Kans., U.S.A. 37°48N 100°21W **82** D3
Cimarron N. Mex., U.S.A. 36°31N 104°55W **131** A6
Cimarron → N. Mex., U.S.A. 36°15N 104°30W **131** A6
Cimarron City Okla., U.S.A. 35°53N 97°36W **107** C6
Cimarron County ☆ Okla., U.S.A. 36°45N 102°30W **107** B1
Cimarron Nat. Grassland Kans., U.S.A. 37°15N 102°0W **82** D1
Cincinnati Iowa, U.S.A. 40°38N 92°56W **81** E6
Cincinnati Ohio, U.S.A. 39°9N 84°27W **86** D2

Cincinnati-Northern Kentucky Int. ✈ (CVG) Ky., U.S.A. 39°3N 84°40W 105 A8
Cinco Manantiales, Parque Natural △ Coahuila, Mexico 28°30N 100°45W 170 B4
Cintalapa Chiapas, Mexico 16°44N 93°43W 178 C3
Circle Alaska, U.S.A. 65°50N 144°4W 135 D11
Circle Mont., U.S.A. 47°25N 105°35W 123 C12
Circle Cliffs Utah, U.S.A. 37°52N 111°15W 129 F4
Circleville Kans., U.S.A. 39°31N 95°52W 82 B8
Circleville Ohio, U.S.A. 39°36N 82°57W 86 D4
Circleville Utah, U.S.A. 38°10N 112°16W 129 E3
Circleville W. Va., U.S.A. 38°40N 79°30W 102 C5
Circleville Mt. Utah, U.S.A. 38°12N 112°24W 129 E3
Cisco Ill., U.S.A. 40°1N 88°44W 84 C5
Cisco Tex., U.S.A. 32°23N 98°59W 109 E9
Cisco Utah, U.S.A. 38°58N 109°19W 129 E6
Cisne Ill., U.S.A. 38°31N 88°26W 84 E5
Cissna Park Ill., U.S.A. 40°34N 87°54W 84 C6
Cistern Tex., U.S.A. 29°49N 97°13W 109 H10
Citaltepec Veracruz, Mexico 21°20N 97°52W 176 D3
Citlaltépetl = Orizaba, Pico de Veracruz, Mexico 18°58N 97°15W 177 F3
Citra Fla., U.S.A. 29°25N 82°7W 114 B6
Citronelle Ala., U.S.A. 31°6N 88°14W 112 E2
Citrus County ☆ Fla., U.S.A. 28°45N 82°30W 114 C6
Citrus Heights Calif., U.S.A. 38°42N 121°17W 126 E5
Citrus Springs Fla., U.S.A. 29°2N 82°27W 114 B6
City Island N.Y., U.S.A. 40°50N 73°47W 97 A4
City of Rocks Nat. Reserve △ Idaho, U.S.A. 42°5N 113°42W 122 G5
City Park Colo., U.S.A. 39°44N 104°56W 134 B2
City Park La., U.S.A. 30°0N 90°5W 117 B2
City View Ont., Canada 45°21N 75°45W 160 B1
Ciudad Acuña Coahuila, Mexico 29°18N 100°55W 170 A4
Ciudad Altamirano Guerrero, Mexico 18°20N 100°40W 175 D7
Ciudad Anáhuac Nuevo León, Mexico 27°14N 100°7W 170 C4
Ciudad Azteca México, Mexico 19°31N 99°2W 181 A3
Ciudad Benito Juárez Monterrey, Mexico 25°37N 100°8W 180 C3
Ciudad Camargo Chihuahua, Mexico 27°40N 105°10W 169 F10
Ciudad Constitución Baja Calif. S., Mexico 25°0N 111°42W 167 J7
Ciudad Cuauhtémoc Chiapas, Mexico 15°37N 92°0W 178 D5
Ciudad Cuauhtémoc Zacatecas, Mexico 22°27N 102°20W 173 E8
Ciudad de Federal, Distrito Federal, Mexico 19°24N 99°9W 181 B3
Ciudad del Carmen Campeche, Mexico 18°38N 91°50W 179 D2
Ciudad del Maíz San Luis Potosí, Mexico 22°24N 99°36W 171 H5
Ciudad Delicias = Delicias Chihuahua, Mexico 28°13N 105°28W 169 E10
Ciudad Deportiva Distrito Federal, Mexico 19°24N 99°5W 181 B3
Ciudad Díaz Ordaz Tamaulipas, Mexico 26°12N 98°28W 170 D6
Ciudad Fernández San Luis Potosí, Mexico 21°57N 100°4W 171 J4
Ciudad Frontera Coahuila, Mexico 26°56N 101°27W 170 D3
Ciudad Granja Jalisco, Mexico 20°39N 103°27W 174 C4
Ciudad Guerrero Chihuahua, Mexico 28°33N 107°30W 169 E8
Ciudad Guerrero Tamaulipas, Mexico 26°34N 99°15W 170 D5
Ciudad Guzmán Jalisco, Mexico 19°41N 103°29W 174 C4
Ciudad Hidalgo Chiapas, Mexico 14°41N 92°9W 178 E4
Ciudad Hidalgo Michoacan, Mexico 19°41N 100°34W 175 C7
Ciudad Insurgentes Baja Calif. S., Mexico 25°13N 111°48W 167 H7
Ciudad Juárez Chihuahua, Mexico 31°44N 106°29W 169 B9
Ciudad Lerdo Durango, Mexico 25°32N 103°32W 173 B7
Ciudad López Mateos México, Mexico 19°33N 99°18W 181 A2
Ciudad Madero Tamaulipas, Mexico 22°19N 97°50W 171 H7
Ciudad Mante Tamaulipas, Mexico 22°44N 98°59W 171 H6
Ciudad Mendoza Veracruz, Mexico 18°48N 97°11W 177 F3
Ciudad Miguel Alemán Tamaulipas, Mexico 26°23N 99°2W 170 D5
Ciudad Nezahualcóyotl México, Mexico 19°24N 99°1W 181 B3
Ciudad Obregón Sonora, Mexico 27°29N 109°56W 168 F6
Ciudad Porfirio Díaz = Piedras Negras Coahuila, Mexico 28°42N 100°31W 170 B4
Ciudad Sahagún Hidalgo, Mexico 19°52N 98°46W 175 C9
Ciudad Satélite México, Mexico 19°30N 99°13W 181 A2
Ciudad Serdán Puebla, Mexico 18°59N 97°27W 177 F3
Ciudad Trujillo = Santo Domingo Dom. Rep. 18°30N 69°59W 183 C6
Ciudad Universitaria México, Mexico 19°20N 99°11W 181 C2
Ciudad Valles San Luis Potosí, Mexico 21°59N 99°1W 171 J5
Ciudad Victoria Tamaulipas, Mexico 23°44N 99°8W 171 H5
Civic Center Park Minn., U.S.A. 44°56N 93°27W 94 B1
Clackamas Oreg., U.S.A. 45°24N 122°34W 132 B2
Clackamas → Oreg., U.S.A. 45°22N 122°36W 121 B3
Clackamas County ☆ Oreg., U.S.A. 45°15N 122°15W 121 B3
Claflin Kans., U.S.A. 38°31N 98°32W 82 C5
Claiborne Ala., U.S.A. 31°33N 87°31W 112 E3
Claiborne Md., U.S.A. 38°50N 76°17W 93 B4
Claiborne, L., U.S.A. 32°45N 93°0W 110 B3
Claiborne County ☆ Miss., U.S.A. 31°58N 90°59W 111 E3
Claiborne County ☆ Tenn., U.S.A. 36°27N 83°34W 105 D9
Claiborne Parish ☆ La., U.S.A. 32°48N 93°0W 110 B2
Clair Engle L. Calif., U.S.A. 40°48N 122°46W 126 C4
Clairambault, L. Qué., Canada 54°29N 69°0W 143 C4
Claire N.B., Canada 47°15N 68°40W 145 D14
Claire, L. Alta., Canada 58°35N 112°5W 157 E10
Claireville Res. Ont., Canada 43°45N 79°39W 161 A1
Clairmont Alta., Canada 55°16N 118°47W 152 C2
Clairton Pa., U.S.A. 40°18N 79°53W 87 D3
Clallam Bay Wash., U.S.A. 48°15N 124°16W 120 B1
Clallam County ☆ Wash., U.S.A. 48°0N 124°0W 120 C2
Clam Gulch Alaska, U.S.A. 60°15N 151°23W 135 F10
Clan Alpine Mts. Nev., U.S.A. 39°40N 117°55W 128 C3
Clancy Mont., U.S.A. 46°28N 111°59W 123 D6
Clandonald Alta., Canada 53°34N 110°44W 152 E10
Clanton Ala., U.S.A. 32°51N 86°38W 112 D4
Clanwilliam Man., Canada 50°22N 99°49W 151 E12
Clapperton I. Ont., Canada 46°0N 82°14W 146 A4
Clara Miss., U.S.A. 31°35N 88°42W 111 E5
Clara City Minn., U.S.A. 44°57N 95°22W 77 F3
Clare Iowa, U.S.A. 42°35N 94°21W 81 C4
Clare Mich., U.S.A. 43°49N 84°46W 79 F7
Clare County ☆ Mich., U.S.A. 44°0N 84°50W 79 F7
Claremont Calif., U.S.A. 34°6N 117°43W 127 J9
Claremont Ill., U.S.A. 38°43N 87°58W 84 E6
Claremont N.H., U.S.A. 43°23N 72°20W 89 C2
Claremont S. Dak., U.S.A. 45°40N 98°1W 76 E7
Claremont Va., U.S.A. 37°14N 76°58W 102 D8
Claremore Okla., U.S.A. 36°19N 95°36W 107 B8
Clarence Iowa, U.S.A. 41°53N 91°4W 81 D7
Clarence La., U.S.A. 31°49N 93°2W 110 C2
Clarence Mo., U.S.A. 39°45N 92°16W 83 B4
Clarence, Port Alaska, U.S.A. 65°15N 166°40W 135 D6
Clarence Hd. Nunavut, Canada 76°47N 77°47W 158 B10
Clarence Town Bahamas 23°6N 74°59W 183 B5
Clarendon N.B., Canada 45°29N 66°26W 141 H3

Clarendon Ark., U.S.A. 34°42N 91°19W 106 D4
Clarendon Pa., U.S.A. 41°47N 79°6W 87 C3
Clarendon Tex., U.S.A. 34°56N 100°53W 108 C7
Clarendon County ☆ S.C., U.S.A. 33°45N 80°10W 103 E5
Clarenville-Shoal Harbour Nfld. & L., Canada 48°10N 54°1W 142 D6
Claresholm Alta., Canada 50°2N 113°33W 153 H7
Clareton Wyo., U.S.A. 43°42N 104°42W 124 C8
Clarinda Iowa, U.S.A. 40°44N 95°2W 81 E3
Clarington Ont., Canada 43°55N 78°41W 147 D8
Clarington Ohio, U.S.A. 39°46N 80°52W 86 D6
Clarion Iowa, U.S.A. 42°44N 93°44W 81 C5
Clarion Pa., U.S.A. 41°13N 79°23W 87 C3
Clarion → Pa., U.S.A. 41°7N 79°41W 87 C3
Clarion County ☆ Pa., U.S.A. 41°5N 79°40W 87 C3
Clarissa Minn., U.S.A. 46°8N 94°57W 77 D4
Clarita Okla., U.S.A. 34°29N 96°26W 107 D7
Clark Mo., U.S.A. 39°17N 92°21W 83 B4
Clark S. Dak., U.S.A. 44°53N 97°44W 76 F8
Clark Wyo., U.S.A. 44°54N 109°9W 124 B3
Clark, Pt. Ont., Canada 44°4N 81°45W 146 C5
Clark Canyon Res. Mont., U.S.A. 44°57N 112°56W 123 F5
Clark County ☆ Ark., U.S.A. 33°55N 93°9W 106 D2
Clark County ☆ Idaho, U.S.A. 44°15N 112°30W 122 E6
Clark County ☆ Ill., U.S.A. 39°20N 87°45W 84 D6
Clark County ☆ Ind., U.S.A. 38°30N 85°40W 85 F5
Clark County ☆ Kans., U.S.A. 37°15N 99°45W 82 D4
Clark County ☆ Ky., U.S.A. 38°0N 84°10W 105 C8
Clark County ☆ Mo., U.S.A. 40°25N 91°40W 83 A5
Clark County ☆ Nev., U.S.A. 36°10N 115°10W 128 F5
Clark County ☆ Ohio, U.S.A. 39°55N 83°49W 86 D3
Clark County ☆ S. Dak., U.S.A. 44°50N 97°44W 76 F8
Clark County ☆ Wash., U.S.A. 45°55N 122°25W 120 D3
Clark County ☆ Wis., U.S.A. 44°40N 90°40W 78 D3
Clark Fork Idaho, U.S.A. 48°9N 116°11W 122 A2
Clark Fork → Idaho, U.S.A. 48°9N 116°5W 122 A2
Clark Mt. Calif., U.S.A. 35°32N 115°35W 127 H11
Clarkdale Ariz., U.S.A. 34°46N 112°3W 130 C3
Clarke City Qué., Canada 50°12N 66°38W 143 C4
Clarke County ☆ Ala., U.S.A. 31°42N 87°47W 112 E3
Clarke County ☆ Ga., U.S.A. 34°0N 83°5W 113 B3
Clarke County ☆ Iowa, U.S.A. 41°0N 93°45W 81 E5
Clarke County ☆ Miss., U.S.A. 32°2N 88°44W 111 D5
Clarke County ☆ Va., U.S.A. 39°9N 77°59W 102 B7
Clarke L. Sask., Canada 54°24N 106°54W 150 A5
Clarkesville Ga., U.S.A. 34°37N 83°31W 113 B3
Clarkfield Minn., U.S.A. 44°48N 95°48W 77 F3
Clarkia Idaho, U.S.A. 47°1N 116°15W 122 B2
Clarkrange Tenn., U.S.A. 36°11N 85°1W 105 D7
Clarks La., U.S.A. 32°2N 92°8W 110 B3
Clarks Nebr., U.S.A. 41°13N 97°50W 80 C8
Clarks → Ky., U.S.A. 37°3N 88°33W 104 C4
Clarks Fork Yellowstone → Wyo., U.S.A. 45°32N 108°50W 123 E9
Clarks Grove Minn., U.S.A. 43°46N 93°20W 77 G5
Clark's Harbour N.S., Canada 43°25N 65°38W 141 K4
Clarks Hill Ind., U.S.A. 40°15N 86°43W 85 C4
Clarks Hill L. = J. Strom Thurmond L. Ga., U.S.A. 33°40N 82°12W 113 C4
Clarks Point Alaska, U.S.A. 58°51N 158°33W 135 G8
Clarks Summit Pa. U.S.A. 41°30N 75°42W 92 A1
Clarksburg Mo., U.S.A. 38°40N 92°40W 83 C4
Clarksburg N.J., U.S.A. 40°12N 74°27W 92 C2
Clarksburg Tenn., U.S.A. 35°52N 88°24W 104 E4
Clarksburg W. Va., U.S.A. 39°17N 80°30W 102 B4
Clarksdale Miss., U.S.A. 34°12N 90°35W 111 B3
Clarksdale Mo., U.S.A. 39°49N 94°33W 83 B2
Clarkson Ky., U.S.A. 37°30N 86°13W 104 C6
Clarkson Nebr., U.S.A. 41°43N 97°7W 80 C8
Clarkston Utah, U.S.A. 41°55N 112°3W 129 B4
Clarkston Wash., U.S.A. 46°25N 117°3W 120 D8
Clarksville Ark., U.S.A. 35°28N 93°28W 106 C2
Clarksville Ind., U.S.A. 38°17N 85°45W 85 F5
Clarksville Iowa, U.S.A. 42°47N 92°40W 81 C6
Clarksville Mich., U.S.A. 39°12N 76°57W 93 A4
Clarksville Mich., U.S.A. 42°50N 85°15W 79 G6
Clarksville Mo., U.S.A. 39°22N 90°54W 83 B6
Clarksville Ohio, U.S.A. 39°24N 83°59W 86 D3
Clarksville Tenn., U.S.A. 36°32N 87°21W 104 D5
Clarksville Tex., U.S.A. 33°37N 95°3W 109 D12
Clarksville Va., U.S.A. 36°37N 78°34W 102 E6
Clarkton N.C., U.S.A. 34°29N 78°39W 103 D7
Clatonia Nebr., U.S.A. 40°28N 96°51W 80 D9
Clatskanie Oreg., U.S.A. 46°6N 123°12W 121 A2
Clatsop County ☆ Oreg., U.S.A. 46°0N 123°43W 121 A2
Claude Tex., U.S.A. 35°7N 101°22W 108 B6
Clavering Ø Greenland 74°15N 21°0W 162 C8
Claxton Ga., U.S.A. 32°10N 81°55W 113 D5
Clay Ky., U.S.A. 37°29N 87°49W 104 C5
Clay W. Va., U.S.A. 38°28N 81°5W 102 C3
Clay Center Kans., U.S.A. 39°23N 97°8W 82 B6
Clay Center Nebr., U.S.A. 40°32N 98°3W 80 D7
Clay City Ill., U.S.A. 38°41N 88°21W 84 E5
Clay City Ind., U.S.A. 39°17N 87°7W 85 D3
Clay County ☆ Ala., U.S.A. 33°16N 85°50W 112 C5
Clay County ☆ Ark., U.S.A. 36°19N 90°36W 106 B5
Clay County ☆ Fla., U.S.A. 30°0N 81°45W 114 B7
Clay County ☆ Ga., U.S.A. 31°30N 85°0W 113 E2
Clay County ☆ Ill., U.S.A. 38°45N 88°30W 84 E5
Clay County ☆ Ind., U.S.A. 39°20N 87°10W 85 D3
Clay County ☆ Iowa, U.S.A. 43°5N 95°10W 81 B3
Clay County ☆ Kans., U.S.A. 39°20N 97°10W 82 B6
Clay County ☆ Ky., U.S.A. 37°10N 83°45W 105 C9
Clay County ☆ Minn., U.S.A. 46°50N 96°30W 77 D2
Clay County ☆ Miss., U.S.A. 33°36N 88°39W 111 C5
Clay County ☆ Mo., U.S.A. 39°20N 94°20W 83 B2
Clay County ☆ Nebr., U.S.A. 40°30N 98°0W 80 D7
Clay County ☆ N.C., U.S.A. 35°5N 83°45W 103 C1
Clay County ☆ S. Dak., U.S.A. 43°0N 97°0W 76 H9
Clay County ☆ Tenn., U.S.A. 36°33N 85°30W 105 D7
Clay County ☆ Tex., U.S.A. 33°49N 98°12W 109 D9
Clay County ☆ W. Va., U.S.A. 38°28N 81°5W 102 C3
Clay L. Ont., Canada 50°3N 93°30W 148 B3
Clay Springs Ariz., U.S.A. 34°22N 110°18W 130 C5
Claymont Del., U.S.A. 39°48N 75°27W 93 A5
Claypool Ariz., U.S.A. 33°25N 110°51W 130 D5
Claysville Pa., U.S.A. 40°7N 80°25W 87 D2
Clayton Del., U.S.A. 39°17N 75°38W 93 B5
Clayton Ga., U.S.A. 34°53N 83°23W 113 B3
Clayton Idaho, U.S.A. 44°16N 114°24W 122 E4
Clayton Ill., U.S.A. 40°2N 90°54W 84 C3
Clayton Ind., U.S.A. 39°41N 86°31W 85 D4

Clayton Iowa, U.S.A. 42°54N 91°9W 81 C7
Clayton Kans., U.S.A. 39°44N 100°11W 82 B3
Clayton La., U.S.A. 31°43N 91°33W 110 C4
Clayton Mo., U.S.A. 38°38N 90°19W 94 B1
Clayton N.C., U.S.A. 35°39N 78°28W 103 C7
Clayton N.J., U.S.A. 39°40N 75°6W 92 C1
Clayton Okla., U.S.A. 34°35N 95°21W 107 D8
Clayton Wis., U.S.A. 45°20N 92°10W 78 C1
Clayton County ☆ Ga., U.S.A. 33°30N 84°20W 113 C2
Clayton County ☆ Iowa, U.S.A. 42°50N 91°20W 81 C7
Clayton L. Va., U.S.A. 37°5N 80°35W 102 D4
Clayton Lake Maine, U.S.A. 46°36N 69°32W 90 B4
Cle Elum Wash., U.S.A. 47°12N 120°56W 120 C5
Clear → Alta., Canada 56°11N 119°42W 152 B1
Clear → Ariz., U.S.A. 34°50N 110°38W 130 C5
Clear, L. Ont., Canada 45°26N 77°12W 147 B9
Clear, L. Ariz., U.S.A. 28°31N 81°24W 115 A2
Clear Boggy Cr. → Okla., U.S.A. 34°3N 95°47W 107 D8
Clear Cr. → Wyo., U.S.A. 44°53N 106°4W 124 B6
Clear Creek County ☆ Colo., U.S.A. 39°40N 105°40W 125 C5
Clear Hills Canada 56°40N 119°30W 152 B1
Clear L. Calif., U.S.A. 39°2N 122°47W 126 D4
Clear L. Idaho, U.S.A. 43°8N 93°26W 81 B5
Clear L. Iowa, U.S.A. 31°53N 93°0W 110 C3
Clear L. Utah, U.S.A. 39°7N 112°38W 129 D3
Clear Lake Ind., U.S.A. 41°44N 84°50W 85 B6
Clear Lake Iowa, U.S.A. 43°8N 93°23W 81 B5
Clear Lake Minn., U.S.A. 45°27N 94°0W 77 E4
Clear Lake S. Dak., U.S.A. 44°45N 96°41W 76 F9
Clear Lake Wis., U.S.A. 45°15N 92°16W 78 C1
Clear Lake Res. Calif., U.S.A. 41°56N 121°5W 126 B5
Clear Spring Md., U.S.A. 39°39N 77°56W 93 A3
Clearbrook Minn., U.S.A. 47°42N 95°26W 77 C3
Clearco W. Va., U.S.A. 38°6N 80°34W 102 C4
Clearfield Iowa, U.S.A. 40°48N 94°29W 81 E4
Clearfield Ky., U.S.A. 38°10N 83°26W 105 B9
Clearfield Pa., U.S.A. 41°2N 78°27W 87 C4
Clearfield Utah, U.S.A. 41°7N 112°2W 129 B3
Clearfield County ☆ Pa., U.S.A. 41°0N 78°35W 87 D4
Clearlake Calif., U.S.A. 38°57N 122°38W 126 E4
Clearmont Mo., U.S.A. 40°31N 95°2W 83 A1
Clearmont Wyo., U.S.A. 44°38N 106°23W 124 B6
Clearview Okla., U.S.A. 35°24N 96°11W 107 C7
Clearwater B.C., Canada 51°38N 120°2W 155 D14
Clearwater Fla., U.S.A. 27°59N 82°48W 115 B2
Clearwater Kans., U.S.A. 37°30N 97°30W 82 D6
Clearwater Nebr., U.S.A. 42°10N 98°11W 80 B7
Clearwater S.C., U.S.A. 33°30N 81°54W 103 E4
Clearwater → Alta., Canada 56°44N 111°23W 152 B9
Clearwater → Alta., Canada 52°22N 114°57W 153 F6
Clearwater → B.C., Canada 51°38N 120°2W 155 D14
Clearwater → Idaho, U.S.A. 46°31N 116°33W 122 C2
Clearwater → Minn., U.S.A. 45°26N 94°16W 77 C2
Clearwater Beach Island Tampa, U.S.A. 27°59N 82°49W 115 A2
Clearwater County ☆ Idaho, U.S.A. 46°50N 115°30W 122 C3
Clearwater County ☆ Minn., U.S.A. 47°30N 95°20W 77 C3
Clearwater L. Mo., U.S.A. 37°8N 90°47W 83 D6
Clearwater Lake Prov. Park △ Man., Canada 54°0N 101°0W 151 A10
Clearwater Mts. Idaho, U.S.A. 46°5N 115°20W 122 C3
Clearwater Nat. Forest Idaho, U.S.A. 46°40N 115°5W 122 C3
Cleburne Tex., U.S.A. 32°21N 97°23W 109 E10
Cleburne County ☆ Ala., U.S.A. 33°39N 85°35W 112 C5
Cleburne County ☆ Ark., U.S.A. 35°30N 92°2W 106 C3
Clem Ga., U.S.A. 33°32N 85°1W 113 C1
Clements Ga., U.S.A. 38°18N 96°44W 82 C7
Clements Md., U.S.A. 38°18N 76°43W 93 B4
Clements Minn., U.S.A. 44°23N 95°3W 77 F3
Clementsport N.S., Canada 44°40N 65°37W 141 J4
Clemmons N.C., U.S.A. 36°1N 80°23W 103 B5
Clemson S.C., U.S.A. 34°41N 82°50W 103 D3
Clendenin W. Va., U.S.A. 38°29N 81°21W 102 C3
Clendinning Park △ B.C., Canada 50°28N 123°44W 154 E11
Cleo Springs Okla., U.S.A. 36°26N 98°29W 107 B5
Clermont Qué., Canada 47°41N 70°14W 145 D12
Clermont Fla., U.S.A. 28°33N 81°46W 114 C7
Clermont Iowa, U.S.A. 43°0N 91°39W 81 C7
Clermont N.J., U.S.A. 39°59N 74°48W 92 C2
Clermont County ☆ Ohio, U.S.A. 39°5N 84°11W 86 D2
Cleveland Ala., U.S.A. 33°59N 86°35W 112 C4
Cleveland Ga., U.S.A. 34°36N 83°46W 113 B3
Cleveland Miss., U.S.A. 33°45N 90°43W 111 C3
Cleveland Minn., U.S.A. 44°19N 93°50W 77 F5
Cleveland N. Dak., U.S.A. 46°54N 99°6W 76 D6
Cleveland Ohio, U.S.A. 41°29N 81°41W 98 A1
Cleveland Okla., U.S.A. 36°19N 96°28W 107 B7
Cleveland Tenn., U.S.A. 35°10N 84°53W 105 E8
Cleveland Tex., U.S.A. 30°21N 95°5W 109 G12
Cleveland Utah, U.S.A. 39°21N 110°51W 129 D5
Cleveland Va., U.S.A. 36°57N 82°9W 102 E4
Cleveland W. Va., U.S.A. 38°44N 80°24W 102 C4
Cleveland Wis., U.S.A. 43°55N 87°45W 78 E6
Cleveland, Mt. Mont., U.S.A. 48°56N 113°51W 123 B4
Cleveland County ☆ Ark., U.S.A. 33°58N 92°11W 106 E3
Cleveland County ☆ N.C., U.S.A. 35°20N 81°40W 103 C4
Cleveland County ☆ Okla., U.S.A. 35°10N 97°20W 107 C6
Cleveland Heights Ohio, U.S.A. 41°31N 81°33W 98 A2
Cleveland Hopkins Int. ✈ (CLE) Ohio, U.S.A. 41°25N 81°51W 86 B5
Cleveland Nat. Forest Calif., U.S.A. 32°45N 116°40W 127 L10
Cleveland Park B.C., Canada 49°22N 123°6W 161 A2
Clever Mo., U.S.A. 37°2N 93°3W 83 D3
Clewiston Fla., U.S.A. 26°45N 80°56W 114 E8
Cliff N. Mex., U.S.A. 32°58N 108°37W 131 E2
Clifford Mich., U.S.A. 43°19N 83°11W 79 F8
Clifford N. Dak., U.S.A. 47°21N 97°24W 76 C8
Cliffside Ont., Canada 43°44N 79°14W 161 A3
Cliffside Park N.J., U.S.A. 40°49N 73°59W 97 B3
Clifftop W. Va., U.S.A. 38°0N 80°56W 102 D4
Clifton Ariz., U.S.A. 33°3N 109°18W 130 D6
Clifton Idaho, U.S.A. 42°11N 112°0W 122 G7
Clifton Ill., U.S.A. 40°56N 87°56W 84 C6
Clifton Kans., U.S.A. 39°34N 97°17W 82 B6
Clifton N.J., U.S.A. 40°37N 74°4W 97 C2
Clifton Tenn., U.S.A. 35°18N 88°1W 104 E4
Clifton Tex., U.S.A. 31°47N 97°35W 109 F10
Clifton Forge Va., U.S.A. 37°49N 79°50W 102 D5
Clifton Heights Mo., U.S.A. 38°36N 90°17W 94 C1
Clifton Heights Pa., U.S.A. 39°56N 75°17W 98 B1
Clifton Park Baltimore, U.S.A. 39°19N 76°34W 99 B2
Clifton Springs N.Y., U.S.A. 42°58N 77°8W 88 C3

Cliftondale Mass., U.S.A. 42°26N 71°0W 96 A2
Clifty Ark., U.S.A. 36°14N 93°48W 106 B2
Climax Sask., Canada 49°10N 108°20W 150 F3
Climax Colo., U.S.A. 39°22N 106°11W 125 C4
Climax Ga., U.S.A. 30°53N 84°26W 113 F2
Climax Kans., U.S.A. 37°43N 96°13W 82 D7
Climax Mich., U.S.A. 42°14N 85°20W 79 G6
Climax Minn., U.S.A. 47°37N 96°49W 77 C2
Clinch → Tenn., U.S.A. 35°53N 84°29W 105 E8
Clinch County ☆ Ga., U.S.A. 31°0N 82°45W 113 E4
Clinchco Va., U.S.A. 37°10N 82°22W 102 D4
Cline Tex., U.S.A. 29°15N 100°5W 109 H7
Clines Corners N. Mex., U.S.A. 35°1N 105°40W 131 B5
Clingmans Dome Tenn., U.S.A. 35°34N 83°30W 105 E8
Clint Tex., U.S.A. 31°35N 106°14W 108 F1
Clinton B.C., Canada 51°6N 121°35W 155 D13
Clinton Ont., Canada 43°37N 81°32W 146 D5
Clinton Ala., U.S.A. 32°58N 88°0W 112 C1
Clinton Ark., U.S.A. 35°36N 92°28W 106 C3
Clinton Conn., U.S.A. 41°17N 72°32W 91 C2
Clinton Ill., U.S.A. 40°9N 88°57W 84 C51
Clinton Ind., U.S.A. 39°40N 87°24W 85 D3
Clinton Iowa, U.S.A. 41°51N 90°12W 81 D8
Clinton Ky., U.S.A. 36°40N 89°0W 104 D4
Clinton La., U.S.A. 30°52N 91°1W 110 D4
Clinton Maine, U.S.A. 44°38N 69°30W 90 D4
Clinton Mass., U.S.A. 42°25N 71°41W 91 B3
Clinton Md., U.S.A. 38°46N 76°54W 93 B4
Clinton Mich., U.S.A. 42°4N 83°58W 79 G8
Clinton Minn., U.S.A. 45°28N 96°26W 77 E2
Clinton Miss., U.S.A. 32°20N 90°20W 111 D3
Clinton Mo., U.S.A. 38°22N 93°46W 83 C3
Clinton Mont., U.S.A. 46°46N 113°43W 123 D4
Clinton N.C., U.S.A. 35°0N 78°22W 103 C7
Clinton N.J., U.S.A. 40°38N 74°55W 92 B2
Clinton N.Y., U.S.A. 43°3N 75°23W 88 C5
Clinton Ohio, U.S.A. 40°56N 81°38W 86 C5
Clinton Okla., U.S.A. 35°31N 98°58W 107 C5
Clinton S.C., U.S.A. 34°29N 81°53W 103 D4
Clinton Tenn., U.S.A. 36°6N 84°8W 105 D8
Clinton Utah, U.S.A. 41°8N 112°3W 129 B3
Clinton Wash., U.S.A. 47°59N 122°21W 120 C3
Clinton Wis., U.S.A. 42°34N 88°52W 78 F5
Clinton, L., U.S.A. 38°8N 85°45W 84 C5
Clinton Colden L. N.W.T., Canada 63°58N 107°27W 157 D11
Clinton County ☆ Ill., U.S.A. 38°35N 89°25W 84 E4
Clinton County ☆ Ind., U.S.A. 40°20N 86°30W 85 C4
Clinton County ☆ Iowa, U.S.A. 41°55N 90°30W 81 D8
Clinton County ☆ Ky., U.S.A. 36°45N 85°10W 105 D7
Clinton County ☆ Mich., U.S.A. 42°55N 84°40W 79 G7
Clinton County ☆ Mo., U.S.A. 39°35N 94°25W 83 B2
Clinton County ☆ N.Y., U.S.A. 44°50N 73°40W 88 B5
Clinton County ☆ Ohio, U.S.A. 39°27N 83°50W 86 D3
Clinton County ☆ Pa., U.S.A. 41°10N 77°50W 87 C5
Clinton L. Kans., U.S.A. 38°55N 95°22W 82 C8
Clintonville N.Y., U.S.A. 44°28N 73°35W 89 B1
Clintonville W. Va., U.S.A. 37°54N 80°36W 102 D4
Clintonville Wis., U.S.A. 44°37N 88°46W 78 D51
Clintwood Va., U.S.A. 37°9N 82°28W 102 D2
Clio Ala., U.S.A. 31°43N 85°37W 112 E5
Clio Iowa, U.S.A. 40°38N 93°27W 81 E5
Clio Mich., U.S.A. 43°11N 83°44W 79 F8
Clio S.C., U.S.A. 34°35N 79°33W 103 D6
Clive Alta., Canada 52°28N 113°27W 153 F7
Clive Iowa, U.S.A. 41°35N 93°43W 81 D5
Clontarf Minn., U.S.A. 45°23N 95°40W 77 E3
Cloquet Minn., U.S.A. 46°43N 92°28W 77 D61
Cloquet → Minn., U.S.A. 46°52N 92°35W 77 D6
Cloud County ☆ Kans., U.S.A. 39°30N 97°45W 82 B6
Cloud Peak Wyo., U.S.A. 44°23N 107°11W 124 B5
Cloudcroft N. Mex., U.S.A. 32°58N 105°45W 131 E5
Clova Qué., Canada 48°7N 75°22W 144 C7
Clover S.C., U.S.A. 35°7N 81°14W 103 C4
Clover Va., U.S.A. 36°50N 78°44W 102 E6
Clover Pt. B.C., Canada 48°24N 123°21W 155 G11
Cloverdale N.B., Canada 46°17N 67°22W 141 G2
Cloverdale Ala., U.S.A. 34°56N 87°46W 112 B3
Cloverdale Calif., U.S.A. 38°48N 123°1W 126 E3
Cloverdale Ind., U.S.A. 39°31N 86°48W 85 D4
Cloverdale Ohio, U.S.A. 41°1N 84°18W 86 B2
Cloverleaf Tex., U.S.A. 29°46N 95°10W 109 H12
Cloverport Ky., U.S.A. 37°50N 86°38W 104 C6
Clovis Calif., U.S.A. 36°49N 119°42W 127 G7
Clovis N. Mex., U.S.A. 34°24N 103°12W 131 C7
Cloyne Ont., Canada 44°49N 77°11W 147 C9
Cluculz L. B.C., Canada 53°53N 123°33W 154 B11
Clute Tex., U.S.A. 29°1N 95°24W 109 H12
Clutier Iowa, U.S.A. 42°4N 92°24W 81 C6
Clyattville Ga., U.S.A. 30°42N 83°19W 113 F3
Clyde Alta., Canada 54°9N 113°39W 152 D7
Clyde Kans., U.S.A. 39°36N 97°24W 82 B6
Clyde N.C., U.S.A. 35°32N 82°55W 103 C3
Clyde N.Y., U.S.A. 43°5N 76°52W 88 B4
Clyde Ohio, U.S.A. 41°18N 82°59W 86 B4
Clyde Tex., U.S.A. 32°24N 99°30W 109 E8
Clyde → N.S., Canada 43°35N 65°27W 141 K4
Clyde → Vt., U.S.A. 44°56N 72°13W 89 B2
Clyde Hill Wash., U.S.A. 47°37N 122°13W 132 C4
Clyde Park Mont., U.S.A. 45°52N 110°37W 123 E7
Clyde River N.S., Canada 43°38N 65°29W 141 K4
Clyde River Nunavut, Canada 70°30N 68°30W 158 C12
Clymer Pa., U.S.A. 40°40N 79°1W 87 D3
Clyo Ga., U.S.A. 32°29N 81°16W 113 D5
Coacalco México, Mexico 19°37N 99°7W 175 C8
Coachella Calif., U.S.A. 33°41N 116°10W 127 K10
Coachella Canal Calif., U.S.A. 32°43N 114°57W 127 L12
Coacoachou, L. Qué., Canada 50°25N 60°14W 143 B7
Coahoma Tex., U.S.A. 32°18N 101°18W 108 E6
Coahoma County ☆ Miss., U.S.A. 34°15N 90°35W 111 B3
Coahuayana → Mexico 18°41N 103°45W 174 D4
Coahuayutla Michoacan, Mexico 18°20N 101°43W 174 D6
Coahuila □ Mexico 27°20N 102°0W 170 C4
Coal → Canada 59°39N 126°57W 157 E7
Coal City Ill., U.S.A. 41°17N 88°17W 84 B5
Coal County ☆ Okla., U.S.A. 34°40N 96°15W 107 D7
Coal Grove Ohio, U.S.A. 38°30N 82°39W 86 E4
Coal Harbour B.C., Canada 50°36N 127°35W 154 C7
Coal Harbour B.C., Canada 49°17N 123°8W 161 B2
Coal Hill Ark., U.S.A. 35°26N 93°40W 106 C2
Coal Valley Nev., U.S.A. 37°57N 115°18W 128 E5
Coalcomán Michoacan, Mexico 18°47N 103°9W 174 D4
Coalcomán → Michoacan, Mexico 18°14N 103°14W 174 D4
Coalcomán, Sa. de Michoacan, Mexico 17°25N 102°55W 174 E5
Coaldale Alta., Canada 49°45N 112°35W 153 J8
Coaldale Colo., U.S.A. 38°22N 105°45W 125 D5
Coaldale Nev., U.S.A. 38°2N 117°54W 128 D3

202 Coalgate INDEX

Coalgate Okla., U.S.A. 34°32N 96°13W 107 D7
Coalhurst Alta., Canada 49°45N 112°56W 153 J8
Coaling Ala., U.S.A. 33°10N 87°20W 112 C3
Coalinga Calif., U.S.A. 36°9N 120°21W 127 G6
Coalmont B.C., Canada 49°32N 120°42W 155 F14
Coalmont Colo., U.S.A. 40°34N 106°27W 125 B4
Coalmont Tenn., U.S.A. 35°20N 85°42W 105 E7
Coalport Pa., U.S.A. 40°45N 78°32W 87 D4
Coalville Utah, U.S.A. 40°55N 111°24W 129 C4
Coamo Puerto Rico 18°5N 66°22W 184 G16
Coarsegold Calif., U.S.A. 37°16N 119°42W 126 F7
Coast Mts. B.C., Canada 55°0N 129°20W 154 B6
Coast Ranges Calif., U.S.A. 39°0N 123°0W 126 D4
Coast Ranges Oreg., U.S.A. 44°0N 123°40W 121 D2
Coatepec Veracruz, Mexico 19°27N 96°58W 176 E4
Coatepeque Guatemala 14°46N 91°55W 182 D1
Coates Minn., U.S.A. 44°43N 93°2W 77 F5
Coatesville Pa., U.S.A. 39°59N 75°50W 87 E7
Coaticook Qué., Canada 45°10N 71°46W 145 F11
Coats Kans., U.S.A. 37°31N 98°50W 82 D5
Coats N.C., U.S.A. 35°25N 78°40W 103 C7
Coats I. Nunavut, Canada 62°30N 83°0W 159 E9
Coatzacoalcos Mexico 18°7N 94°25W 177 F6
Coatzacoalcos → Veracruz, Mexico 18°9N 94°24W 177 F6
Coatzingo Puebla, Mexico 18°37N 98°11W 177 F2
Coatzintla Veracruz, Mexico 20°29N 97°27W 176 D3
Cobá Quintana Roo, Mexico 20°31N 87°45W 179 B6
Cobalt Ont., Canada 47°25N 79°42W 144 D3
Cobalt Idaho, U.S.A. 45°6N 114°14W 122 D4
Cobán Guatemala 15°30N 90°21W 182 C1
Cobaz, L. Qué. Canada 51°15N 60°21W 140 B9
Cobb Calif., U.S.A. 38°49N 122°43W 126 E4
Cobb Ky., U.S.A. 36°59N 87°47W 104 D5
Cobb County ☆ Ga., U.S.A. 33°50N 84°40W 113 C2
Cobb Island Md., U.S.A. 38°16N 76°51W 93 B4
Cobbs Creek Park Pa., U.S.A. 39°58N 75°15W 98 B1
Cobden Ont., Canada 45°38N 76°53W 147 B10
Cobden Ill., U.S.A. 37°32N 89°15W 84 F4
Cobden Minn. U.S.A. 44°17N 94°51W 77 F4
Cobequid B. N.S., Canada 45°21N 63°45W 141 H6
Cobleskill N.Y., U.S.A. 42°41N 74°29W 88 C6
Coboconk Ont., Canada 44°39N 78°48W 147 C8
Cobourg Ont., Canada 43°58N 78°10W 147 D8
Cobre Nev., U.S.A. 41°7N 114°24W 128 A6
Coburg Iowa, U.S.A. 40°55N 95°16W 81 E3
Coburg Oreg., U.S.A. 44°8N 123°4W 121 C2
Coburg I. N.W.T., Canada 75°57N 79°26W 158 B10
Coburn Gore Maine, U.S.A. 45°23N 70°48W 90 C3
Coburn Mt. Maine, U.S.A. 45°28N 70°6W 90 C3
Cocagne N.B., Canada 46°20N 64°37W 141 G5
Cochenour Ont., Canada 51°5N 93°48W 148 A3
Cochise Ariz., U.S.A. 32°7N 109°55W 130 E6
Cochise County ☆ Ariz., U.S.A. 32°0N 109°30W 130 F6
Cochiti Indian Reservation N. Mex., U.S.A. 35°38N 106°22W 131 B4
Cochran Ga., U.S.A. 32°23N 83°21W 113 D3
Cochran Va., U.S.A. 36°51N 77°54W 102 E7
Cochran County ☆ Tex., U.S.A. 33°37N 102°48W 108 D5
Cochrane Alta., Canada 51°11N 114°30W 153 G6
Cochrane Ont., Canada 49°0N 81°0W 144 B1
Cochrane Ala., U.S.A. 33°4N 88°15W 112 C2
Cochrane Wis., U.S.A. 44°14N 91°50W 78 D2
Cochrane → Man., Canada 57°53N 101°34W 157 E12
Cochranton Pa., U.S.A. 41°31N 80°3W 87 C2
Cochranville Pa., U.S.A. 39°54N 75°55W 93 A5
Cockburn I. Ont., Canada 45°55N 83°22W 146 B3
Cocke County ☆ Tenn., U.S.A. 35°58N 83°11W 105 E9
Cockeysville Md., U.S.A. 39°29N 76°39W 93 A4
Cockrell Hill Tex., U.S.A. 32°44N 96°53W 116 B4
Coco → Cent. Amer. 15°0N 83°8W 182 D3
Cocoa Fla., U.S.A. 28°21N 80°44W 114 C8
Cocoa Beach Fla., U.S.A. 28°19N 80°37W 114 C8
Cocodrie La., U.S.A. 29°15N 90°40W 110 E5
Cocodrie, Bayou → La., U.S.A. 31°11N 91°41W 110 C4
Cocohital Tabasco, Mexico 18°23N 93°20W 178 A3
Cocolalla Idaho, U.S.A. 48°6N 116°37W 122 A2
Cocomorachic Chihuahua, Mexico 28°40N 107°55W 169 E8
Coconino County ☆ Ariz., U.S.A. 36°0N 112°0W 130 B4
Coconino Nat. Forest Ariz., U.S.A. 34°45N 111°20W 130 C4
Coconino Plateau Ariz., U.S.A. 35°45N 112°40W 130 B3
Coconut Grove Fla., U.S.A. 25°42N 80°15W 115 D2
Cocos I. Guam 13°14N 144°39E 184 b
Cocula Guerrero, Mexico 18°14N 99°40W 175 D8
Cocula Jalisco, Mexico 20°23N 103°50W 174 B4
Cod, C. Mass., U.S.A. 42°5N 70°10W 91 B4
Cod I. Nfld. & L., Canada 57°47N 61°47W 143 B5
Coderre Sask., Canada 50°11N 106°31W 150 E5
Codette Sask., Canada 53°16N 104°0W 150 B7
Codington County ☆ S. Dak., U.S.A. 44°54N 97°7W 76 F8
Codroy Nfld. & L., Canada 47°53N 59°24W 142 E1
Codroy Pond Nfld. & L., Canada 48°4N 58°52W 142 D2
Cody Nebr., U.S.A. 42°56N 101°15W 80 B4
Cody Wyo., U.S.A. 44°32N 109°3W 124 B3
Cody-Rouge Mich., U.S.A. 42°21N 83°13W 98 A1
Coe Hill Ont., Canada 44°52N 77°50W 147 C9
Coeburn Va., U.S.A. 36°57N 82°28W 102 E2
Coeneo de la Libertad Michoacan, Mexico 19°50N 101°35W 174 C6
Coeur d'Alene Idaho, U.S.A. 47°41N 116°46W 122 B2
Coeur d'Alene → Idaho, U.S.A. 47°45N 116°0W 122 B2
Coeur d'Alene Indian Reservation Idaho, U.S.A. 47°10N 116°55W 122 B2
Coeur d'Alene L. Idaho, U.S.A. 47°32N 116°49W 122 B2
Coeur d'Alene Mts. U.S.A. 47°45N 116°0W 122 B2
Coeur d'Alene Nat. Forest Idaho, U.S.A. 47°55N 116°15W 122 B2
Coffee County ☆ Ala., U.S.A. 31°23N 85°56W 112 E5
Coffee County ☆ Ga., U.S.A. 31°30N 82°50W 113 E4
Coffee County ☆ Tenn., U.S.A. 35°29N 86°5W 104 E6
Coffeen Ill., U.S.A. 39°5N 89°24W 84 D4
Coffeeville Ala., U.S.A. 31°45N 88°5W 112 E2
Coffeeville Miss., U.S.A. 33°59N 89°41W 111 C4
Coffey Mo., U.S.A. 40°6N 94°0W 83 A3
Coffey County ☆ Kans., U.S.A. 38°15N 95°45W 82 C8
Coffeyville Kans., U.S.A. 37°2N 95°37W 82 D8
Cofre de Perote, Cerro Veracruz, Mexico 19°28N 97°0W 176 E3
Cogar Okla., U.S.A. 35°20N 98°8W 107 C5
Cogdell Ga., U.S.A. 31°10N 82°43W 113 E4
Coggon Iowa, U.S.A. 42°17N 91°32W 81 C7
Cogswell N. Dak., U.S.A. 46°7N 97°47W 76 D8
Cohagen Mont., U.S.A. 47°3N 106°37W 123 C11
Cohansey N.J., U.S.A. 39°21N 75°22W 92 C1
Cohasset Mass., U.S.A. 42°14N 70°48W 91 B4
Cohasset Minn., U.S.A. 47°16N 93°38W 77 C5
Cohocton → N.Y., U.S.A. 42°9N 77°6W 88 C3
Cohoes N.Y., U.S.A. 42°46N 73°42W 91 B1
Cohutta Ga., U.S.A. 34°58N 84°57W 113 B2
Coiba, I. de Panama 7°30N 81°40W 182 E3
Coin Iowa, U.S.A. 40°40N 95°14W 81 E3
Coixtlahuaca Oaxaca, Mexico 17°45N 97°18W 177 G3
Cojutepequé El Salv. 13°41N 88°54W 182 D2
Cokato Minn., U.S.A. 45°5N 94°11W 77 E4
Coke County ☆ Tex., U.S.A. 31°54N 100°29W 108 F7
Coker Ala., U.S.A. 33°15N 87°41W 112 C3
Cokeville Wyo., U.S.A. 42°5N 110°57W 124 D2
Colbert Ga., U.S.A. 34°2N 83°13W 113 B3
Colbert Okla., U.S.A. 33°51N 96°30W 107 E7
Colbert County ☆ Ala., U.S.A. 34°44N 87°42W 112 B3
Colborne Ont., Canada 44°0N 77°53W 147 C9
Colbourne Md., U.S.A. 38°15N 75°26W 93 B5
Colburn Idaho, U.S.A. 48°24N 116°32W 122 A2
Colby Kans., U.S.A. 39°24N 101°3W 82 B2
Colby Wash., U.S.A. 47°31N 122°32W 132 C2
Colby Wis., U.S.A. 44°55N 90°19W 78 D3
Colchester Conn., U.S.A. 41°35N 72°20W 91 C2
Colchester Ill., U.S.A. 40°25N 90°48W 84 C3
Colchester Vt., U.S.A. 44°33N 73°9W 89 B1
Colcord Okla., U.S.A. 36°16N 94°42W 107 B9
Colcoyán de las Flores Oaxaca, Mexico 17°17N 98°15W 177 G2
Cold Bay Alaska, U.S.A. 55°12N 162°42W 135 J7
Cold L. Alta., Canada 54°33N 110°5W 152 D10
Cold Lake Alta., Canada 54°27N 110°10W 152 D10
Cold Mt. N.C., U.S.A. 35°25N 82°51W 103 C3
Cold Spring Minn., U.S.A. 45°27N 94°26W 77 E4
Cold Spring N.Y., U.S.A. 41°25N 73°57W 92 A3
Cold Springs Cr. → Wyo., U.S.A. 44°32N 104°6W 124 B8
Coldspring Tex., U.S.A. 30°36N 95°8W 109 G12
Coldstream B.C., Canada 50°13N 119°11W 155 E15
Coldwater Ont., Canada 44°42N 79°40W 146 C7
Coldwater Kans., U.S.A. 37°16N 99°20W 82 D4
Coldwater Mich., U.S.A. 41°57N 85°0W 79 H6
Coldwater Miss., U.S.A. 34°41N 89°59W 111 B4
Coldwater Ohio, U.S.A. 40°29N 84°38W 86 C2
Coldwater → Miss., U.S.A. 34°10N 90°13W 111 B3
Coldwater Cr. → Okla., U.S.A. 36°40N 101°10W 107 B2
Cole Okla., U.S.A. 35°8N 97°33W 107 C6
Cole Camp Mo., U.S.A. 38°28N 93°12W 83 C3
Cole County ☆ Mo., U.S.A. 38°30N 92°15W 83 C4
Colebrook N.H., U.S.A. 44°54N 71°30W 89 B3
Coleman Fla., U.S.A. 28°48N 82°4W 114 C6
Coleman Ga., U.S.A. 31°40N 84°54W 113 E2
Coleman Mich., U.S.A. 43°46N 84°35W 79 F7
Coleman Okla., U.S.A. 34°16N 96°25W 107 D7
Coleman Tex., U.S.A. 31°50N 99°26W 109 F8
Coleman Wis., U.S.A. 45°4N 88°2W 78 C5
Coleman County ☆ Tex., U.S.A. 31°50N 99°30W 109 F8
Colerain N.C., U.S.A. 36°12N 76°46W 103 B9
Coleraine Minn., U.S.A. 47°17N 93°27W 77 C5
Coleridge Nebr., U.S.A. 42°30N 97°13W 80 B8
Coles County ☆ Ill., U.S.A. 39°30N 88°15W 84 D5
Coles Point Va., U.S.A. 38°9N 76°38W 93 B4
Colesburg Iowa, U.S.A. 42°38N 91°12W 81 C7
Colesville Md., U.S.A. 39°5N 77°0W 93 A4
Coleville Sask., Canada 51°43N 109°15W 150 D2
Coleville Calif., U.S.A. 38°34N 119°30W 126 E7
Colfax Calif., U.S.A. 39°6N 120°57W 126 D6
Colfax Ill., U.S.A. 40°34N 88°37W 84 C5
Colfax Ind., U.S.A. 40°12N 86°40W 85 C4
Colfax Iowa, U.S.A. 41°41N 93°14W 81 D5
Colfax La., U.S.A. 31°31N 92°42W 110 C3
Colfax N. Dak., U.S.A. 46°28N 96°53W 76 D9
Colfax Wash., U.S.A. 46°53N 117°22W 120 D8
Colfax Wis., U.S.A. 45°0N 91°44W 78 C2
Colfax County ☆ N. Mex., U.S.A. 36°30N 104°30W 131 A6
Colfax County ☆ Nebr., U.S.A. 41°30N 97°0W 80 C8
Colgate N. Dak., U.S.A. 47°15N 97°39W 76 C8
Colima Colima, Mexico 19°14N 103°43W 174 C4
Colima ☐ Mexico 19°10N 104°0W 174 C4
Colima, Nevado de Jalisco, Mexico 19°33N 103°38W 174 C4
Colima, Volcán de Mexico 19°31N 103°38W 174 C4
Colimilla Guadalajara, Mexico 20°41N 103°12W 180 A2
Colinet Nfld. & L., Canada 47°13N 53°33W 142 E7
Colinton Alta., Canada 54°37N 113°15W 152 D7
Colipa Veracruz, Mexico 19°55N 96°42W 176 E4
Collbran Colo., U.S.A. 39°14N 107°58W 125 C3
College Alaska, U.S.A. 64°52N 147°49W 135 D11
College Corner Ohio, U.S.A. 39°34N 84°49W 86 D2
College Heights Alta., Canada 52°28N 113°45W 153 F7
College Heights Ark., U.S.A. 33°35N 91°48W 106 E4
College Park Ga., U.S.A. 33°39N 84°27W 117 C2
College Park Md., U.S.A. 38°59N 76°55W 99 B4
College Place Wash., U.S.A. 46°3N 118°23W 120 D7
College Point N.Y., U.S.A. 40°47N 73°50W 97 B3
College Station Tex., U.S.A. 30°37N 96°21W 109 G11
Collegedale Tenn., U.S.A. 35°4N 85°3W 105 E7
Collegeville Ind., U.S.A. 40°56N 87°9W 85 C3
Collegeville Pa., U.S.A. 40°11N 75°27W 92 B1
Colleton County ☆ S.C., U.S.A. 33°0N 80°40W 103 F5
Collette N.B., Canada 46°47N 65°27W 141 G4
Colleymount B.C., Canada 54°2N 126°19W 154 A8
Colleyville Tex., U.S.A. 32°52N 97°9W 116 A3
Collier County ☆ Fla., U.S.A. 26°0N 81°30W 114 E7
Collierville Tenn., U.S.A. 35°3N 89°40W 104 E3
Collin County ☆ Tex., U.S.A. 33°6N 96°40W 109 D11
Collingdale Pa., U.S.A. 39°54N 75°16W 98 B1
Collingswood N.J., U.S.A. 39°55N 75°4W 98 B2
Collingsworth County ☆ Tex., U.S.A. 35°0N 100°15W 108 C7
Collingwood Ont., Canada 44°29N 80°13W 146 C6
Collingwood Corner Qué., Canada 45°37N 63°56W 141 H6
Collins Ont., Canada 50°17N 89°27W 148 B7
Collins Ark., U.S.A. 33°32N 91°34W 106 E4
Collins Ga., U.S.A. 32°11N 82°7W 113 D4
Collins Iowa, U.S.A. 41°54N 93°18W 81 D5
Collins Miss., U.S.A. 31°39N 89°33W 111 E4
Collins Mo., U.S.A. 37°54N 93°37W 83 D3
Collins → Tenn., U.S.A. 35°23N 85°34W 105 E7
Collinson Pen. N.W.T., Canada 69°58N 101°24W 158 D5
Collinston La., U.S.A. 32°41N 91°52W 110 B4
Collinsville Ala., U.S.A. 34°16N 85°52W 112 B5
Collinsville Conn., U.S.A. 41°49N 72°55W 91 C2
Collinsville Ill., U.S.A. 38°40N 89°59W 84 E4
Collinsville Miss., U.S.A. 32°30N 88°51W 111 D5
Collinsville Okla., U.S.A. 36°22N 95°51W 107 B8
Collinsville Tex., U.S.A. 33°34N 96°55W 109 D11
Collinsville Va., U.S.A. 36°43N 79°55W 102 E5
Collinwood Tenn., U.S.A. 35°10N 87°44W 104 E5
Collison Ill., U.S.A. 40°14N 87°48W 84 C6
Collyer Kans., U.S.A. 39°2N 100°7W 82 B3
Colma Calif., U.S.A. 37°40N 122°27W 132 B2
Colman S. Dak., U.S.A. 43°59N 96°49W 76 G9
Colmesneil Tex., U.S.A. 30°54N 94°25W 109 G13
Colo Iowa, U.S.A. 42°1N 93°19W 81 C5
Coloma Calif., U.S.A. 38°48N 120°53W 126 E6
Coloma Mich., U.S.A. 42°11N 86°19W 79 G5
Coloma Wis., U.S.A. 44°2N 89°31W 78 D4
Colombia Nuevo León, Mexico 27°42N 99°46W 171 C10
Colombian Basin S. Amer. 14°0N 76°0W 183 D5
Colombier Qué., Canada 48°52N 68°51W 145 C14
Colome S. Dak., U.S.A. 43°16N 99°43W 76 G6
Colón Cuba 22°42N 80°54W 182 B3
Colón Querétaro, Mexico 20°48N 100°3W 175 B7
Colón Panama 9°20N 79°54W 182 E4
Colon Mich., U.S.A. 41°57N 85°19W 79 H6
Colon Nebr., U.S.A. 41°18N 96°37W 80 C9
Colona Colo., U.S.A. 38°20N 107°47W 125 D3
Colona Ill., U.S.A. 41°29N 90°21W 84 B3
Colonet, C. Baja Calif., Mexico 30°57N 116°19W 166 C2
Colonia N.J., U.S.A. 40°34N 74°18W 97 C1
Colonia la Venta Distrito Federal, Mexico 19°20N 99°19W 181 B2
Colonial Beach Va., U.S.A. 38°15N 76°58W 93 B4
Colonial Heights Tenn., U.S.A. 36°29N 82°30W 105 D10
Colonial Heights Va., U.S.A. 37°15N 77°25W 102 D7
Colonial Nat. Historical Park ⌂ Va., U.S.A. 37°13N 76°31W 102 D8
Colonie N.Y., U.S.A. 42°43N 73°50W 88 C7
Colonsay Sask., Canada 51°59N 105°52W 150 D6
Colony Kans., U.S.A. 38°4N 95°22W 82 C8
Colony Okla., U.S.A. 35°23N 98°41W 107 C5
Colorada, L. Coahuila, Mexico 27°32N 103°40W 169 F12
Colorado ☐ U.S.A. 39°30N 105°30W 125 C5
Colorado → Baja Calif., Mexico 31°54N 114°57W 166 B4
Colorado → Tex., U.S.A. 28°36N 95°59W 109 J12
Colorado, Cerro Baja Calif., Mexico 31°28N 115°32W 166 B3
Colorado, Sa. Coahuila, Mexico 28°2N 102°13W 170 B2
Colorado City Ariz., U.S.A. 36°59N 112°59W 130 A3
Colorado City Tex., U.S.A. 32°24N 100°52W 108 E7
Colorado County ☆ Tex., U.S.A. 29°42N 96°33W 109 H11
Colorado Nat. Monument ⌂ Colo., U.S.A. 39°4N 108°42W 125 C2
Colorado Plateau Ariz., U.S.A. 37°0N 111°0W 130 A5
Colorado River Aqueduct Calif., U.S.A. 33°50N 117°23W 127 K9
Colorado River Indian Reservation Ariz., U.S.A. 33°55N 114°25W 130 D1
Colorado Springs Colo., U.S.A. 38°50N 104°49W 125 D6
Colorado Springs Peterson Field ✕ (COS) Colo., U.S.A. 38°49N 104°43W 125 D6
Colotlán Jalisco, Mexico 22°6N 103°16W 173 E7
Colquitt Ga., U.S.A. 31°10N 84°44W 113 E2
Colquitt County ☆ Ga., U.S.A. 31°15N 83°50W 113 E3
Colquitz B.C., Canada 48°29N 123°24W 155 G11
Colrain Mass., U.S.A. 42°41N 72°42W 91 B2
Colstrip Mont., U.S.A. 45°53N 106°38W 123 E11
Colt Ark., U.S.A. 35°8N 90°49W 106 C5
Colter Bay Village Wyo., U.S.A. 43°54N 110°38W 124 C2
Colter Peak Wyo., U.S.A. 44°18N 110°7W 124 B2
Colton Calif., U.S.A. 34°4N 117°20W 127 J9
Colton N.Y., U.S.A. 44°33N 74°56W 88 A6
Colton S. Dak., U.S.A. 43°47N 96°56W 76 G9
Colton Utah, U.S.A. 39°51N 111°0W 129 D5
Colton Wash., U.S.A. 46°34N 117°8W 120 D8
Colts Neck N.J., U.S.A. 40°17N 74°11W 92 B2
Columbia Ala., U.S.A. 31°18N 85°7W 112 E5
Columbia Conn., U.S.A. 41°42N 72°18W 91 C2
Columbia Ill., U.S.A. 38°27N 90°12W 84 E3
Columbia Ky., U.S.A. 37°6N 85°18W 105 C7
Columbia La., U.S.A. 32°6N 92°5W 110 B3
Columbia Md., U.S.A. 39°14N 76°50W 93 A4
Columbia Miss., U.S.A. 31°15N 89°50W 111 E4
Columbia Mo., U.S.A. 38°57N 92°20W 83 C4
Columbia N.C., U.S.A. 35°55N 76°15W 103 C9
Columbia N.J., U.S.A. 40°56N 75°6W 92 B1
Columbia Pa., U.S.A. 40°2N 76°30W 87 D6
Columbia S.C., U.S.A. 34°0N 81°2W 103 D4
Columbia S. Dak., U.S.A. 45°37N 98°19W 76 E7
Columbia Tenn., U.S.A. 35°37N 87°2W 104 E5
Columbia → N. Amer. 46°15N 124°5W 120 D1
Columbia, C. Nunavut, Canada 83°6N 69°57W 158 A12
Columbia, District of ☐ U.S.A. 38°55N 77°0W 93 B4
Columbia, Mt. B.C., Canada 52°8N 117°20W 155 C17
Columbia Basin Wash., U.S.A. 46°45N 119°5W 120 D6
Columbia Bottom Mo., U.S.A. 38°48N 90°9W 94 A3
Columbia City Ind., U.S.A. 41°10N 85°29W 85 B5
Columbia City Oreg., U.S.A. 45°53N 122°49W 121 B3
Columbia County ☆ Ark., U.S.A. 33°16N 93°14W 106 E2
Columbia County ☆ Fla., U.S.A. 30°15N 82°40W 114 A6
Columbia County ☆ Ga., U.S.A. 33°30N 82°10W 113 C4
Columbia County ☆ N.Y., U.S.A. 42°10N 73°40W 88 C7
Columbia County ☆ Oreg., U.S.A. 45°55N 123°0W 121 B2
Columbia County ☆ Pa., U.S.A. 41°10N 76°20W 87 C6
Columbia County ☆ Wash., U.S.A. 46°19N 117°59W 120 D8
Columbia County ☆ Wis., U.S.A. 43°30N 89°20W 78 E4
Columbia Edgewater Oreg., U.S.A. 45°35N 122°48W 132 A2
Columbia Falls Maine, U.S.A. 44°39N 67°44W 90 D6
Columbia Falls Mont., U.S.A. 48°23N 114°11W 123 B3
Columbia Heights Minn., U.S.A. 45°2N 93°14W 94 A2
Columbia L. B.C., Canada 50°15N 115°52W 153 H5
Columbia Mts. B.C., Canada 51°0N 118°0W 155 D16
Columbia Park Minn., U.S.A. 45°1N 93°15W 94 A2
Columbia River Gorge Nat. Scenic Area ⌂ Wash., U.S.A. 45°42N 121°55W 120 E4
Columbia Road Res. S. Dak., U.S.A. 45°40N 98°18W 76 E7
Columbiana Ala., U.S.A. 33°11N 86°36W 112 C4
Columbiana Ohio, U.S.A. 40°53N 80°42W 86 C6
Columbiana County ☆ Ohio, U.S.A. 40°46N 80°46W 86 C6
Columbiaville Mich., U.S.A. 43°9N 83°25W 79 F8
Columbine Colo., U.S.A. 40°56N 106°59W 125 B4
Columbine Valley Colo., U.S.A. 39°36N 105°1W 134 C1
Columbus Ga., U.S.A. 32°28N 84°59W 113 D2
Columbus Ind., U.S.A. 39°13N 85°55W 85 D5
Columbus Kans., U.S.A. 37°10N 94°50W 82 D9
Columbus Ky., U.S.A. 36°46N 89°6W 104 D3
Columbus Miss., U.S.A. 33°30N 88°25W 111 C5
Columbus Mont., U.S.A. 45°38N 109°15W 123 E8
Columbus N.C., U.S.A. 35°15N 82°12W 103 C3
Columbus N. Dak., U.S.A. 48°54N 102°47W 76 B3
Columbus N. Mex., U.S.A. 31°50N 107°38W 131 F3
Columbus Nebr., U.S.A. 41°26N 97°22W 80 C8
Columbus Ohio, U.S.A. 39°58N 83°0W 86 D3
Columbus Tex., U.S.A. 29°42N 96°33W 109 H11
Columbus Wis., U.S.A. 43°21N 89°1W 78 E4
Columbus Air Force Base Miss., U.S.A. 33°31N 88°28W 111 C5
Columbus County ☆ N.C., U.S.A. 34°15N 78°45W 103 D7
Columbus Grove Ohio, U.S.A. 40°55N 84°4W 86 C2
Columbus Int. ✕ (CMH) Ohio, U.S.A. 40°0N 82°53W 86 D4
Columbus Junction Iowa, U.S.A. 41°17N 91°22W 81 D7
Columbus L. Miss., U.S.A. 33°31N 88°29W 111 C5
Columbus Salt Marsh Nev., U.S.A. 38°5N 118°5W 128 D2
Colusa Calif., U.S.A. 39°13N 122°1W 126 D4
Colusa County ☆ Calif., U.S.A. 39°15N 122°15W 126 D4
Colville Wash., U.S.A. 48°33N 117°54W 120 B8
Colville → Alaska, U.S.A. 70°25N 150°30W 135 A10
Colville → Wash., U.S.A. 48°37N 118°5W 120 B7
Colville Indian Reservation Wash., U.S.A. 48°15N 119°0W 120 B7
Colville L. N.W.T., Canada 67°2N 126°7W 156 C7
Colville Lake N.W.T., Canada 67°2N 126°7W 156 C7
Colville Nat. Forest Wash., U.S.A. 48°50N 117°15W 120 B8
Colvos Passage Wash., U.S.A. 47°29N 122°31W 132 D2
Colwell Iowa, U.S.A. 43°9N 92°36W 81 B6
Colwich Kans., U.S.A. 37°47N 97°32W 82 D6
Colwood B.C., Canada 48°26N 123°29W 155 G11
Colwyn Pa., U.S.A. 39°54N 75°15W 98 B1
Comal County ☆ Tex., U.S.A. 29°53N 98°25W 109 H9
Comala Colima, Mexico 19°19N 103°45W 174 C4
Comalcalco Tabasco, Mexico 18°16N 93°13W 178 A3
Comanche Okla., U.S.A. 34°22N 97°58W 107 D6
Comanche Tex., U.S.A. 31°54N 98°36W 109 F9
Comanche County ☆ Kans., U.S.A. 37°15N 99°15W 82 D4
Comanche County ☆ Okla., U.S.A. 34°40N 98°25W 107 D5
Comanche County ☆ Tex., U.S.A. 31°55N 98°35W 109 F9
Comanche Nat. Grassland Colo., U.S.A. 37°20N 103°0W 125 E8
Comayagua Honduras 14°25N 87°37W 182 D2
Combahee → S.C., U.S.A. 32°31N 80°31W 103 F5
Comber Ont., Canada 42°14N 82°33W 146 E4
Combermere Ont., Canada 45°22N 77°37W 147 B9
Come By Chance Nfld. & L., Canada 47°51N 54°0W 142 E6
Comer Ala., U.S.A. 32°2N 85°23W 112 D5
Comer Ga., U.S.A. 34°4N 83°8W 113 B3
Comerío Puerto Rico 18°12N 66°12W 184 G16
Cometa, Pta. Oaxaca, Mexico 15°41N 96°35W 177 J4
Comfort Tex., U.S.A. 29°58N 98°55W 109 H9
Comfrey Minn., U.S.A. 44°7N 94°54W 77 F4
Comitán de Domínguez Chiapas, Mexico 16°15N 92°8W 178 C4
Commack N.Y., U.S.A. 40°51N 73°18W 92 B3
Commanda Ont., Canada 45°57N 79°36W 146 B7
Commerce Calif., U.S.A. 34°0N 118°9W 133 B4
Commerce Ga., U.S.A. 34°12N 83°28W 113 B3
Commerce Mo., U.S.A. 37°9N 89°27W 83 D7
Commerce Okla., U.S.A. 36°56N 94°53W 107 B9
Commerce Tex., U.S.A. 33°15N 95°54W 109 D12
Commerce City Colo., U.S.A. 39°48N 104°56W 134 B2
Commissaires, L. des Qué., Canada 48°10N 72°16W 145 C10
Commissioner I. Man., Canada 52°10N 97°16W 151 C14
Committee B. Nunavut, Canada 68°30N 86°30W 158 D8
Como Colo., U.S.A. 39°19N 105°54W 125 C5
Como Miss., U.S.A. 34°31N 89°56W 111 B4
Como Tex., U.S.A. 33°3N 95°28W 109 D12
Como Park Minn., U.S.A. 44°58N 93°9W 94 B3
Comobabi Mts. Ariz., U.S.A. 32°0N 111°45W 130 E4
Comonfort Guanajuato, Mexico 20°43N 100°46W 175 B7
Comox B.C., Canada 49°42N 124°55W 154 F10
Compass Lake Fla., U.S.A. 30°36N 85°24W 114 A3
Compeer Alta., Canada 51°52N 110°0W 153 G10
Competition Mo., U.S.A. 37°29N 92°26W 83 D4
Compostela Nayarit, Mexico 21°14N 104°55W 172 F6
Comptche Calif., U.S.A. 39°16N 123°35W 126 D3
Compton Qué., Canada 45°14N 71°49W 145 F11
Compton Ark., U.S.A. 36°6N 93°18W 106 B2
Compton Calif., U.S.A. 33°53N 118°13W 127 K8
Comstock Minn., U.S.A. 46°40N 96°45W 77 D2
Comstock Nebr., U.S.A. 41°34N 99°15W 80 C6
Comstock Tex., U.S.A. 29°41N 101°10W 108 H6
Comstock Park Mich., U.S.A. 43°2N 85°40W 79 F6
Conanicut I. R.I., U.S.A. 41°32N 71°21W 91 C3
Conasauga → Ga., U.S.A. 34°33N 84°55W 113 B2
Concan Tex., U.S.A. 29°30N 99°43W 109 H8
Concepción, B. Baja Calif. S., Mexico 26°39N 111°48W 167 G7
Concepción, Pta. Baja Calif. S., Mexico 26°53N 111°50W 167 G7
Concepción de Buenos Aires Jalisco, Mexico 19°58N 103°16W 174 C4
Concepción del Oro Zacatecas, Mexico 24°38N 101°25W 173 C9
Conception, Pt. Calif., U.S.A. 34°27N 120°28W 127 J6
Conception B. Nfld. & L., Canada 47°45N 53°0W 142 E8
Conception I. Bahamas 23°52N 75°9W 183 B4
Conception Junction Mo., U.S.A. 40°16N 94°42W 83 A2
Conchas → N. Mex., U.S.A. 35°23N 104°18W 131 B6
Conchas Dam N. Mex., U.S.A. 35°22N 104°11W 131 B6
Conchas Lake N. Mex., U.S.A. 35°23N 104°11W 131 B6
Conche Nfld. & L., Canada 50°55N 55°58W 142 B5
Concheño → Chihuahua, Mexico 28°3N 108°23W 169 E7
Concho Ariz., U.S.A. 34°28N 109°36W 130 C6
Concho → Tex., U.S.A. 31°34N 99°43W 109 F8
Concho County ☆ Tex., U.S.A. 31°13N 99°51W 109 F8
Conchos → Chihuahua, Mexico 29°35N 104°25W 169 D11
Conchos → Tamaulipas, Mexico 24°55N 97°38W 171 E6
Conconully Wash., U.S.A. 48°34N 119°45W 120 B6
Concord Ont., Canada 43°48N 79°29W 161 A2
Concord Ark., U.S.A. 35°40N 91°51W 106 C4
Concord Calif., U.S.A. 37°59N 122°2W 126 F4
Concord Ga., U.S.A. 33°5N 84°27W 113 C2
Concord Mass., U.S.A. 42°27N 71°20W 91 B3
Concord Md., U.S.A. 38°38N 75°48W 93 B5
Concord Mich., U.S.A. 42°11N 84°38W 79 G7
Concord Mo., U.S.A. 38°32N 90°23W 83 C6
Concord N.C., U.S.A. 35°25N 80°35W 103 C5
Concord N.H., U.S.A. 43°12N 71°32W 89 C3
Concord Vt., U.S.A. 44°26N 71°53W 89 B3
Concordia Sinaloa, Mexico 23°17N 106°4W 172 D4
Concordia Kans., U.S.A. 39°34N 97°40W 82 B6
Concordia Mo., U.S.A. 38°59N 93°34W 83 C3
Concordia Parish ☆ La., U.S.A. 31°38N 91°33W 110 C4
Concrete Wash., U.S.A. 48°32N 121°45W 120 B4
Conda Idaho, U.S.A. 42°44N 111°32W 122 G7
Condado de Sayavedra México, Mexico 19°34N 99°20W 181 A2
Conde S. Dak., U.S.A. 45°9N 98°6W 76 E7
Condon Mont., U.S.A. 47°34N 113°45W 123 C4
Condon Oreg., U.S.A. 45°14N 120°11W 121 B5
Conecuh → Fla., U.S.A. 30°58N 87°13W 114 A1
Conecuh County ☆ Ala., U.S.A. 31°26N 86°57W 112 E4
Conecuh Nat. Forest Ala., U.S.A. 31°2N 86°45W 112 E4
Conejos Durango, Mexico 26°14N 103°53W 173 A7
Conejos Colo., U.S.A. 37°5N 106°1W 125 E4
Conejos → Colo., U.S.A. 37°18N 105°44W 125 E5
Conejos County ☆ Colo., U.S.A. 37°10N 106°10W 125 E4
Conesville Iowa, U.S.A. 41°23N 91°21W 81 D7
Coneto de Comonfort Durango, Mexico 24°58N 104°45W 173 C6
Coney Island N.Y., U.S.A. 40°34N 74°0W 97 C3
Confluence Pa., U.S.A. 39°49N 79°21W 93 A1
Confusion Range Utah, U.S.A. 39°20N 113°40W 129 D2
Congaree → S.C., U.S.A. 33°44N 80°38W 103 E5
Congaree Swamp Nat. Monument ⌂ U.S.A. 33°47N 80°47W 103 E5
Conger Minn., U.S.A. 43°37N 93°32W 77 G5
Congress Ariz., U.S.A. 34°9N 112°51W 130 C3

Congress *Ohio, U.S.A.* 40°56N 82°3W **86** C4
Conicarit *Sonora, Mexico* 27°12N 109°7W **168** F6
Conifer *Colo., U.S.A.* 39°31N 105°18W **125** C5
Coniston *Ont., Canada* 46°29N 80°51W **146** A6
Conkal *Yucatán, Mexico* 21°4N 89°32W **179** A4
Conklin *Alta., Canada* 55°38N 111°5W **152** C9
Conklin *N.Y., U.S.A.* 42°2N 75°49W **88** C5
Conlen *Tex., U.S.A.* 36°14N 102°15W **108** A5
Conley → *Georgia, U.S.A.* 33°40N 84°17W **117** C3
Conn L. *Nunavut, Canada* 70°32N 73°34W **158** C11
Conneaut *Ohio, U.S.A.* 41°57N 80°34W **86** B6
Conneaut Lake *Pa., U.S.A.* 41°36N 80°18W **87** C2
Conneautville *Pa., U.S.A.* 41°45N 80°22W **87** C2
Connecticut □ *Conn., U.S.A.* 41°30N 72°45W **91** C2
Connecticut → *Conn., U.S.A.* 41°16N 72°20W **91** C2
Connell *Wash., U.S.A.* 46°40N 118°52W **120** D7
Connellsville *Pa., U.S.A.* 40°1N 79°35W **87** D3
Conner *Mich., U.S.A.* 42°26N 83°0W **98** A3
Conner *Mont., U.S.A.* 45°56N 114°7W **123** E3
Connersville *Ind., U.S.A.* 39°39N 85°8W **85** D5
Connerville *Okla., U.S.A.* 34°27N 96°38W **107** D7
Connors *N.B., Canada* 47°10N 68°52W **145** D14
Cono, Pta. *Baja Calif., Mexico* 28°59N 114°37W **166** E4
Conover *N.C., U.S.A.* 35°42N 81°13W **103** C4
Conowingo *Md., U.S.A.* 39°40N 76°11W **93** A4
Conquest *Sask., Canada* 51°32N 107°14W **150** D4
Conquista Campesina *Campeche, Mexico* 18°10N 91°15W **179** D2
Conrad *Iowa, U.S.A.* 42°14N 92°52W **81** C6
Conrad *Mont., U.S.A.* 48°10N 111°57W **123** B6
Conrath *Wis., U.S.A.* 45°22N 91°2W **78** C2
Conroe *Tex., U.S.A.* 30°19N 95°27W **109** G12
Conroe, L. *Tex., U.S.A.* 30°21N 95°37W **109** G12
Consecon *Ont., Canada* 44°0N 77°31W **147** D9
Conshohocken *Pa., U.S.A.* 40°4N 75°18W **98** A1
Consort *Alta., Canada* 52°1N 110°46W **153** F10
Constantine *Mich., U.S.A.* 41°50N 85°40W **79** H6
Constantine, C. *Alaska, U.S.A.* 58°24N 158°54W **135** G8
Constitucion de 1857, Parque Nacional △ *Mexico* 32°3N 115°55W **166** A3
Constitution *Georgia, U.S.A.* 33°42N 84°20W **117** B2
Consul *Sask., Canada* 49°20N 109°30W **150** F2
Contact *Nev., U.S.A.* 41°46N 114°45W **128** A6
Contepec *Michoacan, Mexico* 19°57N 100°9W **175** C7
Continental *Ohio, U.S.A.* 41°6N 84°16W **86** B2
Continental Divide *N. Mex., U.S.A.* 35°25N 108°19W **131** B2
Continental L. *Nev., U.S.A.* 41°54N 118°43W **128** A2
Contla *Tlaxcala, Mexico* 19°20N 98°9W **175** C9
Contoocook *N.H., U.S.A.* 43°13N 71°45W **89** C3
Contoocook → *N.H., U.S.A.* 43°27N 71°35W **89** C3
Contoy, I. *Quintana Roo, Mexico* 21°30N 86°48W **179** A7
Contra Costa County ☆ *Calif., U.S.A.* 37°50N 121°50W **126** F5
Contrecoeur *Qué., Canada* 45°51N 73°14W **145** F9
Contreras *N. Mex., U.S.A.* 34°23N 106°49W **131** C4
Controller B. *Alaska, U.S.A.* 60°7N 144°15W **135** F11
Contwoyto L. *N.W.T., Canada* 65°42N 110°50W **157** C10
Convent *La., U.S.A.* 30°1N 90°50W **110** D5
Convention Center *Calif., U.S.A.* 34°3N 118°16W **133** B3
Converse *Ind., U.S.A.* 40°35N 85°52W **85** C5
Converse *La., U.S.A.* 31°47N 93°42W **110** C2
Converse *Tex., U.S.A.* 29°31N 98°18W **116** B4
Converse County ☆ *Wyo., U.S.A.* 43°0N 105°54W **124** D7
Convoy *Ohio, U.S.A.* 40°55N 84°43W **86** C2
Conway *Ark., U.S.A.* 35°5N 92°26W **106** C3
Conway *Fla., U.S.A.* 28°30N 81°19W **115** B2
Conway *Kans., U.S.A.* 38°22N 97°47W **82** C6
Conway *Mo., U.S.A.* 37°30N 92°49W **83** D4
Conway *N.C., U.S.A.* 36°26N 77°14W **103** B8
Conway *N. Dak., U.S.A.* 48°14N 97°41W **76** B8
Conway *N.H., U.S.A.* 43°59N 71°7W **89** C3
Conway *S.C., U.S.A.* 33°51N 79°3W **103** E6
Conway *Tex., U.S.A.* 35°13N 101°23W **108** B6
Conway, L. *Ark., U.S.A.* 34°58N 92°25W **106** D3
Conway, L. *Fla., U.S.A.* 28°28N 81°21W **115** B2
Conway County ☆ *Ark., U.S.A.* 35°10N 92°38W **106** C3
Conway Springs *Kans., U.S.A.* 37°24N 97°39W **82** D6
Conyers *Ga., U.S.A.* 33°40N 84°1W **113** C2
Cook *Minn., U.S.A.* 47°51N 92°41W **77** C61
Cook *Nebr., U.S.A.* 40°31N 96°10W **80** D9
Cook, C. *B.C., Canada* 50°8N 127°55W **154** E7
Cook County ☆ *Ga., U.S.A.* 31°10N 83°30W **113** E3
Cook County ☆ *Ill., U.S.A.* 41°50N 87°45W **84** B6
Cook County ☆ *Minn., U.S.A.* 47°50N 90°30W **77** C8
Cook Forest State Park △ *Pa., U.S.A.* 41°19N 79°9W **87** C3
Cook Inlet *Alaska, U.S.A.* 60°0N 152°0W **135** G10
Cooke City *Mont., U.S.A.* 45°1N 109°56W **123** E8
Cooke County ☆ *Tex., U.S.A.* 33°38N 97°9W **109** D10
Cookes Peak *N. Mex., U.S.A.* 32°32N 107°44W **131** E3
Cookeville *Tenn., U.S.A.* 36°10N 85°30W **105** D7
Cooking L. *Alta., Canada* 53°26N 113°2W **152** E7
Cooks *Mich., U.S.A.* 45°55N 86°29W **79** D5
Cooks Hammock *Fla., U.S.A.* 29°56N 83°17W **114** B5
Cook's Harbour *Nfld. & L., Canada* 51°36N 55°52W **142** A5
Cookshire *Qué., Canada* 45°25N 71°38W **145** F11
Cooksville *Ont., Canada* 43°35N 79°38W **161** B1
Cooksville *Ill., U.S.A.* 40°33N 88°43W **84** C5
Cool *Tex., U.S.A.* 32°49N 98°1W **109** E9
Cool Valley *Mo., U.S.A.* 38°43N 90°18W **94** A2
Cooleemee *N.C., U.S.A.* 35°49N 80°33W **103** C5
Coolidge *Ariz., U.S.A.* 32°59N 111°31W **130** E4
Coolidge *Ga., U.S.A.* 31°1N 83°52W **113** E3
Coolidge *Kans., U.S.A.* 38°0N 102°1W **82** C1
Coolidge *Tex., U.S.A.* 31°45N 96°39W **109** F11
Coolidge Dam *Ariz., U.S.A.* 33°10N 110°32W **130** E5
Coolin *Idaho, U.S.A.* 48°29N 116°51W **122** A2
Coolville *Ohio, U.S.A.* 39°13N 81°48W **86** D5
Coombs *B.C., Canada* 49°18N 124°25W **154** F10
Coon Rapids *Iowa, U.S.A.* 41°53N 94°41W **81** D4
Coon Rapids *Minn., U.S.A.* 45°9N 93°19W **77** E5
Coon Valley *Wis., U.S.A.* 43°42N 91°1W **78** E2
Cooper *Ky., U.S.A.* 36°46N 84°52W **105** D8
Cooper *Tex., U.S.A.* 33°23N 95°42W **109** D12
Cooper → *S.C., U.S.A.* 32°50N 79°56W **103** F6
Cooper City *Fla., U.S.A.* 26°3N 80°16W **115** D3
Cooper County ☆ *Mo., U.S.A.* 38°50N 92°45W **83** C4
Cooper L. *Tex., U.S.A.* 33°19N 95°42W **109** D12
Cooperdale *Ohio, U.S.A.* 40°13N 82°3W **86** C5
Coopersburg *Pa., U.S.A.* 40°31N 75°23W **92** B1
Cooperstown *N. Dak., U.S.A.* 47°27N 98°8W **76** C7
Cooperstown *N.Y., U.S.A.* 42°42N 74°56W **88** C6
Coopersville *Mich., U.S.A.* 43°4N 85°57W **79** F6
Coos Bay *Oreg., U.S.A.* 43°22N 124°13W **121** D1
Coos County ☆ *N.H., U.S.A.* 44°40N 71°15W **89** B3
Coos County ☆ *Oreg., U.S.A.* 43°15N 124°0W **121** D1
Coosa → *Ala., U.S.A.* 32°30N 86°16W **112** D4
Coosa County ☆ *Ala., U.S.A.* 32°53N 86°13W **112** D4
Coosada *Ala., U.S.A.* 32°29N 86°20W **112** D4

Coosawattee → *Ga., U.S.A.* 34°35N 84°55W **113** B2
Copainalá *Chiapas, Mexico* 17°4N 93°18W **178** B3
Copake *N.Y., U.S.A.* 42°7N 73°31W **91** B1
Copala *Guerrero, Mexico* 16°39N 98°59W **175** D9
Copala *Sinaloa, Mexico* 23°23N 105°54W **172** D5
Copalillo *Guerrero, Mexico* 18°2N 99°3W **175** D8
Copalis Beach *Wash., U.S.A.* 47°7N 124°10W **120** C1
Copán *Honduras* 14°50N 89°9W **182** D2
Copan *Okla., U.S.A.* 36°54N 95°56W **107** B8
Copan L. *Okla., U.S.A.* 36°58N 95°57W **107** B8
Copanatoyac *Guerrero, Mexico* 17°15N 98°45W **175** D9
Copano B. *Tex., U.S.A.* 28°5N 97°0W **109** J10
Copco L. *Calif., U.S.A.* 41°59N 122°20W **126** B4
Cope *Colo., U.S.A.* 39°40N 102°51W **125** C8
Copeland *Fla., U.S.A.* 25°57N 81°22W **114** F7
Copeland *Kans., U.S.A.* 37°33N 100°38W **82** D3
Copemish *Mich., U.S.A.* 44°29N 85°55W **79** E6
Copenhagen *N.Y., U.S.A.* 43°54N 75°41W **88** B5
Copiah County ☆ *Miss., U.S.A.* 31°52N 90°24W **111** E3
Copley *Ala., U.S.A.* 32°57N 97°0W **116** A4
Copper → *Alaska, U.S.A.* 60°18N 145°3W **135** F11
Copper Butte *Wash., U.S.A.* 48°42N 118°23W **120** B7
Copper Canyon = Barranca del Cobre, Parque Natural △ *Chihuahua, Mexico* 27°18N 107°40W **169** F8
Copper Center *Alaska, U.S.A.* 61°58N 145°18W **135** F11
Copper City = Invermere *B.C., Canada* 50°30N 116°2W **153** H4
Copper Cliff *Ont., Canada* 46°28N 81°4W **146** A5
Copper Cr. → *Va., U.S.A.* 36°40N 82°44W **102** E2
Copper Harbor *Mich., U.S.A.* 47°28N 87°53W **79** B4
Copperas Cove *Tex., U.S.A.* 31°8N 97°54W **109** F10
Copperhill *Tenn., U.S.A.* 35°0N 84°15W **105** E8
Coppermine = Kugluktuk *Nunavut, Canada* 67°50N 115°5W **156** C9
Coppermine → *Canada* 67°49N 116°4W **156** C9
Copperton *Utah, U.S.A.* 40°33N 112°4W **134** C1
Coquille *Calif., U.S.A.* 43°11N 124°11·W **121** D1
Coquille → *Oreg., U.S.A.* 43°7N 124°26W **121** D1
Coquimatlán *Colima, Mexico* 19°12N 103°48W **174** C4
Coquitlam *B.C., Canada* 49°17N 122°45W **155** F12
Cora *Wyo., U.S.A.* 42°56N 109°59W **124** D3
Cora Island *Mo., U.S.A.* 38°49N 90° 1W **94** A2
Cora L. *Tenn., U.S.A.* 35°0N 90°7W **117** B1
Coral Gables *Fla., U.S.A.* 25°43N 80°16W **115** D1
Coral Harbour *Nunavut, Canada* 64°8N 83°10W **159** F2
Coral Hills *Md., U.S.A.* 38°51N 76°55W **99** B4
Coral Springs *Fla., U.S.A.* 26°16N 80°16W **114** E8
Coralville *Iowa, U.S.A.* 41°40N 91°35W **81** D7
Coralville L. *Iowa, U.S.A.* 41°42N 91°53W **81** D7
Coram *Mont., U.S.A.* 48°25N 114°3W **123** B3
Coram *N.Y., U.S.A.* 40°52N 73°0W **91** D2
Coraopolis *Pa., U.S.A.* 40°31N 80°10W **87** D2
Corbin *Kans., U.S.A.* 37°8N 97°53W **82** D6
Corbin *Ky., U.S.A.* 36°57N 84°6W **105** D8
Corbin *Tex., U.S.A.* 46°23N 112°4W **123** D5
Corcoran *Calif., U.S.A.* 36°6N 119°33W **127** G7
Corcovado, Parque Nac. △ *Costa Rica* 8°33N 83°35W **182** E3
Cordele *Ga., U.S.A.* 31°58N 83°47W **113** E3
Cordell *Okla., U.S.A.* 35°17N 98°59W **107** C5
Cordell Hull L. *Tenn., U.S.A.* 36°17N 85°50W **105** D7
Córdoba *Veracruz, Mexico* 18°53N 96°56W **177** F4
Cordonal *Hidalgo, Mexico* 20°37N 99°7W **175** B8
Cordova *Ala., U.S.A.* 33°46N 87°11W **112** C3
Cordova *Alaska, U.S.A.* 60°33N 145°45W **135** F11
Cordova *Ill., U.S.A.* 41°41N 90°19W **84** B3
Cordova *Nebr., U.S.A.* 40°43N 97°21W **80** D8
Core Banks *N.C., U.S.A.* 34°45N 76°15W **103** D9
Corfu *N.Y., U.S.A.* 42°58N 78°24W **88** C2
Corinna *Maine, U.S.A.* 44°55N 69°16W **90** D4
Corinne *Utah, U.S.A.* 41°33N 112°7W **129** B3
Corinth *Ga., U.S.A.* 33°14N 84°57W **113** C2
Corinth *Ky., U.S.A.* 38°30N 84°34W **105** B8
Corinth *Miss., U.S.A.* 34°56N 88°31W **111** B5
Corinth *N.Y., U.S.A.* 43°15N 73°49W **88** B7
Corinto *Nic.* 12°30N 87°10W **182** D2
Cormack *Nfld. & L., Canada* 49°18N 57°23W **142** C3
Cormorant *Man., Canada* 54°14N 100°35W **151** A11
Cormorant L. *Man., Canada* 54°15N 100°50W **151** A11
Corn *Okla., U.S.A.* 35°24N 98°48W **107** C5
Corn Is. = Maiz, Is. del *Nic* 12°15N 83°4W **182** D3
Cornelia *Ga., U.S.A.* 34°31N 83°32W **113** B3
Cornelius *N.C., U.S.A.* 35°29N 80°52W **103** C5
Cornell *Ill., U.S.A.* 41°0N 88°44W **84** C5
Cornell *Wis., U.S.A.* 45°10N 91°9W **78** C2
Corner Brook *Nfld. & L., Canada* 48°57N 57°58W **142** D3
Cornersville *Tenn., U.S.A.* 35°22N 86°50W **104** E6
Cornerville *Ark., U.S.A.* 33°51N 91°56W **106** E4
Corning *Sask., Canada* 49°58N 102°58W **150** F9
Corning *Ark., U.S.A.* 36°25N 90°35W **106** B51
Corning *Calif., U.S.A.* 39°56N 122°11W **126** D4
Corning *Iowa, U.S.A.* 40°59N 94°44W **81** E4
Corning *Kans., U.S.A.* 39°40N 96°2W **82** B7
Corning *N.Y., U.S.A.* 42°9N 77°3W **88** C3
Corning *Ohio, U.S.A.* 39°36N 82°5W **86** D4
Cornish *Okla., U.S.A.* 34°9N 97°36W **107** D6
Cornish *Utah, U.S.A.* 41°59N 111°57W **129** B4
Cornlea *Nebr., U.S.A.* 41°41N 97°34W **80** C8
Cornucopia *Oreg., U.S.A.* 45°0N 117°12W **121** B8
Cornudas *Tex., U.S.A.* 31°47N 105°28W **108** F2
Cornville *Ariz., U.S.A.* 34°43N 111°55W **130** C4
Cornwall *Ont., Canada* 45°2N 74°44W **147** B12
Cornwall *P.E.I., Canada* 46°14N 63°13W **145** G6
Cornwall *Conn., U.S.A.* 41°50N 73°20W **91** C1
Cornwall *Pa., U.S.A.* 40°17N 76°25W **87** D6
Cornwall *Vt., U.S.A.* 43°56N 73°13W **89** C1
Cornwall Bridge *Conn., U.S.A.* 41°49N 73°22W **91** C1
Cornwallis I. *Nunavut, Canada* 75°8N 95°0W **158** B7
Cornwell *Fla., U.S.A.* 27°23N 81°6W **114** D7
Corona *Calif., U.S.A.* 33°53N 117°34W **127** K9
Corona *N. Mex., U.S.A.* 34°15N 105°36W **131** C5
Coronach *Sask., Canada* 49°7N 105°31W **150** F7
Coronado, B. de *Costa Rica* 9°0N 83°40W **182** E3
Coronado, I. *Baja Calif., Mexico* 29°2N 113°31W **166** D5
Coronado Nat. Forest *Ariz., U.S.A.* 32°10N 110°20W **130** E5
Coronados, I. *Baja Calif. S., Mexico* 26°5N 111°17W **167** G7
Coronados, Is. Los *Baja Calif., Mexico* 32°26N 117°19W **166** A1
Coronation *Alta., Canada* 52°5N 111°27W **153** E10
Coronation Gulf *Nunavut, Canada* 68°25N 110°0W **156** C10
Corozal *Guanajuato, Mexico* 21°20N 101°2W **173** D7
Corozal *Puerto Rico* 18°21N 66°19W **184** G16
Corpus Christi *Tex., U.S.A.* 27°47N 97°24W **109** K10
Corpus Christi, L. *Tex., U.S.A.* 28°2N 97°52W **109** J10

Corpus Christi B. *Tex., U.S.A.* 27°47N 97°22W **109** K10
Corral *Idaho, U.S.A.* 43°21N 114°57W **122** F4
Corral Nuevo *Veracruz, Mexico* 18°7N 95°8W **177** F5
Corralejo *Tamaulipas, Mexico* 24°23N 99°0W **171** F6
Corrales *N. Mex., U.S.A.* 35°14N 106°36W **131** B4
Correctionville *Iowa, U.S.A.* 42°29N 95°47W **81** C3
Corregidora *Querétaro, Mexico* 20°32N 100°27W **175** B7
Correll *Minn., U.S.A.* 45°14N 96°10W **77** E2
Corrientes, C. *Cuba* 21°43N 84°30W **182** B3
Corrientes, C. *Jalisco, Mexico* 20°25N 105°42W **174** B2
Corrigan *Tex., U.S.A.* 31°0N 94°52W **109** G13
Corriganville *Md., U.S.A.* 39°45N 78°17W **93** A2
Corry *Pa., U.S.A.* 41°55N 79°39W **87** C3
Corryton *Tenn., U.S.A.* 36°9N 83°47W **105** D9
Corsica *S. Dak., U.S.A.* 43°25N 98°24W **76** G7
Corsicana *Tex., U.S.A.* 32°6N 96°28W **109** E11
Corson County ☆ *S. Dak., U.S.A.* 45°55N 101°0W **76** E4
Cortaro *Ariz., U.S.A.* 32°21N 111°5W **130** E4
Cortazar *Guanajuato, Mexico* 20°29N 100°56W **175** B7
Cortés, Mar de = California, G. de *Mexico* 27°0N 111°0W **167** F7
Cortes I. *B.C., Canada* 50°7N 124°59W **154** E10
Cortez *Colo., U.S.A.* 37°21N 108°35W **125** E2
Cortez Mts. *Nev., U.S.A.* 40°20N 116°20W **128** B4
Cortland *N.Y., U.S.A.* 42°36N 76°11W **88** C4
Cortland *Nebr., U.S.A.* 40°30N 96°42W **80** D9
Cortland *Ohio, U.S.A.* 41°20N 80°44W **86** B6
Corum *Okla., U.S.A.* 34°22N 98°6W **107** D5
Corunna *Ont., Canada* 42°53N 82°26W **146** E4
Corunna *Mich., U.S.A.* 42°59N 84°7W **79** G7
Corvallis *Mont., U.S.A.* 46°19N 114°7W **123** D3
Corvallis *Oreg., U.S.A.* 44°34N 123°16W **121** C2
Corvette, L. de la *Qué., Canada* 53°25N 74°3W **143** C3
Corwin *Kans., U.S.A.* 37°5N 98°18W **82** D5
Corwith *Iowa, U.S.A.* 42°59N 93°57W **81** C5
Corydon *Ind., U.S.A.* 38°13N 86°7W **85** E4
Corydon *Iowa, U.S.A.* 40°46N 93°19W **81** E5
Corydon *Ky., U.S.A.* 37°44N 87°43W **104** C5
Coryell County ☆ *Tex., U.S.A.* 31°26N 97°45W **109** F10
Cosalá *Sinaloa, Mexico* 24°23N 106°41W **172** C4
Cosamaloapan de Carpio *Veracruz, Mexico* 18°22N 95°48W **177** F5
Coscomatepec *Veracruz, Mexico* 19°4N 97°2W **177** F4
Coshocton *Ohio, U.S.A.* 40°16N 81°51W **86** C5
Coshocton County ☆ *Ohio, U.S.A.* 40°16N 81°51W **86** C5
Cosío *Aguascalientes, Mexico* 22°21N 102°18W **173** E8
Cosmopolis *Wash., U.S.A.* 46°57N 123°46W **120** D2
Coso Junction *Calif., U.S.A.* 36°3N 117°57W **127** G9
Coso Range *Calif., U.S.A.* 36°9N 117°41W **127** G9
Cosoleacaque *Veracruz, Mexico* 18°0N 94°37W **177** F6
Cossatot → *Ark., U.S.A.* 33°48N 94°9W **106** E1
Cost *Tex., U.S.A.* 29°26N 97°32W **109** H10
Costa Azul *Sinaloa, Mexico* 25°7N 108°8W **172** B2
Costa Mesa *Calif., U.S.A.* 33°38N 117°55W **127** K9
Costa Rica ■ *Cent. Amer.* 10°0N 84°0W **182** E3
Costebelle, L. *Qué., Canada* 50°19N 62°23W **140** C7
Costera del Pacífico, Llanura *Sonora, Mexico* 29°0N 111°40W **168** E4
Costilla *N. Mex., U.S.A.* 36°59N 105°32W **131** A5
Costilla County ☆ *Colo., U.S.A.* 37°15N 105°30W **125** E5
Cosumnes → *Calif., U.S.A.* 38°16N 121°26W **126** E5
Cotati *Calif., U.S.A.* 38°20N 122°42W **126** E4
Côte d'Azur *Qué., Canada* 45°29N 75°44W **160** A1
Côte-St-Luc *Qué., Canada* 45°28N 73°39W **160** B3
Coteau des Prairies *S. Dak., U.S.A.* 45°20N 97°50W **76** E8
Coteau du Missouri *N. Dak., U.S.A.* 47°0N 100°0W **76** C5
Cotesfield *Nebr., U.S.A.* 41°22N 98°38W **80** C7
Cotija de la Paz *Michoacan, Mexico* 19°49N 102°43W **174** C5
Cottage Grove *Minn., U.S.A.* 44°50N 92°57W **77** F6
Cottage Grove *Oreg., U.S.A.* 43°48N 123°3W **121** D2
Cottageville *S.C., U.S.A.* 32°56N 80°29W **103** F5
Cottam *Ont., Canada* 42°8N 82°45W **146** E4
Cottle County ☆ *Tex., U.S.A.* 34°0N 100°18W **108** D7
Cotton *Minn., U.S.A.* 47°10N 92°28W **77** C6
Cotton County ☆ *Okla., U.S.A.* 34°15N 98°20W **107** D5
Cotton Plant *Ark., U.S.A.* 35°0N 91°15W **106** C4
Cotton Valley *La., U.S.A.* 32°49N 93°25W **110** B2
Cottondale *Ala., U.S.A.* 33°11N 87°27W **112** C3
Cottondale *Fla., U.S.A.* 30°48N 85°23W **114** A3
Cottonport *La., U.S.A.* 30°59N 92°3W **110** D3
Cottonwood *Ala., U.S.A.* 31°3N 85°18W **112** E5
Cottonwood *Calif., U.S.A.* 34°45N 112°1W **130** C3
Cottonwood *Idaho, U.S.A.* 46°3N 116°21W **122** C2
Cottonwood *Minn., U.S.A.* 44°33N 95°41W **77** F3
Cottonwood *S. Dak., U.S.A.* 43°58N 101°54W **76** G4
Cottonwood → *Kans., U.S.A.* 38°23N 96°3W **82** C7
Cottonwood → *Minn., U.S.A.* 44°17N 94°59W **77** F4
Cottonwood County ☆ *Minn., U.S.A.* 44°0N 95°10W **77** F3
Cottonwood Cove *Nev., U.S.A.* 35°29N 114°41W **128** G6
Cottonwood Cr. → *Tex., U.S.A.* 31°23N 103°46W **108** F4
Cottonwood Falls *Kans., U.S.A.* 38°22N 96°32W **82** C7
Cottonwood Heights *Utah, U.S.A.* 40°37N 111°48W **134** C3
Cottonwood Mt. *Oreg., U.S.A.* 44°10N 117°40W **121** C8
Cottonwood Mts. *Calif., U.S.A.* 36°50N 117°40W **127** G9
Cotuit *Mass., U.S.A.* 41°37N 70°26W **91** C4
Cotulla *Tex., U.S.A.* 28°26N 99°14W **109** J8
Couba Island *La., U.S.A.* 29°48N 90°12W **117** D1
Couderay *Wis., U.S.A.* 45°48N 91°18W **78** C2
Coudersport *Pa., U.S.A.* 41°46N 78°1W **87** C4
Coudres, Île aux *Qué., Canada* 47°24N 70°23W **145** D12
Cougar *Wash., U.S.A.* 46°3N 122°18W **120** D3
Cougar Res. *Oreg., U.S.A.* 44°8N 122°14W **121** C3
Coulee City *Wash., U.S.A.* 47°37N 119°17W **120** C6
Coulee Dam *Wash., U.S.A.* 47°58N 118°58W **120** C7
Coulee Dam Nat. Recr. Area = Lake Roosevelt Nat. Recr. Area → *Wash., U.S.A.* 48°5N 118°14W **120** B7
Coulonge → *Qué., Canada* 45°52N 76°46W **144** F6
Coulterville *Calif., U.S.A.* 37°43N 120°12W **126** F6
Coulterville *Ill., U.S.A.* 38°11N 89°36W **84** E4
Counce *Tenn., U.S.A.* 35°3N 88°16W **104** E4
Council *Alaska, U.S.A.* 64°53N 163°41W **135** D7
Council *Ga., U.S.A.* 30°37N 82°31W **113** F4
Council *Idaho, U.S.A.* 44°44N 116°26W **122** E2
Council Bluffs *Iowa, U.S.A.* 41°16N 95°52W **81** D3
Council Grove *Kans., U.S.A.* 38°40N 96°29W **82** C7
Council Grove Lake *Kans., U.S.A.* 38°41N 96°33W **82** C7
Council Hill *Okla., U.S.A.* 35°31N 95°42W **107** C8
Country Club Hills *Mo., U.S.A.* 38°43N 90°16W **94** A3
Country Homes *Wash., U.S.A.* 47°45N 117°24W **120** C8
Countryside *Ill., U.S.A.* 41°48N 87°55W **84** B6
Country Lake Estates *N.J., U.S.A.* 39°55N 74°32W **92** C2
County Art Museum *Calif., U.S.A.* 34°4N 118°21W **133** B3
Coupeaux, L. *Qué., Canada* 51°27N 63°58W **140** B6

Coupeville *Wash., U.S.A.* 48°13N 122°41W **120** B3
Coupland *Tex., U.S.A.* 30°28N 97°23W **109** G10
Courtenay *B.C., Canada* 49°45N 125°0W **154** F9
Courtenay *N. Dak., U.S.A.* 47°13N 98°34W **76** C7
Courtland *Ont., Canada* 42°51N 80°38W **146** E6
Courtland *Ala., U.S.A.* 34°40N 87°19W **112** B3
Courtland *Calif., U.S.A.* 38°20N 121°34W **126** E5
Courtland *Kans., U.S.A.* 39°47N 97°54W **82** B6
Courtland *Minn., U.S.A.* 44°16N 94°20W **77** F4
Courtland *Miss., U.S.A.* 34°14N 89°57W **111** B4
Courtland *Va., U.S.A.* 36°43N 77°4W **102** E7
Courtright *Ont., Canada* 42°49N 82°28W **146** E4
Courtright Res. *Calif., U.S.A.* 37°5N 118°58W **127** F8
Coushatta *La., U.S.A.* 32°1N 93°21W **110** B2
Coushatta Indian Reservation *La., U.S.A.* 30°13N 92°47W **110** D3
Coutts *Alta., Canada* 49°0N 111°57W **153** J9
Couture, L. *Qué., Canada* 60°7N 75°20W **143** A2
Cove *Ark., U.S.A.* 34°26N 94°25W **106** D1
Cove *Oreg., U.S.A.* 45°18N 117°49W **121** B8
Cove Fort *Utah, U.S.A.* 38°36N 112°35W **129** E3
Cove I. *Ont., Canada* 45°17N 81°44W **146** B5
Covelo *Calif., U.S.A.* 39°48N 123°15W **126** D3
Coventry *Conn., U.S.A.* 41°48N 72°23W **91** C2
Coventry *R.I., U.S.A.* 41°41N 71°34W **91** C3
Coverdale *Ill., U.S.A.* 31°38N 83°58W **113** E3
Covington *Ga., U.S.A.* 33°36N 83°51W **113** C3
Covington *Ind., U.S.A.* 40°9N 87°24W **85** C3
Covington *Ky., U.S.A.* 39°5N 84°30W **105** A8
Covington *La., U.S.A.* 30°29N 90°6W **110** D5
Covington *Mich., U.S.A.* 46°33N 88°32W **79** C3
Covington *Ohio, U.S.A.* 40°7N 84°21W **86** C2
Covington *Okla., U.S.A.* 36°18N 97°35W **107** B6
Covington *Tenn., U.S.A.* 35°34N 89°39W **104** E3
Covington *Va., U.S.A.* 37°47N 79°59W **102** D5
Covington *Wash., U.S.A.* 47°20N 122°6W **132** C5
Covington County ☆ *Ala., U.S.A.* 31°18N 86°29W **112** E4
Covington County ☆ *Miss., U.S.A.* 31°39N 89°33W **111** E4
Cow Cr. → *Kans., U.S.A.* 37°59N 97°50W **82** D6
Cow Cr. → *Oreg., U.S.A.* 42°57N 123°22W **121** E2
Cow Head *Nfld. & L., Canada* 49°55N 57°48W **142** C3
Cowan *Man., Canada* 52°5N 100°45W **151** C11
Cowan *Tenn., U.S.A.* 35°10N 86°1W **104** E6
Cowan L. *Sask., Canada* 54°0N 107°15W **150** A4
Cowansville *Qué., Canada* 45°14N 72°46W **145** F10
Coward *S.C., U.S.A.* 33°58N 79°45W **103** E6
Cowden *Ill., U.S.A.* 39°15N 88°52W **84** D5
Cowdrey *Colo., U.S.A.* 40°52N 106°19W **125** B4
Cowen *W. Va., U.S.A.* 38°25N 80°34W **102** C4
Coweta *Okla., U.S.A.* 35°57N 95°39W **107** C8
Coweta County ☆ *Ga., U.S.A.* 33°20N 84°50W **113** C2
Cowichan L. *B.C., Canada* 48°53N 124°17W **154** G10
Cowles *Nebr., U.S.A.* 40°10N 98°27W **80** D7
Cowley *Alta., Canada* 49°34N 114°5W **153** J6
Cowley *Wyo., U.S.A.* 44°53N 108°28W **124** B4
Cowley County ☆ *Kans., U.S.A.* 37°15N 96°45W **82** D7
Cowlic *Ariz., U.S.A.* 31°48N 111°59W **130** F4
Cowlington *Okla., U.S.A.* 35°17N 94°44W **107** C9
Cowlitz → *Wash., U.S.A.* 46°6N 122°55W **120** D3
Cowlitz County ☆ *Wash., U.S.A.* 46°5N 122°50W **120** D3
Cowpens *S.C., U.S.A.* 35°1N 81°48W **103** C4
Cox City *Okla., U.S.A.* 34°43N 97°44W **107** D6
Cox I. *B.C., Canada* 50°48N 128°36W **154** E6
Coxcatlán *Puebla, Mexico* 18°16N 97°9W **177** F3
Coxcatlán *San Luis Potosí, Mexico* 21°33N 98°55W **171** J6
Cox's Cove *Nfld. & L., Canada* 49°7N 58°5W **142** C2
Coxs Mills *W. Va., U.S.A.* 39°3N 80°50W **102** B4
Coxsackie *N.Y., U.S.A.* 42°21N 73°48W **88** C7
Coy *Ark., U.S.A.* 34°32N 91°53W **106** D4
Coyame *Chihuahua, Mexico* 29°28N 105°6W **169** D10
Coyanosa Draw → *Tex., U.S.A.* 31°18N 103°6W **108** F4
Coyle *Okla., U.S.A.* 35°57N 97°14W **107** C6
Coyoacán *Distrito Federal, Mexico* 19°21N 99°9W **181** B2
Coyote *San Luis Potosí, Mexico* 22°54N 100°35W **171** H4
Coyote N., Mex., U.S.A.* 36°10N 106°37W **131** A4
Coyote, B. *Baja Calif. S., Mexico* 24°30N 110°40W **167** J8
Coyote Canyon *N. Mex., U.S.A.* 35°46N 108°37W **131** B2
Coyote L. *Calif., U.S.A.* 35°4N 116°46W **127** H10
Coyote Res. *Calif., U.S.A.* 37°7N 121°33W **126** F5
Coyote Wash → *Ariz., U.S.A.* 32°41N 114°38W **130** E1
Coyotitán *Sinaloa, Mexico* 23°47N 106°35W **172** D4
Coyuca de Benítez *Guerrero, Mexico* 17°2N 100°4W **175** E7
Coyuca de Catalán *Guerrero, Mexico* 18°20N 100°39W **175** D6
Coyula *Guadalajara, Mexico* 20°39N 103°13W **180** B2
Coyuquilla *Michoacan, Mexico* 18°1N 102°2W **174** D5
Coyutla *Veracruz, Mexico* 20°15N 97°38W **176** D3
Coyville *Kans., U.S.A.* 37°41N 95°54W **82** D8
Cozad *Nebr., U.S.A.* 40°52N 99°59W **80** D6
Cozumel *Quintana Roo, Mexico* 20°31N 86°55W **179** B7
Cozumel, I. de *Quintana Roo, Mexico* 20°30N 86°40W **179** B7
Crab Cr. → *Wash., U.S.A.* 47°1N 119°19W **120** C6
Crab Orchard *Ky., U.S.A.* 37°28N 84°30W **105** C8
Crab Orchard *Nebr., U.S.A.* 40°20N 96°25W **80** D9
Crab Orchard *Tenn., U.S.A.* 35°55N 84°52W **105** E8
Crab Orchard L. *Ill., U.S.A.* 37°43N 89°9W **84** F4
Crab Orchard Nat. Wildlife Refuge △ *Ill., U.S.A.* 37°42N 89°4W **84** F4
Crabtree *Oreg., U.S.A.* 44°38N 122°54W **121** C3
Cracroft Is. *B.C., Canada* 50°32N 126°25W **154** E8
Crafton *Pa., U.S.A.* 40°26N 80°3W **98** B1
Craig *Alaska, U.S.A.* 55°29N 133°9W **135** J14
Craig *Colo., U.S.A.* 40°31N 107°33W **125** B3
Craig *Iowa, U.S.A.* 42°54N 96°19W **81** C2
Craig *Mo., U.S.A.* 40°12N 95°23W **83** A1
Craig *Nebr., U.S.A.* 41°47N 96°31W **80** C9
Craig *Nebr., U.S.A.* 41°47N 96°22W **80** C9
Craig County ☆ *Okla., U.S.A.* 36°45N 95°10W **107** B8
Craig County ☆ *Va., U.S.A.* 37°25N 80°9W **102** D5
Craig Pass *Wyo., U.S.A.* 44°26N 110°43W **124** B2
Craigflower *B.C., Canada* 48°27N 123°26W **155** G11
Craighead County ☆ *Ark., U.S.A.* 35°50N 90°42W **106** C5
Craigmont *Idaho, U.S.A.* 46°15N 116°29W **122** C2
Craigmyle *Alta., Canada* 51°40N 112°15W **153** G8
Craigsville *Va., U.S.A.* 38°5N 79°23W **102** C5
Craik *Sask., Canada* 51°3N 105°49W **150** D6
Cranberry L. *N.Y., U.S.A.* 44°11N 74°50W **88** A6
Cranberry Portage *Man., Canada* 54°35N 101°23W **159** G5
Cranbrook *B.C., Canada* 49°30N 115°46W **153** J5
Crandon *Wis., U.S.A.* 45°34N 88°54W **78** C5
Crandon Park *Fla., U.S.A.* 25°42N 80°9W **115** D3
Crane *Ind., U.S.A.* 38°54N 86°54W **85** E4

Crane Mo., U.S.A. 36°54N 93°34W **83** E3
Crane Mont., U.S.A. 47°35N 104°16W **123** C13
Crane Oreg., U.S.A. 43°25N 118°35W **121** D7
Crane Tex., U.S.A. 31°24N 102°21W **108** F5
Crane County ☆ Tex., U.S.A. 31°24N 102°21W **108** F5
Crane L. Sask., Canada 50°5N 109°5W **150** E2
Crane Mt. Oreg., U.S.A. 42°4N 120°13W **121** E5
Crane Naval Weapons Support Center Ind.,
U.S.A. 38°51N 86°50W **85** E4
Crane Prairie Res. Oreg., U.S.A. 43°45N 121°47W **121** D4
Crane River Man., Canada 51°30N 99°14W **151** D12
Cranfills Gap Tex., U.S.A. 31°46N 97°50W **109** F10
Cranford N.J., U.S.A. 40°40N 74°18W **92** B2
Cranston R.I., U.S.A. 41°47N 71°26W **91** C3
Crapaud P.E., Canada 46°14N 63°30W **141** G6
Crapo Md., U.S.A. 38°18N 76°9W **93** B4
Crary N. Dak. U.S.A. 48°4N 98°38W **76** B7
Crater L. Oreg., U.S.A. 42°56N 122°6W **121** E4
Crater Lake Oreg., U.S.A. 42°54N 122°8W **121** E3
Crater Lake Nat. Park △ Oreg., U.S.A. 42°55N 122°10W **121** E3
Crater of Diamonds State Park △ Ark.,
U.S.A. 34°2N 93°40W **106** D2
Craters of the Moon Nat. Monument △ Idaho,
U.S.A. 43°25N 113°30W **122** F5
Craufurd, C. N.W.T., Canada 73°44N 84°51W **158** C9
Craven Sask., Canada 50°42N 104°49W **150** E7
Craven, L. Qué., Canada 54°20N 76°56W **143** C2
Craven County ☆ N.C., U.S.A. 35°15N 77°10W **103** D8
Crawford Ala., U.S.A. 32°27N 85°11W **112** D5
Crawford Colo., U.S.A. 38°42N 107°37W **125** D3
Crawford Miss., U.S.A. 33°18N 88°37W **111** C5
Crawford Nebr., U.S.A. 42°41N 103°25W **80** B2
Crawford Okla., U.S.A. 35°50N 99°48W **107** C4
Crawford Tex., U.S.A. 31°32N 97°27W **109** F10
Crawford County ☆ Ark., U.S.A. 35°20N 94°18W **106** C1
Crawford County ☆ Ga., U.S.A. 32°50N 84°0W **113** D3
Crawford County ☆ Ill., U.S.A. 39°0N 87°45W **84** D6
Crawford County ☆ Ind., U.S.A. 38°15N 86°25W **85** E4
Crawford County ☆ Iowa, U.S.A. 42°0N 95°20W **81** C3
Crawford County ☆ Kans., U.S.A. 37°30N 94°45W **82** D9
Crawford County ☆ Mich., U.S.A. 44°45N 84°40W **79** E7
Crawford County ☆ Mo., U.S.A. 38°0N 91°20W **83** D5
Crawford County ☆ Ohio, U.S.A. 40°48N 82°59W **86** C4
Crawford County ☆ Pa., U.S.A. 41°45N 80°0W **87** C2
Crawford County ☆ Wis., U.S.A. 43°15N 90°50W **78** E3
Crawford Notch State Park △ N.H.,
U.S.A. 44°11N 71°24W **89** B3
Crawfordsville Ark., U.S.A. 35°14N 90°20W **106** C5
Crawfordsville Ind., U.S.A. 40°2N 86°54W **85** C4
Crawfordsville Iowa, U.S.A. 41°12N 91°32W **81** D7
Crawfordville Fla., U.S.A. 30°11N 84°23W **114** A4
Crawfordville Ga., U.S.A. 33°33N 82°54W **113** C4
Crazy Horse Memorial S. Dak., U.S.A. 43°49N 103°35W **76** G2
Crazy Mts. Mont., U.S.A. 46°12N 110°20W **123** D7
Crazy Woman Cr. → Wyo., U.S.A. 44°29N 106°8W **124** B6
Creagerstown Md., U.S.A. 39°37N 77°22W **93** A3
Creal Springs Ill., U.S.A. 37°37N 88°50W **84** F5
Crean L. Sask., Canada 54°5N 106°9W **150** A5
Creciente, I. Baja Calif. S., Mexico 24°23N 111°42W **167** J7
Cree → Sask., Canada 58°57N 105°47W **157** E11
Cree L. Sask., Canada 57°30N 106°30W **157** E11
Creede Colo., U.S.A. 37°51N 106°56W **125** E4
Creedmoor N.C., U.S.A. 36°7N 78°41W **103** B7
Creek County ☆ Okla., U.S.A. 35°50N 96°20W **107** C7
Creel Chihua ua, Mexico 27°45N 107°38W **169** F8
Creelman Sask., Canada 49°49N 103°18W **150** F8
Creemore Ont., Canada 44°19N 80°6W **146** C6
Creighton Sask., Canada 54°45N 101°54W **157** F12
Creighton Mo., U.S.A. 38°30N 94°4W **83** C2
Creighton Nebr., U.S.A. 42°28N 97°54W **80** B8
Creighton S. Dak., U.S.A. 44°15N 102°12W **76** F3
Crellin Md., U.S.A. 39°25N 79°25W **93** A1
Cremona Alta., Canada 51°33N 114°29W **153** G6
Crenshaw Miss., U.S.A. 34°30N 90°12W **111** B3
Crenshaw County ☆ Ala., U.S.A. 31°43N 86°16W **112** E4
Creole La., U.S.A. 29°49N 93°7W **110** E2
Cresaptown Md., U.S.A. 39°36N 78°50W **93** A2
Cresbard S. Dak., U.S.A. 45°10N 98°57W **76** E7
Crescent Iowa, U.S.A. 41°22N 95°51W **81** D3
Crescent Okla., U.S.A. 35°57N 97°36W **107** C6
Crescent Oreg., U.S.A. 43°28N 121°42W **121** D4
Crescent, L. Fla., U.S.A. 28°30N 81°33W **115** A1
Crescent, L. Wash., U.S.A. 48°4N 123°49W **120** B2
Crescent Beach Fla., U.S.A. 29°46N 81°15W **114** B7
Crescent City Calif., U.S.A. 41°45N 124°12W **126** B2
Crescent City Fla., U.S.A. 29°26N 81°31W **114** B7
Crescent Junction Utah, U.S.A. 38°57N 109°49W **129** E6
Crescent L. Fla., U.S.A. 29°28N 81°30W **114** B7
Crescent Lake Oreg., U.S.A. 43°30N 121°59W **121** D4
Crescent Lake Nat. Wildlife Refuge △ Nebr.,
U.S.A. 41°44N 102°19W **80** C3
Crescent Spur B.C., Canada 53°34N 120°42W **155** B14
Cresco Iowa, U.S.A. 43°22N 92°7W **81** B6
Cresskill N.J., U.S.A. 40°56N 73°57W **97** A3
Cresson Pa., U.S.A. 40°28N 78°36W **87** D4
Crested Butte Colo., U.S.A. 38°52N 106°59W **125** D4
Crestline Ohio, U.S.A. 40°47N 82°44W **86** C4
Creston B.C., Canada 49°10N 116°31W **153** J4
Creston Iowa, U.S.A. 41°4N 94°22W **81** D4
Creston Nebr., U.S.A. 41°42N 97°22W **80** C8
Creston Wash., U.S.A. 47°46N 118°31W **120** C7
Creston Wyo., U.S.A. 41°42N 107°45W **124** E5
Crestone Colo., U.S.A. 37°56N 105°47W **125** E5
Crestview Fla., U.S.A. 30°46N 86°34W **114** A2
Crestwood Ky., U.S.A. 38°19N 85°28W **105** B7
Crestwood Village N.J., U.S.A. 39°56N 74°20W **92** C2
Creswell Oreg., U.S.A. 43°55N 123°1W **121** D2
Creswell B. Nunavut, Canada 72°41N 93°25W **158** C7
Crete Ill., U.S.A. 41°27N 87°38W **84** B6
Crete Nebr., U.S.A. 40°38N 96°58W **80** D9
Creve Coeur Ill., U.S.A. 40°39N 89°35W **84** C4
Crewe Va., U.S.A. 37°10N 78°8W **102** D6
Cricket N.C., U.S.A. 36°11N 81°12W **103** B4
Cricket Mts. Utah, U.S.A. 39°0N 112°58W **129** E3
Crimora Va., U.S.A. 38°9N 78°51W **102** C6
Criner Okla. U.S.A. 34°58N 97°34W **107** D6
Cripple Creek Colo., U.S.A. 38°45N 105°11W **125** D5
Crisfield Md., U.S.A. 37°59N 75°51W **93** C5
Crisp County ☆ Ga., U.S.A. 31°50N 83°50W **113** E3
Crisp Pt. Mich., U.S.A. 46°45N 85°16W **79** C6
Cristo, Sa. Coahuila, Mexico 27°23N 100°58W **170** C3
Cristóbal Colón Tamaulipas, Mexico 25°36N 98°6W **170** E4
Crittenden Ky., U.S.A. 38°47N 84°36W **105** B8
Crittenden County ☆ Ark., U.S.A. 35°14N 90°20W **106** C5
Crittenden County ☆ Ky., U.S.A. 37°20N 88°5W **104** C4
Crivitz Wis., U.S.A. 45°14N 88°1W **78** C5

Croatan Nat. Forest N.C., U.S.A. 34°50N 77°5W **103** D8
Crocheron Md., U.S.A. 38°15N 76°3W **93** B4
Crocker Mo., U.S.A. 37°57N 92°16W **83** D4
Crockett Tex., U.S.A. 31°19N 95°27W **109** F12
Crockett County ☆ Tenn., U.S.A. 35°49N 89°14W **104** E3
Crockett County ☆ Tex., U.S.A. 30°45N 101°30W **108** G6
Crofton B.C., Canada 48°52N 123°38W **155** G11
Crofton Ky., U.S.A. 37°3N 87°29W **104** C5
Crofton Md., U.S.A. 39°1N 76°42W **93** A4
Crofton Nebr., U.S.A. 42°44N 97°30W **80** B8
Croghan N.Y., U.S.A. 43°54N 75°24W **88** B5
Croix, L. La Ont., Canada 48°20N 92°15W **148** D4
Croker, C. Ont., Canada 44°58N 80°59W **146** C6
Cromer Man., Canada 49°44N 101°14W **151** F10
Cromwell Ala., U.S.A. 32°13N 88°17W **112** D2
Cromwell Conn., U.S.A. 41°36N 72°39W **91** C2
Cromwell Minn., U.S.A. 46°41N 92°53W **77** D6
Cromwell Okla., U.S.A. 35°22N 96°29W **107** C7
Cronin, L. Nfld. & L., Canada 48°24N 56°17W **142** D4
Crooked → Oreg., U.S.A. 44°32N 121°16W **121** C4
Crooked Alaska, U.S.A. 61°52N 158°7W **135** F8
Crooked I. Bahamas 22°50N 74°10W **183** B5
Crooked I. Fla., U.S.A. 29°59N 85°31W **114** B3
Crooked Island Passage Bahamas 22°55N 74°35W **183** B5
Crooked L. Fla., U.S.A. 27°48N 81°35W **114** D7
Crooked River Sask., Canada 52°51N 103°44W **150** C8
Crooked River Nat. Grassland Oreg.,
U.S.A. 44°33N 121°7W **121** C4
Crooks S. Dak., U.S.A. 43°40N 96°49W **76** G9
Crookston Minn., U.S.A. 47°47N 96°37W **77** C2
Crookston Nebr., U.S.A. 42°56N 100°45W **80** B5
Crooksville Ohio, U.S.A. 39°46N 82°6W **86** D4
Croom Md., U.S.A. 38°45N 76°46W **93** B4
Cropsey Ill., U.S.A. 40°37N 88°29W **84** C5
Crosby Minn., U.S.A. 46°29N 93°58W **77** D5
Crosby Miss., U.S.A. 31°17N 91°4W **111** E2
Crosby N. Dak., U.S.A. 48°55N 103°18W **76** B2
Crosby Tex., U.S.A. 29°55N 95°4W **109** H12
Crosby, Mt. Wyo., U.S.A. 43°52N 109°20W **124** C3
Crosby County ☆ Tex., U.S.A. 33°40N 101°14W **108** D6
Crosbyton Tex., U.S.A. 33°40N 101°14W **108** D6
Cross Anchor S.C., U.S.A. 34°39N 81°51W **103** C3
Cross City Fla., U.S.A. 29°38N 83°7W **114** B5
Cross County ☆ Ark., U.S.A. 35°14N 90°47W **106** C5
Cross Creek N.B., Canada 46°11N 66°43W **141** G3
Cross Creeks Nat. Wildlife Refuge △ Tenn.,
U.S.A. 36°26N 87°42W **104** D5
Cross Fork Pa., U.S.A. 41°29N 77°49W **87** C5
Cross Hill S.C., U.S.A. 34°18N 81°59W **103** C3
Cross L. Man., Canada 54°45N 97°30W **159** G6
Cross L. Maine, U.S.A. 47°7N 68°20W **90** A5
Cross Lake Man., Canada 54°37N 97°47W **159** G6
Cross Lake Minn., U.S.A. 46°40N 94°7W **77** D4
Cross Plains Tenn., U.S.A. 36°33N 86°42W **104** D6
Cross Plains Tex., U.S.A. 32°8N 99°11W **109** E8
Cross Sound Alaska, U.S.A. 58°0N 135°0W **135** G14
Cross Timbers Mo., U.S.A. 38°1N 93°14W **83** C3
Cross Village Mich., U.S.A. 45°39N 85°2W **79** D6
Crossett Ark., U.S.A. 33°8N 91°58W **106** E4
Crossfield Alta., Canada 51°25N 114°0W **153** G6
Crossroads N. Mex., U.S.A. 33°31N 103°20W **131** D7
Crossville Ala., U.S.A. 34°17N 86°0W **112** B5
Crossville Ill., U.S.A. 38°10N 88°4W **84** E5
Crossville Tenn., U.S.A. 35°57N 85°2W **105** E7
Croswell Mich., U.S.A. 43°16N 82°37W **79** F9
Crotched Mt. N.H., U.S.A. 43°0N 71°52W **89** C3
Crothersville Ind., U.S.A. 38°48N 85°50W **85** E5
Croton-on-Hudson N.Y., U.S.A. 41°12N 73°55W **92** A3
Crouch Idaho, U.S.A. 44°7N 115°58W **122** E3
Crow Agency Mont., U.S.A. 45°36N 107°28W **123** E10
Crow Cr. → Colo., U.S.A. 40°23N 104°29W **125** B6
Crow Creek Indian Reservation S. Dak.,
U.S.A. 44°3N 99°25W **76** F6
Crow Indian Reservation Mont.,
U.S.A. 45°25N 108°0W **123** E10
Crow Wing → Minn., U.S.A. 46°19N 94°20W **77** D4
Crow Wing County ☆ Minn., U.S.A. 46°30N 94°0W **77** D4
Crowder Miss., U.S.A. 34°11N 90°8W **111** B3
Crowder Okla., U.S.A. 35°7N 95°40W **107** C8
Crowell Tex., U.S.A. 33°59N 99°43W **109** D8
Crowheart Wyo., U.S.A. 43°19N 109°12W **124** C3
Crowley Colo., U.S.A. 38°12N 103°51W **125** D7
Crowley La., U.S.A. 30°13N 92°22W **110** D3
Crowley Tex., U.S.A. 32°34N 97°21W **116** C1
Crowley, L. Calif., U.S.A. 37°35N 118°42W **126** F8
Crowley County ☆ Colo., U.S.A. 38°15N 103°45W **125** D7
Crowley Ridge Ark., U.S.A. 35°45N 90°45W **106** C5
Crown City Ohio, U.S.A. 38°36N 82°17W **86** E4
Crown Point Ind., U.S.A. 41°25N 87°22W **85** B3
Crown Point N.Y., U.S.A. 43°57N 73°26W **89** C1
Crown Prince Frederik I. Nunavut,
Canada 70°2N 86°50W **158** C8
Crownpoint N. Mex., U.S.A. 35°41N 108°9W **131** B2
Crows Nest Pk. S. Dak., U.S.A. 44°3N 103°58W **76** F2
Crowsnest Pass Alta.-B.C., Canada 49°40N 114°40W **153** J6
Croydon Flat N.H., U.S.A. 43°25N 72°12W **89** C2
Crozet Va., U.S.A. 38°4N 78°42W **102** C6
Crozier Chan. N.W.T., Canada 76°10N 118°30W **156** A9
Cruces Chihuahua, Mexico 29°26N 107°24W **169** D8
Cruces y Anexas Chihuahua, Mexico 28°43N 104°17W **169** E11
Cruger Miss., U.S.A. 33°19N 90°14W **111** C3
Cruillas Tamaulipas, Mexico 24°45N 98°31W **171** F6
Crum W. Va., U.S.A. 37°57N 82°27W **102** D2
Crump L. Oreg., U.S.A. 42°17N 119°50W **121** E6
Crumpton Md., U.S.A. 39°14N 75°55W **93** A5
Crustepec, Cerro Veracruz, Mexico 21°13N 97°51W **176** C3
Cruz, C. Cuba 19°50N 77°50W **182** C4
Cruz Bay U.S. Virgin Is. 18°20N 64°48W **184** G18
Cruz Grande Guerrero, Mexico 16°44N 99°8W **175** F8
Cruz de Garibay Jalisco, Mexico 19°9N 103°14W **174** C4
Crystal Minn., U.S.A. 45°2N 93°21W **94** A1
Crystal N. Dak., U.S.A. 48°36N 97°40W **76** B8
Crystal → Colo., U.S.A. 39°15N 107°13W **125** C4
Crystal B. Fla., U.S.A. 28°50N 82°45W **114** C6
Crystal Bay Nev., U.S.A. 39°15N 120°0W **128** C1
Crystal Beach Md., U.S.A. 39°26N 75°59W **93** A5
Crystal City Mo., U.S.A. 38°13N 90°23W **83** C6
Crystal City Tex., U.S.A. 28°41N 99°50W **109** J8
Crystal Falls Mich., U.S.A. 46°5N 88°20W **78** B5
Crystal Hill Va., U.S.A. 36°51N 78°55W **102** E6
Crystal L. Mich., U.S.A. 44°40N 86°10W **79** E6
Crystal Lake Fla., U.S.A. 30°26N 85°42W **114** A3

Crystal Lake Ill., U.S.A. 42°14N 88°19W **84** A5
Crystal Lake Iowa, U.S.A. 43°13N 93°47W **81** B5
Crystal River Fla., U.S.A. 28°54N 82°35W **114** C6
Crystal Springs Miss., U.S.A. 31°59N 90°21W **111** E3
Cuajimalpa de Morelos Distrito Federal,
Mexico 19°21N 99°18W **181** B2
Cuajinicuilapa Guerrero, Mexico 16°28N 98°25W **175** F9
Cualác Guerrero, Mexico 17°45N 98°37W **175** E9
Cuarto Dinamo Distrito Federal, Mexico 19°15N 99°17W **181** C2
Cuates de Australia Coahuila, Mexico 26°18N 102°16W **170** D2
Cuatillos Durango, Mexico 24°34N 103°40W **173** B7
Cuatrociénegas, Parque Natural △ Coahuila,
Mexico 26°37N 102°38W **170** D2
Cuauhtémoc Chihuahua, Mexico 28°25N 106°52W **169** E9
Cuauhtémoc Colima, Mexico 19°20N 103°36W **174** C4
Cuauhtémoc Durango, Mexico 24°24N 103°40W **173** C7
Cuauhtémoc México, Mexico 19°25N 99°9W **181** B3
Cuauhtémoc Oaxaca, Mexico 17°7N 94°54W **177** G6
Cuauhtémoc Tamaulipas, Mexico 22°32N 98°6W **171** H6
Cuautepec Guerrero, Mexico 16°14N 98°59W **175** F9
Cuautepec Hidalgo, Mexico 20°2N 98°18W **176** D3
Cuautepec de Madero Distrito Federal,
Mexico 19°33N 99°8W **181** A3
Cuautitlán Jalisco, Mexico 19°26N 104°23W **174** C3
Cuautitlán México, Mexico 19°40N 99°11W **175** C8
Cuautla Jalisco, Mexico 20°11N 104°21W **174** B3
Cuautla Morelos, Mexico 18°48N 98°57W **175** D9
Cub Hill Baltimore, U.S.A. 39°24N 76°30W **99** A2
Cuba Sonora, Mexico 31°7N 111°56W **168** B4
Cuba Ala., U.S.A. 40°30N 90°12W **84** C3
Cuba Ill., U.S.A. 39°48N 97°27W **82** B6
Cuba Kans., U.S.A. 38°4N 91°24W **83** C5
Cuba Mo., U.S.A. 36°1N 107°4W **131** A3
Cuba N. Mex., U.S.A. 42°13N 78°17W **88** C2
Cuba N.Y., U.S.A. 22°0N 79°0W **182** B4
Cuba ■ W. Indies 19°26N 104°23W **174** C3
Cuba City Wis., U.S.A. 42°36N 90°26W **78** F3
Cubabi, Cerro Sonora, Mexico 31°44N 112°46W **168** B3
Cubero N. Mex., U.S.A. 35°5N 107°31W **131** B3
Cucapá, Sa. Baja Calif., Mexico 32°35N 115°40W **166** A3
Cucharas → Colo., U.S.A. 37°55N 104°32W **125** E6
Cuchillo N. Mex., U.S.A. 33°14N 107°22W **131** D3
Cuchillo Parado Chihuahua, Mexico 29°25N 104°52W **169** D11
Cuchumatanes, Sierra de los Guatemala 15°35N 91°25W **182** C1
Cuckoo Va., U.S.A. 37°57N 77°54W **102** D7
Cucurpé Sonora, Mexico 30°20N 110°43W **168** C5
Cudahy Calif., U.S.A. 33°57N 118°11W **133** C3
Cudahy Wis., U.S.A. 42°57N 87°51W **94** C2
Cuddeback L. Calif., U.S.A. 35°18N 117°29W **127** H9
Cudworth Sask., Canada 52°30N 105°44W **150** C6
Cuencamé Durango, Mexico 24°53N 103°42W **173** C7
Cuerámaro Guanajuato, Mexico 20°38N 101°41W **174** B6
Cuerenta Casas Chihuahua, Mexico 29°38N 108°12W **169** D7
Cuernavaca Morelos, Mexico 18°55N 99°15W **175** D8
Cuero Tex., U.S.A. 29°6N 97°17W **109** H10
Cuervo N. Mex., U.S.A. 35°2N 104°25W **131** B6
Cuetzala Guerrero, Mexico 18°8N 99°50W **175** D8
Cuetzalán Puebla, Mexico 20°2N 97°31W **176** D3
Cuichapa Veracruz, Mexico 17°59N 94°15W **177** G6
Cuicuilco, Pirámido de México, Mexico 19°18N 99°11W **181** C2
Cuilapan Oaxaca, Mexico 16°58N 96°46W **177** H4
Cuilco Guatemala 15°24N 91°58W **182** C1
Cuitzeo Michoacan, Mexico 19°59N 101°9W **175** C6
Cuitzeo, L. de Michoacan, Mexico 19°55N 101°5W **175** C6
Cuivre → Mo., U.S.A. 38°56N 90°41W **83** C6
Cuivre River State Park △ Mo., U.S.A. 39°0N 90°56W **83** B6
Culberson County ☆ Tex., U.S.A. 31°30N 104°30W **108** F3
Culbertson Mont., U.S.A. 48°9N 104°31W **123** B13
Culbertson Nebr., U.S.A. 40°14N 100°50W **80** D5
Culdesac Idaho, U.S.A. 46°23N 116°40W **122** C2
Culebra Puerto Rico 18°19N 65°18W **184** G17
Culebra, Cayo Quintana Roo, Mexico 19°43N 87°30W **179** C6
Culebra, Roca Yucatán, Mexico 21°37N 90°30W **179** A3
Culiacán Mexico 24°50N 107°23W **172** C3
Cullen La., U.S.A. 32°58N 93°27W **110** B2
Cullison Kans., U.S.A. 37°38N 98°54W **82** D5
Cullman Ala., U.S.A. 34°11N 86°51W **112** B4
Cullman County ☆ Ala., U.S.A. 34°11N 86°51W **112** B4
Culloden Ga., U.S.A. 32°52N 84°6W **113** D2
Cullom Ill., U.S.A. 40°53N 88°16W **84** C5
Cullomburg Ala., U.S.A. 31°33N 88°18W **112** E2
Cullowhee N.C., U.S.A. 35°19N 83°11W **103** C2
Culmore Va., U.S.A. 38°51N 77°8W **99** B3
Culp Creek Oreg., U.S.A. 43°42N 122°50W **121** D3
Culpeper Va., U.S.A. 38°30N 78°0W **102** C6
Culpeper County ☆ Va., U.S.A. 38°28N 78°0W **102** C6
Culubá Yucatán, Mexico 21°6N 87°54W **179** A6
Culver Ind., U.S.A. 41°13N 86°25W **85** B4
Culver Kans., U.S.A. 38°58N 97°46W **82** C6
Culver Oreg., U.S.A. 44°32N 121°13W **121** C4
Culver City Calif., U.S.A. 34°1N 118°24W **133** B2
Culverton Ga., U.S.A. 33°19N 82°54W **113** C4
Cumberland B.C., Canada 49°40N 125°0W **154** F9
Cumberland Ont., Canada 45°29N 75°24W **147** B11
Cumberland Iowa, U.S.A. 41°16N 94°52W **81** D4
Cumberland Ky., U.S.A. 36°59N 82°59W **105** D10
Cumberland Md., U.S.A. 39°39N 78°46W **93** A2
Cumberland N.C., U.S.A. 35°0N 78°59W **103** C7
Cumberland Ohio, U.S.A. 39°51N 81°40W **86** D5
Cumberland R.I., U.S.A. 41°58N 71°28W **91** C3
Cumberland Wis., U.S.A. 45°32N 92°1W **78** C1
Cumberland → U.S.A. 37°9N 88°25W **104** C4
Cumberland, L. Ky., U.S.A. 36°52N 85°9W **105** D7
Cumberland City Tenn., U.S.A. 36°23N 87°38W **104** D5
Cumberland County ☆ Ill., U.S.A. 39°15N 88°15W **84** D5
Cumberland County ☆ Ky., U.S.A. 36°50N 85°9W **105** D7
Cumberland County ☆ Maine, U.S.A. 43°50N 70°30W **90** E2
Cumberland County ☆ N.C., U.S.A. 35°0N 78°45W **103** D7
Cumberland County ☆ N.J., U.S.A. 39°15N 75°7W **92** D1
Cumberland County ☆ Pa., U.S.A. 40°5N 77°10W **87** D5
Cumberland County ☆ Tenn., U.S.A. 35°57N 84°59W **105** E8
Cumberland County ☆ Va., U.S.A. 37°30N 78°15W **102** D6
Cumberland Falls State Park △ Ky.,
U.S.A. 36°50N 84°20W **105** D8
Cumberland Gap Ky., U.S.A. 36°36N 83°41W **105** D9
Cumberland Gap Nat. Historical Park △ Ky.,
U.S.A. 36°36N 83°40W **105** D9
Cumberland Hill R.I., U.S.A. 41°59N 71°28W **91** C3
Cumberland House Sask., Canada 53°58N 102°15W **151** B9
Cumberland I. Ga., U.S.A. 30°50N 81°25W **113** F5
Cumberland Island Nat. Seashore △ Ga.,
U.S.A. 30°12N 81°24W **113** F5
Cumberland L. Sask., Canada 54°3N 102°18W **151** A9
Cumberland Pen. Nunavut, Canada 67°0N 64°0W **159** D13

Cumberland Plateau U.S.A. 36°0N 85°0W **105** E7
Cumberland Pt. Mich., U.S.A. 47°51N 89°14W **79** B2
Cumberland Sd. Nunavut, Canada 65°30N 66°0W **158** D12
Cumbres de Majalca, Parque Nacional △
Mexico 28°48N 106°30W **169** E9
Cumbres de Monterrey, Parque Nacional △
Nuevo León, Mexico 25°26N 100°25W **180** C1
Cumbres del Ajusco, Parque Nacional △
Distrito Federal, Mexico 19°12N 99°15W **181** C2
Cumby Tex., U.S.A. 33°8N 95°50W **109** D12
Cuming County ☆ Nebr., U.S.A. 41°50N 96°40W **80** C9
Cumming Ga., U.S.A. 34°12N 84°9W **113** B2
Cummins Lakes Park △ B.C., Canada 52°6N 118°3W **155** C16
Cumpas Sonora, Mexico 30°2N 109°48W **168** C6
Cumshewa Inlet B.C., Canada 53°3N 131°50W **154** D3
Cunduacán Tabasco, Mexico 18°4N 93°10W **178** A3
Cunningham Kans., U.S.A. 37°39N 98°26W **82** D5
Cupar Sask., Canada 50°57N 104°10W **150** E7
Cupertino Calif., U.S.A. 37°19N 122°2W **98** E4
Cuprum Idaho, U.S.A. 45°5N 116°41W **122** D2
Cuquío Jalisco, Mexico 20°55N 103°2W **174** B4
Curaçao Neth. Ant. 12°10N 69°0W **183** D6
Curecanti Nat. Recr. Area △ Colo.,
U.S.A. 38°24N 107°25W **125** D3
Curlew Iowa, U.S.A. 42°59N 94°44W **81** C4
Curlew Wash., U.S.A. 48°53N 118°36W **120** B7
Curlew Nat. Grasslands Idaho, U.S.A. 42°13N 112°45W **122** G6
Curran Mich., U.S.A. 44°43N 83°48W **79** E8
Currant Nev., U.S.A. 38°44N 115°28W **128** D5
Currant Mt. Nev., U.S.A. 38°55N 115°25W **128** D5
Current → Ark., U.S.A. 36°15N 90°55W **106** B5
Currie Minn., U.S.A. 44°3N 95°40W **77** F3
Currie Nev., U.S.A. 40°16N 114°45W **128** B6
Currituck N.C., U.S.A. 36°27N 76°1W **103** B10
Currituck County ☆ N.C., U.S.A. 36°20N 76°0W **103** B10
Currituck Sd. N.C., U.S.A. 36°20N 75°52W **103** B10
Curry County ☆ N. Mex., U.S.A. 34°30N 103°15W **131** C7
Curry County ☆ Oreg., U.S.A. 42°20N 124°20W **121** E1
Curryville Mo., U.S.A. 39°21N 91°21W **83** B5
Curtin Oreg., U.S.A. 43°43N 123°12W **121** D2
Curtis Ark., U.S.A. 34°0N 93°2W **106** E2
Curtis Nebr., U.S.A. 40°38N 100°31W **80** D5
Curtis Bay Baltimore, U.S.A. 39°13N 76°33W **99** B2
Curtis Creek → Baltimore, U.S.A. 39°13N 76°33W **99** B2
Curtis L. Nunavut, Canada 66°41N 89°10W **159** D8
Curwensville Pa., U.S.A. 40°58N 78°32W **87** D4
Cusárare Chihuahua, Mexico 27°37N 107°35W **169** F8
Cushing Iowa, U.S.A. 42°28N 95°41W **81** C3
Cushing Nebr., U.S.A. 41°19N 98°22W **80** C7
Cushing Okla., U.S.A. 35°59N 96°46W **107** C7
Cushing Tex., U.S.A. 31°49N 94°51W **109** F13
Cushing, Mt. B.C., Canada 57°35N 126°57W **157** E7
Cushman Ark., U.S.A. 35°53N 91°45W **106** C4
Cushman Oreg., U.S.A. 43°59N 124°3W **121** D1
Cushman, L. Wash., U.S.A. 47°25N 123°13W **120** C2
Cusick Wash., U.S.A. 48°20N 117°18W **120** B8
Cusihuiráchic Chihuahua, Mexico 28°14N 106°50W **169** E9
Cusseta Ga., U.S.A. 32°18N 84°47W **113** D2
Cusson, Pte. Qué., Canada 60°23N 77°46W **143** A2
Custepec Chiapas, Mexico 15°43N 92°58W **178** D3
Custer Mont., U.S.A. 46°8N 107°33W **123** D10
Custer S. Dak., U.S.A. 43°46N 103°36W **76** G2
Custer Wash., U.S.A. 48°55N 122°38W **120** B3
Custer City Okla., U.S.A. 35°40N 98°53W **107** C5
Custer County ☆ Colo., U.S.A. 38°10N 105°20W **125** D5
Custer County ☆ Idaho, U.S.A. 44°0N 114°0W **122** E4
Custer County ☆ Mont., U.S.A. 46°25N 105°30W **123** D12
Custer County ☆ Nebr., U.S.A. 41°30N 99°40W **80** C6
Custer County ☆ Okla., U.S.A. 35°40N 99°0W **107** C5
Custer County ☆ S. Dak., U.S.A. 43°50N 103°30W **76** G2
Custer Nat. Forest Mont., U.S.A. 45°15N 109°50W **123** E8
Custer Nat. Forest S. Dak., U.S.A. 45°30N 103°15W **76** F2
Custer State Park △ S. Dak., U.S.A. 43°42N 103°22W **76** G2
Cut Bank Mont., U.S.A. 48°38N 112°20W **123** B5
Cut Bank Cr. → Mont., U.S.A. 48°29N 112°14W **123** B5
Cut Bank Cr. → N. Dak., U.S.A. 48°10N 100°45W **76** B5
Cut Knife Sask., Canada 52°45N 109°1W **150** C2
Cut Off La., U.S.A. 29°33N 90°20W **110** E5
Cutbank Sask., Canada 51°18N 106°51W **150** D5
Cutbank → Alta., Canada 54°43N 118°32W **152** D2
Cuthbert Ga., U.S.A. 31°46N 84°48W **113** E2
Cutler Calif., U.S.A. 36°31N 119°17W **127** H7
Cutler Ill., U.S.A. 38°2N 89°34W **84** E4
Cutler Maine, U.S.A. 44°40N 67°12W **90** D6
Cutler Park Mass., U.S.A. 42°17N 71°12W **96** B1
Cutler Ridge Fla., U.S.A. 25°35N 80°20W **114** F8
Cutlerville Mich., U.S.A. 42°50N 85°40W **79** G6
Cuttyhunk I. Mass., U.S.A. 41°25N 70°56W **91** C4
Cutzamala Guerrero, Mexico 18°28N 100°34W **175** D7
Cutzamala → Mexico 18°22N 100°39W **175** D7
Cuyahoga → Ohio, U.S.A. 41°30N 81°41W **98** B1
Cuyahoga County ☆ Ohio, U.S.A. 41°23N 81°43W **86** B5
Cuyahoga Falls Ohio, U.S.A. 41°8N 81°29W **86** B5
Cuyahoga Heights Ohio, U.S.A. 41°26N 81°39W **98** B2
Cuyahoga Valley Nat. Park △ Ohio, U.S.A. 41°14N 81°33W **98** B2
Cuyama → Calif., U.S.A. 34°58N 120°38W **127** J6
Cuyamaca State Park △ Calif., U.S.A. 32°56N 116°33W **127** L10
Cuyapaipe Indian Reservation Calif.,
U.S.A. 32°51N 116°23W **127** L10
Cuyuna Range Minn., U.S.A. 46°25N 93°30W **77** D5
Cuyutlán Colima, Mexico 18°55N 104°4W **174** D3
Cygnet Ohio, U.S.A. 41°14N 83°38W **86** B3
Cylinder Iowa, U.S.A. 43°5N 94°33W **81** B4
Cynthia Alta., Canada 53°17N 115°25W **152** E5
Cynthiana Ind., U.S.A. 38°11N 87°43W **85** E3
Cynthiana Ky., U.S.A. 38°23N 84°18W **105** B8
Cypress Ill., U.S.A. 37°22N 89°1W **84** F4
Cypress Creek Nat. Wildlife Refuge △ Ill.,
U.S.A. 37°18N 89°8W **84** F4
Cypress Falls Park B.C., Canada 49°21N 123°12W **161** A1
Cypress Hills Interprovincial Park △ Sask.,
Canada 49°40N 109°30W **150** F2
Cypress River Man., Canada 49°34N 99°5W **151** F12
Cyril Okla., U.S.A. 34°54N 98°12W **107** D5
Cyrus Minn., U.S.A. 45°37N 95°44W **77** E3
Cyrville Ont., Canada 45°25N 75°38W **160** A2
Czar Alta., Canada 52°27N 110°50W **153** F10

D

Dacoma Okla., U.S.A. 36°40N 98°34W **107** B5
Dacono Colo., U.S.A. 40°5N 104°56W **125** B6
Dacula Ga., U.S.A. 33°59N 83°54W **113** B3
Dade City Fla., U.S.A. 28°22N 82°11W **114** C6
Dade County ☆ Ga., U.S.A. 34°53N 85°31W **113** B1
Dade County ☆ Mo., U.S.A. 37°25N 93°50W **83** D3

Dadeville Ala., U.S.A. 32°50N 85°46W 112 D5
Dadeville Mo., U.S.A. 37°29N 93°41W 83 D3
Dafter Mich., U.S.A. 46°22N 84°26W 79 C7
Daggett Mich., U.S.A. 45°28N 87°36W 79 D4
Daggett County ☆ Utah, U.S.A. 40°55N 109°30W 129 C6
Dagsboro Del., U.S.A. 38°33N 75°15W 93 B5
Dahlgren Ill., U.S.A. 38°12N 88°41W 84 E5
Dahlgren Va., U.S.A. 38°20N 77°3W 93 B3
Dahlonega Ga., U.S.A. 34°32N 83°59W 113 B3
Dahlonega Plat. Ga., U.S.A. 34°10N 84°20W 113 B2
Dailey W. Va., U.S.A. 38°48N 79°54W 102 C5
Daingerfield Tex., U.S.A. 33°2N 94°44W 109 D13
Dairy Oreg., U.S.A. 42°14N 121°31W 121 E4
Daisetta Tex., U.S.A. 30°7N 94°39W 109 G13
Daisy Ark., U.S.A. 34°14N 93°45W 106 D2
Daisy Wash., U.S.A. 48°22N 118°10W 120 B7
Dakota Ill., U.S.A. 42°23N 89°32W 84 A4
Dakota Minn., U.S.A. 43°55N 91°22W 77 G7
Dakota City Iowa, U.S.A. 42°43N 94°12W 81 C4
Dakota City Nebr., U.S.A. 42°25N 96°25W 80 B9
Dakota County ☆ Minn., U.S.A. 44°45N 93°0W 77 F5
Dakota County ☆ Nebr., U.S.A. 42°30N 96°30W 80 B9
Dalark Ark., U.S.A. 34°2N 92°53W 106 D3
Dalcour La., U.S.A. 29°48N 89°59W 117 D3
Dale Ind., U.S.A. 38°10N 86°59W 85 E4
Dale Okla., U.S.A. 35°24N 97°3W 107 C6
Dale City Va., U.S.A. 38°38N 77°19W 93 B3
Dale County ☆ Ala., U.S.A. 31°28N 85°39W 112 E5
Dale Hollow L. Tenn., U.S.A. 36°32N 85°27W 105 D7
Daleville Ala., U.S.A. 31°19N 85°43W 112 E5
Daleville Ind., U.S.A. 40°7N 85°33W 85 C5
Daleville Miss., U.S.A. 32°34N 88°41W 111 D5
Dalhart Tex., U.S.A. 36°4N 102°31W 108 A5
Dalhousie N.B., Canada 48°5N 66°26W 141 E3
Dalhousie, C. N.W.T., Canada 70°15N 129°40W 156 B7
Dalkeith Fla., U.S.A. 30°0N 85°9W 114 A3
Dallam County ☆ Tex., U.S.A. 36°15N 102°30W 108 A5
Dallas Ga., U.S.A. 33°55N 84°51W 113 C2
Dallas N.C., U.S.A. 35°19N 81°11W 103 C4
Dallas Oreg., U.S.A. 44°55N 123°19W 121 C2
Dallas Pa., U.S.A. 41°20N 75°58W 87 C7
Dallas S. Dak., U.S.A. 43°14N 99°31W 76 G6
Dallas Tex., U.S.A. 32°47N 96°48W 116 B4
Dallas Wis., U.S.A. 45°16N 91°51W 78 C2
Dallas Center Iowa, U.S.A. 41°41N 93°58W 81 D5
Dallas City Ill., U.S.A. 40°38N 91°10W 84 C2
Dallas County ☆ Ala., U.S.A. 32°25N 87°11W 112 D3
Dallas County ☆ Ark., U.S.A. 33°59N 92°38W 106 E3
Dallas County ☆ Iowa, U.S.A. 41°40N 94°0W 81 D4
Dallas County ☆ Mo., U.S.A. 37°40N 93°0W 83 D3
Dallas County ☆ Tex., U.S.A. 32°50N 96°50W 109 E11
Dallas-Fort Worth Int. ✈ (DFW) Tex., U.S.A. 32°53N 97°2W 116 A3
Dalles, The Oreg., U.S.A. 45°36N 121°10W 121 B4
Dalles Dam, The Wash., U.S.A. 45°37N 121°8W 120 E4
Dalmeny Sask., Canada 52°20N 106°46W 150 C5
Dalton Ont., Canada 48°11N 84°1W 149 D12
Dalton Ga., U.S.A. 34°46N 84°58W 113 B2
Dalton Mass., U.S.A. 42°28N 73°11W 91 B1
Dalton Minn., U.S.A. 46°10N 95°55W 77 D3
Dalton Nebr., U.S.A. 41°25N 102°58W 80 C3
Dalton Ohio, U.S.A. 40°48N 81°42W 86 C5
Dalton Pa., U.S.A. 41°32N 75°44W 92 A1
Dalton, Kap Greenland 69°25N 24°3W 162 D8
Dalton Gardens Idaho, U.S.A. 47°44N 116°46W 122 B2
Dalworthington Gardens Tex., U.S.A. 32°42N 97°9W 116 B3
Daly B. Nunavut, Canada 64°0N 89°45W 159 E8
Daly City Calif., U.S.A. 37°42N 122°27W 132 B2
Damar Kans., U.S.A. 39°19N 99°35W 82 B4
Damasco Chiapas, Mexico 17°10N 91°36W 178 B5
Damascus Ga., U.S.A. 31°18N 84°43W 113 E2
Damascus Md., U.S.A. 39°17N 77°12W 93 A3
Damascus Va., U.S.A. 36°38N 81°47W 102 E3
Dame Marie Haiti 18°36N 74°26W 183 C5
Dameron Md., U.S.A. 38°10N 76°22W 93 B4
Dames Quarter Md., U.S.A. 38°11N 75°54W 93 B5
Damián Carmona San Luis Potosí, Mexico 22°6N 99°17W 171 H5
Dan → Va., U.S.A. 36°42N 78°50W 103 B7
Dan Ryan Woods Ill., U.S.A. 41°44N 87°40W 95 C2
Dana Ind., U.S.A. 39°48N 87°30W 85 D3
Dana Iowa, U.S.A. 42°6N 94°14W 81 C4
Dana, L. Qué., Canada 50°53N 77°20W 143 C2
Dana Point Calif., U.S.A. 33°28N 117°42W 127 K9
Danbury Conn., U.S.A. 41°24N 73°28W 91 C1
Danbury Iowa, U.S.A. 42°14N 95°43W 81 C2
Danbury N.C., U.S.A. 36°25N 80°12W 103 B5
Danbury N.H., U.S.A. 43°32N 71°52W 89 C3
Danbury Nebr., U.S.A. 40°3N 100°25W 80 D5
Danbury Tex., U.S.A. 29°14N 95°21W 109 H12
Danby Vt., U.S.A. 43°20N 72°59W 89 C2
Danby L. Calif., U.S.A. 34°13N 115°5W 127 J11
Dandridge Tenn., U.S.A. 36°1N 83°25W 105 D9
Dane County ☆ Wis., U.S.A. 43°0N 89°29W 78 E4
Danforth Ont., Canada 43°43N 79°16W 161 A3
Danforth Ill., U.S.A. 40°49N 87°59W 84 C6
Danforth Maine, U.S.A. 45°40N 67°52W 90 C6
Danforth Hills Colo., U.S.A. 40°15N 108°0W 125 B2
Dangriga Belize 17°0N 88°13W 182 C2
Dania Beach Fla., U.S.A. 26°3N 80°8W 115 B3
Daniel Wyo., U.S.A. 42°52N 110°4W 124 D2
Daniel Boone Nat. Forest Ky., U.S.A. 37°30N 84°0W 105 C8
Daniels County ☆ Mont., U.S.A. 48°40N 105°20W 123 B12
Daniels Pass Utah, U.S.A. 40°18N 111°10W 129 C4
Danielson Conn., U.S.A. 41°48N 71°53W 91 C3
Danielson Prov. Park △ Sask., Canada 51°16N 106°50W 150 D5
Danielsville Ga., U.S.A. 34°8N 83°13W 113 B3
Danish West Indies = Virgin Is. (U.S.) ☑ W. Indies 18°20N 65°0W 184 G18
Danlí Honduras 14°4N 86°35W 182 D2
Danmark Fjord Greenland 81°30N 22°0W 162 A8
Danmarkshavn Greenland 76°45N 18°50W 162 B9
Dannebrog Nebr., U.S.A. 41°7N 98°33W 80 C7
Dannemora N.Y., U.S.A. 44°43N 73°44W 88 A7
Danskin B.C., Canada 53°59N 125°47W 154 B9
Dansville Mich., U.S.A. 42°34N 84°19W 79 G7
Dansville N.Y., U.S.A. 42°34N 77°42W 88 C3
Dante S. Dak., U.S.A. 43°2N 98°11W 76 G7
Dante Va., U.S.A. 36°59N 82°18W 102 E2
Danvers Ill., U.S.A. 40°32N 89°11W 84 C4
Danvers Mass., U.S.A. 42°34N 70°56W 91 B4
Danvers Minn., U.S.A. 45°17N 95°45W 77 E3
Danville Ark., U.S.A. 35°3N 93°24W 106 C2
Danville Calif., U.S.A. 37°49N 122°0W 126 F5

Danville Ga., U.S.A. 32°37N 83°15W 113 D3
Danville Ill., U.S.A. 40°8N 87°37W 84 C6
Danville Ind., U.S.A. 39°46N 86°32W 85 D4
Danville Iowa, U.S.A. 40°52N 91°19W 81 E7
Danville Kans., U.S.A. 37°17N 97°54W 82 D6
Danville Ky., U.S.A. 37°39N 84°46W 105 C8
Danville Ohio, U.S.A. 40°27N 82°15W 86 C4
Danville Pa., U.S.A. 40°58N 76°37W 87 D6
Danville Va., U.S.A. 36°36N 79°23W 102 E5
Danville Vt., U.S.A. 44°25N 72°9W 89 B2
Danville W. Va., U.S.A. 38°5N 81°50W 102 C3
Danville Wash., U.S.A. 48°59N 118°30W 120 B7
Daphne Ala., U.S.A. 30°36N 87°54W 112 F3
D'Arbonne, Bayou → La., U.S.A. 32°34N 92°7W 110 B3
Darby Mont., U.S.A. 46°1N 114°11W 123 D3
Darby Pa., U.S.A. 39°55N 75°13W 98 B1
Darby, C. Alaska, U.S.A. 64°19N 162°47W 135 D7
Dardanelle Ark., U.S.A. 35°13N 93°9W 106 C2
Dardanelle, L. Ark., U.S.A. 35°14N 93°10W 106 C2
Dare County ☆ N.C., U.S.A. 35°45N 75°40W 103 C10
Darfur Minn., U.S.A. 44°3N 94°50W 77 F4
Darien Conn., U.S.A. 41°5N 73°28W 91 C1
Darien Ga., U.S.A. 31°23N 81°26W 113 E5
Darien Wis., U.S.A. 42°36N 88°43W 78 F5
Darién, G. del Colombia 9°0N 77°0W 182 E4
Darién, Parque Nac. △ Panama 7°36N 77°57W 182 E4
Darién, Serranía del Colombia 8°30N 77°30W 182 E4
Dark Cove Nfld. & L., Canada 48°47N 54°13W 142 D6
Darke County ☆ Ohio, U.S.A. 40°6N 84°38W 86 C2
Darling Miss., U.S.A. 34°22N 90°16W 111 B3
Darling, L. N. Dak., U.S.A. 48°27N 101°35W 76 B4
Darlington Fla., U.S.A. 30°57N 86°3W 114 A2
Darlington Ind., U.S.A. 40°6N 86°47W 85 C4
Darlington La., U.S.A. 30°53N 90°47W 110 D5
Darlington Md., U.S.A. 39°38N 76°12W 93 A4
Darlington S.C., U.S.A. 34°18N 79°52W 103 D6
Darlington Wis., U.S.A. 42°41N 90°7W 78 F3
Darlington County ☆ S.C., U.S.A. 34°20N 80°0W 103 D6
Darmstadt Ind., U.S.A. 38°6N 87°35W 85 E3
Darnestown Md., U.S.A. 39°6N 77°18W 93 A3
Darnley B. N.W.T., Canada 69°30N 123°30W 156 C8
Darr Nebr., U.S.A. 40°49N 99°5W 80 D6
Darrington Wash., U.S.A. 48°15N 121°36W 120 B4
Darrouzett Tex., U.S.A. 36°27N 100°20W 108 A7
Dartmouth N.S., Canada 44°40N 63°30W 141 J6
Dartmouth Mass., U.S.A. 41°34N 71°1W 91 C3
Dartmouth → Qué., Canada 48°53N 64°34W 140 E5
Dasher Ga., U.S.A. 30°45N 83°13W 113 F3
Dassel Minn., U.S.A. 45°5N 94°19W 77 E4
Dasserat, L. Qué., Canada 48°16N 79°25W 144 C3
Dateland Ariz., U.S.A. 32°48N 113°33W 130 E2
Datil N. Mex., U.S.A. 34°9N 107°51W 131 C3
Daulnay N.B., Canada 47°25N 65°28W 141 F4
Dauphin Man., Canada 51°9N 100°5W 151 D11
Dauphin County ☆ Pa., U.S.A. 40°20N 76°55W 87 D6
Dauphin I. Ala., U.S.A. 30°15N 88°11W 112 F2
Dauphin Island Ala., U.S.A. 30°15N 88°7W 112 F2
Dauphin L. Man., Canada 51°20N 99°45W 151 D11
Dauphin River Man., Canada 51°58N 98°4W 151 D13
Davenport Calif., U.S.A. 37°1N 122°12W 126 F4
Davenport Fla., U.S.A. 28°10N 81°36W 114 C7
Davenport Iowa, U.S.A. 41°32N 90°35W 81 D8
Davenport N. Dak., U.S.A. 46°43N 97°4W 76 D8
Davenport Nebr., U.S.A. 42°28N 74°51W 88 C6
Davenport Okla., U.S.A. 35°42N 96°46W 107 C7
Davenport Wash., U.S.A. 47°39N 118°9W 120 C7
Davey Nebr., U.S.A. 40°59N 96°40W 80 D9
David Panama 8°30N 82°30W 182 E3
David Ky., U.S.A. 37°36N 82°54W 105 C10
David City Nebr., U.S.A. 41°15N 97°8W 80 C8
David's Island N.Y., U.S.A. 40°53N 73°46W 97 A4
Davidson Sask., Canada 51°16N 105°59W 150 D6
Davidson N.C., U.S.A. 35°30N 80°51W 103 C4
Davidson Okla., U.S.A. 34°14N 99°5W 107 D4
Davidson, Mt. Calif., U.S.A. 37°44N 122°27W 132 B2
Davidson County ☆ N.C., U.S.A. 35°45N 80°10W 103 C5
Davidson County ☆ Tenn., U.S.A. 36°10N 86°47W 104 C6
Davidson Mts. Alaska, U.S.A. 68°41N 142°22W 135 B12
Davidsonville Md., U.S.A. 38°55N 76°38W 93 B4
Davie Fla., U.S.A. 26°3N 80°14W 115 B2
Davie County ☆ N.C., U.S.A. 35°50N 80°30W 103 C5
Daviess County ☆ Ind., U.S.A. 38°40N 87°5W 85 E3
Daviess County ☆ Ky., U.S.A. 37°40N 87°5W 104 C5
Daviess County ☆ Mo., U.S.A. 40°0N 94°0W 83 B3
Davis Calif., U.S.A. 38°33N 121°44W 126 E5
Davis Ill., U.S.A. 42°25N 89°25W 84 A4
Davis Okla., U.S.A. 34°30N 97°7W 107 D6
Davis S. Dak., U.S.A. 43°16N 96°59W 76 G9
Davis W. Va., U.S.A. 39°8N 79°28W 93 A1
Davis, Lake Calif., U.S.A. 39°53N 120°29W 126 D6
Davis, Mt. Pa., U.S.A. 39°48N 79°10W 87 E3
Davis City Iowa, U.S.A. 40°38N 93°49W 81 E5
Davis County ☆ Iowa, U.S.A. 40°45N 92°25W 81 E6
Davis County ☆ Utah, U.S.A. 41°0N 112°5W 129 C3
Davis Creek Calif., U.S.A. 41°44N 120°22W 126 B6
Davis Dam U.S.A. 35°12N 114°34W 130 B1
Davis Island Tampa, U.S.A. 27°55N 82°27W 115 B4
Davis Junction Ill., U.S.A. 42°6N 89°6W 84 A4
Davis Mts. Tex., U.S.A. 30°50N 103°55W 108 G4
Davis Str. N. Amer. 65°0N 58°0W 158 D14
Davisboro Ga., U.S.A. 32°59N 82°36W 113 D4
Davison Mich., U.S.A. 43°2N 83°31W 79 F8
Davison County ☆ S. Dak., U.S.A. 43°43N 98°2W 76 G8
Davisville Mo., U.S.A. 37°49N 91°11W 83 D5
Davy W. Va., U.S.A. 37°29N 81°39W 102 D3
Davy Crockett Nat. Forest Tex., U.S.A. 31°12N 95°2W 109 F12
Dawes County ☆ Nebr., U.S.A. 42°45N 103°0W 80 B2
Dawn Tex., U.S.A. 34°55N 102°12W 108 C5
Dawson Yukon, Canada 64°10N 139°30W 157 D5
Dawson Ga., U.S.A. 31°46N 84°27W 113 E2
Dawson Minn., U.S.A. 44°56N 96°3W 77 F2
Dawson N. Dak., U.S.A. 46°52N 99°45W 76 D6
Dawson Nebr., U.S.A. 40°8N 95°50W 80 D9
Dawson Tex., U.S.A. 31°54N 96°43W 109 F11
Dawson County ☆ Ga., U.S.A. 34°22N 84°10W 113 B2
Dawson County ☆ Mont., U.S.A. 47°15N 105°0W 123 C13
Dawson County ☆ Nebr., U.S.A. 40°50N 99°45W 80 D6
Dawson County ☆ Tex., U.S.A. 32°44N 101°58W 108 E6
Dawson Creek B.C., Canada 55°45N 120°15W 157 E8
Dawson Inlet Nunavut, Canada 61°50N 93°25W 159 E7

Dawson Range Yukon, Canada 62°35N 138°20W 157 D5
Dawson Springs Ky., U.S.A. 37°10N 87°41W 104 C5
Dawsonville Ga., U.S.A. 34°25N 84°7W 113 B2
Day Fla., U.S.A. 30°12N 83°17W 114 A5
Day County ☆ S. Dak., U.S.A. 45°20N 97°31W 76 E8
Daykin Nebr., U.S.A. 40°21N 97°18W 80 D8
Daysland Alta., Canada 52°50N 112°20W 153 F8
Dayton Iowa, U.S.A. 42°16N 94°4W 81 C4
Dayton Mont., U.S.A. 47°52N 114°17W 123 C3
Dayton Nev., U.S.A. 39°14N 119°36W 128 C1
Dayton Ohio, U.S.A. 39°45N 84°12W 86 D2
Dayton Pa., U.S.A. 40°53N 79°15W 87 D3
Dayton Tenn., U.S.A. 35°30N 85°1W 105 E7
Dayton Tex., U.S.A. 30°3N 94°54W 109 G13
Dayton Va., U.S.A. 38°25N 78°56W 102 C6
Dayton Wash., U.S.A. 46°19N 117°59W 120 D8
Dayton Wyo., U.S.A. 44°53N 107°16W 124 B5
Dayton Int. ✈ (DAY) Ohio, U.S.A. 39°54N 84°13W 86 D2
Daytona Beach Fla., U.S.A. 29°13N 81°1W 114 B7
Dayville Oreg., U.S.A. 44°28N 119°32W 121 C6
Dazey N. Dak., U.S.A. 47°11N 98°12W 76 C7
De Armanville Ala., U.S.A. 33°38N 85°45W 112 C5
De Baca County ☆ N. Mex., U.S.A. 34°15N 104°30W 131 C6
De Bary Fla., U.S.A. 28°54N 81°18W 114 C7
De Beque Colo., U.S.A. 39°20N 108°13W 125 C2
De Forest Wis., U.S.A. 43°15N 89°20W 78 E4
De Funiak Springs Fla., U.S.A. 30°43N 86°7W 114 A2
De Graff Minn., U.S.A. 45°16N 95°28W 77 E3
De Grau Nfld. & L., Canada 48°29N 59°9W 142 D1
De Gray L. Ark., U.S.A. 34°13N 93°7W 106 D2
De Gray Lake Resort State Park △ Ark., U.S.A. 34°15N 93°10W 106 D2
De Kalb Miss., U.S.A. 32°46N 88°39W 111 D5
De Kalb Tex., U.S.A. 33°31N 94°37W 109 D13
De Kalb County ☆ Ala., U.S.A. 34°26N 85°43W 112 B5
De Kalb County ☆ Mo., U.S.A. 39°50N 94°25W 83 B2
De Kalb Junction N.Y., U.S.A. 44°30N 75°17W 88 A5
De Land Fla., U.S.A. 29°2N 81°18W 114 B7
De Leon Tex., U.S.A. 32°7N 98°32W 109 E9
De Leon Springs Fla., U.S.A. 29°7N 81°21W 114 B7
De Long Mts. Alaska, U.S.A. 68°10N 163°30W 135 B7
De Montreville, L. Minn., U.S.A. 45°1N 92°56W 94 A4
De Morbihan, L. Qué., Canada 51°50N 62°54W 140 B7
De Pere Wis., U.S.A. 44°27N 88°4W 78 D5
De Queen Ark., U.S.A. 34°2N 94°21W 106 D1
De Quincy La., U.S.A. 30°27N 93°26W 110 D2
De Ruyter N.Y., U.S.A. 42°46N 75°53W 88 C5
De Smet S. Dak., U.S.A. 44°23N 97°33W 76 F8
De Smet, L. Wyo., U.S.A. 44°29N 106°45W 124 B6
De Soto Ga., U.S.A. 31°54N 84°3W 113 E2
De Soto Iowa, U.S.A. 41°32N 94°1W 81 D4
De Soto Kans., U.S.A. 38°59N 94°58W 82 C9
De Soto Mo., U.S.A. 38°8N 90°34W 83 C61
De Soto Tex., U.S.A. 32°35N 96°51W 116 C5
De Soto Wis., U.S.A. 43°25N 91°12W 78 E2
De Soto City Fla., U.S.A. 27°27N 81°24W 114 D7
De Soto County ☆ Fla., U.S.A. 27°15N 81°45W 114 D7
De Soto County ☆ Miss., U.S.A. 34°53N 90°1W 111 B3
De Soto Nat. Forest Miss., U.S.A. 31°0N 89°0W 111 E4
De Soto Nat. Memorial △ Fla., U.S.A. 27°31N 82°39W 114 D6
De Soto Nat. Wildlife Refuge △ Iowa, U.S.A. 41°30N 96°1W 81 D2
De Soto Parish ☆ La., U.S.A. 32°2N 93°43W 110 B2
De Tour Village Mich., U.S.A. 46°0N 83°56W 79 C8
De Valls Bluff Ark., U.S.A. 34°47N 91°28W 106 D4
De Witt Ark., U.S.A. 34°18N 91°20W 106 D4
De Witt Ill., U.S.A. 40°11N 88°47W 84 C5
De Witt Iowa, U.S.A. 41°49N 90°33W 81 D8
De Witt Mich., U.S.A. 42°51N 84°34W 79 G7
De Witt Nebr., U.S.A. 40°24N 96°55W 80 D9
De Witt County ☆ Ill., U.S.A. 40°10N 88°55W 84 C5
De Witt County ☆ Tex., U.S.A. 29°6N 97°17W 109 H10
Dead L. Fla., U.S.A. 30°10N 85°10W 114 A3
Deadhorse Alaska, U.S.A. 70°11N 148°27W 135 A10
Deadman B. Fla., U.S.A. 29°30N 83°30W 114 A6
Deadwood S. Dak., U.S.A. 44°23N 103°44W 76 F2
Deaf Smith County ☆ Tex., U.S.A. 35°0N 102°30W 108 C5
Deale Md., U.S.A. 38°47N 76°33W 93 B4
Dean → B.C., Canada 52°49N 126°58W 154 C8
Dean Chan. B.C., Canada 52°30N 127°15W 154 C7
Dearborn Mich., U.S.A. 42°19N 83°10W 98 B2
Dearborn Mo., U.S.A. 39°32N 94°46W 83 B2
Dearborn County ☆ Ind., U.S.A. 39°10N 85°0W 85 D6
Dearing Kans., U.S.A. 37°4N 95°43W 82 D8
Deary Idaho, U.S.A. 46°48N 116°32W 122 C2
Deas Island Park B.C., Canada 49°7N 123°4W 161 C2
Dease → B.C., Canada 59°56N 128°32W 157 E7
Dease Arm N.W.T., Canada 66°52N 119°37W 156 C9
Dease Inlet Alaska, U.S.A. 71°2N 155°26W 135 A9
Dease Lake B.C., Canada 58°50N 130°6W 157 E6
Dease Str. Nunavut, Canada 68°50N 107°30W 158 D4
Death Valley Calif., U.S.A. 36°15N 116°50W 127 G10
Death Valley Junction Calif., U.S.A. 36°20N 116°25W 127 G10
Death Valley Nat. Park △ U.S.A. 36°29N 117°6W 127 G9
Deatsville Ala., U.S.A. 32°37N 86°24W 112 D4
Deaver Wyo., U.S.A. 44°54N 108°36W 124 B4
Debden Alta., Canada 53°30N 106°50W 153 E5
Debec N.B., Canada 46°4N 67°41W 141 G2
Debert N.S., Canada 45°26N 63°28W 141 H6
Deblois Maine, U.S.A. 44°45N 68°1W 90 D5
DeBolt Alta., Canada 55°12N 118°1W 152 C2
Decatur Ark., U.S.A. 36°20N 94°28W 106 B1
Decatur Ga., U.S.A. 33°46N 84°16W 117 B3
Decatur Ill., U.S.A. 39°51N 88°57W 84 D5
Decatur Ind., U.S.A. 40°50N 84°56W 85 C6
Decatur Mich., U.S.A. 42°7N 85°58W 79 G6
Decatur Miss., U.S.A. 32°26N 89°7W 111 D4
Decatur Nebr., U.S.A. 42°0N 96°15W 80 C9
Decatur Tenn., U.S.A. 35°31N 84°47W 105 E8
Decatur Tex., U.S.A. 33°14N 97°35W 109 D10
Decatur City Iowa, U.S.A. 40°45N 93°50W 81 E5
Decatur County ☆ Ga., U.S.A. 31°0N 84°35W 113 F2
Decatur County ☆ Ind., U.S.A. 39°15N 85°30W 85 D5
Decatur County ☆ Iowa, U.S.A. 40°45N 93°45W 81 E5
Decatur County ☆ Kans., U.S.A. 39°45N 100°20W 82 B3
Decatur County ☆ Tenn., U.S.A. 35°35N 88°7W 104 E4
Decaturville Tenn., U.S.A. 35°35N 88°7W 104 E4
Decelles, Rés. Qué., Canada 47°42N 78°8W 144 C4
Deception, Mt. Wash., U.S.A. 47°49N 123°14W 120 C2
Deckerville Mich., U.S.A. 43°32N 82°44W 79 F8
Declo Idaho, U.S.A. 42°30N 113°40W 122 G5
Decorah Iowa, U.S.A. 43°18N 91°48W 81 B71

Dededo Guam 13°31N 144°50E 184 b
Dedham Iowa, U.S.A. 41°55N 94°49W 81 D4
Dedham Mass., U.S.A. 42°15N 71°10W 96 B1
Dee Oreg., U.S.A. 43°35N 121°37W 121 D4
Deep → N.C., U.S.A. 35°36N 79°3W 103 C6
Deep Cr. → S. Dak., U.S.A. 45°11N 102°15W 76 E5
Deep Creek L. Md., U.S.A. 39°31N 79°24W 93 A1
Deep Creek Range Utah, U.S.A. 39°50N 113°50W 129 D2
Deep Fork → Okla., U.S.A. 35°28N 95°50W 107 C8
Deep River Conn., U.S.A. 41°23N 72°26W 91 C2
Deep River Iowa, U.S.A. 41°35N 92°22W 81 D6
Deep Run → Baltimore, U.S.A. 37°24N 76°40W 99 B1
Deep Springs L. Calif., U.S.A. 37°20N 118°3W 127 F8
Deepstep Ga., U.S.A. 33°1N 82°58W 113 C4
Deepwater Mo., U.S.A. 38°16N 93°47W 83 C3
Deepwater N.J., U.S.A. 39°41N 75°29W 92 C1
Deer Ark., U.S.A. 35°50N 93°13W 106 C2
Deer, L. Nfld. & L., Canada 49°6N 57°35W 142 D2
Deer Cr. → Ind., U.S.A. 40°34N 86°41W 85 C4
Deer Cr. → Md., U.S.A. 39°40N 76°10W 93 A4
Deer Cr. → Ohio, U.S.A. 39°27N 83°0W 86 D3
Deer Creek Ill., U.S.A. 40°38N 89°20W 84 C4
Deer Creek Okla., U.S.A. 36°48N 97°31W 107 B6
Deer Flat Nat. Wildlife Refuge △ Idaho, U.S.A. 43°18N 116°35W 122 F2
Deer Grove Ill., U.S.A. 41°37N 89°42W 84 B4
Deer I. Alaska, U.S.A. 54°55N 162°18W 135 J7
Deer I. Maine, U.S.A. 44°13N 68°41W 90 D5
Deer Isle Maine, U.S.A. 44°14N 68°41W 90 D5
Deer Lake Nfld. & L., Canada 49°11N 57°27W 142 C3
Deer Lodge Mont., U.S.A. 46°24N 112°44W 123 D5
Deer Lodge County ☆ Mont., U.S.A. 46°0N 113°0W 123 E4
Deer Park Ala., U.S.A. 31°13N 88°19W 112 E2
Deer Park Md., U.S.A. 28°6N 80°54W 114 C8
Deer Park N.Y., U.S.A. 39°25N 79°18W 93 A1
Deer Park Md., U.S.A. 40°46N 73°20W 92 B3
Deer Park Ohio, U.S.A. 39°12N 84°24W 86 D2
Deer Park Wash., U.S.A. 47°57N 117°28W 120 C8
Deer Park Wis., U.S.A. 45°11N 92°23W 78 C1
Deer Pond Nfld. & L., Canada 48°30N 54°45W 142 D6
Deer River Minn., U.S.A. 47°20N 93°48W 77 C5
Deer Trail Colo., U.S.A. 39°37N 104°2W 125 C6
Deer Valley Ariz., U.S.A. 33°41N 112°8W 134 A2
Deer Valley Ariz., U.S.A. 33°43N 112°12W 134 A1
Deerfield Kans., U.S.A. 37°59N 101°8W 82 D2
Deerfield Mass., U.S.A. 42°33N 72°36W 91 B2
Deerfield Mo., U.S.A. 37°50N 94°30W 83 D2
Deerfield S. Dak., U.S.A. 44°1N 103°50W 76 F2
Deerfield Wis., U.S.A. 43°3N 89°5W 78 E4
Deerfield → Mass., U.S.A. 42°35N 72°35W 91 B2
Deerfield Beach Fla., U.S.A. 26°19N 80°6W 114 E8
Deering Alaska, U.S.A. 66°4N 162°42W 135 C7
Deering N. Dak., U.S.A. 48°24N 101°3W 76 B4
Deerlodge Nat. Forest Mont., U.S.A. 46°20N 113°30W 123 D4
Deersville Ohio, U.S.A. 40°18N 81°11W 86 C5
Deerwood Minn., U.S.A. 46°29N 93°54W 77 D5
Deeth Nev., U.S.A. 41°4N 115°17W 128 A5
Defiance Iowa, U.S.A. 41°49N 95°20W 81 D3
Defiance Ohio, U.S.A. 41°17N 84°22W 86 B2
Defiance County ☆ Ohio, U.S.A. 41°23N 84°32W 86 B2
Dégelis Qué., Canada 47°30N 68°35W 145 D14
Degollado Jalisco, Mexico 20°28N 102°9W 174 B5
DeKalb Ill., U.S.A. 41°56N 88°46W 84 B5
DeKalb County ☆ Ga., U.S.A. 33°45N 84°14W 113 C2
DeKalb County ☆ Ill., U.S.A. 41°50N 88°45W 84 B5
DeKalb County ☆ Ind., U.S.A. 41°25N 85°0W 85 B6
DeKalb County ☆ Tenn., U.S.A. 35°58N 85°51W 105 E7
Del City Okla., U.S.A. 35°26N 97°26W 107 C6
Del Mar Calif., U.S.A. 32°58N 117°16W 127 L9
Del Norte Colo., U.S.A. 37°41N 106°21W 125 E4
Del Norte County ☆ Calif., U.S.A. 41°40N 124°0W 126 B1
Del Rio Tex., U.S.A. 29°22N 100°54W 108 H7
Delacroix La., U.S.A. 29°46N 89°45W 110 E6
Delafield Wis., U.S.A. 43°4N 88°24W 78 E5
Delair N.J., U.S.A. 39°58N 75°3W 98 B2
Delamar L. Nev., U.S.A. 37°19N 114°57W 128 E6
Delanco N.J., U.S.A. 40°3N 74°57W 98 B2
Delano Calif., U.S.A. 35°46N 119°15W 127 H7
Delano Minn., U.S.A. 45°2N 93°47W 77 E5
Delano Peak Utah, U.S.A. 38°22N 112°22W 129 D3
Delaplaine Ark., U.S.A. 36°14N 90°44W 106 B5
Delaplane Va., U.S.A. 38°55N 77°55W 93 B3
Delaronde L. Sask., Canada 54°3N 107°3W 150 A4
Delavan Ill., U.S.A. 40°22N 89°33W 84 C4
Delavan Kans., U.S.A. 38°40N 96°49W 82 C7
Delavan Wis., U.S.A. 42°38N 88°39W 78 F51
Delaware Ohio, U.S.A. 40°18N 83°4W 86 C3
Delaware Okla., U.S.A. 36°47N 95°39W 107 B8
Delaware □ U.S.A. 39°0N 75°20W 93 B5
Delaware → U.S.A. 39°15N 75°20W 93 A5
Delaware B. Del., U.S.A. 39°0N 75°10W 93 A5
Delaware City Del., U.S.A. 39°35N 75°36W 93 A5
Delaware County ☆ Ind., U.S.A. 40°15N 85°25W 85 C5
Delaware County ☆ Iowa, U.S.A. 42°30N 91°20W 81 C7
Delaware County ☆ N.Y., U.S.A. 42°15N 75°0W 88 C6
Delaware County ☆ Ohio, U.S.A. 40°18N 83°4W 86 C3
Delaware County ☆ Okla., U.S.A. 36°25N 94°50W 107 B9
Delaware County ☆ Pa., U.S.A. 39°55N 75°23W 87 E7
Delaware Cr. → U.S.A. 32°2N 104°0W 108 E3
Delaware Mts. U.S.A. 31°45N 104°50W 108 F3
Delaware Seashore State Park △ Del., U.S.A. 38°39N 75°4W 93 B5
Delaware Water Gap Nat. Recr. Area △ N.J., U.S.A. 41°10N 74°55W 92 A2
Delbarton W. Va., U.S.A. 37°43N 82°11W 102 D2
Delbrook B.C., Canada 49°21N 123°5W 161 A2
Delburne Alta., Canada 52°12N 113°4W 153 F7
Delcambre La., U.S.A. 29°57N 91°58W 110 E4
Delevan N.Y., U.S.A. 42°29N 78°29W 88 C2
Delgada, Pt. Calif., U.S.A. 40°2N 124°5W 126 C1
Delhi Calif., U.S.A. 37°26N 120°46W 126 F6
Delhi Iowa, U.S.A. 42°26N 91°20W 81 C7
Delhi La., U.S.A. 32°28N 91°30W 110 B4
Delhi N.Y., U.S.A. 42°17N 74°55W 88 C6
Delia Alta., Canada 51°38N 112°23W 153 G8
Delia Kans., U.S.A. 39°15N 95°59W 82 B8
Delicias Chihuahua, Mexico 28°13N 105°28W 169 E10
Delight Ark., U.S.A. 34°2N 93°31W 106 D2
Déline N.W.T., Canada 65°11N 123°25W 157 C8
Delisle Sask., Canada 51°55N 107°8W 150 D4
Dell Mont., U.S.A. 44°44N 112°42W 123 F5
Dell City Tex., U.S.A. 31°56N 105°12W 108 F2
Dell Rapids S. Dak., U.S.A. 43°50N 96°43W 76 G9
Dellwood Minn., U.S.A. 45°6N 92°57W 94 A4
Dellwood Mo., U.S.A. 38°44N 90°17W 94 A2

206 Delmar INDEX

Delmar *Del., U.S.A.* 38°27N 75°35W **93** B5
Delmar *Iowa, U.S.A.* 42°0N 90°37W **81** C8
Delmar *N.Y., U.S.A.* 42°37N 73°47W **88** C7
Delmarva Peninsula *Md., U.S.A.* 38°45N 75°45W **93** B5
Delmont *N.J., U.S.A.* 39°13N 74°57W **92** C2
Delmont *S. Dak., U.S.A.* 43°16N 98°10W **76** G7
Deloit *Iowa, U.S.A.* 42°6N 95°19W **81** C3
Deloraine *Man., Canada* 49°15N 100°29W **151** F11
Delphi *Ind., U.S.A.* 40°36N 86°41W **85** C4
Delphos *Kans., U.S.A.* 39°17N 97°46W **82** B6
Delphos *Ohio, U.S.A.* 40°51N 84°21W **86** C2
Delray *W. Va., U.S.A.* 39°12N 78°36W **102** B6
Delray Beach *Fla., U.S.A.* 26°28N 80°4W **114** E8
Delson *Qué., Canada* 45°22N 73°33W **89** A1
Delta *B.C., Canada* 49°5N 123°5W **161** C2
Delta *Ala., U.S.A.* 33°26N 85°42W **112** C5
Delta *Colo., U.S.A.* 38°44N 108°4W **125** D2
Delta *Mo., U.S.A.* 37°12N 89°44W **83** D7
Delta *Ohio, U.S.A.* 41°34N 84°0W **86** B3
Delta *Utah, U.S.A.* 39°21N 112°35W **129** D3
Delta Beach *Man., Canada* 50°11N 98°19W **151** E13
Delta County ☆ *Colo., U.S.A.* 38°50N 107°50W **125** D3
Delta County ☆ *Mich., U.S.A.* 46°0N 87°0W **79** D5
Delta County ☆ *Tex., U.S.A.* 33°23N 95°42W **109** D12
Delta Junction *Alaska, U.S.A.* 64°2N 145°44W **135** D11
Delta Nat. Forest *Miss., U.S.A.* 32°50N 90°55W **111** D3
Delta Nat. Wildlife Refuge ⌂ *La., U.S.A.* 29°15N 89°15W **110** E6
Deltona *Fla., U.S.A.* 28°54N 81°16W **114** C7
Demarcation Pt. *Alaska, U.S.A.* 69°41N 141°18W **135** B12
Deming *N. Mex., U.S.A.* 32°16N 107°46W **131** E3
Deming *Wash., U.S.A.* 48°50N 122°13W **120** B3
Demopolis *Ala., U.S.A.* 32°31N 87°50W **112** D3
Demorest *Ga., U.S.A.* 34°34N 83°33W **113** B3
Demotte *Ind., U.S.A.* 41°12N 87°12W **85** B3
Dempsey *Okla., U.S.A.* 35°31N 99°49W **107** C4
Denair *Calif., U.S.A.* 37°32N 120°48W **126** F6
Denali = McKinley, Mt. *Alaska, U.S.A.* 63°4N 151°0W **135** E10
Denali ☆ *Alaska, U.S.A.* 61°13N 149°52W **135** F10
Denali Nat. Park and Preserve △ **Denali** △
Alaska, U.S.A. 63°30N 152°0W **135** E10
Denbigh *Ont., Canada* 45°8N 77°15W **147** B9
Denbigh *N. Dak., U.S.A.* 48°19N 100°35W **76** B5
Denbigh, C. *Alaska, U.S.A.* 64°23N 161°32W **135** D7
Dendron *Va., U.S.A.* 37°3N 76°56W **102** D8
Denham *Minn., U.S.A.* 46°22N 92°57W **77** D6
Denham Springs *La., U.S.A.* 30°29N 90°57W **110** D5
Denhoff *N. Dak., U.S.A.* 47°29N 100°16W **76** C5
Denholm *Sask., Canada* 52°39N 108°1W **150** C3
Denio *Nev., U.S.A.* 41°59N 118°38W **128** A2
Denison *Iowa, U.S.A.* 42°1N 95°21W **81** C3
Denison *Kans., U.S.A.* 39°24N 95°38W **82** B8
Denison *Tex., U.S.A.* 33°45N 96°33W **109** D11
Denman Island *B.C., Canada* 49°33N 124°48W **154** F10
Denmark *Kans., U.S.A.* 39°5N 98°17W **82** B5
Denmark *Maine, U.S.A.* 43°58N 70°48W **89** C4
Denmark *S.C., U.S.A.* 33°19N 81°9W **103** E4
Denmark *Wis., U.S.A.* 44°21N 87°50W **78** D6
Dennard *Ark., U.S.A.* 35°46N 92°31W **106** C3
Dennehotso *Ariz., U.S.A.* 36°51N 109°51W **130** A6
Dennis *Kans., U.S.A.* 37°21N 95°25W **82** D8
Dennis *Mass., U.S.A.* 41°44N 70°12W **91** C4
Dennis *Miss., U.S.A.* 34°34N 88°14W **111** B5
Dennis Port *Mass., U.S.A.* 41°39N 70°8W **91** C4
Dennison *Minn., U.S.A.* 44°25N 92°2W **77** F5
Dennison *Ohio, U.S.A.* 40°24N 81°19W **86** C5
Dennisville *N.J., U.S.A.* 39°12N 74°49W **92** C2
Dent *Minn., U.S.A.* 46°33N 95°43W **77** D3
Dent County ☆ *Mo., U.S.A.* 37°35N 91°30W **83** D5
Denton *Ga., U.S.A.* 31°44N 82°42W **113** E4
Denton *Kans., U.S.A.* 39°44N 95°16W **82** B8
Denton *Md., U.S.A.* 38°53N 75°50W **93** B5
Denton *Mont., U.S.A.* 47°19N 109°57W **123** C8
Denton *N.C., U.S.A.* 35°38N 80°6W **103** C5
Denton *Nebr., U.S.A.* 40°44N 96°51W **80** D9
Denton *Tex., U.S.A.* 33°13N 97°8W **109** D10
Denton County ☆ *Tex., U.S.A.* 33°15N 97°10W **109** D10
Denton Cr. → *Tex., U.S.A.* 32°58N 96°57W **109** E11
Dentonia Park *Ont., Canada* 43°42N 79°17W **161** A3
Dentsville *Md., U.S.A.* 38°28N 76°51W **93** B4
Dentsville *S.C., U.S.A.* 34°4N 80°58W **103** D5
Denver *Colo., U.S.A.* 39°42N 104°59W **134** B2
Denver *Ind., U.S.A.* 40°52N 86°5W **85** C4
Denver *Iowa, U.S.A.* 42°40N 92°20W **81** C6
Denver *Pa., U.S.A.* 40°14N 76°8W **87** D6
Denver City *Tex., U.S.A.* 32°58N 102°50W **108** E5
Denver County ☆ *Colo., U.S.A.* 39°45N 105°0W **125** C6
Denver Int. ✈ (DEN) *Colo., U.S.A.* 39°52N 104°40W **125** C6
Denwood = Wainwright *Alta.,*
Canada 52°50N 110°50W **153** F10
Denzil *Sask., Canada* 52°14N 109°39W **150** C2
DePaul University *Ill., U.S.A.* 41°55N 87°39W **95** B3
Depew *Okla., U.S.A.* 35°48N 96°31W **107** C7
Depoe Bay *Oreg., U.S.A.* 44°49N 124°4W **121** C1
Deport *Tex., U.S.A.* 33°32N 95°19W **109** D12
Deposit *N.Y., U.S.A.* 42°4N 75°25W **88** C5
Depue *Ill., U.S.A.* 41°19N 89°19W **84** B4
Derby *Conn., U.S.A.* 41°19N 73°5W **91** C1
Derby *Iowa, U.S.A.* 40°56N 93°27W **81** E5
Derby *Kans., U.S.A.* 37°33N 97°16W **82** D6
Derby *N.Y., U.S.A.* 42°41N 78°58W **88** C2
Derby *Tex., U.S.A.* 28°46N 99°8W **109** J8
Derby Center *Vt., U.S.A.* 44°57N 72°8W **89** B2
Derby Line *Vt., U.S.A.* 45°0N 72°6W **89** B2
Deridder *La., U.S.A.* 30°51N 93°17W **110** D2
Derma *Miss., U.S.A.* 33°51N 89°17W **111** C4
Dermott *Ark., U.S.A.* 33°32N 91°26W **106** E4
Dermott *Tex., U.S.A.* 32°51N 101°1W **108** E6
Dernieres, Isles *La., U.S.A.* 29°2N 90°50W **110** E5
Deroche *B.C., Canada* 49°12N 122°4W **155** F12
Derry *N.H., U.S.A.* 42°53N 71°19W **89** D3
Derwent *Alta., Canada* 53°41N 110°58W **152** E10
Des Allemands *La., U.S.A.* 29°49N 90°28W **110** E5
Des Arc *Ark., U.S.A.* 34°58N 91°30W **106** D4
Des Arc *Mo., U.S.A.* 37°17N 90°38W **83** D6
Des Lacs *N. Dak., U.S.A.* 48°16N 101°34W **76** B4
Des Lacs → *N. Dak., U.S.A.* 48°17N 100°20W **76** B5
Des Lacs Nat. Wildlife Refuge ⌂ *N. Dak.,*
U.S.A. 48°46N 102°6W **76** B3
Des Moines *Iowa, U.S.A.* 41°35N 93°37W **81** D5
Des Moines *N. Mex., U.S.A.* 36°46N 103°50W **131** A7
Des Moines *Wash., U.S.A.* 47°24N 122°19W **132** D4
Des Moines → *Iowa, U.S.A.* 40°23N 91°25W **81** E7
Des Moines ✈ (DSM) *Iowa, U.S.A.* 41°32N 93°40W **81** D5
Des Moines County ☆ *Iowa, U.S.A.* 40°55N 91°10W **81** E7
Des Plaines *Ill., U.S.A.* 42°2N 87°54W **95** A1
Des Plaines → *Ill., U.S.A.* 41°23N 88°15W **84** B5
Desatoya Mts. *Nev., U.S.A.* 39°20N 117°40W **128** C3
Desbarats *Ont., Canada* 46°20N 83°56W **146** A3
Desbiens *Qué., Canada* 48°25N 71°57W **145** C11
Descanso *Calif., U.S.A.* 32°51N 116°37W **127** L10
Descenso, Pta. *Michoacan, Mexico* 17°38N 101°35W **174** E6
Deschaillons-sur-St-Laurent *Qué.,*
Canada 46°32N 72°7W **145** E10
Deschambault *Qué., Canada* 46°39N 71°56W **145** E11
Deschambault L. *Sask., Canada* 54°50N 103°30W **157** F12
Deschambault Lake *Sask., Canada* 54°55N 103°22W **157** F12
Deschênes *Qué., Canada* 45°23N 75°48W **144** F7
Deschutes → *Oreg., U.S.A.* 45°38N 120°55W **121** B5
Deschutes County ☆ *Oreg., U.S.A.* 44°0N 121°30W **121** D4
Deschutes Nat. Forest *Oreg., U.S.A.* 43°40N 121°20W **121** D4
Desdemona *Tex., U.S.A.* 32°16N 98°33W **109** E9
Deseret *Utah, U.S.A.* 39°17N 112°39W **129** D3
Deseret Peak *Utah, U.S.A.* 40°28N 112°38W **129** C3
Deseronto *Ont., Canada* 44°12N 77°3W **147** C9
Desert Center *Calif., U.S.A.* 33°43N 115°24W **127** K11
Desert Hot Springs *Calif., U.S.A.* 33°58N 116°30W **127** K10
Desert L. *Nev., U.S.A.* 36°59N 115°14W **128** F5
Desert Nat. Wildlife Range ⌂ *Nev.,*
U.S.A. 37°8N 115°52W **134** A2
Desert Peak *Utah, U.S.A.* 41°11N 113°22W **129** B2
Desert Ra. *Nev., U.S.A.* 36°55N 115°25W **128** F5
Desert Ranch Res. *Nev., U.S.A.* 41°42N 116°33W **128** A4
Desert Valley *Nev., U.S.A.* 41°10N 118°5W **128** A2
Desert Wetlands Park *Nev., U.S.A.* 36°7N 115°2W **134** C3
Desha *Ark., U.S.A.* 35°44N 91°41W **106** C4
Desha County ☆ *Ark., U.S.A.* 33°48N 91°16W **106** E4
Deshler *Nebr., U.S.A.* 40°9N 97°44W **80** D8
Deshler *Ohio, U.S.A.* 41°13N 83°54W **86** B3
Desierto Central de Baja California, Parque
Natural del ⌂ *Baja Calif., Mexico* 29°40N 114°50W **166** D4
Desierto de los Leones, Parque Nacional △
Distrito Federal, Mexico 19°18N 99°19W **181** C2
Desierto del Carmen, Parque Nacional △
México, Mexico 18°54N 99°37W **175** D8
Desloge *Mo., U.S.A.* 37°51N 90°32W **83** D6
Desmarais *Alta., Canada* 55°56N 113°49W **152** C7
Desmaraisville *Qué., Canada* 49°32N 76°9W **144** B6
Desméloizes *Qué., Canada* 48°57N 79°29W **144** C3
Desolation Sound Marine Park ⌂ *B.C.,*
Canada 50°5N 124°25W **154** E10
Destin *Fla., U.S.A.* 30°24N 86°30W **114** A2
Detour, Pt. *Mich., U.S.A.* 45°40N 86°40W **79** D5
Detroit *Ala., U.S.A.* 34°2N 88°10W **112** B2
Detroit *Mich., U.S.A.* 42°19N 83°12W **98** A2
Detroit *Oreg., U.S.A.* 44°44N 122°9W **121** C3
Detroit *Tex., U.S.A.* 33°40N 95°16W **109** D12
Detroit Beach *Mich., U.S.A.* 41°56N 83°19W **79** H8
Detroit City ✈ (DET) *Mich., U.S.A.* 42°24N 83°0W **98** A2
Detroit Lakes *Minn., U.S.A.* 46°49N 95°51W **77** D3
Detroit Metropolitan Wayne County ✈ (DTW)
Mich., U.S.A. 42°13N 83°21W **79** G8
Deuel County ☆ *Nebr., U.S.A.* 41°10N 102°20W **80** C3
Deuel County ☆ *S. Dak., U.S.A.* 44°45N 96°41W **76** F9
Deux-Loutres, L. aux *Qué., Canada* 51°31N 62°28W **140** B7
Deux-Montagnes *Qué., Canada* 45°32N 73°53W **160** A1
Deux-Montagnes, L. des *Qué., Canada* 45°27N 74°0W **160** B1
Devastation Chan. *B.C., Canada* 53°40N 128°50W **154** B6
Devenyns, L. *Qué., Canada* 47°5N 73°50W **145** D9
Devereux *Ga., U.S.A.* 33°13N 83°5W **113** C3
Devils Den *Calif., U.S.A.* 35°46N 119°58W **127** H7
Devils Hole = Death Valley Nat. Park △
U.S.A. 36°29N 117°6W **127** G9
Devils L. *N. Dak., U.S.A.* 48°2N 98°58W **76** B7
Devils L. *Tex., U.S.A.* 29°34N 100°59W **108** H7
Devils Lake *N. Dak., U.S.A.* 48°7N 98°52W **76** B7
Devil's Lake State Park ⌂ *Wis., U.S.A.* 43°25N 89°42W **78** E4
Devils Paw *B.C., Canada* 58°47N 134°0W **157** E6
Devils Playground *Calif., U.S.A.* 35°0N 115°50W **127** J11
Devils Postpile Nat. Monument ⌂ *Calif.,*
U.S.A. 37°37N 119°5W **126** F7
Devils Tower *Wyo., U.S.A.* 44°35N 104°42W **124** B8
Devils Tower Nat. Monument △ *Wyo.,*
U.S.A. 44°48N 104°55W **124** B8
Devine *Tex., U.S.A.* 29°8N 98°54W **109** H9
Devol *Okla., U.S.A.* 34°11N 98°35W **107** D5
Devon *Alta., Canada* 53°24N 113°44W **152** E7
Devon *Kans., U.S.A.* 37°55N 94°49W **82** D9
Devon *Mont., U.S.A.* 48°28N 111°29W **123** B6
Devon I. *Nunavut, Canada* 75°10N 85°0W **158** B8
Devon Ice Cap *Nunavut, Canada* 75°20N 82°30W **158** B9
Dew *Tex., U.S.A.* 31°36N 96°9W **109** F11
Dewar *Okla., U.S.A.* 35°28N 95°56W **107** C8
Dewberry *Alta., Canada* 53°35N 110°32W **152** E10
Deweese *Nebr., U.S.A.* 40°21N 98°8W **80** D7
Dewey *Puerto Rico* 18°18N 65°18W **184** G17
Dewey *Ariz., U.S.A.* 34°32N 112°15W **130** C3
Dewey *Okla., U.S.A.* 36°48N 95°56W **107** B8
Dewey Beach *Del., U.S.A.* 38°42N 75°5W **93** B5
Dewey County ☆ *Okla., U.S.A.* 36°0N 99°0W **107** C5
Dewey County ☆ *S. Dak., U.S.A.* 45°0N 101°0W **76** E5
Dewey L. *Ky., U.S.A.* 37°44N 82°44W **105** C10
Deweyville *Tex., U.S.A.* 30°18N 93°45W **109** G14
Dewy Rose *Ga., U.S.A.* 34°10N 82°57W **113** B4
Dexter *Ga., U.S.A.* 32°27N 83°4W **113** D3
Dexter *Kans., U.S.A.* 37°11N 96°43W **82** D7
Dexter *Ky., U.S.A.* 36°44N 88°17W **104** D4
Dexter *Maine, U.S.A.* 45°1N 69°18W **90** C4
Dexter *Mich., U.S.A.* 42°20N 83°53W **79** G8
Dexter *Minn., U.S.A.* 43°43N 92°42W **77** G6
Dexter *Mo., U.S.A.* 36°48N 89°57W **83** E7
Dexter *N. Mex., U.S.A.* 33°12N 104°22W **131** D6
Dexter City *Ohio, U.S.A.* 39°39N 81°28W **86** D5
Diablo *Wash., U.S.A.* 48°58N 121°8W **120** B4
Diablo, Pico del *Baja Calif., Mexico* 31°1N 115°28W **166** B3
Diablo, Sierra *Tex., U.S.A.* 31°15N 105°0W **108** F3
Diablo Bolson *Tex., U.S.A.* 31°45N 105°25W **108** F2
Diablo Pt. *N. Marianas* 15°0N 145°35E **184** c
Diablo Range *Calif., U.S.A.* 37°20N 121°25W **126** F5
Diagonal *Iowa, U.S.A.* 40°49N 94°20W **81** E4
Diamond *Mo., U.S.A.* 36°59N 94°19W **83** E2
Diamond, L. *Oreg., U.S.A.* 43°10N 122°9W **121** D3
Diamond City *Alta., Canada* 49°48N 112°51W **153** G8
Diamond Head *Hawai'i, U.S.A.* 21°16N 157°49W **136** K14
Diamond Lake *Oreg., U.S.A.* 43°11N 122°8W **121** D3
Diamond Mts. *Calif., U.S.A.* 40°16N 120°33W **126** C6
Diamond Mts. *Nev., U.S.A.* 39°40N 115°50W **128** C5
Diamond Pk. *Colo., U.S.A.* 40°59N 108°50W **125** B2
Diamond Pk. *Idaho, U.S.A.* 44°9N 113°5W **122** E5
Diamond Springs *Calif., U.S.A.* 38°42N 120°49W **126** E6
Diamond Valley *Nev., U.S.A.* 39°46N 115°58W **128** C5
Diamondhead *Miss., U.S.A.* 30°24N 89°22W **111** F4
Diamondville *Wyo., U.S.A.* 41°47N 110°32W **124** E2
Diana *W. Va., U.S.A.* 38°34N 80°27W **102** C4
Diana B. *Qué., Canada* 61°20N 70°0W **143** A4
Dias Creek *N.J., U.S.A.* 39°8N 74°53W **92** C2
Diaz *Ark., U.S.A.* 35°38N 91°16W **106** C4
Dibble *Okla., U.S.A.* 35°2N 97°38W **107** C6
D'Iberville *Miss., U.S.A.* 30°26N 88°54W **111** F5
Diboll *Tex., U.S.A.* 31°11N 94°47W **109** F13
Dickens *Nebr., U.S.A.* 40°49N 101°2W **80** D4
Dickens *Tex., U.S.A.* 33°37N 100°50W **108** D7
Dickens County ☆ *Tex., U.S.A.* 33°40N 100°50W **108** D7
Dickenson County ☆ *Va., U.S.A.* 37°10N 82°20W **102** D2
Dickey *N. Dak., U.S.A.* 46°32N 98°27W **76** D7
Dickey County ☆ *N. Dak., U.S.A.* 46°2N 98°30W **76** D7
Dickeyville *Wis., U.S.A.* 42°38N 90°36W **78** F3
Dickinson *N. Dak., U.S.A.* 46°53N 102°47W **76** D3
Dickinson *Tex., U.S.A.* 29°28N 95°3W **109** H12
Dickinson County ☆ *Iowa, U.S.A.* 43°20N 95°10W **81** B3
Dickinson County ☆ *Kans., U.S.A.* 38°50N 97°10W **82** C6
Dickinson County ☆ *Mich., U.S.A.* 46°0N 87°50W **79** C4
Dickson *Okla., U.S.A.* 34°11N 96°59W **107** D7
Dickson *Tenn., U.S.A.* 36°5N 87°23W **104** D5
Dickson City *Pa., U.S.A.* 41°28N 75°36W **92** A1
Dickson County ☆ *Tenn., U.S.A.* 36°11N 87°21W **104** D5
Didsbury *Alta., Canada* 51°35N 114°10W **153** G6
Diefenbaker, L. *Sask., Canada* 51°0N 106°55W **150** D5
Diehlstadt *Mo., U.S.A.* 36°58N 89°26W **83** E7
Dieppe *N.B., Canada* 46°6N 64°45W **141** G5
Dierks *Ark., U.S.A.* 34°7N 94°1W **106** D1
Dieterich *Ill., U.S.A.* 39°4N 88°23W **84** D5
Dietrich *Idaho, U.S.A.* 42°55N 114°16W **122** G4
Difficult Run → *Va., U.S.A.* 38°55N 77°18W **99** B2
Digby *N.S., Canada* 44°38N 65°50W **141** J4
Digby Neck *N.S., Canada* 44°30N 66°5W **141** J3
Digges Is. *N.W.T., Canada* 62°40N 77°50W **143** A2
Dighton *Kans., U.S.A.* 38°29N 100°28W **82** C3
Dike *Iowa, U.S.A.* 42°28N 92°38W **81** C6
Dilia *N. Mex., U.S.A.* 35°12N 105°4W **131** B5
Dilke *Sask., Canada* 50°52N 105°15W **150** E6
Dilkon *Ariz., U.S.A.* 35°23N 110°19W **130** B5
Dill City *Okla., U.S.A.* 35°17N 99°8W **107** C4
Dillard *Ga., U.S.A.* 34°58N 83°23W **113** B3
Diller *Nebr., U.S.A.* 40°7N 96°56W **80** D9
Dilley *Tex., U.S.A.* 28°40N 99°10W **109** J8
Dillingham *Alaska, U.S.A.* 59°3N 158°28W **135** G8
Dillingham ☆ *Alaska, U.S.A.* 60°0N 156°0W **135** F8
Dillon *Sask., Canada* 55°56N 108°35W **157** E11
Dillon *Colo., U.S.A.* 39°37N 106°4W **125** C4
Dillon *Mont., U.S.A.* 45°13N 112°38W **123** E5
Dillon *S.C., U.S.A.* 34°25N 79°22W **103** D6
Dillon County ☆ *S.C., U.S.A.* 34°20N 79°20W **103** D6
Dillon L. *Ohio, U.S.A.* 40°0N 82°6W **86** D4
Dillsboro *Ind., U.S.A.* 39°1N 85°4W **85** D5
Dillsburg *Pa., U.S.A.* 40°7N 77°2W **87** D5
Dillwyn *Va., U.S.A.* 37°32N 78°27W **102** D6
Dilworth *Minn., U.S.A.* 46°53N 96°42W **77** D2
Dimas *Sinaloa, Mexico* 23°43N 106°47W **172** D4
Dimmit County ☆ *Tex., U.S.A.* 28°27N 99°46W **109** J8
Dimmitt *Tex., U.S.A.* 34°33N 102°19W **108** C5
Dimock *S. Dak., U.S.A.* 43°29N 97°59W **76** G8
Dinero *Tex., U.S.A.* 28°14N 97°58W **109** J10
Dingwall *N.S., Canada* 46°54N 60°28W **141** G9
Dinnebito Wash → *Ariz., U.S.A.* 35°29N 111°14W **130** B4
Dinorwic *Ont., Canada* 49°41N 92°30W **148** C4
Dinorwic L. *Ont., Canada* 49°37N 92°33W **148** C4
Dinosaur *Colo., U.S.A.* 40°15N 109°1W **125** B1
Dinosaur Nat. Monument ⌂ *Colo.,*
U.S.A. 40°30N 108°45W **125** B2
Dinosaur Prov. Park ⌂ *Alta., Canada* 50°47N 111°30W **153** H9
Dinsmore *Sask., Canada* 51°20N 107°26W **150** D4
Dinuba *Calif., U.S.A.* 36°32N 119°23W **127** G7
Dinwiddie *Va., U.S.A.* 37°5N 77°35W **102** D7
Dinwiddie County ☆ *Va., U.S.A.* 37°5N 77°35W **102** D7
Diomede *Alaska, U.S.A.* 65°47N 169°0W **135** D5
Dionne, L. *Qué., Canada* 49°26N 67°55W **140** D2
Diriamba *Nic.* 11°51N 86°19W **182** D2
Dirty Devil → *Utah, U.S.A.* 37°58N 110°24W **129** F5
Disappointment, C. *Wash., U.S.A.* 46°18N 124°5W **120** D1
Disautel *Wash., U.S.A.* 48°22N 119°14W **120** B6
Dishman *Wash., U.S.A.* 47°39N 117°17W **120** C8
Disko = Qeqertarsuaq *Greenland* 69°45N 53°30W **162** D5
Disko Bugt *Greenland* 69°10N 52°0W **162** D5
Dismal → *Nebr., U.S.A.* 41°50N 100°5W **80** C5
Dismal Swamp *Va., U.S.A.* 36°40N 76°20W **102** E8
Disney *Okla., U.S.A.* 36°29N 95°1W **107** B8
Disney Studios *Calif., U.S.A.* 34°9N 118°19W **133** B3
Disneyland *Calif., U.S.A.* 33°49N 117°55W **127** K9
Disputanta *Va., U.S.A.* 37°8N 77°14W **102** D7
Disraeli *Qué., Canada* 45°54N 71°21W **145** F11
District Heights *Md., U.S.A.* 38°51N 76°53W **99** B4
District of Columbia □ *U.S.A.* 38°55N 77°0W **93** B4
Distrito Federal □ *Mexico* 19°15N 99°10W **175** C8
Divernon *Ill., U.S.A.* 39°34N 89°39W **84** D4
Diversion L. *Tex., U.S.A.* 33°49N 98°56W **109** D9
Divide *Mont., U.S.A.* 45°45N 112°45W **123** E5
Divide County ☆ *N. Dak., U.S.A.* 48°55N 103°30W **76** B2
Dividing Creek *N.J., U.S.A.* 39°16N 75°6W **92** C1
Divisaderos *Sonora, Mexico* 29°33N 109°14W **168** D6
División del Norte *Chihuahua, Mexico* 26°33N 104°22W **169** G11
Dix *Ill., U.S.A.* 38°27N 88°56W **84** E5
Dix *Nebr., U.S.A.* 41°14N 103°29W **80** C2
Dix → *Ky., U.S.A.* 37°49N 84°43W **105** C8
Dixfield *Maine, U.S.A.* 44°32N 70°28W **90** D3
Dixie *Ala., U.S.A.* 31°9N 86°44W **112** E4
Dixie *Ark., U.S.A.* 35°5N 91°22W **106** C4
Dixie *Wash., U.S.A.* 46°8N 118°9W **120** D7
Dixie County ☆ *Fla., U.S.A.* 29°30N 83°15W **114** B5
Dixie Nat. Forest *Utah, U.S.A.* 37°45N 112°15W **129** F3
Dixie Union *Ga., U.S.A.* 31°20N 82°28W **113** E4
Dixmont *Maine, U.S.A.* 44°41N 69°10W **90** D4
Dixon *Calif., U.S.A.* 38°27N 121°49W **126** E5
Dixon *Ill., U.S.A.* 41°50N 89°29W **84** B4
Dixon *Iowa, U.S.A.* 41°45N 90°47W **81** D8
Dixon *Ky., U.S.A.* 37°31N 87°41W **104** C5
Dixon *Mo., U.S.A.* 37°59N 92°6W **83** D4
Dixon *Mont., U.S.A.* 47°19N 114°19W **123** C3
Dixon *N. Mex., U.S.A.* 36°12N 105°53W **131** A5
Dixon *Nebr., U.S.A.* 42°24N 97°2W **80** B8
Dixon *Wyo., U.S.A.* 41°2N 107°32W **124** E5
Dixon County ☆ *Nebr., U.S.A.* 42°30N 96°50W **80** B9
Dixon Entrance *U.S.A.* 54°30N 132°0W **135** J14
Dixons Mills *Ala., U.S.A.* 32°4N 87°47W **112** D3
Dixonville *Alta., Canada* 56°32N 117°40W **152** B3
Dixville *Qué., Canada* 45°4N 71°46W **145** F11
Dixville Notch *N.H., U.S.A.* 44°50N 71°18W **89** B3
Dizney *Ky., U.S.A.* 36°51N 83°7W **105** D9
Doaktown *N.B., Canada* 46°33N 66°8W **141** G3
Dobbin *Tex., U.S.A.* 30°22N 95°46W **109** G12
Dobbs Ferry *N.Y., U.S.A.* 41°1N 73°52W **92** A3
Dobie → *Ont., Canada* 51°41N 90°29W **148** A6
Doboy Sound *Ga., U.S.A.* 31°23N 81°16W **113** E5
Dobson *N.C., U.S.A.* 36°24N 80°43W **103** B5
Doce de Diciembre *Durango, Mexico* 24°42N 103°34W **173** C7
Dockton *Wash., U.S.A.* 47°22N 122°27W **132** D3
Doctor Arroyo *Nuevo León, Mexico* 23°40N 100°11W **171** G4
Doctor Belisario Domínguez *Chihuahua,*
Mexico 28°9N 106°29W **169** E9
Doctor Coss *Nuevo León, Mexico* 25°55N 99°11W **170** E5
Doctor Mora *Guanajuato, Mexico* 21°7N 100°18W **175** A7
Doctor Phillips *Fla., U.S.A.* 28°26N 81°29W **115** B2
Doctors Inlet *Fla., U.S.A.* 30°6N 81°47W **114** A7
Doddridge *Ark., U.S.A.* 33°6N 93°55W **106** E2
Doddridge County ☆ *W. Va., U.S.A.* 39°17N 80°44W **102** B4
Dodge *N. Dak., U.S.A.* 47°18N 102°12W **76** C3
Dodge *Nebr., U.S.A.* 41°43N 96°53W **80** C9
Dodge *Tex., U.S.A.* 30°45N 95°24W **109** G12
Dodge Center *Minn., U.S.A.* 44°2N 92°52W **77** F6
Dodge City *Kans., U.S.A.* 37°45N 100°1W **82** D3
Dodge County ☆ *Ga., U.S.A.* 32°10N 83°10W **113** D3
Dodge County ☆ *Minn., U.S.A.* 44°0N 92°50W **77** G6
Dodge County ☆ *Nebr., U.S.A.* 41°30N 96°40W **80** C9
Dodge County ☆ *Wis., U.S.A.* 43°20N 88°45W **78** E5
Dodger Stadium *Calif., U.S.A.* 34°4N 118°14W **133** B3
Dodgeville *Wis., U.S.A.* 42°58N 90°8W **78** F31
Dodsland *Sask., Canada* 51°50N 108°45W **150** D3
Dodson *La., U.S.A.* 32°5N 92°39W **110** B3
Dodson *Mont., U.S.A.* 48°24N 108°15W **123** B9
Doe Run *Mo., U.S.A.* 37°45N 90°30W **83** D6
Doerun *Ga., U.S.A.* 31°19N 83°55W **113** E3
Dog → *Ont., Canada* 48°32N 89°39W **148** D7
Dog → *Ont., Canada* 47°55N 85°12W **149** E11
Dog Creek *B.C., Canada* 51°35N 122°14W **155** D12
Dog I. *Nfld. & L., Canada* 52°28N 55°40W **143** C6
Dog I. *Fla., U.S.A.* 29°48N 84°36W **114** B4
Dog L. *Man., Canada* 51°2N 98°31W **151** D13
Dog L. *Ont., Canada* 48°48N 89°30W **148** D7
Dog L. *Ont., Canada* 48°17N 84°8W **149** D12
Dohrn Banke *Greenland* 65°55N 25°50W **162** D8
Dolan Springs *Ariz., U.S.A.* 35°36N 114°16W **130** B1
Doland *S. Dak., U.S.A.* 44°54N 98°6W **76** F7
Dolbeau-Mistassini *Qué., Canada* 48°53N 72°14W **145** C10
Doles *Ga., U.S.A.* 31°42N 83°53W **113** E3
Dolgeville *N.Y., U.S.A.* 43°6N 74°46W **88** B6
Dollard *Sask., Canada* 49°37N 108°35W **150** F3
Dollard-des-Ormeaux *Qué., Canada* 45°29N 73°48W **160** A2
Dolliver *Iowa, U.S.A.* 43°28N 94°37W **81** B4
Dolores *Baja Calif. S., Mexico* 25°5N 110°51W **167** H8
Dolores *Chihuahua, Mexico* 28°45N 105°43W **169** E10
Dolores *Colo., U.S.A.* 37°28N 108°30W **125** E2
Dolores → *Utah, U.S.A.* 38°49N 109°17W **129** E6
Dolores County ☆ *Colo., U.S.A.* 37°45N 108°30W **125** E2
Dolores Hidalgo *Guanajuato, Mexico* 21°10N 100°56W **175** A7
Dolphin and Union Str. *N.W.T.,*
Canada 69°5N 114°45W **156** C10
Dolton *Ill., U.S.A.* 41°38N 87°36W **84** B6
Dome, The *Vt., U.S.A.* 42°45N 73°12W **89** D1
Dome Creek *B.C., Canada* 53°44N 121°1W **155** B13
Dominica ■ *W. Indies* 15°20N 61°20W **183** C7
Dominica Passage *W. Indies* 15°10N 61°20W **183** C7
Dominican Rep. ■ *W. Indies* 19°0N 70°30W **183** C5
Dominion *N.S., Canada* 46°13N 60°1W **141** G9
Dominion, C. *N.W.T., Canada* 65°30N 74°28W **159** D11
Dominion City *Man., Canada* 49°9N 97°9W **151** F14
Dominion L. *Nfld. & L., Canada* 52°40N 61°45W **140** A8
Don Martín *Coahuila, Mexico* 27°34N 100°38W **170** C4
Don Mills *Ont., Canada* 43°44N 79°21W **161** A2
Don Pedro Dam *Calif., U.S.A.* 37°43N 120°24W **126** F6
Don Pen. *B.C., Canada* 52°25N 128°12W **154** C6
Dona Ana *N. Mex., U.S.A.* 32°23N 106°49W **131** E4
Dona Ana County ☆ *N. Mex., U.S.A.* 32°20N 107°0W **131** E4
Donahue *Iowa, U.S.A.* 41°42N 90°41W **81** D8
Donald *B.C., Canada* 51°29N 117°10W **155** D17
Donalda *Alta., Canada* 52°35N 112°34W **153** F8
Donaldson *Ark., U.S.A.* 34°14N 92°55W **106** D3
Donaldson *Minn., U.S.A.* 48°35N 96°53W **77** B2
Donaldsonville *La., U.S.A.* 30°6N 90°59W **110** D5
Donalsonville *Ga., U.S.A.* 31°3N 84°53W **113** E2
Donato Guerra *Durango, Mexico* 24°38N 104°38W **173** C6
Donato Guerra *México, Mexico* 19°20N 100°8W **180** b4
Doncaster *Md., U.S.A.* 38°30N 77°15W **93** B3
Dongan Hills *N.Y., U.S.A.* 40°35N 74°5W **97** C2
Donie *Tex., U.S.A.* 31°29N 96°13W **109** F11
Doniphan *Kans., U.S.A.* 39°38N 95°5W **82** B8
Doniphan *Mo., U.S.A.* 36°37N 90°50W **83** E61
Doniphan *Nebr., U.S.A.* 40°46N 98°22W **80** D7
Doniphan County ☆ *Kans., U.S.A.* 39°45N 95°0W **82** B9
Donjek → *Yukon, Canada* 62°36N 140°0W **157** D5
Donley County ☆ *Tex., U.S.A.* 35°0N 100°45W **108** B7
Donna *Tex., U.S.A.* 26°9N 98°4W **108** L9
Donnacona *Qué., Canada* 46°41N 71°41W **145** E11
Donnan *Iowa, U.S.A.* 42°54N 91°53W **81** C7
Donnellson *Iowa, U.S.A.* 40°39N 91°34W **81** E7
Donnelly *Alta., Canada* 55°44N 117°6W **152** C3
Donnelly *Idaho, U.S.A.* 44°44N 116°5W **122** E2
Donnelly *Minn., U.S.A.* 45°42N 96°1W **77** E2
Donner Pass *Calif., U.S.A.* 39°19N 120°20W **126** D6
Donner und Blitzen → *Oreg., U.S.A.* 43°17N 118°49W **121** D7
Donnybrook *N. Dak., U.S.A.* 48°31N 101°53W **76** B4
Donora *Pa., U.S.A.* 40°11N 79°52W **87** D3
Donovan *Ill., U.S.A.* 40°53N 87°37W **84** C6
Donovans *Nfld. & L., Canada* 47°32N 52°50W **142** E8
Doolittle *Mo., U.S.A.* 37°56N 91°53W **83** D5
Dooly County ☆ *Ga., U.S.A.* 32°10N 83°50W **113** D3
Doon *Iowa, U.S.A.* 43°17N 96°14W **81** B2
Door County ☆ *Wis., U.S.A.* 45°0N 87°15W **78** C6
Door Peninsula *Wis., U.S.A.* 44°45N 87°25W **78** D6
Dora *Ala., U.S.A.* 33°44N 87°5W **112** C3
Dora *N. Mex., U.S.A.* 33°56N 103°20W **131** D7
Dora *Oreg., U.S.A.* 43°10N 123°59W **121** D2
Doran *Minn., U.S.A.* 46°11N 96°29W **77** D2
Doraville *Ga., U.S.A.* 33°54N 84°17W **113** C2
Dorcas *W. Va., U.S.A.* 38°56N 79°6W **102** C5
Dorcheat, Bayou → *La., U.S.A.* 32°10N 93°25W **110** B2
Dorchester *N.B., Canada* 45°54N 64°31W **141** H5
Dorchester *Mass., U.S.A.* 42°17N 71°4W **96** B2
Dorchester *N.H., U.S.A.* 43°44N 71°56W **89** C3
Dorchester *Nebr., U.S.A.* 40°39N 97°7W **80** D8
Dorchester *Wis., U.S.A.* 45°0N 90°20W **78** C3
Dorchester, C. *Nunavut, Canada* 65°27N 77°27W **159** D10
Dorchester B. *Mass., U.S.A.* 42°18N 71°1W **96** B2
Dorchester County ☆ *Md., U.S.A.* 38°20N 76°0W **93** B4
Dorchester County ☆ *S.C., U.S.A.* 33°10N 80°30W **103** E5

Dorchester Heights Nat. Historical Site △ *Mass.,*
U.S.A. 42°20N 71°2W **96** B2
Doré L. *Sask., Canada* 54°46N 107°17W **157** F11
Dorena *Oreg., U.S.A.* 43°43N 122°52W **121** D3
Dorion *Ont., Canada* 48°47N 88°39W **148** D8
Dormont *Pa., U.S.A.* 40°23N 80°2W **98** B1
Dorrance *Kans., U.S.A.* 38°51N 98°35W **82** C5
Dorris *Calif., U.S.A.* 41°58N 121°55W **126** B5
Dorset *Ont., Canada* 45°14N 78°54W **144** F4
Dorset *Vt., U.S.A.* 43°15N 73°6W **89** C1
Dortches *N.C., U.S.A.* 36°1N 77°51W **103** B8
Dorton *Ky., U.S.A.* 37°1N 82°35W **105** C10
Dorval *Qué., Canada* 45°26N 73°45W **160** B2
Dorval Int., Montréal ✈ (YUL) *Qué.,*
Canada 45°28N 73°44W **160** B2
Dos Palos *Calif., U.S.A.* 36°59N 120°37W **126** G6
Dos Ríos *México, Mexico* 19°22N 99°1W **181** B1
Dosquet *Qué., Canada* 46°28N 71°32W **145** E11
Doswell *Va., U.S.A.* 37°52N 77°28W **102** D7
Dot Lake *Alaska, U.S.A.* 63°40N 144°4W **135** E11
Dothan *Ala., U.S.A.* 31°13N 85°24W **112** E5
Doting Cove *Nfld. & L., Canada* 49°27N 53°57W **142** C7
Doty *Wash., U.S.A.* 46°38N 123°17W **120** D2
Double Mountain Fork ➛ *Tex., U.S.A.* 33°16N 100°0W **108** D7
Double Springs *Ala., U.S.A.* 34°9N 87°24W **112** B3
Doubletop Pk. *Wyo., U.S.A.* 43°21N 110°17W **124** C2
Dougherty *Iowa, U.S.A.* 42°55N 93°3W **81** C5
Dougherty *Okla., U.S.A.* 34°24N 97°3W **107** D6
Dougherty County ☆ *Ga., U.S.A.* 31°30N 84°15W **113** E2
Douglas *Ont., Canada* 45°31N 76°56W **147** B10
Douglas *Alaska, U.S.A.* 58°17N 134°24W **135** G14
Douglas *Ariz., U.S.A.* 31°21N 109°33W **130** F6
Douglas *Ga., U.S.A.* 31°31N 82°51W **113** E4
Douglas *Mass., U.S.A.* 42°6N 71°45W **91** B3
Douglas *Mich., U.S.A.* 42°39N 86°14W **79** E6
Douglas *Mich., U.S.A.* 44°19N 86°13W **79** E5
Douglas *N. Dak., U.S.A.* 47°51N 101°30W **76** C4
Douglas *Nebr., U.S.A.* 40°36N 96°23W **80** D9
Douglas *Okla., U.S.A.* 36°16N 97°40W **107** B6
Douglas *Wyo., U.S.A.* 42°45N 105°24W **124** D7
Douglas C. *Alaska, U.S.A.* 58°51N 153°15W **135** G6
Douglas Chan. *B.C., Canada* 53°40N 129°20W **154** C2
Douglas City *Calif., U.S.A.* 40°39N 122°57W **126** C4
Douglas County ☆ *Colo., U.S.A.* 39°1N 105°0W **125** C6
Douglas County ☆ *Ga., U.S.A.* 33°40N 84°45W **113** C2
Douglas County ☆ *Ill., U.S.A.* 39°45N 88°15W **84** D5
Douglas County ☆ *Kans., U.S.A.* 38°50N 95°15W **82** C8
Douglas County ☆ *Minn., U.S.A.* 45°50N 95°20W **77** E3
Douglas County ☆ *Mo., U.S.A.* 36°55N 92°30W **83** E4
Douglas County ☆ *Nebr., U.S.A.* 41°15N 96°30W **80** D9
Douglas County ☆ *Nev., U.S.A.* 38°55N 119°45W **128** D1
Douglas County ☆ *Oreg., U.S.A.* 43°15N 123°0W **121** D3
Douglas County ☆ *S. Dak., U.S.A.* 43°25N 98°24W **76** G7
Douglas County ☆ *Wash., U.S.A.* 47°50N 119°45W **120** C6
Douglas County ☆ *Wis., U.S.A.* 46°25N 91°55W **78** B2
Douglas L. *Tenn., U.S.A.* 35°58N 83°32W **105** E9
Douglas Lake *B.C., Canada* 50°10N 120°13W **155** E14
Douglas Park *Ill., U.S.A.* 41°51N 87°42W **95** B2
Douglas Prov. Park △ *Sask., Canada* 51°3N 106°28W **150** D5
Douglas Pt. *Ont., Canada* 44°19N 81°37W **146** C5
Douglass *Kans., U.S.A.* 37°31N 97°1W **82** D6
Douglass *Tex., U.S.A.* 31°40N 94°53W **109** F13
Douglaston *N.Y., U.S.A.* 40°46N 73°44W **97** B4
Douglastown *N.B., Canada* 48°46N 64°24W **140** E5
Douglasville *Ga., U.S.A.* 33°45N 84°45W **113** C2
Dousman *Wis., U.S.A.* 43°1N 88°29W **78** E5
Dove Creek *Colo., U.S.A.* 37°46N 108°54W **125** D2
Dover *Nfld. & L., Canada* 48°53N 53°58W **142** D7
Dover *Ark., U.S.A.* 35°24N 93°7W **106** C2
Dover *Del., U.S.A.* 39°10N 75°32W **93** A5
Dover *Idaho, U.S.A.* 48°15N 116°36W **122** A2
Dover *N.H., U.S.A.* 43°12N 70°56W **89** C4
Dover *N.J., U.S.A.* 40°53N 74°34W **92** B2
Dover *Ohio, U.S.A.* 40°32N 81°29W **86** C5
Dover *Okla., U.S.A.* 35°59N 97°55W **107** C6
Dover *Tenn., U.S.A.* 36°29N 87°50W **104** D5
Dover Air Force Base *Del., U.S.A.* 39°7N 75°29W **93** A5
Dover Downs International Speedway *Del.,*
U.S.A. 39°14N 75°35W **93** A5
Dover-Foxcroft *Maine, U.S.A.* 45°11N 69°13W **90** C4
Dover Plains *N.Y., U.S.A.* 41°43N 73°35W **91** C4
Dow City *Iowa, U.S.A.* 41°56N 95°30W **81** C3
Dowagiac *Mich., U.S.A.* 41°59N 86°6W **79** H5
Dowling Park *Fla., U.S.A.* 30°15N 83°15W **114** A5
Down, L. *Fla., U.S.A.* 28°30N 81°31W **115** A4
Downers Grove *Ill., U.S.A.* 41°48N 88°1W **84** B5
Downey *Calif., U.S.A.* 33°56N 118°9W **133** C4
Downey *Idaho, U.S.A.* 42°26N 112°7W **122** C6
Downieville *Calif., U.S.A.* 39°34N 120°50W **126** D6
Downing *Mo., U.S.A.* 40°29N 92°22W **83** A4
Downingtown *Pa., U.S.A.* 40°0N 75°42W **92** B1
Downs *Ill., U.S.A.* 40°24N 88°52W **84** C5
Downs *Kans., U.S.A.* 39°30N 98°33W **82** B5
Downs Mt. *Wyo., U.S.A.* 43°18N 109°40W **124** C3
Downsview *Ont., Canada* 43°43N 79°30W **161** A1
Downsview ✈ *Ont., Canada* 43°43N 79°29W **161** A2
Downsville *Calif., U.S.A.* 39°35N 77°48W **93** A3
Downsville *N.Y., U.S.A.* 42°5N 75°0W **88** D7
Downton, Mt. *B.C., Canada* 52°42N 124°52W **154** C10
Dows *Iowa, U.S.A.* 42°39N 93°30W **81** C5
Dows L. *Ont., Canada* 45°23N 75°42W **160** B1
Doyle *Calif., U.S.A.* 40°2N 120°6W **126** C6
Doyles *Nfld. & L., Canada* 47°50N 59°12W **142** E1
Doylestown *Ohio, U.S.A.* 40°21N 75°10W **87** D7
Doylestown *Pa., U.S.A.* 40°12N 77°43W **87** D5
Doylestown *Wis., U.S.A.* 43°25N 89°9W **78** E4
Doyleville *Colo., U.S.A.* 38°25N 106°35W **125** D4
Doyline *La., U.S.A.* 32°32N 93°25W **110** B2
Dozier *Ala., U.S.A.* 31°10N 86°28W **112** E4
Dozois, Rés. *Qué., Canada* 47°30N 77°5W **144** D5
Dracut *Mass., U.S.A.* 42°40N 71°18W **91** B3
Dragerton *Utah, U.S.A.* 39°33N 110°25W **129** D5
Dragoon *Ariz., U.S.A.* 32°2N 110°2W **130** E5
Drain *Oreg., U.S.A.* 43°40N 123°19W **121** D2
Drake *Sask., Canada* 51°46N 105°1W **150** D6
Drake *Ariz., U.S.A.* 35°0N 112°20W **130** D3
Drake *N. Dak., U.S.A.* 47°55N 100°23W **76** C5
Drake Pk. *Oreg., U.S.A.* 42°19N 120°7W **121** E5
Drakes Branch *Va., U.S.A.* 36°59N 78°36W **102** E6
Drakesboro *Ky., U.S.A.* 37°13N 87°3W **104** C5
Drakesville *Iowa, U.S.A.* 40°47N 92°31W **81** E6
Draketown *Ga., U.S.A.* 33°50N 85°3W **113** C1
Dranesville *Va., U.S.A.* 39°0N 77°20W **99** A1
Draper *S. Dak., U.S.A.* 43°52N 100°30W **76** G5
Draper *Utah, U.S.A.* 40°31N 111°51W **134** C2

Dravosburg *Pa., U.S.A.* 40°21N 79°53W **98** B2
Drayden *Md., U.S.A.* 38°11N 76°28W **93** B4
Drayton *Ont., Canada* 43°46N 80°40W **146** D6
Drayton *N. Dak., U.S.A.* 48°34N 97°11W **76** B8
Drayton Plains *Mich., U.S.A.* 42°41N 83°23W **79** G8
Drayton Valley *Alta., Canada* 53°12N 114°58W **152** E6
Dresden *Ont., Canada* 42°35N 82°11W **146** E4
Dresden *Kans., U.S.A.* 39°38N 100°26W **82** B3
Dresden *N.Y., U.S.A.* 42°41N 76°58W **88** D4
Dresden *Tenn., U.S.A.* 36°18N 88°42W **104** D4
Dresser *Wis., U.S.A.* 45°20N 92°38W **78** C1
Dretzka Park *Wis., U.S.A.* 43°10N 88°4W **94** A1
Drew *Miss., U.S.A.* 33°49N 90°32W **111** C3
Drew County ☆ *Ark., U.S.A.* 33°35N 91°40W **106** E4
Drews Res. *Oreg., U.S.A.* 42°7N 120°37W **121** E5
Drexel *Mo., U.S.A.* 38°29N 94°37W **83** C2
Drexel Hill *Pa., U.S.A.* 39°56N 75°17W **98** B1
Driftwood *Pa., U.S.A.* 41°20N 78°8W **87** C4
Driggs *Idaho, U.S.A.* 43°44N 111°6W **122** F7
Drinkwater *Sask., Canada* 50°18N 105°8W **150** E6
Dripping Springs *Tex., U.S.A.* 30°12N 98°5W **109** G9
Driscoll *N. Dak., U.S.A.* 46°51N 100°9W **76** D5
Driscoll *Tex., U.S.A.* 27°41N 97°45W **108** K10
Driskill Mt. *La., U.S.A.* 32°25N 92°54W **110** B3
Dronning Ingrid Land *Greenland* 66°25N 52°5W **162** D5
Drowning ➛ *Ont., Canada* 50°54N 84°34W **149** B12
Drumbo *Ont., Canada* 43°16N 80°35W **146** D6
Drumheller *Alta., Canada* 51°25N 112°40W **153** E8
Drummond *N.B., Canada* 47°2N 67°41W **141** F2
Drummond *Idaho, U.S.A.* 43°59N 111°20W **122** F7
Drummond *Mont., U.S.A.* 46°40N 113°9W **123** D4
Drummond *Okla., U.S.A.* 36°18N 98°2W **107** B5
Drummond *Wis., U.S.A.* 46°20N 91°15W **78** B2
Drummond, I. *Mich., U.S.A.* 46°1N 83°39W **79** C8
Drummondville *Qué., Canada* 45°55N 72°25W **145** F10
Drumright *Okla., U.S.A.* 35°59N 96°36W **107** C7
Drury * Mo. , U.S.A.* 38°48N 76°42W **93** A4
Dry Cr. ➛ *Oreg., U.S.A.* 43°34N 117°21W **121** D8
Dry Cr. ➛ *Wyo., U.S.A.* 44°31N 108°33W **124** B4
Dry Creek *La., U.S.A.* 30°40N 93°3W **110** D2
Dry Devils ➛ *Tex., U.S.A.* 29°47N 100°59W **108** H7
Dry Falls Dam *Wash., U.S.A.* 47°37N 119°19W **120** C6
Dry Fork Cheyenne ➛ *Wyo., U.S.A.* 43°26N 105°3W **124** C7
Dry L. *N. Dak., U.S.A.* 48°16N 98°59W **76** B7
Dry Prong *La., U.S.A.* 31°35N 92°32W **110** C3
Dry Ridge *Ky., U.S.A.* 38°41N 84°35W **105** B8
Dry Tortugas *U.S.A.* 24°38N 82°55W **182** B3
Dryberry L. *Ont., Canada* 49°33N 93°53W **148** C3
Dryden *Ont., Canada* 49°47N 92°50W **148** C2
Dryden *N.Y., U.S.A.* 42°30N 76°18W **88** C4
Dryden *Tex., U.S.A.* 30°3N 102°7W **108** G5
Du Bay, L. *Wis., U.S.A.* 44°40N 89°39W **78** D4
Du Bois *Nebr., U.S.A.* 40°2N 96°4W **80** D9
Du Gas, L. *Qué., Canada* 51°26N 60°4W **140** C5
Du Gué ➛ *Qué., Canada* 57°21N 70°45W **143** B3
Du Page County ☆ *Ill., U.S.A.* 41°50N 88°5W **84** B5
Du Quoin *Ill., U.S.A.* 38°1N 89°14W **84** E4
Duarte, Pico *Dom. Rep.* 19°2N 70°59N **183** C5
Dubach *La., U.S.A.* 32°42N 92°39N **110** B3
Dubawnt ➛ *N.W.T., Canada* 64°33N 100°6W **159** E5
Dubawnt L. *Canada* 63°8N 101°28W **159** E5
Dublán *Chihuahua, Mexico* 30°26N 107°55N **168** A3
Dublin *Ga., U.S.A.* 32°32N 82°54W **113** D4
Dublin *Md., U.S.A.* 39°39N 76°16W **93** A4
Dublin *Miss., U.S.A.* 34°4N 90°30W **111** B3
Dublin *N.H., U.S.A.* 42°52N 72°5W **89** D2
Dublin *Ohio, U.S.A.* 40°5N 83°7W **86** C3
Dublin *Tex., U.S.A.* 32°5N 98°21W **109** E9
Dublin *Va., U.S.A.* 37°6N 80°41W **102** D4
Dubois *Idaho, U.S.A.* 44°10N 112°14W **122** F6
Dubois *Ind., U.S.A.* 38°27N 86°48W **85** E4
Dubois *Pa., U.S.A.* 41°7N 78°46W **87** C4
Dubois *Wyo., U.S.A.* 43°33N 109°38W **124** C3
Dubois County ☆ *Ind., U.S.A.* 38°20N 86°50W **85** E4
Dubreuilville *Ont., Canada* 48°21N 84°32W **149** D12
Dubuc *Sask., Canada* 50°41N 102°28W **151** E9
Dubuque *Iowa, U.S.A.* 42°30N 90°41W **81** C8
Dubuque County ☆ *Iowa, U.S.A.* 42°30N 90°54W **81** C8
Dubuque Hills *Ill., U.S.A.* 42°15N 90°0W **84** A3
Duchesne *Utah, U.S.A.* 40°10N 110°24W **129** C5
Duchesne ➛ *Utah, U.S.A.* 40°5N 109°41W **129** C6
Duchesne County ☆ *Utah, U.S.A.* 40°20N 110°30W **129** C5
Duchess *Alta., Canada* 50°43N 111°55W **153** H9
Duck ➛ *Tenn., U.S.A.* 36°2N 87°52W **104** D5
Duck Bay *Man., Canada* 52°10N 100°9W **151** C11
Duck Cr. ➛ *Nev., U.S.A.* 41°55N 116°27W **128** A4
Duck Hill *Miss., U.S.A.* 33°38N 89°43W **111** C4
Duck Lake *Sask., Canada* 52°50N 106°16W **150** C5
Duck Mountain Prov. Park △ *Man.,*
Canada 51°45N 101°0W **151** D10
Duck River *Tenn., U.S.A.* 35°43N 87°16W **104** E5
Duck Valley Indian Reservation *U.S.A.* 41°53N 116°8W **122** H2
Ducktown *Tenn., U.S.A.* 35°3N 84°23W **105** E8
Duckwater *Nev., U.S.A.* 38°55N 115°40W **128** D5
Duckwater Indian Reservation *Nev.,*
U.S.A. 38°56N 115°43W **128** D5
Dudley *Ga., U.S.A.* 32°32N 83°5W **113** D3
Dudley *Mo., U.S.A.* 36°46N 90°8W **83** E6
Dudley *Pa., U.S.A.* 40°12N 78°10W **87** D4
Dudleyville *Ariz., U.S.A.* 32°54N 110°42W **130** E5
Dudswell *Qué., Canada* 45°35N 71°35W **145** F11
Due West *S.C., U.S.A.* 34°20N 82°23W **103** D3
Dufrost, Pte. *Qué., Canada* 60°4N 77°39W **143** A2
Dufur *Oreg., U.S.A.* 45°27N 121°8W **121** B4
Dugdemona ➛ *La., U.S.A.* 31°47N 92°22W **110** C3
Dugger *Ind., U.S.A.* 39°4N 87°18W **85** D3
Dugspur *Va., U.S.A.* 36°49N 80°37W **102** E4
Dugway *Utah, U.S.A.* 40°13N 112°45W **129** C3
Dugway Proving Ground *Utah, U.S.A.* 40°3N 113°1W **129** C2
Duke *Okla., U.S.A.* 34°40N 99°34W **107** D4
Dukes County ☆ *Mass., U.S.A.* 41°23N 70°31W **91** C4
Dulac *La., U.S.A.* 29°23N 90°42W **110** E5
Dulce *N. Mex., U.S.A.* 36°56N 107°0W **131** A3
Dulce, Golfo *Costa Rica* 8°40N 83°20W **182** E3
Dulles Int. ✈ (IAD) *Va., U.S.A.* 38°57N 77°27W **102** C7
Duluth *Ga., U.S.A.* 34°0N 84°9W **113** B2
Duluth *Minn., U.S.A.* 46°47N 92°6W **77** D6
Dumas *Ark., U.S.A.* 33°53N 91°29W **106** E4
Dumas *Tex., U.S.A.* 35°52N 101°58W **108** B4
Dumbell L. *Nfld. & L., Canada* 52°28N 65°45W **140** A4
Dumfries *Va., U.S.A.* 38°34N 77°20W **93** B3
Dumoine ➛ *Qué., Canada* 46°13N 77°51W **144** E5
Dumoine, L. *Qué., Canada* 46°55N 77°55W **144** E5

Dumont *Iowa, U.S.A.* 42°45N 92°58W **81** C6
Dumont *Minn., U.S.A.* 45°43N 96°26W **77** E2
Dumont *N.J., U.S.A.* 40°56N 73°59W **97** A3
Dunbar *Nebr., U.S.A.* 40°38N 96°1W **80** D9
Dunbar *Pa., U.S.A.* 39°58N 79°37W **87** E3
Dunbar *W. Va., U.S.A.* 38°22N 81°45W **102** C3
Dunbarton Center *N.H., U.S.A.* 43°8N 71°38W **89** C3
Duncan *B.C., Canada* 48°45N 123°40W **155** G11
Duncan *Ariz., U.S.A.* 32°43N 109°6W **130** E6
Duncan *Miss., U.S.A.* 34°3N 90°45W **111** B3
Duncan *Nebr., U.S.A.* 41°25N 97°30W **80** C8
Duncan *Okla., U.S.A.* 34°30N 97°57W **107** D6
Duncan *S.C., U.S.A.* 34°56N 82°9W **103** D3
Duncan, L. *Qué., Canada* 53°29N 77°58W **143** C2
Duncan Dam *B.C., Canada* 50°15N 116°56W **155** E18
Duncan Town *Bahamas* 22°15N 75°45W **182** B4
Duncannon *Pa., U.S.A.* 40°23N 77°2W **87** D5
Duncansville *Pa., U.S.A.* 40°25N 78°26W **87** D4
Duncanville *Tex., U.S.A.* 32°39N 96°54W **116** C4
Dunchurch *Ont., Canada* 45°39N 79°51W **146** B7
Duncombe *Iowa, U.S.A.* 42°28N 94°0W **81** C4
Dundalk *Ont., Canada* 44°10N 80°24W **146** C6
Dundalk *Md., U.S.A.* 39°15N 76°31W **93** B2
Dundas = Uummannaq *Greenland* 77°28N 69°13W **162** B4
Dundas *Ont., Canada* 43°17N 79°59W **146** D7
Dundas *Minn., U.S.A.* 44°26N 93°12W **77** F5
Dundas *Va., U.S.A.* 36°55N 78°1W **102** E6
Dundas Pen. *N.W.T., Canada* 74°50N 111°36W **156** B10
Dundee *Iowa, U.S.A.* 42°35N 91°33W **81** C7
Dundee *Ky., U.S.A.* 37°34N 86°46W **104** C6
Dundee *Mich., U.S.A.* 41°57N 83°40W **79** H8
Dundee *Minn., U.S.A.* 43°51N 95°28W **77** G3
Dundee *N.Y., U.S.A.* 42°32N 76°59W **88** C4
Dundurn *Sask., Canada* 51°49N 106°30W **150** D5
Dundy County ☆ *Nebr., U.S.A.* 40°15N 101°45W **80** D4
Dunedin *Fla., U.S.A.* 28°1N 82°46W **115** C2
Dunes City *Oreg., U.S.A.* 43°53N 124°7W **121** D1
Dungannon *Ont., Canada* 43°51N 81°36W **146** D5
Dungannon *Va., U.S.A.* 36°50N 82°28W **102** E2
Dungarvon ➛ *N.B., Canada* 46°49N 65°54W **141** G4
Dungeness *Wash., U.S.A.* 48°9N 123°7W **120** B2
Dunham *Qué., Canada* 45°8N 72°48W **145** F10
Dunière, Réserve Faunique de △ *Qué.,*
Canada 48°38N 66°45W **140** C3
Dunkerton *Iowa, U.S.A.* 42°34N 92°10W **81** C6
Dunkirk *Ind., U.S.A.* 40°23N 85°13W **85** C5
Dunkirk *Mont., U.S.A.* 48°29N 111°40W **123** B6
Dunkirk *N.Y., U.S.A.* 42°29N 79°20W **88** C1
Dunkirk *Ohio, U.S.A.* 40°48N 83°39W **86** C3
Dunklin County ☆ *Mo., U.S.A.* 36°20N 90°0W **83** E6
Dunlap *Ill., U.S.A.* 40°52N 89°40W **84** C4
Dunlap *Ind., U.S.A.* 41°39N 85°56W **85** B5
Dunlap *Iowa, U.S.A.* 41°51N 95°36W **81** D3
Dunlap *Kans., U.S.A.* 38°35N 96°22W **82** C7
Dunlap *Tenn., U.S.A.* 35°23N 85°23W **105** E7
Dunlap *Tex., U.S.A.* 34°8N 100°18W **108** C7
Dunlow *W. Va., U.S.A.* 38°1N 82°26W **102** C2
Dunmor *Ky., U.S.A.* 37°4N 86°59W **104** C6
Dunmore *Alta., Canada* 49°58N 110°36W **153** J10
Dunmore *Pa., U.S.A.* 41°25N 75°38W **92** A1
Dunmore Town *Bahamas* 25°30N 76°39W **182** A4
Dunn *N.C., U.S.A.* 35°19N 78°37W **103** C7
Dunn Center *N. Dak., U.S.A.* 47°21N 102°37W **76** C3
Dunn County ☆ *N. Dak., U.S.A.* 47°15N 102°35W **76** C3
Dunn County ☆ *Wis., U.S.A.* 44°55N 91°50W **78** D2
Dunn Loring *Va., U.S.A.* 38°54N 77°13W **99** B2
Dunnell *Minn., U.S.A.* 43°34N 94°47W **77** G4
Dunnellon *Fla., U.S.A.* 29°3N 82°28W **114** B6
Dunning *Ill., U.S.A.* 41°56N 87°48W **95** B2
Dunning *Nebr., U.S.A.* 41°50N 100°6W **80** C5
Dunnsville *Va., U.S.A.* 37°51N 76°49W **93** C4
Dunnville *Ky., U.S.A.* 37°12N 85°1W **105** C7
Dunrankin ➛ *Ont., Canada* 48°47N 82°51W **149** D14
Dunseith *N. Dak., U.S.A.* 48°50N 100°3W **76** B5
Dunsmuir *Calif., U.S.A.* 41°13N 122°16W **126** B4
Dunster *B.C., Canada* 53°8N 119°50W **155** B15
Dunvegan *Alta., Canada* 55°55N 118°36W **152** C2
Dunville *Nfld. & L., Canada* 47°16N 53°54W **142** E7
Duparquet *Qué., Canada* 48°30N 79°14W **144** D3
Duparquet, L. *Qué., Canada* 48°28N 79°16W **144** C3
Duplin County ☆ *N.C., U.S.A.* 34°50N 78°0W **103** D8
Dupo *Ill., U.S.A.* 38°31N 90°13W **84** E3
Dupont *Colo., U.S.A.* 39°50N 104°54W **134** A2
Dupont *Ind., U.S.A.* 38°53N 85°31W **85** E5
Dupont *Pa., U.S.A.* 41°20N 75°45W **92** A1
Dupont *Wash., U.S.A.* 47°6N 122°38W **120** C3
Dupree *S. Dak., U.S.A.* 45°4N 101°35W **76** E4
Dupuy *Qué., Canada* 48°50N 79°21W **144** C3
Dupuyer *Mont., U.S.A.* 48°13N 112°30W **123** B5
Duquesne *Pa., U.S.A.* 40°22N 79°51W **98** B2
Duran *N. Mex., U.S.A.* 34°28N 105°24W **131** C5
Durand *Ga., U.S.A.* 32°55N 84°46W **113** D2
Durand *Ill., U.S.A.* 42°26N 89°20W **84** A4
Durand *Mich., U.S.A.* 42°55N 83°59W **79** G8
Durand *Wis., U.S.A.* 44°38N 91°58W **78** D21
Durango *Mexico* 24°3N 104°39W **173** C6
Durango *Colo., U.S.A.* 37°16N 107°53W **125** E3
Durango □ *Mexico* 24°50N 105°20W **172** C5
Durant *Iowa, U.S.A.* 41°36N 90°54W **81** D8
Durant *Miss., U.S.A.* 33°4N 89°51W **111** C4
Durant *Okla., U.S.A.* 33°59N 96°25W **107** E7
Durbin *W. Va., U.S.A.* 38°33N 79°50W **102** C5
Durham *Ont., Canada* 44°10N 80°49W **146** C6
Durham *Calif., U.S.A.* 39°39N 121°48W **126** D5
Durham *Conn., U.S.A.* 41°29N 72°41W **91** C2
Durham *Kans., U.S.A.* 38°30N 97°15W **82** C6
Durham *N.C., U.S.A.* 35°59N 78°54W **103** C7
Durham *N.H., U.S.A.* 43°8N 70°56W **89** C4
Durham *Oreg., U.S.A.* 45°24N 122°45W **132** B1
Durham Bridge *N.B., Canada* 46°7N 66°36W **141** G3
Durham County ☆ *N.C., U.S.A.* 36°0N 78°50W **103** C7
Durkee *Oreg., U.S.A.* 44°35N 117°30W **121** C8
Durocher, L. *Qué., Canada* 50°52N 61°12W **140** C8
Dusey ➛ *Ont., Canada* 51°11N 86°21W **149** A10
Dushore *Pa., U.S.A.* 41°31N 76°24W **87** C6
Dusom *La., U.S.A.* 30°14N 92°11W **110** D3
Dustin *Okla., U.S.A.* 35°12N 96°1W **107** C7
Dusty *Wash., U.S.A.* 46°51N 117°38W **120** C8
Dutch Harbor *Alaska, U.S.A.* 53°53N 166°32W **135** K6
Dutch John *Utah, U.S.A.* 40°55N 109°24W **129** C6
Dutch Mills *Ark., U.S.A.* 35°52N 94°29W **106** C1
Dutch Neck *N.J., U.S.A.* 40°17N 74°40W **92** B2
Dutchess County ☆ *N.Y., U.S.A.* 41°45N 73°45W **88** D7
Dutchtown *Mo., U.S.A.* 37°18N 89°42W **83** D7
Dutton *Ont., Canada* 42°39N 81°30W **146** E5
Dutton *Mont., U.S.A.* 47°51N 111°43W **123** C6
Dutton, Mt. *Utah, U.S.A.* 38°1N 112°13W **129** E3

Duval *Sask., Canada* 51°9N 104°59W **150** D7
Duval County ☆ *Fla., U.S.A.* 30°30N 81°30W **114** A7
Duval County ☆ *Tex., U.S.A.* 27°50N 98°30W **109** K9
Duvall *Wash., U.S.A.* 47°45N 121°59W **120** C4
Duvernay *Qué., Canada* 45°35N 73°40W **160** A2
Duxbury *Mass., U.S.A.* 42°2N 70°40W **91** B4
Dwight *Ont., Canada* 45°20N 79°1W **144** F3
Dwight *Ill., U.S.A.* 41°5N 88°26W **84** B5
Dwight *Kans., U.S.A.* 38°50N 96°38W **82** C7
Dwight *N. Dak., U.S.A.* 46°18N 96°44W **76** D8
Dwight *Nebr., U.S.A.* 41°5N 97°1W **80** C8
Dworshak Res. *Idaho, U.S.A.* 46°48N 116°0W **122** C2
Dyer *Nev., U.S.A.* 37°41N 118°5W **128** E2
Dyer *Tenn., U.S.A.* 36°4N 88°59W **104** D4
Dyer B. *Nunavut, Canada* 66°37N 61°16W **158** D13
Dyer B. *N.W.T., Canada* 75°53N 121°42W **156** A8
Dyer County ☆ *Tenn., U.S.A.* 36°0N 89°25W **104** D3
Dyersburg *Tenn., U.S.A.* 36°3N 89°23W **104** D3
Dyersville *Iowa, U.S.A.* 42°29N 91°8W **81** C7
Dyess *Ark., U.S.A.* 35°35N 90°13W **106** C5
Dyess Air Force Base *Tex., U.S.A.* 32°25N 99°51W **109** E8
Dyke *Va., U.S.A.* 38°15N 78°32W **102** C6
Dyment *Ont., Canada* 49°37N 92°18W **148** C4
Dysart *Sask., Canada* 50°57N 104°2W **150** E7
Dysart *Iowa, U.S.A.* 42°10N 92°18W **81** C6
Dzibalchén *Campeche, Mexico* 19°31N 89°45W **179** C3
Dzibilchaltún *Yucatán, Mexico* 21°10N 89°35W **179** A4
Dzibitún *Campeche, Mexico* 19°33N 89°56W **179** C4
Dzidzantún *Yucatán, Mexico* 21°15N 89°3W **179** A4
Dzilam de Bravo *Yucatán, Mexico* 21°24N 88°53W **179** A5
Dzilam González *Yucatán, Mexico* 21°17N 88°56W **179** A5
Dzitás *Yucatán, Mexico* 20°51N 88°31W **179** B5
Dzitbalché *Campeche, Mexico* 20°19N 90°3W **179** B3
Dzonot Carretero *Yucatán, Mexico* 21°25N 87°53W **179** A6
Dzuiché *Quintana Roo, Mexico* 19°54N 88°48W **179** C5

E

E.C. Manning Park △ *B.C., Canada* 49°5N 120°45W **155** F14
E. Carranza, Base Aérea Militar *Guadalajara,*
Mexico 20°45N 103°27W **180** A1
E.G. Simmons Park *Tampa, U.S.A.* 27°46N 82°28W **115** C4
E.V. Spence Res. *Tex., U.S.A.* 31°58N 100°40W **108** F7
Eabamet L. *Ont., Canada* 51°30N 87°46W **149** A9
Eads *Colo., U.S.A.* 38°29N 102°47W **125** D8
Eagar *Ariz., U.S.A.* 34°6N 109°17W **130** D6
Eagle *Alaska, U.S.A.* 64°47N 141°12W **135** D12
Eagle *Colo., U.S.A.* 39°39N 106°50W **125** C4
Eagle *Idaho, U.S.A.* 43°42N 116°21W **122** F2
Eagle *Nebr., U.S.A.* 40°49N 96°26W **80** D9
Eagle *Wis., U.S.A.* 42°53N 88°29W **78** F5
Eagle ➛ *Nfld. & L., Canada* 53°36N 57°26W **143** C6
Eagle ➛ *Colo., U.S.A.* 39°39N 107°4W **125** C3
Eagle, Mt. *U.S. Virgin Is.* 17°46N 64°49W **184** H18
Eagle Bend *Minn., U.S.A.* 46°10N 95°2W **77** E3
Eagle Butte *S. Dak., U.S.A.* 45°0N 101°10W **76** F4
Eagle City *Okla., U.S.A.* 35°56N 98°35W **107** C5
Eagle County ☆ *Colo., U.S.A.* 39°40N 106°50W **125** C4
Eagle Cr. ➛ *Sask., Canada* 52°20N 107°30W **150** C4
Eagle Cr. ➛ *Ky., U.S.A.* 38°36N 85°4W **105** B7
Eagle Grove *Iowa, U.S.A.* 42°40N 93°54W **81** C5
Eagle Harbor *Md., U.S.A.* 38°35N 76°40W **93** B4
Eagle I. *Man., Canada* 45°8N 78°29W **147** B8
Eagle L. *B.C., Canada* 51°55N 124°23W **154** D10
Eagle L. *Ont., Canada* 49°42N 93°13W **148** C3
Eagle L. *Calif., U.S.A.* 40°39N 120°45W **126** C6
Eagle L. *Maine, U.S.A.* 46°20N 69°22W **90** B4
Eagle Lake *Ont., Canada* 45°8N 78°29W **147** B8
Eagle Lake *Maine, U.S.A.* 47°3N 68°36W **90** A5
Eagle Lake *Minn., U.S.A.* 44°10N 93°53W **77** F4
Eagle Lake *Tex., U.S.A.* 29°35N 96°20W **109** H11
Eagle Mills *Ark., U.S.A.* 33°41N 92°43W **106** E3
Eagle Mountain *Calif., U.S.A.* 33°49N 115°27W **127** K11
Eagle Mountain *Minn., U.S.A.* 40°19N 112°0W **129** C3
Eagle Mountain Res. *Tex., U.S.A.* 32°53N 97°28W **109** E10
Eagle Mt. *Minn., U.S.A.* 47°54N 90°34W **77** C4
Eagle Mts. *Tex., U.S.A.* 30°55N 105°5W **108** G2
Eagle Nest N. *Mex., U.S.A.* 36°33N 105°16W **131** A5
Eagle Nest Butte *S. Dak., U.S.A.* 43°27N 101°39W **76** G4
Eagle Pass *Tex., U.S.A.* 28°43N 100°30W **108** J7
Eagle Peak *Calif., U.S.A.* 41°17N 120°12W **126** B6
Eagle Pk. *Calif., U.S.A.* 37°5N 119°1W **127** F7
Eagle Point *Oreg., U.S.A.* 42°28N 122°48W **121** E3
Eagle Point Lake *Minn., U.S.A.* 44°58N 92°54W **94** B4
Eagle River *Ont., Canada* 49°47N 93°12W **148** C3
Eagle River *Mich., U.S.A.* 47°25N 88°18W **79** B3
Eagle River *Wis., U.S.A.* 45°55N 89°15W **78** C41
Eagle Rock *Calif., U.S.A.* 34°8N 118°12W **133** B3
Eagle Rock *Va., U.S.A.* 37°38N 79°48W **102** D5
Eaglehead L. *Ont., Canada* 49°2N 89°12W **148** C7
Eaglesham *Alta., Canada* 55°47N 117°53W **152** C3
Eagletail Mts. *Ariz., U.S.A.* 33°20N 113°30W **130** D2
Eagletown *Okla., U.S.A.* 34°2N 94°34W **107** D9
Eagleville *Calif., U.S.A.* 41°19N 120°7W **126** B6
Eagleville *Mo., U.S.A.* 40°28N 93°59W **83** A3
Eagleville *Tenn., U.S.A.* 35°45N 86°39W **104** E6
Eakly *Okla., U.S.A.* 35°18N 98°34W **107** C5
Ear Falls *Ont., Canada* 50°38N 93°13W **148** B3
Earl, L. *Calif., U.S.A.* 41°50N 124°11W **126** B2
Earl Grey *Sask., Canada* 50°57N 104°43W **150** E7
Earl Park *Ind., U.S.A.* 40°42N 87°25W **85** C3
Earle *Ark., U.S.A.* 35°16N 90°28W **106** C5
Earleville *Md., U.S.A.* 39°24N 75°54W **93** A4
Earlham *Iowa, U.S.A.* 41°30N 94°7W **81** D4
Earlimart *Calif., U.S.A.* 35°53N 119°16W **127** H7
Earlington *Ky., U.S.A.* 37°16N 87°30W **104** C5
Earls Cove *B.C., Canada* 49°45N 124°0W **154** F13
Earlsboro *Okla., U.S.A.* 35°19N 96°49W **107** C7
Earlton *Kans., U.S.A.* 37°35N 95°28W **82** D8
Earltown *N.S., Canada* 45°35N 63°8W **141** H6
Earlville *Ill., U.S.A.* 41°35N 88°55W **84** B5
Earlville *Iowa, U.S.A.* 42°28N 91°16W **81** C7
Earlville *N.Y., U.S.A.* 42°44N 75°33W **88** C5
Early *Iowa, U.S.A.* 42°28N 95°9W **81** C3
Early *Tex., U.S.A.* 31°46N 98°58W **109** F9
Early County ☆ *Ga., U.S.A.* 31°20N 84°50W **113** E2
Earth *Tex., U.S.A.* 34°14N 102°24W **108** C5
Easley *S.C., U.S.A.* 34°50N 82°36W **103** D3
East ➛ *N.Y., U.S.A.* 40°48N 73°48W **92** B3
East Alton *Ill., U.S.A.* 38°53N 90°7W **84** E3
East Angus *Qué., Canada* 45°30N 71°40W **145** F11
East Arlington *Mass., U.S.A.* 42°24N 71°9W **96** A2
East Arlington *Va., U.S.A.* 38°51N 77°4W **99** B3
East Arm Grand Traverse B. *Mich.,*
U.S.A. 44°50N 85°30W **79** E6

East Atlantic Beach N.Y., U.S.A. 40°35N 73°42W **97** C4
East Aurora N.Y., U.S.A. 42°46N 78°37W **88** C2
East B. La., U.S.A. 29°0N 89°15W **110** E6
East B. Tex., U.S.A. 29°30N 94°35W **109** H13
East Baton Rouge Parish ☆ La., U.S.A. 30°30N 91°20W **110** D4
East Bay N.∴, Canada 46°1N 60°25W **141** G9
East Bend N.C., U.S.A. 36°13N 80°31W **103** B5
East Berkshire Vt., U.S.A. 44°56N 72°42W **89** B2
East Berlin Pa., U.S.A. 39°56N 76°59W **87** E6
East Bernard Tex., U.S.A. 29°32N 96°4W **109** H11
East Bernstadt Ky., U.S.A. 37°9N 84°12W **105** C8
East Bethel Minn., U.S.A. 45°19N 93°12W **77** E5
East Boston Mass., U.S.A. 42°22N 71°1W **96** A2
East Brady Pa., U.S.A. 40°59N 79°37W **87** D3
East Branch Clarion River L. Pa., U.S.A. 41°35N 78°35W **87** C4
East Brewton Ala., U.S.A. 31°5N 87°4W **112** E3
East Bridgewater Mass., U.S.A. 42°2N 70°58W **91** B4
East Broughton Qué., Canada 46°14N 71°5W **145** E11
East Brunswick N.J., U.S.A. 40°25N 74°23W **92** B2
East Canton Ohio, U.S.A. 40°47N 81°17W **86** C5
East Canyon Res. Utah, U.S.A. 40°55N 111°36W **134** A4
East Canyon State Park △ Utah, U.S.A. 40°54N 111°35W **134** A4
East Carbon Utah, U.S.A. 39°35N 110°25W **129** D5
East Carroll Parish ☆ La., U.S.A. 32°45N 91°15W **110** B4
East Charleston Vt., U.S.A. 44°49N 71°59W **89** B3
East Chezzetcook N.S., Canada 44°43N 63°14W **141** A2
East Chicago Ind., U.S.A. 41°38N 87°27W **85** B3
East Cleveland Ohio, U.S.A. 41°31N 81°34W **98** A2
East Corinth Vt., U.S.A. 44°5N 72°12W **89** B2
East Cote Blanche B. La., U.S.A. 29°34N 91°38W **110** E4
East Dalhousie N.S., Canada 44°43N 64°48W **141** J5
East Dismal Swamp N.C., U.S.A. 35°43N 76°41W **103** C9
East Don → Ont., Canada 43°48N 79°25W **161** A2
East Don Parkland Ont., Canada 43°47N 79°22W **161** A2
East Dorset Vt., U.S.A. 43°13N 73°0W **89** C2
East Douglas Mass., U.S.A. 42°4N 71°43W **91** B3
East Dublin Ga., U.S.A. 32°32N 82°52W **113** D4
East Dubuque Ill., U.S.A. 42°30N 90°39W **84** A3
East Elmhurst N.Y., U.S.A. 40°45N 73°52W **97** B3
East Ely Nev., U.S.A. 39°15N 114°53W **128** C6
East Fairfield Vt., U.S.A. 44°47N 72°51W **89** B2
East Farnham Qué., Canada 45°14N 72°46W **89** A2
East Felicana Parish ☆ La., U.S.A. 30°47N 91°8W **110** D4
East Flat Rock N.C., U.S.A. 35°17N 82°25W **103** C3
East Fork Juneau → U.S.A. 31°0N 90°50W **111** E3
East Fork Juneau → Idaho, U.S.A. 42°34N 115°38W **122** G3
East Fork Obey → Tenn., U.S.A. 36°37N 85°7W **105** D7
East Fork Sevier → Utah, U.S.A. 38°14N 112°12W **129** E3
East Fork White → Ind., U.S.A. 38°33N 87°14W **85** E3
East Fultonham Ohio, U.S.A. 39°51N 82°8W **86** D4
East Gaffney S.C., U.S.A. 35°5N 81°38W **103** C4
East Glacier Park Mont., U.S.A. 48°27N 113°13W **123** B4
East Grant Conn., U.S.A. 41°57N 72°44W **91** C2
East Grand Forks Minn., U.S.A. 47°56N 97°1W **77** C1
East Grand Rapids Mich., U.S.A. 42°58N 85°37W **79** C6
East Greenville Pa., U.S.A. 40°25N 75°30W **92** B1
East Greenwich R.I., U.S.A. 41°40N 71°27W **91** C3
East Haddam Conn., U.S.A. 41°27N 72°28W **91** C2
East Hampton Conn., U.S.A. 41°35N 72°31W **91** C2
East Hampton N.Y., U.S.A. 40°58N 72°11W **91** D2
East Hartford Conn., U.S.A. 41°46N 72°39W **91** C2
East Haven Conn., U.S.A. 41°17N 72°52W **91** C2
East Haverhill N.H., U.S.A. 44°3N 71°58W **89** B3
East Helena Mont., U.S.A. 46°35N 111°56W **123** D6
East Hills N.Y., U.S.A. 40°47N 73°37W **97** B5
East Holden Maine, U.S.A. 44°44N 68°38W **90** D5
East Hope Idaho, U.S.A. 48°14N 116°17W **122** A2
East Houston Tex., U.S.A. 29°49N 95°16W **116** A3
East Humber → Ont., Canada 43°47N 79°35W **161** A1
East Jordan Mich., U.S.A. 45°10N 85°7W **79** D6
East Kingson N.H., U.S.A. 42°54N 71°2W **89** B3
East Lansowne Pa., U.S.A. 39°56N 75°15W **98** B1
East Lansing Mich., U.S.A. 42°44N 84°29W **79** G7
East Las Vegas = Whitney Nev., U.S.A. 36°4N 115°5W **134** C2
East Lempster N.H., U.S.A. 43°13N 72°13W **89** C2
East Lexington Mass., U.S.A. 42°25N 71°12W **96** A1
East Liberty Ohio, U.S.A. 40°20N 83°35W **86** C3
East Livermore = Livermore Falls Maine, U.S.A. 44°29N 70°11W **90** D3
East Liverpool Ohio, U.S.A. 40°37N 80°35W **86** C6
East Longmeadow Mass., U.S.A. 42°4N 72°31W **91** B2
East Los Angeles Calif., U.S.A. 34°1N 118°10W **133** B3
East Lyme Conn., U.S.A. 41°22N 72°13W **91** C2
East Lynn W. Va., U.S.A. 38°10N 82°23W **102** C2
East Lynn Mo., U.S.A. 38°40N 94°14W **83** C2
East Main = Eastmain Qué., Canada 52°10N 78°30W **143** C2
East Meadow N.Y., U.S.A. 40°43N 73°34W **92** B3
East Middlebury Vt., U.S.A. 43°58N 73°6W **89** C1
East Millcreek Utah, U.S.A. 40°42N 111°48W **134** A4
East Millinocket Maine, U.S.A. 45°38N 68°35W **90** C5
East Milwaukee = Shorewood Wis., U.S.A. 43°5N 87°53W **94** B2
East Moline Ill., U.S.A. 41°32N 90°26W **84** B3
East Naples Fla., U.S.A. 26°8N 81°46W **114** D7
East New Market Md., U.S.A. 38°36N 75°56W **93** B5
East New York N.Y., U.S.A. 40°40N 73°53W **97** B3
East Newark N.J., U.S.A. 40°45N 74°9W **97** B3
East Nishnabotna → Iowa, U.S.A. 40°39N 95°38W **81** E3
East Northport N.Y., U.S.A. 40°53N 73°20W **91** D3
East Norwich N.Y., U.S.A. 40°51N 73°32W **92** B3
East Olympia Wash., U.S.A. 46°58N 122°50W **120** D3
East Orange N.J., U.S.A. 40°46N 74°12W **97** B3
East Palatka Fla., U.S.A. 29°39N 81°36W **114** B7
East Palestine Ohio, U.S.A. 40°50N 80°33W **86** C6
East Park Res. Calif., U.S.A. 39°37N 122°31W **126** D4
East Paterson N.J., U.S.A. 40°54N 74°7W **144** D6
East Peoria Ill., U.S.A. 40°40N 89°34W **84** C4
East Peru Iowa, U.S.A. 41°14N 93°56W **81** D5
East Petersburg Pa., U.S.A. 40°6N 76°21W **87** D6
East Pines Maine, U.S.A. 38°57N 76°54W **99** B4
East Pittsburgh Pa., U.S.A. 40°23N 79°50W **98** B3
East Point Ga., U.S.A. 33°41N 84°25W **117** B2
East Potomac Park D.C., U.S.A. 38°52N 77°1W **99** B3
East Prairie Mo., U.S.A. 36°47N 89°23W **83** E7
East Prospect Pa., U.S.A. 39°58N 76°32W **87** E6
East Providence R.I., U.S.A. 41°49N 71°23W **91** C3
East Pt. B. Virgin Is. 18°40N 64°18W **184** G18
East Pt. N.S., Canada 46°27N 61°58W **141** G8
East Pt. Virgin Is. 17°45N 64°34W **184** H18
East Randolph Vt., U.S.A. 43°56N 72°33W **89** C2
East Range Nev., U.S.A. 40°30N 117°57W **128** B3
East Ridg Tenn., U.S.A. 34°59N 85°13W **105** F7
East River → New York, U.S.A. **96** e3
East Rochester N.Y., U.S.A. 43°7N 77°29W **88** B3
East Rockaway N.Y., U.S.A. 40°38N 73°40W **97** C4

East Rockingham N.C., U.S.A. 34°55N 79°49W **103** D6
East Rupert Vt., U.S.A. 43°16N 73°8W **89** C1
East Rutherford N.J., U.S.A. 40°50N 74°5W **97** A2
East St. Louis Ill., U.S.A. 38°37N 90°9W **94** B3
East Sebago Maine, U.S.A. 43°51N 70°38W **89** C4
East Shoreham N.Y., U.S.A. 40°57N 72°53W **91** D2
East Side Pa., U.S.A. 41°4N 75°46W **92** A1
East Spring Cr. → Colo., U.S.A. 39°30N 102°30W **125** C8
East Stroudsburg Pa., U.S.A. 41°1N 75°11W **87** C7
East Tavaputs Plateau Utah, U.S.A. 39°40N 109°40W **129** D6
East Tawas Mich., U.S.A. 44°17N 83°29W **79** E8
East Thurlow I. B.C., Canada 50°24N 125°25W **154** E9
East Trout L. Sask., Canada 54°22N 105°5W **150** A6
East Troy Wis., U.S.A. 42°47N 88°24W **78** F5
East Vineland N.J., U.S.A. 39°30N 74°55W **92** C2
East Wallingford Vt., U.S.A. 43°25N 72°54W **89** C2
East Wareham Mass., U.S.A. 41°46N 70°40W **91** C4
East Wenatchee Wash., U.S.A. 47°25N 120°18W **120** C5
East Williston N.Y., U.S.A. 40°45N 73°38W **97** B5
East Windsor N.J., U.S.A. 40°17N 74°34W **92** B2
East York Ont., Canada 43°40N 79°22W **161** A2
East Youngstown = Campbell Ohio, U.S.A. 41°5N 80°37W **86** B6
Eastabuchie Miss., U.S.A. 31°26N 89°17W **111** E4
Eastchester N.Y., U.S.A. 40°57N 73°49W **92** B3
Eastchester Bay N.Y., U.S.A. 40°50N 73°48W **97** A4
Eastend Sask., Canada 49°32N 108°50W **150** D2
Eastern Bay Md., U.S.A. 38°50N 76°15W **93** B4
Eastern Neck Nat. Wildlife Refuge △ Md., U.S.A. 39°2N 76°14W **93** A4
Eastern Shore Md., U.S.A. 38°30N 75°50W **93** B5
Easterville Man., Canada 53°8N 99°49W **151** B12
Eastgate Wash., U.S.A. 47°34N 122°9W **132** C5
Eastham Mass., U.S.A. 41°50N 69°58W **91** C5
Easthampton Mass., U.S.A. 42°16N 72°40W **91** B2
Eastlake Mich., U.S.A. 44°15N 86°18W **79** E5
Eastlake Ohio, U.S.A. 41°40N 81°26W **86** B5
Eastland Tex., U.S.A. 32°24N 98°49W **109** E9
Eastland County ☆ Tex., U.S.A. 32°25N 98°50W **109** E9
Eastman Qué., Canada 52°10N 78°30W **143** C2
Eastmain → Qué., Canada 52°27N 78°26W **143** C2
Eastman Qué., Canada 45°18N 72°19W **145** F10
Eastman Wis., U.S.A. 43°10N 91°1W **78** E2
Easton Calif., U.S.A. 36°39N 119°47W **127** G7
Easton Conn., U.S.A. 41°15N 73°18W **91** C1
Easton Ill., U.S.A. 40°14N 89°55W **84** C4
Easton Kans., U.S.A. 39°21N 95°7W **82** B8
Easton Md., U.S.A. 38°47N 76°5W **93** B4
Easton Minn., U.S.A. 43°46N 93°54W **77** G2
Easton Mo., U.S.A. 39°43N 94°39W **83** B2
Easton Pa., U.S.A. 40°41N 75°13W **92** B1
Easton Wash., U.S.A. 47°14N 121°11W **120** C4
Eastover N.C., U.S.A. 35°6N 78°47W **103** C7
Eastover S.C., U.S.A. 33°52N 80°41W **103** E5
Eastpoint Fla., U.S.A. 29°44N 84°53W **114** B4
Eastpoint Park Ont., Canada 43°46N 79°10W **161** A4
Eastport Idaho, U.S.A. 48°59N 116°10W **122** A2
Eastport Maine, U.S.A. 44°56N 67°0W **90** D6
Eastport Mich., U.S.A. 45°6N 85°21W **79** D6
Eastsound Wash., U.S.A. 48°42N 122°55W **120** B3
Eastview Tenn., U.S.A. 35°5N 88°33W **104** E4
Eastville Va., U.S.A. 37°21N 75°57W **102** D9
Eastwood La., U.S.A. 32°33N 93°34W **110** B2
Eaton Colo., U.S.A. 40°32N 104°42W **125** A6
Eaton Ind., U.S.A. 40°21N 85°21W **85** C5
Eaton Ohio, U.S.A. 39°45N 84°38W **86** D2
Eaton County ☆ Mich., U.S.A. 42°35N 84°50W **79** G7
Eaton Rapids Mich., U.S.A. 42°31N 84°39W **79** G7
Eatonia Sask., Canada 51°13N 109°25W **150** D2
Eatonton Ga., U.S.A. 33°20N 83°23W **113** C3
Eatontown N.J., U.S.A. 40°19N 74°4W **92** B2
Eatonville Qué., Canada 47°20N 69°41W **145** D13
Eatonville Wash., U.S.A. 46°52N 122°16W **120** D3
Eau Claire Mich., U.S.A. 41°59N 86°18W **79** H5
Eau Claire Wis., U.S.A. 44°49N 91°30W **78** D2
Eau Claire → Wis., U.S.A. 44°55N 89°35W **78** D4
Eau-Claire, L. à l' Nfld. & L., Canada 52°36N 65°50W **140** A4
Eau-Claire, L. à l' Qué., Canada 56°10N 74°25W **143** B3
Eau Claire County ☆ Wis., U.S.A. 44°45N 91°20W **78** D2
Eau Galle Wis., U.S.A. 44°42N 92°1W **78** D1
Ebano San Luis Potosí, Mexico 22°13N 98°24W **171** H6
Ebensburg Pa., U.S.A. 40°29N 78°44W **87** D4
Ebey's Landing Nat. Historical Reserve △ Wash., U.S.A. 48°12N 122°41W **120** B3
Ebony La., U.S.A. 36°37N 77°59W **102** E7
Ecatepec de Morelos México, Mexico 19°36N 99°3W **181** A3
Ecatzingo México, Mexico 18°58N 98°45W **175** D9
Eccles W. Va., U.S.A. 37°47N 81°16W **102** D3
Echechonee → Ga., U.S.A. 32°39N 83°36W **113** D3
Echo La., U.S.A. 31°29N 85°28W **112** E5
Echo Minn., U.S.A. 44°37N 95°25W **77** F3
Echo Oreg., U.S.A. 45°45N 119°12W **121** B6
Echo Bay N.W.T., Canada 66°5N 117°55W **157** C9
Echo Bay Ont., Canada 46°29N 84°4W **146** A2
Echo Bay N.Y., U.S.A. 40°54N 73°46W **97** A4
Echo Cliffs Ariz., U.S.A. 36°40N 111°35W **130** A4
Echols County ☆ Ga., U.S.A. 30°45N 83°0W **113** F4
Échouani, L. Qué., Canada 47°46N 75°42W **144** D7
Eckley Colo., U.S.A. 40°7N 102°29W **125** B8
Eckville Alta., Canada 52°21N 114°22W **153** F6
Eclectic Ala., U.S.A. 32°38N 86°2W **112** D4
Eclipse Sd. Nunavut, Canada 72°38N 79°0W **158** C10
Economy = Ambridge Pa., U.S.A. 40°36N 80°14W **87** D2
Economy Pa., U.S.A. 39°59N 85°5W **85** D5
Écorce, L. de l' Qué., Canada 47°26N 74°24W **144** D6
Ecru Miss., U.S.A. 34°21N 89°2W **111** B4
Ector County ☆ Tex., U.S.A. 31°46N 102°31W **108** F5
Ecuandureo Michoacan, Mexico 20°10N 102°11W **174** B5
Ecueils, Pte. aux Qué., Canada 59°47N 77°50W **143** B2
Ecum Secum N.S., Canada 44°58N 62°8W **141** J7
Edam Sask., Canada 53°11N 108°46W **150** B3
Edcouch Tex., U.S.A. 26°18N 97°58W **118** L10
Eddy County ☆ N. Dak., U.S.A. 47°50N 99°0W **76** C7
Eddy County ☆ N. Mex., U.S.A. 32°30N 104°20W **131** E6
Eddystone Ill., U.S.A. 37°30N 88°35W **84** F5
Eddyville Iowa, U.S.A. 41°9N 92°38W **81** D6
Eddyville Ky., U.S.A. 37°3N 88°4W **104** D4
Eddyville Nebr., U.S.A. 41°1N 99°38W **80** C6
Eden = Bar Harbor Maine, U.S.A. 44°23N 68°13W **90** D5
Eden Man., Canada 50°23N 99°28W **151** E12
Eden Miss., U.S.A. 32°59N 90°20W **111** D3
Eden N.C., U.S.A. 36°29N 79°53W **103** B6
Eden S. Dak., U.S.A. 45°37N 97°25W **76** E8

Eden Tex., U.S.A. 31°13N 99°51W **109** F8
Eden Wis., U.S.A. 44°42N 72°33W **89** B2
Eden Wis., U.S.A. 43°42N 88°22W **78** E5
Eden Wyo., U.S.A. 42°3N 109°26W **124** D3
Eden Res. Wyo., U.S.A. 42°14N 109°21W **124** D3
Eden Valley Minn., U.S.A. 45°19N 94°33W **77** E4
Edenton N.C., U.S.A. 36°4N 76°39W **103** B9
Edenvale Park Minn., U.S.A. 44°52N 93°27W **94** B1
Edesville Md., U.S.A. 39°9N 76°13W **93** A4
Edgar Nebr., U.S.A. 40°22N 97°58W **80** D8
Edgar Wis., U.S.A. 44°55N 89°59W **78** D4
Edgar County ☆ Ill., U.S.A. 39°40N 87°45W **84** D6
Edgar Springs Mo., U.S.A. 37°42N 91°52W **83** D5
Edgard La., U.S.A. 30°3N 90°34W **110** D5
Edgartown Mass., U.S.A. 41°23N 70°31W **91** C4
Edge Hills Park △ B.C., Canada 51°2N 121°52W **155** D13
Edgecliff Tex., U.S.A. 32°39N 97°20W **116** C1
Edgecombe County ☆ N.C., U.S.A. 35°50N 77°30W **103** C8
Edgefield S.C., U.S.A. 33°47N 81°56W **103** E4
Edgefield County ☆ S.C., U.S.A. 33°50N 82°0W **103** E4
Edgeley Ont., Canada 43°47N 79°31W **161** A1
Edgeley N. Dak., U.S.A. 46°22N 98°43W **76** D7
Edgemar Calif., U.S.A. 39°14N 76°27W **93** A4
Edgemont S. Dak., U.S.A. 43°18N 103°50W **76** G2
Edgemoor Del., U.S.A. 39°45N 75°30W **93** A5
Edgerton Alta., Canada 52°45N 110°27W **153** F10
Edgerton Kans., U.S.A. 38°46N 95°1W **82** C8
Edgerton Minn., U.S.A. 43°53N 96°8W **77** G2
Edgerton Mo., U.S.A. 39°30N 94°38W **83** B2
Edgerton Ohio, U.S.A. 41°27N 84°45W **86** B2
Edgerton Wis., U.S.A. 42°50N 89°4W **78** F4
Edgerton Wyo., U.S.A. 43°25N 106°15W **124** C6
Edgewater B.C., Canada 50°42N 116°5W **153** H4
Edgewater Colo., U.S.A. 39°45N 105°3W **134** B1
Edgewater Fla., U.S.A. 28°59N 80°54W **114** C8
Edgewater Park N.J., U.S.A. 40°4N 74°54W **92** B2
Edgewater Park Ohio, U.S.A. 41°29N 81°43W **98** B1
Edgewood B.C., Canada 49°47N 118°8W **155** F16
Edgewood Fla., U.S.A. 28°29N 81°22W **115** B2
Edgewood Ill., U.S.A. 38°55N 88°40W **84** E5
Edgewood Ind., U.S.A. 39°41N 86°8W **85** D4
Edgewood Iowa, U.S.A. 42°39N 91°24W **81** C7
Edgewood Ky., U.S.A. 39°1N 84°34W **105** A8
Edgewood Md., U.S.A. 39°25N 76°18W **93** A4
Edgewood N. Mex., U.S.A. 35°4N 106°11W **131** B4
Edgewood Pa., U.S.A. 40°25N 79°52W **98** B2
Edgewood Tex., U.S.A. 32°42N 95°53W **109** E12
Edina Minn., U.S.A. 44°53N 93°20W **94** B1
Edina Mo., U.S.A. 40°10N 92°11W **83** A41
Edinboro Pa., U.S.A. 41°52N 80°8W **87** C2
Edinburg Ill., U.S.A. 39°39N 89°23W **84** D4
Edinburg Miss., U.S.A. 32°48N 89°20W **111** D4
Edinburg N. Dak., U.S.A. 48°30N 97°52W **76** B8
Edinburg Tex., U.S.A. 26°18N 98°10W **108** L9
Edinburg Va., U.S.A. 38°49N 78°34W **93** B2
Edinburgh Ind., U.S.A. 39°21N 85°58W **85** D5
Edison Calif., U.S.A. 31°34N 84°44W **113** E2
Edison N.J., U.S.A. 40°31N 74°25W **92** B2
Edison Nebr., U.S.A. 40°17N 99°47W **80** D6
Edison Ohio, U.S.A. 40°33N 82°52W **86** C4
Edison Park Ill., U.S.A. 42°1N 87°48W **95** A2
Edisto → S.C., U.S.A. 32°29N 80°21W **103** F5
Edisto I. S.C., U.S.A. 32°35N 80°20W **103** F5
Edith Tex., U.S.A. 31°54N 100°37W **108** F7
Edmond Kans., U.S.A. 39°37N 99°50W **82** B4
Edmond Okla., U.S.A. 35°39N 97°29W **107** C6
Edmonds Wash., U.S.A. 47°48N 122°22W **132** B3
Edmondson Ark., U.S.A. 35°6N 90°19W **106** C5
Edmondson Md., U.S.A. 38°56N 76°54W **99** B4
Edmonson Tex., U.S.A. 34°17N 101°54W **108** C6
Edmonson County ☆ Ky., U.S.A. 37°10N 86°15W **104** C6
Edmonton Alta., Canada 53°30N 113°30W **152** E7
Edmonton Ky., U.S.A. 36°59N 85°37W **105** D7
Edmonton Int. ✕ (YEG) Alta., Canada 53°21N 113°38W **152** E7
Edmore Mich., U.S.A. 43°25N 85°3W **79** F6
Edmore N. Dak., U.S.A. 48°25N 98°27W **76** B7
Edmunds County ☆ S. Dak., U.S.A. 45°27N 99°20W **76** E6
Edmundson Mo., U.S.A. 38°44N 90°21W **94** A1
Edmundston N.B., Canada 47°23N 68°20W **141** F17
Edna Kans., U.S.A. 37°4N 95°22W **82** D8
Edna Tex., U.S.A. 28°59N 96°39W **109** J11
Edon Ohio, U.S.A. 41°33N 84°46W **86** B2
Edray W. Va., U.S.A. 38°16N 80°6W **102** C4
Edroy Tex., U.S.A. 27°59N 97°41W **109** K10
Edson Alta., Canada 53°35N 116°28W **152** E4
Edson Kans., U.S.A. 39°20N 101°33W **82** B2
Edwall Wash., U.S.A. 47°30N 117°57W **120** C8
Edward Arthur Patterson L. N. Dak., U.S.A. 46°51N 102°51W **76** D3
Edward I. Ont., Canada 48°22N 88°37W **148** D8
Edwards Calif., U.S.A. 34°50N 117°40W **127** J9
Edwards Miss., U.S.A. 32°20N 90°36W **111** D3
Edwards N.Y., U.S.A. 44°20N 75°15W **88** A5
Edwards → Wis., U.S.A. 41°9N 90°50W **84** B4
Edwards Air Force Base Calif., U.S.A. 34°52N 117°56W **127** J9
Edwards County ☆ Ill., U.S.A. 38°25N 88°5W **84** E5
Edwards County ☆ Kans., U.S.A. 37°50N 99°15W **82** D4
Edwards County ☆ Tex., U.S.A. 30°10N 100°13W **108** G7
Edwards Plateau Tex., U.S.A. 30°45N 101°20W **108** G6
Edwardsburg Mich., U.S.A. 41°48N 86°6W **79** H5
Edwardsport Ind., U.S.A. 38°49N 87°15W **85** E3
Edwardsville Ill., U.S.A. 38°49N 89°58W **84** E4
Edziza, Mt. B.C., Canada 57°44N 130°40W **157** E6
Edzná Campeche, Mexico 19°39N 90°19W **179** C2
Edzo N.W.T., Canada 62°49N 116°4W **157** D9
Eek Alaska, U.S.A. 60°14N 162°2W **135** F7
Eel → Calif., U.S.A. 40°38N 124°20W **126** C2
Eel → Ind., U.S.A. 39°7N 86°57W **85** D4
Eel River Crossing N.B., Canada 48°1N 66°25W **141** E3
Effie Minn., U.S.A. 47°50N 93°38W **77** C5
Effigy Mounds Nat. Monument △ Iowa, U.S.A. 43°5N 91°11W **81** B71
Effingham Ill., U.S.A. 39°7N 88°33W **84** E5
Effingham Kans., U.S.A. 39°31N 95°24W **82** B8
Effingham County ☆ Ga., U.S.A. 32°15N 81°15W **113** D5
Effingham County ☆ Ill., U.S.A. 39°5N 88°35W **84** E5
Effingham Falls N.H., U.S.A. 43°47N 71°5W **89** C3
Egan La., U.S.A. 30°13N 92°38W **110** D2
Egan Range Nev., U.S.A. 39°35N 114°55W **128** C6
Eganville Ont., Canada 45°32N 77°5W **147** B9
Egedesminde = Aasiaat Greenland 68°43N 52°56W **162** D5
Egegik Alaska, U.S.A. 58°13N 157°22W **135** G8
Egeland N. Dak., U.S.A. 48°38N 99°6W **76** B6
Egg Harbor Wis., U.S.A. 45°3N 87°17W **78** C6

Eden Tex., U.S.A. 31°13N 99°51W **109** F8
Egg Harbor City N.J., U.S.A. 39°32N 74°39W **92** C2
Egg Island Pt. N.J., U.S.A. 39°11N 75°8W **92** C1
Eglin Air Force Base Fla., U.S.A. 30°28N 86°32W **114** A2
Eglinton I. N.W.T., Canada 75°48N 118°30W **156** A9
Egmont B.C., Canada 49°45N 123°56W **154** F11
Egmont B. P.E.I., Canada 46°29N 64°6W **141** G5
Egmont Channel Tampa, U.S.A. 27°36N 82°47W **115** D2
Egmont Key State Park Tampa, U.S.A. 27°36N 82°46W **115** D2
Egnar Colo., U.S.A. 37°55N 108°56W **125** E9
Eholt B.C., Canada 49°10N 118°34W **155** F16
Ehrenberg Ariz., U.S.A. 33°36N 114°31W **130** D1
Eielson Alaska, U.S.A. 64°40N 147°4W **135** D11
Eitzen Minn., U.S.A. 43°31N 91°28W **77** G7
Ejutla Jalisco, Mexico 19°54N 104°10W **174** C3
Ejutla Oaxaca, Mexico 16°34N 96°44W **177** H4
Ekalaka Mont., U.S.A. 45°53N 104°33W **123** E13
Ekalugad Fiord Nunavut, Canada 68°46N 68°37W **158** D12
Ek'Balam Yucatán, Mexico 20°52N 88°9W **179** B5
Ekka I. N.W.T., Canada 66°19N 122°29W **156** C8
Eklutna Alaska, U.S.A. 61°27N 149°22W **135** F10
Ekron Ky., U.S.A. 37°56N 86°11W **104** C5
Ekwan → Ont., Canada 53°12N 82°15W **159** G9
Ekwok Alaska, U.S.A. 59°22N 157°30W **135** G8
El Abandonado Chihuahua, Mexico 27°49N 107°11W **170** C2
El Aguacate Guadalajara, Mexico 20°42N 103°12W **180** A2
El Aguaje Coahuila, Mexico 24°47N 103°56W **171** F2
El Ahogado, Presa Guadalajara, Mexico 20°32N 103°16W **180** B2
El Alacrán Tabasco, Mexico 18°21N 93°41W **178** A3
El Alamo Baja Calif., Mexico 31°34N 116°2W **166** B2
El Alamo Nuevo León, Mexico 26°29N 99°46W **170** D5
El Alamo, Sa. Sonora, Mexico 30°35N 112°35W **168** C3
El Alhuate Sinaloa, Mexico 24°30N 107°21W **172** C3
El Alicante Coahuila, Mexico 27°56N 103°34W **170** C1
El Arco Baja Calif. S., Mexico 28°1N 113°25W **167** E5
El Arenal Chiapas, Mexico 15°10N 92°42W **178** D3
El Arenal Jalisco, Mexico 20°46N 103°39W **174** B4
El Arenal Michoacan, Mexico 18°7N 102°38W **174** D5
El Bacatete, Sa. Sonora, Mexico 27°54N 110°19W **168** F5
El Barón → Baja Calif., Mexico 31°50N 116°40W **166** B2
El Barreal Chihuahua, Mexico 31°17N 107°10W **169** B8
El Barreal, L. Chihuahua, Mexico 31°7N 107°0W **169** B8
El Barrego → Baja Calif., Mexico 31°25N 114°52W **166** B3
El Barril Baja Calif., Mexico 28°18N 112°55W **167** E4
El Barril San Luis Potosí, Mexico 23°2N 102°8W **171** F2
El Becerro Chihuahua, Mexico 28°37N 104°39W **169** E11
El Berrendo Chihuahua, Mexico 31°20N 108°25W **169** B7
El Bledal Sinaloa, Mexico 24°49N 107°49W **172** C3
El Bluff Nic. 11°59N 83°40W **182** D3
El Bordo Zacatecas, Mexico 22°54N 102°23W **173** E8
El Bosque Chiapas, Mexico 17°4N 92°44W **178** B4
El Brasil Tamaulipas, Mexico 23°20N 97°46W **171** F7
El Cabrito Tamaulipas, Mexico 23°11N 98°29W **171** G6
El Caimanero, L. Sinaloa, Mexico 23°0N 106°7W **172** C4
El Cajon Calif., U.S.A. 32°48N 116°58W **127** L10
El Caldillo Chihuahua, Mexico 26°31N 106°23W **169** G9
El Camarón Oaxaca, Mexico 16°34N 96°2W **177** H4
El Campo Tex., U.S.A. 29°12N 96°16W **109** H11
El Capitan Res. Calif., U.S.A. 32°53N 116°49W **127** L10
El Capulin Guadalajara, Mexico 20°28N 103°16W **180** C2
El Caracol, Presa Guerrero, Mexico 17°57N 99°54W **175** E8
El Carmen Chiapas, Mexico 15°34N 93°7W **178** D3
El Carmen Nuevo León, Mexico 24°36N 100°28W **171** F4
El Carmen → Chihuahua, Mexico 30°42N 106°29W **169** C9
El Carrizal Guerrero, Mexico 17°53N 100°56W **175** E7
El Carrizal Sonora, Mexico 31°5N 111°42W **168** B4
El Carrizalillo Zacatecas, Mexico 23°12N 103°22W **173** D7
El Casco Durango, Mexico 25°34N 104°35W **173** B6
El Castillo Guadalajara, Mexico 20°30N 103°14W **180** B2
El Castillo Sinaloa, Mexico 24°32N 107°43W **172** C3
El Ceborucu, Volcán Nayarit, Mexico 21°9N 104°30W **172** F6
El Cedral Quintana Roo, Mexico 20°21N 87°0W **179** B6
El Cedral Quintana Roo, Mexico 20°56N 87°32W **179** B6
El Centenario Baja Calif. S., Mexico 24°5N 110°26W **167** J8
El Centenario Campeche, Mexico 18°39N 90°10W **179** D3
El Centro Zacatecas, Mexico 23°22N 103°18W **173** D7
El Centro Calif., U.S.A. 32°48N 115°34W **127** L11
El Cerrito Calif., U.S.A. 37°55N 122°19W **126** F4
El Chauz Michoacan, Mexico 18°52N 102°2W **174** D5
El Chico, Parque Nacional △ Hidalgo, Mexico 20°12N 98°43W **175** B9
El Chilacayote Jalisco, Mexico 20°8N 104°39W **174** B3
El Chinal Tabasco, Mexico 18°2N 92°8W **178** A4
El Chinero = La Trinidad Baja Calif., Mexico 31°24N 115°5W **166** B3
El Cielo, Reserva de la Biosfera △ Tamaulipas, Mexico 23°18N 99°12W **171** G5
El Ciento Veintiocho Baja Calif. S., Mexico 24°29N 111°15W **167** J7
El Cimatario, Parque Nacional △ Querétaro, Mexico 20°30N 100°21W **175** B7
El Cinco Coahuila, Mexico 26°47N 103°27W **170** D1
El Claro Sonora, Mexico 30°22N 111°12W **168** C4
El Colomo Colima, Mexico 19°2N 104°15W **174** C3
El Colorado Chihuahua, Mexico 29°53N 108°53W **169** D7
El Colorado Sinaloa, Mexico 25°46N 109°19W **172** B1
El Conejo Baja Calif. S., Mexico 24°7N 110°59W **167** J8
El Consuelo Chihuahua, Mexico 30°47N 105°43W **169** C10
El Control Tamaulipas, Mexico 25°57N 97°48W **170** E7
El Coyote Veracruz, Mexico 18°37N 96°18W **177** F4
El Coyote Coahuila, Mexico 30°48N 112°37W **168** C3
El Coyote, L. Coahuila, Mexico 27°13N 103°15W **170** C1
El Cristo, Vaso Regulador México, Mexico 19°30N 99°5W **181** B2
El Crucero Baja Calif., Mexico 29°15N 114°10W **166** D4
El Cuatro Sinaloa, Mexico 25°14N 108°33W **168** C4
El Cuchijaqui → Sonora, Mexico 26°35N 108°48W **168** F2
El Cuchillo, Presa Nuevo León, Mexico 25°35N 99°10W **170** D5
El Cuervo Chihuahua, Mexico 30°14N 105°10W **169** C10
El Cuervo, L. Chihuahua, Mexico 29°17N 105°57W **169** D10
El Cuyo Yucatán, Mexico 21°31N 87°41W **179** A5
El Cuyo, Pta. Campeche, Mexico 20°5N 90°29W **179** B3
El Descanso, Pta. Baja Calif., Mexico 32°12N 117°4W **166** A1
El Desemboque Sonora, Mexico 30°33N 113°1W **168** C2
El Desemboque Sonora, Mexico 29°30N 112°27W **168** D3
El Diablo, Sa. Chihuahua, Mexico 31°26N 104°10W **169** F11
El Diamante Chiapas, Mexico 16°6N 92°52W **178** C4
El Diamante Durango, Mexico 26°23N 104°20W **173** A6
El Doce Veracruz, Mexico 17°4N 94°13W **177** G6
El Dorado Sinaloa, Mexico 24°17N 107°21W **172** C3
El Dorado Ark., U.S.A. 33°12N 92°40W **106** E4
El Dorado Kans., U.S.A. 37°49N 96°52W **82** D7
El Dorado County ☆ Calif., U.S.A. 38°45N 120°40W **126** E6
El Dorado, L. Kans., U.S.A. 37°51N 96°49W **82** D7
El Dorado Springs Mo., U.S.A. 37°52N 94°1W **83** D2
El Durazno Durango, Mexico 25°14N 104°44W **173** D6
El Durazno Zacatecas, Mexico 24°15N 101°15W **173** C9

El Encinal, Sa. *Sonora, Mexico* 28°45N 109°20W **168** E6
El Espinal *Veracruz, Mexico* 20°16N 97°24W **176** D3
El Espíritu → *Guerrero, Mexico* 18°19N 100°39W **175** D7
El Este, L. *Campeche, Mexico* 18°25N 91°49W **179** D2
El Faro *Michoacan, Mexico* 18°20N 103°29W **174** D4
El Fresnal, Sa. *Chihuahua, Mexico* 31°N 107°40W **169** C8
El Fuerte *Sinaloa, Mexico* 26°25N 108°39W **172** A2
El Gato *Sonora, Mexico* 31°38N 112°0W **168** B3
El Gato → *Coahuila, Mexico* 27°29N 100°55W **170** C4
El Gavilán *Sonora, Mexico* 29°28N 111°45W **168** D4
El Gavilán *Tamaulipas, Mexico* 24°42N 98°59W **171** F6
El Gogorron, Parque Nacional △ *San Luis Potosí, Mexico* 21°49N 100°57W **171** J4
El Golpe *Tabasco, Mexico* 18°20N 93°30W **178** A3
El Grande, Cerro *Chihuahua, Mexico* 31°37N 107°59W **169** B8
El Grullo *Jalisco, Mexico* 19°48N 104°13W **174** C3
El Guasimal *Sinaloa, Mexico* 23°43N 106°18W **172** D4
El Higo *Veracruz, Mexico* 21°46N 98°28W **176** C2
El Huacal *Durango, Mexico* 25°27N 106°10W **172** D4
El Huapango *Tamaulipas, Mexico* 24°38N 98°8W **171** F6
El Huerfanito *Baja Calif., Mexico* 30°8N 114°39W **166** C4
El Humo, Sa. *Sonora, Mexico* 31°20N 111°50W **168** B4
El Indio *Tex., U.S.A.* 28°31N 100°19W **108** J7
El Jaralito *Durango, Mexico* 26°7N 104°10W **173** A6
El Jardal *Honduras* 14°54N 88°50W **182** D2
El Jilguero *Guerrero, Mexico* 17°31N 100°2W **175** E7
El Juento, Volcán *México, Mexico* 19°13N 99°20W **181** C2
El Limón *Sinaloa, Mexico* 19°49N 104°11W **174** C3
El Limón de los Ramos *Sinaloa, Mexico* 24°54N 107°32W **172** C3
El Limón de Papatzingán *Michoacan, Mexico* 19°5N 100°46W **175** C7
El Llano *Nayarit, Mexico* 21°24N 105°11W **172** E6
El Llano → *Chihuahua, Mexico* 30°15N 105°6W **169** C10
El Malpais Nat. Monument △ *U.S.A.* 34°53N 108°0W **131** C2
El Manguito *Chiapas, Mexico* 15°45N 93°31W **178** D3
El Mármol *Guanajuato, Mexico* 20°14N 101°44W **174** B6
El Mezquital *Baja Calif. S., Mexico* 28°17N 113°50W **167** E5
El Mezquite *Tamaulipas, Mexico* 25°4N 97°44W **171** E7
El Mezquite *Zacatecas, Mexico* 23°20N 102°37W **173** D8
El Milagro de Guadalupe *San Luis Potosí, Mexico* 23°8N 100°26W **171** G4
El Mineral el Realito *Guanajuato, Mexico* 21°37N 100°14W **175** A7
El Mineral el Refugio *Guanajuato, Mexico* 21°35N 100°11W **175** A7
El Mirador *Chihuahua, Mexico* 30°52N 107°7W **169** C8
El Mirador *Guadalajara, Mexico* 20°29N 103°30W **180** C1
El Mirage *Ariz., U.S.A.* 33°36N 112°19W **130** D3
El Mirage L. *Calif., U.S.A.* 34°39N 117°37W **127** J9
El Monte *Calif., U.S.A.* 34°4N 118°1W **133** B4
El Moro → *Sonora, Mexico* 28°20N 109°37W **168** E6
El Morro Nat. Monument △ *N. Mex., U.S.A.* 35°2N 108°21W **131** B2
El Naranjo *Campeche, Mexico* 18°2N 91°7W **179** D2
El Naranjo *Durango, Mexico* 24°37N 103°21W **173** C7
El Naranjo *Nayarit, Mexico* 22°1N 104°53W **172** E6
El Naranjo *San Luis Potosí, Mexico* 22°30N 99°21W **171** H5
El Nido *Calif., U.S.A.* 37°8N 120°29W **126** F6
El Nido, Sa. *Chihuahua, Mexico* 29°33N 106°48W **169** D9
El Novillero *Nayarit, Mexico* 22°21N 105°39W **172** E5
El Novillo *Sonora, Mexico* 28°59N 109°37W **168** E6
El Ocotito *Guerrero, Mexico* 17°15N 99°34W **175** E8
El Ojo del Agua *Coahuila, Mexico* 26°20N 103°17W **170** D1
El Oro *México, Mexico* 19°51N 100°7W **175** C7
El Orranteño *Chihuahua, Mexico* 28°10N 105°20W **169** E10
El Oso *Coahuila, Mexico* 26°17N 101°46W **170** D3
El Palmito *Durango, Mexico* 25°38N 105°11W **172** B5
El Papalote *Coahuila, Mexico* 26°27N 102°32W **170** D2
El Parral *Chiapas, Mexico* 16°22N 93°9W **178** C3
El Paso = Derby *Kans., U.S.A.* 37°33N 97°16W **82** D6
El Paso *Ill., U.S.A.* 40°44N 89°1W **84** C4
El Paso *Tex., U.S.A.* 31°45N 106°29W **108** F1
El Paso County ☆ *Colo., U.S.A.* 38°50N 104°30W **125** D6
El Paso County ☆ *Tex., U.S.A.* 31°55N 106°5W **108** F1
El Paso Int. ✈ (ELP) *Tex., U.S.A.* 31°48N 106°23W **108** F1
El Patricio *Sonora, Mexico* 31°34N 112°0W **168** B3
El Pedregal, Parque Nacional △ *Distrito Federal, Mexico* 19°18N 99°12W **181** C2
El Peguis, Sa. *Chihuahua, Mexico* 29°40N 104°48W **169** D11
El Peñol *Chihuahua, Mexico* 29°9N 106°14W **169** D9
El Peñuelo *Nuevo León, Mexico* 24°33N 100°44W **171** F4
El Pequeño *Nuevo León, Mexico* 24°4N 100°15W **171** F4
El Picacho, Cerro *Distrito Federal, Mexico* 19°37N 99°8W **181** A3
El Piche *Tabasco, Mexico* 17°55N 91°1W **178** B5
El Pinacate, Sa. *Sonora, Mexico* 31°45N 113°35W **168** B2
El Pinacate y Gran Desierto de Altar = Gran Desierto del Pinacate, Parque Natural △ *Mexico* 31°51N 113°32W **168** B2
El Pino, Sa. *Chihuahua, Mexico* 28°15N 103°5W **170** B1
El Planchón *Chiapas, Mexico* 16°36N 90°41W **178** C6
El Playón *Sinaloa, Mexico* 25°16N 108°11W **172** B2
El Plomito *Sonora, Mexico* 30°18N 112°22W **168** C3
El Plomo *Sonora, Mexico* 31°15N 112°4W **168** B3
El Pochote *Sonora, Mexico* 27°46N 110°8W **168** F5
El Portal *Calif., U.S.A.* 37°41N 119°47W **126** F7
El Portal *Fla., U.S.A.* 25°51N 80°11W **115** C2
El Porvenir *Chiapas, Mexico* 15°27N 92°16W **178** D7
El Porvenir *Chihuahua, Mexico* 31°15N 105°51W **169** B10
El Porvenir *N. Mex., U.S.A.* 35°43N 105°25W **131** B5
El Porvenir → *Chihuahua, Mexico* 26°59N 106°20W **169** G9
El Potosí, Parque Nacional △ *San Luis Potosí, Mexico* 21°59N 99°58W **171** J5
El Progreso *Honduras* 15°26N 87°51W **182** C2
El Progreso *Coahuila, Mexico* 29°19N 101°39W **170** A3
El Puesto *Jalisco, Mexico* 21°37N 101°58W **174** A6
El Quelite *Sinaloa, Mexico* 23°32N 106°28W **172** D4
El Quince *Guadalajara, Mexico* 20°33N 103°17W **180** B2
El Rajón, Sa. *Sonora, Mexico* 30°30N 112°2W **168** C3
El Ramonal *Campeche, Mexico* 18°22N 89°59W **179** D4
El Rancho Nuevo *Coahuila, Mexico* 25°17N 101°21W **171** E3
El Recodo *Sinaloa, Mexico* 23°24N 106°14W **172** D4
El Reloj *Distrito Federal, Mexico* 19°21N 99°9W **181** C3
El Reno *Okla., U.S.A.* 35°32N 97°57W **107** C6
El Retiro *Baja Calif., Mexico* 31°38N 116°40W **166** B2
El Rio *Calif., U.S.A.* 34°14N 119°10W **127** J7
El Rito *N. Mex., U.S.A.* 36°21N 106°11W **131** A4
El Roble *Zacatecas, Mexico* 23°31N 103°57W **173** D7
El Rodeo *Zacatecas, Mexico* 24°53N 102°11W **173** C8
El Rosario *Baja Calif., Mexico* 30°1N 115°45W **166** B2
El Rosario *Oaxaca, Mexico* 16°52N 97°59W **177** H3
El Rosario *Tlaxcala, Mexico* 19°40N 98°13W **175** C9
El Rosario → *Baja Calif., Mexico* 30°2N 115°48W **166** B2
El Rucio *Zacatecas, Mexico* 23°23N 102°0W **173** D9
El Sabinal, Parque Nacional △ *Nuevo León, Mexico* 26°2N 99°40W **170** D4
El Salado *Coahuila, Mexico* 29°38N 101°45W **170** A3
El Salado *San Luis Potosí, Mexico* 24°18N 100°52W **171** F4
El Salado *Sinaloa, Mexico* 24°30N 107°10W **172** C3
El Salto *Chihuahua, Mexico* 28°30N 108°20W **169** E7
El Salto *Durango, Mexico* 23°47N 105°22W **172** D5
El Salto *Jalisco, Mexico* 20°31N 103°10W **180** B2
El Salvador *Zacatecas, Mexico* 24°31N 100°51W **173** C10
El Salvador ■ *Cent. Amer.* 13°50N 89°0W **182** D2
El Sargento *Baja Calif. S., Mexico* 24°3N 110°11W **167** J8
El Sásabe *Sonora, Mexico* 31°27N 111°31W **168** B4
El Sásabe → *Sonora, Mexico* 30°50N 111°50W **168** C4
El Sauce *Nic.* 13°0N 86°40W **182** D2
El Sauz *Chihuahua, Mexico* 29°3N 106°15W **169** D9
El Sauz *Monterrey, Mexico* 25°52N 100°12W **180** A2
El Sauzalito *Baja Calif. S., Mexico* 25°7N 111°2W **167** H7
El Sereno *Calif., U.S.A.* 34°6N 118°10W **133** B3
El Socorro *Coahuila, Mexico* 27°40N 102°18W **170** C2
El Tajín *Veracruz, Mexico* 20°27N 97°22W **176** D3
El Tecuán *Jalisco, Mexico* 19°28N 103°43W **174** C4
El Tepuche *Sinaloa, Mexico* 24°56N 107°21W **172** C3
El Tigre *Campeche, Mexico* 18°16N 90°33W **179** D3
El Tigre *Nayarit, Mexico* 22°30N 105°21W **172** E5
El Tixquil *Hidalgo, Mexico* 20°44N 99°6W **175** B8
El Triunfo *Chiapas, Mexico* 16°12N 91°51W **178** C4
El Triunfo *Sinaloa, Mexico* 28°52N 111°50W **168** B4
El Triunfo *Tabasco, Mexico* 17°56N 91°9W **178** B5
El Tuito *Jalisco, Mexico* 20°19N 105°22W **174** B2
El Tule *Chihuahua, Mexico* 27°3N 106°16W **169** F9
El Tule *Coahuila, Mexico* 28°31N 101°31W **170** B3
El Tule *Sinaloa, Mexico* 25°39N 107°54W **172** C3
El Tulillo *Zacatecas, Mexico* 22°31N 104°7W **173** E6
El Vado Res. *N. Mex., U.S.A.* 36°36N 106°44W **131** A4
El Veinticuatro *Chihuahua, Mexico* 28°18N 105°55W **169** D10
El Veladero, Parque Nacional △ *Guerrero, Mexico* 16°54N 99°52W **175** F8
El Verde *Guadalajara, Mexico* 20°33N 103°16W **180** B2
El Vergel *Distrito Federal, Mexico* 19°18N 99°5W **181** C3
El Vergelito *Chiapas, Mexico* 16°34N 92°4W **178** C4
El Viejo, Sa. *Sonora, Mexico* 30°15N 112°20W **168** C3
El Vizcaíno *Baja Calif. S., Mexico* 27°46N 114°0W **167** F5
El Yucateco *Tabasco, Mexico* 18°12N 94°1W **178** A2
El Yunque *Puerto Rico* 18°19N 65°48W **184** G17
El Zacatal *Oaxaca, Mexico* 16°57N 95°11W **177** H6
El Zapatero *Durango, Mexico* 24°36N 106°23W **172** C4

Elaho → *B.C., Canada* 50°7N 123°23W **154** E11
Elaine *Ark., U.S.A.* 34°19N 90°51W **106** D3
Elam *Pa., U.S.A.* 39°51N 75°32W **93** A5
Elba *Ala., U.S.A.* 31°25N 86°4W **112** D4
Elba *Idaho, U.S.A.* 42°14N 113°34W **122** G5
Elba *Minn., U.S.A.* 44°5N 92°0W **77** F6
Elba *Nebr., U.S.A.* 41°17N 98°34W **80** C7
Elberfeld *Ind., U.S.A.* 38°10N 87°27W **85** E3
Elberon *Iowa, U.S.A.* 42°0N 92°19W **81** C6
Elbert *Colo., U.S.A.* 39°13N 104°32W **125** C6
Elbert *Tex., U.S.A.* 33°15N 99°0W **109** D9
Elbert, Mt. *Colo., U.S.A.* 39°7N 106°27W **124** C4
Elbert County ☆ *Colo., U.S.A.* 39°20N 104°15W **125** C6
Elbert County ☆ *Ga., U.S.A.* 34°10N 82°50W **113** B4
Elberta *Mich., U.S.A.* 44°37N 86°14W **79** E5
Elberta *Utah, U.S.A.* 39°57N 111°57W **129** D4
Elberton *Ga., U.S.A.* 34°7N 82°52W **113** B4
Elbing *Kans., U.S.A.* 38°3N 97°8W **82** C6
Elbow *Sask., Canada* 51°7N 106°35W **150** D5
Elbow → *Alta., Canada* 51°3N 114°2W **153** G6
Elbow Lake *Minn., U.S.A.* 45°59N 95°58W **77** E3
Elcho *Wis., U.S.A.* 45°26N 89°11W **78** C4
Elderon *Wis., U.S.A.* 44°47N 89°15W **78** D4
Eldersburg *Md., U.S.A.* 39°24N 76°57W **93** A4
Eldon *Iowa, U.S.A.* 40°55N 92°13W **81** E6
Eldon *Mo., U.S.A.* 38°21N 92°35W **83** C4[1]
Eldon *Wash., U.S.A.* 47°33N 123°3W **120** C2
Eldora *Iowa, U.S.A.* 42°22N 93°5W **81** C5
Eldora *N.J., U.S.A.* 39°12N 74°52W **92** C2
Eldorado = Echo Bay *N.W.T., Canada* 66°5N 117°55W **157** C9
Eldorado *Ont., Canada* 44°35N 77°31W **147** C9
Eldorado *Ill., U.S.A.* 37°49N 88°26W **84** F5
Eldorado *Md., U.S.A.* 38°37N 75°48W **93** B5
Eldorado *Ohio, U.S.A.* 39°54N 84°41W **86** D2
Eldorado *Okla., U.S.A.* 34°28N 99°39W **107** D4
Eldorado *Tex., U.S.A.* 30°52N 100°36W **108** G4
Eldorado at Santa Fe *N. Mex., U.S.A.* 35°32N 105°56W **131** B5
Eldorado Nat. Forest *Calif., U.S.A.* 38°50N 120°20W **126** E6
Eldorendo *Ga., U.S.A.* 31°3N 84°39W **113** E2
Eldred *N.Y., U.S.A.* 41°32N 74°53W **92** A2
Eldred *Pa., U.S.A.* 41°58N 78°23W **87** C4
Eldridge *Ala., U.S.A.* 33°55N 87°37W **112** C3
Eldridge *Iowa, U.S.A.* 41°39N 90°35W **81** D8
Eldridge *N. Dak., U.S.A.* 46°54N 98°51W **76** D7
Eleanor *W. Va., U.S.A.* 38°32N 81°56W **102** C3
Eleanor, L. *Calif., U.S.A.* 37°59N 119°53W **126** F7
Eleao *Hawai'i, U.S.A.* 21°27N 157°52W **136** K14
Electra *Tex., U.S.A.* 34°2N 98°55W **109** C9
Electra L. *Colo., U.S.A.* 37°33N 107°48W **125** E3
Electric City *Wash., U.S.A.* 47°56N 119°2W **120** C6
Electric Mills *Miss., U.S.A.* 32°46N 88°28W **111** D5
Elephant Butte *N. Mex., U.S.A.* 33°9N 107°11W **131** D3
Elephant Butte Lake State Park △ *N. Mex., U.S.A.* 33°38N 107°1W **131** D3
Elephant Butte Res. *N. Mex., U.S.A.* 33°9N 107°11W **131** D3
Elephant Mt. *Maine, U.S.A.* 44°46N 70°47W **89** B4
Eleuthera *Bahamas* 25°0N 76°20W **182** B4
Eleva *Wis., U.S.A.* 44°35N 91°29W **78** D2
Eleven Point → *Ark., U.S.A.* 36°9N 91°5W **106** B4
Elevenmile Canyon Res. *Colo., U.S.A.* 38°54N 105°29W **125** C5
Elfin Cove *Alaska, U.S.A.* 58°12N 136°22W **135** G13
Elfrida *Ariz., U.S.A.* 31°41N 109°41W **130** F6
Elgin *Man., Canada* 49°27N 100°16W **151** F11
Elgin *Ont., Canada* 44°36N 76°13W **147** C10
Elgin *Ill., U.S.A.* 42°2N 88°17W **84** A5
Elgin *Iowa, U.S.A.* 42°57N 91°38W **81** C7
Elgin *Kans., U.S.A.* 37°0N 96°17W **82** E7
Elgin *Minn., U.S.A.* 44°8N 92°15W **77** F6
Elgin *N. Dak., U.S.A.* 46°24N 101°51W **76** D4
Elgin *Nebr., U.S.A.* 41°59N 98°5W **80** C7
Elgin *Nev., U.S.A.* 37°21N 114°32W **128** E6
Elgin *Okla., U.S.A.* 34°47N 98°18W **107** D5
Elgin *Oreg., U.S.A.* 45°34N 117°55W **121** D8
Elgin *S.C., U.S.A.* 34°10N 80°48W **103** D5
Elgin *Tex., U.S.A.* 30°21N 97°22W **109** G10
Eli *Nebr., U.S.A.* 42°57N 101°2W **80** B4
Elida *N. Mex., U.S.A.* 33°57N 103°39W **131** D7
Elim *Alaska, U.S.A.* 64°37N 162°15W **135** D7
Eliot *Maine, U.S.A.* 43°7N 70°47W **90** E3
Elizabeth *Colo., U.S.A.* 39°22N 104°36W **125** C6
Elizabeth *Ill., U.S.A.* 42°19N 90°13W **84** A3

Elizabeth *La., U.S.A.* 30°52N 92°48W **110** D3
Elizabeth *Minn., U.S.A.* 46°23N 96°8W **77** D2
Elizabeth *N.J., U.S.A.* 40°39N 74°12W **97** C1
Elizabeth *W. Va., U.S.A.* 39°4N 81°24W **102** B3
Elizabeth, C. *Wash., U.S.A.* 47°21N 124°19W **120** C1
Elizabeth Islands *Mass., U.S.A.* 41°27N 70°47W **91** C4
Elizabeth City *N.C., U.S.A.* 36°18N 76°14W **103** B9
Elizabethton *Tenn., U.S.A.* 36°21N 82°13W **105** D10
Elizabethtown *Ill., U.S.A.* 37°27N 88°18W **84** F5
Elizabethtown *Ky., U.S.A.* 37°42N 85°52W **105** C2
Elizabethtown *N.C., U.S.A.* 34°38N 78°37W **103** D7
Elizabethtown *N.Y., U.S.A.* 44°13N 73°36W **88** C7
Elizabethtown *Pa., U.S.A.* 40°9N 76°36W **87** D6
Elizabethville *Pa., U.S.A.* 40°33N 76°49W **87** D6
Elk *Calif., U.S.A.* 39°8N 123°43W **126** D3
Elk *N. Mex., U.S.A.* 32°57N 105°20W **131** E5
Elk → *B.C., Canada* 49°11N 115°14W **153** J5
Elk → *Ala., U.S.A.* 34°46N 87°16W **112** B3
Elk → *Kans., U.S.A.* 37°15N 95°40W **82** E8
Elk → *Md., U.S.A.* 39°26N 76°1W **93** A4
Elk → *W. Va., U.S.A.* 38°21N 81°38W **102** C3
Elk Basin *Wyo., U.S.A.* 44°58N 108°52W **124** B4
Elk City *Idaho, U.S.A.* 45°50N 115°26W **122** D3
Elk City *Kans., U.S.A.* 37°18N 95°55W **82** D8
Elk City *Okla., U.S.A.* 35°25N 99°25W **107** C4
Elk City Lake *Kans., U.S.A.* 37°17N 95°47W **82** D8
Elk County ☆ *Kans., U.S.A.* 37°30N 96°15W **82** D7
Elk County ☆ *Pa., U.S.A.* 41°35N 78°45W **87** C4
Elk Cr. → *S. Dak., U.S.A.* 44°15N 102°22W **76** F3
Elk Creek *Calif., U.S.A.* 39°36N 122°32W **126** D4
Elk Creek *Nebr., U.S.A.* 40°17N 96°8W **80** D9
Elk Falls *Kans., U.S.A.* 37°22N 96°11W **82** D7
Elk Garden *W. Va., U.S.A.* 39°23N 79°9W **93** A1
Elk Grove *Calif., U.S.A.* 38°25N 121°22W **126** E5
Elk Hill *Pa., U.S.A.* 41°42N 75°32W **87** C7
Elk Horn *Iowa, U.S.A.* 41°36N 95°3W **81** D3
Elk Island Nat. Park △ *Alta., Canada* 53°35N 112°59W **152** E8
Elk L. *Mich., U.S.A.* 44°50N 85°20W **79** E6
Elk Lake *Ont., Canada* 47°40N 80°25W **144** D2
Elk Lakes Park △ *B.C., Canada* 50°30N 115°10W **153** H5
Elk Mound *Wis., U.S.A.* 44°52N 91°42W **78** D2
Elk Mountain *Wyo., U.S.A.* 41°41N 106°25W **124** E6
Elk Mt. *Wyo., U.S.A.* 41°38N 106°32W **124** E6
Elk Neck *Md., U.S.A.* 39°31N 75°57W **93** A5
Elk Point *Alta., Canada* 53°54N 110°55W **152** E10
Elk Point *S. Dak., U.S.A.* 42°41N 96°41W **76** H9
Elk Rapids *Mich., U.S.A.* 44°54N 85°25W **79** E6
Elk Ridge *Utah, U.S.A.* 40°1N 111°41W **129** C4
Elk River *Idaho, U.S.A.* 46°47N 116°11W **122** C2
Elk River *Minn., U.S.A.* 45°18N 93°35W **77** E5
Elk Springs *Colo., U.S.A.* 40°21N 108°27W **125** B2
Elkader *Iowa, U.S.A.* 42°51N 91°24W **81** C7
Elkford *B.C., Canada* 49°52N 114°53W **153** J6
Elkhart *Ill., U.S.A.* 40°1N 89°29W **84** C4
Elkhart *Ind., U.S.A.* 41°41N 85°58W **85** B5
Elkhart *Iowa, U.S.A.* 41°48N 93°31W **81** D5
Elkhart *Kans., U.S.A.* 37°0N 101°54W **82** D2
Elkhart *Tex., U.S.A.* 31°38N 95°35W **109** F12
Elkhart → *Ind., U.S.A.* 41°35N 85°50W **85** B5
Elkhart Lake *Wis., U.S.A.* 43°50N 88°1W **78** E5
Elkhorn *Man., Canada* 49°59N 101°14W **151** F10
Elkhorn *Nebr., U.S.A.* 41°17N 96°14W **80** C9
Elkhorn *Wis., U.S.A.* 42°40N 88°33W **78** F5
Elkhorn → *Nebr., U.S.A.* 41°8N 96°19W **80** C9
Elkhorn City *Ky., U.S.A.* 37°18N 82°21W **105** C10
Elkin *N.C., U.S.A.* 36°15N 80°51W **103** B5
Elkins *Ark., U.S.A.* 36°0N 94°0W **106** B2
Elkins *N. Mex., U.S.A.* 33°42N 104°4W **131** D6
Elkins *W. Va., U.S.A.* 38°55N 79°51W **102** C5
Elkins Park *Pa., U.S.A.* 40°4N 75°7W **98** A2
Elkland *Mo., U.S.A.* 37°27N 93°2W **83** D3
Elkland *Pa., U.S.A.* 41°59N 77°19W **87** C5
Elkmont *Ala., U.S.A.* 34°56N 86°58W **112** B4
Elko *B.C., Canada* 49°20N 115°10W **153** J5
Elko *Minn., U.S.A.* 44°34N 93°19W **77** F5
Elko *Nev., U.S.A.* 40°50N 115°46W **128** B5
Elko County ☆ *Nev., U.S.A.* 41°10N 115°20W **128** A5
Elkol *Wyo., U.S.A.* 41°43N 110°37W **124** E2
Elkridge *Baltimore, U.S.A.* 39°12N 76°42W **99** B1
Elkton *Ky., U.S.A.* 36°49N 87°9W **104** D5
Elkton *Mich., U.S.A.* 43°49N 83°11W **79** F8
Elkton *Oreg., U.S.A.* 43°38N 123°34W **121** D2
Elkton *S. Dak., U.S.A.* 44°14N 96°29W **76** F9
Elkton *Tenn., U.S.A.* 35°3N 86°53W **104** E6
Elkton *Va., U.S.A.* 38°25N 78°37W **102** C6
Elkview *W. Va., U.S.A.* 38°55N 81°40W **102** C3
Elkville *Ill., U.S.A.* 37°55N 89°14W **84** F4
Ellamore *W. Va., U.S.A.* 38°55N 80°5W **102** C4
Ellalville *Ga., U.S.A.* 32°14N 84°19W **113** D2
Ellef Ringnes I. *Nunavut, Canada* 78°30N 102°2W **158** B5
Ellenboro *W. Va., U.S.A.* 39°16N 81°3W **102** B3
Ellenburg *N.Y., U.S.A.* 44°54N 73°48W **88** A7
Ellendale *Del., U.S.A.* 38°48N 75°26W **93** B5
Ellendale *Minn., U.S.A.* 43°52N 93°18W **77** G5
Ellendale *N. Dak., U.S.A.* 46°0N 98°32W **76** D7
Ellenor, L. *Fla., U.S.A.* 28°28N 81°25W **114** B2
Ellensburg *Wash., U.S.A.* 46°59N 120°34W **120** D5
Ellenton *Ga., U.S.A.* 31°11N 83°35W **113** E3
Ellenville *N.Y., U.S.A.* 41°43N 74°24W **88** D6
Ellerbe *N.C., U.S.A.* 35°4N 79°46W **103** C6
Ellesmere I. *Nunavut, Canada* 79°30N 80°0W **158** B10
Ellesmere Island = Quttinirpaaq Nat. Park △ *Nunavut, Canada* 82°13N 72°13W **158** A11
Ellettsville *Ind., U.S.A.* 39°14N 86°38W **85** D4
Ellice → *Nunavut, Canada* 68°2N 103°58W **158** D5
Ellicott *Md., U.S.A.* 39°16N 76°48W **99** A1
Ellicottville *N.Y., U.S.A.* 42°17N 78°40W **88** C2
Ellijay *Ga., U.S.A.* 34°42N 84°29W **113** A2
Ellington *Conn., U.S.A.* 41°54N 72°28W **91** C2
Ellington *Mo., U.S.A.* 37°14N 90°58W **83** D6
Ellington *N.Y., U.S.A.* 42°13N 79°7W **88** C1
Ellinwood *Kans., U.S.A.* 38°21N 98°35W **82** C5
Elliot L. *Man., U.S.A.* 52°54N 95°18W **151** C16
Elliot Lake *Ont., Canada* 46°25N 82°35W **146** A4
Elliott *Iowa, U.S.A.* 41°9N 95°10W **81** D3
Elliott *Md., U.S.A.* 38°24N 75°59W **93** B5
Elliott *Miss., U.S.A.* 33°41N 89°45W **111** C4
Elliott County ☆ *Ky., U.S.A.* 38°5N 83°5W **105** B9
Elliott Bay *Wash., U.S.A.* 47°36N 122°21W **132** C3
Elliott Key *Fla., U.S.A.* 25°27N 80°12W **114** F8
Elliott Knob *Va., U.S.A.* 38°10N 79°19W **102** C5
Ellis *Idaho, U.S.A.* 44°42N 114°3W **122** E4
Ellis *Kans., U.S.A.* 38°56N 99°34W **82** C4
Ellis *Nebr., U.S.A.* 40°13N 96°53W **80** D9

Ellis County ☆ *Kans., U.S.A.* 38°45N 99°15W **82** C4
Ellis County ☆ *Okla., U.S.A.* 36°20N 99°50W **107** B4
Ellis County ☆ *Tex., U.S.A.* 32°24N 96°51W **109** E11
Ellis Grove *Ill., U.S.A.* 38°1N 89°55W **84** E4
Ellis I. *N.J., U.S.A.* 40°41N 74°2W **97** B2
Ellisport *Wash., U.S.A.* 47°25N 122°26W **132** D3
Elliston *Nfld. & L., Canada* 48°38N 53°3W **142** D7
Elliston *Mont., U.S.A.* 46°33N 112°26W **123** D5
Ellisville *Miss., U.S.A.* 31°36N 89°12W **111** E4
Elloree *S.C., U.S.A.* 33°32N 80°34W **103** E5
Ells → *Alta., Canada* 57°18N 111°40W **152** A9
Ellsinore *Mo., U.S.A.* 36°56N 90°45W **83** E6
Ellston *Iowa, U.S.A.* 40°51N 94°7W **81** E4
Ellsworth *Iowa, U.S.A.* 42°19N 93°35W **81** C5
Ellsworth *Kans., U.S.A.* 38°44N 98°14W **82** C5
Ellsworth *Maine, U.S.A.* 44°33N 68°25W **90** D5
Ellsworth *Mich., U.S.A.* 45°10N 85°15W **79** D6
Ellsworth *Minn., U.S.A.* 43°33N 96°1W **77** G2
Ellsworth *Nebr., U.S.A.* 42°4N 102°17W **80** B3
Ellsworth *S. Dak., U.S.A.* 44°9N 103°4W **76** F2
Ellsworth *Wis., U.S.A.* 44°44N 92°29W **78** D1
Ellsworth County ☆ *Kans., U.S.A.* 38°45N 98°15W **82** C5
Ellwood *Ont., Canada* 45°22N 75°40W **160** B2
Ellwood City *Pa., U.S.A.* 40°52N 80°17W **87** D2
Ellzey *Fla., U.S.A.* 29°19N 82°48W **114** B6
Elm → *N. Dak., U.S.A.* 47°17N 96°20W **76** C9
Elm → *S. Dak., U.S.A.* 44°21N 102°42W **76** F3
Elm City *N.C., U.S.A.* 35°48N 77°52W **103** C8
Elm Cr. → *Tex., U.S.A.* 28°42N 99°59W **109** J8
Elm Creek *Nebr., U.S.A.* 40°43N 99°22W **80** D6
Elm Fork Red → *U.S.A.* 34°53N 99°19W **107** D4
Elm Grove *Wis., U.S.A.* 43°2N 88°4W **84** B1
Elm L. *S. Dak., U.S.A.* 45°51N 98°42W **76** E7
Elma *Man., Canada* 49°52N 95°55W **151** F16
Elma *Iowa, U.S.A.* 43°15N 92°26W **81** B6
Elma *Wash., U.S.A.* 47°0N 123°25W **120** C2
Elmdale *Kans., U.S.A.* 38°22N 96°39W **82** C7
Elmendorf *Tex., U.S.A.* 29°15N 98°19W **116** D3
Elmer *Mo., U.S.A.* 39°57N 92°39W **83** B4
Elmer *N.J., U.S.A.* 39°36N 75°10W **92** C1
Elmer *Okla., U.S.A.* 34°29N 99°21W **107** D4
Elmer City *Wash., U.S.A.* 48°0N 118°58W **120** B7
Elmhurst *Ill., U.S.A.* 41°53N 87°56W **84** B6
Elmhurst *N.Y., U.S.A.* 40°44N 73°53W **97** B3
Elmira *Ont., Canada* 43°36N 80°33W **146** D6
Elmira *Idaho, U.S.A.* 48°29N 116°27W **122** A2
Elmira *Mich., U.S.A.* 45°4N 84°51W **79** D7
Elmira *N.Y., U.S.A.* 42°6N 76°48W **88** C4
Elmira Heights *N.Y., U.S.A.* 42°8N 76°50W **88** C4
Elmo *Kans., U.S.A.* 38°41N 97°14W **82** C6
Elmo *Mont., U.S.A.* 47°50N 114°21W **123** C3
Elmo *Utah, U.S.A.* 39°23N 110°49W **129** D5
Elmo *Va., U.S.A.* 36°41N 79°7W **102** E5
Elmodel *Ga., U.S.A.* 31°21N 84°29W **113** E2
Elmont *N.Y., U.S.A.* 40°42N 73°42W **97** B4
Elmore *Ala., U.S.A.* 32°32N 86°19W **112** D4
Elmore *Minn., U.S.A.* 43°30N 94°5W **77** G4
Elmore City *Okla., U.S.A.* 34°37N 97°24W **107** D6
Elmore County ☆ *Ala., U.S.A.* 32°32N 86°51W **112** D4
Elmore County ☆ *Idaho, U.S.A.* 43°30N 115°30W **122** F3
Elmsdale *N.S., Canada* 44°58N 63°30W **141** J6
Elmvale *Ont., Canada* 44°35N 79°52W **146** C7
Elmwood *Ill., U.S.A.* 40°47N 89°58W **84** C4
Elmwood *Nebr., U.S.A.* 40°50N 96°18W **80** D8
Elmwood *Okla., U.S.A.* 36°37N 100°31W **107** B3
Elmwood *Wis., U.S.A.* 44°47N 92°9W **78** D1
Elmwood Park *Ill., U.S.A.* 41°55N 87°48W **92** B6
Elmwood Park *N.J., U.S.A.* 40°54N 74°7W **97** A2
Elmworth *Alta., Canada* 55°3N 119°37W **152** C1
Elnora *Alta., Canada* 51°59N 113°12W **153** G7
Elnora *Ind., U.S.A.* 38°53N 87°5W **85** E3
Elora *Ont., Canada* 43°41N 80°26W **146** D6
Elora *Tenn., U.S.A.* 35°1N 86°21W **104** E6
Eloxochitlán *Puebla, Mexico* 18°31N 96°57W **177** F4
Eloy *Ariz., U.S.A.* 32°45N 111°33W **130** E4
Elphin *Ont., Canada* 44°55N 76°37W **147** C10
Elphinstone *Man., Canada* 50°32N 100°30W **151** E11
Elrosa *Minn., U.S.A.* 45°34N 94°57W **77** E4
Elrose *Sask., Canada* 51°12N 108°0W **150** D3
Elroy *Wis., U.S.A.* 43°45N 90°16W **78** E3
Elsa *Tex., U.S.A.* 26°18N 97°59W **108** L10
Elsah *Ill., U.S.A.* 38°57N 90°21W **84** D3
Elsas *Ont., Canada* 48°32N 82°55W **149** D14
Elsberry *Mo., U.S.A.* 39°10N 90°47W **83** B6
Elsie *Mich., U.S.A.* 43°6N 84°23W **79** F7
Elsie *Nebr., U.S.A.* 40°51N 101°23W **80** D4
Elsinore *Utah, U.S.A.* 38°41N 112°9W **129** E3
Elsinore, L. *Calif., U.S.A.* 33°40N 117°21W **127** K9
Elsmere *Del., U.S.A.* 39°44N 75°35W **93** A5
Elsmere *Nebr., U.S.A.* 42°10N 100°11W **80** B5
Elsworth, L. *Okla., U.S.A.* 34°49N 98°22W **107** D5
Eltinville *N.Y., U.S.A.* 40°33N 74°10W **97** C1
Elton *La., U.S.A.* 30°29N 92°42W **110** D4
Eltopia *Wash., U.S.A.* 46°27N 119°1W **120** D6
Elu Inlet *Nunavut, Canada* 68°30N 106°5W **158** D4
Elverson *Pa., U.S.A.* 40°9N 75°50W **87** D7
Elwell, L. = Tiber Res. *Mont., U.S.A.* 48°19N 111°6W **123** B6
Elwood *Ill., U.S.A.* 41°24N 88°7W **84** B5
Elwood *Ind., U.S.A.* 40°17N 85°50W **85** C5
Elwood *Kans., U.S.A.* 39°45N 94°52W **82** B9
Elwood *Nebr., U.S.A.* 40°35N 99°52W **80** D6
Elwood *Res. *Nebr., U.S.A.* 40°34N 99°55W **80** D6
Ely *Iowa, U.S.A.* 41°52N 91°35W **81** D7
Ely *Minn., U.S.A.* 47°54N 91°52W **77** C7
Ely *Nev., U.S.A.* 39°15N 114°54W **128** C6
Elyria *Kans., U.S.A.* 38°26N 97°38W **82** C6
Elyria *Nebr., U.S.A.* 41°41N 99°0W **80** C7
Elyria *Ohio, U.S.A.* 41°22N 82°7W **86** B4
Emanuel County ☆ *Ga., U.S.A.* 32°40N 82°20W **113** D4
Embarras → *Ill., U.S.A.* 38°39N 87°37W **84** E1
Embarrass *Wis., U.S.A.* 44°40N 88°42W **78** E4
Emblem *Wyo., U.S.A.* 44°30N 108°23W **124** B4
Embro *Ont., Canada* 43°9N 80°54W **146** D6
Emden *Ill., U.S.A.* 40°18N 89°29W **84** C4
Emelle *Ala., U.S.A.* 32°44N 88°19W **112** D2
Emerado *N. Dak., U.S.A.* 47°55N 97°21W **76** C8
Emerald I. *N.W.T., Canada* 76°48N 114°10W **156** A10
Emerald Isle *N.C., U.S.A.* 34°41N 76°57W **103** D9
Emeril *Québec, Canada* 52°47N 66°17W **142** A4
Emerson *Man., Canada* 49°0N 97°10W **151** F14
Emerson *Ark., U.S.A.* 33°6N 93°11W **106** E2
Emerson *Ga., U.S.A.* 34°8N 84°45W **113** B2
Emerson *Nebr., U.S.A.* 42°17N 96°44W **80** B9

Emerson L. *Calif., U.S.A.* 34°27N 116°23W **127** J10
Emery *S. Dak., U.S.A.* 43°36N 97°37W **76** G8
Emery *Utah, U.S.A.* 38°55N 111°15W **129** E4
Emery County ☆ *Utah, U.S.A.* 39°0N 110°45W **129** D4
Emeryville *Calif., U.S.A.* 37°49N 122°17W **132** A3
Emigrant Gap *Calif., U.S.A.* 39°19N 120°38W **126** D6
Emigrant Pass *Nev., U.S.A.* 40°39N 116°16W **128** B4
Emiliano Martínez *Durango, Mexico* 25°26N 105°14W **172** B5
Emiliano Zapata *Chiapas, Mexico* 17°45N 91°46W **178** B5
Emiliano Zapata *Chihuahua, Mexico* 31°35N 106°28W **169** B9
Emiliano Zapata *Coahuila, Mexico* 25°29N 102°56W **170** E2
Emiliano Zapata *Veracruz, Mexico* 20°21N 97°9W **176** D3
Emiliano Zapata *Yucatán, Mexico* 20°13N 89°28W **179** F4
Emilio Carranza *Durango, Mexico* 25°15N 103°55W **173** B7
Emilio Carranza *Veracruz, Mexico* 19°58N 96°35W **176** E4
Emilio Hernández *Hidalgo, Mexico* 20°32N 98°59W **175** B9
Emilio Portes Gil, Presa *Tamaulipas, Mexico* 22°58N 98°46W **171** H6
Emily *Minn. U.S.A.* 46°44N 93°58W **77** D5
Eminence *Mo., U.S.A.* 37°9N 91°21W **83** D5
Eminence *Ky., U.S.A.* 38°22N 85°11W **105** B7
Emiquon Nat. Wildlife Refuge △ *Ill., U.S.A.* 40°20N 90°7W **84** C3
Emlenton *Pa., U.S.A.* 41°11N 79°43W **87** C3
Emmalane *Ga., U.S.A.* 32°46N 82°0W **113** D5
Emmaus *Pa., U.S.A.* 40°32N 75°30W **92** B1
Emmet *Ark., U.S.A.* 33°44N 93°28W **106** E2
Emmet *Nebr., U.S.A.* 42°29N 98°49W **80** B7
Emmet County ☆ *Iowa, U.S.A.* 43°20N 94°41W **81** A4
Emmet County ☆ *Mich., U.S.A.* 45°30N 84°55W **79** D7
Emmetsburg *Iowa, U.S.A.* 43°7N 94°41W **81** B4
Emmett *Idaho, U.S.A.* 43°52N 116°30W **122** F2
Emmett *Kans., U.S.A.* 39°19N 96°3W **82** B7
Emmett *Mich., U.S.A.* 42°59N 82°46W **79** G9
Emmitsburg *Md., U.S.A.* 39°42N 77°20W **93** A3
Emmonak *Alaska, U.S.A.* 62°47N 164°31W **135** E6
Emmons *Minn., U.S.A.* 43°30N 93°29W **77** G5
Emmons County ☆ *N. Dak., U.S.A.* 46°20N 100°10W **76** D5
Emmorton *Md., U.S.A.* 39°30N 76°20W **93** A4
Emo *Ont., Canada* 48°38N 93°50W **148** D3
Emory *Tex., U.S.A.* 32°52N 95°46W **109** E12
Emory → *Tenn., U.S.A.* 35°53N 84°30W **105** E8
Emory Peak *Tex., U.S.A.* 29°15N 103°18W **108** H4
Empalme *Sonora, Mexico* 27°58N 110°51W **168** F5
Empire *Calif., U.S.A.* 37°38N 120°54W **126** F6
Empire *Colo., U.S.A.* 39°46N 105°41W **125** C5
Empire *Ga., U.S.A.* 32°21N 83°18W **113** D3
Empire *La., U.S.A.* 29°23N 89°36W **110** E6
Empire *Mich., U.S.A.* 44°49N 86°4W **79** E5
Empire *Nev., U.S.A.* 40°35N 119°21W **128** B1
Empire City *Okla., U.S.A.* 34°25N 98°2W **107** D5
Empire Res. *Colo., U.S.A.* 40°16N 104°12W **125** B6
Emporia *Kans., U.S.A.* 38°25N 96°11W **82** C7
Emporia *Va., U.S.A.* 36°42N 77°32W **102** E7
Emporium *Pa., U.S.A.* 41°31N 78°14W **87** C4
Empress *Alta., Canada* 50°57N 110°0W **153** H10
Emsdale *Ont., Canada* 45°32N 79°19W **144** F3
Emsworth *Pa., U.S.A.* 40°30N 80°5W **98** A1
Encampment *Wyo., U.S.A.* 41°12N 106°47W **124** E6
Encantada, *L. Baja Calif., Mexico* 30°0N 114°0W **166** D4
Encanto *Calif., U.S.A.* 32°42N 117°2W **133** B2
Encarnación de Díaz *Jalisco, Mexico* 21°31N 102°14W **174** A5
Encinal *Tex., U.S.A.* 28°2N 99°21W **109** J8
Encinillas, *L. Chihuahua, Mexico* 29°29N 106°20W **169** D9
Encinitas *Calif., U.S.A.* 33°3N 117°17W **127** K9
Encino *Calif., U.S.A.* 34°9N 118°28W **133** B2
Encino *N. Mex., U.S.A.* 34°39N 105°28W **131** C6
Encino *Tex., U.S.A.* 26°56N 98°8W **108** L9
Encino Res. *Calif., U.S.A.* 34°8N 118°30W **133** B1
Endako *B.C., Canada* 54°6N 125°2W **154** A9
Endeavor *Wis., U.S.A.* 43°43N 89°28W **78** E4
Endeavour *Sask., Canada* 52°10N 102°39W **150** C9
Enderby *B.C., Canada* 50°35N 119°10W **155** E15
Enderlin *N. Dak., U.S.A.* 46°38N 97°36W **76** D8
Enders *Nebr., U.S.A.* 40°27N 101°32W **80** D4
Enders Res. *Nebr., U.S.A.* 40°25N 101°31W **80** D4
Endicott *Nebr., U.S.A.* 42°6N 97°6W **88** C4
Endicott *Wash., U.S.A.* 46°56N 117°41W **120** D8
Endicott Mts. *Alaska, U.S.A.* 68°0N 152°0W **135** C9
Endwell *N.Y., U.S.A.* 42°6N 76°2W **88** C4
Enfield *N.S., Canada* 44°56N 63°32W **141** J6
Enfield *Conn., U.S.A.* 41°58N 72°36W **91** C2
Enfield *Ill., U.S.A.* 38°6N 88°20W **84** E5
Enfield *N.H., U.S.A.* 43°39N 72°9W **89** C2
Enfield *N.C., U.S.A.* 36°11N 77°41W **103** B8
Enfield Center *N.H., U.S.A.* 43°38N 72°8W **89** C2
Engadine *Mich., U.S.A.* 46°7N 85°34W **79** C6
Engaño, C. *Dom. Rep.* 18°30N 68°20W **183** C6
England *Ark., U.S.A.* 34°33N 91°58W **106** D4
Engle *N. Mex., U.S.A.* 33°4N 107°2W **131** D3
Englebright L. *Calif., U.S.A.* 39°14N 121°16W **126** D5
Englee *Nfld. & L., Canada* 50°45N 56°5W **142** B4
Englefield *Sask., Canada* 52°10N 104°39W **150** C7
Englefield, C. *N.W.T., Canada* 69°49N 85°34W **158** D8
Englehart *Ont., Canada* 47°49N 79°52W **144** D3
Englewood *Colo., U.S.A.* 39°38N 104°59W **134** C1
Englewood *Fla., U.S.A.* 26°58N 82°21W **114** E6
Englewood *Ill., U.S.A.* 41°46N 87°38W **95** C3
Englewood *Kans., U.S.A.* 37°2N 99°59W **82** D4
Englewood *N.J., U.S.A.* 40°54N 73°58W **97** A3
Englewood *Ohio, U.S.A.* 39°53N 84°18W **86** D2
Englewood *Tenn., U.S.A.* 35°26N 84°29W **105** E8
Englewood Cliffs *N.J., U.S.A.* 40°53N 73°59W **97** A3
English *Ind., U.S.A.* 38°20N 86°28W **85** E4
English → *Ont., Canada* 49°12N 91°5W **148** C5
English Bazar *Nfld. & L., Canada* 49°17N 123°10W **161** B2
English Creek *N.J., U.S.A.* 39°24N 74°42W **92** C2
English Harbour East *Nfld. & L., Canada* 47°39N 54°53W **142** D6
English River *Ont., Canada* 49°14N 91°0W **148** C6
English Turn *La., U.S.A.* 29°53N 89°27W **117** C3
Englishtown *N.J., U.S.A.* 40°18N 74°22W **92** B2
Enid *Miss., U.S.A.* 34°7N 89°56W **111** B4
Enid *Okla., U.S.A.* 36°24N 97°53W **107** B6
Enid L. *Miss., U.S.A.* 34°9N 89°54W **111** B4
Enilda *Alta., Canada* 55°25N 116°16W **152** C4
Enloe *Tex., U.S.A.* 33°26N 95°39W **109** D12
Ennadai L. *Nunavut, Canada* 60°58N 101°20W **159** E5
Ennis *Mont., U.S.A.* 45°21N 111°44W **123** E6
Ennis *Tex., U.S.A.* 32°20N 96°38W **109** E11
Ennis L. *Mont., U.S.A.* 45°26N 111°44W **123** E6
Enoch *Utah, U.S.A.* 37°47N 113°2W **129** F2
Enochs *Tex., U.S.A.* 33°52N 102°46W **108** D5
Enola *Nebr., U.S.A.* 41°54N 97°28W **80** C8
Enoree → *S.C., U.S.A.* 34°26N 81°52W **103** D4

Enosburg Falls *Vt., U.S.A.* 44°55N 72°48W **89** B2
Enriquillo *Dom. Rep.* 18°20N 71°57W **183** C5
Enriquillo, L. *Dom. Rep.* 18°20N 72°5W **183** C5
Ensenada *Baja Calif., Mexico* 31°52N 116°37W **166** B2
Ensenada *N. Mex., U.S.A.* 36°44N 106°32W **131** A4
Ensenada de los Muertos *Baja Calif. S., Mexico* 23°59N 109°51W **167** K9
Ensign *Kans., U.S.A.* 37°39N 100°14W **82** D2
Ensley *Fla., U.S.A.* 30°31N 87°16W **114** A1
Enterprise *N.W.T., Canada* 60°47N 115°45W **157** D9
Enterprise *Ala., U.S.A.* 31°19N 85°51W **112** E5
Enterprise *Kans., U.S.A.* 38°54N 97°7W **82** C6
Enterprise *La., U.S.A.* 31°54N 91°53W **110** C4
Enterprise *Miss., U.S.A.* 32°10N 88°49W **111** D5
Enterprise *Nev., U.S.A.* 36°13N 115°14W **134** C1
Enterprise *Oreg., U.S.A.* 45°25N 117°17W **121** B8
Enterprise *Utah, U.S.A.* 37°34N 113°43W **129** F2
Entiako → *B.C., Canada* 53°13N 125°31W **154** B9
Entiako Park ← *B.C., Canada* 53°15N 125°26W **154** B9
Entiat *Wash., U.S.A.* 47°40N 120°13W **120** C5
Enumclaw *Wash., U.S.A.* 47°12N 121°59W **120** C4
Eolia *Mo., U.S.A.* 39°14N 91°1W **83** B5
Eoline *Ala., U.S.A.* 32°59N 87°8W **112** D3
Epatlán *Puebla, Mexico* 18°38N 98°22W **177** F2
Epazoyucan *Hidalgo, Mexico* 20°2N 98°38W **175** B9
Epes *Ala., U.S.A.* 32°42N 88°7W **112** D2
Ephraim *Utah, U.S.A.* 39°22N 111°35W **129** D4
Ephrata *Pa., U.S.A.* 40°11N 76°11W **87** D6
Ephrata *Wash., U.S.A.* 47°19N 119°33W **120** C6
Epleys *Ky., U.S.A.* 36°56N 86°56W **104** D6
Epping *N. Dak., U.S.A.* 48°17N 103°21W **76** B2
Epping *N.H., U.S.A.* 43°2N 71°4W **89** C3
Eppley Airfield, Omaha ✈ (OMA) *Nebr., U.S.A.* 41°18N 95°53W **80** C10
Epps *La., U.S.A.* 32°36N 91°29W **110** B4
Epworth *Iowa, U.S.A.* 42°27N 90°56W **81** C8
Equality *Ill., U.S.A.* 37°44N 88°20W **84** E5
Equinox Mt. *Vt., U.S.A.* 43°11N 73°9W **89** C1
Erath *La., U.S.A.* 29°58N 92°2W **110** E3
Erath County ☆ *Tex., U.S.A.* 32°13N 98°12W **109** E9
Erbacon *W. Va., U.S.A.* 38°31N 80°35W **102** C4
Erda *Utah, U.S.A.* 40°37N 112°18W **129** C3
Eréndira *Baja Calif., Mexico* 31°17N 116°22W **166** B2
Erhard *Minn., U.S.A.* 46°29N 96°6W **77** D2
Éric L. *Qué., Canada* 51°55N 65°36W **140** B4
Erichsen L. *Nunavut, Canada* 70°40N 80°41W **158** C9
Erick *Okla., U.S.A.* 35°13N 99°52W **107** C4
Erickson *Man., Canada* 50°30N 99°55W **151** E12
Ericson *Nebr., U.S.A.* 41°47N 98°41W **80** C7
Eridu *Fla., U.S.A.* 30°18N 83°45W **114** A5
Erie *Colo., U.S.A.* 40°3N 105°3W **125** B5
Erie *Ill., U.S.A.* 41°39N 90°5W **84** B3
Erie *Kans., U.S.A.* 37°34N 95°15W **82** D8
Erie *N. Dak., U.S.A.* 47°7N 97°22W **76** C8
Erie *Pa., U.S.A.* 42°8N 80°5W **87** B2
Erie, L. *N. Amer.* 42°15N 81°0W **146** E5
Erie Canal *N.Y., U.S.A.* 43°5N 78°43W **88** B2
Erie County ☆ *N.Y., U.S.A.* 42°50N 78°45W **88** C2
Erie County ☆ *Ohio, U.S.A.* 41°24N 82°33W **86** B4
Erie County ☆ *Pa., U.S.A.* 42°0N 80°0W **87** C2
Erie Nat. Wildlife Refuge △ *Pa., U.S.A.* 41°36N 79°58W **87** C3
Erieau *Ont., Canada* 42°16N 81°57W **146** E5
Eriksdale *Man., Canada* 50°52N 98°7W **151** E13
Erin *Ont., Canada* 43°45N 80°7W **146** D6
Erin *Tenn., U.S.A.* 36°19N 87°42W **104** D5
Erin Springs *Okla., U.S.A.* 34°49N 97°36W **107** D6
Erlandson, L. *Qué., Canada* 57°3N 68°28W **143** B4
Erlanger *Ky., U.S.A.* 39°1N 84°36W **105** A8
Erling, L. *Ark., U.S.A.* 33°3N 93°32W **106** E2
Erongarícuaro *Michoacan, Mexico* 19°35N 101°43W **174** C6
Errol *N.H., U.S.A.* 44°47N 71°9W **89** B3
Errol Heights *Oreg., U.S.A.* 45°28N 122°36W **132** B2
Erskine *Alta., Canada* 52°20N 112°53W **153** F8
Erskine *Minn., U.S.A.* 47°40N 96°0W **77** C2
Erving *Mass., U.S.A.* 42°36N 72°24W **91** B2
Erwin *N.C., U.S.A.* 35°20N 78°41W **103** C7
Erwin *S. Dak., U.S.A.* 44°29N 97°27W **76** F8
Erwin *Tenn., U.S.A.* 36°9N 82°25W **105** D10
Erwinville *La., U.S.A.* 30°32N 91°24W **110** D4
Esbon *Kans., U.S.A.* 39°49N 98°26W **82** B5
Escalante *Utah, U.S.A.* 37°47N 111°36W **129** F4
Escalante → *Utah, U.S.A.* 37°24N 110°57W **129** F5
Escalante Desert *Utah, U.S.A.* 37°50N 113°20W **129** F2
Escalón *Chihuahua, Mexico* 26°45N 104°20W **169** G11
Escalon *Calif., U.S.A.* 37°48N 121°0W **126** F6
Escambia → *Fla., U.S.A.* 30°32N 87°11W **114** A1
Escambia County ☆ *Ala., U.S.A.* 31°7N 87°4W **112** E3
Escambia County ☆ *Fla., U.S.A.* 30°30N 87°14W **114** A1
Escanaba *Mich., U.S.A.* 45°45N 87°4W **79** D4
Escanaba → *Mich., U.S.A.* 45°47N 87°3W **79** D4
Escárcega *Campeche, Mexico* 18°37N 90°43W **179** D3
Escatawpa → *Miss., U.S.A.* 30°26N 88°33W **111** E5
Escobedo *Coahuila, Mexico* 29°16N 102°9W **170** A2
Escobedo *Guanajuato, Mexico* 20°39N 100°45W **175** B7
Escondido *Calif., U.S.A.* 33°7N 117°5W **127** K9
Escondido → *Quintana Roo, Mexico* 18°30N 88°35W **179** D5
Escuinapa de Hidalgo *Sinaloa, Mexico* 22°50N 105°50W **172** E5
Escuintla *Guatemala* 14°20N 90°48W **182** D1
Escuintla *Chiapas, Mexico* 15°20N 92°38W **178** D3
Eskasoni *N.S., Canada* 45°56N 60°36W **141** H9
Esker *Nfld. & L., Canada* 53°53N 66°25W **143** C4
Eskimo Lakes *N.W.T., Canada* 69°15N 132°17W **156** D6
Eskimo Point = Arviat *Nunavut, Canada* 61°6N 93°59W **159** E7
Eskridge *Kans., U.S.A.* 38°52N 96°6W **82** C7
Esmeralda County ☆ *Nev., U.S.A.* 37°50N 117°45W **128** E3
Esmond *N. Dak., U.S.A.* 48°2N 99°46W **76** B6
Esnagami L. *Ont., Canada* 50°19N 86°51W **149** B10
Esnagi L. *Ont., Canada* 48°36N 84°33W **149** C12
Esom Hill *Ga., U.S.A.* 33°57N 85°23W **113** C1
Españita *Tlaxcala, Mexico* 19°28N 98°24W **175** C9
Espanola *Ont., Canada* 46°15N 81°46W **146** A5
Espanola *Fla., U.S.A.* 29°31N 81°19W **114** B7
Espanola *N. Mex., U.S.A.* 35°59N 106°5W **131** B4
Esparta *Costa Rica* 9°59N 84°40W **182** E3
Esparto *Calif., U.S.A.* 38°42N 122°1W **126** E4
Espenberg, C. *Alaska, U.S.A.* 66°33N 163°36W **135** C7
Esperanza *B.C., Canada* 49°52N 126°43W **154** F8
Esperanza *Puebla, Mexico* 18°52N 97°24W **177** F3
Esperanza *Sonora, Mexico* 27°35N 109°56W **168** F6
Esperanza *Puerto Rico* 18°6N 65°28W **184** G17
Esperanza Inlet *B.C., Canada* 49°51N 126°55W **154** F8
Espinazo *Nuevo León, Mexico* 26°16N 101°6W **170** D3
Espíritu Santo *Zacatecas, Mexico* 22°36N 101°27W **173** E9
Espíritu Santo, B. del *Quintana Roo, Mexico* 19°20N 87°35W **179** C6

Espíritu Santo, I. *Baja Calif. S., Mexico* 24°30N 110°22W **167** J8
Espita *Yucatán, Mexico* 21°1N 88°19W **179** A5
Esqueda *Sonora, Mexico* 30°46N 109°31W **168** C6
Esquimalt *B.C., Canada* 48°26N 123°25W **155** G11
Essex *Ont., Canada* 42°10N 82°49W **146** E4
Essex *Calif., U.S.A.* 34°44N 115°15W **127** J11
Essex *Conn., U.S.A.* 41°21N 72°24W **91** C2
Essex *Ill., U.S.A.* 41°11N 88°11W **84** B5
Essex *Iowa, U.S.A.* 40°50N 95°18W **81** E3
Essex *Md., U.S.A.* 39°19N 76°29W **93** A4
Essex *Mo., U.S.A.* 36°50N 89°8W **83** E7
Essex *Mont., U.S.A.* 48°17N 113°37W **123** B4
Essex *N.Y., U.S.A.* 44°19N 73°21W **89** B1
Essex County ☆ *Mass., U.S.A.* 42°35N 70°50W **91** B4
Essex County ☆ *N.J., U.S.A.* 40°45N 74°15W **92** B2
Essex County ☆ *N.Y., U.S.A.* 44°0N 73°40W **88** A7
Essex County ☆ *Va., U.S.A.* 37°56N 76°52W **102** D8
Essex County ☆ *Vt., U.S.A.* 44°45N 71°45W **89** B3
Essex Fells *N.J., U.S.A.* 40°49N 74°17W **92** B2
Essex Junction *Vt., U.S.A.* 44°29N 73°7W **89** B1
Essexville *Mich., U.S.A.* 43°37N 83°50W **79** F8
Est, Î. de l' *Qué., Canada* 47°37N 61°23W **141** F8
Estacada *Oreg., U.S.A.* 45°17N 122°20W **121** B3
Estación Bamoa *Sinaloa, Mexico* 25°42N 108°21W **172** B2
Estación Camacho *Zacatecas, Mexico* 24°25N 102°18W **173** C8
Estación Catorce *San Luis Potosí, Mexico* 23°41N 100°58W **171** G4
Estación Charcas *San Luis Potosí, Mexico* 23°7N 101°2W **171** G3
Estación Colonias *Chihuahua, Mexico* 29°12N 105°22W **169** D10
Estación Conchos *Chihuahua, Mexico* 27°57N 105°18W **169** F10
Estación Gutiérrez *Zacatecas, Mexico* 23°28N 102°46W **173** D8
Estación Huehuetán *Chiapas, Mexico* 15°1N 92°24W **178** D3
Estación la Colorada *Zacatecas, Mexico* 23°47N 102°24W **173** D8
Estación Macuspana *Tabasco, Mexico* 17°38N 92°32W **178** B4
Estación Marte *Coahuila, Mexico* 25°42N 101°45W **170** E3
Estación Pacheco *Zacatecas, Mexico* 24°0N 102°28W **173** D8
Estación Ruiz *Nayarit, Mexico* 21°56N 105°9W **172** F5
Estación Simón *Durango, Mexico* 24°42N 102°35W **173** C8
Estación Vanegas *San Luis Potosí, Mexico* 23°52N 100°57W **171** G4
Estancia *N. Mex., U.S.A.* 34°46N 106°4W **131** C4
Estanque de Norias *Coahuila, Mexico* 26°29N 101°35W **170** D3
Estanque del León *Coahuila, Mexico* 26°5N 102°12W **170** D2
Estanzuela *Monterrey, Mexico* 25°36N 100°14W **180** C2
Este, Parque Nac. del △ *Dom. Rep.* 18°14N 68°42W **183** C6
Estelí *Nic.* 13°9N 86°22W **182** D2
Estelle *La., U.S.A.* 29°50N 90°6W **117** C2
Estelline *S. Dak., U.S.A.* 44°35N 96°54W **76** F9
Estelline *Tex., U.S.A.* 34°33N 100°26W **108** C7
Estellville *N.J., U.S.A.* 39°23N 74°45W **92** C2
Esterhazy *Sask., Canada* 50°37N 102°5W **151** E9
Estero *Fla., U.S.A.* 26°26N 81°49W **114** E7
Estes Park *Colo., U.S.A.* 40°23N 105°31W **125** B5
Estevan *Sask., Canada* 49°10N 102°59W **150** F9
Estevan Group *B.C., Canada* 53°3N 129°38W **154** B5
Estevan Sd. *B.C., Canada* 53°5N 129°34W **154** B5
Estherville *Iowa, U.S.A.* 43°24N 94°50W **81** A4
Estherwood *La., U.S.A.* 30°11N 92°28W **110** D3
Estill *S.C., U.S.A.* 32°45N 81°15W **103** F4
Estill County ☆ *Ky., U.S.A.* 37°40N 84°0W **105** C9
Estill Springs *Tenn., U.S.A.* 35°16N 86°8W **104** E6
Estrecho, Pta. el *Jalisco, Mexico* 19°20N 104°47W **174** D3
Estrella, Pta. *Baja Calif., Mexico* 30°57N 114°45W **166** C4
Étamamiou *Qué., Canada* 50°18N 59°59W **143** C6
Étang-du-Nord, L. *Qué., Canada* 47°22N 61°57W **141** F8
Etchison *Md., U.S.A.* 39°15N 77°9W **93** A3
Etchojoa *Sonora, Mexico* 26°55N 109°38W **168** G6
Ethan *S. Dak., U.S.A.* 43°33N 97°59W **76** G8
Ethel *La., U.S.A.* 30°47N 91°8W **110** D4
Ethel *Miss., U.S.A.* 33°7N 89°28W **111** C4
Ethel *Mo., U.S.A.* 39°54N 92°45W **83** B4
Ethelbert *Man., Canada* 51°32N 100°25W **151** D11
Ethelsville *Ala., U.S.A.* 33°25N 88°13W **112** C2
Ethete *Wyo., U.S.A.* 43°2N 108°46W **124** C4
Ethridge *Mont., U.S.A.* 48°34N 112°8W **123** B5
Ethridge *Tenn., U.S.A.* 35°19N 87°18W **104** E5
Etna *Calif., U.S.A.* 41°27N 122°54W **126** B4
Etna *Maine, U.S.A.* 44°49N 69°7W **90** D4
Etna *Pa., U.S.A.* 40°30N 79°56W **98** B2
Etna *Utah, U.S.A.* 41°40N 113°58W **129** B2
Etna *Wyo., U.S.A.* 43°5N 111°0W **124** D2
Etobicoke *Ont., Canada* 43°39N 79°34W **161** B1
Etobicoke Cr. → *Ont., Canada* 43°35N 79°32W **161** B1
Etolin Strait *Alaska, U.S.A.* 60°20N 165°15W **135** F6
Eton *Ga., U.S.A.* 34°50N 84°46W **113** B2
Etowah *Tenn., U.S.A.* 35°20N 84°32W **105** E8
Etowah → *Ga., U.S.A.* 34°15N 85°10W **113** B1
Etowah County ☆ *Ala., U.S.A.* 34°0N 86°0W **112** B5
Etta *Miss., U.S.A.* 34°28N 89°14W **111** B4
Etter *Tex., U.S.A.* 36°3N 101°59W **108** A6
Ettrick *Wis., U.S.A.* 44°10N 91°16W **78** D2
Etzatlán *Jalisco, Mexico* 20°46N 104°5W **174** B3
Etzikom *Alta., Canada* 49°29N 111°6W **153** J9
Etzná-Tixmucuy = Edzná *Campeche, Mexico* 19°39N 90°19W **179** C3
Eubank *Ky., U.S.A.* 37°17N 84°40W **105** C8
Euclid *Ohio, U.S.A.* 41°34N 81°32W **86** B5
Eudistes, L. des *Qué., Canada* 50°30N 65°15W **140** C4
Eudora *Ark., U.S.A.* 33°7N 91°16W **106** E4
Eudora *Kans., U.S.A.* 38°57N 95°6W **82** C8
Eufaula *Ala., U.S.A.* 31°54N 85°9W **112** E5
Eufaula *Okla., U.S.A.* 35°17N 95°35W **107** C8
Eufaula L. *Okla., U.S.A.* 35°18N 95°21W **107** C8
Eugene *Mo., U.S.A.* 38°21N 92°24W **83** C4
Eugene *Oreg., U.S.A.* 44°5N 123°4W **121** C2
Euless *Tex., U.S.A.* 32°51N 97°5W **116** A3
Eulonia *Ga., U.S.A.* 31°32N 81°26W **113** E5
Eunice *La., U.S.A.* 30°30N 92°25W **110** D3
Eunice *N. Mex., U.S.A.* 32°26N 103°10W **131** E7
Eupora *Miss., U.S.A.* 33°32N 89°16W **111** C4
Eureka *Nunavut, Canada* 80°0N 85°56W **158** A10
Eureka *Calif., U.S.A.* 40°47N 124°9W **126** C2
Eureka *Ill., U.S.A.* 40°43N 89°16W **84** C4
Eureka *Kans., U.S.A.* 37°49N 96°17W **82** D7
Eureka *Mont., U.S.A.* 48°53N 115°3W **123** B2
Eureka *Nev., U.S.A.* 39°31N 115°58W **128** C5
Eureka *S. Dak., U.S.A.* 45°46N 99°38W **76** E6
Eureka *Utah, U.S.A.* 39°58N 112°7W **129** D3
Eureka *Wash., U.S.A.* 46°18N 118°37W **120** D7
Eureka County ☆ *Nev., U.S.A.* 40°0N 116°10W **128** C4
Eureka Mill *S.C., U.S.A.* 34°43N 81°12W **103** D4
Eureka River *Alta., Canada* 56°27N 118°44W **152** B2
Eureka Sd. *Nunavut, Canada* 79°0N 85°0W **158** B8
Eureka Springs *Ark., U.S.A.* 36°24N 93°44W **106** B2

Eureka Valley *Calif., U.S.A.* 37°7N 117°42W **127** F9
Eustis *Fla., U.S.A.* 28°51N 81°41W **114** C7
Eustis *Maine, U.S.A.* 45°13N 70°29W **90** C3
Eustis *Nebr., U.S.A.* 40°40N 100°2W **80** D5
Eustis, L. *Fla., U.S.A.* 28°55N 81°44W **114** C7
Eutaw *Ala., U.S.A.* 32°50N 87°53W **112** D3
Eutawville *S.C., U.S.A.* 33°24N 80°21W **103** E5
Eutimias *Coahuila, Mexico* 28°19N 102°45W **170** B2
Eutsuk L. *B.C., Canada* 53°20N 126°45W **154** B8
Eva *Ala., U.S.A.* 34°20N 86°46W **112** B4
Evadale *Tex., U.S.A.* 30°21N 94°5W **109** G13
Évain *Qué., Canada* 48°14N 79°9W **144** C3
Evan *Minn., U.S.A.* 44°21N 94°50W **77** F4
Evangeline *La., U.S.A.* 30°16N 92°34W **110** D3
Evangeline Parish ☆ *La., U.S.A.* 30°47N 92°25W **110** D3
Evans *Colo., U.S.A.* 40°23N 104°41W **125** B6
Evans *La., U.S.A.* 30°59N 93°30W **110** D2
Evans, L. *Qué., Canada* 50°50N 77°0W **143** C7
Evans, Mt. *Colo., U.S.A.* 39°35N 105°39W **125** C5
Evans City *Pa., U.S.A.* 40°46N 80°4W **87** D2
Evans County ☆ *Ga., U.S.A.* 32°10N 81°55W **113** D5
Evans Str. *Nunavut, Canada* 63°15N 82°0W **159** E9
Evansburg *Alta., Canada* 53°36N 114°59W **152** E6
Evansdale *Iowa, U.S.A.* 42°30N 92°17W **81** C6
Evanston *Ill., U.S.A.* 42°3N 87°40W **95** A2
Evanston *Ky., U.S.A.* 37°28N 83°2W **105** C9
Evanston *Wyo., U.S.A.* 41°16N 110°58W **124** E2
Evansville *Ark., U.S.A.* 35°48N 94°30W **106** C1
Evansville *Ill., U.S.A.* 38°5N 89°56W **84** E4
Evansville *Ind., U.S.A.* 37°58N 87°35W **85** F3
Evansville *Minn., U.S.A.* 46°0N 95°41W **77** D3
Evansville *Wis., U.S.A.* 42°47N 89°18W **78** F4
Evansville *Wyo., U.S.A.* 42°52N 106°16W **124** D6
Evant *Tex., U.S.A.* 31°29N 98°9W **109** F9
Evart *Mich., U.S.A.* 43°54N 85°7W **79** F6
Evarts *Ky., U.S.A.* 36°52N 83°12W **105** D9
Eveleth *Minn., U.S.A.* 47°28N 92°32W **77** C61
Evelyn *La., U.S.A.* 31°59N 93°27W **110** C2
Evening Shade *Ark., U.S.A.* 36°4N 91°37W **106** B4
Evensville *Tenn., U.S.A.* 35°34N 84°57W **105** E8
Everest *Kans., U.S.A.* 39°41N 95°26W **82** B8
Everett *Ga., U.S.A.* 31°24N 81°38W **113** E5
Everett *Mass., U.S.A.* 42°24N 71°3W **96** A2
Everett *Pa., U.S.A.* 40°1N 78°23W **87** D4
Everett *Wash., U.S.A.* 47°59N 122°12W **120** C3
Everett, Mt. *Mass., U.S.A.* 42°6N 73°26W **91** B1
Everett Mts. *N.W.T., Canada* 62°45N 67°12W **159** E12
Everglades, The *Fla., U.S.A.* 25°50N 81°0W **114** F8
Everglades City *Fla., U.S.A.* 25°52N 81°23W **114** F7
Everglades Nat. Park △ *Fla., U.S.A.* 25°30N 81°0W **114** F8
Everglades Parkway *Fla., U.S.A.* 26°10N 81°0W **114** E7
Evergreen *Ala., U.S.A.* 31°26N 86°57W **112** E4
Evergreen *Colo., U.S.A.* 39°38N 105°19W **125** C5
Evergreen *Mich., U.S.A.* 42°26N 86°12W **98** A1
Evergreen *Mont., U.S.A.* 48°14N 114°17W **123** B3
Evergreen Park *Ill., U.S.A.* 41°43N 87°42W **95** C2
Everly *Iowa, U.S.A.* 43°10N 95°19W **81** A3
Everman *Tex., U.S.A.* 32°37N 97°17W **116** C2
Everson *Wash., U.S.A.* 48°55N 122°20W **120** B3
Everton *Mo., U.S.A.* 37°21N 93°42W **83** D3
'Ewa Beach *Hawai'i, U.S.A.* 21°19N 158°1W **136** K13
'Ewa District *Hawai'i, U.S.A.* 21°25N 158°3W **136** K13
'Ewa Forest Reserve *Hawai'i, U.S.A.* 21°27N 157°53W **136** K14
'Ewa Villages *Hawai'i, U.S.A.* 21°20N 158°3W **136** K13
Ewan *Wash., U.S.A.* 47°7N 117°44W **120** D8
Ewen *Mich., U.S.A.* 46°32N 89°17W **79** C2
Ewing *Ky., U.S.A.* 38°26N 83°52W **105** B9
Ewing *Mo., U.S.A.* 40°6N 91°43W **83** A5
Ewing *N.J., U.S.A.* 40°15N 74°48W **92** B2
Ewing *Nebr., U.S.A.* 42°16N 98°21W **80** B7
Ewing *Va., U.S.A.* 36°38N 83°26W **105** D9
Excello *Mo., U.S.A.* 39°38N 92°29W **83** B4
Excelsior Mts. *Nev., U.S.A.* 38°15N 118°10W **128** D2
Excelsior Springs *Mo., U.S.A.* 39°20N 94°13W **83** B2
Exeland *Wis., U.S.A.* 45°40N 91°15W **78** C2
Exell *Tex., U.S.A.* 35°38N 101°59W **108** A6
Exeter *Ont., Canada* 43°21N 81°29W **146** D5
Exeter *Calif., U.S.A.* 36°18N 119°9W **127** J7
Exeter *Maine, U.S.A.* 44°58N 69°9W **90** D4
Exeter *Mo., U.S.A.* 36°40N 93°56W **83** E3
Exeter *N.H., U.S.A.* 42°59N 70°57W **89** D4
Exeter *Nebr., U.S.A.* 40°39N 97°27W **80** D8
Exeter *Pa., U.S.A.* 41°19N 75°49W **92** A1
Exeter *R.I., U.S.A.* 41°35N 71°32W **91** C3
Exhibition Place *Ont., Canada* 43°38N 79°25W **161** B2
Exira *Iowa, U.S.A.* 41°35N 94°52W **81** D4
Exmore *Va., U.S.A.* 37°32N 75°50W **102** D9
Experiment = Highland Mills *Ga., U.S.A.* 33°17N 84°17W **113** C2
Exploits, B. of *Nfld. & L., Canada* 49°20N 55°0W **142** C6
Exshaw *Alta., Canada* 51°3N 115°9W **153** G5
Exuma Sound *Bahamas* 24°30N 76°20W **182** B4
Eyak *Alaska, U.S.A.* 60°32N 145°36W **135** F11
Eyasi, L. *Tanzania* 3°30N 35°0E
Eyebrow *Sask., Canada* 50°48N 106°9W **150** E5
Eyehill Cr. → *Alta., Canada* 52°14N 110°0W **153** F10
Eyota *Minn., U.S.A.* 43°59N 92°14W **77** G6
Ezequiel Montes *Querétaro, Mexico* 20°40N 99°53W **175** B8

F

F.D. Roosevelt Nat. Historic Site △ *N.Y., U.S.A.* 41°46N 73°56W **88** D7
Fabens *Tex., U.S.A.* 31°30N 106°10W **108** F1
Faber L. *N.W.T., Canada* 63°56N 117°15W **157** D9
Fabius *N.Y., U.S.A.* 42°50N 75°59W **88** C5
Fabre *Qué., Canada* 47°12N 79°22W **144** D3
Fabreville *Qué., Canada* 45°34N 73°51W **160** A2
Faceville *Ga., U.S.A.* 30°45N 84°38W **113** F2
Færingehavn = Kangerluarsoruseq *Greenland* 63°45N 51°27W **162** E5
Fagasa *Amer. Samoa* 14°17S 170°43W **184** e
Faillon, L. *Qué., Canada* 48°21N 76°39W **144** C4
Fair Bluff *N.C., U.S.A.* 34°19N 79°2W **103** D6
Fair Grove *Mo., U.S.A.* 37°23N 93°9W **83** D3
Fair Harbour *B.C., Canada* 50°4N 127°10W **154** E7
Fair Haven *N.J., U.S.A.* 40°22N 74°2W **92** B2
Fair Haven *N.Y., U.S.A.* 43°19N 76°42W **88** B4
Fair Haven *Vt., U.S.A.* 43°36N 73°16W **89** C1
Fair Lawn *N.J., U.S.A.* 40°55N 74°7W **92** A2
Fair Ness *Nunavut, Canada* 63°24N 72°5W **159** E11
Fair Oaks *Okla., U.S.A.* 36°17N 95°50W **107** B8
Fair Plain *Mich., U.S.A.* 42°5N 86°27W **79** G5
Fair Play *Mo., U.S.A.* 37°38N 93°35W **83** D3

Fairbank *Iowa, U.S.A.* 42°38N 92°3W 81 C6
Fairbank *Md., U.S.A.* 38°41N 76°20W 93 B4
Fairbanks *Alaska, U.S.A.* 64°51N 147°43W 135 D11
Fairbanks *Fla., U.S.A.* 29°44N 82°16W 114 B6
Fairbanks North Star ☆ *Alaska, U.S.A.* 64°50N 146°25W 135 D11
Fairborn *Ohio, U.S.A.* 39°49N 84°2W 86 D2
Fairburn *Ga., U.S.A.* 33°34N 84°35W 113 C2
Fairburn *S. Dak., U.S.A.* 43°41N 103°13W 76 G2
Fairbury *Ill., U.S.A.* 40°45N 88°31W 84 C5
Fairbury *Nebr., U.S.A.* 40°8N 97°11W 80 D8
Fairchance *Pa., U.S.A.* 39°49N 79°45W 87 E3
Fairchild *Wis., U.S.A.* 44°36N 90°58W 78 D3
Fairchild Air Force Base *Wash., U.S.A.* 47°38N 117°35W 120 C8
Fairdale *Ky., U.S.A.* 38°6N 85°46W 105 B7
Fairdale *N. Dak., U.S.A.* 48°30N 98°14W 76 B7
Fairfax *Iowa, U.S.A.* 41°55N 91°47W 81 D7
Fairfax *Minn., U.S.A.* 44°32N 94°43W 77 F4
Fairfax *Mo., U.S.A.* 40°20N 95°24W 83 A1
Fairfax *Okla., U.S.A.* 36°34N 96°42W 107 B7
Fairfax *S.C., U.S.A.* 32°59N 81°15W 103 F4
Fairfax *S. Dak., U.S.A.* 43°29N 98°54W 76 G7
Fairfax *Va., U.S.A.* 38°50N 77°19W 99 B2
Fairfax *Vt., U.S.A.* 44°40N 73°1W 89 B1
Fairfax County ☆ *Va., U.S.A.* 38°51N 77°18W 102 D7
Fairfax Station *Va., U.S.A.* 38°48N 77°19W 99 C2
Fairfield *Calif., U.S.A.* 38°15N 122°3W 126 E4
Fairfield *Conn., U.S.A.* 41°9N 73°16W 91 C1
Fairfield *Idaho, U.S.A.* 43°21N 114°44W 122 F4
Fairfield *Ill., U.S.A.* 38°23N 88°22W 84 E5
Fairfield *Iowa, U.S.A.* 40°56N 91°57W 81 E71
Fairfield *Ky., U.S.A.* 37°56N 85°23W 105 C7
Fairfield *Maine, U.S.A.* 44°35N 69°36W 90 D4
Fairfield *Mont., U.S.A.* 47°37N 111°59W 123 C6
Fairfield *N. Dak., U.S.A.* 47°8N 103°14W 76 C2
Fairfield *N.J., U.S.A.* 40°53N 74°18W 97 A1
Fairfield *Nebr., U.S.A.* 40°26N 98°6W 80 D7
Fairfield *Ohio, U.S.A.* 39°20N 84°34W 86 D1
Fairfield *Pa., U.S.A.* 39°47N 77°22W 93 A3
Fairfield *Tex., U.S.A.* 31°44N 96°10W 109 F11
Fairfield *Wash., U.S.A.* 47°23N 117°10W 120 C8
Fairfield County ☆ *Conn., U.S.A.* 41°15N 73°20W 91 C1
Fairfield County ☆ *Ohio, U.S.A.* 39°43N 82°36W 86 D4
Fairfield County ☆ *S.C., U.S.A.* 34°25N 81°10W 103 D4
Fairford *Man., Canada* 51°37N 98°38W 151 D13
Fairground Park *Mo., U.S.A.* 38°39N 90°13W 94 B2
Fairgrove *Mich., U.S.A.* 43°32N 83°33W 79 F8
Fairhaven *Mass., U.S.A.* 41°39N 70°55W 91 C4
Fairhaven *Md., U.S.A.* 38°45N 76°34W 93 B4
Fairhope *Ala., U.S.A.* 30°31N 87°54W 112 F3
Fairhope *Pa., U.S.A.* 39°50N 78°48W 93 A2
Fairland *Ind., U.S.A.* 39°35N 85°52W 85 D5
Fairland *Md., U.S.A.* 39°5N 76°57W 93 A4
Fairland *Okla., U.S.A.* 36°45N 94°51W 107 B9
Fairlee *Md., U.S.A.* 39°13N 76°10W 93 A4
Fairlee *Vt., U.S.A.* 43°54N 72°9W 89 C2
Fairmont *Minn., U.S.A.* 43°39N 94°28W 77 G4
Fairmont *N.C., U.S.A.* 34°30N 79°7W 103 D6
Fairmont *Nebr., U.S.A.* 40°38N 97°35W 80 D8
Fairmont *Okla., U.S.A.* 36°21N 97°43W 107 B6
Fairmont *W. Va., U.S.A.* 39°29N 80°9W 102 B4
Fairmont City *Ill., U.S.A.* 38°38N 90°3W 94 B3
Fairmount *Ga., U.S.A.* 34°26N 84°42W 113 B2
Fairmount *Ill., U.S.A.* 40°3N 87°56W 84 C6
Fairmount *Ind., U.S.A.* 40°25N 85°39W 85 C5
Fairmount *Md., U.S.A.* 38°6N 75°48W 93 B5
Fairmount *N. Dak., U.S.A.* 46°3N 96°36W 76 D9
Fairmount *N.Y., U.S.A.* 43°5N 76°12W 88 B4
Fairmount Heights *Md., U.S.A.* 38°54N 76°54W 99 B4
Fairmount Park *Pa., U.S.A.* 40°1N 75°11W 98 A1
Fairplains *N.C., U.S.A.* 36°12N 81°9W 103 B4
Fairplay *Colo., U.S.A.* 39°15N 106°2W 125 C4
Fairport *Ont., Canada* 43°49N 79°4W 161 A4
Fairport *N.Y., U.S.A.* 43°6N 77°27W 88 B3
Fairport Harbor *Ohio, U.S.A.* 41°45N 81°17W 86 B5
Fairtown *Baltimore, U.S.A.* 39°16N 76°31W 99 B2
Fairvale *N.B., Canada* 45°25N 66°0W 141 H4
Fairview *Alta., Canada* 56°5N 118°25W 152 B2
Fairview *N.S., Canada* 44°40N 63°38W 141 J6
Fairview *Ill., U.S.A.* 40°38N 90°10W 84 C3
Fairview *Kans., U.S.A.* 39°50N 95°44W 82 B8
Fairview *Mich., U.S.A.* 44°44N 84°3W 79 E7
Fairview *Mont., U.S.A.* 47°51N 104°3W 123 C13
Fairview *N.C., U.S.A.* 35°31N 82°24W 103 C3
Fairview *N.J., U.S.A.* 40°23N 74°5W 92 B2
Fairview *N.J., U.S.A.* 40°48N 73°59W 97 B3
Fairview *Okla., U.S.A.* 36°16N 98°29W 107 B5
Fairview *Oreg., U.S.A.* 45°32N 122°26W 121 B3
Fairview *Pa., U.S.A.* 42°2N 80°15W 87 B2
Fairview *S. Dak., U.S.A.* 43°13N 96°29W 76 G9
Fairview *Tenn., U.S.A.* 35°59N 87°7W 104 E5
Fairview Utah, U.S.A. 39°38N 111°26W 129 D4
Fairview *W. Va., U.S.A.* 39°36N 80°15W 102 B4
Fairview, L. *Fla., U.S.A.* 28°35N 81°24W 115 A2
Fairview Park *Ind., U.S.A.* 39°41N 87°25W 85 D3
Fairweather, Mt. *Alaska, U.S.A.* 58°55N 137°32W 135 G13
Fairwood *Wash., U.S.A.* 47°26N 122°9W 132 D5
Faison *N.C., U.S.A.* 35°7N 78°8W 103 C7
Faith *S. Dak., U.S.A.* 45°2N 102°2W 76 E3
Faithorn *Mich., U.S.A.* 45°41N 87°45W 79 D4
Fajardo *Puerto Rico* 18°20N 65°39W 184 G17
Falcon *Colo., U.S.A.* 38°56N 104°37W 125 D6
Falcon, C. *Oreg., U.S.A.* 45°46N 123°59W 121 B2
Falcon Heights *Minn., U.S.A.* 44°59N 93°10W 94 B2
Falcon I. *Ont., Canada* 49°23N 94°45W 148 C2
Falcon Res. *Tex., U.S.A.* 26°34N 99°10W 108 L8
Falconbridge *Ont., Canada* 46°35N 80°45W 146 A6
Falconer *N.Y., U.S.A.* 42°7N 79°12W 88 C1
Falfurrias *Tex., U.S.A.* 27°14N 98°9W 108 K9
Falher *Alta., Canada* 55°44N 117°15W 152 C3
Falkner *Miss., U.S.A.* 34°51N 88°56W 111 B5
Falkville *Ala., U.S.A.* 34°22N 86°55W 112 B4
Fall → *Kans., U.S.A.* 37°24N 95°40W 82 D7
Fall Branch *Tenn., U.S.A.* 36°25N 82°37W 105 D10
Fall Creek *Wis., U.S.A.* 44°46N 91°17W 78 D2
Fall Creek Falls State Park ☐ *Tenn., U.S.A.* 35°39N 85°20W 105 E7
Fall River *Kans., U.S.A.* 37°36N 96°2W 82 D7
Fall River *Mass., U.S.A.* 41°43N 71°10W 91 C3
Fall River *Wis., U.S.A.* 43°23N 89°3W 78 E4
Fall River County ☆ *S. Dak., U.S.A.* 43°10N 103°30W 76 G2
Fall River Lake *Kans., U.S.A.* 37°39N 96°4W 82 D7
Fall River Mills *Calif., U.S.A.* 41°3N 121°26W 126 B5
Fallasbee *W. Va., U.S.A.* 40°20N 80°36W 102 A4
Fallbrook *Calif., U.S.A.* 33°23N 117°15W 127 K9
Fallis *Okla., U.S.A.* 35°45N 97°7W 107 C6

Fallon *Mont., U.S.A.* 46°50N 105°8W 123 D12
Fallon *Nev., U.S.A.* 39°28N 118°47W 128 C2
Fallon County ☆ *Mont., U.S.A.* 46°20N 104°30W 123 D13
Fallon Indian Reservation *Nev., U.S.A.* 39°25N 118°45W 128 C2
Fallon N.A.S. *Nev., U.S.A.* 39°27N 118°44W 128 C2
Falls Church *Va., U.S.A.* 38°53N 77°12W 99 B2
Falls City *Nebr., U.S.A.* 40°3N 95°36W 80 D10
Falls City *Oreg., U.S.A.* 44°52N 123°26W 121 C2
Falls City *Tex., U.S.A.* 28°59N 98°1W 109 J9
Falls County ☆ *Tex., U.S.A.* 31°18N 96°54W 109 F11
Falls Creek *Pa., U.S.A.* 41°9N 78°48W 87 C4
Falls L. *N.C., U.S.A.* 35°57N 78°35W 103 C7
Fallsburg *N.Y., U.S.A.* 38°11N 82°40W 105 B10
Fallstaff *Baltimore, U.S.A.* 39°22N 76°42W 99 A1
Fallston *Md., U.S.A.* 39°31N 76°25W 93 A4
Falmouth *Jamaica* 18°30N 77°40W 182 C4
Falmouth *Fla., U.S.A.* 30°21N 83°8W 114 A5
Falmouth *Ky., U.S.A.* 38°41N 84°20W 105 B8
Falmouth *Maine, U.S.A.* 43°44N 70°14W 90 E3
Falmouth *Mass., U.S.A.* 41°33N 70°37W 91 C4
Falmouth *Mich., U.S.A.* 44°15N 85°5W 79 E6
Falmouth *Va., U.S.A.* 38°20N 77°28W 102 C7
Faloma *Oreg., U.S.A.* 45°36N 122°40W 132 A2
Falsa, Pta. *Baja Calif. S., Mexico* 27°51N 115°3W 167 F3
False Pass *Alaska, U.S.A.* 54°51N 163°25W 135 J7
Falso, C. *Honduras* 15°12N 83°21W 182 C3
Falun *Kans., U.S.A.* 38°40N 97°46W 82 C6
Family L. *Man., Canada* 51°54N 95°27W 151 D16
Fancy Farm *Ky., U.S.A.* 36°48N 88°47W 104 D4
Fannin County ☆ *Ga., U.S.A.* 34°50N 84°15W 113 B2
Fannin County ☆ *Tex., U.S.A.* 33°35N 96°11W 109 D11
Fanny Bay *B.C., Canada* 49°37N 124°48W 154 F10
Fanshawe *Okla., U.S.A.* 34°57N 94°55W 107 D9
Far Mt. *B.C., Canada* 52°47N 125°20W 154 C9
Far Rockaway *N.Y., U.S.A.* 40°36N 73°45W 97 C4
Farallón, Pta. *Jalisco, Mexico* 19°22N 105°2W 174 C2
Farallon de Medinilla *N. Marianas* 16°1N 146°4E 184 a
Farallon de Pajaros *N. Marianas* 20°32N 144°54E 184 a
Farallon Islands Nat. Wildlife Refuge ☐ *Calif., U.S.A.* 37°44N 123°2W 126 F3
Farewell *Alaska, U.S.A.* 62°31N 153°54W 135 E9
Farewell C. = Nunap Isua *Greenland* 59°48N 43°55W 162 F6
Fargo *Ga., U.S.A.* 30°41N 82°34W 113 F4
Fargo *N. Dak., U.S.A.* 46°53N 96°48W 76 D9
Fargo *Okla., U.S.A.* 36°22N 99°37W 107 B4
Faribault *Minn., U.S.A.* 44°18N 93°16W 77 F5
Faribault, L. *Qué., Canada* 59°3N 71°58W 143 B3
Faribault County ☆ *Minn., U.S.A.* 43°45N 94°0W 77 G5
Faride, L. *Qué., Canada* 50°58N 59°55W 140 C10
Farina *Ill., U.S.A.* 38°50N 88°46W 84 E5
Farley *Iowa, U.S.A.* 42°27N 91°0W 81 C7
Farmer City *Ill., U.S.A.* 40°15N 88°39W 84 C5
Farmers Branch *Tex., U.S.A.* 32°55N 96°53W 116 A4
Farmersburg *Ind., U.S.A.* 39°15N 87°23W 85 E3
Farmersville *Calif., U.S.A.* 36°18N 119°12W 127 G7
Farmersville *Ill., U.S.A.* 39°27N 89°39W 84 D4
Farmersville *Tex., U.S.A.* 33°10N 96°22W 109 D11
Farmerville *La., U.S.A.* 32°47N 92°24W 110 B3
Farmingdale *N.J., U.S.A.* 40°12N 74°10W 92 B2
Farmington *B.C., Canada* 55°54N 120°30W 155 B8
Farmington *Ark., U.S.A.* 36°3N 94°15W 106 B1
Farmington *Calif., U.S.A.* 37°55N 120°59W 126 F6
Farmington *Del., U.S.A.* 38°52N 75°35W 93 B5
Farmington *Ga., U.S.A.* 33°47N 83°26W 113 C3
Farmington *Ill., U.S.A.* 40°42N 90°0W 84 C3
Farmington *Iowa, U.S.A.* 40°38N 91°44W 81 E7
Farmington *Maine, U.S.A.* 44°40N 70°9W 90 D3
Farmington *Md., U.S.A.* 39°42N 76°4W 93 A4
Farmington *Minn., U.S.A.* 44°38N 93°8W 77 F5
Farmington *Miss., U.S.A.* 34°56N 88°27W 111 B5
Farmington *Mo., U.S.A.* 37°47N 90°25W 83 D61
Farmington *Mont., U.S.A.* 47°53N 112°10W 123 C5
Farmington *N.H., U.S.A.* 43°24N 71°4W 89 C3
Farmington *N. Mex., U.S.A.* 36°44N 108°12W 131 A2
Farmington *Utah, U.S.A.* 40°59N 111°53W 129 C4
Farmington *Wash., U.S.A.* 47°5N 117°3W 120 C8
Farmington → *Conn., U.S.A.* 41°51N 72°33W 91 C2
Farmville *N.C., U.S.A.* 35°36N 77°35W 103 C7
Farmville *Va., U.S.A.* 37°18N 78°24W 102 D6
Farnam *Nebr., U.S.A.* 40°42N 100°13W 80 D5
Farner *Tenn., U.S.A.* 35°9N 84°19W 105 E8
Farnham *Qué., Canada* 45°17N 72°59W 145 F10
Farnham *Va., U.S.A.* 37°52N 76°33W 93 C4
Farnsworth *Tex., U.S.A.* 36°19N 100°58W 108 A7
Faro *Yukon, Canada* 62°11N 133°22W 157 D6
Faro *Monterrey, Mexico* 25°48N 100°59W 180 B3
Farragut *Iowa, U.S.A.* 40°43N 95°29W 81 E3
Farragut *Tenn., U.S.A.* 35°53N 84°9W 105 E8
Farrell *Pa., U.S.A.* 41°13N 80°30W 87 C2
Farson *Wyo., U.S.A.* 42°7N 109°26W 124 D3
Farvel, Kap = Nunap Isua *Greenland* 59°48N 43°55W 162 F6
Farwell *Mich., U.S.A.* 43°50N 84°52W 79 F7
Farwell *Minn., U.S.A.* 45°45N 95°37W 77 F3
Farwell *Nebr., U.S.A.* 41°13N 98°38W 80 C7
Farwell *Tex., U.S.A.* 34°23N 103°2W 108 C4
Father Marquette Nat. Memorial *Mich., U.S.A.* 45°55N 84°45W 79 D7
Fathom Five Nat. Marine Park ☐ *Ont., Canada* 45°17N 81°40W 146 B5
Fatima *Port., Canada* 47°24N 61°53W 141 F8
Faucett *Mo., U.S.A.* 39°36N 94°48W 83 B2
Faulk County ☆ *S. Dak., U.S.A.* 45°0N 99°9W 76 E6
Faulkner County ☆ *Ark., U.S.A.* 35°10N 92°16W 106 C3
Faulkton *S. Dak., U.S.A.* 45°2N 99°8W 76 E6
Fauquier *B.C., Canada* 49°52N 118°5W 155 F16
Fauquier *Ont., Canada* 49°18N 82°3W 149 C14
Fauquier County ☆ *Va., U.S.A.* 38°43N 77°48W 102 C7
Faust *Alta., Canada* 55°19N 115°38W 152 C5
Faust *Utah, U.S.A.* 40°11N 112°24W 129 C3
Fawcett *Alta., Canada* 54°32N 114°5W 152 D6
Fawcett L. *Alta., Canada* 55°19N 113°53W 152 C7
Fawn → *Ont., Canada* 55°20N 87°35W 159 F8
Fawn Grove *Pa., U.S.A.* 39°44N 76°27W 93 A4
Faxon *Okla., U.S.A.* 34°28N 98°35W 107 D5
Fay *Okla., U.S.A.* 35°49N 98°39W 107 C5
Fayette *Ala., U.S.A.* 33°41N 87°50W 112 C3
Fayette *Iowa, U.S.A.* 42°51N 91°48W 81 C7
Fayette *Mich., U.S.A.* 45°43N 86°40W 79 D5
Fayette *Miss., U.S.A.* 31°43N 91°4W 111 E2
Fayette *Mo., U.S.A.* 39°9N 92°41W 83 B4
Fayette *N.Y., U.S.A.* 42°49N 76°49W 88 C4
Fayette *Ohio, U.S.A.* 41°40N 84°20W 86 B2
Fayette *Utah, U.S.A.* 39°14N 111°51W 129 D4
Fayette County ☆ *Ala., U.S.A.* 33°44N 87°45W 112 C3
Fayette County ☆ *Ga., U.S.A.* 33°25N 84°30W 113 C2
Fayette County ☆ *Ill., U.S.A.* 39°0N 89°0W 84 E4

Fayette County ☆ *Ind., U.S.A.* 39°35N 85°10W 85 D5
Fayette County ☆ *Iowa, U.S.A.* 42°50N 91°50W 81 C7
Fayette County ☆ *Ky., U.S.A.* 38°0N 84°30W 105 B8
Fayette County ☆ *Ohio, U.S.A.* 39°33N 83°26W 86 D3
Fayette County ☆ *Pa., U.S.A.* 40°0N 79°40W 87 E3
Fayette County ☆ *Tenn., U.S.A.* 35°15N 89°21W 104 E3
Fayette County ☆ *Tex., U.S.A.* 29°54N 96°53W 109 H11
Fayette County ☆ *W. Va., U.S.A.* 38°5N 81°9W 102 D3
Fayetteville *Ark., U.S.A.* 36°4N 94°10W 106 B1
Fayetteville *Ga., U.S.A.* 33°27N 84°27W 113 C2
Fayetteville *N.C., U.S.A.* 35°3N 78°53W 103 C7
Fayetteville *N.Y., U.S.A.* 43°2N 76°0W 88 B3
Fayetteville *Pa., U.S.A.* 39°55N 77°33W 87 E5
Fayetteville *Tenn., U.S.A.* 35°9N 86°34W 104 E6
Fayetteville *Tex., U.S.A.* 29°54N 96°41W 109 H11
Fayetteville *W. Va., U.S.A.* 38°3N 81°6W 102 C3
Fear, C. *N.C., U.S.A.* 33°50N 77°58W 103 E8
Feather → *Calif., U.S.A.* 38°47N 121°36W 126 E5
Feather Falls *Calif., U.S.A.* 39°36N 121°16W 126 D5
Featherville *Idaho, U.S.A.* 43°37N 115°15W 122 F3
Federal *Wyo., U.S.A.* 41°16N 105°7W 124 E7
Federal Dam *Minn., U.S.A.* 47°15N 94°14W 77 D4
Federal Heights *Colo., U.S.A.* 39°51N 104°59W 134 A1
Federal Way *Wash., U.S.A.* 47°18N 122°19W 120 C3
Feeding Hills *Mass., U.S.A.* 42°4N 72°41W 91 B2
Felch *Mich., U.S.A.* 46°0N 87°50W 79 C4
Felda *Fla., U.S.A.* 26°34N 81°26W 114 E7
Felicity *Ohio, U.S.A.* 38°51N 84°6W 86 E2
Felipe Carrillo Puerto *Campeche, Mexico* 19°7N 90°32W 179 C3
Felipe Carrillo Puerto *Michoacan, Mexico* 19°7N 102°43W 174 C5
Felipe Carrillo Puerto *Quintana Roo, Mexico* 19°38N 88°3W 179 C5
Felipe Carrillo Puerto *Zacatecas, Mexico* 23°51N 102°6W 173 D6
Felix → *N. Mex., U.S.A.* 33°5N 104°25W 131 D6
Felix, C. *Nunavut, Canada* 69°54N 97°58W 158 D6
Felsenthal Nat. Wildlife Refuge ☐ *Ark., U.S.A.* 33°9N 92°10W 106 E3
Felt *Idaho, U.S.A.* 43°52N 111°11W 122 F7
Felt *Okla., U.S.A.* 36°34N 102°48W 107 B1
Felton *Minn., U.S.A.* 47°5N 96°30W 77 C2
Felton *Pa., U.S.A.* 39°51N 76°34W 87 E6
Fence Lake *N. Mex., U.S.A.* 34°40N 108°40W 131 C2
Fenelon Falls *Ont., Canada* 44°32N 78°45W 147 C8
Fennimore *Wis., U.S.A.* 42°59N 90°39W 78 F3
Fennville *Mich., U.S.A.* 42°36N 86°6W 79 G5
Fenton *Iowa, U.S.A.* 43°13N 94°26W 81 B4
Fenton *La., U.S.A.* 30°22N 92°55W 110 D3
Fenton *Mich., U.S.A.* 42°48N 83°42W 79 G8
Fentress *Tex., U.S.A.* 29°45N 97°47W 109 H10
Fentress County ☆ *Tenn., U.S.A.* 36°25N 85°0W 105 D8
Fenwood *Wis., U.S.A.* 44°52N 90°1W 78 D3
Ferdinand *Idaho, U.S.A.* 46°9N 116°24W 122 C2
Ferdinand *Ind., U.S.A.* 38°14N 86°52W 85 F4
Fergus *Ont., Canada* 43°43N 80°24W 146 D6
Fergus County ☆ *Mont., U.S.A.* 47°30N 109°10W 123 C8
Fergus Falls *Minn., U.S.A.* 46°17N 96°4W 77 D2
Ferguson *Ky., U.S.A.* 37°3N 84°36W 105 C8
Ferguson *Mo., U.S.A.* 38°44N 90°18W 94 A2
Ferguson Lake *Nunavut, Canada* 69°25N 105°15W 158 D4
Ferguson Pt. *B.C., Canada* 49°18N 123°9W 161 B2
Ferintosh *Alta., Canada* 52°46N 112°58W 153 F8
Ferland *Ont., Canada* 50°19N 88°27W 148 B8
Ferme-Neuve *Qué., Canada* 46°42N 75°27W 144 C7
Fermont *Qué., Canada* 52°47N 67°5W 143 C4
Fern Feather *Idaho, U.S.A.* 38°9N 85°36W 105 B7
Fern Ridge L. *Oreg., U.S.A.* 44°7N 123°18W 121 C2
Fernandina Beach *Fla., U.S.A.* 30°40N 81°27W 114 A7
Ferndale *Calif., U.S.A.* 40°35N 124°16W 126 C2
Ferndale *Md., U.S.A.* 39°10N 76°38W 99 B2
Ferndale *Mich., U.S.A.* 42°27N 83°8W 98 A2
Ferndale *Wash., U.S.A.* 48°51N 122°36W 120 B3
Fernie *B.C., Canada* 49°30N 115°5W 153 J5
Fernley *Nev., U.S.A.* 39°36N 119°15W 128 C1
Fernwood *Idaho, U.S.A.* 47°7N 116°24W 122 B2
Fernwood *Miss., U.S.A.* 31°11N 90°27W 111 E3
Fernwood *N.Y., U.S.A.* 43°16N 73°40W 88 B7
Feronia *Ont., Canada* 46°22N 79°19W 146 A7
Ferrelsburg *W. Va., U.S.A.* 38°2N 82°6W 102 C2
Ferriday *La., U.S.A.* 31°38N 91°33W 110 C4
Ferris *Ill., U.S.A.* 40°28N 91°10W 84 C2
Ferris *Tex., U.S.A.* 32°32N 96°40W 109 E11
Ferrisburg *Vt., U.S.A.* 44°12N 73°15W 89 B1
Ferron *Utah, U.S.A.* 39°5N 111°8W 129 D4
Ferrum *Va., U.S.A.* 36°55N 80°1W 102 E4
Ferry County ☆ *Wash., U.S.A.* 48°30N 118°30W 120 B7
Ferry Pass *Fla., U.S.A.* 30°31N 87°13W 114 A1
Ferryland *Nfld. & L., Canada* 47°2N 52°53W 142 E8
Ferrysburg *Mich., U.S.A.* 43°5N 86°13W 79 F5
Ferryville *Wis., U.S.A.* 43°21N 91°6W 78 E2
Fertile *Iowa, U.S.A.* 43°16N 93°25W 81 B5
Fertile *Minn., U.S.A.* 47°32N 96°17W 77 C2
Fessenden *N. Dak., U.S.A.* 47°39N 99°38W 76 C6
Festus *Mo., U.S.A.* 38°13N 90°24W 83 C61
Feuilles → *Qué., Canada* 58°47N 70°4W 143 B3
Feuilles, B. aux *Qué., Canada* 58°55N 69°20W 143 B4
Field *Ont., Canada* 46°31N 80°1W 146 A6
Field *Ky., U.S.A.* 36°54N 83°36W 105 D9
Field Museum of Natural History *Ill., U.S.A.* 41°51N 87°37W 95 B3
Fieldale *Va., U.S.A.* 36°42N 79°56W 102 E5
Fielding *Utah, U.S.A.* 41°49N 112°7W 129 B3
Fieldon *Ill., U.S.A.* 39°6N 90°34W 84 D3
Fields → *La., U.S.A.* 30°32N 93°35W 110 D2
Fields *Oreg., U.S.A.* 42°16N 118°40W 121 E7
Fields Corner *Mass., U.S.A.* 42°18N 71°3W 96 B2
Fields Landing *Calif., U.S.A.* 40°44N 124°13W 126 C2
Fierro *N. Mex., U.S.A.* 32°51N 108°5W 131 E2
Fife *Tex., U.S.A.* 31°24N 99°22W 109 F8
Fife L. *Sask., Canada* 49°14N 105°53W 150 F6
Fife Lake *Mich., U.S.A.* 44°35N 85°21W 79 E6
Fifield *Wis., U.S.A.* 45°53N 90°25W 78 C3
File Axe, L. *Qué., Canada* 50°18N 73°34W 145 A9
Filer *Idaho, U.S.A.* 42°34N 114°37W 122 G4
Fillmore *Sask., Canada* 49°50N 103°25W 150 F8
Fillmore *Calif., U.S.A.* 34°24N 118°55W 127 J8
Fillmore *Utah, U.S.A.* 38°58N 112°20W 129 D3
Fillmore County ☆ *Minn., U.S.A.* 43°40N 92°0W 77 G7
Fillmore County ☆ *Nebr., U.S.A.* 40°30N 97°40W 80 D8
Filomeno Mata *Veracruz, Mexico* 20°12N 97°42W 176 D3
Fils, L. du *Qué., Canada* 46°37N 78°7W 144 E4
Final, Pta. *Baja Calif., Mexico* 29°29N 114°19W 166 D4

Fincastle *Va., U.S.A.* 37°30N 79°53W 102 D5
Finch *Ont., Canada* 45°11N 75°7W 144 F7
Findlater *Sask., Canada* 50°47N 105°24W 150 E6
Findlay *Ill., U.S.A.* 39°31N 88°45W 84 D5
Findlay *Ohio, U.S.A.* 41°2N 83°39W 86 B3
Fine *N.Y., U.S.A.* 44°15N 75°8W 88 A5
Fine Arts, Museum of *Mass., U.S.A.* 42°20N 71°5W 96 A2
Fingal *N. Dak., U.S.A.* 46°46N 97°47W 76 D8
Finger *Tenn., U.S.A.* 35°22N 88°36W 104 E4
Finger Lakes *N.Y., U.S.A.* 42°40N 76°30W 88 C4
Finger Lakes Nat. Forest *N.Y., U.S.A.* 42°31N 76°47W 88 C4
Finisterre *Coahuila, Mexico* 25°59N 103°14W 170 E1
Finksburg *Md., U.S.A.* 39°30N 76°54W 93 A4
Finlay → *B.C., Canada* 57°0N 125°10W 157 E7
Finlayson *Minn., U.S.A.* 46°12N 92°55W 77 D6
Finley *N. Dak., U.S.A.* 47°31N 97°50W 76 C8
Finley *Okla., U.S.A.* 34°20N 95°30W 107 D8
Finmark *Ont., Canada* 48°35N 89°45W 148 D7
Finney *Mich., U.S.A.* 42°24N 82°55W 98 A3
Finney County ☆ *Kans., U.S.A.* 38°0N 100°40W 82 C3
Fire I. *N.Y., U.S.A.* 40°40N 73°11W 88 E7
Fire Island Nat. Seashore ☐ *N.Y., U.S.A.* 40°38N 73°8W 92 B3
Fire River *Ont., Canada* 48°47N 83°21W 149 D13
Firebag → *Alta., Canada* 57°45N 111°21W 152 A9
Firebaugh *Calif., U.S.A.* 36°52N 120°27W 127 G6
First Connecticut L. *N.H., U.S.A.* 45°5N 71°15W 89 A3
First Narrows *B.C., Canada* 49°19N 123°9W 161 B2
Firth *Idaho, U.S.A.* 43°18N 112°11W 122 F6
Firth *Nebr., U.S.A.* 40°33N 96°37W 80 D9
Firth *B.C., Canada* 52°27N 126°13W 154 C8
Fischer *Tex., U.S.A.* 29°58N 98°16W 109 H9
Fish L. *Minn., U.S.A.* 45°5N 93°27W 94 A1
Fish Lake *Minn., U.S.A.* 45°5N 93°27W 94 A1
Fish Lake Regional Park → *Minn., U.S.A.* 45°5N 93°27W 94 A1
Fish Lake Res. *Minn., U.S.A.* 46°57N 92°17W 77 D6
Fish Pt. *Mich., U.S.A.* 43°44N 83°31W 79 F8
Fish River L. *Maine, U.S.A.* 46°50N 68°47W 90 B5
Fish Springs Nat. Wildlife Refuge ☐ *Utah, U.S.A.* 39°51N 113°22W 129 D2
Fisheating Cr. → *Fla., U.S.A.* 26°57N 81°7W 114 E7
Fisher *Ark., U.S.A.* 35°30N 90°58W 106 C5
Fisher *Ill., U.S.A.* 40°19N 88°21W 84 C5
Fisher *La., U.S.A.* 31°30N 93°28W 110 C2
Fisher *Minn., U.S.A.* 47°48N 96°48W 77 C2
Fisher → *Mont., U.S.A.* 48°22N 115°19W 123 B2
Fisher B. *Man., Canada* 51°35N 97°13W 151 D14
Fisher Branch *Man., Canada* 51°5N 97°13W 151 D14
Fisher County ☆ *Tex., U.S.A.* 32°45N 100°23W 108 E7
Fisher Island *Fla., U.S.A.* 25°45N 80°8W 115 D3
Fisher River *Man., Canada* 51°25N 97°21W 151 D14
Fisher Str. *N.W.T., Canada* 63°15N 83°30W 159 E9
Fishermans Island Nat. Wildlife Refuge → *Va., U.S.A.* 37°6N 75°57W 102 D9
Fishers *Ind., U.S.A.* 39°57N 86°0W 85 D4
Fishers I. *N.Y., U.S.A.* 41°15N 72°0W 91 C4
Fishers Peak *Colo., U.S.A.* 37°6N 104°28W 125 E6
Fisherville *Ont., Canada* 43°46N 79°28W 161 A2
Fishing Bridge *Wyo., U.S.A.* 44°29N 110°22W 124 B2
Fishing Creek *Md., U.S.A.* 38°20N 76°14W 93 B4
Fishing Creek → *N.C., U.S.A.* 35°56N 77°31W 103 C8
Fishing L. *Man., Canada* 52°10N 95°24W 151 C16
Fishkill *N.Y., U.S.A.* 41°32N 73°54W 92 A3
Fishlake Nat. Forest *Utah, U.S.A.* 38°40N 112°20W 129 E3
Fishtrap L. *Ky., U.S.A.* 37°25N 82°26W 105 C10
Fiskdale *Mass., U.S.A.* 42°7N 72°7W 91 B2
Fiskenæsset = Qeqertarsuatsiaat *Greenland* 63°5N 50°45W 162 E5
Fitchburg *Mass., U.S.A.* 42°35N 71°48W 91 B3
Fitchburg *Wis., U.S.A.* 42°58N 89°28W 78 F41
Fittstown *Okla., U.S.A.* 34°37N 96°38W 107 D7
Fitz Hugh Sd. *B.C., Canada* 51°40N 127°55W 154 D7
Fitzgerald *Alta., Canada* 59°51N 111°36W 157 E10
Fitzgerald *Ga., U.S.A.* 31°43N 83°15W 113 E3
Fitzgerald B. *Nunavut, Canada* 72°9N 89°45W 158 C8
Fitzhugh *Ark., U.S.A.* 35°22N 91°19W 106 C4
Fitzhugh *Okla., U.S.A.* 34°40N 96°46W 107 D7
Fitzwilliam I. *Ont., Canada* 45°30N 81°45W 146 B5
Five Islands *N.S., Canada* 45°23N 64°6W 141 H5
Flagler *Colo., U.S.A.* 39°18N 103°4W 125 C7
Flagler Beach *Fla., U.S.A.* 29°29N 81°8W 114 B7
Flagler County ☆ *Fla., U.S.A.* 29°30N 81°20W 114 B7
Flagstaff *Ariz., U.S.A.* 35°12N 111°39W 130 B4
Flagstaff L. *Maine, U.S.A.* 45°12N 70°18W 90 C3
Flagstaff L. *Oreg., U.S.A.* 42°35N 119°45W 121 E6
Flaherty I. *N.W.T., Canada* 56°15N 79°15W 143 B2
Flambeau → *Wis., U.S.A.* 45°18N 91°14W 78 C21
Flaming Gorge Dam *Utah, U.S.A.* 40°55N 109°25W 124 E3
Flaming Gorge Nat. Recr. Area ☐ *Wyo., U.S.A.* 41°10N 109°25W 124 E3
Flaming Gorge Res. *Wyo., U.S.A.* 41°10N 109°25W 124 E3
Flamingo *Fla., U.S.A.* 25°8N 80°57W 114 F8
Flamingo *Fla., U.S.A.* 28°22N 81°22W 115 B2
Flanagan *Ill., U.S.A.* 40°53N 88°52W 84 C5
Flanders *N.Y., U.S.A.* 40°54N 72°37W 91 D2
Flandreau *S. Dak., U.S.A.* 44°3N 96°36W 76 F9
Flasher *N. Dak., U.S.A.* 46°27N 101°14W 76 D4
Flat *Alaska, U.S.A.* 62°28N 158°1W 135 E8
Flat → *N.W.T., Canada* 61°33N 125°18W 157 D7
Flat → *Mich., U.S.A.* 42°56N 85°20W 79 G6
Flat → *N.C., U.S.A.* 36°5N 78°49W 103 B7
Flat Bay *Nfld. & L., Canada* 48°24N 58°36W 142 D2
Flat Lake *B.C., Canada* 54°38N 112°54W 152 D8
Flat Lick *Ky., U.S.A.* 36°50N 83°46W 105 D9
Flat River Res. *R.I., U.S.A.* 41°42N 71°37W 91 C3
Flat Rock *Ill., U.S.A.* 38°54N 87°40W 84 E6
Flat Rock *Mich., U.S.A.* 42°6N 83°17W 79 G8
Flat Top Mt. *Colo., U.S.A.* 39°50N 107°11W 125 C3
Flat Tops, The *Colo., U.S.A.* 39°50N 107°0W 125 C3
Flat Woods *Tenn., U.S.A.* 35°29N 87°50W 104 E5
Flatbush *Alta., Canada* 54°42N 114°9W 152 D6
Flatbush *N.Y., U.S.A.* 40°39N 73°56W 97 C3
Flathead → *Mont., U.S.A.* 48°27N 114°47W 123 B3
Flathead County ☆ *Mont., U.S.A.* 48°15N 113°30W 123 B4
Flathead Indian Reservation *Mont., U.S.A.* 47°35N 114°30W 123 C3
Flathead L. *Mont., U.S.A.* 47°51N 114°8W 123 C3
Flathead Nat. Forest *Mont., U.S.A.* 47°50N 113°18W 123 C4
Flatonia *Tex., U.S.A.* 29°41N 97°7W 109 H10
Flatrock → *Ind., U.S.A.* 39°12N 85°56W 85 D5
Flattery, C. *Wash., U.S.A.* 48°23N 124°29W 120 B1
Flatwillow Cr. → *Mont., U.S.A.* 46°56N 107°55W 123 D10
Flatwoods *Ky., U.S.A.* 38°31N 82°43W 105 B10
Flatwoods *La., U.S.A.* 31°24N 92°52W 110 C3

Flatwoods W. Va., U.S.A. 38°43N 80°39W **102** C4
Flaxcombe Sask., Canada 51°29N 109°36W **150** D2
Flaxton N. Dak., U.S.A. 48°54N 102°24W **76** B3
Flaxville Mont., U.S.A. 48°48N 105°11W **123** B12
Fleetwood Pa., U.S.A. 40°27N 75°49W **87** D7
Fleischmanns N.Y., U.S.A. 42°10N 74°32W **88** C6
Fleming Sask., Canada 50°4N 101°31W **151** E10
Fleming Colo., U.S.A. 40°41N 102°50W **125** B8
Fleming County ☆ Ky., U.S.A. 38°20N 83°40W **105** B9
Fleming-Neon Ky., U.S.A. 37°12N 82°42W **105** C10
Flemingsburg Ky., U.S.A. 38°25N 83°45W **105** B9
Flemington N.J., U.S.A. 40°31N 74°52W **92** B2
Flemington W. Va., U.S.A. 39°16N 80°8W **102** B4
Flensburg Minn., U.S.A. 45°57N 94°32W **77** E4
Flesherton Ont., Canada 44°16N 80°33W **146** C6
Fletcher = Aurora Colo., U.S.A. 39°43N 104°49W **134** B3
Fletcher N.C., U.S.A. 35°26N 82°30W **103** C3
Fletcher Okla., U.S.A. 34°50N 98°15W **107** D5
Fletcher Pond Mich., U.S.A. 45°1N 83°47W **79** D8
Fleur de Lys Nfld. & L., Canada 50°7N 56°8W **142** B4
Fleur-de-May, L. Nfld. & L., Canada 52°0N 65°5W **140** B4
Fleurimont Qué., Canada 45°24N 71°51W **145** F11
Flin Flon Man., Canada 54°46N 101°53W **157** F12
Flint Mich., U.S.A. 43°1N 83°41W **79** F8
Flint → Ala., U.S.A. 34°30N 86°30W **112** B4
Flint → Ga., U.S.A. 30°57N 84°34W **113** F2
Flint Cr. → Ala., U.S.A. 34°35N 86°56W **112** B4
Flint Hill Va., U.S.A. 38°46N 78°6W **93** B2
Flint Hills Kans., U.S.A. 38°0N 96°40W **82** D7
Flint L. Nunavut, Canada 69°16N 74°15W **158** D11
Flint L. Ont., Canada 49°52N 85°53W **149** C11
Flint Pk. Calif., U.S.A. 34°9N 118°11W **133** B3
Flintstone Md., U.S.A. 39°42N 78°34W **93** A2
Flippin Ark., U.S.A. 36°17N 92°36W **106** B3
Flomaton Ala., U.S.A. 31°0N 87°16W **112** E3
Flomot Tex., U.S.A. 34°14N 100°59W **108** C7
Floodwood Minn., U.S.A. 46°56N 92°55W **77** D61
Flora Ill., U.S.A. 38°40N 88°29W **84** E5
Flora Ind., U.S.A. 40°33N 86°31W **85** C4
Flora Miss., U.S.A. 32°33N 90°19W **111** D3
Flora Oreg., U.S.A. 45°54N 117°19W **121** B8
Flora Vista N. Mex., U.S.A. 36°48N 108°3W **131** A2
Florahome Fla., U.S.A. 29°44N 81°54W **114** B7
Floral City Fla., U.S.A. 28°45N 82°17W **114** C6
Floral Ark., U.S.A. 35°36N 91°45W **106** C4
Floral City Fla., U.S.A. 28°45N 82°17W **114** C6
Floral Park N.Y., U.S.A. 40°43N 73°42W **97** B4
Florala Ala., U.S.A. 31°0N 86°20W **112** E4
Flordell Hills Mo., U.S.A. 38°43N 90°15W **94** A2
Florence N.S., Canada 46°16N 60°16W **141** G9
Florence Ala., U.S.A. 34°48N 87°41W **112** B3
Florence Ariz., U.S.A. 33°2N 111°23W **130** D4
Florence Ark., U.S.A. 33°46N 91°39W **106** E4
Florence Calif., U.S.A. 33°57N 118°13W **133** C3
Florence Colo., U.S.A. 38°23N 105°8W **125** D5
Florence Kans., U.S.A. 38°15N 96°56W **82** C7
Florence Ky., U.S.A. 39°0N 84°38W **105** B8
Florence Mass., U.S.A. 42°20N 72°40W **91** B2
Florence Md., U.S.A. 39°20N 77°8W **93** A3
Florence Miss., U.S.A. 32°9N 90°8W **111** D3
Florence Mo., U.S.A. 38°35N 92°59W **83** C4
Florence Mont., U.S.A. 46°38N 114°5W **123** D3
Florence Oreg., U.S.A. 43°58N 124°7W **121** D1
Florence S.C., U.S.A. 34°12N 79°46W **103** D6
Florence S. Dak., U.S.A. 45°3N 97°20W **76** E8
Florence Tex., U.S.A. 30°51N 97°48W **109** G10
Florence Wis., U.S.A. 45°56N 88°15W **78** C5
Florence County ☆ S.C., U.S.A. 34°0N 79°45W **103** D6
Florence County ☆ Wis., U.S.A. 45°50N 88°20W **78** C5
Flores Guatemala 16°59N 89°50W **182** C2
Flores, Mercado de México, Mexico 19°19N 99°8W **181** C3
Flores I. B.C. Canada 49°20N 126°10W **154** F8
Flores Island Park ☆ B.C., Canada 49°17N 126°11W **154** F8
Floresville Tex., Canada 29°8N 98°10W **109** H9
Florey Tex., U.S.A. 32°27N 102°36W **108** E5
Florham Park N.J., U.S.A. 40°47N 74°23W **92** B2
Florida Cuba 21°32N 78°14W **182** B4
Florida Puerto Rico 18°22N 66°34W **184** G16
Florida N.Y., U.S.A. 41°20N 74°21W **92** A2
Florida □ U.S.A. 28°0N 82°0W **114** D7
Florida, Straits of U.S.A. 25°0N 80°0W **114** F8
Florida B. U.S.A. 25°0N 80°45W **114** F8
Florida City Fla., U.S.A. 25°27N 80°29W **114** F8
Florida del Norte Tamaulipas, Mexico 25°7N 98°13W **171** E6
Florida Keys Fla., U.S.A. 24°40N 81°0W **114** G8
Florido → Chihuahua, Mexico 27°43N 105°10W **169** F10
Florien La., U.S.A. 31°27N 93°28W **110** C2
Florin Calif., U.S.A. 38°30N 121°24W **126** E5
Floris Iowa, U.S.A. 40°52N 92°20W **81** E6
Florissant Mo., U.S.A. 38°47N 90°19W **94** A1
Florissant Fossil Beds Nat. Monument △ Colo., U.S.A. 38°54N 105°17W **125** D5
Flourtown Pa., U.S.A. 40°6N 75°12W **98** A1
Flower Hill N.Y., U.S.A. 40°48N 73°40W **97** B4
Flower Station Ont., Canada 45°10N 76°41W **147** B10
Flower's Cove Nfld. & L., Canada 51°14N 56°46W **142** A4
Floyd Iowa, U.S.A. 43°8N 92°44W **81** B6
Floyd N. Mex., U.S.A. 34°13N 103°35W **131** C7
Floyd Va., U.S.A. 36°55N 80°19W **102** E4
Floyd → Iowa, U.S.A. 42°29N 96°23W **81** C2
Floyd County ☆ Ga., U.S.A. 34°15N 85°10W **113** B1
Floyd County ☆ Ind., U.S.A. 38°20N 85°55W **85** E5
Floyd County ☆ Iowa, U.S.A. 43°5N 92°45W **81** B6
Floyd County ☆ Ky., U.S.A. 37°30N 82°45W **105** C10
Floyd County ☆ Tex., U.S.A. 34°0N 101°15W **108** C6
Floyd County ☆ Tex., U.S.A. 36°58N 80°25W **102** E4
Floyd Lamb State Park Nev., U.S.A. 36°19N 115°15W **134** A1
Floydada Tex., U.S.A. 33°59N 101°20W **108** D6
Flume, The N.H., U.S.A. 44°6N 71°41W **89** B3
Flushing Mich., U.S.A. 43°4N 83°51W **79** F8
Flushing N.Y., U.S.A. 40°45N 73°49W **97** B4
Flushing Ohio, U.S.A. 40°9N 81°4W **86** C5
Flushing Meadows Corona Park N.Y., U.S.A. 40°44N 73°50W **97** B3
Fluvanna County ☆ Va., U.S.A. 37°52N 78°16W **102** D6
Flynn Tex., U.S.A. 31°15N 96°9W **109** F11
Foam Lake Sask., Canada 51°40N 103°32W **150** D8
Foard City Tex., U.S.A. 33°53N 99°48W **109** D8
Foard County ☆ Tex., U.S.A. 33°59N 99°43W **109** D8
Fogelsville Pa., U.S.A. 40°35N 75°38W **92** B1
Fogo Nfld. & L., Canada 49°43N 54°17W **142** C6
Fogo, C. Nfld. & L., Canada 49°40N 54°5W **142** C7
Fogo I. Nfld. & L., Canada 49°40N 54°5W **142** C6
Foins, L. aux Qué., Canada 47°5N 78°11W **144** D4
Folcroft Pa., U.S.A. 39°53N 75°17W **98** B1
Foley Ala., U.S.A. 30°24N 87°41W **112** F3
Foley Fla., U.S.A. 30°4N 83°32W **114** A5

Foley Minn., U.S.A. 45°40N 93°55W **77** E5
Foley I., N.W.T., Canada 68°32N 75°5W **158** D10
Foleyet Ont., Canada 48°15N 82°25W **149** D12
Folkston Ga., U.S.A. 30°50N 82°0W **113** F4
Folsom La., U.S.A. 30°38N 90°11W **110** D5
Folsom N.J., U.S.A. 39°38N 74°51W **92** C2
Folsom N. Mex., U.S.A. 36°51N 103°55W **131** A7
Folsom W. Va., U.S.A. 39°28N 80°31W **102** B4
Folsom L. Calif., U.S.A. 38°42N 121°9W **126** E5
Fond-du-Lac Sask., Canada 59°19N 107°12W **157** E11
Fond du Lac Wis., U.S.A. 43°47N 88°27W **78** E5
Fond du Lac → Sask., Canada 59°17N 106°0W **157** E11
Fond du Lac County ☆ Wis., U.S.A. 43°40N 88°30W **78** E5
Fond du Lac Indian Reservation Minn., U.S.A. 46°45N 92°40W **77** D6
Fonda Iowa, U.S.A. 42°35N 94°51W **81** C4
Fonda N.Y., U.S.A. 42°57N 74°22W **88** C6
Fonde Ky., U.S.A. 36°36N 83°53W **105** D9
Fonseca, G. de Cent. Amer. 13°10N 87°40W **182** D2
Fontaine N.B., Canada 46°51N 64°58W **141** G5
Fontana Calif., U.S.A. 34°6N 117°26W **127** J9
Fontana Kans., U.S.A. 38°25N 94°51W **82** C9
Fontana Wis., U.S.A. 42°33N 88°35W **78** F5
Fontana L. N.C., U.S.A. 35°27N 83°48W **103** C2
Fontanelle Iowa, U.S.A. 41°17N 94°34W **81** D4
Fontas → B.C., Canada 58°14N 121°48W **157** E8
Fonteneau, L. Qué., Canada 51°55N 61°30W **140** B8
Fontenelle Wyo., U.S.A. 41°59N 110°3W **124** E2
Fontenelle Res. Wyo., U.S.A. 42°1N 110°3W **124** D2
Foosland Ill., U.S.A. 40°22N 88°26W **84** C5
Foothills Alta., Canada 53°4N 116°47W **153** E4
Footville Wis., U.S.A. 42°40N 89°12W **78** F4
Forada Minn., U.S.A. 45°48N 95°21W **77** E3
Foraker Okla., U.S.A. 36°52N 96°34W **107** B7
Foraker, Mt. Alaska, U.S.A. 62°58N 151°24W **135** E10
Forbes N. Dak., U.S.A. 45°57N 98°47W **76** E7
Forbing La., U.S.A. 32°24N 93°44W **110** B2
Ford Kans., U.S.A. 37°38N 99°45W **82** D4
Ford → Mich., U.S.A. 45°41N 87°9W **79** D4
Ford City Calif., U.S.A. 35°9N 119°27W **127** H7
Ford City Pa., U.S.A. 40°46N 79°32W **87** D3
Ford County ☆ Ill., U.S.A. 40°30N 88°10W **84** C5
Ford County ☆ Kans., U.S.A. 37°45N 100°0W **82** D4
Ford Dry L. Calif., U.S.A. 33°37N 114°59W **127** K12
Ford I. Hawai'i, U.S.A. 21°22N 157°58W **136** K14
Ford River Mich., U.S.A. 45°41N 87°8W **79** D4
Fording B.C., Canada 50°12N 114°52W **153** H6
Fordland Mo., U.S.A. 37°9N 92°57W **83** D4
Fordoche La., U.S.A. 30°36N 91°37W **110** D4
Fords Prairie Wash., U.S.A. 46°44N 122°59W **120** D3
Fordsville Ky., U.S.A. 37°38N 86°43W **104** C6
Fordville N. Dak., U.S.A. 48°13N 97°48W **76** B8
Fordyce Ark., U.S.A. 33°49N 92°25W **106** E3
Fordyce Nebr., U.S.A. 42°42N 97°22W **80** B8
Forel, Mt. Greenland 66°52N 36°55W **162** D7
Foreman Ark., U.S.A. 33°43N 94°24W **106** E1
Foremost Alta., Canada 49°26N 111°34W **153** J9
Forest La., U.S.A. 32°47N 91°25W **110** B4
Forest Miss., U.S.A. 32°22N 89°29W **111** D4
Forest Ohio, U.S.A. 40°48N 83°31W **86** C3
Forest → N. Dak., U.S.A. 48°21N 97°9W **76** B8
Forest Acres S.C., U.S.A. 34°1N 80°58W **103** D5
Forest Center Minn., U.S.A. 47°48N 91°19W **77** C7
Forest City Iowa, U.S.A. 43°16N 93°39W **81** B5
Forest City N.C., U.S.A. 35°20N 81°52W **103** C4
Forest City Pa., U.S.A. 41°39N 75°28W **87** C7
Forest County ☆ Pa., U.S.A. 41°30N 79°10W **87** C3
Forest County ☆ Wis., U.S.A. 45°35N 88°45W **78** C5
Forest Dale Vt., U.S.A. 43°48N 73°4W **89** C1
Forest Grove B.C., Canada 51°46N 121°5W **155** D13
Forest Grove Oreg., U.S.A. 45°31N 123°7W **121** B2
Forest Heights Md., U.S.A. 38°48N 77°0W **99** C3
Forest Hill Ont., Canada 43°41N 79°25W **161** A2
Forest Hill La., U.S.A. 31°3N 92°32W **110** C3
Forest Hill Md., U.S.A. 39°35N 76°23W **93** A4
Forest Hill Tex., U.S.A. 32°40N 97°16W **116** B2
Forest Hills N.Y., U.S.A. 40°42N 73°51W **97** B3
Forest Hills Pa., U.S.A. 40°25N 79°51W **98** B2
Forest Home Ala., U.S.A. 31°52N 86°50W **112** E4
Forest Lake Minn., U.S.A. 45°17N 92°59W **77** E6
Forest Park Ga., U.S.A. 33°37N 84°22W **113** C2
Forest Park Ill., U.S.A. 41°51N 87°47W **95** B2
Forest Park Mo., U.S.A. 38°38N 90°16W **94** B2
Forest Park Ohio, U.S.A. 39°17N 84°30W **86** D2
Forest Park Oreg., U.S.A. 45°34N 122°46W **132** A1
Forest View Ill., U.S.A. 41°48N 87°47W **95** C2
Forestbrook S.C., U.S.A. 33°43N 78°58W **103** E7
Forestburg Alta., Canada 52°35N 112°1W **153** F8
Foresthill Calif., U.S.A. 39°1N 120°49W **126** D6
Foreston Minn., U.S.A. 45°44N 93°43W **77** E5
Forestville Qué., Canada 48°48N 69°2W **145** C13
Forestville Md., U.S.A. 38°50N 76°52W **99** B4
Forestville Mich., U.S.A. 43°40N 82°37W **79** F9
Forestville N.Y., U.S.A. 42°28N 79°10W **88** C1
Forestville Ohio, U.S.A. 39°4N 84°20W **86** D2
Forestville Wis., U.S.A. 44°41N 87°29W **78** D6
Forgan Okla., U.S.A. 36°54N 100°32W **107** B3
Forge Village Mass., U.S.A. 42°35N 71°29W **91** B3
Forget Sask., Canada 49°39N 102°52W **150** E8
Forillon, Parc Nat. du △ Qué., Canada 48°46N 64°12W **140** E5
Fork River Man., Canada 51°31N 100°11W **151** C1
Fork Union Va., U.S.A. 37°46N 78°16W **102** D6
Forked Deer → Tenn., U.S.A. 35°56N 89°35W **104** E3
Forked River N.J., U.S.A. 39°50N 74°12W **92** C2
Forkland Ala., U.S.A. 32°39N 87°53W **112** D3
Forks Wash., U.S.A. 47°57N 124°23W **120** C1
Forks, The = Merritt B.C., Canada 50°10N 120°45W **155** E14
Forks of Salmon Calif., U.S.A. 41°16N 123°19W **126** B3
Forkville Miss., U.S.A. 32°28N 89°40W **111** D4
Forman N. Dak., U.S.A. 46°7N 97°38W **76** D8
Forrest Ill., U.S.A. 40°45N 88°25W **84** C5
Forrest N. Mex., U.S.A. 34°48N 103°36W **131** C7
Forrest City Ark., U.S.A. 35°1N 90°47W **106** C5
Forreston Ill., U.S.A. 42°8N 89°35W **84** A4
Forrest County ☆ Miss., U.S.A. 31°10N 89°13W **111** E4
Forreston Tex., U.S.A. 32°13N 96°52W **109** E11
Forsyth Ga., U.S.A. 33°2N 83°56W **113** C3
Forsyth Ill., U.S.A. 39°56N 88°57W **84** D5
Forsyth Mo., U.S.A. 36°41N 93°6W **83** E3
Forsyth Mont., U.S.A. 46°16N 106°41W **123** D11
Forsyth County ☆ Ga., U.S.A. 34°15N 84°5W **113** B2
Forsyth County ☆ N.C., U.S.A. 36°10N 80°15W **103** B5
Forsythe Qué., Canada 48°14N 76°26W **144** C6

Fort A.P. Hill Military Res. Va., U.S.A. 38°7N 77°13W **102** C7
Fort Adams Miss., U.S.A. 31°5N 91°33W **111** E2
Fort Albany Ont., Canada 52°15N 81°35W **159** G9
Fort Alexander Man., Canada 50°36N 96°17W **151** E15
Fort Ann N.Y., U.S.A. 43°25N 73°29W **89** C1
Fort Apache Indian Reservation Ariz., U.S.A. 33°50N 110°0W **130** D6
Fort Ashby W. Va., U.S.A. 39°30N 78°46W **93** A2
Fort Assiniboine Alta., Canada 54°20N 114°45W **152** D6
Fort Atkinson Iowa, U.S.A. 43°9N 91°56W **81** B7
Fort Atkinson Wis., U.S.A. 42°56N 88°50W **78** F5
Fort Belknap Agency Mont., U.S.A. 48°29N 108°45W **123** B9
Fort Belknap Indian Reservation Mont., U.S.A. 48°20N 108°40W **123** B9
Fort Bend County ☆ Tex., U.S.A. 29°34N 95°49W **109** H12
Fort Benning Military Reservation Ga., U.S.A. 32°21N 84°48W **113** D2
Fort Benton Mont., U.S.A. 47°49N 110°40W **123** C7
Fort Berthold Indian Reservation N. Dak., U.S.A. 47°45N 102°15W **76** C3
Fort Bidwell Calif., U.S.A. 41°52N 120°9W **126** B6
Fort Bidwell Indian Reservation Calif., U.S.A. 41°52N 120°12W **126** B6
Fort Bliss Military Reservation U.S.A. 31°49N 106°25W **131** F4
Fort Bowie Nat. Historic Site △ Ariz., U.S.A. 32°9N 109°22W **130** E6
Fort Bragg Calif., U.S.A. 39°26N 123°48W **126** D3
Fort Bragg Military Reservation N.C., U.S.A. 35°9N 79°0W **103** C6
Fort Branch Ind., U.S.A. 38°15N 87°35W **85** E3
Fort Bridger Wyo., U.S.A. 41°19N 110°23W **124** E2
Fort Calhoun Nebr., U.S.A. 41°27N 96°2W **80** C9
Fort Campbell Tenn., U.S.A. 36°38N 87°26W **104** D5
Fort Caroline Nat. Memorial △ U.S.A. 30°23N 81°30W **114** A7
Fort Chaffee Ark., U.S.A. 35°19N 94°18W **106** C1
Fort Chipewyan Alta., Canada 58°42N 111°8W **157** E10
Fort Clatsop Nat. Memorial △ U.S.A. 46°8N 123°53W **121** A2
Fort Cobb Okla., U.S.A. 35°6N 98°26W **107** C5
Fort Cobb Res. Okla., U.S.A. 35°10N 98°27W **107** C5
Fort Coffee Okla., U.S.A. 35°17N 94°35W **107** C9
Fort Collins Colo., U.S.A. 40°35N 105°5W **125** B5
Fort-Coulonge Qué., Canada 45°50N 76°45W **144** F6
Fort Craig Nat. Historic Site △ N. Mex., U.S.A. 33°38N 106°59W **131** D4
Fort Davis Ala., U.S.A. 32°15N 85°43W **112** D5
Fort Davis Tex., U.S.A. 30°35N 103°54W **108** G4
Fort Davis Nat. Historic Site △ Tex., U.S.A. 30°35N 103°54W **108** G4
Fort-de-France Martinique 14°36N 61°2W **183** D7
Fort De Soto Tampa, U.S.A. 27°36N 82°44W **115** D2
Fort De Soto Park Tampa, U.S.A. 27°37N 82°43W **115** D2
Fort Defiance Ariz., U.S.A. 35°45N 109°5W **130** B6
Fort Deposit Ala., U.S.A. 31°59N 86°35W **112** E4
Fort Dick Calif., U.S.A. 41°52N 124°9W **126** B2
Fort Dodge Iowa, U.S.A. 42°30N 94°11W **81** C4
Fort Donelson Nat. Battlefield △ Tenn., U.S.A. 36°29N 87°51W **104** D5
Fort Drum Fla., U.S.A. 27°32N 80°48W **114** D8
Fort Drum Military Reservation N.Y., U.S.A. 44°10N 75°35W **88** A5
Fort Duchesne Utah, U.S.A. 40°17N 109°52W **129** C6
Fort Dupont Park D.C., U.S.A. 38°52N 76°56W **99** B4
Fort Edward N.Y., U.S.A. 43°16N 73°35W **88** B7
Fort Eustis Va., U.S.A. 37°7N 76°34W **102** D8
Fort Fairfield Maine, U.S.A. 46°46N 67°50W **90** B6
Fort Foote Village Md., U.S.A. 38°46N 77°1W **99** C3
Fort Frances Ont., Canada 48°36N 93°24W **148** D3
Fort Franklin = Déline N.W.T., Canada 65°11N 123°25W **157** C8
Fort Fraser B.C., Canada 54°4N 124°33W **154** A10
Fort Frederica Nat. Monument △ Ga., U.S.A. 31°13N 81°23W **113** E5
Fort Gaines Ga., U.S.A. 31°36N 85°3W **113** E1
Fort Garland Colo., U.S.A. 37°26N 105°26W **125** E5
Fort Gay W. Va., U.S.A. 38°7N 82°36W **102** C2
Fort George = Chisasibi Qué., Canada 53°50N 79°0W **143** C2
Fort George = Prince George B.C., Canada 53°55N 122°50W **155** B12
Fort Gibson Okla., U.S.A. 35°48N 95°15W **107** C8
Fort Gibson L. Okla., U.S.A. 35°52N 95°14W **107** C8
Fort Good Hope N.W.T., Canada 66°14N 128°40W **156** C7
Fort Gordon Military Reservation Ga., U.S.A. 33°25N 82°10W **113** C4
Fort Hall Idaho, U.S.A. 43°2N 112°26W **122** F6
Fort Hall Indian Reservation Idaho, U.S.A. 43°2N 112°5W **122** F6
Fort Hancock Tex., U.S.A. 31°18N 105°51W **108** F2
Fort Hill Ohio, U.S.A. 39°7N 84°49W **86** D2
Fort Hood Military Reservation Tex., U.S.A. 31°8N 97°33W **109** F10
Fort Hope Ont., Canada 51°30N 88°0W **149** A9
Fort Huachuca Ariz., U.S.A. 31°35N 110°20W **130** F5
Fort Hunter Liggett Calif., U.S.A. 35°58N 121°12W **127** H5
Fort Irwin Calif., U.S.A. 35°16N 116°41W **127** H10
Fort Jackson Military Reservation S.C., U.S.A. 34°3N 80°55W **103** D5
Fort Jennings Ohio, U.S.A. 40°54N 84°18W **86** C2
Fort Jesup La., U.S.A. 31°37N 93°24W **110** C2
Fort Jones Calif., U.S.A. 41°36N 122°51W **126** B4
Fort Kent Maine, U.S.A. 47°15N 68°36W **90** A5
Fort Klamath Oreg., U.S.A. 42°42N 122°0W **121** E3
Fort Knox Military Reservation Ky., U.S.A. 37°55N 86°5W **104** C6
Fort Laramie Wyo., U.S.A. 42°13N 104°31W **124** D8
Fort Larned Nat. Historic Site △ Kans., U.S.A. 38°11N 99°13W **82** C4
Fort Lauderdale Fla., U.S.A. 26°7N 80°8W **115** B3
Fort Lauderdale Executive ✈ (FXE) Fla., U.S.A. 26°11N 80°10W **115** A2
Fort Lauderdale-Hollywood Int. ✈ (FLL) Fla., U.S.A. 26°4N 80°10W **115** B3
Fort Lawn S.C., U.S.A. 34°42N 80°54W **103** D5
Fort Leavenworth Kans., U.S.A. 39°23N 94°56W **82** B9
Fort Lee N.J., U.S.A. 40°50N 73°58W **97** A3
Fort Leonard Wood Military Reservation Mo., U.S.A. 37°48N 92°10W **83** D4
Fort Lewis Military Reservation Wash., U.S.A. 47°3N 122°35W **120** C3
Fort Liard N.W.T., Canada 60°14N 123°30W **157** D8
Fort Liberté Haiti 19°42N 71°51W **183** C5
Fort Loudon Pa., U.S.A. 39°54N 77°54W **87** E5
Fort Loudoun L. Tenn., U.S.A. 35°47N 84°15W **105** E8
Fort Lupton Colo., U.S.A. 40°5N 104°49W **125** B6
Fort McCoy Wis., U.S.A. 44°0N 90°41W **78** D3
Fort McDermitt Indian Reservation Oreg., U.S.A. 41°56N 117°43W **128** A3

Fort McDowell Indian Reservation Ariz., U.S.A. 33°40N 111°50W **130** D4
Fort MacKay Alta., Canada 57°12N 111°41W **152** A9
Fort Macleod Alta., Canada 49°45N 113°30W **153** J7
Fort McMurray Alta., Canada 56°44N 111°7W **152** B9
Fort McPherson N.W.T., Canada 67°30N 134°55W **156** C6
Fort Madison Iowa, U.S.A. 40°38N 91°27W **81** E71
Fort Matanzas Nat. Monument △ U.S.A. 29°43N 81°14W **114** B7
Fort Meade Fla., U.S.A. 27°45N 81°48W **114** D7
Fort Mill S.C., U.S.A. 35°0N 80°57W **103** C5
Fort Mitchell Ala., U.S.A. 32°20N 85°1W **112** D5
Fort Mohave Indian Reservation Ariz., U.S.A. 34°55N 114°35W **130** C1
Fort Morgan Colo., U.S.A. 40°15N 103°48W **125** B7
Fort Myers Fla., U.S.A. 26°39N 81°52W **114** E7
Fort Myers Beach Fla., U.S.A. 26°26N 81°52W **114** E7
Fort Myers S.W. Florida Regional ✈ (RSW) Fla., U.S.A. 26°32N 81°45W **114** E7
Fort Myers Shores Fla., U.S.A. 26°43N 81°45W **114** E7
Fort Necessity Nat. Battlefield △ Pa., U.S.A. 39°49N 79°36W **87** E3
Fort Nelson B.C., Canada 58°50N 122°44W **157** E8
Fort Nelson → B.C., Canada 59°32N 124°0W **157** E8
Fort Niobrara Nat. Wildlife Refuge △ Nebr., U.S.A. 42°54N 100°28W **80** B3
Fort Norman = Tulita N.W.T., Canada 64°57N 125°30W **157** D7
Fort Ogden Fla., U.S.A. 27°5N 81°57W **114** D7
Fort Oglethorpe Ga., U.S.A. 34°57N 85°16W **113** B1
Fort Payne Ala., U.S.A. 34°26N 85°43W **112** B5
Fort Peck Mont., U.S.A. 48°1N 106°27W **123** B11
Fort Peck Dam Mont., U.S.A. 48°0N 106°26W **123** C11
Fort Peck Indian Reservation Mont., U.S.A. 48°30N 105°30W **123** B12
Fort Peck L. Mont., U.S.A. 48°0N 106°26W **123** C11
Fort Pierce Fla., U.S.A. 27°27N 80°20W **114** D8
Fort Pierre S. Dak., U.S.A. 44°21N 100°22W **76** F5
Fort Pierre Nat. Grassland S. Dak., U.S.A. 44°10N 100°12W **76** F5
Fort Plain N.Y., U.S.A. 42°56N 74°37W **88** C6
Fort Polk Military Reservation La., U.S.A. 31°2N 93°13W **110** C2
Fort Providence N.W.T., Canada 61°3N 117°40W **157** D9
Fort Qu'Appelle Sask., Canada 50°45N 103°50W **150** E8
Fort Raleigh Nat. Historic Site △ N.C., U.S.A. 35°56N 75°43W **103** C11
Fort Randall Dam S. Dak., U.S.A. 43°4N 98°34W **76** G7
Fort Ransom N. Dak., U.S.A. 46°31N 97°56W **76** D8
Fort Recovery Ohio, U.S.A. 40°25N 84°47W **86** C2
Fort Resolution N.W.T., Canada 61°10N 113°40W **157** D10
Fort Riley Kans., U.S.A. 39°10N 96°42W **82** B7
Fort Ripley Minn., U.S.A. 46°10N 94°22W **77** D4
Fort Robinson Nebr., U.S.A. 42°40N 103°28W **80** B2
Fort Rucker Military Reservation Ala., U.S.A. 31°20N 85°43W **112** E5
Fort Rupert = Waskaganish Qué., Canada 51°30N 78°40W **143** C2
Fort St. James B.C., Canada 54°30N 124°10W **157** F8
Fort St. John B.C., Canada 56°15N 120°50W **157** E8
Fort Saskatchewan Alta., Canada 53°40N 113°15W **153** E7
Fort Scott Kans., U.S.A. 37°50N 94°42W **82** D9
Fort Scott Nat. Historic Site △ Kans., U.S.A. 37°51N 94°42W **82** D9
Fort Severn Ont., Canada 56°0N 87°40W **159** F8
Fort Shawnee Ohio, U.S.A. 40°42N 84°7W **86** C2
Fort Sill Military Res. Okla., U.S.A. 34°41N 98°30W **107** D5
Fort Simpson N.W.T., Canada 61°45N 121°15W **157** D8
Fort Smith Alta., Canada 60°0N 111°51W **157** D10
Fort Smith Ark., U.S.A. 35°23N 94°25W **106** C1
Fort Smith Nat. Historic Site △ Ark., U.S.A. 35°23N 94°26W **106** C1
Fort Snelling State Park △ Minn., U.S.A. 44°53N 93°10W **94** B2
Fort Stanton N. Mex., U.S.A. 33°30N 105°31W **131** D5
Fort Stewart Military Reservation Ga., U.S.A. 31°52N 81°37W **113** E5
Fort Stockton Tex., U.S.A. 30°53N 102°53W **108** G5
Fort Sumner N. Mex., U.S.A. 34°28N 104°15W **131** C6
Fort Supply Okla., U.S.A. 36°35N 99°35W **107** B4
Fort Thomas Ky., U.S.A. 39°4N 84°26W **105** A8
Fort Thompson S. Dak., U.S.A. 44°3N 99°26W **76** F6
Fort Totten N. Dak., U.S.A. 47°59N 99°0W **76** C7
Fort Totten Indian Reservation = Spirit Lake Indian Reservation N. Dak., U.S.A. 47°58N 99°0W **76** C7
Fort Towson Okla., U.S.A. 34°1N 95°10W **107** D8
Fort Union Nat. Monument △ N. Mex., U.S.A. 35°54N 105°1W **131** B5
Fort Union Trading Post Nat. Historic Site △ N. Dak., U.S.A. 48°1N 104°1W **76** B1
Fort Valley Ga., U.S.A. 32°33N 83°53W **113** D3
Fort Vancouver Nat. Historic Site △ Wash., U.S.A. 45°37N 122°39W **132** A2
Fort Vermilion Alta., Canada 58°24N 116°0W **157** E9
Fort Walton Beach Fla., U.S.A. 30°25N 86°36W **114** A2
Fort Washakie Wyo., U.S.A. 43°0N 108°53W **124** D4
Fort Washington Md., U.S.A. 38°42N 77°3W **93** B3
Fort Wayne Ind., U.S.A. 41°4N 85°9W **85** B5
Fort White Fla., U.S.A. 29°55N 82°43W **114** B6
Fort Worth Tex., U.S.A. 32°43N 97°19W **116** B2
Fort Worth-Meacham Int. ✈ (FTW) Tex., U.S.A. 32°49N 97°21W **116** B1
Fort Yates N. Dak., U.S.A. 46°5N 100°38W **76** D5
Fort Yukon Alaska, U.S.A. 66°34N 145°16W **135** C11
Fort Yuma Indian Reservation Calif., U.S.A. 32°45N 114°35W **127** L12
Forteau Nfld. & L., Canada 51°28N 56°58W **142** A4
Fortescue N.J., U.S.A. 39°12N 75°12W **92** C1
Fortín Veracruz, Mexico 18°54N 97°0W **177** F4
Fortin, L. Qué., Canada 50°50N 67°46W **140** C2
Fortine Mont., U.S.A. 48°46N 114°54W **123** B3
Fortress Mt. Wyo., U.S.A. 44°9N 109°48W **124** B3
Fortsonia Ga., U.S.A. 34°1N 82°47W **113** B4
Fortuna Calif., U.S.A. 40°36N 124°9W **126** C2
Fortuna Mo., U.S.A. 38°34N 92°48W **83** C4
Fortuna N. Dak., U.S.A. 48°55N 103°47W **76** B2
Fortuna Ledge = Marshall Alaska, U.S.A. 61°53N 162°5W **135** F7
Fortune Nfld. & L., Canada 47°4N 55°50W **142** E5
Fortune B. Nfld. & L., Canada 47°30N 55°22W **142** E5
Fortville Ind., U.S.A. 39°56N 85°51W **85** D5
Fosheim Pen. N.W.T., Canada 80°0N 85°0W **158** B9
Foss Okla., U.S.A. 35°27N 99°10W **107** C4
Foss L. Okla., U.S.A. 35°33N 99°11W **107** C4
Fossil Oreg., U.S.A. 45°0N 120°9W **121** B5
Fossil Butte Nat. Monument △ Wyo., U.S.A. 41°50N 110°27W **124** E2
Fossil L. Oreg., U.S.A. 43°19N 120°25W **121** D5
Fosston Sask., Canada 52°12N 103°49W **150** C8

Fosston *Minn., U.S.A.* 47°35N 95°45W **77** C3
Foster *Qué., Canada* 45°17N 72°30W **145** F10
Foster *Ky., U.S.A.* 38°48N 84°13W **105** B8
Foster *Nebr., U.S.A.* 42°16N 97°40W **80** B8
Foster *Oreg., U.S.A.* 44°25N 122°40W **121** C3
Foster *R.I., U.S.A.* 41°47N 71°44W **91** C3
Foster → *Sask., Canada* 55°47N 105°49W **157** E11
Foster City *Mich., U.S.A.* 45°58N 87°45W **79** D4
Foster County ☆ *N. Dak., U.S.A.* 47°30N 99°00W **76** C7
Foster L. *Oreg., U.S.A.* 42°59N 119°15W **121** E6
Foster Village *Hawai'i, U.S.A.* 21°21N 157°55W **136** K14
Fosters *Ala., U.S.A.* 33°6N 87°41W **112** C3
Fostoria *Iowa, U.S.A.* 43°15N 95°9W **81** B3
Fostoria *Kans., U.S.A.* 39°26N 96°30W **82** B7
Fostoria *Ohio, U.S.A.* 41°10N 83°25W **86** B3
Fouke *Ark., U.S.A.* 33°16N 93°53W **106** E2
Fountain *Colo., U.S.A.* 38°41N 104°42W **125** D6
Fountain *Fla., U.S.A.* 30°29N 85°25W **114** A3
Fountain *Mich., U.S.A.* 44°3N 86°11W **79** E5
Fountain *Minn., U.S.A.* 43°45N 92°8W **77** G6
Fountain City *Ind., U.S.A.* 39°57N 84°55W **85** D6
Fountain City *Wis., U.S.A.* 44°8N 91°43W **78** D2
Fountain County ☆ *Ind., U.S.A.* 40°5N 87°15W **85** C3
Fountain Cr. → *Colo., U.S.A.* 38°15N 104°36W **125** D6
Fountain Green *Utah, U.S.A.* 39°38N 111°38W **129** D4
Fountain Head *Md., U.S.A.* 39°42N 77°42W **93** A3
Fountain Hill *Ark., U.S.A.* 33°21N 91°51W **106** E4
Fountain Hills *Ariz., U.S.A.* 33°37N 111°43W **130** D4
Fountain Inn *S.C., U.S.A.* 34°42N 82°12W **103** D3
Fountain Run *Ky., U.S.A.* 36°43N 85°56W **105** D7
Four Corners *Oreg., U.S.A.* 44°56N 122°58W **121** C3
Four Corners *Wyo., U.S.A.* 44°5N 104°8W **124** B8
Four Corners *Utah, U.S.A.* 37°0N 109°3W **129** F6
Four League B. *La., U.S.A.* 29°20N 91°13W **110** E4
Four Mountains, Is. of *Alaska, U.S.A.* 53°0N 170°0W **135** K5
Four Oaks *N.C., U.S.A.* 35°27N 78°26W **103** C7
Four Town *Minn., U.S.A.* 48°17N 95°20W **77** B3
Fourchu *N.S., Canada* 45°43N 60°17W **141** H9
Fourmont L. *Nfld & L., Canada* 52°5N 60°27W **140** A9
Fournier, L. *Qué., Canada* 51°33N 65°25W **140** B4
Fourteen Mile Pt. *Mich., U.S.A.* 47°0N 89°10W **79** B2
Foux, Cap-à- *Haiti* 19°43N 73°27W **183** C5
Fowblesburg *Md., U.S.A.* 39°34N 76°50W **93** A4
Fowler *Calif., U.S.A.* 36°38N 119°41W **127** G7
Fowler *Colo., U.S.A.* 38°8N 104°2W **125** D6
Fowler *Ind., U.S.A.* 40°37N 87°19W **85** C3
Fowler *Kans., U.S.A.* 37°23N 100°12W **82** D3
Fowler *Mich., U.S.A.* 43°0N 84°45W **79** G7
Fowlerton *Ind., U.S.A.* 40°25N 85°34W **85** C5
Fowlerton *Tex., U.S.A.* 28°28N 98°48W **109** J9
Fowlerville *Mich., U.S.A.* 42°40N 84°4W **79** G7
Fowlstown *Ga., U.S.A.* 30°48N 84°33W **113** F2
Fox *Okla., U.S.A.* 34°22N 97°30W **107** D6
Fox → *Ill., U.S.A.* 41°21N 88°50W **84** B5
Fox → *Mo., U.S.A.* 40°17N 91°30W **83** A5
Fox → *Wis., U.S.A.* 44°32N 88°0W **78** D5
Fox Chapel *Pa., U.S.A.* 40°30N 79°52W **98** A2
Fox Creek *Alta., Canada* 54°24N 116°48W **152** D4
Fox Is. *Alaska, U.S.A.* 53°0N 168°0W **135** K6
Fox Lake *Alta., Canada* 58°28N 114°31W **157** E10
Fox Lake *Ill., U.S.A.* 42°24N 88°11W **84** A5
Fox Lake *Wis., U.S.A.* 43°34N 88°55W **78** E5
Fox Mt. *Yukon, Canada* 61°55N 133°22W **157** D6
Fox Point *Wis., U.S.A.* 43°9N 87°54W **94** B2
Fox Pt. *Wis., U.S.A.* 43°10N 87°52W **94** A2
Fox Valley *Sask., Canada* 50°30N 109°25W **150** E2
Foxboro *Mass., U.S.A.* 42°4N 71°16W **91** B3
Foxe Basin *Nunavut, Canada* 66°0N 77°0W **159** D10
Foxe Chan. *Nunavut, Canada* 65°0N 80°0W **159** E9
Foxe Pen. *Nunavut, Canada* 65°0N 76°0W **159** E10
Foxfield *Colo., U.S.A.* 39°35N 104°47W **134** C3
Foxpark *Wyo., U.S.A.* 41°5N 106°9W **124** E6
Foxville *Ont., Canada* 50°4N 81°38W **149** B15
Foxworth *Miss., U.S.A.* 31°14N 89°52W **111** E4
Foyil *Okla., U.S.A.* 36°26N 95°31W **107** B8
Frametown *W. Va., U.S.A.* 38°38N 80°52W **102** C4
Framingham *Mass., U.S.A.* 42°18N 71°24W **91** B3
Frances *Wash., U.S.A.* 46°33N 123°30W **120** D2
Frances → *Yukon, Canada* 60°16N 129°10W **157** D7
Frances, L. *Mont., U.S.A.* 48°16N 112°13W **123** B5
Frances L. *Yukon, Canada* 61°23N 129°30W **157** D7
Francestown *N.H., U.S.A.* 42°58N 71°48W **89** D3
Francesville *Ind., U.S.A.* 40°59N 86°53W **85** C4
Francis *Sask., Canada* 50°6N 103°52W **150** E8
Francis *Okla., U.S.A.* 34°52N 96°36W **107** D7
Francis *Utah, U.S.A.* 40°37N 111°17W **129** C4
Francis *N.H., U.S.A.* 45°2N 71°20W **89** A3
Francis Case, L. *S. Dak., U.S.A.* 43°4N 98°34W **76** G7
Francis Creek *Wis., U.S.A.* 44°12N 87°44W **78** D6
Francis E. Walter Res. *Pa., U.S.A.* 41°8N 75°44W **92** A1
Francis Marion Nat. Forest *S.C., U.S.A.* 33°10N 79°40W **103** E6
Francisco Ignacio Madero *Chiapas, Mexico* 15°21N 92°24W **178** D3
Francisco Ignacio Madero *Chiapas, Mexico* 16°48N 93°46W **178** C3
Francisco Ignacio Madero *Coahuila, Mexico* 25°48N 103°18W **170** E1
Francisco Ignacio Madero *Durango, Mexico* 24°26N 104°18W **173** C6
Francisco Ignacio Madero *Hidalgo, Mexico* 20°45N 99°19W **175** B8
Francisco Ignacio Madero *Nayarit, Mexico* 21°39N 104°50W **172** F6
Francisco Ignacio Madero *Quintana Roo, Mexico* 20°9N 88°11W **179** B5
Francisco Ignacio Madero *Zacatecas, Mexico* 23°55N 102°56W **173** D8
Francisco Ignacio Madero, Presa *Chihuahua, Mexico* 28°10N 105°37W **169** E10
Francisco R. Serrano *Baja Calif., Mexico* 31°20N 115°33W **166** B3
Francisco Villa *Chiapas, Mexico* 17°0N 93°28W **178** B3
Francisco Zarco *Baja Calif., Mexico* 32°8N 116°34W **166** A2
Francisco Zarco, Presa *Durango, Mexico* 25°16N 103°47W **173** B7
François *Nfld. & L., Canada* 47°35N 56°45W **142** E4
François L. *B.C., Canada* 54°0N 125°30W **154** A9
Franconia *N.H., U.S.A.* 44°14N 71°44W **89** B3
Franconia *Va., U.S.A.* 38°47N 77°7W **99** C3
Francs Pk. *Wyo., U.S.A.* 43°58N 109°20W **124** C3
Frank Church River of No Return Wilderness *Idaho, U.S.A.* 45°41N 114°25W **122** E4
Frank Lloyd Wright Home *Ill., U.S.A.* 41°53N 87°47W **95** B2
Frank Rae, Mt. *Yukon, Canada* 64°28N 138°33W **157** D5
Frankenmuth *Mich., U.S.A.* 43°20N 83°44W **79** F8
Frankewing *Tenn., U.S.A.* 35°12N 86°51W **104** E6

Frankford *Ont., Canada* 44°12N 77°36W **147** C9
Frankford *Del., U.S.A.* 38°31N 75°14W **93** B5
Frankford *Mo., U.S.A.* 39°29N 91°19W **83** B5
Frankford *W. Va., U.S.A.* 37°56N 80°23W **102** D4
Frankfort *Ind., U.S.A.* 40°17N 86°31W **85** C4
Frankfort *Kans., U.S.A.* 39°42N 96°25W **82** B7
Frankfort *Ky., U.S.A.* 38°12N 84°52W **105** B8
Frankfort *Maine, U.S.A.* 44°37N 68°53W **90** E5
Frankfort *Mich., U.S.A.* 44°38N 86°14W **79** E5
Frankfort *Ohio, U.S.A.* 39°24N 83°11W **86** D3
Frankfort *S. Dak., U.S.A.* 44°53N 98°18W **76** F7
Franklin *Ariz., U.S.A.* 32°41N 109°5W **130** E6
Franklin *Ga., U.S.A.* 33°17N 85°6W **113** C1
Franklin *Idaho, U.S.A.* 42°1N 111°48W **122** G7
Franklin *Ill., U.S.A.* 39°37N 90°3W **84** D3
Franklin *Ind., U.S.A.* 39°29N 86°3W **85** D4
Franklin *Kans., U.S.A.* 37°32N 94°42W **82** D9
Franklin *Ky., U.S.A.* 36°43N 86°35W **104** D6
Franklin *La., U.S.A.* 29°48N 91°30W **110** E4
Franklin *Maine, U.S.A.* 44°35N 68°14W **90** E5
Franklin *Mass., U.S.A.* 42°5N 71°24W **91** B3
Franklin *Minn., U.S.A.* 44°32N 94°53W **77** F4
Franklin *N.C., U.S.A.* 35°11N 83°23W **103** C2
Franklin *N.H., U.S.A.* 43°27N 71°39W **89** C3
Franklin *N.J., U.S.A.* 41°7N 74°35W **92** A2
Franklin *N.Y., U.S.A.* 42°21N 75°10W **88** C5
Franklin *Nebr., U.S.A.* 40°6N 98°57W **80** D7
Franklin *Ohio, U.S.A.* 39°34N 84°18W **86** D2
Franklin *Pa., U.S.A.* 41°24N 79°50W **87** C3
Franklin *Tenn., U.S.A.* 35°55N 86°52W **104** E6
Franklin *Tex., U.S.A.* 31°2N 96°29W **109** F11
Franklin *Va., U.S.A.* 36°41N 76°56W **102** E8
Franklin *W. Va., U.S.A.* 38°39N 79°20W **102** C5
Franklin, Pt. *Alaska, U.S.A.* 70°55N 158°48W **135** A8
Franklin B. *N.W.T., Canada* 69°45N 126°0W **156** C7
Franklin County ☆ *Ala., U.S.A.* 34°21N 87°42W **112** B3
Franklin County ☆ *Ark., U.S.A.* 35°29N 93°50W **106** C3
Franklin County ☆ *Fla., U.S.A.* 29°50N 84°45W **114** B4
Franklin County ☆ *Ga., U.S.A.* 34°20N 83°10W **113** B3
Franklin County ☆ *Idaho, U.S.A.* 42°10N 111°50W **122** G7
Franklin County ☆ *Ill., U.S.A.* 38°0N 89°0W **84** E4
Franklin County ☆ *Ind., U.S.A.* 39°25N 85°5W **85** D5
Franklin County ☆ *Iowa, U.S.A.* 42°45N 93°25W **81** C5
Franklin County ☆ *Kans., U.S.A.* 38°30N 95°15W **82** C8
Franklin County ☆ *Ky., U.S.A.* 38°15N 84°55W **105** B8
Franklin County ☆ *Maine, U.S.A.* 45°0N 70°30W **90** D3
Franklin County ☆ *Mass., U.S.A.* 42°30N 72°35W **91** A2
Franklin County ☆ *Miss., U.S.A.* 31°28N 90°54W **111** E3
Franklin County ☆ *Mo., U.S.A.* 38°25N 91°0W **83** C5
Franklin County ☆ *N.C., U.S.A.* 36°0N 78°2CW **103** B7
Franklin County ☆ *N.Y., U.S.A.* 44°30N 74°15W **88** A6
Franklin County ☆ *Nebr., U.S.A.* 40°15N 99°0W **80** D7
Franklin County ☆ *Ohio, U.S.A.* 40°0N 83°4W **86** D3
Franklin County ☆ *Pa., U.S.A.* 39°56N 77°40W **87** E5
Franklin County ☆ *Tenn., U.S.A.* 35°10N 86°1W **104** E6
Franklin County ☆ *Tex., U.S.A.* 33°11N 95°13W **109** D12
Franklin County ☆ *Va., U.S.A.* 37°0N 80°0W **102** E5
Franklin County ☆ *Vt., U.S.A.* 44°50N 72°50W **89** B2
Franklin County ☆ *Wash., U.S.A.* 46°30N 119°0W **120** D7
Franklin D. Roosevelt L. *Wash., U.S.A.* 48°18N 118°9W **120** B7
Franklin Grove *Ill., U.S.A.* 41°51N 89°18W **84** B4
Franklin L. *Nunavut, Canada* 66°56N 96°3W **159** D6
Franklin L. *Nev., U.S.A.* 40°25N 115°22W **128** B5
Franklin Mts. *N.W.T., Canada* 65°0N 125°0W **157** C7
Franklin Parish ☆ *La., U.S.A.* 32°10N 91°43W **110** B4
Franklin Park *Ill., U.S.A.* 41°55N 87°52W **95** B1
Franklin Park *Mass., U.S.A.* 42°18N 71°5W **96** B2
Franklin Park *Va., U.S.A.* 38°55N 77°9W **99** B3
Franklin Res. *Calif., U.S.A.* 34°5N 118°24W **133** B2
Franklin River *B.C., Canada* 49°7N 124°48W **154** F10
Franklin Square *N.Y., U.S.A.* 40°42N 73°40W **99** A4
Franklin Str. *Nunavut, Canada* 72°0N 96°0W **158** C6
Franklinton *La., U.S.A.* 30°51N 90°9W **110** D5
Franklinton *N.C., U.S.A.* 36°6N 78°27W **103** B7
Franklinville *N.J., U.S.A.* 39°37N 75°5W **92** C1
Franklinville *N.Y., U.S.A.* 42°20N 78°27W **88** C2
Frankston *Tex., U.S.A.* 32°3N 95°30W **109** E12
Frankton *Ind., U.S.A.* 40°13N 85°46W **85** C5
Frankville *Ala., U.S.A.* 31°39N 88°9W **112** E2
Frannie *Wyo., U.S.A.* 44°58N 108°37W **124** B4
Franquelin *Qué., Canada* 49°18N 67°54W **140** D2
Franz *Ont., Canada* 48°25N 84°30W **149** D12
Fraser *Colo., U.S.A.* 39°57N 105°49W **125** C5
Fraser → *B.C., Canada* 49°7N 123°11W **155** F11
Fraser → *Nfld. & L., Canada* 56°39N 62°10W **143** B5
Fraser Lake *B.C., Canada* 54°0N 124°50W **154** B10
Fraserdale *Ont., Canada* 49°55N 81°37W **149** C15
Fraserville = Rivière-du-Loup *Qué., Canada* 47°50N 69°30W **145** D13
Fraserwood *Man., Canada* 50°38N 97°13W **151** E14
Frazee *Minn., U.S.A.* 46°44N 95°42W **77** D3
Frazer *Mont., U.S.A.* 48°3N 106°2W **123** B11
Frazer L. *Ont., Canada* 49°15N 88°40W **148** C8
Frazeysburg *Ohio, U.S.A.* 40°7N 82°7W **86** C4
Frazier Park *Calif., U.S.A.* 34°49N 118°56W **127** J8
Fred *Tex., U.S.A.* 30°34N 94°10W **109** G13
Freda *Mich., U.S.A.* 47°8N 88°49W **79** B3
Frederic *Mich., U.S.A.* 44°47N 84°45W **79** E7
Frederic *Wis., U.S.A.* 45°40N 92°28W **78** C1
Frederica *Del., U.S.A.* 39°1N 75°28W **93** A5
Frederick *Colo., U.S.A.* 40°6N 104°56W **125** B6
Frederick *Okla., U.S.A.* 34°23N 99°1W **107** D4
Frederick *S. Dak., U.S.A.* 45°50N 98°31W **76** E7
Frederick County ☆ *Md., U.S.A.* 39°30N 77°25W **93** A3
Frederick County ☆ *Va., U.S.A.* 39°5N 78°13W **102** B6
Frederick E. Hyde Fjord *Greenland* 83°25N 29°0W **162** A8
Fredericksburg *Iowa, U.S.A.* 42°58N 92°12W **81** C6
Fredericksburg *Tex., U.S.A.* 30°16N 98°52W **109** G9
Fredericksburg *Va., U.S.A.* 38°18N 77°28W **102** C7
Fredericksburg and Spotsylvania Nat. Military Park △ *Va., U.S.A.* 38°17N 77°43W **102** C7
Fredericktown *Mo., U.S.A.* 37°34N 90°18W **83** D6
Fredericktown *Ohio, U.S.A.* 40°29N 82°33W **86** C4
Frederickton *N.B., Canada* 45°57N 66°40W **141** H3
Fredericton Junction *N.B., Canada* 45°41N 66°40W **141** H3
Frederika *Iowa, U.S.A.* 42°53N 92°19W **81** C6
Frederikshåb = Paamiut *Greenland* 62°0N 49°43W **162** B5
Frederiksted *U.S. Virgin Is.* 17°43N 64°53W **184** H18
Fredonia *Ariz., U.S.A.* 36°57N 112°32W **130** A3
Fredonia *Kans., U.S.A.* 37°32N 95°49W **82** D8
Fredonia *Ky., U.S.A.* 37°12N 88°4W **104** D4
Fredonia *N. Dak., U.S.A.* 46°20N 99°6W **76** D6
Fredonia *N.Y., U.S.A.* 42°26N 79°20W **88** C1
Fredonia *Pa., U.S.A.* 41°19N 80°16W **87** C2
Fredrica, L. *Fla., U.S.A.* 28°30N 81°18W **115** A3

Freeborn County ☆ *Minn., U.S.A.* 43°40N 93°15W **77** G5
Freeburg *Ill., U.S.A.* 38°26N 89°55W **84** E4
Freeburg *Mo., U.S.A.* 38°19N 91°56W **83** C5
Freedom *Okla., U.S.A.* 36°46N 99°7W **107** B4
Freedom *Wyo., U.S.A.* 42°59N 111°3W **124** D1
Freehold *N.J., U.S.A.* 40°16N 74°17W **92** B2
Freel Pk. *Calif., U.S.A.* 38°51N 119°54W **126** E7
Freeland *Pa., U.S.A.* 41°1N 75°54W **87** C7
Freels, C. *Nfld. & L., Canada* 49°15N 53°30W **142** C7
Freeman *S. Dak., U.S.A.* 43°21N 97°26W **76** G8
Freeman → *Alta., Canada* 54°19N 114°47W **152** D6
Freeman, L. *Ind., U.S.A.* 40°42N 86°45W **85** C4
Freeport *Bahamas* 26°30N 78°47W **182** A4
Freeport *N.S., Canada* 44°15N 66°20W **141** J3
Freeport *Fla., U.S.A.* 30°30N 86°8W **114** A2
Freeport *Ill., U.S.A.* 42°17N 89°36W **84** A4
Freeport *Kans., U.S.A.* 37°12N 97°51W **82** D6
Freeport *Maine, U.S.A.* 43°52N 70°6W **90** E3
Freeport *Mich., U.S.A.* 42°46N 85°19W **79** G6
Freeport *Minn., U.S.A.* 45°40N 94°42W **77** E4
Freeport *N.Y., U.S.A.* 40°39N 73°35W **92** B3
Freeport *Pa., U.S.A.* 40°41N 79°41W **87** D3
Freeport *Tex., U.S.A.* 28°57N 95°21W **109** J12
Freer *Tex., U.S.A.* 27°53N 98°37W **109** K9
Freesoil *Mich., U.S.A.* 44°7N 86°14W **79** E5
Freestone County ☆ *Tex., U.S.A.* 31°44N 96°10W **109** F11
Freistatt *Mo., U.S.A.* 37°1N 93°54W **83** D3
Fremont *Calif., U.S.A.* 37°32N 121°57W **126** F5
Fremont *Ind., U.S.A.* 41°44N 84°56W **85** B6
Fremont *N.C., U.S.A.* 35°33N 77°58W **103** C8
Fremont *Nebr., U.S.A.* 41°26N 96°30W **80** C9
Fremont *Ohio, U.S.A.* 41°21N 83°7W **86** B3
Fremont *Wis., U.S.A.* 44°16N 88°52W **78** D5
Fremont → *Utah, U.S.A.* 38°24N 110°42W **129** E5
Fremont County ☆ *Colo., U.S.A.* 38°30N 105°30W **125** D5
Fremont County ☆ *Idaho, U.S.A.* 44°15N 111°20W **122** E7
Fremont County ☆ *Iowa, U.S.A.* 40°45N 95°35W **81** E3
Fremont County ☆ *Wyo., U.S.A.* 43°0N 108°30W **124** D4
Fremont I. *Utah, U.S.A.* 41°10N 112°21W **129** B3
Fremont Junction *Utah, U.S.A.* 38°45N 111°23W **129** E4
Fremont L. *Wyo., U.S.A.* 42°57N 109°48W **124** D3
Fremont Nat. Forest *Oreg., U.S.A.* 42°20N 120°50W **121** E5
French → *Ont., Canada* 46°2N 80°34W **146** A6
French → *Ont., Canada* 50°40N 80°59W **149** B16
French Broad → *U.S.A.* 35°57N 83°51W **103** C2
French Camp *Calif., U.S.A.* 37°53N 121°16W **126** F5
French Camp *Miss., U.S.A.* 33°18N 89°24W **111** C4
French Cays = Plana Cays *Bahamas* 22°38N 73°30W **183** B5
French Creek *W. Va., U.S.A.* 38°53N 80°18W **102** C4
French Creek → *Pa., U.S.A.* 41°24N 79°50W **87** C3
French Frigate Shoals *Hawai'i, U.S.A.* 23°45N 166°10W **136** G10
French Gulch *Calif., U.S.A.* 40°42N 122°38W **126** C4
French Lick *Ind., U.S.A.* 38°33N 86°37W **85** E4
French Meadows Res. *Calif., U.S.A.* 39°10N 120°40W **126** D6
French Regional Park △ *Minn., U.S.A.* 45°2N 93°26W **94** A1
French River *Ont., Canada* 46°2N 80°34W **146** A6
French River *Minn., U.S.A.* 46°54N 91°54W **77** D7
French Settlement *La., U.S.A.* 30°18N 90°47W **110** D5
Frenchboro *Maine, U.S.A.* 44°7N 68°22W **90** D5
Frenchburg *Ky., U.S.A.* 37°57N 83°38W **105** C9
Frenchglen *Oreg., U.S.A.* 42°50N 118°55W **121** E7
Frenchman Butte *Sask., Canada* 53°35N 109°38W **150** B2
Frenchman Cr. → *N. Amer.* 48°31N 107°10W **123** B10
Frenchman Cr. → *Nebr., U.S.A.* 40°14N 100°50W **80** D5
Frenchman L. *Calif., U.S.A.* 39°54N 120°11W **126** D6
Frenchman L. *Nev., U.S.A.* 36°48N 115°56W **128** C5
Frenchtown *Mont., U.S.A.* 47°1N 114°14W **123** C3
Frenchtown *N.J., U.S.A.* 40°32N 75°4W **92** B1
Frenchville *Maine, U.S.A.* 47°17N 68°23W **90** A5
Fresh Meadows *N.Y., U.S.A.* 40°44N 73°47W **97** B4
Fresh Pond *Mass., U.S.A.* 42°22N 71°9W **96** A2
Fresnillo *Zacatecas, Mexico* 23°10N 102°53W **173** D8
Fresno *Calif., U.S.A.* 36°44N 119°47W **127** G7
Fresno County ☆ *Calif., U.S.A.* 36°40N 120°0W **127** G7
Fresno Res. *Mont., U.S.A.* 48°36N 109°57W **123** B8
Frewsburg *N.Y., U.S.A.* 42°3N 79°10W **88** C1
Friant *Calif., U.S.A.* 36°59N 119°43W **127** G7
Friars Point *Miss., U.S.A.* 34°22N 90°38W **111** B3
Frick Park *Pa., U.S.A.* 40°25N 79°54W **98** B2
Friday Harbor *Wash., U.S.A.* 48°32N 123°1W **120** B2
Fridley *Minn., U.S.A.* 45°5N 93°15W **94** A2
Friend *Kans., U.S.A.* 38°16N 100°55W **82** C3
Friend *Nebr., U.S.A.* 40°38N 97°17W **80** D8
Friendly *Md., U.S.A.* 38°42N 76°59W **93** B4
Friendship *N.Y., U.S.A.* 42°12N 78°8W **88** C2
Friendship *Tenn., U.S.A.* 35°55N 89°14W **104** D3
Friendship *Wis., U.S.A.* 43°58N 89°49W **78** E4
Friendship Hill Nat. Historic Site △ *Pa., U.S.A.* 39°47N 79°56W **87** E3
Friendsville *Md., U.S.A.* 39°40N 79°24W **93** A1
Friendsville *Tenn., U.S.A.* 35°46N 84°8W **105** E8
Fries *Va., U.S.A.* 36°43N 80°59W **102** E4
Friesland *Wis., U.S.A.* 43°35N 89°4W **78** E4
Frio → *Tex., U.S.A.* 28°26N 98°11W **109** J9
Frio County ☆ *Tex., U.S.A.* 28°54N 99°6W **109** J8
Frio Draw → *Tex., U.S.A.* 34°50N 102°19W **108** C5
Friona *Tex., U.S.A.* 34°38N 102°43W **108** C5
Frisco *Colo., U.S.A.* 39°35N 106°6W **125** C4
Frisco City *Ala., U.S.A.* 31°26N 87°24W **112** E3
Frisco Peak *Utah, U.S.A.* 38°31N 113°17W **129** E2
Frissell, Mt. *Conn., U.S.A.* 42°3N 73°28W **91** B1
Fritch *Tex., U.S.A.* 35°38N 101°36W **108** B6
Frobisher *Sask., Canada* 49°12N 102°26W **151** F9
Frobisher B. *Nunavut, Canada* 62°30N 66°0W **159** E12
Frobisher Bay = Iqaluit *Nunavut, Canada* 63°44N 68°31W **159** E12
Frobisher L. *Sask., Canada* 56°20N 108°15W **157** E11
Frog L. *Alta., Canada* 53°55N 110°20W **152** E10
Froid *Mont., U.S.A.* 48°20N 104°30W **123** B13
Fromberg *Mont., U.S.A.* 45°24N 108°54W **123** D9
Front Range *Colo., U.S.A.* 40°25N 105°45W **125** B5
Front Royal *Va., U.S.A.* 38°55N 78°12W **102** B6
Frontenac *Kans., U.S.A.* 37°27N 94°42W **82** D9
Frontenac, Parc de △ *Qué., Canada* 45°52N 71°13W **145** F12
Frontenac Prov. Park △ *Ont., Canada* 44°32N 76°30W **147** C10
Frontera *Tabasco, Mexico* 18°32N 92°38W **178** D4
Frontera Comalapa *Chiapas, Mexico* 15°42N 92°6W **178** D4
Frontera Echeverría *Chiapas, Mexico* 16°49N 90°53W **178** C6
Frontera Hidalgo *Chiapas, Mexico* 14°47N 92°10W **178** E4

Fronteras *Sonora, Mexico* 30°56N 109°31W **168** C6
Frontier *Sask., Canada* 49°12N 108°34W **150** F3
Frontier *Wyo., U.S.A.* 41°49N 110°32W **124** E2
Frontier County ☆ *Nebr., U.S.A.* 40°30N 100°30W **80** D5
Frost *Minn., U.S.A.* 43°35N 93°56W **77** G5
Frost *Tex., U.S.A.* 32°5N 96°49W **109** E11
Frost Place, The *N.H., U.S.A.* 44°13N 71°45W **89** B3
Frostburg *Md., U.S.A.* 39°39N 78°56W **93** A2
Frostproof *Fla., U.S.A.* 27°45N 81°32W **114** D7
Frozen Str. *Nunavut, Canada* 65°45N 84°20W **159** D9
Fruit Cove *Fla., U.S.A.* 30°7N 81°39W **114** A7
Fruita *Colo., U.S.A.* 39°9N 108°44W **125** C2
Fruitdale *Ala., U.S.A.* 31°21N 88°25W **112** E2
Fruitdale *S. Dak., U.S.A.* 44°40N 103°42W **76** F2
Fruithurst *Ala., U.S.A.* 33°44N 85°26W **112** C5
Fruitland *Idaho, U.S.A.* 44°0N 116°55W **122** F2
Fruitland *Iowa, U.S.A.* 41°21N 91°8W **81** D7
Fruitland *Md., U.S.A.* 38°19N 75°37W **93** B5
Fruitland *Mo., U.S.A.* 37°27N 89°38W **83** D7
Fruitland *N. Mex., U.S.A.* 36°44N 108°24W **131** A2
Fruitland *Utah, U.S.A.* 40°13N 110°50W **129** C5
Fruitland Park *Fla., U.S.A.* 28°51N 81°54W **114** C7
Fruitport *Mich., U.S.A.* 43°7N 86°9W **79** F5
Fruitvale *B.C., Canada* 49°7N 117°33W **155** F17
Fruitvale *Idaho, U.S.A.* 44°49N 116°26W **122** E2
Fruitvale *Wash., U.S.A.* 46°37N 120°33W **120** D5
Fry Canyon *Utah, U.S.A.* 37°38N 110°9W **129** F5
Fry L., *Ont., Canada* 51°14N 91°19W **148** A5
Fryeburg *Maine, U.S.A.* 44°1N 70°59W **90** D3
Fuerte → *Sinaloa, Mexico* 25°54N 109°22W **172** B1
Fuertes Brotantes, Parque Nacional △ *Distrito Federal, Mexico* 19°17N 99°11W **181** C2
Fulda *Minn., U.S.A.* 43°53N 95°36W **77** G3
Fulford = North Miami Beach *Fla., U.S.A.* 25°55N 80°9W **115** C2
Fulford Harbour *B.C., Canada* 48°47N 123°27W **155** G11
Fullerton *Baltimore, U.S.A.* 39°22N 76°30W **99** A2
Fullerton *Calif., U.S.A.* 33°53N 117°56W **127** K9
Fullerton *N. Dak., U.S.A.* 46°10N 98°26W **76** D7
Fullerton *Nebr., U.S.A.* 41°22N 97°58W **80** C8
Fullerton, C. *Nunavut, Canada* 63°58N 88°46W **159** D6
Fulton *Ala., U.S.A.* 31°47N 87°44W **112** E3
Fulton *Ark., U.S.A.* 33°37N 93°49W **106** E2
Fulton *Ill., U.S.A.* 41°52N 90°11W **84** B3
Fulton *Kans., U.S.A.* 38°1N 94°43W **82** C9
Fulton *Ky., U.S.A.* 36°30N 88°53W **104** D4
Fulton *Miss., U.S.A.* 34°16N 88°25W **111** B5
Fulton *Mo., U.S.A.* 38°52N 91°57W **83** C5
Fulton *N.Y., U.S.A.* 43°19N 76°25W **88** B4
Fulton *Ohio, U.S.A.* 40°28N 82°50W **86** B4
Fulton *S. Dak., U.S.A.* 43°44N 97°49W **76** G8
Fulton *Tex., U.S.A.* 28°4N 97°2W **109** J10
Fulton County ☆ *Ark., U.S.A.* 36°22N 91°50W **106** B4
Fulton County ☆ *Ga., U.S.A.* 33°40N 84°40W **113** C2
Fulton County ☆ *Ill., U.S.A.* 40°30N 90°10W **84** C3
Fulton County ☆ *Ind., U.S.A.* 41°5N 86°15W **85** B4
Fulton County ☆ *Ky., U.S.A.* 36°32N 89°10W **104** D3
Fulton County ☆ *Ohio, U.S.A.* 41°33N 84°8W **86** B2
Fulton County ☆ *Pa., U.S.A.* 39°55N 78°5W **87** E4
Fultondale *Ala., U.S.A.* 33°37N 86°48W **112** C4
Fults *Ill., U.S.A.* 38°10N 90°13W **84** E3
Fundy, B. of *N.B., Canada* 45°0N 66°0W **141** J3
Fundy Nat. Park △ *N.B., Canada* 45°35N 65°10W **141** H4
Funk *Nebr., U.S.A.* 40°28N 99°15W **80** D6
Funk I. *Nfld. & L., Canada* 49°45N 53°11W **142** C7
Funston *Ga., U.S.A.* 31°12N 83°52W **113** E3
Fuquay-Varina *N.C., U.S.A.* 35°35N 78°48W **103** C7
Furman *S.C., U.S.A.* 32°41N 81°11W **103** F4
Furnas County ☆ *Nebr., U.S.A.* 40°15N 100°0W **80** D6
Fury and Hecla Str. *Nunavut, Canada* 69°56N 84°0W **158** D7
Futiga *Amer. Samoa* 14°21S 170°45W **184** e

G

G. Ross Lord Park *Ont., Canada* 43°47N 79°28W **161** A2
Gabaret I. *Ill., U.S.A.* 38°42N 90°10W **94** A2
Gabarus *N.S., Canada* 45°50N 60°9W **141** H9
Gabbettville *Ga., U.S.A.* 32°57N 85°8W **113** D1
Gabbs *Nev., U.S.A.* 38°52N 117°55W **128** D3
Gabbs Valley *Nev., U.S.A.* 38°51N 118°12W **128** D2
Gabbs Valley Range *Nev., U.S.A.* 38°34N 118°0W **128** D2
Gabilan Range *Calif., U.S.A.* 36°30N 121°15W **126** G5
Gabriel Leyva Solano *Sinaloa, Mexico* 25°40N 108°38W **172** B2
Gabriel Park *Oreg., U.S.A.* 45°28N 122°43W **132** B1
Gabriel Str. *Nunavut, Canada* 61°45N 65°30W **159** E12
Gabriola I. *B.C., Canada* 49°9N 123°47W **155** F11
Gackle *N. Dak., U.S.A.* 46°38N 99°9W **76** D6
Gadsden *Ala., U.S.A.* 34°1N 86°1W **112** B4
Gadsden *Ariz., U.S.A.* 32°33N 114°47W **130** E1
Gadsden *Tenn., U.S.A.* 35°47N 88°59W **104** E4
Gadsden County ☆ *Fla., U.S.A.* 30°30N 84°45W **114** A4
Gadsden Point *Tampa, U.S.A.* 27°49N 82°28W **115** C4
Gaffney *S.C., U.S.A.* 35°5N 81°39W **103** C4
Gage *Okla., U.S.A.* 36°19N 99°45W **107** B4
Gage County ☆ *Nebr., U.S.A.* 40°20N 96°45W **80** D9
Gage Park *Ill., U.S.A.* 41°47N 87°42W **95** C2
Gagetown *N.B., Canada* 45°46N 66°10W **141** H3
Gagnon *Qué., Canada* 51°50N 68°5W **143** C4
Gagnon, L. *Qué., Canada* 46°7N 75°7W **144** C7
Gahanna *Ohio, U.S.A.* 40°1N 82°53W **86** C4
Gail *Tex., U.S.A.* 32°46N 101°27W **108** E6
Gaillarbois, L. *Qué., Canada* 52°0N 67°22W **140** B2
Gaillard, L. *Conn., U.S.A.* 41°21N 72°46W **91** C2
Gaines County ☆ *Tex., U.S.A.* 32°43N 102°39W **108** E5
Gainesboro *Tenn., U.S.A.* 36°21N 85°39W **105** D7
Gainesville *Fla., U.S.A.* 29°40N 82°20W **114** B6
Gainesville *Ga., U.S.A.* 34°18N 83°50W **113** B3
Gainesville *Mo., U.S.A.* 36°36N 92°26W **83** E41
Gainesville *Tex., U.S.A.* 33°38N 97°8W **109** D10
Gainesville *Va., U.S.A.* 38°48N 77°37W **99** C1
Gaithersburg *Md., U.S.A.* 39°8N 77°12W **93** A3
Gakona *Alaska, U.S.A.* 62°18N 145°18W **135** L11
Galahad *Alta., Canada* 52°31N 111°56W **153** F9
Galatia *Ill., U.S.A.* 37°51N 88°37W **84** F5
Galatia *Kans., U.S.A.* 38°38N 98°58W **82** C5
Galax *Va., U.S.A.* 36°40N 80°56W **102** E4
Galeana *Chihuahua, Mexico* 30°7N 107°38W **168** C8
Galeana *Nuevo León, Mexico* 24°50N 100°4W **171** F4
Galena *Alaska, U.S.A.* 64°44N 156°56W **135** D8
Galena *Idaho, U.S.A.* 43°52N 114°39W **122** F4
Galena *Kans., U.S.A.* 37°4N 94°38W **82** D9
Galena *Md., U.S.A.* 39°21N 75°53W **93** A5
Galena *Mo., U.S.A.* 36°48N 93°28W **83** E3
Galena Bay *B.C., Canada* 50°40N 117°51W **155** E17

Galera, Pta. Oaxaca, Mexico 15°58N 97°42W **177 J3**
Galera Pt. Trin. & Tob. 10°49N 60°54W **183 D7**
Galesburg Ill., U.S.A. 40°57N 90°22W **84 C3**
Galesburg Kans., U.S.A. 37°28N 95°21W **82 D8**
Galesburg Mich., U.S.A. 42°17N 85°26W **79 G6**
Galesburg N. Dak., U.S.A. 47°16N 97°24W **76 C8**
Galestown Md., U.S.A. 38°35N 75°42W **93 B5**
Galesville Wis., U.S.A. 44°5N 91°21W **78 D2**
Galeton Colo., U.S.A. 40°31N 104°35W **125 B6**
Galeton Pa., U.S.A. 41°44N 77°39W **87 C5**
Galindo, Barra Veracruz, Mexico 21°14N 97°26W **176 C3**
Galion Ohio, U.S.A. 40°44N 82°47W **86 C4**
Galisteo N. Mex., U.S.A. 35°24N 105°57W **131 B5**
Galiuro Mts. Ariz., U.S.A. 32°30N 110°20W **130 E5**
Gallatin Mo., U.S.A. 39°55N 93°58W **83 B3**
Gallatin Tenn., U.S.A. 36°24N 86°27W **104 D6**
Gallatin Tex., U.S.A. 31°54N 95°9W **109 F12**
Gallatin → Mont., U.S.A. 45°56N 111°30W **123 E6**
Gallatin County ☆ Ill., U.S.A. 37°45N 88°15W **84 F5**
Gallatin County ☆ Ky., U.S.A. 38°45N 84°55W **105 B8**
Gallatin County ☆ Mont., U.S.A. 45°55N 111°15W **123 E6**
Gallatin Gateway Mont., U.S.A. 45°35N 111°12W **123 E6**
Gallatin Nat. Forest Mont., U.S.A. 45°15N 111°15W **123 E7**
Gallatin Range 44°55N 110°53W **123 F7**
Gallia County ☆ Ohio, U.S.A. 38°49N 82°12W **86 E4**
Galliano La., U.S.A. 29°26N 90°18W **110 E5**
Gallinas → N. Mex., U.S.A. 35°0N 104°55W **131 B6**
Gallinas Mts. N. Mex., U.S.A. 34°25N 107°45W **131 C3**
Gallion Ala., U.S.A. 32°30N 87°43W **112 D3**
Gallipolis Ohio, U.S.A. 38°49N 82°12W **86 E4**
Gallman Miss., U.S.A. 31°56N 90°23W **111 E3**
Gallo Mts. N. Mex., U.S.A. 34°5N 108°35W **131 C2**
Galloo I. N.Y., U.S.A. 43°55N 76°25W **88 B4**
Gallup N. Mex., U.S.A. 35°32N 108°45W **131 B2**
Galt Calif., U.S.A. 38°15N 121°18W **126 E5**
Galt Iowa, U.S.A. 42°42N 93°36W **81 C5**
Galt Mo., U.S.A. 40°8N 93°23W **83 A3**
Galva Ill., U.S.A. 41°10N 90°3W **84 B31**
Galva Iowa, U.S.A. 42°30N 95°25W **81 C3**
Galveston Ind., U.S.A. 40°35N 86°11W **85 C4**
Galveston Tex., U.S.A. 29°18N 94°48W **109 H13**
Galveston B. Tex., U.S.A. 29°36N 94°50W **109 H13**
Galveston County ☆ Tex., U.S.A. 29°28N 95°9W **109 H12**
Galveston I. Tex., U.S.A. 29°16N 94°51W **109 H13**
Gamaliel Ark., U.S.A. 36°27N 92°14W **106 B4**
Gamaliel Ky., U.S.A. 36°38N 85°48W **105 D7**
Gambell Alaska, U.S.A. 63°47N 171°45W **135 E5**
Gamber Md., U.S.A. 39°28N 76°56W **93 A4**
Gambier I. B.C., Canada 49°30N 123°23W **155 F11**
Gamerco N. Mex., U.S.A. 35°34N 108°46W **131 B2**
Gammon → Man., Canada 51°24N 95°44W **151 D16**
Ganado Ariz., U.S.A. 35°43N 109°33W **130 B6**
Ganado Tex., U.S.A. 29°2N 96°31W **109 H11**
Gananoque Ont., Canada 44°20N 76°10W **147 C10**
Gandeeville W. Va., U.S.A. 38°42N 81°25W **102 C3**
Gander Nfld. & L., Canada 48°58N 54°35W **142 D6**
Gander → Nfld. & L., Canada 49°16N 54°30W **142 C6**
Gander L. Nfld. & L., Canada 48°58N 54°35W **142 D6**
Gang Ranch B.C., Canada 51°33N 122°20W **155 D12**
Gannett Idaho, U.S.A. 43°22N 114°11W **122 F4**
Gannett Peak Wyo., U.S.A. 43°11N 109°39W **124 C3**
Gannvalley S. Dak., U.S.A. 44°2N 98°59W **76 F7**
Gans Okla., U.S.A. 35°23N 94°42W **107 C9**
Gantt Ala., U.S.A. 31°25N 86°29W **112 E4**
Gantt S.C., U.S.A. 34°48N 82°25W **103 D3**
Gap Mills W. Va., U.S.A. 37°34N 80°24W **102 D4**
Garachiné Panama 8°0N 78°12W **182 E4**
Garambullo Coahuila, Mexico 25°4N 101°30W **173 E2**
Garame de Arriba Durango, Mexico 25°2N 105°30W **172 B5**
Garapan N. Marianas 15°12N 145°43E **184 c**
Garber Iowa, U.S.A. 42°45N 91°16W **81 C7**
Garber Okla., U.S.A. 36°26N 97°35W **107 B6**
Garberville Calif., U.S.A. 40°6N 123°48W **126 C3**
Garcia Colo., U.S.A. 37°0N 105°32W **125 E5**
García de la Cadena Zacatecas, Mexico 21°9N 103°28W **174 A4**
Gardar N. Dak., U.S.A. 48°35N 97°53W **76 B8**
Garden Mich., U.S.A. 45°47N 86°33W **79 D5**
Garden City Ala., U.S.A. 34°1N 86°45W **112 D4**
Garden City Ga., U.S.A. 32°6N 81°9W **113 D5**
Garden City Idaho, U.S.A. 43°38N 116°16W **122 F2**
Garden City Kans., U.S.A. 37°58N 100°53W **82 D3**
Garden City Mo., U.S.A. 38°34N 94°12W **83 C2**
Garden City N.Y., U.S.A. 40°43N 73°38W **97 B5**
Garden City S.C., U.S.A. 33°36N 79°1W **103 E6**
Garden City S. Dak., U.S.A. 44°57N 97°35W **76 E7**
Garden City Tex., U.S.A. 31°52N 101°29W **108 F6**
Garden City Utah, U.S.A. 41°57N 111°24W **129 E4**
Garden County ☆ Nebr., U.S.A. 41°30N 102°15W **80 C3**
Garden District La., U.S.A. 29°55N 90°5W **117 C2**
Garden Grove Calif., U.S.A. 33°47N 117°55W **127 K9**
Garden Grove Iowa, U.S.A. 40°50N 93°36W **81 E5**
Garden Hill Man., Canada 53°53N 94°38W **159 G7**
Garden Home Oreg., U.S.A. 45°27N 122°45W **128 E4**
Garden I. Mich., U.S.A. 45°49N 85°30W **79 D6**
Garden Island B. La., U.S.A. 29°0N 89°0W **117 D4**
Garden Lakes Ga., U.S.A. 34°19N 85°17W **113 B1**
Garden Peninsula Mich., U.S.A. 45°32N 86°38W **79 D5**
Garden Plain Kans., U.S.A. 37°40N 97°41W **82 D6**
Garden Ridge Tex., U.S.A. 29°38N 98°18W **116 B4**
Garden Valley Idaho, U.S.A. 44°6N 115°57W **122 E3**
Garden View Pa., U.S.A. 41°15N 77°22W **87 C5**
Gardena Idaho, U.S.A. 43°58N 116°12W **122 F2**
Gardendale Ala., U.S.A. 33°39N 86°49W **112 C4**
Gardendale Tex., U.S.A. 29°28N 98°21W **116 C3**
Gardenville Baltimore, U.S.A. 39°19N 76°33W **99 B2**
Gardi Ga., U.S.A. 31°32N 81°48W **113 E5**
Gardiner Maine, U.S.A. 44°14N 69°47W **90 D4**
Gardiner Mont., U.S.A. 45°2N 110°42W **123 E7**
Gardiner Oreg., U.S.A. 43°44N 124°7W **121 D1**
Gardiner L. Alta., Canada 57°32N 112°30W **152 A8**
Gardiners B. N.Y., U.S.A. 41°5N 72°5W **91 C2**
Gardiners I. N.Y., U.S.A. 41°6N 72°6W **91 C2**
Gardner Colo., U.S.A. 37°47N 105°10W **125 D5**
Gardner Fla., U.S.A. 27°21N 81°48W **114 D7**
Gardner Ill., U.S.A. 41°11N 88°17W **84 B4**
Gardner Kans., U.S.A. 38°49N 94°56W **82 D6**
Gardner Mass., U.S.A. 42°34N 71°59W **91 B3**
Gardner N. Dak., U.S.A. 47°8N 96°58W **76 C9**
Gardner Canal B.C., Canada 53°27N 128°8W **154 B6**
Gardner L. Maine, U.S.A. 44°45N 67°20W **90 D6**
Gardner Pinnacles Hawai'i, U.S.A. 25°0N 167°55W **136 F10**
Gardnerville Nev., U.S.A. 38°56N 119°45W **128 D1**
Garfield Ark., U.S.A. 36°27N 93°58W **106 B2**
Garfield Kans., U.S.A. 38°5N 99°14W **82 C4**
Garfield Minn., U.S.A. 45°56N 95°30W **77 E3**
Garfield N.J., U.S.A. 40°52N 74°7W **97 A1**

Garfield N. Mex., U.S.A. 32°46N 107°16W **131 E3**
Garfield Wash., U.S.A. 47°1N 117°9W **120 C8**
Garfield County ☆ Colo., U.S.A. 39°30N 108°0W **125 C3**
Garfield County ☆ Mont., U.S.A. 47°15N 107°0W **123 C11**
Garfield County ☆ Nebr., U.S.A. 41°50N 99°0W **80 C7**
Garfield County ☆ Okla., U.S.A. 36°20N 97°45W **107 B6**
Garfield County ☆ Utah, U.S.A. 37°50N 111°20W **129 F4**
Garfield County ☆ Wash., U.S.A. 46°28N 117°36W **120 D8**
Garfield Heights Ohio, U.S.A. 41°25N 81°36W **98 B2**
Garfield Mt. Mont., U.S.A. 44°31N 112°37W **123 F5**
Garfield Park Ill., U.S.A. 41°52N 87°42W **95 B2**
Garfield Park Res. Ohio, U.S.A. 41°26N 81°36W **98 B2**
Garibaldi B.C., Canada 49°58N 123°9W **155 F11**
Garibaldi Oreg., U.S.A. 45°34N 123°55W **121 B2**
Garibaldi, Mt. B.C., Canada 49°50N 123°0W **155 F11**
Garibaldi Park △ B.C., Canada 49°50N 122°40W **155 F12**
Garland Ala., U.S.A. 31°33N 86°50W **112 E4**
Garland Ark., U.S.A. 33°22N 93°43W **106 D2**
Garland Kans., U.S.A. 37°44N 94°37W **82 D9**
Garland N.C., U.S.A. 34°47N 78°24W **103 D7**
Garland Nebr., U.S.A. 40°57N 96°59W **80 D9**
Garland Tex., U.S.A. 32°54N 96°38W **116 A6**
Garland Utah, U.S.A. 41°45N 112°10W **129 D3**
Garland County ☆ Ark., U.S.A. 34°34N 93°10W **106 C2**
Garnavillo Iowa, U.S.A. 42°52N 91°14W **81 C7**
Garneau, L. Qué., Canada 51°43N 63°22W **140 B6**
Garner Iowa, U.S.A. 43°6N 93°36W **81 B5**
Garner N.C., U.S.A. 35°43N 78°37W **103 C7**
Garnet B. Nunavut, Canada 65°18N 75°22W **159 D10**
Garnett Kans., U.S.A. 38°17N 95°14W **82 C8**
Garnish Nfld. & L., Canada 47°14N 55°22W **142 E5**
Garrard County ☆ Ky., U.S.A. 37°35N 84°30W **105 C8**
Garretson S. Dak., U.S.A. 43°43N 96°30W **76 G9**
Garrett Ind., U.S.A. 41°21N 85°8W **85 B5**
Garrett Pa., U.S.A. 39°52N 79°4W **93 A1**
Garrett County ☆ Md., U.S.A. 39°30N 79°20W **93 A1**
Garrison Iowa, U.S.A. 42°9N 92°8W **81 C6**
Garrison Ky., U.S.A. 38°36N 83°10W **105 B9**
Garrison Minn., U.S.A. 46°18N 93°50W **77 D5**
Garrison Mont., U.S.A. 46°31N 112°49W **123 D5**
Garrison N. Dak., U.S.A. 47°40N 101°25W **76 C4**
Garrison Nebr., U.S.A. 41°11N 97°10W **80 C8**
Garrison Tex., U.S.A. 31°49N 94°30W **109 F13**
Garrison Utah, U.S.A. 38°56N 114°2W **129 E1**
Garrison Dam N. Dak., U.S.A. 47°30N 101°25W **76 C4**
Garrison Res. = Sakakawea, L. N. Dak., U.S.A. 47°30N 101°25W **76 C4**
Garry, L. Nunavut, Canada 65°58N 100°18W **159 D5**
Garson L. Alta., Canada 56°19N 110°2W **152 B10**
Garvanza Calif., U.S.A. 34°6N 118°11W **133 B3**
Garvin Okla., U.S.A. 33°57N 94°56W **107 E9**
Garvin County ☆ Okla., U.S.A. 34°45N 97°20W **107 D6**
Garwin Iowa, U.S.A. 42°6N 92°41W **81 C6**
Garwood Tex., U.S.A. 29°27N 96°24W **109 H11**
Gary Ind., U.S.A. 41°36N 87°20W **85 B3**
Gary Minn., U.S.A. 47°22N 96°16W **77 C2**
Gary S. Dak., U.S.A. 44°48N 96°27W **76 F9**
Gary W. Va., U.S.A. 37°22N 81°33W **102 D3**
Garysburg N.C., U.S.A. 36°27N 77°33W **103 B8**
Garza Ayala Nuevo León, Mexico 26°27N 100°5W **170 D4**
Garza County ☆ Tex., U.S.A. 33°12N 101°23W **108 D6**
Garza García Nuevo León, Mexico 25°40N 100°24W **180 C1**
Garza Valdez Tamaulipas, Mexico 24°32N 99°22W **171 F5**
Gas Kans., U.S.A. 37°55N 95°20W **82 D8**
Gas City Ind., U.S.A. 40°29N 85°37W **85 C5**
Gascon N. Mex., U.S.A. 35°53N 105°27W **131 B5**
Gasconade Mo., U.S.A. 38°40N 91°34W **83 C5**
Gasconade → Mo., U.S.A. 38°41N 91°33W **83 C5**
Gasconade County ☆ Mo., U.S.A. 38°25N 91°30W **83 C5**
Gascons Qué., Canada 48°11N 64°51W **140 E5**
Gascoyne N. Dak., U.S.A. 46°7N 103°5W **76 D2**
Gasoriachic Chihuahua, Mexico 27°17N 108°33W **168 F7**
Gasparilla I. Fla., U.S.A. 26°46N 82°16W **114 E6**
Gaspé Qué., Canada 48°52N 64°30W **140 E5**
Gaspé, B. de Qué., Canada 48°46N 64°17W **140 E5**
Gaspé, C. Qué., Canada 48°48N 64°7W **140 E5**
Gaspé Pen. = Gaspésie, Pén. de la Qué., Canada 48°45N 65°40W **140 E4**
Gaspésie, Parc de la Qué., Canada 48°55N 66°10W **140 E3**
Gaspésie, Pén. de la Qué., Canada 48°45N 65°40W **140 E4**
Gasquet Calif., U.S.A. 41°51N 123°58W **126 B3**
Gassaway W. Va., U.S.A. 38°41N 80°47W **102 C4**
Gaston Ind., U.S.A. 40°19N 85°31W **85 C5**
Gaston N.C., U.S.A. 36°30N 77°39W **103 B8**
Gaston S.C., U.S.A. 33°49N 81°5W **103 D4**
Gaston, L. N.C., U.S.A. 36°30N 77°49W **103 B8**
Gaston County ☆ N.C., U.S.A. 35°18N 81°12W **103 C4**
Gastonia N.C., U.S.A. 35°16N 81°11W **103 C4**
Gatchellville Pa., U.S.A. 39°46N 76°28W **93 B4**
Gate Okla., U.S.A. 36°51N 100°4W **107 B3**
Gate City Va., U.S.A. 36°38N 82°35W **102 E2**
Gates N.Y., U.S.A. 43°9N 77°42W **88 C3**
Gates Oreg., U.S.A. 44°45N 122°25W **121 C3**
Gates Tenn., U.S.A. 35°50N 89°24W **104 E3**
Gates County ☆ N.C., U.S.A. 36°25N 76°40W **103 B9**
Gates of the Arctic Nat. Park and Preserve Alaska, U.S.A. 67°45N 153°15W **135 C9**
Gateshead I. N.W.T., Canada 70°36N 100°26W **158 C5**
Gatesville N.C., U.S.A. 36°24N 76°45W **103 B9**
Gatesville Tex., U.S.A. 31°26N 97°45W **109 F10**
Gateway Colo., U.S.A. 38°41N 108°59W **125 D2**
Gateway Nat. Recr. Area △ N.J., U.S.A. 40°26N 74°0W **92 B3**
Gateway Nat. Recr. Area △ N.Y., U.S.A. 40°30N 73°50W **97 C3**
Gateway Park N.Y., U.S.A. 32°43N 96°42W **116 B2**
Gatineau Qué., Canada 45°29N 75°39W **160 A2**
Gatineau → Qué., Canada 45°27N 75°42W **144 F7**
Gatineau, Parc de la △ Qué., Canada 45°40N 76°0W **144 F6**
Gatineau Park Qué., Canada 45°26N 75°45W **160 A1**
Gatlif Ky., U.S.A. 36°41N 84°11W **105 D8**
Gatlinburg Tenn., U.S.A. 35°43N 83°31W **105 E9**
Gato Colo., U.S.A. 37°3N 107°12W **125 E3**
Gauley → W. Va., U.S.A. 38°10N 81°12W **102 C3**
Gauley Bridge W. Va., U.S.A. 38°10N 81°12W **102 C3**
Gauley River Nat. Recr. Area △ W. Va., U.S.A. 38°13N 81°0W **102 C4**
Gaultois Nfld. & L., Canada 47°36N 55°54W **142 E5**
Gavilan N. Mex., U.S.A. 36°24N 107°23W **131 A3**
Gaviota Calif., U.S.A. 34°29N 120°13W **127 J6**
Gay Ga., U.S.A. 33°6N 84°35W **113 C2**
Gay W. Va., U.S.A. 38°44N 81°12W **102 C3**
Gaylord Kans., U.S.A. 39°39N 98°51W **82 B5**
Gaylord Mich., U.S.A. 45°2N 84°41W **79 D7**
Gaylord Minn., U.S.A. 44°33N 94°13W **77 F4**

Gaylordsville Conn., U.S.A. 41°39N 73°29W **91 C1**
Gayot, L. Qué., Canada 55°43N 70°50W **143 B3**
Gays Mills Wis., U.S.A. 43°19N 90°51W **78 E3**
Gayville S. Dak., U.S.A. 42°53N 97°10W **76 H8**
Gazelle Calif., U.S.A. 41°31N 122°31W **126 B4**
Gearhart Oreg., U.S.A. 46°1N 123°55W **121 A2**
Gearhart Mt. Oreg., U.S.A. 42°30N 120°53W **121 E5**
Geary N.B., Canada 45°46N 66°29W **141 H3**
Geary Okla., U.S.A. 35°38N 98°19W **107 C5**
Geary County ☆ Kans., U.S.A. 39°0N 96°45W **82 C7**
Geauga County ☆ Ohio, U.S.A. 41°35N 81°12W **86 B5**
Geddes S. Dak., U.S.A. 43°15N 98°42W **76 G7**
Geiger Ala., U.S.A. 32°52N 88°18W **112 D2**
Geikie → Sask., Canada 57°45N 103°52W **157 E12**
Geikie I. Ont., Canada 50°0N 88°35W **148 E9**
Geistown Pa., U.S.A. 40°18N 78°52W **87 D4**
Gem Alta., Canada 50°57N 112°11W **153 H8**
Gem Kans., U.S.A. 39°26N 100°54W **82 B3**
Gem County ☆ Idaho, U.S.A. 44°0N 116°25W **122 E2**
Gem Lake Minn., U.S.A. 45°3N 93°2W **94 A3**
Gene Autry Okla., U.S.A. 34°19N 97°2W **107 D6**
General Bravo Nuevo León, Mexico 25°48N 99°10W **170 E5**
General Cepeda Coahuila, Mexico 25°21N 101°22W **171 E3**
General Dewitt Spain ✈ Tenn., U.S.A. 32°12N 90°3W **117 A1**
General Enrique Estrada Zacatecas, Mexico 22°59N 102°44W **173 E8**
General Escobedo Durango, Mexico 25°30N 105°15W **172 B5**
General Escobedo Nuevo León, Mexico 25°49N 100°20W **180 B2**
General Francisco Murguía Zacatecas, Mexico 24°0N 103°1W **173 D7**
General Francisco González Villarreal Tamaulipas, Mexico 25°22N 97°53W **170 E7**
General Mariano Escobedo ✈ Monterrey, Mexico 25°46N 100°7W **180 B3**
General Mitchell Int., Milwaukee ✈ (MKE) Wis., U.S.A. 42°57N 87°54W **94 C2**
General Rodrigo M. Quevedo Chihuahua, Mexico 31°46N 107°37W **169 B8**
General Terán Nuevo León, Mexico 25°16N 99°41W **171 E5**
General Treviño Nuevo León, Mexico 26°14N 99°29W **170 D5**
General Trías Chihuahua, Mexico 28°21N 106°22W **169 E9**
General Zuazúa Nuevo León, Mexico 25°54N 100°7W **180 A3**
Genero Codina Zacatecas, Mexico 22°29N 102°27W **173 E8**
Genesee Idaho, U.S.A. 46°33N 116°56W **122 C2**
Genesee → N.Y., U.S.A. 43°16N 77°36W **88 B3**
Genesee County ☆ Mich., U.S.A. 43°0N 83°40W **79 F8**
Genesee County ☆ N.Y., U.S.A. 43°0N 78°10W **88 B2**
Geneseo Ill., U.S.A. 41°27N 90°9W **84 B31**
Geneseo Kans., U.S.A. 38°31N 98°10W **82 C5**
Geneseo N.Y., U.S.A. 42°48N 77°49W **88 C3**
Geneva Ala., U.S.A. 31°2N 85°52W **112 E5**
Geneva Ga., U.S.A. 32°35N 84°33W **113 D2**
Geneva Ill., U.S.A. 41°53N 88°18W **84 B5**
Geneva Ind., U.S.A. 40°36N 84°58W **85 C6**
Geneva Iowa, U.S.A. 42°41N 93°8W **81 C5**
Geneva Minn., U.S.A. 43°49N 93°16W **77 G5**
Geneva N.Y., U.S.A. 42°52N 76°59W **88 C3**
Geneva Nebr., U.S.A. 40°32N 97°36W **80 D8**
Geneva Ohio, U.S.A. 41°48N 80°57W **86 B6**
Geneva County ☆ Ala., U.S.A. 31°6N 85°42W **112 E5**
Genoa Colo., U.S.A. 39°17N 103°30W **125 C7**
Genoa Ill., U.S.A. 42°6N 88°42W **84 A5**
Genoa Nebr., U.S.A. 41°27N 97°44W **80 C8**
Genoa Ohio, U.S.A. 41°31N 83°22W **86 B3**
Genoa Wis., U.S.A. 43°35N 91°13W **78 E2**
Genoa City Wis., U.S.A. 42°30N 88°20W **78 F5**
Genola Minn., U.S.A. 45°58N 94°7W **77 E4**
Gentry Ark., U.S.A. 36°16N 94°29W **106 B1**
Gentry Mo., U.S.A. 40°20N 94°25W **83 A2**
Gentry County ☆ Mo., U.S.A. 40°10N 94°25W **83 A2**
Geographic Center of the 48 Contiguous States Kans., U.S.A. 39°50N 98°35W **82 B5**
Geographical Center of North America N. Dak., U.S.A. 48°21N 99°59W **76 B6**
Geographical Center of the 50 United States S. Dak., U.S.A. 44°58N 103°46W **76 F2**
George Iowa, U.S.A. 43°21N 96°0W **81 B3**
George Wash., U.S.A. 47°5N 119°53W **120 C6**
George → Qué., Canada 58°49N 66°10W **143 D4**
George, L. Fla., U.S.A. 29°17N 81°36W **114 B7**
George, L. Mich., U.S.A. 46°27N 84°8W **79 C7**
George, L. N.Y., U.S.A. 43°37N 73°33W **89 C1**
George Bush Intercontinental, Houston ✈ (IAH) Tex., U.S.A. 29°59N 95°20W **109 H12**
George County ☆ Miss., U.S.A. 30°56N 88°35W **111 F5**
George I. N.W.T., Canada 70°19N 112°2W **156 B10**
George River = Kangiqsualujjuaq Qué., Canada 58°30N 65°59W **143 B4**
George Rogers Clark Nat. Memorial △ Ind., U.S.A. 38°41N 87°32W **85 E3**
George Town Bahamas 23°33N 75°47W **182 B4**
George Town Cayman Is. 19°20N 81°24W **182 C3**
George Washington Birthplace Nat. Monument △ Va., U.S.A. 38°15N 76°56W **102 C8**
George Washington Bridge N.Y., U.S.A. 40°51N 73°57W **97 A3**
George Washington Carter Nat. Monument △ Mo., U.S.A. 36°59N 94°21W **83 E2**
George Washington Nat. Forest U.S.A. 38°15N 79°30W **93 B2**
George West Tex., U.S.A. 28°20N 98°7W **109 J9**
Georgetown Ont., Canada 43°40N 79°56W **146 D7**
Georgetown P.E.I., Canada 46°13N 62°24W **141 G7**
Georgetown Calif., U.S.A. 38°54N 120°50W **126 E6**
Georgetown Colo., U.S.A. 39°42N 105°42W **125 C5**
Georgetown D.C., U.S.A. 38°54N 77°3W **99 B3**
Georgetown Del., U.S.A. 38°41N 75°23W **93 B5**
Georgetown Fla., U.S.A. 29°23N 81°38W **114 B7**
Georgetown Ga., U.S.A. 31°53N 85°6W **113 E1**
Georgetown Idaho, U.S.A. 42°29N 111°22W **122 G7**
Georgetown Ill., U.S.A. 39°59N 87°38W **84 D6**
Georgetown Ky., U.S.A. 38°13N 84°33W **105 B8**
Georgetown La., U.S.A. 31°46N 92°23W **110 C3**
Georgetown Miss., U.S.A. 31°52N 90°10W **111 E3**
Georgetown Ohio, U.S.A. 38°52N 83°54W **86 E3**
Georgetown S.C., U.S.A. 33°23N 79°17W **103 E6**
Georgetown Tex., U.S.A. 30°38N 97°41W **109 G10**
Georgetown County ☆ S.C., U.S.A. 33°30N 79°15W **103 E6**
Georgia □ U.S.A. 32°50N 83°15W **113 D3**
Georgia, Str. of N. Amer. 49°25N 124°0W **154 F11**
Georgia Center Vt., U.S.A. 44°42N 73°9W **89 B1**
Georgia Dome Georgia, U.S.A. 33°45N 84°23W **117 B2**
Georgian Bay Islands Nat. Park △ Ont., Canada 44°53N 79°52W **146 C7**
Georgiana Ala., U.S.A. 31°38N 86°44W **112 E4**

Georgina Ont., Canada 44°15N 79°28W **146 C7**
Georgina I. Ont., Canada 44°22N 79°17W **146 C7**
Gerald Mo., U.S.A. 38°24N 91°20W **83 C5**
Geraldine Mont., U.S.A. 47°36N 110°16W **123 C7**
Gerber Calif., U.S.A. 40°4N 122°9W **126 C4**
Gerber Res. Oreg., U.S.A. 42°12N 121°31W **126 B4**
Gerdine, Mt. Alaska, U.S.A. 61°35N 152°27W **135 F9**
Gering Nebr., U.S.A. 41°50N 103°40W **80 C2**
Gerlach Nev., U.S.A. 40°39N 119°21W **128 E1**
Germain, Grand L. Qué., Canada 51°12N 66°41W **140 B3**
Germania Land Greenland 77°5N 19°30W **162 B9**
Germansen Landing B.C., Canada 55°43N 124°40W **157 E8**
Germantown Ill., U.S.A. 38°33N 89°32W **84 E4**
Germantown Md., U.S.A. 39°10N 77°16W **93 A3**
Germantown Ohio, U.S.A. 39°38N 84°22W **86 D2**
Germantown Tenn., U.S.A. 35°5N 89°49W **104 E3**
Germantown Wis., U.S.A. 43°14N 88°6W **78 E5**
Germfask Mich., U.S.A. 46°15N 85°56W **79 C6**
Geronimo Okla., U.S.A. 34°29N 98°23W **107 D5**
Gerrard B.C., Canada 50°30N 117°17W **155 E17**
Gerty Okla., U.S.A. 34°50N 96°17W **107 D7**
Gervais Lake Minn., U.S.A. 45°1N 93°4W **94 A3**
Getty Center, The Calif., U.S.A. 34°4N 118°29W **133 B2**
Gettysburg Pa., U.S.A. 39°50N 77°14W **93 A3**
Gettysburg S. Dak., U.S.A. 45°1N 99°57W **76 E6**
Gettysburg Nat. Military Park △ Pa., U.S.A. 39°49N 77°13W **87 E3**
Geuda Springs Kans., U.S.A. 37°7N 97°9W **82 D6**
Geyser Mont., U.S.A. 47°16N 110°30W **123 C7**
Geyserville Calif., U.S.A. 38°42N 122°54W **126 E4**
Ghent Ky., U.S.A. 38°44N 85°4W **105 B7**
Ghent Minn., U.S.A. 44°31N 95°54W **77 F3**
Ghent N.Y., U.S.A. 42°20N 73°37W **91 B1**
Ghent W. Va., U.S.A. 37°37N 81°7W **102 D3**
Giant Sequoia Nat. Monument △ Calif., U.S.A. 36°10N 118°35W **127 G8**
Giants Stadium N.J., U.S.A. 40°48N 74°5W **97 A2**
Gibara Cuba 21°9N 76°11W **182 B4**
Gibbon Nebr., U.S.A. 40°45N 98°51W **80 D7**
Gibbon Oreg., U.S.A. 45°42N 118°21W **121 B7**
Gibbons Alta., Canada 53°50N 113°20W **152 E7**
Gibbonsville Idaho, U.S.A. 45°33N 113°56W **122 D5**
Gibbstown N.J., U.S.A. 39°50N 75°18W **92 C1**
Gibraltar Pt. Ont., Canada 43°36N 79°23W **161 B2**
Gibsland La., U.S.A. 32°33N 93°3W **110 B2**
Gibson Ga., U.S.A. 33°14N 82°36W **113 C4**
Gibson La., U.S.A. 29°41N 90°59W **110 E5**
Gibson City Ill., U.S.A. 40°28N 88°22W **84 C5**
Gibson County ☆ Ind., U.S.A. 38°20N 87°35W **85 E3**
Gibson County ☆ Tenn., U.S.A. 36°0N 89°0W **104 D4**
Gibsonburg Ohio, U.S.A. 41°23N 83°19W **86 B3**
Gibsonia Pa., U.S.A. 28°7N 81°58W **114 C7**
Gibsons B.C., Canada 49°24N 123°32W **155 F11**
Gibsonton Fla., U.S.A. 27°51N 82°23W **114 D6**
Giddings Tex., U.S.A. 30°11N 96°56W **109 G11**
Gideon Mo., U.S.A. 36°27N 89°55W **83 E7**
Gifford Fla., U.S.A. 27°40N 80°25W **114 D8**
Gifford Pa., U.S.A. 48°18N 118°9W **102 D4**
Gifford → Nunavut, Canada 70°19N 83°3W **158 C9**
Gifford Pinchot Nat. Forest Wash., U.S.A. 46°15N 121°55W **120 D4**
Gift Lake Alta., Canada 55°53N 115°49W **152 C5**
Gig Harbor Wash., U.S.A. 47°20N 122°34W **132 D2**
Giganta, Sa. de la Baja Calif. S., Mexico 26°0N 111°39W **167 H7**
Gigantes, Llanos de los Chihuahua, Mexico 28°9N 104°45W **169 E11**
Gil I. B.C., Canada 53°12N 129°15W **154 B5**
Gila → Ariz., U.S.A. 32°43N 114°33W **130 E1**
Gila Bend Ariz., U.S.A. 32°57N 112°43W **130 E3**
Gila Bend Indian Reservation Ariz., U.S.A. 33°0N 112°30W **130 D3**
Gila Bend Mts. Ariz., U.S.A. 33°10N 113°0W **130 D3**
Gila Cliff Dwellings Nat. Monument △ N. Mex., U.S.A. 33°12N 108°16W **131 D2**
Gila County ☆ Ariz., U.S.A. 33°30N 110°45W **130 D5**
Gila Mts. Ariz., U.S.A. 33°10N 109°50W **130 D6**
Gila Nat. Forest N. Mex., U.S.A. 33°30N 108°30W **131 D2**
Gila River Indian Reservation Ariz., U.S.A. 33°15N 112°0W **130 D4**
Gilbert Ariz., U.S.A. 33°21N 111°47W **130 D4**
Gilbert Iowa, U.S.A. 42°7N 93°39W **81 C5**
Gilbert La., U.S.A. 32°3N 91°40W **110 B4**
Gilbert Minn., U.S.A. 47°29N 92°28W **77 C6**
Gilbert W. Va., U.S.A. 37°37N 81°52W **102 D3**
Gilbert, Mt. B.C., Canada 50°52N 124°16W **154 E10**
Gilbert Pk. Wash., U.S.A. 46°29N 121°25W **120 D4**
Gilbert Plains Man., Canada 51°9N 100°28W **151 D11**
Gilbertown Ala., U.S.A. 31°53N 88°19W **112 E2**
Gilbertville Mass., U.S.A. 42°19N 72°12W **91 B2**
Gilboa Ohio, U.S.A. 41°1N 83°55W **86 B3**
Gilby N. Dak., U.S.A. 48°5N 97°28W **76 B8**
Gilchrist Oreg., U.S.A. 43°29N 121°41W **121 D4**
Gilchrist Tex., U.S.A. 29°31N 94°29W **109 H13**
Gilchrist County ☆ Fla., U.S.A. 29°45N 82°45W **114 B6**
Gilcrest Colo., U.S.A. 40°17N 104°47W **125 B6**
Gildford Mont., U.S.A. 48°34N 110°18W **123 B7**
Gilead Maine, U.S.A. 44°24N 70°59W **90 D3**
Gilead Nebr., U.S.A. 40°9N 97°25W **80 D8**
Giles County ☆ Tenn., U.S.A. 35°10N 87°0W **104 E4**
Giles County ☆ Va., U.S.A. 37°20N 80°44W **102 D4**
Gilford N.H., U.S.A. 43°33N 71°24W **89 C3**
Gilford I. B.C., Canada 50°40N 126°30W **154 E8**
Gilford Park N.J., U.S.A. 39°58N 74°8W **92 C2**
Gillam Man., Canada 56°20N 94°40W **159 F7**
Gillespie Ill., U.S.A. 39°8N 89°49W **84 D4**
Gillespie County ☆ Tex., U.S.A. 30°16N 98°52W **109 G9**
Gillett Ark., U.S.A. 34°7N 91°23W **106 C5**
Gillett Wis., U.S.A. 44°54N 88°19W **78 D5**
Gillett Grove Iowa, U.S.A. 43°1N 95°2W **81 B3**
Gillette Wyo., U.S.A. 44°18N 105°30W **124 B7**
Gilliam La., U.S.A. 32°50N 93°51W **110 B2**
Gilliam County ☆ Oreg., U.S.A. 45°20N 120°10W **121 A5**
Gillian L. Nunavut, Canada 69°33N 75°30W **158 D10**
Gillies Bay B.C., Canada 49°42N 124°29W **154 F10**
Gillis La., U.S.A. 30°26N 93°14W **110 D2**
Gillis Range Nev., U.S.A. 38°42N 118°21W **128 D2**
Gillsville Ga., U.S.A. 34°18N 83°38W **113 B3**
Gilman Ill., U.S.A. 40°46N 88°0W **84 C6**
Gilman Iowa, U.S.A. 41°53N 92°47W **81 C5**
Gilman Wis., U.S.A. 45°10N 90°48W **78 C3**
Gilman City Mo., U.S.A. 40°8N 93°53W **83 A3**

Gilmanton *N.H., U.S.A.* 43°55'N 71°25'W **89** C3
Gilmer *Tex., U.S.A.* 32°44'N 94°57'W **109** E13
Gilmer County ☆ *Ga., U.S.A.* 34°40'N 84°30'W **113** B2
Gilmer County ☆ *W. Va., U.S.A.* 38°56'N 80°50'W **102** C4
Gilmore *Ark., U.S.A.* 35°25'N 90°17'W **106** C5
Gilmore City *Iowa, U.S.A.* 42°44'N 94°27'W **81** C4
Gilmour *Ont., Canada* 44°48'N 77°37'W **147** C9
Gilnockie Park △ *B.C., Canada* 49°5'N 115°39'W **153** J5
Gilpin County ☆ *Colo., U.S.A.* 39°50'N 105°40'W **125** C5
Gilroy *Calif., U.S.A.* 37°1'N 121°34'W **126** F5
Gilsum *N.H., U.S.A.* 43°3'N 72°16'W **89** C2
Giltner *Nebr., U.S.A.* 40°47'N 98°9'W **80** D7
Girard *Ala., U.S.A.* 33°3'N 81°43'W **113** C5
Girard *Ill., U.S.A.* 39°27'N 89°47'W **84** D4
Girard *Kans., U.S.A.* 37°31'N 94°51'W **82** D9
Girard *Ohio, U.S.A.* 41°9'N 80°42'W **86** B6
Girard *Tex., U.S.A.* 42°0'N 80°19'W **87** C2
Girard *Tex., U.S.A.* 33°22'N 100°40'W **108** F5
Girardville *Qué., Canada* 49°0'N 72°32'W **145** C10
Girdletree *Md., U.S.A.* 38°6'N 75°24'W **93** B5
Girouxville *Alta., Canada* 55°45'N 117°20'W **152** C3
Girvin *Tex., U.S.A.* 31°5'N 102°24'W **108** F5
Gisborne L. *Nfld. & L., Canada* 47°48'N 54°49'W **142** E6
Gjoa Haven *Nunavut, Canada* 68°38'N 95°53'W **158** D6
Glace Bay *N.S., Canada* 46°11'N 59°58'W **141** G10
Glacier *Wash., U.S.A.* 48°53'N 121°57'W **120** B4
Glacier Bay *Alaska, U.S.A.* 58°40'N 136°0'W **135** G14
Glacier Bay Nat. Park and Preserve △ *Alaska, U.S.A.* 58°45'N 136°30'W **135** G13
Glacier County ☆ *Mont., U.S.A.* 48°50'N 112°50'W **123** B5
Glacier Nat. Park △ *B.C., Canada* 51°15'N 117°30'W **155** D17
Glacier Nat. Park △ *Mont., U.S.A.* 48°42'N 113°48'W **123** B4
Glacier Peak *Wash., U.S.A.* 48°7'N 121°7'W **120** B4
Glad Valley *S. Dak., U.S.A.* 45°24'N 101°47'W **76** E4
Gladbrook *Iowa, U.S.A.* 42°11'N 92°43'W **81** C6
Glade *Kans., U.S.A.* 39°41'N 99°19'W **82** B4
Glade Spring *Va., U.S.A.* 36°47'N 81°47'W **102** E3
Glades County ☆ *Fla., U.S.A.* 26°50'N 81°15'W **114** E7
Gladewater *Tex., U.S.A.* 32°33'N 94°56'W **109** E13
Gladmar *Sask., Canada* 49°10'N 104°27'W **150** F7
Gladstone *Man., Canada* 50°13'N 98°57'W **151** E13
Gladstone *Mich., U.S.A.* 45°51'N 87°1'W **79** D4
Gladstone *Mo., U.S.A.* 39°13'N 94°35'W **83** B2
Gladstone *N. Dak., U.S.A.* 46°52'N 102°34'W **76** D3
Gladstone *N. Mex., U.S.A.* 36°18'N 103°58'W **131** A7
Gladstone *Oreg., U.S.A.* 45°22'N 122°35'W **132** B2
Gladstone Park △ *B.C., Canada* 49°18'N 118°15'W **155** F16
Gladwin *Mich., U.S.A.* 43°59'N 84°29'W **79** F7
Gladwin County ☆ *Mich., U.S.A.* 44°0'N 84°25'W **79** F7
Gladwyne *Pa., U.S.A.* 40°2'N 75°16'W **98** A1
Glady *W. Va., U.S.A.* 38°48'N 79°43'W **102** C5
Gladys *Va., U.S.A.* 37°10'N 79°4'W **102** D5
Glamis *Calif., U.S.A.* 32°55'N 115°5'W **127** L11
Glasco *Kans., U.S.A.* 39°22'N 97°50'W **82** B6
Glascock County ☆ *Ga., U.S.A.* 33°15'N 82°40'W **113** C4
Glasford *Ill., U.S.A.* 40°34'N 89°49'W **84** C4
Glasgow *Del., U.S.A.* 39°38'N 75°45'W **93** A5
Glasgow *Ky., U.S.A.* 37°0'N 85°55'W **105** C7
Glasgow *Mo., U.S.A.* 39°14'N 92°51'W **83** B4
Glasgow *Mont., U.S.A.* 48°12'N 106°38'W **123** B11
Glasgow *W. Va., U.S.A.* 37°38'N 79°27'W **102** D5
Glasgow Junction = Park City *Ky., U.S.A.* 37°6'N 86°3'W **104** C6
Glasgow Village *Mo., U.S.A.* 38°45'N 90°11'W **94** A2
Glaslyn *Sask., Canada* 53°22'N 108°21'W **150** B3
Glass Mts. *Tex., U.S.A.* 30°30'N 103°10'W **108** G4
Glassboro *N.J., U.S.A.* 39°42'N 75°7'W **92** C1
Glasscock County ☆ *Tex., U.S.A.* 31°52'N 101°29'W **108** F6
Glassmanor *Md., U.S.A.* 38°49'N 79°50'W **94** C2
Glassport *Pa., U.S.A.* 40°19'N 79°53'W **98** C2
Glastonbury *Conn., U.S.A.* 41°43'N 72°37'W **91** C2
Glazier *Tex., U.S.A.* 36°1'N 100°16'W **108** A7
Gleason *Tenn., U.S.A.* 36°13'N 88°37'W **104** D4
Gleason Lake *Minn., U.S.A.* 44°58'N 93°29'W **94** B1
Glen *Mont., U.S.A.* 45°28'N 112°43'W **123** E5
Glen *N.H., U.S.A.* 44°7'N 71°11'W **89** B3
Glen Allan *Miss., U.S.A.* 33°2'N 91°2'W **111** C2
Glen Alpine *N.C., U.S.A.* 35°44'N 81°47'W **103** C4
Glen Burnie *Md., U.S.A.* 39°10'N 76°37'W **93** A4
Glen Campbell *Pa., U.S.A.* 40°49'N 78°50'W **87** D4
Glen Canyon *Utah, U.S.A.* 37°30'N 110°40'W **130** A4
Glen Canyon Dam *Ariz., U.S.A.* 36°57'N 111°29'W **130** A4
Glen Canyon Nat. Recr. Area △ *Utah, U.S.A.* 37°15'N 111°0'W **129** F5
Glen Cove *N.Y., U.S.A.* 40°51'N 73°38'W **97** A5
Glen Dean *Ky., U.S.A.* 37°39'N 86°32'W **104** C6
Glen Elder *Kans., U.S.A.* 39°30'N 98°18'W **82** B5
Glen Ewen *Sask., Canada* 49°12'N 102°1'W **151** F9
Glen Flora *Tex., U.S.A.* 29°21'N 96°12'W **109** H11
Glen Head *N.Y., U.S.A.* 40°50'N 73°37'W **97** B5
Glen L. *Mich., U.S.A.* 44°52'N 85°59'W **79** E6
Glen Lake *Minn., U.S.A.* 44°54'N 93°27'W **94** B1
Glen Lyon *Pa., U.S.A.* 41°10'N 76°5'W **87** C6
Glen Mar Park *Md., U.S.A.* 38°57'N 77°7'W **99** B3
Glen Martin Nat. Wildlife Refuge △ *Md., U.S.A.* 38°0'N 76°0'W **93** C5
Glen Oaks *N.Y., U.S.A.* 40°44'N 73°42'W **97** B4
Glen Raven *N.C., U.S.A.* 36°31'N 79°29'W **103** B6
Glen Ridge *N.J., U.S.A.* 40°48'N 74°12'W **97** B1
Glen Rock *Pa., U.S.A.* 39°48'N 76°44'W **93** A4
Glen Rose *Tex., U.S.A.* 32°14'N 97°45'W **109** E10
Glen Rouge Park *Ont., Canada* 43°49'N 79°10'W **161** A4
Glen Ullin *N. Dak., U.S.A.* 46°49'N 101°50'W **76** D4
Glenallen *Alaska, U.S.A.* 62°7'N 145°33'W **135** E11
Glenallen *Mo., U.S.A.* 37°19'N 90°2'W **83** D6
Glenarden *Md., U.S.A.* 38°56'N 76°51'W **94** A4
Glenavon *Sask., Canada* 50°12'N 103°8'W **150** E8
Glenboro *Man., Canada* 49°33'N 99°17'W **151** F12
Glenburn *N. Dak., U.S.A.* 48°31'N 101°13'W **76** B4
Glencliff *N.H., U.S.A.* 43°58'N 71°53'W **89** C3
Glencoe *Ont., Canada* 42°45'N 81°43'W **146** C5
Glencoe *Ala., U.S.A.* 33°57'N 85°56'W **112** C5
Glencoe *Ky., U.S.A.* 38°43'N 84°49'W **105** B8
Glencoe *Minn., U.S.A.* 44°46'N 94°9'W **77** F4
Glencoe *Okla., U.S.A.* 36°14'N 96°56'W **107** B7
Glendale *N.S., Canada* 45°49'N 61°18'W **141** H8
Glendale *Ariz., U.S.A.* 33°32'N 112°11'W **134** B1
Glendale *Calif., U.S.A.* 34°9'N 118°15'W **133** B3
Glendale *Fla., U.S.A.* 30°52'N 86°7'W **114** A2
Glendale *Ky., U.S.A.* 37°36'N 85°54'W **105** C7
Glendale *Mo., U.S.A.* 38°35'N 90°22'W **94** B1
Glendale *Nev., U.S.A.* 36°40'N 114°34'W **128** F6
Glendale *Oreg., U.S.A.* 42°44'N 123°26'W **121** E2
Glendale *Pa., U.S.A.* 40°23'N 80°5'W **98** B1
Glendale *Utah, U.S.A.* 37°19'N 112°36'W **129** F3

Glendale *Wis., U.S.A.* 43°8'N 87°56'W **94** B2
Glendale L. *Pa., U.S.A.* 40°42'N 78°32'W **87** D4
Glendevey *Colo., U.S.A.* 40°48'N 105°56'W **125** B5
Glendive *Mont., U.S.A.* 47°7'N 104°43'W **123** C13
Glendo *Wyo., U.S.A.* 42°30'N 105°2'W **124** D7
Glendo Res. *Wyo., U.S.A.* 42°29'N 104°57'W **124** D8
Glendon *Alta., Canada* 54°15'N 111°10'W **152** D9
Glendora *Miss., U.S.A.* 33°50'N 90°18'W **111** C3
Glendora *N.J., U.S.A.* 39°50'N 75°4'W **92** C1
Glenella *Man., Canada* 50°33'N 99°11'W **151** E12
Glenfield *N. Dak., U.S.A.* 47°27'N 98°34'W **76** C7
Glenfield *N.Y., U.S.A.* 43°43'N 75°24'W **88** B5
Glenham *S. Dak., U.S.A.* 45°32'N 100°16'W **76** E5
Glenmont *Ohio, U.S.A.* 40°31'N 82°6'W **86** C4
Glenmora *La., U.S.A.* 30°59'N 92°35'W **110** D3
Glenn *Calif., U.S.A.* 39°31'N 122°1'W **126** D4
Glenn *Mich., U.S.A.* 42°31'N 86°14'W **79** G5
Glenn County ☆ *Calif., U.S.A.* 39°40'N 122°20'W **126** D4
Glenns Ferry *Idaho, U.S.A.* 42°57'N 115°18'W **122** G3
Glennallen *Ga., U.S.A.* 31°56'N 81°56'W **113** E5
Glenolden *Pa., U.S.A.* 39°54'N 75°17'W **98** B1
Glenoma *Wash., U.S.A.* 46°31'N 122°10'W **120** D3
Glenpool *Okla., U.S.A.* 35°58'N 96°1'W **107** C7
Glenrock *Wyo., U.S.A.* 42°52'N 105°52'W **124** D7
Glens Falls *N.Y., U.S.A.* 43°19'N 73°39'W **88** B7
Glenshaw *Pa., U.S.A.* 40°31'N 79°58'W **98** A2
Glenside *Pa., U.S.A.* 40°6'N 75°9'W **98** A2
Glenview *Ill., U.S.A.* 42°3'N 87°48'W **95** A2
Glenview Countryside *Ill., U.S.A.* 42°3'N 87°49'W **95** A2
Glenville *Minn., U.S.A.* 43°34'N 93°17'W **77** G5
Glenville *Nebr., U.S.A.* 40°30'N 98°15'W **80** D7
Glenville *Ohio, U.S.A.* 41°32'N 81°37'W **98** A2
Glenville *W. Va., U.S.A.* 38°56'N 80°50'W **102** C4
Glenwood *Alta., Canada* 49°21'N 113°31'W **153** J7
Glenwood *Nfld. & L., Canada* 49°0'N 54°58'W **142** C6
Glenwood *Ala., U.S.A.* 31°40'N 86°10'W **112** E4
Glenwood *Ark., U.S.A.* 34°20'N 93°33'W **106** D2
Glenwood *Ga., U.S.A.* 32°11'N 82°40'W **113** D4
Glenwood *Hawai'i, U.S.A.* 19°29'N 155°9'W **136** D6
Glenwood *Ind., U.S.A.* 39°37'N 85°18'W **85** D5
Glenwood *Iowa, U.S.A.* 41°3'N 95°45'W **81** D3
Glenwood *Minn., U.S.A.* 45°39'N 95°23'W **77** E3
Glenwood *N. Mex., U.S.A.* 33°19'N 108°53'W **131** D2
Glenwood *Oreg., U.S.A.* 45°39'N 123°16'W **121** B2
Glenwood *Utah, U.S.A.* 38°46'N 111°59'W **129** E4
Glenwood *Wash., U.S.A.* 46°1'N 121°17'W **120** D4
Glenwood City *Wis., U.S.A.* 45°4'N 92°10'W **78** C1
Glenwood Landing *N.Y., U.S.A.* 40°49'N 73°33'W **97** B5
Glenwood Springs *Colo., U.S.A.* 39°33'N 107°19'W **125** C3
Glidden *Iowa, U.S.A.* 42°4'N 94°44'W **81** C4
Glide *Oreg., U.S.A.* 43°18'N 123°6'W **121** D2
Globe *Ariz., U.S.A.* 33°24'N 110°47'W **130** D5
Glorieta *N. Mex., U.S.A.* 35°35'N 105°46'W **131** B5
Gloster *Miss., U.S.A.* 31°12'N 91°1'W **111** E2
Gloucester *Mass., U.S.A.* 42°37'N 70°40'W **91** B4
Gloucester *Va., U.S.A.* 37°25'N 76°32'W **102** D8
Gloucester City *N.J., U.S.A.* 39°53'N 75°7'W **98** B2
Gloucester County ☆ *N.J., U.S.A.* 39°40'N 75°15'W **92** C1
Gloucester County ☆ *Va., U.S.A.* 37°25'N 76°32'W **102** D8
Gloucester Point *Va., U.S.A.* 37°15'N 76°30'W **102** D8
Glover *Mo., U.S.A.* 37°29'N 90°42'W **83** D6
Glover *Vt., U.S.A.* 44°42'N 72°12'W **89** B2
Glover I. *Nfld. & L., Canada* 48°46'N 57°43'W **142** D3
Gloversville *N.Y., U.S.A.* 43°3'N 74°21'W **88** B6
Gloverville = Warrenville *S.C., U.S.A.* 33°33'N 81°48'W **103** E4
Glynn County ☆ *Ga., U.S.A.* 31°10'N 81°30'W **113** E5
Gnadenhutten *Ohio, U.S.A.* 40°22'N 81°26'W **86** C5
Goat Range Park △ *B.C., Canada* 50°17'N 117°17'W **155** E17
Gobernador *N. Mex., U.S.A.* 36°43'N 107°21'W **131** A3
Gobles *Mich., U.S.A.* 42°22'N 85°53'W **79** G6
Godbout *Qué., Canada* 49°20'N 67°38'W **140** D2
Godbout → *Qué., Canada* 49°19'N 67°36'W **140** D2
Goddard *Kans., U.S.A.* 37°39'N 97°34'W **82** D6
Goderich *Ont., Canada* 43°45'N 81°41'W **146** D3
Godfrey *Ill., U.S.A.* 38°58'N 90°11'W **84** E3
Godhavn = Qeqertarsuaq *Greenland* 69°15'N 53°38'W **162** D5
Gods → *Man., Canada* 56°22'N 92°51'W **159** F7
Gods L. *Man., Canada* 54°40'N 94°15'W **159** F7
Gods Mercy, B. of *Nunavut, Canada* 63°30'N 86°10'W **159** E8
Godthåb = Nuuk *Greenland* 64°10'N 51°35'W **162** E5
Goehner *Nebr., U.S.A.* 40°50'N 97°13'W **80** D8
Goéland, L. au *Qué., Canada* 49°50'N 76°48'W **144** B6
Goélands, L. aux *Qué., Canada* 55°27'N 64°17'W **143** B5
Goessel *Kans., U.S.A.* 38°15'N 97°21'W **82** C6
Goetzville *Mich., U.S.A.* 46°3'N 84°5'W **79** C7
Goff *Kans., U.S.A.* 39°40'N 95°56'W **82** B8
Goff Cr. → *Okla., U.S.A.* 36°43'N 101°29'W **107** B2
Goffs *Calif., U.S.A.* 34°55'N 115°4'W **127** J11
Goffstown *N.H., U.S.A.* 43°1'N 71°36'W **89** C3
Gogama *Ont., Canada* 47°35'N 81°43'W **149** E15
Gogebic, L. *Mich., U.S.A.* 46°30'N 89°35'W **79** C21
Gogebic County ☆ *Mich., U.S.A.* 46°25'N 89°45'W **79** C2
Gogebic Range *Mich., U.S.A.* 46°40'N 89°40'W **79** C2
Gogebic Range *Wash., U.S.A.* 47°51'N 121°42'W **120** C4
Golconda *Ill., U.S.A.* 37°22'N 88°29'W **84** F5
Golconda *Nev., U.S.A.* 40°58'N 117°30'W **128** D3
Gold Beach *Oreg., U.S.A.* 42°25'N 124°25'W **121** E1
Gold Coast *Ill., U.S.A.* 41°54'N 87°37'W **95** B3
Gold Creek *Alaska, U.S.A.* 62°46'N 149°41'W **135** E10
Gold Hill *Oreg., U.S.A.* 42°26'N 123°3'W **121** E2
Gold Point *Nev., U.S.A.* 37°21'N 117°22'W **128** E3
Gold River *B.C., Canada* 49°46'N 126°3'W **154** F8
Golden *B.C., Canada* 51°20'N 116°59'W **155** D18
Golden *Idaho, U.S.A.* 45°49'N 115°41'W **122** D3
Golden *Ill., U.S.A.* 40°7'N 91°1'W **84** C2
Golden *Mo., U.S.A.* 36°31'N 93°39'W **83** E3
Golden *N. Mex., U.S.A.* 35°16'N 106°13'W **131** B4
Golden *Okla., U.S.A.* 34°2'N 94°54'W **107** D9
Golden Beach *Fla., U.S.A.* 25°57'N 80°7'W **115** C3
Golden Bridge *B.C., Canada* 50°51'N 120°50'W **155** E12
Golden City *Mo., U.S.A.* 37°24'N 94°5'W **83** D2
Golden Ears Park △ *B.C., Canada* 49°30'N 122°25'W **155** F12
Golden Gate *Calif., U.S.A.* 31°26'N 94°56'W **83** A2
Golden Gate *Fla., U.S.A.* 26°11'N 81°42'W **114** E7
Golden Gate *Ill., U.S.A.* 38°22'N 88°12'W **84** E5
Golden Gate Bridge *Calif., U.S.A.* 37°49'N 122°29'W **132** B2
Golden Gate Nat. Recr. Area △ *Calif., U.S.A.* 37°50'N 122°31'W **132** B2
Golden Gate Park *Calif., U.S.A.* 37°46'N 122°29'W **132** B2
Golden Hinde *B.C., Canada* 49°40'N 125°44'W **154** F9
Golden Lake *Ont., Canada* 45°34'N 77°21'W **144** F5
Golden Meadow *La., U.S.A.* 29°24'N 90°16'W **110** E5
Golden Prairie *Sask., Canada* 50°13'N 109°37'W **150** E2

Golden Spike Nat. Historic Site △ *U.S.A.* 41°37'N 112°33'W **129** B3
Golden Valley *Minn., U.S.A.* 44°59'N 93°21'W **94** B1
Golden Valley *N. Dak., U.S.A.* 47°17'N 102°4'W **76** C3
Golden Valley County ☆ *Mont., U.S.A.* 46°30'N 109°15'W **123** D8
Golden Valley County ☆ *N. Dak., U.S.A.* 47°0'N 103°58'W **76** D2
Goldendale *Wash., U.S.A.* 45°49'N 120°50'W **120** E5
Goldfield *Iowa, U.S.A.* 42°44'N 93°55'W **81** C5
Goldfield *Nev., U.S.A.* 37°42'N 117°14'W **128** E3
Goldonna *La., U.S.A.* 32°1'N 92°54'W **110** B3
Goldsboro *Pa., U.S.A.* 39°2'N 75°47'W **93** A5
Goldsboro *N.C., U.S.A.* 35°23'N 77°59'W **103** C8
Goldsby *Okla., U.S.A.* 35°9'N 97°28'W **107** C6
Goldsmith *Tex., U.S.A.* 31°59'N 102°37'W **108** F5
Goldsmith Ch. *Nunavut, Canada* 73°10'N 106°5'W **158** C4
Goldston *N.C., U.S.A.* 35°36'N 79°20'W **103** C6
Goldthwaite *Tex., U.S.A.* 31°27'N 98°34'W **109** F9
Goleta *Calif., U.S.A.* 34°27'N 119°50'W **127** J7
Golfito *Costa Rica* 8°41'N 83°5'W **182** E3
Golfo de Santa Clara *Sonora, Mexico* 31°45'N 114°33'W **168** B1
Goliad *Tex., U.S.A.* 28°40'N 97°23'W **109** J10
Goliad County ☆ *Tex., U.S.A.* 28°45'N 97°25'W **109** J10
Golovin *Alaska, U.S.A.* 64°33'N 163°2'W **135** D7
Goltry *Okla., U.S.A.* 36°32'N 98°9'W **107** B5
Golva *N. Dak., U.S.A.* 46°44'N 103°59'W **76** D2
Gómez Farías *Chihuahua, Mexico* 29°17'N 107°44'W **169** D8
Gómez Farías *Jalisco, Mexico* 19°47'N 103°29'W **174** C4
Gómez Farías *Tamaulipas, Mexico* 23°3'N 99°9'W **171** G5
Gómez Palacio *Durango, Mexico* 25°34'N 103°30'W **173** B7
Gonaïves *Haiti* 19°20'N 72°42'W **183** C5
Gonâve, G. de la *Haiti* 19°29'N 72°42'W **183** C5
Gonâve, Île de la *Haiti* 18°51'N 73°3'W **183** C5
Gonvick *Minn., U.S.A.* 47°44'N 95°31'W **77** C3
Gonzales *Calif., U.S.A.* 36°30'N 121°26'W **126** G5
Gonzales *La., U.S.A.* 30°14'N 90°55'W **110** D5
Gonzales *Tex., U.S.A.* 29°30'N 97°27'W **109** H10
Gonzales County ☆ *Tex., U.S.A.* 29°26'N 97°32'W **109** H10
González *Tamaulipas, Mexico* 22°48'N 98°25'W **171** H6
Gonzalez *Fla., U.S.A.* 30°35'N 87°17'W **114** A1
González Ortega *Zacatecas, Mexico* 23°58'N 103°26'W **173** D7
González Ortega *Zacatecas, Mexico* 23°11'N 102°28'W **173** D8
Goochland *Va., U.S.A.* 37°41'N 77°53'W **102** D7
Goochland County ☆ *Va., U.S.A.* 37°41'N 77°53'W **102** D7
Good Hope *Ill., U.S.A.* 40°33'N 90°41'W **84** C3
Good Hope Mt. *B.C., Canada* 51°9'N 124°10'W **154** D10
Good Spirit L. *Sask., Canada* 51°34'N 102°40'W **150** D9
Good Spirit Lake Prov. Park △ *Sask., Canada* 51°31'N 102°41'W **150** D9
Good Thunder *Minn., U.S.A.* 44°0'N 94°4'W **77** F4
Goodell *Iowa, U.S.A.* 42°55'N 93°37'W **81** C5
Gooderham *Ont., Canada* 44°54'N 78°21'W **147** C8
Goodeve *Sask., Canada* 51°4'N 103°10'W **150** D8
Goodfellow Air Force Base *Tex., U.S.A.* 31°25'N 100°25'W **108** F7
Goodhue *Minn., U.S.A.* 44°24'N 92°37'W **77** F6
Goodhue County ☆ *Minn., U.S.A.* 44°25'N 92°45'W **77** F6
Gooding *Idaho, U.S.A.* 42°56'N 114°43'W **122** G4
Gooding County ☆ *Idaho, U.S.A.* 43°0'N 115°0'W **122** F4
Goodland *Ind., U.S.A.* 40°46'N 87°18'W **85** C3
Goodland *Kans., U.S.A.* 39°21'N 101°43'W **82** B2
Goodlett *Tex., U.S.A.* 34°20'N 99°53'W **109** C8
Goodlettsville *Tenn., U.S.A.* 36°19'N 86°43'W **104** D6
Goodman *Miss., U.S.A.* 32°58'N 89°55'W **111** D4
Goodman *Mo., U.S.A.* 36°44'N 94°25'W **83** E2
Goodnews Bay *Alaska, U.S.A.* 59°7'N 161°35'W **135** G7
Goodnight *Tex., U.S.A.* 35°2'N 101°11'W **108** B6
Goodrich *Colo., U.S.A.* 40°20'N 104°7'W **125** B6
Goodrich *N. Dak., U.S.A.* 47°29'N 100°8'W **76** C5
Goodrich *Tex., U.S.A.* 30°36'N 94°57'W **109** G13
Goodridge *Minn., U.S.A.* 48°9'N 95°48'W **77** B3
Goodsprings *Nev., U.S.A.* 35°49'N 115°27'W **128** G5
Goodwater *Sask., Canada* 49°24'N 103°42'W **150** F8
Goodwater *Ala., U.S.A.* 33°4'N 86°3'W **112** C4
Goodwell *Okla., U.S.A.* 36°36'N 101°38'W **107** B2
Goodyear *Ariz., U.S.A.* 33°26'N 112°21'W **130** D3
Goose → *Nfld. & L., Canada* 53°20'N 60°35'W **143** C5
Goose → *N. Dak., U.S.A.* 47°28'N 96°52'W **76** C9
Goose Cove East *Nfld. & L., Canada* 51°18'N 55°38'W **142** A5
Goose Creek *S.C., U.S.A.* 32°59'N 80°0'W **113** E6
Goose I. *B.C., Canada* 51°57'N 128°26'W **154** D6
Goose L. *Man., Canada* 54°28'N 101°30'W **151** A10
Goose L. *Calif., U.S.A.* 41°56'N 120°26'W **126** B6
Gooseberry Cr. → *Wyo., U.S.A.* 43°55'N 108°3'W **124** C4
Gorda, Banco *W. Indies* 15°40'N 80°27'W **182** C3
Gorda, Pta. *Nic.* 14°20'N 83°10'W **182** D3
Gorda, Punta *Calif., U.S.A.* 40°16'N 124°22'W **126** C2
Gordo *Ala., U.S.A.* 33°19'N 87°54'W **112** C3
Gordo, Cerro *Baja Calif., Mexico* 32°17'N 116°42'W **166** A2
Gordon → *Sask., Canada* 54°34'N 83°20'W **113** D3
Gordon *Nebr., U.S.A.* 42°48'N 102°12'W **80** B3
Gordon *Ohio, U.S.A.* 39°56'N 84°31'W **86** D2
Gordon *Tex., U.S.A.* 32°33'N 98°22'W **109** E9
Gordon *Wis., U.S.A.* 46°15'N 91°48'W **78** B2
Gordon County ☆ *Ga., U.S.A.* 34°30'N 84°50'W **113** B2
Gordon Cr. → *Nebr., U.S.A.* 42°49'N 100°40'W **80** B5
Gordon Hd. *B.C., Canada* 48°29'N 123°18'W **155** G11
Gordon L. *Alta., Canada* 56°30'N 110°25'W **152** B10
Gordon L. *N.W.T., Canada* 63°5'N 113°11'W **157** D10
Gordonsville *Tenn., U.S.A.* 36°10'N 85°56'W **105** D7
Gordonsville *Va., U.S.A.* 38°9'N 78°11'W **102** C6
Gordonville *Mo., U.S.A.* 37°19'N 89°41'W **83** D8
Gordonville *Tex., U.S.A.* 33°48'N 96°51'W **109** D11
Gore *Va., U.S.A.* 39°16'N 78°30'W **93** A3
Gore Bay *Ont., Canada* 45°57'N 82°28'W **146** B4
Gore Mt. *Vt., U.S.A.* 44°55'N 71°48'W **89** B3
Gore Range *Colo., U.S.A.* 39°50'N 106°25'W **125** C4
Goree *Tex., U.S.A.* 33°28'N 99°31'W **109** D8
Goreville *Ill., U.S.A.* 37°33'N 88°58'W **84** F5
Gorham *Ill., U.S.A.* 37°43'N 89°29'W **84** F4
Gorham *Kans., U.S.A.* 38°53'N 99°1'W **82** C4
Gorham *Maine, U.S.A.* 43°41'N 70°26'W **90** B3
Gorham *N.H., U.S.A.* 44°23'N 71°10'W **89** B3
Gorman *Calif., U.S.A.* 36°2'N 78°49'W **103** B7
Gorman *Tex., U.S.A.* 32°12'N 98°41'W **109** E9
Gortner *Md., U.S.A.* 39°20'N 79°24'W **93** A1
Gorum *La., U.S.A.* 31°26'N 92°56'W **110** C3
Goschen I. *B.C., Canada* 53°48'N 130°33'W **154** B4
Goshen *N.C., U.S.A.* 45°23'N 61°59'W **141** H8
Goshen *Calif., U.S.A.* 36°21'N 119°25'W **127** G7
Goshen *Conn., U.S.A.* 41°50'N 73°14'W **91** C1
Goshen *Ky., U.S.A.* 38°24'N 85°34'W **105** B7
Goshen *N.Y., U.S.A.* 41°24'N 74°20'W **92** A2
Goshen *Oreg., U.S.A.* 43°58'N 123°2'W **121** D2
Goshen *Utah, U.S.A.* 39°57'N 111°54'W **129** D4

Goshen County ☆ *Wyo., U.S.A.* 42°0'N 104°10'W **124** D8
Goshute *Utah, U.S.A.* 39°53'N 114°0'W **129** D1
Goshute Indian Reservation *Nev., U.S.A.* 39°50'N 114°5'W **128** C6
Goshute L. *Nev., U.S.A.* 40°9'N 114°42'W **128** B6
Goshute Mts. *Nev., U.S.A.* 40°15'N 114°19'W **128** B6
Goshute Valley *Nev., U.S.A.* 40°45'N 114°20'W **128** B6
Gosnell *Ark., U.S.A.* 35°58'N 89°58'W **106** C6
Gospel Hump Wilderness *Idaho, U.S.A.* 45°34'N 115°46'W **122** D3
Gosper County ☆ *Nebr., U.S.A.* 40°30'N 99°50'W **80** D6
Gosport *Ind., U.S.A.* 39°21'N 86°40'W **85** C4
Gossville *N.H., U.S.A.* 43°12'N 71°22'W **89** C3
Gotebo *Okla., U.S.A.* 35°4'N 98°53'W **107** C5
Gotha *Fla., U.S.A.* 28°31'N 81°31'W **115** A1
Gotham *Wis., U.S.A.* 43°13'N 90°18'W **78** E3
Gothenburg *Nebr., U.S.A.* 40°56'N 100°10'W **80** D5
Gough *Ga., U.S.A.* 33°6'N 82°14'W **113** C4
Gough L. *Alta., Canada* 52°2'N 112°28'W **153** C8
Gouin, Rés. *Qué., Canada* 48°35'N 74°40'W **144** C8
Goulais → *Ont., Canada* 46°43'N 84°27'W **149** F12
Gould *Ark., U.S.A.* 33°59'N 91°34'W **106** E4
Gould *Okla., U.S.A.* 34°40'N 99°47'W **107** D4
Gould City *Mich., U.S.A.* 46°6'N 85°42'W **79** C6
Gould Mts. *Nfld. & L., Canada* 47°29'N 52°46'W **142** E6
Goulds *Nfld. & L., Canada* 47°29'N 52°46'W **142** E6
Goulds *Fla., U.S.A.* 25°33'N 80°23'W **114** F8
Gouverneur *N.Y., U.S.A.* 44°20'N 75°28'W **88** A5
Govan *Sask., Canada* 51°20'N 105°0'W **150** D7
Gove *Kans., U.S.A.* 38°58'N 100°29'W **82** C3
Gove County ☆ *Kans., U.S.A.* 38°50'N 100°30'W **82** C3
Governor's Harbour *Bahamas* 25°10'N 76°14'W **182** A4
Governors I. *New York, U.S.A.* **96** f1
Govons *Baltimore, U.S.A.* 39°23'N 76°36'W **99** A2
Gowanda *N.Y., U.S.A.* 42°28'N 78°56'W **88** C2
Gower *Mo., U.S.A.* 39°37'N 94°36'W **83** B2
Gowrie *Iowa, U.S.A.* 42°17'N 94°17'W **81** C4
Goyelle, L. *Qué., Canada* 50°47'N 60°45'W **140** C9
Grace *Idaho, U.S.A.* 42°35'N 111°44'W **122** G7
Gracefield *Qué., Canada* 46°6'N 76°3'W **144** E6
Graceland *Tenn., U.S.A.* 35°3'N 90°1'W **104** E2
Gracemont *Okla., U.S.A.* 35°11'N 98°16'W **107** C5
Graceville *Fla., U.S.A.* 30°58'N 85°31'W **114** A3
Graceville *Minn., U.S.A.* 45°34'N 96°26'W **77** E2
Gracewood *Ga., U.S.A.* 33°22'N 82°2'W **113** C4
Gracey *Ky., U.S.A.* 36°53'N 87°40'W **104** D5
Graciano Sánchez *Tamaulipas, Mexico* 22°39'N 98°32'W **171** H6
Graciano Sánchez *Tamaulipas, Mexico* 23°55'N 99°17'W **171** G5
Gracias a Dios, C. *Honduras* 15°0'N 83°10'W **182** D3
Grady *Ala., U.S.A.* 31°59'N 86°3'W **112** E4
Grady *Ark., U.S.A.* 34°5'N 91°42'W **106** D4
Grady *N. Mex., U.S.A.* 34°49'N 103°19'W **131** C7
Grady *Okla., U.S.A.* 34°1'N 97°40'W **107** D6
Grady County ☆ *Ga., U.S.A.* 30°50'N 84°15'W **113** F2
Grady County ☆ *Okla., U.S.A.* 35°0'N 97°50'W **107** C6
Gradyville *Ky., U.S.A.* 37°4'N 85°25'W **105** C7
Graettinger *Iowa, U.S.A.* 43°14'N 94°45'W **81** B4
Graford *Tex., U.S.A.* 32°56'N 98°14'W **109** E9
Grafton *Ill., U.S.A.* 38°58'N 90°26'W **84** E3
Grafton *Iowa, U.S.A.* 43°20'N 93°4'W **81** B5
Grafton *Mass., U.S.A.* 42°12'N 71°41'W **91** B3
Grafton *N. Dak., U.S.A.* 48°25'N 97°25'W **76** B8
Grafton *N.H., U.S.A.* 43°34'N 71°57'W **89** C3
Grafton *N.Y., U.S.A.* 42°46'N 73°27'W **91** B1
Grafton *Ohio, U.S.A.* 41°16'N 82°4'W **86** B4
Grafton *Vt., U.S.A.* 43°10'N 72°37'W **89** C2
Grafton *W. Va., U.S.A.* 39°21'N 80°2'W **102** B4
Grafton *Wis., U.S.A.* 43°19'N 87°57'W **78** E4
Grafton County ☆ *N.H., U.S.A.* 43°50'N 71°45'W **89** C3
Graham *Ont., Canada* 49°20'N 90°30'W **148** C6
Graham *Ga., U.S.A.* 31°50'N 82°35'W **113** D4
Graham *N.C., U.S.A.* 36°5'N 79°25'W **103** B6
Graham *Tex., U.S.A.* 33°6'N 98°35'W **109** D9
Graham, Mt. *Ariz., U.S.A.* 32°42'N 109°52'W **130** E6
Graham County ☆ *Ariz., U.S.A.* 33°0'N 110°0'W **130** E6
Graham County ☆ *Kans., U.S.A.* 39°20'N 99°45'W **82** B4
Graham County ☆ *N.C., U.S.A.* 35°20'N 83°50'W **103** C2
Graham I. *B.C., Canada* 53°40'N 132°30'W **154** B2
Graham I. *Nunavut, Canada* 77°25'N 90°30'W **158** B7
Graham L. *Alta., Canada* 56°35'N 114°33'W **152** B6
Graham L. *Maine, U.S.A.* 44°39'N 68°24'W **90** D5
Grahamdale *Man., Canada* 51°23'N 98°30'W **151** D13
Grain Valley *Mo., U.S.A.* 39°1'N 94°12'W **83** B2
Grainfield *Kans., U.S.A.* 39°7'N 100°28'W **82** B3
Grainger County ☆ *Tenn., U.S.A.* 36°17'N 83°31'W **105** D9
Grainola *Okla., U.S.A.* 36°57'N 96°39'W **107** B7
Grambling *La., U.S.A.* 32°32'N 92°43'W **110** B3
Gramercy *La., U.S.A.* 30°4'N 90°42'W **110** D5
Grampian *Pa., U.S.A.* 40°58'N 78°37'W **87** D4
Gran Desierto del Pinacate, Parque Natural △ *Mexico* 31°51'N 113°32'W **168** B2
Gran Morelos *Chihuahua, Mexico* 28°15'N 106°30'W **169** E9
Granada *Nic.* 11°58'N 86°0'W **182** D2
Granada *Colo., U.S.A.* 38°4'N 102°19'W **125** D8
Granada *Minn., U.S.A.* 43°42'N 94°21'W **77** G4
Granados *Sonora, Mexico* 29°52'N 109°20'W **168** D6
Granbury *Tex., U.S.A.* 32°27'N 97°47'W **109** E10
Granbury, L. *Tex., U.S.A.* 32°22'N 97°41'W **109** E10
Granby *Qué., Canada* 45°25'N 72°45'W **145** F10
Granby *Colo., U.S.A.* 40°5'N 105°56'W **125** B5
Granby *Conn., U.S.A.* 41°57'N 72°47'W **91** C2
Granby *Mo., U.S.A.* 36°55'N 94°15'W **83** E2
Granby → *B.C., Canada* 49°2'N 118°27'W **155** F16
Granby, L. *Colo., U.S.A.* 40°9'N 105°52'W **125** B5
Granby Park △ *B.C., Canada* 49°44'N 118°27'W **155** E16
Grand → *Ont., Canada* 42°51'N 79°34'W **146** E7
Grand → *Mich., U.S.A.* 43°4'N 86°15'W **79** F5
Grand → *Mo., U.S.A.* 39°23'N 93°6'W **83** B3
Grand → *Ohio, U.S.A.* 41°44'N 81°17'W **86** B5
Grand → *S. Dak., U.S.A.* 45°40'N 100°45'W **76** E5
Grand Bahama I. *Bahamas* 26°40'N 78°30'W **182** A4
Grand Bank *Nfld. & L., Canada* 47°6'N 55°48'W **142** E5
Grand Bay *Ala., U.S.A.* 30°29'N 88°21'W **112** F2
Grand Bay-Westfield *N.B., Canada* 45°18'N 66°12'W **141** H3
Grand Blanc *Mich., U.S.A.* 42°56'N 83°38'W **79** F8
Grand-Bourg *Guadeloupe* 15°53'N 61°19'W **183** C7
Grand Bruit *Nfld. & L., Canada* 47°40'N 58°14'W **142** E2
Grand Calumet, Île du *Qué., Canada* 45°44'N 76°41'W **146** E6
Grand Cane *La., U.S.A.* 32°5'N 93°49'W **110** B2
Grand Canyon *Ariz., U.S.A.* 36°3'N 112°9'W **130** A3
Grand Canyon Nat. Park △ *Ariz., U.S.A.* 36°15'N 112°30'W **130** A3
Grand Canyon-Parashant Nat. Monument △ *Ariz., U.S.A.* 36°30'N 113°45'W **130** A2
Grand Cayman *Cayman Is.* 19°20'N 81°20'W **182** C3
Grand Chenier *La., U.S.A.* 29°46'N 92°58'W **110** E3
Grand Coteau *La., U.S.A.* 30°25'N 92°3'W **110** D3
Grand Coulee *Sask., Canada* 50°26'N 104°49'W **150** E7

Grand Coulee Wash., U.S.A. 47°57N 119°0W **120** C6
Grand Coulee Dam Wash., U.S.A. 47°57N 118°59W **120** C7
Grand County ☆ Colo., U.S.A. 40°10N 106°15W **125** B4
Grand County ☆ Utah, U.S.A. 39°0N 109°30W **129** D6
Grand Falls N.B., Canada 47°3N 67°44W **141** F1
Grand Falls-Windsor Nfld. & L., Canada 48°56N 55°40W **142** D5
Grand Forks B.C., Canada 49°0N 118°30W **155** G16
Grand Forks N. Dak., U.S.A. 47°55N 97°3W **76** C8
Grand Forks County ☆ N. Dak., U.S.A. 47°55N 97°22W **76** C8
Grand Harbour N.B., Canada 44°41N 66°46W **141** J3
Grand Haven Mich., U.S.A. 43°4N 86°13W **79** F5
Grand I. Man., Canada 52°51N 100°0W **151** C11
Grand I. La., U.S.A. 29°10N 90°0W **110** E6
Grand I. Mich., U.S.A. 46°31N 86°40W **79** C5
Grand Island Nebr., U.S.A. 40°55N 98°21W **80** D7
Grand Island Nat. Recr. Area △ Mich., U.S.A. 46°31N 86°40W **79** C5
Grand Isle La., U.S.A. 29°14N 90°0W **110** E6
Grand Isle Vt., U.S.A. 44°43N 73°18W **89** B1
Grand Isle County ☆ Vt., U.S.A. 44°57N 73°17W **89** B1
Grand Junction Colo., U.S.A. 39°4N 108°33W **125** C2
Grand Junction Iowa, U.S.A. 42°2N 94°14W **81** C4
Grand Junction Tenn., U.S.A. 35°3N 89°11W **104** E3
Grand L. N.B., Canada 45°57N 66°7W **141** H3
Grand L. Nfld. & L., Canada 49°0N 57°30W **142** D3
Grand L. Nfld. & L., Canada 53°40N 60°30W **143** C5
Grand L. La., U.S.A. 29°55N 92°47W **110** E3
Grand L. Maine, U.S.A. 45°40N 67°50W **90** C6
Grand L. Mich., U.S.A. 45°18N 83°30W **79** D8
Grand L. Ohio, U.S.A. 40°32N 84°25W **86** C2
Grand Lac Victoria Qué., Canada 47°35N 77°35W **144** D5
Grand Lake Colo., U.S.A. 40°15N 105°49W **125** B5
Grand Lake La., U.S.A. 30°2N 93°17W **110** D2
Grand Lake Matagamon Maine, U.S.A. 46°12N 68°47W **90** B5
Grand Lake Seboeis Maine, U.S.A. 46°18N 68°39W **90** B5
Grand Le Pierre Nfld. & L., Canada 47°41N 54°47W **142** E6
Grand Ledge Mich., U.S.A. 42°45N 84°45W **79** G7
Grand Manan Channel Maine, U.S.A. 44°40N 67°0W **90** D7
Grand Manan I. N.B., Canada 44°45N 66°52W **141** J3
Grand Marais Mich., U.S.A. 46°40N 85°59W **79** C6
Grand Marais Minn., U.S.A. 47°45N 90°25W **148** E6
Grand Meadow Minn., U.S.A. 43°42N 92°34W **77** G6
Grand-Mère Qué., Canada 46°36N 72°40W **145** E10
Grand Mesa Colo., U.S.A. 39°0N 108°15W **125** D2
Grand Mesa Nat. Forest Colo., U.S.A. 39°20N 107°50W **125** C3
Grand Piles Qué., Canada 46°40N 72°40W **145** E10
Grand Portage Minn., U.S.A. 47°58N 89°41W **77** C91
Grand Portage Indian Reservation Minn., U.S.A. 47°55N 89°50W **77** C9
Grand Prairie Tex., U.S.A. 32°44N 96°59W **116** B3
Grand Rapids = Wisconsin Rapids Wis., U.S.A. 44°23N 89°49W **78** D4
Grand Rapids Man., Canada 53°12N 99°19W **151** B12
Grand Rapids Mich., U.S.A. 42°58N 85°40W **79** G6
Grand Rapids Minn., U.S.A. 47°14N 93°31W **77** C5
Grand Rapids Ohio, U.S.A. 41°25N 83°52W **86** B3
Grand Rapids ✈ (GRR) Mich., U.S.A. 42°53N 85°31W **79** G6
Grand-Remous Qué., Canada 46°37N 75°54W **144** E7
Grand Ridge Fla., U.S.A. 30°43N 85°1W **114** A3
Grand Ridge Ill., U.S.A. 41°14N 88°50W **84** B5
Grand River Iowa, U.S.A. 40°49N 93°58W **81** E5
Grand River Nat. Grassland S. Dak., U.S.A. 45°47N 102°30W **76** E3
Grand River Ky., U.S.A. 37°1N 88°14W **104** C4
Grand Ronde Oreg., U.S.A. 45°4N 123°37W **121** B2
Grand Ronde → Oreg., U.S.A. 46°5N 117°0W **120** D8
Grand Saline Tex., U.S.A. 32°41N 95°43W **109** E12
Grand Staircase-Escalante Nat. Monument △ Utah, U.S.A. 37°25N 111°33W **129** F4
Grand Teton Wyo., U.S.A. 43°54N 110°50W **124** C2
Grand Teton Nat. Park △ Wyo., U.S.A. 43°50N 110°50W **124** C2
Grand Tower Ill., U.S.A. 37°38N 89°30W **84** F4
Grand Traverse B. Mich., U.S.A. 45°5N 85°35W **79** D6
Grand Traverse County ☆ Mich., U.S.A. 44°40N 85°35W **79** E6
Grand Traverse Indian Reservation Mich., U.S.A. 45°4N 85°40W **79** D6
Grand View Idaho, U.S.A. 42°59N 116°6W **122** G2
Grand Wash Cliffs Ariz., U.S.A. 36°0N 113°50W **130** A2
Grande Baja Calif., Mexico 31°50N 115°15W **166** B3
Grande → Jalisco, Mexico 19°26N 102°44W **174** C5
Grande → Oaxaca, Mexico 17°43N 96°56W **177** G4
Grande, L. Sinaloa, Mexico 22°46N 105°53W **172** E5
Grande, Rio → N. Amer. 25°58N 97°9W **108** M10
Grande-Anse N.B., Canada 47°48N 65°11W **141** F4
Grande Baleine, R. de la → Qué., Canada 55°16N 77°47W **143** B2
Grande Cache Alta., Canada 53°53N 119°8W **152** E1
Grande-Cascapédia Qué., Canada 48°15N 65°54W **140** E4
Grande-Entrée Qué., Canada 47°30N 61°40W **141** F8
Grande-Passe, I. de la Qué., Canada 51°10N 58°35W **143** D6
Grande Pointe Man., Canada 49°46N 97°3W **151** F14
Grande Prairie Alta., Canada 55°10N 118°50W **152** C2
Grande-Rivière Qué., Canada 48°26N 64°30W **140** E5
Grande Ronde → Oreg., U.S.A. 46°5N 116°59W **121** A9
Grande Ronde Indian Reservation Oreg., U.S.A. 45°8N 123°40W **121** B2
Grande-Vallée Qué., Canada 49°14N 65°8W **140** D4
Grandes-Bergeronnes Qué., Canada 48°16N 69°35W **145** C13
Grandfalls Tex., U.S.A. 31°20N 102°51W **108** F5
Grandfield Okla., U.S.A. 34°14N 98°41W **107** D5
Grandin Mo., U.S.A. 36°50N 90°50W **83** E6
Grandin N. Dak., U.S.A. 47°14N 97°0W **76** C9
Grandin, L. N.W.T., Canada 63°59N 119°0W **157** D9
Grandjean Idaho, U.S.A. 44°9N 115°10W **122** E3
Grandmesnil, L. Qué., Canada 51°19N 67°33W **140** B4
Grands-Jardins, Parc des △ Qué., Canada 47°41N 70°51W **145** D12
Grandview Man., Canada 51°10N 100°42W **151** D11
Grandview Iowa, U.S.A. 41°16N 91°11W **81** D7
Grandview Mo., U.S.A. 38°53N 94°32W **83** C2
Grandview Tex., U.S.A. 32°16N 97°11W **109** E10
Grandview Wash., U.S.A. 46°15N 119°54W **120** D6
Grandview Peak Utah, U.S.A. 40°51N 111°45W **134** A3
Granet, L. Qué., Canada 47°47N 77°31W **144** D5
Granger Iowa, U.S.A. 41°45N 86°57W **81** D5
Granger Tex., U.S.A. 30°43N 97°26W **109** G10
Granger Wash., U.S.A. 46°21N 120°11W **120** D5
Granger Wyo., U.S.A. 41°35N 109°58W **124** E3
Grangeville Idaho, U.S.A. 45°56N 116°7W **122** D2
Granisle B.C., Canada 54°53N 126°13W **157** F7
Granite Colo., U.S.A. 39°3N 106°16W **125** C4
Granite Okla., U.S.A. 34°58N 99°23W **107** D4
Granite Oreg., U.S.A. 44°49N 118°25W **121** C7
Granite Utah, U.S.A. 40°34N 111°48W **134** C7

Granite Bay B.C., Canada 50°14N 125°18W **154** E9
Granite City Ill., U.S.A. 38°42N 90°8W **94** A3
Granite County ☆ Mont., U.S.A. 46°25N 113°30W **123** D4
Granite Falls Minn., U.S.A. 44°49N 95°33W **77** F3
Granite Falls N.C., U.S.A. 35°48N 81°26W **103** C4
Granite Falls Wash., U.S.A. 48°5N 121°58W **120** B4
Granite L. Nfld. & L., Canada 48°8N 57°5W **142** D3
Granite Mts. Ariz., U.S.A. 32°20N 113°20W **130** E2
Granite Mts. Wyo., U.S.A. 42°45N 107°30W **124** D5
Granite Pass Wyo., U.S.A. 44°38N 107°30W **124** B5
Granite Peak Mont., U.S.A. 41°40N 117°35W **128** A3
Granite Pk. Mont., U.S.A. 45°10N 109°48W **123** E8
Granite Pt. Nfld. & L., Canada 50°31N 56°17W **142** B4
Granite Pt. Mich., U.S.A. 46°47N 87°36W **79** C4
Granite Quarry N.C., U.S.A. 35°37N 80°26W **103** C5
Granite Range Nev., U.S.A. 40°59N 119°25W **128** B1
Granite Springs Valley Nev., U.S.A. 40°9N 118°25W **128** B2
Graniteville N.Y., U.S.A. 40°37N 74°9W **97** C2
Graniteville S.C., U.S.A. 33°34N 81°49W **103** E4
Graniteville Vt., U.S.A. 44°8N 72°29W **89** B2
Grannis Ark., U.S.A. 34°14N 94°20W **106** D1
Grano N. Dak., U.S.A. 48°37N 101°35W **76** B4
Grant Colo., U.S.A. 39°28N 105°40W **125** C5
Grant Fla., U.S.A. 27°56N 80°32W **114** D8
Grant Iowa, U.S.A. 41°9N 94°59W **81** D4
Grant La., U.S.A. 30°47N 92°57W **110** D3
Grant Mich., U.S.A. 43°20N 85°51W **79** F6
Grant Minn., U.S.A. 45°5N 92°34W **94** A4
Grant Mont., U.S.A. 45°1N 113°4W **123** E4
Grant Nebr., U.S.A. 40°50N 101°43W **80** D4
Grant Okla., U.S.A. 33°57N 95°31W **107** E8
Grant, Mt. Nev., U.S.A. 38°34N 118°48W **128** D2
Grant City Mo., U.S.A. 40°29N 94°25W **83** A2
Grant County ☆ Ark., U.S.A. 34°19N 92°24W **106** D3
Grant County ☆ Ind., U.S.A. 40°30N 85°40W **85** C5
Grant County ☆ Kans., U.S.A. 37°30N 101°15W **82** D2
Grant County ☆ Ky., U.S.A. 38°35N 84°35W **105** B8
Grant County ☆ Minn., U.S.A. 45°55N 96°0W **77** E2
Grant County ☆ N. Dak., U.S.A. 46°15N 101°30W **76** D4
Grant County ☆ N. Mex., U.S.A. 33°0N 108°30W **131** E2
Grant County ☆ Nebr., U.S.A. 41°50N 101°45W **80** D4
Grant County ☆ Okla., U.S.A. 36°50N 97°45W **107** B6
Grant County ☆ Oreg., U.S.A. 44°30N 119°0W **121** C7
Grant County ☆ S. Dak., U.S.A. 45°12N 96°47W **76** E9
Grant County ☆ W. Va., U.S.A. 39°4N 79°4W **102** B5
Grant County ☆ Wash., U.S.A. 47°10N 119°30W **120** C6
Grant County ☆ Wis., U.S.A. 42°50N 90°45W **78** F3
Grant-Kohrs Ranch Nat. Historic Site △ Mont., U.S.A. 46°25N 112°45W **123** D5
Grant Parish ☆ La., U.S.A. 31°32N 92°25W **110** C3
Grant Park Ill., U.S.A. 41°14N 87°39W **84** B6
Grant Park Ill., U.S.A. 41°52N 87°37W **95** B3
Grant Range Nev., U.S.A. 38°30N 115°25W **128** D5
Grantham N.H., U.S.A. 43°29N 72°8W **89** C2
Grants N. Mex., U.S.A. 35°9N 107°52W **131** B3
Grants Pass Oreg., U.S.A. 42°26N 123°19W **121** E2
Grantsburg Wis., U.S.A. 45°47N 92°41W **78** C1
Grantsdale Mont., U.S.A. 46°12N 114°9W **123** D3
Grantsville Md., U.S.A. 39°42N 79°12W **93** A1
Grantsville Utah, U.S.A. 40°36N 112°28W **129** C3
Grantsville W. Va., U.S.A. 38°55N 81°6W **102** C3
Grantville Ga., U.S.A. 33°14N 84°50W **113** C2
Granum Alta., Canada 49°52N 113°30W **153** J7
Granville Ill., U.S.A. 41°16N 89°14W **84** B4
Granville Mass., U.S.A. 42°4N 72°52W **91** B2
Granville N. Dak., U.S.A. 48°16N 100°47W **76** B5
Granville Ohio, U.S.A. 40°4N 82°31W **86** C4
Granville Vt., U.S.A. 43°58N 72°51W **89** C2
Granville County ☆ N.C., U.S.A. 36°20N 78°40W **103** B7
Granville I. B.C., Canada 49°16N 123°8W **161** B2
Granville L. Man., Canada 56°18N 100°30W **159** F5
Grapeland Tex., U.S.A. 31°30N 95°29W **109** F12
Grapevine Tex., U.S.A. 32°56N 97°4W **116** A3
Grapevine L. Tex., U.S.A. 32°58N 97°4W **109** E10
Grapevine Recr. Area Tex., U.S.A. 32°58N 97°3W **116** A3
Gras, L. de N.W.T., Canada 64°30N 110°30W **157** D10
Grasmere Idaho, U.S.A. 42°23N 115°53W **122** G3
Grasonville Md., U.S.A. 38°57N 76°13W **93** B4
Grass Creek Wyo., U.S.A. 43°56N 108°39W **124** C4
Grass Hassock Channel N.Y., U.S.A. 40°36N 73°47W **97** C4
Grass Lake Mich., U.S.A. 42°15N 84°13W **79** G7
Grass Range Mont., U.S.A. 47°2N 108°48W **123** C9
Grass River Prov. Park △ Man., Canada 54°40N 100°50W **151** A11
Grass-Vadnais Regional Park Minn., U.S.A. 45°4N 93°7W **94** A3
Grass Valley Calif., U.S.A. 39°13N 121°4W **126** D3
Grass Valley Oreg., U.S.A. 45°22N 120°47W **121** B5
Grasset, L. Qué., Canada 49°55N 78°10W **144** B4
Grasslands Nat. Park △ Sask., Canada 49°11N 107°38W **150** F4
Grasston Minn., U.S.A. 45°48N 93°9W **77** E5
Grassy Bay N.Y., U.S.A. 40°38N 73°48W **97** C4
Grassy Butte N. Dak., U.S.A. 47°24N 103°15W **76** C2
Grassy Lake Alta., Canada 49°49N 111°43W **153** J9
Gratiot Wis., U.S.A. 42°35N 90°1W **78** F3
Gratiot County ☆ Mich., U.S.A. 43°15N 84°40W **79** F7
Gratz Ky., U.S.A. 38°28N 84°57W **105** B8
Gravel → Qué., Canada 50°2N 66°55W **140** C2
Gravelbourg Sask., Canada 49°50N 106°35W **150** F5
Gravelly Ark., U.S.A. 34°53N 93°41W **106** D3
Gravelly Ra. Mont., U.S.A. 44°49N 111°52W **123** F6
Gravenhurst Ont., Canada 44°52N 79°20W **144** G3
Graves County ☆ Ky., U.S.A. 36°45N 88°40W **104** D4
Gravesend N.Y., U.S.A. 40°36N 73°56W **97** C3
Gravette Ark., U.S.A. 36°25N 94°27W **106** B1
Gravity Iowa, U.S.A. 40°46N 94°45W **81** E4
Gravois, Pointe-à- Haiti 18°15N 73°56W **183** C5
Gravois Mills Mo., U.S.A. 38°19N 92°49W **83** C4
Gray Ga., U.S.A. 33°1N 83°32W **113** C3
Gray Ky., U.S.A. 36°57N 84°0W **105** D9
Gray Tenn., U.S.A. 36°25N 82°29W **105** D10
Gray County ☆ Kans., U.S.A. 37°40N 100°20W **82** D3
Gray County ☆ Tex., U.S.A. 35°26N 100°48W **108** B7
Gray Court S.C., U.S.A. 34°36N 82°7W **103** D3
Gray Hawk Ky., U.S.A. 37°24N 83°56W **105** C9
Gray Summit Mo., U.S.A. 38°29N 90°49W **83** C6
Grayland Wash., U.S.A. 46°49N 124°6W **120** D1
Grayling Alaska, U.S.A. 62°57N 160°3W **135** E7
Grayling Mich., U.S.A. 44°40N 84°43W **79** E7
Grays Harbor Wash., U.S.A. 46°59N 124°1W **120** D1
Grays Harbor County ☆ Wash., U.S.A. 47°15N 123°42W **120** C2
Grays L. Idaho, U.S.A. 43°4N 111°26W **122** F7
Grays Lake Nat. Wildlife Refuge △ Idaho, U.S.A. 43°4N 111°26W **122** F7

Grays River Wash., U.S.A. 46°21N 123°37W **120** D2
Grayslake Ill., U.S.A. 42°21N 88°2W **84** A5
Grayson Sask., Canada 50°45N 102°40W **150** E9
Grayson Ky., U.S.A. 38°20N 82°57W **105** B10
Grayson Okla., U.S.A. 35°32N 95°51W **107** C8
Grayson County ☆ Ky., U.S.A. 37°25N 86°20W **104** C6
Grayson County ☆ Tex., U.S.A. 33°38N 96°36W **109** D11
Grayson County ☆ Va., U.S.A. 36°40N 81°10W **102** E3
Grayson L. Ky., U.S.A. 38°15N 82°59W **105** B10
Grayson Valley Ala., U.S.A. 33°39N 86°38W **112** C4
Graysville Tenn., U.S.A. 35°27N 85°8W **105** C7
Grayton Md., U.S.A. 38°26N 77°13W **93** B3
Grayville Ill., U.S.A. 38°16N 88°0W **84** E5
Great Abaco I. = Abaco I. Bahamas 26°25N 77°10W **182** A4
Great B. N.H., U.S.A. 43°5N 70°53W **89** C4
Great Bahama Bank Bahamas 23°15N 78°0W **182** B3
Great Barrington Mass., U.S.A. 42°12N 73°22W **91** B1
Great Basin Nev., U.S.A. 40°0N 117°0W **128** C4
Great Basin Nat. Park △ Nev., U.S.A. 38°56N 114°15W **128** D6
Great Bay N.J., U.S.A. 39°30N 74°25W **92** C2
Great Bear → N.W.T., Canada 65°0N 124°0W **157** C8
Great Bear L. N.W.T., Canada 65°30N 120°0W **157** C8
Great Bend Kans., U.S.A. 38°22N 98°46W **82** C5
Great Bend N. Dak., U.S.A. 46°9N 96°48W **76** D9
Great Bend Pa., U.S.A. 41°58N 75°45W **87** C7
Great Burnt L. Nfld. & L., Canada 48°20N 56°20W **142** D4
Great Camanoe Br. Virgin Is. 18°30N 64°35W **184** G18
Great Central L. B.C., Canada 49°20N 125°10W **154** F9
Great Central L. B.C., Canada 49°22N 125°10W **154** F9
Great Dismal Swamp Nat. Wildlife Refuge △ Va., U.S.A. 36°35N 76°28W **102** E8
Great Divide Basin Wyo., U.S.A. 42°0N 108°0W **124** D5
Great Duck I. Ont., Canada 45°40N 82°57W **146** B4
Great Egg Harbor → N.J., U.S.A. 39°18N 74°40W **92** C2
Great Exuma I. Bahamas 23°30N 75°50W **182** B4
Great Falls Man., Canada 50°27N 96°1W **151** E15
Great Falls Mont., U.S.A. 47°30N 111°17W **123** C6
Great Falls S.C., U.S.A. 34°34N 80°54W **103** D5
Great Falls Va., U.S.A. 38°59N 77°17W **99** B2
Great Falls Park Md., U.S.A. 38°59N 77°14W **99** B2
Great Guana Cay Bahamas 24°0N 76°20W **182** B4
Great Inagua I. Bahamas 21°0N 73°20W **183** B5
Great Kills N.Y., U.S.A. 40°33N 74°9W **97** C2
Great Kills Harbor N.Y., U.S.A. 40°32N 74°8W **97** C2
Great Kills Park N.Y., U.S.A. 40°32N 74°7W **97** C2
Great L. C.U.S.A. 34°49N 77°2W **103** D8
Great Miami → Ohio, U.S.A. 39°7N 84°49W **86** D2
Great Mills Md., U.S.A. 38°14N 76°30W **93** B4
Great Neck N.Y., U.S.A. 40°47N 73°44W **97** B4
Great Peconic B. N.Y., U.S.A. 40°57N 72°30W **91** D2
Great Pee Dee → S.C., U.S.A. 33°21N 79°10W **103** E6
Great Plains Res. Colo., U.S.A. 38°15N 102°43W **125** D8
Great Pond Maine, U.S.A. 44°57N 68°19W **90** D5
Great Pt. Mass., U.S.A. 41°24N 70°3W **91** C4
Great Quittacas Pond Mass., U.S.A. 41°48N 70°54W **91** C4
Great River Nat. Wildlife Refuge △ Ill., U.S.A. 39°27N 90°58W **84** D3
Great Sacandaga L. N.Y., U.S.A. 43°6N 74°16W **88** B6
Great Salt L. Utah, U.S.A. 41°15N 112°40W **129** B3
Great Salt Lake Desert Utah, U.S.A. 40°50N 113°30W **129** C2
Great Salt Plains L. Okla., U.S.A. 36°45N 98°8W **107** B5
Great Sand Dunes Nat. Monument △ Colo., U.S.A. 37°48N 105°45W **125** E5
Great Sandy Desert Oreg., U.S.A. 43°35N 120°15W **121** D5
Great Sitkin I. Alaska, U.S.A. 52°3N 176°6W **135** K3
Great Slave L. N.W.T., Canada 61°23N 115°38W **157** D9
Great Smoky Mountains Nat. Park △ Tenn., U.S.A. 35°40N 83°40W **103** C2
Great Smoky Mts. Tenn., U.S.A. 35°40N 83°40W **103** C2
Great Snow Mt. B.C., Canada 57°26N 124°0W **157** E8
Great South Bay N.Y., U.S.A. 40°40N 73°15W **92** B3
Great Wass I. Maine, U.S.A. 44°29N 67°36W **90** D6
Great Western Forum Calif., U.S.A. 33°57N 118°20W **133** C2
Great Whale River = Kuujjuarapik Qué., Canada 55°20N 77°35W **143** B2
Great White Heron Nat. Wildlife Refuge △ Fla., U.S.A. 24°45N 81°10W **114** G7
Greater Antilles W. Indies 17°40N 74°0W **183** C5
Greater Buffalo Int. ✈ (BUF) N.Y., U.S.A. 42°56N 78°44W **88** C2
Greater Sudbury = Sudbury Ont., Canada 46°30N 81°0W **146** A5
Greece N.Y., U.S.A. 43°13N 77°41W **88** B3
Greeley Colo., U.S.A. 40°25N 104°42W **125** B6
Greeley Iowa, U.S.A. 42°35N 91°21W **81** C7
Greeley Kans., U.S.A. 38°22N 95°8W **82** C8
Greeley Nebr., U.S.A. 41°33N 98°32W **80** C7
Greeley County ☆ Kans., U.S.A. 38°30N 101°45W **82** C2
Greeley County ☆ Nebr., U.S.A. 41°30N 98°30W **80** C7
Greely Fd. Nunavut, Canada 80°30N 85°0W **158** A9
Green Kans., U.S.A. 39°26N 97°0W **82** B6
Green Ohio, U.S.A. 40°57N 81°29W **86** C5
Green → N.B., Canada 47°18N 68°9W **141** F1
Green → Ill., U.S.A. 41°28N 90°23W **84** B2
Green → Ky., U.S.A. 37°54N 87°30W **104** C5
Green → N. Dak., U.S.A. 46°52N 102°35W **76** D3
Green → Utah, U.S.A. 38°11N 109°53W **129** E6
Green → Wash., U.S.A. 47°28N 122°15W **120** C3
Green B. Nfld. & L., Canada 49°45N 55°55W **142** C5
Green B. Wis., U.S.A. 45°0N 87°30W **78** D6
Green Bank N.J., U.S.A. 39°40N 74°36W **92** C2
Green Bank W. Va., U.S.A. 38°25N 79°50W **102** C5
Green Bay Wis., U.S.A. 44°31N 88°0W **78** D6
Green Camp Ohio, U.S.A. 40°32N 83°5W **86** C3
Green City Mo., U.S.A. 40°16N 92°57W **83** A4
Green County ☆ Ky., U.S.A. 37°15N 85°35W **105** C7
Green County ☆ Wis., U.S.A. 42°45N 89°40W **78** F4
Green Cove Springs Fla., U.S.A. 29°59N 81°42W **114** B7
Green Creek N.J., U.S.A. 39°3N 74°54W **92** D2
Green Forest Ark., U.S.A. 36°20N 93°26W **106** B2
Green Island Iowa, U.S.A. 42°9N 90°20W **81** C8
Green Isle Minn., U.S.A. 44°41N 94°1W **77** F4
Green L. Minn., U.S.A. 45°15N 94°54W **77** E4
Green L. Wis., U.S.A. 43°49N 89°0W **78** E5
Green Lake Sask., Canada 54°17N 107°47W **150** A4
Green Lake Wis., U.S.A. 43°51N 88°58W **78** E5
Green Lake County ☆ Wis., U.S.A. 43°56N 89°0W **78** E5
Green Mountain Nat. Forest Vt., U.S.A. 44°0N 73°0W **89** C2
Green Mts. Vt., U.S.A. 43°45N 72°45W **89** C2
Green Mts. Wyo., U.S.A. 42°23N 107°45W **124** D5
Green Peter L. Oreg., U.S.A. 44°26N 122°37W **121** C3
Green Ridge Mo., U.S.A. 38°37N 93°24W **83** C3
Green Ridge State Forest Md., U.S.A. 39°36N 78°30W **93** A2
Green River Utah, U.S.A. 38°59N 110°10W **129** E5
Green River Wyo., U.S.A. 41°32N 109°28W **124** E3
Green River L. Ky., U.S.A. 37°15N 85°15W **105** C7
Green Spring W. Va., U.S.A. 39°32N 78°37W **93** A2

Green Swamp Fla., U.S.A. 28°12N 81°46W **114** C7
Green Swamp N.C., U.S.A. 34°15N 78°25W **103** D7
Green Tree Pa., U.S.A. 40°24N 80°2W **98** B1
Green Valley Ariz., U.S.A. 31°52N 110°56W **130** F5
Green Valley Ill., U.S.A. 40°24N 89°38W **84** C4
Green Valley Md., U.S.A. 39°19N 77°18W **93** A3
Greenacres Calif., U.S.A. 35°23N 119°7W **127** H7
Greenacres Fla., U.S.A. 26°38N 80°7W **114** E8
Greenback Tenn., U.S.A. 35°30N 84°10W **105** E8
Greenbelt Md., U.S.A. 39°0N 76°53W **99** A4
Greenbrier Ark., U.S.A. 35°14N 92°23W **106** C3
Greenbrier Tenn., U.S.A. 36°26N 86°48W **104** D6
Greenbrier → W. Va., U.S.A. 37°39N 80°53W **102** D4
Greenbrier County ☆ W. Va., U.S.A. 37°56N 80°23W **102** D4
Greenbush Mich., U.S.A. 44°35N 83°19W **79** E8
Greenbush Minn., U.S.A. 48°42N 96°11W **77** B2
Greencastle Ind., U.S.A. 39°38N 86°52W **85** D4
Greencastle Pa., U.S.A. 39°47N 77°44W **93** A3
Greendale Ind., U.S.A. 39°7N 84°52W **86** D2
Greendale Mo., U.S.A. 38°41N 90°18W **94** A2
Greendale Wis., U.S.A. 42°56N 87°59W **94** C2
Greene Iowa, U.S.A. 42°54N 92°48W **81** B5
Greene Maine, U.S.A. 44°12N 70°8W **90** D3
Greene N.Y., U.S.A. 42°20N 75°46W **88** C5
Greene County ☆ Ala., U.S.A. 32°50N 87°53W **112** D3
Greene County ☆ Ark., U.S.A. 36°3N 90°29W **106** B5
Greene County ☆ Ga., U.S.A. 33°30N 83°5W **113** C3
Greene County ☆ Ill., U.S.A. 39°20N 90°20W **84** D3
Greene County ☆ Ind., U.S.A. 39°0N 87°0W **85** D4
Greene County ☆ Iowa, U.S.A. 42°0N 94°25W **81** C4
Greene County ☆ Miss., U.S.A. 31°10N 88°45W **111** E5
Greene County ☆ Mo., U.S.A. 37°15N 93°20W **83** D3
Greene County ☆ N.C., U.S.A. 35°30N 77°40W **103** C8
Greene County ☆ N.Y., U.S.A. 42°20N 74°0W **88** C7
Greene County ☆ Ohio, U.S.A. 39°41N 83°56W **86** D3
Greene County ☆ Pa., U.S.A. 39°55N 80°5W **87** E2
Greene County ☆ Tenn., U.S.A. 36°10N 82°50W **105** D10
Greene County ☆ Va., U.S.A. 38°18N 78°26W **102** C6
Greeneville Tenn., U.S.A. 36°10N 82°50W **105** D10
Greenfield Calif., U.S.A. 36°19N 121°15W **127** G5
Greenfield Ill., U.S.A. 39°21N 90°12W **84** D3
Greenfield Ind., U.S.A. 39°47N 85°46W **85** D5
Greenfield Iowa, U.S.A. 41°18N 94°28W **81** D4
Greenfield Mass., U.S.A. 42°35N 72°36W **91** B2
Greenfield Mo., U.S.A. 37°25N 93°51W **83** D3
Greenfield N.H., U.S.A. 42°55N 71°51W **89** D3
Greenfield Ohio, U.S.A. 39°21N 83°23W **86** D3
Greenfield Okla., U.S.A. 35°44N 98°23W **107** C5
Greenfield Tenn., U.S.A. 36°9N 88°48W **104** D4
Greenfield Wis., U.S.A. 42°57N 88°0W **94** C1
Greenfield Park Qué., Canada 45°29N 73°28W **160** B4
Greenfield Park Wis., U.S.A. 43°0N 88°3W **94** B1
Greenhorn Oreg., U.S.A. 44°42N 118°29W **121** C7
Greenhorn Mts. Calif., U.S.A. 35°51N 118°34W **127** H8
Greenland Mich., U.S.A. 46°47N 89°6W **79** C2
Greenland N.H., U.S.A. 43°4N 70°50W **89** C4
Greenland ☑ N. Amer. 66°0N 45°0W **162** D6
Greenland Sea Arctic 73°0N 10°0W **162** B10
Greenleaf Kans., U.S.A. 39°44N 96°59W **82** B7
Greenlee County ☆ Ariz., U.S.A. 33°0N 109°15W **130** D6
Greenough Mont., U.S.A. 46°55N 113°25W **123** D4
Greenough Pt. Ont., Canada 44°58N 81°26W **146** C5
Greenpoint N.Y., U.S.A. 40°43N 73°57W **97** B3
Greenport N.Y., U.S.A. 41°6N 72°22W **91** C2
Green's Creek Conservation Area Ont., Canada 45°25N 75°35W **160** A2
Greensboro Ala., U.S.A. 32°42N 87°36W **112** D3
Greensboro Ga., U.S.A. 33°35N 83°11W **113** C3
Greensboro Md., U.S.A. 38°58N 75°48W **93** B5
Greensboro N.C., U.S.A. 36°4N 79°48W **103** B6
Greensboro-High Point ✈ (GSO) N.C., U.S.A. 36°5N 79°56W **103** B6
Greensburg Ind., U.S.A. 39°20N 85°29W **85** D5
Greensburg Kans., U.S.A. 37°36N 99°18W **82** D4
Greensburg Ky., U.S.A. 37°16N 85°30W **105** C7
Greensburg La., U.S.A. 30°50N 90°40W **110** D5
Greensburg Pa., U.S.A. 40°18N 79°33W **87** D3
Greenstone Ont., Canada 49°44N 87°10W **149** C9
Greensville County ☆ Va., U.S.A. 36°42N 77°32W **102** E7
Greentown Ind., U.S.A. 40°29N 85°58W **85** C5
Greenup Ill., U.S.A. 39°15N 88°10W **84** D5
Greenup Ky., U.S.A. 38°35N 82°50W **105** B10
Greenup County ☆ Ky., U.S.A. 38°30N 83°0W **105** B9
Greenview Ill., U.S.A. 40°5N 89°44W **84** C4
Greenville Ala., U.S.A. 31°50N 86°38W **112** E4
Greenville Calif., U.S.A. 40°8N 120°57W **126** C6
Greenville Fla., U.S.A. 30°28N 83°38W **114** A5
Greenville Ga., U.S.A. 33°2N 84°43W **113** C2
Greenville Ill., U.S.A. 38°53N 89°25W **84** E4
Greenville Ky., U.S.A. 37°12N 87°11W **104** C5
Greenville Maine, U.S.A. 45°28N 69°35W **90** C4
Greenville Mich., U.S.A. 43°11N 85°15W **79** F6
Greenville Miss., U.S.A. 33°24N 91°4W **111** C2
Greenville Mo., U.S.A. 37°8N 90°27W **83** D61
Greenville N.C., U.S.A. 35°37N 77°23W **103** C8
Greenville N.H., U.S.A. 42°46N 71°49W **89** D3
Greenville Ohio, U.S.A. 40°6N 84°38W **86** C2
Greenville Pa., U.S.A. 41°24N 80°23W **87** C2
Greenville R.I., U.S.A. 41°52N 71°33W **91** C2
Greenville S.C., U.S.A. 34°51N 82°24W **103** D3
Greenville Tex., U.S.A. 33°8N 96°7W **109** D11
Greenville Wis., U.S.A. 44°18N 88°32W **78** D5
Greenville County ☆ S.C., U.S.A. 34°50N 82°20W **103** D3
Greenwald Minn., U.S.A. 45°36N 94°52W **77** E4
Greenwater Lake Prov. Park △ Sask., Canada 52°32N 103°30W **150** C8
Greenway Ark., U.S.A. 36°21N 90°13W **106** B5
Greenwich Conn., U.S.A. 41°2N 73°38W **91** C1
Greenwich N.J., U.S.A. 39°24N 75°21W **92** C1
Greenwich N.Y., U.S.A. 43°5N 73°30W **89** C1
Greenwich Ohio, U.S.A. 41°2N 82°31W **86** B4
Greenwich Village New York, U.S.A. 96 d1
Greenwood B.C., Canada 49°10N 118°40W **155** F16
Greenwood Ark., U.S.A. 35°13N 94°16W **106** C1
Greenwood Del., U.S.A. 38°49N 75°35W **93** B5
Greenwood Ind., U.S.A. 39°37N 86°7W **85** D4
Greenwood Ky., U.S.A. 36°53N 84°30W **105** D8
Greenwood La., U.S.A. 32°27N 93°58W **110** B2
Greenwood Miss., U.S.A. 33°31N 90°11W **111** C3
Greenwood Nebr., U.S.A. 40°58N 96°27W **80** D9

Greenwood S.C., U.S.A. 34°12N 82°10W **103** D3
Greenwood Wis., U.S.A. 44°46N 90°36W **78** D3
Greenwood, L. S.C., U.S.A. 34°11N 81°54W **103** D4
Greenwood Cemetery N.Y., U.S.A. 40°39N 73°59W **97** C3
Greenwood County ☆ Kans., U.S.A. 37°45N 96°15W **82** D7
Greenwood County ☆ S.C., U.S.A. 34°10N 82°5W **103** D3
Greenwood L. U.S.A. 41°10N 74°20W **92** A2
Greenwood Village Colo., U.S.A. 39°37N 104°57W **134** C2
Greenwook Lake N.Y., U.S.A. 41°13N 74°18W **92** A2
Greer County ☆ Okla., U.S.A. 46°24N 116°11W **122** C2
Greer Mo., U.S.A. 36°46N 91°21W **83** E5
Greer S.C., U.S.A. 34°56N 82°14W **103** D3
Greer County ☆ Okla., U.S.A. 35°0N 99°35W **107** D4
Greers Ferry Ark., U.S.A. 35°35N 92°11W **106** C3
Greers Ferry L. Ark., U.S.A. 35°32N 92°10W **106** C3
Greeson, L. Ark., U.S.A. 34°9N 93°43W **106** D2
Gregg County ☆ Tex., U.S.A. 32°30N 94°44W **109** E13
Gregory Ark., U.S.A. 35°9N 91°21W **106** C4
Gregory Mich., U.S.A. 42°28N 84°5W **79** G7
Gregory S. Dak., U.S.A. 43°14N 99°26W **76** G6
Gregory Tex., U.S.A. 27°56N 97°18W **109** K10
Gregory County ☆ S. Dak., U.S.A. 43°11N 99°18W **76** G6
Grenada Calif., U.S.A. 41°39N 122°31W **126** B4
Grenada Miss., U.S.A. 33°47N 89°49W **111** C4
Grenada ■ W. Indies 12°10N 61°40W **183** D7
Grenada County ☆ Miss., U.S.A. 33°47N 89°49W **111** C4
Grenada L. Miss., U.S.A. 33°50N 89°47W **111** C4
Grenadines, The St. Vincent 12°40N 61°20W **183** D7
Grenfell Sask., Canada 50°30N 102°56W **150** E9
Grenola Kans., U.S.A. 37°21N 96°27W **82** D7
Grenora N. Dak., U.S.A. 48°37N 103°56W **76** B2
Grenville Qué., Canada 45°37N 74°36W **144** F8
Grenville N. Mex., U.S.A. 36°36N 103°37W **131** A7
Grenville S. Dak., U.S.A. 45°28N 97°23W **76** E8
Grenville Chan. B.C., Canada 53°40N 129°46W **154** B5
Gres, Pt. au Mich., U.S.A. 43°59N 83°41W **79** F8
Gresham Nebr., U.S.A. 41°2N 97°24W **80** C8
Gresham Oreg., U.S.A. 45°29N 122°25W **132** A2
Gresham Park Georgia, U.S.A. 33°43N 84°20W **117** B2
Gressitt Va., U.S.A. 37°29N 76°43W **102** D8
Gresston Ga., U.S.A. 32°17N 83°15W **113** D3
Gretna Man., Canada 49°1N 97°34W **151** F14
Gretna Fla., U.S.A. 30°37N 84°40W **114** A4
Gretna La., U.S.A. 29°54N 90°3W **117** C2
Gretna Nebr., U.S.A. 41°8N 96°15W **80** C9
Gretna Va., U.S.A. 36°57N 79°22W **102** E5
Gretna City Park La., U.S.A. 29°54N 90°3W **117** C2
Grey ➙ Nfld. & L., Canada 47°34N 57°6W **142** E3
Grey, Pt. B.C., Canada 49°17N 123°14W **161** B1
Grey Eagle Minn., U.S.A. 45°50N 94°45W **77** E4
Grey Forest Tex., U.S.A. 29°36N 98°40W **116** B1
Grey Is. Nfld. & L., Canada 50°50N 55°35W **142** B5
Grey River Nfld. & L., Canada 47°35N 57°6W **142** E3
Greybull Wyo., U.S.A. 44°30N 108°3W **124** B4
Greybull ➙ Wyo., U.S.A. 44°28N 108°3W **124** B4
Greylock, Mt. Mass., U.S.A. 42°38N 73°10W **91** B1
Greynolds Park Fla., U.S.A. 25°56N 80°9W **115** C3
Greystone Colo., U.S.A. 40°37N 108°41W **125** B2
Gribbell I. B.C., Canada 53°23N 129°0W **154** B5
Gridley Calif., U.S.A. 39°22N 121°42W **126** D5
Gridley Ill., U.S.A. 40°45N 88°53W **84** C5
Gridley Kans., U.S.A. 38°6N 95°53W **82** C8
Griffin Ga., U.S.A. 33°15N 84°16W **113** C2
Griffin Ind., U.S.A. 38°12N 87°55W **85** E3
Griffin, L. Fla., U.S.A. 28°52N 81°51W **114** C7
Griffith Ont., Canada 45°15N 77°10W **147** B9
Griffith I. Nunavut, Canada 74°35N 95°30W **158** C6
Griffith I. Ont., Canada 44°50N 80°55W **146** C6
Griffith Park Calif., U.S.A. 34°8N 118°17W **133** B3
Griffithsville W. Va., U.S.A. 38°14N 81°50W **102** C3
Grifton N.C., U.S.A. 35°23N 77°26W **103** C8
Griggs County ☆ N. Dak., U.S.A. 47°34N 98°21W **76** C7
Griggsville Ill., U.S.A. 39°43N 90°43W **84** D3
Grijalva ➙ Tabasco, Mexico 18°36N 92°39W **178** A4
Grimes Iowa, U.S.A. 41°41N 93°47W **81** D5
Grimes County ☆ Tex., U.S.A. 30°29N 95°59W **109** G12
Grimsby Ont., Canada 43°12N 79°34W **146** D7
Grimshaw Alta., Canada 56°10N 117°40W **152** B3
Grimsley Tenn., U.S.A. 36°16N 84°59W **105** D8
Grindstone I. Ont., Canada 44°43N 76°14W **147** C10
Grinnell Iowa, U.S.A. 41°45N 92°43W **81** D61
Grinnell Kans., U.S.A. 39°6N 100°38W **82** B3
Grinnell Pen. Nunavut, Canada 76°40N 95°0W **158** B6
Grise Fiord Nunavut, Canada 76°25N 82°57W **158** B9
Griswold Iowa, U.S.A. 41°14N 95°8W **81** D3
Grizzly Bear Mt. N.W.T., Canada 65°20N 121°0W **157** C8
Groais I. Nfld. & L., Canada 50°55N 55°35W **142** B5
Groesbeck Tex., U.S.A. 31°31N 96°32W **109** F11
Gronlid Sask., Canada 53°6N 104°28W **150** D7
Grønnedal = Kangilinnguit Greenland 61°20N 47°57W **162** E6
Groom Tex., U.S.A. 35°12N 101°6W **108** B6
Groom L. Nev., U.S.A. 37°17N 115°48W **128** E5
Gros-Morne Qué., Canada 49°15N 65°34W **140** D4
Gros Morne Nat. Park Nfld. & L.,
 Canada 49°40N 57°50W **142** C3
Gros Ventre Range Wyo., U.S.A. 43°12N 110°22W **124** C2
Gross Nev., U.S.A. 42°57N 98°34W **80** B7
Grosse Isle Man., Canada 50°4N 97°27W **151** E14
Grosse Point Lighthouse Ill., U.S.A. 42°2N 87°41W **95** A2
Grosse Pointe Mich., U.S.A. 42°24N 82°56W **79** G9
Grosse Tete La., U.S.A. 30°25N 91°26W **110** D4
Grosses-Roches Qué., Canada 48°57N 67°6W **140** E2
Groswater B. Nfld. & L., Canada 54°20N 57°40W **143** C6
Groton Conn., U.S.A. 41°21N 72°5W **91** C2
Groton Mass., U.S.A. 42°37N 71°34W **91** B3
Groton N.Y., U.S.A. 42°36N 76°22W **88** C4
Groton S. Dak., U.S.A. 45°27N 98°6W **76** E7
Groton Vt., U.S.A. 44°12N 72°12W **89** B2
Grottoes Va., U.S.A. 38°16N 78°50W **102** C6
Grouard Mission Alta., Canada 55°33N 116°9W **152** C4
Groundhog ➙ Ont., Canada 48°45N 82°58W **149** D14
Grouse Creek Utah, U.S.A. 41°42N 113°53W **129** B2
Grouse Creek Mts. Utah, U.S.A. 41°30N 113°50W **129** B2
Grovania Ga., U.S.A. 32°22N 83°40W **113** D3
Grove Okla., U.S.A. 36°36N 94°46W **107** B9
Grove, The Ill., U.S.A. 42°5N 87°52W **95** A1
Grove, The Tex., U.S.A. 31°16N 97°32W **109** F10
Grove City Ohio, U.S.A. 39°53N 83°6W **86** D3
Grove City Pa., U.S.A. 41°10N 80°5W **87** C2
Grove Hall Mass., U.S.A. 42°18N 71°4W **96** B2
Grove Hill Ala., U.S.A. 31°42N 87°47W **112** E3
Grove Park Georgia, U.S.A. 33°46N 84°26W **117** B2
Grovedale Alta., Canada 55°3N 118°52W **152** C2
Groveland Calif., U.S.A. 37°50N 120°14W **126** F6
Groveland Fla., U.S.A. 28°34N 81°51W **114** C7
Groveland Mass., U.S.A. 42°46N 71°2W **91** B3

Groveport Ohio, U.S.A. 39°51N 82°53W **86** D4
Grover Colo., U.S.A. 40°52N 104°14W **125** B6
Grover Utah, U.S.A. 38°14N 111°21W **129** E4
Grover Wyo., U.S.A. 42°48N 110°56W **124** D2
Grover Beach Calif., U.S.A. 35°7N 120°37W **127** H6
Grover Hill Ohio, U.S.A. 41°1N 84°29W **86** B2
Groves Tex., U.S.A. 29°57N 93°54W **109** H14
Grovespring Mo., U.S.A. 37°24N 92°37W **83** D4
Groveton N.H., U.S.A. 44°36N 71°31W **89** B3
Groveton Tex., U.S.A. 31°4N 95°8W **109** F12
Groveton Va., U.S.A. 38°46N 77°6W **99** C3
Grovetown Ga., U.S.A. 33°27N 82°12W **113** C4
Growler Mts. Ariz., U.S.A. 32°15N 113°0W **130** E3
Growler Wash ➙ Ariz., U.S.A. 32°40N 113°50W **130** E2
Gruetli-Leager Tenn., U.S.A. 35°22N 85°37W **105** E7
Grulla Tex., U.S.A. 26°16N 98°39W **108** L9
Grundy Va., U.S.A. 37°17N 82°6W **102** D2
Grundy Center Iowa, U.S.A. 42°22N 92°47W **81** C61
Grundy County ☆ Ill., U.S.A. 41°20N 88°25W **84** B5
Grundy County ☆ Iowa, U.S.A. 42°25N 92°45W **81** C6
Grundy County ☆ Mo., U.S.A. 40°5N 93°30W **83** A3
Grundy County ☆ Tenn., U.S.A. 35°25N 85°44W **105** E7
Grundy Prov. Park ◌ Ont., Canada 45°58N 80°30W **146** B6
Grunthal Man., Canada 49°24N 96°51W **151** F15
Gruver Iowa, U.S.A. 43°24N 94°42W **81** B4
Gruver Tex., U.S.A. 36°16N 101°24W **108** A6
Grygla Minn., U.S.A. 48°18N 95°37W **77** B3
Grymes Hill N.Y., U.S.A. 40°36N 74°6W **97** C2
Guacamayita Durango, Mexico 23°21N 104°42W **173** D6
Guacanayabo, G. de Cuba 20°40N 77°20W **182** B4
Guachimetas de Arriba Durango,
 Mexico 24°28N 106°12W **172** C4
Guachimontón Jalisco, Mexico 20°43N 103°51W **174** B4
Guachinango Jalisco, Mexico 20°34N 104°23W **174** B3
Guachochi Chihuahua, Mexico 26°48N 107°7W **169** G8
Guadalajara Jalisco, Mexico 20°40N 103°20W **180** A1
Guadalajara ✈ (GDL) Jalisco, Mexico 20°31N 103°20W **180** A1
Guadalcázar San Luis Potosí, Mexico 22°37N 100°24W **171** H4
Guadalupe = Guadeloupe ☑ W. Indies 16°20N 61°40W **183** C7
Guadalupe Nuevo León, Mexico 25°41N 100°15W **180** C2
Guadalupe Puebla, Mexico 18°5N 98°6W **177** F2
Guadalupe Zacatecas, Mexico 22°45N 102°31W **173** E8
Guadalupe Ariz., U.S.A. 33°22N 111°57W **134** C2
Guadalupe Calif., U.S.A. 34°58N 120°34W **127** J6
Guadalupe ➙ Sonora, Mexico 31°23N 113°6W **168** B2
Guadalupe ➙ Tex., U.S.A. 28°27N 96°47W **109** J11
Guadalupe, Basílica de México, Mexico 19°29N 99°7W **181** B3
Guadalupe, Estancia de Guadalajara,
 Mexico 20°28N 103°11W **180** C2
Guadalupe, Volcan Distrito Federal,
 Mexico 19°19N 99°0W **181** C4
Guadalupe Aguilar Durango, Mexico 24°30N 104°43W **173** C6
Guadalupe County ☆ N. Mex., U.S.A. 35°0N 104°45W **131** C6
Guadalupe County ☆ Tex., U.S.A. 29°34N 97°58W **109** H10
Guadalupe de Bahues Chihuahua,
 Mexico 26°37N 105°11W **169** G10
Guadalupe de Bravo Chihuahua, Mexico 31°23N 106°7W **169** B9
Guadalupe de los Reyes Sinaloa,
 Mexico 24°15N 106°32W **172** C4
Guadalupe del Carricero San Luis Potosí,
 Mexico 23°28N 100°58W **171** G4
Guadalupe Garzarón Zacatecas, Mexico 24°36N 101°12W **173** C9
Guadalupe Mountains Nat. Park △ Tex.,
 U.S.A. 31°40N 104°30W **108** F3
Guadalupe Peak Tex., U.S.A. 31°50N 104°52W **108** F3
Guadalupe Victoria Baja Calif., Mexico 32°29N 115°7W **166** A3
Guadalupe Victoria Chiapas, Mexico 16°27N 93°7W **178** C3
Guadalupe Victoria Durango, Mexico 24°27N 104°7W **173** C6
Guadalupe Victoria Puebla, Mexico 19°18N 97°18W **176** E3
Guadalupe Victoria Tabasco, Mexico 17°37N 93°34W **178** B3
Guadalupe Victoria Tamaulipas, Mexico 23°59N 97°45W **171** E7
Guadalupe y Calvo Chihuahua, Mexico 26°6N 106°53W **169** G9
Guadalupita N. Mex., U.S.A. 36°8N 105°14W **131** A5
Guadeloupe ☑ W. Indies 16°20N 61°4W **183** C7
Guadeloupe Passage W. Indies 16°50N 62°15W **183** C7
Guaguachique Chihuahua, Mexico 27°22N 107°42W **169** F8
Guajardo Baja Calif. S., Mexico 26°33N 112°3W **167** G6
Guajardo Tamaulipas, Mexico 25°23N 97°23W **170** E7
Guaje, L. el Coahuila Mexico 28°0N 103°14W **170** C1
Gualán Guatemala 15°8N 89°22W **182** C2
Guam ☑ Pac. Oc. 13°27N 144°45E **184** b
Guamúchil Sinaloa, Mexico 25°28N 108°6W **172** B2
Guamuchilera Sinaloa, Mexico 24°56N 107°43W **172** B3
Guana I. Br. Virgin Is. 18°30N 64°30W **184** G18
Guanabacoa Cuba 23°8N 82°18W **182** B3
Guanacaste, Cordillera del Costa Rica 10°40N 85°4W **182** D2
Guanacaste, Parque Nac. △ Costa Rica 10°57N 85°30W **182** D2
Guanaceví Durango, Mexico 25°56N 105°57W **172** B5
Guanahani = San Salvador I. Bahamas 24°0N 74°40W **183** B5
Guanajay Cuba 22°56N 82°42W **182** B3
Guanajuato Guanajuato, Mexico 21°1N 101°15W **175** A6
Guanajuato ☑ Mexico 21°0N 101°0W **175** B7
Guane Cuba 22°10N 84°7W **182** B3
Guanica Puerto Rico 17°58N 66°55W **184** H16
Guano L. Oreg., U.S.A. 42°11N 119°32W **126** D6
Guantánamo Cuba 20°10N 75°14W **183** B4
Guantánamo B. Cuba 19°59N 75°10W **183** B4
Guápiles Costa Rica 10°10N 83°46W **182** D3
Guardianes de la Patria Baja Calif.,
 Mexico 32°12N 115°36W **166** A3
Guariche Coahuila, Mexico 25°19N 101°49W **171** E3
Guarisamey Durango, Mexico 25°34N 108°27W **172** B2
Guasizaco Chihuahua, Mexico 27°39N 108°27W **169** F7
Guatemala Guatemala 14°40N 90°22W **182** C1
Guatemala ■ Cent. Amer. 15°40N 90°30W **182** C1
Guatimape Durango, Mexico 24°47N 104°55W **173** C6
Guayalejo ➙ Tamaulipas, Mexico 22°5N 97°55W **171** G7
Guayama Puerto Rico 17°59N 66°7W **184** H16
Guayanés Puerto Rico 18°1N 65°54W **166** D3
Guayanilla Puerto Rico 18°1N 66°47W **184** H16
Guaymas Baja Calif., Mexico 29°59N 115°54W **166** D3
Guaymas Sonora, Mexico 27°56N 110°54W **168** F5
Guaynabo Puerto Rico 18°22N 66°7W **184** G16
Guazapares Chihuahua, Mexico 27°22N 108°15W **169** F7
Guéguen, L. Qué., Canada 48°8N 77°13W **144** C5
Guelph Ont., Canada 43°35N 80°20W **146** D6
Güémez Tamaulipas, Mexico 23°56N 99°0W **171** G6
Guerachi ➙ Chihuahua, Mexico 26°45N 107°32W **169** G8
Guerneville Calif., U.S.A. 38°30N 123°0W **126** E3
Guernsey Sask., Canada 51°53N 105°11W **150** D6
Guernsey Iowa, U.S.A. 41°39N 92°21W **81** D7
Guernsey Wyo., U.S.A. 42°16N 104°45W **124** D8
Guernsey County ☆ Ohio, U.S.A. 40°2N 81°35W **86** C5
Guernsey Res. Wyo., U.S.A. 42°17N 104°46W **124** D8

Guerra Tex., U.S.A. 26°53N 98°54W **108** L9
Guerrero Coahuila, Mexico 28°20N 100°23W **170** B4
Guerrero ☑ Mexico 17°40N 100°0W **175** E8
Guerrero Negro Baja Calif. S., Mexico 27°57N 114°2W **167** F4
Guerrero Negro, L. Baja Calif. S., Mexico 28°2N 114°2W **167** E4
Guevea de Humboldt Oaxaca, Mexico 16°48N 95°22W **177** H6
Gueydan La., U.S.A. 30°2N 92°31W **110** D3
Guffey Colo., U.S.A. 38°45N 105°31W **125** D5
Guffy Peak Wyo., U.S.A. 43°29N 107°54W **124** C5
Guguan N. Marianas 17°18N 145°51E **184** a
Guide Rock Nebr., U.S.A. 40°4N 98°20W **80** D7
Guildhall Vt., U.S.A. 44°34N 71°34W **89** B3
Guilford Conn., U.S.A. 41°17N 72°41W **91** C2
Guilford Maine, U.S.A. 45°10N 69°23W **90** C4
Guilford County ☆ N.C., U.S.A. 36°10N 79°45W **103** B6
Guillaume-Delisle, L. Qué., Canada 56°15N 76°17W **143** B2
Guillermo Blake Aguilar, Presa Sinaloa,
 Mexico 26°10N 108°17W **172** A2
Guillermo Prieto Baja Calif. S., Mexico 27°50N 113°19W **167** F5
Guillermo Zúñiga Tamaulipas, Mexico 24°0N 99°12W **171** G5
Guimbalete Chihuahua Mexico 27°2N 103°44W **169** F12
Guin Ala., U.S.A. 33°58N 87°55W **112** C3
Guinda Calif., U.S.A. 38°50N 122°12W **126** E4
Güines Cuba 22°50N 82°0W **182** B3
Guines, L. Nfld. & L., Canada 52°8N 61°25W **140** A8
Guion Ark., U.S.A. 35°56N 91°57W **106** C4
Gulf Breeze Fla., U.S.A. 30°21N 87°9W **114** E2
Gulf City Fla., U.S.A. 27°42N 82°27W **115** C4
Gulf County ☆ Fla., U.S.A. 29°50N 85°15W **114** B3
Gulf Hammock Fla., U.S.A. 29°15N 82°43W **114** B6
Gulf Islands Nat. Seashore ◌ Ala.,
 U.S.A. 30°10N 87°10W **114** A1
Gulf Shores Ala., U.S.A. 30°17N 87°41W **112** F3
Gulfport Fla., U.S.A. 27°44N 82°42W **115** C2
Gulfport Miss., U.S.A. 30°22N 89°6W **111** F4
Gulkana Alaska, U.S.A. 62°16N 145°23W **135** E11
Gull ➙ Ont., Canada 49°45N 89°0W **148** C7
Gull L. Alta., Canada 52°34N 114°0W **153** F6
Gull L. Minn., U.S.A. 46°25N 94°21W **77** D4
Gull Lake Sask., Canada 50°10N 108°29W **150** E3
Gullivan B. Fla., U.S.A. 25°45N 81°40W **114** F7
Gully Minn., U.S.A. 47°46N 95°37W **77** C3
Gumboro Del., U.S.A. 38°28N 75°22W **93** B5
Gun L. Mich., U.S.A. 42°36N 85°31W **79** G6
Gunisao ➙ Man., Canada 53°56N 97°53W **151** B14
Gunisao L. Man., Canada 53°33N 96°15W **151** B15
Gunnbjørn Fjeld Greenland 68°55N 29°47W **162** D8
Gunnison Colo., U.S.A. 38°33N 106°56W **125** D4
Gunnison Miss., U.S.A. 33°57N 90°57W **111** C3
Gunnison Utah, U.S.A. 39°9N 111°49W **129** D4
Gunnison ➙ Colo., U.S.A. 39°4N 108°35W **125** C2
Gunnison, Mt. Colo., U.S.A. 38°49N 107°23W **125** D4
Gunnison Nat. Forest Colo., U.S.A. 38°40N 107°0W **125** D4
Gunnison County ☆ Colo., U.S.A. 38°30N 107°0W **125** D4
Gunpowder ➙ Md., U.S.A. 39°20N 76°20W **93** A4
Guntersville Ala., U.S.A. 34°21N 86°18W **112** B4
Guntersville L. Ala., U.S.A. 34°25N 86°23W **112** B4
Guntown Miss., U.S.A. 34°27N 88°40W **111** B5
Gurabo Puerto Rico 18°16N 65°58W **184** G17
Gurdon Ark., U.S.A. 33°55N 93°9W **106** E2
Gurley Ala., U.S.A. 34°42N 86°23W **112** B4
Gurley Nebr., U.S.A. 41°19N 102°58W **80** C3
Gurnee Ill., U.S.A. 42°22N 87°55W **84** A6
Gurnet Point Mass., U.S.A. 42°1N 70°34W **91** B4
Gustav Holm, Kap Greenland 66°36N 34°15W **162** D7
Gustavo A. Madero Distrito Federal,
 Mexico 19°29N 99°8W **181** B3
Gustavo Díaz Ordaz, Fresa Sinaloa,
 Mexico 25°55N 107°54W **172** B3
Gustavus Alaska, U.S.A. 58°25N 135°44W **135** G14
Gustine Calif., U.S.A. 37°16N 121°0W **126** F5
Gustine Tex., U.S.A. 31°51N 98°24W **109** F9
Guthrie Ky., U.S.A. 36°39N 87°10W **104** D5
Guthrie Okla., U.S.A. 35°53N 97°25W **107** C6
Guthrie Tex., U.S.A. 33°37N 100°19W **108** D7
Guthrie County ☆ Iowa, U.S.A. 41°41N 94°30W **81** D4
Gutiérrez Zamora Veracruz, Mexico 20°27N 97°5W **176** D4
Guttenberg Iowa, U.S.A. 42°47N 91°6W **81** C71
Guttenberg New York, U.S.A. 96 a1
Guyandotte ➙ W. Va., U.S.A. 38°26N 82°32W **102** C2
Guymon Okla., U.S.A. 36°41N 101°29W **107** B2
Guyot, Mt. Tenn., U.S.A. 35°42N 83°15W **105** E9
Guysborough N.S., Canada 45°23N 61°30W **141** H8
Guyton Ga., U.S.A. 32°20N 81°24W **113** D5
Guzmán, L. de Chihuahua, Mexico 31°20N 107°30W **169** B8
Gwaii Haanas Nat. Park Reserve △ B.C.,
 Canada 52°21N 131°26W **154** C3
Gwinn Mich., U.S.A. 46°19N 87°27W **79** C4
Gwinner N. Dak., U.S.A. 46°14N 97°40W **76** D8
Gwinnett County ☆ Ga., U.S.A. 34°0N 84°0W **113** C2
Gwynns Falls Park Baltimore, U.S.A. 39°18N 76°41W **99** B1
Gyldenløve Fjord Greenland 64°15N 40°30W **162** E6
Gypsum Colo., U.S.A. 39°39N 106°57W **125** C4
Gypsum Kans., U.S.A. 38°42N 97°26W **82** C6
Gypsumville Man., Canada 51°45N 98°40W **151** D13

H

H. Neely Henry L. Ala., U.S.A. 33°55N 86°2W **112** C4
Haakon County ☆ S. Dak., U.S.A. 44°25N 101°35W **76** F4
Haakon VII Topp Jan Mayen, Norway 71°0N 8°20W **162** C10
Habay Alta., Canada 58°50N 118°44W **157** E9
Habersham Ga., U.S.A. 34°36N 83°34W **113** B3
Habersham County ☆ Ga., U.S.A. 34°36N 83°34W **113** B3
Hachita N. Mex., U.S.A. 31°55N 108°19W **131** F2
Hackberry Ariz., U.S.A. 35°22N 113°44W **130** D2
Hackberry La., U.S.A. 30°0N 93°17W **110** D2
Hackensack Minn., U.S.A. 46°56N 94°31W **77** D4
Hackensack N.J., U.S.A. 40°52N 74°4W **97** B2
Hackensack ➙ N.J., U.S.A. 40°42N 74°7W **97** C2
Hackett Ark., U.S.A. 35°11N 94°25W **106** C1
Hackettstown N.J., U.S.A. 40°51N 74°50W **92** B2
Hackleburg Ala., U.S.A. 34°17N 87°50W **112** B3
Hadar Nebr., U.S.A. 42°6N 97°27W **80** B8
Haddam Kans., U.S.A. 39°52N 97°18W **82** B6
Haddock Ga., U.S.A. 33°2N 83°26W **113** C3
Haddon Heights N.J., U.S.A. 39°52N 75°3W **98** B2
Hadlyme Conn., U.S.A. 41°25N 72°25W **91** C2
Ha'ena Hawai'i, U.S.A. 22°14N 159°34W **136** B2
Hafford Sask., Canada 52°43N 107°21W **150** C4
Hagemeister I. Alaska, U.S.A. 58°39N 160°54W **135** G7
Hagensborg B.C., Canada 52°23N 126°30W **154** C8
Hagerman Idaho, U.S.A. 42°49N 114°54W **122** G4
Hagerman N. Mex., U.S.A. 33°7N 104°20W **131** D6

Hagerman Fossil Beds Nat. Monument ◌
 U.S.A. 42°48N 114°57W **122** G4
Hagerman Nat. Wildlife Refuge ◌ Tex.,
 U.S.A. 33°43N 96°47W **109** D11
Hagerstown Ind., U.S.A. 39°55N 85°10W **85** D5
Hagerstown Md., U.S.A. 39°39N 77°43W **93** A3
Hagersville Ont., Canada 42°58N 80°3W **146** E6
Hague N. Dak., U.S.A. 46°2N 99°59W **76** D6
Hague N.Y., U.S.A. 43°45N 73°30W **89** C1
Hague Va., U.S.A. 38°4N 76°39W **102** C8
Hague Park Ont., Canada 43°45N 79°14W **161** A3
Hahira Ga., U.S.A. 30°59N 83°22W **113** F3
Hahnville La., U.S.A. 29°59N 90°25W **110** E5
Haigler Nebr., U.S.A. 40°1N 101°56W **80** D4
Haiku-Pauwela Hawai'i, U.S.A. 20°56N 156°19W **136** C5
Hailey Idaho, U.S.A. 43°31N 114°19W **122** F4
Haileybury Ont., Canada 47°30N 79°38W **144** D3
Haileyville Okla., U.S.A. 34°51N 95°35W **107** D8
Haines Alaska, U.S.A. 59°14N 135°26W **135** G14
Haines Oreg., U.S.A. 44°55N 117°56W **121** C8
Haines ☆ Alaska, U.S.A. 59°15N 135°30W **135** G14
Haines City Fla., U.S.A. 28°7N 81°38W **114** C7
Haines Junction Yukon, Canada 60°45N 137°30W **157** D5
Hainesport N.J., U.S.A. 39°59N 74°50W **92** C2
Haiti ■ W. Indies 19°0N 72°30W **183** C5
Halachó Yucatán, Mexico 20°29N 90°5W **179** B3
Halachó, C. Hawai'i, U.S.A. 21°10N 156°43W **136** B5
Halbrite Sask., Canada 49°30N 103°33W **150** F8
Halbur Iowa, U.S.A. 42°0N 94°59W **81** D4
Haldeman Ky., U.S.A. 38°15N 83°19W **105** B9
Haldimand Ont., Canada 42°59N 79°52W **146** E7
Hale Colo., U.S.A. 39°38N 102°29W **125** C8
Hale Mo., U.S.A. 39°36N 93°20W **83** B3
Hale Center Tex., U.S.A. 34°4N 101°51W **108** C6
Hale County ☆ Ala., U.S.A. 32°42N 87°36W **112** D3
Hale County ☆ Tex., U.S.A. 34°0N 101°55W **108** C6
Haleakalā Nat. Park △ Hawai'i, U.S.A. 20°40N 156°15W **136** C5
Haledon N.J., U.S.A. 40°56N 74°11W **97** A1
Hale'iwa Hawai'i, U.S.A. 21°36N 158°6W **136** J13
Hales Corners Wis., U.S.A. 42°56N 88°2W **94** C1
Halethorpe Md., U.S.A. 39°14N 76°40W **99** B1
Haley N. Dak., U.S.A. 45°58N 103°7W **76** E2
Haleyville Ala., U.S.A. 34°14N 87°37W **112** B3
Haleyville N.J., U.S.A. 39°17N 75°2W **92** C1
Half Island Cove N.S., Canada 45°21N 61°12W **141** H8
Half Moon L. Tex., U.S.A. 34°50N 77°28W **103** D8
Half Way Mo., U.S.A. 37°37N 93°15W **83** D3
Halfmoon Landing Ga., U.S.A. 31°42N 81°16W **113** E5
Halfway Ala., U.S.A. 39°37N 77°46W **93** A3
Halfway L. Nfld. & L., Canada 44°53N 117°7W **121** C8
Halfway ➙ B.C., Canada 56°12N 121°32W **157** E8
Haliburton Ont., Canada 45°3N 78°30W **147** B8
Halifax Mass., U.S.A. 44°38N 63°35W **141** J6
Halifax Mass., U.S.A. 41°59N 70°52W **91** C4
Halifax N.C., U.S.A. 36°20N 77°35W **103** B8
Halifax Pa., U.S.A. 40°28N 76°56W **92** B1
Halifax County ☆ N.C., U.S.A. 36°15N 77°40W **103** B8
Halifax County ☆ Va., U.S.A. 36°55N 79°0W **102** E6
Halifax Int. ✈ (YHZ) N.S., Canada 44°50N 63°30W **141** J6
Halkett, C. Alaska, U.S.A. 70°48N 152°11W **135** A9
Halkirk Alta., Canada 52°17N 112°9W **153** F8
Hall Mont., U.S.A. 46°35N 113°12W **123** D4
Hall County ☆ Ga., U.S.A. 34°15N 83°50W **113** B3
Hall County ☆ Nebr., U.S.A. 40°45N 98°30W **80** D7
Hall County ☆ Tex., U.S.A. 34°30N 100°35W **108** C7
Hall I. Alaska, U.S.A. 60°40N 173°6W **135** F4
Hall L. Nunavut, Canada 68°41N 82°17W **158** D8
Hall Park Okla., U.S.A. 35°14N 97°24W **107** C6
Hall Pen. Nunavut, Canada 63°30N 66°0W **159** D12
Hall Summit La., U.S.A. 32°11N 93°18W **110** B2
Hallam Nebr., U.S.A. 40°32N 96°47W **80** D9
Hallandale Fla., U.S.A. 25°58N 80°8W **115** C3
Hallebourg Ont., Canada 49°40N 83°31W **149** C13
Halleck Nev., U.S.A. 40°57N 115°27W **128** B5
Hallett Okla., U.S.A. 36°16N 96°35W **107** B7
Hallettsville Tex., U.S.A. 29°27N 96°57W **109** H11
Halley Ark., U.S.A. 33°32N 91°24W **106** E4
Halliday N. Dak., U.S.A. 47°21N 102°20W **76** C3
Halligan Res. Colo., U.S.A. 40°53N 105°20W **125** B5
Hallock Minn., U.S.A. 48°47N 96°57W **77** B2
Hallowell Kans., U.S.A. 37°10N 95°3W **82** D8
Hallowell Maine, U.S.A. 44°17N 69°47W **90** D4
Halls Tenn., U.S.A. 35°53N 89°24W **104** E3
Halls Summit Kans., U.S.A. 38°5N 95°41W **82** C8
Hallstead Pa., U.S.A. 41°58N 75°45W **87** C7
Hallsville Mo., U.S.A. 39°7N 92°13W **83** B4
Halltown Pa., U.S.A. 37°21N 93°37W **83** D3
Hallwood Va., U.S.A. 37°53N 75°35W **93** B6
Halma Minn., U.S.A. 48°40N 96°36W **77** B2
Halsey Nebr., U.S.A. 41°54N 100°16W **80** C5
Halsey Oreg., U.S.A. 44°23N 123°7W **121** C2
Halstad Minn., U.S.A. 47°21N 96°50W **77** C2
Halstead Kans., U.S.A. 38°0N 97°31W **82** D6
Haltom City Tex., U.S.A. 32°47N 97°16W **116** B2
Hamber Park ◌ B.C., Canada 52°20N 118°0W **155** C17
Hambleton W. Va., U.S.A. 47°46N 99°31W **76** D6
Hamblen County ☆ Tenn., U.S.A. 36°13N 83°18W **105** D9
Hamburg W., U.S.A. 39°5N 79°39W **102** B5
Hamburg Ark., U.S.A. 33°14N 91°48W **106** E4
Hamburg Conn., U.S.A. 41°23N 72°21W **91** C2
Hamburg Iowa, U.S.A. 40°36N 95°39W **81** E3
Hamburg Minn., U.S.A. 44°44N 93°58W **77** F5
Hamburg N.Y., U.S.A. 41°9N 74°35W **88** C2
Hamburg N.Y., U.S.A. 42°43N 78°50W **88** C2
Hamburg Pa., U.S.A. 40°33N 75°59W **87** D7
Hamden Conn., U.S.A. 41°23N 72°54W **91** C2
Hamer Idaho, U.S.A. 43°56N 112°12W **122** F6
Hamersville Ohio, U.S.A. 38°55N 83°59W **86** E3
Hamilton = Churchill ➙ Nfld. & L.,
 Canada 53°19N 60°10W **143** C5
Hamilton Alta., Canada 43°15N 79°50W **146** D7
Hamilton Alaska, U.S.A. 34°9N 87°59W **112** B3
Hamilton Baltimore, U.S.A. 62°54N 163°53W **135** E7
Hamilton Baltimore, U.S.A. 39°21N 76°33W **99** A2
Hamilton Colo., U.S.A. 40°22N 107°37W **125** B3

Hamilton Ga., U.S.A. 32°45N 84°53W 113 D2
Hamilton Ill., U.S.A. 40°24N 91°21W 84 C2
Hamilton Kan., U.S.A. 37°59N 96°10W 82 D7
Hamilton Maine, U.S.A. 42°38N 70°51W 91 B4
Hamilton Mich., U.S.A. 42°41N 86°0W 79 G6
Hamilton Mo., U.S.A. 39°45N 94°0W 83 B2
Hamilton Mont., U.S.A. 46°15N 114°10W 123 D3
Hamilton N. Dak., U.S.A. 48°48N 97°24W 76 B8
Hamilton N.Y., U.S.A. 42°50N 75°33W 88 C5
Hamilton Ohio, U.S.A. 39°24N 84°34W 86 D2
Hamilton Oreg., U.S.A. 44°44N 119°18W 121 C6
Hamilton Tex., U.S.A. 31°42N 98°7W 109 F9
Hamilton Va., U.S.A. 39°8N 77°40W 93 A3
Hamilton Wash., U.S.A. 48°31N 121°59W 120 B4
Hamilton, L. Ark., U.S.A. 34°26N 93°2W 106 C2
Hamilton City Calif., U.S.A. 39°45N 122°1W 126 D4
Hamilton County ☆ Fla., U.S.A. 30°30N 83°0W 114 A6
Hamilton County ☆ Ill., U.S.A. 38°5N 88°30W 84 E5
Hamilton County ☆ Iowa, U.S.A. 42°20N 93°40W 81 C5
Hamilton County ☆ Kans., U.S.A. 38°0N 101°45W 82 D2
Hamilton County ☆ N.Y., U.S.A. 43°30N 74°30W 88 B6
Hamilton County ☆ Nebr., U.S.A. 40°45N 98°0W 80 D8
Hamilton County ☆ Ohio, U.S.A. 39°13N 84°33W 86 D2
Hamilton County ☆ Tenn., U.S.A. 35°17N 85°10W 105 E7
Hamilton County ☆ Tex., U.S.A. 31°40N 98°8W 109 F9
Hamilton Dome Wyo., U.S.A. 43°46N 108°35W 124 C4
Hamilton Mt. N.Y., U.S.A. 43°25N 74°22W 88 B6
Hamilton Sound Nfld. & L., Canada 49°35N 54°15W 142 C6
Hamiota Man., Canada 50°11N 100°38W 151 E11
Hamler Ohio, U.S.A. 41°14N 84°2W 86 B2
Hamlet Ind., U.S.A. 41°23N 86°35W 85 B4
Hamlet N.C., U.S.A. 34°53N 79°42W 103 D6
Hamlet Nebr., U.S.A. 40°23N 101°14W 80 D4
Hamlin Pa., U.S.A. 41°24N 75°24W 92 A1
Hamlin Tex., U.S.A. 32°53N 100°8W 108 E7
Hamlin W. Va., U.S.A. 38°17N 82°6W 102 C2
Hamlin County ☆ S. Dak., U.S.A. 44°40N 97°13W 76 F8
Hamlin L. Mich., U.S.A. 44°3N 86°28W 79 F5
Hamlin Valley Wash ➤ U.S.A. 38°42N 114°4W 129 E1
Hammel Arverne N.Y., U.S.A. 40°36N 73°48W 97 C4
Hammett Idaho, U.S.A. 42°57N 115°28W 122 G3
Hammon Okla., U.S.A. 35°38N 99°23W 107 C4
Hammond Ill., U.S.A. 39°48N 88°36W 84 D5
Hammond Ind., U.S.A. 41°38N 87°30W 85 B3
Hammond La., U.S.A. 30°30N 90°28W 110 D5
Hammond Minn., U.S.A. 44°13N 92°23W 77 F6
Hammond N.Y., U.S.A. 44°27N 75°42W 88 A5
Hammond B. Mich., U.S.A. 45°31N 84°5W 79 D7
Hammondsport N.Y., U.S.A. 42°25N 77°13W 88 C3
Hammonton N.J., U.S.A. 39°39N 74°48W 92 C2
Hampden Nfld. & L., Canada 49°33N 56°51W 142 C4
Hampden Colo., U.S.A. 39°39N 104°52W 134 C2
Hampden Maine, U.S.A. 44°44N 68°51W 90 D5
Hampden N. Dak., U.S.A. 48°32N 98°40W 76 B7
Hampden County ☆ Mass., U.S.A. 42°10N 72°35W 91 B2
Hampden Sydney Va., U.S.A. 37°14N 78°28W 102 D6
Hampshire Ill., U.S.A. 42°6N 88°32W 84 A5
Hampshire Tenn., U.S.A. 35°36N 87°18W 104 E5
Hampshire County ☆ Mass., U.S.A. 42°22N 72°35W 91 B2
Hampshire County ☆ W. Va., U.S.A. 39°18N 78°38W 102 B6
Hampstead N.B., Canada 45°37N 66°5W 141 H3
Hampstead Qué., Canada 45°28N 73°37W 160 B3
Hampstead Md., U.S.A. 39°37N 76°51W 93 A4
Hampstead N.C., U.S.A. 34°22N 77°44W 103 D8
Hampton N.B., Canada 45°32N 65°51W 141 H4
Hampton Ont., Canada 43°58N 78°45W 147 D8
Hampton Ark., U.S.A. 33°32N 92°28W 106 C3
Hampton Baltimore, U.S.A. 39°25N 76°35W 99 A2
Hampton Conn., U.S.A. 41°47N 72°3W 91 C2
Hampton Fla., U.S.A. 29°52N 82°8W 114 B6
Hampton Ga., U.S.A. 33°23N 84°17W 113 C2
Hampton Iowa, U.S.A. 42°45N 93°13W 81 C5
Hampton Minn., U.S.A. 44°37N 93°0W 77 F6
Hampton N.H., U.S.A. 42°57N 70°50W 89 D4
Hampton N.J., U.S.A. 40°42N 74°58W 92 B2
Hampton Nebr., U.S.A. 40°53N 97°53W 80 D8
Hampton Oreg., U.S.A. 43°40N 120°14W 121 E6
Hampton S.C., U.S.A. 32°50N 81°7W 103 F4
Hampton Tenn., U.S.A. 36°17N 82°10W 105 D10
Hampton Va., U.S.A. 37°2N 76°21W 102 D8
Hampton Bays N.Y., U.S.A. 40°53N 72°30W 91 D2
Hampton County ☆ S.C., U.S.A. 32°50N 81°10W 103 F4
Hampton Springs Fla., U.S.A. 30°5N 83°40W 114 A5
Hams Fork ➤ Wyo., U.S.A. 41°35N 109°57W 124 E3
Hamtramck Mich., U.S.A. 42°23N 83°2W 98 A2
Hāna Hawai'i, U.S.A. 20°45N 155°59W 136 C6
Hanaford Ill., U.S.A. 37°57N 88°50W 84 F5
Hanahan S.C., U.S.A. 32°55N 80°0W 103 F6
Hanalei Hawai'i, U.S.A. 22°12N 159°30W 136 B2
Hanamaulu Hawai'i, U.S.A. 21°59N 159°22W 136 B2
Hanapēpē Hawai'i, U.S.A. 21°55N 159°35W 136 B2
Hanauma B. Hawai'i, U.S.A. 21°15N 157°40W 136 K14
Hanbury ➤ N.W.T., Canada 63°37N 104°34W 157 D12
Hanceville B.C., Canada 51°55N 123°2W 155 D11
Hanceville Ala., U.S.A. 34°4N 86°46W 112 B4
Hancock Iowa, U.S.A. 41°24N 95°21W 81 D3
Hancock Md., U.S.A. 39°42N 78°11W 93 A2
Hancock Mich., U.S.A. 47°8N 88°35W 79 B3
Hancock Minn., U.S.A. 45°30N 95°48W 77 E3
Hancock N.H., U.S.A. 42°57N 71°58W 89 D2
Hancock N.Y., U.S.A. 41°57N 75°17W 88 D5
Hancock Vt., U.S.A. 43°56N 72°51W 89 C2
Hancocks Bridge N.J., U.S.A. 39°31N 75°28W 92 C1
Hand County ☆ S. Dak., U.S.A. 44°31N 98°59W 76 F7
Handel Sask., Canada 52°4N 108°42W 150 C7
Hanford Calif., U.S.A. 36°20N 119°39W 127 G7
Hanford Wash., U.S.A. 46°37N 119°19W 120 D6
Hanford Reach Nat. Monument △ U.S.A. 46°40N 119°30W 120 D6
Hanford Site, U.S. Dept. of Energy Wash., U.S.A. 46°35N 119°23W 120 D6
Hangman Cr ➤ Wash., U.S.A. 47°40N 117°27W 120 C8

Hankinson N. Dak., U.S.A. 46°4N 96°54W 76 D9
Hanksville Utah, U.S.A. 38°22N 110°43W 129 E5
Hanley Sask., Canada 51°38N 106°26W 150 D5
Hanley Falls Minn., U.S.A. 44°42N 95°37W 77 F3
Hanley Hills Mo., U.S.A. 38°41N 90°19W 94 A2
Hanlon Ont., Canada 43°38N 79°39W 161 B1
Hanna Alta., Canada 51°40N 111°54W 153 G9
Hanna Ind., U.S.A. 41°25N 86°47W 85 B4
Hanna La., U.S.A. 31°58N 93°21W 110 C2
Hanna Okla., U.S.A. 35°12N 95°53W 107 C8
Hanna Utah, U.S.A. 40°26N 110°48W 129 C5
Hanna Wyo., U.S.A. 41°52N 106°34W 124 E6
Hanna City Ill., U.S.A. 40°42N 89°48W 84 C4
Hannaford N. Dak., U.S.A. 47°19N 98°11W 76 C7
Hannah N. Dak., U.S.A. 48°58N 98°42W 76 B7
Hannahville Indian Reservation Mich., U.S.A. 45°43N 87°25W 79 D4
Hannibal Mo., U.S.A. 39°42N 91°22W 83 B5
Hannibal N.Y., U.S.A. 43°19N 76°35W 88 B4
Hannover N. Dak., U.S.A. 47°7N 101°26W 76 C4
Hanover Ont., Canada 44°9N 81°2W 146 C5
Hanover Baltimore, U.S.A. 39°11N 76°43W 99 B1
Hanover Ill., U.S.A. 42°15N 90°17W 84 A3
Hanover Ind., U.S.A. 38°43N 85°28W 85 E5
Hanover Kans., U.S.A. 39°54N 96°53W 82 B7
Hanover Maine, U.S.A. 44°30N 70°42W 89 C2
Hanover Mass., U.S.A. 42°7N 70°49W 91 B4
Hanover Mich., U.S.A. 42°6N 84°33W 79 G7
Hanover Minn., U.S.A. 45°10N 93°40W 77 E5
Hanover Mont., U.S.A. 47°7N 109°33W 123 C8
Hanover N.H., U.S.A. 43°42N 72°17W 89 C2
Hanover N. Mex., U.S.A. 32°48N 108°6W 131 E2
Hanover Ohio, U.S.A. 40°4N 82°16W 86 C4
Hanover Pa., U.S.A. 39°48N 76°59W 93 A4
Hanover Va., U.S.A. 37°46N 77°22W 102 D7
Hanover County ☆ Va., U.S.A. 37°46N 77°29W 102 D7
Hanoverton Ohio, U.S.A. 40°45N 80°56W 86 C6
Hans Lollik I. U.S. Virgin Is. 18°24N 64°53W 184 G18
Hansboro N. Dak., U.S.A. 48°57N 99°23W 76 B6
Hansen Idaho, U.S.A. 42°32N 114°18W 122 G4
Hansen Park Wis., U.S.A. 43°4N 88°1W 94 B1
Hansford County ☆ Tex., U.S.A. 36°10N 101°30W 108 A6
Hanska Minn., U.S.A. 44°9N 94°30W 77 F4
Hanson Fla., U.S.A. 30°34N 83°21W 114 A5
Hanson Ky., U.S.A. 37°25N 87°29W 104 C5
Hanson County ☆ S. Dak., U.S.A. 43°39N 97°47W 76 G8
Hanston Kans., U.S.A. 38°7N 99°43W 82 C4
Hant's Harbour Nfld. & L., Canada 48°1N 53°16W 142 D7
Hantsport N.S., Canada 45°4N 64°11W 141 H5
Hantzsch ➤ Nunavut, Canada 67°32N 72°25W 158 D11
Hapeville Ga., U.S.A. 33°39N 84°24W 117 C2
Happy Tex., U.S.A. 34°45N 101°51W 108 C6
Happy Camp Calif., U.S.A. 41°48N 123°23W 126 B3
Happy Jack Ariz., U.S.A. 34°45N 111°24W 130 D4
Happy Valley Oreg., U.S.A. 45°26N 122°31W 132 B2
Happy Valley-Goose Bay Nfld. & L., Canada 53°15N 60°20W 143 C5
Harahan La., U.S.A. 29°56N 90°12W 117 C1
Haralson La., U.S.A. 33°14N 84°34W 113 C2
Haralson County ☆ Ga., U.S.A. 33°45N 85°10W 113 C1
Harbeson Del., U.S.A. 38°43N 75°17W 93 B5
Harbor Beach Mich., U.S.A. 43°51N 82°39W 79 F9
Harbor Bluffs Tampa, U.S.A. 24°54N 87°49W 115 B2
Harbor Hills N.Y., U.S.A. 40°47N 73°44W 97 B4
Harbor Springs Mich., U.S.A. 45°26N 85°0W 79 D7
Harborcreek Pa., U.S.A. 42°10N 79°57W 87 B3
Harbour Oreg., U.S.A. 42°3N 124°16W 121 E1
Harbour Breton Nfld. & L., Canada 47°29N 55°50W 142 E5
Harbour Deep Nfld. & L., Canada 50°25N 56°32W 142 B4
Harbour Grace Nfld. & L., Canada 47°40N 53°22W 142 E7
Harbour Heights Fla., U.S.A. 26°59N 82°0W 114 E7
Harcones Nuevo León, Mexico 27°10N 100°25W 170 C4
Harcourt N.B., Canada 46°27N 65°15W 141 G4
Harcourt Iowa, U.S.A. 42°16N 94°11W 81 C4
Harcuvar Mts. Ariz., U.S.A. 34°0N 113°30W 130 D2
Hardee County ☆ Fla., U.S.A. 27°30N 81°45W 114 D7
Hardeeville S.C., U.S.A. 32°17N 81°5W 103 F4
Hardeman County ☆ Tenn., U.S.A. 35°6N 89°0W 104 E4
Hardeman County ☆ Tex., U.S.A. 34°20N 99°50W 109 C8
Hardesty Okla., U.S.A. 36°37N 101°12W 107 B2
Hardin Ill., U.S.A. 39°10N 90°37W 84 D3
Hardin Ky., U.S.A. 36°46N 88°18W 104 D4
Hardin Mont., U.S.A. 45°44N 107°37W 123 E10
Hardin Tex., U.S.A. 30°9N 94°44W 109 G13
Hardin County ☆ Ill., U.S.A. 37°30N 88°15W 84 F5
Hardin County ☆ Iowa, U.S.A. 42°25N 93°15W 81 C5
Hardin County ☆ Ky., U.S.A. 37°40N 86°0W 104 C6
Hardin County ☆ Ohio, U.S.A. 40°42N 83°47W 86 C3
Hardin County ☆ Tenn., U.S.A. 35°14N 88°15W 104 E4
Hardin County ☆ Tex., U.S.A. 30°22N 94°19W 109 G13
Harding Minn., U.S.A. 46°7N 94°2W 77 D4
Harding, L. Ala., U.S.A. 32°40N 85°5W 112 D5
Harding County ☆ N. Mex., U.S.A. 36°0N 104°0W 131 B7
Harding County ☆ S. Dak., U.S.A. 45°30N 103°30W 76 E2
Hardinge B. N.W.T., Canada 76°28N 101°40W 156 A8
Hardinsburg Ind., U.S.A. 38°28N 86°17W 85 E4
Hardinsburg Ky., U.S.A. 37°47N 86°28W 104 C6
Hardisty Alta., Canada 52°40N 111°18W 153 F9
Hardisty L. N.W.T., Canada 64°30N 117°45W 157 D9
Hardman Oreg., U.S.A. 45°10N 119°41W 121 B6
Hardtner Kans., U.S.A. 37°1N 98°39W 82 E5
Hardwick Ga., U.S.A. 33°3N 83°14W 113 C3
Hardwick Mass., U.S.A. 42°21N 72°12W 91 B2
Hardwick Minn., U.S.A. 43°47N 96°12W 77 G2
Hardwick Vt., U.S.A. 44°30N 72°22W 89 B2
Hardwicke I. B.C., Canada 50°27N 125°50W 154 E9
Hardwicke Island B.C., Canada 50°26N 125°55W 154 E9
Hardwood Ridge N.B., Canada 46°19N 66°1W 141 G3
Hardy Ark., U.S.A. 36°19N 91°29W 106 B4
Hardy Nebr., U.S.A. 47°12N 111°47W 123 C6
Hardy Nebr., U.S.A. 40°1N 97°56W 80 D8
Hardy County ☆ W. Va., U.S.A. 39°0N 78°55W 102 C6
Hardy Dam Pond Mich., U.S.A. 43°30N 85°37W 79 F6
Hare B. Nfld. & L., Canada 51°15N 55°45W 142 A5
Hare Bay Nfld. & L., Canada 48°51N 54°1W 142 D7
Hare Indian ➤ N.W.T., Canada 66°17N 128°37W 156 C7
Harford County ☆ Md., U.S.A. 39°35N 76°25W 93 A4
Hargill Tex., U.S.A. 26°27N 98°1W 108 L9
Harker Heights Tex., U.S.A. 31°5N 97°40W 109 F10
Harkers Island N.C., U.S.A. 34°42N 76°34W 103 D9
Harlan Iowa, U.S.A. 41°39N 95°19W 81 D3
Harlan Kans., U.S.A. 39°36N 98°46W 82 B5
Harlan County ☆ Ky., U.S.A. 36°51N 83°19W 105 D9
Harlan County ☆ Nebr., U.S.A. 40°15N 99°30W 80 D6

Harlan County Lake Nebr., U.S.A. 40°4N 99°13W 80 D6
Harlem Fla., U.S.A. 26°44N 80°57W 114 E8
Harlem Ga., U.S.A. 33°25N 82°19W 113 C4
Harlem Mont., U.S.A. 48°32N 108°47W 123 B9
Harlem New York, U.S.A. 96 a3
Harleyville S.C., U.S.A. 33°13N 80°27W 103 E5
Harlingen Tex., U.S.A. 26°12N 97°42W 108 L10
Harlowton Mont., U.S.A. 46°26N 109°50W 123 D8
Harman W. Va., U.S.A. 38°55N 79°32W 102 C5
Harmon Ill., U.S.A. 41°43N 89°33W 84 B4
Harmon County ☆ Okla., U.S.A. 34°45N 99°50W 107 D4
Harmon L. Ont., Canada 49°56N 90°13W 148 C6
Harmony Ind., U.S.A. 39°32N 87°4W 85 D3
Harmony Maine, U.S.A. 44°58N 69°33W 90 D4
Harmony Md., U.S.A. 38°47N 75°53W 93 B5
Harmony Minn., U.S.A. 43°33N 92°1W 77 G6
Harnett County ☆ N.C., U.S.A. 35°20N 78°50W 103 C7
Harney Md., U.S.A. 39°44N 77°13W 93 A3
Harney, L. Fla., U.S.A. 28°45N 81°3W 114 C7
Harney Basin Oreg., U.S.A. 43°0N 119°30W 121 D6
Harney County ☆ Oreg., U.S.A. 43°0N 119°0W 121 D6
Harney L. Oreg., U.S.A. 43°14N 119°8W 121 D6
Harney Peak S. Dak., U.S.A. 43°52N 103°32W 76 G2
Haro Str. B.C., Canada 48°30N 123°15W 155 G11
Harold Fla., U.S.A. 30°40N 86°53W 114 A2
Harp L. Nfld. & L., Canada 55°5N 61°50W 143 B5
Harper Iowa, U.S.A. 41°22N 92°3W 81 D6
Harper Kans., U.S.A. 37°17N 98°1W 82 D5
Harper Oreg., U.S.A. 43°52N 117°37W 121 D8
Harper Tex., U.S.A. 30°18N 99°15W 109 G8
Harper, Mt. Alaska, U.S.A. 64°14N 143°51W 135 D12
Harper County ☆ Kans., U.S.A. 37°15N 98°0W 82 D5
Harper County ☆ Okla., U.S.A. 36°50N 99°40W 107 B4
Harper L. Calif., U.S.A. 35°1N 117°17W 127 H9
Harpers Ferry Iowa, U.S.A. 43°12N 91°9W 81 B7
Harpers Ferry W. Va., U.S.A. 39°20N 77°44W 93 A3
Harpers Ferry Nat. Historical Park △ W. Va., U.S.A. 39°19N 77°45W 102 B7
Harpersville Ala., U.S.A. 33°21N 86°26W 112 C4
Harpeth ➤ Tenn., U.S.A. 36°18N 87°10W 104 D5
Harqualala Mts. Ariz., U.S.A. 33°45N 113°20W 130 D2
Harrah Okla., U.S.A. 35°29N 97°10W 107 C6
Harrah Wash., U.S.A. 46°24N 120°33W 120 D5
Harrell Ark., U.S.A. 33°31N 92°24W 106 E3
Harricana ➤ Qué., Canada 50°56N 79°32W 144 A3
Harriet, L. Minn., U.S.A. 44°55N 93°18W 94 B2
Harriman Tenn., U.S.A. 35°56N 84°33W 105 E8
Harriman Res. Vt., U.S.A. 42°48N 72°55W 89 D2
Harriman State Park △ N.Y., U.S.A. 41°13N 74°5W 88 D6
Harrington Del., U.S.A. 38°56N 75°35W 93 B5
Harrington Maine, U.S.A. 44°37N 67°49W 90 D6
Harrington Wash., U.S.A. 47°29N 118°15W 120 C7
Harrington Harbour Qué., Canada 50°31N 59°30W 143 C6
Harris Sask., Canada 51°44N 107°35W 150 D4
Harris Kans., U.S.A. 38°19N 95°26W 82 C8
Harris Minn., U.S.A. 45°35N 92°58W 77 E6
Harris Mo., U.S.A. 40°18N 93°21W 83 A3
Harris Okla., U.S.A. 33°45N 94°44W 107 E9
Harris County ☆ Ga., U.S.A. 32°40N 84°50W 113 D2
Harris County ☆ Tex., U.S.A. 29°46N 95°22W 109 H12
Harris Pt. Ont., Canada 43°6N 82°9W 146 D4
Harrisburg Ark., U.S.A. 35°34N 90°43W 106 C5
Harrisburg Ill., U.S.A. 37°44N 88°32W 84 F51
Harrisburg Mo., U.S.A. 39°9N 92°28W 83 B4
Harrisburg N.C., U.S.A. 35°19N 80°39W 103 C5
Harrisburg Nebr., U.S.A. 41°33N 103°44W 80 C2
Harrisburg Oreg., U.S.A. 44°16N 123°10W 121 C2
Harrisburg Pa., U.S.A. 40°16N 76°53W 87 D6
Harrisburg S. Dak., U.S.A. 43°26N 96°42W 76 G9
Harrison Ark., U.S.A. 36°14N 93°7W 106 B2
Harrison Ga., U.S.A. 32°50N 82°43W 113 D4
Harrison Idaho, U.S.A. 47°27N 116°47W 122 B2
Harrison Mich., U.S.A. 44°1N 84°48W 79 E7
Harrison Mont., U.S.A. 45°42N 111°47W 123 E6
Harrison Nebr., U.S.A. 42°41N 103°53W 80 B2
Harrison Ohio, U.S.A. 39°16N 84°49W 86 D2
Harrison, C. Nfld. & L., Canada 54°55N 57°55W 143 C6
Harrison Bay Alaska, U.S.A. 70°40N 151°0W 135 A10
Harrison County ☆ Ind., U.S.A. 38°10N 86°10W 85 E4
Harrison County ☆ Iowa, U.S.A. 41°40N 95°50W 81 D3
Harrison County ☆ Ky., U.S.A. 38°25N 84°20W 105 B8
Harrison County ☆ Miss., U.S.A. 30°30N 89°7W 111 F4
Harrison County ☆ Mo., U.S.A. 40°20N 94°0W 83 A3
Harrison County ☆ Ohio, U.S.A. 40°18N 81°11W 86 C5
Harrison County ☆ Tex., U.S.A. 32°33N 94°23W 109 E13
Harrison County ☆ W. Va., U.S.A. 39°17N 80°30W 102 B4
Harrison Hot Springs B.C., Canada 49°18N 121°47W 155 F13
Harrisonburg La., U.S.A. 31°46N 91°49W 110 C4
Harrisonburg Va., U.S.A. 38°27N 78°52W 102 C6
Harrisonville Mo., U.S.A. 38°39N 94°21W 83 C2
Harriston Ont., Canada 43°57N 80°53W 146 D6
Harriston Miss., U.S.A. 31°44N 91°2W 111 E2
Harrisville Mich., U.S.A. 44°39N 83°17W 79 E8
Harrisville N.Y., U.S.A. 44°9N 75°19W 88 A5
Harrisville R.I., U.S.A. 41°58N 71°41W 91 C3
Harrisville W. Va., U.S.A. 39°13N 81°3W 102 B3
Harrod Ohio, U.S.A. 40°43N 83°56W 86 C3
Harrodsburg Ky., U.S.A. 37°46N 84°51W 105 C8
Harrogate Tenn., U.S.A. 36°35N 83°40W 105 D9
Harrold S. Dak., U.S.A. 44°31N 99°44W 76 F6
Harrow Ont., Canada 42°2N 82°55W 146 E4
Harrowsmith Ont., Canada 44°24N 76°40W 147 C10
Harry S. Moss Park Tex., U.S.A. 32°53N 96°44W 116 A5
Harry S. Truman Res. Mo., U.S.A. 38°16N 93°24W 83 C3
Harry Strunk L. Nebr., U.S.A. 40°23N 100°13W 80 D5
Hart Tex., U.S.A. 34°23N 102°7W 108 C5
Hart ➤ Yukon, Canada 65°51N 136°22W 156 C5
Hart County ☆ Ga., U.S.A. 34°15N 83°0W 113 B4
Hart County ☆ Ky., U.S.A. 37°20N 85°50W 105 C7
Hart I. N.Y., U.S.A. 40°51N 73°46W 97 A4
Hart L. Oreg., U.S.A. 42°25N 119°51W 121 E6
Hart Mt. Oreg., U.S.A. 42°27N 119°55W 121 E6
Hartell Alta., Canada 50°36N 114°14W 153 H6
Hartfield Va., U.S.A. 37°33N 76°27W 102 D8
Hartford Ala., U.S.A. 31°6N 85°42W 112 E5
Hartford Conn., U.S.A. 41°46N 72°41W 91 C2
Hartford Iowa, U.S.A. 41°28N 93°24W 81 D5
Hartford Ky., U.S.A. 37°27N 86°55W 104 C5
Hartford Mich., U.S.A. 42°13N 86°10W 79 G5
Hartford N.Y., U.S.A. 43°22N 73°24W 89 C1

Hartford S. Dak., U.S.A. 43°38N 96°57W 76 G9
Hartford Tenn., U.S.A. 35°49N 83°9W 105 E9
Hartford Wis., U.S.A. 43°19N 88°22W 78 E5
Hartford Bradley Int. ✈ (BDL) Conn., U.S.A. 41°56N 72°41W 91 C2
Hartford City Ind., U.S.A. 40°27N 85°22W 85 C5
Hartford County ☆ Conn., U.S.A. 41°45N 72°45W 91 C2
Hartington Nebr., U.S.A. 42°37N 97°16W 80 B8
Hartland N.B., Canada 46°20N 67°32W 141 G2
Hartland Maine, U.S.A. 44°53N 69°27W 90 D4
Hartland Minn., U.S.A. 43°48N 93°29W 77 G5
Hartland Vt., U.S.A. 43°32N 72°24W 89 C2
Hartland Wis., U.S.A. 43°6N 88°21W 78 E5
Hartley Iowa, U.S.A. 43°11N 95°29W 81 B3
Hartley Tex., U.S.A. 35°53N 102°24W 108 B5
Hartley County ☆ Tex., U.S.A. 35°50N 102°30W 108 B5
Hartline Wash., U.S.A. 47°41N 119°6W 120 C6
Hartly Del., U.S.A. 39°10N 75°43W 93 A5
Hartman Colo., U.S.A. 38°7N 102°13W 125 D8
Hartney Man., Canada 49°30N 100°35W 151 F11
Hartsburg Mo., U.S.A. 38°42N 92°19W 83 C4
Hartsel Colo., U.S.A. 39°1N 105°48W 125 C5
Hartselle Ala., U.S.A. 34°27N 86°56W 112 B4
Hartsfield-Atlanta Int. ✈ (ATL) Ga., U.S.A. 33°38N 84°26W 117 C2
Hartshorne Okla., U.S.A. 34°51N 95°34W 107 D8
Hartsville S.C., U.S.A. 34°23N 80°4W 103 D5
Hartsville Tenn., U.S.A. 36°24N 86°10W 104 D6
Hartville Mo., U.S.A. 37°15N 92°31W 83 D4
Hartville Ohio, U.S.A. 40°58N 81°20W 86 C5
Hartville Wyo., U.S.A. 42°20N 104°44W 124 D8
Hartwell Ga., U.S.A. 34°21N 82°56W 113 B4
Hartwell L. S.C., U.S.A. 34°21N 82°49W 103 D3
Hartwick Iowa, U.S.A. 41°47N 92°21W 81 D6
Harty Ont., Canada 49°29N 82°41W 149 C14
Harvard Idaho, U.S.A. 46°55N 116°44W 122 C2
Harvard Ill., U.S.A. 42°25N 88°37W 84 A5
Harvard Nebr., U.S.A. 40°37N 98°6W 80 D7
Harvard, Mt. Colo., U.S.A. 38°56N 106°19W 125 D4
Harvard University Mass., U.S.A. 42°22N 71°7W 96 A2
Harvey N.B., Canada 45°43N 67°1W 141 H2
Harvey Ark., U.S.A. 34°51N 93°44W 106 D2
Harvey Ill., U.S.A. 41°36N 87°50W 84 B6
Harvey La., U.S.A. 29°54N 90°4W 117 C2
Harvey N. Dak., U.S.A. 47°47N 99°56W 76 C6
Harvey Cedars N.J., U.S.A. 39°43N 74°11W 92 C2
Harvey County ☆ Kans., U.S.A. 38°0N 97°20W 82 D6
Harveys Lake Pa., U.S.A. 41°23N 76°1W 87 C6
Harveyville Kans., U.S.A. 38°47N 95°58W 82 C8
Harwich Mass., U.S.A. 41°41N 70°5W 91 C4
Harwinton Conn., U.S.A. 41°46N 73°4W 91 C1
Harwood Mo., U.S.A. 37°57N 94°9W 83 D2
Harwood Tex., U.S.A. 29°40N 97°30W 109 H10
Harwood Heights Ill., U.S.A. 41°57N 87°46W 95 B2
Harwood Park Baltimore, U.S.A. 39°11N 76°44W 99 B1
Hasbrouck Heights N.J., U.S.A. 40°51N 74°6W 97 A2
Haskell Ark., U.S.A. 34°30N 92°38W 106 D3
Haskell Okla., U.S.A. 35°50N 95°40W 107 C8
Haskell Tex., U.S.A. 33°10N 99°44W 108 D8
Haskell County ☆ Kans., U.S.A. 37°30N 100°45W 82 D3
Haskell County ☆ Okla., U.S.A. 35°10N 95°10W 107 C8
Haskell County ☆ Tex., U.S.A. 33°12N 99°45W 108 D8
Haskins Ohio, U.S.A. 41°28N 83°42W 86 B3
Haslet Tex., U.S.A. 32°59N 97°21W 109 E10
Hassayampa ➤ Ariz., U.S.A. 33°19N 112°42W 130 D3
Hassel Sd. Nunavut, Canada 78°18N 98°46W 158 B6
Hastings Ont., Canada 44°18N 77°57W 147 C9
Hastings Fla., U.S.A. 29°43N 81°31W 114 B7
Hastings Iowa, U.S.A. 41°1N 95°30W 81 D3
Hastings Mich., U.S.A. 42°39N 85°17W 79 G6
Hastings Minn., U.S.A. 44°44N 92°51W 77 F61
Hastings Nebr., U.S.A. 40°35N 98°23W 80 D7
Hastings Okla., U.S.A. 34°14N 98°7W 107 D5
Hastings Park B.C., Canada 49°17N 123°3W 161 B2
Hasty Colo., U.S.A. 38°7N 102°58W 125 D8
Haswell Colo., U.S.A. 38°27N 103°10W 125 D7
Hat Cr. ➤ S. Dak., U.S.A. 43°15N 103°37W 76 G2
Hatch N. Mex., U.S.A. 32°40N 107°9W 131 E3
Hatch Utah, U.S.A. 37°39N 112°26W 129 F3
Hatch Wash ➤ Utah, U.S.A. 38°35N 109°35W 129 E6
Hatchet Cr. ➤ Ala., U.S.A. 32°51N 86°27W 112 D4
Hatchie ➤ Tenn., U.S.A. 35°35N 89°53W 104 E3
Hatchie Nat. Wildlife Refuge △ Tenn., U.S.A. 35°30N 89°13W 104 E3
Hatchineha, L. Fla., U.S.A. 28°2N 81°25W 114 C7
Hatfield Ark., U.S.A. 34°29N 94°23W 106 D1
Hatfield Ind., U.S.A. 37°54N 87°14W 85 F3
Hatfield Mass., U.S.A. 42°22N 72°36W 91 B2
Hatfield Minn., U.S.A. 43°58N 96°12W 77 G2
Hatfield Pa., U.S.A. 40°17N 75°18W 92 B1
Hatillo Puerto Rico 18°29N 66°50W 184 G16
Hato Mayor Dom. Rep. 18°46N 69°15W 183 C6
Hatteras N.C., U.S.A. 35°13N 75°42W 103 C10
Hatteras, C. N.C., U.S.A. 35°14N 75°32W 103 C10
Hatteras I. N.C., U.S.A. 35°30N 75°28W 103 C10
Hattiesburg Miss., U.S.A. 31°20N 89°17W 111 E4
Hattieville Ark., U.S.A. 35°17N 92°47W 106 C3
Hatton Ala., U.S.A. 34°34N 87°25W 112 B3
Hatton N. Dak., U.S.A. 47°38N 97°27W 76 C8
Hatton Wash., U.S.A. 46°47N 118°50W 120 D7
Haubstadt Ind., U.S.A. 38°12N 87°34W 85 E3
Haugan Mont., U.S.A. 47°23N 115°24W 123 C2
Haugen Wis., U.S.A. 45°37N 91°46W 78 C2
Haughton La., U.S.A. 32°32N 93°30W 110 B2
Haultain ➤ Sask., Canada 55°51N 106°46W 157 E11
Hauser Oreg., U.S.A. 43°30N 124°13W 121 D1
Haut, I. au Maine, U.S.A. 44°3N 68°38W 90 D5
Hautes-Gorges-de-la-Rivière-Malbaie, Parc des △ Qué., Canada 47°56N 70°31W 145 D12
Hau'ula Hawai'i, U.S.A. 21°37N 157°55W 136 J14
Havana = La Habana Cuba 23°8N 82°22W 182 B3
Havana Ark., U.S.A. 35°7N 93°33W 106 C2
Havana Fla., U.S.A. 30°37N 84°25W 114 A4
Havana Ill., U.S.A. 40°18N 90°4W 84 C31
Havana Kans., U.S.A. 37°6N 95°57W 82 E7
Havana N. Dak., U.S.A. 45°57N 97°37W 76 E8
Havasu, L. Ariz., U.S.A. 34°18N 114°28W 130 C1
Havasu Cr. ➤ Ariz., U.S.A. 36°19N 112°46W 130 A3
Havasupai Indian Reservation Ariz., U.S.A. 36°15N 112°35W 130 A3
Havelock N.B., Canada 46°2N 65°24W 141 G4
Havelock Ont., Canada 44°26N 77°53W 147 C9
Havelock N.C., U.S.A. 34°53N 76°54W 103 D9
Havelock N. Dak., U.S.A. 46°29N 102°45W 76 D3

Haven *Kans., U.S.A.* 37°54N 97°47W **82** D6
Havensville *Kans., U.S.A.* 39°31N 96°5W **82** B7
Haverford *Pa., U.S.A.* 40°0N 75°17W **98** A1
Haverhill *Fla., U.S.A.* 26°42N 80°7W **114** E8
Haverhill *Mass., U.S.A.* 42°47N 71°5W **91** B3
Haverhill *N.H., U.S.A.* 44°3N 72°4W **89** B2
Haverstraw *N.Y., U.S.A.* 41°12N 73°58W **92** A3
Havertown *Pa., U.S.A.* 39°58N 75°18W **98** B1
Haviland *Kans., U.S.A.* 37°37N 99°6W **82** D4
Havre *Mont., U.S.A.* 48°33N 109°41W **123** B8
Havre-Aubert *Qué., Canada* 47°12N 61°56W **141** F8
Havre-Aubert, Î. *Qué., Canada* 47°13N 61°57W **141** F8
Havre-aux-Maisons *Qué., Canada* 47°24N 61°49W **141** F8
Havre-aux-Maisons, Î. du *Qué., Canada* 47°25N 61°42W **141** F8
Havre de Grace *Md., U.S.A.* 39°33N 76°6W **93** A4
Havre-St.-Pierre *Qué., Canada* 50°18N 63°33W **143** C5
Haw → *N.C., U.S.A.* 35°36N 79°3W **103** C6
Haw Knob *N.C., U.S.A.* 35°19N 84°2W **103** C1
Hawai'i *Hawai'i, U.S.A.* 19°30N 155°30W **136** D6
Hawai'i □ *Hawai'i, U.S.A.* 19°30N 156°30W **136** D5
Hawai'i County ☆ *Hawai'i, U.S.A.* 19°30N 155°30W **136** D6
Hawai'i Volcanoes Nat. Park △ *Hawai'i,*
U.S.A. 19°25N 155°18W **136** D6
Hawaiian Is. *Pac. Oc.* 20°30N 156°0W **136** G12
Hawarden *Sask., Canada* 51°25N 106°36W **150** D5
Hawarden *Iowa, U.S.A.* 43°0N 96°29W **81** B2
Hawesville *Ky., U.S.A.* 37°54N 86°45W **104** C6
Hawi *Hawai'i, U.S.A.* 20°14N 155°50W **136** C6
Hawk Junction *Ont., Canada* 48°5N 84°38W **149** D12
Hawk Point *Mo., U.S.A.* 38°58N 91°8W **83** C5
Hawk Springs *Wyo., U.S.A.* 41°47N 104°16W **124** E8
Hawke's Bay *Nfld. & L., Canada* 50°36N 57°10W **142** B3
Hawkesbury I. *B.C., Canada* 53°37N 129°3W **154** B5
Hawkeye *Iowa, U.S.A.* 42°56N 91°57W **81** C7
Hawkins *Tex., U.S.A.* 32°35N 95°12W **109** E12
Hawkins *Wis., U.S.A.* 45°31N 90°43W **78** C3
Hawkins County ☆ *Tenn., U.S.A.* 36°24N 83°1W **105** D9
Hawkinsville *Ga., U.S.A.* 32°17N 83°28W **113** D3
Hawks *Mich., U.S.A.* 45°18N 83°53W **79** D8
Hawksbill *Va., U.S.A.* 38°34N 78°27W **102** C6
Hawksbill Mt. *N.C., U.S.A.* 35°55N 81°53W **103** C4
Hawley *Minn., U.S.A.* 46°53N 96°19W **77** D2
Hawley *Pa., U.S.A.* 41°28N 75°11W **92** A1
Hawley *Tex., U.S.A.* 32°37N 99°49W **109** E8
Haworth *Okla., U.S.A.* 33°51N 94°39W **107** E9
Hawthorne *Fla., U.S.A.* 29°36N 82°5W **114** B6
Hawthorne *N.Y., U.S.A.* 41°6N 73°48W **92** A3
Hawthorne *Nev., U.S.A.* 38°32N 118°38W **128** D2
Hawthorne Army Depot *Nev., U.S.A.* 38°29N 118°38W **128** D2
Hawthorne Racecourse *Ill., U.S.A.* 41°49N 87°44W **95** C2
Haxtun *Colo., U.S.A.* 40°39N 102°38W **125** B8
Hay *Wash., U.S.A.* 46°41N 117°55W **120** D8
Hay → *Alta., Canada* 60°50N 116°26W **157** D9
Hay → *Wis., U.S.A.* 44°59N 91°51W **78** D2
Hay, C. *N.W.T., Canada* 74°25N 113°0W **156** B10
Hay Cove *N.S., Canada* 45°45N 60°44W **141** H9
Hay I. *Ont., Canada* 44°53N 80°58W **146** C6
Hay Lakes *Alta., Canada* 53°12N 113°2W **153** E7
Hay River *N.W.T., Canada* 60°51N 115°44W **157** D9
Hay Springs *Nebr., U.S.A.* 42°41N 102°41W **80** B3
Hayden *Ariz., U.S.A.* 33°0N 110°47W **130** D5
Hayden *Colo., U.S.A.* 40°30N 107°16W **125** B3
Hayden *Idaho, U.S.A.* 47°46N 116°47W **122** B2
Hayden *N. Mex., U.S.A.* 35°59N 103°31W **131** B7
Hayden Peak *Idaho, U.S.A.* 42°59N 116°40W **122** G2
Hayes *Ind., U.S.A.* 30°7N 92°55W **110** D3
Hayes *S. Dak., U.S.A.* 44°23N 101°1W **76** F4
Hayes → *Man., Canada* 57°3N 92°12W **159** F7
Hayes → *Nunavut, Canada* 67°8N 95°17W **159** D6
Hayes, Mt. *Alaska, U.S.A.* 63°37N 146°43W **135** E11
Hayes Center *Nebr., U.S.A.* 40°31N 101°1W **80** D4
Hayes County ☆ *Nebr., U.S.A.* 40°30N 101°0W **80** D4
Hayesville *Iowa, U.S.A.* 41°16N 92°15W **81** D6
Hayesville *N.C., U.S.A.* 35°3N 83°49W **103** C2
Hayesville *Oreg., U.S.A.* 44°59N 122°59W **121** C3
Hayfield *Minn., U.S.A.* 43°53N 92°51W **77** G6
Hayford *Ill., U.S.A.* 41°45N 87°42W **95** C2
Hayford Peak *Nev., U.S.A.* 36°39N 115°12W **128** F5
Haylow *Ga., U.S.A.* 30°50N 82°54W **113** F4
Haymarket *Va., U.S.A.* 38°49N 77°38W **93** B3
Haynes *Ark., U.S.A.* 34°54N 90°47W **106** D5
Haynes *N. Dak., U.S.A.* 45°59N 102°28W **76** E3
Haynesville *La., U.S.A.* 32°58N 93°8W **110** B2
Haynesville *Maine, U.S.A.* 45°50N 67°59W **90** C6
Haynesville *Va., U.S.A.* 37°57N 76°40W **93** C4
Hayneville *Ala., U.S.A.* 32°11N 86°35W **112** D4
Hayneville *Ga., U.S.A.* 32°23N 83°37W **113** D3
Hays *Alta., Canada* 50°6N 111°48W **153** H9
Hays *Kans., U.S.A.* 38°53N 99°20W **82** C4
Hays Canyon Ra. *Nev., U.S.A.* 41°25N 119°53W **128** A1
Hays County ☆ *Tex., U.S.A.* 29°59N 97°53W **109** H10
Haysi *Va., U.S.A.* 37°12N 82°18W **102** D2
Haystack Peak *Utah, U.S.A.* 39°50N 113°55W **129** D2
Haysville *Kans., U.S.A.* 37°34N 97°21W **82** D6
Hayti *Mo., U.S.A.* 36°14N 89°44W **83** E7
Hayti *S. Dak., U.S.A.* 44°40N 97°13W **76** F8
Hayward *Calif., U.S.A.* 37°40N 122°4W **126** F4
Hayward *Minn., U.S.A.* 43°39N 93°15W **77** G5
Hayward *Wis., U.S.A.* 46°1N 91°29W **78** B2
Haywood County ☆ *N.C., U.S.A.* 35°30N 83°0W **103** C3
Haywood County ☆ *Tenn., U.S.A.* 35°36N 89°16W **104** E3
Hazard *Ky., U.S.A.* 37°15N 83°12W **105** C9
Hazard *Nebr., U.S.A.* 41°6N 99°9W **80** C6
Hazardville *Conn., U.S.A.* 41°59N 72°32W **91** C2
Hazel *Ky., U.S.A.* 36°30N 88°20W **104** D4
Hazel *S. Dak., U.S.A.* 44°46N 97°23W **76** F8
Hazel → *N.W.T., Canada* 38°33N 77°51W **102** C7
Hazel Green *Ala., U.S.A.* 34°56N 86°34W **112** B4
Hazel Green *Wis., U.S.A.* 42°32N 90°26W **78** F3
Hazel Park *Mich., U.S.A.* 42°27N 83°6W **98** A2
Hazel Run *Minn., U.S.A.* 44°45N 95°43W **77** F3
Hazelton *B.C., Canada* 55°20N 127°42W **157** E7
Hazelton *Idaho, U.S.A.* 42°36N 114°8W **122** G4
Hazelton *Kans., U.S.A.* 37°5N 98°24W **82** D5
Hazelton *N. Dak., U.S.A.* 46°29N 100°17W **76** D5
Hazelton Peak *Wyo., U.S.A.* 44°6N 107°3W **124** B5
Hazelwood *Mo., U.S.A.* 38°46N 90°22W **94** A1
Hazen *Ark., U.S.A.* 34°47N 91°35W **106** D4
Hazen *N. Dak., U.S.A.* 47°18N 101°38W **76** C4
Hazen *Nev., U.S.A.* 39°34N 119°3W **128** C1
Hazen, L. *Nunavut, Canada* 81°47N 71°1W **158** A11
Hazen Str. *Canada* 77°15N 109°0W **156** A11
Hazenmore *Sask., Canada* 49°42N 107°8W **150** F4
Hazlehurst *Ga., U.S.A.* 31°52N 82°36W **113** E4
Hazlehurst *Miss., U.S.A.* 31°52N 90°24W **111** E3

Hazlet *Sask., Canada* 50°24N 108°36W **150** E3
Hazlet *N.J., U.S.A.* 40°25N 74°12W **92** B2
Hazleton *Ind., U.S.A.* 38°29N 87°33W **85** E3
Hazleton *Iowa, U.S.A.* 42°37N 91°54W **81** C6
Hazleton *Pa., U.S.A.* 40°57N 75°59W **87** D7
Hazlettville *Del., U.S.A.* 39°9N 75°40W **93** A5
He Devil *Idaho, U.S.A.* 45°21N 116°33W **122** D2
Head of St. Margarets Bay *N.S., Canada* 44°41N 63°55W **141** J6
Headland *Ala., U.S.A.* 31°21N 85°21W **112** E5
Headquarters *Idaho, U.S.A.* 46°38N 115°48W **122** C2
Headrick *Okla., U.S.A.* 34°38N 99°9W **107** D4
Healdsburg *Calif., U.S.A.* 38°37N 122°52W **126** E4
Healdton *Okla., U.S.A.* 34°14N 97°29W **107** D6
Healdville *Vt., U.S.A.* 43°25N 72°45W **89** C2
Healy *Alaska, U.S.A.* 63°52N 148°58W **135** E10
Healy *Kans., U.S.A.* 38°36N 100°37W **82** C3
Heard County ☆ *Ga., U.S.A.* 33°15N 85°0W **113** C1
Hearne *Tex., U.S.A.* 30°53N 96°36W **109** G11
Hearst *Ont., Canada* 49°40N 83°41W **149** C13
Heart → *N. Dak., U.S.A.* 46°46N 100°50W **76** D5
Heart L. *Alta., Canada* 55°2N 111°50W **152** C9
Heart L. *Wyo., U.S.A.* 44°16N 110°29W **124** B2
Heart's Content *Nfld. & L., Canada* 47°54N 53°27W **142** E7
Heartwell *Nebr., U.S.A.* 40°34N 98°47W **80** D7
Heath *Ohio, U.S.A.* 40°2N 82°27W **86** D5
Heath Springs *S.C., U.S.A.* 34°36N 80°40W **103** C5
Heath Steele *N.B., Canada* 47°17N 66°5W **141** F3
Heatherton *N.S., Canada* 45°35N 61°47W **141** H8
Heatherton *Nfld. & L., Canada* 48°17N 58°45W **142** D2
Heatherwood = Edson *Alta., Canada* 53°35N 116°28W **152** E4
Heathsville *Va., U.S.A.* 37°55N 76°29W **93** C4
Heavener *Okla., U.S.A.* 34°53N 94°36W **107** D9
Hebbardsville *Ky., U.S.A.* 37°47N 87°23W **104** C5
Hebbronville *Tex., U.S.A.* 27°18N 98°41W **108** K9
Heber *Ariz., U.S.A.* 34°26N 110°36W **130** C5
Heber *Calif., U.S.A.* 32°44N 115°32W **127** L11
Heber City *Utah, U.S.A.* 40°31N 111°25W **129** C4
Heber Springs *Ark., U.S.A.* 35°30N 92°2W **106** C4
Hebert *Sask., Canada* 50°30N 107°10W **150** E4
Hebgen L. *Mont., U.S.A.* 44°52N 111°20W **123** F6
Hebo *Oreg., U.S.A.* 45°14N 123°52W **121** B2
Hebron *N.S., Canada* 43°53N 66°5W **141** K3
Hebron *Nfld. & L., Canada* 58°5N 62°30W **143** B5
Hebron *Conn., U.S.A.* 41°39N 72°22W **91** C2
Hebron *Ill., U.S.A.* 42°28N 88°26W **84** A5
Hebron *Ind., U.S.A.* 41°19N 87°12W **85** B3
Hebron *Md., U.S.A.* 38°25N 75°41W **93** B5
Hebron *N. Dak., U.S.A.* 46°54N 102°3W **76** D3
Hebron *N.H., U.S.A.* 43°42N 71°48W **89** C3
Hebron *Nebr., U.S.A.* 40°10N 97°35W **80** D8
Hebron Fd. *Nfld. & L., Canada* 58°9N 62°45W **143** B5
Hecate I. *B.C., Canada* 51°42N 128°0W **154** D7
Hecate Str. *B.C., Canada* 53°10N 130°30W **154** B4
Hecelchakán *Campeche, Mexico* 20°10N 90°8W **179** B3
Hecla *S. Dak., U.S.A.* 45°53N 98°9W **76** E7
Hecla and Griper B. *Canada* 76°0N 109°35W **156** A11
Hecla-Grindstone Prov. Park △ *Man.,*
Canada 51°15N 96°45W **151** D15
Hecla I. *Man., Canada* 51°10N 96°43W **151** D15
Hector *Ark., U.S.A.* 35°28N 92°59W **106** C3
Hector *Minn., U.S.A.* 44°45N 94°43W **77** F4
Hedgesville *W. Va., U.S.A.* 39°31N 77°58W **93** A3
Hedionda Grande *Coahuila, Mexico* 25°7N 100°5´W **171** A4
Hedley *B.C., Canada* 49°22N 120°4W **155** F14
Hedley *Tex., U.S.A.* 34°52N 100°39W **108** C3
Hedley B. *N.W.T., Canada* 72°31N 108°12W **158** C4
Hedrick *Iowa, U.S.A.* 41°11N 92°19W **81** D6
Hedwig Village *Tex., U.S.A.* 29°46N 95°31W **116** B1
He'eia *Hawai'i, U.S.A.* 21°25N 157°48W **136** K14
Heffley Creek *B.C., Canada* 50°52N 120°16W **155** E14
Heflin *Ala., U.S.A.* 33°39N 85°35W **112** C5
Heiberger *Ala., U.S.A.* 32°46N 87°17W **112** D3
Heidelberg *Minn., U.S.A.* 44°30N 93°38W **77** F5
Heidelberg *Miss., U.S.A.* 31°53N 88°56W **111** E5
Heidelberg *Pa., U.S.A.* 40°23N 80°8W **98** B1
Heidrick *Ky., U.S.A.* 36°52N 83°54W **105** D9
Height of the Rockies Park △ *B.C.,*
Canada 50°30N 115°15W **153** H5
Heilprin Land *Greenland* 82°5N 33°0W **162** A7
Heisler *Alta., Canada* 52°41N 112°13W **153** F8
Heizer *Kans., U.S.A.* 38°25N 98°53W **82** C5
Helemano → *Hawai'i, U.S.A.* 21°35N 158°7W **136** J13
Helen *Ga., U.S.A.* 34°42N 83°44W **113** B3
Helen *Md., U.S.A.* 38°22N 76°42W **93** B4
Helena *Ala., U.S.A.* 33°18N 86°51W **112** C4
Helena *Ark., U.S.A.* 34°32N 90°36W **106** D5
Helena *Calif., U.S.A.* 40°47N 123°8W **126** C3
Helena *Ga., U.S.A.* 32°5N 82°55W **113** D3
Helena *Mont., U.S.A.* 46°36N 112°2W **123** D5
Helena I. *Nunavut, Canada* 76°39N 101°4W **158** B5
Helena Nat. Forest *Mont., U.S.A.* 46°30N 111°30W **123** D6
Hélène de Champlain, Pa △ *Qué.,*
Canada 45°31N 73°32W **160** A3
Helene L. *Sask., Canada* 53°33N 108°12W **150** B3
Heliotrope Mt. *Utah, U.S.A.* 39°7N 111°27W **129** D4
Helix *Oreg., U.S.A.* 45°51N 118°39W **121** B7
Hell Cr. → *Colo., U.S.A.* 39°30N 102°30W **125** C8
Hellertown *Pa., U.S.A.* 40°35N 75°21W **92** B1
Hells Canyon *Oreg., U.S.A.* 45°10N 116°50W **121** B9
Hells Canyon Nat. Recr. Area △ *Oreg.,*
U.S.A. 45°30N 117°45W **121** B8
Helmville *Mont., U.S.A.* 46°52N 112°58W **123** D5
Helotes *Tex., U.S.A.* 29°34N 98°41W **116** B1
Helper *Utah, U.S.A.* 39°41N 110°51W **129** D5
Helton *Ky., U.S.A.* 36°58N 83°24W **105** D9
Hematite *Mo., U.S.A.* 38°12N 90°29W **83** C6
Hemet *Calif., U.S.A.* 33°45N 116°58W **127** K10
Hemford *N.S., Canada* 44°30N 64°47W **141** J5
Hemingford *Nebr., U.S.A.* 42°19N 103°4W **80** B2
Hemingway *S.C., U.S.A.* 33°45N 79°27W **103** E6
Hemmingford *Qué., Canada* 45°3N 73°35W **145** F9
Hemphill *Tex., U.S.A.* 31°20N 93°51W **109** F14
Hemphill County ☆ *Tex., U.S.A.* 35°55N 100°15W **108** B7
Hempstead *N.Y., U.S.A.* 40°42N 73°37W **97** B5
Hempstead *Tex., U.S.A.* 30°6N 96°5W **109** G11
Hempstead County ☆ *Ark., U.S.A.* 33°40N 93°36W **106** E2
Hempstead Harbor *N.Y., U.S.A.* 40°49N 73°39W **97** B5
Henagar *Ala., U.S.A.* 34°38N 85°46W **112** B5
Henderson *Ga., U.S.A.* 32°21N 83°47W **113** D3
Henderson *Iowa, U.S.A.* 41°8N 95°26W **81** D3
Henderson *Ky., U.S.A.* 37°50N 87°35W **104** C5
Henderson *Md., U.S.A.* 39°6N 75°47W **93** A5
Henderson *N.C., U.S.A.* 36°20N 78°25W **103** B7
Henderson *Nebr., U.S.A.* 40°47N 97°49W **80** D8

Henderson *Nev., U.S.A.* 36°2N 114°58W **134** D2
Henderson *Tenn., U.S.A.* 35°26N 88°38W **104** E4
Henderson *Tex., U.S.A.* 32°9N 94°48W **109** E13
Henderson, Mt. *B.C., Canada* 54°16N 128°4W **154** A6
Henderson County ☆ *Ill., U.S.A.* 40°50N 90°55W **84** C3
Henderson County ☆ *Ky., U.S.A.* 37°45N 87°35W **104** C5
Henderson County ☆ *N.C., U.S.A.* 35°15N 82°30W **103** C3
Henderson County ☆ *Tenn., U.S.A.* 35°39N 88°24W **104** E4
Henderson County ☆ *Tex., U.S.A.* 32°12N 95°51W **109** E12
Henderson Executive ✈ *Nev., U.S.A.* 35°59N 115°8W **134** D2
Hendersonville *N.C., U.S.A.* 35°19N 82°28W **103** C3
Hendersonville *Tenn., U.S.A.* 36°18N 86°37W **104** D6
Hendley *Nebr., U.S.A.* 40°8N 99°58W **80** D6
Hendricks *Minn., U.S.A.* 44°30N 96°25W **77** F2
Hendricks County ☆ *Ind., U.S.A.* 39°45N 86°30W **85** D4
Hendrix Lake *B.C., Canada* 52°5N 120°48W **155** C14
Hendrum *Minn., U.S.A.* 47°16N 96°49W **77** C2
Hendry County ☆ *Fla., U.S.A.* 26°30N 81°20W **114** E7
Henefer *Utah, U.S.A.* 41°1N 111°30W **129** B4
Henlopen, C. *Del., U.S.A.* 38°48N 75°6W **93** B5
Hennepin *Ill., U.S.A.* 41°15N 89°21W **84** B4
Hennepin *Okla., U.S.A.* 34°31N 97°21W **107** D6
Hennepin Canal *Ill., U.S.A.* 41°29N 90°12W **84** B3
Hennepin County ☆ *Minn., U.S.A.* 45°0N 93°30W **77** E5
Hennessey *Okla., U.S.A.* 36°6N 97°54W **107** B6
Henniker *N.H., U.S.A.* 43°11N 71°50W **89** C3
Henning *Ill., U.S.A.* 40°18N 87°42W **84** C6
Henning *Minn., U.S.A.* 46°19N 95°27W **77** D3
Henning *Tenn., U.S.A.* 35°41N 89°34W **104** E3
Henrico County ☆ *Va., U.S.A.* 37°33N 77°20W **102** D7
Henrietta *N.C., U.S.A.* 35°15N 81°48W **103** C4
Henrietta *N.Y., U.S.A.* 43°4N 77°37W **88** B3
Henrietta *Tex., U.S.A.* 33°49N 98°12W **109** D9
Henrietta Maria, C. *Ont., Canada* 55°9N 82°20W **159** F9
Henriette *Minn., U.S.A.* 45°53N 93°7W **77** E5
Henrieville *Utah, U.S.A.* 37°30N 112°0W **129** F4
Henry *Ill., U.S.A.* 41°7N 89°22W **84** B4
Henry *Nebr., U.S.A.* 41°58N 104°4W **80** C1
Henry *S. Dak., U.S.A.* 44°53N 97°28W **76** F8
Henry *Tenn., U.S.A.* 36°12N 88°25W **104** D4
Henry, C. *Va., U.S.A.* 36°56N 76°1W **102** E8
Henry County ☆ *Ala., U.S.A.* 31°34N 85°15W **112** E5
Henry County ☆ *Ga., U.S.A.* 33°25N 84°5W **113** C2
Henry County ☆ *Ill., U.S.A.* 41°20N 90°0W **84** B3
Henry County ☆ *Ind., U.S.A.* 39°55N 85°25W **85** D5
Henry County ☆ *Iowa, U.S.A.* 41°0N 91°30W **81** D7
Henry County ☆ *Ky., U.S.A.* 38°25N 85°10W **105** B7
Henry County ☆ *Mo., U.S.A.* 38°25N 93°45W **83** C3
Henry County ☆ *Ohio, U.S.A.* 41°19N 84°2W **86** B2
Henry County ☆ *Tenn., U.S.A.* 36°18N 88°19W **104** D4
Henry County ☆ *Va., U.S.A.* 36°50N 79°56W **102** E5
Henry Kater, C. *N.W.T., Canada* 69°8N 66°30W **158** D12
Henry Kater Pen. *Nunavut, Canada* 69°23N 68°4W **158** D12
Henry Mts. *Utah, U.S.A.* 38°0N 110°50W **129** E5
Henrys Fork → *Idaho, U.S.A.* 43°57N 111°45W **122** F7
Henrys Lake *Idaho, U.S.A.* 44°36N 111°21W **122** F7
Henryville *Qué., Canada* 45°8N 73°11W **145** F9
Henshaw *Ky., U.S.A.* 37°37N 88°3W **104** C4
Henshaw, L. *Calif., U.S.A.* 33°15N 116°45W **127** K10
Hensler *N. Dak., U.S.A.* 47°16N 101°5W **76** C4
Henson Cr. → *Md., U.S.A.* 38°47N 76°58W **99** C4
Hepburn *Iowa, U.S.A.* 40°51N 95°1W **81** E3
Hephzibah *Ga., U.S.A.* 33°19N 82°6W **113** C4
Hepler *Kans., U.S.A.* 37°40N 94°58W **82** D9
Heppner *Oreg., U.S.A.* 45°21N 119°33W **121** B6
Hepworth *Ont., Canada* 44°37N 81°9W **146** C5
Herbert Hoover Nat. Historic Site △ *Iowa,*
U.S.A. 41°40N 91°21W **81** D7
Herbert I. *Alaska, U.S.A.* 52°45N 170°7W **135** K5
Herbert Inlet *B.C., Canada* 49°20N 125°58W **154** F9
Herbes, Point aux *La., U.S.A.* 29°56N 90°10W **117** B3
Herculaneum *Mo., U.S.A.* 38°16N 90°23W **83** C6
Hércules *Coahuila, Mexico* 28°6N 103°46W **169** E12
Hereford *Colo., U.S.A.* 40°57N 104°18W **125** B6
Hereford *Md., U.S.A.* 39°35N 76°40W **93** A4
Hereford *Tex., U.S.A.* 34°49N 102°24W **108** C5
Hereford, Mt. *Qué., Canada* 45°5N 71°36W **145** F11
Herington *Kans., U.S.A.* 38°40N 96°57W **82** C7
Heriot Bay *B.C., Canada* 50°7N 125°13W **154** E9
Herkimer *Kans., U.S.A.* 39°54N 96°43W **82** B7
Herkimer *N.Y., U.S.A.* 43°2N 74°59W **88** B6
Herkimer County ☆ *N.Y., U.S.A.* 43°0N 75°0W **88** B6
Herman *Minn., U.S.A.* 45°49N 96°9W **77** E2
Herman *Nebr., U.S.A.* 41°40N 96°13W **80** C9
Hermann *Mo., U.S.A.* 38°42N 91°27W **83** C5
Hermansville *Mich., U.S.A.* 45°42N 87°36W **79** D4
Hermantown *Minn., U.S.A.* 46°50N 92°15W **77** D6
Hermanville *Miss., U.S.A.* 31°58N 90°50W **111** E3
Hermiston *Oreg., U.S.A.* 45°51N 119°17W **121** B6
Hermitage *Nfld. & L., Canada* 47°33N 55°56W **142** E5
Hermitage *Ark., U.S.A.* 33°27N 92°10W **106** E3
Hermitage *Mo., U.S.A.* 37°56N 93°19W **83** D3
Hermitage *Pa., U.S.A.* 41°14N 80°27W **87** C2
Hermleigh *Tex., U.S.A.* 32°38N 100°46W **108** E7
Hermon *N.Y., U.S.A.* 44°28N 75°14W **88** A5
Hermosa *S. Dak., U.S.A.* 43°50N 103°12W **76** G2
Hermosillo *Sonora, Mexico* 29°10N 111°0W **168** D5
Hernando *Miss., U.S.A.* 34°50N 90°0W **111** B3
Hernando County ☆ *Fla., U.S.A.* 28°35N 82°30W **114** C6
Herndon *Kans., U.S.A.* 39°55N 100°47W **82** B3
Herndon *Ky., U.S.A.* 36°44N 87°34W **104** D5
Herndon *Pa., U.S.A.* 40°43N 76°51W **87** D6
Herndon *Va., U.S.A.* 38°58N 77°23W **102** C7
Herod *Ga., U.S.A.* 31°42N 84°26W **113** E2
Héroes de Churubusco *Distrito Federal,*
Mexico 19°21N 99°6W **181** B3
Heroica Caborca = Caborca *Sonora,*
Mexico 30°37N 112°6W **168** C3
Heroica Nogales = Nogales *Sonora,*
Mexico 31°19N 110°56W **168** B5
Heron *Mont., U.S.A.* 48°3N 115°57W **123** B2
Heron Bay *Ont., Canada* 48°40N 86°25W **149** D10
Heron L. *N. Mex., U.S.A.* 36°41N 106°43W **131** A4
Heron Lake *Minn., U.S.A.* 43°48N 95°19W **77** G3
Heron Park *Ont., Canada* 45°23N 75°41W **160** B1
Herons, Î. aux *Qué., Canada* 45°25N 73°34W **160** B3
Herreid *S. Dak., U.S.A.* 45°50N 100°4W **76** E5
Herrero, Pta. *Quintana Roo, Mexico* 19°17N 87°27W **179** C6
Herrick *S. Dak., U.S.A.* 43°7N 99°11W **76** G6
Herricks *N.Y., U.S.A.* 40°45N 73°40W **97** B5
Herrin *Ill., U.S.A.* 37°48N 89°2W **84** F41
Herring Cove *N.S., Canada* 44°34N 63°34W **141** J6

Herring Run Park *Baltimore, U.S.A.* 39°19N 76°33W **99** B2
Herrington L. *Ky., U.S.A.* 37°45N 84°44W **105** C8
Herschel *Sask., Canada* 51°38N 108°21W **150** D3
Herschel I. *Yukon, Canada* 69°35N 139°5W **156** C5
Herscher *Ill., U.S.A.* 41°3N 88°6W **84** B5
Hershey *Mich., U.S.A.* 43°51N 85°27W **79** F6
Hershey *Nebr., U.S.A.* 41°10N 101°0W **80** C5
Hershey *Pa., U.S.A.* 40°17N 76°39W **87** D6
Hershey Park *Pa., U.S.A.* 40°17N 76°39W **87** D6
Hertford *N.C., U.S.A.* 36°11N 76°28W **103** B9
Hertford County ☆ *N.C., U.S.A.* 36°20N 77°0W **103** B8
Hesperia *Calif., U.S.A.* 34°25N 117°18W **127** J8
Hesperia *Mich., U.S.A.* 43°34N 86°3W **79** F5
Hesperus *Colo., U.S.A.* 37°17N 108°2W **125** E2
Hesquiat Peninsula Park △ *B.C.,*
Canada 49°26N 126°31W **154** F8
Hess → *Yukon, Canada* 63°33N 133°59W **157** D6
Hessel *Mich., U.S.A.* 46°0N 84°26W **79** C7
Hessmer *La., U.S.A.* 31°3N 92°8W **110** C3
Hesston *Kans., U.S.A.* 38°8N 97°26W **82** C6
Hetch Hetchy Aqueduct *Calif., U.S.A.* 37°29N 122°19W **126** F4
Hetch Hetchy Res. *Calif., U.S.A.* 37°57N 119°47W **126** E6
Hettinger *N. Dak., U.S.A.* 46°0N 102°42W **76** D3
Hettinger County ☆ *N. Dak., U.S.A.* 46°25N 102°30W **76** D3
Heuvelton *N.Y., U.S.A.* 44°37N 75°25W **88** A5
Hewett, C. *Nunavut, Canada* 70°16N 67°45W **158** C12
Hewins *Kans., U.S.A.* 37°3N 96°25W **82** D7
Hewitt *Minn., U.S.A.* 46°20N 95°5W **77** D3
Hewitt *Tex., U.S.A.* 31°28N 97°12W **109** F10
Hewlett Neck *N.Y., U.S.A.* 40°37N 73°41W **97** C4
Hext *Tex., U.S.A.* 30°52N 99°32W **109** G8
Heyburn *Idaho, U.S.A.* 42°34N 113°46W **122** G5
Heyburn L. *Okla., U.S.A.* 35°57N 96°18W **107** C7
Heyworth *Ill., U.S.A.* 40°19N 88°59W **84** C5
Hialeah *Fla., U.S.A.* 25°51N 80°16W **115** C1
Hiattville *Kans., U.S.A.* 37°43N 94°52W **82** D9
Hiawassa, L. *Fla., U.S.A.* 28°33N 81°28W **115** A3
Hiawassee *Ga., U.S.A.* 34°58N 83°46W **113** B3
Hiawatha *Iowa, U.S.A.* 42°2N 91°41W **81** C7
Hiawatha *Kans., U.S.A.* 39°51N 95°32W **82** B8
Hiawatha *Utah, U.S.A.* 39°29N 111°1W **129** D4
Hiawatha Nat. Forest *Mich., U.S.A.* 46°15N 86°40W **79** C5
Hibben I. *B.C., Canada* 53°0N 132°18W **154** C2
Hibbing *Minn., U.S.A.* 47°25N 92°56W **77** C6
Hickam Air Force Base *Hawai'i,*
U.S.A. 21°20N 157°56W **136** K14
Hickam Housing *Hawai'i, U.S.A.* 21°21N 157°57W **136** K14
Hickman *Del., U.S.A.* 38°50N 75°42W **93** B5
Hickman *Ky., U.S.A.* 36°34N 89°11W **104** D3
Hickman *Nebr., U.S.A.* 40°37N 96°38W **80** D9
Hickman County ☆ *Ky., U.S.A.* 36°40N 89°0W **104** D4
Hickman County ☆ *Tenn., U.S.A.* 35°47N 87°28W **104** E5
Hickman's Harbour *Nfld. & L., Canada* 48°6N 53°44W **142** D7
Hickok *Kans., U.S.A.* 37°34N 101°14W **82** D2
Hickory *Ky., U.S.A.* 36°48N 88°40W **104** D4
Hickory *Miss., U.S.A.* 32°19N 89°2W **111** D4
Hickory *N.C., U.S.A.* 35°44N 81°21W **103** C4
Hickory *Okla., U.S.A.* 34°33N 96°52W **107** D7
Hickory, L. *N.C., U.S.A.* 35°49N 81°12W **103** C4
Hickory County ☆ *Mo., U.S.A.* 37°55N 93°15W **83** D3
Hickory Flat *Miss., U.S.A.* 34°37N 89°11W **111** B4
Hickory Hills *Ill., U.S.A.* 41°43N 87°49W **95** C2
Hickory Plains *Ark., U.S.A.* 34°59N 91°44W **106** C4
Hickory Ridge *Ark., U.S.A.* 35°24N 90°58W **106** C5
Hickory Run State Park △ *Pa., U.S.A.* 41°2N 75°41W **87** C7
Hickory Valley *Tenn., U.S.A.* 35°9N 89°8W **104** E3
Hickory Withe *Tenn., U.S.A.* 35°14N 89°35W **104** E3
Hicksville *N.Y., U.S.A.* 40°46N 73°32W **92** B3
Hicksville *Ohio, U.S.A.* 41°18N 84°46W **86** B2
Hico *Tex., U.S.A.* 31°59N 98°2W **109** F9
Hidalgo *Chihuahua, Mexico* 30°33N 107°54W **169** C8
Hidalgo *Coahuila, Mexico* 25°29N 103°9W **171** B4
Hidalgo *Durango, Mexico* 24°9N 104°35W **173** C6
Hidalgo *Nuevo León, Mexico* 25°59N 100°27W **170** E4
Hidalgo *Zacatecas, Mexico* 23°59N 102°43W **173** D8
Hidalgo *Zacatecas, Mexico* 23°59N 103°40W **173** D7
Hidalgo *Ill., U.S.A.* 39°9N 88°9W **84** E5
Hidalgo □ *Mexico* 20°30N 99°0W **175** B3
Hidalgo County ☆ *N. Mex., U.S.A.* 32°0N 108°45W **131** F2
Hidalgo County ☆ *Tex., U.S.A.* 26°25N 98°10W **108** L9
Hidalgo del Parral *Chihuahua, Mexico* 26°56N 105°40W **169** G10
Hidalgotitlán *Veracruz, Mexico* 17°47N 94°38W **177** G6
Hidden Falls-Crosby Farm Regional Park △
Minn., U.S.A. 44°54N 93°9W **94** B3
Higbee *Mo., U.S.A.* 39°19N 92°31W **83** B4
Higgins *Tex., U.S.A.* 36°7N 100°2W **108** B6
Higgins L. *Mich., U.S.A.* 44°29N 84°43W **79** E7
Higginsport *Ohio, U.S.A.* 38°47N 83°58W **86** E3
Higginsville *Mo., U.S.A.* 39°4N 93°43W **83** B3
High Bridge *N.J., U.S.A.* 40°40N 74°54W **92** B2
High Desert *Oreg., U.S.A.* 43°40N 120°20W **121** D5
High Hill *Mo., U.S.A.* 38°53N 91°23W **83** C5
High I. *Mich., U.S.A.* 45°42N 85°41W **79** D6
High Island *Tex., U.S.A.* 29°34N 94°24W **109** H13
High Level *Alta., Canada* 58°31N 117°8W **157** E9
High Park *Ont., Canada* 43°38N 79°27W **161** B2
High Point *N.C., U.S.A.* 35°57N 80°0W **103** C5
High Point *Tampa, U.S.A.* 27°54N 82°42W **115** B2
High Prairie *Alta., Canada* 55°30N 116°30W **152** C4
High Pt. *N.J., U.S.A.* 41°19N 74°40W **92** A2
High River *Alta., Canada* 50°30N 113°50W **153** H7
High Rock L. *N.C., U.S.A.* 35°36N 80°14W **103** C5
High Rock L. *Nev., U.S.A.* 41°17N 119°17W **128** A1
High Rolls *N. Mex., U.S.A.* 32°57N 105°50W **131** E5
High Springs *Fla., U.S.A.* 29°50N 82°36W **114** B6
Highgate Center *Vt., U.S.A.* 44°56N 73°3W **89** B1
Highland *Ill., U.S.A.* 34°38N 117°23W **127** J9
Highland *Ill., U.S.A.* 38°44N 89°41W **84** E4
Highland *Ind., U.S.A.* 41°33N 87°28W **85** B3
Highland *Kans., U.S.A.* 39°52N 95°16W **82** B8
Highland *N.Y., U.S.A.* 41°43N 73°58W **88** D7
Highland *Wis., U.S.A.* 43°5N 90°22W **78** E3
Highland Beach *Md., U.S.A.* 38°56N 76°28W **93** B4
Highland City *Fla., U.S.A.* 27°58N 81°53W **114** D7
Highland County ☆ *Ohio, U.S.A.* 39°12N 83°37W **86** D3
Highland County ☆ *Va., U.S.A.* 38°25N 79°35W **102** C5
Highland Cr. → *Ont., Canada* 43°45N 79°13W **161** A3
Highland Creek *Ont., Canada* 43°46N 79°8W **161** A3
Highland Falls *N.Y., U.S.A.* 41°22N 73°58W **92** A3
Highland Heights *Ky., U.S.A.* 29°15N 95°25W **116** A2
Highland Hills *Ont., Canada* 41°51N 88°1W **84** B5
Highland Home *Ala., U.S.A.* 31°57N 86°19W **112** E4
Highland Lakes *N.J., U.S.A.* 41°11N 74°28W **92** A2
Highland Mills *Ga., U.S.A.* 33°17N 84°17W **113** C2

Highland Park Ont., Canada 45°22N 75°45W 160 B1
Highland Park Calif., U.S.A. 34°7N 118°13W 133 B3
Highland Park Ill., U.S.A. 42°11N 87°48W 84 A6
Highland Park Mich., U.S.A. 42°24N 83°5W 98 A2
Highland Park Pa., U.S.A. 40°28N 79°55W 98 B2
Highland Park Tex., U.S.A. 32°50N 96°47W 116 B5
Highland Springs Va., U.S.A. 37°33N 77°20W 102 D7
Highland View Fla., U.S.A. 29°50N 85°19W 114 B3
Highlands = Fort Thomas Ky., U.S.A. 39°4N 84°26W 105 A8
Highlands N.C., U.S.A. 35°3N 83°12W 103 C2
Highlands N.J., U.S.A. 40°24N 73°59W 92 B3
Highlands County ☆ Fla., U.S.A. 27°20N 81°20W 114 D7
Highlands Ranch Colo., U.S.A. 39°33N 104°58W 134 C2
Highlandtown Baltimore, U.S.A. 39°17N 76°34W 99 B2
Highmore S. Dak., U.S.A. 44°31N 99°27W 76 F6
Highridge Alta., Canada 54°3N 114°8W 152 D6
Hightstown N.J., U.S.A. 40°16N 74°31W 92 B2
Highway City Calif., U.S.A. 36°49N 119°43W 127 G7
Highwood Mont., U.S.A. 47°30N 110°30W 105 E9
Higuera de Zaragoza Sinaloa, Mexico 25°59N 109°18W 172 B1
Higueras Nuevo León, Mexico 25°27N 100°0W 170 E5
Higuero, Pta. Puerto Rico 18°22N 67°16W 184 G15
Higüey Dom. Rep. 18°37N 68°42W 183 C6
Hiko Nev., U.S.A. 37°32N 115°14W 128 E5
Hiland Wyo., U.S.A. 43°7N 107°21W 124 C5
Hilda Alta., Canada 50°28N 110°3W 153 H10
Hildale Utah, U.S.A. 37°0N 112°58W 129 F3
Hilden N.S., Canada 45°18N 63°18W 141 H6
Hildreth Nebr., U.S.A. 40°20N 99°3W 80 D6
Hilgard Oreg., U.S.A. 45°21N 118°14W 121 B7
Hill City Idaho, U.S.A. 43°18N 115°3W 122 F3
Hill City Kans., U.S.A. 39°22N 99°51W 82 B4
Hill City Minn., U.S.A. 46°59N 93°36W 77 D5
Hill City S. Dak., U.S.A. 43°56N 103°35W 76 G2
Hill Country Village Tex., U.S.A. 29°34N 98°29W 116 B2
Hill County ☆ Mont., U.S.A. 48°40N 110°0W 123 B7
Hill County ☆ Tex., U.S.A. 32°1N 97°8W 109 E10
Hill Cr. → Utah, U.S.A. 39°55N 109°40W 129 D6
Hill Island L. → N.W.T., Canada 60°30N 109°50W 157 D11
Hill Spring Alta., Canada 49°17N 113°38W 153 J7
Hill-Stead Museum Conn., U.S.A. 41°43N 72°49W 91 C2
Hillcrest Heights Md., U.S.A. 38°49N 76°57W 99 C4
Hilliard Fla., U.S.A. 30°41N 81°55W 114 A7
Hilliard Ohio, U.S.A. 40°2N 83°10W 86 C3
Hilliards Pa., U.S.A. 41°5N 79°50W 87 C3
Hillister Tex., U.S.A. 30°40N 94°23W 109 G13
Hillman Mich., U.S.A. 45°4N 83°54W 79 D8
Hillman Minn., U.S.A. 46°0N 93°53W 77 E5
Hillmond Sask., Canada 53°26N 109°41W 150 B2
Hillrose Colo., U.S.A. 40°20N 103°31W 125 B7
Hills Iowa, U.S.A. 41°33N 91°32W 81 D7
Hills Minn., U.S.A. 43°32N 96°21W 77 G2
Hills Creek L. Oreg., U.S.A. 43°43N 122°26W 121 D3
Hillsboro = Deerfield Beach Fla., U.S.A. 26°19N 80°6W 114 E8
Hillsboro Ill., U.S.A. 33°11N 83°38W 113 C3
Hillsboro Ill., U.S.A. 39°9N 89°29W 84 D4
Hillsboro Kans., U.S.A. 38°21N 97°12W 82 C6
Hillsboro Md., U.S.A. 38°55N 75°50W 93 B5
Hillsboro Mo., U.S.A. 38°14N 90°34W 83 C6
Hillsboro N. Dak., U.S.A. 47°26N 97°3W 76 C8
Hillsboro N. Mex., U.S.A. 32°55N 107°34W 131 E3
Hillsboro Ohio, U.S.A. 39°12N 83°37W 86 D3
Hillsboro Oreg., U.S.A. 45°31N 122°59W 121 B3
Hillsboro Tex., U.S.A. 32°1N 97°8W 109 E10
Hillsboro Va., U.S.A. 39°12N 77°43W 93 A3
Hillsboro W. Va., U.S.A. 38°8N 80°13W 102 C4
Hillsboro Wis., U.S.A. 43°39N 90°21W 78 E3
Hillsboro Canal Fla., U.S.A. 26°30N 80°15W 114 E8
Hillsborough N.B., Canada 45°55N 64°39W 141 H5
Hillsborough Grenada 12°28N 61°28W 183 D7
Hillsborough N.C., U.S.A. 36°5N 79°7W 103 B6
Hillsborough N.H., U.S.A. 43°7N 71°54W 89 C3
Hillsborough B. P.E.I., Canada 46°8N 63°5W 141 G6
Hillsborough Bay Tampa, U.S.A. 27°50N 82°26W 115 B4
Hillsborough County ☆ Fla., U.S.A. 27°50N 82°20W 114 D6
Hillsborough County ☆ N.H., U.S.A. 42°50N 71°45W 89 D3
Hillsborough Land = Belle Glade Fla., U.S.A. 26°41N 80°40W 114 E8
Hillsborough Upper Village N.H., U.S.A. 43°9N 71°58W 89 C3
Hillsdale Ill., U.S.A. 41°37N 90°11W 84 B3
Hillsdale Kans., U.S.A. 38°40N 94°51W 82 C9
Hillsdale Mich., U.S.A. 41°56N 84°38W 79 H7
Hillsdale Mo., U.S.A. 38°41N 90°17W 94 A2
Hillsdale N.Y., U.S.A. 42°11N 73°32W 91 B1
Hillsdale Okla., U.S.A. 36°34N 97°59W 107 B6
Hillsdale County ☆ Mich., U.S.A. 41°50N 84°40W 79 H7
Hillside Ariz., U.S.A. 34°25N 112°55W 130 C3
Hillside N.J., U.S.A. 40°42N 74°13W 97 B1
Hillside N.Y., U.S.A. 40°42N 73°40W 97 B4
Hillside Manor N.Y., U.S.A. 40°45N 73°40W 97 B4
Hillsmere Shores Md., U.S.A. 38°56N 76°32W 93 B4
Hillsport Ont., Canada 49°27N 85°34W 149 C11
Hillsville Va., U.S.A. 36°46N 80°44W 102 E4
Hilltonia Ga., U.S.A. 32°53N 81°40W 113 D5
Hilltop Minn., U.S.A. 45°3N 93°14W 94 A2
Hillview Ky., U.S.A. 38°5N 85°49W 105 B7
Hillwood Va., U.S.A. 38°52N 77°9W 99 B3
Hilo Hawai'i, U.S.A. 19°44N 155°5W 136 D6
Hilo ✈ (ITO Hawai'i, U.S.A. 19°43N 155°2W 136 D6
Hilo B. Hawai'i, U.S.A. 19°45N 155°5W 136 D6
Hilshire Village Tex., U.S.A. 29°47N 95°29W 116 B2
Hilt Calif., U.S.A. 41°50N 122°37W 126 B4
Hilton N.Y., U.S.A. 43°17N 77°48W 88 B3
Hilton Beach Ont., Canada 46°15N 83°53W 146 A3
Hilton Head Island S.C., U.S.A. 32°13N 80°45W 103 F5
Hinche Haiti 19°9N 72°1W 183 C5
Hinckley Ill., U.S.A. 41°46N 88°38W 84 B5
Hinckley Minn., U.S.A. 46°1N 92°56W 77 D61
Hinckley Utah, U.S.A. 39°20N 112°40W 129 D3
Hinckley Res. N.Y., U.S.A. 43°19N 75°7W 88 B5
Hindman Ky., U.S.A. 37°20N 82°59W 105 C10
Hinds County ☆ Miss., U.S.A. 32°16N 90°25W 111 D3
Hinds L. Nfld. & L., Canada 48°58N 57°0W 142 D4
Hindsboro Ill., U.S.A. 39°41N 88°8W 84 D5
Hines Fla., U.S.A. 29°45N 83°14W 114 B5
Hines Creek Alta., Canada 56°20N 118°40W 152 B2
Hinesburg Vt., U.S.A. 44°18N 73°6W 89 B1
Hineston La., U.S.A. 31°9N 92°46W 110 C3
Hinesville Ga., U.S.A. 31°51N 81°36W 113 E5
Hingham Mass., U.S.A. 42°14N 70°54W 91 B4
Hingham Mont., U.S.A. 48°33N 110°25W 123 B7
Hinsdale Mass., U.S.A. 42°26N 73°8W 91 B1
Hinsdale Mont., U.S.A. 48°24N 107°5W 123 B10
Hinsdale N.H., U.S.A. 42°47N 72°29W 89 D2
Hinsdale County ☆ Colo., U.S.A. 37°50N 107°20W 125 E3

Hinson Fla., U.S.A. 30°39N 84°25W 114 A4
Hinton Alta., Canada 53°26N 117°34W 152 E3
Hinton Iowa, U.S.A. 42°38N 96°18W 81 C2
Hinton Okla., U.S.A. 35°28N 98°21W 107 C5
Hinton W. Va., U.S.A. 37°40N 80°54W 102 D4
Hiram Ohio, U.S.A. 41°19N 81°9W 86 B5
Hispaniola W. Indies 19°0N 71°0W 183 C5
History Center Georgia, U.S.A. 33°45N 84°22W 117 B2
Hitchcock Sask., Canada 49°14N 103°7W 150 F8
Hitchcock Okla., U.S.A. 35°58N 98°21W 107 C5
Hitchcock S. Dak., U.S.A. 44°38N 98°25W 76 F7
Hitchcock Tex., U.S.A. 29°21N 95°1W 109 H12
Hitchcock County ☆ Nebr., U.S.A. 40°15N 101°0W 80 D4
Hitchins Ky., U.S.A. 38°17N 82°55W 105 B10
Hitchita Okla., U.S.A. 35°31N 95°44W 107 C8
Hiwassee Va., U.S.A. 36°58N 80°43W 102 E4
Hiwassee → Tenn., U.S.A. 35°19N 84°47W 105 E8
Hiwassee L. N.C., U.S.A. 35°9N 84°11W 103 C1
Hixon B.C., Canada 53°25N 122°35W 155 B12
Hixton Wis., U.S.A. 44°23N 91°1W 78 D2
Hoback → Wyo., U.S.A. 43°19N 110°34W 124 C2
Hoback Junction Wyo., U.S.A. 43°5N 110°34W 124 C2
Hoback Pk. Wyo., U.S.A. 41°32N 87°15W 85 B3
Hobart Ind., U.S.A. 41°32N 87°15W 85 B3
Hobart N.Y., U.S.A. 42°22N 74°40W 88 C6
Hobart Okla., U.S.A. 35°1N 99°6W 107 C4
Hobbs N. Mex., U.S.A. 32°42N 103°8W 131 E7
Hobe Sound Fla., U.S.A. 27°4N 80°8W 114 D8
Hoberg Mo., U.S.A. 37°4N 93°51W 83 D3
Hoboken Ga., U.S.A. 31°11N 82°8W 113 E4
Hoboken New York 96 d1
Hobson Ky., U.S.A. 37°25N 85°22W 105 C7
Hobson Mont., U.S.A. 47°0N 109°52W 123 C8
Hobson L. B.C., Canada 52°35N 120°15W 155 C14
Hocabá Yucatán, Mexico 20°49N 89°15W 179 A4
Hochelaga Qué., Canada 45°32N 73°33W 160 A3
Hochheim Tex., U.S.A. 29°19N 97°17W 109 H10
Hockessin Del., U.S.A. 39°47N 75°42W 93 A4
Hocking → Ohio, U.S.A. 39°12N 81°45W 86 D5
Hocking County ☆ Ohio, U.S.A. 39°32N 82°25W 86 D4
Hockley = Levelland Tex., U.S.A. 33°35N 102°23W 108 D5
Hockley County ☆ Tex., U.S.A. 33°35N 102°23W 108 D5
Hoctún Yucatán, Mexico 20°52N 89°12W 179 B4
Hodge La., U.S.A. 32°17N 92°43W 110 B3
Hodgeman County ☆ Kans., U.S.A. 38°0N 100°0W 82 C4
Hodgenville Ky., U.S.A. 37°34N 85°44W 105 C7
Hodges S.C., U.S.A. 34°17N 82°15W 103 D3
Hodges Hill Nfld. & L., Canada 49°4N 55°53W 142 C5
Hodgeville Sask., Canada 50°7N 106°58W 150 E5
Hodgkins Ill., U.S.A. 41°46N 87°53W 95 C1
Hodgson Man., Canada 51°13N 97°36W 151 D14
Hoehne Colo., U.S.A. 37°17N 104°23W 125 E6
Hoffman Ill., U.S.A. 38°32N 89°16W 84 D4
Hoffman Minn., U.S.A. 45°50N 95°48W 77 E3
Hoffman Okla., U.S.A. 35°29N 95°51W 107 C8
Hoffman I. N.Y., U.S.A. 40°34N 74°3W 97 C2
Hog I. Mich., U.S.A. 45°48N 85°22W 79 D6
Hog I. Va., U.S.A. 37°26N 75°42W 102 D9
Hogansville Ga., U.S.A. 33°10N 84°55W 113 C2
Hogback Mt. Mont., U.S.A. 44°54N 112°7W 123 F5
Hogback Mt. Nebr., U.S.A. 41°44N 103°42W 80 C2
Hogeland Mont., U.S.A. 48°51N 108°40W 123 B9
Hogsty Reef Bahamas 21°41N 73°48W 183 B5
Hogup Mts. Utah, U.S.A. 41°30N 113°7W 129 B2
Hoh → Wash., U.S.A. 47°45N 124°29W 120 C1
Hoh Indian Reservation Wash., U.S.A. 47°44N 124°25W 120 C1
Hohenwald Tenn., U.S.A. 35°33N 87°33W 104 E5
Hohokam Pima Nat. Monument △ Ariz., U.S.A. 33°11N 111°56W 130 D4
Hoisington Kans., U.S.A. 38°31N 98°47W 82 C5
Hokah Minn., U.S.A. 43°46N 91°21W 77 G7
Hoke County ☆ N.C., U.S.A. 35°0N 79°15W 103 C6
Holberg B.C., Canada 50°40N 128°0W 154 E6
Holbox, I. Quintana Roo, Mexico 21°33N 87°15W 179 A6
Holbrook Ariz., U.S.A. 34°54N 110°10W 130 C5
Holbrook Idaho, U.S.A. 42°10N 112°39W 122 G6
Holbrook Mass., U.S.A. 42°9N 71°1W 91 B3
Holbrook N.Y., U.S.A. 40°49N 73°5W 92 B3
Holbrook Nebr., U.S.A. 40°18N 100°1W 80 D5
Holchit, Pta. Yucatán, Mexico 21°37N 88°8W 179 A5
Holcomb Kans., U.S.A. 37°59N 100°59W 82 D3
Holcomb Miss., U.S.A. 33°46N 89°59W 111 C4
Holcomb Mo., U.S.A. 36°24N 90°2W 83 E6
Holcomb N.Y., U.S.A. 42°54N 77°25W 88 C3
Holcombe Flowage Wis., U.S.A. 45°13N 91°8W 78 C2
Holden Alta., Canada 53°13N 112°11W 152 E8
Holden Mass., U.S.A. 42°21N 71°52W 91 B3
Holden Mo., U.S.A. 38°43N 94°0W 83 C3
Holden Utah, U.S.A. 39°6N 112°16W 129 D3
Holden, L. Fla., U.S.A. 28°30N 81°23W 115 B2
Holden Beach N.C., U.S.A. 33°55N 78°15W 103 E7
Holdenville Okla., U.S.A. 35°5N 96°24W 107 C7
Holder Fla., U.S.A. 28°58N 82°25W 114 C6
Holderness N.H., U.S.A. 43°43N 71°37W 89 C3
Holdfast Sask., Canada 50°58N 105°25W 150 E6
Holdingford Minn., U.S.A. 45°44N 94°28W 77 E4
Holdrege Nebr., U.S.A. 40°26N 99°23W 80 D6
Holgate N.J., U.S.A. 39°33N 74°15W 92 C2
Holgate Ohio, U.S.A. 41°15N 84°8W 86 B2
Holguín Cuba 20°50N 76°20W 182 B4
Holiday Fla., U.S.A. 28°11N 82°44W 114 C6
Holiday Park Fla., U.S.A. 26°8N 80°7W 115 B3
Holinshead L. Ont., Canada 49°39N 89°40W 148 C1
Holladay Tenn., U.S.A. 35°52N 88°9W 104 E4
Holladay Utah, U.S.A. 40°40N 111°49W 134 C3
Holland Ark., U.S.A. 35°10N 92°16W 106 C3
Holland Ga., U.S.A. 34°21N 85°22W 113 B1
Holland Iowa, U.S.A. 42°24N 92°48W 81 C6
Holland Mich., U.S.A. 42°47N 86°7W 79 G5
Holland Minn., U.S.A. 44°6N 96°11W 77 F2
Holland Mo., U.S.A. 36°3N 89°52W 83 E7
Holland Tex., U.S.A. 30°53N 97°24W 109 G10
Holland Patent N.Y., U.S.A. 43°14N 75°15W 88 B5
Hollandale Minn., U.S.A. 43°46N 93°12W 77 G5
Hollandale Wis., U.S.A. 42°53N 89°56W 78 F4
Hollansburg Ohio, U.S.A. 39°59N 84°50W 86 D2
Hollenberg Kans., U.S.A. 39°58N 96°59W 82 B7
Holley N.Y., U.S.A. 30°27N 86°54W 114 A2
Holley Oreg., U.S.A. 44°21N 122°47W 121 C3
Holliday Tex., U.S.A. 33°49N 98°42W 109 D9
Hollidaysburg Pa., U.S.A. 40°26N 78°24W 87 C6
Hollins Va., U.S.A. 37°20N 79°57W 102 D5
Hollis Ark., U.S.A. 34°52N 93°7W 106 D2

Hollis Kans., U.S.A. 39°38N 97°33W 82 B6
Hollis N.H., U.S.A. 42°45N 71°36W 89 D3
Hollis N.Y., U.S.A. 40°42N 73°46W 97 B4
Hollis Okla., U.S.A. 34°41N 99°55W 107 D4
Hollister Calif., U.S.A. 36°51N 121°24W 126 G5
Hollister Idaho, U.S.A. 42°21N 114°35W 122 G4
Hollister Mo., U.S.A. 36°38N 93°12W 83 E3
Hollister Okla., U.S.A. 34°21N 98°52W 107 D5
Holliston Mass., U.S.A. 42°12N 71°26W 91 B3
Holloman Air Force Base N. Mex., U.S.A. 32°50N 106°4W 131 E4
Hollow Rock Tenn., U.S.A. 36°2N 88°16W 104 D4
Holloway Minn., U.S.A. 45°15N 95°55W 77 E3
Holly Colo., U.S.A. 38°3N 102°7W 125 D8
Holly Mich., U.S.A. 42°48N 83°38W 79 G8
Holly Bluff Miss., U.S.A. 32°49N 90°43W 111 D3
Holly Grove Ark., U.S.A. 34°36N 91°12W 106 D4
Holly Hill Fla., U.S.A. 29°16N 81°3W 114 B7
Holly Hill S.C., U.S.A. 33°19N 80°25W 103 E5
Holly Pond Ala., U.S.A. 34°10N 86°37W 112 B4
Holly Ridge N.C., U.S.A. 34°30N 77°33W 103 D8
Holly Springs Ga., U.S.A. 34°10N 84°30W 113 B2
Holly Springs Miss., U.S.A. 34°46N 89°27W 111 B4
Holly Springs N.C., U.S.A. 35°39N 78°50W 103 C7
Holly Springs Nat. Forest Miss., U.S.A. 34°44N 89°8W 111 B4
Hollywood Ala., U.S.A. 34°44N 85°59W 112 B5
Hollywood Calif., U.S.A. 34°5N 118°19W 133 B3
Hollywood Fla., U.S.A. 26°0N 80°8W 115 B3
Hollywood Md., U.S.A. 38°21N 76°34W 93 B4
Hollywood S.C., U.S.A. 32°44N 80°15W 103 F5
Hollywood Bowl Calif., U.S.A. 34°7N 118°20W 133 B2
Hollywood Park Tex., U.S.A. 29°36N 98°29W 116 B2
Holman N.W.T., Canada 70°44N 117°44W 156 B9
Holman Field = St. Paul Downtown ✈ Minn., U.S.A. 44°56N 93°3W 94 B3
Holmen Wis., U.S.A. 43°58N 91°15W 78 E21
Holmes, Mt. Wyo., U.S.A. 44°49N 110°51W 124 B2
Holmes Beach Fla., U.S.A. 27°31N 82°43W 114 D6
Holmes County ☆ Fla., U.S.A. 30°50N 85°45W 114 A3
Holmes County ☆ Miss., U.S.A. 33°7N 90°3W 111 C3
Holmes County ☆ Ohio, U.S.A. 40°33N 81°55W 86 C5
Holmes Cr. → Fla., U.S.A. 30°30N 85°50W 114 A3
Holmes Run Acres Va., U.S.A. 38°51N 77°13W 99 B2
Holmesville Ohio, U.S.A. 40°38N 81°56W 86 C5
Holopaw Fla., U.S.A. 28°8N 81°5W 114 C7
Holstein Iowa, U.S.A. 42°29N 95°33W 81 C2
Holstein Nebr., U.S.A. 40°28N 98°39W 80 D7
Holsteinsborg = Sisimiut Greenland 66°40N 53°30W 162 D5
Holston → Tenn., U.S.A. 35°58N 83°51W 105 E9
Holt Ala., U.S.A. 33°14N 87°29W 112 C3
Holt Fla., U.S.A. 30°43N 86°45W 114 A2
Holt Mich., U.S.A. 42°39N 84°31W 79 G7
Holt Minn., U.S.A. 48°18N 96°11W 77 B2
Holt Mo., U.S.A. 39°27N 94°21W 83 B2
Holt County ☆ Mo., U.S.A. 40°5N 95°10W 83 A1
Holt County ☆ Nebr., U.S.A. 42°30N 98°45W 80 B7
Holton Nfld. & L., Canada 54°31N 57°12W 143 C6
Holton Ind., U.S.A. 39°5N 85°23W 85 D5
Holton Kans., U.S.A. 39°28N 95°44W 82 B8
Holts Summit Mo., U.S.A. 38°38N 92°7W 83 C4
Holtville Calif., U.S.A. 32°49N 115°23W 127 L11
Holualoa Hawai'i, U.S.A. 19°37N 155°57W 136 D6
Holy Cross Alaska, U.S.A. 62°12N 159°46W 135 E8
Holyoke Colo., U.S.A. 40°35N 102°18W 125 B8
Holyoke Mass., U.S.A. 42°12N 72°37W 91 B2
Holyrood Nfld. & L., Canada 47°27N 53°8W 142 E7
Holyrood Kans., U.S.A. 38°35N 98°25W 82 C5
Homathko → B.C., Canada 51°0N 124°56W 154 D10
Home Kans., U.S.A. 39°51N 96°31W 82 B7
Home B. Nunavut, Canada 68°40N 67°10W 158 D12
Homedale Idaho, U.S.A. 43°37N 116°56W 122 F2
Homeland Ga., U.S.A. 30°51N 82°1W 113 F4
Homeland Park S.C., U.S.A. 34°28N 82°40W 103 D3
Homer Alaska, U.S.A. 59°39N 151°33W 135 G10
Homer Ga., U.S.A. 34°20N 83°30W 113 B3
Homer La., U.S.A. 32°48N 93°4W 110 B2
Homer Mich., U.S.A. 42°9N 84°49W 79 G7
Homer N.Y., U.S.A. 42°38N 76°11W 88 C4
Homer Nebr., U.S.A. 42°19N 96°29W 80 B9
Homer City Pa., U.S.A. 40°32N 79°10W 87 D3
Homer Youngs Pk. Mont., U.S.A. 45°19N 113°41W 123 E4
Homerville Ga., U.S.A. 31°2N 82°45W 113 E4
Homestead Fla., U.S.A. 25°28N 80°29W 114 F8
Homestead Oreg., U.S.A. 45°2N 116°51W 121 B9
Homestead Pa., U.S.A. 40°24N 79°54W 98 B2
Homestead Nat. Monument of America Nebr., U.S.A. 40°17N 96°50W 80 D9
Hometown Ill., U.S.A. 41°44N 87°42W 95 C2
Homewood Ala., U.S.A. 33°29N 86°47W 112 C4
Homewood Ill., U.S.A. 41°34N 87°40W 84 B6
Hominy Okla., U.S.A. 36°25N 96°24W 107 B7
Homochitto → Miss., U.S.A. 31°13N 91°32W 111 E2
Homochitto Nat. Forest Miss., U.S.A. 31°15N 90°45W 111 E3
Homosassa Springs Fla., U.S.A. 28°48N 82°35W 114 C6
Hon Ark., U.S.A. 34°56N 94°11W 106 D1
Honaker Va., U.S.A. 37°1N 81°59W 102 D3
Hōnaunau Hawai'i, U.S.A. 19°26N 155°55W 136 D6
Honda, Bahía Cuba 22°54N 83°10W 182 B3
Hondo Alta., Canada 55°4N 114°2W 152 C6
Hondo N. Mex., U.S.A. 33°24N 105°16W 131 D5
Hondo Tex., U.S.A. 29°21N 99°9W 109 H8
Hondo → N. Mex., U.S.A. 33°20N 104°25W 131 D5
Hondo, Río → Belize 18°25N 88°21W 179 D5
Hondo, Río → Calif., U.S.A. 34°2N 118°15W 133 B4
Honduras ■ Cent. Amer. 14°40N 86°30W 182 D2
Honduras, G. de Caribbean 16°50N 87°0W 182 C2
Honea Path S.C., U.S.A. 34°27N 82°24W 103 D3
Honesdale Pa., U.S.A. 41°34N 75°16W 87 C7
Honey Brook Pa., U.S.A. 40°6N 75°55W 87 D7
Honey Grove Tex., U.S.A. 33°35N 95°55W 109 D12
Honey Harbour Ont., Canada 44°52N 79°49W 146 B7
Honey Island Tex., U.S.A. 30°24N 94°27W 109 G13
Honey L. Calif., U.S.A. 40°15N 120°19W 126 C6
Honeyville Fla., U.S.A. 30°3N 85°11W 114 A3
Honeyville Utah, U.S.A. 41°38N 112°4W 129 B3
Honga Md., U.S.A. 38°19N 76°14W 93 B4
Honguedo, Détroit d' Qué., Canada 49°15N 64°0W 140 D6
Honka'a Hawai'i, U.S.A. 20°5N 155°28W 136 C6
Honokahua Hawai'i, U.S.A. 21°0N 156°40W 136 B4
Honokai Hale Hawai'i, U.S.A. 21°20N 158°6W 136 K13
Honolulu Hawai'i, U.S.A. 21°19N 157°52W 136 K14
Honolulu District ☆ Hawai'i, U.S.A. 21°18N 157°46W 136 K14
Honolulu Int. ✈ (HNL) Hawai'i, U.S.A. 21°19N 157°55W 136 K14

Honolulu Watershed Forest Reserve Hawai'i, U.S.A. 21°21N 157°48W 136 K14
Honomu Hawai'i, U.S.A. 19°52N 155°7W 136 D6
Honor Mich., U.S.A. 44°40N 86°1W 79 E5
Honoré Mercier, Pont Qué., Canada 45°24N 73°39W 160 B3
Honouliuli Hawai'i, U.S.A. 21°22N 158°2W 136 K13
Honouliuli Forest Reserve Hawai'i, U.S.A. 21°25N 158°4W 136 K13
Honu'apo B. Hawai'i, U.S.A. 19°5N 155°33W 136 D6
Hood → Nunavut, Canada 67°26N 108°53W 156 C11
Hood, Mt. Oreg., U.S.A. 45°23N 121°42W 121 B4
Hood Canal Wash., U.S.A. 47°35N 123°0W 120 C2
Hood County ☆ Tex., U.S.A. 32°27N 97°47W 109 E10
Hood River Oreg., U.S.A. 45°43N 121°31W 121 B4
Hood River County ☆ Oreg., U.S.A. 45°30N 121°20W 121 B4
Hoodsport Wash., U.S.A. 47°24N 123°9W 120 C2
Hooker Okla., U.S.A. 36°52N 101°13W 107 B2
Hooker County ☆ Nebr., U.S.A. 41°50N 101°0W 80 B4
Hooker L. Ont., Canada 50°35N 91°1W 148 B5
Hooks Tex., U.S.A. 33°28N 94°16W 109 D13
Hooksett N.H., U.S.A. 43°5N 71°30W 89 C3
Hool Campeche, Mexico 19°31N 90°27W 179 C3
Ho'olehua Hawai'i, U.S.A. 21°10N 157°5W 136 B4
Hoonah Alaska, U.S.A. 58°7N 135°27W 135 G14
Hoopa Calif., U.S.A. 41°3N 123°41W 126 B3
Hoopa Valley Indian Reservation Calif., U.S.A. 41°10N 123°45W 126 B3
Hooper Colo., U.S.A. 37°45N 105°53W 125 E5
Hooper Nebr., U.S.A. 41°37N 96°33W 80 C9
Hooper Wash., U.S.A. 46°45N 118°9W 120 D7
Hooper Bay Alaska, U.S.A. 61°32N 166°6W 135 E6
Hooper Str. Md., U.S.A. 38°15N 76°5W 93 B4
Hoopersville Md., U.S.A. 38°16N 76°11W 93 B4
Hoopeston Ill., U.S.A. 40°28N 87°40W 84 C6
Hoople N. Dak., U.S.A. 48°32N 97°38W 76 B8
Hoosac Range U.S.A. 42°45N 73°2W 91 B1
Hoosic → N.Y., U.S.A. 42°56N 73°21W 91 B1
Hoosick Falls N.Y., U.S.A. 42°54N 73°21W 91 B1
Hoosier Nat. Forest Ind., U.S.A. 38°30N 86°35W 85 E4
Hoover Ala., U.S.A. 33°24N 86°49W 112 C4
Hoover Dam U.S.A. 36°1N 114°44W 130 A1
Hoover Res. Ohio, U.S.A. 40°7N 82°53W 86 C4
Hooversville Pa., U.S.A. 40°9N 78°55W 87 D4
Hop Bottom Pa., U.S.A. 41°42N 75°46W 87 C7
Hopatcong N.J., U.S.A. 40°55N 74°40W 92 B2
Hopatcong, L. N.J., U.S.A. 40°55N 74°38W 92 B2
Hope B.C., Canada 49°25N 121°25W 155 F13
Hope Ariz., U.S.A. 33°43N 113°42W 130 D2
Hope Ark., U.S.A. 33°40N 93°36W 106 E2
Hope Ind., U.S.A. 39°18N 85°46W 85 D5
Hope Kans., U.S.A. 38°41N 97°5W 82 C6
Hope N. Dak., U.S.A. 47°19N 97°43W 76 C8
Hope N. Mex., U.S.A. 32°49N 104°44W 131 E6
Hope R.I., U.S.A. 41°44N 71°34W 91 C3
Hope, Pt. Alaska, U.S.A. 68°21N 166°47W 135 B6
Hope I. B.C., Canada 50°55N 127°53W 154 E7
Hope I. Ont., Canada 44°55N 80°11W 146 C6
Hope Mills N.C., U.S.A. 34°59N 78°57W 103 D7
Hope Town Bahamas 26°35N 76°57W 182 A4
Hope Valley R.I., U.S.A. 41°30N 71°43W 91 C3
Hopedale Nfld. & L., Canada 55°28N 60°13W 143 B5
Hopedale Ill., U.S.A. 40°25N 89°25W 84 C4
Hopelawn N.J., U.S.A. 40°31N 74°17W 97 C1
Hopelchén Campeche, Mexico 19°46N 89°51W 179 C4
Hopes Advance, C. Qué., Canada 61°4N 69°34W 143 A4
Hopes Advance B. Qué., Canada 59°20N 69°44W 143 A4
Hopeton Okla., U.S.A. 36°41N 98°40W 107 B5
Hopewell N.S., Canada 45°29N 62°42W 141 H7
Hopewell Tenn., U.S.A. 35°14N 84°53W 105 E8
Hopewell Va., U.S.A. 37°18N 77°17W 102 D7
Hopewell Cape N.B., Canada 45°51N 64°35W 141 H5
Hopewell Culture Nat. Historical Park △ Ohio, U.S.A. 39°17N 82°55W 86 D4
Hopewell Furnace Nat. Historical Park △ Pa., U.S.A. 40°12N 75°47W 87 D7
Hopewell Is. Nunavut, Canada 58°24N 78°10W 159 F10
Hopi Indian Reservation Ariz., U.S.A. 35°45N 110°30W 130 B5
Hopkins Mich., U.S.A. 42°37N 85°46W 79 G6
Hopkins Minn., U.S.A. 44°55N 93°27W 94 B1
Hopkins Mo., U.S.A. 40°33N 94°49W 83 A2
Hopkins County ☆ Ky., U.S.A. 37°20N 87°30W 104 C5
Hopkins County ☆ Tex., U.S.A. 33°8N 95°36W 109 D12
Hopkinsville Ky., U.S.A. 36°52N 87°29W 104 C5
Hopkinton Iowa, U.S.A. 42°21N 91°15W 81 C7
Hopkinton Mass., U.S.A. 42°14N 71°31W 91 B3
Hopkinton N.H., U.S.A. 43°12N 71°41W 89 C3
Hopkinton R.I., U.S.A. 41°28N 71°48W 91 C3
Hopland Calif., U.S.A. 38°58N 123°7W 126 E3
Hoquiam Wash., U.S.A. 46°59N 123°53W 120 D2
Horace Kans., U.S.A. 38°29N 101°47W 82 C2
Horace N. Dak., U.S.A. 46°45N 96°54W 76 D9
Horatio Ark., U.S.A. 33°56N 94°21W 106 E1
Horconcitos Veracruz, Mexico 21°51N 97°43W 176 C2
Hordville Nebr., U.S.A. 41°5N 97°53W 80 C8
Horicon Wis., U.S.A. 43°27N 88°38W 78 E5
Horicon Nat. Wildlife Refuge △ Wis., U.S.A. 43°35N 88°38W 78 E5
Hormigas Coahuila, Mexico 27°46N 103°56W 169 F12
Hormigueros Puerto Rico 18°8N 67°8W 184 G15
Horn → N.W.T., Canada 61°30N 118°1W 157 D9
Horn I. Miss., U.S.A. 30°14N 88°39W 111 F3
Horn Lake Miss., U.S.A. 34°58N 90°2W 111 B3
Horn Plateau N.W.T., Canada 62°15N 119°15W 157 D9
Horn Pond Mass., U.S.A. 42°28N 71°9W 96 A1
Hornaday → N.W.T., Canada 69°19N 123°48W 156 C8
Hornbeak Tenn., U.S.A. 36°20N 89°18W 104 D3
Hornbeck La., U.S.A. 31°20N 93°24W 110 C2
Hornbrook Calif., U.S.A. 41°55N 122°33W 126 B4
Hornell N.Y., U.S.A. 42°20N 77°40W 88 C3
Hornepayne Ont., Canada 49°14N 84°48W 149 C12
Hornersville Mo., U.S.A. 36°3N 90°7W 83 E6
Hornick Iowa, U.S.A. 42°14N 96°6W 81 C2
Hornillos Sinaloa, Mexico 26°28N 108°27W 172 A2
Hornings Mills Ont., Canada 44°9N 80°12W 146 C6
Hornitos Calif., U.S.A. 37°30N 120°14W 126 F6
Hornsby Tenn., U.S.A. 35°14N 88°50W 104 E4
Horry County ☆ S.C., U.S.A. 33°50N 79°0W 103 D7
Horse → N.W.T., Canada 58°5N 103°19W 157 D7
Horse Cave Ky., U.S.A. 37°11N 85°54W 105 C7
Horse Cr. → Fla., U.S.A. 27°6N 81°58W 114 D7
Horse Cr. → Nebr., U.S.A. 37°46N 93°53W 83 D3
Horse Cr. → Wyo., U.S.A. 41°57N 103°58W 124 E7
Horse Creek Wyo., U.S.A. 41°25N 105°11W 124 E7
Horse Creek Res. Colo., U.S.A. 38°10N 104°3W 125 D7
Horse Heaven Hills Wash., U.S.A. 46°3N 119°30W 120 D6
Horse I. Man., Canada 53°20N 99°6W 151 B12

Horse Is. Nfld. & L., Canada 50°15N 55°50W 142 B5
Horse L. Calif., U.S.A. 40°40N 120°31W 126 C6
Horse Pasture Va., U.S.A. 36°38N 79°57W 102 E5
Horsefly B.C., Canada 52°20N 121°25W 155 C13
Horsefly L. B.C., Canada 52°25N 121°0W 155 C13
Horsehead L. N. Dak., U.S.A. 47°3N 99°47W 76 C6
Horseheads N.Y., U.S.A. 42°10N 76°49W 88 C4
Horseshoe Bend Ark., U.S.A. 36°14N 91°46W 106 B4
Horseshoe Bend Idaho, U.S.A. 43°55N 116°12W 122 F2
Horseshoe Bend Nat. Military Park △ Ala., U.S.A. 32°59N 85°44W 112 D5
Horseshoe Lake Ill., U.S.A. 38°41N 90°5W 94 A3
Horseshoe Lake State Park △ Ill., U.S.A. 38°41N 90°5W 94 B3
Horseshoe Res. Ariz., U.S.A. 34°2N 111°42W 130 C4
Hortense Ga., U.S.A. 31°20N 81°57W 113 E5
Horton Ark., U.S.A. 39°40N 95°32W 82 B8
Horton → N.W.T., Canada 69°56N 126°52W 156 C7
Horton L. N.W.T., Canada 67°29N 122°31W 156 C8
Hortonville Wis., U.S.A. 44°20N 88°38W 78 D5
Horwood Nfld. & L., Canada 49°27N 54°32W 142 C6
Horwood L. Ont., Canada 48°5N 82°20W 149 D14
Hosford Fla., U.S.A. 30°23N 84°48W 114 A4
Hoskins Nebr., U.S.A. 42°7N 97°18W 80 B8
Hoskins Oreg., U.S.A. 44°41N 123°28W 121 C2
Hoskinston Ky., U.S.A. 37°5N 83°24W 105 C9
Hosmer S. Dak., U.S.A. 45°34N 99°28W 76 E6
Hospers Iowa, U.S.A. 43°4N 95°54W 81 B3
Hostotipaquillo Jalisco, Mexico 21°4N 104°4W 174 A3
Hot Creek Range Nev., U.S.A. 38°40N 116°20W 128 D4
Hot Spring County ☆ Ark., U.S.A. 34°14N 92°55W 106 D3
Hot Springs = Truth or Consequences N. Mex., U.S.A. 33°8N 107°15W 131 D3
Hot Springs Ark., U.S.A. 34°31N 93°30W 106 D2
Hot Springs Mont., U.S.A. 47°37N 114°40W 123 C4
Hot Springs N.C., U.S.A. 35°54N 82°50W 103 C3
Hot Springs S. Dak., U.S.A. 43°26N 103°29W 76 G2
Hot Springs Va., U.S.A. 38°0N 79°50W 102 D5
Hot Springs County ☆ Wyo., U.S.A. 43°55N 108°30W 124 C4
Hot Springs Nat. Park △ Ark., U.S.A. 34°31N 93°0W 106 D2
Hot Springs Village Ark., U.S.A. 34°40N 93°0W 106 D3
Hot Sulphur Springs Colo., U.S.A. 40°4N 106°6W 125 B4
Hotchkiss Colo., U.S.A. 38°48N 107°43W 125 D3
Hotchkiss → Alta., Canada 57°2N 117°28W 152 A3
Hotevilla Ariz., U.S.A. 35°56N 110°41W 130 B5
Hottah L. N.W.T., Canada 65°4N 118°30W 157 C9
Hotte, Massif de la Haiti 18°30N 73°45W 182 C5
Houck Ariz., U.S.A. 35°20N 109°10W 130 B6
Houghton Mich., U.S.A. 47°7N 88°34W 79 B3
Houghton N.Y., U.S.A. 42°25N 78°10W 88 C2
Houghton County ☆ Mich., U.S.A. 47°0N 88°45W 79 C3
Houghton L. Mich., U.S.A. 44°21N 84°44W 79 E7
Houghton Lake Mich., U.S.A. 44°18N 84°45W 79 E7
Houlton Maine, U.S.A. 46°8N 67°51W 90 B6
Houma La., U.S.A. 29°36N 90°43W 110 E5
Housatonic Mass., U.S.A. 42°16N 73°22W 91 B1
Housatonic → Conn., U.S.A. 41°10N 73°7W 91 C1
House N. Mex., U.S.A. 34°39N 103°54W 131 C7
House Range Utah, U.S.A. 39°30N 113°20W 129 D2
Houston B.C., Canada 54°25N 126°39W 157 F7
Houston Ark., U.S.A. 35°2N 92°42W 106 C3
Houston Fla., U.S.A. 30°15N 82°54W 114 A6
Houston Minn., U.S.A. 43°46N 91°34W 77 G7
Houston Miss., U.S.A. 33°54N 89°0W 111 C4
Houston Mo., U.S.A. 37°22N 91°58W 83 D5
Houston Tex., U.S.A. 29°45N 95°21W 116 B2
Houston → La., U.S.A. 30°16N 93°13W 110 D2
Houston, L. Tex., U.S.A. 29°55N 95°8W 109 H12
Houston County ☆ Ala., U.S.A. 31°11N 85°14W 112 E5
Houston County ☆ Ga., U.S.A. 32°20N 83°45W 113 D3
Houston County ☆ Minn., U.S.A. 43°35N 91°30W 77 G7
Houston County ☆ Tenn., U.S.A. 36°19N 87°42W 104 D5
Houston County ☆ Tex., U.S.A. 31°19N 95°21W 109 F12
Houston George Bush Intercontinental ✈ (IAH) Tex., U.S.A. 29°59N 95°20W 109 H12
Houston William P. Hobby ✈ (HOU) Tex., U.S.A. 29°38N 95°16W 116 C3
Houstonia Mo., U.S.A. 38°54N 93°22W 83 C3
Hoved I. Nunavut, Canada 77°32N 85°9W 158 B8
Hoven S. Dak., U.S.A. 45°15N 99°47W 76 E6
Hovenweep Nat. Monument △ Colo., U.S.A. 37°20N 109°0W 125 E2
Hovgaard Ø Greenland 79°55N 18°50W 162 B9
Hovland Minn., U.S.A. 47°51N 89°58W 77 C9
Howard Colo., U.S.A. 38°27N 105°50W 125 D5
Howard Ga., U.S.A. 32°36N 84°23W 113 D2
Howard Kans., U.S.A. 37°28N 96°16W 82 D7
Howard Pa., U.S.A. 41°1N 77°40W 87 C5
Howard S. Dak., U.S.A. 44°1N 97°32W 76 F8
Howard Wis., U.S.A. 44°33N 88°4W 78 D5
Howard Beach N.Y., U.S.A. 40°39N 73°50W 97 C3
Howard City Mich., U.S.A. 43°24N 85°28W 79 F6
Howard County ☆ Ark., U.S.A. 34°7N 94°1W 106 D1
Howard County ☆ Ind., U.S.A. 40°30N 86°10W 85 C4
Howard County ☆ Iowa, U.S.A. 43°20N 92°20W 81 B6
Howard County ☆ Md., U.S.A. 39°15N 77°0W 93 A4
Howard County ☆ Mo., U.S.A. 39°10N 92°40W 83 B4
Howard County ☆ Nebr., U.S.A. 41°15N 98°30W 80 C7
Howard County ☆ Tex., U.S.A. 32°15N 101°28W 108 E6
Howard Draw → Tex., U.S.A. 30°10N 101°35W 108 G6
Howard Hanson Res. Wash., U.S.A. 47°17N 121°47W 120 C4
Howard Lake Minn., U.S.A. 45°4N 94°4W 77 E4
Howard Prairie L. Oreg., U.S.A. 42°13N 122°22W 121 E3
Howe Idaho, U.S.A. 43°48N 113°0W 122 F5
Howe Ind., U.S.A. 41°43N 85°25W 85 B5
Howe Okla., U.S.A. 34°57N 94°38W 107 D9
Howe Tex., U.S.A. 33°30N 96°37W 109 D11
Howe I. Ont., Canada 44°16N 76°17W 147 C10
Howe Sd. B.C., Canada 49°35N 123°15W 155 F11
Howell Mich., U.S.A. 42°36N 83°56W 79 G8
Howell Utah, U.S.A. 41°48N 112°27W 129 B3
Howell County ☆ Mo., U.S.A. 36°45N 91°50W 83 E5
Howells Nebr., U.S.A. 41°44N 97°0W 80 C9
Howes S. Dak., U.S.A. 44°37N 102°3W 76 F3
Howes Mill Mo., U.S.A. 37°38N 91°16W 83 D5
Howland Maine, U.S.A. 45°14N 68°40W 90 C5
Howland I. Pac. Oc. 0°48N 176°38W 184 D6
Howley Nfld. & L., Canada 49°12N 57°2W 142 C3
Hoxie Ark., U.S.A. 36°3N 90°59W 106 B5
Hoxie Kans., U.S.A. 39°21N 100°26W 82 B3
Hoyanco Sinaloa, Mexico 26°22N 107°1W 172 A2
Hoyleton Ill., U.S.A. 38°27N 89°16W 84 E4
Hoyt Colo., U.S.A. 40°1N 104°50W 125 B6
Hoyt Kans., U.S.A. 39°15N 95°43W 82 B8
Hoyt Lakes Minn., U.S.A. 47°32N 92°8W 77 C6
Huacales, Cerro los Zacatecas, Mexico 22°21N 101°30W 173 E9

Huacasco Jalisco, Mexico 22°13N 103°6W 173 E7
Huachichil Coahuila, Mexico 25°11N 100°50W 171 E4
Huachinera Sonora, Mexico 30°9N 108°55W 168 C7
Huachuca City Ariz., U.S.A. 31°34N 110°21W 130 F5
Huajicori Nayarit, Mexico 22°44N 105°21W 172 E5
Huajimic Nayarit, Mexico 21°42N 104°20W 172 F6
Huajuapán de León Oaxaca, Mexico 17°48N 97°46W 177 G3
Huajumbaro Michoacan, Mexico 19°52N 100°36W 175 C7
Hualahuises Nuevo León, Mexico 24°53N 99°41W 171 F5
Hualālai Hawai'i, U.S.A. 19°42N 155°52W 136 D6
Hualapai Indian Reservation Ariz., U.S.A. 35°45N 113°20W 130 B2
Hualapai Mts. Ariz., U.S.A. 34°45N 113°30W 130 C2
Hualapai Peak Ariz., U.S.A. 35°5N 113°54W 130 B2
Hualula Hidalgo, Mexico 20°45N 98°47W 175 B9
Huamantla Tlaxcala, Mexico 19°19N 97°56W 175 C10
Huamuxtitlán Guerrero, Mexico 17°49N 98°34W 175 E9
Huandacareó Michoacan, Mexico 19°59N 101°17W 175 C6
Huanímaro Guanajuato, Mexico 20°23N 101°31W 174 B6
Huaniqueo de Morales Michoacan, Mexico 19°55N 101°31W 174 C6
Huanusco Zacatecas, Mexico 21°46N 102°59W 173 F8
Huapacal Tabasco, Mexico 17°55N 93°45W 178 B3
Huásabas Granados Sonora, Mexico 29°57N 109°13W 168 D6
Huatabampo Sonora, Mexico 26°50N 109°38W 168 G6
Huatamote → Baja Calif., Mexico 30°50N 114°43W 166 C4
Huatusco de Chicuellar Veracruz, Mexico 19°9N 96°57W 177 E4
Huauchinango Puebla, Mexico 20°12N 98°3W 176 D2
Huautla Hidalgo, Mexico 21°3N 98°16W 175 A9
Huautla de Jiménez Oaxaca, Mexico 18°8N 96°51W 177 F4
Huayacocotla Veracruz, Mexico 20°33N 98°29W 176 D1
Huaymil Campeche, Mexico 20°27N 90°25W 179 B3
Hubbard Sask., Canada 51°8N 103°22W 150 D8
Hubbard Iowa, U.S.A. 42°18N 93°18W 81 C5
Hubbard Nebr., U.S.A. 42°23N 96°36W 80 B9
Hubbard Ohio, U.S.A. 41°9N 80°34W 86 B6
Hubbard Oreg., U.S.A. 45°11N 122°48W 121 B3
Hubbard Tex., U.S.A. 31°51N 96°48W 109 F11
Hubbard, Mt. N. Amer. 60°19N 139°4W 157 D5
Hubbard County ☆ Minn., U.S.A. 47°10N 94°50W 77 C4
Hubbard Creek L. Tex., U.S.A. 32°50N 98°58W 109 E9
Hubbard L. Mich., U.S.A. 44°48N 83°34W 79 E8
Hubbards N.S., Canada 44°38N 64°4W 141 J5
Hubbardston Mass., U.S.A. 42°28N 72°0W 91 B3
Hubbardton Vt., U.S.A. 43°42N 73°12W 89 C1
Hubbell Mich., U.S.A. 47°11N 88°26W 79 B3
Hubbell Nebr., U.S.A. 40°1N 97°29W 80 D8
Hubbell Trading Post Nat. Historic Site △ Ariz., U.S.A. 35°43N 109°33W 130 B6
Huber Heights Ohio, U.S.A. 39°50N 84°5W 86 D2
Huddy Ky., U.S.A. 37°36N 82°17W 105 C10
Hudson Ont., Canada 50°6N 92°9W 148 B4
Hudson Colo., U.S.A. 40°4N 104°38W 125 B6
Hudson Fla., U.S.A. 28°22N 82°42W 114 C6
Hudson Iowa, U.S.A. 42°24N 92°28W 81 C6
Hudson Kans., U.S.A. 38°6N 98°40W 82 C5
Hudson Maine, U.S.A. 45°0N 68°53W 90 C5
Hudson Mass., U.S.A. 42°23N 71°34W 91 B3
Hudson Md., U.S.A. 38°36N 76°15W 93 B4
Hudson Mich., U.S.A. 41°51N 84°21W 79 H7
Hudson N.C., U.S.A. 35°51N 81°30W 103 C4
Hudson N.H., U.S.A. 42°46N 71°23W 89 D2
Hudson N.Y., U.S.A. 42°15N 73°46W 88 C7
Hudson Ohio, U.S.A. 41°14N 81°26W 86 B5
Hudson S. Dak., U.S.A. 43°8N 96°27W 76 G9
Hudson Wis., U.S.A. 44°58N 92°45W 78 D11
Hudson Wyo., U.S.A. 42°54N 108°35W 124 D4
Hudson → N.Y., U.S.A. 40°42N 74°2W 88 E6
Hudson, L. Okla., U.S.A. 36°14N 95°11W 107 B8
Hudson Bay Nunavut, Canada 60°0N 86°0W 159 E8
Hudson Bay Sask., Canada 52°51N 102°23W 151 C9
Hudson County ☆ N.J., U.S.A. 40°45N 74°5W 92 B2
Hudson Falls N.Y., U.S.A. 43°18N 73°35W 88 B7
Hudson Str. Nunavut, Canada 62°0N 70°0W 159 E11
Hudson's Hope B.C., Canada 56°0N 121°54W 157 E8
Hudsonville Mich., U.S.A. 42°52N 85°52W 79 G6
Hudspeth County ☆ Tex., U.S.A. 31°30N 105°30W 108 F2
Hudwin L. Man., Canada 53°12N 95°41W 151 B16
Hueco Mts. Tex., U.S.A. 31°53N 105°58W 108 F2
Huehuetán Chiapas, Mexico 15°5N 92°22W 178 D4
Huehuetenango Guatemala 15°20N 91°28W 182 C1
Huehuetla Hidalgo, Mexico 20°28N 98°3W 175 B9
Huehuetlán el Chico Puebla, Mexico 18°44N 98°10W 177 F2
Huejotitán Chihuahua, Mexico 27°4N 106°12W 169 F9
Huejotzingo Puebla, Mexico 19°10N 98°24W 177 F2
Huejúcar Jalisco, Mexico 22°21N 103°13W 173 E7
Huejuquilla Jalisco, Mexico 22°36N 103°52W 173 E7
Huejutla de Reyes Hidalgo, Mexico 21°8N 98°25W 175 A9
Hueneme = Port Hueneme Calif., U.S.A. 34°7N 119°12W 127 J7
Huépac Sonora, Mexico 29°54N 110°10W 168 D5
Huerfano → Colo., U.S.A. 38°14N 104°15W 125 D6
Huerfano County ☆ Colo., U.S.A. 37°40N 104°50W 125 E6
Huetamo Michoacan, Mexico 18°35N 100°53W 175 D7
Hueyapán de Ocampo Veracruz, Mexico 18°7N 95°9W 177 F5
Hueytamalco Puebla, Mexico 19°57N 97°17W 176 D3
Hueytown Ala., U.S.A. 33°27N 86°59W 112 C4
Huffman Tex., U.S.A. 30°1N 95°6W 109 G12
Hugh Butler L. Nebr., U.S.A. 40°21N 100°39W 80 D5
Hugh Taylor Birch State Rec. Area △ Fla., U.S.A. 26°8N 80°6W 115 B3
Hughes Alaska, U.S.A. 66°3N 154°15W 135 C9
Hughes Ark., U.S.A. 34°57N 90°28W 106 D5
Hughes County ☆ Okla., U.S.A. 35°2N 96°15W 107 C7
Hughes County ☆ S. Dak., U.S.A. 44°30N 100°0W 76 F6
Hughes Springs Tex., U.S.A. 33°0N 94°38W 109 E13
Hughesville Md., U.S.A. 38°32N 76°47W 93 B4
Hughesville Mo., U.S.A. 38°50N 93°18W 83 C3
Hughson Calif., U.S.A. 37°36N 120°52W 126 F6
Hugo Colo., U.S.A. 39°8N 103°28W 125 C6
Hugo Okla., U.S.A. 34°1N 95°31W 107 D8
Hugo L. Okla., U.S.A. 34°3N 95°27W 107 D8
Hugoton Kans., U.S.A. 37°11N 101°21W 82 D2
Huguenot N.Y., U.S.A. 40°32N 74°11W 97 C1
Huguenot Park N.Y., U.S.A. 40°33N 74°11W 97 C1
Huhi Yucatán, Mexico 20°43N 89°10W 179 A4
Huichapán Hidalgo, Mexico 20°23N 99°39W 175 B8
Huimanguillo Tabasco, Mexico 17°51N 93°23W 178 B3
Huimilpan Querétaro, Mexico 20°22N 100°17W 175 B7
Huinala Monterrey, Mexico 25°44N 100°10W 180 B3
Huitiupán Chiapas, Mexico 17°13N 92°39W 178 C4
Huitussi Sinaloa, Mexico 25°30N 108°31W 172 B2
Huitzila Zacatecas, Mexico 21°12N 103°37W 174 A4

Huitzuco Guerrero, Mexico 18°18N 99°21W 175 D8
Huivulai, I. Sonora. Mexico 27°3N 109°59W 168 F6
Huixquilucan de Degollado México, Mexico 19°23N 99°27W 181 B1
Huixtán Chiapas, Mexico 16°46N 92°27W 178 C4
Huixtla Chiapas, Mexico 15°9N 92°28W 178 D4
Hulah L. Okla., U.S.A. 36°56N 96°5W 107 B7
Hulbert Mich., U.S.A. 46°21N 85°9W 79 C6
Hulbert Okla., U.S.A. 35°56N 95°9W 107 C8
Hulett Wyo., U.S.A. 44°41N 104°36W 124 B8
Huletts Landing N.Y., U.S.A. 43°38N 73°30W 89 C1
Hull Qué., Canada 45°26N 75°43W 160 A1
Hull Fla., U.S.A. 27°7N 81°56W 114 D7
Hull Ill., U.S.A. 39°43N 91°13W 84 D2
Hull Iowa, U.S.A. 43°11N 96°8W 81 B2
Hull Mass., U.S.A. 42°18N 70°54W 91 B4
Humacao Puerto Rico 18°9N 65°50W 184 G17
Humansville Mo., U.S.A. 37°48N 93°35W 83 D3
Humaya → Mexico 24°49N 107°24W 172 C3
Humber → Ont., Canada 43°38N 79°28W 161 B2
Humber Arm South Nfld. & L., Canada 49°1N 58°7W 142 C2
Humber B. Ont., Canada 43°37N 79°27W 161 B2
Humber Bay Ont., Canada 43°38N 79°29W 161 B2
Humber Bay Park Ont., Canada 43°37N 79°28W 161 B2
Humber College Ont., Canada 43°35N 79°30W 161 B1
Humber Summit Ont., Canada 43°45N 79°32W 161 A1
Humber Valley Village Ont., Canada 43°40N 79°31W 161 A1
Humberlea Ont., Canada 43°43N 79°31W 161 A1
Humberwood Park Ont., Canada 43°44N 79°37W 161 A1
Humble Tex., U.S.A. 30°0N 95°18W 109 H12
Humble City N. Mex., U.S.A. 32°47N 103°13W 131 E7
Humboldt Sask., Canada 52°15N 105°9W 150 C6
Humboldt Ariz., U.S.A. 34°30N 112°14W 130 C3
Humboldt Ill., U.S.A. 39°36N 88°19W 84 D5
Humboldt Iowa, U.S.A. 42°44N 94°13W 81 C4
Humboldt Kans., U.S.A. 37°49N 95°26W 82 D8
Humboldt Nebr., U.S.A. 40°10N 95°57W 80 D10
Humboldt S. Dak., U.S.A. 43°39N 97°5W 76 G8
Humboldt Tenn., U.S.A. 35°50N 88°55W 104 E4
Humboldt → Nev., U.S.A. 39°59N 118°36W 128 C2
Humboldt B. Calif., U.S.A. 40°45N 124°10W 126 C2
Humboldt County ☆ Calif., U.S.A. 40°50N 124°0W 126 C3
Humboldt County ☆ Iowa, U.S.A. 42°50N 94°10W 81 C4
Humboldt County ☆ Nev., U.S.A. 41°20N 118°10W 128 A2
Humboldt Gletscher = Sermersuaq Greenland 79°30N 62°0W 162 B4
Humboldt Nat. Forest Nev., U.S.A. 41°45N 115°30W 128 A5
Humboldt Park Ill., U.S.A. 41°54N 87°42W 95 B2
Humboldt Peak Colo., U.S.A. 37°59N 105°33W 125 E5
Humboldt Range Nev., U.S.A. 40°20N 118°10W 128 B2
Humboldt Redwoods State Park △ Calif., U.S.A. 40°19N 123°59W 126 C3
Humboldt Salt Marsh Nev., U.S.A. 39°50N 117°55W 128 C3
Humboldt Sink Nev., U.S.A. 39°50N 118°15W 128 C2
Humboldt-Toiyabe Nat. Forest Nev., U.S.A. 38°40N 117°0W 128 D4
Hume Mo., U.S.A. 38°6N 94°34W 83 C2
Hume Va., U.S.A. 38°50N 78°0W 93 B3
Hume → N.W.T., Canada 66°1N 129°8W 156 C7
Humeston Iowa, U.S.A. 40°52N 93°30W 81 E5
Humnoke Ark., U.S.A. 34°33N 91°45W 106 D4
Humphrey Ark., U.S.A. 34°25N 91°43W 106 D4
Humphrey Idaho, U.S.A. 44°29N 112°14W 122 E6
Humphrey Nebr., U.S.A. 41°42N 97°7W 80 C8
Humphreys Okla., U.S.A. 34°33N 99°14W 107 D4
Humphreys, Mt. Calif., U.S.A. 37°17N 118°40W 127 F8
Humphreys County ☆ Miss., U.S.A. 33°6N 90°30W 111 C3
Humphreys County ☆ Tenn., U.S.A. 36°5N 87°48W 104 D5
Humphreys Peak Ariz., U.S.A. 35°21N 111°41W 130 B4
Hundred W. Va., U.S.A. 39°41N 80°28W 102 B4
Hundred and Fifty Mile House B.C., Canada 52°7N 121°57W 155 C13
Hundred Mile House B.C., Canada 51°38N 121°18W 155 D13
Hungry Horse Mont., U.S.A. 48°23N 114°4W 123 B3
Hungry Horse Res. Mont., U.S.A. 48°21N 114°1W 123 B3
Hunnewell Kans., U.S.A. 37°1N 97°25W 82 D6
Hunnewell Mo., U.S.A. 39°40N 91°52W 83 B5
Hunt Tex., U.S.A. 30°4N 99°20W 109 G8
Hunt County ☆ Tex., U.S.A. 33°8N 96°7W 109 D11
Hunt Mt. Wyo., U.S.A. 44°55N 107°59W 124 B5
Hunter Ark., U.S.A. 35°3N 91°8W 106 C4
Hunter Kans., U.S.A. 39°14N 98°24W 82 B5
Hunter N. Dak., U.S.A. 47°12N 97°13W 76 C8
Hunter N.Y., U.S.A. 42°13N 74°13W 88 C6
Hunter Okla., U.S.A. 36°34N 97°40W 107 B6
Hunter I. B.C., Canada 51°55N 128°0W 154 D6
Hunterdon County ☆ N.J., U.S.A. 40°30N 75°0W 92 B2
Hunters Wash., U.S.A. 48°7N 118°12W 120 B7
Hunters Creek Village Tex., U.S.A. 29°46N 95°30W 116 B2
Hunters Pt. Calif., U.S.A. 37°43N 122°21W 132 B2
Hunters Valley Pa., U.S.A. 38°54N 77°1W 99 B2
Huntersville N.C., U.S.A. 35°25N 80°51W 103 C5
Huntertown Ind., U.S.A. 41°14N 85°10W 85 B5
Huntingburg Ind., U.S.A. 38°18N 86°57W 85 E4
Huntingdon Qué., Canada 45°6N 74°10W 145 F8
Huntingdon Pa., U.S.A. 40°30N 78°1W 87 D4
Huntingdon Tenn., U.S.A. 36°0N 88°26W 104 E4
Huntingdon County ☆ Pa., U.S.A. 40°15N 78°0W 87 D5
Huntington = Shelton Conn., U.S.A. 41°19N 73°5W 91 C1
Huntington Ark., U.S.A. 35°5N 94°16W 106 C1
Huntington Ind., U.S.A. 40°53N 85°30W 85 C5
Huntington Mass., U.S.A. 42°14N 72°53W 91 B2
Huntington N.Y., U.S.A. 40°52N 73°26W 91 D1
Huntington Oreg., U.S.A. 44°21N 117°16W 121 C8
Huntington Tex., U.S.A. 31°17N 94°34W 109 F13
Huntington Utah, U.S.A. 39°20N 110°58W 129 D5
Huntington W. Va., U.S.A. 38°25N 82°27W 102 C2
Huntington → Nev., U.S.A. 39°7N 115°43W 128 B5
Huntington = Utah, U.S.A. 39°0N 110°55W 129 D5
Huntington Beach Calif., U.S.A. 33°40N 118°5W 127 K8
Huntington County ☆ Ind., U.S.A. 40°50N 85°30W 85 C5
Huntington Park Calif., U.S.A. 33°58N 118°13W 133 C3
Huntington Station N.Y., U.S.A. 40°51N 73°25W 92 B3
Huntington Woods Mich., U.S.A. 42°28N 83°10W 98 A1
Huntland Tenn., U.S.A. 35°3N 86°16W 104 E6
Huntley Ill., U.S.A. 42°10N 88°26W 84 A5
Huntley Mont., U.S.A. 45°54N 108°1W 124 C6
Huntley Nebr., U.S.A. 40°13N 99°18W 80 D6
Hunts Point Wash., U.S.A. 47°38N 122°13W 132 C4
Huntsville Ont., Canada 45°20N 79°14W 146 B7
Huntsville Ala., U.S.A. 34°44N 86°35W 112 B4
Huntsville Ark., U.S.A. 36°5N 93°44W 106 B2

Huntsville Ky., U.S.A. 37°10N 86°53W 104 C6
Huntsville Mo., U.S.A. 39°26N 92°33W 83 B4
Huntsville Ohio, U.S.A. 40°26N 83°48W 86 C3
Huntsville Tenn., U.S.A. 36°25N 84°29W 105 D8
Huntsville Tex., U.S.A. 30°43N 95°33W 109 G12
Huntsville Utah, U.S.A. 41°16N 111°46W 129 B4
Hunucmá Yucatán, Mexico 21°1N 89°52W 179 A4
Hupel B.C., Canada 50°37N 118°44W 155 E16
Hurdsfield N. Dak., U.S.A. 47°26N 99°55W 76 C6
Hurley Miss., U.S.A. 30°40N 88°30W 111 F5
Hurley Mo., U.S.A. 36°56N 93°30W 83 E3
Hurley N. Mex., U.S.A. 32°42N 108°8W 131 E2
Hurley N.Y., U.S.A. 41°55N 74°4W 88 D6
Hurley S. Dak., U.S.A. 43°17N 97°5W 76 G8
Hurley Wis., U.S.A. 46°27N 90°11W 78 B3
Hurlock Md., U.S.A. 38°38N 75°52W 93 B5
Huron Calif., U.S.A. 36°12N 120°6W 127 G6
Huron Kans., U.S.A. 39°38N 95°21W 82 B8
Huron Ohio, U.S.A. 41°24N 82°33W 86 B4
Huron S. Dak., U.S.A. 44°22N 98°13W 76 F7
Huron → Mich., U.S.A. 42°2N 83°11W 79 G8
Huron, L. Mich., U.S.A. 44°30N 82°40W 146 C4
Huron Bay Mich., U.S.A. 46°54N 88°13W 79 C3
Huron Beach Mich., U.S.A. 45°30N 84°6W 79 D7
Huron County ☆ Mich., U.S.A. 43°50N 83°0W 79 F9
Huron County ☆ Ohio, U.S.A. 41°15N 82°33W 86 B4
Huron East Ont., Canada 43°37N 81°18W 146 D5
Huron Mts. Mich., U.S.A. 46°50N 88°0W 79 C4
Huron Nat. Forest Mich., U.S.A. 44°30N 84°0W 79 E8
Huron Potawatomi Indian Reservation Mich., U.S.A. 42°5N 85°16W 79 G6
Hurricane Utah, U.S.A. 37°11N 113°17W 129 F2
Hurricane W. Va., U.S.A. 38°26N 82°1W 102 C2
Hurricane Cliffs Ariz., U.S.A. 36°45N 113°20W 130 A2
Hurricane L. N. Dak., U.S.A. 48°26N 99°31W 76 B6
Hurst Tex., U.S.A. 32°49N 97°10W 116 B3
Hurstville Iowa, U.S.A. 42°6N 90°41W 81 C8
Hurt Va., U.S.A. 37°6N 79°18W 102 D5
Hurtsboro Ala., U.S.A. 32°15N 85°25W 112 D5
Huslia Alaska, U.S.A. 65°41N 156°24W 135 D8
Hussar Alta., Canada 51°3N 112°41W 153 G8
Hustisford Wis., U.S.A. 43°23N 88°36W 78 E5
Hustle Va., U.S.A. 38°3N 77°4W 93 B3
Hustonville Ky., U.S.A. 37°28N 84°49W 105 C8
Husum Wash., U.S.A. 45°48N 121°29W 120 E4
Hutch Mt. Ariz., U.S.A. 34°47N 111°22W 130 C4
Hutchins Tex., U.S.A. 32°38N 96°42W 116 C5
Hutchinson Kans., U.S.A. 38°5N 97°56W 82 C6
Hutchinson Minn., U.S.A. 44°54N 94°22W 77 F4
Hutchinson County ☆ S. Dak., U.S.A. 43°25N 97°48W 76 G8
Hutchinson County ☆ Tex., U.S.A. 35°50N 101°30W 108 B6
Hutsonville Ill., U.S.A. 39°7N 87°40W 84 D6
Hutte Sauvage, L. de la Qué., Canada 56°15N 64°45W 143 B5
Huttig Ark., U.S.A. 33°2N 92°11W 106 E3
Hutto Tex., U.S.A. 30°33N 97°33W 109 G10
Hutton Md., U.S.A. 39°25N 79°28W 93 A1
Huttonsville W. Va., U.S.A. 38°43N 79°59W 102 C5
Huxford Ala., U.S.A. 31°13N 87°28W 112 E3
Huxley Iowa, U.S.A. 41°54N 93°36W 81 D5
Huyett Md., U.S.A. 39°40N 77°20W 93 A3
Hyak Wash., U.S.A. 47°24N 121°24W 120 C4
Hyannis Mass., U.S.A. 41°39N 70°17W 91 C4
Hyannis Nebr., U.S.A. 42°0N 101°46W 80 C4
Hyas Sask., Canada 51°54N 102°16W 151 D9
Hyattsville Md., U.S.A. 38°57N 76°57W 99 B4
Hyattville Wyo., U.S.A. 44°15N 107°36W 124 B5
Hybart Ala., U.S.A. 31°50N 87°23W 112 E3
Hyco L. N.C., U.S.A. 36°31N 79°3W 103 B6
Hydaburg Alaska, U.S.A. 55°15N 132°50W 135 J14
Hyde County ☆ N.C., U.S.A. 35°30N 76°20W 103 C9
Hyde County ☆ S. Dak., U.S.A. 44°31N 99°27W 76 F6
Hyde Park Ill., U.S.A. 41°47N 87°35W 95 C3
Hyde Park Mass., U.S.A. 42°15N 71°7W 96 B2
Hyde Park N.Y., U.S.A. 41°47N 73°56W 88 D7
Hyde Park Vt., U.S.A. 44°36N 72°37W 89 B2
Hyden Ky., U.S.A. 37°10N 83°22W 105 C9
Hydes Md., U.S.A. 39°30N 76°29W 93 A4
Hydro Okla., U.S.A. 35°33N 98°39W 107 C5
Hygiene Colo., U.S.A. 40°11N 105°11W 125 B5
Hyland → Canada 59°52N 128°12W 157 E7
Hymera Ind., U.S.A. 39°11N 87°18W 85 D3
Hymers Ont., Canada 48°18N 89°43W 148 D7
Hyndman Pa., U.S.A. 39°49N 78°43W 93 A2
Hyndman Peak Idaho, U.S.A. 43°45N 114°8W 122 F4
Hyrum Utah, U.S.A. 41°38N 111°51W 129 B4
Hysham Mont., U.S.A. 46°18N 107°14W 123 D10
Hythe Alta., Canada 55°20N 119°33W 152 C1

I

Iaeger W. Va., U.S.A. 37°28N 81°49W 102 D3
Iamonia L. Fla., U.S.A. 30°38N 84°14W 114 A4
Ian Calder L. Nunavut, Canada 66°28N 97°22W 159 D6
Ian L. B.C., Canada 53°50N 132°45W 154 B2
Iatan Mo., U.S.A. 39°29N 94°59W 83 B2
Iatt L., U.S.A. 31°35N 92°40W 110 C3
Ibapah Utah, U.S.A. 40°2N 113°59W 129 C2
Ibapah Pk. Utah, U.S.A. 40°2N 113°53W 129 C2
Ibarra Guanajuato, Mexico 21°29N 101°33W 174 A6
Iberia Mo., U.S.A. 38°5N 92°18W 83 C4
Iberia Parish ☆ La., U.S.A. 30°1N 91°49W 110 D4
Iberville Qué., Canada 45°19N 73°17W 145 F9
Iberville, Lac d' Qué., Canada 55°55N 73°15W 143 B3
Iberville, Mt. d' Nfld. & L., Canada 58°50N 63°50W 143 B5
Iberville Parish ☆ La., U.S.A. 30°17N 91°14W 110 D4
Icard N.C., U.S.A. 35°44N 81°28W 103 C4
Ice Harbor Dam Wash., U.S.A. 46°15N 118°53W 120 D7
Icy C. Alaska, U.S.A. 70°20N 161°52W 135 A7
Ida La., U.S.A. 41°55N 83°34W 79 H8
Ida County ☆ Iowa, U.S.A. 42°25N 95°30W 81 C3
Ida Grove Iowa, U.S.A. 42°21N 95°28W 81 C3
Idabel Okla., U.S.A. 33°54N 94°50W 107 E9
Idaho □ U.S.A. 45°0N 115°0W 122 E4
Idaho City Idaho, U.S.A. 43°50N 115°50W 122 F3
Idaho County ☆ Idaho, U.S.A. 45°35N 115°30W 122 D3
Idaho Falls Idaho, U.S.A. 43°30N 112°2W 122 F6
Idaho Nat. Engineering Laboratory Idaho, U.S.A. 43°38N 112°45W 122 F6
Idaho Springs Colo., U.S.A. 39°45N 105°31W 125 C5
Idalia Colo., U.S.A. 39°42N 102°18W 125 C8
Idalou Tex., U.S.A. 33°40N 101°41W 108 D6
Idana Kans., U.S.A. 39°22N 97°16W 82 B6
Idanha Oreg., U.S.A. 44°42N 122°5W 121 C3
Ideal Ga., U.S.A. 32°22N 84°11W 113 D2
Ideal S. Dak., U.S.A. 43°33N 99°54W 76 G6
Ider Ala., U.S.A. 34°43N 85°41W 112 B5

Ídolo, I. del *Veracruz, Mexico* 21°25N 97°27W **176 C3**
Idria *Calif., U.S.A.* 36°25N 120°41W **127 G6**
Igiugig *Alaska, U.S.A.* 59°20N 155°55W **135 G9**
Igloolik *Nunavut, Canada* 69°20N 81°49W **158 D9**
Igluligaarjuk = Chesterfield Inlet *Nunavut, Canada* 63°30N 90°45W **159 E7**
Iglulik = Igloolik *Nunavut, Canada* 69°20N 81°49W **158 D9**
Ignace *Ont., Canada* 49°30N 91°40W **148 C1**
Ignacio *Colo., U.S.A.* 37°7N 107°38W **125 E3**
Ignacio Allende *Durango, Mexico* 24°28N 104°0W **173 C7**
Ignacio Allende *Tabasco, Mexico* 18°21N 92°51W **178 A4**
Ignacio Allende *Zacatecas, Mexico* 21°30N 103°24W **173 F7**
Ignacio de la Llave *Veracruz, Mexico* 18°43N 95°59W **177 F5**
Ignacio Ramírez *Sonora, Mexico* 28°43N 111°20W **168 E4**
Ignacio Zaragoza *Chiapas, Mexico* 16°1N 92°35W **178 C4**
Ignacio Zaragoza *Chiapas, Mexico* 16°35N 93°21W **178 C3**
Ignacio Zaragoza *Chihuahua, Mexico* 29°40N 107°43W **169 D8**
Ignacio Zaragoza *Chihuahua, Mexico* 30°12N 108°18W **169 D7**
Ignacio Zaragoza *Coahuila, Mexico* 25°21N 103°9W **171 E1**
Ignacio Zaragoza *Sonora, Mexico* 32°18N 114°12W **168 A1**
Ignacio Zaragoza *Tamaulipas, Mexico* 23°12N 98°46W **175 D6**
Igornachoix Bay *Nfld. & L., Canada* 50°40N 57°25W **142 B3**
Iguala *Guerrero, Mexico* 18°21N 99°32W **175 D8**
Igualapa *Guerrero, Mexico* 16°44N 98°36W **175 F9**
Ihlen *Minn., U.S.A.* 43°55N 96°22W **77 G2**
Ikalukutiiak *Nunavut, Canada* 69°10N 105°0W **158 D4**
Ikparjuk = Arctic Bay *Nunavut, Canada* 73°1N 85°7W **158 C8**
Île-à-la-Crosse *Sask., Canada* 55°27N 107°53W **157 E11**
Île-à-la-Crosse, Lac *Sask., Canada* 55°40N 107°45W **157 E11**
Île-Anticosti Réserve Faunique de l' △ *Qué., Canada* 49°30N 62°50W **140 D7**
Île-Perrot *Qué., Canada* 45°22N 73°57W **160 B1**
Îles, L. des *Qué., Canada* 46°20N 75°18W **144 C7**
Ilfeld *N. Mex., U.S.A.* 35°25N 105°34W **131 B5**
Iliamna *Alaska, U.S.A.* 59°45N 154°55W **135 G9**
Iliamna L. *Alaska, U.S.A.* 59°30N 155°0W **135 G9**
Iliff *Colo., U.S.A.* 40°45N 103°4W **125 E7**
Ilio Pt. *Hawai'i, U.S.A.* 21°13N 157°16W **136 K4**
Ilion *N.Y., U.S.A.* 43°1N 75°2W **88 B5**
Illescas *San Luis Potosí, Mexico* 23°13N 102°7W **171 G2**
Illinois □ *U.S.A.* 40°15N 89°30W **84 C4**
Illinois → *Ill., U.S.A.* 38°58N 90°28W **84 E3**
Illinois → *Okla., U.S.A.* 35°30N 95°9W **107 C8**
Illinois → *Oreg., U.S.A.* 42°33N 124°3W **121 E1**
Illinois at Chicago, University of *Ill., U.S.A.* 41°52N 87°38W **95 B3**
Illinois Institute of Technology *Ill., U.S.A.* 41°50N 87°37W **95 B3**
Illinois Peak *U.S.A.* 47°2N 115°4W **123 C2**
Illiopolis *Ill., U.S.A.* 39°51N 89°15W **84 D4**
Illukotat → *Qué., Canada* 60°48N 78°11W **143 A2**
Illulissat *Greenland* 69°12N 51°10W **162 D5**
Ilwaco *Wash., U.S.A.* 46°19N 124°3W **120 D1**
Imala *Sinaloa, Mexico* 24°53N 107°13W **172 C3**
Imbler *Oreg., U.S.A.* 45°28N 117°58W **121 B8**
Imboden *Ark., U.S.A.* 36°12N 91°11W **106 B4**
Imlay *Nev., U.S.A.* 40°40N 118°9W **128 B2**
Imlay City *Mich., U.S.A.* 43°2N 83°5W **79 F8**
Immokalee *Fla., U.S.A.* 26°25N 81°25W **114 E7**
Imnaha *Oreg., U.S.A.* 45°34N 116°50W **121 B9**
Imnaha → *Oreg., U.S.A.* 45°49N 116°46W **121 B9**
Imogene *Iowa, U.S.A.* 40°53N 95°29W **81 E3**
Imperial *Sask., Canada* 51°21N 105°28W **150 D6**
Imperial *Calif., U.S.A.* 32°51N 115°34W **127 L11**
Imperial *Nebr., U.S.A.* 40°31N 101°39W **80 D4**
Imperial, Pt. *Ariz., U.S.A.* 36°15N 111°57W **130 A4**
Imperial Beach *Calif., U.S.A.* 32°35N 117°6W **133 C2**
Imperial County ☆ *Calif., U.S.A.* 33°0N 115°20W **127 K11**
Imperial Dam *Ariz., U.S.A.* 32°55N 114°25W **130 E1**
Imperial Res. *Ariz., U.S.A.* 32°53N 114°28W **130 E1**
Imperial Valley *Calif., U.S.A.* 33°0N 115°30W **127 L11**
Imuris *Sonora, Mexico* 30°47N 110°52W **168 C5**
Ina, L. *U.S.A.* 38°9N 88°54W **84 E5**
Inarajan *Guam* 13°16N 144°45E **184 b**
Inchelium *Wash., U.S.A.* 48°18N 118°12W **120 B7**
Incline Village *Nev., U.S.A.* 39°10N 119°58W **128 C1**
Indé *Durango, Mexico* 25°54N 105°13W **172 B5**
Independence *Calif., U.S.A.* 36°48N 118°12W **127 G8**
Independence *Iowa, U.S.A.* 42°28N 91°54W **81 C7**
Independence *Kans., U.S.A.* 37°14N 95°42W **82 D8**
Independence *Ky., U.S.A.* 38°57N 84°33W **105 B8**
Independence *Miss., U.S.A.* 34°42N 89°49W **111 B4**
Independence *Mo., U.S.A.* 39°6N 94°25W **83 B2**
Independence *Ohio, U.S.A.* 41°22N 81°38W **98 B2**
Independence *Va., U.S.A.* 44°51N 123°11W **121 C2**
Independence *Va., U.S.A.* 36°37N 81°9W **102 E3**
Independence *Wis., U.S.A.* 44°22N 91°25W **78 D2**
Independence County ☆ *Ark., U.S.A.* 35°46N 91°39W **106 C4**
Independence Cr. → *Tex., U.S.A.* 30°27N 101°44W **108 G6**
Independence Fjord *Greenland* 82°10N 29°0W **162 A8**
Independence Mts. *Nev., U.S.A.* 41°20N 116°0W **128 A4**
Independence Pass *Colo., U.S.A.* 39°7N 106°33W **125 C4**
Independencia y Libertad *Durango, Mexico* 24°2N 104°19W **173 C6**
Index *Wash., U.S.A.* 47°50N 121°33W **120 C4**
Indiahoma *Okla., U.S.A.* 34°37N 98°45W **107 D5**
Indialantic *Fla., U.S.A.* 28°6N 80°34W **114 D8**
Indian → *Fla., U.S.A.* 27°59N 80°34W **114 D8**
Indian → *N.Y., U.S.A.* 44°39N 103°19W **76 F2**
Indian Cr. → *S. Dak., U.S.A.* 44°39N 103°19W **76 F2**
Indian Cr. → *Tenn., U.S.A.* 35°23N 88°9W **104 E4**
Indian Creek Village *Fla., U.S.A.* 25°52N 80°8W **115 C3**
Indian Harbour *Nfld. & L., Canada* 54°27N 57°13W **143 C6**
Indian Harbour Beach *Fla., U.S.A.* 28°10N 80°35W **114 D8**
Indian Head *Sask., Canada* 50°30N 103°41W **150 D8**
Indian Head *Md., U.S.A.* 38°38N 77°12W **93 B3**
Indian Heights *Ind., U.S.A.* 40°26N 86°10W **85 C4**
Indian L. *Mich., U.S.A.* 45°59N 86°20W **79 C4**
Indian L. *Ohio, U.S.A.* 40°30N 83°53W **86 C3**
Indian Lake *N.Y., U.S.A.* 43°47N 74°16W **88 B6**
Indian Mills → *N.Y., U.S.A.* 39°48N 74°46W **92 C2**
Indian Mounds Park *Minn., U.S.A.* 44°56N 93°3W **94 B3**
Indian Peak *Utah, U.S.A.* 38°16N 113°53W **129 F2**
Indian Peak Range = Needle Range *Utah, U.S.A.* 38°25N 113°55W **129 E2**
Indian River *Mich., U.S.A.* 45°25N 84°37W **79 D7**
Indian River Bay *Del., U.S.A.* 38°36N 75°4W **93 B5**
Indian River County ☆ *Fla., U.S.A.* 27°40N 80°45W **114 D8**
Indian River Shores *Fla., U.S.A.* 27°43N 80°23W **114 D8**
Indian Rock *Wash., U.S.A.* 45°59N 120°49W **120 E5**
Indian Rocks Beach *Fla., U.S.A.* 27°51N 82°50W **115 B1**
Indian Shores *Tampa, U.S.A.* 27°51N 82°50W **115 B1**
Indian Springs *Nev., U.S.A.* 36°35N 115°40W **128 F5**
Indian Township Indian Reservation *Maine, U.S.A.* 45°18N 67°30W **90 C6**

Indian Trail *N.C., U.S.A.* 35°5N 80°40W **103 C5**
Indian Valley *Idaho, U.S.A.* 44°33N 116°26W **122 E2**
Indian Valley Res. *Calif., U.S.A.* 39°5N 122°32W **126 D4**
Indian Village *Kans., U.S.A.* 37°5N 95°38W **82 D8**
Indiana → *Pa., U.S.A.* 40°37N 79°9W **87 D3**
Indiana □ *U.S.A.* 40°0N 86°0W **85 C5**
Indiana County ☆ *Pa., U.S.A.* 40°45N 79°0W **87 D3**
Indiana Dunes Nat. Lakeshore △ *Ind., U.S.A.* 41°40N 87°0W **85 B3**
Indiana Motor Speedway *Ind., U.S.A.* 39°48N 86°14W **85 D4**
Indianapolis *Ind., U.S.A.* 39°46N 86°9W **85 D4**
Indianapolis Int. ✈ (IND) *Ind., U.S.A.* 39°43N 86°17W **85 D4**
Indianola *Iowa, U.S.A.* 33°27N 90°39W **111 C3**
Indianola *Miss., U.S.A.* 33°27N 90°39W **111 C3**
Indianola *Nebr., U.S.A.* 40°14N 100°25W **80 D5**
Indianola *Okla., U.S.A.* 35°10N 95°46W **107 C8**
Indianola *Wash., U.S.A.* 47°44N 122°31W **132 B2**
Indiantown *Fla., U.S.A.* 27°1N 80°28W **114 D8**
Industry *Ill., U.S.A.* 40°20N 90°36W **84 C3**
Industry *Kans., U.S.A.* 39°8N 97°10W **82 B6**
Industry *Tex., U.S.A.* 29°58N 96°30W **109 H11**
Inez *Ky., U.S.A.* 37°52N 82°32W **105 C10**
Inferior, L. *Oaxaca, Mexico* 16°20N 94°40W **177 H6**
Infiernillo, Presa del *Michoacan, Mexico* 18°35N 101°50W **174 D6**
Ingalls *Ark., U.S.A.* 33°23N 92°9W **106 E3**
Ingalls *Mo., U.S.A.* 37°50N 100°27W **82 D3**
Ingersoll *Ont., Canada* 43°4N 80°55W **146 D6**
Ingham County ☆ *Mich., U.S.A.* 42°35N 84°30W **79 F7**
Inglefield Land *Greenland* 78°30N 70°0W **162 B4**
Ingleside *Md., U.S.A.* 39°6N 75°53W **93 A5**
Ingleside *Tex., U.S.A.* 27°53N 97°13W **109 K10**
Inglewood *Calif., U.S.A.* 33°58N 118°21W **133 C3**
Inglewood *Nebr., U.S.A.* 41°25N 96°30W **80 C9**
Inglis *Fla., U.S.A.* 29°2N 82°40W **114 B6**
Ingolf Fjord *Greenland* 80°35N 17°30W **162 A9**
Ingomar *N.S., Canada* 43°34N 65°22W **141 A4**
Ingomar *Mont., U.S.A.* 46°35N 107°23W **123 D10**
Ingonish *N.S., Canada* 46°42N 60°18W **141 G9**
Ingonish Beach *N.S., Canada* 46°38N 60°25W **141 G9**
Ingram *Pa., U.S.A.* 40°26N 80°4W **98 B1**
Ingram *Tex., U.S.A.* 30°5N 99°14W **109 G8**
Ingram *Wis., U.S.A.* 45°31N 90°49W **78 C3**
Inkerman *N.B., Canada* 47°40N 64°49W **141 F5**
Inklin → *N. Amer.* 58°50N 133°10W **157 E6**
Inkom *Idaho, U.S.A.* 42°48N 112°15W **122 G6**
Inkster *N. Dak., U.S.A.* 48°9N 97°39W **76 B8**
Inland *Ala., U.S.A.* 33°50N 86°30W **112 C4**
Inlet *N.Y., U.S.A.* 43°45N 74°48W **88 B6**
Inman *Kans., U.S.A.* 38°14N 97°47W **82 C6**
Inman *Nebr., U.S.A.* 42°23N 98°32W **80 B7**
Inman *S.C., U.S.A.* 35°3N 82°5W **103 C3**
Innerkip *Ont., Canada* 43°13N 80°42W **146 D6**
Innetalling I. *N.W.T., Canada* 56°0N 79°0W **143 B2**
Innisfail *Alta., Canada* 52°2N 113°57W **152 C6**
Innisfree *Alta., Canada* 53°22N 111°32W **152 E9**
Innoko Nat. Wildlife Refuge △ *Alaska, U.S.A.* 63°20N 158°25W **135 E8**
Inola *Okla., U.S.A.* 36°9N 95°31W **107 B8**
Inoucdjouac = Inukjuak *Qué., Canada* 58°25N 78°15W **143 B2**
Insurgente J. M. Morelos y Pavón, Parque Nacional △ *Michoacan, Mexico* 19°36N 100°57W **175 D7**
Intata Reach *B.C., Canada* 53°38N 125°30W **154 B9**
Intercession City *Fla., U.S.A.* 28°16N 81°31W **114 C7**
Interior *S. Dak., U.S.A.* 43°44N 101°59W **76 G4**
Interlachen *Fla., U.S.A.* 29°37N 81°53W **114 B7**
Interlaken *N.Y., U.S.A.* 42°37N 76°44W **88 C4**
International Falls *Minn., U.S.A.* 48°36N 93°25W **77 B5**
International Peace Garden *N. Dak., U.S.A.* 49°0N 100°4W **76 B5**
Intervale *N.H., U.S.A.* 44°6N 71°8W **89 B3**
Intracoastal City *La., U.S.A.* 29°47N 92°9W **110 E3**
Inukjuak *Qué., Canada* 58°25N 78°15W **143 B2**
Inuvik *N.W.T., Canada* 68°16N 133°40W **156 C6**
Inver Grove Heights *Minn., U.S.A.* 44°51N 93°1W **77 F3**
Invermay *Sask., Canada* 51°48N 103°9W **150 D8**
Invermere *B.C., Canada* 50°30N 116°2W **153 H4**
Inverness *N.S., Canada* 46°15N 61°19W **141 G8**
Inverness *Ala., U.S.A.* 32°1N 85°45W **112 D5**
Inverness *Baltimore, U.S.A.* 39°15N 76°29W **99 B3**
Inverness *Calif., U.S.A.* 38°6N 122°51W **126 E4**
Inverness *Fla., U.S.A.* 28°50N 82°20W **114 C6**
Inverness *Miss., U.S.A.* 33°21N 90°35W **111 C3**
Inwood *Man., Canada* 50°30N 97°30W **151 E14**
Inwood *Iowa, U.S.A.* 43°19N 96°26W **81 C1**
Inwood *N.Y., U.S.A.* 40°37N 73°44W **97 C4**
Inwood *W. Va., U.S.A.* 39°21N 78°2W **93 A2**
Inyan Kara Mt. *Wyo., U.S.A.* 44°13N 104°21W **124 B8**
Inyo County ☆ *Calif., U.S.A.* 36°30N 117°40W **127 G9**
Inyo Mts. *Calif., U.S.A.* 36°40N 118°0W **127 G8**
Inyo Nat. Forest *U.S.A.* 37°30N 118°15W **127 F8**
Inyokern *Calif., U.S.A.* 35°39N 117°49W **127 H9**
Iola *Ill., U.S.A.* 38°50N 88°38W **84 E5**
Iola *Kans., U.S.A.* 37°55N 95°24W **82 D8**
Iola *Wis., U.S.A.* 44°30N 89°8W **78 D4**
Iolani Palace *Hawai'i, U.S.A.* 21°18N 157°51W **136 K14**
Iona *N.S., Canada* 45°58N 60°48W **141 H9**
Iona *Idaho, U.S.A.* 43°32N 111°56W **122 F7**
Iona *Minn., U.S.A.* 43°55N 95°47W **77 G3**
Iona I. *B.C., Canada* 43°33N 99°26W **76 G6**
Iona Beach Regional Park *B.C., Canada* 49°13N 123°12W **161 B1**
Iona I. *B.C., Canada* 49°13N 123°12W **161 B1**
Ione *Calif., U.S.A.* 38°21N 120°56W **126 E6**
Ione *Oreg., U.S.A.* 45°30N 119°50W **121 B6**
Ione *Wash., U.S.A.* 48°45N 117°25W **120 B8**
Ionia *Kans., U.S.A.* 39°40N 98°21W **82 B5**
Ionia *Mich., U.S.A.* 42°59N 85°4W **79 G6**
Ionia *Mo., U.S.A.* 38°30N 93°19W **83 C3**
Ionia County ☆ *Mich., U.S.A.* 42°55N 85°5W **79 G6**
Iosco County ☆ *Mich., U.S.A.* 44°20N 83°40W **79 E8**
Iota *La., U.S.A.* 30°20N 92°30W **110 D3**
Iowa *La., U.S.A.* 30°14N 93°1W **110 D2**
Iowa □ *U.S.A.* 42°18N 93°30W **81 C5**
Iowa → *Iowa, U.S.A.* 41°10N 91°1W **81 D7**
Iowa City *Iowa, U.S.A.* 41°40N 91°32W **81 D7**
Iowa County ☆ *Iowa, U.S.A.* 41°40N 92°0W **81 D6**
Iowa County ☆ *Wis., U.S.A.* 43°0N 90°10W **78 F3**
Iowa Falls *Iowa, U.S.A.* 42°31N 93°16W **81 C5**
Iowa Indian Reservation *U.S.A.* 39°59N 95°21W **82 B8**
Iowa Park *Tex., U.S.A.* 33°57N 98°40W **109 D9**
Ipava *Ill., U.S.A.* 40°21N 90°19W **84 C3**
Ipswich *Mass., U.S.A.* 42°41N 70°50W **91 B4**
Ipswich *S. Dak., U.S.A.* 45°27N 99°2W **76 E6**

Ipswich B. *Mass., U.S.A.* 42°41N 70°42W **91 B4**
Iqaluit *Nunavut, Canada* 63°44N 68°31W **159 E12**
Ira *Tex., U.S.A.* 32°35N 101°0W **108 E6**
Iraan *Tex., U.S.A.* 30°55N 101°54W **108 G6**
Irapuato *Guanajuato, Mexico* 20°41N 101°28W **175 B6**
Irasburg *Vt., U.S.A.* 44°48N 73°47W **89 B1**
Iredell *Tex., U.S.A.* 31°59N 97°52W **109 F10**
Iredell County ☆ *N.C., U.S.A.* 35°45N 80°50W **103 C5**
Irene *S. Dak., U.S.A.* 43°5N 97°9W **76 G8**
Ireton *Iowa, U.S.A.* 42°58N 96°19W **81 C2**
Irimbo *Michoacan, Mexico* 19°43N 100°29W **175 C7**
Irion County ☆ *Tex., U.S.A.* 31°15N 101°0W **108 F7**
Iriona *Honduras* 15°57N 85°11W **182 C2**
Irish, Mt. *Nev., U.S.A.* 37°39N 115°24W **128 E5**
Irma *Alta., Canada* 52°55N 111°14W **153 F9**
Irma, L. *Fla., U.S.A.* 28°35N 81°16W **115 A4**
Irmo *S.C., U.S.A.* 34°5N 81°11W **103 D4**
Iron Belt *Wis., U.S.A.* 46°24N 90°19W **78 B3**
Iron Bridge *Ont., Canada* 46°17N 83°14W **146 A3**
Iron City *Ga., U.S.A.* 31°1N 84°49W **113 E2**
Iron City *Tenn., U.S.A.* 35°1N 87°35W **104 E5**
Iron County ☆ *Mich., U.S.A.* 46°15N 88°35W **79 C3**
Iron County ☆ *Mo., U.S.A.* 37°30N 90°40W **83 D6**
Iron County ☆ *Utah, U.S.A.* 37°50N 113°20W **129 F2**
Iron County ☆ *Wis., U.S.A.* 46°15N 90°15W **78 B3**
Iron Junction *Minn., U.S.A.* 47°25N 92°36W **77 C6**
Iron Mountain *Mich., U.S.A.* 45°49N 88°4W **79 D3**
Iron Mountain *Mo., U.S.A.* 37°37N 90°40W **83 D6**
Iron Mountain *Utah, U.S.A.* 37°37N 113°23W **129 F2**
Iron Mountain *Wyo., U.S.A.* 41°33N 105°13W **124 E7**
Iron Mts. *Va., U.S.A.* 36°40N 81°45W **103 B4**
Iron Ridge *Wis., U.S.A.* 43°24N 88°32W **78 E5**
Iron River *Mich., U.S.A.* 46°6N 88°39W **79 C31**
Iron River *Wis., U.S.A.* 46°34N 91°24W **78 B2**
Iron Springs *Alta., Canada* 49°56N 112°41W **153 J8**
Irondale *Ala., U.S.A.* 33°32N 86°42W **112 C4**
Irondale *Mo., U.S.A.* 37°50N 90°41W **83 D6**
Irondale *Ohio, U.S.A.* 40°34N 80°44W **86 C6**
Irondequoit *N.Y., U.S.A.* 43°13N 77°35W **88 B3**
Ironside *Ont., Canada* 45°28N 75°44W **160 A1**
Ironside *Oreg., U.S.A.* 44°19N 117°57W **121 C8**
Ironsides *Md., U.S.A.* 38°30N 77°12W **93 B3**
Ironton *Minn., U.S.A.* 46°28N 93°59W **77 D5**
Ironton *Mo., U.S.A.* 37°36N 90°38W **83 D61**
Ironton *Ohio, U.S.A.* 38°32N 82°41W **86 E4**
Ironwood *Mich., U.S.A.* 46°27N 90°9W **79 C1**
Ironwood Forest Nat. Monument △ *U.S.A.* 32°32N 111°28W **130 E4**
Iroquois *Ont., Canada* 44°51N 75°19W **147 C11**
Iroquois *Ill., U.S.A.* 40°50N 87°35W **84 C6**
Iroquois *S. Dak., U.S.A.* 44°22N 97°51W **76 F8**
Iroquois → *N.W.T., Canada* 68°5N 129°26W **156 C7**
Iroquois → *Ill., U.S.A.* 41°5N 87°49W **85 B3**
Iroquois County ☆ *Ill., U.S.A.* 40°45N 87°50W **84 C6**
Iroquois Falls *Ont., Canada* 48°46N 80°41W **144 C2**
Iroquois Nat. Wildlife Refuge △ *N.Y., U.S.A.* 43°7N 78°21W **88 B2**
Iroquois Point *Hawai'i, U.S.A.* 21°19N 157°58W **136 K14**
Irricana *Alta., Canada* 51°19N 113°37W **153 G7**
Irrigon *Oreg., U.S.A.* 45°54N 119°30W **121 B6**
Irvine *Ky., U.S.A.* 37°42N 83°58W **105 C9**
Irvine *Calif., U.S.A.* 33°41N 117°46W **127 K9**
Irving *Ill., U.S.A.* 39°12N 89°24W **84 D4**
Irving *Tex., U.S.A.* 32°48N 96°56W **116 B4**
Irving Park *Ill., U.S.A.* 41°57N 87°42W **95 B2**
Irvington *Ill., U.S.A.* 38°26N 89°10W **84 E4**
Irvington *N.Y., U.S.A.* 40°43N 74°14W **97 B1**
Irvington *N.J., U.S.A.* 40°43N 74°14W **97 B1**
Irvona *Pa., U.S.A.* 40°46N 78°33W **87 D4**
Irwin *Iowa, U.S.A.* 41°47N 95°12W **81 D3**
Irwin County ☆ *Ga., U.S.A.* 31°40N 83°15W **113 E3**
Irwinton *Ga., U.S.A.* 32°49N 83°10W **113 D3**
Irwinville *Ga., U.S.A.* 31°39N 83°23W **113 E3**
Isabel *Kans., U.S.A.* 37°28N 98°33W **82 D5**
Isabel *S. Dak., U.S.A.* 45°24N 101°26W **76 E4**
Isabel, I. *Nayarit, Mexico* 21°51N 105°55W **172 F5**
Isabel Segunda *Puerto Rico* 18°9N 65°27W **184 G17**
Isabela *Puerto Rico* 18°30N 67°2W **184 G15**
Isabelia, Cord. *Nic.* 13°30N 85°25W **182 D2**
Isabella County ☆ *Mich., U.S.A.* 43°40N 84°50W **79 F7**
Isabella Indian Reservation *Mich., U.S.A.* 43°36N 84°42W **79 F7**
Isabella L. *Calif., U.S.A.* 35°39N 118°28W **127 H8**
Isabelle, Pt. *Mich., U.S.A.* 47°21N 87°56W **79 B4**
Isachsen, C. *Nunavut, Canada* 79°20N 105°28W **158 B4**
Isanti *Minn., U.S.A.* 45°29N 93°15W **77 E5**
Isanti County ☆ *Minn., U.S.A.* 45°30N 93°15W **77 E5**
Ishpeming *Mich., U.S.A.* 46°29N 87°40W **79 C4**
Iskut → *B.C., Canada* 56°45N 131°49W **157 E6**
Isla *Veracruz, Mexico* 18°4N 95°33W **177 F5**
Isla Aguada *Campeche, Mexico* 18°47N 91°28W **179 D2**
Isla Ángel de la Guarda, Parque Natural △ *Baja California, Mexico* 29°30N 113°30W **166 D5**
Isla Coiba, Parque Nac. △ *Panama* 7°33N 81°36W **182 E4**
Isla de Arena *Campeche, Mexico* 20°42N 90°26W **179 D3**
Isla Isabel, Parque Nacional △ *Nayarit, Mexico* 21°54N 105°58W **172 F5**
Isla la Peña *Nayarit, Mexico* 21°33N 105°16W **172 F5**
Isla Vista *Calif., U.S.A.* 34°25N 119°53W **127 J7**
Islamorada *Fla., U.S.A.* 24°56N 80°37W **114 G8**
Island Beach *N.J., U.S.A.* 39°50N 74°5W **92 C2**
Island Beach State Park △ *N.J., U.S.A.* 39°51N 74°6W **92 C2**
Island Channel *N.Y., U.S.A.* 40°36N 73°53W **97 C3**
Island City *Oreg., U.S.A.* 45°20N 118°3W **121 B7**
Island County ☆ *Wash., U.S.A.* 48°10N 122°35W **120 B3**
Island Creek *Md., U.S.A.* 38°37N 76°35W **93 B4**
Island Falls *Ont., Canada* 49°35N 81°20W **144 B1**
Island Falls *Maine, U.S.A.* 46°1N 68°16W **90 B5**
Island Heights *N.J., U.S.A.* 39°57N 74°9W **92 C2**
Island L. *Man., Canada* 53°47N 94°25W **159 G7**
Island Lake *Minn., U.S.A.* 54°51N 113°33W **152 D7**
Island Lake Res. *Minn., U.S.A.* 47°48N 94°19W **77 C4**
Island Lake Res. *Minn., U.S.A.* 47°0N 92°14W **77 C6**
Island Park *Idaho, U.S.A.* 44°24N 111°19W **122 F7**
Island Park *Idaho, U.S.A.* 44°36N 73°39W **97 C3**
Island Park Res. *Idaho, U.S.A.* 44°25N 111°24W **122 F7**
Island Pond *Nfld. & L., Canada* 48°25N 56°6W **142 C2**
Island Pond *Vt., U.S.A.* 44°49N 71°53W **89 B3**
Islands, B. of *Nfld. & L., Canada* 49°11N 58°15W **142 C2**
Islay *Alta., Canada* 53°24N 110°33W **152 E10**
Isle *Minn., U.S.A.* 46°8N 93°28W **77 D5**
Isle aux Morts *Nfld. & L., Canada* 47°35N 59°0W **142 C2**
Isle La Motte *Vt., U.S.A.* 44°52N 73°18W **89 B1**
Isle of Hope *Ga., U.S.A.* 31°58N 81°5W **113 E5**

Isle of Palms *S.C., U.S.A.* 32°47N 79°48W **103 F6**
Isle of Wight *Va., U.S.A.* 36°54N 76°43W **102 E8**
Isle of Wight Bay *Md., U.S.A.* 38°22N 75°6W **93 B5**
Isle of Wight County ☆ *Va., U.S.A.* 36°54N 76°43W **102 E8**
Isle Pierre *B.C., Canada* 53°57N 123°16W **154 B11**
Isle Royale Nat. Park △ *Mich., U.S.A.* 48°0N 88°55W **79 A31**
Isles, L. des *Ont., Canada* 49°10N 89°44W **148 C7**
Islesboro I. *Maine, U.S.A.* 44°19N 68°54W **90 D5**
Isleta Indian Reservation *N. Mex., U.S.A.* 34°55N 106°45W **131 C4**
Isleton *Calif., U.S.A.* 38°10N 121°37W **126 E5**
Islington *Ont., Canada* 43°38N 79°30W **161 C5**
Ismay *Mont., U.S.A.* 46°30N 104°48W **123 D13**
Isola *Miss., U.S.A.* 33°16N 90°35W **111 C3**
Israel → *N.H., U.S.A.* 44°29N 71°35W **89 B3**
Issaquah *Wash., U.S.A.* 47°32N 122°2W **120 C3**
Issaquena County ☆ *Miss., U.S.A.* 32°54N 91°3W **111 C2**
Issoudun *Qué., Canada* 46°35N 71°38W **145 E11**
Issue *U.S.A.* 38°16N 76°53W **93 B4**
Istanbul *N. Mt. Alaska, U.S.A.* 69°12N 143°48W **135 B12**
Istokpoga, L. *Fla., U.S.A.* 27°23N 81°17W **114 D7**
Italy *Tex., U.S.A.* 32°10N 97°9W **109 E10**
Itasca *Tex., U.S.A.* 32°10N 97°9W **109 E10**
Itasca, L. *Minn., U.S.A.* 47°13N 95°12W **77 C3**
Itasca County ☆ *Minn., U.S.A.* 47°25N 93°25W **77 C5**
Itasca State Park *Minn., U.S.A.* 47°12N 95°12W **77 C3**
Itawamba County ☆ *Miss., U.S.A.* 34°16N 88°25W **111 B5**
Itcha Ilgachuz Park △ *B.C., Canada* 52°42N 124°58W **154 C10**
Itchen L. *N.W.T., Canada* 65°35N 112°25W **157 C10**
Ithaca *Mich., U.S.A.* 43°18N 84°36W **79 F7**
Ithaca *N.Y., U.S.A.* 42°27N 76°30W **88 C4**
Ithaca *Nebr., U.S.A.* 41°10N 96°33W **80 C9**
Itkilik → *Alaska, U.S.A.* 70°9N 150°56W **135 A10**
Itomamo, L. *Qué., Canada* 49°11N 70°28W **145 B12**
Itta Bena *Miss., U.S.A.* 33°30N 90°20W **111 C3**
Ittoqqortoormiit *Greenland* 70°20N 23°0W **162 C8**
Ituna *Sask., Canada* 51°10N 103°24W **150 D8**
Iturbide *Campeche, Mexico* 19°40N 89°37W **179 C4**
Iturbide *Nuevo León, Mexico* 24°44N 99°54W **171 F5**
Itxlahuacán del Río *Jalisco, Mexico* 20°52N 103°18W **174 B4**
Iuka *Kans., U.S.A.* 37°44N 98°44W **82 D5**
Iuka *Miss., U.S.A.* 34°49N 88°12W **111 B5**
Iuka *Mo., U.S.A.* 34°19N 82°40W **103 D3**
Ivan *Ark., U.S.A.* 33°55N 92°26W **106 E3**
Ivanhoe *Calif., U.S.A.* 36°23N 119°13W **127 G7**
Ivanhoe *Minn., U.S.A.* 44°28N 96°15W **77 F2**
Ivanhoe *N.C., U.S.A.* 36°50N 80°58W **102 E4**
Ivanof Bay *Alaska, U.S.A.* 55°54N 159°29W **135 J8**
Ivesdale *Ill., U.S.A.* 39°57N 88°28W **84 D5**
Ivins *Utah, U.S.A.* 37°10N 113°41W **129 F2**
Ivittuut *Greenland* 61°14N 48°12W **162 E6**
Ivor *Va., U.S.A.* 36°54N 76°54W **102 E8**
Ivujivik *Qué., Canada* 62°24N 77°55W **143 A2**
Ivvavik Nat. Park △ *Yukon, Canada* 69°6N 139°30W **156 C5**
Ivydale *W. Va., U.S.A.* 38°32N 81°2W **102 C3**
Ixcamilpa *Puebla, Mexico* 18°3N 98°41W **177 F2**
Ixcapuzalco *Guerrero, Mexico* 18°32N 99°53W **175 D8**
Ixcateopan *Guerrero, Mexico* 18°30N 99°46W **175 D8**
Ixcatepec *Guerrero, Mexico* 18°30N 100°6W **175 D7**
Ixhil *Quintana Roo, Mexico* 20°27N 87°54W **179 B6**
Ixhuatlán *Veracruz, Mexico* 20°42N 98°0W **177 E2**
Ixmiquilpan *Hidalgo, Mexico* 20°29N 99°14W **175 B8**
Ixtaczoquitlán *Veracruz, Mexico* 18°52N 97°3W **177 F3**
Ixtalahuite, Pta. *Oaxaca, Mexico* 15°40N 96°30W **177 J4**
Ixtapa *Chiapas, Mexico* 16°48N 92°53W **178 C3**
Ixtapa *Jalisco, Mexico* 20°42N 105°11W **174 B2**
Ixtapaluca *México, Mexico* 19°18N 98°53W **175 C9**
Ixtapán de la Concepción *Nayarit, Mexico* 21°19N 105°10W **172 F5**
Ixtapán de la Sal *México, Mexico* 18°50N 99°41W **175 D8**
Ixtapán del Oro *México, Mexico* 19°16N 100°14W **175 C7**
Ixtepec *Oaxaca, Mexico* 16°34N 95°6W **177 H5**
Ixtlahuaca *México, Mexico* 19°34N 99°46W **175 C8**
Ixtlahuacán *Colima, Mexico* 18°59N 103°45W **174 D4**
Ixtlán de Juárez *Oaxaca, Mexico* 17°20N 96°30W **177 H4**
Ixtlán del Río *Nayarit, Mexico* 21°2N 104°22W **172 F6**
Izabal, L. de *Guatemala* 15°30N 89°10W **182 C2**
Izamal *Yucatán, Mexico* 20°56N 89°1W **179 B4**
Izapa *Chiapas, Mexico* 14°58N 92°11W **178 E4**
Izard County ☆ *Ark., U.S.A.* 36°4N 91°54W **106 B4**
Izembek Nat. Wildlife Refuge △ *Alaska, U.S.A.* 55°15N 162°45W **135 J7**
Iztacalco *Distrito Federal, Mexico* 19°23N 99°5W **181 B3**
Iztaccihuatl y Popocatépetl, Parque Nacional △ *Mexico* 19°10N 98°38W **177 E2**
Iztapalapa *Distrito Federal, Mexico* 19°21N 99°6W **181 B3**
Izúcar de Matamoros *Puebla, Mexico* 18°36N 98°28W **177 F2**

J

J.B. Thomas, L. *Tex., U.S.A.* 32°36N 101°8W **108 E6**
J. Clark Salyer Nat. Wildlife Reserve △ *N. Dak., U.S.A.* 48°37N 100°40W **76 B5**
J.F.K. Int. ✈ (JFK) *N.Y., U.S.A.* 40°38N 73°47W **97 C4**
J. Percy Priest L. *Tenn., U.S.A.* 36°9N 86°37W **104 D6**
J. Strom Thurmond L. *Ga., U.S.A.* 33°40N 82°12W **113 C4**
Jaab L. *Ont., Canada* 51°10N 82°58W **149 A14**
Jacala *Hidalgo, Mexico* 21°1N 99°11W **175 A8**
Jacinto City *Tex., U.S.A.* 29°46N 95°14W **116 B3**
Jack County ☆ *Tex., U.S.A.* 33°13N 98°10W **109 D9**
Jack Creek *Nev., U.S.A.* 41°30N 116°6W **128 A4**
Jack Lee, L. *Ark., U.S.A.* 33°15N 92°8W **106 E3**
Jackfish L. *Sask., Canada* 53°9N 108°29W **150 B3**
Jackman *Maine, U.S.A.* 45°37N 70°15W **90 C3**
Jackpot *Nev., U.S.A.* 41°59N 114°40W **128 A6**
Jacks Fork → *Mo., U.S.A.* 37°12N 91°18W **83 D5**
Jacksboro *Tenn., U.S.A.* 36°20N 84°11W **105 D8**
Jacksboro *Tex., U.S.A.* 33°13N 98°10W **109 D9**
Jackson *Ala., U.S.A.* 31°31N 87°53W **112 C3**
Jackson *Calif., U.S.A.* 38°21N 120°46W **126 E6**
Jackson *Ga., U.S.A.* 33°18N 83°57W **113 C3**
Jackson *Ky., U.S.A.* 37°33N 83°23W **105 C9**
Jackson *La., U.S.A.* 30°50N 91°13W **110 D4**
Jackson *Mich., U.S.A.* 42°15N 84°24W **79 G7**
Jackson *Minn., U.S.A.* 43°37N 95°1W **77 G3**
Jackson *Miss., U.S.A.* 32°18N 90°12W **111 D3**
Jackson *Mo., U.S.A.* 37°23N 89°40W **83 D8**
Jackson *N.C., U.S.A.* 36°23N 77°25W **103 B8**
Jackson *N.J., U.S.A.* 44°10N 71°11W **89 B3**
Jackson *Nebr., U.S.A.* 40°6N 74°23W **92 B2**
Jackson *Ohio, U.S.A.* 39°3N 82°39W **86 D4**
Jackson *S.C., U.S.A.* 33°20N 81°47W **103 E4**
Jackson *Tenn., U.S.A.* 35°37N 88°49W **104 E4**

Jackson Wis., U.S.A. 43°19N 88°10W 78 E5
Jackson Wyo., U.S.A. 43°29N 110°46W 124 C2
Jackson County ☆ Ala., U.S.A. 34°40N 86°2W 112 B4
Jackson County ☆ Ark., U.S.A. 35°37N 91°16W 106 C4
Jackson County ☆ Colo., U.S.A. 40°45N 106°20W 125 B4
Jackson County ☆ Fla., U.S.A. 30°45N 85°15W 114 A3
Jackson County ☆ Ga., U.S.A. 34°10N 83°30W 113 B3
Jackson County ☆ Ill., U.S.A. 37°45N 89°25W 84 F4
Jackson County ☆ Ind., U.S.A. 38°55N 86°0W 85 E4
Jackson County ☆ Iowa, U.S.A. 42°10N 90°35W 81 C8
Jackson County ☆ Kans., U.S.A. 39°20N 95°45W 82 B8
Jackson County ☆ Ky., U.S.A. 37°25N 84°0W 105 C8
Jackson County ☆ Mich., U.S.A. 42°15N 84°30W 79 G7
Jackson County ☆ Minn., U.S.A. 43°40N 95°10W 77 G3
Jackson County ☆ Miss., U.S.A. 30°32N 88°42W 111 F2
Jackson County ☆ Mo., U.S.A. 39°0N 94°20W 83 E2
Jackson County ☆ N.C., U.S.A. 35°20N 83°10W 103 C2
Jackson County ☆ Ohio, U.S.A. 39°3N 82°39W 86 D4
Jackson County ☆ Okla., U.S.A. 34°30N 99°25W 107 D4
Jackson County ☆ Oreg., U.S.A. 42°20N 122°45W 121 E3
Jackson County ☆ S. Dak., U.S.A. 43°45N 101°45W 76 G4
Jackson County ☆ Tenn., U.S.A. 36°21N 85°39W 105 D7
Jackson County ☆ Tex., U.S.A. 28°59N 96°39W 109 J11
Jackson County ☆ W. Va., U.S.A. 38°49N 81°43W 102 C3
Jackson County ☆ Wis., U.S.A. 44°20N 90°45W 78 C3
Jackson Heights N.Y., U.S.A. 40°44N 73°53W 97 B3
Jackson Hole Wyo., U.S.A. 43°36N 110°51W 124 C2
Jackson Junction Iowa, U.S.A. 43°7N 92°2W 81 B6
Jackson L. Fla., U.S.A. 30°30N 84°17W 114 A4
Jackson L. Ga., U.S.A. 33°19N 83°50W 113 C3
Jackson Mts. Nev., U.S.A. 41°51N 118°33W 128 A2
Jackson Parish ☆ La., U.S.A. 32°15N 92°43W 110 B3
Jackson Park Ill., U.S.A. 41°46N 87°34W 95 C3
Jackson Park Wis., U.S.A. 42°57N 87°57W 94 C2
Jackson Res. Colo., U.S.A. 40°22N 104°6W 125 B6
Jackson's Arm Nfld. & L., Canada 49°52N 56°47W 142 C4
Jacksonville Ala., U.S.A. 33°49N 85°46W 112 C5
Jacksonville Ark., U.S.A. 34°52N 92°7W 106 D3
Jacksonville Fla., U.S.A. 30°20N 81°39W 114 A7
Jacksonville Ga., U.S.A. 31°49N 82°59W 113 E4
Jacksonville Ill., U.S.A. 39°44N 90°14W 84 D3
Jacksonville N.C., U.S.A. 34°45N 77°26W 103 D8
Jacksonville Ohio, U.S.A. 39°29N 82°5W 86 D4
Jacksonville Oreg., U.S.A. 42°19N 122°57W 121 E3
Jacksonville Tex., U.S.A. 31°58N 95°17W 109 F12
Jacksonville Vt., U.S.A. 42°47N 72°49W 89 D2
Jacksonville Beach Fla., U.S.A. 30°17N 81°24W 114 A7
Jacksonville Int. ✈ (JAX) Fla., U.S.A. 30°30N 81°41W 114 A7
Jacmel Haiti 18°14N 72°32W 183 C5
Jacob Lake Ariz., U.S.A. 36°43N 112°13W 130 A3
Jacob Riis Park N.Y., U.S.A. 40°33N 73°52W 97 C3
Jacobsville Md., U.S.A. 39°7N 76°31W 93 A4
Jacobus Pa., U.S.A. 39°52N 76°42W 93 A4
Jacomulco Veracruz, Mexico 19°16N 96°44W 176 E4
Jacona de Plancarte Michoacan, Mexico 19°57N 102°16W 174 C5
Jacques-Cartier Qué., Canada 45°31N 73°27W 160 A3
Jacques-Cartier → Qué., Canada 46°40N 71°45W 145 E11
Jacques-Cartier, Dét. de Qué., Canada 50°0N 63°30W 143 C5
Jacques-Cartier, L. Qué., Canada 47°35N 71°13W 145 C11
Jacques-Cartier, Mt. Qué., Canada 48°57N 66°0W 140 E4
Jacques-Cartier, Parc de △ Qué., Canada 47°15N 71°33W 145 D11
Jacques-Cartier, Pont Qué., Canada 45°31N 73°32W 160 A3
Jacquet River N.B., Canada 47°55N 66°0W 141 F3
Jacumba Calif., U.S.A. 32°37N 116°11W 127 L10
Jacumé Baja Calif., Mexico 32°36N 116°10W 166 A2
Jaffrey N.H., U.S.A. 42°49N 72°2W 89 D2
Jagüey, Pta. Sonora, Mexico 30°47N 113°12W 168 C2
Jagüey Grande Cuba 22°35N 81°7W 182 B3
Jaina, I. Campeche, Mexico 20°15N 90°30W 179 B3
Jakin Ga., U.S.A. 31°6N 84°59W 113 E2
Jakobshavn = Illulissat Greenland 69°12N 51°10W 162 D5
Jal N. Mex., U.S.A. 32°7N 103°12W 131 E7
Jala Nayarit, Mexico 21°6N 104°26W 172 F6
Jalaihai Pt. Guam 13°18N 144°46E 184 b
Jalapa Guatemala 14°39N 89°59W 182 D2
Jalapa Oaxaca, Mexico 18°4N 96°32W 177 F4
Jalapa Tabasco, Mexico 17°43N 92°49W 178 B4
Jalapa del Marques Oaxaca, Mexico 16°26N 95°25W 177 H5
Jalapa Enríquez = Xalapa Veracruz, Mexico 19°32N 96°55W 176 E4
Jalcocotán Nayarit, Mexico 21°28N 105°7W 172 F5
Jalisco □ Mexico 20°20N 103°40W 174 B4
Jalostotitlán Jalisco, Mexico 21°12N 102°28W 174 A5
Jalpa Coahuila, Mexico 25°34N 101°45W 170 E3
Jalpa Zacatecas, Mexico 21°38N 102°58W 173 F8
Jalpa de Méndez Tabasco, Mexico 18°11N 93°4W 178 A3
Jalpan Querétaro, Mexico 21°14N 99°29W 175 A8
Jáltipan de Morelos Veracruz, Mexico 17°58N 94°43W 177 G6
Jaltocán Hidalgo, Mexico 21°8N 98°32W 175 A9
Jamaica Iowa, U.S.A. 41°51N 94°18W 81 D4
Jamaica Vt., U.S.A. 43°13N 72°46W 89 C2
Jamaica ■ W. Indies 18°10N 77°30W 182 C4
Jamaica B. N.Y., U.S.A. 40°36N 73°50W 97 C3
Jamaica Channel Jamaica 17°0N 76°0W 183 C4
Jamaica Plain Mass., U.S.A. 42°18N 71°6W 96 B2
Jamapa Veracruz, Mexico 19°3N 96°25W 177 E4
Jamay Jalisco, Mexico 20°18N 102°43W 174 B5
James Ga., U.S.A. 32°58N 83°29W 113 D3
James → Mo., U.S.A. 36°45N 93°30W 83 E3
James → S. Dak., U.S.A. 42°52N 97°18W 76 H8
James → Va., U.S.A. 36°56N 76°27W 102 E8
James, L. N.C., U.S.A. 35°44N 81°54W 103 C4
James B. Nunavut, Canada 54°0N 80°0W 159 G9
James City N.C., U.S.A. 35°5N 77°2W 103 C8
James City County ☆ Va., U.S.A. 37°16N 76°40W 102 D8
James Island S.C., U.S.A. 32°45N 79°55W 103 F6
James River N.S., Canada 45°35N 62°7W 141 H7
James Ross Str. Nunavut, Canada 69°40N 96°10W 158 A13
Jameson Land Greenland 71°0N 23°30W 162 C8
Jamesport Mo., U.S.A. 39°58N 93°48W 83 B3
Jamestown = Wawa Ont., Canada 47°59N 84°47W 149 E12
Jamestown Calif., U.S.A. 37°57N 120°26W 126 D4
Jamestown Ind., U.S.A. 39°56N 86°38W 85 D4
Jamestown Kans., U.S.A. 39°36N 97°52W 82 B6
Jamestown Ky., U.S.A. 36°59N 85°4W 105 D7
Jamestown La., U.S.A. 32°21N 93°13W 110 B2
Jamestown N. Dak., U.S.A. 46°54N 98°42W 76 B5
Jamestown N.Y., U.S.A. 42°6N 79°14W 88 C1
Jamestown Ohio, U.S.A. 39°39N 83°39W 86 D3
Jamestown R.I., U.S.A. 41°30N 71°22W 91 C3
Jamestown Tenn., U.S.A. 36°26N 84°56W 105 D8
Jamestown Va., U.S.A. 37°12N 79°46W 102 D5

Jamestown Res. N. Dak., U.S.A. 46°56N 98°43W 76 D7
Jamesville N.C., U.S.A. 35°49N 76°54W 103 C9
Jamieson Oreg., U.S.A. 44°11N 117°26W 121 C8
Jane Mo., U.S.A. 36°33N 94°18W 83 E2
Jane, L. Minn., U.S.A. 45°1N 92°55W 94 A4
Jane Lew W. Va., U.S.A. 39°7N 80°25W 102 B4
Janes I. Del., U.S.A. 38°0N 75°51W 93 C5
Janesville Calif., U.S.A. 40°18N 120°32W 126 C6
Janesville Iowa, U.S.A. 42°39N 92°28W 81 C6
Janesville Minn., U.S.A. 44°7N 93°42W 77 F5
Janesville Wis., U.S.A. 42°41N 89°1W 78 F4
Janos Chihuahua, Mexico 30°54N 108°10W 169 C7
Jansen Sask., Canada 51°54N 104°45W 150 D7
Jansen Colo., U.S.A. 37°9N 104°32W 125 E6
Jantetelco Morelos, Mexico 18°34N 98°46W 175 D9
Jaqué Panama 7°27N 78°8W 182 E4
Jaral Guanajuato, Mexico 21°41N 101°1W 175 A6
Jaral del Progreso Guanajuato, Mexico 20°23N 101°5W 175 B6
Jarales N. Mex., U.S.A. 34°37N 106°46W 131 B4
Jarbidge Nev., U.S.A. 41°52N 115°26W 128 A5
Jarbidge → Idaho, U.S.A. 42°20N 115°39W 122 G3
Jarboesville = Lexington Park Md., U.S.A. 38°16N 76°27W 93 B4
Jardines de la Reina, Arch. de los Cuba 20°50N 78°50W 182 B4
Jardines de la Silla Monterey, Mexico 25°38N 100°11W 180 C2
Jarratt Va., U.S.A. 36°48N 77°28W 102 E7
Jarrettsville Md., U.S.A. 39°36N 76°29W 93 A4
Jarvis Ont., Canada 42°53N 80°6W 146 E6
Jarvis I. Pac. Oc. 0°15S 160°5W 184 E7
Jas Punta Quintana Roo, Mexico 18°25N 87°56W 179 D6
Jasonville Ind., U.S.A. 39°10N 87°12W 85 D3
Jasper Alta., Canada 52°55N 118°5W 153 F2
Jasper Ont., Canada 44°52N 75°57W 147 C11
Jasper Ala., U.S.A. 33°50N 87°17W 112 C3
Jasper Ark., U.S.A. 36°1N 93°11W 106 B2
Jasper Fla., U.S.A. 30°31N 82°57W 114 A6
Jasper Ga., U.S.A. 34°28N 84°26W 113 B2
Jasper Ind., U.S.A. 38°24N 86°56W 85 E4
Jasper Minn., U.S.A. 43°51N 96°24W 77 G2
Jasper Mo., U.S.A. 37°20N 94°18W 83 D2
Jasper Tenn., U.S.A. 35°5N 85°38W 105 D7
Jasper Tex., U.S.A. 30°56N 94°1W 109 G13
Jasper County ☆ Ga., U.S.A. 33°20N 83°45W 113 C3
Jasper County ☆ Ill., U.S.A. 39°0N 88°10W 84 E5
Jasper County ☆ Ind., U.S.A. 41°0N 87°5W 85 B3
Jasper County ☆ Iowa, U.S.A. 41°40N 93°0W 81 D5
Jasper County ☆ Miss., U.S.A. 32°2N 89°2W 111 D4
Jasper County ☆ Mo., U.S.A. 37°10N 94°20W 83 D2
Jasper County ☆ S.C., U.S.A. 32°30N 81°0W 103 F4
Jasper County ☆ Tex., U.S.A. 30°40N 93°59W 109 G14
Jasper Nat. Park △ Alta., Canada 52°50N 118°8W 153 F2
Jataté → Chiapas, Mexico 16°15N 91°17W 178 C5
Jaumave Tamaulipas, Mexico 23°25N 99°23W 171 G5
Java S. Dak., U.S.A. 45°30N 99°53W 76 E6
Java Va., U.S.A. 36°50N 79°14W 102 E5
Jay Fla., U.S.A. 30°57N 87°9W 114 A1
Jay Maine, U.S.A. 44°30N 70°13W 90 D3
Jay N.Y., U.S.A. 44°20N 73°45W 88 A7
Jay Okla., U.S.A. 36°25N 94°48W 107 B9
Jay County ☆ Ind., U.S.A. 40°25N 85°0W 85 C6
Jay Em Wyo., U.S.A. 42°28N 104°22W 124 D8
Jay Peak Vt., U.S.A. 44°55N 72°32W 89 B2
Jaype Idaho, U.S.A. 46°32N 115°50W 122 C3
Jayton Tex., U.S.A. 33°15N 100°34W 108 E7
Jazminal Coahuila, Mexico 24°52N 101°24W 171 F3
Jean Nev., U.S.A. 35°47N 115°20W 128 J11
Jean Tex., U.S.A. 33°18N 98°37W 109 D9
Jean Lafitte Nat. Historical Park △ La., U.S.A. 29°51N 90°9W 117 D2
Jean Marie River N.W.T., Canada 61°32N 120°38W 157 D8
Jean-Rabel Haiti 19°50N 73°5W 183 C5
Jeanerette La., U.S.A. 29°55N 91°40W 110 E4
Jeanetta Tex., U.S.A. 29°43N 95°31W 116 B1
Jeannette, L. Ont., Canada 51°5N 92°5W 148 A4
Jecopaco Sonora, Mexico 27°12N 109°46W 168 F6
Jedway B.C., Canada 52°17N 131°14W 154 C3
Jeff Davis County ☆ Ga., U.S.A. 31°50N 82°45W 113 E4
Jeff Davis County ☆ Tex., U.S.A. 30°55N 104°5W 108 G3
Jeffers Minn., U.S.A. 44°3N 95°12W 77 F3
Jefferson Colo., U.S.A. 39°23N 105°48W 125 C5
Jefferson Iowa, U.S.A. 42°1N 94°23W 81 C4
Jefferson La., U.S.A. 29°57N 90°9W 117 B2
Jefferson Maine, U.S.A. 44°13N 69°27W 90 D4
Jefferson Md., U.S.A. 39°22N 77°32W 93 A3
Jefferson N.C., U.S.A. 36°25N 81°28W 103 B4
Jefferson Ohio, U.S.A. 41°44N 80°46W 86 B6
Jefferson Okla., U.S.A. 36°43N 97°48W 107 B6
Jefferson Oreg., U.S.A. 44°43N 123°1W 121 C2
Jefferson S.C., U.S.A. 34°39N 80°23W 103 D5
Jefferson S. Dak., U.S.A. 42°36N 96°34W 76 H9
Jefferson Tex., U.S.A. 32°46N 94°21W 109 E13
Jefferson Wis., U.S.A. 43°0N 88°48W 78 F5
Jefferson → Mont., U.S.A. 45°56N 111°31W 123 E6
Jefferson, Mt. Nev., U.S.A. 38°47N 116°56W 128 D4
Jefferson, Mt. Oreg., U.S.A. 44°41N 121°48W 121 C4
Jefferson City Mo., U.S.A. 38°34N 92°10W 83 C4
Jefferson City Tenn., U.S.A. 36°7N 83°30W 105 D9
Jefferson County ☆ Ala., U.S.A. 33°31N 86°48W 112 C4
Jefferson County ☆ Ark., U.S.A. 34°15N 92°0W 106 D3
Jefferson County ☆ Colo., U.S.A. 39°40N 105°15W 125 C5
Jefferson County ☆ Fla., U.S.A. 30°20N 84°0W 114 A5
Jefferson County ☆ Ga., U.S.A. 32°55N 82°25W 113 C4
Jefferson County ☆ Idaho, U.S.A. 43°50N 112°20W 122 F6
Jefferson County ☆ Ill., U.S.A. 38°20N 88°55W 84 E5
Jefferson County ☆ Ind., U.S.A. 38°40N 85°25W 85 E5
Jefferson County ☆ Iowa, U.S.A. 41°0N 92°0W 81 D7
Jefferson County ☆ Kans., U.S.A. 39°15N 95°30W 82 B8
Jefferson County ☆ Ky., U.S.A. 38°10N 85°40W 105 B7
Jefferson County ☆ Miss., U.S.A. 31°43N 91°4W 111 E2
Jefferson County ☆ Mo., U.S.A. 38°15N 90°30W 83 C6
Jefferson County ☆ Mont., U.S.A. 46°8N 112°0W 123 D6
Jefferson County ☆ N.Y., U.S.A. 44°0N 76°0W 88 B5
Jefferson County ☆ Nebr., U.S.A. 40°5N 97°10W 80 D8
Jefferson County ☆ Ohio, U.S.A. 40°25N 80°54W 86 C6
Jefferson County ☆ Okla., U.S.A. 34°10N 97°50W 107 D6
Jefferson County ☆ Oreg., U.S.A. 44°40N 121°10W 121 C4
Jefferson County ☆ Pa., U.S.A. 41°5N 79°0W 87 C4
Jefferson County ☆ Tenn., U.S.A. 36°7N 83°30W 105 D9
Jefferson County ☆ Tex., U.S.A. 29°55N 94°15W 109 H13
Jefferson County ☆ W. Va., U.S.A. 39°17N 77°52W 102 B7
Jefferson County ☆ Wash., U.S.A. 47°50N 123°45W 120 C2
Jefferson County ☆ Wis., U.S.A. 43°0N 88°45W 78 F5
Jefferson Davis County ☆ Miss., U.S.A. 31°36N 89°52W 111 E4

Jefferson Davis Parish ☆ La., U.S.A. 30°14N 92°49W 110 D3
Jefferson Nat. Forest La., U.S.A. 37°10N 81°15W 102 D3
Jefferson Parish ☆ La., U.S.A. 29°44N 90°8W 110 E5
Jefferson Park Ill., U.S.A. 41°58N 87°46W 95 B2
Jefferson Valley N.Y., U.S.A. 41°20N 73°47W 92 A3
Jeffersonton Va., U.S.A. 38°38N 77°55W 102 C7
Jeffersontown Ky., U.S.A. 38°12N 85°35W 105 B7
Jeffersonville Ga., U.S.A. 32°41N 83°20W 113 D3
Jeffersonville Ind., U.S.A. 38°17N 85°44W 85 E5
Jeffersonville Ky., U.S.A. 37°59N 83°51W 105 C9
Jeffersonville Ohio, U.S.A. 39°39N 83°34W 86 D3
Jeffersonville Vt., U.S.A. 44°40N 72°50W 89 B2
Jeffrey City Wyo., U.S.A. 42°30N 107°49W 124 D5
Jeffrey Res. Nebr., U.S.A. 40°58N 100°24W 80 D5
Jekyll I. Ga., U.S.A. 31°4N 81°25W 113 E5
Jellico Tenn., U.S.A. 36°35N 84°8W 105 D8
Jellicoe Ont., Canada 49°40N 87°30W 149 C9
Jemez Indian Reservation N. Mex., U.S.A. 35°40N 106°50W 131 B4
Jemez Mts. N. Mex., U.S.A. 35°45N 106°35W 131 B4
Jemez Pueblo N. Mex., U.S.A. 35°37N 106°44W 131 B4
Jemez Springs N. Mex., U.S.A. 35°46N 106°42W 131 B4
Jemison Ala., U.S.A. 32°58N 86°45W 112 D4
Jena Fla., U.S.A. 29°40N 83°22W 114 B5
Jena La., U.S.A. 31°41N 92°8W 110 C3
Jenison Mich., U.S.A. 42°54N 85°47W 79 G6
Jenkins Ky., U.S.A. 37°10N 82°38W 105 C10
Jenkins Minn., U.S.A. 46°39N 94°20W 77 D4
Jenkins N.J., U.S.A. 39°42N 74°32W 92 C2
Jenkins County ☆ Ga., U.S.A. 32°45N 82°0W 113 D4
Jenkintown Pa., U.S.A. 40°5N 75°7W 92 B4
Jenks Okla., U.S.A. 36°1N 95°58W 107 B8
Jenner Calif., U.S.A. 38°27N 123°7W 126 E3
Jennings Fla., U.S.A. 30°36N 83°6W 114 A5
Jennings Kans., U.S.A. 39°41N 100°18W 82 B3
Jennings La., U.S.A. 30°13N 92°40W 110 D3
Jennings Mo., U.S.A. 38°43N 90°15W 94 A2
Jennings Okla., U.S.A. 36°11N 96°34W 107 B7
Jennings County ☆ Ind., U.S.A. 39°0N 85°40W 85 D5
Jennings Lodge Oreg., U.S.A. 45°23N 122°36W 132 E2
Jenny Lind I. Nunavut, Canada 68°43N 101°58W 158 B10
Jens Munk I. Nunavut, Canada 69°39N 80°4W 158 D9
Jensen Utah, U.S.A. 40°22N 109°20W 129 C6
Jensen Beach Fla., U.S.A. 27°15N 80°14W 114 D8
Jerauld County ☆ S. Dak., U.S.A. 44°0N 98°40W 76 F7
Jerécuaro Guanajuato, Mexico 20°9N 100°13W 175 B7
Jérémie Haiti 18°40N 74°10W 183 C5
Jeremy Point Mass., U.S.A. 41°53N 70°4W 91 C4
Jerez → Zacatecas, Mexico 22°28N 103°13W 173 E7
Jerez de García Salinas Zacatecas, Mexico 22°39N 103°0W 173 E8
Jericho Beach Park B.C., Canada 49°16N 123°12W 161 B1
Jerico Springs Mo., U.S.A. 37°37N 94°1W 83 D2
Jerimoth Hill R.I., U.S.A. 41°51N 71°47W 91 C3
Jermyn Pa., U.S.A. 41°32N 75°33W 92 A1
Jermyn Tex., U.S.A. 33°16N 98°23W 109 D9
Jerome Ont., Canada 47°37N 82°14W 149 E14
Jerome Ariz., U.S.A. 34°45N 112°7W 130 C3
Jerome Ark., U.S.A. 33°24N 91°28W 106 E4
Jerome Idaho, U.S.A. 42°44N 114°31W 122 G4
Jerome County ☆ Idaho, U.S.A. 42°42N 114°15W 122 G4
Jerry City Ohio, U.S.A. 41°15N 83°36W 86 B3
Jersey Ark., U.S.A. 33°26N 92°19W 106 E3
Jersey Ga., U.S.A. 33°43N 83°47W 113 C3
Jersey County ☆ Ill., U.S.A. 39°5N 90°20W 84 D3
Jersey Shore Pa., U.S.A. 41°12N 77°15W 87 C5
Jersey Village Tex., U.S.A. 29°53N 95°33W 116 A1
Jerseyside Nfld. & L., Canada 47°16N 53°58W 142 E7
Jerseyville Ill., U.S.A. 39°7N 90°20W 84 D3
Jerusalem Ohio, U.S.A. 39°58N 81°5W 86 C6
Jervis Inlet B.C., Canada 50°0N 123°57W 154 F11
Jessamine Fla., U.S.A. 28°28N 81°23W 115 B2
Jessamine County ☆ Ky., U.S.A. 37°50N 84°35W 105 C8
Jessieville Ark., U.S.A. 34°42N 93°4W 106 D2
Jessup Md., U.S.A. 39°9N 76°46W 93 A4
Jesup Ga., U.S.A. 31°36N 81°53W 113 E5
Jesup Iowa, U.S.A. 42°29N 92°4W 81 C6
Jesup, L. Fla., U.S.A. 28°43N 81°14W 114 C7
Jésus, Î. Qué., Canada 45°36N 73°44W 160 A2
Jesús Carranza Veracruz, Mexico 17°26N 95°2W 177 G5
Jesús García Sonora, Mexico 30°45N 112°23W 168 C3
Jesús María Aguascalientes, Mexico 21°57N 102°20W 173 F8
Jesús María Jalisco, Mexico 20°37N 102°7W 174 B5
Jesús María Nayarit, Mexico 22°1N 104°31W 172 E6
Jesús María → Mexico 21°57N 104°31W 172 F6
Jesús María Garza Chiapas, Mexico 16°22N 93°18W 178 C3
Jet Okla., U.S.A. 36°40N 98°11W 107 B5
Jetmore Kans., U.S.A. 38°4N 99°54W 82 C4
Jewel Cave Nat. Monument △ S. Dak., U.S.A. 43°45N 103°48W 76 G2
Jewell Iowa, U.S.A. 42°20N 93°39W 81 C5
Jewell Kans., U.S.A. 39°40N 98°10W 82 B5
Jewell County ☆ Kans., U.S.A. 39°45N 98°10W 82 B5
Jewell Ridge Va., U.S.A. 37°11N 81°47W 102 D3
Jewett Ill., U.S.A. 39°13N 88°15W 84 D5
Jewett Ohio, U.S.A. 40°22N 81°2W 86 C5
Jewett Tex., U.S.A. 31°22N 96°9W 109 F11
Jewett City Conn., U.S.A. 41°36N 71°59W 91 C3
Jicarilla Indian Reservation N. Mex., U.S.A. 36°45N 107°0W 131 A4
Jicarón, I. Panama 7°10N 81°50W 182 E3
Jigger La., U.S.A. 32°2N 91°45W 110 B4
Jiggs Nev., U.S.A. 40°26N 115°40W 128 C5
Jilotepec México, Mexico 19°58N 99°32W 175 C8
Jilotlán de los Dolores Jalisco, Mexico 19°12N 103°13W 174 C4
Jim Hogg County ☆ Tex., U.S.A. 27°0N 98°45W 108 K9
Jim Thorpe Pa., U.S.A. 40°52N 75°44W 92 B1
Jim Wells County ☆ Tex., U.S.A. 28°0N 98°0W 109 K9
Jiménez Chihuahua, Mexico 27°8N 104°54W 169 F11
Jiménez Coahuila, Mexico 29°2N 100°41W 170 A4
Jiménez del Téul Zacatecas, Mexico 23°15N 103°47W 173 D7
Jimmy Carter Nat. Historic Site △ Ga., U.S.A. 32°2N 84°25W 113 D2
Jimulco, Sa. Coahuila, Mexico 25°15N 103°19W 171 A3
Jinotega Nic. 13°6N 85°59W 182 D2
Jinotepe Nic. 11°50N 86°10W 182 D2
Jiquilpan Michoacán, Mexico 19°59N 102°43W 174 C5
Jiquipilas Chiapas, Mexico 16°40N 93°39W 178 C3
Jitotol Chiapas, Mexico 17°3N 92°52W 178 B4
Jitzamuri, B. Mexico 26°15N 109°16W 172 A1
Jo Daviess County ☆ Ill., U.S.A. 42°20N 90°10W 84 A3
Joanna S.C., U.S.A. 34°25N 81°49W 103 D4
Joaquín Tex., U.S.A. 31°58N 94°3W 109 F13
Joaquín Amaro Zacatecas, Mexico 21°56N 103°6W 173 F7

Jocassee, L. S.C., U.S.A. 34°58N 82°56W 103 D3
Jococuistle Durango, Mexico 23°15N 105°21W 172 D5
Jocotepec Jalisco, Mexico 20°18N 103°26W 174 B4
Jocotitlán México, Mexico 19°42N 99°48W 175 C7
Joe Batt's Arm-Barr'd Islands-Shoal Bay Nfld. & L., Canada 49°44N 54°10W 142 C6
Joe Pool Lake Tex., U.S.A. 32°38N 96°59W 116 C4
Joes Colo., U.S.A. 39°39N 102°41W 125 C8
Joffre, Mt. B.C., Canada 50°32N 115°13W 153 H5
Joggins N.S., Canada 45°42N 64°27W 141 H5
Jogues Ont., Canada 49°36N 83°45W 149 C13
Johanna, L. Minn., U.S.A. 45°2N 93°10W 94 A2
Johannesburg Calif., U.S.A. 35°22N 117°38W 127 H9
John C. Stennis Space Center Miss., U.S.A. 30°23N 89°37W 111 F4
John D. Rockefeller Jr. Memorial Parkway Wyo., U.S.A. 44°5N 110°44W 124 B2
John Day Oreg., U.S.A. 44°25N 118°57W 121 C7
John Day → Oreg., U.S.A. 45°44N 120°39W 121 B5
John Day Dam Wash., U.S.A. 45°44N 120°41W 120 C5
John Day Fossil Beds Nat. Monument Clarno △ Oreg., U.S.A. 44°55N 120°28W 121 C5
John Day Fossil Beds Nat. Monument Painted Hills △ Oreg., U.S.A. 44°39N 120°15W 121 C5
John Day Fossil Beds Nat. Monument Sheep Rock △ Oreg., U.S.A. 44°33N 119°30W 121 C6
John Dickinson Plantation Del., U.S.A. 39°10N 75°31W 93 A5
John D'Or Prairie Alta., Canada 58°30N 115°8W 157 E9
John F. Kennedy Nat. Historic Site △ Mass., U.S.A. 42°20N 71°7W 96 A2
John F. Kennedy Space Center U.S.A. 28°40N 80°42W 114 C8
John H. Kerr Res. N.C., U.S.A. 36°36N 78°18W 103 B7
John Heinz Nat. Wildlife Refuge △ Pa., U.S.A. 39°53N 75°17W 98 B1
John Hendrey Park B.C., Canada 49°15N 123°5W 161 B2
John McLaren Park Calif., U.S.A. 37°43N 122°24W 132 B2
John Martin Res. Colo., U.S.A. 38°4N 102°56W 125 D8
John Redmond Res. Kans., U.S.A. 38°14N 95°46W 82 C8
John W. Flanagan Res. Va., U.S.A. 37°15N 82°22W 102 D2
John Wayne, Santa Ana ✈ (SNA) Calif., U.S.A. 33°41N 117°52W 127 K9
Johns I. S.C., U.S.A. 32°47N 80°7W 103 F5
Johnson Nebr., U.S.A. 40°25N 96°0W 80 D10
Johnson Vt., U.S.A. 44°38N 72°41W 89 B2
Johnson City Kans., U.S.A. 37°34N 101°45W 82 D2
Johnson City N.Y., U.S.A. 42°7N 75°58W 88 C5
Johnson City Tenn., U.S.A. 36°19N 82°21W 105 D10
Johnson City Tex., U.S.A. 30°17N 98°25W 109 G9
Johnson County ☆ Ark., U.S.A. 35°28N 93°28W 106 C2
Johnson County ☆ Ga., U.S.A. 32°45N 82°40W 113 D4
Johnson County ☆ Ill., U.S.A. 37°30N 88°50W 84 F5
Johnson County ☆ Ind., U.S.A. 39°30N 86°5W 85 D4
Johnson County ☆ Iowa, U.S.A. 41°40N 91°35W 81 D7
Johnson County ☆ Kans., U.S.A. 38°45N 94°45W 82 C9
Johnson County ☆ Ky., U.S.A. 37°50N 82°50W 105 C10
Johnson County ☆ Mo., U.S.A. 38°50N 93°45W 83 C3
Johnson County ☆ Nebr., U.S.A. 40°20N 96°15W 80 D9
Johnson County ☆ Tenn., U.S.A. 36°29N 81°48W 105 D11
Johnson County ☆ Tex., U.S.A. 32°21N 97°23W 109 E10
Johnson County ☆ Wyo., U.S.A. 44°0N 106°35W 124 B6
Johnson Draw → Tex., U.S.A. 30°8N 101°7W 108 G6
Johnson L. Nebr., U.S.A. 40°42N 99°49W 80 D6
Johnsonburg N.J., U.S.A. 40°58N 74°53W 92 B2
Johnsonburg Pa., U.S.A. 41°29N 78°41W 87 C4
Johnsondale Calif., U.S.A. 35°58N 118°32W 127 H8
Johnsons Crossing Yukon, Canada 60°29N 133°18W 157 D6
Johnson's Shut-Ins State Park △ Mo., U.S.A. 37°32N 90°51W 83 D6
Johnsonville S.C., U.S.A. 33°49N 79°27W 103 E6
Johnston Iowa, U.S.A. 41°40N 93°42W 81 D5
Johnston R.I., U.S.A. 41°50N 71°30W 91 C3
Johnston S.C., U.S.A. 33°50N 81°48W 103 E4
Johnston City Ill., U.S.A. 37°49N 88°56W 84 F5
Johnston County ☆ N.C., U.S.A. 35°30N 78°20W 103 C7
Johnston County ☆ Okla., U.S.A. 34°20N 96°40W 107 D7
Johnston I. Pac. Oc. 17°10N 169°8W 184 C8
Johnston Str. B.C., Canada 50°28N 126°0W 154 E8
Johnstown Colo., U.S.A. 40°20N 104°54W 125 B6
Johnstown N.Y., U.S.A. 43°0N 74°22W 88 B6
Johnstown Nebr., U.S.A. 42°34N 100°3W 80 B5
Johnstown Ohio, U.S.A. 40°9N 82°41W 86 C4
Johnstown Pa., U.S.A. 40°20N 78°55W 87 D4
Johnstown Flood Nat. Memorial △ Pa., U.S.A. 40°20N 78°46W 87 D4
Joice Iowa, U.S.A. 43°22N 93°27W 81 B5
Joiner Ark., U.S.A. 35°31N 90°9W 106 C5
Joir → Qué., Canada 51°59N 60°12W 140 F4
Jojutla Morelos, Mexico 18°37N 99°11W 175 D8
Joliet Ill., U.S.A. 41°32N 88°5W 84 B5
Joliet Mont., U.S.A. 45°29N 108°58W 123 E9
Joliette Qué., Canada 46°3N 73°24W 145 E12
Jolley Iowa, U.S.A. 42°29N 94°43W 81 C4
Jonacatepec Morelos, Mexico 18°41N 98°48W 175 D9
Jones La., U.S.A. 32°58N 91°39W 110 B4
Jones Okla., U.S.A. 35°34N 97°17W 107 C6
Jones County ☆ Ga., U.S.A. 33°0N 83°30W 113 D3
Jones County ☆ Iowa, U.S.A. 42°5N 91°5W 81 C7
Jones County ☆ Miss., U.S.A. 31°36N 89°12W 111 E4
Jones County ☆ N.C., U.S.A. 35°0N 77°30W 103 C8
Jones County ☆ S. Dak., U.S.A. 44°0N 100°50W 76 F5
Jones County ☆ Tex., U.S.A. 32°45N 99°54W 108 E7
Jones Falls → Baltimore, U.S.A. 39°18N 76°37W 99 A1
Jones Sound Nunavut, Canada 76°0N 85°0W 158 B8
Jones Springs W. Va., U.S.A. 39°29N 78°6W 93 A2
Jonesboro Ark., U.S.A. 35°50N 90°42W 106 C5
Jonesboro Ga., U.S.A. 33°31N 84°22W 113 C2
Jonesboro Ill., U.S.A. 37°27N 89°16W 84 F4
Jonesboro Ind., U.S.A. 40°29N 85°38W 85 C5
Jonesboro La., U.S.A. 32°15N 92°43W 110 B2
Jonesboro Tex., U.S.A. 31°37N 97°53W 109 F10
Jonesborough Tenn., U.S.A. 36°18N 82°29W 105 D10
Jonesburg Mo., U.S.A. 38°51N 91°18W 83 C5
Jonesport Maine, U.S.A. 44°32N 67°37W 90 D6
Jonestown Miss., U.S.A. 34°19N 90°27W 111 B3
Jonestown Pa., U.S.A. 40°25N 76°29W 87 D6
Jonesville La., U.S.A. 31°38N 91°49W 110 C4
Jonesville Mich., U.S.A. 41°59N 84°40W 79 H7
Jonesville S.C., U.S.A. 34°50N 81°41W 103 D4
Jonesville Va., U.S.A. 36°41N 83°7W 102 E1
Jonquière Qué., Canada 48°27N 71°14W 145 C11
Jonuta Tabasco, Mexico 18°5N 92°8W 178 A4
Joplin Mo., U.S.A. 37°6N 94°31W 83 D2
Joplin Mont., U.S.A. 48°34N 110°46W 123 B7
Joppa Ill., U.S.A. 37°12N 88°51W 84 F5

Joppatowne Md., U.S.A. 39°27N 76°21W 93 A4
Joquicingo Mexico, Mexico 19°4N 99°32W 175 C8
Jordan Minn., U.S.A. 44°40N 93°38W 77 F5
Jordan Mont., U.S.A. 47°19N 106°55W 123 C11
Jordan N.Y., U.S.A. 43°4N 76°29W 88 B4
Jordan → Utah, U.S.A. 40°49N 112°8W 129 C3
Jordan, L., Canada 44°5N 65°14W 141 J4
Jordan, L. Alta., U.S.A. 32°37N 86°15W 112 D4
Jordan Falls N.S., Canada 43°49N 65°14W 141 K4
Jordan River State Park △ Utah,
   U.S.A. 40°47N 111°46W 134 B2
Jordan Valley Oreg., U.S.A. 42°59N 117°3W 121 E4
Jorgen Brønl and Fjord Greenland 82°30N 29°0W 162 A8
Jornado del Muerto N. Mex., U.S.A. 33°15N 106°50W 131 D4
José Azueta Veracruz, Mexico 18°4N 95°43W 177 F5
José López Portillo, Presa Sinaloa,
   Mexico 24°36N 106°45W 172 C4
José María Morelos Jalisco, Mexico 19°39N 105°9W 174 C2
José María Morelos Quintana Roo,
   Mexico 19°45N 88°47W 179 C5
José María Morelos y Pavón Campeche,
   Mexico 19°5N 90°44W 179 C3
Josefa Ortiz de Dominguez, Presa Sinaloa,
   Mexico 26°30N 108°42W 172 A2
Joseph Oreg., U.S.A. 45°21N 117°14W 121 B8
Joseph Utah, U.S.A. 38°38N 112°13W 129 E3
Joseph, L. Nfld. & L., Canada 52°45N 65°18W 143 C4
Joseph, L. Ont., Canada 45°10N 79°44W 144 F3
Joseph, Petit ac Nfld. & L., Canada 52°36N 65°5W 140 A4
Joseph City Ariz., U.S.A. 34°57N 110°20W 130 C5
Joseph Cr. → Wash., U.S.A. 46°3N 117°1W 120 D8
Josephine, L. Minn., U.S.A. 45°2N 93°9W 94 A3
Josephine County ☆ Oreg., U.S.A. 42°20N 123°40W 121 E2
Joshua Tex., U.S.A. 32°28N 97°23W 109 E10
Joshua Tree Calif., U.S.A. 34°8N 116°19W 127 J10
Joshua Tree Nat. Park △ Calif., U.S.A. 33°55N 116°0W 127 K11
Jost Van Dyke I. Br. Virgin Is. 18°29N 64°47W 184 G18
Jourdanton Tex., U.S.A. 28°55N 98°33W 109 J9
Joussard Alta., Canada 55°22N 115°50W 152 C5
Jovellanos Cuba 22°40N 81°10W 182 B3
Joy Ill., U.S.A. 41°12N 90°53W 84 B3
Joy B. Qué., Canada 61°30N 72°0W 143 A3
Joyce Wash., U.S.A. 48°8N 123°44W 120 B2
Juab County ☆ Utah, U.S.A. 39°40N 113°0W 129 D3
Juan Aldam a Zacatecas, Mexico 24°19N 103°21W 173 C7
Juan de Fuca, Str. of N. Amer. 48°15N 124°0W 154 G10
Juan de la Cruz Borrego Coahuila,
   Mexico 28°5N 103°18W 170 B1
Juan Diaz Covarrubias Veracruz, Mexico 18°9N 95°11W 177 F5
Juan Escutia México, Mexico 19°25N 99°43W 181 A3
Juan González Romero México, Mexico 19°30N 99°3W 181 A3
Juan Ixcaquixtla Puebla, Mexico 18°27N 97°49W 177 F3
Juan José Ríos Sinaloa, Mexico 25°45N 108°49W 172 B2
Juan Mata Ortiz Chihuahua, Mexico 30°8N 108°4W 169 C4
Juan Perez Sd. B.C., Canada 52°32N 131°30W 154 C2
Juan Ramírez, I. Veracruz, Mexico 21°45N 97°28W 176 C3
Juan Rodríguez Clara Veracruz, Mexico 17°59N 95°25W 177 F4
Juana Días Puerto Rico 18°3N 66°31W 184 G16
Juanacatlán Jalisco, Mexico 20°31N 103°10W 180 B3
Juárez Chiapas, Mexico 17°39N 93°10W 178 B3
Juárez Chihuahua, Mexico 30°19N 108°5W 169 C7
Juárez Coahuila, Mexico 27°37N 100°44W 170 C4
Juárez, Sa. de Baja Calif., Mexico 16°30N 95°28W 177 H5
Juárez, Sa. de Baja Calif., Mexico 32°0N 115°50W 166 B3
Juárez Int. ✈ (MEX) Distrito Federal,
   Mexico 19°25N 99°5W 181 B3
Jubilee L. Nfld. & L., Canada 48°3N 55°11W 142 D5
Júcaro Cuba 21°37N 78°51W 182 B4
Juchipila Zacatecas, Mexico 21°25N 103°7W 173 F7
Juchipila → Mexico 21°4N 103°22W 174 A4
Juchique Veracruz, Mexico 19°51N 96°41W 176 E4
Juchitán de Zaragoza Oaxaca, Mexico 16°26N 95°1W 175 H9
Juchitlán Jalisco, Mexico 16°37N 98°52W 175 F9
Juchitlán Jalisco, Mexico 20°4N 104°5W 174 B3
Jud N. Dak., U.S.A. 46°32N 98°54W 78 D7
Jude I. Nfld. & L., Canada 47°15N 54°49W 142 E6
Judge Daly Promontory Nunavut,
   Canada 81°15N 67°0W 158 A12
Judique N.S. Canada 45°52N 61°30W 141 H8
Judith → Mont., U.S.A. 47°44N 109°39W 123 C8
Judith, Pt. R.I., U.S.A. 41°22N 71°29W 91 C3
Judith Basin County ☆ Mont., U.S.A. 46°55N 110°10W 123 C7
Judith Gap Mont., U.S.A. 46°41N 109°45W 123 D8
Judith Mts. Mont., U.S.A. 47°15N 109°20W 123 C8
Judsonia Ark., U.S.A. 35°16N 91°38W 106 C4
Juigalpa Nic. 12°6N 85°26W 182 D2
Julesburg Colo., U.S.A. 40°59N 102°16W 125 B8
Julesburg Res. Colo., U.S.A. 40°56N 102°38W 125 B8
Julian Nebr. U.S.A. 40°31N 95°52W 80 D10
Julian, L. Qué., Canada 54°25N 79°7W 143 B2
Julianehåb = Qaqortoq Greenland 60°43N 46°0W 162 E6
Juliette, L. Ga., U.S.A. 33°2N 83°50W 113 C3
Julimes Chihuahua, Mexico 28°25N 105°27W 169 E10
Jumentos Cays Bahamas 23°0N 75°40W 182 B4
Jump → Wis., U.S.A. 45°1N 91°5W 78 C2
Jumpertown Miss., U.S.A. 34°43N 88°40W 111 B5
Juncos Puerto Rico 18°14N 65°55W 184 G17
Junction Tex., U.S.A. 30°29N 99°46W 109 G8
Junction Utah, U.S.A. 38°14N 112°13W 129 E3
Junction City Ga., U.S.A. 32°36N 84°28W 113 D2
Junction City Kans., U.S.A. 39°2N 96°50W 82 B7
Junction City Ky., U.S.A. 37°35N 84°48W 105 C8
Junction City La., U.S.A. 33°1N 92°43W 110 B3
Junction City Oreg., U.S.A. 44°13N 123°12W 121 C2
Junction City Wis., U.S.A. 44°35N 89°46W 78 D4
Junction Sheep Range Park △ B.C.,
   Canada 51°48N 122°25W 155 D12
June Lake Calif., U.S.A. 37°47N 119°4W 126 F7
Juneau Alaska, U.S.A. 58°18N 134°25W 135 G14
Juneau Wis., U.S.A. 43°24N 88°42W 78 E3
Juneau County ☆ Wis., U.S.A. 43°50N 90°10W 78 E3
Juneau Park Wis., U.S.A. 58°25N 134°20W 135 G14
Jungapeo Michoacan, Mexico 19°27N 100°29W 175 C7
Juniata Nebr., U.S.A. 40°35N 98°30W 80 D7
Juniata Pa., U.S.A. 40°24N 77°1W 87 D5
Juniata County ☆ Pa., U.S.A. 40°45N 77°55W 87 D5
Junior W. Va., U.S.A. 38°59N 79°57W 93 A5
Juniper N.B., Canada 46°33N 67°13W 141 G2
Juniper Ga., U.S.A. 32°32N 84°36W 113 D2
Juniper Mt. Ariz., U.S.A. 35°10N 113°0W 130 B3
Juno Tex., U.S.A. 30°9N 101°7W 108 G6
Juno Beach Fla., U.S.A. 26°52N 80°3W 114 E8
Juntura Oreg., U.S.A. 43°45N 118°5W 121 D7
Jupiter Fla., U.S.A. 26°57N 80°6W 114 E8
Jupiter → Qué., Canada 49°29N 63°37W 140 D6

Juquila Mixes Oaxaca, Mexico 16°58N 95°55W 177 H5
Juskatla B.C., Canada 53°37N 132°18W 154 B2
Justice Ill., U.S.A. 41°44N 87°49W 95 C2
Justin Tex., U.S.A. 33°5N 97°18W 109 D10
Juticalpa Honduras 14°40N 86°12W 182 D2
Juventino Rosas Guanajuato, Mexico 20°39N 101°0W 175 B7
Juventud, I. de la Cuba 21°40N 82°40W 182 B3

K

Kaaawa Hawai'i, U.S.A. 21°33N 157°51W 136 J14
Ka'ala Hawai'i, U.S.A. 21°31N 158°9W 136 J13
Ka'alu'alu B. Hawai'i, U.S.A. 18°58N 155°37W 136 E6
Kabah Yucatán, Mexico 20°15N 89°41W 179 B4
Kabetogama L. Minn., U.S.A. 48°28N 93°1W 77 B3
Kabinakagami → Ont., Canada 50°25N 84°20W 149 B12
Kabinakagami L. Ont., Canada 48°54N 84°25W 149 D12
Kachess L. Wash., U.S.A. 47°20N 121°15W 120 C4
Kackley Kans., U.S.A. 39°42N 97°51W 82 B6
Kadiak I. = Kodiak I. Alaska, U.S.A. 57°30N 152°45W 135 H9
Kadoka S. Dak., U.S.A. 43°50N 101°31W 76 G4
Ka'ena Hawai'i, U.S.A. 21°34N 158°14W 136 J13
Ka'ena Pt. Hawai'i, U.S.A. 21°35N 158°17W 136 J13
Kagamil I. Alaska, U.S.A. 53°0N 169°43W 135 K5
Kagawong L. Ont., Canada 45°54N 82°15W 146 B4
Kagianagami L. Ont., Canada 50°57N 87°50W 149 B9
Kagiano L. Ont., Canada 49°16N 86°26W 149 C10
Kahalu'u Hawai'i, U.S.A. 21°27N 157°50W 136 K14
Kahana Hawai'i, U.S.A. 21°33N 157°53W 136 J14
Kahana B. Hawai'i, U.S.A. 21°35N 157°55W 136 J14
Kahana Valley State Park △ Hawai'i,
   U.S.A. 21°32N 157°53W 136 J14
Kahlotus Wash., U.S.A. 46°39N 118°33W 120 D7
Kahnawake Qué., Canada 45°24N 73°40W 160 B2
Kahoka Mo., U.S.A. 40°25N 91°44W 83 A51
Kaho'olawe Hawai'i, U.S.A. 20°33N 156°37W 136 C5
Kahuku Hawai'i, U.S.A. 21°41N 157°57W 136 J14
Kahuku Pt. Hawai'i, U.S.A. 21°43N 157°59W 136 J14
Kahului Hawai'i, U.S.A. 20°54N 156°28W 136 C5
Kahului ✈ (OGG) Hawai'i, U.S.A. 20°54N 156°26W 136 C5
Kaibab Ariz., U.S.A. 36°54N 112°44W 130 A3
Kaibab Indian Reservation Ariz.,
   U.S.A. 36°55N 112°40W 130 A3
Kaibab Nat. Forest Ariz., U.S.A. 36°35N 112°15W 130 A3
Kaibab Plateau Ariz., U.S.A. 36°45N 112°15W 130 A3
Kaibito Ariz., U.S.A. 36°35N 111°4W 130 A4
Kaibito Plateau Ariz., U.S.A. 36°30N 111°15W 130 A4
Kailua Hawai'i, U.S.A. 19°39N 155°59W 136 D6
Kailua Hawai'i, U.S.A. 21°24N 157°44W 136 K14
Kailua B. Hawai'i, U.S.A. 21°25N 157°40W 136 K14
Kaiparowits Plateau Utah, U.S.A. 37°30N 111°35W 129 F4
Kaipokok B. Nfld. & L., Canada 54°54N 59°47W 143 C6
Kaiwi Channel Hawai'i, U.S.A. 21°15N 157°30W 136 K14
Kaiyuh Mts. Alaska, U.S.A. 64°30N 158°0W 135 D8
Kakabeka Falls Ont., Canada 48°24N 89°37W 148 D7
Kakagi L. Ont., Canada 49°13N 93°52W 148 C3
Kake Alaska, U.S.A. 56°59N 133°57W 135 G14
Kakhonak Alaska, U.S.A. 59°26N 154°51W 135 G9
Kakisa → N.W.T., Canada 61°3N 117°10W 157 D9
Kakisa L. N.W.T., Canada 60°56N 117°43W 157 D9
Kaktovik Alaska, U.S.A. 70°8N 143°38W 135 A12
Kakwa → Alta., Canada 54°37N 118°28W 152 D2
Kakwa Wildland Prov. Park △ Alta.,
   Canada 54°5N 119°55W 152 D1
Kalaallit Nunaat = Greenland ☑
   N. Amer. 66°0N 45°0W 162 D6
Kaladar Ont., Canada 44°37N 77°5W 147 C9
Kalae Hawai'i, U.S.A. 18°55N 155°41W 136 E6
Kalaheo Hawai'i, U.S.A. 21°56N 159°32W 136 B2
Kalama Wash., U.S.A. 46°1N 122°51W 120 D3
Kalamazoo Mich., U.S.A. 42°17N 85°35W 79 G6
Kalamazoo → Mich., U.S.A. 42°40N 86°10W 79 G5
Kalamazoo County ☆ Mich., U.S.A. 42°15N 85°30W 79 G6
Kalaoa Hawai'i, U.S.A. 19°43N 155°58W 136 D6
Kalaupapa Hawai'i, U.S.A. 21°12N 156°59W 136 B5
Kalaupapa Nat. Historical Park △
   Hawai'i, U.S.A. 21°10N 156°59W 136 B5
Kalawao County ☆ Hawai'i, U.S.A. 21°11N 156°58W 136 B5
Kaleden B.C., Canada 49°24N 119°36W 155 F15
Kaleva Mich., U.S.A. 44°22N 86°1W 79 F5
Kalida Ohio, U.S.A. 40°59N 84°12W 86 C2
Kalihi Hawai'i, U.S.A. 21°20N 157°52W 136 K14
Kalihi Valley Hawai'i, U.S.A. 21°20N 157°52W 136 K14
Kalispel Indian Reservation Wash.,
   U.S.A. 48°23N 117°17W 120 B8
Kalispell Mont., U.S.A. 48°12N 114°19W 123 B3
Kalkaska Mich., U.S.A. 44°44N 85°11W 79 E6
Kalkaska County ☆ Mich., U.S.A. 44°45N 85°5W 79 E6
Kalohi Channel Hawai'i, U.S.A. 21°0N 157°0W 136 C5
Kaloko-Honokōhau Nat. Historical Park △
   U.S.A. 19°40N 156°1W 136 D5
Kalona Iowa, U.S.A. 41°29N 91°43W 81 D7
Kaltag Alaska, U.S.A. 64°20N 158°43W 135 D8
Kalvesta Kans., U.S.A. 38°4N 100°18W 82 C3
Kamakou Hawai'i, U.S.A. 21°7N 156°52W 136 B5
Kamalō Hawai'i, U.S.A. 21°3N 156°52W 136 B5
Kamananui → Hawai'i, U.S.A. 21°35N 158°4W 136 J13
Kamas Utah, U.S.A. 40°38N 111°17W 129 C4
Kamela Oreg., U.S.A. 45°26N 118°24W 121 B7
Kamiah Idaho, U.S.A. 46°14N 116°2W 122 C2
Kamilukuak L. Nunavut, Canada 62°22N 101°40W 159 E5
Kaminak L. Nunavut, Canada 62°10N 95°0W 159 E7
Kaminuriak L. Nunavut, Canada 62°57N 95°46W 159 E6
Kamishak Bay Alaska, U.S.A. 59°15N 153°45W 135 G9
Kamloops B.C., Canada 50°40N 120°20W 155 E14
Kamloops L. B.C., Canada 50°45N 120°40W 155 E14
Kamo'oloa Hawai'i, U.S.A. 21°34N 158°7W 136 J13
Kampsville Ill., U.S.A. 39°18N 90°37W 84 D3
Kamrar Iowa, U.S.A. 42°24N 93°44W 81 C5
Kamsack Sask., Canada 51°34N 101°54W 151 D10
Kanaaupscow Qué., Canada 54°2N 76°30W 143 C2
Kanaaupscow → Qué., Canada 53°39N 77°9W 143 C2
Kanab Utah, U.S.A. 37°3N 112°32W 129 F3
Kanab Cr. → Ariz., U.S.A. 36°24N 112°38W 130 A3
Kanabec County ☆ Minn., U.S.A. 45°55N 93°20W 77 E5
Kanaga I. Alaska, U.S.A. 51°45N 177°22W 135 L3
Kanairiktok → Nfld. & L., Canada 55°2N 60°18W 143 B5
Kanakanak Alaska, U.S.A. 59°0N 158°30W 135 G8
Kanarraville Utah, U.S.A. 37°32N 113°11W 129 F2
Kanasin Yucatán, Mexico 20°56N 89°34W 179 B4
Kanata Ont., Canada 45°20N 75°59W 147 B11
Kanawha Iowa, U.S.A. 42°56N 93°48W 81 C5
Kanawha → W. Va., U.S.A. 38°50N 82°9W 102 C2

Kanawha County ☆ W. Va., U.S.A. 38°21N 81°38W 102 C3
Kandiyohi County ☆ Minn., U.S.A. 45°10N 95°0W 77 E4
Kane Ill., U.S.A. 39°11N 90°21W 84 D3
Kane Pa., U.S.A. 41°40N 78°49W 87 C4
Kane Wyo., U.S.A. 44°51N 108°12W 124 B4
Kane Basin Greenland 79°1N 70°0W 162 B4
Kane County ☆ Ill., U.S.A. 41°50N 88°25W 84 B5
Kane County ☆ Utah, U.S.A. 37°15N 112°0W 129 F4
Kaneilio Pt. Hawai'i, U.S.A. 21°27N 158°12W 136 K13
Kāne'ohe Hawai'i, U.S.A. 21°25N 157°48W 136 K14
Kāne'ohe B. Hawai'i, U.S.A. 21°30N 157°50W 136 K14
Kaneohe Marine Corps Air Station Hawai'i,
   U.S.A. 21°27N 157°46W 136 K14
Kangaamiut Greenland 65°50N 53°20W 162 D5
Kangerdlugssuak Greenland 68°10N 32°20W 162 D7
Kangerluarsoruseq Greenland 63°45N 51°27W 162 E5
Kangerluarsoruset = Kangerluarsoruseq
   Greenland 63°45N 51°27W 162 E5
Kangerlussuaq Greenland 66°59N 50°40W 162 E5
Kangersuatsiaq Greenland 72°23N 55°32W 158 C14
Kangikajik Greenland 70°7N 22°0W 162 C8
Kangilinnguit Greenland 61°20N 47°57W 162 E6
Kangiqliniq = Rankin Inlet Nunavut,
   Canada 62°30N 93°0W 159 E7
Kangiqsualujjuaq Qué., Canada 58°30N 65°59W 143 B4
Kangiqsujuaq Qué., Canada 61°30N 72°0W 143 A3
Kangiqtugaapik = Clyde River Nunavut,
   Canada 70°30N 68°30W 158 C12
Kangirsuk Qué., Canada 60°0N 70°0W 143 A4
Kaniapiskau = Caniapiscau → Qué.,
   Canada 56°40N 69°30W 143 B4
Kaniapiskau, L. = Caniapiscau, L. de Qué.,
   Canada 54°10N 69°55W 143 C4
Kaniksu Nat. Forest Idaho, U.S.A. 48°50N 116°30W 122 A2
Kankakee Ill., U.S.A. 41°7N 87°52W 84 B6
Kankakee → Ill., U.S.A. 41°23N 88°15W 84 B5
Kankakee County ☆ Ill., U.S.A. 41°10N 87°50W 84 B6
Kannapolis N.C., U.S.A. 35°30N 80°37W 103 C5
Kanopolis Kans., U.S.A. 38°43N 98°9W 82 C5
Kanopolis Lake Kans., U.S.A. 38°37N 97°58W 82 C6
Kanorado Kans., U.S.A. 39°20N 102°2W 82 B1
Kanosh Utah, U.S.A. 38°48N 112°26W 129 E3
Kansas Ill., U.S.A. 39°33N 87°56W 84 D6
Kansas Okla., U.S.A. 36°12N 94°48W 107 B9
Kansas □ U.S.A. 38°30N 99°0W 82 C5
Kansas → Kans., U.S.A. 39°7N 94°37W 82 B9
Kansas City Kans., U.S.A. 39°7N 94°38W 83 B2
Kansas City Mo., U.S.A. 39°6N 94°35W 83 B2
Kansas City Int. ✈ (MCI) Mo., U.S.A. 39°17N 94°43W 83 B2
Kantishna Alaska, U.S.A. 63°31N 150°57W 135 E10
Kantishna → Alaska, U.S.A. 64°45N 149°58W 135 D10
Kantunil Yucatán, Mexico 20°48N 89°2W 179 B4
Kantunilkin Quintana Roo, Mexico 21°7N 87°28W 179 A6
Kanuti Nat. Wildlife Refuge △ Alaska,
   U.S.A. 66°25N 151°50W 135 C10
Kanxoc Yucatán, Mexico 20°6N 88°4W 179 B5
Kapaa Hawai'i, U.S.A. 22°5N 159°19W 136 A2
Kapahulu Hawai'i, U.S.A. 21°16N 157°49W 136 K14
Kapapa I. Hawai'i, U.S.A. 21°29N 157°48W 136 K14
Kapikotongwa → Ont., Canada 50°39N 86°43W 149 B10
Kaplan La., U.S.A. 30°0N 92°17W 110 E3
Kapoho Hawai'i, U.S.A. 19°30N 154°50W 136 D7
Kaposvar Cr. → Sask., Canada 50°31N 101°55W 151 E10
Kapowsin Wash., U.S.A. 46°59N 122°13W 120 D3
Kapuskasing Ont., Canada 49°25N 82°30W 149 C14
Kapuskasing → Ont., Canada 49°49N 82°0W 149 C14
Karlsruhe N. Dak., U.S.A. 48°6N 100°37W 76 B5
Karlstad Minn., U.S.A. 48°35N 96°31W 77 B2
Karnack Tex., U.S.A. 57°34N 154°28W 135 F19
Karluk Alaska, U.S.A. 32°40N 94°10W 109 E13
Karnak Ill., U.S.A. 37°18N 88°58W 84 F5
Karnes City Tex., U.S.A. 28°53N 97°54W 109 J10
Karnes County ☆ Tex., U.S.A. 28°49N 97°51W 109 J10
Kasaan Alaska, U.S.A. 55°32N 132°24W 135 J15
Kasba L. Nunavut, Canada 60°20N 102°10W 157 D12
Kashabowie Ont., Canada 48°40N 90°26W 148 D6
Kasilof Alaska, U.S.A. 60°23N 151°18W 135 F10
Kaskaskia → Ill., U.S.A. 37°58N 89°57W 84 F41
Kaskattama → Man., Canada 57°3N 90°4W 159 F7
Kaslo B.C., Canada 49°55N 116°55W 155 F18
Kasson Minn., U.S.A. 44°2N 92°45W 77 F61
Katahdin, Mt. Maine, U.S.A. 45°54N 68°56W 90 C5
Katalla Alaska, U.S.A. 60°12N 144°31W 135 F11
Kathleen Fla., U.S.A. 28°7N 82°2W 114 C6
Kathryn N. Dak., U.S.A. 46°41N 97°58W 76 D8
Katimik L. Man., Canada 52°53N 99°21W 151 C12
Katmai Nat. Park and Preserve △ Alaska,
   U.S.A. 58°20N 155°0W 135 G9
Katy Tex., U.S.A. 29°47N 95°49W 109 H12
Kau Hawai'i, U.S.A. 19°21N 155°19W 136 D6
Ka'ū Desert Hawai'i, U.S.A. 19°20N 155°30W 136 D6
Kaua'i Hawai'i, U.S.A. 22°3N 159°30W 136 A2
Kauai Channel Hawai'i, U.S.A. 21°45N 158°50W 136 B3
Kauai Island Lihue Municipal ✈ (LIH) Hawai'i,
   U.S.A. 21°58N 159°20W 136 B2
Kaufman Tex., U.S.A. 32°35N 96°19W 109 E11
Kaufman County ☆ Tex., U.S.A. 32°35N 96°20W 109 E11
Kauhola Pt. Hawai'i, U.S.A. 20°15N 155°47W 136 B6
Kaukauna Wis., U.S.A. 44°17N 88°17W 78 D5
Kaukonahua → Hawai'i, U.S.A. 21°35N 158°7W 136 J13
Ka'ula I. Hawai'i, U.S.A. 21°40N 160°33W 136 B1
Kaulakahi Channel Hawai'i, U.S.A. 22°0N 159°55W 136 B2
Kaumalapau Hawai'i, U.S.A. 20°47N 156°59W 136 C5
Kaunā Pt. Hawai'i, U.S.A. 19°2N 155°53W 136 D6
Kaunakakai Hawai'i, U.S.A. 21°6N 157°1W 136 B4
Kaupō Hawai'i, U.S.A. 20°38N 156°8W 136 C5
Kaw City Okla., U.S.A. 36°46N 96°53W 107 B7
Kaw L. Okla., U.S.A. 36°50N 97°0W 107 B6
Kawagama L. Ont., Canada 45°18N 78°45W 144 F4
Kawaihae B. Hawai'i, U.S.A. 20°0N 155°50W 136 C6
Kawaihae Pt. Hawai'i, U.S.A. 21°4N 160°12W 136 B1
Kawaikini Hawai'i, U.S.A. 22°5N 159°29W 136 A2
Kawailoa Hawai'i, U.S.A. 21°36N 158°5W 136 J13
Kawailoa Beach Hawai'i, U.S.A. 21°37N 158°5W 136 J13
Kawailoa Forest Reserve Hawai'i,
   U.S.A. 21°38N 158°0W 136 J14
Kawawachikamach Qué., Canada 54°48N 66°50W 143 C4
Kaweah, L. Calif., U.S.A. 36°28N 118°52W 127 J8
Kaweenakumik L. Man., Canada 52°50N 99°30W 151 C12
Kawela Hawai'i, U.S.A. 21°42N 158°1W 136 J13
Kawick Pk. Nev., U.S.A. 38°0N 116°5W 126 F10
Kawkawlin Mich., U.S.A. 43°39N 83°57W 79 F8
Kay County ☆ Okla., U.S.A. 36°50N 97°10W 107 B6
Kayak I. Alaska, U.S.A. 59°56N 144°23W 135 G11
Kaycee Wyo., U.S.A. 43°43N 106°38W 124 C1
Kayenta Ariz., U.S.A. 36°44N 110°15W 130 A5
Kaylor S. Dak., U.S.A. 43°11N 97°50W 76 G8

Kaysville Utah, U.S.A. 41°2N 111°56W 129 B4
Kazan → Nunavut, Canada 64°2N 95°29W 159 E6
Kea'au Hawai'i, U.S.A. 19°37N 155°2W 136 D6
Keachie La., U.S.A. 32°11N 93°54W 110 B2
Keahi Pt. Hawai'i, U.S.A. 21°19N 157°59W 136 K14
Keahole Pt. Hawai'i, U.S.A. 19°44N 156°4W 136 D5
Kealaikahiki Channel Hawai'i, U.S.A. 20°35N 156°50W 136 C5
Kealakekua Hawai'i, U.S.A. 19°31N 155°55W 136 D6
Kealia Hawai'i, U.S.A. 19°24N 155°53W 136 D6
Keams Canyon Ariz., U.S.A. 35°49N 110°12W 130 B5
Kearney N.J., U.S.A. 40°27N 74°8W 92 B2
Kearney Ont., Canada 45°33N 79°13W 146 B7
Kearney Mo., U.S.A. 39°22N 94°22W 83 B2
Kearney Nebr., U.S.A. 40°42N 99°5W 80 D6
Kearney County ☆ Nebr., U.S.A. 40°30N 99°0W 80 D7
Kearneysville W. Va., U.S.A. 39°23N 77°53W 93 A3
Kearns Utah, U.S.A. 40°39N 111°59W 134 C1
Kearny Ariz., U.S.A. 33°3N 110°55W 130 D5
Kearny N.J., U.S.A. 40°46N 74°8W 92 B2
Kearny County ☆ Kans., U.S.A. 38°0N 101°15W 82 C2
Kearsarge, Mt. N.H., U.S.A. 43°22N 71°50W 89 C2
Keating Oreg., U.S.A. 44°53N 117°28W 121 C8
Keats Kans., U.S.A. 39°14N 96°43W 82 B7
Keawakapu Hawai'i, U.S.A. 20°43N 156°27W 136 C5
Kechika → B.C., Canada 59°41N 127°12W 157 E7
Keddie Calif., U.S.A. 40°1N 120°58W 126 C6
Kedgwick N.B., Canada 47°40N 67°20W 141 G2
Keedysville Md., U.S.A. 39°29N 77°40W 93 A3
Keefers B.C., Canada 50°1N 121°32W 155 E13
Keefeton Okla., U.S.A. 35°36N 95°21W 107 C8
Ke'ehi Lagoon Hawai'i, U.S.A. 21°20N 157°54W 136 K14
Keele → N.W.T., Canada 64°25N 124°48W 157 D6
Keele Pk. Yukon, Canada 63°26N 130°19W 157 D6
Keele → N.W.T., Canada 44°15N 78°10W 147 C8
Keene Ont., Canada 47°56N 102°56W 76 C3
Keene N. Dak., U.S.A. 42°56N 72°17W 89 D2
Keene N.H., U.S.A. 32°24N 97°20W 109 E10
Keene Tex., U.S.A. 40°7N 104°31W 125 B6
Keenesburg Colo., U.S.A. 38°21N 87°52W 84 E6
Keensburg Ill., U.S.A. 44°29N 73°30W 89 B1
Keeseville N.Y., U.S.A. 47°24N 93°5W 77 C5
Keewatin Minn., U.S.A. 51°45N 88°38W 148 A5
Keezhik L. Ont., Canada 50°9N 61°18W 143 C5
Kegaska Qué., Canada 50°20N 61°25W 148 C6
Kégaska, L. Qué., Canada 58°40N 66°0W 143 B4
Keglo B. Qué., Canada 19°23N 154°55W 136 D7
Kehena Hawai'i, U.S.A. 19°31N 155°58W 136 D6
Keikiwaha Pt. Hawai'i, U.S.A. 35°40N 90°6W 106 C5
Keiser Ark., U.S.A. 64°20N 122°15W 157 D6
Keith Arm N.W.T., Canada 41°15N 101°40W 80 C4
Keith County ☆ Nebr., U.S.A. 39°48N 99°56W 82 C4
Keith Sebelius L. Kans., U.S.A. 41°9N 90°56W 84 B4
Keithsburg Ill., U.S.A. 44°57N 123°1W 121 C2
Keizer Oreg., U.S.A. 44°25N 65°25W 141 J3
Kejimkujik Nat. Park △ N.S., Canada 73°30N 24°30W 162 C8
Kejserr Franz Joseph Fd. Greenland 21°58N 159°43W 136 B2
Kekaha Hawai'i, U.S.A. 32°42N 96°36W 116 B6
Kelberg Tex., U.S.A. 38°30N 88°54W 84 E5
Kell Ill., U.S.A. 31°50N 81°15W 113 C5
Keller Ga., U.S.A. 32°56N 97°15W 116 A2
Keller Tex., U.S.A. 48°5N 118°41W 120 B7
Keller Wash., U.S.A. 63°57N 121°35W 157 D8
Keller L. N.W.T., Canada 40°43N 94°3W 81 E4
Kellerton Iowa, U.S.A. 35°22N 100°30W 108 B7
Kellerville Tex., U.S.A. 68°20N 90°6W 158 D7
Kellet, C. N.W.T., Canada 72°0N 126°0W 156 B7
Kellett Str. N.W.T., Canada 75°45N 117°30W 156 A4
Kelley Iowa, U.S.A. 41°57N 93°40W 81 D5
Kelleys I. Ohio, U.S.A. 41°36N 82°42W 86 B4
Kelliher Sask., Canada 51°16N 103°44W 150 D8
Kelliher Minn., U.S.A. 47°57N 94°27W 77 C4
Kellogg Idaho, U.S.A. 47°32N 116°7W 122 B2
Kellogg Iowa, U.S.A. 41°43N 92°54W 81 D6
Kellogg Minn., U.S.A. 44°18N 91°59W 77 F7
Kellyville Okla., U.S.A. 35°57N 96°13W 107 C7
Kelowna B.C., Canada 49°50N 119°25W 155 F15
Kelsey Bay B.C., Canada 50°25N 126°0W 154 E4
Kelseyville Calif., U.S.A. 38°59N 122°50W 126 E4
Kelso Ark., U.S.A. 33°48N 91°16W 106 D4
Kelso Wash., U.S.A. 46°9N 122°54W 120 D3
Kelvin I. Ont., Canada 49°51N 88°40W 148 C8
Kelvington Sask., Canada 52°10N 103°30W 150 C8
Kelwood Man., Canada 50°37N 99°28W 151 C12
Kemah Tex., U.S.A. 29°32N 95°1W 109 H12
Kemano B.C., Canada 53°35N 128°0W 154 B7
Kemblesville Pa., U.S.A. 39°45N 75°50W 93 B5
Kemmerer Wyo., U.S.A. 41°48N 110°32W 124 E2
Kemp Okla., U.S.A. 33°46N 96°21W 107 E7
Kemp Tex., U.S.A. 32°26N 96°14W 109 E11
Kemp, L. Tex., U.S.A. 33°46N 99°9W 108 D7
Kemper County ☆ Miss., U.S.A. 32°46N 88°33W 111 B5
Kempt, L. Qué., Canada 47°25N 74°22W 145 D8
Kempton Ill., U.S.A. 40°56N 88°14W 84 C5
Kempton Ind., U.S.A. 40°17N 86°14W 85 C4
Kemptown N.S., Canada 45°28N 63°5W 141 H6
Kemptown Md., U.S.A. 39°20N 77°3W 93 A3
Kemptville Ont., Canada 45°0N 75°38W 147 B11
Kenab Plateau Ariz., U.S.A. 36°40N 113°0W 129 F2
Kenai Alaska, U.S.A. 60°33N 151°16W 135 F10
Kenai Fjords Nat. Park △ Alaska,
   U.S.A. 59°40N 149°50W 135 G10
Kenai Mts. Alaska, U.S.A. 60°0N 150°0W 135 G10
Kenai Nat. Wildlife Refuge △ Alaska,
   U.S.A. 60°20N 150°30W 135 F10
Kenai Peninsula ☆ Alaska, U.S.A. 60°25N 151°15W 135 F10
Kenansville Fla., U.S.A. 27°53N 80°59W 114 D8
Kenansville N.C., U.S.A. 34°58N 77°58W 103 D8
Kenaston Sask., Canada 51°30N 106°17W 150 D5
Kenbridge Va., U.S.A. 36°58N 78°8W 102 D6
Kendall Fla., U.S.A. 25°40N 80°19W 115 D1
Kendall Kans., U.S.A. 37°56N 101°33W 82 E2
Kendall Wis., U.S.A. 43°48N 90°21W 78 E3
Kendall, C. Nunavut, Canada 63°36N 87°19W 159 E11
Kendall County ☆ Ill., U.S.A. 41°35N 88°25W 84 B5
Kendall County ☆ Tex., U.S.A. 29°57N 98°48W 109 H9
Kendall Park N.J., U.S.A. 40°25N 74°34W 92 B2
Kendallville Ind., U.S.A. 41°27N 85°16W 85 B5
Kendleton Tex., U.S.A. 29°26N 96°0W 109 H12
Kendrick Fla., U.S.A. 29°15N 82°10W 114 B6
Kendrick Idaho, U.S.A. 46°37N 116°39W 122 C2
Kendrick Okla., U.S.A. 35°47N 96°56W 107 C7
Kenedy Tex., U.S.A. 28°49N 97°51W 109 J10
Kenedy County ☆ Tex., U.S.A. 27°0N 97°40W 108 K10
Kenefic Okla., U.S.A. 34°10N 96°22W 107 D7
Kenefick Tex., U.S.A. 30°7N 94°52W 109 G13

Kenesaw Nebr., U.S.A. 40°37N 98°39W 80 D7
Kenilworth N.J., U.S.A. 40°40N 74°17W 97 B1
Kenly N.C., U.S.A. 35°36N 78°7W 103 C7
Kenmare N. Dak., U.S.A. 48°41N 102°5W 76 B3
Kenmore N.Y., U.S.A. 42°58N 78°52W 88 C2
Kenmore Wash., U.S.A. 47°45N 122°14W 132 B4
Kenna N. Mex., U.S.A. 33°51N 103°46W 131 D7
Kenna W. Va., U.S.A. 38°41N 81°40W 102 C3
Kennaday Peak Wyo., U.S.A. 41°27N 106°31W 124 E6
Kennard Nebr., U.S.A. 41°28N 96°12W 80 C9
Kennard Tex., U.S.A. 31°22N 95°11W 109 F12
Kennebago L. Maine, U.S.A. 45°6N 70°44W 89 A4
Kennebec S. Dak., U.S.A. 43°54N 99°52W 76 G6
Kennebec → Maine, U.S.A. 43°45N 69°46W 90 E4
Kennebec County ☆ Maine, U.S.A. 44°20N 69°50W 90 D4
Kennebecasis → N.B., Canada 45°19N 66°4W 141 H3
Kennebunk Maine, U.S.A. 43°23N 70°33W 90 E3
Kennebunkport Maine, U.S.A. 43°21N 70°28W 90 E3
Kennedale Tex., U.S.A. 32°38N 97°13W 116 C2
Kennedy Sask., Canada 50°1N 102°21W 151 E9
Kennedy Ala., U.S.A. 33°35N 87°59W 112 C3
Kennedy Minn., U.S.A. 48°39N 96°54W 77 B2
Kennedy, C. = Canaveral, C. Fla., U.S.A. 28°27N 80°32W 114 C8
Kennedy, Mt. B.C., Canada 50°50N 125°33W 154 E9
Kennedy Entrance Alaska, U.S.A. 59°1N 152°0W 135 G10
Kennedy I. B.C., Canada 54°3N 130°11W 154 A4
Kennedy Kanal Arctic 80°50N 66°0W 162 A4
Kennedy L. B.C., Canada 49°3N 125°32W 154 F9
Kennedy Space Center U.S.A. 28°40N 80°42W 114 C8
Kennedyville Md., U.S.A. 39°18N 75°58W 93 A5
Kenner La., U.S.A. 29°59N 90°14W 117 B1
Kennesaw Ga., U.S.A. 34°1N 84°37W 113 B2
Kennetcook Qué., Canada 45°11N 63°44W 141 H6
Kenneth City Tampa, U.S.A. 27°48N 82°43W 115 C2
Kennett Mo., U.S.A. 36°14N 90°3W 83 E6
Kennett Square Pa., U.S.A. 39°51N 75°43W 93 A5
Kennewick Wash., U.S.A. 46°12N 119°7W 120 D6
Kenney Ill., U.S.A. 40°6N 89°5W 84 C4
Keno Oreg., U.S.A. 42°8N 121°56W 121 E4
Keno Hill Yukon, Canada 63°57N 135°18W 157 D5
Kenogami → Ont., Canada 51°6N 84°28W 149 A12
Kénogami, L. Qué., Canada 48°20N 71°23W 145 C11
Kenogami Lake Qué., Canada 48°6N 80°12W 144 C2
Kenora Ont., Canada 49°47N 94°29W 148 C2
Kenosha Wis., U.S.A. 42°35N 87°49W 78 F6
Kenosha County ☆ Wis., U.S.A. 42°35N 87°50W 78 F6
Kenova W. Va., U.S.A. 38°24N 82°35W 102 C2
Kensal N. Dak., U.S.A. 47°18N 98°44W 76 C7
Kensett Ark., U.S.A. 35°14N 91°40W 106 C4
Kensett Iowa, U.S.A. 43°21N 93°13W 81 B5
Kensington P.E.I., Canada 46°28N 63°34W 141 G6
Kensington Conn., U.S.A. 41°38N 72°46W 91 C2
Kensington Kans., U.S.A. 39°46N 99°2W 82 B4
Kensington Md., U.S.A. 39°2N 77°5W 93 A3
Kensington Minn., U.S.A. 45°47N 95°42W 77 E3
Kensington N.Y., U.S.A. 40°38N 73°57W 97 C3
Kent Conn., U.S.A. 41°44N 73°29W 91 C1
Kent Iowa, U.S.A. 40°57N 94°28W 81 E4
Kent Minn., U.S.A. 46°26N 96°41W 77 D2
Kent Ohio, U.S.A. 41°9N 81°22W 86 B5
Kent Oreg., U.S.A. 45°12N 120°42W 121 B5
Kent Tex., U.S.A. 31°4N 104°13W 108 F3
Kent Wash., U.S.A. 47°22N 122°14W 132 D4
Kent City Mich., U.S.A. 43°13N 85°45W 79 F6
Kent County ☆ Del., U.S.A. 39°10N 75°30W 93 A5
Kent County ☆ Md., U.S.A. 39°15N 76°6W 93 A5
Kent County ☆ Mich., U.S.A. 43°0N 85°35W 79 F6
Kent County ☆ R.I., U.S.A. 41°35N 71°40W 91 C3
Kent County ☆ Tex., U.S.A. 33°10N 100°45W 108 D7
Kent I. Md., U.S.A. 38°52N 76°18W 93 B4
Kent Junction N.B., Canada 46°35N 65°20W 141 G4
Kent Pen. Nunavut, Canada 68°30N 107°0W 158 D4
Kent Village Md., U.S.A. 38°55N 76°53W 99 B4
Kentland Ind., U.S.A. 40°46N 87°27W 85 C3
Kentmore Park Md., U.S.A. 39°22N 75°58W 93 A5
Kenton Del., U.S.A. 39°14N 75°40W 93 A5
Kenton Mich., U.S.A. 46°28N 88°54W 79 C3
Kenton Ohio, U.S.A. 40°39N 83°37W 86 C5
Kenton Okla., U.S.A. 36°54N 102°58W 107 B1
Kenton Tenn., U.S.A. 36°12N 89°1W 104 D3
Kenton County ☆ Ky., U.S.A. 38°55N 84°32W 105 B8
Kentucky □ U.S.A. 37°0N 84°0W 105 C8
Kentucky → Ky., U.S.A. 38°41N 85°11W 105 B7
Kentucky L. Ky., U.S.A. 37°1N 88°16W 104 C4
Kentville N.S., Canada 45°6N 64°29W 141 H5
Kentwood La., U.S.A. 30°56N 90°31W 110 D5
Kentwood Mich., U.S.A. 42°52N 85°39W 79 G6
Kenville Man., Canada 52°0N 101°20W 151 D10
Kenwood Baltimore, U.S.A. 39°20N 76°30W 99 B2
Kenyon Minn., U.S.A. 44°16N 92°59W 77 F6
Keo Ark., U.S.A. 34°36N 92°1W 106 D3
Keokuk Iowa, U.S.A. 40°24N 91°24W 81 E7
Keokuk County ☆ Iowa, U.S.A. 41°20N 92°10W 81 D6
Keosauqua Iowa, U.S.A. 40°44N 91°58W 81 E7
Keota Colo., U.S.A. 40°42N 104°5W 125 B6
Keota Iowa, U.S.A. 41°22N 91°57W 81 D7
Keota Okla., U.S.A. 35°15N 94°55W 107 C9
Kepuhi Pt. Hawai'i, U.S.A. 21°29N 158°14W 136 K13
Kerby Oreg., U.S.A. 42°12N 123°39W 121 E2
Keremeos B.C., Canada 49°13N 119°50W 155 F15
Kerens Tex., U.S.A. 32°8N 96°14W 109 E11
Kerkhoven Minn., U.S.A. 45°12N 95°19W 77 E3
Kerman Calif., U.S.A. 36°43N 120°4W 127 G6
Kermit Tex., U.S.A. 31°52N 103°6W 108 F4
Kermit W. Va., U.S.A. 37°50N 82°24W 102 D2
Kern County ☆ Calif., U.S.A. 35°20N 118°30W 127 H8
Kern Park Wis., U.S.A. 43°5N 87°53W 94 B2
Kernersville N.C., U.S.A. 36°7N 80°4W 103 B5
Kernville Calif., U.S.A. 35°45N 118°26W 127 H8
Kerr County ☆ Tex., U.S.A. 30°0N 99°21W 109 G8
Kerrick Minn., U.S.A. 46°20N 92°35W 77 D6
Kerrick Tex., U.S.A. 36°30N 102°15W 108 A5
Kerrobert Sask., Canada 51°56N 109°8W 150 D2
Kerrville Tex., U.S.A. 30°3N 99°8W 109 G8
Kersey Colo., U.S.A. 40°23N 104°34W 125 B6
Kershaw S.C., U.S.A. 34°33N 80°35W 103 D5
Kershaw County ☆ S.C., U.S.A. 34°20N 80°40W 103 D5
Keswick = Georgina Ont., Canada 44°15N 79°28W 146 C7
Keshena Wis., U.S.A. 44°53N 88°39W 78 D5
Ketchikan Alaska, U.S.A. 55°21N 131°39W 135 J15
Ketchikan Gateway ☆ Alaska, U.S.A. 55°50N 131°25W 135 J15
Ketchum Idaho, U.S.A. 43°41N 114°22W 122 F4
Ketchum Okla., U.S.A. 36°32N 95°1W 107 B8

Kettering Md., U.S.A. 38°53N 76°49W 99 B5
Kettering Ohio, U.S.A. 39°41N 84°10W 86 D2
Kettle → N. Amer. 48°41N 118°7W 155 G16
Kettle → Minn., U.S.A. 45°52N 92°46W 77 E6
Kettle, Île Qué., Canada 45°28N 75°59W 160 A2
Kettle Cr. → Pa., U.S.A. 41°18N 77°51W 87 C5
Kettle Falls Wash., U.S.A. 48°37N 118°3W 120 B7
Kettle Pt. Ont., Canada 43°13N 82°1W 146 D4
Kettle River Minn., U.S.A. 46°29N 92°53W 77 D6
Kettle River Range Wash., U.S.A. 48°30N 118°40W 120 B7
Kettleman City Calif., U.S.A. 36°1N 119°58W 127 G7
Keuka L. N.Y., U.S.A. 42°30N 77°9W 88 C5
Kevil Ky., U.S.A. 37°5N 88°53W 104 C4
Kevin Mont., U.S.A. 48°45N 111°58W 123 B6
Kew Gardens Ont., Canada 43°39N 79°18W 161 A3
Kewanee Ill., U.S.A. 41°14N 89°56W 84 B4
Kewanna Ind., U.S.A. 41°1N 86°25W 85 B4
Kewaskum Wis., U.S.A. 43°31N 88°14W 78 E5
Kewaunee Wis., U.S.A. 44°27N 87°31W 78 D6
Kewaunee County ☆ Wis., U.S.A. 44°30N 87°40W 78 D6
Keweenaw B. Mich., U.S.A. 47°0N 88°15W 79 C3
Keweenaw County ☆ Mich., U.S.A. 47°20N 88°5W 79 B3
Keweenaw Nat. Historic Park Mich., U.S.A. 47°9N 88°33W 79 B3
Keweenaw Pen. Mich., U.S.A. 47°15N 88°15W 79 B3
Keweenaw Pt. Mich., U.S.A. 47°25N 87°43W 79 B4
Key Tex., U.S.A. 32°44N 101°48W 108 D6
Key Biscayne Fla., U.S.A. 25°41N 80°9W 115 D3
Key Colony Beach Fla., U.S.A. 24°43N 80°57W 114 G8
Key Harbour Ont., Canada 45°50N 80°45W 146 B6
Key Largo Fla., U.S.A. 25°5N 80°27W 114 F8
Key West Fla., U.S.A. 24°33N 81°48W 114 G7
Key West Nat. Wildlife Refuge Fla., U.S.A. 24°33N 82°2W 114 G6
Keya Paha → Nebr., U.S.A. 42°54N 99°0W 80 B6
Keya Paha County ☆ Nebr., U.S.A. 42°50N 99°40W 80 B6
Keyapaha S. Dak., U.S.A. 43°7N 100°8W 76 G5
Keyes Okla., U.S.A. 36°49N 102°15W 107 B1
Keyesport Ill., U.S.A. 38°45N 89°17W 84 E4
Keyhole Reservoir Wyo., U.S.A. 44°21N 104°51W 124 B8
Keymar Md., U.S.A. 39°38N 77°16W 93 A3
Keyport N.J., U.S.A. 40°26N 74°12W 92 B2
Keyport Wash., U.S.A. 47°42N 122°37W 132 B2
Keyser W. Va., U.S.A. 39°26N 78°59W 93 A2
Keystone Iowa, U.S.A. 42°0N 92°2W 81 C6
Keystone Nebr., U.S.A. 41°13N 101°35W 80 C4
Keystone S. Dak., U.S.A. 43°54N 103°25W 76 G2
Keystone Heights Fla., U.S.A. 29°47N 82°2W 114 B6
Keystone L. Okla., U.S.A. 36°15N 96°25W 107 B7
Keystone Peak Ariz., U.S.A. 31°53N 111°13W 130 F4
Keysville Ga., U.S.A. 33°14N 82°14W 113 C4
Keysville Va., U.S.A. 37°2N 78°29W 102 D6
Keytesville Mo., U.S.A. 39°26N 92°56W 83 B4
Kezar Falls Maine, U.S.A. 43°48N 70°53W 90 E3
Khedive Sask., Canada 49°37N 104°31W 150 F7
Kiamichi → Okla., U.S.A. 33°58N 95°14W 107 E8
Kiamichi Mt. Okla., U.S.A. 34°38N 94°35W 107 D9
Kiamichi Mts. Okla., U.S.A. 34°37N 95°0W 107 D9
Kiana Alaska, U.S.A. 66°58N 160°26W 135 C7
Kianuko Park → B.C., Canada 49°26N 116°28W 153 J4
Kiawah Island S.C., U.S.A. 32°36N 80°5W 103 F5
Kickapoo Wis., U.S.A. 43°5N 90°55W 78 E3
Kickapoo, L. Tex., U.S.A. 33°40N 98°47W 109 D9
Kickapoo Indian Reservation Kans., U.S.A. 39°40N 95°50W 82 B8
Kicking Horse Pass B.C., Canada 51°28N 116°16W 155 D18
Kidder Mo., U.S.A. 39°47N 94°6W 83 B2
Kidder County ☆ N. Dak., U.S.A. 47°0N 99°55W 76 D6
Kief N. Dak., U.S.A. 47°51N 100°31W 76 C5
Kiefer Okla., U.S.A. 35°57N 96°4W 107 C7
Kiel Wis., U.S.A. 43°55N 88°2W 78 E5
Kiester Minn., U.S.A. 43°32N 93°43W 77 G5
Kiglapait Mts. Nfld. & L., Canada 57°6N 61°22W 143 B5
Kihei Hawai'i, U.S.A. 20°47N 156°28W 136 C5
Kiholo B. Hawai'i, U.S.A. 19°50N 155°55W 136 D6
Kihuic Yucatán, Mexico 20°4N 89°32W 179 B4
Kijik Alaska, U.S.A. 60°20N 154°20W 135 F9
Kikerk L. Nunavut, Canada 67°18N 113°12W 156 C10
Kikino Alta., Canada 54°27N 112°8W 152 D8
Kikkertoksoak I. N.W.T., Canada 58°50N 65°50W 143 B4
Kila Mont., U.S.A. 48°7N 114°27W 123 B3
Kilauea Hawai'i, U.S.A. 22°13N 159°25W 136 A2
Kilauea Caldera Hawai'i, U.S.A. 19°25N 155°17W 136 D6
Kilbourne Ill., U.S.A. 40°9N 90°1W 84 C3
Kilbourne La., U.S.A. 33°0N 91°20W 110 A4
Kilbride Nfld. & L., Canada 47°32N 52°45W 142 E8
Kilbuck Mts. Alaska, U.S.A. 60°36N 159°53W 135 F8
Kildala Arm B.C., Canada 53°50N 128°29W 154 B6
Kildare Ga., U.S.A. 32°32N 81°27W 113 D5
Kilgore Idaho, U.S.A. 44°24N 111°54W 122 E7
Kilgore Tex., U.S.A. 32°23N 94°53W 109 E13
Kilian I. Nunavut, Canada 73°35N 107°53W 158 C4
Kilkenny Minn., U.S.A. 44°19N 93°34W 77 F5
Kill Devil Hills N.C., U.S.A. 36°1N 75°39W 103 B10
Kill Van Kull → N.Y., U.S.A. 40°39N 74°5W 97 C2
Kilala L. Ont., Canada 49°5N 86°32W 149 C10
Killaloe Ont., Canada 45°33N 77°25W 144 F5
Killaly Sask., Canada 50°45N 102°50W 150 E9
Killam Alta., Canada 52°47N 111°51W 153 F9
Killarney B.C., Canada 49°16N 123°1W 161 B2
Killarney Man., Canada 49°10N 99°40W 151 F12
Killarney Ont., Canada 45°55N 81°30W 146 B5
Killarney Prov. Park → Ont., Canada 46°2N 81°35W 146 A5
Killbuck Ohio, U.S.A. 40°30N 81°59W 86 C5
Killbuck Cr. → Ohio, U.S.A. 40°30N 81°59W 86 C5
Killdeer Sask., Canada 49°6N 106°22W 150 F5
Killdeer N. Dak., U.S.A. 47°22N 102°45W 76 C3
Killen Ala., U.S.A. 34°52N 87°32W 112 B3
Killingly Conn., U.S.A. 41°50N 71°55W 91 C3
Killingworth Conn., U.S.A. 41°21N 72°30W 91 C2
Killiniq I. Nfld. & L., Canada 60°24N 64°37W 143 A3
Kilmar Qué., Canada 45°46N 74°37W 144 F8
Kilmarnock Va., U.S.A. 37°43N 76°23W 93 C4
Kilmichael Miss., U.S.A. 33°27N 89°34W 111 C4
Kilometro Noventa y Uno Chihuahua, Mexico 28°7N 105°36W 169 E10
Kim Colo., U.S.A. 37°15N 103°21W 125 E7
Kimball Nebr., U.S.A. 41°14N 103°40W 80 C2
Kimball S. Dak., U.S.A. 43°45N 98°57W 76 G7
Kimball W. Va., U.S.A. 37°26N 81°30W 102 D3
Kimball County ☆ Nebr., U.S.A. 41°15N 103°40W 80 C2
Kimballton Iowa, U.S.A. 41°38N 95°4W 81 D3

Kimberley B.C., Canada 49°40N 115°59W 153 J5
Kimberling City Mo., U.S.A. 36°38N 93°25W 83 E3
Kimberly Idaho, U.S.A. 42°32N 114°22W 122 G4
Kimberly Oreg., U.S.A. 44°46N 119°39W 121 C6
Kimble County ☆ Tex., U.S.A. 30°29N 99°46W 109 G8
Kimbolton Ohio, U.S.A. 40°9N 81°34W 86 C5
Kimbrough Ala., U.S.A. 32°2N 87°34W 112 D3
Kimiwan L. Alta., Canada 55°45N 116°55W 152 C4
Kimmirut Nunavut, Canada 62°50N 69°50W 159 E12
Kimsquit B.C., Canada 52°45N 126°57W 154 C6
Kinard Fla., U.S.A. 30°16N 85°15W 114 A3
Kinbasket L. B.C., Canada 52°0N 118°10W 155 C16
Kincaid Ill., U.S.A. 39°35N 89°25W 84 D4
Kincaid Kans., U.S.A. 38°5N 95°9W 82 C8
Kincardine Ont., Canada 44°10N 81°40W 146 C5
Kinchafoonee Cr. → Ga., U.S.A. 31°38N 84°10W 113 E2
Kinchil Yucatán, Mexico 20°55N 89°57W 179 B4
Kincolith B.C., Canada 55°0N 129°57W 157 F7
Kinde Mich., U.S.A. 43°56N 83°0W 79 F8
Kinderhook N.Y., U.S.A. 42°24N 73°42W 91 B1
Kindersley Sask., Canada 51°30N 109°10W 150 D2
Kindred N. Dak., U.S.A. 46°39N 97°1W 76 D8
King N.C., U.S.A. 36°17N 80°22W 103 B5
King and Queen County ☆ Va., U.S.A. 37°40N 76°53W 102 D8
King and Queen Court House Va., U.S.A. 37°40N 76°53W 93 C4
King Christian I. Nunavut, Canada 77°48N 101°40W 158 B5
King City Calif., U.S.A. 36°13N 121°8W 127 G5
King City Mo., U.S.A. 40°3N 94°31W 83 A2
King County ☆ Tex., U.S.A. 33°37N 100°19W 108 D7
King County ☆ Wash., U.S.A. 47°25N 121°40W 120 C4
King County Int. ✈ (BFI) Wash., U.S.A. 47°31N 122°18W 132 C4
King Cove Alaska, U.S.A. 55°3N 162°19W 135 J7
King Frederik VI Land = Kong Frederik VI Kyst Greenland 63°0N 43°0W 162 E6
King George Va., U.S.A. 38°16N 77°11W 93 B3
King George County ☆ Va., U.S.A. 38°16N 77°11W 102 D7
King George Is. Nunavut, Canada 57°20N 80°30W 143 B1
King I. B.C., Canada 52°10N 127°40W 154 B6
King of Prussia Pa., U.S.A. 40°5N 75°23W 92 B1
King Range Nat. Conservation Area Calif., U.S.A. 40°10N 124°8W 126 C2
King Salmon Alaska, U.S.A. 58°42N 156°40W 135 G8
King William Va., U.S.A. 37°41N 77°1W 102 D7
King William County ☆ Va., U.S.A. 37°41N 77°1W 102 D7
King William I. Nunavut, Canada 69°10N 97°25W 158 D6
Kingait = Cape Dorset Nunavut, Canada 64°14N 76°32W 159 E10
Kingaok = Bathurst Inlet Nunavut, Canada 66°50N 108°1W 156 C11
Kingcome Inlet B.C., Canada 50°56N 126°29W 154 E8
Kingfield Maine, U.S.A. 44°58N 70°9W 90 D3
Kingfisher Okla., U.S.A. 35°52N 97°56W 107 C6
Kingfisher County ☆ Okla., U.S.A. 36°0N 98°0W 107 C6
Kingman Ariz., U.S.A. 35°12N 114°4W 130 B1
Kingman Kans., U.S.A. 37°39N 98°7W 82 D5
Kingman County ☆ Kans., U.S.A. 37°30N 98°0W 82 D5
Kings → Ark., U.S.A. 36°30N 93°35W 106 B2
Kings → Calif., U.S.A. 36°3N 119°50W 127 G7
Kings → Nev., U.S.A. 41°31N 118°8W 128 A2
Kings Canyon Nat. Park △ Calif., U.S.A. 36°50N 118°40W 127 G8
Kings County ☆ Calif., U.S.A. 36°0N 119°50W 127 G7
Kings County ☆ N.Y., U.S.A. 40°37N 73°55W 88 E7
Kings Mountain N.C., U.S.A. 35°15N 81°20W 103 C4
Kings Park Va., U.S.A. 38°48N 77°17W 99 C2
Kings Park West Va., U.S.A. 38°48N 77°18W 99 C2
Kings Peak Utah, U.S.A. 40°46N 110°23W 129 C5
King's Point Nfld. & L., Canada 49°35N 56°11W 142 C4
King's Point N.Y., U.S.A. 40°49N 73°44W 97 B4
Kings Valley Oreg., U.S.A. 44°42N 123°26W 121 C2
Kingsburg Calif., U.S.A. 36°31N 119°33W 127 G7
Kingsbury N.Y., U.S.A. 43°22N 73°32W 89 C1
Kingsbury County ☆ S. Dak., U.S.A. 44°23N 97°33W 76 F8
Kingsdown Kans., U.S.A. 37°32N 99°46W 82 D4
Kingsey Falls Qué., Canada 45°51N 72°4W 145 F10
Kingsford Mich., U.S.A. 45°48N 88°4W 79 D3
Kingsford Heights Ind., U.S.A. 41°29N 86°42W 85 B4
Kingsgate B.C., Canada 49°1N 116°11W 153 J4
Kingsland Ark., U.S.A. 33°52N 92°18W 106 E3
Kingsland Ga., U.S.A. 30°48N 81°41W 113 F5
Kingsland Tex., U.S.A. 30°40N 98°26W 109 G9
Kingsley Iowa, U.S.A. 42°35N 95°58W 81 C2
Kingsley Mich., U.S.A. 44°35N 85°32W 79 E6
Kingsmere L. Sask., Canada 54°6N 106°27W 150 A5
Kingsmill Tex., U.S.A. 35°29N 101°4W 108 B6
Kingsport Tenn., U.S.A. 36°33N 82°33W 105 D10
Kingston N.S., Canada 44°59N 64°57W 141 J5
Kingston Ont., Canada 44°14N 76°30W 147 C10
Kingston Jamaica 18°0N 76°50W 182 C4
Kingston Ark., U.S.A. 36°3N 93°31W 106 B2
Kingston Ga., U.S.A. 34°14N 84°57W 113 B2
Kingston Ky., U.S.A. 37°39N 84°15W 105 C8
Kingston Mass., U.S.A. 41°59N 70°43W 91 B4
Kingston Md., U.S.A. 38°5N 75°46W 93 B5
Kingston Mich., U.S.A. 43°25N 83°11W 79 F8
Kingston Minn., U.S.A. 45°12N 94°19W 77 E4
Kingston N.H., U.S.A. 42°56N 71°3W 89 D3
Kingston N.Y., U.S.A. 41°56N 73°59W 88 D7
Kingston Ohio, U.S.A. 39°28N 82°55W 86 D4
Kingston Okla., U.S.A. 33°59N 96°45W 107 E7
Kingston Pa., U.S.A. 41°16N 75°54W 87 C8
Kingston R.I., U.S.A. 41°29N 71°30W 91 C3
Kingston Tenn., U.S.A. 35°52N 84°31W 105 D8
Kingston Utah, U.S.A. 38°13N 112°11W 129 E3
Kingston Wash., U.S.A. 47°47N 122°29W 132 B3
Kingston Pk. Calif., U.S.A. 35°44N 115°55W 127 H11
Kingston Springs Tenn., U.S.A. 36°6N 87°7W 104 D5
Kingstown St. Vincent 13°10N 61°10W 183 D7
Kingstree S.C., U.S.A. 33°40N 79°50W 103 E6
Kingsville Ont., Canada 42°2N 82°45W 146 E4
Kingsville Md., U.S.A. 39°27N 76°25W 99 A4
Kingsville Mo., U.S.A. 38°45N 94°4W 83 C2
Kingsville Tex., U.S.A. 27°31N 97°52W 108 K10
Kingsway Qué., Canada 43°38N 79°32W 161 B1
Kingwood Tex., U.S.A. 30°3N 95°16W 109 G12
Kingwood W. Va., U.S.A. 39°28N 79°41W 102 B5
Kinistino Sask., Canada 52°57N 105°2W 150 C6
Kinkaid L. Ill., U.S.A. 37°40N 89°25W 84 F4
Kinkora P.E.I., Canada 46°19N 63°36W 141 G6

Kinloch Mo., U.S.A. 38°44N 90°19W 94 A2
Kinmount Ont., Canada 44°48N 78°45W 147 C8
Kinmundy Ill., U.S.A. 38°46N 88°51W 84 E5
Kinnear Wyo., U.S.A. 43°9N 108°41W 124 C4
Kinnelon N.J., U.S.A. 40°58N 74°22W 92 B2
Kinney Minn., U.S.A. 47°31N 92°44W 77 C6
Kinney County ☆ Tex., U.S.A. 29°19N 100°25W 108 H7
Kino Nuevo Sonora, Mexico 28°52N 112°3W 168 E3
Kinoje Lakes Ont., Canada 51°35N 81°48W 149 A15
Kinsale Va., U.S.A. 38°2N 76°35W 93 B4
Kinsley Kans., U.S.A. 37°55N 99°25W 82 D4
Kinston Ala., U.S.A. 31°13N 86°10W 112 E4
Kinston N.C., U.S.A. 35°16N 77°35W 103 C8
Kinta Okla., U.S.A. 35°8N 95°14W 107 C8
Kinuso Alta., Canada 55°20N 115°25W 152 C4
Kinzua Oreg., U.S.A. 44°59N 120°3W 121 C5
Kiosk Ont., Canada 46°6N 78°53W 147 A8
Kiowa Colo., U.S.A. 39°21N 104°28W 125 C6
Kiowa Kans., U.S.A. 37°1N 98°29W 82 D5
Kiowa Okla., U.S.A. 34°43N 95°54W 107 D8
Kiowa County ☆ Colo., U.S.A. 38°25N 102°50W 125 D8
Kiowa County ☆ Kans., U.S.A. 37°30N 99°15W 82 D4
Kiowa County ☆ Okla., U.S.A. 35°0N 99°0W 107 D5
Kiowa Cr. → Colo., U.S.A. 40°20N 104°5W 125 B6
Kiowa Cr. → Okla., U.S.A. 36°24N 100°0W 107 B4
Kipapa → Hawai'i, U.S.A. 21°24N 158°1W 136 K13
Kipawa Qué., Canada 46°47N 78°59W 144 E4
Kipawa, L. Qué., Canada 46°50N 79°0W 144 E4
Kipling Sask., Canada 50°6N 102°38W 150 E9
Kipling Heights Ont., Canada 43°43N 79°34W 161 A1
Kipnuk Alaska, U.S.A. 59°56N 164°3W 135 G6
Kipp Kans., U.S.A. 38°47N 97°27W 82 C6
Kippens Nfld. & L., Canada 48°33N 58°38W 142 D2
Kiptopeke Va., U.S.A. 37°8N 75°58W 102 D9
Kirby Tex., U.S.A. 29°27N 98°23W 116 D2
Kirby W. Va., U.S.A. 39°11N 78°44W 93 A2
Kirby Wyo., U.S.A. 43°48N 108°11W 124 C4
Kirbyville Tex., U.S.A. 30°40N 93°54W 109 G14
Kirk Colo., U.S.A. 39°37N 102°36W 125 C8
Kirk Oreg., U.S.A. 42°45N 121°50W 121 E4
Kirkfield Ont., Canada 44°34N 78°59W 147 C8
Kirkland Ariz., U.S.A. 34°25N 112°43W 130 C3
Kirkland Ill., U.S.A. 42°6N 88°51W 84 A5
Kirkland Tex., U.S.A. 34°23N 100°4W 109 C7
Kirkland Wash., U.S.A. 47°40N 122°12W 132 B4
Kirkland Junction Ariz., U.S.A. 34°22N 112°40W 130 C3
Kirklin Ind., U.S.A. 40°12N 86°22W 85 C4
Kirkman Iowa, U.S.A. 41°44N 95°16W 81 D3
Kirkmansville Ky., U.S.A. 37°1N 87°15W 104 C5
Kirksey Ky., U.S.A. 36°42N 88°24W 104 C4
Kirksville Mo., U.S.A. 40°12N 92°35W 83 A4
Kirkwood Del., U.S.A. 39°34N 75°42W 93 A5
Kirkwood Ill., U.S.A. 40°52N 90°45W 84 C3
Kirkwood Mo., U.S.A. 38°35N 90°24W 83 C6
Kirkwood Pa., U.S.A. 39°51N 76°5W 93 A4
Kiron Iowa, U.S.A. 42°12N 95°20W 81 C3
Kirtland N. Mex., U.S.A. 36°44N 108°21W 131 A2
Kirwin Kans., U.S.A. 39°40N 99°7W 82 B4
Kirwin Res. Kans., U.S.A. 39°40N 99°8W 82 B4
Kiryas Joel N.Y., U.S.A. 41°21N 74°10W 92 A2
Kisalaya Nic. 14°40N 84°3W 182 D3
Kisatchie La., U.S.A. 31°25N 93°10W 110 C2
Kisatchie Nat. Forest La., U.S.A. 31°45N 92°30W 110 C3
Kisbey Sask., Canada 49°39N 102°40W 150 F9
Kiska I. Alaska, U.S.A. 51°59N 177°30E 135 L2
Kiskitto L. Man., Canada 54°16N 98°30W 151 A13
Kiskittogisu L. Man., Canada 54°13N 98°20W 151 A13
Kismet Kans., U.S.A. 37°12N 100°42W 82 D3
Kissena Park N.Y., U.S.A. 40°44N 73°48W 97 B4
Kissimmee Fla., U.S.A. 28°18N 81°24W 114 C7
Kissimmee → Fla., U.S.A. 27°9N 80°52W 114 D8
Kissimmee, L. Fla., U.S.A. 27°55N 81°17W 114 D7
Kit Carson Colo., U.S.A. 38°46N 102°48W 125 D8
Kit Carson County ☆ Colo., U.S.A. 39°15N 102°30W 125 C8
Kitaa □ Greenland 70°0N 47°0W 162 C6
Kitamaat Village B.C., Canada 53°59N 128°39W 154 B6
Kitchener Ont., Canada 43°27N 80°29W 146 D6
Kitimat B.C., Canada 54°3N 128°38W 154 A6
Kitimat Arm B.C., Canada 53°55N 128°42W 154 B6
Kitimat Ranges B.C., Canada 54°0N 129°15W 154 B5
Kitkatla B.C., Canada 53°47N 130°25W 154 B4
Kitsap County ☆ Wash., U.S.A. 47°40N 122°45W 120 C3
Kitscoty Alta., Canada 53°20N 110°20W 152 E10
Kittanning Pa., U.S.A. 40°49N 79°31W 87 D2
Kittatinny Mt. N.J., U.S.A. 41°19N 74°39W 92 A2
Kittery Maine, U.S.A. 43°5N 70°45W 90 E3
Kittitas Wash., U.S.A. 46°59N 120°25W 120 C5
Kittitas County ☆ Wash., U.S.A. 47°10N 120°30W 120 C5
Kitts Hummock Del., U.S.A. 39°8N 75°25W 93 A5
Kittson County ☆ Minn., U.S.A. 48°50N 96°50W 77 B2
Kitzmiller Md., U.S.A. 39°23N 79°10W 93 A1
Kivalina Alaska, U.S.A. 67°44N 164°33W 135 C6
Klamath Calif., U.S.A. 41°32N 124°2W 126 B2
Klamath → Calif., U.S.A. 41°33N 124°5W 126 B2
Klamath County ☆ Oreg., U.S.A. 42°40N 121°40W 121 E4
Klamath Falls Oreg., U.S.A. 42°13N 121°46W 121 E4
Klamath Marsh Oreg., U.S.A. 43°0N 121°40W 121 E4
Klamath Mts. Calif., U.S.A. 41°50N 123°20W 126 B3
Klamath Nat. Forest Calif., U.S.A. 41°30N 123°20W 126 B3
Klamath River Calif., U.S.A. 41°52N 122°50W 126 B4
Klawock Alaska, U.S.A. 55°33N 133°6W 135 J14
Kleberg County ☆ Tex., U.S.A. 27°31N 97°52W 108 K10
Kleczkowski, L. Qué., Canada 50°48N 63°27W 140 C6
Kleena Kleene B.C., Canada 52°0N 124°59W 154 C8
Klein Mont., U.S.A. 46°24N 108°33W 123 D9
Kleindale B.C., Canada 49°38N 123°58W 154 F12
Klemme Iowa, U.S.A. 43°1N 93°36W 81 B5
Kletzsch Park Wis., U.S.A. 43°8N 87°55W 94 B2
Klickitat Wash., U.S.A. 45°49N 121°9W 120 E4
Klickitat → Wash., U.S.A. 45°42N 121°17W 120 E4
Klickitat County ☆ Wash., U.S.A. 45°55N 120°30W 120 E5
Klinaklini → B.C., Canada 51°21N 125°40W 154 D9
Klondike Yukon, Canada 64°3N 139°26W 157 D5
Klondike Goldrush Nat. Historical Park U.S.A. 59°27N 135°19W 135 G14
Klotz, L. Qué., Canada 60°32N 70°40W 143 A3
Kluane L. Yukon, Canada 61°15N 138°40W 157 D5
Kluane Nat. Park △ Yukon, Canada 60°45N 139°30W 157 D5
Kluskoil Lake Park △ B.C., Canada 53°13N 123°54W 154 B11
Knapp Wis., U.S.A. 44°57N 92°5W 78 D1
Knee L. Man., Canada 54°54N 94°45W 159 F7
Kneeland Calif., U.S.A. 40°45N 123°59W 126 C3
Knewstubb L. B.C., Canada 53°33N 124°55W 154 B10
Knierim Iowa, U.S.A. 42°27N 94°27W 81 C4

Knife ➤ N. Dak., U.S.A. 47°17N 101°20W 76 C4
Knife River Minn., U.S.A. 46°57N 91°47W 77 D7
Knife River Indian Village Nat. Historic Site △ N. Dak., U.S.A. 47°20N 101°23W 76 C4
Knight I. Alaska, U.S.A. 60°21N 147°45W 135 F11
Knight Inlet B.C., Canada 50°45N 125°40W 154 E9
Knightdale N.C., U.S.A. 35°47N 78°29W 103 C7
Knights Landing Calif., U.S.A. 38°48N 121°43W 126 E5
Knightstown Ind., U.S.A. 39°48N 85°32W 85 D5
Knob Lake = Kawawachikamach Qué., Canada 54°48N 66°50W 143 C4
Knob Lick Ky., U.S.A. 37°56N 85°54W 105 C7
Knob Lick Mo., U.S.A. 37°41N 90°22W 83 D6
Knob Noster Mo., U.S.A. 38°46N 93°33W 83 C3
Knobel Ark., U.S.A. 36°19N 90°36W 106 B5
Knott County ☆ Ky., U.S.A. 37°20N 83°00W 105 C10
Knowles Okla., U.S.A. 36°53N 100°12W 107 B3
Knowlton Qué., Canada 45°13N 72°31W 145 F10
Knox Ind., U.S.A. 41°18N 86°37W 85 B4
Knox N. Dak., U.S.A. 48°20N 99°41W 76 B5
Knox Pa., U.S.A. 41°14N 79°32W 87 C3
Knox, C. B.C., Canada 54°11N 133°5W 154 C1
Knox City Mo., U.S.A. 40°9N 92°1W 83 A4
Knox City Tex., U.S.A. 33°25N 99°49W 109 D8
Knox County ☆ Ill., U.S.A. 40°55N 90°10W 84 C3
Knox County ☆ Ind., U.S.A. 38°40N 87°25W 85 E3
Knox County ☆ Ky., U.S.A. 36°55N 83°50W 105 D9
Knox County ☆ Maine, U.S.A. 44°5N 69°5W 90 D4
Knox County ☆ Mo., U.S.A. 40°10N 92°10W 83 A4
Knox County ☆ Nebr., U.S.A. 42°40N 97°50W 80 B8
Knox County ☆ Ohio, U.S.A. 40°23N 82°29W 86 C4
Knox County ☆ Tenn., U.S.A. 36°0N 84°0W 105 D8
Knox County ☆ Tex., U.S.A. 33°35N 99°48W 109 D8
Knoxville Ga., U.S.A. 32°47N 83°59W 113 D3
Knoxville Ill., U.S.A. 40°55N 90°17W 84 C3
Knoxville Iowa, U.S.A. 41°19N 93°6W 81 D5
Knoxville Pa., U.S.A. 41°57N 77°27W 87 C5
Knoxville Tenn., U.S.A. 35°58N 83°56W 105 E9
Knoxville McGhee Tyson ✈ (TYS) Tenn., U.S.A. 35°49N 83°59W 105 E9
Knud Rasmussen Land Greenland 78°0N 60°0W 162 B4
Koartac = Quaqtaq Qué., Canada 60°55N 69°40W 143 A4
Kobuk Alaska, U.S.A. 66°55N 156°52W 135 C8
Kobuk ➤ Alaska, U.S.A. 66°54N 160°38W 135 C7
Kobuk Valley Nat. Park △ Alaska, U.S.A. 67°0N 160°0W 135 C7
Koch I. Nunavut, Canada 69°38N 78°20W 158 D10
Kodiak Alaska, U.S.A. 57°47N 152°24W 135 H9
Kodiak I. Alaska, U.S.A. 57°30N 152°45W 135 H9
Kodiak Island ☆ Alaska, U.S.A. 57°30N 153°30W 135 H9
Koehn Dry L. Calif., U.S.A. 35°20N 117°53W 127 H9
Kofa Mts. Ariz., U.S.A. 33°15N 113°40W 130 D2
Kofa Nat. Wildlife Refuge △ Ariz., U.S.A. 33°15N 113°50W 130 D2
Kogaluc ➤ Nfld. & L., Canada 56°12N 61°44W 143 B5
Kogaluc, B. Qué., Canada 59°10N 78°40W 143 B2
Kohala Forest Reserve Hawai'i, U.S.A. 20°9N 155°4W 136 C6
Kohala Mts. Hawai'i, U.S.A. 20°5N 155°45W 136 C6
Kohler Wis., U.S.A. 43°44N 87°47W 78 E6
Kohlman Lake Minn., U.S.A. 45°1N 93°3W 94 A3
Kohunlich Quintana Roo, Mexico 18°22N 88°47W 179 D5
Kokanee Glacier Park △ B.C., Canada 49°47N 117°10W 155 F17
Köke'e State Park △ Hawai'i, U.S.A. 22°6N 159°40W 136 A2
Koko Head Hawai'i, U.S.A. 21°16N 157°43W 136 K14
Kokomo Ind. U.S.A. 40°29N 86°8W 85 C4
Kokomo Miss., U.S.A. 31°12N 90°0W 111 E3
Koksoak ➤ Qué., Canada 58°30N 68°10W 143 B4
Koliganek Alaska, U.S.A. 59°48N 157°25W 135 G8
Koloa Hawai'i, U.S.A. 21°55N 159°28W 136 B2
Komatke Ariz., U.S.A. 33°17N 112°10W 134 D2
Kona ✈ (KOA) Hawai'i, U.S.A. 19°44N 156°3W 136 D5
Könähuanu Hawai'i, U.S.A. 21°21N 157°47W 136 K14
Konawa Okla., U.S.A. 34°58N 96°45W 107 D7
Kong Christian IX Land Greenland 68°0N 36°0W 162 D7
Kong Christian X Land Greenland 74°0N 29°0W 162 C8
Kong Frederik IX Land Greenland 67°0N 52°0W 162 D6
Kong Frederik VI Kyst Greenland 63°0N 43°0W 162 E6
Kong Frederik VIII Land Greenland 78°30N 26°0W 162 B8
Kong Karls Land Svalbard 79°0N 28°0E 162 B13
Kong Oscar Fjord Greenland 72°20N 24°0W 162 C8
Koocanusa, — B.C., Canada 49°20N 115°15W 153 J5
Koochiching County ☆ Minn., U.S.A. 48°15N 93°50W 77 B5
Ko'olau Range Hawai'i, U.S.A. 21°35N 157°50W 136 J14
Ko'olauloa District Hawai'i, U.S.A. 21°35N 157°55W 136 J14
Ko'olaupoko District Hawai'i, U.S.A. 21°25N 157°50W 136 K14
Koosharem Utah, U.S.A. 38°31N 111°53W 129 E4
Kooskia Idaho, U.S.A. 46°9N 115°59W 122 C3
Kootenai Idaho, U.S.A. 48°0N 116°30W 122 A2
Kootenai County ☆ Idaho, U.S.A. 47°45N 116°30W 122 B2
Kootenai Nat. Forest Mont., U.S.A. 48°30N 115°40W 123 B2
Kootenay ➤ B.C., Canada 49°45N 116°50W 155 F18
Kootenay Nat. Park △ B.C., Canada 51°0N 116°0W 153 G4
Kopka ➤ Ont., Canada 50°4N 89°1W 148 B7
Kopomá Yucatán, Mexico 20°38N 89°55W 179 B4
Kopperston W. Va., U.S.A. 37°45N 81°35W 102 D3
Kormak Ont. Canada 47°38N 82°59W 149 E14
Koroc ➤ Qué., Canada 58°50N 65°50W 143 B4
Korona Fla., U.S.A. 29°25N 81°12W 114 B7
Kosciusko Miss., U.S.A. 33°4N 89°35W 111 C4
Kosciusko County ☆ Ind., U.S.A. 41°15N 85°50W 85 B5
Koshkonong Mo., U.S.A. 36°36N 91°39W 83 E5
Koshkonong L. Wis., U.S.A. 42°52N 88°58W 78 F5
Kosse Tex., U.S.A. 31°18N 96°38W 109 F11
Kossuth Miss., U.S.A. 34°52N 88°39W 111 B5
Kossuth County ☆ Iowa, U.S.A. 43°15N 94°10W 81 B4
Kotcho L. B.C., Canada 59°7N 121°12W 157 E8
Kotlik Alaska, U.S.A. 63°2N 163°33W 135 E7
Kotzebue Alaska, U.S.A. 66°53N 162°39W 135 C7
Kotzebue Sound Alaska, U.S.A. 66°20N 163°00W 135 C7
Kouchibouguac Nat. Park △ N.B., Canada 46°50N 65°0W 141 G5
Koukdjuak ➤ Nunavut, Canada 66°43N 73°0W 159 D11
Koukdjuak, Great Plain of the Nunavut, Canada 66°25N 72°50W 159 D11
Kountze Tex. U.S.A. 30°22N 94°19W 109 G13
Kouts Ind., U.S.A. 41°18N 87°2W 85 B4
Kovik, B. Qué., Canada 61°35N 77°36W 143 A2
Kowkash Ont., Canada 50°20N 87°12W 149 B9
Koyuk Alaska, U.S.A. 64°56N 161°9W 135 D7
Koyukuk Alaska, U.S.A. 64°53N 157°42W 135 D8
Koyukuk ➤ Alaska, U.S.A. 64°55N 157°32W 135 D8
Koyukuk Nat. Wildlife Refuge △ Alaska, U.S.A. 65°30N 156°30W 135 D8
Kramer N. Dak., U.S.A. 48°42N 100°43W 76 B5
Kranzburg S. Dak., U.S.A. 44°54N 96°55W 76 F9

Kraulshavn = Nuussuaq Greenland 74°8N 57°3W 162 C5
Krebs Okla., U.S.A. 34°56N 95°43W 107 D8
Kremlin Okla., U.S.A. 36°33N 97°50W 107 B6
Kremmling Colo., U.S.A. 40°4N 106°24W 125 B4
Kress Tex., U.S.A. 34°22N 101°45W 108 C6
Krusenstern, C. Nunavut, Canada 68°24N 113°54W 156 C10
Krusenstern, C. Alaska, U.S.A. 67°8N 163°45W 135 C7
Krydor Sask., Canada 52°47N 107°4W 150 C4
Ku Tree Res. Hawai'i, U.S.A. 21°30N 157°59W 136 J14
Kualapu'u Hawai'i, U.S.A. 21°9N 157°2W 136 B4
Kualoa Pt. Hawai'i, U.S.A. 21°31N 157°50W 136 B1
Kuapā Pond Hawai'i, U.S.A. 21°17N 157°43W 136 K14
Kuehn Mont., U.S.A. 45°49N 107°5W 123 D10
Kugaaruk = Pelly Bay Nunavut, Canada 68°38N 89°50W 158 D8
Kugluktuk Nunavut, Canada 67°50N 115°5W 156 C9
Kugong I. N.W.T., Canada 56°18N 79°50W 143 B1
Kuiu I. Alaska, U.S.A. 57°45N 134°10W 135 H14
Kukuihaele Hawai'i, U.S.A. 20°5N 155°35W 136 C6
Kukukus L. Ont. Canada 49°47N 91°41W 148 C5
Kulkayu = Hartley Bay B.C., Canada 53°25N 129°15W 154 B5
Kulm N. Dak., U.S.A. 46°18N 98°57W 76 D7
Kumakahi, C. Hawai'i, U.S.A. 19°31N 154°49W 136 D7
Kuna Idaho, U.S.A. 43°30N 116°25W 122 F2
Kunghit I. B.C., Canada 52°6N 131°3W 154 C3
Kunia Hawai'i, U.S.A. 21°28N 158°4W 136 K13
Kunkletown Pa., U.S.A. 40°51N 75°27W 92 B1
Kūpikipiki'ö Pt. Hawai'i, U.S.A. 21°15N 157°47W 136 K14
Kupreanof I. Alaska, U.S.A. 56°50N 133°30W 135 H14
Kure I. Hawai'i, U.S.A. 28°25N 178°25W 136 F8
Kuroki Sask., Canada 51°52N 103°29W 150 D8
Kurthwood La., U.S.A. 31°20N 93°10W 110 C2
Kurtistown Hawai'i, U.S.A. 19°36N 155°4W 136 D6
Kusawa L. Yukon, Canada 60°20N 136°13W 157 D5
Kuskokwim ➤ Alaska, U.S.A. 60°5N 162°25W 135 F7
Kuskokwim B. Alaska, U.S.A. 59°45N 162°25W 135 G7
Kuskokwim Mts. Alaska, U.S.A. 62°30N 156°0W 135 E9
Kuttawa Ky., U.S.A. 37°4N 88°7W 104 C4
Kutztown Pa., U.S.A. 40°31N 75°47W 92 B1
Kuujjuaq Qué., Canada 58°6N 68°15W 143 B4
Kuujjuarapik Qué., Canada 55°20N 77°35W 143 B2
Kuzitrin ➤ Alaska, U.S.A. 65°10N 165°25W 135 D6
Kvichak B. Alaska, U.S.A. 58°48N 157°35W 135 G8
Kvitøya Svalbard 80°8N 32°35E 162 A14
Kwataboahegan ➤ Ont., Canada 51°9N 80°50W 149 A16
Kwethluk Alaska, U.S.A. 60°49N 161°26W 135 F7
Kwigillingok Alaska, U.S.A. 59°51N 163°8W 135 G7
Kwinitsa B.C., Canada 54°19N 129°22W 154 A5
Kyburz Calif., U.S.A. 38°47N 120°18W 126 E6
Kykotsmovi Village Ariz., U.S.A. 35°52N 110°37W 130 B5
Kyle Sask., Canada 50°50N 108°2W 150 D3
Kyle S. Dak., U.S.A. 43°26N 102°10W 76 E3
Kyle Tex., U.S.A. 29°59N 97°53W 109 H10
Kynoch Inlet B.C., Canada 52°45N 128°0W 154 C7
Kyuquot B.C., Canada 50°2N 127°22W 154 E7
Kyuquot Sound Canada 50°2N 127°22W 154 E7

L

La Aguada Quintana Roo, Mexico 19°57N 88°32W 179 C5
La Aguja Baja Calif. S., Mexico 23°59N 110°53W 167 K8
La Alameda Guadalajara, Mexico 20°30N 103°15W 180 C2
La Amistad, Parque Internacional △ Cent. Amer. 9°28N 83°18W 182 E3
La Angostura Sonora, Mexico 30°26N 109°22W 168 C4
La Angostura, Cerro Chiapas, Mexico 15°54N 93°10W 178 D3
La Antigua Veracruz, Mexico 19°19N 96°19W 176 E4
La Ascensión Nuevo León, Mexico 24°20N 99°55W 171 F5
La Ballena Baja Calif. S., Mexico 26°22N 112°39W 167 G6
La Barca Jalisco, Mexico 20°17N 102°34W 174 B5
La Barge Wyo., U.S.A. 42°16N 110°12W 124 D2
La Belle Fla., U.S.A. 26°46N 81°26W 114 E7
La Biche, L. Alta., Canada 54°50N 112°3W 152 D8
La Bocana Baja Calif., Mexico 29°26N 114°53W 166 D3
La Bocana Baja Calif., Mexico 31°34N 116°41W 166 B2
La Bocana ➤ Baja Calif., Mexico 29°26N 115°7W 166 D3
La Bocana, Estero Baja Calif. S., Mexico 26°47N 113°43W 167 G5
La Boquilla ➤ Coahuila, Mexico 29°11N 102°58W 170 B1
La Boquilla del Conchos Chihuahua, Mexico 27°32N 105°21W 169 F10
La Broquerie Man., Canada 49°25N 96°30W 151 F15
La Bufadora Baja Calif., Mexico 31°45N 116°46W 166 B2
La Caja Colima, Mexico 19°21N 103°47W 174 C4
La Calerilla Guadalajara, Mexico 20°33N 103°24W 180 B1
La Cañada Querétaro, Mexico 20°37N 100°19W 175 B7
La Candelaria Zacatecas, Mexico 24°28N 101°51W 173 C9
La Capilla de los Remedios Chihuahua, Mexico 28°7N 106°57W 169 E9
La Casa Colorada, Cerro Chihuahua, Mexico 27°4N 108°20W 169 F7
La Catarina, Sa. Chihuahua, Mexico 29°18N 107°48W 169 D8
La Ceiba Honduras 15°40N 86°50W 182 C2
La Center Ky., U.S.A. 37°4N 88°58W 104 C4
La Center Wash., U.S.A. 45°52N 122°40W 120 B3
La Chorrera Panama 8°53N 79°47W 182 E4
La Choya Sonora, Mexico 31°20N 113°40W 168 B2
La Ciénaga Oaxaca, Mexico 16°55N 96°47W 177 H4
La Cienega N. Mex., U.S.A. 35°34N 106°4W 131 B4
La Cieneguita Durango, Mexico 24°34N 105°1W 172 C5
La Colorada Sonora, Mexico 28°49N 110°36W 168 C5
La Coma Tamaulipas, Mexico 24°37N 97°57W 171 F7
La Compañía Oaxaca, Mexico 16°34N 96°49W 177 H4
La Concepción Sinaloa, Mexico 23°23N 106°9W 172 D4
La Concepción Panama 8°31N 82°37W 182 E3
La Conception Qué., Canada 46°9N 74°42W 144 E8
La Conchas Sonora, Mexico 28°21N 111°20W 168 E4
La Conner Wash., U.S.A. 48°23N 122°30W 120 B3
La Constitución Chihuahua, Mexico 29°55N 107°48W 169 D8
La Crescent Minn., U.S.A. 43°50N 91°18W 77 G1
La Croix, L. Minn., U.S.A. 48°20N 92°10W 77 B6
La Crosse Fla., U.S.A. 29°51N 82°24W 114 B6
La Crosse Kans., U.S.A. 38°32N 99°18W 82 C4
La Crosse Va., U.S.A. 36°42N 78°6W 102 E6
La Crosse Wash., U.S.A. 46°49N 117°53W 120 C8
La Crosse Wis., U.S.A. 43°48N 91°15W 78 E4
La Crosse County ☆ Wis., U.S.A. 44°0N 91°0W 78 E4
La Cruz Costa Rica 11°4N 85°39W 182 D2
La Cruz Chihuahua, Mexico 27°52N 105°12W 169 F10
La Cruz Guadalajara, Mexico 20°9N 103°12W 180 B2

La Cruz Sinaloa, Mexico 23°55N 106°54W 172 D4
La Cruz de Loreto Jalisco, Mexico 20°0N 105°27W 174 C2
La Cuchilla Tabasco, Mexico 17°49N 91°14W 178 B5
La Cuesta Jalisco, Mexico 20°9N 104°49W 174 B3
La Cygne Kans., U.S.A. 38°21N 94°46W 82 C9
La Cygnes L. Kans., U.S.A. 38°20N 94°33W 82 C9
La Désirade Guadeloupe 16°18N 61°3W 183 C7
La Discordia Sonora, Mexico 31°1N 111°55W 168 B4
La Doré Qué., Canada 48°43N 72°39W 145 C10
La Encantada Coahuila, Mexico 28°35N 102°27W 170 B2
La Encantada Coahuila, Mexico 28°22N 102°35W 170 B2
La Escopeta Baja Calif., Mexico 23°14N 109°34W 167 K9
La Esmeralda Chihuahua, Mexico 29°18N 108°25W 169 D7
La Esperanza Cuba 22°46N 83°44W 182 B3
La Esperanza Honduras 14°15N 88°10W 182 D2
La Esperanza, Sa. Chihuahua, Mexico 30°1N 104°52W 169 C11
La Farge Wis., U.S.A. 43°35N 90°38W 78 E3
La Fayette Ga., U.S.A. 34°42N 85°17W 113 B1
La Fayette Ky., U.S.A. 36°40N 87°40W 104 D5
La Follette Tenn., U.S.A. 36°23N 84°7W 105 D8
La Fontaine Ind., U.S.A. 40°40N 85°43W 85 C5
La Florida Coahuila, Mexico 28°37N 102°58W 170 B2
La Fragua, Sa. Coahuila, Mexico 26°45N 102°28W 170 D2
La Galissonnière, L. Qué., Canada 51°25N 62°0W 140 B7
La Garita Colo., U.S.A. 37°50N 106°15W 125 E4
La Gloria, Sa. Coahuila, Mexico 26°45N 101°10W 170 D3
La Gloria, Sa. Sonora, Mexico 30°50N 112°10W 168 C3
La Golondrina Sonora, Mexico 30°3N 112°23W 168 C3
La Goma Durango, Mexico 25°29N 103°42W 173 B7
La Grande Oreg., U.S.A. 45°20N 118°5W 121 B7
La Grande Wash., U.S.A. 46°50N 122°19W 120 D3
La Grande Deux, Rés. Qué., Canada 53°40N 76°55W 143 C2
La Grande Quatre, Rés. Qué., Canada 54°0N 73°15W 143 C3
La Grande Trois, Rés. Qué., Canada 53°46N 75°30W 143 C2
La Grange Ark., U.S.A. 34°39N 90°44W 106 D5
La Grange Ga., U.S.A. 33°2N 85°2W 113 C1
La Grange Ill., U.S.A. 41°48N 87°53W 95 C1
La Grange Ky., U.S.A. 38°24N 85°22W 105 B7
La Grange Mo., U.S.A. 40°3N 91°35W 83 A5
La Grange N.C., U.S.A. 35°19N 77°47W 103 C8
La Grange Tenn., U.S.A. 35°3N 89°15W 104 E3
La Grange Tex., U.S.A. 29°54N 96°52W 109 H11
La Grange Wyo., U.S.A. 41°38N 104°10W 124 E8
La Grange Park Ill., U.S.A. 41°48N 87°51W 95 C1
La Guadeloupe Qué., Canada 45°57N 70°56W 145 F12
La Guajolota Durango, Mexico 22°56N 104°52W 173 E6
La Guardia, New York ✈ (LGA) N.Y., U.S.A. 40°46N 73°52W 98 B3
La Habana Cuba 23°8N 82°22W 182 B3
La Harpe Ill., U.S.A. 40°35N 90°58W 84 C3
La Harpe Kans., U.S.A. 37°55N 95°18W 82 D8
La Have ➤ N.S., Canada 44°14N 64°20W 141 J5
La Herradura San Luis Potosí, Mexico 23°1N 101°45W 171 G3
La Higuera ➤ Sonora, Mexico 29°21N 109°42W 168 D6
La Huacana Michoacan, Mexico 18°58N 101°49W 174 D6
La Huerta Jalisco, Mexico 19°29N 104°36W 174 C3
La Hulería Tabasco, Mexico 17°59N 91°23W 178 A5
La Independencia Chiapas, Mexico 16°15N 92°1W 178 D4
La Inmaculada Sonora, Mexico 29°55N 111°48W 168 D4
La Isabela Dom. Rep. 19°58N 71°2W 183 C5
La Jara Colo., U.S.A. 37°16N 105°58W 125 E5
La Jara N. Mex., U.S.A. 36°5N 106°58W 131 A4
La Jolla Calif., U.S.A. 32°50N 117°16W 133 A1
La Jolla Indian Reservation Calif., U.S.A. 33°16N 116°52W 127 K10
La Joya Baja Calif., Mexico 32°29N 111°1W 166 A1
La Joya Chihuahua, Mexico 28°5N 106°16W 169 E9
La Joya N. Mex., U.S.A. 34°21N 106°51W 131 C4
La Joya Tex., U.S.A. 26°14N 98°27W 108 L9
La Junta Colo., U.S.A. 37°59N 103°33W 125 E7
La Lágrima, Sa. Chihuahua, Mexico 30°15N 105°20W 169 C10
La Laguna Guerrero, Mexico 17°45N 99°45W 175 E8
La Laguna Zacatecas, Mexico 24°15N 103°8W 173 C7
La Lagunita Durango, Mexico 26°2N 106°29W 172 A4
La Laja Jalisco, Mexico 20°35N 104°32W 174 B3
La Leche, L. Tex., U.S.A. 27°14N 102°53W 170 C2
La Libertad = Puerto Libertad Sonora, Mexico 29°55N 112°43W 168 D3
La Libertad Guatemala 16°47N 90°7W 182 C1
La Libertad Chiapas, Mexico 17°41N 91°43W 178 B5
La Libertad Chiapas, Mexico 27°37N 106°49W 169 F9
La Libertad, Sa. Baja Calif., Mexico 28°45N 114°0W 166 E5
La Linda Coahuila, Mexico 29°26N 102°48W 170 A2
La Loche Sask., Canada 56°29N 109°26W 157 E11
La Loma México, Mexico 19°31N 99°11W 181 A2
La Luz Coahuila, Mexico 25°47N 102°10W 172 B4
La Luz N. Mex., U.S.A. 32°59N 105°57W 131 E5
La Madera N. Mex., U.S.A. 36°23N 106°3W 131 A4
La Madera, Sa. Coahuila, Mexico 27°6N 102°30W 170 C2
La Magdalena Chihuahua, Mexico 26°52N 106°20W 169 G9
La Magdalena Chichicaspa México, Mexico 19°26N 99°19W 181 B2
La Malbaie Qué., Canada 47°40N 70°10W 145 D12
La Malinche, Parque Nacional △ Mexico 19°15N 98°3W 175 C9
La Mancha, L. Durango, Mexico 24°37N 102°37W 173 C8
La Manga Sonora, Mexico 29°8N 111°3W 168 D4
La Margarita del Norte Coahuila, Mexico 26°27N 102°53W 170 D2
La Marque Tex., U.S.A. 29°23N 94°58W 109 H13
La Marquesa, Parque Nacional △ México, Mexico 19°20N 99°21W 175 C8
La Martre Qué., Canada 49°12N 66°10W 140 D3
La Martre, L. N.W.T., Canada 63°15N 117°55W 156 D8
La Mesa Baja Calif., Mexico 32°30N 116°57W 166 A2
La Mesa Calif., U.S.A. 32°46N 117°1W 133 A2
La Mesa N. Mex., U.S.A. 32°16N 106°48W 131 E4
La Mesa del Huracán Chihuahua, Mexico 29°40N 108°15W 169 D7
La Mesa del Rodeo Durango, Mexico 24°47N 106°46W 172 C4
La Mesilla N. Mex., U.S.A. 32°16N 106°48W 131 E4
La Mira Michoacan, Mexico 18°0N 102°19W 174 D5
La Misa Sonora, Mexico 28°23N 110°19W 168 C5
La Mocha Sonora, Mexico 29°0N 111°40W 168 D4
La Moille Ill., U.S.A. 41°32N 89°17W 84 B4
La Moine ➤ Ill., U.S.A. 39°59N 90°31W 84 D3
La Monte Mo., U.S.A. 38°46N 93°26W 83 C3
La Mora Coahuila, Mexico 27°44N 102°10W 170 C2
La Mora Michoacan, Mexico 19°20N 100°31W 175 C7
La Mothe, L. Qué., Canada 48°46N 71°9W 145 C11
La Moure N. Dak., U.S.A. 46°21N 98°18W 76 D7
La Moure County ☆ N. Dak., U.S.A. 46°23N 98°29W 76 D7
La Muralla Guanajuato, Mexico 20°48N 101°42W 174 B6

La Nariz, Cerro Coahuila, Mexico 26°6N 100°59W 170 D4
La Nopalera Distrito Federal, Mexico 19°18N 99°5W 181 C3
La Noria Sinaloa, Mexico 23°30N 106°18W 172 D4
La Paila, Sa. Coahuila, Mexico 25°50N 101°36W 170 E3
La Palma Nayarit, Mexico 21°59N 105°22W 172 F5
La Palma Sonora, Mexico 28°40N 110°59W 168 E5
La Palma Tabasco, Mexico 17°27N 91°7W 178 B5
La Palma Panama 8°15N 78°0W 182 E4
La Palma Ariz., U.S.A. 32°53N 111°31W 130 E4
La Palmas, Cerro Distrito Federal, Mexico 19°15N 99°20W 181 C2
La Palomas Baja Calif. S., Mexico 24°43N 113°25W 167 F5
La Palotada ➤ Chihuahua, Mexico 31°7N 108°34W 169 B7
La Partida Baja Calif. S., Mexico 25°36N 103°19W 170 E1
La Patrie Qué., Canada 45°24N 71°15W 145 F11
La Paz Honduras 14°20N 87°47W 182 D2
La Paz Baja Calif. S., Mexico 24°10N 110°18W 167 J8
La Paz San Luis Potosí, Mexico 23°41N 100°42W 171 G4
La Paz Ariz., U.S.A. 33°37N 113°53W 130 D2
La Paz Centro Nic. 12°20N 86°41W 182 D2
La Peña Tamaulipas, Mexico 23°22N 98°9W 171 G6
La Perla Chihuahua, Mexico 28°18N 104°32W 169 E11
La Pesca Tamaulipas, Mexico 23°46N 97°47W 171 G7
La Piedad Michoacan, Mexico 20°21N 102°0W 174 B6
La Pine Oreg., U.S.A. 43°40N 121°30W 121 D4
La Pinta Chihuahua, Mexico 29°12N 107°40W 169 D8
La Plant S. Dak., U.S.A. 45°9N 100°39W 76 E5
La Plata Md., U.S.A. 38°32N 76°59W 93 B4
La Plata Mo., U.S.A. 40°2N 92°29W 83 A4
La Plata N. Mex., U.S.A. 36°56N 108°12W 131 A2
La Plata County ☆ Colo., U.S.A. 37°15N 107°50W 125 E3
La Pocatière Qué., Canada 47°22N 70°2W 145 D12
La Poile Nfld. & L., Canada 47°41N 58°24W 142 E2
La Polka Chiapas, Mexico 15°57N 93°39W 178 D3
La Porte Ind., U.S.A. 41°36N 86°43W 85 B4
La Porte City Iowa, U.S.A. 42°19N 92°12W 81 C6
La Poza Grande Baja Calif. S., Mexico 25°50N 112°2W 167 H6
La Prairie Qué., Canada 45°25N 73°29W 160 B4
La Presa Baja Calif. S., Mexico 32°28N 116°55W 166 A2
La Presa Baja Calif. S., Mexico 24°51N 111°5W 167 J7
La Presa Nayarit, Mexico 21°46N 105°13W 172 F5
La Providencia Coahuila, Mexico 27°5N 103°31W 170 C1
La Providencia Durango, Mexico 26°41N 105°59W 172 A5
La Pryor Tex., U.S.A. 28°57N 99°51W 109 J8
La Puente N. Mex., U.S.A. 36°42N 106°36W 131 A4
La Punta Guadalajara, Mexico 20°34N 103°12W 180 B2
La Purísima Baja Calif. S., Mexico 26°10N 112°4W 167 G6
La Purisma Zacatecas, Mexico 22°4N 101°24W 173 E9
La Push Wash., U.S.A. 47°55N 124°38W 120 C1
La Rastra Sinaloa, Mexico 23°4N 105°32W 172 D5
La Reforma Chihuahua, Mexico 26°58N 108°9W 169 G7
La Reine Qué., Canada 48°50N 79°30W 144 C3
La Ribera Baja Calif. S., Mexico 23°35N 109°34W 167 K9
La Romaine Qué., Canada 50°13N 60°40W 143 C5
La Romana Dom. Rep. 18°27N 68°57W 183 C6
La Ronge Sask., Canada 55°5N 105°20W 157 E11
La Rue Ohio, U.S.A. 40°35N 83°23W 86 C3
La Rumorosa Baja Calif., Mexico 32°34N 116°6W 166 A2
La Sal Utah, U.S.A. 38°19N 109°15W 129 E6
La Sal Mts. Utah, U.S.A. 38°30N 109°10W 129 E6
La Salle Colo., U.S.A. 40°21N 104°42W 125 B6
La Salle Ill., U.S.A. 41°20N 89°6W 84 B4
La Salle Minn., U.S.A. 44°4N 94°33W 77 F4
La Salle County ☆ Ill., U.S.A. 41°20N 88°50W 84 B4
La Salle County ☆ Tex., U.S.A. 28°26N 99°14W 109 J8
La Salle Parish ☆ La., U.S.A. 31°41N 92°8W 110 C3
La Sarre Qué., Canada 48°45N 79°15W 144 C3
La Scie Nfld. & L., Canada 49°57N 55°36W 142 C5
La Silla, Cerro de Monterrey, Mexico 25°37N 100°13W 180 D2
La Soledad Coahuila, Mexico 26°48N 101°42W 170 D3
La Soledad Durango, Mexico 25°14N 107°8W 172 B3
La Soledad N. Mex., U.S.A. 34°20N 100°34W 171 F4
La Solidaridad Iberoamericana, Parque de Guadalajara, Mexico 20°39N 103°17W 180 B2
La Soufrière St. Vincent 13°20N 61°11W 183 D7
La Suerte Baja Calif., Mexico 30°34N 115°19W 166 C3
La Tabatière Qué., Canada 50°50N 58°58W 142 B2
La Tinaja Veracruz, Mexico 18°35N 96°28W 177 F4
La Tortuga Venezuela 11°0N 65°22W 183 D6
La Trasquila Chihuahua, Mexico 29°45N 107°55W 169 D8
La Trinidad Baja Calif., Mexico 31°24N 115°55W 166 B3
La Trinitaria Chiapas, Mexico 16°7N 92°3W 178 D4
La Tuque Qué., Canada 47°30N 72°50W 145 D10
La Unión El Salv. 13°20N 87°50W 182 D2
La Unión Guerrero, Mexico 17°58N 101°49W 174 E6
La Unión Nuevo León, Mexico 25°45N 98°45W 171 E7
La Unión Nuevo León, Mexico 26°11N 100°29W 170 D4
La Unión Nuevo León, Mexico 23°51N 100°9W 171 G4
La Unión Quintana Roo, Mexico 17°50N 88°50W 179 E5
La Unión N. Mex., U.S.A. 31°57N 106°40W 131 F4
La Unión del Cuatro Guadalajara, Mexico 20°31N 103°21W 180 B1
La Vale Md., U.S.A. 39°40N 78°48W 93 A2
La Valle Wis., U.S.A. 43°35N 90°8W 78 E3
La Vega Dom. Rep. 19°20N 70°30W 183 C5
La Venta Tabasco, Mexico 18°5N 94°3W 178 A2
La Vérendrye, Réserve Faunique △ Qué., Canada 47°20N 76°40W 144 D6
La Vergne Tenn., U.S.A. 36°1N 86°35W 104 D6
La Verkin Utah, U.S.A. 37°12N 113°16W 129 F2
La Vernia Tex., U.S.A. 29°21N 98°7W 109 H9
La Veta Colo., U.S.A. 37°31N 105°0W 125 E6
La Victoria San Luis Potosí, Mexico 23°38N 101°23W 171 G3
La Vieja, L. Chihuahua, Mexico 30°15N 107°12W 169 C8
La Vista Nebr., U.S.A. 41°11N 96°2W 80 C9
La Yesca Nayarit, Mexico 21°19N 104°1W 172 F6
Labadieville La., U.S.A. 29°50N 90°57W 110 E5
Laberge, L. Yukon, Canada 61°11N 135°12W 157 C6
Labette County ☆ Kans., U.S.A. 37°15N 95°15W 82 D8
Labná Yucatán, Mexico 20°9N 89°33W 179 B4
Labor de Santa Bárbara Zacatecas, Mexico 23°0N 103°13W 173 E7
Labrador City Nfld. & L., Canada 52°57N 66°55W 143 C4
Labrieville Qué., Canada 49°18N 69°34W 145 B13
Lac Allard Qué., Canada 50°33N 63°24W 143 C5
Lac-au-Saumon Qué., Canada 48°25N 67°22W 140 D3
Lac-aux-Sables Qué., Canada 46°51N 72°24W 145 C10
Lac-Beauchamp, Parc du Qué., Canada 45°29N 75°37W 160 A2
Lac-Bouchette Qué., Canada 48°16N 72°11W 145 C10
Lac Brochet Man., Canada 58°37N 101°29W 159 E15
Lac Courte Oreilles Indian Reservation Wis., U.S.A. 45°50N 91°15W 78 C2
Lac-des-Écorces Qué., Canada 46°34N 75°22W 144 E7

Lac du Bonnet *Man., Canada* 50°15N 96°4W **151** E15
Lac du Flambeau *Wis., U.S.A.* 45°58N 89°53W **78** C4
Lac du Flambeau Indian Reservation *Wis., U.S.A.* 46°0N 89°50W **78** B4
Lac-Édouard *Qué., Canada* 47°40N 72°16W **145** D10
Lac-Etchemin *Qué., Canada* 46°24N 70°30W **145** E12
La Biche *Alta., Canada* 54°45N 111°58W **152** D9
Lac la Hache *B.C., Canada* 51°49N 121°27W **155** D13
Lac la Martre = Wha Ti *N.W.T., Canada* 63°8N 117°16W **157** D9
Lac-Leamy, Parc *Qué., Canada* 45°27N 75°43W **160** A1
Lac-Mégantic *Qué., Canada* 45°35N 70°53W **145** F12
Lac qui Parle County ☆ *Minn., U.S.A.* 44°55N 96°0W **77** F2
Lac-Ste-Marie *Qué., Canada* 45°57N 75°57W **144** F7
Lac Vieux Desert Indian Reservation *Mich., U.S.A.* 46°10N 89°9W **79** C2
Lacantún → *Chiapas, Mexico* 16°36N 90°39W **178** C6
Lacanuá *Chiapas, Mexico* 16°41N 91°6W **178** C6
Lacassine, Bayou → *La., U.S.A.* 30°19N 92°53W **110** D3
Lacey *Wash., U.S.A.* 47°7N 122°49W **120** C3
Lacey Spring *Va., U.S.A.* 38°32N 78°46W **99** B2
Lachine *Qué., Canada* 45°26N 73°42W **160** B2
Lachine *Mich., U.S.A.* 45°4N 83°43W **79** D8
Lachine, Canal de *Qué., Canada* 45°26N 73°38W **160** B3
Lachute *Qué., Canada* 45°39N 74°21W **145** F8
Lackawanna *N.Y., U.S.A.* 42°50N 78°50W **88** C2
Lackawanna → *Pa., U.S.A.* 41°20N 75°48W **92** A1
Lackawanna County ☆ *Pa., U.S.A.* 41°30N 75°50W **87** C7
Lackawaxen → *Pa., U.S.A.* 41°29N 74°59W **92** A2
Lackland City *Tex., U.S.A.* 29°23N 98°38W **116** C2
Laclede County ☆ *Mo., U.S.A.* 37°40N 92°35W **83** D4
Laclu *Ont., Canada* 49°46N 94°41W **148** C2
Lacolle *Qué., Canada* 45°5N 73°22W **145** F9
Lacombe *Alta., Canada* 52°30N 113°44W **153** F7
Lacombe *La., U.S.A.* 30°19N 89°56W **110** D6
Lacon *Ill., U.S.A.* 41°2N 89°24W **84** B4
Lacona *Iowa, U.S.A.* 41°12N 93°23W **81** D5
Laconia *Ind., U.S.A.* 38°2N 86°5W **85** E4
Laconia *N.H., U.S.A.* 43°32N 71°28W **89** C3
Lacoochee *Fla., U.S.A.* 28°28N 82°11W **114** C6
Lacreek L. *S. Dak., U.S.A.* 43°7N 101°33W **76** G4
Lacs-Albanel-Mistassini et Waconichi, Réserve Faunique des △ *Qué., Canada* 51°8N 74°25W **145** A8
Ladd *Ill., U.S.A.* 41°23N 89°13W **84** B4
Ladder Cr. → *Kans., U.S.A.* 38°45N 100°52W **82** C3
Laddonia *Mo., U.S.A.* 39°15N 91°39W **83** B5
Ladelle *Ark., U.S.A.* 33°28N 91°48W **106** E4
Ladera Heights *Calif., U.S.A.* 33°59N 118°22W **133** C2
Ladoga *Ind., U.S.A.* 39°55N 86°48W **85** D4
Ladonia *Tex., U.S.A.* 33°25N 95°57W **109** D12
Ladson *S.C., U.S.A.* 32°59N 80°6W **103** F5
Ladue *Mo., U.S.A.* 38°38N 90°22W **94** B1
Lady Lake *Fla., U.S.A.* 28°55N 81°55W **114** C7
Ladysmith *B.C., Canada* 49°0N 123°49W **154** G11
Ladysmith *Wis., U.S.A.* 45°28N 91°12W **78** C2
Lae 'o Kākā *Hawai'i, U.S.A.* 20°31N 156°53W **136** C5
Lae 'o Kealaikahiki *Hawai'i, U.S.A.* 20°32N 156°42W **136** C5
Lafayette *Ala., U.S.A.* 32°54N 85°24W **112** D5
Lafayette *Calif., U.S.A.* 37°53N 122°7W **126** F4
Lafayette *Colo., U.S.A.* 39°58N 105°12W **125** C5
Lafayette *Ind., U.S.A.* 40°25N 86°54W **85** C4
Lafayette *La., U.S.A.* 30°14N 92°1W **110** D3
Lafayette *Minn., U.S.A.* 44°27N 94°24W **77** F4
Lafayette *Ohio, U.S.A.* 40°46N 83°57W **86** C3
Lafayette *Oreg., U.S.A.* 45°15N 123°7W **121** B2
LaFayette *Tenn., U.S.A.* 36°31N 86°2W **104** D6
Lafayette, Mt. *N.H., U.S.A.* 44°10N 71°38W **89** B3
Lafayette County ☆ *Ark., U.S.A.* 33°22N 93°43W **106** E2
Lafayette County ☆ *Fla., U.S.A.* 30°0N 83°0W **114** B5
Lafayette County ☆ *Miss., U.S.A.* 34°22N 89°31W **111** B4
Lafayette County ☆ *Mo., U.S.A.* 39°5N 93°45W **83** B3
Lafayette County ☆ *Wis., U.S.A.* 42°35N 90°10W **78** F3
Lafayette Hill *Pa., U.S.A.* 40°4N 75°15W **98** A1
Lafayette Parish ☆ *La., U.S.A.* 30°14N 92°1W **110** D3
Laflamme → *Qué., Canada* 49°17N 77°9W **144** B5
Lafleche *Sask., Canada* 49°45N 106°40W **150** F5
Laforce *Qué., Canada* 47°32N 78°44W **144** D4
Lafourche, Bayou → *La., U.S.A.* 29°5N 90°14W **110** E5
Lafourche Parish ☆ *La., U.S.A.* 29°34N 90°23W **110** E5
Lages Station *Nev., U.S.A.* 40°4N 114°37W **128** B6
Laggan = Lake Louise *Alta., Canada* 51°30N 116°10W **153** G4
Lagona = Laguna Beach *Calif., U.S.A.* 33°33N 117°47W **127** K9
Lagos de Moreno *Jalisco, Mexico* 21°21N 101°55W **174** A6
Lagrange *Maine, U.S.A.* 45°11N 68°54W **90** C5
Lagrange *Ohio, U.S.A.* 41°14N 82°7W **86** B4
Lagrange *Ind., U.S.A.* 41°39N 85°25W **85** B5
Lagrange County ☆ *Ind., U.S.A.* 41°35N 85°25W **85** B5
Laguasima *Nayarit, Mexico* 22°25N 105°17W **172** E6
Laguna *N. Mex., Mexico* 35°2N 107°25W **131** B3
Laguna, Sa. de la *Baja Calif. S., Mexico* 23°35N 109°55W **167** K9
Laguna Atascosa Nat. Wildlife Refuge △ *Tex., U.S.A.* 26°17N 97°23W **109** L10
Laguna Beach *Calif., U.S.A.* 33°33N 117°47W **127** K9
Laguna Beach *Fla., U.S.A.* 30°14N 85°55W **114** A3
Laguna Canachi *Sinaloa, Mexico* 24°4N 107°6W **172** C3
Laguna del Mante *San Luis Potosí, Mexico* 22°13N 98°59W **171** H6
Laguna del Tigre, Parque Nac. △ *Guatemala* 17°32N 90°56W **182** C1
Laguna Grande *Zacatecas, Mexico* 22°27N 103°30W **173** E7
Laguna Indian Reservation *N. Mex., U.S.A.* 35°0N 107°20W **131** C3
Laguna Mts. *Calif., U.S.A.* 33°0N 116°40W **127** K10
Laguna San Ignacio *Baja Calif. S., Mexico* 26°54N 113°8W **167** G5
Laguna Seca *Durango, Mexico* 25°53N 106°9W **172** B4
Lagunas de Chacahua, Parque Nacional △ *Oaxaca, Mexico* 16°47N 97°2W **177** H3
Lagunas de Montebello, Parque Nacional △ *Chiapas, Mexico* 16°4N 91°42W **178** C5
Lagunas de Zempoala △ *México, Mexico* 19°6N 99°18W **175** C8
Lagunera, Región *Coahuila, Mexico* 25°35N 103°3W **170** E1
Lagunillas *Michoacán, Mexico* 19°4N 101°26W **175** C6
Lagunillas *San Luis Potosí, Mexico* 21°24N 99°35W **171** J5
Lagunitas *Sonora, Mexico* 32°20N 114°52W **168** A1
Lahaina *Hawai'i, U.S.A.* 20°53N 156°41W **136** C5
Lahontan Res. *Nev., U.S.A.* 39°28N 119°4W **128** C2
Lahilahi Pt. *Hawai'i, U.S.A.* 21°28N 158°13W **136** K13
Lahoma *Okla., U.S.A.* 36°23N 98°5W **107** B5
Lai'ie *Hawai'i, U.S.A.* 21°39N 157°56W **136** J14
Laingsburg *Mich., U.S.A.* 42°54N 84°21W **79** G7

Lair *Ky., U.S.A.* 38°20N 84°18W **105** B8
Laird *Sask., Canada* 52°43N 106°35W **150** C5
Lajitas *Tex., U.S.A.* 29°16N 103°46W **108** H4
Lake *Miss., U.S.A.* 32°21N 89°20W **111** D4
Lake *Wyo., U.S.A.* 44°33N 110°24W **124** B2
Lake Alfred *Fla., U.S.A.* 28°6N 81°44W **114** C7
Lake Alma *Sask., Canada* 49°9N 104°12W **150** F7
Lake and Peninsula ☆ *Alaska, U.S.A.* 57°0N 158°0W **135** H8
Lake Andes *S. Dak., U.S.A.* 43°9N 98°32W **76** G7
Lake Ann *Mich., U.S.A.* 44°43N 85°51W **79** E6
Lake Arthur *La., U.S.A.* 30°5N 92°41W **110** D3
Lake Arthur *N. Mex., U.S.A.* 33°0N 104°22W **131** D5
Lake Benton *Minn., U.S.A.* 44°15N 96°17W **77** F2
Lake Bird *Fla., U.S.A.* 30°14N 83°37W **114** A5
Lake Bronson *Minn., U.S.A.* 48°44N 96°40W **77** B2
Lake Buena Vista *Fla., U.S.A.* 28°23N 81°32W **115** B1
Lake Butler *Fla., U.S.A.* 30°1N 82°21W **114** B6
Lake Cain Hills *Fla., U.S.A.* 28°29N 81°28W **115** B2
Lake Carmel *N.Y., U.S.A.* 41°28N 73°40W **92** A3
Lake Charles *La., U.S.A.* 30°14N 93°13W **110** D2
Lake Chelan Nat. Recr. Area △ *Wash., U.S.A.* 48°25N 120°52W **120** B5
Lake City *Ark., U.S.A.* 35°49N 90°26W **106** C5
Lake City *Calif., U.S.A.* 41°39N 120°13W **126** B6
Lake City *Colo., U.S.A.* 38°2N 107°19W **125** D3
Lake City *Fla., U.S.A.* 30°11N 82°38W **114** A6
Lake City *Iowa, U.S.A.* 42°16N 94°44W **81** C4
Lake City *Kans., U.S.A.* 37°21N 98°49W **82** D5
Lake City *Mich., U.S.A.* 44°20N 85°13W **79** E6
Lake City *Minn., U.S.A.* 44°27N 92°16W **77** F61
Lake City *Pa., U.S.A.* 42°1N 80°21W **87** B2
Lake City *S.C., U.S.A.* 33°52N 79°45W **103** E6
Lake City *Tenn., U.S.A.* 36°13N 84°9W **105** D8
Lake Clark Nat. Park and Preserve △ *Alaska, U.S.A.* 61°0N 154°0W **135** F9
Lake Clear *N.Y., U.S.A.* 44°22N 74°14W **88** A6
Lake County ☆ *Calif., U.S.A.* 39°5N 122°45W **126** D4
Lake County ☆ *Colo., U.S.A.* 39°10N 106°20W **125** C4
Lake County ☆ *Fla., U.S.A.* 28°45N 81°45W **114** C7
Lake County ☆ *Ill., U.S.A.* 42°20N 86°0W **84** A5
Lake County ☆ *Ind., U.S.A.* 41°25N 87°25W **85** B3
Lake County ☆ *Mich., U.S.A.* 44°0N 85°50W **79** F6
Lake County ☆ *Minn., U.S.A.* 47°30N 91°20W **77** C6
Lake County ☆ *Mont., U.S.A.* 47°40N 114°10W **123** C3
Lake County ☆ *Ohio, U.S.A.* 41°40N 81°21W **86** B5
Lake County ☆ *Oreg., U.S.A.* 42°45N 120°20W **121** D3
Lake County ☆ *S. Dak., U.S.A.* 44°0N 97°7W **76** F8
Lake County ☆ *Tenn., U.S.A.* 36°23N 89°23W **104** D3
Lake Cowichan *B.C., Canada* 48°49N 124°3W **154** G10
Lake Crystal *Minn., U.S.A.* 44°6N 94°13W **77** F4
Lake Delton *Wis., U.S.A.* 43°35N 89°47W **78** E4
Lake Elmo *Minn., U.S.A.* 44°59N 92°54W **94** B4
Lake Elmo Regional Park *Minn., U.S.A.* 44°59N 92°55W **94** B4
Lake Elsinore *Calif., U.S.A.* 33°38N 117°20W **127** K9
Lake Fairfax Park *Va., U.S.A.* 38°57N 77°19W **99** B2
Lake Forest *Ill., U.S.A.* 42°15N 87°50W **84** A6
Lake Forest Park *Wash., U.S.A.* 47°45N 122°13W **132** B4
Lake Fork *Idaho, U.S.A.* 44°50N 116°5W **122** E2
Lake Fork → *Utah, U.S.A.* 40°13N 110°7W **129** C5
Lake Geneva *Wis., U.S.A.* 42°36N 88°26W **78** F5
Lake George *Colo., U.S.A.* 38°59N 105°22W **125** D5
Lake George *Minn., U.S.A.* 47°12N 94°59W **77** C4
Lake George *N.Y., U.S.A.* 43°26N 73°43W **88** B7
Lake Hamilton *Ark., U.S.A.* 34°25N 93°6W **106** D2
Lake Harbor *Fla., U.S.A.* 26°42N 80°43W **114** E8
Lake Harbour = Kimmirut *Nunavut, Canada* 62°50N 69°50W **159** E12
Lake Havasu City *Ariz., U.S.A.* 34°27N 114°22W **130** C1
Lake Helen *Fla., U.S.A.* 28°59N 81°14W **114** C7
Lake Hill *B.C., Canada* 48°28N 123°22W **155** G11
Lake Hughes *Calif., U.S.A.* 34°41N 118°25W **127** J8
Lake Isabella *Calif., U.S.A.* 35°38N 118°28W **127** H8
Lake Jackson *Tex., U.S.A.* 29°3N 95°27W **109** H12
Lake Lenore *Sask., Canada* 52°24N 104°59W **150** C7
Lake Lenore Caves *Wash., U.S.A.* 47°28N 119°3W **120** C6
Lake Lillian *Minn., U.S.A.* 44°57N 94°53W **77** F4
Lake Linden *Mich., U.S.A.* 47°11N 88°24W **79** B3
Lake Louise *Alta., Canada* 51°30N 116°10W **153** G4
Lake Lure *N.C., U.S.A.* 35°26N 82°12W **103** C3
Lake Mary *Fla., U.S.A.* 28°46N 81°19W **114** C7
Lake Mason Nat. Wildlife Refuge △ *Mont., U.S.A.* 46°38N 108°44W **123** D9
Lake Mead *Nev., U.S.A.* 36°1N 114°44W **128** F6
Lake Mead Nat. Recr. Area △ *Ariz., U.S.A.* 36°30N 114°22W **130** A1
Lake Meredith Nat. Recr. Area △ *Tex., U.S.A.* 35°50N 101°50W **108** B6
Lake Mills *Iowa, U.S.A.* 43°25N 93°32W **81** B5
Lake Mills *Wis., U.S.A.* 43°5N 88°55W **78** E5
Lake Mohawk *N.J., U.S.A.* 41°1N 74°39W **92** A2
Lake Montezuma *Ariz., U.S.A.* 34°38N 111°47W **130** C4
Lake Murray *Calif., U.S.A.* 32°46N 117°2W **133** E2
Lake Nebagamon *Wis., U.S.A.* 46°31N 91°42W **78** B2
Lake Norden *S. Dak., U.S.A.* 44°35N 97°13W **76** F8
Lake Odessa *Mich., U.S.A.* 42°47N 85°8W **79** G6
Lake of the Woods County ☆ *Minn., U.S.A.* 48°40N 94°50W **77** B4
Lake of the Woods Prov. Park △ *Ont., Canada* 49°4N 94°31W **148** C2
Lake Ophelia Nat. Wildlife Refuge △ *La., U.S.A.* 31°15N 91°55W **110** C4
Lake Orion *Mich., U.S.A.* 42°47N 83°14W **79** G8
Lake Oswego *Oreg., U.S.A.* 45°25N 122°40W **132** B1
Lake Ozark *Mo., U.S.A.* 38°12N 92°38W **83** C4
Lake Park *Fla., U.S.A.* 26°48N 80°3W **114** E8
Lake Park *Ga., U.S.A.* 30°41N 83°11W **113** F3
Lake Park *Iowa, U.S.A.* 43°27N 95°19W **81** B3
Lake Park *Minn., U.S.A.* 46°53N 96°5W **77** D2
Lake Park *Wis., U.S.A.* 43°4N 87°52W **92** A2
Lake Placid *Fla., U.S.A.* 27°18N 81°22W **114** D7
Lake Placid *N.Y., U.S.A.* 44°17N 73°59W **88** A7
Lake Pleasant *N.Y., U.S.A.* 43°28N 74°25W **88** B6
Lake Preston *S. Dak., U.S.A.* 44°22N 97°23W **76** F8
Lake Providence *La., U.S.A.* 32°48N 91°10W **110** B4
Lake Range *Nev., U.S.A.* 40°10N 119°20W **128** B1
Lake Roosevelt Nat. Recr. Area △ *Wash., U.S.A.* 48°5N 118°14W **120** B7
Lake St. Peter *Ont., Canada* 45°18N 78°2W **147** B8
Lake Seminole Park *Tampa, U.S.A.* 27°51N 82°46W **115** B2
Lake Shore *Md., U.S.A.* 39°7N 76°29W **93** A4
Lake Stevens *Wash., U.S.A.* 48°1N 122°4W **120** B3
Lake Success *N.Y., U.S.A.* 40°46N 73°43W **97** B4
Lake Superior Prov. Park △ *Ont., Canada* 47°45N 84°45W **149** E12
Lake Traverse Indian Reservation *N. Dak., U.S.A.* 46°0N 97°10W **76** E8

Lake Valley *Nev., U.S.A.* 38°20N 114°30W **128** D6
Lake View *Nev., U.S.A.* 35°54N 90°27W **106** C5
Lake View *Iowa, U.S.A.* 42°18N 95°3W **81** C3
Lake View *S.C., U.S.A.* 34°21N 79°10W **103** D6
Lake Villa *Ill., U.S.A.* 42°25N 88°5W **84** A5
Lake Village *Ark., U.S.A.* 33°20N 91°17W **106** E4
Lake Wales *Fla., U.S.A.* 27°54N 81°35W **114** D7
Lake Wilson *Minn., U.S.A.* 43°59N 95°57W **77** G3
Lake Worth *Fla., U.S.A.* 26°37N 80°3W **114** E8
Lakecreek *Oreg., U.S.A.* 42°26N 122°37W **121** E3
Lakefield *Ont., Canada* 44°25N 78°16W **147** C8
Lakefield *Minn., U.S.A.* 43°41N 95°10W **77** G3
Lakefront State Park △ *Ohio, U.S.A.* 41°32N 81°39W **98** A2
Lakehurst *N.J., U.S.A.* 40°1N 74°19W **92** B2
Lakeland *Fla., U.S.A.* 28°3N 81°57W **114** C7
Lakeland *Ga., U.S.A.* 31°2N 83°4W **113** E3
Lakeland *Tenn., U.S.A.* 35°14N 89°44W **104** E3
Lakeland Prov. Park △ *Alta., Canada* 54°45N 111°33W **152** D9
Lakemont *Ga., U.S.A.* 34°47N 83°25W **113** B3
Lakemont *Pa., U.S.A.* 40°28N 78°24W **87** D5
Lakeport *Calif., U.S.A.* 39°3N 122°55W **126** D4
Lakeport *Mich., U.S.A.* 43°7N 82°30W **79** F9
Lakeshore *Calif., U.S.A.* 37°15N 119°12W **127** F7
Lakeshore *Miss., U.S.A.* 30°15N 89°26W **111** F4
Lakeside *Calif., U.S.A.* 32°52N 116°55W **127** L10
Lakeside *Colo., U.S.A.* 39°46N 105°3W **134** B1
Lakeside *Mont., U.S.A.* 48°1N 114°14W **123** B3
Lakeside *Nebr., U.S.A.* 42°3N 102°26W **80** B3
Lakeside *Oreg., U.S.A.* 43°35N 124°11W **121** D1
Lakeside *Utah, U.S.A.* 41°13N 112°52W **129** B3
Lakeside *Va., U.S.A.* 37°37N 77°28W **102** D7
Laketon *Tex., U.S.A.* 35°33N 100°38W **108** B7
Laketown *Utah, U.S.A.* 41°49N 111°19W **129** B4
Lakeview *Ill., U.S.A.* 41°56N 87°38W **95** B3
Lakeview *Mich., U.S.A.* 43°27N 85°17W **79** F6
Lakeview *Mont., U.S.A.* 44°36N 111°49W **123** F6
Lakeview *Ohio, U.S.A.* 40°29N 83°56W **86** C3
Lakeview *Oreg., U.S.A.* 42°11N 120°21W **121** E5
Lakeview *Tex., U.S.A.* 34°40N 100°42W **108** C7
Lakeville *Conn., U.S.A.* 41°58N 73°26W **91** C4
Lakeville *Ind., U.S.A.* 41°31N 86°16W **85** B4
Lakeville *Mass., U.S.A.* 41°50N 70°55W **91** C4
Lakeville *Minn., U.S.A.* 44°39N 93°14W **77** F5
Lakewood *Colo., U.S.A.* 39°42N 105°4W **134** B1
Lakewood *N.J., U.S.A.* 40°6N 74°13W **92** B2
Lakewood *N. Mex., U.S.A.* 32°38N 104°23W **131** E6
Lakewood *N.Y., U.S.A.* 42°6N 79°19W **87** C2
Lakewood *Ohio, U.S.A.* 41°28N 81°47W **98** B1
Lakewood *Wash., U.S.A.* 48°9N 122°13W **120** B3
Lakewood *Wis., U.S.A.* 45°18N 88°31W **78** C5
Lakewood Park *Fla., U.S.A.* 27°33N 80°24W **114** D8
Lakewood Park *Georgia, U.S.A.* 33°43N 84°24W **117** B2
Lakin *Kans., U.S.A.* 37°57N 101°15W **82** D2
Lakota *Iowa, U.S.A.* 43°23N 94°6W **81** B4
Lakota *N. Dak., U.S.A.* 48°2N 98°21W **76** B7
Lamadrid *Coahuila, Mexico* 27°3N 101°47W **170** C3
Lamaline *Nfld. & L., Canada* 46°52N 55°49W **142** F5
Lamar *Ark., U.S.A.* 35°27N 93°23W **106** C2
Lamar *Colo., U.S.A.* 38°5N 102°37W **125** D8
Lamar *Miss., U.S.A.* 34°55N 89°19W **111** B4
Lamar *Mo., U.S.A.* 37°30N 94°16W **83** D2
Lamar *Nebr., U.S.A.* 40°34N 101°59W **80** D4
Lamar *Okla., U.S.A.* 35°6N 96°8W **107** C7
Lamar *S.C., U.S.A.* 34°10N 80°4W **103** D5
Lamar County ☆ *Ala., U.S.A.* 33°45N 88°7W **112** C2
Lamar County ☆ *Ga., U.S.A.* 33°5N 84°10W **113** C2
Lamar County ☆ *Miss., U.S.A.* 31°9N 89°25W **111** E4
Lamar County ☆ *Tex., U.S.A.* 33°40N 95°33W **109** D12
Lamb County ☆ *Tex., U.S.A.* 34°0N 102°15W **108** D5
Lambert *Miss., U.S.A.* 34°12N 90°16W **111** B3
Lambert *Mont., U.S.A.* 47°41N 104°37W **123** C13
Lambert-St. Louis Int. ✈ (STL) *Mo., U.S.A.* 38°45N 90°22W **94** A1
Lamberton *Minn., U.S.A.* 44°14N 95°16W **77** F3
Lambertville *Mich., U.S.A.* 41°46N 83°35W **79** H8
Lambertville *N.J., U.S.A.* 40°22N 74°57W **92** B2
Lambeth *Ont., Canada* 42°54N 81°18W **146** E5
Lambton, C. *N.W.T., Canada* 71°5N 123°9W **156** B8
Lambton Mills *Ont., Canada* 43°39N 79°30W **161** B1
Lambton Shores *Ont., Canada* 43°10N 81°56W **146** D5
Lame Deer *Mont., U.S.A.* 45°37N 106°40W **123** E11
Lamèque *N.B., Canada* 47°45N 64°38W **141** F5
Lamèque, Î. *N.B., Canada* 47°50N 64°38W **141** F5
Lamesa *Tex., U.S.A.* 32°44N 101°58W **108** E6
Lamine → *Mo., U.S.A.* 38°59N 92°51W **83** C4
Lamison *Ala., U.S.A.* 32°7N 87°34W **112** D3
Lamlam, Mt. *Guam* 13°22N 144°41E **184** b
Lamoille *Nev., U.S.A.* 40°44N 115°29W **128** B5
Lamoille → *Vt., U.S.A.* 44°38N 73°13W **89** B1
Lamoille County ☆ *Vt., U.S.A.* 44°40N 72°40W **89** B2
Lamona *Wash., U.S.A.* 47°22N 118°29W **120** C7
Lamoni *Iowa, U.S.A.* 40°37N 93°56W **81** E5
Lamont *Alta., Canada* 53°46N 112°50W **152** E8
Lamont *Calif., U.S.A.* 35°15N 118°55W **127** H8
Lamont *Fla., U.S.A.* 30°23N 83°49W **114** A5
Lamont *Iowa, U.S.A.* 42°36N 91°39W **81** C7
Lamont *Kans., U.S.A.* 38°7N 96°2W **82** C7
Lamont *Miss., U.S.A.* 33°32N 91°5W **111** C2
Lamont *Okla., U.S.A.* 36°42N 97°30W **107** B6
Lamont *Wash., U.S.A.* 47°12N 117°54W **120** C8
Lampacitos *Nuevo León, Mexico* 24°14N 99°42W **171** F5
Lampasas *Tex., U.S.A.* 31°4N 98°11W **109** F9
Lampasas → *Tex., U.S.A.* 30°59N 97°24W **109** G10
Lampasas County ☆ *Tex., U.S.A.* 31°5N 98°10W **109** F9
Lampazos de Naranjo *Nuevo León, Mexico* 27°1N 100°31W **170** C4
Lampman *Sask., Canada* 49°25N 102°50W **150** F9
Lamy *N. Mex., U.S.A.* 35°29N 105°53W **131** B5
Lanagan *Mo., U.S.A.* 36°37N 94°27W **83** E2
Lāna'i *Hawai'i, U.S.A.* 20°50N 156°55W **136** C5
Lāna'i City *Hawai'i, U.S.A.* 20°50N 156°55W **136** C5
Lāna'ihale *Hawai'i, U.S.A.* 20°49N 156°53W **136** C5
Lanark *Ont., Canada* 45°1N 76°22W **144** F6
Lanark *Ill., U.S.A.* 42°6N 89°50W **84** A4
Lanark Village *Fla., U.S.A.* 29°53N 84°36W **114** B4
Lancaster *Ont., Canada* 45°10N 74°30W **144** F8
Lancaster *Calif., U.S.A.* 34°42N 118°8W **127** J8
Lancaster *Ky., U.S.A.* 37°37N 84°35W **105** C8
Lancaster *Minn., U.S.A.* 48°52N 96°48W **77** B2
Lancaster *Mo., U.S.A.* 40°31N 92°32W **83** A4

Lancaster *N.H., U.S.A.* 44°29N 71°34W **89** B3
Lancaster *N.Y., U.S.A.* 42°54N 78°40W **88** C2
Lancaster *Ohio, U.S.A.* 39°43N 82°36W **86** D4
Lancaster *Pa., U.S.A.* 40°2N 76°19W **87** D6
Lancaster *S.C., U.S.A.* 34°43N 80°46W **103** D5
Lancaster *S.C., U.S.A.* 32°35N 96°45W **116** C5
Lancaster *Va., U.S.A.* 37°46N 76°28W **93** C4
Lancaster *Wis., U.S.A.* 42°51N 90°43W **78** F3
Lancaster County ☆ *Nebr., U.S.A.* 40°45N 96°45W **80** D9
Lancaster County ☆ *Pa., U.S.A.* 40°0N 76°19W **87** E6
Lancaster County ☆ *S.C., U.S.A.* 34°40N 80°40W **103** D5
Lancaster County ☆ *Va., U.S.A.* 37°45N 76°30W **102** C8
Lancaster Sd. *Nunavut, Canada* 74°13N 84°0W **158** C9
Lance Creek *Wyo., U.S.A.* 43°2N 104°39W **124** C8
Land Between the Lakes Nat. Recr. Area △ *U.S.A.* 36°25N 88°0W **104** D4
Land O'Lakes *Fla., U.S.A.* 28°13N 82°27W **114** C6
Landa *N. Dak., U.S.A.* 48°54N 100°55W **76** B5
Landa de Matamoros *Querétaro, Mexico* 21°13N 99°20W **175** A8
Landenburg *Pa., U.S.A.* 39°47N 75°46W **93** A5
Lander *Wyo., U.S.A.* 42°50N 108°44W **124** D4
Lander County ☆ *Nev., U.S.A.* 40°0N 117°0W **128** C4
Landfall *Minn., U.S.A.* 44°55N 92°58W **94** B4
Landis *Sask., Canada* 52°12N 108°27W **150** C3
Landis *N.C., U.S.A.* 35°33N 80°37W **103** C5
Landisville *N.J., U.S.A.* 39°32N 75°40W **93** B5
Landover Hills *Md., U.S.A.* 38°56N 76°54W **99** B4
Landrienne *Qué., Canada* 48°30N 77°50W **144** C5
Landrum *S.C., U.S.A.* 35°11N 82°11W **103** C3
Lands End *N.W.T., Canada* 76°22N 122°37W **158** B1
Lane *Kans., U.S.A.* 38°26N 95°5W **82** C8
Lane *S. Dak., U.S.A.* 44°4N 98°26W **76** F7
Lane County ☆ *Kans., U.S.A.* 38°30N 100°30W **82** C3
Lane County ☆ *Oreg., U.S.A.* 44°0N 123°0W **121** D2
Lanesboro *Iowa, U.S.A.* 42°11N 94°41W **81** C4
Lanesboro *Minn., U.S.A.* 43°43N 91°58W **77** G7
Lanesborough *Mass., U.S.A.* 42°31N 73°14W **91** B1
Lanett *Ala., U.S.A.* 32°52N 85°12W **112** D5
Lang Bay *B.C., Canada* 49°45N 124°21W **154** F10
Langara I. *B.C., Canada* 54°14N 133°1W **154** A1
Langdon *Kans., U.S.A.* 37°51N 98°19W **82** D5
Langdon *N. Dak., U.S.A.* 48°45N 98°22W **76** B7
Langenburg *Sask., Canada* 50°51N 101°43W **151** D12
Langford *B.C., Canada* 48°27N 123°29W **155** G11
Langford *S. Dak., U.S.A.* 45°36N 97°50W **76** E8
Langham *Sask., Canada* 52°22N 106°58W **150** C5
Langhorne *Pa., U.S.A.* 40°10N 74°55W **92** B2
Langlade *St-P. & M.* 46°50N 56°20W **142** F4
Langlade County ☆ *Wis., U.S.A.* 45°13N 89°5W **78** C4
Langley *B.C., Canada* 49°7N 122°39W **155** F12
Langley *Ark., U.S.A.* 34°19N 93°51W **106** D2
Langley *Okla., U.S.A.* 36°28N 95°3W **107** B8
Langley *Va., U.S.A.* 38°57N 77°11W **99** B2
Langley *Wash., U.S.A.* 48°2N 122°24W **120** B3
Langley Park *Md., U.S.A.* 38°59N 76°58W **99** B4
Langlois *Oreg., U.S.A.* 42°56N 124°27W **121** E1
Langruth *Man., Canada* 50°23N 98°40W **151** E13
Langston *Okla., U.S.A.* 35°59N 97°18W **107** C6
Langtry *Tex., U.S.A.* 29°49N 101°34W **108** G6
L'Anguille → *Ark., U.S.A.* 34°44N 90°40W **106** D5
Lanham *Md., U.S.A.* 38°59N 76°51W **99** B4
Lanier County ☆ *Ga., U.S.A.* 31°0N 83°5W **113** E3
Lanigan *Sask., Canada* 51°51N 105°2W **150** D6
L'Annociation *Qué., Canada* 46°25N 74°55W **144** E8
Lansdale *Pa., U.S.A.* 40°14N 75°17W **92** B1
Lansdowne *Ont., Canada* 44°24N 76°1W **147** C10
Lansdowne *Md., U.S.A.* 39°14N 76°39W **99** B2
Lansford *N. Dak., U.S.A.* 48°38N 101°23W **76** B4
Lansford *Pa., U.S.A.* 40°50N 75°53W **87** D7
Lansing *Ont., Canada* 43°45N 79°24W **161** A2
Lansing *Ill., U.S.A.* 41°34N 87°33W **84** B6
Lansing *Iowa, U.S.A.* 43°22N 91°13W **81** B7
Lansing *Kans., U.S.A.* 39°15N 94°54W **82** B9
Lansing *Mich., U.S.A.* 42°44N 84°33W **79** G7
Lansing → *Yukon, Canada* 63°44N 133°28W **156** C6
Lantana *Fla., U.S.A.* 26°35N 80°3W **114** E8
Lantzville *B.C., Canada* 49°15N 124°5W **154** F10
Lanz I. *B.C., Canada* 50°49N 128°41W **154** E6
Laona *Wis., U.S.A.* 45°34N 88°40W **78** C5
Lapeer *Mich., U.S.A.* 43°3N 83°19W **79** F8
Lapeer County ☆ *Mich., U.S.A.* 43°3N 83°15W **79** F8
Lapel *Ind., U.S.A.* 40°4N 85°51W **85** C5
Laplace *La., U.S.A.* 30°4N 90°29W **110** D5
LaPorte *Ind., U.S.A.* 41°36N 86°43W **85** B4
Laporte *Minn., U.S.A.* 47°13N 94°45W **77** C4
Laporte *Pa., U.S.A.* 41°25N 76°30W **87** C6
LaPorte County ☆ *Ind., U.S.A.* 41°30N 86°45W **85** B4
Lappans *Md., U.S.A.* 39°33N 77°43W **93** A3
Lapwai *Idaho, U.S.A.* 46°24N 116°48W **122** C2
Laramie *Wyo., U.S.A.* 41°19N 105°35W **124** E8
Laramie → *Wyo., U.S.A.* 42°13N 104°33W **124** D8
Laramie County ☆ *Wyo., U.S.A.* 41°15N 104°40W **124** E8
Laramie Mts. *Wyo., U.S.A.* 42°0N 105°30W **124** E7
Laramie Pk. *Wyo., U.S.A.* 42°17N 105°27W **124** D7
Larchmont *N.Y., U.S.A.* 40°55N 73°45W **97** A4
Larchwood *Iowa, U.S.A.* 43°27N 96°26W **81** B2
Larder Lake *Ont., Canada* 48°5N 79°40W **144** C4
Lardo *Idaho, U.S.A.* 44°55N 116°8W **122** E2
L'Ardoise *N.S., Canada* 45°37N 60°45W **141** H9
Laredo *Mo., U.S.A.* 40°2N 93°27W **83** A3
Laredo *Tex., U.S.A.* 27°30N 99°30W **108** K8
Laredo Sd. *B.C., Canada* 52°30N 128°53W **154** C6
Lares *Puerto Rico* 18°18N 66°53W **184** G16
Larga, Laguna *Tex., U.S.A.* 27°30N 97°25W **109** K10
Largo *Fla., U.S.A.* 27°54N 82°47W **115** B2
Largo, Key *Fla., U.S.A.* 25°15N 80°15W **114** F8
Largo Cr. → *N. Mex., U.S.A.* 34°30N 108°51W **131** C2
Larimer County ☆ *Colo., U.S.A.* 40°40N 105°20W **125** B5
Larimore *N. Dak., U.S.A.* 47°54N 97°38W **76** C8
Lark *N. Dak., U.S.A.* 46°27N 101°24W **76** D4
Lark *Tex., U.S.A.* 35°12N 101°14W **108** B6
Lark *Utah, U.S.A.* 40°32N 112°6W **129** C3
Lark Harbour *Nfld. & L., Canada* 49°6N 58°23W **142** D5
Larkins = South Miami *Fla., U.S.A.* 25°42N 80°17W **115** D1
Larkspur *Colo., U.S.A.* 39°14N 104°53W **125** C6
Larned *Kans., U.S.A.* 38°11N 99°6W **82** C4

Larose *La., U.S.A.* 29°34N 90°23W **110** E5
Larrabee *Iowa, U.S.A.* 42°52N 95°33W **81** C3
Larrainzar *Chiapas, Mexico* 16°53N 92°42W **178** C4
Larrys River *N.S., Canada* 45°13N 61°23W **141** H8
Larsen Bay *Alaska, U.S.A.* 57°32N 153°59W **135** H9
Larsen Sound *Nunavut, Canada* 70°30N 98°45W **158** C6
Larson *N. Dak., U.S.A.* 48°53N 102°52W **76** B3
Larue *Ont., Canada* 51°17N 94°40W **148** A2
Larus *L. Ont., Canada* 51°17N 94°40W **148** A2
Las Almejas, E. *Baja Calif. S., Mexico* 24°33N 111°42W **167** J7
Las Ánimas *Colo., U.S.A.* 38°4N 103°13W **125** D7
Las Ánimas, I. *Baja Calif., Mexico* 28°43N 112°58W **166** E6
Las Ánimas, Pta. *Baja Calif., Mexico* 28°51N 113°16W **166** E5
Las Animas County ☆ *Colo., U.S.A.* 37°15N 104°00W **125** E7
Las Arenitas *Sinaloa, Mexico* 24°22N 107°23W **172** C3
Las Calabazas *Baja Calif., Mexico* 32°18N 116°33W **166** A2
Las Calenturas *Sonora, Mexico* 30°37N 112°22W **168** C3
Las Cañas *Michoacan, Mexico* 18°34N 101°58W **174** D6
Las Choapas *Veracruz, Mexico* 17°55N 94°7W **177** G6
Las Coloradas *Yucatán, Mexico* 21°36N 87°59W **179** A6
Las Cruces *N. Mex., U.S.A.* 32°19N 106°47W **131** E4
Las Cuatas *Chiapas, Mexico* 30°3N 105°59W **169** C10
Las Cuevas *Baja Calif. S., Mexico* 23°32N 109°41W **167** K9
Las Delicias *Chiapas, Mexico* 15°58N 91°51W **178** D5
Las Enchilayas *Sonora, Mexico* 30°55N 112°45W **168** C3
Las Esperanza *Durango, Mexico* 25°52N 104°50W **173** B6
Las Glorias *Sinaloa, Mexico* 25°17N 108°30W **172** B2
Las Guacamayas, Cerro *Chihuahua, Mexico* 30°32N 108°38W **168** C7
Las Herrera *Durango, Mexico* 25°10N 105°33W **172** B5
Las Hormigas *Nuevo León, Mexico* 25°27N 98°39W **170** E6
Las Juntas, Presa *Sinaloa, Mexico* 24°00N 106°18W **172** D4
Las Lagunas *Baja Calif. S., Mexico* 23°31N 109°29W **167** K9
Las Lajitas *Sinaloa, Mexico* 26°5N 109°22W **172** A1
Las Lomas *Calif., U.S.A.* 38°41N 123°8W **126** E3
Las Margaritas *Chiapas, Mexico* 16°19N 91°59W **178** C5
Las Margaritas *Durango, Mexico* 23°18N 104°17W **173** D6
Las Mesas *Michoacan, Mexico* 19°4N 100°23W **175** C7
Las Milpas *Sonora, Mexico* 26°48N 109°50W **168** G6
Las Nopaleras, Cerro *Coahuila, Mexico* 25°8N 103°15W **171** E1
Las Norias *Coahuila, Mexico* 27°33N 103°30W **170** C1
Las Nutrias *N. Mex., U.S.A.* 34°28N 106°46W **131** C4
Las Palmas *Oaxaca, Mexico* 16°27N 94°35W **177** H6
Las Palomas *Chihuahua, Mexico* 26°32N 107°00W **169** G8
Las Palomas *Baja Calif., Mexico* 32°18N 116°33W **166** A2
Las Pampas *Chihuahua, Mexico* 27°30N 104°45W **169** F11
Las Pampas, Sa. *Chihuahua, Mexico* 27°20N 104°45W **169** F11
Las Piedras *Puerto Rico* 18°11N 65°52W **184** G17
Las Puentes *Sinaloa, Mexico* 24°31N 107°34W **172** C3
Las Rosas *Chiapas, Mexico* 16°24N 92°23W **178** C4
Las Tablas *Panama* 7°49N 80°14W **182** E3
Las Toronjas *Chiapas, Mexico* 15°57N 92°59W **178** D3
Las Tortugas *Durango, Mexico* 26°28N 103°45W **173** A7
Las Tunas *Cuba* 20°58N 76°59W **182** B4
Las Tunas, Sa. *Chihuahua, Mexico* 29°40N 107°15W **169** D8
Las Tunitas *Baja Calif. S., Mexico* 24°49N 110°50W **167** J8
Las Varas *Chihuahua, Mexico* 29°30N 108°3W **169** D7
Las Varas *Nayarit, Mexico* 21°10N 105°10W **172** E5
Las Vegas *N. Mex., U.S.A.* 35°36N 105°13W **131** B5
Las Vegas *Nev., U.S.A.* 36°10N 115°8W **134** B2
Las Vegas, L. *Nev., U.S.A.* 36°8N 114°58W **134** C3
Las Vegas Bay *Nev., U.S.A.* 36°7N 114°51W **134** C3
Las Vegas-Dunes Recreation Lands *Nev., U.S.A.* 36°17N 114°55W **134** B3
Las Vegas McCarran Int. ✈ (LAS) *Nev., U.S.A.* 36°5N 115°9W **134** C2
Las Vigas *Guerrero, Mexico* 16°46N 99°14W **175** F8
Lasalle *Que., Canada* 45°26N 73°38W **160** B3
LaSalle Street Station *Ill., U.S.A.* 41°52N 87°37W **95** B3
Lashburn *Sask., Canada* 53°10N 109°40W **150** D2
Lasqueti *B.C., Canada* 49°30N 124°21W **154** F10
Lasqueti I. *B.C., Canada* 49°29N 124°16W **154** F10
Lassen County ☆ *Calif., U.S.A.* 40°45N 120°30W **126** C6
Lassen Nat. Forest *Calif., U.S.A.* 40°30N 121°15W **126** C5
Lassen Pk. *Calif., U.S.A.* 40°29N 121°30W **126** C5
Lassen Volcanic Nat. Park and Wilderness △ *Calif., U.S.A.* 40°30N 121°20W **126** C5
Last Chance *Colo., U.S.A.* 39°44N 103°36W **125** C7
Last Chance Cr. → *Utah, U.S.A.* 38°33N 111°21W **129** E4
Last Chance Range *Calif., U.S.A.* 36°55N 117°36W **127** G9
Last Mountain L. *Sask., Canada* 51°5N 105°14W **150** D6
Lastrup *Minn., U.S.A.* 46°2N 94°4W **77** D4
Lata Mt. *Amer. Samoa* 14°14S 169°27W **184** f
Latah *Wash., U.S.A.* 47°17N 117°9W **120** C8
Latah County ☆ *Idaho, U.S.A.* 46°45N 116°52W **122** C2
Latchford *Ont., Canada* 47°20N 79°50W **144** D3
Laterrière *Que., Canada* 48°18N 71°7W **145** C11
Latham *Ill., U.S.A.* 39°58N 89°10W **84** D4
Latham *Kans., U.S.A.* 37°32N 96°38W **82** D7
Lathrop *Calif., U.S.A.* 37°49N 121°16W **126** F5
Lathrop *Mo., U.S.A.* 39°33N 94°20W **83** B2
Lathrup Village *Mich., U.S.A.* 42°46N 93°22W **98** A1
Latimer *Iowa, U.S.A.* 42°46N 93°22W **81** C5
Latimer *Kans., U.S.A.* 38°44N 96°51W **82** C7
Latimer County ☆ *Okla., U.S.A.* 34°50N 95°10W **107** D8
Laton *Calif., U.S.A.* 36°26N 119°41W **127** G7
Latrobe *Pa., U.S.A.* 40°19N 79°23W **87** D3
Latta *S.C., U.S.A.* 34°21N 79°26W **103** D6
Latulipe *Que. Canada* 47°26N 79°2W **144** D3
Lauderdale *Minn., U.S.A.* 44°59N 93°12W **94** B2
Lauderdale *Miss., U.S.A.* 32°31N 88°31W **111** D5
Lauderdale County ☆ *Ala., U.S.A.* 34°56N 87°46W **112** B3
Lauderdale County ☆ *Miss., U.S.A.* 32°22N 88°42W **111** D5
Lauderdale County ☆ *Tenn., U.S.A.* 35°45N 89°23W **104** E3
Lauderdale Lakes *Fla., U.S.A.* 26°9N 80°12W **115** B1
Lauderhill *Fla., U.S.A.* 26°9N 80°12W **115** B2
Lauge Koch Kyst *Greenland* 75°45N 57°45W **158** B14
Laughing Fish Pt. *Mich., U.S.A.* 46°32N 87°1W **79** C4
Laughlin *Nev., U.S.A.* 35°10N 114°34W **128** G6
Laughlin Pk. *N. Mex., U.S.A.* 36°40N 104°10W **131** A6
Laulau, Bahia *N. Marianas* 15°8N 145°45E **184** c
Laura *Ohio, U.S.A.* 39°59N 84°22W **86** D2
Laurel *Del., U.S.A.* 38°33N 75°34W **93** B5
Laurel *Fla., U.S.A.* 27°8N 82°27W **114** D6
Laurel *Ind., U.S.A.* 39°30N 85°11W **85** D5
Laurel *Iowa, U.S.A.* 41°53N 92°55W **81** D6
Laurel *Md., U.S.A.* 39°6N 76°51W **93** A4
Laurel *Miss., U.S.A.* 31°41N 89°8W **111** E4
Laurel *Mont., U.S.A.* 45°40N 108°46W **123** E9
Laurel *Nebr., U.S.A.* 42°26N 97°6W **80** B8
Laurel Bay *S.C., U.S.A.* 32°27N 80°47W **103** F5
Laurel County ☆ *Ky., U.S.A.* 37°5N 84°10W **105** C8
Laurel Hill *Fla., U.S.A.* 30°57N 86°27W **112** A4
Laurel Hill *Pa., U.S.A.* 40°14N 79°6W **87** D3
Laurel River L. *Ky., U.S.A.* 36°57N 84°10W **105** D8
Laureldale *N.J., U.S.A.* 39°30N 74°41W **92** C2

Laureldale *Pa., U.S.A.* 40°23N 75°55W **87** D7
Laureles y Góngora I *Nayarit, Mexico* 21°39N 105°23W **172** F5
Laurelton *N.Y., U.S.A.* 40°40N 73°45W **97** B4
Laurelville *Ohio, U.S.A.* 39°28N 82°44W **86** D4
Laurens *Iowa, U.S.A.* 42°51N 94°52W **81** C4
Laurens *S.C., U.S.A.* 34°30N 82°1W **103** D3
Laurens County ☆ *Ga., U.S.A.* 32°30N 83°0W **113** C3
Laurens County ☆ *S.C., U.S.A.* 34°30N 82°0W **103** D4
Laurentides, Réserve Faunique des △ *Que., Canada* 47°45N 71°15W **145** D11
Laurie *Mo., U.S.A.* 38°12N 92°50W **83** C4
Laurier *Man., Canada* 50°53N 99°33W **151** E12
Laurier-Station *Que., Canada* 46°32N 71°38W **145** E11
Laurierville *Que., Canada* 46°18N 71°39W **145** E11
Laurinburg *N.C., U.S.A.* 34°47N 79°28W **103** D6
Laurium *Mich., U.S.A.* 47°14N 88°27W **79** B3
Lava Beds Nat. Monument △ *Calif., U.S.A.* 41°40N 121°30W **126** B5
Lava Hot Springs *Idaho, U.S.A.* 42°37N 112°1W **122** G6
Lavaca *Ark., U.S.A.* 35°20N 94°10W **106** C1
Lavaca → *Tex., U.S.A.* 28°41N 96°35W **109** J11
Lavaca County ☆ *Tex., U.S.A.* 29°27N 96°57W **109** H11
Laval-des-Rapides *Que., Canada* 45°33N 73°42W **160** A2
Laval Ouest *Que., Canada* 45°33N 73°52W **160** A1
Laval-sur-le-Lac *Que., Canada* 45°32N 73°52W **160** A1
Lavallette *N.J., U.S.A.* 39°58N 74°4W **92** C2
Lavaltrie *Que., Canada* 45°53N 73°17W **145** F9
Lavant Station *Ont., Canada* 45°3N 76°42W **147** B10
Laveen *Ariz., U.S.A.* 33°21N 112°12W **134** C1
Laverlochère *Que., Canada* 47°26N 79°18W **144** D3
Laverne *Okla., U.S.A.* 36°43N 99°54W **107** B4
Lavic *L. Calif., U.S.A.* 34°40N 116°21W **127** J10
Lavieille, L. *Ont., Canada* 45°51N 78°14W **147** B8
Lavillette *N.B., Canada* 47°16N 65°18W **141** F4
Lavina *Mont., U.S.A.* 46°18N 108°56W **123** D9
Lavon L. *Tex., U.S.A.* 33°2N 96°28W **109** D11
Lavonia *Ga., U.S.A.* 34°26N 83°6W **113** B3
Lavoy *Alta., Canada* 53°27N 111°52W **152** E9
Lawen *Oreg., U.S.A.* 43°27N 118°48W **121** D7
Lawler *Iowa, U.S.A.* 43°4N 92°9W **81** B6
Lawn *Nfld. & L., Canada* 46°57N 55°35W **142** F5
Lawn *Tex., U.S.A.* 32°8N 99°45W **109** E8
Lawndale *Ind., U.S.A.* 41°50N 87°42W **95** D2
Lawne L. *Fla., U.S.A.* 28°33N 81°26W **115** A2
Lawrence *Ind., U.S.A.* 39°50N 86°2W **85** D4
Lawrence *Kans., U.S.A.* 38°58N 95°14W **82** C8
Lawrence *Mass., U.S.A.* 42°43N 71°10W **91** B3
Lawrence *Mich., U.S.A.* 42°13N 86°3W **79** G5
Lawrence *N.Y., U.S.A.* 40°36N 73°43W **97** C5
Lawrence *Nebr., U.S.A.* 40°18N 98°16W **80** D7
Lawrence County ☆ *Ala., U.S.A.* 34°29N 87°18W **112** B3
Lawrence County ☆ *Ark., U.S.A.* 36°0N 91°0W **106** B4
Lawrence County ☆ *Ill., U.S.A.* 38°45N 87°45W **84** E6
Lawrence County ☆ *Ind., U.S.A.* 38°50N 86°30W **85** E4
Lawrence County ☆ *Ky., U.S.A.* 38°5N 82°45W **105** B9
Lawrence County ☆ *Miss., U.S.A.* 31°33N 90°7W **111** E3
Lawrence County ☆ *Mo., U.S.A.* 37°10N 93°50W **83** D3
Lawrence County ☆ *Ohio, U.S.A.* 38°32N 82°41W **86** E4
Lawrence County ☆ *Pa., U.S.A.* 41°0N 80°15W **87** D2
Lawrence County ☆ *S. Dak., U.S.A.* 44°23N 103°44W **76** F2
Lawrence County ☆ *Tenn., U.S.A.* 35°14N 87°20W **104** E5
Lawrence Creek *Okla., U.S.A.* 36°5N 96°26W **107** B7
Lawrence Heights *Ont., Canada* 43°43N 79°25W **161** A2
Lawrence J. Timmerman ✈ (MWC) *Wis., U.S.A.* 43°6N 88°2W **94** B1
Lawrence Station *N.B., Canada* 45°26N 67°11W **141** H2
Lawrenceburg *Ind., U.S.A.* 39°6N 84°52W **85** D6
Lawrenceburg *Ky., U.S.A.* 38°2N 84°54W **105** B8
Lawrenceburg *Tenn., U.S.A.* 35°14N 87°20W **104** E5
Lawrencetown *N.S., Canada* 44°53N 65°10W **141** J4
Lawrenceville *Ga., U.S.A.* 33°57N 83°59W **113** C3
Lawrenceville *Ill., U.S.A.* 38°44N 87°41W **84** E6
Lawrenceville *N.J., U.S.A.* 40°18N 74°44W **92** B2
Lawrenceville *Pa., U.S.A.* 41°59N 77°8W **87** C5
Lawrenceville *Va., U.S.A.* 36°46N 77°51W **102** E7
Lawson *Mo., U.S.A.* 39°26N 94°12W **83** B2
Lawtey *Fla., U.S.A.* 30°3N 82°5W **114** A6
Lawton *Mich., U.S.A.* 42°10N 85°50W **79** G6
Lawton *N. Dak., U.S.A.* 48°18N 98°22W **76** B7
Lawton *Okla., U.S.A.* 34°37N 98°25W **107** D6
Lay *Colo., U.S.A.* 40°32N 107°53W **125** B3
Laysan I. *Hawai'i, U.S.A.* 25°50N 171°50W **136** F9
Layton *Fla., U.S.A.* 24°50N 80°47W **114** G8
Layton *N.J., U.S.A.* 41°13N 74°50W **92** A2
Layton *Utah, U.S.A.* 41°4N 111°58W **129** F4
Laytonsville *Md., U.S.A.* 39°13N 77°9W **93** A3
Laytonville *Calif., U.S.A.* 39°41N 123°29W **126** D3
Lázaro Cárdenas *Baja Calif., Mexico* 31°25N 115°43W **166** B3
Lázaro Cárdenas *Chiapas, Mexico* 16°39N 93°48W **178** C3
Lázaro Cárdenas *Chihuahua, Mexico* 29°7N 107°5W **169** D8
Lázaro Cárdenas *Jalisco, Mexico* 19°48N 105°9W **172** F6
Lázaro Cárdenas *Michoacan, Mexico* 17°55N 102°11W **174** E5
Lázaro Cárdenas *Quintana Roo, Mexico* 18°59N 88°13W **179** C5
Lázaro Cárdenas *Tabasco, Mexico* 18°10N 93°34W **178** A3
Lázaro Cárdenas *Veracruz, Mexico* 22°15N 98°8W **176** B2
Lázaro Cárdenas, Presa *Durango, Mexico* 25°36N 105°3W **172** B5
Lazear *Colo., U.S.A.* 38°47N 107°47W **125** D3
Le Bic *Que., Canada* 48°20N 68°41W **145** C14
Le Breton, L. *Que., Canada* 51°53N 60°9W **140** B9
Le Center *Minn., U.S.A.* 44°23N 93°44W **77** F5
Le Claire *Iowa, U.S.A.* 41°36N 90°21W **81** D8
Le Doré, L. *Que., Canada* 51°71N 61°23W **140** B8
Le Flore County ☆ *Okla., U.S.A.* 35°0N 94°45W **107** D9
Le François *Martinique* 14°38N 60°57W **183** D7
Le Grand *Calif., U.S.A.* 37°14N 120°15W **126** F6
Le Grand *Iowa, U.S.A.* 42°0N 92°47W **81** C6
Le Loup *Kans., U.S.A.* 38°42N 95°4W **82** C8
Le Mars *Iowa, U.S.A.* 42°47N 96°10W **81** C2
Le Moule *Guadeloupe* 16°20N 61°22W **183** C7
Le Moyen *La., U.S.A.* 30°48N 92°40W **110** D3
Le Raysville *Pa., U.S.A.* 41°51N 76°11W **87** C6
Le Roy *Ill., U.S.A.* 40°21N 88°46W **84** C5
Le Roy *Kans., U.S.A.* 38°5N 95°38W **82** C8
Le Roy *Mich., U.S.A.* 44°2N 85°27W **79** E6
Le Roy *Minn., U.S.A.* 43°31N 92°30W **77** G6
Le Roy *N.Y., U.S.A.* 42°58N 78°0W **88** C2
Le Roy *Pa., U.S.A.* 41°41N 76°43W **87** C6
Le Roy, L. *Que., Canada* 51°10N 61°53W **140** B8
Le Sueur *Minn., U.S.A.* 44°28N 93°55W **77** F5
Le Sueur County ☆ *Minn., U.S.A.* 44°23N 93°45W **77** F5
Lea County ☆ *N. Mex., U.S.A.* 32°50N 103°30W **131** E7
Leach I. *Ont., Canada* 47°28N 84°57W **149** E12
Leachville *Ark., U.S.A.* 35°56N 90°16W **106** C5
Lead *S. Dak., U.S.A.* 44°21N 103°46W **76** F2

Lead Hill *Ark., U.S.A.* 36°25N 92°55W **106** B3
Lead Hill *Mo., U.S.A.* 37°6N 92°38W **83** D4
Leadbetter Pt. *Wash., U.S.A.* 46°39N 124°3W **120** D1
Leader *Sask., Canada* 50°50N 109°30W **150** E2
Leadore *Idaho, U.S.A.* 44°41N 113°21W **122** E5
Leadpoint *Wash., U.S.A.* 48°55N 117°35W **120** B8
Leadville *Colo., U.S.A.* 39°15N 106°18W **125** C4
Leadwood *Mo., U.S.A.* 37°52N 90°36W **83** D6
Leaf → *Miss., U.S.A.* 30°59N 88°44W **111** F5
Leaf *L. Sask., Canada* 53°11N 102°8W **151** B9
Leaf Rapids *Man., Canada* 56°30N 99°59W **159** F6
League City *Tex., U.S.A.* 29°31N 95°6W **109** H12
Leake County ☆ *Miss., U.S.A.* 32°42N 89°38W **111** D4
Leakesville *Miss., U.S.A.* 31°9N 88°33W **111** E5
Leaksville = Eden *N.C., U.S.A.* 36°29N 79°53W **103** B6
Lealman *Tampa, U.S.A.* 27°49N 82°40W **115** C3
Leamington *Ont., Canada* 42°3N 82°36W **146** E4
Leamington *Utah, U.S.A.* 39°32N 112°17W **129** D3
Leamy, L. *Que., Canada* 45°27N 75°43W **160** A1
Leary *Ga., U.S.A.* 31°29N 84°31W **113** E2
Leasburg *Mo., U.S.A.* 38°5N 91°18W **83** C5
Leaside *Ont., Canada* 43°42N 79°22W **161** A2
Leask *Sask., Canada* 53°5N 106°45W **150** B5
Leatherwood *Ky., U.S.A.* 37°2N 83°11W **105** C9
Leavenworth *Ind., U.S.A.* 38°12N 86°21W **85** E4
Leavenworth *Kans., U.S.A.* 39°19N 94°55W **82** B9
Leavenworth *Wash., U.S.A.* 47°36N 120°40W **120** C5
Leavenworth County ☆ *Kans., U.S.A.* 39°15N 95°0W **82** B9
Leavittsburg *Ohio, U.S.A.* 41°14N 80°53W **86** B6
Leawood *Kans., U.S.A.* 38°58N 94°37W **82** C9
Lebam *Wash., U.S.A.* 46°34N 123°33W **120** D2
Lebanon *Conn., U.S.A.* 41°38N 72°13W **91** C2
Lebanon *Ind., U.S.A.* 40°3N 86°28W **85** C4
Lebanon *Kans., U.S.A.* 39°49N 98°33W **82** B5
Lebanon *Ky., U.S.A.* 37°34N 85°15W **105** C7
Lebanon *Mo., U.S.A.* 37°41N 92°40W **83** D4
Lebanon *N.H., U.S.A.* 43°39N 72°15W **91** C2
Lebanon *Nebr., U.S.A.* 40°3N 100°17W **80** D5
Lebanon *Ohio, U.S.A.* 39°26N 84°13W **86** D2
Lebanon *Okla., U.S.A.* 33°59N 96°55W **107** E7
Lebanon *Oreg., U.S.A.* 44°32N 122°55W **121** C3
Lebanon *Pa., U.S.A.* 40°20N 76°26W **87** D6
Lebanon *S. Dak., U.S.A.* 45°4N 99°46W **76** E6
Lebanon *Tenn., U.S.A.* 36°12N 86°18W **104** D6
Lebanon *Va., U.S.A.* 36°54N 82°5W **102** E2
Lebanon County ☆ *Pa., U.S.A.* 40°20N 76°25W **87** D6
Lebanon Junction *Ky., U.S.A.* 37°50N 85°44W **105** C7
Lebanon State Forest *N.J., U.S.A.* 39°53N 74°30W **92** C2
Lebanon Station *Fla., U.S.A.* 29°10N 82°37W **114** B6
Lebec *Calif., U.S.A.* 34°51N 118°52W **127** J8
Lebel-sur-Quévillon *Que., Canada* 49°3N 76°59W **144** B6
Lebo *Kans., U.S.A.* 38°25N 95°51W **82** C8
Lecompte *La., U.S.A.* 31°6N 92°24W **110** C3
Lecompton *Kans., U.S.A.* 39°3N 95°24W **82** B8
Leduc *Alta., Canada* 53°15N 113°30W **152** E7
Ledyard *Iowa, U.S.A.* 43°25N 94°10W **81** B4
Lee → *Fla., U.S.A.* 30°25N 83°18W **114** A5
Lee *Ill., U.S.A.* 41°48N 88°56W **84** B5
Lee *Maine, U.S.A.* 45°22N 68°17W **90** C5
Lee *Mass., U.S.A.* 42°19N 73°15W **91** B1
Lee *Nev., U.S.A.* 40°34N 115°36W **128** B5
Lee City *Ky., U.S.A.* 37°44N 83°29W **105** C9
Lee County ☆ *Ala., U.S.A.* 32°39N 85°23W **112** D5
Lee County ☆ *Ark., U.S.A.* 34°46N 90°46W **106** D5
Lee County ☆ *Ga., U.S.A.* 31°45N 84°5W **113** E2
Lee County ☆ *Ill., U.S.A.* 41°45N 89°20W **84** B4
Lee County ☆ *Iowa, U.S.A.* 40°40N 91°30W **81** E7
Lee County ☆ *Ky., U.S.A.* 37°35N 83°45W **105** C9
Lee County ☆ *Miss., U.S.A.* 34°16N 88°43W **111** B5
Lee County ☆ *N.C., U.S.A.* 35°30N 79°10W **103** C6
Lee County ☆ *S.C., U.S.A.* 34°10N 80°15W **103** D5
Lee County ☆ *Tex., U.S.A.* 30°17N 96°58W **109** G11
Lee County ☆ *Va., U.S.A.* 36°45N 83°5W **102** E1
Lee Vining *Calif., U.S.A.* 37°58N 119°7W **126** F7
Leech L. *Sask., Canada* 51°5N 102°28W **150** D9
Leech L. *Minn., U.S.A.* 47°10N 94°24W **77** C4
Leech Lake Indian Reservation *Minn., U.S.A.* 47°20N 94°10W **77** C4
Leedey *Okla., U.S.A.* 35°52N 99°21W **107** C4
Leeds *Ala., U.S.A.* 33°33N 86°33W **112** C4
Leeds *Maine, U.S.A.* 44°18N 70°7W **90** D3
Leeds *N. Dak., U.S.A.* 48°17N 99°27W **76** B6
Leeds *Utah, U.S.A.* 37°14N 113°22W **129** F2
Leektown *N.J., U.S.A.* 39°36N 74°26W **92** C2
Leelanau County ☆ *Mich., U.S.A.* 44°55N 85°50W **79** E6
Leelanau L. *Mich., U.S.A.* 44°55N 85°43W **79** E6
Lee's Summit *Mo., U.S.A.* 38°55N 94°23W **83** C2
Leesburg *Fla., U.S.A.* 28°49N 81°53W **114** C7
Leesburg *Ga., U.S.A.* 31°44N 84°10W **113** E2
Leesburg *N.J., U.S.A.* 39°15N 74°59W **92** C2
Leesburg *Ohio, U.S.A.* 39°21N 83°33W **86** D3
Leesburg *Va., U.S.A.* 39°7N 77°34W **93** A3
Leesport *Pa., U.S.A.* 40°27N 75°58W **87** D7
Leesville *La., U.S.A.* 31°8N 93°16W **110** C2
Leesville *Ohio, U.S.A.* 40°27N 81°13W **86** C5
Leesville *S.C., U.S.A.* 33°55N 81°31W **103** D4
Leesville *Va., U.S.A.* 37°5N 79°25W **102** D5
Leeton *Mo., U.S.A.* 38°35N 93°42W **83** C3
Leetonia *Minn., U.S.A.* 47°32N 92°59W **77** C6
Leetonia *Ohio, U.S.A.* 40°53N 80°45W **86** C6
Leeward Is. *Atl. Oc.* 16°30N 63°30W **183** C7
Leewood *W. Va., U.S.A.* 38°4N 81°27W **102** C3
Leflore *Okla., U.S.A.* 34°54N 94°59W **107** D9
Leflore County ☆ *Miss., U.S.A.* 33°30N 90°20W **111** C3
Lefors *Tex., U.S.A.* 35°26N 100°48W **108** B7
Lefroy *Ont., Canada* 44°16N 79°34W **146** C4
Legal *Alta., Canada* 53°55N 113°35W **152** E7
Leggett *Calif., U.S.A.* 39°52N 123°43W **126** D3
Leggett *Tex., U.S.A.* 30°49N 94°52W **109** G13
Lehi *Utah, U.S.A.* 40°24N 111°51W **129** C4
Lehigh *Iowa, U.S.A.* 42°22N 94°3W **81** C4
Lehigh *Kans., U.S.A.* 38°23N 97°18W **82** C6
Lehigh *Okla., U.S.A.* 34°28N 96°13W **107** D7
Lehigh → *Pa., U.S.A.* 40°41N 75°12W **92** A1
Lehigh Acres *Fla., U.S.A.* 26°36N 81°39W **114** E7
Lehigh County ☆ *Pa., U.S.A.* 40°40N 75°50W **87** D7
Lehr *N. Dak., U.S.A.* 46°17N 99°21W **76** B6
Lehua *Hawai'i, U.S.A.* 22°1N 160°6W **136** A1
Leicester *Mass., U.S.A.* 42°15N 71°55W **91** B3
Leicester *Vt., U.S.A.* 43°53N 73°8W **89** C1
Leidy, Mt. *Wyo., U.S.A.* 43°44N 110°24W **124** C2
Leigh *Nebr., U.S.A.* 41°42N 97°14W **80** C8

Leighton *Ala., U.S.A.* 34°42N 87°32W **112** B3
Leighton *Iowa, U.S.A.* 41°20N 92°47W **81** D6
Leipsic *Del., U.S.A.* 39°14N 75°31W **93** A5
Leipsic *Ohio, U.S.A.* 41°6N 83°59W **86** B3
Leisure City *Fla., U.S.A.* 25°30N 80°26W **114** F8
Leitchfield *Ky., U.S.A.* 37°29N 86°18W **104** C6
Leiter *Wyo., U.S.A.* 44°43N 106°16W **124** B6
Leitersburg *Md., U.S.A.* 39°42N 77°37W **93** A3
Leith *N. Dak., U.S.A.* 46°22N 101°38W **76** D4
Lejeune *Que., Canada* 47°46N 68°34W **145** C14
Lela *Tex., U.S.A.* 35°14N 100°21W **108** B7
Leland *Ill., U.S.A.* 41°37N 88°48W **84** B4
Leland *Iowa, U.S.A.* 43°20N 93°38W **81** B5
Leland *Mich., U.S.A.* 45°1N 85°45W **79** D6
Leland *Miss., U.S.A.* 33°24N 90°54W **111** C3
Leland *N.C., U.S.A.* 34°15N 78°3W **103** D7
Leland *Wash., U.S.A.* 47°53N 122°53W **120** C3
Leleiwi Pt. *Hawai'i, U.S.A.* 19°44N 155°0W **136** D7
Lelia Lake *Tex., U.S.A.* 34°54N 100°46W **108** C7
Lemberg *Sask., Canada* 50°44N 103°12W **150** E8
Lemhi *Idaho, U.S.A.* 45°12N 113°53W **122** D5
Lemhi → *Idaho, U.S.A.* 45°12N 113°53W **122** D5
Lemhi County ☆ *Idaho, U.S.A.* 45°0N 114°0W **122** E4
Lemhi Ra. *Idaho, U.S.A.* 44°0N 113°0W **122** E5
Lemieux *Que., Canada* 46°18N 72°7W **145** E10
Lemieux, L. *Que., Canada* 50°19N 74°38W **144** A8
Lemieux Is. *N.W.T., Canada* 63°40N 64°20W **159** E13
Lemington *Vt., U.S.A.* 44°51N 71°36W **89** B3
Lemitar *N. Mex., U.S.A.* 34°10N 106°55W **131** C4
Lemmon *S. Dak., U.S.A.* 45°57N 102°10W **76** E3
Lemmon, L. *Tex., U.S.A.* 32°41N 96°44W **116** B5
Lemoine, L. *Que., Canada* 48°0N 78°0W **144** C5
Lemon Grove *Calif., U.S.A.* 32°44N 117°1W **133** B2
Lemont *Ill., U.S.A.* 40°48N 77°49W **87** D5
Lemoore *Calif., U.S.A.* 36°18N 119°46W **127** G7
Lemoyne *Que., Canada* 45°29N 73°29W **160** B4
Lemoyne *Nebr., U.S.A.* 41°17N 101°49W **80** C4
Lempster *N.H., U.S.A.* 43°15N 72°12W **89** C2
Lena *Ill., U.S.A.* 42°23N 89°49W **84** A4
Lena *Miss., U.S.A.* 32°36N 89°36W **111** D4
Lena, Mt. *Utah, U.S.A.* 40°50N 109°20W **129** C6
Lenapah *Okla., U.S.A.* 36°51N 95°38W **107** B8
Lenawee County ☆ *Mich., U.S.A.* 41°50N 84°5W **79** H7
Lennep *Mont., U.S.A.* 46°25N 110°33W **123** D7
Lennox *Calif., U.S.A.* 33°56N 118°20W **133** C2
Lennox *S. Dak., U.S.A.* 43°21N 96°53W **76** G9
Lennoxville *Que., Canada* 45°22N 71°51W **89** A3
Lenoir *N.C., U.S.A.* 35°55N 81°32W **103** C4
Lenoir City *Tenn., U.S.A.* 35°48N 84°16W **105** E8
Lenoir County ☆ *N.C., U.S.A.* 35°10N 77°40W **103** C8
Lenora *Kans., U.S.A.* 39°37N 100°0W **82** B3
Lenore *Idaho, U.S.A.* 46°31N 116°33W **122** C2
Lenore L. *Sask., Canada* 52°30N 104°59W **150** C7
Lenox *Ga., U.S.A.* 31°16N 83°28W **113** E3
Lenox *Iowa, U.S.A.* 40°53N 94°34W **81** E4
Lenox *Mass., U.S.A.* 42°22N 73°17W **91** B1
Lenox *Mo., U.S.A.* 37°39N 91°46W **83** D5
Lenwood *Calif., U.S.A.* 34°53N 117°7W **127** J9
Leo-Cedarville *Ind., U.S.A.* 41°13N 85°1W **85** B5
Leola *S. Dak., U.S.A.* 45°43N 98°56W **76** E7
Leoma *Tenn., U.S.A.* 35°10N 87°21W **104** E5
Leominster *Mass., U.S.A.* 42°32N 71°46W **91** B3
León *Guanajuato, Mexico* 21°6N 101°41W **174** C4
León *Nic.* 12°20N 86°51W **182** D2
Leon *Iowa, U.S.A.* 40°44N 93°45W **81** E5
Leon *Kans., U.S.A.* 37°42N 96°46W **82** D7
Leon *Okla., U.S.A.* 33°53N 97°26W **107** E6
Leon → *Tex., U.S.A.* 31°14N 97°28W **109** F10
Leon County ☆ *Fla., U.S.A.* 30°30N 84°15W **114** A4
Leon County ☆ *Tex., U.S.A.* 31°16N 95°59W **109** F12
Leon Valley *Tex., U.S.A.* 29°29N 98°39W **116** E2
Leona *Tex., U.S.A.* 39°47N 95°19W **82** B8
Leona *Tex., U.S.A.* 31°9N 95°58W **109** F12
Leona → *Tex., U.S.A.* 28°45N 99°11W **109** J8
Leona Vicario *Quintana Roo, Mexico* 21°0N 87°11W **179** B6
Leonard *Minn., U.S.A.* 47°39N 95°16W **77** C3
Leonard *N. Dak., U.S.A.* 46°39N 97°15W **76** D8
Leonard *Tex., U.S.A.* 33°23N 96°15W **109** D11
Leonardtown *Md., U.S.A.* 38°17N 76°38W **93** B4
Leonardville *Kans., U.S.A.* 39°22N 96°51W **82** B7
Leone *Amer. Samoa* 14°23S 170°48W **184** e
Leonia *Fla., U.S.A.* 30°55N 86°14W **114** A2
Leonia *N.J., U.S.A.* 40°51N 73°59W **97** A3
Leopoldo Sánchez *Sinaloa, Mexico* 25°7N 108°12W **172** C2
Leoti *Kans., U.S.A.* 38°29N 101°21W **82** C2
Leoville *Sask., Canada* 53°39N 107°33W **150** B4
Lepanto *Ark., U.S.A.* 35°37N 90°20W **106** C5
Lepreau *N.B., Canada* 45°10N 66°28W **141** H3
Lerdo de Tejada *Veracruz, Mexico* 18°37N 95°31W **177** F5
Lerma → *Mexico* 20°13N 102°46W **174** D5
Lerna *Ill., U.S.A.* 39°25N 88°17W **84** D5
Leroux Wash → *Ariz., U.S.A.* 34°50N 110°10W **134** D5
Leroy *Sask., Canada* 52°0N 104°44W **150** C7
Léry *Que., Canada* 45°21N 73°48W **160** B3
Les Cayes *Haiti* 18°15N 73°46W **183** C5
Les Coteaux *Que., Canada* 45°15N 74°13W **160** B3
Les Éboulements *Que., Canada* 47°28N 70°21W **145** D12
Les Escoumins *Que., Canada* 48°21N 69°24W **145** C13
Les Étroits *Que., Canada* 47°24N 68°54W **145** D14
Les Laurentides *Que., Canada* 47°13N 74°23W **145** D8
Les Méchins *Que., Canada* 48°59N 66°59W **140** E2
Les Notre-Dame *Que., Canada* 48°10N 68°0W **140** E2
Lesage *W. Va., U.S.A.* 38°30N 82°18W **102** C2
Leslie *Ark., U.S.A.* 35°50N 92°34W **106** C3
Leslie *Ga., U.S.A.* 31°57N 84°5W **113** E2
Leslie *Idaho, U.S.A.* 43°52N 113°28W **122** F5
Leslie County ☆ *Ky., U.S.A.* 37°5N 83°25W **105** C9
Leslieville *Alta., Canada* 52°23N 114°38W **152** D6
Lesser Antilles *W. Indies* 15°0N 61°0W **183** D7
Lesser Slave L. *Alta., Canada* 55°30N 115°25W **152** C5
Lesser Slave Lake Prov. Park △ *Alta., Canada* 55°26N 114°49W **152** C6
Lesslie *S.C., U.S.A.* 34°55N 80°59W **103** D4
Lester *W. Va., U.S.A.* 37°44N 81°18W **102** D3
Lester B. Pearson Int., Toronto ✈ (YYZ) *Ont., Canada* 43°46N 79°35W **161** A1
Lestershire = Johnson City *N.Y., U.S.A.* 42°7N 75°58W **88** C5
Lestock *Sask., Canada* 51°19N 103°59W **150** D8
Letart Falls *Ohio, U.S.A.* 38°54N 81°56W **86** E5
Letcher *S. Dak., U.S.A.* 43°54N 98°9W **76** F7
Letcher County ☆ *Ky., U.S.A.* 37°5N 82°55W **105** C10

Letchworth State Park △ N.Y., U.S.A. 42°37N 78°0W **88** C2
Letha Idaho, U.S.A. 43°54N 116°39W **122** F2
Lethbridge Alta., Canada 49°45N 112°45W **153** J8
Lethbridge Nfld. & L., Canada 48°22N 53°52W **142** D7
Letohatchee Ala., U.S.A. 32°8N 86°29W **112** D4
Letterkenny Army Depot Pa., U.S.A. 40°2N 77°37W **87** D5
Letts Iowa, U.S.A. 41°20N 91°14W **81** D7
Leucadia Calif., U.S.A. 33°4N 117°18W **127** K9
Leupp Corner Ariz., U.S.A. 35°N 110°52W **130** B5
Leusoalii Amer. Samoa 14°14S 169°25W **184** f
Levack Ont., Canada 46°38N 81°23W **146** A5
Levan Utah, U.S.A. 39°33N 111°52W **129** D4
Leveaux Mt. Minn., U.S.A. 47°37N 90°48W **77** C8
Levelland Tex., U.S.A. 33°35N 102°23W **108** D5
Levelock Alaska, U.S.A. 59°7N 156°51W **135** G8
Levering Mich., U.S.A. 45°38N 84°47W **79** D7
Lévis Qué., Canada 46°48N 71°9W **145** E11
Levisa Fork → Ky., U.S.A. 38°8N 82°37W **105** B10
Levittown N.Y., U.S.A. 40°44N 73°31W **92** B3
Levittown Pa., U.S.A. 40°9N 74°51W **92** B2
Levy N. Mex., U.S.A. 36°5N 104°41W **131** A6
Levy County ☆ Fla., U.S.A. 29°15N 82°45W **114** B6
Lewellen Nebr., U.S.A. 41°20N 102°9W **80** C3
Lewes Del., U.S.A. 38°46N 75°9W **93** B5
Lewis Iowa, U.S.A. 41°18N 95°5W **81** D3
Lewis Kans., U.S.A. 37°56N 99°15W **82** D4
Lewis N.Y., U.S.A. 44°17N 73°34W **89** B1
Lewis → Wash., U.S.A. 45°51N 122°48W **120** E3
Lewis, Mt. Nev., U.S.A. 40°24N 116°52W **128** B4
Lewis and Clark County ☆ Mont., U.S.A. 47°25N 112°35W **123** C5
Lewis and Clark L. U.S.A. 42°52N 97°48W **80** B8
Lewis and Clark Nat. Forest Mont., U.S.A. 47°30N 112°55W **123** C5
Lewis and Clark Nat. Historic Trail △ U.S.A. 43°30N 99°20W **76** G8
Lewis County ☆ Idaho, U.S.A. 46°15N 116°29W **122** C2
Lewis County ☆ Ky., U.S.A. 38°30N 83°25W **105** B9
Lewis County ☆ Mo., U.S.A. 40°5N 91°40W **83** A5
Lewis County ☆ N.Y., U.S.A. 43°45N 75°30W **88** B5
Lewis County ☆ Tenn., U.S.A. 35°33N 87°30W **104** E5
Lewis County ☆ W. Va., U.S.A. 39°2N 80°28W **102** B4
Lewis County ☆ Wash., U.S.A. 46°30N 122°0W **120** D3
Lewis Hills Nfld. & L., Canada 48°48N 58°30W **142** D2
Lewis L. Wyo., U.S.A. 44°18N 110°38W **124** B2
Lewis Range Mont., U.S.A. 48°5N 113°5W **123** B4
Lewis Run Pa., U.S.A. 41°52N 78°40W **87** C4
Lewis Smith L. Ala., U.S.A. 33°56N 87°6W **112** C3
Lewisburg Ky., U.S.A. 36°59N 86°57W **104** D6
Lewisburg Ohio, U.S.A. 39°51N 84°33W **86** D2
Lewisburg Pa., U.S.A. 40°58N 76°54W **87** D6
Lewisburg Tenn., U.S.A. 35°27N 86°48W **104** E6
Lewisburg W. Va., U.S.A. 37°48N 80°27W **102** D4
Lewisdale Md., U.S.A. 38°58N 76°59W **99** B4
Lewisetta Va., U.S.A. 38°0N 76°28W **93** B4
Lewisport Ky., U.S.A. 37°56N 86°54W **104** C6
Lewisporte Nfld. & L., Canada 49°15N 55°3W **142** C5
Lewiston Calif., U.S.A. 40°43N 122°48W **126** C4
Lewiston Idaho, U.S.A. 46°25N 117°1W **122** C1
Lewiston Maine, U.S.A. 44°6N 70°13W **90** D3
Lewiston Mich., U.S.A. 44°53N 84°18W **79** E7
Lewiston Minn., U.S.A. 43°59N 91°52W **77** G7
Lewiston N.C., U.S.A. 36°7N 77°10W **103** B8
Lewiston N.Y., U.S.A. 43°11N 79°3W **88** B1
Lewiston Nebr., U.S.A. 40°14N 96°25W **80** D9
Lewiston Utah, U.S.A. 41°59N 111°51W **129** B4
Lewiston Woodville N.C., U.S.A. 36°7N 77°11W **103** B8
Lewistown Ill., U.S.A. 40°24N 90°9W **84** C3
Lewistown Md., U.S.A. 39°32N 77°25W **93** A3
Lewistown Mo., U.S.A. 40°5N 91°49W **83** A5
Lewistown Mont., U.S.A. 47°4N 109°26W **123** C8
Lewistown Pa., U.S.A. 40°36N 77°34W **87** D5
Lewisville N.B., Canada 46°6N 64°46W **141** G5
Lewisville Ark., U.S.A. 33°22N 93°35W **106** E2
Lewisville Minn., U.S.A. 43°55N 94°26W **77** G4
Lewisville N.C., U.S.A. 36°6N 80°25W **103** B5
Lewisville Ohio, U.S.A. 39°46N 81°13W **86** D5
Lewisville Tex., U.S.A. 33°5N 97°0W **109** D11
Lewisville, L. Tex., U.S.A. 33°4N 96°58W **109** D11
Lexington Ala., U.S.A. 34°58N 87°22W **112** B3
Lexington Ga., U.S.A. 33°52N 83°7W **113** C3
Lexington Ill., U.S.A. 40°39N 88°47W **84** C51
Lexington Ky., U.S.A. 38°3N 84°30W **105** B8
Lexington Mass., U.S.A. 42°25N 71°12W **96** A1
Lexington Mich., U.S.A. 43°16N 82°32W **79** F9
Lexington Miss., U.S.A. 33°7N 90°3W **111** C3
Lexington Mo., U.S.A. 39°11N 93°52W **83** A3
Lexington N.C., U.S.A. 35°49N 80°15W **103** C5
Lexington Nebr., U.S.A. 40°47N 99°45W **80** D6
Lexington Ohio, U.S.A. 40°41N 82°35W **86** C4
Lexington Okla., U.S.A. 35°1N 97°20W **107** C6
Lexington Oreg., U.S.A. 45°27N 119°42W **121** B6
Lexington S.C., U.S.A. 33°59N 81°11W **103** E4
Lexington Tenn., U.S.A. 35°39N 88°24W **104** E4
Lexington Tex., U.S.A. 30°25N 97°1W **109** G10
Lexington Va., U.S.A. 37°47N 79°27W **102** D5
Lexington Wash., U.S.A. 46°11N 122°54W **120** D3
Lexington Blue Grass Ky., U.S.A. 37°43N 84°14W **105** C8
Lexington County ☆ S.C., U.S.A. 33°50N 81°10W **103** E4
Lexington Park Md., U.S.A. 38°16N 76°27W **93** B4
Liard → Canada 61°51N 121°18W **157** D8
Liard River B.C., Canada 59°25N 126°5W **157** E7
Libby Mont., U.S.A. 48°23N 115°33W **123** B2
Libby Dam Mont., U.S.A. 48°24N 115°19W **123** B2
Liberal Kans., U.S.A. 37°3N 100°55W **82** D3
Liberal Mo., U.S.A. 37°34N 94°31W **83** D2
Liberia Costa Rica 10°40N 85°30W **182** D2
Liberty Sask., Canada 51°8N 105°26W **150** D6
Liberty Ill., U.S.A. 39°53N 91°6W **84** C2
Liberty Ind., U.S.A. 39°38N 84°56W **85** D6
Liberty Kans., U.S.A. 37°9N 95°36W **82** D8
Liberty Ky., U.S.A. 37°19N 84°56W **105** C8
Liberty Maine, U.S.A. 44°24N 69°18W **90** D4
Liberty Miss., U.S.A. 31°10N 90°49W **111** E3
Liberty Mo., U.S.A. 39°15N 94°25W **83** B2
Liberty N.C., U.S.A. 35°51N 79°34W **103** C6
Liberty N.Y., U.S.A. 41°48N 74°45W **88** D6
Liberty Nebr., U.S.A. 40°5N 96°29W **80** D9
Liberty Okla., U.S.A. 35°52N 95°59W **107** C8
Liberty Pa., U.S.A. 41°34N 77°6W **87** C5
Liberty S.C., U.S.A. 34°48N 82°42W **103** D2
Liberty Tenn., U.S.A. 36°1N 85°58W **105** D7
Liberty Tex., U.S.A. 30°3N 94°48W **109** G13
Liberty Wash., U.S.A. 47°14N 120°42W **120** C5

Liberty Center Ohio, U.S.A. 41°27N 84°1W **86** B2
Liberty County ☆ Fla., U.S.A. 30°15N 85°0W **114** A4
Liberty County ☆ Ga., U.S.A. 31°50N 81°30W **113** E5
Liberty County ☆ Mont., U.S.A. 48°40N 111°0W **123** B7
Liberty County ☆ Tex., U.S.A. 30°7N 94°52W **109** G13
Liberty Hill Tex., U.S.A. 30°40N 97°55W **109** G10
Liberty I. N.Y., U.S.A. 40°41N 74°2W **97** B2
Liberty-Newark Int. ✈ (EWR) N.J., U.S.A. 40°42N 74°10W **97** B1
Liberty Res. Md., U.S.A. 39°23N 76°54W **93** A4
Liberty State Park △ N.J., U.S.A. 40°42N 74°2W **97** B2
Libertytown Md., U.S.A. 39°30N 77°15W **93** A3
Libertytown Md., U.S.A. 38°18N 75°18W **93** B5
Libertyville Ill., U.S.A. 42°18N 87°57W **84** A6
Libertyville Iowa, U.S.A. 40°57N 92°3W **81** E6
Libres Puebla, Mexico 19°28N 97°40W **176** D3
Licking Mo., U.S.A. 37°30N 91°54W **83** D5
Licking → Ky., U.S.A. 39°6N 84°30W **105** A8
Licking County ☆ Ohio, U.S.A. 40°3N 82°24W **86** C4
Lida Nev., U.S.A. 37°28N 117°30W **128** E3
Lidderdale Iowa, U.S.A. 42°8N 94°47W **81** C4
Liddon G. N.W.T., Canada 75°3N 113°0W **156** A10
Lidgerwood N. Dak., U.S.A. 46°5N 97°9W **76** D8
Lido Beach N.Y., U.S.A. 40°35N 73°37W **97** C5
Liebenthal Kans., U.S.A. 38°39N 99°19W **82** C4
Lièvre → Qué., Canada 45°31N 75°26W **144** F7
Lièvres, Î. aux Qué., Canada 47°50N 69°44W **145** D13
Lighthouse Park B.C., Canada 49°20N 123°14W **161** B1
Lighthouse Point Fla., U.S.A. 26°15N 80°7W **114** E8
Lighthouse Pt. Fla., U.S.A. 29°54N 84°21W **114** B4
Lightning Cr. → Wyo., U.S.A. 43°11N 104°44W **124** C8
Lignite N. Dak., U.S.A. 48°53N 102°34W **76** B3
Lignum Va., U.S.A. 38°25N 77°50W **102** C7
Ligonier Ind., U.S.A. 41°28N 85°35W **85** B5
Ligonier Pa., U.S.A. 40°15N 79°14W **87** D3
Lihue Hawai'i, U.S.A. 21°59N 159°23W **136** B2
Likely B.C., Canada 52°37N 121°35W **155** C13
Likely Calif., U.S.A. 41°14N 120°30W **126** B6
Lilbourn Mo., U.S.A. 36°36N 89°37W **83** E7
Liliba Sonora, Mexico 27°19N 110°29W **168** F5
Lillian L. = Le Doré, L. Qué., Canada 51°17N 61°23W **140** B8
Lillie La., U.S.A. 32°56N 92°39W **110** B3
Lillington N.C., U.S.A. 35°24N 78°49W **103** C7
Lilly Pa., U.S.A. 40°26N 78°37W **87** D4
Lilly S. Dak., U.S.A. 45°11N 97°41W **76** E8
Lily Wis., U.S.A. 45°18N 88°51W **78** C5
Lilydale Minn., U.S.A. 44°54N 93°7W **94** B3
Lima Ill., U.S.A. 40°11N 91°23W **84** C2
Lima Mont., U.S.A. 44°38N 112°36W **123** F5
Lima N.Y., U.S.A. 42°55N 77°37W **88** C3
Lima Ohio, U.S.A. 40°44N 84°6W **86** C2
Lima Okla., U.S.A. 35°10N 96°36W **107** C7
Lima Oreg., U.S.A. 44°24N 117°13W **121** C8
Lime Ridge Wis., U.S.A. 43°28N 9C°9W **78** E3
Lime Springs Iowa, U.S.A. 43°27N 92°17W **81** B6
Lime Village Alaska, U.S.A. 61°21N 155°28W **135** F9
Limerick Sask., Canada 49°39N 106°16W **150** F5
Limerick Maine, U.S.A. 43°41N 70°48W **90** D2
Limestone Fla., U.S.A. 27°22N 81°54W **114** D7
Limestone Maine, U.S.A. 46°55N 67°50W **90** B6
Limestone N.Y., U.S.A. 42°2N 78°38W **88** C2
Limestone, L. Tex., U.S.A. 31°25N 96°22W **109** F11
Limestone B. Man., Canada 53°50N 98°53W **151** B13
Limestone County ☆ Ala. U.S.A. 34°48N 86°53W **112** B4
Limestone County ☆ Tex., U.S.A. 31°39N 96°31W **109** F11
Limestone Hill = Lackawanna N.Y., U.S.A. 42°50N 78°50W **88** C2
Limoges Ont., Canada 45°20N 75°13W **144** F7
Limón Costa Rica 10°0N 83°2W **182** E3
Limon Colo., U.S.A. 39°16N 103°41W **125** C7
Limones Quintana Roo, Mexico 19°4N 88°12W **179** D5
Linares Nuevo León, Mexico 24°52N 99°34W **171** F5
Linaria Alta., Canada 54°19N 114°8W **152** D6
Linch Wyo., U.S.A. 43°37N 106°12W **124** C6
Lincoln = Beamsville Ont., Canada 43°12N 79°28W **146** D7
Lincoln Ala., U.S.A. 33°37N 86°7W **112** C4
Lincoln Ark., U.S.A. 35°57N 94°25W **106** C1
Lincoln Calif., U.S.A. 38°54N 121°17W **126** E5
Lincoln Del., U.S.A. 38°52N 75°25W **93** B5
Lincoln Ill., U.S.A. 40°9N 89°22W **84** C4
Lincoln Iowa, U.S.A. 42°16N 92°42W **81** C6
Lincoln Kans., U.S.A. 39°3N 98°9W **82** B5
Lincoln Maine, U.S.A. 45°22N 68°30W **90** C5
Lincoln Mich., U.S.A. 44°41N 83°25W **79** E8
Lincoln Mo., U.S.A. 38°23N 93°20W **83** C3
Lincoln Mont., U.S.A. 46°58N 112°41W **123** D5
Lincoln N. Dak., U.S.A. 46°45N 100°44W **76** D5
Lincoln N.H., U.S.A. 44°3N 71°40W **89** B3
Lincoln N. Mex., U.S.A. 33°30N 105°23W **131** D5
Lincoln Nebr., U.S.A. 40°49N 96°41W **80** D9
Lincoln Wash., U.S.A. 47°50N 118°25W **120** C7
Lincoln Boyhood Nat. Memorial △ Ind., U.S.A. 38°7N 86°59W **85** E4
Lincoln City Oreg., U.S.A. 44°57N 124°1W **121** C1
Lincoln County ☆ Ark., U.S.A. 33°56N 91°45W **106** E4
Lincoln County ☆ Colo., U.S.A. 39°0N 103°20W **125** D7
Lincoln County ☆ Ga., U.S.A. 33°45N 82°20W **113** C4
Lincoln County ☆ Idaho, U.S.A. 43°0N 114°0W **122** G4
Lincoln County ☆ Kans., U.S.A. 39°0N 98°10W **82** B5
Lincoln County ☆ Ky., U.S.A. 37°25N 84°40W **105** C8
Lincoln County ☆ Maine, U.S.A. 44°0N 69°30W **90** D4
Lincoln County ☆ Minn., U.S.A. 44°25N 96°16W **77** F2
Lincoln County ☆ Miss., U.S.A. 31°35N 90°26W **111** E3
Lincoln County ☆ Mo., U.S.A. 39°0N 91°0W **83** B5
Lincoln County ☆ Mont., U.S.A. 48°45N 115°30W **123** B2
Lincoln County ☆ N.C., U.S.A. 35°31N 81°1W **103** C4
Lincoln County ☆ N. Mex., U.S.A. 33°40N 105°30W **131** D5
Lincoln County ☆ Nev., U.S.A. 37°50N 115°0W **128** E6
Lincoln County ☆ Okla., U.S.A. 35°40N 96°55W **107** C7
Lincoln County ☆ Oreg., U.S.A. 44°40N 123°55W **121** C2
Lincoln County ☆ S. Dak., U.S.A. 43°21N 96°53W **76** G9
Lincoln County ☆ Tenn., U.S.A. 35°9N 86°34W **104** E6
Lincoln County ☆ W. Va., U.S.A. 38°14N 81°59W **102** C3
Lincoln County ☆ Wash., U.S.A. 47°45N 118°30W **120** C7
Lincoln County ☆ Wis., U.S.A. 45°20N 89°45W **78** C4
Lincoln County ☆ Wyo., U.S.A. 42°0N 110°30W **124** D2
Lincoln Creek Parkway Wis., U.S.A. 45°20N 88°20W **94** A2
Lincoln Hav = Lincoln Sea Arctic 84°0N 55°0W **162** A5
Lincoln Heights Calif., U.S.A. 34°4N 118°12W **133** B3
Lincoln Memorial D.C., U.S.A. 38°52N 77°4W **99** B3

Lincoln Nat. Forest N. Mex., U.S.A. 32°45N 105°40W **131** E5
Lincoln Parish ☆ La., U.S.A. 32°33N 92°38W **110** B3
Lincoln Park Calif., U.S.A. 37°47N 122°30W **132** B1
Lincoln Park Colo., U.S.A. 38°25N 105°10W **125** D5
Lincoln Park Ga., U.S.A. 32°52N 84°20W **113** D2
Lincoln Park Ill., U.S.A. 41°57N 87°38W **95** B3
Lincoln Park Mich., U.S.A. 42°15N 83°11W **79** G8
Lincoln Park N.J., U.S.A. 40°55N 74°18W **97** A1
Lincoln Park Wis., U.S.A. 43°6N 87°55W **94** B2
Lincoln Park Zoo Ill., U.S.A. 41°55N 87°38W **95** B3
Lincoln Sea Arctic 84°0N 55°0W **162** A5
Lincolnton Ga., U.S.A. 33°48N 82°29W **113** C4
Lincolnton N.C., U.S.A. 35°29N 81°16W **103** C4
Lincolnville N.S., Canada 45°30N 61°33W **141** H8
Lincolnville Kans., U.S.A. 38°30N 96°58W **82** C7
Lincolnville Maine, U.S.A. 44°17N 69°1W **90** D4
Lincolnwood Ill., U.S.A. 42°1N 87°43W **95** A2
Lind Wash., U.S.A. 46°58N 118°37W **120** D7
Linda Calif., U.S.A. 39°8N 121°34W **126** D5
Lindale Ga., U.S.A. 34°11N 85°11W **113** B1
Lindale Tex., U.S.A. 32°31N 95°25W **109** E12
Lindavista Chiapas, Mexico 17°24N 91°30W **178** B5
Lindell Beach B.C., Canada 49°2N 122°1W **155** F12
Linden = Gladstone Mo., U.S.A. 39°13N 94°35W **83** B2
Linden Alta., Canada 51°36N 113°28W **153** G7
Linden Ala., U.S.A. 32°18N 87°48W **112** D3
Linden Calif., U.S.A. 38°1N 121°5W **126** E5
Linden Ind., U.S.A. 40°11N 86°54W **85** C4
Linden Iowa, U.S.A. 41°39N 94°16W **81** D4
Linden Mich., U.S.A. 42°49N 83°47W **79** G8
Linden N.J., U.S.A. 40°37N 74°14W **97** C1
Linden Tenn., U.S.A. 35°37N 87°50W **104** E5
Linden Tex., U.S.A. 33°1N 94°22W **109** D13
Linden Wis., U.S.A. 42°55N 90°16W **78** F3
Lindenhurst N.Y., U.S.A. 40°41N 73°23W **92** B3
Lindenow Fjord Greenland 60°30N 43°25W **162** E6
Lindenwold N.J., U.S.A. 39°49N 74°59W **92** C2
Lindley N.Y., U.S.A. 42°1N 77°8W **88** C3
Lindon Colo., U.S.A. 39°44N 103°24W **125** C7
Lindon Utah, U.S.A. 40°21N 111°43W **129** C4
Lindsay Ont., Canada 44°22N 78°43W **147** C8
Lindsay Calif., U.S.A. 36°12N 119°5W **127** G7
Lindsay Nebr., U.S.A. 41°42N 97°42W **80** C8
Lindsay Okla., U.S.A. 34°50N 97°38W **107** D6
Lindsborg Kans., U.S.A. 38°35N 97°40W **82** C6
Lindy Nebr., U.S.A. 42°44N 97°44W **80** B8
Linesville Pa., U.S.A. 41°39N 80°26W **87** C2
Lineville Ala., U.S.A. 33°19N 85°45W **112** C5
Lineville Iowa, U.S.A. 40°35N 93°32W **81** E5
Lingle Wyo., U.S.A. 42°8N 104°21W **124** D8
Linglestown Pa., U.S.A. 40°20N 76°47W **87** D6
Link L. B.C., Canada 52°25N 127°40W **154** C7
Linn Kans., U.S.A. 39°41N 97°5W **82** B6
Linn Mo., U.S.A. 38°29N 91°51W **83** C5
Linn Tex., U.S.A. 26°34N 98°7W **108** L9
Linn W. Va., U.S.A. 39°0N 80°43W **102** B4
Linn County ☆ Iowa, U.S.A. 42°5N 91°35W **81** C7
Linn County ☆ Kans., U.S.A. 38°15N 94°45W **82** C9
Linn County ☆ Mo., U.S.A. 39°50N 93°10W **83** B3
Linn County ☆ Oreg., U.S.A. 44°30N 122°20W **121** C3
Linn Creek Mo., U.S.A. 38°2N 92°43W **83** C4
Linn Grove Iowa, U.S.A. 42°53N 95°15W **81** C3
Linn Valley Kans., U.S.A. 38°23N 94°42W **82** C9
Linndale Ohio, U.S.A. 41°26N 81°46W **98** B1
Linneus Maine, U.S.A. 46°18N 67°52W **90** B6
Linneus Mo., U.S.A. 39°53N 93°11W **83** B3
Lino Lakes Minn., U.S.A. 45°12N 93°6W **77** E5
Linthicum Balt'more, U.S.A. 39°12N 76°39W **99** B1
Lintlaw Sask., Canada 52°4N 103°14W **150** C8
Linton Qué., Canada 47°15N 72°16W **145** D10
Linton Ind., U.S.A. 39°2N 87°10W **85** D3
Linton N. Dak., U.S.A. 46°16N 100°14W **76** D5
Linwood Ont., Canada 43°35N 80°43W **146** D6
Linwood Kans., U.S.A. 39°0N 95°2W **82** B8
Linwood N.J., U.S.A. 39°21N 74°34W **92** C2
Linwood Nebr., U.S.A. 41°25N 96°56W **80** C9
Lion's Head Ont., Canada 44°58N 81°15W **146** C5
Lipscomb Tex., U.S.A. 36°14N 100°16W **108** A7
Lipscomb County ☆ Tex., U.S.A. 36°15N 100°15W **108** A7
Lipton Sask., Canada 50°54N 103°51W **150** D8
Liquillo, Sierra de Puerto Rico 18°20N 65°47W **184** G17
Lisbon Ill., U.S.A. 41°29N 88°29W **84** B5
Lisbon Maine, U.S.A. 44°2N 70°6W **90** D3
Lisbon N. Dak., U.S.A. 46°27N 97°41W **76** D8
Lisbon N.H., U.S.A. 44°13N 71°55W **89** B3
Lisbon N.Y., U.S.A. 44°44N 75°19W **88** A5
Lisbon Ohio, U.S.A. 40°46N 80°46W **86** C6
Lisbon Falls Maine, U.S.A. 44°0N 70°4W **90** D3
Lisburne, C. Alaska, U.S.A. 68°53N 166°13W **135** B6
Lisco Nebr., U.S.A. 41°30N 102°37W **80** C3
Lisianski I. Hawai'i, U.S.A. 26°2N 174°0W **136** F9
L'Isle Verte Qué., Canada 48°1N 69°20W **145** C13
Lisman Ala., U.S.A. 32°10N 88°15W **112** D2
Lismore Minn., U.S.A. 43°45N 95°57W **77** G3
Listowel Ont., Canada 43°44N 80°58W **146** D6
Litchfield Conn., U.S.A. 41°45N 73°11W **91** C1
Litchfield Ill., U.S.A. 39°11N 89°39W **84** D4
Litchfield Mich., U.S.A. 42°3N 84°46W **79** G7
Litchfield Minn., U.S.A. 45°8N 94°32W **77** E4
Litchfield Nebr., U.S.A. 41°10N 99°9W **80** C6
Litchfield County ☆ Conn., U.S.A. 41°40N 73°15W **91** C1
Litchfield Park Ariz., U.S.A. 33°30N 112°22W **130** D3
Litchville N. Dak., U.S.A. 46°39N 98°12W **76** D7
Lititz Pa., U.S.A. 40°9N 76°18W **87** D6
Little → Ark., U.S.A. 33°45N 94°3W **106** E1
Little → Ga., U.S.A. 30°46N 83°30W **113** F3
Little → La., U.S.A. 31°40N 92°20W **110** C3
Little → N.C., U.S.A. 35°18N 78°42W **103** C7
Little → Tex., U.S.A. 30°51N 96°41W **109** G11
Little Abaco Bahamas 26°50N 77°30W **182** A4
Little Abitibi → Ont., Canada 50°29N 81°32W **149** B15
Little America Wyo., U.S.A. 41°33N 109°52W **124** E3
Little Arkansas → Kans., U.S.A. 37°41N 97°21W **82** D6
Little Bay Nfld. & L., Canada 49°36N 55°57W **142** C5
Little Beaver Cr. → Ohio, U.S.A. 40°35N 80°34W **86** C6
Little Belt Mts. Mont., U.S.A. 46°40N 110°45W **123** D7
Little Bighorn → Mont., U.S.A. 45°44N 107°34W **123** E10
Little Bighorn Battlefield Nat. Monument △ Mont., U.S.A. 45°34N 107°25W **123** E10
Little Black → Ark., U.S.A. 36°25N 90°49W **106** B5
Little Blue → Kans., U.S.A. 39°42N 96°41W **82** B7

Little Bow → Alta., Canada 49°53N 112°29W **153** J8
Little Burnt Bay Nfld. & L., Canada 49°25N 55°5W **142** C5
Little Cadotte → Alta., Canada 56°41N 117°6W **152** B3
Little Calumet → Ill., U.S.A. 41°39N 87°34W **95** D3
Little Canada Minn., U.S.A. 45°1N 93°5W **94** A3
Little Cayman Cayman Is. 19°41N 80°3W **182** C3
Little Chute Wis., U.S.A. 44°17N 88°16W **78** D5
Little City Okla., U.S.A. 34°5N 96°36W **107** D7
Little Colorado → Ariz., U.S.A. 36°12N 111°48W **130** A4
Little Creek Del., U.S.A. 39°10N 75°27W **93** A5
Little Current Ont., Canada 45°55N 82°0W **146** B5
Little Current → Ont., Canada 50°57N 84°36W **149** B12
Little Diomede I. Alaska, U.S.A. 65°45N 168°56W **135** D5
Little Dover N.S., Canada 45°15N 61°3W **141** H8
Little Dry Creek Mont., U.S.A. 47°21N 106°22W **123** C11
Little Eagle S. Dak., U.S.A. 45°40N 100°49W **76** E3
Little Egg Harbor → N.J., U.S.A. 39°35N 74°18W **92** C2
Little Falls Minn., U.S.A. 45°59N 94°22W **77** E4
Little Falls N.J., U.S.A. 40°52N 74°12W **97** A1
Little Falls N.Y., U.S.A. 43°3N 74°51W **88** C6
Little Ferry N.J., U.S.A. 40°50N 74°2W **97** A2
Little Fork → Minn., U.S.A. 48°31N 93°35W **77** B5
Little Fort B.C., Canada 51°26N 120°13W **155** D14
Little Goose Dam Wash., U.S.A. 46°35N 118°1W **120** D7
Little Grand Rapids Man., Canada 52°0N 95°29W **151** C16
Little Haiti Fla., U.S.A. 25°50N 80°11W **115** C2
Little Havana Fla., U.S.A. 25°47N 80°15W **115** D1
Little Haw Cr. → Fla., U.S.A. 29°23N 81°24W **114** B7
Little Humboldt → Nev., U.S.A. 41°1N 117°43W **128** A3
Little Inagua I. Bahamas 21°40N 73°50W **183** B5
Little Kanawha → W. Va., U.S.A. 39°16N 81°34W **102** B3
Little Lake Calif., U.S.A. 35°56N 117°55W **127** H9
Little Lake Conway Fla., U.S.A. 28°29N 81°21W **115** D2
Little Lost → Idaho, U.S.A. 43°46N 112°58W **122** F6
Little Mecatina = Petit-Mécatina → Qué., Canada 50°40N 59°30W **143** C6
Little Medicine Bow → Wyo., U.S.A. 41°58N 106°17W **124** E6
Little Menomonee River Parkway Wis., U.S.A. 43°4N 88°2W **94** B1
Little Missouri → Ark., U.S.A. 33°49N 92°54W **106** E3
Little Missouri → N. Dak., U.S.A. 47°36N 102°25W **76** C3
Little Missouri Badlands N. Dak., U.S.A. 47°5N 103°45W **76** C2
Little Muddy → N. Dak., U.S.A. 48°11N 103°36W **76** B2
Little Narrows N.S., Canada 45°59N 60°59W **141** H9
Little Neck N.Y., U.S.A. 40°45N 73°44W **97** B4
Little Pic → Ont., Canada 48°48N 86°37W **149** D10
Little Powder → Mont., U.S.A. 45°28N 105°20W **123** E12
Little Quill L. Sask., Canada 51°55N 104°5W **150** D7
Little Red → Ark., U.S.A. 35°11N 91°27W **106** C4
Little Red School House Nature Center Ill., U.S.A. 41°42N 87°51W **95** C1
Little River Ark., U.S.A. 38°24N 98°1W **82** C5
Little River Canyon Nat. Preserve △ Ala., U.S.A. 34°25N 85°37W **112** B5
Little River County ☆ Ark., U.S.A. 33°40N 94°9W **106** E1
Little River Indian Reservation Mich., U.S.A. 44°16N 86°15W **79** E5
Little Rock Ark., U.S.A. 34°45N 92°17W **106** D3
Little Rock Air Force Base Ark., U.S.A. 34°54N 92°9W **106** D3
Little Rocky Mts. Mont., U.S.A. 47°55N 108°33W **123** C9
Little Rouge → Ont., Canada 43°45N 79°11W **161** A4
Little Sable Pt. Mich., U.S.A. 43°38N 86°33W **79** F5
Little Salt → Utah, U.S.A. 37°55N 112°53W **129** F3
Little Sioux → Iowa, U.S.A. 41°48N 96°4W **81** D2
Little Sitkin I. Alaska, U.S.A. 51°57N 178°31E **135** L2
Little Smoky → Alta., Canada 54°44N 117°11W **152** D3
Little Snake → Colo., U.S.A. 40°27N 108°26W **125** B2
Little Tallapoosa → Ala., U.S.A. 33°19N 85°34W **112** C5
Little Tennessee → Tenn., U.S.A. 35°47N 84°16W **105** E8
Little Traverse B. Mich., U.S.A. 45°25N 85°10W **79** D6
Little Traverse Bay Indian Reservation Mich., U.S.A. 45°20N 84°58W **79** D7
Little Valley N.Y., U.S.A. 42°15N 78°48W **88** C2
Little White → Ill., U.S.A. 37°55N 88°55W **84** F5
Little White → S. Dak., U.S.A. 43°40N 100°40W **76** G5
Little Wood → Idaho, U.S.A. 42°57N 114°21W **122** G4
Little York N.Y., U.S.A. 41°1N 90°45W **84** B2
Little York Ind., U.S.A. 38°42N 85°54W **85** E5
Littlefield Tex., U.S.A. 33°55N 102°20W **108** D5
Littlefork Minn., U.S.A. 48°24N 93°34W **77** B5
Littlerock Calif., U.S.A. 34°31N 117°59W **127** J8
Littlerock Wash., U.S.A. 46°54N 123°1W **120** D2
Littlestown Pa., U.S.A. 39°45N 77°5W **93** A3
Littleton Colo., U.S.A. 39°36N 105°0W **134** C1
Littleton Ill., U.S.A. 40°14N 90°37W **84** C3
Littleton Maine, U.S.A. 46°14N 67°51W **90** B6
Littleton N.H., U.S.A. 44°18N 71°46W **89** B3
Littleton W. Va., U.S.A. 39°42N 80°32W **102** B4
Littleton Common Mass., U.S.A. 42°33N 71°28W **91** B3
Littleville Ala., U.S.A. 34°35N 87°41W **112** B3
Live Oak Calif., U.S.A. 39°17N 121°40W **126** D5
Live Oak Fla., U.S.A. 30°18N 82°59W **114** A6
Live Oak Tex., U.S.A. 29°33N 98°20W **116** B3
Live Oak County ☆ Tex., U.S.A. 28°20N 98°7W **109** J9
Lively Ont., Canada 46°26N 81°9W **146** A5
Livengood Alaska, U.S.A. 65°32N 148°33W **135** D10
Livermore Calif., U.S.A. 37°41N 121°47W **126** F5
Livermore Iowa, U.S.A. 42°52N 94°11W **81** C4
Livermore Ky., U.S.A. 37°29N 87°8W **104** C5
Livermore, Mt. Tex., U.S.A. 30°38N 104°11W **108** G3
Livermore Falls Maine, U.S.A. 44°29N 70°11W **90** D3
Liverpool N.S., Canada 44°5N 64°41W **141** J5
Liverpool N.Y., U.S.A. 43°6N 76°13W **88** B4
Liverpool Pa., U.S.A. 40°34N 76°59W **87** D6
Liverpool, C. N.W.T., Canada 73°38N 78°6W **158** C10
Liverpool Bay N.W.T., Canada 70°0N 128°0W **156** B7
Livingston Guatemala 15°50N 88°50W **182** C2
Livingston Ala., U.S.A. 32°35N 88°11W **112** D2
Livingston Calif., U.S.A. 37°23N 120°43W **126** F6
Livingston Ill., U.S.A. 38°58N 89°46W **84** E4
Livingston La., U.S.A. 30°30N 90°45W **110** D5
Livingston Mont., U.S.A. 45°40N 110°34W **123** E7
Livingston N.J., U.S.A. 40°48N 74°19W **92** B2
Livingston Tenn., U.S.A. 36°23N 85°19W **105** D7
Livingston Tex., U.S.A. 30°43N 94°56W **109** G13
Livingston, L. Tex., U.S.A. 30°50N 95°10W **109** G12
Livingston County ☆ Ill., U.S.A. 40°55N 88°50W **84** C5
Livingston County ☆ Ky., U.S.A. 37°10N 88°20W **104** C4

230 Livingston County
INDEX

Livingston County ☆ *Mich., U.S.A.* 42°35N 83°55W **79** G8
Livingston County ☆ *Mo., U.S.A.* 39°50N 93°30W **83** B3
Livingston County ☆ *N.Y., U.S.A.* 42°40N 77°45W **88** C3
Livingston Manor *N.Y., U.S.A.* 41°54N 74°50W **88** D6
Livingston Parish ☆ *La., U.S.A.* 30°30N 90°45W **110** D5
Livingstone *N.J., U.S.A.* 40°48N 74°17W **97** B1
Livonia *Ind., U.S.A.* 38°33N 86°17W **85** E4
Livonia *La., U.S.A.* 30°34N 91°33W **110** D4
Livonia *Mich. U.S.A.* 42°23N 83°23W **79** G8
Livonia *Mo., U.S.A.* 40°30N 92°42W **83** A4
Livonia *N.Y., U.S.A.* 42°49N 77°40W **88** C3
Lizard Cr. → *Iowa, U.S.A.* 42°30N 94°14W **81** C4
Lizella *Ga., U.S.A.* 32°48N 83°49W **113** D3
Lizemores *W. Va., U.S.A.* 38°20N 81°11W **102** C3
Llano *Tex., U.S.A.* 30°45N 98°41W **109** G9
Llano → *Tex., U.S.A.* 30°39N 98°26W **109** G9
Llano County ☆ *Tex., U.S.A.* 30°45N 98°41W **109** G9
Llano Estacado *Tex., U.S.A.* 33°30N 103°0W **108** D5
Llano Grande *Durango, Mexico* 23°27N 105°5W **172** D5
Llera de Canales *Tamaulipas, Mexico* 23°19N 99°1W **171** G5
Lloydminster *Sask., Canada* 53°17N 110°0W **150** B2
Lloyds *Md., U.S.A.* 38°36N 76°12W **93** B4
Lloyds → *Nfld. & L., Canada* 48°35N 57°15W **142** D3
Loa *Utah, U.S.A.* 38°24N 111°39W **129** E4
Loami *Ill., U.S.A.* 39°40N 89°51W **84** D4
Lobelville *Tenn., U.S.A.* 35°46N 87°47W **104** E5
Lobos, Cayo *Quintana Roo, Mexico* 18°22N 87°24W **179** D6
Lobos, I. *Baja Calif., Mexico* 30°5N 114°30W **166** C4
Lobos, I. *Sonora, Mexico* 27°20N 110°36W **168** F5
Lobos, I. *Veracruz, Mexico* 21°28N 97°8W **176** C3
Lobos, Pt. *Calif., U.S.A.* 37°46N 122°30W **132** B1
Loch Raven *Md., U.S.A.* 39°26N 76°33W **93** A4
Lochbuie *Colo., U.S.A.* 40°0N 104°43W **125** C6
Lochearn *Md., U.S.A.* 39°20N 76°42W **99** A1
Lochloosa L. *Fla., U.S.A.* 29°30N 82°7W **114** B6
Lochsa → *Idaho, U.S.A.* 46°9N 115°36W **122** C3
Lock Haven *Pa., U.S.A.* 41°8N 77°28W **87** C5
Lock Springs *Mo., U.S.A.* 39°51N 93°47W **83** B3
Lockeford *Calif., U.S.A.* 38°10N 121°9W **126** E5
Lockeport *N.S., Canada* 43°47N 65°4W **141** K4
Lockesburg *Ark., U.S.A.* 33°58N 94°10W **106** E1
Lockhart *Tex. U.S.A.* 29°53N 97°40W **109** H10
Lockington *Ohio, U.S.A.* 40°12N 84°14W **86** C2
Lockney *Tex. U.S.A.* 34°7N 101°27W **108** C6
Lockport *Ill., U.S.A.* 41°35N 88°3W **84** B5
Lockport *La., U.S.A.* 29°39N 90°33W **110** E5
Lockport *N.Y., U.S.A.* 43°10N 78°42W **88** B2
Lockridge *Iowa, U.S.A.* 40°59N 91°45W **81** E7
Lockwood *Mo., U.S.A.* 37°23N 93°57W **83** D3
Loco *Okla., U.S.A.* 34°19N 97°41W **107** D6
Locust Cr. → *Mo., U.S.A.* 39°40N 93°17W **83** B3
Locust Fork → *Ala., U.S.A.* 33°33N 87°11W **112** C3
Locust Grove *Ga., U.S.A.* 33°21N 84°7W **113** C2
Locust Grove *Okla., U.S.A.* 36°12N 95°10W **107** B8
Locust Manor *N.Y., U.S.A.* 40°41N 73°46W **97** B4
Locust Valley *N.Y., U.S.A.* 40°52N 73°35W **97** A5
Loda *Ill., U.S.A.* 40°31N 88°4W **84** C5
Lodge → *Mont., U.S.A.* 48°35N 109°12W **123** B8
Lodge Grass *Mont., U.S.A.* 45°19N 107°22W **123** E10
Lodgepole *Alta., Canada* 53°6N 115°19W **153** E5
Lodgepole *Nebr., U.S.A.* 41°9N 102°38W **80** C3
Lodgepole *S. Dak., U.S.A.* 45°48N 102°40W **76** E3
Lodgepole → *Nebr., U.S.A.* 41°2N 102°10W **80** C3
Lodgepole Cr. → *U.S.A.* 40°57N 102°23W **125** B8
Lodi *Calif., U.S.A.* 38°8N 121°16W **126** E5
Lodi *N.J., U.S.A.* 40°52N 74°5W **97** A2
Lodi *Ohio, U.S.A.* 41°2N 82°1W **86** B4
Lodi *Wis., U.S.A.* 43°19N 89°32W **78** E4
Lofall *Wash., U.S.A.* 47°48N 122°39W **132** B2
Log Lane Village *Colo., U.S.A.* 40°17N 103°51W **125** B7
Logan *Iowa, U.S.A.* 41°39N 95°47W **81** D3
Logan *Kans., U.S.A.* 39°40N 99°34W **82** B4
Logan *N. Mex., U.S.A.* 35°22N 103°25W **131** B7
Logan *Ohio, U.S.A.* 39°32N 82°25W **86** D4
Logan *Utah, U.S.A.* 41°44N 111°50W **129** B4
Logan *W. Va. U.S.A.* 37°51N 81°59W **102** D3
Logan, Mt. *Qué., Canada* 48°53N 66°38W **140** E3
Logan, Mt. *Yukon, Canada* 60°34N 140°23W **157** D4
Logan County ☆ *Ark., U.S.A.* 35°18N 93°44W **106** C2
Logan County ☆ *Colo., U.S.A.* 40°45N 103°0W **125** B7
Logan County ☆ *Ill., U.S.A.* 41°10N 89°20W **84** B4
Logan County ☆ *Kans., U.S.A.* 39°0N 101°0W **82** C2
Logan County ☆ *Ky., U.S.A.* 36°50N 86°50W **104** D6
Logan County ☆ *N. Dak., U.S.A.* 46°28N 99°25W **76** D6
Logan County ☆ *Nebr., U.S.A.* 41°30N 100°30W **80** C5
Logan County ☆ *Ohio, U.S.A.* 40°22N 83°46W **86** C3
Logan County ☆ *Okla., U.S.A.* 36°0N 97°30W **107** C6
Logan County ☆ *W. Va., U.S.A.* 37°58N 82°0W **102** D3
Logan Cr. → *Nebr., U.S.A.* 41°37N 96°30W **80** C9
Logan I. *Ont Canada* 50°7N 88°27W **148** B8
Logan Int., Boston ✈ **(BOS)** *Mass., U.S.A.* 42°22N 71°1W **96** A2
Logan Lake *B.C., Canada* 50°30N 120°48W **155** E14
Logan Martin L. *Ala., U.S.A.* 33°26N 86°20W **112** C4
Logan Square *Ill., U.S.A.* 41°55N 87°42W **95** B2
Logandale *Nev., U.S.A.* 36°36N 114°29W **128** F6
Logansport *Ind., U.S.A.* 40°45N 86°22W **85** C4
Logansport *La., U.S.A.* 31°58N 94°0W **110** C2
Loganton *Pa., U.S.A.* 41°2N 77°19W **87** C5
Loganville *Wis., U.S.A.* 43°27N 90°2W **78** E3
Loggieville *N.B., Canada* 47°4N 65°23W **141** F4
Logy Bay *Nfld. & L., Canada* 47°38N 52°40W **142** E8
Lohrville *Iowa, U.S.A.* 42°17N 94°33W **81** C4
Lois *Tex., U.S.A.* 29°49N 95°30W **116** A1
Loks Land *Nunavut, Canada* 62°26N 64°38W **159** E13
Lola *Ky., U.S.A.* 37°19N 88°18W **104** C4
Lola, Mt. *Calif., U.S.A.* 39°26N 120°22W **126** D6
Loleta *Calif., U.S.A.* 40°38N 124°13W **126** C2
Lolita *Tex., U.S.A.* 28°50N 96°33W **109** J11
Lolo *Mont., U.S.A.* 46°45N 114°5W **123** D3
Lolo Hot Springs *Mont., U.S.A.* 46°44N 114°32W **123** D3
Lolo Nat. Forest *Mont., U.S.A.* 47°8N 114°40W **123** C3
Lolo Pass *U.S.A.* 46°38N 114°35W **122** C4
Lolo Peak *Mont., U.S.A.* 46°41N 114°14W **123** D3
Loltún *Yucatán, Mexico* 20°15N 89°30W **179** B4
Loma *Colo., U.S.A.* 39°12N 108°49W **125** C2
Loma *Mont. U.S.A.* 47°56N 110°30W **123** C7
Loma *N. Dak. U.S.A.* 48°38N 98°32W **76** B7
Loma, Pt. *Calif., U.S.A.* 32°42N 117°14W **133** C1
Loma Blanca *Chihuahua, Mexico* 29°38N 105°32W **169** D10
Loma Bonita *Oaxaca, Mexico* 18°7N 95°53W **177** F5
Loma Bonita *Veracruz, Mexico* 17°48N 94°48W **177** G6
Loma de Vaca Escondido *México, Mexico* 19°33N 99°19W **181** A2
Loma Prieta *Calif., U.S.A.* 37°6N 121°50W **126** F5
Loman *Minn., U.S.A.* 48°31N 93°49W **77** B5
Lomas Alegres *Tabasco, Mexico* 17°34N 92°36W **178** B4
Lomas Chapultepec *Distrito Federal, Mexico* 19°25N 99°12W **181** B2
Lomas de Arena *Chihuahua, Mexico* 30°35N 104°56W **169** C11
Lomas de San Angel Inn *Distrito Federal, Mexico* 19°20N 99°13W **181** B2
Lomas de Tejeda *Guadalajara, Mexico* 20°28N 103°24W **180** C1
Lomax *Ill., U.S.A.* 40°41N 91°4W **84** C2
Lombardia *Michoacan, Mexico* 19°8N 102°3W **174** C5
Lometa *Tex., U.S.A.* 31°13N 98°24W **109** F9
Lomond *Alta., Canada* 50°24N 112°36W **153** H8
Lompoc *Calif., U.S.A.* 34°38N 120°28W **127** J6
Lomus Reforma *Distrito Federal, Mexico* 19°24N 99°14W **181** B2
Lonaconing *Md., U.S.A.* 39°34N 78°59W **93** A2
London *Ont., Canada* 42°59N 81°15W **146** E5
London *Ark., U.S.A.* 35°20N 93°15W **106** C2
London *Ky., U.S.A.* 37°8N 84°5W **105** C8
London *Ohio, U.S.A.* 39°53N 83°27W **86** D3
London Mills *Ill., U.S.A.* 40°43N 90°11W **84** C3
Londonderry *Qué., Canada* 45°29N 63°36W **141** H6
Londonderry *N.H., U.S.A.* 42°52N 71°22W **89** D3
Londonderry *Ohio, U.S.A.* 39°16N 82°48W **86** D4
Londonderry *Vt., U.S.A.* 43°14N 72°48W **89** C2
Londontowne *Md., U.S.A.* 38°55N 76°33W **93** B4
Lone Butte *B.C., Canada* 51°33N 121°12W **155** D13
Lone Grove *Okla., U.S.A.* 34°11N 97°15W **107** D6
Lone Mountain *Tenn., U.S.A.* 36°24N 83°35W **105** D9
Lone Mt. *S. Dak., U.S.A.* 45°23N 103°44W **76** E2
Lone Oak *Ky., U.S.A.* 37°2N 88°40W **104** C4
Lone Oak *Tex., U.S.A.* 33°0N 95°57W **109** E12
Lone Peak *Utah, U.S.A.* 40°31N 111°45W **134** C3
Lone Peak Wilderness *Utah, U.S.A.* 40°30N 111°42W **134** C3
Lone Pine *Alta., Canada* 54°18N 115°7W **152** D5
Lone Pine *Calif., U.S.A.* 36°36N 118°4W **127** G8
Lone Rock *Sask., Canada* 53°3N 109°53W **150** B2
Lone Star *Tex., U.S.A.* 32°55N 94°43W **109** E13
Lone Tree *Iowa, U.S.A.* 41°29N 91°26W **81** D7
Lone Wolf *Okla., U.S.A.* 34°59N 99°15W **107** D4
Lonejack *Mo., U.S.A.* 38°52N 94°10W **83** C2
Lonely I. *Ont., Canada* 45°34N 81°28W **146** B5
Lonepine *Mont., U.S.A.* 47°42N 114°38W **123** C3
Lonerock *Oreg., U.S.A.* 45°5N 119°53W **121** B6
Long B. *S.C., U.S.A.* 33°35N 78°45W **103** E7
Long Beach *Calif., U.S.A.* 33°46N 118°11W **127** K8
Long Beach *Miss., U.S.A.* 30°21N 89°9W **111** F4
Long Beach *N.Y., U.S.A.* 40°35N 73°39W **97** C5
Long Beach *Wash., U.S.A.* 46°21N 124°3W **120** D1
Long Beach I. *N.J., U.S.A.* 39°42N 74°6W **92** C2
Long Branch *Ont., Canada* 43°35N 79°31W **161** B1
Long Branch *N.J., U.S.A.* 40°18N 74°0W **92** B3
Long Branch L. *Mo., U.S.A.* 39°50N 92°30W **83** B4
Long Brook → *Va., U.S.A.* 38°49N 77°15W **99** C2
Long County ☆ *Ga., U.S.A.* 31°45N 81°45W **113** E5
Long Cr. → *Sask., Canada* 49°7N 102°59W **150** F9
Long Creek *Oreg., U.S.A.* 44°43N 119°6W **121** C6
Long I. *Bahamas* 23°20N 75°10W **183** B4
Long I. *Nfld. & L., Canada* 47°34N 55°59W **142** E5
Long I. *Nunavut, Canada* 54°50N 79°20W **143** C2
Long I. *N.Y., U.S.A.* 40°45N 73°30W **92** B3
Long Island *Kans., U.S.A.* 39°57N 99°32W **82** B4
Long Island City *N.Y., U.S.A.* 40°45N 73°56W **97** B3
Long Island Sd. *N.Y., U.S.A.* 41°10N 73°0W **91** C2
Long L. *Alta., Canada* 54°22N 112°46W **152** D8
Long L. *Ont., Canada* 49°30N 86°50W **149** C10
Long L. *Maine, U.S.A.* 44°2N 70°39W **89** B4
Long L. *Maine, U.S.A.* 47°13N 68°15W **90** A5
Long L. *Maine, U.S.A.* 46°43N 69°23W **90** B4
Long L. *Mich., U.S.A.* 45°13N 83°29W **79** D8
Long L. *N. Dak., U.S.A.* 46°44N 100°6W **76** D5
Long L. *N.Y., U.S.A.* 44°1N 74°24W **88** A6
Long L. *Wash., U.S.A.* 47°50N 117°51W **120** C8
Long L. *Wis., U.S.A.* 45°45N 91°45W **78** C2
Long Lake *N.Y., U.S.A.* 43°58N 74°25W **88** B6
Long Lake *Wash., U.S.A.* 47°29N 122°35W **132** D2
Long Lake Regional Park ⌂ *Minn., U.S.A.* 45°3N 93°11W **94** A2
Long Mt. *Mo., U.S.A.* 36°43N 92°31W **83** E4
Long Pine *Nebr., U.S.A.* 42°32N 99°42W **80** B6
Long Point *Ill., U.S.A.* 41°0N 88°54W **84** B5
Long Point B. *Ont., Canada* 42°40N 80°10W **146** E6
Long Pond *Mass., U.S.A.* 41°48N 70°56W **91** C4
Long Prairie *Minn., U.S.A.* 45°59N 94°52W **77** E4
Long Prairie → *Minn., U.S.A.* 46°20N 94°36W **77** D4
Long Pt. *Minn., U.S.A.* 48°59N 94°59W **77** B4
Long Pt. *Man., Canada* 53°2N 98°25W **151** B13
Long Pt. *Nfld. & L., Canada* 48°47N 58°46W **142** D2
Long Pt. *Ont., Canada* 42°35N 80°2W **146** E6
Long Range Mts. *Nfld. & L., Canada* 49°30N 57°30W **142** C3
Long Reach *N.B., Canada* 45°28N 66°5W **141** H3
Long Ridge *Ky., U.S.A.* 38°35N 84°49W **105** B8
Long Valley *S. Dak., U.S.A.* 43°28N 101°29W **76** G4
Longboat Key *Fla., U.S.A.* 27°23N 82°39W **114** D6
Longbranch *Wash., U.S.A.* 47°13N 122°46W **120** C3
Longdale *Okla., U.S.A.* 36°8N 98°33W **107** B5
Longford *Kans., U.S.A.* 39°10N 97°20W **82** B6
Longjohn Slough *Ill., U.S.A.* 41°42N 87°52W **95** C1
Longlegged L. *Ont., Canada* 50°46N 94°8W **148** B2
Longmeadow *Mass., U.S.A.* 42°3N 72°34W **91** B2
Longmont *Colo., U.S.A.* 40°10N 105°6W **125** B5
Longridge *Md., U.S.A.* 38°16N 75°37W **93** B5
Longs Pk. *Colo., U.S.A.* 40°15N 105°37W **125** B5
Longstreet *La., U.S.A.* 32°6N 93°57W **110** B2
Longton *Kans., U.S.A.* 37°23N 96°5W **82** D7
Longtown *Mo., U.S.A.* 37°40N 89°47W **83** D7
Longue-Pointe *Qué., Canada* 45°35N 73°31W **160** A3
Longue-Pointe-de-Mingan *Qué., Canada* 50°16N 64°9W **140** C5
Longue-Rive *Qué., Canada* 48°33N 69°15W **145** C13
Longueuil *Qué., Canada* 45°31N 73°29W **160** A4
Longueuil-St-Hubert = St-Hubert *Qué., Canada* 45°29N 73°25W **160** B4
Longview *Alta., Canada* 50°32N 114°10W **153** H6
Longview *Ill., U.S.A.* 39°53N 88°4W **84** D5
Longview *Tex., U.S.A.* 32°30N 94°44W **109** E13
Longview *Wash., U.S.A.* 46°8N 122°57W **120** D3
Longville *La., U.S.A.* 30°36N 93°14W **110** D2
Longville *Minn., U.S.A.* 46°59N 94°13W **77** D4
Longwood *Fla., U.S.A.* 28°42N 81°21W **114** C7
Longwoods *Md., U.S.A.* 38°52N 76°5W **93** B4
Lonoke *Ark., U.S.A.* 34°47N 91°54W **106** D4
Lonoke County ☆ *Ark., U.S.A.* 34°47N 91°54W **106** D4
Lonsdale *Minn., U.S.A.* 44°29N 93°26W **77** F5
Loogootee *Ind., U.S.A.* 38°41N 86°55W **85** E4
Lookeba *Okla., U.S.A.* 35°22N 98°22W **107** C5
Looking Glass → *Mich., U.S.A.* 42°52N 84°54W **79** G7
Lookout *Calif., U.S.A.* 41°13N 121°9W **126** B5
Lookout, C. *N.C., U.S.A.* 34°35N 76°32W **103** D9
Lookout, C. *Oreg., U.S.A.* 45°20N 124°1W **121** B1
Lookout, Pt. *Mich., U.S.A.* 44°3N 83°35W **79** E8
Lookout Mountain *Tenn., U.S.A.* 34°59N 85°21W **105** F7
Lookout Mt. *Ala., U.S.A.* 34°20N 85°45W **112** B5
Lookout Mt. *Idaho, U.S.A.* 47°5N 115°58W **122** B3
Lookout Mt. *N. Mex., U.S.A.* 35°13N 108°13W **131** B2
Lookout Mt. *Oreg., U.S.A.* 44°21N 121°31W **121** C4
Lookout Pass *U.S.A.* 47°27N 115°42W **122** B3
Lookout Point Res. *Oreg., U.S.A.* 43°55N 122°45W **121** D3
Loomis *Nebr., U.S.A.* 40°29N 99°31W **80** D6
Loomis *Wash., U.S.A.* 48°49N 119°38W **120** B6
Loon → *Alta., Canada* 57°8N 115°3W **152** A5
Loon L. *Maine, U.S.A.* 46°8N 69°36W **90** B4
Loon Lake *Alta., Canada* 56°33N 115°24W **152** B5
Loon Lake *Sask., Canada* 54°2N 109°10W **150** A2
Loon Lake *Wash., U.S.A.* 48°4N 117°38W **120** B8
Loos *B.C., Canada* 53°36N 120°42W **155** B14
Loosahatchie Bar *Tenn., U.S.A.* 35°11N 90°4W **117** A1
Lopez I. *Wash., U.S.A.* 48°29N 122°54W **120** B3
Lopez Pt. *Calif., U.S.A.* 36°1N 121°34W **127** G5
Lorain *Ohio, U.S.A.* 41°28N 82°11W **86** B4
Lorain County ☆ *Ohio, U.S.A.* 41°14N 82°7W **86** B4
Loraine *Ill., U.S.A.* 40°9N 91°13W **84** C2
Loraine *Tex., U.S.A.* 32°25N 100°43W **108** E7
Lord Mayor B. *Nunavut, Canada* 69°44N 92°2W **158** D7
Lord's Cove *Nfld. & L., Canada* 46°53N 55°40W **142** F5
Lords Valley *Pa., U.S.A.* 41°22N 75°4W **92** A1
Lordsburg *N. Mex., U.S.A.* 32°21N 108°43W **131** E2
Lore City *Ohio, U.S.A.* 39°59N 81°28W **86** D5
Loreauville *La., U.S.A.* 30°3N 91°44W **110** D4
Loreburn *Sask., Canada* 51°13N 106°36W **150** D5
Lorenzo *Idaho, U.S.A.* 43°44N 111°52W **122** F7
Lorenzo *Tex., U.S.A.* 33°40N 101°32W **108** D6
Loreto *Baja Calif. S., Mexico* 26°0N 111°21W **167** G7
Loreto *Zacatecas, Mexico* 22°16N 101°59W **173** E9
Loretta *Kans., U.S.A.* 38°39N 99°12W **82** C4
Lorette *Man., Canada* 49°44N 96°52W **151** F15
Loretteville *Qué., Canada* 46°51N 71°21W **145** E11
Loretto *Ky., U.S.A.* 37°38N 85°24W **105** C7
Loretto *Tenn., U.S.A.* 35°5N 87°26W **104** E5
Loretto *Va., U.S.A.* 38°5N 77°3W **93** B3
Lorimor *Iowa, U.S.A.* 41°8N 94°3W **81** D4
Loris *S.C., U.S.A.* 34°4N 78°53W **103** D7
Lorman *Miss., U.S.A.* 31°49N 91°3W **111** E2
Lorne *N.B., Canada* 47°53N 66°8W **141** F3
Lorraine = Baker *Mont., U.S.A.* 46°22N 104°17W **123** D13
Lorraine *Kans., U.S.A.* 38°34N 98°19W **82** C5
Lorrainville *Qué., Canada* 47°21N 79°23W **144** D3
Lorton *Nebr., U.S.A.* 40°35N 96°1W **80** D9
Lorton *Va., U.S.A.* 38°42N 77°14W **93** B3
Los Alamos *Calif., U.S.A.* 34°44N 120°17W **127** J6
Los Alamos *N. Mex., U.S.A.* 35°53N 106°19W **131** B4
Los Alamos County ☆ *N. Mex., U.S.A.* 35°55N 106°15W **131** B4
Los Alamos de Márquez *Coahuila, Mexico* 28°46N 103°28W **170** B1
Los Aldamas *Nuevo León, Mexico* 26°3N 99°11W **170** D5
Los Altos *Veracruz, Mexico* 19°27N 97°11W **176** E3
Los Angeles *Baja Calif. S., Mexico* 27°30N 113°18W **167** F5
Los Angeles *Calif., U.S.A.* 34°4N 118°15W **127** J8
Los Angeles Aqueduct *Calif., U.S.A.* 35°22N 118°5W **127** H8
Los Angeles County ☆ *Calif., U.S.A.* 34°20N 118°10W **127** J8
Los Angeles Int. ✈ **(LAX)** *Calif., U.S.A.* 33°57N 118°25W **133** C2
Los Arrieros *Sonora, Mexico* 28°18N 111°2W **168** E4
Los Azabaches *Baja Calif. S., Mexico* 24°20N 110°15W **167** J8
Los Aztecas *Tamaulipas, Mexico* 22°30N 98°37W **171** H6
Los Banos *Calif., U.S.A.* 37°4N 120°51W **126** F6
Los Charcos → *Chihuahua, Mexico* 30°33N 106°30W **169** C9
Los Chaves *N. Mex., U.S.A.* 34°44N 106°44W **131** C4
Los Chiles *Costa Rica* 11°2N 84°43W **182** D3
Los Colomos, Parque de *Guadalajara, Mexico* 20°43N 103°23W **180** A1
Los Coyotes Indian Reservation *Calif., U.S.A.* 33°17N 116°33W **127** K10
Los Dinamos, Parque Nacional △ *Distrito Federal, Mexico* 19°16N 99°16W **181** C2
Los Frailes *Durango, Mexico* 25°37N 106°56W **172** B4
Los Frailes, Picacho *Sinaloa, Mexico* 23°53N 106°2W **172** D4
Los Fresnos *Tex., U.S.A.* 26°4N 97°29W **108** L10
Los Galenos *Monterrey, Mexico* 25°53N 100°21W **180** A1
Los Gatos *Calif., U.S.A.* 37°14N 121°59W **126** F5
Los Gavilanes *Baja Calif. S., Mexico* 27°32N 113°42W **167** F5
Los Gavilanes *Guadalajara, Mexico* 20°34N 103°26W **180** B1
Los Haïtises, Parque Nac. △ *Dom. Rep.* 19°4N 69°36W **183** C6
Los Hermanos Is. *Venezuela* 11°45N 64°25W **183** D7
Los Herreras *Nuevo León, Mexico* 25°55N 99°24W **170** E5
Los Hoyos *Sonora, Mexico* 30°10N 109°47W **168** C6
Los Jazmines, Presa *Distrito Federal, Mexico* 19°25N 99°15W **181** B2
Los Juncos → *Chihuahua, Mexico* 30°47N 106°42W **169** C9
Los Lentiscos *Baja Calif. S., Mexico* 27°32N 114°28W **167** F4
Los Lirios *Coahuila, Mexico* 25°23N 100°34W **170** E4
Los Lirios *Quintana Roo, Mexico* 19°4N 88°45W **179** C5
Los Loera → *Chihuahua, Mexico* 26°37N 107°13W **169** G8
Los Lunas *N. Mex., U.S.A.* 34°48N 106°44W **131** C4
Los Mármoles, Parque Nacional △ *Hidalgo, Mexico* 20°53N 99°12W **175** B8
Los Médanos *Sonora, Mexico* 27°10N 110°20W **168** F5
Los Mochis *Sinaloa, Mexico* 25°45N 108°57W **172** B2
Los Molinos *Sonora, Mexico* 31°9N 111°45W **168** B4
Los Molinos *Calif., U.S.A.* 40°1N 122°6W **126** C4
Los Montoyas *N. Mex., U.S.A.* 35°25N 105°12W **131** B5
Los Naranjos *Durango, Mexico* 23°21N 105°30W **172** D5
Los Naranjos *Monterrey, Mexico* 25°51N 100°22W **180** A1
Los Naranjos *Veracruz, Mexico* 18°21N 96°10W **177** F4
Los Nietos *Calif., U.S.A.* 33°57N 118°4W **133** C4
Los Novillos, Parque Nacional △ *Coahuila, Mexico* 29°22N 101°40W **170** A3
Los Olivos *Calif., U.S.A.* 34°40N 120°7W **127** J6
Los Olmos Cr. → *Tex., U.S.A.* 27°16N 97°44W **109** K10
Los Osos *Calif., U.S.A.* 35°19N 120°50W **127** H6
Los Padillas *N. Mex., U.S.A.* 34°57N 106°42W **131** C4
Los Padres National Forest *Calif., U.S.A.* 34°40N 119°40W **127** J7
Los Palacios *Cuba* 22°35N 83°15W **182** B3
Los Pericos *Oaxaca, Mexico* 16°48N 94°7W **177** H6
Los Pinitos *Sonora, Mexico* 29°55N 111°28W **168** D4
Los Pinos → *Colo., U.S.A.* 36°56N 107°36W **125** F3
Los Pirules *México, Mexico* 19°25N 99°2W **181** B3
Los Planes *Baja Calif. S., Mexico* 23°57N 109°58W **167** K9
Los Prietos → *Chihuahua, Mexico* 29°28N 106°21W **169** D9
Los Ramones *Nuevo León, Mexico* 25°42N 99°37W **170** E5
Los Ranchos de Albuquerque *N. Mex., U.S.A.* 35°10N 106°39W **131** B4
Los Remedios *San Luis Potosí, Mexico* 22°55N 101°19W **171** H3
Los Reyes *México, Mexico* 19°21N 99°6W **181** B3
Los Reyes Acaquilpan *México, Mexico* 19°22N 98°59W **181** B4
Los Reyes de Salgado *Michoacan, Mexico* 19°35N 102°29W **174** C5
Los Rodríguez *Guanajuato, Mexico* 21°3N 100°38W **175** A7
Los Roques Is. *Venezuela* 11°50N 66°45W **183** D6
Los Sauces *Guerrero, Mexico* 18°17N 99°50W **175** D8
Los Toriles *Nayarit, Mexico* 21°4N 104°20W **172** F6
Los Troncones *Sinaloa, Mexico* 25°45N 107°55W **172** B3
Los Vidrios *Sonora, Mexico* 32°2N 113°26W **168** A2
Losantville *Ind., U.S.A.* 40°2N 85°11W **85** C5
Lost → *Ind., U.S.A.* 38°33N 86°49W **85** E4
Lost → *Oreg., U.S.A.* 41°56N 121°30W **121** F4
Lost → *W. Va., U.S.A.* 39°4N 78°39W **102** B6
Lost Brook Preserve *N.J., U.S.A.* 40°56N 73°56W **97** A3
Lost City *W. Va., U.S.A.* 38°56N 78°50W **102** C6
Lost Creek *W. Va., U.S.A.* 39°10N 80°21W **102** B4
Lost Hills *Calif., U.S.A.* 35°37N 119°41W **127** H7
Lost Nation *Iowa, U.S.A.* 41°58N 90°49W **81** D8
Lost Peak *Utah, U.S.A.* 37°29N 113°55W **129** F2
Lost River *Idaho, U.S.A.* 43°41N 113°22W **122** F5
Lost River Range *Idaho, U.S.A.* 44°8N 113°47W **122** E5
Lost Springs *Kans., U.S.A.* 38°34N 96°58W **82** C7
Lost Springs *Wyo., U.S.A.* 42°46N 104°56W **124** D8
Lost Trail Pass *U.S.A.* 45°42N 113°57W **122** D5
Lostine *Oreg., U.S.A.* 45°29N 117°26W **121** B8
Lostwood *N. Dak., U.S.A.* 48°29N 102°25W **76** B3
Lostwood Nat. Wildlife Reserve ⌂ *N. Dak., U.S.A.* 48°40N 102°30W **76** B3
Lothair *Mont., U.S.A.* 48°28N 111°14W **123** B6
Lott *Tex., U.S.A.* 31°12N 97°2W **109** F10
Lottsburg *Va., U.S.A.* 37°58N 76°31W **93** C4
Loudon *N.H., U.S.A.* 43°16N 71°27W **89** C3
Loudon *Tenn., U.S.A.* 35°45N 84°20W **105** E8
Loudon County ☆ *Tenn., U.S.A.* 35°45N 84°20W **105** E8
Loudonville *Ohio, U.S.A.* 40°38N 82°14W **86** C4
Loudoun County ☆ *Va., U.S.A.* 39°5N 77°50W **102** B7
Lougheed *Alta., Canada* 52°44N 111°33W **153** F9
Lougheed I. *Nunavut, Canada* 77°26N 105°6W **158** B4
Loughman *Fla., U.S.A.* 28°14N 81°34W **114** C7
Louin *Miss., U.S.A.* 32°4N 89°16W **111** D4
Louis Armstrong New Orleans Int. ✈ **(MSY)** *La., U.S.A.* 30°0N 90°15W **117** C1
Louis Creek *B.C., Canada* 51°8N 120°7W **155** D14
Louis XIV, Pte. *Qué., Canada* 54°37N 79°45W **143** C2
Louisa *Ky., U.S.A.* 38°7N 82°36W **105** B10
Louisa *Va., U.S.A.* 38°1N 78°0W **102** C7
Louisa County ☆ *Iowa, U.S.A.* 41°15N 91°15W **81** D7
Louisa County ☆ *Va., U.S.A.* 38°1N 78°0W **102** D7
Louisbourg *N.S., Canada* 45°55N 60°0W **141** H10
Louisburg *Kans., U.S.A.* 38°37N 94°41W **82** C9
Louisburg *Minn., U.S.A.* 45°10N 96°10W **77** E2
Louisburg *Mo., U.S.A.* 37°46N 93°8W **83** D3
Louisburg *N.C., U.S.A.* 36°6N 78°18W **103** B7
Louisdale *N.S., Canada* 45°36N 61°4W **141** H8
Louise *Miss., U.S.A.* 32°59N 90°35W **111** D3
Louise *Tex., U.S.A.* 29°6N 96°24W **109** H11
Louise, L. *Fla., U.S.A.* 28°28N 81°32W **115** B1
Louise I. *B.C., Canada* 52°55N 131°50W **154** C3
Louiseville *Qué., Canada* 46°20N 72°56W **145** E10
Louisiana *Mo., U.S.A.* 39°27N 91°3W **83** B51
Louisiana □ *U.S.A.* 30°50N 92°0W **110** D3
Louisville *Ala., U.S.A.* 31°47N 85°33W **112** E5
Louisville *Colo., U.S.A.* 39°59N 105°8W **125** C5
Louisville *Ga., U.S.A.* 33°0N 82°25W **113** D4
Louisville *Ill., U.S.A.* 38°46N 88°30W **84** E5
Louisville *Kans., U.S.A.* 39°15N 96°18W **82** B7
Louisville *Ky., U.S.A.* 38°15N 85°46W **105** B7
Louisville *Miss., U.S.A.* 33°7N 89°3W **111** C4
Louisville *Nebr., U.S.A.* 41°0N 96°10W **80** D9
Louisville *Ohio, U.S.A.* 40°50N 81°16W **86** C5
Louisville Int. ✈ **(SDF)** *Ky., U.S.A.* 38°10N 85°44W **105** B7
Loup → *Nebr., U.S.A.* 41°24N 97°19W **80** C8
Loup City *Nebr., U.S.A.* 41°17N 98°58W **80** C7
Loup County ☆ *Nebr., U.S.A.* 41°50N 99°30W **80** C6
Loups Marins, Lacs des *Qué., Canada* 56°30N 73°45W **143** B3
Lourdes *Nfld. & L., Canada* 48°39N 59°0W **142** D2
Loutre, Bayou → *La., U.S.A.* 32°41N 92°8W **110** B3
Louvale *Ga., U.S.A.* 32°10N 84°50W **113** D2
Louvicourt *Qué., Canada* 48°4N 77°23W **144** C5
Louviers *Colo., U.S.A.* 39°28N 105°1W **125** C5
Love *Sask., Canada* 53°29N 104°10W **150** B7
Love County ☆ *Okla., U.S.A.* 34°0N 97°15W **107** E6
Love Point *Md., U.S.A.* 39°2N 76°19W **93** A4
Lovelady *Tex., U.S.A.* 31°8N 95°27W **109** F12
Loveland *Colo., U.S.A.* 40°24N 105°5W **125** B5
Loveland *Ohio, U.S.A.* 39°16N 84°16W **86** D2
Loveland *Okla., U.S.A.* 34°18N 98°46W **107** D5
Loveland Pass *Colo., U.S.A.* 39°40N 105°53W **125** C5
Lovell *Maine, U.S.A.* 44°8N 70°54W **90** D3
Lovell *Wyo., U.S.A.* 44°50N 108°24W **124** B4
Lovells *Mich., U.S.A.* 44°48N 84°29W **79** E7
Lovelock *Nev., U.S.A.* 40°11N 118°28W **128** B2
Loverna *Sask., Canada* 51°40N 110°0W **150** D2
Loves Park *Ill., U.S.A.* 42°19N 89°3W **84** A4
Lovett *Ga., U.S.A.* 32°38N 82°46W **113** D4
Lovettsville *Va., U.S.A.* 39°16N 77°38W **93** A3
Lovilia *Iowa, U.S.A.* 41°8N 92°55W **81** D6
Loving *N. Mex., U.S.A.* 32°17N 104°6W **131** E6
Loving County ☆ *Tex., U.S.A.* 31°42N 103°36W **108** F4
Lovingston *Va., U.S.A.* 37°46N 78°52W **102** D6
Lovington *Ill., U.S.A.* 39°43N 88°38W **84** D5
Lovington *N. Mex., U.S.A.* 32°57N 103°21W **131** E7
Low *Qué., Canada* 45°50N 75°58W **144** F7
Low, C. *N.W.T., Canada* 63°7N 85°18W **159** E8
Low Desert *Oreg., U.S.A.* 43°27N 120°27W **121** D5
Low L. *Qué., Canada* 55°54N 61°7W **143** B4
Lowden *Iowa, U.S.A.* 41°52N 90°56W **81** D8
Lowe Farm *Man., Canada* 49°21N 97°35W **151** F14
Lowell *Ark., U.S.A.* 36°15N 94°8W **106** B1
Lowell *Fla., U.S.A.* 29°20N 82°12W **114** B6
Lowell *Idaho, U.S.A.* 46°9N 115°36W **122** C3
Lowell *Ind., U.S.A.* 41°18N 87°25W **85** B3
Lowell *Mass., U.S.A.* 42°38N 71°19W **91** B3
Lowell *Oreg., U.S.A.* 43°55N 122°47W **121** D3
Lowell *Vt., U.S.A.* 44°48N 72°27W **89** B2
Lowell, L. *Idaho, U.S.A.* 43°35N 116°44W **122** F2
Lower Alkali L. *Calif., U.S.A.* 41°16N 120°2W **126** B6
Lower Arrow L. *B.C., Canada* 49°40N 118°5W **155** F16
Lower B. *N.Y., U.S.A.* 40°32N 74°5W **97** C2
Lower Brule *S. Dak., U.S.A.* 44°5N 99°34W **76** F6
Lower Brule Indian Reservation *S. Dak., U.S.A.* 44°5N 100°0W **76** F6
Lower California = Baja California *Mexico* 31°10N 115°12W **166** E5

Lower Crab Cr. → Wash., U.S.A. 46°49N 119°55W 120 D6
Lower Elwha Indian Reservation Wash., U.S.A. 48°8N 123°33W 120 B2
Lower Gilmanton N.H., U.S.A. 43°24N 71°24W 89 C3
Lower Granite L. Wash., U.S.A. 46°26N 117°14W 120 D8
Lower Kalskag Alaska, U.S.A. 61°31N 160°22W 135 F7
Lower Klamath L. Calif., U.S.A. 41°57N 121°42W 126 B5
Lower Lake Calif., U.S.A. 38°55N 122°37W 126 E4
Lower Lonsdale B.C., Canada 49°19N 123°4W 161 B2
Lower Manitou L. Ont., Canada 49°15N 93°0W 148 C4
Lower Marlboro Md., U.S.A. 38°39N 76°41W 93 B4
Lower Monumental Dam Wash., U.S.A. 46°32N 118°33W 120 D7
Lower New York B. = Lower B. N.Y., U.S.A. 40°32N 74°5W 97 C2
Lower Nicola B.C., Canada 50°12N 120°54W 155 E14
Lower Paia Hawai'i, U.S.A. 20°55N 156°23W 136 C5
Lower Post B.C., Canada 59°58N 128°30W 157 E7
Lower Red L. Minn., U.S.A. 47°58N 95°0W 77 C4
Lower Sioux Indian Reservation Minn., U.S.A. 44°32N 94°59W 77 F4
Lower Suwannee Nat. Wildlife Refuge △ Fla., U.S.A. 29°20N 83°8W 114 B5
Lower Tsitika River Park △ B.C., Canada 50°27N 126°35W 154 E8
Lower West Pubnico N.S., Canada 43°38N 65°48W 141 K4
Lower Woods Harbour N.S., Canada 43°31N 65°44W 141 K4
Lowes Ky., U.S.A. 36°53N 88°46W 104 D4
Lowes Crossroads Del., U.S.A. 38°34N 75°24W 93 B5
Lowman Idaho, U.S.A. 44°5N 115°37W 122 E3
Lowmoor Va., U.S.A. 37°47N 79°53W 102 D5
Lowndes County ☆ Ala., U.S.A. 32°11N 86°35W 112 D4
Lowndes County ☆ Ga., U.S.A. 30°50N 83°15W 113 F3
Lowndes County ☆ Miss., U.S.A. 33°30N 88°25W 111 C5
Lowndesboro Ala., U.S.A. 32°17N 86°37W 112 D4
Lowry Minn., U.S.A. 45°42N 95°31W 77 E3
Lowry S. Dak., U.S.A. 45°20N 99°59W 76 E6
Lowry City Mo., U.S.A. 38°8N 93°44W 83 C3
Lowther Ont., Canada 49°32N 83°2W 149 C13
Lowther I. Nunavut, Canada 74°33N 97°30W 158 C6
Lowville N.Y., U.S.A. 43°47N 75°29W 88 B5
Loxley Ala., U.S.A. 30°37N 87°45W 112 F3
Loyal Okla., U.S.A. 35°59N 98°6W 107 C5
Loyal Wis., U.S.A. 44°44N 90°30W 78 D3
Loyal Valley Tex., U.S.A. 30°35N 99°0W 109 G9
Loyall Ky., U.S.A. 36°51N 83°22W 105 D9
Loyalton Calif., U.S.A. 39°41N 120°14W 126 D6
Loyalton S. Dak., U.S.A. 45°17N 99°17W 76 E6
Loyola University Ill., U.S.A. 42°0N 87°39W 95 B3
Lu Verne Iowa, U.S.A. 42°55N 94°5W 81 C4
Lua Makiki Hawai'i, U.S.A. 20°33N 156°37W 136 C5
Lualualei Naval Reserve Hawai'i, U.S.A. 21°27N 158°6W 136 K13
Lubbock Tex., U.S.A. 33°35N 101°51W 108 D6
Lubbock County ☆ Tex., U.S.A. 33°35N 101°50W 108 D6
Lubec Maine, U.S.A. 44°52N 66°59W 90 D7
Lubicon L. Alta., Canada 56°23N 115°56W 152 B5
Lubicon Lake Alta., Canada 56°22N 115°52W 152 B5
Lublin Wis., U.S.A. 45°5N 90°43W 78 C2
Lucama N.C., U.S.A. 35°39N 78°0W 103 C7
Lucan Ont., Canada 43°11N 81°24W 146 D5
Lucania, Mt. Yukon, Canada 61°1N 140°27W 157 D4
Lucas Kans., U.S.A. 39°4N 98°32W 82 B5
Lucas Ky., U.S.A. 36°53N 86°2W 104 D6
Lucas Ohio, U.S.A. 40°42N 82°25W 86 C4
Lucas County ☆ Iowa, U.S.A. 41°0N 93°20W 81 E5
Lucas County ☆ Ohio, U.S.A. 41°31N 83°48W 86 B3
Lucasville Ohio, U.S.A. 38°53N 82°59W 86 E4
Luce County ☆ Mich., U.S.A. 46°30N 85°30W 79 C6
Lucea Jamaica 18°27N 78°10W 182 C4
Lucedale Miss., U.S.A. 30°56N 88°35W 111 F5
Lucenilla, Península Sinaloa, Mexico 24°29N 107°46W 172 C3
Lucerne = Lake Worth Fla., U.S.A. 26°37N 80°3W 114 E8
Lucerne B.C., Canada 52°52N 118°33W 155 C16
Lucerne Calif., U.S.A. 39°6N 122°48W 126 D4
Lucerne Colo., U.S.A. 40°29N 104°41W 125 B6
Lucerne Wyo., U.S.A. 43°44N 108°11W 124 C4
Lucerne L. Calif., U.S.A. 34°31N 116°58W 127 J10
Lucerne Valley Calif., U.S.A. 34°27N 116°57W 127 J10
Lucero, L. N. Mex., U.S.A. 32°42N 106°27W 131 E4
Luceville Qué., Canada 48°32N 68°22W 145 C14
Lucile Idaho, U.S.A. 45°32N 116°18W 122 D2
Luck Wis., U.S.A. 45°35N 92°29W 78 C1
Luck L. Sask., Canada 51°5N 107°5W 150 D4
Luckey Ohio, U.S.A. 41°27N 83°29W 86 B3
Lucknow Ont., Canada 43°57N 81°31W 146 D5
Lucky Lake Sask., Canada 50°59N 107°8W 150 E4
Lucy, L. Fla., U.S.A. 28°34N 81°29W 115 A2
Ludden N. Dak., U.S.A. 46°1N 98°7W 76 F7
Ludell Kans., U.S.A. 39°52N 100°58W 82 B3
Ludington Mich., U.S.A. 43°57N 86°27W 79 F5
Ludlow N.B., Canada 46°29N 66°21W 141 G3
Ludlow Calif., U.S.A. 34°43N 116°10W 127 J10
Ludlow Colo., U.S.A. 37°20N 104°35W 125 E6
Ludlow Ill., U.S.A. 40°23N 88°8W 84 C5
Ludlow Mass., U.S.A. 42°10N 72°29W 91 B2
Ludlow Miss., U.S.A. 32°34N 89°43W 111 D4
Ludlow Mo., U.S.A. 39°39N 93°42W 83 B3
Ludlow S. Dak., U.S.A. 45°50N 103°23W 76 E2
Ludlow Vt., U.S.A. 43°24N 72°42W 89 C2
Ludowici Ga., U.S.A. 31°43N 81°45W 113 E5
Lueders Tex., U.S.A. 32°48N 99°37W 109 E8
Lugoff S.C., U.S.A. 34°13N 80°40W 103 D5
Luis Echeverría Alvarez Quintana Roo, Mexico 18°39N 88°14W 179 D5
Luis L. León, Presa Chihuahua, Mexico 28°57N 105°37W 172 B3
Luis Lopez N. Mex., U.S.A. 33°59N 106°53W 131 D4
Luis Moya Zacatecas, Mexico 22°25N 102°15W 173 E8
Luis Munoz Marin Int., San Juan ✈ (SJU) Puerto Rico 18°26N 66°0W 184 G16
Lukachukai Ariz., U.S.A. 36°25N 109°15W 130 A2
Luke Md., U.S.A. 39°30N 79°5W 93 A1
Lukeville Ariz., U.S.A. 31°53N 112°49W 130 F3
Lula Ark., U.S.A. 34°23N 83°40W 113 B3
Lula Miss., U.S.A. 34°27N 90°29W 111 B3
Luling Tex., U.S.A. 29°41N 97°39W 109 H10
Lulu Fla., U.S.A. 30°6N 82°29W 114 A6
Lulu I. B.C., Canada 49°10N 123°6W 161 C2
Lumber → N.C., U.S.A. 34°12N 79°10W 103 D6
Lumber City Ga., U.S.A. 31°56N 82°41W 113 E4
Lumberport W. Va., U.S.A. 39°22N 80°21W 102 B4
Lumberton Miss., U.S.A. 31°0N 89°27W 111 E4
Lumberton N.C., U.S.A. 34°37N 79°0W 103 D7

Lumberton N. Mex. U.S.A. 36°56N 106°56W 131 A4
Lumberton Tex., U.S.A. 30°16N 94°12W 109 G13
Lumby B.C., Canada 50°15N 118°58W 155 E16
Lummi Indian Reservation Wash., U.S.A. 48°52N 122°32W 120 B3
Lumpkin Ga., U.S.A. 32°3N 84°48W 113 D2
Lumpkin County ☆ Ga., U.S.A. 34°40N 84°0W 113 B3
Lumsden Nfld. & L., Canada 49°19N 53°37W 142 C7
Lumsden Sask., Canada 50°39N 104°52W 150 E7
Luna N. Mex., U.S.A. 33°49N 108°57W 131 D2
Luna County ☆ N. Mex., U.S.A. 32°15N 107°45W 131 E3
Luna Pier Mich., U.S.A. 41°48N 83°29W 79 H8
Lund B.C., Canada 49°59N 124°45W 154 F10
Lund Nev., U.S.A. 38°52N 115°0W 128 D5
Lund Utah, U.S.A. 38°0N 113°26W 129 E2
Lundar Man., Canada 50°42N 98°2W 151 E13
Lundbreck Alta., Canada 49°35N 114°10W 153 J6
Lunenburg N.S., Canada 44°22N 64°18W 141 J5
Lunenburg Va., U.S.A. 36°58N 78°16W 102 E6
Lunenburg Vt., U.S.A. 44°26N 71°42W 89 B3
Lunenburg County ☆ Va., U.S.A. 36°58N 78°16W 102 E6
Luning Nev., U.S.A. 38°30N 118°11W 128 D2
Lupton Ariz., U.S.A. 35°21N 109°4W 130 B6
Lupus Mo., U.S.A. 38°51N 92°27W 83 C4
Luquillo Puerto Rico 18°23N 65°43W 184 G17
Luray Kans., U.S.A. 39°7N 98°41W 82 B5
Luray Mo., U.S.A. 40°27N 91°53W 83 A5
Luray Va., U.S.A. 38°40N 78°28W 93 B2
Lusby Md., U.S.A. 38°22N 76°26W 93 B4
Luseland Sask., Canada 52°5N 109°24W 150 C2
Lushton Nebr., U.S.A. 40°43N 97°44W 80 D8
Lusk Wyo., U.S.A. 42°46N 104°27W 124 D8
Lutcher La., U.S.A. 30°2N 90°42W 110 D5
Luther Iowa, U.S.A. 41°58N 93°49W 81 D5
Luther Mich., U.S.A. 44°2N 85°41W 79 E6
Luther Okla., U.S.A. 35°40N 97°12W 107 C6
Luthersville Ga., U.S.A. 33°13N 84°45W 113 C2
Lutherville-Timonium Md., U.S.A. 39°25N 76°38W 99 A2
Lutie Tex., U.S.A. 35°1N 100°13W 108 B7
Lutselk'e N.W.T., Canada 62°24N 110°44W 157 D10
Lutsen Minn., U.S.A. 47°39N 90°41W 77 C8
Luttrell Tenn., U.S.A. 36°12N 83°45W 105 D9
Lutz Fla., U.S.A. 28°9N 82°28W 114 C6
Luverne Ala., U.S.A. 31°43N 86°13W 112 E4
Luverne Minn., U.S.A. 43°39N 96°13W 77 G2
Luverne N. Dak., U.S.A. 47°16N 97°55W 76 C8
Luxapallila Cr. → U.S.A. 33°27N 88°26W 111 C6
Luxemburg Iowa, U.S.A. 42°36N 91°5W 81 C7
Luxemburg Wis., U.S.A. 44°33N 87°42W 78 D6
Luxora Ark., U.S.A. 35°45N 89°56W 106 C6
Luzerne County ☆ Pa., U.S.A. 41°10N 76°0W 87 C7
Lyal I. Ont., Canada 44°57N 81°24W 146 C5
Lycan Colo., U.S.A. 37°37N 102°12W 125 E8
Lycoming County ☆ Pa., U.S.A. 41°20N 77°0W 87 C5
Lyell I. B.C., Canada 52°40N 131°35W 154 C3
Lyells Va., U.S.A. 38°0N 76°44W 93 C4
Lyerly Ga., U.S.A. 34°24N 85°24W 113 B1
Lyford Tex., U.S.A. 26°25N 97°48W 108 L10
Lykens Pa., U.S.A. 40°34N 76°42W 87 D6
Lyle Minn., U.S.A. 43°30N 92°57W 77 G6
Lyles Tenn., U.S.A. 35°55N 87°21W 104 E5
Lyman Miss., U.S.A. 30°30N 89°7W 111 F4
Lyman Nebr., U.S.A. 41°55N 104°2W 80 C1
Lyman Utah, U.S.A. 38°24N 111°35W 129 E4
Lyman Wash., U.S.A. 48°32N 122°4W 120 B3
Lyman Wyo., U.S.A. 41°20N 110°18W 124 C4
Lyman County ☆ S. Dak., U.S.A. 44°0N 100°0W 76 G6
Lyman L. Ariz., U.S.A. 34°22N 109°23W 130 C6
Lymburn Alta., Canada 55°21N 119°47W 152 C1
Lyme N.H., U.S.A. 43°48N 72°9W 89 C2
Lynbrook N.Y., U.S.A. 40°39N 73°41W 99 C2
Lynch Ky., U.S.A. 36°58N 82°54W 105 D10
Lynch Nebr., U.S.A. 42°50N 98°28W 80 B7
Lynchburg Ohio, U.S.A. 39°15N 83°48W 86 D3
Lynchburg S.C., U.S.A. 34°3N 80°4W 103 D5
Lynchburg Tenn., U.S.A. 35°17N 86°22W 104 E6
Lynchburg Va., U.S.A. 37°25N 79°9W 102 D5
Lynches → S.C., U.S.A. 33°50N 79°22W 103 E6
Lynd Minn., U.S.A. 44°23N 95°54W 77 F3
Lynden Wash., U.S.A. 48°57N 122°27W 120 B3
Lyndhurst N.J., U.S.A. 40°49N 74°7W 97 B2
Lyndon Ill., U.S.A. 41°43N 89°56W 84 B4
Lyndon Kans., U.S.A. 38°37N 95°41W 82 C8
Lyndon Vt., U.S.A. 44°31N 72°1W 89 B2
Lyndon B. Johnson, L. Tex., U.S.A. 30°33N 98°20W 109 G9
Lyndon B. Johnson Nat. Grassland Tex., U.S.A. 33°25N 97°37W 109 D10
Lyndon B. Johnson Nat. Historical Park △ Tex., U.S.A. 30°15N 98°25W 109 G9
Lyndon Station Wis., U.S.A. 43°43N 89°54W 78 E4
Lyndonville N.Y., U.S.A. 43°20N 78°23W 88 B2
Lyndonville Vt., U.S.A. 44°31N 72°1W 89 B2
Lynn Ala., U.S.A. 34°3N 87°33W 112 B3
Lynn Ind., U.S.A. 40°3N 84°6W 85 C6
Lynn Mass., U.S.A. 42°28N 70°57W 91 B4
Lynn Utah, U.S.A. 41°53N 113°45W 129 B2
Lynn Canal Alaska, U.S.A. 58°50N 135°15W 135 G14
Lynn Canyon Park B.C., Canada 42°20N 123°1W 161 A2
Lynn County ☆ Tex., U.S.A. 33°10N 101°48W 108 D6
Lynn Haven Fla., U.S.A. 30°15N 85°39W 114 A3
Lynn Headwaters Regional Park B.C., Canada 49°22N 123°1W 161 A2
Lynn Lake Man., Canada 56°51N 101°3W 159 F5
Lynn Valley B.C., Canada 49°20N 123°2W 161 A2
Lynn Woods Res. Mass., U.S.A. 42°29N 71°0W 96 A2
Lynndyl Utah, U.S.A. 39°31N 112°22W 129 D3
Lynne Fla., U.S.A. 29°12N 81°55W 114 B7
Lynnfield Mass., U.S.A. 42°32N 71°3W 91 B3
Lynnville Ind., U.S.A. 38°12N 87°18W 85 E3
Lynnville Ky., U.S.A. 36°34N 88°34W 104 D4
Lynnville Tenn., U.S.A. 35°23N 87°0W 104 E5
Lynnwood Wash., U.S.A. 47°49N 122°18W 132 A3
Lynx L. N.W.T., Canada 62°25N 106°15W 157 D11
Lynxville Wis., U.S.A. 43°15N 91°2W 78 E2
Lyon Miss., U.S.A. 34°13N 90°33W 111 B3
Lyon, C. N.W.T., Canada 69°50N 122°57W 156 C8
Lyon County ☆ Iowa, U.S.A. 43°20N 96°10W 81 B2
Lyon County ☆ Kans., U.S.A. 38°30N 96°10W 82 C7
Lyon County ☆ Ky., U.S.A. 37°0N 88°5W 104 D3
Lyon County ☆ Minn., U.S.A. 44°25N 95°50W 77 F3
Lyon County ☆ Nev., U.S.A. 38°45N 119°10W 128 D2
Lyon Inlet Nunavut, Canada 66°32N 83°53W 159 D9
Lyon Mountain N.Y., U.S.A. 44°43N 73°55W 88 A7
Lyons Colo., U.S.A. 40°14N 105°16W 125 B5

Lyons Ga., U.S.A. 32°12N 82°19W 113 D4
Lyons Ill., U.S.A. 41°48N 87°49W 95 C2
Lyons Ind., U.S.A. 38°59N 87°5W 85 E3
Lyons Kans., U.S.A. 38°21N 98°12W 82 C5
Lyons N.Y., U.S.A. 43°5N 77°0W 88 B4
Lyons Nebr., U.S.A. 41°56N 96°28W 80 C9
Lyons Ohio, U.S.A. 41°42N 84°4W 86 B2
Lyons Oreg., U.S.A. 44°47N 122°37W 121 C3
Lyons Tex., U.S.A. 30°23N 96°34W 109 G11
Lyons Falls N.Y., U.S.A. 43°37N 75°22W 88 B5
Lysite Wyo., U.S.A. 43°16N 107°41W 124 C5
Lyster Qué., Canada 46°22N 71°37W 145 E11
Lytle Tex., U.S.A. 29°14N 98°48W 109 H9
Lytton B.C., Canada 50°13N 121°31W 155 E13
Lytton Iowa, U.S.A. 42°25N 94°51W 81 C4

M

Ma-Me-O Beach Alta., Canada 52°58N 113°59W 153 F7
Maarmorilik Greenland 71°3N 51°0W 162 C5
Mabank Tex., U.S.A. 32°22N 96°6W 109 E11
Mabel Minn., U.S.A. 43°32N 91°46W 77 G7
Mabel, L. Fla., U.S.A. 28°25N 81°32W 115 B1
Mabel L. B.C., Canada 50°35N 118°43W 155 E16
Maben W. Va., U.S.A. 37°38N 81°23W 102 D3
Maberly Ont., Canada 44°50N 76°32W 147 C10
Mableton Ga., U.S.A. 33°49N 84°35W 113 C2
Mabou N.S., Canada 46°4N 61°29W 141 G8
Mabton Wash., U.S.A. 46°13N 120°0W 120 D5
McAdam N.B., Canada 45°36N 67°20W 141 H2
McAdoo Pa., U.S.A. 40°55N 75°59W 87 D7
McAlester Okla., U.S.A. 34°56N 95°46W 107 D8
Macalister B.C., Canada 52°27N 122°32W 155 C12
McAlister N. Mex., U.S.A. 34°42N 103°47W 131 C7
McAllen Tex., U.S.A. 26°12N 98°14W 108 L9
McAllister Park Tex., U.S.A. 29°33N 98°23W 116 B3
McAlpin Fla., U.S.A. 30°8N 82°57W 114 A6
MacAlpine L. N.W.T., Canada 66°32N 102°45W 159 D5
Macamic Qué., Canada 48°45N 79°0W 144 C3
Macapule, I. Sinaloa, Mexico 25°21N 108°40W 172 B2
McArthur Calif., U.S.A. 41°3N 121°24W 126 B5
McArthur Ohio, U.S.A. 39°15N 82°29W 86 D4
Macaulay Pt. B.C., Canada 48°25N 123°24W 155 G11
McAuley Man., Canada 50°16N 101°23W 151 E10
McBain Mich., U.S.A. 44°12N 85°13W 79 E6
McBride B.C., Canada 53°20N 120°19W 155 B14
McBride Mo., U.S.A. 37°50N 89°50W 83 D7
McBride Okla., U.S.A. 33°54N 96°36W 107 E7
McBrides Mich., U.S.A. 43°21N 85°2W 79 F6
McCall Idaho, U.S.A. 44°55N 116°6W 122 E2
McCall Creek Miss., U.S.A. 31°31N 90°42W 111 E3
McCallsburg Iowa, U.S.A. 42°10N 93°23W 81 C5
McCallum Nfld. & L., Canada 47°38N 56°14W 142 E4
McCamey Tex., U.S.A. 31°8N 102°14W 108 F5
McCammon Idaho, U.S.A. 42°39N 112°12W 122 G6
Maccan N.S., Canada 45°43N 64°15W 141 H5
McCandless Pa., U.S.A. 40°30N 80°4W 98 B2
McCarran Int., Las Vegas ✈ (LAS) Nev., U.S.A. 36°5N 115°9W 134 C2
McCarthy Alaska, U.S.A. 61°26N 142°56W 135 F12
McCarty Park Wis., U.S.A. 42°59N 88°0W 94 C1
McCartys N. Mex., U.S.A. 35°4N 107°41W 131 B3
McCauley I. B.C., Canada 53°40N 130°15W 154 B4
McCaysville Ga., U.S.A. 34°59N 84°23W 113 B2
McClain County ☆ Okla., U.S.A. 35°0N 97°30W 107 D6
McClave Colo., U.S.A. 38°8N 102°51W 125 D8
McCleary Wash., U.S.A. 47°3N 123°16W 120 C2
McClelland Iowa, U.S.A. 41°20N 95°41W 81 D3
McClelland L. Alta., Canada 57°29N 111°20W 152 A9
McClellanville S.C., U.S.A. 33°5N 79°28W 103 E6
M'Clintock Chan. Nunavut, Canada 72°0N 102°0W 158 C5
McCloud Calif., U.S.A. 41°15N 122°8W 126 B4
McClure Ohio, U.S.A. 41°22N 83°57W 86 B3
McClure Pa., U.S.A. 40°42N 77°19W 87 D5
McClure Va., U.S.A. 37°6N 82°23W 102 D2
McClure, L. Calif., U.S.A. 37°35N 120°16W 126 F6
M'Clure Str. N.W.T., Canada 75°0N 119°0W 156 B9
McClusky N. Dak., U.S.A. 47°29N 100°27W 76 C5
McColl S.C., U.S.A. 34°40N 79°33W 103 D6
McComb Miss., U.S.A. 31°15N 90°27W 111 E3
McComb Ohio, U.S.A. 41°7N 83°48W 86 B3
McCone County ☆ Mont., U.S.A. 47°40N 105°50W 123 C12
McConnell Air Force Base Kans., U.S.A. 37°40N 97°16W 82 D6
McConnellsburg Pa., U.S.A. 39°56N 77°59W 87 E5
McConnelsville Ohio, U.S.A. 39°39N 81°51W 86 D5
McCook Ill., U.S.A. 41°47N 87°49W 95 C2
McCook Nebr., U.S.A. 40°12N 100°38W 80 D5
McCook County ☆ S. Dak., U.S.A. 43°44N 97°23W 76 G8
McCool Miss., U.S.A. 33°12N 89°21W 111 C4
McCool Junction Nebr., U.S.A. 40°45N 97°36W 80 D8
McCormick S.C., U.S.A. 33°55N 82°17W 103 E3
McCormick County ☆ S.C., U.S.A. 33°50N 82°15W 103 E3
McCoy Colo., U.S.A. 39°55N 106°44W 125 C4
McCracken Kans., U.S.A. 38°36N 99°34W 82 C4
McCracken County ☆ Ky., U.S.A. 37°5N 88°45W 104 C4
McCreary Man., Canada 50°47N 99°29W 151 E12
McCreary County ☆ Ky., U.S.A. 36°45N 84°30W 105 D8
McCrory Ark., U.S.A. 35°16N 91°12W 106 C4
McCulloch County ☆ Tex., U.S.A. 31°9N 99°20W 109 F8
McCullough Ra. Nev., U.S.A. 35°45N 115°5W 128 G5
McCune Kans., U.S.A. 37°21N 95°1W 82 D8
McCurtain Okla., U.S.A. 35°9N 94°58W 107 D9
McCurtain County ☆ Okla., U.S.A. 34°10N 94°45W 107 D9
McDade Tex., U.S.A. 30°17N 97°14W 109 G10
McDame B.C., Canada 59°44N 128°59W 157 E7
McDavid Fla., U.S.A. 30°52N 87°19W 114 A1
McDermitt Nev., U.S.A. 41°59N 117°43W 128 A3
Macdiarmid Ont., Canada 49°26N 88°8W 148 C8
MacDill Air Force Base Tampa, U.S.A. 27°50N 82°30W 115 C2
Macdoel Calif., U.S.A. 41°50N 122°0W 126 B4
Macdona Tex., U.S.A. 29°19N 98°41W 116 C1
McDonald Kans., U.S.A. 39°47N 101°22W 82 B2
McDonald N. Mex., U.S.A. 33°50N 103°19W 131 D7
McDonald, L. Mont., U.S.A. 48°35N 113°56W 123 B4
McDonald Cartier Int., Ottawa ✈ (YOW) Ont., Canada 45°19N 75°40W 147 B11
McDonald County ☆ Mo., U.S.A. 36°40N 94°20W 83 E2
McDonough Ga., U.S.A. 33°27N 84°9W 113 C2
McDonough County ☆ Ill., U.S.A. 40°30N 90°40W 84 C3
McDougal Ark., U.S.A. 36°26N 90°23W 106 B5
McDougall, Mt. Wyo., U.S.A. 42°54N 110°36W 124 C2
McDowell Va., U.S.A. 38°20N 79°29W 102 C5
McDowell County ☆ N.C., U.S.A. 35°40N 82°0W 103 C4

McDowell County ☆ W. Va., U.S.A. 37°22N 81°33W 102 D3
McDuffie County ☆ Ga., U.S.A. 33°20N 82°25W 113 C4
Macedonia Ill., U.S.A. 38°3N 88°42W 84 E5
Macedonia Iowa, U.S.A. 41°12N 95°25W 81 D3
Macedonia Ohio, U.S.A. 41°19N 81°31W 98 B5
Maceo Ky., U.S.A. 37°51N 87°0W 104 C6
Maces Bay N.B., Canada 45°6N 66°29W 141 H3
McEwen Tenn., U.S.A. 36°7N 87°38W 104 D5
McFadden Wyo., U.S.A. 41°39N 106°8W 124 E6
McFaddin Tex., U.S.A. 28°33N 97°1W 109 J10
McFaddin Nat. Wildlife Refuge △ Tex., U.S.A. 29°39N 94°3W 109 H13
McFall Nev., U.S.A. 40°7N 94°13W 83 A2
McFarland Calif., U.S.A. 35°41N 119°14W 127 H7
McFarland Kans., U.S.A. 39°3N 96°14W 82 B7
McFarland Mich., U.S.A. 46°11N 87°15W 79 C4
McFarland Wis., U.S.A. 43°1N 89°17W 78 E4
McGee Sask., Canada 59°12N 107°58W 157 E11
McGee Creek L. Okla., U.S.A. 34°22N 95°38W 107 D8
McGehee Ark., U.S.A. 33°38N 91°24W 106 E4
McGhee Tyson, Knoxville ✈ (TYS) Tenn., U.S.A. 35°49N 83°59W 105 E9
McGill Nev., U.S.A. 39°23N 114°47W 128 C6
McGill University Montréal, Canada 160 b1
McGrath Alaska, U.S.A. 62°58N 155°36W 135 E9
McGrath Minn., U.S.A. 46°14N 93°16W 77 D5
McGraw N.Y., U.S.A. 42°36N 76°8W 88 C4
MacGregor Man., Canada 49°57N 98°48W 151 F13
McGregor Iowa, U.S.A. 43°1N 91°11W 81 B7
McGregor N. Dak., U.S.A. 48°36N 102°56W 76 B3
McGregor Tex., U.S.A. 31°27N 97°24W 109 F10
McGregor → B.C., Canada 54°11N 122°2W 157 F8
McGregor L. Alta., Canada 50°25N 112°52W 153 H8
McGrew Nebr., U.S.A. 41°45N 103°25W 80 C2
McGuffey Ohio, U.S.A. 40°42N 83°47W 86 C2
McHenry Ill., U.S.A. 42°21N 88°16W 84 A5
McHenry Ky., U.S.A. 37°22N 86°55W 104 C6
McHenry Md., U.S.A. 39°36N 79°22W 93 A1
McHenry Miss., U.S.A. 30°43N 89°9W 111 F4
McHenry N. Dak., U.S.A. 47°35N 98°35W 76 C7
McHenry County ☆ Ill., U.S.A. 42°20N 88°25W 84 A5
McHenry County ☆ N. Dak., U.S.A. 48°20N 100°45W 76 B5
Machesney Park Ill., U.S.A. 42°21N 89°2W 84 A4
Machias Maine, U.S.A. 44°43N 67°28W 90 D6
Machias N.Y., U.S.A. 42°25N 78°29W 88 C2
Machias → Maine, U.S.A. 44°43N 67°22W 90 D6
Machona, L. Tabasco, Mexico 18°20N 93°40W 178 A3
McIntire Iowa, U.S.A. 43°26N 92°36W 81 B6
McIntosh Ala., U.S.A. 31°16N 88°2W 112 E2
McIntosh Minn., U.S.A. 47°38N 95°53W 77 C3
McIntosh N. Mex., U.S.A. 34°52N 106°3W 131 C4
McIntosh S. Dak., U.S.A. 45°55N 101°21W 76 E4
McIntosh County ☆ Ga., U.S.A. 31°30N 81°25W 113 E5
McIntosh County ☆ N. Dak., U.S.A. 46°2N 99°20W 76 D6
McIntosh County ☆ Okla., U.S.A. 35°20N 95°40W 107 C8
McIntyre Ga., U.S.A. 32°51N 83°11W 113 D3
McIntyre B. B.C., Canada 54°5N 132°0W 154 A3
Mack Colo., U.S.A. 39°13N 108°52W 125 C2
MacKay Alta., Canada 53°39N 115°35W 153 F6
MacKay Idaho, U.S.A. 43°55N 113°37W 122 F5
MacKay → Alta., Canada 57°10N 111°38W 152 A9
MacKay L. N.W.T., Canada 63°55N 110°25W 157 D10
McKay L. Ont., Canada 49°37N 86°25W 149 C10
McKean County ☆ Pa., U.S.A. 41°50N 78°45W 87 C4
McKeand → Nunavut, Canada 65°34N 67°55W 159 D12
McKee Ky., U.S.A. 37°25N 84°0W 105 C9
McKee City N.J., U.S.A. 39°26N 74°37W 92 C2
McKee Cr. → Ill., U.S.A. 39°46N 90°36W 84 D3
McKees Rocks Pa., U.S.A. 40°27N 80°3W 98 B1
McKeesport Pa., U.S.A. 40°20N 79°51W 98 B2
McKellar Ont., Canada 45°30N 79°55W 146 B7
McKenney Va., U.S.A. 36°59N 77°43W 102 E7
Mackenzie B.C., Canada 55°20N 123°5W 157 E8
Mackenzie Ala., U.S.A. 31°33N 86°43W 112 E4
Mackenzie Mich., U.S.A. 42°21N 83°9W 98 A1
Mackenzie Mo., U.S.A. 38°34N 90°19W 94 B2
Mackenzie N. Dak., U.S.A. 46°50N 100°29W 76 C5
Mackenzie Tenn., U.S.A. 36°8N 88°31W 104 D4
Mackenzie → N.W.T., Canada 69°10N 134°20W 156 C6
Mackenzie → Oreg., U.S.A. 44°7N 123°6W 121 C2
Mackenzie Bay Canada 69°0N 137°30W 156 C5
Mackenzie Bridge Oreg., U.S.A. 44°11N 122°10W 121 C3
Mackenzie County ☆ N. Dak., U.S.A. 47°55N 103°30W 76 C2
Mackenzie King I. N.W.T., Canada 77°45N 111°0W 156 A10
Mackenzie L. Sask., Canada 54°12N 102°30W 150 B9
Mackenzie Mts. Canada 64°0N 130°0W 157 D7
McKibben Tex., U.S.A. 36°8N 100°20W 108 A6
Mackinac, Straits of Mich., U.S.A. 45°50N 84°40W 79 D7
Mackinac County ☆ Mich., U.S.A. 46°5N 85°0W 79 C7
Mackinac Island Mich., U.S.A. 45°51N 84°37W 79 D7
Mackinaw Ill., U.S.A. 40°32N 89°21W 84 C4
Mackinaw → Ill., U.S.A. 40°33N 89°44W 84 C4
Mackinaw City Mich., U.S.A. 45°47N 84°44W 79 D7
McKinley, Mt. Alaska, U.S.A. 63°4N 151°0W 135 E10
McKinley County ☆ N. Mex., U.S.A. 35°30N 108°0W 131 B2
McKinley Park Alaska, U.S.A. 63°44N 148°55W 135 E10
McKinley Park Ill., U.S.A. 41°49N 87°40W 95 C2
McKinley Sea Arctic 82°0N 0°0 162 A11
McKinleyville Calif., U.S.A. 40°57N 124°6W 126 C2
McKinney Mt. Tex., U.S.A. 33°12N 96°37W 109 D11
McKinney Mt. Tex., U.S.A. 29°50N 103°47W 108 H4
McKinnon Ga., U.S.A. 31°25N 81°56W 113 E5
McKittrick Calif., U.S.A. 35°18N 119°37W 127 H7
McKittrick Mo., U.S.A. 38°44N 91°27W 83 C5
Macklin Sask., Canada 52°20N 109°56W 150 C2
Macksburg Iowa, U.S.A. 41°13N 94°11W 81 D4
Macksville Kans., U.S.A. 37°58N 98°58W 82 D5
McLain Miss., U.S.A. 31°7N 88°50W 111 E5
McLaughlin S. Dak., U.S.A. 45°49N 100°49W 76 E5
McLean Sask., Canada 50°31N 104°4W 150 E7
McLean Ill., U.S.A. 40°19N 89°10W 84 C4
McLean Nebr., U.S.A. 42°23N 97°28W 80 B8
McLean Tex., U.S.A. 35°14N 100°36W 108 B7
McLean Va., U.S.A. 38°56N 77°10W 99 B2
McLean County ☆ Ill., U.S.A. 40°30N 88°50W 84 C5
McLean County ☆ Ky., U.S.A. 37°30N 87°15W 104 C5
McLean County ☆ N. Dak., U.S.A. 47°30N 101°10W 76 C4
Maclean Str. N.W.T., Canada 77°30N 103°30W 158 B5
Macleansboro Ill., U.S.A. 38°6N 88°32W 84 E5
MacLennan Res. Colo., U.S.A. 39°34N 105°1W 134 C1
McLennan Alta., Canada 55°42N 116°50W 152 C4
McLennan County ☆ Tex., U.S.A. 31°33N 97°9W 109 F10
MacLeod = Fort Macleod Alta., Canada 49°45N 113°30W 153 J7
McLeod N. Dak., U.S.A. 46°24N 97°18W 76 D8

McLeod → *Alta., Canada* 54°9N 115°44W **152** D5
MacLeod, B. *N.W.T., Canada* 62°53N 110°0W **157** D10
McLeod County ☆ *Minn., U.S.A.* 44°50N 94°15W **77** F4
McLoud *Okla., U.S.A.* 35°26N 97°46W **107** C6
McLoughlin, Mt. *Oreg., U.S.A.* 42°27N 122°19W **121** E3
McLure *B.C., Canada* 51°2N 120°13W **155** D14
McLouth *Kan., U.S.A.* 39°12N 95°13W **82** B8
Maclovio Herrera *Chihuahua, Mexico* 29°5N 105°8W **169** D10
McLure *B.C., Canada* 51°2N 120°13W **155** D14
McMichael C → *Pa., U.S.A.* 40°59N 75°11W **92** B1
Macmillan Pass *Canada* 63°15N 130°2W **157** D6
McMinn County ☆ *Tenn., U.S.A.* 35°27N 84°36W **105** E8
McMinnville *Oreg., U.S.A.* 45°13N 123°12W **121** B2
McMinnville *Tenn., U.S.A.* 35°41N 85°46W **105** E7
McMorran *Sask., Canada* 51°19N 108°42W **150** D3
McMullen County ☆ *Tex., U.S.A.* 28°28N 98°33W **109** J9
McMurray = Fort McMurray *Alta.,*
  Canada 56°44N 111°7W **152** B9
McMurray *Wash., U.S.A.* 48°19N 122°14W **132** B4
McNab *Ark., U.S.A.* 33°40N 93°50W **106** E2
McNairy County ☆ *Tenn., U.S.A.* 35°10N 88°36W **104** E4
McNary *Ariz., U.S.A.* 34°4N 109°51W **130** C6
McNary *Tex., U.S.A.* 31°15N 105°48W **108** F2
McNaughton L. *Nunavut, Canada* 67°20N 98°25W **158** D6
McNeal *Ariz., U.S.A.* 31°36N 109°40W **130** F6
McNeil *Ark., U.S.A.* 33°21N 93°13W **106** E2
McNeill *Miss., U.S.A.* 30°40N 89°38W **111** F4
MacNutt *Sask., Canada* 51°5N 101°36W **151** D10
Macomb *Ill., U.S.A.* 40°27N 90°40W **84** C3
Macomb *Okla., U.S.A.* 35°10N 97°0W **107** C6
Macomb County ☆ *Mich., U.S.A.* 42°40N 83°0W **79** G9
Macon *Ga., U.S.A.* 32°51N 83°38W **113** D3
Macon *Ill., U.S.A.* 39°43N 89°0W **84** D5
Macon *Miss., U.S.A.* 33°7N 88°34W **111** C5
Macon *Mo., U.S.A.* 39°44N 92°28W **83** B41
Macon *Nebr., U.S.A.* 40°13N 98°55W **80** D7
Macon, Bayou → *La., U.S.A.* 31°55N 91°33W **110** C4
Macon County ☆ *Ala., U.S.A.* 32°25N 85°42W **112** D5
Macon County ☆ *Ga., U.S.A.* 32°20N 84°0W **113** D2
Macon County ☆ *Ill., U.S.A.* 39°50N 89°0W **84** D5
Macon County ☆ *Mo., U.S.A.* 39°50N 92°30W **83** B4
Macon County ☆ *N.C., U.S.A.* 35°10N 83°30W **103** C2
Macon County ☆ *Tenn., U.S.A.* 36°31N 86°2W **104** D6
Maconí *Querétaro, Mexico* 20°50N 99°23W **176** A4
Macoun *Sask., Canada* 49°19N 103°16W **150** F8
Macoupin County ☆ *Ill., U.S.A.* 39°20N 89°55W **84** D4
MacPherson = Kapuskasing *Ont.,*
  Canada 49°25N 82°30W **149** C14
McPherson *Kans., U.S.A.* 38°22N 97°40W **82** C6
McPherson County ☆ *Kans., U.S.A.* 38°20N 97°40W **82** C6
McPherson County ☆ *Nebr., U.S.A.* 41°30N 101°0W **80** C4
McPherson County ☆ *S. Dak., U.S.A.* 45°46N 99°0W **76** E6
McQuady *Ky., U.S.A.* 37°42N 86°31W **104** C6
McRae *Ark., U.S.A.* 35°7N 91°49W **106** C4
McRae *Ga., U.S.A.* 32°4N 82°54W **113** D4
McRoberts *Ky., U.S.A.* 37°12N 82°40W **105** C10
McSherrytown *Pa., U.S.A.* 39°48N 77°1W **93** A3
McTavish Arm *N.W.T., Canada* 66°6N 119°0W **156** C9
MacTier *Ont., Canada* 45°8N 79°47W **146** B7
Mactún *Tabasco, Mexico* 17°35N 91°17W **178** B5
Macungie *Pa., U.S.A.* 40°31N 75°33W **92** B1
Macuspana *Tabasco, Mexico* 17°46N 92°36W **178** B4
Macuyú *Coahuila, Mexico* 25°20N 101°37W **171** E3
McVeigh *Ky., U.S.A.* 37°32N 82°15W **105** C10
McVeytown *Pa., U.S.A.* 40°30N 77°45W **87** D5
McVicar Arm *N.W.T., Canada* 65°20N 120°10W **157** C8
McVille *N. Dak., U.S.A.* 47°46N 98°11W **76** C7
Macwahoc *Maine, U.S.A.* 45°38N 68°16W **90** C5
McWilliams *Ala., U.S.A.* 31°50N 87°6W **112** E3
Macy *Nebr., U.S.A.* 42°7N 96°21W **80** B9
Mad → *Calif., U.S.A.* 40°57N 124°7W **126** C2
Mad → *Ohio, U.S.A.* 39°46N 84°12W **86** D2
Mad → *Vt., U.S.A.* 44°18N 72°41W **89** B2
Mad River Glen *Vt., U.S.A.* 44°12N 72°55W **89** B2
Madagascar, Arrecife *Yucatán, Mexico* 21°29N 90°19W **179** A3
Madame, I. *N.S., Canada* 45°30N 60°58W **141** H9
Madawaska *Ont., Canada* 45°30N 78°0W **144** F5
Madawaska *Maine, U.S.A.* 47°21N 68°20W **90** A5
Madawaska → *Ont., Canada* 45°27N 76°21W **147** B10
Maddock *N. Dak., U.S.A.* 47°58N 99°32W **76** C6
Maddox *Md., U.S.A.* 38°20N 76°48W **93** B4
Maddox Cove *Nfld. & L., Canada* 47°28N 52°42W **142** E8
Madeira Beach *Fla., U.S.A.* 27°47N 82°47W **115** C2
Madeira Park *B.C., Canada* 49°37N 124°0W **154** F10
Madeleine → *Qué., Canada* 49°15N 65°19W **140** D4
Madeleine, Îs. de la *Qué., Canada* 47°30N 61°40W **141** F8
Madeleine-Centre *Qué., Canada* 49°15N 65°22W **140** D4
Madelia *Minn., U.S.A.* 44°3N 94°25W **77** F4
Madeline *Calif., U.S.A.* 41°3N 120°28W **126** B6
Madeline I. *Wis., U.S.A.* 46°49N 90°42W **78** B3
Madera *Chihuahua, Mexico* 29°12N 108°7W **169** D7
Madera *Calif., U.S.A.* 36°57N 120°3W **127** G6
Madera County ☆ *Calif., U.S.A.* 37°15N 119°35W **126** F7
Madill *Okla., U.S.A.* 34°6N 96°46W **107** D7
Madín *México, Mexico* 19°32N 99°16W **181** A2
Madín, L. *México, Mexico* 19°31N 99°16W **181** A2
Madison *Ala., U.S.A.* 34°42N 86°45W **112** B4
Madison *Ark., U.S.A.* 35°1N 90°43W **106** C5
Madison *Fla., U.S.A.* 30°28N 83°25W **114** A5
Madison *Ga., U.S.A.* 33°36N 83°28W **113** C3
Madison *Ill., U.S.A.* 38°40N 90°9W **94** A3
Madison *Ind., U.S.A.* 38°44N 85°23W **85** E5
Madison *Kans., U.S.A.* 38°8N 96°8W **82** C7
Madison *Maine, U.S.A.* 44°48N 69°53W **90** D4
Madison *Md., U.S.A.* 38°30N 76°13W **93** B4
Madison *Minn., U.S.A.* 45°1N 96°11W **77** E2
Madison *Miss., U.S.A.* 32°28N 90°7W **111** D3
Madison *N.C., U.S.A.* 36°23N 79°58W **103** B6
Madison *N.J., U.S.A.* 40°46N 74°25W **92** B2
Madison *Nebr., U.S.A.* 41°50N 97°27W **80** C8
Madison *Ohio, U.S.A.* 41°46N 81°3W **86** B5
Madison *S. Dak., U.S.A.* 44°0N 97°7W **76** D8
Madison *Tenn., U.S.A.* 36°16N 86°42W **104** D6
Madison *Va., U.S.A.* 38°23N 78°15W **102** C5
Madison *W. Va., U.S.A.* 38°4N 81°49W **102** C3
Madison *Wis., U.S.A.* 43°4N 89°24W **78** E4
Madison → *Mont., U.S.A.* 45°56N 111°31W **123** E6
Madison County ☆ *Ala., U.S.A.* 34°44N 86°35W **112** B4
Madison County ☆ *Ark., U.S.A.* 36°0N 93°45W **106** B2
Madison County ☆ *Fla., U.S.A.* 30°30N 83°30W **114** A5
Madison County ☆ *Ga., U.S.A.* 34°10N 83°10W **113** B3
Madison County ☆ *Idaho, U.S.A.* 43°55N 111°50W **122** F7
Madison County ☆ *Ill., U.S.A.* 38°50N 89°55W **84** E4
Madison County ☆ *Ind., U.S.A.* 40°10N 85°45W **85** C5
Madison County ☆ *Iowa, U.S.A.* 41°20N 94°0W **81** D5

Madison County ☆ *Ky., U.S.A.* 37°40N 84°20W **105** C8
Madison County ☆ *Miss., U.S.A.* 32°37N 90°2W **111** D3
Madison County ☆ *Mo., U.S.A.* 37°30N 90°20W **83** D6
Madison County ☆ *Mont., U.S.A.* 45°12N 112°0W **123** E6
Madison County ☆ *N.C., U.S.A.* 35°50N 82°50W **103** C3
Madison County ☆ *N.Y., U.S.A.* 43°0N 75°45W **88** C5
Madison County ☆ *Nebr., U.S.A.* 41°50N 97°30W **80** C8
Madison County ☆ *Ohio, U.S.A.* 39°53N 83°27W **86** D3
Madison County ☆ *Tenn., U.S.A.* 35°37N 88°49W **104** E4
Madison County ☆ *Tex., U.S.A.* 31°0N 96°0W **109** G12
Madison County ☆ *Va., U.S.A.* 38°23N 78°15W **102** C6
Madison Heights *Va., U.S.A.* 37°25N 79°8W **102** D5
Madison Lake *Minn., U.S.A.* 44°12N 93°49W **77** F5
Madison Mills *Ohio, U.S.A.* 39°39N 83°20W **86** D3
Madison Parish ☆ *La., U.S.A.* 32°25N 91°11W **110** B4
Madison Range *Mont., U.S.A.* 45°15N 111°30W **123** E6
Madisonville *Ky., U.S.A.* 37°20N 87°30W **104** C5
Madisonville *La., U.S.A.* 30°24N 90°10W **110** D5
Madisonville *Tenn., U.S.A.* 35°31N 84°22W **105** E8
Madisonville *Tex., U.S.A.* 30°57N 95°55W **109** G12
Madoc *Ont., Canada* 44°30N 77°28W **147** C9
Madras *Oreg., U.S.A.* 44°38N 121°8W **121** C4
Madre, L. *Tex., U.S.A.* 25°15N 97°30W **108** L10
Madre del Sur, Sierra *Mexico* 17°30N 100°0W **175** F8
Madre Occidental, Sierra *Mexico* 27°0N 107°0W **172** C5
Madre Oriental, Sierra *Mexico* 25°0N 100°0W **171** H5
Madrid *Colima, Mexico* 19°4N 103°52W **174** C4
Madrid *Ala., U.S.A.* 31°2N 85°24W **112** E5
Madrid *Iowa, U.S.A.* 41°53N 93°49W **81** D5
Madrid *N. Mex., U.S.A.* 35°24N 106°9W **131** B4
Madrid *N.Y., U.S.A.* 44°45N 75°8W **88** A5
Madrid *Nebr., U.S.A.* 40°51N 101°33W **80** D4
Madsen *Ont., Canada* 50°58N 93°55W **148** B3
Maeser *Utah, U.S.A.* 40°28N 109°35W **129** C6
Maestra, Sierra *Cuba* 20°15N 77°0W **182** B4
Maeystown *Ill., U.S.A.* 38°10N 90°14W **84** E3
Mafeking *Man., Canada* 52°40N 101°10W **151** C10
Magaguadavic *N.B., Canada* 45°42N 67°12W **141** H2
Magaguadavic → *N.B., Canada* 45°7N 66°54W **141** H3
Magaguadavic L. *N.B., Canada* 45°43N 67°12W **141** H2
Magallanes, Sa. *Sonora, Mexico* 30°50N 109°50W **168** C5
Magazine *Ark., U.S.A.* 35°9N 93°48W **106** C2
Magazine Mt. *Ark., U.S.A.* 35°10N 93°41W **106** C2
Magdalen Is. = Madeleine, Îs. de la *Qué.,*
  Canada 47°30N 61°40W **141** F8
Magdalena *Jalisco, Mexico* 20°55N 103°57W **174** B4
Magdalena *N. Mex., U.S.A.* 34°7N 107°15W **131** C3
Magdalena, B. *Baja Calif. S., Mexico* 24°35N 112°0W **167** J7
Magdalena, I. *Baja Calif. S., Mexico* 24°55N 112°15W **167** J6
Magdalena, Llano de *Baja Calif. S.,*
  Mexico 25°0N 111°25W **167** J7
Magdalena Contreras *Distrito Federal,*
  Mexico 19°20N 99°13W **181** C2
Magdalena de Kino *Sonora, Mexico* 30°38N 110°57W **168** C5
Magdalena Jaltepec *Oaxaca, Mexico* 17°25N 97°13W **177** G3
Magdalena Mts. *N. Mex., U.S.A.* 33°45N 107°15W **131** D3
Magdalena Petlacalco *Distrito Federal,*
  Mexico 19°14N 99°11W **181** C2
Magdalena Tequisistlán *Oaxaca, Mexico* 16°22N 95°45W **177** H5
Magdaleno Cedillo *Tamaulipas, Mexico* 22°48N 99°56W **171** H5
Magee *Miss., U.S.A.* 31°52N 89°44W **111** E4
Maggiore, L. *Tampa, U.S.A.* 27°44N 82°39W **115** C3
Magic Res. *Idaho, U.S.A.* 43°15N 114°22W **122** F4
Magiscatzin *Tamaulipas, Mexico* 22°48N 98°42W **171** H6
Magna *Utah, U.S.A.* 40°42N 112°6W **134** B1
Magnet *Nebr., U.S.A.* 42°27N 97°28W **80** B8
Magnetawan *Ont., Canada* 45°40N 79°39W **146** B7
Magnetic Pole (North) *Canada* 82°42N 114°24W **158** B5
Magnolia *Ark., U.S.A.* 33°16N 93°14W **106** D2
Magnolia *Del., U.S.A.* 39°4N 75°29W **93** A5
Magnolia *Iowa, U.S.A.* 41°42N 95°52W **81** D3
Magnolia *Ky., U.S.A.* 37°27N 85°45W **105** C7
Magnolia *Miss., U.S.A.* 31°9N 90°28W **111** E3
Magnolia *N.C., U.S.A.* 34°54N 78°3W **103** D7
Magnolia *Ohio, U.S.A.* 40°39N 81°18W **86** C5
Magnolia *Tex., U.S.A.* 30°13N 95°45W **109** G12
Magoffin County ☆ *Ky., U.S.A.* 37°45N 83°5W **105** C9
Magog *Qué., Canada* 45°18N 72°9W **145** F10
Magog, L. *Qué., Canada* 45°18N 72°9W **89** A2
Magozal *Veracruz, Mexico* 21°34N 97°59W **176** D3
Magpie → *Ont., Canada* 50°19N 64°30W **140** C5
Magpie *Ont., Canada* 47°56N 84°50W **149** E12
Magpie → *Qué., Canada* 50°19N 64°27W **140** C5
Magpie, L. *Qué., Canada* 51°0N 64°41W **140** B5
Magpie Ouest → *Qué., Canada* 52°0N 65°0W **143** C5
Magrath *Alta., Canada* 49°25N 112°50W **153** A8
Maguarichic *Chihuahua, Mexico* 27°50N 108°0W **169** F8
Maguey, Cerro el *Guerrero, Mexico* 17°15N 98°51W **175** E9
Magueyal *Coahuila, Mexico* 27°7N 102°51W **170** C2
Maguse L. *Nunavut, Canada* 61°37N 95°10W **159** E6
Maguse Pt. *Nunavut, Canada* 61°20N 93°50W **159** E7
Mahaffey *Pa., U.S.A.* 40°53N 78°44W **87** D4
Mahanoy City *Pa., U.S.A.* 40°49N 76°9W **87** D6
Mahaska *Kans., U.S.A.* 39°59N 97°20W **82** B6
Mahaska County ☆ *Iowa, U.S.A.* 41°20N 92°40W **81** D6
Mahatta River *B.C., Canada* 50°22N 127°47W **154** E7
Mahnomen *Minn., U.S.A.* 47°19N 95°58W **77** C3
Mahnomen County ☆ *Minn., U.S.A.* 47°20N 95°45W **77** C3
Mahogany Mts. *Oreg., U.S.A.* 43°14N 117°15W **121** D8
Mahomet *Ill., U.S.A.* 40°12N 88°24W **84** C5
Mahone Bay *N.S., Canada* 44°27N 64°23W **141** J5
Mahoning County ☆ *Ohio, U.S.A.* 41°6N 80°48W **86** B6
Mahood Falls *B.C., Canada* 51°50N 120°38W **155** D14
Mahood L. *B.C., Canada* 51°50N 120°23W **155** D14
Mahopac *N.Y., U.S.A.* 41°22N 73°45W **92** A3
Mahtomedi *Minn., U.S.A.* 45°3N 92°57W **94** A4
Maicasagi → *Qué., Canada* 49°58N 76°33W **144** B6
Maida *N. Dak., U.S.A.* 48°58N 98°33W **76** B6
Maiden Rock *Wis., U.S.A.* 44°34N 92°18W **78** D1
Maidstone *Sask., Canada* 53°5N 109°20W **150** B2
Ma'ili *Hawai'i, U.S.A.* 21°25N 158°11W **136** K13
Ma'ili Pt. *Hawai'i, U.S.A.* 21°24N 158°11W **136** K13
Main-à-Dieu *N.S., Canada* 46°0N 59°51W **141** H10
Main Brook *Nfld. & L., Canada* 51°11N 56°1W **142** A4
Main Centre *Sask., Canada* 50°35N 107°21W **150** E4
Main Pass *La., U.S.A.* 29°15N 89°14W **110** E6
Maine □ *U.S.A.* 45°20N 69°0W **90** C5
Maini *Cuba* 20°17N 74°9W **183** B5
Maisi, Pta. de *Cuba* 20°10N 74°10W **183** B5
Maisonnette *N.B., Canada* 47°49N 65°0W **141** F4
Maisonneuve, Parc *Qué., Canada* 45°32N 73°33W **160** A3
Maisonneuve *Qué., Canada* 45°32N 73°33W **160** A3
Maitland *N.S., Canada* 45°19N 63°30W **141** H6
Maitland *Mo., U.S.A.* 40°12N 95°5W **83** A1

Maitland Bridge *N.S., Canada* 44°27N 65°12W **141** J4
Maiz, Is. del *Nic.* 12°15N 83°4W **182** D3
Maizaga *Oaxaca, Mexico* 18°18N 96°34W **177** F4
Majahual *Quintana Roo, Mexico* 18°43N 87°43W **179** D6
Majahual *Sinaloa, Mexico* 22°48N 106°2W **172** E4
Major *Sask., Canada* 51°52N 109°37W **150** D2
Major County ☆ *Okla., U.S.A.* 36°15N 98°30W **107** B5
Majors Place *Nev., U.S.A.* 39°2N 114°35W **128** C6
Makah Indian Reservation *Wash.,*
  U.S.A. 48°23N 124°29W **120** B1
Mākaha *Hawai'i, U.S.A.* 21°29N 158°13W **136** K13
Makahoa Pt. *Hawai'i, U.S.A.* 21°41N 157°56W **136** J14
Makahuena Pt. *Hawai'i, U.S.A.* 21°52N 159°27W **136** B2
Makakilo City *Hawai'i, U.S.A.* 21°22N 158°5W **136** K13
Makanda *Ill., U.S.A.* 37°37N 89°13W **84** F4
Makapu'u Pt. *Hawai'i, U.S.A.* 21°19N 157°39W **136** K14
Makawao *Hawai'i, U.S.A.* 20°52N 156°17W **136** C5
Makkovik *Nfld. & L., Canada* 55°10N 59°10W **143** B6
Makokibatan L. *Ont., Canada* 51°17N 87°20W **149** A9
Makoti *N. Dak., U.S.A.* 47°58N 101°48W **76** C4
Mākua *Hawai'i, U.S.A.* 21°32N 158°13W **136** J13
Mākua Kea'au Forest Reserve *Hawai'i,*
  U.S.A. 21°30N 158°12W **136** J13
Makua Military Reservation *Hawai'i,*
  U.S.A. 21°32N 158°14W **136** J13
Makushin Volcano *Alaska, U.S.A.* 53°53N 166°55W **135** K6
Mala, Pta. *Panama* 7°28N 80°2W **182** E3
Malabar *Fla., U.S.A.* 28°0N 80°34W **114** D8
Malachi *Ont., Canada* 49°56N 94°59W **148** C2
Malad City *Idaho, U.S.A.* 42°12N 112°15W **122** G6
Malae Pt. *Hawai'i, U.S.A.* 20°7N 155°53W **136** C6
Malaga *N. Mex., U.S.A.* 32°14N 104°4W **131** E6
Malaga *Ohio, U.S.A.* 39°51N 81°9W **86** D5
Malakoff *Tex., U.S.A.* 32°10N 96°1W **109** E11
Malartic *Qué., Canada* 48°9N 78°9W **144** C4
Malartic, L. *Qué., Canada* 48°15N 78°5W **144** C4
Malaspina Glacier *Alaska, U.S.A.* 59°50N 140°30W **135** G12
Malcolm *Nebr., U.S.A.* 40°54N 96°52W **80** D9
Malcolm I. *B.C., Canada* 50°38N 127°0W **154** E8
Malcom *Iowa, U.S.A.* 41°43N 92°33W **81** D6
Malden *Ill., U.S.A.* 41°25N 89°22W **84** B4
Malden *Mass., U.S.A.* 42°26N 71°3W **96** A2
Malden *Mo., U.S.A.* 36°34N 89°57W **83** E7
Maldonado, Pta. *Guerrero, Mexico* 16°20N 98°33W **177** H2
Malheur → *Oreg., U.S.A.* 44°4N 116°59W **121** D8
Malheur County ☆ *Oreg., U.S.A.* 43°15N 117°45W **121** D8
Malheur L. *Oreg., U.S.A.* 43°20N 118°48W **121** D7
Malheur Nat. Forest *Oreg., U.S.A.* 44°10N 119°15W **121** C6
Maligne L. *Alta., Canada* 52°40N 117°31W **153** F3
Malin *Oreg., U.S.A.* 42°1N 121°24W **121** E4
Malinalco *Mexico, Mexico* 19°0N 99°26W **175** D8
Malinaltepec *Guerrero, Mexico* 17°3N 98°40W **175** E9
Malinta *Ohio, U.S.A.* 41°19N 84°2W **86** B2
Maljamar *N. Mex., U.S.A.* 32°50N 103°46W **131** E7
Mallaig *Alta., Canada* 54°13N 111°22W **152** D9
Mallard *Iowa, U.S.A.* 42°56N 94°41W **81** C4
Mallery L. *Nunavut, Canada* 63°59N 98°23W **159** E6
Mallorytown *Ont., Canada* 44°29N 75°53W **147** C11
Malmesbury *Ont., Canada* 41°16N 96°43W **80** C9
Malmstrom Air Force Base *Mont.,*
  U.S.A. 47°30N 111°11W **123** C6
Malone *Fla., U.S.A.* 30°57N 85°10W **114** A3
Malone *N.Y., U.S.A.* 44°51N 74°18W **88** A6
Malone *Tenn., U.S.A., Ky., U.S.A.* 35°5N 87°2W **104** C5
Maloney, L. *Nebr., U.S.A.* 41°3N 100°48W **80** C5
Malott *Wash., U.S.A.* 48°17N 119°42W **120** B6
Maloy *Iowa, U.S.A.* 40°40N 94°25W **81** E4
Malpais, The *N. Mex., U.S.A.* 33°43N 105°56W **131** D5
Malpaso *Zacatecas, Mexico* 22°37N 102°46W **173** E8
Malpaso, Presa = Netzahualcóyotl, Presa
  Chiapas, Mexico 17°8N 93°35W **178** B3
Malta *Idaho, U.S.A.* 42°18N 113°22W **122** G5
Malta *Ill., U.S.A.* 41°56N 88°52W **84** B5
Malta *Mont., U.S.A.* 48°21N 107°52W **123** B10
Maltby *Wash., U.S.A.* 47°48N 122°6W **132** B5
Malton *Ont., Canada* 43°42N 79°38W **161** A1
Malvern *Ont., Canada* 43°47N 79°13W **161** A3
Malvern *Ark., U.S.A.* 34°22N 92°49W **106** D3
Malvern *Iowa, U.S.A.* 41°0N 95°35W **81** E3
Malvern *Ohio, U.S.A.* 40°42N 81°11W **86** C5
Malvern *Pa., U.S.A.* 40°2N 75°31W **92** B1
Malverne *N.Y., U.S.A.* 40°40N 73°40W **97** B4
Māmala B. *Hawai'i, U.S.A.* 21°15N 157°55W **136** K14
Mamantel *Campeche, Mexico* 18°33N 91°5W **179** D2
Mamaroneck *N.Y., U.S.A.* 40°57N 73°44W **97** A4
Mamaroneck Harbor *N.Y., U.S.A.* 40°56N 73°42W **97** A4
Mameigwess L. *Ont., Canada* 49°34N 91°49W **148** C5
Mammoth *Ariz., U.S.A.* 32°43N 110°39W **130** E5
Mammoth Cave Nat. Park △ *Ky.,*
  U.S.A. 37°8N 86°13W **104** C6
Mammoth Hot Springs *Wyo., U.S.A.* 44°59N 110°42W **124** B2
Mammoth Lakes *Calif., U.S.A.* 37°39N 118°59W **126** F8
Mammoth Pool Res. *Calif., U.S.A.* 37°20N 119°19W **126** F7
Mammoth Spring *Ark., U.S.A.* 36°30N 91°33W **106** B4
Mamou *La., U.S.A.* 30°38N 92°25W **110** D3
Man *W. Va., U.S.A.* 37°45N 81°53W **102** D3
Mana *Hawai'i, U.S.A.* 22°2N 159°47W **136** A2
Managua *Nic.* 12°6N 86°20W **182** D2
Managua, L. de *Nic.* 12°20N 86°30W **182** D2
Manahawkin *N.J., U.S.A.* 39°42N 74°16W **92** C2
Manalapan *N.J., U.S.A.* 40°15N 74°24W **92** B2
Mānana I. *Hawai'i, U.S.A.* 21°20N 157°40W **136** K14
Manasquan *N.J., U.S.A.* 40°6N 74°2W **92** B2
Manasquan → *N.J., U.S.A.* 40°6N 74°2W **92** B2
Manassa *Colo., U.S.A.* 37°11N 105°56W **125** D5
Manassas *Va., U.S.A.* 38°45N 77°28W **93** B3
Manassas Park *Va., U.S.A.* 38°47N 77°28W **93** B3
Manatee County ☆ *Fla., U.S.A.* 27°30N 82°30W **115** C3
Manati *Puerto Rico* 18°26N 66°29W **184** G16
Manawa *Wis., U.S.A.* 44°28N 88°55W **78** D5
Mancelona *Mich., U.S.A.* 44°54N 85°4W **79** E6
Mancha, Pta. *Veracruz, Mexico* 19°37N 96°22W **176** E4
Manchester *Calif., U.S.A.* 38°58N 123°41W **126** E3
Manchester *Conn., U.S.A.* 41°47N 72°31W **91** C2
Manchester *Ga., U.S.A.* 32°51N 84°37W **113** D2
Manchester *Iowa, U.S.A.* 42°29N 91°27W **81** C71
Manchester *Ky., U.S.A.* 37°9N 83°46W **105** C9
Manchester *Md., U.S.A.* 39°40N 76°53W **93** A4
Manchester *Mich., U.S.A.* 42°9N 84°2W **79** G7
Manchester *N.H., U.S.A.* 42°59N 71°28W **89** B3
Manchester *Ohio, U.S.A.* 38°41N 83°36W **86** E3
Manchester *Okla., U.S.A.* 36°59N 98°2W **107** B5
Manchester *Tenn., U.S.A.* 35°29N 86°5W **104** E6

Manchester *Wash., U.S.A.* 47°33N 122°32W **132** C2
Manchester-by-the-Sea *Mass., U.S.A.* 42°35N 70°46W **91** B4
Manchester Center *Vt., U.S.A.* 43°10N 73°4W **89** C1
Mancos *Colo., U.S.A.* 37°21N 108°18W **125** E2
Mandan *N. Dak., U.S.A.* 46°50N 100°54W **76** D5
Mandaree *N. Dak., U.S.A.* 47°43N 102°41W **76** C3
Manderson *Wyo., U.S.A.* 44°16N 107°58W **124** B5
Mandeville *La., U.S.A.* 30°22N 90°4W **110** D5
Mandinga, L. *Veracruz, Mexico* 19°0N 96°4W **177** F4
Maneadero = Rodolfo Sánchez Taboada
  Baja Calif., Mexico 31°45N 116°35W **166** B2
Mangham *La., U.S.A.* 32°19N 91°47W **110** B4
Mango *Fla., U.S.A.* 27°59N 82°18W **114** D6
Mangohick *Va., U.S.A.* 37°49N 77°16W **93** C3
Mangum *Okla., U.S.A.* 34°53N 99°30W **107** D4
Manhasset *N.Y., U.S.A.* 40°47N 73°42W **97** B4
Manhasset Bay *N.Y., U.S.A.* 40°50N 73°43W **97** B4
Manhasset Hills *N.Y., U.S.A.* 40°45N 73°40W **97** B4
Manhattan *Kans., U.S.A.* 39°11N 96°35W **82** B7
Manhattan *Mont., U.S.A.* 45°51N 111°20W **123** E6
Manhattan *Nev., U.S.A.* 38°32N 117°4W **128** D3
Manhattan *New York, U.S.A.* **96** d2
Manhattan Beach *Calif., U.S.A.* 33°53N 118°25W **133** D2
Manic 2, Rés. *Qué., Canada* 49°30N 68°24W **145** B14
Manic 3, Rés. *Qué., Canada* 50°0N 68°40W **145** B14
Manicouagan → *Qué., Canada* 49°30N 68°30W **145** B14
Manicouagan, Rés. *Qué., Canada* 51°5N 68°40W **143** C4
Manifest *La., U.S.A.* 31°43N 91°58W **110** C4
Manigotagan *Man., Canada* 51°6N 96°18W **151** D15
Manigotagan L. *Man., Canada* 50°52N 95°37W **151** E16
Maniitsoq *Greenland* 65°26N 52°55W **162** D5
Manila *Ark., U.S.A.* 35°53N 90°10W **106** C5
Manila *Utah, U.S.A.* 40°59N 109°43W **129** C6
Manilla *Iowa, U.S.A.* 41°53N 95°14W **81** D3
Maninel, Volcan *Distrito Federal, Mexico* 19°14N 99°12W **181** C2
Manistee *Mich., U.S.A.* 44°15N 86°19W **79** E5
Manistee → *Mich., U.S.A.* 44°15N 86°21W **79** E5
Manistee County ☆ *Mich., U.S.A.* 44°20N 86°10W **79** E5
Manistee Nat. Forest *Mich., U.S.A.* 44°0N 86°0W **79** E5
Manistique *Mich., U.S.A.* 45°57N 86°15W **79** D5
Manistique → *Mich., U.S.A.* 45°57N 86°15W **79** D5
Manistique L. *Mich., U.S.A.* 46°15N 85°46W **79** C6
Manito *Ill., U.S.A.* 40°26N 89°47W **84** C4
Manitoba □ *Man., Canada* 53°30N 97°0W **151** B14
Manitoba, L. *Man., Canada* 51°0N 98°45W **151** E13
Manitou *Man., Canada* 49°15N 98°32W **151** F13
Manitou *Qué., Canada* 50°18N 65°15W **140** C4
Manitou *Okla., U.S.A.* 34°30N 98°59W **107** D5
Manitou → *Qué., Canada* 50°18N 65°15W **140** C4
Manitou, L. *Ont., Canada* 45°51N 82°0W **146** B3
Manitou, L. *Qué., Canada* 50°55N 65°17W **143** C4
Manitou Beach *Mich., U.S.A.* 41°58N 84°19W **79** H7
Manitou I. *Mich., U.S.A.* 47°25N 87°37W **79** B4
Manitou Springs *Colo., U.S.A.* 38°52N 104°55W **125** D6
Manitoulin I. *Ont., Canada* 45°40N 82°30W **146** B4
Manitouwadge *Ont., Canada* 49°8N 85°48W **149** C11
Manitowaning *Ont., Canada* 45°46N 81°49W **146** B5
Manitowish *Wis., U.S.A.* 46°8N 90°0W **78** B3
Manitowish Waters *Wis., U.S.A.* 46°9N 89°53W **78** B4
Manitowoc *Wis., U.S.A.* 44°5N 87°40W **78** D6
Manitowoc County ☆ *Wis., U.S.A.* 44°10N 87°50W **78** D6
Maniwaki *Qué., Canada* 46°23N 75°58W **144** E7
Mankato *Kans., U.S.A.* 39°47N 98°13W **82** B5
Mankato *Minn., U.S.A.* 44°10N 94°0W **77** F4
Mankota *Sask., Canada* 49°25N 107°5W **150** F4
Manley *Nebr., U.S.A.* 40°55N 96°10W **80** D9
Manley Hot Springs *Alaska, U.S.A.* 65°0N 150°38W **135** D10
Manlio Fabio Altamirano *Veracruz,*
  Mexico 19°5N 96°19W **177** F4
Manlius *Ill., U.S.A.* 41°27N 89°40W **84** B4
Manlius *N.Y., U.S.A.* 43°0N 75°59W **88** C5
Manly *Iowa, U.S.A.* 43°17N 93°12W **81** B5
Mann, L. *Fla., U.S.A.* 28°32N 81°35W **115** A2
Mannford *Okla., U.S.A.* 36°8N 96°24W **107** B7
Manning *Alta., Canada* 56°53N 117°39W **152** B3
Manning *Iowa, U.S.A.* 41°55N 95°3W **81** D3
Manning *N. Dak., U.S.A.* 47°14N 102°46W **76** C3
Manning *S.C., U.S.A.* 33°42N 80°13W **103** E5
Manning Park *B.C., Canada* 49°4N 120°47W **155** F14
Mannington *W. Va., U.S.A.* 39°32N 80°21W **102** B4
Mann's Chinese Theatre *Calif., U.S.A.* 34°6N 118°20W **133** B2
Manns Harbor *N.C., U.S.A.* 35°53N 75°46W **103** C10
Mannsville *N.Y., U.S.A.* 43°43N 76°4W **88** B4
Mannville *Alta., Canada* 53°20N 111°10W **152** E9
Manokin *Md., U.S.A.* 38°5N 75°55W **93** B5
Manokotak *Alaska, U.S.A.* 58°58N 159°3W **135** G8
Manor *Sask., Canada* 49°36N 102°5W **151** F19
Manorhaven *N.Y., U.S.A.* 40°50N 73°42W **97** A4
Manotick *Ont., Canada* 45°13N 75°41W **147** B11
Manouane *Qué., Canada* 47°13N 74°23W **145** D8
Manouane, L. *Qué., Canada* 50°45N 70°45W **143** C4
Manouane, L. *Qué., Canada* 47°33N 74°6W **145** D8
Manseau *Qué., Canada* 46°22N 72°0W **145** E11
Mansel I. *Nunavut, Canada* 62°0N 80°0W **159** E10
Mansfield *Ark., U.S.A.* 35°4N 94°15W **106** C1
Mansfield *Conn., U.S.A.* 41°46N 72°14W **91** C2
Mansfield *Ga., U.S.A.* 33°31N 83°44W **113** C3
Mansfield *Ill., U.S.A.* 40°13N 88°31W **84** C5
Mansfield *La., U.S.A.* 32°2N 93°43W **110** B2
Mansfield *Mass., U.S.A.* 42°2N 71°13W **91** B3
Mansfield *Mo., U.S.A.* 37°6N 92°35W **83** D4
Mansfield *Ohio, U.S.A.* 40°45N 82°31W **86** C4
Mansfield *Pa., U.S.A.* 41°48N 77°5W **87** C5
Mansfield *S. Dak., U.S.A.* 45°13N 98°18W **76** D6
Mansfield *Tex., U.S.A.* 36°11N 88°17W **104** D4
Mansfield *Wash., U.S.A.* 47°49N 119°38W **120** C6
Mansfield, Mt. *Vt., U.S.A.* 44°33N 72°49W **89** B2
Mansfield Hollow L. *Conn., U.S.A.* 41°45N 72°11W **91** C2
Manson *Iowa, U.S.A.* 42°32N 94°32W **81** C4
Manson *Wash., U.S.A.* 47°53N 120°9W **120** C5
Mansura *La., U.S.A.* 31°4N 92°3W **110** C3
Mantador *N. Dak., U.S.A.* 46°10N 96°59W **76** D9
Manteca *Calif., U.S.A.* 37°48N 121°13W **126** F5
Mantee *Miss., U.S.A.* 33°44N 89°3W **111** C4
Manteno *Ill., U.S.A.* 41°15N 87°50W **84** B6
Manteo *N.C., U.S.A.* 35°55N 75°40W **103** C10
Manter *Kans., U.S.A.* 37°31N 101°53W **82** D2
Manti *Utah, U.S.A.* 39°16N 111°38W **129** D8
Manti-la Sal Nat. Forest *Utah, U.S.A.* 39°30N 109°50W **129** C6
Mantoloking *N.J., U.S.A.* 40°4N 74°4W **92** B2
Manton *Mich., U.S.A.* 44°25N 85°24W **79** E6

Mantorville Minn., U.S.A. 44°5N 92°45W 77 F6
Mantua Ohio, U.S.A. 41°17N 81°14W 86 B5
Mantua Utah, U.S.A. 41°30N 111°57W 129 B4
Manu'a Is. Amer. Samoa 14°13S 169°35W 184 f
Manuel Tamaulipas, Mexico 22°44N 98°19W 171 H6
Manuel Benavides Chihuahua, Mexico 29°8N 103°55W 169 D12
Manuel Doblado Guanajuato, Mexico 20°44N 101°56W 174 B6
Manuel M. Diéguez Jalisco, Mexico 19°35N 102°55W 174 C5
Manuelito N. Mex., U.S.A. 35°24N 109°0W 131 B2
Manuels N.B., Canada 47°3N 64°59W 141 F5
Manvel N. Dak., U.S.A. 48°5N 97°11W 76 B8
Manvel Tex., U.S.A. 29°28N 95°21W 109 H12
Manville N.J., U.S.A. 40°33N 74°35W 92 B2
Manville Wyo., U.S.A. 42°47N 104°37W 124 D8
Many La., U.S.A. 31°34N 93°29W 110 C2
Many Farms Ariz., U.S.A. 36°21N 109°37W 130 A6
Many Island L. Alta., Canada 50°8N 110°3W 153 H10
Manyberries Alta., Canada 49°24N 110°42W 153 J10
Manzanar Nat. Historic Site △ Calif., U.S.A. 36°44N 118°9W 127 G8
Manzanillo Cuba 20°20N 77°31W 182 B4
Manzanillo Colima, Mexico 19°3N 104°20W 174 C3
Manzanillo, B. de Colima, Mexico 19°1N 104°27W 174 C3
Manzanillo, Pta. Panama 9°30N 79°40W 182 E4
Manzanita Oreg., U.S.A. 45°43N 123°56W 121 B2
Manzano Indian Reservation Calif., U.S.A. 32°45N 116°20W 127 L10
Manzano Mts. N. Mex., U.S.A. 34°40N 106°20W 131 C4
Manzanola Colo., U.S.A. 38°6N 103°52W 125 D7
Mapastepec Chiapas, Mexico 15°26N 92°54W 178 D4
Mapimí Durango, Mexico 25°49N 103°51W 173 B7
Mapimí, Bolsón de Mexico 27°0N 104°15W 169 G11
Maple → Iowa, U.S.A. 42°0N 95°59W 81 C3
Maple → Mich., U.S.A. 42°59N 84°57W 79 G7
Maple → N. Dak., U.S.A. 46°56N 96°55W 76 D9
Maple → S. Dak., U.S.A. 45°48N 98°38W 76 E7
Maple Bay B.C., Canada 48°48N 123°37W 155 G11
Maple Creek Sask., Canada 49°55N 109°29W 150 F2
Maple Falls Wash., U.S.A. 48°56N 122°5W 120 B3
Maple Heights Ohio, U.S.A. 41°24N 81°33W 98 B2
Maple Hill Kans., U.S.A. 39°5N 96°2W 82 B7
Maple Rapids Mich., U.S.A. 43°6N 84°42W 79 F7
Maple Shade N.J., U.S.A. 39°57N 74°58W 92 C2
Maplesville Ala., U.S.A. 32°47N 86°52W 112 D4
Mapleton Iowa, U.S.A. 42°10N 95°47W 81 C3
Mapleton Kans., U.S.A. 38°1N 94°53W 82 C9
Mapleton Minn., U.S.A. 43°56N 93°57W 77 G5
Mapleton N. Dak., U.S.A. 46°53N 97°3W 76 D8
Mapleton Oreg., U.S.A. 44°2N 123°52W 121 C2
Mapleton Utah, U.S.A. 40°8N 111°35W 129 C4
Maplewood B.C., Canada 49°18N 123°0W 161 B2
Maplewood Minn., U.S.A. 44°59N 93°1W 94 A3
Maplewood Mo., U.S.A. 38°36N 90°19W 94 B1
Maplewood N.J., U.S.A. 40°44N 74°16W 97 B1
Maquoketa Iowa, U.S.A. 42°4N 90°40W 81 C8
Maquoketa → Iowa, U.S.A. 42°11N 90°19W 81 C8
Maquon Ill., U.S.A. 40°48N 90°10W 84 D6
Mar-Mac N.C., U.S.A. 35°20N 78°3W 103 C7
Mar Negro, L. Tamaulipas, Mexico 25°53N 97°9W 171 E9
Marais des Cygnes → U.S.A. 38°3N 94°17W 82 C9
Maramec Okla., U.S.A. 36°15N 96°41W 107 B7
Marana Ariz., U.S.A. 32°27N 111°13W 130 E4
Marathon Ont., Canada 48°44N 86°23W 149 D10
Marathon Fla., U.S.A. 24°43N 81°5W 114 G7
Marathon Iowa, U.S.A. 42°52N 94°59W 81 C4
Marathon N.Y., U.S.A. 42°27N 76°2W 88 C4
Marathon Tex., U.S.A. 30°12N 103°15W 108 G4
Marathon City Wis., U.S.A. 44°56N 89°50W 78 D4
Marathon County ☆ Wis., U.S.A. 44°50N 89°45W 78 D4
Maravatío Michoacan, Mexico 19°54N 100°27W 175 C7
Maravillas Chihuahua, Mexico 27°22N 104°29W 169 F11
Maravillas Cr. → Tex., U.S.A. 29°34N 102°47W 108 H5
Marble Ark., U.S.A. 36°8N 93°35W 106 B2
Marble Colo., U.S.A. 39°4N 107°12W 125 C3
Marble Canyon Ariz., U.S.A. 36°49N 111°38W 130 A4
Marble City Okla., U.S.A. 35°35N 94°49W 107 C9
Marble Falls Tex., U.S.A. 30°35N 98°16W 109 F8
Marble Hill Mo., U.S.A. 37°18N 89°58W 83 D7
Marble I. Nunavut, Canada 62°41N 91°8W 159 E7
Marble Range Park △ B.C., Canada 51°11N 121°49W 155 D13
Marble Rock Iowa, U.S.A. 42°58N 92°52W 81 C6
Marbled B.C., Canada 50°15N 116°58W 155 E18
Marblehead Mass., U.S.A. 42°29N 70°51W 91 B4
Marblehead Ohio, U.S.A. 41°32N 82°44W 86 B4
Marblemount Wash., U.S.A. 48°32N 121°26W 120 B3
Marbleton Wyo., U.S.A. 42°34N 110°7W 124 D2
Marbury Md., U.S.A. 38°35N 77°10W 93 B3
Marceau, L. Qué., Canada 51°25N 66°48W 140 B3
Marcelin Sask., Canada 52°55N 106°47W 150 C5
Marceline Mo., U.S.A. 39°43N 92°57W 83 B4
Marcellus Mich., U.S.A. 42°2N 85°49W 79 G6
Marcellus N.Y., U.S.A. 42°59N 76°20W 88 C4
Marcellus Wash., U.S.A. 47°14N 118°24W 120 C7
Marco Island Fla., U.S.A. 25°58N 81°44W 114 F7
Marcola Oreg., U.S.A. 44°10N 122°52W 121 C3
Marcus Iowa, U.S.A. 42°50N 95°48W 81 C3
Marcus Wash., U.S.A. 48°40N 118°4W 120 B7
Marcus Baker, Mt. Alaska, U.S.A. 61°26N 147°45W 135 F11
Marcy, Mt. N.Y., U.S.A. 44°7N 73°56W 88 A7
Mardela Springs Md., U.S.A. 38°28N 75°45W 93 B5
Marengo Sask., Canada 51°29N 109°47W 150 D2
Marengo Ill., U.S.A. 42°15N 88°37W 84 A5
Marengo Ind., U.S.A. 38°22N 86°21W 85 E4
Marengo Iowa, U.S.A. 41°48N 92°4W 81 D61
Marengo Ohio, U.S.A. 40°24N 82°49W 86 C4
Marengo Wash., U.S.A. 47°1N 118°12W 120 C7
Marengo County ☆ Ala., U.S.A. 32°18N 87°48W 112 D3
Marenisco Mich., U.S.A. 46°23N 89°45W 79 C2
Marfa Tex., U.S.A. 30°19N 104°1W 108 G2
Margaree Forks N.S., Canada 46°20N 61°5W 141 G8
Margaret Bay B.C., Canada 51°21N 127°35W 154 D7
Margaretville N.Y., U.S.A. 42°9N 74°39W 88 C6
Margate Fla., U.S.A. 26°15N 80°12W 114 E8
Margate City N.J., U.S.A. 39°20N 74°30W 92 D2
Margo Sask., Canada 51°49N 103°20W 150 D8
Marguerite B.C., Canada 52°30N 122°25W 155 C12
Maria Qué., Canada 48°10N 65°59W 140 E4
María Cleofas, I. Nayarit, Mexico 21°16N 106°14W 172 F4
María Lombardo de Caso Oaxaca, Mexico 17°27N 95°27W 177 G5
María Madre, I. Nayarit, Mexico 21°35N 106°32W 172 F4
María Magdalena, I. Nayarit, Mexico 21°25N 106°24W 172 F4
Marian, L. Fla., U.S.A. 27°53N 81°6W 114 D7
Mariana Islands N. Marianas 15°15N 145°48E 184 a

Mariana Trench Pac. Oc. 13°0N 145°0E 184 a
Marianna Ark., U.S.A. 34°46N 90°46W 106 D5
Marianna Fla., U.S.A. 30°46N 85°14W 114 A3
Marianna Pa., U.S.A. 40°2N 80°6W 87 D2
Marias → Mont., U.S.A. 47°56N 110°30W 123 C7
Marías, Is. Nayarit, Mexico 21°25N 106°28W 172 F4
Mariato, Punta Panama 7°12N 80°52W 182 E3
Maricao Puerto Rico 18°11N 66°59W 184 G16
Maricopa Ariz., U.S.A. 33°4N 112°3W 130 D3
Maricopa Calif., U.S.A. 35°4N 119°24W 127 H7
Maricopa County ☆ Ariz., U.S.A. 33°15N 112°30W 130 D3
Maricopa Indian Reservation Ariz., U.S.A. 33°0N 112°1W 130 E3
Maricopa Mts. Ariz., U.S.A. 33°0N 112°30W 130 E3
Maricopa Village Ariz., U.S.A. 33°22N 112°14W 134 C1
Maricourt Qué., Canada 56°34N 70°49W 143 B3
Marie-Galante Guadeloupe 15°56N 61° 6W 183 C7
Marie L. Alta., Canada 54°38N 110°18W 152 D10
Mariecourt = Kangiqsujuaq Qué., Canada 61°30N 72°0W 143 A3
Marienthal Kans., U.S.A. 38°29N 101°13W 82 C2
Marienville Pa., U.S.A. 41°28N 79°8W 87 C3
Maries → Mo., U.S.A. 38°30N 92°1W 83 C4
Maries County ☆ Mo., U.S.A. 38°10N 91°55W 83 C5
Marietta Ga., U.S.A. 33°57N 84°33W 113 C2
Marietta Miss., U.S.A. 34°30N 88°28W 111 B5
Marietta Ohio, U.S.A. 39°25N 81°27W 86 D5
Marietta Okla., U.S.A. 33°56N 97°7W 107 E6
Marietta S.C., U.S.A. 35°1N 82°30W 103 C3
Marietta Wash., U.S.A. 48°47N 122°35W 120 B3
Marieville Qué., Canada 45°26N 73°10W 145 F9
Marín Nuevo León, Mexico 25°52N 100°3W 170 E4
Marin City Calif., U.S.A. 37°52N 122°30W 132 A1
Marin County ☆ Calif., U.S.A. 38°0N 122°45W 126 E4
Marin Pen. Calif., U.S.A. 37°50N 122°30W 132 A1
Marina Calif., U.S.A. 36°41N 121°43W 126 G5
Marina del Rey Calif., U.S.A. 33°58N 118°27W 133 C2
Marine Ill., U.S.A. 38°47N 89°47W 84 E4
Marine on St. Croix Minn., U.S.A. 45°12N 92°46W 77 E6
Marine Park N.Y., U.S.A. 40°36N 73°55W 97 C3
Marineland Fla., U.S.A. 29°40N 81°13W 114 B7
Mariners Harbor N.Y., U.S.A. 40°38N 74°9W 97 C2
Marinette Wis., U.S.A. 45°6N 87°38W 78 C6
Marinette County ☆ Wis., U.S.A. 45°25N 88°10W 78 C5
Maringouin La., U.S.A. 30°29N 91°3W 110 D4
Marion Ala., U.S.A. 32°38N 87°19W 112 D3
Marion Ark., U.S.A. 35°13N 90°12W 106 C5
Marion Idaho, U.S.A. 42°17N 113°55W 122 G5
Marion Ill., U.S.A. 37°44N 88°56W 84 F5
Marion Ind., U.S.A. 40°32N 85°40W 85 C5
Marion Iowa, U.S.A. 42°2N 91°36W 81 C71
Marion Kans., U.S.A. 38°21N 97°1W 82 C6
Marion Ky., U.S.A. 37°20N 88°5W 104 C4
Marion La., U.S.A. 32°54N 92°15W 110 B3
Marion Mass., U.S.A. 41°42N 70°46W 91 C4
Marion Md., U.S.A. 38°2N 75°46W 93 B5
Marion Mich., U.S.A. 44°6N 85°9W 79 E6
Marion Miss., U.S.A. 32°25N 88°39W 111 D5
Marion Mont., U.S.A. 48°6N 114°40W 123 B3
Marion N.C., U.S.A. 35°41N 82°1W 103 C3
Marion N. Dak., U.S.A. 46°37N 98°2W 76 D7
Marion Nebr., U.S.A. 40°1N 100°23W 80 D5
Marion Ohio, U.S.A. 40°35N 83°8W 86 C3
Marion S.C., U.S.A. 34°11N 79°24W 103 D6
Marion S. Dak., U.S.A. 43°25N 97°16W 76 G8
Marion Va., U.S.A. 36°50N 81°31W 102 E3
Marion Wis., U.S.A. 44°39N 88°54W 78 D5
Marion, L. S.C., U.S.A. 33°28N 80°10W 103 E5
Marion County ☆ Ala., U.S.A. 34°9N 87°59W 112 B3
Marion County ☆ Ark., U.S.A. 36°14N 92°41W 106 B3
Marion County ☆ Fla., U.S.A. 29°15N 82°0W 114 B7
Marion County ☆ Ga., U.S.A. 32°25N 84°35W 113 D2
Marion County ☆ Ill., U.S.A. 38°40N 88°55W 84 E5
Marion County ☆ Ind., U.S.A. 39°45N 86°10W 85 D4
Marion County ☆ Iowa, U.S.A. 41°20N 93°5W 81 D5
Marion County ☆ Kans., U.S.A. 38°20N 97°0W 82 C6
Marion County ☆ Ky., U.S.A. 37°30N 85°15W 105 C7
Marion County ☆ Miss., U.S.A. 31°15N 89°50W 111 E4
Marion County ☆ Mo., U.S.A. 39°50N 91°35W 83 B5
Marion County ☆ Ohio, U.S.A. 40°35N 83°8W 86 C3
Marion County ☆ Oreg., U.S.A. 44°50N 122°50W 121 C3
Marion County ☆ S.C., U.S.A. 34°10N 79°20W 103 D6
Marion County ☆ Tenn., U.S.A. 35°5N 85°38W 105 E7
Marion County ☆ Tex., U.S.A. 32°46N 94°21W 109 E13
Marion County ☆ W. Va., U.S.A. 39°29N 80°9W 102 B4
Marion Junction Ala., U.S.A. 32°26N 87°14W 112 D3
Marion Lake Kans., U.S.A. 38°22N 97°5W 82 C6
Marionville Mo., U.S.A. 37°0N 93°38W 83 E3
Mariposa Calif., U.S.A. 37°29N 119°58W 126 F7
Mariposa County ☆ Calif., U.S.A. 37°30N 120°0W 126 F7
Mariscala Oaxaca, Mexico 17°53N 98°7W 177 G2
Marissa Ill., U.S.A. 38°15N 89°45W 84 E4
Mark Twain L. Mo., U.S.A. 39°28N 91°55W 83 B5
Mark Twain Nat. Forest △ Mo., U.S.A. 36°50N 92°0W 83 E5
Mark Twain Nat. Wildlife Refuge △ Iowa, U.S.A. 41°17N 91°6W 81 D7
Markdale Ont., Canada 44°19N 80°39W 146 C6
Marked Tree Ark., U.S.A. 35°32N 90°25W 106 C5
Markerville Alta., Canada 52°7N 114°10W 153 F6
Markesan Wis., U.S.A. 43°42N 88°59W 78 E5
Markham Ont., Canada 43°52N 79°16W 161 A3
Markham Tex., U.S.A. 28°58N 96°4W 109 J11
Markland Wood Ont., Canada 43°38N 79°34W 161 B1
Markle Ind., U.S.A. 40°50N 85°20W 85 C5
Markleeville Calif., U.S.A. 38°42N 119°47W 126 E7
Markleville Ind., U.S.A. 39°59N 85°37W 85 D5
Markleysburg Pa., U.S.A. 39°44N 79°27W 87 E3
Marks Miss., U.S.A. 34°16N 90°16W 111 B3
Marks Butte Colo., U.S.A. 40°53N 102°23W 125 B8
Markstay Ont., Canada 46°29N 80°32W 146 A6
Marksville La., U.S.A. 31°8N 92°4W 110 C3
Marland Okla., U.S.A. 36°34N 97°9W 107 B6
Marlbank Ont., Canada 44°26N 77°6W 147 C9
Marlboro N.J., U.S.A. 40°19N 74°15W 92 B2
Marlboro N.Y., U.S.A. 41°36N 73°59W 97 A5
Marlboro County ☆ S.C., U.S.A. 34°40N 79°40W 103 D6
Marlborough Conn., U.S.A. 41°38N 72°27W 91 C2
Marlborough Mass., U.S.A. 42°21N 71°33W 91 B3
Marlborough Mo., U.S.A. 30°34N 90°20W 94 B1
Marlborough N.H., U.S.A. 42°54N 72°13W 89 D2
Marlette Mich., U.S.A. 43°20N 83°5W 79 F8
Marlin Tex., U.S.A. 31°18N 96°54W 109 F11
Marlin Wash., U.S.A. 47°25N 119°6W 120 C6
Marlow Ga., U.S.A. 32°16N 81°23W 113 D5

Marlow N.H., U.S.A. 43°9N 72°12W 89 C2
Marlow Okla., U.S.A. 34°39N 97°58W 107 D6
Marlton N.J., U.S.A. 39°54N 74°55W 92 C2
Marmaduke Ark., U.S.A. 36°11N 90°23W 106 B5
Marmarth N. Dak., U.S.A. 46°18N 103°54W 76 D2
Marmora Ont., Canada 44°28N 77°41W 147 C9
Marmora Ont., Canada 39°16N 74°39W 92 D2
Marne Iowa, U.S.A. 41°27N 95°6W 81 D3
Maro Reef Hawai'i, U.S.A. 25°25N 170°35W 136 F9
Maroa Ill., U.S.A. 40°2N 88°57W 84 D5
Maroma, Pta. Quintana Roo, Mexico 20°44N 86°58W 179 B7
Marpole B.C., Canada 49°12N 123°8W 161 B2
Marquand Mo., U.S.A. 37°26N 90°10W 83 D6
Marquelia Guerrero, Mexico 16°36N 98°48W 175 F9
Marqués de Comillas, Parque Natural △ Chiapas, Mexico 16°16N 90°39W 178 C6
Marquesas Keys Fla., U.S.A. 24°35N 82°10W 114 G6
Marquette Man., Canada 50°4N 97°44W 151 E14
Marquette Iowa, U.S.A. 43°3N 91°11W 81 B7
Marquette Kans., U.S.A. 38°33N 97°50W 82 C6
Marquette Nebr., U.S.A. 41°0N 98°1W 80 D7
Marquette Mich., U.S.A. 46°33N 87°24W 79 C4
Marquette, L. Qué., Canada 48°54N 73°54W 145 C9
Marquette County ☆ Mich., U.S.A. 46°20N 87°30W 79 C4
Marquette County ☆ Wis., U.S.A. 43°50N 89°25W 78 E4
Marquette I. Mich., U.S.A. 45°58N 84°24W 79 D7
Marquette Park Ill., U.S.A. 41°46N 87°42W 98 C1
Marquez Tex., U.S.A. 31°14N 96°15W 109 F11
Marrero La., U.S.A. 29°53N 90°6W 117 C2
Marrowbone Ky., U.S.A. 36°50N 85°30W 105 D7
Mars Pa., U.S.A. 40°42N 80°1W 87 D2
Mars Hill Maine, U.S.A. 46°31N 67°52W 90 B6
Mars Hill N.C., U.S.A. 35°50N 82°33W 103 C3
Marsden Sask., Canada 52°52N 109°49W 150 C2
Marseilles Ill., U.S.A. 41°20N 88°43W 84 B5
Marseilles Ohio, U.S.A. 40°42N 83°24W 86 C3
Marsh I., La., U.S.A. 29°34N 91°53W 110 E4
Marsh Pass Ariz., U.S.A. 36°36N 110°35W 130 A5
Marsh Peak Utah, U.S.A. 40°43N 109°50W 129 C6
Marsha, L. Fla., U.S.A. 28°29N 81°29W 115 B2
Marshall Sask., Canada 53°11N 109°47W 150 C2
Marshall Alaska, U.S.A. 61°53N 162°5W 135 F7
Marshall Ark., U.S.A. 35°55N 92°38W 106 C3
Marshall Ill., U.S.A. 39°23N 87°42W 84 D6
Marshall Ind., U.S.A. 39°51N 87°11W 85 D3
Marshall Mich., U.S.A. 42°16N 84°58W 79 G7
Marshall Minn., U.S.A. 44°27N 95°47W 77 F3
Marshall Mo., U.S.A. 39°7N 93°12W 83 B3
Marshall N.C., U.S.A. 35°48N 82°41W 103 C3
Marshall Okla., U.S.A. 36°9N 97°38W 107 B6
Marshall Tex., U.S.A. 32°33N 94°23W 109 E13
Marshall Va., U.S.A. 38°52N 77°51W 93 B3
Marshall County ☆ Ala., U.S.A. 34°21N 86°18W 112 B4
Marshall County ☆ Ill., U.S.A. 41°0N 89°20W 84 B4
Marshall County ☆ Ind., U.S.A. 41°20N 86°15W 85 B4
Marshall County ☆ Iowa, U.S.A. 42°0N 93°0W 81 D5
Marshall County ☆ Kans., U.S.A. 39°45N 96°30W 82 B7
Marshall County ☆ Ky., U.S.A. 36°55N 88°20W 104 D4
Marshall County ☆ Minn., U.S.A. 48°15N 96°15W 77 B2
Marshall County ☆ Miss., U.S.A. 34°46N 89°27W 111 A4
Marshall County ☆ Okla., U.S.A. 34°0N 96°50W 107 D7
Marshall County ☆ S. Dak., U.S.A. 45°48N 97°45W 76 E8
Marshall County ☆ Tenn., U.S.A. 35°28N 86°48W 104 E6
Marshall County ☆ W. Va., U.S.A. 39°50N 80°34W 102 B4
Marshallberg N.C., U.S.A. 34°44N 76°31W 103 D9
Marshalltown Iowa, U.S.A. 42°3N 92°55W 81 C61
Marshallville Ga., U.S.A. 32°27N 83°56W 113 D3
Marshallville Ohio, U.S.A. 40°54N 81°44W 86 C5
Marshfield = Coos Bay Oreg., U.S.A. 43°22N 124°13W 121 D1
Marshfield Mo., U.S.A. 37°15N 92°54W 83 D41
Marshfield Vt., U.S.A. 44°20N 72°20W 89 B2
Marshfield Wis., U.S.A. 44°40N 90°10W 78 D3
Marshfield Hills Mass., U.S.A. 42°9N 70°44W 91 B4
Marshville N.C., U.S.A. 35°0N 80°25W 103 C5
Marshyhope → Md., U.S.A. 38°32N 75°45W 93 B5
Marsing Idaho, U.S.A. 43°33N 116°48W 122 F2
Marsoui Qué., Canada 49°13N 66°4W 140 D2
Marston Mo., U.S.A. 36°31N 89°37W 83 E7
Marston L. Colo., U.S.A. 39°38N 105°3W 134 C1
Mart Tex., U.S.A. 31°33N 96°50W 109 F11
Marte R. Gomez, Presa Tamaulipas, Mexico 26°10N 99°0W 170 D6
Martelle Iowa, U.S.A. 42°1N 91°22W 81 C7
Marten River Ont., Canada 46°44N 79°49W 146 A7
Martensdale Iowa, U.S.A. 41°23N 93°45W 81 D5
Martha Lake Wash., U.S.A. 47°50N 122°14W 132 A4
Martha's Vineyard Mass., U.S.A. 41°25N 70°38W 91 C4
Marthasville Mo. U.S.A. 38°38N 91°4W 83 C5
Marthaville La., U.S.A. 31°44N 93°24W 110 C2
Martin Ky., U.S.A. 37°34N 82°45W 105 C10
Martin La., U.S.A. 32°5N 93°13W 110 B2
Martin Mich., U.S.A. 42°32N 85°39W 79 G6
Martin N. Dak., U.S.A. 47°50N 100°7W 76 C5
Martin S. Dak., U.S.A. 43°11N 101°44W 76 G3
Martin Tenn., U.S.A. 36°21N 88°51W 104 D41
Martin County ☆ Fla., U.S.A. 27°10N 80°20W 114 D8
Martin County ☆ Ind., U.S.A. 38°40N 86°50W 85 E4
Martin County ☆ Ky., U.S.A. 37°45N 82°30W 105 C10
Martin County ☆ Minn., U.S.A. 43°40N 94°30W 77 G4
Martin County ☆ N.C., U.S.A. 35°45N 77°0W 103 C8
Martin County ☆ Tex., U.S.A. 32°18N 101°58W 108 E5
Martin L. Ala., U.S.A. 32°41N 85°55W 112 D5
Martin Luther King Nat. Historic Site △ Georgia, U.S.A. 33°45N 84°22W 117 B2
Martin Pt. Alaska, U.S.A. 70°8N 143°16W 135 A12
Martin Van Buren Nat. Historic Site △ N.Y., U.S.A. 42°23N 73°42W 88 C7
Martinecock N.Y. U.S.A. 40°51N 73°35W 97 A5
Martinez Calif., U.S.A. 38°1N 122°8W 126 E4
Martinez Ga., U.S.A. 33°31N 82°5W 113 C4
Martínez de la Torre Veracruz, Mexico 20°4N 97°3W 176 D2
Martinez Lake Ariz., U.S.A. 32°59N 114°29W 130 E1
Martinique ☒ W. Indies 14°40N 61°0W 183 D7
Martinique Passage W. Indies 15°15N 61°0W 183 D7
Martins Ferry Ohio, U.S.A. 40°6N 80°44W 86 C6
Martinsburg Md., U.S.A. 39°10N 77°28W 93 A3
Martinsburg Mo., U.S.A. 39°5N 91°39W 83 B5
Martinsburg Nebr., U.S.A. 42°30N 96°50W 80 B9
Martinsburg Ohio, U.S.A. 40°16N 82°21W 86 C4

Martinsburg Pa., U.S.A. 40°19N 78°20W 87 D4
Martinsburg W. Va., U.S.A. 39°27N 77°58W 93 A3
Martinsdale Mont., U.S.A. 46°28N 110°18W 123 D7
Martinsville Ill., U.S.A. 39°20N 87°53W 84 D6
Martinsville Ind., U.S.A. 39°26N 86°25W 85 D4
Martinsville Va., U.S.A. 36°41N 79°52W 102 E5
Martinton Ill., U.S.A. 40°55N 87°44W 84 C6
Maruchin Campeche, Mexico 18°17N 89°53W 179 D4
Marvel Colo., U.S.A. 37°7N 108°8W 125 E2
Marvell Ark., U.S.A. 34°33N 90°55W 106 D5
Marvin S. Dak., U.S.A. 45°16N 96°55W 76 E8
Marvine, Mt. Utah, U.S.A. 38°40N 111°39W 129 E4
Marwayne Alta., Canada 53°32N 110°20W 152 E10
Mary S. Young State Park △ Oreg., U.S.A. 45°22N 122°37W 132 E2
Maryhill Wash., U.S.A. 45°41N 120°49W 120 E5
Maryland □ U.S.A. 39°0N 76°30W 93 A3
Maryland City Md., U.S.A. 39°6N 76°50W 93 A4
Maryland Line Md., U.S.A. 39°43N 76°40W 93 A4
Maryland Point Md., U.S.A. 38°22N 77°14W 93 B3
Maryneal Tex., U.S.A. 32°14N 100°27W 108 E7
Marys → Nev., U.S.A. 41°4N 115°16W 128 A5
Marys Corner Wash., U.S.A. 46°33N 122°49W 120 D3
Marys Pk. Oreg., U.S.A. 44°30N 123°33W 121 C2
Marystown Nfld. & L., Canada 47°10N 55°10W 142 E5
Marysvale Utah, U.S.A. 38°27N 112°14W 129 E3
Marysville Calif., U.S.A. 39°9N 121°35W 126 D5
Marysville Kans., U.S.A. 39°51N 96°39W 82 B7
Marysville Mich., U.S.A. 42°54N 82°29W 79 G9
Marysville Ohio, U.S.A. 40°14N 83°22W 86 C3
Marysville Pa., U.S.A. 40°21N 76°56W 87 D6
Marysville Wash., U.S.A. 48°3N 122°11W 120 B3
Maryvale Ariz., U.S.A. 33°30N 112°10W 134 C1
Maryville Mo., U.S.A. 40°21N 94°52W 83 A2
Maryville Tenn., U.S.A. 35°46N 83°58W 105 E9
Masalog Pt. N. Marianas 15°1N 145°40E 184 c
Masardis Maine, U.S.A. 46°30N 68°22W 90 B5
Masaryktown Fla., U.S.A. 28°27N 82°27W 114 C6
Masaya Nic. 12°0N 86°7W 182 D2
Mascareñas Veracruz, Mexico 21°40N 98°0W 176 C2
Mascot Tenn., U.S.A. 36°4N 83°45W 105 D9
Mascota Jalisco, Mexico 20°32N 104°49W 174 B3
Mascouche Qué., Canada 45°45N 73°36W 145 F9
Mascual Guadalajara, Mexico 20°46N 103°17W 180 A2
Mashantucket Pequot Indian Reservation Conn., U.S.A. 41°27N 71°58W 91 C3
Mashpee Mass., U.S.A. 41°39N 70°29W 91 C4
Masiaca Sonora, Mexico 26°45N 109°18W 168 G6
Maskell Nebr., U.S.A. 42°41N 96°59W 80 B9
Maskinongé Qué., Canada 46°14N 73°1W 145 E9
Mason Ill., U.S.A. 38°57N 88°38W 84 E5
Mason Mich., U.S.A. 42°35N 84°27W 79 G7
Mason N.H., U.S.A. 42°45N 71°47W 89 D3
Mason Ohio, U.S.A. 39°22N 84°19W 86 D2
Mason Tenn., U.S.A. 35°25N 89°32W 104 E3
Mason Tex., U.S.A. 30°45N 99°14W 109 G8
Mason W. Va., U.S.A. 39°1N 82°2W 102 B2
Mason Wis., U.S.A. 46°26N 91°4W 78 B2
Mason City Ill., U.S.A. 40°12N 89°42W 84 C4
Mason City Iowa, U.S.A. 43°9N 93°12W 81 B5
Mason City Nebr., U.S.A. 41°13N 99°18W 80 C6
Mason County ☆ Ill., U.S.A. 40°15N 89°50W 84 C4
Mason County ☆ Ky., U.S.A. 38°35N 83°50W 105 B9
Mason County ☆ Mich., U.S.A. 44°0N 86°15W 79 F5
Mason County ☆ Tex., U.S.A. 30°45N 99°15W 109 G8
Mason County ☆ Wash., U.S.A. 47°20N 123°10W 120 C2
Mason Springs Md., U.S.A. 38°36N 77°10W 93 B3
Masonboro N.C., U.S.A. 34°11N 77°51W 103 D8
Masontown Pa., U.S.A. 39°50N 79°54W 87 E3
Masontown W. Va., U.S.A. 39°33N 79°48W 102 B5
Masonville Iowa, U.S.A. 42°29N 91°36W 81 C7
Maspeth N.Y., U.S.A. 40°43N 73°55W 97 B3
Mass City Mich., U.S.A. 46°46N 89°5W 79 C2
Massabesic L. N.H., U.S.A. 43°0N 71°23W 89 C3
Massac County ☆ Ill., U.S.A. 37°15N 88°45W 84 F5
Massachusetts □ U.S.A. 42°30N 72°0W 91 B2
Massachusetts B. Mass., U.S.A. 42°25N 70°50W 91 B4
Massachusetts Inst. of Tech. Mass., U.S.A. 42°21N 71°5W 96 A2
Massacre L. Nev., U.S.A. 41°39N 119°36W 128 A1
Massapequa N.Y., U.S.A. 40°41N 73°29W 92 B3
Massawippi, L. Qué., Canada 45°13N 72°0W 89 A3
Massena Iowa, U.S.A. 41°15N 94°46W 81 D4
Massena N.Y., U.S.A. 44°56N 74°54W 88 A6
Masset B.C., Canada 54°2N 132°10W 154 A2
Masset Inlet B.C., Canada 53°43N 132°20W 154 B2
Massey Ont., Canada 46°12N 82°5W 146 A4
Massey → Ont., Canada 39°18N 75°49W 93 A5
Massey I. Nunavut, Canada 76°0N 103°0W 158 B5
Massey Sd. Nunavut, Canada 78°30N 94°0W 158 B7
Massillon Ohio, U.S.A. 40°48N 81°32W 86 C5
Masson-Angers Qué., Canada 45°32N 75°25W 144 F7
Massueville Qué., Canada 45°55N 72°56W 145 F10
Mastens Corner Del., U.S.A. 38°57N 75°37W 93 B5
Masters Colo., U.S.A. 40°18N 104°15W 125 B6
Mastic N.Y., U.S.A. 40°47N 72°54W 88 E8
Mastigouche, Réserve Faunique △ Qué., Canada 46°33N 73°41W 145 E9
Mata de Labra Tamaulipas, Mexico 22°26N 98°7W 171 H6
Matachic Chihuahua, Mexico 28°51N 107°45W 169 E8
Matador Tex., U.S.A. 34°1N 100°49W 108 C7
Matagalpa Nic. 13°0N 85°58W 182 D2
Matagami Qué., Canada 49°45N 77°34W 143 D2
Matagami, L. Qué., Canada 49°50N 77°40W 143 D2
Matagorda Tex., U.S.A. 28°42N 95°58W 109 J12
Matagorda B. Tex., U.S.A. 28°40N 96°12W 109 J11
Matagorda County ☆ Tex., U.S.A. 28°45N 96°0W 109 J11
Matagorda Peninsula Tex., U.S.A. 28°15N 96°30W 109 J12
Matamec, L. Qué., Canada 50°21N 65°58W 140 C4
Matamoros Coahuila, Mexico 25°32N 103°15W 170 E1
Matamoros Durango, Mexico 25°21N 105°27W 172 E5
Matamoros Tamaulipas, Mexico 25°53N 97°30W 170 E7
Matane Qué., Canada 48°50N 67°33W 140 E2
Matane Qué., Canada 48°50N 67°35W 140 E2
Matane, Réserve Faunique de □ Qué., Canada 48°40N 67°0W 140 E3

Matanuska-Susitna ☆ *Alaska, U.S.A.* 62°30N 150°0W **135** E10
Matanzas *Cuba* 23°0N 81°40W **182** B3
Matapé → *Sonora, Mexico* 28°15N 110°42W **168** E5
Matapédia *N.B., Canada* 48°0N 66°59W **141** F3
Matapédia, L. *Qué., Canada* 48°35N 67°35W **140** E2
Matasaguas, Sa. *Chihuahua, Mexico* 29°20N 104°38W **169** D11
Matatula, C. *Amer. Samoa* 14°15S 170°33W **184** e
Matawan *N.J., U.S.A.* 40°25N 74°14W **92** B2
Matawin → *Qué., Canada* 46°54N 72°56W **145** E10
Matawin, Rés. *Qué., Canada* 46°46N 73°50W **145** E9
Matchi-Manitou, L. *Qué., Canada* 48°11N 99°19W **181** C2
Matehuala *San Luis Potosí, Mexico* 23°39N 100°39W **171** G4
Matewan *W. Va., U.S.A.* 37°37N 82°10W **102** D2
Mateo, Cerro *Distrito Federal, Mexico* 19°11N 99°9W **181** C2
Matfield Green *Kans., U.S.A.* 38°9N 96°31W **82** C7
Matheson *Colo., U.S.A.* 39°10N 103°59W **125** C7
Matheson Island *Man., Canada* 51°45N 96°56W **151** D15
Mathews *Va., U.S.A.* 37°26N 76°19W **102** D8
Mathews, L. *Calif., U.S.A.* 33°51N 117°27W **127** K9
Mathews County ☆ *Va., U.S.A.* 37°26N 76°19W **102** D8
Mathias *W. Va., U.S.A.* 38°53N 78°52W **102** C6
Mathis *Tex., U.S.A.* 28°6N 97°50W **109** J10
Mathiston *Miss., U.S.A.* 33°32N 89°7W **111** C4
Matías Romero *Oaxaca, Mexico* 16°53N 95°2W **177** H5
Matinenda L. *Ont., Canada* 46°22N 82°57W **146** A4
Matinicus *Maine, U.S.A.* 43°52N 68°54W **90** E5
Matinicus I. *Maine, U.S.A.* 43°52N 68°54W **90** E5
Matlapa *San Luis Potosí, Mexico* 21°19N 98°49W **171** J6
Matlock *Iowa, U.S.A.* 43°15N 95°56W **81** B3
Matoaka *W. Va., U.S.A.* 37°25N 81°15W **102** D3
Mattagami → *Ont., Canada* 50°43N 81°29W **149** B15
Mattagami L. *Ont., Canada* 47°54N 81°35W **149** E15
Mattamuskeet, L. *N.C., U.S.A.* 35°30N 76°12W **103** C9
Mattapan *Mass., U.S.A.* 42°16N 71°6W **96** D2
Mattapoisett *Mass., U.S.A.* 41°40N 70°49W **91** C4
Mattaponi → *Va., U.S.A.* 37°31N 76°47W **102** D8
Mattawa *Wash., U.S.A.* 46°44N 119°54W **120** D6
Mattawamkeag *Maine, U.S.A.* 45°32N 68°21W **90** C5
Mattawitchewan → *Ont., Canada* 49°52N 83°12W **149** C13
Matterhorn *Nev., U.S.A.* 41°49N 115°23W **128** A5
Matthew Town *Bahamas* 20°57N 73°40W **183** C5
Matthews *Ind., U.S.A.* 40°23N 85°30W **85** C5
Matthews *Md., U.S.A.* 38°49N 75°57W **93** B5
Matthews *Mo., U.S.A.* 36°46N 89°35W **83** E7
Matthews *N.C., U.S.A.* 35°7N 80°43W **103** C5
Matthews Pk. *Ariz., U.S.A.* 36°20N 109°8W **130** A6
Mattice *Ont., Canada* 49°40N 83°20W **149** C13
Mattituck *N.Y., U.S.A.* 40°59N 72°32W **91** D2
Mattole → *Calif., U.S.A.* 40°18N 124°21W **126** C2
Mattoon *Ill., U.S.A.* 39°29N 88°23W **84** D5
Mattson *Miss., U.S.A.* 34°6N 90°31W **111** B3
Matunuck R.I., U.S.A. 41°23N 71°32W **91** C3
Maud *Okla., U.S.A.* 35°8N 96°46W **107** C7
Maud *Tex., U.S.A.* 33°20N 94°21W **109** D13
Maug Is. *N. Marianas* 20°1N 145°13E **184** a
Maugerville *N.B., Canada* 45°52N 66°27W **141** H3
Maui *Hawai'i, U.S.A.* 20°48N 156°20W **136** C5
Mauldin *S.C., U.S.A.* 34°47N 82°19W **103** B3
Maumee *Ohio, U.S.A.* 41°34N 83°39W **86** B3
Maumee → *Ohio, U.S.A.* 41°42N 83°28W **86** B3
Maumelle *Ark., U.S.A.* 34°52N 92°24W **106** D3
Maumelle, L. *Ark., U.S.A.* 34°52N 92°24W **106** D3
Mauna Kea *Hawai'i, U.S.A.* 19°50N 155°28W **136** D6
Mauna Kea Forest Reserve *Hawai'i, U.S.A.* 19°52N 155°26W **136** D6
Mauna Loa *Hawai'i, U.S.A.* 19°30N 155°35W **136** D6
Mauna Loa Forest Reserve *Hawai'i, U.S.A.* 19°35N 155°33W **136** D6
Maunabo *Puerto Rico* 18°1N 65°54W **184** G17
Maunaloa *Hawai'i, U.S.A.* 21°8N 157°13W **136** B4
Maunalua B. *Hawai'i, U.S.A.* 21°15N 157°45W **136** K14
Maunawili *Hawai'i, U.S.A.* 21°23N 157°46W **136** K14
Maunie *Ill., U.S.A.* 38°2N 88°3W **84** E5
Maunoir, L. *N.W.T., Canada* 67°30N 124°55W **156** C8
Maupin *Oreg., U.S.A.* 45°11N 121°5W **121** B4
Maurepas, L. *La., U.S.A.* 30°15N 90°30W **110** D3
Maurice *La., U.S.A.* 30°7N 92°7W **110** D3
Maurice → *N.J., U.S.A.* 39°13N 75°2W **92** C1
Mauriceville *Tex., U.S.A.* 30°12N 93°52W **109** G14
Mauricie, Parc Nat. de la △ *Qué., Canada* 46°45N 73°0W **145** E10
Maurine *S. Dak., U.S.A.* 45°1N 102°35W **76** E3
Maury → *Va., U.S.A.* 37°50N 79°25W **102** D5
Maury City *Tenn., U.S.A.* 35°49N 89°14W **104** E3
Maury County ☆ *Tenn., U.S.A.* 35°37N 87°2W **104** E5
Maury Island *Wash., U.S.A.* 47°22N 122°25W **132** D3
Mauston *Wis., U.S.A.* 43°48N 90°5W **78** E31
Maverick County ☆ *Tex., U.S.A.* 28°55N 100°8W **108** J7
Mavillette *N.S., Canada* 44°6N 66°11W **141** J3
Max *N. Dak., U.S.A.* 47°49N 101°18W **76** C4
Maxbass *N. Dak., U.S.A.* 48°43N 101°9W **76** B4
Maxcanú *Yucatán, Mexico* 20°35N 90°0W **179** B4
Maxeys *Ga., U.S.A.* 33°45N 83°11W **113** C3
Maxton *N.C., U.S.A.* 34°44N 79°21W **103** D6
Maxville *Ont., Canada* 45°17N 74°51W **144** F8
Maxville *Mont., U.S.A.* 46°28N 113°14W **123** D4
Maxwell *Calif., U.S.A.* 39°17N 122°11W **126** D4
Maxwell *Iowa, U.S.A.* 41°53N 93°24W **81** D5
Maxwell *N. Mex., U.S.A.* 36°32N 104°33W **131** A6
Maxwell *Nebr., U.S.A.* 41°5N 100°31W **80** D6
May *Idaho, U.S.A.* 44°36N 113°55W **122** E5
May *Okla., U.S.A.* 36°37N 99°45W **107** B4
May, C. *N.J., U.S.A.* 38°56N 74°58W **92** D2
May Mt. *Idaho, U.S.A.* 44°41N 113°50W **122** E5
May Pen *Jamaica* 17°58N 77°15W **182** C4
Maya Mts. *Belize* 16°30N 89°0W **182** C2
Mayaguana *Bahamas* 22°30N 72°44W **183** B5
Mayagüez *Puerto Rico* 18°12N 67°9W **184** G15
Mayapán *Yucatán, Mexico* 20°29N 89°11W **179** B4
Mayapán *Yucatán, Mexico* 20°35N 89°29W **179** B4
Mayarí *Cuba* 20°40N 75°41W **183** B4
Maybell *Colo., U.S.A.* 40°31N 108°5W **125** B2
Maybeury *W. Va., U.S.A.* 37°22N 81°22W **102** D3
Maybrook *N.Y., U.S.A.* 41°29N 74°13W **92** B2
Mayer *Ariz., U.S.A.* 34°24N 112°14W **130** C3
Mayersville *Miss., U.S.A.* 32°54N 91°3W **111** C2
Mayerthorpe *Alta., Canada* 53°57N 115°8W **152** E5
Mayes County ☆ *Okla., U.S.A.* 36°15N 95°10W **107** B8
Mayesville *S.C., U.S.A.* 34°0N 80°12W **103** D5
Mayetta *Kans., U.S.A.* 39°20N 95°43W **82** B8
Mayetta *N.J., U.S.A.* 39°40N 74°18W **92** C2
Mayfair *Tex., U.S.A.* 29°41N 95°19W **116** B3
Mayfield *Ga., U.S.A.* 33°21N 82°48W **113** C4

Mayfield *Idaho, U.S.A.* 43°25N 115°54W **122** F3
Mayfield *Kans., U.S.A.* 37°16N 97°33W **82** D6
Mayfield *Ky., U.S.A.* 36°44N 88°38W **104** D4
Mayfield *Utah, U.S.A.* 39°7N 111°43W **129** D4
Mayhill *N. Mex., U.S.A.* 32°53N 105°29W **131** E4
Maymont *Sask., Canada* 52°34N 107°42W **150** C4
Maynard *Ark., U.S.A.* 36°25N 90°54W **106** B5
Maynard *Iowa, U.S.A.* 42°47N 91°53W **81** C7
Maynard *Mass., U.S.A.* 42°26N 71°27W **91** B3
Maynardville *Tenn., U.S.A.* 36°15N 83°48W **105** D9
Mayne *B.C., Canada* 48°52N 123°17W **155** G11
Mayo *Yukon, Canada* 63°38N 135°57W **157** D5
Mayo *Fla., U.S.A.* 30°3N 83°10W **114** A5
Mayo *S.C., U.S.A.* 35°5N 81°52W **103** C4
Mayo → *Sonora, Mexico* 26°45N 109°47W **168** G6
Mayo Res. *N.C., U.S.A.* 36°32N 78°53W **103** B6
Mayodan *N.C., U.S.A.* 36°25N 79°58W **103** B6
Mayoworth *Wyo., U.S.A.* 43°50N 106°47W **124** C6
Mayport Naval Station *Fla., U.S.A.* 30°24N 81°25W **114** A7
Mayran, Desierto de *Mexico* 25°53N 103°8W **170** E1
Mays Landing *N.J., U.S.A.* 39°27N 74°44W **92** C2
Mays Lick *Ky., U.S.A.* 38°31N 83°50W **105** B9
Maysville *Ga., U.S.A.* 34°15N 83°34W **113** B3
Maysville *Ky., U.S.A.* 38°39N 83°46W **105** B9
Maysville *Mo., U.S.A.* 39°53N 94°22W **83** B2
Maysville *N.C., U.S.A.* 34°54N 77°14W **103** D8
Maysville *Okla., U.S.A.* 34°49N 97°24W **107** D6
Maysville *W. Va., U.S.A.* 39°7N 79°10W **93** A1
Mayview *Mo., U.S.A.* 39°3N 93°50W **83** B3
Mayville *Mich., U.S.A.* 43°20N 83°21W **79** F8
Mayville *N. Dak., U.S.A.* 47°30N 97°20W **76** C8
Mayville *N.Y., U.S.A.* 42°15N 79°30W **88** C1
Mayville *Wis., U.S.A.* 43°30N 88°33W **78** E5
Maywood *Calif., U.S.A.* 33°59N 118°12W **133** C3
Maywood *Ill., U.S.A.* 41°52N 87°51W **95** B1
Maywood *N.J., U.S.A.* 40°53N 74°3W **97** A2
Maywood Park *Oreg., U.S.A.* 45°33N 122°33W **132** A2
Maywood Park Race Track *Ill., U.S.A.* 41°54N 87°50W **95** B1
Maza *N. Dak., U.S.A.* 48°22N 99°12W **76** B6
Mazama *Wash., U.S.A.* 48°36N 120°24W **120** B5
Mazamitla *Jalisco, Mexico* 19°55N 103°2W **174** C4
Mazapil *Zacatecas, Mexico* 24°39N 101°34W **173** C9
Mazatán *Chiapas, Mexico* 14°52N 92°27W **178** E4
Mazatán *Sonora, Mexico* 29°0N 110°8W **168** E5
Mazatenango *Guatemala* 14°35N 91°30W **182** D1
Mazatepec *Puebla, Mexico* 20°2N 97°24W **176** B3
Mazatlán *Guerrero, Mexico* 17°26N 99°28W **175** E8
Mazatlán *Sinaloa, Mexico* 23°13N 106°25W **172** D4
Mazatzal Mts. *Ariz., U.S.A.* 34°0N 111°30W **130** D4
Mazenod *Sask., Canada* 49°52N 106°13W **150** F5
Mazie *Ky., U.S.A.* 38°2N 82°58W **105** B10
Mazie *Okla., U.S.A.* 36°6N 95°22W **107** B8
Mazomanie *Wis., U.S.A.* 43°11N 89°48W **78** E4
Mazon *Ill., U.S.A.* 41°14N 88°25W **95** C1
Meacham *Sask., Canada* 52°6N 105°45W **150** C6
Meacham *Oreg., U.S.A.* 45°31N 118°25W **121** B7
Mead *Nebr., U.S.A.* 41°14N 96°29W **80** C9
Mead *Okla., U.S.A.* 34°0N 96°31W **107** E7
Mead *Wash., U.S.A.* 47°46N 117°21W **120** C8
Mead, L. *Nev., U.S.A.* 36°0N 114°44W **130** A1
Meade = Atqasuk → *Alaska, U.S.A.* 70°52N 155°54W **135** A9
Meade *Kans., U.S.A.* 37°17N 100°20W **82** D3
Meade County ☆ *Kans., U.S.A.* 37°15N 100°20W **82** D3
Meade County ☆ *Ky., U.S.A.* 37°55N 86°10W **104** C6
Meade County ☆ *S. Dak., U.S.A.* 44°30N 102°30W **76** F3
Meade River = Atqasuk *Alaska, U.S.A.* 70°28N 157°24W **135** A8
Meadow *S. Dak., U.S.A.* 45°32N 102°13W **76** E3
Meadow *Tex., U.S.A.* 33°20N 102°12W **108** D5
Meadow → *W. Va., U.S.A.* 38°13N 80°57W **102** C4
Meadow Bridge *W. Va., U.S.A.* 37°52N 80°51W **102** D4
Meadow Brook Park *Minn., U.S.A.* 44°55N 93°21W **94** B1
Meadow Grove *Nebr., U.S.A.* 42°2N 97°44W **80** B8
Meadow L. *Sask., Canada* 54°7N 108°26W **150** A3
Meadow Lake *Sask., Canada* 54°10N 108°26W **150** A3
Meadow Lake *N.Y., U.S.A.* 40°44N 73°50W **97** B3
Meadow Park *Minn., U.S.A.* 44°57N 93°26W **94** B1
Meadow Valley Wash → *Nev., U.S.A.* 36°40N 114°34W **128** F6
Meadow Vista *Calif., U.S.A.* 39°6N 121°1W **126** D4
Meadowdale *Wyo., U.S.A.* 42°33N 104°42W **124** D8
Meadowlands *Ont., Canada* 45°21N 75°45W **160** B1
Meadowlands *Minn., U.S.A.* 47°4N 92°44W **77** C6
Meadows *N.H., U.S.A.* 44°21N 71°28W **89** B3
Meadowview *Va., U.S.A.* 36°46N 81°52W **102** E2
Meadville *Miss., U.S.A.* 31°28N 90°54W **111** E3
Meadville *Mo., U.S.A.* 39°47N 93°18W **83** B3
Meadville *Pa., U.S.A.* 41°39N 80°9W **87** C2
Meaford *Ont., Canada* 44°36N 80°35W **146** C6
Meagher County ☆ *Mont., U.S.A.* 46°40N 110°57W **123** C8
Meaghers Grant *N.S., Canada* 44°55N 63°15W **141** J6
Meander River *Alta., Canada* 59°2N 117°42W **152** B6
Meansville *Ga., U.S.A.* 33°3N 84°18W **113** C2
Meares I. *B.C., Canada* 49°12N 125°50W **154** F9
Meath Park *Sask., Canada* 53°27N 105°22W **150** C6
Mebane *N.C., U.S.A.* 36°6N 79°16W **103** B6
Mecapalapa *Puebla, Mexico* 20°32N 97°50W **176** D3
Mecatán *Nayarit, Mexico* 21°32N 105°7W **172** F5
Mecatina, Little → *Nfld. & L., Canada* 52°0N 60°15W **140** A9
Mecayapán *Veracruz, Mexico* 18°13N 94°50W **177** F6
Mecca *Calif., U.S.A.* 33°34N 116°5W **127** K10
Mechanic Falls *Maine, U.S.A.* 44°7N 70°24W **90** D3
Mechanicsburg *Ohio, U.S.A.* 40°4N 83°33W **86** C3
Mechanicsburg *Pa., U.S.A.* 40°13N 77°1W **87** E6
Mechanicsville *Iowa, U.S.A.* 41°54N 91°16W **81** D7
Mechanicsville *Md., U.S.A.* 38°26N 76°44W **93** B4
Mechanicville *N.Y., U.S.A.* 42°54N 73°41W **91** B1
Mecklenburg County ☆ *N.C., U.S.A.* 35°15N 80°45W **103** C5
Mecklenburg County ☆ *Va., U.S.A.* 36°55N 78°20W **102** E6
Meckling *S. Dak., U.S.A.* 42°51N 97°4W **76** H8
Mecosta *Mich., U.S.A.* 43°37N 85°14W **79** F6
Mecosta County ☆ *Mich., U.S.A.* 43°37N 85°19W **79** F6
Medanales *N. Mex., U.S.A.* 36°11N 106°11W **131** A4
Medart *Fla., U.S.A.* 30°5N 84°23W **114** A4
Medaryville *Ind., U.S.A.* 41°5N 86°55W **85** B4
Medellín *Veracruz, Mexico* 19°2N 96°7W **177** E4
Medfield *Mass., U.S.A.* 42°11N 71°18W **91** B3
Medford *Mass., U.S.A.* 42°25N 71°7W **96** A2
Medford *Minn., U.S.A.* 44°11N 93°15W **77** F5
Medford *N.J., U.S.A.* 39°54N 74°50W **92** C2

Medford *N.Y., U.S.A.* 40°49N 73°0W **92** B3
Medford *Okla., U.S.A.* 36°48N 97°44W **107** B6
Medford *Oreg., U.S.A.* 42°19N 122°52W **121** E3
Medford *Wis., U.S.A.* 45°9N 90°20W **78** C3
Medford Lakes *N.J., U.S.A.* 39°52N 74°48W **92** C2
Media *Pa., U.S.A.* 39°55N 75°23W **92** C1
Mediapolis *Iowa, U.S.A.* 41°0N 91°10W **81** E7
Medias Aguas *Veracruz, Mexico* 17°40N 95°2W **177** G5
Medical Lake *Wash., U.S.A.* 47°34N 117°41W **120** C8
Medicine Bow *Wyo., U.S.A.* 41°54N 106°12W **124** E6
Medicine Bow → *Wyo., U.S.A.* 42°0N 106°40W **124** D6
Medicine Bow Mts. *U.S.A.* 40°40N 106°0W **125** B5
Medicine Bow Nat. Forest *Wyo., U.S.A.* 42°20N 105°38W **124** D7
Medicine Cr. → *Mo., U.S.A.* 39°43N 93°24W **83** B3
Medicine Cr. → *Nebr., U.S.A.* 40°17N 100°10W **80** D5
Medicine Hat *Alta., Canada* 50°0N 110°45W **153** H10
Medicine L. *Minn., U.S.A.* 45°0N 93°25W **94** A1
Medicine Lake *Mont., U.S.A.* 48°28N 104°24W **123** B13
Medicine Lake *Minn., U.S.A.* 44°59N 93°24W **94** A1
Medicine Lodge *Kans., U.S.A.* 37°17N 98°35W **82** D5
Medicine Lodge → *Kans., U.S.A.* 36°49N 98°20W **82** C5
Medicine Park *Okla., U.S.A.* 34°44N 98°30W **107** D5
Medina *N. Dak., U.S.A.* 46°54N 99°18W **76** D6
Medina *N.Y., U.S.A.* 43°13N 78°23W **88** B2
Medina *Ohio, U.S.A.* 41°8N 81°52W **86** B5
Medina *Tenn., U.S.A.* 35°48N 88°46W **104** E4
Medina *Tex., U.S.A.* 29°48N 99°15W **109** H8
Medina *Wash., U.S.A.* 47°37N 122°13W **132** C4
Medina County ☆ *Ohio, U.S.A.* 41°8N 81°52W **86** B5
Medina County ☆ *Tex., U.S.A.* 29°21N 99°9W **109** H8
Medora *Ill., U.S.A.* 39°11N 90°9W **84** D3
Medora *Ind., U.S.A.* 38°49N 86°10W **85** E4
Medora *N. Dak., U.S.A.* 46°55N 103°31W **76** D2
Medstead *Sask., Canada* 53°19N 108°5W **150** C3
Meductic *N.B., Canada* 46°0N 67°29W **141** H2
Medway *Mass., U.S.A.* 42°8N 71°24W **91** B3
Medway → *N.S., Canada* 44°8N 64°36W **141** J5
Meeker *Colo., U.S.A.* 40°2N 107°55W **125** B3
Meeker *Okla., U.S.A.* 35°30N 96°54W **107** C7
Meeker County ☆ *Minn., U.S.A.* 45°10N 94°30W **77** E4
Meeks Bay *Calif., U.S.A.* 39°2N 120°8W **126** D6
Meelpaeg L. *Nfld. & L., Canada* 48°15N 56°30W **142** D4
Meeteetse *Wyo., U.S.A.* 44°9N 108°52W **124** B4
Meeks L. *Calif., U.S.A.* 41°52N 122°4W **126** B4
Mégantic, L. *Qué., Canada* 45°32N 70°53W **145** F12
Mégantic, Mt. *Qué., Canada* 45°28N 71°9W **145** F11
Megargel *Tex., U.S.A.* 33°27N 98°56W **109** D9
Mégiscane → *Qué., Canada* 48°29N 75°38W **144** C7
Mégiscane, L. *Qué., Canada* 48°35N 75°55W **144** C7
Megueyera, Cerro la *Michoacan, Mexico* 18°25N 102°34W **174** D5
Mehatl Creek Park △ *B.C., Canada* 50°3N 122°2W **155** E12
Meherrin → *Va., U.S.A.* 36°26N 76°57W **102** E8
Mehlville *Mo., U.S.A.* 38°31N 90°19W **83** C61
Meighen I. *Nunavut, Canada* 80°0N 99°30W **158** A5
Meigs *Ga., U.S.A.* 31°4N 84°6W **113** E2
Meigs County ☆ *Ohio, U.S.A.* 39°3N 82°8W **86** D4
Meigs County ☆ *Tenn., U.S.A.* 35°31N 84°47W **105** E8
Meija, I. *Baja Calif., Mexico* 29°36N 113°37W **166** D5
Mékinac, L. *Qué., Canada* 47°3N 72°41W **145** D10
Mekinock *N. Dak., U.S.A.* 48°1N 97°22W **76** B8
Mekoryuk *Alaska, U.S.A.* 60°23N 166°11W **135** F6
Melb *Idaho, U.S.A.* 43°23N 116°32W **122** F2
Melbourne *Ark., U.S.A.* 36°4N 91°54W **106** B4
Melbourne *Fla., U.S.A.* 28°5N 80°37W **114** C8
Melbourne *Iowa, U.S.A.* 41°57N 93°6W **81** D5
Melbourne *Nunavut, Canada* 68°30N 104°45W **158** C3
Melcher-Dallas *Iowa, U.S.A.* 41°14N 93°15W **81** D5
Melchor Múzquiz *Coahuila, Mexico* 27°53N 101°31W **170** C2
Melchor Ocampo *Durango, Mexico* 25°22N 105°16W **172** B5
Melchor Ocampo *Nuevo León, Mexico* 26°4N 99°10W **173** D9
Melchor Ocampo *Zacatecas, Mexico* 24°51N 101°39W **173** C9
Meldrum Bay *Ont., Canada* 45°56N 83°6W **146** B3
Meldrum Creek *B.C., Canada* 52°6N 122°21W **155** C12
Mélèzes → *Qué., Canada* 57°40N 69°29W **143** B4
Melfa *Va., U.S.A.* 37°39N 75°45W **102** D9
Melfort *Sask., Canada* 52°50N 104°37W **150** C7
Melissa *Tex., U.S.A.* 33°17N 96°34W **109** D11
Melita *Man., Canada* 49°15N 101°0W **151** F11
Melitota *Md., U.S.A.* 39°16N 76°9W **93** A4
Mellen *Wis., U.S.A.* 46°20N 90°40W **78** B31
Mellette *S. Dak., U.S.A.* 45°9N 98°30W **76** E7
Mellette County ☆ *S. Dak., U.S.A.* 43°35N 101°0W **76** G5
Mellott *Ind., U.S.A.* 40°10N 87°9W **85** C3
Mellwood *Ark., U.S.A.* 34°12N 90°56W **106** D5
Melrose *Iowa, U.S.A.* 40°59N 93°3W **81** E5
Melrose *Mass., U.S.A.* 42°27N 71°2W **96** A2
Melrose *Minn., U.S.A.* 45°40N 94°49W **77** E4
Melrose *Mont., U.S.A.* 45°38N 112°41W **123** E5
Melrose *N. Mex., U.S.A.* 34°26N 103°38W **131** C7
Melrose *N.Y., U.S.A.* 42°51N 73°37W **91** B1
Melrose *N.Y., U.S.A.* 40°49N 73°55W **97** B3
Melrose *Wis., U.S.A.* 44°8N 91°1W **78** D2
Melrose Park *Fla., U.S.A.* 26°6N 80°11W **115** B3
Melrose Park *Ill., U.S.A.* 41°53N 87°50W **95** B1
Melrose Park *Pa., U.S.A.* 40°3N 75°7W **98** A2
Melstone *Mont., U.S.A.* 46°36N 107°52W **123** D10
Melstrand *Mich., U.S.A.* 46°28N 86°25W **79** C5
Melton Hill L. *Tenn., U.S.A.* 35°53N 84°18W **105** E8
Melvern *Kans., U.S.A.* 38°30N 95°38W **82** C8
Melvern Lake *Kans., U.S.A.* 38°30N 95°44W **82** C8
Melville *Sask., Canada* 50°55N 102°50W **150** E8
Melville, L. *Nfld. & L., Canada* 53°30N 60°0W **143** C6
Melville B. *Greenland* 75°30N 63°0W **162** B4
Melville Hills *Canada* 68°57N 120°45W **156** C8
Melville I. *Canada* 75°30N 112°0W **156** A10
Melville Pen. *Nunavut, Canada* 68°0N 84°0W **158** D8
Melville Sd. *Nunavut, Canada* 68°10N 107°0W **158** D4
Melvin *Ala., U.S.A.* 31°55N 88°27W **112** E2
Melvin *Ill., U.S.A.* 40°34N 88°15W **84** C5
Melvin *Tex., U.S.A.* 31°12N 99°35W **109** F8
Melvin Village *N.H., U.S.A.* 43°42N 71°29W **89** C3
Melvina *Wis., U.S.A.* 43°48N 90°47W **78** E3
Melvindale *Mich., U.S.A.* 42°17N 83°10W **98** B2
Memorial Park *Tex., U.S.A.* 29°45N 95°26W **116** A2
Memphis *Fla., U.S.A.* 27°32N 82°34W **114** D6
Memphis *Mich., U.S.A.* 42°54N 82°46W **79** F9
Memphis *Mo., U.S.A.* 40°28N 92°10W **83** A4
Memphis *Nebr., U.S.A.* 41°6N 96°26W **80** C9
Memphis *Tenn., U.S.A.* 35°8N 90°2W **117** B1

Memphis *Tex., U.S.A.* 34°44N 100°33W **108** C7
Memphis Int. ✈ (MEM) *Tenn., U.S.A.* 35°3N 89°59W **117** B2
Memphrémagog, L. *N. Amer.* 45°8N 72°17W **145** F10
Memramcook *N.B., Canada* 45°58N 64°35W **141** H5
Mena *Ark., U.S.A.* 34°35N 94°15W **106** D1
Menahga *Minn., U.S.A.* 46°45N 95°6W **77** D3
Menan *Idaho, U.S.A.* 43°43N 111°59W **122** F7
Menard *Mont., U.S.A.* 45°59N 111°10W **123** D6
Menard *Tex., U.S.A.* 30°55N 99°47W **109** G8
Menard County ☆ *Ill., U.S.A.* 40°0N 89°50W **84** C4
Menard County ☆ *Tex., U.S.A.* 30°55N 99°47W **109** G8
Ménascouagama, L. *Qué., Canada* 51°13N 61°52W **140** B8
Menasha *Wis., U.S.A.* 44°13N 88°26W **78** D5
Mendenhall *Miss., U.S.A.* 31°58N 89°52W **111** E4
Mendenhall, C. *Alaska, U.S.A.* 59°45N 166°10W **135** G6
Mendham *Sask., Canada* 50°46N 109°40W **150** E2
Mendham *N.J., U.S.A.* 40°47N 74°36W **92** B2
Mendocino *Calif., U.S.A.* 39°19N 123°48W **126** D3
Mendocino, C. *Calif., U.S.A.* 40°26N 124°25W **126** C2
Mendocino, L. *Calif., U.S.A.* 39°12N 123°11W **126** D3
Mendocino County ☆ *Calif., U.S.A.* 39°0N 123°20W **126** D3
Mendocino Nat. Forest *Calif., U.S.A.* 39°45N 122°50W **126** D4
Mendon *Mich., U.S.A.* 42°0N 85°27W **79** G6
Mendon *Mo., U.S.A.* 39°36N 93°8W **83** B3
Mendon *Ohio, U.S.A.* 40°40N 84°31W **86** C2
Mendon *Vt., U.S.A.* 43°40N 72°54W **89** C2
Mendota *Calif., U.S.A.* 36°45N 120°23W **127** G6
Mendota *Ill., U.S.A.* 41°33N 89°7W **84** B4
Mendota *Minn., U.S.A.* 44°53N 93°9W **94** B3
Mendota, L. *Wis., U.S.A.* 43°7N 89°25W **78** E4
Mendota Heights *Minn., U.S.A.* 44°53N 93°9W **94** B3
Menifee County ☆ *Ky., U.S.A.* 37°55N 83°35W **105** C9
Menihek *Nfld. & L., Canada* 54°28N 56°36W **143** C6
Menihek L. *Nfld. & L., Canada* 54°0N 56°0W **143** C4
Ménistouc, L. *Qué., Canada* 52°52N 66°29W **140** A3
Menlo *Iowa, U.S.A.* 41°31N 94°24W **81** D4
Menlo *Kans., U.S.A.* 39°21N 100°43W **82** B3
Menlo *Wash., U.S.A.* 46°38N 123°39W **120** D2
Menlo Park *Calif., U.S.A.* 37°27N 122°12W **126** F4
Menlo Park Terrace *N.J., U.S.A.* 40°33N 74°19W **97** C1
Menno *S. Dak., U.S.A.* 43°14N 97°34W **76** G8
Meno *Okla., U.S.A.* 36°23N 98°11W **107** B5
Menominee *Mich., U.S.A.* 45°6N 87°37W **79** D4
Menominee → *U.S.A.* 45°6N 87°35W **79** D4
Menominee County ☆ *Mich., U.S.A.* 45°30N 87°40W **79** D4
Menominee County ☆ *Wis., U.S.A.* 45°0N 88°45W **78** C5
Menominee Ind. Reservation *Wis., U.S.A.* 45°0N 88°45W **78** C5
Menominee Ra. *Mich., U.S.A.* 46°0N 88°10W **79** B3
Menomonee Falls *Wis., U.S.A.* 43°10N 88°7W **94** B1
Menomonie *Wis., U.S.A.* 44°53N 91°55W **78** D2
Mentasta Lake *Alaska, U.S.A.* 62°55N 143°45W **135** E12
Mentone *Ind., U.S.A.* 41°10N 86°2W **85** B4
Mentone *Tex., U.S.A.* 31°42N 103°36W **108** F4
Mentor *Minn., U.S.A.* 47°42N 96°9W **77** C2
Mentor *Ohio, U.S.A.* 41°40N 81°21W **86** B5
Mentor-on-the-Lake *Ohio, U.S.A.* 41°43N 81°22W **86** B5
Meoqui *Chihuahua, Mexico* 28°17N 105°29W **169** D10
Meota *Sask., Canada* 53°2N 108°37W **150** B4
Mequon *Wis., U.S.A.* 43°14N 87°59W **78** E6
Mer Rouge *La., U.S.A.* 32°47N 91°48W **110** B4
Meramec → *Mo., U.S.A.* 38°24N 90°21W **83** C6
Meramec State Park △ *Mo., U.S.A.* 38°13N 91°5W **83** C5
Merasheen I. *Nfld. & L., Canada* 47°25N 54°15W **142** E6
Meraux *La., U.S.A.* 29°55N 89°56W **117** C3
Merced *Calif., U.S.A.* 37°18N 120°29W **126** F6
Merced → *Calif., U.S.A.* 37°21N 120°59W **126** F6
Merced, L. *Calif., U.S.A.* 37°43N 122°29W **132** B2
Merced County ☆ *Calif., U.S.A.* 37°15N 120°30W **126** F6
Mercedes *Tex., U.S.A.* 26°9N 97°55W **108** L10
Mercenarios, Pta. *Baja Calif. S., Mexico* 26°20N 111°23W **167** G7
Mercer *Maine, U.S.A.* 44°41N 69°56W **90** D4
Mercer *Mo., U.S.A.* 40°31N 93°32W **83** A3
Mercer *N. Dak., U.S.A.* 47°29N 100°43W **76** C5
Mercer *Pa., U.S.A.* 41°14N 80°15W **87** C2
Mercer *Tenn., U.S.A.* 35°29N 89°2W **104** E3
Mercer *Wis., U.S.A.* 46°10N 90°4W **78** B3
Mercer County ☆ *Ill., U.S.A.* 41°15N 90°40W **84** B3
Mercer County ☆ *Ky., U.S.A.* 37°50N 84°50W **105** C8
Mercer County ☆ *Mo., U.S.A.* 40°25N 93°30W **83** A3
Mercer County ☆ *N. Dak., U.S.A.* 47°15N 102°0W **76** C4
Mercer County ☆ *N.J., U.S.A.* 40°15N 74°40W **92** B2
Mercer County ☆ *Ohio, U.S.A.* 40°33N 84°35W **86** C2
Mercer County ☆ *Pa., U.S.A.* 41°15N 80°10W **87** C2
Mercer County ☆ *W. Va., U.S.A.* 37°22N 81°6W **102** D3
Mercer Island *Wash., U.S.A.* 47°34N 122°13W **132** C4
Mercersburg *Pa., U.S.A.* 39°50N 77°54W **93** A3
Mercerville *N.J., U.S.A.* 40°14N 74°41W **92** B2
Merchantville *N.J., U.S.A.* 39°56N 75°4W **98** B2
Mercier *Qué., Canada* 45°19N 73°45W **145** F9
Mercoal *Alta., Canada* 53°10N 117°5W **152** E4
Mercury *Nev., U.S.A.* 36°40N 115°59W **128** F5
Mercy, C. *Nunavut, Canada* 65°0N 63°30W **159** E13
Mercy B. *N.W.T., Canada* 74°5N 119°0W **156** B9
Meredith *Colo., U.S.A.* 39°22N 106°51W **125** C4
Meredith *N.H., U.S.A.* 43°39N 71°30W **89** C3
Meredith, L. *Colo., U.S.A.* 38°12N 103°43W **125** D7
Meredith, L. *Tex., U.S.A.* 35°43N 101°33W **108** B6
Meredosia *Ill., U.S.A.* 39°50N 90°34W **84** D3
Meredosia Nat. Wildlife Refuge △ *Ill., U.S.A.* 39°53N 90°34W **84** D3
Mérida *Baja Calif., Mexico* 32°41N 114°55W **166** A4
Mérida *Yucatán, Mexico* 20°58N 89°37W **179** B4
Meriden *Conn., U.S.A.* 41°32N 72°48W **91** C2
Meriden *Iowa, U.S.A.* 42°48N 95°38W **81** C3
Meriden *Kans., U.S.A.* 39°11N 95°34W **82** B8
Meriden *N.H., U.S.A.* 43°32N 72°16W **89** C2
Meriden *Wyo., U.S.A.* 41°33N 104°19W **124** E8
Meridian *Ga., U.S.A.* 31°27N 81°23W **113** E5
Meridian *Idaho, U.S.A.* 43°37N 116°24W **122** F2
Meridian *Miss., U.S.A.* 32°22N 88°42W **111** D5
Meridian *Okla., U.S.A.* 35°48N 97°15W **107** C6
Meridian *Tex., U.S.A.* 31°56N 97°39W **109** F10
Meridianville *Ala., U.S.A.* 34°51N 86°34W **112** B4
Merigold *Miss., U.S.A.* 33°50N 90°44W **111** C3
Merigomish *N.S., Canada* 45°38N 62°26W **141** H7
Meriwether County ☆ *Ga., U.S.A.* 33°0N 84°40W **113** C2
Merizo *Guam* 13°16N 144°40E **184** b
Merkel *Tex., U.S.A.* 32°28N 100°1W **109** E7
Merlin *Ont., Canada* 42°14N 82°14W **146** E3
Merlin *Oreg., U.S.A.* 42°31N 123°25W **121** E2
Mermentau *La., U.S.A.* 30°11N 92°35W **110** D2
Merna *Nebr., U.S.A.* 41°29N 99°46W **80** C6
Merrick *N.Y., U.S.A.* 40°40N 73°33W **92** B3

Merrick County ☆ *Nebr., U.S.A.* 41°15N 98°0W **80** C7
Merrickville *Ont., Canada* 44°55N 75°50W **147** C11
Merricourt *N. Dak., U.S.A.* 46°12N 98°46W **76** D7
Merrill *Iowa, U.S.A.* 42°43N 96°15W **81** C2
Merrill *Mich., U.S.A.* 43°25N 84°20W **79** F7
Merrill *Miss., U.S.A.* 30°59N 88°43W **111** F5
Merrill *Oreg., U.S.A.* 42°1N 121°36W **121** E4
Merrill *Wis., U.S.A.* 45°11N 89°41W **78** C4
Merrillan *Wis., U.S.A.* 44°27N 90°50W **78** D3
Merrillville *Ga., U.S.A.* 30°57N 83°53W **113** F3
Merrillville *Ind., U.S.A.* 41°29N 87°20W **85** B3
Merrimac *Mass., U.S.A.* 42°50N 71°0W **91** B3
Merrimac *Wis., U.S.A.* 43°22N 89°37W **78** E4
Merrimack *N.H., U.S.A.* 42°49N 70°49W **89** D4
Merrimack *N.H., U.S.A.* 42°52N 71°30W **89** D3
Merrimack → *Mass., U.S.A.* 42°49N 70°49W **89** D4
Merrimack County ☆ *N.H., U.S.A.* 43°15N 71°45W **89** C3
Merriman *Nebr., U.S.A.* 42°55N 101°42W **80** B4
Merrionette Park *Ill., U.S.A.* 41°41N 87°40W **95** C2
Merritt *B.C., Canada* 50°10N 120°45W **155** E14
Merritt *Wash., U.S.A.* 47°47N 120°50W **120** C4
Merritt Island *Fla., U.S.A.* 28°21N 80°42W **114** C8
Merritt Island Nat. Wildlife Refuge △ *Fla., U.S.A.* 28°40N 80°42W **114** C8
Merritt Res. *Nebr., U.S.A.* 42°38N 100°53W **80** B5
Merry I. *N.W.T., Canada* 55°29N 77°31W **143** B2
Merryville *La., U.S.A.* 30°45N 93°33W **110** D2
Mersey → *N.S., Canada* 44°2N 64°43W **141** J5
Mershon *Ga., U.S.A.* 31°28N 82°15W **113** E4
Mertzon *Tex., U.S.A.* 31°16N 100°49W **108** F7
Merville *B.C., Canada* 49°48N 125°3W **154** F9
Mervin *Sask., Canada* 53°20N 108°53W **150** B3
Mesa *Ariz., U.S.A.* 33°25N 111°50W **130** D4
Mesa *Colo., U.S.A.* 39°10N 108°8W **125** C2
Mesa *Idaho, U.S.A.* 44°38N 116°27W **122** E2
Mesa *Wash., U.S.A.* 46°35N 119°0W **120** D6
Mesa County ☆ *Colo., U.S.A.* 39°0N 108°30W **125** C2
Mesa de los Rios *Nayarit, Mexico* 22°50N 105°6W **172** E5
Mesa del Nayar *Nayarit, Mexico* 22°16N 104°35W **172** E6
Mesa del Seri *Sonora, Mexico* 29°8N 110°50W **168** D5
Mesa Tres Rios *Sonora, Mexico* 29°52N 108°44W **168** D7
Mesa Verde *Colo., U.S.A.* 37°15N 108°45W **125** E2
Mesa Verde Nat. Park △ *Colo., U.S.A.* 37°11N 108°29W **125** E2
Mesabi Iron Range *Minn., U.S.A.* 47°40N 92°45W **77** C6
Mescalero *N. Mex., U.S.A.* 33°9N 105°46W **131** D5
Mescalero Apache Indian Reservation *N. Mex., U.S.A.* 33°12N 105°40W **131** D5
Meservey *Iowa, U.S.A.* 42°55N 93°29W **81** C5
Mesgouez, L. *Qué., Canada* 51°20N 75°0W **143** C2
Mesick *Mich., U.S.A.* 44°24N 85°43W **79** E6
Mesilinka → *B.C., Canada* 56°6N 124°30W **157** E8
Mesita *Colo., U.S.A.* 37°6N 105°36W **125** E5
Mesita *N. Mex., U.S.A.* 35°1N 107°19W **131** B3
Mesquite *N. Mex., U.S.A.* 32°10N 106°42W **131** E4
Mesquite *Nev., U.S.A.* 36°48N 114°4W **128** F6
Mesquite *Tex., U.S.A.* 32°46N 96°36W **109** E11
Mesquite L. *Calif., U.S.A.* 35°43N 115°35W **127** H11
Messines *Qué., Canada* 46°14N 76°2W **144** E6
Mestersvig *Greenland* 72°10N 23°40W **162** C8
Meta *S. Dak., U.S.A.* 38°19N 92°10W **83** C4
Meta Incognita Pen. *Nunavut, Canada* 62°45N 68°30W **159** E12
Metairie *La., U.S.A.* 29°59N 90°9W **117** B2
Metaline *Wash., U.S.A.* 48°51N 117°23W **120** B8
Metaline Falls *Wash., U.S.A.* 48°52N 117°22W **120** B8
Metamora *Ill., U.S.A.* 40°47N 89°22W **84** C4
Metamora *Mich., U.S.A.* 42°57N 83°17W **79** G8
Metamoras *Pa., U.S.A.* 41°22N 74°42W **92** A2
Metcalf *Ga., U.S.A.* 30°43N 83°59W **113** F3
Metcalf *Ill., U.S.A.* 39°48N 87°48W **84** D6
Metcalfe County ☆ *Ky., U.S.A.* 37°0N 85°40W **105** D7
Meteghan *N.S., Canada* 44°11N 66°10W **141** J3
Metepec *Hidalgo, Mexico* 20°14N 98°19W **175** B9
Metepec *México, Mexico* 19°15N 99°36W **175** C8
Methow *Wash., U.S.A.* 48°8N 120°0W **120** B6
Methow → *Wash., U.S.A.* 48°5N 119°55W **120** B6
Methuen *Mass., U.S.A.* 42°44N 71°11W **91** B3
Métis-sur-Mer *Qué., Canada* 48°40N 67°59W **140** E2
Metlakatla *Alaska, U.S.A.* 55°8N 131°35W **135** J15
Metlaltoyuca *Puebla, Mexico* 20°44N 97°51W **176** D3
Metlatonoc *Guerrero, Mexico* 17°11N 98°20W **175** E9
Metolius *Oreg., U.S.A.* 44°35N 121°11W **121** C4
Metro Toronto Zoo *Ont., Canada* 43°48N 79°10W **161** A3
Metropolis *Ill., U.S.A.* 37°9N 88°44W **84** F5
Metter *Ga., U.S.A.* 32°24N 82°3W **113** D4
Metuchen *N.J., U.S.A.* 40°32N 74°22W **92** B2
Metz *Mo., U.S.A.* 37°59N 94°27W **83** D2
Metzger *Oreg., U.S.A.* 45°26N 122°45W **132** B1
Metzquititlán *Hidalgo, Mexico* 20°33N 98°23W **175** B9
Metztitlán *Hidalgo, Mexico* 20°36N 98°45W **175** B9
Mexcaltepec, Cerro *Guerrero, Mexico* 17°4N 98°53W **175** E9
Mexcaltitán *Nayarit, Mexico* 21°55N 105°31W **172** F5
Mexia *Tex., U.S.A.* 31°41N 96°29W **109** F11
Mexicali *Mexico* 32°40N 115°30W **166** A3
Mexican Hat *Utah, U.S.A.* 37°9N 109°52W **129** F6
Mexican Springs *N. Mex., U.S.A.* 35°47N 108°50W **131** B2
Mexican Water *Ariz., U.S.A.* 36°57N 109°32W **130** A6
Mexicanos, L. de los *Chihuahua, Mexico* 28°9N 106°57W **169** E9
México *Distrito Federal, Mexico* 19°24N 99°9W **175** C8
Mexico *Ind., U.S.A.* 40°49N 86°7W **85** C4
Mexico *Maine, U.S.A.* 44°34N 70°33W **90** D3
Mexico *Mo., U.S.A.* 39°10N 91°53W **83** B51
Mexico *N.Y., U.S.A.* 43°28N 76°14W **88** B4
México □ *Mexico* 19°20N 99°30W **175** C8
Mexico ■ *Cent. Amer.* 25°0N 105°0W **164** C4
México, Ciudad de *Distrito Federal, Mexico* 19°24N 99°9W **175** C8
Mexico B. *N.Y., U.S.A.* 43°35N 76°20W **88** B4
Mexico Beach *Fla., U.S.A.* 29°57N 85°25W **114** B3
Mexico City Int. ✈ (MEX) *Distrito Federal, Mexico* 19°25N 99°5W **181** B3
Mexquitic de Carmona *San Luis Potosí, Mexico* 22°16N 101°7W **171** H3
Mexticacán *Jalisco, Mexico* 21°13N 102°43W **174** A5
Meyerland *Tex., U.S.A.* 29°41N 95°28W **116** B2
Meyers Chuck *Alaska, U.S.A.* 55°45N 132°15W **135** J14
Meyersdale *Pa., U.S.A.* 39°49N 79°2W **93** A1
Meyronne *Sask., Canada* 49°39N 106°50W **150** F5
Mezacalapa → *Tabasco, Mexico* 17°22N 93°23W **178** B2
Mezcala → *Guerrero, Mexico* 17°58N 99°42W **175** E8
Mezontepec, Cerro *Distrito Federal, Mexico* 19°11N 99°14W **181** C2
Mezquital *Durango, Mexico* 23°29N 104°23W **173** D6
Mezquital *Tamaulipas, Mexico* 25°15N 97°26W **171** E7
Mezquital → *Mexico* 22°15N 104°54W **172** E6
Mezquital del Oro *Zacatecas, Mexico* 21°10N 103°23W **174** A4

Mezquitic *Jalisco, Mexico* 22°23N 103°41W **173** E7
Miacatlán *Morelos, Mex.* 18°46N 99°17W **175** D8
Miahuatlán *Oaxaca, Mexico* 16°20N 96°36W **177** H4
Miami *Ariz., U.S.A.* 33°24N 110°52W **130** D5
Miami *Fla., U.S.A.* 25°46N 80°11W **115** D2
Miami *Mo., U.S.A.* 39°19N 93°14W **83** B3
Miami *N. Mex., U.S.A.* 36°21N 104°48W **131** A6
Miami *Tex., U.S.A.* 35°42N 100°38W **108** B7
Miami → *Fla., U.S.A.* 25°46N 80°1W **115** D1
Miami Beach *Fla., U.S.A.* 25°47N 80°7W **115** D3
Miami Canal *Fla., U.S.A.* 26°30N 80°45W **114** E8
Miami County ☆ *Ind., U.S.A.* 40°45N 86°0W **85** C4
Miami County ☆ *Kans., U.S.A.* 38°30N 94°45W **82** C9
Miami County ☆ *Ohio, U.S.A.* 40°9N 84°15W **86** C2
Miami-Dade County ☆ *Fla., U.S.A.* 25°30N 80°30W **114** F8
Miami Int. ✈ (MIA) *Fla., U.S.A.* 25°48N 80°17W **115** D1
Miami Lakes *Fla., U.S.A.* 25°54N 80°18W **115** C1
Miami Shores *Fla., U.S.A.* 25°51N 80°11W **115** D1
Miami Springs *Fla., U.S.A.* 25°49N 80°17W **115** D1
Miamisburg *Ohio, U.S.A.* 39°38N 84°17W **86** D2
Mica Creek *B.C., Canada* 52°2N 118°35W **155** C16
Micanopy *Fla., U.S.A.* 29°30N 82°17W **114** B6
Micco *Fla., U.S.A.* 27°53N 80°30W **114** D8
Miccosukee *Fla., U.S.A.* 30°36N 84°3W **114** A4
Miccosukee I. *Fla., U.S.A.* 30°33N 83°53W **114** A3
Miccosukee Indian Reservation *Fla., U.S.A.* 25°46N 80°46W **114** F8
Michelsen, C. *Nunavut, Canada* 70°42N 103°3W **158** C5
Michie *Tenn., U.S.A.* 35°3N 88°26W **104** E4
Michigamme, L. *Mich., U.S.A.* 46°32N 88°5W **79** C3
Michigamme Res. *Mich., U.S.A.* 46°10N 88°10W **79** C3
Michigan *N. Dak., U.S.A.* 48°1N 98°7W **76** B7
Michigan □ *U.S.A.* 44°0N 85°0W **79** F7
Michigan, L. *Mich., U.S.A.* 44°0N 87°0W **79** F5
Michigan Center *Mich., U.S.A.* 42°14N 84°20W **79** G7
Michigan City *Ind., U.S.A.* 41°43N 86°54W **85** B4
Michigan City *Miss., U.S.A.* 34°59N 89°15W **111** B4
Michigan I. *Wis., U.S.A.* 46°59N 90°29W **78** B3
Michigan Islands Nat. Wildlife Refuge △ *Mich., U.S.A.* 45°42N 85°50W **79** D6
Michigantown *Ind., U.S.A.* 40°20N 86°24W **85** C4
Michipicoten *Ont., Canada* 47°55N 84°55W **149** E12
Michipicoten B. *Ont., Canada* 47°53N 84°53W **149** E12
Michipicoten I. *Ont., Canada* 47°40N 85°40W **149** E11
Michoacán □ *Mexico* 19°10N 101°5CW **174** C6
Mico, Pta. *Nic.* 12°0N 83°30W **182** D3
Midale *Sask., Canada* 49°25N 103°20W **150** F8
Middle → *Minn., U.S.A.* 48°22N 97°5W **77** B1
Middle Alkali L. *Calif., U.S.A.* 41°27N 120°5W **126** B6
Middle Bass I. *Ohio, U.S.A.* 41°41N 82°48W **86** A4
Middle Bay *Qué., Canada* 51°28N 57°30W **142** A3
Middle Bay *N.Y., U.S.A.* 40°37N 73°36W **97** C5
Middle Branch → *Baltimore, U.S.A.* 39°15N 76°37W **99** B2
Middle Concho → *Tex., U.S.A.* 31°27N 100°25W **108** F7
Middle Falls *N.Y., U.S.A.* 43°6N 73°32W **89** C1
Middle Feather → *Calif., U.S.A.* 38°33N 121°30W **126** E5
Middle Fork Forked Deer → *Tenn., U.S.A.* 36°1N 89°13W **104** D3
Middle Fork John Day → *Oreg., U.S.A.* 44°45N 119°38W **121** C6
Middle Fork Powder → *Wyo., U.S.A.* 43°42N 106°33W **124** C6
Middle Fork Sappa Cr. → *Kans., U.S.A.* 39°42N 100°5W **82** B3
Middle Granville *N.Y., U.S.A.* 43°26N 73°17W **89** C1
Middle Island *N.Y., U.S.A.* 40°53N 72°56W **91** D2
Middle Lake *Sask., Canada* 52°29N 105°18W **150** C6
Middle Loup → *Nebr., U.S.A.* 41°17N 98°24W **80** C7
Middle Musquodoboit *N.S., Canada* 45°3N 63°9W **141** H6
Middle Pease → *Tex., U.S.A.* 34°15N 100°7W **108** C7
Middle Point *Ohio, U.S.A.* 40°51N 84°27W **86** C2
Middle Ridge Wildlife Reserve △ *Nfld. & L., Canada* 48°15N 55°16W **142** D5
Middle River *Md., U.S.A.* 39°20N 76°27W **93** A4
Middle River *Minn., U.S.A.* 48°26N 96°10W **77** B2
Middle Valley *Tenn., U.S.A.* 35°12N 85°11W **105** E7
Middle Village *N.Y., U.S.A.* 40°43N 73°52W **97** B3
Middleboro *W. Va., U.S.A.* 39°30N 80°54W **102** B4
Middleburg *Fla., U.S.A.* 30°4N 81°52W **114** A7
Middleburg *Pa., U.S.A.* 40°47N 77°3W **87** D5
Middleburg *Va., U.S.A.* 38°58N 77°44W **93** B3
Middleburg Heights *Ohio, U.S.A.* 41°22N 81°48W **98** C5
Middleburgh *N.Y., U.S.A.* 42°36N 74°20W **88** C6
Middlebury *Conn., U.S.A.* 41°32N 73°7W **91** C1
Middlebury *Ind., U.S.A.* 41°41N 85°42W **85** B5
Middlebury *Vt., U.S.A.* 44°1N 73°10W **89** B1
Middlefield *Mass., U.S.A.* 42°20N 73°2W **91** B1
Middlefield *Ohio, U.S.A.* 41°28N 81°5W **86** B5
Middlegate *Nev., U.S.A.* 39°17N 118°2W **128** C2
Middleport *N.Y., U.S.A.* 43°13N 78°29W **88** B2
Middleport *Ohio, U.S.A.* 39°0N 82°3W **86** D4
Middlesboro *Ky., U.S.A.* 36°36N 83°43W **105** D9
Middlesex *Belize* 17°2N 88°31W **182** C2
Middlesex *N.C., U.S.A.* 35°47N 78°12W **103** C7
Middlesex County ☆ *Conn., U.S.A.* 41°25N 72°30W **91** C2
Middlesex County ☆ *Mass., U.S.A.* 42°20N 71°15W **91** B3
Middlesex County ☆ *N.J., U.S.A.* 40°30N 74°25W **92** B2
Middlesex County ☆ *Va., U.S.A.* 37°36N 76°36W **102** D8
Middlesex Fells Reservation *Mass., U.S.A.* 42°27N 71°6W **96** A2
Middleton *N.S., Canada* 44°57N 65°4W **141** J4
Middleton *Idaho, U.S.A.* 43°42N 116°37W **122** F2
Middleton *Mass., U.S.A.* 42°36N 71°1W **91** B3
Middleton *Mich., U.S.A.* 43°11N 84°43W **79** F7
Middleton *Tenn., U.S.A.* 35°4N 88°53W **104** E4
Middleton I. *Alaska, U.S.A.* 59°26N 146°20W **135** G11
Middletown *Calif., U.S.A.* 38°45N 122°37W **126** E4
Middletown *Conn., U.S.A.* 41°34N 72°39W **91** C2
Middletown *Del., U.S.A.* 39°27N 75°43W **93** A5
Middletown *Ill., U.S.A.* 40°11N 89°35W **84** C4
Middletown *Ind., U.S.A.* 40°3N 85°32W **85** C5
Middletown *Md., U.S.A.* 39°27N 77°33W **93** A3
Middletown *Mo., U.S.A.* 39°8N 91°25W **83** B5
Middletown *N.J., U.S.A.* 40°24N 74°9W **92** B2
Middletown *N.Y., U.S.A.* 41°27N 74°25W **92** A1
Middletown *Ohio, U.S.A.* 39°31N 84°24W **86** D2
Middletown *Pa., U.S.A.* 40°12N 76°44W **87** D6
Middletown *R.I., U.S.A.* 41°32N 71°17W **91** C3
Middletown *Va., U.S.A.* 39°2N 78°17W **93** A2
Middletown Springs *Vt., U.S.A.* 43°28N 73°8W **89** C1
Middleville *Mich., U.S.A.* 42°43N 85°28W **79** G6
Middleville *N.Y., U.S.A.* 43°8N 74°58W **88** B6
Middlewood *N.S., Canada* 44°14N 64°34W **141** J4
Midland *Ont., Canada* 44°45N 79°50W **146** D4
Midland *Calif., U.S.A.* 33°52N 114°48W **127** K12

Midland *Md., U.S.A.* 39°37N 78°55W **93** A2
Midland *Mich., U.S.A.* 43°37N 84°14W **79** F7
Midland *Oreg., U.S.A.* 42°8N 121°49W **121** E4
Midland *S. Dak., U.S.A.* 44°4N 101°10W **76** F4
Midland *Tex., U.S.A.* 32°0N 102°3W **108** F5
Midland Beach *N.Y., U.S.A.* 40°34N 74°6W **97** C2
Midland City *Ala., U.S.A.* 31°19N 85°30W **112** C5
Midland County ☆ *Mich., U.S.A.* 43°35N 84°20W **79** F7
Midland County ☆ *Tex., U.S.A.* 32°0N 102°0W **108** F5
Midlothian *Md., U.S.A.* 39°40N 78°58W **93** A2
Midlothian *Tex., U.S.A.* 32°30N 97°0W **109** E11
Midlothian *Va., U.S.A.* 37°30N 77°28W **102** D7
Midnight *Miss., U.S.A.* 33°3N 90°35W **111** C3
Midvale *Idaho, U.S.A.* 44°28N 116°44W **122** E2
Midvale *Ohio, U.S.A.* 40°26N 81°23W **86** C5
Midvale *Utah, U.S.A.* 40°36N 111°53W **134** C2
Midville *Ga., U.S.A.* 32°49N 82°14W **113** D4
Midway *B.C., Canada* 49°1N 118°48W **155** F16
Midway *Ala., U.S.A.* 32°5N 85°31W **112** D5
Midway *Fla., U.S.A.* 30°30N 84°27W **114** A4
Midway *Ky., U.S.A.* 31°48N 81°26W **113** E5
Midway *Ky., U.S.A.* 38°9N 84°41W **105** B8
Midway *Utah, U.S.A.* 40°31N 111°28W **129** C4
Midway *Tex., U.S.A.* 31°2N 95°45W **109** F12
Midway City *Calif., U.S.A.* 33°44N 117°59W **133** D7
Midwest *Wyo., U.S.A.* 43°25N 106°16W **124** C6
Midwest City *Okla., U.S.A.* 35°27N 97°24W **107** C6
Mier *Tamaulipas, Mexico* 26°26N 99°9W **170** D5
Mier y Noriega *Nuevo León, Mexico* 23°25N 100°7W **171** G4
Miesville *Minn., U.S.A.* 44°36N 92°49W **77** F6
Miette Hotsprings *Alta., Canada* 53°8N 117°46W **152** D3
Mifflin *Ohio, U.S.A.* 40°46N 82°22W **86** C4
Mifflin County ☆ *Pa., U.S.A.* 40°45N 77°45W **87** D5
Mifflinburg *Pa., U.S.A.* 40°55N 77°3W **87** D5
Mifflintown *Pa., U.S.A.* 40°34N 77°24W **87** D5
Miguel Alemán *Sonora, Mexico* 28°50N 111°30W **168** E4
Miguel Alemán, Presa *Oaxaca, Mexico* 18°15N 96°32W **177** F4
Miguel Auza *Zacatecas, Mexico* 24°19N 103°25W **173** C7
Miguel Hidalgo *Durango, Mexico* 24°40N 104°43W **173** C6
Miguel Hidalgo *Jalisco, Mexico* 19°25N 104°54W **174** C3
Miguel Hidalgo *México, Mexico* 19°25N 99°12W **181** B2
Miguel Hidalgo, Int. ✈ (EDL) *Guadalajara, Mexico* 20°31N 103°19W **180** B2
Miguel Hidalgo, Presa *Sinaloa, Mexico* 26°30N 108°34W **172** A2
Mikkalo *Oreg., U.S.A.* 45°28N 120°14W **121** B5
Mikkwa → *Alta., Canada* 58°25N 114°46W **152** A6
Milaca *Minn., U.S.A.* 45°45N 93°39W **77** E5
Milam *Tex., U.S.A.* 31°26N 93°51W **109** F14
Milam County ☆ *Tex., U.S.A.* 30°51N 96°59W **109** G11
Milan *Ga., U.S.A.* 32°1N 83°4W **113** D3
Milan *Ill., U.S.A.* 41°27N 90°34W **84** B3
Milan *Ind., U.S.A.* 39°7N 85°8W **85** D5
Milan *Mich., U.S.A.* 42°5N 83°41W **79** G8
Milan *Mo., U.S.A.* 40°12N 93°7W **83** A3
Milan *N.H., U.S.A.* 44°36N 71°12W **89** B3
Milan *N. Mex., U.S.A.* 35°9N 107°54W **131** B3
Milan *Ohio, U.S.A.* 41°18N 82°37W **86** B4
Milan *Tenn., U.S.A.* 35°55N 88°46W **104** E4
Milan *Wash., U.S.A.* 47°58N 117°20W **120** C8
Milan Arsenal *Tenn., U.S.A.* 35°52N 88°43W **104** E4
Milbank *S. Dak., U.S.A.* 45°13N 96°38W **76** E8
Milbanke Sd. *B.C., Canada* 52°19N 128°33W **154** C6
Milbridge *Maine, U.S.A.* 44°32N 67°53W **90** D6
Milburn *Nebr., U.S.A.* 41°43N 99°44W **80** C6
Milburn *Okla., U.S.A.* 34°14N 96°33W **107** D7
Milden *Sask., Canada* 51°29N 107°32W **150** D4
Mildmay *Ont., Canada* 44°3N 81°7W **146** C3
Mildred *Kans., U.S.A.* 38°1N 95°10W **82** C8
Miles *Tex., U.S.A.* 31°36N 100°11W **108** F7
Miles *Wash., U.S.A.* 47°55N 118°18W **120** C7
Miles City *Mont., U.S.A.* 46°25N 105°51W **123** D12
Milesburg *Pa., U.S.A.* 40°57N 77°47W **87** D5
Milestone *Sask., Canada* 49°59N 104°31W **150** F7
Milford *Baltimore, U.S.A.* 39°20N 76°44W **99** A1
Milford *Calif., U.S.A.* 40°10N 120°22W **126** C6
Milford *Conn., U.S.A.* 41°14N 73°3W **91** C1
Milford *Del., U.S.A.* 38°55N 75°26W **93** B5
Milford *Ga., U.S.A.* 31°23N 84°33W **113** E2
Milford *Ill., U.S.A.* 40°38N 87°42W **84** C6
Milford *Ind., U.S.A.* 41°25N 85°51W **85** B5
Milford *Iowa, U.S.A.* 43°19N 95°9W **81** B3
Milford *Kans., U.S.A.* 39°10N 96°55W **82** B7
Milford *Ky., U.S.A.* 38°35N 84°9W **105** B8
Milford *Maine, U.S.A.* 44°57N 68°39W **90** D5
Milford *Mass., U.S.A.* 42°8N 71°31W **91** B3
Milford *Mich., U.S.A.* 42°35N 83°36W **79** G8
Milford *Mo., U.S.A.* 37°35N 94°9W **83** D2
Milford *N.H., U.S.A.* 42°50N 71°39W **89** D3
Milford *N.J., U.S.A.* 40°34N 75°6W **92** B1
Milford *N.Y., U.S.A.* 42°35N 74°57W **88** C6
Milford *Nebr., U.S.A.* 40°47N 97°3W **80** D8
Milford *Pa., U.S.A.* 41°19N 74°48W **92** A2
Milford *Utah, U.S.A.* 38°24N 113°1W **129** D2
Milford Center *Ohio, U.S.A.* 40°11N 83°26W **86** C3
Milford Lake *Kans., U.S.A.* 39°5N 96°54W **82** B7
Milford Station *N.S., Canada* 45°3N 63°26W **141** H6
Mililani Town *Hawai'i, U.S.A.* 21°28N 158°1W **136** K13
Milk River *Alta., Canada* 49°10N 112°5W **153** J8
Mill → *Mich., U.S.A.* 43°2N 82°35W **79** F9
Mill City *Nev., U.S.A.* 40°41N 118°4W **128** B2
Mill City *Oreg., U.S.A.* 44°45N 122°29W **121** C3
Mill Creek *W. Va., U.S.A.* 38°44N 79°58W **102** C5
Mill Creek *Wash., U.S.A.* 47°51N 122°12W **132** A4
Mill Hall *Pa., U.S.A.* 41°6N 77°29W **87** C5
Mill I. *Nunavut, Canada* 63°58N 77°47W **159** E10
Mill Shoals *Ill., U.S.A.* 38°15N 88°21W **84** E5
Mill Stream Run Reservation *Ohio, U.S.A.* 41°19N 81°48W **98** C1
Mill Village *N.S., Canada* 44°9N 64°39W **141** J5
Millard *Mo., U.S.A.* 40°7N 92°33W **83** A4
Millard County ☆ *Utah, U.S.A.* 39°0N 113°0W **129** D3
Millboro *S. Dak., U.S.A.* 43°4N 99°58W **76** G6
Millboro *Va., U.S.A.* 37°59N 79°36W **102** D5
Millbourne *Pa., U.S.A.* 39°58N 75°15W **98** B1
Millbridge *Ont., Canada* 44°41N 77°36W **147** C9
Millbrook *Ont., Canada* 44°10N 78°29W **147** C8
Millbrook *N.Y., U.S.A.* 41°47N 73°42W **88** D7
Millbury *Mass., U.S.A.* 42°12N 71°46W **91** B3
Millcreek *Utah, U.S.A.* 40°41N 111°52W **134** B2
Mille Lacs, L. des *Ont., Canada* 48°45N 90°35W **148** D6
Mille Lacs County ☆ *Minn., U.S.A.* 45°50N 93°45W **77** E5
Mille Lacs Indian Reservation *Minn., U.S.A.* 46°8N 93°45W **77** D5

Mille Lacs L. *Minn., U.S.A.* 46°15N 93°39W **77** D5
Milledgeville *Ga., U.S.A.* 33°5N 83°14W **113** C3
Milledgeville *Ill., U.S.A.* 41°58N 89°46W **84** B4
Milledgeville *Ohio, U.S.A.* 39°36N 83°35W **86** D3
Milledgeville *Tenn., U.S.A.* 35°22N 88°22W **104** E4
Millen *Ga., U.S.A.* 32°48N 81°57W **113** D5
Millennium Dallas ✈ *Tex., U.S.A.* 32°44N 96°56W **116** B4
Miller *Kans., U.S.A.* 38°33N 95°59W **82** C8
Miller *Mo., U.S.A.* 37°13N 93°50W **83** D3
Miller *Nebr., U.S.A.* 40°56N 99°23W **80** D6
Miller *S. Dak., U.S.A.* 44°31N 98°59W **76** F7
Miller County ☆ *Ark., U.S.A.* 33°10N 93°58W **106** E2
Miller County ☆ *Ga., U.S.A.* 31°10N 84°45W **113** E2
Miller County ☆ *Mo., U.S.A.* 38°15N 92°25W **83** C4
Miller Meadow *Ill., U.S.A.* 41°51N 87°49W **95** B2
Millerand *Qué., Canada* 47°13N 61°59W **141** F8
Millers → *Mass., U.S.A.* 42°35N 72°30W **91** B2
Millers Creek Res. *Tex., U.S.A.* 33°30N 99°20W **109** D8
Millers Falls *Mass., U.S.A.* 42°35N 72°30W **91** B2
Millers Ferry *Ala., U.S.A.* 32°6N 87°22W **112** D3
Millers Tavern *Va., U.S.A.* 37°50N 76°57W **93** C4
Millersburg *Ind., U.S.A.* 41°32N 85°42W **85** B5
Millersburg *Iowa, U.S.A.* 41°34N 92°10W **81** D6
Millersburg *Ky., U.S.A.* 38°18N 84°9W **105** B8
Millersburg *Mich., U.S.A.* 45°20N 84°4W **79** D7
Millersburg *Ohio, U.S.A.* 40°33N 81°55W **86** C5
Millersburg *Pa., U.S.A.* 40°32N 76°58W **87** D6
Millersport *Ohio, U.S.A.* 39°54N 82°32W **86** D4
Millersville *Md., U.S.A.* 39°4N 76°39W **93** A4
Millersville *Ohio, U.S.A.* 40°0N 76°22W **87** E6
Millersville *Pa., U.S.A.* 40°0N 76°22W **87** E6
Millersville *Tenn., U.S.A.* 36°22N 86°43W **104** D6
Millerton *Iowa, U.S.A.* 40°51N 93°18W **81** E5
Millerton *N.Y., U.S.A.* 41°57N 73°31W **91** C1
Millerton *Okla., U.S.A.* 33°59N 95°1W **107** E8
Millerton L. *Calif., U.S.A.* 37°1N 119°41W **127** F7
Millertown *Nfld. & L., Canada* 48°49N 56°33W **142** D4
Milles Isles, R. des → *Qué., Canada* 45°34N 73°50W **160** A1
Millet *Alta., Canada* 53°6N 113°28W **153** E7
Millett *Tex., U.S.A.* 28°35N 99°12W **109** J8
Millheim *Pa., U.S.A.* 40°54N 77°29W **87** D5
Milligan *Fla., U.S.A.* 30°45N 86°38W **114** A2
Milligan *Nebr., U.S.A.* 40°30N 97°23W **80** D8
Millington *Md., U.S.A.* 39°16N 75°50W **93** A5
Millington *Mich., U.S.A.* 43°17N 83°32W **79** F8
Millington *Tenn., U.S.A.* 35°20N 89°53W **104** E2
Millinocket *Maine, U.S.A.* 45°39N 68°43W **90** C5
Millinocket L. *Maine, U.S.A.* 45°46N 68°48W **90** C5
Millis *Mass., U.S.A.* 42°10N 71°22W **91** B3
Millport *Ala., U.S.A.* 33°34N 88°5W **112** C2
Millry *Ala., U.S.A.* 31°38N 88°19W **112** E2
Mills *N. Mex., U.S.A.* 36°5N 104°15W **131** A6
Mills *Nebr., U.S.A.* 42°57N 99°27W **80** B6
Mills *Wyo., U.S.A.* 42°50N 106°22W **124** D6
Mills County ☆ *Iowa, U.S.A.* 41°0N 95°35W **81** D3
Mills County ☆ *Tex., U.S.A.* 31°27N 98°34W **109** F9
Mills L. *N.W.T., Canada* 61°30N 118°20W **157** D9
Millsap *Tex., U.S.A.* 32°45N 98°1W **109** E9
Millsboro *Del., U.S.A.* 38°36N 75°18W **93** B5
Millstadt *Ill., U.S.A.* 38°28N 90°6W **84** D3
Millstream *N.B., Canada* 48°2N 67°2W **141** E2
Milltown *Ind., U.S.A.* 38°21N 86°17W **85** E4
Milltown *S. Dak., U.S.A.* 43°25N 97°43W **76** G7
Milltown *Wis., U.S.A.* 45°32N 92°30W **78** C1
Milltown-Head of Bay d'Espoir *Nfld. & L., Canada* 47°56N 55°45W **142** E5
Millvale *Pa., U.S.A.* 40°28N 79°58W **98** B2
Millville *N.B., Canada* 46°8N 67°12W **141** G2
Millville *Del., U.S.A.* 38°35N 75°8W **93** B5
Millville *Iowa, U.S.A.* 42°42N 91°6W **81** C7
Millville *Ky., U.S.A.* 38°8N 84°49W **105** B8
Millville *Mass., U.S.A.* 42°2N 71°35W **91** B3
Millville *N.J., U.S.A.* 39°24N 75°2W **92** C1
Millville *Pa., U.S.A.* 41°7N 76°32W **87** C6
Millwood *Ga., U.S.A.* 31°16N 82°40W **113** E4
Millwood *Md., U.S.A.* 38°52N 76°52W **99** B4
Millwood *Va., U.S.A.* 39°4N 78°2W **93** A2
Millwood L. *Ark., U.S.A.* 47°41N 117°17W **120** C8
Millwood L. *Ark., U.S.A.* 33°42N 93°58W **106** E2
Milmay *N.J., U.S.A.* 39°26N 74°52W **92** C2
Milne Land *Greenland* 70°40N 26°30W **162** C8
Milner *Colo., U.S.A.* 40°29N 107°1W **125** B3
Milnesand *N. Mex., U.S.A.* 33°39N 103°20W **131** D7
Milnor *N. Dak., U.S.A.* 46°16N 97°27W **76** D8
Milo *Alta., Canada* 50°34N 112°53W **153** H8
Milo *Iowa, U.S.A.* 41°17N 93°27W **81** D5
Milo *Maine, U.S.A.* 45°15N 68°59W **90** C5
Milo *Mo., U.S.A.* 37°45N 94°18W **83** D2
Milo *Oreg., U.S.A.* 42°56N 123°39W **121** E2
Miloli'i *Hawai'i, U.S.A.* 19°11N 155°55W **136** D6
Milpa Alta *Distrito Federal, Mexico* 19°11N 99°1W **181** C3
Milpillas *Chihuahua, Mexico* 27°13N 108°40W **168** F7
Milpitas *Calif., U.S.A.* 37°26N 121°55W **126** F5
Milroy *Ind., U.S.A.* 39°30N 85°28W **85** D5
Milroy *Minn., U.S.A.* 44°25N 95°33W **77** F3
Milroy *Pa., U.S.A.* 40°43N 77°35W **87** D5
Milton *N.S., Canada* 44°4N 64°45W **141** J5
Milton *Ont., Canada* 43°31N 79°53W **146** D7
Milton *Del., U.S.A.* 38°47N 75°19W **93** B5
Milton *Ill., U.S.A.* 39°34N 90°39W **84** D3
Milton *Iowa, U.S.A.* 40°41N 92°10W **81** E6
Milton *Kans., U.S.A.* 37°26N 97°46W **82** D6
Milton *Ky., U.S.A.* 38°43N 85°22W **105** B7
Milton *Mass., U.S.A.* 42°15N 71°4W **96** B2
Milton *N. Dak., U.S.A.* 48°38N 98°3W **76** B7
Milton *N.H., U.S.A.* 43°25N 70°59W **89** C4
Milton *Pa., U.S.A.* 41°1N 76°51W **87** C6
Milton *Vt., U.S.A.* 44°38N 73°7W **89** B1
Milton *W. Va., U.S.A.* 38°26N 82°8W **102** C2
Milton *Wis., U.S.A.* 42°47N 88°56W **78** F4
Milton-Freewater *Oreg., U.S.A.* 45°56N 118°23W **121** B7
Miltona *Minn., U.S.A.* 46°3N 95°18W **77** D3
Miltonvale *Kans., U.S.A.* 39°21N 97°27W **82** B6
Milverton *Ont., Canada* 43°34N 80°55W **146** D6
Milwaukee *Wis., U.S.A.* 43°2N 87°54W **94** A2
Milwaukee → *Wis., U.S.A.* 43°2N 87°54W **94** A2
Milwaukee Bay *Wis., U.S.A.* 43°1N 87°53W **94** B2
Milwaukee County ☆ *Wis., U.S.A.* 43°0N 88°0W **78** F4
Milwaukee Deep *Atl. Oc.* 19°50N 68°0W **183** C6
Milwaukee General Mitchell Int. ✈ (MKE) *Wis., U.S.A.* 42°57N 87°54W **94** C2
Mimbres *N. Mex., U.S.A.* 32°51N 107°59W **131** D2
Mimbres Mts. *N. Mex., U.S.A.* 32°50N 107°45W **131** E3

Mimico Ont., Canada 43°36N 79°29W **161** B2
Mimico Creek → Ont., Canada 43°37N 79°28W **161** B2
Mimingeash P.E.I., Canada 46°53N 64°14W **141** G5
Miminiska L. Ont., Canada 51°55N 88°37W **148** A8
Mims Fla., U.S.A. 28°40N 80°51W **114** C8
Mina Nuevo León, Mexico 26°1N 100°32W **170** D4
Mina Nev., U.S.A. 38°24N 118°7W **128** D2
Minago → Man., Canada 54°33N 98°59W **151** A13
Minaki Ont., Canada 49°59N 94°40W **148** C2
Minam Oreg., U.S.A. 45°38N 117°43W **121** B8
Minas, Sierra de las Guatemala 15°9N 89°31W **182** C2
Minas Basin U.S., Canada 45°20N 64°12W **141** H5
Minas Channel N.S., Canada 45°15N 64°45W **141** H5
Minas de Barroterán Coahuila, Mexico 27°41N 101°18W **170** C3
Minatare Nebr., U.S.A. 41°49N 103°30W **80** C2
Minatitlán Colima, Mexico 19°22N 104°4W **174** C3
Minatitlán Veracruz, Mexico 17°59N 94°31W **177** G6
Minburn Iowa, U.S.A. 41°45N 94°2W **81** D4
Minco Okla., U.S.A. 35°19N 97°57W **107** C6
Mindemoya Ont., Canada 45°44N 82°10W **146** B4
Minden Ont., Canada 44°55N 78°43W **147** C8
Minden Iowa, U.S.A. 41°28N 95°32W **81** D3
Minden La., U.S.A. 32°37N 93°17W **110** B2
Minden Nebr., U.S.A. 40°30N 98°57W **80** D7
Minden Nev., U.S.A. 38°57N 119°46W **128** D1
Minden City Mich., U.S.A. 43°40N 82°47W **79** F9
Mindenmines Mo., U.S.A. 37°28N 94°35W **83** D2
Mine, L. de la Qué., Canada 50°51N 64°43W **140** C5
Mine Centre Ont., Canada 48°45N 92°37W **148** D4
Minebank Run → Baltimore, U.S.A. 39°25N 76°32W **99** A2
Mineola N.Y. U.S.A. 40°44N 73°38W **97** B5
Mineola Tex., U.S.A. 32°40N 95°29W **109** E12
Miner Mo., U.S.A. 36°53N 89°32W **83** E7
Miner → Yukon, Canada 66°30N 138°25W **156** C5
Miner County ☆ S. Dak., U.S.A. 44°1N 97°36W **76** F8
Mineral Calif., U.S.A. 40°21N 121°36W **126** C5
Mineral Va., U.S.A. 38°1N 77°55W **102** C7
Mineral Wash., U.S.A. 46°43N 122°11W **120** D3
Mineral Bluff Ga., U.S.A. 34°55N 84°17W **113** B2
Mineral County ☆ Colo., U.S.A. 37°40N 106°50W **125** E4
Mineral County ☆ Mont., U.S.A. 47°4N 115°0W **123** C3
Mineral County ☆ Nev., U.S.A. 38°30N 118°25W **128** D2
Mineral County ☆ W. Va., U.S.A. 39°21N 79°0W **102** B6
Mineral de Cucharas Nayarit, Mexico 22°49N 105°17W **172** E5
Mineral del Monte Hidalgo, Mexico 20°8N 98°40W **175** B9
Mineral la Luz Coahuila, Mexico 27°36N 101°29W **170** C3
Mineral Mts. Utah, U.S.A. 38°30N 112°45W **129** F7
Mineral Point Mo., U.S.A. 37°57N 90°44W **83** D6
Mineral Point Wis., U.S.A. 42°52N 90°11W **78** F3
Mineral Springs Ark., U.S.A. 33°53N 93°55W **106** C2
Mineral Wells Tex., U.S.A. 32°48N 98°7W **109** E9
Minersville Pa., U.S.A. 40°41N 76°16W **87** D6
Minersville Utah, U.S.A. 38°13N 112°56W **129** E3
Minerva N.Y., U.S.A. 43°47N 73°59W **88** B7
Minerva Ohio, U.S.A. 40°44N 81°6W **86** C5
Mineville N.Y., U.S.A. 44°6N 73°31W **89** B1
Mingan Qué., Canada 50°20N 64°0W **143** C5
Mingan → Qué., Canada 50°18N 63°59W **140** C6
Mingan, Île de Qué., Canada 50°12N 63°45W **140** C6
Mingo Co. ☆ W. Va., U.S.A. 37°43N 82°11W **102** D2
Mingo Junction Ohio, U.S.A. 40°19N 80°37W **86** C6
Mingo L. Nunavut, Canada 64°30N 72°10W **159** E11
Minidoka Idaho, U.S.A. 42°45N 113°29W **122** G5
Minidoka County ☆ Idaho, U.S.A. 42°50N 113°38W **122** G5
Minidoka Nat. Wildlife Refuge △ Idaho,
  U.S.A. 42°40N 113°23W **122** G5
Minier Ill., U.S.A. 40°26N 89°19W **84** C4
Miniota Man., Canada 50°8N 101°2W **151** E10
Minipi L. Nfld. & L., Canada 52°25N 60°45W **140** A9
Miniss L. Ont., Canada 50°48N 90°50W **148** B6
Minitonas Man., Canada 52°5N 101°2W **151** C10
Minneapolis Kans., U.S.A. 39°8N 97°42W **82** D8
Minneapolis Minn., U.S.A. 44°57N 93°16W **94** B2
Minneapolis Crystal ✈ (MIC) Minn.,
  U.S.A. 45°3N 93°23W **94** A1
Minneapolis-St. Paul Int. ✈ (MSP) Minn.,
  U.S.A. 44°53N 93°13W **94** B2
Minnedosa Man., Canada 50°14N 99°50W **151** E12
Minnehaha County ☆ S. Dak., U.S.A. 43°40N 96°49W **76** G9
Minnehaha Regional Park △ Minn.,
  U.S.A. 44°53N 93°12W **94** B2
Minneiska Minn., U.S.A. 44°12N 91°52W **77** F7
Minneola Kans., U.S.A. 37°26N 100°1W **82** D3
Minneota Minn., U.S.A. 44°34N 95°59W **77** F3
Minnesota → Minn., U.S.A. 46°0N 94°15W **77** F4
Minnesota → Minn., U.S.A. 44°54N 93°9W **77** F5
Minnesota City Minn., U.S.A. 44°6N 91°46W **77** F7
Minnesota Lake Minn., U.S.A. 43°51N 93°50W **77** G5
Minnetex Tex., U.S.A. 29°36N 95°21W **116** C2
Minnetonka Minn., U.S.A. 44°55N 93°42W **94** B2
Minnetonka, L. Minn., U.S.A. 44°54N 93°38W **94** B1
Minnewaukan N. Dak., U.S.A. 48°4N 99°15W **76** B6
Minnitaki L. Ont., Canada 49°57N 92°10W **148** C4
Minong Wis., U.S.A. 46°6N 91°49W **78** B2
Minonk Ill., U.S.A. 40°54N 89°2W **84** C4
Minooka Ill., U.S.A. 41°27N 88°16W **84** B5
Minor Hill Tenn., U.S.A. 35°4N 87°9W **104** C5
Minoru Park B.C., Canada 49°9N 123°9W **161** C2
Minot N. Dak., U.S.A. 48°14N 101°18W **76** B4
Minster Ohio, U.S.A. 40°24N 84°23W **86** C2
Minstrel Island B.C., Canada 50°37N 126°18W **154** E8
Mint Hill N.C., U.S.A. 35°13N 80°41W **103** C5
Minter City Miss., U.S.A. 33°45N 90°19W **111** C3
Minto → Canada 46°5N 66°5W **141** G3
Minto Alaska, U.S.A. 64°53N 149°10W **135** D10
Minto N. Dak., U.S.A. 48°17N 97°22W **76** B8
Minto, L. Qué., Canada 57°13N 75°0W **143** B3
Minto Hd. Nunavut, Canada 73°5N 102°17W **158** C5
Minto Inlet N.W.T., Canada 71°20N 117°0W **156** B9
Minton Sask., Canada 49°10N 104°35W **150** F7
Minturn Colo., U.S.A. 39°35N 106°26W **125** C4
Minuteman Missile Nat. Historic Site △ S. Dak.,
  U.S.A. 43°55N 102°8W **76** G3
Mio Mich., U.S.A. 44°39N 84°8W **79** E7
Miquelon Qué., Canada 49°25N 76°27W **144** B6
Miquelon St-P. & M. 47°8N 56°22W **142** E4
Miquihuana Tamaulipas, Mexico 23°34N 99°47W **171** G5
Mira N.S., Canada 46°2N 59°58W **141** G10
Mira → N.S., Canada 46°1N 59°58W **141** G10
Mira por vos Cay Bahamas 22°9N 74°30W **183** B5
Mirador Chiapas, Mexico 16°49N 93°8W **178** C3
Mirador-Río Azul, Parque Nac. △
  Guatemala 17°45N 89°50W **182** C1
Miramar Fla., U.S.A. 25°59N 80°13W **115** C1
Miramar L. Chiapas, Mexico 16°25N 91°15W **178** C5

Miramichi N.B., Canada 47°2N 65°28W **141** F4
Miramichi, Little S.W. → N.B., Canada 46°58N 65°40W **141** G4
Miramichi, N.W. → N.B., Canada 46°57N 65°50W **141** G4
Miramichi, S.W. → N.B., Canada 46°58N 65°38W **141** G4
Miramichi B. N.B., Canada 47°15N 65°0W **141** F4
Mirando City Tex., U.S.A. 27°26N 99°0W **108** K9
Misantla Veracruz, Mexico 19°56N 96°50W **176** E4
Miscou Centre N.B., Canada 47°57N 64°34W **141** F5
Miscou I. N.B., Canada 47°57N 64°31W **141** F5
Miscouche P.E.I., Canada 46°26N 63°52W **141** G6
Misehkow → Ont., Canada 51°26N 89°11W **148** A7
Mishawaka Ind., U.S.A. 41°40N 86°11W **85** B4
Misión de Santa Gertrudis Baja Calif.,
  Mexico 28°5N 113°4W **167** E5
Miskitos, Cayos Nic. 14°26N 82°50W **182** D3
Misquah Hills Minn., U.S.A. 47°50N 90°30W **77** C8
Misquamicut R.I., U.S.A. 41°20N 71°49W **91** C3
Missanabie Ont., Canada 48°20N 84°6W **149** D12
Missaukee County ☆ Mich., U.S.A. 44°20N 85°10W **79** E6
Missinaibi → Ont., Canada 50°43N 81°29W **149** B15
Missinaibi L. Ont., Canada 48°23N 83°40W **149** D13
Missinaibi Lake Prov. Park △ Ont.,
  Canada 48°25N 83°30W **149** D13
Mission B.C., Canada 49°10N 122°15W **155** F12
Mission Calif., U.S.A. 37°44N 122°25W **132** B2
Mission S. Dak., U.S.A. 43°18N 100°39W **76** G5
Mission Tex., U.S.A. 26°13N 98°20W **108** L9
Mission Bay Calif., U.S.A. 32°46N 117°14W **133** B1
Mission Bay Park Calif., U.S.A. 32°46N 117°13W **133** B1
Mission Mt. Okla., U.S.A. 36°2N 94°35W **107** B9
Mission Ridge S. Dak., U.S.A. 44°42N 100°47W **76** F5
Mission Trails Regional Park △ Calif.,
  U.S.A. 32°47N 117°2W **133** A2
Mission Viejo Calif., U.S.A. 33°36N 117°40W **127** K9
Missipuskiow → Sask., Canada 53°53N 103°18W **150** B8
Missisicabi → Qué., Canada 51°14N 79°31W **143** C2
Missisquoi → Vt., U.S.A. 45°0N 73°8W **89** B1
Missisquoi, B. N. Amer. 45°2N 73°9W **89** A1
Missisquoi B. Vt., U.S.A. 45°0N 73°8W **89** A1
Missisquoi Nat. Wildlife Refuge △ Vt.,
  U.S.A. 44°57N 73°10W **89** B1
Mississagi → Ont., Canada 46°15N 83°9W **146** A3
Mississagi Prov. Park △ Ont., Canada 46°30N 82°40W **146** A3
Mississauga Ont., Canada 43°32N 79°35W **161** B1
Mississinewa L. Ind., U.S.A. 40°42N 85°52W **85** C5
Mississippi □ U.S.A. 33°0N 90°0W **111** D4
Mississippi → La., U.S.A. 29°9N 89°15W **110** E6
Mississippi Choctaw Indian Reservation Miss.,
  U.S.A. 32°48N 89°7W **111** D4
Mississippi County ☆ Ark., U.S.A. 35°45N 90°5W **106** C5
Mississippi County ☆ Mo., U.S.A. 36°50N 89°15W **83** E7
Mississippi L. Ont., Canada 45°5N 76°10W **144** F6
Mississippi River Delta La., U.S.A. 29°10N 89°15W **110** E6
Mississippi Sd. Miss., U.S.A. 30°20N 89°0W **111** F5
Missoula Mont., U.S.A. 46°52N 114°1W **123** D3
Missoula County ☆ Mont., U.S.A. 47°4N 114°0W **123** C4
Missouri □ U.S.A. 38°25N 92°30W **83** C4
Missouri → U.S.A. 38°49N 90°7W **83** C6
Missouri Buttes Wyo., U.S.A. 44°37N 104°47W **124** B8
Missouri City Mo., U.S.A. 39°14N 94°18W **83** B2
Missouri City Tex., U.S.A. 29°37N 95°32W **116** C1
Missouri Nat. Scenic River △ U.S.A. 42°48N 97°25W **80** B8
Missouri Valley Iowa, U.S.A. 41°34N 95°53W **81** D3
Mistanipisipou → Qué., Canada 51°32N 61°50W **140** B8
Mistaouac, L. Qué., Canada 49°25N 78°41W **144** B4
Mistassin I. Qué., Canada 52°35N 78°33W **144** C2
Mistassibi → Qué., Canada 48°53N 72°13W **145** C10
Mistassibi Nord-Est → Qué., Canada 49°31N 71°56W **145** B11
Mistassini → Qué., Canada 48°42N 72°20W **145** C10
Mistassini, L. Qué., Canada 51°0N 73°30W **143** C3
Mistatim Sask., Canada 52°52N 103°22W **150** C8
Misteriosa Bank W. Indies 18°50N 83°50W **182** C2
Mistissini Qué., Canada 50°24N 73°56W **143** C3
Misty Fjords Nat. Monument △ Alaska,
  U.S.A. 55°40N 130°40W **135** J15
Mita, Pta. Nayarit, Mexico 20°47N 105°33W **172** G5
Mitchell Ont., Canada 43°28N 81°12W **146** D5
Mitchell Ga., U.S.A. 33°13N 82°42W **113** C4
Mitchell Ind., U.S.A. 38°44N 86°28W **85** E4
Mitchell Iowa, U.S.A. 43°19N 92°53W **81** B6
Mitchell Nebr., U.S.A. 41°57N 103°49W **80** C2
Mitchell Oreg., U.S.A. 44°34N 120°9W **121** C5
Mitchell S. Dak., U.S.A. 43°43N 98°2W **76** G7
Mitchell, L. Mich., U.S.A. 44°15N 85°30W **79** E6
Mitchell, Mt. N.C., U.S.A. 35°46N 82°16W **103** C3
Mitchell County ☆ Ga., U.S.A. 31°15N 84°10W **113** E2
Mitchell County ☆ Iowa, U.S.A. 43°20N 92°45W **81** B6
Mitchell County ☆ Kans., U.S.A. 39°30N 98°10W **82** B5
Mitchell County ☆ N.C., U.S.A. 36°5N 82°9W **103** B3
Mitchell County ☆ Tex., U.S.A. 32°24N 100°52W **108** E7
Mitchell I. B.C., Canada 49°12N 123°5W **161** B2
Mitchell L. B.C., Canada 52°52N 120°37W **155** C14
Mitchell L. Ala., U.S.A. 32°48N 86°27W **112** D4
Mitchell Lake Tex., U.S.A. 29°18N 98°29W **116** D3
Mitchell Museum of the American Indian Ill.,
  U.S.A. 42°4N 87°43W **95** A2
Mitchellsburg Ky., U.S.A. 37°36N 84°57W **105** C8
Mitchellville Iowa, U.S.A. 41°40N 93°22W **81** D5
Mitchinamecus, Rés. Qué., Canada 47°19N 75°9W **144** D7
Mitla Oaxaca, Mexico 16°57N 96°24W **177** H4
Mittimatalik = Pond Inlet Nunavut,
  Canada 72°40N 77°0W **158** C10
Mixcoac Distrito Federal, Mexico 19°23N 99°11W **181** B2
Mixistlán Oaxaca, Mexico 17°1N 96°5W **177** G4
Mixquiahuala Hidalgo, Mexico 20°14N 99°13W **175** B8
Mixtlán Jalisco, Mexico 20°26N 104°25W **174** B3
Mize Miss., U.S.A. 31°52N 89°33W **111** E4
Mizpah Minn., U.S.A. 47°55N 94°12W **77** C4
Mizpah → Mont., U.S.A. 46°14N 105°42W **124** D12
Moa Cuba 20°40N 74°56W **183** B4
Moab Utah, U.S.A. 38°35N 109°33W **129** D9
Moapa Nev., U.S.A. 36°40N 114°37W **128** F6
Moapa River Indian Reservation Nev.,
  U.S.A. 36°36N 114°45W **128** F6
Mobeetie Tex., U.S.A. 35°31N 100°26W **108** B7
Moberly Mo., U.S.A. 39°25N 92°26W **83** B4
Mobile Ala., U.S.A. 30°41N 88°3W **112** F2
Mobile Ariz., U.S.A. 33°3N 112°16W **130** D3
Mobile → Ala., U.S.A. 30°39N 88°2W **112** F2
Mobile B. Ala., U.S.A. 30°30N 88°0W **112** F3
Mobile County ☆ Ala., U.S.A. 30°41N 88°3W **112** F2
Mobridge S. Dak., U.S.A. 45°32N 100°26W **76** E5
Moca Puerto Rico 18°24N 67°10W **184** G15
Moccasin Ariz., U.S.A. 36°55N 112°46W **130** A3

Moccasin Gap Va., U.S.A. 36°38N 82°33W **102** E2
Mochomos, Cerro Sonora, Mexico 28°20N 109°25W **168** E6
Mocksville N.C., U.S.A. 35°54N 80°34W **103** C5
Moclips Wash., U.S.A. 47°14N 124°13W **120** C1
Mocorito Sinaloa, Mexico 25°29N 107°55W **172** B3
Moctezuma Chihuahua, Mexico 30°12N 106°26W **169** C9
Moctezuma San Luis Potosí, Mexico 22°45N 101°5W **171** H3
Moctezuma Sonora, Mexico 29°48N 109°42W **168** D6
Moctezuma → San Luis Potosí, Mexico 21°59N 98°34W **175** A9
Moctezuma → Sonora, Mexico 29°9N 109°40W **168** D6
Model Colo., U.S.A. 37°22N 104°15W **125** E6
Modena Utah, U.S.A. 37°48N 113°56W **129** F2
Modesto Calif., U.S.A. 37°39N 121°0W **126** D5
Modoc Ga., U.S.A. 32°37N 82°19W **113** D4
Modoc County ☆ Calif., U.S.A. 41°40N 120°50W **126** B6
Modoc Nat. Forest Calif., U.S.A. 41°30N 121°0W **126** B6
Modoc Point Oreg., U.S.A. 42°27N 121°52W **121** E4
Moenkopi Ariz., U.S.A. 36°7N 111°13W **130** A4
Moenkopi Wash → Ariz., U.S.A. 35°50N 111°20W **130** B4
Moffat Colo., U.S.A. 37°58N 105°56W **125** E5
Moffat County ☆ Colo., U.S.A. 40°45N 108°10W **125** B2
Mogollon N. Mex., U.S.A. 33°25N 108°40W **131** D2
Mogollon Plateau Ariz., U.S.A. 34°30N 111°0W **130** C5
Mogollon Rim Ariz., U.S.A. 34°10N 110°50W **130** C5
Mohall N. Dak., U.S.A. 48°46N 101°31W **76** B4
Mohave → Ariz., U.S.A. 35°12N 114°34W **130** B1
Mohave County ☆ Ariz., U.S.A. 35°0N 114°0W **130** B1
Mohave, Mts. Ariz., U.S.A. 34°35N 114°10W **130** C1
Mohawk Mich., U.S.A. 47°18N 88°21W **79** B3
Mohawk N.Y., U.S.A. 43°0N 75°0W **88** C6
Mohawk → N.Y., U.S.A. 42°47N 73°41W **88** C7
Mohawk Mts. Ariz., U.S.A. 32°30N 113°35W **130** E2
Mohawksin, L. Wis., U.S.A. 45°38N 89°43W **78** C4
Mohican → Ohio, U.S.A. 40°22N 82°10W **86** C4
Mohican, C. Alaska, U.S.A. 60°12N 167°25W **135** F6
Mohon Pk. → Ariz., U.S.A. 34°57N 113°9W **130** C2
Moira → Ont., Canada 44°21N 77°24W **147** C9
Moisie Qué., Canada 50°12N 66°1W **143** C4
Moisie → Qué., Canada 50°14N 66°5W **140** C3
Mojave Calif., U.S.A. 35°3N 118°10W **127** H8
Mojave → Calif., U.S.A. 35°6N 116°4W **127** H10
Mojave Desert Calif., U.S.A. 35°0N 116°30W **127** H10
Mojave Nat. Preserve △ U.S.A. 35°7N 115°32W **127** H11
Mojikit L. Ont., Canada 50°40N 88°15W **148** B8
Mokane Mo., U.S.A. 38°41N 91°53W **83** C5
Mōkapu Peninsula Hawai'i, U.S.A. 21°25N 157°45W **136** K14
Mokelumne → Calif., U.S.A. 38°13N 121°28W **126** C6
Mokelumne Hill Calif., U.S.A. 38°18N 120°43W **126** C6
Mōkōlea Rock Hawai'i, U.S.A. 21°27N 157°44W **136** K14
Mokuauia I. Hawai'i, U.S.A. 21°40N 157°56W **136** J14
Mokulua Is. Hawai'i, U.S.A. 21°24N 157°43W **136** K14
Mokumanu Hawai'i, U.S.A. 21°28N 157°43W **136** K14
Molalla Oreg., U.S.A. 45°9N 122°35W **121** B3
Molango Hidalgo, Mexico 20°47N 98°43W **175** B9
Molas, Pta. Quintana Roo, Mexico 20°35N 86°45W **179** B7
Molena Ga., U.S.A. 33°1N 84°30W **113** C2
Moline Ill., U.S.A. 41°30N 90°31W **84** B3
Moline Kans., U.S.A. 37°22N 96°18W **82** D7
Moline Acres Mo., U.S.A. 38°45N 90°15W **94** A2
Molino Fla., U.S.A. 30°43N 87°20W **114** A1
Molino de Rosas Distrito Federal, Mexico 19°21N 99°14W **181** B2
Moloka'i Hawai'i, U.S.A. 21°8N 157°0W **136** B4
Molokai I. Hawai'i, U.S.A. 20°38N 156°30W **136** C5
Molokini I. Hawai'i, U.S.A. 20°38N 156°30W **136** C5
Molson L. Man., Canada 54°22N 96°40W **151** A15
Molybdenite Mt. Wash., U.S.A. 48°42N 117°15W **120** B8
Momax Zacatecas, Mexico 21°55N 103°18W **173** F7
Momence Ill., U.S.A. 41°10N 87°40W **84** B6
Mona Utah, U.S.A. 39°49N 111°51W **129** D4
Mona, Canal de la = Mona Passage
  W. Indies 18°30N 67°45W **183** C6
Mona, Isla Puerto Rico 18°5N 67°54W **183** C6
Mona, Pta. Costa Rica 9°37N 82°36W **182** E3
Mona Passage W. Indies 18°30N 67°45W **183** C6
Monadnock, Mt. N.H., U.S.A. 42°52N 72°7W **89** D2
Monahans Tex., U.S.A. 31°36N 102°54W **108** F5
Monango N. Dak., U.S.A. 46°10N 98°36W **76** D7
Monarch Alta., Canada 49°48N 113°7W **153** D7
Monarch S.C., U.S.A. 34°43N 81°36W **103** D4
Monarch Mt. B.C., Canada 51°55N 125°57W **154** D9
Monarch Pass Colo., U.S.A. 38°30N 106°20W **125** D4
Monashee Mts. B.C., Canada 51°0N 118°43W **155** D16
Monashee Park △ B.C., Canada 50°30N 118°15W **155** E16
Moncks Corner S.C., U.S.A. 33°12N 80°1W **103** E5
Monclova Campeche, Mexico 18°4N 90°51W **179** D3
Monclova Coahuila, Mexico 26°54N 101°25W **170** D3
Moncouche, L. Qué., Canada 48°45N 70°42W **145** C12
Moncton N.B., Canada 46°7N 64°51W **141** G5
Mondamin Iowa, U.S.A. 41°42N 96°1W **81** D2
Mondonac, L. Qué., Canada 47°24N 73°58W **145** D9
Mondovi Wis., U.S.A. 44°34N 91°40W **78** C2
Monero N. Mex., U.S.A. 36°55N 106°52W **131** A4
Monessen Pa., U.S.A. 40°9N 79°53W **87** D3
Moneta Iowa, U.S.A. 43°13N 95°24W **81** B3
Moneta Wyo., U.S.A. 43°9N 107°43W **124** C5
Monett Mo., U.S.A. 36°55N 93°55W **83** E3
Monette Ark., U.S.A. 35°53N 90°21W **106** C5
Monhegan I. Maine, U.S.A. 43°46N 69°19W **90** E4
Moniac Ga., U.S.A. 30°31N 82°14W **113** F4
Monico Wis., U.S.A. 45°35N 89°9W **78** C4
Monida Mont., U.S.A. 44°34N 112°19W **123** F5
Monida Pass U.S.A. 44°34N 112°18W **122** G6
Moniteau County ☆ Mo., U.S.A. 38°35N 92°35W **83** C4
Monitor Alta., Canada 51°58N 110°33W **153** C10
Monitor Wash., U.S.A. 47°29N 120°25W **120** C5
Monitor Range Nev., U.S.A. 38°40N 116°48W **128** D5
Monkey River Belize 16°22N 88°29W **182** C2
Monkstown Nfld. & L., Canada 47°56N 54°26W **142** E6
Monkstown Tex., U.S.A. 33°48N 95°56W **109** D12
Monkton Ont., Canada 43°35N 81°5W **146** D5
Monkton Md., U.S.A. 39°35N 76°37W **93** A4
Monmouth Ill., U.S.A. 40°55N 90°39W **84** C3
Monmouth Oreg., U.S.A. 44°51N 123°14W **121** C2
Monmouth County ☆ N.J., U.S.A. 40°15N 74°15W **92** B3
Monmouth Junction N.J., U.S.A. 40°23N 74°33W **92** B2
Monmouth Mt. B.C., Canada 51°0N 124°0W **154** D11
Mono County ☆ Calif., U.S.A. 38°0N 119°0W **126** D7
Mono L. Calif., U.S.A. 38°1N 119°1W **126** E7
Monocacy → Md., U.S.A. 39°13N 77°27W **93** A3
Monolith Calif., U.S.A. 35°7N 118°22W **127** H8
Monomoy I. Mass., U.S.A. 41°36N 69°59W **91** C5
Monomoy Nat. Wildlife Refuge △ Mass.,
  U.S.A. 41°29N 69°58W **91** C5
Monomoy Point Mass., U.S.A. 41°33N 70°2W **91** C4

Monon Ind., U.S.A. 40°52N 86°53W **85** C4
Monona Iowa, U.S.A. 43°3N 91°23W **81** B7
Monona Wis., U.S.A. 43°4N 89°20W **78** E4
Monona County ☆ Iowa, U.S.A. 42°0N 96°0W **81** D3
Monongah W. Va., U.S.A. 39°28N 80°13W **102** B4
Monongahela Pa., U.S.A. 40°12N 79°56W **87** D3
Monongahela → Pa., U.S.A. 40°27N 80°1W **87** D2
Monongahela Nat. Forest W. Va.,
  U.S.A. 38°30N 79°57W **102** C5
Monongalia County ☆ W. Va., U.S.A. 39°39N 80°1W **102** B4
Monowi Nebr., U.S.A. 42°50N 98°20W **80** B7
Monroe Ark., U.S.A. 34°44N 91°6W **106** D4
Monroe Ga., U.S.A. 33°47N 83°43W **113** C3
Monroe Ind., U.S.A. 40°45N 84°56W **85** C6
Monroe Iowa, U.S.A. 41°31N 93°6W **81** D5
Monroe La., U.S.A. 32°30N 92°7W **110** B3
Monroe Mich., U.S.A. 41°55N 83°24W **79** H8
Monroe N.C., U.S.A. 34°59N 80°33W **103** D5
Monroe N.Y., U.S.A. 41°20N 74°11W **92** A2
Monroe Nebr., U.S.A. 41°27N 97°36W **80** C8
Monroe Ohio, U.S.A. 39°27N 84°22W **86** C1
Monroe Okla., U.S.A. 34°59N 94°30W **107** D9
Monroe Oreg., U.S.A. 44°19N 123°18W **121** C2
Monroe S. Dak., U.S.A. 43°29N 97°13W **76** G8
Monroe Utah, U.S.A. 38°38N 112°7W **129** E3
Monroe Va., U.S.A. 37°30N 79°8W **102** C5
Monroe Wash., U.S.A. 47°51N 121°58W **120** C4
Monroe Wis., U.S.A. 42°36N 89°38W **78** F4
Monroe, L. Fla., U.S.A. 28°50N 81°19W **114** C7
Monroe City Mo., U.S.A. 39°39N 91°44W **83** B51
Monroe County ☆ Ala., U.S.A. 31°31N 87°20W **112** E3
Monroe County ☆ Ark., U.S.A. 34°42N 91°19W **106** D4
Monroe County ☆ Fla., U.S.A. 25°30N 81°0W **114** F7
Monroe County ☆ Ga., U.S.A. 33°0N 83°55W **113** C3
Monroe County ☆ Ill., U.S.A. 38°15N 90°10W **84** E3
Monroe County ☆ Ind., U.S.A. 39°10N 86°30W **85** E4
Monroe County ☆ Iowa, U.S.A. 41°0N 92°50W **81** E6
Monroe County ☆ Ky., U.S.A. 36°45N 85°45W **105** D7
Monroe County ☆ Mich., U.S.A. 41°50N 83°35W **79** H8
Monroe County ☆ Miss., U.S.A. 33°49N 88°33W **111** C5
Monroe County ☆ Mo., U.S.A. 39°30N 92°0W **83** B4
Monroe County ☆ N.Y., U.S.A. 43°10N 77°40W **88** B3
Monroe County ☆ Ohio, U.S.A. 39°46N 81°7W **86** D5
Monroe County ☆ Pa., U.S.A. 41°5N 75°15W **87** C7
Monroe County ☆ Tenn., U.S.A. 35°31N 84°22W **105** E8
Monroe County ☆ W. Va., U.S.A. 37°36N 80°33W **102** D4
Monroe County ☆ Wis., U.S.A. 43°50N 90°40W **78** E3
Monroeton Pa., U.S.A. 41°43N 76°29W **87** C6
Monroeville Ala., U.S.A. 31°31N 87°20W **112** E3
Monroeville Ind., U.S.A. 40°59N 84°52W **85** C6
Monroeville Ohio, U.S.A. 41°15N 82°42W **86** B4
Monroeville Pa., U.S.A. 40°26N 79°45W **87** D3
Monrovia Calif., U.S.A. 34°9N 118°0W **133** B4
Monsey N.Y., U.S.A. 41°7N 74°4W **92** A2
Monson Maine, U.S.A. 45°17N 69°30W **90** C4
Monson Mass., U.S.A. 42°6N 72°19W **91** B2
Mont Alto Pa., U.S.A. 39°51N 77°34W **93** A3
Mont-Bleu Qué., Canada 45°27N 75°45W **160** A1
Mont-Carmel Qué., Canada 47°26N 69°52W **145** D13
Mont Ida Kans., U.S.A. 38°13N 95°22W **82** C8
Mont-Joli Qué., Canada 48°37N 68°10W **145** C14
Mont-Laurier Qué., Canada 46°35N 75°30W **144** E7
Mont-Louis Qué., Canada 49°15N 65°44W **140** D4
Mont-Royal Qué., Canada 45°30N 73°38W **160** A3
Mont-Royal, Parc Qué., Canada 45°30N 73°36W **160** A3
Mont St-Pierre Qué., Canada 49°13N 65°49W **140** D4
Mont-Tremblant Qué., Canada 46°13N 74°36W **144** E8
Mont-Tremblant, Parc de Récr. du Qué.,
  Canada 46°30N 74°30W **145** E8
Mont Vernon N.H., U.S.A. 42°50N 71°42W **89** D3
Montagne, Parc de la Qué., Canada 45°27N 75°45W **160** A1
Montague P.E.I., Canada 46°10N 62°39W **141** G7
Montague Mass., U.S.A. 42°32N 72°32W **91** B2
Montague Mich., U.S.A. 43°25N 86°22W **79** F5
Montague Tex., U.S.A. 33°42N 97°48W **109** D10
Montague County ☆ Tex., U.S.A. 33°47N 97°44W **109** D10
Montague, I. Baja Calif., Mexico 31°45N 114°48W **166** B4
Montague I. Alaska, U.S.A. 60°0N 147°30W **135** G11
Montalba Tex., U.S.A. 31°53N 95°44W **109** F12
Montana □ U.S.A. 47°0N 110°0W **123** C7
Montana City Mont., U.S.A. 46°32N 111°56W **123** D6
Montauk N.Y., U.S.A. 41°3N 71°57W **91** C3
Montauk Pt. N.Y., U.S.A. 41°4N 71°51W **91** C3
Montbello Colo., U.S.A. 39°47N 104°49W **134** B3
Montcalm County ☆ Mich., U.S.A. 43°15N 85°10W **79** F6
Montcerf Qué., Canada 46°32N 76°3W **144** E6
Montcevelles, L. Qué., Canada 51°7N 60°38W **140** B9
Montclair N.J., U.S.A. 40°49N 74°12W **97** B1
Monte Albán Oaxaca, Mexico 17°2N 96°46W **177** H4
Monte Blanco Veracruz, Mexico 18°58N 97°2W **177** F3
Monte Cristi Dom. Rep. 19°52N 71°39W **183** C5
Monte Escobedo Zacatecas, Mexico 22°18N 103°34W **173** E7
Monte Grande Tabasco, Mexico 17°56N 92°16W **178** B4
Monte Pio Veracruz, Mexico 18°38N 95°5W **177** F5
Monte Redondo Chihuahua, Mexico 27°38N 105°37W **169** F10
Monte Vista Colo., U.S.A. 37°35N 106°9W **125** E4
Monteagle Tenn., U.S.A. 35°15N 85°50W **105** E7
Montebello Qué., Canada 45°40N 74°55W **144** F8
Montebello Calif., U.S.A. 34°1N 118°8W **133** B4
Montecito Calif., U.S.A. 34°26N 119°40W **127** J7
Montego Bay Jamaica 18°28N 77°55W **182** C4
Montello Nev., U.S.A. 41°16N 114°12W **128** A6
Montello Wis., U.S.A. 43°48N 89°20W **78** E4
Montemorelos Nuevo León, Mexico 25°12N 99°49W **171** E5
Monterde, Sa. Chihuahua, Mexico 27°45N 108°25W **169** F7
Monterey Ind., U.S.A. 41°11N 86°30W **85** B4
Monterey Calif., U.S.A. 36°37N 121°55W **126** D3
Monterey Mass., U.S.A. 42°11N 73°13W **91** B1
Monterey Tenn., U.S.A. 36°9N 85°16W **105** D7
Monterey Va., U.S.A. 38°25N 79°35W **102** C5
Monterey B. Calif., U.S.A. 36°45N 122°0W **126** D3
Monterey County ☆ Calif., U.S.A. 36°15N 121°20W **126** D4
Monterey Park Calif., U.S.A. 34°3N 118°7W **133** B4
Monterrey Baja Calif., Mexico 32°34N 115°4W **166** A3
Monterrey Nuevo León, Mexico 25°40N 100°19W **180** B2
Montes Azules, Reserva de la Biosfera △
  Chiapas, Mexico 16°30N 91°10W **178** C5
Montesano Wash., U.S.A. 46°59N 123°36W **120** D2
Montevallo Ala., U.S.A. 33°6N 86°52W **112** C4

Montevideo *Minn., U.S.A.* 44°57N 95°43W **77** F3
Monteview *Idaho, U.S.A.* 43°56N 112°32W **122** F6
Montezuma *Ga., U.S.A.* 32°18N 84°2W **113** D2
Montezuma *Ind., U.S.A.* 39°48N 87°22W **85** D3
Montezuma *Iowa, U.S.A.* 41°35N 92°32W **81** D61
Montezuma *Kans., U.S.A.* 37°36N 100°27W **82** D3
Montezuma Castle Nat. Monument △ *Ariz., U.S.A.* 34°39N 111°45W **130** C4
Montezuma County ☆ *Colo., U.S.A.* 37°20N 108°30W **125** D2
Montezuma Cr. ➜ *Utah, U.S.A.* 37°17N 109°20W **129** F6
Montezuma Creek *Utah, U.S.A.* 37°16N 109°19W **129** F6
Montfort *Wis., U.S.A.* 42°58N 90°26W **78** F3
Montgomery *Ala., U.S.A.* 32°23N 86°19W **112** D4
Montgomery *La., U.S.A.* 31°40N 92°53W **110** C3
Montgomery *Minn., U.S.A.* 44°26N 93°35W **77** F5
Montgomery *N.Y., U.S.A.* 41°32N 74°14W **92** A2
Montgomery *Pa., U.S.A.* 41°10N 76°53W **87** C6
Montgomery *Tex., U.S.A.* 30°23N 95°42W **109** G12
Montgomery *W. Va., U.S.A.* 38°11N 81°19W **102** C3
Montgomery Center *Vt., U.S.A.* 44°53N 73°40W **89** B1
Montgomery City *Mo., U.S.A.* 38°59N 91°30W **83** C51
Montgomery County ☆ *Ala., U.S.A.* 32°15N 86°18W **112** D4
Montgomery County ☆ *Ark., U.S.A.* 34°34N 93°38W **106** D2
Montgomery County ☆ *Ga., U.S.A.* 32°15N 82°35W **113** D4
Montgomery County ☆ *Ill., U.S.A.* 39°10N 89°30W **84** D4
Montgomery County ☆ *Ind., U.S.A.* 40°5N 86°55W **85** C4
Montgomery County ☆ *Iowa, U.S.A.* 41°0N 95°9W **81** D3
Montgomery County ☆ *Kans., U.S.A.* 37°15N 95°45W **82** D8
Montgomery County ☆ *Ky., U.S.A.* 38°0N 83°55W **105** B9
Montgomery County ☆ *Md., U.S.A.* 39°15N 77°15W **93** A3
Montgomery County ☆ *Miss., U.S.A.* 33°29N 89°44W **111** C4
Montgomery County ☆ *Mo., U.S.A.* 38°55N 91°30W **83** C5
Montgomery County ☆ *N.C., U.S.A.* 35°20N 79°50W **103** C6
Montgomery County ☆ *N.Y., U.S.A.* 42°50N 74°30W **88** C6
Montgomery County ☆ *Ohio, U.S.A.* 39°45N 84°12W **86** D2
Montgomery County ☆ *Pa., U.S.A.* 40°10N 75°10W **87** D7
Montgomery County ☆ *Tenn., U.S.A.* 36°32N 87°21W **104** D5
Montgomery County ☆ *Tex., U.S.A.* 30°19N 95°27W **109** G12
Montgomery County ☆ *Va., U.S.A.* 37°8N 80°25W **102** D4
Montgomery Field *Calif., U.S.A.* 32°48N 117°8W **133** B2
Montgomery Pass *Nev., U.S.A.* 37°58N 118°20W **128** E2
Montgomery Village *Md., U.S.A.* 39°12N 77°13W **93** A3
Monticello *Ark., U.S.A.* 33°38N 91°47W **106** E4
Monticello *Fla., U.S.A.* 30°33N 83°52W **114** A5
Monticello *Ga., U.S.A.* 33°18N 83°40W **113** C3
Monticello *Ill., U.S.A.* 40°1N 88°34W **84** C5
Monticello *Ind., U.S.A.* 40°45N 86°46W **85** C4
Monticello *Iowa, U.S.A.* 42°15N 91°12W **81** C71
Monticello *Ky., U.S.A.* 36°50N 84°51W **105** D8
Monticello *Maine, U.S.A.* 46°19N 67°51W **90** B6
Monticello *Minn., U.S.A.* 45°18N 93°48W **77** E5
Monticello *Miss., U.S.A.* 31°33N 90°7W **111** E3
Monticello *Mo., U.S.A.* 40°7N 91°43W **83** A5
Monticello *N. Mex., U.S.A.* 33°24N 107°27W **131** D3
Monticello *N.Y., U.S.A.* 41°39N 74°42W **88** D6
Monticello *Utah, U.S.A.* 37°52N 109°21W **129** F8
Monticello *Wis., U.S.A.* 42°45N 89°36W **78** F4
Monticello *Va., U.S.A.* 38°0N 78°27W **102** D6
Montmagny *Qué., Canada* 46°58N 70°34W **145** E12
Montmartre *Sask., Canada* 50°14N 103°27W **150** E8
Montmorency County ☆ *Mich., U.S.A.* 45°0N 84°10W **79** D7
Montour *Idaho, U.S.A.* 43°55N 116°20W **122** F2
Montour *Iowa, U.S.A.* 41°59N 92°43W **81** D6
Montour County ☆ *Pa., U.S.A.* 41°0N 76°40W **87** D6
Montour Falls *N.Y., U.S.A.* 42°21N 76°51W **88** C4
Montoursville *Pa., U.S.A.* 41°15N 76°55W **87** C6
Montoya *N. Mex., U.S.A.* 35°6N 104°4W **131** B6
Montpelier *Idaho, U.S.A.* 42°19N 111°18W **122** G7
Montpelier *Ind., U.S.A.* 40°33N 85°17W **85** C5
Montpelier *La., U.S.A.* 30°41N 90°39W **110** D5
Montpelier *Miss., U.S.A.* 33°43N 88°57W **111** C5
Montpelier *N. Dak., U.S.A.* 46°42N 98°35W **76** D7
Montpelier *Ohio, U.S.A.* 41°35N 84°37W **86** B2
Montpelier *Va., U.S.A.* 37°49N 77°41W **102** D7
Montpelier *Vt., U.S.A.* 44°16N 72°35W **89** B2
Montréal *Qué., Canada* 45°30N 73°33W **160** A3
Montreal ➜ *Ont., Canada* 47°14N 84°39W **149** E12
Montréal, Î. de *Qué., Canada* 45°30N 73°40W **160** A3
Montréal, Université de *Qué., Canada* 45°29N 73°37W **160** B3
Montréal Dorval Int. ✈ (YUL) *Qué., Canada* 45°28N 73°44W **160** B2
Montreal Est *Qué., Canada* 45°37N 73°31W **160** A3
Montreal I. *Ont., Canada* 47°19N 84°44W **149** E12
Montreal L. *Sask., Canada* 54°20N 105°45W **150** A6
Montreal Lake *Sask., Canada* 54°3N 105°46W **150** A6
Montréal-Nord *Qué., Canada* 45°36N 73°36W **160** A3
Montréal-Ouest *Qué., Canada* 45°27N 73°39W **160** B2
Montreat *N.C., U.S.A.* 35°39N 82°15W **103** C3
Montreuil, L. *Qué., Canada* 50°12N 77°40W **144** A5
Montrose *B.C., Canada* 49°5N 117°35W **155** F17
Montrose *Ark., U.S.A.* 33°18N 91°30W **106** E4
Montrose *Colo., U.S.A.* 38°29N 107°53W **125** D3
Montrose *Ill., U.S.A.* 39°10N 88°23W **84** D5
Montrose *Iowa, U.S.A.* 40°31N 91°25W **81** E7
Montrose *Mich., U.S.A.* 43°11N 83°54W **79** F8
Montrose *Miss., U.S.A.* 32°8N 89°14W **111** D4
Montrose *Mo., U.S.A.* 38°16N 93°59W **83** C3
Montrose *Pa., U.S.A.* 41°50N 75°53W **87** C7
Montrose *S. Dak., U.S.A.* 43°42N 97°11W **76** G8
Montrose *W. Va., U.S.A.* 39°4N 79°49W **102** B5
Montrose County ☆ *Colo., U.S.A.* 38°30N 108°15W **125** D2
Montross *Va., U.S.A.* 38°6N 76°50W **93** B4
Monts, Pte. des *Qué., Canada* 49°20N 67°12W **140** D2
Monts-Valin, Parc des △ *Qué., Canada* 48°37N 70°48W **145** C12
Montserrat ☒ *W. Indies* 16°40N 62°10W **183** C7
Montserrat, I. *Baja Calif. S., Mexico* 25°40N 111°0W **167** H7
Montvale *Va., U.S.A.* 37°23N 79°44W **102** D5
Montville *Conn., U.S.A.* 41°27N 72°8W **91** C2
Monument *Colo., U.S.A.* 39°6N 104°52W **125** C6
Monument *Kans., U.S.A.* 39°6N 101°1W **82** B2
Monument *Oreg., U.S.A.* 44°49N 119°25W **121** C6
Monument Draw ➜ *Tex., U.S.A.* 32°29N 102°20W **108** E5
Monument Pk. *Idaho, U.S.A.* 42°17N 114°14W **122** G4
Monument Pass *Ariz., U.S.A.* 36°58N 110°5W **130** A5
Monument Valley *Ariz., U.S.A.* 36°56N 110°5W **130** A5
Moodus *Conn., U.S.A.* 41°30N 72°25W **91** C2
Moody *Ala., U.S.A.* 33°35N 86°29W **112** C4
Moody *Mo., U.S.A.* 36°32N 91°59W **83** E5
Moody *Tex., U.S.A.* 31°18N 97°21W **109** F10
Moody Air Force Base *Ga., U.S.A.* 30°58N 83°12W **113** F3
Moody County ☆ *S. Dak., U.S.A.* 44°3N 96°36W **76** F9
Moodyville = North Vancouver *B.C., Canada* 49°19N 123°4W **161** B2
Mooers *N.Y., U.S.A.* 44°58N 73°35W **89** B1
Mooleyville *Ky., U.S.A.* 38°1N 86°28W **104** B6

Moomaw, L. *Va., U.S.A.* 37°57N 79°57W **102** D5
Moon L. *Calif., U.S.A.* 41°10N 120°22W **126** B6
Moon Res. *Oreg., U.S.A.* 43°24N 119°24W **121** D6
Moonachie *N.J., U.S.A.* 40°50N 74°2W **97** A2
Moonbeam *Ont., Canada* 49°20N 82°10W **149** C14
Mooney's Bay *Ont., Canada* 45°22N 75°41W **160** B1
Mooney's Bay Park *Ont., Canada* 45°22N 75°41W **160** B1
Moorcroft *Wyo., U.S.A.* 44°16N 104°57W **124** B8
Moore *Idaho, U.S.A.* 43°44N 113°22W **122** F5
Moore *Mont., U.S.A.* 46°59N 109°42W **123** D8
Moore *Okla., U.S.A.* 35°20N 97°29W **107** C6
Moore *Tex., U.S.A.* 29°3N 99°1W **109** H8
Moore *Utah, U.S.A.* 38°58N 111°10W **129** E4
Moore County ☆ *N.C., U.S.A.* 35°20N 79°20W **103** C6
Moore County ☆ *Tenn., U.S.A.* 35°17N 86°24W **104** D3
Moore County ☆ *Tex., U.S.A.* 35°55N 101°59W **108** B6
Moore Haven *Fla., U.S.A.* 26°50N 81°6W **114** E7
Moore Res. *N.H., U.S.A.* 44°20N 71°53W **89** B3
Moorefield *Nebr., U.S.A.* 40°41N 100°24W **80** D5
Moorefield *W. Va., U.S.A.* 39°4N 78°58W **93** A2
Mooreland *Okla., U.S.A.* 36°26N 99°12W **107** B4
Moores Creek Nat. Battlefield △ *N.C., U.S.A.* 34°27N 78°7W **103** D7
Moores Mill *N.B., Canada* 45°18N 67°17W **141** H2
Moores Mill *Ala., U.S.A.* 34°51N 86°31W **112** B4
Moorestown *N.J., U.S.A.* 39°58N 74°57W **92** C2
Mooresville *Ind., U.S.A.* 39°37N 86°22W **85** D4
Mooresville *N.C., U.S.A.* 35°35N 80°48W **103** C5
Mooreton *N. Dak., U.S.A.* 46°16N 96°53W **76** D9
Moorhead *Iowa, U.S.A.* 41°56N 95°51W **81** D3
Moorhead *Minn., U.S.A.* 46°53N 96°45W **77** D2
Moorhead *Miss., U.S.A.* 33°27N 90°30W **111** C3
Mooringsport *La., U.S.A.* 32°41N 93°58W **110** B2
Moorland *Iowa, U.S.A.* 42°26N 94°18W **81** C4
Moose *Wyo., U.S.A.* 43°39N 110°43W **124** C2
Moose ➜ *Ont., Canada* 51°20N 80°25W **149** A16
Moose ➜ *Maine, U.S.A.* 45°41N 69°45W **90** C4
Moose ➜ *N.Y., U.S.A.* 43°38N 75°24W **88** C5
Moose ➜ *Vt., U.S.A.* 44°24N 72°1W **89** B2
Moose Creek *Ont., Canada* 45°15N 74°58W **147** B12
Moose Factory *Ont., Canada* 51°16N 80°32W **149** A16
Moose Heights *B.C., Canada* 53°4N 122°31W **155** B12
Moose I. *Man., Canada* 51°42N 97°10W **151** C14
Moose Jaw *Sask., Canada* 50°24N 105°30W **150** E6
Moose Jaw ➜ *Sask., Canada* 50°34N 105°18W **150** E6
Moose L. *Alta., Canada* 54°15N 110°55W **152** D10
Moose L. *Man., Canada* 53°46N 100°8W **151** B11
Moose Lake *Minn., U.S.A.* 46°27N 92°46W **77** D61
Moose Mountain Cr. ➜ *Sask., Canada* 49°13N 102°12W **150** F9
Moose Mountain Prov. Park △ *Sask., Canada* 49°48N 102°25W **151** F9
Moose Pass *Alaska, U.S.A.* 60°29N 149°22W **135** F10
Moose River *Ont., Canada* 50°48N 81°17W **149** B15
Moose River *Maine, U.S.A.* 45°39N 70°16W **90** C3
Mooselookmeguntic L. *Maine, U.S.A.* 44°55N 70°45W **90** D3
Moosic *Pa., U.S.A.* 41°21N 75°44W **92** A1
Moosilauke, Mt. *N.H., U.S.A.* 44°3N 71°40W **89** B3
Moosomin *Sask., Canada* 50°9N 101°40W **151** E10
Moosonee *Ont., Canada* 51°17N 80°39W **149** A16
Moosup *Conn., U.S.A.* 41°43N 71°53W **91** C3
Mora *Minn., U.S.A.* 45°53N 93°18W **77** E5
Mora *N. Mex., U.S.A.* 35°58N 105°20W **131** B5
Mora ➜ *N. Mex., U.S.A.* 35°35N 104°25W **131** B6
Mora County ☆ *N. Mex., U.S.A.* 36°0N 104°58W **131** B6
Morada *Calif., U.S.A.* 38°2N 121°15W **126** E5
Morales *Tex., U.S.A.* 29°8N 96°46W **109** H11
Morales, L. *Tamaulipas, Mexico* 23°35N 97°47W **171** G7
Moran *Kans., U.S.A.* 37°55N 95°10W **82** D8
Moran *Mich., U.S.A.* 46°0N 84°50W **79** C7
Moran *Tex., U.S.A.* 32°33N 99°10W **109** E8
Moran *Wyo., U.S.A.* 43°50N 110°31W **124** C2
Morant Cays *Jamaica* 17°22N 76°0W **182** C4
Morant Pt. *Jamaica* 17°55N 76°12W **182** C4
Moravia *Iowa, U.S.A.* 40°53N 92°49W **81** E6
Moravia *N.Y., U.S.A.* 42°43N 76°25W **88** C4
Morden *Man., Canada* 49°15N 98°10W **151** F13
Moreau ➜ *S. Dak., U.S.A.* 45°18N 100°43W **76** E5
Morehead *Ky., U.S.A.* 38°11N 83°26W **105** B9
Morehead City *N.C., U.S.A.* 34°43N 76°43W **103** D9
Morehouse *Mo., U.S.A.* 36°51N 89°41W **83** E7
Morehouse Parish ☆ *La., U.S.A.* 32°47N 91°48W **110** A3
Moreland *Ga., U.S.A.* 33°17N 84°46W **113** C2
Moreland *Ky., U.S.A.* 37°30N 84°49W **105** C8
Morelia *Michoacan, Mexico* 19°42N 101°7W **175** C6
Morell *P.E.I., Canada* 46°25N 62°42W **141** G7
Morelos *Baja Calif. S., Mexico* 28°19N 114°5W **167** E4
Morelos *Chihuahua, Mexico* 26°42N 107°40W **169** G8
Morelos *Coahuila, Mexico* 28°25N 100°53W **170** B4
Morelos *Coahuila, Mexico* 28°0N 101°43W **170** C3
Morelos *Coahuila, Mexico* 29°6N 102°26W **170** A2
Morelos *Durango, Mexico* 25°45N 105°15W **172** B5
Morelos *Sonora, Mexico* 30°50N 109°13W **168** C6
Morelos *Sonora, Mexico* 31°12N 110°14W **168** B5
Morelos *Zacatecas, Mexico* 22°53N 102°37W **173** E8
Morelos ☐ *Mexico* 18°45N 99°0W **175** D9
Morenci *Ariz., U.S.A.* 33°5N 109°22W **130** D6
Morenci *Mich., U.S.A.* 41°43N 84°13W **79** H7
Moreno Valley *Calif., U.S.A.* 33°56N 117°14W **127** K9
Moresby I. *B.C., Canada* 52°30N 131°40W **154** C2
Morevain Falls *N.C., U.S.A.* 36°6N 81°11W **103** B4
Morfin Chávez *Zacatecas, Mexico* 23°11N 102°46W **173** D8
Morgan *Ga., U.S.A.* 31°32N 84°36W **113** E2
Morgan *Ky., U.S.A.* 38°36N 84°24W **105** B8
Morgan *Minn., U.S.A.* 44°25N 94°56W **77** F4
Morgan *Utah, U.S.A.* 41°2N 111°41W **129** B4
Morgan *Vt., U.S.A.* 44°53N 73°2W **89** B1
Morgan, Arboretum *Qué., Canada* 45°24N 73°58W **160** A2
Morgan, Mt. *Calif., U.S.A.* 37°31N 118°47W **127** F8
Morgan City *Ala., U.S.A.* 34°28N 86°34W **112** B4
Morgan City *La., U.S.A.* 29°42N 91°12W **110** E4
Morgan City *Miss., U.S.A.* 33°23N 90°21W **111** C3
Morgan County ☆ *Ala., U.S.A.* 34°27N 86°56W **112** B4
Morgan County ☆ *Colo., U.S.A.* 40°15N 103°50W **125** B7
Morgan County ☆ *Ga., U.S.A.* 33°40N 83°25W **113** C3
Morgan County ☆ *Ill., U.S.A.* 39°45N 90°0W **84** D3
Morgan County ☆ *Ind., U.S.A.* 39°30N 86°25W **85** D4
Morgan County ☆ *Ky., U.S.A.* 37°55N 83°15W **105** C9
Morgan County ☆ *Mo., U.S.A.* 38°25N 92°50W **83** C4
Morgan County ☆ *Ohio, U.S.A.* 39°39N 81°51W **86** D5
Morgan County ☆ *Tenn., U.S.A.* 36°6N 84°36W **105** D8
Morgan County ☆ *Utah, U.S.A.* 41°10N 111°45W **129** B4
Morgan County ☆ *W. Va., U.S.A.* 39°35N 78°16W **102** B6
Morgan Hill *Calif., U.S.A.* 37°8N 121°39W **126** F5

Morgan L. *N. Mex., U.S.A.* 36°52N 108°41W **131** A2
Morgan Mill *Tex., U.S.A.* 32°23N 98°10W **109** E9
Morgan Park *Ill., U.S.A.* 41°41N 87°38W **95** C3
Morganfield *Ky., U.S.A.* 37°41N 87°55W **104** C5
Morganton *Ga., U.S.A.* 34°53N 84°15W **113** B2
Morganton *N.C., U.S.A.* 35°45N 81°41W **103** C4
Morgantown *Ind., U.S.A.* 39°22N 86°16W **85** D4
Morgantown *Ky., U.S.A.* 37°13N 86°41W **104** C6
Morgantown *Md., U.S.A.* 38°21N 76°58W **93** B4
Morgantown *Miss., U.S.A.* 31°18N 89°55W **111** E4
Morgantown *Miss., U.S.A.* 31°34N 91°21W **111** E2
Morgantown *Ohio, U.S.A.* 39°8N 83°12W **86** D3
Morgantown *W. Va., U.S.A.* 39°38N 79°57W **102** B5
Morganville *Kans., U.S.A.* 39°28N 97°12W **82** B6
Morganza *La., U.S.A.* 30°44N 91°36W **110** D4
Moriah, Mt. *Nev., U.S.A.* 39°17N 114°12W **128** C6
Moriarty *N. Mex., U.S.A.* 34°59N 106°3W **131** C4
Morice ➜ *B.C., Canada* 54°12N 127°5W **154** A7
Morice L. *B.C., Canada* 53°50N 127°40W **154** B7
Morin-Heights *Qué., Canada* 45°54N 74°15W **145** F8
Morinville *Alta., Canada* 53°49N 113°41W **152** E7
Moris *Chihuahua, Mexico* 28°10N 108°32W **168** E7
Morland *Kans., U.S.A.* 39°21N 100°5W **82** B3
Morley *Mich., U.S.A.* 43°29N 85°27W **79** F6
Morley *Mo., U.S.A.* 37°3N 89°37W **83** D7
Mormon L. *Ariz., U.S.A.* 34°57N 111°29W **130** C4
Mormon Lake *Ariz., U.S.A.* 34°55N 111°28W **130** C4
Mormon Mts. *Nev., U.S.A.* 37°0N 114°0W **128** F6
Morning Sun *Iowa, U.S.A.* 41°5N 91°15W **81** D7
Morningside *Md., U.S.A.* 38°49N 76°53W **99** C4
Morningside Park *Ont., Canada* 43°47N 79°12W **161** A3
Morningside Park *Fla., U.S.A.* 28°26N 81°24W **115** B2
Moro *Ark., U.S.A.* 34°48N 90°59W **106** D5
Moro *Oreg., U.S.A.* 45°29N 120°44W **121** B5
Moro ➜ *Ark., U.S.A.* 33°17N 92°21W **106** E3
Morocco *Ind., U.S.A.* 40°57N 87°27W **85** C3
Moroleón *Guanajuato, Mexico* 20°8N 101°12W **175** B6
Morón *Cuba* 22°8N 78°39W **182** B4
Morongo Indian Reservation *Calif., U.S.A.* 33°57N 116°49W **127** K10
Moroni *Utah, U.S.A.* 39°32N 111°35W **129** D4
Morral *Ohio, U.S.A.* 40°41N 83°13W **86** C2
Morrill *Kans., U.S.A.* 39°56N 95°42W **82** B8
Morrill *Nebr., U.S.A.* 41°58N 103°56W **80** C2
Morrill County ☆ *Nebr., U.S.A.* 41°45N 103°0W **80** C3
Morrilton *Ark., U.S.A.* 35°9N 92°44W **106** C3
Morrin *Alta., Canada* 51°40N 112°47W **153** G8
Morris *Man., Canada* 49°25N 97°22W **151** F14
Morris *Conn., U.S.A.* 41°43N 73°15W **91** C1
Morris *Ga., U.S.A.* 31°48N 84°57W **113** E2
Morris *Ill., U.S.A.* 41°22N 88°26W **84** B5
Morris *Minn., U.S.A.* 45°35N 95°55W **77** E3
Morris *N.Y., U.S.A.* 42°33N 75°15W **88** C5
Morris *Okla., U.S.A.* 35°36N 95°51W **107** C8
Morris ➜ *Man., Canada* 49°21N 97°21W **151** F14
Morris County ☆ *Kans., U.S.A.* 38°30N 96°40W **82** C7
Morris County ☆ *N.J., U.S.A.* 40°45N 74°30W **92** B2
Morris County ☆ *Tex., U.S.A.* 33°2N 94°44W **109** D13
Morris Jesup, Kap *Greenland* 83°40N 34°0W **82** C5
Morrisburg *Ont., Canada* 44°55N 75°7W **147** C11
Morrison *Ill., U.S.A.* 41°49N 89°58W **84** B4
Morrison *Okla., U.S.A.* 36°18N 97°1W **107** B6
Morrison *Tenn., U.S.A.* 35°36N 85°55W **105** E7
Morrison County ☆ *Minn., U.S.A.* 46°0N 94°10W **77** E4
Morrisonville *Ill., U.S.A.* 39°25N 89°27W **84** D4
Morrisonville *N.Y., U.S.A.* 44°42N 73°33W **89** B1
Morristown *Ariz., U.S.A.* 33°51N 112°37W **130** D3
Morristown *Ind., U.S.A.* 39°40N 85°42W **85** D5
Morristown *Minn., U.S.A.* 44°14N 93°27W **77** F5
Morristown *N.J., U.S.A.* 40°48N 74°29W **92** B2
Morristown *N.Y., U.S.A.* 44°35N 75°39W **88** A5
Morristown *S. Dak., U.S.A.* 45°56N 101°43W **76** E4
Morristown *Tenn., U.S.A.* 36°13N 83°18W **105** D9
Morristown *Vt., U.S.A.* 44°33N 72°37W **89** B2
Morrisville *Mo., U.S.A.* 37°29N 93°25W **83** D3
Morrisville *N.C., U.S.A.* 35°49N 78°50W **103** C7
Morrisville *N.Y., U.S.A.* 42°53N 75°35W **88** C5
Morrisville *Pa., U.S.A.* 40°13N 74°47W **92** B2
Morrisville *Vt., U.S.A.* 44°34N 72°36W **89** B2
Morro Bay *Calif., U.S.A.* 35°22N 120°51W **127** H6
Morro Santo Domingo *Baja Calif. S., Mexico* 28°12N 114°8W **167** E4
Morrosquillo, G. de *Colombia* 9°35N 75°40W **182** E4
Morrow *La., U.S.A.* 30°50N 92°5W **110** D3
Morrow *Ohio, U.S.A.* 39°21N 84°8W **86** D2
Morrow County ☆ *Ohio, U.S.A.* 40°33N 82°50W **86** C4
Morrow County ☆ *Oreg., U.S.A.* 45°35N 119°40W **121** B6
Morrowville *Kans., U.S.A.* 39°51N 97°10W **82** B6
Morse *La., U.S.A.* 30°7N 92°30W **110** D3
Morse *Sask., Canada* 50°25N 107°3W **150** E4
Morse Bluff *Nebr., U.S.A.* 41°26N 96°46W **80** C9
Morson *Ont., Canada* 49°6N 94°19W **148** C2
Mortlach *Sask., Canada* 50°27N 106°4W **150** E5
Morton *Ill., U.S.A.* 40°37N 89°28W **84** C4
Morton *Minn., U.S.A.* 44°33N 94°59W **77** F4
Morton *Miss., U.S.A.* 32°21N 89°39W **111** D4
Morton *Tex., U.S.A.* 33°44N 102°46W **108** D5
Morton *Wash., U.S.A.* 46°34N 122°17W **120** D3
Morton County ☆ *Kans., U.S.A.* 37°15N 101°45W **82** D2
Morton County ☆ *N. Dak., U.S.A.* 46°45N 101°30W **76** D4
Morton Grove *Ill., U.S.A.* 42°2N 87°46W **95** A2
Mortons Gap *Ky., U.S.A.* 37°14N 87°28W **104** C5
Morven *Ga., U.S.A.* 30°57N 83°30W **113** F3
Morven *N.C., U.S.A.* 34°52N 80°0W **103** D5
Morven *N.C., U.S.A.* 37°58N 78°28W **102** D6
Mosby *Mont., U.S.A.* 47°0N 107°52W **123** C10
Mosca *Colo., U.S.A.* 37°39N 105°52W **125** D3
Moscow *Idaho, U.S.A.* 46°44N 117°0W **122** C2
Moscow *Kans., U.S.A.* 37°20N 101°12W **82** D2
Moscow *Ky., U.S.A.* 36°37N 89°2W **104** D3
Moscow *Ohio, U.S.A.* 38°52N 84°14W **86** E2
Moscow *Pa., U.S.A.* 41°20N 75°31W **92** A1
Moscow *Tenn., U.S.A.* 35°4N 89°24W **104** E3
Moscow Mills *Mo., U.S.A.* 38°57N 90°55W **83** C6
Moselle *Miss., U.S.A.* 31°30N 89°17W **111** E4
Mosenthein Island *Ill., U.S.A.* 38°43N 90°5W **94** A2
Moses Inlet *B.C., Canada* 51°47N 127°23W **154** D7
Moses Lake *Wash., U.S.A.* 47°8N 119°17W **120** C6
Moshannon State Forest *Pa., U.S.A.* 41°7N 78°29W **87** C4
Mosheim *Tenn., U.S.A.* 36°11N 82°57W **105** D10
Mosher *Ont., Canada* 48°42N 84°12W **149** D12
Mosher *S. Dak., U.S.A.* 43°28N 100°18W **76** G5

Mosier *Oreg., U.S.A.* 45°41N 121°24W **121** B4
Mosinee *Wis., U.S.A.* 44°47N 89°43W **78** D4
Mosley Cr. ➜ *B.C., Canada* 51°18N 124°50W **154** C6
Mosquero *N. Mex., U.S.A.* 35°47N 103°58W **131** B7
Mosquitera, L. *Quintana Roo, Mexico* 19°12N 87°33W **179** C6
Mosquitia *Honduras* 15°20N 84°10W **182** C3
Mosquito, Pta. *Yucatán, Mexico* 21°34N 87°48W **179** A6
Mosquito B. *Qué., Canada* 61°10N 78°0W **143** A2
Mosquito Coast = Mosquitia *Honduras* 15°20N 84°10W **182** C3
Mosquito Creek L. *Ohio, U.S.A.* 41°18N 80°46W **86** E6
Mosquitos, G. de los *Panama* 9°15N 81°10W **182** E3
Moss *Tenn., U.S.A.* 36°36N 85°37W **105** D7
Moss Bluff *La., U.S.A.* 30°18N 93°11W **110** D2
Moss Landing *Calif., U.S.A.* 36°48N 121°47W **126** G5
Moss Point *Miss., U.S.A.* 30°25N 88°30W **111** F5
Mossbank *Sask., Canada* 49°56N 105°56W **150** F6
Mossy ➜ *Sask., Canada* 54°5N 102°58W **150** A9
Mossy Head *Fla., U.S.A.* 30°45N 86°19W **114** A2
Mossyrock *Wash., U.S.A.* 46°32N 122°29W **120** D3
Motagua ➜ *Guatemala* 15°44N 88°14W **182** C2
Motley *Minn., U.S.A.* 46°20N 94°40W **77** D4
Motley County ☆ *Tex., U.S.A.* 34°5N 100°58W **108** D7
Motozintla de Mendoza *Chiapas, Mexico* 15°22N 92°14W **178** D4
Mott *N. Dak., U.S.A.* 46°23N 102°20W **76** D3
Motte, L. la *Qué., Canada* 48°20N 78°2W **144** C4
Motters *Md., U.S.A.* 39°40N 77°20W **93** A3
Motul *Yucatán, Mexico* 21°6N 89°17W **179** A4
Mouchalagane ➜ *Qué., Canada* 50°56N 68°41W **143** C12
Mouchoir Bank *W. Indies* 20°57N 70°47W **183** B5
Moulton *Ala., U.S.A.* 34°29N 87°18W **112** B3
Moulton *Iowa, U.S.A.* 40°41N 92°41W **81** E6
Moulton *Tex., U.S.A.* 29°35N 97°9W **109** H10
Moultonborough *N.H., U.S.A.* 43°45N 71°10W **89** C3
Moultrie *Ga., U.S.A.* 31°11N 83°47W **113** E3
Moultrie, L. *S.C., U.S.A.* 33°20N 80°5W **103** E5
Moultrie County ☆ *Ill., U.S.A.* 39°40N 88°35W **84** D5
Mound *La., U.S.A.* 32°21N 91°1W **110** B4
Mound Bayou *Miss., U.S.A.* 33°53N 90°44W **111** C3
Mound City *Ill., U.S.A.* 37°5N 89°10W **84** F4
Mound City *Kans., U.S.A.* 38°8N 94°49W **82** C9
Mound City *Mo., U.S.A.* 40°7N 95°14W **83** A1
Mound City *S. Dak., U.S.A.* 45°44N 100°4W **76** E5
Mound Valley *Kans., U.S.A.* 37°12N 95°24W **82** D8
Moundridge *Kans., U.S.A.* 38°12N 97°31W **82** C6
Mounds *Ill., U.S.A.* 37°7N 89°12W **84** F4
Mounds *Okla., U.S.A.* 35°53N 96°4W **107** C7
Moundsville *W. Va., U.S.A.* 39°55N 80°44W **102** B4
Moundville *Ala., U.S.A.* 33°1N 87°37W **112** C3
Moundville *Mo., U.S.A.* 37°46N 94°27W **83** D2
Mount Airy *Md., U.S.A.* 39°22N 77°10W **93** A3
Mount Airy *N.C., U.S.A.* 36°31N 80°37W **103** B5
Mount Albert *Ont., Canada* 44°8N 79°19W **146** C7
Mount Angel *Oreg., U.S.A.* 45°4N 122°48W **121** B3
Mount Assiniboine Park △ *B.C., Canada* 50°53N 115°39W **153** H5
Mount Auburn *Iowa, U.S.A.* 42°15N 92°6W **81** C6
Mount Ayr *Ill., U.S.A.* 40°57N 87°18W **85** C3
Mount Ayr *Iowa, U.S.A.* 40°43N 94°14W **81** E4
Mount Baker Nat. Recr. Area △ *Wash., U.S.A.* 47°44N 121°48W **120** C4
Mount Baker-Snoqualmie Nat. Forest *Wash., U.S.A.* 48°10N 121°15W **120** B4
Mount Bennett Hills *Idaho, U.S.A.* 43°13N 115°5W **122** F3
Mount Blanchard *Ohio, U.S.A.* 40°54N 83°34W **86** C3
Mount Brydges *Ont., Canada* 42°54N 81°29W **146** D3
Mount Calm *Tex., U.S.A.* 31°46N 96°53W **109** F11
Mount Carleton Prov. Park △ *N.B., Canada* 47°25N 66°55W **141** F3
Mount Carmel *Ill., U.S.A.* 38°25N 87°46W **84** E6
Mount Carmel *Pa., U.S.A.* 40°47N 76°26W **87** D6
Mount Carmel *Utah, U.S.A.* 37°15N 112°40W **129** F3
Mount Carroll *Ill., U.S.A.* 42°6N 89°59W **84** A4
Mount Clemens *Mich., U.S.A.* 42°35N 82°53W **79** G9
Mount Dennis *Ont., Canada* 43°40N 79°28W **161** A2
Mount Desert I. *Maine, U.S.A.* 44°21N 68°20W **90** D5
Mount Dora *Fla., U.S.A.* 28°48N 81°38W **114** C7
Mount Dora *N. Mex., U.S.A.* 36°31N 103°29W **131** A7
Mount Eaton *Ohio, U.S.A.* 40°42N 81°42W **86** C5
Mount Eden *Ky., U.S.A.* 38°3N 85°9W **105** B7
Mount Enterprise *Tex., U.S.A.* 31°55N 94°41W **109** F13
Mount Ephraim *N.J., U.S.A.* 39°52N 75°5W **98** B2
Mount Erie *Ill., U.S.A.* 38°31N 88°14W **84** E5
Mount Etna *Ind., U.S.A.* 40°45N 85°34W **85** C5
Mount Forest *Ont., Canada* 43°59N 80°43W **146** D6
Mount Gay *W. Va., U.S.A.* 37°51N 82°1W **102** D2
Mount Gilead *N.C., U.S.A.* 35°13N 80°0W **103** C6
Mount Gilead *Ohio, U.S.A.* 40°33N 82°50W **86** C4
Mount Greenwood *Ill., U.S.A.* 41°42N 87°42W **95** C2
Mount Holly *N.C., U.S.A.* 35°18N 81°1W **103** C4
Mount Holly *N.J., U.S.A.* 39°59N 74°47W **92** C2
Mount Holly Springs *Pa., U.S.A.* 40°7N 77°12W **87** D5
Mount Hood Memorial Park △ *Mass., U.S.A.* 42°26N 71°1W **96** A2
Mount Hood Nat. Forest *Oreg., U.S.A.* 45°15N 122°0W **121** B4
Mount Hope *W. Va., U.S.A.* 37°54N 81°10W **102** D3
Mount Horeb *Wis., U.S.A.* 43°1N 89°44W **78** E4
Mount Ida *Ark., U.S.A.* 34°34N 93°38W **106** D2
Mount Jackson *Va., U.S.A.* 38°45N 78°39W **93** B2
Mount Jewett *Pa., U.S.A.* 41°44N 78°39W **87** C4
Mount Joy *Pa., U.S.A.* 40°7N 76°30W **87** D6
Mount Judge Howay Park △ *B.C., Canada* 49°30N 122°18W **155** F12
Mount Juliet *Tenn., U.S.A.* 36°12N 86°31W **104** D6
Mount Ka'ala Nat. Area Reserve △ *Hawai'i, U.S.A.* 21°31N 158°7W **136** J13
Mount Kisco *N.Y., U.S.A.* 41°12N 73°44W **92** A3
Mount Laguna *Calif., U.S.A.* 32°52N 116°25W **127** L10
Mount Lebanon *Pa., U.S.A.* 40°21N 80°2W **98** B1
Mount Liberty *Ohio, U.S.A.* 40°21N 82°38W **86** C4
Mount McGuire *Idaho, U.S.A.* 45°10N 114°36W **122** D4
Mount McKinley = Denali Nat. Park and Preserve △*Denali* △ *Alaska, U.S.A.* 63°30N 152°0W **135** E10
Mount Moriah *Nfld. & L., Canada* 48°58N 58°2W **142** D2
Mount Moriah *Mo., U.S.A.* 40°20N 93°48W **83** A3
Mount Morris *Ill., U.S.A.* 42°3N 89°26W **84** A4
Mount Morris *Mich., U.S.A.* 43°7N 83°42W **79** F8
Mount Morris *N.Y., U.S.A.* 42°44N 77°52W **88** C3
Mount Morris L. *N.Y., U.S.A.* 42°44N 77°54W **88** C3
Mount Nebo *Pa., U.S.A.* 39°53N 76°20W **93** A4
Mount Olive *Ala., U.S.A.* 39°4N 89°44W **84** D4
Mount Olive *Miss., U.S.A.* 31°46N 89°39W **111** E4
Mount Olive *N.C., U.S.A.* 35°12N 78°4W **103** C7
Mount Oliver *Pa., U.S.A.* 40°24N 79°59W **98** B2
Mount Olivet *Ky., U.S.A.* 38°32N 84°2W **105** B8
Mount Olympus *Utah, U.S.A.* 40°41N 111°47W **134** B3

Mount Olympus Wilderness *Utah,*
U.S.A. .... 40°39N 111°43W **134 B3**
Mount Orab *Ohio, U.S.A.* ...... 39°2N 83°55W **86 D3**
Mount Pearl *Nfld. & L., Canada* 47°31N 52°47W **142 E8**
Mount Pleasant *Ark., U.S.A.* .. 35°58N 91°45W **106 C4**
Mount Pleasant *Del., U.S.A.* ... 39°32N 75°43W **93 A5**
Mount Pleasant *Iowa, U.S.A.* .. 40°58N 91°33W **81 E71**
Mount Pleasant *Mich., U.S.A.* . 43°36N 84°46W **79 F7**
Mount Pleasant *Miss., U.S.A.* . 34°57N 89°31W **111 B4**
Mount Pleasant *Pa., U.S.A.* .... 40°9N 79°33W **87 D3**
Mount Pleasant *S.C., U.S.A.* ... 32°47N 79°52W **103 F6**
Mount Pleasant *Tenn., U.S.A.* . 35°32N 87°12W **104 E5**
Mount Pleasant *Tex., U.S.A.* ... 33°9N 94°58W **109 D13**
Mount Pleasant *Utah, U.S.A.* .. 39°33N 111°27W **129 D4**
Mount Poconos *Pa., U.S.A.* ..... 41°7N 75°22W **92 A4**
Mount Prospect *Ill., U.S.A.* .... 42°4N 87°56W **84 A6**
Mount Pulaski *Ill., U.S.A.* ...... 40°1N 89°17W **84 C4**
Mount Rainier *Md., U.S.A.* ..... 38°56N 76°57W **99 B4**
Mount Rainier Nat. Park △ *Wash.,*
U.S.A. .... 46°55N 121°50W **120 D4**
Mount Revelstoke Nat. Park △ *B.C.,*
Canada .... 51°5N 118°30W **155 D16**
Mount Robson Park △ *B.C., Canada* 51°50N 119°0W **155 C16**
Mount Rushmore Nat. Memorial △ *S. Dak.,*
U.S.A. .... 43°53N 103°27W **76 G2**
Mount St. Helens Nat. Volcanic Monument △
Wash., U.S.A. .... 46°14N 122°11W **120 D3**
Mount Savage *Md., U.S.A.* ...... 39°42N 78°53W **93 A2**
Mount Seymour Prov. Park △ *B.C.,*
Canada .... 49°20N 123°0W **161 B3**
Mount Shasta *Calif., U.S.A.* ... 41°19N 122°19W **126 B4**
Mount Snow Resort *Vt., U.S.A.* 42°58N 72°54W **89 D2**
Mount Solo *Va., U.S.A.* .... 38°21N 79°5W **102 C5**
Mount Sterling *Ill., U.S.A.* ..... 39°59N 90°45W **84 D31**
Mount Sterling *Ky., U.S.A.* ..... 38°4N 83°56W **105 B9**
Mount Sterling *Ohio, U.S.A.* ... 39°43N 83°16W **86 D3**
Mount Stewart *P.E.I., Canada* . 46°22N 62°52W **141 G7**
Mount Storm *W. Va., U.S.A.* ... 39°17N 79°15W **93 A1**
Mount Storm L. *W. Va., U.S.A.* 39°13N 79°16W **93 A1**
Mount Summit *Ind., U.S.A.* .... 40°0N 85°23W **85 C5**
Mount Sumpee *Ind., U.S.A.* .... 43°19N 72°6W **89 C2**
Mount Tabor Park *Oreg., U.S.A.* 45°30N 122°35W **132 A2**
Mount Tolmie *B.C., Canada* ..... 48°28N 123°20W **155 G11**
Mount Uniacke *N.S., Canada* .... 44°54N 63°50W **141 J6**
Mount Union *Iowa, U.S.A.* ...... 41°3N 91°23W **81 D7**
Mount Union *Pa., U.S.A.* .... 40°23N 77°53W **87 D5**
Mount Vernon *Ala., U.S.A.* ...... 31°5N 88°1W **112 E2**
Mount Vernon *Ark., U.S.A.* ..... 35°14N 92°8W **106 C3**
Mount Vernon *Ga., U.S.A.* ...... 32°11N 82°36W **113 D4**
Mount Vernon *Ill., U.S.A.* .... 38°19N 88°55W **84 E5**
Mount Vernon *Ind., U.S.A.* ...... 37°56N 87°54W **85 F3**
Mount Vernon *Iowa, U.S.A.* ..... 41°55N 91°23W **81 D7**
Mount Vernon *Ky., U.S.A.* .... 37°21N 84°21W **105 C8**
Mount Vernon *Md., U.S.A.* ...... 38°47N 77°6W **93 B3**
Mount Vernon *Mo., U.S.A.* ...... 37°6N 93°49W **83 D3**
Mount Vernon *N.Y., U.S.A.* ..... 40°54N 73°49W **97 A4**
Mount Vernon *Ohio, U.S.A.* ..... 40°23N 82°29W **86 C4**
Mount Vernon *Oreg., U.S.A.* .... 44°25N 119°7W **121 C6**
Mount Vernon *S. Dak., U.S.A.* . 43°43N 98°16W **76 G7**
Mount Vernon *Tenn., U.S.A.* ... 35°25N 84°22W **105 E8**
Mount Vernon *Tex., U.S.A.* ..... 33°11N 95°13W **109 D12**
Mount Vernon *Wash., U.S.A.* ... 48°25N 122°20W **120 B3**
Mount Washington Cog Railway *N.H.,*
U.S.A. .... 44°17N 71°21W **89 B3**
Mount Wolf *Pa., U.S.A.* .... 40°4N 76°43W **87 D6**
Mount Zion *Ill., U.S.A.* .... 39°46N 88°53W **84 D5**
Mountain *J. Dak., U.S.A.* .... 48°41N 97°52W **76 B8**
Mountain *Wis., U.S.A.* .... 45°11N 88°28W **78 C5**
Mountain ➤ *N.W.T., Canada* .... 65°41N 128°50W **157 C7**
Mountain Brook *Ala., U.S.A.* ... 33°30N 86°45W **112 C4**
Mountain City *Ga., U.S.A.* ...... 34°55N 83°23W **113 B3**
Mountain City *Nev., U.S.A.* .... 41°50N 115°58W **122 A5**
Mountain City *Tenn., U.S.A.* ... 36°29N 81°48W **105 D11**
Mountain Creek *Ala., U.S.A.* ... 32°43N 86°29W **112 D4**
Mountain Creek L. *Tex., U.S.A.* 32°43N 96°56W **116 B4**
Mountain Creek Lake Park *Tex.,*
U.S.A. .... 32°41N 96°58W **116 B4**
Mountain Grove *Mo., U.S.A.* ... 37°8N 92°16W **83 D41**
Mountain Home *Ark., U.S.A.* ... 36°20N 92°23W **106 B31**
Mountain Home *Idaho, U.S.A.* . 43°8N 115°41W **122 F3**
Mountain Home *N.C., U.S.A.* ... 35°23N 82°30W **103 C3**
Mountain Home *Tex., U.S.A.* ... 30°10N 99°22W **109 G8**
Mountain Home *Wyo., U.S.A.* .. 41°0N 106°10W **124 E6**
Mountain Home Air Force Base *Idaho,*
U.S.A. .... 43°3N 115°51W **122 F3**
Mountain Iron *Minn., U.S.A.* ... 47°32N 92°37W **77 C61**
Mountain Lake *Minn., U.S.A.* .. 43°57N 94°56W **77 G4**
Mountain Lake Park *Md., U.S.A.* 39°24N 79°23W **93 A1**
Mountain Meadows Res. *Calif., U.S.A.* 40°17N 120°49W **126 C6**
Mountain Park *Okla., U.S.A.* .... 34°42N 98°57W **107 D5**
Mountain Pine *Ark., U.S.A.* ..... 34°34N 93°10W **106 D2**
Mountain View *Alta., Canada* ... 49°8N 113°36W **153 J7**
Mountain View *Ark., U.S.A.* ..... 35°52N 92°7W **106 C3**
Mountain View *Calif., U.S.A.* ... 37°23N 122°5W **126 F4**
Mountain View *Colo., U.S.A.* .... 39°46N 105°3W **134 B1**
Mountain View *Hawai'i, U.S.A.* 19°33N 155°7W **136 D6**
Mountain View *Mo., U.S.A.* ...... 37°0N 91°42W **83 D5**
Mountain View *N.J., U.S.A.* ...... 40°55N 74°15W **97 A1**
Mountain View *Wyo., U.S.A.* .... 41°16N 110°20W **124 E2**
Mountain Village *Alaska, U.S.A.* 62°5N 163°43W **135 E7**
Mountainair *N. Mex., U.S.A.* ... 34°31N 106°15W **131 C4**
Mountainaire *Ariz., U.S.A.* ...... 35°9N 111°40W **130 B4**
Mountainburg *Ark., U.S.A.* ...... 35°38N 94°10W **106 C1**
Mountlake Terrace *Wash., U.S.A.* 47°47N 122°18W **132 B3**
Mountrail County ☆ *N. Dak., U.S.A.* 48°10N 102°30W **76 B3**
Mousie *Ky., U.S.A.* .... 37°25N 82°53W **105 C10**
Moville *Iowa, U.S.A.* .... 42°29N 96°4W **81 C2**
Moweaqua *Ill., U.S.A.* .... 39°38N 89°1W **84 D4**
Mower County ☆ *Minn., U.S.A.* 43°40N 92°45W **77 G6**
Mowrystown *Ohio, U.S.A.* .... 39°2N 83°45W **86 D3**
Moxee City *Wash., U.S.A.* .... 46°33N 120°23W **120 D5**
Moyahua de Estrada *Zacatecas, Mexico* 21°16N 103°11W **173 F7**
Moyers *Okla., U.S.A.* .... 34°19N 95°39W **107 D8**
Moyie *Idaho, U.S.A.* .... 48°43N 116°11W **122 A1**
Moyie Springs *Idaho, U.S.A.* .... 48°44N 116°11W **122 A1**
Mozhabong L. *Ont., Canada* ..... 46°58N 82°30W **149 F14**
Muchalat Inlet *B.C., Canada* .... 49°38N 126°15W **154 F8**
Muckalee Cr. ➤ *Ga., U.S.A.* ..... 31°38N 84°9W **113 E2**
Mud ➤ *Ky., U.S.A.* .... 37°38N 86°54W **104 C6**
Mud Butte *S. Dak., U.S.A.* ...... 45°0N 102°54W **76 E3**
Mud Cr. ➤ *Okla., U.S.A.* .... 33°55N 97°28W **107 E6**
Mud Cr. ➤ *S. Dak., U.S.A.* ...... 45°11N 98°24W **76 E7**
Mud I. *N.S., Canada* .... 43°28N 65°59W **141 K4**

Mud L. *Fla., U.S.A.* .... 28°23N 81°17W **115 B3**
Mud L. *Nev., U.S.A.* .... 37°52N 117°4W **128 E3**
Mud Lake Res. *S. Dak., U.S.A.* . 45°47N 98°15W **76 E7**
Muddy ➤ *Nev., U.S.A.* .... 36°31N 114°24W **128 F6**
Muddy Boggy Cr. ➤ *Okla., U.S.A.* 34°3N 95°47W **107 D8**
Muddy Cr. ➤ *Utah, U.S.A.* ...... 38°24N 110°42W **129 E5**
Muddy Cr. ➤ *Wyo., U.S.A.* ...... 41°35N 109°58W **124 E3**
Muddy Creek Res. *Colo., U.S.A.* 38°15N 107°4W **125 E7**
Muddy Gap *Wyo., U.S.A.* .... 42°21N 107°28W **124 D5**
Muddy L. *Sask., Canada* .... 52°19N 109°6W **150 C2**
Muddy Mts. *Nev., U.S.A.* .... 36°24N 114°39W **128 F6**
Muenster *Sask., Canada* .... 52°12N 105°0W **150 C7**
Muenster *Tex., U.S.A.* .... 33°39N 97°23W **109 D10**
Muerto, Mar *Oaxaca, Mexico* ... 16°10N 94°10W **177 H6**
Muertos, B. de los *Baja Calif. S., Mexico* 23°55N 109°45W **167 K9**
Muhlenberg County ☆ *Ky., U.S.A.* 37°10N 87°10W **104 C5**
Muir *Mich., U.S.A.* .... 43°0N 84°56W **79 F7**
Muir Woods Nat. Monument △ *Calif.,*
U.S.A. .... 37°55N 122°35W **126 F4**
Mujeres, B. *Quintana Roo, Mexico* 21°15N 86°46W **179 A7**
Mujeres, I. *Quintana Roo, Mexico* 21°13N 86°43W **179 A7**
Mukilteo *Wash., U.S.A.* .... 47°57N 122°18W **120 C3**
Mukutawa ➤ *Man., Canada* ..... 53°10N 97°24W **151 B14**
Mukwonago *Wis., U.S.A.* .... 42°52N 88°20W **78 F5**
Mul *Yucatán, Mexico* .... 20°10N 88°42W **179 B5**
Mulatos *Sonora, Mexico* .... 28°39N 108°51W **168 E7**
Mulatos ➤ *Mexico* .... 28°58N 108°46W **168 E7**
Mulberry *Ark., U.S.A.* .... 35°30N 94°3W **106 C1**
Mulberry *Fla., U.S.A.* .... 27°54N 81°59W **114 D7**
Mulberry *Ind., U.S.A.* .... 40°21N 86°40W **85 C4**
Mulberry *N.C., U.S.A.* .... 36°14N 81°11W **103 B4**
Mulberry Fork ➤ *Ala., U.S.A.* .. 33°33N 87°11W **112 C3**
Mulberry Grove *Ill., U.S.A.* ..... 38°56N 89°16W **84 E4**
Mulchatna ➤ *Alaska, U.S.A.* .... 59°40N 157°7W **135 G8**
Muldoon *Tex., U.S.A.* .... 29°49N 97°4W **109 H10**
Muldraugh *Ky., U.S.A.* .... 37°56N 85°59W **105 C7**
Muldrow *Okla., U.S.A.* .... 35°24N 94°36W **107 C9**
Mule Creek *N. Mex., U.S.A.* ..... 33°7N 108°57W **131 D2**
Mule Creek Junction *Wyo., U.S.A.* 43°23N 104°13W **124 C8**
Mulegé *Baja Calif. S., Mexico* .. 26°53N 111°59W **167 G7**
Muleshoe *Tex., U.S.A.* .... 34°13N 102°43W **108 B5**
Muleshoe Nat. Wildlife Refuge △ *Tex.,*
U.S.A. .... 33°58N 102°44W **108 D5**
Mulgrave *N.S., Canada* .... 45°38N 61°31W **141 H8**
Mulhall *Okla., U.S.A.* .... 36°4N 97°25W **107 B6**
Mullan *Idaho, U.S.A.* .... 47°28N 115°48W **122 B3**
Mullen *Nebr., U.S.A.* .... 42°3N 101°1W **80 B4**
Mullens *W. Va., U.S.A.* .... 37°35N 81°23W **102 D5**
Mullet L. *Mich., U.S.A.* .... 45°31N 84°31W **79 D7**
Mullett Lake *Mich., U.S.A.* ..... 45°34N 84°32W **79 D7**
Mullica ➤ *N.J., U.S.A.* .... 39°33N 74°25W **92 C2**
Mullin *Tex., U.S.A.* .... 31°33N 98°40W **109 F9**
Mullins *S.C., U.S.A.* .... 34°12N 79°15W **103 D6**
Mullinville *Kans., U.S.A.* .... 37°35N 99°29W **82 D4**
Mulvane *Kans., U.S.A.* .... 37°29N 97°15W **82 D6**
Muna *Yucatán, Mexico* .... 20°29N 89°43W **179 B4**
Muncie *Ind., U.S.A.* .... 40°12N 85°23W **85 C5**
Muncy *Pa., U.S.A.* .... 41°12N 76°47W **87 C6**
Mundare *Alta., Canada* .... 53°35N 112°20W **152 E8**
Munday *Tex., U.S.A.* .... 33°27N 99°38W **108 D8**
Mundelein *Ill., U.S.A.* .... 42°16N 88°0W **84 A5**
Munden *Kans., U.S.A.* .... 39°55N 97°32W **82 B6**
Munford *Tenn., U.S.A.* .... 35°27N 89°49W **104 E3**
Munfordville *Ky., U.S.A.* .... 37°16N 85°54W **105 C7**
Munhall *Pa., U.S.A.* .... 40°23N 79°54W **98 B2**
Munich *N. Dak., U.S.A.* .... 48°40N 98°50W **76 B7**
Municipal Park *Minn., U.S.A.* .. 44°52N 93°22W **94 B1**
Munising *Mich., U.S.A.* .... 46°25N 86°40W **79 C5**
Munjor *Kans., U.S.A.* .... 38°49N 99°16W **82 C4**
Munnsville *N.Y., U.S.A.* .... 42°59N 75°35W **88 C7**
Munsey Park *N.Y., U.S.A.* .... 40°47N 73°40W **97 B4**
Munson *Alta., Canada* .... 51°34N 112°45W **153 G8**
Munson *Fla., U.S.A.* .... 30°52N 86°52W **114 A2**
Munsungan L. *Maine, U.S.A.* ... 46°22N 69°0W **90 B5**
Murchison ➤ *Nunavut, Canada* . 68°35N 93°35W **158 D7**
Murchison I. *Ont., Canada* ...... 50°0N 88°21W **148 C8**
Murdo *S. Dak., U.S.A.* .... 43°53N 100°43W **76 G5**
Murdochville *Qué., Canada* ...... 48°58N 65°30W **140 E4**
Murdock *Kans., U.S.A.* .... 37°37N 97°56W **82 D6**
Murdock *Minn., U.S.A.* .... 45°13N 95°24W **77 E3**
Murdock *Nebr., U.S.A.* .... 40°55N 96°17W **80 D9**
Murdock Park *Utah, U.S.A.* ..... 40°41N 111°36W **134 B4**
Murfreesboro *Ark., U.S.A.* ...... 34°4N 93°41W **106 D2**
Murfreesboro *N.C., U.S.A.* ...... 36°27N 77°6W **103 B8**
Murfreesboro *Tenn., U.S.A.* ..... 35°51N 86°24W **104 E6**
Muriel L. *Alta., Canada* .... 54°9N 110°40W **152 D10**
Murphy *Idaho, U.S.A.* .... 43°13N 116°33W **122 F2**
Murphy *N.C., U.S.A.* .... 38°29N 90°29W **83 C6**
Murphy *Oreg., U.S.A.* .... 42°21N 123°20W **121 E2**
Murphy L. *B.C., Canada* .... 52°3N 121°15W **155 C13**
Murphy's Station = Sunnyvale *Calif.,*
U.S.A. .... 37°23N 122°2W **126 F4**
Murphysboro *Ill., U.S.A.* .... 37°46N 89°20W **84 F4**
Murray *Iowa, U.S.A.* .... 41°3N 93°57W **81 D5**
Murray *Ky., U.S.A.* .... 36°37N 88°19W **104 D4**
Murray *Utah, U.S.A.* .... 40°40N 111°53W **134 C2**
Murray, L. *Okla., U.S.A.* .... 34°2N 97°3W **107 D6**
Murray, L. *S.C., U.S.A.* .... 34°3N 81°13W **103 C5**
Murray City *Ohio, U.S.A.* .... 39°31N 82°10W **86 D4**
Murray County ☆ *Ga., U.S.A.* .. 34°50N 84°45W **113 B2**
Murray County ☆ *Minn., U.S.A.* 44°0N 95°45W **77 F3**
Murray County ☆ *Okla., U.S.A.* 34°30N 97°0W **107 D6**
Murray Harbour *P.E.I., Canada* 46°0N 62°28W **141 H7**
Murray River *P.E.I., Canada* .... 46°1N 62°37W **141 G7**
Murrayville *Ill., U.S.A.* .... 39°35N 90°15W **84 D3**
Murrells Inlet *S.C., U.S.A.* .... 33°33N 79°2W **103 E6**
Murtaugh *Idaho, U.S.A.* .... 42°30N 114°10W **122 G4**
Murtle L. *B.C., Canada* .... 52°8N 119°38W **155 C15**
Murval L. *B.C., Canada* .... 32°2N 94°8W **109 E13**
Muscatatuck ➤ *Ind., U.S.A.* ..... 38°46N 86°10W **85 E4**
Muscatatuck Nat. Wildlife Refuge △ *Ind.,*
U.S.A. .... 38°56N 85°49W **85 E5**
Muscatine *Iowa, U.S.A.* .... 41°25N 91°3W **81 D71**
Muscatine County ☆ *Iowa, U.S.A.* 41°30N 91°0W **81 D7**
Muscle Shoals *Ala., U.S.A.* ...... 34°45N 87°40W **112 B3**
Muscoda *Wis., U.S.A.* .... 43°11N 90°27W **78 E3**
Muscogee County ☆ *Ga., U.S.A.* 32°30N 84°58W **113 D2**
Musconetcong ➤ *N.J., U.S.A.* ... 40°36N 75°11W **92 B1**
Muscotah *Kans., U.S.A.* .... 39°33N 95°31W **82 B8**
Musella *Ga., U.S.A.* .... 32°48N 84°2W **113 D2**
Musgrave Harbour *Nfld. & L., Canada* 49°27N 53°58W **142 C7**
Mushaboom *N.S., Canada* .... 44°51N 62°32W **141 J7**

Muskeg B. *Minn., U.S.A.* .... 48°55N 95°10W **77 B3**
Muskeg L. *Minn., U.S.A.* .... 49°0N 90°2W **148 C6**
Muskeg River *Alta., Canada* ..... 53°55N 118°39W **152 E2**
Muskeget Channel *Mass., U.S.A.* 41°25N 70°25W **91 C4**
Muskego *Wis., U.S.A.* .... 42°55N 88°8W **78 F5**
Muskegon *Mich., U.S.A.* .... 43°14N 86°16W **79 F5**
Muskegon ➤ *Mich., U.S.A.* ...... 43°14N 86°21W **79 F5**
Muskegon County ☆ *Mich., U.S.A.* 43°15N 86°15W **79 F5**
Muskegon Heights *Mich., U.S.A.* 43°12N 86°16W **79 F5**
Muskingum ➤ *Ohio, U.S.A.* ...... 40°3N 81°59W **86 C5**
Muskingum County ☆ *Ohio, U.S.A.* 39°56N 82°1W **86 D4**
Muskogee *Okla., U.S.A.* .... 35°45N 95°22W **107 C8**
Muskogee County ☆ *Okla., U.S.A.* 35°40N 95°25W **107 C8**
Muskoka, L. *Ont., Canada* .... 45°0N 79°25W **146 C7**
Muskrat Cr. ➤ *Wyo., U.S.A.* ..... 43°9N 108°12W **124 C4**
Muskwa ➤ *Alta., Canada* .... 56°15N 113°48W **152 B7**
Muskwa ➤ *B.C., Canada* .... 58°47N 122°48W **157 E8**
Muskwa L. *Alta., Canada* .... 56°9N 114°38W **152 B6**
Musquanousse, L. *Qué., Canada* 50°22N 61°5W **140 C8**
Musquaro *Qué., Canada* .... 50°10N 61°3W **140 C8**
Musquaro, L. *Qué., Canada* ...... 50°38N 61°5W **143 C5**
Musquash *N.B., Canada* .... 45°11N 66°19W **141 H3**
Musquodoboit Harbour *N.S., Canada* 44°50N 63°9W **141 J6**
Mussel Fork ➤ *Mo., U.S.A.* ...... 39°26N 92°57W **83 B4**
Mussel Inlet *B.C., Canada* .... 52°53N 128°7W **154 C6**
Musselshell ➤ *Mont., U.S.A.* .... 47°21N 107°57W **123 C10**
Musselshell County ☆ *Mont., U.S.A.* 46°35N 108°30W **123 D9**
Mustang *Okla., U.S.A.* .... 35°24N 97°42W **107 C6**
Mustang Draw ➤ *Tex., U.S.A.* ... 31°58N 102°40W **108 F5**
Mustang I. *Tex., U.S.A.* .... 27°52N 97°3W **109 K10**
Mustinka ➤ *Minn., U.S.A.* .... 45°45N 96°38W **77 E2**
Mutual *Ohio, U.S.A.* .... 40°5N 83°38W **86 C3**
Mutual *Okla., U.S.A.* .... 36°14N 99°9W **107 B4**
Muy Muy *Nic.* .... 12°39N 85°36W **182 D2**
Muyil *Quintana Roo, Mexico* ..... 20°4N 87°37W **179 B6**
Muzon, C. *Alaska, U.S.A.* .... 54°40N 132°42W **135 J14**
Myakka ➤ *Fla., U.S.A.* .... 26°56N 82°11W **114 E6**
Myakka City *Fla., U.S.A.* .... 27°21N 82°10W **114 D6**
Myerstown *Pa., U.S.A.* .... 40°22N 76°19W **87 D6**
Mylius Erichsen Land *Greenland* 81°30N 27°0W **162 A8**
Mylo *N. Dak., U.S.A.* .... 48°38N 99°37W **76 B6**
Myrnam *Alta., Canada* .... 53°40N 111°14W **152 E9**
Myrtle *Miss., U.S.A.* .... 34°34N 89°7W **111 B4**
Myrtle *Mo., U.S.A.* .... 36°31N 91°16W **83 E5**
Myrtle *Tex., U.S.A.* .... 29°39N 95°24W **116 C2**
Myrtle *W. Va., U.S.A.* .... 37°46N 82°12W **102 D2**
Myrtle Beach *S.C., U.S.A.* .... 33°42N 78°53W **103 E7**
Myrtle Creek *Oreg., U.S.A.* ...... 43°1N 123°17W **121 D2**
Myrtle Grove *Fla., U.S.A.* .... 30°23N 87°17W **114 A1**
Myrtle Grove *N.C., U.S.A.* .... 34°8N 77°53W **103 D8**
Myrtle Point *Oreg., U.S.A.* .... 43°4N 124°8W **121 D1**
Myrtlewood *Ala., U.S.A.* .... 32°16N 87°57W **112 D3**
Mystic *Conn., U.S.A.* .... 41°21N 71°58W **91 C3**
Mystic *Iowa, U.S.A.* .... 40°47N 92°57W **81 E6**
Mystic ➤ *Mass., U.S.A.* .... 42°22N 71°3W **96 A2**
Mystic Island *N.J., U.S.A.* .... 39°34N 74°22W **92 C2**
Mystic Seaport *Conn., U.S.A.* ... 41°22N 71°58W **91 C3**
Myton *Utah, U.S.A.* .... 40°12N 110°4W **129 C5**

N

N.A.S.A. Michoud Facility *La., U.S.A.* 30°1N 89°55W **117 B3**
N.A.S.A. Space Center = John C. Stennis Space
Center *Miss., U.S.A.* .... 30°23N 89°37W **111 F4**
N.A.S.A. Wallops I. *Va., U.S.A.* 37°50N 75°30W **102 D9**
Nä'älehu *Hawai'i, U.S.A.* .... 19°4N 155°35W **136 D6**
Nabalam *Yucatán, Mexico* .... 20°56N 88°1W **179 B5**
Nabesna *Alaska, U.S.A.* .... 62°22N 143°0W **135 E12**
Nabisipi ➤ *Qué., Canada* .... 50°14N 62°13W **143 C5**
Nabor Carrillo, Laguna *México, Mexico* 19°28N 98°59W **181 B4**
Nacajuca *Tabasco, Mexico* .... 18°8N 93°1W **178 A3**
Nacaome *Honduras* .... 13°31N 87°30W **182 D2**
Nacha, L. la *Tamaulipas, Mexico* 24°52N 97°51W **171 F7**
Naches *Wash., U.S.A.* .... 46°44N 120°42W **120 D5**
Naches ➤ *Wash., U.S.A.* .... 46°38N 120°31W **120 D5**
Nachicapau, L. *Qué., Canada* .... 56°40N 68°5W **143 B4**
Nachvak Fd. *Nfld. & L., Canada* 59°3N 63°45W **143 B5**
Nackawic *N.B., Canada* .... 45°59N 67°17W **141 H2**
Naco *Sonora, Mexico* .... 31°19N 109°56W **168 B6**
Naco *Ariz., U.S.A.* .... 31°21N 109°57W **130 F6**
Nacogdoches *Tex., U.S.A.* .... 31°36N 94°39W **109 F13**
Nacogdoches County ☆ *Tex., U.S.A.* 31°35N 94°40W **109 F13**
Nácori Chico *Sonora, Mexico* .... 29°40N 108°57W **168 D7**
Nacori Grande *Sonora, Mexico* .. 29°4N 110°3W **168 D5**
Nacozari de García *Sonora, Mexico* 30°25N 109°38W **168 C6**
Nacupétaro *Michoacan, Mexico* . 19°4N 101°10W **175 C6**
Nadadores *Coahuila, Mexico* ..... 27°3N 101°36W **170 C3**
Nadadores ➤ *Coahuila, Mexico* .. 27°28N 100°43W **170 C4**
Nadern Harb. *B.C., Canada* ...... 54°0N 132°36W **154 A2**
Nadina ➤ *B.C., Canada* .... 53°58N 126°30W **154 B7**
Nadina L. *B.C., Canada* .... 53°53N 127°2W **154 B7**
Nadine *N. Mex., U.S.A.* .... 32°37N 103°8W **131 E7**
Naftan Pt. *N. Marianas* .... 15°5N 145°45E **184 c**
Nagagami ➤ *Ont., Canada* .... 49°40N 84°40W **149 C12**
Nagagami L. *Ont., Canada* .... 49°25N 85°1W **149 C11**
Nagagamisis L. *Ont., Canada* .... 49°28N 84°40W **149 C12**
Nagai I. *Alaska, U.S.A.* .... 55°5N 160°0W **135 J8**
Nagas Pt. *B.C., Canada* .... 52°12N 131°22W **154 C3**
Nagasin L. *Ont., Canada* .... 47°48N 83°37W **149 E13**
Nageezi *N. Mex., U.S.A.* .... 36°16N 107°45W **131 A3**
Nags Head *N.C., U.S.A.* .... 35°57N 75°38W **103 C10**
Nagua *Dom. Rep.* .... 19°23N 69°50W **183 C6**
Naguabo *Puerto Rico* .... 18°13N 65°44W **184 G17**
Nahanni Butte *N.W.T., Canada* . 61°2N 123°31W **157 D8**
Nahanni Nat. Park △ *N.W.T., Canada* 61°36N 125°41W **157 D8**
Nahant *Mass., U.S.A.* .... 42°25N 70°54W **91 B4**
Nahma *Mich., U.S.A.* .... 45°50N 86°40W **79 D5**
Nahuatzen *Michoacan, Mexico* .. 19°40N 101°55W **174 C6**
Nahunta *Ga., U.S.A.* .... 31°12N 81°59W **113 E5**
Naicá *Chihuahua, Mexico* .... 27°53N 105°31W **169 F10**
Naicam *Sask., Canada* .... 52°30N 104°30W **150 C7**
Naikoon Park △ *B.C., Canada* ... 53°55N 131°55W **154 B3**
Nain *Nfld. & L., Canada* .... 56°34N 61°40W **143 B5**
Nain *N. Mex., U.S.A.* .... 39°14N 78°12W **93 A2**
Nairn *La., U.S.A.* .... 29°26N 89°37W **110 E6**
Nairn Centre *Ont., Canada* ...... 46°20N 81°35W **146 A5**
Nakalele Pt. *Hawai'i, U.S.A.* ..... 21°2N 156°35W **136 B5**
Nakina *Ont., Canada* .... 50°10N 86°40W **149 B10**
Naknek *Alaska, U.S.A.* .... 58°44N 157°1W **135 G8**
Nakusp *B.C., Canada* .... 50°20N 117°45W **155 E17**
Nallen *W. Va., U.S.A.* .... 38°5N 80°53W **102 C4**
Namakan L. *Ont., Canada* .... 48°27N 92°35W **148 D4**
Nambe Indian Reservation *N. Mex.,*
U.S.A. .... 35°52N 105°52W **131 B5**

Namekagon ➤ *Wis., U.S.A.* ...... 46°5N 92°6W **78 B1**
Namew L. *Sask., Canada* .... 54°14N 101°56W **151 A10**
Namiquipa *Chihuahua, Mexico* .. 29°15N 107°25W **169 E8**
Nampa *Alta., Canada* .... 56°2N 117°8W **152 B3**
Nampa *Idaho, U.S.A.* .... 43°34N 116°34W **122 F2**
Namu *B.C., Canada* .... 51°52N 127°50W **154 D7**
Namur *Qué., Canada* .... 45°54N 74°56W **144 F8**
Namur L. *Alta., Canada* .... 57°25N 112°40W **152 A8**
Nanacamilpa *Tlaxcala, Mexico* .. 19°45N 98°31W **175 C9**
Nanaimo *B.C., Canada* .... 49°10N 124°0W **154 F11**
Nänäkuli *Hawai'i, U.S.A.* .... 21°24N 158°9W **136 K13**
Nance County ☆ *Nebr., U.S.A.* .. 41°25N 98°0W **80 C8**
Nanchital *Veracruz, Mexico* ...... 18°4N 94°24W **177 F6**
Nancy *Ky., U.S.A.* .... 37°4N 84°45W **105 C8**
Nanika L. *B.C., Canada* .... 53°47N 127°38W **154 B7**
Nanisivik *Nunavut, Canada* ...... 73°2N 84°33W **158 C7**
Nanjemoy *Md., U.S.A.* .... 38°27N 77°13W **93 B3**
Nanortalik *Greenland* .... 60°10N 45°17W **162 E6**
Nansen Land *Greenland* .... 83°0N 43°0W **162 A6**
Nansen Sd. *Nunavut, Canada* ... 81°0N 91°0W **158 C17**
Nantahala Nat. Forest *N.C., U.S.A.* 35°15N 83°30W **103 C2**
Nanticoke *Md., U.S.A.* .... 38°16N 75°54W **93 B5**
Nanticoke *Pa., U.S.A.* .... 41°12N 76°0W **87 C6**
Nanticoke ➤ *Md., U.S.A.* .... 38°16N 75°56W **93 B5**
Nanton *Alta., Canada* .... 50°21N 113°46W **153 H7**
Nantucket *Mass., U.S.A.* .... 41°17N 70°6W **91 C4**
Nantucket County ☆ *Mass., U.S.A.* 41°15N 70°5W **91 C4**
Nantucket Harbor *Mass., U.S.A.* 41°17N 70°6W **91 C4**
Nantucket I. *Mass., U.S.A.* ...... 41°16N 70°5W **91 C4**
Nantucket Sd. *Mass., U.S.A.* .... 41°30N 70°15W **91 C4**
Nanty Glo *Pa., U.S.A.* .... 40°28N 78°50W **87 D4**
Naococane, L. *Qué., Canada* ..... 52°50N 70°45W **143 C3**
Naolinco de Victoria *Veracruz, Mexico* 19°39N 96°53W **176 C4**
Naomi Peak *Utah, U.S.A.* .... 41°55N 111°41W **129 B4**
Napa *Calif., U.S.A.* .... 38°18N 122°17W **126 E4**
Napa County ☆ *Calif., U.S.A.* ... 38°30N 122°20W **126 E4**
Napaimiut *Alaska, U.S.A.* .... 61°33N 158°42W **135 F8**
Napakiak *Alaska, U.S.A.* .... 60°42N 161°57W **135 F7**
Napaktulik L. *N.W.T., Canada* .. 65°30N 113°55W **156 C10**
Näpali Coast *Hawai'i, U.S.A.* .... 22°11N 159°39W **136 A2**
Napanee *Ont., Canada* .... 44°15N 77°0W **147 C10**
Napartokh B. *Nfld. & L., Canada* 58°1N 62°19W **143 B5**
Napaskiak *Alaska, U.S.A.* .... 60°43N 161°55W **135 F7**
Napavine *Wash., U.S.A.* .... 46°35N 122°54W **120 D3**
Napeague B. *N.Y., U.S.A.* .... 41°2N 72°2W **91 C2**
Naper *Nebr., U.S.A.* .... 42°58N 99°6W **80 B6**
Naperville *Ill., U.S.A.* .... 41°46N 88°9W **84 B5**
Napierville *Qué., Canada* .... 45°11N 73°25W **145 F6**
Napili-Honokowai *Hawai'i, U.S.A.* 20°58N 156°39W **136 C5**
Naples *Fla., U.S.A.* .... 26°8N 81°48W **114 E7**
Naples *Idaho, U.S.A.* .... 48°34N 116°24W **122 A2**
Naples *N.Y., U.S.A.* .... 42°37N 77°24W **88 C3**
Naples *Tex., U.S.A.* .... 33°12N 94°41W **109 D13**
Naples *Utah, U.S.A.* .... 40°26N 109°30W **129 C6**
Naples Park *Fla., U.S.A.* .... 26°17N 81°46W **114 E7**
Napoleanville *La., U.S.A.* .... 29°56N 91°2W **110 E4**
Napoleon *Ind., U.S.A.* .... 39°12N 85°20W **85 D5**
Napoleon *N. Dak., U.S.A.* .... 46°30N 99°46W **76 D6**
Napoleon *Ohio, U.S.A.* .... 41°23N 84°8W **86 B2**
Naponee *Nebr., U.S.A.* .... 40°5N 99°9W **80 D6**
Nappanee *Ind., U.S.A.* .... 41°27N 86°0W **85 B5**
Nara Visa *N. Mex., U.S.A.* .... 35°37N 103°6W **131 B7**
Naramata *B.C., Canada* .... 49°36N 119°35W **155 F15**
Naranjo *Sinaloa, Mexico* .... 25°48N 108°31W **172 B2**
Naranjo ➤ *Jalisco, Mexico* .... 19°30N 103°37W **174 C4**
Naranjos *Veracruz, Mexico* .... 21°21N 97°41W **176 C3**
Narberth *Pa., U.S.A.* .... 40°0N 75°13W **98 A1**
Nardin *Okla., U.S.A.* .... 36°47N 97°27W **107 B6**
Nares Str. *Arctic* .... 80°0N 70°0W **162 B3**
Narka *Kans., U.S.A.* .... 39°58N 97°25W **82 B6**
Narragansett Bay *R.I., U.S.A.* ... 41°36N 71°19W **91 C3**
Narragansett Pier *R.I., U.S.A.* ... 41°26N 71°27W **91 C3**
Narraway ➤ *Alta., Canada* .... 55°44N 119°55W **152 C1**
Narrow Hills Prov. Park △ *Sask.,*
Canada .... 54°0N 104°37W **150 A7**
Narrows *Va., U.S.A.* .... 37°20N 80°49W **102 D4**
Narrows, The *N.Y., U.S.A.* ...... 40°37N 74°3W **97 C2**
Narsaq *Greenland* .... 60°54N 46°4W **162 E6**
Naruna *Va., U.S.A.* .... 37°6N 79°0W **102 D6**
Naschitti *N. Mex., U.S.A.* .... 36°4N 108°41W **131 A2**
Naselle *Wash., U.S.A.* .... 46°22N 123°49W **120 D2**
Nash *Okla., U.S.A.* .... 36°40N 98°3W **107 B5**
Nash County ☆ *N.C., U.S.A.* .... 36°0N 78°0W **103 B8**
Nash Creek *N.B., Canada* .... 47°56N 66°6W **141 F3**
Nash Stream Forest *N.H., U.S.A.* 44°42N 71°25W **89 B3**
Nashawena I. *Mass., U.S.A.* ..... 41°26N 70°53W **91 C4**
Nashoba *Okla., U.S.A.* .... 34°29N 95°13W **107 D8**
Nashua *Iowa, U.S.A.* .... 42°57N 92°32W **81 C6**
Nashua *Minn., U.S.A.* .... 46°2N 96°19W **77 D2**
Nashua *Mont., U.S.A.* .... 48°8N 106°22W **123 B11**
Nashua *N.H., U.S.A.* .... 42°45N 71°28W **89 D3**
Nashville *Ark., U.S.A.* .... 33°57N 93°51W **106 E2**
Nashville *Ga., U.S.A.* .... 31°12N 83°15W **113 E3**
Nashville *Ill., U.S.A.* .... 38°21N 89°23W **84 E4**
Nashville *Ind., U.S.A.* .... 39°12N 86°15W **85 D4**
Nashville *Kans., U.S.A.* .... 37°27N 98°25W **82 D5**
Nashville *Mich., U.S.A.* .... 42°36N 85°5W **79 G6**
Nashville *Mo., U.S.A.* .... 37°33N 94°30W **83 D2**
Nashville *N.C., U.S.A.* .... 35°58N 77°58W **103 C8**
Nashville *Ohio, U.S.A.* .... 40°36N 82°7W **86 C4**
Nashville *Tenn., U.S.A.* .... 36°10N 86°47W **104 D6**
Nashville ✈ (BNA) *Tenn., U.S.A.* 36°7N 86°41W **104 D6**
Nashwaak Bridge *N.B., Canada* 46°14N 66°37W **141 G3**
Nashwauk *Minn., U.S.A.* .... 47°23N 93°10W **77 C5**
Naskaupi ➤ *Nfld. & L., Canada* . 53°47N 60°51W **143 B5**
Nass ➤ *B.C., Canada* .... 55°0N 129°40W **157 E7**
Nassau *Bahamas* .... 25°5N 77°20W **182 A4**
Nassau *Minn., U.S.A.* .... 45°4N 96°26W **77 E2**
Nassau *N.Y., U.S.A.* .... 42°31N 73°37W **91 B1**
Nassau County ☆ *Fla., U.S.A.* ... 30°40N 81°45W **114 A7**
Nassau County ☆ *N.Y., U.S.A.* .. 40°45N 73°40W **88 E7**
Nassawadox *Va., U.S.A.* .... 37°28N 75°52W **102 D9**
Nastapoka ➤ *Qué., Canada* ...... 56°55N 76°33W **143 B2**
Nastapoka, Is. *Nunavut, Canada* 56°55N 76°50W **143 B2**
Natal *B.C., Canada* .... 49°43N 114°51W **153 J6**
Natalbany ➤ *La., U.S.A.* .... 30°20N 90°30W **110 D5**
Natalia *Tex., U.S.A.* .... 29°11N 98°52W **109 H9**
Natalkuz L. *B.C., Canada* .... 53°36N 125°2W **154 B9**
Natashquan *Qué., Canada* .... 50°14N 61°46W **143 C5**
Natashquan ➤ *Qué., Canada* ..... 50°7N 61°50W **143 C5**
Natashquan, Pte. *Qué., Canada* . 50°7N 61°40W **143 C5**
Natashquan-Est ➤ *Qué., Canada* 51°20N 61°40W **140 B8**
Natchez Nat. Historical Park △ *Miss.,*
U.S.A. .... 31°30N 91°23W **111 E2**

Natchez *La., U.S.A.* 31°41N 93°3W **110 C2**
Natchez *Miss., U.S.A.* 31°34N 91°24W **111 E2**
Natchez Trace Parkway *U.S.A.* 31°37N 91°16W **111 D3**
Natchez Trace State Park △ *Tenn., U.S.A.* 35°47N 88°17W **104 E4**
Natchitoches *La., U.S.A.* 31°46N 93°5W **110 C2**
Natchitoches Parish ☆ *La., U.S.A.* 31°41N 93°3W **110 C2**
Nathrop *Colo., U.S.A.* 38°45N 106°5W **125 D4**
Natick *Mass., U.S.A.* 42°16N 71°19W **91 B3**
Nation → *B.C., Canada* 55°30N 123°32W **157 E8**
National Arboretum *D.C., U.S.A.* 38°54N 76°59W **99 B3**
National Bison Range △ *Mont., U.S.A.* 47°20N 114°14W **123 C3**
National City *Calif., U.S.A.* 32°40N 117°6W **127 N9**
National Elk Refuge △ *Wyo., U.S.A.* 43°38N 110°35W **124 C2**
National Key Deer Refuge △ *Fla., U.S.A.* 24°43N 81°30W **114 G7**
National Zoological Park *D.C., U.S.A.* 38°55N 77°4W **99 B3**
Natividad, I. *Baja Calif. S., Mexico* 27°52N 115°11W **167 F3**
Natoma *Kans., U.S.A.* 39°11N 99°2W **82 B4**
Natora *Sonora, Mexico* 29°2N 108°55W **168 B7**
Natrona *Wyo., U.S.A.* 43°2N 104°49W **124 C8**
Natrona County ☆ *Wyo., U.S.A.* 43°0N 107°0W **124 D6**
Natrona Heights *Pa., U.S.A.* 40°37N 79°44W **87 D2**
Natural Bridge *Ala., U.S.A.* 34°6N 87°36W **112 B3**
Natural Bridge *Va., U.S.A.* 37°38N 79°33W **102 D5**
Natural Bridges Nat. Monument △ *Utah, U.S.A.* 37°36N 110°0W **129 F5**
Naturita *Colo., U.S.A.* 38°14N 108°34W **125 D2**
Naubinway *Mich., U.S.A.* 46°6N 85°27W **79 C6**
Naucalpan de Juárez *México, Mexico* 19°28N 99°14W **181 B2**
Nautla *Veracruz, Mexico* 20°13N 96°47W **176 D4**
Nautla, Barra de *Veracruz, Mexico* 20°15N 96°45W **176 D4**
Nauvoo *Ala., U.S.A.* 33°59N 87°29W **112 C3**
Nauvoo *Ill., U.S.A.* 40°33N 91°23W **84 C2**
Nava *Coahuila, Mexico* 28°25N 100°45W **170 B4**
Navajo *N. Mex., U.S.A.* 35°7N 109°32W **130 B6**
Navajo *N. Mex., U.S.A.* 35°54N 109°2W **131 B1**
Navajo County ☆ *Ariz., U.S.A.* 36°0N 110°20W **130 B5**
Navajo Cr. → *Ariz., U.S.A.* 36°59N 111°24W **130 A4**
Navajo Indian Reservation *Ariz., U.S.A.* 35°20N 110°0W **130 B6**
Navajo Mt. *Utah, U.S.A.* 37°2N 110°52W **129 F5**
Navajo Nat. Monument △ *Ariz., U.S.A.* 36°41N 110°32W **130 A5**
Navajo Res. *N. Mex., U.S.A.* 36°48N 107°36W **131 A3**
Navarre *Fla., U.S.A.* 30°24N 86°52W **114 A2**
Navarre *Ohio, U.S.A.* 40°43N 81°31W **91 C4**
Navarro → *Calif., U.S.A.* 39°11N 123°45W **126 D3**
Navarro County ☆ *Tex., U.S.A.* 32°6N 96°28W **109 E11**
Navarro Mills L. *Tex., U.S.A.* 31°57N 96°42W **109 F11**
Navasota *Tex., U.S.A.* 30°23N 96°5W **109 G11**
Navasota → *Tex., U.S.A.* 30°21N 96°10W **109 G11**
Navassa I. *W. Indies* 18°30N 75°0W **183 C5**
Navidad *Jalisco, Mexico* 20°34N 104°40W **174 B3**
Navidad → *Tex., U.S.A.* 28°50N 96°35W **109 J11**
Navidad Bank *W. Indies* 20°0N 68°58W **183 B6**
Navojoa *Sonora, Mexico* 27°6N 109°26W **168 F6**
Navolato *Sinaloa, Mexico* 24°47N 107°42W **172 C3**
Navy Pier *Ill., U.S.A.* 41°53N 87°36W **95 B3**
Nayarit □ *Mexico* 22°0N 105°0W **172 F6**
Naylor *Mo., U.S.A.* 36°34N 90°36W **83 E6**
Nazareno *Durango, Mexico* 25°23N 103°27W **170 E1**
Nazareth *Pa., U.S.A.* 40°44N 75°19W **92 B1**
Nazareth *Tex., U.S.A.* 34°33N 102°6W **108 C5**
Nazas *Durango, Mexico* 25°14N 104°12W **173 B6**
Nazas → *Durango, Mexico* 25°12N 104°12W **173 B6**
Nazko *B.C., Canada* 53°1N 123°37W **154 B11**
Nazko → *B.C., Canada* 53°7N 123°34W **154 B11**
Nazko Lake Park △ *B.C., Canada* 52°26N 123°33W **154 C11**
Neah Bay *Wash., U.S.A.* 48°22N 124°37W **120 B1**
Neal *Kans., U.S.A.* 37°50N 96°5W **82 D7**
Neal Smith Nat. Wildlife Refuge △ *Iowa, U.S.A.* 41°35N 93°15W **81 D5**
Nealtican *Puebla, Mexico* 19°3N 98°25W **177 E2**
Near Is. *Alaska, U.S.A.* 52°30N 174°0E **135 K1**
Near North *Ill., U.S.A.* 41°54N 87°38W **95 B3**
Nebo *Ill., U.S.A.* 39°27N 90°47W **84 D3**
Nebo *La., U.S.A.* 31°35N 92°9W **110 C3**
Nebo, Mt. *Utah, U.S.A.* 39°49N 111°46W **129 D4**
Nebraska □ *U.S.A.* 41°30N 99°30W **80 C6**
Nebraska City *Nebr., U.S.A.* 40°41N 95°52W **80 D10**
Nebraska Nat. Forest *Nebr., U.S.A.* 42°45N 103°10W **80 B2**
Necedah *Wis., U.S.A.* 44°2N 90°4W **78 D31**
Necedah Nat. Wildlife Refuge △ *Wis., U.S.A.* 44°9N 90°11W **78 D3**
Nechako → *B.C., Canada* 53°55N 122°42W **155 B12**
Nechako Res. *B.C., Canada* 53°42N 127°30W **154 B7**
Neche *N. Dak., U.S.A.* 48°59N 97°33W **76 B8**
Neches → *Tex., U.S.A.* 29°58N 93°51W **109 H14**
Necker I. *Hawai'i, U.S.A.* 23°35N 164°42W **136 G11**
Nederland *Colo., U.S.A.* 39°58N 105°31W **125 C5**
Nederland *Tex., U.S.A.* 29°59N 94°0W **109 H13**
Needham *Mass., U.S.A.* 42°17N 71°14W **96 B1**
Needham Heights *Mass., U.S.A.* 42°17N 71°14W **96 B1**
Needle Range *Utah, U.S.A.* 38°25N 113°55W **129 E2**
Needles *B.C., Canada* 49°53N 118°7W **155 F16**
Needles *Calif., U.S.A.* 34°51N 114°37W **127 J12**
Needmore *Ga., U.S.A.* 30°41N 82°43W **113 F4**
Needmore *Pa., U.S.A.* 39°51N 78°9W **93 A2**
Needville *Tex., U.S.A.* 29°24N 95°50W **109 H12**
Neely *Miss., U.S.A.* 31°10N 88°45W **111 E5**
Neelyville *Mo., U.S.A.* 36°34N 90°30W **83 E6**
Neenah *Wis., U.S.A.* 44°11N 88°28W **78 D5**
Neepawa *Man., Canada* 50°15N 99°30W **151 E12**
Negaunee *Mich., U.S.A.* 46°30N 87°36W **79 C4**
Negreet *La., U.S.A.* 31°28N 93°35W **110 C2**
Negril *Jamaica* 18°22N 78°20W **182 C4**
Neguac *N.B., Canada* 47°15N 65°5W **141 F4**
Nehalem *Oreg., U.S.A.* 45°43N 123°54W **121 B2**
Nehalem → *Oreg., U.S.A.* 45°40N 123°56W **121 B2**
Nehawka *Nebr., U.S.A.* 40°50N 95°59W **80 D10**
Neidpath *Sask., Canada* 50°12N 107°20W **150 E4**
Neihart *Mont., U.S.A.* 46°56N 110°44W **123 D7**
Neilburg *Sask., Canada* 52°20N 109°38W **150 C2**
Neillsville *Wis., U.S.A.* 44°34N 90°36W **78 D31**
Neils Harbour *N.S., Canada* 46°48N 60°20W **141 G9**
Neilton *Wash., U.S.A.* 47°25N 123°53W **120 C2**
Nejanilini L. *Man., Canada* 59°33N 97°48W **159 F6**

Nekoma *Kans., U.S.A.* 38°28N 99°27W **82 C4**
Nekoma *N. Dak., U.S.A.* 48°35N 98°22W **76 B7**
Nekoosa *Wis., U.S.A.* 44°19N 89°54W **78 D4**
Neligh *Nebr., U.S.A.* 42°8N 98°2W **80 B7**
Nellis Air Force Base *Nev., U.S.A.* 36°14N 115°2W **134 B2**
Nellis Air Force Range Complex *Nev., U.S.A.* 37°15N 116°30W **128 E4**
Nelson *B.C., Canada* 49°30N 117°20W **155 F17**
Nelson *Ariz., U.S.A.* 35°31N 113°19W **130 B2**
Nelson *Mo., U.S.A.* 38°59N 93°3W **83 C3**
Nelson *N.H., U.S.A.* 42°58N 72°8W **89 D2**
Nelson *Nebr., U.S.A.* 40°12N 98°4W **80 D7**
Nelson *Nev., U.S.A.* 35°42N 114°49W **128 G6**
Nelson *Wis., U.S.A.* 44°25N 92°0W **78 D2**
Nelson → *Man., Canada* 54°33N 98°2W **159 G6**
Nelson Canyon Park *B.C., Canada* 49°22N 123°13W **161 A1**
Nelson County ☆ *Ky., U.S.A.* 37°50N 85°30W **105 C7**
Nelson County ☆ *N. Dak., U.S.A.* 48°0N 98°5W **76 B7**
Nelson County ☆ *Va., U.S.A.* 37°50N 78°52W **102 D6**
Nelson Forks *B.C., Canada* 59°30N 124°0W **157 E8**
Nelson House *Man., Canada* 55°47N 98°51W **159 F6**
Nelson-Miramichi *N.B., Canada* 46°59N 65°34W **141 G4**
Nelson Res. *Mont., U.S.A.* 48°32N 107°31W **123 B10**
Nelsonville *Ohio, U.S.A.* 39°28N 82°13W **86 D4**
Nemah *Wash., U.S.A.* 46°31N 123°53W **120 D2**
Nemaha *Iowa, U.S.A.* 42°31N 95°6W **81 C3**
Nemaha *Nebr., U.S.A.* 40°20N 95°41W **80 D10**
Nemaha County ☆ *Kans., U.S.A.* 39°45N 96°3W **82 B8**
Nemaha County ☆ *Nebr., U.S.A.* 40°20N 95°45W **80 D10**
Nemegosenda L. *Ont., Canada* 48°0N 83°7W **149 D13**
Némiscachingue, L. *Qué., Canada* 47°25N 74°30W **144 D8**
Nemiscau *Qué., Canada* 51°18N 76°54W **143 C2**
Nemiscau L. *Qué., Canada* 51°25N 76°40W **143 C2**
Nenana *Alaska, U.S.A.* 64°34N 149°5W **135 D10**
Nenzel *Nebr., U.S.A.* 42°56N 101°6W **80 B4**
Neodesha *Kans., U.S.A.* 37°25N 95°41W **82 D8**
Neoga *Ill., U.S.A.* 39°19N 88°27W **84 D5**
Neola *Iowa, U.S.A.* 41°27N 95°37W **81 D3**
Neola *Utah, U.S.A.* 40°26N 110°2W **129 C5**
Neopit *Wis., U.S.A.* 44°59N 88°50W **78 D5**
Neosho *Mo., U.S.A.* 36°52N 94°22W **83 E2**
Neosho → *Okla., U.S.A.* 36°48N 95°18W **107 B8**
Neosho County ☆ *Kans., U.S.A.* 37°30N 95°15W **82 D8**
Neosho Falls *Kans., U.S.A.* 37°59N 95°33W **82 D8**
Neosho Rapids *Kans., U.S.A.* 38°22N 95°55W **82 C8**
Nephi *Utah, U.S.A.* 39°43N 111°50W **129 D4**
Nepisiguit → *N.B., Canada* 47°37N 65°38W **141 F4**
Neppel = Moses Lake *Wash., U.S.A.* 47°8N 119°17W **120 C6**
Neptune *N.J., U.S.A.* 40°13N 74°2W **92 B2**
Neptune Beach *Fla., U.S.A.* 30°19N 81°24W **114 A7**
Néret, L. *Qué., Canada* 54°45N 70°44W **143 C3**
Nerstrand *Minn., U.S.A.* 44°20N 93°4W **77 F5**
Nesbit *Miss., U.S.A.* 34°53N 90°1W **111 B3**
Neshoba *Miss., U.S.A.* 32°37N 89°8W **111 D4**
Neshoba County ☆ *Miss., U.S.A.* 32°46N 89°7W **111 D4**
Neshaminy Cr. → *Pa., U.S.A.* 40°4N 74°55W **92 B2**
Ness City *Kans., U.S.A.* 38°27N 99°54W **82 C4**
Ness County ☆ *Kans., U.S.A.* 38°30N 100°0W **82 C4**
Nestaocano → *Qué., Canada* 49°38N 73°28W **145 B9**
Nestor Falls *Ont., Canada* 49°7N 93°56W **148 D3**
Netarts *Oreg., U.S.A.* 45°26N 123°57W **121 B2**
Netawaka *Kans., U.S.A.* 39°36N 95°43W **82 B8**
Netcong *N.J., U.S.A.* 40°54N 74°42W **92 B2**
Net L. *Minn., U.S.A.* 48°7N 93°7W **77 B5**
Nettilling L. *Nunavut, Canada* 66°30N 71°0W **159 D11**
Nettleton *Miss., U.S.A.* 34°5N 88°37W **111 B5**
Netzahualcóyotl *Tabasco, Mexico* 17°42N 91°27W **178 B5**
Netzahualcóyotl, Presa *Chiapas, Mexico* 17°8N 93°35W **178 B3**
Neudorf *Sask., Canada* 50°43N 103°1W **150 E8**
Neuse → *N.C., U.S.A.* 35°6N 76°29W **103 C9**
Neuville *Tex., U.S.A.* 31°41N 94°9W **109 F13**
Nevada *Iowa, U.S.A.* 42°1N 93°27W **81 C5**
Nevada *Mo., U.S.A.* 37°51N 94°22W **83 D2**
Nevada □ *U.S.A.* 39°0N 117°0W **128 D4**
Nevada City *Calif., U.S.A.* 39°16N 121°1W **126 D5**
Nevada County ☆ *Ark., U.S.A.* 33°36N 93°17W **106 E2**
Nevada County ☆ *Calif., U.S.A.* 39°15N 121°0W **126 D6**
Nevado de Colima = Volcán de Colima, Parque Nacional △ *Jalisco, Mexico* 19°30N 103°40W **174 C4**
Nevado de Toluca, Parque Nacional △ *México, Mexico* 19°8N 99°45W **175 C8**
Neveros *Durango, Mexico* 23°46N 105°44W **172 D5**
Neversink → *N.Y., U.S.A.* 41°21N 74°42W **88 D6**
Neversink Res. *N.Y., U.S.A.* 41°48N 74°42W **88 D6**
Neville *Sask., Canada* 49°58N 107°39W **150 F4**
Nevis *St. Kitts & Nevis* 17°0N 62°30W **183 C7**
Nevis *Minn., U.S.A.* 46°58N 94°51W **77 D4**
New → *Fla., U.S.A.* 29°50N 84°40W **114 B4**
New → *N.C., U.S.A.* 34°32N 77°20W **103 C8**
New → *Tenn., U.S.A.* 36°25N 84°37W **105 D8**
New → *W. Va., U.S.A.* 38°10N 81°12W **102 C3**
New Aiyansh *B.C., Canada* 55°12N 129°4W **157 E7**
New Albany *Ind., U.S.A.* 38°18N 85°49W **85 E7**
New Albany *Kans., U.S.A.* 37°34N 95°56W **82 D8**
New Albany *Miss., U.S.A.* 34°29N 89°0W **111 B5**
New Albany *Pa., U.S.A.* 41°36N 76°27W **87 C6**
New Albin *Iowa, U.S.A.* 43°30N 91°17W **81 B7**
New Alluwe *Okla., U.S.A.* 36°37N 95°29W **107 B8**
New Almelo *Kans., U.S.A.* 39°36N 100°0W **82 B3**
New Athens *Ill., U.S.A.* 38°19N 89°53W **84 E4**
New Athens *Ohio, U.S.A.* 40°11N 81°0W **86 C5**
New Auburn *Minn., U.S.A.* 44°40N 94°14W **77 F4**
New Auburn *Wis., U.S.A.* 45°12N 91°33W **78 C2**
New Augusta *Miss., U.S.A.* 31°12N 89°2W **111 E4**
New Baden *Ill., U.S.A.* 38°32N 89°42W **84 E4**
New Baltimore *Mich., U.S.A.* 42°41N 82°44W **79 G9**
New Baltimore *Va., U.S.A.* 38°59N 78°46W **87 E4**
New Barbadoes = Hackensack *N.J.,*
New Bavaria *Ohio, U.S.A.* 41°12N 84°10W **86 B2**
New Bedford *Mass., U.S.A.* 41°38N 70°56W **91 C4**
New Berlin = North Canton *Ohio, U.S.A.* 40°53N 81°24W **86 C5**
New Berlin *Ill., U.S.A.* 39°44N 89°55W **84 D4**
New Berlin *N.Y., U.S.A.* 42°37N 75°20W **88 C5**
New Berlin *Wis., U.S.A.* 42°59N 88°6W **78 F5**
New Bern *N.C., U.S.A.* 35°7N 77°3W **103 C8**
New Bethlehem *Pa., U.S.A.* 41°0N 79°20W **87 D3**
New Bloomfield *Mo., U.S.A.* 38°43N 92°5W **83 C4**
New Bloomfield *Pa., U.S.A.* 40°25N 77°11W **87 D5**
New Boston *Ill., U.S.A.* 41°10N 91°0W **84 C3**
New Boston *Mass., U.S.A.* 42°6N 73°5W **91 B1**
New Boston *N.H., U.S.A.* 42°59N 71°41W **89 D3**
New Boston *Ohio, U.S.A.* 38°45N 82°56W **86 E4**

New Boston *Tex., U.S.A.* 33°28N 94°25W **109 D13**
New Braunfels *Tex., U.S.A.* 29°42N 98°8W **109 H9**
New Bremen *Ohio, U.S.A.* 40°26N 84°23W **86 C2**
New Brigden *Alta., Canada* 51°42N 110°29W **153 G10**
New Brighton *Minn., U.S.A.* 45°3N 93°12W **94 A2**
New Brighton *N.Y., U.S.A.* 40°38N 74°5W **97 C2**
New Britain *Conn., U.S.A.* 41°40N 72°47W **91 C2**
New Brockton *Ala., U.S.A.* 31°23N 85°56W **112 E5**
New Brookland = West Columbia *S.C., U.S.A.* 33°59N 81°4W **103 E4**
New Brunswick *N.J., U.S.A.* 40°30N 74°27W **92 B2**
New Brunswick □ *Canada* 46°50N 66°30W **141 G3**
New Buffalo *Mich., U.S.A.* 41°47N 86°45W **79 H5**
New Bullards Bar Dam *Calif., U.S.A.* 39°24N 121°9W **126 D5**
New Cambria *Kans., U.S.A.* 38°53N 97°30W **82 C6**
New Canaan *Conn., U.S.A.* 41°9N 73°30W **91 C1**
New Canton *Va., U.S.A.* 37°42N 78°18W **102 D6**
New Carlisle *Ohio, U.S.A.* 39°56N 84°2W **86 D2**
New Carrollton *Md., U.S.A.* 38°58N 76°53W **99 B4**
New Castle *Colo., U.S.A.* 39°34N 107°32W **125 C3**
New Castle *Del., U.S.A.* 39°40N 75°34W **93 A5**
New Castle *Ind., U.S.A.* 39°55N 85°22W **85 D5**
New Castle *Ky., U.S.A.* 38°26N 85°10W **105 B7**
New Castle *Pa., U.S.A.* 41°0N 80°21W **87 D2**
New Castle *Va., U.S.A.* 37°30N 80°7W **102 D4**
New Castle County ☆ *Del., U.S.A.* 39°30N 75°40W **93 A5**
New Church *Va., U.S.A.* 37°59N 75°32W **93 C5**
New City *N.Y., U.S.A.* 41°9N 73°59W **92 A3**
New Concord *Ky., U.S.A.* 36°33N 88°9W **104 D4**
New Concord *Ohio, U.S.A.* 39°59N 81°54W **86 D5**
New Cumberland *W. Va., U.S.A.* 40°30N 80°36W **102 A4**
New Deal *Tex., U.S.A.* 33°44N 101°50W **108 D5**
New Denmark *N.B., Canada* 47°2N 67°38W **141 F2**
New Denver *B.C., Canada* 50°0N 117°25W **155 F17**
New Don Pedro Res. *Calif., U.S.A.* 37°43N 120°24W **126 F6**
New Dorp *N.Y., U.S.A.* 40°34N 74°7W **97 C2**
New Dorp Beach *N.Y., U.S.A.* 40°33N 74°6W **97 C2**
New Edinburg *Ark., U.S.A.* 33°46N 92°14W **106 E3**
New Effington *S. Dak., U.S.A.* 45°51N 96°55W **76 E9**
New Egypt *N.J., U.S.A.* 40°4N 74°32W **92 B2**
New Ellenton *S.C., U.S.A.* 33°28N 81°41W **103 E4**
New England *N. Dak., U.S.A.* 46°32N 102°52W **76 D3**
New Era *Mich., U.S.A.* 43°36N 86°21W **79 F5**
New Fairfield *Conn., U.S.A.* 41°27N 73°14W **91 C1**
New Florence *Mo., U.S.A.* 38°55N 91°27W **83 C5**
New Florence *Pa., U.S.A.* 40°23N 79°5W **87 D3**
New Fork Lakes *Wyo., U.S.A.* 43°6N 109°57W **124 C3**
New Franklin *Mo., U.S.A.* 39°1N 92°44W **83 C4**
New Freedom *Pa., U.S.A.* 39°44N 76°42W **93 A4**
New Germany *N.S., Canada* 44°33N 64°43W **141 J5**
New Glarus *Wis., U.S.A.* 42°49N 89°38W **78 F4**
New Glasgow *N.S., Canada* 45°35N 62°36W **141 H7**
New Hamburg *Ont., Canada* 43°23N 80°42W **146 D6**
New Hampshire □ *U.S.A.* 44°0N 71°30W **89 C3**
New Hampton *Iowa, U.S.A.* 43°3N 92°19W **81 B61**
New Hampton *Mo., U.S.A.* 40°16N 94°12W **83 A2**
New Hampton *N.H., U.S.A.* 43°36N 71°39W **89 C3**
New Hanover County ☆ *N.C., U.S.A.* 34°15N 77°50W **103 D8**
New Harbour *Nfld., Canada* 45°13N 61°29W **141 H8**
New Harmony *Ind., U.S.A.* 38°8N 87°56W **85 E3**
New Harmony *Utah, U.S.A.* 37°29N 113°19W **129 F2**
New Hartford *Conn., U.S.A.* 41°53N 72°59W **91 C2**
New Hartford *Iowa, U.S.A.* 42°34N 92°37W **81 C6**
New Hartford *N.Y., U.S.A.* 43°4N 75°18W **88 B5**
New Haven *Conn., U.S.A.* 41°18N 72°55W **91 C2**
New Haven *Ill., U.S.A.* 37°55N 88°8W **84 F5**
New Haven *Ind., U.S.A.* 41°4N 85°1W **85 B5**
New Haven *Ky., U.S.A.* 37°40N 85°36W **105 C7**
New Haven *Mich., U.S.A.* 42°44N 82°48W **79 G9**
New Haven *Mo., U.S.A.* 38°37N 91°13W **83 C5**
New Haven *N.Y., U.S.A.* 43°29N 76°19W **88 B4**
New Haven *W. Va., U.S.A.* 38°59N 81°58W **102 C3**
New Haven County ☆ *Conn., U.S.A.* 41°25N 72°50W **91 C2**
New Hebron *Miss., U.S.A.* 31°44N 89°59W **111 E4**
New Hogan L. *Calif., U.S.A.* 38°9N 120°49W **126 E6**
New Holland *Ohio, U.S.A.* 39°33N 83°15W **86 D3**
New Holland *Pa., U.S.A.* 40°6N 76°5W **87 D6**
New Holstein *Wis., U.S.A.* 43°57N 88°5W **78 E5**
New Hope *Ala., U.S.A.* 34°32N 86°24W **112 B4**
New Hope *Minn., U.S.A.* 45°2N 93°23W **94 A1**
New Hope *Pa., U.S.A.* 40°22N 74°57W **92 B2**
New Houlka *Miss., U.S.A.* 34°2N 89°1W **111 B4**
New Hyde Park *N.Y., U.S.A.* 40°44N 73°41W **97 B4**
New Iberia *La., U.S.A.* 30°1N 91°49W **110 D4**
New Ipswich *N.H., U.S.A.* 42°46N 71°51W **89 D3**
New Jersey □ *U.S.A.* 40°0N 74°30W **92 B2**
New Johnsonville *Tenn., U.S.A.* 36°1N 87°58W **104 D5**
New Kensington *Pa., U.S.A.* 40°34N 79°46W **87 D3**
New Kent *Va., U.S.A.* 37°31N 76°59W **102 D8**
New Kent County ☆ *Va., U.S.A.* 37°31N 76°59W **102 D8**
New L. *N.C., U.S.A.* 35°39N 76°13W **103 C9**
New Leipzig *N. Dak., U.S.A.* 46°22N 101°57W **76 D4**
New Lexington *Ohio, U.S.A.* 39°43N 82°13W **86 D4**
New Lisbon *Wis., U.S.A.* 43°53N 90°10W **78 E3**
New Liskeard *Ont., Canada* 47°31N 79°41W **144 D3**
New Llano *La., U.S.A.* 31°7N 93°16W **110 C2**
New London *Conn., U.S.A.* 41°22N 72°6W **91 C2**
New London *Iowa, U.S.A.* 40°55N 91°24W **81 E7**
New London *Md., U.S.A.* 39°25N 77°9W **93 A3**
New London *Minn., U.S.A.* 45°18N 94°56W **77 E4**
New London *Mo., U.S.A.* 39°35N 91°24W **83 B5**
New London *N.H., U.S.A.* 43°25N 71°59W **89 C3**
New London *Ohio, U.S.A.* 41°5N 82°24W **86 C4**
New London *Wis., U.S.A.* 44°23N 88°45W **78 D51**
New London County ☆ *Conn., U.S.A.* 41°30N 72°15W **91 C2**
New Madison *Ohio, U.S.A.* 39°58N 84°43W **86 D2**
New Madrid *Mo., U.S.A.* 36°36N 89°32W **83 E7**
New Madrid County ☆ *Mo., U.S.A.* 36°36N 89°34W **83 E7**
New Market *Ala., U.S.A.* 34°55N 86°26W **112 B4**
New Market *Ind., U.S.A.* 39°57N 86°55W **85 D4**
New Market *Iowa, U.S.A.* 40°44N 94°54W **81 E3**
New Market *Md., U.S.A.* 39°23N 77°16W **93 A3**
New Market *Tenn., U.S.A.* 36°6N 83°33W **105 D9**
New Market *Va., U.S.A.* 38°39N 78°40W **102 C6**
New Marlborough *Mass., U.S.A.* 42°7N 73°14W **91 B1**
New Martinsville *W. Va., U.S.A.* 39°39N 80°52W **102 B4**
New Matamoras *Ohio, U.S.A.* 39°31N 81°4W **86 D5**
New Meadows *Idaho, U.S.A.* 44°58N 116°18W **122 E2**
New Melle *Mo., U.S.A.* 38°43N 90°53W **83 C6**
New Melones Dam *Calif., U.S.A.* 37°57N 120°32W **126 F6**
New Melones L. *Calif., U.S.A.* 37°57N 120°31W **126 F6**
New Mexico □ *U.S.A.* 34°30N 106°0W **131 C5**
New Miami *Ohio, U.S.A.* 39°26N 84°32W **86 D2**
New Milford *Conn., U.S.A.* 41°35N 73°25W **91 C1**

New Milford *Pa., U.S.A.* 41°52N 75°44W **87 C7**
New Munich *Minn., U.S.A.* 45°38N 94°45W **77 E4**
New Norway *Alta., Canada* 52°52N 112°57W **153 F8**
New Orleans *La., U.S.A.* 29°57N 90°4W **117 C2**
New Orleans Int. ✈ (MSY) *La., U.S.A.* 30°0N 90°15W **117 C1**
New Oxford *Pa., U.S.A.* 39°52N 77°4W **93 A3**
New Paltz *N.Y., U.S.A.* 41°45N 74°5W **88 D6**
New Paris *Ind., U.S.A.* 41°30N 85°50W **85 B5**
New Paris *Ohio, U.S.A.* 39°51N 84°48W **86 D2**
New Pekin *Ind., U.S.A.* 38°30N 86°0W **85 E4**
New Philadelphia *Ohio, U.S.A.* 40°30N 81°27W **86 C5**
New Pine Creek *Oreg., U.S.A.* 42°0N 120°18W **121 E5**
New Plymouth *Idaho, U.S.A.* 43°58N 116°49W **122 F2**
New Point *Va., U.S.A.* 37°21N 76°17W **102 D8**
New Port Richey *Fla., U.S.A.* 28°16N 82°43W **114 C6**
New Prague *Minn., U.S.A.* 44°32N 93°35W **77 F5**
New Preston *Conn., U.S.A.* 41°40N 73°21W **91 C1**
New Princeton *Oreg., U.S.A.* 43°15N 118°35W **121 D7**
New Providence *Bahamas* 25°25N 78°35W **182 A4**
New Providence *Ind., U.S.A.* 38°28N 85°57W **85 E5**
New Raymer *Colo., U.S.A.* 40°36N 103°51W **125 B7**
New Richland *Minn., U.S.A.* 43°54N 93°30W **77 G5**
New Richmond *Qué., Canada* 48°15N 65°45W **141 F5**
New Richmond *Ohio, U.S.A.* 38°57N 84°17W **86 E2**
New Richmond *Wis., U.S.A.* 45°7N 92°32W **78 C11**
New Riegel *Ohio, U.S.A.* 41°3N 83°19W **86 B3**
New River → *Fla., U.S.A.* 26°6N 80°6W **115 B3**
New River Gorge Nat. River △ *W. Va., U.S.A.* 37°53N 81°5W **102 D3**
New Roads *La., U.S.A.* 30°42N 91°26W **110 D4**
New Rochelle *N.Y., U.S.A.* 40°55N 73°46W **97 A4**
New Rockford *N. Dak., U.S.A.* 47°41N 99°8W **76 C6**
New Ross *N.S., Canada* 44°44N 64°27W **141 J5**
New Salem *Mass., U.S.A.* 42°30N 72°20W **91 B2**
New Salem *N. Dak., U.S.A.* 46°51N 101°25W **76 D4**
New Sarepta *Alta., Canada* 53°16N 113°8W **152 F4**
New Sharon *Iowa, U.S.A.* 41°28N 92°39W **81 D6**
New Smyrna Beach *Fla., U.S.A.* 29°1N 80°56W **114 B8**
New Springville *N.Y., U.S.A.* 40°35N 74°9W **97 C2**
New Straitsville *Ohio, U.S.A.* 39°35N 82°14W **86 D4**
New Stuyahok *Alaska, U.S.A.* 59°29N 157°20W **135 G8**
New Tazewell *Tenn., U.S.A.* 36°27N 83°36W **105 D9**
New Tecumseth *Ont., Canada* 44°9N 79°52W **146 C7**
New Toronto *Ont., Canada* 43°35N 79°30W **161 B1**
New Town *N. Dak., U.S.A.* 47°59N 102°30W **76 C2**
New Tripoli *Pa., U.S.A.* 40°41N 75°45W **92 B1**
New Tulsa *Okla., U.S.A.* 36°9N 95°48W **107 B8**
New Ulm *Minn., U.S.A.* 44°19N 94°28W **77 F4**
New Underwood *S. Dak., U.S.A.* 44°6N 102°50W **76 E2**
New Utrecht *N.Y., U.S.A.* 40°36N 73°59W **97 C3**
New Vienna *Iowa, U.S.A.* 42°33N 91°7W **81 C7**
New Vienna *Ohio, U.S.A.* 39°19N 83°42W **86 D3**
New Vineyard *Maine, U.S.A.* 44°48N 70°7W **90 D3**
New Virginia *Iowa, U.S.A.* 41°11N 93°44W **81 D5**
New Washington *Ohio, U.S.A.* 40°58N 82°51W **86 C4**
New Waterford *N.S., Canada* 46°13N 60°4W **141 G9**
New Waverly *Tex., U.S.A.* 30°32N 95°29W **109 G12**
New Westminster *B.C., Canada* 49°13N 122°55W **155 F12**
New Whiteland *Ind., U.S.A.* 39°33N 86°5W **85 D4**
New Windsor *Md., U.S.A.* 39°34N 77°9W **93 A3**
New Windsor *N.Y., U.S.A.* 41°29N 74°1W **92 A2**
New World I. *Nfld. & L., Canada* 49°35N 54°40W **142 C6**
New York □ *U.S.A.* 40°43N 74°0W **88 E7**
New York County ☆ *N.Y., U.S.A.* 40°45N 73°59W **88 E7**
New York J.F. Kennedy Int. ✈ (JFK) *N.Y., U.S.A.* 40°38N 73°47W **97 C4**
New York La Guardia ✈ (LGA) *N.Y., U.S.A.* 40°46N 73°52W **97 B3**
New York Mills *Minn., U.S.A.* 46°31N 95°22W **77 D3**
New York Mts. *Calif., U.S.A.* 35°0N 115°20W **127 H11**
Newark *Ark., U.S.A.* 35°42N 91°27W **106 C4**
Newark *Calif., U.S.A.* 37°32N 122°2W **126 F4**
Newark *Del., U.S.A.* 39°41N 75°46W **93 A5**
Newark *Md., U.S.A.* 38°15N 75°17W **93 B6**
Newark *N.J., U.S.A.* 40°44N 74°10W **97 B1**
Newark *N.Y., U.S.A.* 43°3N 77°6W **88 B3**
Newark *Ohio, U.S.A.* 40°3N 82°24W **86 C4**
Newark *Tex., U.S.A.* 33°0N 97°29W **109 D10**
Newark B. *N.J., U.S.A.* 40°40N 74°8W **97 B2**
Newark L. *Nev., U.S.A.* 39°42N 115°44W **128 C5**
Newark Liberty Int. ✈ (EWR) *N.J., U.S.A.* 40°42N 74°10W **97 B1**
Newark Valley *N.Y., U.S.A.* 42°14N 76°11W **88 C4**
Newaygo *Mich., U.S.A.* 43°25N 85°48W **79 F6**
Newaygo County ☆ *Mich., U.S.A.* 43°30N 85°50W **79 F6**
Newberg *Oreg., U.S.A.* 45°18N 122°58W **121 B3**
Newbern *Ala., U.S.A.* 32°36N 87°32W **112 D3**
Newbern *Tenn., U.S.A.* 36°7N 89°16W **104 D3**
Newberry *Fla., U.S.A.* 29°39N 82°37W **114 B6**
Newberry *Ind., U.S.A.* 38°55N 87°1W **85 E3**
Newberry *Mich., U.S.A.* 46°21N 85°30W **79 C6**
Newberry *S.C., U.S.A.* 34°17N 81°37W **103 D4**
Newberry County ☆ *S.C., U.S.A.* 34°20N 81°40W **103 D4**
Newberry Nat. Volcanic Monument △ *Oreg., U.S.A.* 43°43N 121°14W **121 D4**
Newberry Springs *Calif., U.S.A.* 34°50N 116°41W **127 J10**
Newboro L. *Ont., Canada* 44°38N 76°20W **147 C10**
Newbrook *Alta., Canada* 54°24N 112°57W **152 D8**
Newburg *Md., U.S.A.* 38°22N 76°37W **93 B4**
Newburg *Mo., U.S.A.* 37°55N 91°54W **83 D5**
Newburg *N. Dak., U.S.A.* 48°43N 100°55W **76 B5**
Newburg *W. Va., U.S.A.* 39°23N 79°51W **102 B5**
Newburgh *Ont., Canada* 44°19N 76°52W **147 C10**
Newburgh *Ind., U.S.A.* 37°57N 87°24W **85 F3**
Newburgh *N.Y., U.S.A.* 41°30N 74°1W **92 A2**
Newburgh Heights *Ohio, U.S.A.* 41°27N 81°39W **98 B1**
Newbury *N.H., U.S.A.* 43°19N 72°3W **89 C2**
Newburyport *Mass., U.S.A.* 42°49N 70°53W **91 B4**
Newcastle *N.B., Canada* 47°1N 65°38W **141 F4**
Newcastle *Calif., U.S.A.* 38°53N 121°8W **126 E5**
Newcastle *Maine, U.S.A.* 44°2N 69°32W **90 D3**
Newcastle *Nebr., U.S.A.* 42°39N 96°52W **80 B9**
Newcastle *Okla., U.S.A.* 35°15N 97°36W **107 C6**
Newcastle *Tex., U.S.A.* 33°12N 98°44W **109 D9**
Newcastle *Utah, U.S.A.* 37°40N 113°33W **129 F2**
Newcastle *Wash., U.S.A.* 47°30N 122°9W **132 C5**
Newcastle *Wyo., U.S.A.* 43°50N 104°11W **124 C8**
Newcastle Bridge *N.B., Canada* 46°5N 66°3W **141 G3**
Newcomb *Md., U.S.A.* 38°45N 76°12W **93 B4**
Newcomb *N. Mex., U.S.A.* 36°17N 108°42W **131 A2**
Newcomb *N.Y., U.S.A.* 43°58N 74°10W **88 B6**
Newcomerstown *Ohio, U.S.A.* 40°16N 81°36W **86 C5**

Newell Ark., U.S.A. 33°10N 92°45W 106 E3
Newell Iowa, U.S.A. 42°36N 95°0W 81 C3
Newell S. Dak., U.S.A. 44°43N 103°25W 76 F2
Newell W. Va., U.S.A. 40°37N 80°36W 102 A4
Newell, L. Alta., Canada 50°26N 111°55W 135 H9
Newellton La., U.S.A. 32°4N 91°14W 110 B4
Newenham, C. Alaska, U.S.A. 58°39N 162°11W 135 F7
Newfane N.Y., U.S.A. 43°17N 78°43W 88 B2
Newfane Vt., U.S.A. 42°59N 72°39W 89 D2
Newfield N.J., U.S.A. 39°33N 75°1W 91 C4
Newfolden Minn., U.S.A. 48°21N 96°20W 77 B2
Newfound L. N.H., U.S.A. 43°40N 71°47W 89 C3
Newfoundland Canada 49°0N 55°0W 142 D4
Newfoundland Pa., U.S.A. 41°18N 75°19W 92 A1
Newfoundland & Labrador □ Canada 52°0N 58°0W 142 B5
Newfoundland Evaporation Basin Utah, U.S.A. 40°50N 113°26W 129 C2
Newfoundland Mts. Utah, U.S.A. 41°10N 113°20W 129 B2
Newgate B.C., Canada 49°2N 115°12W 153 J5
Newhalem Wash., U.S.A. 48°40N 121°15W 120 B4
Newhalen Alaska, U.S.A. 59°43N 154°54W 135 G9
Newhall Iowa, U.S.A. 41°59N 91°59W 81 D7
Newington Conn., U.S.A. 41°43N 72°45W 91 C2
Newington Ga., U.S.A. 32°35N 81°30W 113 D5
Newkirk N. Mex., U.S.A. 35°4N 104°16W 131 B6
Newkirk Okla., U.S.A. 36°53N 97°3W 107 B6
Newland N.C., U.S.A. 36°5N 81°56W 103 B4
Newland Va., U.S.A. 38°3N 76°52W 93 B4
Newman Calif., U.S.A. 37°19N 121°1W 126 F5
Newman Ill., U.S.A. 39°48N 87°59W 84 D6
Newman Grove Nebr., U.S.A. 41°45N 97°47W 80 C8
Newmans L. Fla., U.S.A. 29°40N 82°12W 114 B6
Newmarket Ont., Canada 44°3N 79°28W 146 C7
Newmarket N.H., U.S.A. 43°5N 70°56W 89 C4
Newnan Ga., U.S.A. 33°23N 84°48W 113 C2
Newnan Qué., Canada 48°16N 64°45W 140 E5
Newport Ark., U.S.A. 35°37N 91°16W 106 C4
Newport Del., U.S.A. 39°43N 75°37W 93 A5
Newport Ind., U.S.A. 39°53N 87°25W 85 D3
Newport Ky., U.S.A. 39°5N 84°29W 104 A5
Newport Maine, U.S.A. 44°50N 69°17W 90 D4
Newport Mich., U.S.A. 42°0N 83°19W 79 H8
Newport Minn., U.S.A. 44°52N 92°59W 94 B4
Newport N.C., U.S.A. 34°48N 76°52W 103 D9
Newport N.H., U.S.A. 43°22N 72°10W 89 C2
Newport N.J., U.S.A. 39°18N 75°11W 92 C1
Newport Nebr., U.S.A. 42°36N 99°20W 80 B6
Newport Oreg., U.S.A. 44°39N 124°3W 121 C1
Newport Pa., U.S.A. 40°29N 77°8W 87 D5
Newport R.I., U.S.A. 41°29N 71°19W 91 C3
Newport Tenn., U.S.A. 35°58N 83°11W 105 E9
Newport Vt., U.S.A. 44°56N 72°13W 89 B2
Newport Wash., U.S.A. 48°11N 117°3W 120 B8
Newport Beach Calif., U.S.A. 33°37N 117°56W 127 K9
Newport County ☆ R.I., U.S.A. 41°30N 71°20W 91 C3
Newport News Va., U.S.A. 36°58N 76°25W 102 E8
Newsoms Va., U.S.A. 36°38N 77°9W 102 E7
Newtok Alaska, U.S.A. 60°56N 164°38W 135 F6
Newton Ga., U.S.A. 31°19N 84°20W 113 E2
Newton Ill., U.S.A. 38°59N 88°10W 84 E5
Newton Iowa, U.S.A. 41°42N 93°3W 81 D5
Newton Kans., U.S.A. 38°3N 97°21W 82 C6
Newton Mass., U.S.A. 42°21N 71°12W 96 B1
Newton Miss., U.S.A. 32°19N 89°10W 111 D4
Newton N.C., U.S.A. 35°40N 81°13W 103 C4
Newton N.J., U.S.A. 41°3N 74°45W 92 A2
Newton Tex., U.S.A. 30°51N 93°46W 109 G14
Newton Utah, U.S.A. 41°52N 112°0W 129 B3
Newton County ☆ Ark., U.S.A. 35°50N 93°13W 106 C2
Newton County ☆ Ga., U.S.A. 33°30N 83°50W 113 C3
Newton County ☆ Ind., U.S.A. 41°0N 87°25W 85 B3
Newton County ☆ Miss., U.S.A. 32°26N 89°7W 111 D4
Newton County ☆ Mo., U.S.A. 36°55N 94°20W 83 E2
Newton County ☆ Tex., U.S.A. 30°32N 93°49W 109 G14
Newton Falls N.Y., U.S.A. 44°13N 74°59W 88 A6
Newton Falls Ohio, U.S.A. 41°11N 80°59W 86 B6
Newton L. Ill., U.S.A. 38°55N 88°14W 84 E5
Newtonbrook Ont., Canada 43°47N 79°24W 161 A2
Newtonia Mo., U.S.A. 36°53N 94°11W 83 E2
Newtonsville Ohio, U.S.A. 39°11N 84°5W 86 D2
Newtontoppen Svalbard 79°0N 17°30E 162 B12
Newtonville Ala., U.S.A. 33°33N 87°48W 112 C3
Newtonville Mass., U.S.A. 42°20N 71°11W 96 A1
Newtown Nfld. & L., Canada 49°12N 53°31W 142 C7
Newtown Conn., U.S.A. 41°25N 73°19W 91 C1
Newtown Mo., U.S.A. 40°22N 93°20W 83 A3
Newtown Pa., U.S.A. 40°14N 74°57W 92 B2
Newtown Va., U.S.A. 37°55N 77°8W 93 C3
Newville Pa., U.S.A. 40°10N 77°24W 87 D5
Ney Ohio, U.S.A. 41°23N 84°32W 86 B2
Nez Perce County ☆ Idaho, U.S.A. 46°10N 116°55W 122 C2
Nez Perce Indian Reservation Idaho, U.S.A. 46°15N 116°30W 122 C2
Nezahualcóyotl México, Mexico 19°23N 99°0W 175 C9
Nezperce Idaho, U.S.A. 46°14N 116°14W 122 C2
Nezperce Nat. Forest Idaho, U.S.A. 45°50N 115°20W 122 D3
Nezpique, Bayou → La., U.S.A. 30°11N 92°34W 110 D3
Niagara N. Dak., U.S.A. 48°0N 97°58W 76 C8
Niagara Wis., U.S.A. 45°46N 88°0W 78 C5
Niagara N.Y., U.S.A. 43°16N 79°4W 88 B1
Niagara County ☆ N.Y., U.S.A. 43°15N 78°45W 88 B2
Niagara Falls Ont., Canada 43°7N 79°5W 146 D7
Niagara Falls N.Y., U.S.A. 43°5N 79°4W 88 B1
Niagara-on-the-Lake Ont., Canada 43°15N 79°4W 146 D7
Niangua → Mo., U.S.A. 37°23N 92°50W 83 D4
Niangua Mo., U.S.A. 38°58N 92°48W 83 C4
Niantic Conn., U.S.A. 41°20N 72°11W 91 C2
Niarada Mont., U.S.A. 47°49N 114°36W 123 C3
Nicaragua ■ Cent. Amer. 11°40N 85°30W 182 D2
Nicaragua, L. de Nic. 12°0N 85°30W 182 D2
Nicatous L. Maine, U.S.A. 45°5N 68°9W 90 C5
Nice Calif., U.S.A. 39°7N 122°51W 126 E3
Niceville Fla., U.S.A. 30°31N 86°30W 114 A2
Nicholás Canal W. Indies 23°30N 80°5W 182 B3
Nicholas County ☆ Ky., U.S.A. 38°20N 84°0W 105 B9
Nicholas County ☆ W. Va., U.S.A. 38°17N 80°51W 102 C4
Nicholasville Ky., U.S.A. 37°53N 84°34W 105 C8
Nicholls Ga., U.S.A. 31°31N 82°38W 113 E4
Nichols Iowa, U.S.A. 41°29N 91°19W 81 D7
Nichols S.C., U.S.A. 34°14N 79°9W 103 D6
Nichols Wis., U.S.A. 44°40N 88°28W 78 D5
Nicholson Ga., U.S.A. 34°7N 83°26W 113 B3

Nicholson Miss., U.S.A. 30°29N 89°43W 111 F4
Nichupté, L. Quintana Roo, Mexico 21°7N 86°47W 179 A7
Nickel Creek Tex., U.S.A. 31°55N 104°45W 108 F3
Nickerson Kans., U.S.A. 38°8N 98°5W 82 C5
Nickerson Nebr., U.S.A. 41°32N 96°28W 80 C9
Nicodemus Kans., U.S.A. 39°24N 99°37W 82 B4
Nicodemus Nat. Historic Site △ Kans., U.S.A. 39°23N 99°37W 82 B4
Nicola B.C., Canada 50°12N 120°40W 155 E14
Nicola L. B.C., Canada 50°10N 120°32W 155 E14
Nicolás Bravo Durango, Mexico 24°59N 104°45W 173 C6
Nicolás Bravo Quintana Roo, Mexico 18°29N 88°55W 179 D5
Nicolás Flores Hidalgo, Mexico 20°46N 99°9W 175 B8
Nicolás R. Casillas Guadalajara, Mexico 20°33N 103°28W 180 B1
Nicolet Qué., Canada 46°17N 72°35W 145 C10
Nicolet Nat. Forest Wis., U.S.A. 45°35N 88°45W 78 C5
Nicollet Minn., U.S.A. 44°17N 94°11W 77 F4
Nicollet County ☆ Minn., U.S.A. 44°20N 94°15W 77 F4
Nicolls Town Bahamas 25°8N 78°0W 182 A4
Nicoya Costa Rica 10°9N 85°27W 182 D2
Nicoya, G. de Costa Rica 10°0N 85°0W 182 E3
Nicoya, Pen. de Costa Rica 9°45N 85°40W 182 E2
Nielsville Minn., U.S.A. 47°32N 96°49W 77 C2
Nigei I. B.C., Canada 50°53N 127°43W 154 E7
Nighthawk Wash., U.S.A. 48°58N 119°38W 120 B6
Nightmute Alaska, U.S.A. 60°29N 164°44W 135 F6
Nihoa Hawai'i, U.S.A. 23°6N 161°58W 136 G11
Ni'ihau Hawai'i, U.S.A. 21°54N 160°9W 136 B1
Nikep Md., U.S.A. 39°32N 79°1W 93 A1
Nikiski Alaska, U.S.A. 61°4N 151°18W 135 F10
Nikolai Alaska, U.S.A. 62°58N 154°10W 135 E9
Nikolski Alaska, U.S.A. 52°56N 168°52W 135 K5
Niland Calif., U.S.A. 33°14N 115°31W 127 K11
Niles Ill., U.S.A. 42°1N 87°48W 95 A2
Niles Kans., U.S.A. 38°58N 97°28W 82 C6
Niles Mich., U.S.A. 41°50N 86°15W 79 H5
Niles Ohio, U.S.A. 41°11N 80°46W 86 B6
Niles Center = Skokie Ill., U.S.A. 42°2N 87°43W 95 A2
Niltepec Oaxaca, Mexico 16°34N 94°37W 177 H6
Nimpkish → B.C., Canada 50°34N 126°58W 154 E8
Nimpkish L. B.C., Canada 50°25N 126°59W 154 E8
Nimpkish Lake Park △ B.C., Canada 50°20N 127°0W 154 E7
Nimpo L. B.C., Canada 52°20N 125°10W 154 C9
Nimpo Lake B.C., Canada 52°20N 125°9W 154 C9
Nimrod Minn., U.S.A. 46°38N 94°53W 77 D4
Nimrod L. Ark., U.S.A. 34°57N 93°10W 106 D2
Nimún, Pta. Campeche, Mexico 20°46N 90°25W 179 B3
Nina Bang L. Nunavut, Canada 70°52N 79°24W 158 C10
Ninaview Colo., U.S.A. 37°39N 103°15W 125 E7
Nine Mile Cr. → Utah, U.S.A. 39°50N 109°53W 129 D6
Ninette Man., Canada 49°24N 99°38W 151 F12
Ninety Six S.C., U.S.A. 34°11N 82°1W 103 D3
Ninety Six Nat. Historical Site △ S.C., U.S.A. 34°9N 82°1W 103 D3
Ninini Pt. Hawai'i, U.S.A. 21°58N 159°20W 136 B2
Ninnekah Okla., U.S.A. 34°57N 97°56W 107 D6
Ninnescah → Kans., U.S.A. 37°20N 97°10W 82 D6
Niños Héroes de Chapultepec Sinaloa, Mexico 26°19N 108°54W 172 A2
Niobrara Nebr., U.S.A. 42°45N 98°2W 80 B7
Niobrara → Nebr., U.S.A. 42°46N 98°3W 80 B7
Niobrara County ☆ Wyo., U.S.A. 43°0N 104°25W 124 C8
Niobrara Nat. Scenic River → Nebr., U.S.A. 42°48N 98°7W 80 B7
Nioman Qué., Canada 50°25N 66°5W 143 C4
Niota Tenn., U.S.A. 35°31N 84°33W 105 E8
Nipawin Sask., Canada 53°20N 104°0W 150 B7
Nipekamew → Sask., Canada 54°59N 104°52W 150 A7
Nipigon Ont., Canada 49°0N 88°17W 148 C8
Nipigon → Ont., Canada 48°57N 88°14W 148 D8
Nipigon, L. Ont., Canada 49°50N 88°30W 148 C8
Nipigon B. Ont., Canada 48°53N 87°50W 149 D9
Nipishish L. Nfld. & L., Canada 54°12N 60°45W 143 C5
Nipisi L. Alta., Canada 55°47N 114°57W 152 C6
Nipissing, L. Ont., Canada 46°20N 80°0W 146 A7
Nipissis → Qué., Canada 50°30N 66°5W 143 C4
Nipissis, L. Qué., Canada 51°20N 66°10W 140 D3
Nipisso, L. Qué., Canada 50°52N 65°50W 140 C4
Nipomo Calif., U.S.A. 35°3N 120°29W 127 H6
Nippers Harbour Nfld. & L., Canada 49°48N 55°52W 142 C5
Nipton Calif., U.S.A. 35°28N 115°16W 127 H11
Nisland S. Dak., U.S.A. 44°40N 103°33W 76 F2
Nisling → Yukon, Canada 62°29N 139°28W 157 D5
Nisqually Wash., U.S.A. 47°3N 122°42W 120 C3
Nisqually → Wash., U.S.A. 47°7N 122°42W 120 C3
Nisswa Minn., U.S.A. 46°31N 94°17W 77 D4
Nisula Mich., U.S.A. 46°46N 88°48W 79 C3
Nitchequon Qué., Canada 53°10N 70°58W 140 B3
Nith → Ont., Canada 43°12N 80°23W 146 D6
Nitinat B.C., Canada 48°56N 124°29W 154 G10
Nitinat L. B.C., Canada 48°45N 124°45W 154 G10
Nitro W. Va., U.S.A. 38°25N 81°51W 102 C3
Nitta Yuma Miss., U.S.A. 33°2N 90°51W 111 C3
Nitun, Pta. Campeche, Mexico 20°1N 90°29W 179 B3
Niu Valley Hawai'i, U.S.A. 21°19N 157°44W 136 K14
Niverville Man., Canada 49°36N 97°3W 151 F14
Niverville Qué., Canada 42°26N 73°40W 91 B1
Niwot Colo., U.S.A. 40°6N 105°10W 125 B5
Nixa Mo., U.S.A. 37°3N 93°18W 83 D3
Nixon Tex., U.S.A. 29°16N 97°46W 109 H10
Nizuc, Pta. Quintana Roo, Mexico 21°2N 86°48W 179 A7
Noank Conn., U.S.A. 41°19N 72°1W 91 C2
Noatak Alaska, U.S.A. 67°34N 162°58W 135 C7
Noatak Nat. Preserve △ Alaska, U.S.A. 68°10N 160°0W 135 B8
Nobel Ont., Canada 45°25N 80°6W 146 B6
Noble Ill., U.S.A. 38°42N 88°14W 84 E5
Noble La., U.S.A. 31°41N 93°41W 110 C2
Noble Okla., U.S.A. 35°8N 97°24W 107 C6
Noble County ☆ Ind., U.S.A. 41°25N 85°25W 85 B5
Noble County ☆ Ohio, U.S.A. 39°45N 81°31W 86 D5
Noble County ☆ Okla., U.S.A. 36°20N 97°10W 107 B6
Nobleford Alta., Canada 49°53N 113°3W 153 J7
Nobles County ☆ Minn., U.S.A. 43°45N 95°45W 77 G3
Noblesville Ind., U.S.A. 40°3N 86°1W 85 C4
Nocatee Fla., U.S.A. 27°10N 81°53W 114 D7
Nochistlán de Mejía Zacatecas, Mexico 21°22N 102°51W 173 D8
Nockamixon Lake Pa., U.S.A. 40°28N 75°11W 92 B1
Nocona Tex., U.S.A. 33°47N 97°44W 109 D10
Nodaway → Iowa, U.S.A. 40°56N 94°54W 83 A2
Nodaway Mo., U.S.A. 39°54N 94°58W 83 A2
Nodaway County ☆ Mo., U.S.A. 40°20N 94°54W 83 A2
Node Wyo., U.S.A. 42°43N 104°18W 124 D8
Noel Qué., Canada 45°18N 63°45W 141 H6
Noel Mo., U.S.A. 36°33N 94°29W 83 E2
Noëlville Ont., Canada 46°8N 80°26W 146 A6

Nogal N. Mex., U.S.A. 33°33N 105°42W 131 D5
Nogal → Chihuahua, Mexico 29°25N 104°13W 169 D11
Nogales Durango, Mexico 24°59N 104°43W 173 C6
Nogales Sonora, Mexico 31°19N 110°56W 168 B5
Nogales Veracruz, Mexico 18°49N 97°10W 177 F3
Nogales Ariz., U.S.A. 31°21N 110°56W 130 F5
Nohcacab Yucatán, Mexico 20°2N 89°22W 179 B4
Nohili Pt. Hawai'i, U.S.A. 22°4N 159°47W 136 A2
Noirclair, L. Qué., Canada 50°38N 60°23W 140 C9
Noire → Qué., Canada 45°54N 76°57W 144 F4
Nokesville Va., U.S.A. 38°42N 77°35W 93 B3
Nokomis Sask., Canada 51°35N 105°0W 150 D7
Nokomis Fla., U.S.A. 27°7N 82°27W 114 D6
Nokomis Ill., U.S.A. 39°18N 89°18W 84 D4
Nokomis, L. Wis., U.S.A. 45°34N 93°14W 94 B2
Nokomis-Hiawatha Regional Park △ Minn., U.S.A. 44°55N 93°15W 98 E2
Nolan County ☆ Tex., U.S.A. 32°28N 100°25W 108 E7
Nolensville Tenn., U.S.A. 35°57N 86°40W 104 E6
Nolichucky → Tenn., U.S.A. 36°5N 83°14W 105 D9
Nolin River L. Ky., U.S.A. 37°17N 86°15W 104 C6
Noma Fla., U.S.A. 30°59N 85°37W 114 A3
Nomans Land Mass., U.S.A. 41°15N 70°49W 91 C4
Nomans Land Nat. Wildlife Refuge △ Mass., U.S.A. 41°15N 70°49W 91 C4
Nombre de Dios Durango, Mexico 23°51N 104°14W 173 D6
Nombre de Dios Panama 9°34N 79°28W 182 E4
Nome Alaska, U.S.A. 64°30N 165°25W 135 D6
Nome N. Dak., U.S.A. 46°41N 97°49W 76 D8
Nome Tex., U.S.A. 30°2N 94°25W 109 G12
Nome ☆ Alaska, U.S.A. 64°50N 163°45W 135 D7
Nominingue Qué., Canada 46°24N 75°2W 144 E7
Nominingue, L. Qué., Canada 46°26N 74°59W 144 E8
Nona, L. Fla., U.S.A. 28°24N 81°16W 115 B3
Nonacho L. N.W.T., Canada 61°42N 109°40W 157 D11
Nonoava Chihuahua, Mexico 27°28N 106°44W 169 F9
Nondalton Alaska, U.S.A. 60°0N 154°51W 135 F9
Nooksack Wash., U.S.A. 48°56N 122°19W 120 B3
Noonan N. Dak., U.S.A. 48°54N 103°1W 76 B2
Noorvik Alaska, U.S.A. 66°50N 161°3W 135 C7
Nootka B.C., Canada 49°38N 126°38W 154 F8
Nootka I. B.C., Canada 49°32N 126°42W 154 F8
Nopah Range Calif., U.S.A. 36°10N 116°10W 127 G10
Nopaltepec México, Mexico 19°47N 98°43W 175 C9
Nopiming Prov. Park △ Man., Canada 50°30N 95°37W 151 E16
Nora Nebr., U.S.A. 40°10N 97°58W 80 D8
Nora Springs Iowa, U.S.A. 43°9N 93°0W 81 B6
Noralee B.C., Canada 53°59N 126°29W 154 B8
Noranda = Rouyn-Noranda Qué., Canada 48°20N 79°0W 144 C3
Norborne Mo., U.S.A. 39°18N 93°40W 83 B3
Norcatur Kans., U.S.A. 39°50N 100°11W 82 B3
Norco Calif., U.S.A. 33°56N 117°33W 127 K9
Norcross Ga., U.S.A. 33°56N 84°13W 113 C2
Norcross Minn., U.S.A. 45°52N 96°12W 77 E2
Nord, Grand L. du Qué., Canada 50°40N 67°6W 140 C2
Nord, Petit L. du Qué., Canada 50°50N 67°10W 140 C2
Nord-og-Østgrønland, Nationalparken i △ Greenland 76°0N 35°0W 162 C7
Nordegg Alta., Canada 52°29N 116°5W 153 F4
Norden Nebr., U.S.A. 42°50N 100°5W 80 B5
Nordenskiold → Yukon, Canada 62°6N 136°18W 157 D5
Nordgrønland = Avannaarsua □ Greenland 80°0N 55°0W 162 B5
Nordheim Tex., U.S.A. 28°55N 97°37W 109 J10
Nordman Idaho, U.S.A. 48°38N 116°57W 122 A2
Nordostrundingen Greenland 81°22N 11°40W 162 A9
Nordre Strømfjord Greenland 67°10N 53°30W 162 C5
Noremberga Ont., Canada 48°59N 80°43W 144 C2
Norfolk Ont., Canada 42°50N 80°23W 146 E6
Norfolk Conn., U.S.A. 41°59N 73°12W 91 C1
Norfolk N.Y., U.S.A. 44°50N 75°1W 88 A5
Norfolk Nebr., U.S.A. 42°2N 97°25W 80 C8
Norfolk Va., U.S.A. 36°50N 76°17W 102 E8
Norfolk County ☆ Mass., U.S.A. 42°10N 71°20W 91 B3
Norfolk Int. ✈ (ORF) Va., U.S.A. 36°54N 76°12W 102 E8
Norfork Ark., U.S.A. 36°13N 92°17W 106 B3
Norfork L. Ark., U.S.A. 36°15N 92°14W 106 B3
Norge Okla., U.S.A. 34°59N 98°0W 107 D6
Noria de los Angeles Zacatecas, Mexico 22°27N 101°53W 173 E9
Norias Tex., U.S.A. 26°47N 97°47W 108 L10
Norias del Caballo Coahuila, Mexico 27°43N 103°3W 170 C1
Norlina N.C., U.S.A. 36°27N 78°12W 103 B7
Normal Ill., U.S.A. 40°31N 88°59W 84 C5
Norman Ark., U.S.A. 34°27N 93°41W 106 D2
Norman Nebr., U.S.A. 40°29N 98°48W 80 D7
Norman Okla., U.S.A. 35°13N 97°26W 107 C6
Norman, L. N.C., U.S.A. 35°26N 80°57W 103 C5
Norman County ☆ Minn., U.S.A. 47°20N 96°30W 77 C2
Norman Park Ga., U.S.A. 31°16N 83°41W 113 E3
Norman Wells N.W.T., Canada 65°17N 126°51W 157 C7
Normandie Qué., Canada 48°49N 72°31W 145 C10
Normandy Mo., U.S.A. 38°43N 90°17W 94 A2
Normandy Tex., U.S.A. 28°55N 100°36W 108 J7
Normandy L. Tenn., U.S.A. 35°28N 86°15W 104 E6
Normandy Park Wash., U.S.A. 47°26N 122°20W 132 C3
Normangee Tex., U.S.A. 31°2N 96°7W 109 F11
Norman's Cove-St. Philip's Nfld. & L., Canada 47°33N 53°40W 142 E7
Normétal Qué., Canada 49°0N 79°22W 144 C3
Norphlet Ark., U.S.A. 33°19N 92°40W 106 E3
Norquay Sask., Canada 51°53N 102°5W 151 D9
Norridge Ill., U.S.A. 41°57N 87°49W 95 B2
Norridgewock Maine, U.S.A. 44°43N 69°47W 90 D4
Norris Mont., U.S.A. 45°34N 111°41W 123 E6
Norris S. Dak., U.S.A. 43°26N 101°12W 76 G4
Norris Tenn., U.S.A. 36°12N 84°4W 105 D8
Norris Arm Nfld. & L., Canada 49°5N 55°15W 142 C5
Norris City Ill., U.S.A. 37°59N 88°20W 84 F5
Norris L. Tenn., U.S.A. 36°14N 84°6W 105 D8
Norris Point Nfld. & L., Canada 49°31N 57°53W 142 C3
Norristown Pa., U.S.A. 40°7N 75°21W 92 B1
Norte ✈ (NTR) Monterrey, Mexico 25°51N 100°14W 180 A2
Norte, Cayo Quintana Roo, Mexico 18°45N 87°19W 179 D6
Norte de Chiapas, Mts. del Chiapas, Mexico 16°50N 91°40W 178 C4
Norte de Chiapas, Sa. del Chiapas, Mexico 17°15N 92°30W 178 B4
North S.C., U.S.A. 33°37N 81°6W 103 E4
North → Nfld. & L., Canada 50°50N 61°0W 143 C5
North → W. Va., U.S.A. 39°25N 78°25W 93 A2
North, C. N.S., Canada 47°2N 60°20W 141 F9
North Adams Mass., U.S.A. 42°42N 73°7W 91 B1

North Adams Mich., U.S.A. 41°58N 84°32W 79 H7
North Amherst Mass., U.S.A. 42°25N 72°32W 91 B2
North Andover Mass., U.S.A. 42°42N 71°8W 91 B3
North Anna → Va., U.S.A. 37°48N 77°25W 102 D7
North Arlington N.J., U.S.A. 40°47N 74°7W 97 B2
North Arm N.W.T., Canada 62°0N 114°30W 157 D10
North Arm Fraser River → B.C., Canada 49°13N 123°12W 161 B2
North Atlanta Ga., U.S.A. 33°52N 84°21W 113 C2
North Attleboro Mass., U.S.A. 41°59N 71°20W 91 C3
North Augusta S.C., U.S.A. 33°30N 81°59W 103 E4
North Aulatsivik I. Nfld. & L., Canada 59°46N 64°5W 143 B5
North Baltimore Ohio, U.S.A. 41°11N 83°41W 86 B3
North Bass I. Ohio, U.S.A. 41°40N 82°56W 86 B4
North Battleford Sask., Canada 52°50N 108°17W 150 C3
North Bay Ont., Canada 46°20N 79°30W 146 A7
North Bay Village Fla., U.S.A. 25°50N 80°9W 115 C3
North Beach Md., U.S.A. 38°43N 76°32W 93 B4
North Beach Peninsula Wash., U.S.A. 46°30N 124°2W 120 D1
North Belcher Is. N.W.T., Canada 56°45N 79°50W 158 D8
North Bend B.C., Canada 49°50N 121°27W 155 F13
North Bend Nebr., U.S.A. 41°28N 96°47W 80 C9
North Bend Oreg., U.S.A. 43°24N 124°14W 121 D1
North Bend Wash., U.S.A. 47°30N 121°47W 120 C4
North Bennington Vt., U.S.A. 42°56N 73°15W 89 D1
North Bergen N.J., U.S.A. 40°48N 74°0W 97 B2
North Berwick Maine, U.S.A. 43°18N 70°44W 89 C4
North Bonneville Wash., U.S.A. 45°39N 121°57W 120 E4
North Braddock Pa., U.S.A. 40°23N 79°50W 98 B2
North Branch Mich., U.S.A. 43°14N 83°12W 79 F8
North Branch Minn., U.S.A. 45°31N 92°59W 77 E6
North Branch Chicago River → Ill., U.S.A. 41°53N 87°42W 95 B2
North Branch Elkhorn → Nebr., U.S.A. 41°59N 97°27W 80 C8
North Branch Potomac → U.S.A. 39°32N 78°35W 93 A2
North Branford Conn., U.S.A. 41°20N 72°46W 91 C2
North Brookfield Mass., U.S.A. 42°16N 72°5W 91 B2
North Brunswick N.J., U.S.A. 40°28N 74°28W 92 B2
North Buck L. Alta., Canada 54°41N 112°32W 152 D8
North Buena Vista Iowa, U.S.A. 42°41N 90°58W 81 C8
North Butte Wyo., U.S.A. 43°54N 105°57W 124 C7
North C. N.B., Canada 47°5N 64°0W 141 F8
North Caldwell N.J., U.S.A. 40°51N 74°15W 97 A1
North Canadian → Okla., U.S.A. 35°22N 95°37W 107 C8
North Canton Ohio, U.S.A. 40°53N 81°24W 86 C5
North Cape May N.J., U.S.A. 38°59N 74°57W 92 D2
North Caribou L. Ont., Canada 52°50N 90°40W 159 G7
North Carolina □ U.S.A. 35°30N 80°0W 103 C6
North Cascades Nat. Park △ Wash., U.S.A. 48°45N 121°10W 120 B4
North Channel Ont., Canada 46°0N 83°0W 146 A3
North Charleston N.H., U.S.A. 43°18N 72°24W 89 C2
North Charleston S.C., U.S.A. 32°53N 79°58W 103 F6
North Chelmsford Mass., U.S.A. 42°38N 71°23W 91 B3
North Chicago Ill., U.S.A. 42°19N 87°51W 84 A6
North Chichester R.I., U.S.A. 43°15N 71°22W 89 C3
North College Hill Ohio, U.S.A. 39°13N 84°33W 86 D2
North Collins N.Y., U.S.A. 42°36N 78°56W 88 C2
North Concho → Tex., U.S.A. 31°27N 100°25W 108 F7
North Conway N.H., U.S.A. 44°3N 71°8W 89 B3
North Cowichan B.C., Canada 48°50N 123°41W 155 G11
North Creek N.Y., U.S.A. 43°42N 73°59W 88 B7
North Crossett Ark., U.S.A. 33°10N 91°56W 106 E4
North Dakota □ U.S.A. 47°30N 100°15W 76 C5
North Dartmouth Mass., U.S.A. 41°36N 70°59W 91 C4
North Decatur Georgia, U.S.A. 33°48N 84°17W 117 B3
North Dighton Mass., U.S.A. 41°50N 71°10W 91 C3
North Druid Hills Ga., U.S.A. 33°49N 84°17W 117 B3
North East Md., U.S.A. 39°36N 75°57W 93 A5
North East Pa., U.S.A. 42°13N 79°50W 87 B3
North East Cape Fear → N.C., U.S.A. 34°11N 77°57W 103 D8
North Eastham Mass., U.S.A. 41°52N 69°59W 91 C5
North Easton Mass., U.S.A. 42°4N 71°6W 91 B3
North English Iowa, U.S.A. 41°31N 92°5W 81 D6
North Enid Okla., U.S.A. 36°26N 97°52W 107 B6
North Fabius → Mo., U.S.A. 39°54N 91°30W 83 B3
North Fairfield Ohio, U.S.A. 41°6N 82°37W 86 B4
North Folk Holston → Va., U.S.A. 36°33N 82°37W 102 E2
North Fond du Lac Wis., U.S.A. 43°48N 88°29W 78 E5
North Fork Idaho, U.S.A. 45°25N 113°59W 122 D5
North Fork, Salt → Mo., U.S.A. 39°26N 91°53W 83 B5
North Fork American → Calif., U.S.A. 38°57N 120°59W 126 E6
North Fork Bad → S. Dak., U.S.A. 44°10N 101°40W 76 F4
North Fork Cimarron → Kans., U.S.A. 37°15N 102°9W 82 D1
North Fork Cuivre → Mo., U.S.A. 39°2N 90°59W 83 B6
North Fork Edisto → S.C., U.S.A. 33°16N 80°54W 103 E5
North Fork Feather → Calif., U.S.A. 38°33N 121°30W 126 E5
North Fork Forked Deer → Tenn., U.S.A. 36°0N 89°26W 104 D3
North Fork Grand → S. Dak., U.S.A. 45°47N 102°16W 76 E3
North Fork Humboldt → Nev., U.S.A. 41°0N 115°30W 128 B5
North Fork John Day → Oreg., U.S.A. 44°45N 119°33W 121 C6
North Fork Kentucky → Ky., U.S.A. 37°28N 83°40W 105 C9
North Fork Licking → Ky., U.S.A. 38°35N 84°12W 105 B8
North Fork Moreau → S. Dak., U.S.A. 45°9N 102°50W 76 E3
North Fork Red → U.S.A. 34°24N 99°14W 107 D4
North Fork Shenandoah → Va., U.S.A. 38°59N 78°22W 102 C6
North Fork Shoshone → Wyo., U.S.A. 44°29N 109°18W 124 B3
North Fork Smoky Hill → Kans., U.S.A. 38°54N 101°18W 82 C2
North Fork Solomon → Kans., U.S.A. 39°28N 98°26W 82 B5
North Fork South Platte → Colo., U.S.A. 39°25N 105°12W 125 C5
North Fort Myers Fla., U.S.A. 26°41N 81°53W 114 E7
North Fox I. Mich., U.S.A. 45°29N 85°47W 79 D6
North Freedom Wis., U.S.A. 43°28N 89°52W 78 E4
North French → Ont., Canada 51°10N 80°50W 149 A16
North Gower Ont., Canada 45°8N 75°43W 147 B11
North Grafton Mass., U.S.A. 42°14N 71°42W 91 B2
North Grant N.S., Canada 45°40N 62°2W 141 H7
North Greenfield = West Allis Wis., U.S.A. 43°1N 88°0W 94 B1
North Grosvenor Dale Conn., U.S.A. 41°59N 71°54W 91 C3
North Hackensack N.J., U.S.A. 40°54N 74°2W 97 A2
North Hampton N.H., U.S.A. 42°58N 70°50W 89 C4
North Hartsville S.C., U.S.A. 34°24N 80°4W 103 D5
North Hatley Qué., Canada 45°17N 71°58W 145 F11
North Haven Conn., U.S.A. 41°23N 72°52W 91 C2
North Haven Maine, U.S.A. 44°8N 68°53W 90 D5
North Head N.B., Canada 44°46N 66°45W 141 J3
North Head Nfld. & L., Canada 47°29N 52°38W 142 E8
North Hero Vt., U.S.A. 44°49N 73°18W 89 B1
North Highlands Calif., U.S.A. 38°40N 121°23W 126 E5
North Hills N.Y., U.S.A. 40°46N 73°40W 97 B5
North Hollywood Calif., U.S.A. 34°9N 118°23W 133 B2
North Hoosick N.Y., U.S.A. 42°55N 73°21W 91 B1

North Houston *Tex., U.S.A.* 29°55N 95°30W **116** A2
North I. *S.C., U.S.A.* 33°17N 79°11W **103** E6
North Java *N.Y., U.S.A.* 42°41N 78°20W **88** C2
North Judson *Ind., U.S.A.* 41°13N 86°46W **85** B4
North Kent I. *Nunavut, Canada* 76°40N 90°8W **158** B7
North Kingstown *R.I., U.S.A.* 41°33N 71°28W **91** C3
North Kingsville *Ohio, U.S.A.* 41°54N 80°42W **86** B6
North Knife → *Man., Canada* 58°53N 94°45W **159** F7
North Knife L. *Man., Canada* 58°5N 97°4W **159** F6
North L. *Tex., U.S.A.* 32°56N 96°58W **116** A4
North La Veta Pass *Colo., U.S.A.* 37°36N 105°13W **125** E5
North Lake Park *Iowa, U.S.A.* 32°55N 96°58W **116** A4
North Las Vegas *Nev., U.S.A.* 36°11N 115°7W **134** B1
North Las Vegas ✈ (VGT) *Nev., U.S.A.* 36°12N 115°11W **134** B1
North Lewisburg *Ohio, U.S.A.* 40°13N 83°33W **86** C3
North Lexington *Mass., U.S.A.* 42°27N 71°14W **96** A1
North Liberty *Ind., U.S.A.* 41°32N 86°26W **85** B4
North Liberty *Iowa, U.S.A.* 41°46N 91°35W **81** D7
North Little Rock *Ark., U.S.A.* 34°45N 92°16W **106** D3
North Logan *Utah, U.S.A.* 41°46N 111°48W **129** B4
North Lonsdale *B.C., Canada* 49°20N 123°4W **161** A2
North Loon Mt. *Idaho, U.S.A.* 45°7N 115°52W **122** D3
North Loup *Nebr., U.S.A.* 41°30N 98°46W **80** C7
North Loup → *Nebr., U.S.A.* 41°17N 98°24W **80** C7
North Magnetic Pole *Canada* 82°42N 114°24W **158** B5
North Manchester *Ind., U.S.A.* 41°0N 85°46W **85** B5
North Manitou L. *Mich., U.S.A.* 45°7N 85°58W **79** D6
North Manitou I. *Mich., U.S.A.* 45°7N 86°1W **79** D5
North Mankato *Minn., U.S.A.* 44°10N 94°2W **77** F4
North Miami *Fla., U.S.A.* 25°53N 80°11W **115** C2
North Miami *Okla., U.S.A.* 36°55N 94°53W **107** B9
North Miami Beach *Fla., U.S.A.* 25°55N 80°9W **115** C2
North Middletown *Ky., U.S.A.* 38°9N 84°7W **105** B8
North Moose L. *Man., Canada* 54°4N 100°12W **151** A11
North Mountain Recreation Area *Ariz., U.S.A.* 33°35N 112°4W **134** B2
North Muskegon *Mich., U.S.A.* 43°15N 86°17W **79** F5
North Myrtle Beach *S.C., U.S.A.* 33°48N 78°42W **103** E7
North Naples *Fla., U.S.A.* 26°12N 81°48W **114** E7
North New Hyde Park *N.Y., U.S.A.* 40°44N 73°41W **97** B4
North Oaks *Minn., U.S.A.* 45°6N 93°5W **94** A3
North Ogden *Utah, U.S.A.* 41°19N 111°58W **129** B4
North Olmsted *Ohio, U.S.A.* 41°25N 81°56W **86** B5
North Palisade *Calif., U.S.A.* 37°6N 118°31W **127** F8
North Pass *La., U.S.A.* 29°12N 89°2W **110** E6
North Pease → *Tex., U.S.A.* 34°15N 100°7W **108** C7
North Pelham *N.Y., U.S.A.* 40°54N 73°49W **97** A4
North Perry *Ohio, U.S.A.* 41°47N 81°8W **86** B5
North Perry ✈ *Fla., U.S.A.* 26°0N 80°14W **115** B2
North Plains *N. Mex., U.S.A.* 34°45N 108°10W **131** C2
North Plains *Oreg., U.S.A.* 45°37N 123°0W **121** B3
North Platte *Nebr., U.S.A.* 41°8N 100°46W **80** C5
North Platte → *Nebr., U.S.A.* 41°7N 100°42W **80** C5
North Platte Nat. Wildlife Refuge △ *Nebr., U.S.A.* 41°36N 103°29W **80** C2
North Pole *Alaska, U.S.A.* 64°45N 147°21W **135** D11
North Port *Fla., U.S.A.* 27°3N 82°14W **114** D6
North Portal *Sask., Canada* 49°0N 102°33W **151** F9
North Powder *Oreg., U.S.A.* 45°2N 117°55W **121** B8
North Prairie *Wis., U.S.A.* 42°56N 88°24W **78** F5
North Providence *R.I., U.S.A.* 41°50N 71°25W **91** C3
North Quincy *Mass., U.S.A.* 42°16N 71°1W **96** B2
North Ram → *Alta., Canada* 52°16N 114°38W **153** F6
North Redington Beach *Tampa, U.S.A.* 27°48N 82°49W **115** C2
North Res. *Mass., U.S.A.* 42°27N 71°6W **96** A2
North Richland Hills *Tex., U.S.A.* 32°50N 97°13W **116** A2
North Rim *Ariz., U.S.A.* 36°12N 112°3W **130** A3
North Riverside *Ill., U.S.A.* 41°50N 87°48W **95** B2
North Royalton *Ohio, U.S.A.* 41°18N 81°43W **98** C1
North Rustico *P.E.I., Canada* 46°27N 63°19W **141** G6
North St. Paul *Minn., U.S.A.* 45°1N 92°59W **94** A4
North Salem *Ind., U.S.A.* 39°52N 86°39W **85** D4
North Salt Lake *Utah, U.S.A.* 40°50N 111°54W **134** A1
North Santiam → *Oreg., U.S.A.* 44°41N 123°0W **121** C3
North Saskatchewan → *Sask., Canada* 53°15N 105°5W **150** B6
North Saugus *Mass., U.S.A.* 42°29N 71°0W **96** A2
North Schell Peak *Nev., U.S.A.* 39°25N 114°36W **128** C6
North Sea *N.Y., U.S.A.* 40°56N 72°25W **91** D2
North Shapleigh *Maine, U.S.A.* 43°36N 70°53W **89** C4
North Shore *Hawai'i, U.S.A.* 21°39N 158°30W **136** J13
North Shore Channel → *Ill., U.S.A.* 41°58N 87°42W **95** B2
North Sioux City *S. Dak., U.S.A.* 42°32N 96°29W **76** H9
North Slope ☆ *Alaska, U.S.A.* 69°15N 152°0W **135** B9
North Spicer I. *Nunavut, Canada* 68°33N 78°45W **158** D10
North Springfield *Pa., U.S.A.* 41°59N 80°26W **87** C2
North Springfield *Vt., U.S.A.* 43°20N 72°32W **89** B3
North Star *Alta., Canada* 56°51N 117°38W **152** B3
North Station *Boston, U.S.A.* **96** a2
North Stratford *N.H., U.S.A.* 44°45N 71°38W **89** B3
North Sulphur → *Tex., U.S.A.* 33°23N 95°18W **109** D12
North Sutton *N.H., U.S.A.* 43°22N 71°56W **89** C3
North Sydney *N.S., Canada* 46°12N 60°15W **141** G9
North Syracuse *N.Y., U.S.A.* 43°8N 76°7W **88** B4
North Terre Haute *Ind., U.S.A.* 39°31N 87°22W **85** D3
North Thompson → *B.C., Canada* 50°40N 120°20W **155** E14
North Tonawanda *N.Y., U.S.A.* 43°2N 78°53W **88** B2
North Troy *Vt., U.S.A.* 45°0N 72°24W **89** B2
North Truro *Mass., U.S.A.* 42°2N 70°5W **91** B4
North Twin I. *N.W.T., Canada* 53°20N 80°0W **143** C1
North Twin L. *Nfld. & L., Canada* 49°16N 55°56W **142** C5
North Umpqua → *Oreg., U.S.A.* 43°16N 123°27W **121** D2
North Union = Shaker Heights *Ohio, U.S.A.* 41°28N 81°32W **98** A2
North Valley Stream *N.Y., U.S.A.* 40°41N 73°42W **97** B4
North Vancouver *B.C., Canada* 49°19N 123°4W **161** B2
North Vernon *Ind., U.S.A.* 39°0N 85°38W **85** D5
North Wabasca L. *Alta., Canada* 56°0N 113°55W **152** B7
North Wales *Pa., U.S.A.* 40°13N 75°17W **92** B1
North Washington *Iowa, U.S.A.* 43°9N 92°13W **81** B6
North Waterford *Maine, U.S.A.* 44°14N 70°46W **89** B4
North West River *Nfld. & L., Canada* 53°30N 60°10W **143** C5
North Wichita → *Tex., U.S.A.* 33°43N 99°29W **109** D8
North Wildwood *N.J., U.S.A.* 39°0N 74°48W **92** D2
North Wilkesboro *N.C., U.S.A.* 36°10N 81°9W **103** B4
North Windham *Maine, U.S.A.* 43°50N 70°26W **90** E3
North Wolf Cr. → *S. Dak., U.S.A.* 44°42N 98°46W **76** F7
North Yakima = Yakima *Wash., U.S.A.* 46°36N 120°31W **120** D5
North York *Ont., Canada* 43°45N 79°27W **161** A4
Northampton *Mass., U.S.A.* 42°19N 72°38W **91** B2
Northampton *Pa., U.S.A.* 40°41N 75°30W **92** B1
Northampton County ☆ *N.C., U.S.A.* 36°20N 77°30W **103** B8
Northampton County ☆ *Pa., U.S.A.* 40°50N 75°20W **87** D7

Northampton County ☆ *Va., U.S.A.* 37°15N 75°55W **102** D9
Northborough *Mass., U.S.A.* 42°19N 71°39W **91** B3
Northbridge *Mass., U.S.A.* 42°9N 71°39W **91** B3
Northeast C. *Alaska, U.S.A.* 63°18N 168°42W **135** E5
Northeast Providence Chan. *W. Indies* 26°0N 76°0W **182** A4
Northeastern University *Mass., U.S.A.* 42°20N 71°4W **96** C1
Northern Cambria *Pa., U.S.A.* 40°40N 78°47W **87** D4
Northern Cheyenne Indian Reservation *Mont., U.S.A.* 45°30N 106°40W **123** E11
Northern Indian L. *Man., Canada* 57°20N 97°20W **159** F6
Northern Light L. *Ont., Canada* 48°15N 90°39W **148** D6
Northern Marianas ☑ *Pac. Oc.* 17°0N 145°0E **184** a
Northern Virginia Regional Park △ *Va., U.S.A.* 38°55N 77°6W **99** B3
Northfield *Maine, U.S.A.* 44°52N 67°34W **90** D6
Northfield *Mass., U.S.A.* 42°42N 72°27W **91** B2
Northfield *Minn., U.S.A.* 44°27N 93°9W **77** F5
Northfield *N.H., U.S.A.* 43°26N 71°36W **89** C3
Northfield *N.J., U.S.A.* 39°22N 74°33W **92** C2
Northfield *Vt., U.S.A.* 44°9N 72°40W **89** B2
Northford *Conn., U.S.A.* 41°24N 72°43W **91** C1
Northgate *N. Dak., U.S.A.* 48°59N 102°1W **76** B3
Northglenn *Colo., U.S.A.* 39°53N 104°59W **134** A2
Northlake *Ill., U.S.A.* 41°54N 87°53W **95** B1
Northmount *Ont., Canada* 43°46N 79°23W **161** A2
Northome *Minn., U.S.A.* 47°52N 94°17W **77** C4
Northport *Ala., U.S.A.* 33°14N 87°35W **112** C3
Northport *Mich., U.S.A.* 45°8N 85°37W **79** D6
Northport *N.Y., U.S.A.* 40°54N 73°2W **91** D1
Northport *Nebr., U.S.A.* 41°41N 103°5W **80** C2
Northport *Wash., U.S.A.* 48°55N 117°48W **120** B8
Northridge *Ohio, U.S.A.* 39°59N 83°46W **86** D3
Northrop *Minn., U.S.A.* 43°44N 94°26W **77** G4
Northumberland *Pa., U.S.A.* 40°54N 76°48W **87** D6
Northumberland County ☆ *Pa., U.S.A.* 40°55N 76°55W **87** D6
Northumberland County ☆ *Va., U.S.A.* 37°55N 76°29W **102** D8
Northumberland Str. *N.S., Canada* 46°20N 64°0W **141** G6
Northview *Mo., U.S.A.* 37°17N 93°0W **83** D4
Northville *N.Y., U.S.A.* 43°13N 74°11W **88** B6
Northville *S. Dak., U.S.A.* 45°9N 98°35W **76** E7
Northway *Alaska, U.S.A.* 62°58N 141°56W **135** C12
Northwest Arctic ☆ *Alaska, U.S.A.* 66°50N 161°0W **135** C7
Northwest Gander → *Nfld. & L., Canada* 48°55N 55°2W **142** D5
Northwest Providence Channel *W. Indies* 26°0N 78°0W **182** A4
Northwest Territories ☑ *Canada* 63°0N 118°0W **157** D9
Northwestern Station *Ill., U.S.A.* 41°52N 87°38W **95** B3
Northwestern University *Ill., U.S.A.* 42°3N 87°40W **95** A2
Northwind Ridge *Arctic* 77°50N 155°10W **156** A1
Northwood *Iowa, U.S.A.* 43°27N 93°13W **81** B5
Northwood *N. Dak., U.S.A.* 47°44N 97°34W **76** C8
Northwood *N.H., U.S.A.* 43°12N 71°9W **89** C3
Northwood Park *Ont., Canada* 43°45N 79°30W **161** A1
Northwoods *Mo., U.S.A.* 38°42N 90°17W **94** A2
Norton *N.B., Canada* 45°38N 65°42W **141** H4
Norton *Kans., U.S.A.* 39°50N 99°53W **82** B4
Norton *Mass., U.S.A.* 41°58N 71°11W **91** C3
Norton *Vt., U.S.A.* 45°0N 71°48W **89** B3
Norton B. *Alaska, U.S.A.* 64°45N 161°15W **135** D7
Norton County ☆ *Kans., U.S.A.* 39°45N 99°50W **82** B4
Norton Pk. *Idaho, U.S.A.* 43°46N 114°39W **122** F4
Norton Sd. *Alaska, U.S.A.* 63°50N 164°0W **135** D7
Norton Shores *Mich., U.S.A.* 43°10N 86°16W **79** F5
Nortonville *Kans., U.S.A.* 39°25N 95°20W **82** B8
Nortonville *Ky., U.S.A.* 37°12N 87°27W **104** C5
Norwalk *Calif., U.S.A.* 33°54N 118°4W **127** K8
Norwalk *Conn., U.S.A.* 41°7N 73°22W **91** C1
Norwalk *Iowa, U.S.A.* 41°29N 93°41W **81** D5
Norwalk *Ohio, U.S.A.* 41°15N 82°37W **86** B4
Norwalk *Wis., U.S.A.* 43°50N 90°37W **78** E3
Norway *Iowa, U.S.A.* 41°54N 91°55W **81** D7
Norway *Kans., U.S.A.* 39°42N 97°47W **82** B6
Norway *Maine, U.S.A.* 44°13N 70°32W **90** D3
Norway *Mich., U.S.A.* 45°47N 87°55W **79** D4
Norway B. *Nunavut, Canada* 71°6N 104°28W **158** C5
Norway House *Man., Canada* 53°59N 97°50W **151** B14
Norwegian B. *Nunavut, Canada* 77°30N 90°0W **158** B7
Norwell *Mass., U.S.A.* 42°10N 70°48W **91** B4
Norwich *Ont., Canada* 42°59N 80°36W **146** E6
Norwich *Conn., U.S.A.* 41°31N 72°5W **91** C2
Norwich *Kans., U.S.A.* 37°27N 97°51W **82** D6
Norwich *N.Y., U.S.A.* 42°32N 75°32W **88** C5
Norwich *Vt., U.S.A.* 43°42N 72°18W **89** C2
Norwood *Ont., Canada* 44°23N 77°59W **147** C9
Norwood *Colo., U.S.A.* 38°8N 108°20W **125** D2
Norwood *La., U.S.A.* 30°58N 91°6W **110** D4
Norwood *Mass., U.S.A.* 42°12N 71°12W **91** B3
Norwood *Mo., U.S.A.* 37°7N 92°24W **83** D4
Norwood *N.C., U.S.A.* 35°14N 80°7W **103** C5
Norwood *N.Y., U.S.A.* 44°45N 75°0W **88** a4
Norwood *Ohio, U.S.A.* 39°9N 84°27W **86** D2
Norwood → *Wyo., U.S.A.* 44°17N 107°58W **124** B5
Norwood Park *Ill., U.S.A.* 41°59N 87°48W **95** B2
Norwood-Young America *Minn., U.S.A.* 44°46N 93°55W **77** F5
Norwoodville *Iowa, U.S.A.* 41°39N 93°33W **81** D5
Notasulga *Ala., U.S.A.* 32°34N 85°41W **112** D5
Notch Peak *Utah, U.S.A.* 39°9N 113°25W **129** D2
Notikewin → *Alta., Canada* 57°2N 117°38W **152** A3
Notikewin Prov. Park △ *Alta., Canada* 57°14N 117°9W **152** A3
Notre-Dame *N.B., Canada* 46°18N 64°46W **141** E8
Notre-Dame, Basilique *Montréal, Canada* **160** c3
Notre-Dame, Île *Qué., Canada* 45°29N 73°31W **160** A3
Notre Dame B. *Nfld. & L., Canada* 49°45N 55°30W **142** C5
Notre-Dame-de-Grace *Qué., Canada* 45°28N 73°38W **160** B3
Notre-Dame-de-Koartac = Quaqtaq *Qué., Canada* 60°55N 69°40W **143** A4
Notre Dame de Lourdes *Man., Canada* 49°32N 98°33W **151** F13
Notre-Dame-des-Bois *Qué., Canada* 45°24N 71°4W **145** F11
Notre-Dame-d'Ivugivic = Ivujivik *Qué., Canada* 62°24N 77°55W **143** A2
Notre-Dame-du-Bon-Conseil *Qué., Canada* 46°0N 72°21W **145** F10
Notre-Dame-du-Laus *Qué., Canada* 46°5N 75°37W **144** E7
Notre-Dame-du-Portage *Qué., Canada* 47°46N 69°37W **145** D13
Notrees *Tex., U.S.A.* 31°55N 102°48W **116** C5
Nottawasaga B. *Ont., Canada* 44°35N 80°15W **146** C5
Nottaway = Sennettere *Qué., Canada* 48°25N 77°15W **144** C5
Nottaway → *Qué., Canada* 5°22N 78°55W **143** C2
Nottely L. *Ga., U.S.A.* 34°58N 84°5W **113** B2
Nottingham *N.H., U.S.A.* 43°7N 71°6W **89** C3
Nottingham *N.Y., U.S.A.* 39°25N 76°1W **93** A4
Nottingham I. *Nunavut, Canada* 63°20N 77°55W **159** E10

Nottoway → *Va., U.S.A.* 36°33N 76°55W **102** E8
Nottoway County ☆ *Va., U.S.A.* 37°8N 78°5W **102** D6
Nottoway Court House *Va., U.S.A.* 37°8N 78°5W **102** D6
Notukeu Cr. → *Sask., Canada* 49°56N 106°29W **150** F5
Notus *Idaho, U.S.A.* 43°43N 116°48W **122** F2
Nouveau Comptoir = Wemindji *Qué., Canada* 53°0N 78°49W **143** C2
Nouvelle *N.B., Canada* 48°8N 66°19W **141** E3
Nouvelle → *N.B., Canada* 48°5N 66°19W **141** E3
Nouvelle France, C. de *Qué., Canada* 62°27N 73°42W **143** A3
Nova Scotia ☑ *Canada* 45°10N 63°0W **141** J5
Nova Zembla I. *N.W.T., Canada* 72°11N 74°50W **158** C11
Novar *Ont., Canada* 45°27N 79°15W **146** B7
Novato *Calif., U.S.A.* 38°6N 122°35W **126** E4
Novinger *Mo., U.S.A.* 40°14N 92°43W **83** A4
Nowata *Okla., U.S.A.* 36°42N 95°38W **107** B8
Nowata County ☆ *Okla., U.S.A.* 36°50N 95°40W **107** B8
Nowater Cr. → *Wyo., U.S.A.* 43°57N 108°0W **124** C5
Nowitna Nat. Wildlife Refuge △ *Alaska, U.S.A.* 64°40N 154°16W **135** D9
Noxapater *Miss., U.S.A.* 33°1N 89°1W **111** C4
Noxon Res. *Mont., U.S.A.* 47°57N 115°44W **123** C2
Noxubee → *U.S.A.* 32°50N 88°10W **112** D2
Noxubee County ☆ *Miss., U.S.A.* 33°7N 88°34W **111** C5
Noyes *Minn., U.S.A.* 49°0N 97°12W **77** B1
Nubieber *Calif., U.S.A.* 41°6N 121°11W **126** B5
Nuckolls County ☆ *Nebr., U.S.A.* 40°15N 98°0W **80** E8
Nucla *Colo., U.S.A.* 38°16N 108°33W **125** D2
Nuctunich, Pta. *Quintana Roo, Mexico* 21°27N 87°11W **179** A4
Nueces → *Tex., U.S.A.* 27°51N 97°30W **109** K10
Nueces County ☆ *Tex., U.S.A.* 27°47N 97°40W **109** K10
Nueltin L. *Canada* 60°30N 99°30W **159** E6
Nueva Atzacoalco *Distrito Federal, Mexico* 19°29N 99°4W **181** B3
Nueva Ciudad Guerrero *Tamaulipas, Mexico* 26°34N 99°12W **170** D5
Nueva Cuadrilla *Michoacán, Mexico* 18°4N 101°32W **174** D6
Nueva Esperanza *Quintana Roo, Mexico* 18°9N 89°9W **179** D4
Nueva Esperanza *Tabasco, Mexico* 17°20N 91°4W **178** B5
Nueva Gerona *Cuba* 21°53N 82°49W **182** B3
Nueva Italia *Michoacán, Mexico* 19°1N 102°6W **174** C5
Nueva Rosita *Coahuila, Mexico* 27°57N 101°13W **170** C3
Nueva San Salvador *El Salv.* 13°40N 89°18W **182** D2
Nueva Tenochtitlán *Distrito Federal, Mexico* 19°27N 99°5W **181** B3
Nuevitas *Cuba* 21°30N 77°20W **182** B4
Nuevo América *Chiapas, Mexico* 15°57N 92°26W **178** D3
Nuevo Anáhuac *Nuevo León, Mexico* 27°14N 100°9W **170** C4
Nuevo Casas Grandes *Chihuahua, Mexico* 30°25N 107°55W **169** C8
Nuevo Coahuila *Campeche, Mexico* 17°55N 90°51W **179** E3
Nuevo Cuauhtémoc *Chihuahua, Mexico* 31°30N 107°15W **169** B8
Nuevo Delicias *Coahuila, Mexico* 26°14N 102°48W **170** D2
Nuevo Guerrero *Chiapas, Mexico* 17°1N 91°19W **178** B5
Nuevo Ideal *Durango, Mexico* 24°55N 105°7W **172** C5
Nuevo Ixcatlán *Veracruz, Mexico* 17°38N 95°27W **177** G5
Nuevo Laredo *Tamaulipas, Mexico* 27°30N 99°31W **170** C5
Nuevo León ☑ *Mexico* 25°20N 100°0W **171** E5
Nuevo México *Chiapas, Mexico* 16°27N 93°26W **178** C3
Nuevo México *Guadalajara, Mexico* 20°45N 103°26W **180** A1
Nuevo Momón *Chiapas, Mexico* 16°20N 91°44W **178** C5
Nuevo Morelos *Tamaulipas, Mexico* 22°32N 99°12W **171** H5
Nuevo Padilla *Tamaulipas, Mexico* 24°1N 98°47W **171** F6
Nuevo Progreso *Tamaulipas, Mexico* 26°3N 97°56W **170** D7
Nuevo Progreso *Tamaulipas, Mexico* 23°11N 97°56W **171** G7
Nuevo Progresso *Campeche, Mexico* 18°37N 92°17W **179** D1
Nuevo Reforma *Coahuila, Mexico* 27°28N 102°6W **170** C2
Nuevo San Miguel Zapotitlán *Sinaloa, Mexico* 25°56N 109°3W **172** B1
Nuevo Urecho *Michoacán, Mexico* 19°8N 101°53W **174** C6
Nuevo X-Can *Yucatán, Mexico* 20°51N 87°40W **179** B6
Nulato *Alaska, U.S.A.* 64°43N 158°6W **135** D8
Nulhegan → *Vt., U.S.A.* 44°45N 71°38W **89** B3
Nulki L. *B.C., Canada* 53°55N 124°7W **154** B4
Numa *Iowa, U.S.A.* 40°41N 92°59W **81** E6
Numarán *Michoacán, Mexico* 20°15N 101°56W **174** B6
Nunaksaluk I. *Nfld. & L., Canada* 55°49N 60°20W **143** B5
Nunap Isua *Greenland* 59°48N 43°55W **162** F6
Nunavut ☑ *Canada* 66°0N 85°0W **158** C7
Nunda *N.Y., U.S.A.* 42°35N 77°56W **88** C3
Nunda *S. Dak., U.S.A.* 44°10N 97°1W **76** F8
Nungesser L. *Ont., Canada* 51°28N 93°30W **148** A3
Nunivak I. *Alaska, U.S.A.* 60°10N 166°30W **135** F6
Nunn *Colo., U.S.A.* 40°42N 104°47W **125** B6
Nunnelly *Tenn., U.S.A.* 35°52N 87°28W **104** C5
Nuntsi Park → *B.C., Canada* 51°45N 123°47W **154** D11
Nuri *Sonora, Mexico* 28°5N 109°22W **168** C3
Nursery *Tex., U.S.A.* 28°56N 97°6W **109** J10
Nut L. *Sask., Canada* 52°22N 103°42W **150** C8
Nutak *Nfld. & L., Canada* 57°28N 61°59W **143** B5
Nutley *N.J., U.S.A.* 40°49N 74°9W **97** B2
Nutrioso *Ariz., U.S.A.* 33°57N 109°13W **130** D6
Nuuk *Greenland* 64°10N 51°35W **162** C5
Nuussuaq *Greenland* 74°8N 57°3W **162** C5
Nu'uuli *Amer. Samoa* 14°19S 170°42W **184** e
Nyack *N.Y., U.S.A.* 41°5N 73°55W **92** A3
Nye County ☆ *Nev., U.S.A.* 38°0N 116°40W **128** D4
Nyeboe Land *Greenland* 82°0N 57°0W **162** A5
Nyssa *Oreg., U.S.A.* 43°53N 117°0W **121** D8

O

O.C. Fisher L. *Tex., U.S.A.* 31°29N 100°29W **108** F7
O.H. Ivie Res. *Tex., U.S.A.* 31°34N 99°41W **108** F8
Oacoma *S. Dak., U.S.A.* 43°48N 99°24W **76** D6
Oahe, L. *U.S.A.* 44°27N 100°24W **76** F5
Oahe Dam *S. Dak., U.S.A.* 44°27N 100°24W **76** F5
O'ahu *Hawai'i, U.S.A.* 21°28N 157°58W **136** K14
Oak *Nebr., U.S.A.* 40°14N 97°54W **80** E8
Oak Bay *B.C., Canada* 48°26N 123°18W **155** G11
Oak Bay *N.B., Canada* 45°14N 67°12W **141** H2
Oak Bluffs *Mass., U.S.A.* 41°27N 70°34W **91** C5
Oak City *Utah, U.S.A.* 39°22N 112°20W **129** D3
Oak Cr. → *Ariz., U.S.A.* 34°45N 111°55W **130** C4
Oak Creek *Colo., U.S.A.* 40°16N 106°57W **125** B4
Oak Creek *Wis., U.S.A.* 42°52N 87°55W **78** F9
Oak Grove *Georgia, U.S.A.* 33°50N 84°18W **117** A3
Oak Grove *Ky., U.S.A.* 36°40N 87°26W **104** D4
Oak Grove *La., U.S.A.* 32°52N 91°23W **110** B4
Oak Grove *Mo., U.S.A.* 39°0N 94°8W **83** C2
Oak Grove *Oreg., U.S.A.* 45°25N 122°38W **121** B2
Oak Grove *Tenn., U.S.A.* 36°25N 82°55W **105** D10
Oak Grove *Va., U.S.A.* 38°11N 77°0W **93** B4

Oak Harbor *Ohio, U.S.A.* 41°30N 83°9W **86** B3
Oak Harbor *Wash., U.S.A.* 48°18N 122°39W **120** B3
Oak Hill *N.B., Canada* 45°20N 67°20W **141** H2
Oak Hill *Fla., U.S.A.* 28°52N 80°51W **114** C8
Oak Hill *Kans., U.S.A.* 39°15N 97°21W **82** B6
Oak Hill *Mass., U.S.A.* 42°18N 71°10W **96** B1
Oak Hill *Ohio, U.S.A.* 38°54N 82°35W **86** E4
Oak Hill *Tenn., U.S.A.* 36°5N 86°47W **104** D6
Oak Hill *W. Va., U.S.A.* 37°59N 81°9W **102** D3
Oak Island *N.C., U.S.A.* 33°55N 78°10W **103** E7
Oak Lake *Man., Canada* 49°46N 100°38W **151** F11
Oak Lawn *Ill., U.S.A.* 41°42N 87°45W **95** C2
Oak Orchard *Del., U.S.A.* 38°36N 75°12W **93** B5
Oak Park *Ga., U.S.A.* 32°22N 82°19W **113** D4
Oak Park *Ill., U.S.A.* 41°52N 87°47W **95** B2
Oak Park *Mich., U.S.A.* 42°27N 83°10W **98** B1
Oak Point *Man., Canada* 50°30N 98°1W **151** E13
Oak Ridge *La., U.S.A.* 32°38N 91°47W **110** B4
Oak Ridge *Mo., U.S.A.* 37°30N 89°44W **83** D7
Oak Ridge *Tenn., U.S.A.* 36°1N 84°16W **105** D3
Oak River *Man., Canada* 50°8N 100°26W **151** E11
Oak Vale *Miss., U.S.A.* 31°26N 89°58W **111** E4
Oak Valley *Kans., U.S.A.* 37°20N 96°1W **82** D7
Oak View *Calif., U.S.A.* 34°24N 119°18W **127** J7
Oak View *Md., U.S.A.* 39°1N 76°58W **99** A4
Oakbank *Man., Canada* 49°57N 96°51W **151** F15
Oakboro *N.C., U.S.A.* 35°13N 80°20W **103** C5
Oakdale *Calif., U.S.A.* 37°46N 120°51W **126** F6
Oakdale *Georgia, U.S.A.* 33°51N 84°30W **117** A2
Oakdale *Ill., U.S.A.* 38°16N 89°30W **84** E4
Oakdale *La., U.S.A.* 30°49N 92°40W **110** D3
Oakdale *Minn., U.S.A.* 44°57N 92°57W **94** B4
Oakdale *Nebr., U.S.A.* 42°4N 97°58W **80** B8
Oakdale Park *Minn., U.S.A.* 45°1N 92°57W **94** B1
Oakes *N. Dak., U.S.A.* 46°8N 98°6W **76** D7
Oakesdale *Wash., U.S.A.* 47°8N 117°15W **120** C8
Oakfield *Ga., U.S.A.* 31°47N 83°58W **113** E3
Oakfield *N.Y., U.S.A.* 43°4N 78°16W **88** B2
Oakfield *Wis., U.S.A.* 43°41N 88°33W **78** E5
Oakford *Ill., U.S.A.* 40°6N 89°58W **84** C4
Oakgrove *Ark., U.S.A.* 36°27N 93°26W **106** B3
Oakhurst *Calif., U.S.A.* 37°19N 119°40W **126** F7
Oakhurst *N.J., U.S.A.* 40°16N 74°1W **92** B2
Oakhurst *Okla., U.S.A.* 36°5N 96°4W **107** B7
Oakland *Ark., U.S.A.* 36°28N 92°35W **106** B3
Oakland *Calif., U.S.A.* 37°48N 122°18W **132** B3
Oakland *Ill., U.S.A.* 39°39N 88°2W **84** D5
Oakland *Iowa, U.S.A.* 41°19N 95°23W **81** D3
Oakland *Ky., U.S.A.* 36°52N 86°15W **104** C6
Oakland *Maine, U.S.A.* 44°33N 69°43W **90** D4
Oakland *Md., U.S.A.* 39°25N 79°24W **93** A1
Oakland *Miss., U.S.A.* 34°3N 89°55W **111** B4
Oakland *Nebr., U.S.A.* 38°34N 90°23W **94** B1
Oakland *N.J., U.S.A.* 41°2N 74°14W **92** A2
Oakland *Nebr., U.S.A.* 41°50N 96°28W **80** C8
Oakland *Okla., U.S.A.* 34°7N 96°49W **107** D7
Oakland *Oreg., U.S.A.* 43°25N 123°18W **121** D2
Oakland *Pa., U.S.A.* 41°57N 75°37W **87** C7
Oakland *Tenn., U.S.A.* 35°14N 89°31W **104** C3
Oakland City *Ind., U.S.A.* 38°20N 87°21W **85** E3
Oakland County ☆ *Mich., U.S.A.* 42°35N 83°20W **79** G8
Oakland Gardens *N.Y., U.S.A.* 40°44N 73°44W **97** B4
Oakland Int. ✈ (OAK) *Calif., U.S.A.* 37°43N 122°13W **126** F4
Oakland Park *Fla., U.S.A.* 26°10N 80°7W **115** A3
Oaklawn *Kans., U.S.A.* 37°36N 97°18W **82** D6
Oaklawn *Md., U.S.A.* 38°46N 76°56W **99** C4
Oakley *Idaho, U.S.A.* 42°15N 113°53W **122** G5
Oakley *Kans., U.S.A.* 39°8N 100°51W **82** B3
Oakley *Mich., U.S.A.* 43°9N 84°10W **79** F7
Oakley *Utah, U.S.A.* 40°43N 111°18W **129** C4
Oaklyn *Pa., U.S.A.* 39°54N 75°5W **92** B2
Oakman *Ala., U.S.A.* 33°43N 87°23W **112** C3
Oakmont *Pa., U.S.A.* 40°31N 79°50W **98** A2
Oakridge *Oreg., U.S.A.* 43°45N 122°28W **121** D3
Oaks *Okla., U.S.A.* 36°10N 94°51W **107** B9
Oakton *Ky., U.S.A.* 36°40N 89°4W **104** D3
Oakton *Ind., U.S.A.* 38°52N 87°27W **85** E3
Oakville *Ont., Canada* 43°27N 79°41W **146** D7
Oakville *Conn., U.S.A.* 41°36N 73°5W **91** C1
Oakville *Iowa, U.S.A.* 41°6N 91°3W **81** D7
Oakville *Wash., U.S.A.* 46°51N 123°14W **120** D2
Oakwood *N.Y., U.S.A.* 40°33N 74°6W **97** C2
Oakwood *Ohio, U.S.A.* 41°6N 84°23W **86** B2
Oakwood *Okla., U.S.A.* 35°56N 98°42W **107** C5
Oakwood *Tex., U.S.A.* 41°1N 80°23W **87** C2
Oakwood *Tex., U.S.A.* 31°35N 95°51W **109** F12
Oakwood Beach *N.Y., U.S.A.* 40°33N 74°7W **97** C2
Oark *Ark., U.S.A.* 35°41N 93°35W **106** B3
Oasis *Nev., U.S.A.* 41°2N 114°29W **128** A6
Oatman *Ariz., U.S.A.* 35°1N 114°19W **130** B1
Oaxaca *Oaxaca, Mexico* 17°3N 96°43W **177** G4
Oaxaca ☑ *Mexico* 17°0N 96°30W **177** H4
Oba *Ont., Canada* 49°4N 84°7W **149** D8
Oba L. *Ont., Canada* 48°40N 84°16W **149** D12
Obakamiga L. *Ont., Canada* 49°9N 85°9W **149** C11
Obalski, L. *Qué., Canada* 48°43N 77°58W **144** C5
Obamsca, L. *Qué., Canada* 50°24N 78°16W **144** A4
Oban *Ont., Canada* 48°13N 77°21W **144** C5
Obatanga Prov. Park △ *Ont., Canada* 48°20N 85°10W **149** D11
Obayos *Coahuila, Mexico* 27°26N 101°24W **170** C3
Obayos, Sa. *Coahuila, Mexico* 27°35N 101°37W **170** C3
Obed *Alta., Canada* 53°30N 117°10W **152** E3
Obed → *Tenn., U.S.A.* 36°5N 84°39W **105** D8
Obedjiwan *Qué., Canada* 48°40N 74°56W **144** C8
Oberlin *Kans., U.S.A.* 39°49N 100°32W **82** B3
Oberlin *La., U.S.A.* 30°37N 92°46W **110** D3
Oberlin *Ohio, U.S.A.* 41°18N 82°13W **86** B4
Oberon *N. Dak., U.S.A.* 47°55N 99°24W **76** C6
Obert *Nebr., U.S.A.* 42°41N 97°2W **80** B8
Obion *Tenn., U.S.A.* 36°16N 89°12W **104** D3
Obion → *Tenn., U.S.A.* 36°20N 89°39W **104** C3
Obion County ☆ *Tenn., U.S.A.* 36°20N 89°10W **104** D3
Oblong *Ill., U.S.A.* 38°59N 87°55W **84** D6
Obonga L. *Ont., Canada* 49°57N 89°22W **148** C7
O'Brien *Fla., U.S.A.* 30°2N 82°57W **114** A6
O'Brien *Oreg., U.S.A.* 42°4N 123°42W **121** E2
O'Brien County ☆ *Iowa, U.S.A.* 43°5N 95°35W **81** B3
Obscura, Sierra *N. Mex., U.S.A.* 33°45N 106°25W **131** D4
Observatorio de Arecibo *Puerto Rico* 18°21N 66°45W **184** G16

Obsidian *Idaho, U.S.A.* 44°51N 114°51W **122** E4
Ocala *Fla., U.S.A.* 29°11N 82°8W **114** B6
Ocampo *Chihuahua, Mexico* 28°11N 108°23W **169** E7
Ocampo *Coahuila, Mexico* 27°20N 102°21W **170** C2
Ocampo *Guanajuato, Mexico* 21°39N 101°30W **175** A6
Ocampo *Tamaulipas, Mexico* 22°50N 99°20W **171** H5
Ocate *N. Mex., U.S.A.* 36°11N 105°3W **131** A5
Ocate → *N. Mex., U.S.A.* 36°10N 104°30W **131** A6
Occoquan Ca. → *Va., U.S.A.* 38°39N 77°14W **93** B3
Ocean Beach *Calif., U.S.A.* 32°44N 117°15W **133** B1
Ocean Bluff *Mass., U.S.A.* 42°6N 70°39W **91** B4
Ocean City *Md., U.S.A.* 38°20N 75°5W **93** B5
Ocean City *N.J., U.S.A.* 39°17N 74°35W **92** C2
Ocean City *Wash., U.S.A.* 47°4N 124°10W **120** C1
Ocean County ☆ *N.J., U.S.A.* 39°50N 74°15W **92** C2
Ocean Falls *B.C., Canada* 52°18N 127°48W **154** C7
Ocean L. *Wyo., U.S.A.* 43°12N 108°36W **124** C4
Ocean Park *Wash., U.S.A.* 46°30N 124°3W **120** D1
Ocean Pines *Md., U.S.A.* 38°24N 75°9W **93** B5
Ocean Springs *Miss., U.S.A.* 30°25N 88°50W **111** F5
Oceana *W. Va., U.S.A.* 37°42N 81°38W **102** D3
Oceana County ☆ *Mich., U.S.A.* 43°40N 86°20W **79** F5
Oceano *Calif., U.S.A.* 35°6N 120°37W **127** H6
Oceanport *N.J., U.S.A.* 40°19N 74°3W **92** B2
Oceanside *Calif., U.S.A.* 33°12N 117°23W **127** K9
Oceanside *N.Y., U.S.A.* 40°38N 73°37W **97** C5
Oceanville *N.J., U.S.A.* 39°28N 74°28W **92** C2
Ochelata *Okla., U.S.A.* 36°36N 95°59W **107** B8
Ocheyedan *Iowa, U.S.A.* 43°25N 95°32W **81** B3
Ocheyedan Mound *Iowa, U.S.A.* 43°24N 95°31W **81** B3
Ochiltree County ☆ *Tex., U.S.A.* 36°10N 100°55W **108** A7
Ochlocknee *Ga., U.S.A.* 30°58N 84°3W **113** F2
Ochlockonee → *Fla., U.S.A.* 29°59N 84°26W **114** B4
Ochoco Mts. *Oreg., U.S.A.* 44°30N 120°35W **121** C5
Ochoco Nat. Forest *Oreg., U.S.A.* 44°20N 120°15W **121** C5
Ochopee *Fla., U.S.A.* 25°54N 81°18W **114** F7
Ochre River *Man., Canada* 51°4N 99°47W **151** D12
Ocilla *Ga., U.S.A.* 31°36N 83°15W **113** E3
Ocmulgee → *Ga., U.S.A.* 31°58N 82°33W **113** E4
Ocoee *Fla., U.S.A.* 28°34N 81°32W **115** A1
Ocoee *Tenn., U.S.A.* 35°7N 84°43W **105** E8
Ocoee → *Tenn., U.S.A.* 35°12N 84°39W **105** E8
Ocoee, L. *Tenn., U.S.A.* 35°6N 84°39W **105** E8
Oconee *Ill., U.S.A.* 39°17N 89°7W **84** D4
Oconee → *Ga., U.S.A.* 31°58N 82°33W **113** E4
Oconee, L. *Ga., U.S.A.* 33°28N 83°15W **113** C3
Oconee County ☆ *Ga., U.S.A.* 33°50N 83°25W **113** C3
Oconee County ☆ *S.C., U.S.A.* 34°45N 83°0W **103** D2
Oconee Nat. Forest *Ga., U.S.A.* 33°15N 83°45W **113** C3
Oconomowoc *Wis., U.S.A.* 43°7N 88°30W **78** E51
Oconto *Nebr., U.S.A.* 41°9N 99°46W **80** C6
Oconto *Wis., U.S.A.* 44°53N 87°52W **78** D6
Oconto → *Wis., U.S.A.* 44°53N 87°50W **78** D6
Oconto County ☆ *Wis., U.S.A.* 45°0N 88°15W **78** D5
Oconto Falls *Wis., U.S.A.* 44°52N 88°9W **78** D5
Ocosingo *Chiapas, Mexico* 16°53N 92°6W **178** C4
Ocotal *Nic.* 13°41N 86°31W **182** D2
Ocotlán *Jalisco, Mexico* 20°21N 102°46W **174** B5
Ocotlán *Oaxaca, Mexico* 16°48N 96°40W **177** H4
Ocoyucan *Puebla, Mexico* 18°59N 98°17W **177** F2
Ocozocoautla *Chiapas, Mexico* 16°46N 93°22W **178** C3
Ocracoke *N.C., U.S.A.* 35°7N 75°58W **103** C10
Ocracoke I. *N.C., U.S.A.* 35°10N 75°50W **103** C10
Octavia *Nebr., U.S.A.* 41°21N 97°4W **80** C8
Ocuiltzapotlán *Tabasco, Mexico* 18°8N 92°54W **178** C6
Ocumicho *Michoacan, Mexico* 19°46N 102°13W **174** C5
Odebolt *Iowa, U.S.A.* 42°19N 95°15W **81** C3
Odell *Ill., U.S.A.* 41°0N 88°31W **84** B5
Odell *Nebr., U.S.A.* 40°3N 96°48W **80** D9
Odell *Oreg., U.S.A.* 45°38N 121°32W **121** B4
Odell *Tex., U.S.A.* 34°21N 99°25W **109** C8
Odem *Tex., U.S.A.* 27°57N 97°35W **109** K10
Oden *Ark., U.S.A.* 34°37N 93°47W **106** D2
Odenton *Md., U.S.A.* 39°5N 76°42W **93** A4
Odessa *Ont., Canada* 44°17N 76°43W **147** C10
Odessa *Sask., Canada* 50°17N 103°47W **150** E8
Odessa *Del., U.S.A.* 39°27N 75°40W **93** A5
Odessa *Minn., U.S.A.* 45°16N 96°20W **77** E2
Odessa *Mo., U.S.A.* 39°0N 93°57W **83** C3
Odessa *N.Y., U.S.A.* 42°20N 76°47W **88** C4
Odessa *Tex., U.S.A.* 31°52N 102°23W **108** F5
Odessa *Wash., U.S.A.* 47°20N 118°41W **120** C7
Odin, Mt. *Nunavut, Canada* 66°33N 65°26W **158** D12
Odon *Ind., U.S.A.* 38°51N 86°59W **85** E4
O'Donnel *Tex., U.S.A.* 32°58N 101°50W **108** E6
Odum *Ga., U.S.A.* 31°40N 82°2W **113** E4
Oelrichs *S. Dak., U.S.A.* 43°11N 103°14W **76** G2
Oelwein *Iowa, U.S.A.* 42°41N 91°55W **81** C71
O'Fallon *Ill., U.S.A.* 38°49N 90°42W **83** G6
O'Fallon *Mark Mo., U.S.A.* 38°40N 90°13W **94** A2
Offerle *Kans., U.S.A.* 37°54N 99°33W **82** D4
Ofu *Amer. Samoa* 14°11S 169°41W **184** f
Ogahalla *Ont., Canada* 50°6N 85°51W **149** B11
Ogallah *Kans., U.S.A.* 38°59N 99°44W **82** C4
Ogallala *Nebr., U.S.A.* 41°8N 101°43W **80** C4
Ogascanan, L. *Qué., Canada* 47°5N 78°25W **144** D4
Ogden *Ark., U.S.A.* 33°35N 94°3W **106** E1
Ogden *Iowa, U.S.A.* 42°2N 94°2W **81** C4
Ogden *Kans., U.S.A.* 39°7N 96°43W **82** B7
Ogden *Utah, U.S.A.* 41°13N 111°58W **129** B4
Ogden Peak *Ill., U.S.A.* 41°46N 87°39W **95** C2
Ogdensburg *N.J., U.S.A.* 41°5N 74°36W **92** A2
Ogdensburg *N.Y., U.S.A.* 44°42N 75°30W **88** A5
Ogeechee → *Ga., U.S.A.* 31°50N 81°3W **113** E5
Ogema *Sask., Canada* 49°35N 104°55W **150** F7
Ogema *Wis., U.S.A.* 45°36N 90°13W **73** C8
Ogemaw *Ark., U.S.A.* 33°36N 93°18W **106** E2
Ogemaw County ☆ *Mich., U.S.A.* 44°15N 84°10W **79** E7
Ogilvie *Minn., U.S.A.* 45°50N 93°26W **77** E5
Ogilvie *Yukon, Canada* 65°51N 137°15W **156** C4
Ogilvie Mts. *N.W.T., Canada* 65°0N 140°0W **157** D5
Oglala *S. Dak., U.S.A.* 43°11N 102°44W **76** G3
Oglala Nat. Grassland *Nebr., U.S.A.* 42°55N 103°45W **80** B2
Ogle County ☆ *Ill., U.S.A.* 42°0N 89°20W **84** A4
Oglesby *Ill., U.S.A.* 41°18N 89°4W **84** B4
Oglesby *Tex., U.S.A.* 31°25N 97°30W **109** F10
Oglethorpe *Ga., U.S.A.* 32°18N 84°4W **113** D2
Oglethorpe County ☆ *Ga., U.S.A.* 33°50N 83°5W **113** C4
Ogoki *Ont., Canada* 51°38N 85°58W **149** A11
Ogoki → *Ont., Canada* 51°38N 85°57W **149** A11
Ogoki L. *Ont., Canada* 50°50N 87°10W **149** B9
Ogoki Res. *Ont., Canada* 50°45N 88°15W **148** B8
Ogontz *Maine, U.S.A.* 40°6N 75°6W **98** A2
Ogunquit *Maine, U.S.A.* 43°15N 70°36W **89** C4
O'Hare Int., Chicago ✈ (ORD) *Ill., U.S.A.* 41°59N 87°54W **95** B1

Ohatchee *Ala., U.S.A.* 33°47N 86°0W **112** C5
Ohio *Colo., U.S.A.* 38°34N 106°37W **125** D4
Ohio *Ill., U.S.A.* 41°34N 89°28W **84** B4
Ohio □ *U.S.A.* 40°15N 82°45W **86** C4
Ohio → *Ohio, U.S.A.* 36°59N 89°8W **104** D3
Ohio City *Ohio, U.S.A.* 40°46N 84°37W **86** C2
Ohio City *Ohio, U.S.A.* 41°29N 81°42W **98** B1
Ohio County ☆ *Ind., U.S.A.* 38°55N 85°0W **85** E6
Ohio County ☆ *Ky., U.S.A.* 37°30N 86°50W **104** C6
Ohio County ☆ *W. Va., U.S.A.* 40°6N 80°34W **102** A4
Ohio River Islands Nat. Wildlife Refuge △ *U.S.A.* 39°25N 81°12W **102** B3
Ohiopyle *Pa., U.S.A.* 39°52N 79°30W **93** A1
Ohiopyle State Park △ *Pa., U.S.A.* 39°50N 79°26W **93** A1
Ohioville *Pa., U.S.A.* 40°41N 80°30W **87** D2
Ohoopee → *Ga., U.S.A.* 31°54N 82°8W **113** E4
Oies, I. aux *Qué., Canada* 47°4N 70°33W **145** D12
Oil City *Calif., U.S.A.* 32°45N 93°58W **110** B2
Oil City *Pa., U.S.A.* 41°26N 79°42W **87** C3
Oil Springs *Ont., Canada* 42°47N 82°7W **146** E4
Oil Springs Indian Reservation N.Y., U.S.A. 42°14N 78°18W **88** C2
Oil Trough *Ark., U.S.A.* 35°38N 91°28W **106** C4
Oildale *Calif., U.S.A.* 35°25N 119°1W **127** H7
Oilmont *Mont., U.S.A.* 48°44N 111°51W **123** B6
Oilton *Okla., U.S.A.* 36°5N 96°35W **107** B7
Ojai *Calif., U.S.A.* 34°27N 119°15W **127** J7
Ojinaga *Chihuahua, Mexico* 29°34N 104°25W **169** D11
Ojo Caliente *Zacatecas, Mexico* 22°34N 102°15W **173** E8
Ojo Caliente *N. Mex., U.S.A.* 36°18N 106°3W **131** A4
Ojo de Agua de Palmillas *Sinaloa, Mexico* 22°37N 105°37W **172** E5
Ojo de Liebre, L. *Baja Calif. S., Mexico* 27°45N 114°15W **167** F4
Ojo del Carrizo *Chihuahua, Mexico* 29°58N 105°16W **169** D10
Ojo del Diablo, L. *Chihuahua, Mexico* 30°40N 106°55W **169** C9
Ojo Feliz *N. Mex., U.S.A.* 36°4N 105°7W **131** A5
Ojo Sarco *N. Mex., U.S.A.* 36°7N 105°47W **131** A5
Ojos Azules *Chihuahua, Mexico* 29°18N 106°46W **169** D9
Ojuelos de Jalisco *Jalisco, Mexico* 21°51N 101°35W **174** A6
Okabena *Minn., U.S.A.* 43°44N 95°19W **77** G3
Okak *Nfld. & L., Canada* 57°33N 61°54W **143** B5
Okak Is. *Nfld. & L., Canada* 57°30N 61°30W **143** B5
Okaloosa County ☆ *Fla., U.S.A.* 30°30N 86°40W **114** A2
Okanagan Falls *B.C., Canada* 49°21N 119°34W **155** F15
Okanagan L. *B.C., Canada* 50°0N 119°30W **155** F15
Okanagan Mountain Park △ *B.C., Canada* 49°45N 119°30W **155** F15
Okanogan *Wash., U.S.A.* 48°22N 119°35W **120** B6
Okanogan → *Wash., U.S.A.* 48°6N 119°44W **120** B6
Okanogan County ☆ *Wash., U.S.A.* 48°30N 120°0W **120** B6
Okanogan Nat. Forest *Wash., U.S.A.* 48°30N 120°10W **120** B5
Okarche *Okla., U.S.A.* 35°44N 97°58W **107** C6
Okatibbee L. *Miss., U.S.A.* 32°29N 88°48W **111** D5
Okaton *S. Dak., U.S.A.* 43°53N 100°53W **76** G5
Okay *Okla., U.S.A.* 35°51N 95°19W **107** C8
Okeechobee *Fla., U.S.A.* 27°15N 80°50W **114** D8
Okeechobee, L. *Fla., U.S.A.* 27°0N 80°50W **114** E8
Okeechobee County ☆ *Fla., U.S.A.* 27°30N 81°0W **114** D8
Okeene *Okla., U.S.A.* 36°7N 98°19W **107** B5
Okefenokee Nat. Wildlife Refuge △ *U.S.A.* 30°45N 82°18W **113** F4
Okefenokee Swamp *Ga., U.S.A.* 30°40N 82°20W **113** F4
Okemah *Okla., U.S.A.* 35°26N 96°19W **107** C7
Okemo Mt. *Vt., U.S.A.* 43°24N 72°45W **89** C2
Okemos *Mich., U.S.A.* 42°43N 84°26W **79** G2
Okfuskee County ☆ *Okla., U.S.A.* 35°25N 96°15W **107** C7
Oklahoma □ *U.S.A.* 35°20N 97°30W **107** C6
Oklahoma City ★ *U.S.A.* 35°30N 97°30W **107** C6
Oklahoma City Will Rogers ✈ (OKC) *Okla., U.S.A.* 35°24N 97°36W **107** C6
Oklahoma County ☆ *Okla., U.S.A.* 35°35N 97°20W **107** C6
Oklaunion *Tex., U.S.A.* 34°8N 99°9W **109** C8
Oklawaha → *Fla., U.S.A.* 29°28N 81°41W **114** B7
Oklawaha, L. *Fla., U.S.A.* 29°30N 81°45W **114** B7
Oklee *Minn., U.S.A.* 47°50N 95°51W **77** C3
Okmulgee *Okla., U.S.A.* 35°37N 95°58W **107** C8
Okmulgee County ☆ *Okla., U.S.A.* 35°40N 96°0W **107** C8
Okoboji *Iowa, U.S.A.* 43°23N 95°8W **81** B3
Okolona *Ark., U.S.A.* 34°0N 93°0W **106** E2
Okolona *Ky., U.S.A.* 38°8N 85°41W **105** B7
Okolona *Miss., U.S.A.* 34°0N 88°45W **111** B5
Oktaha *Okla., U.S.A.* 35°35N 95°29W **107** C8
Oktibbeha County ☆ *Miss., U.S.A.* 33°28N 88°49W **111** C5
Ola *Ark., U.S.A.* 35°2N 93°13W **106** C2
Ola *Idaho, U.S.A.* 44°11N 116°18W **122** E2
Olalla *Wash., U.S.A.* 47°25N 122°32W **132** D2
Olamon *Maine, U.S.A.* 45°7N 68°37W **90** C5
Olancha *Calif., U.S.A.* 36°17N 118°1W **127** G8
Olancha Pk. *Calif., U.S.A.* 36°16N 118°7W **127** G8
Olanchito *Honduras* 15°30N 86°30W **182** C2
Olanta *S.C., U.S.A.* 33°56N 79°56W **103** E6
Olathe *Colo., U.S.A.* 38°36N 107°59W **125** D3
Olathe *Kans., U.S.A.* 38°53N 94°49W **82** C7
Olberg *Ariz., U.S.A.* 32°58N 111°41W **130** D4
Old Bahama Chan. = Bahama, Canal Viejo de *W. Indies* 22°10N 77°30W **182** B4
Old Bridge *N.J., U.S.A.* 40°25N 74°22W **92** B2
Old City Hall *Ont., Canada* 43°39N 79°23W **161** B2
Old Crow *Yukon, Canada* 67°30N 139°55W **156** C5
Old Faithful *Wyo., U.S.A.* 44°28N 110°50W **124** B2
Old Fields *W. Va., U.S.A.* 39°8N 78°57W **93** A2
Old Forge *N.Y., U.S.A.* 43°43N 74°58W **88** B6
Old Forge *Pa., U.S.A.* 41°22N 75°45W **92** A1
Old Fort *N.C., U.S.A.* 35°38N 82°11W **103** C3
Old Fort York *Ont., Canada* 43°39N 79°24W **161** B2
Old Harbor *Alaska, U.S.A.* 57°12N 153°18W **135** H9
Old Harbour *Jamaica* 17°56N 77°6W **182** a
Old Hickory L. *Tenn., U.S.A.* 36°18N 86°40W **104** D6
Old Horse Springs *N. Mex., U.S.A.* 33°55N 108°14W **131** D2
Old Lyme *Conn., U.S.A.* 41°19N 72°20W **91** C2
Old Mines *Mo., U.S.A.* 38°1N 90°45W **83** C6
Old Monroe *Mo., U.S.A.* 38°56N 90°45W **83** A5
Old Ocean *Tex., U.S.A.* 29°5N 95°45W **109** H12
Old Orchard Beach *Maine, U.S.A.* 43°31N 70°23W **90** E3
Old Perlican *Nfld. & L., Canada* 48°5N 53°1W **142** D7
Old Saybrook *Conn., U.S.A.* 41°18N 72°23W **91** C2
Old Speck Mt. *Maine, U.S.A.* 44°34N 70°57W **90** D3
Old Tampa Bay *Tampa, U.S.A.* 27°54N 82°35W **115** B3
Old Tampa Bay Park *Tampa, U.S.A.* 28°1N 82°38W **115** A3
Old Tavern *La., U.S.A.* 38°50N 77°49W **93** B3
Old Town *Fla., U.S.A.* 29°36N 82°59W **114** B6
Old Town *Ill., U.S.A.* 41°58N 87°37W **95** B3
Old Town *Maine, U.S.A.* 44°56N 68°39W **90** D5

Old Washington *Ohio, U.S.A.* 40°2N 81°27W **86** C5
Old Wives I. *Sask., Canada* 50°5N 106°0W **150** E6
Old Woman Mts. *Calif., U.S.A.* 34°20N 115°0W **127** J11
Oldenburg *Ind., U.S.A.* 39°21N 85°12W **85** D5
Oldham *S. Dak., U.S.A.* 44°14N 97°19W **76** F8
Oldham County ☆ *Ky., U.S.A.* 38°25N 85°30W **105** B7
Oldham County ☆ *Tex., U.S.A.* 35°30N 102°30W **108** B5
Oldhams *Va., U.S.A.* 38°0N 76°40W **93** B4
Oldman → *Alta., Canada* 49°57N 111°42W **153** J9
Olds *Alta., Canada* 51°50N 114°10W **153** G6
Oldsmar *Fla., U.S.A.* 28°2N 82°39W **115** A3
Oldtown *Md., U.S.A.* 39°33N 78°37W **93** A2
Ole Romer Land *Greenland* 74°10N 24°30W **162** C8
Olean *Mo., U.S.A.* 38°25N 92°32W **83** C4
Olean *N.Y., U.S.A.* 42°5N 78°26W **88** C2
O'Leary *P.E.I., Canada* 46°42N 64°13W **141** G5
Olentangy → *Ohio, U.S.A.* 39°57N 77°10W **86** C3
Oleta River State Rec. Area *Fla., U.S.A.* 25°55N 80°8W **115** C3
Olex *Oreg., U.S.A.* 45°30N 120°11W **121** B5
Olga *La., U.S.A.* 49°47N 77°15W **143** D2
Olga, Mt. = Kata Tjuta *Australia* 49°13N 119°37W **155** F15
Oliver *B.C., Canada* 49°13N 119°37W **155** F15
Oliver *La., U.S.A.* 32°31N 81°32W **113** D5
Oliver County ☆ *N. Dak., U.S.A.* 47°2N 101°5W **76** C4
Oliver Springs *Tenn., U.S.A.* 36°3N 84°20W **105** D8
Olivet *Kans., U.S.A.* 38°29N 95°45W **82** C8
Olivet *Md., U.S.A.* 38°20N 76°26W **93** B4
Olivet *Mich., U.S.A.* 42°27N 84°56W **79** G2
Olivet *S. Dak., U.S.A.* 43°14N 97°40W **76** G8
Olivette *Mo., U.S.A.* 38°39N 90°22W **94** A1
Olivia *Minn., U.S.A.* 44°47N 94°59W **77** F4
Olivia *L., Fla., U.S.A.* 28°31N 81°31W **115** A1
Olla *La., U.S.A.* 31°54N 92°14W **110** C3
Ollie *Iowa, U.S.A.* 41°12N 92°6W **81** D6
Olmos Basin Park *Tex., U.S.A.* 29°29N 98°28W **116** B2
Olmos Park *Tex., U.S.A.* 29°28N 98°28W **116** C2
Olmstead *Ky., U.S.A.* 36°45N 87°1W **104** D5
Olmsted *Ill., U.S.A.* 37°11N 89°5W **84** F4
Olmsted County ☆ *Minn., U.S.A.* 44°0N 92°30W **77** G6
Olney *Ill., U.S.A.* 38°44N 88°5W **84** D5
Olney *Md., U.S.A.* 39°9N 77°4W **93** A3
Olney *Mont., U.S.A.* 48°33N 114°35W **123** B3
Olney *Tex., U.S.A.* 33°22N 98°45W **109** D9
Olney Springs *Colo., U.S.A.* 38°10N 103°57W **125** D7
Ololizqui, Volcan *Distrito Federal, Mexico* 19°14N 99°11W **181** C2
Olomane → *Qué., Canada* 50°14N 60°37W **143** C5
Olomatlán *Puebla, Mexico* 17°57N 98°15W **177** G2
Olosega *Amer. Samoa* 14°10S 169°37W **184** f
Olowalu *Hawai'i, U.S.A.* 20°49N 156°38W **136** C5
Olpe *Kans., U.S.A.* 38°16N 96°10W **82** C7
Olsburg *Kans., U.S.A.* 39°26N 96°37W **82** B7
Olson, L. *Minn., U.S.A.* 45°1N 92°56W **94** A4
Olton *Tex., U.S.A.* 34°11N 102°8W **108** C5
Olustee *Fla., U.S.A.* 30°12N 82°26W **114** A6
Olustee *Okla., U.S.A.* 34°33N 99°25W **107** D4
Olympia *Wash., U.S.A.* 47°3N 122°53W **120** C3
Olympia, L. *Calif., U.S.A.* 28°34N 81°31W **115** A1
Olympian Village *Mo., U.S.A.* 38°8N 90°27W **83** C6
Olympic Mts. *Wash., U.S.A.* 47°55N 123°45W **120** C2
Olympic Nat. Forest *Wash., U.S.A.* 47°25N 123°35W **120** C2
Olympic Nat. Park △ *Wash., U.S.A.* 48°16N 124°40W **120** B1
Olympic Stadium = Turner Field *Georgia, U.S.A.* 33°44N 84°23W **117** B2
Olympique, Stade *Qué., Canada* 45°33N 73°33W **160** A3
Olympus, Mt. *Utah, U.S.A.* 40°39N 111°46W **134** C3
Olympus, Mt. *Wash., U.S.A.* 47°48N 123°43W **120** C2
Omaha *Ark., U.S.A.* 36°27N 93°11W **106** B2
Omaha *Nebr., U.S.A.* 41°17N 95°58W **80** C10
Omaha *Tex., U.S.A.* 33°11N 94°45W **109** D13
Omaha Eppley Airfield ✈ (OMA) *Nebr., U.S.A.* 41°18N 95°53W **80** C10
Omaha Indian Reservation *Nebr., U.S.A.* 42°0N 96°30W **80** B9
Omak *Wash., U.S.A.* 48°25N 119°31W **120** B6
Omak L. *Wash., U.S.A.* 48°17N 119°24W **120** B6
Omak Mt. *Wash., U.S.A.* 48°17N 119°18W **120** B6
Omega *Ga., U.S.A.* 31°21N 83°36W **113** E3
Omemee *Ont., Canada* 44°18N 78°33W **147** C8
Omemee *N. Dak., U.S.A.* 48°42N 100°22W **76** B5
Omer *Mich., U.S.A.* 44°3N 83°51W **79** E8
Ometepe, I. de *Nic.* 11°32N 85°35W **182** D2
Ometepec *Guerrero, Mexico* 16°41N 98°25W **175** F9
Omineca *B.C., Canada* 56°3N 124°16W **157** E8
Omineca Mts. *B.C., Canada* 56°30N 125°30W **157** E7
Omitlán → *Guerrero, Mexico* 16°59N 99°56W **175** F9
Ommaney, C. *Alaska, U.S.A.* 56°10N 134°40W **135** H14
Ommanney B. *N.W.T., Canada* 73°0N 101°0W **158** C5
Ompompanoosuc → *Vt., U.S.A.* 43°45N 72°14W **89** C2
Omps → *Va., U.S.A.* 39°30N 78°17W **93** A2
Omro *Wis., U.S.A.* 44°2N 88°45W **78** D5
Ona *Wis., U.S.A.* 27°29N 81°55W **114** D7
Onaga *Kans., U.S.A.* 39°29N 96°10W **82** B7
Onaka *S. Dak., U.S.A.* 45°11N 99°28W **76** E6
Onakawana *Ont., Canada* 50°36N 81°27W **149** B15
Onalaska *Wis., U.S.A.* 43°53N 91°14W **78** E21
Onaman *Ont., Canada* 49°59N 88°0W **149** C9
Onaman L. *Ont., Canada* 50°0N 87°26W **149** C9
Onamia *Minn., U.S.A.* 46°4N 93°40W **77** E5
Onancock *Va., U.S.A.* 37°43N 75°45W **102** D9
Onanole *Man., Canada* 50°37N 99°58W **151** E12
Onaping *Ont., Canada* 46°37N 81°18W **146** A5
Onaping → *Ont., Canada* 46°37N 81°18W **146** A5
Onaping L. *Ont., Canada* 47°3N 81°30W **149** E15
Onarga *Ill., U.S.A.* 40°43N 88°1W **84** C5
Onatchiway, L. *Qué., Canada* 49°3N 71°5W **145** B11
Onavas *Sonora, Mexico* 28°31N 109°35W **168** E6
Onawa *Iowa, U.S.A.* 42°2N 96°6W **81** C2
Onaway *Idaho, U.S.A.* 46°56N 116°53W **122** D2
Onaway *Mich., U.S.A.* 45°21N 84°14W **79** D7
Oneco *Fla., U.S.A.* 27°25N 82°31W **114** D6
Oneida *Ill., U.S.A.* 41°4N 90°13W **84** B3
Oneida *Iowa, U.S.A.* 42°23N 91°21W **81** C7
Oneida *Kans., U.S.A.* 39°52N 95°56W **82** B8
Oneida *N.Y., U.S.A.* 43°6N 75°39W **88** B5
Oneida *Tenn., U.S.A.* 36°30N 84°31W **105** D8
Oneida County ☆ *Idaho, U.S.A.* 42°10N 112°30W **122** G6
Oneida County ☆ *N.Y., U.S.A.* 43°20N 75°30W **88** B5

Oneida County ☆ *Wis., U.S.A.* 45°40N 89°35W **78** C4
Oneida Indian Reservation *N.Y., U.S.A.* 43°1N 75°38W **88** B5
Oneida Indian Reservation *Wis., U.S.A.* 43°12N 88°10W **78** D5
Oneida L. *N.Y., U.S.A.* 43°13N 75°54W **88** B5
O'Neill *Nebr., U.S.A.* 42°27N 98°39W **80** B7
Onekama *Mich., U.S.A.* 44°22N 86°12W **79** E5
Oneonta *Ala., U.S.A.* 33°57N 86°28W **112** C4
Oneonta *N.Y., U.S.A.* 42°27N 75°4W **88** C5
Onida *S. Dak., U.S.A.* 44°42N 100°4W **76** F5
Onion Lake *Sask., Canada* 53°43N 110°0W **150** B2
Onley *Va., U.S.A.* 37°41N 75°43W **102** D9
Ono *Calif., U.S.A.* 40°29N 122°37W **126** C4
Onondaga County ☆ *N.Y., U.S.A.* 43°0N 76°15W **88** B4
Onondaga Indian Reservation *N.Y., U.S.A.* 42°55N 76°10W **88** C4
Onoway *Alta., Canada* 53°42N 114°12W **152** E6
Onset *Mass., U.S.A.* 41°45N 70°39W **91** B6
Onslow *Iowa, U.S.A.* 42°6N 91°1W **81** C7
Onslow B. *N.C., U.S.A.* 34°20N 77°15W **103** D8
Onslow County ☆ *N.C., U.S.A.* 34°50N 77°30W **103** D8
Ontario *Calif., U.S.A.* 34°4N 117°39W **127** J9
Ontario *Oreg., U.S.A.* 44°2N 116°58W **121** C10
Ontario *Wis., U.S.A.* 43°45N 90°35W **78** E3
Ontario □ *Canada* 48°0N 83°0W **148** B6
Ontario, L. *N. Amer.* 43°20N 78°0W **147** C7
Ontario County ☆ *N.Y., U.S.A.* 42°50N 77°20W **88** C3
Ontario Int. ✈ (ONT) *Calif., U.S.A.* 34°3N 117°36W **127** J9
Ontario Science Centre *Ont., Canada* 43°43N 79°20W **161** A2
Ontonagon *Mich., U.S.A.* 46°52N 89°19W **79** C2
Ontonagon → *Mich., U.S.A.* 46°40N 89°25W **79** C2
Ontonagon Indian Reservation *Mich., U.S.A.* 46°29N 89°6W **79** C2
'Ō'ōkala *Hawai'i, U.S.A.* 20°1N 155°17W **136** D6
Oolitic *Ind., U.S.A.* 38°54N 86°31W **85** E4
Oologah *Okla., U.S.A.* 36°27N 95°43W **107** B8
Oologah L. *Okla., U.S.A.* 36°26N 95°41W **107** B8
Oona River *B.C., Canada* 53°57N 130°16W **154** B4
Oostburg *Wis., U.S.A.* 43°37N 87°48W **78** E6
Ootsa L. *B.C., Canada* 53°50N 126°2W **154** C4
Ootsa Lake *B.C., Canada* 53°50N 126°5W **154** C4
Opa-Locka *Fla., U.S.A.* 25°54N 80°15W **115** C1
Opa-Locka ✈ (OPF) *Fla., U.S.A.* 25°54N 80°16W **115** C1
Opal *Wyo., U.S.A.* 41°46N 110°20W **124** C2
Opasatika, L. *Qué., Canada* 48°5N 79°18W **144** C3
Opasatika *Ont., Canada* 49°30N 82°50W **149** C14
Opasatika → *Ont., Canada* 50°25N 82°25W **149** B14
Opasatika L. *Ont., Canada* 49°4N 83°6W **149** C13
Opataca, L. *Qué., Canada* 50°22N 74°54W **144** A8
Opawica → *Qué., Canada* 49°35N 75°55W **144** B7
Opelika *Ala., U.S.A.* 32°39N 85°23W **112** D5
Opelousas *La., U.S.A.* 30°32N 92°5W **110** D3
Opémisca, L. *Qué., Canada* 49°56N 74°52W **143** D3
Opeongo L. *Ont., Canada* 45°42N 78°23W **147** B8
Opequon → *W. Va., U.S.A.* 39°31N 77°52W **93** A3
Opheim *Mont., U.S.A.* 48°51N 106°24W **123** B11
Ophir *Alaska, U.S.A.* 63°10N 156°31W **135** E9
Ophir *Oreg., U.S.A.* 42°34N 124°23W **121** E1
Opichén *Yucatán, Mexico* 20°33N 89°51W **179** B4
Opihikao *Hawai'i, U.S.A.* 19°26N 154°53W **136** D7
Opinaca → *Qué., Canada* 52°15N 78°2W **143** C2
Opinaca, Rés. *Qué., Canada* 52°39N 76°20W **143** C2
Opiscotéo, L. *Qué., Canada* 53°10N 68°10W **143** C4
Opocopa, L. *Qué., Canada* 52°38N 66°58W **143** C4
Opodepe *Sonora, Mexico* 29°55N 110°39W **168** D5
Opopeo *Michoacan, Mexico* 19°25N 101°37W **174** C6
Opp *Ala., U.S.A.* 31°17N 86°16W **112** E4
Opportunity *Mont., U.S.A.* 46°6N 112°50W **123** D5
Opportunity *Wash., U.S.A.* 47°39N 117°15W **120** C8
Optima *Okla., U.S.A.* 36°46N 101°21W **107** B2
Optima L. *Okla., U.S.A.* 36°40N 101°8W **107** B2
Optima Nat. Wildlife Refuge △ *Okla., U.S.A.* 36°48N 101°19W **107** B2
Oquawka *Ill., U.S.A.* 40°56N 90°57W **84** C3
Oquirrh *Utah, U.S.A.* 40°37N 112°11W **134** C1
Oquitoa *Sonora, Mexico* 30°44N 111°41W **168** C4
Quossoc *Maine, U.S.A.* 44°58N 70°46W **89** B4
Oracle *Ariz., U.S.A.* 32°37N 110°46W **130** E5
Oran *Mo., U.S.A.* 37°5N 89°39W **83** D7
Orange *Calif., U.S.A.* 33°47N 117°51W **127** K9
Orange *Conn., U.S.A.* 41°17N 73°2W **91** C1
Orange *Mass., U.S.A.* 42°35N 72°19W **91** B3
Orange *N.J., U.S.A.* 40°46N 74°13W **97** B1
Orange *Tex., U.S.A.* 30°6N 93°44W **109** G14
Orange *Va., U.S.A.* 38°15N 78°7W **102** C6
Orange Beach *Ala., U.S.A.* 30°18N 87°34W **112** F3
Orange Bowl Stadium *Fla., U.S.A.* 25°46N 80°14W **115** C2
Orange City *Fla., U.S.A.* 28°57N 81°18W **114** C7
Orange City *Iowa, U.S.A.* 43°0N 96°4W **81** B2
Orange County ☆ *Calif., U.S.A.* 33°30N 117°45W **127** K9
Orange County ☆ *Fla., U.S.A.* 28°30N 81°15W **114** C7
Orange County ☆ *Ind., U.S.A.* 38°30N 86°30W **85** E4
Orange County ☆ *N.C., U.S.A.* 36°0N 79°10W **103** B6
Orange County ☆ *N.Y., U.S.A.* 41°20N 74°15W **88** D6
Orange County ☆ *Tex., U.S.A.* 30°12N 93°52W **109** G14
Orange County ☆ *Va., U.S.A.* 38°15N 78°7W **102** C6
Orange County ☆ *Vt., U.S.A.* 44°0N 72°20W **89** B2
Orange Cove *Calif., U.S.A.* 36°38N 119°19W **127** G7
Orange Grove *Tex., U.S.A.* 27°58N 97°56W **109** K10
Orange L. *Fla., U.S.A.* 29°25N 82°13W **114** B6
Orange Park *Fla., U.S.A.* 30°10N 81°42W **114** A7
Orange Res. *N.J., U.S.A.* 40°45N 74°17W **97** B1
Orangeburg *S.C., U.S.A.* 33°30N 80°52W **103** E5
Orangeburg County ☆ *S.C., U.S.A.* 33°20N 80°30W **103** E5
Orangevale *Calif., U.S.A.* 38°41N 121°13W **126** E5
Orangeville *Ont., Canada* 43°55N 80°5W **146** D6
Orangeville *Pa., U.S.A.* 41°5N 76°25W **87** C6
Orangeville *Utah, U.S.A.* 39°14N 111°3W **129** D4
Oranjestad *Aruba* 12°32N 70°2W **183** D5
Orbisonia *Pa., U.S.A.* 40°15N 77°54W **87** D5
Orcas I. *Wash., U.S.A.* 48°42N 122°56W **120** B3
Orchard *Colo., U.S.A.* 40°20N 104°7W **125** B6
Orchard *Idaho, U.S.A.* 43°19N 116°2W **122** F2
Orchard *Iowa, U.S.A.* 43°14N 92°47W **81** B6
Orchard *Nebr., U.S.A.* 42°20N 98°15W **80** B7
Orchard City *Colo., U.S.A.* 38°50N 107°58W **125** D3
Orchard Homes *Mont., U.S.A.* 46°55N 114°4W **123** D3
Orchard Mesa *Colo., U.S.A.* 39°3N 108°33W **125** C2
Orchard Park *N.Y., U.S.A.* 42°46N 78°45W **88** C2
Orchard Valley *Wyo., U.S.A.* 41°6N 104°49W **124** E8
Orchards *Wash., U.S.A.* 45°40N 122°33W **132** C5
Orchila, I. *Venezuela* 11°48N 66°10W **183** D6
Orcutt *Calif., U.S.A.* 34°52N 120°27W **127** J6
Ord *Nebr., U.S.A.* 41°36N 98°56W **80** C7
Ord, Mt. *Tex., U.S.A.* 30°18N 103°30W **108** G4

Ord Mts. *Calif., U.S.A.* 34°39N 116°45W **127** J10
Orderville *Utah, U.S.A.* 37°17N 112°38W **129** F3
Ordway *Colo., U.S.A.* 38°13N 103°46W **125** D7
Oreana *Idaho, U.S.A.* 43°3N 116°24W **122** F2
Oreana *Ill., U.S.A.* 39°56N 88°52W **84** D5
Oreana *Nev., U.S.A.* 40°20N 118°19W **128** B2
Oregon *Ill., U.S.A.* 42°1N 89°20W **84** A41
Oregon *Mo., U.S.A.* 39°59N 95°9W **83** B1
Oregon *Ohio, U.S.A.* 41°38N 83°25W **86** B3
Oregon *Wis., U.S.A.* 42°56N 89°23W **78** F4
Oregon □ *U.S.A.* 44°0N 121°0W **121** D4
Oregon Butte *Idaho, U.S.A.* 45°31N 115°40W **122** D3
Oregon Butte *Wash., U.S.A.* 46°7N 117°41W **120** D8
Oregon Caves Nat. Monument △ *Oreg., U.S.A.* 42°6N 123°24W **121** E2
Oregon City *Oreg., U.S.A.* 45°21N 122°36W **121** B3
Oregon County ☆ *Mo., U.S.A.* 36°40N 91°25W **83** E5
Oregon Dunes Nat. Recr. Area △ *Oreg., U.S.A.* 43°40N 124°10W **121** D1
Oreland *Pa., U.S.A.* 40°7N 75°10W **98** A1
Orem *Utah, U.S.A.* 40°19N 111°42W **129** C4
Orestes Pereyra *Durango, Mexico* 26°30N 105°39W **172** A5
Organ *N. Mex., U.S.A.* 32°26N 106°36W **131** E4
Organ Pipe Cactus Nat. Monument △ *Ariz., U.S.A.* 32°0N 112°52W **130** E3
Organos, Pta. los *Michoacan, Mexico* 17°50N 101°45W **174** E6
Orick *Calif., U.S.A.* 41°17N 124°4W **126** B2
Orient *Iowa, U.S.A.* 41°12N 94°25W **81** D4
Orient *Maine, U.S.A.* 45°49N 67°50W **90** C6
Orient *N.Y., U.S.A.* 41°8N 72°18W **91** C2
Orient *S. Dak., U.S.A.* 44°54N 99°5W **76** F6
Orient *Wash., U.S.A.* 48°52N 118°12W **120** B7
Orient Heights *Mass., U.S.A.* 42°23N 70°59W **96** A3
Oriental *Puebla, Mexico* 19°22N 97°37W **176** E3
Oriental *N.C., U.S.A.* 35°2N 76°42W **103** C9
Orillia *Ont., Canada* 44°40N 79°24W **146** C7
Orin *Wyo., U.S.A.* 42°39N 105°12W **124** D7
Orinda *Calif., U.S.A.* 37°52N 122°10W **126** F4
Orion *Ala., U.S.A.* 31°58N 86°0W **112** E5
Orion *Ill., U.S.A.* 41°21N 90°23W **84** B3
Orion *Okla., U.S.A.* 36°13N 98°47W **107** B5
Oriska *N. Dak., U.S.A.* 46°56N 97°47W **76** D8
Oriskany *N.Y., U.S.A.* 43°10N 75°20W **88** B5
Orizaba *Veracruz, Mexico* 18°51N 97°6W **177** F3
Orizaba, Pico de *Veracruz, Mexico* 18°58N 97°15W **177** F3
Orla *Tex., U.S.A.* 31°50N 103°55W **108** F4
Orland *Calif., U.S.A.* 39°45N 122°12W **126** D4
Orland Park *Ill., U.S.A.* 41°38N 87°52W **84** B6
Orlando *Fla., U.S.A.* 28°32N 81°22W **115** A2
Orlando *Okla., U.S.A.* 36°9N 97°23W **107** B6
Orlando Executive ✈ *Fla., U.S.A.* 28°32N 81°20W **115** A2
Orlando Int. ✈ (MCO) *Fla., U.S.A.* 28°26N 81°19W **115** B3
Orlean *Va., U.S.A.* 38°45N 77°58W **93** B3
Orleans *Calif., U.S.A.* 41°18N 123°32W **126** B3
Orleans *Ind., U.S.A.* 38°40N 86°27W **85** E4
Orleans *Iowa, U.S.A.* 43°27N 95°6W **81** B3
Orleans *Mass., U.S.A.* 41°47N 69°59W **91** C5
Orleans *Nebr., U.S.A.* 40°8N 99°27W **80** D6
Orleans *Vt., U.S.A.* 44°49N 72°12W **89** B2
Orléans, Î. d' *Qué., Canada* 46°54N 70°58W **145** E12
Orleans County ☆ *N.Y., U.S.A.* 43°15N 78°10W **88** B2
Orleans County ☆ *Vt., U.S.A.* 44°45N 72°15W **89** B2
Orleans Parish ☆ *La., U.S.A.* 29°58N 90°4W **110** E5
Orlinda *Tenn., U.S.A.* 36°36N 86°43W **104** D6
Orlovista *Fla., U.S.A.* 28°32N 81°27W **115** A2
Ormiston *Sask., Canada* 49°44N 105°24W **150** F6
Ormond Beach *Fla., U.S.A.* 29°17N 81°3W **114** B7
Ormond-by-the-Sea *Fla., U.S.A.* 29°21N 81°4W **114** B7
Ormsby *Minn., U.S.A.* 43°51N 94°42W **77** G4
Ormstown *Qué., Canada* 45°8N 74°0W **145** F9
Oro Grande *Calif., U.S.A.* 34°36N 117°20W **127** J9
Oro Valley *Ariz., U.S.A.* 32°26N 110°58W **130** D6
Orofino *Idaho, U.S.A.* 46°29N 116°15W **122** C2
Orogrande *Idaho, U.S.A.* 45°42N 115°33W **122** D3
Orogrande *N. Mex., U.S.A.* 32°24N 106°5W **131** E4
Oromocto *N.B., Canada* 45°54N 66°29W **141** H3
Oromocto L. *N.B., Canada* 45°36N 67°0W **141** H3
Orono *Ont., Canada* 43°59N 78°37W **147** D8
Orono *Maine, U.S.A.* 44°53N 68°40W **90** D5
Oronoco *Minn., U.S.A.* 44°10N 92°32W **77** F6
Orote Pen. *Guam* 13°26N 144°38E **184** b
Orovada *Nev., U.S.A.* 41°34N 117°47W **128** A3
Oroville *Calif., U.S.A.* 39°31N 121°33W **126** D5
Oroville *Wash., U.S.A.* 48°56N 119°26W **120** B6
Oroville, L. *Calif., U.S.A.* 39°33N 121°29W **126** D5
Oroville Dam *Calif., U.S.A.* 39°33N 121°29W **126** D5
Orpha *Wyo., U.S.A.* 42°51N 105°30W **124** D7
Orr *Minn., U.S.A.* 48°3N 92°50W **77** B6
Orr *Okla., U.S.A.* 34°2N 97°32W **107** D6
Orrick *Mo., U.S.A.* 39°13N 94°7W **83** B2
Orrin *N. Dak., U.S.A.* 48°6N 100°10W **76** B5
Orrville *Ala., U.S.A.* 32°19N 87°15W **112** D4
Orrville *Ohio, U.S.A.* 40°50N 81°46W **86** C5
Orting *Wash., U.S.A.* 47°6N 122°12W **120** C3
Ortiz *Sonora, Mexico* 28°17N 110°43W **168** E5
Ortley *S. Dak., U.S.A.* 45°20N 97°12W **76** E8
Ortonville *Minn., U.S.A.* 45°19N 96°27W **77** E2
Orwell *Ohio, U.S.A.* 41°32N 80°52W **86** B6
Osa, Pen. de *Costa Rica* 8°0N 84°0W **182** E3
Osage *Ark., U.S.A.* 36°11N 93°24W **106** B2
Osage *Iowa, U.S.A.* 43°17N 92°49W **81** B61
Osage *Okla., U.S.A.* 36°19N 96°24W **107** B7
Osage *W. Va., U.S.A.* 39°39N 80°1W **102** B4
Osage *Wyo., U.S.A.* 43°59N 104°25W **124** C8
Osage ➜ *Mo., U.S.A.* 38°36N 91°57W **83** C51
Osage Beach *Mo., U.S.A.* 38°9N 92°37W **83** C4
Osage City *Kans., U.S.A.* 38°38N 95°50W **82** C8
Osage County ☆ *Kans., U.S.A.* 38°40N 95°40W **82** C8
Osage County ☆ *Mo., U.S.A.* 38°30N 91°45W **83** C5
Osage County ☆ *Okla., U.S.A.* 36°40N 96°30W **107** B7
Osage Fork ➜ *Mo., U.S.A.* 37°46N 92°26W **83** D4
Osage Indian Reservation *Okla., U.S.A.* 36°35N 96°20W **107** B7
Osakis *Minn., U.S.A.* 45°52N 95°9W **77** E3
Osakis, L. *Minn., U.S.A.* 45°54N 95°7W **77** E3
Osawatomie *Kans., U.S.A.* 38°31N 94°57W **82** C9
Osawin ➜ *Ont., Canada* 49°45N 85°19W **149** C11
Osborne *Kans., U.S.A.* 39°26N 98°42W **82** B5
Osborne County ☆ *Kans., U.S.A.* 39°30N 98°45W **82** B5
Osburn *Idaho, U.S.A.* 47°30N 115°59W **122** B3
Oscar Soto Maynes *Chihuahua, Mexico* 29°3N 107°28W **169** D8
Osceola *Ark., U.S.A.* 35°42N 89°58W **106** C6
Osceola *Iowa, U.S.A.* 41°2N 93°46W **81** D5
Osceola *Mo., U.S.A.* 38°3N 93°42W **83** C3

Osceola *Nebr., U.S.A.* 41°11N 97°33W **80** C8
Osceola *Wis., U.S.A.* 45°19N 92°42W **78** C1
Osceola County ☆ *Fla., U.S.A.* 28°0N 81°0W **114** C7
Osceola County ☆ *Iowa, U.S.A.* 43°20N 95°35W **81** B3
Osceola County ☆ *Mich., U.S.A.* 44°0N 85°20W **79** F6
Osceola Mills *Pa., U.S.A.* 40°51N 78°16W **87** D4
Osceola Nat. Forest *Fla., U.S.A.* 30°20N 82°30W **114** A6
Oscoda *Mich., U.S.A.* 44°26N 83°20W **79** E7
Oscoda County ☆ *Mich., U.S.A.* 44°40N 84°0W **79** E7
Oscuro *N. Mex., U.S.A.* 33°29N 106°33W **131** D4
Osgood *Ind., U.S.A.* 39°8N 85°18W **85** D5
Osgood *Ohio, U.S.A.* 40°20N 84°30W **86** C2
Osgood Mts. *Nev., U.S.A.* 41°10N 117°20W **128** A3
Osgoode *Ont., Canada* 45°8N 75°36W **147** B11
Oshawa *Ont., Canada* 43°50N 78°50W **147** D8
Oshkosh *Nebr., U.S.A.* 41°24N 102°21W **80** C3
Oshkosh *Wis., U.S.A.* 44°1N 88°33W **78** D1
Osierfield *Ga., U.S.A.* 31°40N 83°7W **113** E3
Oskaloosa *Iowa, U.S.A.* 41°18N 92°39W **81** D6
Oskaloosa *Kans., U.S.A.* 39°13N 95°19W **82** B8
Oskélanéo *Qué., Canada* 48°5N 75°15W **144** C7
Osler *Sask., Canada* 52°22N 106°33W **150** C5
Oslo *Minn., U.S.A.* 48°12N 97°8W **77** B1
Osmond *Nebr., U.S.A.* 42°22N 97°36W **80** B8
Osnabrock *N. Dak., U.S.A.* 48°40N 98°9W **76** B7
Osnaburgh House *Ont., Canada* 51°14N 90°14W **148** A6
Osnaburgh L. *Ont., Canada* 51°12N 90°9W **148** A6
Osoyoos *B.C., Canada* 49°0N 119°30W **155** F15
Osoyoos L. *B.C., Canada* 49°0N 119°27W **155** G15
Osprey *Fla., U.S.A.* 27°12N 82°29W **114** D6
Ossabaw I. *Ga., U.S.A.* 31°50N 81°5W **113** E5
Ossabaw Sd. *Ga., U.S.A.* 31°50N 81°6W **113** E5
Osseo *Minn., U.S.A.* 41°53N 84°33W **79** H7
Osseo *Wis., U.S.A.* 44°35N 91°13W **78** D2
Ossian *Ind., U.S.A.* 40°53N 85°1W **85** C5
Ossian *Iowa, U.S.A.* 43°9N 91°43W **81** B7
Ossineke *Mich., U.S.A.* 44°55N 83°26W **79** E8
Ossining *N.Y., U.S.A.* 41°10N 73°55W **92** A3
Ossipee *N.H., U.S.A.* 43°41N 71°7W **89** C3
Ossipee L. *N.H., U.S.A.* 43°42N 71°11W **89** C3
Ossokmanuan L. *Nfld. & L., Canada* 53°25N 65°0W **143** C5
Ostaboningue, L. *Qué., Canada* 47°9N 78°53W **144** D4
Ostego L. *Mich., U.S.A.* 44°55N 84°42W **79** E7
Osterville *Mass., U.S.A.* 41°38N 70°22W **91** C4
Østgrønland = Tunu □ *Greenland* 75°0N 30°0W **162** C7
Ostión, L. *Veracruz, Mexico* 18°11N 94°38W **177** F6
Ostrander *Minn., U.S.A.* 43°37N 92°26W **77** G6
Ostuacán *Chiapas, Mexico* 17°22N 93°18W **150** C5
O'Sullivan Dam *Wash., U.S.A.* 46°59N 119°16W **120** D6
O'Sullivan L. *Ont., Canada* 50°25N 87°2W **149** B9
Oswegatchie ➜ *N.Y., U.S.A.* 44°42N 75°30W **88** A5
Oswego *Ill., U.S.A.* 41°41N 88°21W **84** B5
Oswego *Kans., U.S.A.* 37°10N 95°6W **82** D8
Oswego *N.Y., U.S.A.* 43°27N 76°31W **88** B4
Oswego *N.Y., U.S.A.* 43°27N 76°30W **88** B4
Oswego, L. *Oreg., U.S.A.* 45°25N 122°40W **132** B1
Oswego County ☆ *N.Y., U.S.A.* 43°25N 76°10W **88** B4
Osyka *Miss., U.S.A.* 31°0N 90°28W **111** E3
Otáez *Durango, Mexico* 24°42N 106°0W **172** C5
Otatlán ➜ *Guerrero, Mexico* 17°59N 100°5W **175** E7
Otay Mesa *Calif., U.S.A.* 32°40N 117°3W **133** C2
Otego *N.Y., U.S.A.* 42°24N 75°10W **88** C5
Otelnuk, L. *Qué., Canada* 56°9N 68°12W **143** B4
Otero County ☆ *Colo., U.S.A.* 38°0N 103°45W **125** E7
Otero County ☆ *N. Mex., U.S.A.* 32°30N 105°45W **131** E5
Oteros ➜ *Chihuahua, Mexico* 27°29N 108°30W **168** F7
Othello *Wash., U.S.A.* 46°50N 119°10W **120** D6
Otho *Iowa, U.S.A.* 42°25N 94°9W **81** C4
Othón P. Blanco *Quintana Roo, Mexico* 19°35N 89°4W **179** C4
Otinapa *Durango, Mexico* 24°1N 105°2W **172** C5
Otis *Colo., U.S.A.* 40°9N 102°58W **125** B8
Otis *Kans., U.S.A.* 38°32N 99°3W **82** C4
Otis *Mass., U.S.A.* 42°12N 73°6W **91** B1
Otish, Mts. *Qué., Canada* 52°22N 70°30W **143** C3
Otisville *Mich., U.S.A.* 43°10N 83°31W **79** F8
Otisville *N.Y., U.S.A.* 41°28N 74°32W **92** A2
Oto *Iowa, U.S.A.* 42°17N 95°54W **81** C3
Otoe *Nebr., U.S.A.* 40°43N 96°7W **80** D9
Otoe County ☆ *Nebr., U.S.A.* 40°40N 96°0W **80** D9
Otongo *Hidalgo, Mexico* 20°58N 98°45W **175** B9
Otosquen *Sask., Canada* 53°17N 102°1W **151** B9
Otsego *Mich., U.S.A.* 42°27N 85°42W **79** G6
Otsego County ☆ *Mich., U.S.A.* 45°0N 84°40W **79** D7
Otsego County ☆ *N.Y., U.S.A.* 42°40N 75°0W **88** C5
Otsego L. *N.Y., U.S.A.* 42°45N 74°52W **88** C6
Ottawa = Outaouais ➜ *Qué., Canada* 45°27N 74°8W **145** E8
Ottawa *Ill., U.S.A.* 41°21N 88°51W **84** B5
Ottawa *Kans., U.S.A.* 38°37N 95°16W **82** C8
Ottawa *Ohio, U.S.A.* 41°1N 84°3W **86** B2
Ottawa County ☆ *Kans., U.S.A.* 39°15N 97°45W **82** B6
Ottawa County ☆ *Mich., U.S.A.* 42°50N 86°0W **79** G6
Ottawa County ☆ *Ohio, U.S.A.* 41°30N 83°9W **86** B3
Ottawa County ☆ *Okla., U.S.A.* 36°50N 94°50W **107** B9
Ottawa Is. *N.W.T., Canada* 59°35N 80°10W **143** B1
Ottawa McDonald Cartier Int. ✈ (YOW) *Ont., Canada* 45°19N 75°40W **147** B11
Ottawa Nat. Forest *Mich., U.S.A.* 46°30N 89°30W **79** C2
Ottawa Nat. Wildlife Refuge △ *Ohio, U.S.A.* 41°36N 83°13W **86** B3
Otter *Mont., U.S.A.* 45°12N 106°12W **123** E11
Otter Cr. ➜ *Utah, U.S.A.* 38°10N 112°2W **129** E3
Otter Cr. ➜ *Vt., U.S.A.* 44°13N 73°17W **89** B1
Otter Creek *Fla., U.S.A.* 29°19N 82°46W **114** B6
Otter Creek Res. *Utah, U.S.A.* 38°10N 112°1W **129** E3
Otter Lake *Ill., U.S.A.* 39°28N 89°56W **84** D4
Otter Lake *Mich., U.S.A.* 43°13N 83°28W **79** F8
Otter Rapids *Ont., Canada* 50°11N 81°39W **149** B15
Otter Tail ➜ *Minn., U.S.A.* 46°16N 96°36W **77** D2
Otter Tail County ☆ *Minn., U.S.A.* 46°20N 95°45W **77** D3
Otter Tail L. *Minn., U.S.A.* 46°24N 95°40W **77** D3
Otterbein *Ind., U.S.A.* 40°29N 87°6W **85** C3
Ottertail *Minn., U.S.A.* 46°26N 95°33W **77** D3
Otterville *Ont., Canada* 42°55N 80°36W **146** E6
Otterville *Mo., U.S.A.* 38°42N 93°0W **83** C4
Otto *Wyo., U.S.A.* 44°24N 108°16W **124** B4
Otto Fiord *Nunavut, Canada* 81°2N 87°0W **158** A8
Ottosen *Iowa, U.S.A.* 42°54N 94°23W **81** C4
Ottumwa *Iowa, U.S.A.* 41°1N 92°25W **81** D6
Otway *Ohio, U.S.A.* 38°52N 83°11W **86** E3
Otzolotepec *México, Mexico* 19°31N 99°31W **175** D7
Otzoloapan *México, Mexico* 19°10N 100°16W **175** D7
Ouachita ➜ *La., U.S.A.* 31°38N 91°49W **110** C4
Ouachita, L. *Ark., U.S.A.* 34°34N 93°12W **106** D2
Ouachita County ☆ *Ark., U.S.A.* 33°35N 92°50W **106** E2

Ouachita Mts. *Ark., U.S.A.* 34°30N 94°30W **107** D9
Ouachita Nat. Forest *Ark., U.S.A.* 34°42N 93°48W **106** D2
Ouachita Nat. Forest *Okla., U.S.A.* 34°50N 94°50W **107** D9
Ouachita Parish ☆ *La., U.S.A.* 32°30N 92°7W **110** B3
Ouareau ➜ *Qué., Canada* 46°17N 74°9W **145** E8
Ouasiemsca ➜ *Qué., Canada* 49°0N 72°30W **145** B10
Ouest, Pte. de l' *Qué., Canada* 49°52N 64°40W **140** D5
Ouray *Colo., U.S.A.* 38°1N 107°40W **125** D3
Ouray *Utah, U.S.A.* 40°6N 109°41W **129** C6
Ouray County ☆ *Colo., U.S.A.* 38°10N 107°45W **125** D3
Outagamie County ☆ *Wis., U.S.A.* 44°20N 88°30W **78** D1
Outaouais ➜ *Qué., Canada* 45°27N 74°8W **145** E8
Outardes ➜ *Qué., Canada* 50°20N 69°10W **145** A13
Outardes 4, Rés. aux *Qué., Canada* 50°11N 69°13W **145** A13
Outer I. = Grande-Passe I. de la *Qué., Canada* 51°10N 58°35W **143** C6
Outer I. *Wis., U.S.A.* 47°2N 90°26W **78** A3
Outer Mission *Calif., U.S.A.* 37°43N 122°26W **132** E2
Outer Santa Barbara Passage *Calif., U.S.A.* 33°15N 118°40W **127** K8
Outlook *Sask., Canada* 51°30N 107°0W **150** D4
Outlook *Mont., U.S.A.* 48°53N 104°47W **123** B13
Outlook Pk. *Nunavut, Canada* 79°45N 91°23W **158** B7
Outremont *Qué., Canada* 45°31N 73°36W **160** A3
Ouzinkie *Alaska, U.S.A.* 57°56N 152°30W **135** H9
Oval Pk. *Wash., U.S.A.* 48°17N 120°25W **120** B5
Ovando *Mont., U.S.A.* 47°1N 113°8W **123** C4
Overbrook *Kans., U.S.A.* 38°47N 95°33W **82** C8
Overflow Nat. Wildlife Refuge △ *Ark., U.S.A.* 33°4N 91°41W **106** E4
Overflowing ➜ *Man., Canada* 53°8N 101°5W **151** B10
Overland *Mo., U.S.A.* 38°42N 90°21W **94** A1
Overland Park *Kans., U.S.A.* 38°58N 94°40W **82** C9
Overlea *Md., U.S.A.* 39°21N 76°31W **99** A2
Overly *N. Dak., U.S.A.* 48°41N 100°9W **76** B5
Overton *Nebr., U.S.A.* 40°44N 99°32W **80** D6
Overton *Nev., U.S.A.* 36°33N 114°27W **128** F6
Overton *Tex., U.S.A.* 32°16N 94°59W **109** E13
Overton County ☆ *Tenn., U.S.A.* 36°23N 85°19W **105** D7
Overton Park *Tenn., U.S.A.* 35°8N 89°59W **117** B2
Ovett *Miss., U.S.A.* 31°29N 89°2W **111** E4
Ovid *Colo., U.S.A.* 40°58N 102°23W **125** B8
Ovid *Mich., U.S.A.* 43°1N 84°22W **79** F7
Ovid *N.Y., U.S.A.* 42°41N 76°49W **88** C4
Oviedo *Fla., U.S.A.* 28°40N 81°13W **114** C7
Owanka *S. Dak., U.S.A.* 44°1N 102°35W **76** F3
Owasa *Iowa, U.S.A.* 42°39N 93°12W **81** C5
Owasco L. *N.Y., U.S.A.* 42°50N 76°31W **88** C4
Owasso *Okla., U.S.A.* 36°16N 95°51W **107** B8
Owatonna *Minn., U.S.A.* 44°5N 93°14W **77** F5
Owego *N.Y., U.S.A.* 42°6N 76°16W **88** C4
Owen *Wis., U.S.A.* 44°57N 90°33W **78** D3
Owen County ☆ *Ind., U.S.A.* 39°20N 86°50W **85** D4
Owen County ☆ *Ky., U.S.A.* 38°30N 84°55W **105** B6
Owen Sound *Ont., Canada* 44°35N 80°55W **146** C6
Owens ➜ *Calif., U.S.A.* 36°32N 117°59W **127** G9
Owens L. *Calif., U.S.A.* 36°26N 117°57W **127** G9
Owensboro *Ky., U.S.A.* 37°46N 87°7W **104** C4
Owensville *Ind., U.S.A.* 38°16N 87°41W **85** E3
Owensville *Mo., U.S.A.* 38°21N 91°30W **83** C5
Owensville *Ohio, U.S.A.* 39°7N 84°8W **86** D2
Owenton *Ky., U.S.A.* 38°32N 84°50W **105** B6
Owenton *N.Y., U.S.A.* 42°37N 76°6W **93** C3
Owikeno L. *B.C., Canada* 51°40N 126°50W **154** D8
Owings Mills *Md., U.S.A.* 39°25N 76°47W **99** A4
Owingsville *Ky., U.S.A.* 38°9N 83°46W **105** B9
Owl ➜ *Man., Canada* 57°51N 92°44W **159** F7
Owl Creek Mts. *Wyo., U.S.A.* 43°40N 108°55W **124** C4
Owls Head *Maine, U.S.A.* 44°5N 69°4W **90** D4
Owosso *Mich., U.S.A.* 43°0N 84°10W **79** F7
Owsley County ☆ *Ky., U.S.A.* 37°25N 83°40W **105** C9
Owyhee *Nev., U.S.A.* 41°57N 116°6W **128** A4
Owyhee ➜ *Oreg., U.S.A.* 43°49N 117°2W **121** D8
Owyhee, L. *Oreg., U.S.A.* 43°38N 117°14W **121** D8
Owyhee County ☆ *Idaho, U.S.A.* 42°45N 116°20W **122** G2
Owyhee Desert *Nev., U.S.A.* 41°40N 116°50W **128** A4
Owyhee Mts. *Idaho, U.S.A.* 42°45N 116°30W **122** G2
Ox Cr. ➜ *N. Dak., U.S.A.* 48°35N 100°8W **76** B5
Oxbow *Sask., Canada* 49°14N 102°10W **151** F9
Oxbow *Maine, U.S.A.* 46°25N 68°28W **90** B5
Oxchuc *Chiapas, Mexico* 16°47N 92°20W **178** C4
Oxford *Qué., Canada* 45°44N 63°52W **141** H6
Oxford *Ala., U.S.A.* 33°36N 85°51W **112** D5
Oxford *Ark., U.S.A.* 36°13N 91°56W **106** B4
Oxford *Ind., U.S.A.* 40°31N 87°15W **85** C3
Oxford *Iowa, U.S.A.* 41°43N 91°47W **81** D7
Oxford *Kans., U.S.A.* 37°17N 97°10W **82** D6
Oxford *La., U.S.A.* 31°56N 93°38W **110** C2
Oxford *Maine, U.S.A.* 44°8N 70°30W **90** D3
Oxford *Mass., U.S.A.* 42°7N 71°52W **91** B3
Oxford *Mich., U.S.A.* 42°49N 83°16W **79** F8
Oxford *Miss., U.S.A.* 34°22N 89°31W **111** B4
Oxford *N.C., U.S.A.* 36°19N 78°35W **103** B7
Oxford *N.Y., U.S.A.* 42°27N 75°36W **88** C5
Oxford *Nebr., U.S.A.* 40°15N 99°38W **80** D6
Oxford *Ohio, U.S.A.* 39°31N 84°45W **86** D2
Oxford *Pa., U.S.A.* 39°47N 75°59W **93** B5
Oxford *Wis., U.S.A.* 43°47N 89°34W **78** E4
Oxford County ☆ *Maine, U.S.A.* 44°30N 70°30W **90** D3
Oxford Junction *Iowa, U.S.A.* 41°59N 90°57W **81** D8
Oxford L. *Man., Canada* 54°51N 95°37W **159** G6
Oxford Pk. *Idaho, U.S.A.* 42°16N 112°2W **129** B4
Oxkutzcab *Yucatán, Mexico* 20°18N 89°25W **179** B4
Oxnard *Calif., U.S.A.* 34°12N 119°11W **127** J7
Oxon Hill *Md., U.S.A.* 38°48N 76°59W **99** C4
Oyama *B.C., Canada* 50°7N 119°22W **155** E15
Oyameyo, Volcan *Distrito Federal, Mexico* 19°11N 99°11W **181** C2
Oyen *Alta., Canada* 51°22N 110°28W **153** D12
Oyster Bay *N.Y., U.S.A.* 40°52N 73°32W **91** D1
Oyster Harbour = Ladysmith *B.C., Canada* 49°0N 123°49W **154** G9
Ozan *Ark., U.S.A.* 33°51N 93°43W **106** E2
Ozark *Ala., U.S.A.* 31°28N 85°39W **112** E5
Ozark *Ark., U.S.A.* 35°29N 93°50W **106** C2
Ozark *Mo., U.S.A.* 37°1N 93°12W **83** D3
Ozark County ☆ *Mo., U.S.A.* 36°40N 92°25W **83** E4
Ozark Folk Center State Park △ *Ark., U.S.A.* 35°53N 92°7W **106** C3

Ozark Lake *Ark., U.S.A.* 35°30N 94°10W **106** C1
Ozark Nat. Forest *Ark., U.S.A.* 35°40N 93°20W **106** C2
Ozark Nat. Scenic Riverways △ *Mo., U.S.A.* 37°25N 91°12W **83** D5
Ozark Plateau *Mo., U.S.A.* 37°20N 91°40W **83** E3
Ozarks, L. of the *Mo., U.S.A.* 38°12N 92°38W **83** C4
Ozaukee County ☆ *Wis., U.S.A.* 43°20N 88°0W **78** E6
Ozawkie *Kans., U.S.A.* 39°14N 95°28W **82** B8
Ozette, L. *Wash., U.S.A.* 48°6N 124°38W **120** B1
Ozette Indian Reservation *Wash., U.S.A.* 48°10N 124°34W **120** B1
Ozona *Tex., U.S.A.* 30°43N 101°12W **108** G6
Ozona *Tenn., U.S.A.* 35°53N 84°49W **105** E8
Ozone Park *N.Y., U.S.A.* 40°40N 73°50W **97** B3
Ozuluama *Veracruz, Mexico* 21°40N 97°51W **176** C3
Ozumba *México, Mexico* 19°3N 98°46W **175** C9

P

Paamiut *Greenland* 62°0N 49°43W **162** E6
Pa'auilo *Hawai'i, U.S.A.* 20°2N 155°22W **136** C6
Pabellón de Arteaga *Aguascalientes, Mexico* 22°10N 102°21W **173** E8
Pabellónes, Ensenada de *Sinaloa, Mexico* 24°27N 107°36W **172** C3
Pabelo *Jalisco, Mexico* 19°53N 104°39W **174** C3
Pablo *Mont., U.S.A.* 47°36N 114°7W **123** C3
Pabos Mills *Qué., Canada* 48°19N 64°42W **140** E5
Pace *Fla., U.S.A.* 30°36N 87°10W **114** A1
Pachuca *Hidalgo, Mexico* 20°7N 98°44W **175** B9
Pachuquilla *Hidalgo, Mexico* 20°5N 98°41W **175** B9
Pachuta *Miss., U.S.A.* 32°2N 88°53W **111** D5
Pacific *Mo., U.S.A.* 38°29N 90°45W **83** C6
Pacific Beach *Calif., U.S.A.* 32°47N 117°14W **133** B1
Pacific Beach *Wash., U.S.A.* 47°13N 124°12W **120** C1
Pacific City = Huntington Beach *Calif., U.S.A.* 33°40N 118°5W **127** K8
Pacific City *Oreg., U.S.A.* 45°12N 123°57W **121** B2
Pacific County ☆ *Wash., U.S.A.* 46°30N 123°55W **120** D2
Pacific Grove *Calif., U.S.A.* 36°38N 121°56W **126** G5
Pacific Heights *Calif., U.S.A.* 37°47N 122°26W **132** E2
Pacific Junction *Iowa, U.S.A.* 41°1N 95°48W **81** D3
Pacific Manor *Calif., U.S.A.* 37°38N 122°27W **132** G2
Pacific Palisades *Calif., U.S.A.* 34°2N 118°32W **133** B1
Pacific Palisades *Hawai'i, U.S.A.* 21°25N 157°58W **136** K14
Pacific Rim Nat. Park Reserve △ *B.C., Canada* 48°40N 124°45W **154** G10
Pacific Spirit Regional Park *B.C., Canada* 49°15N 123°3W **161** B1
Pacifica *Calif., U.S.A.* 37°37N 122°27W **132** G2
Packanack Lake *N.J., U.S.A.* 40°56N 94°13W **97** A1
Packenham *Ont., Canada* 45°22N 76°25W **147** B10
Packwood *Iowa, U.S.A.* 41°8N 92°5W **81** D6
Packwood *Wash., U.S.A.* 46°36N 121°40W **120** D4
Pacolet *S.C., U.S.A.* 34°54N 81°46W **103** D4
Pacquet *Nfld. & L., Canada* 50°0N 55°53W **142** C5
Pacula *Hidalgo, Mexico* 21°3N 99°18W **175** A8
Paddle Prairie *Alta., Canada* 57°57N 117°29W **157** E9
Paden *N. Mex., U.S.A.* 35°30N 96°34W **107** C7
Paden City *W. Va., U.S.A.* 39°36N 80°56W **102** B4
Padre I. *Tex., U.S.A.* 27°10N 97°25W **108** K10
Padre Island Nat. Seashore △ *U.S.A.* 27°0N 97°25W **108** K10
Padroni *Colo., U.S.A.* 40°47N 103°10W **125** B7
Paducah *Ky., U.S.A.* 37°5N 88°37W **104** C4
Paducah *Tex., U.S.A.* 34°1N 100°18W **108** C7
Pagan *N. Marianas* 18°7N 145°46E **184** a
Page *Ariz., U.S.A.* 36°57N 111°27W **130** A4
Page *N. Dak., U.S.A.* 47°10N 97°34W **76** C8
Page *Nebr., U.S.A.* 42°26N 98°25W **80** B7
Page *Okla., U.S.A.* 34°45N 94°40W **107** D9
Page City *Kans., U.S.A.* 39°5N 101°9W **82** B2
Page County ☆ *Iowa, U.S.A.* 40°45N 95°10W **81** E3
Page County ☆ *Va., U.S.A.* 38°40N 78°28W **102** C6
Pagedale *Mo., U.S.A.* 38°41N 90°18W **94** B2
Pageland *S.C., U.S.A.* 34°46N 80°24W **103** D5
Pago B. *Guam* 13°25N 144°47E **184** b
Pago Pago *Amer. Samoa* 14°16S 170°43W **184** e
Pago Pago Harbor *Amer. Samoa* 14°17S 170°40W **184** e
Pagosa Springs *Colo., U.S.A.* 37°16N 107°1W **125** E3
Paguate *N. Mex., U.S.A.* 35°8N 107°23W **131** B3
Pagwa River *Ont., Canada* 50°2N 85°14W **149** B10
Pagwachuan ➜ *Ont., Canada* 50°12N 84°43W **149** B12
Pāhala *Hawai'i, U.S.A.* 19°12N 155°29W **136** D6
Pahaska *Wyo., U.S.A.* 44°30N 109°58W **124** B3
Pāhoa *Hawai'i, U.S.A.* 19°30N 154°57W **136** D7
Pahokee *Fla., U.S.A.* 26°50N 80°40W **114** E8
Pahrangat Ra. *Nev., U.S.A.* 37°15N 115°20W **128** E5
Pahroc Ra. *Nev., U.S.A.* 37°45N 114°50W **128** E6
Pahrump *Nev., U.S.A.* 36°12N 115°59W **128** F5
Pahute Mesa *Nev., U.S.A.* 37°20N 116°45W **128** E4
Pahvant Range *Utah, U.S.A.* 39°10N 112°5W **129** D3
Paia *Hawai'i, U.S.A.* 20°54N 156°22W **136** C5
Paige *Tex., U.S.A.* 30°13N 97°7W **109** G10
Pailolo Channel *Hawai'i, U.S.A.* 21°0N 156°40W **136** B5
Paimpont, L. *Qué., Canada* 50°28N 61°34W **140** C8
Paincourtville *La., U.S.A.* 29°59N 91°3W **110** E4
Painesdale *Mich., U.S.A.* 47°3N 88°40W **79** B3
Painesville *Ohio, U.S.A.* 41°43N 81°15W **86** B5
Paint ➜ *Mich., U.S.A.* 45°58N 88°15W **79** C3
Paint Cr. ➜ *Ohio, U.S.A.* 39°15N 83°20W **86** D3
Paint Hills = Wemindji *Qué., Canada* 53°0N 78°49W **143** C2
Paint Rock *Ala., U.S.A.* 34°40N 86°20W **112** B4
Paint Rock *Tex., U.S.A.* 31°31N 99°55W **109** F8
Paint Rock ➜ *Ala., U.S.A.* 34°28N 86°28W **112** B4
Painted Desert *Ariz., U.S.A.* 36°0N 111°0W **130** B5
Painted Post *N.Y., U.S.A.* 42°10N 77°6W **88** C3
Paintsville *Ky., U.S.A.* 37°49N 82°48W **105** C10
Paintsville L. *Ky., U.S.A.* 37°50N 82°52W **105** C10
Paisley *Ont., Canada* 44°18N 81°16W **146** C5
Paisley *Oreg., U.S.A.* 42°42N 120°32W **121** E5
Paiute Indian Reservation *Utah, U.S.A.* 37°10N 113°46W **129** F2
Pajapan *Veracruz, Mexico* 18°15N 94°42W **177** F6
Pajarito *N. Mex., U.S.A.* 34°59N 106°43W **131** C4
Pajaritos *Nayarit, Mexico* 22°28N 105°32W **172** E5
Pájaros, Pta. *Quintana Roo, Mexico* 19°36N 87°25W **179** C6
Pájaros Azules, Sa. *Coahuila, Mexico* 27°3N 100°58W **170** C4
Pakashkan L. *Ont., Canada* 49°21N 90°18W **148** C5
Pakenham *Ont., Canada* 45°18N 76°18W **144** F6
Pakwash L. *Ont., Canada* 50°45N 93°30W **148** B3
Pala Indian Reservation *Calif., U.S.A.* 33°22N 116°58W **127** K10
Palacios *Tex., U.S.A.* 28°42N 96°13W **109** J11
Palamos = General Rodrigo M. Quevedo *Chihuahua, Mexico* 31°46N 107°37W **169** B8

Palaoa Pt. *Hawai'i, U.S.A.* 20°44N 156°58W **136** C5
Palatine *Ill., U.S.A.* 42°7N 88°3W **84** A5
Palatka *Fla., U.S.A.* 29°39N 81°38W **114** B7
Palco *Kans., U.S.A.* 39°15N 99°34W **82** B4
Palen Dry L. *Calif., U.S.A.* 33°46N 115°13W **127** K11
Palenque *Chiapas, Mexico* 17°29N 92°1W **178** B4
Palenque, Parque Nacional △ *Chiapas, Mexico* 17°30N 92°3W **178** B4
Palermo *Calif., U.S.A.* 39°26N 121°33W **126** D5
Palermo *N. Dak., U.S.A.* 48°21N 102°14W **76** B3
Palestine *Ark., U.S.A.* 34°58N 90°54W **106** D5
Palestine *Ill., U.S.A.* 39°0N 87°37W **84** D6
Palestine *Ohio, U.S.A.* 40°3N 84°45W **86** C2
Palestine *Tex., U.S.A.* 31°46N 95°38W **109** F12
Palestine, L. *Tex., U.S.A.* 32°6N 95°27W **109** E12
Palikea *Hawai'i, U.S.A.* 21°26N 158°6W **136** K13
Palisade *Colo., U.S.A.* 39°7N 108°21W **125** C2
Palisade *Nebr., U.S.A.* 40°21N 101°7W **80** D4
Palisades *Idaho, U.S.A.* 43°21N 111°13W **122** F7
Palisades *Wash., U.S.A.* 47°25N 119°54W **120** C6
Palisades Park *N.J., U.S.A.* 40°50N 74°1W **97** A2
Palisades Res. *Idaho, U.S.A.* 43°20N 111°12W **122** F7
Palito Blanco *Tex., U.S.A.* 27°35N 98°11W **108** K9
Palizada *Campeche, Mexico* 18°15N 92°5W **179** D1
Palizada, I. *Oaxaca, Mexico* 16°9N 94°12W **177** H6
Palm Bay *Fla., U.S.A.* 28°2N 80°35W **114** C8
Palm Beach *Fla., U.S.A.* 26°43N 80°2W **114** E8
Palm Beach County ☆ *Fla., U.S.A.* 26°45N 80°20W **114** E8
Palm Beach Gardens *Fla., U.S.A.* 26°49N 80°8W **114** E8
Palm Beach Int. ✈ (PBI) *Fla., U.S.A.* 26°41N 80°6W **114** E8
Palm City *Calif., U.S.A.* 32°35N 117°5W **133** C2
Palm Coast *Fla., U.S.A.* 29°35N 81°12W **114** B7
Palm Desert *Calif., U.S.A.* 33°43N 116°22W **127** K10
Palm Harbor *Fla., U.S.A.* 28°5N 82°46W **114** C6
Palm Springs *Calif., U.S.A.* 33°50N 116°33W **127** K10
Palm Valley *Fla., U.S.A.* 30°11N 81°23W **114** A7
Palma Soriano *Cuba* 20°15N 76°0W **182** B4
Palmar, Península el *Campeche, Mexico* 18°50N 91°27W **179** D2
Palmar Chico *Mexico* 18°42N 100°22W **175** D7
Palmar Grande *de México, Mexico* 18°36N 100°24W **175** D7
Palmarolle *Qué., Canada* 48°40N 79°12W **144** C3
Palmas, B. *Baja Calif. S., Mexico* 23°40N 109°40W **167** K9
Palmdale *Calif., U.S.A.* 34°35N 118°7W **127** J8
Palmdale *Fla., U.S.A.* 26°57N 81°19W **114** D7
Palmer *Alaska, U.S.A.* 61°36N 149°7W **135** F10
Palmer *Iowa, U.S.A.* 42°38N 94°36W **81** C4
Palmer *Kans., U.S.A.* 39°38N 97°8W **82** B6
Palmer *Mass., U.S.A.* 42°9N 72°20W **91** B2
Palmer *Nebr., U.S.A.* 41°13N 98°13W **80** C7
Palmer *Tenn., U.S.A.* 35°21N 85°34W **105** E7
Palmer Lake *Colo., U.S.A.* 39°7N 104°55W **125** C6
Palmer Park *Colo., U.S.A.* 38°55N 76°52W **99** B4
Palmers Crossing *Miss., U.S.A.* 31°16N 89°15W **111** E4
Palmerston *Ont., Canada* 43°50N 80°51W **146** D6
Palmerton *Pa., U.S.A.* 40°48N 75°37W **92** B1
Palmetto *Fla., U.S.A.* 27°31N 82°34W **114** D6
Palmetto *Ga., U.S.A.* 33°31N 84°40W **113** C2
Palmetto *La., U.S.A.* 30°43N 91°55W **110** D4
Palmillas *Tamaulipas, Mexico* 23°18N 99°33W **171** G5
Palmyra *Ill., U.S.A.* 39°26N 90°0W **84** D4
Palmyra *Ind., U.S.A.* 38°24N 86°7W **85** E4
Palmyra *Mo., U.S.A.* 39°48N 91°32W **83** B51
Palmyra *N. J., U.S.A.* 40°0N 75°1W **98** B2
Palmyra *Nebr., U.S.A.* 40°42N 96°23W **80** D9
Palmyra *Pa., U.S.A.* 40°18N 76°36W **87** D6
Palmyra *Va., U.S.A.* 37°52N 78°16W **102** D6
Palmyra I. *Pac. Oc.* 5°52N 162°5W **184** D7
Palo *Iowa, U.S.A.* 42°4N 91°48W **81** C7
Palo Alto *Aguascalientes, Mexico* 21°56N 101°59W **173** F9
Palo Alto *Aguascalientes, Mexico* 22°1N 102°41W **173** E8
Palo Alto *Calif., U.S.A.* 37°27N 122°10W **126** F4
Palo Alto County ☆ *Iowa, U.S.A.* 43°5N 94°40W **81** B4
Palo Duro → *Tex., U.S.A.* 35°0N 101°55W **108** B6
Palo Pinto *Tex., U.S.A.* 32°46N 98°18W **109** E9
Palo Pinto County ☆ *Tex., U.S.A.* 32°45N 98°20W **109** E9
Palo Verde *Guanajuato, Mexico* 20°20N 101°51W **174** B6
Palo Verde *Ariz., U.S.A.* 33°21N 112°41W **130** D3
Palo Verde *Calif., U.S.A.* 33°26N 114°44W **127** K12
Palo Verde, Parque Nac. △ *Costa Rica* 10°21N 85°21W **182** D2
Palomar *Ont., Canada* 48°10N 82°16W **149** D14
Palomares *Oaxaca, Mexico* 17°9N 95°4W **177** G5
Palomas *Durango, Mexico* 25°8N 106°10W **172** B4
Palomas, L. *Chihuahua, Mexico* 26°48N 103°55W **169** G12
Palos Heights *Ill., U.S.A.* 41°39N 87°47W **95** D2
Palos Hills *Ill., U.S.A.* 41°42N 87°49W **95** C2
Palos Hills Forest *Ill., U.S.A.* 41°40N 87°52W **95** C1
Palos Park *Ill., U.S.A.* 41°40N 87°50W **95** C1
Palouse *Wash., U.S.A.* 46°55N 117°4W **120** D8
Palouse → *Wash., U.S.A.* 46°35N 118°13W **120** D7
Pamlico → *N.C., U.S.A.* 35°20N 76°28W **103** C9
Pamlico County ☆ *N.C., U.S.A.* 35°10N 76°45W **103** C9
Pamlico Sd. *N.C., U.S.A.* 35°20N 76°0W **103** C10
Pampa *Tex., U.S.A.* 35°32N 100°58W **108** B7
Pamplico *S.C., U.S.A.* 34°0N 79°34W **103** E6
Pamplin *Va., U.S.A.* 37°16N 78°41W **102** D6
Pamunkey → *Va., U.S.A.* 37°32N 76°48W **102** D8
Pana *Ill., U.S.A.* 39°23N 89°5W **84** D4
Panabá *Yucatán, Mexico* 21°17N 88°16W **179** A5
Panaca *Nev., U.S.A.* 37°47N 114°23W **128** E6
Panacea *Fla., U.S.A.* 30°2N 84°23W **114** A4
Panache, L. *Ont., Canada* 46°15N 81°20W **146** A5
Panalachic *Chihuahua, Mexico* 27°40N 107°29W **169** F8
Panamá *Panama* 9°0N 79°25W **182** E4
Panama *Nebr., U.S.A.* 40°36N 96°31W **80** D9
Panama *Okla., U.S.A.* 35°10N 94°40W **107** C9
Panama *Cent. Amer.* 8°48N 79°55W **182** E4
Panamá, G. de *Panama* 8°4N 79°20W **182** E4
Panama, Isthmus of *Cent. Amer.* 9°0N 79°0W **182** E4
Panama Canal *Panama* 9°10N 79°37W **182** E4
Panama City *Fla., U.S.A.* 30°10N 85°40W **114** A3
Panama City Beach *Fla., U.S.A.* 30°11N 85°48W **114** A3
Panamint Range *Calif., U.S.A.* 36°20N 117°20W **127** G9
Panamint Valley *Calif., U.S.A.* 36°15N 117°20W **127** G9
Pancake Range *Nev., U.S.A.* 38°30N 115°50W **128** D5
Pancho Villa *Chihuahua, Mexico* 30°50N 108°40W **168** F4
Pandora *Costa Rica* 9°43N 83°3W **182** E3
Pandora *Ohio, U.S.A.* 40°57N 83°58W **86** C3
Pangburn *Ark., U.S.A.* 35°26N 91°50W **106** C4
Pangman *Sask., Canada* 49°39N 104°40W **150** F7
Pangnirtung *Nunavut, Canada* 66°8N 65°43W **159** D12
Panguitch *Utah, U.S.A.* 37°50N 112°26W **129** F3
Panhandle *Tex., U.S.A.* 35°21N 101°23W **108** B6
Päni'au *Hawai'i, U.S.A.* 21°56N 160°5W **136** B1
Panindícuaro *Michoacan, Mexico* 19°59N 101°46W **174** C6
Pannirtuq = Pangnirtung *Nunavut, Canada* 66°8N 65°43W **159** D12

Panny → *Alta., Canada* 57°8N 114°51W **152** A6
Panola *Ala., U.S.A.* 32°57N 88°16W **112** D2
Panola County ☆ *Miss., U.S.A.* 34°19N 89°57W **111** B4
Panola County ☆ *Tex., U.S.A.* 32°9N 94°20W **109** E13
Panora *Iowa, U.S.A.* 41°42N 94°22W **81** D4
Panorama Pt. *Nebr., U.S.A.* 41°0N 104°2W **80** C1
Pantego *Tex., U.S.A.* 32°42N 97°9W **116** B3
Panthersville *Georgia, U.S.A.* 33°43N 84°16W **117** B3
Pantelhó *Chiapas, Mexico* 17°0N 92°28W **178** C4
Pantitlán *Distrito Federal, Mexico* 19°24N 99°4W **181** B3
Pánuco *Veracruz, Mexico* 22°3N 98°10W **176** B2
Pánuco *Zacatecas, Mexico* 22°53N 102°31W **173** E8
Pánuco → *Veracruz, Mexico* 22°16N 97°47W **176** B3
Pánuco de Coronado *Durango, Mexico* 24°32N 104°20W **173** C6
Paola *Kans., U.S.A.* 38°35N 94°53W **82** D9
Paoli *Colo., U.S.A.* 40°37N 102°28W **125** B8
Paoli *Ind., U.S.A.* 38°33N 86°28W **85** E4
Paoli *Okla., U.S.A.* 34°50N 97°15W **107** D6
Paonia *Colo., U.S.A.* 38°52N 107°36W **125** D3
Päpä *Hawai'i, U.S.A.* 19°13N 155°52W **136** D6
Päpa'aloa *Hawai'i, U.S.A.* 19°59N 155°13W **136** D6
Papagayo *Guerrero, Mexico* 16°46N 99°43W **175** F8
Papagayo, G. de *Costa Rica* 10°30N 85°50W **182** D2
Papago Park *Ariz., U.S.A.* 33°27N 111°56W **134** C3
Päpa'ikou *Hawai'i, U.S.A.* 19°47N 155°6W **136** D6
Papaloapán → *Veracruz, Mexico* 18°42N 95°38W **177** F5
Papanoa, B. *Guerrero, Mexico* 17°20N 101°6W **175** E6
Papanoa, Pta. *Guerrero, Mexico* 17°17N 101°4W **175** E6
Papantla *Veracruz, Mexico* 20°27N 97°19W **176** D3
Papawai Pt. *Hawai'i, U.S.A.* 20°47N 156°32W **136** C5
Papigochic → *Chihuahua, Mexico* 29°9N 109°7W **169** D8
Papillion *Nebr., U.S.A.* 41°9N 96°3W **80** D9
Papineau *Ill., U.S.A.* 40°58N 87°43W **84** C6
Papineau-Labelle, Réserve Faunique de △ *Qué., Canada* 46°10N 75°15W **144** E7
Papineauville *Qué., Canada* 45°37N 75°1W **144** F7
Paquetville *N.B., Canada* 47°40N 65°5W **141** F4
Paquimé *Chihuahua, Mexico* 30°20N 108°0W **169** C8
Paracho *Michoacan, Mexico* 19°39N 102°4W **174** C5
Parachute *Colo., U.S.A.* 39°27N 108°3W **125** C2
Parácuaro *Guanajuato, Mexico* 20°9N 100°46W **175** B7
Parácuaro *Michoacan, Mexico* 19°7N 102°12W **174** C5
Parade *S. Dak., U.S.A.* 45°1N 100°6W **76** E4
Paradis *Qué., Canada* 48°15N 76°35W **144** C6
Paradise *Nfld. & L., Canada* 47°32N 52°53W **142** E8
Paradise *Calif., U.S.A.* 39°46N 121°37W **126** D5
Paradise *Kans., U.S.A.* 39°7N 98°55W **82** B5
Paradise *Mich., U.S.A.* 46°38N 85°2W **79** C6
Paradise *Mont., U.S.A.* 47°23N 114°48W **123** C3
Paradise *Nev., U.S.A.* 36°5N 115°8W **134** C2
Paradise *Utah, U.S.A.* 41°34N 111°50W **129** B4
Paradise → *Nfld. & L., Canada* 53°27N 57°19W **143** C6
Paradise Hill *Sask., Canada* 53°32N 109°28W **150** B2
Paradise Hill *Okla., U.S.A.* 35°40N 95°5W **107** C8
Paradise Hills *Okla., U.S.A.* 32°40N 117°3W **133** B2
Paradise Valley *Alta., Canada* 53°2N 110°17W **153** E10
Paradise Valley *Ariz., U.S.A.* 33°31N 111°56W **134** B3
Paradise Valley *Ariz., U.S.A.* 33°36N 112°0W **134** A3
Paradise Valley *Nev., U.S.A.* 41°30N 117°32W **128** A3
Paradise Valley *Wyo., U.S.A.* 42°49N 106°23W **124** D6
Paragon *Ind., U.S.A.* 39°24N 86°34W **85** D4
Paragonah *Utah, U.S.A.* 37°53N 112°46W **129** F3
Paragould *Ark., U.S.A.* 36°3N 90°29W **106** B5
Paraíso *Colima, Mexico* 18°53N 103°58W **174** D4
Paraíso *Tabasco, Mexico* 18°24N 93°14W **178** B3
Paraíso → *Baja Calif. S., Mexico* 28°22N 114°5W **167** E4
Parás *Nuevo León, Mexico* 26°30N 99°31W **170** D5
Paramount Studios *Calif., U.S.A.* 34°5N 118°19W **133** B3
Paramus *N.J., U.S.A.* 40°56N 74°2W **97** A2
Parás *Nuevo León, Mexico* 26°30N 99°31W **170** D5
Parchment *Mich., U.S.A.* 42°20N 85°34W **79** G6
Parco = Sinclair *Wyo., U.S.A.* 41°47N 107°7W **124** E5
Pardee Res. *Calif., U.S.A.* 38°16N 120°51W **126** E6
Pardeeville *Wis., U.S.A.* 43°32N 89°18W **78** E4
Paredón *Chiapas, Mexico* 16°2N 93°52W **178** C3
Paredón *Coahuila, Mexico* 25°56N 100°58W **170** E4
Parent *Qué., Canada* 47°55N 74°35W **144** D8
Parent, L. *Qué., Canada* 48°31N 77°1W **144** C5
Parguera *Puerto Rico* 17°59N 67°3W **184** b
Parham *Ont., Canada* 44°39N 76°43W **147** C10
Paria → *Ariz., U.S.A.* 36°52N 111°36W **130** A4
Paria Plateau *Ariz., U.S.A.* 36°50N 111°50W **130** A4
Paris *Ont., Canada* 43°12N 80°25W **146** D6
Paris *Ark., U.S.A.* 35°18N 93°44W **106** C2
Paris *Idaho, U.S.A.* 42°14N 111°24W **122** G7
Paris *Ill., U.S.A.* 39°36N 87°42W **84** D6
Paris *Ky., U.S.A.* 38°13N 84°15W **105** B8
Paris *Maine, U.S.A.* 44°16N 70°30W **90** D3
Paris *Miss., U.S.A.* 34°11N 89°27W **111** B4
Paris *Mo., U.S.A.* 39°29N 92°0W **83** B5
Paris *Tenn., U.S.A.* 36°18N 88°19W **104** D4
Paris *Tex., U.S.A.* 33°40N 95°33W **109** D12
Parish *N.Y., U.S.A.* 43°25N 76°8W **88** B4
Parishville *N.Y., U.S.A.* 44°38N 74°49W **88** A6
Park *Kans., U.S.A.* 39°7N 100°22W **82** B3
Park → *N. Dak., U.S.A.* 48°28N 97°9W **76** B8
Park City *Kans., U.S.A.* 37°48N 97°20W **82** D6
Park City *Ky., U.S.A.* 37°6N 86°3W **104** C6
Park City *Mont., U.S.A.* 45°38N 108°55W **123** E8
Park City *Utah, U.S.A.* 40°39N 111°30W **129** C4
Park Falls *Wis., U.S.A.* 45°56N 90°27W **78** C3
Park Forest *Ill., U.S.A.* 41°29N 87°40W **84** B6
Park Hills *Mo., U.S.A.* 37°51N 90°51W **83** D61
Park Range *Colo., U.S.A.* 40°41N 106°41W **125** B4
Park Rapids *Minn., U.S.A.* 46°55N 95°4W **77** D3
Park Ridge *Ill., U.S.A.* 42°2N 87°51W **95** A1
Park Ridge *N.J., U.S.A.* 41°2N 74°2W **97** A2
Park River *N. Dak., U.S.A.* 48°24N 97°45W **76** B8
Park Valley *Utah, U.S.A.* 41°49N 113°20W **129** B2
Park View *Iowa, U.S.A.* 41°42N 90°33W **81** D8
Parkchester *N.Y., U.S.A.* 40°49N 73°50W **97** B3
Parkdale *Ont., Canada* 43°38N 79°27W **161** B2
Parkdale *Ark., U.S.A.* 33°7N 91°33W **106** E4
Parkdale *Oreg., U.S.A.* 45°31N 121°36W **121** B4
Parke County ☆ *Ind., U.S.A.* 39°45N 87°10W **85** D3
Parker *Ariz., U.S.A.* 34°9N 114°17W **130** C1
Parker *Colo., U.S.A.* 39°31N 104°46W **125** C6
Parker *Kans., U.S.A.* 38°18N 95°0W **82** C8
Parker *S. Dak., U.S.A.* 43°24N 97°8W **76** G8
Parker *Wash., U.S.A.* 46°30N 120°28W **120** D5
Parker, C. *Nunavut, Canada* 75°13N 79°30W **158** B10
Parker City *Ind., U.S.A.* 40°11N 85°12W **85** C5

Parker County ☆ *Tex., U.S.A.* 32°46N 97°48W **109** E10
Parker Dam *Ariz., U.S.A.* 34°18N 114°8W **130** C1
Parker River Nat. Wildlife Refuge △ *Mass., U.S.A.* 42°45N 70°49W **91** B4
Parkers Prairie *Minn., U.S.A.* 46°9N 95°20W **77** D3
Parkersburg *Ill., U.S.A.* 38°36N 88°3W **84** E5
Parkersburg *Iowa, U.S.A.* 42°35N 92°47W **81** C6
Parkersburg *W. Va., U.S.A.* 39°16N 81°34W **102** B3
Parkerview *Sask., Canada* 51°21N 103°18W **150** D8
Parkerville *Kans., U.S.A.* 38°46N 96°40W **82** C7
Parkesburg *Pa., U.S.A.* 39°58N 75°55W **87** E7
Parkfield *Calif., U.S.A.* 35°54N 120°26W **127** H6
Parkhill *Ont., Canada* 43°15N 81°38W **146** D5
Parkin *Ark., U.S.A.* 35°16N 90°34W **106** C5
Parkland *Ont., Canada* 45°23N 75°40W **160** B2
Parkland *Wash., U.S.A.* 47°9N 122°26W **120** C3
Parklawn *Va., U.S.A.* 38°50N 77°7W **99** B3
Parkrose *Oreg., U.S.A.* 45°34N 122°33W **121** B3
Parks *Ark., U.S.A.* 34°48N 93°58W **106** D2
Parks *Nebr., U.S.A.* 40°3N 101°44W **80** D4
Parks L. *Ont., Canada* 49°27N 87°38W **149** C12
Parkside *Sask., Canada* 53°10N 106°33W **150** B5
Parkside *Calif., U.S.A.* 37°44N 122°29W **132** C2
Parksley *Va., U.S.A.* 37°47N 75°39W **93** C5
Parkston *S. Dak., U.S.A.* 43°24N 97°59W **76** G8
Parksville *B.C., Canada* 49°20N 124°21W **154** F12
Parkton *N.C., U.S.A.* 39°40N 76°40W **93** A4
Parkville *Md., U.S.A.* 39°22N 76°32W **99** A2
Parkville *N.Y., U.S.A.* 40°38N 73°57W **97** C3
Parkway *Calif., U.S.A.* 38°32N 121°26W **126** E5
Parle, L. qui *Minn., U.S.A.* 45°1N 95°52W **77** E3
Parleys Summit *Utah, U.S.A.* 40°45N 111°37W **134** E4
Parlier *Calif., U.S.A.* 36°37N 119°32W **127** G7
Parma *Idaho, U.S.A.* 43°47N 116°57W **122** F2
Parma *Mich., U.S.A.* 42°16N 84°36W **79** G7
Parma *Mo., U.S.A.* 36°37N 89°48W **83** E7
Parma *Ohio, U.S.A.* 41°24N 81°43W **98** B1
Parma Heights *Ohio, U.S.A.* 41°23N 81°45W **98** B1
Parmelee *S. Dak., U.S.A.* 43°19N 101°2W **76** G4
Parmer County ☆ *Tex., U.S.A.* 34°38N 102°45W **108** C5
Parnell *Iowa, U.S.A.* 41°35N 92°0W **81** D7
Parnell *Mo., U.S.A.* 40°26N 94°37W **83** A4
Parol *Md., U.S.A.* 38°59N 76°32W **93** B4
Parowan *Utah, U.S.A.* 37°51N 112°50W **129** F3
Parral *Chihuahua, Mexico* 27°39N 105°7W **169** F10
Parramore I. *Va., U.S.A.* 37°32N 75°39W **102** D9
Parras *Coahuila, Mexico* 25°25N 102°11W **170** E2
Parras, Sa. de *Coahuila, Mexico* 25°24N 102°45W **170** E2
Parrilla *Tabasco, Mexico* 17°55N 92°55W **178** B4
Parris I. *S.C., U.S.A.* 32°20N 80°41W **103** F5
Parrish *Ala., U.S.A.* 33°44N 87°17W **112** C3
Parrish *Fla., U.S.A.* 27°35N 82°26W **114** D6
Parrott *Ga., U.S.A.* 31°54N 84°31W **113** E2
Parrsboro *N.S., Canada* 45°30N 64°25W **141** H5
Parry, C. *N.W.T., Canada* 70°20N 123°38W **156** B8
Parry B. *Nunavut, Canada* 68°6N 81°40W **158** D9
Parry Channel *Nunavut, Canada* 74°15N 94°0W **158** C7
Parry Is. *Canada* 77°0N 110°0W **156** A10
Parry Pen. *N.W.T., Canada* 69°45N 124°45W **156** C8
Parry Sound *Ont., Canada* 45°20N 80°0W **146** B6
Parshall *Colo., U.S.A.* 40°3N 106°11W **125** B4
Parshall *N. Dak., U.S.A.* 47°57N 102°8W **76** C3
Parsippany *N.J., U.S.A.* 40°52N 74°26W **92** B2
Parsnip → *B.C., Canada* 55°10N 123°2W **157** E8
Parson *B.C., Canada* 51°5N 116°37W **155** D18
Parsons *Kans., U.S.A.* 37°20N 95°16W **82** D8
Parsons *Tenn., U.S.A.* 35°39N 88°8W **104** E4
Parsons *W. Va., U.S.A.* 39°6N 79°41W **102** B5
Parson's Pond *Nfld. & L., Canada* 50°2N 57°43W **142** B3
Parsonsburg *Md., U.S.A.* 38°22N 75°28W **93** B5
Partida, I. *Baja Calif., Mexico* 28°55N 113°5W **166** E5
Partida, I. *Baja Calif. S., Mexico* 24°34N 110°24W **167** J8
Partridge *Kans., U.S.A.* 37°58N 98°5W **82** D5
Partridge → *Ont., Canada* 51°19N 80°18W **149** A16
Partridge Pt. *Nfld. & L., Canada* 50°10N 56°10W **142** B4
Pas, The *Man., Canada* 53°45N 101°15W **151** B10
Pasadena *Nfld. & L., Canada* 49°1N 57°36W **142** C3
Pasadena *Calif., U.S.A.* 34°9N 118°8W **133** B4
Pasadena *Tex., U.S.A.* 29°43N 95°13W **109** H12
Pasayten → *N. Amer.* 49°9N 120°36W **120** A5
Pascagoula *Miss., U.S.A.* 30°21N 88°33W **111** F5
Pascagoula → *Miss., U.S.A.* 30°23N 88°37W **111** F5
Pasco *Wash., U.S.A.* 46°14N 119°6W **120** D6
Pasco County ☆ *Fla., U.S.A.* 28°20N 82°30W **114** C6
Pascoag *R.I., U.S.A.* 41°57N 71°42W **91** C3
Pasfield L. *Sask., Canada* 58°24N 105°20W **157** E11
Paskenta *Calif., U.S.A.* 39°53N 122°33W **126** D4
Paso de Cuarenta *Jalisco, Mexico* 21°31N 101°45W **174** A6
Paso de Ovejas *Veracruz, Mexico* 19°17N 96°26W **176** E4
Paso de Piedras, Presa *Veracruz, Mexico* 21°43N 98°8W **176** C2
Paso de San Antonio *Chihuahua, Mexico* 28°59N 103°45W **169** E12
Paso de San Antonio *San Luis Potosí, Mexico* 22°0N 100°22W **171** J4
Paso del Macho *Veracruz, Mexico* 18°58N 96°43W **177** F4
Paso Robles *Calif., U.S.A.* 35°38N 120°41W **127** H6
Paspébiac *N.B., Canada* 48°3N 65°17W **141** E4
Pasqual, B. *Baja Calif. S., Mexico* 25°31N 111°6W **167** H7
Pasquotank County ☆ *N.C., U.S.A.* 36°15N 76°10W **103** B9
Pass Christian *Miss., U.S.A.* 30°19N 89°15W **111** F4
Pass Island *Nfld. & L., Canada* 47°30N 56°12W **142** E4
Passaconaway *N.H., U.S.A.* 43°59N 71°22W **89** C3
Passadumkeag *Maine, U.S.A.* 45°11N 68°37W **90** C5
Passage Pt. *N.W.T., Canada* 73°29N 115°16W **156** B9
Passaic *Mo., U.S.A.* 38°19N 94°21W **83** C2
Passaic *N.J., U.S.A.* 40°51N 74°7W **97** A2
Passaic → *N.J., U.S.A.* 40°42N 74°10W **97** B2
Passaic County ☆ *N.J., U.S.A.* 41°0N 74°20W **92** B1
Passumpsic → *Vt., U.S.A.* 44°18N 72°3W **89** C2
Pasteur, L. *Qué., Canada* 50°13N 66°58W **140** C3
Pastol B. *Alaska, U.S.A.* 63°7N 163°15W **135** E7
Pastor Ortiz *Guanajuato, Mexico* 20°18N 101°37W **174** B6
Pastora Peak *Ariz., U.S.A.* 36°47N 109°10W **130** A6
Pastura *N. Mex., U.S.A.* 34°47N 104°57W **131** C6
Pat Mayse L. *Tex., U.S.A.* 33°51N 95°33W **109** D12
Patagonia *Ariz., U.S.A.* 31°33N 110°45W **130** F5
Patapsco *Md., U.S.A.* 39°32N 76°54W **93** A4
Patapsco → *Md., U.S.A.* 39°9N 76°26W **93** A4
Pataskala *Ohio, U.S.A.* 40°0N 82°40W **86** C4
Patch Grove *Wis., U.S.A.* 42°56N 90°58W **78** F3
Patchogue *N.Y., U.S.A.* 40°46N 73°1W **92** B3
Pateros *Wash., U.S.A.* 48°3N 119°54W **120** B6
Paterson *N.J., U.S.A.* 40°54N 74°9W **97** A2
Paterson *Wash., U.S.A.* 45°56N 119°36W **120** E6

Patesville *Ky., U.S.A.* 37°47N 86°43W **104** C6
Pathfinder Res. *Wyo., U.S.A.* 42°28N 106°51W **124** D6
Pati Pt. *Guam* 13°35N 144°57E **184** b
Patillas *Puerto Rico* 18°1N 66°1W **184** G16
Patoka *Ill., U.S.A.* 38°45N 89°6W **84** E4
Patoka *Ind., U.S.A.* 38°24N 87°35W **85** E3
Patoka → *Ind., U.S.A.* 38°24N 87°45W **85** E3
Patoka L. *Ind., U.S.A.* 38°20N 86°40W **85** E4
Paton *Iowa, U.S.A.* 42°10N 94°16W **81** C4
Patos, I. *Sonora, Mexico* 29°17N 112°26W **168** D3
Patricia *Tex., U.S.A.* 32°33N 102°1W **108** E5
Patrick County ☆ *Va., U.S.A.* 36°55N 80°10W **102** E4
Patrick's Cove *Nfld. & L., Canada* 47°3N 54°7W **142** E6
Patsaliga Cr. → *Ala., U.S.A.* 31°22N 86°31W **112** E4
Patten *Maine, U.S.A.* 46°0N 68°38W **90** B5
Patterson *Calif., U.S.A.* 37°28N 121°8W **126** F5
Patterson *Ga., U.S.A.* 31°23N 82°8W **113** E4
Patterson *Idaho, U.S.A.* 44°32N 113°43W **122** E5
Patterson *La., U.S.A.* 29°42N 91°18W **110** E4
Patterson *N.Y., U.S.A.* 41°31N 73°36W **91** C1
Patterson, Pt. *Mich., U.S.A.* 45°58N 85°39W **79** D6
Patterson Cr. → *W. Va., U.S.A.* 39°34N 78°44W **93** A2
Pattison *Miss., U.S.A.* 31°53N 90°53W **111** E3
Patton = Monroeville *Pa., U.S.A.* 40°26N 79°45W **87** D3
Patton *Pa., U.S.A.* 40°38N 78°39W **87** D4
Pattonsburg *Mo., U.S.A.* 40°3N 94°8W **83** A2
Patuca → *Honduras* 15°50N 84°18W **182** C3
Patuca, Parque Nac. △ *Honduras* 14°30N 85°30W **182** D2
Patuca, Punta *Honduras* 15°49N 84°14W **182** D3
Patuxent → *Md., U.S.A.* 38°18N 76°25W **93** B4
Patuxent Nat. Wildlife Refuge △ *Md., U.S.A.* 39°6N 76°48W **93** A4
Patuxent River Naval Air Station *Md., U.S.A.* 38°17N 76°27W **93** B4
Pátzcuaro *Michoacan, Mexico* 19°31N 101°38W **174** C6
Pátzcuaro, L. de *Michoacan, Mexico* 19°35N 101°40W **174** C6
Paul *Idaho, U.S.A.* 42°36N 113°47W **122** G5
Paul I. *Nfld. & L., Canada* 56°30N 61°20W **143** B5
Paul-Sauvé, L. *Qué., Canada* 50°15N 78°20W **144** C6
Paul Smiths *N.Y., U.S.A.* 44°26N 74°15W **88** A6
Paulatuk *N.W.T., Canada* 69°25N 124°0W **156** C8
Paulden *Ariz., U.S.A.* 34°53N 112°28W **130** C3
Paulding *Miss., U.S.A.* 32°2N 89°2W **111** D4
Paulding *Ohio, U.S.A.* 41°8N 84°35W **86** B2
Paulding County ☆ *Ga., U.S.A.* 34°0N 84°50W **113** C2
Paulding County ☆ *Ohio, U.S.A.* 41°8N 84°35W **86** B2
Paulina *Oreg., U.S.A.* 44°8N 119°58W **121** C6
Paulina Marsh *Oreg., U.S.A.* 43°15N 121°0W **121** C4
Paulina Pk. *Oreg., U.S.A.* 43°41N 121°15W **121** C4
Paulins Kill → *N.J., U.S.A.* 40°55N 75°7W **92** B1
Paullina *Iowa, U.S.A.* 42°59N 95°41W **81** C3
Pauls Valley *Okla., U.S.A.* 34°44N 97°13W **107** D6
Paulsboro *N.J., U.S.A.* 39°50N 75°15W **92** C1
Paupack *Pa., U.S.A.* 41°22N 75°12W **92** A1
Pavillion *Wyo., U.S.A.* 43°15N 108°42W **124** C4
Pavo *Ga., U.S.A.* 30°58N 83°45W **113** F3
Paw Paw *Ill., U.S.A.* 41°41N 88°59W **84** B5
Paw Paw *Mich., U.S.A.* 42°13N 85°53W **79** G6
Paw Paw *W. Va., U.S.A.* 39°32N 78°28W **93** A2
Paw Paw Lake *Mich., U.S.A.* 42°13N 86°16W **79** G5
Pawcatuck *Conn., U.S.A.* 41°22N 71°52W **91** C2
Pawhuska *Okla., U.S.A.* 36°40N 96°20W **107** B7
Pawlet *Vt., U.S.A.* 43°20N 73°12W **89** C1
Pawling *N.Y., U.S.A.* 41°34N 73°36W **91** C1
Pawnee *Ill., U.S.A.* 39°36N 89°35W **84** D4
Pawnee *Okla., U.S.A.* 36°20N 96°48W **107** B7
Pawnee → *Kans., U.S.A.* 38°10N 99°15W **82** C4
Pawnee City *Nebr., U.S.A.* 40°7N 96°9W **80** D9
Pawnee County ☆ *Kans., U.S.A.* 38°10N 99°15W **82** C4
Pawnee County ☆ *Nebr., U.S.A.* 40°10N 96°20W **80** D9
Pawnee County ☆ *Okla., U.S.A.* 36°20N 96°50W **107** B7
Pawnee Cr. → *Colo., U.S.A.* 40°34N 103°14W **125** B7
Pawnee Nat. Grassland *Colo., U.S.A.* 40°40N 104°20W **125** B6
Pawnee Rock *Kans., U.S.A.* 38°16N 99°1W **82** C4
Pawtuckaway State Park △ *N.H., U.S.A.* 43°7N 71°11W **89** C3
Pawtucket *R.I., U.S.A.* 41°53N 71°23W **91** C3
Paxico *Kans., U.S.A.* 39°4N 96°10W **82** B7
Paxson *Alaska, U.S.A.* 63°2N 145°30W **135** E11
Paxton *Ill., U.S.A.* 40°27N 88°6W **84** C5
Paxton *Ind., U.S.A.* 42°19N 71°56W **91** B3
Paxton *Nebr., U.S.A.* 41°7N 101°21W **80** C4
Payette *Idaho, U.S.A.* 44°5N 116°56W **122** E2
Payette → *Idaho, U.S.A.* 44°5N 116°57W **122** E2
Payette County ☆ *Idaho, U.S.A.* 44°0N 116°55W **122** E2
Payette Nat. Forest *Idaho, U.S.A.* 45°10N 115°30W **122** D3
Payne *Ohio, U.S.A.* 41°5N 84°44W **86** B2
Payne, B. *Qué., Canada* 60°0N 69°43W **143** B4
Payne, L *Qué., Canada* 59°25N 74°0W **143** B3
Payne Bay = Kangirsuk *Qué., Canada* 60°0N 70°0W **143** B4
Payne, L. *Qué., Canada* 59°30N 74°30W **143** B3
Paynesville *Minn., U.S.A.* 45°23N 94°43W **77** E4
Payo Obispo = Chetumal *Quintana Roo, Mexico* 18°30N 88°20W **179** D5
Payson *Ariz., U.S.A.* 34°14N 111°20W **130** C4
Payson *Ill., U.S.A.* 39°49N 91°15W **84** D2
Payson *Utah, U.S.A.* 40°3N 111°44W **129** C4
Paz → *Guatemala* 13°44N 90°10W **182** D1
Paz, B. de la *Baja Calif. S., Mexico* 24°9N 110°25W **167** J8
Pe Ell *Wash., U.S.A.* 46°34N 123°18W **120** D2
Pea → *Ala., U.S.A.* 31°1N 85°51W **112** E5
Pea Ridge *Ark., U.S.A.* 36°27N 94°7W **106** B1
Peabody *Kans., U.S.A.* 38°10N 97°7W **82** C6
Peabody *Mass., U.S.A.* 42°31N 70°56W **91** B4
Peace → *Alta., Canada* 59°0N 111°25W **157** E10
Peace → *Fla., U.S.A.* 26°56N 82°6W **114** E6
Peace Dale *R.I., U.S.A.* 41°27N 71°30W **91** C3
Peace Point *Alta., Canada* 59°7N 112°27W **157** E10
Peace River *Alta., Canada* 56°15N 117°18W **152** B3
Peach County ☆ *Ga., U.S.A.* 32°30N 83°50W **113** D3
Peach Creek *W. Va., U.S.A.* 37°53N 81°59W **102** D3
Peach Orchard *Ark., U.S.A.* 36°17N 90°40W **106** B5
Peach Springs *Ariz., U.S.A.* 35°32N 113°25W **130** B2
Peachland *B.C., Canada* 49°47N 119°45W **155** F15
Peachtree City *Ga., U.S.A.* 33°25N 84°35W **113** C2
Peale, Mt. *Utah, U.S.A.* 38°26N 109°14W **129** E6
Pearblossom *Calif., U.S.A.* 34°30N 117°55W **127** J9
Pearce *Ariz., U.S.A.* 31°54N 109°49W **130** F6
Pearisburg *Va., U.S.A.* 37°20N 80°44W **102** D4
Pearl *Ont., Canada* 48°40N 88°40W **149** D12
Pearl *Ill., U.S.A.* 39°28N 90°38W **84** D3
Pearl *Miss., U.S.A.* 32°18N 90°12W **111** D3
Pearl → *Miss., U.S.A.* 30°11N 89°32W **111** F4

Pearl and Hermes Reef *Hawai'i, U.S.A.* 27°55N 175°45W 136 F8
Pearl City *Hawai'i, U.S.A.* 21°24N 157°59W 136 K14
Pearl City *Ill., U.S.A.* 42°16N 89°50W 84 A4
Pearl Harbor *Hawai'i, U.S.A.* 21°21N 157°57W 136 K14
Pearl Harbor Nat. Wildlife Refuge △ *Hawai'i,*
  U.S.A. 21°23N 157°59W 136 K14
Pearl River *La., U.S.A.* 30°23N 89°45W 110 D6
Pearl River *N.Y., U.S.A.* 41°4N 74°2W 97 A4
Pearl River County ☆ *Miss., U.S.A.* 30°40N 89°38W 111 F4
Pearland *Tex., U.S.A.* 29°33N 95°17W 116 C3
Pearsall *Tex., U.S.A.* 28°54N 99°6W 109 J8
Pearson *Ga., U.S.A.* 31°18N 82°51W 113 E4
Pearson Int. Toronto ✕ (YYZ) *Ont.,*
  Canada 43°46N 79°35W 161 A1
Peary Chan. *Nunavut, Canada* 79°40N 101°30W 158 B5
Peary Land *Greenland* 82°40N 33°0W 162 A7
Pease *Minn., U.S.A.* 45°42N 93°39W 77 E5
Pease → *Tex., U.S.A.* 34°12N 99°2W 109 C8
Peawanuck *Ont., Canada* 55°15N 85°12W 159 F11
Pebble Beach *Calif., U.S.A.* 36°34N 121°57W 126 G5
Pecan Island *La., U.S.A.* 29°39N 92°27W 110 E3
Pecatonica *Ill., U.S.A.* 42°19N 89°22W 84 A4
Pecatonica → *Ill., U.S.A.* 42°26N 89°12W 84 A4
Peck *Mich., U.S.A.* 43°16N 82°49W 79 F9
Peckerwood L. *Ark., U.S.A.* 34°40N 91°30W 106 D4
Pecos *N. Mex., U.S.A.* 35°35N 105°41W 131 B5
Pecos *Tex., U.S.A.* 31°26N 103°30W 108 F4
Pecos → *N. Mex., U.S.A.* 29°42N 101°22W 108 H6
Pecos County ☆ *Tex., U.S.A.* 30°53N 102°53W 108 G5
Pecos Nat. Historical Park △ *N. Mex.,*
  U.S.A. 35°33N 105°41W 131 B5
Pecos Plains *N. Mex., U.S.A.* 33°15N 104°10W 131 D6
Peculiar *Mo., U.S.A.* 38°43N 94°28W 83 C2
Pedernales *Dom. Rep.* 18°2N 71°44W 183 C5
Pedernales *Michoacan, Mexico* 19°8N 101°28W 175 C6
Pedernales → *Tex., U.S.A.* 30°26N 98°4W 109 G9
Pedregal de San Angel, Jardines del
  Distrito Federal, Mexico 19°19N 99°12W 181 C2
Pedro Antonio de los Santos *San Luis Potosí,*
  Mexico 21°36N 98°58W 171 J6
Pedro Bank *W. Indies* 17°5N 78°20W 182 C4
Pedro Cays *Jamaica* 17°5N 77°48W 182 C4
Pee Dee = Great Pee Dee → *S.C.,*
  U.S.A. 33°21N 79°10W 103 E6
Peebles *Ohio, U.S.A.* 38°57N 83°24W 86 E3
Peekskill *N.Y., U.S.A.* 41°17N 73°55W 92 A3
Peel → *Canada* 67°0N 135°0W 156 C6
Peel Pt. *N.W.T., Canada* 73°22N 114°30W 156 B10
Peel Sd. *Nunavut, Canada* 73°0N 96°0W 158 C6
Peerless *Mont., U.S.A.* 48°47N 105°50W 123 B12
Peerless L. *Alta., Canada* 56°40N 114°35W 152 B6
Peerless Lake *Alta., Canada* 56°37N 114°40W 152 B6
Peers *Alta., Canada* 53°40N 116°0W 152 C4
Peetz *Colo., U.S.A.* 40°58N 103°7W 125 D7
Peever *S. Dak., U.S.A.* 45°33N 96°57W 76 F9
Peggs *Okla., U.S.A.* 36°5N 95°6W 107 B8
Peggys Cove *N.S., Canada* 44°30N 63°55W 141 J6
Pegram *Tenn., U.S.A.* 36°6N 87°3W 104 D5
Pékans → *Qué., Canada* 52°12N 66°49W 140 A3
Pekin *Ill., U.S.A.* 40°35N 89°40W 84 C4
Pekin *N. Dak., U.S.A.* 47°48N 98°20W 76 C7
Pelahatchie *Miss., U.S.A.* 32°19N 89°48W 111 D4
Pelée, Mt. *Martinique* 14°48N 61°10W 183 D7
Pelee, Pt. *Ont., Canada* 41°54N 82°31W 146 F4
Pelee I. *Ont., Canada* 41°47N 82°40W 146 F4
Pelham *Ont., Canada* 43°3N 79°21W 146 D7
Pelham *Ala., U.S.A.* 33°44N 85°48W 112 C5
Pelham *Ga., U.S.A.* 31°8N 84°9W 113 E2
Pelham *Mass., U.S.A.* 42°24N 72°24W 91 B2
Pelham *N.H., U.S.A.* 42°44N 71°20W 89 D3
Pelham *N.Y., U.S.A.* 40°54N 73°48W 97 A4
Pelham Bay Park *N.Y., U.S.A.* 40°51N 73°48W 97 A4
Pelham Manor *N.Y., U.S.A.* 40°53N 73°48W 97 A4
Pelican *Alaska, U.S.A.* 57°58N 136°14W 135 H13
Pelican *La., U.S.A.* 31°53N 93°35W 110 C2
Pélican, L. du *Qué., Canada* 59°47N 73°35W 143 B3
Pelican L. *Alta., Canada* 55°48N 113°15W 152 C7
Pelican L. *Man., Canada* 52°28N 100°20W 151 C11
Pelican L. *Minn., U.S.A.* 48°4N 92°55W 77 B6
Pelican Narrows *Sask., Canada* 55°10N 102°56W 157 E12
Pelican Rapids *Man., Canada* 52°45N 100°42W 151 C11
Pelican Rapids *Minn., U.S.A.* 46°34N 96°5W 77 D2
Pelicano, I. *Sonora, Mexico* 34°5N 114°36W 168 B1
Pelicano, Is. el *Baja Calif. S., Mexico* 26°55N 113°10W 167 G5
Pell City *Ala., U.S.A.* 33°35N 86°17W 112 C4
Pella *Iowa, U.S.A.* 41°25N 92°55W 81 D61
Pellston *Mich., U.S.A.* 45°33N 84°47W 79 D7
Pellville *Ky., U.S.A.* 37°45N 86°49W 104 C6
Pelly *Sask., Canada* 51°52N 101°56W 151 D10
Pelly → *Yukon, Canada* 62°47N 137°19W 157 D5
Pelly B. *Nunavut, Canada* 68°53N 89°51W 158 D7
Pelly Bay *Nunavut, Canada* 68°38N 89°50W 158 D8
Pelly Crossing *N.W.T., Canada* 62°49N 136°34W 157 D5
Pelly L. *Nunavut, Canada* 66°0N 102°0W 159 D5
Pelly Mts. *Yukon, Canada* 61°40N 132°30W 157 D6
Peloncillo Mts. *Ariz., U.S.A.* 32°20N 109°20W 130 E6
Pemadumcook L. *Maine, U.S.A.* 45°42N 68°57W 90 C5
Pemberton *B.C., Canada* 50°25N 122°50W 155 E12
Pemberton *Minn., U.S.A.* 44°1N 93°47W 77 F5
Pemberton *N.J., U.S.A.* 39°58N 74°41W 92 C2
Pemberville *Ohio, U.S.A.* 41°25N 83°28W 86 B3
Pembina *N. Dak., U.S.A.* 48°58N 97°15W 76 B8
Pembina → *Alta., Canada* 54°45N 114°17W 152 D6
Pembina → *N. Dak., U.S.A.* 48°58N 97°14W 76 B8
Pembina County ☆ *N. Dak., U.S.A.* 48°48N 97°37W 76 B8
Pembine *Wis., U.S.A.* 45°38N 87°59W 78 C6
Pembroke *Ont., Canada* 45°50N 77°7W 147 B9
Pembroke *Ga., U.S.A.* 32°8N 81°37W 113 D5
Pembroke *Ky., U.S.A.* 36°47N 87°21W 104 D5
Pembroke *Mass., U.S.A.* 42°5N 70°48W 91 B4
Pembroke *Mich., U.S.A.* 42°26N 83°11W 98 A2
Pembroke *N.C., U.S.A.* 34°41N 79°12W 103 D6
Pembroke Pines *Fla., U.S.A.* 26°0N 80°13W 115 B1
Pemigewasset → *N.H., U.S.A.* 43°26N 71°40W 89 C3
Pemiscot County ☆ *Mo., U.S.A.* 36°5N 89°50W 83 E7
Pen Argyl *Pa., U.S.A.* 40°52N 75°16W 92 B2
Peña Nevada, Cerro *Nuevo León, Mexico* 23°46N 99°52W 171 G5
Penacook *N.H., U.S.A.* 43°15N 71°40W 89 C3
Penalosa *Kans., U.S.A.* 37°43N 98°19W 82 D5
Peñamiller *Querétaro, Mexico* 21°3N 99°49W 175 A8
Peñasco *N. Mex., U.S.A.* 36°10N 105°41W 131 A5
Peñasco → *N. Mex., U.S.A.* 32°40N 104°25W 131 E6
Pend Oreille → *Wash., U.S.A.* 49°4N 117°37W 120 A8
Pend Oreille, L. *Idaho, U.S.A.* 48°0N 116°21W 122 A2

Pend Oreille County ☆ *Wash., U.S.A.* 48°30N 117°10W 120 B8
Pender *Nebr., U.S.A.* 42°7N 96°43W 80 B9
Pender County ☆ *N.C., U.S.A.* 34°30N 78°0W 103 D8
Pendergrass *Ga., U.S.A.* 34°10N 83°41W 113 B3
Pendleton *Ind., U.S.A.* 40°5N 85°45W 85 D5
Pendleton *Oreg., U.S.A.* 45°40N 118°47W 121 B7
Pendleton County ☆ *Ky., U.S.A.* 38°40N 84°20W 105 B8
Pendleton County ☆ *W. Va., U.S.A.* 38°47N 79°17W 102 C5
Pendroy *Mont., U.S.A.* 48°4N 112°18W 123 B6
Penelope *Tex., U.S.A.* 31°52N 96°56W 109 F11
Penetanguishene *Nfld. & L., Canada* 47°36N 52°45W 142 E8
Penetanguishene *Ont., Canada* 44°50N 79°55W 146 C7
Penfield *Pa., U.S.A.* 41°13N 78°25W 87 C4
Penhold *Alta., Canada* 52°8N 113°52W 153 F7
Peñitas, Presa *Chiapas, Mexico* 17°25N 93°27W 178 B3
Pénjamillo *Michoacan, Mexico* 20°6N 101°54W 174 B6
Pénjamo *Guanajuato, Mexico* 20°26N 101°44W 174 B6
Penn = Penn Hills *Pa., U.S.A.* 40°28N 79°52W 87 D3
Penn Hills *Pa., U.S.A.* 40°28N 79°52W 87 D3
Penn Wynne *Pa., U.S.A.* 39°59N 75°16W 98 B1
Penn Yan *N.Y., U.S.A.* 42°40N 77°3W 88 C3
Pennant *Sask., Canada* 50°32N 108°14W 150 D3
Pennell, Mt. *Utah, U.S.A.* 37°58N 110°47W 129 F5
Penniac *N.B., Canada* 46°2N 66°34W 141 G3
Pennington *Ala., U.S.A.* 32°13N 88°3W 112 D2
Pennington *N.J., U.S.A.* 40°19N 74°48W 92 B2
Pennington County ☆ *Minn., U.S.A.* 48°5N 96°0W 77 B2
Pennington County ☆ *S. Dak., U.S.A.* 44°0N 103°0W 76 G2
Pennington Gap *Va., U.S.A.* 36°46N 83°2W 102 E1
Pennock *Minn., U.S.A.* 45°9N 95°10W 77 E3
Penns Grove *N.J., U.S.A.* 39°44N 75°28W 92 C1
Pennsauken *N.J., U.S.A.* 39°58N 75°3W 98 B2
Pennsboro *W. Va., U.S.A.* 39°17N 80°58W 102 B4
Pennsburg *Pa., U.S.A.* 40°23N 75°29W 92 B1
Pennsville *Pa., U.S.A.* 39°39N 75°31W 92 C1
Pennsylvania □ *U.S.A.* 40°45N 77°30W 87 D5
Pennville *Ind., U.S.A.* 40°30N 85°9W 85 C5
Penny *B.C., Canada* 53°51N 121°20W 155 B13
Penny Ice Cap *Nunavut, Canada* 67°17N 66°13W 158 D12
Penny Str. *Nunavut, Canada* 76°30N 97°0W 158 B6
Pennypack Park *Pa., U.S.A.* 40°3N 75°2W 98 A2
Pennyrile State Forest *Ky., U.S.A.* 37°11N 87°33W 104 C5
Penobscot → *Maine, U.S.A.* 44°30N 68°48W 90 D5
Penobscot B. *Maine, U.S.A.* 44°35N 68°50W 90 D5
Penobscot County ☆ *Maine, U.S.A.* 45°0N 69°0W 90 C5
Peñón Blanco *Durango, Mexico* 24°47N 104°2W 173 C6
Penonomé *Panama* 8°31N 80°21W 182 E3
Penrose *N. Mex., U.S.A.* 36°26N 105°1W 125 D5
Penrose *Tex., U.S.A.* 31°45N 102°36W 108 F5
Pensacola *Fla., U.S.A.* 30°25N 87°13W 114 A1
Pensacola *Okla., U.S.A.* 36°28N 95°7W 107 B8
Pensacola B. *Fla., U.S.A.* 30°25N 87°5W 114 A1
Pense *Sask., Canada* 50°25N 104°59W 150 E7
Pentagon *Va., U.S.A.* 38°53N 77°3W 99 B3
Pentecôte → *Qué., Canada* 49°46N 67°10W 140 D2
Pentecôte, L. *Qué., Canada* 49°53N 67°20W 140 D2
Penticton *B.C., Canada* 49°30N 119°38W 155 F15
Pentwater *Mich., U.S.A.* 43°47N 86°26W 79 F5
Penwell *Tex., U.S.A.* 31°45N 102°36W 108 F5
Peoria *Ariz., U.S.A.* 33°43N 112°14W 134 A1
Peoria *Ill., U.S.A.* 40°42N 89°36W 84 C4
Peoria *Okla., U.S.A.* 36°54N 94°41W 107 B9
Peoria County ☆ *Ill., U.S.A.* 40°45N 89°45W 84 C4
Peoria Heights *Ill., U.S.A.* 40°45N 89°35W 84 C4
Peotone *Ill., U.S.A.* 41°20N 87°48W 84 B6
Pep *N. Mex., U.S.A.* 33°50N 103°20W 131 D7
Pepacton Res. *N.Y., U.S.A.* 42°5N 74°58W 88 C6
Pepeekeo *Hawai'i, U.S.A.* 19°51N 155°6W 136 D6
Pepin *Wis., U.S.A.* 44°27N 92°9W 78 D1
Pepin County ☆ *Wis., U.S.A.* 44°30N 92°10W 78 D1
Pepperell *Mass., U.S.A.* 42°40N 71°35W 91 B3
Pequannock *N.J., U.S.A.* 40°57N 74°18W 92 B2
Pequeña, Pta. *Baja Calif. S., Mexico* 26°15N 112°30W 167 G6
Pequest → *N.J., U.S.A.* 40°50N 75°5W 92 B1
Pequop Mts. *Nev., U.S.A.* 40°45N 114°40W 128 B6
Pequot Lakes *Minn., U.S.A.* 46°36N 94°19W 77 D4
Peralta *N. Mex., U.S.A.* 34°50N 106°41W 131 C4
Percé *Qué., Canada* 48°31N 64°13W 140 E5
Perdido *Ala., U.S.A.* 31°0N 87°38W 112 E3
Perdido → *Ala., U.S.A.* 30°27N 87°23W 112 F3
Perdido, L. el *San Luis Potosí, Mexico* 23°17N 101°43W 171 G3
Perdido B. *Ala., U.S.A.* 30°20N 87°30W 112 F3
Perdue *Sask., Canada* 52°0N 107°33W 150 C4
Perham *Minn., U.S.A.* 46°36N 95°34W 77 D3
Peribán de Ramos *Michoacan, Mexico* 19°30N 102°25W 174 C5
Péribonka *Qué., Canada* 48°46N 72°3W 145 C10
Péribonka → *Qué., Canada* 48°45N 72°5W 143 D3
Péribonka, L. *Qué., Canada* 50°1N 71°10W 145 A11
Pericos *Sinaloa, Mexico* 25°3N 107°42W 172 B3
Peridot *Ariz., U.S.A.* 33°18N 110°28W 130 D5
Perkasie *Pa., U.S.A.* 40°22N 75°18W 92 B1
Perkins *Okla., U.S.A.* 35°58N 97°2W 107 C6
Perkins County ☆ *Nebr., U.S.A.* 40°45N 101°45W 80 D4
Perkins County ☆ *S. Dak., U.S.A.* 45°30N 102°30W 76 E3
Perkinston *Miss., U.S.A.* 30°47N 89°8W 111 F4
Perkiomen → *Pa., U.S.A.* 40°7N 75°28W 92 B1
Perley *Minn., U.S.A.* 47°11N 96°48W 77 C2
Perma *Mont., U.S.A.* 47°22N 114°35W 123 C3
Pernell *Okla., U.S.A.* 34°39N 97°31W 107 D6
Perote *Veracruz, Mexico* 19°34N 97°14W 176 D3
Perquimans County ☆ *N.C., U.S.A.* 36°10N 76°30W 103 B9
Perrin *Tex., U.S.A.* 33°2N 98°4W 109 D9
Perrine *Fla., U.S.A.* 25°36N 80°21W 114 F8
Perris *Calif., U.S.A.* 33°47N 117°14W 127 K9
Perro, L. del *N. Mex., U.S.A.* 34°41N 105°58W 131 C5
Perry *Ark., U.S.A.* 35°3N 92°48W 106 C3
Perry *Fla., U.S.A.* 30°7N 83°35W 114 A5
Perry *Ga., U.S.A.* 32°28N 83°44W 113 D3
Perry *Ill., U.S.A.* 39°47N 90°45W 84 D3
Perry *Iowa, U.S.A.* 41°51N 94°6W 81 D4
Perry *Kans., U.S.A.* 39°5N 95°24W 82 B8
Perry *Maine, U.S.A.* 44°58N 67°5W 90 D6
Perry *Mich., U.S.A.* 42°50N 84°13W 79 G7
Perry *Mo., U.S.A.* 39°26N 91°40W 83 B5
Perry *N.Y., U.S.A.* 42°43N 78°0W 88 C2
Perry *Okla., U.S.A.* 36°17N 97°14W 107 B6
Perry *Utah, U.S.A.* 41°28N 112°2W 129 B3
Perry County ☆ *Ala., U.S.A.* 32°38N 87°19W 112 D3
Perry County ☆ *Ark., U.S.A.* 35°0N 92°48W 106 D3
Perry County ☆ *Ill., U.S.A.* 38°5N 89°20W 84 E4
Perry County ☆ *Ind., U.S.A.* 38°5N 86°40W 85 E4
Perry County ☆ *Ky., U.S.A.* 37°15N 83°13W 105 C9

Perry County ☆ *Miss., U.S.A.* 31°12N 89°2W 111 E4
Perry County ☆ *Mo., U.S.A.* 37°45N 89°50W 83 D7
Perry County ☆ *Ohio, U.S.A.* 39°43N 82°13W 86 D4
Perry County ☆ *Pa., U.S.A.* 40°35N 77°5W 87 D5
Perry County ☆ *Tenn., U.S.A.* 35°39N 87°50W 104 E5
Perry Hall *Md., U.S.A.* 39°25N 76°28W 93 A4
Perry Lake *Kans., U.S.A.* 39°7N 95°26W 82 B8
Perrydale *Oreg., U.S.A.* 45°3N 123°16W 121 B2
Perrysburg *Ohio, U.S.A.* 41°34N 83°38W 86 B3
Perrysville *Ohio, U.S.A.* 40°40N 82°19W 86 C4
Perrysville *Pa., U.S.A.* 40°32N 80°1W 98 A1
Perryton *Tex., U.S.A.* 36°24N 100°48W 108 A7
Perryville *Alaska, U.S.A.* 55°55N 159°9W 135 J8
Perryville *Ark., U.S.A.* 35°0N 92°48W 106 C3
Perryville *Ky., U.S.A.* 37°39N 84°57W 105 C8
Perryville *Md., U.S.A.* 39°34N 76°4W 93 A4
Perryville *Mo., U.S.A.* 37°43N 89°52W 83 D7
Pershing *Mich., U.S.A.* 46°23N 88°48W 78 B5
Pershing County ☆ *Nev., U.S.A.* 40°20N 118°10W 128 B2
Persia *Iowa, U.S.A.* 41°35N 95°33W 81 D3
Person County ☆ *N.C., U.S.A.* 36°20N 79°0W 103 B7
Perth *Ont., Canada* 44°55N 76°15W 147 C10
Perth *Kans., U.S.A.* 37°11N 97°3W 82 D6
Perth *N. Dak., U.S.A.* 48°43N 99°28W 76 B6
Perth Amboy *N.J., U.S.A.* 40°30N 74°15W 97 C1
Perth-Andover *N.B., Canada* 46°44N 67°42W 141 G2
Peru *Ill., U.S.A.* 41°20N 89°8W 84 B4
Peru *Ind., U.S.A.* 40°45N 86°4W 85 C4
Peru *Kans., U.S.A.* 37°5N 96°6W 82 D7
Peru *N.Y., U.S.A.* 44°35N 73°32W 89 B1
Peru *Nebr., U.S.A.* 40°29N 95°44W 80 D10
Peru *Vt., U.S.A.* 43°14N 72°54W 89 C2
Peshtigo *Wis., U.S.A.* 45°3N 87°45W 78 C6
Peshtigo → *Wis., U.S.A.* 44°58N 87°40W 78 D6
Pesotum *Ill., U.S.A.* 39°55N 88°16W 84 D5
Pesqueira *Sonora, Mexico* 29°23N 110°54W 168 D5
Pesquería *Nuevo León, Mexico* 25°45N 100°4W 170 E4
Pesquería → *Nuevo León, Mexico* 25°53N 99°11W 170 E5
Petacalco, B. de *Guerrero, Mexico* 17°57N 102°5W 174 E5
Petal *Miss., U.S.A.* 31°21N 89°16W 111 E4
Petalcingo *Chiapas, Mexico* 17°1N 92°27W 178 B4
Petaluma *Calif., U.S.A.* 38°14N 122°39W 126 E4
Petatlán *Guerrero, Mexico* 17°31N 101°16W 175 E6
Petawawa *Ont., Canada* 45°54N 77°17W 147 B9
Petcacab *Quintana Roo, Mexico* 19°16N 88°12W 179 C5
Petén Itzá, L. *Guatemala* 16°58N 89°50W 182 C2
Petenwell L. *Wis., U.S.A.* 44°4N 90°1W 78 D3
Peter I. *Br. Virgin Is.* 18°22N 64°35W 184 G18
Peter Lougheed Prov. Park △ *Alta.,*
  Canada 50°42N 115°10W 153 H5
Peter O. Knight ✕ *Tampa, U.S.A.* 27°54N 82°26W 115 B4
Peter Pond L. *Sask., Canada* 55°55N 108°44W 157 E11
Peterbell *Ont., Canada* 48°36N 83°21W 149 D13
Peterborough *Ont., Canada* 44°20N 78°20W 147 C8
Peterborough *N.H., U.S.A.* 42°53N 71°57W 89 D3
Peterman *Ala., U.S.A.* 31°35N 87°16W 112 E3
Petermann Bjerg *Greenland* 73°7N 28°25W 162 C8
Petermann Gletscher *Greenland* 80°30N 60°0W 162 A4
Peters, L. *Qué., Canada* 59°41N 70°53W 143 B3
Petersburg *Alaska, U.S.A.* 56°48N 132°58W 135 H14
Petersburg *Ill., U.S.A.* 40°1N 89°51W 84 C4
Petersburg *Ind., U.S.A.* 38°30N 87°17W 85 E3
Petersburg *Mich., U.S.A.* 41°54N 83°43W 79 H8
Petersburg *N. Dak., U.S.A.* 48°0N 98°0W 76 C7
Petersburg *N.J., U.S.A.* 39°15N 74°42W 92 C2
Petersburg *N.Y., U.S.A.* 42°44N 73°20W 91 B1
Petersburg *Nebr., U.S.A.* 41°51N 98°5W 80 C7
Petersburg *Ohio, U.S.A.* 40°55N 80°32W 86 C6
Petersburg *Pa., U.S.A.* 40°34N 78°3W 87 D4
Petersburg *Tenn., U.S.A.* 35°19N 86°38W 104 E6
Petersburg *Tex., U.S.A.* 33°52N 101°36W 108 D6
Petersburg *Va., U.S.A.* 37°14N 77°24W 102 D7
Petersburg *W. Va., U.S.A.* 39°1N 79°5W 102 B5
Petersfield *Mass., U.S.A.* 50°18N 96°58W 151 E15
Petersham *Mass., U.S.A.* 42°29N 72°11W 91 B2
Peterson *Iowa, U.S.A.* 42°55N 95°21W 81 C3
Peterson *Minn., U.S.A.* 43°47N 91°50W 77 G7
Peterson Field, Colorado Springs ✕ (COS) *Colo.,*
  U.S.A. 38°49N 104°43W 125 D6
Peterstown *W. Va., U.S.A.* 37°24N 80°48W 102 D4
Petersville *Ky., U.S.A.* 38°27N 83°30W 105 B9
Peterview *Nfld. & L., Canada* 49°7N 55°21W 142 C5
Petit Bois I. *Miss., U.S.A.* 30°12N 88°26W 111 F5
Petit-Cap *Qué., Canada* 49°3N 64°30W 140 D5
Petit-de-Grat *N.S., Canada* 45°30N 60°58W 141 H9
Petit Étang *N.S., Canada* 46°39N 60°58W 141 G8
Petit Goâve *Haiti* 18°27N 72°51W 183 C5
Petit Jean State Park △ *Ark., U.S.A.* 35°7N 92°56W 106 C3
Petit Lac Manicouagan *Qué., Canada* 51°25N 67°40W 140 B2
Petit Manan Pt. *Maine, U.S.A.* 44°24N 67°54W 90 D6
Petit-Mécatina → *Qué., Canada* 50°40N 59°30W 143 C6
Petit-Mécatina, Î. du *Qué., Canada* 50°30N 59°25W 143 C6
Petit-Rocher *N.B., Canada* 47°46N 65°43W 141 F4
Petit-Saguenay *Qué., Canada* 48°15N 70°4W 145 C12
Petitcodiac *N.B., Canada* 45°57N 65°11W 141 H4
Petite-Rivière *Qué., Canada* 47°20N 70°33W 145 C12
Petite Rivière Bridge *N.S., Canada* 44°14N 64°27W 141 J5
Petitot → *B.C., Canada* 60°14N 123°29W 157 D8
Petitsikapau L. *Nfld. & L., Canada* 54°37N 66°25W 143 C4
Peto *Yucatán, Mexico* 20°8N 88°55W 179 B5
Petoskey *Mich., U.S.A.* 45°22N 84°57W 79 D7
Petrified Forest Nat. Park △ *Ariz.,*
  U.S.A. 35°0N 109°30W 130 B6
Petroglyph Nat. Monument △ *N. Mex.,*
  U.S.A. 35°10N 106°43W 131 B4
Petroleum *W. Va., U.S.A.* 39°11N 81°16W 102 B3
Petroleum County ☆ *Mont., U.S.A.* 47°7N 108°25W 123 C9
Petrolia *Ont., Canada* 42°54N 82°9W 146 E4
Petrolia *Kans., U.S.A.* 37°45N 95°29W 82 D8
Petrolia *Tex., U.S.A.* 34°1N 98°14W 109 C9
Petros *Tenn., U.S.A.* 36°6N 84°27W 105 D8
Pettibone *N. Dak., U.S.A.* 47°7N 99°31W 76 C6
Pettis County ☆ *Mo., U.S.A.* 38°40N 93°15W 83 C3
Pettus *Tex., U.S.A.* 28°37N 97°48W 109 J10
Petty Harbour Long Pond *Nfld. & L.,*
  Canada 47°31N 52°58W 142 E8
Pettys Island *N.J., U.S.A.* 39°57N 75°9W 98 B2
Pfeifer *Kans., U.S.A.* 38°43N 99°10W 82 C4
Phalen, L. *Minn., U.S.A.* 44°59N 93°3W 94 B3
Phalen Park *Minn., U.S.A.* 44°59N 93°3W 94 B3
Pharr *Tex., U.S.A.* 26°12N 98°11W 108 L9
Pheba *Miss., U.S.A.* 33°35N 88°57W 111 C5
Phelps *Ky., U.S.A.* 37°32N 82°9W 105 C10

Phelps *N.Y., U.S.A.* 42°58N 77°3W 88 C3
Phelps *Wis., U.S.A.* 46°4N 89°5W 78 B4
Phelps County ☆ *Mo., U.S.A.* 37°55N 91°45W 83 D5
Phelps County ☆ *Nebr., U.S.A.* 40°30N 99°30W 80 D6
Phelps L. *Sask., Canada* 59°15N 103°15W 157 E12
Phelps L. *N.C., U.S.A.* 35°46N 76°27W 103 C9
Phenix *Va., U.S.A.* 37°5N 78°45W 102 D6
Phenix City *Ala., U.S.A.* 32°28N 85°0W 112 D5
Phil Campbell *Ala., U.S.A.* 34°21N 87°42W 112 B3
Philadelphia *Miss., U.S.A.* 32°46N 89°7W 111 D4
Philadelphia *N.Y., U.S.A.* 44°9N 75°43W 88 A5
Philadelphia *Pa., U.S.A.* 39°57N 75°9W 98 B1
Philadelphia □ *Pa., U.S.A.* 35°41N 84°24W 105 E8
Philadelphia County ☆ *Pa., U.S.A.* 39°57N 75°10W 98 B1
Philadelphia Int. ✕ (PHL) *Pa., U.S.A.* 39°51N 75°18W 98 B1
Philip *S. Dak., U.S.A.* 44°2N 101°40W 76 F4
Philip Smith Mts. *Alaska, U.S.A.* 68°0N 148°0W 135 C10
Philippi *W. Va., U.S.A.* 39°9N 80°3W 102 B4
Philip's L. *Oreg., U.S.A.* 45°25N 123°13W 121 B2
Philipsburg *Qué., Canada* 45°2N 73°5W 145 F9
Philipsburg *Mont., U.S.A.* 46°20N 113°18W 123 D4
Philipsburg *Pa., U.S.A.* 40°54N 78°13W 87 D4
Phillips *Maine, U.S.A.* 44°49N 70°21W 90 D3
Phillips *Nebr., U.S.A.* 40°54N 98°13W 80 D7
Phillips *Okla., U.S.A.* 34°30N 96°12W 107 D7
Phillips *Tex., U.S.A.* 35°42N 101°22W 108 B6
Phillips *Wis., U.S.A.* 45°42N 90°24W 78 C3
Phillips County ☆ *Ark., U.S.A.* 34°19N 90°51W 106 D5
Phillips County ☆ *Colo., U.S.A.* 40°40N 102°20W 125 D8
Phillips County ☆ *Kans., U.S.A.* 39°45N 99°15W 82 B4
Phillips County ☆ *Mont., U.S.A.* 48°12N 108°0W 123 B10
Phillips Inlet *Nunavut, Canada* 82°5N 86°10W 158 A4
Phillipsburg *Ga., U.S.A.* 31°25N 83°30W 113 E3
Phillipsburg *Kans., U.S.A.* 39°45N 99°19W 82 B4
Phillipsburg *Mo., U.S.A.* 37°33N 92°47W 83 D4
Phillipsburg *N.J., U.S.A.* 40°42N 75°12W 92 B1
Philmont *N.Y., U.S.A.* 42°15N 73°39W 88 C7
Philo *Calif., U.S.A.* 39°4N 123°26W 126 D3
Philo *Ill., U.S.A.* 40°1N 88°9W 84 C5
Philomath *Ga., U.S.A.* 33°44N 82°59W 113 C4
Philomath *Oreg., U.S.A.* 44°32N 123°22W 121 C2
Philpott Res. *Va., U.S.A.* 36°47N 80°2W 102 E4
Phippsburg *Colo., U.S.A.* 40°14N 106°57W 125 B4
Phoenix *Ariz., U.S.A.* 33°26N 112°4W 134 C2
Phoenix *La., U.S.A.* 29°39N 89°56W 110 E6
Phoenix *N.Y., U.S.A.* 43°14N 76°18W 88 B4
Phoenix *Oreg., U.S.A.* 42°16N 122°49W 121 E3
Phoenix Sky Harbour ✕ (PHX) *Ariz.,*
  U.S.A. 33°26N 112°5W 134 C2
Phoenixville *Pa., U.S.A.* 40°8N 75°31W 92 B1
Piapot *Sask., Canada* 49°59N 109°8W 150 F2
Piashti, L. *Qué., Canada* 50°29N 62°52W 140 C7
Piatt County ☆ *Ill., U.S.A.* 40°0N 88°35W 84 C5
Piaxtla *Puebla, Mexico* 18°12N 98°14W 177 F2
Piaxtla → *Sinaloa, Mexico* 23°42N 106°49W 172 D4
Pic → *Ont., Canada* 48°36N 86°18W 149 D10
Pic I. *Ont., Canada* 48°43N 86°37W 149 D10
Picacho *Ariz., U.S.A.* 32°43N 111°30W 130 E4
Picacho *N. Mex., U.S.A.* 33°21N 105°9W 131 D5
Picacho Pass *Ariz., U.S.A.* 32°40N 111°25W 130 E4
Picachos, Sa. los *Michoacan, Mexico* 18°50N 101°30W 174 D6
Picayune *Miss., U.S.A.* 30°32N 89°41W 111 F4
Piccadilly *Nfld. & L., Canada* 48°34N 58°55W 142 D2
Piceance Cr. → *Colo., U.S.A.* 40°5N 108°14W 125 B2
Pich *Campeche, Mexico* 19°31N 90°4W 179 C3
Picher *Okla., U.S.A.* 36°59N 94°50W 107 B9
Pichilingue *Baja Calif. S., Mexico* 24°15N 110°20W 167 J8
Pichucalco *Chiapas, Mexico* 17°31N 93°4W 178 B3
Pickaway County ☆ *Ohio, U.S.A.* 39°43N 82°59W 86 D4
Pickens *Ark., U.S.A.* 33°51N 91°29W 106 E4
Pickens *Miss., U.S.A.* 32°53N 89°58W 111 D4
Pickens *Okla., U.S.A.* 34°23N 95°0W 107 D8
Pickens *S.C., U.S.A.* 34°53N 82°42W 103 C3
Pickens *W. Va., U.S.A.* 38°39N 80°13W 102 C4
Pickens County ☆ *Ala., U.S.A.* 33°16N 88°6W 112 C2
Pickens County ☆ *Ga., U.S.A.* 34°30N 84°25W 113 B2
Pickens County ☆ *S.C., U.S.A.* 34°50N 82°45W 103 C3
Pickerel L. *Ont., Canada* 48°40N 91°25W 148 D5
Pickering *Mo., U.S.A.* 40°27N 94°49W 83 A2
Pickerington *Ohio, U.S.A.* 39°53N 82°45W 86 D4
Pickett County ☆ *Tenn., U.S.A.* 36°34N 85°8W 105 D7
Pickford *Mich., U.S.A.* 46°10N 84°22W 79 C7
Pickle Lake *Ont., Canada* 51°30N 90°12W 148 A6
Pickrell *Nebr., U.S.A.* 40°23N 96°44W 80 D9
Pickstown *S. Dak., U.S.A.* 43°4N 98°32W 76 G7
Pickwick L. *Ala., U.S.A.* 35°4N 88°15W 112 A2
Pico Bonito, Parque Nac. △ *Honduras* 15°34N 86°48W 182 C2
Pico de Orizaba, Parque Nacional △ *Puebla,*
  Mexico 19°0N 97°20W 177 E3
Pico de Tancítaro, Parque Nacional △
  Michoacan, Mexico 19°21N 102°20W 174 C5
Pico Rivera *Calif., U.S.A.* 33°59N 118°5W 133 C4
Picton *Ont., Canada* 44°1N 77°9W 147 C9
Pictou *N.S., Canada* 45°41N 62°42W 141 H7
Pictou I. *N.S., Canada* 45°49N 62°33W 141 H7
Picture Butte *Alta., Canada* 49°55N 112°45W 153 J8
Pictured Rocks Nat. Lakeshore △ *Mich.,*
  U.S.A. 46°30N 86°30W 79 C5
Picuris Indian Reservation *N. Mex.,*
  U.S.A. 36°12N 105°48W 131 A5
Pie I. *Ont., Canada* 48°15N 89°6W 148 D7
Pie Town *N. Mex., U.S.A.* 34°18N 108°9W 131 C2
Piedmont *Ala., U.S.A.* 33°55N 85°37W 112 C5
Piedmont *Kans., U.S.A.* 37°37N 96°22W 82 D7
Piedmont *Okla., U.S.A.* 35°39N 97°44W 107 C6
Piedmont *Mo., U.S.A.* 37°9N 90°42W 83 D6
Piedmont *Oreg., U.S.A.* 45°33N 122°40W 132 A1
Piedmont *S.C., U.S.A.* 34°42N 82°28W 103 D3
Piedmont *S. Dak., U.S.A.* 44°14N 103°24W 76 F2
Piedmont *W. Va., U.S.A.* 39°29N 79°3W 93 A1
Piedmont L. *Ohio, U.S.A.* 40°11N 81°13W 86 C6
Piedmont Nat. Wildlife Refuge △ *Ga.,*
  U.S.A. 33°8N 83°45W 113 C3
Piedras, I. *Campeche, Mexico* 20°23N 90°38W 179 B3
Piedra, Península la *Sinaloa, Mexico* 23°8N 106°21W 172 D4
Piedra, Pta. de *Tamaulipas, Mexico* 22°59N 97°45W 171 F7
Piedras Negras *Coahuila, Mexico* 28°42N 100°31W 170 B4
Piedras Negras *Veracruz, Mexico* 18°46N 96°11W 177 F4
Piedritas *Coahuila, Mexico* 28°46N 103°4W 170 B1
Pierce *Colo., U.S.A.* 40°38N 104°45W 125 B6
Pierce *Nebr., U.S.A.* 42°12N 97°32W 80 B8
Pierce City *Mo., U.S.A.* 36°57N 94°0W 83 E3
Pierce County ☆ *Ga., U.S.A.* 31°20N 82°10W 113 E4

Pierce County ☆ N. Dak., U.S.A. 48°0N 100°0W **76 B5**
Pierce County ☆ Nebr., U.S.A. 42°20N 97°40W **80 B8**
Pierce County ☆ Wash., U.S.A. 47°0N 122°0W **120 C3**
Pierce County ☆ Wis., U.S.A. 44°45N 92°25W **78 D1**
Pierceland Sask., Canada 54°20N 109°46W **157 F11**
Pierceton Ind., U.S.A. 41°12N 85°42W **85 B5**
Pierceville Kans., U.S.A. 37°53N 100°40W **82 D3**
Piercy Calif., U.S.A. 39°59N 123°48W **126 D3**
Pierre S. Dak., U.S.A. 44°22N 100°21W **76 F5**
Pierre Elliott-Trudeau ✈ (YUL) Qué., Canada 45°28N 73°44W **160 B2**
Pierre Part La., U.S.A. 29°58N 91°12W **110 E4**
Pierrefonds Qué., Canada 45°29N 73°51W **160 B1**
Pierreville Qué., Canada 46°4N 72°49W **145 E10**
Pierron Ill., U.S.A. 38°47N 89°36W **84 E4**
Pierson Man., Canada 49°11N 101°15W **151 F10**
Pierson Fla., U.S.A. 29°14N 81°28W **114 B7**
Pierson Iowa, U.S.A. 42°33N 95°52W **81 C3**
Pierz Minn., U.S.A. 45°59N 94°6W **77 E4**
Pigeon La., U.S.A. 30°4N 91°17W **110 D4**
Pigeon Mich., U.S.A. 43°50N 83°16W **79 F8**
Pigeon → Ind., U.S.A. 41°47N 85°49W **85 B5**
Pigeon → Tenn., U.S.A. 36°2N 83°17W **105 D9**
Pigeon Cove Mass., U.S.A. 42°41N 70°38W **91 B4**
Pigeon Cr. → Ala., U.S.A. 31°20N 86°42W **112 E4**
Pigeon Falls Wis., U.S.A. 44°26N 91°13W **78 D2**
Pigeon Forge Tenn., U.S.A. 35°48N 83°33W **105 E9**
Pigeon L. Alta., Canada 53°1N 114°2W **153 E6**
Pigeon L. Ont., Canada 44°27N 78°30W **147 C8**
Pigg → Va., U.S.A. 37°0N 79°29W **102 E5**
Piggott Ark. U.S.A. 36°23N 90°11W **106 B51**
Pigs Eye Lake Minn., U.S.A. 44°54N 93°4W **94 B3**
Pihuamo Jalisco, Mexico 19°15N 103°23W **174 C4**
Pijijiapan Chiapas, Mexico 15°42N 93°14W **178 D3**
Pike County ☆ Ala., U.S.A. 31°48N 85°58W **112 E5**
Pike County ☆ Ark., U.S.A. 34°14N 93°45W **106 D2**
Pike County ☆ Ga., U.S.A. 33°5N 84°20W **113 C2**
Pike County ☆ Ill., U.S.A. 39°35N 90°50W **84 D3**
Pike County ☆ Ind., U.S.A. 38°25N 87°10W **85 E3**
Pike County ☆ Ky., U.S.A. 37°30N 82°25W **105 C10**
Pike County ☆ Miss., U.S.A. 31°15N 90°27W **111 E3**
Pike County ☆ Mo., U.S.A. 39°20N 91°10W **83 B5**
Pike County ☆ Ohio, U.S.A. 39°4N 83°1W **86 D3**
Pike County ☆ Pa., U.S.A. 41°20N 75°0W **87 C8**
Pike Nat. Forest Colo., U.S.A. 39°15N 105°20W **125 C5**
Pike River Qué., Canada 45°4N 73°6W **89 A1**
Pike Road Ala., U.S.A. 32°17N 86°6W **112 D4**
Pikes Peak Colo., U.S.A. 38°50N 105°3W **125 D5**
Pikesville Md., U.S.A. 39°22N 76°43W **99 A1**
Piketon Ohio, U.S.A. 39°4N 83°1W **86 D3**
Pikeville Ky., U.S.A. 37°29N 82°31W **105 C10**
Pikeville N.C., U.S.A. 35°30N 77°59W **103 C8**
Pikeville Tenn., U.S.A. 35°36N 85°11W **105 E7**
Pilares, Sa. Chihuahua, Mexico 30°20N 104°55W **169 C11**
Pilger Nebr., U.S.A. 42°0N 97°3W **80 B8**
Pillager Minn., U.S.A. 46°20N 94°28W **77 D4**
Pillsbury N. Dak., U.S.A. 47°13N 97°48W **76 C8**
Pillsbury, L. Calif., U.S.A. 39°25N 122°57W **126 D4**
Pillsbury State Forest Minn., U.S.A. 46°25N 94°26W **77 D4**
Pillsbury State Park △ N.H., U.S.A. 43°14N 72°6W **91 C2**
Pilón → Tamaulipas, Mexico 23°58N 98°42W **171 G6**
Pilot Butte Sask., Canada 50°28N 104°25W **150 E7**
Pilot Grove Mo., U.S.A. 38°53N 92°55W **83 C4**
Pilot Knob Ark., U.S.A. 35°42N 93°57W **106 C2**
Pilot Knob Ky., U.S.A. 36°50N 86°41W **104 D6**
Pilot Knob Mo., U.S.A. 37°40N 90°40W **83 D6**
Pilot Mound Man., Canada 49°15N 98°54W **151 F13**
Pilot Mountain N.C., U.S.A. 36°23N 80°28W **103 B5**
Pilot Pk. Nev., U.S.A. 41°1N 114°5W **128 A6**
Pilot Pk. Wyo., U.S.A. 44°58N 109°53W **124 B3**
Pilot Point Alaska, U.S.A. 57°34N 157°35W **135 H8**
Pilot Point Tex., U.S.A. 33°24N 96°58W **109 D11**
Pilot Rock Oreg., U.S.A. 45°29N 118°50W **121 B7**
Pilot Station Alaska, U.S.A. 61°56N 162°53W **135 F7**
Pim I. Nunavut, Canada 78°44N 74°25W **158 B11**
Pima Ariz., U.S.A. 32°54N 109°50W **130 E6**
Pima County ☆ Ariz., U.S.A. 32°0N 112°0W **130 E4**
Pimmit Hills Va., U.S.A. 38°54N 77°12W **99 B2**
Pin-Blanc, → du Qué., Canada 46°45N 78°8W **144 E4**
Pinacate, Cerro del Sonora, Mexico 31°45N 113°30W **168 B2**
Pinal County ☆ Ariz., U.S.A. 33°0N 111°15W **130 E4**
Pinal de Amoles Querétaro, Mexico 21°8N 99°42W **175 A8**
Pinaleno Mts. Ariz., U.S.A. 32°45N 110°0W **130 E6**
Pinar del Río Cuba 22°26N 83°40W **182 B3**
Pinardville N.H., U.S.A. 42°59N 71°30W **89 D3**
Pinawa Man., Canada 50°9N 95°50W **151 E16**
Pincher Creek Alta., Canada 49°30N 113°57W **153 J7**
Pinckard Ala., U.S.A. 31°19N 85°33W **112 E5**
Pinckneyville Ill., U.S.A. 38°5N 89°23W **84 E4**
Pinconning Mich., U.S.A. 43°51N 83°58W **79 F8**
Pindall Ark., U.S.A. 36°4N 92°53W **106 B3**
Pine Ariz., U.S.A. 34°23N 111°27W **130 C4**
Pine Oreg., U.S.A. 44°42N 117°12W **121 C8**
Pine → B.C., Canada 56°8N 120°43W **157 E8**
Pine → Mich., U.S.A. 43°35N 84°8W **79 F7**
Pine → Mich., U.S.A. 44°14N 85°54W **79 E6**
Pine, C. Nfld. & L., Canada 46°37N 53°32W **142 F7**
Pine Apple Ala., U.S.A. 31°52N 87°0W **112 E4**
Pine Barrens N.J., U.S.A. 39°30N 74°30W **92 C2**
Pine Bluff Ark., U.S.A. 34°13N 92°1W **106 D3**
Pine Bluff Arsenal Ark., U.S.A. 34°19N 92°6W **106 D3**
Pine Bluffs Wyo., U.S.A. 41°11N 104°4W **124 E8**
Pine Bush N.Y., U.S.A. 41°36N 74°17W **88 D2**
Pine Castle Fla., U.S.A. 28°28N 81°22W **115 B2**
Pine City Minn., U.S.A. 45°50N 92°59W **77 E6**
Pine City Wash., U.S.A. 47°12N 117°31W **120 C8**
Pine County ☆ Minn., U.S.A. 46°5N 92°50W **77 D6**
Pine Cr. → Nev., U.S.A. 40°36N 116°12W **128 B4**
Pine Cr. → Pa., U.S.A. 41°10N 77°16W **87 C5**
Pine Creek Okla., U.S.A. 34°7N 95°5W **107 D8**
Pine Dock Man., Canada 51°38N 96°48W **151 D15**
Pine Falls Man., Canada 50°34N 96°11W **151 E16**
Pine Flat L. Calif., U.S.A. 36°50N 119°20W **127 J7**
Pine Forest Range Nev., U.S.A. 41°45N 118°50W **128 A2**
Pine Grove Ont., Canada 43°47N 79°34W **161 A1**
Pine Grove La., U.S.A. 30°43N 90°45W **110 D3**
Pine Grove Pa., U.S.A. 40°33N 76°23W **87 D6**
Pine Grove W. Va., U.S.A. 39°34N 80°41W **102 B4**
Pine Grove Park Ont., Canada 45°22N 75°37W **160 B2**
Pine Haven Wyo., U.S.A. 44°21N 104°49W **124 B8**
Pine Hill Ala., U.S.A. 31°59N 87°35W **112 E4**
Pine Hills Fla., U.S.A. 28°33N 81°27W **115 A2**
Pine Hills N.J., U.S.A. 39°47N 74°59W **92 C2**
Pine I. Fla., U.S.A. 26°36N 82°7W **114 E6**

Pine Island Minn., U.S.A. 44°12N 92°39W **77 F6**
Pine Knot Ky., U.S.A. 36°39N 84°26W **105 D8**
Pine Lawn Mo., U.S.A. 38°41N 90°16W **94 A2**
Pine Level Ala., U.S.A. 32°4N 86°4W **112 D4**
Pine Level N.C., U.S.A. 35°31N 78°14W **103 C7**
Pine Log Ga., U.S.A. 34°21N 84°44W **113 B2**
Pine Mountain Ga., U.S.A. 32°49N 84°51W **113 D2**
Pine Mt. Ga., U.S.A. 32°49N 84°50W **113 D2**
Pine Mt. Ky., U.S.A. 37°0N 83°45W **105 D9**
Pine Mt. Wyo., U.S.A. 41°2N 109°1W **124 E3**
Pine Plains N.Y., U.S.A. 42°59N 73°39W **91 B1**
Pine Point N.W.T., Canada 60°50N 114°28W **157 D10**
Pine Prairie La., U.S.A. 30°47N 92°25W **110 D3**
Pine Ridge S. Dak., U.S.A. 43°2N 102°33W **76 G3**
Pine Ridge Indian Reservation S. Dak., U.S.A. 43°30N 102°0W **76 G3**
Pine River Man., Canada 51°45N 100°30W **151 D11**
Pine River Minn., U.S.A. 46°43N 94°24W **77 D4**
Pine Springs Minn., U.S.A. 45°2N 92°57W **94 A4**
Pine Springs Tex., U.S.A. 31°54N 104°49W **108 F3**
Pine Valley Utah, U.S.A. 38°20N 113°45W **129 E2**
Pinebluff N.C., U.S.A. 35°6N 79°28W **103 C6**
Pinecone Burke Park △ B.C., Canada 49°32N 122°41W **155 F12**
Pinecrest Fla., U.S.A. 25°40N 80°18W **115 D1**
Pinedale Fla., U.S.A. 36°50N 119°48W **127 G7**
Pinedale Wyo., U.S.A. 42°52N 109°52W **124 D3**
Pinehouse L. Sask., Canada 55°32N 106°35W **157 E11**
Pinehouse Lake Sask., Canada 55°32N 106°35W **157 E11**
Pinehurst Ga., U.S.A. 32°12N 83°46W **113 D3**
Pinehurst Idaho, U.S.A. 45°15N 116°20W **122 D2**
Pinehurst L. Alta., Canada 54°39N 111°25W **152 D9**
Pineland Tex., U.S.A. 31°15N 93°58W **109 F14**
Pinellas County ☆ Fla., U.S.A. 28°0N 82°45W **114 C6**
Pinellas Nat. Wildlife Refuge △ Tampa, U.S.A. 27°39N 82°41W **115 C2**
Pinellas Park Fla., U.S.A. 27°50N 82°41W **115 B2**
Pinellas Point Fla., U.S.A. 27°42N 82°38W **115 C2**
Pines, Lake O' The Tex., U.S.A. 32°45N 94°30W **109 E13**
Pinetop-Lakeside Ariz., U.S.A. 34°9N 109°58W **130 C6**
Pinetops N.C., U.S.A. 35°46N 77°38W **103 C8**
Pinetta Fla., U.S.A. 30°36N 83°21W **114 A5**
Pineview Ga., U.S.A. 32°7N 83°30W **113 D3**
Pineville Ky., U.S.A. 36°46N 83°42W **105 D9**
Pineville La., U.S.A. 31°19N 92°26W **110 C3**
Pineville Mo., U.S.A. 36°36N 94°23W **83 E2**
Pineville N.C., U.S.A. 35°4N 80°53W **103 C3**
Pineville W. Va., U.S.A. 37°35N 81°32W **102 D3**
Pinewood S.C., U.S.A. 33°44N 80°27W **103 E5**
Pinewood Park Fla., U.S.A. 25°52N 80°13W **115 C2**
Piney → Mo., U.S.A. 37°54N 92°4W **83 D4**
Piney → Tenn., U.S.A. 35°49N 87°34W **104 E5**
Piney Buttes Mont., U.S.A. 47°35N 106°45W **123 C11**
Piney Green N.C., U.S.A. 34°43N 77°19W **103 D8**
Piney Grove Md., U.S.A. 39°42N 78°24W **93 A2**
Piney Point Md., U.S.A. 38°9N 76°31W **93 B4**
Piney Point Village Tex., U.S.A. 29°45N 95°31W **116 B1**
Piney Pt. Fla., U.S.A. 29°46N 83°35W **114 B5**
Piney River → Va., U.S.A. 37°42N 79°1W **102 D5**
Piney Run → Va., U.S.A. 38°58N 77°14W **99 B2**
Piney Woods Miss., U.S.A. 32°2N 90°0W **111 D3**
Pingree N. Dak., U.S.A. 47°10N 98°55W **76 C7**
Pink Okla., U.S.A. 35°18N 97°6W **107 C6**
Pink Cliffs Utah, U.S.A. 37°25N 112°20W **129 F3**
Pink Hill N.C., U.S.A. 35°3N 77°45W **103 C8**
Pinnacle Buttes Wyo., U.S.A. 43°44N 109°57W **124 C3**
Pinnacle Peak Wyo., U.S.A. 43°23N 110°32W **124 C2**
Pinnacles Nat. Monument △ Calif., U.S.A. 36°25N 121°12W **127 G5**
Pino → Baja Calif., Mexico 31°44N 116°40W **166 B2**
Pinola Miss., U.S.A. 31°53N 89°58W **111 D3**
Pinon Ariz., U.S.A. 36°6N 110°14W **130 A5**
Pinon N. Mex., U.S.A. 32°37N 105°24W **131 E5**
Pinos Zacatecas, Mexico 22°18N 101°34W **173 E9**
Pinos, Mt. Calif., U.S.A. 34°49N 119°8W **127 J7**
Pins, Pte. aux Ont., Canada 42°15N 81°51W **146 E5**
Pinson Ala., U.S.A. 33°41N 86°41W **112 C4**
Pinson Tenn., U.S.A. 35°29N 88°43W **104 E4**
Pinta, Sierra Ariz., U.S.A. 32°15N 113°30W **130 E2**
Pinware Nfld. & L., Canada 51°37N 56°42W **142 A4**
Pinware → Nfld. & L., Canada 51°39N 56°42W **142 A4**
Pioche Nev., U.S.A. 37°56N 114°27W **128 E6**
Pioneer Iowa, U.S.A. 42°39N 94°23W **81 C4**
Pioneer La., U.S.A. 32°44N 91°26W **110 B4**
Pioneer Ohio, U.S.A. 41°41N 84°33W **86 B2**
Pioneer Tenn., U.S.A. 36°25N 84°19W **105 D8**
Pioneer Mts. Idaho, U.S.A. 43°38N 113°52W **122 F5**
Pioneer Mts. Mont., U.S.A. 45°29N 112°58W **123 C5**
Pipe Creek Tex., U.S.A. 29°43N 98°56W **109 H9**
Pipe Spring Nat. Monument △ Ariz., U.S.A. 36°50N 112°55W **130 A3**
Pipestem L. N. Dak., U.S.A. 46°57N 98°45W **76 D7**
Pipestone Minn., U.S.A. 44°0N 96°19W **77 F2**
Pipestone County ☆ Minn., U.S.A. 44°0N 96°15W **77 F2**
Pipestone Cr. → Man., Canada 49°38N 100°15W **151 F11**
Pipestone Nat. Monument △ Minn., U.S.A. 43°58N 96°14W **77 G2**
Pipmuacan, Rés. Qué., Canada 49°45N 70°30W **145 B12**
Piqua Kans., U.S.A. 37°56N 95°32W **82 D8**
Piqua Ohio, U.S.A. 40°9N 84°15W **86 C2**
Pirtleville Ariz., U.S.A. 31°21N 109°34W **130 F6**
Piscataquis → Maine, U.S.A. 45°15N 68°58W **90 C5**
Piscataquis County ☆ Maine, U.S.A. 46°0N 69°0W **90 C4**
Piscataway Md., U.S.A. 38°42N 76°58W **93 B4**
Piscataway N.J., U.S.A. 40°34N 74°27W **92 B2**
Pisek N. Dak., U.S.A. 48°19N 97°43W **76 B8**
Pisgah Iowa, U.S.A. 41°50N 95°55W **81 D3**
Pisgah Md., U.S.A. 38°32N 77°9W **93 B3**
Pisgah, Mt. N.H., U.S.A. 44°59N 71°13W **89 B3**
Pisgah Nat. Forest N.C., U.S.A. 35°50N 82°0W **103 C3**
Pisgah State Park △ N.H., U.S.A. 42°50N 72°27W **89 D2**
Pisinimo Ariz., U.S.A. 32°2N 112°19W **130 E3**
Pismo Beach Calif., U.S.A. 35°9N 120°38W **127 H6**
Piste Yucatán, Mexico 20°42N 88°35W **179 B5**
Pistol River Oreg., U.S.A. 42°17N 124°24W **121 E1**
Pistolet B. Nfld. & L., Canada 51°35N 55°45W **142 A5**
Pit → Calif., U.S.A. 40°47N 122°6W **126 C4**
Pitchfork Wyo., U.S.A. 44°6N 109°5W **124 B3**
Piti Guam 13°28N 144°41E **184 b**
Pitiquito Sonora, Mexico 30°41N 112°5W **168 C3**
Pitkin Colo., U.S.A. 38°37N 106°31W **125 D4**
Pitkin La., U.S.A. 30°56N 92°57W **110 D3**
Pitkin County ☆ Colo., U.S.A. 39°10N 106°50W **125 C4**
Pitman N.J., U.S.A. 39°44N 75°8W **92 C1**

Pitt County ☆ N.C., U.S.A. 35°30N 77°20W **103 C8**
Pitt I. B.C., Canada 53°30N 129°50W **154 B5**
Pitt L. B.C., Canada 49°25N 122°32W **155 F12**
Pittock Oreg., U.S.A. 40°29N 80°5W **98 B1**
Pittsboro Ind., U.S.A. 39°52N 86°28W **85 D4**
Pittsboro Miss., U.S.A. 33°56N 89°20W **111 C4**
Pittsboro N.C., U.S.A. 35°43N 79°11W **103 C6**
Pittsburg Calif., U.S.A. 38°2N 121°53W **126 E5**
Pittsburg Ill., U.S.A. 37°47N 88°51W **84 F5**
Pittsburg Kans., U.S.A. 37°25N 94°42W **82 D9**
Pittsburg N.H., U.S.A. 45°3N 71°24W **89 A3**
Pittsburg Okla., U.S.A. 34°43N 95°52W **107 D8**
Pittsburg Tex., U.S.A. 33°0N 94°59W **109 D13**
Pittsburgh Pa., U.S.A. 40°26N 79°58W **98 B1**
Pittsburgh Int. ✈ (PIT) Pa., U.S.A. 40°29N 80°14W **87 D2**
Pittsfield Ill., U.S.A. 39°36N 90°49W **84 D31**
Pittsfield Maine, U.S.A. 44°47N 69°23W **90 D4**
Pittsfield Mass., U.S.A. 42°27N 73°15W **91 B1**
Pittsfield N.H., U.S.A. 43°18N 71°20W **89 C3**
Pittsfield Vt., U.S.A. 43°46N 72°48W **89 C2**
Pittsford Vt., U.S.A. 43°42N 73°3W **89 C1**
Pittston Pa., U.S.A. 41°19N 75°47W **92 A1**
Pittstown N.J., U.S.A. 40°36N 74°56W **92 B2**
Pittsview Ala., U.S.A. 32°11N 85°10W **112 D5**
Pittsville Md., U.S.A. 38°24N 75°52W **93 B5**
Pittsville Mo., U.S.A. 38°50N 94°0W **83 C3**
Pittsville Wis., U.S.A. 44°27N 90°8W **78 D3**
Pittsylvania County ☆ Va., U.S.A. 36°55N 79°15W **102 E5**
Piumafua Mt. Amer. Samoa 14°11S 169°37W **184 f**
Piute County ☆ Utah, U.S.A. 38°20N 112°10W **129 E3**
Piute Pk. Calif., U.S.A. 35°27N 118°23W **127 H8**
Pivabiska → Ont., Canada 50°13N 82°52W **149 B14**
Pixley Calif., U.S.A. 35°58N 119°18W **127 H7**
Pixoyal Campeche, Mexico 18°56N 90°37W **179 D3**
Placedo Tex., U.S.A. 28°41N 96°50W **109 J11**
Placentia Nfld. & L., Canada 47°20N 54°0W **142 E7**
Placentia B. Nfld. & L., Canada 47°0N 54°40W **142 E6**
Placer County ☆ Calif., U.S.A. 39°10N 120°30W **126 D6**
Placeres del Oro Guerrero, Mexico 18°15N 100°55W **175 D7**
Placerville Calif., U.S.A. 38°44N 120°48W **126 E6**
Placerville Colo., U.S.A. 38°1N 108°3W **125 D2**
Placerville Idaho, U.S.A. 43°57N 115°57W **122 F3**
Placetas Cuba 22°15N 79°44W **182 B4**
Placid, L. Fla., U.S.A. 27°15N 81°22W **114 D7**
Placitas N. Mex., U.S.A. 35°18N 106°25W **131 A4**
Plain City Ohio, U.S.A. 40°6N 83°16W **86 C3**
Plain City Utah, U.S.A. 41°18N 112°6W **129 B3**
Plain Dealing La., U.S.A. 32°54N 93°42W **110 B2**
Plainfield Conn., U.S.A. 41°41N 71°56W **91 C3**
Plainfield Ind., U.S.A. 39°42N 86°24W **85 D4**
Plainfield Iowa, U.S.A. 42°51N 92°32W **81 C6**
Plainfield Mass., U.S.A. 42°31N 72°57W **91 B2**
Plainfield N.H., U.S.A. 43°32N 72°21W **89 C2**
Plainfield N.J., U.S.A. 40°37N 74°25W **92 B2**
Plainfield Vt., U.S.A. 44°17N 72°26W **89 B2**
Plainfield Wis., U.S.A. 44°13N 89°30W **78 D4**
Plainfield Heights Mich., U.S.A. 43°1N 85°37W **79 F6**
Plains Kans., U.S.A. 37°16N 100°35W **82 D3**
Plains Mont., U.S.A. 47°28N 114°53W **123 C3**
Plains Tex., U.S.A. 33°11N 102°50W **108 D5**
Plains, The Va., U.S.A. 38°52N 77°47W **93 B3**
Plainview Ark., U.S.A. 34°59N 93°18W **106 C2**
Plainview Minn., U.S.A. 44°10N 92°10W **77 F6**
Plainview N.Y., U.S.A. 40°46N 73°29W **92 B3**
Plainview Nebr., U.S.A. 42°21N 97°47W **80 B8**
Plainview Tex., U.S.A. 34°11N 101°43W **108 C6**
Plainville Conn., U.S.A. 41°41N 72°51W **91 C2**
Plainville Ind., U.S.A. 38°48N 87°9W **85 E3**
Plainville Kans., U.S.A. 39°14N 99°18W **82 B4**
Plainville Mass., U.S.A. 42°0N 71°20W **91 B3**
Plainwell Mich., U.S.A. 42°27N 85°38W **79 G6**
Plaistow N.H., U.S.A. 42°50N 71°6W **89 D3**
Plamondon Alta., Canada 54°51N 112°32W **152 D8**
Plana Cays Bahamas 22°38N 73°30W **183 B5**
Planada Calif., U.S.A. 37°16N 120°19W **126 F6**
Plandome N.Y., U.S.A. 40°48N 73°42W **97 B4**
Plandome Heights N.Y., U.S.A. 40°48N 73°42W **97 B4**
Plankinton S. Dak., U.S.A. 43°43N 98°29W **76 G7**
Plano Ill., U.S.A. 41°40N 88°32W **84 B5**
Plano Tex., U.S.A. 33°1N 96°42W **109 D11**
Plant City Fla., U.S.A. 28°1N 82°7W **114 C6**
Plantation Fla., U.S.A. 26°7N 80°14W **115 B2**
Plantersville Ala., U.S.A. 32°40N 86°56W **112 D4**
Plantersville Miss., U.S.A. 34°12N 88°40W **111 B5**
Plantón Sánchez Veracruz, Mexico 21°17N 98°21W **176 D2**
Plantsite Ariz., U.S.A. 33°2N 109°21W **130 D6**
Plaquemine La., U.S.A. 30°17N 91°14W **110 D4**
Plaquemines Parish ☆ La., U.S.A. 29°29N 89°42W **110 E6**
Plaster Rock N.B., Canada 46°53N 67°22W **141 G2**
Plateros Zacatecas, Mexico 23°13N 102°51W **173 D8**
Platina Calif., U.S.A. 40°22N 122°53W **126 C4**
Platinum Alaska, U.S.A. 59°1N 161°49W **135 G7**
Platte → Mo., U.S.A. 39°16N 94°50W **83 B2**
Platte → Nebr., U.S.A. 41°4N 95°53W **80 C10**
Platte Center Nebr., U.S.A. 41°32N 97°29W **80 C8**
Platte City Mo., U.S.A. 39°22N 94°47W **83 B2**
Platte County ☆ Mo., U.S.A. 39°20N 94°45W **83 B2**
Platte County ☆ Nebr., U.S.A. 41°30N 97°30W **80 C8**
Platte County ☆ Wyo., U.S.A. 42°0N 105°0W **124 E8**
Platteville Colo., U.S.A. 40°13N 104°49W **125 B6**
Platteville Wis., U.S.A. 42°44N 90°29W **78 F31**
Plattsburg Mo., U.S.A. 39°34N 94°27W **83 B2**
Plattsburgh N.Y., U.S.A. 44°42N 73°28W **89 B1**
Plattsmouth Nebr., U.S.A. 41°1N 95°53W **80 C10**
Playa Algodones Sonora, Mexico 27°58N 111°8W **168 F4**
Playa Colorada, B. Sinaloa, Mexico 25°14N 108°22W **172 B2**
Playa Corrida de San Juan, Pta. la Michoacan, Mexico 18°35N 103°42W **174 D4**
Playa de Piedra Tabasco, Mexico 17°33N 93°26W **178 B3**
Playa del Carmen Quintana Roo, Mexico 20°37N 87°4W **179 B6**
Playa Lauro Villar Tamaulipas, Mexico 25°49N 97°8W **170 E7**
Playa Vicente Veracruz, Mexico 17°50N 95°49W **176 E4**
Playas L. N. Mex., U.S.A. 31°51N 108°35W **131 F2**
Playgreen L. Man., Canada 54°0N 98°15W **151 B13**
Plaza N. Dak., U.S.A. 48°1N 101°58W **76 B4**
Plaza Wash., U.S.A. 47°19N 117°23W **120 C8**
Plaza Larga Cr. → N. Mex., U.S.A. 35°14N 103°57W **131 B7**
Pleasant, L. Ariz., U.S.A. 33°51N 112°16W **130 D3**
Pleasant B. Mass., U.S.A. 41°40N 69°57W **91 C5**
Pleasant Dale Nebr., U.S.A. 40°48N 96°56W **80 D9**

Pleasant Gap Pa., U.S.A. 40°52N 77°44W **87 D5**
Pleasant Garden N.C., U.S.A. 35°58N 79°46W **103 C6**
Pleasant Grove Utah, U.S.A. 40°22N 111°44W **129 C3**
Pleasant Hill Calif., U.S.A. 37°57N 122°4W **126 F4**
Pleasant Hill Ill., U.S.A. 39°27N 90°52W **84 D3**
Pleasant Hill Iowa, U.S.A. 41°35N 93°31W **81 D5**
Pleasant Hill La., U.S.A. 31°49N 93°31W **110 C2**
Pleasant Hill Mo., U.S.A. 38°47N 94°16W **83 C2**
Pleasant Hill N. Mex., U.S.A. 34°31N 103°4W **131 C7**
Pleasant Hill Ohio, U.S.A. 40°3N 84°21W **86 C2**
Pleasant Hill Tenn., U.S.A. 35°59N 85°12W **105 E7**
Pleasant Hill L. Ohio, U.S.A. 40°37N 82°19W **86 C4**
Pleasant Hills Pa., U.S.A. 40°20N 79°57W **98 B1**
Pleasant Lake Minn., U.S.A. 45°30N 94°17W **77 E4**
Pleasant Lake Minn., U.S.A. 45°5N 93°5W **94 A3**
Pleasant Plains Ark., U.S.A. 35°33N 91°38W **106 C4**
Pleasant Plains Ill., U.S.A. 39°52N 89°55W **84 D4**
Pleasant Point Indian Reservation Maine, U.S.A. 44°57N 67°3W **90 D6**
Pleasant Prairie Wis., U.S.A. 42°33N 87°56W **78 F6**
Pleasant Ridge Mich., U.S.A. 42°28N 83°8W **98 A2**
Pleasant Site Ala., U.S.A. 34°33N 88°4W **112 B4**
Pleasant View Colo., U.S.A. 37°35N 108°46W **125 E2**
Pleasant View Tenn., U.S.A. 36°24N 87°2W **104 D5**
Pleasant View Utah, U.S.A. 41°19N 112°0W **129 B3**
Pleasant View Wash., U.S.A. 46°29N 118°20W **120 D7**
Pleasantdale Sask., Canada 52°35N 104°30W **150 C7**
Pleasanton Iowa, U.S.A. 40°35N 93°45W **81 E5**
Pleasanton Kans., U.S.A. 38°11N 94°43W **82 C9**
Pleasanton N. Mex., U.S.A. 33°17N 108°53W **131 D2**
Pleasanton Nebr., U.S.A. 40°58N 99°5W **80 D6**
Pleasanton Tex., U.S.A. 28°58N 98°29W **109 J9**
Pleasants County ☆ W. Va., U.S.A. 39°22N 81°12W **102 B3**
Pleasantville Iowa, U.S.A. 41°23N 93°18W **81 D5**
Pleasantville N.J., U.S.A. 39°24N 74°32W **92 C2**
Pleasantville N.Y., U.S.A. 41°8N 73°48W **92 A3**
Pleasantville Ohio, U.S.A. 39°49N 82°32W **86 D4**
Pleasure Ridge Park Ky., U.S.A. 38°9N 85°50W **105 B8**
Pleasureville Ky., U.S.A. 38°21N 85°7W **105 B7**
Pledger L. Ont., Canada 50°53N 83°42W **149 B13**
Plenty Sask., Canada 51°47N 108°38W **150 D3**
Plentywood Mont., U.S.A. 48°47N 104°34W **123 B13**
Plessisville Qué., Canada 46°14N 71°47W **145 E11**
Plétipi, L. Qué., Canada 51°44N 70°6W **143 C3**
Plevna Ont., Canada 44°58N 76°59W **147 C10**
Plevna Kans., U.S.A. 37°59N 98°19W **82 D5**
Plevna Mont., U.S.A. 46°25N 104°31W **123 D13**
Plimoth Plantation Mass., U.S.A. 41°56N 70°37W **91 C4**
Plomosa Chihuahua, Mexico 29°5N 105°15W **169 D10**
Plover Iowa, U.S.A. 42°53N 94°38W **81 C4**
Plover Wis., U.S.A. 44°27N 89°32W **78 D4**
Plover → Wis., U.S.A. 44°29N 89°35W **78 D4**
Plum Pa., U.S.A. 40°29N 79°47W **87 D3**
Plum City Wis., U.S.A. 44°38N 92°11W **78 D1**
Plum Coulee Man., Canada 49°11N 97°45W **151 F14**
Plum Cr. → S. Dak., U.S.A. 44°13N 100°45W **76 F5**
Plum I. Mass., U.S.A. 42°45N 70°48W **91 B4**
Plum I. N.Y., U.S.A. 41°11N 72°12W **91 C2**
Plum Point Md., U.S.A. 38°37N 76°32W **93 B4**
Plum Springs Ky., U.S.A. 37°0N 86°20W **104 D6**
Plumas Man., Canada 50°23N 99°5W **151 E12**
Plumas County ☆ Calif., U.S.A. 40°0N 121°0W **126 D5**
Plumas Nat. Forest Calif., U.S.A. 39°50N 120°40W **126 D6**
Plumerville Ark., U.S.A. 35°10N 92°38W **106 C3**
Plummer Idaho, U.S.A. 47°20N 116°53W **122 B2**
Plummer Minn., U.S.A. 47°55N 96°3W **77 C2**
Plunkett Sask., Canada 51°55N 105°27W **150 D6**
Plush Oreg., U.S.A. 42°25N 119°54W **121 E6**
Plutarco Elías Calles Baja Calif. S., Mexico 23°11N 110°9W **167 K8**
Plutarco Elías Calles, Presa del Sonora, Mexico 29°10N 109°40W **168 D6**
Plymouth Calif., U.S.A. 38°29N 120°51W **126 E6**
Plymouth Ill., U.S.A. 40°18N 90°58W **84 C3**
Plymouth Ind., U.S.A. 41°21N 86°19W **85 B4**
Plymouth Iowa, U.S.A. 43°15N 93°7W **81 B5**
Plymouth Kans., U.S.A. 38°25N 96°20W **82 C7**
Plymouth Mass., U.S.A. 41°57N 70°40W **91 C4**
Plymouth Minn., U.S.A. 45°1N 93°27W **94 A1**
Plymouth N.C., U.S.A. 35°52N 76°43W **103 C9**
Plymouth N.H., U.S.A. 43°46N 71°41W **89 C3**
Plymouth Nebr., U.S.A. 40°18N 96°59W **80 D9**
Plymouth Pa., U.S.A. 41°14N 75°57W **87 C7**
Plymouth Utah, U.S.A. 41°53N 112°9W **129 B3**
Plymouth Vt., U.S.A. 43°34N 72°45W **89 C2**
Plymouth Wis., U.S.A. 43°45N 87°59W **78 E6**
Plymouth Bay Mass., U.S.A. 41°57N 70°37W **91 C4**
Plymouth County ☆ Iowa, U.S.A. 42°45N 96°10W **81 C2**
Plymouth County ☆ Mass., U.S.A. 41°45N 70°45W **91 C4**
Plymouth Creek Park Minn., U.S.A. 45°1N 93°28W **94 A1**
Plymouth Meeting Pa., U.S.A. 40°6N 75°16W **98 A1**
Plympton N.S., Canada 44°30N 65°55W **141 J4**
Plympton-Wyoming Ont., Canada 42°57N 82°7W **146 E4**
Poanas Durango, Mexico 25°46N 103°37W **173 B7**
Poarch Creek Indian Reservation Ala., U.S.A. 31°10N 87°35W **112 E3**
Poca W. Va., U.S.A. 38°28N 81°49W **102 C3**
Pocahontas Ark., U.S.A. 36°16N 90°58W **106 B51**
Pocahontas Ill., U.S.A. 38°50N 89°33W **84 E4**
Pocahontas Iowa, U.S.A. 42°44N 94°40W **81 C4**
Pocahontas County ☆ Iowa, U.S.A. 42°45N 94°40W **81 C4**
Pocahontas County ☆ W. Va., U.S.A. 38°10N 80°2W **102 C4**
Pocasset Mass., U.S.A. 41°41N 70°37W **91 C4**
Pocasset Okla., U.S.A. 35°12N 98°0W **107 C6**
Pocatalico W. Va., U.S.A. 38°29N 81°40W **102 C3**
Pocatalico → W. Va., U.S.A. 38°29N 81°49W **102 C3**
Pocatello Idaho, U.S.A. 42°52N 112°27W **122 G6**
Pocola Okla., U.S.A. 35°14N 94°29W **107 C9**
Pocomoke → Md., U.S.A. 37°58N 75°39W **93 C5**
Pocomoke City Md., U.S.A. 38°5N 75°34W **93 B5**
Pocomoke Sd. Va., U.S.A. 37°50N 75°50W **93 C5**
Pocomoke State Forest Md., U.S.A. 38°9N 75°32W **93 B5**
Pocono Mts. Pa., U.S.A. 41°7N 75°22W **92 A1**
Pocono Pines Pa., U.S.A. 41°6N 75°27W **92 A1**
Pocono Summit Pa., U.S.A. 41°7N 75°23W **92 A1**
Poestenkill N.Y., U.S.A. 42°41N 73°34W **91 B1**
Pogamasing Ont., Canada 46°55N 81°50W **146 A6**
Pohénégamook Qué., Canada 47°28N 69°13W **145 D13**
Pohick Creek → Va., U.S.A. 38°48N 77°15W **99 C2**
Pōhue B. Hawai'i, U.S.A. 19°0N 155°48W **136 E6**
Poinsett, L. S. Dak., U.S.A. 44°34N 97°5W **76 F8**
Poinsett County ☆ Ark., U.S.A. 35°34N 90°39W **106 C5**
Point Arena Calif., U.S.A. 38°55N 123°41W **126 E3**
Point au Fer I. La., U.S.A. 29°18N 91°15W **110 E4**
Point Baker Alaska, U.S.A. 56°21N 133°37W **135 H14**

Point Blank *Tex., U.S.A.* 30°45N 95°13W **109** G12
Point Clear *Ala., U.S.A.* 30°28N 87°55W **112** F3
Point Comfort *Tex., U.S.A.* 28°41N 96°33W **109** J11
Point Hope *Alaska, U.S.A.* 68°21N 166°47W **135** B6
Point L. *N.W.T., Canada* 65°15N 113°4W **157** C10
Point Lay *Alaska, U.S.A.* 69°46N 163°3W **135** B7
Point Leamington *Nfld. & L., Canada* 49°20N 55°24W **142** C5
Point Lookout *Md., U.S.A.* 38°5N 76°18W **93** B4
Point Marion *Pa., U.S.A.* 39°44N 79°54W **87** E3
Point of Rocks *Wyo., U.S.A.* 41°41N 108°47W **124** E4
Point Pelee Nat. Park △ *Ont., Canada* 41°57N 82°31W **146** F4
Point Pleasant *N.J., U.S.A.* 40°5N 74°4W **92** B2
Point Pleasant *W. Va., U.S.A.* 38°51N 82°8W **102** C2
Point Reyes Nat. Seashore △ *Calif., U.S.A.* 38°10N 122°55W **126** E4
Point Roberts *Wash., U.S.A.* 48°59N 123°4W **120** B2
Pointe-à-la-Frégate *Qué., Canada* 49°12N 64°55W **140** D5
Pointe à la Hache *La., U.S.A.* 29°35N 89°48W **111** E5
Pointe-à-Maurier *Qué., Canada* 50°20N 59°48W **140** C10
Pointe-à-Pitre *Guadeloupe* 16°10N 61°32W **183** C7
Pointe au Baril Station *Ont., Canada* 45°35N 80°23W **146** B6
Pointe-au-Pic = La Malbaie *Qué., Canada* 47°40N 70°10W **145** D12
Pointe-aux-Anglais *Qué., Canada* 49°41N 67°10W **140** D2
Pointe-aux-Outardes *Qué., Canada* 49°3N 68°26W **145** B14
Pointe Aux Pins *Mich., U.S.A.* 45°44N 84°29W **79** D7
Pointe-Aux-Trembles *Qué., Canada* 45°38N 73°30W **160** A3
Pointe-Claire *Qué., Canada* 45°26N 73°50W **145** F9
Pointe Coupee Parish ☆ *La., U.S.A.* 30°36N 91°37W **110** D4
Pointe du Bois *Man., Canada* 50°18N 95°33W **151** E16
Pointe-Gatineau *Ont., Canada* 45°27N 75°41W **160** A1
Pointe-Lebel *Qué., Canada* 49°10N 68°12W **145** B14
Pointe-Parent *Qué., Canada* 50°8N 61°47W **140** D5
Pointe-Sapin *N.B., Canada* 46°58N 64°50W **141** G5
Pointe-Taillon, Parc de la △ *Qué., Canada* 48°42N 71°58W **145** C11
Pointe-Verte *N.B., Canada* 47°51N 65°46W **141** F4
Poisson Blanc, L. *Qué., Canada* 46°0N 75°45W **144** F7
Pojoaque *N. Mex., U.S.A.* 35°54N 106°1W **131** B4
Pojoaque Indian Reservation *N. Mex., U.S.A.* 35°54N 106°1W **131** B4
Poka'i B. *Hawai'i, U.S.A.* 21°27N 158°12W **136** K13
Pokegama L. *Minn., U.S.A.* 47°12N 93°35W **77** C5
Polacca *Ariz., U.S.A.* 35°50N 110°23W **130** B5
Polacca Wash ➤ *Ariz., U.S.A.* 35°22N 110°50W **130** B5
Poland *N.Y., U.S.A.* 43°14N 75°4W **88** C5
Poland *Ohio, U.S.A.* 41°1N 80°37W **86** B6
Pole Mt. *Wyo., U.S.A.* 41°14N 105°23W **124** E7
Polk *Nebr., U.S.A.* 41°4N 97°46W **80** C8
Polk *Ohio, U.S.A.* 40°57N 82°13W **86** C4
Polk *Pa., U.S.A.* 41°22N 79°56W **87** C3
Polk City *Fla., U.S.A.* 28°11N 81°49W **114** C7
Polk City *Iowa, U.S.A.* 41°46N 93°43W **81** D5
Polk County ☆ *Ark., U.S.A.* 34°35N 94°15W **106** D1
Polk County ☆ *Fla., U.S.A.* 28°0N 81°45W **114** D7
Polk County ☆ *Ga., U.S.A.* 34°0N 85°10W **113** B1
Polk County ☆ *Iowa, U.S.A.* 41°40N 93°35W **81** D5
Polk County ☆ *Minn., U.S.A.* 47°40N 96°30W **77** C2
Polk County ☆ *Mo., U.S.A.* 37°35N 93°25W **83** D3
Polk County ☆ *N.C., U.S.A.* 35°15N 82°10W **103** C3
Polk County ☆ *Nebr., U.S.A.* 41°15N 97°40W **80** C8
Polk County ☆ *Oreg., U.S.A.* 44°55N 123°20W **121** C2
Polk County ☆ *Tenn., U.S.A.* 35°10N 84°39W **105** E8
Polk County ☆ *Tex., U.S.A.* 30°43N 94°56W **109** G13
Polk County ☆ *Wis., U.S.A.* 45°30N 92°30W **78** C1
Polkton *N.C., U.S.A.* 35°1N 80°12W **103** C5
Polkville *Miss., U.S.A.* 32°11N 89°42W **111** D4
Polkville *N.C., U.S.A.* 35°25N 81°39W **103** C4
Pollock *Idaho, U.S.A.* 45°19N 116°21W **122** D2
Pollock *La., U.S.A.* 31°32N 92°25W **110** C3
Pollock *Mo., U.S.A.* 40°21N 93°5W **83** A3
Pollock *S. Dak., U.S.A.* 45°55N 100°17W **76** E5
Pollock Pines *Calif., U.S.A.* 38°46N 120°34W **126** E6
Polo *Ill., U.S.A.* 41°59N 89°35W **84** B4
Polo *Mo., U.S.A.* 39°33N 94°3W **83** B2
Polotitlán *México, Mexico* 20°13N 99°49W **175** B8
Polson *Mont., U.S.A.* 47°41N 114°9W **123** C3
Poltimore *Qué., Canada* 45°47N 75°43W **144** F7
Polvadera *N. Mex., U.S.A.* 34°12N 106°55W **131** C4
Polvorillas *Chihuahua, Mexico* 28°48N 104°14W **169** E11
Polynesian Cultural Center *Hawai'i, U.S.A.* 21°38N 157°55W **136** J14
Pom, L. *Campeche, Mexico* 18°35N 92°12W **179** D1
Pomeroy *Iowa, U.S.A.* 42°33N 94°41W **81** C4
Pomeroy *Ohio, U.S.A.* 39°2N 82°2W **86** D4
Pomeroy *Wash., U.S.A.* 46°28N 117°36W **120** D8
Pomfret *Conn., U.S.A.* 41°54N 71°58W **91** C3
Pomfret *Md., U.S.A.* 38°30N 77°2W **93** B3
Pomme de Terre ➤ *Minn., U.S.A.* 45°10N 96°54W **77** C2
Pomme de Terre ➤ *Mo., U.S.A.* 38°11N 93°25W **83** C3
Pomme de Terre L. *Mo., U.S.A.* 37°54N 93°19W **83** D3
Pomona *Calif., U.S.A.* 34°4N 117°45W **127** J9
Pomona *Kans., U.S.A.* 38°36N 95°27W **82** C8
Pomona *Md., U.S.A.* 39°10N 76°7W **93** A4
Pomona *Mo., U.S.A.* 36°52N 91°55W **83** E5
Pomona *N.J., U.S.A.* 39°29N 74°35W **92** C2
Pomona Lake *Kans., U.S.A.* 38°39N 95°34W **82** C8
Pomona Park *Fla., U.S.A.* 29°30N 81°36W **114** B7
Pompano Beach *Fla., U.S.A.* 26°14N 80°7W **115** A3
Pompeys Pillar *Mont., U.S.A.* 45°59N 107°57W **123** E10
Pompeys Pillar Nat. Monument △ *Mont., U.S.A.* 46°0N 108°0W **123** D10
Pompton Lakes *N.J., U.S.A.* 41°0N 74°17W **92** B2
Pomuch *Campeche, Mexico* 20°8N 90°11W **179** B3
Ponass L. *Sask., Canada* 52°16N 103°58W **150** C8
Ponca *Nebr., U.S.A.* 42°34N 96°43W **80** B9
Ponca City *Okla., U.S.A.* 36°42N 97°5W **107** B6
Ponca Cr. ➤ *Nebr., U.S.A.* 42°48N 98°5W **80** B7
Ponce *Puerto Rico* 18°1N 66°37W **184** G16
Ponce de Leon *Fla., U.S.A.* 30°44N 85°56W **114** A3
Ponce de Leon B. *Fla., U.S.A.* 25°15N 81°10W **114** F7
Ponce Inlet *Fla., U.S.A.* 29°6N 80°56W **114** B8
Poncha Springs *Colo., U.S.A.* 38°31N 106°5W **125** D4
Ponchatoula *La., U.S.A.* 30°26N 90°26W **110** D5
Poncheville, L. *Qué., Canada* 50°10N 76°55W **143** C2
Poncitlán *Jalisco, Mexico* 20°22N 102°55W **174** B5
Pond *Calif., U.S.A.* 35°43N 119°20W **127** H7
Pond ➤ *Ky., U.S.A.* 37°32N 87°21W **104** C3
Pond Creek *Okla., U.S.A.* 36°40N 97°48W **107** B6
Pond Eddy *N.Y., U.S.A.* 41°26N 74°49W **92** A2
Pond Inlet *Nunavut, Canada* 72°40N 77°0W **158** C10
Ponderay *N. Mex., U.S.A.* 48°12N 116°33W **122** C5
Ponderosa *N. Mex., U.S.A.* 35°40N 106°40W **131** B4
Pondosa *Calif., U.S.A.* 41°12N 121°41W **126** B5
Ponds, I. of *Nfld. & L., Canada* 53°27N 55°52W **143** C6

Poneto *Ind., U.S.A.* 40°39N 85°13W **85** C5
Ponoka *Alta., Canada* 52°42N 113°40W **153** F7
Pont-Rouge *Qué., Canada* 46°45N 71°42W **145** E11
Pont-Viau *Qué., Canada* 45°35N 73°41W **160** A2
Pontchartrain, L. *La., U.S.A.* 30°5N 90°5W **110** D5
Ponte Vedra Beach *Fla., U.S.A.* 30°15N 81°23W **114** A7
Pontiac *Ill., U.S.A.* 40°53N 88°38W **84** C5
Pontiac *Mich., U.S.A.* 42°38N 83°8W **79** G8
Pontotoc *Miss., U.S.A.* 34°15N 89°0W **111** B5
Pontotoc *Tex., U.S.A.* 30°55N 99°0W **109** H8
Pontotoc County ☆ *Miss., U.S.A.* 34°15N 89°0W **111** B5
Pontotoc County ☆ *Okla., U.S.A.* 34°45N 96°45W **107** D7
Pontypool *Ont., Canada* 44°6N 78°38W **147** C8
Poole *Ky., U.S.A.* 37°38N 87°39W **104** C5
Poole *Nebr., U.S.A.* 40°59N 98°58W **80** D7
Pooler *Ga., U.S.A.* 32°7N 81°15W **113** D5
Pooles I. *Md., U.S.A.* 39°17N 76°6W **93** A4
Poolesville *Md., U.S.A.* 39°9N 77°25W **93** A3
Pooley I. *B.C., Canada* 52°45N 128°15W **154** C6
Poorman *Alaska, U.S.A.* 64°5N 155°33W **135** D9
Pope *Miss., U.S.A.* 34°13N 89°57W **111** B4
Pope County ☆ *Ark., U.S.A.* 35°28N 92°59W **106** C3
Pope County ☆ *Ill., U.S.A.* 37°25N 88°35W **84** F5
Pope County ☆ *Minn., U.S.A.* 45°40N 95°25W **77** C3
Pope Cr. ➤ *Ill., U.S.A.* 41°8N 90°58W **84** B3
Popejoy *Iowa, U.S.A.* 42°36N 93°26W **81** C5
Popes Creek *Md., U.S.A.* 38°24N 76°58W **93** B4
Poplar *Wis., U.S.A.* 46°35N 91°48W **78** B2
Poplar ➤ *Man., Canada* 53°0N 97°19W **151** C14
Poplar ➤ *Mont., U.S.A.* 48°5N 105°11W **123** B12
Poplar Bluff *Mo., U.S.A.* 36°46N 90°24W **83** E6
Poplar Grove *Ill., U.S.A.* 42°22N 88°49W **84** A5
Poplar Grove Nat. Cemetery *Va., U.S.A.* 37°10N 77°26W **102** D7
Poplar Head = Dothan *Ala., U.S.A.* 31°13N 85°24W **112** E5
Poplar Hill *Va., U.S.A.* 37°13N 80°44W **102** D4
Poplar I. *Md., U.S.A.* 38°46N 76°23W **93** B4
Poplar Mt. *Ky., U.S.A.* 36°43N 85°3W **105** D7
Poplar Plains *Ky., U.S.A.* 38°21N 83°41W **105** B9
Poplar Point *Man., Canada* 50°4N 97°59W **151** E14
Poplar River *Man., Canada* 52°59N 97°16W **151** C14
Poplarfield *Man., Canada* 50°53N 97°36W **151** C14
Poplarville *Miss., U.S.A.* 30°51N 89°32W **111** F4
Popo Agie ➤ *Wyo., U.S.A.* 43°1N 108°21W **124** C4
Popocatépetl, Volcán *Puebla, Mexico* 19°2N 98°38W **177** E2
Popolnah *Yucatán, Mexico* 21°0N 87°35W **179** B6
Poquetanuck *Conn., U.S.A.* 41°29N 72°3W **91** C2
Poquonock Bridge *Conn., U.S.A.* 41°19N 72°11W **91** C2
Poquoson *Va., U.S.A.* 37°8N 76°24W **102** D8
Porcher I. *B.C., Canada* 53°50N 130°30W **154** B4
Porcupine *Ont., Canada* 48°30N 81°11W **144** C1
Porcupine *S. Dak., U.S.A.* 43°14N 102°13W **76** G3
Porcupine ➤ *Sask., Canada* 59°11N 104°46W **157** E12
Porcupine ➤ *Alaska, U.S.A.* 66°34N 145°19W **135** C11
Porcupine ➤ *Qué., Canada* 48°7N 106°20W **123** B11
Porcupine Hills *Canada* 52°33N 101°22W **151** C10
Porcupine Mountains Wilderness State Park △ *Mich., U.S.A.* 46°47N 89°41W **79** C2
Porcupine Mts. *Mich., U.S.A.* 46°47N 89°44W **79** C3
Porcupine Plain *Sask., Canada* 52°36N 103°15W **150** C8
Porphyry Pk. *Mont., U.S.A.* 47°14N 109°18W **123** C8
Porquis Junction *Qué., Canada* 48°42N 80°47W **144** C2
Port Alberni *B.C., Canada* 49°14N 124°50W **154** F10
Port Alexander *Alaska, U.S.A.* 56°15N 134°38W **135** H14
Port Alfred *Qué., Canada* 48°18N 70°53W **145** C12
Port Alice *B.C., Canada* 50°20N 127°25W **154** E7
Port Allegany *Pa., U.S.A.* 41°48N 78°17W **87** C4
Port Allen *La., U.S.A.* 30°27N 91°12W **110** D4
Port Angeles *Wash., U.S.A.* 48°7N 123°27W **120** B2
Port Antonio *Jamaica* 18°10N 76°26W **182** C4
Port Aransas *Tex., U.S.A.* 27°50N 97°4W **109** K10
Port Arthur *Tex., U.S.A.* 29°54N 93°56W **109** H14
Port au Choix *Nfld. & L., Canada* 50°43N 57°22W **142** B3
Port au Port *Nfld. & L., Canada* 48°33N 58°43W **142** D2
Port au Port B. *Nfld. & L., Canada* 48°40N 58°50W **142** D2
Port au Port Pen. *Nfld. & L., Canada* 48°35N 59°0W **142** D2
Port-au-Prince *Haiti* 18°40N 72°20W **183** C5
Port Austin *Mich., U.S.A.* 44°3N 83°1W **79** E8
Port Barre *La., U.S.A.* 30°34N 91°57W **110** D4
Port Blandford *Nfld. & L., Canada* 48°20N 54°10W **142** D6
Port Burwell *Ont., Canada* 42°40N 80°48W **146** E6
Port Byron *Ill., U.S.A.* 41°36N 90°20W **84** B3
Port Carling *Ont., Canada* 45°7N 79°35W **146** B7
Port-Cartier *Qué., Canada* 50°2N 66°50W **143** C4
Port-Cartier-Sept-Îles, Réserve Faunique de △ *Qué., Canada* 50°30N 67°20W **140** C2
Port Charlotte *Fla., U.S.A.* 26°59N 82°6W **114** E6
Port Chester *N.Y., U.S.A.* 41°0N 73°40W **88** E7
Port Clements *B.C., Canada* 53°40N 132°10W **154** B2
Port Clinton *Ohio, U.S.A.* 41°31N 82°56W **86** B4
Port Clyde *Maine, U.S.A.* 43°56N 69°16W **90** E4
Port Colborne *Ont., Canada* 42°50N 79°10W **146** E7
Port Columbus Int. ✈ (CMH) *Ohio, U.S.A.* 40°0N 82°53W **86** D4
Port Credit *Ont., Canada* 43°33N 79°35W **146** D7
Port-Daniel, Réserve Faunique de △ *Qué., Canada* 48°11N 64°58W **140** E5
Port-de-Paix *Haiti* 19°50N 72°50W **183** C5
Port Dover *Ont., Canada* 42°47N 80°12W **146** E6
Port Dufferin *N.S., Canada* 44°55N 62°23W **141** J7
Port Edward *B.C., Canada* 54°12N 130°10W **154** A4
Port Edwards *Wis., U.S.A.* 44°21N 89°52W **78** D4
Port Elgin *N.B., Canada* 46°3N 64°5W **141** G5
Port Elgin *Ont., Canada* 44°25N 81°25W **146** C5
Port Elizabeth *N.J., U.S.A.* 39°19N 74°59W **92** C2
Port Essington *B.C., Canada* 54°9N 129°58W **154** A5
Port Ewen *N.Y., U.S.A.* 41°54N 73°59W **88** D7
Port Fourchon *La., U.S.A.* 29°6N 90°11W **110** E5
Port Gamble *Wash., U.S.A.* 47°51N 122°34W **132** A2
Port Gibson *Miss., U.S.A.* 31°58N 90°59W **111** E3
Port Greville *N.S., Canada* 45°24N 64°33W **141** H5
Port Hadlock *Wash., U.S.A.* 48°2N 122°45W **120** B3
Port Hardy *B.C., Canada* 50°41N 127°30W **154** E7
Port Harrison = Inukjuak *Qué., Canada* 58°25N 78°15W **143** D2
Port Hastings *N.S., Canada* 45°39N 61°24W **141** H8
Port Hawkesbury *N.S., Canada* 45°36N 61°22W **141** H8
Port Heiden *Alaska, U.S.A.* 56°55N 158°41W **135** H8
Port Henry *N.Y., U.S.A.* 44°3N 73°28W **89** B1
Port Hood *N.S., Canada* 46°0N 61°32W **141** G8
Port Hope *Ont., Canada* 43°56N 78°20W **147** D8
Port Hope *Mich., U.S.A.* 43°57N 82°43W **79** F9
Port Hope Simpson *Nfld. & L., Canada* 52°33N 56°18W **143** C6
Port Howe *N.S., Canada* 45°51N 63°45W **141** H6
Port Hueneme *Calif., U.S.A.* 34°7N 119°12W **127** J7
Port Huron *Mich., U.S.A.* 42°58N 82°26W **79** G9

Port Isabel *Tex., U.S.A.* 26°5N 97°12W **108** L10
Port Jefferson *N.Y., U.S.A.* 40°57N 73°3W **91** D1
Port Jefferson *Ohio, U.S.A.* 40°20N 84°6W **86** C2
Port Jervis *N.Y., U.S.A.* 41°22N 74°41W **92** A2
Port Kent *N.Y., U.S.A.* 44°32N 73°24W **89** B1
Port Lavaca *Tex., U.S.A.* 28°37N 96°38W **109** J11
Port Leyden *N.Y., U.S.A.* 43°35N 75°21W **88** B5
Port Lions *Alaska, U.S.A.* 57°52N 152°53W **135** H9
Port Loring *Ont., Canada* 45°55N 80°0W **146** B6
Port Lorne *N.S., Canada* 44°57N 65°16W **141** J4
Port Louisa Nat. Wildlife Refuge △ *Ill., U.S.A.* 41°6N 90°57W **84** B3
Port Ludlow *Wash., U.S.A.* 47°56N 122°41W **120** C3
Port McNeill *B.C., Canada* 50°35N 127°6W **154** E7
Port Mansfield *Tex., U.S.A.* 26°34N 97°26W **108** L10
Port Mayaca *Fla., U.S.A.* 26°59N 80°36W **114** E8
Port Medway *N.S., Canada* 44°8N 64°34W **141** J5
Port Mellon *B.C., Canada* 49°32N 123°31W **155** F11
Port-Menier *Qué., Canada* 49°51N 64°15W **140** D4
Port Moller *Alaska, U.S.A.* 55°59N 160°34W **135** J7
Port Moody *B.C., Canada* 49°17N 122°51W **155** F12
Port Morant *Jamaica* 17°54N 76°19W **182** C4
Port Mouton *N.S., Canada* 43°58N 64°50W **141** K5
Port Neches *Tex., U.S.A.* 30°0N 93°59W **109** H14
Port Newark *N.J., U.S.A.* 40°41N 74°7W **97** B2
Port Norris *N.J., U.S.A.* 39°15N 75°2W **92** C1
Port Nouveau-Québec = Kangiqsualujjuaq *Qué., Canada* 58°30N 65°59W **143** B4
Port O'Connor *Tex., U.S.A.* 28°27N 96°24W **109** J11
Port of Portland *Oreg., U.S.A.* 45°34N 122°43W **132** A1
Port of Spain *Trin. & Tob.* 10°40N 61°31W **183** D7
Port Orange *Fla., U.S.A.* 29°9N 80°59W **114** B8
Port Orchard *Wash., U.S.A.* 47°32N 122°38W **132** C2
Port Orford *Oreg., U.S.A.* 42°45N 124°30W **121** E1
Port Penn *Del., U.S.A.* 39°31N 75°35W **93** A5
Port Perry *Ont., Canada* 44°6N 78°56W **147** C8
Port Reading *N.J., U.S.A.* 40°34N 74°15W **97** C1
Port Renfrew *B.C., Canada* 48°30N 124°20W **154** G10
Port Republic *Md., U.S.A.* 38°30N 76°33W **93** B4
Port Republic *N.J., U.S.A.* 39°31N 74°29W **92** C2
Port Richey *Fla., U.S.A.* 28°16N 82°43W **114** C6
Port Richmond *N.Y., U.S.A.* 40°38N 74°7W **97** C2
Port Rowan *Ont., Canada* 42°40N 80°30W **146** E6
Port Royal *N.S., Canada* 44°43N 65°36W **141** J4
Port Royal *Ky., U.S.A.* 38°33N 85°5W **105** B7
Port Royal *S.C., U.S.A.* 32°23N 80°42W **103** F5
Port Royal *Va., U.S.A.* 38°10N 77°12W **93** B3
Port Royal Sd. *S.C., U.S.A.* 32°15N 80°40W **103** F5
Port St. Joe *Fla., U.S.A.* 29°49N 85°18W **114** B3
Port St. John *Fla., U.S.A.* 28°29N 80°47W **114** C8
Port St. Lucie *Fla., U.S.A.* 27°18N 80°21W **114** D8
Port Salerno *Fla., U.S.A.* 27°9N 80°12W **114** D8
Port Sanilac *Mich., U.S.A.* 43°26N 82°33W **79** F9
Port Saunders *Nfld. & L., Canada* 50°40N 57°18W **142** B3
Port Severn *Ont., Canada* 44°48N 79°43W **146** C7
Port Simpson *B.C., Canada* 54°30N 130°20W **157** F6
Port Stanley *Ont., Canada* 42°40N 81°10W **146** E5
Port Sulphur *La., U.S.A.* 29°29N 89°42W **110** E6
Port Susan *Wash., U.S.A.* 48°5N 122°15W **120** B3
Port Tobacco *Md., U.S.A.* 38°27N 77°2W **93** B3
Port Townsend *Wash., U.S.A.* 48°7N 122°45W **120** B3
Port Union *Ont., Canada* 43°47N 79°7W **161** A4
Port Vincent *La., U.S.A.* 30°20N 90°51W **110** D5
Port Vue *Pa., U.S.A.* 40°20N 79°52W **98** B2
Port Washington *N.Y., U.S.A.* 40°49N 73°41W **97** B2
Port Washington *Ohio, U.S.A.* 40°20N 81°31W **86** C5
Port Washington *Wis., U.S.A.* 43°23N 87°53W **78** E6
Port Washington North *N.Y., U.S.A.* 40°50N 73°42W **97** A4
Port Wentworth *Ga., U.S.A.* 32°9N 81°10W **113** D5
Port Wing *Wis., U.S.A.* 46°47N 91°23W **78** B2
Portage *Ind., U.S.A.* 41°34N 87°11W **85** B3
Portage *Maine, U.S.A.* 46°46N 68°29W **90** B5
Portage *Mich., U.S.A.* 42°12N 85°35W **79** G6
Portage *Utah, U.S.A.* 41°59N 112°14W **129** B3
Portage *Wis., U.S.A.* 43°33N 89°28W **78** E4
Portage ➤ *Ohio, U.S.A.* 41°31N 83°5W **86** B3
Portage B. *Man., Canada* 51°33N 98°50W **151** D13
Portage County ☆ *Ohio, U.S.A.* 41°9N 81°15W **86** B5
Portage County ☆ *Wis., U.S.A.* 44°25N 89°30W **78** D4
Portage la Prairie *Man., Canada* 49°58N 98°18W **151** F13
Portage Park *Ill., U.S.A.* 41°56N 87°45W **95** B2
Portageville *Mo., U.S.A.* 36°26N 89°42W **83** E11
Portal *Ariz., U.S.A.* 31°55N 109°9W **130** F6
Portal *N. Dak., U.S.A.* 48°59N 102°33W **76** B3
Portales *N. Mex., U.S.A.* 34°11N 103°20W **131** C7
Porter *Minn., U.S.A.* 44°38N 96°10W **77** F2
Porter *Okla., U.S.A.* 35°52N 95°31W **107** C8
Porter, L. *Fla., U.S.A.* 28°30N 81°19W **115** A3
Porter County ☆ *Ind., U.S.A.* 41°25N 87°5W **85** B3
Porterville *Calif., U.S.A.* 36°4N 119°1W **127** H8
Porterville *Miss., U.S.A.* 32°41N 88°28W **111** D5
Portezuelo, Cerro El *Baja Calif., Mexico* 30°22N 115°0W **166** C3
Porthill *Idaho, U.S.A.* 48°59N 116°30W **122** C4
Portis *Kans., U.S.A.* 39°34N 98°41W **82** B5
Portland *Ont., Canada* 44°42N 76°12W **147** C10
Portland *Ark., U.S.A.* 33°14N 91°31W **106** E4
Portland *Conn., U.S.A.* 41°34N 72°38W **91** C2
Portland *Fla., U.S.A.* 30°31N 86°12W **114** A2
Portland *Ind., U.S.A.* 40°26N 84°59W **85** C6
Portland *Maine, U.S.A.* 43°39N 70°16W **90** E2
Portland *Mich., U.S.A.* 42°52N 84°54W **79** G7
Portland *Mo., U.S.A.* 38°43N 91°43W **83** C5
Portland *N. Dak., U.S.A.* 47°30N 97°22W **76** C8
Portland *Oreg., U.S.A.* 45°32N 122°37W **132** A1
Portland *Pa., U.S.A.* 40°55N 75°6W **92** B1
Portland *Tenn., U.S.A.* 36°35N 86°31W **104** D6
Portland *Tex., U.S.A.* 27°53N 97°20W **109** K10
Portland Creek Pond *Nfld. & L., Canada* 50°15N 57°32W **142** B3
Portland Int. ✈ (PDX) *Oreg., U.S.A.* 45°35N 122°36W **132** A2
Portland Prom. *Qué., Canada* 58°40N 78°33W **143** D2
Portneuf *Qué., Canada* 46°43N 71°55W **145** E11
Portneuf ➤ *Qué., Canada* 48°38N 69°5W **145** C13
Portneuf ➤ *Idaho, U.S.A.* 42°55N 112°35W **122** G7
Portneuf, Réserve Faunique de △ *Qué., Canada* 47°10N 72°25W **145** D10
Portneuf Range *Idaho, U.S.A.* 42°50N 112°0W **122** G7
Portobelo *Panama* 9°35N 79°42W **182** E4
Portola *Calif., U.S.A.* 39°49N 120°28W **126** D6
Portrero *Calif., U.S.A.* 37°46N 122°25W **132** E4
Portsmouth *Dominica* 15°34N 61°27W **183** C7
Portsmouth *N.H., U.S.A.* 43°5N 70°45W **89** C4

Portsmouth *Ohio, U.S.A.* 38°44N 82°57W **86** E4
Portsmouth *R.I., U.S.A.* 41°36N 71°15W **91** C3
Portsmouth *Va., U.S.A.* 36°58N 76°23W **102** E8
Portville *N.Y., U.S.A.* 42°3N 78°20W **88** C2
Porum *Okla., U.S.A.* 35°22N 95°16W **107** C8
Posen *Mich., U.S.A.* 45°16N 83°42W **79** D8
Posey County ☆ *Ind., U.S.A.* 38°0N 87°50W **85** F3
Poseyville *Ind., U.S.A.* 38°10N 87°47W **85** E3
Possum Kingdom L. *Tex., U.S.A.* 32°52N 98°26W **109** E9
Post *Oreg., U.S.A.* 44°10N 120°29W **121** C5
Post Falls *Idaho, U.S.A.* 47°43N 116°57W **122** B2
Post Tex., U.S.A. 33°12N 101°23W **108** D6
Posta de Jihuites *Durango, Mexico* 25°44N 105°37W **172** B5
Poste-de-la-Baleine = Kuujjuarapik *Qué., Canada* 55°20N 77°35W **143** B2
Poston *Ariz., U.S.A.* 54°0N 114°24W **130** C1
Posts *Calif., U.S.A.* 36°14N 121°46W **126** G5
Potatch ➤ *Idaho, U.S.A.* 46°26N 116°47W **122** C2
Pot Mt. *Idaho, U.S.A.* 46°44N 115°24W **122** C3
Potagannissing B. *Mich., U.S.A.* 46°5N 83°50W **79** C8
Potatch ➤ *Idaho, U.S.A.* 46°26N 116°47W **122** C2
Potawatomi Indian Reservation *Wis., U.S.A.* 45°27N 88°35W **78** C5
Poteau *Okla., U.S.A.* 35°3N 94°37W **107** C9
Poteau ➤ *Okla., U.S.A.* 35°23N 94°26W **107** C9
Poteet *Tex., U.S.A.* 29°2N 98°35W **109** H9
Poterdale *Ga., U.S.A.* 33°35N 83°54W **113** C3
Potholes Res. *Wash., U.S.A.* 46°59N 119°16W **120** D6
Potlatch *Idaho, U.S.A.* 46°55N 116°54W **122** C2
Potomac *Ill., U.S.A.* 40°18N 87°48W **84** C6
Potomac *Md., U.S.A.* 38°59N 77°13W **99** A2
Potomac ➤ *Md., U.S.A.* 38°0N 76°23W **93** B4
Potomac Heights *Md., U.S.A.* 38°36N 77°8W **93** B3
Potosi *Mo., U.S.A.* 37°56N 90°47W **83** D6
Potosí, B. *Michoacan, Mexico* 17°35N 101°35W **174** E6
Potosí, Pta. el *Guerrero, Mexico* 17°33N 101°27W **175** E6
Potrero Chico, Parque Recreativo *Monterrey, Mexico* 25°53N 100°26W **180** A1
Potrero del Llano *Durango, Mexico* 26°7N 105°13W **172** A5
Potrero Pt. *Calif., U.S.A.* 37°45N 122°22W **132** E2
Potsdam *N.Y., U.S.A.* 44°40N 74°59W **88** A6
Pottawatomie County ☆ *Kans., U.S.A.* 39°20N 96°15W **82** B7
Pottawatomie County ☆ *Okla., U.S.A.* 35°10N 97°0W **107** C7
Pottawattamie County ☆ *Iowa, U.S.A.* 41°20N 95°30W **81** D3
Potter *Kans., U.S.A.* 39°26N 95°9W **82** B8
Potter *Nebr., U.S.A.* 41°13N 103°19W **80** C2
Potter County ☆ *Pa., U.S.A.* 41°50N 78°0W **87** C5
Potter County ☆ *S. Dak., U.S.A.* 45°0N 100°0W **76** E6
Potter County ☆ *Tex., U.S.A.* 35°25N 101°50W **108** B6
Potterville *La., U.S.A.* 32°31N 84°7W **113** D2
Potterville *Mich., U.S.A.* 42°38N 84°45W **79** G7
Potts Camp *Miss., U.S.A.* 34°39N 89°18W **111** B4
Pottsboro *Tex., U.S.A.* 33°46N 96°40W **109** D11
Pottstown *Pa., U.S.A.* 40°15N 75°39W **92** B1
Pottsville *Pa., U.S.A.* 40°41N 76°12W **87** D6
Poтуро *Michoacan, Mexico* 18°48N 101°38W **174** D6
Potwin *Kans., U.S.A.* 37°56N 97°1W **82** D6
Pouch Cove *Nfld. & L., Canada* 47°46N 52°46W **142** E8
Poughkeepsie *N.Y., U.S.A.* 41°42N 73°56W **88** D7
Poulan *La., U.S.A.* 31°31N 83°47W **113** E3
Poulin-de-Courval, L. *Qué., Canada* 48°52N 70°27W **145** C12
Poulsbo *Wash., U.S.A.* 47°44N 122°38W **132** B2
Poultney *Vt., U.S.A.* 43°31N 73°14W **89** C1
Pound *Va., U.S.A.* 37°8N 82°36W **102** D2
Pound *Wis., U.S.A.* 45°6N 88°2W **78** D5
Poutrincourt, L. *Qué., Canada* 49°11N 74°7W **145** B8
Poverty Point Nat. Monument △ *La., U.S.A.* 32°39N 91°24W **110** B4
Povungnituk = Puvirnituq *Qué., Canada* 60°2N 77°10W **143** A2
Powassan *Ont., Canada* 46°5N 79°25W **146** A7
Poway *Calif., U.S.A.* 32°58N 117°2W **127** L9
Powder ➤ *Mont., U.S.A.* 46°45N 105°26W **123** D12
Powder ➤ *Oreg., U.S.A.* 44°45N 117°3W **121** C8
Powder Horn Park *Minn., U.S.A.* 44°56N 93°15W **94** B2
Powder River *Wyo., U.S.A.* 43°2N 106°59W **124** C6
Powder River County ☆ *Mont., U.S.A.* 45°20N 105°40W **123** E12
Powder River Pass *Wyo., U.S.A.* 44°9N 107°5W **124** B5
Powder Springs *Ga., U.S.A.* 33°52N 84°41W **113** C2
Powderhorn *Colo., U.S.A.* 38°17N 107°7W **125** D3
Powell *Idaho, U.S.A.* 46°35N 114°43W **122** C4
Powell *Ohio, U.S.A.* 40°18N 81°42W **86** C5
Powell *Tenn., U.S.A.* 36°2N 83°55W **105** C9
Powell *Wyo., U.S.A.* 44°45N 108°46W **124** B4
Powell ➤ *Tenn., U.S.A.* 36°29N 83°52W **105** D9
Powell, L. *Utah, U.S.A.* 36°57N 111°29W **129** G4
Powell Butte *Oreg., U.S.A.* 44°15N 121°1W **121** C4
Powell Butte Park *Oreg., U.S.A.* 45°29N 122°30W **132** B2
Powell County ☆ *Ky., U.S.A.* 37°50N 83°50W **105** C9
Powell County ☆ *Mont., U.S.A.* 46°50N 113°0W **123** D6
Powell L. *B.C., Canada* 50°2N 124°25W **154** E10
Powell River *B.C., Canada* 49°50N 124°35W **154** F10
Powellville *Md., U.S.A.* 38°20N 75°22W **93** B5
Powelton *Ga., U.S.A.* 33°26N 82°52W **113** C4
Power County ☆ *Idaho, U.S.A.* 42°50N 112°50W **122** G6
Power House = Drayton Valley *Alta., Canada* 53°12N 114°58W **152** E6
Powers *Mich., U.S.A.* 45°41N 87°32W **79** D5
Powers *Oreg., U.S.A.* 42°53N 124°4W **121** E1
Powers Lake *N. Dak., U.S.A.* 48°34N 102°39W **76** B3
Powersville *Mo., U.S.A.* 40°33N 93°15W **83** A3
Poweshiek County ☆ *Iowa, U.S.A.* 41°40N 92°30W **81** D6
Powhatan *La., U.S.A.* 36°5N 91°7W **106** B4
Powhatan *Va., U.S.A.* 37°32N 77°55W **102** D7
Powhatan County ☆ *Va., U.S.A.* 37°35N 77°55W **102** D7
Powhatan Point *Ohio, U.S.A.* 39°50N 80°49W **86** D6
Powhattan *Kans., U.S.A.* 39°46N 95°38W **82** B8
Pownal *Vt., U.S.A.* 42°46N 73°14W **89** D1
Poxyaxum *Campeche, Mexico* 19°45N 90°20W **179** C3
Poydras *La., U.S.A.* 29°52N 89°53W **117** C3
Poygan L. *Wis., U.S.A.* 44°19N 88°50W **78** D5
Poynette *Wis., U.S.A.* 43°24N 89°24W **78** E4
Poza Rica *Veracruz, Mexico* 20°33N 97°27W **178** D3
Pozo Coyote *Sonora, Mexico* 29°38N 112°22W **168** D3
Pozuelos *San Luis Potosí, Mexico* 22°6N 101°7W **171** H3
Prado Churubusco *Distrito Federal, Mexico* 19°20N 99°8W **181** B3
Prague *Nebr., U.S.A.* 41°19N 96°49W **80** C9
Prague *Okla., U.S.A.* 35°29N 96°41W **107** C7
Praires, R. des ➤ *Qué., Canada* 45°38N 73°36W **160** A3
Prairie Band of the Potawatomi Indian Reservation *Kans., U.S.A.* 39°20N 95°52W **82** B8
Prairie City *Iowa, U.S.A.* 41°36N 93°14W **81** D5

Prairie City *Oreg., U.S.A.* 44°28N 118°43W 121 C7
Prairie City *S.Dak., U.S.A.* 45°32N 102°48W 76 E3
Prairie Coun. ☆ *Ark., U.S.A.* 34°47N 91°35W 106 D4
Prairie Coun. ☆ *Mont., U.S.A.* 46°57N 105°30W 123 D12
Prairie Dog C. ➜ *Kans., U.S.A.* 40°0N 99°18W 82 B4
Prairie Dog Town Fork Red ➜ *U.S.A.* 34°34N 99°58W 108 C7
Prairie du Chien *Wis., U.S.A.* 43°3N 91°9W 78 E2
Prairie du Rocher *Ill., U.S.A.* 38°5N 90°6W 84 B4
Prairie du Sac *Wis., U.S.A.* 43°17N 89°43W 78 E4
Prairie Farm *Wis., U.S.A.* 45°14N 91°59W 78 C2
Prairie Grove *Ark., U.S.A.* 35°59N 94°19W 106 C1
Prairie Hill *Mo., U.S.A.* 39°31N 92°44W 83 B4
Prairie Home *Mo., U.S.A.* 38°49N 92°35W 83 C4
Prairie Island Indian Reservation *Minn., U.S.A.* 44°39N 92°39W 77 F6
Prairie View *Kans., U.S.A.* 39°50N 99°34W 82 B4
Prairie View *Tex., U.S.A.* 30°6N 95°59W 109 G12
Prairie Village *Kans., U.S.A.* 38°58N 94°38W 82 C9
Pratt *Kans., U.S.A.* 37°39N 98°44W 82 D5
Pratt County ☆ *Kans., U.S.A.* 37°35N 98°45W 82 D5
Prattville *Ala., U.S.A.* 32°28N 86°29W 112 D4
Práxedis G. Guerrero *Chihuahua, Mexico* 31°22N 106°0W 169 B9
Preble *N.Y., U.S.A.* 42°44N 76°9W 88 C7
Preble County ☆ *Ohio, U.S.A.* 39°45N 84°38W 86 D2
Preeceville *Sask., Canada* 51°57N 102°40W 150 D9
Preissac, L. *Qué., Canada* 48°20N 78°20W 144 C4
Prelate *Sask., Canada* 50°51N 109°24W 150 E2
Premont *Tex., U.S.A.* 27°22N 98°7W 108 K9
Prentice *Wis., U.S.A.* 45°33N 90°17W 78 C31
Prentiss *Miss., U.S.A.* 31°36N 89°52W 111 E4
Prentiss County ☆ *Miss., U.S.A.* 34°39N 88°34W 111 B5
Presa de Guadalupe *San Luis Potosí, Mexico* 22°52N 100°8W 171 H4
Presa de la Amistad, Parque Natural △ *Coahuila, Mexico* 29°30N 101°15W 170 A3
Presa de San Pedro *Coahuila, Mexico* 24°41N 101°3W 171 F3
Presa Verde *San Luis Potosí, Mexico* 24°0N 100°42W 171 F4
Prescott *Ont., Canada* 44°45N 75°30W 147 C11
Prescott *Ariz., U.S.A.* 34°33N 112°28W 130 C3
Prescott *Ark., U.S.A.* 33°48N 93°23W 106 E2
Prescott *Iowa, U.S.A.* 41°1N 94°37W 81 D4
Prescott *Kans., U.S.A.* 38°4N 94°42W 82 C9
Prescott *Mich., U.S.A.* 44°11N 83°56W 79 E8
Prescott *Wash., U.S.A.* 46°3N 122°53W 121 A3
Prescott *Wash., U.S.A.* 46°18N 118°19W 120 D7
Prescott *Wis., U.S.A.* 44°45N 92°48W 78 D1
Prescott I. *B.C., Canada* 54°6N 130°37W 154 A4
Prescott I. *Nunavut, Canada* 73°3N 96°50W 158 C6
Prescott Nat. Forest *Ariz., U.S.A.* 34°30N 112°30W 130 C3
Prescott Valley *Ariz., U.S.A.* 34°40N 112°18W 130 C3
Presho *S. Dak., U.S.A.* 43°54N 100°3W 76 G5
Presidente Calles, Presa *Aguascalientes, Mexico* 22°9N 102°27W 173 E8
Presidente Juárez *Quintana Roo, Mexico* 19°18N 88°34W 179 C5
Presidential Lakes Estates *N.J., U.S.A.* 39°54N 74°35W 92 C2
Presidents I. *Tenn., U.S.A.* 35°6N 90°6W 117 B1
Presidio *Tex., U.S.A.* 29°34N 104°22W 108 H3
Presidio County ☆ *Tex., U.S.A.* 30°0N 104°0W 108 G3
Presidio *Sinaloa, Mexico* 23°6N 106°17W 172 D4
Presque I. ➜ *U.S.A.* 42°10N 80°6W 87 B2
Presque Isle *Maine, U.S.A.* 46°41N 68°1W 90 B5
Presque Isle *Mich., U.S.A.* 45°18N 83°29W 79 D8
Presque Isle County ☆ *Mich., U.S.A.* 45°15N 84°0W 79 D8
Preston *Ga., U.S.A.* 32°4N 84°32W 113 D2
Preston *Idaho, U.S.A.* 42°6N 111°53W 122 G7
Preston *Iowa, U.S.A.* 42°3N 90°24W 81 C8
Preston *Kans., U.S.A.* 37°46N 98°33W 82 D5
Preston *Md. U.S.A.* 38°43N 75°55W 93 B5
Preston *Minn., U.S.A.* 43°40N 92°5W 77 G6
Preston *Miss., U.S.A.* 32°53N 88°50W 111 D5
Preston *Nev., U.S.A.* 38°55N 115°4W 128 D5
Preston *Okla., U.S.A.* 35°43N 95°59W 107 C8
Preston County ☆ *W. Va., U.S.A.* 39°31N 79°48W 102 B5
Preston City *Conn., U.S.A.* 41°33N 72°57W 91 C2
Preston County ☆ *W. Va., U.S.A.* 39°31N 79°48W 105 C10
Prestonsburg *Ky., U.S.A.* 37°40N 82°47W 105 C10
Pretty Prairie *Kans., U.S.A.* 37°47N 98°1W 82 D5
Prettyboy Res. *Md., U.S.A.* 39°37N 76°43W 93 A4
Préville *Qué. Canada* 45°28N 73°29W 160 B4
Prewitt *N. Mex., U.S.A.* 35°22N 108°3W 131 B2
Prewitt Res. *Colo., U.S.A.* 40°26N 103°22W 125 B7
Pribilof Is. *Alaska, U.S.A.* 57°0N 170°0W 135 H5
Price *Qué., Canada* 48°36N 68°7W 140 E1
Price *Md., U.S.A.* 39°6N 75°58W 93 A5
Price *Tex., U.S.A.* 32°8N 94°57W 109 E13
Price *Utah, U.S.A.* 39°36N 110°49W 129 D5
Price ➜ *Utah, U.S.A.* 39°10N 110°6W 129 D5
Price County ☆ *Wis., U.S.A.* 45°45N 90°20W 78 C3
Price I. *B.C. Canada* 52°23N 128°41W 154 C6
Prichard *Ala., U.S.A.* 30°44N 88°5W 112 F2
Prichard *W.Va., U.S.A.* 38°15N 82°36W 102 C2
Priddy *Tex., U.S.A.* 31°41N 98°31W 109 F9
Pride *Ky., U.S.A.* 37°34N 87°53W 104 C4
Priest ➜ *Idaho, U.S.A.* 48°12N 116°54W 122 A2
Priest L. *Idaho, U.S.A.* 48°35N 116°52W 122 A2
Priest Rapids Dam *Wash., U.S.A.* 46°39N 119°54W 120 D6
Priest River *Idaho, U.S.A.* 48°11N 116°55W 122 A2
Prime Hook Nat. Wildlife Refuge △ *Del., U.S.A.* 38°55N 75°18W 93 B5
Primera *Tex., U.S.A.* 26°13N 97°45W 108 L10
Primghar *Iowa, U.S.A.* 43°5N 95°38W 81 B3
Primm *Nev., U.S.A.* 35°37N 115°23W 128 G5
Primo Tapia *Baja Calif., Mexico* 32°16N 116°54W 166 A2
Primrose *Nebr., U.S.A.* 41°38N 98°14W 80 C7
Primrose L. *Sask., Mexico* 54°55N 109°45W 157 F11
Prince *Sask. Canada* 52°58N 108°23W 150 C3
Prince Albert *Sask., Canada* 53°15N 105°50W 150 B6
Prince Albert Nat. Park △ *Sask., Canada* 54°0N 106°25W 150 B5
Prince Albert Pen. *N.W.T., Canada* 72°30N 116°0W 156 B9
Prince Albert Sd. *N.W.T., Canada* 70°25N 115°0W 156 B9
Prince Alfred, C. *N.W.T., Canada* 74°20N 124°40W 156 B8
Prince Charles I. *Nunavut, Canada* 67°47N 76°12W 158 D12
Prince Edward County ☆ *Va., U.S.A.* 37°15N 78°25W 102 D6
Prince Edward I. □ *Canada* 46°20N 63°20W 141 G6
Prince Edward Island Nat. Park △ *P.E.I., Canada* 46°26N 63°12W 141 G6
Prince Edward Pt. *Ont., Canada* 43°56N 76°52W 147 D10
Prince Frederick *Md., U.S.A.* 38°33N 76°35W 93 B4
Prince George *B.C., Canada* 53°55N 122°50W 155 B12
Prince George *Va., U.S.A.* 37°13N 77°17W 102 D7
Prince George County ☆ *Va., U.S.A.* 37°13N 77°17W 102 D7
Prince Georges County ☆ *Md., U.S.A.* 38°45N 76°50W 93 B4
Prince Gustaf Adolf Sea *N.W.T., Canada* 78°30N 107°0W 158 B4
Prince of Wales, C. *Qué., Canada* 61°37N 71°30W 143 A3
Prince of Wales, C. *Alaska, U.S.A.* 65°36N 168°5W 135 D5

Prince of Wales I. *Nunavut, Canada* 73°0N 99°0W 158 C6
Prince of Wales I. *Alaska, U.S.A.* 55°47N 132°50W 135 J14
Prince of Wales Icefield *Nunavut, Canada* 78°15N 79°0W 158 B10
Prince of Wales-Outer Ketchikan ☆ *Alaska, U.S.A.* 55°30N 132°0W 135 J15
Prince of Wales Str. *N.W.T., Canada* 73°0N 117°0W 156 B9
Prince Patrick I. *N.W.T., Canada* 77°0N 120°0W 156 A9
Prince Regent Inlet *Nunavut, Canada* 73°0N 90°0W 158 C8
Prince Rupert *B.C., Canada* 54°20N 130°20W 154 A4
Prince William County ☆ *Va., U.S.A.* 38°45N 77°29W 102 C7
Prince William Forest Park △ *Va., U.S.A.* 38°35N 77°24W 102 C7
Prince William Sd. *Alaska, U.S.A.* 60°40N 147°0W 135 F11
Princess Anne *Md., U.S.A.* 38°12N 75°42W 93 B5
Princess Margaret Range *N.W.T., Canada* 80°30N 92°0W 158 A7
Princess Royal Chan. *B.C., Canada* 53°0N 128°40W 154 B6
Princess Royal I. *B.C., Canada* 53°0N 128°40W 154 B6
Princeton *B.C., Canada* 49°27N 120°30W 155 F14
Princeton *Calif., U.S.A.* 39°24N 122°1W 126 D4
Princeton *Ill., U.S.A.* 41°23N 89°28W 84 B4
Princeton *Ind., U.S.A.* 38°21N 87°34W 85 E3
Princeton *Iowa, U.S.A.* 41°40N 90°20W 81 D8
Princeton *Kans., U.S.A.* 38°29N 95°16W 82 C8
Princeton *Ky., U.S.A.* 37°7N 87°53W 104 C3
Princeton *Maine, U.S.A.* 45°13N 67°34W 90 C6
Princeton *Mass., U.S.A.* 42°27N 71°55W 91 B3
Princeton *Mich., U.S.A.* 46°17N 87°29W 79 C4
Princeton *Minn., U.S.A.* 45°34N 93°35W 77 E5
Princeton *Mo., U.S.A.* 40°24N 93°35W 83 A3
Princeton *N.C., U.S.A.* 35°28N 78°10W 103 C7
Princeton *N.J., U.S.A.* 40°21N 74°39W 92 B2
Princeton *W. Va., U.S.A.* 37°22N 81°6W 102 D3
Princeton *Wis., U.S.A.* 43°51N 89°8W 78 E4
Princeville *Qué., Canada* 46°10N 71°53W 145 E11
Princeville *Hawai'i, U.S.A.* 22°13N 159°29W 136 A2
Princeville *Ill., U.S.A.* 40°56N 89°46W 84 C4
Principe Chan. *B.C., Canada* 53°28N 130°0W 154 B4
Prineville *Oreg., U.S.A.* 44°18N 120°51W 121 C5
Prineville Res. *Oreg., U.S.A.* 44°7N 120°47W 121 C5
Pringle *S. Dak., U.S.A.* 43°37N 103°36W 76 G2
Pringle *Tex., U.S.A.* 35°57N 101°27W 108 B6
Prins Christian Sund *Greenland* 60°4N 43°10W 162 E6
Prins Karls Forland *Svalbard* 78°30N 11°0E 162 B12
Prinsburg *Minn., U.S.A.* 44°56N 95°11W 77 F3
Prinzapolca *Nic.* 13°20N 83°35W 182 D3
Prior Lake *Minn., U.S.A.* 44°43N 93°25W 77 F5
Pritchett *Colo., U.S.A.* 37°22N 102°52W 125 E8
Procter *B.C., Canada* 49°37N 116°57W 155 F18
Proctor *Colo., U.S.A.* 40°48N 102°57W 125 B8
Proctor *Minn., U.S.A.* 46°45N 92°14W 77 D6
Proctor *Vt., U.S.A.* 43°40N 73°2W 89 C1
Proctor *W. Va., U.S.A.* 39°43N 80°49W 102 B4
Proctor L. *Tex., U.S.A.* 31°58N 98°29W 109 F9
Proctorsville *Vt., U.S.A.* 43°23N 72°40W 89 C2
Proctorville *Ohio, U.S.A.* 38°26N 82°23W 86 E4
Progreso *Baja Calif., Mexico* 32°38N 115°40W 166 A3
Progreso *Chihuahua, Mexico* 30°25N 107°17W 169 C8
Progreso *Coahuila, Mexico* 27°28N 100°59W 170 D4
Progreso *Hidalgo, Mexico* 20°15N 99°12W 175 B8
Progreso *Yucatán, Mexico* 21°20N 89°40W 179 A4
Progreso Nacional *Distrito Federal, Mexico* 19°30N 99°9W 181 A3
Promise City *Iowa, U.S.A.* 40°45N 93°9W 81 E5
Promontory Mts. *Utah, U.S.A.* 41°30N 112°30W 129 B3
Prophet ➜ *B.C., Canada* 58°48N 122°40W 157 E8
Prophet River *B.C., Canada* 58°6N 122°43W 157 E8
Prophetstown *Ill., U.S.A.* 41°40N 89°56W 84 B4
Prospect *Conn., U.S.A.* 41°30N 72°59W 91 C2
Prospect *Ky., U.S.A.* 38°21N 85°37W 105 B7
Prospect *Ohio, U.S.A.* 40°27N 83°11W 86 C3
Prospect *Oreg., U.S.A.* 42°45N 122°29W 121 E3
Prospect *Pa., U.S.A.* 40°54N 80°3W 87 D2
Prospect Hill Park *Mass., U.S.A.* 42°23N 71°13W 96 A1
Prospect Park *N.J., U.S.A.* 40°56N 74°10W 97 A1
Prospect Park *N.Y., U.S.A.* 40°39N 73°58W 97 C3
Prospect Pt. *U.S.A.* 49°19N 123°8W 161 B2
Prosperity *S.C., U.S.A.* 34°21N 81°32W 103 D4
Prosser *Nebr., U.S.A.* 40°41N 98°34W 80 D7
Prosser *Wash., U.S.A.* 46°12N 119°46W 120 D6
Protection *Kans., U.S.A.* 37°12N 99°29W 82 D4
Protem *Mo., U.S.A.* 36°32N 92°51W 83 E4
Protivin *Iowa, U.S.A.* 43°13N 92°6W 81 B6
Providence *Baltimore, U.S.A.* 39°25N 76°33W 99 A2
Providence *Ky., U.S.A.* 37°24N 87°46W 104 C5
Providence *R.I., U.S.A.* 41°49N 71°24W 91 C3
Providence *Utah, U.S.A.* 41°43N 111°49W 129 B4
Providence Bay *Ont., Canada* 45°41N 82°15W 146 B4
Providence County ☆ *R.I., U.S.A.* 41°50N 71°40W 91 C3
Providence Mts. *Calif., U.S.A.* 35°10N 115°15W 127 H11
Providencia, I. de *Colombia* 13°25N 81°26W 182 D3
Provincetown *Mass., U.S.A.* 42°3N 70°11W 91 B4
Provo *S. Dak., U.S.A.* 43°12N 103°50W 76 G2
Provo *Utah, U.S.A.* 40°14N 111°39W 129 C4
Prowers County ☆ *Colo., U.S.A.* 38°0N 102°30W 125 E8
Prudence I. *R.I., U.S.A.* 41°37N 71°19W 91 C3
Prudhoe Bay *Alaska, U.S.A.* 70°18N 148°22W 135 A10
Prud'homme *Sask., Canada* 52°20N 105°54W 150 C6
Prue *Okla., U.S.A.* 36°15N 96°16W 107 B7
Pryor *Okla., U.S.A.* 36°19N 95°19W 107 B8
Pryor Mts. *Mont., U.S.A.* 45°15N 108°30W 123 E9
Pua'ena Pt. *Hawai'i, U.S.A.* 21°36N 158°6W 136 J13
Puckaway L. *Wis., U.S.A.* 43°45N 89°10W 78 E4
Puckett *Miss., U.S.A.* 32°5N 89°47W 111 D4
Pucnachén *Campeche, Mexico* 20°22N 90°13W 179 B3
Puebla *Puebla, Mexico* 19°3N 98°12W 177 E2
Puebla □ *Mexico* 18°50N 98°0W 177 F3
Pueblillo *Veracruz, Mexico* 20°15N 97°14W 176 D3
Pueblo *Colo., U.S.A.* 38°16N 104°37W 125 D6
Pueblo Colorado Wash ➜ *Ariz., U.S.A.* 35°5N 110°22W 130 B5
Pueblo County ☆ *Colo., U.S.A.* 38°15N 104°30W 125 D6
Pueblo Mt. *Oreg., U.S.A.* 42°6N 118°39W 121 E7
Pueblo Mts. *Oreg., U.S.A.* 42°6N 118°43W 121 E7
Pueblo Nuevo *Durango, Mexico* 23°23N 105°23W 172 D5
Pueblo Nuevo Jolistahuacán *Chiapas, Mexico* 17°6N 92°53W 178 B4
Pueblo Viejo *Sinaloa, Mexico* 25°57N 109°3W 172 C3
Pueblo Viejo *Veracruz, Mexico* 19°48N 96°51W 176 E4
Pueblo Viejo, L. *Veracruz, Mexico* 22°10N 97°54W 176 C4
Pueblo West *Colo., U.S.A.* 38°20N 104°43W 125 D6
Pueblo Yaqui *Sonora, Mexico* 27°20N 110°2W 168 F5
Puente de Ixtla *Morelos, Mexico* 18°38N 99°19W 175 D8

Pueo Pt. *Hawai'i, U.S.A.* 21°54N 160°4W 136 B1
Puerca, Pta. *Puerto Rico* 18°13N 65°36W 184 G17
Puerco ➜ *Ariz., U.S.A.* 34°54N 110°23W 130 C5
Puerco ➜ *N. Mex., U.S.A.* 34°22N 107°50W 131 C3
Puertecitos *Baja Calif., Mexico* 30°22N 114°40W 166 C4
Puerto Ángel *Oaxaca, Mexico* 15°40N 96°29W 177 J4
Puerto Arista *Chiapas, Mexico* 15°56N 93°48W 178 D3
Puerto Armuelles *Panama* 8°20N 82°51W 182 E3
Puerto Arturo *Quintana Roo, Mexico* 19°38N 89°5W 179 C4
Puerto Barrios *Guatemala* 15°40N 88°32W 182 C2
Puerto Bravo *Quintana Roo, Mexico* 18°47N 87°40W 179 D6
Puerto Cabezas *Nic.* 14°0N 83°30W 182 D3
Puerto Cabo Gracias á Dios *Nic.* 15°0N 83°10W 182 D3
Puerto Canoas *Baja Calif., Mexico* 29°26N 115°8W 166 D3
Puerto Castilla *Honduras* 16°0N 86°0W 182 C2
Puerto Chale *Baja Calif. S., Mexico* 24°26N 111°33W 167 J7
Puerto Cortés *Costa Rica* 8°55N 84°0W 182 E3
Puerto Cortés *Honduras* 15°51N 88°0W 182 C2
Puerto Cortés *Baja Calif. S., Mexico* 24°28N 111°50W 167 J7
Puerto de Luna *N. Mex., U.S.A.* 35°50N 104°37W 131 B6
Puerto del Gallo *Guerrero, Mexico* 17°30N 100°11W 175 F7
Puerto Escondido *Baja Calif. S., Mexico* 27°35N 114°46W 167 F4
Puerto Escondido *Oaxaca, Mexico* 15°50N 97°3W 177 J3
Puerto Juárez *Quintana Roo, Mexico* 21°11N 86°49W 179 A7
Puerto Libertad *Sonora, Mexico* 29°55N 112°43W 168 D3
Puerto Lobos *Sonora, Mexico* 30°25N 112°55W 168 D3
Puerto Madero *Chiapas, Mexico* 14°44N 92°25W 178 E4
Puerto Manatí *Cuba* 21°22N 76°50W 182 B4
Puerto Mexico = Coatzacoalcos *Mexico* 18°7N 94°25W 177 F6
Puerto Modero *Zacatecas, Mexico* 23°43N 101°56W 173 D9
Puerto Morazán *Nic.* 12°51N 87°11W 182 D2
Puerto Morelos *Quintana Roo, Mexico* 20°50N 86°52W 179 B7
Puerto Morro Redondo *Baja Calif. S., Mexico* 28°2N 115°11W 167 E3
Puerto Padre *Cuba* 21°13N 76°35W 182 B4
Puerto Peñasco *Sonora, Mexico* 31°20N 113°33W 168 B2
Puerto Plata *Dom. Rep.* 19°48N 70°45W 183 C5
Puerto Quepos *Costa Rica* 9°29N 84°6W 182 E3
Puerto Rico ☑ *W. Indies* 18°15N 66°45W 184 G16
Puerto Rico Trench *Atl. Oc.* 19°50N 66°0W 183 C6
Puerto San Andrecito *Baja Calif. S., Mexico* 25°49N 112°8W 167 H6
Puerto Vallarta *Jalisco, Mexico* 20°37N 105°15W 174 B2
Puerto Vallarta ✈ (PVR) *Jalisco, Mexico* 20°39N 105°15W 174 B2
Puget Sound *Wash., U.S.A.* 47°50N 122°30W 120 C3
Pugwash *Qué., Canada* 45°51N 63°40W 141 H6
Pukalani *Hawai'i, U.S.A.* 20°51N 156°20W 136 C5
Pukaskwa ➜ *Ont., Canada* 48°0N 85°53W 149 D11
Pukaskwa Nat. Park △ *Ont., Canada* 48°20N 86°0W 149 D11
Pukatawagan *Man., Canada* 55°45N 101°20W 157 E12
Püko'o *Hawai'i, U.S.A.* 21°4N 156°48W 136 B5
Pulaski *Ill., U.S.A.* 37°12N 89°10W 84 F4
Pulaski *Iowa, U.S.A.* 40°45N 92°12W 81 E6
Pulaski *Miss., U.S.A.* 32°16N 89°36W 111 D4
Pulaski *N.Y., U.S.A.* 43°34N 76°8W 88 B6
Pulaski *Tenn., U.S.A.* 35°12N 87°2W 104 E5
Pulaski *Va., U.S.A.* 37°3N 80°47W 102 D4
Pulaski County ☆ *Ark., U.S.A.* 34°45N 92°20W 106 D3
Pulaski County ☆ *Ga., U.S.A.* 32°15N 83°30W 113 D3
Pulaski County ☆ *Ill., U.S.A.* 37°15N 89°5W 84 F4
Pulaski County ☆ *Ind., U.S.A.* 41°0N 86°40W 85 B4
Pulaski County ☆ *Ky., U.S.A.* 37°5N 84°35W 105 C8
Pulaski County ☆ *Mo., U.S.A.* 37°50N 92°10W 83 D4
Pulaski County ☆ *Va., U.S.A.* 37°0N 80°45W 102 D4
Pullman *Wash., U.S.A.* 46°44N 117°10W 120 D8
Pullman Historic District *Ill., U.S.A.* 41°41N 87°36W 95 C3
Púlpito, Pta. *Baja Calif. S., Mexico* 26°31N 111°28W 167 G7
Pulticub, Pta. *Quintana Roo, Mexico* 19°7N 87°32W 179 C6
Pumphrey *Baltimore, U.S.A.* 39°13N 76°38W 99 B2
Pumpkin Creek *Mont., U.S.A.* 46°15N 105°45W 123 D12
Pumpville *Tex., U.S.A.* 29°53N 101°45W 108 H6
Puna Forest Reserve *Hawai'i, U.S.A.* 19°34N 154°59W 136 D7
Punalu'u *Hawai'i, U.S.A.* 21°35N 157°53W 136 J14
Pungo *N.C., U.S.A.* 35°23N 76°33W 103 C9
Pungo L. *N.C., U.S.A.* 35°42N 76°33W 103 C9
Punnichy *Sask., Canada* 51°23N 104°18W 150 D7
Punta, Cerro de *Puerto Rico* 18°10N 66°37W 184 G16
Punta Abreojos *Baja Calif., Mexico* 26°42N 113°35W 167 G5
Punta Allen *Quintana Roo, Mexico* 19°48N 87°28W 179 C6
Punta Caracol *Quintana Roo, Mexico* 20°54N 86°51W 179 B7
Punta Chueca *Sonora, Mexico* 29°1N 112°10W 168 D3
Punta Colonet *Baja Calif., Mexico* 31°5N 116°11W 166 B2
Punta de Agua ➜ *Tex., U.S.A.* 35°32N 102°27W 108 B5
Punta de Mita *Nayarit, Mexico* 20°46N 105°30W 172 G5
Punta Estrella *Quintana Roo, Mexico* 19°34N 87°26W 179 C6
Punta Flor *Chiapas, Mexico* 16°6N 93°58W 178 C3
Punta Gorda *Belize* 16°10N 88°45W 182 C2
Punta Gorda *Fla., U.S.A.* 26°56N 82°3W 114 E6
Punta Prieta *Baja Calif., Mexico* 28°58N 114°17W 166 C4
Punta Prieta *Baja Calif. S., Mexico* 27°1N 114°1W 167 F4
Punta Rassa *Fla., U.S.A.* 26°26N 81°59W 114 E7
Punta Rossa *Costa Rica* 8°0N 84°50W 182 E3
Puntzi L. *B.C., Canada* 52°12N 124°2W 154 C10
Puolo Pt. *Hawai'i, U.S.A.* 21°54N 159°36W 136 B2
Pūpūkea *Hawai'i, U.S.A.* 21°40N 158°3W 136 J13
Purcell *Okla., U.S.A.* 35°1N 97°22W 107 C6
Purcell Mts. *B.C., Canada* 48°30N 116°0W 123 D2
Purcellville *Va., U.S.A.* 39°8N 77°43W 93 A3
Purdin *Mo., U.S.A.* 39°57N 93°10W 83 B3
Purdon *Tex., U.S.A.* 31°57N 96°37W 109 F11
Purdy *Mo., U.S.A.* 36°49N 93°55W 83 E3
Purdy *Okla., U.S.A.* 34°43N 97°35W 107 D6
Purdy *Wash., U.S.A.* 47°23N 122°37W 132 D2
Purépero de Echaiz *Michoacan, Mexico* 19°54N 102°0W 174 C6
Purgatoire ➜ *Colo., U.S.A.* 38°4N 103°11W 125 D7
Purgatory Park *Minn., U.S.A.* 44°54N 93°30W 94 B3
Purgitsville *W. Va., U.S.A.* 39°14N 78°55W 93 A2
Purificación *Jalisco, Mexico* 19°43N 104°38W 174 C5
Purísima de Bustos *Guanajuato, Mexico* 21°2N 101°55W 174 A6
Purísima de Conchos *Nuevo León, Mexico* 24°55N 99°15W 171 F3
Puruándiro *Michoacan, Mexico* 20°6N 101°32W 174 B6
Puruarican *Michoacan, Mexico* 19°5N 101°32W 174 C6
Purvis *Miss., U.S.A.* 31°9N 89°25W 111 E4
Puryear *Tenn., U.S.A.* 36°27N 88°20W 104 D4
Pushaw L. *Maine, U.S.A.* 44°56N 68°48W 90 D5
Pushmataha County ☆ *Okla., U.S.A.* 34°25N 95°20W 107 D8
Put-in-Bay *Ohio, U.S.A.* 41°39N 82°49W 86 B4
Puta *Oaxaca, Mexico* 16°27N 97°56W 177 G3
Putnam *Conn., U.S.A.* 41°55N 71°55W 91 C3
Putnam *Okla., U.S.A.* 35°51N 98°58W 107 C5

Putnam *Tex., U.S.A.* 32°22N 99°12W 109 E8
Putnam County ☆ *Fla., U.S.A.* 29°35N 81°45W 114 B7
Putnam County ☆ *Ga., U.S.A.* 33°20N 83°15W 113 C3
Putnam County ☆ *Ill., U.S.A.* 41°10N 89°15W 84 B4
Putnam County ☆ *Ind., U.S.A.* 39°40N 86°50W 85 D4
Putnam County ☆ *Mo., U.S.A.* 40°30N 93°0W 83 A4
Putnam County ☆ *N.Y., U.S.A.* 41°25N 73°45W 88 D7
Putnam County ☆ *Ohio, U.S.A.* 40°59N 84°12W 86 C2
Putnam County ☆ *Tenn., U.S.A.* 36°10N 85°30W 105 D7
Putnam County ☆ *W. Va., U.S.A.* 38°32N 81°54W 102 C3
Putnam Lake *N.Y., U.S.A.* 41°28N 73°33W 91 C1
Putney *Ga., U.S.A.* 31°29N 84°8W 113 E2
Putney *S. Dak., U.S.A.* 45°34N 98°11W 76 E7
Putney *Vt., U.S.A.* 42°58N 72°31W 89 D2
Putty Hill *Baltimore, U.S.A.* 39°22N 76°30W 99 A2
Pu'uanahulu *Hawai'i, U.S.A.* 19°49N 155°51W 136 D6
Pu'uhonua o Hōnaunau Nat. Historical Park △ *Hawai'i, U.S.A.* 19°25N 155°54W 136 D6
Pu'uka'aumakua *Hawai'i, U.S.A.* 21°30N 157°54W 136 J14
Pu'ukeahiakahoe *Hawai'i, U.S.A.* 21°23N 157°49W 136 K14
Pu'ukoholā Heiau Nat. Historic Site △ *U.S.A.* 20°1N 155°49W 136 C6
Pu'ula'ula *Hawai'i, U.S.A.* 20°42N 156°15W 136 C5
Puunene *Hawai'i, U.S.A.* 20°53N 156°23W 136 C5
Pu'uoke'oke'o *Hawai'i, U.S.A.* 19°13N 155°44W 136 D6
Pu'uwai *Hawai'i, U.S.A.* 21°54N 160°12W 136 B1
Puvirnituq *Qué., Canada* 60°2N 77°10W 143 A2
Puvirnituq ➜ *Qué., Canada* 60°3N 77°15W 143 A2
Puvirnituq, B. de *Qué., Canada* 60°0N 77°30W 143 B2
Puvirnituq, Mts. de *Qué., Canada* 61°22N 75°55W 143 A2
Puxico *Mo., U.S.A.* 36°57N 90°10W 83 E6
Puxmetacán ➜ *Oaxaca, Mexico* 17°22N 95°36W 177 G5
Puyallup *Wash., U.S.A.* 47°12N 122°18W 120 C3
Puyallup Indian Reservation *Wash., U.S.A.* 47°14N 122°17W 120 C3
Puyjalon, L. *Qué., Canada* 50°30N 63°25W 140 C6
Pymatuning Res. *Ohio, U.S.A.* 41°30N 80°28W 86 B6
Pymatuning State Park △ *Pa., U.S.A.* 41°37N 80°24W 87 C2
Pyote *Tex., U.S.A.* 31°32N 103°8W 108 F4
Pyramid L. *Nev., U.S.A.* 40°1N 119°35W 128 B1
Pyramid Lake Indian Reservation *Nev., U.S.A.* 40°20N 119°35W 128 B1
Pyramid Mts. *N. Mex., U.S.A.* 32°12N 108°43W 131 E2
Pyramid Pk. *Wyo., U.S.A.* 43°27N 110°28W 124 C2

Q

Qaanaaq *Greenland* 77°40N 69°0W 162 B4
Qamanirjuaq L. = Kaminuriak L. *Nunavut, Canada* 62°57N 95°46W 159 E6
Qamani'tuaq = Baker Lake *Nunavut, Canada* 64°20N 96°3W 159 E6
Qaqortoq *Greenland* 60°43N 46°0W 162 E6
Qasigiannguit *Greenland* 68°50N 51°18W 162 D5
Qausiuittuq = Resolute *Nunavut, Canada* 74°42N 94°54W 158 C7
Qeqertarsuaq *Greenland* 69°45N 53°30W 162 D5
Qeqertarsuaq *Greenland* 69°15N 53°38W 162 D5
Qeqertarsuatsiaat *Greenland* 63°5N 50°45W 162 E5
Qiajivik *Nunavut, Canada* 72°10N 75°54W 158 C10
Qikiqtarjuaq *Nunavut, Canada* 67°33N 63°0W 158 D13
Qikirtaluq, Î. *Qué., Canada* 59°5N 69°15W 143 B4
Qirniraujaq, Pte. *Qué., Canada* 58°35N 68°1W 143 B4
Quabbin Res. *Mass., U.S.A.* 42°20N 72°20W 91 B2
Quadra I. *B.C., Canada* 50°10N 125°15W 154 D9
Quail *Tex., U.S.A.* 34°55N 100°30W 108 C7
Quakertown *Pa., U.S.A.* 40°26N 75°21W 87 D7
Qualicum Beach *B.C., Canada* 49°22N 124°26W 154 F10
Quamba *Minn., U.S.A.* 45°55N 93°10W 77 E5
Quanah *Tex., U.S.A.* 34°18N 99°44W 109 C8
Quantico *Md., U.S.A.* 38°23N 75°44W 93 B5
Quantico U.S.M.C. Base *Va., U.S.A.* 38°30N 77°17W 102 C7
Quapaw *Okla., U.S.A.* 36°58N 94°50W 107 B9
Qu'Appelle *Sask., Canada* 50°33N 103°53W 150 E8
Qu'Appelle ➜ *Sask., Canada* 50°26N 101°19W 151 E10
Quaqtaq *Qué., Canada* 60°55N 69°40W 143 A4
Quarryville *N.B., Canada* 46°50N 65°47W 141 G4
Quarryville *Pa., U.S.A.* 39°54N 76°10W 93 A4
Quartz Hill *Calif., U.S.A.* 34°39N 118°13W 127 J8
Quartz Mt. *Okla., U.S.A.* 34°54N 99°19W 107 D4
Quartzsite *Ariz., U.S.A.* 33°40N 114°13W 130 D1
Quasqueton *Iowa, U.S.A.* 42°24N 91°46W 81 C7
Quathiaski Cove *B.C., Canada* 50°3N 125°12W 154 D9
Quatsino *B.C., Canada* 50°30N 127°40W 154 E7
Quatsino Sd. *B.C., Canada* 50°25N 127°58W 154 E7
Quay *N. Mex., U.S.A.* 34°56N 103°45W 131 C7
Quay County ☆ *N. Mex., U.S.A.* 35°0N 103°30W 131 B7
Québec *Qué., Canada* 46°52N 71°13W 145 E11
Québec □ *Canada* 48°0N 74°0W 144 C6
Québec Int. ✈ (YQB) *Qué., Canada* 46°51N 71°19W 145 E11
Quebradillas *Puerto Rico* 18°29N 66°56W 184 G16
Quechee *Vt., U.S.A.* 43°40N 72°25W 89 C2
Quechultenango *Guerrero, Mexico* 17°25N 99°23W 175 E8
Queen Anne *Md., U.S.A.* 38°55N 75°57W 93 B5
Queen Anne County ☆ *Md., U.S.A.* 39°10N 76°0W 93 A5
Queen Charlotte City *B.C., Canada* 53°15N 132°2W 154 B2
Queen Charlotte Is. *B.C., Canada* 53°20N 132°10W 154 B2
Queen Charlotte Mts. *B.C., Canada* 53°5N 132°15W 154 B2
Queen Charlotte Sd. *B.C., Canada* 51°0N 128°0W 154 D5
Queen City *Mo., U.S.A.* 40°25N 92°34W 83 A4
Queen City *Tex., U.S.A.* 33°9N 94°9W 109 D13
Queen Creek *Ariz., U.S.A.* 33°15N 111°35W 130 D4
Queen Elizabeth Is. *Canada* 76°0N 95°0W 158 B3
Queen Elizabeth Park *B.C., Canada* 49°15N 123°17W 161 B2
Queen Maud G. *Nunavut, Canada* 68°15N 102°30W 156 C12
Queens *N.S., Canada* 44°14N 65°0W 141 J5
Queens Chan. *Nunavut, Canada* 76°11N 96°0W 158 B6
Queens County ☆ *N.Y., U.S.A.* 40°40N 73°50W 88 E7
Queens Sd. *B.C., Canada* 51°57N 128°20W 154 D6
Queens Village *N.Y., U.S.A.* 40°43N 73°44W 97 B4
Queensland *Ga., U.S.A.* 31°46N 83°14W 113 E3
Queenstown *N.B., Canada* 45°41N 66°14W 141 H3
Queenstown *Md., U.S.A.* 38°59N 76°9W 93 B4
Queets ➜ *Wash., U.S.A.* 47°33N 124°21W 120 C1
Quemado *N. Mex., U.S.A.* 34°20N 108°30W 131 C1
Quemado *Tex., U.S.A.* 28°56N 100°37W 108 J7
Quenemo *Kans., U.S.A.* 38°35N 95°30W 82 C8
Quentin *Miss., U.S.A.* 31°31N 90°45W 111 E3
Queréndaro *Michoacan, Mexico* 19°48N 100°53W 175 C7
Querétaro *Querétaro, Mexico* 20°36N 100°23W 175 A7
Querétaro □ *Mexico* 21°0N 99°55W 175 B8
Quesería *Colima, Mexico* 19°22N 103°35W 174 C4
Quesnel *B.C., Canada* 53°0N 122°30W 155 C12

Quesnel → B.C., Canada 52°58N 122°29W 155 C12
Quesnel L. B.C., Canada 52°30N 121°20W 155 C13
Questa N. Mex., U.S.A. 36°42N 105°36W 131 A5
Quetico Prov. Park △ Ont., Canada 48°30N 91°45W 148 D5
Quetzala → Guerrero, Mexico 16°35N 98°30W 175 F9
Quevedo, Península Sinaloa, Mexico 24°10N 107°18W 172 C3
Quévillon, L. Qué., Canada 49°4N 76°57W 144 B6
Quezaltenango Guatemala 14°50N 91°30W 182 D1
Quiahuiztlán Veracruz, Mexico 19°40N 96°25W 176 E4
Quidi Vidi Nfld. & L., Canada 47°35N 52°41W 142 E8
Quidnet Mass., U.S.A. 41°18N 69°58W 91 C5
Quilcene Wash., U.S.A. 47°49N 122°53W 120 C3
Quilchena B.C., Canada 50°10N 120°30W 155 E14
Quileute Indian Reservation Wash., U.S.A. 47°54N 124°37W 120 C1
Quill Lakes Sask., Canada 51°55N 104°13W 150 C7
Quimby Iowa, U.S.A. 42°38N 95°38W 81 C3
Quimichis Nayarit, Mexico 22°21N 105°32W 172 E5
Quinault Wash., U.S.A. 47°28N 123°51W 120 C2
Quinault → Wash., U.S.A. 47°21N 124°18W 120 C1
Quinault Indian Reservation Wash., U.S.A. 47°30N 124°5W 120 C1
Quinby S.C., U.S.A. 34°14N 79°44W 103 D6
Quincy Calif., U.S.A. 39°56N 120°57W 126 D6
Quincy Fla., U.S.A. 30°35N 84°34W 114 A4
Quincy Ill., U.S.A. 39°56N 91°23W 84 D2
Quincy Mass., U.S.A. 42°14N 71°0W 96 B2
Quincy Mich., U.S.A. 41°57N 84°53W 79 H7
Quincy Ohio, U.S.A. 40°18N 83°58W 86 C3
Quincy Wash., U.S.A. 47°14N 119°51W 120 C6
Quincy B. Mass., U.S.A. 42°16N 70°59W 96 B3
Quincy Res. Colo., U.S.A. 39°38N 104°46W 134 C3
Quinebaug Conn., U.S.A. 42°1N 71°57W 91 B3
Quinebaug → Conn., U.S.A. 41°33N 72°3W 91 C2
Quinhagak Alaska, U.S.A. 59°45N 161°54W 135 C7
Quinlan Okla., U.S.A. 36°27N 99°3W 107 B4
Quinlan Tex., U.S.A. 32°55N 96°8W 109 E11
Quinn → Nev., U.S.A. 40°53N 119°3W 128 B1
Quintana Roo Chiapas, Mexico 16°40N 93°42W 178 C3
Quintana Roo Yucatán, Mexico 20°52N 88°38W 179 B5
Quintana Roo □ Mexico 19°40N 88°30W 179 C5
Quintana Roo, Parque Natural de △ Quintana Roo, Mexico 20°15N 87°45W 179 B6
Quinte West Ont., Canada 44°10N 77°34W 147 C9
Quinter Kans., U.S.A. 39°4N 100°14W 82 B3
Quinton Sask., Canada 51°23N 104°24W 150 D7
Quinton Okla., U.S.A. 35°7N 95°22W 107 C8
Quinwood W. Va., U.S.A. 38°4N 80°42W 102 C4
Quinze, L. des Qué., Canada 47°35N 79°5W 144 D3
Quiriego Sonora, Mexico 27°31N 109°16W 168 F6
Quiroga Michoacan, Mexico 19°40N 101°31W 174 C6
Quitaque Tex., U.S.A. 34°22N 101°4W 108 C6
Quitman Ark., U.S.A. 35°23N 92°13W 106 C3
Quitman Ga., U.S.A. 30°47N 83°34W 113 F3
Quitman La., U.S.A. 32°21N 92°43W 110 B3
Quitman Miss., U.S.A. 32°2N 88°44W 111 D5
Quitman Tex., U.S.A. 32°48N 95°27W 109 E12
Quitman County ☆ Ga., U.S.A. 31°50N 85°0W 113 E2
Quitman County ☆ Miss., U.S.A. 34°12N 90°17W 111 B3
Quitman Mts. Tex., U.S.A. 31°0N 105°16W 108 F2
Quivira Nat. Wildlife Refuge △ Kans., U.S.A. 38°11N 98°31W 82 C5
Qulin Mo., U.S.A. 36°36N 90°15W 83 E6
Quoich → Nunavut, Canada 64°0N 93°30W 159 E7
Quonochontaug R.I., U.S.A. 41°21N 71°43W 91 C3
Qurlutuq → Qué., Canada 58°57N 66°50W 143 B4
Quttinirpaaq Nat. Park △ Nunavut, Canada 82°13N 72°13W 158 A11
Quyon Qué., Canada 45°31N 76°14W 144 F6

R

R.D. Bailey L. W. Va., U.S.A. 37°36N 81°49W 102 D3
Raanes Pen. N.W.T., Canada 78°30N 85°45W 158 B8
Rabbit Cr. → S. Dak., U.S.A. 45°13N 102°10W 76 E3
Rabbit Ears Pass Colo., U.S.A. 40°23N 106°37W 125 B4
Rabbit Lake Sask., Canada 53°8N 107°46W 150 B4
Rabón, L. el Tamaulipas, Mexico 25°27N 97°23W 170 E7
Rabun County ☆ Ga., U.S.A. 34°50N 83°30W 113 B3
Raccoon → Iowa, U.S.A. 41°35N 93°37W 81 D5
Raccoon Cr. → Ohio, U.S.A. 40°20N 82°24W 86 C4
Race, C. Nfld. & L., Canada 46°40N 53°5W 142 F7
Race Point Mass., U.S.A. 42°4N 70°14W 91 B4
Raceland Ky., U.S.A. 38°32N 82°44W 105 B10
Raceland La., U.S.A. 29°44N 90°36W 110 E5
Racepond Ga., U.S.A. 31°1N 82°8W 113 E4
Rachel Nev., U.S.A. 37°39N 115°45W 128 E5
Racine Minn., U.S.A. 43°48N 92°31W 77 G6
Racine Wis., U.S.A. 42°44N 87°47W 78 F6
Racine → Wis., U.S.A. 42°45N 88°5W 78 F5
Racine L. Ont., Canada 48°2N 83°20W 149 D13
Raco Mich., U.S.A. 46°23N 84°43W 79 C7
Radcliff Ky., U.S.A. 37°51N 85°57W 105 C7
Radcliffe Iowa, U.S.A. 42°19N 93°25W 81 C5
Radcliffe College Mass., U.S.A. 42°22N 71°7W 96 A2
Radford Va., U.S.A. 37°8N 80°34W 102 D4
Radisson Sask., Canada 52°30N 107°20W 150 C4
Radisson Wis., U.S.A. 45°45N 91°14W 78 C2
Radium Kans., U.S.A. 38°12N 98°56W 82 C5
Radium Hot Springs B.C., Canada 50°35N 116°2W 153 H4
Radium Springs N. Mex., U.S.A. 32°30N 106°55W 131 E4
Radnor Ohio, U.S.A. 40°23N 83°9W 86 C3
Radnor Pa., U.S.A. 40°3N 75°22W 92 B1
Radville Sask., Canada 49°30N 104°15W 150 F7
Rae Alta., Canada 54°4N 112°57W 152 D8
Rae N.W.T., Canada 62°50N 116°3W 157 D9
Rae → Nunavut, Canada 67°55N 115°31W 156 C9
Rae Isthmus Nunavut, Canada 66°40N 87°30W 159 D8
Rae Lakes N.W.T., Canada 64°7N 117°21W 157 D9
Rae Str. Nunavut, Canada 68°50N 94°51W 158 D7
Raeford N.C., U.S.A. 34°59N 79°13W 103 D6
Rafael Delgado Veracruz, Mexico 18°46N 97°1W 177 F3
Raft → Idaho, U.S.A. 42°33N 113°12W 122 G5
Raft River Mts. Utah, U.S.A. 41°55N 113°25W 129 B2
Ragan Nebr., U.S.A. 40°19N 99°15W 80 D6
Ragland Ala., U.S.A. 33°45N 86°9W 112 C4
Ragley La., U.S.A. 30°30N 93°15W 110 D2
Rago Kans., U.S.A. 37°26N 98°4W 82 D5
Rahway N.J., U.S.A. 40°36N 74°16W 97 C1
Railroad Valley Nev., U.S.A. 38°25N 115°40W 128 D5
Rainbow Bridge Nat. Monument △ U.S.A. 37°5N 110°58W 129 F5
Rainbow City Ala., U.S.A. 33°57N 86°5W 112 C4
Rainbow Lake Alta., Canada 58°30N 119°23W 157 E9

Rainbow Plateau Ariz., U.S.A. 36°55N 111°0W 130 A5
Rainelle W. Va., U.S.A. 37°58N 80°47W 102 D4
Raines Tenn., U.S.A. 35°2N 90°3W 117 B1
Rainier Wash., U.S.A. 46°53N 122°41W 120 D3
Rainier, Mt. Wash., U.S.A. 46°52N 121°46W 120 D4
Rains S.C., U.S.A. 34°6N 79°19W 103 D6
Rains County ☆ Tex., U.S.A. 32°52N 95°46W 109 E12
Rainsburg Pa., U.S.A. 39°54N 78°30W 87 E4
Rainsville Ala., U.S.A. 34°30N 85°50W 112 B5
Rainy → Ont., Canada 48°43N 94°29W 148 D2
Rainy → Mich., U.S.A. 48°50N 94°42W 77 B4
Rainy L. Ont., Canada 48°42N 93°10W 148 D2
Raisin → Mich., U.S.A. 41°54N 83°20W 79 H8
Rake Iowa, U.S.A. 43°35N 93°50W 81 B5
Raleigh Nfld. & L., Canada 51°34N 55°44W 142 A5
Raleigh Fla., U.S.A. 29°25N 82°32W 114 B6
Raleigh Ga., U.S.A. 32°56N 84°38W 113 D2
Raleigh Miss., U.S.A. 32°2N 89°30W 111 D4
Raleigh N.C., U.S.A. 35°47N 78°39W 103 C7
Raleigh N. Dak., U.S.A. 46°20N 101°20W 76 D4
Raleigh Tenn., U.S.A. 35°12N 89°54W 117 A2
Raleigh B. N.C., U.S.A. 34°50N 76°15W 103 D9
Raleigh County ☆ W. Va., U.S.A. 37°45N 81°10W 102 D3
Raleigh-Durham Int. ✈ (RDU) N.C., U.S.A. 35°52N 78°47W 103 C7
Raleigh Hills Oreg., U.S.A. 45°28N 122°45W 132 B1
Ralls Tex., U.S.A. 33°41N 101°24W 108 D6
Ralls County ☆ Mo., U.S.A. 39°30N 91°30W 83 B5
Ralston Alta., Canada 50°15N 111°10W 153 H9
Ralston Nebr., U.S.A. 41°12N 96°3W 80 C9
Ralston Okla., U.S.A. 36°30N 96°44W 107 B7
Ralston Pa., U.S.A. 41°30N 76°57W 87 C6
Ralston Wyo., U.S.A. 44°43N 108°52W 124 B4
Ram → Alta., Canada 52°23N 115°25W 153 F5
Rama Sask., Canada 51°46N 103°0W 150 D9
Rama Nic. 12°9N 84°15W 182 D3
Ramah Nfld. & L., Canada 58°52N 63°15W 143 B5
Ramah Colo., U.S.A. 39°7N 104°10W 125 C6
Ramah N. Mex., U.S.A. 35°8N 108°29W 131 B2
Ramah B. Nfld. & L., Canada 58°52N 63°13W 143 B5
Ramea Nfld. & L., Canada 47°31N 57°23W 142 E3
Ramea Is. Nfld. & L., Canada 47°31N 57°22W 142 E3
Ramer Ala., U.S.A. 32°3N 86°13W 112 D4
Ramer Tenn., U.S.A. 35°4N 88°37W 104 E4
Ramiro Caballero, Presa Tamaulipas, Mexico 22°37N 98°42W 171 H6
Ramon N. Mex., U.S.A. 34°14N 104°54W 131 C6
Ramón Corona Campeche, Mexico 19°28N 89°28W 179 C4
Ramón Corona Durango, Mexico 24°13N 103°37W 173 C7
Ramona Calif., U.S.A. 33°2N 116°52W 127 K10
Ramona Kans., U.S.A. 38°36N 97°4W 82 C6
Ramona Okla., U.S.A. 36°32N 95°55W 107 B8
Ramona S. Dak., U.S.A. 44°7N 97°13W 76 F8
Ramore Ont., Canada 48°30N 80°25W 144 C2
Ramos → Durango, Mexico 25°23N 105°3W 172 B5
Ramos Arizpe Coahuila, Mexico 25°33N 100°58W 170 E4
Ramos Arizpe Coahuila, Mexico 25°41N 101°23W 170 E3
Rampart Alaska, U.S.A. 65°30N 150°10W 135 D10
Ramparts → N.W.T., Canada 66°11N 129°2W 156 C7
Ramsay Mich., U.S.A. 46°28N 90°0W 79 C2
Ramsay Mont., U.S.A. 46°1N 112°42W 123 D5
Ramsay I. B.C., Canada 52°33N 131°23W 154 C3
Ramseur N.C., U.S.A. 35°44N 79°39W 103 C6
Ramsey Ont., Canada 47°25N 82°20W 149 E14
Ramsey Ill., U.S.A. 39°8N 89°7W 84 D4
Ramsey Minn., U.S.A. 45°15N 92°58W 77 E6
Ramsey N.J., U.S.A. 41°4N 74°9W 92 A2
Ramsey County ☆ Minn., U.S.A. 45°0N 93°5W 77 F5
Ramsey County ☆ N. Dak., U.S.A. 48°15N 98°50W 76 B7
Ramsey L. Ont., Canada 47°13N 82°15W 149 E14
Ranchester Wyo., U.S.A. 44°54N 107°10W 124 B5
Rancho Cordova Calif., U.S.A. 38°36N 121°18W 126 E5
Rancho Cucamonga Calif., U.S.A. 34°10N 117°30W 127 J9
Rancho Grande Zacatecas, Mexico 23°32N 102°57W 173 D8
Ranchos de Taos N. Mex., U.S.A. 36°22N 105°37W 131 A5
Rand → Alta., Canada 40°27N 71°2W 93 B7
Rand W. Va., U.S.A. 38°13N 81°34W 102 C3
Randalia Iowa, U.S.A. 42°52N 91°53W 81 C7
Randall Iowa, U.S.A. 42°14N 93°35W 81 C5
Randall Kans., U.S.A. 39°38N 98°3W 82 B5
Randall Minn., U.S.A. 46°5N 94°30W 77 D4
Randall County ☆ Tex., U.S.A. 34°59N 101°55W 108 C6
Randallstown Md., U.S.A. 39°22N 76°48W 93 A4
Randle Wash., U.S.A. 46°32N 121°57W 120 D4
Randleman N.C., U.S.A. 35°49N 79°48W 103 C6
Randlett Okla., U.S.A. 34°11N 98°28W 107 D5
Randlett Utah, U.S.A. 40°14N 109°48W 129 C6
Randolph Iowa, U.S.A. 40°52N 95°34W 81 E3
Randolph Kans., U.S.A. 39°26N 96°46W 82 B7
Randolph Maine, U.S.A. 44°14N 69°46W 90 D4
Randolph Mass., U.S.A. 42°10N 71°2W 91 B4
Randolph Miss., U.S.A. 34°11N 89°10W 111 B4
Randolph N.Y., U.S.A. 42°10N 78°59W 88 C2
Randolph Nebr., U.S.A. 42°23N 97°22W 80 B8
Randolph Utah, U.S.A. 41°40N 111°11W 129 B4
Randolph Vt., U.S.A. 43°55N 72°40W 89 C2
Randolph Air Force Base Tex., U.S.A. 29°31N 98°16W 116 B4
Randolph Center Vt., U.S.A. 43°55N 72°37W 89 C2
Randolph County ☆ Ala., U.S.A. 33°20N 85°25W 112 C5
Randolph County ☆ Ark., U.S.A. 36°20N 91°0W 106 B5
Randolph County ☆ Ga., U.S.A. 31°45N 84°45W 113 E2
Randolph County ☆ Ill., U.S.A. 38°0N 89°50W 84 E4
Randolph County ☆ Ind., U.S.A. 40°10N 85°0W 85 C6
Randolph County ☆ Mo., U.S.A. 39°25N 92°30W 83 B4
Randolph County ☆ N.C., U.S.A. 35°40N 79°50W 103 C6
Randolph County ☆ W. Va., U.S.A. 38°45N 80°0W 102 C5
Random I. Nfld. & L., Canada 48°8N 53°44W 142 D7
Random Lake Wis., U.S.A. 43°33N 87°58W 78 E6
Randville Mich., U.S.A. 46°0N 88°3W 79 C3
Ranfurly Alta., Canada 53°25N 111°41W 152 E9
Rangeley Maine, U.S.A. 44°58N 70°39W 90 D1
Rangeley L. Maine, U.S.A. 44°55N 70°43W 90 D1
Rangely Colo., U.S.A. 40°5N 108°48W 125 B2
Ranger Ga., U.S.A. 34°30N 84°43W 113 B2
Ranger Tex., U.S.A. 32°28N 98°41W 109 E9
Ranger L. Ont., Canada 46°52N 83°35W 149 F13
Rankin Ill., U.S.A. 40°28N 87°54W 84 C6
Rankin Pa., U.S.A. 40°24N 79°53W 86 E3
Rankin Tex., U.S.A. 31°13N 101°56W 108 F6
Rankin County ☆ Miss., U.S.A. 32°15N 90°0W 111 D4
Rankin Inlet Nunavut, Canada 62°30N 93°0W 159 E7
Ransom Kans., U.S.A. 38°38N 99°56W 82 C4

Ransom County ☆ N. Dak., U.S.A. 46°30N 97°40W 76 D8
Ranson W. Va., U.S.A. 39°18N 77°52W 93 A3
Rantoul Ill., U.S.A. 40°19N 88°9W 84 C5
Rantoul Kans., U.S.A. 38°33N 95°7W 82 C8
Rapelje Mont., U.S.A. 45°58N 109°14W 123 E8
Raper, C. Nunavut, Canada 69°44N 67°6W 158 D12
Rapid → Minn., U.S.A. 48°42N 94°26W 77 B4
Rapid City Man., Canada 50°7N 100°2W 151 E11
Rapid City S. Dak., U.S.A. 44°5N 103°14W 76 F2
Rapid Cr. → S. Dak., U.S.A. 43°54N 102°37W 76 G3
Rapid River Mich., U.S.A. 45°55N 86°58W 79 D5
Rapidan → Va., U.S.A. 38°22N 77°37W 102 C7
Rapide-Blanc Qué., Canada 47°48N 73°2W 145 D9
Rapide-Sept Qué., Canada 47°46N 78°19W 144 D4
Rapides-des-Joachims Qué., Canada 46°13N 77°43W 144 E5
Rapides Parish ☆ La., U.S.A. 31°15N 92°30W 110 C3
Rappahannock → Va., U.S.A. 37°34N 76°18W 93 C4
Rappahannock County ☆ Va., U.S.A. 38°40N 78°10W 102 C6
Raquette → N.Y., U.S.A. 45°0N 74°42W 88 A6
Rarden Ohio, U.S.A. 38°55N 83°12W 86 E3
Raritan N.J., U.S.A. 40°34N 74°38W 92 B2
Raritan → N.J., U.S.A. 40°29N 74°17W 92 B2
Raritan Bay N.J., U.S.A. 40°27N 74°15W 92 B2
Rasa, I. Baja Calif., Mexico 28°50N 112°57W 166 E6
Raspberry Pk. Ark., U.S.A. 34°23N 94°0W 106 D2
Rat → Man., Canada 49°35N 97°10W 151 F14
Rat I. Alaska, U.S.A. 51°48N 178°15E 135 L2
Rat Islands Alaska, U.S.A. 52°0N 178°0E 135 L2
Ratcliff Tex., U.S.A. 31°24N 95°8W 109 F12
Rathbun Iowa, U.S.A. 40°50N 92°52W 81 E6
Rathbun L. Iowa, U.S.A. 40°54N 93°5W 81 E5
Rathdrum Idaho, U.S.A. 47°49N 116°54W 122 B2
Ratliff City Okla., U.S.A. 34°25N 97°30W 107 D6
Raton N. Mex., U.S.A. 36°54N 104°24W 131 A6
Raton, Cueva del Baja Calif. S., Mexico 27°32N 113°0W 167 F5
Raton Pass U.S.A. 37°0N 104°30W 125 F6
Rats, R. aux → Qué., Canada 48°53N 72°14W 145 C10
Rattan Okla., U.S.A. 34°12N 95°25W 107 D8
Rattlesnake Cr. → Oreg., U.S.A. 42°44N 117°47W 121 E8
Rattlesnake Hills Wash., U.S.A. 46°31N 120°20W 120 D5
Rattlesnake Hills Wyo., U.S.A. 42°45N 107°10W 124 D5
Ratz, Mt. B.C., Canada 57°23N 132°12W 157 E6
Raudales de Malpaso Chiapas, Mexico 17°27N 93°39W 178 B3
Ravalli Mont., U.S.A. 47°17N 114°11W 123 C3
Ravalli County ☆ Mont., U.S.A. 46°0N 114°0W 123 C3
Raven Va., U.S.A. 37°5N 81°51W 102 D3
Ravena N.Y., U.S.A. 42°28N 73°49W 88 C7
Ravendale Calif., U.S.A. 40°48N 120°22W 126 C6
Ravenel S.C., U.S.A. 32°46N 80°15W 103 F5
Ravenna Ky., U.S.A. 37°41N 83°57W 105 C9
Ravenna Mich., U.S.A. 43°11N 85°56W 79 F5
Ravenna Nebr., U.S.A. 41°1N 98°55W 80 C7
Ravenna Ohio, U.S.A. 41°9N 81°15W 86 B5
Ravenna Tex., U.S.A. 33°40N 96°15W 109 D11
Ravenswood W. Va., U.S.A. 38°57N 81°46W 102 C3
Ravenwood Mo., U.S.A. 40°22N 94°41W 83 A2
Ravia Okla., U.S.A. 34°15N 96°45W 107 D7
Ravinia S. Dak., U.S.A. 43°8N 98°26W 76 G7
Rawdon Qué., Canada 46°3N 73°40W 145 E9
Rawlins Wyo., U.S.A. 41°47N 107°14W 124 E5
Rawlins County ☆ Kans., U.S.A. 39°45N 101°0W 82 B2
Rawson Vt., U.S.A. 43°10N 72°50W 89 C2
Ray Minn., U.S.A. 48°25N 93°13W 77 B5
Ray N. Dak., U.S.A. 48°21N 103°10W 76 B2
Ray, C. Nfld. & L., Canada 47°33N 59°15W 142 E1
Ray City Ga., U.S.A. 31°5N 83°11W 113 E3
Ray County ☆ Mo., U.S.A. 39°20N 94°0W 83 B3
Ray Mts. Alaska, U.S.A. 66°0N 152°0W 135 D10
Ray Roberts L. Tex., U.S.A. 33°20N 97°2W 109 D10
Rayle Ga., U.S.A. 33°48N 82°54W 113 C4
Raymond Alta., Canada 49°30N 112°35W 153 J8
Raymond Calif., U.S.A. 37°13N 119°54W 126 F7
Raymond Ga., U.S.A. 33°20N 84°43W 113 C2
Raymond Ill., U.S.A. 39°19N 89°34W 84 D4
Raymond Kans., U.S.A. 38°17N 98°25W 82 C5
Raymond Minn., U.S.A. 45°2N 95°14W 77 E3
Raymond Miss., U.S.A. 32°16N 90°25W 111 D3
Raymond N.H., U.S.A. 43°2N 71°11W 89 D3
Raymond Nebr., U.S.A. 40°57N 96°47W 80 D9
Raymond S. Dak., U.S.A. 44°53N 97°56W 76 F8
Raymond Wash., U.S.A. 46°41N 123°44W 120 D2
Raymondville Mo., U.S.A. 37°20N 91°50W 83 D5
Raymondville Tex., U.S.A. 26°29N 97°47W 108 L10
Raymore Sask., Canada 51°25N 104°31W 150 D7
Raymore Mo., U.S.A. 38°48N 94°27W 83 C2
Rayne La., U.S.A. 30°14N 92°16W 110 D3
Raynham Center Mass., U.S.A. 41°55N 71°3W 91 C3
Rayón Chiapas, Mexico 17°12N 93°0W 178 B2
Rayón San Luis Potosí, Mexico 21°51N 99°40W 171 J5
Rayón Sonora, Mexico 29°43N 110°35W 168 D5
Rayones Nuevo León, Mexico 25°1N 100°5W 171 E4
Raystown Branch → Pa., U.S.A. 40°27N 77°59W 87 D5
Raystown L. Pa., U.S.A. 40°25N 78°5W 87 D4
Raytown Mo., U.S.A. 39°1N 94°28W 83 B2
Rayville La., U.S.A. 32°29N 91°46W 110 B4
Rayville Mo., U.S.A. 39°21N 94°4W 83 B2
Reach II Recreation Area Ariz., U.S.A. 33°37N 111°53W 134 A3
Reader W. Va., U.S.A. 39°36N 80°46W 102 B4
Reading Kans., U.S.A. 38°31N 95°58W 82 C8
Reading Mass., U.S.A. 42°32N 71°6W 91 B3
Reading Mich., U.S.A. 41°50N 84°45W 79 H7
Reading Ohio, U.S.A. 39°13N 84°26W 86 D2
Reading Pa., U.S.A. 40°20N 75°56W 87 D7
Readland Ark., U.S.A. 33°4N 91°13W 106 E4
Readsboro Vt., U.S.A. 42°46N 72°57W 89 D2
Readstown Wis., U.S.A. 43°27N 90°45W 78 E3
Reagan County ☆ Tex., U.S.A. 31°25N 101°34W 108 F6
Real County ☆ Tex., U.S.A. 29°55N 99°59W 108 H8
Real de Catorce San Luis Potosí, Mexico 23°42N 100°54W 171 G4
Realitos Tex., U.S.A. 27°27N 98°32W 108 K9
Reams, L. Fla., U.S.A. 28°31N 81°34W 115 D1
Reardan Wash., U.S.A. 47°40N 117°53W 120 C8
Rebecca Ga., U.S.A. 31°48N 83°29W 113 E3
Rebeico Sonora, Mexico 28°53N 109°45W 168 E6
Rector Ark., U.S.A. 36°16N 90°17W 106 B6
Red → Ky., U.S.A. 37°56N 83°45W 105 C8
Red → Tenn., U.S.A. 36°32N 87°22W 104 D5
Red → Tex., U.S.A. 31°1N 91°45W 110 C4
Red Bank N.J., U.S.A. 40°21N 74°5W 92 B2
Red Bank Tenn., U.S.A. 35°7N 85°17W 105 E7
Red Bay Nfld. & L., Canada 51°44N 56°25W 142 A4

Red Bay Ala., U.S.A. 34°27N 88°7W 112 B2
Red Bird Okla., U.S.A. 35°54N 95°36W 107 C8
Red Bluff Calif., U.S.A. 40°11N 122°15W 126 C4
Red Bluff Res. N. Mex., U.S.A. 31°54N 103°55W 131 F7
Red Boiling Springs Tenn., U.S.A. 36°32N 85°51W 105 D7
Red Bud Ill., U.S.A. 38°13N 89°59W 84 E4
Red Cedar → Wis., U.S.A. 44°42N 91°53W 78 D2
Red Cliff Colo., U.S.A. 39°31N 106°22W 125 C4
Red Cliff Ind. Reservation Wis., U.S.A. 46°50N 90°47W 78 B3
Red Cloud Nebr., U.S.A. 40°5N 98°32W 80 D7
Red Cr. → Miss., U.S.A. 30°41N 88°40W 111 F5
Red Deer → Alta., Canada 52°20N 113°50W 153 F7
Red Deer → Alta., Canada 50°58N 110°0W 153 H10
Red Deer → Man., Canada 52°53N 101°1W 151 C10
Red Deer L. Alta., Canada 52°43N 113°2W 153 F7
Red Deer L. Man., Canada 52°55N 101°20W 151 C10
Red Devil Alaska, U.S.A. 61°46N 157°19W 135 F8
Red Feather Lakes Colo., U.S.A. 40°48N 105°35W 125 B5
Red Head Fla., U.S.A. 30°29N 85°51W 114 A3
Red Hills Kans., U.S.A. 37°20N 98°50W 82 D5
Red Hook N.Y., U.S.A. 41°55N 73°53W 88 D7
Red I. Nfld. & L., Canada 47°23N 54°10W 142 E6
Red Indian L. Nfld. & L., Canada 48°35N 57°0W 142 D2
Red L. Ont., Canada 51°3N 93°49W 148 C3
Red L. Ariz., U.S.A. 35°40N 114°4W 130 B1
Red L. S. Dak., U.S.A. 43°44N 99°13W 76 G6
Red Lake Ont., Canada 51°3N 93°49W 148 C3
Red Lake Minn., U.S.A. 47°53N 95°1W 77 C3
Red Lake → Minn., U.S.A. 47°55N 97°1W 77 C1
Red Lake County ☆ Minn., U.S.A. 47°50N 96°9W 77 C2
Red Lake Falls Minn., U.S.A. 47°53N 96°16W 77 C2
Red Lake Indian Reservation Minn., U.S.A. 48°30N 94°30W 77 B4
Red Lake Road Ont., Canada 49°59N 93°25W 148 C3
Red Level Ala., U.S.A. 31°24N 86°36W 112 E4
Red Lion N.J., U.S.A. 39°53N 74°45W 92 C2
Red Lion Pa., U.S.A. 39°54N 76°36W 93 A4
Red Lodge Mont., U.S.A. 45°11N 109°15W 123 E8
Red Mountain Calif., U.S.A. 35°37N 117°38W 127 H9
Red Oak Iowa, U.S.A. 41°1N 95°14W 81 D3
Red Oak N.C., U.S.A. 36°2N 77°54W 103 B8
Red Oak Okla., U.S.A. 34°57N 95°5W 107 D8
Red Pass B.C., Canada 53°0N 119°0W 155 C15
Red River N. Mex., U.S.A. 36°42N 105°22W 131 A5
Red River County ☆ Tex., U.S.A. 33°37N 95°3W 109 D12
Red River Hot Springs Idaho, U.S.A. 45°47N 115°12W 122 D3
Red River of the North → N. Amer. 49°0N 97°15W 151 F14
Red River Parish ☆ La., U.S.A. 32°1N 93°21W 110 B2
Red River Valley Minn., U.S.A. 48°0N 96°50W 77 C2
Red Rock B.C., Canada 53°42N 122°40W 155 B12
Red Rock Ont., Canada 48°55N 88°15W 148 D8
Red Rock Okla., U.S.A. 36°36N 109°3W 130 A6
Red Rock Mont., U.S.A. 44°55N 112°50W 123 E5
Red Rock Okla., U.S.A. 36°28N 97°11W 107 B6
Red Rock L. Iowa, U.S.A. 41°22N 92°59W 81 D61
Red Rock Canyon Nat. Conservation Area △ Nev., U.S.A. 36°6N 115°28W 128 F5
Red Rock Cr. → Okla., U.S.A. 36°30N 96°59W 107 B7
Red Rock Lakes Nat. Wildlife Refuge △ Mont., U.S.A. 44°38N 111°45W 123 F6
Red Springs N.C., U.S.A. 34°49N 79°11W 103 D6
Red Springs Tex., U.S.A. 33°37N 99°25W 109 D8
Red Willow County ☆ Nebr., U.S.A. 40°15N 100°30W 80 D5
Red Willow Cr. → Nebr., U.S.A. 40°13N 100°29W 80 D5
Red Wing Minn., U.S.A. 44°34N 92°31W 77 F6
Redbay Fla., U.S.A. 30°35N 85°57W 114 A3
Redberry L. Sask., Canada 52°45N 107°14W 150 C4
Redbird Wyo., U.S.A. 43°15N 104°17W 124 C8
Redcliff Alta., Canada 50°10N 110°50W 153 H10
Reddell La., U.S.A. 30°40N 92°25W 110 D3
Reddick Fla., U.S.A. 29°22N 82°12W 114 B6
Reddick Ill., U.S.A. 41°6N 88°15W 84 B5
Redding Conn., U.S.A. 40°35N 122°24W 126 C4
Redding Calif., U.S.A. 41°18N 73°23W 91 C1
Redding Iowa, U.S.A. 40°36N 94°23W 81 E4
Redding Ridge Conn., U.S.A. 41°19N 73°21W 91 C1
Redditt Ont., Canada 49°59N 94°24W 148 C2
Redfield Ark., U.S.A. 34°27N 92°11W 106 D3
Redfield Iowa, U.S.A. 41°35N 94°12W 81 D4
Redfield S. Dak., U.S.A. 37°50N 94°53W 82 D8
Redfield S. Dak., U.S.A. 44°53N 98°31W 76 F7
Redford Tex., U.S.A. 29°27N 104°11W 108 H3
Redig S. Dak., U.S.A. 45°16N 103°33W 76 E2
Redington Beach Tampa, U.S.A. 27°48N 82°48W 115 C2
Redington Shores Tampa, U.S.A. 27°49N 82°49W 115 C2
Redkey Ind., U.S.A. 40°21N 85°9W 85 C5
Redlands Calif., U.S.A. 34°4N 117°11W 127 J9
Redman Point Bar Tenn., U.S.A. 35°31N 90°5W 117 A1
Redmesa Colo., U.S.A. 37°6N 108°11W 125 E2
Redmon Ill., U.S.A. 39°39N 87°52W 84 D6
Redmond Oreg., U.S.A. 44°17N 121°11W 121 C4
Redmond Utah, U.S.A. 39°0N 111°52W 129 D4
Redmond Wash., U.S.A. 47°40N 122°7W 132 B5
Redonda Antigua & B. 16°58N 62°19W 183 C7
Redonda Is. B.C., Canada 50°15N 124°50W 154 E10
Redondo, Cabo Baja Calif. S., Mexico 24°34N 112°5W 167 J6
Redondo Beach Calif., U.S.A. 33°50N 118°23W 127 K8
Redoubt Volcano Alaska, U.S.A. 60°29N 152°45W 135 F9
Redrock N. Mex., U.S.A. 32°41N 108°44W 131 E2
Redstone B.C., Canada 52°8N 123°42W 154 C11
Redstone → N.W.T., Canada 39°11N 107°14W 125 C3
Redstone → N.W.T., Canada 64°17N 124°32W 157 D8
Redstone Arsenal Ala., U.S.A. 34°35N 86°41W 112 B4
Redstone Cr. → S. Dak., U.S.A. 44°4N 98°5W 76 F7
Redvers Sask., Canada 49°35N 101°40W 151 F10
Redwater → Mont., U.S.A. 48°3N 105°13W 123 B12
Redwater → Alta., Canada 55°2N 119°5W 152 E7
Redwood Miss., U.S.A. 32°29N 90°48W 111 D3
Redwood → Minn., U.S.A. 44°34N 95°5W 77 F3
Redwood City Calif., U.S.A. 37°30N 122°15W 126 F4
Redwood County ☆ Minn., U.S.A. 44°20N 95°15W 77 F3
Redwood Cr. → Calif., U.S.A. 41°18N 124°5W 126 B2
Redwood Falls Minn., U.S.A. 44°32N 95°7W 77 F3
Redwood Nat. Park △ Calif., U.S.A. 41°40N 124°5W 126 B2
Ree Heights S. Dak., U.S.A. 44°31N 99°12W 76 F6
Reece Kans., U.S.A. 37°48N 96°22W 82 D7
Reed Kans., U.S.A. 37°51N 87°21W 104 C5
Reed Okla., U.S.A. 34°54N 99°42W 107 D4
Reed City Mich., U.S.A. 43°53N 85°31W 79 F6
Reed L. Sask., Canada 46°7N 102°57W 76 D3
Reeders Pa., U.S.A. 41°1N 75°20W 92 A1
Reedley Calif., U.S.A. 36°36N 119°27W 127 G7
Reeds Mo., U.S.A. 37°7N 94°10W 83 D2
Reeds Pk. N. Mex., U.S.A. 33°9N 107°51W 131 D3

Reeds Spring Mo., U.S.A. 36°45N 93°23W 83 E3
Reedsburg Wis., U.S.A. 43°32N 90°0W 78 E31
Reedsport Oreg., U.S.A. 43°42N 124°6W 121 D1
Reedsville W. Va., U.S.A. 39°31N 79°48W 102 B5
Reedy W. Va., U.S.A. 38°54N 81°26W 102 C3
Reelfoot L. Tenn., U.S.A. 36°25N 89°22W 104 D3
Reese Mich., U.S.A. 43°27N 83°42W 79 F8
Reese Nev., U.S.A. 40°48N 117°4W 128 B3
Reeves La., U.S.A. 30°31N 93°3W 110 D2
Reeves County ☆ Tex., U.S.A. 31°13N 103°45W 108 F4
Reform Ala., U.S.A. 33°23N 88°1W 112 C2
Reforma Chiapas, Mexico 17°56N 93°10W 178 B3
Reforma Quintana Roo, Mexico 18°45N 88°31W 179 D5
Reforma de Pineda Oaxaca, Mexico 16°24N 94°28W 177 H6
Refugio Tex., U.S.A. 28°18N 97°17W 109 J10
Refugio County ☆ Tex., U.S.A. 28°14N 97°20W 109 J10
Regan N. Dak., U.S.A. 47°10N 100°32W 76 C5
Regent N. Dak., U.S.A. 46°25N 102°33W 76 D3
Regina Sask., Canada 50°27N 104°35W 150 E7
Regina N. Mex., U.S.A. 36°11N 106°57W 131 A4
Regina Beach Sask., Canada 50°47N 105°0W 150 E7
Register Ga., U.S.A. 32°22N 81°53W 113 D5
Rego Park N.Y., U.S.A. 40°43N 73°51W 97 B3
Regocijo Durango, Mexico 23°35N 105°11W 172 D5
Rehoboth Mass., U.S.A. 41°50N 71°15W 91 C3
Rehoboth N. Mex., U.S.A. 35°32N 108°30W 131 B2
Rehoboth Bay Del., U.S.A. 38°40N 75°6W 93 B5
Rehoboth Beach Del., U.S.A. 38°43N 75°15W 93 B5
Reid L. Sask., Canada 50°0N 108°9W 150 E3
Reid Lake B.C., Canada 53°58N 123°6W 154 B11
Reidland Ky., U.S.A. 37°1N 88°32W 104 C4
Reidsville Ga., U.S.A. 32°6N 82°7W 113 D4
Reidsville N.C., U.S.A. 36°21N 79°40W 103 B6
Reinbeck Iowa, U.S.A. 42°19N 92°36W 81 C6
Reindeer I. Man., Canada 52°30N 98°0W 151 C14
Reindeer L. Sask., Canada 57°15N 102°15W 157 E12
Reinland Man., Canada 49°2N 97°52W 151 F14
Reisterstown Md., U.S.A. 39°28N 76°50W 99 A4
Reliance N.W., Canada 63°0N 109°20W 157 D11
Reliance Del., U.S.A. 38°38N 75°43W 93 B5
Reliance S. Dak., U.S.A. 43°53N 99°36W 76 G6
Reliance Wyo. U.S.A. 41°40N 109°12W 124 E3
Rembrandt Iowa, U.S.A. 42°50N 95°10W 81 B4
Remedios Panama 8°15N 81°50W 182 E3
Remedios, Parque Nacional de los △ Mexico 19°28N 99°17W 181 B2
Remer Minn., U.S.A. 47°4N 93°55W 77 C5
Rémigny Qué., Canada 47°46N 79°12W 144 D3
Remington Ind., U.S.A. 40°46N 87°9W 85 C3
Remington Va., U.S.A. 38°32N 77°49W 102 C7
Remmel Mt. Wash., U.S.A. 48°58N 120°9W 120 B5
Remsen Iowa, U.S.A. 42°49N 95°58W 81 C3
Remsen N.Y., U.S.A. 43°20N 75°11W 88 B5
Renata B.C., Canada 49°27N 118°7W 155 F16
Rencontre East Nfld. & L., Canada 47°38N 55°12W 142 E5
Rend Lake Ill., U.S.A. 38°2N 88°58W 84 E5
René-Levasseur, Î. Qué., Canada 51°20N 68°40W 143 C4
Renews Nfld. & L., Canada 46°56N 52°56W 142 F8
Renfrew Ont., Canada 45°30N 76°40W 147 B10
Renfroe Ga., U.S.A. 32°14N 84°43W 113 D2
Renfrow Okla., U.S.A. 36°56N 97°39W 107 B6
Renick W. Va., U.S.A. 38°1N 80°22W 102 C4
Renland Greenland 71°10N 26°30W 162 C8
Rennell Sd. B.C., Canada 53°23N 132°35W 154 B2
Rennie Man., Canada 49°51N 95°33W 151 F16
Rennison I. B.C., Canada 52°50N 129°20W 154 C3
Reno Nev., U.S.A. 39°31N 119°48W 128 C1
Reno ✈ (RNC) Nev., U.S.A. 39°30N 119°46W 128 C1
Reno County ☆ Kans., U.S.A. 38°0N 98°0W 82 C5
Renovo Pa., U.S.A. 41°20N 77°45W 87 C5
Rensselaer Ind., U.S.A. 40°57N 87°9W 85 C3
Rensselaer N.Y., U.S.A. 42°38N 73°45W 88 C7
Rensselaer County ☆ N.Y., U.S.A. 42°40N 73°30W 88 C7
Rentiesville Okla., U.S.A. 35°35N 95°30W 107 C8
Renton Wash., U.S.A. 47°28N 122°12W 132 D4
Rentz Ga., U.S.A. 32°25N 82°59W 113 D4
Renville Minn., U.S.A. 44°48N 95°13W 77 F3
Renville County ☆ Minn., U.S.A. 44°45N 95°0W 77 F4
Renville County ☆ N. Dak., U.S.A. 48°37N 101°35W 76 B4
Renwick Iowa, U.S.A. 42°50N 93°59W 81 C5
Repentigny Qué., Canada 45°44N 73°28W 145 F9
Repton Ala., U.S.A. 31°25N 87°14W 112 E3
Republic Kans., U.S.A. 39°55N 97°49W 82 B6
Republic Mich., U.S.A. 46°25N 87°59W 79 C4
Republic Mo., U.S.A. 37°7N 93°29W 83 D3
Republic Ohio, U.S.A. 41°8N 83°1W 86 B3
Republic Wash., U.S.A. 48°39N 118°44W 120 B7
Republic County ☆ Kans., U.S.A. 39°45N 97°40W 82 B6
Republican → Kans., U.S.A. 39°4N 96°48W 82 B7
Republican City Nebr., U.S.A. 40°6N 99°13W 80 D6
Repulse Bay Nunavut, Canada 66°30N 86°30W 159 D13
Reserve Sask., Canada 52°28N 102°39W 150 C9
Reserve Kans., U.S.A. 39°59N 95°34W 82 B8
Reserve La., U.S.A. 30°3N 90°33W 110 D5
Reserve N. Mex., U.S.A. 33°43N 108°45W 131 D2
Residencial Chiluca México, Mexico 19°33N 99°17W 181 A2
Resolute Nunavut, Canada 74°42N 94°54W 158 C7
Resolution I. Nunavut, Canada 61°30N 65°0W 159 E13
Restigouche → N.B., Canada 47°50N 67°0W 141 F2
Reston Man., Canada 49°33N 101°6W 151 F10
Reston Va., U.S.A. 38°57N 77°20W 99 B2
Retalhuleu Guatemala 14°33N 91°46W 182 D1
Retsil Wash. U.S.A. 47°32N 122°36W 132 C2
Reva S. Dak., U.S.A. 45°32N 103°5W 76 E2
Revelstoke B.C., Canada 51°0N 118°10W 155 E16
Revere Mass., U.S.A. 42°25N 71°0W 96 A2
Revere Mo., U.S.A. 40°35N 91°41W 83 A5
Revillo S. Dak., U.S.A. 45°1N 96°34W 76 E9
Revolución Durango, Mexico 26°12N 105°9W 172 C5
Revolución Mexicana Chiapas, Mexico 16°10N 93°4W 178 C3
Rewey Wis., U.S.A. 42°51N 90°24W 78 E1
Rexburg Idaho, U.S.A. 43°49N 111°47W 122 F7
Rexdale Ont., Canada 43°43N 79°35W 161 A1
Rexford Kans., U.S.A. 39°28N 100°45W 82 B3
Rexford Mont., U.S.A. 48°53N 115°12W 123 B2
Rexton N.B., Canada 46°39N 64°52W 141 G5
Rexton Mich., U.S.A. 46°10N 85°14W 79 D4
Rey, I. del Panama 8°20N 78°30W 182 E4
Rey, I. del Coahuila, Mexico 27°1N 103°0W 170 C1
Reydon Okla., U.S.A. 35°39N 99°55W 107 C4
Reyes, Pt. Calif., U.S.A. 38°0N 123°0W 126 B5
Reyno Ark., U.S.A. 36°22N 90°45W 106 B5
Reynolds Man., Canada 49°40N 95°55W 151 F16
Reynolds Ga., U.S.A. 32°33N 84°6W 113 D2

Reynolds Ill., U.S.A. 41°20N 90°40W 84 B3
Reynolds Ind., U.S.A. 40°45N 86°52W 85 C4
Reynolds N. Dak., U.S.A. 47°40N 97°7W 76 C8
Reynolds Nebr., U.S.A. 40°4N 97°20W 80 D8
Reynolds Channel N.Y., U.S.A. 40°35N 73°40W 97 C4
Reynolds County ☆ Mo., U.S.A. 37°20N 91°0W 83 D6
Reynoldsburg Ohio, U.S.A. 39°57N 82°48W 86 D4
Reynoldsville Ga., U.S.A. 30°51N 84°47W 113 F2
Reynoldsville Pa., U.S.A. 41°6N 78°53W 87 C4
Reynosa Tamaulipas, Mexico 26°7N 98°18W 170 D6
Reynosa Tamaulipas Distrito Federal, Mexico 19°30N 99°10W 181 A2
Rhame N. Dak., U.S.A. 46°14N 103°39W 76 D2
Rhea County ☆ Tenn., U.S.A. 35°30N 85°0W 105 E8
Rhein Sask., Canada 51°25N 102°15W 151 D9
Rhine Ga., U.S.A. 31°59N 83°12W 113 E3
Rhinebeck N.Y., U.S.A. 41°56N 73°55W 88 D7
Rhinelander Wis., U.S.A. 45°38N 89°25W 78 C4
Rhode Island R.I., U.S.A. 41°30N 71°15W 91 C3
Rhode Island □ U.S.A. 41°40N 71°30W 91 C3
Rhode Island Sd. R.I., U.S.A. 41°20N 71°10W 91 C3
Rhodes Pk. Idaho, U.S.A. 46°40N 114°47W 122 C4
Rhodhiss L. N.C., U.S.A. 35°47N 81°26W 103 C4
Rhododendron Oreg., U.S.A. 45°20N 121°55W 121 B4
Rhome Tex., U.S.A. 33°3N 97°28W 109 D10
Ría Celestún, Parque Natural △ Yucatán, Mexico 21°0N 90°20W 179 A3
Ría Lagartos, Parque Natural △ Yucatán, Mexico 21°30N 87°45W 179 A6
Rib Lake Wis., U.S.A. 45°19N 90°12W 78 C3
Ribera N. Mex., U.S.A. 35°23N 105°27W 131 B5
Ribstone Cr. → Alta., Canada 52°52N 110°5W 153 F10
Ricardo Tex., U.S.A. 27°25N 97°51W 108 K10
Ricardo Flores Magón Chihuahua, Mexico 29°56N 106°57W 169 D9
Rice Calif., U.S.A. 34°5N 114°51W 127 J12
Rice Minn., U.S.A. 45°45N 94°13W 77 E4
Rice Tex., U.S.A. 32°14N 96°30W 109 E11
Rice Va., U.S.A. 37°17N 78°18W 102 D6
Rice County ☆ Kans., U.S.A. 38°25N 98°10W 82 C5
Rice County ☆ Minn., U.S.A. 44°20N 93°15W 77 F5
Rice L. Ont., Canada 44°12N 78°10W 147 C8
Rice Lake Wis., U.S.A. 45°30N 91°44W 78 C2
Riceboro Ga., U.S.A. 31°44N 81°26W 113 E5
Riceton Sask., Canada 50°7N 104°19W 150 E7
Riceville Iowa, U.S.A. 43°22N 92°33W 81 B6
Riceville Tenn., U.S.A. 35°23N 84°42W 105 E8
Rich Miss., U.S.A. 34°25N 90°27W 111 B3
Rich, C. Ont., Canada 44°43N 80°38W 146 C6
Rich County ☆ Utah, U.S.A. 41°30N 111°10W 129 B4
Rich Fountain Mo., U.S.A. 38°24N 91°53W 83 C5
Rich Hill Mo., U.S.A. 38°6N 94°22W 83 C2
Rich Square N.C., U.S.A. 36°16N 77°17W 103 B8
Rich Valley Alta., Canada 53°51N 114°21W 152 F8
Richard B. Russell L. Ga., U.S.A. 34°5N 82°38W 113 B4
Richard Collinson Inlet N.W.T., Canada 72°46N 113°54W 156 B10
Richards Mo., U.S.A. 37°54N 94°33W 83 D2
Richards Tex., U.S.A. 30°32N 95°51W 109 G12
Richards I. N.W.T., Canada 68°0N 135°0W 156 C6
Richardson Tex., U.S.A. 32°56N 96°43W 116 A5
Richardson → Alta., Canada 58°25N 111°14W 157 E10
Richardson County ☆ Nebr., U.S.A. 40°15N 95°45W 80 D10
Richardson Is. Nunavut, Canada 68°33N 110°45W 156 C10
Richardson Lakes Maine, U.S.A. 44°46N 70°58W 90 D3
Richardson Mts. N.W.T., Canada 68°20N 135°45W 156 C5
Richardson N. Dak., U.S.A. 46°53N 102°19W 76 D3
Richboro Pa., U.S.A. 40°13N 75°1W 92 B1
Riche, Pte. Nfld. & L., Canada 50°42N 57°25W 142 B3
Richelieu → Qué., Canada 45°28N 73°18W 89 A1
Richey Mont., U.S.A. 47°39N 105°4W 123 C12
Richfield Idaho, U.S.A. 43°3N 114°9W 122 F4
Richfield Kans., U.S.A. 37°16N 101°47W 82 D2
Richfield Minn., U.S.A. 44°53N 93°16W 94 B2
Richfield Pa., U.S.A. 40°41N 77°7W 87 D5
Richfield Utah, U.S.A. 38°46N 112°5W 129 E3
Richfield Springs N.Y., U.S.A. 42°51N 74°59W 88 C6
Richford Vt., U.S.A. 45°0N 72°40W 89 B2
Richgrove Calif., U.S.A. 35°48N 119°7W 127 H7
Richibucto N.B., Canada 46°42N 64°54W 141 G5
Richland Ga., U.S.A. 32°5N 84°40W 113 D2
Richland Mich., U.S.A. 42°22N 85°27W 79 G6
Richland Mo., U.S.A. 37°51N 92°26W 83 D4
Richland Nebr., U.S.A. 41°26N 97°13W 80 C8
Richland Oreg., U.S.A. 44°46N 117°10W 121 C8
Richland Tex., U.S.A. 31°57N 96°26W 109 F11
Richland Wash., U.S.A. 46°17N 119°18W 120 D6
Richland Center Wis., U.S.A. 43°21N 90°23W 78 E3
Richland Chambers Res. Tex., U.S.A. 32°0N 96°12W 109 F11
Richland County ☆ Ill., U.S.A. 38°45N 88°5W 84 E5
Richland County ☆ Mont., U.S.A. 47°48N 104°40W 123 C13
Richland County ☆ N. Dak., U.S.A. 46°15N 97°0W 76 D9
Richland County ☆ Ohio, U.S.A. 40°45N 82°31W 86 C4
Richland County ☆ S.C., U.S.A. 34°10N 81°0W 103 D5
Richland County ☆ Wis., U.S.A. 43°20N 90°30W 78 E3
Richland Cr. → Tenn., U.S.A. 35°2N 86°56W 104 E6
Richland Hills Tex., U.S.A. 32°48N 97°13W 116 B2
Richland Parish ☆ La., U.S.A. 32°22N 91°52W 110 B4
Richland Springs Tex., U.S.A. 31°16N 98°57W 109 F9
Richlands Va., U.S.A. 37°6N 81°48W 102 D3
Richmond B.C., Canada 49°10N 123°7W 161 C2
Richmond Ont., Canada 45°11N 75°50W 147 B11
Richmond Qué., Canada 45°40N 72°9W 145 F10
Richmond Calif., U.S.A. 37°56N 122°21W 126 F4
Richmond Ill., U.S.A. 42°29N 88°18W 84 A5
Richmond Ind., U.S.A. 39°50N 84°53W 85 D6
Richmond Kans., U.S.A. 38°24N 95°15W 82 C8
Richmond Ky., U.S.A. 37°45N 84°18W 105 C8
Richmond Maine, U.S.A. 44°5N 69°48W 90 D4
Richmond Mich., U.S.A. 42°49N 82°45W 79 G9
Richmond Mo., U.S.A. 39°17N 93°58W 83 B3
Richmond N.H., U.S.A. 42°45N 72°16W 91 B2
Richmond Tex., U.S.A. 29°35N 95°46W 109 H12
Richmond Utah, U.S.A. 41°56N 111°48W 129 B4
Richmond Vt., U.S.A. 44°24N 72°59W 89 B2
Richmond ✈ (RIC) Va., U.S.A. 37°30N 77°19W 102 D7
Richmond County ☆ Ga., U.S.A. 33°15N 82°5W 113 C4
Richmond County ☆ N.C., U.S.A. 35°0N 79°45W 103 D6
Richmond County ☆ N.Y., U.S.A. 40°40N 74°15W 88 E6
Richmond County ☆ Va., U.S.A. 37°58N 76°46W 102 D7
Richmond Heights Fla., U.S.A. 25°38N 80°23W 114 F8

Richmond Heights Mo., U.S.A. 38°37N 90°19W 94 B2
Richmond Hill Ont., Canada 43°52N 79°27W 146 D7
Richmond Hill Ga., U.S.A. 31°56N 81°18W 113 E5
Richmond Hill N.Y., U.S.A. 40°41N 73°51W 97 B3
Richmond Nature Park B.C., Canada 49°10N 123°7W 161 C2
Richmond Valley N.Y., U.S.A. 40°31N 74°13W 97 C1
Richmondville N.Y., U.S.A. 42°38N 74°34W 88 C6
Richmound Sask., Canada 50°27N 109°45W 150 E2
Richton Miss., U.S.A. 31°16N 88°56W 111 E5
Richville Minn., U.S.A. 46°31N 95°38W 77 D3
Richville N.Y., U.S.A. 44°25N 75°22W 88 A5
Richwood La., U.S.A. 32°27N 92°5W 110 B3
Richwood Ohio, U.S.A. 40°26N 83°18W 86 C3
Richwood W. Va., U.S.A. 38°14N 80°32W 102 C4
Richwoods Mo., U.S.A. 38°10N 90°50W 83 C6
Ricketts Iowa, U.S.A. 42°8N 95°35W 81 C3
Ricketts Glen State Park △ Pa., U.S.A. 41°19N 76°16W 87 C6
Rico Colo., U.S.A. 37°42N 108°2W 125 D2
Riddle Idaho, U.S.A. 42°11N 116°7W 122 G2
Riddle Oreg., U.S.A. 42°57N 123°22W 121 E2
Rideau → Ont., Canada 45°27N 75°42W 160 B1
Riderwood Baltimore, U.S.A. 39°24N 76°38W 99 A2
Ridge Md., U.S.A. 38°8N 76°24W 93 B4
Ridge → Ont., Canada 50°25N 84°20W 149 B12
Ridge Farm Ill., U.S.A. 39°54N 87°39W 84 D6
Ridge Spring S.C., U.S.A. 33°51N 81°40W 103 D4
Ridgecrest Calif., U.S.A. 35°38N 117°40W 127 H9
Ridgedale Sask., Canada 53°0N 104°10W 150 B7
Ridgefield Conn., U.S.A. 41°17N 73°30W 91 C1
Ridgefield Wash., U.S.A. 45°49N 122°45W 120 D3
Ridgefield Park N.J., U.S.A. 40°52N 74°1W 97 A2
Ridgeland Miss., U.S.A. 32°26N 90°8W 111 D3
Ridgeland S.C., U.S.A. 32°29N 80°59W 103 F5
Ridgely Md., U.S.A. 45°12N 91°54W 78 C2
Ridgely Tenn., U.S.A. 36°16N 89°29W 104 D3
Ridgetown Ont., Canada 42°26N 81°52W 146 E5
Ridgeville Ind., U.S.A. 40°18N 85°2W 85 C5
Ridgeville S.C., U.S.A. 33°6N 80°19W 103 D5
Ridgeway Iowa, U.S.A. 43°18N 91°59W 81 B7
Ridgeway Mo., U.S.A. 40°23N 93°57W 83 A3
Ridgeway Ohio, U.S.A. 40°31N 83°35W 86 C3
Ridgeway S.C., U.S.A. 34°18N 80°58W 103 D5
Ridgeway Va., U.S.A. 36°35N 79°52W 102 E5
Ridgeway Wis., U.S.A. 43°19N 90°1W 78 E3
Ridgewood N.J., U.S.A. 40°59N 74°7W 92 B2
Ridgewood N.Y., U.S.A. 40°42N 73°53W 97 B3
Ridgway Colo., U.S.A. 38°9N 107°46W 125 D3
Ridgway Ill., U.S.A. 37°48N 88°16W 84 F5
Ridgway Pa., U.S.A. 41°25N 78°44W 87 C4
Riding Mountain Nat. Park △ Man., Canada 50°50N 100°0W 151 E11
Rienzi Miss., U.S.A. 34°46N 88°32W 111 B5
Rieth Oreg., U.S.A. 45°40N 118°54W 121 B7
Riffe L. Wash., U.S.A. 46°32N 122°26W 120 D3
Rifle Colo., U.S.A. 39°32N 107°47W 125 C3
Rifle → Mich., U.S.A. 44°0N 83°49W 79 E8
Rigby Idaho, U.S.A. 43°40N 111°55W 122 F7
Riggins Idaho, U.S.A. 45°25N 116°19W 122 D2
Rigolet Nfld. & L., Canada 54°10N 58°23W 143 C6
Rikers I. N.Y., U.S.A. 40°47N 73°53W 97 B3
Riley Ind., U.S.A. 39°23N 87°18W 85 D3
Riley Kans., U.S.A. 39°18N 96°50W 82 B7
Riley Oreg., U.S.A. 43°32N 119°28W 121 D6
Riley County ☆ Kans., U.S.A. 39°20N 96°40W 82 B7
Rileyville Va., U.S.A. 38°46N 78°23W 93 B2
Rillito Ariz., U.S.A. 32°25N 111°9W 130 E4
Rimbey Alta., Canada 52°35N 114°15W 153 F6
Rimersburg Pa., U.S.A. 41°3N 79°30W 87 C3
Rimouski Qué., Canada 48°27N 68°30W 145 C14
Rimouski → Qué., Canada 48°27N 68°32W 145 C14
Rimouski, Réserve Faunique de △ Qué., Canada 48°0N 68°15W 145 C14
Rimouski-Est Qué., Canada 48°28N 68°31W 145 C14
Rimrock Wash., U.S.A. 46°40N 121°7W 120 D4
Rinard Iowa, U.S.A. 42°20N 94°29W 81 C4
Rincon Puerto Rico 18°20N 67°15W 184 G15
Rincon Ga., U.S.A. 32°18N 81°14W 113 D5
Rincón de las Bayas, B. Tamaulipas, Mexico 25°15N 97°45W 171 E7
Rincón de López Colima, Mexico 19°2N 103°56W 174 C4
Rincón de Romos Aguascalientes, Mexico 22°14N 102°18W 173 E8
Rincón Juárez Oaxaca, Mexico 16°17N 94°21W 177 H6
Rincón Moreno Oaxaca, Mexico 16°14N 95°28W 177 H6
Rinconada → Baja Calif., Mexico 29°17N 114°52W 166 D4
Rindge N.H., U.S.A. 42°45N 72°1W 89 D2
Rineyville Ky., U.S.A. 37°45N 85°59W 105 C7
Ringgold Ga., U.S.A. 34°55N 85°7W 113 B1
Ringgold La., U.S.A. 32°20N 93°17W 110 B2
Ringgold Nebr., U.S.A. 41°31N 100°47W 80 C5
Ringgold County ☆ Iowa, U.S.A. 40°45N 94°15W 81 E4
Ringling Mont., U.S.A. 46°16N 110°49W 123 D7
Ringling Okla., U.S.A. 34°11N 97°36W 107 D6
Ringoes N.J., U.S.A. 40°26N 74°52W 92 B2
Ringsted Iowa, U.S.A. 43°18N 94°31W 81 B4
Ringwood Okla., U.S.A. 36°23N 98°15W 107 B5
Ringwood N.J., U.S.A. 41°7N 74°15W 92 A2
Rio Ill., U.S.A. 41°7N 90°24W 83 B1
Rio Wis., U.S.A. 43°27N 89°14W 78 E4
Río Arriba County ☆ N. Mex., U.S.A. 36°30N 106°45W 131 A4
Río Blanco Chiapas, Mexico 16°39N 93°2W 178 C3
Río Blanco Colo., U.S.A. 39°44N 107°57W 125 C3
Río Blanco County ☆ Colo., U.S.A. 40°0N 108°15W 125 C3
Río Bravo Tamaulipas, Mexico 25°59N 98°6W 170 E6
Rio Claro Trin. & Tob. 10°20N 61°25W 183 D7
Rio Communities N. Mex., U.S.A. 34°40N 106°43W 126 C5
Río Dell Calif., U.S.A. 40°30N 124°6W 126 C2
Río Dulce, Parque Nac. △ Guatemala 15°43N 88°50W 182 C2
Rio Grande Oaxaca, Mexico 16°1N 97°37W 177 H3
Río Grande Puebla, Mexico 18°39N 98°20W 177 F2
Rio Grande Nic. 12°54N 83°50W 182 D3
Río Grande Puerto Rico 18°23N 65°50W 184 G17
Rio Grande N.J., U.S.A. 39°1N 74°53W 92 C2
Río Grande → N. Amer. 25°58N 97°9W 108 M10
Rio Grande City Tex., U.S.A. 26°23N 98°49W 108 L9
Río Grande County ☆ Colo., U.S.A. 37°40N 106°20W 125 E4
Río Grande de Santiago → Nayarit, Mexico 21°36N 105°26W 172 F5
Rio Grande Nat. Forest Colo., U.S.A. 37°30N 106°30W 125 E4
Hato Panama 8°22N 80°10W 182 E3
Río Hondo Tex., U.S.A. 26°14N 97°35W 108 L10
Río Indio, Pta. Quintana Roo, Mexico 18°50N 87°38W 179 D6
Río Lagartos Yucatán, Mexico 21°36N 88°10W 179 A5

Río Lagartos, Estero Yucatán, Mexico 21°37N 87°55W 179 A6
Río Platano, Reserva de la Biosfera de △ Honduras 15°45N 85°0W 182 C2
Río San Rodrigo-El Burro, Parque Natural △ Coahuila, Mexico 28°57N 101°53W 170 B3
Río Verde Quintana Roo, Mexico 19°5N 89°2W 179 C4
Río Verde San Luis Potosí, Mexico 21°56N 99°59W 171 J5
Río Vista Calif., U.S.A. 38°10N 121°42W 126 E5
Riondel B.C., Canada 49°46N 116°51W 155 F18
Ripley Ont., Canada 44°4N 81°35W 146 C5
Ripley Calif., U.S.A. 33°32N 114°39W 127 K12
Ripley Ill., U.S.A. 40°1N 90°38W 84 C3
Ripley Miss., U.S.A. 34°44N 88°57W 111 B5
Ripley N.Y., U.S.A. 42°16N 79°43W 88 C1
Ripley Ohio, U.S.A. 38°45N 83°51W 86 E3
Ripley Okla., U.S.A. 36°1N 96°54W 107 B7
Ripley Tenn., U.S.A. 35°45N 89°32W 104 D3
Ripley W. Va., U.S.A. 38°49N 81°43W 102 C3
Ripley County ☆ Ind., U.S.A. 39°5N 85°15W 85 D5
Ripley County ☆ Mo., U.S.A. 36°40N 90°50W 83 E6
Ripogenus Dam Maine, U.S.A. 45°53N 69°11W 90 C4
Ripon Qué., Canada 45°45N 75°10W 147 B10
Ripon Calif., U.S.A. 37°44N 121°7W 126 F5
Ripon Wis., U.S.A. 43°51N 88°50W 78 E5
Rippey Iowa, U.S.A. 41°56N 94°12W 81 D4
Rippon W. Va., U.S.A. 39°13N 77°54W 93 A3
Ririe Idaho, U.S.A. 43°38N 111°47W 122 F7
Ririe Res. Idaho, U.S.A. 43°36N 111°33W 122 F7
Risco Mo., U.S.A. 36°33N 89°49W 83 E7
Rising City Nebr., U.S.A. 41°12N 97°8W 80 C8
Rising Fawn Ga., U.S.A. 34°46N 85°32W 113 B1
Rising Star Tex., U.S.A. 32°6N 98°58W 109 E9
Rising Sun Ind., U.S.A. 38°57N 84°51W 85 E6
Rising Sun Md., U.S.A. 39°42N 76°4W 93 A4
Rison Ark., U.S.A. 33°58N 92°11W 106 D3
Rita Blanca Cr. → Tex., U.S.A. 35°40N 102°29W 108 B5
Rita Blanca Nat. Grassland Tex., U.S.A. 36°20N 102°30W 108 A5
Ritchie Md., U.S.A. 38°52N 76°51W 99 B4
Ritchie County ☆ W. Va., U.S.A. 39°13N 81°3W 102 B3
Ritchie L. Nfld. & L., Canada 52°58N 66°1W 140 A3
Ritidian Pt. Guam 13°39N 144°51E 184 b
Ritter, Mt. Calif., U.S.A. 37°41N 119°12W 126 F7
Rittman Ohio, U.S.A. 40°58N 81°47W 86 C5
Ritzville Wash., U.S.A. 47°8N 118°23W 120 D7
Riva Md., U.S.A. 38°57N 76°35W 93 B4
Riva Palacio Chihuahua, Mexico 28°33N 106°30W 169 E9
Rivanna → Va., U.S.A. 37°45N 78°10W 102 D6
Rivas Nic. 11°30N 85°50W 182 D2
Rive Sud, Canal de la → Qué., Canada 45°24N 73°31W 160 B3
River Edge N.J., U.S.A. 40°56N 74°1W 97 A2
River Falls Ala., U.S.A. 31°21N 86°32W 112 E4
River Falls Wis., U.S.A. 44°52N 92°38W 78 D1
River Forest Ill., U.S.A. 41°53N 87°49W 95 B2
River Grove Ill., U.S.A. 41°55N 87°50W 95 B1
River Hebert N.S., Canada 45°42N 64°23W 141 H5
River Hills Wis., U.S.A. 43°10N 87°55W 94 B2
River John N.S., Canada 45°45N 63°3W 141 H6
River Jordan B.C., Canada 48°26N 124°3W 154 E3
River of Ponds Nfld. & L., Canada 50°32N 57°24W 142 B3
River of Ponds L. Nfld. & L., Canada 50°30N 57°20W 142 B3
River Ridge La., U.S.A. 29°57N 90°12W 117 C1
River Rouge Mich., U.S.A. 42°16N 83°8W 98 B2
River Rouge Park Mich., U.S.A. 42°18N 83°14W 98 A1
River Valley Ont., Canada 46°35N 80°11W 146 A6
Riverbank Calif., U.S.A. 37°44N 120°56W 126 F6
Rivercrest Man., Canada 50°0N 97°3W 151 E14
Riverdale Calif., U.S.A. 36°26N 119°52W 127 G7
Riverdale Ga., U.S.A. 33°34N 84°25W 113 C2
Riverdale Md., U.S.A. 38°57N 76°56W 99 B4
Riverdale N. Dak., U.S.A. 47°30N 101°22W 76 C4
Riverdale N.Y., U.S.A. 40°59N 74°17W 97 A3
Riverdale Wash., U.S.A. 40°47N 99°10W 80 D6
Riverdale Park Ont., Canada 43°40N 79°21W 161 A2
Rivergrove Oreg., U.S.A. 45°23N 122°43W 132 B1
Riverhead Nfld. & L., Canada 46°58N 53°31W 142 F7
Riverhead N.Y., U.S.A. 40°55N 72°40W 91 D2
Riverhurst Sask., Canada 50°55N 106°50W 150 E5
Rivers Man., Canada 50°2N 100°14W 151 E11
Rivers, L. of the Sask., Canada 49°49N 105°44W 150 F6
Rivers Inlet B.C., Canada 51°42N 127°15W 154 D7
Riverside Calif., U.S.A. 33°59N 117°22W 127 K9
Riverside Ill., U.S.A. 41°49N 87°49W 95 C2
Riverside Iowa, U.S.A. 41°29N 91°35W 81 D7
Riverside Md., U.S.A. 38°22N 77°11W 93 B3
Riverside N.J., U.S.A. 40°2N 74°58W 92 B2
Riverside N. Mex., U.S.A. 32°50N 104°17W 131 E6
Riverside Tex., U.S.A. 30°51N 95°24W 109 G12
Riverside Wash., U.S.A. 48°30N 119°30W 120 B6
Riverside Wyo., U.S.A. 41°13N 106°47W 124 E6
Riverside-Albert N.B., Canada 45°42N 64°45W 141 H5
Riverside County ☆ Calif., U.S.A. 33°45N 116°0W 127 K11
Riverside Res. Colo., U.S.A. 40°20N 104°15W 125 B6
Riverton Man., Canada 51°1N 97°0W 151 D14
Riverton Ill., U.S.A. 39°51N 89°33W 84 D4
Riverton Iowa, U.S.A. 40°41N 95°34W 81 E3
Riverton Kans., U.S.A. 37°5N 94°42W 82 D9
Riverton Oreg., U.S.A. 43°10N 124°12W 121 D1
Riverton Utah, U.S.A. 40°31N 111°56W 104 C2
Riverton W. Va., U.S.A. 38°45N 79°26W 102 C5
Riverton Wyo., U.S.A. 43°2N 108°23W 124 C4
Riverview N.B., Canada 46°4N 64°48W 141 G5
Riverview Ont., Canada 42°54N 75°39W 160 B2
Riverview Fla., U.S.A. 27°52N 82°20W 114 E6
Riverview Mo., U.S.A. 38°44N 90°12W 94 A2
Riverview Park Pa., U.S.A. 40°28N 80°1W 98 B1
Rivesville W. Va., U.S.A. 39°32N 80°7W 102 B4
Riviera Qué., Canada 45°34N 114°35W 130 B1
Riviera Tex., U.S.A. 27°18N 97°49W 108 K10
Riviera Beach Fla., U.S.A. 26°47N 80°3W 114 E9
Riviera Beach Md., U.S.A. 39°10N 76°31W 93 B4
Rivière-à-Pierre Qué., Canada 46°59N 72°11W 145 E12
Rivière-au-Renard Qué., Canada 48°59N 64°23W 140 C5
Rivière-au-Tonnerre Qué., Canada 50°16N 64°47W 140 C7
Rivière-aux-Graines Qué., Canada 50°7N 65°11W 140 C6
Rivière-aux-Rats Qué., Canada 47°13N 72°53W 145 D11
Rivière-Bersimis Qué., Canada 48°56N 68°42W 145 C14
Rivière-Bleue Qué., Canada 47°26N 69°3W 145 D13

Rivière-de-la-Chaloupe *Qué., Canada* 49°8N 62°32W **140** D7
Rivière-des-Prairies *Qué., Canada* 45°38N 73°34W **160** A3
Rivière-du-Loup *Qué., Canada* 47°50N 69°30W **145** D13
Rivière-du-Portage *N.B., Canada* 47°25N 64°56W **141** F5
Rivière-Ouelle *Qué., Canada* 47°26N 70°1W **145** D12
Rivière-Pentecôte *Qué., Canada* 49°57N 67°1W **140** D2
Rivière-Pigou *Qué., Canada* 50°16N 65°35W **140** C4
Rivière-Pilote *Martinique* 14°26N 60°53W **183** D7
Rivière-St-Jean *Qué., Canada* 50°17N 64°19W **140** C5
Rivière Verte *N.B., Canada* 47°19N 68°9W **141** F1
Rixeyville *Va., U.S.A.* 38°35N 77°59W **102** C7
Roach L. *Nev., U.S.A.* 35°41N 115°22W **128** G5
Roachdale *Ind., U.S.A.* 39°51N 86°48W **85** D4
Road Town *Br. Virgin Is.* 18°27N 64°37W **184** G18
Roan Cliffs *Colo., U.S.A.* 39°20N 108°40W **125** C2
Roan Cliffs *Utah, U.S.A.* 39°20N 109°40W **129** D6
Roan Cr. → *Colo., U.S.A.* 39°20N 108°13W **125** C2
Roan Mountain *Tenn., U.S.A.* 36°12N 82°4W **105** D10
Roan Plateau *Colo., U.S.A.* 39°35N 108°40W **125** C2
Roan Plateau *Utah, U.S.A.* 39°20N 109°20W **129** D6
Roane County ☆ *Tenn., U.S.A.* 35°52N 84°31W **105** E8
Roane County ☆ *W. Va., U.S.A.* 38°48N 81°21W **102** C3
Roanoke *Ala., U.S.A.* 33°9N 85°22W **112** C5
Roanoke *Ill., U.S.A.* 40°48N 89°12W **84** C4
Roanoke *Ind., U.S.A.* 40°58N 85°22W **85** C5
Roanoke *Tex., U.S.A.* 33°0N 97°10W **109** D10
Roanoke *Va., U.S.A.* 37°16N 79°56W **102** D5
Roanoke → *N.C., U.S.A.* 35°57N 76°42W **103** C9
Roanoke County ☆ *Va., U.S.A.* 37°16N 79°56W **102** D5
Roanoke I. *N.C., U.S.A.* 35°53N 75°39W **103** C10
Roanoke Rapids *N.C., U.S.A.* 36°28N 77°40W **103** B8
Roanoke Rapids L. *N.C., U.S.A.* 36°29N 77°40W **103** B8
Roaring Spring *Pa., U.S.A.* 40°20N 78°24W **87** D4
Roaring Springs *Tex., U.S.A.* 33°54N 100°52W **108** D7
Roatán *Honduras* 16°18N 86°35W **182** C2
Robards *Ky., U.S.A.* 37°41N 87°33W **104** C5
Robb *Alta., Canada* 53°13N 116°58W **152** E4
Robbins *Ill., U.S.A.* 41°38N 87°42W **95** D2
Robbins *N.C., U.S.A.* 35°26N 79°35W **103** C6
Robbins *Tenn., U.S.A.* 36°21N 84°35W **105** D8
Robbinsdale *Minn., U.S.A.* 45°1N 93°19W **94** A2
Robbinsville *N.C., U.S.A.* 35°19N 83°48W **103** C2
Robco L. *Tenn., U.S.A.* 35°0N 90°7W **117** B1
Robe-Noire, L. de la *Qué., Canada* 50°42N 62°42W **140** C7
Robersonville *N.C., U.S.A.* 35°50N 77°15W **103** C8
Robert E. Lee Park *Baltimore, U.S.A.* 39°23N 76°39W **99** A2
Robert Lee *Tex., U.S.A.* 31°54N 100°29W **108** F7
Robert S. Kerr L. *Okla., U.S.A.* 35°21N 94°47W **107** C9
Roberta *Ga., U.S.A.* 32°43N 84°1W **113** D2
Roberts *Idaho, U.S.A.* 43°43N 112°8W **122** F6
Roberts *Ill., U.S.A.* 40°37N 88°11W **84** C5
Roberts *Mont., U.S.A.* 45°22N 109°10W **123** E8
Roberts, Mt. *Alaska, U.S.A.* 60°2N 166°16W **135** F6
Robert's Arm *Nfld. & L., Canada* 49°29N 55°49W **142** C5
Roberts County ☆ *S. Dak., U.S.A.* 45°33N 96°57W **76** E9
Roberts County ☆ *Tex., U.S.A.* 35°55N 100°55W **108** B7
Roberts Creek *B.C., Canada* 49°26N 123°38W **155** F11
Robertsdale *Ala., U.S.A.* 30°33N 87°43W **112** F3
Robertson *Mo., U.S.A.* 38°44N 90°22W **94** A1
Robertson *Wyo., U.S.A.* 41°11N 110°25W **124** E2
Robertson County ☆ *Ky., U.S.A.* 38°30N 84°5W **105** B8
Robertson County ☆ *Tenn., U.S.A.* 36°31N 86°53W **104** D6
Robertson County ☆ *Tex., U.S.A.* 31°2N 96°29W **109** F11
Robertsonville *Qué., Canada* 46°9N 71°13W **145** E11
Robbinsville *N.J., U.S.A.* 40°21N 74°17W **92** B2
Robertville *N.B., Canada* 47°42N 65°46W **141** F4
Roberval *Qué., Canada* 48°32N 72°15W **145** C10
Robeson Chan. *N. Amer.* 82°0N 61°30W **162** A4
Robeson County ☆ *N.C., U.S.A.* 34°30N 79°10W **103** D6
Robesonia *Pa., U.S.A.* 40°21N 76°8W **87** D6
Robins *Iowa, U.S.A.* 42°4N 91°40W **81** C7
Robinson *Ill., U.S.A.* 39°0N 87°44W **84** E6
Robinson *Kans., U.S.A.* 39°49N 95°25W **82** B8
Robinson *N. Dak., U.S.A.* 47°9N 99°47W **76** C6
Robinson *Tex., U.S.A.* 31°28N 97°7W **109** F10
Robinson, L. *S.C., U.S.A.* 34°30N 80°12W **103** D5
Robinson Mt. *Mont., U.S.A.* 48°58N 115°25W **123** B2
Robinsonville *Miss., U.S.A.* 34°49N 90°19W **111** B3
Roblin *Man., Canada* 51°14N 101°21W **151** D10
Robsart *Sask., Canada* 49°23N 109°17W **150** F2
Robson, Mt. *B.C., Canada* 53°10N 119°10W **155** B15
Robstown *Tex., U.S.A.* 27°47N 97°40W **109** K10
Roby *Mo., U.S.A.* 37°31N 92°8W **83** D4
Roby *Tex., U.S.A.* 32°45N 100°23W **108** E7
Roca *Nebr., U.S.A.* 40°39N 96°40W **80** D9
Roca Partida *Veracruz, Mexico* 18°42N 95°5W **177** F5
Roca Partida, Pta. *Veracruz, Mexico* 18°42N 95°10W **177** F5
Rocanville *Sask., Canada* 50°23N 101°42W **151** E10
Rochdale *Mass., U.S.A.* 42°12N 71°54W **91** B3
Roche Percee *Sask., Canada* 49°4N 102°48W **150** F9
Rochéachic *Chihuahua, Mexico* 27°5N 107°12W **169** F8
Rochebaucourt *Qué., Canada* 48°41N 77°30W **144** C5
Rochelle *Ga., U.S.A.* 31°57N 83°27W **113** E3
Rochelle *Ill., U.S.A.* 41°56N 89°4W **84** B41
Rochelle *Tex., U.S.A.* 31°14N 99°13W **109** F8
Rochelle Park *N.J., U.S.A.* 40°54N 74°4W **97** A2
Rocheport *Mo., U.S.A.* 38°59N 92°34W **83** C4
Rochester *Alta., Canada* 54°22N 113°27W **152** D7
Rochester *Ill., U.S.A.* 39°45N 89°32W **84** D4
Rochester *Ind., U.S.A.* 41°4N 86°13W **85** B4
Rochester *Ky., U.S.A.* 37°13N 86°53W **104** C6
Rochester *Mass., U.S.A.* 41°44N 70°49W **91** C4
Rochester *Minn., U.S.A.* 44°1N 92°28W **77** F6
Rochester *N.H., U.S.A.* 43°18N 70°59W **89** C4
Rochester *N.Y., U.S.A.* 43°10N 77°37W **88** B3
Rochester *Ohio, U.S.A.* 41°8N 82°18W **86** B4
Rochester *Tex., U.S.A.* 33°19N 99°51W **109** D8
Rochester *Vt., U.S.A.* 43°51N 72°48W **89** C2
Rochester *Wash., U.S.A.* 46°49N 123°6W **120** D2
Rochester Hills *Mich., U.S.A.* 42°41N 83°8W **79** G8
Rochester Park *Tex., U.S.A.* 32°43N 96°44W **116** B5
Rock *Mich., U.S.A.* 46°4N 87°10W **79** C4
Rock → *Yukon, Canada* 60°7N 127°7W **157** D7
Rock → *Ill., U.S.A.* 41°29N 90°37W **84** B3
Rock Cave *W. Va., U.S.A.* 38°50N 80°21W **102** C4
Rock County ☆ *Minn., U.S.A.* 43°45N 96°15W **77** G2
Rock County ☆ *Nebr., U.S.A.* 42°30N 99°30W **80** B6
Rock County ☆ *Wis., U.S.A.* 42°45N 89°10W **78** F4
Rock Cr. → *D.C., U.S.A.* 38°54N 77°3W **99** B3
Rock Cr. → *Ill., U.S.A.* 41°42N 90°3W **84** B3
Rock Cr. → *Mont., U.S.A.* 46°43N 113°40W **123** D4
Rock Cr. → *Mont., U.S.A.* 48°27N 107°6W **123** B10
Rock Cr. → *Nev., U.S.A.* 40°39N 116°55W **128** B4
Rock Cr. → *Oreg., U.S.A.* 45°34N 120°25W **121** B5
Rock Cr. → *S. Dak., U.S.A.* 43°44N 97°58W **76** G8
Rock Cr. → *Utah, U.S.A.* 40°17N 110°30W **129** C5
Rock Creek *B.C., Canada* 49°4N 119°0W **155** F16
Rock Creek *Minn., U.S.A.* 45°45N 92°58W **77** E6
Rock Creek *Ohio, U.S.A.* 41°40N 80°52W **86** B6
Rock Creek Butte *Oreg., U.S.A.* 44°49N 118°7W **121** C7
Rock Creek Park *D.C., U.S.A.* 38°56N 77°2W **99** B3
Rock Falls *Ill., U.S.A.* 41°47N 89°41W **84** B41
Rock Falls *Iowa, U.S.A.* 43°13N 93°5W **81** B5
Rock Forest *Qué., Canada* 45°21N 71°59W **145** F11
Rock Hall *Md., U.S.A.* 39°8N 76°14W **93** A4
Rock Hill *Mo., U.S.A.* 38°36N 90°22W **94** B1
Rock Hill *S.C., U.S.A.* 34°56N 81°1W **103** D4
Rock I. *Wis., U.S.A.* 45°25N 86°49W **78** C7
Rock Island *Ill., U.S.A.* 41°30N 90°34W **84** B3
Rock Island *Okla., U.S.A.* 35°10N 94°28W **107** C9
Rock Island *Wash., U.S.A.* 47°22N 120°8W **120** C5
Rock Island County ☆ *Ill., U.S.A.* 41°25N 90°30W **84** B3
Rock Island Dam *Wash., U.S.A.* 47°23N 120°4W **120** C5
Rock L. *N. Dak., U.S.A.* 48°50N 99°12W **76** B6
Rock L. *Wash., U.S.A.* 47°11N 117°41W **120** C8
Rock Point *Ariz., U.S.A.* 36°43N 109°38W **130** A6
Rock Point *Md., U.S.A.* 38°16N 76°50W **93** B4
Rock Port *Mo., U.S.A.* 40°25N 95°31W **83** A1
Rock Rapids *Iowa, U.S.A.* 43°26N 96°10W **81** B2
Rock River *Wyo., U.S.A.* 41°44N 105°58W **124** E7
Rock Sound *Bahamas* 24°54N 76°12W **182** B4
Rock Spring *Ga., U.S.A.* 34°50N 85°14W **113** B1
Rock Springs *Mont., U.S.A.* 46°49N 106°15W **123** D11
Rock Springs *Wyo., U.S.A.* 41°35N 109°14W **124** E3
Rock Valley *Iowa, U.S.A.* 43°12N 96°18W **81** B2
Rockaway Beach *Oreg., U.S.A.* 45°37N 123°57W **121** B2
Rockaway Inlet *N.Y., U.S.A.* 40°34N 73°54W **97** C3
Rockaway Pt. *N.Y., U.S.A.* 40°33N 73°54W **97** C3
Rockbridge *Ill., U.S.A.* 39°16N 90°12W **84** D3
Rockbridge County ☆ *Va., U.S.A.* 37°55N 79°20W **102** D5
Rockcastle → *Ky., U.S.A.* 36°58N 84°21W **105** D8
Rockcastle County ☆ *Ky., U.S.A.* 37°20N 84°20W **105** C8
Rockcliffe Park *Ont., Canada* 45°27N 75°41W **160** A1
Rockdale *Tex., U.S.A.* 30°39N 97°0W **109** G11
Rockdale County ☆ *Ga., U.S.A.* 33°40N 84°0W **113** C2
Rockefeller Center *New York, U.S.A.* **96** c2
Rockefeller Park *Ohio, U.S.A.* 41°31N 81°37W **98** A2
Rockford *Ala., U.S.A.* 32°53N 86°13W **112** D4
Rockford *Ill., U.S.A.* 42°16N 89°6W **84** A4
Rockford *Iowa, U.S.A.* 43°3N 92°57W **81** B6
Rockford *Mich., U.S.A.* 43°7N 85°34W **79** F6
Rockford *Minn., U.S.A.* 45°5N 93°44W **77** E5
Rockford *Ohio, U.S.A.* 40°41N 84°39W **86** C2
Rockford *Wash., U.S.A.* 47°27N 117°8W **120** C8
Rockglen *Sask., Canada* 49°11N 105°57W **150** F6
Rockham *S. Dak., U.S.A.* 44°55N 98°49W **76** F7
Rockingham *N.C., U.S.A.* 34°57N 79°46W **103** D6
Rockingham *Vt., U.S.A.* 43°11N 72°29W **89** C2
Rockingham County ☆ *N.C., U.S.A.* 36°20N 79°50W **103** B6
Rockingham County ☆ *N.H., U.S.A.* 43°0N 71°10W **89** D3
Rockingham County ☆ *Va., U.S.A.* 38°27N 78°52W **102** C6
Rocklake *N. Dak., U.S.A.* 48°47N 99°15W **76** B6
Rockland *Ont., Canada* 45°33N 75°17W **144** F7
Rockland *Idaho, U.S.A.* 42°34N 112°53W **122** G6
Rockland *Maine, U.S.A.* 44°6N 69°7W **90** D4
Rockland *Mass., U.S.A.* 42°8N 70°55W **91** B4
Rockland *Mich., U.S.A.* 46°44N 89°11W **79** C21
Rockland *Wis., U.S.A.* 43°54N 90°55W **78** E3
Rockland County ☆ *N.Y., U.S.A.* 41°10N 74°5W **88** D6
Rockledge *Fla., U.S.A.* 28°20N 80°43W **114** C8
Rockledge *Pa., U.S.A.* 40°4N 75°5W **98** A2
Rocklin *Calif., U.S.A.* 38°48N 121°14W **126** E5
Rockmart *Ga., U.S.A.* 34°0N 85°3W **113** B1
Rockport *Calif., U.S.A.* 39°44N 123°49W **126** D3
Rockport *Ind., U.S.A.* 37°53N 87°3W **85** F3
Rockport *Mass., U.S.A.* 42°39N 70°37W **91** B4
Rockport *Tex., U.S.A.* 28°2N 97°3W **109** J10
Rockport *Wash., U.S.A.* 48°29N 121°36W **120** B4
Rocksprings *Tex., U.S.A.* 30°1N 100°13W **108** G7
Rockton *Ill., U.S.A.* 42°27N 89°4W **84** A4
Rockville *Conn., U.S.A.* 41°52N 72°28W **91** C2
Rockville *Ind., U.S.A.* 39°46N 87°14W **85** D3
Rockville *Md., U.S.A.* 39°5N 77°9W **93** A3
Rockville *Mo., U.S.A.* 38°4N 94°5W **83** C2
Rockville *Nebr., U.S.A.* 41°7N 98°50W **80** C7
Rockville *Utah, U.S.A.* 37°10N 113°2W **129** F2
Rockville Centre *N.Y., U.S.A.* 40°39N 73°33W **97** C5
Rockwall *Tex., U.S.A.* 32°56N 96°28W **109** E11
Rockwall County ☆ *Tex., U.S.A.* 32°56N 96°28W **109** E11
Rockwell *Iowa, U.S.A.* 42°59N 93°11W **81** C5
Rockwell *N.C., U.S.A.* 35°33N 80°25W **103** C5
Rockwell City *Iowa, U.S.A.* 42°24N 94°38W **81** C4
Rockwood *Ont., Canada* 43°37N 80°8W **146** D6
Rockwood *Maine, U.S.A.* 45°41N 69°45W **90** C4
Rockwood *Pa., U.S.A.* 39°55N 79°9W **87** E3
Rockwood *Tenn., U.S.A.* 35°52N 84°41W **105** E8
Rocky *Okla., U.S.A.* 35°9N 99°3W **107** C4
Rocky → *Alta., Canada* 53°8N 117°59W **153** E3
Rocky → *N.C., U.S.A.* 35°37N 79°9W **103** C6
Rocky → *N.C., U.S.A.* 35°9N 80°5W **103** C5
Rocky Boy *Mont., U.S.A.* 48°16N 109°47W **123** B8
Rocky Boy's Indian Reservation *Mont., U.S.A.* 48°25N 109°30W **123** B8
Rocky Comfort Cr. → *Ga., U.S.A.* 32°59N 82°25W **113** D4
Rocky Ford *Colo., U.S.A.* 38°3N 103°43W **125** D7
Rocky Ford *Ga., U.S.A.* 32°40N 81°50W **113** D5
Rocky Fork L. *Ohio, U.S.A.* 39°11N 83°26W **86** D3
Rocky Harbour *Nfld. & L., Canada* 49°36N 57°55W **142** C3
Rocky Hill *Conn., U.S.A.* 41°40N 72°39W **91** C2
Rocky Island L. *Ont., Canada* 46°55N 83°0W **149** F14
Rocky Lane *Alta., Canada* 58°31N 116°22W **157** E9
Rocky Mount *N.C., U.S.A.* 35°57N 77°48W **103** C8
Rocky Mount *Va., U.S.A.* 37°12N 79°57W **102** D5
Rocky Mountain Arsenal Nat. Wildlife Area △ *Colo., U.S.A.* 39°50N 104°50W **134** A2
Rocky Mountain House *Alta., Canada* 52°22N 114°55W **153** F6
Rocky Mountain Nat. Park △ *Colo., U.S.A.* 40°25N 105°45W **125** B5
Rocky Mts. *N. Amer.* 49°0N 115°0W **157** E8
Rocky Reach Dam *Wash., U.S.A.* 47°32N 120°18W **120** C5
Rocky Ridge *Md., U.S.A.* 39°38N 77°20W **93** A3
Rocky Ridge *Utah, U.S.A.* 39°56N 111°50W **129** D4
Rocky Run → *Va., U.S.A.* 38°58N 77°14W **99** B2
Rocky Top *Oreg., U.S.A.* 44°47N 122°17W **121** C3
Rockyford *Alta., Canada* 51°14N 113°10W **153** G7
Roddickton *Nfld. & L., Canada* 50°51N 56°8W **142** B4
Rodemacher, L. *La., U.S.A.* 31°23N 92°43W **110** C3
Rodeo *Durango, Mexico* 25°11N 104°4W **173** B6
Rodeo *N. Mex., U.S.A.* 31°50N 109°2W **131** F1
Roderick I. *B.C., Canada* 52°38N 128°22W **154** C6
Rodessa *La., U.S.A.* 32°58N 93°59W **110** B2
Rodgers Forge *Baltimore, U.S.A.* 39°22N 76°36W **99** A2
Rodman *Iowa, U.S.A.* 43°2N 94°32W **81** B4
Rodney *Ont., Canada* 42°34N 81°41W **146** E5
Rodney *Iowa, U.S.A.* 42°12N 95°57W **81** C3
Rodolfo Sánchez Taboada *Baja Calif., Mexico* 31°45N 116°35W **166** B2
Roebling *N.J., U.S.A.* 40°7N 74°47W **92** B2
Roes Welcome Sd. *Nunavut, Canada* 65°0N 87°0W **159** E8
Roff *Okla., U.S.A.* 34°38N 96°50W **107** D7
Roger, L. *Qué., Canada* 47°50N 78°59W **144** D4
Roger Mills County ☆ *Okla., U.S.A.* 35°45N 99°45W **107** C4
Roger Williams Park Zoo *R.I., U.S.A.* 41°46N 71°24W **91** C3
Rogers *Ark., U.S.A.* 36°20N 94°7W **106** B1
Rogers *La., U.S.A.* 31°32N 92°14W **110** C3
Rogers *N. Dak., U.S.A.* 47°4N 98°12W **76** C7
Rogers *Nebr., U.S.A.* 41°28N 96°55W **80** C9
Rogers *Tex., U.S.A.* 30°56N 97°14W **109** G10
Rogers, Mt. *Va., U.S.A.* 36°40N 81°33W **102** E3
Rogers City *Mich., U.S.A.* 45°25N 83°49W **79** D8
Rogers County ☆ *Okla., U.S.A.* 36°20N 95°40W **107** B8
Rogers L. *Calif., U.S.A.* 34°55N 117°50W **127** J9
Rogers Lake *Minn., U.S.A.* 44°52N 93°8W **94** B3
Rogers Park *Ill., U.S.A.* 42°0N 87°40W **95** A3
Rogerson *Idaho, U.S.A.* 42°13N 114°36W **122** G4
Rogersville *N.B., Canada* 46°44N 65°26W **141** G4
Rogersville *Ala., U.S.A.* 34°50N 87°18W **112** B3
Rogersville *Mo., U.S.A.* 37°7N 93°3W **83** D3
Rogersville *Tenn., U.S.A.* 36°24N 83°1W **105** D9
Roggan L. *Qué., Canada* 54°8N 77°50W **143** C2
Roggan River *Qué., Canada* 54°25N 79°32W **143** C2
Roggen *Colo., U.S.A.* 40°10N 104°22W **125** B6
Rogue → *Oreg., U.S.A.* 42°26N 124°26W **121** E1
Rogue River *Oreg., U.S.A.* 42°26N 123°10W **121** E2
Rogue River Nat. Forest *Oreg., U.S.A.* 42°54N 122°22W **121** E3
Rohault, L. *Qué., Canada* 49°23N 74°20W **145** B8
Rohnerville *Calif., U.S.A.* 40°34N 124°8W **126** C2
Rojas *Durango, Mexico* 23°51N 104°3W **173** D6
Rojo, C. *Veracruz, Mexico* 21°33N 97°20W **176** C3
Roland *Man., Canada* 49°22N 97°56W **151** F14
Roland *Iowa, U.S.A.* 42°10N 93°30W **81** C5
Roland *Okla., U.S.A.* 35°25N 94°31W **107** C9
Roland, L. *Baltimore, U.S.A.* 39°22N 76°38W **99** A2
Rolette *N. Dak., U.S.A.* 48°40N 99°51W **76** B6
Rolette County ☆ *N. Dak., U.S.A.* 48°55N 99°55W **76** B6
Rolfe *Iowa, U.S.A.* 42°49N 94°31W **81** C4
Roll *Ariz., U.S.A.* 32°45N 113°59W **130** E2
Rolla *Kans., U.S.A.* 37°7N 101°38W **82** D2
Rolla *Mo., U.S.A.* 37°57N 91°46W **83** D5
Rolla *N. Dak., U.S.A.* 48°52N 99°37W **76** B6
Rollet *Qué., Canada* 47°55N 79°15W **144** D3
Rolling Fork *Miss., U.S.A.* 32°55N 90°53W **111** D3
Rolling Fork → *Ky., U.S.A.* 37°55N 85°50W **105** C7
Rolling Hills *Alta., Canada* 50°13N 111°46W **153** H9
Rollingbay *Wash., U.S.A.* 47°39N 122°30W **132** C2
Roma-Los Saenz *Tex., U.S.A.* 26°24N 99°1W **108** L8
Romain, C. *S.C., U.S.A.* 33°0N 79°22W **103** F6
Romaine → *Qué., Canada* 50°18N 63°47W **143** C5
Romano, C. *Fla., U.S.A.* 25°51N 81°41W **114** F7
Romano, Cayo *Cuba* 22°0N 77°30W **182** B4
Romanzof C. *Alaska, U.S.A.* 61°49N 166°6W **135** F6
Rome *Ga., U.S.A.* 34°15N 85°10W **113** B1
Rome *Ill., U.S.A.* 40°53N 89°30W **84** C4
Rome *N.Y., U.S.A.* 43°13N 75°27W **88** B5
Rome *Pa., U.S.A.* 41°51N 76°21W **87** C6
Rome City *Ind., U.S.A.* 41°30N 85°23W **85** B5
Romeo *Colo., U.S.A.* 37°10N 105°59W **125** E5
Romeo *Mich., U.S.A.* 42°48N 83°1W **79** G8
Romeoville *Ill., U.S.A.* 41°39N 88°3W **84** B5
Romero *Tex., U.S.A.* 35°44N 102°56W **108** B5
Romeroville *N. Mex., U.S.A.* 35°31N 105°15W **131** B5
Romita *Guanajuato, Mexico* 20°53N 101°31W **174** B6
Romney *W. Va., U.S.A.* 39°21N 78°45W **93** A2
Ronald Reagan National, Washington ✈ (DCA) *Va., U.S.A.* 38°51N 77°2W **99** B3
Ronan *Mont., U.S.A.* 47°32N 114°6W **123** C3
Roncador, Cayos *Colombia* 13°32N 80°4W **182** D3
Ronceverte *W. Va., U.S.A.* 37°45N 80°28W **102** D4
Rondeau Prov. Park △ *Ont., Canada* 42°19N 81°51W **146** E5
Rondout Res. *N.Y., U.S.A.* 41°50N 74°29W **88** D6
Ronge, L. la *Sask., Canada* 55°6N 105°17W **157** E11
Ronkonkoma *N.Y., U.S.A.* 40°48N 73°7W **92** B3
Roodhouse *Ill., U.S.A.* 39°29N 90°24W **84** D3
Roof Butte *Ariz., U.S.A.* 36°28N 109°5W **130** A6
Rooks County ☆ *Kans., U.S.A.* 39°20N 99°15W **82** B4
Roopville *Ga., U.S.A.* 33°27N 85°8W **113** C1
Roosevelt *Ariz., U.S.A.* 33°41N 111°9W **130** D4
Roosevelt *Minn., U.S.A.* 48°48N 95°6W **77** B3
Roosevelt *N.Y., U.S.A.* 40°40N 73°35W **97** B5
Roosevelt *Okla., U.S.A.* 34°51N 99°1W **107** D4
Roosevelt *Utah, U.S.A.* 40°18N 109°59W **129** C6
Roosevelt County ☆ *Mont., U.S.A.* 48°20N 105°20W **123** B12
Roosevelt County ☆ *N. Mex., U.S.A.* 34°0N 103°30W **131** D7
Roosevelt Nat. Forest *Colo., U.S.A.* 40°45N 105°40W **125** B5
Roosevelt Park *Pa., U.S.A.* 39°54N 75°10W **98** B1
Roosville *B.C., Canada* 49°0N 115°3W **153** J5
Root → *N.W.T., Canada* 62°26N 123°18W **157** D8
Root → *Minn., U.S.A.* 43°46N 91°51W **77** G7
Root River Parkway *Wis., U.S.A.* 42°55N 88°0W **94** C1
Roper *N.C., U.S.A.* 35°53N 76°37W **103** C9
Ropesville *Tex., U.S.A.* 33°26N 102°9W **108** D5
Roqueta, I. *Guerrero, Mexico* 16°51N 99°54W **175** F8
Rorketon *Man., Canada* 51°24N 99°35W **151** D12
Rosa, L. *Bahamas* 21°0N 73°30W **183** B5
Rosales *Chihuahua, Mexico* 28°12N 105°33W **169** E10
Rosalia *Wash., U.S.A.* 47°14N 117°22W **120** C8
Rosalind *Alta., Canada* 52°47N 112°27W **153** F8
Rosalind Bank *W. Indies* 16°30N 80°30W **182** C3
Rosamond *Calif., U.S.A.* 34°52N 118°10W **127** J8
Rosamond L. *Calif., U.S.A.* 34°50N 118°4W **127** J8
Rosamorada *Nayarit, Mexico* 22°4N 105°4W **172** E5
Rosario *Sinaloa, Mexico* 22°58N 105°53W **172** E5
Rosario *Sonora, Mexico* 27°50N 109°22W **168** F6
Rosario *Sonora, Mexico* 28°30N 111°30W **168** E4
Rosario, B. *Baja Calif., Mexico* 29°55N 115°45W **166** D3
Rosario, I. el *Tabasco, Mexico* 17°52N 93°48W **178** B3
Rosarito *Baja Calif., Mexico* 28°38N 114°1W **166** E4
Rosarito *Baja Calif., Mexico* 32°20N 117°2W **166** A1
Rosarito *Baja Calif. S., Mexico* 26°27N 111°38W **167** G7
Rosarito, Pta. *Baja Calif., Mexico* 28°33N 114°10W **166** E4
Rosburg *Wash., U.S.A.* 46°20N 123°38W **120** D2
Roscoe *Ill., U.S.A.* 42°25N 89°1W **84** A4
Roscoe *S. Dak., U.S.A.* 45°27N 99°20W **76** E6
Roscoe *Tex., U.S.A.* 32°27N 100°32W **108** E7
Roscommon *Mich., U.S.A.* 44°30N 84°35W **79** E7
Roscommon County ☆ *Mich., U.S.A.* 44°15N 84°40W **79** E7
Rose *Nebr., U.S.A.* 42°11N 99°32W **80** B6
Rose, L. *Fla., U.S.A.* 28°32N 81°30W **115** A1
Rose, Mt. *Nev., U.S.A.* 39°21N 119°55W **128** C1
Rose Blanche-Harbour Le Cou *Nfld. & L., Canada* 47°38N 58°45W **142** E2
Rose Bowl *Calif., U.S.A.* 34°9N 118°10W **133** B4
Rose Bud *Ark., U.S.A.* 35°20N 92°5W **106** C3
Rose City *Mich., U.S.A.* 44°25N 84°7W **79** E7
Rose Creek *Minn., U.S.A.* 43°36N 92°50W **77** G6
Rose Harbour *B.C., Canada* 52°15N 131°10W **154** C3
Rose Hill *Ill., U.S.A.* 39°6N 88°9W **84** D5
Rose Hill *Iowa, U.S.A.* 41°19N 92°28W **81** D6
Rose Hill *Kans., U.S.A.* 37°34N 97°7W **82** D6
Rose Hill *N.C., U.S.A.* 34°50N 78°2W **103** D7
Rose Hill *Va., U.S.A.* 36°40N 83°22W **102** E1
Rose Hill *Va., U.S.A.* 38°47N 77°6W **99** C3
Rose Pk. *Ariz., U.S.A.* 33°25N 109°21W **130** D6
Rose Pt. *B.C., Canada* 54°11N 131°39W **154** A3
Rose Valley *Sask., Canada* 52°19N 103°49W **150** C8
Roseau *Dominica* 15°17N 61°24W **183** C7
Roseau *Minn., U.S.A.* 48°51N 95°46W **77** B3
Roseau → *Minn., U.S.A.* 49°0N 96°30W **77** B2
Roseau County ☆ *Minn., U.S.A.* 48°45N 95°50W **77** B3
Rosebank *N.Y., U.S.A.* 40°36N 74°4W **97** C2
Roseboro *N.C., U.S.A.* 34°58N 78°31W **103** D7
Rosebud *Mo., U.S.A.* 38°23N 91°25W **83** C5
Rosebud *Mont., U.S.A.* 46°16N 106°27W **123** D11
Rosebud *S. Dak., U.S.A.* 43°14N 100°51W **76** G5
Rosebud *Tex., U.S.A.* 31°4N 96°59W **109** F11
Rosebud → *Alta., Canada* 51°25N 112°38W **153** G8
Rosebud County ☆ *Mont., U.S.A.* 46°30N 106°45W **123** D11
Rosebud Creek *Mont., U.S.A.* 46°16N 106°29W **123** D11
Rosebud Indian Reservation *S. Dak., U.S.A.* 43°10N 101°0W **76** G5
Roseburg *Oreg., U.S.A.* 43°13N 123°20W **121** D2
Rosebush *Mich., U.S.A.* 43°42N 84°46W **79** F7
Rosedal La Candelaria *Distrito Federal, Mexico* 19°20N 99°10W **181** B2
Rosedale *Md., U.S.A.* 39°19N 76°30W **99** B2
Rosedale *Miss., U.S.A.* 33°51N 91°2W **111** C2
Rosedale *N.Y., U.S.A.* 40°39N 73°44W **97** C4
Rosedale *Okla., U.S.A.* 34°55N 97°11W **107** D6
Rosedale *W. Va., U.S.A.* 38°44N 80°57W **102** C4
Roseglen *N. Dak., U.S.A.* 47°45N 101°50W **76** C4
Roseisle *Man., Canada* 49°30N 98°20W **151** F13
Roseland *Ill., U.S.A.* 41°42N 87°37W **95** C3
Roseland *La., U.S.A.* 30°46N 90°31W **110** D5
Roseland *N.J., U.S.A.* 40°49N 74°17W **97** B1
Roseland *Nebr., U.S.A.* 40°28N 98°34W **80** D7
Roselle *N.J., U.S.A.* 40°39N 74°15W **97** C1
Roselle Park *N.J., U.S.A.* 40°39N 74°15W **97** C1
Rosemary *Alta., Canada* 50°46N 112°5W **153** H8
Rosemead *Calif., U.S.A.* 34°4N 118°4W **133** B4
Rosemère *Qué., Canada* 45°38N 73°48W **160** A2
Rosemont *Qué., Canada* 45°34N 73°33W **160** A3
Rosemont *Ill., U.S.A.* 41°59N 87°53W **95** B1
Rosemont *Md., U.S.A.* 39°20N 77°37W **93** A3
Rosemount *Minn., U.S.A.* 44°45N 93°8W **77** F5
Rosenberg *Tex., U.S.A.* 29°34N 95°49W **109** H12
Rosenhayn *N.J., U.S.A.* 39°29N 75°8W **92** C1
Rosepine *La., U.S.A.* 30°55N 93°17W **110** D2
Rosetown *Sask., Canada* 51°35N 107°59W **150** D4
Rosette *Utah, U.S.A.* 41°49N 113°25W **129** B2
Roseville *Calif., U.S.A.* 38°45N 121°17W **126** E5
Roseville *Ill., U.S.A.* 40°44N 90°40W **84** C3
Roseville *Mich., U.S.A.* 42°30N 82°56W **79** G9
Roseville *Minn., U.S.A.* 45°0N 93°9W **94** A2
Roseville *Ohio, U.S.A.* 39°49N 82°5W **86** D4
Roseville *Pa., U.S.A.* 41°52N 76°57W **87** C6
Rosharon *Tex., U.S.A.* 29°21N 95°28W **109** H12
Rosholt *S. Dak., U.S.A.* 45°52N 96°44W **76** E9
Rosholt *Wis., U.S.A.* 44°38N 89°18W **78** D4
Rosiclare *Ill., U.S.A.* 37°26N 88°21W **84** F5
Rosier *Ga., U.S.A.* 32°59N 82°15W **113** D4
Roslindale *Mass., U.S.A.* 42°17N 71°7W **96** B2
Roslyn *N.Y., U.S.A.* 40°47N 73°39W **97** B5
Roslyn *S. Dak., U.S.A.* 45°30N 97°29W **76** E8
Roslyn *Wash., U.S.A.* 47°13N 120°59W **120** C5
Roslyn Estates *N.Y., U.S.A.* 40°47N 73°39W **97** B5
Roslyn Harbor *N.Y., U.S.A.* 40°48N 73°39W **97** B5
Rosman *N.C., U.S.A.* 35°9N 82°49W **103** C3
Ross *N. Dak., U.S.A.* 48°19N 102°33W **76** B3
Ross → *Yukon, Canada* 61°59N 132°25W **157** D6
Ross Barnett Res. *Miss., U.S.A.* 32°24N 90°4W **111** D3
Ross County ☆ *Ohio, U.S.A.* 39°20N 82°59W **86** D4
Ross L. *Wash., U.S.A.* 48°44N 121°4W **120** B4
Ross Lake Nat. Recr. Area △ *Wash., U.S.A.* 48°43N 121°4W **120** B4
Ross River *Yukon, Canada* 62°30N 131°30W **157** D6
Rossburg *Ohio, U.S.A.* 40°17N 84°38W **86** C2
Rossburn *Man., Canada* 50°40N 100°49W **151** E11
Rosseau *Ont., Canada* 45°16N 79°39W **146** B7
Rosseau, L. *Ont., Canada* 45°10N 79°35W **146** B7
Rossford *Ohio, U.S.A.* 41°36N 83°34W **86** B3
Rossie *Iowa, U.S.A.* 43°1N 95°11W **81** B3
Rossignol, L. *Qué., Canada* 52°43N 73°40W **143** C3
Rossignol L. *N.S., Canada* 44°12N 65°10W **141** J4
Rossiter *Pa., U.S.A.* 40°54N 78°56W **87** D4
Rossland *B.C., Canada* 49°6N 117°50W **155** F17
Rosslyn *Va., U.S.A.* 38°53N 77°4W **99** B3
Rosslyn Farms *Pa., U.S.A.* 40°23N 80°5W **98** B1
Rossmore *Ont., Canada* 44°8N 77°23W **147** C9
Rossport *Ont., Canada* 48°50N 87°30W **149** D9
Rosston *Ark., U.S.A.* 33°36N 93°17W **106** E2
Rosston *Okla., U.S.A.* 36°49N 99°56W **107** B4
Rossville *Baltimore, U.S.A.* 39°20N 76°28W **99** A3
Rossville *Ga., U.S.A.* 34°59N 85°17W **113** B1
Rossville *Ill., U.S.A.* 40°23N 87°40W **84** C6
Rossville *Ind., U.S.A.* 40°25N 86°36W **85** C4
Rossville *Kans., U.S.A.* 39°8N 95°57W **82** B8
Rossville *N.Y., U.S.A.* 40°33N 74°12W **97** C1
Rosthern *Sask., Canada* 52°40N 106°20W **150** C5
Roswell *Ga., U.S.A.* 34°2N 84°22W **113** B2
Roswell *N. Mex., U.S.A.* 33°24N 104°32W **131** D6
Rota *N. Marianas* 14°9N 145°12E **184** a
Rotan *Tex., U.S.A.* 32°51N 100°28W **108** E7
Rothesay *N.B., Canada* 45°23N 66°0W **141** H3
Rothrock State Forest *Pa., U.S.A.* 40°43N 77°49W **87** D5
Rothsay *Minn., U.S.A.* 46°28N 96°17W **77** D2
Rothschild *Wis., U.S.A.* 44°53N 89°37W **78** D4
Rothwell Heights *Ont., Canada* 45°27N 75°37W **160** A2
Rotonda *Fla., U.S.A.* 26°53N 82°17W **114** E6
Rotterdam *N.Y., U.S.A.* 42°48N 74°1W **88** C6
Rouge → *Qué., Canada* 45°17N 74°10W **144** F8

Rouge Hill Ont., Canada 43°48N 79°6W 161 A4
Rouge-Matawie, Réserve Faunique △ Qué., Canada 46°51N 74°31W 145 E8
Rough → Ky., U.S.A. 37°29N 87°8W 104 C5
Rough River L. Ky., U.S.A. 37°37N 86°30W 104 C6
Rouleau Sask., Canada 50°10N 104°56W 150 E7
Roulette Pa., U.S.A. 41°47N 78°9W 87 C4
Round Hill Alta, Canada 53°10N 112°38W 153 E8
Round Hill N.S., Canada 44°46N 65°24W 141 J4
Round Hill Va., U.S.A. 39°8N 77°46W 93 A3
Round L. Ont., Canada 45°38N 77°30W 147 B9
Round Lake Minn., U.S.A. 43°32N 95°28W 77 G3
Round Mountain Nev., U.S.A. 38°43N 117°4W 128 D3
Round Mountain Tex., U.S.A. 30°26N 98°21W 109 G9
Round Oak Ga., U.S.A. 33°7N 83°37W 113 C3
Round Pond Nfld. & L., Canada 48°11N 56°0W 142 D4
Round Rock Ariz., U.S.A. 36°31N 109°28W 130 A6
Round Rock Tex., U.S.A. 30°31N 97°41W 109 G10
Round Top Tex., U.S.A. 30°4N 96°42W 109 G11
Round Valley Indian Reservation Calif., U.S.A. 39°50N 123°20W 126 D3
Round Valley Res. N.J., U.S.A. 40°37N 74°51W 92 B2
Roundup Mont., U.S.A. 46°27N 108°33W 123 D9
Rouses Point N.Y., U.S.A. 44°59N 73°22W 89 B1
Rouseville Pa., U.S.A. 41°28N 79°42W 87 C3
Routhierville Qué., Canada 48°11N 67°9W 140 E2
Routt County ☆ Colo., U.S.A. 40°30N 107°0W 125 B4
Routt Nat. Forest Colo., U.S.A. 40°45N 107°0W 125 B4
Rouvray, L. Qué., Canada 49°18N 70°49W 145 B12
Rouyn-Noranda Qué., Canada 48°20N 79°0W 144 C3
Rouzerville Pa., U.S.A. 39°44N 77°32W 93 A3
Rover Tenn., U.S.A. 35°40N 86°36W 104 E6
Rowan Iowa, U.S.A. 42°45N 93°33W 81 C5
Rowan County ☆ Ky., U.S.A. 38°10N 83°25W 105 B9
Rowan County ☆ N.C., U.S.A. 35°40N 80°30W 103 C5
Rowe N. Mex., U.S.A. 35°30N 105°41W 131 B5
Rowena Tex., U.S.A. 31°39N 100°3W 109 F7
Rowland N.C., U.S.A. 34°32N 79°18W 103 D6
Rowlesburg W. Va., U.S.A. 39°21N 79°40W 102 B5
Rowley Iowa, U.S.A. 42°22N 91°51W 81 C7
Rowley Utah, U.S.A. 40°54N 112°46W 129 C3
Rowley I. N.W.T., Canada 69°6N 77°52W 158 D10
Roxana Del., U.S.A. 38°30N 75°10W 93 B5
Roxboro Qué., Canada 45°30N 73°48W 160 A2
Roxboro N.C., U.S.A. 36°24N 78°59W 103 B7
Roxbury Conn., U.S.A. 41°45N 73°11W 91 C1
Roxbury Kans., U.S.A. 38°33N 97°26W 82 C6
Roxbury Mass., U.S.A. 42°19N 71°5W 96 B2
Roxbury N.Y., U.S.A. 42°17N 74°34W 88 C6
Roxbury N.Y., U.S.A. 40°33N 73°53W 97 C3
Roxbury Vt., U.S.A. 44°8N 72°44W 89 B2
Roxie Miss., U.S.A. 31°30N 91°4W 111 E2
Roxton Tex., U.S.A. 33°33N 95°44W 109 D12
Roxton Falls Qué., Canada 45°34N 72°31W 145 F10
Roxton Pond Qué., Canada 45°28N 72°40W 145 F10
Roy Mont., U.S.A. 47°20N 108°58W 123 C9
Roy N. Mex., U.S.A. 35°57N 104°12W 131 B6
Roy Utah, U.S.A. 41°10N 112°2W 129 B3
Roy Wash., U.S.A. 47°0N 122°33W 120 D3
Royal Iowa, U.S.A. 43°4N 95°17W 81 B3
Royal, Mt. Ont., Canada 49°56N 88°48W 148 C8
Royal Center Ind., U.S.A. 40°52N 86°30W 85 C4
Royal City Wash., U.S.A. 46°54N 119°38W 120 D6
Royal Geographical Society Is. Nunavut, Canada 68°56N 100°15W 158 D5
Royal Oak B.C., Canada 48°29N 123°23W 155 G11
Royal Oak Md., U.S.A. 38°44N 76°11W 93 B4
Royal Oak Mich., U.S.A. 42°30N 83°9W 79 G8
Royal Palm Beach Fla., U.S.A. 26°42N 80°14W 114 E8
Royale, Isle Mich., U.S.A. 48°0N 88°54W 79 B3
Royalston Mass., U.S.A. 42°40N 72°12W 91 B2
Royalton Minn., U.S.A. 45°50N 94°18W 77 E4
Royalty Tex., U.S.A. 31°22N 102°52W 108 F5
Royersford Pa., U.S.A. 40°11N 75°33W 92 B1
Royse City Tex., U.S.A. 32°59N 96°20W 109 E11
Royston Ga., U.S.A. 34°17N 83°7W 113 B3
Roza Canal Wash., U.S.A. 46°35N 120°23W 120 D5
Rozel Kans., U.S.A. 38°12N 99°24W 82 C4
Rozet Wyo., U.S.A. 44°17N 105°12W 124 B7
Rubonia Tampa, U.S.A. 27°34N 82°33W 115 D3
Ruby Alaska, U.S.A. 64°45N 155°30W 135 D9
Ruby Beach = Jacksonville Beach Fla., U.S.A. 30°17N 81°24W 114 A7
Ruby Dome Nev., U.S.A. 40°37N 115°28W 128 B5
Ruby L. Nev., U.S.A. 40°10N 115°28W 128 B5
Ruby Lake Nat. Wildlife Refuge △ Nev., U.S.A. 40°12N 115°28W 128 B5
Ruby Mts. Nev., U.S.A. 40°30N 115°28W 128 B5
Ruby Valley Nev., U.S.A. 40°30N 115°21W 128 B5
Rudolph Wis., U.S.A. 44°30N 89°48W 78 D4
Rudy Ark., U.S.A. 35°31N 94°16W 106 C1
Rudyard Mich., U.S.A. 46°14N 84°36W 79 C7
Rudyard Mont., U.S.A. 48°34N 110°33W 123 B7
Ruel Ont., Canada 47°15N 81°28W 149 E15
Ruffling Pt. Br. Virgin Is. 18°44N 64°27W 184 G18
Rufus Oreg., U.S.A. 45°42N 120°44W 121 B5
Rugby N. Dak., U.S.A. 48°22N 100°0W 76 B6
Rugby Tenn., U.S.A. 35°12N 90°0W 117 A2
Ruidosa Tex., U.S.A. 29°59N 104°41W 108 H3
Ruidoso N. Mex., U.S.A. 33°20N 105°41W 131 D5
Ruidoso Downs N. Mex., U.S.A. 33°20N 105°32W 131 D5
Ruisseau-Vert Qué., Canada 49°24N 68°28W 145 B14
Ruiz Cortines Sinaloa, Mexico 25°41N 108°42W 172 B2
Rule Tex., U.S.A. 33°11N 99°54W 109 D8
Ruleville Miss., U.S.A. 33°44N 90°33W 111 C3
Rulo Nebr., U.S.A. 40°3N 95°26W 80 D10
Rum → Minn., U.S.A. 45°11N 93°23W 77 E5
Rum Cay Bahamas 23°40N 74°58W 183 B5
Rumbley Md., U.S.A. 38°6N 75°51W 93 B5
Rumford Maine, U.S.A. 44°33N 70°33W 90 D3
Rumney N. Dak., U.S.A. 43°47N 71°49W 89 C3
Rump Mt. Maine, U.S.A. 45°12N 71°4W 90 C2
Rumsey Alta, Canada 51°51N 112°48W 153 G8
Rumson N.J., U.S.A. 40°23N 74°0W 92 B3
Runge Tex., U.S.A. 28°53N 97°43W 109 J10
Runnells Iowa, U.S.A. 41°31N 93°21W 81 D5
Runnels County ☆ Tex., U.S.A. 31°51N 99°57W 109 F8
Running Water → Tex., U.S.A. 34°0N 101°30W 108 D6
Rupert Idaho, U.S.A. 42°37N 113°41W 122 G5
Rupert Vt., U.S.A. 43°16N 73°13W 89 C1
Rupert → Qué., Canada 51°29N 78°45W 143 C2
Rupert B. Qué., Canada 51°35N 79°0W 143 C2
Rupert House = Waskaganish Qué., Canada 51°30N 78°40W 143 C2

Rural Retreat Va., U.S.A. 36°54N 81°17W 102 E3
Rusagonis N.B., Canada 45°48N 66°37W 141 H3
Rush Ky., U.S.A. 38°20N 82°46W 105 B10
Rush Center Kans., U.S.A. 38°28N 99°19W 82 C4
Rush City Minn., U.S.A. 45°41N 92°58W 77 E6
Rush County ☆ Ind., U.S.A. 39°35N 85°58W 85 E5
Rush County ☆ Kans., U.S.A. 38°30N 99°15W 82 C4
Rush Cr. → Colo., U.S.A. 38°22N 102°32W 125 D8
Rush L. Ont., Canada 47°47N 82°11W 149 E14
Rush Lake Sask., Canada 50°24N 107°24W 150 E4
Rush Springs Okla., U.S.A. 34°47N 97°58W 107 D6
Rush Valley Utah, U.S.A. 40°22N 112°27W 129 C3
Rushford Minn., U.S.A. 43°49N 91°46W 77 G7
Rushoon Nfld. & L., Canada 47°21N 54°55W 142 E6
Rushville Ill., U.S.A. 40°7N 90°34W 84 C3
Rushville Ind., U.S.A. 39°37N 85°27W 85 E5
Rushville Mo., U.S.A. 39°35N 95°1W 83 B1
Rushville Nebr., U.S.A. 42°43N 102°28W 80 B3
Rusk Tex., U.S.A. 31°48N 95°9W 109 F12
Rusk County ☆ Tex., U.S.A. 32°9N 94°48W 109 E13
Rusk County ☆ Wis., U.S.A. 45°25N 91°10W 78 C2
Ruskin Fla., U.S.A. 27°43N 82°26W 115 C4
Ruskin Nebr., U.S.A. 40°9N 97°52W 80 D8
Ruso N. Dak., U.S.A. 47°50N 100°56W 76 C6
Russell Qué., Canada 45°18N 75°19W 144 F7
Russell Fla., U.S.A. 30°3N 81°45W 114 A7
Russell Iowa, U.S.A. 40°59N 93°12W 81 E5
Russell Kans., U.S.A. 38°54N 98°52W 82 C5
Russell Ky., U.S.A. 38°31N 82°43W 105 B10
Russell Minn., U.S.A. 44°19N 95°57W 77 F3
Russell, L. N.W.T., Canada 75°15N 117°40W 156 A9
Russell Cave Nat. Monument △ Ala., U.S.A. 34°59N 85°49W 112 B5
Russell County ☆ Ala., U.S.A. 32°18N 85°10W 112 D5
Russell County ☆ Kans., U.S.A. 39°0N 98°45W 82 C5
Russell County ☆ Ky., U.S.A. 37°0N 85°0W 105 C7
Russell County ☆ Va., U.S.A. 37°0N 82°0W 102 E3
Russell Cr. → Ky., U.S.A. 37°14N 85°30W 105 C7
Russell L. N.W.T., Canada 74°0N 98°25W 158 C6
Russell L. = Richard B. Russell L. Ga., U.S.A. 34°2N 82°38W 113 B4
Russell Springs Kans., U.S.A. 38°55N 101°11W 82 C2
Russell Springs Ky., U.S.A. 37°3N 85°5W 105 C7
Russellville Ala., U.S.A. 34°30N 87°44W 112 B3
Russellville Ark., U.S.A. 35°17N 93°8W 106 C2
Russellville Ky., U.S.A. 36°51N 86°53W 104 D6
Russellville Mo., U.S.A. 38°31N 92°26W 83 C4
Russellville Ohio, U.S.A. 38°52N 83°47W 86 E3
Russellville Pa., U.S.A. 39°51N 75°57W 93 A5
Russellville Tenn., U.S.A. 36°15N 83°12W 105 D9
Russian → Calif., U.S.A. 38°27N 123°8W 126 E3
Russian Mission Alaska, U.S.A. 61°47N 161°19W 135 F7
Russiaville Ind., U.S.A. 40°25N 86°16W 85 C4
Rustburg Va., U.S.A. 37°17N 79°6W 102 D5
Ruston La., U.S.A. 32°32N 92°38W 110 B3
Ruth Miss., U.S.A. 31°23N 90°19W 111 E3
Ruth Nev., U.S.A. 39°17N 114°59W 128 C6
Rutherford N.J., U.S.A. 40°49N 74°6W 97 B2
Rutherford Tenn., U.S.A. 36°8N 88°59W 104 D4
Rutherford County ☆ N.C., U.S.A. 35°20N 81°50W 103 C4
Rutherford County ☆ Tenn., U.S.A. 35°51N 86°24W 104 E6
Rutherford Fork → Tenn., U.S.A. 36°16N 89°1W 104 D3
Rutherfordton N.C., U.S.A. 35°22N 81°58W 103 C4
Ruthsburg Md., U.S.A. 39°0N 75°58W 93 B5
Ruthton Minn., U.S.A. 44°11N 96°6W 77 F2
Ruthven Va., U.S.A. 43°8N 94°54W 81 B3
Rutland Ill., U.S.A. 40°59N 89°3W 84 C4
Rutland Mass., U.S.A. 42°23N 71°57W 91 B3
Rutland N. Dak., U.S.A. 46°3N 97°30W 76 D8
Rutland Ohio, U.S.A. 39°3N 82°8W 86 D4
Rutland S. Dak., U.S.A. 44°5N 96°58W 76 F9
Rutland Vt., U.S.A. 43°37N 72°58W 89 C2
Rutland County ☆ Vt., U.S.A. 43°35N 73°0W 89 C1
Rutledge Ga., U.S.A. 33°38N 83°37W 113 C3
Rutledge Mo., U.S.A. 46°16N 92°52W 77 D6
Rutledge Tenn., U.S.A. 36°17N 83°31W 105 D9
Ruxton Baltimore, U.S.A. 39°24N 76°38W 99 A2
Ryan Iowa, U.S.A. 42°21N 91°29W 81 C7
Ryan Okla., U.S.A. 34°1N 97°57W 107 D6
Ryan Park Wyo., U.S.A. 41°19N 106°31W 124 E6
Ryans B. Nfld. & L., Canada 59°35N 64°33W 143 B5
Rycroft Alta., Canada 55°45N 118°40W 152 C2
Ryder N. Dak., U.S.A. 47°55N 101°40W 76 C4
Ryderwood Wash., U.S.A. 46°23N 123°3W 120 D2
Rye Ark., U.S.A. 33°45N 91°59W 106 C4
Rye Colo., U.S.A. 37°55N 104°56W 125 E6
Rye N.H., U.S.A. 42°59N 70°50W 89 C4
Rye Beach N.H., U.S.A. 42°59N 70°46W 89 C4
Rye Patch Res. Nev., U.S.A. 40°28N 118°19W 128 B2
Ryegate Mont., U.S.A. 46°18N 109°15W 123 D8
Ryley Alta., Canada 53°17N 112°26W 152 E8

S

Saanich B.C., Canada 48°29N 123°26W 155 G11
Saba W. Indies 17°38N 63°14W 183 C7
Sabana, Arch. de Cuba 23°0N 80°0W 182 B3
Sábana de la Mar Dom. Rep. 19°7N 69°24W 183 C6
Sábana Grande Guerrero, Mexico 18°10N 99°33W 175 D8
Sábana Grande Zacatecas, Mexico 24°30N 101°45W 173 C9
Sabana Grande Puerto Rico 18°5N 66°58W 184 G16
Sabancuy Campeche, Mexico 18°58N 91°11W 179 D7
Sabaneta Pt. N. Marianas 15°17N 145°49E 184 c
Sabanilla Tabasco, Mexico 17°20N 92°38W 178 B4
Sabetha Kans., U.S.A. 39°54N 95°48W 82 B8
Sabin Minn., U.S.A. 46°47N 96°39W 77 D2
Sabina Ohio, U.S.A. 39°29N 83°38W 86 D3
Sabinal Tex., U.S.A. 29°19N 99°28W 109 H8
Sabinas Coahuila, Mexico 27°51N 101°7W 170 C3
Sabinas → Coahuila, Mexico 27°37N 100°42W 170 C4
Sabinas → Nuevo León, Mexico 26°50N 99°55W 170 D5
Sabinas Hidalgo Nuevo León, Mexico 26°30N 100°10W 170 D4
Sabine → La., U.S.A. 29°59N 93°47W 110 E2
Sabine County ☆ Tex., U.S.A. 31°20N 93°51W 109 F14
Sabine L. La., U.S.A. 29°53N 93°51W 110 E2
Sabine Nat. Forest Tex., U.S.A. 31°38N 94°0W 109 F14
Sabine Nat. Wildlife Refuge △ La., U.S.A. 29°52N 93°30W 110 E2
Sabine Parish ☆ La., U.S.A. 31°38N 93°39W 110 C3
Sabine Pass Tex., U.S.A. 29°44N 93°54W 109 H14
Sabinoso N. Mex., U.S.A. 35°42N 104°34W 131 B6
Sable → Qué., Canada 55°30N 68°21W 143 B4
Sable, C. Canada 43°29N 65°38W 141 K4
Sable, C. Fla., U.S.A. 25°9N 81°8W 114 F7
Sable River N.S., Canada 43°51N 65°3W 141 K4

Sables, R. aux → Ont., Canada 46°13N 82°3W 146 A4
Sabourin, L. Qué., Canada 47°58N 77°41W 144 D5
Sabula Iowa, U.S.A. 42°4N 90°10W 81 C8
Sabula Mo., U.S.A. 38°1N 93°43W 83 D4
Sac → Mo., U.S.A. 38°1N 93°43W 83 D4
Sac and Fox Indian Reservation U.S.A. 39°59N 95°31W 82 B8
Sac and Fox/Mesquakie Indian Reservation Iowa, U.S.A. 41°59N 92°39W 81 D6
Sac City Iowa, U.S.A. 42°25N 95°0W 81 C3
Sac County ☆ Iowa, U.S.A. 42°25N 95°5W 81 C3
Sacajawea, L. Wash., U.S.A. 46°20N 118°45W 120 D7
Sacajawea Peak Oreg., U.S.A. 45°15N 117°17W 121 B8
Sacalum Yucatán, Mexico 20°29N 89°35W 179 B4
Sacaton Ariz., U.S.A. 33°5N 111°44W 130 D4
Sachigo → Ont., Canada 55°6N 88°58W 159 F8
Sachigo, L. Ont., Canada 53°50N 92°12W 159 G7
Sachs Harbour N.W.T., Canada 71°59N 125°15W 156 B7
Sackets Harbor N.Y., U.S.A. 43°57N 76°7W 88 B4
Sackville N.B., Canada 45°54N 64°22W 141 H5
Saco Ala., U.S.A. 31°57N 85°49W 112 C5
Saco Maine, U.S.A. 43°30N 70°27W 90 E3
Saco Mont., U.S.A. 48°28N 107°21W 123 B10
Saco → Maine, U.S.A. 43°28N 70°23W 90 E3
Sacramento Coahuila, Mexico 27°1N 101°41W 170 C3
Sacramento Calif., U.S.A. 38°35N 121°29W 126 E5
Sacramento Ky., U.S.A. 37°25N 87°16W 104 C5
Sacramento N. Mex., U.S.A. 32°48N 105°34W 131 E5
Sacramento → Calif., U.S.A. 38°3N 121°56W 126 E5
Sacramento County ☆ Calif., U.S.A. 38°20N 121°20W 126 E5
Sacramento Int. ✈ (SMF) Calif., U.S.A. 38°42N 121°35W 126 E5
Sacramento Mts. N. Mex., U.S.A. 32°30N 105°30W 131 E5
Sacramento Valley Calif., U.S.A. 39°30N 122°0W 126 D5
Sacramento Wash → Ariz., U.S.A. 34°43N 114°28W 130 C1
Sacré-Coeur Qué., Canada 48°14N 69°48W 145 C13
Saddle Brook N.J., U.S.A. 40°53N 74°5W 97 A2
Saddle Mt. Oreg., U.S.A. 45°58N 123°41W 121 B2
Saddle Mt. Wyo., U.S.A. 44°43N 109°56W 124 B3
Saddle Mts. Wash., U.S.A. 46°55N 120°0W 120 D5
Saddle Rock N.Y., U.S.A. 40°47N 73°44W 97 B4
Sadieville Ky., U.S.A. 38°23N 84°32W 105 B8
Sadorus Ill., U.S.A. 39°58N 88°21W 84 D5
Saegertown Pa., U.S.A. 41°43N 80°9W 87 C2
Safety Harbor Tampa, U.S.A. 27°59N 82°41W 115 A2
Safford Ariz., U.S.A. 32°50N 109°43W 130 E6
Sag Harbor N.Y., U.S.A. 41°0N 72°18W 91 D2
Sagadahoc County ☆ Maine, U.S.A. 44°0N 70°0W 90 E4
Sagamore Mass., U.S.A. 41°45N 70°33W 91 C4
Sagamore Hill Nat. Historic Site △ N.Y., U.S.A. 40°53N 73°30W 88 E7
Sagamore Hills Ohio, U.S.A. 41°18N 81°34W 98 B2
Saganaga L. Ont., Canada 48°14N 90°52W 148 D6
Saganash L. Ont., Canada 49°4N 82°35W 149 C14
Saganashkee Slough Ill., U.S.A. 41°41N 87°53W 95 C1
Sagavanirktok → Alaska, U.S.A. 70°19N 147°53W 135 A11
Sage Wyo., U.S.A. 41°49N 110°58W 124 E2
Sage Cr. → Mont., U.S.A. 47°16N 109°43W 123 C8
Sagerton Tex., U.S.A. 33°5N 99°58W 109 D8
Sageville Iowa, U.S.A. 42°32N 90°43W 81 C8
Saginaw Mich., U.S.A. 43°26N 83°56W 79 F8
Saginaw Tex., U.S.A. 32°51N 97°21W 116 A1
Saginaw → Mich., U.S.A. 43°39N 83°51W 79 F8
Saginaw B. Mich., U.S.A. 43°50N 83°40W 79 F8
Saginaw County ☆ Mich., U.S.A. 43°20N 84°0W 79 F7
Saglek L. Nfld. & L., Canada 58°30N 63°0W 143 B5
Saglek Fd. Nfld. & L., Canada 58°29N 63°15W 143 B5
Saglouc = Salluit Qué., Canada 62°14N 75°38W 143 A2
Sagola Mich., U.S.A. 46°5N 88°5W 79 C3
Sagua la Grande Cuba 22°50N 80°10W 182 B3
Saguache Colo., U.S.A. 38°5N 106°8W 125 D4
Saguache County ☆ Colo., U.S.A. 38°10N 106°15W 125 D4
Saguaro Nat. Park △ Ariz., U.S.A. 32°12N 110°38W 130 E5
Saguenay → Qué., Canada 48°17N 70°17W 145 C12
Saguenay, Parc du △ Qué., Canada 48°17N 70°17W 145 C12
Sahuaripa Sonora, Mexico 29°3N 109°14W 168 D6
Sahuarita Ariz., U.S.A. 31°57N 110°58W 130 F5
Sahuaro Sonora, Mexico 31°6N 112°58W 168 B3
Sahuayo de Díaz Michoacan, Mexico 20°4N 102°43W 174 B5
Sailor Springs Ill., U.S.A. 38°46N 88°22W 84 E5
Sailor's Creek Battlefield Historic State Park △ Va., U.S.A. 37°17N 78°12W 102 D6
Sain Alto Zacatecas, Mexico 23°35N 103°15W 173 D7
St-Adalbert Qué., Canada 46°51N 69°53W 145 E13
St-Agapit Qué., Canada 46°34N 71°26W 145 E11
St. Alban's Nfld. & L., Canada 47°51N 55°50W 142 E5
St. Albans N.Y., U.S.A. 40°41N 73°45W 97 B4
St. Albans Vt., U.S.A. 44°49N 73°5W 89 B1
St. Albans W. Va., U.S.A. 38°23N 81°50W 102 C3
St. Albert Alta., Canada 53°37N 113°32W 152 E7
St-Alexandre Qué., Canada 47°41N 69°38W 145 D13
St-Alexandre Qué., Canada 45°14N 73°7W 89 A1
St-Alexis-des-Monts Qué., Canada 46°28N 73°8W 145 E9
St-Ambroise Qué., Canada 48°33N 71°20W 145 C11
St-Anaclet Qué., Canada 48°29N 68°26W 145 C14
St. André N.B., Canada 47°8N 67°45W 141 F2
St-André Qué., Canada 47°41N 69°44W 145 D13
St-André-Avellin Qué., Canada 45°43N 75°3W 144 F7
St-André-Est Qué., Canada 45°34N 74°20W 145 F8
St. Andrew Sd. Ga., U.S.A. 30°58N 81°25W 113 F5
St. Andrews N.B., Canada 45°7N 67°5W 141 H2
St. Andrew's Nfld. & L., Canada 47°46N 59°15W 142 E1
St. Andrews S.C., U.S.A. 32°47N 80°0W 103 F5
St. Andrews B. Fla., U.S.A. 30°5N 85°52W 114 A3
St-Anicet Qué., Canada 45°8N 74°22W 145 F8
St. Anne Ill., U.S.A. 41°1N 87°43W 84 B6
St. Anns B. N.S., Canada 46°22N 60°25W 141 G9
St. Ann's Bay Jamaica 18°26N 77°12W 182 C4
St-Anselme Qué., Canada 46°37N 70°58W 145 E12
St. Ansgar Iowa, U.S.A. 43°23N 92°55W 81 B6
St. Anthony Nfld. & L., Canada 51°22N 55°35W 142 A5
St. Anthony Idaho, U.S.A. 43°58N 111°41W 122 F7
St. Anthony Minn., U.S.A. 45°1N 93°13W 94 A2
St-Antoine N.B., Canada 46°22N 64°45W 141 G5
St-Antonin Qué., Canada 47°46N 69°29W 145 D13
St-Aubert Qué., Canada 47°11N 70°13W 145 D12
St-Augustin Qué., Canada 51°13N 58°38W 142 A2
St. Augustine Fla., U.S.A. 29°54N 81°19W 114 B7
St. Augustine Beach Fla., U.S.A. 29°51N 81°16W 114 B7
St. Augustine Shores Fla., U.S.A. 29°49N 81°19W 114 B7
St-Barthélemy W. Indies 17°50N 62°50W 183 C7
St-Basile N.B., Canada 47°21N 68°14W 141 F1
St-Basile Qué., Canada 46°45N 71°49W 145 E11
St. Benedict Sask., Canada 52°34N 105°23W 150 D7

St. Benedict Kans., U.S.A. 39°53N 96°6W 82 B7
St. Bernard La., U.S.A. 29°52N 89°51W 117 C3
St. Bernard Parish ☆ La., U.S.A. 29°55N 89°10W 110 E6
St. Bernard's-Jacques Fontaine Nfld. & L., Canada 47°31N 54°55W 142 E6
St. Brendan's Nfld. & L., Canada 48°52N 53°40W 142 D7
St. Bride's Nfld. & L., Canada 46°56N 54°10W 142 F6
St. Brieux Sask., Canada 52°38N 104°54W 150 D7
St-Bruno Qué., Canada 48°28N 71°39W 145 C11
St-Bruno-de-Guigues Qué., Canada 47°28N 79°26W 144 D3
St-Bruno-de-Montarville Qué., Canada 45°32N 73°21W 160 A4
St-Casimir Qué., Canada 46°40N 72°8W 145 E10
St. Catharines Ont., Canada 43°10N 79°15W 146 D7
St. Catherines I. Ga., U.S.A. 31°40N 81°10W 113 E5
St. Charles Ark., U.S.A. 34°23N 91°8W 106 C4
St. Charles Idaho, U.S.A. 42°7N 111°23W 122 G7
St. Charles Ill., U.S.A. 41°54N 88°19W 84 B5
St. Charles Iowa, U.S.A. 41°17N 93°49W 81 D5
St. Charles Ky., U.S.A. 37°11N 87°33W 104 C5
St. Charles Md., U.S.A. 38°36N 76°56W 93 B4
St. Charles Mich., U.S.A. 43°18N 84°9W 79 F7
St. Charles Minn., U.S.A. 43°58N 92°4W 77 G6
St. Charles Mo., U.S.A. 38°47N 90°29W 83 C6
St. Charles S. Dak., U.S.A. 43°5N 99°6W 76 G6
St. Charles Va., U.S.A. 36°48N 83°4W 102 E1
St-Charles-Borromée Qué., Canada 46°3N 73°28W 145 E9
St. Charles County ☆ Mo., U.S.A. 38°45N 90°40W 83 C6
St-Charles-de-Drummond Qué., Canada 45°54N 72°28W 145 F10
St. Charles Parish ☆ La., U.S.A. 29°59N 90°25W 110 E5
St. Christopher-Nevis = St. Kitts & Nevis ■ W. Indies 17°20N 62°40W 183 C7
St-Chrysostôme Qué., Canada 45°6N 73°46W 145 F9
St. Clair Ga., U.S.A. 33°9N 82°13W 113 C4
St. Clair Mich., U.S.A. 42°50N 82°30W 79 G9
St. Clair Minn., U.S.A. 44°5N 93°51W 77 F5
St. Clair Mo., U.S.A. 38°21N 90°59W 83 C6
St. Clair Pa., U.S.A. 40°43N 76°12W 87 D6
St. Clair → Mich., U.S.A. 42°38N 82°31W 79 G9
St. Clair, L. N. Amer. 42°27N 82°39W 146 E4
St. Clair County ☆ Ala., U.S.A. 33°35N 86°17W 112 C4
St. Clair County ☆ Ill., U.S.A. 38°30N 89°55W 84 E4
St. Clair County ☆ Mich., U.S.A. 43°0N 82°30W 79 G9
St. Clair County ☆ Mo., U.S.A. 38°0N 93°45W 83 C3
St. Clair Shores Mich., U.S.A. 42°30N 82°53W 79 G9
St. Clairsville Ohio, U.S.A. 40°5N 80°54W 86 C5
St. Claude Man., Canada 49°40N 98°20W 151 F13
St. Cloud Fla., U.S.A. 28°15N 81°17W 114 C7
St. Cloud Minn., U.S.A. 45°34N 94°10W 77 E4
St-Coeur de Marie Qué., Canada 48°39N 71°43W 145 C11
St-Côme Qué., Canada 46°16N 73°47W 145 E9
St-Côme-Linière Qué., Canada 46°4N 70°32W 145 E12
St. Croix N.B., Canada 45°34N 67°26W 141 H2
St. Croix U.S. Virgin Is. 17°45N 64°45W 183 C7
St. Croix → Maine, U.S.A. 45°4N 67°5W 141 H2
St. Croix → Wis., U.S.A. 44°45N 92°48W 78 D1
St. Croix, L. Minn., U.S.A. 44°52N 92°45W 77 F6
St. Croix County ☆ Wis., U.S.A. 45°0N 92°20W 78 C1
St. Croix Falls Wis., U.S.A. 45°24N 92°38W 78 C1
St. Croix Flowage Wis., U.S.A. 46°15N 91°56W 78 B2
St. Croix I. Puerto Rico 17°45N 64°45W 184 G18
St. Croix Indian Reservation Wis., U.S.A. 45°46N 92°20W 78 C1
St. Croix Island Int. Historic Site △ N. Amer. 45°8N 67°8W 90 C6
St. Croix Nat. Scenic Riverway △ Wis., U.S.A. 46°6N 91°23W 78 B2
St-Cyrille-de-L'Islet Qué., Canada 47°2N 70°17W 145 D12
St. David Ariz., U.S.A. 31°54N 110°13W 130 F5
St. David Ill., U.S.A. 40°30N 90°3W 84 C3
St. David's Nfld. & L., Canada 48°12N 58°52W 142 D2
St-Dominique-du-Rosaire Qué., Canada 48°46N 78°7W 144 C4
St-Donat Qué., Canada 46°19N 74°13W 145 E8
St. Donatus Iowa, U.S.A. 42°22N 90°33W 81 C8
St. Edward Nebr., U.S.A. 41°34N 97°52W 80 C8
St. Eleanors P.E.I., Canada 46°25N 63°49W 141 G6
St. Elias, Mt. Alaska, U.S.A. 60°18N 140°56W 135 F12
St. Elias Mts. N. Amer. 60°33N 139°28W 157 D5
St. Elizabeth Mo., U.S.A. 38°15N 92°16W 83 C4
St. Elmo Ill., U.S.A. 39°2N 88°51W 84 D5
St-Éloi Qué., Canada 48°2N 69°14W 145 C13
St-Éleuthère Qué., Canada 47°30N 69°15W 145 D13
St-Éphrem-de-Tring Qué., Canada 46°2N 70°59W 145 E12
St. Eugène Ont., Canada 45°30N 74°28W 144 F8
St-Eugène Qué., Canada 47°33N 68°55W 145 D14
St. Eustache Man., Canada 49°59N 97°47W 151 F14
St-Eustache Qué., Canada 45°34N 73°54W 160 A1
St. Eustatius W. Indies 17°20N 63°0W 183 C7
St. Fabien Qué., Canada 48°18N 68°52W 145 C14
St-Faustin-Lac-Carré Qué., Canada 46°7N 74°29W 145 E8
St-Félicien Qué., Canada 48°40N 72°25W 145 C10
St-Félix-de-Valois Qué., Canada 46°10N 73°26W 145 E9
St. Ferdinand = Florissant Mo., U.S.A. 38°47N 90°19W 94 A1
St-Ferdinand Qué., Canada 46°6N 71°34W 145 E11
St. Frances S. Dak., U.S.A. 43°9N 100°54W 76 G5
St. Francis Kans., U.S.A. 39°46N 101°48W 82 B2
St. Francis Maine, U.S.A. 47°10N 68°54W 90 A5
St. Francis Minn., U.S.A. 45°23N 93°22W 77 E5
St. Francis Wis., U.S.A. 42°58N 87°52W 94 C2
St. Francis → Ark., U.S.A. 34°38N 90°36W 106 D4
St. Francis County ☆ Ark., U.S.A. 35°1N 90°47W 106 C4
St. Francisville Ill., U.S.A. 38°36N 87°39W 84 E6
St. Francisville La., U.S.A. 30°47N 91°23W 110 D4
St-François Qué., Canada 46°48N 70°49W 145 E12
St-François → Qué., Canada 46°7N 72°55W 145 E10
St-François, L. Qué., Canada 45°10N 74°22W 145 F8
St. François County ☆ Mo., U.S.A. 37°50N 90°30W 83 D6
St-François-du-Lac Qué., Canada 46°5N 72°50W 145 E10
St. François Mts. Mo., U.S.A. 37°30N 90°35W 83 D6
St-François Xavier Man., Canada 49°55N 97°32W 151 F14
St. Froid, L. Maine, U.S.A. 46°57N 68°37W 90 B5
St-Gabriel Qué., Canada 46°17N 73°24W 145 E9
St. Gabriel La., U.S.A. 30°16N 91°6W 110 D4
St-Gabriel-de-Gaspé Qué., Canada 48°31N 64°32W 140 E5
St-Gaudens Nat. Historic Park △ N.H., U.S.A. 43°30N 72°22W 89 C2
St-Gédéon Qué., Canada 48°30N 71°46W 145 C11
St-Gédéon-de-Beauce Qué., Canada 45°45N 70°40W 145 F12
St. Genevieve County ☆ Mo., U.S.A. 37°50N 90°10W 83 D6
St. George Ont., Canada 43°15N 80°15W 146 D6
St. George Ont., Canada 43°15N 80°15W 146 D6
St. George Kans., U.S.A. 39°12N 96°25W 82 B7
St. George S.C., U.S.A. 33°11N 80°35W 103 E5

St. George *Utah, U.S.A.* 37°6N 113°35W **129** F2
St. George, C. *Nfld. & L., Canada* 48°30N 59°16W **142** D1
St. George, C. *Nfld. & L., Canada* 29°40N 85°5W **114** B3
St. George, Pt. *Calif., U.S.A.* 41°47N 124°15W **126** B2
St. George I. *Alaska, U.S.A.* 56°35N 169°35W **135** H5
St. George I. *Fla., U.S.A.* 29°35N 84°55W **114** B4
St. George's *Grenada* 12°5N 61°43W **183** D7
St. George's B. *Nfld. & L., Canada* 48°24N 58°53W **142** D2
St. Georges *Qué., Canada* 46°8N 70°40W **145** E12
St. George's Bay *N.S., Canada* 45°45N 61°45W **141** H8
St-Godefroi *N.B., Canada* 48°5N 65°6W **141** G4
St. Helen *Mich., U.S.A.* 44°22N 84°25W **79** F7
St. Helena *Calif., U.S.A.* 38°30N 122°28W **126** E4
St. Helena *Nebr., U.S.A.* 42°49N 97°15W **80** B8
St. Helena Parish ☆ *La., U.S.A.* 30°50N 90°40W **110** D5
St. Helena Sd. *S.C., U.S.A.* 32°15N 80°25W **103** F5
St. Helens *Oreg., U.S.A.* 45°52N 122°48W **121** B3
St. Helens, Mt. *Wash., U.S.A.* 46°12N 122°12W **120** D3
St. Henry *Ohio, U.S.A.* 40°25N 84°38W **86** C2
St. Hilaire *Minn., U.S.A.* 48°1N 96°14W **77** B2
St-Hilarion *Qué., Canada* 47°34N 70°24W **145** D12
St-Honoré *Qué., Canada* 48°32N 71°5W **145** C11
St-Hubert *Qué., Canada* 45°29N 73°25W **160** B4
St-Hubert-de-Témiscouata *Qué.,
 Canada* 47°49N 69°9W **145** D13
St-Hyacinthe *Qué., Canada* 45°40N 72°58W **145** F10
St-Ignace *N.B., Canada* 46°42N 65°5W **141** G4
St. Ignace *Mich., U.S.A.* 45°52N 84°44W **79** D7
St. Ignace I. *Ont., Canada* 48°45N 88°50W **149** D9
St. Ignatius *Mont., U.S.A.* 47°19N 114°6W **123** C3
St-Isidore *N.B., Canada* 47°33N 65°2W **141** F4
St-Isidore *Qué., Canada* 45°20N 73°42W **145** F9
St-Jacques *N.B., Canada* 47°26N 68°23W **141** F1
St-Jacques → *Qué., Canada* 45°26N 73°29W **160** B4
St. James *Mich., U.S.A.* 45°45N 85°31W **79** D6
St. James *Minn., U.S.A.* 43°59N 94°38W **77** G4
St. James *Mo., U.S.A.* 38°0N 91°37W **83** D5
St. James *N.Y., U.S.A.* 40°53N 73°9W **91** D1
St. James City *Fla., U.S.A.* 26°29N 82°5W **114** E6
St. James Parish ☆ *La., U.S.A.* 30°1N 90°50W **110** D5
St. Jean *Mich., U.S.A.* 42°22N 83°0W **98** A3
St-Jean → *Qué., Canada* 48°46N 64°26W **140** E5
St-Jean → *Qué., Canada* 50°17N 64°20W **140** C5
St-Jean, L. *Qué., Canada* 48°40N 72°0W **145** C11
St-Jean Baptiste *Man., Canada* 49°15N 97°20W **151** F14
St-Jean-Baptiste-de-Restigouche *N.B.,
 Canada* 47°46N 67°13W **141** F2
St-Jean-de-Dieu *Qué., Canada* 48°0N 69°3W **145** C13
St-Jean-Port-Joli *Qué., Canada* 47°15N 70°13W **145** D12
St-Jean-sur-Richelieu *Qué., Canada* 45°20N 73°20W **145** F9
St-Jérôme *Qué., Canada* 45°47N 74°0W **145** F9
St. Jo *Tex., U.S.A.* 33°42N 97°31W **109** D10
St-Joachim *Qué., Canada* 47°4N 70°50W **145** D12
St. Joe *Ark., U.S.A.* 36°2N 92°48W **106** B3
St. Joe *Idaho, U.S.A.* 47°19N 116°21W **122** B2
St. Joe → *Idaho, U.S.A.* 47°24N 116°45W **122** B2
St. Joe Mt. *Idaho, U.S.A.* 47°25N 116°0W **122** B2
St. Joe Nat. Forest *Idaho, U.S.A.* 47°15N 115°30W **122** B3
St. John *N.B., Canada* 45°20N 66°8W **141** H3
St. John *Kans., U.S.A.* 38°0N 98°46W **82** C5
St. John *Mo., U.S.A.* 38°42N 90°20W **94** A1
St. John *N. Dak., U.S.A.* 48°57N 99°43W **76** B6
St. John *Wash., U.S.A.* 47°6N 117°35W **120** C8
St. John → *N. Amer.* 45°12N 66°5W **141** H3
St. John, C. *Nfld. & L., Canada* 50°0N 55°32W **142** B5
St. John, L. *Nfld. & L., Canada* 48°23N 54°41W **142** D6
St. John B. *Nfld. & L., Canada* 50°55N 57°9W **142** B3
St. John Harbour *N.B., Canada* 45°15N 66°4W **141** H3
St. John I. *Nfld. & L., Canada* 50°49N 57°14W **142** B3
St. John I. *U.S. Virgin Is.* 18°20N 64°42W **184** G18
St. John the Baptist Parish ☆ *La., U.S.A.* 30°3N 90°33W **110** D5
St. John's *Antigua & B.* 17°6N 61°51W **183** C7
St. John's *Nfld. & L., Canada* 47°35N 52°40W **142** E8
St. Johns *Ariz., U.S.A.* 34°30N 109°22W **130** C6
St. Johns *Mich., U.S.A.* 43°0N 84°33W **79** G7
St. Johns *Oreg., U.S.A.* 45°35N 122°45W **132** A1
St. Johns → *Fla., U.S.A.* 30°24N 81°24W **114** A7
St. John's B. *Nfld. & L., Canada* 47°34N 52°42W **142** E8
St. Johns County ☆ *Fla., U.S.A.* 29°45N 81°25W **114** B7
St. John's East *Nfld. & L., Canada* 47°38N 52°42W **142** E8
St. John's North *Nfld. & L., Canada* 47°35N 52°42W **142** E8
St. John's South *Nfld. & L., Canada* 47°30N 52°42W **142** E8
St. Johnsbury *Vt., U.S.A.* 44°25N 72°1W **89** B2
St. Joseph *Ill., U.S.A.* 40°7N 88°2W **84** C4
St. Joseph *La., U.S.A.* 31°55N 91°14W **110** D4
St. Joseph *Mich., U.S.A.* 42°6N 86°29W **79** G5
St. Joseph *Minn., U.S.A.* 45°34N 94°19W **77** E4
St. Joseph *Mo., U.S.A.* 39°46N 94°50W **83** B2
St. Joseph *Tenn., U.S.A.* 35°2N 87°30W **104** E5
St. Joseph → *Ind., U.S.A.* 41°5N 85°58W **85** B5
St. Joseph → *Mich., U.S.A.* 42°7N 86°29W **79** G5
St. Joseph, I. *Ont., Canada* 46°12N 83°58W **146** A3
St. Joseph, L. *Ont., Canada* 51°10N 90°35W **148** A6
St. Joseph B. *Fla., U.S.A.* 29°47N 85°21W **114** B3
St. Joseph County ☆ *Ind., U.S.A.* 41°35N 86°15W **85** B4
St. Joseph Sound *Tampa, U.S.A.* 28°5N 82°48W **115** A2
St-Jude *Qué., Canada* 45°46N 72°59W **145** F10
St. Kitts & Nevis ■ *W. Indies* 17°20N 62°40W **183** C7
St-Lambert *Qué., Canada* 45°30N 73°29W **160** A4
St. Landry Parish ☆ *La., U.S.A.* 30°40N 92°0W **110** D4
St. Laurent *Man., Canada* 50°25N 97°58W **151** E14
St-Laurent *Qué., Canada* 45°30N 73°43W **160** A2
St-Laurent *Nfld. & L., Canada* 46°54N 55°23W **142** F5
St. Lawrence *S. Dak., U.S.A.* 44°31N 98°56W **76** F7
St. Lawrence → *Canada* 49°30N 66°0W **140** D3
St. Lawrence, Gulf of *Canada* 48°25N 62°0W **140** E7
St. Lawrence County ☆ *N.Y., U.S.A.* 44°30N 75°0W **88** A6
St. Lawrence I. *Alaska, U.S.A.* 63°30N 170°30W **135** E5
St. Lawrence Islands Nat. Park △ *Ont.,
 Canada* 44°27N 75°52W **147** C11
St-Lazare *Man., Canada* 50°27N 101°18W **151** E10
St. Leo *Minn., U.S.A.* 44°43N 96°3W **77** F2
St-Léolin *N.B., Canada* 47°46N 65°10W **141** F4
St-Léon-le-Grand *Qué., Canada* 48°23N 67°30W **140** E2
St-Léonard *N.B., Canada* 47°12N 67°58W **141** F2
St-Léonard *Qué., Canada* 45°35N 73°34W **160** A3
St-Léonard-de-Portneuf *Qué., Canada* 46°53N 71°55W **145** E11
St. Lewis → *Nfld. & L., Canada* 52°26N 56°11W **143** C6
St. Libory *Nebr., U.S.A.* 41°5N 98°12W **80** C7

St-Lin-Laurentides *Qué., Canada* 45°51N 73°46W **145** F9
St. Louis *P.E.I., Canada* 46°53N 64°8W **141** G5
St. Louis *Sask., Canada* 52°55N 105°49W **150** C6
St. Louis *Mich., U.S.A.* 43°25N 84°36W **79** F7
St. Louis *Mo., U.S.A.* 38°37N 90°11W **94** B2
St. Louis *Okla., U.S.A.* 35°5N 96°53W **107** C7
St. Louis → *Minn., U.S.A.* 46°44N 92°9W **77** D61
St-Louis, L. *Qué., Canada* 45°24N 73°48W **160** B2
St. Louis County ☆ *Minn., U.S.A.* 47°40N 92°20W **77** C6
St. Louis County ☆ *Mo., U.S.A.* 38°40N 90°25W **83** C6
St-Louis-de-France *Qué., Canada* 46°25N 72°36W **145** E10
St-Louis-de-Kent *N.B., Canada* 46°44N 64°58W **141** G5
St-Louis Lambert Int. ✈ (STL) *Mo.,
 U.S.A.* 38°45N 90°22W **94** A1
St. Louis Park *Minn., U.S.A.* 45°56N 93°21W **94** B1
St. Louisville *Ohio, U.S.A.* 40°10N 82°25W **86** C4
St-Luc *Qué., Canada* 45°22N 73°18W **145** F9
St-Luc-de-Matane *Qué., Canada* 48°48N 67°28W **140** E2
St. Lucia ■ *W. Indies* 14°0N 60°57W **183** D7
St. Lucia Channel *W. Indies* 14°15N 61°0W **183** D7
St. Lucie *Fla., U.S.A.* 27°29N 80°20W **114** D8
St. Lucie Canal *Fla., U.S.A.* 27°10N 80°18W **114** D8
St. Lucie County ☆ *Fla., U.S.A.* 27°25N 80°30W **114** D8
St-Ludger *Qué., Canada* 45°45N 70°42W **145** F12
St-Ludger-de-Milot *Qué., Canada* 48°54N 71°43W **145** C11
St. Lunaire-Griquet *Nfld. & L., Canada* 51°31N 55°28W **142** A5
St. Maarten ☐ *W. Indies* 18°0N 63°5W **183** C7
St-Magloire *Qué., Canada* 46°35N 70°17W **145** E12
St. Malo *Man., Canada* 49°19N 96°57W **151** F15
St-Marc *Haiti* 19°10N 72°41W **183** C5
St. Margarets *N.B., Canada* 46°54N 65°11W **141** G4
St. Maries *Idaho, U.S.A.* 47°19N 116°35W **122** B2
St. Maries → *Idaho, U.S.A.* 47°19N 116°33W **122** B2
St. Marks *Fla., U.S.A.* 30°9N 84°12W **114** A4
St. Marks → *Fla., U.S.A.* 30°8N 84°12W **114** A4
St. Marks Nat. Wildlife Refuge △ *Fla.,
 U.S.A.* 30°7N 84°7W **114** A4
St-Martin *Qué., Canada* 45°35N 73°43W **160** A2
St-Martin, L. *Man., Canada* 51°40N 98°3CW **151** D13
St. Martin I. *Mich., U.S.A.* 45°30N 86°46W **79** D5
St. Martin Parish ☆ *La., U.S.A.* 30°7N 91°50W **110** D4
St. Martins *N.B., Canada* 45°22N 65°34W **141** H4
St-Martinville *La., U.S.A.* 30°7N 91°50W **110** D4
St. Mary *Mo., U.S.A.* 37°53N 89°57W **83** D7
St. Mary → *B.C., Canada* 49°37N 115°58W **153** J5
St. Mary L. *Mont., U.S.A.* 48°39N 113°34W **123** B4
St. Mary Parish ☆ *La., U.S.A.* 29°48N 91°30W **110** E4
St. Mary Res. *Alta., Canada* 49°20N 113°11W **153** J7
St. Marys *Ont., Canada* 43°20N 81°10W **146** D5
St. Mary's *Alaska, U.S.A.* 62°4N 163°10W **135** E7
St. Marys *Ga., U.S.A.* 30°44N 81°33W **113** F5
St. Marys *Iowa, U.S.A.* 41°19N 93°44W **81** D5
St. Marys *Kans., U.S.A.* 39°12N 96°4W **82** B7
St. Marys *Ohio, U.S.A.* 40°33N 84°24W **86** C2
St. Marys *Pa., U.S.A.* 41°26N 78°34W **87** C4
St. Marys *W. Va., U.S.A.* 39°23N 81°12W **102** B3
St. Marys → *N.S., Canada* 45°2N 61°53W **141** H8
St. Marys → *Ga., U.S.A.* 30°43N 81°27W **113** F5
St. Marys → *Ind., U.S.A.* 41°5N 85°8W **85** B5
St. Marys → *W. Va., U.S.A.* 46°0N 83°55W **79** D8
St. Mary's, C. *Nfld. & L., Canada* 46°50N 54°12W **142** F6
St. Mary's Alpine Park △ *B.C., Canada* 49°50N 116°25W **153** J4
St. Marys Bay *N.S., Canada* 44°25N 66°10W **141** J3
St. Mary's City *Md., U.S.A.* 38°11N 76°26W **93** B4
St. Marys County ☆ *Md., U.S.A.* 38°15N 76°40W **93** B4
St. Matthew I. *Alaska, U.S.A.* 60°24N 172°42W **135** F4
St. Matthews *Ky., U.S.A.* 38°15N 85°39W **105** B7
St. Matthews *S.C., U.S.A.* 33°40N 80°46W **103** E5
St-Maurice → *Qué., Canada* 46°21N 72°31W **145** E10
St-Maurice, Réserve Faunique du △ *Qué.,
 Canada* 47°5N 73°15W **145** D9
St. Meinrad *Ind., U.S.A.* 38°10N 86°49W **85** E4
St. Michael *Alaska, U.S.A.* 63°29N 162°2W **135** E7
St. Michael *Minn., U.S.A.* 45°13N 93°40W **77** E5
St. Michaels *Md., U.S.A.* 38°47N 76°14W **93** B4
St-Michel *Qué., Canada* 45°34N 73°37W **160** A3
St-Michel-des-Saints *Qué., Canada* 46°41N 73°55W **145** E9
St-Nazaire *Qué., Canada* 45°44N 72°37W **145** F10
St. Nazianz *Wis., U.S.A.* 44°0N 87°55W **78** E6
St-Nicolas *Qué., Canada* 46°42N 71°24W **145** E11
St-Noël *Qué., Canada* 48°35N 67°50W **140** E2
St-Octave-de-l'Avenir *Qué., Canada* 49°0N 66°33W **140** E3
St. Olaf *Iowa, U.S.A.* 42°56N 91°23W **81** C7
St-Omer *Qué., Canada* 47°3N 69°43W **145** D13
St. Onge *S. Dak., U.S.A.* 44°33N 103°43W **76** F2
St-Ours *Qué., Canada* 45°53N 73°9W **145** F9
St-Pacôme *Qué., Canada* 47°24N 69°58W **145** D13
St-Pamphile *Qué., Canada* 46°58N 69°48W **145** E13
St. Paris *Ohio, U.S.A.* 40°8N 83°58W **86** C3
St-Pascal *Qué., Canada* 47°32N 69°48W **145** D13
St-Patrice *Qué., Canada* 46°22N 77°20W **144** E5
St. Patrick Peak *Mont., U.S.A.* 46°59N 114°51W **123** D3
St. Paul *Alta., Canada* 54°0N 111°17W **152** D9
St. Paul *Alaska, U.S.A.* 57°7N 170°17W **135** H5
St. Paul *Ark., U.S.A.* 35°50N 93°46W **106** C2
St. Paul *Ind., U.S.A.* 39°26N 85°38W **85** D5
St. Paul *Iowa, U.S.A.* 40°46N 91°31W **81** E7
St. Paul *Kans., U.S.A.* 37°31N 95°10W **82** D8
St. Paul *Minn., U.S.A.* 44°56N 93°5W **94** B3
St. Paul *Nebr., U.S.A.* 41°13N 98°27W **80** C7
St. Paul *Va., U.S.A.* 36°54N 82°19W **102** E2
St-Paul → *Qué., Canada* 51°27N 57°42W **143** C6
St-Paul-de-Montminy *Qué., Canada* 46°44N 70°22W **145** E12
St. Paul Downtown ✈ *Minn., U.S.A.* 44°56N 93°3W **94** B3
St. Paul I. *N.S., Canada* 47°12N 60°9W **141** F9
St. Paul I. *Alaska, U.S.A.* 57°10N 170°15W **135** H5
St-Paulin *Qué., Canada* 46°25N 73°1W **145** E9
St. Pauls *Nfld. & L., Canada* 49°52N 57°48W **142** C3
St. Pauls *N.C., U.S.A.* 34°48N 78°58W **103** D7
St. Peter *Ill., U.S.A.* 38°52N 88°51W **84** E5
St. Peter *Minn., U.S.A.* 44°20N 93°57W **77** F5
St. Peters *N.S., Canada* 45°40N 60°53W **141** H9
St. Peters *P.E.I., Canada* 46°25N 62°35W **141** G7
St. Peters *Mo., U.S.A.* 38°48N 90°37W **83** C6
St. Petersburg *Fla., U.S.A.* 27°46N 82°40W **115** C3
St. Petersburg-Clearwater Int. ✈ (PIE) *Tampa,
 U.S.A.* 27°54N 82°41W **115** B2
St-Philémon *Qué., Canada* 46°41N 70°23W **145** E12
St. Phillip *Mont., U.S.A.* 46°50N 104°9W **123** D13
St-Pie *Qué., Canada* 45°30N 72°54W **145** F10
St-Pierre *Qué., Canada* 45°27N 73°38W **160** B3
St-Pierre *St-P. & M.* 46°46N 56°12W **142** F4
St-Pierre, Î. *St-P. & M.* 46°47N 56°11W **142** F4

St-Pierre, L. *Qué., Canada* 50°8N 68°26W **145** A14
St-Pierre, L. *Qué., Canada* 46°12N 72°52W **145** E10
St-Pierre-de-la-Pointe-aux-Esquimaux =
 Havre-St.-Pierre *Qué., Canada* 50°18N 63°33W **143** C5
St-Pierre-et-Miquelon ☐ *N. Amer.* 46°55N 56°10W **142** F4
St-Pierre-Jolys *Man., Canada* 49°26N 96°59W **151** F15
St-Prime *Qué., Canada* 48°35N 72°20W **145** C10
St-Prosper *Qué., Canada* 46°13N 70°29W **145** E12
St-Quentin *N.B., Canada* 47°30N 67°23W **141** F2
St-Raphaël *Qué., Canada* 46°48N 70°45W **145** E12
St-Raymond *Qué., Canada* 46°54N 71°50W **145** E10
St. Regis *Mont., U.S.A.* 47°18N 115°6W **123** C2
St. Regis Falls *N.Y., U.S.A.* 44°41N 74°33W **88** A6
St. Regis Indian Reservation *N. Amer.* 44°59N 74°39W **88** A6
St-Rémi *Qué., Canada* 45°16N 73°37W **145** F9
St-Rémi-d'Amherst *Qué., Canada* 46°1N 74°46W **144** E8
St. Robert *Mo., U.S.A.* 37°50N 92°11W **83** D4
St-Roch-Aulnaies *Qué., Canada* 47°18N 70°12W **145** E12
St-Romuald *Qué., Canada* 46°46N 71°20W **145** E11
St-Sauveur *N.B., Canada* 47°32N 65°20W **141** F4
St-Sébastien *Qué., Canada* 45°4N 70°58W **145** F12
St-Siméon *N.B., Canada* 48°5N 65°36W **141** F4
St-Siméon *Qué., Canada* 47°51N 69°54W **145** D13
St-Simon *Qué., Canada* 48°12N 69°3W **145** C13
St. Simons I. *Ga., U.S.A.* 31°12N 81°15W **113** E5
St. Simons Island *Ga., U.S.A.* 31°9N 81°22W **113** E5
St. Stephen *N.B., Canada* 45°16N 67°17W **141** H2
St. Stephen *S.C., U.S.A.* 33°24N 79°55W **103** E6
St. Tammany Parish ☆ *La., U.S.A.* 30°29N 90°2W **110** D5
St. Thomas = Charlotte Amalie
 U.S. Virgin Is. 18°21N 64°56W **184** G18
St. Thomas *Ont., Canada* 42°45N 81°10W **146** E5
St. Thomas *Mo., U.S.A.* 38°23N 92°13W **83** C4
St. Thomas *N. Dak., U.S.A.* 48°37N 97°27W **76** B8
St. Thomas I. *U.S. Virgin Is.* 18°20N 64°55W **184** G18
St-Tite *Qué., Canada* 46°45N 72°34W **145** E9
St-Tite-des-Caps *Qué., Canada* 47°8N 70°47W **145** D12
St-Ulric *Qué., Canada* 48°47N 67°42W **140** E2
St-Urbain *Qué., Canada* 47°33N 70°32W **145** D12
St-Vianney *Qué., Canada* 48°37N 67°25W **140** E2
St. Victor *Sask., Canada* 49°56N 105°59W **150** F6
St. Vincent *Minn., U.S.A.* 48°58N 97°14W **77** B1
St. Vincent & the Grenadines ■
 W. Indies 13°0N 61°10W **183** D7
St-Vincent-de-Paul *Qué., Canada* 45°36N 73°39W **160** A3
St. Vincent I. *Fla., U.S.A.* 29°42N 85°3W **114** B3
St. Vincent Passage *W. Indies* 13°30N 61°0W **183** D7
St. Vincent's *Nfld. & L., Canada* 46°48N 53°38W **142** F7
St. Vrain *N. Mex., U.S.A.* 34°25N 103°29W **131** C7
St. Walburg *Sask., Canada* 53°39N 109°12W **150** D2
St. Xavier University *Ill., U.S.A.* 41°42N 87°42W **95** C2
St-Yvon *Qué., Canada* 49°10N 64°48W **140** D5
Ste-Adèle *Qué., Canada* 45°57N 74°7W **145** F8
Ste. Agathe *Man., Canada* 49°34N 97°11W **151** F14
Ste-Agathe *Qué., Canada* 46°23N 71°25W **145** E11
Ste-Agathe-des-Monts *Qué., Canada* 46°3N 74°17W **145** E8
Ste-Angèle-de-Mérici *Qué., Canada* 48°32N 68°5W **140** E1
Ste. Anne, L. *Alta., Canada* 53°42N 114°25W **152** E6
Ste-Anne, L. *Qué., Canada* 50°0N 67°42W **140** C2
Ste-Anne de Beaupré *Qué., Canada* 47°2N 70°58W **145** D12
Ste-Anne-de-Bellevue *Qué., Canada* 45°24N 73°56W **160** B1
Ste-Anne-de-Madawaska *N.B., Canada* 47°3N 67°42W **141** F1
Ste-Anne-de-Portneuf *Qué., Canada* 48°38N 69°6W **145** C13
Ste-Anne-des-Monts-Tourelle *Qué.,
 Canada* 49°8N 66°30W **140** D3
Ste-Anne-des-Plaines *Qué., Canada* 45°47N 73°49W **145** F9
Ste. Anne-du-Lac *Qué., Canada* 46°48N 75°25W **144** E7
Ste-Apolline *Qué., Canada* 46°48N 70°12W **145** E12
Ste-Blandine *Qué., Canada* 48°22N 68°28W **145** C14
Ste-Brigide-d'Iberville *Qué., Canada* 45°19N 73°4W **89** A1
Ste-Catherine *Qué., Canada* 45°24N 73°34W **160** B3
Ste-Claire *Qué., Canada* 46°36N 70°51W **145** E12
Ste-Croix *Qué., Canada* 46°38N 71°44W **145** E11
Ste-Dorothée *Qué., Canada* 45°32N 73°49W **160** A2
Ste-Famille *Qué., Canada* 46°58N 70°58W **145** E12
Ste-Félicité *Qué., Canada* 48°54N 67°20W **140** E2
Ste-Florence *Qué., Canada* 48°16N 67°14W **140** E2
Ste-Foy *Qué., Canada* 46°47N 71°17W **145** E11
Ste-Françoise *Qué., Canada* 48°6N 69°4W **145** C13
Ste-Geneviève *Qué., Canada* 45°29N 73°52W **160** B1
Ste. Genevieve *Mo., U.S.A.* 37°59N 90°2W **83** D6
Ste-Hélène, Î. *Qué., Canada* 45°31N 73°32W **160** A3
Ste-Julie *Qué., Canada* 45°35N 73°20W **160** A4
Ste-Justine *Qué., Canada* 46°24N 70°21W **145** E12
Ste-Marguerite → *Qué., Canada* 50°9N 66°36W **143** C4
Ste-Marie *Qué., Canada* 46°26N 71°0W **145** E12
Ste. Marie *Martinique* 14°48N 61°1W **183** D7
Ste. Marie *Ill., U.S.A.* 38°56N 88°1W **84** E5
Ste-Marthe-sur-le-Lac *Qué., Canada* 45°32N 73°56W **160** A1
Ste-Monique *Qué., Canada* 48°44N 71°51W **145** C11
Ste-Rose *Qué., Canada* 45°36N 73°47W **160** A2
Ste. Rose *Guadeloupe* 16°20N 61°45W **183** C7
Ste. Rose du Lac *Man., Canada* 51°4N 99°30W **151** D12
Ste-Sabine *Qué., Canada* 45°15N 73°2W **145** F9
Ste-Thècle *Qué., Canada* 46°49N 72°31W **145** E9
Ste-Thérèse-Ouest *Qué., Canada* 45°36N 73°51W **160** A1
Saintes, Îs. des *Guadeloupe* 15°50N 61°35W **183** D7
Saipan *N. Marianas* 15°12N 145°45E **184** c
Saipan Channel *N. Marianas* 15°5N 145°41E **184** c
Sairs, L. *Qué., Canada* 46°49N 78°26W **144** E4
Sakakawea, L. *N. Dak., U.S.A.* 47°30N 101°25W **76** C4
Sakami → *Qué., Canada* 53°40N 76°40W **143** C2
Sakami, L. *Qué., Canada* 53°15N 77°0W **143** C2
Saks *Ala., U.S.A.* 33°42N 85°50W **112** C5
Salaberry-de-Valleyfield *Qué., Canada* 45°15N 74°8W **145** F8
Salada, L. *Baja Calif., Mexico* 32°20N 115°40W **166** A3
Salado *Ark., U.S.A.* 35°42N 91°36W **106** C4
Salado → *Oaxaca, Mexico* 17°55N 96°59W **177** D4
Salado, Rio → *N. Mex., U.S.A.* 33°16N 106°52W **131** C4
Salado, Valle del *Mex.co* 23°56N 101°15W **171** G3
Salamanca *Guanajuato, Mexico* 20°34N 101°12W **176** B6
Salamanca *N.Y., U.S.A.* 42°10N 78°43W **88** C2
Salamonia *Ind., U.S.A.* 40°23N 84°52W **85** C6
Salamonie, L. *Ind., U.S.A.* 40°46N 85°37W **85** C5
Sale City *Ga., U.S.A.* 31°16N 84°1W **113** E2
Sale Creek *Tenn., U.S.A.* 35°23N 85°5W **112** B6
Salem *Ala., U.S.A.* 32°36N 85°14W **112** D5
Salem *Ark., U.S.A.* 36°22N 91°50W **106** B4
Salem *Ark., U.S.A.* 34°38N 92°33W **106** D3
Salem *Conn., U.S.A.* 41°28N 72°16W **91** C2
Salem *Ill., U.S.A.* 38°38N 88°57W **84** E51
Salem *Ind., U.S.A.* 38°36N 86°6W **85** E4
Salem *Iowa, U.S.A.* 40°51N 91°38W **81** E7

Salem *Ky., U.S.A.* 37°16N 88°15W **104** C4
Salem *Mass., U.S.A.* 42°31N 70°53W **91** B4
Salem *Md., U.S.A.* 38°32N 75°35W **93** B5
Salem *Mo., U.S.A.* 37°39N 91°32W **83** D5
Salem *N.C., U.S.A.* 35°42N 81°42W **103** C4
Salem *N.H., U.S.A.* 42°45N 71°12W **89** D3
Salem *N.J., U.S.A.* 39°34N 75°28W **92** C1
Salem *N. Mex., U.S.A.* 32°42N 107°13W **131** E4
Salem *N.Y., U.S.A.* 43°10N 73°20W **89** C1
Salem *Nebr., U.S.A.* 40°5N 95°43W **80** D10
Salem *Ohio, U.S.A.* 40°54N 80°52W **86** C6
Salem *Oreg., U.S.A.* 44°56N 123°2W **121** C2
Salem *S. Dak., U.S.A.* 43°44N 97°23W **76** G8
Salem *Utah, U.S.A.* 40°3N 111°40W **129** C4
Salem *Va., U.S.A.* 37°18N 80°3W **102** D4
Salem *W. Va., U.S.A.* 39°17N 80°34W **102** B4
Salem County ☆ *N.J., U.S.A.* 39°30N 75°20W **92** C1
Salem Plateau *Mo., U.S.A.* 37°30N 91°30W **83** D5
Saliaca *I. Sinaloa, Mexico* 25°11N 108°20W **172** B2
Salida *Colo., U.S.A.* 38°32N 106°0W **125** D5
Salina *Ariz., U.S.A.* 36°1N 109°52W **130** A6
Salina *Kans., U.S.A.* 38°50N 97°37W **82** C6
Salina *Okla., U.S.A.* 36°18N 95°9W **107** B8
Salina *Utah, U.S.A.* 38°58N 111°51W **129** E4
Salina, Pta. *Sonora, Mexico* 31°4N 113°9W **168** B2
Salina Cruz *Oaxaca, Mexico* 16°10N 95°12W **177** E5
Salinas *Puerto Rico* 17°59N 66°18W **184** H16
Salinas *Calif., U.S.A.* 36°40N 121°39W **126** G5
Salinas → *Calif., U.S.A.* 36°45N 121°48W **126** G5
Salinas, B. de *Nic.* 11°4N 85°45W **182** D2
Salinas de Hidalgo *San Luis Potosí,
 Mexico* 22°38N 101°43W **171** H3
Salinas Pk. *N. Mex., U.S.A.* 33°22N 106°35W **131** D4
Salinas Pueblo Missions Nat. Monument △
 U.S.A. 34°6N 106°4W **131** C4
Salinas Valley *Calif., U.S.A.* 36°15N 121°15W **127** G5
Salinas Victoria *Nuevo León, Mexico* 25°58N 100°48W **170** E4
Saline *La., U.S.A.* 32°10N 93°0W **110** B3
Saline *Mich., U.S.A.* 42°10N 83°47W **79** G8
Saline → *Ark., U.S.A.* 33°10N 92°8W **106** E3
Saline → *Ark., U.S.A.* 33°44N 93°58W **106** E2
Saline → *Ill., U.S.A.* 37°35N 88°9W **84** F5
Saline → *Kans., U.S.A.* 38°52N 97°30W **82** C6
Saline Bayou → *La., U.S.A.* 31°45N 92°58W **110** C3
Saline County ☆ *Ark., U.S.A.* 34°34N 92°35W **106** D3
Saline County ☆ *Ill., U.S.A.* 37°45N 88°30W **84** F5
Saline County ☆ *Kans., U.S.A.* 38°45N 97°40W **82** C6
Saline County ☆ *Mo., U.S.A.* 39°10N 93°10W **83** B3
Saline County ☆ *Nebr., U.S.A.* 40°30N 97°10W **80** D8
Saline L. *La., U.S.A.* 31°52N 92°54W **110** C3
Saline Valley *Calif., U.S.A.* 36°50N 117°50W **127** G9
Salineno *Tex., U.S.A.* 26°31N 99°7W **108** L8
Salisbury *N.B., Canada* 46°2N 65°3W **141** G4
Salisbury *Conn., U.S.A.* 41°59N 73°25W **91** C1
Salisbury *Mass., U.S.A.* 42°51N 70°49W **91** B4
Salisbury *Md., U.S.A.* 38°22N 75°36W **93** B5
Salisbury *Mo., U.S.A.* 39°25N 92°48W **83** B4
Salisbury *N.C., U.S.A.* 35°40N 80°29W **103** C5
Salisbury *N.H., U.S.A.* 43°22N 71°42W **89** C3
Salisbury *Pa., U.S.A.* 39°45N 79°5W **93** A1
Salisbury *Vt., U.S.A.* 43°53N 73°6W **89** C1
Salisbury *Nunavut, Canada* 63°30N 77°0W **159** E10
Salisbury Heights *N.H., U.S.A.* 43°24N 71°44W **89** C3
Salish Mts. *Mont., U.S.A.* 48°30N 115°0W **123** B3
Salitpa *Ala., U.S.A.* 31°37N 88°1W **112** E2
Salix *Iowa, U.S.A.* 42°19N 96°17W **81** C2
Salkehatchie → *S.C., U.S.A.* 32°37N 80°53W **103** F5
Salkum *Wash., U.S.A.* 46°32N 122°38W **120** D3
Salladasburg *Pa., U.S.A.* 41°17N 77°14W **87** C3
Salliq = Coral Harbour *Nunavut, Canada* 64°8N 83°10W **159** E9
Sallisaw *Okla., U.S.A.* 35°28N 94°47W **107** C9
Sally's Cove *Nfld. & L., Canada* 49°44N 57°56W **142** C3
Salmo *B.C., Canada* 49°10N 117°20W **155** F17
Salmon *Idaho, U.S.A.* 45°11N 113°54W **122** D5
Salmon → *N.B., Canada* 46°6N 65°56W **141** G4
Salmon → *Idaho, U.S.A.* 45°51N 116°47W **122** D2
Salmon Arm *B.C., Canada* 50°40N 119°15W **155** E15
Salmon Falls → *N.H., U.S.A.* 43°12N 70°50W **89** C4
Salmon Falls Cr. → *Idaho, U.S.A.* 42°43N 114°51W **122** G4
Salmon Middle Fork → *Idaho, U.S.A.* 45°18N 114°36W **122** D4
Salmon Mt. *N.H., U.S.A.* 45°14N 71°8W **89** A3
Salmon Mts. *Calif., U.S.A.* 41°0N 123°30W **126** B3
Salmon Nat. Forest *Idaho, U.S.A.* 45°15N 114°30W **122** D4
Salmon River *N.S., Canada* 44°3N 66°10W **141** J3
Salmon River Mts. *Idaho, U.S.A.* 44°50N 115°30W **122** E3
Salmon River Res. *N.Y., U.S.A.* 43°32N 75°55W **88** B5
Salmon South Fork → *Idaho, U.S.A.* 45°23N 115°31W **122** D3
Salome *Ariz., U.S.A.* 33°47N 113°37W **130** D2
Salpiuedes, Canal *Baja Calif., Mexico* 28°38N 113°0W **166** E6
Salsipuedes, Pta. *Baja Calif., Mexico* 31°59N 116°43W **166** B2
Salt → *Ariz., U.S.A.* 33°23N 112°19W **130** D3
Salt → *Ky., U.S.A.* 38°0N 85°57W **105** C7
Salt → *Mo., U.S.A.* 39°29N 91°4W **83** B5
Salt → *Wyo., U.S.A.* 43°10N 111°4W **124** C1
Salt Basin *Tex., U.S.A.* 31°42N 105°2W **108** F2
Salt Cr. → *Ill., U.S.A.* 40°8N 89°50W **84** C4
Salt Cr. → *N. Mex., U.S.A.* 33°33N 104°35W **131** D6
Salt Cr. → *Ohio, U.S.A.* 38°58N 83°1W **86** E3
Salt Cr. → *Wyo., U.S.A.* 43°41N 106°20W **124** C6
Salt Draw → *Tex., U.S.A.* 31°19N 103°28W **108** F4
Salt Flat *Tex., U.S.A.* 31°45N 105°5W **108** F2
Salt Fork → *Tex., U.S.A.* 33°16N 100°0W **108** D7
Salt Fork Arkansas → *Okla., U.S.A.* 36°36N 97°3W **107** B7
Salt Fork L. *Ohio, U.S.A.* 40°3N 81°30W **86** C5
Salt Fork Red → *Okla., U.S.A.* 34°27N 99°21W **107** D4
Salt Fork State Park △ *Ohio, U.S.A.* 40°8N 81°30W **86** C5
Salt L. *Hawai'i, U.S.A.* 21°21N 157°55W **136** K14
Salt L. *N. Mex., U.S.A.* 32°18N 104°0W **131** C7
Salt L. *N. Mex., U.S.A.* 34°5N 103°4W **131** C7
Salt Lake City *Utah, U.S.A.* 40°45N 111°53W **134** B1
Salt Lake City Int. ✈ (SLC) *Utah,
 U.S.A.* 40°47N 111°58W **134** B2
Salt Lake County ☆ *Utah, U.S.A.* 40°40N 112°0W **129** C3
Salt Lick *Ky., U.S.A.* 38°7N 83°37W **105** B9
Salt Marsh L. *Utah, U.S.A.* 39°29N 113°55W **129** D2
Salt Plains Nat. Wildlife Refuge △ *Okla.,
 U.S.A.* 36°44N 98°13W **107** B5
Salt River Canyon *Ariz., U.S.A.* 33°50N 110°40W **130** D5
Salt River Indian Reservation *Ariz.,
 U.S.A.* 33°35N 111°50W **130** D4
Salt Springs *Fla., U.S.A.* 29°21N 81°44W **114** B7
Saltair *B.C., Canada* 48°57N 123°46W **154** G11
Saltcoats *Sask., Canada* 51°5N 102°15W **151** D9

Saltery Bay B.C., Canada 49°47N 124°10W **154** F10
Saltillo Coahuila, Mexico 25°25N 101°0W **170** E4
Saltillo Miss., U.S.A. 34°23N 88°41W **111** B5
Saltillo Pa., U.S.A. 40°13N 78°1W **87** D4
Saltillo Tenn., U.S.A. 35°23N 88°13W **104** E4
Salto Chico Sinaloa, Mexico 24°8N 106°59W **172** C4
Salto de Agua Chiapas, Mexico 17°37N 92°22W **178** B4
Salto del Agua San Luis Potosí, Mexico 22°36N 99°24W **171** H5
Salton City Calif., U.S.A. 33°18N 115°57W **127** K11
Salton Sea Calif., U.S.A. 33°15N 115°45W **127** K11
Saltville Va., U.S.A. 36°53N 81°46W **102** E3
Saluda S.C., U.S.A. 34°0N 81°46W **103** D4
Saluda Va., U.S.A. 37°36N 76°36W **102** D8
Saluda → S.C., U.S.A. 34°1N 81°4W **103** D4
Saluda → S.C., U.S.A. 34°0N 81°45W **103** D4
Saluda County ☆ S.C., U.S.A. 34°0N 81°45W **103** D4
Salus Ark., U.S.A. 35°44N 93°24W **106** C2
Salvador Sask., Canada 52°10N 109°32W **150** C2
Salvador, El ■ Cent. Amer. 13°50N 89°0W **182** D2
Salvador, L. La., U.S.A. 29°43N 90°15W **117** D1
Salvatierra Guanajuato, Mexico 20°13N 100°53W **175** B7
Salyersville Ky., U.S.A. 37°45N 83°4W **105** C9
Sam Houston Nat. Forest Tex., U.S.A. 30°32N 95°29W **109** G12
Sam Rayburn Res. Tex., U.S.A. 31°4N 94°5W **109** F13
Samahil Yucatan, Mexico 20°53N 89°53W **179** B4
Samalayuca Chihuahua, Mexico 31°21N 106°28W **169** B9
Samana Cay Bahamas 23°3N 73°45W **183** B5
Samaria Idaho, U.S.A. 42°7N 112°20W **122** G6
Sambro N.S., Canada 44°28N 63°36W **141** J6
Samburg Tenn., U.S.A. 36°23N 89°21W **104** D3
Samish B. Wash., U.S.A. 48°36N 122°31W **120** B3
Sammamish, L. Wash., U.S.A. 47°36N 122°5W **132** C5
Samoset Fla., U.S.A. 27°28N 82°33W **114** D6
Sampson County ☆ N.C., U.S.A. 35°0N 78°30W **103** C7
Samson Ala., U.S.A. 31°7N 86°3W **112** E4
Samuel R. McKelvie Nat. Forest Nebr., U.S.A. 42°40N 101°0W **80** B4
Samuel Smith Park Ont., Canada 43°35N 79°30W **161** B1
San Acacia N.Mex., U.S.A. 34°15N 106°54W **131** C4
San Agustín Jalisco, Mexico 20°37N 102°47W **174** B5
San Agustin, Plains of N.Mex., U.S.A. 33°45N 108°15W **131** D2
San Alberto Coahuila, Mexico 25°11N 101°17W **170** C3
San Andreas Calif., U.S.A. 38°12N 120°41W **126** E6
San Andrés Oaxaca, Mexico 16°55N 97°41W **177** H3
San Andrés, I. de Caribbean 12°42N 81°46W **182** D3
San Andrés, I. Tamaulipas, Mexico 22°40N 97°52W **171** H7
San Andrés Ahuayucan Distrito Federal, Mexico 19°13N 99°6W **181** C3
San Andres Mts. N.Mex., U.S.A. 33°0N 106°30W **131** E4
San Andres Pk. N.Mex., U.S.A. 32°41N 106°32W **131** E4
San Andrés Totoltepec Distrito Federal, Mexico 19°15N 99°10W **181** C2
San Andrés Tuxtla Veracruz, Mexico 18°27N 95°13W **177** F5
San Angel Distrito Federal, Mexico 19°20N 99°11W **181** B2
San Angelo Tex., U.S.A. 31°28N 100°26W **108** F7
San Anselmo Calif., U.S.A. 37°59N 122°34W **126** F4
San Antonino Monte Verde Oaxaca, Mexico 17°33N 97°44W **177** G3
San Antonio Belize 16°15N 89°2W **182** C2
San Antonio Baja Calif. S., Mexico 23°47N 110°5W **167** K8
San Antonio Chihuahua, Mexico 28°54N 103°19W **169** E12
San Antonio N.Mex., U.S.A. 33°55N 106°52W **131** D4
San Antonio Tex., U.S.A. 29°25N 98°29W **116** C3
San Antonio → Tex., U.S.A. 28°30N 96°54W **109** J11
San Antonio, C. de Cuba 21°50N 84°57W **182** B3
San Antonio, Pta. Baja Calif., Mexico 35°48N 120°53W **127** H6
San Antonio Sa. de Sonora, Mexico 29°45N 115°43W **166** B3
San Antonio B. Tex., U.S.A. 28°20N 96°45W **109** J11
San Antonio de las Alazanas Coahuila, Mexico 25°16N 100°36W **171** E4
San Antonio de los Baños Cuba 22°54N 82°31W **182** B3
San Antonio de Trojes San Luis Potosí, Mexico 22°43N 100°13W **171** H4
San Antonio del Potrero Chihuahua, Mexico 27°0N 105°45W **169** G10
San Antonio del Salero Nuevo León, Mexico 24°27N 100°15W **171** F4
San Antonio Int. ✈ (SAT) Tex., U.S.A. 29°32N 98°28W **116** B3
San Antonio Missions Nat. Historical Park ○ Tex., U.S.A. 29°23N 98°29W **116** C3
San Antonio Mt. Tex., U.S.A. 32°0N 105°30W **108** F2
San Antonio Tecómitl Distrito Federal, Mexico 19°14N 99°0W **181** C4
San Ardo Calif., U.S.A. 36°1N 120°54W **127** G6
San Augustine Tex., U.S.A. 31°32N 94°7W **109** F13
San Augustine County ☆ Tex., U.S.A. 31°30N 94°9W **109** F13
San Bartolo Baja Calif. S., Mexico 23°45N 109°51W **167** K9
San Bartolo San Luis Potosí, Mexico 22°18N 100°42W **171** H4
San Bartolo Morelos México, Mexico 17°49N 99°41W **175** C8
San Bartolo Soyaltepec Oaxaca, Mexico 17°36N 97°16W **177** G3
San Bartolomé Coatepec México, Mexico 19°24N 99°18W **181** B2
San Bartolomé Loxicha Oaxaca, Mexico 15°58N 96°43W **177** J4
San Bartolomé Xicomulco Distrito Federal, Mexico 19°13N 99°5W **181** C3
San Benito Sonora, Mexico 29°45N 111°48W **168** D4
San Benito Tex., U.S.A. 26°8N 97°38W **108** L10
San Benito, Is. Baja Calif. S., Mexico 28°20N 115°31W **167** E3
San Benito County ☆ Calif., U.S.A. 36°30N 121°0W **127** G5
San Bernardino Nat. Forest Calif., U.S.A. 34°10N 116°50W **127** J10
San Bernard → Tex., U.S.A. 28°52N 95°27W **109** J12
San Bernard Nat. Wildlife Refuge ○ Tex., U.S.A. 28°51N 95°32W **109** J12
San Bernardino Calif., U.S.A. 34°7N 117°19W **127** J9
San Bernardino County ☆ Calif., U.S.A. 34°45N 116°0W **127** J11
San Bernardino de Milpillas Chico Durango, Mexico 23°23N 105°10W **172** D5
San Bernardino Mts. Calif., U.S.A. 34°10N 116°45W **127** J10
San Bernardo Durango, Mexico 26°0N 105°33W **172** B5
San Bernardo Sonora, Mexico 27°24N 108°50W **168** F7
San Blas Coahuila, Mexico 27°25N 101°40W **170** C2
San Blas Nayarit, Mexico 21°31N 105°16W **172** F5
San Blas Sinaloa, Mexico 26°5N 108°46W **172** A2
San Blas, Arch. de Panama 9°50N 78°31W **182** E4
San Blas, C. Fla., U.S.A. 29°40N 85°21W **114** B3
San Borja Baja Calif. S., Mexico 28°47N 113°55W **166** E5
San Borja, Sa. de Baja Calif., Mexico 28°42N 113°47W **166** E5
San Bruno Baja Calif. S., Mexico 27°11N 112°12W **167** F6
San Bruno Calif., U.S.A. 37°38N 122°25W **126** F4
San Bruno, Pt. Calif., U.S.A. 37°39N 122°22W **132** C2
San Bruno Mt. Calif., U.S.A. 37°41N 122°26W **132** B2

San Buenaventura = Ventura Calif., U.S.A. 34°17N 119°18W **127** J7
San Buenaventura Baja Calif. S., Mexico 26°38N 111°52W **167** G7
San Buenaventura Coahuila, Mexico 27°5N 101°32W **170** C3
San Carlos Baja Calif., Mexico 29°39N 115°29W **166** D3
San Carlos Baja Calif. S., Mexico 24°47N 112°7W **167** J6
San Carlos Coahuila, Mexico 29°1N 100°51W **170** A4
San Carlos Sonora, Mexico 27°59N 111°4W **168** F4
San Carlos Tamaulipas, Mexico 24°36N 98°51W **171** F6
San Carlos Nic. 11°12N 84°50W **182** D3
San Carlos Ariz., U.S.A. 33°21N 110°27W **130** D5
San Carlos L. Ariz., U.S.A. 33°11N 110°32W **130** D5
San Carlos Park Fla., U.S.A. 26°28N 81°49W **114** E7
San Carlos Yautepec Oaxaca, Mexico 16°31N 96°6W **177** H4
San Carlos, B. Baja Calif. S., Mexico 27°53N 112°46W **167** F6
San Carlos, Cerro Sonora, Mexico 31°17N 112°33W **168** B3
San Carlos, Pta. Sonora, Mexico 29°38N 115°31W **166** D3
San Carlos Indian Reservation Ariz., U.S.A. 33°25N 110°0W **130** D6
San Cayetano Nayarit, Mexico 22°27N 105°41W **172** E5
San Ciro de Acosta San Luis Potosí, Mexico 21°39N 99°49W **171** J5
San Clara Man., Canada 51°29N 101°26W **151** D10
San Clemente Calif., U.S.A. 33°26N 117°37W **127** K9
San Clemente I. Calif., U.S.A. 32°53N 118°29W **127** L8
San Clemente Island Calif., U.S.A. 32°54N 118°30W **127** L8
San Cristóbal Dom. Rep. 18°25N 70°6W **183** C5
San Cristóbal N.Mex., U.S.A. 36°36N 105°39W **131** A5
San Cristóbal Baja Calif. S., Mexico 27°23N 114°38W **167** F4
San Cristóbal de la Barranca Jalisco, Mexico 21°3N 103°26W **174** A4
San Cristóbal de las Casas Chiapas, Mexico 16°45N 92°38W **178** C4
San Cristóbal Texcalucan México, Mexico 19°25N 99°21W **181** B1
San Cristobal Wash → Ariz., U.S.A. 32°45N 113°45W **130** E2
San Diego Calif., U.S.A. 32°42N 117°9W **133** B2
San Diego Tex., U.S.A. 27°46N 98°14W **109** K9
San Diego → Michoacan, Mexico 18°55N 101°11W **175** D6
San Diego, I. Baja Calif. S., Mexico 25°11N 110°42W **167** H8
San Diego, Sa. Sonora, Mexico 30°30N 109°5W **168** C6
San Diego Bay Calif., U.S.A. 32°39N 117°8W **133** C2
San Diego County ☆ Calif., U.S.A. 33°0N 117°15W **127** K10
San Diego de Alcalá Chihuahua, Mexico 28°35N 105°34W **169** E10
San Diego de Alcalá Durango, Mexico 24°28N 105°12W **172** C5
San Diego de Alejandría Jalisco, Mexico 21°26N 102°6W **174** B5
San Diego de la Unión Guanajuato, Mexico 21°28N 100°52W **175** A7
San Diego Int. ✈ (SAN) Calif., U.S.A. 32°44N 117°11W **133** B2
San Diego la Mesa Tochimiltzingo Puebla, Mexico 18°49N 98°19W **177** F2
San Dimas Durango, Mexico 24°8N 105°58W **172** C5
San Eduardo Chihuahua, Mexico 29°42N 105°14W **169** E10
San Elizario Tex., U.S.A. 31°35N 106°16W **108** F1
San Emeterio Sonora, Mexico 31°40N 112°51W **168** B3
San Esteban Sonora, Mexico 29°29N 102°3W **170** A2
San Esteban, I. Sonora, Mexico 28°42N 112°36W **168** E3
San Evaristo Baja Calif. S., Mexico 24°55N 110°45W **167** J8
San Felipe Baja Calif., Mexico 31°1N 114°52W **166** B4
San Felipe Guanajuato, Mexico 21°29N 101°13W **175** A6
San Felipe Yucatan, Mexico 21°34N 88°14W **179** A5
San Felipe → Calif., U.S.A. 33°10N 115°49W **127** K11
San Felipe, B. Baja Calif., Mexico 30°58N 114°45W **166** C4
San Felipe, Parque Natural ○ Yucatán, Mexico 21°27N 88°39W **179** A5
San Felipe, Sa. Baja Calif., Mexico 30°55N 115°10W **166** C3
San Felipe Aztatán Nayarit, Mexico 22°23N 105°24W **172** E5
San Felipe de Jesús Sonora, Mexico 29°52N 110°15W **168** D5
San Felipe del Progreso México, Mexico 19°41N 99°57W **175** C8
San Felipe Indian Reservation N.Mex., U.S.A. 35°26N 106°31W **131** B4
San Felipe Nuevo Mercurio Zacatecas, Mexico 24°14N 102°8W **173** C8
San Felipe Orizatlán Hidalgo, Mexico 21°11N 98°37W **175** A9
San Felipe Pueblo N.Mex., U.S.A. 35°26N 106°27W **131** B4
San Fermín Durango, Mexico 26°20N 104°49W **173** A6
San Fernando Chiapas, Mexico 16°52N 93°13W **178** C3
San Fernando Tamaulipas, Mexico 24°51N 98°10W **171** F6
San Fernando Trin. & Tob. 10°16N 61°28W **183** D7
San Fernando Calif., U.S.A. 34°17N 118°26W **127** J8
San Fernando → Baja Calif., Mexico 29°45N 115°40W **166** D3
San Fidel N.Mex., U.S.A. 35°5N 107°36W **131** B3
San Francisco Durango, Mexico 23°58N 105°47W **172** D5
San Francisco Guadalajara, Mexico 20°33N 103°10W **180** B2
San Francisco Nuevo León, Mexico 24°42N 99°40W **171** F5
San Francisco Yucatán, Mexico 20°42N 88°29W **179** B5
San Francisco → Ariz., U.S.A. 32°59N 109°22W **130** E6
San Francisco, Barra Oaxaca, Mexico 16°12N 94°55W **177** H6
San Francisco, I. Baja Calif. S., Mexico 24°41N 110°35W **167** J8
San Francisco, Sa. Baja Calif. S., Mexico 27°43N 113°10W **167** F5
San Francisco B. Calif., U.S.A. 37°39N 122°14W **132** B3
San Francisco Chimalpa México, Mexico 19°26N 99°20W **181** B2
San Francisco County ☆ Calif., U.S.A. 37°47N 122°25W **126** F4
San Francisco Cr. → Tex., U.S.A. 29°53N 102°19W **108** H5
San Francisco Culhuacán Distrito Federal, Mexico 19°19N 99°8W **181** C3
San Francisco de Asís Durango, Mexico 25°29N 104°51W **173** B6
San Francisco de Borja Chihuahua, Mexico 27°53N 106°41W **169** F9
San Francisco de Conchos Chihuahua, Mexico 27°35N 105°19W **169** F10
San Francisco de los Romo Aguascalientes, Mexico 22°9N 102°16W **173** E8
San Francisco de Macorís Dom. Rep. 19°19N 70°15W **183** C5
San Francisco del Barrial Coahuila, Mexico 25°11N 102°8W **171** E2
San Francisco del Oro Chihuahua, Mexico 26°52N 105°51W **169** G10
San Francisco del Rincón Guanajuato, Mexico 21°1N 101°51W **174** A6
San Francisco Int. ✈ (SFO) Calif., U.S.A. 37°37N 122°22W **126** F4
San Francisco Ixhuatán Oaxaca, Mexico 16°21N 94°29W **177** H6
San Francisco Ixtacamatitlán Puebla, Mexico 19°38N 97°49W **176** E3
San Francisco Logueche Oaxaca, Mexico 16°21N 96°23W **177** H4
San Francisco Mts. Ariz., U.S.A. 35°15N 111°45W **130** B4
San Francisco Mts. N.Mex., U.S.A. 33°45N 108°50W **131** D2
San Francisco Pujiltic Chiapas, Mexico 16°17N 92°27W **178** C4

San Francisco Tesistán Jalisco, Mexico 20°47N 103°29W **174** B4
San Francisco Tlalnepantla Distrito Federal, Mexico 19°12N 99°7W **181** C3
San Francisco Tlaltenco Distrito Federal, Mexico 19°18N 99°0W **181** C4
San Francisquito Baja Calif. S., Mexico 28°25N 112°52W **166** E6
San Francisquito, Pta. Baja Calif., Mexico 28°26N 112°51W **166** E6
San Gabriel Calif., U.S.A. 34°5N 118°5W **133** B4
San Gabriel Calif., U.S.A. 33°58N 118°5W **133** B4
San Gabriel → Tex., U.S.A. 30°46N 97°1W **109** G10
San Gabriel Chilac Puebla, Mexico 18°19N 97°21W **177** F3
San Gabriel Mts. Calif., U.S.A. 34°17N 117°38W **127** J9
San German Puerto Rico 18°4N 67°4W **184** G15
San Gorgonio Mt. Calif., U.S.A. 34°6N 116°50W **127** J10
San Gregorio Calif., U.S.A. 37°20N 122°24W **132** C2
San Gregorio → Durango, Mexico 24°40N 106°28W **172** C4
San Gregorio Atlapulco Distrito Federal, Mexico 19°16N 99°3W **181** C3
San Hipólito, B. Baja Calif. S., Mexico 26°57N 113°55W **167** G5
San Ignacio Belize 17°10N 89°5W **182** C2
San Ignacio Baja Calif. S., Mexico 27°27N 112°51W **167** F6
San Ignacio Sinaloa, Mexico 23°55N 106°37W **172** D4
San Ignacio Sinaloa, Mexico 25°31N 108°53W **172** B2
San Ignacio Sonora, Mexico 27°25N 110°16W **168** F5
San Ignacio → Sonora, Mexico 29°53N 112°40W **168** D3
San Ignacio, I. de Sinaloa, Mexico 30°30N 108°55W **172** B2
San Ignacio, L. Baja Calif. S., Mexico 26°54N 113°13W **167** G5
San Ildefonso Indian Reservation N.Mex., U.S.A. 35°53N 106°8W **131** B4
San Isabel Nat. Forest Colo., U.S.A. 38°0N 105°2W **125** E5
San Isidro Baja Calif. S., Mexico 26°12N 112°2W **167** G6
San Isidro Campeche, Mexico 18°38N 91°4W **179** C2
San Isidro Chiapas, Mexico 15°44N 93°21W **178** D3
San Isidro Chihuahua, Mexico 31°33N 106°18W **169** B9
San Isidro Guadalajara, Mexico 20°45N 103°23W **180** A1
San Isidro Sonora, Mexico 30°48N 112°22W **168** C3
San Isidro Tex., U.S.A. 26°43N 98°27W **108** L9
San Isidro → Baja Calif., Mexico 31°17N 116°22W **166** B3
San Jacinto México, Mexico 19°21N 99°19W **181** B2
San Jacinto Calif., U.S.A. 33°47N 116°57W **127** K10
San Jacinto County ☆ Tex., U.S.A. 30°36N 95°8W **109** G12
San Jacinto Mts. Calif., U.S.A. 33°45N 116°40W **127** K10
San Javier Chiapas, Mexico 16°48N 91°6W **178** C5
San Javier Monterrey, Mexico 25°53N 100°15W **180** A2
San Javier Sonora, Mexico 28°35N 109°45W **168** F6
San Javier → Baja Calif. S., Mexico 25°28N 112°4W **167** H6
San Jerónimo Durango, Mexico 23°49N 105°33W **172** D5
San Jerónimo Guerrero, Mexico 17°8N 100°28W **175** E7
San Jerónimo Zacatecas, Mexico 22°41N 102°29W **173** E8
San Jerónimo Lidice Distrito Federal, Mexico 19°19N 99°14W **181** C2
San Jerónimo Taviche Oaxaca, Mexico 16°44N 96°35W **177** H4
San Jerónimo Xayacaylán Puebla, Mexico 18°14N 97°55W **177** F3
San Joaquín Querétaro, Mexico 20°35N 99°54W **175** B8
San Joaquin Calif., U.S.A. 36°36N 120°11W **127** G6
San Joaquin County ☆ Calif., U.S.A. 37°50N 121°15W **126** F5
San Joaquin Valley Calif., U.S.A. 37°20N 121°0W **126** F5
San Jon N.Mex., U.S.A. 35°6N 103°20W **131** B7
San Jorge, B. de Sonora, Mexico 31°20N 113°20W **168** B2
San Jorge, I. Sonora, Mexico 30°57N 113°15W **168** C2
San José Costa Rica 9°55N 84°2W **182** E3
San José Guatemala 14°0N 90°50W **182** D1
San José Campeche, Mexico 18°27N 91°28W **179** D2
San Jose N. Marianas 14°58N 145°37E **184** c
San José de Jesús Sonora, Mexico 27°20N 121°53W **126** F5
San Jose III., U.S.A. 40°18N 89°36W **84** C4
San Jose → N.Mex., U.S.A. 34°25N 106°45W **131** C4
San José, I. Baja Calif. S., Mexico 25°0N 110°38W **167** H8
San José, Pta. Baja Calif., Mexico 31°28N 116°37W **166** B2
San José Baqueachi Chihuahua, Mexico 27°38N 107°1W **169** F8
San José Carbonerillas Zacatecas, Mexico 24°29N 101°27W **173** C9
San José Chiltepec Oaxaca, Mexico 17°57N 96°11W **177** G4
San José de Aura Coahuila, Mexico 27°36N 101°21W **170** C3
San José de Bavicora Chihuahua, Mexico 29°15N 107°46W **169** D8
San José de Carranza Coahuila, Mexico 27°49N 103°35W **170** C1
San José de Comondú Baja Calif. S., Mexico 26°3N 111°50W **167** G7
San José de Gracia Aguascalientes, Mexico 22°8N 102°23W **173** E8
San José de Gracia Baja Calif. S., Mexico 26°34N 112°45W **167** G6
San José de Guajademi Baja Calif. S., Mexico 24°36N 112°9W **167** J6
San José de la Boca Durango, Mexico 25°20N 105°47W **172** B5
San José de la Brecha Sinaloa, Mexico 25°21N 108°25W **172** B2
San José de la Noria Baja Calif. S., Mexico 25°24N 111°6W **167** H7
San José de Moradillos Sonora, Mexico 28°36N 110°30W **168** E5
San José del Cabo Baja Calif. S., Mexico 23°3N 109°41W **167** K9
San José del Cabo, B. Baja Calif. S., Mexico 22°56N 109°42W **167** K9
San José del Prisco, Sa. Chihuahua, Mexico 30°0N 105°50W **169** C10
San José El Barranco Sinaloa, Mexico 25°41N 107°9W **172** B3
San José Guacayvo Chihuahua, Mexico 27°43N 107°52W **169** F8
San Jose Int. ✈ (SJC) Calif., U.S.A. 37°22N 121°55W **126** F5
San José Iturbide Guanajuato, Mexico 21°0N 100°23W **175** B7
San José Miahuatlán Puebla, Mexico 18°20N 97°17W **177** F3
San José Río Hondo México, Mexico 19°26N 99°14W **181** B2
San José Río Manso Oaxaca, Mexico 17°40N 95°54W **177** G4
San José Tenango Oaxaca, Mexico 18°8N 96°43W **177** F4
San José y Anexas Chihuahua, Mexico 28°52N 107°15W **169** E8
San Juan Coahuila, Mexico 27°0N 101°53W **170** C3
San Juan Oaxaca, Mexico 17°52N 96°16W **177** G2
San Juan Sonora, Mexico 30°48N 112°9W **168** C3
San Juan Puerto Rico 18°28N 66°7W **184** G16
San Juan → Coahuila, Mexico 25°51N 101°7W **170** C3
San Juan → Nic. 10°56N 83°42W **182** D3
San Juan → Utah, U.S.A. 37°16N 110°26W **129** F5
San Juan, Pta. Veracruz, Mexico 18°17N 94°37W **177** F6
San Juan, Sa. Sonora, Mexico 31°0N 111°35W **168** B4
San Juan Basin N.Mex., U.S.A. 36°20N 108°10W **131** A2
San Juan Bautista = Villahermosa Tabasco, Mexico 17°59N 92°55W **178** B4
San Juan Bautista Campeche, Mexico 19°53N 89°59W **179** C4

San Juan Bautista Oaxaca, Mexico 16°32N 98°19W **177** H2
San Juan Bautista Calif., U.S.A. 36°51N 121°32W **126** G5
San Juan Bautista, B. Baja Calif. S., Mexico 28°1N 112°49W **167** E6
San Juan Bautista Cuicatlán Oaxaca, Mexico 17°48N 96°58W **177** G4
San Juan Cacahuatepec Oaxaca, Mexico 16°37N 98°7W **177** H2
San Juan Cancuc Chiapas, Mexico 16°53N 92°22W **178** C4
San Juan Capistrano Calif., U.S.A. 33°30N 117°40W **127** K9
San Juan Chiquihuitlán Oaxaca, Mexico 17°57N 96°44W **177** G4
San Juan County ☆ Colo., U.S.A. 37°50N 107°40W **125** E3
San Juan County ☆ N.Mex., U.S.A. 36°30N 108°30W **131** A2
San Juan County ☆ Utah, U.S.A. 38°0N 109°30W **129** F6
San Juan County ☆ Wash., U.S.A. 48°32N 123°5W **120** B2
San Juan Cr. → Calif., U.S.A. 35°40N 120°22W **127** H6
San Juan de Abajo Nayarit, Mexico 20°49N 105°12W **172** G5
San Juan de Ahrocados, Lago Zacatecas, Mexico 24°2N 102°17W **173** C8
San Juan de Aragón Distrito Federal, Mexico 19°28N 99°4W **181** B3
San Juan de Aragón, Parque Distrito Federal, Mexico 19°27N 99°4W **181** B3
San Juan de Guadelupe Durango, Mexico 24°38N 102°44W **173** C8
San Juan de la Costa Baja Calif. S., Mexico 24°20N 110°41W **167** J8
San Juan de los Charcos Zacatecas, Mexico 25°3N 102°36W **173** B8
San Juan de los Lagos Jalisco, Mexico 21°15N 102°18W **174** A5
San Juan de Sabinas Coahuila, Mexico 27°55N 101°18W **170** C3
San Juan de Villa Hermosa = Villahermosa Tabasco, Mexico 17°59N 92°55W **178** B4
San Juan del Norte Nic. 10°58N 83°40W **182** D3
San Juan del Norte, B. de Nic. 11°0N 83°40W **182** D3
San Juan del Río Durango, Mexico 24°47N 104°27W **173** C6
San Juan del Río Querétaro, Mexico 20°23N 100°0W **175** B8
San Juan del Sur Nic. 11°20N 85°51W **182** D2
San Juan Evangelista Veracruz, Mexico 17°54N 95°9W **177** F5
San Juan Guichicovi Oaxaca, Mexico 16°58N 95°6W **177** H5
San Juan I. Wash., U.S.A. 48°32N 123°5W **120** B2
San Juan Indian Reservation N.Mex., U.S.A. 36°3N 106°4W **131** A4
San Juan Island Nat. Historical Park ○ Wash., U.S.A. 48°35N 123°8W **120** B2
San Juan Ixtacala México, Mexico 19°31N 99°10W **181** A2
San Juan Ixtayopan Distrito Federal, Mexico 19°15N 99°0W **181** C4
San Juan Lalana Oaxaca, Mexico 17°28N 95°54W **177** G5
San Juan Luis Munoz Marin Int. ✈ (SJU) Puerto Rico 18°26N 66°0W **184** G16
San Juan Mazatlán Oaxaca, Mexico 17°2N 95°27W **177** G5
San Juan Mts. Colo., U.S.A. 37°30N 107°0W **125** E4
San Juan Nat. Forest Colo., U.S.A. 37°30N 108°0W **125** E3
San Juan Pueblo N.Mex., U.S.A. 36°3N 106°4W **131** A4
San Juan Quiotepec Oaxaca, Mexico 17°36N 96°35W **177** G4
San Juan Teita Oaxaca, Mexico 17°6N 97°25W **177** H3
San Juan Tepenahuac Distrito Federal, Mexico 19°11N 98°59W **181** C4
San Juan Toltotepec México, Mexico 19°28N 99°15W **181** B2
San Juan Volador Veracruz, Mexico 18°16N 94°37W **177** F6
San Juanico Baja Calif. S., Mexico 26°16N 112°29W **167** G6
San Juanico, B. Baja Calif. S., Mexico 26°26N 111°25W **167** G7
San Juanico, B. Baja Calif. S., Mexico 26°14N 112°27W **167** G6
San Juanito Chihuahua, Mexico 27°58N 107°36W **169** F8
San Juanito, I. Nayarit, Mexico 21°43N 106°38W **172** F4
San Julian Jalisco, Mexico 21°1N 102°14W **174** A5
San Leandro Calif., U.S.A. 37°42N 122°9W **126** F4
San Lorenzo San Luis Potosí, Mexico 22°33N 100°40W **171** H4
San Lorenzo N.Mex., U.S.A. 32°49N 107°55W **131** E3
San Lorenzo → Nuevo León, Mexico 25°7N 98°32W **171** E6
San Lorenzo, I. Baja Calif., Mexico 28°38N 112°51W **166** E6
San Lorenzo Acopilco México, Mexico 19°20N 99°21W **181** C1
San Lorenzo Texmelucan Oaxaca, Mexico 16°36N 97°11W **177** H3
San Lorenzo Tezonco Distrito Federal, Mexico 19°19N 99°3W **181** C3
San Lorenzo Tlacoyucan Distrito Federal, Mexico 19°11N 99°2W **181** C3
San Lucas = Cabo San Lucas Baja Calif. S., Mexico 22°53N 109°54W **167** L9
San Lucas Michoacan, Mexico 18°36N 100°48W **175** D7
San Lucas Calif., U.S.A. 36°8N 121°1W **127** G5
San Lucas, C. Baja Calif. S., Mexico 22°52N 109°53W **167** L9
San Luis Pinar del Rio, Cuba 22°17N 83°46W **182** B3
San Luis Guatemala 16°14N 89°27W **182** C2
San Luis Coahuila, Mexico 25°45N 102°29W **170** E2
San Luis Ariz., U.S.A. 32°29N 114°47W **130** E1
San Luis Colo., U.S.A. 37°12N 105°25W **125** E5
San Luis, I. Baja Calif., Mexico 29°58N 114°26W **166** D4
San Luis Acatlán Guerrero, Mexico 16°48N 98°55W **177** H2
San Luis Amatlán Oaxaca, Mexico 16°25N 96°30W **177** H4
San Luis Cr. → Colo., U.S.A. 37°42N 105°44W **125** E5
San Luis de la Loma Guerrero, Mexico 17°18N 100°55W **175** E7
San Luis de la Paz Guanajuato, Mexico 21°18N 100°31W **175** A7
San Luis del Cordero Durango, Mexico 25°26N 104°18W **173** B6
San Luis Gonzaga Sonora, Mexico 29°51N 114°20W **166** D4
San Luis Gonzaga Baja Calif. S., Mexico 24°55N 111°20W **167** J7
San Luis Gonzaga, B. Baja Calif., Mexico 29°48N 114°22W **166** D4
San Luis Gonzaga, I. Baja Calif. S., Mexico 25°17N 110°40W **167** H8
San Luis Obispo Calif., U.S.A. 35°17N 120°40W **127** H6
San Luis Obispo County ☆ Calif., U.S.A. 35°30N 120°30W **127** H6
San Luis Peak Colo., U.S.A. 37°59N 106°56W **125** E4
San Luis Potosí San Luis Potosí, Mexico 22°9N 100°59W **171** H4
San Luis Potosí □ Mexico 23°0N 101°0W **171** H4
San Luis Res. Calif., U.S.A. 37°4N 121°5W **126** F5
San Luis Rey → Calif., U.S.A. 33°12N 117°24W **127** K9
San Luis Río Colorado Mexico 32°29N 114°58W **168** A1
San Luis San Pedro Guerrero, Mexico 17°18N 100°53W **175** E7
San Luis Tlaxialtemalco Distrito Federal, Mexico 19°16N 99°1W **181** C3
San Luis Valley Colo., U.S.A. 37°45N 105°50W **125** E5
San Luisito Sonora, Mexico 31°18N 112°28W **168** B3
San Manuel Ariz., U.S.A. 32°36N 110°38W **130** D5
San Marcos Guatemala 14°59N 91°52W **182** D1
San Marcos Guerrero, Mexico 16°48N 99°21W **175** E8
San Marcos Jalisco, Mexico 20°47N 104°11W **174** B3
San Marcos Calif., U.S.A. 33°9N 117°10W **109** H10
San Marcos, I. Baja Calif. S., Mexico 27°13N 112°6W **167** F6
San Marcos y Pinos, Sa. Coahuila, Mexico 26°28N 101°47W **170** D3

San Marino *Calif., U.S.A.* 34°7N 118°5W **133** B4
San Martín *Zacatecas, Mexico* 22°14N 101°22W **173** E9
San Martin *Calif., U.S.A.* 37°5N 121°37W **126** F5
San Martin, I. *Baja Calif., Mexico* 30°28N 116°8W **166** C2
San Martín Chalchicuautla *San Luis Potosí, Mexico* 21°23N 98°39W **171** J6
San Martín de Bolaños *Jalisco, Mexico* 21°29N 103°58W **173** F7
San Martín de Hidalgo *Jalisco, Mexico* 20°27N 103°57W **174** B4
San Martín Texmelucan *Puebla, Mexico* 19°17N 98°26W **176** E2
San Mateo *Calif., U.S.A.* 37°34N 122°19W **126** F4
San Mateo *N. Mex., U.S.A.* 35°20N 107°39W **131** B3
San Mateo County ☆ *Calif., U.S.A.* 37°30N 122°25W **126** F4
San Mateo del Mar *Oaxaca, Mexico* 16°12N 95°0W **177** H6
San Mateo Mts. *N. Mex., U.S.A.* 33°45N 107°25W **131** D3
San Mateo Tlaltenango *Distrito Federal, Mexico* 19°20N 99°16W **181** B2
San Mateo Xalpa *Distrito Federal, Mexico* 19°14N 99°8W **181** C2
San Miguel *El Salv.* 13°30N 88°12W **182** D2
San Miguel *Campeche, Mexico* 17°54N 90°31W **179** E3
San Miguel *Chihuahua, Mexico* 28°18N 104°17W **169** E11
San Miguel *Chihuahua, Mexico* 28°15N 107°23W **169** E8
San Miguel *Coahuila, Mexico* 28°37N 102°57W **170** B2
San Miguel *Jalisco, Mexico* 19°39N 104°45W **174** C3
San Miguel *Monterrey, Mexico* 25°43N 100°10W **180** B2
San Miguel *Panama* 8°27N 78°55W **182** E4
San Miguel *Calif., U.S.A.* 35°45N 120°42W **127** H6
San Miguel *N. Mex., U.S.A.* 32°9N 106°44W **131** E4
San Miguel → *Chihuahua, Mexico* 26°55N 107°56W **169** G8
San Miguel → *Colo., U.S.A.* 38°23N 108°48W **125** D2
San Miguel, Cabo *Baja Calif. S., Mexico* 28°12N 112°48W **167** E6
San Miguel, Pta. *Baja Calif., Mexico* 31°53N 116°46W **166** B2
San Miguel Ahuehuetitlán *Oaxaca, Mexico* 17°37N 98°21W **177** G2
San Miguel Ajusco *Distrito Federal, Mexico* 19°13N 99°11W **181** C2
San Miguel Chicohua *Oaxaca, Mexico* 17°38N 97°10W **177** G3
San Miguel County ☆ *Colo., U.S.A.* 38°0N 108°30W **125** D1
San Miguel County ☆ *N. Mex., U.S.A.* 35°30N 105°0W **131** B6
San Miguel de Allende *Guanajuato, Mexico* 20°55N 100°45W **175** B7
San Miguel de Cruces *Durango, Mexico* 24°25N 105°53W **172** C5
San Miguel de Horcasitas *Sonora, Mexico* 29°30N 110°43W **168** D5
San Miguel de los Garza *Monterrey, Mexico* 25°50N 100°24W **180** B1
San Miguel de Temoaya *Durango, Mexico* 23°18N 104°30W **173** D6
San Miguel del Cantil *Durango, Mexico* 24°56N 106°16W **172** C4
San Miguel del Puerto *Oaxaca, Mexico* 15°55N 96°10W **177** J4
San Miguel el Alto *Jalisco, Mexico* 21°1N 102°21W **174** A5
San Miguel Huaistita *Jalisco, Mexico* 22°3N 104°19W **173** E6
San Miguel I. *Calif., U.S.A.* 34°2N 120°23W **133** E3
San Miguel Suchixtepec *Oaxaca, Mexico* 16°5N 96°28W **177** H4
San Miguel Talea *Oaxaca, Mexico* 17°12N 96°14W **177** G4
San Miguel Topilejo *Distrito Federal, Mexico* 19°12N 99°9W **181** C3
San Miguel Totolapán *Guerrero, Mexico* 18°8N 100°23W **175** D7
San Miguel Xicalco *Distrito Federal, Mexico* 19°15N 99°10W **181** C3
San Miguelito *Sonora, Mexico* 30°32N 108°55W **168** C7
San Nicolás *Sonora, Mexico* 28°25N 109°10W **168** E6
San Nicolás *Tamaulipas, Mexico* 24°41N 98°48W **171** F6
San Nicolás de los Garza *Nuevo León, Mexico* 25°45N 100°18W **180** B1
San Nicolas I. *Calif., U.S.A.* 33°15N 119°30W **127** K7
San Nicolas Island *Calif., U.S.A.* 33°15N 119°30W **127** K7
San Nicolás Tolentino *San Luis Potosí, Mexico* 22°16N 100°34W **171** H4
San Nicolás Totolapan *Distrito Federal, Mexico* 19°18N 99°15W **181** C2
San Pablo *Calif., U.S.A.* 37°58N 122°21W **126** F4
San Pablo B. *Calif., U.S.A.* 38°5N 122°20W **126** E4
San Pablo Chimalpa *Distrito Federal, Mexico* 19°21N 99°19W **181** B2
San Pablo Etla *Oaxaca, Mexico* 17°8N 96°46W **177** G4
San Pablo Huitzo *Oaxaca, Mexico* 17°15N 96°52W **177** G4
San Pablo Huixtepec *Oaxaca, Mexico* 16°50N 96°46W **177** H4
San Pablo Oztotepec *Distrito Federal, Mexico* 19°11N 99°5W **181** C3
San Patricio *N. Mex., U.S.A.* 33°25N 105°20W **131** D5
San Patricio County ☆ *Tex., U.S.A.* 28°2N 97°31W **109** J10
San Patricio Melaque *Jalisco, Mexico* 19°14N 104°44W **174** C3
San Pedrito *Querétaro, Mexico* 20°19N 100°19W **175** B7
San Pedro *Baja Calif., Mexico* 28°29N 113°24W **166** E5
San Pedro *Baja Calif. S., Mexico* 23°55N 110°17W **167** K8
San Pedro *Sonora, Mexico* 30°47N 112°34W **168** C3
San Pedro *Tabasco, Mexico* 17°46N 91°9W **178** B5
San Pedro *Tex., U.S.A.* 27°48N 97°41W **109** K10
San Pedro → *Chihuahua, Mexico* 28°21N 105°25W **169** E10
San Pedro → *Chihuahua, Mexico* 30°56N 108°8W **169** C7
San Pedro → *Ariz., U.S.A.* 32°59N 110°47W **130** E5
San Pedro Amuzgos *Oaxaca, Mexico* 16°38N 98°5W **177** H2
San Pedro Atocpan *Distrito Federal, Mexico* 19°13N 99°2W **181** C3
San Pedro Atoyac *Oaxaca, Mexico* 16°31N 97°59W **177** H3
San Pedro Atzumba *Puebla, Mexico* 18°8N 97°34W **177** F3
San Pedro Channel *Calif., U.S.A.* 33°30N 118°25W **127** K8
San Pedro de la Cueva *Sonora, Mexico* 29°18N 109°44W **168** D6
San Pedro de las Colonias *Coahuila, Mexico* 25°45N 102°59W **170** E2
San Pedro de Macorís *Dom. Rep.* 18°30N 69°18W **183** C6
San Pedro del Gallo *Durango, Mexico* 25°33N 104°18W **173** B6
San Pedro del Norte *Nic.* 13°4N 84°33W **182** D3
San Pedro Denxhi *Querétaro, Mexico* 20°15N 99°55W **181** A4
San Pedro Huamelula *Oaxaca, Mexico* 16°2N 95°40W **177** H5
San Pedro Huazalingo *Hidalgo, Mexico* 20°57N 98°30W **175** B9
San Pedro Juchatenga *Oaxaca, Mexico* 16°22N 97°5W **177** H3
San Pedro Lagunillas *Nayarit, Mexico* 21°13N 104°46W **172** F6
San Pedro Mártir *Baja Calif., Mexico* 31°3N 115°28W **166** B3
San Pedro Mártir *Distrito Federal, Mexico* 19°16N 99°10W **181** C2
San Pedro Mártir, Sa. de *Baja Calif., Mexico* 30°45N 115°13W **166** C3
San Pedro Naranjestil *Michoacan, Mexico* 18°18N 103°7W **174** D4
San Pedro Nolasco, I. *Sonora, Mexico* 24°58N 111°25W **168** F4
San Pedro Ocampo = Melchor Ocampo *Zacatecas, Mexico* 24°51N 101°39W **173** C9
San Pedro Pochutla *Oaxaca, Mexico* 15°44N 96°28W **177** J4
San Pedro Quiatoni *Oaxaca, Mexico* 16°47N 96°2W **177** H4
San Pedro Sula *Honduras* 15°30N 88°0W **182** C2
San Pedro Tapanatepec *Oaxaca, Mexico* 16°21N 94°12W **177** H6
San Pedro Tláhuac *Distrito Federal, Mexico* 19°17N 99°0W **181** C4

San Pedro Totolapan *Oaxaca, Mexico* 16°40N 96°18W **177** H4
San Pedro Tututepec *Oaxaca, Mexico* 16°9N 97°38W **177** H3
San Pedro Villa de Mitla *Oaxaca, Mexico* 16°55N 96°24W **177** H4
San Pedro y San Pablo → *Tabasco, Mexico* 18°38N 92°29W **178** A4
San Pedro y San Pablo Ayutla *Oaxaca, Mexico* 17°2N 96°4W **177** G4
San Pedro Zacatenco *Distrito Federal, Mexico* 19°30N 99°6W **181** A3
San Perlita *Tex., U.S.A.* 26°30N 97°39W **108** L10
San Pitch → *Utah, U.S.A.* 39°3N 111°51W **129** D4
San Quintín *Baja Calif. S., Mexico* 23°42N 110°23W **167** K8
San Quintín *Chiapas, Mexico* 16°24N 91°20W **178** C5
San Quintín, C. *Baja Calif., Mexico* 30°21N 116°0W **166** C2
San Rafael *Baja Calif. S., Mexico* 27°10N 114°8W **167** F4
San Rafael *Chihuahua, Mexico* 27°28N 107°53W **169** F8
San Rafael *Nuevo León, Mexico* 23°31N 100°13W **171** G4
San Rafael *Nuevo León, Mexico* 25°1N 100°33W **171** E4
San Rafael *Veracruz, Mexico* 20°11N 96°52W **176** D4
San Rafael *Calif., U.S.A.* 37°58N 122°32W **126** F4
San Rafael *N. Mex., U.S.A.* 35°7N 107°53W **131** B3
San Rafael → *Baja Calif. Mexico* 30°58N 116°16W **166** C2
San Rafael → *Utah, U.S.A.* 38°47N 110°7W **129** E5
San Rafael, B. *Baja Calif., Mexico* 28°30N 113°4W **166** E5
San Rafael Champa *Mexico, Mexico* 19°27N 99°15W **181** B2
San Rafael de los Moreno *Jalisco, Mexico* 20°6N 105°10W **174** B2
San Rafael Desert *Utah, U.S.A.* 38°41N 110°26W **129** E5
San Rafael Hills *Calif., U.S.A.* 34°10N 118°12W **133** A3
San Rafael Mts. *Calif., U.S.A.* 34°40N 119°50W **127** J7
San Rafael Swell *Utah, U.S.A.* 38°45N 110°45W **129** E5
San Rodrigo → *Coahuila, Mexico* 28°54N 100°37W **170** B4
San Rolando *Tamaulipas, Mexico* 22°54N 98°51W **171** H6
San Roque *Monterrey, Mexico* 25°36N 100°9W **180** C3
San Roque, Pta. *Baja Calif. S., Mexico* 27°11N 114°27W **167** F4
San Saba *Tex., U.S.A.* 31°12N 98°43W **109** F9
San Saba → *Tex., U.S.A.* 31°15N 98°36W **109** F9
San Saba County ☆ *Tex., U.S.A.* 31°13N 98°47W **109** F9
San Salvador *El Salv.* 13°40N 89°10W **182** D2
San Salvador *Hidalgo, Mexico* 20°17N 99°0W **175** B9
San Salvador Cuauhtenco *Distrito Federal, Mexico* 19°12N 99°7W **181** C3
San Salvador el Seco *Puebla, Mexico* 19°8N 97°39W **177** E3
San Salvador I. *Bahamas* 24°0N 74°40W **183** B5
San Sebastián *Jalisco, Mexico* 20°47N 104°51W **174** B3
San Sebastián *Veracruz, Mexico* 21°13N 98°7W **176** C2
San Sebastián *Puerto Rico* 18°20N 66°59W **184** G16
San Sebastián El Grande *Jalisco, Mexico* 20°32N 103°25W **180** B1
San Sebastián Río Hondo *Oaxaca, Mexico* 16°11N 96°28W **177** H4
San Simeon *Calif., U.S.A.* 35°39N 121°11W **127** H5
San Simon *Ariz., U.S.A.* 32°16N 109°14W **130** E6
San Simón → *Baja Calif., Mexico* 30°30N 115°44W **166** C3
San Simon → *Ariz., U.S.A.* 32°50N 109°39W **130** E6
San Simon Wash → *Ariz., U.S.A.* 31°45N 112°25W **130** F3
San Simón Zahuatlán *Oaxaca, Mexico* 17°50N 98°1W **177** G2
San Telmo *Baja Calif., Mexico* 30°58N 116°6W **166** C2
San Tiburcio *Zacatecas, Mexico* 24°8N 101°32W **173** C9
San Vicente *Baja Calif., Mexico* 31°20N 116°11W **166** B2
San Vicente *Nayarit, Mexico* 21°58N 105°19W **172** F5
San Vicente *San Luis Potosí, Mexico* 24°10N 100°55W **171** F4
San Vicente *San Luis Potosí, Mexico* 21°44N 98°34W **171** J6
San Vicente Coatlán *Oaxaca, Mexico* 16°24N 96°51W **177** H4
San Vicente Lachixio *Oaxaca, Mexico* 16°43N 97°2W **177** H3
San Vito *Costa Rica* 8°50N 82°58W **182** E3
San Xavier Tohono O'odham Indian Reservation *Ariz., U.S.A.* 32°10N 111°0W **130** E4
San Ygnacio *Tex., U.S.A.* 27°3N 99°26W **108** K8
San Ysidro *Calif., U.S.A.* 32°33N 117°2W **133** C2
San Ysidro *N. Mex., U.S.A.* 35°34N 106°46W **131** B4
San Zacarías *Baja Calif. S., Mexico* 27°8N 112°55W **167** F6
Sanak I. *Alaska, U.S.A.* 54°25N 162°40W **135** J7
Sanalona *Sinaloa, Mexico* 24°47N 107°8W **172** C3
Sanalona, Presa *Sinaloa, Mexico* 24°49N 107°7W **172** C3
Sanatoga *Pa., U.S.A.* 40°15N 75°36W **92** B1
Sanborn *Iowa, U.S.A.* 43°11N 95°39W **81** B3
Sanborn *N. Dak., U.S.A.* 46°57N 98°14W **76** D7
Sanborn County ☆ *S. Dak., U.S.A.* 44°0N 98°0W **76** D7
Sanbornville *N.H., U.S.A.* 43°33N 71°2W **89** C3
Sánchez *Dom. Rep.* 19°15N 69°36W **183** C6
Sánchez Magallanes *Tabasco, Mexico* 18°17N 93°54W **178** A3
Sancti Spíritus *Cuba* 21°52N 79°33W **182** B4
Sand → *U.S.A.* 54°23N 111°2W **152** C6
Sand Arroyo Cr. → *U.S.A.* 37°22N 102°8W **82** D1
Sand Cr. → *Ind., U.S.A.* 39°3N 85°51W **85** D5
Sand Cr. → *S. Dak., U.S.A.* 45°7N 103°17W **76** E2
Sand Cr. → *Wyo., U.S.A.* 43°20N 105°2W **124** C7
Sand Draw *Wyo., U.S.A.* 42°46N 108°11W **124** E4
Sand Fork *W. Va., U.S.A.* 38°55N 80°45W **102** C4
Sand Hill → *Minn., U.S.A.* 47°36N 96°52W **77** C2
Sand Hills *Calif., U.S.A.* 32°50N 115°0W **127** L11
Sand Hills *Nebr., U.S.A.* 42°10N 101°30W **80** B4
Sand I. *Hawai'i, U.S.A.* 21°19N 157°53W **136** K14
Sand I. *Oreg., U.S.A.* 43°35N 122°33W **132** A2
Sand I. *Wis., U.S.A.* 46°59N 90°58W **78** B3
Sand Key *Tampa, U.S.A.* 27°54N 82°50W **115** B1
Sand Key Park *Tampa, U.S.A.* 27°58N 82°50W **115** B1
Sand L. *Ont., Canada* 50°10N 94°35W **148** B2
Sand Lake *Mich., U.S.A.* 43°18N 85°31W **79** F6
Sand Lake → *Mich., U.S.A.* 42°38N 73°32W **91** B1
Sand Lake Nat. Wildlife Refuge △ *S. Dak., U.S.A.* 45°48N 98°13W **76** E7
Sand Point *Alaska, U.S.A.* 55°20N 160°30W **135** J7
Sand Pt. *Mich., U.S.A.* 43°53N 83°24W **79** F8
Sand Springs *Okla., U.S.A.* 36°9N 96°7W **107** B7
Sand Tank Mts. *Ariz., U.S.A.* 32°45N 112°30W **130** E3
Sandbank L. *Ont., Canada* 51°8N 82°41W **149** A14
Sandborn *Ind., U.S.A.* 38°54N 87°11W **85** E3
Sanders *Ariz., U.S.A.* 35°13N 109°20W **130** B6
Sanders County ☆ *Mont., U.S.A.* 47°40N 115°30W **123** C2
Sanderson *Fla., U.S.A.* 30°15N 82°16W **114** A6
Sanderson *Tex., U.S.A.* 30°9N 102°24W **108** G5
Sandersville *Ga., U.S.A.* 32°59N 82°48W **113** G4
Sandersville *Miss., U.S.A.* 31°47N 89°2W **111** E4
Sandia *Tex., U.S.A.* 28°1N 97°53W **109** J10
Sandia, Cerro La *Baja Calif., Mexico* 28°27N 113°33W **166** E5
Sandia Indian Reservation *N. Mex., U.S.A.* 35°15N 106°33W **131** B4
Sandia La Victoria *Nuevo León, Mexico* 24°11N 100°4W **171** F4
Sandias *Durango, Mexico* 25°15N 105°37W **172** B5
Sandoval *Ill., U.S.A.* 38°37N 89°7W **84** E4
Sandoval County ☆ *N. Mex., U.S.A.* 35°45N 106°45W **131** A4
Sandpoint *Idaho, U.S.A.* 48°17N 116°33W **122** A2
Sands Point *N.Y., U.S.A.* 40°52N 73°41W **97** A4

Sands Point Preserve *N.Y., U.S.A.* 40°51N 73°43W **97** A4
Sandspit *B.C., Canada* 53°14N 131°49W **154** B3
Sandston *Va., U.S.A.* 37°31N 77°19W **102** D7
Sandstone *Minn., U.S.A.* 46°8N 92°52W **77** D6
Sandtown *Del., U.S.A.* 39°4N 75°44W **93** A5
Sandusky *Mich., U.S.A.* 43°25N 82°50W **79** F9
Sandusky *Ohio, U.S.A.* 41°27N 82°42W **86** B4
Sandusky → *Ohio, U.S.A.* 41°27N 83°0W **86** B3
Sandusky B. *Ohio, U.S.A.* 41°29N 82°50W **86** B4
Sandusky County ☆ *Ohio, U.S.A.* 41°21N 83°7W **86** B3
Sandwich *Ill., U.S.A.* 41°39N 88°37W **84** B5
Sandwich *Mass., U.S.A.* 41°46N 70°30W **91** C4
Sandwich B. *Nfld. & L., Canada* 53°40N 57°15W **143** C6
Sandy *Oreg., U.S.A.* 45°24N 122°16W **132** A3
Sandy *Utah, U.S.A.* 40°35N 111°53W **129** D4 (edit: 41°6N 78°46W?)

Sandy Pa., U.S.A. 41°6N 78°46W **87** C4
Sandy Bay *Man., Canada* 50°33N 98°38W **151** E13
Sandy Bay *Sask., Canada* 55°31N 102°19W **157** E12
Sandy Cay *Long I., Bahamas* 23°13N 75°18W **183** B4
Sandy Cove *Nfld. & L., Canada* 51°21N 56°40W **142** A4
Sandy Cr. → *Wyo., U.S.A.* 41°51N 109°47W **124** E3
Sandy Creek *Mont., U.S.A.* 44°41N 112°10W **123** F5
Sandy Creek *N.Y., U.S.A.* 43°39N 76°5W **88** B4
Sandy Creek *Pa., U.S.A.* 40°28N 79°50W **98** B2
Sandy Hill *Ont., Canada* 45°25N 75°41W **160** A1
Sandy Hook *Ky., U.S.A.* 38°5N 83°8W **105** B9
Sandy Hook *Miss., U.S.A.* 31°2N 89°49W **111** E4
Sandy L. *Alta., Canada* 55°50N 113°25W **152** C7
Sandy L. *Alta., Canada* 53°41N 114°2W **152** E6
Sandy L. *Nfld. & L., Canada* 49°15N 57°0W **142** C4
Sandy L. *Ont., Canada* 53°2N 93°0W **159** G2
Sandy Lake *Ont., Canada* 53°0N 93°15W **159** G2
Sandy Lake Indian Reservation *Minn., U.S.A.* 46°51N 93°19W **77** D5
Sandy Point *N.S., Canada* 43°42N 65°19W **141** K4
Sandy Springs *Ga., U.S.A.* 33°56N 84°23W **113** C2
Sandy Valley *Nev., U.S.A.* 35°49N 115°38W **128** G5
Sandybeach L. *Ont., Canada* 49°49N 92°21W **148** C4
Sandyville *W. Va., U.S.A.* 38°54N 81°40W **102** C3
Sangamon → *Ill., U.S.A.* 40°1N 90°26W **84** C3
Sangamon County ☆ *Ill., U.S.A.* 39°45N 89°40W **84** D4
Sanger *Calif., U.S.A.* 36°42N 119°33W **127** G7
Sanger *Tex., U.S.A.* 33°22N 97°10W **109** D10
Sangre de Cristo *N. Mex., U.S.A.* 36°40N 105°15W **131** A5
Sangre de Cristo Mts. *U.S.A.* 37°30N 105°20W **125** E5
Sangudo *Alta., Canada* 53°50N 114°54W **152** E6
Sanibel *Fla., U.S.A.* 26°27N 82°1W **114** E6
Sanibel I. *Fla., U.S.A.* 26°26N 82°6W **114** E6
Sanikiluaq *Nunavut, Canada* 56°32N 79°14W **159** F10
Sanilac County ☆ *Mich., U.S.A.* 43°25N 82°50W **79** F9
Sanirajak *Nunavut, Canada* 68°46N 81°12W **158** D9
Sanmaur *Qué., Canada* 47°54N 73°47W **145** D9
Sanostee *N. Mex., U.S.A.* 36°25N 108°52W **131** A2
Sanpete County ☆ *Utah, U.S.A.* 39°30N 111°40W **129** D4
Sanpoil → *Wash., U.S.A.* 47°57N 118°41W **120** C7
Sans Bois Mts. *Okla., U.S.A.* 35°1N 95°13W **107** C8
Sanscartier, Parc *Qué., Canada* 45°28N 75°38W **160** A2
Sansom Park *Tex., U.S.A.* 32°48N 97°24W **116** B1
Sant Joseph County ☆ *Mich., U.S.A.* 41°50N 85°30W **79** H6
Santa *Idaho, U.S.A.* 47°9N 116°27W **122** B2
Santa Ana *El Salv.* 14°0N 89°31W **182** D2
Santa Ana *Oaxaca, Mexico* 16°20N 96°44W **177** H4
Santa Ana *Sonora, Mexico* 30°33N 111°7W **168** C4
Santa Ana *Calif., U.S.A.* 33°46N 117°52W **127** K9
Santa Ana, B. *Baja Calif. S., Mexico* 27°40N 112°36W **167** F6
Santa Ana Indian Reservation *N. Mex., U.S.A.* 35°26N 106°37W **131** B4
Santa Ana John Wayne ✈ (SNA) *Calif., U.S.A.* 33°41N 117°52W **127** K9
Santa Ana Maya *Michoacan, Mexico* 20°1N 101°2W **175** B6
Santa Ana Mts. *Calif., U.S.A.* 33°40N 117°30W **127** K9
Santa Ana Pueblo *N. Mex., U.S.A.* 35°26N 106°37W **131** B4
Santa Ana Tepetitlán *Guadalajara, Mexico* 20°37N 103°27W **180** B1
Santa Ana Tlacotenco *Distrito Federal, Mexico* 19°11N 99°0W **181** C4
Santa Ana Travela *Oaxaca, Mexico* 16°40N 95°54W **177** H6
Santa Anita *Coahuila, Mexico* 28°19N 103°31W **170** B1
Santa Anita *Guadalajara, Mexico* 20°33N 103°27W **180** B1
Santa Anna *Tex., U.S.A.* 31°45N 99°20W **109** F8
Santa Bárbara *Honduras* 14°53N 88°14W **182** C2
Santa Bárbara *Chihuahua, Mexico* 26°48N 105°49W **169** G10
Santa Barbara *Calif., U.S.A.* 34°25N 119°42W **127** J7
Santa Barbara Channel *Calif., U.S.A.* 34°15N 120°0W **127** J7
Santa Barbara County ☆ *Calif., U.S.A.* 34°40N 120°0W **127** J6
Santa Barbara I. *Calif., U.S.A.* 33°29N 119°2W **127** K7
Santa Catalina, Gulf of *Calif., U.S.A.* 33°10N 117°50W **127** K9
Santa Catalina, I. *Baja Calif. S., Mexico* 25°40N 110°47W **167** H8
Santa Catalina Mts. *Ariz., U.S.A.* 32°35N 110°50W **130** E5
Santa Catalina Quieri *Oaxaca, Mexico* 16°19N 96°16W **177** H4
Santa Catarina *Baja Calif., Mexico* 29°42N 115°8W **166** D3
Santa Catarina *Guanajuato, Mexico* 21°9N 100°5W **175** A7
Santa Catarina *San Luis Potosí, Mexico* 25°41N 100°28W **180** B1
Santa Catarina Juquila *Oaxaca, Mexico* 16°14N 97°18W **177** H3
Santa Catarina Loxicha *Oaxaca, Mexico* 16°4N 96°46W **177** H4
Santa Catarina Zapoquila *Oaxaca, Mexico* 18°4N 97°35W **177** F3
Santa Cecilia Tepetlapa *Distrito Federal, Mexico* 19°14N 99°5W **181** C3
Santa Clara *Cuba* 22°20N 80°0W **182** B4
Santa Clara *Baja Calif., Mexico* 31°5N 115°17W **166** B3
Santa Clara *Durango, Mexico* 24°29N 103°21W **173** C7
Santa Clara *México, Mexico* 19°33N 99°4W **181** A3
Santa Clara *Calif., U.S.A.* 37°21N 121°57W **126** F5
Santa Clara *N. Mex., U.S.A.* 32°47N 108°9W **131** D2
Santa Clara *N.Y., U.S.A.* 44°38N 74°27W **88** A6
Santa Clara *Oreg., U.S.A.* 44°6N 123°8W **132** B2
Santa Clara *Utah, U.S.A.* 37°8N 113°39W **129** F2
Santa Clara → *Chihuahua, Mexico* 29°51N 107°6W **169** D8
Santa Clara County ☆ *Calif., U.S.A.* 37°15N 121°40W **126** F5
Santa Clara de González *Nuevo León, Mexico* 24°39N 100°1W **171** F4
Santa Clara Indian Reservation *N. Mex., U.S.A.* 35°26N 106°11W **131** B4

Santa Clara Pueblo *N. Mex., U.S.A.* 35°58N 106°5W **131** B4
Santa Clara Valley *Calif., U.S.A.* 36°50N 121°30W **126** G5
Santa Clarita *Calif., U.S.A.* 34°24N 118°33W **127** J8
Santa Claus *Ind., U.S.A.* 38°7N 86°55W **85** E4
Santa Cruz *Costa Rica* 10°15N 85°35W **182** D2
Santa Cruz *Nayarit, Mexico* 21°58N 105°37W **172** F5
Santa Cruz *Calif., U.S.A.* 36°58N 122°1W **126** G4
Santa Cruz → *Chihuahua, Mexico* 27°55N 109°3W **169** F9
Santa Cruz, I. *Baja Calif. S., Mexico* 25°17N 110°43W **167** H8
Santa Cruz Acalpixca *Distrito Federal, Mexico* 19°15N 99°4W **181** C3
Santa Cruz County ☆ *Ariz., U.S.A.* 31°30N 110°45W **130** F5
Santa Cruz County ☆ *Calif., U.S.A.* 37°3N 122°0W **126** G5
Santa Cruz de Bravo = Felipe Carrillo Puerto *Quintana Roo, Mexico* 19°38N 88°3W **179** C5
Santa Cruz del Norte *Cuba* 23°9N 81°55W **182** B3
Santa Cruz del Sur *Cuba* 20°44N 78°0W **182** B4
Santa Cruz del Valle *Guadalajara, Mexico* 20°32N 103°26W **180** B1
Santa Cruz Huatulco *Oaxaca, Mexico* 15°46N 96°7W **177** J4
Santa Cruz I. *Calif., U.S.A.* 34°1N 119°43W **127** J7
Santa Cruz José María *Sonora, Mexico* 31°14N 110°35W **168** B5
Santa Cruz Meyehualco *Distrito Federal, Mexico* 19°20N 99°1W **181** B3
Santa Cruz Mts. *Calif., U.S.A.* 37°15N 122°0W **126** F4
Santa Cruz Wash → *Ariz., U.S.A.* 33°23N 112°12W **130** D3
Santa Domingo, Cay *Bahamas* 21°25N 75°15W **182** B4
Santa Elena *Coahuila, Mexico* 27°27N 102°33W **170** C2
Santa Elena *Yucatán, Mexico* 20°20N 89°39W **179** B4
Santa Elena *Tex., U.S.A.* 26°46N 98°29W **108** L9
Santa Elena → *Mexico* 26°30N 103°50W **169** G12
Santa Elena, C. *Costa Rica* 10°54N 85°56W **182** D2
Santa Fe *Chihuahua, Mexico* 28°33N 104°3W **169** E11
Santa Fe *N. Mex., U.S.A.* 35°41N 105°57W **131** B5
Santa Fe Baldy *N. Mex., U.S.A.* 35°50N 105°46W **131** B5
Santa Fe County ☆ *N. Mex., U.S.A.* 35°30N 106°0W **131** B4
Santa Fe del Pino *Coahuila, Mexico* 28°39N 103°13W **170** B1
Santa Fe L. *Fla., U.S.A.* 29°45N 82°5W **114** B6
Santa Fe Nat. Forest *N. Mex., U.S.A.* 36°3N 106°42W **131** A4
Santa Fe Springs *Calif., U.S.A.* 33°56N 118°3W **133** C4
Santa Gertrudis *Baja Calif. S., Mexico* 23°11N 110°8W **167** K8
Santa Gertrudis *Chihuahua, Mexico* 27°49N 105°44W **169** F10
Santa Gertrudis *Jalisco, Mexico* 20°5N 104°45W **174** B3
Santa Inés, B. *Baja Calif. S., Mexico* 26°59N 111°59W **167** G7
Santa Inés, I. *Baja Calif. S., Mexico* 28°15N 112°52W **167** E6
Santa Inés, I. *Baja Calif. S., Mexico* 27°3N 111°58W **167** F7
Santa Inés Ahuatempan *Puebla, Mexico* 18°25N 98°1W **177** F2
Santa Isabel *Baja Calif. S., Mexico* 25°56N 111°38W **167** H7
Santa Isabel *Chihuahua, Mexico* 28°14N 104°51W **169** E11
Santa Isabel *San Luis Potosí, Mexico* 23°10N 100°50W **171** G4
Santa Isabel *Puerto Rico* 17°58N 66°24W **184** H16
Santa Lucía *Durango, Mexico* 23°37N 105°31W **172** D5
Santa Lucía de la Sierra *Zacatecas, Mexico* 22°27N 104°13W **173** E6
Santa Lucia Range *Calif., U.S.A.* 36°0N 121°20W **127** H5
Santa Margarita, I. *Baja Calif. S., Mexico* 24°27N 111°50W **167** J7
Santa Margarita, Sa. de *Sonora, Mexico* 30°4N 110°2W **168** C5
Santa Margarita L. *Calif., U.S.A.* 35°20N 120°30W **127** H6
Santa María *Sonora, Mexico* 28°57N 111°50W **180** a3
Santa María *Ariz., U.S.A.* 33°25N 112°12W **134** C1
Santa María *Calif., U.S.A.* 34°57N 120°26W **127** J6
Santa María → *Chihuahua, Mexico* 31°0N 107°14W **169** C8
Santa María → *San Luis Potosí, Mexico* 21°37N 99°15W **171** J5
Santa María → *Ariz., U.S.A.* 34°19N 114°31W **130** C1
Santa María, B. *Baja Calif., Mexico* 30°40N 114°40W **166** C4
Santa María, B. *Baja Calif. S., Mexico* 30°30N 115°55W **166** C3
Santa María, B. *Baja Calif. S., Mexico* 24°45N 112°0W **167** J6
Santa María, B. de *Sinaloa, Mexico* 25°4N 108°6W **172** B2
Santa María, I. *Sinaloa, Mexico* 25°39N 109°4W **172** B1
Santa María, L. de *Chihuahua, Mexico* 31°7N 107°16W **169** B8
Santa María Acu *Yucatán, Mexico* 20°33N 90°0W **179** B3
Santa María Ayoquezco *Oaxaca, Mexico* 16°42N 96°51W **177** H4
Santa María Aztahuacan *Distrito Federal, Mexico* 19°21N 99°1W **181** B3
Santa María Chichotla *Oaxaca, Mexico* 18°12N 96°48W **177** F4
Santa María Chimalapa *Oaxaca, Mexico* 16°55N 94°41W **177** H6
Santa María de Cuevas *Chihuahua, Mexico* 27°55N 106°23W **169** F9
Santa María de los Ángeles *Jalisco, Mexico* 22°11N 103°14W **173** E7
Santa María de Mohovano *Durango, Mexico* 26°39N 103°38W **173** A7
Santa María de Ocotán *Durango, Mexico* 22°51N 104°51W **173** E6
Santa María del Oro *Durango, Mexico* 25°56N 105°23W **172** B5
Santa María del Oro *Nayarit, Mexico* 21°20N 104°35W **172** F6
Santa María del Río *San Luis Potosí, Mexico* 21°48N 100°45W **171** J4
Santa María Ecatepec *Oaxaca, Mexico* 16°17N 95°53W **177** H5
Santa María Huatulco *Oaxaca, Mexico* 15°50N 96°17W **177** J4
Santa María Ixcatlán *Oaxaca, Mexico* 17°52N 97°10W **177** G3
Santa María Nativitas *Distrito Federal, Mexico* 19°15N 99°5W **181** C3
Santa María Tecomavaca *Oaxaca, Mexico* 17°57N 97°1W **177** G3
Santa María Totolapilla *Oaxaca, Mexico* 16°37N 95°37W **177** H6
Santa María Tulpetlac *México, Mexico* 19°35N 99°4W **181** A3
Santa María Xadoni *Oaxaca, Mexico* 16°46N 98°0W **177** H3
Santa María Zacatepec *Oaxaca, Mexico* 16°46N 98°0W **177** H3
Santa María Zoquitlán *Oaxaca, Mexico* 16°33N 96°23W **177** H4
Santa Martha *Sonora, Mexico* 29°8N 111°33W **168** D4
Santa Martha, Cerro *Veracruz, Mexico* 18°19N 94°51W **177** F6
Santa Martha Acatitla *Distrito Federal, Mexico* 19°22N 99°2W **181** B3
Santa Matilde *Chihuahua, Mexico* 27°8N 108°23W **169** F7
Santa Mónica *Coahuila, Mexico* 28°38N 103°4W **170** B1
Santa Monica *Calif., U.S.A.* 34°1N 118°29W **133** B2
Santa Monica B. *Calif., U.S.A.* 33°56N 118°28W **127** K8
Santa Monica Mountains Nat. Recr. Area △ *Calif., U.S.A.* 34°4N 118°44W **127** J8
Santa Monica Mts. *Calif., U.S.A.* 34°4N 118°44W **133** B2
Santa Paula *Calif., U.S.A.* 34°21N 119°4W **127** J7
Santa Rita *Guam* 13°23N 144°40E **184** b
Santa Rita *Baja Calif. S., Mexico* 23°40N 110°30W **167** K8
Santa Rita *Nuevo León, Mexico* 24°12N 100°30W **171** F4
Santa Rita *Mont., U.S.A.* 48°42N 112°19W **123** B5
Santa Rita del Rucio *San Luis Potosí, Mexico* 23°5N 100°17W **171** G4
Santa Rosa *Coahuila, Mexico* 28°37N 101°44W **170** B4
Santa Rosa *Guanajuato, Mexico* 21°5N 101°11W **175** A6
Santa Rosa *Guerrero, Mexico* 17°23N 101°4W **175** E6
Santa Rosa *Monterrey, Mexico* 25°49N 100°14W **180** B2
Santa Rosa *Quintana Roo, Mexico* 19°58N 88°15W **179** C5
Santa Rosa *Sonora, Mexico* 28°25N 109°8W **168** E6

Santa Rosa Zacatecas, Mexico 22°56N 103°6W 173 E7
Santa Rosa Ariz., U.S.A. 32°19N 112°2W 130 E3
Santa Rosa Calif., U.S.A. 38°26N 122°43W 126 E4
Santa Rosa N. Mex., U.S.A. 34°57N 104°41W 131 C6
Santa Rosa Tex., U.S.A. 26°16N 97°50W 108 L10
Santa Rosa, L. Quintana Roo, Mexico 19°31N 87°28W 179 C6
Santa Rosa, Mt. Guam 13°32N 144°55E 184 b
Santa Rosa, Sa. Coahuila, Mexico 28°18N 101°49W 170 B3
Santa Rosa, Sa. Sonora, Mexico 30°5N 111°35W 168 C4
Santa Rosa and San Jacinto Mountains Nat. Monument ⌂ U.S.A. 33°28N 116°20W 127 J8
Santa Rosa Beach Fla., U.S.A. 30°22N 86°14W 114 A2
Santa Rosa County ☆ Fla., U.S.A. 30°45N 87°0W 114 A2
Santa Rosa de Copán Honduras 14°47N 88°46W 182 D2
Santa Rosa de Jauregui Querétaro, Mexico 20°45N 100°27W 175 B7
Santa Rosa I. Calif., U.S.A. 33°58N 120°6W 127 K6
Santa Rosa I. Fla., U.S.A. 30°20N 86°50W 114 A2
Santa Rosa Indian Reservation Calif., U.S.A. 33°34N 116°32W 127 K10
Santa Rosa L. N. Mex., U.S.A. 35°2N 104°41W 131 B6
Santa Rosa Mts. Calif., U.S.A. 33°20N 116°15W 127 K10
Santa Rosa Range Nev., U.S.A. 41°45N 117°40W 128 A3
Santa Rosa Wash → Ariz., U.S.A. 33°0N 112°0W 130 E4
Santa Rosa Xochiac Distrito Federal, Mexico 19°20N 99°18W 181 C2
Santa Rosalía Baja Calif. S., Mexico 27°19N 112°17W 167 F6
Santa Rosalía Baja Calif., Mexico 28°40N 114°14W 166 E4
Santa Rosalía, B. Baja Calif., Mexico 28°37N 114°13W 166 E4
Santa Rosalía, Pta. Baja Calif., Mexico 28°39N 114°16W 166 E4
Santa Tecla = Nueva San Salvador El Salv. 13°40N 89°18W 182 D2
Santa Teresa Nayarit, Mexico 22°28N 104°44W 172 E6
Santa Teresa Tamaulipas, Mexico 25°17N 97°51W 171 E7
Santa Teresa, Pta. Baja Calif. S., Mexico 26°45N 111°38W 167 G7
Santa Teresa N. Mex., U.S.A. 31°51N 106°38W 131 F4
Santa Ursula Xitla Distrito Federal, Mexico 19°16N 99°11W 181 C2
Santa Ynez Calif., U.S.A. 34°37N 120°5W 127 J6
Santa Ynez → Calif., U.S.A. 34°41N 120°36W 127 J6
Santa Ynez Mts. Calif., U.S.A. 34°30N 120°0W 127 J7
Santa Ysabel Indian Reservation Calif., U.S.A. 33°10N 116°40W 127 K10
Santander Jiménez Tamaulipas, Mexico 24°13N 98°28W 171 F6
Santanilla, Is. Honduras 17°22N 83°57W 182 C3
Santaquin Utah, U.S.A. 39°59N 111°47W 129 D4
Santaren Channel W. Indies 24°0N 79°30W 182 B4
Santa's Village N.H., U.S.A. 44°27N 71°32W 89 B3
Sante Genevieve Mo., U.S.A. 37°59N 90°3W 83 D6
Santee Calif., U.S.A. 32°50N 116°58W 133 A2
Santee Nebr., U.S.A. 42°51N 97°50W 80 B8
Santee S.C., U.S.A. 33°29N 80°29W 103 E5
Santee → S.C., U.S.A. 33°7N 79°17W 103 E6
Santee Indian Reservation Nebr., U.S.A. 42°50N 97°50W 80 B8
Santee Lake Calif., U.S.A. 32°50N 117°0W 133 A2
Santiago Baja Calif. S., Mexico 23°28N 109°43W 167 K9
Santiago Colima, Mexico 19°7N 104°21W 174 C3
Santiago Nuevo León, Mexico 25°27N 100°9W 170 E4
Santiago Panama 8°0N 81°0W 182 E3
Santiago → Durango, Mexico 25°11N 105°26W 172 B5
Santiago Acahualtepec Distrito Federal, Mexico 19°21N 99°0W 181 B3
Santiago Amoltepec Oaxaca, Mexico 16°38N 97°30W 177 H3
Santiago Astata Oaxaca, Mexico 15°59N 95°40W 177 J5
Santiago Atzuquilla Oaxaca, Mexico 17°57N 97°58W 177 G3
Santiago de Anaya Hidalgo, Mexico 20°22N 98°56W 175 B9
Santiago de Cuba Cuba 20°0N 75°49W 182 C4
Santiago de los Caballeros Dom. Rep. 19°30N 70°40W 183 C5
Santiago Domingo Xagacia Oaxaca, Mexico 17°8N 96°17W 177 G4
Santiago Huauclilla Oaxaca, Mexico 17°28N 97°4W 177 H3
Santiago Ixcuintepec Oaxaca, Mexico 16°56N 95°38W 177 H6
Santiago Ixcuintla Nayarit, Mexico 21°49N 105°13W 172 F5
Santiago Jamiltepec Oaxaca, Mexico 16°35N 97°49W 177 H3
Santiago Jamiltepec Oaxaca, Mexico 16°17N 97°49W 177 H3
Santiago Jxtlahuaca Oaxaca, Mexico 17°20N 98°1W 177 G2
Santiago Llano Grande Oaxaca, Mexico 16°28N 98°11W 177 H2
Santiago Maravatío Guanajuato, Mexico 20°10N 101°0W 175 B7
Santiago Miahuatlán Puebla, Mexico 18°34N 97°26W 177 F3
Santiago Minas Oaxaca, Mexico 16°26N 97°13W 177 H3
Santiago Mts. Tex., U.S.A. 29°55N 103°22W 108 H4
Santiago Papasquiaro Durango, Mexico 25°2N 105°25W 172 B5
Santiago Peak Tex., U.S.A. 29°47N 103°25W 108 H4
Santiago Tenotepa Nacional Oaxaca, Mexico 16°19N 98°1W 177 H2
Santiago Quiotepec Oaxaca, Mexico 17°55N 96°57W 177 G4
Santiago Tangamandapio Michoacan, Mexico 19°57N 102°26W 174 C5
Santiago Tepalcatlalpan Distrito Federal, Mexico 19°15N 99°8W 181 C3
Santiago Tepatlaxco México, Mexico 19°28N 99°20W 181 B1
Santiago Tilantongo Oaxaca, Mexico 17°17N 97°20W 177 H3
Santiago Tulyehualco Distrito Federal, Mexico 19°15N 99°1W 181 C3
Santiago Tuxtla Veracruz, Mexico 18°28N 95°18W 177 F5
Santiago Yancuitlalpan México, Mexico 19°23N 99°19W 181 B2
Santiago Yaveo Oaxaca, Mexico 17°20N 95°42W 177 G5
Santiago Yosondúa Oaxaca, Mexico 16°53N 97°34W 177 H3
Santiago Zacatepec Oaxaca, Mexico 17°11N 95°51W 177 H6
Santiaguillo, L. de Durango, Mexico 24°48N 104°48W 173 C6
Santiam → Oreg., U.S.A. 44°25N 121°55W 121 C4
Santo Domingo Dom. Rep. 18°30N 69°59W 183 C6
Santo Domingo Baja Calif. Mexico 28°12N 114°2W 167 F2
Santo Domingo Baja Calif. S., Mexico 25°29N 111°55W 167 H7
Santo Domingo Oaxaca, Mexico 16°48N 104°28W 173 H6
Santo Domingo Oaxaca, Mexico 16°34N 94°51W 177 H6
Santo Domingo Nic. 12°14N 84°59W 182 D3
Santo Domingo → Baja Calif., Mexico 30°43N 116°4W 166 C3
Santo Domingo Indian Reservation N. Mex., U.S.A. 35°30N 106°30W 131 B4
Santo Domingo Pueblo N. Mex., U.S.A. 35°31N 106°22W 131 B4
Santo Domingo Tehuantepec Oaxaca, Mexico 16°20N 95°14W 177 H5
Santo Tomás Baja Calif. Mexico 31°33N 116°24W 166 B2
Santo Tomás → Baja Calif. Mexico 31°34N 116°42W 166 B2
Santo Tomás, Pta. Baja Calif. Mexico 31°33N 116°42W 166 B2
Santos Reyes Nopala Oaxaca, Mexico 16°6N 97°10W 177 H3
Saona I. Dom. Rep. 18°10N 68°40W 183 C6
Sapello N. Mex., U.S.A. 35°46N 105°15W 131 B5
Sapello L. Ga., U.S.A. 31°25N 81°12W 113 E5
Sapello Island Ga., U.S.A. 31°23N 81°17W 113 E5

Sapelo Sound Ga., U.S.A. 31°30N 81°10W 113 E5
Sappa Cr. → Nebr., U.S.A. 40°7N 99°39W 80 D6
Sappho Wash., U.S.A. 48°4N 124°16W 120 B1
Sapulpa Okla., U.S.A. 35°59N 96°5W 107 C7
Sara, L. Ill., U.S.A. 39°8N 88°36W 84 D5
Saragosa Tex., U.S.A. 31°2N 103°39W 108 F4
Sarah Miss., U.S.A. 34°34N 90°13W 111 B3
Saraland Ala., U.S.A. 30°50N 88°4W 112 F2
Saranac Mich., U.S.A. 42°56N 85°13W 79 G6
Saranac → N.Y., U.S.A. 44°39N 73°45W 88 A7
Saranac Lake N.Y., U.S.A. 44°20N 74°10W 88 A6
Saranac Lakes N.Y., U.S.A. 44°20N 74°28W 88 A6
Sarasota Fla., U.S.A. 27°20N 82°32W 114 D6
Sarasota County ☆ Fla., U.S.A. 27°15N 82°20W 114 D6
Saratoga Calif., U.S.A. 37°16N 122°2W 126 F4
Saratoga Ind., U.S.A. 40°14N 84°55W 85 C6
Saratoga Wyo., U.S.A. 41°27N 106°49W 124 E6
Saratoga County ☆ N.Y., U.S.A. 43°10N 73°50W 88 B7
Saratoga L. N.Y., U.S.A. 43°1N 73°45W 88 B7
Saratoga Nat. Historical Park ⌂ N.Y., U.S.A. 43°0N 73°38W 88 C7
Saratoga Springs N.Y., U.S.A. 43°5N 73°47W 88 B7
Sarcobatus Flat Nev., U.S.A. 37°10N 116°58W 128 E4
Sarcoxie Mo., U.S.A. 37°3N 94°7W 83 D2
Sardinas Durango, Mexico 26°7N 105°32W 172 A5
Sardinia Ohio, U.S.A. 39°0N 83°49W 86 E3
Sardis Ala., U.S.A. 32°17N 86°59W 112 D4
Sardis Ga., U.S.A. 32°58N 81°46W 113 D5
Sardis Miss., U.S.A. 34°26N 89°55W 111 B4
Sardis Tenn., U.S.A. 35°27N 88°18W 104 E4
Sardis L. Miss., U.S.A. 34°25N 89°48W 111 B4
Sardis L. Okla., U.S.A. 34°40N 95°25W 107 D8
Sarepta La., U.S.A. 32°54N 93°27W 110 B2
Sarepta N.Y., U.S.A. 34°7N 89°17W 111 B4
Sargeant Minn., U.S.A. 43°48N 92°48W 77 G6
Sargent Ga., U.S.A. 33°26N 84°52W 113 C2
Sargent Nebr., U.S.A. 41°39N 99°22W 80 C6
Sargent County ☆ N. Dak., U.S.A. 46°30N 97°45W 76 D8
Sargents Colo., U.S.A. 38°25N 106°24W 125 D4
Sáric Sonora, Mexico 31°8N 111°21W 168 B4
Sarigan N. Marianas 16°43N 145°47E 184 a
Sarita Tex., U.S.A. 27°13N 97°47W 108 K10
Sarles N. Dak., U.S.A. 48°58N 99°0W 76 B7
Sarnia Ont., Canada 42°58N 82°23W 146 E4
Sarpy County ☆ Nebr., U.S.A. 41°10N 96°10W 80 C9
Sartell Minn., U.S.A. 45°37N 94°12W 77 E4
Sasabe Ariz., U.S.A. 31°29N 111°33W 130 F4
Sasaginnigak L. Man., Canada 51°36N 95°39W 151 D16
Sasakwa Okla., U.S.A. 34°57N 96°31W 107 D7
Saseginaga, L. Qué., Canada 47°6N 78°35W 144 D4
Saskatchewan □ Sask., Canada 54°40N 106°0W 150 B3
Saskatchewan → Sask., Canada 53°37N 100°40W 151 B11
Saskatchewan Landing Prov. Park ⌂ Sask., Canada 50°38N 107°59W 150 E4
Saskatoon Sask., Canada 52°10N 106°38W 150 C5
Saspamco Tex., U.S.A. 29°14N 98°17W 116 D4
Sassafras Md., U.S.A. 39°22N 75°20W 93 A5
Sassafras Mt. S.C., U.S.A. 35°4N 82°47W 103 C3
Sasser Ga., U.S.A. 31°43N 84°21W 113 E2
Satanta Kans., U.S.A. 37°26N 100°59W 82 D3
Satartia Miss., U.S.A. 32°40N 90°33W 111 D3
Satellite Beach Fla., U.S.A. 28°10N 80°36W 114 C8
Satevó Chihuahua, Mexico 27°57N 106°7W 169 F9
Satilla → Ga., U.S.A. 30°59N 81°29W 113 E5
Satolah Ga., U.S.A. 34°59N 83°11W 113 B3
Satsuma Ala., U.S.A. 30°51N 88°4W 112 F2
Saturna B.C., Canada 48°47N 123°11W 155 G11
Satus Pass Wash., U.S.A. 45°59N 120°39W 120 E5
Saubosq, L. Qué., Canada 51°30N 64°53W 140 B5
Sauceda Coahuila, Mexico 25°46N 101°19W 170 D4
Sauceda Mts. Ariz., U.S.A. 32°35N 112°35W 130 E3
Saucier Miss., U.S.A. 30°39N 89°8W 111 F4
Saucillo Chihuahua, Mexico 28°1N 105°17W 169 E10
Saugatuck Mich., U.S.A. 42°40N 86°12W 79 G5
Saugatuck → Conn., U.S.A. 41°7N 73°22W 91 C1
Saugeen → Ont., Canada 44°30N 81°22W 146 C5
Saugerties N.Y., U.S.A. 42°5N 73°57W 88 C7
Sauget Ill., U.S.A. 38°35N 90°11W 94 B3
Saugus Mass., U.S.A. 42°28N 71°0W 96 A2
Saugus → Mass., U.S.A. 42°27N 70°58W 96 A2
Sauk → Wash., U.S.A. 48°29N 121°36W 120 B4
Sauk Centre Minn., U.S.A. 45°44N 94°57W 77 E4
Sauk City Wis., U.S.A. 43°17N 89°43W 78 E4
Sauk County ☆ Wis., U.S.A. 43°25N 89°50W 78 E4
Sauk Rapids Minn., U.S.A. 45°35N 94°10W 77 E4
Saukville Wis., U.S.A. 43°23N 87°56W 78 E6
Saulnierville N.S., Canada 44°16N 66°8W 141 J3
Saulsbury Tenn., U.S.A. 35°3N 89°5W 104 E3
Sault-au-Récollet Qué., Canada 45°35N 73°39W 160 A3
Sault aux Cochons → Qué., Canada 48°44N 69°4W 145 C13
Sault Ste. Marie Ont., Canada 46°30N 84°20W 146 A2
Sault Ste. Marie Mich., U.S.A. 46°30N 84°21W 79 C7
Saumons → Qué., Canada 49°25N 62°15W 140 D7
Saumur, L. Qué., Canada 51°16N 62°49W 140 B7
Saunders County ☆ Nebr., U.S.A. 41°15N 96°40W 80 C9
Saunemin Ill., U.S.A. 40°54N 88°24W 84 C5
Sauquoit N.Y., U.S.A. 43°5N 75°16W 88 C5
Sausalito Calif., U.S.A. 37°51N 122°29W 132 A2
Sauvage, L. Qué., Canada 50°6N 74°30W 144 A8
Sauz Mocho Durango, Mexico 24°39N 103°39W 173 C7
Savá Honduras 15°32N 86°15W 182 C2
Savage Md., U.S.A. 39°8N 76°50W 93 A4
Savage Miss., U.S.A. 34°38N 90°13W 111 B3
Savage Mont., U.S.A. 47°27N 104°21W 123 C13
Savage River State Forest Md., U.S.A. 39°41N 79°12W 93 A1
Savagetown Wyo., U.S.A. 43°52N 105°47W 124 C7
Savanna Ill., U.S.A. 42°5N 90°8W 84 A31
Savanna Okla., U.S.A. 34°50N 95°50W 107 D8
Savanna-la-Mar Jamaica 18°10N 78°10W 182 C4
Savannah → Ga., U.S.A. 32°5N 81°6W 113 D5
Savannah Mo., U.S.A. 39°56N 94°50W 83 B2
Savannah Ohio, U.S.A. 40°58N 82°22W 86 C4
Savannah Tenn., U.S.A. 35°14N 88°15W 104 E4
Savannah → Ga., U.S.A. 32°2N 80°53W 103 F5
Savannah Beach = Tybee Island Ga., U.S.A. 32°1N 80°51W 113 D6
Savannah River Plant S.C., U.S.A. 33°15N 81°35W 103 E4
Savant L. Ont., Canada 50°16N 90°44W 148 B6
Savant Lake Ont., Canada 50°14N 90°40W 148 B6
Savona B.C., Canada 50°45N 120°50W 155 E14
Savonburg Kans., U.S.A. 37°45N 95°9W 82 D8
Savoonga Alaska, U.S.A. 63°42N 170°29W 135 E5
Savoy Ill., U.S.A. 40°3N 88°15W 84 C5

Sawatch Range Colo., U.S.A. 39°0N 106°30W 125 D4
Sawpit Colo., U.S.A. 37°56N 108°6W 125 E2
Sawtooth City Idaho, U.S.A. 43°54N 114°50W 122 F4
Sawtooth Mts. Minn., U.S.A. 47°30N 91°0W 77 C8
Sawtooth Nat. Forest Utah, U.S.A. 41°54N 113°29W 122 H5
Sawtooth Nat. Recr. Area ⌂ Idaho, U.S.A. 44°0N 114°50W 122 E4
Sawtooth Range Idaho, U.S.A. 44°3N 114°58W 122 E4
Sawtooth Wilderness Idaho, U.S.A. 43°59N 115°4W 122 F3
Sawyer Kans., U.S.A. 37°30N 98°41W 82 D5
Sawyer Mich., U.S.A. 41°53N 86°35W 79 H5
Sawyer N. Dak., U.S.A. 48°5N 101°3W 76 B4
Sawyer Okla., U.S.A. 34°1N 95°23W 107 D8
Sawyer County ☆ Wis., U.S.A. 45°50N 91°0W 78 C3
Sawyers Bar Calif., U.S.A. 41°18N 123°7W 126 B3
Sawyerville Qué., Canada 45°20N 71°34W 145 F11
Saxapahaw N.C., U.S.A. 35°57N 79°19W 103 C6
Saxis Va., U.S.A. 37°55N 75°43W 93 C5
Saxonburg Pa., U.S.A. 40°45N 79°49W 87 D3
Saxton Ky., U.S.A. 36°38N 84°7W 105 D8
Saxton Pa., U.S.A. 40°13N 78°15W 87 D4
Sayabec Qué., Canada 48°35N 67°41W 140 E2
Saybrook Ill., U.S.A. 40°26N 88°32W 84 C5
Sayers Tex., U.S.A. 29°22N 98°17W 116 C4
Sayil Yucatán, Mexico 20°8N 89°40W 179 B4
Saylorsburg Pa., U.S.A. 40°54N 75°19W 92 B1
Saylorville L. Iowa, U.S.A. 41°48N 93°46W 81 D5
Sayre Okla., U.S.A. 35°18N 99°38W 107 C4
Sayre Pa., U.S.A. 41°59N 76°32W 87 C6
Sayreville N.J., U.S.A. 40°28N 74°22W 92 B2
Sayula Jalisco, Mexico 19°52N 103°36W 174 C4
Sayula de Alemán Veracruz, Mexico 17°52N 94°57W 177 G6
Sayulita Nayarit, Mexico 20°52N 105°27W 172 G5
Sayville N.Y., U.S.A. 40°44N 73°5W 92 B3
Scaggsville Md., U.S.A. 39°9N 76°54W 93 A4
Scales Mound Ill., U.S.A. 42°29N 90°15W 84 A3
Scammon Kans., U.S.A. 37°17N 94°49W 82 D9
Scammon Bay Alaska, U.S.A. 61°51N 165°35W 135 F6
Scandia Alta., Canada 50°20N 112°2W 153 H8
Scandia Kans., U.S.A. 39°48N 97°47W 82 B6
Scandinavia Wis., U.S.A. 44°27N 89°9W 78 D4
Scanlon Minn., U.S.A. 46°42N 92°26W 77 D5
Scappoose Oreg., U.S.A. 45°45N 122°53W 121 B3
Scarborough Ont., Canada 43°44N 79°14W 161 A3
Scarborough Trin. & Tob. 11°11N 60°42W 183 D7
Scarborough Maine, U.S.A. 43°35N 70°19W 90 E3
Scarborough Bluffs Ont., Canada 43°42N 79°14W 161 A3
Scarsdale N.Y., U.S.A. 29°50N 89°58W 117 C3
Scarsdale N.Y., U.S.A. 40°59N 73°49W 92 B3
Scarville Iowa, U.S.A. 43°28N 93°37W 81 B5
Scatarie I. N.S., Canada 46°0N 59°44W 141 G10
Scenic S. Dak., U.S.A. 43°47N 102°33W 76 G3
Scenic Woods Tex., U.S.A. 29°51N 95°18W 116 A3
Sceptre Sask., Canada 50°51N 109°15W 150 E2
Schaller Iowa, U.S.A. 42°30N 95°18W 81 C3
Schaumburg Ill., U.S.A. 42°2N 88°5W 84 A5
Schefferville = Kawawachikamach Qué., Canada 54°48N 66°50W 143 C4
Schell City Mo., U.S.A. 38°1N 94°7W 83 C2
Schell Creek Ra. Nev., U.S.A. 39°25N 114°40W 128 C6
Schellsburg Pa., U.S.A. 40°3N 78°39W 87 D4
Schenectady N.Y., U.S.A. 42°49N 73°57W 88 C7
Schenectady County ☆ N.Y., U.S.A. 42°50N 74°0W 88 C7
Schenley Park Pa., U.S.A. 40°25N 79°56W 98 B2
Schererville Ind., U.S.A. 41°29N 87°27W 85 B3
Scherr W. Va., U.S.A. 39°12N 79°10W 93 A1
Schertz Tex., U.S.A. 29°33N 98°16W 116 B4
Schiller Park Ill., U.S.A. 41°56N 87°52W 95 B1
Schiller Woods Ill., U.S.A. 41°57N 87°51W 95 B1
Schlater Miss., U.S.A. 33°39N 90°21W 111 C3
Schleicher County ☆ Tex., U.S.A. 30°52N 100°36W 108 G7
Schleswig Iowa, U.S.A. 42°10N 95°26W 81 C3
Schley County ☆ Ga., U.S.A. 32°15N 84°15W 113 D2
Schoen Lake Park ⌂ B.C., Canada 50°11N 126°14W 154 E8
Schoenchen Kans., U.S.A. 38°43N 99°20W 82 C4
Schofield Wis., U.S.A. 44°54N 89°36W 78 D4
Schofield Barracks Hawai'i, U.S.A. 21°29N 158°7W 136 K13
Schoharie N.Y., U.S.A. 42°40N 74°19W 88 C6
Schoharie County ☆ N.Y., U.S.A. 42°35N 74°30W 88 C6
Schoharie Cr. → N.Y., U.S.A. 42°57N 74°18W 88 C6
Schoharie Res. N.Y., U.S.A. 42°22N 74°26W 88 C6
Schoodic L. Maine, U.S.A. 45°23N 68°56W 90 C5
Schoolcraft Mich., U.S.A. 42°7N 85°38W 79 G6
Schoolcraft County ☆ Mich., U.S.A. 46°10N 86°15W 79 C5
Schreiber Ont., Canada 48°45N 87°20W 149 D6
Schriever La., U.S.A. 29°45N 90°49W 110 E5
Schroon L. N.Y., U.S.A. 43°47N 73°47W 88 B7
Schroon Lake N.Y., U.S.A. 43°50N 73°46W 88 B7
Schulenburg Tex., U.S.A. 29°41N 96°54W 109 H11
Schuler Alta., Canada 50°20N 110°6W 153 H10
Schultz L. Nunavut, Canada 64°45N 97°30W 159 E6
Schumacher Ont., Canada 48°30N 81°16W 149 D15
Schurz Nev., U.S.A. 38°57N 118°49W 128 D2
Schuyler Nebr., U.S.A. 41°27N 97°4W 80 C8
Schuyler Va., U.S.A. 37°47N 78°42W 102 D6
Schuyler County ☆ Ill., U.S.A. 40°10N 90°40W 84 C3
Schuyler County ☆ Mo., U.S.A. 40°25N 92°30W 83 A4
Schuyler County ☆ N.Y., U.S.A. 42°20N 76°50W 88 C4
Schuylkill → Pa., U.S.A. 39°53N 75°12W 87 E7
Schuylkill County ☆ Pa., U.S.A. 40°48N 76°10W 87 D6
Schuylkill Haven Pa., U.S.A. 40°37N 76°11W 87 D6
Schwatka Mts. Alaska, U.S.A. 67°20N 156°30W 135 C8
Schweitzer Mt. Idaho, U.S.A. 48°23N 116°37W 122 A2
Science and Industry, Museum of Ill., U.S.A. 41°47N 87°34W 95 C3
Science Hill Ky., U.S.A. 37°11N 84°38W 105 C8
Scio Ohio, U.S.A. 40°24N 81°5W 86 D5
Scio Oreg., U.S.A. 44°42N 122°51W 121 C3
Scioto → Ohio, U.S.A. 38°44N 83°1W 86 E3
Scioto County ☆ Ohio, U.S.A. 38°53N 82°59W 86 E4
Scipio Okla., U.S.A. 35°3N 95°58W 107 C8
Scipio Utah, U.S.A. 39°15N 112°6W 129 D3
Scitrek Museum Georgia, U.S.A. 33°46N 84°22W 117 B2
Scituate Mass., U.S.A. 42°12N 70°44W 91 B4
Scituate Res. R.I., U.S.A. 41°45N 71°35W 91 C3
Scobey Mont., U.S.A. 48°47N 105°25W 123 B12
Scofield Utah, U.S.A. 39°44N 111°10W 129 D4
Scofield Res. Utah, U.S.A. 39°49N 111°8W 129 D4
Scooba Miss., U.S.A. 32°50N 88°29W 111 D5
Scoresby, C. Nunavut, Canada 71°43N 93°41W 158 C7
Scoresby Sund Greenland 70°28N 21°46W 162 C8
Scoresbysund = Ittoqqortoormiit Greenland 70°20N 23°0W 162 C8

Scotch Plains N.J., U.S.A. 40°39N 74°24W 92 B2
Scotchtown N.Y., U.S.A. 41°29N 74°22W 92 A2
Scotia Calif., U.S.A. 40°29N 124°6W 126 C2
Scotia N.Y., U.S.A. 42°50N 73°58W 88 C7
Scotia Nebr., U.S.A. 41°28N 98°42W 80 C7
Scotland Ont., Canada 43°1N 80°22W 146 D6
Scotland Ark., U.S.A. 35°32N 92°37W 106 C3
Scotland Conn., U.S.A. 41°42N 72°7W 91 C2
Scotland Md., U.S.A. 38°5N 76°22W 93 B4
Scotland S. Dak., U.S.A. 43°9N 97°43W 76 G8
Scotland County ☆ Mo., U.S.A. 40°25N 92°10W 83 A4
Scotland County ☆ N.C., U.S.A. 34°50N 79°30W 103 D6
Scotland Neck N.C., U.S.A. 36°8N 77°25W 103 B8
Scotlandville La., U.S.A. 30°31N 91°11W 110 D4
Scotrun Pa., U.S.A. 41°4N 75°19W 92 A1
Scotstown Qué., Canada 45°32N 71°17W 145 F11
Scott Sask., Canada 52°22N 108°50W 150 C3
Scott Ark., U.S.A. 34°42N 92°6W 106 D3
Scott La., U.S.A. 30°14N 92°6W 110 D3
Scott Miss., U.S.A. 33°36N 91°5W 111 C2
Scott Ohio, U.S.A. 40°59N 84°35W 86 C2
Scott → La., U.S.A. 41°48N 123°2W 126 B4
Scott, Mt. Oreg., U.S.A. 42°56N 122°1W 121 E3
Scott Air Force Base Ill., U.S.A. 38°34N 89°51W 84 E4
Scott Bar Mts. Calif., U.S.A. 41°50N 123°0W 126 B4
Scott Chan. B.C., Canada 50°45N 128°30W 154 E6
Scott City Kans., U.S.A. 38°29N 100°54W 82 C3
Scott City Mo., U.S.A. 37°12N 89°30W 83 D7
Scott County ☆ Ark., U.S.A. 34°54N 94°5W 106 D1
Scott County ☆ Ill., U.S.A. 39°40N 90°30W 84 D3
Scott County ☆ Ind., U.S.A. 38°40N 85°45W 85 E5
Scott County ☆ Iowa, U.S.A. 41°35N 90°35W 81 D8
Scott County ☆ Kans., U.S.A. 38°30N 101°0W 82 C3
Scott County ☆ Ky., U.S.A. 38°15N 84°35W 105 B8
Scott County ☆ Minn., U.S.A. 44°40N 93°30W 77 F5
Scott County ☆ Miss., U.S.A. 32°22N 89°29W 111 D4
Scott County ☆ Mo., U.S.A. 37°0N 89°35W 83 E7
Scott County ☆ Tenn., U.S.A. 36°25N 84°29W 105 D8
Scott County ☆ Va., U.S.A. 36°55N 82°45W 102 E2
Scott Is. B.C., Canada 50°48N 128°40W 154 E6
Scott Islands Park ⌂ B.C., Canada 50°48N 128°40W 154 E6
Scott-Jonction Qué., Canada 46°30N 71°4W 145 E11
Scott L. Sask., Canada 59°55N 106°18W 157 E11
Scott Mts. Calif., U.S.A. 41°15N 122°45W 126 B4
Scott Peak Idaho, U.S.A. 44°21N 112°49W 122 E6
Scottdale Georgia, U.S.A. 33°47N 84°16W 117 B3
Scottdale Pa., U.S.A. 40°6N 79°35W 87 D3
Scotts Bluff County ☆ Nebr., U.S.A. 41°50N 103°40W 80 C2
Scotts Bluff Nat. Monument ⌂ Nebr., U.S.A. 41°50N 103°40W 80 C2
Scotts Hill Tenn., U.S.A. 35°31N 88°15W 104 E4
Scotts Valley Calif., U.S.A. 37°3N 122°1W 126 F4
Scottsbluff Nebr., U.S.A. 41°52N 103°40W 80 C2
Scottsboro Ala., U.S.A. 34°40N 86°2W 112 B4
Scottsburg Ind., U.S.A. 38°41N 85°47W 85 E5
Scottsburg Oreg., U.S.A. 43°39N 123°49W 121 D2
Scottsburg Va., U.S.A. 36°45N 78°48W 102 E6
Scottsdale Ariz., U.S.A. 33°40N 111°53W 134 A3
Scottsdale ✈ (SCF) Ariz., U.S.A. 33°37N 111°54W 134 B3
Scottsville Kans., U.S.A. 39°32N 97°57W 82 B6
Scottsville Ky., U.S.A. 36°45N 86°11W 104 D6
Scottsville Va., U.S.A. 37°48N 78°30W 102 D6
Scottville Mich., U.S.A. 43°58N 86°17W 79 F5
Scotty's Junction Nev., U.S.A. 37°18N 117°3W 128 E3
Scranton Iowa, U.S.A. 42°1N 94°33W 81 C4
Scranton Kans., U.S.A. 38°47N 95°44W 82 C8
Scranton N. Dak., U.S.A. 46°9N 103°9W 76 D2
Scranton Pa., U.S.A. 41°25N 75°40W 92 A1
Scranton S.C., U.S.A. 33°55N 79°45W 103 E6
Screven Ga., U.S.A. 31°29N 82°1W 113 E4
Screven County ☆ Ga., U.S.A. 32°45N 81°40W 113 D5
Scribner Nebr., U.S.A. 41°40N 96°40W 80 C9
Scugog L. Ont., Canada 44°10N 78°55W 147 C8
Scurry County ☆ Tex., U.S.A. 32°44N 100°55W 108 E7
Sea Breeze N.J., U.S.A. 39°18N 75°20W 92 C1
Sea Bright N.J., U.S.A. 40°22N 73°59W 92 B3
Sea Cliff N.Y., U.S.A. 40°50N 73°38W 97 A5
Sea I. B.C., Canada 49°11N 123°10W 161 B2
Sea Isle City N.J., U.S.A. 39°9N 74°42W 92 C2
Sea World Calif., U.S.A. 32°46N 117°14W 127 L9
Seaboard N.C., U.S.A. 36°29N 77°26W 103 B8
Seabrook Md., U.S.A. 38°58N 76°49W 99 B5
Seabrook N.H., U.S.A. 42°53N 70°52W 90 E4
Seabrook Island S.C., U.S.A. 29°34N 95°2W 109 H12
Seacliff Calif., U.S.A. 32°35N 80°10W 103 F5
Seadrift Tex., U.S.A. 37°47N 122°28W 132 B2
Seaford Del., U.S.A. 28°25N 96°43W 109 J11
Seaford Va., U.S.A. 38°39N 75°37W 93 B5
Seaforth Ont., Canada 37°12N 76°26W 102 D8
Seaforth Minn., U.S.A. 43°35N 81°25W 146 D5
Seagate N.Y., U.S.A. 44°29N 95°20W 77 F3
Seager Wheeler L. Sask., Canada 54°17N 103°31W 150 A8
Seagoville Tex., U.S.A. 32°38N 96°32W 109 E11
Seagraves Tex., U.S.A. 32°57N 102°34W 108 E5
Seahorse L. Nfld. & L., Canada 52°12N 65°48W 140 A4
Seal → Man., Canada 59°4N 94°48W 159 F7
Seal Cove N.B., Canada 44°39N 66°51W 141 J3
Seal Cove Nfld. & L., Canada 47°29N 56°4W 142 C4
Seal Cove Nfld. & L., Canada 49°57N 56°22W 142 C4
Seal I. Maine, U.S.A. 43°53N 68°45W 90 E5
Seal L. Nfld. & L., Canada 54°20N 61°30W 143 B6
Seale Ala., U.S.A. 32°18N 85°10W 112 D5
Sealy Tex., U.S.A. 29°47N 96°9W 109 H11
Seaman Ohio, U.S.A. 38°57N 83°34W 86 E3
Seaman Ra. Nev., U.S.A. 37°50N 115°8W 128 E6
Searchlight Nev., U.S.A. 35°28N 114°55W 128 G6
Searchmont Ont., Canada 46°47N 84°3W 149 F12
Searcy Ark., U.S.A. 35°15N 91°44W 106 C4
Searcy County ☆ Ark., U.S.A. 35°55N 92°38W 106 C3
Searles L. Calif., U.S.A. 35°44N 117°21W 127 H9
Searsboro Iowa, U.S.A. 41°35N 92°42W 81 D6
Searsburg Vt., U.S.A. 42°53N 72°58W 89 D2
Searsport Maine, U.S.A. 44°28N 68°56W 90 D5
Seaside Calif., U.S.A. 36°37N 121°50W 126 G5
Seaside Oreg., U.S.A. 46°0N 123°56W 121 B2
Seaside Heights N.J., U.S.A. 39°55N 74°6W 92 C2
Seaside Park N.J., U.S.A. 38°53N 76°53W 99 B4
Seat Pleasant Md., U.S.A. 38°53N 76°53W 99 B4
SeaTac Wash., U.S.A. 47°27N 122°19W 132 D1
Seattle Wash., U.S.A. 47°36N 122°19W 132 C1
Seattle-Tacoma Int. ✈ (SEA) Wash., U.S.A. 47°27N 122°18W 132 D4
Seaville N.J., U.S.A. 39°12N 74°42W 92 C2
Seba Beach Alta., Canada 53°35N 114°47W 152 E6

Sebago L. Maine, U.S.A. 43°52N 70°34W 90 E3
Sebastian Fla., U.S.A. 27°49N 80°28W 114 D8
Sebastian, C. Oreg., U.S.A. 42°20N 124°26W 121 E1
Sebastian County ☆ Ark., U.S.A. 35°10N 94°10W 106 C1
Sebastián Vizcaíno, B. Baja Calif., Mexico 28°0N 114°30W 167 F4
Sebastopol Calif., U.S.A. 38°24N 122°49W 126 E4
Sebastopol Miss., U.S.A. 32°34N 89°20W 111 D4
Sebec L. Maine, U.S.A. 45°16N 69°15W 90 C4
Sebeka Minn., U.S.A. 46°38N 95°5W 77 D3
Sebewaing Mich., U.S.A. 43°44N 83°27W 79 F8
Seboeis Maine, U.S.A. 45°22N 68°43W 90 C5
Seboeis L. Maine, U.S.A. 45°28N 68°53W 90 C5
Seboomook L. Maine, U.S.A. 45°56N 69°51W 90 C4
Sebree Ky., U.S.A. 37°36N 87°32W 104 C5
Sebrell Va., U.S.A. 36°47N 77°8W 102 E7
Sebring Fla., U.S.A. 27°30N 81°27W 114 D7
Sebringville Ont., Canada 43°24N 81°4W 146 D5
Secaucus N.J., U.S.A. 40°47N 74°3W 97 B2
Sechelt B.C., Canada 49°25N 123°42W 154 F11
Second Connecticut L. N.H., U.S.A. 45°9N 71°10W 89 A3
Second Mesa Ariz., U.S.A. 35°48N 110°30W 130 B5
Second Narrows B.C., Canada 49°18N 123°2W 161 B2
Secor Ill., U.S.A. 40°45N 89°8W 84 C4
Secretary Md., U.S.A. 38°37N 75°57W 93 B5
Section Ala., U.S.A. 34°35N 85°59W 112 B5
Security Colo., U.S.A. 38°45N 104°45W 125 C6
Sedalia Colo., U.S.A. 39°26N 104°58W 125 C6
Sedalia Mo., U.S.A. 38°42N 93°14W 83 C3
Sedan Kans., U.S.A. 37°8N 96°11W 82 D7
Sedan Minn., U.S.A. 45°35N 95°15W 77 E3
Sedan N. Mex., U.S.A. 36°9N 103°8W 131 A7
Sedgewick Alta., Canada 52°48N 111°41W 153 F9
Sedgwick Colo., U.S.A. 40°56N 102°32W 125 B8
Sedgwick Kans., U.S.A. 37°55N 97°26W 82 D6
Sedgwick Maine, U.S.A. 44°18N 68°37W 90 D5
Sedgwick County ☆ Colo., U.S.A. 40°50N 102°15W 125 B8
Sedgwick County ☆ Kans., U.S.A. 37°30N 97°20W 82 D6
Sedley Sask., Canada 50°10N 104°0W 150 E8
Sedona Ariz., U.S.A. 34°52N 111°46W 130 C4
Sedro-Woolley Wash., U.S.A. 48°30N 122°14W 120 B3
Seedskadee Nat. Wildlife Refuge ○ Wyo., U.S.A. 41°49N 109°48W 124 E3
Seekonk Mass., U.S.A. 41°49N 71°20W 91 C3
Seeley Lake Mont., U.S.A. 47°11N 113°29W 123 C4
Seeley's Bay Ont., Canada 44°29N 76°14W 147 C10
Seelyville Ind., U.S.A. 39°30N 87°16W 85 D3
Segovia = Coco → Cent. Amer. 15°0N 83°8W 182 D3
Seguam I. Alaska, U.S.A. 52°19N 172°30W 135 K4
Seguam Pass Alaska, U.S.A. 52°0N 172°30W 135 K4
Seguin Tex., U.S.A. 29°34N 97°58W 109 H10
Seibert Colo., U.S.A. 39°18N 102°53W 125 C8
Seiling Okla., U.S.A. 36°9N 98°56W 107 B5
Selah Wash., U.S.A. 46°39N 120°32W 120 D5
Selawik Alaska, U.S.A. 66°36N 160°0W 135 C8
Selawik L. Alaska, U.S.A. 66°30N 160°45W 135 C7
Selawik Nat. Wildlife Refuge ○ Alaska, U.S.A. 66°35N 159°10W 135 C8
Selby S. Dak., U.S.A. 45°31N 100°2W 76 E5
Selbyville Del., U.S.A. 38°28N 75°14W 93 B5
Selden Kans., U.S.A. 39°33N 100°34W 82 B3
Selden N.Y., U.S.A. 40°52N 73°2W 91 D1
Seldovia Alaska, U.S.A. 59°26N 151°43W 135 G10
Selfridge N. Dak., U.S.A. 46°2N 100°56W 76 D5
Seligman Ariz., U.S.A. 35°20N 112°53W 130 D3
Seligman Mo., U.S.A. 36°31N 93°56W 83 E3
Selinsgrove Pa., U.S.A. 40°48N 76°52W 87 D6
Selkirk Man., Canada 50°10N 96°55W 151 E15
Selkirk Ont., Canada 42°49N 79°56W 146 E7
Selkirk Kans., U.S.A. 38°29N 101°32W 82 C2
Selkirk I. = Horse I. Man., Canada 53°20N 99°6W 151 B12
Selkirk Mts. Idaho, U.S.A. 48°30N 116°40W 122 A2
Sellers S.C., U.S.A. 34°17N 79°28W 103 D6
Sellersburg Ind., U.S.A. 38°24N 85°45W 85 E5
Sells Ariz., U.S.A. 31°55N 111°53W 130 F4
Selma Ala., U.S.A. 32°25N 87°1W 112 D3
Selma Ark., U.S.A. 33°42N 91°34W 106 E4
Selma Calif., U.S.A. 36°34N 119°37W 127 G6
Selma N.C., U.S.A. 35°32N 78°17W 103 C7
Selma Oreg., U.S.A. 42°17N 123°37W 121 E2
Selma Tex., U.S.A. 29°35N 98°18W 116 B4
Selman Okla., U.S.A. 36°48N 99°30W 107 B4
Selmer Tenn., U.S.A. 35°10N 88°36W 104 E4
Selway → Idaho, U.S.A. 46°9N 115°36W 122 C3
Selway-Bitterroot Wilderness Idaho, U.S.A. 46°1N 114°49W 122 C4
Selwyn L. Canada 60°0N 104°30W 157 D12
Selwyn Mts. Canada 63°0N 130°0W 157 D6
Selz N. Dak., U.S.A. 47°52N 99°54W 76 C6
Semans Sask., Canada 51°25N 104°44W 150 D7
Semichi Is. Alaska, U.S.A. 52°42N 174°0E 135 K1
Seminary Miss., U.S.A. 31°34N 89°30W 111 E4
Seminoe Dam Wyo., U.S.A. 42°9N 106°54W 124 D6
Seminoe Res. Wyo., U.S.A. 42°9N 106°55W 124 D6
Seminole Fla., U.S.A. 27°50N 82°47W 115 B2
Seminole Okla., U.S.A. 35°14N 96°41W 107 C7
Seminole Tex., U.S.A. 32°43N 102°39W 108 E5
Seminole, L. Ga., U.S.A. 30°43N 84°52W 113 F2
Seminole County ☆ Fla., U.S.A. 28°40N 81°15W 114 C7
Seminole County ☆ Ga., U.S.A. 31°0N 84°55W 113 F2
Seminole County ☆ Okla., U.S.A. 35°10N 96°40W 107 C7
Seminole Draw → Tex., U.S.A. 32°27N 102°20W 108 E5
Semisopochnoi I. Alaska, U.S.A. 51°55N 179°36E 135 L2
Semmes Ala., U.S.A. 30°47N 88°16W 112 F2
Senachwine L. Ill., U.S.A. 41°10N 89°18W 84 B4
Senath Mo., U.S.A. 36°8N 90°10W 83 E6
Senatobia Miss., U.S.A. 34°37N 89°58W 111 B4
Seneca Ill., U.S.A. 41°19N 88°37W 84 B5
Seneca Kans., U.S.A. 39°50N 96°4W 82 B7
Seneca Md., U.S.A. 39°5N 77°20W 93 A3
Seneca Mo., U.S.A. 36°51N 94°37W 83 E2
Seneca Nebr., U.S.A. 42°3N 100°50W 80 B5
Seneca Oreg., U.S.A. 44°8N 118°58W 121 C7
Seneca S.C., U.S.A. 34°41N 82°57W 103 D3
Seneca S. Dak., U.S.A. 45°4N 99°31W 76 E6
Seneca County ☆ N.Y., U.S.A. 42°45N 76°45W 88 C4
Seneca County ☆ Ohio, U.S.A. 41°7N 83°11W 86 B3
Seneca Falls N.Y., U.S.A. 42°55N 76°48W 88 C4
Seneca L. N.Y., U.S.A. 42°40N 76°54W 88 C4
Seneca Rocks W. Va., U.S.A. 38°50N 79°23W 102 C5
Sénécal L. Nfld. & L., Canada 52°5N 63°20W 140 A6
Senecaville L. Ohio, U.S.A. 39°55N 81°25W 86 D6
Seney Mich., U.S.A. 46°21N 85°57W 79 C6
Seney Nat. Wildlife Refuge ○ Mich., U.S.A. 46°16N 86°6W 79 C5

Sénguio Michoacan, Mexico 19°44N 100°21W 175 C7
Senneterre Qué., Canada 48°25N 77°5W 144 C5
Senoia Ga., U.S.A. 33°18N 84°33W 113 C2
Señor Quintana Roo, Mexico 19°50N 88°9W 179 C5
Sentinel Okla., U.S.A. 35°9N 99°1W 107 C4
Sentinel Butte N. Dak., U.S.A. 46°55N 103°51W 76 D2
Separ N. Mex., U.S.A. 32°12N 108°25W 131 E2
Separation L. Ont., Canada 50°14N 94°5W 148 B2
Sept-Îles Qué., Canada 50°13N 66°22W 143 C4
Sepulga → Ala., U.S.A. 31°11N 86°46W 112 E4
Sepulveda Flood Control Basin Calif., U.S.A. 34°10N 118°28W 133 A2
Sequart L. Nfld. & L., Canada 52°26N 63°47W 140 A6
Sequatchie → Tenn., U.S.A. 35°1N 85°38W 105 E7
Sequatchie County ☆ Tenn., U.S.A. 35°23N 85°23W 105 E7
Sequim Wash., U.S.A. 48°5N 123°6W 120 B2
Sequoia Nat. Forest Calif., U.S.A. 36°0N 118°20W 127 G8
Sequoia Nat. Park △ Calif., U.S.A. 36°30N 118°30W 127 G8
Sequoyah Nat. Wildlife Refuge ○ Okla., U.S.A. 35°27N 95°1W 107 C8
Serafina N. Mex., U.S.A. 35°24N 105°19W 131 B5
Sergeant Bluff Iowa, U.S.A. 42°24N 96°22W 81 C2
Sérigny → Qué., Canada 56°47N 66°0W 143 B4
Sermersuaq Greenland 79°30N 62°0W 162 B4
Serpent Mound Ohio, U.S.A. 39°1N 83°26W 86 D3
Serramonte Calif., U.S.A. 37°39N 122°28W 132 C2
Serranilla Bank W. Indies 15°50N 80°0W 182 C4
Sesser Ill., U.S.A. 38°5N 89°1W 84 E4
Seth Ward Tex., U.S.A. 34°13N 101°42W 108 C6
Seton L. B.C., Canada 50°42N 122°8W 155 E12
Seton Portage B.C., Canada 50°42N 122°17W 155 E12
Settlement, The Br. Virgin Is. 18°43N 64°22W 184 G18
Seul, Lac Ont., Canada 50°20N 92°30W 148 B4
Seul Choix Pt. Mich., U.S.A. 45°55N 85°55W 79 D6
Seven Corners Va., U.S.A. 38°53N 77°9W 99 B3
Seven Devils Mts. Idaho, U.S.A. 44°54N 116°42W 122 D1
Seven Hills Ohio, U.S.A. 41°23N 81°40W 98 B1
Seven Islands = Sept-Îles Qué., Canada 50°13N 66°22W 143 C4
Seven Islands B. Nfld. & L., Canada 59°25N 63°45W 143 B5
Seven River N. Mex., U.S.A. 32°36N 104°25W 131 E6
Seven Sisters B.C., Canada 54°56N 128°1W 157 F7
Seven Sisters Falls Man., Canada 50°7N 96°2W 151 E15
Seven Troughs Range Nev., U.S.A. 40°30N 118°40W 128 B2
Seven Valleys Pa., U.S.A. 39°51N 76°46W 93 A4
Seventy Mile House B.C., Canada 51°18N 121°23W 155 D13
Severn → Ont., Canada 56°2N 87°36W 159 F8
Severna Park Md., U.S.A. 39°4N 76°33W 93 A4
Severy Kans., U.S.A. 37°37N 96°4W 82 D7
Sevier → Utah, U.S.A. 39°4N 113°6W 129 D2
Sevier Bridge Res. Utah, U.S.A. 39°22N 112°2W 129 D3
Sevier County ☆ Ark., U.S.A. 33°58N 94°10W 106 E1
Sevier County ☆ Tenn., U.S.A. 35°48N 83°33W 105 E9
Sevier County ☆ Utah, U.S.A. 38°45N 111°50W 129 E4
Sevier Desert Utah, U.S.A. 39°40N 112°45W 129 D3
Sevier L. Utah, U.S.A. 38°54N 113°9W 129 E2
Sevier Plateau Utah, U.S.A. 38°20N 112°10W 129 E3
Sevierville Tenn., U.S.A. 35°52N 83°34W 105 E9
Seville Fla., U.S.A. 29°19N 81°30W 114 B7
Seville Ga., U.S.A. 31°58N 83°36W 113 E3
Seville Ohio, U.S.A. 41°1N 81°52W 98 C2
Sewanee Tenn., U.S.A. 35°12N 85°55W 105 E7
Seward Alaska, U.S.A. 60°7N 149°27W 135 F10
Seward Ill., U.S.A. 42°14N 89°22W 84 A4
Seward Kans., U.S.A. 38°11N 98°48W 82 C5
Seward Nebr., U.S.A. 40°55N 97°6W 80 D8
Seward Pa., U.S.A. 40°25N 79°1W 87 D3
Seward County ☆ Kans., U.S.A. 37°15N 100°45W 82 D3
Seward County ☆ Nebr., U.S.A. 40°50N 97°10W 80 D8
Seward Peninsula Alaska, U.S.A. 65°30N 166°0W 135 D6
Sewaren N.J., U.S.A. 40°33N 74°15W 97 C1
Sewickley Pa., U.S.A. 40°32N 80°12W 87 D2
Sexsmith Alta., Canada 55°21N 118°47W 152 C2
Sextin → Durango, Mexico 25°41N 105°5W 172 B5
Seybaplaya Campeche, Mexico 19°39N 90°40W 179 C3
Seybaplaya, Pta. Campeche, Mexico 19°39N 90°41W 179 C3
Seyé Yucatán, Mexico 20°50N 89°22W 179 B4
Seymour Conn., U.S.A. 41°24N 73°4W 91 C1
Seymour Ind., U.S.A. 38°58N 85°53W 85 E5
Seymour Iowa, U.S.A. 40°45N 93°7W 81 E5
Seymour Mo., U.S.A. 37°9N 92°43W 83 D4
Seymour Tenn., U.S.A. 35°53N 83°43W 105 E9
Seymour Tex., U.S.A. 33°35N 99°16W 109 D8
Seymour Wis., U.S.A. 44°31N 88°20W 78 D5
Seymour Arm B.C., Canada 51°15N 118°57W 155 D16
Seymour Inlet B.C., Canada 51°3N 127°0W 154 D7
Seymourville La., U.S.A. 30°16N 91°14W 110 D4
Shabogamo L. Nfld. & L., Canada 53°15N 66°30W 143 C4
Shabuskwia L. Ont., Canada 51°15N 89°0W 148 A8
Shackelford County ☆ Tex., U.S.A. 32°45N 99°18W 109 E8
Shadehill S. Dak., U.S.A. 45°45N 102°12W 76 E3
Shady Cove Oreg., U.S.A. 42°37N 122°49W 121 E3
Shady Dale Ga., U.S.A. 33°24N 83°36W 113 C3
Shady Grove Fla., U.S.A. 30°17N 83°38W 114 A5
Shady Grove Ky., U.S.A. 37°20N 87°53W 104 C4
Shady Point Okla., U.S.A. 35°8N 94°40W 107 C9
Shady Side Md., U.S.A. 38°50N 76°31W 93 B4
Shady Spring W. Va., U.S.A. 37°42N 81°6W 102 D3
Shadyside Ohio, U.S.A. 39°58N 80°45W 86 D6
Shafer, L. Ind., U.S.A. 40°46N 86°46W 85 C4
Shafter Calif., U.S.A. 35°30N 119°16W 127 H7
Shafter Tex., U.S.A. 29°49N 104°18W 108 H3
Shaftsbury Vt., U.S.A. 43°1N 73°11W 89 C1
Shageluk Alaska, U.S.A. 62°41N 159°34W 135 E8
Shaker Heights Ohio, U.S.A. 41°28N 81°32W 98 A2
Shakespeare I. Ont., Canada 49°38N 88°25W 148 C8
Shakopee Minn., U.S.A. 44°48N 93°32W 77 F5
Shaktoolik Alaska, U.S.A. 64°20N 161°9W 135 C8
Shalalth B.C., Canada 50°43N 122°13W 155 E12
Shaler Mts. Canada 71°54N 111°35W 156 B11
Shallotte N.C., U.S.A. 33°58N 78°23W 103 E7
Shallow Lake Ont., Canada 44°36N 81°5W 146 C5
Shallow Water Kans., U.S.A. 38°23N 100°55W 82 C3
Shallowater Tex., U.S.A. 33°36N 102°0W 108 D5
Shamattawa Man., Canada 55°51N 92°5W 159 F21
Shambaugh Iowa, U.S.A. 40°42N 95°5W 81 E2
Shamokin Pa., U.S.A. 40°47N 76°34W 87 D6
Shamrock Sask., Canada 50°10N 106°37W 150 E5
Shamrock Okla., U.S.A. 35°56N 96°34W 107 C7
Shamrock Tex., U.S.A. 35°13N 100°15W 108 B7
Shandon Calif., U.S.A. 35°39N 120°23W 127 H6
Shaniko Oreg., U.S.A. 45°0N 120°45W 121 B5
Shannon Greenland 75°10N 18°30W 162 B9
Shannon Ga., U.S.A. 34°20N 85°4W 113 B1

Shannon Ill., U.S.A. 42°9N 89°44W 84 A4
Shannon Miss., U.S.A. 34°7N 88°43W 111 B5
Shannon, L. Wash., U.S.A. 48°33N 121°45W 120 B4
Shannon County ☆ Mo., U.S.A. 37°10N 91°20W 83 D5
Shannon County ☆ S. Dak., U.S.A. 43°15N 102°35W 76 G3
Shannon L. Ont., Canada 49°48N 83°24W 149 C13
Shannontown S.C., U.S.A. 33°53N 80°21W 103 D5
Shapleigh Maine, U.S.A. 43°32N 70°51W 89 C4
Sharbot Lake Ont., Canada 44°46N 76°41W 147 C10
Sharkey County ☆ Miss., U.S.A. 32°55N 90°53W 111 D3
Sharon Conn., U.S.A. 41°53N 73°29W 91 C1
Sharon Kans., U.S.A. 37°15N 98°25W 82 D5
Sharon Mass., U.S.A. 42°7N 71°11W 91 B3
Sharon Miss., U.S.A. 32°40N 89°56W 111 D4
Sharon N. Dak., U.S.A. 47°36N 97°54W 76 C8
Sharon Okla., U.S.A. 36°17N 99°20W 107 B4
Sharon Pa., U.S.A. 41°14N 80°31W 87 C2
Sharon Tenn., U.S.A. 36°14N 88°50W 104 D4
Sharon Vt., U.S.A. 43°47N 72°25W 89 C2
Sharon Wis., U.S.A. 42°30N 88°44W 78 F5
Sharon Hill Pa., U.S.A. 39°54N 75°16W 98 B1
Sharon Springs Kans., U.S.A. 38°54N 101°45W 82 C2
Sharonville Ohio, U.S.A. 39°16N 84°25W 86 D2
Sharp County ☆ Ark., U.S.A. 36°4N 91°37W 106 B4
Sharp Mt. Yukon, Canada 67°11N 138°42W 156 C5
Sharp, L. S. Dak., U.S.A. 44°1N 99°23W 76 F6
Sharpes Fla., U.S.A. 28°26N 80°46W 114 C8
Sharps Va., U.S.A. 37°49N 76°42W 93 C4
Sharpsburg Iowa, U.S.A. 40°48N 94°38W 81 E4
Sharpsburg Ky., U.S.A. 38°12N 83°56W 105 B9
Sharpsburg Md., U.S.A. 39°28N 77°45W 93 A3
Sharpsburg N.C., U.S.A. 35°53N 77°50W 103 C8
Sharpsburg Pa., U.S.A. 40°29N 79°55W 98 B2
Sharpsville Ind., U.S.A. 40°23N 86°5W 85 C4
Sharpsville Pa., U.S.A. 41°15N 80°29W 87 C2
Sharptown Md., U.S.A. 38°35N 75°45W 93 B5
Shasta Calif., U.S.A. 40°36N 122°29W 126 C4
Shasta, Mt. Calif., U.S.A. 41°25N 122°12W 126 B4
Shasta County ☆ Calif., U.S.A. 40°40N 122°0W 126 C5
Shasta Dam Calif., U.S.A. 40°43N 122°25W 126 C4
Shasta L. Calif., U.S.A. 40°43N 122°25W 126 C4
Shasta Lake Calif., U.S.A. 40°41N 122°22W 126 C4
Shasta Nat. Forest Calif., U.S.A. 41°10N 122°20W 126 B4
Shattuck Okla., U.S.A. 36°16N 99°53W 107 B4
Shaunavon Sask., Canada 49°35N 108°25W 150 F3
Shavano Park Tex., U.S.A. 29°35N 98°33W 116 B2
Shaver L. Calif., U.S.A. 37°9N 119°18W 127 F7
Shaw Miss., U.S.A. 33°36N 90°41W 111 C3
Shawanaga Ont., Canada 45°31N 80°17W 146 B6
Shawangunk Mts. N.Y., U.S.A. 41°35N 74°30W 88 D6
Shawano Wis., U.S.A. 44°47N 88°36W 78 D5
Shawano County ☆ Wis., U.S.A. 44°45N 88°40W 78 D5
Shawinigan Qué., Canada 46°35N 72°50W 145 C10
Shawinigan-Sud Qué., Canada 46°31N 72°45W 145 C10
Shawnee Ga., U.S.A. 32°29N 81°25W 113 D5
Shawnee Kans., U.S.A. 39°1N 94°43W 82 B9
Shawnee Ohio, U.S.A. 39°36N 82°13W 86 D4
Shawnee Okla., U.S.A. 35°20N 96°55W 107 C7
Shawnee County ☆ Kans., U.S.A. 39°0N 95°45W 82 C8
Shawnee Nat. Forest Ill., U.S.A. 37°40N 88°20W 84 F5
Shawnee State Forest Ohio, U.S.A. 38°43N 83°13W 86 E3
Shawneetown Ill., U.S.A. 37°42N 88°8W 84 F5
Shawville Qué., Canada 45°36N 76°30W 144 F6
Shea Stadium N.Y., U.S.A. 40°45N 73°51W 97 B3
Shebandowan Ont., Canada 48°38N 90°4W 148 D6
Sheboygan Wis., U.S.A. 43°46N 87°45W 78 E6
Sheboygan County ☆ Wis., U.S.A. 43°45N 87°50W 78 E6
Sheboygan Falls Wis., U.S.A. 43°44N 87°49W 78 E6
Shedd Oreg., U.S.A. 44°28N 123°7W 121 C2
Shediac N.B., Canada 46°14N 64°32W 141 G5
Sheen, L. Fla., U.S.A. 28°25N 81°31W 115 A5
Sheenjek → Alaska, U.S.A. 66°45N 144°33W 135 C11
Sheep Hole Mts. Calif., U.S.A. 34°10N 115°40W 127 J11
Sheep Mt. Colo., U.S.A. 39°55N 107°8W 125 C3
Sheep Mt. Wyo., U.S.A. 43°31N 110°28W 124 C2
Sheep Range Nev., U.S.A. 36°35N 115°15W 128 F5
Sheep Springs N. Mex., U.S.A. 36°9N 108°42W 131 A2
Sheepshead Bay N.Y., U.S.A. 40°35N 73°55W 97 C3
Sheepshead Mts. Oreg., U.S.A. 42°54N 118°9W 121 E7
Sheet Harbour N.S., Canada 44°56N 62°31W 141 J7
Sheffield Ala., U.S.A. 34°46N 87°41W 112 B3
Sheffield Ill., U.S.A. 41°21N 89°44W 84 B4
Sheffield Iowa, U.S.A. 42°54N 93°13W 81 C5
Sheffield Mass., U.S.A. 42°5N 73°21W 91 B1
Sheffield Pa., U.S.A. 41°42N 79°3W 87 C3
Sheffield L. Nfld. & L., Canada 49°20N 56°34W 142 C4
Sheguiandah Ont., Canada 45°54N 81°55W 146 B4
Sheho Sask., Canada 51°35N 103°13W 150 D8
Shelbiana Ky., U.S.A. 37°26N 82°30W 105 C10
Shelbina Mo., U.S.A. 39°47N 92°2W 83 B4
Shelburn Ind., U.S.A. 39°11N 87°24W 85 D3
Shelburne N.S., Canada 43°47N 65°20W 141 K4
Shelburne Ont., Canada 44°4N 80°15W 146 C6
Shelburne Vt., U.S.A. 44°23N 73°14W 89 B1
Shelburne Falls Mass., U.S.A. 42°36N 72°45W 91 B2
Shelburne Museum Vt., U.S.A. 44°23N 73°14W 89 B1
Shelby Iowa, U.S.A. 41°31N 95°27W 81 D2
Shelby Mich., U.S.A. 43°37N 86°22W 79 F5
Shelby Miss., U.S.A. 33°57N 90°46W 111 C3
Shelby Mont., U.S.A. 48°30N 111°51W 123 B6
Shelby N.C., U.S.A. 35°17N 81°32W 103 C4
Shelby Nebr., U.S.A. 41°12N 97°26W 80 C8
Shelby Ohio, U.S.A. 40°53N 82°40W 86 C4
Shelby County ☆ Ala., U.S.A. 33°15N 86°49W 112 C4
Shelby County ☆ Ill., U.S.A. 39°30N 88°50W 85 D5
Shelby County ☆ Ind., U.S.A. 39°30N 85°50W 85 D5
Shelby County ☆ Iowa, U.S.A. 41°40N 95°20W 81 D2
Shelby County ☆ Ky., U.S.A. 38°10N 85°10W 105 B7
Shelby County ☆ Mo., U.S.A. 39°50N 92°0W 83 B4
Shelby County ☆ Ohio, U.S.A. 40°17N 84°9W 86 C2
Shelby County ☆ Tenn., U.S.A. 35°5N 89°59W 104 E2
Shelby County ☆ Tex., U.S.A. 31°48N 94°11W 109 F13
Shelbyville Ill., U.S.A. 39°24N 88°48W 84 D5
Shelbyville Ind., U.S.A. 39°31N 85°47W 85 D5
Shelbyville Ky., U.S.A. 38°13N 85°14W 105 B7
Shelbyville Mo., U.S.A. 39°48N 92°2W 83 B4
Shelbyville Tenn., U.S.A. 35°29N 86°28W 104 E6
Shelbyville Tex., U.S.A. 31°46N 94°5W 109 F13
Shelbyville, L. Ill., U.S.A. 39°26N 88°46W 85 D5
Sheldahl Iowa, U.S.A. 41°52N 93°42W 81 D5
Sheldon Iowa, U.S.A. 43°11N 95°51W 81 B2
Sheldon Mo., U.S.A. 37°40N 94°18W 83 D2
Sheldon N. Dak., U.S.A. 46°35N 97°30W 76 D8
Sheldon Vt., U.S.A. 44°53N 72°56W 89 B2

Sheldon Wis., U.S.A. 45°19N 90°58W 78 C3
Sheldon Nat. Wildlife Refuge ○ Nev., U.S.A. 41°48N 119°12W 128 A1
Sheldon Point Alaska, U.S.A. 62°32N 164°52W 135 E6
Sheldrake Qué., Canada 50°20N 64°51W 143 C5
Shelikof Strait Alaska, U.S.A. 57°30N 155°0W 135 H9
Shell Wyo., U.S.A. 44°32N 107°47W 124 B5
Shell Beach = Huntington Beach Calif., U.S.A. 33°40N 118°5W 127 K8
Shell Lake Sask., Canada 53°19N 107°2W 150 B4
Shell Lake Wis., U.S.A. 45°45N 91°55W 78 C2
Shell Rock Iowa, U.S.A. 42°43N 92°35W 81 C6
Shell Rock → Iowa, U.S.A. 42°35N 92°28W 81 C6
Shellbrook Sask., Canada 53°13N 106°24W 150 B5
Shelley B.C., Canada 54°0N 122°37W 155 B12
Shelley Idaho, U.S.A. 43°23N 112°7W 122 F6
Shellman Ga., U.S.A. 31°46N 84°37W 113 E2
Shellman Bluff Ga., U.S.A. 31°35N 81°19W 113 E5
Shellmouth Man., Canada 50°56N 101°29W 151 E10
Shellsburg Iowa, U.S.A. 42°6N 91°52W 81 D7
Shelly Minn., U.S.A. 47°28N 96°49W 77 C2
Shelter Bay = Port-Cartier Qué., Canada 50°2N 66°50W 143 C4
Shelter I. N.Y., U.S.A. 41°4N 72°20W 91 C2
Shelton Conn., U.S.A. 41°19N 73°5W 91 C1
Shelton Nebr., U.S.A. 40°47N 98°44W 80 D7
Shelton Wash., U.S.A. 47°13N 123°6W 120 C2
Shenandoah Iowa, U.S.A. 40°46N 95°22W 81 E3
Shenandoah Pa., U.S.A. 40°49N 76°12W 87 D6
Shenandoah Va., U.S.A. 38°29N 78°37W 102 C6
Shenandoah → Va., U.S.A. 39°19N 77°44W 102 B7
Shenandoah County ☆ Va., U.S.A. 38°53N 78°30W 102 C6
Shenandoah Mts. Va., U.S.A. 38°40N 79°15W 102 C5
Shenandoah Nat. Park △ Va., U.S.A. 38°35N 78°22W 93 B2
Shepherd Mich., U.S.A. 43°32N 84°41W 79 F7
Shepherd Mont., U.S.A. 45°57N 108°21W 123 E9
Shepherd Tex., U.S.A. 30°31N 95°1W 109 G12
Shepherdstown W. Va., U.S.A. 39°26N 77°48W 93 A3
Shepherdsville Ky., U.S.A. 37°59N 85°43W 105 C7
Sheppard Air Force Base Tex., U.S.A. 33°57N 98°30W 109 D9
Sherando Va., U.S.A. 37°59N 78°57W 102 D6
Sherard Miss., U.S.A. 34°13N 90°42W 111 B3
Sherard, C. Nunavut, Canada 74°36N 80°13W 158 C9
Sherbrooke Qué., Canada 45°28N 71°57W 145 F11
Sherburn Minn., U.S.A. 43°39N 94°43W 77 G4
Sherburne N.Y., U.S.A. 42°41N 75°30W 88 C5
Sherburne Vt., U.S.A. 43°10N 72°47W 89 C2
Sherburne County ☆ Minn., U.S.A. 45°20N 93°45W 77 E5
Sheridan Ark., U.S.A. 34°19N 92°24W 106 D3
Sheridan Colo., U.S.A. 39°38N 105°1W 134 C1
Sheridan Ill., U.S.A. 41°32N 88°41W 84 B5
Sheridan Ind., U.S.A. 40°8N 86°13W 85 C4
Sheridan Mich., U.S.A. 43°13N 85°4W 79 F6
Sheridan Mo., U.S.A. 40°31N 94°37W 83 A2
Sheridan Mont., U.S.A. 45°27N 112°12W 123 E5
Sheridan Oreg., U.S.A. 45°6N 123°24W 121 B2
Sheridan Wyo., U.S.A. 44°48N 106°58W 124 B6
Sheridan County ☆ Kans., U.S.A. 39°20N 100°30W 82 B3
Sheridan County ☆ Mont., U.S.A. 48°48N 104°30W 123 B13
Sheridan County ☆ N. Dak., U.S.A. 47°45N 100°20W 76 C6
Sheridan County ☆ Nebr., U.S.A. 42°30N 102°20W 80 B3
Sheridan County ☆ Wyo., U.S.A. 44°50N 106°45W 124 B6
Sheridan L. B.C., Canada 51°31N 120°54W 155 D14
Sheridan Lake Colo., U.S.A. 38°28N 102°18W 125 D8
Sheridan Park Wis., U.S.A. 42°34N 87°49W 94 C2
Sherman Conn., U.S.A. 41°35N 73°30W 91 C1
Sherman Ill., U.S.A. 39°54N 89°36W 84 C4
Sherman Miss., U.S.A. 34°22N 88°50W 111 B5
Sherman N.Y., U.S.A. 42°10N 79°36W 88 C1
Sherman Tex., U.S.A. 33°38N 96°36W 109 D11
Sherman Basin Nunavut, Canada 67°4N 97°35W 158 D6
Sherman County ☆ Kans., U.S.A. 39°20N 101°45W 82 B2
Sherman County ☆ Nebr., U.S.A. 41°15N 99°0W 80 C7
Sherman County ☆ Oreg., U.S.A. 45°30N 120°40W 121 B5
Sherman County ☆ Tex., U.S.A. 36°10N 101°58W 108 A6
Sherman Oaks Calif., U.S.A. 34°8N 118°29W 133 B2
Sherman Park Ill., U.S.A. 41°47N 87°39W 95 C2
Sherman Pk. Idaho, U.S.A. 42°28N 111°33W 122 G7
Sherman Res. Nebr., U.S.A. 41°18N 98°53W 80 C7
Sherman Station Maine, U.S.A. 45°54N 68°26W 90 C5
Sherrard Ill., U.S.A. 41°19N 90°31W 84 B3
Sherrelwood Colo., U.S.A. 39°50N 105°0W 134 C1
Sherrill Ark., U.S.A. 34°23N 91°57W 106 D4
Sherwood Ark., U.S.A. 34°48N 92°16W 106 D3
Sherwood Md., U.S.A. 38°46N 76°19W 93 B4
Sherwood N. Dak., U.S.A. 48°57N 101°38W 76 B4
Sherwood Ohio, U.S.A. 41°17N 84°33W 86 B2
Sherwood Oreg., U.S.A. 45°21N 122°50W 121 B3
Sherwood Tenn., U.S.A. 35°5N 85°56W 105 E7
Sherwood, L. Fla., U.S.A. 24°33N 81°48W 115 A2
Sherwood Park Alta., Canada 53°31N 113°19W 152 E7
Sheslay B.C., Canada 58°48N 132°5W 157 E6
Shetek, L. Minn., U.S.A. 44°6N 95°42W 77 F3
Shetucket → Conn., U.S.A. 41°39N 72°6W 91 C2
Shevlin Minn., U.S.A. 47°32N 95°15W 77 C3
Sheyenne N. Dak., U.S.A. 47°50N 99°7W 76 C6
Sheyenne → N. Dak., U.S.A. 47°2N 96°50W 76 C9
Sheyenne L. N. Dak., U.S.A. 47°42N 100°12W 76 C5
Sheyenne Nat. Grassland N. Dak., U.S.A. 46°25N 97°20W 76 D8
Shiawassee → Mich., U.S.A. 43°23N 83°58W 79 F8
Shiawassee County ☆ Mich., U.S.A. 42°55N 84°10W 79 G7
Shiawassee Nat. Wildlife Refuge ○ Mich., U.S.A. 43°21N 84°1W 79 F7
Shibogama L. Ont., Canada 53°35N 88°15W 159 G8
Shickley Nebr., U.S.A. 40°25N 97°43W 80 D8
Shickshinny Pa., U.S.A. 41°9N 76°9W 87 C6
Shickshock Mts. = Chic-Chocs, Mts. Qué., Canada 48°55N 66°0W 140 C4
Shidler Okla., U.S.A. 36°47N 96°40W 107 B7
Shidler Res. Okla., U.S.A. 36°50N 96°40W 107 B7
Shields Kans., U.S.A. 38°37N 100°27W 82 C3
Shields Mich., U.S.A. 43°25N 84°3W 79 F7
Shillington Pa., U.S.A. 40°18N 75°58W 87 D7
Shiloh Ga., U.S.A. 32°49N 84°42W 113 D2
Shiloh N.J., U.S.A. 39°28N 75°18W 92 C1
Shiloh Ohio, U.S.A. 40°58N 82°36W 86 C4
Shiloh Nat. Military Park ○ Tenn., U.S.A. 35°8N 88°20W 104 E4
Shin Pond Maine, U.S.A. 46°6N 68°33W 90 B5
Shiner Tex., U.S.A. 29°26N 97°10W 109 H10
Shinglehouse Pa., U.S.A. 41°58N 78°12W 87 C4
Shingler Ga., U.S.A. 31°35N 83°47W 113 E3
Shingleton Mich., U.S.A. 46°21N 86°28W 79 C5
Shingletown Calif., U.S.A. 40°30N 121°53W 126 C5

258 Shinnston INDEX

Shinnston *W. Va., U.S.A.* 39°24N 80°18W **102** B4
Shiocton *Wis., U.S.A.* 44°27N 88°35W **78** D5
Ship Bottom *N.J., U.S.A.* 39°39N 74°11W **92** C2
Ship I. *Miss., U.S.A.* 30°13N 88°55W **111** F5
Ship Rock *N. Mex., U.S.A.* 36°41N 108°50W **131** A2
Shipman *Ill., U.S.A.* 39°7N 90°3W **84** D3
Shipman *Va., U.S.A.* 37°43N 78°51W **102** D6
Shippagan *N.B., Canada* 47°45N 64°45W **141** F5
Shippensburg *Pa., U.S.A.* 40°3N 77°31W **87** D5
Shippenville *Pa., U.S.A.* 41°15N 79°28W **87** C3
Shiprock *N. Mex., U.S.A.* 36°47N 108°41W **131** A2
Shipshewana *Ind., U.S.A.* 41°41N 85°35W **85** B5
Shirley *Ark., U.S.A.* 35°39N 92°19W **106** C3
Shirley *Ind., U.S.A.* 39°53N 85°35W **85** D5
Shirley *Mass., U.S.A.* 42°33N 71°39W **91** B3
Shirley Basin *Wyo., U.S.A.* 42°20N 106°10W **124** D6
Shirley City = Woodlawn *Md., U.S.A.* 39°19N 76°43W **99** B1
Shirley Mills *Maine, U.S.A.* 45°22N 69°37W **90** C4
Shishaldin Volcano *Alaska, U.S.A.* 54°45N 163°58W **135** J7
Shishmaref *Alaska, U.S.A.* 66°15N 166°4W **135** C6
Shively *Ky., U.S.A.* 38°12N 85°49W **105** B7
Shivwits Plateau *Ariz., U.S.A.* 36°15N 113°30W **130** A2
Shoal Cr. → *Ill., U.S.A.* 38°28N 89°35W **84** E4
Shoal Cr. → *Mo., U.S.A.* 39°44N 93°32W **83** B3
Shoal Cr. → *Tenn., U.S.A.* 34°50N 87°33W **104** F5
Shoal L. *Ont., Canada* 49°33N 95°1W **148** C1
Shoal Lake *Man., Canada* 50°30N 100°35W **151** E11
Shoals *Ind., U.S.A.* 38°40N 86°47W **85** E4
Shoals Prov. Park, The △ *Ont., Canada* 47°50N 83°50W **149** E13
Shoalwater Indian Reservation *Wash., U.S.A.* 46°44N 124°1W **120** D1
Shoemakersville *Pa., U.S.A.* 40°30N 75°58W **87** D7
Shonto *Ariz., U.S.A.* 36°36N 110°39W **130** A5
Shopville *Ky., U.S.A.* 37°9N 84°29W **105** C8
Shoreacres *Tex., U.S.A.* 29°36N 95°1W **109** H12
Shoreham *Vt., U.S.A.* 43°54N 73°19W **89** C1
Shoreline *Wash., U.S.A.* 47°45N 122°20W **132** B3
Shorewood *Wis., U.S.A.* 43°5N 87°53W **94** B2
Short Gap *W. Va., U.S.A.* 39°33N 78°49W **93** A2
Shorter *Ala., U.S.A.* 32°24N 85°57W **112** D5
Shorterville *Ala., U.S.A.* 31°34N 85°6W **112** E5
Shortsville *N.Y., U.S.A.* 42°57N 77°14W **88** C3
Shoshone *Calif., U.S.A.* 35°58N 116°16W **127** H10
Shoshone *Idaho, U.S.A.* 42°56N 114°25W **122** G4
Shoshone → *Wyo., U.S.A.* 44°52N 108°11W **124** B4
Shoshone Basin *Wyo., U.S.A.* 43°5N 108°5W **124** C4
Shoshone County ☆ *Idaho, U.S.A.* 47°30N 116°0W **122** B3
Shoshone Falls *Idaho, U.S.A.* 42°36N 114°24W **122** G4
Shoshone L. *Wyo., U.S.A.* 44°22N 110°43W **124** B2
Shoshone Mts. *Nev., U.S.A.* 39°20N 117°25W **128** C3
Shoshone Nat. Forest *Wyo., U.S.A.* 44°20N 109°45W **124** B3
Shoshone Range *Nev., U.S.A.* 40°20N 116°50W **128** B4
Shoshoni *Wyo., U.S.A.* 43°14N 108°7W **124** C4
Shoup *Idaho, U.S.A.* 45°23N 114°17W **122** D4
Shoveltown *Mo., U.S.A.* 38°48N 90°16W **94** A2
Show Low *Ariz., U.S.A.* 34°15N 110°2W **130** C5
Showell *Md., U.S.A.* 38°24N 75°13W **93** B5
Shreve *Ohio, U.S.A.* 40°41N 82°1W **86** C4
Shreveport *La., U.S.A.* 32°31N 93°45W **110** B2
Shrewsbury *Mass., U.S.A.* 42°18N 71°43W **91** B3
Shrewsbury *Mo., U.S.A.* 38°35N 90°20W **94** B2
Shrewsbury *Pa., U.S.A.* 39°46N 76°41W **93** A4
Shubenacadie *N.S., Canada* 45°5N 63°24W **141** H6
Shubert *Nebr., U.S.A.* 40°14N 95°41W **80** D10
Shubuta *Miss., U.S.A.* 31°52N 88°42W **111** E5
Shuksan, Mt. *Wash., U.S.A.* 48°50N 121°36W **120** B4
Shullsburg *Wis., U.S.A.* 42°35N 90°13W **78** F3
Shumagin Is. *Alaska, U.S.A.* 55°7N 160°30W **135** J7
Shungnak *Alaska, U.S.A.* 66°52N 157°9W **135** C8
Shuqualak *Miss., U.S.A.* 32°59N 88°34W **111** D5
Shushan *N.Y., U.S.A.* 43°5N 73°21W **89** C1
Shuswap L. *B.C., Canada* 50°55N 119°3W **155** E15
Shutesbury *Mass., U.S.A.* 42°25N 72°25W **91** B2
Shuyak I. *Alaska, U.S.A.* 58°31N 152°30W **135** G9
Sian Ka'an, Reserva de la Biósfera △ *Mexico* 19°35N 87°40W **179** C6
Siasconset *Mass., U.S.A.* 41°16N 69°58W **91** C5
Sibley *Ill., U.S.A.* 40°35N 88°23W **84** C5
Sibley *Iowa, U.S.A.* 43°24N 95°45W **81** B3
Sibley *La., U.S.A.* 32°33N 93°18W **110** B2
Sibley *Miss., U.S.A.* 31°23N 91°24W **111** E2
Sibley County ☆ *Minn., U.S.A.* 44°35N 94°15W **77** F4
Sicamous *B.C., Canada* 50°49N 119°0W **155** E16
Sicily Island *La., U.S.A.* 31°51N 91°40W **110** C4
Sideburned L. *Ont., Canada* 47°45N 83°15W **149** E13
Sidell *Ill., U.S.A.* 39°55N 87°49W **84** D6
Siding No 1 = Ponoka *Alta., Canada* 52°42N 113°40W **153** F7
Sidnaw *Mich., U.S.A.* 46°30N 88°43W **79** C3
Sidney *B.C., Canada* 48°39N 123°24W **155** G11
Sidney *Man., Canada* 49°54N 99°4W **151** F12
Sidney *Ark., U.S.A.* 36°0N 91°40W **106** B4
Sidney *Ill., U.S.A.* 40°1N 88°4W **84** C5
Sidney *Iowa, U.S.A.* 40°45N 95°39W **81** E3
Sidney *Mont., U.S.A.* 47°43N 104°9W **123** C13
Sidney *N.Y., U.S.A.* 42°19N 75°24W **88** C5
Sidney *Nebr., U.S.A.* 41°8N 102°59W **80** C3
Sidney *Ohio, U.S.A.* 40°17N 84°9W **86** C2
Sidney Lanier, L. *Ga., U.S.A.* 34°10N 84°4W **113** B2
Sidon *Miss., U.S.A.* 33°25N 90°12W **111** C3
Sierra Blanca *Tex., U.S.A.* 31°11N 105°22W **108** F2
Sierra Blanca Peak *N. Mex., U.S.A.* 33°23N 105°49W **131** D5
Sierra City *Calif., U.S.A.* 39°34N 120°38W **126** D6
Sierra County ☆ *Calif., U.S.A.* 39°40N 121°30W **126** D5
Sierra County ☆ *N. Mex., U.S.A.* 33°0N 107°0W **131** D3
Sierra de Baoruco, Parque Nac. de △ *Dom. Rep.* 18°10N 71°25W **183** C5
Sierra de la Paila, Parque Natural △ *Coahuila, Mexico* 25°36N 102°7W **170** E2
Sierra de San Pedro Mártir, Parque Nacional △ *Baja Calif., Mexico* 31°10N 115°30W **166** B3
Sierra del Carmen, Parque Natural △ *Coahuila, Mexico* 29°17N 101°14W **170** A3
Sierra Madre *Calif., U.S.A.* 34°9N 118°3W **133** B4
Sierra Madre *Wyo., U.S.A.* 41°15N 107°5W **124** E5
Sierra Madre del Sur *Mexico* 18°45N 104°40W **174** D4
Sierra Madre Mts. *Calif., U.S.A.* 34°54N 119°51W **127** J7
Sierra Madre Occidental *Mexico* 27°0N 107°0W **172** C5
Sierra Madre Oriental *Mexico* 25°0N 100°0W **171** H5
Sierra Mojada *Coahuila, Mexico* 27°18N 103°41W **170** C1
Sierra Morena *Chiapas, Mexico* 16°8N 93°35W **178** C3
Sierra Nat. Forest *Calif., U.S.A.* 37°15N 119°10W **127** F7
Sierra Nevada *Calif., U.S.A.* 39°0N 120°30W **126** D6
Sierra Vista *Ariz., U.S.A.* 31°33N 110°18W **130** F5
Sierraville *Calif., U.S.A.* 39°36N 120°22W **126** D6
Sierra *Calif., U.S.A.* 40°15N 120°6W **126** C6
Siesta Key *Fla., U.S.A.* 27°18N 82°33W **114** D6
Sifton *Man., Canada* 51°21N 100°8W **151** D11
Sifton Pass *B.C., Canada* 57°52N 126°15W **157** E7
Signal Mountain *Tenn., U.S.A.* 35°7N 85°21W **105** E7
Signal Pk. *Ariz., U.S.A.* 33°20N 114°2W **130** D1
Signal Pk. *Utah, U.S.A.* 37°19N 113°29W **129** F2
Sigourney *Iowa, U.S.A.* 41°20N 92°12W **81** D6
Sigsbee *Ga., U.S.A.* 31°16N 83°52W **113** E3
Sigurd *Utah, U.S.A.* 38°50N 111°58W **129** E4
Sigutlat L. *B.C., Canada* 52°57N 126°12W **154** C8
Sihoplaya, Pta. *Campeche, Mexico* 19°35N 90°43W **179** C3
Sikanni Chief *B.C., Canada* 57°14N 122°42W **157** E8
Sikanni Chief → *B.C., Canada* 57°47N 122°15W **157** E8
Sikes *La., U.S.A.* 32°5N 92°29W **110** B3
Sikeston *Mo., U.S.A.* 36°53N 89°35W **83** E7
Sil Nakya *Ariz., U.S.A.* 32°13N 111°49W **130** E4
Silacayoapan *Oaxaca, Mexico* 17°30N 98°9W **177** G2
Silao *Guanajuato, Mexico* 20°56N 101°26W **175** B6
Silas *Ala., U.S.A.* 31°46N 88°20W **112** E2
Siler City *N.C., U.S.A.* 35°44N 79°28W **103** C6
Siletz *Oreg., U.S.A.* 44°43N 123°55W **121** C2
Siletz → *Oreg., U.S.A.* 44°54N 124°1W **121** C1
Siletz Indian Reservation *Oreg., U.S.A.* 44°47N 123°48W **121** C2
Silo *Okla., U.S.A.* 34°3N 96°29W **107** D7
Siloam Springs *Ark., U.S.A.* 36°11N 94°32W **106** B1
Silsbee *Tex., U.S.A.* 30°21N 94°11W **109** G13
Silt *Colo., U.S.A.* 39°33N 107°40W **125** C3
Siltcoos L. *Oreg., U.S.A.* 43°53N 124°6W **121** D1
Siltepec *Chiapas, Mexico* 15°39N 92°17W **178** D4
Silver *Tex., U.S.A.* 32°4N 100°40W **108** E7
Silver, L. *Fla., U.S.A.* 28°35N 81°23W **115** A2
Silver Bank *W. Indies* 20°30N 69°45W **183** B6
Silver Bank Passage *W. Indies* 20°0N 70°0W **183** B5
Silver Bay *Minn., U.S.A.* 47°18N 91°16W **77** C7
Silver Bell *Ariz., U.S.A.* 32°23N 111°30W **130** E4
Silver Bow County ☆ *Mont., U.S.A.* 45°48N 112°45W **123** E5
Silver City *Iowa, U.S.A.* 41°7N 95°39W **81** D3
Silver City *Mich., U.S.A.* 46°50N 89°35W **79** C2
Silver City *Miss., U.S.A.* 33°6N 90°30W **111** C3
Silver City *N. Mex., U.S.A.* 32°46N 108°17W **131** E2
Silver Cliff *Colo., U.S.A.* 38°8N 105°27W **125** D5
Silver Cr. → *Ariz., U.S.A.* 34°44N 110°2W **130** C5
Silver Cr. → *Ill., U.S.A.* 38°20N 89°53W **84** E4
Silver Cr. → *Oreg., U.S.A.* 43°16N 119°13W **121** D6
Silver Creek *Miss., U.S.A.* 31°36N 89°59W **111** E4
Silver Creek *N.Y., U.S.A.* 42°33N 79°10W **88** C1
Silver Creek *Nebr., U.S.A.* 41°19N 97°40W **80** C8
Silver Dollar City *Mo., U.S.A.* 36°40N 93°20W **83** E3
Silver Fork *Utah, U.S.A.* 40°37N 111°36W **134** C4
Silver Hill *Md., U.S.A.* 38°49N 76°55W **99** C4
Silver L. *N.H., U.S.A.* 43°52N 71°10W **89** C3
Silver L. *Oreg., U.S.A.* 43°22N 119°25W **121** D6
Silver L. *Oreg., U.S.A.* 43°6N 120°53W **121** D5
Silver L. *Wash., U.S.A.* 46°17N 122°47W **120** D3
Silver Lake *Calif., U.S.A.* 35°21N 116°7W **127** H10
Silver Lake *Kans., U.S.A.* 39°6N 95°52W **82** B8
Silver Lake *Minn., U.S.A.* 44°54N 94°12W **77** F4
Silver Lake *Oreg., U.S.A.* 43°8N 121°3W **121** D4
Silver Lake *Wis., U.S.A.* 44°4N 89°14W **78** D4
Silver Peak *Nev., U.S.A.* 37°45N 117°38W **128** E3
Silver Peak Ra. *U.S.A.* 37°45N 117°45W **128** E3
Silver Ridge *Man., Canada* 50°48N 98°52W **151** E13
Silver Run *Md., U.S.A.* 39°42N 77°3W **93** A3
Silver Spring *Md., U.S.A.* 38°59N 77°2W **99** A3
Silver Springs *Fla., U.S.A.* 29°13N 82°3W **114** B6
Silver Springs *Nev., U.S.A.* 39°25N 119°14W **128** C1
Silver Star Park △ *B.C., Canada* 50°23N 119°5W **155** E15
Silver Water *Ont., Canada* 45°52N 82°52W **146** B4
Silverdale *Kans., U.S.A.* 37°3N 96°54W **82** D7
Silverthorne *Colo., U.S.A.* 39°38N 106°4W **125** C4
Silverthrone Glacier *B.C., Canada* 51°26N 125°53W **154** D9
Silvertip Mt. *B.C., Canada* 49°10N 121°13W **155** F13
Silverton *B.C., Canada* 49°57N 117°21W **155** F17
Silverton *Colo., U.S.A.* 37°49N 107°40W **125** E3
Silverton *N.J., U.S.A.* 40°1N 74°10W **92** B2
Silverton *Oreg., U.S.A.* 45°1N 122°47W **121** B3
Silverton *Tex., U.S.A.* 34°28N 101°19W **108** C6
Silverton *Wash., U.S.A.* 48°5N 121°35W **120** B4
Silverwood *Idaho, U.S.A.* 47°56N 116°42W **122** B2
Silvies → *Oreg., U.S.A.* 43°34N 119°2W **121** D6
Silvis *Ill., U.S.A.* 41°31N 90°25W **84** B3
Simard, L. *Qué., Canada* 47°40N 78°40W **144** D4
Simcoe, L. *Ont., Canada* 44°25N 79°20W **146** C7
Simi Valley *Calif., U.S.A.* 34°16N 118°47W **127** J8
Simla *Colo., U.S.A.* 39°9N 104°5W **125** C6
Simmesport *La., U.S.A.* 30°59N 91°49W **110** D4
Simmie *Sask., Canada* 49°56N 108°6W **150** F3
Simmler *Calif., U.S.A.* 35°21N 119°59W **127** H7
Simms *Mont., U.S.A.* 47°30N 111°56W **123** C6
Simnasho *Oreg., U.S.A.* 44°58N 121°21W **121** C4
Simojovel *Chiapas, Mexico* 17°12N 92°38W **178** B4
Simón Bolívar *Durango, Mexico* 24°41N 103°14W **173** C7
Simonette → *Alta., Canada* 55°9N 118°15W **152** C2
Simonhouse *Man., Canada* 54°26N 101°23W **151** A10
Simonton Lake *Ind., U.S.A.* 41°44N 85°59W **85** B5
Simpson *Sask., Canada* 51°27N 105°27W **150** D6
Simpson *Kans., U.S.A.* 39°23N 97°56W **82** B6
Simpson *La., U.S.A.* 31°16N 93°1W **110** C2
Simpson County ☆ *Ky., U.S.A.* 36°45N 86°35W **104** D6
Simpson County ☆ *Miss., U.S.A.* 31°53N 89°58W **111** E4
Simpson I. *Ont., Canada* 48°46N 87°41W **149** D9
Simpson Park Mts. *Nev., U.S.A.* 39°50N 116°35W **128** C4
Simpson Pen. *Nunavut, Canada* 68°34N 88°45W **158** D8
Simpsonville *S.C., U.S.A.* 34°44N 82°15W **103** D3
Sims *Ill., U.S.A.* 38°22N 88°32W **84** E5
Simsbury *Conn., U.S.A.* 41°53N 72°48W **91** C2
Sinai *S. Dak., U.S.A.* 44°15N 97°3W **76** F8
Sinaloa □ *Mexico* 25°0N 107°30W **172** C3
Sinaloa → *Sinaloa, Mexico* 25°18N 108°27W **172** B2
Sinaloa de Leyva *Sinaloa, Mexico* 25°50N 108°14W **172** B2
Sinanché *Yucatán, Mexico* 21°13N 89°11W **179** A4
Sinclair *Wyo., U.S.A.* 41°47N 107°7W **124** E5
Sinclair, L. *Ga., U.S.A.* 33°8N 83°12W **113** C3
Sinclair Pass *B.C., Canada* 50°40N 115°58W **153** H5
Sinclairville *N.Y., U.S.A.* 42°16N 79°16W **88** C1
Sing Sing = Ossining *N.Y., U.S.A.* 41°10N 73°55W **92** A3
Singac *N.J., U.S.A.* 40°53N 74°14W **97** A1
Singer *La., U.S.A.* 30°39N 93°25W **110** D2
Singuilucan *Hidalgo, Mexico* 19°58N 98°31W **175** C9
Sinking Spring *Ohio, U.S.A.* 39°4N 83°23W **86** D3
Sinnemahoning *Pa., U.S.A.* 41°19N 78°6W **87** C4
Sintaluta *Sask., Canada* 50°29N 103°27W **150** E8
Sinton *Tex., U.S.A.* 28°2N 97°31W **109** J10
Siorapaluk *Greenland* 77°47N 70°45W **158** B11
Sioux Center *Iowa, U.S.A.* 43°5N 96°11W **81** B2
Sioux City *Iowa, U.S.A.* 42°30N 96°24W **81** C2
Sioux County ☆ *Iowa, U.S.A.* 43°5N 96°10W **81** B2
Sioux County ☆ *N. Dak., U.S.A.* 46°0N 101°0W **76** D5
Sioux County ☆ *Nebr., U.S.A.* 42°30N 103°45W **80** B2
Sioux Falls *S. Dak., U.S.A.* 43°33N 96°44W **76** G9
Sioux Lookout *Ont., Canada* 50°10N 91°50W **148** B5
Sioux Narrows *Ont., Canada* 49°25N 94°10W **148** C2
Sioux Rapids *Iowa, U.S.A.* 42°53N 95°9W **81** C3
Sipiwesk L. *Man., Canada* 55°5N 97°35W **159** F6
Sipsey → *Ala., U.S.A.* 33°0N 88°10W **112** C2
Siqueiros *Sinaloa, Mexico* 23°19N 106°15W **172** D4
Siquia → *Nic.* 12°10N 84°20W **182** D3
Siquirres *Costa Rica* 10°6N 83°30W **182** D3
Sir Francis Drake, Mt. *B.C., Canada* 50°49N 124°48W **154** E10
Sir James MacBrien, Mt. *N.W.T., Canada* 62°7N 127°41W **157** D7
Sir Sandford, Mt. *B.C., Canada* 51°40N 117°52W **155** D17
Siren *Wis., U.S.A.* 45°47N 92°24W **78** C1
Sirmans *Fla., U.S.A.* 30°21N 83°39W **114** A5
Sirmilik Nat. Park △ *Nunavut, Canada* 72°50N 80°35W **158** C9
Sisal *Yucatán, Mexico* 21°10N 90°2W **179** A3
Sisal, Arrecife *Yucatán, Mexico* 21°25N 90°18W **179** A3
Sisbicchén *Yucatán, Mexico* 20°49N 87°56W **179** B6
Sisimiut *Greenland* 66°40N 53°30W **162** D5
Siskiyou County ☆ *Calif., U.S.A.* 41°40N 122°40W **126** B4
Siskiyou Mts. *U.S.A.* 42°0N 122°40W **126** B3
Siskiyou Nat. Forest *Oreg., U.S.A.* 42°20N 124°0W **121** E2
Siskiyou Summit *Oreg., U.S.A.* 42°3N 122°48W **121** E3
Sisoguichi *Chihuahua, Mexico* 27°48N 107°31W **169** F8
Sisquoc → *Calif., U.S.A.* 34°54N 120°18W **127** J6
Sisseton *S. Dak., U.S.A.* 45°40N 97°3W **76** E8
Sisseton Indian Reservation = Lake Traverse Indian Reservation *N. Dak., U.S.A.* 46°0N 97°10W **76** E8
Sisson = Mount Shasta *Calif., U.S.A.* 41°19N 122°19W **126** B4
Sissonville *W. Va., U.S.A.* 38°32N 81°38W **102** C3
Sister Bay *Wis., U.S.A.* 45°11N 87°7W **78** C6
Sisters *Oreg., U.S.A.* 44°18N 121°33W **121** C4
Sistersville *W. Va., U.S.A.* 39°34N 80°59W **102** B4
Sitidgi L. *N.W.T., Canada* 68°33N 132°42W **156** C6
Sitka *Alaska, U.S.A.* 57°3N 135°20W **135** H14
Sitka *Kans., U.S.A.* 37°11N 99°39W **82** D4
Sitka ☆ *Alaska, U.S.A.* 57°10N 135°20W **135** H14
Sitka Nat. Historical Park △ *Alaska, U.S.A.* 57°3N 135°19W **135** H14
Sitkinak I. *Alaska, U.S.A.* 56°33N 154°10W **135** H9
Siufaalete Pt. *Amer. Samoa* 14°17S 169°29W **184** f
Siuna *Nic.* 13°37N 84°45W **182** D3
Siuslaw → *Oreg., U.S.A.* 44°1N 124°8W **121** C1
Siuslaw Nat. Forest *Oreg., U.S.A.* 44°15N 123°50W **121** C2
Six Flags Great Adventure *N.J., U.S.A.* 40°10N 74°27W **92** B2
Six Gun City *N.H., U.S.A.* 44°25N 71°29W **89** B3
Six Rivers Nat. Forest *Calif., U.S.A.* 41°0N 123°3W **126** C3
Skagit → *Wash., U.S.A.* 48°23N 122°22W **120** B3
Skagit B. *Wash., U.S.A.* 48°22N 122°34W **120** B3
Skagit County ☆ *Wash., U.S.A.* 48°30N 121°30W **120** B4
Skagit Valley Park △ *B.C., Canada* 49°7N 121°10W **155** F13
Skagway *Alaska, U.S.A.* 59°28N 135°19W **135** G14
Skagway-Hoonah-Angoon ☆ *Alaska, U.S.A.* 58°45N 136°15W **135** G13
Skamania County ☆ *Wash., U.S.A.* 46°0N 122°0W **120** D4
Skaneateles *N.Y., U.S.A.* 42°57N 76°26W **88** C4
Skanee *Mich., U.S.A.* 46°52N 88°13W **79** C3
Skedee *Okla., U.S.A.* 36°23N 96°42W **107** B7
Skeena → *B.C., Canada* 54°9N 130°5W **154** A4
Skeena Mts. *B.C., Canada* 56°40N 128°30W **157** E7
Skellytown *Tex., U.S.A.* 35°34N 101°11W **108** B6
Skiatook *Okla., U.S.A.* 36°22N 96°0W **107** B7
Skiatook L. *Okla., U.S.A.* 36°20N 96°10W **107** B7
Skidegate *B.C., Canada* 53°15N 132°1W **154** B2
Skidmore *Mo., U.S.A.* 40°17N 95°5W **83** A1
Skidmore *Tex., U.S.A.* 28°15N 97°41W **109** J10
Skidway Lake *Mich., U.S.A.* 44°11N 84°2W **79** E7
Skihist, Mt. *B.C., Canada* 50°12N 121°54W **155** E13
Skillet Fork → *Ill., U.S.A.* 38°5N 88°5W **84** E5
Skokie *Ill., U.S.A.* 42°2N 87°43W **95** A2
Skokie → *Ill., U.S.A.* 42°3N 87°46W **95** A2
Skokie Heritage Museum *Ill., U.S.A.* 42°2N 87°44W **95** A2
Skowhegan *Maine, U.S.A.* 44°46N 69°43W **90** D4
Skownan *Man., Canada* 51°58N 99°35W **151** D12
Skull Valley *Ariz., U.S.A.* 34°30N 112°41W **130** C3
Skull Valley Indian Reservation *Utah, U.S.A.* 40°24N 112°45W **129** C3
Skuna → *Miss., U.S.A.* 33°54N 89°41W **111** C4
Skunk → *Iowa, U.S.A.* 40°42N 91°7W **81** E7
Sky Lake *Fla., U.S.A.* 28°27N 81°23W **115** B2
Skykomish *Wash., U.S.A.* 47°42N 121°22W **120** C4
Skykomish → *Wash., U.S.A.* 47°49N 122°3W **120** C3
Skyland *Georgia, U.S.A.* 33°53N 84°19W **117** A3
Skyline *Ala., U.S.A.* 34°49N 86°7W **112** B4
Skyline *Calif., U.S.A.* 32°42N 117°1W **133** B2
Skyway *Wash., U.S.A.* 47°29N 122°15W **132** C4
Slagle *La., U.S.A.* 31°12N 93°8W **110** C2
Slanesville *W. Va., U.S.A.* 39°22N 78°31W **93** A2
Slate Creek *Idaho, U.S.A.* 45°38N 116°17W **122** D2
Slate Is. *Ont., Canada* 48°40N 87°0W **149** D10
Slate Spring *Miss., U.S.A.* 33°44N 89°22W **111** C4
Slater *Iowa, U.S.A.* 41°53N 93°41W **81** D5
Slater *Mo., U.S.A.* 39°13N 93°4W **83** B3
Slater *Wyo., U.S.A.* 41°52N 104°49W **124** E8
Slatington *Pa., U.S.A.* 40°45N 75°37W **92** B1
Slaton *Tex., U.S.A.* 33°26N 101°39W **108** D6
Slaughter *La., U.S.A.* 30°43N 91°9W **110** D4
Slaughter Beach *Del., U.S.A.* 38°52N 75°18W **93** B5
Slaughters *Ky., U.S.A.* 37°29N 87°30W **104** C5
Slaughterville *Okla., U.S.A.* 35°5N 97°20W **107** C6
Slave → *Canada* 61°18N 113°39W **157** D10
Slave Lake *Alta., Canada* 55°17N 114°43W **152** C6
Slayton *Minn., U.S.A.* 43°59N 95°45W **77** G3
Sledge *Miss., U.S.A.* 34°26N 90°13W **111** B3
Sleeper *Mo., U.S.A.* 37°46N 92°36W **83** D4
Sleeping Bear Dunes Nat. Lakeshore △ *Mich., U.S.A.* 44°50N 86°5W **79** E5
Sleeping Bear Pt. *Mich., U.S.A.* 44°55N 86°3W **79** E5
Sleeping Giant Prov. Park △ *Ont., Canada* 48°26N 88°46W **148** D8
Sleepy Eye *Minn., U.S.A.* 44°18N 94°43W **77** F4
Sleetmute *Alaska, U.S.A.* 61°42N 157°10W **135** F8
Slemp *Ky., U.S.A.* 37°5N 83°6W **105** C9
Slick *Okla., U.S.A.* 35°47N 96°16W **107** C7
Slick Rock *Colo., U.S.A.* 38°3N 108°54W **125** D2
Slide Mt. *N.Y., U.S.A.* 42°0N 74°25W **88** D6
Slidell *La., U.S.A.* 30°17N 89°47W **110** D6
Sligo *Pa., U.S.A.* 41°6N 79°29W **87** C3
Slim Buttes *S. Dak., U.S.A.* 45°20N 103°15W **76** E2
Slippery Rock *Pa., U.S.A.* 41°4N 80°3W **87** C2
Sloan *Iowa, U.S.A.* 42°14N 96°14W **81** C2
Sloan *Nev., U.S.A.* 35°57N 115°13W **128** G5
Sloat *Calif., U.S.A.* 39°52N 120°44W **126** D6
Slocan *B.C., Canada* 49°48N 117°28W **155** F17
Slocan L. *B.C., Canada* 49°50N 117°23W **155** F17
Slocan Park *B.C., Canada* 49°31N 117°37W **155** F17
Slocomb *Ala., U.S.A.* 31°7N 85°36W **112** E5
Slocum *R.I., U.S.A.* 41°32N 71°31W **91** C3
Slope County ☆ *N. Dak., U.S.A.* 46°20N 103°30W **76** D2
Smackover *Ark., U.S.A.* 33°22N 92°44W **106** E3
Small, C. *Maine, U.S.A.* 43°42N 69°51W **90** E4
Smallwood Res. *Qué., Canada* 54°5N 64°30W **143** C5
Smarr *Ga., U.S.A.* 32°59N 83°53W **113** D3
Smarts Mt. *N.H., U.S.A.* 43°48N 72°3W **89** C2
Smartville *Calif., U.S.A.* 39°13N 121°18W **126** D5
Smeaton *Sask., Canada* 53°30N 104°49W **150** B7
Smethport *Pa., U.S.A.* 41°49N 78°27W **87** C4
Smiley *Sask., Canada* 51°38N 109°29W **150** D2
Smiley *Tex., U.S.A.* 29°16N 97°38W **109** H10
Smith *Alta., Canada* 55°10N 114°0W **152** C6
Smith *Nev., U.S.A.* 38°48N 119°20W **128** D1
Smith → *Mont., U.S.A.* 47°25N 111°29W **123** C6
Smith → *N.C., U.S.A.* 36°27N 79°43W **103** B6
Smith Arm *N.W.T., Canada* 66°15N 123°0W **156** C8
Smith B. *Alaska, U.S.A.* 70°30N 154°20W **135** A9
Smith Bay *Nunavut, Canada* 77°4N 78°40W **158** B10
Smith Center *Kans., U.S.A.* 39°47N 98°47W **82** B5
Smith County ☆ *Kans., U.S.A.* 39°45N 98°45W **82** B5
Smith County ☆ *Miss., U.S.A.* 32°1N 89°23W **111** D4
Smith County ☆ *Tenn., U.S.A.* 36°5N 85°57W **105** D7
Smith County ☆ *Tex., U.S.A.* 32°21N 95°18W **109** E12
Smith Forest Preserve *Ill., U.S.A.* 41°59N 87°45W **95** B2
Smith I. *Nunavut, Canada* 60°45N 78°25W **143** C6
Smith I. *Md., U.S.A.* 38°0N 76°0W **93** B4
Smith I. *N.C., U.S.A.* 33°53N 77°59W **103** E8
Smith I. *Va., U.S.A.* 37°9N 75°53W **102** D9
Smith Lake *Oreg., U.S.A.* 45°36N 122°43W **132** A1
Smith Mountain L. *Va., U.S.A.* 37°2N 79°30W **102** D5
Smith Pk. *Idaho, U.S.A.* 48°51N 116°40W **122** A2
Smith River *Calif., U.S.A.* 41°56N 124°9W **126** B2
Smith River Nat. Recr. Area △ *U.S.A.* 41°55N 124°0W **126** B2
Smith Sd. *N. Amer.* 78°25N 74°0W **162** B3
Smithburg *N.J., U.S.A.* 40°13N 74°21W **92** B2
Smithburg *W. Va., U.S.A.* 39°17N 80°44W **102** B4
Smithdale *Miss., U.S.A.* 31°20N 90°41W **111** E3
Smithers *B.C., Canada* 54°45N 127°10W **157** F7
Smithfield *N.C., U.S.A.* 35°31N 78°21W **103** C7
Smithfield *Nebr., U.S.A.* 40°34N 99°45W **80** D6
Smithfield *R.I., U.S.A.* 41°55N 71°33W **91** C3
Smithfield *Utah, U.S.A.* 41°50N 111°50W **129** B4
Smithfield *Va., U.S.A.* 36°59N 76°38W **102** E8
Smithland *Iowa, U.S.A.* 42°14N 95°56W **81** C3
Smithland *Ky., U.S.A.* 37°9N 88°24W **104** C4
Smiths *Ala., U.S.A.* 32°32N 85°6W **112** D5
Smiths Cove *N.S., Canada* 44°37N 65°42W **141** J4
Smiths Falls *Ont., Canada* 44°55N 76°0W **147** C10
Smiths Ferry *Idaho, U.S.A.* 44°18N 116°5W **122** E2
Smiths Grove *Ky., U.S.A.* 37°3N 86°12W **104** C6
Smithsburg *Md., U.S.A.* 39°39N 77°35W **93** A3
Smithton *Mo., U.S.A.* 38°41N 93°5W **83** C3
Smithtown *N.Y., U.S.A.* 40°51N 73°12W **91** D1
Smithville *Ont., Canada* 43°6N 79°33W **146** D7
Smithville *Ga., U.S.A.* 31°54N 84°15W **113** E2
Smithville *Md., U.S.A.* 38°46N 75°45W **93** B5
Smithville *Miss., U.S.A.* 34°4N 88°23W **111** B5
Smithville *Mo., U.S.A.* 39°23N 94°35W **83** B2
Smithville *Okla., U.S.A.* 34°28N 94°39W **107** D9
Smithville *Tenn., U.S.A.* 35°58N 85°49W **105** E7
Smithville *Tex., U.S.A.* 30°1N 97°10W **109** G10
Smithville *W. Va., U.S.A.* 39°4N 81°6W **102** B3
Smoaks *S.C., U.S.A.* 33°5N 80°49W **103** E5
Smoke Creek Desert *Nev., U.S.A.* 40°30N 119°40W **128** B1
Smokey Point *Wash., U.S.A.* 48°9N 122°11W **120** B3
Smoky → *Alta., Canada* 56°10N 117°21W **152** B3
Smoky Dome *Idaho, U.S.A.* 43°30N 114°56W **122** F4
Smoky Hill → *Kans., U.S.A.* 39°4N 96°48W **82** B7
Smoky Hills *Kans., U.S.A.* 39°15N 99°30W **82** B4
Smoky Lake *Alta., Canada* 54°10N 112°30W **152** D8
Smoky Mts. *Idaho, U.S.A.* 43°40N 114°38W **122** F4
Smolan *Kans., U.S.A.* 38°44N 97°41W **82** C6
Smoot *Wyo., U.S.A.* 42°37N 110°55W **124** D2
Smooth Rock Falls *Ont., Canada* 49°17N 81°37W **149** C15
Smoothrock L. *Ont., Canada* 50°30N 89°30W **148** B7
Smoothstone L. *Sask., Canada* 54°40N 106°50W **157** F11
Smugglers Notch Resort *Vt., U.S.A.* 44°33N 72°47W **89** B2
Smyrna *Del., U.S.A.* 39°18N 75°36W **93** A5
Smyrna *Ga., U.S.A.* 33°53N 84°31W **113** C2
Smyrna *Tenn., U.S.A.* 35°59N 86°31W **104** E6
Smyrna Mills *Maine, U.S.A.* 46°8N 68°10W **90** B5
Smyth County ☆ *Va., U.S.A.* 36°55N 81°25W **102** E3
Snail Lake *Minn., U.S.A.* 45°4N 93°7W **94** A3
Snake → *Yukon, Canada* 65°59N 134°12W **156** C6
Snake → *Idaho, U.S.A.* 46°12N 119°2W **120** D6
Snake → *Minn., U.S.A.* 48°26N 97°7W **77** B1
Snake → *Minn., U.S.A.* 45°49N 92°46W **77** E6
Snake → *Nebr., U.S.A.* 42°47N 100°47W **80** B5
Snake Creek Canal *Fla., U.S.A.* 25°57N 80°19W **115** C2
Snake Mts. *Nev., U.S.A.* 41°25N 115°0W **128** A6
Snake Range *Nev., U.S.A.* 39°0N 114°20W **128** D6
Snake River Birds of Prey Nat. Conservation Area △ *Idaho, U.S.A.* 43°10N 116°19W **122** F2
Snake River Plain *Idaho, U.S.A.* 42°50N 114°0W **122** G4
Snake River Ra. *Idaho, U.S.A.* 43°23N 111°5W **122** F7
Snake Valley *Utah, U.S.A.* 39°30N 113°55W **129** D2
Snakeden Branch → *Va., U.S.A.* 38°55N 77°18W **99** B1
Snare Lakes = Wekweètì *N.W.T., Canada* 64°11N 114°10W **157** D10
Sneads Ferry *N.C., U.S.A.* 34°33N 77°24W **103** D8
Sneedville *Tenn., U.S.A.* 36°32N 83°13W **105** D9
Snelling *Calif., U.S.A.* 37°31N 120°26W **126** F6
Snellville *Ga., U.S.A.* 33°51N 84°1W **113** C2
Snipe L. *Alta., Canada* 55°7N 116°47W **152** C4
Snohomish *Wash., U.S.A.* 47°55N 122°6W **120** C3
Snohomish County ☆ *Wash., U.S.A.* 48°0N 121°30W **120** B4
Snoqualmie *Wash., U.S.A.* 47°31N 121°49W **120** C4
Snoqualmie Pass *Wash., U.S.A.* 47°25N 121°25W **120** C4
Snover *Mich., U.S.A.* 43°28N 82°58W **79** F9
Snow Hill *Ala., U.S.A.* 32°0N 87°0W **112** D4
Snow Hill *Md., U.S.A.* 38°11N 75°24W **93** B5
Snow Hill *N.C., U.S.A.* 35°27N 77°40W **103** C8
Snow King *Wyo., U.S.A.* 43°28N 110°46W **124** C2
Snow Lake *Man., Canada* 54°52N 100°3W **159** G5
Snow Mt. *Calif., U.S.A.* 39°23N 122°45W **126** D4
Snow Mt. *Maine, U.S.A.* 45°18N 70°48W **90** C3
Snow Pk. *Wash., U.S.A.* 48°35N 118°29W **120** B7
Snow Shoe *Pa., U.S.A.* 41°2N 77°57W **87** C5

Snow Water L. *Nev., U.S.A.* 40°48N 114°59W **128** B6
Snowball *Ark., U.S.A.* 35°55N 92°49W **106** C3
Snowbird L. *N.W.T., Canada* 60°45N 103°0W **157** D12
Snowdoun *Ala., U.S.A.* 32°15N 86°18W **112** D4
Snowdrift = Łutselk'e *N.W.T., Canada* 62°24N 110°44W **157** D10
Snowflake *Man., Canada* 49°3N 98°39W **151** F13
Snowflake *Ariz., U.S.A.* 34°30N 110°5W **130** C5
Snowmass *Colo., U.S.A.* 39°20N 106°59W **125** E4
Snowmass Mt. *Colo., U.S.A.* 39°8N 107°5W **125** D4
Snowshoe Pk. *Mont., U.S.A.* 48°13N 115°41W **123** B2
Snowshoe Ski Resort *W. Va., U.S.A.* 38°25N 80°0W **102** C4
Snowville *Utah, U.S.A.* 41°58N 112°43W **129** B3
Snowy Mt. *N.Y., U.S.A.* 43°42N 74°23W **88** B6
Snowyside Pk. *Idaho, U.S.A.* 43°57N 114°58W **122** F4
Snug Corner *Bahamas* 22°33N 73°52W **183** B5
Snug Harbor *Tampa, U.S.A.* 27°12N 82°13W **115** B3
Snyder *Nebr., U.S.A.* 41°43N 96°47W **80** C9
Snyder *Okla., U.S.A.* 34°40N 98°57W **107** D5
Snyder *Tex., U.S.A.* 32°44N 100°55W **108** E7
Snyder County ☆ *Pa., U.S.A.* 40°50N 77°0W **87** D5
Soap Lake *Wash., U.S.A.* 47°23N 119°29W **120** C6
Socastee *S.C., U.S.A.* 33°41N 78°59W **103** E7
Social Circle *Ga., U.S.A.* 33°39N 83°43W **113** C3
Society Hill *Ala., U.S.A.* 32°26N 85°27W **112** D5
Society Hill *S.C., U.S.A.* 34°31N 79°51W **103** D6
Socoltenango *Chiapas, Mexico* 16°13N 92°15W **178** C4
Socorro *Coahuila, Mexico* 26°56N 102°24W **170** D2
Socorro *N. Mex., U.S.A.* 34°4N 106°54W **131** C4
Socorro *Tex., U.S.A.* 31°39N 106°18W **108** F1
Socorro County ☆ *N. Mex., U.S.A.* 34°0N 107°0W **131** C4
Soda Creek *B.C., Canada* 52°21N 122°17W **155** C12
Soda L. *Calif., U.S.A.* 35°10N 116°4W **127** H10
Soda Springs *Calif., U.S.A.* 39°20N 120°23W **126** D6
Soda Springs *Idaho, U.S.A.* 42°39N 111°36W **122** G7
Sodaville *Oreg., U.S.A.* 44°29N 122°52W **121** D3
Soddy-Daisy *Tenn., U.S.A.* 35°17N 85°10W **105** E7
Sodus *N.Y., U.S.A.* 43°14N 77°4W **88** B3
Sodus Point *N.Y., U.S.A.* 43°16N 76°59W **88** B4
Soeurs, Î. des *Qué., Canada* 45°27N 73°32W **160** B3
Sointula *B.C., Canada* 50°38N 127°0W **154** E7
Sol Duc → *Wash., U.S.A.* 47°55N 124°32W **120** C1
Sola de Vega *Oaxaca, Mexico* 16°33N 96°58W **177** H4
Solana Beach *Calif., U.S.A.* 32°58N 117°16W **127** L9
Solano County ☆ *Calif., U.S.A.* 38°20N 121°54W **126** E5
Soldier *Iowa, U.S.A.* 41°59N 95°46W **81** D3
Soldier *Kans., U.S.A.* 39°32N 95°58W **82** B8
Soldier Summit *Utah, U.S.A.* 39°56N 111°5W **129** D4
Soldiers Grove *Wis., U.S.A.* 43°24N 90°47W **78** E3
Soldotna *Alaska, U.S.A.* 60°29N 151°3W **135** F10
Soledad *Calif., U.S.A.* 36°26N 121°20W **126** G5
Soledad de Doblado *Veracruz, Mexico* 19°3N 96°25W **177** E4
Soledad de Graciano Sánchez *San Luis Potosí, Mexico* 22°12N 100°57W **171** H4
Solen *N. Dak., U.S.A.* 46°23N 100°48W **76** D5
Solferino *Quintana Roo, Mexico* 21°21N 87°28W **179** A6
Solis, Presa *Guanajuato, Mexico* 20°2N 100°37W **175** B7
Sololá *Guatemala* 14°49N 91°10W **182** D1
Solomon *Ariz., U.S.A.* 32°49N 109°38W **130** E6
Solomon *Kans., U.S.A.* 38°55N 97°22W **82** C6
Solomon → *Kans., U.S.A.* 38°55N 97°22W **82** C6
Solomon, N. Fork → *Kans., U.S.A.* 39°29N 98°26W **82** B5
Solomon, S. Fork → *Kans., U.S.A.* 39°25N 99°12W **82** B4
Solomons *Md., U.S.A.* 38°19N 76°27W **93** B4
Solon *Iowa, U.S.A.* 41°48N 91°30W **81** D7
Solon *Maine, U.S.A.* 44°57N 69°52W **90** D4
Solon Springs *Wis., U.S.A.* 46°22N 91°49W **78** B21
Solvang *Calif., U.S.A.* 34°36N 120°8W **127** J6
Solvay *N.Y., U.S.A.* 43°3N 76°13W **88** B4
Sombra *Ont., Canada* 42°43N 82°29W **146** E4
Sombrerete *Zacatecas, Mexico* 23°38N 103°39W **173** D7
Sombrero *Anguilla* 18°37N 63°30W **183** C7
Somers *Conn., U.S.A.* 41°59N 72°27W **91** C2
Somers *Iowa, U.S.A.* 42°23N 94°26W **81** C4
Somers *Mont., U.S.A.* 48°5N 114°13W **123** B3
Somers Point *N.J., U.S.A.* 39°20N 74°36W **92** C2
Somerset *Man., Canada* 49°25N 98°39W **151** F13
Somerset *Colo., U.S.A.* 38°56N 107°28W **125** D3
Somerset *Ky., U.S.A.* 37°5N 84°36W **105** C8
Somerset *Mass., U.S.A.* 41°47N 71°8W **91** C3
Somerset *Md., U.S.A.* 38°57N 77°5W **99** B3
Somerset *Mich., U.S.A.* 42°3N 84°23W **79** G7
Somerset *Ohio, U.S.A.* 39°48N 82°18W **86** D4
Somerset *Pa., U.S.A.* 40°1N 79°5W **87** D3
Somerset *Tex., U.S.A.* 29°14N 98°40W **109** H9
Somerset County ☆ *Maine, U.S.A.* 45°30N 70°0W **90** C4
Somerset County ☆ *Md., U.S.A.* 38°10N 75°50W **93** B5
Somerset County ☆ *N.J., U.S.A.* 40°35N 74°35W **92** B2
Somerset County ☆ *Pa., U.S.A.* 40°0N 79°0W **87** D3
Somerset I. *Nunavut, Canada* 73°30N 93°0W **158** C7
Somerset Res. *Vt., U.S.A.* 43°0N 72°57W **89** C2
Somersworth *N.H., U.S.A.* 43°16N 70°52W **89** C4
Somerton *Ariz., U.S.A.* 32°36N 114°43W **130** E1
Somervell County ☆ *Tex., U.S.A.* 32°14N 97°45W **109** E10
Somerville *Mass., U.S.A.* 42°23N 71°5W **96** A2
Somerville *N.J., U.S.A.* 40°35N 74°38W **92** B2
Somerville *Ohio, U.S.A.* 39°34N 84°38W **86** D2
Somerville *Tenn., U.S.A.* 35°15N 89°21W **104** E3
Somerville *Tex., U.S.A.* 30°21N 96°32W **109** G11
Somerville L. *Tex., U.S.A.* 30°19N 96°31W **109** G11
Somes Bar *Calif., U.S.A.* 41°23N 123°29W **126** B3
Somoto *Nic.* 13°28N 86°37W **182** D2
Soná *Panama* 8°0N 81°20W **182** E3
Sondheimer *La., U.S.A.* 32°33N 91°11W **110** B4
Søndre Strømfjord = Kangerlussuaq *Greenland* 66°59N 50°40W **162** D5
Sonningdale *Sask., Canada* 52°23N 107°44W **150** C4
Sonny Bono Nat. Wildlife Refuge △ *Calif., U.S.A.* 33°15N 115°40W **127** K11
Sonoma *Calif., U.S.A.* 38°18N 122°28W **126** E4
Sonoma, L. *Calif., U.S.A.* 38°43N 123°1W **126** E3
Sonoma County ☆ *Calif., U.S.A.* 38°30N 123°0W **126** E3
Sonoma Peak *Nev., U.S.A.* 40°52N 117°36W **128** B3
Sonora *N.S., Canada* 45°4N 61°54W **141** H8
Sonora *Calif., U.S.A.* 37°59N 120°23W **126** F6
Sonora *Ky., U.S.A.* 37°32N 85°54W **105** C7
Sonora *Tex., U.S.A.* 30°34N 100°39W **108** G7
Sonora □ *Mexico* 29°20N 110°40W **168** D5
Sonora → *Mexico* 29°5N 110°55W **168** D5
Sonora I. *B.C., Canada* 50°22N 125°15W **154** E9
Sonoran Desert *Ariz., U.S.A.* 33°40N 113°30W **130** D2
Sonoran Desert Nat. Monument △ *Ariz., U.S.A.* 33°10N 112°45W **130** D3
Sonoyta *Sonora, Mexico* 31°51N 112°50W **168** B3
Sonoyta → *Sonora, Mexico* 31°16N 113°26W **168** B2
Sonsonate *El Salv.* 13°43N 89°44W **182** D2

Sontag *Miss., U.S.A.* 31°39N 90°12W **111** E3
Sony Picture Studio *Calif., U.S.A.* 34°1N 118°4W **133** B2
Sooke *B.C., Canada* 48°13N 123°43W **155** G11
Sooner L. *Okla., U.S.A.* 36°28N 95°53W **107** B8
Sopchoppy *Fla., U.S.A.* 30°4N 84°29W **114** A4
Soper *Okla., U.S.A.* 34°2N 95°42W **107** D8
Sophia *W. Va., U.S.A.* 37°42N 81°15W **102** D3
Sop's Arm *Nfld. & L., Canada* 49°46N 56°56W **142** C4
Sorel-Tracy *Qué., Canada* 46°0N 73°10W **145** E9
Sorento *Ill., U.S.A.* 39°1N 89°35W **84** D4
Sorrento *B.C., Canada* 50°53N 119°28W **155** E15
Sorrento *La., U.S.A.* 30°11N 90°51W **110** D5
Soscumica, L. *Qué., Canada* 50°15N 77°27W **143** C2
Soso *Miss., U.S.A.* 31°45N 89°17W **111** E4
Soteapan *Veracruz, Mexico* 18°14N 94°52W **177** F6
Soto la Marina *Tamaulipas, Mexico* 23°46N 98°3W **171** G6
Soto la Marina → *Tamaulipas, Mexico* 23°45N 97°45W **171** G7
Soto la Marina, Barra *Tamaulipas, Mexico* 24°5N 97°44W **171** F7
Sotuta *Yucatán, Mexico* 20°36N 89°1W **179** B4
Souderton *Pa., U.S.A.* 40°19N 75°19W **92** B1
Soufrière *St. Lucia* 13°51N 61°3W **183** D7
Sougahatchee Cr. → *Ala., U.S.A.* 32°36N 85°54W **112** D5
Souhegan → *N.H., U.S.A.* 42°51N 71°29W **89** D3
Sound Beach *N.Y., U.S.A.* 40°57N 72°58W **91** D2
Sounding Cr. → *Alta., Canada* 52°6N 110°28W **153** F10
Sounding L. *Alta., Canada* 52°8N 110°29W **153** F10
Soundview *N.Y., U.S.A.* 40°49N 73°53W **97** B3
Sour Lake *Tex., U.S.A.* 30°9N 94°2EW **109** G13
Souris *P.E.I., Canada* 46°21N 62°15W **141** G7
Souris *N. Dak., U.S.A.* 48°55N 100°40W **76** B5
Souris → *N. Amer.* 49°40N 99°34W **151** F12
Souris → *N. Amer.* 49°0N 100°57W **76** B5
South → *N.C., U.S.A.* 34°20N 78°3W **103** D7
South Amboy *N.J., U.S.A.* 40°29N 74°18W **92** B2
South Anna → *Va., U.S.A.* 37°48N 77°25W **102** D7
South Arm Park *B.C., Canada* 49°7N 123°8W **161** C2
South Ashburnham *Mass., U.S.A.* 42°37N 71°57W **96** B1
South Aulatsivik I. *Nfld. & L., Canada* 56°45N 61°30W **143** B5
South B. *Nunavut, Canada* 63°58N 83°30W **159** E9
South Baldy Pk. *N. Mex., U.S.A.* 34°6N 107°11W **131** C3
South Baltimore *Baltimore, U.S.A.* 39°16N 76°36W **99** B2
South Barre *Mass., U.S.A.* 42°23N 72°6W **96** B2
South Bass I. *Ohio, U.S.A.* 41°39N 82°49W **86** B4
South Bay *Fla., U.S.A.* 26°40N 80°43W **114** E8
South Baymouth *Ont., Canada* 45°33N 82°1W **146** B4
South Beach *Fla., U.S.A.* 25°46N 80°7W **115** D3
South Beach *N.Y., U.S.A.* 40°35N 74°4W **97** C2
South Beach *Wash., U.S.A.* 47°34N 122°30W **132** C3
South Beloit *Ill., U.S.A.* 42°29N 89°2W **84** A4
South Bend *Ind., U.S.A.* 41°41N 86°15W **85** A4
South Bend *Wash., U.S.A.* 46°40N 123°48W **120** D2
South Bend Park *Georgia, U.S.A.* 33°42N 84°23W **117** B2
South Bentinck Arm *B.C., Canada* 52°7N 126°47W **154** C8
South Berwick *Maine, U.S.A.* 43°14N 70°49W **89** C4
South Bloomfield *Ohio, U.S.A.* 39°43N 82°59W **86** D4
South Boardman *Mich., U.S.A.* 44°38N 85°17W **79** E6
South Boston *Mass., U.S.A.* 42°20N 71°2W **96** A2
South Boston *Va., U.S.A.* 36°42N 78°54W **102** E6
South Branch *Nfld. & L., Canada* 47°55N 59°2W **142** E1
South Branch Potomac → *W. Va., U.S.A.* 39°32N 78°35W **102** B6
South Branch Two → *Minn., U.S.A.* 48°46N 96°56W **77** B2
South Brook *Nfld. & L., Canada* 49°26N 56°5W **142** C4
South Burlington *Vt., U.S.A.* 44°28N 73°13W **89** B1
South C. = Kalae *Hawai'i, U.S.A.* 18°55N 155°4'W **136** E6
South Carolina □ *U.S.A.* 34°0N 81°0W **103** E5
South Carthage *Tenn., U.S.A.* 36°15N 85°57W **105** D7
South Carver *Mass., U.S.A.* 41°51N 70°54W **91** C4
South Chaplin *Conn., U.S.A.* 41°46N 72°9W **91** C2
South Charleston *Ohio, U.S.A.* 39°50N 83°38W **86** D3
South Charleston *W. Va., U.S.A.* 38°22N 81°44W **102** C3
South Charlestown *N.H., U.S.A.* 43°12N 72°26W **89** C2
South China *Maine, U.S.A.* 44°24N 69°34W **90** D4
South Cle Elum *Wash., U.S.A.* 47°11N 120°57W **120** C5
South Coffeyville *Okla., U.S.A.* 36°59N 95°37W **107** B8
South Colton *N.Y., U.S.A.* 44°30N 74°54W **88** A6
South Congaree *S.C., U.S.A.* 33°53N 81°5W **103** E4
South Dakota □ *U.S.A.* 44°15N 100°0W **76** F6
South Dartmouth *Mass., U.S.A.* 41°36N 70°57W **91** C4
South Dayton *N.Y., U.S.A.* 42°22N 79°3W **88** C1
South Daytona *Fla., U.S.A.* 29°10N 81°0W **114** B7
South Decatur *Georgia, U.S.A.* 33°44N 84°16W **117** B3
South Deerfield *Mass., U.S.A.* 42°29N 72°37W **89** C2
South Deerfield *N.H., U.S.A.* 43°6N 71°13W **89** C3
South Deering *Ill., U.S.A.* 41°42N 87°33W **95** C3
South Easton *Mass., U.S.A.* 42°3N 71°5W **91** B3
South Egremont *Mass., U.S.A.* 42°10N 73°25W **91** C1
South El Monte *Calif., U.S.A.* 34°3N 118°2W **133** B4
South English *Iowa, U.S.A.* 41°27N 92°5W **81** D6
South Fabius → *Mo., U.S.A.* 39°54N 91°30W **83** B5
South Fallsburg *N.Y., U.S.A.* 41°43N 74°38W **88** D6
South Floral Park *N.Y., U.S.A.* 40°43N 73°42W **97** B4
South Fork *Colo., U.S.A.* 37°40N 106°37W **125** E4
South Fork *Pa., U.S.A.* 40°22N 78°48W **87** D4
South Fork American → *Calif., U.S.A.* 38°57N 120°59W **126** E5
South Fork Edisto → *S.C., U.S.A.* 33°16N 80°54W **103** E5
South Fork Forked Deer → *Tenn., U.S.A.* 36°0N 89°26W **104** E3
South Fork Grand → *S. Dak., U.S.A.* 45°43N 102°17W **76** E3
South Fork Indian Reservation *Nev., U.S.A.* 40°45N 115°40W **128** B5
South Fork John Day → *Oreg., U.S.A.* 44°28N 119°31W **121** C6
South Fork Kentucky → *Ky., U.S.A.* 37°34N 83°43W **105** C9
South Fork Milk → *Mont., U.S.A.* 48°4N 106°19W **123** B11
South Fork Moreau → *S. Dak., U.S.A.* 45°0N 102°50W **76** E3
South Fork Obion → *Tenn., U.S.A.* 36°12N 88°56W **104** D4
South Fork Owyhee → *Idaho, U.S.A.* 42°16N 116°53W **122** G2
South Fork Powder → *Wyo., U.S.A.* 43°40N 106°30W **124** C6
South Fork Republican → *Nebr., U.S.A.* 40°3N 101°31W **82** A2
South Fork Sappa Cr. → *Kans., U.S.A.* 39°47N 100°35W **82** B3
South Fork Selway → *Idaho, U.S.A.* 46°10N 115°58W **122** C3
South Fork Shenandoah → *Va., U.S.A.* 38°57N 78°12W **102** C6
South Fork Shoshone → *Wyo., U.S.A.* 44°27N 109°14W **124** B3
South Fork Solomon → *Kans., U.S.A.* 39°28N 98°26W **82** B5
South Fork South Branch Potomac → *W. Va., U.S.A.* 39°5N 78°59W **102** B6
South Fork Spring → *Ark., U.S.A.* 36°19N 91°30W **106** B4
South Fox I. *Mich., U.S.A.* 45°25N 85°51W **79** D5
South Fulton *Tenn., U.S.A.* 36°30N 88°52W **104** D4
South Gate *Calif., U.S.A.* 33°56N 118°12W **133** C3
South Gillies *Ont., Canada* 48°14N 89°42W **148** D7
South Gorin *Mo., U.S.A.* 40°22N 92°1W **83** A4
South Grand → *Mo., U.S.A.* 38°17N 93°25W **83** C3
South Greensburg *Pa., U.S.A.* 40°17N 79°33W **87** D3

South Hadley *Mass., U.S.A.* 42°16N 72°35W **91** B2
South Hadley Falls *Mass., U.S.A.* 42°14N 72°36W **91** B2
South Hamilton *Mass., U.S.A.* 42°37N 70°53W **91** B4
South Haven *Kans., U.S.A.* 37°3N 97°24W **82** D6
South Haven *Mich., U.S.A.* 42°24N 86°16W **79** G5
South Hd. *Nfld. & L., Canada* 49°9N 58°22W **142** C2
South Heart *N. Dak., U.S.A.* 46°52N 102°59W **76** D3
South Heart → *Alta., Canada* 55°34N 116°11W **152** C4
South Hempstead *N.Y., U.S.A.* 40°40N 73°36W **97** B5
South Henik L. *Nunavut, Canada* 61°30N 97°20W **159** E6
South Hero *Vt., U.S.A.* 44°39N 73°19W **89** B1
South Hill *Va., U.S.A.* 36°44N 78°8W **102** E6
South Holston L. *Tenn., U.S.A.* 36°31N 82°5W **105** D10
South Hooksett *N.H., U.S.A.* 43°2N 71°26W **89** C3
South Hutchinson *Kans., U.S.A.* 38°2N 97°56W **82** C6
South I. *N.Y., U.S.A.* 33°10N 79°14W **103** E6
South Indian Lake *Man., Canada* 56°47N 98°56W **159** B9
South Jacksonville *Ill., U.S.A.* 39°44N 90°12W **84** D3
South Jordan *Utah, U.S.A.* 40°33N 111°55W **134** C2
South Lake Tahoe *Calif., U.S.A.* 38°57N 119°59W **126** E7
South Lancaster *Mass., U.S.A.* 42°27N 71°41W **91** B3
South Lawn *Md., U.S.A.* 38°47N 77°0W **99** C3
South Lebanon *Ohio, U.S.A.* 39°22N 84°13W **86** D2
South Loup → *Nebr., U.S.A.* 41°4N 98°39W **80** C7
South Lyon *Mich., U.S.A.* 42°28N 83°39W **79** G8
South Manitou I. *Mich., U.S.A.* 45°2N 86°8W **79** D5
South Marsh I. *La., U.S.A.* 38°6N 76°2W **93** B4
South Merrimack *N.H., U.S.A.* 42°49N 71°34W **89** D3
South Miami *Fla., U.S.A.* 25°42N 80°17W **115** D1
South Middleboro *Mass., U.S.A.* 41°45N 70°50W **91** C4
South Milwaukee *Wis., U.S.A.* 42°55N 87°52W **78** F6
South Moose L. *Man., Canada* 53°49N 100°1W **151** B11
South Mountain *Ariz., U.S.A.* 33°22N 112°4W **134** C2
South Mountain *Md., U.S.A.* 39°30N 77°40W **93** A3
South Mountain *Pa., U.S.A.* 39°51N 77°29W **93** A3
South Mountain *Utah, U.S.A.* 40°28N 112°2W **134** D1
South Mountain Park *Ariz., U.S.A.* 33°20N 112°8W **134** D2
South Mountain Reservation N.J., *U.S.A.* 40°45N 74°17W **97** B1
South Mountains *Ariz., U.S.A.* 33°19N 112°4W **134** D2
South Mt. *Idaho, U.S.A.* 42°44N 116°54W **122** G2
South Nahanni → *N.W.T., Canada* 61°3N 123°21W **157** D8
South Nation → *Ont., Canada* 45°34N 75°6W **147** B11
South Negril Pt. *Jamaica* 18°16N 78°22W **182** C4
South Newport *Ga., U.S.A.* 31°38N 81°24W **113** E5
South Newtane *Vt., U.S.A.* 42°55N 72°42W **89** D2
South of Market *Calif., U.S.A.* 37°46N 122°24W **132** B2
South Ogden *Utah, U.S.A.* 41°12N 111°58W **129** B4
South Orange *N.J., U.S.A.* 40°44N 74°15W **97** B1
South Otselic *N.Y., U.S.A.* 42°39N 75°47W **88** C5
South Ozone Park *N.Y., U.S.A.* 40°41N 73°49W **97** B4
South Paris *Maine, U.S.A.* 44°14N 70°31W **90** D3
South Park *Pa., U.S.A.* 40°18N 79°59W **98** C1
South Pasadena *Calif., U.S.A.* 34°7N 118°9W **133** B4
South Pasadena *Tampa, U.S.A.* 27°45N 82°44W **115** C2
South Pass *La., U.S.A.* 29°3N 89°12W **110** E6
South Pass *Wyo., U.S.A.* 42°22N 108°55W **124** D4
South Pass City *Wyo., U.S.A.* 42°28N 108°48W **124** D4
South Pekin *Ill., U.S.A.* 40°30N 89°39W **84** C4
South Pittsburg *Tenn., U.S.A.* 35°1N 85°42W **105** E7
South Platte → *Nebr., U.S.A.* 41°7N 100°42W **80** C5
South Point *Ohio, U.S.A.* 38°25N 82°35W **86** E4
South Pomfret *Vt., U.S.A.* 43°40N 72°33W **89** C2
South Ponte Vedra Beach *Fla., U.S.A.* 30°3N 81°20W **114** A7
South Porcupine *Ont., Canada* 48°30N 81°12W **144** C1
South Portland *Maine, U.S.A.* 43°38N 70°15W **90** E3
South Range *Mich., U.S.A.* 47°4N 88°38W **79** B3
South Res. *Mass., U.S.A.* 42°26N 71°6W **96** A2
South River *Ont., Canada* 45°52N 79°23W **146** B7
South River *N.J., U.S.A.* 40°27N 74°23W **92** B2
South Royalton *Vt., U.S.A.* 43°49N 72°32W **89** C2
South St. Paul *Minn., U.S.A.* 44°53N 93°2W **94** B3
South St. Paul Municipal ✈ *Minn., U.S.A.* 44°51N 93°1W **94** B3
South Salt Lake *Utah, U.S.A.* 40°43N 111°53W **134** B2
South San Francisco *Calif., U.S.A.* 37°38N 122°26W **132** C2
South San Gabriel *Calif., U.S.A.* 34°3N 118°6W **133** B4
South Sanford *Maine, U.S.A.* 43°25N 70°45W **89** C4
South Saskatchewan → *Sask., Canada* 53°15N 105°5W **150** B6
South Seaville *N.J., U.S.A.* 39°11N 74°46W **92** C2
South Shore *Ill., U.S.A.* 41°45N 87°34W **95** C3
South Shore *Ky., U.S.A.* 38°43N 82°59W **105** B9
South Shore *S. Dak., U.S.A.* 45°7N 96°56W **76** E9
South Shore Park *Wis., U.S.A.* 42°57N 87°52W **94** A2
South Sioux City *Nebr., U.S.A.* 42°28N 96°24W **80** B9
South Sister *Oreg., U.S.A.* 44°4N 121°51W **121** C4
South Skunk → *Iowa, U.S.A.* 41°15N 92°2W **81** D6
South Slocan *B.C., Canada* 49°28N 117°31W **155** F17
South Spicer I. *Nunavut, Canada* 68°16N 79°0W **158** D10
South Stoddard *N.H., U.S.A.* 43°4N 72°7W **89** C2
South Strafford *Vt., U.S.A.* 43°49N 72°23W **89** C2
South Sulphur → *Tex., U.S.A.* 33°23N 95°18W **109** D12
South Thompson → *B.C., Canada* 50°40N 120°20W **155** E14
South Torrington *Wyo., U.S.A.* 42°3N 104°11W **124** D8
South Tucson *Ariz., U.S.A.* 32°12N 110°58W **130** E5
South Twin I. *N.W.T., Canada* 53°7N 79°52W **143** C2
South Umpqua → *Oreg., U.S.A.* 43°16N 123°27W **121** D2
South Valley *N. Mex., U.S.A.* 35°1N 106°41W **131** B4
South Valley Stream *N.Y., U.S.A.* 40°39N 73°43W **97** C4
South Venice *Fla., U.S.A.* 27°3N 82°25W **114** D6
South Wabasca L. *Alta., Canada* 55°55N 113°45W **152** C7
South Wayne *Wis., U.S.A.* 42°34N 89°53W **78** F4
South Weare *N.H., U.S.A.* 43°5N 71°45W **89** C3
South Webster *Ohio, U.S.A.* 38°49N 82°44W **86** E4
South Wellfleet *Mass., U.S.A.* 41°55N 69°58W **91** C5
South West City *Mo., U.S.A.* 36°31N 94°37W **83** E2
South West Port Mouton *N.S., Canada* 43°54N 64°49W **141** K5
South Whitley *Ind., U.S.A.* 41°5N 85°38W **85** B5
South Williamson *Ky., U.S.A.* 37°40N 82°17W **105** C10
South Williamsport *Pa., U.S.A.* 41°13N 77°0W **87** C6
South Windsor *Conn., U.S.A.* 41°49N 72°37W **91** C2
South Woodstock *Vt., U.S.A.* 43°35N 72°32W **89** C2
South Yarmouth *Mass., U.S.A.* 41°40N 70°10W **91** C5
South Zanesville *Ohio, U.S.A.* 39°54N 82°2W **86** D4
Southampton *N.S., Canada* 45°35N 64°15W **141** H5
Southampton *Ont., Canada* 44°30N 81°25W **146** C5
Southampton *Mass., U.S.A.* 42°14N 72°44W **91** B2
Southampton *N.Y., U.S.A.* 40°53N 72°23W **91** D2
Southampton, C. *Nunavut, Canada* 62°8N 83°43W **159** E9
Southampton County ☆ *Va., U.S.A.* 36°43N 77°4W **102** E7
Southampton I. *Nunavut, Canada* 64°30N 84°0W **159** E9
Southard *Okla., U.S.A.* 36°4N 98°29W **107** B5
Southaven *Miss., U.S.A.* 34°59N 90°0W **117** C2
Southbank *B.C., Canada* 54°2N 125°46W **154** A9
Southbeach *Oreg., U.S.A.* 44°37N 124°3W **121** C1

Southbridge *Mass., U.S.A.* 42°5N 72°2W **91** B2
Southbury *Conn., U.S.A.* 41°29N 73°13W **91** C1
Southeast C. *Alaska, U.S.A.* 62°56N 169°39W **135** E5
Southeast Fairbanks ☆ *Alaska, U.S.A.* 63°45N 143°15W **135** E12
Southend *Sask., Canada* 56°19N 103°22W **157** E12
Southern California, University of *Calif., U.S.A.* 34°1N 118°17W **133** B3
Southern Indian L. *Man., Canada* 57°10N 98°30W **159** F6
Southern Pines *N.C., U.S.A.* 35°11N 79°24W **103** C6
Southern Ute Indian Reservation *Colo., U.S.A.* 37°10N 107°30W **125** E3
Southey *Sask., Canada* 50°56N 104°30W **150** E7
Southfield *Mich., U.S.A.* 42°28N 83°15W **98** A1
Southington *Conn., U.S.A.* 41°36N 72°53W **91** C2
Southlake *Tex., U.S.A.* 32°56N 97°8W **116** A3
Southland *Tex., U.S.A.* 33°22N 101°33W **108** D6
Southold *N.Y., U.S.A.* 41°4N 72°26W **91** D2
Southport *N.C., U.S.A.* 33°55N 78°1W **112** C4
Southport *N.Y., U.S.A.* 42°3N 76°49W **88** C4
Southside *Ala., U.S.A.* 33°55N 86°1W **112** C4
Southside *W. Va., U.S.A.* 38°43N 81°58W **102** C3
Southside Place *Tex., U.S.A.* 29°42N 95°26W **116** B2
Southton *Tex., U.S.A.* 29°17N 98°25W **116** D3
Southwest Florida Int. ✈ (RSW) *Fla., U.S.A.* 26°32N 81°45W **114** E7
Southwest Harbor *Maine, U.S.A.* 44°17N 68°20W **90** D5
Southwest Museum *Calif., U.S.A.* 34°6N 118°13W **133** B3
Southwest Pass *La., U.S.A.* 29°56N 89°17W **116** B4
Southwest Pt. *U.S. Virgin Is.* 17°40N 64°55W **184** H18
Southwick *Mass., U.S.A.* 42°3N 72°46W **91** B2
Southwood Acres *Conn., U.S.A.* 41°59N 72°32W **91** C2
Southworth *Wash., U.S.A.* 47°30N 122°30W **132** C2
Sovereign *Sask., Canada* 51°31N 107°43W **150** D4
Sowden L. *Ont., Canada* 49°32N 91°12W **148** C5
Soyopa *Sonora, Mexico* 28°45N 109°38W **168** E6
Spalding *Sask., Canada* 52°20N 104°30W **150** C7
Spalding *Idaho, U.S.A.* 46°27N 116°49W **122** C2
Spalding *Nebr., U.S.A.* 41°42N 98°22W **80** C7
Spalding County ☆ *Ga., U.S.A.* 33°15N 84°15W **113** C2
Spallumcheen *B.C., Canada* 50°26N 119°13W **155** E15
Spanaway *Wash., U.S.A.* 47°6N 122°26W **120** C3
Spangle *Wash., U.S.A.* 47°26N 117°23W **120** C8
Spaniard's Bay *Nfld. & L., Canada* 47°38N 53°20W **142** E7
Spanish *Ont., Canada* 46°12N 82°20W **146** A4
Spanish → *Ont., Canada* 46°11N 82°19W **146** A4
Spanish Fork *Utah, U.S.A.* 40°7N 111°39W **129** C4
Spanish Fort *Ala., U.S.A.* 30°40N 87°53W **112** F3
Spanish Lake *Mo., U.S.A.* 38°47N 90°12W **94** A2
Spanish Lake County Park △ *Mo., U.S.A.* 38°47N 90°12W **94** A2
Spanish Town *Br. Virgin Is.* 17°43N 64°26W **184** H18
Spanish Town *Jamaica* 18°0N 76°57W **182** C4
Sparkman *Ark., U.S.A.* 33°55N 92°51W **106** E3
Sparks *Ga., U.S.A.* 31°11N 83°26W **113** E3
Sparks *Nebr., U.S.A.* 42°56N 100°15W **80** B5
Sparks *Nev., U.S.A.* 39°32N 119°45W **128** C1
Sparks *Okla., U.S.A.* 35°37N 96°50W **107** C7
Sparland *Ill., U.S.A.* 41°2N 89°26W **84** B4
Sparlingville *Mich., U.S.A.* 42°58N 82°32W **79** G9
Sparr *Fla., U.S.A.* 29°20N 82°7W **114** B6
Sparrows Point *Md., U.S.A.* 39°13N 76°28W **99** B3
Sparrows Pt. *Baltimore, U.S.A.* 39°12N 76°29W **99** B3
Sparta *Ga., U.S.A.* 33°17N 82°58W **113** C4
Sparta *Ill., U.S.A.* 38°8N 89°42W **84** E4
Sparta *Ky., U.S.A.* 38°41N 84°54W **105** B8
Sparta *Mich., U.S.A.* 43°10N 85°42W **79** F6
Sparta *Mo., U.S.A.* 37°0N 93°5W **83** D3
Sparta *N.C., U.S.A.* 36°30N 81°7W **103** B4
Sparta *N.J., U.S.A.* 41°2N 74°38W **92** B3
Sparta *Tenn., U.S.A.* 35°56N 85°28W **105** E7
Sparta *Va., U.S.A.* 38°0N 77°14W **93** C3
Sparta *Wis., U.S.A.* 43°56N 90°49W **78** E3
Spartanburg *S.C., U.S.A.* 34°56N 81°57W **103** B4
Spartanburg County ☆ *S.C., U.S.A.* 34°50N 82°0W **103** D4
Spartansburg *Pa., U.S.A.* 41°49N 79°41W **87** C3
Sparwood *B.C., Canada* 49°44N 114°53W **153** J6
Spaulding *Okla., U.S.A.* 35°1N 96°26W **107** C7
Spavinaw *Okla., U.S.A.* 36°23N 95°3W **107** B8
Speaks *Tex., U.S.A.* 29°15N 96°42W **109** H11
Spear, C. *Nfld. & L., Canada* 47°31N 52°37W **142** E8
Spearfish *S. Dak., U.S.A.* 44°30N 103°52W **76** E2
Spearman *Tex., U.S.A.* 36°12N 101°12W **108** A6
Spearsville *La., U.S.A.* 32°56N 92°36W **110** B3
Spearville *Kans., U.S.A.* 37°51N 99°45W **82** D4
Spectacle I. *Mass., U.S.A.* 42°19N 70°59W **96** A3
Speculator *N.Y., U.S.A.* 43°30N 74°22W **88** B6
Speed *Kans., U.S.A.* 39°41N 99°25W **82** B4
Speed *Ind., U.S.A.* 39°48N 86°16W **85** D4
Speer *N.Y., U.S.A.* 42°13N 76°30W **88** C4
Speers *Sask., Canada* 52°43N 107°34W **150** C4
Speightstown *Barbados* 13°15N 59°39W **183** D8
Spence Bay = Taloyoak *Nunavut, Canada* 69°32N 93°32W **158** D7
Spencer *Idaho, U.S.A.* 44°22N 112°11W **122** E6
Spencer *Ind., U.S.A.* 39°17N 86°46W **85** D4
Spencer *Iowa, U.S.A.* 43°9N 95°9W **81** B3
Spencer *Mass., U.S.A.* 42°15N 71°59W **91** B2
Spencer *N.Y., U.S.A.* 42°13N 76°30W **88** C4
Spencer *Nebr., U.S.A.* 42°53N 98°42W **80** B7
Spencer *Ohio, U.S.A.* 41°6N 82°8W **86** B4
Spencer *Okla., U.S.A.* 35°31N 97°23W **107** C6
Spencer *S. Dak., U.S.A.* 43°44N 97°36W **76** G8
Spencer *Tenn., U.S.A.* 35°45N 85°28W **105** E7
Spencer *W. Va., U.S.A.* 38°48N 81°21W **102** C3
Spencer *Wis., U.S.A.* 44°46N 90°18W **78** D3
Spencer County ☆ *Ind., U.S.A.* 38°0N 87°0W **85** F3
Spencer County ☆ *Ky., U.S.A.* 38°0N 85°20W **105** B7
Spencerport *N.Y., U.S.A.* 43°11N 77°48W **88** B4
Spencerville *Ont., Canada* 44°51N 75°33W **147** C11
Spencerville *Ohio, U.S.A.* 40°43N 84°21W **86** D2
Spencerville *Okla., U.S.A.* 34°8N 95°21W **107** D8
Spences Bridge *B.C., Canada* 50°25N 121°20W **155** E13
Sperling *Man., Canada* 49°30N 97°42W **151** F14
Sperry *Okla., U.S.A.* 36°18N 95°59W **107** B8
Sperryville *Va., U.S.A.* 38°39N 78°14W **102** C6
Spiceland *Ind., U.S.A.* 39°50N 85°26W **85** D5
Spicer *Minn., U.S.A.* 45°14N 94°56W **77** C3
Spickard *Mo., U.S.A.* 40°14N 93°36W **83** A3
Spillimacheen *B.C., Canada* 50°54N 116°22W **155** E18
Spink *S. Dak., U.S.A.* 42°36N 96°45W **76** H9
Spink County ☆ *S. Dak., U.S.A.* 45°0N 98°18W **76** F7
Spirit L. *Idaho, U.S.A.* 47°58N 116°52W **122** B2
Spirit Lake *Idaho, U.S.A.* 47°58N 116°52W **122** B2
Spirit Lake *Iowa, U.S.A.* 43°26N 95°6W **81** B3
Spirit Lake Indian Reservation *N. Dak., U.S.A.* 47°58N 99°0W **76** C7

Spirit River *Alta., Canada* 55°45N 118°50W **152** C2
Spiritwood *Sask., Canada* 53°24N 107°33W **150** B4
Spiritwood *N. Dak., U.S.A.* 46°56N 98°30W **76** D7
Spiro *Okla., U.S.A.* 35°15N 94°37W **107** C9
Splendora *Tex., U.S.A.* 30°14N 95°10W **109** G12
Split L. *Man., Canada* 56°8N 96°15W **159** F6
Split Lake *Man., Canada* 56°8N 96°15W **159** F6
Spofford *Tex., U.S.A.* 29°10N 100°25W **108** H7
Spokane *Wash., U.S.A.* 47°40N 117°24W **120** C8
Spokane → *Wash., U.S.A.* 47°54N 118°20W **120** C7
Spokane County ☆ *Wash., U.S.A.* 47°35N 117°25W **120** C8
Spokane Indian Reservation *Wash., U.S.A.* 47°57N 118°0W **120** C7
Spokane Int. ✈ (GEG) *Wash., U.S.A.* 47°37N 117°32W **120** C8
Spoon → *Ill., U.S.A.* 40°19N 90°4W **84** C3
Spooner *Wis., U.S.A.* 45°50N 91°53W **78** C2
Sportsman Acres *Okla., U.S.A.* 36°15N 95°16W **107** B8
Spot Pond *Mass., U.S.A.* 42°26N 71°4W **96** A2
Spotswood *N.J., U.S.A.* 40°23N 74°23W **92** B2
Spotsylvania *Va., U.S.A.* 38°12N 77°36W **102** C7
Spotsylvania County ☆ *Va., U.S.A.* 38°12N 77°36W **102** C7
Spotted Horse *Wyo., U.S.A.* 44°43N 105°50W **124** B7
Spotted Ra. *Nev., U.S.A.* 36°48N 115°48W **128** F5
Spragge *Ont., Canada* 46°15N 82°40W **146** A4
Sprague *Man., Canada* 49°2N 95°38W **151** F16
Sprague *Nebr., U.S.A.* 40°38N 96°45W **80** D9
Sprague *Wash., U.S.A.* 47°18N 117°59W **120** C8
Sprague → *Oreg., U.S.A.* 42°34N 121°51W **121** E4
Sprague Rive *Oreg., U.S.A.* 42°27N 121°30W **121** E4
Spray *Oreg., U.S.A.* 44°50N 119°48W **121** C6
Sprigg's Pt. *Nfld. & L., Canada* 52°52N 55°40W **142** E8
Spring *Tex., U.S.A.* 30°5N 95°25W **109** G12
Spring → *Mo., U.S.A.* 37°5N 94°45W **83** D2
Spring Butte *Wyo., U.S.A.* 41°51N 108°53W **124** E4
Spring City *Pa., U.S.A.* 40°11N 75°33W **92** B1
Spring City *Tenn., U.S.A.* 35°42N 84°52W **105** E8
Spring City *Utah, U.S.A.* 39°29N 111°30W **129** D4
Spring Coulee *Alta., Canada* 49°20N 113°3W **153** J7
Spring Cr. → *Ga., U.S.A.* 30°54N 84°45W **113** F2
Spring Cr. → *N. Dak., U.S.A.* 47°15N 101°48W **76** C4
Spring Cr. → *Nebr., U.S.A.* 40°20N 101°6W **80** D4
Spring Cr. → *Nev., U.S.A.* 39°55N 117°50W **128** C3
Spring Cr. → *S. Dak., U.S.A.* 45°45N 100°18W **76** E5
Spring Cr. → *S. Dak., U.S.A.* 43°52N 102°42W **76** G3
Spring Creek *Nev., U.S.A.* 40°44N 115°35W **128** B5
Spring Glen *Utah, U.S.A.* 39°40N 110°51W **129** D5
Spring Green *Wis., U.S.A.* 43°11N 90°4W **78** E3
Spring Grove *Minn., U.S.A.* 43°34N 91°38W **77** G7
Spring Grove *Pa., U.S.A.* 39°52N 76°52W **93** A4
Spring Hill *Ala., U.S.A.* 31°42N 85°58W **112** C5
Spring Hill *Ark., U.S.A.* 33°35N 93°39W **106** E2
Spring Hill *Fla., U.S.A.* 28°27N 82°41W **114** C6
Spring Hill *Iowa, U.S.A.* 41°25N 93°39W **81** C5
Spring Hill *Minn., U.S.A.* 45°32N 94°50W **77** E4
Spring Hill *Tenn., U.S.A.* 35°45N 86°56W **104** E6
Spring Hope *N.C., U.S.A.* 35°57N 78°6W **103** C7
Spring Lake *Mich., U.S.A.* 43°5N 86°12W **79** F5
Spring Lake *N.C., U.S.A.* 35°10N 78°58W **103** C7
Spring Lake *N.J., U.S.A.* 40°9N 74°2W **92** B2
Spring Mts. *Nev., U.S.A.* 36°0N 115°45W **128** F5
Spring Valle *Sask., Canada* 49°56N 105°24W **150** F6
Spring Valle *Calif., U.S.A.* 32°44N 116°59W **133** B2
Spring Valle *Ill., U.S.A.* 41°20N 89°12W **84** B4
Spring Valle *Minn., U.S.A.* 43°41N 92°23W **77** G6
Spring Valle *N.Y., U.S.A.* 41°7N 74°3W **92** A2
Spring Valle *Nev., U.S.A.* 39°10N 114°25W **128** C6
Spring Valle *Nev., U.S.A.* 36°6N 115°14W **134** C1
Spring Valle *Tex., U.S.A.* 29°47N 95°30W **116** B1
Spring Valle *Wis., U.S.A.* 44°51N 92°14W **78** D1
Springbrook *Iowa, U.S.A.* 42°10N 90°29W **81** C8
Springdale *Nfld. & L., Canada* 49°30N 56°6W **142** C4
Springdale *Ark., U.S.A.* 36°11N 94°8W **106** B1
Springdale *Ohio, U.S.A.* 39°17N 84°29W **86** D2
Springdale *Utah, U.S.A.* 37°10N 113°0W **129** F3
Springdale *Wash., U.S.A.* 48°4N 117°45W **120** B8
Springer *N. Mex., U.S.A.* 36°22N 104°36W **131** A6
Springerton *Ill., U.S.A.* 38°11N 88°21W **84** E5
Springerville *Ariz., U.S.A.* 34°8N 109°17W **130** C6
Springfield *N.S., Canada* 44°38N 64°52W **141** J5
Springfield *Ont., Canada* 42°50N 80°56W **146** E6
Springfield *Colo., U.S.A.* 37°24N 102°37W **125** E8
Springfield *Fla., U.S.A.* 30°10N 85°37W **114** A3
Springfield *Ga., U.S.A.* 32°22N 81°18W **113** D5
Springfield *Idaho, U.S.A.* 43°5N 112°41W **122** F6
Springfield *Ill., U.S.A.* 39°48N 89°39W **84** D4
Springfield *Ky., U.S.A.* 37°41N 85°13W **105** C7
Springfield *La., U.S.A.* 30°26N 90°33W **110** D5
Springfield *Maine, U.S.A.* 45°24N 68°8W **90** C5
Springfield *Mass., U.S.A.* 42°6N 72°35W **91** B2
Springfield *Mich., U.S.A.* 42°20N 85°14W **79** G6
Springfield *Minn., U.S.A.* 44°14N 94°59W **77** F4
Springfield *Mo., U.S.A.* 37°13N 93°17W **83** D3
Springfield *N.J., U.S.A.* 44°43N 74°18W **97** B1
Springfield *Nebr., U.S.A.* 41°5N 96°8W **80** C9
Springfield *Ohio, U.S.A.* 39°55N 83°49W **86** D3
Springfield *Oreg., U.S.A.* 44°3N 123°1W **121** C2
Springfield *Pa., U.S.A.* 39°56N 75°19W **92** C1
Springfield *S.C., U.S.A.* 33°30N 81°17W **103** E4
Springfield *S. Dak., U.S.A.* 42°49N 97°54W **76** H8
Springfield *Tenn., U.S.A.* 36°31N 86°53W **104** C6
Springfield *Va., U.S.A.* 38°46N 77°10W **99** C2
Springfield *Vt., U.S.A.* 43°18N 72°29W **89** C2
Springfield *W. Va., U.S.A.* 39°27N 78°42W **93** A2
Springfield, L. *Ill., U.S.A.* 39°46N 89°36W **84** D4
Springhill *La., U.S.A.* 33°0N 93°28W **110** B2
Springhouse *B.C., Canada* 51°56N 122°7W **155** D12
Springlake *Tex., U.S.A.* 34°14N 102°18W **108** C5
Springport *Mich., U.S.A.* 42°22N 84°42W **79** G7
Springside *Sask., Canada* 51°21N 102°43W **150** D9
Springtown *Tex., U.S.A.* 32°58N 97°41W **109** E10
Springvale *Ga., U.S.A.* 31°50N 84°53W **113** E2
Springvale *Maine, U.S.A.* 43°28N 70°48W **90** E3
Springview *Nebr., U.S.A.* 42°50N 99°45W **80** B6
Springville *Ala., U.S.A.* 33°46N 86°29W **112** C4
Springville *Calif., U.S.A.* 36°8N 118°49W **127** G8
Springville *Iowa, U.S.A.* 42°3N 91°27W **81** C7
Springville *N.Y., U.S.A.* 42°31N 78°40W **88** D5
Springville *Utah, U.S.A.* 40°10N 111°37W **129** C4
Springwater *Sask., Canada* 51°58N 108°23W **150** D3
Sproat L. *B.C., Canada* 49°17N 125°2W **154** F9
Sproul State Forest *Pa., U.S.A.* 41°11N 77°49W **87** C5
Spruce Grove *Alta., Canada* 53°32N 113°55W **152** E7
Spruce I. *Man., Canada* 53°5N 100°40W **151** B11

Spruce Knob *W. Va., U.S.A.* 38°42N 79°32W **102** C5
Spruce Knob-Seneca Rocks Nat. Recr. Area ○ *W. Va., U.S.A.* 38°59N 79°30W **102** C5
Spruce Mts. *Ariz., U.S.A.* 34°28N 112°24W **130** C3
Spruce Pine *N.C., U.S.A.* 35°55N 82°4W **103** C3
Spruce Woods Prov. Park ○ *Man., Canada* 49°43N 99°5W **151** F12
Sprucedale *Ont., Canada* 45°29N 79°28W **146** B7
Spur *Tex., U.S.A.* 33°28N 100°52W **108** D7
Spurlockville *W. Va., U.S.A.* 38°8N 82°1W **102** C2
Spuzzum *B.C., Canada* 49°37N 121°23W **155** F13
Spy Hill *Man., Canada* 52°22N 101°26W **151** C10
Squa Pan L. *Maine, U.S.A.* 46°31N 68°13W **90** B5
Squam L. *N.H., U.S.A.* 43°45N 71°32W **89** C3
Squamish *B.C., Canada* 49°45N 123°10W **155** F11
Squamish → *B.C., Canada* 49°45N 123°8W **155** F11
Squantum *Mass., U.S.A.* 42°17N 71°0W **96** B2
Square Butte Cr. → *N. Dak., U.S.A.* 46°55N 100°55W **76** D5
Square Islands *Nfld. & L., Canada* 52°47N 55°47W **143** C6
Square L. *Maine, U.S.A.* 47°11N 68°20W **90** A5
Squatec *Qué., Canada* 47°53N 68°43W **145** D14
Squaw Lake *Minn., U.S.A.* 47°38N 94°8W **77** C4
Squaw Peak Recreation Area *Ariz., U.S.A.* 33°34N 112°0W **134** B2
Squaw Valley *Calif., U.S.A.* 36°44N 119°15W **127** G7
Squaxin Island Indian Reservation *Wash., U.S.A.* 47°12N 122°55W **120** C3
Squibnocket Point *Mass., U.S.A.* 41°18N 70°47W **91** C4
Squire *W. Va., U.S.A.* 37°14N 81°37W **102** D3
Squires *Mo., U.S.A.* 36°51N 92°37W **83** E4
Stacy *Minn., U.S.A.* 45°24N 92°59W **77** E6
Stacyville *Iowa, U.S.A.* 43°26N 92°47W **81** B6
Stafford *Conn., U.S.A.* 41°59N 72°17W **91** C2
Stafford *Kans., U.S.A.* 37°58N 98°36W **82** D5
Stafford *Tex., U.S.A.* 29°36N 95°33W **116** C1
Stafford *Va., U.S.A.* 38°25N 77°25W **102** C7
Stafford County ☆ *Kans., U.S.A.* 38°0N 98°45W **82** C5
Stafford County ☆ *Va., U.S.A.* 38°25N 77°25W **102** C7
Stafford Springs *Conn., U.S.A.* 41°57N 72°18W **91** C2
Stambaugh *Mich., U.S.A.* 46°5N 88°38W **79** C3
Stamford *Conn., U.S.A.* 41°3N 73°32W **91** C1
Stamford *N.Y., U.S.A.* 42°25N 74°38W **88** D6
Stamford *Nebr., U.S.A.* 40°8N 99°36W **80** D6
Stamford *S. Dak., U.S.A.* 43°53N 101°5W **76** G4
Stamford *Tex., U.S.A.* 32°57N 99°48W **109** E8
Stamford *Vt., U.S.A.* 42°45N 73°4W **89** D1
Stamford, L. *Tex., U.S.A.* 33°4N 99°34W **109** D8
Stamping Ground *Ky., U.S.A.* 38°16N 84°41W **105** B8
Stamps *Ark., U.S.A.* 33°22N 93°30W **106** E2
Stanardsville *Va., U.S.A.* 38°18N 78°26W **102** C6
Stanberry *Mo., U.S.A.* 40°13N 94°35W **83** A2
Standard *Alta., Canada* 51°7N 112°59W **153** G8
Standing Rock *N. Mex., U.S.A.* 35°48N 108°22W **131** B2
Standing Rock Indian Reservation *S. Dak., U.S.A.* 45°45N 101°10W **76** E4
Standing Stone State Park ○ *Tenn., U.S.A.* 36°28N 85°25W **105** D7
Standish *Calif., U.S.A.* 40°22N 120°25W **126** C6
Standish *Mich., U.S.A.* 43°59N 83°57W **79** F8
Standrod *Utah, U.S.A.* 41°59N 113°25W **129** B2
Stanfield *Ariz., U.S.A.* 32°53N 111°58W **130** E4
Stanfield *Oreg., U.S.A.* 45°47N 119°13W **121** B6
Stanford *Ky., U.S.A.* 37°32N 84°40W **105** C8
Stanford *Mont., U.S.A.* 47°9N 110°13W **123** C7
Stanhope *Iowa, U.S.A.* 42°17N 93°48W **81** C5
Stanislaus → *Calif., U.S.A.* 37°40N 121°14W **126** F5
Stanislaus County ☆ *Calif., U.S.A.* 37°30N 121°0W **126** F6
Stanislaus Nat. Forest *Calif., U.S.A.* 38°10N 120°0W **126** E6
Stanley *N.B., Canada* 46°20N 66°44W **141** G3
Stanley *Idaho, U.S.A.* 44°13N 114°56W **122** E4
Stanley *Kans., U.S.A.* 37°50N 87°15W **104** C5
Stanley *Ky., U.S.A.* 37°50N 87°11W **104** C5
Stanley *La., U.S.A.* 31°58N 93°54W **110** C2
Stanley *N.C., U.S.A.* 35°21N 81°6W **103** C4
Stanley *N. Dak., U.S.A.* 48°19N 102°23W **76** B3
Stanley *N. Mex., U.S.A.* 35°9N 105°59W **131** B5
Stanley *Va., U.S.A.* 38°35N 78°30W **102** C6
Stanley *Wis., U.S.A.* 44°58N 90°56W **78** D3
Stanley County ☆ *S. Dak., U.S.A.* 44°30N 101°0W **76** F5
Stanley Mission *Sask., Canada* 55°25N 104°33W **157** E12
Stanley Park *B.C., Canada* 49°18N 123°8W **161** B2
Stanleyville *N.C., U.S.A.* 36°12N 80°17W **103** B5
Stanly County ☆ *N.C., U.S.A.* 35°20N 80°10W **103** C5
Stannards *N.Y., U.S.A.* 42°5N 77°55W **88** C3
Stansbury I. *Utah, U.S.A.* 40°50N 112°30W **129** C3
Stanstead *Qué., Canada* 45°7N 72°12W **145** F10
Stanton *Iowa, U.S.A.* 40°59N 95°6W **81** E3
Stanton *Ky., U.S.A.* 37°54N 83°52W **105** C9
Stanton *Mich., U.S.A.* 43°18N 85°5W **79** F6
Stanton *Mo., U.S.A.* 38°17N 91°6W **83** C5
Stanton *N. Dak., U.S.A.* 47°19N 101°23W **76** C4
Stanton *Nebr., U.S.A.* 41°57N 97°14W **80** C8
Stanton *Tenn., U.S.A.* 35°28N 89°24W **104** E3
Stanton *Tex., U.S.A.* 32°8N 101°48W **108** E6
Stanton County ☆ *Kans., U.S.A.* 37°30N 101°45W **82** D2
Stanton County ☆ *Nebr., U.S.A.* 41°50N 97°10W **80** C8
Stanwood *Wash., U.S.A.* 48°15N 122°23W **120** B3
Staplehurst *Nebr., U.S.A.* 40°58N 97°10W **80** D8
Stapleton *Ala., U.S.A.* 30°45N 87°48W **112** F3
Stapleton *Colo., U.S.A.* 39°46N 104°52W **134** B2
Stapleton *N.Y., U.S.A.* 40°36N 74°5W **97** C2
Stapleton *Nebr., U.S.A.* 41°29N 100°31W **80** C5
Stapylton B. *Nunavut, Canada* 68°52N 116°15W **156** C9
Star *N.C., U.S.A.* 35°24N 79°47W **103** C6
Star City *Sask., Canada* 52°50N 104°20W **150** C7
Star City *Ark., U.S.A.* 33°56N 91°51W **106** E4
Star City *Ind., U.S.A.* 40°58N 86°33W **85** C4
Star Lake *N.Y., U.S.A.* 44°10N 75°2W **88** A5
Star Prairie *Wis., U.S.A.* 45°12N 92°32W **78** C1
Starbuck *Man., Canada* 49°46N 97°37W **151** F14
Starbuck *Minn., U.S.A.* 45°37N 95°32W **77** E3
Starbuck *Wash., U.S.A.* 46°31N 118°7W **120** C7
Stark *Kans., U.S.A.* 37°42N 95°9W **82** D8
Stark County ☆ *Ill., U.S.A.* 41°5N 89°45W **84** B4
Stark County ☆ *N. Dak., U.S.A.* 46°55N 102°30W **76** D3
Stark County ☆ *Ohio, U.S.A.* 40°48N 81°22W **86** C5
Starke *Fla., U.S.A.* 29°57N 82°7W **114** B6
Starke County ☆ *Ind., U.S.A.* 41°15N 86°40W **85** B4
Starks *La., U.S.A.* 30°19N 93°40W **110** D2
Starkville *Colo., U.S.A.* 37°8N 104°30W **125** E6
Starkville *Miss., U.S.A.* 33°28N 88°49W **111** C5
Starkweather *N. Dak., U.S.A.* 48°27N 98°53W **76** B7

Starr County ☆ *Tex., U.S.A.* 26°30N 98°50W **108** L9
Starrs Mill *Ga., U.S.A.* 33°19N 84°31W **113** C2
Starrucca *Pa., U.S.A.* 41°54N 75°28W **87** C7
Starvation Res. *Utah, U.S.A.* 40°15N 110°30W **129** C5
State Center *Iowa, U.S.A.* 42°1N 93°10W **81** C5
State College *Pa., U.S.A.* 40°48N 77°52W **87** D5
State Line *Miss., U.S.A.* 31°26N 88°28W **111** E5
Staten I. *N.Y., U.S.A.* 40°35N 74°9W **97** C2
Staten Island Zoo *N.Y., U.S.A.* 40°38N 74°6W **97** C2
Statenville *Ga., U.S.A.* 30°42N 83°2W **113** F3
Statesboro *Ga., U.S.A.* 32°27N 81°47W **113** D5
Statesville *N.C., U.S.A.* 35°47N 80°53W **103** C5
Statham *Ga., U.S.A.* 33°58N 83°35W **113** C3
Statia = St. Eustatius *W. Indies* 17°20N 63°0W **183** C7
Statue of Liberty *N.J., U.S.A.* 40°41N 74°2W **97** B2
Staunton *Ill., U.S.A.* 39°1N 89°47W **84** D4
Staunton *Va., U.S.A.* 38°9N 79°4W **102** C5
Stave L. *B.C., Canada* 49°22N 122°17W **155** F12
Stavely *Alta., Canada* 50°10N 113°38W **153** H7
Stayner *Ont., Canada* 44°25N 80°5W **146** C6
Stayton *Oreg., U.S.A.* 44°48N 122°48W **121** C3
Staytonville *Del., U.S.A.* 38°50N 75°32W **93** B5
Stead *N. Mex., U.S.A.* 36°6N 103°12W **131** A7
Steamboat Canyon *Ariz., U.S.A.* 35°45N 109°51W **130** B6
Steamboat Rock *Ariz., U.S.A.* 42°25N 93°4W **81** C5
Steamboat Springs *Colo., U.S.A.* 40°29N 106°50W **125** B4
Stearns *Ky., U.S.A.* 36°42N 84°29W **105** D8
Stearns County ☆ *Minn., U.S.A.* 45°35N 94°30W **77** E4
Stebbins *Alaska, U.S.A.* 63°31N 162°17W **135** E7
Stedman *N.C., U.S.A.* 35°0N 78°41W **103** D7
Steele *Ala., U.S.A.* 33°56N 86°12W **112** C4
Steele *Mo., U.S.A.* 36°5N 89°50W **83** E7
Steele *N. Dak., U.S.A.* 46°51N 99°55W **76** D6
Steele, Mt. *Wyo., U.S.A.* 41°50N 107°0W **124** E5
Steele City *Nebr., U.S.A.* 40°2N 97°2W **80** D8
Steele County ☆ *Minn., U.S.A.* 44°0N 93°10W **77** F5
Steele County ☆ *N. Dak., U.S.A.* 47°31N 97°50W **76** C8
Steeleville *Ill., U.S.A.* 38°0N 89°40W **84** E4
Steelton *Pa., U.S.A.* 40°14N 76°50W **87** D6
Steelville *Mo., U.S.A.* 37°58N 91°22W **83** D5
Steen *Minn., U.S.A.* 43°31N 96°16W **77** G2
Steens Mt. *Oreg., U.S.A.* 42°35N 118°40W **121** E7
Steensby Inlet *N.W.T., Canada* 70°15N 78°35W **158** C10
Steenstrup Gletscher *Greenland* 75°15N 57°0W **162** B5
Steep Rock *Man., Canada* 51°30N 98°48W **151** D13
Steer, L. *Tex., U.S.A.* 28°31N 81°30W **115** A2
Stefansson I. *N.W.T., Canada* 73°20N 105°45W **158** C4
Stegman = Artesia *N. Mex., U.S.A.* 32°51N 104°24W **131** E6
Stehekin *Wash., U.S.A.* 48°19N 120°39W **120** B5
Stein Valley Park ○ *B.C., Canada* 50°16N 122°2W **155** E12
Steinauer *Nebr., U.S.A.* 40°12N 96°14W **80** D9
Steinbach *Man., Canada* 49°32N 96°40W **151** F15
Steinhatchee *Fla., U.S.A.* 29°40N 83°23W **114** B5
Stella *Mo., U.S.A.* 36°46N 94°12W **83** E2
Stella *Nebr., U.S.A.* 40°14N 95°46W **80** D10
Stellarton *N.S., Canada* 45°32N 62°30W **141** H7
Stemmers → *Baltimore, U.S.A.* 39°19N 76°28W **99** A2
Stephen *Minn., U.S.A.* 48°27N 96°53W **77** B2
Stephens *Ark., U.S.A.* 33°25N 93°4W **106** E2
Stephens City *Va., U.S.A.* 39°5N 78°13W **93** A2
Stephens County ☆ *Ga., U.S.A.* 34°35N 83°15W **113** B3
Stephens County ☆ *Okla., U.S.A.* 34°30N 97°50W **107** D6
Stephens County ☆ *Tex., U.S.A.* 32°45N 98°54W **109** E9
Stephens I. *B.C., Canada* 54°10N 130°45W **154** A4
Stephens Knob *Ky., U.S.A.* 36°37N 84°20W **105** D8
Stephenson *Mich., U.S.A.* 45°25N 87°36W **79** D4
Stephenson County ☆ *Ill., U.S.A.* 42°20N 89°40W **84** A4
Stephentown *N.Y., U.S.A.* 42°33N 73°22W **91** B1
Stephenville *Nfld. & L., Canada* 48°31N 58°35W **142** D2
Stephenville *Tex., U.S.A.* 32°13N 98°12W **109** E9
Stephenville Crossing *Nfld. & L., Canada* 48°30N 58°26W **142** D2
Steps Pt. *Amer. Samoa* 14°23S 170°45W **184** e
Steptoe *Wash., U.S.A.* 47°0N 117°21W **120** D8
Steptoe Valley *Nev., U.S.A.* 39°50N 114°45W **128** C6
Sterling *Alaska, U.S.A.* 60°32N 150°46W **135** F10
Sterling *Colo., U.S.A.* 40°37N 103°13W **125** B7
Sterling *Ga., U.S.A.* 31°16N 81°34W **113** E5
Sterling *Idaho, U.S.A.* 43°2N 112°44W **122** F6
Sterling *Ill., U.S.A.* 41°48N 89°42W **84** B4
Sterling *Kans., U.S.A.* 38°13N 98°12W **82** C5
Sterling *Mass., U.S.A.* 42°26N 71°46W **91** B3
Sterling *Mich., U.S.A.* 44°2N 84°2W **79** E7
Sterling *N. Dak., U.S.A.* 46°49N 100°17W **76** D5
Sterling *Nebr., U.S.A.* 40°28N 96°23W **80** D9
Sterling *Okla., U.S.A.* 34°45N 98°10W **107** D5
Sterling *Utah, U.S.A.* 39°12N 111°42W **129** D4
Sterling City *Tex., U.S.A.* 31°51N 101°0W **108** F7
Sterling County ☆ *Tex., U.S.A.* 32°0N 101°0W **108** F7
Sterling Heights *Mich., U.S.A.* 42°35N 83°2W **79** G8
Sterling Res. *Colo., U.S.A.* 40°47N 103°16W **125** B7
Sterlington *La., U.S.A.* 32°42N 92°5W **110** B3
Stetsonville *Wis., U.S.A.* 45°4N 90°19W **78** C3
Stettler *Alta., Canada* 52°19N 112°40W **153** F8
Steuben *Mich., U.S.A.* 46°11N 86°27W **79** C5
Steuben *Wis., U.S.A.* 43°11N 90°52W **78** E3
Steuben County ☆ *Ind., U.S.A.* 41°40N 85°0W **85** B6
Steuben County ☆ *N.Y., U.S.A.* 42°15N 77°20W **88** C3
Steubenville *Ky., U.S.A.* 36°53N 84°48W **105** D8
Steubenville *Ohio, U.S.A.* 40°22N 80°37W **86** C6
Stevens *Ont., Canada* 49°33N 85°49W **149** C11
Stevens County ☆ *Kans., U.S.A.* 37°15N 101°20W **82** D2
Stevens County ☆ *Minn., U.S.A.* 45°40N 96°0W **77** E2
Stevens County ☆ *Wash., U.S.A.* 48°30N 118°0W **120** B8
Stevens Pottery *Ga., U.S.A.* 32°57N 83°17W **113** D3
Stevens Village *Alaska, U.S.A.* 66°1N 149°6W **135** C10
Stevenson *Ala., U.S.A.* 34°52N 85°50W **112** B5
Stevenson *Baltimore, U.S.A.* 39°24N 76°42W **99** A1
Stevenson *Wash., U.S.A.* 45°42N 121°53W **120** E4
Stevenson I. *Man., Canada* 53°55N 96°0W **151** B15
Stevensville *Md., U.S.A.* 38°59N 76°19W **93** B4
Stevensville *Mich., U.S.A.* 42°1N 86°31W **79** G4
Stevensville *Mont., U.S.A.* 46°30N 114°5W **123** D3
Steveston *B.C., Canada* 49°8N 123°11W **161** C1
Steward *Ill., U.S.A.* 41°51N 89°1W **84** B4
Stewardson *Ill., U.S.A.* 39°16N 88°38W **84** D5
Stewart *B.C., Canada* 55°56N 129°57W **157** E7
Stewart *Minn., U.S.A.* 44°43N 94°29W **77** F4
Stewart *Miss., U.S.A.* 33°27N 89°26W **111** C4
Stewart → *Yukon, Canada* 63°19N 139°26W **157** D5
Stewart B. McKinney Nat. Wildlife Refuge ○ *Conn., U.S.A.* 41°12N 73°7W **91** C1

Stewart County ☆ *Ga., U.S.A.* 32°5N 84°50W **113** D2
Stewart County ☆ *Tenn., U.S.A.* 36°20N 87°55W **104** D5
Stewart Crossing *Yukon, Canada* 63°22N 136°40W **157** D5
Stewart Manor *N.Y., U.S.A.* 40°43N 73°41W **97** B1
Stewart Valley *Sask., Canada* 50°36N 107°48W **150** E4
Stewarts Point *Calif., U.S.A.* 38°39N 123°24W **126** E3
Stewartstown *N.H., U.S.A.* 45°0N 71°31W **89** B3
Stewartstown *Pa., U.S.A.* 39°45N 76°36W **93** A4
Stewartsville *Mo., U.S.A.* 39°45N 94°30W **83** B2
Stewartville *Minn., U.S.A.* 43°51N 92°29W **77** G6
Stewiacke *N.S., Canada* 45°9N 63°22W **141** H6
Stibnite *Idaho, U.S.A.* 44°54N 115°20W **122** E3
Stickney *Ill., U.S.A.* 41°49N 87°46W **95** C2
Stickney *S. Dak., U.S.A.* 43°35N 98°26W **76** G7
Stidham *Okla., U.S.A.* 35°22N 95°42W **107** C8
Stigler *Okla., U.S.A.* 35°15N 95°8W **107** C8
Stikine → *B.C., Canada* 56°40N 132°30W **157** E6
Stikine Range *B.C., Canada* 59°0N 129°0W **157** C7
Stiles *Tex., U.S.A.* 31°25N 101°34W **108** F6
Stilesville *Ind., U.S.A.* 39°38N 86°38W **85** D4
Still Pond *Md., U.S.A.* 39°20N 76°3W **93** A4
Stillhouse Hollow L. *Tex., U.S.A.* 31°2N 97°32W **109** F10
Stillmore *Ga., U.S.A.* 32°27N 82°13W **113** D4
Stillwater *Nev., U.S.A.* 39°31N 118°33W **128** C2
Stillwater *Okla., U.S.A.* 36°7N 97°4W **107** B6
Stillwater County ☆ *Mont., U.S.A.* 45°48N 109°15W **123** E8
Stillwater Nat. Wildlife Refuge ○ *Nev., U.S.A.* 39°33N 118°29W **128** C2
Stillwater Range *Nev., U.S.A.* 39°50N 118°5W **128** C2
Stillwater Res. *N.Y., U.S.A.* 43°54N 75°3W **88** B5
Stillwell *Ga., U.S.A.* 32°23N 81°15W **113** D5
Stilwell *Kans., U.S.A.* 38°46N 94°39W **82** C9
Stilwell *Okla., U.S.A.* 35°49N 94°38W **107** C9
Stinnett *Tex., U.S.A.* 35°50N 101°27W **108** B6
Stinson Lake *N.H., U.S.A.* 43°51N 71°48W **89** C3
Stirling *Alta., Canada* 49°30N 112°30W **153** J8
Stirling *Ont., Canada* 44°18N 77°33W **147** C9
Stirling City *Calif., U.S.A.* 39°54N 121°32W **126** D5
Stirrat *W. Va., U.S.A.* 37°44N 82°0W **102** D3
Stirupa → *Chihuahua, Mexico* 28°45N 107°58W **169** E8
Stites *Idaho, U.S.A.* 46°6N 115°59W **122** C3
Stittsville *Ont., Canada* 45°15N 75°55W **144** F7
Stock Island *Fla., U.S.A.* 24°32N 81°34W **114** G4
Stockbridge *Ga., U.S.A.* 33°33N 84°14W **113** C2
Stockbridge *Mass., U.S.A.* 42°17N 73°19W **91** B1
Stockbridge *Mich., U.S.A.* 42°27N 84°11W **79** G7
Stockbridge-Munsee Indian Reservation *Wis., U.S.A.* 44°50N 88°50W **78** D5
Stockdale *Tex., U.S.A.* 29°14N 97°58W **109** H10
Stockett *Mont., U.S.A.* 47°21N 111°10W **123** C6
Stockham *Nebr., U.S.A.* 40°43N 97°56W **80** D8
Stockholm *Sask., Canada* 50°39N 102°18W **151** E9
Stockholm *Maine, U.S.A.* 47°3N 68°8W **90** A5
Stockholm *S. Dak., U.S.A.* 45°6N 96°48W **76** E9
Stockholm *Wis., U.S.A.* 44°29N 92°16W **78** D1
Stockland *Ill., U.S.A.* 40°37N 87°36W **84** C6
Stockley *Del., U.S.A.* 38°40N 75°20W **93** B5
Stockport *Iowa, U.S.A.* 40°51N 91°50W **81** E7
Stockport *Ohio, U.S.A.* 39°33N 81°48W **86** D5
Stockton *Ala., U.S.A.* 31°0N 87°52W **112** F3
Stockton *Calif., U.S.A.* 37°58N 121°17W **126** F5
Stockton *Ill., U.S.A.* 42°21N 90°1W **84** A3
Stockton *Kans., U.S.A.* 39°26N 99°16W **82** B4
Stockton *Md., U.S.A.* 38°3N 75°25W **93** B5
Stockton *Minn., U.S.A.* 44°2N 91°46W **77** F7
Stockton *Mo., U.S.A.* 37°42N 93°48W **83** D3
Stockton *N.J., U.S.A.* 40°24N 74°58W **92** B2
Stockton *Utah, U.S.A.* 40°27N 112°22W **129** C3
Stockton I. *Wis., U.S.A.* 46°57N 90°35W **78** B3
Stockton L. *Mo., U.S.A.* 37°40N 93°45W **83** D3
Stockton Plateau *U.S.A.* 30°30N 102°30W **108** G5
Stockville *Nebr., U.S.A.* 40°32N 100°23W **80** D5
Stoddard *Wis., U.S.A.* 43°40N 91°13W **78** E2
Stoddard County ☆ *Mo., U.S.A.* 36°50N 90°0W **83** E7
Stokes Bay *Ont., Canada* 45°0N 81°28W **146** B5
Stokes County ☆ *N.C., U.S.A.* 36°20N 80°10W **103** B5
Stone *Ky., U.S.A.* 42°1N 112°42W **122** G6
Stone Canyon Res. *Calif., U.S.A.* 34°6N 118°27W **133** B2
Stone County ☆ *Ark., U.S.A.* 35°52N 92°7W **106** C3
Stone County ☆ *Miss., U.S.A.* 30°47N 89°8W **111** F4
Stone County ☆ *Mo., U.S.A.* 36°45N 93°25W **83** E3
Stone Harbor *N.J., U.S.A.* 39°3N 74°45W **92** C2
Stone Mountain *Ga., U.S.A.* 33°49N 84°10W **113** C2
Stone Mountain Park ○ *Ga., U.S.A.* 33°48N 84°8W **113** C2
Stone Mt. *Vt., U.S.A.* 44°34N 71°40W **89** B3
Stoneboro *Pa., U.S.A.* 41°20N 80°7W **87** C2
Stoneham *Colo., U.S.A.* 40°36N 103°40W **125** B7
Stoneham *Mass., U.S.A.* 42°29N 71°5W **96** A2
Stoner *Colo., U.S.A.* 37°35N 108°19W **125** E2
Stones River Nat. Battlefield ○ *Tenn., U.S.A.* 35°53N 86°26W **104** E6
Stoneville *N.C., U.S.A.* 36°28N 79°54W **103** B6
Stoneville *S. Dak., U.S.A.* 44°44N 102°39W **76** F3
Stonewall *Man., Canada* 50°10N 97°19W **151** E14
Stonewall *Ark., U.S.A.* 36°14N 90°32W **106** B5
Stonewall *Colo., U.S.A.* 37°9N 105°1W **125** E6
Stonewall *La., U.S.A.* 32°17N 93°50W **110** B2
Stonewall *Miss., U.S.A.* 32°8N 88°47W **111** D5
Stonewall *Okla., U.S.A.* 34°39N 96°32W **107** D7
Stonewall County ☆ *Tex., U.S.A.* 33°8N 100°14W **108** D7
Stonewall Jackson L. *W. Va., U.S.A.* 38°58N 80°29W **102** C4
Stonewood *W. Va., U.S.A.* 39°15N 80°19W **102** B4
Stoney Creek *Ont., Canada* 43°14N 79°45W **92** A3
Stonington *Colo., U.S.A.* 37°18N 102°11W **125** E8
Stonington *Ill., U.S.A.* 39°44N 89°12W **84** D4
Stonington *Maine, U.S.A.* 44°9N 68°40W **90** D5
Stony Brook *N.Y., U.S.A.* 40°56N 73°8W **88** E7
Stony Brook Res. *Mass., U.S.A.* 42°15N 71°15W **96** B1
Stony Creek *N.Y., U.S.A.* 36°57N 77°24W **102** E7
Stony Creek → *Ill., U.S.A.* 41°38N 87°41W **95** C2
Stony Gorge Res. *Calif., U.S.A.* 39°35N 122°32W **126** D4
Stony I. *N.Y., U.S.A.* 43°54N 76°20W **88** B4
Stony L. *Man., Canada* 58°51N 98°40W **159** F7
Stony L. *Ont., Canada* 44°30N 78°5W **147** C8
Stony Mountain *Man., Canada* 50°5N 97°13W **151** E14
Stony Plain *Alta., Canada* 53°32N 114°0W **152** E7
Stony Point *N.C., U.S.A.* 35°52N 81°3W **103** C4
Stony Point *N.Y., U.S.A.* 41°14N 73°59W **92** A3
Stony Pt. *N.Y., U.S.A.* 43°50N 76°18W **88** B4
Stony Rapids *Sask., Canada* 59°16N 105°50W **157** E11
Stony Ridge *Ohio, U.S.A.* 41°31N 83°30W **86** B3
Stony River *Alaska, U.S.A.* 61°47N 156°35W **135** E8

Stonyford *Calif., U.S.A.* 39°23N 122°33W **126** D4
Stor I. *Nunavut, Canada* 79°0N 85°50W **158** B8
Store Koldewey *Greenland* 76°30N 19°0W **162** B9
Storey County ☆ *Nev., U.S.A.* 39°30N 119°35W **128** C1
Storkerson B. *N.W.T., Canada* 72°56N 124°50W **156** B8
Storkerson Pen. *Nunavut, Canada* 72°30N 106°30W **158** C4
Storm L. *Iowa, U.S.A.* 42°38N 95°13W **81** C3
Storm Lake *Iowa, U.S.A.* 42°39N 95°13W **81** C3
Stormy L. *Ont., Canada* 49°23N 92°18W **148** C4
Stormy Mt. *Wash., U.S.A.* 47°54N 120°21W **120** C5
Storrs *Conn., U.S.A.* 41°49N 72°15W **91** C2
Story *Wyo., U.S.A.* 44°35N 106°53W **124** B6
Story City *Iowa, U.S.A.* 42°11N 93°36W **81** C5
Story County ☆ *Iowa, U.S.A.* 42°0N 93°25W **81** D5
Stotesbury *Mo., U.S.A.* 37°59N 94°34W **83** D2
Stouffville *Ont., Canada* 43°58N 79°15W **146** D7
Stoughton *Sask., Canada* 49°40N 103°0W **150** F18
Stoughton *Mass., U.S.A.* 42°8N 71°6W **91** B3
Stoughton *Wis., U.S.A.* 42°55N 89°13W **78** F4
Stout *Iowa, U.S.A.* 42°32N 92°43W **81** C6
Stoutland *Mo., U.S.A.* 37°49N 92°31W **83** D4
Stoutsville *Mo., U.S.A.* 39°33N 91°51W **83** B5
Stoutsville *Ohio, U.S.A.* 39°36N 82°50W **86** D4
Stovall *Ga., U.S.A.* 32°58N 84°51W **113** D2
Stovall *N.C., U.S.A.* 36°27N 78°35W **103** B7
Stover *Mo., U.S.A.* 38°27N 92°59W **83** C4
Stow *Ohio, U.S.A.* 41°10N 81°27W **86** B5
Stowe *Pa., U.S.A.* 40°15N 75°41W **92** B1
Stowe *Vt., U.S.A.* 44°28N 72°41W **89** B2
Stowell *Tex., U.S.A.* 29°47N 94°23W **109** H13
Strafford *Mo., U.S.A.* 37°16N 93°7W **83** D3
Strafford *N.H., U.S.A.* 43°19N 71°12W **89** C3
Strafford County ☆ *N.H., U.S.A.* 43°15N 71°0W **89** C3
Strandburg *S. Dak., U.S.A.* 45°3N 96°46W **76** E9
Strandquist *Minn., U.S.A.* 48°29N 96°27W **77** B2
Strang *Nebr., U.S.A.* 40°25N 97°35W **80** D8
Stranraer *Sask., Canada* 51°43N 108°29W **150** D3
Strasbourg *Sask., Canada* 51°4N 104°55W **150** D7
Strasburg *Colo., U.S.A.* 39°44N 104°20W **125** C6
Strasburg *Mo., U.S.A.* 38°46N 94°10W **83** C2
Strasburg *N. Dak., U.S.A.* 46°8N 100°10W **76** D5
Strasburg *Ohio, U.S.A.* 40°36N 81°32W **86** C5
Strasburg *Va., U.S.A.* 38°59N 78°22W **93** B2
Stratford *Ont., Canada* 43°23N 81°0W **146** D6
Stratford *Calif., U.S.A.* 36°11N 119°49W **127** G7
Stratford *Conn., U.S.A.* 41°12N 73°8W **91** C1
Stratford *Iowa, U.S.A.* 42°16N 93°56W **81** C5
Stratford *N.H., U.S.A.* 44°42N 71°36W **89** B3
Stratford *N.J., U.S.A.* 39°50N 75°1W **92** C1
Stratford *Okla., U.S.A.* 34°48N 96°58W **107** D7
Stratford *S. Dak., U.S.A.* 45°19N 98°18W **76** E7
Stratford *Tex., U.S.A.* 36°20N 102°4W **108** A5
Stratford *Wis., U.S.A.* 44°48N 90°4W **78** D3
Stratham *N.H., U.S.A.* 43°3N 70°55W **89** C4
Strathcona *Minn., U.S.A.* 48°33N 96°10W **77** B2
Strathcona Park △ *B.C., Canada* 49°38N 125°40W **154** F9
Strathmere *N.J., U.S.A.* 39°12N 74°40W **92** C2
Strathmore *Alta., Canada* 51°5N 113°18W **153** G7
Strathmore *Calif., U.S.A.* 36°9N 119°4W **127** G7
Strathnaver *B.C., Canada* 53°20N 122°33W **155** B12
Strathroy *Ont., Canada* 42°58N 81°38W **146** E5
Stratton *Ont., Canada* 48°41N 94°10W **148** D2
Stratton *Colo., U.S.A.* 39°19N 102°36W **125** C8
Stratton *Maine, U.S.A.* 45°8N 70°26W **90** C3
Stratton *Nebr., U.S.A.* 40°9N 101°14W **80** D4
Stratton Meadows *Colo., U.S.A.* 38°45N 104°48W **125** D6
Stratton Mt. *Vt., U.S.A.* 43°4N 72°55W **89** C2
Strawberry *Ark., U.S.A.* 35°58N 91°19W **106** C4
Strawberry *Calif., U.S.A.* 38°48N 120°9W **126** E6
Strawberry → *Ark., U.S.A.* 35°53N 91°13W **106** C4
Strawberry → *Utah, U.S.A.* 40°10N 110°24W **129** C5
Strawberry Banke Museum *N.H., U.S.A.* 43°4N 70°44W **89** C4
Strawberry Mt. *Oreg., U.S.A.* 44°19N 118°43W **121** C7
Strawberry Point *Iowa, U.S.A.* 42°41N 91°32W **81** C7
Strawberry Res. *Utah, U.S.A.* 40°8N 111°9W **129** C4
Strawn *Ill., U.S.A.* 40°39N 88°24W **84** C5
Strawn *Tex., U.S.A.* 32°33N 98°30W **109** E9
Streator *Ill., U.S.A.* 41°8N 88°50W **84** B51
Streeman *Tex., U.S.A.* 31°53N 96°19W **109** F11
Streeter *N. Dak., U.S.A.* 46°39N 99°21W **76** D6
Streetsboro *Ohio, U.S.A.* 41°14N 81°21W **86** B5
Streetsville *Ont., Canada* 43°35N 79°42W **146** D7
Stringer *Miss., U.S.A.* 31°52N 89°16W **111** E4
Stringtown *Okla., U.S.A.* 34°28N 96°3W **107** D7
Strip, The *Nev., U.S.A.* 36°7N 119°10W **134** C2
Strome *Alta., Canada* 52°48N 112°4W **153** F8
Stromsburg *Nebr., U.S.A.* 41°7N 97°36W **80** C8
Strong *Ark., U.S.A.* 33°7N 92°21W **106** E3
Strong → *Miss., U.S.A.* 31°51N 90°8W **111** E3
Strong City *Kans., U.S.A.* 38°24N 96°32W **82** C7
Strong City *Okla., U.S.A.* 35°40N 99°36W **107** C4
Strongfield *Sask., Canada* 51°20N 106°35W **150** D5
Stronghurst *Ill., U.S.A.* 40°45N 90°55W **84** C3
Stroud *Ont., Canada* 44°19N 79°37W **146** C7
Stroud *Okla., U.S.A.* 35°45N 96°40W **107** C7
Stroudsburg *Pa., U.S.A.* 40°59N 75°12W **92** B1
Strum *Wis., U.S.A.* 44°33N 91°24W **78** D2
Struthers *Ohio, U.S.A.* 41°4N 80°39W **86** B6
Stryker *Mont., U.S.A.* 48°41N 114°46W **123** B3
Stryker *Ohio, U.S.A.* 41°30N 84°25W **86** B2
Stuart *Fla., U.S.A.* 27°12N 80°15W **114** D8
Stuart *Iowa, U.S.A.* 41°30N 94°19W **81** D4
Stuart *Nebr., U.S.A.* 42°36N 99°8W **80** B6
Stuart *Va., U.S.A.* 36°38N 80°16W **102** E4
Stuart, Mt. *Wash., U.S.A.* 47°29N 120°54W **120** C5
Stuart I. *Alaska, U.S.A.* 63°35N 162°30W **135** E7
Stuart L. *B.C., Canada* 54°30N 124°30W **157** F8
Stuarts Draft *Va., U.S.A.* 38°2N 79°2W **102** D5
Studio City *Calif., U.S.A.* 34°8N 118°24W **133** B2
Studley *Kans., U.S.A.* 39°21N 100°10W **82** B3
Study Butte *Tex., U.S.A.* 29°19N 103°31W **108** H4
Stuie *B.C., Canada* 52°22N 126°4W **154** C8
Stump L. *N. Dak., U.S.A.* 47°54N 98°24W **76** C7
Sturgeon *Mo., U.S.A.* 39°14N 92°17W **83** B4
Sturgeon → *Ont., Canada* 46°35N 80°11W **146** A6
Sturgeon → *Mich., U.S.A.* 45°23N 105°52W **79** D7
Sturgeon → *Mich., U.S.A.* 47°2N 88°39W **79** D3
Sturgeon B. *Man., Canada* 52°0N 97°50W **151** C14
Sturgeon B. *Mich., U.S.A.* 45°45N 85°0W **79** D6
Sturgeon Bay *Wis., U.S.A.* 44°50N 87°23W **79** D4
Sturgeon Falls *Ont., Canada* 46°25N 79°57W **146** A7
Sturgeon L. *Alta., Canada* 55°6N 117°32W **152** C3

Sturgeon L. *Ont., Canada* 44°28N 78°43W **147** C8
Sturgeon L. *Ont., Canada* 50°0N 90°45W **148** B6
Sturgeon L. *Ont., Canada* 48°29N 91°38W **148** D5
Sturgeon Lake *Minn., U.S.A.* 46°23N 92°49W **77** D6
Sturgis *Sask., Canada* 51°56N 102°36W **150** D9
Sturgis *Ky., U.S.A.* 37°33N 87°59W **104** C5
Sturgis *Mich., U.S.A.* 41°48N 85°25W **79** H6
Sturgis *Miss., U.S.A.* 33°21N 89°3W **111** C4
Sturgis *S. Dak., U.S.A.* 44°25N 103°31W **76** F2
Sturtevant *Wis., U.S.A.* 42°42N 87°54W **78** F6
Stutsman County ☆ *N. Dak., U.S.A.* 47°0N 99°0W **76** C6
Stuttgart *Ark., U.S.A.* 34°30N 91°33W **106** D4
Styx → *Ala., U.S.A.* 30°31N 87°27W **112** F3
Suaqui Grande *Sonora, Mexico* 28°24N 109°54W **168** E6
Sublett Ra. *Idaho, U.S.A.* 42°18N 112°55W **122** G6
Sublette *Ill., U.S.A.* 41°39N 89°14W **84** B4
Sublette *Kans., U.S.A.* 37°29N 100°51W **82** D3
Sublette County ☆ *Wyo., U.S.A.* 43°0N 110°0W **124** D3
Sucarnoochee → *Ala., U.S.A.* 32°25N 88°2W **112** D2
Success *Sask., Canada* 50°28N 108°6W **150** E3
Success *Ark., U.S.A.* 36°27N 90°43W **106** B5
Success, L. *Calif., U.S.A.* 36°4N 118°55W **127** G8
Success, Mt. *N.H., U.S.A.* 44°27N 71°5W **89** B4
Suchiapa *Chiapas, Mexico* 16°37N 93°5W **178** C3
Suchil *Durango, Mexico* 23°39N 103°54W **173** D7
Suchitoto *El Salv.* 13°56N 89°0W **182** D2
Sud, Pte. du *Qué., Canada* 49°3N 62°14W **140** D7
Sud-Ouest, Pte. *Qué., Canada* 49°23N 63°33W **140** D6
Sudan *Tex., U.S.A.* 34°4N 102°31W **108** C5
Sudbury *Ont., Canada* 46°30N 81°0W **146** A5
Sudbury *Mass., U.S.A.* 42°22N 71°24W **91** B3
Sudlersville *Md., U.S.A.* 39°11N 75°52W **93** A5
Sue, L. *Fla., U.S.A.* 28°34N 81°21W **115** A2
Suffern *N.Y., U.S.A.* 41°7N 74°9W **92** A2
Suffield *Alta., Canada* 50°12N 111°10W **153** H9
Suffield *Conn., U.S.A.* 41°59N 72°39W **91** C2
Suffolk *Va., U.S.A.* 36°44N 76°35W **102** E8
Suffolk County ☆ *Mass., U.S.A.* 42°21N 71°5W **91** B3
Suffolk County ☆ *N.Y., U.S.A.* 40°50N 73°0W **88** E8
Sugar → *Ill., U.S.A.* 42°26N 89°12W **84** A4
Sugar → *N.H., U.S.A.* 43°24N 72°24W **89** C2
Sugar City *Colo., U.S.A.* 38°14N 103°40W **125** D7
Sugar City *Idaho, U.S.A.* 43°52N 111°44W **122** F7
Sugar Cr. → *Ill., U.S.A.* 40°9N 89°38W **84** C4
Sugar Cr. → *Ill., U.S.A.* 40°50N 87°45W **84** C6
Sugar Cr. → *Ind., U.S.A.* 39°51N 87°21W **85** D3
Sugar Grove *Ohio, U.S.A.* 39°38N 82°33W **86** D4
Sugar Grove *Pa., U.S.A.* 41°59N 79°22W **87** C3
Sugar Hill *Ga., U.S.A.* 34°6N 84°2W **113** B2
Sugar I. *Mich., U.S.A.* 46°25N 84°12W **79** C7
Sugar L. *B.C., Canada* 50°24N 118°30W **155** E16
Sugar Land *Tex., U.S.A.* 29°37N 95°38W **109** H12
Sugar Mountain *N.C., U.S.A.* 36°8N 81°52W **103** B4
Sugar Notch *Pa., U.S.A.* 41°11N 75°55W **87** C7
Sugarbowl-Grizzly Den Park △ *B.C., Canada* 53°51N 121°39W **155** B13
Sugarcreek *Ohio, U.S.A.* 40°30N 81°38W **86** C5
Sugarcreek *Pa., U.S.A.* 41°25N 79°53W **87** C3
Sugarloaf Head *Nfld. & L., Canada* 47°37N 52°39W **142** E8
Sugarloaf Mt. *Maine, U.S.A.* 45°2N 70°19W **90** C3
Sugarloaf Mt. *Okla., U.S.A.* 35°2N 94°28W **107** C9
Sugartown *La., U.S.A.* 30°50N 93°1W **110** D2
Sugarville *Utah, U.S.A.* 39°28N 112°39W **129** D3
Sugden *Okla., U.S.A.* 34°5N 97°59W **107** D6
Suggi L. *Sask., Canada* 54°22N 102°47W **150** A9
Sugluk = Salluit *Qué., Canada* 62°14N 75°38W **143** A2
Suisun B. *Calif., U.S.A.* 38°5N 122°0W **126** E5
Suisun City *Calif., U.S.A.* 38°15N 122°2W **126** E4
Suitland *Md., U.S.A.* 38°50N 76°55W **99** B4
Sukkertoppen = Maniitsoq *Greenland* 65°26N 52°55W **162** D5
Sulaco → *Honduras* 15°2N 87°44W **182** C2
Sulligent *Ala., U.S.A.* 33°54N 88°8W **112** C2
Sullivan *Qué., Canada* 48°7N 77°50W **144** C5
Sullivan *Ill., U.S.A.* 39°36N 88°37W **84** D51
Sullivan *Ind., U.S.A.* 39°6N 87°24W **85** D3
Sullivan *Ky., U.S.A.* 37°30N 87°57W **104** C5
Sullivan *Mo., U.S.A.* 38°13N 91°10W **83** C51
Sullivan Bay *B.C., Canada* 50°55N 126°50W **154** E8
Sullivan County ☆ *Ind., U.S.A.* 39°5N 87°25W **85** D3
Sullivan County ☆ *Mo., U.S.A.* 40°10N 93°5W **83** A3
Sullivan County ☆ *N.H., U.S.A.* 43°20N 72°15W **89** C2
Sullivan County ☆ *N.Y., U.S.A.* 41°45N 74°45W **88** D6
Sullivan County ☆ *Pa., U.S.A.* 41°30N 76°35W **87** C6
Sullivan County ☆ *Tenn., U.S.A.* 36°32N 82°19W **105** D10
Sullivan L. *Alta., Canada* 52°0N 112°0W **153** F8
Sully *Iowa, U.S.A.* 41°34N 92°50W **81** D5
Sully County ☆ *S. Dak., U.S.A.* 44°45N 100°0W **76** F5
Sulphur *La., U.S.A.* 30°14N 93°23W **110** D2
Sulphur *Okla., U.S.A.* 34°31N 96°58W **107** D7
Sulphur → *S. Dak., U.S.A.* 33°7N 93°52W **106** C2
Sulphur → *Tex., U.S.A.* 44°45N 100°20W **76** F5
Sulphur Draw → *Tex., U.S.A.* 33°12N 102°17W **108** D5
Sulphur Rock *Ark., U.S.A.* 35°45N 91°30W **106** C4
Sulphur Springs *Ind., U.S.A.* 36°29N 94°28W **86** B1
Sulphur Springs *Ind., U.S.A.* 40°0N 85°27W **85** C5
Sulphur Springs *Tex., U.S.A.* 33°8N 95°36W **109** D12
Sulphur Springs Draw → *Tex., U.S.A.* 32°12N 101°36W **108** E6
Sulphur Springs Range *Nev., U.S.A.* 40°15N 116°0W **128** B5
Sultan *Ont., Canada* 47°36N 82°47W **149** E14
Sultan *Wash., U.S.A.* 47°52N 121°49W **120** C4
Sultepec *México, Mexico* 18°52N 99°57W **175** D8
Sumas *Wash., U.S.A.* 48°59N 122°15W **120** B3
Sumatra *Fla., U.S.A.* 30°1N 84°59W **114** A4
Sumatra *Mont., U.S.A.* 46°37N 107°33W **123** D10
Summer I. *Mich., U.S.A.* 45°34N 86°39W **79** D5
Summer Lake *Oreg., U.S.A.* 42°58N 120°47W **121** E5
Summerdale *Ala., U.S.A.* 30°28N 87°55W **112** F3
Summerfield *Kans., U.S.A.* 39°59N 96°21W **82** B7
Summerfield *N.C., U.S.A.* 36°13N 79°54W **103** B6
Summerfield *Ohio, U.S.A.* 39°48N 81°20W **86** D5
Summerfield *Tex., U.S.A.* 34°44N 102°31W **108** C5
Summerford *Nfld. & L., Canada* 49°29N 54°47W **142** C6
Summerland *B.C., Canada* 49°32N 119°41W **155** F15
Summerland Key *Fla., U.S.A.* 24°40N 81°27W **114** G7
Summers County ☆ *W. Va., U.S.A.* 37°40N 80°54W **102** D4
Summerside *P.E.I., Canada* 46°24N 63°47W **141** G6
Summersville *Mo., U.S.A.* 37°11N 91°40W **83** D5
Summersville *W. Va., U.S.A.* 38°17N 80°51W **102** C4
Summersville L. *W. Va., U.S.A.* 38°13N 80°53W **102** C4
Summerton *S.C., U.S.A.* 33°36N 80°20W **103** D5
Summertown *Ga., U.S.A.* 32°45N 82°16W **113** D4
Summertown *Tenn., U.S.A.* 35°26N 87°18W **104** E5

Summerville *Nfld. & L., Canada* 48°27N 53°33W **142** D7
Summerville *Ont., Canada* 43°37N 79°33W **161** B1
Summerville *Ga., U.S.A.* 34°29N 85°21W **113** B1
Summerville *Oreg., U.S.A.* 45°29N 118°0W **121** B7
Summerville *S.C., U.S.A.* 33°1N 80°11W **103** E5
Summit *Alaska, U.S.A.* 63°20N 149°7W **135** E10
Summit *Ill., U.S.A.* 41°47N 87°47W **95** C2
Summit *Miss., U.S.A.* 31°17N 90°28W **111** E3
Summit *N.J., U.S.A.* 40°43N 74°22W **92** B2
Summit *Okla., U.S.A.* 35°40N 95°26W **107** C8
Summit *Oreg., U.S.A.* 44°38N 123°35W **121** C2
Summit *S. Dak., U.S.A.* 45°18N 97°2W **76** E8
Summit *Utah, U.S.A.* 37°48N 112°56W **129** F3
Summit County ☆ *Colo., U.S.A.* 39°30N 106°0W **125** C4
Summit County ☆ *Ohio, U.S.A.* 41°8N 81°29W **86** B5
Summit County ☆ *Utah, U.S.A.* 40°55N 111°0W **129** C4
Summit L. *Nev., U.S.A.* 41°31N 119°4W **128** A1
Summit Lake *B.C., Canada* 54°20N 122°40W **157** F8
Summit Lake Indian Reservation *Nev., U.S.A.* 41°33N 119°2W **128** A1
Summit Mt. *Nev., U.S.A.* 39°23N 116°28W **128** C4
Summit Peak *Colo., U.S.A.* 37°21N 106°42W **125** E4
Summit Point *Utah, U.S.A.* 38°3N 109°7W **129** E6
Sumner *Iowa, U.S.A.* 42°51N 92°6W **81** C61
Sumner *Miss., U.S.A.* 33°58N 90°22W **111** C3
Sumner *Mo., U.S.A.* 39°39N 93°15W **83** B3
Sumner *Nebr., U.S.A.* 40°57N 99°31W **80** D6
Sumner, L. *N. Mex., U.S.A.* 34°40N 104°25W **131** C6
Sumner County ☆ *Kans., U.S.A.* 37°15N 97°20W **82** D6
Sumner County ☆ *Tenn., U.S.A.* 36°24N 86°27W **104** D6
Sumpter *Oreg., U.S.A.* 44°45N 118°12W **121** C7
Sumrall *Miss., U.S.A.* 31°25N 89°33W **111** E4
Sumter *S.C., U.S.A.* 33°55N 80°21W **103** D5
Sumter County ☆ *Ala., U.S.A.* 32°35N 88°11W **112** D2
Sumter County ☆ *Fla., U.S.A.* 28°45N 82°10W **114** C6
Sumter County ☆ *Ga., U.S.A.* 32°0N 84°10W **113** D2
Sumter County ☆ *S.C., U.S.A.* 33°50N 80°30W **103** E5
Sumter Nat. Forest *S.C., U.S.A.* 34°50N 83°0W **103** D2
Sun *La., U.S.A.* 30°39N 89°54W **110** D6
Sun → *Mont., U.S.A.* 47°29N 111°19W **123** C6
Sun City *Ariz., U.S.A.* 33°35N 112°16W **134** B1
Sun City *Calif., U.S.A.* 33°42N 117°11W **127** K9
Sun City *Kans., U.S.A.* 37°23N 98°55W **82** D5
Sun City *Tampa, U.S.A.* 27°40N 82°28W **115** C4
Sun City Center *Fla., U.S.A.* 27°43N 82°21W **114** D6
Sun City West *Ariz., U.S.A.* 33°40N 112°20W **130** D3
Sun Lakes *Ariz., U.S.A.* 33°10N 111°52W **130** D4
Sun Prairie *Wis., U.S.A.* 43°11N 89°13W **78** E4
Sun River *Mont., U.S.A.* 47°32N 111°43W **123** C6
Sun Valley *Idaho, U.S.A.* 43°42N 114°21W **122** F4
Sun Valley *Nev., U.S.A.* 39°36N 119°46W **128** C1
Sunapee *N.H., U.S.A.* 43°23N 72°7W **89** C2
Sunapee L. *N.H., U.S.A.* 43°23N 72°5W **89** C2
Sunbright *Tenn., U.S.A.* 36°15N 84°40W **105** D8
Sunburg *Minn., U.S.A.* 45°21N 95°14W **77** E3
Sunburst *Mont., U.S.A.* 48°53N 111°55W **123** B6
Sunbury *Ohio, U.S.A.* 40°15N 82°52W **86** C4
Sunbury *Pa., U.S.A.* 40°52N 76°48W **87** D6
Suncook *N.H., U.S.A.* 43°8N 71°27W **89** C3
Suncook → *N.H., U.S.A.* 43°8N 71°28W **89** C3
Suncrest *B.C., Canada* 49°13N 123°1W **161** B2
Sundance *Man., Canada* 56°32N 94°4W **159** F7
Sundance *Wyo., U.S.A.* 44°24N 104°23W **124** B8
Sunderland *Ont., Canada* 44°16N 79°4W **147** C7
Sunderland *Md., U.S.A.* 38°40N 76°36W **93** B4
Sundown *Man., Canada* 49°6N 96°16W **151** F15
Sundre *Alta., Canada* 51°49N 114°38W **153** G6
Sundridge *Ont., Canada* 45°45N 79°25W **146** B7
Sunfish Lake *Minn., U.S.A.* 44°52N 93°5W **94** B3
Sunfish Park *Minn., U.S.A.* 45°0N 92°56W **94** A4
Sunflower *Miss., U.S.A.* 33°33N 90°32W **111** C3
Sunflower, Mt. *Kans., U.S.A.* 39°6N 102°2W **82** B1
Sunflower County ☆ *Miss., U.S.A.* 33°44N 90°33W **111** C3
Sunland Park *N. Mex., U.S.A.* 31°50N 106°40W **131** F4
Sunman *Ind., U.S.A.* 39°14N 85°6W **85** D5
Sunny Brae *N.S., Canada* 45°24N 62°30W **141** H7
Sunny Corner *N.B., Canada* 46°57N 65°49W **141** G4
Sunny Side *Tex., U.S.A.* 29°39N 95°22W **116** B2
Sunnyside *Nfld. & L., Canada* 47°51N 53°55W **142** E7
Sunnyside *Calif., U.S.A.* 32°40N 117°0W **133** B2
Sunnyside *Nev., U.S.A.* 38°25N 115°1W **128** D5
Sunnyside *Utah, U.S.A.* 39°34N 110°23W **129** D5
Sunnyside *Wash., U.S.A.* 46°20N 120°0W **120** D6
Sunnyslope *Ariz., U.S.A.* 33°33N 112°3W **134** B2
Sunnyvale *Calif., U.S.A.* 37°23N 122°2W **126** F4
Sunol *Calif., U.S.A.* 41°9N 102°46W **80** D3
Sunray *Okla., U.S.A.* 34°25N 97°58W **107** D6
Sunray *Tex., U.S.A.* 36°1N 101°49W **108** A6
Sunrise *Minn., U.S.A.* 26°8N 80°14W **115** B2
Sunrise *Wyo., U.S.A.* 42°20N 104°42W **124** D8
Sunrise Manor *Nev., U.S.A.* 36°12N 115°4W **134** B2
Sunrise Mountain Natural Area *Nev., U.S.A.* 36°12N 114°58W **134** B3
Sunrise Mt. *Nev., U.S.A.* 36°13N 114°38W **134** B3
Sunset *Ark., U.S.A.* 35°13N 90°12W **106** C5
Sunset *La., U.S.A.* 30°25N 92°4W **110** D3
Sunset Beach *Hawai'i, U.S.A.* 21°40N 158°3W **136** J13
Sunset Crater Volcano Nat. Monument △ *Ariz., U.S.A.* 35°20N 111°20W **130** B4
Sunset Park *N.Y., U.S.A.* 40°38N 73°59W **97** C3
Sunset Park *Nev., U.S.A.* 36°3N 115°6W **134** C2
Suntrana *Alaska, U.S.A.* 63°52N 148°51W **135** E10
Sunwapta Pass *Alta., Canada* 52°13N 117°10W **153** F3
Supai *Ariz., U.S.A.* 36°15N 112°41W **130** B3
Superior *Ariz., U.S.A.* 33°18N 111°6W **130** D4
Superior *Iowa, U.S.A.* 43°26N 94°57W **81** B4
Superior *Nebr., U.S.A.* 40°1N 98°4W **80** D7
Superior *Wyo., U.S.A.* 41°46N 108°58W **124** E4
Superior, L. *Oaxaca, Mexico* 16°20N 94°55W **177** H6
Superior, L. *N. Amer.* 47°0N 87°0W **149** E9
Superior Nat. Forest *Minn., U.S.A.* 47°45N 91°30W **77** C6
Suquamish *Wash., U.S.A.* 47°44N 122°33W **120** C3
Sur, Pt. *Calif., U.S.A.* 36°18N 121°54W **126** G5
Sur, Pta. *Quintana Roo, Mexico* 20°20N 87°0W **179** B6
Surazo *Zacatecas, Mexico* 22°36N 103°5W **173** E7
Susupuato *Michoacan, Mexico* 19°13N 100°24W **175** C7
Sutcliffe *Nev., U.S.A.* 39°57N 119°36W **128** C1
Sutherland *Iowa, U.S.A.* 42°58N 95°29W **81** C3
Sutherland *Nebr., U.S.A.* 41°10N 101°8W **80** C4
Sutherland Res. *Nebr., U.S.A.* 41°6N 101°10W **80** C4
Sutherlin *Oreg., U.S.A.* 43°23N 123°19W **121** D2
Sutter *Calif., U.S.A.* 39°10N 121°45W **126** D5
Sutter Buttes *Calif., U.S.A.* 39°12N 121°49W **126** D5
Sutter County ☆ *Calif., U.S.A.* 39°0N 121°45W **126** D5
Sutter Creek *Calif., U.S.A.* 38°24N 120°48W **126** E6
Suttle *Ala., U.S.A.* 32°32N 87°11W **112** D3
Sutton *Ont., Canada* 44°18N 79°22W **146** C7
Sutton *Qué., Canada* 45°6N 72°37W **145** F10
Sutton *Mass., U.S.A.* 42°9N 71°46W **91** B3
Sutton *N. Dak., U.S.A.* 47°24N 98°27W **76** C7
Sutton *Nebr., U.S.A.* 40°36N 97°52W **80** D8
Sutton *Vt., U.S.A.* 44°39N 72°3W **89** B2
Sutton *W. Va., U.S.A.* 38°40N 80°43W **102** C4
Sutton, Mts. *Qué., Canada* 45°5N 72°32W **89** A2
Sutton B. *Mich., U.S.A.* 44°59N 85°37W **79** E6
Sutton County ☆ *Tex., U.S.A.* 30°34N 100°39W **108** G7
Sutton L. *Ont., Canada* 54°15N 84°42W **159** G9
Sutton L. *W. Va., U.S.A.* 38°40N 80°41W **102** C4
Sutwik I. *Alaska, U.S.A.* 56°34N 157°12W **135** H8
Suwannee *Fla., U.S.A.* 29°20N 83°9W **114** B5
Suwannee → *Fla., U.S.A.* 29°17N 83°10W **114** B5
Suwannee County ☆ *Fla., U.S.A.* 30°15N 83°0W **114** A6
Suwannee Sd. *Fla., U.S.A.* 29°20N 83°15W **114** B5
Sverdrup Chan. *Nunavut, Canada* 79°56N 96°25W **158** B6
Sverdrup Is. *Nunavut, Canada* 79°0N 97°0W **158** B6
Swain *Ark., U.S.A.* 35°51N 93°20W **106** C2
Swain County ☆ *N.C., U.S.A.* 35°30N 83°20W **103** C2
Swainsboro *Ga., U.S.A.* 32°36N 82°20W **113** D4
Swaledale *Iowa, U.S.A.* 42°59N 93°19W **81** C5
Swampscott *Mass., U.S.A.* 42°28N 70°53W **91** B4
Swan → *Alta., Canada* 55°30N 115°18W **152** C5
Swan → *Man., Canada* 52°30N 100°45W **151** C11
Swan Cr. → *Mo., U.S.A.* 36°41N 93°6W **83** E3
Swan Hills *Alta., Canada* 54°43N 115°24W **152** D5
Swan Is. = Santanilla, Is. *Honduras* 17°22N 83°57W **182** C3
Swan L. *Man., Canada* 52°30N 100°40W **151** C11
Swan L. *S. Dak., U.S.A.* 45°17N 99°51W **76** E6
Swan Lake *Mont., U.S.A.* 47°56N 113°51W **123** C4
Swan Ra. *Mont., U.S.A.* 48°0N 113°45W **123** C4
Swan River *Man., Canada* 52°10N 101°16W **151** C10
Swan River *Minn., U.S.A.* 47°5N 93°12W **77** C5
Swan Valley *Idaho, U.S.A.* 43°27N 111°20W **122** F7
Swandale *W. Va., U.S.A.* 38°30N 80°57W **102** C4
Swannanoa *N.C., U.S.A.* 35°36N 82°24W **103** C3
Swanquarter *N.C., U.S.A.* 35°25N 76°20W **103** C9
Swans I. *Maine, U.S.A.* 44°10N 68°26W **90** D5
Swansboro *N.C., U.S.A.* 34°39N 77°7W **103** D8
Swansea *Ont., Canada* 43°38N 79°28W **161** B2
Swansea *S.C., U.S.A.* 33°44N 81°6W **103** D4
Swanson L. *Nebr., U.S.A.* 40°10N 101°4W **80** D4
Swanton *Md., U.S.A.* 39°27N 79°14W **93** A1
Swanton *Vt., U.S.A.* 44°55N 73°8W **89** B1
Swanville *Minn., U.S.A.* 45°55N 94°38W **77** E4
Swarthmore *Pa., U.S.A.* 39°54N 75°21W **92** C1
Swartswood *N.J., U.S.A.* 41°8N 74°50W **92** A2
Swartz Creek *Mich., U.S.A.* 42°58N 83°50W **79** G8
Swasey Peak *Utah, U.S.A.* 39°23N 113°19W **129** D2
Swastika *Ont., Canada* 48°7N 80°6W **144** C2
Swayzee *Ind., U.S.A.* 40°30N 85°50W **85** C5
Swea City *Iowa, U.S.A.* 43°23N 94°19W **81** B4
Swedeborg *Mo., U.S.A.* 37°55N 92°20W **83** D4
Sweden *Maine, U.S.A.* 46°57N 68°8W **90** B5
Swedesboro *N.J., U.S.A.* 39°45N 75°19W **92** C1
Swedish Knoll *Utah, U.S.A.* 39°16N 111°26W **129** D4
Sweeny *Tex., U.S.A.* 29°3N 95°42W **109** H12
Sweet Air Md., U.S.A. 39°31N 76°32W **93** A4
Sweet Briar Station *Va., U.S.A.* 37°33N 79°4W **102** D5
Sweet Grass *Mont., U.S.A.* 48°59N 111°58W **123** B6
Sweet Grass County ☆ *Mont., U.S.A.* 46°0N 110°0W **123** E8
Sweet Home *Ark., U.S.A.* 34°41N 92°15W **106** D3
Sweet Home *Oreg., U.S.A.* 44°24N 122°44W **121** C3
Sweet Springs *Mo., U.S.A.* 38°58N 93°25W **83** C3
Sweet Springs *W. Va., U.S.A.* 37°38N 80°14W **102** D4
Sweet Water *Ala., U.S.A.* 32°6N 87°52W **112** D3
Sweetwater *Tenn., U.S.A.* 35°36N 84°28W **105** E8
Sweetwater *Tex., U.S.A.* 32°28N 100°24W **108** E7
Sweetwater → *Wyo., U.S.A.* 42°31N 107°2W **124** D5
Sweetwater County ☆ *Wyo., U.S.A.* 42°0N 109°0W **124** E4
Sweetwater L. *N. Dak., U.S.A.* 48°3N 98°50W **76** B7
Sweetwater Marsh Nat. Wildlife Refuge △ *Calif., U.S.A.* 32°38N 117°6W **133** C2
Sweetwater Res. *Calif., U.S.A.* 32°41N 117°0W **133** B3
Sweetwater Station *Wyo., U.S.A.* 42°32N 108°11W **124** D4
Swenson *Tex., U.S.A.* 33°13N 100°19W **108** D7
Swift County ☆ *Minn., U.S.A.* 45°15N 95°45W **77** E3
Swift Current *Nfld. & L., Canada* 47°53N 54°14W **142** E7
Swift Current *Sask., Canada* 50°20N 107°45W **150** E4
Swift Current → *Sask., Canada* 50°38N 107°44W **150** E4
Swift Res. *Wash., U.S.A.* 46°4N 122°3W **120** D3
Swifton *Ark., U.S.A.* 35°49N 91°8W **106** C4
Swinburne I. *N.Y., U.S.A.* 40°33N 74°3W **97** C2
Swindle, I. *B.C., Canada* 52°30N 128°35W **154** C6
Swink *Colo., U.S.A.* 38°1N 103°38W **125** D7
Swinomish Indian Reservation *Wash., U.S.A.* 48°23N 122°32W **120** B3

Swisher Iowa, U.S.A. 41°50N 91°42W **81** D7
Swisher County ☆ Tex., U.S.A. 34°32N 101°46W **108** C6
Swisshome Oreg., U.S.A. 44°4N 123°48W **121** C2
Swissvale Pa., U.S.A. 40°25N 79°52W **98** B2
Switzerland County ☆ Ind., U.S.A. 38°50N 85°0W **85** E6
Swords Ga., U.S.A. 33°33N 83°18W **113** C3
Swoyerville Pa., U.S.A. 41°18N 75°53W **87** C7
Sycamore Ga., U.S.A. 31°40N 83°38W **113** E3
Sycamore Ill., U.S.A. 41°59N 88°41W **84** B5
Sycamore Kans., U.S.A. 37°20N 95°43W **82** D8
Sycamore Ohio, U.S.A. 40°57N 83°10W **86** C3
Sycan Marsh Oreg., U.S.A. 42°45N 121°5W **121** E4
Sydenham ➔ Ont., Canada 42°33N 82°25W **146** E4
Sydney N.S., Canada 46°7N 60°7W **141** G9
Sydney N. Dak. U.S.A. 46°44N 98°46W **76** D7
Sydney L. Ont. Canada 50°41N 94°25W **148** B2
Sydney Mines N.S., Canada 46°18N 60°15W **141** G9
Sydney River N.S., Canada 46°7N 60°10W **141** G9
Sydproven = Alluitsup Paa Greenland 60°30N 45°35W **162** E6
Sykeston N. Dak., U.S.A. 47°28N 99°24W **76** C6
Sykesville Md., U.S.A. 39°22N 76°58W **93** A4
Sykesville Pa., U.S.A. 41°3N 78°50W **87** C4
Sylacauga Ala., U.S.A. 33°10N 86°15W **112** C2
Sylva N.C., U.S.A. 35°23N 83°13W **103** C2
Sylvan Pa., U.S.A. 39°45N 78°1W **93** A2
Sylvan Grove Kans., U.S.A. 39°1N 98°24W **82** B5
Sylvan L. Alta., Canada 52°21N 114°10W **153** F6
Sylvan Lake Alta., Canada 52°20N 114°3W **153** F6
Sylvania Sask. Canada 52°42N 104°0W **150** C8
Sylvania Ga., U.S.A. 32°45N 81°38W **113** D5
Sylvania Ohio, U.S.A. 41°43N 83°42W **86** B3
Sylvarena Miss., U.S.A. 32°1N 89°23W **111** D4
Sylvester Ga., U.S.A. 31°32N 83°50W **113** E3
Sylvester Tex. U.S.A. 32°43N 100°15W **108** E7
Sylvia Kans., U.S.A. 37°57N 98°25W **82** D5
Symerton Ill., U.S.A. 41°20N 88°3W **84** B5
Symmes Cr. ➔ Ohio, U.S.A. 38°26N 82°27W **86** E4
Symsonia Ky., U.S.A. 36°55N 88°31W **104** D4
Syracuse Ind., U.S.A. 41°26N 85°45W **85** B5
Syracuse Kans., U.S.A. 37°59N 101°45W **82** D2
Syracuse Mo., U.S.A. 38°40N 92°53W **83** C4
Syracuse N.Y., U.S.A. 43°3N 76°9W **88** B4
Syracuse Nebr., U.S.A. 40°39N 96°11W **80** D9
Syracuse ✈ (SYR) N.Y., U.S.A. 43°7N 76°6W **88** B4
Syria Va., U.S.A. 38°29N 78°20W **102** C6
Syringa Park ➔ B.C., Canada 49°23N 117°54W **155** F17

T

T.O. Fuller State Park ➔ Tenn., U.S.A. 35°3N 90°7W **117** B1
Tabasará, Serranía de Panama 8°35N 81°40W **182** E3
Tabasco Zacatecas, Mexico 21°52N 102°55W **173** F8
Tabasco ☐ Mexico 18°0N 92°40W **178** B4
Tabernash Colo., U.S.A. 39°57N 105°52W **125** C5
Tabiona Utah, U.S.A. 40°21N 110°43W **129** C5
Table B. Nfld. & L., Canada 53°40N 56°25W **143** C6
Table I. Nunavut, Canada 77°12N 95°28W **158** B6
Table Mt. Ariz., U.S.A. 32°49N 110°31W **130** E5
Table Mt. S. Dak., U.S.A. 45°55N 103°48W **76** E2
Table Rock Nebr., U.S.A. 40°11N 96°6W **80** D9
Table Rock Wyo., U.S.A. 41°37N 108°23W **124** E4
Table Rock L. Mo., U.S.A. 36°36N 93°19W **83** E3
Table Top Ariz., U.S.A. 32°45N 112°8W **130** E3
Tabor Iowa, U.S.A. 40°54N 95°40W **81** E3
Tabor Minn., U.S.A. 48°5N 96°52W **77** B2
Tabor S. Dak., U.S.A. 42°57N 97°40W **76** H8
Tabor City N.C., U.S.A. 34°10N 78°52W **103** D7
Tabusintac N.B., Canada 47°20N 65°1W **141** F4
Tacámbaro de Codallos Michoacan, Mexico 19°14N 101°28W **175** C6
Tachick L. B.C., Canada 53°57N 124°13W **154** B10
Tacna Ariz. U.S.A. 32°41N 113°59W **130** E2
Tacoh Campeche, Mexico 19°47N 89°52W **179** C4
Tacoma Wash., U.S.A. 47°14N 122°26W **120** C3
Taconic Ra. U.S.A. 42°40N 73°18W **91** B1
Taconite Harbor Minn., U.S.A. 47°32N 90°55W **77** C8
Tacotalpa Tabasco, Mexico 17°36N 92°49W **178** B4
Tacuba Distrito Federal, Mexico 19°26N 99°11W **181** B2
Tacubaya Distrito Federal, Mexico 19°24N 99°9W **181** B2
Tadoule L. Man., Canada 58°36N 98°20W **159** F6
Tadoussac Qué., Canada 48°11N 69°42W **145** C13
Tafetán Michoacan, Mexico 19°26N 100°54W **175** C7
Taft Calif., U.S.A. 35°8N 119°28W **127** H7
Taft Fla., U.S.A. 28°25N 81°21W **115** B2
Taft Okla., U.S.A. 35°46N 95°32W **107** C8
Taft Tenn., U.S.A. 35°1N 86°43W **104** E6
Taft Tex., U.S.A. 27°59N 97°24W **109** K10
Tafton Pa., U.S.A. 41°24N 75°11W **92** A1
Tagpocha, Mt. N. Marianas 15°11N 145°44E **184** c
Tahdziú Yucatán, Mexico 20°12N 88°57W **179** B5
Tahgong Pt. N. Marianas 15°6N 145°39E **184** c
Tahlequah Okla., U.S.A. 35°55N 94°58W **107** C9
Tahoe, L. U.S.A. 39°6N 120°2W **126** D6
Tahoe City Calif., U.S.A. 39°10N 120°9W **126** D6
Tahoe L. Nunavut, Canada 70°5N 108°45W **158** C4
Tahoe Nat. Forest Calif., U.S.A. 39°20N 120°30W **126** D6
Tahoka Tex., U.S.A. 33°10N 101°48W **108** D6
Taholah Wash., U.S.A. 47°21N 124°17W **120** C1
Tahquamenon ➔ Mich., U.S.A. 46°34N 85°2W **79** C8
Tahsis B.C., Canada 49°55N 126°40W **154** F8
Tahsish-Kwois Park ➔ B.C., Canada 50°11N 127°9W **154** E7
Tahtsa L. B.C., Canada 53°42N 127°27W **154** B7
Taiban N. Mex., U.S.A. 34°26N 104°1W **131** C6
Tajique N. Mex., U.S.A. 34°44N 106°17W **131** C4
Tajirachi Chihuahua, Mexico 28°1N 107°10W **169** E8
Tajitos Sonora, Mexico 30°57N 112°20W **168** C3
Takla L. B.C., Canada 55°15N 125°45W **157** E7
Takla Landing B.C., Canada 55°30N 125°50W **157** E7
Takoma Park Md., U.S.A. 38°58N 77°0W **93** A4
Takysie Lake B.C., Canada 53°53N 125°53W **154** B9
Tala Jalisco, Mexico 20°40N 103°42W **174** B4
Talala Okla., U.S.A. 36°32N 95°42W **107** B8
Talamanca, Cordillera de Cent. Amer. 9°20N 83°0W **182** E3
Talbot County ☆ Ga., U.S.A. 32°45N 84°40W **113** D2
Talbot County ☆ Md., U.S.A. 38°45N 76°5W **93** B5
Talbot Inlet Nunavut, Canada 77°55N 77°40W **158** B10
Talbot L. Man., Canada 54°0N 99°55W **151** A12
Talbotton Ga., U.S.A. 32°41N 84°32W **113** D2
Talcayuca Hidalgo, Mexico 19°57N 98°54W **175** C9
Talchichilte, I. Sinaloa, Mexico 24°55N 108°7W **172** C2
Talco Tex., U.S.A. 33°22N 95°6W **109** D12
Talent Oreg., U.S.A. 42°15N 122°47W **121** E3
Taliaferro County ☆ Ga., U.S.A. 33°35N 82°50W **113** C4

Taliesin Wis., U.S.A. 43°8N 90°4W **78** E3
Talihina Okla., U.S.A. 34°45N 95°3W **107** D8
Talkeetna Alaska, U.S.A. 62°20N 150°6W **135** E10
Talking Rock Ga., U.S.A. 34°31N 84°30W **113** B2
Talladega Ala., U.S.A. 33°26N 86°6W **112** C4
Talladega County ☆ Ala., U.S.A. 33°26N 86°6W **112** C4
Talladega Cr. ➔ Ala., U.S.A. 33°18N 86°22W **112** C4
Talladega Nat. Forest Ala., U.S.A. 32°55N 87°15W **112** D3
Tallahala Cr. ➔ Miss., U.S.A. 31°12N 89°5W **111** E4
Tallahassee Fla., U.S.A. 30°27N 84°17W **114** A4
Tallahatchie ➔ Miss., U.S.A. 33°33N 90°10W **111** C3
Tallahatchie County ☆ Miss., U.S.A. 33°58N 90°2W **111** C3
Tallapoosa Ga., U.S.A. 33°45N 85°17W **113** C1
Tallapoosa ➔ Ala., U.S.A. 32°30N 86°16W **112** D4
Tallapoosa County ☆ Ala., U.S.A. 32°50N 85°46W **112** D5
Tallassee Ala., U.S.A. 32°32N 85°54W **112** D5
Talleyville Del., U.S.A. 39°48N 75°33W **93** A5
Tallgrass Prairie Nat. Preserve ➔ Kans., U.S.A. 38°26N 96°34W **82** C7
Tallmadge Ohio, U.S.A. 41°6N 81°27W **86** B5
Tallula Ill., U.S.A. 39°56N 89°56W **84** D4
Tallulah La., U.S.A. 32°25N 91°11W **110** B4
Tallulah Falls Ga., U.S.A. 34°44N 83°24W **113** B3
Talmage Kans., U.S.A. 39°2N 97°16W **82** B6
Talmage Nebr., U.S.A. 40°32N 96°1W **80** D9
Talofofo Guam 13°21N 144°45E **184** b
Taloga Okla., U.S.A. 36°2N 98°58W **107** B5
Taloyoak Nunavut, Canada 69°32N 93°32W **158** D7
Talpa de Allende Jalisco, Mexico 20°23N 104°51W **174** B3
Talquin, L. Fla., U.S.A. 30°23N 84°39W **114** A4
Taltson ➔ N.W.T., Canada 61°24N 112°46W **157** D10
Talunkwan I. B.C., Canada 52°50N 131°45W **154** C3
Tama Iowa, U.S.A. 41°58N 92°35W **81** C6
Tama County ☆ Iowa, U.S.A. 42°5N 92°30W **81** C6
Tamaha Okla., U.S.A. 35°20N 94°59W **107** C9
Tamaqua Pa., U.S.A. 40°48N 75°58W **87** D7
Tamarac Fla., U.S.A. 26°12N 80°15W **115** A1
Tamarac Nat. Wildlife Refuge ➔ Minn., U.S.A. 47°2N 95°36W **77** C3
Tamarack Idaho, U.S.A. 44°57N 116°23W **122** E2
Tamarack Minn., U.S.A. 46°39N 93°8W **77** D5
Tamaroa Ill., U.S.A. 38°8N 89°14W **84** E4
Tamasopo San Luis Potosí, Mexico 21°55N 99°24W **171** J5
Tamaulipas ☐ Mexico 24°0N 98°45W **171** G6
Tamazula Durango, Mexico 24°57N 106°57W **172** C4
Tamazula de Gordiano Jalisco, Mexico 19°38N 103°15W **174** C4
Tamazunchale San Luis Potosí, Mexico 21°16N 98°47W **171** J6
Tameapa Sinaloa, Mexico 25°39N 107°22W **172** B3
Tamesí ➔ Tamaulipas, Mexico 22°13N 97°52W **171** H7
Tamiahua Veracruz, Mexico 21°16N 97°27W **176** C3
Tamiahua, L. de Veracruz, Mexico 21°35N 97°35W **176** C3
Tamiami Canal Fla., U.S.A. 25°50N 81°0W **114** F8
Tamms Ill., U.S.A. 37°14N 89°16W **84** F4
Tamora Nebr., U.S.A. 40°54N 97°14W **80** D8
Tampa Fla., U.S.A. 27°56N 82°27W **115** B3
Tampa Kans., U.S.A. 38°33N 97°9W **82** C6
Tampa B. Fla., U.S.A. 27°50N 82°30W **115** C3
Tampa B. Fla., U.S.A. 27°59N 82°33W **115** B3
Tampa Int. ✈ (TPA) Fla., U.S.A. 27°59N 82°33W **115** B3
Tampacán San Luis Potosí, Mexico 21°25N 98°44W **171** J6
Tampalam Quintana Roo, Mexico 19°9N 87°33W **179** C6
Tampamolón San Luis Potosí, Mexico 21°34N 98°49W **171** J6
Tampaón ➔ San Luis Potosí, Mexico 21°58N 98°39W **171** J6
Tampico Tamaulipas, Mexico 22°13N 97°51W **171** H7
Tampico Ill., U.S.A. 41°38N 89°47W **84** B4
Tampico Alto Veracruz, Mexico 22°7N 97°48W **176** B3
Tampico L. San Luis Potosí, Mexico 21°59N 98°41W **176** A3
Tamuín San Luis Potosí, Mexico 22°0N 98°45W **171** J6
Tamulte de las Sabanas Tabasco, Mexico 18°13N 92°47W **178** A4
Tamuning Guam 13°29N 144°47E **184** b
Tamworth Ont., Canada 44°29N 77°0W **147** C10
Tamworth N.H., U.S.A. 43°50N 71°18W **89** C3
Tanacross Alaska, U.S.A. 63°23N 143°21W **135** E12
Tanaga I. Alaska, U.S.A. 51°48N 177°53W **135** L3
Tanaga Volcano Alaska, U.S.A. 51°53N 178°8W **135** L3
Tanana Alaska, U.S.A. 65°10N 152°4W **135** D9
Tanana ➔ Alaska, U.S.A. 65°10N 151°58W **135** D10
Tanapag N. Marianas 15°14N 145°45E **184** c
Tancítaro Michoacan, Mexico 19°23N 102°23W **174** C5
Tancoco Veracruz, Mexico 21°17N 97°47W **176** C3
Taney County ☆ Mo., U.S.A. 36°40N 93°0W **83** E3
Taneytown Md., U.S.A. 39°40N 77°11W **93** A3
Taneyville Mo., U.S.A. 36°44N 93°2W **83** E3
Tangancicuaro Michoacan, Mexico 19°54N 102°8W **174** C5
Tangelo Park Fla., U.S.A. 28°27N 81°26W **115** B2
Tangent Oreg., U.S.A. 44°33N 123°7W **121** C2
Tangier N.S., Canada 44°48N 62°42W **141** J7
Tangier I. Va., U.S.A. 37°50N 75°59W **93** C5
Tangier Sd. Md., U.S.A. 38°0N 75°57W **93** B5
Tangipahoa La., U.S.A. 30°53N 90°31W **110** D5
Tangipahoa ➔ La., U.S.A. 30°20N 90°16W **110** D5
Tangipahoa Parish ☆ La., U.S.A. 30°30N 90°28W **110** D5
Tanhuijo, Arrecife de Veracruz, Mexico 21°8N 97°15W **176** C3
Tankersley Tex., U.S.A. 31°21N 100°39W **108** F7
Tankuché Campeche, Mexico 20°20N 90°12W **179** B3
Tanlajas San Luis Potosí, Mexico 21°40N 98°53W **171** J6
Tanner W. Va., U.S.A. 38°59N 80°57W **102** C4
Tanners Lake Minn., U.S.A. 44°57N 92°58W **94** B4
Tanque de Dolores San Luis Potosí, Mexico 23°40N 101°9W **171** G3
Tanque del Cerro Coahuila, Mexico 24°38N 100°49W **171** F4
Tanque Nuevo Coahuila, Mexico 26°38N 102°11W **170** D2
Tanque Nuevo San Luis Potosí, Mexico 24°22N 100°57W **171** F4
Tanquian San Luis Potosí, Mexico 21°36N 98°40W **171** J6
Tantallon Sask., Canada 50°32N 101°50W **151** E10
Tantalus Park ➔ B.C., Canada 49°50N 123°17W **155** F11
Tantoyuca Veracruz, Mexico 21°21N 98°14W **176** C2
Tanu I. B.C., Canada 52°46N 131°40W **154** C3
Taopi Minn., U.S.A. 43°34N 92°38W **77** G6
Taos County ☆ N. Mex., U.S.A. 36°30N 105°35W **131** A5
Taos Indian Reservation N. Mex., U.S.A. 36°35N 105°25W **131** A5
Taos Pueblo N. Mex., U.S.A. 36°24N 105°33W **131** A5
Tapachula Chiapas, Mexico 14°54N 92°17W **178** E4
Tapalpa Jalisco, Mexico 19°56N 103°46W **174** C4
Tapijulapa Tabasco, Mexico 17°28N 92°47W **178** B4
Tapilula Chiapas, Mexico 17°14N 93°0W **178** B3
Tappahannock Va., U.S.A. 37°56N 76°52W **93** C4
Tappan L. Ohio, U.S.A. 40°22N 81°14W **86** C5
Tappen N. Dak., U.S.A. 46°52N 99°38W **76** D6
Tapuatapu, C. Amer. Samoa 14°20S 170°47E **184** e
Tar ➔ N.C., U.S.A. 35°33N 77°6W **103** C8
Tara Ont., Canada 44°28N 81°9W **146** C5
Tarandacuao Guanajuato, Mexico 20°0N 100°31W **175** C7

Tarboro Ga., U.S.A. 31°1N 81°48W **113** E5
Tarboro N.C., U.S.A. 35°54N 77°32W **103** C8
Taretán Michoacan, Mexico 19°20N 101°55W **174** C6
Targhee Nat. Forest Idaho, U.S.A. 44°30N 111°20W **122** E7
Targhee Pass U.S.A. 44°40N 111°16W **122** E7
Tarimbaro Michoacan, Mexico 19°47N 101°8W **175** C6
Tarimoro Guanajuato, Mexico 20°17N 100°45W **175** B7
Tarkio Mo., U.S.A. 40°27N 95°23W **83** A1
Tarkio Mont., U.S.A. 47°1N 114°44W **123** C3
Tarkio ➔ Mo., U.S.A. 40°27N 95°23W **83** A1
Tarlton Ohio, U.S.A. 39°33N 82°47W **86** D4
Tarnov Nebr., U.S.A. 41°37N 97°30W **80** C8
Tarpon Springs Fla., U.S.A. 28°9N 82°45W **114** C6
Tarrant City Ala., U.S.A. 33°34N 86°47W **112** C4
Tarrant County ☆ Tex., U.S.A. 32°44N 97°9W **109** E10
Tarryall Colo., U.S.A. 39°7N 105°29W **125** C5
Tarryall Cr. ➔ Colo., U.S.A. 39°5N 105°19W **125** C5
Tarrytown Ga., U.S.A. 32°19N 82°34W **113** D4
Tarrytown N.Y., U.S.A. 41°4N 73°52W **92** A3
Tarzan Tex., U.S.A. 32°18N 101°58W **108** E6
Tasajeras Sinaloa, Mexico 26°47N 108°16W **169** G7
Taschereau Qué., Canada 48°40N 78°40W **144** C4
Taseko ➔ B.C., Canada 52°8N 123°45W **154** C11
Taseko L. B.C., Canada 51°15N 123°35W **154** C1
Tasiilaq Greenland 65°40N 37°20W **162** D7
Tasiujaq Qué., Canada 58°42N 69°56W **143** B4
Tasquillo Hidalgo, Mexico 20°38N 99°12W **175** B8
Tassialuk, L. Qué., Canada 59°3N 74°0W **143** B3
Tasu B.C., Canada 52°45N 132°5W **154** C2
Tasu Sd. B.C., Canada 52°47N 132°2W **154** C2
Tatahuicapa Veracruz, Mexico 18°15N 94°46W **177** F6
Tatalpetec Oaxaca, Mexico 16°18N 97°13W **177** H3
Tatamagouche N.S., Canada 45°43N 63°18W **141** H6
Tate ➔ Ga., U.S.A. 34°25N 84°23W **113** B2
Tate County ☆ Miss., U.S.A. 34°37N 89°58W **111** B4
Tathlina L. N.W.T., Canada 60°33N 117°39W **157** D9
Tatitlek Alaska, U.S.A. 60°52N 146°41W **135** F11
Tatla L. B.C., Canada 52°0N 124°20W **154** D10
Tatlayoko L. B.C., Canada 51°35N 124°24W **154** D10
Tatnam, C. Man., Canada 57°16N 91°0W **159** F7
Tattnall County ☆ Ga., U.S.A. 32°0N 82°0W **113** D4
Tatuk, L. B.C., Canada 53°32N 124°14W **154** B10
Tatum N. Mex., U.S.A. 33°16N 103°19W **131** D7
Tatum Okla., U.S.A. 32°19N 94°31W **109** E13
Tatum Cr. ➔ Ga., U.S.A. 30°43N 82°32W **113** F4
Ta'ū Amer. Samoa 14°15S 169°30W **184** f
Taum Sauk Mt. Mo., U.S.A. 37°34N 90°44W **83** D6
Taunton Mass., U.S.A. 41°54N 71°6W **91** E5
Taunton Minn., U.S.A. 44°36N 96°4W **77** F2
Taunton Lake N.J., U.S.A. 39°51N 74°52W **92** C2
Taverner B. Nunavut, Canada 67°12N 72°25W **158** D11
Tavernier Fla., U.S.A. 25°1N 80°31W **114** F8
Tavistock Ont., Canada 43°19N 80°50W **146** D6
Tawakoni, L. Tex., U.S.A. 32°49N 95°55W **109** E12
Tawas City Mich., U.S.A. 44°16N 83°31W **79** E8
Taxco Guerrero, Mexico 18°33N 99°36W **175** D8
Taylor Ariz., U.S.A. 34°28N 110°5W **130** C5
Taylor Ark., U.S.A. 33°6N 93°28W **106** E2
Taylor Fla., U.S.A. 30°26N 82°18W **114** A6
Taylor Mich., U.S.A. 42°14N 83°16W **79** G8
Taylor Miss., U.S.A. 34°16N 89°35W **111** B4
Taylor N. Dak., U.S.A. 46°54N 102°26W **76** D3
Taylor Nebr., U.S.A. 41°46N 99°23W **80** C6
Taylor Tex., U.S.A. 30°34N 97°25W **109** G10
Taylor Wis., U.S.A. 44°19N 91°7W **78** D2
Taylor ➔ Colo., U.S.A. 38°32N 106°55W **125** D4
Taylor, Mt. N. Mex., U.S.A. 35°14N 107°37W **131** B3
Taylor County ☆ Fla., U.S.A. 30°0N 83°30W **114** A5
Taylor County ☆ Ga., U.S.A. 32°35N 84°15W **113** D2
Taylor County ☆ Iowa, U.S.A. 40°45N 94°40W **81** E4
Taylor County ☆ Ky., U.S.A. 37°20N 85°20W **105** C7
Taylor County ☆ Tex., U.S.A. 32°21N 99°53W **109** E8
Taylor County ☆ W. Va., U.S.A. 39°21N 80°2W **102** B4
Taylor County ☆ Wis., U.S.A. 45°10N 90°30W **78** C3
Taylor Park Res. Colo., U.S.A. 38°49N 106°36W **125** D4
Taylor Ridge Ga., U.S.A. 34°35N 85°12W **113** B1
Taylors S.C., U.S.A. 34°55N 82°18W **103** C3
Taylors Bridge Del., U.S.A. 39°23N 75°36W **93** A5
Taylors Island Md., U.S.A. 38°28N 76°18W **93** B4
Taylorsville Ind., U.S.A. 39°27N 77°9W **93** A3
Taylorsville Ky., U.S.A. 38°2N 85°21W **105** B7
Taylorsville Miss., U.S.A. 31°50N 89°26W **111** E4
Taylorsville N.C., U.S.A. 35°55N 81°11W **103** C4
Taylorsville Utah, U.S.A. 40°40N 111°56W **134** C2
Taylorville Ill., U.S.A. 39°33N 89°18W **84** D4
Tayoltita Durango, Mexico 24°5N 105°56W **172** C5
Tazewell Tenn., U.S.A. 36°27N 83°34W **105** D9
Tazewell Va., U.S.A. 37°7N 81°31W **102** D3
Tazewell County ☆ Ill., U.S.A. 40°30N 89°30W **84** C4
Tazewell County ☆ Va., U.S.A. 37°7N 81°31W **102** D3
Tazin ➔ Canada 59°48N 109°55W **157** E11
Tazin L. Sask., Canada 59°44N 108°42W **157** E11
Tazlina Alaska, U.S.A. 62°4N 146°27W **135** E11
Tchula Miss., U.S.A. 33°11N 90°13W **111** C3
Tea S. Dak., U.S.A. 43°27N 96°50W **76** G9
Teabo Yucatán, Mexico 20°24N 89°17W **179** B4
Teacapan Sinaloa, Mexico 22°33N 105°45W **172** E5
Teacapan, Estero Nayarit, Mexico 22°26N 105°40W **172** E5
Teague Tex., U.S.A. 31°38N 96°17W **109** F11
Teahwhit Head Wash., U.S.A. 47°52N 124°37W **120** C1
Teaneck N.J., U.S.A. 40°53N 74°1W **97** A2
Teapa Tabasco, Mexico 17°33N 92°57W **178** B4
Teatlalco Puebla, Mexico 18°28N 98°47W **177** F2
Tecalitlan Jalisco, Mexico 19°26N 103°16W **174** C4
Tecamachalco México, Mexico 19°25N 99°14W **181** B2
Tecamachalco Puebla, Mexico 18°53N 97°44W **177** F3
Tecate Baja Calif., Mexico 32°34N 116°38W **166** A2
Techaluta Jalisco, Mexico 20°4N 103°33W **174** B4
Tecoh Yucatán, Mexico 20°55N 89°30W **179** B4
Tecolote Canyon Natural Park ➔ Calif., U.S.A. 32°46N 117°11W **133** B1
Tecolotlán Jalisco, Mexico 20°13N 104°3W **174** B3
Tecolutilla Tabasco, Mexico 18°17N 93°19W **178** A3
Tecolutla Veracruz, Mexico 20°30N 97°0W **176** D3
Tecolutla, Barra de Veracruz, Mexico 20°34N 97°0W **176** D3
Tecomán Colima, Mexico 18°55N 103°53W **174** C4
Tecomate, L. Guerrero, Mexico 16°42N 99°0W **175** F8
Tecomatlán Puebla, Mexico 18°7N 98°18W **177** F2
Tecopa Calif., U.S.A. 35°51N 116°13W **127** H10
Tecoripa Sonora, Mexico 28°37N 109°57W **168** E6
Tecozautla Hidalgo, Mexico 20°32N 99°38W **175** B8
Tecpan de Galeana Guerrero, Mexico 17°15N 100°41W **175** E7

Tecpatán Chiapas, Mexico 17°8N 93°18W **178** B3
Tecuala Nayarit, Mexico 22°23N 105°27W **172** E5
Tecuanapa Guerrero, Mexico 17°0N 99°15W **175** F8
Tecumseh Ont., Canada 42°19N 82°54W **146** E4
Tecumseh Mich., U.S.A. 42°0N 83°57W **79** H8
Tecumseh Nebr., U.S.A. 40°22N 96°11W **80** D9
Tecumseh Okla., U.S.A. 35°15N 96°56W **107** C7
Tecumseh, Mt. N.H., U.S.A. 43°57N 71°34W **89** C3
Ted Williams Tunnel Mass., U.S.A. 42°21N 71°1W **96** A2
Tee Lake Qué., Canada 46°40N 79°0W **144** E3
Teec Nos Pos Ariz., U.S.A. 36°55N 109°6W **130** A6
Teepee Creek Alta., Canada 55°22N 118°24W **152** C2
Teeswater Ont., Canada 43°59N 81°17W **146** D5
Tegucigalpa Honduras 14°5N 87°14W **182** D2
Tehachapi Calif., U.S.A. 35°8N 118°27W **127** H8
Tehachapi Mts. Calif., U.S.A. 35°0N 118°30W **127** J8
Tehachapi Pass Calif., U.S.A. 35°6N 118°18W **127** H8
Tehama Calif., U.S.A. 40°2N 122°7W **126** C4
Tehama County ☆ Calif., U.S.A. 40°5N 122°15W **159** C4
Tehek L. Nunavut, Canada 64°55N 95°38W **159** E5
Tehuacán Puebla, Mexico 18°27N 97°23W **177** F3
Tehuantepec Oaxaca, Mexico 16°20N 95°14W **177** J5
Tehuantepec, G. de Mexico 15°50N 95°12W **177** J5
Tehuantepec, Istmo de Mexico 17°15N 94°30W **177** G6
Tehuipango Veracruz, Mexico 18°31N 97°4W **177** F3
Tehuitzingo Puebla, Mexico 18°21N 98°16W **177** F2
Tejában de la Rosita Coahuila, Mexico 25°15N 103°13W **171** E1
Tejamén Durango, Mexico 24°48N 105°7W **172** C5
Tejar Veracruz, Mexico 19°3N 96°10W **177** E4
Tejon Pass Calif., U.S.A. 34°49N 118°53W **127** J8
Tejupan, Pta. Michoacan, Mexico 18°20N 103°31W **174** D4
Tejupilco México, Mexico 18°54N 100°9W **175** D7
Tekamah Nebr., U.S.A. 41°47N 96°13W **80** C9
Tekanto Yucatán, Mexico 21°1N 89°6W **179** A4
Tekax Yucatán, Mexico 20°12N 89°17W **179** B4
Tekit Yucatán, Mexico 20°32N 89°20W **179** B4
Tekoa Wash., U.S.A. 47°14N 117°4W **120** C8
Tekonsha Mich., U.S.A. 42°5N 84°59W **79** G7
Tela Honduras 15°40N 87°28W **182** C2
Telchac Puerto Yucatán, Mexico 21°21N 89°16W **179** A4
Telegraph Cove B.C., Canada 50°32N 126°50W **154** E8
Telegraph Creek B.C., Canada 58°0N 131°10W **157** E6
Telescope Pk. Calif., U.S.A. 36°10N 117°5W **127** G9
Telfair County ☆ Ga., U.S.A. 31°55N 83°0W **113** E4
Telida Alaska, U.S.A. 63°23N 153°16W **135** E9
Tell City Ind., U.S.A. 37°57N 86°46W **85** F4
Teller Alaska, U.S.A. 65°16N 166°22W **135** D6
Teller County ☆ Colo., U.S.A. 38°50N 105°10W **125** D5
Tellico L. Tenn., U.S.A. 35°21N 84°17W **105** E8
Tellico Plains Tenn., U.S.A. 35°22N 84°18W **105** E8
Telluride Colo., U.S.A. 37°56N 107°49W **125** E3
Telocaset Oreg., U.S.A. 45°6N 117°49W **121** B8
Telogia Fla., U.S.A. 30°21N 84°49W **114** A4
Teloloapán Guerrero, Mexico 18°21N 99°51W **175** D8
Temascal Oaxaca, Mexico 18°14N 96°25W **177** F4
Temascalcingo México, Mexico 19°55N 100°0W **175** C7
Temascaltepec México, Mexico 19°2N 100°3W **175** C7
Temascaltepec ➔ Mexico 18°47N 100°41W **175** D7
Temax Yucatán, Mexico 21°9N 88°56W **179** A5
Temblor Range Calif., U.S.A. 35°20N 119°50W **127** H7
Temecula Calif., U.S.A. 33°30N 117°9W **127** K9
Témiscamie ➔ Qué., Canada 50°59N 73°5W **143** C3
Témiscaming Qué., Canada 46°44N 79°5W **144** E3
Témiscamingue, L. Qué., Canada 47°10N 79°25W **144** D3
Temoac Morelos, Mexico 18°49N 98°45W **175** D9
Témoris Chihuahua, Mexico 27°16N 108°15W **169** F7
Temosachic Chihuahua, Mexico 28°57N 107°51W **169** E8
Temozón Yucatán, Mexico 20°48N 88°13W **179** A5
Tempe Ariz., U.S.A. 33°24N 111°54W **134** C3
Temperance Mich., U.S.A. 41°47N 83°34W **79** H8
Temperance Vale N.B., Canada 46°4N 67°15W **141** G2
Temperanceville Va., U.S.A. 37°54N 75°33W **93** C5
Tempiute Nev., U.S.A. 37°39N 115°38W **128** E5
Temple N.H., U.S.A. 42°48N 71°50W **89** D3
Temple Okla., U.S.A. 34°16N 98°14W **107** D5
Temple Tex., U.S.A. 31°6N 97°21W **109** F10
Temple City Calif., U.S.A. 34°6N 118°3W **133** B4
Temple Hill Ky., U.S.A. 36°53N 85°51W **105** D7
Temple Hills Md., U.S.A. 38°48N 76°56W **99** C4
Temple Terrace Fla., U.S.A. 28°2N 82°24W **115** B3
Templeman, Mt. B.C., Canada 50°42N 117°12W **155** E17
Templeton Calif., U.S.A. 35°33N 120°42W **127** H6
Templeton Mass., U.S.A. 42°33N 72°4W **91** B2
Templeton-Ouest Qué., Canada 45°29N 75°34W **160** A1
Tempoal ➔ Veracruz, Mexico 21°4N 98°23W **176** C2
Tempoal de Sánchez Veracruz, Mexico 21°31N 98°23W **176** C2
Ten Mile L. Nfld. & L., Canada 51°6N 56°42W **142** A4
Ten Mile Pond Nfld. & L., Canada 49°11N 54°0W **142** C6
Ten Sleep Wyo., U.S.A. 44°2N 107°27W **124** B5
Ten Thousand Is. Fla., U.S.A. 25°55N 81°45W **114** F7
Tenabo Campeche, Mexico 20°3N 90°13W **179** B3
Tenacatita Jalisco, Mexico 19°17N 104°52W **174** C3
Tenacatita, B. Jalisco, Mexico 19°17N 104°50W **174** C3
Tenafly N.J., U.S.A. 40°54N 73°58W **97** A3
Tenaha Tex., U.S.A. 31°57N 94°15W **109** F13
Tenakee Springs Alaska, U.S.A. 57°47N 135°13W **135** H14
Tenampa Veracruz, Mexico 20°13N 104°10W **174** B3
Tenampa Tamaulipas, Mexico 25°10N 98°24W **170** E6
Tenampulco Puebla, Mexico 20°10N 97°24W **176** D3
Tenango del Valle México, Mexico 19°7N 99°33W **175** C8
Tenayuca, Piramide de México, Mexico 19°31N 99°10W **181** A2
Tendoy Idaho, U.S.A. 44°57N 113°38W **122** E5
Tenejapa Chiapas, Mexico 16°49N 92°31W **178** C4
Tenino Wash., U.S.A. 46°51N 122°51W **120** D3
Tenkiller Ferry L. Okla., U.S.A. 35°35N 95°2W **107** C8
Tennant Iowa, U.S.A. 41°35N 95°26W **81** D3
Tennessee Ill., U.S.A. 40°18N 90°52W **84** C3
Tennessee ☐ U.S.A. 36°0N 86°30W **104** C4
Tennessee ➔ Tenn., U.S.A. 34°4N 88°34W **104** C4
Tennessee Pass Colo., U.S.A. 39°22N 106°19W **125** C4
Tennessee Ridge Tenn., U.S.A. 36°19N 87°47W **104** D5
Tennessee-Tombigbee Waterway U.S.A. 32°50N 88°10W **111** C6
Tennille Ga., U.S.A. 32°56N 82°48W **113** D4
Tennyson Ind., U.S.A. 38°5N 87°7W **85** F3
Tennyson Wis., U.S.A. 42°41N 90°46W **78** F3
Tenosique Tabasco, Mexico 17°29N 91°26W **178** B2
Tensas ➔ La., U.S.A. 31°38N 91°40W **110** C4
Tensas Parish ☆ La., U.S.A. 32°0N 91°20W **110** B4
Tensas River Nat. Wildlife Refuge ➔ La., U.S.A. 32°10N 91°27W **110** B4
Tensaw ➔ Ala., U.S.A. 30°41N 88°0W **112** F3
Tensed Idaho, U.S.A. 47°10N 116°55W **122** B2
Tenstrike Minn., U.S.A. 47°39N 94°41W **77** C4
Teoca, Volcan Distrito Federal, Mexico 19°12N 99°9W **181** C3
Teocaltiche Jalisco, Mexico 21°26N 102°35W **174** A5

Teocelo *Veracruz, Mexico* 19°23N 96°58W **176** E4
Teocuitlatlán de Corona *Jalisco, Mexico* 20°7N 103°24W **174** B4
Teolocholco *Tlaxcala, Mexico* 19°15N 98°2W **175** C9
Teopantlán *Puebla, Mexico* 18°43N 98°15W **177** F2
Teopisca *Chiapas, Mexico* 16°31N 92°29W **178** C4
Teotihuacán *México, Mexico* 19°42N 98°52W **175** C9
Teotitlán del Camino *Oaxaca, Mexico* 18°6N 97°3W **177** F3
Tepalcatepec *Michoacan, Mexico* 19°11N 102°51W **174** D3
Tepalcates *Distrito Federal, Mexico* 19°23N 99°3W **181** B3
Tepalcingo *Morelos, Mexico* 18°36N 98°51W **175** D9
Tepatitán *Tabasco, Mexico* 17°50N 92°22W **178** B4
Tepatitlán de Morelos *Jalisco, Mexico* 20°49N 102°44W **174** B5
Tepatlaxco *Puebla, Mexico* 19°5N 97°58W **177** E3
Tepeaca *Puebla, Mexico* 18°58N 97°54W **177** F3
Tepechitlán *Zacatecas, Mexico* 21°40N 103°20W **173** F7
Tepecoacuilco *Guerrero, Mexico* 18°18N 99°29W **175** D8
Tepeguajes *Tamaulipas, Mexico* 23°30N 97°47W **171** G7
Tepehuanes *Durango, Mexico* 25°21N 105°44W **172** D5
Tepeji del Río *Hidalgo, Mexico* 19°54N 99°21W **175** C8
Tepelmeme *Oaxaca, Mexico* 17°54N 97°21W **177** G3
Tepepan *Distrito Federal, Mexico* 19°17N 99°9W **181** C3
Tepetlaoxtoc *México, Mexico* 19°35N 98°49W **175** C9
Tepetongo *Zacatecas, Mexico* 22°28N 103°9W **173** F7
Tepetzintla *Veracruz, Mexico* 21°10N 97°50W **176** C3
Tepexco *Puebla, Mexico* 18°38N 98°41W **177** F2
Tepeyac, Parque Nacional △ *Distrito Federal, Mexico* 19°30N 99°7W **181** B3
Tepic = Nayarit □ *Mexico* 22°0N 105°0W **172** F6
Tepic *Nayarit, Mexico* 21°30N 104°54W **172** F6
Tepich *Quintana Roo, Mexico* 20°16N 88°16W **179** B5
Tepoca, Pta. *Sonora, Mexico* 29°55N 112°45W **168** D3
Tepotzotlán *México, Mexico* 19°43N 99°14W **175** C8
Tepozteco, Parque Nacional △ *Morelos, Mexico* 19°0N 99°7W **175** D8
Tepoztlán *Morelos, Mexico* 19°0N 99°6W **175** D8
Tepuxtepec, Presa de *Michoacan, Mexico* 20°3N 100°16W **175** B7
Tequesquitlán *Jalisco, Mexico* 19°28N 104°38W **174** C3
Tequila *Jalisco, Mexico* 20°54N 103°47W **174** B4
Tequilita *Nayarit, Mexico* 21°5N 104°49W **172** F6
Tequisquiapan *Querétaro, Mexico* 20°31N 99°52W **175** B8
Tequixquitla *Tlaxcala, Mexico* 19°20N 97°39W **175** C10
Terence Bay *N.S., Canada* 44°28N 63°43W **141** J6
Terlingua *Tex., U.S.A.* 29°19N 103°36W **108** H4
Terlingua Cr. → *Tex., U.S.A.* 29°10N 103°36W **108** H4
Terlton *Okla., U.S.A.* 36°8N 96°29W **107** B7
Términos, L. de *Campeche, Mexico* 18°37N 91°33W **178** C2
Terra Alta *W. Va., U.S.A.* 39°27N 79°33W **93** A1
Terra Bella *Calif., U.S.A.* 35°58N 119°3W **127** H7
Terra Ceia *Tampa, U.S.A.* 27°34N 82°34W **115** D3
Terra Nova *Nfld. & L., Canada* 48°30N 54°13W **142** D6
Terra Nova → *Nfld. & L., Canada* 48°40N 54°0W **142** D6
Terra Nova Nat. Park △ *Nfld. & L., Canada* 48°33N 53°55W **142** D7
Terrace *B.C., Canada* 54°30N 128°35W **157** F7
Terrace Bay *Ont., Canada* 48°47N 87°5W **149** D9
Terral *Okla., U.S.A.* 33°54N 97°57W **107** E6
Terre des Hommes *Qué., Canada* 45°31N 73°32W **160** A3
Terre Haute *Ind., U.S.A.* 39°28N 87°25W **85** D3
Terrebonne *Qué., Canada* 45°42N 73°38W **145** F9
Terrebonne *Oreg., U.S.A.* 44°21N 121°11W **121** C4
Terrebonne B. *La., U.S.A.* 29°5N 90°35W **110** E5
Terrebonne Parish ☆ *La., U.S.A.* 29°20N 91°0W **110** E5
Terrell *Tex., U.S.A.* 32°44N 96°17W **109** E11
Terrell County ☆ *Ga., U.S.A.* 31°50N 84°25W **113** E2
Terrell County ☆ *Tex., U.S.A.* 30°0N 102°0W **108** G6
Terrell Hills *Tex., U.S.A.* 29°28N 98°27W **116** B3
Terrenceville *Nfld. & L., Canada* 47°40N 54°44W **142** E6
Terreton *Idaho, U.S.A.* 43°51N 112°26W **122** F6
Terril *Iowa, U.S.A.* 43°18N 94°58W **81** B4
Terry *La., U.S.A.* 32°56N 91°21W **110** B4
Terry *Miss., U.S.A.* 32°6N 90°18W **111** D3
Terry *Mont., U.S.A.* 46°47N 105°19W **123** D12
Terry County ☆ *Tex., U.S.A.* 33°11N 102°17W **108** D5
Terry Pk. *S. Dak., U.S.A.* 44°19N 103°50W **76** F2
Terrytown *La., U.S.A.* 29°54N 90°1W **117** C2
Terrytown *Nebr., U.S.A.* 41°51N 103°40W **80** D2
Terryville *Conn., U.S.A.* 41°41N 73°3W **91** C1
Tescott *Kans., U.S.A.* 39°1N 97°53W **82** B6
Teshekpuk L. *Alaska, U.S.A.* 70°35N 153°26W **135** A9
Teslin *Yukon, Canada* 60°10N 132°43W **157** D6
Teslin → *Canada* 61°34N 134°35W **157** D6
Teslin L. *Canada* 60°15N 132°57W **157** D6
Tessik L. *Nunavut, Canada* 64°49N 75°22W **159** E10
Testigos, Is. Los *Venezuela* 11°23N 63°7W **183** D7
Tesuque *N. Mex., U.S.A.* 35°46N 105°55W **131** B5
Tesuque Indian Reservation *N. Mex., U.S.A.* 35°48N 105°58W **131** B5
Tetachuck L. *B.C., Canada* 53°18N 125°55W **154** B9
Tête-à-la-Baleine *Qué., Canada* 50°41N 59°20W **142** B1
Tête Jaune Cache *B.C., Canada* 52°58N 119°26W **155** C15
Tetela de Ocampo *Puebla, Mexico* 19°49N 97°48W **176** E3
Teterboro ✈ (TEB) *N.J., U.S.A.* 40°51N 74°3W **97** A2
Tetipac *Guerrero, Mexico* 18°39N 99°38W **175** D8
Tetiz *Yucatán, Mexico* 20°58N 89°57W **179** B4
Tetla *Tlaxcala, Mexico* 19°28N 98°5W **175** C9
Tetlin *Alaska, U.S.A.* 63°8N 142°31W **135** E12
Tetlin Junction *Alaska, U.S.A.* 63°19N 142°36W **135** E12
Tetlin Nat. Wildlife Refuge △ *Alaska, U.S.A.* 62°40N 141°50W **135** E12
Teton *Idaho, U.S.A.* 43°53N 111°40W **122** F7
Teton → *Idaho, U.S.A.* 43°54N 111°51W **122** F7
Teton → *Mont., U.S.A.* 47°56N 110°31W **123** C7
Teton County ☆ *Idaho, U.S.A.* 43°55N 111°5W **122** F7
Teton County ☆ *Mont., U.S.A.* 47°52N 112°20W **123** C5
Teton County ☆ *Wyo., U.S.A.* 44°0N 110°30W **124** C2
Teton Pass *Wyo., U.S.A.* 43°30N 110°57W **124** C2
Teton Range *Wyo., U.S.A.* 43°45N 111°0W **124** C2
Teton Village *Wyo., U.S.A.* 43°35N 110°51W **124** C2
Tetonia *Idaho, U.S.A.* 43°49N 111°10W **122** F7
Tetrahedron Park △ *B.C., Canada* 49°36N 123°35W **155** F11
Tetu L. *Ont., Canada* 50°11N 95°2W **148** B1
Teuhtli, Volcan *Distrito Federal, Mexico* 19°14N 99°2W **181** C3
Teúl de González Ortega *Zacatecas, Mexico* 21°28N 103°29W **173** F7
Teulon *Man., Canada* 50°23N 97°16W **151** E14
Teutopolis *Ill., U.S.A.* 39°8N 88°29W **84** D5
Tewaukon, L. *N. Dak., U.S.A.* 46°0N 97°22W **76** E8
Tewksbury *Mass., U.S.A.* 42°37N 71°14W **91** B3
Texada I. *B.C., Canada* 49°40N 124°25W **154** F10
Texana, L. *Tex., U.S.A.* 29°0N 96°35W **109** J11
Texarkana *Ark., U.S.A.* 33°26N 94°2W **106** E1
Texarkana *Tex., U.S.A.* 33°26N 94°3W **109** D13
Texas □ *U.S.A.* 31°40N 98°30W **109** F9
Texas City *Tex., U.S.A.* 29°24N 94°54W **109** H13

Texas County ☆ *Mo., U.S.A.* 37°20N 92°0W **83** D5
Texas County ☆ *Okla., U.S.A.* 36°45N 101°30W **107** B2
Texas Point Nat. Wildlife Refuge △ *Tex., U.S.A.* 29°42N 93°54W **109** H14
Texcaltitlán *México, Mexico* 18°54N 99°59W **175** D8
Texcoco *Chihuahua, Mexico* 28°6N 104°20W **169** E11
Texcoco *México, Mexico* 19°31N 98°53W **175** C9
Texcoco, L. de *México, Mexico* 19°30N 99°0W **181** B3
Texhoma *Okla., U.S.A.* 36°30N 101°47W **107** B2
Texhuacán *Veracruz, Mexico* 18°37N 97°2W **177** F3
Texico *N. Mex., U.S.A.* 34°24N 103°3W **131** C7
Texline *Tex., U.S.A.* 36°23N 103°2W **108** A4
Texola *Okla., U.S.A.* 35°12N 99°59W **107** C4
Texoma, L. *Tex., U.S.A.* 33°50N 96°34W **109** D11
Texon *Tex., U.S.A.* 31°13N 101°42W **108** F6
Teya *Yucatán, Mexico* 21°5N 89°6W **179** A4
Teyra, Pico de *Zacatecas, Mexico* 24°35N 102°11W **173** C8
Teziutlán *Puebla, Mexico* 19°49N 97°21W **176** E3
Tezoatlán de Segura y Luna *Oaxaca, Mexico* 17°39N 97°48W **177** G3
Tezonapa *Veracruz, Mexico* 18°35N 96°42W **177** F4
Tezontepec *Hidalgo, Mexico* 20°12N 99°6W **175** B8
Tha-anne → *Nunavut, Canada* 60°31N 94°37W **159** E7
Thackerville *Okla., U.S.A.* 33°48N 97°9W **107** E6
Thalia *Tex., U.S.A.* 33°59N 99°32W **109** D8
Thalmann *Ga., U.S.A.* 31°18N 81°41W **113** E5
Thames → *Ont., Canada* 42°20N 82°25W **146** E4
Thames → *Conn., U.S.A.* 41°18N 72°5W **91** C2
Thamesford *Ont., Canada* 43°4N 81°0W **146** D3
Thamesville *Ont., Canada* 42°33N 81°59W **146** E5
Thatcher *Ariz., U.S.A.* 32°51N 109°46W **130** E5
Thatcher *Colo., U.S.A.* 37°33N 104°7W **125** E6
Thawville *Ill., U.S.A.* 40°41N 88°7W **84** C5
Thaxton *Miss., U.S.A.* 34°18N 89°11W **111** B4
Thayer *Kans., U.S.A.* 37°29N 95°28W **82** D8
Thayer *Mo., U.S.A.* 36°31N 91°33W **83** E51
Thayer *Nebr., U.S.A.* 40°58N 97°30W **80** D8
Thayer County ☆ *Nebr., U.S.A.* 40°15N 97°40W **80** D8
Thayne *Wyo., U.S.A.* 42°55N 111°0W **124** D2
The Everglades *Fla., U.S.A.* 25°50N 81°0W **114** F8
The Glebe *Ont., Canada* 45°24N 75°41W **160** B1
The Pas *Man., Canada* 53°45N 101°15W **151** B10
Thebes *Ill., U.S.A.* 37°13N 89°28W **84** F4
Thedford *Nebr., U.S.A.* 41°59N 100°35W **80** C5
Thelon → *Canada* 64°16N 96°4W **159** E6
Theodore *Sask., Canada* 51°26N 102°55W **150** D9
Theodore *Ala., U.S.A.* 30°33N 88°11W **112** F2
Theodore Roosevelt L. *Ariz., U.S.A.* 33°40N 111°10W **130** D4
Theodore Roosevelt Nat. Park △ *N. Dak., U.S.A.* 47°0N 103°25W **76** D2
Theodore Wirth Regional Park △ *Minn., U.S.A.* 44°59N 93°19W **94** B2
Theodosia *Mo., U.S.A.* 36°35N 92°39W **83** E4
Theresa *N.Y., U.S.A.* 44°13N 75°48W **88** A5
Theressa *Fla., U.S.A.* 29°50N 82°4W **114** B6
Theriot *La., U.S.A.* 29°28N 90°45W **110** E5
Therma = Eagle Nest *N. Mex., U.S.A.* 36°33N 105°16W **131** A5
Thermal *Calif., U.S.A.* 33°39N 116°9W **127** K10
Thermalito *Calif., U.S.A.* 39°31N 121°36W **126** D5
Thermopolis *Wyo., U.S.A.* 43°39N 108°13W **124** C4
Thesiger B. *N.W.T., Canada* 71°30N 124°5W **156** B8
Thessalon *Ont., Canada* 46°20N 83°30W **146** A3
Thetford Mines *Qué., Canada* 46°8N 71°18W **145** E11
Thévet, L. *Qué., Canada* 51°50N 64°12W **140** A8
Thibodaux *La., U.S.A.* 29°48N 90°49W **110** E5
Thief → *Minn., U.S.A.* 48°7N 96°10W **77** B2
Thief L. *Minn., U.S.A.* 48°30N 95°54W **77** B2
Thief River Falls *Minn., U.S.A.* 48°7N 96°10W **77** B2
Thielsen, Mt. *Oreg., U.S.A.* 43°9N 122°4W **121** D3
Thirtymile Cr. → *N. Dak., U.S.A.* 46°22N 102°4W **76** D3
Thistle *Utah, U.S.A.* 39°59N 111°30W **129** D4
Thistletown *Ont., Canada* 43°44N 79°34W **161** A1
Thlewiaza → *Nunavut, Canada* 60°29N 94°4C W **159** E7
Thoa → *N.W.T., Canada* 60°31N 109°47W **157** D11
Thomas *Md., U.S.A.* 38°36N 76°18W **93** B4
Thomas *Okla., U.S.A.* 35°45N 98°45W **107** C5
Thomas *W. Va., U.S.A.* 39°9N 79°30W **93** A1
Thomas A. Edison, L. *Calif., U.S.A.* 37°25N 119°0W **127** F7
Thomas County ☆ *Ga., U.S.A.* 30°50N 83°55W **113** F3
Thomas County ☆ *Kans., U.S.A.* 39°20N 101°0W **82** B2
Thomas County ☆ *Nebr., U.S.A.* 41°50N 100°30W **80** C5
Thomas Hill Res. *Mo., U.S.A.* 39°34N 92°33W **83** B4
Thomas Hubbard, C. *N.W.T., Canada* 82°0N 94°25W **158** A7
Thomasboro *Ill., U.S.A.* 40°15N 88°11W **84** C5
Thomaston *Ala., U.S.A.* 32°16N 87°38W **112** D3
Thomaston *Conn., U.S.A.* 41°41N 73°4W **91** C1
Thomaston *Ga., U.S.A.* 32°53N 84°20W **113** D2
Thomaston *Maine, U.S.A.* 44°5N 69°11W **90** D4
Thomaston *N.Y., U.S.A.* 40°47N 73°42W **97** B4
Thomastown *Miss., U.S.A.* 32°52N 89°40W **111** D4
Thompson *Man., Canada* 55°45N 97°52W **159** F6
Thompson *Iowa, U.S.A.* 43°22N 93°46W **81** B5
Thompson *N. Dak., U.S.A.* 47°47N 97°6W **76** D8
Thompson *Pa., U.S.A.* 41°52N 75°3⁴W **87** C7
Thompson → *B.C., Canada* 50°15N 121°24W **155** E13
Thompson → *Iowa, U.S.A.* 39°46N 93°37W **83** B3
Thompson, L. *S. Dak., U.S.A.* 44°15N 97°28W **76** F8
Thompson Falls *Mont., U.S.A.* 47°36N 115°21W **123** C2
Thompson L. *Maine, U.S.A.* 42°19N 70°59W **96** B3
Thompson Pk. *Calif., U.S.A.* 41°0N 123°2W **126** B3
Thompson Sound *B.C., Canada* 50°48N 126°1W **154** E8
Thompson Springs *Utah, U.S.A.* 38°58N 109°43W **129** E6
Thompsons Cr. → *Miss., U.S.A.* 31°10N 88°55W **111** E5
Thompsonville *Ill., U.S.A.* 37°55N 88°46W **84** F5
Thompsonville *Mich., U.S.A.* 44°31N 85°56W **79** E6
Thomson *Ga., U.S.A.* 33°28N 82°30W **113** C4
Thomson *Ill., U.S.A.* 41°58N 90°6W **84** B3
Thoreau *N. Mex., U.S.A.* 35°24N 108°13W **131** B2
Thorhild *Alta., Canada* 54°10N 113°7W **152** D7
Thorn *N. Dak., U.S.A.* 33°57N 89°6W **111** C4
Thornapple → *Mich., U.S.A.* 42°56N 85°28W **79** G6
Thornapple → *Wis., U.S.A.* 45°28N 91°16W **78** C2
Thornburg *Iowa, U.S.A.* 41°27N 92°20W **81** C8
Thornburg *Pa., U.S.A.* 40°26N 80°4W **98** B1
Thornburg *Va., U.S.A.* 38°8N 77°31W **92** C7
Thornburg Road *Nfld. & L., Canada* 47°35N 52°51W **142** E8
Thornbury *Ont., Canada* 44°34N 80°26W **146** C6
Thorncliffe *Ont., Canada* 43°42N 79°20W **161** A2
Thorndale *Tex., U.S.A.* 30°37N 97°12W **109** G10
Thornhill *Man., Canada* 49°12N 98°14W **151** F13
Thornhill *Ont., Canada* 43°48N 79°25W **161** A2

Thornhurst *Pa., U.S.A.* 41°11N 75°35W **92** A1
Thornton *Colo., U.S.A.* 39°52N 104°58W **134** A2
Thornton *Idaho, U.S.A.* 43°45N 111°51W **122** F7
Thornton *Iowa, U.S.A.* 42°57N 93°23W **81** C5
Thornton *Miss., U.S.A.* 33°5N 90°19W **111** C3
Thornton *Tex., U.S.A.* 31°25N 96°34W **109** F11
Thornton *Wash., U.S.A.* 47°7N 117°23W **120** C8
Thorntown *Ind., U.S.A.* 40°8N 86°36W **85** C4
Thornville *Ohio, U.S.A.* 39°54N 82°25W **86** D4
Thorny *Mt. Mo., U.S.A.* 37°6N 91°10W **83** D5
Thorold *Ont., Canada* 43°7N 79°12W **146** D7
Thorp *Wash., U.S.A.* 47°4N 120°40W **120** C5
Thorp *Wis., U.S.A.* 44°58N 90°48W **78** B3
Thorsby *Alta., Canada* 53°14N 114°3W **152** E6
Thorsby *Ala., U.S.A.* 32°55N 86°43W **112** D4
Thousand Hills State Park △ *Mo., U.S.A.* 40°11N 92°39W **83** A4
Thousand Islands *N.Y., U.S.A.* 44°20N 76°0W **88** A4
Thousand Oaks *Calif., U.S.A.* 34°10N 118°50W **127** J8
Thousand Springs Cr. → *U.S.A.* 41°17N 113°51W **129** B2
Thrall *Tex., U.S.A.* 30°35N 97°18W **109** G10
Three Creek *Idaho, U.S.A.* 42°4N 115°10W **122** G3
Three Forks *Mont., U.S.A.* 45°54N 111°33W **123** E6
Three Hills *Alta., Canada* 51°43N 113°15W **153** G7
Three Lakes *Wis., U.S.A.* 45°48N 89°10W **78** C4
Three Mile Plains *N.S., Canada* 44°58N 64°7W **141** J5
Three Oaks *Mich., U.S.A.* 41°48N 86°36W **79** H5
Three Rivers *Calif., U.S.A.* 36°26N 118°54W **127** G8
Three Rivers *Mich., U.S.A.* 41°57N 85°38W **79** H6
Three Rivers *N. Mex., U.S.A.* 33°19N 106°5W **131** D4
Throckmorton *Tex., U.S.A.* 33°11N 99°11W **109** D8
Throckmorton County ☆ *Tex., U.S.A.* 33°10N 99°10W **109** D8
Throgs Neck *N.Y., U.S.A.* 40°48N 73°49W **97** B4
Thudaka Peak *B.C., Canada* 57°56N 126°51W **157** E7
Thule = Qaanaaq *Greenland* 77°40N 69°0W **162** B4
Thule Air Base = Uummannaq *Greenland* 77°28N 69°13W **162** B4
Thunder B. *Mich., U.S.A.* 45°0N 83°20W **79** E8
Thunder Basin Nat. Grassland *Wyo., U.S.A.* 43°45N 105°5W **124** C7
Thunder Bay *Ont., Canada* 48°20N 89°15W **148** D7
Thunder Butte *S. Dak., U.S.A.* 45°19N 101°53W **76** E4
Thunder Cr. → *Sask., Canada* 50°23N 105°32W **150** E6
Thunder Hawk *S. Dak., U.S.A.* 45°56N 101°58W **76** E4
Thunderbird, L. *Okla., U.S.A.* 35°14N 97°18W **107** C6
Thunderbird Park *Ariz., U.S.A.* 33°41N 112°11W **134** A1
Thunderbolt *Ga., U.S.A.* 32°3N 81°4W **113** D5
Thunderhead, L. *Mo., U.S.A.* 40°30N 93°1W **83** A3
Thurman *Iowa, U.S.A.* 40°49N 95°45W **81** E3
Thurmont *Md., U.S.A.* 39°37N 77°25W **93** A3
Thurso *Qué., Canada* 45°36N 75°15W **144** F7
Thurston *Nebr., U.S.A.* 42°11N 96°42W **80** B9
Thurston County ☆ *Nebr., U.S.A.* 42°15N 96°40W **80** B9
Thurston County ☆ *Wash., U.S.A.* 46°58N 122°59W **120** D3
Thutade L. *B.C., Canada* 57°0N 126°55W **157** E7
Tía Chena, Cerro *Nuevo León, Mexico* 26°7N 100°35W **170** D4
Tianguistenco *México, Mexico* 19°13N 99°28W **175** C8
Tianguistengo *Hidalgo, Mexico* 20°44N 98°38W **175** B9
Tibbie *Ala., U.S.A.* 31°22N 88°15W **112** E2
Tiber Res. *Mont., U.S.A.* 48°19N 111°6W **123** B6
Tibet, L. *Fla., U.S.A.* 28°27N 81°31W **115** B1
Tiburon *Calif., U.S.A.* 37°52N 122°27W **132** A2
Tiburón, Cerro el *Sinaloa, Mexico* 24°19N 106°56W **172** C4
Tiburón, I. *Sonora, Mexico* 29°0N 112°25W **168** D3
Ticaboo *Utah, U.S.A.* 37°40N 110°42W **129** F5
Tice *Fla., U.S.A.* 26°40N 81°49W **114** E7
Tichnor *Ark., U.S.A.* 34°8N 91°16W **106** D4
Tickfaw *La., U.S.A.* 30°21N 90°28W **110** D5
Ticomán *Distrito Federal, Mexico* 19°31N 99°8W **181** A3
Ticonderoga *N.Y., U.S.A.* 43°51N 73°26W **89** C1
Ticul *Yucatán, Mexico* 20°24N 89°32W **179** B4
Tide Head *N.B., Canada* 47°59N 66°47W **141** F3
Tidewater *Oreg., U.S.A.* 37°51N 76°42W **93** G4
Tidioute *Pa., U.S.A.* 41°41N 79°24W **87** C3
Tidmore = Seminole *Okla., U.S.A.* 35°14N 96°41W **107** C7
Tidnish *N.S., Canada* 45°59N 64°1W **141** H5
Tie Plant *Miss., U.S.A.* 33°44N 89°47W **111** C4
Tie Siding *Wyo., U.S.A.* 41°5N 105°30W **124** E7
Tierra Amarilla *N. Mex., U.S.A.* 36°42N 106°33W **131** A4
Tierra Blanca *Guanajuato, Mexico* 21°7N 100°57W **175** A7
Tierra Blanca *Veracruz, Mexico* 18°27N 96°21W **177** F4
Tierra Blanca Cr. → *Tex., U.S.A.* 34°58N 101°55W **108** C6
Tierra Colorada *Guerrero, Mexico* 17°11N 99°32W **175** E8
Tierra Nueva *San Luis Potosí, Mexico* 21°40N 100°35W **171** J4
Tierra Verde *Tampa, U.S.A.* 27°41N 82°43W **115** C2
Tierrasanta *Calif., U.S.A.* 32°49N 117°6W **133** B2
Tieton *Wash., U.S.A.* 46°42N 120°46W **120** D5
Tiffany *Colo., U.S.A.* 37°2N 107°33W **125** E3
Tiffin *Iowa, U.S.A.* 41°42N 91°40W **81** D7
Tiffin *Ohio, U.S.A.* 41°7N 83°11W **86** B3
Tiffin → *Ohio, U.S.A.* 41°17N 84°23W **86** B2
Tift County ☆ *Ga., U.S.A.* 31°30N 83°30W **113** E3
Tifton *Ga., U.S.A.* 31°27N 83°31W **113** E3
Tigalda I. *Alaska, U.S.A.* 54°6N 165°5W **135** J6
Tigard *Oreg., U.S.A.* 45°26N 122°46W **132** B1
Tiger *Wash., U.S.A.* 48°42N 117°24W **120** B8
Tignall *Ga., U.S.A.* 33°52N 82°44W **113** C4
Tignish *P.E.I., Canada* 46°58N 64°2W **141** G5
Tihuatlán *Veracruz, Mexico* 20°43N 97°32W **176** D3
Tijeras *N. Mex., U.S.A.* 35°5N 106°23W **131** B4
Tijuana *Baja Calif., Mexico* 32°32N 117°1W **166** A1
Tijuana → *Calif., U.S.A.* 32°33N 117°6W **133** C2
Tijuana ✈ (TIJ) *Baja Calif., Mexico* 32°30N 116°58W **166** A2
Tikal *Guatemala* 17°13N 89°24W **182** C2
Tikchik Lakes *Alaska, U.S.A.* 60°0N 159°0W **135** G8
Tikirarjuaq = Whale Cove *Nunavut, Canada* 62°10N 92°34W **159** E7
Tilapa *Puebla, Mexico* 18°35N 98°33W **177** F2
Tilbury *Ont., Canada* 42°17N 82°26W **146** E4
Tilden *Ill., U.S.A.* 38°13N 89°41W **84** E4
Tilden *Nebr., U.S.A.* 42°3N 97°50W **80** B8
Tilden *Tex., U.S.A.* 28°28N 98°33W **109** J9
Tilghman *Md., U.S.A.* 38°43N 76°20W **93** B4
Tiline *Ky., U.S.A.* 37°11N 88°15W **104** C4
Tillamook *Oreg., U.S.A.* 45°27N 123°51W **121** B2
Tillamook B. *Oreg., U.S.A.* 45°30N 123°53W **121** B2
Tillamook County ☆ *Oreg., U.S.A.* 45°20N 123°45W **121** B2
Tillamook Head *Oreg., U.S.A.* 45°57N 123°58W **121** B1
Tillar *Ark., U.S.A.* 33°41N 91°27W **106** E4
Tiller *Oreg., U.S.A.* 42°56N 122°57W **121** E3
Tillery, L. *N.C., U.S.A.* 35°12N 80°4W **103** C5

Tilley *Alta., Canada* 50°27N 111°39W **153** H9
Tillman County ☆ *Okla., U.S.A.* 34°25N 99°0W **107** D4
Tillmans Corner *Ala., U.S.A.* 30°46N 88°8W **112** F2
Tillsonburg *Ont., Canada* 42°53N 80°44W **146** E6
Tilston *Man., Canada* 49°23N 101°19W **151** F10
Tilton *Calif., U.S.A.* 34°40N 84°56W **113** B2
Tilton *Ill., U.S.A.* 40°6N 87°38W **84** C6
Tilton *N.H., U.S.A.* 43°27N 71°36W **89** C3
Tilzapotla *Morelos, Mexico* 18°30N 99°16W **175** D8
Timagami, L. *Ont., Canada* 47°0N 80°10W **144** E2
Timbalier B. *La., U.S.A.* 29°3N 90°20W **110** E5
Timbalier I. *La., U.S.A.* 29°3N 90°28W **110** E5
Timber Lake *S. Dak., U.S.A.* 45°26N 101°5W **76** E4
Timberlea *N.S., Canada* 44°40N 63°45W **141** J6
Timberville *Va., U.S.A.* 38°38N 78°46W **102** C6
Timbo *Ark., U.S.A.* 35°52N 92°19W **106** C3
Timiskaming, L. = Témiscamingue, L. *Qué., Canada* 47°10N 79°25W **144** D3
Timken *Kans., U.S.A.* 38°29N 99°11W **82** C4
Timken Wildlife Management Area *La., U.S.A.* 29°48N 90°12W **117** D1
Timmins *Ont., Canada* 48°28N 81°25W **144** C1
Timmonsville *S.C., U.S.A.* 34°8N 79°57W **103** D6
Timms Hill *Wis., U.S.A.* 45°27N 90°12W **78** C3
Timnath *Colo., U.S.A.* 40°32N 104°59W **125** B6
Timpas *Colo., U.S.A.* 37°49N 103°46W **125** E7
Timpson *Tex., U.S.A.* 31°54N 94°24W **109** F13
Tims Ford L. *Tenn., U.S.A.* 35°15N 86°10W **104** E3
Timucuan Ecological and Historical Preserve △ *Fla., U.S.A.* 30°28N 81°27W **114** A7
Timucuy *Yucatán, Mexico* 20°49N 89°31W **179** B4
Tin Mt. *Calif., U.S.A.* 36°50N 117°10W **127** G9
Tina *Mo., U.S.A.* 39°32N 93°27W **83** B3
Tindall *Mo., U.S.A.* 40°10N 93°36W **83** A3
Tinemaha Res. *Calif., U.S.A.* 37°3N 118°13W **127** F8
Tingley *Iowa, U.S.A.* 40°51N 94°12W **81** E4
Tingmerkpuk Mt. *Alaska, U.S.A.* 68°34N 162°28W **135** B7
Tingüindín *Michoacan, Mexico* 19°45N 102°29W **174** C5
Tinmouth *Vt., U.S.A.* 43°26N 73°4W **89** C1
Tinnie *N. Mex., U.S.A.* 33°22N 105°14W **131** D5
Tinsley *Miss., U.S.A.* 32°44N 90°28W **111** D3
Tinsman *Ark., U.S.A.* 33°38N 92°21W **106** E3
Tintagel *B.C., Canada* 54°12N 125°35W **154** A9
Tintah *Minn., U.S.A.* 46°1N 96°19W **77** D2
Tintero, Presa el *Chihuahua, Mexico* 29°32N 107°42W **169** D8
Tinton Falls *N.J., U.S.A.* 40°18N 74°6W **92** D7
Tinum *Yucatán, Mexico* 20°46N 88°23W **179** B5
Tioga *N. Dak., U.S.A.* 48°24N 102°56W **76** B3
Tioga *Pa., U.S.A.* 41°55N 77°8W **87** C5
Tioga *Tex., U.S.A.* 33°28N 96°55W **109** D11
Tioga *W. Va., U.S.A.* 38°25N 80°40W **102** C4
Tioga County ☆ *N.Y., U.S.A.* 42°10N 76°20W **88** C4
Tioga County ☆ *Pa., U.S.A.* 41°50N 77°10W **87** C5
Tioga Pass *Calif., U.S.A.* 37°54N 119°15W **126** F7
Tionesta *Pa., U.S.A.* 41°30N 79°28W **87** C3
Tipler *Wis., U.S.A.* 45°55N 88°38W **78** C5
Tipp City *Ohio, U.S.A.* 39°58N 84°11W **86** D2
Tippah County ☆ *Miss., U.S.A.* 34°44N 88°57W **111** B5
Tippecanoe → *Ind., U.S.A.* 40°30N 86°45W **85** C4
Tippecanoe County ☆ *Ind., U.S.A.* 40°25N 86°55W **85** C4
Tipton *Calif., U.S.A.* 36°4N 119°19W **127** G7
Tipton *Ind., U.S.A.* 40°17N 86°2W **85** C4
Tipton *Iowa, U.S.A.* 41°46N 91°8W **81** D7
Tipton *Kans., U.S.A.* 39°21N 98°28W **82** B5
Tipton *Mo., U.S.A.* 38°39N 92°47W **83** C4
Tipton *Okla., U.S.A.* 34°30N 99°9W **107** D4
Tipton County ☆ *Ind., U.S.A.* 40°20N 86°5W **85** C4
Tipton County ☆ *Tenn., U.S.A.* 35°29N 89°43W **104** E3
Tipton Mt. *Ariz., U.S.A.* 35°32N 114°12W **130** B1
Tiptonville *Tenn., U.S.A.* 36°23N 89°29W **104** D31
Tiqua Indian Reservation *Tex., U.S.A.* 31°41N 106°19W **108** F1
Tiquicheo *Michoacan, Mexico* 18°53N 100°44W **175** D7
Tiquimul *Campeche, Mexico* 19°47N 90°13W **179** C3
Tisdale *Sask., Canada* 52°50N 104°0W **150** D7
Tishomingo *Miss., U.S.A.* 34°38N 88°14W **111** B5
Tishomingo *Okla., U.S.A.* 34°14N 96°41W **107** D7
Tishomingo County ☆ *Miss., U.S.A.* 34°49N 88°12W **111** B5
Tishomingo Nat. Wildlife Refuge △ *Okla., U.S.A.* 34°11N 96°39W **107** D7
Tiskilwa *Ill., U.S.A.* 41°18N 89°30W **84** B4
Titonka *Iowa, U.S.A.* 43°14N 94°3W **81** B4
Tittabawassee → *Mich., U.S.A.* 43°23N 83°59W **79** F8
Titus County ☆ *Tex., U.S.A.* 33°9N 94°58W **109** D13
Titusville *Fla., U.S.A.* 28°37N 80°49W **114** C8
Titusville *Pa., U.S.A.* 41°38N 79°41W **87** C3
Tiverton *N.S., Canada* 44°23N 66°13W **141** J3
Tiverton *Ont., Canada* 44°16N 81°32W **146** C5
Tiverton *R.I., U.S.A.* 41°38N 71°12W **91** C3
Tiverton Four Corners *R.I., U.S.A.* 41°34N 71°11W **91** C3
Tivoli *Tex., U.S.A.* 28°27N 96°53W **109** J11
Tixcacalcupul *Yucatán, Mexico* 20°32N 88°16W **179** B5
Tixcancal *Yucatán, Mexico* 21°3N 87°51W **179** A6
Tixkokob *Yucatán, Mexico* 21°0N 89°24W **179** B4
Tixmehuac *Yucatán, Mexico* 20°15N 89°6W **179** B4
Tixmul *Quintana Roo, Mexico* 19°26N 88°16W **179** C5
Tixtla *Guerrero, Mexico* 17°35N 99°26W **175** E8
Tixtlancoyan *Guerrero, Mexico* 17°35N 98°23W **177** G2
Tizapán *Distrito Federal, Mexico* 19°19N 99°13W **181** C2
Tizapán el Alto *Jalisco, Mexico* 20°10N 103°4W **174** B4
Tizayuca *Hidalgo, Mexico* 19°51N 99°9W **175** C8
Tizimín *Yucatán, Mexico* 21°9N 88°9W **179** A5
Tizupán *Michoacan, Mexico* 18°14N 103°7W **174** D4
Tlachichilco *Veracruz, Mexico* 20°38N 98°10W **176** D2
Tlachichuca *Puebla, Mexico* 19°7N 97°24W **177** E3
Tlacoachistlahuaca *Guerrero, Mexico* 16°50N 98°19W **175** F9
Tlacolula de Matamoros *Oaxaca, Mexico* 16°57N 96°29W **177** H4
Tlacotalpán *Veracruz, Mexico* 18°37N 95°40W **177** F4
Tlacotepec *Guerrero, Mexico* 17°46N 99°59W **175** E8
Tlacotepec *Puebla, Mexico* 18°38N 97°37W **177** F3
Tlacuapa *Guerrero, Mexico* 17°17N 98°45W **175** F10
Tláhuac *Distrito Federal, Mexico* 19°17N 99°0W **181** C3
Tláhuac, Parque *Distrito Federal, Mexico* 19°17N 99°2W **181** C3
Tlahualilo, Sa. de *Coahuila, Mexico* 26°7N 103°19W **170** D1
Tlahualilo de Zaragoza *Durango, Mexico* 26°7N 103°27W **173** A7
Tlahuelilpan *Hidalgo, Mexico* 20°8N 99°14W **175** B8
Tlajomulco de Zúñiga *Jalisco, Mexico* 20°28N 103°27W **180** C1
Tlalchapa *Guerrero, Mexico* 18°24N 100°28W **175** D7
Tlalixcoyan *Guerrero, Mexico* 18°24N 100°28W **175** D7
Tlalixtaquilla *Guerrero, Mexico* 17°35N 98°23W **177** G2
Tlalnepantla *México, Mexico* 19°32N 99°11W **181** A2
Tlalnepantla → *Distrito Federal, Mexico* 19°30N 99°18W **181** A2

Tlalpan *Distrit. Federal, Mexico* 19°18N 99°10W **181** C2
Tlalpujahua *Michoacan, Mexico* 19°48N 100°10W **175** C7
Tlaltenango de Sánchez Román *Zacatecas, Mexico* 21°47N 103°19W **173** F7
Tlaltizapán *Morelos, Mexico* 18°41N 99°7W **175** D8
Tlalmanalco *México, Mexico* 19°12N 98°50W **175** C9
Tlanalapa *Hidalgo, Mexico* 19°49N 98°36W **175** C9
Tlanchinol *Hidalgo, Mexico* 21°0N 98°39W **175** B9
Tlapa de Comonfort *Guerrero, Mexico* 17°33N 98°33W **175** E9
Tlapacoyan *Veracruz, Mexico* 19°58N 97°13W **176** E3
Tlapaneco → *Guerrero, Mexico* 17°55N 98°48W **175** E9
Tlapehuala *Guerrero, Mexico* 18°13N 100°31W **175** D7
Tlaquepaque *Jalisco, Mexico* 20°39N 103°19W **180** B1
Tlatlauquitepec *Puebla, Mexico* 19°51N 97°29W **176** E3
Tlatlaya *México, Mexico* 18°31N 100°15W **175** D7
Tlaxcala *Tlaxcala, Mexico* 19°19N 98°14W **175** C9
Tlaxcala □ *Mexico* 19°37N 98°7W **175** C9
Tlaxco *Tlaxcala, Mexico* 19°37N 98°7W **175** C9
Tlaxiaco *Oaxaca, Mexico* 17°25N 97°35W **177** G3
Tlayacapan *Morelos, Mexico* 18°59N 98°59W **175** D9
Tlell *B.C., Canada* 53°34N 131°56W **154** B3
Toad → *B.C., Canada* 59°25N 124°57W **157** E8
Toad River *B.C., Canada* 58°51N 125°14W **157** E7
Toana Range *Nev., U.S.A.* 40°50N 114°20W **128** B6
Toano *Va., U.S.A.* 37°23N 76°48W **102** D8
Toast *N.C., U.S.A.* 36°30N 80°38W **103** B5
Toba Inlet *B.C., Canada* 50°25N 124°35W **154** E10
Tobago *Trin. & Tob.* 11°10N 60°30W **183** D7
Tobermory *Ont., Canada* 45°12N 81°40W **146** B5
Tobias *Nebr., U.S.A.* 40°25N 97°20W **80** D8
Tobin, Mt. *Nev., U.S.A.* 40°23N 117°31W **128** B3
Tobin L. *Sask., Canada* 53°35N 103°30W **150** B8
Tobin Range *Nev., U.S.A.* 40°20N 117°30W **128** B3
Tobique → *N.B., Canada* 46°46N 67°42W **141** G2
Toby Creek → *B.C., Canada* 50°20N 116°25W **155** E18
Tobyhanna → *Pa., U.S.A.* 41°11N 75°25W **92** A1
Toccoa *Ga., U.S.A.* 34°35N 83°19W **113** B3
Toccopola *Miss., U.S.A.* 34°15N 89°14W **111** B4
Tochapán *Puebla, Mexico* 18°55N 97°38W **177** F3
Tochtepec *Puebla, Mexico* 18°50N 97°50W **177** F3
Toco Hills *Georgia, U.S.A.* 33°49N 84°20W **117** B2
Tocumbo *Michoacan, Mexico* 19°42N 102°32W **174** C5
Todd County ☆ *Ky., U.S.A.* 36°50N 87°10W **104** D5
Todd County ☆ *Minn., U.S.A.* 46°10N 94°50W **77** D4
Todd County ☆ *S. Dak., U.S.A.* 43°5N 101°0W **76** G5
Toddville *Md., U.S.A.* 38°18N 76°4W **93** B4
Todos Santos *Baja Calif. S., Mexico* 23°26N 110°13W **167** K8
Todos Santos, B. *Baja Calif., Mexico* 31°48N 116°42W **166** B2
Todos Santos, I. de *Baja Calif., Mexico* 31°48N 116°48W **166** B2
Todt Hill *N.Y., U.S.A.* 40°36N 74°6W **97** C2
Tofield *Alta., Canada* 53°25N 112°40W **152** E8
Tofino *B.C., Canada* 49°11N 125°55W **154** F9
Tofte *Minn., U.S.A.* 47°35N 90°50W **77** C8
Togiak *Alaska, U.S.A.* 59°4N 160°24W **135** G7
Togiak Nat. Wildlife Refuge △ *Alaska, U.S.A.* 59°20N 160°15W **135** G7
Togo *Sask., Canada* 51°24N 101°35W **151** D10
Togowatee Pass *Wyo., U.S.A.* 43°45N 110°4W **124** C2
Tohatchi *N. Mex., U.S.A.* 35°52N 108°47W **131** B2
Tohono O'odam Indian Reservation *Ariz., U.S.A.* 32°15N 112°0W **130** E4
Tohopekaliga, East L. *Fla., U.S.A.* 28°18N 81°15W **114** C7
Tohopekaliga, L. *Fla., U.S.A.* 28°12N 81°24W **114** C7
Toiyabe Range *Nev., U.S.A.* 39°30N 117°0W **128** C3
Tok *Alaska, U.S.A.* 63°20N 142°59W **135** E12
Tokeland *Wash., U.S.A.* 46°42N 123°59W **120** D2
Tokio, Parque Natural △ *Coahuila, Mexico* 24°50N 100°52W **171** F4
Toksook Ba. *Alaska, U.S.A.* 60°32N 165°0W **135** F6
Tolageak *Alaska, U.S.A.* 70°3N 162°27W **135** A7
Tolar *N. Mex., U.S.A.* 34°27N 103°56W **131** C7
Tolbert *Tex., U.S.A.* 34°13N 99°24W **109** C8
Tolchester Beach *Md., U.S.A.* 39°13N 76°14W **93** A4
Toledo *Ill., U.S.A.* 39°16N 88°15W **84** D5
Toledo *Iowa, U.S.A.* 42°0N 92°35W **81** C6
Toledo *Ohio, U.S.A.* 41°39N 83°33W **86** B3
Toledo *Oreg., U.S.A.* 44°37N 123°56W **121** C2
Toledo *Wash., U.S.A.* 46°26N 122°51W **120** D3
Toledo Bend Res. *La., U.S.A.* 31°11N 93°34W **110** C2
Toledo Bend Reservoir Dam *La., U.S.A.* 31°12N 93°34W **110** C2
Tolimán *Jalisco, Mexico* 19°35N 103°57W **174** C4
Tolimán *Querétaro, Mexico* 20°53N 99°54W **175** B8
Tolland *Conn., U.S.A.* 41°52N 72°22W **91** C2
Tolland County ☆ *Conn., U.S.A.* 41°45N 72°20W **91** C2
Tollesboro *Ky., U.S.A.* 38°34N 83°34W **105** B9
Tolleson *Ariz., U.S.A.* 33°27N 112°15W **134** C1
Tolley *N. Dak., U.S.A.* 48°44N 101°50W **76** B4
Tolna *N. Dak., U.S.A.* 47°48N 98°26W **76** C7
Tolono *Ill., U.S.A.* 39°59N 88°16W **84** D5
Tolstoi *Man., Canada* 49°5N 96°49W **151** F15
Tolu *Ky., U.S.A.* 37°26N 88°15W **104** C4
Toluca *Méx., Mexico* 19°17N 99°40W **175** C8
Toluca *Ill., U.S.A.* 41°0N 89°8W **84** C4
Toluca, Volcán Nevado de *México, Mexico* 19°8N 99°44W **175** C8
Tom *Okla., U.S.A.* 33°44N 94°35W **107** E9
Tom Bass Regional Park △ *Tex., U.S.A.* 29°35N 95°22W **116** C2
Tom Green County ☆ *Tex., U.S.A.* 31°28N 100°26W **108** F7
Tom Steed Res. *Okla., U.S.A.* 34°46N 98°50W **107** D5
Tomah *Wis., U.S.A.* 43°59N 90°30W **78** E3
Tomahawk *Wis., U.S.A.* 45°28N 89°44W **78** C41
Tomahawk *Oreg., U.S.A.* 45°36N 122°39W **94** E2
Tomales *Calif., U.S.A.* 38°14N 122°59W **126** E4
Tomás Garrido *Quintana Roo, Mexico* 18°1N 89°4W **179** D4
Tomatlán *Jalisco, Mexico* 19°56N 105°15W **174** C2
Tomball *Tex., U.S.A.* 30°6N 95°37W **109** G12
Tombigbee → *Ala., U.S.A.* 31°8N 87°57W **112** B3
Tombigbee Nat. Forest *Miss., U.S.A.* 33°56N 88°56W **111** C5
Tombstone *Ariz., U.S.A.* 31°43N 110°4W **130** F5
Tome *N. Mex., U.S.A.* 34°44N 106°44W **131** C4
Tomichi → *Colo., U.S.A.* 38°31N 106°58W **125** D4
Tomiko L. *Ont., Canada* 46°32N 79°49W **146** A7
Tommy Thompson Park *Ont., Canada* 43°38N 79°20W **161** B3
Tomochic *Chihuahua, Mexico* 28°22N 107°51W **169** E8
Tomochic → *Chihuahua, Mexico* 28°28N 107°50W **169** E8
Tompkins *Sask., Canada* 50°4N 108°47W **150** E3
Tompkins County ☆ *N.Y., U.S.A.* 42°30N 76°30W **88** C4
Tompkinsville *Ky., U.S.A.* 36°42N 85°41W **105** D7
Tompkinsville *Md., U.S.A.* 38°18N 76°54W **93** B4
Toms → *Ala., U.S.A.* 39°57N 74°7W **92** C2
Toms Brook *Va., U.S.A.* 38°57N 78°26W **93** B2
Toms River *N.J., U.S.A.* 39°58N 74°12W **92** C2
Tonalá *Chiapas, Mexico* 16°4N 93°45W **178** D3
Tonalá *Jalisco, Mexico* 20°37N 103°14W **180** B2
Tonalea *Ariz., U.S.A.* 36°17N 110°56W **130** A5

Tonasket *Wash., U.S.A.* 48°42N 119°26W **120** B6
Tonatico *México, Mexico* 18°48N 99°40W **175** D8
Tonawanda *N.Y., U.S.A.* 43°1N 78°53W **88** B2
Tonawanda Indian Reservation *N.Y., U.S.A.* 43°5N 78°25W **88** B2
Tonaya *Jalisco, Mexico* 19°51N 103°58W **174** C4
Tonganoxie *Kans., U.S.A.* 39°7N 95°5W **82** B8
Tongass Nat. Forest *Alaska, U.S.A.* 54°45N 133°0W **135** J14
Tongue → *Mont., U.S.A.* 46°25N 105°52W **123** D12
Tongue → *N. Dak., U.S.A.* 48°5N 96°48W **76** B8
Tongue River Res. *Mont., U.S.A.* 45°8N 106°46W **123** E11
Tonica *Ill., U.S.A.* 41°13N 89°4W **84** B4
Tonila *Jalisco, Mexico* 19°26N 103°31W **174** C4
Toniná *Chiapas, Mexico* 16°53N 91°57W **178** C5
Tonina, Boca la *Sinaloa, Mexico* 24°34N 107°57W **172** C3
Tonkawa *Okla., U.S.A.* 36°41N 97°18W **107** B6
Tonopah *Ariz., U.S.A.* 33°30N 112°56W **130** D3
Tonopah *Nev., U.S.A.* 38°4N 117°14W **128** D3
Tonosí *Panama* 7°20N 80°20W **182** E3
Tonsina *Alaska, U.S.A.* 61°39N 145°11W **135** F11
Tonto Cr. → *Ariz., U.S.A.* 33°45N 111°10W **130** D4
Tonto Nat. Forest *Ariz., U.S.A.* 34°0N 111°20W **130** D4
Tonto Nat. Monument △ *Ariz., U.S.A.* 33°39N 111°7W **130** D4
Tony *Wis., U.S.A.* 45°29N 91°0W **78** C3
Tooele *Utah, U.S.A.* 40°32N 112°18W **129** C3
Tooele County ☆ *Utah, U.S.A.* 40°25N 113°0W **129** C3
Toole County ☆ *Mont., U.S.A.* 48°48N 111°50W **123** B6
Toombs County ☆ *Ga., U.S.A.* 32°10N 82°15W **113** D4
Toone *Tenn., U.S.A.* 35°21N 88°57W **104** E4
Top of the World Park △ *B.C., Canada* 49°51N 115°35W **153** J5
Topanga State Park △ *Calif., U.S.A.* 34°7N 118°31W **133** B1
Topawa *Ariz., U.S.A.* 31°48N 111°51W **130** F4
Topaz L. *Nev., U.S.A.* 38°41N 119°33W **128** D1
Topeka *Ind., U.S.A.* 41°32N 85°32W **85** B5
Topeka *Kans., U.S.A.* 39°3N 95°40W **82** B8
Topia *Durango, Mexico* 25°13N 106°34W **172** B4
Topock *Calif., U.S.A.* 34°46N 114°29W **130** C1
Topolobampo *Sinaloa, Mexico* 25°36N 109°3W **172** B1
Topolobampo, B. de *Sinaloa, Mexico* 25°37N 109°1W **172** B1
Toponas *Colo., U.S.A.* 40°4N 106°48W **125** B4
Toppenish *Wash., U.S.A.* 46°23N 120°19W **120** D5
Topsfield *Maine, U.S.A.* 45°25N 67°44W **90** C6
Topsfield *Mass., U.S.A.* 42°38N 70°57W **91** B4
Topton *Pa., U.S.A.* 40°30N 75°42W **92** B1
Toquerville *Utah, U.S.A.* 37°15N 113°17W **129** F2
Toquima Range *Nev., U.S.A.* 38°55N 116°50W **128** D4
Torbay *Nfld. & L., Canada* 47°40N 52°42W **142** E8
Torch → *Sask., Canada* 53°50N 103°5W **150** B8
Torch L. *Mich., U.S.A.* 45°0N 85°18W **79** E6
Tordilla, Sa. *Sonora, Mexico* 29°45N 112°30W **168** B3
Tordo, Barra el *Tamaulipas, Mexico* 23°4N 97°45W **171** G7
Torngat Mts. *Nfld. & L., Canada* 59°0N 63°40W **143** B5
Tornillo *Tex., U.S.A.* 31°27N 106°5W **108** F1
Toro, I. el *Veracruz, Mexico* 21°35N 97°29W **176** C3
Toro *Sask., Canada* 50°50N 103°33W **130** D4
Toronto *Ont., Canada* 43°39N 79°20W **161** B2
Toronto *Iowa, U.S.A.* 41°54N 90°52W **81** D8
Toronto *Kans., U.S.A.* 37°48N 95°57W **82** D8
Toronto *Ohio, U.S.A.* 40°28N 80°36W **86** C6
Toronto *S. Dak., U.S.A.* 44°34N 96°39W **76** F9
Toronto, Univ. of *Ont., Canada* 43°39N 79°23W **161** B2
Toronto City Centre ✈ (YTZ) *Ont., Canada* 43°38N 79°24W **161** B2
Toronto Harbour *Ont., Canada* 43°38N 79°21W **161** B2
Toronto Is. *Ont., Canada* 43°37N 79°23W **161** B2
Toronto Lake *Kans., U.S.A.* 37°46N 95°57W **82** D8
Toronto Lester B. Pearson Int. ✈ (YYZ) *Ont., Canada* 43°46N 79°35W **161** A1
Torquay *Sask., Canada* 49°9N 103°30W **150** F8
Torrance *Calif., U.S.A.* 33°50N 118°20W **127** K8
Torrance County ☆ *N. Mex., U.S.A.* 34°40N 106°0W **131** C5
Torreón *Coahuila, Mexico* 25°33N 103°26W **170** E1
Torreon *N. Mex., U.S.A.* 35°48N 107°13W **131** B3
Torreón de Mata *Chihuahua, Mexico* 26°48N 105°25W **169** G10
Torres Martinez Indian Reservation *Calif., U.S.A.* 33°29N 116°5W **127** K10
Torrey *Utah, U.S.A.* 38°18N 111°25W **129** E4
Torrington *Alta., Canada* 51°48N 113°35W **153** G7
Torrington *Conn., U.S.A.* 41°48N 73°7W **91** C1
Torrington *Wyo., U.S.A.* 42°4N 104°11W **124** D8
Tortilla Flat *Ariz., U.S.A.* 33°32N 111°23W **130** D4
Tortola *Br. Virgin Is.* 18°19N 64°45W **184** G18
Tortue, Î. de la *Haiti* 20°5N 72°57W **183** B5
Tortuga, I. *Baja Calif. S., Mexico* 27°26N 111°52W **167** F7
Tortuga, I. la *Veracruz, Mexico* 22°20N 98°7W **176** B2
Tortugas, B. *Baja Calif. S., Mexico* 27°42N 114°53W **167** F4
Tortugas, Presa *Sinaloa, Mexico* 23°7N 105°53W **172** D5
Tortuguero, Parque Nac. △ *Costa Rica* 10°31N 83°29W **182** D3
Tosanachic *Chihuahua, Mexico* 28°33N 108°1W **169** E7
Toston *Mont., U.S.A.* 46°11N 111°26W **123** D6
Totatiche *Jalisco, Mexico* 21°56N 103°27W **173** F7
Totoltepec *Puebla, Mexico* 18°14N 97°52W **177** F3
Totonicapán *Guatemala* 14°58N 91°12W **182** D1
Tototepec *Oaxaca, Mexico* 17°15N 96°2W **177** G4
Tototlán del Oro *Jalisco, Mexico* 20°7N 104°31W **174** B3
Totowa *N.J., U.S.A.* 40°54N 74°12W **97** A1
Tottenham *Ont., Canada* 44°1N 79°49W **146** C7
Touchet → *Wash., U.S.A.* 46°2N 118°40W **120** D7
Toughy *Nebr., U.S.A.* 41°8N 96°50W **80** C9
Toulnustouc → *Qué., Canada* 49°35N 68°24W **140** D1
Toulnustouc Nord-Est → *Qué., Canada* 50°56N 67°44W **140** C2
Toulon *Ill., U.S.A.* 41°6N 89°52W **84** B4
Tournament Players Club of Michigan *Mich., U.S.A.* 42°31N 83°12W **98** B3
Toutle → *Wash., U.S.A.* 46°19N 122°55W **120** D3
Towanda *Kans., U.S.A.* 37°48N 97°0W **82** D7
Towanda *Pa., U.S.A.* 41°46N 76°27W **87** C6
Towaoc *Colo., U.S.A.* 37°12N 108°44W **125** E2
Tower *Minn., U.S.A.* 47°48N 92°17W **77** C61
Tower City *N. Dak., U.S.A.* 46°56N 97°40W **76** D8
Tower City *Pa., U.S.A.* 40°35N 76°33W **87** D6
Tower Hill *Ill., U.S.A.* 39°23N 88°58W **84** D5
Tower Junction *Wyo., U.S.A.* 44°55N 110°25W **124** B2
Town Creek *Ala., U.S.A.* 34°41N 87°24W **112** B3
Towner *N. Dak., U.S.A.* 48°21N 100°25W **76** B5
Towner County ☆ *N. Dak., U.S.A.* 48°45N 99°0W **76** B6
Townley *N.J., U.S.A.* 40°41N 74°14W **97** B1
Towns *Ga., U.S.A.* 32°0N 82°45W **113** D4
Towns County ☆ *Ga., U.S.A.* 34°55N 83°45W **113** B3
Townsend *Del., U.S.A.* 39°24N 75°41W **93** A5
Townsend *Ga., U.S.A.* 31°33N 81°31W **113** E5

Townsend *Mass., U.S.A.* 42°40N 71°42W **91** B3
Townsend *Mont., U.S.A.* 46°19N 111°31W **123** D6
Townshend *Vt., U.S.A.* 43°3N 72°41W **89** C2
Townville *Pa., U.S.A.* 41°41N 79°53W **87** C3
Towson *Md., U.S.A.* 39°24N 76°36W **99** A2
Toxey *Ala., U.S.A.* 31°55N 88°19W **112** C2
Toyah *Tex., U.S.A.* 31°19N 103°48W **108** F4
Toyah → *Tex., U.S.A.* 31°18N 103°27W **108** F4
Toyah L. *Tex., U.S.A.* 31°15N 103°20W **108** F4
Toyahvale *Tex., U.S.A.* 30°57N 103°47W **108** G4
Tracadie-Sheila *N.B., Canada* 47°30N 64°55W **141** F5
Tracy *N.B., Canada* 45°41N 66°41W **141** H3
Tracy *Calif., U.S.A.* 37°44N 121°26W **126** E5
Tracy *Minn., U.S.A.* 44°14N 95°37W **77** F3
Tracy City *Tenn., U.S.A.* 35°16N 85°44W **105** E7
Tracyton *Wash., U.S.A.* 47°36N 122°39W **132** C2
Tradewater → *Ky., U.S.A.* 37°31N 88°3W **104** C4
Traer *Iowa, U.S.A.* 42°12N 92°28W **81** C6
Trafalgar *Ind., U.S.A.* 39°25N 86°9W **85** D4
Trail *B.C., Canada* 49°5N 117°40W **155** F17
Trail *Minn., U.S.A.* 47°47N 95°42W **77** C3
Trail of Tears Nat. Historic Trail *Ark., U.S.A.* 35°45N 93°30W **106** C2
Traill County ☆ *N. Dak., U.S.A.* 47°30N 97°20W **76** C8
Traill Ø *Greenland* 72°30N 23°0W **162** C8
Trammel *La., U.S.A.* 37°1N 82°18W **102** D2
Trammel Cr. → *Ky., U.S.A.* 36°53N 86°23W **104** D6
Tramping Lake *Sask., Canada* 52°8N 108°57W **150** C3
Tranquillity *Calif., U.S.A.* 36°39N 120°15W **127** G6
Trans-Alaska Pipeline *Alaska, U.S.A.* 70°11N 148°27W **135** A10
Transylvania *La., U.S.A.* 32°41N 91°11W **110** B4
Transylvania County ☆ *N.C., U.S.A.* 35°10N 82°50W **103** C3
Trappe *Md., U.S.A.* 38°40N 76°4W **93** B4
Trapper Pk. *Mont., U.S.A.* 45°54N 114°18W **123** E3
Trask Mt. *Oreg., U.S.A.* 45°22N 123°27W **121** B2
Traskwood *Ark., U.S.A.* 34°27N 92°39W **106** D3
Travelers Rest *S.C., U.S.A.* 34°58N 82°27W **103** D3
Travers Res. *Alta., Canada* 50°12N 112°51W **153** H8
Traverse, L. → *Calif., U.S.A.* 45°46N 96°38W **77** E2
Traverse City *Mich., U.S.A.* 44°46N 85°38W **79** E6
Traverse County ☆ *Minn., U.S.A.* 45°45N 96°25W **77** E2
Traverse Mountains *Utah, U.S.A.* 40°29N 111°49W **134** D3
Traverse Pt. *Mich., U.S.A.* 47°9N 88°14W **79** B3
Travis *Calif., U.S.A.* 40°35N 74°11W **97** C1
Travis, L. *Tex., U.S.A.* 30°24N 97°55W **109** G10
Travis County ☆ *Tex., U.S.A.* 30°17N 97°45W **109** G10
Treasure County ☆ *Mont., U.S.A.* 46°15N 107°20W **123** D10
Treasure I. *Calif., U.S.A.* 37°49N 122°22W **132** B2
Treasure I. *Fla., U.S.A.* 30°5N 90°6W **117** B1
Treasure Island *Fla., U.S.A.* 27°46N 82°46W **115** C2
Tree Tops Park *Fla., U.S.A.* 26°4N 80°16W **118** B1
Treece *Kans., U.S.A.* 37°0N 94°51W **82** D9
Trego *Mont., U.S.A.* 48°42N 114°52W **123** B3
Trego County ☆ *Kans., U.S.A.* 38°55N 99°50W **82** C4
Treherne *Man., Canada* 49°38N 98°42W **151** F13
Trejos *Jalisco, Mexico* 20°47N 103°11W **174** B4
Tremblant, Mt. *Qué., Canada* 46°16N 74°35W **144** E8
Trementina *N. Mex., U.S.A.* 35°28N 104°32W **131** B6
Tremont *Ill., U.S.A.* 40°28N 89°29W **84** C4
Tremont *Miss., U.S.A.* 34°14N 88°16W **111** B5
Tremont *N.Y., U.S.A.* 40°50N 73°52W **97** A3
Tremonton *Utah, U.S.A.* 41°43N 112°10W **129** B3
Trempealeau *Wis., U.S.A.* 44°0N 91°26W **78** D2
Trempealeau County ☆ *Wis., U.S.A.* 44°15N 91°20W **78** D2
Trenary *Mich., U.S.A.* 46°12N 86°58W **79** C5
Trenche → *Qué., Canada* 47°46N 72°53W **145** D10
Trent *S. Dak., U.S.A.* 43°54N 96°39W **76** F9
Trent → *Ont., Canada* 44°6N 77°34W **147** C9
Trent → *Tex., U.S.A.* 35°5N 77°2W **103** C8
Trente et Un Milles, L. des *Qué., Canada* 46°12N 75°49W **144** E7
Trenton = Quinte West *Ont., Canada* 44°10N 77°34W **147** C9
Trenton *Fla., U.S.A.* 45°37N 62°38W **141** H7
Trenton *Fla., U.S.A.* 29°37N 82°49W **114** B6
Trenton *Ga., U.S.A.* 34°52N 85°31W **113** B1
Trenton *Ill., U.S.A.* 38°36N 89°41W **84** E4
Trenton *Maine, U.S.A.* 44°27N 68°22W **90** D5
Trenton *Mich., U.S.A.* 42°8N 83°11W **79** G8
Trenton *Mo., U.S.A.* 40°5N 93°37W **83** A3
Trenton *N.C., U.S.A.* 35°4N 77°21W **103** C8
Trenton *N. Dak., U.S.A.* 48°4N 103°51W **76** B2
Trenton *N.J., U.S.A.* 40°14N 74°46W **92** B2
Trenton *Nebr., U.S.A.* 40°11N 101°1W **80** D4
Trenton *Ohio, U.S.A.* 39°29N 84°28W **86** D2
Trenton *Tenn., U.S.A.* 35°59N 88°56W **104** E4
Trenton *Utah, U.S.A.* 41°55N 111°57W **129** B4
Trentwood *Wash., U.S.A.* 47°42N 117°13W **120** C8
Trepassey *Nfld. & L., Canada* 46°43N 53°25W **142** F7
Trepassey B. *Nfld. & L., Canada* 46°37N 53°30W **142** F7
Tres Garantías *Quintana Roo, Mexico* 18°14N 89°11W **179** D5
Tres Ojitos *Chihuahua, Mexico* 28°50N 108°17W **169** E7
Tres Palos, L. *Guerrero, Mexico* 16°47N 99°41W **175** F8
Tres Picos *Chiapas, Mexico* 15°52N 93°32W **178** D3
Tres Picos, Cerro *Chihuahua, Mexico* 29°12N 107°34W **169** D8
Tres Piedras *N. Mex., U.S.A.* 36°39N 105°58W **131** A5
Tres Pinos *Calif., U.S.A.* 36°48N 121°19W **126** G5
Tres Valles *Veracruz, Mexico* 18°15N 96°8W **177** F4
Tres Virgenes, Volcán de las *Baja Calif. S., Mexico* 27°27N 112°34W **167** F6
Treutlen County ☆ *Ga., U.S.A.* 32°24N 82°34W **113** D4
Trève, L. la *Qué., Canada* 49°56N 75°30W **144** B7
Trevorton *Pa., U.S.A.* 40°47N 76°41W **87** D6
Trexlertown *Pa., U.S.A.* 40°33N 75°36W **92** B1
Treynor *Iowa, U.S.A.* 41°14N 95°36W **81** D3
Trezevant *Tenn., U.S.A.* 36°1N 88°37W **104** D4
Tri-City *Oreg., U.S.A.* 42°59N 123°19W **121** E2
Triangle *Va., U.S.A.* 38°33N 77°20W **93** B3
Triángulos, Arrecifes *Campeche, Mexico* 20°52N 92°11W **179** B1
Tribbey *Okla., U.S.A.* 35°7N 97°4W **107** C6
Tribly *Okla., U.S.A.* 28°28N 82°12W **114** B6
Tribune *Sask., Canada* 49°15N 103°49W **150** F8
Tribune *Kans., U.S.A.* 38°28N 101°45W **82** C2
Trident *Mont., U.S.A.* 45°57N 111°28W **123** E6
Trident Peak *Nev., U.S.A.* 41°54N 118°25W **128** A2
Trigg County ☆ *Ky., U.S.A.* 36°50N 87°50W **104** D5
Trigo Mountains *Ariz., U.S.A.* 33°15N 114°40W **130** D1
Trimble *Mo., U.S.A.* 39°28N 94°34W **83** B2
Trimble *Tenn., U.S.A.* 36°12N 89°11W **104** D3
Trimble County ☆ *Ky., U.S.A.* 38°35N 85°20W **105** B7
Trimont *Minn., U.S.A.* 43°46N 94°43W **77** G4
Trinchera *Colo., U.S.A.* 37°2N 104°3W **125** E6
Trincheras *Sonora, Mexico* 30°24N 111°32W **168** C4
Tring-Jonction *Qué., Canada* 46°16N 70°59W **145** E12
Trinidad *Cuba* 21°48N 80°0W **182** B4
Trinidad *Trin. & Tob.* 10°30N 61°15W **183** D7

Trinidad *Calif., U.S.A.* 41°4N 124°9W **126** B2
Trinidad *Colo., U.S.A.* 37°10N 104°31W **125** E6
Trinidad *D.C., U.S.A.* 38°54N 76°59W **99** B4
Trinidad *Tex., U.S.A.* 32°9N 96°6W **109** E11
Trinidad & Tobago ■ *W. Indies* 10°30N 61°20W **183** D7
Trinidad Head *Calif., U.S.A.* 41°3N 124°9W **126** B2
Trinity *Nfld. & L., Canada* 48°59N 53°55W **142** D7
Trinity *N.C., U.S.A.* 35°54N 79°59W **103** C6
Trinity → *Calif., U.S.A.* 30°57N 95°22W **109** G12
Trinity → *Calif., U.S.A.* 41°11N 123°42W **126** B3
Trinity B. *Nfld. & L., Canada* 48°20N 53°10W **142** D7
Trinity Center *Calif., U.S.A.* 40°59N 122°41W **126** C3
Trinity County ☆ *Calif., U.S.A.* 40°40N 123°0W **126** C3
Trinity County ☆ *Tex., U.S.A.* 31°4N 95°8W **109** F12
Trinity Dam *Calif., U.S.A.* 40°48N 122°46W **126** C4
Trinity Is. *Alaska, U.S.A.* 56°33N 154°25W **135** H9
Trinity Mt. *Idaho, U.S.A.* 43°36N 115°26W **122** F3
Trinity Mts. *Calif., U.S.A.* 41°12N 122°40W **126** C4
Trinity Nat. Forest *Calif., U.S.A.* 40°40N 123°15W **126** C3
Trinity Range *Nev., U.S.A.* 40°10N 118°40W **128** B2
Trinity River Greenbelt Park *Tex., U.S.A.* 32°45N 96°48W **116** B4
Trinway *Ohio, U.S.A.* 40°9N 82°1W **86** C4
Trion *Ga., U.S.A.* 34°33N 85°19W **113** B1
Triplett *Mo., U.S.A.* 39°30N 93°12W **83** B3
Tripoli *Iowa, U.S.A.* 42°49N 92°16W **81** C6
Tripp *S. Dak., U.S.A.* 43°13N 97°58W **76** G8
Tripp County ☆ *S. Dak., U.S.A.* 43°20N 100°0W **76** G6
Triquet, L. *Qué., Canada* 50°42N 59°47W **140** C10
Triton *Nfld. & L., Canada* 49°31N 55°37W **142** C5
Triumph *La., U.S.A.* 29°20N 89°30W **110** E6
Trochu *Alta., Canada* 51°50N 113°13W **153** G7
Trodely I. *N.W.T., Canada* 52°15N 79°26W **143** C2
Troilus, L. *Qué., Canada* 50°50N 74°35W **143** C3
Trois-Pistoles *Qué., Canada* 48°5N 69°10W **145** C13
Trois Pitons, Morne *Dominica* 15°22N 61°20W **183** C7
Trois-Rivières *Qué., Canada* 46°25N 72°34W **145** E10
Trois-Rivières-Ouest *Qué., Canada* 46°21N 72°35W **145** E10
Trojes *Michoacan, Mexico* 18°55N 103°19W **174** D4
Trona *Calif., U.S.A.* 35°46N 117°23W **127** H9
Troncoso *Zacatecas, Mexico* 22°37N 102°28W **173** E8
Tropic *Utah, U.S.A.* 37°37N 112°5W **129** F3
Trotwood *Ohio, U.S.A.* 39°48N 84°18W **86** D2
Troup *Tex., U.S.A.* 32°9N 95°7W **109** E12
Troup County ☆ *Ga., U.S.A.* 33°0N 85°0W **113** C1
Trousdale *Kans., U.S.A.* 37°49N 99°5W **82** D4
Trousdale County ☆ *Tenn., U.S.A.* 36°24N 86°10W **104** D6
Trout → *N.W.T., Canada* 61°19N 119°51W **157** D9
Trout Cr. → *B.C., Canada* 42°23N 118°3W **121** E7
Trout Cr. → *Oreg., U.S.A.* 44°48N 121°3W **121** C4
Trout Creek *Mich., U.S.A.* 46°29N 89°1W **79** C2
Trout Creek *Mont., U.S.A.* 47°50N 115°36W **123** C2
Trout Creek *Utah, U.S.A.* 39°42N 113°50W **129** D2
Trout Creek Mts. *Oreg., U.S.A.* 42°6N 118°18W **121** E7
Trout L. *N.W.T., Canada* 60°40N 121°14W **157** D8
Trout L. *Ont., Canada* 51°20N 93°15W **148** A3
Trout L. *Minn., U.S.A.* 47°59N 92°18W **77** C6
Trout Lake *B.C., Canada* 50°35N 117°25W **157** D9
Trout Lake *N.W.T., Canada* 56°30N 114°32W **157** D8
Trout Lake *Mich., U.S.A.* 46°12N 85°1W **79** C6
Trout Lake Wash. *L., U.S.A.* 46°0N 121°32W **120** E4
Trout Pk. *Wyo., U.S.A.* 44°36N 109°32W **124** B3
Trout River *Nfld. & L., Canada* 49°29N 58°8W **142** C2
Troutdale *Oreg., U.S.A.* 45°32N 122°23W **121** B3
Troutdale *Va., U.S.A.* 36°42N 81°26W **102** E3
Troutman *N.C., U.S.A.* 35°42N 80°53W **103** C5
Troutmans *N.C., U.S.A.* 35°42N 80°53W **103** C5
Troutville *Va., U.S.A.* 37°25N 79°53W **102** D5
Troy *N.S., Canada* 45°42N 61°24W **141** H8
Troy *Ala., U.S.A.* 31°48N 85°58W **112** E5
Troy *Idaho, U.S.A.* 46°44N 116°46W **122** C2
Troy *Ind., U.S.A.* 37°59N 86°55W **85** F4
Troy *Kans., U.S.A.* 39°47N 95°5W **82** B8
Troy *Mich., U.S.A.* 42°37N 83°9W **79** G8
Troy *Mo., U.S.A.* 38°59N 90°59W **83** C61
Troy *Mont., U.S.A.* 48°28N 115°53W **123** B2
Troy *N.C., U.S.A.* 35°22N 79°53W **103** C6
Troy *N.H., U.S.A.* 42°49N 72°11W **89** D2
Troy *N.Y., U.S.A.* 42°44N 73°41W **91** B1
Troy *Ohio, U.S.A.* 40°2N 84°12W **86** C2
Troy *Oreg., U.S.A.* 45°57N 117°27W **121** B8
Troy *Pa., U.S.A.* 41°47N 76°47W **87** C6
Troy *S. Dak., U.S.A.* 45°2N 96°52W **76** F9
Troy *Tenn., U.S.A.* 36°20N 89°10W **104** D3
Troy *Tex., U.S.A.* 31°12N 97°18W **109** G10
Troy *Vt., U.S.A.* 44°52N 72°25W **89** B2
Troy Peak *Nev., U.S.A.* 38°19N 115°30W **128** D5
Truchas *N. Mex., U.S.A.* 36°3N 105°49W **131** A5
Truchas Pk. *N. Mex., U.S.A.* 35°58N 105°39W **131** B5
Truckee *Calif., U.S.A.* 39°20N 120°11W **126** D6
Truckee → *Nev., U.S.A.* 39°51N 119°24W **128** C1
Trudeau ✈ (YUL) *Qué., Canada* 45°28N 73°44W **160** B2
Truesdale *Iowa, U.S.A.* 42°44N 95°11W **81** C3
Truite, L. à la *Qué., Canada* 47°20N 78°20W **144** D4
Trujillo *Honduras* 16°0N 86°0W **182** C2
Trujillo *N. Mex., U.S.A.* 35°32N 104°42W **131** B6
Trujillo, Mte. = Duarte, Pico *Dom. Rep.* 19°2N 70°59W **183** C5
Trujillo Alto *Puerto Rico* 18°21N 66°1W **184** G16
Truman *Minn., U.S.A.* 43°50N 94°26W **77** G4
Trumann *Ark., U.S.A.* 35°41N 90°31W **106** C5
Trumansburg *N.Y., U.S.A.* 42°33N 76°40W **88** C4
Trumbull *Conn., U.S.A.* 41°15N 73°12W **91** C1
Trumbull *Nebr., U.S.A.* 40°41N 98°16W **80** D7
Trumbull, Mt. *N. Mex., U.S.A.* 36°25N 113°19W **130** A2
Trumbull County ☆ *Ohio, U.S.A.* 41°14N 80°49W **86** B6
Truro *N.S., Canada* 45°21N 63°14W **141** H6
Truro *Mass., U.S.A.* 42°0N 70°3W **91** C4
Truscott *Tex., U.S.A.* 33°45N 99°49W **109** D8
Trussville *Ala., U.S.A.* 33°37N 86°35W **112** C4
Truth or Consequences *N. Mex., U.S.A.* 33°8N 107°15W **131** D3
Truxton *Ariz., U.S.A.* 35°29N 113°34W **130** B2
Truxton *Nebr., U.S.A.* 41°33N 100°57W **80** C5
Tryon *Okla., U.S.A.* 35°52N 96°58W **107** C7
Tryon Creek State Park △ *Oreg., U.S.A.* 45°25N 122°40W **132** B1
Tsacha L. *B.C., Canada* 53°3N 124°50W **154** D10
Tsaile *Ariz., U.S.A.* 36°17N 109°10W **130** A6
Tsala Apopka L. *Fla., U.S.A.* 28°53N 82°19W **114** C6
Tschida, L. *N. Dak., U.S.A.* 46°37N 101°55W **76** D4
Tsiigehtchic *N.W.T., Canada* 67°15N 134°0W **156** C6
Tsil-os Park △ *B.C., Canada* 51°9N 123°59W **154** D11
Tsitsutl Pk. *B.C., Canada* 52°43N 125°47W **154** C9
Tsuniah L. *B.C., Canada* 51°33N 124°4W **154** D10
Tualatin *Oreg., U.S.A.* 45°23N 122°45W **132** B1

Tuba City *Ariz., U.S.A.* 36°8N 111°14W 130 A4
Tubac *Ariz., U.S.A.* 31°37N 111°3W 130 F4
Tubutama *Sonora, Mexico* 30°53N 111°29W 168 C4
Tucannon → *Wash., U.S.A.* 46°33N 118°11W 120 D7
Tuckahoe *N.J., U.S.A.* 39°17N 74°45W 92 C2
Tuckahoe → *Md., U.S.A.* 39°0N 75°56W 93 B5
Tucker *Ark., U.S.A.* 34°26N 91°57W 106 D4
Tucker *Ga., U.S.A.* 33°51N 84°13W 113 C2
Tucker County ☆ *W. Va., U.S.A.* 39°9N 79°30W 102 B5
Tuckerman *Ark., U.S.A.* 35°44N 91°12W 106 C4
Tuckernuck Island *Mass., U.S.A.* 41°18N 70°15W 91 C4
Tuckerton *N.J., U.S.A.* 39°36N 74°20W 92 C2
Tucson *Ariz., U.S.A.* 32°13N 110°58W 130 E5
Tucson Int. ✈ (TUS) *Ariz., U.S.A.* 32°7N 110°56W 130 E5
Tucumcari *N. Mex., U.S.A.* 35°10N 103°44W 131 B7
Tucumcari Cr. → *N. Mex., U.S.A.* 35°20N 103°15W 131 B7
Tudor, L. *Qué., Canada* 55°50N 65°25W 143 B4
Tuftonboro *N.H., U.S.A.* 43°42N 71°13W 89 C3
Tufts University *Mass., U.S.A.* 42°24N 71°7W 96 A2
Tug Fork → *W. Va., U.S.A.* 38°7N 82°36W 102 C2
Tugaske *Sask., Canada* 50°52N 106°17W 150 C5
Tugidak I. *Alaska, U.S.A.* 56°30N 154°40W 135 H9
Tukarak I. *N.W.T., Canada* 56°15N 78°45W 143 B2
Tuktoyaktuk *N.W.T., Canada* 69°27N 133°2W 156 C6
Tuktut Nogait Nat. Park △ *N.W.T., Canada* 69°15N 122°0W 156 C8
Tukwila *Wash., U.S.A.* 47°28N 122°15W 132 D4
Tula *Amer. Samoa* 14°15S 170°34W 184 e
Tula *Hidalgo, Mexico* 20°3N 99°21W 175 B8
Tula *Tamaulipas, Mexico* 23°0N 99°43W 171 G5
Tula *Miss., U.S.A.* 34°14N 89°22W 111 B4
Tulalip Indian Reservation *Wash., U.S.A.* 48°4N 122°13W 120 B3
Tulancingo *Hidalgo, Mexico* 20°5N 98°22W 175 B9
Tulancingo *Oaxaca, Mexico* 17°46N 97°26W 177 G3
Tulare *Calif., U.S.A.* 36°13N 119°21W 127 G7
Tulare *S. Dak., U.S.A.* 44°44N 98°31W 76 F7
Tulare County ☆ *Calif., U.S.A.* 36°10N 118°50W 127 G8
Tulare Lake Bed *Calif., U.S.A.* 36°0N 119°48W 127 H7
Tularosa *N. Mex., U.S.A.* 33°5N 106°1W 131 D4
Tularosa Mts. *N. Mex., U.S.A.* 33°45N 108°40W 131 D2
Tularosa Valley *N. Mex., U.S.A.* 32°45N 106°0W 131 E4
Tule → *Calif., U.S.A.* 36°3N 119°50W 127 G7
Tule Cr. → *Tex., U.S.A.* 34°40N 101°14W 108 C6
Tule L. *Calif., U.S.A.* 41°53N 121°30W 126 B5
Tule Lake Nat. Wildlife Refuge △ *Calif., U.S.A.* 41°52N 121°30W 126 B5
Tule River Indian Reservation *Calif., U.S.A.* 36°0N 118°50W 127 H8
Tule Valley *Utah, U.S.A.* 39°25N 113°30W 129 D2
Tulelake *Calif., U.S.A.* 41°57N 121°29W 126 B5
Tulemalu L. *Nunavut, Canada* 62°58N 99°25W 159 E6
Tulia *Tex., U.S.A.* 34°32N 101°46W 108 C6
Tulija → *Tabasco, Mexico* 17°38N 92°28W 178 B4
Tulita *N.W.T., Canada* 64°57N 125°30W 157 D7
Tullahassee *Okla., U.S.A.* 35°50N 95°26W 107 C8
Tullahoma *Tenn., U.S.A.* 35°22N 86°13W 104 E6
Tulloch Res. *Calif., U.S.A.* 37°53N 120°36W 126 F6
Tullos *La., U.S.A.* 31°49N 92°19W 110 C3
Tully *N.Y., U.S.A.* 42°48N 76°7W 88 C4
Tulsa *Okla., U.S.A.* 36°10N 95°55W 107 B8
Tulsa County ☆ *Okla., U.S.A.* 36°0N 95°55W 107 B8
Tulsa Int. ✈ (TUL) *Okla., U.S.A.* 36°12N 95°53W 107 B8
Tulsayab, Pta. *Quintana Roo, Mexico* 20°16N 87°22W 179 B6
Tultepec *México, Mexico* 19°40N 99°8W 175 C8
Tuluksak *Alaska, U.S.A.* 61°6N 160°58W 135 F7
Tulum *Quintana Roo, Mexico* 20°13N 87°28W 179 B6
Tuma → *Nic.* 13°6N 84°35W 182 D3
Tumacacori Nat. Historic Park △ *U.S.A.* 31°35N 111°6W 130 F4
Tumbalá *Chiapas, Mexico* 17°18N 92°19W 178 B4
Tumbiscatio de Ruiz *Michoacan, Mexico* 18°31N 102°21W 174 D5
Tumbledown Mt. *Maine, U.S.A.* 45°27N 70°28W 90 C3
Tumbler Ridge *B.C., Canada* 55°8N 121°0W 157 E8
Tumon B. *Guam* 13°31N 144°48E 184 b
Tumwater *Wash., U.S.A.* 47°1N 122°54W 120 C3
Tunas de Zaza *Cuba* 21°39N 79°34W 182 B4
Tungla *Nic.* 13°24N 84°21W 182 D3
Tungsten *N.W.T., Canada* 61°57N 128°16W 157 D7
Tunica *La., U.S.A.* 30°56N 91°33W 110 D4
Tunica *Miss., U.S.A.* 34°41N 90°23W 111 B3
Tunica-Biloxi Indian Reservation *La., U.S.A.* 31°7N 92°3W 110 C3
Tunica County ☆ *Miss., U.S.A.* 34°41N 90°23W 111 B3
Tunis Mills *Md., U.S.A.* 38°49N 76°10W 93 B4
Tunkás *Yucatán, Mexico* 20°54N 88°45W 179 B5
Tunkhannock *Pa., U.S.A.* 41°32N 75°57W 87 C7
Tunnel Hill *Ill., U.S.A.* 37°32N 88°50W 84 F5
Tunnelton *W. Va., U.S.A.* 39°24N 79°45W 102 B5
Tuntutuliak *Alaska, U.S.A.* 60°22N 162°38W 135 F7
Tunu □ *Greenland* 75°0N 30°0W 162 C7
Tununak *Alaska, U.S.A.* 60°37N 165°15W 135 F6
Tunungayualok I. *Nfld. & L., Canada* 56°0N 61°0W 143 B5
Tuolumne *Calif., U.S.A.* 37°58N 120°15W 126 F6
Tuolumne County ☆ *Calif., U.S.A.* 38°0N 120°0W 126 E7
Tupátaro *Guanajuato, Mexico* 20°35N 101°38W 174 B6
Tupelo *Miss., U.S.A.* 34°16N 88°43W 111 B5
Tupelo *Okla., U.S.A.* 34°36N 96°26W 107 D7
Tupelo Nat. Battlefield △ *Miss., U.S.A.* 34°15N 88°14W 111 B5
Tupper L. *N.Y., U.S.A.* 44°14N 74°35W 88 A6
Tupper Lake *N.Y., U.S.A.* 44°14N 74°28W 88 A6
Turbeville *S.C., U.S.A.* 33°54N 80°1W 103 E5
Turbeville *Va., U.S.A.* 36°37N 79°2W 102 E5
Turgeon → *Qué., Canada* 50°0N 78°56W 144 B4
Turgeon, L. *Qué., Canada* 49°2N 79°4W 144 B3
Turicato *Michoacan, Mexico* 19°4N 101°24W 175 C6
Turin *Alta., Canada* 49°58N 112°31W 153 J8
Turin *Iowa, U.S.A.* 42°1N 95°58W 81 C3
Turkey *Tex., U.S.A.* 34°24N 100°54W 108 C7
Turkey → *Iowa, U.S.A.* 42°43N 91°2W 81 C7
Turkey Cr. → *Okla., U.S.A.* 35°58N 97°56W 107 C6
Turkey Creek *La., U.S.A.* 30°53N 92°25W 110 D3
Turkey L. *Fla., U.S.A.* 28°30N 81°28W 115 A2
Turkey Lake Park *Fla., U.S.A.* 28°30N 81°28W 115 A2
Turkey Mt. *Tex., U.S.A.* 29°22N 100°12W 108 H7
Turkey Ridge *S. Dak., U.S.A.* 43°25N 97°25W 76 G8
Turks & Caicos Is. ☑ *W. Indies* 21°20N 71°20W 183 B5
Turks Island Passage *W. Indies* 21°30N 71°30W 183 B5
Turlock *Calif., U.S.A.* 37°30N 120°51W 126 F6
Turlock L. *Calif., U.S.A.* 37°37N 120°34W 126 F6
Turnagain → *B.C., Canada* 59°12N 127°35W 157 E7
Turneffe Is. *Belize* 17°20N 87°50W 182 C2
Turner *Mich., U.S.A.* 44°9N 83°47W 79 E8
Turner *Mont., U.S.A.* 48°51N 108°24W 123 B9

Turner *Oreg., U.S.A.* 44°51N 122°57W 121 C3
Turner *Wash., U.S.A.* 46°25N 117°51W 120 D8
Turner County ☆ *Ga., U.S.A.* 31°45N 83°45W 113 E3
Turner County ☆ *S. Dak., U.S.A.* 43°17N 97°5W 76 G8
Turner Field *Georgia, U.S.A.* 33°44N 84°23W 117 B2
Turner Valley *Alta., Canada* 50°40N 114°17W 153 H6
Turners Falls *Mass., U.S.A.* 42°36N 72°33W 91 B2
Turnerville *Wyo., U.S.A.* 42°52N 113°54W 124 D2
Turnor L. *Sask., Canada* 56°35N 108°35W 157 E11
Turnour I. *B.C., Canada* 50°36N 125°27W 154 E8
Turon *Kans., U.S.A.* 37°48N 98°26W 82 D5
Turpin *Okla., U.S.A.* 36°52N 100°52W 107 B3
Turrell *Ark., U.S.A.* 35°23N 90°15W 106 C5
Turtle → *Ont., Canada* 48°51N 92°45W 148 D4
Turtle → *N. Dak., U.S.A.* 48°19N 97°8W 76 B8
Turtle → *S. Dak., U.S.A.* 44°55N 98°29W 76 F7
Turtle-Flambeau Flowage *Wis., U.S.A.* 46°4N 90°14W 78 B3
Turtle L. *Sask., Canada* 53°36N 108°38W 150 B3
Turtle Lake *Minn., U.S.A.* 45°5N 93°7W 94 A3
Turtle Lake *N. Dak., U.S.A.* 47°31N 100°53W 76 C5
Turtle Lake *Wis., U.S.A.* 45°24N 92°8W 78 C1
Turtle Mountain Indian Reservation *N. Dak., U.S.A.* 48°58N 99°58W 76 B6
Turtle Mountains *N. Dak., U.S.A.* 48°58N 100°0W 76 B6
Turtle Mt. Prov. Park △ *Man., Canada* 49°3N 100°15W 151 F11
Turtle River *Minn., U.S.A.* 47°35N 94°46W 77 C4
Turtleford *Sask., Canada* 53°23N 108°57W 150 B3
Turuachi → *Chihuahua, Mexico* 26°30N 106°50W 169 G9
Tusayan *Ariz., U.S.A.* 35°58N 112°8W 130 B3
Tuscaloosa *Ala., U.S.A.* 33°12N 87°34W 112 C3
Tuscaloosa, L. *Ala., U.S.A.* 33°16N 87°30W 112 C3
Tuscaloosa County ☆ *Ala., U.S.A.* 33°11N 87°27W 112 C3
Tuscarawas → *Ohio, U.S.A.* 40°24N 81°25W 86 C5
Tuscarawas County ☆ *Ohio, U.S.A.* 40°22N 81°26W 86 C5
Tuscarora *Nev., U.S.A.* 41°19N 116°14W 128 A4
Tuscarora Indian Reservation *N.Y., U.S.A.* 43°10N 78°55W 88 B2
Tuscarora Mt. *Pa., U.S.A.* 40°55N 77°55W 87 D5
Tuscarora Mts. *Nev., U.S.A.* 41°0N 116°20W 128 B4
Tuscola *Ill., U.S.A.* 39°48N 88°17W 84 D5
Tuscola *Tex., U.S.A.* 32°12N 99°48W 109 E8
Tuscola County ☆ *Mich., U.S.A.* 43°25N 83°20W 79 F8
Tusculum *Tenn., U.S.A.* 36°10N 82°46W 105 D10
Tuscumbia *Ala., U.S.A.* 34°44N 87°42W 112 B3
Tuscumbia *Mo., U.S.A.* 38°14N 92°28W 83 C4
Tushar Mts. *Utah, U.S.A.* 38°20N 112°30W 129 E3
Tushka *Okla., U.S.A.* 34°19N 96°10W 107 D7
Tuskahoma *Okla., U.S.A.* 34°37N 95°17W 107 D8
Tuskegee *Ala., U.S.A.* 32°25N 85°42W 112 D5
Tuskegee Nat. Forest *Ala., U.S.A.* 32°29N 85°35W 112 D5
Tusket *N.S., Canada* 43°52N 65°58W 141 K4
Tusket → *N.S., Canada* 43°41N 65°57W 141 K4
Tusket Wedge = Wedgeport *N.S., Canada* 43°44N 65°59W 141 K4
Tustin *Mich., U.S.A.* 44°6N 85°28W 79 E6
Tuttle *N. Dak., U.S.A.* 47°9N 100°0W 76 C6
Tuttle *Okla., U.S.A.* 35°17N 97°49W 107 C6
Tuttle Creek L. *Kans., U.S.A.* 39°15N 96°36W 82 B7
Tutuaca → *Chihuahua, Mexico* 29°10N 108°54W 168 D7
Tutuila *Amer. Samoa* 14°19S 170°50W 184 e
Tutwiler *Miss., U.S.A.* 34°1N 90°26W 111 B3
Tuweep *Ariz., U.S.A.* 36°25N 113°4W 130 A2
Tuxcacuesco *Jalisco, Mexico* 19°44N 103°59W 174 C4
Tuxedo Park *N.Y., U.S.A.* 41°12N 74°11W 92 A2
Tuxford *Sask., Canada* 50°34N 105°35W 150 E6
Tuxpan *Jalisco, Mexico* 19°33N 103°24W 174 C4
Tuxpan *Michoacan, Mexico* 19°34N 100°28W 175 C7
Tuxpan *Nayarit, Mexico* 21°57N 105°18W 172 F5
Tuxpan *Veracruz, Mexico* 20°57N 97°24W 176 D3
Tuxpan, Arrecife *Veracruz, Mexico* 21°2N 97°11W 176 D3
Tuxpan, Barra de *Veracruz, Mexico* 20°59N 97°8W 176 D3
Tuxtepec *Oaxaca, Mexico* 18°6N 96°7W 177 F4
Tuxtla Chico *Chiapas, Mexico* 14°57N 92°10W 178 E4
Tuxtla Gutiérrez *Chiapas, Mexico* 16°45N 93°7W 178 C3
Tuya → *B.C., Canada* 58°2N 130°51W 157 E6
Tuzantán *Chiapas, Mexico* 15°9N 92°25W 178 D3
Tuzantla *Michoacan, Mexico* 19°13N 100°35W 175 C7
Tuzigoot Nat. Monument △ *Ariz., U.S.A.* 34°46N 112°2W 130 C3
Twain Harte *Calif., U.S.A.* 38°2N 120°14W 126 F6
Tweed *Ont., Canada* 44°29N 77°19W 147 C9
Tweedside *N.B., Canada* 45°38N 67°14W 141 H2
Tweedsmuir *Sask., Canada* 53°34N 105°57W 150 B6
Tweedsmuir Park △ *B.C., Canada* 53°0N 126°20W 154 B8
Twelve Mile L. *Sask., Canada* 49°29N 106°14W 150 F5
Twentynine Palms *Calif., U.S.A.* 34°8N 116°3W 127 J10
Twentynine Palms Indian Reservation *Calif., U.S.A.* 34°7N 116°3W 127 J10
Twiggs County ☆ *Ga., U.S.A.* 32°40N 83°30W 113 D3
Twillingate *Nfld. & L., Canada* 49°42N 54°45W 142 C6
Twin Bridges *Mont., U.S.A.* 45°33N 112°20W 123 E5
Twin Brooks *S. Dak., U.S.A.* 45°12N 96°47W 76 E9
Twin Buttes Res. *Tex., U.S.A.* 31°22N 100°32W 108 F7
Twin City *Ga., U.S.A.* 32°35N 82°10W 113 D4
Twin Falls *Idaho, U.S.A.* 42°34N 114°28W 122 G4
Twin Falls County ☆ *Idaho, U.S.A.* 42°30N 114°45W 122 G4
Twin Hills *Alaska, U.S.A.* 59°23N 159°56W 135 G8
Twin Lake *Mich., U.S.A.* 43°22N 86°0W 79 F5
Twin Lakes *Colo., U.S.A.* 39°5N 106°23W 125 C4
Twin Lakes *Colo., U.S.A.* 30°43N 83°13W 113 F3
Twin Lakes *Mich., U.S.A.* 46°54N 88°51W 79 C3
Twin Lakes *Minn., U.S.A.* 43°34N 93°25W 77 G5
Twin Lakes *N. Mex., U.S.A.* 35°43N 108°46W 131 B2
Twin Lakes *Pa., U.S.A.* 41°23N 74°54W 92 A2
Twin Mountain *N.H., U.S.A.* 44°16N 71°32W 89 B3
Twin Mts. *Tex., U.S.A.* 30°25N 103°50W 108 G4
Twin Peaks *Calif., U.S.A.* 37°45N 122°28W 133 B2
Twin Peaks *Idaho, U.S.A.* 44°35N 114°29W 122 E4
Twin Peaks *Utah, U.S.A.* 40°35N 111°43W 134 C3
Twin Peaks Wilderness *Utah, U.S.A.* 40°36N 111°43W 134 C3
Twin Rivers *Calif., U.S.A.* 40°15N 74°32W 92 B2
Twin Valley *Minn., U.S.A.* 47°16N 96°16W 77 C2
Twinsburg *Ohio, U.S.A.* 41°19N 81°26W 86 B5
Twisp *Wash., U.S.A.* 48°22N 120°7W 120 B5
Twitchell Res. *Calif., U.S.A.* 34°59N 120°19W 127 J6
Twitty *Tex., U.S.A.* 35°19N 100°14W 108 B7
Two Butte Cr. → *Colo., U.S.A.* 38°2N 102°9W 125 D8
Two Buttes *Colo., U.S.A.* 37°34N 102°24W 125 D8
Two Buttes Res. *Colo., U.S.A.* 37°38N 102°32W 125 E8
Two Harbors *Minn., U.S.A.* 47°1N 91°40W 77 C7
Two Hills *Alta., Canada* 53°43N 111°52W 152 E9
Two Medicine → *Mont., U.S.A.* 48°29N 112°14W 123 B5
Two Rivers *Wis., U.S.A.* 44°9N 87°34W 78 D6
Two Rivers Nat. Wildlife Refuge △ *Ill., U.S.A.* 38°57N 90°31W 84 E3

Two Taverns *Pa., U.S.A.* 39°47N 77°10W 93 A3
Ty Ty *Ga., U.S.A.* 31°28N 83°39W 113 E3
Tyaskin *Md., U.S.A.* 38°18N 75°52W 93 B5
Tybee Island *Ga., U.S.A.* 32°1N 80°51W 113 D6
Tye *Tex., U.S.A.* 32°27N 99°52W 109 E8
Tygart L. *W. Va., U.S.A.* 39°19N 80°2W 102 B4
Tygart Valley → *W. Va., U.S.A.* 39°28N 80°9W 102 B4
Tyger → *S.C., U.S.A.* 34°28N 81°26W 103 D4
Tygh Valley *Oreg., U.S.A.* 45°15N 121°10W 121 B4
Tyler *Minn., U.S.A.* 44°17N 96°8W 77 F2
Tyler *Tex., U.S.A.* 32°21N 95°18W 109 E12
Tyler *Wash., U.S.A.* 47°26N 117°47W 120 C8
Tyler County ☆ *Tex., U.S.A.* 30°47N 94°25W 109 G13
Tyler County ☆ *W. Va., U.S.A.* 39°30N 80°54W 102 B4
Tylertown *Miss., U.S.A.* 31°7N 90°9W 111 E3
Tymochtee → *Ohio, U.S.A.* 40°57N 83°16W 86 C3
Tynan *Tex., U.S.A.* 28°10N 97°45W 109 J10
Tyndall *Man., Canada* 50°5N 96°40W 151 E15
Tyndall *S. Dak., U.S.A.* 43°0N 97°50W 76 G8
Tyndall Air Force Base *Fla., U.S.A.* 30°3N 85°40W 114 A3
Tyne Valley *P.E.I., Canada* 46°35N 63°56W 141 G6
Tyngsborough *Mass., U.S.A.* 42°40N 71°25W 91 B3
Tyonek *Alaska, U.S.A.* 61°4N 151°8W 135 F10
Tyro *Ark., U.S.A.* 33°50N 91°43W 106 E4
Tyro *Kans., U.S.A.* 37°2N 95°49W 82 D8
Tyrone *N. Mex., U.S.A.* 32°40N 108°22W 131 E2
Tyrone *Okla., U.S.A.* 36°57N 101°4W 107 B2
Tyrone *Pa., U.S.A.* 40°40N 78°14W 87 D4
Tyronza *Ark., U.S.A.* 35°29N 90°22W 106 C5
Tyrrell County ☆ *N.C., U.S.A.* 35°50N 76°10W 103 C9
Tyson *N.C., U.S.A.* 43°27N 72°44W 89 C2
Tysons Corner *Va., U.S.A.* 38°55N 77°13W 99 B2
Tzendales *Chiapas, Mexico* 16°19N 91°7W 178 C5
Tzimol *Chiapas, Mexico* 16°16N 92°16W 178 C4
Tzintzuntzán *Michoacan, Mexico* 19°38N 101°35W 174 C6
Tziscao *Chiapas, Mexico* 16°10N 91°42W 178 C5
Tztitzio *Michoacan, Mexico* 19°34N 100°55W 175 C7
Tzucacab *Yucatán, Mexico* 20°4N 89°3W 179 B4

U

U.L. Bend Nat. Wildlife Refuge △ *Mont., U.S.A.* 47°40N 107°55W 123 C10
U.S.A. = United States of America ■ *N. Amer.* 37°0N 96°0W 72 C7
U.S. Air Force Academy *Colo., U.S.A.* 38°59N 104°51W 125 D6
U.S. Cellular Field *Ill., U.S.A.* 41°50N 87°37W 95 C3
U.S.S. Arizona Memorial △ *U.S.A.* 21°22N 157°57W 136 K14
U.S. Virgin Is. ☑ *W. Indies* 18°20N 65°0W 184 G18
Uaxactún *Guatemala* 17°25N 89°29W 182 C2
Uayma *Yucatán, Mexico* 20°44N 88°19W 179 B5
Ubly *Mich., U.S.A.* 43°43N 82°56W 79 F9
Ucluelet *B.C., Canada* 48°57N 125°32W 154 G9
Ucon *Idaho, U.S.A.* 43°36N 111°58W 122 F7
Ucross *Wyo., U.S.A.* 44°34N 106°32W 124 B6
Ucú *Yucatán, Mexico* 21°2N 89°45W 179 A4
Ucum *Quintana Roo, Mexico* 19°15N 89°20W 179 C4
Udall *Kans., U.S.A.* 37°23N 97°7W 82 D6
Udell *Iowa, U.S.A.* 40°47N 92°45W 81 E6
Uehling *Nebr., U.S.A.* 41°44N 96°30W 80 C9
Uhrichsville *Ohio, U.S.A.* 40°24N 81°21W 86 C5
Uinta → *Utah, U.S.A.* 40°14N 109°51W 129 C6
Uinta County ☆ *Wyo., U.S.A.* 41°15N 110°30W 124 E2
Uinta Mts. *Utah, U.S.A.* 40°45N 110°30W 129 C5
Uinta Nat. Forest *Utah, U.S.A.* 40°32N 111°39W 129 C4
Uintah and Ouray Indian Reservation *Utah, U.S.A.* 40°15N 110°20W 129 C5
Uintah County ☆ *Utah, U.S.A.* 40°20N 109°30W 129 C6
Uivuk, C. *Nfld. & L., Canada* 58°29N 62°34W 143 B5
Ukiah *Calif., U.S.A.* 39°9N 123°13W 126 D3
Ukiah *Oreg., U.S.A.* 45°8N 118°56W 121 B7
Ulak I. *Alaska, U.S.A.* 51°22N 178°57W 135 L3
Ulen *Minn., U.S.A.* 47°5N 96°16W 77 C2
Ullin *Ill., U.S.A.* 37°17N 89°11W 84 F4
Ulster County ☆ *N.Y., U.S.A.* 41°50N 74°15W 88 D6
Ultima Agua *Baja Calif. S. Mexico* 25°33N 111°17W 167 H7
Ulupalakua Ranch *Hawai'i, U.S.A.* 20°39N 156°24W 136 C5
Ulysses *Kans., U.S.A.* 37°35N 101°22W 82 D2
Ulysses *Nebr., U.S.A.* 41°4N 97°12W 80 C8
Ulysses *Pa., U.S.A.* 41°54N 77°46W 87 C5
Ulysses S. Grant Nat. Historic Site △ *Mo., U.S.A.* 38°33N 90°28W 83 C6
Umán *Yucatán, Mexico* 20°53N 89°45W 179 B4
Umatac *Guam* 13°18N 144°39E 184 b
Umatilla *Oreg., U.S.A.* 45°55N 119°21W 121 B6
Umatilla → *Oreg., U.S.A.* 45°55N 119°20W 121 B6
Umatilla, L. *Wash., U.S.A.* 45°53N 119°40W 120 E6
Umatilla County ☆ *Oreg., U.S.A.* 45°40N 118°45W 121 B7
Umatilla Indian Reservation *Oreg., U.S.A.* 45°41N 118°31W 121 B7
Umatilla Nat. Forest *Oreg., U.S.A.* 45°38N 118°11W 121 C7
Umbarger *Tex., U.S.A.* 34°57N 102°7W 108 C5
Umbagog L. *N.H., U.S.A.* 44°46N 71°3W 89 B3
Umfreville L. *Ont., Canada* 50°18N 94°45W 148 B2
Umiat *Alaska, U.S.A.* 69°22N 152°8W 135 B9
Umingmaktok *Nunavut, Canada* 67°41N 107°56W 158 D4
Umiujaq *Qué., Canada* 56°33N 76°33W 143 B2
Umnak I. *Alaska, U.S.A.* 53°15N 168°20W 135 K5
Umpire *Ark., U.S.A.* 34°17N 94°3W 106 D1
Umpqua *Oreg., U.S.A.* 43°25N 123°28W 121 D2
Umpqua → *Oreg., U.S.A.* 43°40N 124°12W 121 D1
Umpqua Nat. Forest *Oreg., U.S.A.* 43°10N 122°40W 121 D3
Uña de Gato *Nuevo León, Mexico* 26°13N 100°14W 170 D4
Unadilla *Ga., U.S.A.* 32°16N 83°44W 113 D3
Unadilla *N.Y., U.S.A.* 42°20N 75°19W 88 C5
Unadilla *Nebr., U.S.A.* 40°41N 96°16W 80 D9
Unadilla → *N.Y., U.S.A.* 42°20N 75°25W 88 C5
Unalakleet *Alaska, U.S.A.* 63°52N 160°47W 135 E7
Unalaska *Alaska, U.S.A.* 53°53N 166°32W 135 K6
Unalaska I. *Alaska, U.S.A.* 53°35N 166°50W 135 K6
Uncompahgre → *Colo., U.S.A.* 38°45N 108°6W 125 D2
Uncompahgre Nat. Forest *Colo., U.S.A.* 38°30N 108°30W 125 D2
Uncompahgre Peak *Colo., U.S.A.* 38°4N 107°28W 125 D3
Uncompahgre Plateau *Colo., U.S.A.* 38°20N 108°5W 125 D2
Underground Atlanta *Georgia, U.S.A.* 33°45N 84°24W 117 B2
Underhill *Vt., U.S.A.* 44°32N 72°56W 89 B2
Underhill, L. *Fla., U.S.A.* 28°32N 81°20W 115 A3
Underwood *Iowa, U.S.A.* 41°23N 95°41W 81 D2
Underwood *N. Dak., U.S.A.* 47°27N 101°8W 76 C4
Unga I. *Alaska, U.S.A.* 55°15N 160°40W 135 J7
Ungava, Pén. d' *Qué., Canada* 60°0N 74°0W 143 B3
Ungava B. *Nfld. & L., Canada* 59°30N 67°30W 143 B4
Unicoi *Tenn., U.S.A.* 36°12N 82°21W 105 D10
Unicoi County ☆ *Tenn., U.S.A.* 36°9N 82°25W 105 D10

Unidad Santa Fe *Distrito Federal, Mexico* 19°23N 99°13W 181 B2
Unidos Venceremos *Durango, Mexico* 23°58N 105°28W 172 D5
Unimak I. *Alaska, U.S.A.* 54°45N 164°0W 135 J7
Unimak Pass *Alaska, U.S.A.* 54°15N 164°30W 135 J6
Union *Ala., U.S.A.* 32°59N 87°54W 112 D3
Union *Iowa, U.S.A.* 42°15N 93°4W 81 C5
Union *Maine, U.S.A.* 44°13N 69°17W 90 D4
Union *Miss., U.S.A.* 32°34N 89°7W 111 D4
Union *Mo., U.S.A.* 38°27N 91°0W 83 C51
Union *N.J., U.S.A.* 40°41N 74°15W 97 B1
Union *Nebr., U.S.A.* 40°49N 95°55W 80 D10
Union *Oreg., U.S.A.* 45°13N 117°52W 121 B8
Union *S.C., U.S.A.* 34°43N 81°37W 103 D4
Union *W. Va., U.S.A.* 37°36N 80°33W 102 D4
Union *Wash., U.S.A.* 47°22N 123°6W 120 C2
Union Bay *B.C., Canada* 49°35N 124°53W 154 F10
Union Bridge *Md., U.S.A.* 39°34N 77°11W 93 A3
Union Center *S. Dak., U.S.A.* 44°34N 102°40W 76 F3
Union Center *Wis., U.S.A.* 43°41N 90°16W 78 E3
Union Church *Miss., U.S.A.* 31°41N 90°47W 111 E3
Union City *Calif., U.S.A.* 37°36N 122°1W 126 F4
Union City *Ga., U.S.A.* 33°35N 84°33W 113 C2
Union City *Ind., U.S.A.* 40°12N 84°49W 85 C6
Union City *Mich., U.S.A.* 42°4N 85°8W 79 G6
Union City *New York, U.S.A.* 96 b1
Union City *Ohio, U.S.A.* 40°12N 84°48W 85 C6
Union City *Okla., U.S.A.* 35°23N 97°57W 107 C6
Union City *Pa., U.S.A.* 41°54N 79°51W 87 C3
Union City *Tenn., U.S.A.* 36°26N 89°3W 104 D3
Union County ☆ *Ark., U.S.A.* 33°12N 92°40W 106 E3
Union County ☆ *Fla., U.S.A.* 30°0N 82°25W 114 A6
Union County ☆ *Ga., U.S.A.* 34°50N 84°0W 113 B3
Union County ☆ *Ill., U.S.A.* 37°30N 89°15W 84 F4
Union County ☆ *Ind., U.S.A.* 39°35N 84°55W 85 D6
Union County ☆ *Iowa, U.S.A.* 41°0N 94°15W 81 E4
Union County ☆ *Ky., U.S.A.* 37°40N 87°55W 104 C5
Union County ☆ *Miss., U.S.A.* 34°29N 89°0W 111 B5
Union County ☆ *N.C., U.S.A.* 35°0N 80°40W 103 D5
Union County ☆ *N.J., U.S.A.* 40°40N 74°20W 92 B2
Union County ☆ *N. Mex., U.S.A.* 36°30N 103°30W 131 A7
Union County ☆ *Ohio, U.S.A.* 40°14N 83°22W 86 C3
Union County ☆ *Oreg., U.S.A.* 45°15N 118°0W 121 B8
Union County ☆ *Pa., U.S.A.* 41°0N 77°0W 87 D5
Union County ☆ *S.C., U.S.A.* 34°45N 81°45W 103 D4
Union County ☆ *S. Dak., U.S.A.* 42°51N 96°45W 76 H9
Union County ☆ *Tenn., U.S.A.* 36°15N 83°48W 105 D9
Union Creek *Calif., U.S.A.* 42°55N 122°27W 121 E3
Union Dale *Pa., U.S.A.* 41°43N 75°30W 87 C7
Unión de San Antonio *Jalisco, Mexico* 21°6N 102°1W 174 A5
Union Flat Cr. → *U.S.A.* 46°49N 118°0W 120 D8
Union Gap *Wash., U.S.A.* 46°33N 120°28W 120 C5
Union Grove *Wis., U.S.A.* 42°41N 88°3W 78 F5
Unión Hidalgo *Oaxaca, Mexico* 16°30N 94°51W 177 H6
Union Hills *Ariz., U.S.A.* 33°43N 112°3W 134 A2
Union I. *B.C., Canada* 50°0N 127°16W 154 F7
Unión Juárez *Chiapas, Mexico* 15°4N 92°5W 178 D4
Union L. *N.J., U.S.A.* 39°24N 75°3W 92 C1
Union Parish ☆ *La., U.S.A.* 32°47N 92°24W 110 B3
Union Park *Fla., U.S.A.* 28°34N 81°17W 114 C7
Union Point *Ga., U.S.A.* 33°37N 83°4W 113 C3
Union Port *N.Y., U.S.A.* 40°49N 73°50W 97 B3
Union Slough Nat. Wildlife Refuge △ *Iowa, U.S.A.* 43°17N 94°7W 81 B4
Union Springs *Ala., U.S.A.* 32°9N 85°43W 112 D5
Union Springs *N.Y., U.S.A.* 42°51N 76°42W 88 C4
Union Star *Mo., U.S.A.* 39°59N 94°36W 83 B2
Union Station *Ont., Canada* 43°39N 79°23W 161 B2
Union Valley Res. *Calif., U.S.A.* 38°52N 120°26W 126 E6
Unión y Progreso *Durango, Mexico* 25°14N 104°59W 173 B6
Uniondale *Ind., U.S.A.* 40°50N 85°15W 85 C5
Uniontown *Ala., U.S.A.* 32°27N 87°31W 112 D3
Uniontown *Kans., U.S.A.* 37°51N 94°59W 82 D9
Uniontown *Ky., U.S.A.* 37°47N 87°56W 104 C5
Uniontown *Pa., U.S.A.* 39°54N 79°44W 87 E3
Uniontown *Wash., U.S.A.* 46°32N 117°5W 120 D8
Unionville *Conn., U.S.A.* 41°45N 72°53W 91 C2
Unionville *Ga., U.S.A.* 31°26N 83°30W 113 E3
Unionville *Iowa, U.S.A.* 40°49N 92°42W 81 E6
Unionville *Md., U.S.A.* 39°28N 77°12W 93 A3
Unionville *Mich., U.S.A.* 43°39N 83°28W 79 F8
Unionville *Mo., U.S.A.* 40°29N 93°1W 83 A3
Unionville *N.Y., U.S.A.* 41°18N 74°34W 92 A2
Unionville *Nev., U.S.A.* 40°27N 118°8W 128 B2
Unionville *Pa., U.S.A.* 40°55N 77°53W 87 D5
Unionville *Va., U.S.A.* 39°54N 79°54W 93 A5
Unionville *Va., U.S.A.* 38°16N 77°58W 102 C7
Uniopolis *Ohio, U.S.A.* 40°36N 84°5W 86 C2
United Center *Ill., U.S.A.* 41°53N 87°41W 95 B2
United States of America ■ *N. Amer.* 37°0N 96°0W 72 C7
United States Range *N.W.T., Canada* 82°25N 68°0W 158 A12
Unity *Sask., Canada* 52°30N 109°5W 150 C2
Unity *Maine, U.S.A.* 44°37N 69°20W 90 D4
Unity *Md., U.S.A.* 39°13N 77°5W 93 A3
Unity *Oreg., U.S.A.* 44°26N 118°12W 121 C7
Unity *Wis., U.S.A.* 44°51N 90°19W 78 D3
Universal City *Tex., U.S.A.* 29°32N 98°17W 116 B4
Universal Studios *Calif., U.S.A.* 34°9N 118°21W 133 B2
University City *Calif., U.S.A.* 32°51N 117°12W 133 A1
University City *Mo., U.S.A.* 38°39N 90°19W 98 A3
University Gardens *N.Y., U.S.A.* 40°46N 73°43W 97 B4
University Hill *B.C., Canada* 49°16N 123°15W 161 B1
University Park ☆ *Ill., U.S.A.* 41°25N 87°44W 84 B6
University Park *Md., U.S.A.* 38°58N 76°56W 99 B4
University Park *N.Y., U.S.A.* 40°30N 73°30W 97 B3
University Park *Tex., U.S.A.* 32°51N 96°48W 116 A5
University Place *Wash., U.S.A.* 47°14N 122°33W 120 C3
Upatoi Cr. → *Ga., U.S.A.* 32°22N 84°58W 113 D2
Upernavik *Greenland* 72°49N 56°20W 162 C5
Upernavik Kujalleq *Greenland* 72°10N 55°30W 158 C14
Upham *N. Dak., U.S.A.* 48°35N 100°44W 76 B5
Upland *Calif., U.S.A.* 34°6N 117°39W 127 J9
Upland *Ind., U.S.A.* 40°28N 85°30W 85 C5
Upland *Nebr., U.S.A.* 40°19N 98°54W 80 D7
Upolu Pt. *Hawai'i, U.S.A.* 20°16N 155°52W 136 C6
Upper Alkali L. *Calif., U.S.A.* 41°47N 120°8W 126 B6
Upper Arlington *Ohio, U.S.A.* 40°0N 83°4W 86 C3
Upper Arrow L. *B.C., Canada* 50°30N 117°50W 155 E17
Upper B. *N.Y., U.S.A.* 40°40N 74°4W 97 C2
Upper Blackville *N.B., Canada* 46°39N 65°55W 141 H4
Upper Campbell L. *B.C., Canada* 49°55N 125°39W 154 F9
Upper Crossroads *Md., U.S.A.* 39°33N 76°29W 93 A4
Upper Darby *Pa., U.S.A.* 39°55N 75°16W 98 B1
Upper Delaware Scenic & Recr. River △ *N.Y., U.S.A.* 41°40N 75°3W 88 D5

Upper Duck Island Ont., Canada 45°28N 75°37W 160 A2
Upper Goose L. Ont., Canada 51°43N 92°43W 148 A4
Upper Humber → Nfld. & L., Canada 49°11N 57°28W 142 C3
Upper Iowa → Iowa, U.S.A. 43°29N 91°14W 81 B7
Upper Klamath → Oreg., U.S.A. 42°25N 121°55W 121 E4
Upper Lake Calif., U.S.A. 39°10N 122°54W 126 D4
Upper Lillooet Park △ B.C., Canada 50°39N 123°36W 154 E11
Upper Manitou → Ont., Canada 49°24N 92°48W 148 C4
Upper Marlboro Md., U.S.A. 38°49N 76°45W 93 B4
Upper Mississippi River Nat. Wildlife & Fish Refuge △ Iowa, U.S.A. 42°57N 91°9W 81 C7
Upper Missouri Breaks Nat. Monument △ Mont., U.S.A. 47°50N 109°55W 123 C8
Upper Musquodoboit N.S., Canada 45°10N 62°58W 141 H7
Upper New York B. = Upper B. N.Y., U.S.A. 40°40N 74°3W 97 C2
Upper Ouachita Nat. Wildlife Refuge △ La., U.S.A. 32°57N 92°8W 110 B3
Upper Peoria L. Ill., U.S.A. 40°55N 89°27W 84 C4
Upper Red L. Minn., U.S.A. 48°8N 94°45W 77 B4
Upper St. Clair Pa., U.S.A. 40°20N 80°5W 98 C1
Upper Sandusky Ohio, U.S.A. 40°50N 83°17W 86 C3
Upper Seymour Prov. Park △ Alta., Canada 49°5N 113°52W 153 J7
Upper Sioux Indian Reservation Minn., U.S.A. 44°46N 95°31W 77 F3
Upper Souris Nat. Wildlife Refuge △ N. Dak., U.S.A. 48°35N 101°38W 76 B4
Upper Stewiacke N.S., Canada 45°13N 63°0W 141 H7
Upper Tract W. Va., U.S.A. 38°47N 79°17W 102 C5
Upperville Va., U.S.A. 39°0N 77°53W 93 B3
Upsala Ont., Canada 49°3N 90°28W 148 C6
Upshur County ☆ Tex., U.S.A. 32°44N 94°57W 109 E13
Upshur County ☆ W. Va., U.S.A. 39°0N 80°8W 102 C4
Upson Wis., U.S.A. 46°22N 90°24W 78 B2
Upson County ☆ Ga., U.S.A. 32°50N 84°20W 113 D2
Upton Qué., Canada 45°39N 72°41W 145 F10
Upton Ky., U.S.A. 37°28N 85°54W 105 C7
Upton Maine, U.S.A. 44°42N 71°1W 90 D2
Upton Mass., U.S.A. 42°11N 71°37W 91 B3
Upton Wyo., U.S.A. 44°6N 104°38W 124 B8
Upton County ☆ Tex., U.S.A. 31°15N 102°0W 108 F6
Uptown Ill., U.S.A. 41°58N 87°40W 95 B2
Uqsuqtuuq = Gjoa Haven Nunavut, Canada 68°38N 95°53W 158 D6
Urania La., U.S.A. 31°52N 92°18W 110 C3
Uranium City Sask., Canada 59°34N 108°37W 157 E11
Uravan Colo., U.S.A. 38°22N 108°44W 125 D2
Urbana Ark., U.S.A. 33°10N 92°27W 106 C3
Urbana Ill., U.S.A. 40°7N 88°12W 84 C5
Urbana Iowa, U.S.A. 42°13N 91°52W 81 C7
Urbana Mo., U.S.A. 37°51N 93°10W 83 D3
Urbana Ohio, U.S.A. 40°7N 83°45W 86 C3
Urbandale Iowa, U.S.A. 41°38N 93°43W 81 C5
Urbank Minn., U.S.A. 46°8N 95°31W 77 D3
Ures Sonora, Mexico 29°26N 110°24W 168 D5
Uriah Ala., U.S.A. 31°18N 87°30W 112 C3
Uriangato Guanajuato, Mexico 20°9N 101°11W 175 B6
Urich Mo., U.S.A. 38°28N 94°2W 83 C2
Urique Chihuahua, Mexico 27°13N 107°55W 169 F8
Urique → Chihuahua, Mexico 26°29N 107°58W 169 G8
Uroyan, Montañas de Puerto Rico 18°12N 67°0W 184 G16
Ursa Ill., U.S.A. 40°4N 91°22W 84 C2
Ursina Pa., U.S.A. 39°49N 79°20W 93 A1
Ursine Nev., U.S.A. 37°59N 114°13W 128 E6
Ursula Chan. B.C., Canada 53°25N 128°55W 154 B6
Ursulo Galván Veracruz, Mexico 19°24N 96°21W 176 E4
Uruachic Chihuahua, Mexico 27°52N 108°14W 169 F7
Uruapan Michoacan, Mexico 19°24N 102°3W 174 C5
Usher Fla., U.S.A. 29°24N 82°49W 114 B6
Usk B.C., Canada 54°38N 128°26W 157 F7
Usk Wash., U.S.A. 48°19N 117°17W 120 B8
Usulután El Salv. 13°25N 88°28W 182 D2
Usumacinta Tabasco, Mexico 17°33N 91°29W 178 B5
Usumacinta → Mexico 18°24N 92°38W 178 A4
Utah □ U.S.A. 39°20N 111°30W 129 D4
Utah County ☆ Utah, U.S.A. 40°10N 111°50W 129 C4
Utah L. Utah, U.S.A. 40°12N 111°48W 129 C4
Utah Test Range North Utah, U.S.A. 41°7N 113°11W 129 B2
Utah Test Range South Utah, U.S.A. 40°30N 113°50W 129 C2
Utatlan Guatemala 15°2N 91°11W 182 C1
Ute Iowa, U.S.A. 42°3N 95°42W 81 C3
Ute Creek → N. Mex., U.S.A. 35°21N 103°50W 131 B7
Ute L. N. Mex., U.S.A. 35°21N 103°27W 131 B7
Ute Mountain Indian Reservation Colo., U.S.A. 37°13N 108°41W 125 E2
Ute Park N. Mex., U.S.A. 36°34N 105°6W 131 A5
Utica Kans., U.S.A. 38°39N 100°10W 82 C3
Utica Miss., U.S.A. 32°7N 90°37W 111 D3
Utica N.Y., U.S.A. 43°6N 75°14W 88 B5
Utica Nebr., U.S.A. 40°54N 97°21W 80 D8
Utica Ohio, U.S.A. 40°14N 82°27W 86 C4
Utica S. Dak., U.S.A. 42°59N 97°30W 76 H8
Utikuma L. Alta., Canada 55°50N 115°30W 152 C5
Utleyville Colo., U.S.A. 37°17N 103°4W 125 E7
Utopia Tex., U.S.A. 29°37N 99°32W 109 H8
Utuado Puerto Rico 18°16N 66°42W 184 G16
Uummann Greenland 70°58N 52°17W 158 C15
Uummann Greenland 77°28N 69°13W 162 B4
Uummannasuaq = Nunap Isua Greenland 59°48N 43°55W 162 F6
Uvada Utah, U.S.A. 37°43N 114°3W 129 F1
Uvalda Ga., U.S.A. 32°2N 82°31W 113 D4
Uvalde Tex., U.S.A. 29°13N 99°47W 109 H8
Uvalde County ☆ Tex., U.S.A. 29°30N 99°43W 109 H8
Uvas, Sierra de las N. Mex., U.S.A. 32°29N 107°12W 131 E3
Uwharrie N.C., U.S.A. 35°21N 80°3W 103 C5
Uwharrie Nat. Forest N.C., U.S.A. 35°20N 80°0W 103 C6
Uxbridge Ont., Canada 44°6N 79°7W 146 C5
Uxbridge Mass., U.S.A. 42°5N 71°38W 91 B3
Uxmal Yucatán, Mexico 20°22N 89°46W 179 D4
Uxpanapa → Veracruz, Mexico 17°58N 94°29W 177 G6
Uyak Alask., U.S.A. 57°38N 154°0W 135 H9

V

Vaca Pinta Cerro la Michoacan, Mexico 18°43N 102°58W 174 D5
Vacas, Arroyo de las → Coahuila, Mexico 29°19N 100°54W 170 A4
Vacaville Calif., U.S.A. 38°21N 121°59W 126 E5
Vache, Î. Haiti 18°2N 73°35W 183 C5
Vacherie La., U.S.A. 30°0N 90°48W 110 E5
Vachon → Qué., Canada 59°58N 72°24W 143 B3
Vader Wash., U.S.A. 46°24N 122°58W 120 D3

Vadnais, L. Minn., U.S.A. 45°3N 93°5W 94 A3
Vadnais Heights Minn., U.S.A. 45°3N 93°4W 94 A3
Vado N. Mex., U.S.A. 32°7N 106°40W 131 E4
Vado Hondo Sinaloa, Mexico 23°52N 106°15W 172 D4
Vaiden Miss., U.S.A. 33°20N 89°45W 111 C4
Vail Ariz., U.S.A. 32°3N 110°43W 130 E5
Vail Colo., U.S.A. 39°40N 106°20W 125 C4
Vail Iowa, U.S.A. 42°4N 95°12W 81 C3
Val-Alain Qué., Canada 46°24N 71°45W 145 E11
Val-Barrette Qué., Canada 46°30N 75°21W 144 E7
Val-Brillant Qué., Canada 48°32N 67°33W 140 F2
Val Caron Ont., Canada 46°37N 81°1W 146 A5
Val-des-Bois Qué., Canada 45°54N 75°35W 144 F7
Val-d'Espoir Qué., Canada 48°31N 64°24W 140 E5
Val-d'Or Qué., Canada 48°7N 77°47W 144 C5
Val Marie Sask., Canada 49°15N 107°45W 150 F4
Val Rita Ont., Canada 49°22N 82°33W 149 C14
Val Tétreault Qué., Canada 45°26N 75°45W 160 A1
Val Verde County ☆ Tex., U.S.A. 30°0N 101°0W 108 H6
Valatie N.Y., U.S.A. 42°25N 73°41W 88 C7
Valcourt Qué., Canada 45°29N 72°18W 145 F11
Valders Wis., U.S.A. 44°4N 87°53W 78 D6
Valdes I. B.C., Canada 49°4N 123°39W 155 F11
Valdez Alaska, U.S.A. 61°7N 146°16W 135 F11
Valdez N. Mex., U.S.A. 36°32N 105°35W 131 A5
Valdez-Cordova ☆ Alaska, U.S.A. 61°30N 144°30W 135 F11
Valdosta Ga., U.S.A. 30°50N 83°17W 113 F3
Vale Oreg., U.S.A. 43°59N 117°15W 121 D8
Vale S. Dak., U.S.A. 44°37N 103°24W 76 F2
Vale Va., U.S.A. 38°55N 77°20W 99 B1
Valemount B.C., Canada 52°50N 119°15W 155 D14
Valencia N. Mex., U.S.A. 34°48N 106°43W 131 C4
Valencia County ☆ N. Mex., U.S.A. 34°45N 107°0W 131 C4
Valentín, Barra Guerrero, Mexico 17°28N 101°15W 175 E6
Valentin Ariz., U.S.A. 35°23N 113°40W 130 B2
Valentine Nebr., U.S.A. 42°52N 100°33W 80 B5
Valentine Tex., U.S.A. 30°35N 104°30W 108 G3
Valentine Nat. Wildlife Refuge △ Nebr., U.S.A. 42°31N 100°36W 80 B5
Valentines Va., U.S.A. 36°35N 77°50W 102 E7
Valeria Iowa, U.S.A. 41°44N 93°20W 81 D5
Valerio Chihuahua, Mexico 27°39N 106°6W 169 F9
Válgame Dios Sinaloa, Mexico 26°7N 107°32W 172 A3
Valier Ill., U.S.A. 38°1N 89°3W 84 E4
Valier Mont., U.S.A. 48°18N 112°16W 123 B5
Valladolid Yucatán, Mexico 20°41N 88°12W 179 D4
Valle Sonora, Mexico 30°50N 111°16W 168 C4
Valle de Allende Chihuahua, Mexico 26°56N 105°24W 169 G10
Valle de Bravo México, Mexico 19°11N 100°8W 175 C7
Valle de Guadalupe Jalisco, Mexico 21°0N 102°38W 174 B5
Valle de Juárez Jalisco, Mexico 19°55N 102°53W 174 C5
Valle de Santiago Guanajuato, Mexico 20°23N 101°12W 175 B6
Valle de Zaragoza Chihuahua, Mexico 27°25N 105°50W 169 F10
Valle del Rosario Chihuahua, Mexico 27°19N 106°18W 169 F9
Valle Hermosa Quintana Roo, Mexico 19°11N 88°32W 179 C5
Valle Hermoso Tamaulipas, Mexico 25°35N 97°40W 171 E6
Valle Hermoso Tamaulipas, Mexico 23°40N 99°45W 171 G5
Valle las Palmas Baja Calif., Mexico 32°23N 116°47W 166 A2
Valle Nacional Oaxaca, Mexico 17°47N 96°18W 177 E4
Valle Verde Sonora, Mexico 28°44N 111°44W 168 E4
Vallecillos Nuevo León, Mexico 26°40N 99°58W 170 D4
Vallecito Colo., U.S.A. 37°23N 107°35W 125 E3
Vallecito Res. Colo., U.S.A. 37°23N 107°34W 125 E3
Vallecitos Guerrero, Mexico 17°56N 101°20W 175 E6
Vallée-Jonction Qué., Canada 46°22N 70°55W 145 E12
Vallejo Calif., U.S.A. 38°7N 122°14W 126 E4
Valles Mines Mo., U.S.A. 38°2N 90°30W 83 C6
Valley Ala., U.S.A. 32°49N 85°11W 112 D5
Valley Nebr., U.S.A. 41°19N 96°21W 80 C9
Valley Wash., U.S.A. 48°11N 117°44W 120 B8
Valley Wyo., U.S.A. 44°9N 109°36W 124 B3
Valley Center Calif., U.S.A. 33°13N 117°2W 127 K9
Valley Center Kans., U.S.A. 37°50N 97°22W 82 D6
Valley City N. Dak., U.S.A. 46°55N 98°0W 76 D8
Valley County ☆ Idaho, U.S.A. 44°45N 115°30W 122 E3
Valley County ☆ Mont., U.S.A. 48°35N 106°30W 123 B11
Valley County ☆ Nebr., U.S.A. 41°30N 99°0W 80 C7
Valley Falls Kans., U.S.A. 39°21N 95°28W 82 B8
Valley Falls N.Y., U.S.A. 42°54N 73°34W 91 B1
Valley Falls Oreg., U.S.A. 42°29N 120°17W 121 E5
Valley Falls R.I., U.S.A. 41°54N 71°24W 91 C3
Valley Forge Nat. Historical Park △ Pa., U.S.A. 40°6N 75°27W 87 D7
Valley Grove W. Va., U.S.A. 40°6N 80°34W 102 A4
Valley Head Ala., U.S.A. 34°34N 85°37W 112 B5
Valley Head W. Va., U.S.A. 38°33N 80°2W 102 C4
Valley Junction = West Des Moines Iowa, U.S.A. 41°35N 93°43W 81 D5
Valley Lee Md., U.S.A. 38°12N 76°31W 93 B4
Valley Mills Tex., U.S.A. 31°40N 97°28W 109 F10
Valley of Fire State Park △ Nev., U.S.A. 36°26N 114°29W 128 F6
Valley Park Miss., U.S.A. 32°38N 90°52W 111 D3
Valley Park Mo., U.S.A. 38°33N 90°29W 83 C6
Valley Springs Calif., U.S.A. 38°12N 120°50W 126 E6
Valley Station Ky., U.S.A. 38°6N 85°52W 105 B7
Valley Stream N.Y., U.S.A. 40°39N 73°42W 97 C4
Valley Stream State Park △ N.Y., U.S.A. 40°40N 73°41W 97 B4
Valley View Ohio, U.S.A. 41°23N 81°36W 98 B2
Valley View Pa., U.S.A. 40°39N 76°33W 87 D6
Valley View Tex., U.S.A. 33°29N 97°10W 109 D10
Valleyview Alta., Canada 55°5N 117°17W 152 C4
Valliant Okla., U.S.A. 34°0N 95°6W 107 E8
Valmeyer Ill., U.S.A. 38°18N 90°19W 84 E3
Valmy Nev., U.S.A. 40°48N 117°9W 128 B3
Valois, Baie de Qué., Canada 45°26N 73°47W 160 B2
Valora Ont., Canada 49°46N 91°13W 148 C5
Valparaíso Zacatecas, Mexico 22°46N 103°34W 173 E7
Valparaiso Fla., U.S.A. 30°29N 86°30W 114 A2
Valparaiso Ind., U.S.A. 41°28N 87°4W 85 B3
Valparaiso Nebr., U.S.A. 41°5N 96°50W 80 C9
Valsequillo, Presa Puebla, Mexico 18°55N 98°10W 177 F2
Valtierrilla Guanajuato, Mexico 20°30N 101°10W 175 B6
Van Alstyne Tex., U.S.A. 33°25N 96°35W 109 D11
Van Anda B.C., Canada 49°46N 124°33W 154 F10
Van Bruyssel Qué., Canada 47°56N 72°9W 145 D10
Van Buren = Kettering Ohio, U.S.A. 39°41N 84°10W 86 D2
Van Buren Ark., U.S.A. 35°26N 94°21W 106 C1
Van Buren Ind., U.S.A. 40°37N 85°30W 85 C5

Van Buren Maine, U.S.A. 47°10N 67°58W 90 A6
Van Buren Mo., U.S.A. 37°0N 91°1W 83 E5
Van Buren Ohio, U.S.A. 41°8N 83°39W 86 B3
Van Buren County ☆ Ark., U.S.A. 35°36N 92°28W 106 C3
Van Buren County ☆ Iowa, U.S.A. 40°45N 91°55W 81 E7
Van Buren County ☆ Mich., U.S.A. 42°20N 85°50W 79 G6
Van Buren County ☆ Tenn., U.S.A. 35°45N 85°28W 105 E7
Van Horn Tex., U.S.A. 31°3N 104°50W 108 F3
Van Horne Iowa, U.S.A. 42°1N 92°5W 81 C6
Van Meter Iowa, U.S.A. 41°32N 93°57W 81 D5
Van Tassell Wyo., U.S.A. 42°40N 104°5W 124 D8
Van Vleet Miss., U.S.A. 33°59N 88°54W 111 C5
Van Wert Iowa, U.S.A. 40°52N 93°48W 81 E5
Van Wert Ohio, U.S.A. 40°52N 84°35W 86 C2
Van Wert County ☆ Ohio, U.S.A. 40°52N 84°35W 86 C2
Van Zandt County ☆ Tex., U.S.A. 32°33N 95°52W 109 E12
Vanceboro Maine, U.S.A. 45°34N 67°26W 90 C6
Vanceboro N.C., U.S.A. 35°19N 77°9W 103 C8
Vanceburg Ky., U.S.A. 38°36N 83°19W 105 B9
Vancleave Miss., U.S.A. 30°32N 88°41W 111 F5
Vancleve Ky., U.S.A. 37°38N 83°25W 105 C9
Vancorum Colo., U.S.A. 38°14N 108°36W 125 D2
Vancourt Tex., U.S.A. 31°21N 100°11W 108 F7
Vancouver B.C., Canada 49°15N 123°7W 161 B2
Vancouver Wash., U.S.A. 45°38N 122°40W 132 A2
Vancouver, Mt. Alaska, U.S.A. 60°20N 139°41W 135 F13
Vancouver Harbour B.C., Canada 49°18N 123°6W 161 B2
Vancouver I. B.C., Canada 49°50N 126°0W 154 F9
Vancouver I. Ranges B.C., Canada 49°30N 125°40W 154 F9
Vancouver Int. ✈ (YVR) B.C., Canada 49°10N 123°10W 161 B2
Vandalia Ill., U.S.A. 38°58N 89°6W 84 E4
Vandalia Mo., U.S.A. 39°19N 91°29W 83 B5
Vandalia Ohio, U.S.A. 39°54N 84°12W 86 D2
Vandemere N.C., U.S.A. 35°11N 76°41W 103 C9
Vandenberg Air Force Base Calif., U.S.A. 34°47N 120°32W 127 J6
Vandenberg Village Calif., U.S.A. 34°43N 120°28W 127 J6
Vanderbilt Mich., U.S.A. 45°9N 84°40W 79 D7
Vanderburgh County ☆ Ind., U.S.A. 38°5N 87°35W 85 G3
Vandercook Lake Mich., U.S.A. 42°12N 84°23W 79 G7
Vandergrift Pa., U.S.A. 40°36N 79°34W 87 D3
Vanderhoof B.C., Canada 54°0N 124°0W 154 A10
Vanderpool Tex., U.S.A. 29°45N 99°33W 109 H8
Vandry Qué., Canada 47°52N 73°34W 145 D9
Vanduser Mo., U.S.A. 36°59N 89°42W 83 E7
Vanguard Sask., Canada 49°55N 107°20W 150 F4
Vanier Ont., Canada 45°27N 75°40W 147 B11
Vanier, I. Nunavut, Canada 76°10N 103°15W 158 B5
Vankleek Hill Ont., Canada 45°32N 74°40W 147 B12
Vanoss Okla., U.S.A. 34°46N 96°52W 107 D7
Vanscoy Sask., Canada 52°0N 106°59W 150 C5
Vansittart I. N.W.T., Canada 65°50N 84°0W 159 D9
Vapor, L. el Campeche, Mexico 18°20N 91°50W 178 D2
Varadito, Pta. Sinaloa, Mexico 24°48N 108°5W 172 C2
Vardaman Miss., U.S.A. 33°53N 89°11W 111 C4
Varejonal Sinaloa, Mexico 25°6N 107°22W 172 B3
Vargas I. B.C., Canada 49°11N 125°59W 154 F9
Varina Iowa, U.S.A. 42°40N 94°54W 81 C4
Varna Ill., U.S.A. 41°2N 89°14W 84 B4
Varnado La., U.S.A. 30°54N 89°50W 110 D6
Varnville S.C., U.S.A. 32°51N 81°5W 103 F4
Vars Ont., Canada 45°21N 75°21W 144 F7
Vasconcelos Veracruz, Mexico 17°34N 94°44W 177 G6
Vashon Wash., U.S.A. 47°26N 122°27W 132 D3
Vashon Heights Wash., U.S.A. 47°30N 122°27W 132 C3
Vashon Island Wash., U.S.A. 47°25N 122°28W 132 D3
Vass N.C., U.S.A. 35°15N 79°17W 103 C6
Vassar Qué., Canada 58°14N 77°56W 144 C5
Vassar Man., Canada 49°10N 95°55W 151 F16
Vassar Kans., U.S.A. 38°42N 95°37W 82 C8
Vassar Mich., U.S.A. 43°22N 83°35W 79 F8
Vassia Amer. Samoa 14°15S 170°40W 184 e
Vaudreuil-Dorion Qué., Canada 45°23N 74°3W 145 F8
Vaughan Ont., Canada 43°50N 79°32W 161 A1
Vaughan Miss., U.S.A. 32°48N 90°3W 111 D3
Vaughn Mont., U.S.A. 47°33N 111°33W 123 C6
Vaughn N. Mex., U.S.A. 34°36N 105°13W 131 C5
Vauxhall Alta., Canada 50°5N 112°9W 153 H8
Vavenby B.C., Canada 51°36N 119°43W 155 D15
Veblen S. Dak., U.S.A. 45°52N 97°17W 76 E8
Veedersburg Ind., U.S.A. 40°7N 87°16W 85 C3
Vega Tex., U.S.A. 35°15N 102°26W 108 D5
Vega, L. la Jalisco, Mexico 20°36N 103°50W 174 B4
Vega Alta Puerto Rico 18°25N 66°20W 184 G16
Vega Baja Puerto Rico 18°27N 66°23W 184 G16
Vega de Alatorre Veracruz, Mexico 20°2N 96°38W 176 D4
Vegas Verde = North Las Vegas Nev., U.S.A. 36°11N 115°7W 134 B1
Vegreville Alta., Canada 53°30N 112°5W 152 E8
Veguita N. Mex., U.S.A. 34°31N 106°46W 131 C4
Veinte de Noviembre Chiapas, Mexico 16°32N 92°53W 178 C4
Veinte Séptimos de Enero Baja Calif., Mexico 31°7N 116°20W 166 B2
Veintiocho de Agosto Coahuila, Mexico 25°37N 102°6W 170 E2
Velardeña Durango, Mexico 25°4N 103°44W 173 D7
Velas, C. Costa Rica 10°21N 85°52W 182 D2
Velasco Suárez Chiapas, Mexico 16°49N 91°15W 178 C5
Velma Okla., U.S.A. 34°28N 97°40W 107 D6
Velva N. Dak., U.S.A. 48°4N 100°56W 76 B5
Venado San Luis Potosí, Mexico 22°56N 101°6W 171 H3
Venados, I. Sinaloa, Mexico 23°15N 106°28W 172 D4
Venango County ☆ Pa., U.S.A. 41°20N 79°50W 87 C3
Vencedores Durango, Mexico 24°55N 105°43W 172 C5
Venedocia Ohio, U.S.A. 40°47N 84°28W 86 C2
Veneta Oreg., U.S.A. 44°3N 123°21W 121 D3
Venetian Islands Fla., U.S.A. 25°47N 80°9W 115 D3
Venetie Alaska, U.S.A. 67°1N 146°25W 135 C11
Venezuelan Basin Cent. Amer. 15°0N 68°0W 183 E7
Venice Calif., U.S.A. 33°59N 118°27W 133 C2
Venice Fla., U.S.A. 27°6N 82°27W 114 D6
Venice Ill., U.S.A. 38°40N 90°10W 94 B3
Venice La., U.S.A. 29°17N 89°22W 110 E6
Venleer Tenn., U.S.A. 36°14N 87°27W 104 D5
Venosta Qué., Canada 45°56N 76°1W 144 F6
Ventana, I. Sinaloa, Mexico 24°46N 108°3W 172 C2
Venton City N.J., U.S.A. 38°12N 75°18W 93 B5
Ventucopa Calif., U.S.A. 34°50N 119°29W 127 J7
Ventura Calif., U.S.A. 34°17N 119°18W 127 J7
Ventura County ☆ Calif., U.S.A. 34°30N 119°0W 127 J7
Venustiano Carranza Baja Calif., Mexico 30°25N 115°53W 166 C3

Venustiano Carranza Chiapas, Mexico 16°21N 92°33W 178 C4
Venustiano Carranza Chiapas, Mexico 17°20N 92°13W 178 B4
Venustiano Carranza Distrito Federal, Mexico 19°25N 99°5W 181 B3
Venustiano Carranza Jalisco, Mexico 19°44N 103°47W 174 C4
Venustiano Carranza Michoacan, Mexico 20°5N 102°38W 174 B5
Venustiano Carranza Puebla, Mexico 20°32N 97°39W 176 D3
Venustiano Carranza, Presa Coahuila, Mexico 27°30N 100°37W 170 C4
Vera Okla., U.S.A. 36°27N 95°53W 107 B8
Veracruz Veracruz, Mexico 19°11N 96°8W 177 E5
Veracruz □ Mexico 19°0N 96°15W 177 F4
Veracruzano, Parque Nacional Sistema Arrecifal △ Veracruz, Mexico 19°10N 96°5W 177 E5
Verbena Ala., U.S.A. 32°45N 86°31W 112 D4
Verda La., U.S.A. 31°42N 92°46W 110 C3
Verde → Chihuahua, Mexico 26°39N 107°11W 169 G8
Verde → Jalisco, Mexico 20°42N 103°14W 174 B4
Verde → Oaxaca, Mexico 15°59N 97°50W 177 J3
Verde → Ariz., U.S.A. 33°33N 111°40W 130 D4
Verde, Cay Bahamas 23°0N 75°5W 182 B4
Verde Grande Tamaulipas, Mexico 24°6N 97°56W 171 F7
Verdel Nebr., U.S.A. 42°49N 98°12W 80 B7
Verden Okla., U.S.A. 35°5N 98°5W 107 C5
Verdi Nev., U.S.A. 39°31N 119°59W 128 C1
Verdigre Nebr., U.S.A. 42°36N 98°2W 80 B7
Verdigre Cr. → Nebr., U.S.A. 42°42N 98°3W 80 B7
Verdigris → Okla., U.S.A. 35°48N 95°19W 107 C8
Verdon Nebr., U.S.A. 40°9N 95°43W 80 D10
Verdugo Mts. Calif., U.S.A. 34°10N 118°16W 133 A2
Verdun Qué., Canada 45°27N 73°35W 160 B3
Veregin Sask., Canada 51°35N 102°5W 151 D9
Vergas Minn., U.S.A. 46°40N 95°48W 77 D3
Vergennes Vt., U.S.A. 44°10N 73°15W 89 B1
Verlo Sask., Canada 50°19N 108°35W 150 E3
Vermejo → N. Mex., U.S.A. 36°25N 104°30W 131 A6
Vermeulle, L. Qué., Canada 54°43N 69°24W 143 C4
Vermilion Alta., Canada 53°20N 110°50W 152 E10
Vermilion Ill., U.S.A. 39°35N 87°35W 84 D6
Vermilion Ohio, U.S.A. 41°25N 82°22W 86 B4
Vermilion → Alta., Canada 53°22N 110°51W 152 E10
Vermilion → Ill., U.S.A. 41°19N 89°4W 84 B4
Vermilion B. La., U.S.A. 29°42N 92°0W 110 E4
Vermilion Bay Ont., Canada 49°51N 93°34W 148 C2
Vermilion Cliffs Utah, U.S.A. 37°10N 112°30W 129 F3
Vermilion Cliffs Nat. Monument △ Ariz., U.S.A. 36°54N 112°5W 130 A3
Vermilion County ☆ Ill., U.S.A. 40°10N 87°45W 84 C6
Vermilion L. Ont., Canada 50°3N 92°13W 148 B4
Vermilion L. Minn., U.S.A. 47°53N 92°26W 77 C6
Vermilion Parish ☆ La., U.S.A. 29°55N 92°15W 110 E3
Vermilion Pass B.C., Canada 51°15N 116°2W 155 D18
Vermilion Ra. Minn., U.S.A. 47°50N 92°0W 77 C6
Vermillion S. Dak., U.S.A. 42°47N 96°56W 76 H9
Vermillion → S. Dak., U.S.A. 42°44N 96°53W 76 H9
Vermillion Bluffs Colo., U.S.A. 40°50N 108°20W 125 B2
Vermillion County ☆ Ind., U.S.A. 39°50N 87°30W 85 D3
Vermont □ U.S.A. 44°0N 73°0W 89 B2
Verona Fla., U.S.A. 27°23N 82°16W 114 D6
Vernal Utah, U.S.A. 40°27N 109°32W 129 C6
Verndale Minn., U.S.A. 46°24N 95°1W 77 D3
Verner Ont., Canada 46°25N 80°8W 146 A6
Vernon B.C., Canada 50°20N 119°15W 155 E15
Vernon Ala., U.S.A. 33°45N 88°7W 112 C2
Vernon Calif., U.S.A. 34°0N 118°13W 133 B2
Vernon Colo., U.S.A. 39°57N 102°19W 125 C8
Vernon Conn., U.S.A. 41°50N 72°28W 91 C2
Vernon Fla., U.S.A. 30°37N 85°43W 114 A3
Vernon Ill., U.S.A. 38°48N 89°5W 84 E4
Vernon Ind., U.S.A. 38°59N 85°36W 85 E5
Vernon N.J., U.S.A. 41°12N 74°29W 92 A2
Vernon Tex., U.S.A. 34°9N 99°17W 109 C8
Vernon Utah, U.S.A. 40°6N 112°26W 129 C3
Vernon Center Minn., U.S.A. 43°58N 94°10W 77 G4
Vernon County ☆ Mo., U.S.A. 37°50N 94°20W 83 D2
Vernon County ☆ Wis., U.S.A. 43°30N 90°50W 78 E3
Vernon L. La., U.S.A. 31°11N 93°12W 110 C2
Vernon Parish ☆ La., U.S.A. 31°9N 93°16W 110 C2
Vernonia Oreg., U.S.A. 45°52N 123°11W 121 B2
Vernon Mich., U.S.A. 42°19N 83°7W 98 B2
Vero Beach Fla., U.S.A. 27°38N 80°24W 115 C4
Véron, L. Nfld. & L., Canada 51°48N 65°7W 140 B4
Verona Ont., Canada 44°29N 76°42W 147 C10
Verona Miss., U.S.A. 34°12N 88°43W 111 B5
Verona N. Dak., U.S.A. 46°22N 98°4W 76 D7
Verona N.J., U.S.A. 40°49N 74°14W 97 B1
Verona Pa., U.S.A. 40°30N 79°50W 98 A2
Verona Va., U.S.A. 38°12N 79°0W 102 C5
Verona Wis., U.S.A. 42°59N 89°32W 78 F4
Verrazano Narrows Bridge N.Y., U.S.A. 40°36N 74°2W 97 C2
Verret, L. La., U.S.A. 29°53N 91°10W 110 E4
Versailles Conn., U.S.A. 41°36N 72°2W 91 C2
Versailles Ill., U.S.A. 39°53N 90°39W 84 D3
Versailles Ind., U.S.A. 39°4N 85°15W 85 D5
Versailles Ky., U.S.A. 38°3N 84°44W 105 B8
Versailles Mo., U.S.A. 38°26N 92°51W 83 C4
Versailles Ohio, U.S.A. 40°13N 84°29W 86 C2
Vert I. Ont., Canada 48°55N 88°3W 148 D8
Verte, Î. Qué., Canada 48°2N 69°26W 145 C13
Vesper Kans., U.S.A. 39°2N 98°17W 82 B5
Vesper Wis., U.S.A. 44°29N 89°58W 78 D4
Vesta Ga., U.S.A. 33°58N 82°56W 113 C4
Vesta Nebr., U.S.A. 40°21N 96°20W 80 D9
Vestavia Hills Ala., U.S.A. 33°27N 86°47W 112 C4
Vestgrønland = Kitaa □ Greenland 70°0N 47°0W 162 C6
Veta Grande Zacatecas, Mexico 22°52N 102°32W 173 E8
Vetal S. Dak., U.S.A. 43°13N 101°23W 76 G3
Veteran Alta., Canada 52°0N 111°7W 153 F9
Veterans Memorial County Park △ Mo., U.S.A. 38°48N 90°15W 94 A2
Vevay Ind., U.S.A. 38°45N 85°4W 85 E5
Vibank Sask., Canada 50°20N 103°56W 150 E8
Viborg S. Dak., U.S.A. 43°10N 97°5W 76 G8
Viburnum Mo., U.S.A. 37°43N 91°8W 83 D5
Vicam Sonora, Mexico 27°35N 110°20W 168 F5
Vicco Ky., U.S.A. 37°13N 83°4W 105 C9
Vicente Guerrero Baja Calif., Mexico 30°45N 116°0W 166 C2
Vicente Guerrero Chiapas, Mexico 16°41N 93°15W 178 C3
Vicente Guerrero Durango, Mexico 23°45N 103°59W 173 D7
Vicente Guerrero Puebla, Mexico 18°33N 97°11W 177 F3

Vicente Guerrero *Sonora, Mexico* 30°50N 112°53W **168** C3
Vicente Guerrero *Tabasco, Mexico* 18°27N 92°58W **178** A4
Vicente Guerrero *Tlaxcala, Mexico* 19°8N 98°10W **175** C9
Vicente Guerrero, Presa *Tamaulipas, Mexico* 23°57N 98°42W **171** G6
Viceroy *Sask., Canada* 49°28N 105°22W **150** F6
Vici *Okla., U.S.A.* 36°9N 99°18W **107** B4
Vick *Ark., U.S.A.* 33°20N 92°6W **106** E3
Vicksburg *Ariz., U.S.A.* 33°45N 113°45W **130** D2
Vicksburg *Mich., U.S.A.* 42°7N 85°32W **79** G6
Vicksburg *Miss., U.S.A.* 32°21N 90°53W **111** D3
Vicksburg Nat. Military Park △ *Miss., U.S.A.* 32°21N 90°51W **111** D3
Victor *Colo., U.S.A.* 38°43N 105°9W **125** D5
Victor *Idaho, U.S.A.* 43°36N 111°7W **122** F7
Victor *Iowa, U.S.A.* 41°44N 92°18W **81** D6
Victor *Mont., U.S.A.* 46°25N 114°9W **123** D3
Victor, L. *Qué., Canada* 50°35N 61°50W **140** C8
Victoria *Nfld. & L., Canada* 48°30N 123°25W **155** G11
Victoria *Nfld. & L., Canada* 47°46N 53°14W **142** E7
Victoria *Guanajuato, Mexico* 21°23N 100°12W **175** A7
Victoria *Ill., U.S.A.* 41°2N 90°6W **84** B3
Victoria *Kans., U.S.A.* 38°52N 99°9W **82** C4
Victoria *Tex., U.S.A.* 28°48N 97°0W **109** L6
Victoria *Va., U.S.A.* 36°59N 78°8W **102** E6
Victoria, Grand L. *Qué., Canada* 47°31N 77°30W **144** D5
Victoria, Pont *Qué., Canada* 45°29N 73°32W **160** B3
Victoria Beach *Man., Canada* 50°40N 96°35W **151** E15
Victoria County ☆ *Tex., U.S.A.* 28°45N 96°55W **109** J11
Victoria de Durango = Durango *Mexico* 24°3N 104°39W **173** C6
Victoria de las Tunas = Las Tunas *Cuba* 20°58N 76°59W **182** B4
Victoria Harbour *Ont., Canada* 44°45N 79°45W **146** C7
Victoria I. *Canada* 71°0N 111°0W **156** B10
Victoria L. *Nfld. & L., Canada* 48°20N 57°27W **142** D3
Victoria Pk. *Alta., Canada* 49°18N 114°8W **152** E6
Victoria Pk. *B.C., Canada* 50°3N 126°5W **154** E8
Victoria Str. *N.W.T., Canada* 69°31N 100°30W **158** D5
Victoriaville *Qué., Canada* 46°4N 71°56W **145** E11
Victorville *Calif., U.S.A.* 34°32N 117°18W **127** J9
Vidal *Calif., U.S.A.* 34°7N 114°31W **127** J12
Vidal Junction *Calif., U.S.A.* 34°11N 114°34W **127** J12
Vidalia *Ga., U.S.A.* 32°13N 82°25W **113** D4
Vidalia *La., U.S.A.* 31°34N 91°26W **110** C4
Vidauri *Tex., U.S.A.* 28°26N 97°8W **109** J10
Vidette *La., U.S.A.* 33°2N 82°15W **113** C4
Vidor *Tex., U.S.A.* 30°7N 94°1W **109** G13
Vieja, Sierra *Tex., U.S.A.* 30°35N 104°40W **108** G3
Vienna *Ont., Canada* 42°41N 80°48W **146** E6
Vienna *Ga., U.S.A.* 32°6N 83°47W **113** D3
Vienna *Ill., U.S.A.* 37°25N 88°54W **84** F51
Vienna *Md., U.S.A.* 38°29N 75°50W **93** B5
Vienna *Mo., U.S.A.* 38°11N 91°57W **83** C51
Vienna *S. Dak., U.S.A.* 44°42N 97°30W **76** F8
Vienna *Va., U.S.A.* 38°54N 77°16W **99** B2
Vienna *W. Va., U.S.A.* 39°20N 81°33W **102** B3
Viento, L. el *Tabasco, Mexico* 18°13N 92°38W **178** A4
Vientos, Paso de los *Caribbean* 20°0N 74°0W **183** C5
Vieques *Puerto Rico* 18°8N 65°25W **184** G17
Viesca *Coahuila, Mexico* 25°21N 102°48W **171** E2
Vietnam Veterans Memorial *D.C., U.S.A.* 38°53N 77°2W **99** B3
Vietnam War Museum *Ill., U.S.A.* 41°58N 87°39W **95** B3
Vieux Desert, L. *Mich., U.S.A.* 46°8N 89°7W **79** C2
View Park *Calif., U.S.A.* 34°0N 118°20W **133** B3
Vigía Grande, Península *Quintana Roo, Mexico* 19°40N 87°27W **179** C6
Vigo County ☆ *Ind., U.S.A.* 39°25N 87°25W **85** D3
Vigo Park *Tex., U.S.A.* 34°39N 101°30W **108** C6
Viking *Alta., Canada* 53°7N 111°50W **153** E9
Viking *Minn., U.S.A.* 48°13N 96°24W **77** B2
Vilas *Colo., U.S.A.* 37°22N 102°27W **125** E8
Vilas *S. Dak., U.S.A.* 44°1N 97°36W **76** F8
Vilas County ☆ *Wis., U.S.A.* 46°0N 89°30W **78** B4
Villa Acuña *Veracruz, Mexico* 18°31N 95°47W **177** F5
Villa Ahumada *Chihuahua, Mexico* 30°37N 106°31W **169** C9
Villa Ahumada y Anexas *Chihuahua, Mexico* 30°31N 106°50W **169** C9
Villa Alta *Oaxaca, Mexico* 17°5N 96°0W **177** G5
Villa Cecilia = Ciudad Madero *Tamaulipas, Mexico* 22°19N 97°50W **171** H7
Villa Chacaltongo *Oaxaca, Mexico* 17°3N 97°35W **177** G3
Villa Comaltitlán *Chiapas, Mexico* 15°13N 92°35W **178** D4
Villa Coronado *Chihuahua, Mexico* 26°45N 105°10W **169** G10
Villa Corzo *Chiapas, Mexico* 16°10N 93°12W **178** C3
Villa Cuauhtémoc *Veracruz, Mexico* 22°11N 97°50W **176** B3
Villa de Acala *Chiapas, Mexico* 16°34N 92°48W **178** C4
Villa de Allende *México, Mexico* 19°23N 100°9W **175** C7
Villa de Álvarez *Colima, Mexico* 19°15N 103°44W **174** C4
Villa de Arriaga *San Luis Potosí, Mexico* 21°56N 101°20W **171** J3
Villa de Bustamante *Tamaulipas, Mexico* 23°26N 99°47W **171** G5
Villa de Casas *Tamaulipas, Mexico* 23°44N 98°43W **171** G6
Villa de Cos *Zacatecas, Mexico* 23°17N 102°21W **173** D8
Villa de Costa Rica *Sinaloa, Mexico* 24°35N 107°38W **172** C3
Villa de García *Nuevo León, Mexico* 25°49N 100°35W **170** E4
Villa de Guadalupe *Distrito Federal, Mexico* 19°29N 99°6W **181** B3
Villa de Guadalupe *San Luis Potosí, Mexico* 23°22N 100°46W **171** G4
Villa de Méndez *Tamaulipas, Mexico* 25°7N 98°34W **171** E6
Villa de Ramos *San Luis Potosí, Mexico* 22°50N 101°56W **171** H3
Villa de Reyes *San Luis Potosí, Mexico* 21°48N 100°56W **171** J4
Villa de Tamazulapan *Oaxaca, Mexico* 17°40N 97°35W **177** G3
Villa de Tezantepec *Hidalgo, Mexico* 19°48N 98°53W **175** C9
Villa del Rio *Chiapas, Mexico* 16°44N 93°55W **178** C3
Villa Escalante *Michoacan, Mexico* 19°24N 101°39W **174** C6
Villa Escobedo *Coahuila, Mexico* 27°13N 101°21W **170** C3
Villa Flores *Chiapas, Mexico* 16°14N 93°14W **178** C3
Villa García *Zacatecas, Mexico* 22°13N 101°57W **173** E9
Villa González Ortega *Zacatecas, Mexico* 22°31N 101°54W **173** E9
Villa Grove *Colo., U.S.A.* 38°15N 105°59W **125** D5
Villa Grove *Ill., U.S.A.* 39°52N 88°10W **84** D5
Villa Guadalupe *Sonora, Mexico* 27°10N 110°10W **168** F5
Villa Guadalupe *Sonora, Mexico* 30°52N 112°58W **168** C3
Villa Guerrero *Jalisco, Mexico* 21°59N 103°36W **173** F7
Villa Guerrero *México, Mexico* 18°58N 99°38W **175** D8
Villa Guerrero *Veracruz, Mexico* 17°36N 95°12W **177** G5
Villa Hidalgo *Chiapas, Mexico* 16°18N 93°9W **178** C3
Villa Hidalgo *Coahuila, Mexico* 27°46N 99°50W **170** C3
Villa Hidalgo *Durango, Mexico* 26°16N 104°54W **173** A6
Villa Hidalgo *Jalisco, Mexico* 21°40N 102°36W **174** A5
Villa Hidalgo *Nayarit, Mexico* 21°40N 104°54W **173** F5
Villa Hidalgo *San Luis Potosí, Mexico* 22°27N 100°42W **171** H4
Villa Hidalgo *Sonora, Mexico* 30°7N 109°20W **168** C6

Villa Hidalgo *Tamaulipas, Mexico* 24°15N 99°26W **171** F5
Villa Hidalgo *Zacatecas, Mexico* 22°21N 101°42W **173** E9
Villa Jesús María *Baja Calif. S., Mexico* 28°18N 114°0W **167** E5
Villa Juanita *Veracruz, Mexico* 17°49N 95°14W **177** G5
Villa Juárez *Durango, Mexico* 25°30N 103°35W **173** B7
Villa Juárez *San Luis Potosí, Mexico* 22°23N 100°16W **171** H4
Villa Juárez *Sinaloa, Mexico* 24°39N 107°34W **172** D3
Villa Juárez *Sonora, Mexico* 27°7N 109°52W **168** F6
Villa López *Chihuahua, Mexico* 27°0N 105°2W **169** G10
Villa Madero *Michoacan, Mexico* 19°24N 101°16W **175** C6
Villa Mainero *Tamaulipas, Mexico* 24°34N 99°36W **171** F5
Villa Matamoros *Chihuahua, Mexico* 26°47N 105°35W **169** G10
Villa Morelos *Baja Calif. S., Mexico* 24°54N 111°38W **167** J7
Villa Moros *Sinaloa, Mexico* 24°40N 107°41W **172** C3
Villa Nicolas Romero *México, Mexico* 19°38N 99°19W **175** C8
Villa Ocampo *Durango, Mexico* 26°27N 105°31W **172** A5
Villa Pesqueria *Sonora, Mexico* 29°8N 109°59W **168** D6
Villa Progreso *Querétaro, Mexico* 20°38N 99°48W **175** B8
Villa Rica *Ga., U.S.A.* 33°44N 84°55W **113** C2
Villa Santo Domingo *San Luis Potosí, Mexico* 23°20N 101°44W **171** G3
Villa Unión *Coahuila, Mexico* 28°15N 100°43W **170** B4
Villa Unión *Durango, Mexico* 23°58N 104°2W **173** D6
Villa Unión *Sinaloa, Mexico* 23°12N 106°14W **172** D4
Villa Victoria *México, Mexico* 19°26N 100°0W **175** C8
Villa Victoria *Michoacan, Mexico* 18°47N 103°24W **174** D4
Villa Zaragoza *San Luis Potosí, Mexico* 22°2N 100°44W **171** H4
Village, The *Okla., U.S.A.* 35°35N 97°33W **107** C6
Village of Superior *Wis., U.S.A.* 46°40N 92°6W **78** B1
Villagrán *Guanajuato, Mexico* 20°31N 100°59W **175** B7
Villagrán *Sonora, Mexico* 31°39N 113°6W **168** B2
Villagrán *Tamaulipas, Mexico* 24°29N 99°29W **171** F5
Villahermosa *Tabasco, Mexico* 17°59N 92°55W **178** B4
Villalba *Puerto Rico* 18°8N 66°30W **184** G16
Villaldama *Nuevo León, Mexico* 26°30N 100°26W **170** D4
Villamar *Michoacan, Mexico* 19°59N 102°35W **174** C5
Villanueva *Zacatecas, Mexico* 22°21N 102°53W **173** E8
Villanueva *N. Mex., U.S.A.* 35°16N 105°22W **131** B5
Villard *Minn., U.S.A.* 45°43N 95°16W **77** E3
Villas *N.J., U.S.A.* 39°2N 74°56W **92** C2
Ville-Marie *Qué., Canada* 47°20N 79°30W **144** D3
Ville Platte *La., U.S.A.* 30°41N 92°17W **110** D3
Villebon, L. *Qué., Canada* 47°58N 77°17W **144** D5
Villegreen *Colo., U.S.A.* 37°18N 103°31W **125** E7
Villemontel *Qué., Canada* 48°38N 78°22W **144** C4
Villisca *Iowa, U.S.A.* 40°56N 94°59W **81** E4
Vilna *Alta., Canada* 54°7N 111°55W **152** D9
Vilonia *Ark., U.S.A.* 35°5N 92°13W **106** C3
Vimont *Qué., Canada* 45°36N 73°43W **160** A2
Vina *Ala., U.S.A.* 34°23N 88°4W **112** B2
Vinalhaven *Maine, U.S.A.* 44°3N 68°50W **90** D5
Vinalhaven I. *Maine, U.S.A.* 44°5N 68°51W **90** D5
Vincennes *Ind., U.S.A.* 38°41N 87°32W **85** E3
Vincent *Ala., U.S.A.* 33°23N 86°25W **112** C4
Vincent *Iowa, U.S.A.* 42°36N 94°1W **81** C4
Vincentown *N.J., U.S.A.* 39°56N 74°45W **92** C2
Vine Grove *Ky., U.S.A.* 37°49N 85°59W **105** C7
Vineland *Fla., U.S.A.* 28°23N 81°30W **115** B1
Vineland *N.J., U.S.A.* 39°29N 75°2W **92** C1
Vinemont *Ala., U.S.A.* 34°15N 86°52W **112** B4
Vineyard Haven *Mass., U.S.A.* 41°27N 70°36W **91** C4
Vineyard Sd. *Mass., U.S.A.* 41°25N 70°45W **91** C4
Vining *Minn., U.S.A.* 46°16N 95°32W **77** D3
Vinings *Georgia, U.S.A.* 33°53N 84°29W **117** A2
Vinita *Okla., U.S.A.* 36°39N 95°9W **107** B8
Vinita Park *Mo., U.S.A.* 38°41N 90°20W **94** B1
Vinson *Okla., U.S.A.* 34°54N 99°52W **107** D4
Vinton *Calif., U.S.A.* 39°48N 120°10W **126** D6
Vinton *Iowa, U.S.A.* 42°10N 92°1W **81** C61
Vinton *La., U.S.A.* 30°11N 93°35W **110** D2
Vinton *Ohio, U.S.A.* 38°59N 82°21W **86** E4
Vinton *Va., U.S.A.* 37°17N 79°54W **102** D5
Vinton County ☆ *Ohio, U.S.A.* 39°15N 82°29W **86** D4
Viola *Ark., U.S.A.* 36°24N 91°59W **106** B4
Viola *Del., U.S.A.* 39°5N 75°34W **93** A5
Viola *Ill., U.S.A.* 41°12N 90°35W **84** B3
Viola *Kans., U.S.A.* 37°29N 97°39W **82** D6
Viola *Tenn., U.S.A.* 35°32N 85°52W **105** E7
Viola *Wis., U.S.A.* 43°31N 90°40W **78** E3
Violet *La., U.S.A.* 29°53N 89°53W **117** C3
Virago Sd. *B.C., Canada* 54°0N 132°30W **154** A2
Virden *Man., Canada* 49°50N 100°56W **151** F11
Virden *Ill., U.S.A.* 39°30N 89°46W **84** D4
Virden *N. Mex., U.S.A.* 32°41N 109°0W **131** E2
Virgenes, C. *Baja Calif. S., Mexico* 27°31N 112°21W **167** F6
Virgil *Ill., U.S.A.* 37°59N 96°1W **82** D7
Virgil *S. Dak., U.S.A.* 44°17N 98°26W **76** F7
Virgilina *Va., U.S.A.* 36°33N 78°47W **102** E6
Virgin → *Utah, U.S.A.* 36°28N 114°21W **128** F6
Virgin *Utah, U.S.A.* 37°12N 113°11W **129** F2
Virgin Gorda *Br. Virgin Is.* 18°30N 64°26W **184** G18
Virgin Is. (British) ☑ *W. Indies* 18°30N 64°30W **184** G18
Virgin Is. (U.S.) ☑ *W. Indies* 18°20N 65°0W **184** G18
Virgin Islands Nat. Park △ *U.S. Virgin Is.* 18°21N 64°43W **184** G18
Virgin Mts. *Ariz., U.S.A.* 36°45N 113°45W **130** A2
Virginia *Idaho, U.S.A.* 42°30N 112°10W **122** G6
Virginia *Ill., U.S.A.* 39°57N 90°13W **84** D3
Virginia *Minn., U.S.A.* 47°31N 92°32W **77** C6
Virginia ☑ *U.S.A.* 37°30N 78°45W **102** D6
Virginia, L. *Fla., U.S.A.* 28°35N 81°20W **115** A2
Virginia Beach *Va., U.S.A.* 36°44N 76°0W **102** E9
Virginia City *Mont., U.S.A.* 45°18N 111°56W **123** E6
Virginia City *Nev., U.S.A.* 39°19N 119°39W **128** C1
Virginia Falls *N.W.T., Canada* 61°38N 125°42W **157** D7
Virginia Gardens *Fla., U.S.A.* 25°48N 80°18W **115** D1
Virginia Key *Fla., U.S.A.* 25°44N 80°8W **115** D3
Virginia Mts. *Nev., U.S.A.* 39°50N 119°30W **128** C1
Virginiatown *Ont., Canada* 48°9N 79°36W **144** C3
Viroqua *Wis., U.S.A.* 43°34N 90°53W **78** E3
Visalia *Calif., U.S.A.* 36°20N 119°18W **127** D7
Viscount *Sask., Canada* 51°57N 105°39W **150** D6
Viscount Melville Sd. *Canada* 74°10N 108°0W **156** B11
Visitacion Valley *Calif., U.S.A.* 37°42N 122°23W **132** B2
Vista *Calif., U.S.A.* 33°12N 117°14W **127** K9
Vista *Mo., U.S.A.* 37°58N 93°40W **83** D3
Vista Grove *Georgia, U.S.A.* 33°51N 84°16W **117** A3
Vivian *La., U.S.A.* 32°53N 93°59W **110** B2
Vivian *S. Dak., U.S.A.* 43°56N 100°18W **76** G5
Vizcaíno, Desierto de *Mexico* 27°30N 113°45W **167** F5
Vogar *Man., Canada* 50°57N 98°39W **151** E13
Voisey B. *Nfld. & L., Canada* 55°15N 61°50W **143** B5
Volborg *Mont., U.S.A.* 45°51N 105°41W **123** C12
Volcán de Colima, Parque Nacional △ *Jalisco, Mexico* 19°30N 103°40W **174** C4

Volcano *Hawai'i, U.S.A.* 19°26N 155°14W **136** D6
Volga *Iowa, U.S.A.* 42°48N 91°33W **81** C7
Volga *S. Dak., U.S.A.* 44°19N 96°56W **76** F9
Volin *S. Dak., U.S.A.* 42°58N 97°11W **76** H8
Voltaire *N. Dak., U.S.A.* 48°2N 100°47W **76** A4
Voltaire → *Wash., U.S.A.* 46°20N 120°30W **120** C5
Voluntown *Conn., U.S.A.* 41°34N 71°52W **91** C3
Volusia County ☆ *Fla., U.S.A.* 29°0N 81°15W **114** B7
Von Ormy *Tex., U.S.A.* 29°17N 98°38W **116** D2
Vona *Colo., U.S.A.* 39°18N 102°45W **125** C8
Vonda *Sask., Canada* 52°19N 106°6W **150** C5
Vonore *Tenn., U.S.A.* 35°36N 84°14W **105** E8
Voorheesville *N.Y., U.S.A.* 42°39N 73°56W **88** C7
Voyageurs Nat. Park △ *Minn., U.S.A.* 48°32N 93°0W **77** B6
Vulcan *Alta., Canada* 50°25N 113°15W **153** H7
Vulcan *Mich., U.S.A.* 45°47N 87°53W **79** D4
Vulture Mts. *Ariz., U.S.A.* 33°45N 112°50W **130** D3
Vuntut Nat. Park △ *Yukon, Canada* 68°25N 139°41W **156** C5
Vya *Nev., U.S.A.* 41°35N 119°52W **128** A1

W

W. Kerr Scott Res. *N.C., U.S.A.* 36°10N 81°20W **103** B4
Wabakimi L. *Ont., Canada* 50°38N 89°45W **148** B7
Wabakimi Prov. Park △ *Ont., Canada* 50°39N 89°29W **148** B7
Wabamun *Alta., Canada* 53°33N 114°28W **152** E6
Wabamun L. *Alta., Canada* 53°32N 114°35W **152** E6
Wabano → *Qué., Canada* 48°20N 74°3W **145** C8
Wabasca → *Alta., Canada* 58°22N 115°20W **152** A5
Wabasca-Desmarais *Alta., Canada* 55°57N 113°56W **152** C7
Wabash *Ind., U.S.A.* 40°48N 85°49W **85** C5
Wabash → *Ind., U.S.A.* 37°48N 88°2W **85** F2
Wabash County ☆ *Ill., U.S.A.* 38°30N 87°50W **84** E6
Wabash County ☆ *Ind., U.S.A.* 40°50N 85°45W **85** C5
Wabasha *Minn., U.S.A.* 44°23N 92°2W **77** F6
Wabasha County ☆ *Minn., U.S.A.* 44°15N 92°15W **77** F6
Wabaskang L. *Ont., Canada* 50°26N 93°13W **148** B3
Wabassi → *Ont., Canada* 51°45N 86°20W **149** A10
Wabasso *Fla., U.S.A.* 27°45N 80°26W **114** D8
Wabasso *Minn., U.S.A.* 44°24N 95°15W **77** F3
Wabatongushi L. *Ont., Canada* 48°26N 84°13W **149** D12
Wabaunsee *Kans., U.S.A.* 39°9N 96°21W **82** B7
Wabaunsee County ☆ *Kans., U.S.A.* 39°0N 96°15W **82** C7
Wabeno *Wis., U.S.A.* 45°26N 88°39W **78** C5
Wabigoon *Ont., Canada* 49°43N 92°35W **148** C4
Wabigoon L. *Ont., Canada* 49°44N 92°44W **148** C4
Wabimeig L. *Ont., Canada* 51°28N 85°36W **149** A11
Wabinosh L. *Ont., Canada* 50°5N 89°0W **148** B8
Wabuk Pt. *Ont., Canada* 55°20N 85°5W **159** F8
Wabush *Nfld. & L., Canada* 52°55N 66°52W **143** C4
Wabuska *Nev., U.S.A.* 39°9N 119°11W **128** C1
Waccamaw, L. *N.C., U.S.A.* 34°18N 78°31W **103** D7
Waccasassa B. *Fla., U.S.A.* 29°10N 82°50W **114** B6
Wachapreague *Va., U.S.A.* 37°36N 75°42W **102** D9
Wachusett Res. *Mass., U.S.A.* 42°24N 71°41W **91** B3
Wacissa *Fla., U.S.A.* 30°22N 83°59W **114** A5
Waco *Qué., Canada* 51°27N 65°37W **143** C4
Waco *Nebr., U.S.A.* 40°54N 97°28W **80** D8
Waco *Tex., U.S.A.* 31°33N 97°9W **109** F10
Waco L. *Tex., U.S.A.* 31°35N 97°12W **109** F10
Waconda Lake *Kans., U.S.A.* 39°29N 98°19W **82** B5
Waconia *Minn., U.S.A.* 44°51N 93°47W **77** F5
Waconichi, L. *Qué., Canada* 50°8N 74°0W **145** A8
Wacouno → *Qué., Canada* 50°54N 65°57W **140** C4
Waddington *N.Y., U.S.A.* 44°52N 75°12W **88** A5
Waddington, Mt. *B.C., Canada* 51°23N 125°15W **154** D4
Wade Hampton ☆ *Alaska, U.S.A.* 62°15N 163°0W **135** E7
Wadena *Sask., Canada* 51°57N 103°47W **150** D8
Wadena *Minn., U.S.A.* 46°26N 95°8W **77** D3
Wadena County ☆ *Minn., U.S.A.* 46°30N 95°0W **77** D4
Wadesboro *N.C., U.S.A.* 34°58N 80°5W **103** D5
Wadhams *B.C., Canada* 51°30N 127°30W **154** D7
Wading River *N.J., U.S.A.* 39°38N 74°31W **92** C2
Wadley *Ala., U.S.A.* 33°7N 85°34W **112** C5
Wadley *Ga., U.S.A.* 32°52N 82°24W **113** D4
Wadlin L. *Alta., Canada* 57°44N 115°35W **152** A5
Wadsworth *Nev., U.S.A.* 39°38N 119°17W **128** C1
Wadsworth *Ohio, U.S.A.* 41°2N 81°44W **86** B5
Wadsworth *Tex., U.S.A.* 28°50N 95°56W **109** J12
Wadsworth Atheneum *Conn., U.S.A.* 41°46N 72°40W **91** C2
Waelder *Tex., U.S.A.* 29°42N 97°18W **109** H10
Wagener *S.C., U.S.A.* 33°39N 81°22W **103** E4
Wager B. *Nunavut, Canada* 65°26N 88°40W **159** D8
Waggaman *La., U.S.A.* 29°55N 90°12W **117** C1
Wagner *S. Dak., U.S.A.* 43°5N 98°18W **76** G7
Wagon Mound *N. Mex., U.S.A.* 36°1N 104°42W **131** A5
Wagon Wheel Gap *Colo., U.S.A.* 37°46N 106°49W **125** E4
Wagoner *Okla., U.S.A.* 35°58N 95°22W **107** C8
Wagoner County ☆ *Okla., U.S.A.* 36°0N 95°30W **107** B8
Wagontire *Oreg., U.S.A.* 43°15N 119°52W **121** D6
Wagontire Mt. *Oreg., U.S.A.* 43°19N 119°52W **121** D6
Wah Wah Mts. *Utah, U.S.A.* 38°25N 113°40W **129** E2
Wahiawā *Hawai'i, U.S.A.* 21°30N 158°2W **136** K13
Wahiawā District ☆ *Hawai'i, U.S.A.* 21°31N 157°58W **136** J14
Wahiawā Res. *Hawai'i, U.S.A.* 21°30N 158°3W **136** K13
Wahkiakum County ☆ *Wash., U.S.A.* 46°10N 123°30W **120** D2
Wahkon *Minn., U.S.A.* 46°7N 93°31W **77** D5
Wahoo *Nebr., U.S.A.* 41°13N 96°37W **80** C9
Wahpeton *N. Dak., U.S.A.* 46°16N 96°36W **76** D9
Wai'ale'ale *Hawai'i, U.S.A.* 22°4N 159°30W **136** A2
Waialae *Hawai'i, U.S.A.* 21°41N 158°1W **136** J13
Waialua *Hawai'i, U.S.A.* 21°34N 158°8W **136** J13
Waialua District ☆ *Hawai'i, U.S.A.* 21°35N 158°5W **136** J13
Wai'anae Coast *Hawai'i, U.S.A.* 21°27N 158°11W **136** K13
Wai'anae District ☆ *Hawai'i, U.S.A.* 21°28N 158°10W **136** K13
Wai'anae Range *Hawai'i, U.S.A.* 21°30N 158°10W **136** K13
Waiawa → *Hawai'i, U.S.A.* 21°23N 157°59W **136** K14
Waihee-Waiehu *Hawai'i, U.S.A.* 20°56N 156°31W **136** C5
Waikīkī *Hawai'i, U.S.A.* 21°17N 157°50W **136** K14
Waikoloa Village *Hawai'i, U.S.A.* 19°57N 155°49W **136** D5
Wailea-Makena *Hawai'i, U.S.A.* 20°40N 156°27W **136** C5
Wailua *Hawai'i, U.S.A.* 22°3N 159°20W **136** A2
Wailua *Hawai'i, U.S.A.* 20°51N 156°9W **136** C6
Wailuku *Hawai'i, U.S.A.* 20°53N 156°30W **136** C5
Waimalu *Hawai'i, U.S.A.* 21°24N 157°57W **136** K14
Waimānalo *Hawai'i, U.S.A.* 21°20N 157°43W **136** K14
Waimānalo B. *Hawai'i, U.S.A.* 21°20N 157°40W **136** K14
Waimānalo Beach *Hawai'i, U.S.A.* 21°20N 157°42W **136** K14
Waimano → *Hawai'i, U.S.A.* 21°23N 157°59W **136** K14
Waimea *Hawai'i, U.S.A.* 21°58N 159°40W **136** B2
Waimea B. *Hawai'i, U.S.A.* 21°40N 158°5W **136** J13
Waimea Canyon *Hawai'i, U.S.A.* 22°0N 159°39W **136** A2
Wainwright *Alta., Canada* 52°50N 110°50W **153** F10
Wainwright *Alaska, U.S.A.* 70°38N 160°2W **135** A7

Wainwright *Okla., U.S.A.* 35°37N 95°34W **107** C8
Waipahu *Hawai'i, U.S.A.* 21°23N 158°1W **136** K13
Waipi'o *Hawai'i, U.S.A.* 21°25N 158°0W **136** K14
Waipi'o Acres *Hawai'i, U.S.A.* 21°28N 158°1W **136** K13
Waipi'o Peninsula *Hawai'i, U.S.A.* 21°20N 158°0W **136** K14
Waita Res. *Hawai'i, U.S.A.* 21°55N 159°28W **136** B2
Waite *Maine, U.S.A.* 45°20N 67°42W **90** C6
Waite Park *Minn., U.S.A.* 45°33N 94°14W **77** E4
Waiteville *W. Va., U.S.A.* 37°28N 80°25W **102** D4
Waits → *Vt., U.S.A.* 43°59N 72°8W **89** C2
Waitsburg *Wash., U.S.A.* 46°16N 118°9W **120** D7
Waitsfield *Vt., U.S.A.* 44°42N 72°50W **89** B2
Waka *Tex., U.S.A.* 36°17N 101°3W **108** A6
Wakami Lake Prov. Park △ *Ont., Canada* 47°29N 82°50W **149** E14
Wakarusa *Ind., U.S.A.* 41°32N 86°1W **85** B4
Wakaw *Sask., Canada* 52°39N 105°44W **150** C6
Wake County ☆ *N.C., U.S.A.* 35°40N 78°45W **103** C7
Wake Forest *N.C., U.S.A.* 35°59N 78°30W **103** C7
Wake I. *Pac. Oc.* 19°18N 166°36E **184** C5
WaKeeney *Kans., U.S.A.* 39°1N 99°53W **82** B4
Wakefield *Qué., Canada* 45°38N 75°56W **144** F7
Wakefield *Kans., U.S.A.* 39°13N 97°1W **82** B6
Wakefield *Mass., U.S.A.* 42°30N 71°5W **96** A2
Wakefield *Mich., U.S.A.* 46°29N 89°56W **79** C2
Wakefield *N.H., U.S.A.* 43°35N 71°4W **89** C3
Wakefield *Nebr., U.S.A.* 42°16N 96°52W **80** B9
Wakefield *Pa., U.S.A.* 39°46N 76°11W **93** C3
Wakefield *R.I., U.S.A.* 41°26N 71°30W **91** C3
Wakefield *Va., U.S.A.* 36°58N 76°59W **102** E8
Wakeham *Qué., Canada* 48°50N 64°34W **140** E5
Wakeham Bay = Maricourt *Qué., Canada* 56°34N 70°49W **143** B3
Wakita *Okla., U.S.A.* 36°53N 97°55W **107** B6
Wakomata L. *Ont., Canada* 46°34N 83°22W **146** A3
Wakonda *S. Dak., U.S.A.* 43°0N 97°6W **76** G8
Wakpala *S. Dak., U.S.A.* 45°40N 100°32W **76** E5
Wakuach, L. *Qué., Canada* 55°34N 67°32W **143** B4
Wakulla *Fla., U.S.A.* 30°14N 84°14W **114** A4
Wakulla Beach *Fla., U.S.A.* 30°6N 84°16W **114** A4
Wakulla County ☆ *Fla., U.S.A.* 30°15N 84°20W **114** A4
Walcott *Iowa, U.S.A.* 41°35N 90°47W **81** D8
Walcott *N. Dak., U.S.A.* 46°33N 96°56W **76** D9
Walcott *Wyo., U.S.A.* 41°46N 106°51W **124** E6
Walcott, L. *Idaho, U.S.A.* 42°40N 113°29W **122** G5
Waldeck *Sask., Canada* 50°22N 107°36W **150** E4
Walden *Colo., U.S.A.* 40°44N 106°17W **125** B4
Walden *N.Y., U.S.A.* 41°34N 74°11W **88** D6
Walden *Tenn., U.S.A.* 35°10N 85°18W **105** E7
Walden Res. *Colo., U.S.A.* 40°43N 106°17W **125** B4
Walden Ridge *Tenn., U.S.A.* 35°30N 85°15W **105** E7
Waldheim *Sask., Canada* 52°39N 106°37W **150** C5
Waldo *Ark., U.S.A.* 33°21N 93°18W **106** E2
Waldo *Fla., U.S.A.* 29°48N 82°10W **114** B6
Waldo *Maine, U.S.A.* 44°31N 69°5W **90** D4
Waldo *Ohio, U.S.A.* 40°28N 83°5W **86** C3
Waldo County ☆ *Maine, U.S.A.* 44°25N 69°0W **90** D4
Waldo L. *Oreg., U.S.A.* 43°44N 122°2W **121** D3
Waldoboro *Maine, U.S.A.* 44°6N 69°23W **90** D4
Waldorf *Md., U.S.A.* 38°38N 76°55W **93** B4
Waldorf *Minn., U.S.A.* 43°56N 93°42W **77** G5
Waldport *Oreg., U.S.A.* 44°26N 124°4W **121** C1
Waldron *Ark., U.S.A.* 34°54N 94°5W **106** D1
Waldron *Ind., U.S.A.* 39°27N 85°40W **85** D5
Waldron *Mich., U.S.A.* 41°44N 84°25W **79** H7
Waldwick *N.J., U.S.A.* 41°1N 74°7W **92** A2
Wales *Alaska, U.S.A.* 65°37N 168°5W **135** D5
Wales *Mass., U.S.A.* 42°4N 72°13W **91** B2
Wales *N. Dak., U.S.A.* 48°54N 98°36W **76** B7
Wales *Utah, U.S.A.* 39°29N 111°38W **129** D4
Wales I. *Nunavut, Canada* 62°0N 72°30W **143** A3
Wales I. *Nunavut, Canada* 68°1N 86°40W **158** D8
Walford *Iowa, U.S.A.* 41°53N 91°50W **81** D7
Walhachin *B.C., Canada* 50°45N 120°59W **155** E14
Walhalla *N. Dak., U.S.A.* 48°55N 97°55W **76** B8
Walhalla *S.C., U.S.A.* 34°46N 83°4W **103** D2
Walk, L. *Tex., U.S.A.* 29°31N 100°59W **108** H7
Walker *Iowa, U.S.A.* 42°17N 91°47W **81** C7
Walker *Mich., U.S.A.* 42°58N 85°46W **79** G6
Walker *Minn., U.S.A.* 47°6N 94°35W **77** C4
Walker *Mo., U.S.A.* 37°54N 94°14W **83** D2
Walker → *Nev., U.S.A.* 38°54N 118°47W **128** D2
Walker, L. *Qué., Canada* 50°20N 67°11W **143** C4
Walker County ☆ *Ala., U.S.A.* 33°50N 87°17W **112** C3
Walker County ☆ *Ga., U.S.A.* 34°45N 85°15W **113** B1
Walker County ☆ *Tex., U.S.A.* 30°43N 95°33W **109** G12
Walker L. *Nev., U.S.A.* 38°42N 118°43W **128** D2
Walker River Indian Reservation *Nev., U.S.A.* 39°0N 118°50W **128** D2
Walkers Pt. *Maine, U.S.A.* 43°21N 70°28W **90** E3
Walkersville *Md., U.S.A.* 39°29N 77°21W **93** A3
Walkerton *Ont., Canada* 44°10N 81°10W **146** C5
Walkerton *Ind., U.S.A.* 41°28N 86°29W **85** B4
Walkertown *N.C., U.S.A.* 36°10N 80°10W **103** B5
Walkerville *Mich., U.S.A.* 43°43N 86°8W **79** F5
Wall *Tex., U.S.A.* 31°22N 100°18W **108** F7
Wall *Tex., U.S.A.* 31°22N 100°18W **108** F7
Wall Lake *Iowa, U.S.A.* 42°16N 95°5W **81** C3
Walla Walla → *Wash., U.S.A.* 46°4N 118°20W **120** D7
Walla Walla *Wash., U.S.A.* 46°3N 118°25W **120** D7
Walla Walla County ☆ *Wash., U.S.A.* 46°18N 118°37W **120** D7
Wallace *N.S., Canada* 45°48N 63°29W **141** H6
Wallace *Idaho, U.S.A.* 47°28N 115°56W **122** C3
Wallace *Kans., U.S.A.* 38°58N 101°36W **82** C2
Wallace *Nebr., U.S.A.* 40°50N 101°10W **80** D4
Wallace County ☆ *Kans., U.S.A.* 38°50N 101°45W **82** C2
Wallace Mt. *Alta., Canada* 54°58N 115°48W **152** D5
Wallaceburg *Ont., Canada* 42°34N 82°23W **146** E4
Walland *Tenn., U.S.A.* 35°44N 83°49W **105** E9
Wallenpaupack, L. *Pa., U.S.A.* 41°25N 75°15W **92** A1
Waller *Tex., U.S.A.* 30°4N 95°56W **109** G12
Waller County ☆ *Tex., U.S.A.* 30°0N 96°0W **109** G11
Wallingford *Conn., U.S.A.* 41°27N 72°50W **91** C2
Wallingford *Iowa, U.S.A.* 43°19N 94°48W **81** B4
Wallingford *Vt., U.S.A.* 43°28N 72°58W **89** D2
Wallington *N.J., U.S.A.* 40°51N 74°6W **97** A2
Wallis *Tex., U.S.A.* 29°38N 96°4W **109** H11
Wallisville L. *Tex., U.S.A.* 29°57N 94°54W **109** H13
Wallkill → *N.Y., U.S.A.* 41°51N 74°3W **88** D6
Walloon L. *Mich., U.S.A.* 45°17N 85°0W **79** D7
Wallops I. *Va., U.S.A.* 37°51N 75°28W **93** E5

Wallowa *Oreg., L.S.A.* 45°34N 117°32W **121** B8
Wallowa → *Oreg., U.S.A.* 45°43N 117°47W **121** B8
Wallowa County ☆ *Oreg., U.S.A.* 45°30N 117°10W **121** B8
Wallowa Mts. *U.S.A.* 45°20N 117°30W **121** B8
Wallowa-Whitman Nat. Forest *Oreg.,*
U.S.A. 45°15N 117°20W **121** B8
Walls *Miss., U.S.A.* 34°58N 90°9W **111** B3
Wallsburg *Utah, U.S.A.* 40°23N 111°25W **129** C4
Wallula *Wash., U.S.A.* 46°5N 118°54W **120** D7
Wallula, L. *Wash., U.S.A.* 46°2N 118°59W **120** D7
Walnut *Ill., U.S.A.* 41°33N 89°36W **84** B4
Walnut *Iowa, U.S.A.* 41°29N 95°13W **81** D3
Walnut *Kans., U.S.A.* 37°36N 95°5W **82** D8
Walnut *Miss., U.S.A.* 34°57N 88°54W **111** B5
Walnut → *Kans., U.S.A.* 37°3N 97°0W **82** D6
Walnut Canyon Nat. Monument △ *Ariz.,*
U.S.A. 35°15N 111°20W **130** B4
Walnut Cove *N.C., U.S.A.* 36°18N 80°9W **103** B5
Walnut Cr. → *Kans., U.S.A.* 38°21N 98°41W **82** C5
Walnut Cr. → *Ohio, U.S.A.* 39°41N 82°59W **86** D4
Walnut Creek *Calif., U.S.A.* 37°54N 122°4W **126** F4
Walnut Creek *N.C., U.S.A.* 35°18N 77°52W **103** C8
Walnut Grove *Ala., U.S.A.* 34°4N 86°18W **112** B4
Walnut Grove *Miss., U.S.A.* 32°36N 89°28W **111** D4
Walnut Grove *Mo., U.S.A.* 37°25N 93°33W **83** D3
Walnut Hill *Fla., U.S.A.* 30°53N 87°30W **114** A1
Walnut Ridge *Ark., U.S.A.* 36°4N 90°57W **106** B51
Walnut Spring *Tex., U.S.A.* 32°3N 97°45W **109** E10
Walpole *Mass., U.S.A.* 42°9N 71°15W **91** B3
Walpole *N.H., U.S.A.* 43°5N 72°26W **89** C2
Walsenburg *Colo., U.S.A.* 37°38N 104°47W **125** E6
Walsh *Alta., Canada* 49°57N 110°3W **153** J10
Walsh *Colo., U.S.A.* 37°23N 102°17W **125** E8
Walsh County ☆ *N. Dak., U.S.A.* 48°24N 97°45W **76** B8
Walt Disney World *Fla., U.S.A.* 28°22N 81°33W **115** B1
Walter Chandler Park *Tenn., U.S.A.* 35°1N 90°3W **117** B1
Walter D. Stone Memorial Zoo *Mass.,*
U.S.A. 42°28N 71°6W **96** A2
Walter F. George Res. *U.S.A.* 31°38N 85°4W **112** E5
Walterboro *S.C., U.S.A.* 32°55N 80°40W **103** F5
Walters *Okla., U.S.A.* 34°22N 98°19W **107** D5
Walterville *Oreg., U.S.A.* 44°4N 122°48W **121** C3
Walthall *Miss., U.S.A.* 33°37N 89°17W **111** C4
Walthall County ☆ *Miss., U.S.A.* 31°7N 90°9W **111** E3
Waltham *Qué., Canada* 45°57N 76°57W **144** F6
Waltham *Maine, U.S.A.* 44°43N 68°20W **90** D5
Waltham *Mass., U.S.A.* 42°23N 71°14W **96** A1
Walthill *Nebr., U.S.A.* 42°9N 96°30W **80** B9
Waltman *Wyo., U.S.A.* 43°4N 107°12W **124** C5
Walton *N.S., Canada* 45°14N 64°0W **141** H5
Walton *Ind., U.S.A.* 40°40N 86°15W **85** C4
Walton *Kans., U.S.A.* 38°7N 97°15W **82** C6
Walton *Ky., U.S.A.* 38°52N 84°37W **105** B8
Walton *N.Y., U.S.A.* 42°10N 75°8W **88** C5
Walton County ☆ *Fla., U.S.A.* 30°30N 86°10W **114** A2
Walton County ☆ *Ga., U.S.A.* 33°45N 83°45W **113** C3
Waltonville *Ill., U.S.A.* 38°13N 89°2W **84** E4
Walworth County ☆ *S. Dak., U.S.A.* 45°30N 100°0W **76** E6
Walworth County ☆ *Wis., U.S.A.* 42°40N 88°30W **78** F5
Wamac *Ill., U.S.A.* 38°31N 89°8W **84** E4
Wamego *Kans., U.S.A.* 39°12N 96°18W **82** B7
Wampsville *N.Y., U.S.A.* 43°5N 75°42W **88** B5
Wampum *Pa., U.S.A.* 40°54N 80°21W **87** D2
Wamsutter *Wyo., U.S.A.* 41°40N 107°58W **124** E5
Wanamingo *Minn., U.S.A.* 44°18N 92°47W **77** F6
Wanapitei → *Ont., Canada* 46°2N 80°51W **146** A6
Wanapitei L. *Ont., Canada* 46°45N 80°40W **146** A6
Wanapum Dam *Wash., U.S.A.* 46°52N 119°58W **120** D6
Wanaque *N.J., U.S.A.* 41°2N 74°18W **92** A2
Wanaque Res. *N.J., U.S.A.* 41°2N 74°18W **92** A2
Wanatah *Ind., U.S.A.* 41°26N 86°54W **85** B4
Wanblee *S. Dak., U.S.A.* 43°34N 101°40W **76** G4
Wanchese *N.C., U.S.A.* 35°51N 75°38W **103** C10
Wanda *Minn., U.S.A.* 44°19N 95°13W **77** F3
Wandel Sea = McKinley Sea *Arctic* 82°0N 0°0 **162** A11
Wanette *Okla., U.S.A.* 34°58N 97°2W **107** D6
Wango *Md., U.S.A.* 38°20N 75°25W **93** B5
Wanham *Alta., Canada* 55°44N 118°24W **152** C2
Wanless *Man., Canada* 54°11N 101°21W **151** A10
Wann *Okla., U.S.A.* 36°55N 95°48W **107** B8
Wapack Nat. Wildlife Refuge △ *N.H.,*
U.S.A. 42°53N 71°52W **89** D3
Wapakoneta *Ohio, U.S.A.* 40°34N 84°12W **86** C2
Wapanuck *Okla., U.S.A.* 34°23N 96°26W **107** D7
Wapato *Wash., U.S.A.* 46°27N 120°25W **120** D5
Wapella *Sask., Canada* 50°16N 101°58W **151** E10
Wapello *Iowa, U.S.A.* 41°11N 91°11W **81** D7
Wapello County ☆ *Iowa, U.S.A.* 41°0N 92°25W **81** E6
Wapinitia Pass *Oreg., U.S.A.* 45°14N 121°42W **121** B4
Wapiti *Wyo., U.S.A.* 44°28N 109°26W **124** B3
Wapiti → *Alta., Canada* 55°5N 118°18W **152** C2
Wappapello L. *Mo., U.S.A.* 36°56N 90°17W **83** E6
Wappingers Falls *N.Y., U.S.A.* 41°36N 73°55W **88** D7
Wapsipinicon → *Iowa, U.S.A.* 41°44N 90°19W **81** D81
War *W. Va., U.S.A.* 37°18N 81°41W **102** D3
War in the Pacific Nat. Hist. Park △
Guam 13°24N 144°39E **184** b
Warburg *Alta., Canada* 53°11N 114°19W **153** C6
Ward *Ark., U.S.A.* 35°2N 91°57W **106** C4
Ward *S. Dak., U.S.A.* 44°9N 96°28W **76** F9
Ward County ☆ *N. Dak., U.S.A.* 48°5N 101°30W **76** B4
Ward County ☆ *Tex., U.S.A.* 31°32N 103°8W **108** F4
Wardell *Mo., U.S.A.* 36°21N 89°49W **83** E7
Wardensville *W. Va., U.S.A.* 39°5N 78°36W **93** A2
Wardlow *Alta., Canada* 50°56N 111°31W **153** H9
Wardner *Idaho, U.S.A.* 49°25N 115°26W **153** J5
Wardsville *Mo., U.S.A.* 38°29N 92°11W **83** C4
Ware *B.C., Canada* 57°26N 125°41W **157** E7
Ware *Mass., U.S.A.* 42°16N 72°14W **91** B2
Ware → *Mass., U.S.A.* 42°11N 72°22W **91** B2
Ware County ☆ *Ga., U.S.A.* 31°10N 82°20W **113** E4
Ware Shoals *S.C., U.S.A.* 34°24N 82°15W **103** D3
Wareham *Mass., U.S.A.* 41°46N 70°43W **91** C4
Warehouse Point *Conn., U.S.A.* 41°56N 72°37W **91** C2
Waresboro *Ga., U.S.A.* 31°15N 82°29W **113** E4
Warfield *B.C., Canada* 49°6N 117°46W **155** F17
Warfield *Ky., U.S.A.* 37°51N 82°25W **105** C10
Warm Lake *Idaho, U.S.A.* 44°39N 115°40W **122** E3
Warm Springs *Ga., U.S.A.* 32°53N 84°41W **113** D2
Warm Springs *Nev., U.S.A.* 38°10N 116°20W **128** D4
Warm Springs *Oreg., U.S.A.* 44°46N 121°16W **121** C4
Warm Springs → *Oreg., U.S.A.* 44°51N 121°4W **121** C4

Warm Springs Indian Reservation *Oreg.,*
U.S.A. 45°0N 121°25W **121** C4
Warm Springs Res. *Oreg., U.S.A.* 43°35N 118°13W **121** D7
Warman *Sask., Canada* 52°19N 106°30W **150** C5
Warminster *Pa., U.S.A.* 40°12N 75°6W **87** D7
Warner *Alta., Canada* 49°17N 112°12W **153** J8
Warner *N.H., U.S.A.* 43°17N 71°49W **89** C2
Warner *Okla., U.S.A.* 35°30N 95°18W **107** C8
Warner *S. Dak., U.S.A.* 45°20N 98°30W **76** E7
Warner Brothers Studios *Calif., U.S.A.* 34°9N 118°20W **133** B2
Warner Mts. *Calif., U.S.A.* 41°40N 120°15W **126** B6
Warner Robins *Ga., U.S.A.* 32°37N 83°36W **113** D3
Warner Springs *Calif., U.S.A.* 33°17N 116°38W **127** K10
Warner Valley *Oreg., U.S.A.* 42°35N 119°50W **121** E6
Warr Acres *Okla., U.S.A.* 35°31N 97°37W **107** C6
Warren *Ont., Canada* 46°27N 80°18W **146** A6
Warren *Ark., U.S.A.* 33°37N 92°4W **106** E3
Warren *Conn., U.S.A.* 41°44N 73°21W **91** C1
Warren *Idaho, U.S.A.* 45°16N 115°41W **122** D3
Warren *Ill., U.S.A.* 42°29N 90°0W **84** A4
Warren *Ind., U.S.A.* 40°41N 85°26W **85** C5
Warren *Mich., U.S.A.* 42°28N 83°1W **98** A2
Warren *Minn., U.S.A.* 48°12N 96°46W **77** B2
Warren *N.H., U.S.A.* 43°56N 71°54W **89** C3
Warren *Ohio, U.S.A.* 41°14N 80°49W **86** B6
Warren *Pa., U.S.A.* 41°51N 79°9W **87** C3
Warren *R.I., U.S.A.* 41°43N 71°17W **91** C3
Warren *Tex., U.S.A.* 30°37N 94°24W **109** G13
Warren *Vt., U.S.A.* 44°7N 72°50W **89** B2
Warren County ☆ *Ga., U.S.A.* 33°20N 82°40W **113** C4
Warren County ☆ *Ill., U.S.A.* 40°50N 90°35W **84** C3
Warren County ☆ *Ind., U.S.A.* 40°20N 87°25W **85** C3
Warren County ☆ *Iowa, U.S.A.* 41°20N 93°35W **81** D5
Warren County ☆ *Ky., U.S.A.* 37°0N 86°25W **104** C6
Warren County ☆ *Miss., U.S.A.* 32°21N 90°53W **111** D3
Warren County ☆ *Mo., U.S.A.* 38°45N 91°10W **83** C5
Warren County ☆ *N.C., U.S.A.* 36°15N 78°0W **103** B7
Warren County ☆ *N.J., U.S.A.* 40°50N 75°0W **92** B2
Warren County ☆ *N.Y., U.S.A.* 43°35N 73°45W **88** B7
Warren County ☆ *Ohio, U.S.A.* 39°26N 84°13W **86** D2
Warren County ☆ *Pa., U.S.A.* 41°50N 79°15W **87** C3
Warren County ☆ *Tenn., U.S.A.* 35°41N 85°46W **105** E7
Warren County ☆ *Va., U.S.A.* 38°55N 78°12W **102** C6
Warren Grove *N.J., U.S.A.* 39°44N 74°22W **92** C2
Warren Pks. *Wyo., U.S.A.* 44°29N 104°28W **124** B8
Warrens *Wis., U.S.A.* 44°8N 90°30W **78** D3
Warrensburg *Ill., U.S.A.* 39°56N 89°4W **84** D4
Warrensburg *Mo., U.S.A.* 38°46N 93°44W **83** C3
Warrensburg *N.Y., U.S.A.* 43°29N 73°46W **88** B7
Warrenton *Ga., U.S.A.* 33°24N 82°40W **113** C4
Warrenton *Mo., U.S.A.* 38°49N 91°9W **83** C5
Warrenton *N.C., U.S.A.* 36°24N 78°9W **103** B7
Warrenton *Oreg., U.S.A.* 46°10N 123°56W **121** A2
Warrenton *Va., U.S.A.* 38°43N 77°48W **93** A3
Warrenville *S.C., U.S.A.* 33°33N 81°48W **103** E4
Warrick County ☆ *Ind., U.S.A.* 38°5N 87°15W **85** F3
Warrington *Fla., U.S.A.* 30°23N 87°17W **114** A1
Warrior *Ala., U.S.A.* 33°49N 86°49W **112** C4
Warroad *Minn., U.S.A.* 48°54N 95°19W **77** B3
Warsaw *Ill., U.S.A.* 40°22N 91°26W **84** C2
Warsaw *Ind., U.S.A.* 41°14N 85°51W **85** B5
Warsaw *Ky., U.S.A.* 38°47N 84°54W **105** B8
Warsaw *Mo., U.S.A.* 38°15N 93°23W **83** C3
Warsaw *N.C., U.S.A.* 35°0N 78°5W **103** C7
Warsaw *N.Y., U.S.A.* 42°45N 78°8W **88** C2
Warsaw *Va., U.S.A.* 37°58N 76°46W **102** D8
Wartburg *Tenn., U.S.A.* 36°6N 84°36W **105** D8
Warthen *Ga., U.S.A.* 33°6N 82°48W **113** C4
Wartrace *Tenn., U.S.A.* 35°32N 86°20W **104** E6
Warwick *Qué., Canada* 31°50N 83°57W **113** E3
Warwick *Md., U.S.A.* 39°25N 75°47W **93** A5
Warwick *N. Dak., U.S.A.* 47°51N 98°43W **76** C7
Warwick *N.Y., U.S.A.* 41°16N 74°22W **92** A2
Warwick *Okla., U.S.A.* 35°41N 97°0W **107** C7
Warwick *R.I., U.S.A.* 41°42N 71°28W **91** C3
Wasaga Beach *Ont., Canada* 44°31N 80°1W **146** C6
Wasatch-Cache Nat. Forest *Utah,*
U.S.A. 41°14N 111°25W **134** B3
Wasatch County ☆ *Utah, U.S.A.* 40°20N 111°15W **129** C4
Wasatch Plateau *Utah, U.S.A.* 39°20N 111°30W **129** D4
Wasatch Ra. *Utah, U.S.A.* 40°0N 111°30W **134** B4
Wasco *Calif., U.S.A.* 35°36N 119°20W **127** H7
Wasco *Oreg., U.S.A.* 45°36N 120°42W **121** B5
Wasco County ☆ *Oreg., U.S.A.* 45°15N 121°15W **121** B4
Waseca *Sask., Canada* 53°6N 109°28W **150** B2
Waseca *Minn., U.S.A.* 44°5N 93°30W **77** F5
Waseca County ☆ *Minn., U.S.A.* 44°0N 93°30W **77** F5
Washago *Ont., Canada* 44°45N 79°20W **146** C7
Washakie County ☆ *Wyo., U.S.A.* 44°0N 107°40W **124** C5
Washburn *Ill., U.S.A.* 40°55N 89°17W **84** C4
Washburn *Maine, U.S.A.* 46°47N 68°9W **90** B5
Washburn *Mo., U.S.A.* 36°35N 93°58W **83** E3
Washburn *N. Dak., U.S.A.* 47°17N 101°2W **76** C4
Washburn *Tex., U.S.A.* 35°11N 101°34W **108** B6
Washburn *Wis., U.S.A.* 46°40N 90°54W **78** B3
Washburn, Mt. *Wyo., U.S.A.* 44°48N 110°26W **124** B2
Washburn County ☆ *Wis., U.S.A.* 45°50N 91°50W **78** C2
Washburn L. *Nunavut, Canada* 70°3N 107°30W **158** C4
Washi L. *Ont., Canada* 51°24N 87°2W **149** A9
Washicoutal, L. *Qué., Canada* 50°20N 60°10W **140** C9
Washington *Ark., U.S.A.* 33°47N 93°41W **106** E2
Washington *Conn., U.S.A.* 41°39N 73°19W **91** C1
Washington *D.C., U.S.A.* 38°53N 77°2W **99** B3
Washington *Ga., U.S.A.* 33°44N 82°44W **113** C4
Washington *Ill., U.S.A.* 40°42N 89°24W **84** C4
Washington *Ind., U.S.A.* 38°40N 87°10W **85** E3
Washington *Iowa, U.S.A.* 41°18N 91°42W **81** D7
Washington *Kans., U.S.A.* 39°49N 97°3W **82** B6
Washington *Ky., U.S.A.* 38°37N 83°49W **105** B9
Washington *Maine, U.S.A.* 44°16N 69°22W **90** D4
Washington *Miss., U.S.A.* 31°35N 91°18W **111** E2
Washington *Mo., U.S.A.* 38°33N 91°1W **83** C51
Washington *N.C., U.S.A.* 35°33N 77°3W **103** C8
Washington *N.H., U.S.A.* 43°11N 72°6W **89** C2
Washington *N.J., U.S.A.* 40°46N 74°59W **92** B2
Washington *Nebr., U.S.A.* 41°24N 96°13W **80** C9
Washington *Okla., U.S.A.* 35°4N 97°29W **107** C6
Washington *Pa., U.S.A.* 40°10N 80°15W **87** D2
Washington *Utah, U.S.A.* 37°8N 113°31W **129** F2
Washington *Va., U.S.A.* 38°43N 78°10W **93** B2
Washington □ *U.S.A.* 47°30N 120°30W **120** C5
Washington, Lake *Wash., U.S.A.* 47°37N 122°15W **132** B4
Washington, Mt. *N.H., U.S.A.* 44°16N 71°18W **89** B3

Washington County ☆ *Ala., U.S.A.* 31°22N 88°15W **112** E2
Washington County ☆ *Ark., U.S.A.* 36°4N 94°10W **106** B1
Washington County ☆ *Colo., U.S.A.* 40°0N 103°10W **125** C7
Washington County ☆ *Fla., U.S.A.* 30°30N 85°45W **114** A3
Washington County ☆ *Ga., U.S.A.* 33°0N 82°50W **113** C4
Washington County ☆ *Idaho, U.S.A.* 44°30N 116°50W **122** E2
Washington County ☆ *Ill., U.S.A.* 38°20N 89°25W **84** E4
Washington County ☆ *Ind., U.S.A.* 38°35N 86°5W **85** E4
Washington County ☆ *Iowa, U.S.A.* 41°20N 91°40W **81** D7
Washington County ☆ *Kans., U.S.A.* 39°45N 97°0W **82** B6
Washington County ☆ *Ky., U.S.A.* 37°45N 85°10W **105** C8
Washington County ☆ *Maine, U.S.A.* 45°0N 67°30W **90** C6
Washington County ☆ *Md., U.S.A.* 39°40N 78°0W **93** A3
Washington County ☆ *Minn., U.S.A.* 45°10N 92°55W **77** E6
Washington County ☆ *Miss., U.S.A.* 33°16N 90°53W **111** C3
Washington County ☆ *Mo., U.S.A.* 38°0N 90°50W **83** D5
Washington County ☆ *N.C., U.S.A.* 35°50N 76°30W **103** C9
Washington County ☆ *N.Y., U.S.A.* 43°20N 73°25W **88** B7
Washington County ☆ *Nebr., U.S.A.* 41°30N 96°15W **80** C9
Washington County ☆ *Ohio, U.S.A.* 39°25N 81°27W **86** D5
Washington County ☆ *Okla., U.S.A.* 36°40N 95°55W **107** B8
Washington County ☆ *Oreg., U.S.A.* 45°30N 123°0W **121** B2
Washington County ☆ *Pa., U.S.A.* 40°8N 80°8W **87** D2
Washington County ☆ *R.I., U.S.A.* 41°30N 71°40W **91** C3
Washington County ☆ *Tenn., U.S.A.* 36°18N 82°29W **105** D10
Washington County ☆ *Tex., U.S.A.* 30°10N 96°24W **109** G11
Washington County ☆ *Utah, U.S.A.* 37°20N 113°30W **129** F2
Washington County ☆ *Va., U.S.A.* 36°55N 82°0W **102** E3
Washington County ☆ *Vt., U.S.A.* 44°15N 72°40W **89** B2
Washington County ☆ *Wis., U.S.A.* 43°20N 88°15W **78** E5
Washington Court House *Ohio, U.S.A.* 39°32N 83°26W **86** D3
Washington Dulles Int. ✈ (IAD) *Va.,*
U.S.A. 38°57N 77°27W **102** C7
Washington Grove *Md., U.S.A.* 39°8N 77°11W **93** A3
Washington Heights *N.Y., U.S.A.* 40°51N 73°56W **97** A3
Washington I. *Wis., U.S.A.* 45°23N 86°54W **78** C7
Washington Island *Wis., U.S.A.* 45°24N 86°56W **78** C7
Washington Land *Greenland* 80°30N 66°0W **162** A4
Washington Parish ☆ *La., U.S.A.* 30°51N 90°9W **110** D5
Washington Park *Ill., U.S.A.* 38°38N 90°5W **94** B3
Washington Park *Ill., U.S.A.* 41°47N 87°36W **95** C3
Washington Park *Oreg., U.S.A.* 45°30N 122°42W **132** A1
Washington Park *Wis., U.S.A.* 43°4N 87°58W **94** B2
Washington Ronald Reagan National ✈ (DCA)
Va., U.S.A. 38°51N 77°2W **99** B3
Washington Terrace *Utah, U.S.A.* 41°11N 111°59W **129** B4
Washingtonville *N.Y., U.S.A.* 41°26N 74°10W **92** A2
Washita → *Okla., U.S.A.* 34°8N 96°36W **107** D7
Washita Battlefield Nat. Historic Site △ *Okla.,*
U.S.A. 35°57N 99°42W **107** C4
Washita County ☆ *Okla., U.S.A.* 35°15N 99°0W **107** C5
Washoe City *Nev., U.S.A.* 39°19N 119°49W **128** C1
Washoe County ☆ *Nev., U.S.A.* 41°0N 119°40W **128** B1
Washoe L. *Nev., U.S.A.* 39°16N 119°48W **128** C1
Washougal *Wash., U.S.A.* 45°35N 122°21W **120** E3
Washta *Iowa, U.S.A.* 42°35N 95°43W **81** C3
Washtenaw County ☆ *Mich., U.S.A.* 42°15N 83°50W **79** E8
Washtucna *Wash., U.S.A.* 46°45N 118°19W **120** D7
Wasilla *Alaska, U.S.A.* 61°35N 149°26W **135** F10
Waskada *Man., Canada* 49°6N 100°48W **151** F11
Waskaganish *Qué., Canada* 51°30N 78°40W **143** C2
Waskatenau *Alta., Canada* 54°7N 112°47W **152** D8
Waskesiu L. *Sask., Canada* 53°58N 106°12W **150** B5
Waskesiu Lake *Sask., Canada* 53°55N 106°5W **150** B5
Waskish *Minn., U.S.A.* 48°10N 94°31W **77** B4
Waskom *Tex., U.S.A.* 32°29N 94°4W **109** E13
Wassaw I. *Ga., U.S.A.* 31°53N 80°58W **113** E6
Wassaw Sd. *Ga., U.S.A.* 31°55N 80°55W **113** E6
Wassuk Range *Nev., U.S.A.* 38°40N 118°50W **128** D2
Wasta *S. Dak., U.S.A.* 44°4N 102°27W **76** F3
Waswanipi *Qué., Canada* 49°40N 76°29W **143** D2
Waswanipi → *Qué., Canada* 49°40N 76°25W **143** D2
Waswanipi, L. *Qué., Canada* 49°35N 76°40W **144** B6
Watauga *Tenn., U.S.A.* 36°22N 82°18W **105** D10
Watauga *Tex., U.S.A.* 32°51N 97°15W **116** A2
Watauga County ☆ *N.C., U.S.A.* 36°15N 81°45W **103** B4
Watauga → *Tenn., U.S.A.* 36°19N 82°7W **105** D10
Water Valley *Ky., U.S.A.* 36°34N 88°49W **104** D4
Water Valley *Miss., U.S.A.* 34°10N 89°38W **111** B4
Waterboro *Maine, U.S.A.* 43°32N 70°43W **89** C4
Waterbury *Conn., U.S.A.* 41°33N 73°3W **91** C1
Waterbury *Nebr., U.S.A.* 42°27N 96°44W **80** B9
Waterbury *Vt., U.S.A.* 44°20N 72°46W **89** B2
Waterbury Center *Vt., U.S.A.* 44°23N 72°46W **89** B2
Waterbury Res. *Vt., U.S.A.* 44°23N 72°46W **89** B2
Waterdown *Ont., Canada* 43°20N 79°53W **146** D7
Wateree → *S.C., U.S.A.* 33°45N 80°37W **103** E5
Wateree, L. *S.C., U.S.A.* 34°20N 80°42W **103** D5
Waterflow *N. Mex., U.S.A.* 36°45N 108°27W **131** A2
Waterford *Ont., Canada* 42°56N 80°17W **146** E6
Waterford *Calif., U.S.A.* 37°38N 120°46W **126** F4
Waterford *Conn., U.S.A.* 41°20N 72°9W **91** C2
Waterford *Maine, U.S.A.* 44°14N 70°46W **90** D3
Waterford *Mich., U.S.A.* 42°45N 83°32W **79** G8
Waterford *Miss., U.S.A.* 34°39N 89°28W **111** B4
Waterford *N.Y., U.S.A.* 42°48N 73°41W **91** B1
Waterford *Pa., U.S.A.* 41°57N 79°59W **87** C2
Waterford *Va., U.S.A.* 39°11N 77°37W **93** A3
Waterford *Wis., U.S.A.* 42°46N 88°13W **78** F5
Waterford → *Nfld. & L., Canada* 47°33N 52°43W **142** E8
Watergap *Ky., U.S.A.* 37°38N 82°45W **105** C10
Waterhen L. *Man., Canada* 52°10N 99°40W **151** C12
Waterloo *Ont., Canada* 43°30N 80°32W **146** D6
Waterloo *Qué., Canada* 45°22N 72°32W **145** F10
Waterloo *Ala., U.S.A.* 34°55N 88°4W **112** B2
Waterloo *Ark., U.S.A.* 33°33N 93°15W **106** E2
Waterloo *Iowa, U.S.A.* 42°30N 92°21W **81** C6
Waterloo *Ill., U.S.A.* 38°20N 90°9W **84** E4
Waterloo *Mont., U.S.A.* 45°43N 112°12W **123** E5
Waterloo *N.Y., U.S.A.* 42°54N 76°52W **88** C4
Waterloo *Oreg., U.S.A.* 44°30N 122°49W **121** C3
Waterloo *Wis., U.S.A.* 43°11N 88°59W **78** E5
Waterman *Ill., U.S.A.* 41°46N 88°47W **84** B5
Waterproof *La., U.S.A.* 31°48N 91°23W **110** C4
Waters *Mich., U.S.A.* 44°53N 84°42W **79** E7
Watersmeet *Mich., U.S.A.* 46°16N 89°11W **79** C2
Waterton Park *Alta., Canada* 49°5N 113°52W **153** J7
Watertown *Conn., U.S.A.* 41°36N 73°7W **91** C1
Watertown *Fla., U.S.A.* 30°11N 82°36W **114** A6
Watertown *Mass., U.S.A.* 42°22N 71°10W **96** A1
Watertown *N.Y., U.S.A.* 43°59N 75°55W **88** B5
Watertown *S. Dak., U.S.A.* 44°54N 97°7W **76** E9
Watertown *Tenn., U.S.A.* 36°6N 86°9W **104** D6
Watertown *Wis., U.S.A.* 43°12N 88°43W **78** E5

Waterville *N.S., Canada* 45°3N 64°41W **141** H5
Waterville *Qué., Canada* 45°16N 71°54W **145** F11
Waterville *Kans., U.S.A.* 39°42N 96°45W **82** B7
Waterville *Maine, U.S.A.* 44°33N 69°38W **90** D4
Waterville *Minn., U.S.A.* 44°13N 93°34W **77** F5
Waterville *N.Y., U.S.A.* 42°56N 75°23W **88** C5
Waterville *Ohio, U.S.A.* 41°30N 83°43W **86** B3
Waterville *Vt., U.S.A.* 44°42N 72°47W **89** B2
Waterville *Wash., U.S.A.* 47°39N 120°4W **120** C5
Waterville Valley *N.H., U.S.A.* 43°57N 71°31W **89** C3
Watford *Ont., Canada* 42°57N 81°53W **146** E5
Watford City *N. Dak., U.S.A.* 47°48N 103°17W **76** C2
Wathaman → *Sask., Canada* 57°16N 102°59W **157** E12
Wathena *Kans., U.S.A.* 39°46N 94°57W **82** B9
Watkins *Minn., U.S.A.* 45°19N 94°24W **77** E4
Watkins Glen *N.Y., U.S.A.* 42°23N 76°52W **88** C4
Watkinsville *Ga., U.S.A.* 33°52N 83°25W **113** C3
Watling I. = San Salvador I. *Bahamas* 24°0N 74°40W **183** B5
Watonga *Okla., U.S.A.* 35°51N 98°25W **107** C5
Watonwan County ☆ *Minn., U.S.A.* 44°0N 94°40W **77** F4
Watova *Okla., U.S.A.* 36°37N 95°39W **107** B8
Watrous *Sask., Canada* 51°40N 105°25W **150** D6
Watrous *N. Mex., U.S.A.* 35°48N 104°59W **131** B6
Watseka *Ill., U.S.A.* 40°47N 87°44W **84** C6
Watson *Sask., Canada* 52°10N 104°30W **150** C7
Watson *Ark., U.S.A.* 33°54N 91°15W **106** E4
Watson *Ill., U.S.A.* 39°2N 88°34W **84** D5
Watson *Minn., U.S.A.* 45°1N 95°48W **77** E3
Watson *Mo., U.S.A.* 40°29N 95°40W **83** A1
Watson Lake *Yukon, Canada* 60°6N 128°49W **157** D7
Watsontown *Pa., U.S.A.* 41°5N 76°52W **87** D6
Watsonville *Calif., U.S.A.* 36°55N 121°45W **126** G5
Watts *Okla., U.S.A.* 36°7N 94°34W **107** B9
Watts Bar L. *Tenn., U.S.A.* 35°37N 84°47W **105** E8
Wattsburg *Pa., U.S.A.* 42°0N 79°49W **87** B3
Watuppa Pond *Mass., U.S.A.* 41°42N 71°6W **91** C3
Waubamik *Ont., Canada* 45°27N 80°1W **146** B6
Waubaushene *Ont., Canada* 44°45N 79°42W **146** C7
Waubay *S. Dak., U.S.A.* 45°20N 97°18W **76** E8
Waubay L. *S. Dak., U.S.A.* 45°25N 97°24W **76** E8
Waubun *Minn., U.S.A.* 47°11N 95°57W **77** C3
Wauchula *Fla., U.S.A.* 27°33N 81°49W **114** C4
Waucoba Mt. *Calif., U.S.A.* 37°1N 118°0W **127** F9
Waucoma *Iowa, U.S.A.* 43°2N 92°1W **81** B6
Waugh *Man., Canada* 49°40N 95°11W **151** F16
Waugoshance Pt. *Mich., U.S.A.* 45°46N 85°1W **79** D6
Waukee *Iowa, U.S.A.* 41°37N 93°53W **81** D5
Waukeenah *Fla., U.S.A.* 30°25N 83°57W **114** A5
Waukegan *Ill., U.S.A.* 42°22N 87°50W **84** A6
Waukesha *Wis., U.S.A.* 43°1N 88°14W **78** E5
Waukesha County ☆ *Wis., U.S.A.* 43°0N 88°15W **78** F5
Waukomis *Okla., U.S.A.* 36°17N 97°54W **107** B6
Waukon *Iowa, U.S.A.* 43°16N 91°29W **81** B71
Wauna *Wash., U.S.A.* 47°22N 122°38W **132** D2
Waunakee *Wis., U.S.A.* 43°11N 89°27W **78** E4
Wauneta *Nebr., U.S.A.* 40°25N 101°23W **80** D4
Waupaca *Wis., U.S.A.* 44°21N 89°5W **78** D4
Waupaca County ☆ *Wis., U.S.A.* 44°25N 89°0W **78** D5
Waupun *Wis., U.S.A.* 43°38N 88°44W **78** E5
Waurika *Okla., U.S.A.* 34°10N 98°0W **107** D5
Waurika L. *Okla., U.S.A.* 34°10N 98°3W **107** D5
Wausa *Nebr., U.S.A.* 42°30N 97°32W **80** B8
Wausau *Fla., U.S.A.* 30°38N 85°35W **114** A3
Wausau *Wis., U.S.A.* 44°58N 89°38W **78** D4
Wausaukee *Wis., U.S.A.* 45°23N 87°57W **78** D8
Wauseon *Ohio, U.S.A.* 41°33N 84°8W **86** B2
Waushara County ☆ *Wis., U.S.A.* 44°10N 89°15W **78** D4
Wautoma *Wis., U.S.A.* 44°4N 89°18W **78** D4
Wauwatosa *Wis., U.S.A.* 43°2N 88°0W **94** B1
Wauzeka *Wis., U.S.A.* 43°5N 90°53W **78** E3
Waveland *Ind., U.S.A.* 39°53N 87°3W **85** D3
Waveland *Miss., U.S.A.* 30°17N 89°23W **111** F4
Waverley *N.S., Canada* 44°47N 63°36W **141** J6
Waverley *Mass., U.S.A.* 42°23N 71°10W **96** A1
Waverley Hall *Ga., U.S.A.* 32°41N 84°44W **113** D2
Waverly *Ala., U.S.A.* 32°44N 85°35W **112** D5
Waverly *Fla., U.S.A.* 27°59N 81°37W **114** C4
Waverly *Ga., U.S.A.* 31°6N 81°43W **113** E5
Waverly *Ill., U.S.A.* 39°36N 89°57W **84** D4
Waverly *Iowa, U.S.A.* 42°44N 92°29W **81** C61
Waverly *Kans., U.S.A.* 38°23N 95°36W **82** C8
Waverly *Minn., U.S.A.* 37°43N 87°48W **104** C5
Waverly *Mo., U.S.A.* 39°13N 93°31W **83** B3
Waverly *N.Y., U.S.A.* 42°1N 76°32W **88** C4
Waverly *Nebr., U.S.A.* 40°55N 96°32W **80** D9
Waverly *Ohio, U.S.A.* 39°8N 82°59W **86** D4
Waverly *Tenn., U.S.A.* 36°5N 87°48W **104** D5
Waverly *Va., U.S.A.* 37°2N 77°6W **93** C2
Waverly *Wash., U.S.A.* 47°21N 117°14W **120** C8
Wawa *Ont., Canada* 47°59N 84°47W **149** E12
Wawagosic → *Qué., Canada* 49°58N 79°34W **143** D2
Wawanesa *Man., Canada* 49°36N 99°40W **151** F12
Wawang L. *Ont., Canada* 49°25N 90°34W **148** C6
Wawasee, L. *Ind., U.S.A.* 41°24N 85°42W **85** B5
Wawona *Calif., U.S.A.* 37°32N 119°39W **126** F7
Wawota *Sask., Canada* 49°54N 102°2W **151** F9
Waxahachie *Tex., U.S.A.* 32°24N 96°51W **109** E11
Waxhaw *N.C., U.S.A.* 34°56N 80°45W **103** D5
Wayagamac, L. *Qué., Canada* 47°21N 72°39W **145** D10
Wayan *Idaho, U.S.A.* 42°58N 111°23W **122** G7
Waycross *Ga., U.S.A.* 31°13N 82°21N **113** E4
Wayland *Iowa, U.S.A.* 41°8N 91°40W **81** D7
Wayland *Ky., U.S.A.* 37°27N 82°48W **105** C10
Wayland *Mass., U.S.A.* 42°21N 71°20W **91** B3
Wayland *Mich., U.S.A.* 42°40N 85°39W **79** G6
Wayne *Kans., U.S.A.* 39°43N 97°33W **82** B6
Wayne *N.J., U.S.A.* 40°55N 74°16W **97** A1
Wayne *Ohio, U.S.A.* 41°18N 83°29W **86** B3
Wayne *W. Va., U.S.A.* 38°13N 82°27W **102** C2
Wayne County ☆ *Ga., U.S.A.* 31°30N 82°0W **113** E5
Wayne County ☆ *Ill., U.S.A.* 38°25N 88°25W **84** E5
Wayne County ☆ *Ind., U.S.A.* 39°50N 85°0W **85** D6
Wayne County ☆ *Iowa, U.S.A.* 40°45N 93°20W **81** E5
Wayne County ☆ *Ky., U.S.A.* 36°45N 84°50W **105** D8
Wayne County ☆ *Mich., U.S.A.* 42°15N 83°15W **79** G8
Wayne County ☆ *Miss., U.S.A.* 31°40N 88°39W **111** E5
Wayne County ☆ *Mo., U.S.A.* 37°5N 90°30W **83** D6
Wayne County ☆ *N.C., U.S.A.* 35°20N 78°0W **103** C7
Wayne County ☆ *N.Y., U.S.A.* 43°10N 77°0W **88** B4
Wayne County ☆ *Nebr., U.S.A.* 42°15N 97°5W **80** B8
Wayne County ☆ *Ohio, U.S.A.* 40°48N 81°56W **86** C5
Wayne County ☆ *Pa., U.S.A.* 41°35N 75°15W **87** C7
Wayne County ☆ *Tenn., U.S.A.* 35°10N 87°44W **104** E5

Wayne County ☆ Utah, U.S.A. 38°15N 111°0W 129 E5
Wayne County ☆ W. Va., U.S.A. 38°13N 82°27W 102 C2
Wayne County, Detroit ✕ (DTW) Mich., U.S.A. 42°13N 83°21W 79 G8
Wayne Nat. Forest Ohio, U.S.A. 39°33N 81°4W 86 D5
Waynesboro Ga., U.S.A. 33°6N 82°1W 113 C4
Waynesboro Miss., U.S.A. 31°40N 88°39W 111 E5
Waynesboro Pa., U.S.A. 39°45N 77°35W 93 A3
Waynesboro Tenn., U.S.A. 35°19N 87°46W 104 E5
Waynesboro Va., U.S.A. 38°4N 78°53W 102 C6
Waynesburg Pa., U.S.A. 39°54N 80°11W 87 E2
Waynesville Ill., U.S.A. 40°15N 89°8W 84 C4
Waynesville Mo., U.S.A. 37°50N 92°12W 83 D4
Waynesville N.C., U.S.A. 35°28N 82°58W 103 C3
Waynesville Ohio, U.S.A. 39°32N 84°5W 86 D2
Waynetown Ind., U.S.A. 40°5N 87°4W 85 C3
Waynoka Okla., U.S.A. 36°35N 98°53W 107 B5
Wayside Ga., U.S.A. 33°4N 83°37W 113 C3
Wayside Miss., U.S.A. 33°16N 91°2W 111 C2
Wayzata Minn., U.S.A. 44°58N 93°30W 94 B1
Weakley County ☆ Tenn., U.S.A. 36°14N 88°50W 104 D4
Weare N.H., U.S.A. 43°6N 71°44W 89 C3
Weatherby Mo., U.S.A. 39°55N 94°14W 83 B2
Weatherford Okla., U.S.A. 35°32N 98°43W 107 C5
Weatherford Tex., U.S.A. 32°46N 97°48W 109 E10
Weatherly Pa., U.S.A. 40°57N 75°50W 92 B1
Weaubleau Mo., U.S.A. 37°54N 93°32W 83 D3
Weaverville Calif., U.S.A. 40°44N 122°56W 126 C4
Weaverville N.C., U.S.A. 35°42N 82°34W 103 C3
Webb Sask., Canada 50°11N 108°12W 150 E3
Webb Iowa, U.S.A. 42°57N 95°1W 81 C3
Webb Miss., U.S.A. 33°57N 90°21W 111 C3
Webb City Mo., U.S.A. 37°9N 94°28W 83 D2
Webb City Okla., U.S.A. 36°48N 96°42W 107 B7
Webb County ☆ Tex., U.S.A. 27°30N 99°10W 109 K8
Webber Kans., U.S.A. 39°56N 98°2W 82 B5
Webbers Falls Okla., U.S.A. 35°31N 95°8W 107 C8
Webbville Ky., U.S.A. 38°11N 82°52W 105 B10
Webbwood Ont., Canada 46°16N 81°52W 146 A5
Webequie Ont., Canada 52°59N 87°21W 159 G8
Weber → U.S.A. 41°13N 112°8W 129 B3
Weber County ☆ Utah, U.S.A. 41°20N 111°40W 129 B4
Webster Fla., U.S.A. 28°37N 82°3W 114 C6
Webster Iowa, U.S.A. 41°26N 92°10W 81 D6
Webster Mass., U.S.A. 42°3N 71°53W 91 B3
Webster N. Dak., U.S.A. 48°17N 98°53W 76 B7
Webster N.Y., U.S.A. 43°13N 77°26W 88 B3
Webster S. Dak., U.S.A. 45°20N 97°31W 76 E8
Webster Wis., U.S.A. 45°53N 92°22W 78 C1
Webster City Iowa, U.S.A. 42°28N 93°49W 81 C5
Webster County ☆ Ga., U.S.A. 32°0N 84°35W 113 E2
Webster County ☆ Iowa, U.S.A. 42°25N 94°10W 81 C4
Webster County ☆ Ky., U.S.A. 37°30N 87°40W 104 C5
Webster County ☆ Miss., U.S.A. 33°37N 89°17W 111 C4
Webster County ☆ Mo., U.S.A. 37°15N 92°50W 83 D4
Webster County ☆ Nebr., U.S.A. 40°15N 98°30W 80 D7
Webster County ☆ W. Va., U.S.A. 38°29N 80°25W 102 C4
Webster Groves Mo., U.S.A. 38°35N 90°21W 94 B1
Webster Parish ☆ La., U.S.A. 32°40N 93°20W 110 B2
Webster Ra. Idaho, U.S.A. 42°46N 111°11W 122 G7
Webster Res. Kans., U.S.A. 39°25N 99°26W 82 B4
Webster Springs W. Va., U.S.A. 38°29N 80°25W 102 C4
Websters Mill Pa., U.S.A. 39°52N 78°2W 93 A2
Weddington N.C., U.S.A. 35°1N 80°46W 103 C5
Wedgeport N.S., Canada 43°44N 65°59W 141 K4
Wedowee Ala., U.S.A. 33°19N 85°29W 112 C5
Weed Calif., U.S.A. 41°25N 122°23W 126 B4
Weed N. Mex., U.S.A. 32°48N 105°31W 131 E5
Weed Heights Nev., U.S.A. 38°59N 119°13W 128 D1
Weedon Qué., Canada 45°42N 71°27W 145 F11
Weedon Island Preserve Tampa, U.S.A. 27°50N 82°36W 115 B3
Weedsport N.Y., U.S.A. 43°3N 76°34W 88 B4
Weedville Pa., U.S.A. 41°17N 78°30W 87 C4
Weehawken New York, U.S.A. 96 b1
Weekapaug R.I., U.S.A. 41°20N 71°45W 91 C3
Weekes Sask., Canada 52°34N 102°52W 150 C9
Weekstown N.J., U.S.A. 39°37N 74°37W 92 C2
Weeping Water Nebr., U.S.A. 40°52N 96°8W 80 D9
Weigelstown Pa., U.S.A. 39°59N 76°49W 87 E6
Weimar Calif., U.S.A. 39°2N 120°59W 126 D6
Weimar Tex., U.S.A. 29°42N 96°47W 109 H11
Weinberg-King State Park ⌂ Ill., U.S.A. 40°14N 90°54W 84 C3
Weiner Ark., U.S.A. 35°37N 90°54W 106 C5
Weippe Idaho, U.S.A. 46°23N 115°56W 122 C3
Weir Kans., U.S.A. 37°19N 94°46W 82 D9
Weir Ky., U.S.A. 37°7N 87°13W 104 C5
Weir Miss., U.S.A. 33°16N 89°18W 111 C4
Weir, L. Fla., U.S.A. 29°0N 81°57W 114 B7
Weir River Man., Canada 56°49N 94°6W 159 F7
Weirdale Sask., Canada 53°27N 105°15W 150 B6
Weirsdale Fla., U.S.A. 28°59N 81°55W 114 C7
Weirton W. Va., U.S.A. 40°24N 80°35W 102 A4
Weiser Idaho, U.S.A. 44°15N 116°58W 122 E2
Weiser → Idaho, U.S.A. 44°14N 116°58W 122 E2
Weiss L. Ala., U.S.A. 34°8N 85°48W 112 B5
Weissert Nebr., U.S.A. 41°28N 99°27W 80 C6
Wekweti N.W.T., Canada 64°11N 114°10W 157 D10
Welby Colo., U.S.A. 39°50N 104°57W 134 A2
Welch Okla., U.S.A. 36°52N 95°6W 107 B8
Welch Tex., U.S.A. 32°56N 102°8W 108 E5
Welch W. Va., U.S.A. 37°26N 81°35W 102 D3
Welcome Md., U.S.A. 38°28N 77°8W 93 B3
Welcome Minn., U.S.A. 43°40N 94°37W 77 G4
Welcome N.C., U.S.A. 35°55N 80°15W 103 C5
Weld Maine, U.S.A. 44°42N 70°25W 90 D3
Weld County ☆ Colo., U.S.A. 40°45N 104°15W 125 B6
Welda Kans., U.S.A. 38°10N 95°18W 82 C8
Weldon Sask., Canada 53°1N 105°8W 150 B6
Weldon Ill., U.S.A. 40°7N 88°45W 84 C5
Weldon Iowa, U.S.A. 40°54N 93°44W 81 E5
Weldon N.C., U.S.A. 36°25N 77°36W 103 B8
Weldon → Mo., U.S.A. 40°6N 93°39W 83 A3
Weldon Spring Mo., U.S.A. 38°43N 90°41W 83 C6
Weleetka Okla., U.S.A. 35°20N 96°8W 107 C7
Welland Ont., Canada 43°0N 79°15W 146 E7
Wellborn Tex., U.S.A. 30°32N 96°18W 109 G11
Wellersburg Pa., U.S.A. 39°44N 78°51W 93 A2
Wellesley Mass., U.S.A. 42°17N 71°17W 91 B3
Wellesley Hills Mass., U.S.A. 42°18N 71°16W 96 B1
Wellfleet Mass., U.S.A. 41°56N 70°2W 91 C4
Wellfleet Nebr., U.S.A. 40°45N 100°44W 80 D5
Wellford Va., U.S.A. 37°53N 76°46W 93 C4
Wellington Ont., Canada 43°57N 77°20W 147 D9
Wellington P.E.I., Canada 46°27N 64°0W 141 G5
Wellington Colo., U.S.A. 40°42N 105°0W 125 B5
Wellington Ill., U.S.A. 40°32N 87°41W 84 C6
Wellington Kans., U.S.A. 37°16N 97°24W 82 D6
Wellington Maine, U.S.A. 45°2N 69°36W 90 C4
Wellington Mass., U.S.A. 42°24N 71°5W 96 A2
Wellington Mo., U.S.A. 39°8N 93°59W 83 B3
Wellington Nev., U.S.A. 38°45N 119°23W 128 D1
Wellington Ohio, U.S.A. 41°10N 82°13W 86 B4
Wellington Tex., U.S.A. 34°51N 100°13W 108 C7
Wellington Utah, U.S.A. 39°32N 110°44W 129 D5
Wellington Chan. Nunavut, Canada 75°0N 93°0W 158 B7
Wellman Iowa, U.S.A. 41°28N 91°50W 81 D7
Wellman Tex., U.S.A. 33°3N 102°26W 108 D5
Wellpinit Wash., U.S.A. 47°53N 117°59W 120 C8
Wells B.C., Canada 53°6N 121°36W 155 B13
Wells Kans., U.S.A. 39°5N 97°33W 82 B6
Wells Maine, U.S.A. 43°20N 70°35W 90 E3
Wells Minn., U.S.A. 43°45N 93°44W 77 G5
Wells N.Y., U.S.A. 43°24N 74°17W 88 B6
Wells Nev., U.S.A. 41°7N 114°58W 128 A6
Wells Tex., U.S.A. 31°29N 94°56W 109 F13
Wells Vt., U.S.A. 43°25N 73°10W 89 C1
Wells → Vt., U.S.A. 44°10N 72°3W 89 B2
Wells County ☆ Ind., U.S.A. 40°45N 85°15W 85 C5
Wells County ☆ N. Dak., U.S.A. 47°35N 99°45W 76 C6
Wells Dam Wash., U.S.A. 47°57N 119°52W 120 C6
Wells Gray Park ⌂ B.C., Canada 52°30N 120°15W 155 C14
Wellsboro Pa., U.S.A. 41°45N 77°18W 87 C5
Wellsburg Iowa, U.S.A. 42°26N 92°56W 81 C6
Wellsburg N.Y., U.S.A. 42°1N 76°44W 88 C4
Wellsburg W. Va., U.S.A. 40°16N 80°37W 102 A4
Wellsford Kans., U.S.A. 37°37N 99°2W 82 D4
Wellston = Warner Robins Ga., U.S.A. 32°37N 83°36W 113 D3
Wellston Mo., U.S.A. 38°40N 90°17W 94 B2
Wellston Ohio, U.S.A. 39°7N 82°32W 86 D4
Wellston Okla., U.S.A. 35°42N 97°4W 107 C6
Wellsville Kans., U.S.A. 38°43N 95°5W 82 C8
Wellsville Mo., U.S.A. 39°4N 91°34W 83 B5
Wellsville N.Y., U.S.A. 42°7N 77°57W 88 C3
Wellsville Ohio, U.S.A. 40°36N 80°39W 86 C6
Wellsville Pa., U.S.A. 40°3N 76°56W 87 D6
Wellsville Utah, U.S.A. 41°38N 111°56W 129 B4
Wellton Ariz., U.S.A. 32°40N 114°8W 130 E1
Welsford N.B., Canada 45°27N 66°20W 141 H3
Welsh La., U.S.A. 30°14N 92°49W 110 D3
Welton Iowa, U.S.A. 41°55N 90°36W 81 D8
Wembley Alta., Canada 55°9N 119°8W 152 C1
Wemindji Qué., Canada 53°0N 78°49W 143 C2
Wenasaga → Ont., Canada 50°38N 93°10W 148 B3
Wenatchee Wash., U.S.A. 47°25N 120°19W 120 C5
Wenatchee → Wash., U.S.A. 47°27N 120°19W 120 C5
Wenatchee Mts. Wash., U.S.A. 47°15N 120°30W 120 C5
Wenatchee Nat. Forest Wash., U.S.A. 47°55N 120°55W 120 C5
Wendell Idaho, U.S.A. 42°47N 114°42W 122 G4
Wendell Minn., U.S.A. 46°2N 96°6W 77 D2
Wendell N.H., U.S.A. 43°22N 72°9W 89 C2
Wenden Ariz., U.S.A. 33°49N 113°33W 130 D2
Wendover Utah, U.S.A. 40°44N 114°2W 129 C1
Wenebegon → Ont., Canada 46°53N 83°12W 149 F13
Wenebegon L. Ont., Canada 47°23N 83°6W 149 E13
Wenona Ill., U.S.A. 41°3N 89°3W 84 B4
Wenona Md., U.S.A. 38°8N 75°57W 93 B5
Wentworth Qué., Canada 45°38N 63°33W 141 H6
Wentworth Mo., U.S.A. 36°59N 94°4W 83 E2
Wentworth N.C., U.S.A. 36°24N 79°46W 103 B6
Wentworth N.H., U.S.A. 43°52N 71°55W 89 C3
Wentworth S. Dak., U.S.A. 43°59N 96°57W 76 G9
Wentworth, L. N.H., U.S.A. 43°35N 71°3W 89 C3
Wentzville Mo., U.S.A. 38°49N 90°51W 83 C6
Weott Calif., U.S.A. 40°20N 123°55W 126 C3
Werley Wis., U.S.A. 43°1N 90°45W 78 E3
Wernecke Mts. Yukon, Canada 64°50N 134°15W 157 D6
Weskan Kans., U.S.A. 38°52N 101°57W 82 C2
Weslaco Tex., U.S.A. 26°10N 97°58W 108 L10
Weslemkoon L. Ont., Canada 45°2N 77°25W 147 B9
Wesley Ga., U.S.A. 32°29N 82°20W 113 D4
Wesley Iowa, U.S.A. 43°5N 93°59W 81 B5
Wesley Maine, U.S.A. 44°57N 67°40W 90 D6
Wesleyville Pa., U.S.A. 42°9N 80°1W 87 B3
Wessington S. Dak., U.S.A. 44°27N 98°42W 76 F7
Wessington Springs S. Dak., U.S.A. 44°5N 98°34W 76 F7
Wesson Ark., U.S.A. 33°7N 92°46W 106 E3
Wesson Miss., U.S.A. 31°42N 90°24W 111 E3
West Miss., U.S.A. 33°12N 89°47W 111 C4
West Tex., U.S.A. 31°48N 97°6W 109 F10
West → Vt., U.S.A. 42°52N 72°33W 89 D2
West Alexandria Ohio, U.S.A. 39°45N 84°32W 86 D2
West Allis Wis., U.S.A. 43°1N 88°0W 94 B1
West Arlington Vt., U.S.A. 43°8N 73°12W 89 C1
West Arm Grand Traverse B. Mich., U.S.A. 44°50N 85°40W 79 E6
West Arm Park ⌂ B.C., Canada 49°30N 117°7W 155 F17
West B. Fla., U.S.A. 30°10N 85°45W 114 A3
West B. La., U.S.A. 29°3N 89°22W 110 E6
West B. Tex., U.S.A. 29°14N 95°0W 109 H13
West Babylon N.Y., U.S.A. 40°42N 73°21W 92 B3
West Baton Rouge Parish ☆ La., U.S.A. 30°27N 91°12W 110 D4
West Bay B.C., Canada 49°20N 123°12W 161 B1
West Bend Iowa, U.S.A. 42°57N 94°27W 81 C4
West Bend Wis., U.S.A. 43°25N 88°11W 78 E5
West Blocton Ala., U.S.A. 33°7N 87°7W 112 C3
West Bountiful Utah, U.S.A. 40°53N 111°54W 134 A2
West Boylston Mass., U.S.A. 42°22N 71°47W 91 B3
West Branch Iowa, U.S.A. 41°40N 91°20W 81 D7
West Branch Mich., U.S.A. 44°17N 84°14W 79 E7
West Branch Susquehanna → Pa., U.S.A. 40°53N 76°48W 87 D6
West Bridgewater Mass., U.S.A. 42°1N 71°0W 91 B4
West Brookfield Mass., U.S.A. 42°14N 72°9W 91 B2
West Burke Vt., U.S.A. 44°39N 71°59W 89 B3
West Burlington Iowa, U.S.A. 40°49N 91°9W 81 E7
West Caldwell N.J., U.S.A. 40°50N 74°18W 97 A1
West Campton N.H., U.S.A. 43°40N 71°41W 89 C3
West Canaan N.H., U.S.A. 43°40N 72°2W 89 C2
West Cape May N.J., U.S.A. 38°56N 74°56W 92 D2
West Carroll Parish ☆ La., U.S.A. 32°48N 91°27W 110 B4
West Carthage N.Y., U.S.A. 43°59N 75°37W 88 B5
West Chazy N.Y., U.S.A. 44°49N 73°28W 89 B1
West Chester Iowa, U.S.A. 41°20N 91°49W 81 D7
West Chester Pa., U.S.A. 39°58N 75°36W 92 C1
West Columbia S.C., U.S.A. 33°59N 81°4W 103 E4
West Columbia Tex., U.S.A. 29°9N 95°39W 109 H12
West Concord Minn., U.S.A. 44°9N 92°54W 77 F6
West Cote Blanche B. La., U.S.A. 29°45N 91°55W 110 E4
West Covina Calif., U.S.A. 34°4N 117°54W 127 J9
West Creek N.J., U.S.A. 39°38N 74°18W 92 C2
West Cummington Mass., U.S.A. 42°29N 72°57W 91 B2
West Dalhousie N.S., Canada 44°43N 65°13W 141 J4
West Delta Park Oreg., U.S.A. 45°35N 122°42W 132 A1
West Des Moines Iowa, U.S.A. 41°35N 93°43W 81 D5
West Don → Ont., Canada 43°44N 79°24W 161 A2
West Dover Vt., U.S.A. 42°56N 72°51W 89 D2
West Dummerston Vt., U.S.A. 42°55N 72°38W 89 D2
West Elk Mts. Colo., U.S.A. 38°35N 107°15W 125 D3
West Elkton Ohio, U.S.A. 39°35N 84°33W 86 D2
West End Bahamas 26°41N 78°58W 182 A4
West Fairlee Vt., U.S.A. 43°54N 72°16W 89 C2
West Fargo N. Dak., U.S.A. 46°52N 96°54W 76 D9
West Feliciana Parish ☆ La., U.S.A. 30°50N 91°23W 110 D4
West Fork → W. Va., U.S.A. 39°28N 80°9W 102 B4
West Fork Amite → U.S.A. 31°0N 90°50W 111 E3
West Fork Poplar → Mont., U.S.A. 48°31N 105°22W 123 B12
West Fork Trinity → Tex., U.S.A. 32°48N 96°54W 109 E11
West Forks Maine, U.S.A. 45°20N 69°58W 90 C4
West Frankfort Ill., U.S.A. 37°54N 88°55W 84 F5
West Glacier Mont., U.S.A. 48°30N 113°59W 123 B4
West Grand L. Maine, U.S.A. 45°14N 67°51W 90 C6
West Green Ga., U.S.A. 31°37N 82°44W 113 E4
West Grove Pa., U.S.A. 39°49N 75°49W 87 E7
West Hamlin W. Va., U.S.A. 38°17N 82°12W 102 C2
West Hartford Conn., U.S.A. 41°45N 72°44W 91 C2
West Haven Conn., U.S.A. 41°17N 72°57W 91 C2
West Hebron N.Y., U.S.A. 43°14N 73°23W 89 C1
West Helena Ark., U.S.A. 34°33N 90°38W 106 D5
West Hempstead N.Y., U.S.A. 40°42N 73°39W 97 B5
West Hill Ont., Canada 43°46N 79°10W 161 A3
West Hollywood Calif., U.S.A. 34°5N 118°21W 133 B2
West Homestead Pa., U.S.A. 40°23N 79°54W 98 B2
West Indies Cent. Amer. 15°0N 65°0W 183 D7
West Jefferson N.C., U.S.A. 36°24N 81°30W 103 B4
West Jordan Utah, U.S.A. 40°36N 111°56W 134 C1
West Kingston R.I., U.S.A. 41°29N 71°34W 91 C3
West Lafayette Ind., U.S.A. 40°27N 86°55W 85 C4
West Lebanon Ind., U.S.A. 40°16N 87°23W 85 C3
West Liberty Iowa, U.S.A. 41°34N 91°16W 81 D7
West Liberty Ky., U.S.A. 37°55N 83°16W 105 C9
West Liberty Ohio, U.S.A. 40°15N 83°45W 86 C3
West Liberty W. Va., U.S.A. 40°10N 80°36W 102 A4
West Line Mo., U.S.A. 38°38N 94°35W 83 C2
West Linn Oreg., U.S.A. 45°21N 122°36W 132 B2
West Lorne Ont., Canada 42°36N 81°36W 146 E5
West Los Angeles, University of Calif., U.S.A. 34°7N 118°23W 133 C2
West Louisville Ky., U.S.A. 37°42N 87°17W 104 C5
West Mansfield Ohio, U.S.A. 40°24N 83°33W 86 C3
West Mayfield Pa., U.S.A. 40°47N 80°20W 87 D2
West Medford Mass., U.S.A. 42°25N 71°7W 96 A2
West Memphis Ark., U.S.A. 35°8N 90°11W 117 B1
West Miami Fla., U.S.A. 25°45N 80°17W 115 D1
West Mifflin Pa., U.S.A. 40°21N 79°52W 98 B2
West Milan N.H., U.S.A. 44°37N 71°18W 89 B3
West Milford N.J., U.S.A. 41°8N 74°22W 92 A2
West Milford W. Va., U.S.A. 39°12N 80°24W 102 B4
West Millgrove Ohio, U.S.A. 41°15N 83°30W 86 B3
West Milton Ohio, U.S.A. 39°58N 84°20W 86 D2
West Milwaukee Wis., U.S.A. 43°0N 87°58W 94 B2
West Mineral Kans., U.S.A. 37°17N 94°55W 82 D9
West Monroe La., U.S.A. 32°31N 92°9W 110 B3
West Mts. Idaho, U.S.A. 44°28N 116°14W 122 E2
West New York New York, U.S.A. 96 a1
West Newbury Mass., U.S.A. 42°48N 71°0W 91 B4
West Newfield Maine, U.S.A. 43°39N 70°55W 89 C4
West Nishnabotna → Iowa, U.S.A. 40°39N 95°38W 81 E3
West Nueces → Tex., U.S.A. 29°16N 99°56W 109 H8
West Odessa Tex., U.S.A. 31°50N 102°30W 108 F5
West of Twin Peaks Calif., U.S.A. 37°43N 122°27W 132 B2
West Okoboji L. Iowa, U.S.A. 43°23N 95°9W 81 B3
West Orange N.J., U.S.A. 40°47N 74°14W 97 B1
West Orange Tex., U.S.A. 30°5N 93°46W 109 G14
West Ossipee N.H., U.S.A. 43°48N 71°12W 89 C3
West Palm Beach Fla., U.S.A. 26°43N 80°3W 114 E8
West Palm Beach Canal Fla., U.S.A. 26°40N 80°15W 114 E8
West Palm Beach Int. ✕ (PBI) Fla., U.S.A. 26°41N 80°6W 114 E8
West Park Pa., U.S.A. 40°28N 80°4W 98 B1
West Paterson N.J., U.S.A. 40°53N 74°11W 97 A1
West Pawlet Vt., U.S.A. 43°21N 73°15W 89 C1
West Pensacola Fla., U.S.A. 30°25N 87°16W 114 A1
West Plains Mo., U.S.A. 36°44N 91°51W 83 E5
West Plymouth N.H., U.S.A. 43°45N 71°45W 89 C3
West Point Calif., U.S.A. 38°24N 120°32W 126 E6
West Point Ga., U.S.A. 32°53N 85°11W 113 D1
West Point Ill., U.S.A. 40°15N 91°11W 84 C2
West Point Iowa, U.S.A. 40°43N 91°27W 81 E7
West Point Ky., U.S.A. 37°59N 85°57W 105 C7
West Point Miss., U.S.A. 33°36N 88°39W 111 C5
West Point N.Y., U.S.A. 41°24N 73°58W 88 D7
West Point Nebr., U.S.A. 41°51N 96°43W 80 C9
West Point Va., U.S.A. 37°32N 76°48W 102 D8
West Point L. Ga., U.S.A. 33°8N 85°0W 113 C1
West Point Military Academy N.Y., U.S.A. 41°22N 73°57W 88 D7
West Portland Oreg., U.S.A. 45°27N 122°43W 132 B1
West Pt. = Ouest, Pte. de l' Qué., Canada 49°52N 64°40W 140 D5
West Richland Wash., U.S.A. 46°18N 119°20W 120 D6
West Rindge N.H., U.S.A. 42°47N 72°3W 89 D2
West River Md., U.S.A. 38°52N 76°31W 93 B4
West Road → B.C., Canada 53°18N 122°53W 154 B11
West Rouge Ont., Canada 43°48N 79°7W 161 A4
West Roxbury Mass., U.S.A. 42°16N 71°9W 96 B2
West Rutland Vt., U.S.A. 43°36N 73°3W 89 C1
West Sacramento Calif., U.S.A. 38°35N 121°32W 126 E5
West St. Paul Minn., U.S.A. 44°54N 93°5W 94 B3
West Salem Ill., U.S.A. 38°31N 88°1W 84 E5
West Salem Ohio, U.S.A. 40°58N 82°7W 86 C4
West Salem Wis., U.S.A. 43°54N 91°5W 78 E2
West Seneca N.Y., U.S.A. 42°51N 78°48W 88 C2
West Siloam Springs Okla., U.S.A. 36°12N 94°39W 107 B9
West Slope Oreg., U.S.A. 45°29N 122°45W 132 B1
West Springfield Mass., U.S.A. 42°6N 72°38W 91 B2
West Springfield Va., U.S.A. 38°47N 77°13W 99 C2
West Stewartstown N.H., U.S.A. 44°59N 71°32W 89 B3
West Tavaputs Plateau Utah, U.S.A. 39°50N 110°20W 129 D5
West Terre Haute Ind., U.S.A. 39°28N 87°27W 85 D3
West Thompson Res. Conn., U.S.A. 41°57N 71°54W 91 C3
West Thorton N.H., U.S.A. 43°55N 71°42W 89 C3
West Thumb Wyo., U.S.A. 44°25N 110°34W 124 B2
West Thurlow I. B.C., Canada 50°25N 125°35W 154 E9
West Tisbury Mass., U.S.A. 41°23N 70°41W 91 C4
West Topsham Vt., U.S.A. 44°7N 72°19W 89 B2
West Town Ill., U.S.A. 41°53N 87°42W 95 B2
West Union Iowa, U.S.A. 42°57N 91°49W 81 C7
West Union Minn., U.S.A. 45°48N 95°5W 77 E3
West Union Ohio, U.S.A. 38°48N 83°33W 86 E3
West Union W. Va., U.S.A. 39°18N 80°47W 102 B4
West Unity Ohio, U.S.A. 41°35N 84°26W 86 B2
West University Place Tex., U.S.A. 29°43N 95°26W 116 B2
West Valley City Utah, U.S.A. 40°42N 111°58W 134 B1
West Vancouver B.C., Canada 49°22N 123°10W 161 B1
West View Pa., U.S.A. 40°31N 80°2W 98 A1
West Virginia □ U.S.A. 38°45N 80°30W 102 C4
West Warwick R.I., U.S.A. 41°43N 71°32W 91 C3
West Wendover Nev., U.S.A. 40°44N 114°4W 128 B6
West Winfield N.Y., U.S.A. 42°53N 75°12W 88 C5
West Yarmouth Mass., U.S.A. 41°39N 70°15W 91 C4
West Yellowstone Mont., U.S.A. 44°40N 111°6W 123 F6
West York Pa., U.S.A. 39°57N 76°46W 87 E6
Westbank B.C., Canada 49°50N 119°38W 155 F15
Westbay Fla., U.S.A. 30°18N 85°52W 114 A3
Westboro Mo., U.S.A. 40°32N 95°19W 83 A1
Westborough Mass., U.S.A. 42°16N 71°37W 91 B3
Westbourne Man., Canada 50°8N 98°35W 151 E13
Westbridge B.C., Canada 49°10N 118°58W 155 F16
Westbrook Conn., U.S.A. 41°17N 72°27W 91 C2
Westbrook Maine, U.S.A. 43°41N 70°22W 90 E3
Westbrook Minn., U.S.A. 44°3N 95°26W 77 F3
Westbrook Tex., U.S.A. 32°21N 101°1W 108 E6
Westby Mont., U.S.A. 48°52N 104°3W 123 B13
Westby Wis., U.S.A. 43°39N 90°51W 78 E3
Westchester Calif., U.S.A. 33°57N 118°23W 133 C2
Westchester Ill., U.S.A. 41°51N 87°53W 95 B1
Westchester N.Y., U.S.A. 40°51N 73°51W 97 A3
Westchester County ☆ N.Y., U.S.A. 41°40N 73°45W 88 D7
Westcliffe Colo., U.S.A. 38°9N 105°28W 125 D5
Westend Calif., U.S.A. 35°42N 117°24W 127 H9
Westerly R.I., U.S.A. 41°22N 71°50W 91 C3
Western Nebr., U.S.A. 40°24N 97°12W 80 D8
Western Addition Calif., U.S.A. 37°47N 122°25W 132 B2
Western Duck I. Ont., Canada 45°45N 83°0W 146 B3
Western Grove Ark., U.S.A. 36°6N 92°57W 106 B3
Western Pen. Ont., Canada 49°30N 94°50W 148 C2
Western Shore N.S., Canada 44°32N 64°19W 141 J5
Western Sierra Madre = Madre Occidental, Sierra Mexico 27°0N 107°0W 172 C5
Westernport Md., U.S.A. 39°29N 79°3W 93 A1
Westerville Nebr., U.S.A. 41°24N 99°23W 80 C6
Westerville Ohio, U.S.A. 40°8N 82°56W 86 C4
Westfall Oreg., U.S.A. 43°59N 117°48W 121 D8
Westfield Ill., U.S.A. 39°27N 88°0W 84 D5
Westfield Ind., U.S.A. 40°2N 86°8W 85 C4
Westfield Iowa, U.S.A. 42°45N 96°36W 81 C2
Westfield Maine, U.S.A. 46°34N 67°55W 90 B6
Westfield Mass., U.S.A. 42°7N 72°45W 91 B2
Westfield N.J., U.S.A. 40°39N 74°21W 92 B2
Westfield N.Y., U.S.A. 42°20N 79°35W 88 C1
Westfield Pa., U.S.A. 41°55N 77°32W 87 C5
Westfield Wis., U.S.A. 43°53N 89°30W 78 E4
Westfield → Mass., U.S.A. 42°5N 72°35W 91 B2
Westfir Oreg., U.S.A. 43°46N 122°31W 121 D3
Westford Mass., U.S.A. 42°35N 71°26W 91 B3
Westgate Iowa, U.S.A. 42°46N 92°0W 81 C6
Westgate Md., U.S.A. 38°57N 77°6W 99 B3
Westhoff Tex., U.S.A. 29°12N 97°28W 109 H10
Westhope N. Dak., U.S.A. 48°55N 101°1W 76 B4
Westlake Calif., U.S.A. 37°42N 122°29W 132 B2
Westlake La., U.S.A. 30°15N 93°59W 110 D2
Westland Mich., U.S.A. 42°15N 83°20W 79 G8
Westlock Alta., Canada 54°9N 113°55W 152 D7
Westlynn B.C., Canada 49°19N 123°1W 161 B2
Westminster Calif., U.S.A. 33°45N 118°0W 127 K8
Westminster Colo., U.S.A. 39°50N 105°2W 134 A1
Westminster Mass., U.S.A. 42°33N 71°55W 91 B3
Westminster Md., U.S.A. 39°34N 76°59W 93 A4
Westminster S.C., U.S.A. 34°40N 83°6W 103 D2
Westminster Vt., U.S.A. 43°5N 72°27W 89 C2
Westmont N.J., U.S.A. 39°54N 75°2W 98 B2
Westmont Pa., U.S.A. 40°19N 78°58W 87 D4
Westmore Vt., U.S.A. 44°50N 72°3W 89 B2
Westmoreland Kans., U.S.A. 39°24N 96°25W 82 B7
Westmoreland N.H., U.S.A. 42°57N 72°25W 89 D2
Westmoreland Tenn., U.S.A. 36°34N 86°15W 104 D6
Westmoreland Va., U.S.A. 38°4N 76°34W 93 B4
Westmoreland County ☆ Pa., U.S.A. 40°20N 79°25W 87 D3
Westmoreland County ☆ Va., U.S.A. 38°6N 76°50W 102 C8
Westmorland Calif., U.S.A. 33°2N 115°37W 127 K11
Westmount Qué., Canada 45°29N 73°35W 160 B3
Weston Ont., Canada 43°42N 79°30W 161 A1
Weston Colo., U.S.A. 37°8N 104°48W 125 E6
Weston Mass., U.S.A. 42°22N 71°16W 91 B3
Weston Mo., U.S.A. 39°25N 94°54W 83 B2
Weston Nebr., U.S.A. 41°12N 96°45W 80 C9
Weston Oreg., U.S.A. 45°49N 118°26W 121 B7
Weston Vt., U.S.A. 43°18N 72°38W 89 C2
Weston W. Va., U.S.A. 39°2N 80°28W 102 B4
Weston Wyo., U.S.A. 44°38N 105°20W 124 B7
Weston County ☆ Wyo., U.S.A. 43°55N 104°35W 124 C8
Weston I. N.W.T., Canada 52°33N 79°36W 143 C2
Westover Md., U.S.A. 38°7N 75°42W 93 B5
Westover Pa., U.S.A. 40°45N 78°40W 87 D4
Westover W. Va., U.S.A. 39°38N 79°58W 102 B5
Westover Air Reserve Base Mass., U.S.A. 42°13N 72°29W 91 B2
Westphalia Mich., U.S.A. 42°56N 84°48W 79 G7
Westphalia Mo., U.S.A. 38°26N 92°0W 83 C4
Westpoint Tenn., U.S.A. 35°8N 87°32W 104 E5
Westport N.S., Canada 44°15N 66°22W 141 J3
Westport Nfld. & L., Canada 49°47N 56°38W 142 C4
Westport Ont., Canada 44°40N 76°25W 147 C10
Westport Calif., U.S.A. 39°38N 123°47W 126 D3
Westport Conn., U.S.A. 41°9N 73°22W 91 C1
Westport Ind., U.S.A. 39°11N 85°34W 85 D5
Westport Minn., U.S.A. 45°43N 95°10W 77 E3
Westport N.H., U.S.A. 42°49N 72°20W 89 D2
Westport N.Y., U.S.A. 44°11N 73°26W 89 B1
Westport Okla., U.S.A. 36°8N 96°20W 107 B7
Westport Oreg., U.S.A. 46°8N 123°23W 121 A2
Westport Wash., U.S.A. 46°53N 124°6W 120 D1
Westray Man., Canada 53°36N 101°24W 151 B10
Westree Ont., Canada 47°26N 81°34W 149 E15
Westview Baltimore, U.S.A. 39°17N 76°44W 99 B1
Westville N.S., Canada 45°34N 62°43W 141 H7
Westville Fla., U.S.A. 30°46N 85°51W 114 A3
Westville Ill., U.S.A. 40°2N 87°38W 84 C6
Westville Ind., U.S.A. 41°32N 86°54W 85 B4
Westville N.J., U.S.A. 39°52N 75°7W 98 B2
Westville Okla., U.S.A. 35°58N 94°40W 107 C9
Westville S.C., U.S.A. 34°27N 80°36W 103 D5

Westwego *La.*, *U.S.A.* 29°54N 90°8W **117** C2
Westwold *B.C.*, *Canada* 50°28N 119°45W **155** E15
Westwood *Calif.*, *U.S.A.* 40°18N 121°0W **126** C6
Westwood *Ky.*, *U.S.A.* 38°30N 82°50W **105** B10
Westwood *Mass.*, *U.S.A.* 42°13N 71°14W **91** B3
Westwood *Md.*, *U.S.A.* 38°40N 76°45W **93** B4
Westwood *N.J.*, *U.S.A.* 40°58N 74°2W **92** B2
Westwood Lakes *Fla.*, *U.S.A.* 25°44N 80°23W **114** F8
Westwood Village *Calif.*, *U.S.A.* 34°3N 118°26W **133** B2
Westwood Village *Tex.*, *U.S.A.* 29°24N 98°37W **116** C2
Wet Mts. *Colo.*, *U.S.A.* 38°0N 105°10W **125** E5
Wetaskiwin *Alta.*, *Canada* 52°55N 113°24W **153** F7
Wethersfield *Conn.*, *U.S.A.* 41°42N 72°40W **91** C2
Wetmore *Colo.*, *U.S.A.* 38°14N 105°5W **125** D5
Wetmore *Kans.*, *U.S.A.* 39°38N 95°49W **82** B8
Wetumka *Okla.*, *U.S.A.* 35°14N 96°15W **107** C7
Wetumpka *Ala.*, *U.S.A.* 32°32N 86°13W **112** D4
Wetzel County ☆ *W. Va.*, *U.S.A.* 39°34N 80°41W **102** B4
Wevok *Alaska*, *U.S.A.* 68°53N 166°13W **135** B6
Wewahitchka *Fla.*, *U.S.A.* 30°7N 85°12W **114** A3
Wewoka *Okla.*, *U.S.A.* 35°9N 96°30W **107** C7
Wexford *Ont.*, *Canada* 43°45N 79°18W **161** A3
Wexford County ☆ *Mich.*, *U.S.A.* 44°20N 85°40W **79** E6
Weyauwega *Wis.*, *U.S.A.* 44°19N 88°56W **78** D5
Weyburn *Sask.*, *Canada* 49°40N 103°50W **150** F8
Weyerhaeuser *Wis.*, *U.S.A.* 45°26N 91°25W **78** C2
Weymouth *N.S.*, *Canada* 44°30N 66°1W **141** J3
Weymouth *Mass.*, *U.S.A.* 42°13N 70°58W **91** B4
Wha Ti *N.W.T.*, *Canada* 63°8N 117°16W **157** D9
Whalan *Minn.*, *U.S.A.* 43°44N 91°55W **77** G7
Whale → *Que.*, *Canada* 58°15N 67°40W **143** B4
Whale Cove *Nunavut*, *Canada* 62°10N 92°34W **159** E7
Whaletown *B.C.*, *Canada* 50°7N 125°2W **154** E9
Whaleysville *Md.*, *U.S.A.* 38°24N 75°18W **93** B5
Wharncliffe *W. Va.*, *U.S.A.* 37°33N 81°58W **102** D3
Wharton *N.J.*, *U.S.A.* 40°54N 74°35W **92** B2
Wharton *Ohio*, *U.S.A.* 40°52N 83°28W **86** C3
Wharton *Tex.*, *U.S.A.* 29°19N 96°6W **109** H11
Wharton County ☆ *Tex.*, *U.S.A.* 29°12N 96°16W **109** H11
Wharton L. *Nunavut*, *Canada* 64°1N 99°50W **159** E6
Wharton State Forest *N.J.*, *U.S.A.* 39°45N 74°40W **92** D2
What Cheer *Iowa*, *U.S.A.* 41°24N 92°21W **81** D6
Whatcom = Bellingham *Wash.*, *U.S.A.* 48°46N 122°29W **120** B3
Whatcom, L. *Wash.*, *U.S.A.* 48°44N 122°20W **120** B3
Whatcom County ☆ *Wash.*, *U.S.A.* 48°56N 122°0W **120** B4
Whately *Mass.*, *U.S.A.* 42°26N 72°38W **91** B2
Whatley *Ala.*, *U.S.A.* 31°39N 87°42W **112** E3
Wheat Ridge *Colo.*, *U.S.A.* 39°45N 105°4W **134** B1
Wheatcroft *Ky.*, *U.S.A.* 37°30N 87°52W **104** C5
Wheatland *Calif.*, *U.S.A.* 39°1N 121°25W **126** D5
Wheatland *Ind.*, *U.S.A.* 38°40N 87°19W **85** E3
Wheatland *Iowa*, *U.S.A.* 41°50N 90°51W **81** D8
Wheatland *Mo.*, *U.S.A.* 37°57N 93°24W **83** D3
Wheatland *Wyo.*, *U.S.A.* 42°3N 104°58W **124** D8
Wheatland County ☆ *Mont.*, *U.S.A.* 46°30N 109°50W **123** D8
Wheatland Res. No.2 *Wyo.*, *U.S.A.* 41°50N 105°38W **124** E7
Wheatley *Ont.*, *Canada* 42°6N 82°27W **146** E4
Wheatley *Ark.*, *U.S.A.* 34°55N 91°7W **106** D4
Wheaton *Ill.*, *U.S.A.* 41°52N 88°6W **84** B5
Wheaton *Kans.*, *U.S.A.* 39°30N 96°19W **82** B7
Wheaton *Md.*, *U.S.A.* 39°3N 77°3W **93** A3
Wheaton *Minn.*, *U.S.A.* 45°48N 96°30W **77** E2
Wheaton *Mo.*, *U.S.A.* 36°46N 94°3W **83** E2
Wheeler *Ill.*, *U.S.A.* 39°3N 88°19W **84** D5
Wheeler *Kans.*, *U.S.A.* 39°46N 101°43W **82** B2
Wheeler *Miss.*, *U.S.A.* 34°35N 88°37W **111** B5
Wheeler *Oreg.*, *U.S.A.* 45°41N 123°53W **121** B2
Wheeler *Tex.*, *U.S.A.* 35°27N 100°16W **108** B7
Wheeler *Wis.*, *U.S.A.* 45°3N 91°55W **78** C2
Wheeler → *Qué.*, *Canada* 57°2N 67°13W **143** B4
Wheeler County ☆ *Ga.*, *U.S.A.* 32°5N 82°45W **113** D4
Wheeler County ☆ *Nebr.*, *U.S.A.* 41°50N 98°30W **80** C7
Wheeler County ☆ *Oreg.*, *U.S.A.* 44°45N 120°0W **121** C6
Wheeler County ☆ *Tex.*, *U.S.A.* 35°30N 100°15W **108** B7
Wheeler L. *Ala.*, *U.S.A.* 34°48N 87°23W **112** B3
Wheeler Pk. *Calif.*, *U.S.A.* 40°6N 120°41W **126** C6
Wheeler Pk. *N. Mex.*, *U.S.A.* 36°34N 105°25W **131** A5
Wheeler Pk. *Nev.*, *U.S.A.* 38°57N 114°15W **128** D6
Wheeler Ridge *Calif.*, *U.S.A.* 35°0N 118°57W **127** H8
Wheelersburg *Ohio*, *U.S.A.* 38°44N 82°51W **86** E4
Wheeling *Ill.*, *U.S.A.* 42°8N 87°55W **84** A6
Wheeling *W. Va.*, *U.S.A.* 40°4N 80°43W **102** A4
Wheelock *N. Dak.*, *U.S.A.* 48°18N 103°15W **76** B2
Wheelwright *Ky.*, *U.S.A.* 37°20N 82°43W **105** C10
Whelen Springs *Ark.*, *U.S.A.* 33°50N 93°7W **106** E2
Whidbey I. *Wash.*, *U.S.A.* 48°12N 122°17W **120** B3
Whigham *Ga.*, *U.S.A.* 30°53N 84°19W **113** F2
Whiskey Pk. *Wyo.*, *U.S.A.* 42°18N 107°35W **124** D5
Whiskeytown-Shasta-Trinity Nat. Recr.
  Area △ *Calif.*, *U.S.A.* 40°45N 122°15W **126** C4
Whispering Pines *N.C.*, *U.S.A.* 35°17N 79°26W **103** C6
Whistler *B.C.*, *Canada* 50°7N 122°58W **155** E12
Whitaker *Pa.*, *U.S.A.* 40°23N 79°53W **98** B2
Whitakers *N.C.*, *U.S.A.* 36°6N 77°43W **103** B8
Whitbourne *Nfld. & L.*, *Canada* 47°25N 53°32W **142** E7
Whitby *Ont.*, *Canada* 43°52N 78°56W **147** D8
White *Ga.*, *U.S.A.* 34°17N 84°45W **113** B2
White *S. Dak.*, *U.S.A.* 44°26N 96°39W **76** F9
White → *Ont.*, *Canada* 48°33N 86°16W **149** D10
White → *Yukon*, *Canada* 63°11N 139°35W **157** D5
White → *Ariz.*, *U.S.A.* 33°44N 110°13W **130** D5
White → *Ark.*, *U.S.A.* 33°57N 91°5W **106** E4
White → *Ind.*, *U.S.A.* 38°25N 87°45W **85** E3
White → *Nev.*, *U.S.A.* 37°19N 115°8W **128** E5
White → *Oreg.*, *U.S.A.* 45°14N 121°1W **121** B4
White → *S. Dak.*, *U.S.A.* 43°42N 99°27W **76** G6
White → *Tex.*, *U.S.A.* 33°14N 100°56W **108** D7
White → *Utah*, *U.S.A.* 40°4N 109°41W **129** C6
White → *Vt.*, *U.S.A.* 43°37N 72°20W **89** C2
White → *Wash.*, *U.S.A.* 47°50N 120°48W **120** C5
White → *Wash.*, *U.S.A.* 47°12N 122°15W **120** C3
White B. *Nfld. & L.*, *Canada* 50°0N 56°35W **142** C4
White Bear *Sask.*, *Canada* 50°53N 108°13W **150** E3
White Bear L. *Minn.*, *U.S.A.* 45°4N 92°58W **94** A4
White Bear Lake *Minn.*, *U.S.A.* 45°4N 93°0W **94** A3
White Bird *Idaho*, *U.S.A.* 45°46N 116°18W **122** D2
White Bluff *Tenn.*, *U.S.A.* 36°6N 87°13W **104** B6
White Butte *N. Dak.*, *U.S.A.* 46°23N 103°18W **76** D2
White Butte *S. Dak.*, *U.S.A.* 45°56N 102°22W **76** E3
White Canyon *Utah*, *U.S.A.* 37°57N 110°26W **129** F5
White Castle *La.*, *U.S.A.* 30°10N 91°9W **110** D4
White Center *Wash.*, *U.S.A.* 47°31N 122°21W **132** C3
White City *Fla.*, *U.S.A.* 29°55N 85°13W **114** B3
White City *Fla.*, *U.S.A.* 27°22N 80°20W **114** D8
White City *Kans.*, *U.S.A.* 38°48N 96°44W **82** C7

White City *Oreg.*, *U.S.A.* 42°26N 122°51W **121** E3
White Cloud *Kans.*, *U.S.A.* 39°59N 95°18W **82** B8
White Cloud *Mich.*, *U.S.A.* 43°33N 85°46W **79** F6
White County ☆ *Ark.*, *U.S.A.* 35°15N 91°44W **106** C4
White County ☆ *Ga.*, *U.S.A.* 34°40N 83°45W **113** B3
White County ☆ *Ill.*, *U.S.A.* 38°5N 88°10W **84** E5
White County ☆ *Ind.*, *U.S.A.* 40°45N 86°50W **85** C4
White County ☆ *Tenn.*, *U.S.A.* 35°56N 85°28W **105** E7
White Deer *Tex.*, *U.S.A.* 35°26N 101°10W **108** B6
White Earth *N. Dak.*, *U.S.A.* 48°23N 102°46W **76** B3
White Earth → *N. Dak.*, *U.S.A.* 48°9N 102°42W **76** B3
White Earth Indian Reservation *Minn.*,
  U.S.A. 47°20N 95°45W **77** C3
White Fox *Sask.*, *Canada* 53°27N 104°5W **150** B7
White Hall *Ala.*, *U.S.A.* 32°20N 86°43W **112** D3
White Hall *Ark.*, *U.S.A.* 34°16N 92°5W **106** D3
White Hall *Ill.*, *U.S.A.* 39°26N 90°24W **84** D31
White Haven *Pa.*, *U.S.A.* 41°4N 75°47W **92** A1
White Hill *N.S.*, *Canada* 46°42N 60°36W **141** G9
White Horse *N.J.*, *U.S.A.* 40°11N 74°42W **92** B2
White House *Tenn.*, *U.S.A.* 36°28N 86°39W **104** D6
White I. *Nunavut*, *Canada* 65°47N 84°54W **159** D9
White L. *Ont.*, *Canada* 45°18N 76°31W **144** F6
White L. *Ont.*, *Canada* 48°47N 85°37W **149** D11
White L. *La.*, *U.S.A.* 29°44N 92°30W **110** E3
White Lake *N.C.*, *U.S.A.* 34°39N 78°30W **103** D7
White Lake *S. Dak.*, *U.S.A.* 43°44N 98°43W **76** G7
White Lake *Wis.*, *U.S.A.* 45°10N 88°46W **78** C5
White Lakes *N. Mex.*, *U.S.A.* 35°12N 105°47W **131** B5
White Mountain *Alaska*, *U.S.A.* 64°41N 163°24W **135** D7
White Mountain Nat. Forest *N.H.*,
  U.S.A. 44°35N 71°23W **89** B3
White Mountain Peak *Calif.*, *U.S.A.* 37°38N 118°15W **127** F8
White Mountains Nat. Recr. Area △ *Alaska*,
  U.S.A. 65°30N 147°40W **135** D11
White Mts. *Alaska*, *U.S.A.* 65°30N 146°30W **135** D11
White Mts. *Ariz.*, *U.S.A.* 34°0N 109°40W **130** D6
White Mts. *Calif.*, *U.S.A.* 37°30N 118°15W **127** F8
White Mts. *N.H.*, *U.S.A.* 44°15N 71°15W **89** B3
White Oak *Ga.*, *U.S.A.* 31°2N 81°43W **113** E5
White Oak *Tex.*, *U.S.A.* 32°32N 94°52W **109** E13
White Oak Cr. → *Tex.*, *U.S.A.* 33°14N 94°42W **109** D13
White Oak Lake *Ark.*, *U.S.A.* 33°42N 93°5W **106** E2
White Otter L. *Ont.*, *Canada* 49°5N 91°55W **148** C5
White Owl *S. Dak.*, *U.S.A.* 44°36N 102°26W **76** F3
White Owl L. *Ont.*, *Canada* 47°10N 82°35W **149** E14
White Pass *Wash.*, *U.S.A.* 46°38N 121°24W **120** D4
White Pigeon *Mich.*, *U.S.A.* 41°48N 85°39W **79** H6
White Pine *Mich.*, *U.S.A.* 46°45N 89°35W **79** C2
White Pine *Mont.*, *U.S.A.* 47°45N 115°29W **123** C2
White Pine *Tenn.*, *U.S.A.* 36°7N 83°17W **105** D9
White Pine County ☆ *Nev.*, *U.S.A.* 39°30N 115°0W **128** C6
White Pine Range *Nev.*, *U.S.A.* 39°10N 115°22W **128** C6
White Plains *Ga.*, *U.S.A.* 33°28N 83°1W **113** C3
White Plains *Md.*, *U.S.A.* 38°36N 76°55W **93** B4
White Plains *N.Y.*, *U.S.A.* 41°2N 73°46W **92** A3
White River *Ont.*, *Canada* 48°35N 85°20W **149** D11
White River *S. Dak.*, *U.S.A.* 43°34N 100°45W **76** G5
White River Junction *Vt.*, *U.S.A.* 43°39N 72°19W **89** C2
White River Nat. Forest *Colo.*, *U.S.A.* 39°20N 106°45W **125** C4
White River Nat. Wildlife Refuge △ *Ark.*,
  U.S.A. 34°18N 91°5W **106** D4
White River Res. *Tex.*, *U.S.A.* 33°27N 101°5W **108** D6
White River Valley *Nev.*, *U.S.A.* 38°6N 114°58W **128** D6
White Rock *B.C.*, *Canada* 49°2N 122°48W **155** F12
White Rock *Ky.*, *U.S.A.* 36°40N 83°27W **105** D9
White Rock *N. Mex.*, *U.S.A.* 35°50N 106°12W **131** B4
White Rock Cr. → *Kans.*, *U.S.A.* 39°55N 97°50W **82** B6
White Rock Lake *Tex.*, *U.S.A.* 32°48N 96°43W **116** A5
White Rocks Nat. Recr. Area △ *Vt.*,
  U.S.A. 43°22N 72°55W **89** C2
White Salmon *Wash.*, *U.S.A.* 45°44N 121°29W **120** E4
White Sands *N. Mex.*, *U.S.A.* 32°23N 106°29W **131** D4
White Sands Missile Range *N. Mex.*,
  U.S.A. 33°0N 106°25W **131** E4
White Sands Nat. Monument △ *N. Mex.*,
  U.S.A. 32°46N 106°20W **131** D4
White Shield *N. Dak.*, *U.S.A.* 47°40N 101°51W **76** C4
White Signal *N. Mex.*, *U.S.A.* 32°33N 108°22W **131** E2
White Springs *Fla.*, *U.S.A.* 30°20N 82°45W **114** A6
White Stone *Va.*, *U.S.A.* 37°39N 76°23W **102** D8
White Sulphur Springs *Mont.*, *U.S.A.* 46°33N 110°54W **123** D7
White Sulphur Springs *W. Va.*, *U.S.A.* 37°48N 80°18W **102** D4
White Swan *Wash.*, *U.S.A.* 46°23N 120°44W **120** D5
White Woman Cr. → *U.S.A.* 38°26N 100°54W **82** C3
Whiteburg *Md.*, *U.S.A.* 38°12N 75°32W **93** B5
Whiteclay *Nebr.*, *U.S.A.* 42°57N 102°33W **80** B3
Whiteclay L. *Ont.*, *Canada* 50°53N 88°45W **148** B8
Whitecourt *Alta.*, *Canada* 54°10N 115°45W **153** D3
Whiteface *Tex.*, *U.S.A.* 33°36N 102°37W **108** D5
Whiteface → *Minn.*, *U.S.A.* 46°58N 92°48W **77** D6
Whiteface Mt. *N.Y.*, *U.S.A.* 44°22N 73°54W **88** A7
Whiteface Res. *Minn.*, *U.S.A.* 47°17N 92°11W **77** C6
Whitefield *Maine*, *U.S.A.* 44°10N 69°38W **90** D4
Whitefield *N.H.*, *U.S.A.* 44°23N 71°37W **89** B3
Whitefish *Ont.*, *Canada* 46°23N 81°19W **146** A5
Whitefish *Mont.*, *U.S.A.* 48°25N 114°20W **123** B3
Whitefish → *Mich.*, *U.S.A.* 45°55N 86°57W **79** D5
Whitefish B. *Mich.*, *U.S.A.* 46°40N 84°55W **79** D7
Whitefish B. *Wis.*, *U.S.A.* 43°7N 87°53W **94** B2
Whitefish Bay *Wis.*, *U.S.A.* 43°6N 87°54W **94** B2
Whitefish Falls *Ont.*, *Canada* 46°7N 81°44W **146** A5
Whitefish L. *N.W.T.*, *Canada* 62°41N 106°48W **157** D11
Whitefish Point *Mich.*, *U.S.A.* 46°46N 84°57W **79** C7
Whitefish Pt. *Mich.*, *U.S.A.* 46°45N 84°59W **79** C7
Whiteford *Md.*, *U.S.A.* 39°42N 76°21W **93** A4
Whitegull, L. = Goélands, L. aux *Qué.*,
  Canada 55°27N 64°17W **143** B5
Whitehall *Mich.*, *U.S.A.* 43°24N 86°21W **79** F5
Whitehall *Mont.*, *U.S.A.* 45°52N 112°6W **123** E5
Whitehall *N.Y.*, *U.S.A.* 43°33N 73°24W **89** C1
Whitehall *Pa.*, *U.S.A.* 40°38N 75°30W **92** B1
Whitehall *Pa.*, *U.S.A.* 40°21N 79°59W **98** B2
Whitehall *Wis.*, *U.S.A.* 44°22N 91°19W **78** D2
Whitehorse *Yukon*, *Canada* 60°43N 135°3W **157** D5
Whitehouse *Ohio*, *U.S.A.* 41°31N 83°48W **86** B3
Whiteland *Ind.*, *U.S.A.* 39°33N 86°5W **85** D4
Whitelaw *Wis.*, *U.S.A.* 44°9N 87°49W **78** D6
Whitemouth *Man.*, *Canada* 49°57N 95°58W **151** F16
Whitemouth → *Man.*, *Canada* 50°7N 96°2W **151** E15
Whitemouth L. *Man.*, *Canada* 49°15N 95°40W **151** F16
Whiteriver *Ariz.*, *U.S.A.* 33°50N 109°58W **130** D6

Whiterocks *Utah*, *U.S.A.* 40°28N 109°56W **129** C6
Whites City *N. Mex.*, *U.S.A.* 32°11N 104°22W **131** E5
Whitesand → *Sask.*, *Canada* 51°34N 102°56W **150** D9
Whitesboro *N.Y.*, *U.S.A.* 43°7N 75°18W **88** B5
Whitesboro *Okla.*, *U.S.A.* 34°41N 94°53W **107** D9
Whitesboro *Tex.*, *U.S.A.* 33°39N 96°54W **109** D11
Whitesburg *Ky.*, *U.S.A.* 37°7N 82°49W **105** C10
Whiteshell Prov. Park △ *Man.*, *Canada* 50°0N 95°40W **151** E16
Whiteside County ☆ *Ill.*, *U.S.A.* 41°45N 89°55W **84** B4
Whitestone *N.J.*, *U.S.A.* 40°47N 73°39W **97** B4
Whitestone → *Yukon*, *Canada* 66°30N 138°0W **156** C5
Whitestown *Ind.*, *U.S.A.* 40°0N 86°21W **85** D4
Whitesville *Ky.*, *U.S.A.* 37°41N 86°52W **104** C6
Whitesville *W. Va.*, *U.S.A.* 37°59N 81°32W **102** D3
Whiteswan L. *Sask.*, *Canada* 54°5N 105°10W **150** A6
Whiteswan Lake Park △ *B.C.*, *Canada* 50°9N 115°30W **155** E19
Whitetail *Mont.*, *U.S.A.* 48°54N 105°10W **123** B12
Whiteville *N.C.*, *U.S.A.* 34°20N 78°42W **103** D7
Whiteville *Tenn.*, *U.S.A.* 35°20N 89°9W **104** E3
Whitewater *Kans.*, *U.S.A.* 37°58N 97°9W **82** D6
Whitewater *Mo.*, *U.S.A.* 37°14N 89°48W **83** D7
Whitewater *Mont.*, *U.S.A.* 48°46N 107°38W **123** B10
Whitewater *Wis.*, *U.S.A.* 42°50N 88°44W **78** F5
Whitewater → *Sask.*, *Canada* 49°0N 108°0W **150** G4
Whitewater B. *Fla.*, *U.S.A.* 25°15N 81°0W **114** F8
Whitewater Baldy *N. Mex.*, *U.S.A.* 33°20N 108°39W **131** D2
Whitewater L. *Ont.*, *Canada* 50°50N 89°10W **148** B7
Whitewood *Sask.*, *Canada* 50°20N 102°20W **151** E9
Whitewood *S. Dak.*, *U.S.A.* 44°28N 103°39W **76** F2
Whitewright *Tex.*, *U.S.A.* 33°31N 96°24W **109** D11
Whitfield County ☆ *Ga.*, *U.S.A.* 34°50N 84°55W **113** B2
Whiting *Ind.*, *U.S.A.* 41°41N 87°30W **85** B3
Whiting *Iowa*, *U.S.A.* 42°8N 96°9W **81** C2
Whiting *Kans.*, *U.S.A.* 39°35N 95°37W **82** B8
Whiting *Maine*, *U.S.A.* 44°48N 67°11W **90** D6
Whiting *N.J.*, *U.S.A.* 39°57N 74°23W **92** C2
Whiting *Vt.*, *U.S.A.* 43°50N 73°12W **89** C1
Whiting *Wis.*, *U.S.A.* 44°30N 89°34W **78** D4
Whitinsville *Mass.*, *U.S.A.* 42°7N 71°40W **91** B3
Whitlash *Mont.*, *U.S.A.* 48°55N 111°15W **123** B6
Whitley City *Ky.*, *U.S.A.* 36°44N 84°29W **105** D8
Whitley County ☆ *Ind.*, *U.S.A.* 41°10N 85°30W **85** B5
Whitley County ☆ *Ky.*, *U.S.A.* 36°45N 84°10W **105** D8
Whitman *Mass.*, *U.S.A.* 42°5N 70°56W **91** B4
Whitman *Nebr.*, *U.S.A.* 42°3N 101°31W **80** B4
Whitman Air Force Base *Mo.*, *U.S.A.* 38°44N 93°31W **83** C3
Whitman County ☆ *Wash.*, *U.S.A.* 47°0N 117°30W **120** D8
Whitman Mission Nat. Historic Site △ *Wash.*,
  U.S.A. 46°2N 118°28W **120** D7
Whitmire *S.C.*, *U.S.A.* 34°30N 81°37W **103** D4
Whitmore *Calif.*, *U.S.A.* 40°38N 121°55W **126** B4
Whitmore Village *Hawai'i*, *U.S.A.* 21°31N 158°1W **136** J13
Whitney *Ont.*, *Canada* 45°31N 78°14W **144** F4
Whitney *Nebr.*, *U.S.A.* 42°47N 103°15W **80** B2
Whitney *Nev.*, *U.S.A.* 36°4N 115°5W **134** C2
Whitney *Tex.*, *U.S.A.* 31°57N 97°19W **109** F10
Whitney, L. *Tex.*, *U.S.A.* 31°52N 97°22W **109** F10
Whitney, Mt. *Calif.*, *U.S.A.* 36°35N 118°18W **127** G8
Whitney Point *N.Y.*, *U.S.A.* 42°20N 75°58W **88** C5
Whitsett *Tex.*, *U.S.A.* 28°38N 98°16W **109** J9
Whittemore *Iowa*, *U.S.A.* 43°4N 94°26W **81** B4
Whittemore *Mich.*, *U.S.A.* 44°14N 83°48W **79** E8
Whittier *Alaska*, *U.S.A.* 60°47N 148°41W **135** F10
Whittier *Calif.*, *U.S.A.* 33°58N 118°2W **133** C4
Whittlesey, Mt. *Wis.*, *U.S.A.* 46°18N 90°37W **78** B3
Whitwell *Tenn.*, *U.S.A.* 35°12N 85°31W **105** E7
Wholdaia L. *N.W.T.*, *Canada* 60°43N 104°20W **157** D12
Whycocomagh *N.S.*, *Canada* 45°59N 61°7W **141** H8
Wiarton *Ont.*, *Canada* 44°40N 81°10W **146** C5
Wibaux *Mont.*, *U.S.A.* 46°59N 104°11W **123** D13
Wibaux County ☆ *Mont.*, *U.S.A.* 46°50N 104°20W **123** D13
Wichita *Kans.*, *U.S.A.* 37°42N 97°20W **82** D6
Wichita → *Tex.*, *U.S.A.* 34°4N 98°10W **109** C9
Wichita County ☆ *Kans.*, *U.S.A.* 38°30N 101°20W **82** C2
Wichita County ☆ *Tex.*, *U.S.A.* 33°57N 98°40W **109** D9
Wichita Falls *Tex.*, *U.S.A.* 33°54N 98°30W **109** D9
Wichita Mountains Nat. Wildlife Refuge △
  Okla., *U.S.A.* 34°46N 98°42W **107** D5
Wichita Mts. *Okla.*, *U.S.A.* 34°50N 98°45W **107** D5
Wick *W. Va.*, *U.S.A.* 39°25N 80°58W **102** B4
Wicked Pt. *Ont.*, *Canada* 43°52N 77°15W **147** D9
Wickenburg *Ariz.*, *U.S.A.* 33°58N 112°44W **130** D3
Wickes *Ark.*, *U.S.A.* 34°18N 94°20W **106** D1
Wickham *Qué.*, *Canada* 45°45N 72°30W **145** F10
Wickiup Res. *Oreg.*, *U.S.A.* 43°41N 121°41W **121** D4
Wickliffe *Ky.*, *U.S.A.* 36°58N 89°5W **104** D3
Wickliffe *Ohio*, *U.S.A.* 41°36N 81°28W **86** B5
Wicomico → *Md.*, *U.S.A.* 38°13N 75°55W **93** B5
Wicomico Church *Md.*, *U.S.A.* 37°49N 76°23W **93** C4
Wicomico County ☆ *Md.*, *U.S.A.* 38°25N 75°45W **93** B5
Wiggins *Colo.*, *U.S.A.* 40°14N 104°4W **125** B6
Wiggins *Miss.*, *U.S.A.* 30°51N 89°8W **111** F4
Wiggins *Miss.*, *U.S.A.* 32°42N 89°38W **111** D4
Wikwemikong *Ont.*, *Canada* 45°48N 81°43W **146** B5
Wilbarger County ☆ *Tex.*, *U.S.A.* 34°9N 99°17W **109** C8
Wilber *Nebr.*, *U.S.A.* 40°29N 96°58W **80** D9
Wilberforce *Ont.*, *Canada* 45°2N 78°13W **144** F4
Wilbraham *Mass.*, *U.S.A.* 42°7N 72°26W **91** B2
Wilbur *Oreg.*, *U.S.A.* 43°19N 123°21W **121** D2
Wilbur *Wash.*, *U.S.A.* 47°46N 118°42W **120** C7
Wilburton *Okla.*, *U.S.A.* 34°55N 95°19W **107** D8
Wilcox *Sask.*, *Canada* 50°6N 104°44W **150** E7
Wilcox *Nebr.*, *U.S.A.* 40°22N 99°10W **80** D6
Wilcox *Pa.*, *U.S.A.* 41°35N 78°41W **87** C4
Wilcox County ☆ *Ala.*, *U.S.A.* 31°59N 87°17W **112** E3
Wilcox County ☆ *Ga.*, *U.S.A.* 31°59N 83°25W **113** D3
Wild Horse *Colo.*, *U.S.A.* 38°50N 103°0W **125** D8
Wild Horse Hill *Nebr.*, *U.S.A.* 41°55N 101°56W **80** C4
Wild Horse Res. *Nev.*, *U.S.A.* 41°41N 115°51W **128** A5
Wild Rice → *Minn.*, *U.S.A.* 47°20N 96°50W **77** C2
Wild Rice → *N. Dak.*, *U.S.A.* 46°45N 96°47W **76** D9
Wild Rose *Wis.*, *U.S.A.* 44°11N 89°15W **78** D4
Wildcat Cr. → *Ind.*, *U.S.A.* 40°28N 86°52W **85** C4
Wildcat Hill Prov. Park △ *Sask.*,
  Canada 53°14N 102°28W **150** B9
Wilder *Idaho*, *U.S.A.* 43°41N 116°55W **122** F2
Wilder *Minn.*, *U.S.A.* 43°50N 95°12W **77** G3
Wilder *Vt.*, *U.S.A.* 43°40N 72°19W **89** C2
Wildersville *Tenn.*, *U.S.A.* 35°47N 88°22W **104** E4
Wilderville *Oreg.*, *U.S.A.* 42°23N 123°28W **121** E2
Wildgoose L. *Ont.*, *Canada* 49°44N 87°11W **149** C9
Wildhay → *Alta.*, *Canada* 53°59N 117°20W **152** D2
Wildhorse Cr. → *Okla.*, *U.S.A.* 34°32N 97°10W **107** D6
Wildorado *Tex.*, *U.S.A.* 35°13N 102°12W **108** B5

Wildrose *N. Dak.*, *U.S.A.* 48°38N 103°11W **76** B2
Wildwood *Alta.*, *Canada* 53°37N 115°14W **152** D2
Wildwood *Fla.*, *U.S.A.* 28°52N 82°2W **114** C6
Wildwood *N.J.*, *U.S.A.* 38°59N 74°50W **92** D2
Wildwood Crest *N.J.*, *U.S.A.* 38°58N 74°50W **92** D2
Wiley *Colo.*, *U.S.A.* 38°10N 102°40W **125** D8
Wiley City *Wash.*, *U.S.A.* 46°33N 120°42W **120** D5
Wilkes-Barre *Pa.*, *U.S.A.* 41°15N 75°53W **87** C7
Wilkes County ☆ *Ga.*, *U.S.A.* 33°50N 82°45W **113** C4
Wilkes County ☆ *N.C.*, *U.S.A.* 36°10N 81°10W **103** B4
Wilkesboro *N.C.*, *U.S.A.* 36°9N 81°10W **103** B4
Wilkesboro Res. = W. Kerr Scott Res. *N.C.*,
  U.S.A. 36°10N 81°20W **103** B4
Wilket Creek Park *Ont.*, *Canada* 43°43N 79°21W **161** A2
Wilkie *Sask.*, *Canada* 52°27N 108°42W **150** D3
Wilkin County ☆ *Minn.*, *U.S.A.* 46°20N 96°25W **77** D2
Wilkins Str. *Canada* 78°5N 111°55W **156** A10
Wilkinsburg *Pa.*, *U.S.A.* 40°26N 79°52W **98** B2
Wilkinson County ☆ *Ga.*, *U.S.A.* 32°45N 83°10W **113** C3
Wilkinson County ☆ *Miss.*, *U.S.A.* 31°6N 91°18W **111** E2
Will County ☆ *Ill.*, *U.S.A.* 41°25N 88°0W **84** B6
Will Rogers, Oklahoma City ✈ (OKC) *Okla.*,
  U.S.A. 35°24N 97°36W **107** C6
Will Rogers State Historical Park △ *Calif.*,
  U.S.A. 34°2N 118°30W **133** B1
Willacoochee *Ga.*, *U.S.A.* 31°20N 83°3W **113** E3
Willacy County ☆ *Tex.*, *U.S.A.* 26°29N 97°47W **108** L10
Willamette → *Oreg.*, *U.S.A.* 45°39N 122°46W **132** A1
Willamette Heights *Oreg.*, *U.S.A.* 45°32N 122°42W **132** A1
Willamette Nat. Forest *Oreg.*, *U.S.A.* 44°20N 122°10W **121** C3
Willamina *Oreg.*, *U.S.A.* 45°5N 123°29W **121** B2
Willapa B. *Wash.*, *U.S.A.* 46°40N 124°0W **120** D1
Willard *Colo.*, *U.S.A.* 40°33N 103°29W **125** B7
Willard *Mo.*, *U.S.A.* 37°18N 93°26W **83** D3
Willard *N. Mex.*, *U.S.A.* 34°36N 106°2W **131** C4
Willard *Ohio*, *U.S.A.* 41°3N 82°44W **86** B4
Willard *Utah*, *U.S.A.* 41°25N 112°2W **129** B3
Willards *Md.*, *U.S.A.* 38°24N 75°21W **93** B5
Willcox *Ariz.*, *U.S.A.* 32°15N 109°50W **130** E6
Willcox Playa *Ariz.*, *U.S.A.* 32°8N 109°51W **130** E6
Willemstad *Neth. Ant.* 12°5N 68°55W **183** D6
Willernie *Minn.*, *U.S.A.* 45°3N 92°57W **94** A4
Willey *Iowa*, *U.S.A.* 41°59N 94°49W **81** D4
William → *Sask.*, *Canada* 59°8N 109°19W **157** E11
William A. Switzer Prov. Park △ *Alta.*,
  Canada 53°30N 117°48W **152** E3
William B. Bankhead Nat. Forest *Ala.*,
  U.S.A. 34°10N 87°15W **112** B3
William 'Bill' Dannelly Res. *Ala.*, *U.S.A.* 32°6N 87°24W **112** D3
William L. *Man.*, *Canada* 53°54N 99°21W **151** B12
William P. Hobby, Houston ✈ (HOU) *Tex.*,
  U.S.A. 29°38N 95°16W **116** C3
Williams *Ariz.*, *U.S.A.* 35°15N 112°11W **130** B3
Williams *Calif.*, *U.S.A.* 39°9N 122°9W **126** D4
Williams *Minn.*, *U.S.A.* 48°45N 94°54W **77** B4
Williams → *Ark.*, *U.S.A.* 43°12N 72°27W **89** C2
Williams County ☆ *N. Dak.*, *U.S.A.* 48°20N 103°30W **76** B2
Williams County ☆ *Ohio*, *U.S.A.* 41°35N 84°37W **86** B2
Williams Fork → *Colo.*, *U.S.A.* 40°28N 107°40W **125** B3
Williams Fork Res. *Colo.*, *U.S.A.* 40°0N 106°8W **125** C4
Williams L. *Ont.*, *Canada* 51°48N 90°45W **148** A6
Williams Lake *B.C.*, *Canada* 52°10N 122°10W **155** C12
Williamsbridge *N.Y.*, *U.S.A.* 40°52N 73°51W **97** A3
Williamsburg *Fla.*, *U.S.A.* 28°24N 81°28W **115** B2
Williamsburg *Iowa*, *U.S.A.* 41°40N 92°1W **81** D6
Williamsburg *Kans.*, *U.S.A.* 38°29N 95°28W **82** C8
Williamsburg *Ky.*, *U.S.A.* 36°44N 84°10W **105** D8
Williamsburg *Mass.*, *U.S.A.* 42°23N 72°44W **91** B2
Williamsburg *Md.*, *U.S.A.* 38°40N 75°50W **93** B5
Williamsburg *New York*, *U.S.A.* **96** f3
Williamsburg *Ohio*, *U.S.A.* 39°3N 84°4W **86** D2
Williamsburg *Pa.*, *U.S.A.* 40°28N 78°12W **87** D4
Williamsburg *Va.*, *U.S.A.* 37°16N 76°43W **102** D8
Williamsburg County ☆ *S.C.*, *U.S.A.* 33°40N 79°40W **103** E6
Williamsfield *Ill.*, *U.S.A.* 40°55N 90°1W **84** C3
Williamson *Ga.*, *U.S.A.* 33°11N 84°22W **113** C2
Williamson *Iowa*, *U.S.A.* 41°5N 93°15W **81** D5
Williamson *N.Y.*, *U.S.A.* 43°14N 77°11W **88** B3
Williamson *W. Va.*, *U.S.A.* 37°41N 82°17W **102** D2
Williamson → *Oreg.*, *U.S.A.* 42°28N 121°57W **121** E4
Williamson County ☆ *Ill.*, *U.S.A.* 37°40N 88°55W **84** F5
Williamson County ☆ *Tenn.*, *U.S.A.* 35°55N 86°52W **104** E6
Williamson County ☆ *Tex.*, *U.S.A.* 30°38N 97°41W **109** G10
Williamsport *Ind.*, *U.S.A.* 40°17N 87°17W **85** C3
Williamsport *Md.*, *U.S.A.* 39°37N 77°50W **93** A3
Williamsport *Ohio*, *U.S.A.* 39°35N 83°7W **86** D3
Williamsport *Pa.*, *U.S.A.* 41°15N 77°1W **87** C5
Williamston *Mich.*, *U.S.A.* 42°41N 84°17W **79** G7
Williamston *N.C.*, *U.S.A.* 35°51N 77°4W **103** C8
Williamston *S.C.*, *U.S.A.* 34°37N 82°29W **103** D3
Williamstown *Ky.*, *U.S.A.* 38°38N 84°34W **105** D8
Williamstown *Mass.*, *U.S.A.* 42°43N 73°12W **91** B1
Williamstown *N.J.*, *U.S.A.* 39°40N 74°59W **92** C2
Williamstown *N.Y.*, *U.S.A.* 43°26N 75°53W **88** B5
Williamstown *W. Va.*, *U.S.A.* 39°24N 81°27W **102** B3
Williamsville *Del.*, *U.S.A.* 38°27N 75°8W **93** B5
Williamsville *Ill.*, *U.S.A.* 39°57N 89°33W **84** D4
Williamsville *Mo.*, *U.S.A.* 36°58N 90°33W **83** E6
Williford *Ark.*, *U.S.A.* 36°15N 91°21W **106** B4
Willimantic *Conn.*, *U.S.A.* 41°43N 72°13W **91** C2
Willimantic → *Conn.*, *U.S.A.* 41°43N 72°12W **91** C2
Willingboro *N.J.*, *U.S.A.* 40°3N 74°54W **92** B2
Willingdon *Alta.*, *Canada* 53°50N 112°8W **152** E8
Willis *Kans.*, *U.S.A.* 39°43N 95°31W **82** B8
Willis *Tex.*, *U.S.A.* 30°25N 95°29W **109** G12
Willis, L. *Tex.*, *U.S.A.* 28°23N 81°28W **115** B3
Williston *Fla.*, *U.S.A.* 29°23N 82°27W **114** B6
Williston *Md.*, *U.S.A.* 38°48N 75°52W **93** B5
Williston *N. Dak.*, *U.S.A.* 48°9N 103°37W **76** B2
Williston *S.C.*, *U.S.A.* 33°24N 81°25W **103** E4
Williston *Tenn.*, *U.S.A.* 35°9N 89°22W **104** E3
Williston *Vt.*, *U.S.A.* 44°25N 73°10W **89** B1
Williston L. *B.C.*, *Canada* 56°0N 124°0W **157** E8
Williston Park *N.Y.*, *U.S.A.* 40°45N 73°38W **97** B5
Willisville *Ill.*, *U.S.A.* 37°59N 89°35W **84** F4
Willits *Calif.*, *U.S.A.* 39°25N 123°21W **126** D3
Willmar *Minn.*, *U.S.A.* 45°7N 95°3W **77** E3
Willmore Park *Mo.*, *U.S.A.* 38°34N 90°17W **94** B2
Willmore Wilderness Prov. Park △ *Alta.*,
  Canada 53°45N 119°30W **152** E1
Willoughby *Ohio*, *U.S.A.* 41°39N 81°24W **86** B5
Willoughby *Vt.*, *U.S.A.* 44°45N 72°34W **89** B2
Willow *Alaska*, *U.S.A.* 61°45N 150°3W **135** F10
Willow *Ark.*, *U.S.A.* 34°8N 92°45W **106** D3
Willow *Okla.*, *U.S.A.* 35°3N 99°31W **107** C4

Willow Bunch Sask., Canada 49°20N 105°35W 150 F6
Willow Bunch L. Sask., Canada 49°27N 105°27W 150 F6
Willow City N. Dak., U.S.A. 48°36N 100°18W 76 B5
Willow Cr. → Oreg., U.S.A. 45°48N 120°1W 121 B5
Willow Cr. → Oreg., U.S.A. 44°0N 117°13W 121 C8
Willow Cr. → Utah, U.S.A. 40°2N 109°45W 129 C6
Willow Creek Calif., U.S.A. 40°56N 123°38W 126 C3
Willow Creek Res. Nev., U.S.A. 41°14N 116°32W 128 A4
Willow Grove Del., U.S.A. 39°8N 75°39W 93 A5
Willow Grove Pa., U.S.A. 40°9N 75°7W 92 B1
Willow L. Alta., Canada 56°27N 111°8W 152 B9
Willow L. N.W.T., Canada 62°10N 119°8W 157 D9
Willow L. Wyo., U.S.A. 43°0N 109°52W 124 C3
Willow Lake S. Dak., U.S.A. 44°38N 97°38W 76 F8
Willow Ranch Calif., U.S.A. 41°54N 120°21W 126 B6
Willow Res. Wis., U.S.A. 45°43N 89°51W 78 C4
Willow River Minn., U.S.A. 46°19N 92°51W 77 D6
Willow Springs Ill., U.S.A. 41°44N 87°51W 95 C1
Willow Springs Mo., U.S.A. 37°0N 91°58W 83 E5
Willowbrook Sask., Canada 51°12N 102°48W 150 D9
Willowbrook Kans., U.S.A. 38°8N 97°57W 82 C6
Willowbrook N.Y., U.S.A. 40°36N 74°8W 97 C2
Willowdale Ont., Canada 43°46N 79°25W 161 A2
Willowdale Oreg., U.S.A. 44°48N 120°57W 121 C5
Willowick Ohio, U.S.A. 41°38N 81°28W 86 B5
Willowlake → N.W.T., Canada 62°42N 123°8W 157 D8
Willows Calif., U.S.A. 39°31N 122°12W 126 D4
Wills Cr. → Ohio, U.S.A. 40°9N 81°54W 86 C5
Wills Point Tex., U.S.A. 32°43N 96°1W 109 E11
Willsboro N.Y., U.S.A. 44°21N 73°24W 89 B1
Willshire Ohio, U.S.A. 40°45N 84°48W 86 C2
Wilma Fla., U.S.A. 30°9N 84°58W 114 A4
Wilmar Ark., U.S.A. 33°38N 91°56W 106 E4
Wilmer Ala., U.S.A. 30°49N 88°22W 112 F2
Wilmer Tex., U.S.A. 32°35N 96°41W 116 C5
Wilmette Ill., U.S.A. 42°4N 87°42W 95 A2
Wilmington Del., U.S.A. 39°45N 75°33W 93 A5
Wilmington Ill., U.S.A. 41°18N 88°9W 84 B5
Wilmington Mass., U.S.A. 42°33N 71°10W 91 B3
Wilmington N.C., U.S.A. 34°14N 77°55W 103 D8
Wilmington Ohio, U.S.A. 39°27N 83°50W 86 D3
Wilmington Vt., U.S.A. 42°52N 72°52W 89 D2
Wilmont Minn., U.S.A. 43°46N 95°50W 77 G3
Wilmore Kans., U.S.A. 37°20N 99°13W 82 D4
Wilmore Ky., U.S.A. 37°52N 84°40W 105 C8
Wilmot Ark., U.S.A. 33°4N 91°34W 106 E4
Wilmot Kans., U.S.A. 37°22N 96°53W 82 D7
Wilmot P.E.I., Canada 46°2N 62°30W 141 G7
Wilmot S. Dak., U.S.A. 45°25N 96°52W 76 E9
Wilsall Mont., U.S.A. 45°59N 110°38W 123 E7
Wilson Ark., U.S.A. 35°34N 90°3W 106 C5
Wilson Kans., U.S.A. 38°50N 98°29W 82 C5
Wilson La., U.S.A. 30°55N 91°7W 110 D4
Wilson N.C., U.S.A. 35°44N 77°55W 103 D8
Wilson N.Y., U.S.A. 43°19N 78°50W 88 B2
Wilson Okla., U.S.A. 34°10N 97°26W 107 D6
Wilson Tex., U.S.A. 33°19N 101°44W 108 D6
Wilson → Oreg., U.S.A. 45°29N 123°53W 121 B2
Wilson, C. Nunavut, Canada 66°59N 81°27W 159 D9
Wilson, Mt. Colo., U.S.A. 37°50N 107°59W 125 E3
Wilson County ☆ Kans., U.S.A. 37°30N 95°45W 82 D8
Wilson County ☆ N.C., U.S.A. 35°45N 78°0W 103 C7
Wilson County ☆ Tenn., U.S.A. 36°12N 86°18W 104 D6
Wilson County ☆ Tex., U.S.A. 29°8N 98°10W 109 H9
Wilson Creek B.C., Canada 49°27N 123°43W 154 F11
Wilson Creek Wash., U.S.A. 47°25N 119°7W 120 C6
Wilson Creek Ra. Nev., U.S.A. 38°12N 114°18W 128 D6
Wilson L. Ala., U.S.A. 34°48N 87°38W 112 B3
Wilson Lake Kans., U.S.A. 38°58N 98°30W 82 C5
Wilson Landing B.C., Canada 50°0N 119°30W 155 F15
Wilsons Beach N.B., Canada 44°56N 66°56W 141 J3
Wilsons Creek Nat. Battlefield △ Mo., U.S.A. 37°6N 93°25W 83 D3
Wilsons Mills Maine, U.S.A. 44°57N 71°2W 90 D2
Wilsonville Ala., U.S.A. 33°14N 86°29W 112 C4
Wilsonville Nebr., U.S.A. 40°7N 100°7W 80 D5
Wilsonville Oreg., U.S.A. 45°18N 122°46W 121 B3
Wilton Ark., U.S.A. 33°45N 94°9W 106 E1
Wilton Conn., U.S.A. 41°12N 73°26W 91 C1
Wilton Iowa, U.S.A. 41°35N 91°1W 81 D7
Wilton Maine, U.S.A. 44°36N 70°14W 90 D3
Wilton Minn., U.S.A. 47°30N 95°0W 77 C3
Wilton N. Dak., U.S.A. 47°10N 100°47W 76 C5
Wilton N.H., U.S.A. 42°51N 71°44W 89 D3
Wilton Wis., U.S.A. 43°49N 90°32W 78 E3
Wilton Manors Fla., U.S.A. 26°9N 80°8W 115 B3
Wimbledon N. Dak., U.S.A. 47°10N 98°28W 76 C7
Winagami L. Alta., Canada 55°37N 116°44W 152 C4
Winamac Ind., U.S.A. 41°3N 86°36W 85 B4
Winchendon Mass., U.S.A. 42°41N 72°3W 91 B2
Winchester Ont., Canada 45°6N 75°21W 147 B11
Winchester Ark., U.S.A. 33°47N 91°29W 106 E4
Winchester Idaho, U.S.A. 46°14N 116°38W 122 C2
Winchester Ill., U.S.A. 39°38N 90°27W 84 D3
Winchester Ind., U.S.A. 40°10N 84°59W 85 C6
Winchester Ky., U.S.A. 37°59N 84°11W 105 C8
Winchester Mass., U.S.A. 42°26N 71°8W 94 A2
Winchester N.H., U.S.A. 42°46N 72°23W 89 D2
Winchester Nev., U.S.A. 36°7N 115°7W 134 C2
Winchester Ohio, U.S.A. 38°56N 83°39W 86 E3
Winchester Tenn., U.S.A. 35°11N 86°7W 104 E6
Winchester Va., U.S.A. 39°11N 78°10W 93 A8
Winchester Wyo., U.S.A. 43°52N 108°10W 124 C4
Winchester Bay Oreg., U.S.A. 43°41N 124°10W 121 D1
Wind → Yukon, Canada 65°50N 135°18W 156 C5
Wind → Wyo., U.S.A. 43°12N 108°12W 124 C4
Wind Cave Nat. Park △ S. Dak., U.S.A. 43°33N 103°17W 76 G2
Wind Gap Pa., U.S.A. 40°51N 75°18W 92 B1
Wind Mt. N. Mex., U.S.A. 32°2N 105°31W 131 E5
Wind Point Wis., U.S.A. 42°47N 87°46W 78 F6
Wind River Indian Reservation Wyo., U.S.A. 43°20N 109°0W 124 C4
Wind River Pk. Wyo., U.S.A. 42°42N 109°7W 124 C4
Wind River Range Wyo., U.S.A. 43°0N 109°30W 124 C3
Windber Pa., U.S.A. 40°14N 78°50W 87 D4
Windcrest Tex., U.S.A. 29°31N 98°19W 116 B3
Windemere L. Ont., Canada 47°58N 83°47W 149 E13
Winder Ga., U.S.A. 34°0N 83°45W 113 B3
Windermere B.C., Canada 50°28N 115°59W 153 H5
Windermere Fla., U.S.A. 28°29N 81°32W 115 E1
Windfall Ind., U.S.A. 40°22N 85°57W 85 C5
Windham N.H., U.S.A. 42°48N 71°18W 89 D3
Windham County ☆ Conn., U.S.A. 41°45N 72°0W 91 C2

Windham County ☆ Vt., U.S.A. 43°0N 72°45W 89 D1
Windigo Mich., U.S.A. 47°55N 89°9W 79 B2
Windigo → Qué., Canada 47°46N 73°19W 145 D9
Winding Stair Mountain Nat. Recr. Area △ Okla., U.S.A. 34°45N 94°47W 107 D9
Windom Kans., U.S.A. 38°23N 97°55W 82 C6
Windom Minn., U.S.A. 43°52N 95°7W 77 G3
Windom Pk. Colo., U.S.A. 37°35N 107°35W 125 E3
Window Rock Ariz., U.S.A. 35°41N 109°3W 130 B6
Windsor N.S., Canada 44°59N 64°5W 141 J5
Windsor Ont., Canada 42°18N 83°0W 98 B2
Windsor Qué., Canada 45°34N 72°0W 145 F11
Windsor Calif., U.S.A. 38°33N 122°49W 126 E4
Windsor Colo., U.S.A. 40°29N 104°54W 125 B6
Windsor Conn., U.S.A. 41°50N 72°39W 91 C2
Windsor Ill., U.S.A. 39°26N 86°36W 84 D5
Windsor Mo., U.S.A. 38°32N 93°31W 83 C3
Windsor N.C., U.S.A. 36°0N 76°57W 103 C9
Windsor Va., U.S.A. 36°49N 76°45W 102 E8
Windsor Vt., U.S.A. 43°29N 72°24W 89 C2
Windsor, Gare Montréal, Canada 160 c2
Windsor County ☆ Vt., U.S.A. 43°35N 72°35W 89 C2
Windsor Forest Ga., U.S.A. 31°59N 81°5W 113 E5
Windsor Heights Nfld. & L., Canada 47°36N 52°49W 142 E8
Windsor Hills Calif., U.S.A. 33°59N 118°22W 133 C2
Windsor L. Nfld. & L., Canada 47°36N 52°48W 142 E8
Windsor Locks Conn., U.S.A. 41°56N 72°38W 91 C2
Windthorst Sask., Canada 50°6N 102°50W 150 E9
Windthorst Tex., U.S.A. 33°34N 98°26W 109 D9
Windward Is. W. Indies 13°0N 61°0W 183 D7
Windward Passage = Vientos, Paso de los Caribbean 20°0N 74°0W 183 C5
Windy L. Sask., Canada 54°22N 102°55W 150 A9
Windy Pk. Wash., U.S.A. 48°56N 119°58W 120 B6
Winefred L. Alta., Canada 55°30N 110°30W 152 C10
Winema Nat. Forest Oreg., U.S.A. 43°10N 121°50W 121 D4
Winfield Alta., Canada 52°58N 114°26W 153 F6
Winfield B.C., Canada 50°2N 119°24W 155 E15
Winfield Iowa, U.S.A. 41°7N 91°26W 81 D7
Winfield Kans., U.S.A. 37°15N 96°59W 82 D7
Winfield Ala., U.S.A. 33°56N 87°49W 112 C3
Winfield Md., U.S.A. 39°26N 77°4W 93 A3
Winfield Mo., U.S.A. 39°0N 90°44W 83 C6
Winfield N.J., U.S.A. 40°38N 74°17W 97 C1
Winfield Tenn., U.S.A. 36°33N 84°27W 105 D8
Winfield W. Va., U.S.A. 38°32N 81°54W 102 C3
Wing N. Dak., U.S.A. 47°9N 100°17W 76 C5
Wingate Ind., U.S.A. 40°10N 87°4W 85 C3
Wingate N.C., U.S.A. 34°59N 80°26W 103 D5
Wingdale N.Y., U.S.A. 41°39N 73°34W 91 C1
Winger Minn., U.S.A. 47°32N 95°59W 77 C3
Wingham Ont., Canada 43°55N 81°20W 146 D5
Wingo Ky., U.S.A. 36°39N 88°44W 104 D4
Winifred Mont., U.S.A. 47°34N 109°23W 123 C8
Winigan Mo., U.S.A. 40°3N 92°54W 83 A4
Winisk → Ont., Canada 55°17N 85°5W 159 F8
Wink Tex., U.S.A. 31°45N 103°9W 108 F4
Winkelman Ariz., U.S.A. 32°59N 110°46W 130 D3
Winkler Man., Canada 49°10N 97°56W 151 F14
Winkler County ☆ Tex., U.S.A. 31°52N 103°6W 108 F4
Winlock Wash., U.S.A. 46°30N 122°56W 120 D3
Winn Parish ☆ La., U.S.A. 31°56N 92°38W 110 C3
Winnebago Ill., U.S.A. 42°16N 89°15W 84 A4
Winnebago Minn., U.S.A. 43°46N 94°10W 77 G4
Winnebago Nebr., U.S.A. 42°14N 96°28W 80 B9
Winnebago, L. Wis., U.S.A. 44°0N 88°26W 78 E5
Winnebago County ☆ Ill., U.S.A. 42°20N 89°1CW 84 A4
Winnebago County ☆ Iowa, U.S.A. 43°20N 93°40W 81 B5
Winnebago County ☆ Wis., U.S.A. 44°0N 88°45W 78 D5
Winnebago Indian Reservation Nebr., U.S.A. 42°15N 96°40W 80 B9
Winneconne Wis., U.S.A. 44°7N 88°43W 78 D5
Winnemucca Nev., U.S.A. 40°58N 117°44W 128 B3
Winnemucca L. Nev., U.S.A. 40°7N 119°21W 128 B1
Winner S. Dak., U.S.A. 43°22N 99°52W 76 G6
Winneshiek County ☆ Iowa, U.S.A. 43°15N 91°50W 81 B7
Winnetka Ill., U.S.A. 42°6N 87°44W 95 A2
Winnetoon Nebr., U.S.A. 42°31N 97°58W 80 B8
Winnett Mont., U.S.A. 47°0N 108°21W 123 D9
Winnfield La., U.S.A. 31°56N 92°38W 110 C3
Winnibigoshish, L. Minn., U.S.A. 47°27N 94°13W 77 C4
Winnie Tex., U.S.A. 29°49N 94°23W 109 H13
Winnipeg Man., Canada 49°54N 97°9W 151 F14
Winnipeg → Man., Canada 50°38N 96°19W 151 E15
Winnipeg, L. Man., Canada 52°0N 97°0W 151 C14
Winnipeg Beach Man., Canada 50°30N 96°58W 151 E15
Winnipeg Int. ✈ (YWG) Man., Canada 49°55N 97°15W 151 F14
Winnipegosis Man., Canada 51°39N 99°55W 151 D12
Winnipegosis L. Man., Canada 52°30N 100°0W 151 C12
Winnipesaukee N.H., U.S.A. 43°40N 71°20W 89 C3
Winnipesaukee, L. N.H., U.S.A. 43°38N 71°21W 89 C3
Winnisquam L. N.H., U.S.A. 43°33N 71°31W 89 C3
Winnsboro La., U.S.A. 32°10N 91°43W 110 B4
Winnsboro S.C., U.S.A. 34°23N 81°5W 103 D4
Winnsboro Tex., U.S.A. 32°58N 95°17W 109 E12
Winokapau L. Nfld. & L., Canada 53°15N 62°50W 143 C5
Winona Kans., U.S.A. 39°4N 101°15W 82 B2
Winona Minn., U.S.A. 44°3N 91°39W 77 F7
Winona Miss., U.S.A. 33°29N 89°44W 111 C4
Winona Mo., U.S.A. 37°1N 91°20W 83 D5
Winona Wash., U.S.A. 46°57N 117°48W 120 D8
Winona County ☆ Minn., U.S.A. 44°0N 91°50W 77 G7
Winona Lake Ind., U.S.A. 41°14N 85°49W 85 B5
Winooski Vt., U.S.A. 44°29N 73°11W 89 B1
Winooski → Vt., U.S.A. 44°32N 73°17W 89 B1
Winside Nebr., U.S.A. 42°11N 97°10W 80 B8
Winslow = Bainbridge Island Wash., U.S.A. 47°38N 122°32W 132 C2
Winslow Ariz., U.S.A. 35°2N 110°42W 130 B5
Winslow Ark., U.S.A. 35°48N 94°8W 106 C1
Winslow Ind., U.S.A. 38°23N 87°13W 85 E3
Winslow Maine, U.S.A. 44°33N 69°37W 90 D4
Winslow Nebr., U.S.A. 41°37N 96°30W 80 C9
Winsted Conn., U.S.A. 41°55N 73°4W 91 C1
Winsted Minn., U.S.A. 44°58N 94°3W 77 F4
Winston N. Mex., U.S.A. 33°20N 107°39W 131 D3
Winston Oreg., U.S.A. 43°7N 123°25W 121 D2
Winston County ☆ Ala., U.S.A. 34°9N 87°24W 112 B3
Winston County ☆ Miss., U.S.A. 33°7N 89°3W 111 C4
Winston-Salem N.C., U.S.A. 36°6N 80°15W 103 B5
Winter Wis., U.S.A. 45°49N 91°1W 78 C2
Winter Garden Fla., U.S.A. 28°34N 81°35W 114 D2
Winter Harbor Maine, U.S.A. 44°24N 68°5W 90 D5
Winter Harbour B.C., Canada 50°31N 128°2W 154 E6
Winter Haven Fla., U.S.A. 28°1N 81°44W 114 C7

Winter I. Nunavut, Canada 66°16N 83°4W 159 D9
Winter Park Colo., U.S.A. 39°53N 105°46W 125 C5
Winter Park Fla., U.S.A. 28°36N 81°20W 114 C7
Winterhaven Calif., U.S.A. 32°44N 114°38W 127 L12
Wintering L. Ont., Canada 49°26N 87°16W 149 C9
Winters Calif., U.S.A. 38°32N 121°58W 126 E5
Winters Tex., U.S.A. 31°58N 99°58W 109 F8
Winterset Iowa, U.S.A. 41°20N 94°1W 81 D4
Wintersville Ohio, U.S.A. 40°23N 80°42W 86 C6
Winterton Nfld. & L., Canada 47°58N 53°20W 142 E7
Winterville Maine, U.S.A. 46°58N 68°34W 90 B5
Winterville N.C., U.S.A. 35°32N 77°24W 103 C8
Winthrop Ark., U.S.A. 33°50N 94°21W 106 E1
Winthrop Iowa, U.S.A. 42°28N 91°44W 81 C7
Winthrop Maine, U.S.A. 44°18N 69°58W 90 D4
Winthrop Minn., U.S.A. 44°32N 94°22W 77 F4
Winthrop Wash., U.S.A. 48°28N 120°10W 120 B5
Winthrop Harbor Ill., U.S.A. 42°29N 87°50W 84 A6
Winton Calif., U.S.A. 37°23N 120°37W 126 F6
Winton Minn., U.S.A. 47°56N 91°48W 77 C7
Winton N.C., U.S.A. 36°24N 76°56W 103 B9
Wiota Iowa, U.S.A. 41°24N 94°54W 81 D4
Wiota Wis., U.S.A. 42°39N 89°57W 78 F4
Wirt County ☆ W. Va., U.S.A. 39°4N 81°24W 102 B3
Wiscasset Maine, U.S.A. 44°0N 69°40W 90 E4
Wisconsin □ U.S.A. 44°45N 89°30W 78 D4
Wisconsin → Wis., U.S.A. 43°0N 91°15W 78 E21
Wisconsin, L. Wis., U.S.A. 43°19N 89°44W 78 E4
Wisconsin Dells Wis., U.S.A. 43°38N 89°46W 78 E4
Wisconsin Rapids Wis., U.S.A. 44°23N 89°49W 78 D4
Wisdom Mont., U.S.A. 45°37N 113°27W 123 E4
Wise Va., U.S.A. 36°59N 82°35W 102 E2
Wise County ☆ Tex., U.S.A. 33°14N 97°35W 109 D10
Wise County ☆ Va., U.S.A. 37°0N 82°45W 102 E2
Wise River Mont., U.S.A. 45°48N 112°57W 123 E5
Wiseman Alaska, U.S.A. 67°25N 150°6W 135 C10
Wiseton Sask., Canada 51°19N 107°39W 150 D4
Wishek N. Dak., U.S.A. 46°16N 99°33W 76 D6
Wishon Res. Calif., U.S.A. 36°50N 118°50W 127 G8
Wishram Wash., U.S.A. 45°40N 120°58W 120 E5
Wisner La., U.S.A. 31°59N 91°39W 110 C4
Wisner Nebr., U.S.A. 41°59N 96°55W 80 C9
Wissota L. Wis., U.S.A. 44°56N 91°20W 78 D2
Wister Okla., U.S.A. 34°58N 94°43W 107 D9
Withee Wis., U.S.A. 45°17N 88°1W 79 D3
Witherbee N.Y., U.S.A. 44°5N 73°32W 89 B1
Withington Mt. N. Mex., U.S.A. 33°53N 107°29W 131 D3
Withlacoochee → Fla., U.S.A. 29°0N 82°45W 114 C6
Withlacoochee → Fla., U.S.A. 30°24N 83°10W 114 A5
Withrow Wash., U.S.A. 47°42N 119°48W 120 C6
Witless Bay Nfld. & L., Canada 47°17N 52°50W 142 E8
Witt Ill., U.S.A. 39°15N 89°21W 84 D4
Witten S. Dak., U.S.A. 43°26N 100°5W 76 G5
Wittenberg Mo., U.S.A. 37°39N 89°31W 83 D7
Wittenberg Wis., U.S.A. 44°49N 89°10W 78 D4
Wittman Md., U.S.A. 38°48N 76°18W 93 B4
Wittmann Ariz., U.S.A. 33°47N 112°32W 130 D3
Wixom Mich., U.S.A. 42°32N 83°32W 79 G8
Wixom L. Mich., U.S.A. 43°50N 84°20W 79 F7
Woburn Ont., Canada 43°46N 79°12W 161 A3
Woburn Mass., U.S.A. 42°29N 71°9W 96 A2
Wolbach Nebr., U.S.A. 41°24N 98°24W 80 C7
Wolcott Colo., U.S.A. 39°42N 106°40W 125 C4
Wolcott Conn., U.S.A. 41°36N 72°59W 91 C2
Wolcott Ind., U.S.A. 40°46N 87°3W 85 C3
Wolcott N.Y., U.S.A. 43°13N 76°49W 88 B4
Wolcottville Ind., U.S.A. 41°32N 85°22W 85 B5
Wold Cr. → S. Dak., U.S.A. 44°42N 98°40W 76 F7
Wolf → Miss., U.S.A. 30°22N 89°18W 111 F4
Wolf → Tenn., U.S.A. 35°10N 89°54W 104 E3
Wolf → Wis., U.S.A. 44°5N 88°41W 78 D5
Wolf Bay Qué., Canada 50°16N 60°8W 140 C9
Wolf Cr. → Mont., U.S.A. 47°37N 109°38W 123 C8
Wolf Creek Mont., U.S.A. 47°0N 112°4W 123 C5
Wolf Creek Oreg., U.S.A. 42°42N 123°24W 121 E2
Wolf Creek Pass Colo., U.S.A. 37°29N 106°48W 125 E4
Wolf L. Alta., Canada 54°42N 110°57W 152 D10
Wolf Lake Mich., U.S.A. 43°15N 86°7W 79 F5
Wolf Lake Minn., U.S.A. 46°48N 95°21W 77 D3
Wolf Mts. Mont., U.S.A. 45°12N 107°8W 123 E10
Wolf Point Mont., U.S.A. 48°5N 105°39W 123 B12
Wolf Trap Farm Park Va., U.S.A. 38°56N 77°17W 99 B2
Wolfdale Pa., U.S.A. 40°12N 80°17W 87 D2
Wolfe City Tex., U.S.A. 33°22N 96°4W 109 D11
Wolfe County ☆ Ky., U.S.A. 37°45N 83°30W 105 C9
Wolfe I. Ont., Canada 44°7N 76°20W 147 C10
Wolfeboro N.H., U.S.A. 43°35N 71°13W 89 C3
Wolfforth Tex., U.S.A. 33°30N 102°1W 108 D5
Wolford N. Dak., U.S.A. 48°30N 99°42W 76 B6
Wolfsville Md., U.S.A. 39°37N 77°35W 93 A3
Wolfville N.S., Canada 45°5N 64°22W 141 H5
Wollaston Mass., U.S.A. 42°15N 71°2W 96 B2
Wollaston, C. N.W.T., Canada 71°7N 118°4W 156 B7
Wollaston Forland Greenland 74°25N 19°40W 162 C9
Wollaston L. Sask., Canada 58°7N 103°10W 157 E12
Wollaston Lake Sask., Canada 58°3N 103°33W 157 E12
Wollaston Pen. Canada 69°30N 115°0W 156 C10
Wolseley Sask., Canada 50°25N 103°15W 150 E8
Wolsey S. Dak., U.S.A. 44°25N 98°28W 76 F7
Wolstenholme, C. Qué., Canada 62°35N 77°30W 143 A2
Wolverine Mich., U.S.A. 45°17N 84°36W 79 D7
Wolverine Minn., U.S.A. 46°34N 96°44W 77 D2
Wolverine Peak Wyo., U.S.A. 42°59N 109°22W 124 D3
Wonalancet N.H., U.S.A. 43°44N 71°21W 89 C3
Wood S. Dak., U.S.A. 43°30N 100°29W 76 G5
Wood → Sask., Canada 50°8N 106°13W 150 E5
Wood → Nebr., U.S.A. 41°2N 98°5W 80 C7
Wood Buffalo Nat. Park △ Alta., Canada 59°0N 113°41W 157 E10
Wood County ☆ Ohio, U.S.A. 41°23N 83°39W 86 B3
Wood County ☆ Tex., U.S.A. 32°48N 95°27W 109 E12
Wood County ☆ W. Va., U.S.A. 39°14N 81°34W 102 B3
Wood County ☆ Wis., U.S.A. 44°20N 90°0W 78 D4
Wood Lake Minn., U.S.A. 44°39N 95°32W 77 F3
Wood Lake Nebr., U.S.A. 42°38N 100°14W 80 B5
Wood Ridge N.J., U.S.A. 40°50N 74°4W 97 A2
Wood River Ill., U.S.A. 38°52N 90°5W 84 E3
Wood River Nebr., U.S.A. 40°49N 98°36W 80 C7
Woodall Mt. Miss., U.S.A. 34°47N 88°15W 111 B5
Woodberry Ark., U.S.A. 33°35N 92°31W 106 E3
Woodbine Ga., U.S.A. 30°58N 81°44W 113 F5

Woodbine Iowa, U.S.A. 41°44N 95°43W 81 D3
Woodbine Kans., U.S.A. 38°48N 96°57W 82 C7
Woodbine Ky., U.S.A. 36°54N 84°5W 105 D8
Woodbine Md., U.S.A. 39°22N 77°4W 93 A3
Woodbine N.J., U.S.A. 39°15N 74°49W 92 C2
Woodbine Race Track Ont., Canada 43°43N 79°36W 161 A1
Woodbourne N.Y., U.S.A. 41°46N 74°36W 88 D6
Woodbridge Ont., Canada 43°47N 79°36W 161 A1
Woodbridge Conn., U.S.A. 41°21N 73°2W 91 C1
Woodbridge N.J., U.S.A. 40°33N 74°17W 97 C1
Woodbridge Va., U.S.A. 38°40N 77°15W 93 B3
Woodburn Ind., U.S.A. 41°8N 84°51W 85 B6
Woodburn Iowa, U.S.A. 41°1N 93°36W 81 D5
Woodburn Ky., U.S.A. 36°50N 86°32W 104 D6
Woodburn Oreg., U.S.A. 45°9N 122°51W 121 B3
Woodbury Conn., U.S.A. 41°33N 73°13W 91 C1
Woodbury Ga., U.S.A. 32°59N 84°35W 113 D2
Woodbury Ky., U.S.A. 37°11N 86°38W 104 C6
Woodbury Minn., U.S.A. 44°55N 92°57W 94 B4
Woodbury N.J., U.S.A. 39°50N 75°9W 92 C1
Woodbury Tenn., U.S.A. 35°50N 86°4W 104 E6
Woodbury County ☆ Iowa, U.S.A. 42°25N 96°0W 81 C2
Wooden Shoe Mich., U.S.A. 43°59N 84°21W 79 F7
Woodfibre B.C., Canada 49°41N 123°15W 155 F11
Woodfin N.C., U.S.A. 35°38N 82°36W 103 C3
Woodford Vt., U.S.A. 42°52N 73°6W 89 D1
Woodford County ☆ Ill., U.S.A. 40°50N 89°10W 84 C4
Woodford County ☆ Ky., U.S.A. 38°0N 84°45W 105 B8
Woodfords Calif., U.S.A. 38°47N 119°50W 126 E7
Woodhaven N.Y., U.S.A. 40°41N 73°51W 97 B3
Woodhull Ill., U.S.A. 41°11N 90°20W 84 B3
Woodinville Wash., U.S.A. 47°45N 122°9W 132 B3
Woodlake Calif., U.S.A. 36°25N 119°6W 127 G7
Woodland Calif., U.S.A. 38°41N 121°46W 126 E5
Woodland Ill., U.S.A. 40°43N 87°44W 84 C6
Woodland Maine, U.S.A. 45°9N 67°25W 90 C6
Woodland Miss., U.S.A. 33°47N 89°3W 111 C4
Woodland Tex., U.S.A. 33°48N 95°17W 109 D12
Woodland Wash., U.S.A. 45°54N 122°45W 120 E3
Woodland Beach Del., U.S.A. 39°20N 75°28W 93 A5
Woodland Caribou Prov. Park △ Ont., Canada 51°0N 94°45W 148 A2
Woodland Park Colo., U.S.A. 38°57N 105°12W 125 D5
Woodlands Man., Canada 50°12N 97°40W 151 E14
Woodlands, The Tex., U.S.A. 30°9N 95°29W 109 G12
Woodlawn Md., U.S.A. 39°19N 76°43W 99 B1
Woodlynne N.J., U.S.A. 39°54N 75°5W 92 B1
Woodman Wis., U.S.A. 43°7N 90°48W 78 E3
Woodmere N.Y., U.S.A. 40°37N 73°42W 97 C4
Woodmont Md., U.S.A. 38°59N 77°5W 99 B3
Woodmoor Baltimore, U.S.A. 39°20N 76°44W 99 B1
Woodpecker B.C., Canada 53°30N 122°40W 155 B12
Woodridge Man., Canada 49°20N 96°9W 151 F15
Woodridge N.Y., U.S.A. 41°43N 74°34W 88 D6
Woodrow N.Y., U.S.A. 40°32N 74°11W 97 C1
Woodrow Tex., U.S.A. 33°27N 101°50W 108 D6
Woodruff Kans., U.S.A. 39°59N 99°19W 82 B4
Woodruff S.C., U.S.A. 34°45N 82°2W 103 D3
Woodruff Utah, U.S.A. 41°31N 111°10W 129 B4
Woodruff Wis., U.S.A. 45°54N 89°42W 78 C4
Woodruff, L. Fla., U.S.A. 29°6N 81°24W 114 B7
Woodruff County ☆ Ark., U.S.A. 35°9N 91°21W 106 C4
Woodruff Narrows Res. Wyo., U.S.A. 41°31N 111°1W 124 E1
Woods, L. Nfld. & L., Canada 54°30N 65°13W 143 C4
Woods, L. of the Canada 49°15N 94°45W 148 C2
Woods, L. of the Minn., U.S.A. 49°0N 95°0W 77 A4
Woods County ☆ Okla., U.S.A. 36°45N 98°50W 107 B5
Woods Cross Utah, U.S.A. 40°52N 111°53W 134 A2
Woods Hole Mass., U.S.A. 41°31N 70°40W 91 C4
Woods Landing Wyo., U.S.A. 41°7N 106°1W 124 E6
Woods Res. Tenn., U.S.A. 35°18N 86°5W 105 E7
Woodsboro Md., U.S.A. 39°32N 77°19W 93 A3
Woodsboro Tex., U.S.A. 28°14N 97°20W 109 J10
Woodsfield Ohio, U.S.A. 39°46N 81°7W 86 D5
Woodside N.Y., U.S.A. 40°44N 73°54W 97 B3
Woodson Ark., U.S.A. 34°32N 92°13W 106 D3
Woodson Tex., U.S.A. 33°1N 99°3W 109 D8
Woodson County ☆ Kans., U.S.A. 37°50N 95°45W 82 D8
Woodson Terrace Mo., U.S.A. 38°43N 90°21W 94 A1
Woodstock N.B., Canada 46°11N 67°37W 141 G2
Woodstock Ont., Canada 43°10N 80°45W 146 D6
Woodstock Conn., U.S.A. 41°56N 72°55W 91 C2
Woodstock Ga., U.S.A. 34°6N 84°31W 113 B2
Woodstock Ill., U.S.A. 42°19N 88°27W 84 A5
Woodstock N.H., U.S.A. 43°57N 71°42W 89 C3
Woodstock N.Y., U.S.A. 42°2N 74°7W 88 C6
Woodstock Ohio, U.S.A. 40°10N 83°32W 86 C3
Woodstock Vt., U.S.A. 38°53N 78°30W 93 B2
Woodstock Vt., U.S.A. 43°37N 72°31W 89 C2
Woodston Kans., U.S.A. 39°27N 99°6W 82 B4
Woodstown N.J., U.S.A. 39°39N 75°20W 92 C1
Woodsville N.H., U.S.A. 44°9N 72°2W 89 C2
Woodville Ala., U.S.A. 34°38N 86°17W 112 B4
Woodville Fla., U.S.A. 30°19N 84°15W 114 A4
Woodville Ga., U.S.A. 33°40N 83°7W 113 C3
Woodville Miss., U.S.A. 31°6N 91°18W 111 E3
Woodville Okla., U.S.A. 33°58N 96°39W 107 E7
Woodville Tex., U.S.A. 30°47N 94°25W 109 G13
Woodward Iowa, U.S.A. 41°51N 93°55W 81 D5
Woodward Okla., U.S.A. 36°26N 99°24W 107 B4
Woodward County ☆ Okla., U.S.A. 36°25N 99°15W 107 B4
Woodway Tex., U.S.A. 31°30N 97°13W 109 F10
Woodway Wash., U.S.A. 47°47N 122°22W 132 B3
Woodworth La., U.S.A. 31°9N 92°30W 110 C3
Woodworth N. Dak., U.S.A. 47°9N 99°23W 76 C6
Woody Creek Colo., U.S.A. 39°17N 106°54W 125 C4
Woody Point Nfld. & L., Canada 49°30N 57°55W 142 C2
Woolridge Mo., U.S.A. 38°55N 92°32W 83 C4
Woolstock Iowa, U.S.A. 42°34N 93°51W 81 C5
Woolwine Va., U.S.A. 36°47N 80°17W 102 E4
Woonsocket R.I., U.S.A. 42°0N 71°31W 91 C3
Woonsocket S. Dak., U.S.A. 44°3N 98°17W 76 F7
Wooster Ark., U.S.A. 35°12N 92°27W 106 C3
Wooster Ohio, U.S.A. 40°48N 81°56W 86 C5
Worcester Mass., U.S.A. 42°16N 71°48W 91 B3
Worcester N.Y., U.S.A. 42°36N 74°45W 88 C6
Worcester Vt., U.S.A. 44°24N 72°34W 89 B1
Worcester County ☆ Mass., U.S.A. 42°25N 72°0W 91 B2
Worcester County ☆ Md., U.S.A. 38°15N 75°20W 93 B5
Worcester Mts. Vt., U.S.A. 44°27N 72°36W 89 B2
Worden Ill., U.S.A. 38°56N 89°50W 84 E4
Worden Mont., U.S.A. 45°58N 108°10W 123 E9
Worden Oreg., U.S.A. 42°2N 121°52W 121 E4
Worland Wyo., U.S.A. 44°1N 107°57W 124 B5

World Trade Center, site of former N.Y.,
U.S.A. 40°42N 74°0W **97** B2
Worley Idaho, U.S.A. 47°24N 116°55W **122** B2
Woronoco Mass., U.S.A. 42°10N 72°50W **91** B2
Worsley Alta., Canada 56°31N 119°8W **152** B1
Worth Ill., U.S.A. 41°41N 87°47W **95** C2
Worth Mo., U.S.A. 40°24N 94°27W **83** A2
Worth County ☆ Ga., U.S.A. 31°30N 83°50W **113** E3
Worth County ☆ Iowa, U.S.A. 43°20N 93°15W **81** B5
Worth County ☆ Mo., U.S.A. 40°30N 94°25W **83** A2
Wortham Tex., U.S.A. 31°47N 96°28W **109** F11
Worthing S. Dak., U.S.A. 43°20N 96°46W **76** G9
Worthington Ind., U.S.A. 39°7N 86°59W **85** D4
Worthington Iowa, U.S.A. 42°24N 91°7W **81** C7
Worthington Minn., U.S.A. 43°37N 95°36W **77** G3
Worthington Ohio, U.S.A. 40°5N 83°1W **86** C3
Worthington Pa., U.S.A. 40°50N 79°38W **87** D3
Worton Md., U.S.A. 39°17N 76°6W **93** A4
Woss B.C., Canada 50°13N 126°35W **154** E8
Woss L. B.C., Canada 50°7N 126°36W **154** E8
Woss Lake Park ☐ B.C., Canada 50°4N 126°37W **154** E8
Wottonville Qué., Canada 45°44N 71°48W **145** F11
Wounded Knee S. Dak., U.S.A. 43°8N 102°22W **76** G3
Wrangell Alaska, U.S.A. 56°28N 132°23W **135** H14
Wrangell Mts. Alaska, U.S.A. 61°30N 142°0W **135** F12
Wrangell-Petersburg ☆ Alaska, U.S.A. 56°30N 133°0W **135** H14
Wrangell-St. Elias Nat. Park and Preserve △
Alaska, U.S.A. 61°0N 142°0W **135** F12
Wray Colo., U.S.A. 40°5N 102°13W **125** B8
Wren Ala., U.S.A. 34°26N 87°18W **112** B3
Wren Ohio, U.S.A. 40°48N 84°47W **86** C2
Wrens Ga., U.S.A. 33°12N 82°23W **113** C4
Wren's Nest Georgia, U.S.A. 33°44N 84°25W **112** B2
Wrenshall Minn., U.S.A. 46°37N 92°23W **77** D6
Wrentham Mass., U.S.A. 42°4N 71°20W **91** B3
Wright Fla., U.S.A. 30°27N 86°38W **114** A2
Wright Kans., U.S.A. 37°47N 99°54W **82** D4
Wright Wyo., U.S.A. 43°45N 105°28W **124** C7
Wright Brothers Nat. Memorial △ N.C.,
U.S.A. 36°1N 75°40W **103** B10
Wright City Mo., U.S.A. 38°50N 91°1W **83** C5
Wright City Okla., U.S.A. 34°5N 95°0W **107** D9
Wright County ☆ Iowa, U.S.A. 42°45N 93°40W **81** C5
Wright County ☆ Minn., U.S.A. 45°10N 94°0W **77** E5
Wright County ☆ Mo., U.S.A. 37°15N 92°30W **83** D4
Wright Patman L. Tex., U.S.A. 33°19N 94°10W **109** D13
Wrightson, Mt. Ariz., U.S.A. 31°42N 110°51W **130** F5
Wrightstown N.J., U.S.A. 40°2N 74°37W **92** B2
Wrightstown Wis., U.S.A. 44°20N 88°10W **78** D5
Wrightsville Ark., U.S.A. 34°36N 92°13W **106** D3
Wrightsville Ga., U.S.A. 32°44N 82°43W **113** D4
Wrightsville Beach N.C., U.S.A. 34°12N 77°48W **103** D8
Wrightwood Calif., U.S.A. 34°22N 117°38W **127** J9
Wrigley N.W.T., Canada 63°16N 123°37W **157** D8
Wrigley Tenn., U.S.A. 35°54N 87°21W **104** E5
Wrigley Field Ill., U.S.A. 41°56N 87°39W **95** B3
Wrottesley, C. N.W.T., Canada 74°32N 121°33W **156** B8
Wroxton Sask., Canada 51°14N 101°53W **151** D10
Wulff Land Greenland 82°0N 49°0W **162** A6
Wupatki Nat. Monument △ Ariz.,
U.S.A. 35°35N 111°20W **130** B4
Wyaconda Mo., U.S.A. 40°24N 91°55W **83** A5
Wyalusing Pa., U.S.A. 41°40N 76°16W **87** C6
Wyandot County ☆ Ohio, U.S.A. 40°50N 83°17W **86** C3
Wyandotte Mich., U.S.A. 42°12N 83°9W **79** G8
Wyandotte Okla., U.S.A. 36°48N 94°44W **107** B9
Wyandotte County ☆ Kans., U.S.A. 39°10N 94°45W **82** B9
Wyarno Wyo., U.S.A. 44°49N 106°46W **124** B6
Wyatt Mo., U.S.A. 32°9N 92°42W **110** B3
Wyatt Mo., U.S.A. 36°55N 89°13W **83** E7
Wyeville Wis., U.S.A. 44°2N 90°23W **78** D3
Wykoff Minn., U.S.A. 43°42N 92°16W **77** G6
Wylie Tex., U.S.A. 33°1N 96°33W **109** D11
Wylie, L. S.C., U.S.A. 35°1N 81°1W **103** C4
Wylliesburg Va., U.S.A. 36°51N 78°35W **102** E6
Wymark Sask., Canada 50°7N 107°44W **150** E4
Wymore Nebr., U.S.A. 40°7N 96°40W **80** D9
Wyncote Pa., U.S.A. 40°5N 75°9W **98** A2
Wyndmere N. Dak., U.S.A. 46°16N 97°9W **76** D8
Wyniatt B. N.W.T., Canada 72°45N 110°30W **156** B10
Wynndel B.C., Canada 49°11N 116°33W **153** J4
Wynne Ark., U.S.A. 35°14N 90°47W **106** C5
Wynnewood Okla., U.S.A. 34°39N 97°10W **107** D6
Wynnewood Pa., U.S.A. 40°0N 75°16W **98** B1
Wynona Okla., U.S.A. 36°33N 96°20W **107** B7
Wynot Nebr., U.S.A. 42°45N 97°10W **80** B7
Wynyard Sask., Canada 51°45N 104°10W **150** D7
Wyocena Wis., U.S.A. 43°30N 89°17W **78** E4
Wyoconda → Mo., U.S.A. 40°2N 91°34W **83** A5
Wyodak Wyo., U.S.A. 44°17N 105°22W **124** B7
Wyoming = Plympton-Wyoming Ont.,
Canada 42°57N 82°7W **146** E4
Wyoming Del., U.S.A. 39°7N 75°34W **93** A5
Wyoming Ill., U.S.A. 41°4N 89°47W **84** B4
Wyoming Iowa, U.S.A. 42°4N 91°0W **81** C8
Wyoming Mich., U.S.A. 42°54N 85°42W **79** G6
Wyoming ☐ U.S.A. 43°0N 107°30W **124** C5
Wyoming County ☆ N.Y., U.S.A. 42°40N 78°15W **88** C2
Wyoming County ☆ Pa., U.S.A. 41°30N 76°5W **87** C6
Wyoming County ☆ W. Va., U.S.A. 37°35N 81°32W **102** D3
Wyoming Pk. Wyo., U.S.A. 42°36N 110°37W **124** D2
Wyoming Range Wyo., U.S.A. 42°55N 110°52W **124** D2
Wyomissing Pa., U.S.A. 40°20N 75°59W **87** D7
Wythe County ☆ Va., U.S.A. 37°0N 81°5W **102** E3
Wytheville Va., U.S.A. 36°57N 81°5W **102** E3

X

X-Catzim Yucatán, Mexico 20°43N 87°53W **179** B6
X-Hasil Yucatán, Mexico 20°29N 88°25W **179** B5
X-Pichil Quintana Roo, Mexico 19°41N 88°25W **179** C5
X-Uilub Quintana Roo, Mexico 20°25N 88°1W **179** B5
X.L. Ranch Indian Reservation Calif.,
U.S.A. 41°34N 120°26W **126** B6
Xalancocotla = Cuarto Dinamo Distrito Federal,
Mexico 19°15N 99°17W **181** C2
Xalapa Veracruz, Mexico 19°32N 96°55W **176** E4
Xalisco Nayarit, Mexico 21°27N 104°54W **172** F6
Xalitla Guerrero, Mexico 18°0N 99°33W **175** E8
Xalostoc Tlaxcala, Mexico 19°23N 98°5W **175** C9
Xalpatláhuac Guerrero, Mexico 17°29N 98°37W **175** E9
Xaltepec Volcan Distrito Federal, Mexico 19°19N 99°2W **181** C3
Xayacatán Puebla, Mexico 18°15N 97°58W **177** F3
Xcalak Quintana Roo, Mexico 18°16N 87°50W **179** D6
Xcalakdzonot Yucatán, Mexico 20°27N 88°35W **179** B5

Xcalumkin Campeche, Mexico 20°8N 90°4W **179** B3
Xcaret Quintana Roo, Mexico 20°33N 87°11W **179** B6
Xcayal, Pta. Quintana Roo, Mexico 18°25N 87°46W **179** D6
Xel-Há Quintana Roo, Mexico 20°27N 87°18W **179** B6
Xenia Ill., U.S.A. 38°38N 88°38W **84** E5
Xenia Ohio, U.S.A. 39°41N 83°56W **86** D3
Xichú Guanajuato, Mexico 21°25N 100°4W **175** A7
Xico Veracruz, Mexico 19°25N 97°0W **176** E4
Xicoténcatl Tamaulipas, Mexico 23°0N 98°56W **171** H6
Xicotepec Puebla, Mexico 20°16N 97°57W **176** D3
Xicotlán Puebla, Mexico 18°4N 98°32W **177** F2
Xictle, Volcan Distrito Federal, Mexico 19°15N 99°13W **181** C2
Xilitla San Luis Potosí, Mexico 21°20N 98°58W **171** J6
Xitla Distrito Federal, Mexico 19°16N 99°12W **181** C2
Xiutetelco Puebla, Mexico 19°47N 97°19W **176** E3
Xochiapa Veracruz, Mexico 17°39N 95°45W **177** G5
Xochiatipan Hidalgo, Mexico 20°50N 98°16W **175** B9
Xochihuehuetlán Guerrero, Mexico 17°55N 98°26W **175** E9
Xochimilco Distrito Federal, Mexico 19°16N 99°7W **181** C3
Xochimilco, Parque Ecológico Distrito Federal,
Mexico 19°18N 99°5W **181** C3
Xochistlahuaca Guerrero, Mexico 16°47N 98°15W **175** F9
Xochitepec Distrito Federal, Mexico 19°17N 99°9W **181** C3
Xochitepec Morelos, Mexico 18°45N 99°20W **175** D8
Xochitlán Puebla, Mexico 18°42N 97°47W **177** F3
Xochob Campeche, Mexico 19°21N 89°48W **179** C4
Xococatlán Oaxaca, Mexico 17°2N 96°43W **177** G4
Xoxhen, Pta. Campeche, Mexico 19°14N 90°55W **179** C3
Xpujil Campeche, Mexico 18°33N 89°26W **179** D4
Xul Yucatán, Mexico 20°8N 89°32W **179** B4
Xul-Ha Quintana Roo, Mexico 18°33N 88°28W **179** D5

Y

Yaak Mont., U.S.A. 48°50N 115°43W **123** B2
Yabucoa Puerto Rico 18°3N 65°53W **184** G17
Yachats Oreg., U.S.A. 44°19N 124°6W **121** C1
Yacolt Wash., U.S.A. 45°51N 122°24W **120** E3
Yadkin → N.C., U.S.A. 35°23N 80°4W **103** C5
Yadkin County ☆ N.C., U.S.A. 36°10N 80°40W **103** B5
Yadkinville N.C., U.S.A. 36°8N 80°39W **103** B5
Yago Nayarit, Mexico 21°50N 105°4W **172** F5
Yah-Tah-Hey N. Mex., U.S.A. 35°38N 108°47W **131** B2
Yahk B.C., Canada 49°6N 116°10W **153** J4
Yahualica de González Gallo Jalisco,
Mexico 21°8N 102°51W **174** A5
Yajalón Chiapas, Mexico 17°14N 92°20W **178** B4
Yakama Indian Reservation Wash.,
U.S.A. 46°10N 120°30W **120** D5
Yakima Wash., U.S.A. 46°36N 120°31W **120** D5
Yakima → Wash., U.S.A. 46°15N 119°14W **120** D6
Yakima County ☆ Wash., U.S.A. 46°30N 121°0W **120** D5
Yakima Training Center Wash.,
U.S.A. 46°38N 120°25W **120** D5
Yakutat Alaska, U.S.A. 59°33N 139°44W **135** G13
Yakutat ☆ Alaska, U.S.A. 59°40N 139°8W **135** G13
Yakutat B. Alaska, U.S.A. 59°45N 140°45W **135** G12
Yalahán, L. Quintana Roo, Mexico 21°30N 87°15W **179** A6
Yale B.C., Canada 49°34N 121°25W **155** F13
Yale Ill., U.S.A. 39°7N 88°2W **84** D5
Yale Iowa, U.S.A. 41°47N 94°21W **81** D4
Yale Mich., U.S.A. 43°8N 82°48W **79** F9
Yale Okla., U.S.A. 36°7N 96°42W **107** B7
Yale S. Dak., U.S.A. 44°26N 97°59W **76** F8
Yale Va., U.S.A. 36°51N 77°17W **102** E7
Yale L. Wash., U.S.A. 45°58N 122°20W **120** E3
Yalobusha → Miss., U.S.A. 33°33N 90°10W **111** C3
Yalobusha County ☆ Miss., U.S.A. 33°59N 89°41W **111** C4
Yamaska Qué., Canada 46°0N 72°55W **145** G10
Yamhill County ☆ Oreg., U.S.A. 45°15N 123°10W **121** B2
Yampa Colo., U.S.A. 40°9N 106°55W **125** B4
Yampa → Colo., U.S.A. 40°32N 108°59W **125** B2
Yamsay Mt. Oreg., U.S.A. 42°56N 121°22W **121** E4
Yancey Tex., U.S.A. 29°8N 99°9W **109** H8
Yancey County ☆ N.C., U.S.A. 35°50N 82°20W **103** C3
Yanceyville N.C., U.S.A. 36°24N 79°20W **103** B6
Yankee Stadium N.Y., U.S.A. 40°49N 73°55W **97** B3
Yankton S. Dak., U.S.A. 42°53N 97°23W **76** H8
Yankton County ☆ S. Dak., U.S.A. 43°0N 97°30W **76** G8
Yankton Indian Reservation S. Dak.,
U.S.A. 43°5N 98°20W **76** G7
Yanush Okla., U.S.A. 34°43N 95°19W **107** D8
Yaqui → Sonora, Mexico 27°37N 110°39W **168** F5
Yaquina B. Oreg., U.S.A. 44°37N 124°1W **121** C1
Yaquina Head Oreg., U.S.A. 44°41N 124°5W **121** C1
Yarbo Ala., U.S.A. 31°32N 88°1W **112** E2
Yardville N.J., U.S.A. 40°11N 74°40W **92** B2
Yarker Ont., Canada 44°23N 76°46W **147** C10
Yarmouth N.S., Canada 43°50N 66°7W **141** K3
Yarmouth Maine, U.S.A. 43°48N 70°11W **90** E3
Yarmouth Port Mass., U.S.A. 34°13N 112°45W **130** D3
Yarrow Point Wash., U.S.A. 47°38N 122°12W **132** C4
Yasinski, L. Qué., Canada 53°16N 77°35W **143** C2
Yates Center Kans., U.S.A. 37°53N 95°44W **82** D8
Yates City Ill., U.S.A. 40°47N 90°1W **84** C3
Yates County ☆ N.Y., U.S.A. 42°40N 77°10W **88** C3
Yatesboro Pa., U.S.A. 40°48N 79°20W **87** D3
Yatesville L. Ky., U.S.A. 38°8N 82°41W **105** B10
Yathkyed L. Nunavut, Canada 62°40N 98°0W **159** E6
Yauco Puerto Rico 18°2N 66°51W **184** G16
Yautepec Morelos, Mexico 18°53N 99°4W **175** D8
Yavapai County ☆ Ariz., U.S.A. 34°30N 112°30W **130** C3
Yávaros Sonora, Mexico 26°42N 109°31W **168** G6
Yaxcabá Yucatán, Mexico 20°32N 88°50W **179** B5
Yaxchilán Chiapas, Mexico 16°54N 90°58W **178** C6
Yaxuná Yucatán, Mexico 20°32N 88°39W **179** B5
Yazoo → Miss., U.S.A. 32°22N 90°54W **111** D3
Yazoo City Miss., U.S.A. 32°51N 90°25W **111** D3
Yazoo County ☆ Miss., U.S.A. 32°50N 90°25W **111** D3
Yeadon Pa., U.S.A. 39°56N 75°16W **98** B1
Yeager Okla., U.S.A. 35°9N 96°21W **107** C7
Yecapixtla Morelos, Mexico 18°53N 99°4W **175** D8
Yecorata Sinaloa, Mexico 26°25N 108°14W **172** A2
Yécora Sonora, Mexico 28°20N 108°58W **168** E7
Yeehaw Junction Fla., U.S.A. 27°42N 80°54W **114** D8
Yell County ☆ Ark., U.S.A. 35°3N 93°24W **106** C2
Yellow → Fla., U.S.A. 30°30N 87°0W **114** A4
Yellow → Ind., U.S.A. 41°16N 86°50W **85** B4
Yellow → Wis., U.S.A. 46°1N 92°28W **77** C6
Yellow → Wis., U.S.A. 43°54N 89°59W **78** E4
Yellow Creek Sask., Canada 52°35N 105°15W **150** C6
Yellow Grass Sask., Canada 49°48N 104°10W **150** F7
Yellow Jacket Colo., U.S.A. 37°32N 108°43W **125** E2
Yellow Medicine County ☆ Minn.,
U.S.A. 44°40N 95°45W **77** F3

Yellow Pine Idaho, U.S.A. 44°58N 115°30W **122** E3
Yellow Spring W. Va., U.S.A. 39°11N 78°31W **93** A2
Yellow Springs Ohio, U.S.A. 39°48N 83°53W **86** D3
Yellowhead Pass B.C., Canada 52°53N 118°25W **155** C16
Yellowknife N.W.T., Canada 62°27N 114°29W **157** D10
Yellowknife → N.W.T., Canada 62°31N 114°19W **157** D10
Yellowstone → Mont., U.S.A. 47°59N 103°59W **123** C14
Yellowstone County ☆ Mont., U.S.A. 46°10N 108°0W **123** D10
Yellowstone L. Wyo., U.S.A. 44°27N 110°22W **124** B2
Yellowstone Nat. Park △ Wyo., U.S.A. 44°40N 110°30W **124** B2
Yellville Ark., U.S.A. 36°14N 92°41W **106** B3
Yelm Wash., U.S.A. 46°57N 122°36W **120** D3
Yelverton B. Nunavut, Canada 82°23N 83°18W **158** A9
Yemassee S.C., U.S.A. 32°41N 80°51W **103** F5
Yeoman Ind., U.S.A. 40°40N 86°44W **85** C4
Yerba Buena I. Calif., U.S.A. 37°48N 122°21W **132** B2
Yerbanis Durango, Mexico 24°45N 103°50W **173** C7
Yerbitas Chihuahua, Mexico 26°7N 106°50W **169** G9
Yerington Nev., U.S.A. 38°59N 119°10W **128** D1
Yermo Calif., U.S.A. 34°54N 116°50W **127** J10
Yeso N. Mex., U.S.A. 34°26N 104°37W **131** C6
Yetter Iowa, U.S.A. 42°19N 94°51W **81** C4
Yigo Guam 13°32N 144°53E **184** b
Ymir B.C., Canada 49°17N 117°13W **155** F17
Yoakum Tex., U.S.A. 29°17N 97°9W **109** H10
Yoakum County ☆ Tex., U.S.A. 33°11N 102°50W **108** D5
Yockanookany → Miss., U.S.A. 32°40N 89°41W **111** D4
Yocona → Miss., U.S.A. 34°11N 90°10W **111** B3
Yoder Wyo., U.S.A. 41°55N 104°18W **124** E8
Yogana Oaxaca, Mexico 16°28N 96°48W **177** H4
Yohaltum Campeche, Mexico 19°1N 90°0W **179** C3
Yoho Nat. Park △ B.C., Canada 51°25N 116°30W **155** D18
Yojoa, L. de Honduras 14°53N 88°0W **182** D2
Yolaina, Cordillera de Nic. 11°30N 84°0W **182** D3
Yolo County ☆ Calif., U.S.A. 38°45N 121°50W **126** E5
Yona Guam 13°25N 144°46E **184** b
Yoncalla Oreg., U.S.A. 43°36N 123°17W **121** D2
Yonkers N.Y., U.S.A. 40°56N 73°52W **97** A3
York Ont., Canada 43°40N 79°26W **161** A2
York Ala., U.S.A. 32°29N 88°18W **112** D2
York N. Dak., U.S.A. 48°19N 99°34W **76** B6
York Nebr., U.S.A. 40°52N 97°36W **80** D8
York Pa., U.S.A. 39°58N 76°44W **87** E6
York S.C., U.S.A. 35°0N 81°12W **103** C4
York → Qué., Canada 48°49N 64°34W **140** E5
York → Va., U.S.A. 37°15N 76°23W **102** D8
York, Kap Greenland 75°55N 66°25W **162** B4
York County ☆ Maine, U.S.A. 43°25N 70°50W **90** E3
York County ☆ Nebr., U.S.A. 40°45N 97°40W **80** D8
York County ☆ Pa., U.S.A. 39°58N 76°44W **87** E6
York County ☆ S.C., U.S.A. 34°55N 81°10W **103** D4
York County ☆ Va., U.S.A. 37°14N 76°30W **102** D8
York Mills Ont., Canada 43°45N 79°22W **161** A2
York Springs Pa., U.S.A. 40°0N 77°7W **87** D5
York University Ont., Canada 43°43N 79°22W **161** A1
York Village Maine, U.S.A. 43°9N 70°39W **90** E3
Yorkton Sask., Canada 51°11N 102°28W **151** D9
Yorktown Ark., U.S.A. 34°1N 91°49W **106** D4
Yorktown Ind., U.S.A. 40°10N 85°30W **85** C5
Yorktown N.Y., U.S.A. 41°18N 73°49W **92** A3
Yorktown Tex., U.S.A. 28°59N 97°30W **109** J10
Yorktown Va., U.S.A. 37°14N 76°30W **102** D8
Yorktown Heights N.Y., U.S.A. 41°16N 73°47W **92** A3
Yorkville Calif., U.S.A. 33°55N 84°58W **113** C2
Yorkville Ill., U.S.A. 41°38N 88°27W **84** B5
Yoro Honduras 15°9N 87°7W **182** C2
Yosemite Ky., U.S.A. 37°21N 84°50W **105** C8
Yosemite Nat. Park △ Calif., U.S.A. 37°45N 119°40W **126** F7
Yosemite Village Calif., U.S.A. 37°45N 119°35W **126** F7
Yost Utah, U.S.A. 41°58N 113°33W **129** B2
Youbou B.C., Canada 48°53N 124°13W **154** G10
Youghiogheny → Pa., U.S.A. 40°22N 79°52W **87** D3
Youghiogheny River Lake Md., U.S.A. 39°48N 79°22W **93** A1
Young Sask., Canada 51°47N 105°45W **150** D6
Young County ☆ Tex., U.S.A. 33°11N 98°44W **109** D9
Young Harris Ga., U.S.A. 34°56N 83°51W **113** B3
Youngs, Lake Wash., U.S.A. 47°25N 122°7W **132** D5
Youngstown Alta., Canada 51°35N 111°10W **153** G9
Youngstown Fla., U.S.A. 30°22N 85°26W **114** A3
Youngstown N.Y., U.S.A. 43°15N 79°3W **88** B1
Youngstown Ohio, U.S.A. 41°6N 80°39W **86** B6
Youngsville La., U.S.A. 30°3N 92°0W **110** D4
Youngsville N. Mex., U.S.A. 36°11N 106°34W **131** A4
Youngsville Pa., U.S.A. 41°51N 79°19W **87** C3
Youngtown Ariz., U.S.A. 33°35N 112°18W **134** B1
Youngwood Pa., U.S.A. 40°14N 79°34W **87** D3
Yountville Calif., U.S.A. 38°24N 122°22W **126** E4
Ypsilanti Mich., U.S.A. 42°14N 83°37W **79** G8
Ypsilanti N. Dak., U.S.A. 46°47N 98°34W **76** D7
Yreka Calif., U.S.A. 41°44N 122°38W **126** B4
Yuba Wis., U.S.A. 43°33N 90°26W **78** E3
Yuba City Calif., U.S.A. 39°8N 121°37W **126** D5
Yuba County ☆ Calif., U.S.A. 39°15N 121°30W **126** D5
Yucatán ☐ Mexico 20°50N 89°0W **179** B5
Yucatán, Canal de Caribbean 22°0N 86°30W **182** B2
Yucatán, Península de Mexico 19°30N 89°0W **179** C5
Yucatan Basin Cent. Amer. 19°0N 86°0W **182** C3
Yucatan Channel = Yucatán, Canal de
Caribbean 22°0N 86°30W **182** B2
Yucca Ariz., U.S.A. 34°52N 114°9W **130** C1
Yucca House Nat. Monument △ Colo.,
U.S.A. 37°16N 108°38W **125** E2
Yucca L. Nev., U.S.A. 36°57N 116°2W **128** F4
Yucca Valley Calif., U.S.A. 34°8N 116°27W **127** J10
Yuhalixqui, Volcan Distrito Federal,
Mexico 19°19N 99°4W **181** C3
Yukon Okla., U.S.A. 35°31N 97°45W **107** C6
Yukon → Alaska, U.S.A. 62°32N 163°54W **135** E7
Yukon-Charley Rivers Nat. Preserve △ Alaska,
U.S.A. 65°15N 144°0W **135** D12
Yukon Delta Nat. Wildlife Refuge △ Alaska,
U.S.A. 61°0N 163°0W **135** F7
Yukon Flats Alaska, U.S.A. 66°40N 145°45W **135** C11
Yukon Harbor Wash., U.S.A. 47°31N 122°32W **132** C2
Yukon-Koyukuk ☆ Alaska, U.S.A. 65°42N 152°30W **135** D9
Yukon Territory ☐ Canada 63°0N 135°0W **157** D5
Yulee Fla., U.S.A. 30°38N 81°36W **114** F4
Yum Balam, Parque Natural △ Quintana Roo,
Mexico 21°15N 87°20W **179** A6
Yuma Ariz., U.S.A. 32°43N 114°37W **130** E1
Yuma Colo., U.S.A. 40°8N 102°43W **125** B8
Yuma, B. de Dom. Rep. 18°20N 68°35W **183** C6
Yuma County ☆ Ariz., U.S.A. 33°0N 114°0W **130** E2
Yuma County ☆ Colo., U.S.A. 40°0N 102°20W **125** C8

Yuma Desert Ariz., U.S.A. 32°25N 114°30W **130** E1
Yunaska I. Alaska, U.S.A. 52°38N 170°40W **135** K5
Yurécuaro Michoacan, Mexico 20°20N 102°18W **174** B5
Yuriria Guanajuato, Mexico 20°12N 101°9W **175** B6
Yuriria, L. de Guanajuato, Mexico 20°15N 101°6W **175** B6
Yuscarán Honduras 13°58N 86°45W **182** D2
Yutan Nebr., U.S.A. 41°15N 96°24W **80** C9

Z

Zaachila Oaxaca, Mexico 16°57N 96°45W **177** H4
Zac Pol Campeche, Mexico 20°15N 90°27W **179** B3
Zacamulpa México, Mexico 19°21N 99°20W **181** B1
Zacapa Guatemala 14°59N 89°31W **182** D2
Zacapetec Morelos, Mexico 18°39N 99°12W **175** D8
Zacapoaxtla Puebla, Mexico 19°53N 97°35W **176** D3
Zacapu Michoacan, Mexico 19°50N 101°43W **174** C6
Zacata Va., U.S.A. 38°7N 76°47W **93** B4
Zacatal, Pta. Campeche, Mexico 18°36N 91°52W **179** D2
Zacatal, Pta. Campeche, Mexico 18°32N 91°51W **179** D2
Zacatecas Monterrey, Mexico 25°49N 100°8W **180** B4
Zacatecas Zacatecas, Mexico 22°47N 102°35W **173** E8
Zacatecas ☐ Mexico 23°0N 103°0W **173** E7
Zacatecoluca El Salv. 13°29N 88°51W **182** D2
Zacatelco Tlaxcala, Mexico 19°14N 98°14W **175** C9
Zacatlán Puebla, Mexico 19°56N 97°58W **176** E3
Zacatón San Luis Potosí, Mexico 22°51N 102°3W **171** H2
Zachary La., U.S.A. 30°39N 91°9W **110** D4
Zacoalco de Torres Jalisco, Mexico 20°14N 103°35W **174** C4
Zacualpan Colima, Mexico 19°19N 103°50W **174** C4
Zacualpan Guerrero, Mexico 17°7N 100°20W **175** E7
Zacualpan Nayarit, Mexico 21°15N 105°10W **172** F5
Zacualtipán Hidalgo, Mexico 20°39N 98°36W **175** B9
Zahl N. Dak., U.S.A. 48°34N 103°42W **76** B2
Zaleski Ohio, U.S.A. 39°17N 82°24W **86** D4
Zalma Mo., U.S.A. 37°9N 90°5W **83** D6
Zamach, Pta. Quintana Roo, Mexico 19°56N 87°27W **179** C6
Zamora Michoacan, Mexico 19°59N 102°16W **174** C5
Zamorano, Cerro el Querétaro, Mexico 20°54N 100°12W **175** B7
Zanatepec Oaxaca, Mexico 16°29N 94°21W **177** H6
Zanesville Ohio, U.S.A. 39°56N 82°1W **86** D4
Zap N. Dak., U.S.A. 47°17N 101°55W **76** C4
Zapata Tex., U.S.A. 26°55N 99°16W **108** L8
Zapata County ☆ Tex., U.S.A. 27°0N 99°0W **108** K8
Zapopán Jalisco, Mexico 20°43N 103°24W **180** A1
Zapote de Santa Cruz del Valle Guadalajara,
Mexico 20°31N 103°18W **180** B2
Zapotiltic Jalisco, Mexico 19°37N 103°26W **174** C4
Zapotitlán Distrito Federal, Mexico 19°18N 99°3W **181** C3
Zapotitlán de Valdillo Jalisco, Mexico 19°31N 103°44W **174** C4
Zapotitlán Lagunas Oaxaca, Mexico 17°38N 98°19W **177** G2
Zapotitlán Tablas Guerrero, Mexico 17°13N 98°59W **175** E9
Zapotlán del Rey Jalisco, Mexico 20°27N 102°55W **174** B6
Zapotlanejo Jalisco, Mexico 20°38N 103°4W **174** B4
Zaragoza Chiapas, Mexico 15°7N 92°18W **178** D3
Zaragoza Coahuila, Mexico 28°29N 100°55W **170** B4
Zaragoza Durango, Mexico 25°7N 103°22W **173** B7
Zaragoza Nuevo León, Mexico 23°58N 99°46W **171** G5
Zaragoza Puebla, Mexico 18°3N 98°27W **177** F2
Zaragoza San Luis Potosí, Mexico 24°2N 101°4W **171** F3
Zautla Puebla, Mexico 19°43N 97°40W **176** D3
Zavala County ☆ Tex., U.S.A. 28°57N 99°51W **109** J8
Zavalla Tex., U.S.A. 31°10N 94°26W **109** F13
Zealand N.B., Canada 45°57N 66°56W **141** G3
Zealandia Sask., Canada 51°37N 107°45W **150** D4
Zearing Iowa, U.S.A. 42°10N 93°18W **81** C5
Zeballos B.C., Canada 49°59N 126°50W **154** F8
Zebulon Ga., U.S.A. 33°6N 84°21W **113** C2
Zeeland Mich., U.S.A. 42°49N 86°1W **79** G5
Zeeland N. Dak., U.S.A. 45°58N 99°50W **76** E6
Zeigler Ill., U.S.A. 37°54N 89°3W **84** F4
Zelienople Pa., U.S.A. 40°48N 80°8W **87** D2
Zell S. Dak., U.S.A. 44°54N 98°44W **76** F7
Zempoala Hidalgo, Mexico 19°55N 98°40W **175** C9
Zempoala Veracruz, Mexico 19°27N 96°23W **176** E4
Zempoala, Pta. Veracruz, Mexico 19°28N 96°19W **176** E4
Zenda Kans., U.S.A. 37°27N 98°17W **82** D5
Zenon Park Sask., Canada 53°4N 103°45W **150** B8
Zephyr Cove Nev., U.S.A. 39°0N 119°57W **128** C1
Zephyr Field La., U.S.A. 30°1N 90°5W **117** C1
Zephyrhills Fla., U.S.A. 28°14N 82°11W **114** C6
Zeta L. Nunavut, Canada 70°54N 106°25W **158** C4
Zia Indian Reservation N. Mex., U.S.A. 35°30N 106°50W **131** B4
Zicuirán Michoacan, Mexico 18°54N 101°47W **174** D6
Ziebach County ☆ S. Dak., U.S.A. 45°0N 101°50W **76** F4
Zihuatanejo Michoacan, Mexico 17°39N 101°33W **174** E6
Zillah Wash., U.S.A. 46°24N 120°16W **120** D5
Zimapán Hidalgo, Mexico 20°45N 99°21W **175** B8
Zimapán, Presa Hidalgo, Mexico 20°37N 99°24W **175** B8
Zimatlán Oaxaca, Mexico 16°52N 96°47W **177** H4
Zimmerman Minn., U.S.A. 45°37N 93°34W **77** E5
Zinacantán Chiapas, Mexico 16°45N 92°42W **178** C4
Zinacantepec México, Mexico 19°17N 99°44W **174** C7
Zinacatepec Puebla, Mexico 18°20N 97°15W **177** F3
Zinapécuaro Michoacan, Mexico 19°52N 100°49W **175** C7
Zion Ill., U.S.A. 42°27N 87°50W **84** A6
Zion Nat. Park △ Utah, U.S.A. 37°15N 113°5W **129** F2
Zion Res. Ariz., U.S.A. 34°37N 109°29W **130** D8
Zionsville Ind., U.S.A. 39°57N 86°16W **85** D4
Ziquítaro Michoacan, Mexico 20°4N 101°54W **174** B6
Zirándaro Guerrero, Mexico 18°27N 100°59W **175** D7
Zirándaro Monterrey, Mexico 25°48N 100°9W **180** C3
Zirkel, Mt. Colo., U.S.A. 40°50N 106°40W **125** B4
Zitácuaro Michoacan, Mexico 19°24N 100°22W **175** C7
Zitlala Guerrero, Mexico 17°38N 99°5W **175** E8
Zoh-Laguna Campeche, Mexico 18°36N 89°25W **179** D4
Zolfo Springs Fla., U.S.A. 27°30N 81°48W **114** D7
Zona del Silencio Coahuila, Mexico 26°50N 103°36W **170** D1
Zongolica Veracruz, Mexico 18°40N 96°59W **176** E4
Zontecomatlán Veracruz, Mexico 20°46N 98°21W **176** D2
Zoquitlán Puebla, Mexico 18°20N 97°1W **177** F3
Zucualpan México, Mexico 18°43N 99°47W **175** D8
Zumbro → Minn., U.S.A. 44°17N 92°26W **77** F6
Zumbro Falls Minn., U.S.A. 44°17N 92°26W **77** F6
Zumbrota Minn., U.S.A. 44°18N 92°40W **77** F6
Zumpahuacán México, Mexico 18°51N 99°34W **175** D8
Zumpango México, Mexico 19°48N 99°6W **175** C8
Zumpango del Río Guerrero, Mexico 17°40N 99°31W **175** E8
Zuni → Ariz., U.S.A. 34°59N 109°40W **130** C6
Zuni Indian Reservation N. Mex.,
U.S.A. 35°0N 108°50W **131** C2
Zuni Mts. N. Mex., U.S.A. 35°10N 108°30W **131** B3
Zuni Pueblo N. Mex., U.S.A. 35°4N 108°51W **131** B2
Zurich Kans., U.S.A. 39°14N 99°26W **82** B4
Zwingle Iowa, U.S.A. 42°18N 90°41W **81** C8
Zwolle La., U.S.A. 31°38N 93°39W **110** C2